# CONTENTS

# THE
# OFFICIAL
# TCCB
# CRICKET
# STATISTICS
# 1991

# THE OFFICIAL TCCB CRICKET STATISTICS 1991

Compiled
by
Richard Lockwood

Macdonald
Queen Anne Press

A QUEEN ANNE PRESS BOOK

© Lennard Associates Ltd 1991

First published in 1991 by
Queen Anne Press, a division of
Macdonald & Co (Publishers) Ltd
165 Great Dover Street
London SE1 4YA

A member of the Maxwell Macmillan Pergamon Publishing Corporation

British Library Cataloguing in Publication Data
is available

Made by Lennard Associates Ltd
Mackerye End, Harpenden
Herts AL5 5DR

Photograhs by David Munden Photography
Designed by Forest Publication Services
Cover design by Cooper Wilson
Typesetting by Leaside Graphics
Printed and bound in England by
Butler & Tanner Ltd, Frome and London

## EDITOR'S PREFACE

## THE TCCB / BULL COMPUTER OFFICIAL
## STATISTICS SERVICE

The TCCB Official Cricket Statistics for the 1991 English season is the product of my work as editor of the TCCB / Bull Computer Official Statistics Service, now in its second year of operation, which provides a computer database dedicated to English cricket. I would like to thank all those who have helped in the creation and the successful operation of the Service and in the production of this book. I would particularly like to recognise the contribution made by the county scorers who have been of great assistance in the checking of all the match scorecards.


Richard Lockwood

# INTRODUCTION

Graham Gooch and Viv Richards at Headingley. The Test
series was a memorable one for both captains.

## 1991 - GOOCH LEADS FROM THE FRONT

Although not as rich in statistical achievement as the run-filled 1990 season, the summer of '91 was in many ways a memorable one. Capacity crowds watched the most competitive Test series contested in England in the last 20 years. The home side began at Headingley by gaining their first victory over West Indies in a home Test for 22 years and finished by drawing level in the series with a five-wicket victory at The Oval, after enjoying the rare treat of forcing the West Indians to follow on. On the domestic front the battle for the County Championship held the attention until the completion of the final round of matches, Essex just edging out Warwickshire, leaders for most of the season. Holding centre stage in both cricketing theatres was Graham Gooch, captain of England and Essex, who inspired his country and his county to achieve greatness by the power of his own personal example.

It was his masterful unbeaten 154 in the second innings of the Headingley Test, as he became the fifth Englishman to carry his bat in a Test match, that brought the belief back into the England team after they had endured an appalling winter in Australia. With the captain overcoming all that Curtly Ambrose and his fellow fast bowlers could hurl at him on an untrustworthy pitch, a narrow first innings advantage was converted into a winning lead, as the West Indian batsmen could not come to terms with the English seam attack. The 115-run win was England's first

# INTRODUCTION

over West Indies at home since Ray Illingworth led England to victory at Headingley in 1969.

The Lord's Test was transformed by another outstanding individual performance, this time from Robin Smith. West Indies, thanks to Carl Hooper's first Test 100 against England, had quickly taken the initiative, and England were in grave danger of complete collapse at 84 for five in reply to 419, but Smith, often hitting the ball with almost unbelievable force, made the highest score of his Test career as the last five wickets added 270. Although the last two days were ruined by some of the worst of a dreadful June's weather, England had remained in control of the series.

West Indies' fightback gathered force at Trent Bridge and Edgbaston as the third and fourth Tests resembled so many of those played between the two countries in the previous two series in England: Ambrose was the most lethal of the fast bowlers, carving through the England frontline batting like a knife through butter, but his assistants also caused plenty of problems. Phil DeFreitas, at Trent Bridge, and Chris Lewis, at Edgbaston, both batted with character to score their first Test match fifties and to avert total surrender, but West Indies won both Tests with ease, by nine and seven wickets, Viv Richards taking his side into a two-one lead with a monumental straight six off Richard Illingworth as he left Edgbaston secure in the knowledge that he would never lose a Test series as West Indies captain.

England looked a beaten side, Atherton, Lamb and Hick, enduring a horrendous first series in Test cricket, were barely able to muster 10 runs an innings apiece over the four Tests. Drastic measures were required. A remodelled batting line-up, a new wicket-keeper, an attacking spin bowler and the recall to arms of Ian Botham, who had been denied an earlier entry into the series by an injury suffered during the first Texaco Trophy match, all paid dividends as England's victory at The Oval brought their first drawn series against West Indies since Tony Greig's men levelled the series in the Caribbean in 1973-74.

Robin Smith completed his second 100 of the series as England passed 400 for the first time in a Test against West Indies since The Oval Test of 1976. 15 years ago, this did not save them from a heavy defeat, but it was to be very different in 1991. Phil Tufnell changed the character of the match within a handful of overs. He claimed six wickets for four runs either side of the lunch interval, as a full house Saturday crowd watched in stunned amazement. West Indies' last seven wickets surrendered for 18 runs, Desmond Haynes was left stranded on 75, and the visitors were asked to follow on 243 runs behind.

While Richie Richardson, now fully at ease in English conditions, and Viv Richards, looking to bring his Test career to a close in the grand manner, were together West Indies were far from out of the match. The West Indian captain's final Test innings came to a close on 62 and he received a standing ovation as he bade an emotional farewell to the Test arena he had dominated for almost 17 years, but Richardson remained to make his 14th Test 100, and it was only when DeFreitas, England's best bowler throughout the series, and David Lawrence, their most enthusiastic, combined to bring the West Indies second innings to a close early on the fifth morning that an England victory became a realistic target. Alec Stewart and

# INTRODUCTION

Mark Ramprakash calmed English nerves with a courageous fifth-wicket stand to level the scores but it was left to the old-stager Ian Botham to hit the winning runs.

England completed the summer's programme of international cricket with a 130-run victory over Sri Lanka at Lord's, a match that will be remembered most for Alec Stewart's maiden Test 100, a career best bowling performance from DeFreitas and 174 from Gooch, his 15th Test 100 as he became the fifth English batsman to score 7,000 runs in Test cricket. This third Test victory of the season added to their 3-0 victory in the Texaco Trophy ended a highly satisfactory summer for the England captain and his men.

The race for the Britannic Assurance Championship developed into an intriguing contest between Warwickshire and Essex. Andy Lloyd's side headed the table from the early stages and so effective was their fast bowling attack that by August their advantage stood at 51 points. But as Warwickshire, sensing their first county title since 1972, began to falter Essex, by far the strongest all-round team, grew in strength. By winning six out of their last seven matches, they replaced Warwickshire at the top of the table and stayed there.

Although Warwickshire kept up the pressure by rediscovering their winning formula, the destination of the Championship title was effectively decided by the extraordinary events of the opening day of Essex's match against Middlesex at Chelmsford: the 1990 champions were dismissed for 51, the season's lowest total, and Essex reached 385 for three, Gooch leading the way with an unbeaten double century. Two days later he was celebrating Essex's fifth Championship success in 13 seasons.

The Refuge Assurance League also developed into a two-horse race, Nottinghamshire overhauling Lancashire in the final stages. The two knockout competitions both saw new champions: Worcestershire won a Lord's final for the first time when they defeated Lancashire in the Benson & Hedges Cup final, and Hampshire, at last getting beyond the semi-final stage, won the NatWest Trophy with a thrilling victory over Surrey.

The 1991 first-class season saw the pendulum swing back from the batsman-friendly days of 1990. Fast bowlers Waqar Younis, the most devasting bowler on the county circuit for several seasons who claimed 113 Championship victims, Neil Foster, who also took 100 first-class wickets, and Allan Donald, the spearhead of Warwickshire's Championship campaign, all proved match-winners for their counties.

Although Jimmy Cook recorded the highest aggregate (2755) in an English season since the reduction of the County Championship in 1969, taking his three-year total for Somerset to 7604, only Mike Gatting and Mohammad Azharuddin also completed 2,000 first-class runs, compared to the ten batsmen who managed to do so in 1990; the 18 double centuries and 315 centuries were a considerable reduction from 1990's high watermarks of 32 and 428 respectively. Yet the 1991 batting statistics still compared more than favourably with any season in the 1980s.

The debate over the structure of English domestic cricket continued unabated and largely unacted upon. Much of the mid-season three-day programme was affected by poor weather, and match after match was decided by declaration,

forfeiture and manipulation; yet the combination of a dry final month and the return to four-day cricket saw only one of the last 29 matches fail to bring a positive result: a contrast, even allowing for an unpredictable climate, that should not be ignored. Yet the only change in the fixture list for 1992 is the welcome entry of Durham into the County Championship.

Change may not be delayed for long, as even a summer of success for the national side cannot disguise the underlying weaknesses in the English game. Gooch himself was the only current England player in the top 15 of the batting averages, along with seven overseas batsmen, three Englishmen currently ineligible and two nearing or past retirement. The bowling situation was just as worrying. Waqar Younis, Ambrose, Donald and Foster dominated the list with only DeFreitas, Lawrence and Tufnell making an effective contribution among England-qualified bowlers.

But the abiding memory of the summer was of Graham Gooch, leading from the front, and he thoroughly deserves to look back with pride on the most satisfying season of his career.

# THE
# SCORECARDS

# THE OPENING FIRST-CLASS MATCHES

## CAMBRIDGE U vs. LANCASHIRE

at Fenner's on 13th, 14th, 15th April 1991
Toss : Lancashire. Umpires : G.I.Burgess and M.J.Kitchen
Match drawn

### LANCASHIRE

| | | | | |
|---|---|---|---|---|
| G.D.Mendis | c Turner b Arscott | 44 | not out | 127 |
| G.Fowler | c Arscott b Bush | 63 | c Crawley b Lowrey | 25 |
| M.A.Atherton | st Turner b Pearson | 138 | | |
| N.H.Fairbrother * | c Bush b Waller | 23 | (3) retired hurt/ill | 25 |
| G.D.Lloyd | c Morris b Johnson | 70 | (4) c Turner b Bush | 39 |
| M.Watkinson | b Pearson | 10 | (5) not out | 35 |
| P.A.J.DeFreitas | b Pearson | 39 | | |
| W.K.Hegg + | not out | 26 | | |
| G.Yates | not out | 11 | | |
| J.D.Fitton | | | | |
| P.J.W.Allott | | | | |
| Extras | (b 8,lb 9,w 1,nb 1) | 19 | (lb 1,nb 3) | 4 |
| TOTAL | (for 7 wkts dec) | 443 | (for 2 wkts dec) | 255 |

### CAMBRIDGE U

| | | | | |
|---|---|---|---|---|
| G.W.Jones | c Hegg b Allott | 1 | c Hegg b DeFreitas | 0 |
| R.I.Clitheroe | c Lloyd b DeFreitas | 8 | not out | 22 |
| J.P.Crawley | b Watkinson | 83 | b Allott | 30 |
| R.J.Turner *+ | lbw b DeFreitas | 43 | | |
| M.J.Lowrey | c Fowler b DeFreitas | 43 | not out | 2 |
| M.J.Morris | c Hegg b Watkinson | 0 | (4) c Allott b Fitton | 0 |
| J.P.Arscott | not out | 35 | | |
| R.M.Pearson | c Mendis b Yates | 2 | | |
| R.B.Waller | c Allott b Fitton | 2 | | |
| S.W.Johnson | c DeFreitas b Yates | 14 | | |
| D.J.Bush | c Hegg b Yates | 5 | | |
| Extras | (b 4,lb 11) | 15 | (b 4) | 4 |
| TOTAL | | 251 | (for 3 wkts) | 58 |

| CAMBRIDGE U | O | M | R | W | O | M | R | W |
|---|---|---|---|---|---|---|---|---|
| Bush | 22 | 7 | 78 | 1 | 11 | 0 | 45 | 1 |
| Waller | 18 | 1 | 84 | 1 | 6 | 2 | 23 | 0 |
| Johnson | 24 | 3 | 88 | 1 | 6 | 1 | 38 | 0 |
| Arscott | 12 | 2 | 44 | 1 | 2 | 0 | 5 | 0 |
| Pearson | 38 | 6 | 124 | 3 | 24 | 5 | 76 | 0 |
| Lowrey | 1 | 0 | 8 | 0 | 18 | 3 | 67 | 1 |

| LANCASHIRE | O | M | R | W | O | M | R | W |
|---|---|---|---|---|---|---|---|---|
| DeFreitas | 23 | 5 | 62 | 3 | 6 | 2 | 19 | 1 |
| Allott | 15 | 5 | 23 | 1 | 4 | 1 | 4 | 1 |
| Watkinson | 22 | 7 | 52 | 2 | 4 | 2 | 5 | 0 |
| Fitton | 19 | 1 | 60 | 1 | 2 | 1 | 2 | 1 |
| Yates | 17.2 | 7 | 39 | 3 | 8 | 2 | 24 | 0 |

| FALL OF WICKETS | LAN | CAM | LAN | CAM |
|---|---|---|---|---|
| 1st | 84 | 7 | 99 | 2 |
| 2nd | 133 | 21 | 200 | 48 |
| 3rd | 173 | 103 | | 54 |
| 4th | 307 | 189 | | |
| 5th | 328 | 189 | | |
| 6th | 377 | 193 | | |
| 7th | 414 | 212 | | |
| 8th | | 215 | | |
| 9th | | 242 | | |
| 10th | | 251 | | |

## CAMBRIDGE U vs. NORTHANTS

at Fenner's on 16th, 17th, 18th April 1991
Toss : Cambridge U. Umpires : G.I.Burgess and M.J.Kitchen
Match drawn

### NORTHANTS

| | | | | |
|---|---|---|---|---|
| A.Fordham | c Waller b Arscott | 81 | | |
| N.A.Felton | c Clitheroe b Waller | 12 | not out | 26 |
| R.J.Bailey * | c Crawley b Jenkins | 21 | | |
| D.J.Capel | c Crawley b Pearson | 100 | | |
| R.G.Williams | not out | 101 | | |
| K.M.Curran | b Lowrey | 79 | | |
| A.L.Penberthy | not out | 2 | | |
| D.Ripley + | | | (1) not out | 38 |
| J.G.Thomas | | | | |
| J.P.Taylor | | | | |
| N.G.B.Cook | | | | |
| Extras | (b 5,lb 2,w 1) | 8 | (lb 2) | 2 |
| TOTAL | (for 5 wkts dec) | 404 | (for 0 wkts) | 66 |

### CAMBRIDGE U

| | | | |
|---|---|---|---|
| G.W.Jones | c Ripley b Taylor | 5 | |
| R.I.Clitheroe | b Cook | 8 | |
| R.H.J.Jenkins | c Cook b Thomas | 20 | |
| R.M.Pearson | b Taylor | 0 | |
| J.P.Crawley | c Ripley b Taylor | 39 | |
| R.J.Turner *+ | retired hurt | 0 | |
| M.J.Lowrey | b Penberthy | 51 | |
| M.J.Morris | lbw b Cook | 0 | |
| J.P.Arscott | c Ripley b Thomas | 12 | |
| S.W.Johnson | b Penberthy | 20 | |
| R.B.Waller | not out | 4 | |
| Extras | (b 7,lb 7,nb 1) | 15 | |
| TOTAL | | 174 | |

| CAMBRIDGE U | O | M | R | W | O | M | R | W |
|---|---|---|---|---|---|---|---|---|
| Jenkins | 19 | 3 | 71 | 1 | 8 | 0 | 17 | 0 |
| Johnson | 15.1 | 2 | 76 | 0 | 5 | 0 | 42 | 0 |
| Waller | 11 | 1 | 75 | 1 | | | | |
| Arscott | 3 | 0 | 26 | 1 | | | | |
| Pearson | 24 | 2 | 115 | 1 | 2 | 0 | 5 | 0 |
| Lowrey | 7 | 1 | 34 | 1 | | | | |

| NORTHANTS | O | M | R | W | O | M | R | W |
|---|---|---|---|---|---|---|---|---|
| Taylor | 18 | 3 | 56 | 3 | | | | |
| Thomas | 15 | 5 | 21 | 2 | | | | |
| Cook | 15 | 8 | 25 | 2 | | | | |
| Williams | 4 | 2 | 3 | 0 | | | | |
| Penberthy | 10.4 | 3 | 24 | 2 | | | | |
| Capel | 4 | 1 | 5 | 0 | | | | |
| Curran | 10 | 5 | 16 | 0 | | | | |
| Bailey | 4 | 0 | 10 | 0 | | | | |

| FALL OF WICKETS | NOR | CAM | NOR | CAM |
|---|---|---|---|---|
| 1st | 48 | 9 | | |
| 2nd | 107 | 23 | | |
| 3rd | 139 | 23 | | |
| 4th | 267 | 54 | | |
| 5th | 400 | 88 | | |
| 6th | | 106 | | |
| 7th | | 129 | | |
| 8th | | 169 | | |
| 9th | | 174 | | |
| 10th | | | | |

## OXFORD U vs. HAMPSHIRE

at The Parks on 13th, 15th, 16th April 1991
Toss : Oxford U. Umpires : J.H.Hampshire and R.C.Tolchard
Match drawn

### OXFORD U

| | | | | |
|---|---|---|---|---|
| R.E.Morris | lbw b James | 5 | (7) lbw b Bakker | 0 |
| R.R.Montgomerie | c Middleton b James | 10 | (1) lbw b Bakker | 88 |
| C.Gupte | c Aymes b Maru | 15 | (2) b Connor | 0 |
| G.Lovell | c Terry b Ayling | 18 | c Maru b Ayling | 41 |
| G.J.Turner * | lbw b Ayling | 9 | c Aymes b James | 11 |
| D.Pfaff | not out | 48 | lbw b Maru | 50 |
| M.J.Russell | c Aymes b Maru | 13 | (8) c James b Maru | 0 |
| D.Sandiford + | c Nicholas b Maru | 0 | (3) b Connor | 10 |
| H.Davies | c Aymes b Connor | 0 | not out | 19 |
| R.MacDonald | c Smith b Maru | 20 | not out | 5 |
| B.Wood | b Ayling | 0 | | |
| Extras | (lb 4,nb 5) | 9 | (b 4,lb 7,nb 3) | 14 |
| TOTAL | | 147 | (for 8 wkts) | 238 |

### HAMPSHIRE

| | | | |
|---|---|---|---|
| V.P.Terry | retired hurt | 4 | |
| C.L.Smith | b Turner | 200 | |
| T.C.Middleton | c Sandiford b MacDonald | 2 | |
| M.C.J.Nicholas * | c Montgomerie b MacDonald | 7 | |
| K.D.James | c & b Turner | 47 | |
| J.R.Ayling | not out | 52 | |
| A.N Aymes + | not out | 52 | |
| R.J.Maru | | | |
| C.A.Connor | | | |
| P.J.Bakker | | | |
| Aqib Javed | | | |
| Extras | (lb 4,nb 1) | 5 | |
| TOTAL | (for 4 wkts dec) | 369 | |

| HAMPSHIRE | O | M | R | W | O | M | R | W |
|---|---|---|---|---|---|---|---|---|
| Aqib Javed | 11 | 1 | 27 | 0 | 14 | 2 | 43 | 0 |
| Bakker | 12 | 7 | 18 | 0 | 18 | 6 | 42 | 2 |
| James | 13 | 6 | 25 | 2 | 14 | 6 | 33 | 1 |
| Connor | 15 | 4 | 40 | 1 | 16 | 5 | 38 | 2 |
| Maru | 18 | 4 | 17 | 4 | 29 | 9 | 47 | 2 |
| Ayling | 12.2 | 5 | 16 | 3 | 13 | 8 | 24 | 1 |

| OXFORD U | O | M | R | W | O | M | R | W |
|---|---|---|---|---|---|---|---|---|
| MacDonald | 30 | 10 | 81 | 2 | | | | |
| Wood | 12 | 3 | 41 | 0 | | | | |
| Turner | 31 | 7 | 105 | 2 | | | | |
| Davies | 17.1 | 2 | 78 | 0 | | | | |
| Lovell | 8 | 2 | 36 | 0 | | | | |
| Gupte | 5 | 1 | 24 | 0 | | | | |

| FALL OF WICKETS | OXF | HAM | OXF | HAM |
|---|---|---|---|---|
| 1st | 9 | 20 | 2 | |
| 2nd | 21 | 36 | 19 | |
| 3rd | 39 | 142 | 122 | |
| 4th | 58 | 291 | 145 | |
| 5th | 63 | | 171 | |
| 6th | 105 | | 171 | |
| 7th | 107 | | 172 | |
| 8th | 114 | | 225 | |
| 9th | 147 | | | |
| 10th | 147 | | | |

## MCC vs. MIDDLESEX

at Lord's on 16th, 17th, 18th, 19th April 1991
Toss : MCC. Umpires : D.J.Constant and A.G.T.Whitehead
Match drawn

### MIDDLESEX

| | | | |
|---|---|---|---|
| M.A.Roseberry | lbw b Thorpe | 98 | |
| J.C.Pooley | b Munton | 17 | |
| I.J.F.Hutchinson | c Morris b Thorpe | 70 | |
| M.R.Ramprakash | c Rhodes b Illingworth | 28 | |
| K.R.Brown | c Hick b Pick | 44 | |
| P.R.Downton + | c Fairbrother b Watkin | 32 | |
| J.E.Emburey * | c Bicknell b Watkin | 4 | |
| N.F.Williams | run out | 29 | |
| D.W.Headley | b Pick | 0 | |
| P.C.R.Tufnell | c Hussain b Munton | 34 | |
| N.G.Cowans | not out | 4 | |
| Extras | (b 2,lb 12,nb 3) | 17 | |
| TOTAL | | 377 | |

### MCC

| | | | |
|---|---|---|---|
| D.J.Bicknell | c Headley b Williams | 44 | |
| H.Morris * | c Roseberry b Williams | 44 | |
| G.A.Hick | c Downton b Cowans | 58 | |
| N.H.Fairbrother | b Headley | 5 | |
| N.Hussain | not out | 47 | |
| G.P.Thorpe | not out | 37 | |
| S.J.Rhodes + | | | |
| R.K.Illingworth | | | |
| R.A.Pick | | | |
| S.L.Watkin | | | |
| T.A.Munton | | | |
| Extras | (lb 7,nb 8) | 15 | |
| TOTAL | (for 4 wkts) | 250 | |

| MCC | O | M | R | W | O | M | R | W |
|---|---|---|---|---|---|---|---|---|
| Pick | 27 | 4 | 95 | 2 | | | | |
| Watkin | 30 | 7 | 88 | 2 | | | | |
| Munton | 31.1 | 7 | 68 | 2 | | | | |
| Thorpe | 15 | 2 | 48 | 2 | | | | |
| Illingworth | 22 | 2 | 46 | 1 | | | | |
| Hick | 4 | 0 | 18 | 0 | | | | |

| MIDDLESEX | O | M | R | W | O | M | R | W |
|---|---|---|---|---|---|---|---|---|
| Cowans | 16 | 6 | 38 | 1 | | | | |
| Williams | 18 | 2 | 70 | 2 | | | | |
| Headley | 20.1 | 7 | 78 | 1 | | | | |
| Emburey | 11 | 4 | 38 | 0 | | | | |
| Tufnell | 13 | 7 | 15 | 0 | | | | |
| Ramprakash | 1 | 0 | 4 | 0 | | | | |

| FALL OF WICKETS | MID | MCC | MID | MCC |
|---|---|---|---|---|
| 1st | 38 | 78 | | |
| 2nd | 189 | 124 | | |
| 3rd | 202 | 145 | | |
| 4th | 246 | 180 | | |
| 5th | 292 | | | |
| 6th | 308 | | | |
| 7th | 317 | | | |
| 8th | 318 | | | |
| 9th | 373 | | | |
| 10th | 377 | | | |

# THE OPENING FIRST-CLASS MATCHES

## OXFORD U vs. GLAMORGAN

at The Parks on 17th, 18th, 19th April 1991
Toss : Oxford U.  Umpires : J.H.Hampshire and R.C.Tolchard
Match drawn

**OXFORD U**

| | | |
|---|---|---|
| R.E.Morris | c Maynard b Bastien | 30 |
| R.R.Montgomerie | lbw b Dennis | 0 |
| C.Gupte | c Metson b Bastien | 1 |
| G.Lovell | lbw b Foster | 17 |
| G.J.Turner * | c Metson b Dennis | 94 |
| D.Pfaff | c Metson b Smith | 16 |
| S.Warley | c Metson b Frost | 3 |
| D.Sandiford + | lbw b Frost | 32 |
| H.Davies | c Metson b Frost | 0 |
| R.MacDonald | c Metson b Dennis | 4 |
| B.Wood | not out | 2 |
| Extras | (b 1,lb 3,w 1,nb 14) | 19 |
| TOTAL | | 218 |

**GLAMORGAN**

| | | |
|---|---|---|
| A.R.Butcher * | not out | 25 |
| P.A.Cottey | not out | 9 |
| G.C.Holmes | | |
| M.P.Maynard | | |
| I.Smith | | |
| R.D.B.Croft | | |
| C.P.Metson + | | |
| S.J.Dennis | | |
| S.Bastien | | |
| D.J.Foster | | |
| M.Frost | | |
| Extras | | 0 |
| TOTAL | (for 0 wkts) | 34 |

| GLAMORGAN | O | M | R | W | O | M | R | W |
|---|---|---|---|---|---|---|---|---|
| Frost | 17 | 5 | 29 | 3 | | | | |
| Dennis | 17.3 | 7 | 31 | 3 | | | | |
| Bastien | 14 | 5 | 40 | 2 | | | | |
| Foster | 13 | 1 | 61 | 1 | | | | |
| Smith | 6 | 1 | 24 | 1 | | | | |
| Croft | 15 | 7 | 29 | 0 | | | | |

| OXFORD U | O | M | R | W | O | M | R | W |
|---|---|---|---|---|---|---|---|---|
| MacDonald | 4.4 | 1 | 15 | 0 | | | | |
| Wood | 4 | 0 | 19 | 0 | | | | |

**FALL OF WICKETS**

| | OXF | GLA | OXF | GLA |
|---|---|---|---|---|
| 1st | 3 | | | |
| 2nd | 18 | | | |
| 3rd | 51 | | | |
| 4th | 58 | | | |
| 5th | 83 | | | |
| 6th | 86 | | | |
| 7th | 191 | | | |
| 8th | 196 | | | |
| 9th | 215 | | | |
| 10th | 218 | | | |

## CAMBRIDGE U vs. ESSEX

at Fenner's on 19th, 20th, 22nd April 1991
Toss : Essex.  Umpires : H.D.Bird and R.A.White
Essex won by 350 runs

**ESSEX**

| | | | | | |
|---|---|---|---|---|---|
| G.A.Gooch * | retired hurt | 101 | | | |
| N.Shahid | c Johnson b Lyons | 83 | | | |
| P.J.Prichard | not out | 55 | (6) not out | | 18 |
| Salim Malik | b Arscott | 40 | c Johnson b Pearson | | 32 |
| J.P.Stephenson | not out | 16 | (1) c Jenkins b Bush | | 84 |
| D.R.Pringle | | | (2) b Arscott | | 52 |
| M.A.Garnham + | | | (3) not out | | 102 |
| N.A.Foster | | | (5) c sub b Pearson | | 2 |
| T.D.Topley | | | | | |
| M.C.Ilott | | | | | |
| P.M.Such | | | | | |
| Extras | (b 8,lb 5,w 1,nb 2) | 16 | (lb 1,w 1,nb 6) | | 8 |
| TOTAL | (for 2 wkts dec) | 311 | (for 4 wkts dec) | | 298 |

**CAMBRIDGE U**

| | | | | | |
|---|---|---|---|---|---|
| G.E.Thwaites | b Foster | 19 | c Garnham b Pringle | | 6 |
| R.I.Clitheroe + | c Gooch b Ilott | 13 | c Pringle b Ilott | | 4 |
| J.P.Crawley * | c Garnham b Topley | 39 | c Pringle b Stephenson | | 54 |
| M.J.Lowrey | lbw b Pringle | 0 | c Shahid b Such | | 9 |
| R.J.Lyons | c Gooch b Foster | 20 | c Salim Malik b Stephenson | | 18 |
| M.J.Morris | b Topley | 2 | c Salim Malik b Foster | | 15 |
| J.P.Arscott | c Salim Malik b Foster | 0 | lbw b Stephenson | | 0 |
| R.H.J.Jenkins | b Foster | 5 | lbw b Stephenson | | 0 |
| R.M.Pearson | b Such | 0 | c Pringle b Foster | | 15 |
| S.W.Johnson | not out | 4 | not out | | 18 |
| D.J.Bush | c Topley b Such | 0 | b Ilott | | 3 |
| Extras | (b 1,lb 1,nb 1) | 3 | (b 4,lb 5,nb 3) | | 12 |
| TOTAL | | 105 | | | 154 |

| CAMBRIDGE U | O | M | R | W | O | M | R | W |
|---|---|---|---|---|---|---|---|---|
| Jenkins | 16 | 1 | 61 | 0 | 14 | 1 | 53 | 0 |
| Bush | 9 | 1 | 42 | 0 | 13 | 1 | 66 | 1 |
| Pearson | 18 | 3 | 77 | 0 | 23 | 5 | 88 | 2 |
| Johnson | 8 | 0 | 33 | 0 | 12 | 2 | 69 | 0 |
| Lowrey | 7 | 0 | 42 | 0 | | | | |
| Lyons | 4 | 0 | 26 | 1 | | | | |
| Arscott | 6 | 1 | 17 | 1 | 4 | 0 | 21 | 1 |

| ESSEX | O | M | R | W | O | M | R | W |
|---|---|---|---|---|---|---|---|---|
| Foster | 17 | 7 | 29 | 4 | 9 | 2 | 32 | 2 |
| Ilott | 12 | 4 | 32 | 1 | 9.4 | 3 | 30 | 2 |
| Pringle | 7 | 1 | 18 | 1 | 9 | 7 | 4 | 1 |
| Topley | 7 | 1 | 19 | 2 | 7 | 2 | 28 | 0 |
| Such | 5 | 3 | 5 | 2 | 10 | 3 | 21 | 1 |
| Stephenson | | | | | 9 | 2 | 30 | 4 |

**FALL OF WICKETS**

| | ESS | CAM | ESS | CAM |
|---|---|---|---|---|
| 1st | 209 | 22 | 118 | 9 |
| 2nd | 282 | 52 | 166 | 25 |
| 3rd | | 55 | 231 | 44 |
| 4th | | 88 | 239 | 88 |
| 5th | | 90 | | 95 |
| 6th | | 91 | | 99 |
| 7th | | 100 | | 99 |
| 8th | | 101 | | 119 |
| 9th | | 105 | | 134 |
| 10th | | 105 | | 154 |

## HEADLINES

### 13th - 16th April

• The longest first-class season of this century got under way on 13th April with traditional opening matches at Fenner's and the The Parks.

• Michael Atherton quickly made his mark by becoming the first batsman to reach three figures as Lancashire amassed 443 for seven declared against Cambridge University, but Atherton's fellow old boy of Manchester G.S., John Crawley, responded with 83 in his first innings for the University.

• Chris Smith also made the most of his first innings of the season, making exactly 200 of Hampshire's 369 for four declared against an Oxford University side with as many as seven new faces. Oxford were able to hold out for a draw thanks to 88 from Richard Montgomerie who made an encouraging start to his first-class career.

• First-class débuts: G.W.Jones, R.I.Clitheroe, R.M.Pearson, R.B.Waller (Cambridge U), R.R.Montgomerie, C.Gupte, G.Lovell, D.Pfaff, D.Sandiford, R.MacDonald, B.Wood (Oxford U).

### 16th - 19th April

• The annual MCC vs. Champion County encounter took place at Lord's with the St John's Wood weather at its most inhospitable, cold and gloomy when play was possible at all. A second-wicket stand of 151 between Mike Roseberry and Ian Hutchinson formed the basis for Middlesex's total of 377, while in MCC's reply Graeme Hick managed 58 in his first innings as an England-qualified player. Dean Headley, boasting a vintage cricketing pedigree, was a new face in the Middlesex side and he made a good impression on his first-class début, claiming the wicket of Neil Fairbrother.

• David Capel and Richard Williams both hit centuries for Northamptonshire against Cambridge University at Fenner's and two of the county's new recruits also caught the eye: Kevin Curran made 79 and Paul Taylor took three wickets.

• Only the opening day survived at The Parks, where Oxford University were bowled out for 218 by Glamorgan despite an innings of 94 , his best in first-class cricket, from new captain Graeme Turner.

• First-class débuts: D.W.Headley (Middlesex), S.Warley (Oxford U).

### 19th - 22nd April

• Essex became the first county to gain a first-class victory by beating Cambridge University by 350 runs at Fenner's, clearly displaying their credentials as Championship contenders on each of the three days. Graham Gooch, quickly into his stride with his 84th first-class hundred, and Nadeem Shahid provided an opening stand of 209 in the first innings, John Stephenson and Derek Pringle one of 118 in the second, before Mike Garnham scored his maiden first-class century. Six bowlers shared the wickets, Stephenson returning career-best figures of 4 for 30.

• First-class débuts: G.E.Thwaites and R.J.Lyons (Cambridge U)

# REFUGE ASSURANCE LEAGUE

## GLAMORGAN vs. NORTHANTS

at Cardiff on 21st April 1991
Toss: N'hants. Umps: D.R.Shepherd and A.G.T.Whitehead
N'hants won on faster scoring rate. Glam 0pts, N'hants 4pts

### GLAMORGAN

| | | |
|---|---|---|
| A.R.Butcher * | b Taylor | 77 |
| H.Morris | c Lamb b Taylor | 2 |
| M.P.Maynard | c Baptiste b Curran | 13 |
| R.J.Shastri | not out | 64 |
| I.Smith | c Thomas b Williams | 6 |
| G.C.Holmes | not out | 13 |
| R.D.B.Croft | | |
| C.P.Metson + | | |
| S.L.Watkin | | |
| S.R.Barwick | | |
| M.Frost | | |
| Extras | (b 1,lb 9,w 1) | 11 |
| TOTAL | (40 overs)(for 4 wkts) | 186 |

### NORTHANTS

| | | |
|---|---|---|
| A.Fordham | c Barwick b Watkin | 3 |
| R.J.Bailey | run out | 8 |
| A.J.Lamb * | lbw b Watkin | 2 |
| D.J.Capel | b Watkin | 20 |
| K.M.Curran | c Metson b Barwick | 13 |
| R.G.Williams | not out | 66 |
| E.A.E.Baptiste | run out | 11 |
| D.Ripley + | b Frost | 14 |
| J.G.Thomas | c Butcher b Barwick | 5 |
| N.G.B.Cook | c Morris b Barwick | 6 |
| J.P.Taylor | not out | 2 |
| Extras | (b 1,lb 15,w 4,nb 1) | 21 |
| TOTAL | (35.5 overs)(for 9 wkts) | 171 |

| NORTHANTS | O | M | R | W | FALL OF WICKETS | | |
|---|---|---|---|---|---|---|---|
| | | | | | | GLA | NOR |
| Baptiste | 8 | 0 | 39 | 0 | | | |
| Thomas | 4 | 0 | 27 | 0 | 1st | 32 | 7 |
| Curran | 8 | 0 | 37 | 1 | 2nd | 54 | 20 |
| Taylor | 8 | 0 | 27 | 2 | 3rd | 131 | 20 |
| Cook | 5 | 0 | 19 | 0 | 4th | 150 | 51 |
| Williams | 7 | 0 | 27 | 1 | 5th | | 64 |
| | | | | | 6th | | 80 |
| GLAMORGAN | O | M | R | W | 7th | | 126 |
| Frost | 8 | 1 | 24 | 1 | 8th | | 141 |
| Watkin | 8 | 0 | 30 | 3 | 9th | | 155 |
| Barwick | 8 | 0 | 30 | 3 | 10th | | |
| Shastri | 8 | 0 | 31 | 0 | | | |
| Croft | 2 | 0 | 16 | 0 | | | |
| Holmes | 1.5 | 0 | 24 | 0 | | | |

## HAMPSHIRE vs. YORKSHIRE

at Southampton on 21st April 1991
Toss : Yorkshire. Umpires : A.A.Jones and P.B.Wight
Hampshire won by 49 runs. Hampshire 4 pts, Yorks 0 pts

### HAMPSHIRE

| | | |
|---|---|---|
| T.C.Middleton | c Fletcher b Hartley | 22 |
| C.L.Smith | c Moxon b Hartley | 86 |
| D.I.Gower | c Sharp b Sidebottom | 45 |
| J.R.Wood | c & b Fletcher | 14 |
| M.C.J.Nicholas * | not out | 22 |
| J.R.Ayling | not out | 2 |
| K.D.James | | |
| A.N Aymes + | | |
| C.A.Connor | | |
| Aqib Javed | | |
| S.D.Udal | | |
| Extras | (lb 3,w 2,nb 1) | 6 |
| TOTAL | (39 overs)(for 4 wkts) | 197 |

### YORKSHIRE

| | | |
|---|---|---|
| M.D.Moxon * | c Aymes b James | 15 |
| A.A.Metcalfe | c Aymes b Connor | 7 |
| R.J.Blakey + | b Udal | 24 |
| K.Sharp | c Wood b James | 41 |
| P.E.Robinson | run out | 15 |
| D.Byas | lbw b James | 2 |
| P.J.Hartley | b Aqib Javed | 8 |
| P.W.Jarvis | st Aymes b Ayling | 4 |
| A.Sidebottom | not out | 7 |
| S.D.Fletcher | b Aqib Javed | 1 |
| M.A.Robinson | not out | 2 |
| Extras | (lb 18,w 4) | 22 |
| TOTAL | (39 overs)(for 9 wkts) | 148 |

| YORKSHIRE | O | M | R | W | FALL OF WICKETS | | |
|---|---|---|---|---|---|---|---|
| | | | | | | HAM | YOR |
| Jarvis | 7 | 2 | 27 | 0 | | | |
| Sidebottom | 8 | 0 | 42 | 1 | 1st | 40 | 27 |
| Robinson M.A. | 8 | 0 | 45 | 0 | 2nd | 142 | 31 |
| Hartley | 8 | 0 | 36 | 2 | 3rd | 160 | 78 |
| Fletcher | 8 | 0 | 44 | 1 | 4th | 190 | 102 |
| | | | | | 5th | | 120 |
| HAMPSHIRE | O | M | R | W | 6th | | 123 |
| James | 8 | 0 | 24 | 3 | 7th | | 129 |
| Aqib Javed | 8 | 0 | 21 | 2 | 8th | | 137 |
| Connor | 7 | 0 | 25 | 1 | 9th | | 139 |
| Ayling | 8 | 0 | 33 | 1 | 10th | | |
| Udal | 8 | 0 | 27 | 1 | | | |

## LEICESTERSHIRE vs. DERBYSHIRE

at Leicester on 21st April 1991
Toss : Leicestershire. Umpires : B.Leadbeater and R.Palmer
Derby won on faster scoring rate. Leics 0 pts, Derby 4 pts

### DERBYSHIRE

| | | |
|---|---|---|
| K.J.Barnett * | c Mullally b Potter | 46 |
| P.D.Bowler + | c Willey b Mullally | 77 |
| J.E.Morris | c Whitaker b Wilkinson | 26 |
| M.Azharuddin | run out | 11 |
| B.Roberts | c Maguire b Mullally | 0 |
| T.J.G.O'Gorman | not out | 10 |
| C.J.Adams | not out | 4 |
| D.E.Malcolm | | |
| S.J.Base | | |
| M.Jean-Jacques | | |
| O.H.Mortensen | | |
| Extras | (lb 8,w 1) | 9 |
| TOTAL | (36.3 overs)(for 5 wkts) | 183 |

### LEICESTERSHIRE

| | | |
|---|---|---|
| T.J.Boon | lbw b Mortensen | 22 |
| N.E.Briers * | c Azharuddin b Mortensen | 21 |
| J.J.Whitaker | c Barnett b Malcolm | 22 |
| C.C.Lewis | c Bowler b Malcolm | 1 |
| L.Potter | run out | 12 |
| P.Willey | c Barnett b Base | 1 |
| J.D.R.Benson | c Barnett b Base | 0 |
| P.Whitticase + | not out | 0 |
| C.Wilkinson | not out | 3 |
| J.N.Maguire | | |
| A.D.Mullally | | |
| Extras | (b 1,lb 6,w 11) | 18 |
| TOTAL | (20 overs)(for 7 wkts) | 100 |

| LEICS | O | M | R | W | FALL OF WICKETS | | |
|---|---|---|---|---|---|---|---|
| | | | | | | DER | LEI |
| Lewis | 6.3 | 0 | 21 | 0 | | | |
| Mullally | 8 | 0 | 31 | 2 | 1st | 102 | 51 |
| Maguire | 6 | 0 | 25 | 0 | 2nd | 147 | 51 |
| Wilkinson | 6 | 0 | 28 | 1 | 3rd | 166 | 55 |
| Willey | 6 | 0 | 33 | 0 | 4th | 167 | 86 |
| Potter | 4 | 0 | 37 | 1 | 5th | 172 | 87 |
| | | | | | 6th | | 90 |
| DERBYSHIRE | O | M | R | W | 7th | | 95 |
| Mortensen | 8 | 0 | 36 | 2 | 8th | | |
| Jean-Jacques | 2 | 0 | 13 | 0 | 9th | | |
| Malcolm | 8 | 0 | 39 | 2 | 10th | | |
| Base | 2 | 0 | 5 | 2 | | | |

## GLOUCS vs. MIDDLESEX

at Bristol on 21st April 1991
Toss : Middlesex. Umpires : J.H.Harris and K.J.Lyons
Middlesex won by 80 runs. Gloucs 0 pts, Middlesex 4 pts

### MIDDLESEX

| | | |
|---|---|---|
| M.W.Gatting * | run out | 111 |
| M.A.Roseberry | c Wright b Babington | 2 |
| M.R.Ramprakash | not out | 111 |
| K.R.Brown | not out | 8 |
| P.R.Downton + | | |
| J.E.Emburey | | |
| N.F.Williams | | |
| P.N.Weekes | | |
| D.W.Headley | | |
| C.W.Taylor | | |
| N.G.Cowans | | |
| Extras | (lb 6,nb 1) | 7 |
| TOTAL | (40 overs)(for 2 wkts) | 239 |

### GLOUCS

| | | |
|---|---|---|
| R.J.Scott | c Downton b Taylor | 44 |
| C.W.J.Athey | run out | 1 |
| A.J.Wright * | c Roseberry b Williams | 1 |
| M.W.Alleyne | st Downton b Emburey | 48 |
| J.W.Lloyds | c Taylor b Emburey | 11 |
| P.W.Romaines | st Downton b Emburey | 13 |
| R.C.Russell + | b Cowans | 12 |
| D.V.Lawrence | c Williams b Cowans | 9 |
| D.R.Gilbert | c Weekes b Emburey | 0 |
| A.M.Smith | not out | 0 |
| A.M.Babington | c Ramprakash b Cowans | 6 |
| Extras | (lb 3,w 10,nb 1) | 14 |
| TOTAL | (32.5 overs) | 159 |

| GLOUCS | O | M | R | W | FALL OF WICKETS | | |
|---|---|---|---|---|---|---|---|
| | | | | | | MID | GLO |
| Gilbert | 8 | 0 | 47 | 0 | | | |
| Babington | 8 | 0 | 33 | 1 | 1st | 10 | 15 |
| Lawrence | 8 | 0 | 52 | 0 | 2nd | 204 | 26 |
| Smith | 6 | 0 | 36 | 0 | 3rd | | 82 |
| Scott | 4 | 0 | 23 | 0 | 4th | | 116 |
| Alleyne | 6 | 0 | 42 | 0 | 5th | | 116 |
| | | | | | 6th | | 141 |
| MIDDLESEX | O | M | R | W | 7th | | 148 |
| Williams | 7 | 1 | 26 | 1 | 8th | | 148 |
| Cowans | 6.5 | 0 | 33 | 3 | 9th | | 152 |
| Emburey | 7 | 0 | 39 | 4 | 10th | | 159 |
| Headley | 8 | 0 | 38 | 0 | | | |
| Taylor | 4 | 0 | 20 | 1 | | | |

## LANCASHIRE vs. NOTTS

at Old Trafford on 21st April 1991
Toss : Notts. Umpires : J.C.Balderstone and J.D.Bond
Notts won by 9 wickets. Lancashire 0 pts, Notts 4 pts

### LANCASHIRE

| | | |
|---|---|---|
| G.D.Mendis | c Robinson b Crawley | 34 |
| G.Fowler | c French b Evans | 36 |
| M.A.Atherton | c Johnson b Hemmings | 45 |
| N.H.Fairbrother * | run out | 4 |
| G.D.Lloyd | lbw b Hemmings | 2 |
| M.Watkinson | c Broad b Stephenson | 25 |
| Wasim Akram | c Hemmings b Stephenson | 12 |
| P.A.J.DeFreitas | b Evans | 7 |
| W.K.Hegg + | c Johnson b Evans | 7 |
| I.D.Austin | not out | 4 |
| P.J.W.Allott | not out | 1 |
| Extras | (lb 2,w 6,nb 1) | 9 |
| TOTAL | (40 overs)(for 9 wkts) | 186 |

### NOTTS

| | | |
|---|---|---|
| B.C.Broad | not out | 100 |
| D.W.Randall | c Atherton b Allott | 49 |
| R.T.Robinson * | not out | 29 |
| P.Johnson | | |
| M.A.Crawley | | |
| M.Saxelby | | |
| K.P.Evans | | |
| F.D.Stephenson | | |
| B.N.French + | | |
| E.E.Hemmings | | |
| K.E.Cooper | | |
| Extras | (lb 6,w 1,nb 5) | 12 |
| TOTAL | (37.5 overs)(for 1 wkt) | 190 |

| NOTTS | O | M | R | W | FALL OF WICKETS | | |
|---|---|---|---|---|---|---|---|
| | | | | | | LAN | NOT |
| Stephenson | 8 | 0 | 41 | 2 | | | |
| Cooper | 5 | 0 | 19 | 0 | 1st | 60 | 106 |
| Saxelby | 8 | 0 | 37 | 0 | 2nd | 90 | |
| Evans | 7 | 0 | 46 | 3 | 3rd | 105 | |
| Crawley | 4 | 0 | 20 | 1 | 4th | 116 | |
| Hemmings | 8 | 1 | 21 | 2 | 5th | 137 | |
| | | | | | 6th | 158 | |
| LANCASHIRE | O | M | R | W | 7th | 173 | |
| Allott | 8 | 0 | 30 | 1 | 8th | 176 | |
| DeFreitas | 8 | 1 | 30 | 0 | 9th | 183 | |
| Watkinson | 8 | 0 | 40 | 0 | 10th | | |
| Wasim Akram | 6.5 | 0 | 54 | 0 | | | |
| Austin | 7 | 0 | 30 | 0 | | | |

## SURREY vs. SOMERSET

at The Oval on 21st April 1991
Toss : Somerset. Umpires : D.J.Constant and M.J.Kitchen
Som won on faster scoring rate. Surrey 0 pts, Som 4 pts

### SURREY

| | | |
|---|---|---|
| A.J.Stewart + | c Tavare b Rose | 14 |
| A.D.Brown | run out | 3 |
| G.P.Thorpe | c Hayhurst b Beal | 8 |
| D.M.Ward | b Lefebvre | 51 |
| M.A.Lynch | c Burns b Rose | 9 |
| J.D.Robinson | not out | 55 |
| I.A.Greig * | c Burns b Beal | 30 |
| C.K.Bullen | not out | 2 |
| M.P.Bicknell | | |
| Waqar Younis | | |
| A.J.Murphy | | |
| Extras | (lb 7,w 6,nb 4) | 17 |
| TOTAL | (40 overs)(for 6 wkts) | 189 |

### SOMERSET

| | | |
|---|---|---|
| S.J.Cook | b Waqar Younis | 31 |
| R.J.Bartlett | c Stewart b Waqar Younis | 34 |
| C.J.Tavare * | c Stewart b Thorpe | 0 |
| R.J.Harden | c Robinson b Thorpe | 2 |
| G.D.Rose | b Thorpe | 2 |
| A.N.Hayhurst | c Stewart b Waqar Younis | 1 |
| N.D.Burns + | b Waqar Younis | 5 |
| R.P.Lefebvre | not out | 15 |
| N.A.Mallender | run out | 0 |
| D.A.Graveney | not out | 4 |
| D.Beal | | |
| Extras | (b 1,lb 7,w 2) | 10 |
| TOTAL | (21.4 overs)(for 8 wkts) | 104 |

| SOMERSET | O | M | R | W | FALL OF WICKETS | | |
|---|---|---|---|---|---|---|---|
| | | | | | | SUR | SOM |
| Mallender | 8 | 0 | 38 | 0 | | | |
| Lefebvre | 8 | 0 | 27 | 1 | 1st | 6 | 73 |
| Rose | 8 | 0 | 30 | 2 | 2nd | 28 | 74 |
| Beal | 8 | 0 | 40 | 2 | 3rd | 30 | 76 |
| Hayhurst | 8 | 0 | 47 | 0 | 4th | 69 | 79 |
| | | | | | 5th | 129 | 84 |
| SURREY | O | M | R | W | 6th | 180 | 84 |
| Bicknell | 4 | 0 | 24 | 0 | 7th | | 85 |
| Murphy | 6 | 0 | 21 | 0 | 8th | | 85 |
| Waqar Younis | 7.4 | 0 | 30 | 4 | 9th | | |
| Thorpe | 4 | 0 | 21 | 3 | 10th | | |

# REFUGE ASSURANCE LEAGUE

## WARWICKSHIRE vs. SUSSEX

at Edgbaston on 21st April 1991
Toss : Sussex. Umpires : J.H.Hampshire and B.Hassan
Warwicks won by 21 runs. Warwicks 4 pts, Sussex 0 pts

**WARWICKSHIRE**

| | | |
|---|---|---|
| D.A.Reeve | c Dodemaide b Jones | 10 |
| Asif Din | c North b Pigott | 3 |
| P.A.Smith | c Smith b Pigott | 44 |
| D.P.Ostler | b Pigott | 15 |
| N.M.K.Smith | c & b Jones | 1 |
| T.A.Lloyd * | not out | 7 |
| R.G.Twose | not out | 0 |
| P.C.L.Holloway + | | |
| G.C.Small | | |
| A.A.Donald | | |
| T.A.Munton | | |
| Extras | (lb 3,w 6) | 9 |
| TOTAL | (10 overs)(for 5 wkts) | 89 |

**SUSSEX**

| | | |
|---|---|---|
| N.J.Lenham | c & b Donald | 3 |
| D.M.Smith | c Ostler b Smith N.M.K. | 23 |
| I.J.Gould + | run out | 21 |
| A.P.Wells * | run out | 8 |
| A.C.S.Pigott | c Twose b Donald | 5 |
| J.A.North | not out | 1 |
| K.Greenfield | | |
| A.I.C.Dodemaide | | |
| E.S.H.Giddins | | |
| I.D.K.Salisbury | | |
| A.N.Jones | | |
| Extras | (lb 5,w 2) | 7 |
| TOTAL | (10 overs)(for 5 wkts) | 68 |

| SUSSEX | O | M | R | W | FALL OF WICKETS | | |
|---|---|---|---|---|---|---|---|
| | | | | | | WAR | SUS |
| North | 1 | 0 | 12 | 0 | | | |
| Jones | 2 | 0 | 13 | 2 | 1st | 14 | 4 |
| Pigott | 2 | 0 | 11 | 3 | 2nd | 18 | 49 |
| Giddins | 2 | 0 | 19 | 0 | 3rd | 76 | 54 |
| Dodemaide | 2 | 0 | 20 | 0 | 4th | 82 | 67 |
| Salisbury | 1 | 0 | 11 | 0 | 5th | 82 | 68 |
| | | | | | 6th | | |
| WARWICKS | O | M | R | W | 7th | | |
| Donald | 2 | 0 | 7 | 2 | 8th | | |
| Munton | 2 | 0 | 16 | 0 | 9th | | |
| Small | 2 | 0 | 8 | 0 | 10th | | |
| Smith N.M.K. | 2 | 0 | 14 | 1 | | | |
| Reeve | 2 | 0 | 18 | 0 | | | |

## WORCESTERSHIRE vs. KENT

at Worcester on 21st April 1991
Toss : Kent. Umpires : B.J.Meyer and R.C.Tolchard
Worcs won on faster scoring rate. Worcs 4 pts, Kent 0 pts

**WORCESTERSHIRE**

| | | |
|---|---|---|
| T.S.Curtis | c Davis b Igglesden | 70 |
| T.M.Moody | b Igglesden | 160 |
| G.A.Hick | c Davis b Igglesden | 8 |
| I.T.Botham | b Igglesden | 20 |
| D.B.D'Oliveira | not out | 9 |
| P.A.Neale * | not out | 5 |
| M.J.Weston | | |
| S.J.Rhodes + | | |
| R.K.Illingworth | | |
| S.R.Lampitt | | |
| N.V.Radford | | |
| Extras | (b 1,lb 5,w 5) | 11 |
| TOTAL | (40 overs)(for 4 wkts) | 283 |

**KENT**

| | | |
|---|---|---|
| N.R.Taylor | c Weston b Botham | 62 |
| M.R.Benson * | lbw b Radford | 12 |
| T.R.Ward | c Curtis b Botham | 40 |
| G.R.Cowdrey | c Radford b Lampitt | 0 |
| C.S.Cowdrey | c Neale b Botham | 24 |
| M.V.Fleming | b Lampitt | 26 |
| S.A.Marsh + | c Hick b Radford | 27 |
| R.M.Ellison | not out | 12 |
| R.P.Davis | lbw b Radford | 7 |
| T.A.Merrick | run out | 1 |
| A.P.Igglesden | c D'Oliveira b Moody | 1 |
| Extras | (b 2,lb 10,w 6) | 18 |
| TOTAL | (38 overs) | 230 |

| KENT | O | M | R | W | FALL OF WICKETS | | |
|---|---|---|---|---|---|---|---|
| | | | | | | WOR | KEN |
| Igglesden | 8 | 0 | 59 | 4 | | | |
| Ellison | 8 | 0 | 47 | 0 | 1st | 198 | 25 |
| Merrick | 8 | 1 | 38 | 0 | 2nd | 242 | 99 |
| Fleming | 8 | 0 | 56 | 0 | 3rd | 256 | 103 |
| Davis | 5 | 0 | 40 | 0 | 4th | 273 | 137 |
| Cowdrey C.S. | 3 | 0 | 37 | 0 | 5th | | 164 |
| | | | | | 6th | | 208 |
| WORCS | O | M | R | W | 7th | | 210 |
| Radford | 8 | 0 | 46 | 3 | 8th | | 225 |
| Weston | 6 | 0 | 26 | 0 | 9th | | 227 |
| Illingworth | 3 | 0 | 32 | 0 | 10th | | 230 |
| Lampitt | 8 | 0 | 42 | 2 | | | |
| Botham | 8 | 0 | 34 | 3 | | | |
| Moody | 5 | 0 | 38 | 1 | | | |

## HEADLINES

### Refuge Assurance League

### 21st April

• Australian Tom Moody produced the day's most outstanding performance, hitting 160, his first Sunday League century, in his first innings for Worcestershire in county cricket in their convincing victory over Kent. He completely overshadowed Tim Curtis, who helped him add 198 for the first wicket, Graeme Hick and Ian Botham. The Worcestershire first four must now look a forbidding sight to opposition bowlers, so congratulations to Alan Igglesden for dismissing all four.

• Mike Gatting and Mark Ramprakash shared an exhilarating second-wicket stand of 194 in Middlesex's victory over Gloucestershire at Bristol, Gatting hitting his fifth Sunday hundred and his young partner, looking to move closer to England selection, his second. Two of John Emburey's four wickets were stumpings as the home side could reach only 159.

• Lancashire, the most formidable one-day side in the country in recent seasons, were comprehensively outplayed by Nottinghamshire at Old Trafford, Chris Broad scoring his fourth Sunday League 100 in a convincing nine-wicket victory.

• Defending champions Derbyshire almost suffered a similar fate in a rain-affected match at Leicester, but Leicestershire, requiring only 101 in 20 overs for victory, were just contained by the accuracy of Ole Mortensen and Devon Malcolm.

• Somerset gained a narrow victory over Surrey at The Oval on faster scoring rate after withstanding a devastating spell from Waqar Younis which saw the visitors collapse from 73 for no wicket to 83 for eight. Jonathan Robinson had earlier made his first Sunday fifty.

• Northamptonshire only beat Glamorgan at Cardiff by reaching a reduced target with a last-wicket stand of 16 between Richard Williams and Paul Taylor after Steve Watkin and Steve Barwick had given Glamorgan the advantage with three wickets apiece.

• Hampshire also won by virtue of superior run-rate, but their victory over Yorkshire at Southampton was more clearcut, Chris Smith hitting 86 and David Gower 45 as they added 102 for the second wicket and Kevan James marking his return to fitness with three for 24.

• The day's other winners were Warwickshire who beat Sussex by 21 runs at Edgbaston in a 10-over match.

# BENSON & HEDGES CUP

## GLOUCS vs. COMBINED U
at Bristol on 23rd April 1991
Toss : Gloucs. Umpires : G.I.Burgess and K.J.Lyons
Gloucs won by 66 runs. Gloucs 2 pts, Combined U 0 pts
Man of the match: D.V.Lawrence

### GLOUCS
| | | |
|---|---|---|
| G.D.Hodgson | c Knight b Hallett | 7 |
| R.J.Scott | c Holloway b MacDonald | 29 |
| A.J.Wright * | c Crawley b MacDonald | 13 |
| C.W.J.Athey | c Holloway b MacDonald | 0 |
| M.W.Alleyne | b MacDonald | 6 |
| J.W.Lloyds | c Knight b Turner | 19 |
| R.C.Russell + | c Jenkins b Turner | 25 |
| D.V.Lawrence | c Knight b MacDonald | 23 |
| D.R.Gilbert | c Holloway b MacDonald | 1 |
| A.M.Smith | run out | 8 |
| A.M.Babington | not out | 1 |
| Extras | (b 3,lb 4,w 9,nb 1) | 17 |
| TOTAL | (50.5 overs) | 149 |

### COMBINED U
| | | |
|---|---|---|
| R.E.Morris | c Lloyds b Lawrence | 19 |
| N.V.Knight * | c Alleyne b Lawrence | 36 |
| J.P.Crawley | b Lawrence | 0 |
| J.I.Longley | lbw b Lawrence | 1 |
| G.J.Turner | c Russell b Gilbert | 8 |
| P.C.L.Holloway + | b Lawrence | 0 |
| P.J.Rendell | b Lawrence | 0 |
| R.MacDonald | c Smith b Lloyds | 5 |
| J.C.Hallett | b Lloyds | 0 |
| A.R.Hansford | b Lloyds | 0 |
| R.H.J.Jenkins | not out | 0 |
| Extras | (lb 4,w 6,nb 4) | 14 |
| TOTAL | (38 overs) | 83 |

| COMBINED U | O | M | R | W | | FALL OF WICKETS | |
|---|---|---|---|---|---|---|---|
| | | | | | | GLO | COM |
| Hansford | 8.5 | 1 | 21 | 0 | | | |
| Hallett | 11 | 0 | 32 | 1 | 1st | 13 | 50 |
| MacDonald | 10 | 1 | 36 | 6 | 2nd | 49 | 53 |
| Jenkins | 11 | 1 | 35 | 0 | 3rd | 50 | 60 |
| Turner | 10 | 2 | 18 | 2 | 4th | 59 | 67 |
| | | | | | 5th | 66 | 69 |
| GLOUCS | O | M | R | W | 6th | 96 | 69 |
| Gilbert | 11 | 2 | 34 | 1 | 7th | 132 | 76 |
| Lawrence | 11 | 3 | 20 | 6 | 8th | 133 | 80 |
| Babington | 7 | 3 | 11 | 0 | 9th | 141 | 80 |
| Lloyds | 9 | 2 | 14 | 3 | 10th | 149 | 83 |

## SOMERSET vs. MIDDLESEX
at Taunton on 23rd April 1991
Toss : Middlesex. Umpires : K.E.Palmer and D.R.Shepherd
Middlesex won by 8 wickets. Somerset 0 pts, Middx 2 pts
Man of the match: M.W.Gatting

### SOMERSET
| | | |
|---|---|---|
| S.J.Cook | b Emburey | 41 |
| P.M.Roebuck | run out | 61 |
| R.J.Harden | c Ramprakash b Emburey | 3 |
| G.D.Rose | c Downton b Williams | 11 |
| C.J.Tavare * | c Downton b Tufnell | 1 |
| A.N.Hayhurst | c Downton b Cowans | 32 |
| N.D.Burns + | c Tufnell b Cowans | 37 |
| R.P.Lefebvre | st Downton b Emburey | 5 |
| N.A.Mallender | c Cowans b Emburey | 1 |
| D.A.Graveney | not out | 3 |
| D.Beal | b Emburey | 1 |
| Extras | (b 1,lb 6,w 4,nb 1) | 12 |
| TOTAL | (55 overs) | 208 |

### MIDDLESEX
| | | |
|---|---|---|
| M.W.Gatting * | b Beal | 112 |
| J.C.Pooley | b Mallender | 2 |
| M.R.Ramprakash | not out | 78 |
| K.R.Brown | not out | 0 |
| M.A.Roseberry | | |
| P.R.Downton + | | |
| J.E.Emburey | | |
| N.F.Williams | | |
| D.W.Headley | | |
| P.C.R.Tufnell | | |
| N.G.Cowans | | |
| Extras | (lb 10,w 3,nb 5) | 18 |
| TOTAL | (45.1 overs)(for 2 wkts) | 210 |

| MIDDLESEX | O | M | R | W | | FALL OF WICKETS | |
|---|---|---|---|---|---|---|---|
| | | | | | | SOM | MID |
| Williams | 11 | 0 | 26 | 1 | | | |
| Cowans | 11 | 1 | 49 | 2 | 1st | 101 | 8 |
| Headley | 11 | 2 | 48 | 0 | 2nd | 107 | 206 |
| Tufnell | 11 | 0 | 41 | 1 | 3rd | 116 | |
| Emburey | 11 | 0 | 37 | 5 | 4th | 123 | |
| | | | | | 5th | 127 | |
| SOMERSET | O | M | R | W | 6th | 187 | |
| Mallender | 10 | 2 | 45 | 1 | 7th | 200 | |
| Lefebvre | 8 | 2 | 22 | 0 | 8th | 204 | |
| Beal | 8 | 1 | 51 | 1 | 9th | 206 | |
| Rose | 7 | 0 | 31 | 0 | 10th | 208 | |
| Graveney | 7 | 0 | 33 | 0 | | | |
| Hayhurst | 5.1 | 0 | 18 | 0 | | | |

## SURREY vs. ESSEX
at The Oval on 23rd, 24th April 1991
Toss : Surrey. Umpires : J.C.Balderstone and J.H.Harris
Essex won by 53 runs. Surrey 0 pts, Essex 2 pts
Man of the match: Salim Malik

### ESSEX
| | | |
|---|---|---|
| G.A.Gooch * | c Greig b Feltham | 34 |
| J.P.Stephenson | c & b Bullen | 73 |
| P.J.Prichard | c & b Feltham | 10 |
| Salim Malik | not out | 90 |
| N.Hussain | c Stewart b Bicknell M.P. | 1 |
| D.R.Pringle | run out | 25 |
| N.Shahid | run out | 8 |
| M.A.Garnham + | not out | 6 |
| N.A.Foster | | |
| M.C.Ilott | | |
| P.M.Such | | |
| Extras | (lb 7,w 7) | 14 |
| TOTAL | (55 overs)(for 6 wkts) | 261 |

### SURREY
| | | |
|---|---|---|
| D.J.Bicknell | lbw b Such | 43 |
| G.P.Thorpe | c Pringle b Ilott | 3 |
| A.J.Stewart + | c Prichard b Such | 30 |
| D.M.Ward | b Ilott | 41 |
| M.A.Lynch | lbw b Pringle | 0 |
| I.A.Greig * | c Stephenson b Gooch | 47 |
| M.A.Feltham | c Gooch b Foster | 4 |
| C.K.Bullen | c Stephenson b Salim Malik | 16 |
| M.P.Bicknell | c Stephenson b Ilott | 6 |
| Waqar Younis | not out | 5 |
| A.J.Murphy | not out | 0 |
| Extras | (lb 6,w 7) | 13 |
| TOTAL | (55 overs)(for 9 wkts) | 208 |

| SURREY | O | M | R | W | | FALL OF WICKETS | |
|---|---|---|---|---|---|---|---|
| | | | | | | ESS | SUR |
| Waqar Younis | 11 | 0 | 63 | 0 | | | |
| Bicknell M.P. | 11 | 0 | 55 | 1 | 1st | 82 | 13 |
| Murphy | 11 | 1 | 46 | 0 | 2nd | 96 | 67 |
| Feltham | 11 | 1 | 45 | 2 | 3rd | 160 | 91 |
| Thorpe | 4 | 0 | 16 | 0 | 4th | 161 | 92 |
| Bullen | 7 | 0 | 29 | 1 | 5th | 212 | 172 |
| | | | | | 6th | 237 | 177 |
| ESSEX | O | M | R | W | 7th | | 177 |
| Foster | 11 | 3 | 26 | 1 | 8th | | 193 |
| Ilott | 11 | 3 | 34 | 3 | 9th | | 208 |
| Gooch | 9 | 0 | 52 | 1 | 10th | | |
| Such | 11 | 1 | 52 | 2 | | | |
| Pringle | 9 | 0 | 25 | 1 | | | |
| Stephenson | 2 | 0 | 6 | 0 | | | |
| Salim Malik | 2 | 0 | 7 | 1 | | | |

## DERBYSHIRE vs. NORTHANTS
at Derby on 23rd April 1991
Toss : Derby. Umpires : H.D.Bird and B.Hassan
Northants won by 66 runs. Derby 0 pts, Northants 2 pts
Man of the match: J.G.Thomas

### NORTHANTS
| | | |
|---|---|---|
| A.Fordham | c Bowler b Mortensen | 1 |
| N.A.Felton | c Barnett b Base | 23 |
| R.J.Bailey | c Morris b Mortensen | 38 |
| A.J.Lamb * | c Azharuddin b Malcolm | 45 |
| D.J.Capel | c Roberts b Base | 3 |
| K.M.Curran | b Warner | 26 |
| R.G.Williams | c Azharuddin b Barnett | 22 |
| E.A.E.Baptiste | not out | 15 |
| J.G.Thomas | not out | 4 |
| D.Ripley + | | |
| J.P.Taylor | | |
| Extras | (b 1,lb 6,w 7) | 14 |
| TOTAL | (55 overs)(for 7 wkts) | 191 |

### DERBYSHIRE
| | | |
|---|---|---|
| K.J.Barnett * | c Ripley b Thomas | 6 |
| P.D.Bowler + | c Ripley b Thomas | 5 |
| J.E.Morris | c Felton b Thomas | 0 |
| M.Azharuddin | b Capel | 29 |
| B.Roberts | c Ripley b Thomas | 2 |
| T.J.G.O'Gorman | b Capel | 49 |
| C.J.Adams | b Taylor | 0 |
| A.E.Warner | c Bailey b Capel | 0 |
| D.E.Malcolm | c Williams b Thomas | 14 |
| S.J.Base | b Capel | 7 |
| O.H.Mortensen | not out | 4 |
| Extras | (lb 4,w 5) | 9 |
| TOTAL | (38.3 overs) | 125 |

| DERBYSHIRE | O | M | R | W | | FALL OF WICKETS | |
|---|---|---|---|---|---|---|---|
| | | | | | | NOR | DER |
| Mortensen | 11 | 5 | 16 | 2 | | | |
| Warner | 11 | 4 | 25 | 1 | 1st | 4 | 12 |
| Base | 11 | 0 | 40 | 2 | 2nd | 43 | 12 |
| Malcolm | 11 | 1 | 42 | 1 | 3rd | 93 | 13 |
| Roberts | 4 | 0 | 26 | 0 | 4th | 108 | 20 |
| Barnett | 7 | 1 | 35 | 1 | 5th | 134 | 96 |
| | | | | | 6th | 156 | 97 |
| NORTHANTS | O | M | R | W | 7th | 181 | 98 |
| Thomas | 9.3 | 1 | 29 | 5 | 8th | | 98 |
| Taylor | 11 | 3 | 14 | 1 | 9th | | 110 |
| Curran | 3 | 0 | 15 | 0 | 10th | | 125 |
| Capel | 11 | 1 | 37 | 4 | | | |
| Baptiste | 4 | 0 | 26 | 0 | | | |

## KENT vs. LEICESTERSHIRE
at Canterbury on 23rd April 1991
Toss : Leics. Umpires : M.J.Kitchen and D.O.Oslear
Kent won by 74 runs. Kent 2 pts, Leicestershire 0 pts
Man of the match: M.R.Benson

### KENT
| | | |
|---|---|---|
| N.R.Taylor | c Wilkinson b Lewis | 1 |
| M.R.Benson * | c Briers b Maguire | 76 |
| T.R.Ward | b Mullally | 87 |
| G.R.Cowdrey | not out | 70 |
| C.S.Cowdrey | b Lewis | 4 |
| M.V.Fleming | b Lewis | 8 |
| S.A.Marsh + | not out | 23 |
| R.M.Ellison | | |
| M.J.McCague | | |
| T.A.Merrick | | |
| A.P.Igglesden | | |
| Extras | (b 1,lb 10,w 15,nb 2) | 28 |
| TOTAL | (55 overs)(for 5 wkts) | 297 |

### LEICESTERSHIRE
| | | |
|---|---|---|
| L.Potter | c Cowdrey C.S. b Igglesden | 6 |
| N.E.Briers * | c Marsh b McCague | 12 |
| J.J.Whitaker | b Merrick | 100 |
| P.Willey | c Cowdrey G.R. b Fleming | 36 |
| C.C.Lewis | c Taylor b Fleming | 5 |
| J.D.R.Benson | b McCague | 27 |
| P.Whitticase + | c Marsh b Merrick | 2 |
| C.Wilkinson | not out | 9 |
| J.N.Maguire | c Taylor b Igglesden | 2 |
| A.D.Mullally | c & b Igglesden | 5 |
| T.J.Boon | absent hurt | |
| Extras | (lb 8,w 10,nb 1) | 19 |
| TOTAL | (54.5 overs) | 223 |

| LEICESTERSHIRE | O | M | R | W | | FALL OF WICKETS | |
|---|---|---|---|---|---|---|---|
| | | | | | | KEN | LEI |
| Lewis | 11 | 0 | 62 | 3 | | | |
| Mullally | 11 | 0 | 45 | 1 | 1st | 4 | 20 |
| Maguire | 11 | 3 | 59 | 1 | 2nd | 174 | 25 |
| Wilkinson | 11 | 0 | 58 | 0 | 3rd | 188 | 112 |
| Willey | 6 | 0 | 33 | 0 | 4th | 201 | 126 |
| Benson | 5 | 0 | 29 | 0 | 5th | 221 | 199 |
| | | | | | 6th | | 205 |
| KENT | O | M | R | W | 7th | | 207 |
| McCague | 11 | 1 | 53 | 2 | 8th | | 210 |
| Igglesden | 10.5 | 1 | 32 | 3 | 9th | | 223 |
| Ellison | 11 | 0 | 44 | 0 | 10th | | |
| Merrick | 11 | 2 | 34 | 2 | | | |
| Fleming | 11 | 0 | 52 | 2 | | | |

## SCOTLAND vs. LANCASHIRE
at Forfar on 23rd April 1991
Toss : Lancashire. Umpires : J.H.Hampshire and R.Julian
Lancs won by 7 wickets. Scotland 0 pts, Lancashire 2 pts
Man of the match: P.A.J.DeFreitas

### SCOTLAND
| | | |
|---|---|---|
| I.L.Philip | lbw b DeFreitas | 0 |
| B.M.W.Patterson | c Atherton b DeFreitas | 2 |
| G.Salmond | c Fairbrother b DeFreitas | 6 |
| G.N.Reifer | lbw b Watkinson | 25 |
| O.Henry * | c Hegg b Watkinson | 4 |
| A.B.Russell | c Hegg b DeFreitas | 31 |
| J.W.Govan | b Austin | 18 |
| D.J.Haggo + | not out | 22 |
| A.W.Bee | b Austin | 13 |
| D.Cowan | not out | 3 |
| J.D.Moir | | |
| Extras | (lb 9,w 21,nb 5) | 35 |
| TOTAL | (55 overs)(for 8 wkts) | 163 |

### LANCASHIRE
| | | |
|---|---|---|
| G.D.Mendis | c Philip b Cowan | 63 |
| G.Fowler | c Reifer b Govan | 45 |
| M.A.Atherton | c Haggo b Cowan | 10 |
| N.H.Fairbrother * | not out | 22 |
| M.Watkinson | not out | 15 |
| N.J.Speak | | |
| Wasim Akram | | |
| P.A.J.DeFreitas | | |
| W.K.Hegg + | | |
| I.D.Austin | | |
| P.J.W.Allott | | |
| Extras | (lb 1,w 8) | 9 |
| TOTAL | (46.2 overs)(for 3 wkts) | 164 |

| LANCASHIRE | O | M | R | W | | FALL OF WICKETS | |
|---|---|---|---|---|---|---|---|
| | | | | | | SCO | LAN |
| DeFreitas | 11 | 5 | 21 | 4 | | | |
| Allott | 11 | 3 | 21 | 0 | 1st | 0 | 97 |
| Wasim Akram | 11 | 0 | 32 | 0 | 2nd | 6 | 115 |
| Watkinson | 11 | 2 | 30 | 2 | 3rd | 9 | 132 |
| Austin | 11 | 0 | 50 | 2 | 4th | 43 | |
| | | | | | 5th | 68 | |
| SCOTLAND | O | M | R | W | 6th | 116 | |
| Bee | 4 | 0 | 18 | 0 | 7th | 123 | |
| Moir | 8 | 1 | 26 | 0 | 8th | 154 | |
| Reifer | 8.2 | 2 | 27 | 0 | 9th | | |
| Cowan | 9 | 0 | 47 | 2 | 10th | | |
| Govan | 11 | 4 | 26 | 1 | | | |
| Henry | 6 | 1 | 19 | 0 | | | |

# BENSON & HEDGES CUP

## MINOR COUNTIES vs. GLAMORGAN
at Trowbridge on 23rd April 1991
Toss : Min Counties. Umpires : B.Dudleston and B.J.Meyer
Glam won by 17 runs. Minor Counties 0 pts, Glam 2 pts
Man of the match: R.J.Shastri

**GLAMORGAN**

| | | |
|---|---|---|
| A.R.Butcher * | c Roberts b Greensword | 25 |
| H.Morris | c Fothergill b Taylor | 1 |
| R.J.Shastri | not out | 138 |
| M.P.Maynard | c Brown b Greensword | 7 |
| I.Smith | run out | 2 |
| G.C.Holmes | c Mack b Green | 34 |
| R.D.B.Croft | c Fothergill b Green | 0 |
| C.P.Metson + | b Taylor | 0 |
| S.L.Watkin | not out | 5 |
| S.R.Barwick | | |
| M.Frost | | |
| Extras | (b 4,lb 11,w 5,nb 1) | 21 |
| TOTAL | (55 overs)(for 7 wkts) | 233 |

**MINOR COUNTIES**

| | | |
|---|---|---|
| G.K.Brown | b Barwick | 2 |
| M.J.Roberts | c Shastri b Croft | 40 |
| N.A.Folland | c Barwick b Croft | 45 |
| J.D.Love | c Butcher b Watkin | 81 |
| S.G.Plumb | b Watkin | 23 |
| S.Greensword * | run out | 3 |
| A.R.Fothergill + | lbw b Frost | 0 |
| R.A.Evans | b Watkin | 5 |
| C.R.Green | not out | 0 |
| N.R.Taylor | not out | 1 |
| A.J.Mack | | |
| Extras | (lb 9,w 7) | 16 |
| TOTAL | (55 overs)(for 8 wkts) | 216 |

| MIN. COUNTIES | O | M | R | W | FALL OF WICKETS | GLA | MIN |
|---|---|---|---|---|---|---|---|
| Taylor | 11 | 4 | 33 | 2 | | | |
| Mack | 11 | 3 | 49 | 0 | 1st | 7 | 6 |
| Green | 10 | 0 | 55 | 2 | 2nd | 68 | 76 |
| Greensword | 11 | 3 | 31 | 2 | 3rd | 84 | 108 |
| Evans | 10 | 0 | 35 | 0 | 4th | 109 | 174 |
| Plumb | 2 | 0 | 15 | 0 | 5th | 190 | 180 |
| | | | | | 6th | 191 | 186 |
| GLAMORGAN | O | M | R | W | 7th | 202 | 215 |
| Watkin | 11 | 4 | 28 | 3 | 8th | | 215 |
| Frost | 11 | 1 | 45 | 1 | 9th | | |
| Barwick | 10 | 3 | 31 | 1 | 10th | | |
| Shastri | 11 | 1 | 36 | 0 | | | |
| Croft | 9 | 0 | 49 | 2 | | | |
| Smith | 3 | 0 | 18 | 0 | | | |

## HAMPSHIRE vs. NOTTS
at Southampton on 23rd April 1991
Toss : Notts. Umpires : R.Palmer and R.C.Tolchard
Hampshire won by 4 runs. Hampshire 2 pts, Notts 0 pts
Man of the match: C.L.Smith

**HAMPSHIRE**

| | | |
|---|---|---|
| T.C.Middleton | b Cooper | 60 |
| C.L.Smith | not out | 121 |
| D.I.Gower | c French b Hemmings | 5 |
| J.R.Wood | c Randall b Hemmings | 0 |
| M.C.J.Nicholas * | b Pick | 50 |
| J.R.Ayling | not out | 3 |
| K.D.James | | |
| A.N Aymes + | | |
| C.A.Connor | | |
| S.D.Udal | | |
| Aqib Javed | | |
| Extras | (lb 17,w 4,nb 4) | 25 |
| TOTAL | (55 overs)(for 4 wkts) | 264 |

**NOTTS**

| | | |
|---|---|---|
| B.C.Broad | b Connor | 8 |
| M.Newell | c Wood b Udal | 18 |
| R.T.Robinson * | st Aymes b Ayling | 54 |
| P.Johnson | c Middleton b Ayling | 24 |
| D.W.Randall | c & b Connor | 5 |
| M.Saxelby | lbw b Udal | 32 |
| F.D.Stephenson | c Connor b Aqib Javed | 14 |
| B.N.French + | not out | 37 |
| E.E.Hemmings | c Connor b Udal | 9 |
| K.E.Cooper | run out | 0 |
| R.A.Pick | not out | 25 |
| Extras | (b 2,lb 14,w 17,nb 1) | 34 |
| TOTAL | (55 overs)(for 9 wkts) | 260 |

| NOTTS | O | M | R | W | FALL OF WICKETS | HAM | NOT |
|---|---|---|---|---|---|---|---|
| Stephenson | 11 | 0 | 56 | 0 | | | |
| Pick | 11 | 0 | 61 | 1 | 1st | 163 | 11 |
| Cooper | 11 | 2 | 42 | 1 | 2nd | 168 | 52 |
| Saxelby | 11 | 1 | 39 | 0 | 3rd | 168 | 116 |
| Hemmings | 11 | 0 | 49 | 2 | 4th | 257 | 126 |
| | | | | | 5th | | 135 |
| HAMPSHIRE | O | M | R | W | 6th | | 160 |
| Aqib Javed | 11 | 2 | 35 | 1 | 7th | | 194 |
| Connor | 11 | 1 | 50 | 2 | 8th | | 212 |
| James | 11 | 0 | 55 | 0 | 9th | | 216 |
| Udal | 11 | 1 | 48 | 3 | 10th | | |
| Ayling | 11 | 0 | 56 | 2 | | | |

## HEADLINES

### Benson & Hedges Cup

### 23rd - 24th April

•Bowlers held sway over the batsmen at Bristol where Gloucestershire beat the Combined Universities by 66 runs, after being given a fright by Rob MacDonald who returned the best figures by a Universities bowler in the history of the competition, but the students found David Lawrence an even more daunting proposition as he recorded his best B & H figures.

•Runs were little easier to come across at Derby, where Northamptonshire struggled to free themselves of the shackles imposed by the Derbyshire bowlers, then dismissed the home side for 125 as Greg Thomas, with career-best figures, and David Capel shared nine wickets.

•Middlesex enjoyed a comfortable eight-wicket victory over Somerset at Taunton after John Emburey achieved his best figures in the competiton to restrict Somerset to 208 and Mike Gatting, with his third B & H hundred, and Mark Ramprakash, with his highest score, added 198 for the second wicket.

•Salim Malik took the Gold Award in his first match in the competition after scoring an unbeaten 90 in Essex's 53-run victory over Surrey at The Oval. Mark Ilott also impressed with his best B & H figures.

•Kent made the highest total of the round (297 for five) against Leicestershire at Canterbury, Mark Benson and Trevor Ward sharing a second-wicket stand of 170 and Graham Cowdrey making a personal best. James Whitaker's first B & H century was to no avail as the home side were victors by 74 runs.

•1990 B & H winners Lancashire made a successful start to their defence of the trophy with a straightforward seven-wicket win over Scotland at Forfar, Phil DeFreitas taking four for 21 to restrict the Scots to 163 for eight.

•The closest contest came at Southampton where Hampshire defeated Nottinghamshire by four runs. Chris Smith, continuing his outstanding start to the season, and Tony Middleton opened with 163 for Hampshire, but it was only a last-wicket stand of 44 between Bruce French and Andy Pick that brought Notts close to their target.

•Minor Counties gave a good account of themselves at Trowbridge. Glamorgan were grateful for 138 not out from Ravi Shastri, his first B & H hundred, which took them to 233 for seven in their 55 overs. Then Jim Love hit 81 in his first match for Minor Counties to launch a spirited response.

# BENSON & HEDGES CUP

## WORCESTERSHIRE vs. GLOUCS

at Worcester on 25th, 26th April 1991
Toss : Worcestershire. Umpires : A.A.Jones and N.T.Plews
Worcestershire won by 6 wickets. Worcs 2 pts, Gloucs 0 pts
Man of the match: S.R.Lampitt

### GLOUCS

| | | |
|---|---|---|
| G.D.Hodgson | c D'Oliveira b Newport | 9 |
| R.J.Scott | c Curtis b Radford | 10 |
| A.J.Wright * | c Rhodes b Moody | 36 |
| C.W.J.Athey | c Hick b Lampitt | 5 |
| M.W.Alleyne | c Hick b Lampitt | 0 |
| J.W.Lloyds | c Lampitt b Moody | 24 |
| R.C.Russell + | c Newport b Radford | 51 |
| D.V.Lawrence | c Hick b Radford | 10 |
| D.R.Gilbert | c Curtis b Lampitt | 16 |
| A.M.Smith | not out | 3 |
| A.M.Babington | c Moody b Lampitt | 8 |
| Extras | (b 1,lb 9,w 8,nb 7) | 25 |
| TOTAL | (54.1 overs) | 197 |

### WORCESTERSHIRE

| | | |
|---|---|---|
| T.S.Curtis | c Russell b Smith | 36 |
| T.M.Moody | c Lloyds b Lawrence | 21 |
| G.A.Hick | b Lawrence | 56 |
| D.B.D'Oliveira | c Hodgson b Scott | 6 |
| P.A.Neale * | not out | 48 |
| I.T.Botham | not out | 18 |
| S.J.Rhodes + | | |
| P.J.Newport | | |
| R.K.Illingworth | | |
| S.R.Lampitt | | |
| N.V.Radford | | |
| Extras | (lb 9,w 1,nb 3) | 13 |
| TOTAL | (53.5 overs)(for 4 wkts) | 198 |

| WORCS | O | M | R | W | FALL OF WICKETS | | |
|---|---|---|---|---|---|---|---|
| | | | | | | GLO | WOR |
| Radford | 11 | 2 | 40 | 3 | 1st | 17 | 39 |
| Newport | 11 | 1 | 30 | 1 | 2nd | 32 | 105 |
| Lampitt | 10.1 | 2 | 46 | 4 | 3rd | 52 | 114 |
| Botham | 11 | 1 | 28 | 0 | 4th | 52 | 140 |
| Moody | 6 | 0 | 22 | 2 | 5th | 98 | |
| Illingworth | 5 | 0 | 21 | 0 | 6th | 120 | |
| | | | | | 7th | 145 | |
| GLOUCS | O | M | R | W | 8th | 181 | |
| Gilbert | 11 | 0 | 36 | 0 | 9th | 186 | |
| Lawrence | 11 | 3 | 35 | 2 | 10th | 197 | |
| Babington | 11 | 3 | 27 | 0 | | | |
| Smith | 11 | 2 | 30 | 1 | | | |
| Scott | 7.5 | 0 | 42 | 1 | | | |
| Alleyne | 2 | 0 | 19 | 0 | | | |

## MIDDLESEX vs. SURREY

at Lord's on 25th April 1991
Toss : Middlesex. Umpires : B.Dudleston and M.J.Kitchen
Surrey won by 75 runs. Middlesex 0 pts, Surrey 2 pts
Man of the match: A.J.Stewart

### SURREY

| | | |
|---|---|---|
| D.J.Bicknell | b Williams | 1 |
| M.A.Lynch | c Downton b Headley | 20 |
| A.J.Stewart + | c Emburey b Tufnell | 55 |
| D.M.Ward | run out | 46 |
| G.P.Thorpe | c Weekes b Tufnell | 40 |
| I.A.Greig * | b Cowans | 38 |
| J.D.Robinson | c Ramprakash b Cowans | 4 |
| M.P.Bicknell | b Cowans | 7 |
| J.Boiling | not out | 3 |
| Waqar Younis | c Brown b Tufnell | 3 |
| A.J.Murphy | | |
| Extras | (lb 9,w 6,nb 3) | 18 |
| TOTAL | (55 overs)(for 9 wkts) | 235 |

### MIDDLESEX

| | | |
|---|---|---|
| M.W.Gatting * | b Murphy | 34 |
| J.C.Pooley | b Waqar Younis | 8 |
| M.R.Ramprakash | c Robinson b Bicknell M.P. | 2 |
| K.R.Brown | c Bicknell D.J. b Boiling | 25 |
| P.N.Weekes | lbw b Murphy | 0 |
| P.R.Downton + | not out | 35 |
| J.E.Emburey | c Stewart b Bicknell M.P. | 9 |
| N.F.Williams | c Stewart b Bicknell M.P. | 6 |
| D.W.Headley | b Robinson | 26 |
| P.C.R.Tufnell | run out | 1 |
| N.G.Cowans | c Thorpe b Robinson | 5 |
| Extras | (lb 3,w 6) | 9 |
| TOTAL | (45.2 overs) | 160 |

| MIDDLESEX | O | M | R | W | FALL OF WICKETS | | |
|---|---|---|---|---|---|---|---|
| | | | | | | SUR | MID |
| Cowans | 11 | 1 | 42 | 3 | 1st | 10 | 26 |
| Williams | 11 | 2 | 37 | 1 | 2nd | 41 | 29 |
| Headley | 11 | 0 | 54 | 1 | 3rd | 113 | 55 |
| Emburey | 11 | 1 | 43 | 0 | 4th | 151 | 55 |
| Tufnell | 11 | 0 | 50 | 3 | 5th | 206 | 87 |
| | | | | | 6th | 215 | 102 |
| SURREY | O | M | R | W | 7th | 227 | 111 |
| Bicknell M.P. | 11 | 1 | 28 | 3 | 8th | 228 | 153 |
| Waqar Younis | 8 | 0 | 32 | 1 | 9th | 235 | 154 |
| Robinson | 8.2 | 1 | 31 | 2 | 10th | | 160 |
| Murphy | 9 | 2 | 23 | 2 | | | |
| Boiling | 9 | 0 | 43 | 1 | | | |

## COMBINED U vs. DERBYSHIRE

at The Parks on 25th April 1991
Toss : Derby. Umpires : J.H.Harris and P.B.Wight
Derby won by 206 runs. Combined U 0 pts, Derby 2 pts
Man of the match: P.D.Bowler

### DERBYSHIRE

| | | |
|---|---|---|
| K.J.Barnett * | c Hallett b Turner | 82 |
| P.D.Bowler + | c Rendell b Jenkins | 100 |
| J.E.Morris | c Knight b Rendell | 71 |
| M.Azharuddin | not out | 44 |
| D.E.Malcolm | b Hansford | 15 |
| A.E.Warner | not out | 35 |
| B.Roberts | | |
| T.J.G.O'Gorman | | |
| C.J.Adams | | |
| S.J.Base | | |
| O.H.Mortensen | | |
| Extras | (lb 4,w 4,nb 11) | 19 |
| TOTAL | (55 overs)(for 4 wkts) | 366 |

### COMBINED U

| | | |
|---|---|---|
| R.E.Morris | c Roberts b Mortensen | 12 |
| N.V.Knight * | b Mortensen | 5 |
| J.P.Crawley | c Adams b Malcolm | 18 |
| J.I.Longley | c Bowler b Malcolm | 6 |
| G.J.Turner | not out | 70 |
| P.C.L.Holloway + | c Azharuddin b Barnett | 27 |
| P.J.Rendell | c Bowler b Roberts | 8 |
| R.MacDonald | not out | 1 |
| J.C.Hallett | | |
| A.R.Hansford | | |
| R.H.J.Jenkins | | |
| Extras | (b 3,lb 3,w 6,nb 1) | 13 |
| TOTAL | (55 overs)(for 6 wkts) | 160 |

| COMBINED U | O | M | R | W | FALL OF WICKETS | | |
|---|---|---|---|---|---|---|---|
| | | | | | | DER | COM |
| Hansford | 11 | 2 | 55 | 1 | 1st | 177 | 19 |
| Hallett | 11 | 0 | 43 | 0 | 2nd | 233 | 20 |
| Turner | 11 | 0 | 61 | 1 | 3rd | 278 | 37 |
| MacDonald | 9 | 0 | 90 | 0 | 4th | 302 | 66 |
| Jenkins | 7 | 0 | 58 | 1 | 5th | | 121 |
| Rendell | 6 | 0 | 55 | 1 | 6th | | 147 |
| | | | | | 7th | | |
| DERBYSHIRE | O | M | R | W | 8th | | |
| Mortensen | 7 | 2 | 16 | 2 | 9th | | |
| Warner | 6 | 2 | 14 | 0 | 10th | | |
| Base | 5 | 0 | 24 | 0 | | | |
| Malcolm | 6 | 1 | 14 | 2 | | | |
| Azharuddin | 11 | 0 | 29 | 0 | | | |
| Barnett | 11 | 2 | 28 | 1 | | | |
| Morris | 4 | 0 | 14 | 0 | | | |
| Roberts | 3 | 1 | 11 | 1 | | | |
| Adams | 1 | 0 | 3 | 0 | | | |
| O'Gorman | 1 | 0 | 1 | 0 | | | |

## SUSSEX vs. LEICESTERSHIRE

at Hove on 25th April 1991
Toss : Leicestershire. Umpires : R.Palmer and R.C.Tolchard
Sussex won by 72 runs. Sussex 2 pts, Leicestershire 0 pts
Man of the match: P.W.G.Parker

### SUSSEX

| | | |
|---|---|---|
| D.M.Smith | c Briers b Willey | 76 |
| J.W.Hall | c Potter b Benson | 43 |
| P.W.G.Parker * | run out | 87 |
| A.P.Wells | not out | 23 |
| K.Greenfield | not out | 0 |
| A.I.C.Dodemaide | | |
| J.A.North | | |
| P.Moores + | | |
| A.C.S.Pigott | | |
| I.D.K.Salisbury | | |
| A.N.Jones | | |
| Extras | (b 2,lb 19,w 10,nb 3) | 34 |
| TOTAL | (55 overs)(for 3 wkts) | 263 |

### LEICESTERSHIRE

| | | |
|---|---|---|
| L.Potter | c Parker b Jones | 2 |
| N.E.Briers * | b Salisbury | 46 |
| J.J.Whitaker | c Moores b Jones | 2 |
| P.Willey | c Greenfield b Dodemaide | 4 |
| J.D.R.Benson | c & b Pigott | 3 |
| C.C.Lewis | c Moores b Jones | 8 |
| P.N.Hepworth | b Greenfield | 33 |
| P.Whitticase + | c Greenfield b North | 31 |
| J.N.Maguire | b Pigott | 35 |
| D.J.Millns | not out | 11 |
| A.D.Mullally | c Greenfield b Pigott | 1 |
| Extras | (lb 4,w 11) | 15 |
| TOTAL | (50.4 overs) | 191 |

| LEICS | O | M | R | W | FALL OF WICKETS | | |
|---|---|---|---|---|---|---|---|
| | | | | | | SUS | LEI |
| Lewis | 11 | 0 | 53 | 0 | 1st | 94 | 4 |
| Millns | 9 | 3 | 39 | 0 | 2nd | 202 | 19 |
| Maguire | 11 | 2 | 43 | 0 | 3rd | 260 | 37 |
| Mullally | 11 | 0 | 63 | 0 | 4th | | 40 |
| Willey | 11 | 1 | 34 | 1 | 5th | | 51 |
| Benson | 2 | 0 | 10 | 1 | 6th | | 111 |
| | | | | | 7th | | 111 |
| SUSSEX | O | M | R | W | 8th | | 157 |
| Jones | 9 | 0 | 33 | 3 | 9th | | 189 |
| Dodemaide | 7 | 3 | 17 | 1 | 10th | | 191 |
| Pigott | 8.4 | 2 | 29 | 3 | | | |
| Salisbury | 8 | 0 | 32 | 1 | | | |
| North | 10 | 0 | 41 | 1 | | | |
| Greenfield | 8 | 0 | 35 | 1 | | | |

## WARWICKSHIRE vs. ESSEX

at Edgbaston on 25th April 1991
Toss : Essex. Umpires : K.J.Lyons and B.J.Meyer
Essex won by 12 runs. Warwickshire 0 pts, Essex 2 pts
Man of the match: J.P.Stephenson

### ESSEX

| | | |
|---|---|---|
| G.A.Gooch * | c Moles b Munton | 26 |
| J.P.Stephenson | c Lloyd b Donald | 142 |
| P.J.Prichard | c Small b Moles | 38 |
| Salim Malik | b Donald | 72 |
| D.R.Pringle | not out | 9 |
| N.Hussain | not out | 2 |
| N.Shahid | | |
| M.A.Garnham + | | |
| N.A.Foster | | |
| T.D.Topley | | |
| P.M.Such | | |
| Extras | (b 6,lb 4,w 7,nb 1) | 18 |
| TOTAL | (55 overs)(for 4 wkts) | 307 |

### WARWICKSHIRE

| | | |
|---|---|---|
| A.J.Moles | c Hussain b Foster | 19 |
| Asif Din | lbw b Gooch | 34 |
| T.A.Lloyd * | c Salim Malik b Pringle | 58 |
| P.A.Smith | c Garnham b Gooch | 3 |
| D.A.Reeve | run out | 80 |
| D.P.Ostler | b Pringle | 45 |
| N.M.K.Smith | c Prichard b Pringle | 23 |
| M.Burns + | c Hussain b Foster | 3 |
| G.C.Small | c Such b Pringle | 2 |
| T.A.Munton | b Pringle | 6 |
| A.A.Donald | not out | 6 |
| Extras | (lb 9,w 6,nb 1) | 16 |
| TOTAL | (54.2 overs) | 295 |

| WARWICKS | O | M | R | W | FALL OF WICKETS | | |
|---|---|---|---|---|---|---|---|
| | | | | | | ESS | WAR |
| Donald | 11 | 0 | 78 | 2 | 1st | 44 | 24 |
| Small | 11 | 0 | 43 | 0 | 2nd | 114 | 87 |
| Reeve | 11 | 0 | 64 | 0 | 3rd | 294 | 99 |
| Munton | 11 | 0 | 40 | 1 | 4th | 295 | 159 |
| Smith N.M.K. | 4 | 0 | 32 | 0 | 5th | | 237 |
| Moles | 4 | 1 | 19 | 1 | 6th | | 268 |
| Smith P.A. | 3 | 0 | 21 | 0 | 7th | | 278 |
| | | | | | 8th | | 283 |
| ESSEX | O | M | R | W | 9th | | 283 |
| Pringle | 10.2 | 1 | 51 | 5 | 10th | | 295 |
| Foster | 11 | 0 | 52 | 2 | | | |
| Topley | 9 | 0 | 57 | 0 | | | |
| Such | 10 | 0 | 47 | 0 | | | |
| Gooch | 11 | 0 | 54 | 2 | | | |
| Stephenson | 3 | 0 | 25 | 0 | | | |

## NOTTS vs. YORKSHIRE

at Trent Bridge on 25th April 1991
Toss : Yorkshire. Umpires : D.J.Constant and B.Leadbeater
Notts won by 7 wickets. Notts 2 pts, Yorkshire 0 pts
Man of the match: F.D.Stephenson

### YORKSHIRE

| | | |
|---|---|---|
| M.D.Moxon * | b Stephenson | 95 |
| A.A.Metcalfe | b Evans | 20 |
| D.Byas | lbw b Stephenson | 47 |
| R.J.Blakey + | c Randall b Stephenson | 39 |
| P.E.Robinson | b Stephenson | 0 |
| K.Sharp | b Evans | 0 |
| P.Carrick | c French b Cooper | 2 |
| P.J.Hartley | c Johnson b Stephenson | 13 |
| P.W.Jarvis | not out | 3 |
| S.D.Fletcher | not out | 2 |
| M.A.Robinson | | |
| Extras | (lb 10,w 2,nb 1) | 13 |
| TOTAL | (55 overs)(for 8 wkts) | 234 |

### NOTTS

| | | |
|---|---|---|
| B.C.Broad | not out | 108 |
| D.W.Randall | c Blakey b Hartley | 86 |
| R.T.Robinson * | b Jarvis | 27 |
| P.Johnson | c Metcalfe b Robinson M.A. | 4 |
| M.A.Crawley | not out | 0 |
| M.Saxelby | | |
| K.P.Evans | | |
| F.D.Stephenson | | |
| B.N.French + | | |
| E.E.Hemmings | | |
| K.E.Cooper | | |
| Extras | (lb 5,w 5) | 10 |
| TOTAL | (54.2 overs)(for 3 wkts) | 235 |

| NOTTS | O | M | R | W | FALL OF WICKETS | | |
|---|---|---|---|---|---|---|---|
| | | | | | | YOR | NOT |
| Stephenson | 11 | 5 | 30 | 5 | 1st | 60 | 179 |
| Cooper | 10 | 2 | 27 | 1 | 2nd | 169 | 227 |
| Evans | 11 | 0 | 50 | 2 | 3rd | 176 | 232 |
| Saxelby | 6 | 0 | 43 | 0 | 4th | 178 | |
| Hemmings | 11 | 0 | 52 | 0 | 5th | 179 | |
| Crawley | 6 | 0 | 22 | 0 | 6th | 182 | |
| | | | | | 7th | 216 | |
| YORKSHIRE | O | M | R | W | 8th | 232 | |
| Jarvis | 10.2 | 2 | 34 | 1 | 9th | | |
| Robinson M.A. | 11 | 0 | 52 | 1 | 10th | | |
| Fletcher | 11 | 2 | 40 | 0 | | | |
| Hartley | 11 | 0 | 56 | 1 | | | |
| Carrick | 11 | 0 | 48 | 0 | | | |

# BENSON & HEDGES CUP

## LANCASHIRE vs. KENT

at Old Trafford on 25th April 1991
Toss : Kent. Umpires : J.H.Hampshire and R.Julian
Lancashire won by 6 wickets. Lancashire 2 pts, Kent 0 pts
Man of the match: P.A.J.DeFreitas

**KENT**

| | | |
|---|---|---|
| N.R.Taylor | b DeFreitas | 9 |
| M.R.Benson * | c Allott b DeFreitas | 4 |
| T.R.Ward | c Hegg b Allott | 1 |
| G.R.Cowdrey | c Mendis b Watkinson | 10 |
| C.S.Cowdrey | c Fairbrother b Allott | 0 |
| M.V.Fleming | c Fairbrother b Allott | 8 |
| S.A.Marsh + | c Mendis b DeFreitas | 71 |
| R.M.Ellison | c DeFreitas b Watkinson | 6 |
| M.J.McCague | c Mendis b Watkinson | 12 |
| T.A.Merrick | not out | 22 |
| A.P.Igglesden | c Yates b DeFreitas | 3 |
| Extras | (lb 6,w 11,nb 4) | 21 |
| TOTAL | (53.4 overs) | 167 |

**LANCASHIRE**

| | | |
|---|---|---|
| G.D.Mendis | b Merrick | 22 |
| G.Fowler | c Ward b McCague | 1 |
| M.A.Atherton | c Marsh b McCague | 22 |
| N.H.Fairbrother * | c Marsh b Ellison | 46 |
| M.Watkinson | not out | 22 |
| Wasim Akram | not out | 45 |
| P.A.J.DeFreitas | | |
| W.K.Hegg + | | |
| G.Yates | | |
| I.D.Austin | | |
| P.J.W.Allott | | |
| Extras | (lb 6,w 6) | 12 |
| TOTAL | (37.3 overs)(for 4 wkts) | 170 |

| LANCASHIRE | O | M | R | W | FALL OF WICKETS | | |
|---|---|---|---|---|---|---|---|
| | | | | | | KEN | LAN |
| DeFreitas | 10.4 | 3 | 15 | 4 | | | |
| Allott | 11 | 4 | 17 | 3 | 1st | 7 | 3 |
| Watkinson | 11 | 1 | 42 | 3 | 2nd | 14 | 31 |
| Wasim Akram | 11 | 1 | 49 | 0 | 3rd | 14 | 98 |
| Austin | 10 | 1 | 38 | 0 | 4th | 14 | 98 |
| | | | | | 5th | 26 | |
| KENT | O | M | R | W | 6th | 40 | |
| McCague | 7 | 1 | 32 | 2 | 7th | 57 | |
| Igglesden | 10 | 0 | 48 | 0 | 8th | 83 | |
| Merrick | 10 | 0 | 30 | 1 | 9th | 163 | |
| Ellison | 8 | 1 | 45 | 1 | 10th | 167 | |
| Fleming | 2.3 | 0 | 9 | 0 | | | |

## MINOR COUNTIES vs. HAMPSHIRE

at Trowbridge on 25th, 26th April 1991
Toss : Min Counties. Umpires : G.I.Burgess and J.W.Holder
Hants won by 8 wickets. Minor Counties 0 pts, Hants 2 pts
Man of the match: J.R.Wood

**MINOR COUNTIES**

| | | |
|---|---|---|
| G.K.Brown | st Aymes b Connor | 82 |
| M.J.Roberts | lbw b Aqib Javed | 4 |
| N.A.Folland | b Aqib Javed | 0 |
| J.D.Love | st Aymes b Bakker | 75 |
| S.G.Plumb | not out | 23 |
| A.R.Fothergill + | b Aqib Javed | 5 |
| R.A.Evans | not out | 5 |
| S.Greensword * | | |
| C.R.Green | | |
| N.R.Taylor | | |
| A.J.Mack | | |
| Extras | (b 4,lb 4,w 9,nb 3) | 20 |
| TOTAL | (55 overs)(for 5 wkts) | 214 |

**HAMPSHIRE**

| | | |
|---|---|---|
| T.C.Middleton | run out | 40 |
| C.L.Smith | not out | 78 |
| D.I.Gower | c Roberts b Greensword | 6 |
| J.R.Wood | not out | 70 |
| M.C.J.Nicholas * | | |
| J.R.Ayling | | |
| A.N Aymes + | | |
| C.A.Connor | | |
| S.D.Udal | | |
| Aqib Javed | | |
| P.J.Bakker | | |
| Extras | (lb 9,w 11,nb 1) | 21 |
| TOTAL | (49.5 overs)(for 2 wkts) | 215 |

| HAMPSHIRE | O | M | R | W | FALL OF WICKETS | | |
|---|---|---|---|---|---|---|---|
| | | | | | | MIN | HAM |
| Bakker | 11 | 3 | 21 | 1 | | | |
| Aqib Javed | 11 | 0 | 43 | 3 | 1st | 7 | 76 |
| Ayling | 11 | 0 | 28 | 0 | 2nd | 9 | 99 |
| Connor | 11 | 0 | 64 | 1 | 3rd | 163 | |
| Udal | 11 | 2 | 50 | 0 | 4th | 199 | |
| | | | | | 5th | 204 | |
| MIN.COUNTIES | O | M | R | W | 6th | | |
| Taylor | 9 | 2 | 41 | 0 | 7th | | |
| Green | 10.5 | 0 | 35 | 0 | 8th | | |
| Mack | 10 | 1 | 48 | 0 | 9th | | |
| Greensword | 11 | 2 | 35 | 1 | 10th | | |
| Evans | 9 | 1 | 47 | 0 | | | |

# HEADLINES

### Benson & Hedges Cup

### 25th April

• Derbyshire recorded the highest total in the 20 years of the Benson & Hedges Cup when they reached 366 for four against Combined Universities at The Parks. Kim Barnett and Peter Bowler, who hit his second B & H century, shared an opening stand of 177, which was quickly built upon by John Morris and Mohammad Azharuddin. Graeme Turner gained some consolation for the students with a career best 70* as all ten Derbyshire outfielders were given a bowl.

• Worcestershire moved to the top of Group A with their six-wicket win over Gloucestershire at Worcester, Stuart Lampitt returning career-best figures as Gloucestershire were bowled out for 197, even after Jack Russell had made his first fifty in B & H cricket.

• Essex achieved their second victory to head Group B when they had the better of a run-feast at Edgbaston. Essex's total reached 307 for four, John Stephenson hitting his highest B & H score and sharing a third wicket stand of 180 with Salim Malik, but so well did Warwickshire keep up the chase that Essex were certain of victory only when Dermot Reeve was run out for a career-best 80. Derek Pringle's figures of 5 for 51 were his best in the competition.

• Middlesex suffered their first defeat of the season at the hands of neighbours Surrey at Lord's when they found a target of 236 beyond them, their batting in the absence of Haynes and Roseberry dangerously over-reliant on the efforts of Gatting and Ramprakash.

• In Group C Lancashire gave another highly efficient display to defeat Kent by six wickets at Old Trafford. The seam bowling of DeFreitas, Allott and Watkinson proved irresistible as Kent lost their first eight wickets for 83, but a career-best 71 from Steve Marsh at least brought a measure of respectability to their total.

• Paul Parker made his highest score in the B & H Cup as Sussex defeated Leicestershire by 72 runs at Hove, the visitors losing their first five wickets for 51 as they chased a target of 264.

• Chris Smith passed the fifty mark for the fourth time in as many innings but he was outshone by Julian Wood who contributed 70 to a partnership of 116 to take Hampshire to the top of Group D with an eight-wicket win over Minor Counties at Trowbridge.

• Chris Broad, who scored his second one-day 100 of the season, and Derek Randall shared an opening stand of 177 to set Nottinghamshire well on the way to a seven-wicket victory over Yorkshire at Trent Bridge. Franklyn Stephenson had earlier produced his best B & H bowling figures.

# REFUGE ASSURANCE LEAGUE

## ESSEX vs. YORKSHIRE

at Chelmsford on 28th April 1991
Toss : Yorkshire. Umpires : K.J.Lyons and P.B.Wight
Essex won by 9 wickets. Essex 4 pts, Yorkshire 0 pts

### YORKSHIRE

| | | |
|---|---|---|
| M.D.Moxon * | c Garnham b Ilott | 6 |
| A.A.Metcalfe | c Garnham b Ilott | 3 |
| R.J.Blakey + | lbw b Gooch | 18 |
| D.Byas | c Ilott b Gooch | 5 |
| P.E.Robinson | run out | 20 |
| K.Sharp | c Such b Gooch | 37 |
| P.W.Jarvis | c Garnham b Pringle | 5 |
| P.Carrick | not out | 20 |
| A.Sidebottom | c Garnham b Pringle | 6 |
| S.D.Fletcher | not out | 11 |
| M.A.Robinson | | |
| Extras | (lb 4,w 14) | 18 |
| TOTAL | (40 overs)(for 8 wkts) | 149 |

### ESSEX

| | | |
|---|---|---|
| G.A.Gooch * | not out | 59 |
| J.P.Stephenson | c Blakey b Fletcher | 32 |
| Salim Malik | not out | 48 |
| P.J.Prichard | | |
| N.Hussain | | |
| N.Shahid | | |
| D.R.Pringle | | |
| M.A.Garnham + | | |
| T.D.Topley | | |
| M.C.Ilott | | |
| P.M.Such | | |
| Extras | (b 1,lb 8,w 2,nb 3) | 14 |
| TOTAL | (33.3 overs)(for 1 wkt) | 153 |

| ESSEX | O | M | R | W | FALL OF WICKETS | | |
|---|---|---|---|---|---|---|---|
| | | | | | | YOR | ESS |
| Pringle | 8 | 1 | 28 | 2 | 1st | 11 | 56 |
| Ilott | 6 | 0 | 26 | 2 | 2nd | 17 | |
| Gooch | 8 | 1 | 25 | 3 | 3rd | 28 | |
| Topley | 6 | 0 | 18 | 0 | 4th | 48 | |
| Stephenson | 4 | 0 | 19 | 0 | 5th | 74 | |
| Such | 8 | 0 | 29 | 0 | 6th | 99 | |
| | | | | | 7th | 116 | |
| YORKSHIRE | O | M | R | W | 8th | 128 | |
| Jarvis | 8 | 1 | 39 | 0 | 9th | | |
| Sidebottom | 8 | 0 | 26 | 0 | 10th | | |
| Fletcher | 8 | 1 | 37 | 1 | | | |
| Robinson M.A. | 6 | 1 | 25 | 0 | | | |
| Carrick | 2 | 0 | 10 | 0 | | | |
| Moxon | 1.3 | 0 | 7 | 0 | | | |

## LEICESTERSHIRE vs. GLAMORGAN

at Leicester on 28th April 1991
Toss : Glamorgan. Umpires : H.D.Bird and J.D.Bond
Leicestershire won by 13 runs. Leics 4 pts, Glamorgan 0 pts

### LEICESTERSHIRE

| | | |
|---|---|---|
| P.Whitticase * | run out | 8 |
| N.E.Briers * | lbw b Watkin | 11 |
| J.J.Whitaker | c Frost b Watkin | 73 |
| P.Willey | c Metson b Shastri | 27 |
| C.C.Lewis | c Barwick b Croft | 8 |
| L.Potter | lbw b Barwick | 45 |
| J.D.R.Benson | not out | 14 |
| P.N.Hepworth | run out | 5 |
| J.N.Maguire | not out | 2 |
| C.Wilkinson | | |
| L.Tennant | | |
| Extras | (lb 8,w 6) | 14 |
| TOTAL | (40 overs)(for 7 wkts) | 207 |

### GLAMORGAN

| | | |
|---|---|---|
| H.Morris * | c Lewis b Benson | 62 |
| P.A.Cottey | lbw b Lewis | 3 |
| M.P.Maynard | lbw b Maguire | 2 |
| R.J.Shastri | c Benson b Maguire | 5 |
| G.C.Holmes | b Lewis | 72 |
| I.Smith | not out | 27 |
| R.D.B.Croft + | c Benson b Maguire | 6 |
| C.P.Metson | not out | 1 |
| S.L.Watkin | | |
| S.R.Barwick | | |
| M.Frost | | |
| Extras | (lb 4,w 11,nb 1) | 16 |
| TOTAL | (40 overs)(for 6 wkts) | 194 |

| GLAMORGAN | O | M | R | W | FALL OF WICKETS | | |
|---|---|---|---|---|---|---|---|
| | | | | | | LEI | GLA |
| Watkin | 8 | 2 | 28 | 2 | 1st | 21 | 8 |
| Frost | 8 | 0 | 48 | 0 | 2nd | 21 | 15 |
| Barwick | 8 | 0 | 29 | 1 | 3rd | 75 | 22 |
| Shastri | 8 | 0 | 38 | 1 | 4th | 91 | 131 |
| Croft | 7 | 0 | 49 | 1 | 5th | 176 | 185 |
| Smith | 1 | 0 | 7 | 0 | 6th | 188 | 192 |
| LEICS | O | M | R | W | 7th | 204 | |
| Lewis | 8 | 2 | 33 | 2 | 8th | | |
| Maguire | 8 | 0 | 31 | 3 | 9th | | |
| Wilkinson | 8 | 0 | 39 | 0 | 10th | | |
| Tennant | 6 | 0 | 30 | 0 | | | |
| Willey | 5 | 0 | 25 | 0 | | | |
| Benson | 5 | 0 | 32 | 1 | | | |

## NOTTS vs. WARWICKSHIRE

at Trent Bridge on 28th April 1991
Toss : Warwickshire. Umpires : D.O.Oslear and K.E.Palmer
Notts won by 82 runs. Notts 4 pts, Warwickshire 0 pts

### NOTTS

| | | |
|---|---|---|
| B.C.Broad | c Piper b Munton | 2 |
| D.W.Randall | c & b Smith N.M.K. | 32 |
| R.T.Robinson * | c & b Munton | 3 |
| P.Johnson | c Smith P.A. b Small | 80 |
| M.A.Crawley | b Smith P.A. | 29 |
| M.Saxelby | c Piper b Smith P.A. | 0 |
| F.D.Stephenson | not out | 36 |
| K.P.Evans | not out | 14 |
| B.N.French + | | |
| E.E.Hemmings | | |
| K.E.Cooper | | |
| Extras | (b 1,lb 8,w 5,nb 2) | 16 |
| TOTAL | (40 overs)(for 6 wkts) | 212 |

### WARWICKSHIRE

| | | |
|---|---|---|
| A.J.Moles | b Cooper | 0 |
| Asif Din | b Stephenson | 6 |
| T.A.Lloyd * | lbw b Hemmings | 45 |
| P.A.Smith | c Robinson b Hemmings | 15 |
| D.A.Reeve | b Crawley | 17 |
| D.P.Ostler | b Crawley | 16 |
| N.M.K.Smith | c Broad b Hemmings | 8 |
| K.J.Piper + | st French b Hemmings | 1 |
| G.C.Small | b Stephenson | 1 |
| A.A.Donald | c Broad b Stephenson | 7 |
| T.A.Munton | not out | 3 |
| Extras | (lb 6,w 1,nb 4) | 11 |
| TOTAL | (35.2 overs) | 130 |

| WARWICKS | O | M | R | W | FALL OF WICKETS | | |
|---|---|---|---|---|---|---|---|
| | | | | | | NOT | WAR |
| Munton | 8 | 1 | 35 | 2 | 1st | 12 | 0 |
| Donald | 8 | 0 | 41 | 0 | 2nd | 20 | 17 |
| Smith P.A. | 8 | 0 | 36 | 2 | 3rd | 75 | 76 |
| Small | 8 | 0 | 37 | 1 | 4th | 149 | 77 |
| Moles | 4 | 0 | 24 | 0 | 5th | 155 | 108 |
| Smith N.M.K. | 4 | 0 | 30 | 1 | 6th | 156 | 111 |
| NOTTS | O | M | R | W | 7th | | 119 |
| Cooper | 8 | 1 | 20 | 1 | 8th | | 119 |
| Stephenson | 5.2 | 0 | 17 | 3 | 9th | | 127 |
| Saxelby | 4 | 0 | 20 | 0 | 10th | | 130 |
| Evans | 4 | 0 | 16 | 0 | | | |
| Hemmings | 8 | 0 | 26 | 4 | | | |
| Crawley | 6 | 0 | 25 | 2 | | | |

## LANCASHIRE vs. NORTHANTS

at Old Trafford on 28th April 1991
Toss : Lancashire. Umpires : M.J.Kitchen and B.J.Meyer
Lancashire won by 5 wickets. Lancs 4 pts, Northants 0 pts

### NORTHANTS

| | | |
|---|---|---|
| A.Fordham | c Hegg b Allott | 12 |
| R.J.Bailey | b Austin | 99 |
| A.J.Lamb * | b DeFreitas | 13 |
| D.J.Capel | c Fowler b DeFreitas | 53 |
| R.G.Williams | not out | 16 |
| E.A.E.Baptiste | not out | 5 |
| A.L.Penberthy | | |
| D.Ripley + | | |
| J.G.Thomas | | |
| N.G.B.Cook | | |
| J.P.Taylor | | |
| Extras | (b 2,lb 13,w 5,nb 1) | 21 |
| TOTAL | (40 overs)(for 4 wkts) | 219 |

### LANCASHIRE

| | | |
|---|---|---|
| G.Fowler | c Ripley b Taylor | 52 |
| M.A.Atherton | b Thomas | 25 |
| G.D.Lloyd | c Cook b Capel | 71 |
| N.H.Fairbrother * | not out | 39 |
| M.Watkinson | c Penberthy b Taylor | 4 |
| Wasim Akram | c Bailey b Capel | 6 |
| P.A.J.DeFreitas | not out | 6 |
| W.K.Hegg + | | |
| G.Yates | | |
| I.D.Austin | | |
| P.J.W.Allott | | |
| Extras | (b 1,lb 12,w 5,nb 1) | 19 |
| TOTAL | (39.1 overs)(for 5 wkts) | 222 |

| LANCASHIRE | O | M | R | W | FALL OF WICKETS | | |
|---|---|---|---|---|---|---|---|
| | | | | | | NOR | LAN |
| DeFreitas | 8 | 0 | 39 | 2 | 1st | 19 | 50 |
| Allott | 8 | 0 | 27 | 1 | 2nd | 40 | 121 |
| Watkinson | 8 | 0 | 53 | 0 | 3rd | 163 | 180 |
| Wasim Akram | 8 | 1 | 33 | 0 | 4th | 211 | 189 |
| Austin | 6 | 0 | 32 | 1 | 5th | | 195 |
| Yates | 2 | 0 | 20 | 0 | 6th | | |
| | | | | | 7th | | |
| NORTHANTS | O | M | R | W | 8th | | |
| Taylor | 8 | 1 | 27 | 2 | 9th | | |
| Baptiste | 7.1 | 0 | 34 | 0 | 10th | | |
| Cook | 8 | 0 | 36 | 0 | | | |
| Thomas | 8 | 0 | 47 | 1 | | | |
| Capel | 6 | 0 | 43 | 2 | | | |
| Williams | 2 | 0 | 22 | 0 | | | |

## MIDDLESEX vs. SURREY

at Lord's on 28th April 1991
Toss : Middlesex. Umpires : B.Hassan and A.A.Jones
Surrey won by 4 wickets. Middlesex 0 pts, Surrey 4 pts

### MIDDLESEX

| | | |
|---|---|---|
| M.W.Gatting * | b Boiling | 22 |
| J.C.Pooley | c Robinson b Waqar Younis | 42 |
| K.R.Brown | not out | 81 |
| M.Keech | c Bicknell b Greig | 36 |
| P.R.Downton + | c Waqar Younis b Bicknell | 5 |
| P.N.Weekes | c Ward b Greig | 5 |
| J.E.Emburey | not out | 16 |
| D.W.Headley | | |
| S.P.Hughes | | |
| P.C.R.Tufnell | | |
| C.W.Taylor | | |
| Extras | (b 4,lb 7,w 5) | 16 |
| TOTAL | (40 overs)(for 5 wkts) | 221 |

### SURREY

| | | |
|---|---|---|
| M.A.Lynch | c Keech b Taylor | 5 |
| A.D.Brown | b Tufnell | 15 |
| A.J.Stewart + | c Brown b Tufnell | 71 |
| D.M.Ward | c Brown b Tufnell | 7 |
| G.P.Thorpe | b Hughes | 2 |
| I.A.Greig * | not out | 68 |
| J.D.Robinson | b Hughes | 26 |
| M.P.Bicknell | not out | 7 |
| J.Boiling | | |
| Waqar Younis | | |
| A.J.Murphy | | |
| Extras | (lb 15,w 5,nb 3) | 23 |
| TOTAL | (38.2 overs)(for 6 wkts) | 224 |

| SURREY | O | M | R | W | FALL OF WICKETS | | |
|---|---|---|---|---|---|---|---|
| | | | | | | MID | SUR |
| Bicknell | 7 | 0 | 37 | 1 | 1st | 67 | 6 |
| Murphy | 8 | 1 | 31 | 0 | 2nd | 71 | 49 |
| Robinson | 5 | 0 | 34 | 0 | 3rd | 151 | 59 |
| Waqar Younis | 8 | 1 | 41 | 1 | 4th | 159 | 67 |
| Boiling | 3 | 0 | 21 | 1 | 5th | 166 | 128 |
| Thorpe | 2 | 0 | 16 | 0 | 6th | | 198 |
| Greig | 7 | 0 | 30 | 2 | 7th | | |
| | | | | | 8th | | |
| MIDDLESEX | O | M | R | W | 9th | | |
| Headley | 8 | 0 | 41 | 0 | 10th | | |
| Taylor | 7.2 | 0 | 50 | 1 | | | |
| Tufnell | 8 | 0 | 28 | 3 | | | |
| Hughes | 8 | 0 | 46 | 2 | | | |
| Emburey | 7 | 0 | 44 | 0 | | | |

## SOMERSET vs. SUSSEX

at Taunton on 28th April 1991
Toss : Som. Umps : J.C.Balderstone and A.G.T.Whitehead
Somerset won by 3 wickets. Somerset 4 pts, Sussex 0 pts

### SUSSEX

| | | |
|---|---|---|
| D.M.Smith | c Rose b Lefebvre | 48 |
| J.W.Hall | b Graveney | 50 |
| P.W.G.Parker * | run out | 3 |
| A.P.Wells | c & b Rose | 38 |
| K.Greenfield | b Lefebvre | 5 |
| J.A.North | c Cook b Rose | 5 |
| A.C.S.Pigott | run out | 14 |
| P.Moores + | b Lefebvre | 12 |
| I.D.K.Salisbury | run out | 2 |
| A.N.Jones | not out | 0 |
| R.A.Bunting | not out | 1 |
| Extras | (b 1,lb 7,w 1,nb 1) | 10 |
| TOTAL | (39 overs)(for 9 wkts) | 188 |

### SOMERSET

| | | |
|---|---|---|
| S.J.Cook | c Parker b Jones | 33 |
| R.J.Bartlett | c Moores b Pigott | 26 |
| C.J.Tavare * | b Salisbury | 15 |
| R.J.Harden | c Moores b Jones | 15 |
| N.D.Burns + | c Moores b North | 6 |
| G.D.Rose | b Bunting | 50 |
| A.N.Hayhurst | not out | 26 |
| R.P.Lefebvre | c Wells b North | 4 |
| I.G.Swallow | not out | 4 |
| N.A.Mallender | | |
| D.A.Graveney | | |
| Extras | (lb 1,w 11) | 12 |
| TOTAL | (38.3 overs)(for 7 wkts) | 191 |

| SOMERSET | O | M | R | W | FALL OF WICKETS | | |
|---|---|---|---|---|---|---|---|
| | | | | | | SUS | SOM |
| Mallender | 8 | 0 | 37 | 0 | 1st | 83 | 42 |
| Lefebvre | 8 | 1 | 29 | 3 | 2nd | 88 | 78 |
| Rose | 5 | 0 | 40 | 2 | 3rd | 132 | 90 |
| Swallow | 3 | 0 | 16 | 0 | 4th | 142 | 102 |
| Hayhurst | 8 | 0 | 25 | 0 | 5th | 158 | 111 |
| Graveney | 7 | 0 | 33 | 1 | 6th | 158 | 179 |
| | | | | | 7th | 183 | 186 |
| SUSSEX | O | M | R | W | 8th | 185 | |
| Jones | 8 | 0 | 49 | 2 | 9th | 186 | |
| Bunting | 5 | 0 | 27 | 1 | 10th | | |
| Pigott | 8 | 0 | 30 | 1 | | | |
| Salisbury | 8 | 1 | 16 | 1 | | | |
| North | 5 | 0 | 39 | 2 | | | |
| Greenfield | 4.3 | 0 | 29 | 0 | | | |

| REFUGE ASSURANCE LEAGUE | BRITANNIC ASS. CHAMPIONSHIP |

## HEADLINES

### Refuge Assurance League

### 28th April

• Nottinghamshire and Somerset were the only counties with two victories in the Refuge League after the second round of matches. Nottinghamshire had an easy 82-run win over Warwickshire at Trent Bridge, Paul Johnson (80) and Eddie Hemmings (4 for 26) playing the match-winning roles.

• Somerset defeated Sussex at Taunton by three wickets with only three balls to spare, Roland Lefebvre pegging back the visitors after Jamie Hall had made his first Sunday League fifty and Graham Rose and Andy Hayhurst reviving Somerset from 111 for five.

• Essex opened their Refuge campaign with a nine-wicket victory over Yorkshire that owed much to Graham Gooch who claimed three wickets and hit an unbeaten 59.

• Northamptonshire made Lancashire work hard for their first Sunday victory at Old Trafford, Rob Bailey's 99 helping the visitors to a healthy 219 for four, but Lancashire's first four batsmen all contributed and the target was reached with five balls and five wickets to spare.

• Leicestershire's first Sunday success came at the expense of Glamorgan, John Maguire, Leicester's new overseas signing, taking 3 for 31 as the home side won by 13 runs.

• Surrey recorded their second victory in three days over Middlesex, Ian Greig guiding them to their target after Philip Tufnell had returned his best Sunday League figures.

## SOMERSET vs. SUSSEX

at Taunton on 27th, 29th (np), 30th (np) April, 1st May 1991
Toss : Somerset. Umpires : J.C.Balderstone and A.G.T.Whitehead
Match drawn. Somerset 4 pts (Bt: 2, Bw: 2), Sussex 8 pts (Bt: 4, Bw: 4)

**SOMERSET**

| | | |
|---|---|---|
| S.J.Cook | b Pigott | 57 |
| P.M.Roebuck | c Smith b Jones | 18 |
| A.N.Hayhurst | c Hall b Salisbury | 32 |
| C.J.Tavare * | c Moores b North | 25 |
| R.J.Harden | c Moores b North | 19 |
| N.D.Burns + | c Smith b Donelan | 7 |
| G.D.Rose | c Salisbury b Donelan | 13 |
| R.P.Lefebvre | c Greenfield b Pigott | 16 |
| I.G.Swallow | c Greenfield b Pigott | 4 |
| N.A.Mallender | lbw b North | 15 |
| D.A.Graveney | not out | 4 |
| Extras | (lb 8,w 4,nb 7) | 19 |
| TOTAL | | 229 |

**SUSSEX**

| | | |
|---|---|---|
| D.M.Smith | b Swallow | 53 |
| J.W.Hall | not out | 117 |
| P.W.G.Parker * | st Burns b Swallow | 11 |
| A.P.Wells | b Swallow | 3 |
| J.A.North | c Harden b Mallender | 15 |
| P.Moores + | c Swallow b Rose | 69 |
| A.C.S.Pigott | not out | 5 |
| K.Greenfield | | |
| I.D.K.Salisbury | | |
| B.T.P.Donelan | | |
| A.N.Jones | | |
| Extras | (lb 10,w 1,nb 16) | 27 |
| TOTAL | (for 5 wkts) | 300 |

| SUSSEX | O | M | R | W | O | M | R | W |
|---|---|---|---|---|---|---|---|---|
| Jones | 13 | 2 | 28 | 1 | | | | |
| Pigott | 21 | 6 | 36 | 3 | | | | |
| North | 15.3 | 2 | 54 | 3 | | | | |
| Salisbury | 23 | 7 | 64 | 1 | | | | |
| Donelan | 16 | 4 | 39 | 2 | | | | |
| SOMERSET | O | M | R | W | O | M | R | W |
| Mallender | 16 | 3 | 33 | 1 | | | | |
| Rose | 19 | 2 | 90 | 1 | | | | |
| Graveney | 5 | 5 | 0 | 0 | | | | |
| Swallow | 20 | 3 | 43 | 3 | | | | |
| Lefebvre | 15 | 2 | 50 | 0 | | | | |
| Roebuck | 17 | 3 | 54 | 0 | | | | |
| Hayhurst | 3 | 0 | 20 | 0 | | | | |

FALL OF WICKETS

| | SOM | SUS | SOM | SUS |
|---|---|---|---|---|
| 1st | 51 | 120 | | |
| 2nd | 103 | 147 | | |
| 3rd | 123 | 153 | | |
| 4th | 152 | 193 | | |
| 5th | 167 | 290 | | |
| 6th | 175 | | | |
| 7th | 193 | | | |
| 8th | 207 | | | |
| 9th | 210 | | | |
| 10th | 229 | | | |

## WARWICKSHIRE vs. LANCASHIRE

at Edgbaston on 27th, 29th (np), 30th April, 1st May 1991
Toss : Lancashire. Umpires : J.H.Hampshire and B.Leadbeater
Match drawn. Warwickshire 2 pts (Bt: 1, Bw: 1), Lancashire 7 pts (Bt: 4, Bw: 3)
100 overs scores : Lancashire 340 for 4

**LANCASHIRE**

| | | |
|---|---|---|
| G.D.Mendis | lbw b Smith | 113 |
| G.Fowler | c Moles b Small | 35 |
| M.A.Atherton | c Ostler b Moles | 10 |
| N.H.Fairbrother * | c Small b Reeve | 121 |
| N.J.Speak | not out | 37 |
| M.Watkinson | b Small | 30 |
| Wasim Akram | | |
| P.A.J.DeFreitas | | |
| W.K.Hegg + | | |
| G.Yates | | |
| P.J.W.Allott | | |
| Extras | (b 13,lb 11,w 1,nb 6) | 31 |
| TOTAL | (for 5 wkts dec) | 377 |

**WARWICKSHIRE**

| | | |
|---|---|---|
| A.J.Moles | c Fairbrother b Yates | 51 |
| Asif Din | c Hegg b Allott | 15 |
| T.A.Lloyd * | c Wasim Akram b Yates | 19 |
| P.A.Smith | c & b Wasim Akram | 27 |
| D.A.Reeve | not out | 20 |
| D.P.Ostler | b Yates | 9 |
| K.J.Piper + | lbw b DeFreitas | 6 |
| G.C.Small | b Speak | 2 |
| T.A.Munton | not out | 0 |
| A.R.K.Pierson | | |
| A.A.Donald | | |
| Extras | (b 3,lb 11,w 1,nb 5) | 20 |
| TOTAL | (for 7 wkts) | 169 |

| WARWICKS | O | M | R | W | O | M | R | W |
|---|---|---|---|---|---|---|---|---|
| Donald | 17 | 2 | 58 | 0 | | | | |
| Small | 21 | 5 | 67 | 2 | | | | |
| Munton | 20 | 3 | 83 | 0 | | | | |
| Reeve | 19 | 6 | 42 | 1 | | | | |
| Pierson | 15 | 5 | 49 | 0 | | | | |
| Moles | 8 | 2 | 14 | 1 | | | | |
| Smith | 10 | 1 | 40 | 1 | | | | |
| LANCASHIRE | O | M | R | W | O | M | R | W |
| Wasim Akram | 14 | 3 | 33 | 1 | | | | |
| DeFreitas | 22 | 8 | 45 | 1 | | | | |
| Allott | 8 | 1 | 30 | 1 | | | | |
| Yates | 22 | 6 | 47 | 3 | | | | |
| Speak | 0.1 | 0 | 0 | 1 | | | | |

FALL OF WICKETS

| | LAN | WAR | LAN | WAR |
|---|---|---|---|---|
| 1st | 111 | 25 | | |
| 2nd | 150 | 62 | | |
| 3rd | 224 | 119 | | |
| 4th | 324 | 123 | | |
| 5th | 377 | 148 | | |
| 6th | | 165 | | |
| 7th | | 169 | | |
| 8th | | | | |
| 9th | | | | |
| 10th | | | | |

# BRITANNIC ASSURANCE CHAMPIONSHIP

## HAMPSHIRE vs. KENT

at Southampton on 27th, 28th, 29th (np), 30th (np) April, 1st May 1991
Toss : Kent. Umpires : J.H.Harris and N.T.Plews
Match drawn. Hampshire 1 pt (Bt: 0, Bw: 1), Kent 5 pts (Bt: 4, Bw: 1)
100 overs scores : Kent 318 for 3

**KENT**

| | | |
|---|---|---|
| N.R.Taylor | lbw b Bakker | 3 |
| M.R.Benson * | c Nicholas b Bakker | 257 |
| T.R.Ward | c Aymes b Aqib Javed | 35 |
| G.R.Cowdrey | c Gower b Maru | 0 |
| C.S.Cowdrey | c Maru b Nicholas | 97 |
| R.M.Ellison | lbw b Bakker | 1 |
| R.P.Davis | b Aqib Javed | 0 |
| C.Penn | c Middleton b Bakker | 37 |
| T.A.Merrick | not out | 9 |
| A.P.Igglesden | c Bakker b Ayling | 7 |
| S.A.Marsh + | absent hurt | |
| Extras | (b 10,lb 10,w 3,nb 13) | 36 |
| TOTAL | | 482 |

**HAMPSHIRE**

| | | |
|---|---|---|
| T.C.Middleton | c Cowdrey G.R. b Merrick | 15 |
| C.L.Smith | c Taylor b Merrick | 19 |
| D.I.Gower | c Benson b Merrick | 11 |
| J.R.Wood | b Merrick | 25 |
| M.C.J.Nicholas * | not out | 5 |
| J.R.Ayling | | |
| K.D.James | | |
| A.N Aymes + | | |
| R.J.Maru | | |
| P.J.Bakker | | |
| Aqib Javed | | |
| Extras | (b 6,lb 5,nb 2) | 13 |
| TOTAL | (for 4 wkts) | 88 |

| HAMPSHIRE | O | M | R | W | O | M | R | W |
|---|---|---|---|---|---|---|---|---|
| Aqib Javed | 33 | 6 | 103 | 2 | | | | |
| Bakker | 32 | 5 | 95 | 4 | | | | |
| Maru | 31 | 8 | 86 | 1 | | | | |
| James | 17 | 5 | 59 | 0 | | | | |
| Ayling | 22.4 | 3 | 64 | 1 | | | | |
| Wood | 6 | 0 | 17 | 0 | | | | |
| Nicholas | 8 | 0 | 38 | 1 | | | | |

| KENT | O | M | R | W | O | M | R | W |
|---|---|---|---|---|---|---|---|---|
| Merrick | 11 | 3 | 37 | 4 | | | | |
| Igglesden | 8 | 0 | 34 | 0 | | | | |
| Penn | 3 | 0 | 6 | 0 | | | | |

| FALL OF WICKETS | | | | |
|---|---|---|---|---|
| | KEN | HAM | KEN | HAM |
| 1st | 10 | 40 | | |
| 2nd | 98 | 52 | | |
| 3rd | 101 | 57 | | |
| 4th | 325 | 88 | | |
| 5th | 343 | | | |
| 6th | 346 | | | |
| 7th | 455 | | | |
| 8th | 464 | | | |
| 9th | 482 | | | |
| 10th | | | | |

## DERBYSHIRE vs. NORTHANTS

at Derby on 27th, 29th (np), 30th (np) April, 1st (np) May 1991
Toss : Derby. Umpires : D.J.Constant and K.E.Palmer
Match drawn. Derby 1 pt (Bt: 0, Bw: 1), Northants 4 pts (Bt: 4, Bw: 0)
100 overs scores : Northants 311 for 3

**NORTHANTS**

| | | |
|---|---|---|
| A.Fordham | c Krikken b Mortensen | 131 |
| N.A.Felton | c Bowler b Base | 9 |
| R.J.Bailey | lbw b Azharuddin | 83 |
| A.J.Lamb * | not out | 74 |
| D.J.Capel | lbw b Jean-Jacques | 16 |
| R.G.Williams | not out | 11 |
| E.A.E.Baptiste | | |
| D.Ripley + | | |
| J.G.Thomas | | |
| N.G.B.Cook | | |
| J.P.Taylor | | |
| Extras | (lb 4,w 3,nb 16) | 23 |
| TOTAL | (for 4 wkts) | 347 |

**DERBYSHIRE**

| | |
|---|---|
| K.J.Barnett * | |
| P.D.Bowler | |
| J.E.Morris | |
| M.Azharuddin | |
| T.J.G.O'Gorman | |
| C.J.Adams | |
| K.M.Krikken + | |
| A.E.Warner | |
| M.Jean-Jacques | |
| S.J.Base | |
| O.H.Mortensen | |
| Extras | |
| TOTAL | |

| DERBYSHIRE | O | M | R | W | O | M | R | W |
|---|---|---|---|---|---|---|---|---|
| Mortensen | 22 | 6 | 62 | 1 | | | | |
| Jean-Jacques | 28 | 5 | 81 | 1 | | | | |
| Base | 29 | 5 | 88 | 1 | | | | |
| Warner | 22 | 5 | 60 | 0 | | | | |
| Azharuddin | 14 | 1 | 52 | 1 | | | | |

| NORTHANTS | O | M | R | W | O | M | R | W |
|---|---|---|---|---|---|---|---|---|

| FALL OF WICKETS | | | | |
|---|---|---|---|---|
| | NOR | DER | NOR | DER |
| 1st | 47 | | | |
| 2nd | 207 | | | |
| 3rd | 274 | | | |
| 4th | 314 | | | |
| 5th | | | | |
| 6th | | | | |
| 7th | | | | |
| 8th | | | | |
| 9th | | | | |
| 10th | | | | |

## WORCESTERSHIRE vs. GLOUCS

at Worcester on 27th, 28th, 29th (np), 30th (np) April, 1st May 1991
Toss : Gloucs. Umpires : G.I.Burgess and D.R.Shepherd
Match drawn. Worcestershire 5 pts (Bt: 3, Bw: 2), Gloucs 5 pts (Bt: 4, Bw: 1)
100 overs scores : Gloucs 301 for 5

**GLOUCS**

| | | |
|---|---|---|
| G.D.Hodgson | c Rhodes b Newport | 65 |
| R.J.Scott | st Rhodes b Botham | 127 |
| A.J.Wright * | c Hick b Radford | 30 |
| C.W.J.Athey | c Botham b Lampitt | 56 |
| M.W.Alleyne | lbw b Radford | 2 |
| J.W.Lloyds | lbw b Botham | 4 |
| R.C.Russell + | b Botham | 64 |
| D.V.Lawrence | c Moody b Lampitt | 23 |
| D.R.Gilbert | c Curtis b Botham | 16 |
| A.M.Smith | not out | 3 |
| A.M.Babington | c Lord b Botham | 13 |
| Extras | (b 5,lb 16,w 6,nb 20) | 47 |
| TOTAL | | 450 |

**WORCESTERSHIRE**

| | | |
|---|---|---|
| T.S.Curtis | lbw b Babington | 49 |
| G.J.Lord | b Gilbert | 29 |
| G.A.Hick | b Babington | 14 |
| T.M.Moody | not out | 82 |
| P.A.Neale * | lbw b Babington | 29 |
| I.T.Botham | not out | 39 |
| S.J.Rhodes + | | |
| R.K.Illingworth | | |
| P.J.Newport | | |
| S.R.Lampitt | | |
| N.V.Radford | | |
| Extras | (lb 8,nb 5) | 13 |
| TOTAL | (for 4 wkts) | 255 |

| WORCS | O | M | R | W | O | M | R | W |
|---|---|---|---|---|---|---|---|---|
| Radford | 28 | 2 | 94 | 2 | | | | |
| Newport | 25 | 2 | 85 | 1 | | | | |
| Lampitt | 34 | 10 | 75 | 2 | | | | |
| Botham | 34.2 | 8 | 125 | 5 | | | | |
| Illingworth | 14 | 4 | 40 | 0 | | | | |
| Hick | 6 | 2 | 10 | 0 | | | | |

| GLOUCS | O | M | R | W | O | M | R | W |
|---|---|---|---|---|---|---|---|---|
| Lawrence | 12 | 1 | 50 | 0 | | | | |
| Gilbert | 15.1 | 2 | 78 | 1 | | | | |
| Babington | 20 | 4 | 55 | 3 | | | | |
| Smith | 7 | 1 | 34 | 0 | | | | |
| Lloyds | 10 | 0 | 30 | 0 | | | | |

| FALL OF WICKETS | | | | |
|---|---|---|---|---|
| | GLO | WOR | GLO | WOR |
| 1st | 179 | 77 | | |
| 2nd | 247 | 91 | | |
| 3rd | 247 | 103 | | |
| 4th | 249 | 167 | | |
| 5th | 260 | | | |
| 6th | 385 | | | |
| 7th | 413 | | | |
| 8th | 426 | | | |
| 9th | 430 | | | |
| 10th | 450 | | | |

## ESSEX vs. SURREY

at Chelmsford on 27th, 29th, 30th (np), 1st (np) May 1991
Toss : Essex. Umpires : K.J.Lyons and P.B.Wight
Match drawn. Essex 6 pts (Bt: 2, Bw: 4), Surrey 4 pts (Bt: 3, Bw: 1)

**SURREY**

| | | |
|---|---|---|
| D.J.Bicknell | not out | 145 |
| M.A.Lynch | lbw b Pringle | 11 |
| A.J.Stewart | c Hussain b Pringle | 19 |
| D.M.Ward | c Garnham b Topley | 30 |
| G.P.Thorpe | c Garnham b Topley | 0 |
| J.D.Robinson | c Pringle b Foster | 15 |
| I.A.Greig * | c Gooch b Topley | 0 |
| N.F.Sargeant + | lbw b Topley | 11 |
| M.P.Bicknell | c Garnham b Topley | 6 |
| A.J.Murphy | lbw b Foster | 2 |
| A.G.Robson | b Andrew | 0 |
| Extras | (b 3,lb 4,w 4,nb 18) | 29 |
| TOTAL | | 268 |

**ESSEX**

| | | |
|---|---|---|
| G.A.Gooch * | c Sargeant b Murphy | 3 |
| J.P.Stephenson | c Lynch b Greig | 85 |
| T.D.Topley | c Lynch b Bicknell M.P. | 29 |
| P.J.Prichard | not out | 45 |
| Salim Malik | lbw b Greig | 0 |
| N.Hussain | not out | 19 |
| N.Shahid | | |
| D.R.Pringle | | |
| M.A.Garnham + | | |
| N.A.Foster | | |
| S.J.W.Andrew | | |
| Extras | (b 4,lb 17,w 6,nb 3) | 30 |
| TOTAL | (for 4 wkts) | 211 |

| ESSEX | O | M | R | W | O | M | R | W |
|---|---|---|---|---|---|---|---|---|
| Foster | 23 | 4 | 61 | 2 | | | | |
| Pringle | 29 | 6 | 74 | 2 | | | | |
| Andrew | 19 | 2 | 55 | 1 | | | | |
| Topley | 23 | 3 | 71 | 5 | | | | |

| SURREY | O | M | R | W | O | M | R | W |
|---|---|---|---|---|---|---|---|---|
| Bicknell M.P. | 24 | 7 | 44 | 1 | | | | |
| Murphy | 25 | 5 | 57 | 1 | | | | |
| Robson | 15 | 4 | 31 | 0 | | | | |
| Robinson | 2 | 0 | 15 | 0 | | | | |
| Thorpe | 5 | 0 | 18 | 0 | | | | |
| Greig | 7 | 2 | 25 | 2 | | | | |

| FALL OF WICKETS | | | | |
|---|---|---|---|---|
| | SUR | ESS | SUR | ESS |
| 1st | 17 | 11 | | |
| 2nd | 61 | 111 | | |
| 3rd | 120 | 185 | | |
| 4th | 124 | 191 | | |
| 5th | 166 | | | |
| 6th | 178 | | | |
| 7th | 214 | | | |
| 8th | 228 | | | |
| 9th | 252 | | | |
| 10th | 268 | | | |

# BRITANNIC ASSURANCE CHAMPIONSHIP

## LEICESTERSHIRE vs. GLAMORGAN ━━━━━

at Leicester on 27th, 29th (np), 30th April, 1st (np) May 1991
Toss : Glamorgan.  Umpires : H.D.Bird and J.D.Bond
Match drawn.  Leicestershire 4 pts (Bt: 0, Bw: 4), Glamorgan 1 pt (Bt: 1, Bw: 0)

### GLAMORGAN

| | | | | |
|---|---|---|---|---|
| H.Morris * | b Lewis | 11 | not out | 15 |
| P.A.Cottey | c Whitticase b Lewis | 3 | not out | 16 |
| R.J.Shastri | c Whitticase b Millns | 0 | | |
| M.P.Maynard | c Lewis b Millns | 41 | | |
| G.C.Holmes | c Whitticase b Lewis | 18 | | |
| I.Smith | lbw b Maguire | 39 | | |
| R.D.B.Croft | c Willey b Lewis | 15 | | |
| C.P.Metson + | c Benson b Lewis | 0 | | |
| S.L.Watkin | not out | 13 | | |
| S.R.Barwick | c Briers b Maguire | 5 | | |
| M.Frost | lbw b Millns | 0 | | |
| Extras | (lb 9,w 1,nb 6) | 16 | | 0 |
| TOTAL | | 161 | (for 0 wkts) | 31 |

### LEICESTERSHIRE

| | | |
|---|---|---|
| P.N.Hepworth | not out | 29 |
| N.E.Briers * | not out | 42 |
| J.J.Whitaker | | |
| P.Willey | | |
| L.Potter | | |
| C.C.Lewis | | |
| J.D.R.Benson | | |
| P.Whitticase + | | |
| J.N.Maguire | | |
| D.J.Millns | | |
| A.D.Mullally | | |
| Extras | (lb 5,w 1) | 6 |
| TOTAL | (for 0 wkts dec) | 77 |

| LEICS | O | M | R | W | O | M | R | W | | FALL OF WICKETS | | | |
|---|---|---|---|---|---|---|---|---|---|---|---|---|---|
| Lewis | 22 | 7 | 35 | 5 | 4 | 0 | 8 | 0 | | | GLA | LEI GLA | LEI |
| Millns | 11.5 | 2 | 41 | 3 | 6 | 0 | 15 | 0 | 1st | | 9 | | |
| Maguire | 15 | 6 | 35 | 2 | 5 | 4 | 4 | 0 | 2nd | | 10 | | |
| Mullally | 16 | 6 | 40 | 0 | 2 | 1 | 4 | 0 | 3rd | | 23 | | |
| Potter | 2 | 1 | 1 | 0 | | | | | 4th | | 79 | | |
| | | | | | | | | | 5th | | 79 | | |
| GLAMORGAN | O | M | R | W | O | M | R | W | 6th | | 104 | | |
| Watkin | 14 | 2 | 29 | 0 | | | | | 7th | | 104 | | |
| Frost | 10 | 2 | 16 | 0 | | | | | 8th | | 145 | | |
| Barwick | 9 | 4 | 12 | 0 | | | | | 9th | | 157 | | |
| Croft | 8 | 3 | 9 | 0 | | | | | 10th | | 161 | | |
| Shastri | 2 | 0 | 6 | 0 | | | | | | | | | |

## MIDDLESEX vs. YORKSHIRE ━━━━━

at Lord's on 27th, 29th, 30th (np) April, 1st (np) May 1991
Toss : Yorkshire.  Umpires : B.Hassan and A.A.Jones
Match drawn.  Middlesex 1 pt (Bt: 0, Bw: 1), Yorkshire 3 pts (Bt: 2, Bw: 1)
100 overs scores : Yorkshire 208 for 4

### YORKSHIRE

| | | |
|---|---|---|
| M.D.Moxon * | b Cowans | 15 |
| A.A.Metcalfe | c Downton b Headley | 18 |
| D.Byas | c Downton b Headley | 32 |
| R.J.Blakey + | c Downton b Headley | 97 |
| P.E.Robinson | c Downton b Tufnell | 10 |
| S.A.Kellett | run out | 42 |
| P.Carrick | c Gatting b Emburey | 0 |
| P.W.Jarvis | not out | 22 |
| P.J.Hartley | b Headley | 1 |
| J.D.Batty | c Cowans b Taylor | 0 |
| M.A.Robinson | c Brown b Headley | 8 |
| Extras | (b 1,lb 11,nb 2) | 14 |
| TOTAL | | 259 |

### MIDDLESEX

| | | |
|---|---|---|
| I.J.F.Hutchinson | lbw b Jarvis | 1 |
| J.C.Pooley | c Blakey b Robinson M.A. | 3 |
| M.W.Gatting * | not out | 25 |
| M.R.Ramprakash | lbw b Jarvis | 0 |
| K.R.Brown | not out | 12 |
| P.R.Downton + | | |
| J.E.Emburey | | |
| D.W.Headley | | |
| C.W.Taylor | | |
| P.C.R.Tufnell | | |
| N.G.Cowans | | |
| Extras | | 0 |
| TOTAL | (for 3 wkts) | 41 |

| MIDDLESEX | O | M | R | W | O | M | R | W | | FALL OF WICKETS | | | |
|---|---|---|---|---|---|---|---|---|---|---|---|---|---|
| Cowans | 18 | 2 | 44 | 1 | | | | | | | YOR | MID YOR | MID |
| Taylor | 20 | 2 | 57 | 1 | | | | | 1st | | 26 | 4 | |
| Headley | 18 | 5 | 46 | 5 | | | | | 2nd | | 38 | 4 | |
| Emburey | 32 | 13 | 55 | 1 | | | | | 3rd | | 125 | 4 | |
| Tufnell | 27 | 10 | 45 | 1 | | | | | 4th | | 141 | | |
| | | | | | | | | | 5th | | 224 | | |
| YORKSHIRE | O | M | R | W | O | M | R | W | 6th | | 225 | | |
| Jarvis | 6 | 1 | 25 | 2 | | | | | 7th | | 227 | | |
| Robinson M.A. | 6 | 2 | 16 | 1 | | | | | 8th | | 229 | | |
| Hartley | 1 | 1 | 0 | 0 | | | | | 9th | | 240 | | |
| | | | | | | | | | 10th | | 259 | | |

## HEADLINES

### Britannic Assurance Championship

### 27th April - 1st May

- The first round of Championship matches was ruined by appalling weather, little cricket being possible anywhere on Monday, Tuesday or Wednesday, with the inevitable result that all eight matches were drawn.

- The matches at Southampton and Worcester were least badly affected, by virtue of Sunday play which allowed two uninterrupted days. Kent's Mark Benson took full advantage against Hampshire, compiling a career-best 257 to begin his first season as Kent captain in imperious fashion. Former captain Chris Cowdrey gave him good support in a fourth-wicket stand of 224 as Kent's total reached 482.  Tony Merrick's four wickets put Hampshire under considerable pressure by the end of the second day, but there was to be no resumption.

- Worcestershire's contest against Gloucestershire didn't get beyond the second day either, to the chagrin of Tom Moody who was denied the opportunity of scoring a century on his Championship début for Worcestershire as he had done for Warwickshire in 1990. Gloucestershire could be pleased with their early efforts, totalling 450 after a stand of 179 from new opening pair Dean Hodgson and Richard Scott, who hit 127 on his début for the county.

- Derbyshire's match with Northamptonshire was restricted to the first day, Alan Fordham starting his Championship season with 131 and Rob Bailey and Allan Lamb also making runs in a total of 347 for four.

- Despite the efforts of Darren Bicknell, who carried his bat with 145 out of Surrey's total of 268, Essex were building a strong position when rain ended play midway through the second day.

- Chris Lewis had put Leicestershire in command at Leicester with figures of 5 for 35 as Glamorgan were dismissed for 161 on the opening day, but even a declaration from Nigel Briers could not resurrect the match after the elements had had their say.

- The story was similar at Lord's where the champions were under pressure from Yorkshire's seam bowlers when the weather intervened at lunch on the second day. Dean Headley marked his Championship début with five wickets for 46, but Mike Gatting had been faced with a considerable challenge when Middlesex lost their first three wickets for four runs.

- Sussex were the only side able to achieve maximum bonus points, dismissing Somerset for 229 on the first day then, when play resumed on the fourth day, reaching 300 for five thanks to 117* from Jamie Hall.

- Gehan Mendis hit his second first-class hundred of the season, Neil Fairbrother his first, as Lancashire enjoyed excellent conditions on the opening day at Edgbaston, but Warwickshire found batting more difficult on the third and fourth days, managing a solitary batting point.

- First-class débuts: A.M.Smith (Gloucestershire), A.G.Robson (Surrey).

# OTHER FIRST-CLASS MATCH

## OXFORD U vs. NOTTS

at The Parks on 27th, 29th (np), 30th (np) April 1991
Toss : Notts.  Umpires : R.Julien and G.A.Stickley
Match drawn

**NOTTS**

| | | |
|---|---|---|
| P.Pollard | lbw b Oppenheimer | 20 |
| M.Newell | lbw b Turner | 91 |
| M.A.Crawley | c Montgomerie b Gupte | 112 |
| P.Johnson * | not out | 97 |
| M.Saxelby | c Sandiford b Gupte | 13 |
| K.P.Evans | c Sandiford b Lovell | 13 |
| D.J.R.Martindale | not out | 4 |
| C.W.Scott + | | |
| M.G.Field-Buss | | |
| R.A.Pick | | |
| J.A.Afford | | |
| Extras | (b 11,lb 1,w 6) | 18 |
| TOTAL | (for 5 wkts) | 368 |

**OXFORD U**

R.E.Morris
R.R.Montgomerie
C.Gupte
G.Lovell
G.J.Turner *
D.Pfaff
D.A.Hagan
D.Sandiford +
J.M.E.Oppenheimer
R.MacDonald
B.Wood
Extras
TOTAL

| OXFORD U | O | M | R | W | | O | M | R | W | FALL OF WICKETS | | | | |
|---|---|---|---|---|---|---|---|---|---|---|---|---|---|---|
| | | | | | | | | | | | NOT | OXF | NOT | OXF |
| MacDonald | 23 | 8 | 55 | 0 | | | | | | 1st | 40 | | | |
| Wood | 19 | 3 | 74 | 0 | | | | | | 2nd | 206 | | | |
| Oppenheimer | 19 | 2 | 75 | 1 | | | | | | 3rd | 257 | | | |
| Turner | 29 | 6 | 92 | 1 | | | | | | 4th | 285 | | | |
| Pfaff | 2 | 0 | 6 | 0 | | | | | | 5th | 348 | | | |
| Gupte | 9 | 1 | 41 | 2 | | | | | | 6th | | | | |
| Lovell | 4 | 0 | 13 | 1 | | | | | | 7th | | | | |
| | | | | | | | | | | 8th | | | | |
| NOTTS | O | M | R | W | | O | M | R | W | 9th | | | | |
| | | | | | | | | | | 10th | | | | |

Mark Crawley (left), who enjoyed his return to The Parks, and Mike Newell (right), who was also in the runs.

# BENSON & HEDGES CUP

## GLOUCS vs. NORTHANTS

at Bristol on 2nd May 1991
Toss : Gloucs. Umpires : R.Julian and A.G.T.Whitehead
Gloucs won by 7 wickets. Gloucs 2 pts, Northants 0 pts
Man of the match: A.J.Wright

### NORTHANTS

| | | |
|---|---|---|
| A.Fordham | lbw b Gilbert | 0 |
| N.A.Felton | c Russell b Lawrence | 22 |
| R.J.Bailey | c Athey b Lawrence | 15 |
| A.J.Lamb * | b Lawrence | 0 |
| D.J.Capel | run out | 42 |
| R.G.Williams | c & b Alleyne | 29 |
| E.A.E.Baptiste | c & b Babington | 11 |
| D.Ripley + | not out | 36 |
| J.G.Thomas | c Athey b Lawrence | 3 |
| N.G.B.Cook | run out | 1 |
| J.P.Taylor | not out | |
| Extras | (b 1,lb 5,w 3,nb 1) | 10 |
| TOTAL | (55 overs)(for 9 wkts) | 170 |

### GLOUCS

| | | |
|---|---|---|
| G.D.Hodgson | c Taylor b Thomas | 3 |
| R.J.Scott | st Ripley b Williams | 46 |
| A.J.Wright * | c Lamb b Taylor | 81 |
| C.W.J.Athey | not out | 22 |
| R.C.Russell + | not out | 0 |
| M.W.Alleyne | | |
| J.W.Lloyds | | |
| D.V.Lawrence | | |
| D.R.Gilbert | | |
| A.M.Smith | | |
| A.M.Babington | | |
| Extras | (lb 10,w 9) | 19 |
| TOTAL | (53.1 overs)(for 3 wkts) | 171 |

| GLOUCS | O | M | R | W | FALL OF WICKETS | | |
|---|---|---|---|---|---|---|---|
| | | | | | | NOR | GLO |
| Gilbert | 11 | 1 | 31 | 1 | 1st | 0 | 10 |
| Babington | 11 | 3 | 24 | 1 | 2nd | 36 | 86 |
| Lawrence | 11 | 1 | 44 | 4 | 3rd | 40 | 165 |
| Smith | 11 | 0 | 26 | 0 | 4th | 44 | |
| Scott | 3 | 0 | 15 | 0 | 5th | 92 | |
| Alleyne | 8 | 0 | 24 | 1 | 6th | 110 | |
| | | | | | 7th | 138 | |
| NORTHANTS | O | M | R | W | 8th | 147 | |
| Thomas | 10 | 3 | 22 | 1 | 9th | 158 | |
| Taylor | 11 | 3 | 25 | 1 | 10th | | |
| Baptiste | 6.1 | 0 | 38 | 0 | | | |
| Capel | 11 | 1 | 29 | 0 | | | |
| Cook | 4 | 1 | 16 | 0 | | | |
| Williams | 11 | 2 | 31 | 1 | | | |

## LEICESTERSHIRE vs. SCOTLAND

at Leicester on 2nd May 1991
Toss : Leics. Umpires : B.Leadbeater and P.B.Wight
Leicestershire won by 45 runs. Leics 2 pts, Scotland 0 pts
Man of the match: T.J.Boon

### LEICESTERSHIRE

| | | |
|---|---|---|
| T.J.Boon | c Haggo b Cowan | 103 |
| N.E.Briers * | c Haggo b Reifer | 36 |
| J.J.Whitaker | c Reifer b Bee | 84 |
| P.Willey | b Cowan | 0 |
| L.Potter | not out | 3 |
| J.D.R.Benson | not out | 6 |
| P.N.Hepworth | | |
| P.Whitticase + | | |
| C.Wilkinson | | |
| J.N.Maguire | | |
| D.J.Millns | | |
| Extras | (lb 6,w 4,nb 1) | 11 |
| TOTAL | (55 overs)(for 4 wkts) | 243 |

### SCOTLAND

| | | |
|---|---|---|
| I.L.Philip | c Whitticase b Wilkinson | 35 |
| B.M.W.Patterson | run out | 12 |
| G.N.Reifer | c Millns b Wilkinson | 31 |
| R.G.Swan | lbw b Wilkinson | 55 |
| A.B.Russell | lbw b Hepworth | 2 |
| O.Henry * | c Wilkinson b Hepworth | 22 |
| J.W.Govan | st Whitticase b Hepworth | 10 |
| A.W.Bee | c Briers b Millns | 3 |
| D.J.Haggo + | not out | 10 |
| D.Cowan | c Maguire b Hepworth | 0 |
| J.D.Moir | not out | 6 |
| Extras | (lb 6,w 6) | 12 |
| TOTAL | (55 overs)(for 9 wkts) | 198 |

| SCOTLAND | O | M | R | W | FALL OF WICKETS | | |
|---|---|---|---|---|---|---|---|
| | | | | | | LEI | SCO |
| Moir | 11 | 6 | 16 | 0 | 1st | 71 | 47 |
| Bee | 6 | 0 | 38 | 1 | 2nd | 231 | 51 |
| Cowan | 8 | 0 | 54 | 2 | 3rd | 231 | 138 |
| Reifer | 9 | 0 | 36 | 1 | 4th | 232 | 144 |
| Henry | 11 | 0 | 43 | 0 | 5th | | 144 |
| Govan | 10 | 0 | 50 | 0 | 6th | | 176 |
| | | | | | 7th | | 179 |
| LEICS | O | M | R | W | 8th | | 182 |
| Maguire | 6 | 0 | 25 | 0 | 9th | | 182 |
| Millns | 7 | 0 | 25 | 1 | | | |
| Wilkinson | 11 | 1 | 46 | 3 | | | |
| Willey | 11 | 3 | 15 | 0 | | | |
| Potter | 9 | 0 | 42 | 0 | | | |
| Hepworth | 11 | 1 | 39 | 4 | | | |

## WARWICKSHIRE vs. SOMERSET

at Edgbaston on 2nd May 1991
Toss : Somerset. Umpires : D.O.Oslear and R.Palmer
Warwicks won by 33 runs. Warwicks 2 pts, Somerset 0 pts
Man of the match: Asif Din

### WARWICKSHIRE

| | | |
|---|---|---|
| A.J.Moles | st Burns b Swallow | 65 |
| Asif Din | c Cook b Mallender | 137 |
| T.A.Lloyd * | c Hayhurst b Beal | 40 |
| P.A.Smith | lbw b Lefebvre | 5 |
| D.A.Reeve | b Beal | 19 |
| D.P.Ostler | run out | 12 |
| K.J.Piper + | not out | 6 |
| P.A.Booth | | |
| G.C.Small | | |
| A.A.Donald | | |
| T.A.Munton | | |
| Extras | (b 4,lb 12,w 2,nb 1) | 19 |
| TOTAL | (55 overs)(for 6 wkts) | 303 |

### SOMERSET

| | | |
|---|---|---|
| S.J.Cook | b Booth | 58 |
| P.M.Roebuck | b Munton | 11 |
| A.N.Hayhurst | c Lloyd b Donald | 70 |
| C.J.Tavare * | c Lloyd b Donald | 53 |
| G.D.Rose | c Munton b Donald | 2 |
| R.J.Harden | c Smith b Reeve | 21 |
| N.D.Burns + | b Donald | 21 |
| R.P.Lefebvre | c & b Reeve | 2 |
| I.G.Swallow | b Reeve | 3 |
| N.A.Mallender | run out | 1 |
| D.Beal | not out | 0 |
| Extras | (b 9,lb 10,w 5,nb 4) | 28 |
| TOTAL | (54.2 overs) | 270 |

| SOMERSET | O | M | R | W | FALL OF WICKETS | | |
|---|---|---|---|---|---|---|---|
| | | | | | | WAR | SOM |
| Mallender | 11 | 1 | 47 | 1 | 1st | 146 | 36 |
| Rose | 10 | 1 | 38 | 0 | 2nd | 238 | 100 |
| Lefebvre | 11 | 1 | 59 | 1 | 3rd | 256 | 207 |
| Beal | 8 | 0 | 63 | 2 | 4th | 277 | 213 |
| Swallow | 10 | 0 | 58 | 1 | 5th | 286 | 255 |
| Roebuck | 5 | 0 | 22 | 0 | 6th | 303 | 257 |
| | | | | | 7th | | 262 |
| WARWICKS | O | M | R | W | 8th | | 264 |
| Munton | 11 | 0 | 48 | 1 | 9th | | 267 |
| Donald | 11 | 0 | 55 | 4 | 10th | | 270 |
| Small | 11 | 1 | 52 | 0 | | | |
| Reeve | 9.2 | 0 | 43 | 3 | | | |
| Booth | 7 | 0 | 35 | 1 | | | |
| Smith | 5 | 0 | 18 | 0 | | | |

## COMBINED U vs. WORCESTERSHIRE

at Fenner's on 2nd May 1991
Toss : Worcestershire. Umpires : J.D.Bond and B.Hassan
Worcs won by 6 wickets. Combined U 0 pts, Worcs 2 pts
Man of the match: T.M.Moody

### COMBINED U

| | | |
|---|---|---|
| R.E.Morris | c Rhodes b Radford | 6 |
| N.V.Knight * | lbw b Radford | 9 |
| J.P.Crawley | lbw b Botham | 0 |
| J.I.Longley | run out | 47 |
| G.J.Turner | c D'Oliveira b Newport | 12 |
| P.C.L.Holloway + | c D'Oliveira b Lampitt | 22 |
| R.Macdonald | not out | 5 |
| J.C.Hallett | c Botham b Newport | 5 |
| R.H.J.Jenkins | c Rhodes b Radford | 9 |
| A.R.Hansford | not out | 13 |
| R.M.Pearson | | |
| Extras | (lb 7,w 3,nb 3) | 13 |
| TOTAL | (55 overs)(for 8 wkts) | 148 |

### WORCESTERSHIRE

| | | |
|---|---|---|
| T.S.Curtis | c Jenkins b MacDonald | 2 |
| T.M.Moody | c Longley b Hallett | 50 |
| G.A.Hick | lbw b Hallett | 55 |
| D.B.D'Oliveira | b Hallett | 8 |
| P.A.Neale * | not out | 8 |
| I.T.Botham | not out | 16 |
| S.J.Rhodes + | | |
| R.K.Illingworth | | |
| P.J.Newport | | |
| S.R.Lampitt | | |
| N.V.Radford | | |
| Extras | (lb 4,w 6) | 10 |
| TOTAL | (32.1 overs)(for 4 wkts) | 149 |

| WORCS | O | M | R | W | FALL OF WICKETS | | |
|---|---|---|---|---|---|---|---|
| | | | | | | COM | WOR |
| Radford | 11 | 5 | 22 | 3 | 1st | 16 | 9 |
| Botham | 11 | 5 | 26 | 1 | 2nd | 17 | 104 |
| Illingworth | 11 | 1 | 28 | 0 | 3rd | 17 | 116 |
| Lampitt | 11 | 1 | 29 | 1 | 4th | 33 | 128 |
| Newport | 11 | 2 | 36 | 2 | 5th | 92 | |
| | | | | | 6th | 113 | |
| COMBINED U | O | M | R | W | 7th | 118 | |
| Hansford | 6 | 0 | 31 | 0 | 8th | 131 | |
| MacDonald | 6 | 0 | 31 | 1 | 9th | | |
| Pearson | 6 | 0 | 24 | 0 | 10th | | |
| Hallett | 10.1 | 0 | 36 | 3 | | | |
| Jenkins | 4 | 0 | 23 | 0 | | | |

## ESSEX vs. MIDDLESEX

at Chelmsford on 2nd May 1991
Toss : Essex. Umpires : G.I.Burgess and R.A.White
Essex won by 3 wickets. Essex 2 pts, Middlesex 0 pts
Man of the match: N.A.Foster

### MIDDLESEX

| | | |
|---|---|---|
| M.W.Gatting * | lbw b Ilott | 6 |
| J.C.Pooley | lbw b Foster | 1 |
| M.R.Ramprakash | run out | 33 |
| K.R.Brown | lbw b Stephenson | 20 |
| M.Keech | run out | 37 |
| P.R.Downton + | c Shahid b Foster | 58 |
| J.E.Emburey | st Garnham b Such | 6 |
| N.F.Williams | c Prichard b Pringle | 1 |
| R.M.Ellcock | run out | 0 |
| D.W.Headley | run out | 2 |
| P.C.R.Tufnell | not out | 0 |
| Extras | (lb 2,w 15,nb 5) | 22 |
| TOTAL | (54 overs) | 186 |

### ESSEX

| | | |
|---|---|---|
| G.A.Gooch * | c Downton b Ellcock | 29 |
| J.P.Stephenson | c Downton b Emburey | 23 |
| P.J.Prichard | lbw b Emburey | 31 |
| Salim Malik | b Emburey | 3 |
| N.Hussain | b Williams | 0 |
| N.Shahid | c Gatting b Williams | 0 |
| D.R.Pringle | not out | 36 |
| M.A.Garnham + | c Keech b Headley | 8 |
| N.A.Foster | not out | 39 |
| M.C.Ilott | | |
| P.M.Such | | |
| Extras | (b 1,lb 4,w 10,nb 6) | 21 |
| TOTAL | (47.1 overs)(for 7 wkts) | 190 |

| ESSEX | O | M | R | W | FALL OF WICKETS | | |
|---|---|---|---|---|---|---|---|
| | | | | | | MID | ESS |
| Ilott | 10 | 1 | 32 | 1 | 1st | 4 | 59 |
| Foster | 10 | 1 | 28 | 2 | 2nd | 13 | 93 |
| Pringle | 9 | 1 | 32 | 1 | 3rd | 68 | 100 |
| Gooch | 9 | 0 | 41 | 0 | 4th | 76 | 101 |
| Stephenson | 5 | 0 | 17 | 1 | 5th | 137 | 101 |
| Such | 11 | 1 | 34 | 1 | 6th | 172 | 105 |
| | | | | | 7th | 178 | 121 |
| MIDDLESEX | O | M | R | W | 8th | 182 | |
| Ellcock | 10 | 0 | 55 | 1 | 9th | 184 | |
| Williams | 11 | 4 | 19 | 2 | 10th | 186 | |
| Headley | 9.1 | 1 | 34 | 1 | | | |
| Tufnell | 6 | 0 | 37 | 0 | | | |
| Emburey | 11 | 2 | 40 | 3 | | | |

## KENT vs. SUSSEX

at Canterbury on 2nd May 1991
Toss : Sussex. Umpires : A.A.Jones and M.J.Kitchen
Kent won by 4 wickets. Kent 2 pts, Sussex 0 pts
Man of the match: C.S.Cowdrey

### SUSSEX

| | | |
|---|---|---|
| D.M.Smith | lbw b Igglesden | 4 |
| J.W.Hall | lbw b Ellison | 8 |
| P.W.G.Parker * | lbw b Ellison | 1 |
| A.P.Wells | c & b Ealham | 66 |
| M.P.Speight | run out | 35 |
| J.A.North | run out | 13 |
| P.Moores + | c Ellison b Fleming | 20 |
| A.C.S.Pigott | b Igglesden | 16 |
| I.D.K.Salisbury | not out | 17 |
| B.T.P.Donelan | not out | 8 |
| A.N.Jones | | |
| Extras | (b 1,lb 23,w 5,nb 1) | 30 |
| TOTAL | (55 overs)(for 8 wkts) | 218 |

### KENT

| | | |
|---|---|---|
| N.R.Taylor | b North | 21 |
| M.R.Benson * | b Salisbury | 28 |
| T.R.Ward | c Wells b Salisbury | 38 |
| G.R.Cowdrey | c Moores b Pigott | 18 |
| C.S.Cowdrey | not out | 57 |
| M.V.Fleming | c Smith b Jones | 0 |
| V.J.Wells + | c Moores b Salisbury | 25 |
| R.M.Ellison | not out | 7 |
| M.A.Ealham | | |
| T.A.Merrick | | |
| A.P.Igglesden | | |
| Extras | (lb 16,w 11,nb 1) | 28 |
| TOTAL | (54.4 overs)(for 6 wkts) | 222 |

| KENT | O | M | R | W | FALL OF WICKETS | | |
|---|---|---|---|---|---|---|---|
| | | | | | | SUS | KEN |
| Ellison | 11 | 5 | 19 | 2 | 1st | 12 | 58 |
| Igglesden | 11 | 2 | 35 | 2 | 2nd | 17 | 62 |
| Ealham | 11 | 0 | 46 | 1 | 3rd | 18 | 111 |
| Merrick | 11 | 0 | 53 | 0 | 4th | 101 | 153 |
| Fleming | 11 | 0 | 41 | 1 | 5th | 122 | 154 |
| | | | | | 6th | 153 | 201 |
| SUSSEX | O | M | R | W | 7th | 183 | |
| Jones | 10.4 | 1 | 41 | 1 | 8th | 191 | |
| Pigott | 11 | 1 | 41 | 1 | 9th | | |
| Donelan | 11 | 0 | 54 | 0 | 10th | | |
| North | 11 | 1 | 30 | 1 | | | |
| Salisbury | 11 | 0 | 40 | 3 | | | |

# BENSON & HEDGES CUP

## HAMPSHIRE vs. GLAMORGAN

at Southampton on 2nd May 1991
Toss : Glam. Umpires : J.C.Balderstone and D.R.Shepherd
Hampshire won by 59 runs. Hants 2 pts, Glamorgan 0 pts
Man of the match: C.L.Smith

### HAMPSHIRE

| | | |
|---|---|---|
| T.C.Middleton | c Roberts b Smith | 54 |
| C.L.Smith | b Barwick | 142 |
| D.I.Gower | b Frost | 63 |
| M.C.J.Nicholas * | not out | 15 |
| J.R.Wood | lbw b Barwick | 6 |
| J.R.Ayling | not out | 5 |
| A.N Aymes + | | |
| C.A.Connor | | |
| S.D.Udal | | |
| P.J.Bakker | | |
| Aqib Javed | | |
| Extras | (b 4,lb 5,w 5) | 14 |
| TOTAL | (55 overs)(for 4 wkts) | 299 |

### GLAMORGAN

| | | |
|---|---|---|
| A.R.Butcher * | c Gower b Udal | 70 |
| H.Morris | c Aymes b Bakker | 3 |
| A.Dale | c Middleton b Ayling | 19 |
| M.P.Maynard | b Connor | 6 |
| G.C.Holmes | c Aymes b Connor | 1 |
| I.Smith | b Bakker | 51 |
| M.L.Roberts + | c & b Udal | 1 |
| S.J.Dennis | c Bakker b Connor | 50 |
| S.L.Watkin | c Middleton b Nicholas | 15 |
| S.R.Barwick | not out | 1 |
| M.Frost | c Wood b Nicholas | 0 |
| Extras | (b 1,lb 7,w 9,nb 6) | 23 |
| TOTAL | (55 overs) | 240 |

| GLAMORGAN | O | M | R | W | FALL OF WICKETS | | |
|---|---|---|---|---|---|---|---|
| | | | | | | HAM | GLA |
| Watkin | 11 | 0 | 69 | 0 | | | |
| Frost | 11 | 2 | 50 | 1 | 1st | 140 | 18 |
| Barwick | 11 | 0 | 61 | 2 | 2nd | 264 | 86 |
| Dennis | 11 | 1 | 29 | 0 | 3rd | 274 | 107 |
| Dale | 4 | 0 | 30 | 0 | 4th | 289 | 111 |
| Smith | 7 | 0 | 51 | 1 | 5th | | 111 |
| | | | | | 6th | | 117 |
| HAMPSHIRE | O | M | R | W | 7th | | 193 |
| Aqib Javed | 9 | 1 | 30 | 0 | 8th | | 230 |
| Bakker | 11 | 2 | 37 | 2 | 9th | | 239 |
| Connor | 11 | 0 | 54 | 3 | 10th | | 240 |
| Ayling | 9 | 0 | 51 | 1 | | | |
| Udal | 11 | 2 | 33 | 2 | | | |
| Nicholas | 4 | 0 | 27 | 2 | | | |

## YORKSHIRE vs. MINOR COUNTIES

at Headingley on 2nd May 1991
Toss : Yorkshire. Umpires : H.D.Bird and K.E.Palmer
Yorks won by 7 wickets. Yorks 2 pts, Minor Counties 0 pts
Man of the match: M.D.Moxon

### MINOR COUNTIES

| | | |
|---|---|---|
| G.K.Brown | c Fletcher b Pickles | 6 |
| M.J.Roberts | c Blakey b Jarvis | 6 |
| N.A.Folland | c Fletcher b Pickles | 54 |
| J.D.Love | not out | 80 |
| S.G.Plumb | c Blakey b Robinson M.A. | 0 |
| D.R.Thomas | b Jarvis | 6 |
| A.R.Fothergill + | not out | 15 |
| S.Greensword * | | |
| R.A.Evans | | |
| N.R.Taylor | | |
| A.J.Mack | | |
| Extras | (lb 6,w 9) | 15 |
| TOTAL | (55 overs)(for 5 wkts) | 182 |

### YORKSHIRE

| | | |
|---|---|---|
| M.D.Moxon * | b Greensword | 65 |
| A.A.Metcalfe | not out | 92 |
| D.Byas | run out | 3 |
| R.J.Blakey + | c Folland b Greensword | 0 |
| P.E.Robinson | not out | 11 |
| S.A.Kellett | | |
| P.W.Jarvis | | |
| C.S.Pickles | | |
| S.D.Fletcher | | |
| J.D.Batty | | |
| M.A.Robinson | | |
| Extras | (lb 6,w 6,nb 1) | 13 |
| TOTAL | (53.2 overs)(for 3 wkts) | 184 |

| YORKSHIRE | O | M | R | W | FALL OF WICKETS | | |
|---|---|---|---|---|---|---|---|
| | | | | | | MIN | YOR |
| Jarvis | 11 | 5 | 27 | 2 | 1st | 11 | 135 |
| Fletcher | 11 | 3 | 26 | 0 | 2nd | 20 | 148 |
| Robinson M.A. | 11 | 2 | 33 | 1 | 3rd | 138 | 160 |
| Pickles | 11 | 0 | 49 | 2 | 4th | 138 | |
| Batty | 11 | 2 | 41 | 0 | 5th | 160 | |
| | | | | | 6th | | |
| MIN. COUNTIES | O | M | R | W | 7th | | |
| Taylor | 10.2 | 3 | 36 | 0 | 8th | | |
| Mack | 9 | 2 | 32 | 0 | 9th | | |
| Thomas | 11 | 0 | 49 | 0 | 10th | | |
| Evans | 11 | 0 | 37 | 0 | | | |
| Greensword | 11 | 3 | 21 | 2 | | | |
| Plumb | 1 | 0 | 3 | 0 | | | |

# HEADLINES

## Benson & Hedges Cup

### 2nd - 3rd May

• Worcestershire gained their second win in Group A, restricting Combined Universities to 148 for eight and needing only 32.1 overs to reach their target, Graeme Hick and Tom Moody both making fifties.

• Gloucestershire kept their qualification hopes alive by beating Northamptonshire by seven wickets. David Lawrence took his tally to 12 wickets in three B & H matches and Tony Wright hit 81 to secure victory.

• Essex became the first side to qualify from Group B, after their three-wicket victory over Middlesex in a match of fluctuating fortunes. Middlesex's total of 186 had looked a modest one until Essex lost six wickets for 28 runs to stand at 121 for seven, but Derek Pringle and Neil Foster came to the rescue with an unbroken eighth-wicket stand of 69.

• Warwickshire this time had the better of another high-scoring match at Edgbaston, Asif Din making the highest score by a Warwickshire batsman in B & H cricket as they reached 303 for six against a weakened Somerset attack. Although the visitors passed 200 with only two wickets down they lost momentum and wickets to fall 33 runs short.

• Kent gained their second win in Group C, overcoming Sussex by four wickets with two balls to spare. Chris Cowdrey calmed Kentish nerves with an unbeaten 57 after Ian Salisbury had returned his best B & H figures.

• Leicestershire gained their first victory at the third attempt by defeating Scotland by 45 runs, Tim Boon and James Whitaker adding 160 for the second wicket.

• Hampshire continued to lead Group D with a 59-run victory over Glamorgan, as Chris Smith made his second B & H 100 of the season in a formidable 299 for four. Ian Smith and Simon Dennis both made their first B & H fifties for Glamorgan

• Jim Love hit an unbeaten 80 for Minor Counties on his return to Headingley but it was to no avail as Martyn Moxon and Ashley Metcalfe helped Yorkshire to their first victory with an opening stand of 135.

## NORTHANTS vs. COMBINED U

at Northampton on 4th May 1991
Toss : Combined U. Umpires : A.A.Jones and K.E.Palmer
Northants won by 6 wickets. N'hants 2 pts, Comb U 0 pts
Man of the match: A.Fordham

### COMBINED U

| | | |
|---|---|---|
| R.E.Morris | b Penberthy | 7 |
| N.V.Knight * | c Ripley b Penberthy | 12 |
| J.P.Crawley | c Ripley b Thomas | 40 |
| J.I.Longley | run out | 9 |
| G.J.Turner | not out | 80 |
| I.Fletcher | c Ripley b Williams | 9 |
| P.C.L.Holloway + | run out | 10 |
| R.MacDonald | | |
| J.C.Hallett | | |
| A.R.Hansford | | |
| R.H.J.Jenkins | | |
| Extras | (b 1,lb 8,w 8,nb 2) | 19 |
| TOTAL | (55 overs)(for 6 wkts) | 186 |

### NORTHANTS

| | | |
|---|---|---|
| A.Fordham | not out | 93 |
| N.A.Felton | c Fletcher b Hallett | 20 |
| R.J.Bailey | c Holloway b Hallett | 1 |
| A.J.Lamb * | c Knight b MacDonald | 34 |
| D.J.Capel | run out | 11 |
| R.G.Williams | not out | 17 |
| E.A.E.Baptiste | | |
| A.L.Penberthy | | |
| D.Ripley + | | |
| J.G.Thomas | | |
| J.P.Taylor | | |
| Extras | (lb 2,w 7,nb 2) | 11 |
| TOTAL | (43.4 overs)(for 4 wkts) | 187 |

| NORTHANTS | O | M | R | W | FALL OF WICKETS | | |
|---|---|---|---|---|---|---|---|
| | | | | | | COM | NOR |
| Thomas | 11 | 1 | 30 | 1 | 1st | 22 | 54 |
| Baptiste | 10 | 3 | 24 | 0 | 2nd | 23 | 56 |
| Taylor | 10 | 3 | 37 | 0 | 3rd | 49 | 122 |
| Penberthy | 9 | 3 | 22 | 2 | 4th | 106 | 135 |
| Capel | 4 | 0 | 20 | 0 | 5th | 142 | |
| Williams | 11 | 0 | 44 | 1 | 6th | 186 | |
| | | | | | 7th | | |
| COMBINED U | O | M | R | W | 8th | | |
| Hansford | 7 | 0 | 18 | 0 | 9th | | |
| Hallett | 11 | 0 | 38 | 2 | 10th | | |
| MacDonald | 11 | 0 | 59 | 1 | | | |
| Turner | 9.4 | 2 | 41 | 0 | | | |
| Jenkins | 4 | 0 | 25 | 0 | | | |
| Knight | 1 | 0 | 4 | 0 | | | |

## WORCESTERSHIRE vs. DERBYSHIRE

at Worcester on 4th May 1991
Toss : Worcestershire. Umpires : J.H.Harris and B.Hassan
Worcestershire won by 7 wickets. Worcs 2 pts, Derby 0 pts
Man of the match: T.M.Moody

### DERBYSHIRE

| | | |
|---|---|---|
| K.J.Barnett * | c Radford b Lampitt | 66 |
| P.D.Bowler + | c Hick b Radford | 29 |
| J.E.Morris | b Lampitt | 18 |
| M.Azharuddin | run out | 30 |
| B.Roberts | c Newport b Dilley | 24 |
| T.J.G.O'Gorman | lbw b Newport | 6 |
| C.J.Adams | not out | 16 |
| A.E.Warner | c Rhodes b Dilley | 4 |
| D.E.Malcolm | b Lampitt | 8 |
| S.J.Base | run out | 1 |
| O.H.Mortensen | lbw b Radford | 2 |
| Extras | (lb 8,w 1,nb 10) | 19 |
| TOTAL | (53 overs) | 223 |

### WORCESTERSHIRE

| | | |
|---|---|---|
| T.S.Curtis | b Warner | 30 |
| T.M.Moody | not out | 110 |
| G.A.Hick | b Roberts | 6 |
| D.B.D'Oliveira | c Bowler b Mortensen | 17 |
| I.T.Botham | not out | 35 |
| P.A.Neale * | | |
| S.J.Rhodes + | | |
| P.J.Newport | | |
| S.R.Lampitt | | |
| N.V.Radford | | |
| G.R.Dilley | | |
| Extras | (b 1,lb 11,w 14,nb 3) | 29 |
| TOTAL | (51.3 overs)(for 3 wkts) | 227 |

| WORCS | O | M | R | W | FALL OF WICKETS | | |
|---|---|---|---|---|---|---|---|
| | | | | | | DER | WOR |
| Dilley | 11 | 0 | 57 | 2 | 1st | 73 | 75 |
| Radford | 10 | 2 | 36 | 2 | 2nd | 104 | 87 |
| Botham | 11 | 0 | 40 | 0 | 3rd | 133 | 126 |
| Lampitt | 10 | 0 | 46 | 3 | 4th | 176 | |
| Newport | 11 | 0 | 36 | 1 | 5th | 188 | |
| | | | | | 6th | 192 | |
| DERBYSHIRE | O | M | R | W | 7th | 201 | |
| Malcolm | 11 | 1 | 46 | 0 | 8th | 218 | |
| Mortensen | 11 | 0 | 47 | 1 | 9th | 219 | |
| Base | 11 | 1 | 44 | 0 | 10th | 223 | |
| Warner | 9.3 | 0 | 34 | 1 | | | |
| Roberts | 6 | 0 | 32 | 1 | | | |
| Azharuddin | 3 | 0 | 12 | 0 | | | |

# BENSON & HEDGES CUP

## MIDDLESEX vs. WARWICKSHIRE

at Lord's on 4th, 6th May 1991
Toss : Middlesex. Umpires : J.D.Bond and P.B.Wight
Warwicks won by 39 runs. Middx 0 pts, Warwicks 2 pts
Man of the match: P.A.Smith

### WARWICKSHIRE

| | | |
|---|---|---|
| A.J.Moles | c Williams b Headley | 51 |
| Asif Din | run out | 97 |
| P.A.Smith | c Downton b Williams | 34 |
| T.A.Lloyd * | c & b Embury | 0 |
| D.A.Reeve | c Headley b Cowans | 12 |
| D.P.Ostler | c Embury b Cowans | 7 |
| K.J.Piper + | run out | 7 |
| G.C.Small | c Ramprakash b Cowans | 1 |
| P.A.Booth | run out | 11 |
| A.A.Donald | not out | 2 |
| T.A.Munton | not out | 2 |
| Extras | (lb 7,w 5,nb 1) | 13 |
| TOTAL | (55 overs)(for 9 wkts) | 237 |

### MIDDLESEX

| | | |
|---|---|---|
| I.J.F.Hutchinson | c Piper b Smith | 8 |
| M.W.Gatting * | c Piper b Reeve | 17 |
| M.R.Ramprakash | b Smith | 7 |
| K.R.Brown | c Reeve b Smith | 12 |
| M.Keech | c Reeve b Smith | 47 |
| P.R.Downton + | c Piper b Reeve | 41 |
| J.E.Emburey | b Reeve | 23 |
| N.F.Williams | c Donald b Small | 3 |
| D.W.Headley | c Ostler b Munton | 2 |
| P.C.R.Tufnell | run out | 18 |
| N.G.Cowans | not out | 0 |
| Extras | (b 2,lb 6,w 11,nb 1) | 20 |
| TOTAL | (51.3 overs) | 198 |

| MIDDLESEX | O | M | R | W | FALL OF WICKETS | | |
|---|---|---|---|---|---|---|---|
| | | | | | | WAR | MID |
| Cowans | 11 | 0 | 39 | 3 | 1st | 120 | 34 |
| Williams | 11 | 2 | 41 | 1 | 2nd | 186 | 36 |
| Headley | 11 | 1 | 44 | 1 | 3rd | 187 | 55 |
| Emburey | 11 | 0 | 47 | 1 | 4th | 202 | 57 |
| Tufnell | 11 | 0 | 59 | 0 | 5th | 206 | 132 |
| | | | | | 6th | 213 | 153 |
| WARWICKSHIRE | O | M | R | W | 7th | 219 | 161 |
| Donald | 9 | 1 | 32 | 0 | 8th | 232 | 166 |
| Munton | 11 | 2 | 27 | 1 | 9th | 232 | 198 |
| Smith | 11 | 1 | 28 | 3 | 10th | | 198 |
| Reeve | 9.3 | 0 | 48 | 3 | | | |
| Small | 11 | 0 | 55 | 1 | | | |

## SOMERSET vs. SURREY

at Taunton on 4th May 1991
Toss : Somerset. Umpires : K.J.Lyons and D.R.Shepherd
Somerset won by 4 wickets. Somerset 2 pts, Surrey 0 pts
Man of the match: S.J.Cook

### SURREY

| | | |
|---|---|---|
| D.J.Bicknell | run out | 11 |
| J.D.Robinson | c Tavare b Swallow | 35 |
| A.J.Stewart + | not out | 110 |
| D.M.Ward | b Rose | 28 |
| G.P.Thorpe | c Swallow b Lefebvre | 41 |
| I.A.Greig * | c Lefebvre b Rose | 4 |
| M.A.Feltham | c Tavare b Lefebvre | 2 |
| C.K.Bullen | c Mallender b Lefebvre | 0 |
| M.P.Bicknell | | |
| Waqar Younis | | |
| A.J.Murphy | | |
| Extras | (lb 5,w 6,nb 2) | 13 |
| TOTAL | (55 overs)(for 7 wkts) | 244 |

### SOMERSET

| | | |
|---|---|---|
| S.J.Cook | c Bullen b Feltham | 76 |
| P.M.Roebuck | b Waqar Younis | 0 |
| R.J.Harden | c & b Waqar Younis | 1 |
| C.J.Tavare * | b Murphy | 39 |
| R.J.Bartlett | b Waqar Younis | 14 |
| N.D.Burns + | not out | 43 |
| G.D.Rose | b Bicknell M.P. | 23 |
| R.P.Lefebvre | not out | 21 |
| I.G.Swallow | | |
| M.W.Cleal | | |
| N.A.Mallender | | |
| Extras | (b 4,lb 10,w 15) | 29 |
| TOTAL | (53.2 overs)(for 6 wkts) | 246 |

| SOMERSET | O | M | R | W | FALL OF WICKETS | | |
|---|---|---|---|---|---|---|---|
| | | | | | | SUR | SOM |
| Mallender | 10 | 0 | 54 | 0 | 1st | 31 | 1 |
| Rose | 11 | 1 | 48 | 2 | 2nd | 68 | 11 |
| Swallow | 11 | 1 | 31 | 1 | 3rd | 133 | 110 |
| Lefebvre | 11 | 1 | 44 | 3 | 4th | 226 | 134 |
| Cleal | 4 | 0 | 21 | 0 | 5th | 231 | 157 |
| Roebuck | 8 | 0 | 41 | 0 | 6th | 243 | 212 |
| | | | | | 7th | 244 | |
| SURREY | O | M | R | W | 8th | | |
| Waqar Younis | 11 | 2 | 29 | 3 | 9th | | |
| Bicknell M.P. | 11 | 0 | 49 | 1 | 10th | | |
| Feltham | 10.2 | 0 | 58 | 1 | | | |
| Murphy | 11 | 0 | 48 | 1 | | | |
| Bullen | 6 | 0 | 29 | 0 | | | |
| Thorpe | 4 | 0 | 19 | 0 | | | |

## YORKSHIRE vs. HAMPSHIRE

at Headingley on 4th May 1991
Toss : Hants. Umpires : B.Dudleston and J.H.Hampshire
Yorkshire won by 189 runs. Yorks 2 pts, Hampshire 0 pts
Man of the match: A.Sidebottom

### YORKSHIRE

| | | |
|---|---|---|
| M.D.Moxon * | b Connor | 24 |
| A.A.Metcalfe | c & b Udal | 37 |
| D.Byas | c Ayling b Aqib Javed | 92 |
| R.J.Blakey + | c Smith b Ayling | 20 |
| P.E.Robinson | b Connor | 43 |
| P.W.Jarvis | c Ayling b Aqib Javed | 0 |
| P.J.Hartley | c Wood b Aqib Javed | 1 |
| S.A.Kellett | not out | 0 |
| A.Sidebottom | | |
| J.D.Batty | | |
| S.D.Fletcher | | |
| Extras | (lb 7,w 13,nb 2) | 22 |
| TOTAL | (55 overs)(for 7 wkts) | 239 |

### HAMPSHIRE

| | | |
|---|---|---|
| T.C.Middleton | b Jarvis | 2 |
| C.L.Smith | c Robinson b Sidebottom | 1 |
| D.I.Gower | lbw b Jarvis | 5 |
| J.R.Wood | c Robinson b Sidebottom | 14 |
| M.C.J.Nicholas * | run out | 0 |
| J.R.Ayling | lbw b Sidebottom | 2 |
| A.N Aymes + | c Robinson b Hartley | 10 |
| S.D.Udal | c Moxon b Sidebottom | 1 |
| C.A.Connor | c Blakey b Hartley | 3 |
| P.J.Bakker | b Fletcher | 7 |
| Aqib Javed | not out | 0 |
| Extras | (w 1,nb 4) | 5 |
| TOTAL | (27.2 overs) | 50 |

| HAMPSHIRE | O | M | R | W | FALL OF WICKETS | | |
|---|---|---|---|---|---|---|---|
| | | | | | | YOR | HAM |
| Aqib Javed | 11 | 2 | 51 | 3 | 1st | 42 | 2 |
| Bakker | 11 | 1 | 54 | 0 | 2nd | 106 | 11 |
| Connor | 11 | 2 | 59 | 2 | 3rd | 165 | 11 |
| Ayling | 11 | 0 | 51 | 1 | 4th | 228 | 14 |
| Udal | 11 | 3 | 17 | 1 | 5th | 231 | 24 |
| | | | | | 6th | 237 | 29 |
| YORKSHIRE | O | M | R | W | 7th | 239 | 33 |
| Jarvis | 7 | 2 | 13 | 2 | 8th | | 43 |
| Sidebottom | 11 | 5 | 19 | 4 | 9th | | 46 |
| Hartley | 7 | 3 | 7 | 2 | 10th | | 50 |
| Fletcher | 2.2 | 0 | 11 | 1 | | | |

## LEICESTERSHIRE vs. LANCASHIRE

at Leicester on 4th May 1991
Toss : Lancashire. Umpires : J.W.Holder and R.A.White
Lancashire won by 7 wickets. Leics 0 pts, Lancashire 2 pts
Man of the match: P.J.W.Allott

### LEICESTERSHIRE

| | | |
|---|---|---|
| T.J.Boon | run out | 16 |
| N.E.Briers * | c Austin b Allott | 9 |
| J.J.Whitaker | lbw b Allott | 1 |
| P.Willey | c Hegg b Austin | 29 |
| L.Potter | b Allott | 54 |
| P.N.Hepworth | b Fitton | 9 |
| P.Whitticase + | not out | 34 |
| J.N.Maguire | b Allott | 0 |
| C.Wilkinson | not out | 19 |
| D.J.Millns | | |
| A.D.Mullally | | |
| Extras | (b 4,lb 5,w 11,nb 1) | 21 |
| TOTAL | (55 overs)(for 7 wkts) | 192 |

### LANCASHIRE

| | | |
|---|---|---|
| G.D.Mendis | c Boon b Hepworth | 36 |
| G.Fowler | c Briers b Maguire | 17 |
| M.A.Atherton | c Hepworth b Willey | 74 |
| N.H.Fairbrother * | not out | 53 |
| G.D.Lloyd | not out | 1 |
| P.A.J.DeFreitas | | |
| W.K.Hegg + | | |
| G.Yates | | |
| I.D.Austin | | |
| J.D.Fitton | | |
| P.J.W.Allott | | |
| Extras | (lb 4,w 7,nb 1) | 12 |
| TOTAL | (53.5 overs)(for 3 wkts) | 193 |

| LANCASHIRE | O | M | R | W | FALL OF WICKETS | | |
|---|---|---|---|---|---|---|---|
| | | | | | | LEI | LAN |
| DeFreitas | 11 | 3 | 37 | 0 | 1st | 12 | 42 |
| Allott | 11 | 4 | 23 | 4 | 2nd | 16 | 69 |
| Yates | 11 | 3 | 35 | 0 | 3rd | 41 | 189 |
| Austin | 11 | 1 | 41 | 1 | 4th | 88 | |
| Fitton | 11 | 0 | 47 | 1 | 5th | 111 | |
| | | | | | 6th | 148 | |
| LEICS | O | M | R | W | 7th | 148 | |
| Mullally | 11 | 2 | 26 | 0 | 8th | | |
| Millns | 7 | 0 | 37 | 0 | 9th | | |
| Wilkinson | 9 | 2 | 26 | 0 | 10th | | |
| Maguire | 9 | 2 | 27 | 1 | | | |
| Willey | 8.5 | 0 | 29 | 1 | | | |
| Hepworth | 9 | 1 | 44 | 1 | | | |

## SUSSEX vs. SCOTLAND

at Hove on 4th, 5th May 1991
Toss : Scotland. Umpires : D.J.Constant and R.C.Tolchard
Sussex won by 4 runs. Sussex 2 pts, Scotland 0 pts
Man of the match: D.M.Smith

### SUSSEX

| | | |
|---|---|---|
| D.M.Smith | b Bee | 102 |
| J.W.Hall | run out | 28 |
| P.W.G.Parker * | c Cowan b Bee | 35 |
| A.P.Wells | c Govan b Henry | 0 |
| M.P.Speight | run out | 6 |
| J.A.North | st Haggo b Moir | 22 |
| A.C.S.Pigott | c Russell b Moir | 2 |
| P.Moores + | st Haggo b Bee | 9 |
| I.D.K.Salisbury | c Russell b Bee | 5 |
| A.N.Jones | not out | 0 |
| R.A.Bunting | not out | 1 |
| Extras | (b 3,lb 9,w 4) | 16 |
| TOTAL | (55 overs)(for 9 wkts) | 226 |

### SCOTLAND

| | | |
|---|---|---|
| I.L.Philip | c Moores b Jones | 2 |
| B.M.W.Patterson | c Pigott b Jones | 0 |
| G.N.Reifer | c Salisbury b Bunting | 76 |
| G.Salmond | run out | 24 |
| A.B.Russell | c Pigott b Jones | 45 |
| O.Henry * | c Smith b Salisbury | 32 |
| J.W.Govan | run out | 9 |
| D.J.Haggo + | b Pigott | 1 |
| A.W.Bee | not out | 1 |
| J.D.Moir | | |
| D.Cowan | | |
| Extras | (b 1,lb 9,w 22) | 32 |
| TOTAL | (55 overs)(for 8 wkts) | 222 |

| SCOTLAND | O | M | R | W | FALL OF WICKETS | | |
|---|---|---|---|---|---|---|---|
| | | | | | | SUS | SCO |
| Reifer | 9 | 2 | 30 | 0 | 1st | 74 | 1 |
| Moir | 11 | 1 | 47 | 2 | 2nd | 134 | 3 |
| Govan | 10 | 0 | 52 | 0 | 3rd | 140 | 73 |
| Henry | 11 | 1 | 31 | 1 | 4th | 150 | 160 |
| Cowan | 5 | 1 | 23 | 0 | 5th | 202 | 187 |
| Bee | 9 | 0 | 31 | 4 | 6th | 204 | 218 |
| | | | | | 7th | 211 | 221 |
| SUSSEX | O | M | R | W | 8th | 223 | 222 |
| Jones | 11 | 3 | 43 | 3 | 9th | 225 | |
| Bunting | 11 | 1 | 34 | 1 | 10th | | |
| Pigott | 11 | 1 | 34 | 1 | | | |
| North | 11 | 0 | 57 | 0 | | | |
| Salisbury | 11 | 1 | 44 | 1 | | | |

## GLAMORGAN vs. NOTTS

at Cardiff on 4th May 1991
Toss : Notts. Umpires : J.C.Balderstone and D.O.Oslear
Glamorgan won by 1 run. Glamorgan 2 pts, Notts 0 pts
Man of the match: R.T.Robinson

### GLAMORGAN

| | | |
|---|---|---|
| A.R.Butcher * | run out | 57 |
| H.Morris | c French b Stephenson | 3 |
| R.J.Shastri | lbw b Evans | 16 |
| M.P.Maynard | c Randall b Saxelby | 62 |
| G.C.Holmes | b Hemmings | 22 |
| I.Smith | !bw b Evans | 36 |
| M.L.Roberts + | lbw b Evans | 0 |
| S.J.Dennis | c Randall b Evans | 5 |
| S.L.Watkin | c & b Stephenson | 5 |
| S.R.Barwick | not out | 4 |
| M.Frost | not out | 0 |
| Extras | (lb 8,w 6,nb 5) | 19 |
| TOTAL | (55 overs)(for 9 wkts) | 229 |

### NOTTS

| | | |
|---|---|---|
| B.C.Broad | c Smith b Frost | 0 |
| D.W.Randall | c Roberts b Watkin | 14 |
| R.T.Robinson * | b Frost | 116 |
| P.Johnson | c Maynard b Shastri | 14 |
| M.A.Crawley | c & b Barwick | 58 |
| M.Saxelby | c Maynard b Frost | 5 |
| F.D.Stephenson | not out | 4 |
| K.P.Evans | not out | 5 |
| B.N.French + | | |
| E.E.Hemmings | | |
| K.E.Cooper | | |
| Extras | (lb 9,w 3) | 12 |
| TOTAL | (55 overs)(for 6 wkts) | 228 |

| NOTTS | O | M | R | W | FALL OF WICKETS | | |
|---|---|---|---|---|---|---|---|
| | | | | | | GLA | NOT |
| Stephenson | 11 | 1 | 46 | 2 | 1st | 15 | 0 |
| Cooper | 10 | 1 | 34 | 0 | 2nd | 56 | 29 |
| Evans | 11 | 0 | 43 | 4 | 3rd | 97 | 53 |
| Saxelby | 9 | 0 | 36 | 1 | 4th | 153 | 200 |
| Hemmings | 11 | 1 | 46 | 1 | 5th | 207 | 214 |
| Crawley | 3 | 0 | 16 | 0 | 6th | 207 | 214 |
| | | | | | 7th | 218 | |
| GLAMORGAN | O | M | R | W | 8th | 221 | |
| Frost | 9 | 1 | 38 | 3 | 9th | 225 | |
| Dennis | 11 | 1 | 41 | 0 | 10th | | |
| Watkin | 11 | 3 | 42 | 1 | | | |
| Barwick | 10 | 1 | 42 | 1 | | | |
| Shastri | 11 | 0 | 40 | 1 | | | |
| Butcher | 3 | 0 | 16 | 0 | | | |

| B & H CUP | REFUGE ASSURANCE LEAGUE |
|---|---|

## HEADLINES

### Benson & Hedges Cup

### 4th - 6th May

• Tom Moody took Worcestershire to their third successive B & H victory and a guaranteed place in the quarter-finals. His unbeaten 110* was his first hundred in the competition as he dominated an unbroken stand of 101 with Ian Botham that ensured success.

• Northamptonshire kept alive their chance of qualification by beating Combined Universities. Graeme Turner improved his personal best for the students but 93 not out from Alan Fordham saw Northants to victory.

• Warwickshire gave themselves a good chance of qualifying by inflicting on Middlesex their third successive B & H defeat. Asif Din and Andy Moles shared their second consecutive 100 partnership as Warwicks reached 237 for nine, then Paul Smith reduced the home side from 34 for nought to 57 for four.

• Surrey's chances faded when they were beaten by Somerset after Alec Stewart had put them in a strong position with his first B & H century. However, Jimmy Cook laid a secure foundation for Somerset with 76, and Neil Burns saw them home.

• Lancashire made almost certain of a place in the quarter-finals with their third victory, again requiring a relatively modest total after Leicestershire struggled for runs against the miserly Paul Allott.

• Sussex just kept their hopes alive by defeating Scotland by four runs at Hove. The home side totalled 226 for nine, and the Scots, led by George Reifer, took up the challenge which failed only in the final over.

• Yorkshire beat Hampshire in convincing style. David Byas's 92 formed the backbone for the home side's total of 239 for seven, Hampshire were demolished for 50, the lowest total in B & H history.

• Glamorgan ensured that either they or Yorkshire qualify for the quarter-finals by defeating Nottinghamshire by one run. Notts had seemed well in control while Tim Robinson and Mark Crawley were adding 147 for the fourth wicket, but with their dismissals Notts lost all momentum and Glamorgan were able to hold on.

### GLAMORGAN vs. NOTTS
at Cardiff on 5th May 1991
Toss : Glam. Umpires : J.C.Balderstone and D.O.Oslear
Notts won by 4 wickets. Glamorgan 0 pts, Notts 4 pts

**GLAMORGAN**
| | | |
|---|---|---|
| A.R.Butcher * | b Saxelby | 77 |
| H.Morris | c Hemmings b Evans | 46 |
| M.P.Maynard | not out | 57 |
| I.Smith | not out | 28 |
| G.C.Holmes | | |
| R.D.B.Croft | | |
| A.Dale | | |
| M.L.Roberts + | | |
| S.L.Watkin | | |
| S.R.Barwick | | |
| M.Frost | | |
| Extras | (lb 8,w 4,nb 3) | 15 |
| TOTAL | (40 overs)(for 2 wkts) | 223 |

**NOTTS**
| | | |
|---|---|---|
| B.C.Broad | c Morris b Smith | 108 |
| D.W.Randall | lbw b Croft | 24 |
| R.T.Robinson * | c Watkin b Smith | 10 |
| P.Johnson | c Roberts b Frost | 22 |
| M.Saxelby | run out | 19 |
| F.D.Stephenson | run out | 15 |
| B.N.French + | not out | 8 |
| M.A.Crawley | not out | 5 |
| K.P.Evans | | |
| E.E.Hemmings | | |
| K.E.Cooper | | |
| Extras | (b 1,lb 6,w 6,nb 1) | 14 |
| TOTAL | (39 overs)(for 6 wkts) | 225 |

| NOTTS | O | M | R | W | FALL OF WICKETS | | |
|---|---|---|---|---|---|---|---|
| | | | | | | GLA | NOT |
| Cooper | 8 | 1 | 40 | 0 | 1st | 104 | 59 |
| Stephenson | 8 | 1 | 42 | 0 | 2nd | 146 | 87 |
| Saxelby | 8 | 1 | 36 | 1 | 3rd | | 144 |
| Hemmings | 6 | 1 | 27 | 0 | 4th | | 188 |
| Evans | 8 | 0 | 54 | 1 | 5th | | 204 |
| Crawley | 2 | 0 | 16 | 0 | 6th | | 218 |
| GLAMORGAN | O | M | R | W | 7th | | |
| Frost | 8 | 0 | 41 | 1 | 8th | | |
| Watkin | 7 | 0 | 33 | 0 | 9th | | |
| Dale | 2 | 0 | 16 | 0 | 10th | | |
| Barwick | 1 | 0 | 8 | 0 | | | |
| Croft | 8 | 0 | 39 | 1 | | | |
| Smith | 8 | 0 | 49 | 2 | | | |
| Butcher | 5 | 0 | 32 | 0 | | | |

### DERBYSHIRE vs. HAMPSHIRE
at Derby on 5th May 1991
Toss : Derby. Umpires : H.D.Bird and B.Leadbeater
Derby won by 4 wickets. Derby 4 pts, Hampshire 0 pts

**HAMPSHIRE**
| | | |
|---|---|---|
| V.P.Terry | c Bowler b Mortensen | 5 |
| C.L.Smith | run out | 29 |
| D.I.Gower | b Warner | 37 |
| J.R.Wood | c Warner b Roberts | 19 |
| M.C.J.Nicholas * | c Azharuddin b Malcolm | 23 |
| K.D.James | c Warner b Base | 12 |
| A.N Aymes + | not out | 17 |
| S.D.Udal | c Azharuddin b Warner | 6 |
| C.A.Connor | not out | 0 |
| P.J.Bakker | | |
| Aqib Javed | | |
| Extras | (b 3,lb 6,w 9) | 18 |
| TOTAL | (40 overs)(for 7 wkts) | 166 |

**DERBYSHIRE**
| | | |
|---|---|---|
| K.J.Barnett * | run out | 11 |
| P.D.Bowler + | b James | 8 |
| J.E.Morris | st Aymes b Udal | 32 |
| M.Azharuddin | lbw b Connor | 9 |
| B.Roberts | run out | 12 |
| T.J.G.O'Gorman | c Smith b James | 22 |
| C.J.Adams | not out | 34 |
| A.E.Warner | not out | 22 |
| D.E.Malcolm | | |
| S.J.Base | | |
| O.H.Mortensen | | |
| Extras | (lb 7,w 9,nb 1) | 17 |
| TOTAL | (39.1 overs)(for 6 wkts) | 167 |

| DERBYSHIRE | O | M | R | W | FALL OF WICKETS | | |
|---|---|---|---|---|---|---|---|
| | | | | | | HAM | DER |
| Base | 8 | 1 | 27 | 1 | 1st | 12 | 22 |
| Mortensen | 8 | 2 | 27 | 1 | 2nd | 76 | 27 |
| Malcolm | 8 | 0 | 35 | 1 | 3rd | 81 | 57 |
| Warner | 8 | 2 | 34 | 2 | 4th | 106 | 71 |
| Roberts | 8 | 1 | 34 | 1 | 5th | 125 | 91 |
| HAMPSHIRE | O | M | R | W | 6th | 155 | 128 |
| James | 8 | 1 | 29 | 2 | 7th | 165 | |
| Aqib Javed | 7.1 | 1 | 26 | 0 | 8th | | |
| Bakker | 8 | 1 | 31 | 0 | 9th | | |
| Connor | 8 | 0 | 48 | 1 | 10th | | |
| Udal | 8 | 2 | 26 | 1 | | | |

### MIDDLESEX vs. NORTHANTS
at Lord's on 5th May 1991
Match abandoned (without a ball bowled).
Middlesex 2 pts, Northants 2 pts

### GLOUCS vs. WORCESTERSHIRE
at Bristol on 5th May 1991
Toss : Gloucs. Umpires : M.J.Kitchen and R.Palmer
Worcs won by 10 wickets. Gloucs 0 pts, Worcs 4 pts

**GLOUCS**
| | | |
|---|---|---|
| R.J.Scott | c Rhodes b Weston | 32 |
| C.W.J.Athey | c & b Illingworth | 26 |
| A.J.Wright * | c Curtis b Illingworth | 23 |
| M.W.Alleyne | c Weston b Newport | 44 |
| J.J.E.Hardy | run out | 20 |
| P.W.Romaines | not out | 27 |
| R.C.Russell + | c Weston b Radford | 4 |
| D.V.Lawrence | c D'Oliveira b Radford | 0 |
| D.R.Gilbert | not out | 10 |
| M.C.J.Ball | | |
| A.M.Babington | | |
| Extras | (b 1,w 5,nb 1) | 7 |
| TOTAL | (39 overs)(for 7 wkts) | 193 |

**WORCESTERSHIRE**
| | | |
|---|---|---|
| T.S.Curtis | not out | 61 |
| T.M.Moody | not out | 128 |
| G.A.Hick | | |
| I.T.Botham | | |
| D.B.D'Oliveira | | |
| P.A.Neale * | | |
| M.J.Weston | | |
| S.J.Rhodes + | | |
| R.K.Illingworth | | |
| P.J.Newport | | |
| N.V.Radford | | |
| Extras | (lb 6,w 1,nb 1) | 8 |
| TOTAL | (29.4 overs)(for 0 wkts) | 197 |

| WORCS | O | M | R | W | FALL OF WICKETS | | |
|---|---|---|---|---|---|---|---|
| | | | | | | GLO | WOR |
| Newport | 8 | 0 | 47 | 1 | 1st | 52 | |
| Weston | 8 | 1 | 24 | 1 | 2nd | 67 | |
| Radford | 8 | 0 | 37 | 2 | 3rd | 98 | |
| Illingworth | 8 | 1 | 37 | 2 | 4th | 148 | |
| Botham | 7 | 0 | 47 | 0 | 5th | 149 | |
| GLOUCS | O | M | R | W | 6th | 161 | |
| Gilbert | 8 | 0 | 38 | 0 | 7th | 161 | |
| Babington | 6.4 | 0 | 48 | 0 | 8th | | |
| Lawrence | 8 | 0 | 42 | 0 | 9th | | |
| Ball | 2 | 0 | 19 | 0 | 10th | | |
| Alleyne | 3 | 0 | 33 | 0 | | | |
| Scott | 2 | 0 | 11 | 0 | | | |

| REFUGE ASSURANCE LEAGUE | B & H CUP |
| --- | --- |

## ESSEX vs. LEICESTERSHIRE

at Chelmsford on 5th May 1991
Match abandoned. Essex 2 pts, Leicestershire 2 pts

## HEADLINES

### Refuge Assurance League

### 5th May

• Half the day's programme was washed out, as all three matches in the South East were abandoned without a ball bowled, but Nottinghamshire took advantage of better weather at Cardiff to take an early lead in the Refuge table. Their third successive victory was achieved largely thanks to Chris Broad's highest Sunday score, and the visitors had an over in hand when they overhauled Glamorgan's total.

• Worcestershire had almost 10 overs to spare when they defeated Gloucestershire by 10 wickets at Bristol, Tom Moody again batting in the most commanding fashion to record his second successive Sunday 100 as he and Tim Curtis shared an unbeaten opening stand of 197 in just 29.4 overs.

• Derbyshire also registered their second Sunday victory of the season, beating Hampshire by four wickets at Derby in a low-scoring contest in which David Gower's 37 was the highest individual score.

## KENT vs. WARWICKSHIRE

at Canterbury on 5th May 1991
Match abandoned. Kent 2 pts, Warwickshire 2 pts

K

## NORTHANTS vs. WORCESTERSHIRE

at Northampton on 7th May 1991
Toss : Worcs. Umpires : D.J.Constant and J.W.Holder
Northants won by 75 runs. Northants 2 pts, Worcs 0 pts
Man of the match: A.Fordham

NORTHANTS
| A.Fordham | run out | 70 |
| --- | --- | --- |
| N.A.Felton | lbw b Dilley | 10 |
| R.J.Bailey | c Rhodes b Dilley | 55 |
| A.J.Lamb * | c Moody b Weston | 23 |
| D.J.Capel | c Newport b Botham | 27 |
| R.G.Williams | not out | 28 |
| E.A.E.Baptiste | c Illingworth b Botham | 2 |
| D.Ripley + | b Botham | 5 |
| J.G.Thomas | c Newport b Dilley | 3 |
| N.G.B.Cook | b Dilley | 0 |
| J.P.Taylor | not out | 1 |
| Extras | (b 1,lb 9,w 12,nb 2) | 24 |
| TOTAL | (55 overs)(for 9 wkts) | 248 |

WORCESTERSHIRE
| T.S.Curtis | b Taylor | 11 |
| --- | --- | --- |
| T.M.Moody | b Baptiste | 17 |
| G.A.Hick | c Felton b Taylor | 4 |
| D.B.D'Oliveira | b Cook | 21 |
| I.T.Botham | c Fordham b Capel | 0 |
| P.A.Neale * | not out | 52 |
| M.J.Weston | run out | 30 |
| S.J.Rhodes + | not out | 13 |
| R.K.Illingworth | | |
| P.J.Newport | | |
| G.R.Dilley | | |
| Extras | (b 1,lb 10,w 14) | 25 |
| TOTAL | (55 overs)(for 6 wkts) | 173 |

| WORCS | O | M | R | W | FALL OF WICKETS | | |
| --- | --- | --- | --- | --- | --- | --- | --- |
| | | | | | | NOR | WOR |
| Dilley | 11 | 1 | 35 | 4 | 1st | 29 | 32 |
| Botham | 11 | 1 | 46 | 3 | 2nd | 132 | 32 |
| Newport | 11 | 0 | 64 | 0 | 3rd | 157 | 50 |
| Illingworth | 11 | 0 | 52 | 0 | 4th | 180 | 58 |
| Weston | 11 | 0 | 41 | 1 | 5th | 211 | 65 |
| NORTHANTS | O | M | R | W | 6th | 222 | 146 |
| Thomas | 8 | 0 | 38 | 0 | 7th | 237 | |
| Baptiste | 11 | 2 | 30 | 1 | 8th | 246 | |
| Taylor | 10 | 0 | 30 | 2 | 9th | 247 | |
| Capel | 4 | 0 | 9 | 1 | 10th | | |
| Cook | 11 | 1 | 21 | 1 | | | |
| Williams | 11 | 0 | 34 | 0 | | | |

## DERBYSHIRE vs. GLOUCS

at Derby on 6th, 7th May 1991
Toss : Derby. Umpires : B.Dudleston and D.O.Oslear
Derby won on faster scoring rate. Derby 2 pts, Gloucs 0 pts
Man of the match: K.J.Barnett

GLOUCS
| R.J.Scott | c Bowler b Warner | 14 |
| --- | --- | --- |
| C.W.J.Athey | b Mortensen | 81 |
| A.J.Wright * | c & b Azharuddin | 45 |
| J.J.E.Hardy | b Barnett | 6 |
| M.W.Alleyne | c Barnett b Malcolm | 1 |
| P.W.Romaines | c Bowler b Malcolm | 22 |
| R.C.Russell + | c O'Gorman b Warner | 9 |
| D.V.Lawrence | not out | 18 |
| D.R.Gilbert | run out | 8 |
| A.M.Babington | c Barnett b Base | 4 |
| A.M.Smith | not out | 1 |
| Extras | (lb 5,w 8,nb 2) | 15 |
| TOTAL | (55 overs)(for 9 wkts) | 224 |

DERBYSHIRE
| K.J.Barnett * | b Smith | 102 |
| --- | --- | --- |
| P.D.Bowler + | lbw b Gilbert | 7 |
| J.E.Morris | b Babington | 0 |
| M.Azharuddin | c Russell b Lawrence | 22 |
| B.Roberts | c Romaines b Babington | 49 |
| T.J.G.O'Gorman | not out | 23 |
| C.J.Adams | run out | 2 |
| A.E.Warner | not out | 0 |
| D.E.Malcolm | | |
| S.J.Base | | |
| O.H.Mortensen | | |
| Extras | (b 2,lb 11,w 6) | 19 |
| TOTAL | (55 overs)(for 6 wkts) | 224 |

| DERBYSHIRE | O | M | R | W | FALL OF WICKETS | | |
| --- | --- | --- | --- | --- | --- | --- | --- |
| | | | | | | GLO | DER |
| Mortensen | 11 | 3 | 36 | 1 | 1st | 37 | 20 |
| Base | 9 | 3 | 26 | 1 | 2nd | 133 | 21 |
| Warner | 11 | 0 | 57 | 2 | 3rd | 151 | 67 |
| Barnett | 11 | 1 | 34 | 1 | 4th | 153 | 186 |
| Malcolm | 11 | 0 | 49 | 2 | 5th | 165 | 216 |
| Azharuddin | 2 | 0 | 17 | 1 | 6th | 189 | 219 |
| GLOUCS | O | M | R | W | 7th | 193 | |
| Gilbert | 11 | 2 | 37 | 1 | 8th | 217 | |
| Babington | 11 | 0 | 49 | 2 | 9th | 222 | |
| Lawrence | 11 | 0 | 38 | 1 | 10th | | |
| Smith | 11 | 0 | 39 | 1 | | | |
| Alleyne | 5 | 0 | 24 | 0 | | | |
| Scott | 6 | 0 | 24 | 0 | | | |

# BENSON & HEDGES CUP

## HEADLINES

### Benson & Hedges Cup

### 7th - 8th May

• The final round of the B & H qualifiying matches saw the normal scramble for the remaining quarter-final places, calculators and slide rules being employed to compare run-rates. Northamptonshire caused the day's major surprise at Worcester by reducing Worcestershire to 65 for five in reply to their own total of 248 for nine. Phil Neale was forced to concede his side's first defeat of the season in order to concentrate on maintaining a superior run-rate: Northants duly joined Worcestershire in the quarter-finals.

• Although neither Derbyshire nor Gloucestershire could now qualify, they produced an exciting finish to their match at Derby, the home side winning by losing fewer wickets after Kim Barnett had compiled his third B & H 100.

• Essex completed their fourth successive win to head Group B, Graham Gooch and John Stephenson making victory over Somerset at Chelmsford a formality with an opening stand of 151.

• The major excitement came in the group's other match at The Oval where Surrey made a last desperate effort to claim the second qualifying position. The first part of their attempt went exactly to plan as their bowlers limited Warwickshire to 184 for seven in their 55 overs; Surrey now had 22.3 overs to reach their target and a quickfire sixth-wicket stand of 90 between Jonathan Robinson and Darren Bicknell certainly had Warwickshire pulses racing, but Tim Munton and Dermot Reeve shared eight wickets as the visitors fought back to claim a remarkable one-run victory and a place in the quarter-finals.

• Lancashire made sure of their place in the quarter-final draw in less frenetic fashion by outplaying Sussex at Old Trafford to gain their fourth win by 123 runs. Their total of 330 for four was the best by the county in a completed B & H match, and Graeme Fowler's 136 was the highest score by a Lancashire player in all one-day cricket, last year's performances against Hampshire not being allowed official status. Michael Atherton's 91 was also a career best and Neil Farbrother pitched in with 50 in six overs. Sussex's Ian Salisbury probably deserved a medal for conceding only 33 runs from his 11 overs, and Jamie Hall could also be pleased with a best B & H score of 71.

• Kent confirmed second place in the group with a comfortable 130-run win over Scotland in Glasgow, Neil Taylor hitting his fifth B & H century as the visitors made the most of their long journey with their best total in the competition. Determined resistance from the Scotish lower-order at least avoided a rout.

• Glamorgan and Yorkshire were effectively playing off for top spot in Group D at Cardiff with the losers failing even to qualify for the quarter-finals, and it was the visitors who came out on top, thanks to a marvellous opening stand of 213 between Martyn Moxon, who was only one run short of Geoffrey Boycott's individual record for the county, and Ashley Metcalfe. Glamorgan's openers also shared a century partnership and Alan Butcher went on to complete his first B & H 100, but it wasn't enough to prevent Yorkshire joining Hampshire in the quarter-finals.

• Nottinghamshire finished their B & H campaign with victory over Minor Counties at Trent Bridge, Paul Johnson's century bringing their total to 279 for five, but it was the Minor Counties' Neil Folland who took the individual honours with his first 100 in senior cricket.

## ESSEX vs. SOMERSET

at Chelmsford on 7th, 8th May 1991
Toss : Essex. Umpires : J.D.Bond and N.T.Plews
Essex won by 8 wickets. Essex 2 pts, Somerset 0 pts
Man of the match: G.A.Gooch

### SOMERSET

| | | |
|---|---|---|
| S.J.Cook | c & b Gooch | 38 |
| P.M.Roebuck | run out | 2 |
| R.J.Harden | c Garnham b Ilott | 1 |
| C.J.Tavare * | lbw b Such | 46 |
| R.J.Bartlett | lbw b Gooch | 14 |
| N.D.Burns + | c Garnham b Pringle | 9 |
| G.D.Rose | c Garnham b Pringle | 1 |
| R.P.Lefebvre | not out | 23 |
| I.G.Swallow | c Garnham b Pringle | 2 |
| M.W.Cleal | lbw b Foster | 18 |
| N.A.Mallender | not out | 2 |
| Extras | (b 1,lb 4,w 10,nb 3) | 18 |
| TOTAL | (55 overs)(for 9 wkts) | 174 |

### ESSEX

| | | |
|---|---|---|
| G.A.Gooch * | c Burns b Mallender | 72 |
| J.P.Stephenson | c Bartlett b Rose | 60 |
| P.J.Prichard | not out | 12 |
| Salim Malik | not out | 12 |
| N.Hussain | | |
| N.Shahid | | |
| D.R.Pringle | | |
| M.A.Garnham + | | |
| N.A.Foster | | |
| M.C.Ilott | | |
| P.M.Such | | |
| Extras | (lb 4,w 4,nb 11) | 19 |
| TOTAL | (37.5 overs)(for 2 wkts) | 175 |

| ESSEX | O | M | R | W | | FALL OF WICKETS | |
|---|---|---|---|---|---|---|---|
| | | | | | | SOM | ESS |
| Foster | 11 | 1 | 41 | 1 | | | |
| Ilott | 10 | 2 | 35 | 1 | 1st | 8 | 151 |
| Pringle | 11 | 1 | 31 | 3 | 2nd | 12 | 152 |
| Gooch | 11 | 1 | 19 | 2 | 3rd | 69 | |
| Such | 11 | 1 | 34 | 1 | 4th | 96 | |
| Stephenson | 1 | 0 | 9 | 0 | 5th | 122 | |
| | | | | | 6th | 123 | |
| SOMERSET | O | M | R | W | 7th | 124 | |
| Mallender | 10 | 0 | 35 | 1 | 8th | 131 | |
| Rose | 10.5 | 0 | 55 | 1 | 9th | 166 | |
| Lefebvre | 8 | 2 | 25 | 0 | 10th | | |
| Cleal | 6 | 0 | 34 | 0 | | | |
| Swallow | 3 | 0 | 22 | 0 | | | |

## SURREY vs. WARWICKSHIRE

at The Oval on 7th May 1991
Toss : Surrey. Umpires : K.E.Palmer and A.G.T.Whitehead
Warwickshire won by 1 run. Surrey 0 pts, Warwicks 2 pts
Man of the match: D.A.Reeve

### WARWICKSHIRE

| | | |
|---|---|---|
| A.J.Moles | run out | 21 |
| J.D.Ratcliffe | c Greig b Murphy | 29 |
| T.A.Lloyd * | c Robinson b Greig | 32 |
| P.A.Smith | b Boiling | 17 |
| D.A.Reeve | b Greig | 13 |
| D.P.Ostler | b Robinson | 28 |
| R.G.Twose | run out | 5 |
| K.J.Piper + | not out | 11 |
| P.A.Booth | not out | 4 |
| A.A.Donald | | |
| T.A.Munton | | |
| Extras | (b 4,lb 11,w 8,nb 1) | 24 |
| TOTAL | (55 overs)(for 7 wkts) | 184 |

### SURREY

| | | |
|---|---|---|
| A.D.Brown | c Booth b Reeve | 37 |
| I.A.Greig * | c Moles b Donald | 4 |
| A.J.Stewart + | b Munton | 0 |
| D.M.Ward | c Booth b Donald | 5 |
| G.P.Thorpe | c Piper b Reeve | 28 |
| J.D.Robinson | c Moles b Reeve | 38 |
| D.J.Bicknell | c Booth b Reeve | 53 |
| M.P.Bicknell | c Ostler b Munton | 4 |
| J.Boiling | c Moles b Munton | 7 |
| A.J.Murphy | b Munton | 1 |
| Waqar Younis | not out | 0 |
| Extras | (b 1,lb 3,w 2) | 6 |
| TOTAL | (31.4 overs) | 183 |

| SURREY | O | M | R | W | | FALL OF WICKETS | |
|---|---|---|---|---|---|---|---|
| | | | | | | WAR | SUR |
| Waqar Younis | 5.4 | 0 | 16 | 0 | 1st | 57 | 5 |
| Bicknell M.P. | 8 | 1 | 26 | 0 | 2nd | 58 | 7 |
| Murphy | 10 | 1 | 34 | 1 | 3rd | 85 | 30 |
| Robinson | 11 | 2 | 29 | 1 | 4th | 127 | 66 |
| Boiling | 11 | 0 | 38 | 1 | 5th | 140 | 80 |
| Greig | 9.2 | 0 | 26 | 2 | 6th | 151 | 170 |
| | | | | | 7th | 177 | 170 |
| WARWICKS | O | M | R | W | 8th | | 179 |
| Donald | 7 | 0 | 55 | 2 | 9th | | 182 |
| Munton | 7.4 | 0 | 35 | 4 | 10th | | 183 |
| Booth | 6 | 0 | 46 | 0 | | | |
| Reeve | 11 | 0 | 43 | 4 | | | |

# BENSON & HEDGES CUP

## LANCASHIRE vs. SUSSEX
at Old Trafford on 7th May 1991
Toss : Sussex. Umpires : B.Leadbeater and R.A.White
Lancashire won by 123 runs. Lancashire 2 pts, Sussex 0 pts
Man of the match: G.Fowler

**LANCASHIRE**

|  | | |
|---|---|---|
| G.D.Mendis | lbw b Salisbury | 31 |
| G.Fowler | c Moores b North | 136 |
| M.A.Atherton | c Bunting b Giddins | 91 |
| N.H.Fairbrother * | c Salisbury b North | 50 |
| G.D.Lloyd | not out | 6 |
| Wasim Akram | not out | 6 |
| P.A.J.DeFreitas | | |
| W.K.Hegg + | | |
| G.Yates | | |
| I.D.Austin | | |
| P.J.W.Allott | | |
| Extras | (lb 5,w 5) | 10 |
| TOTAL | (55 overs)(for 4 wkts) | 330 |

**SUSSEX**

|  | | |
|---|---|---|
| D.M.Smith | lbw b Wasim Akram | 27 |
| J.W.Hall | c Atherton b Yates | 71 |
| M.P.Speight | c Atherton b Wasim Akram | 1 |
| A.P.Wells * | c Mendis b Yates | 7 |
| K.Greenfield | c Hegg b Wasim Akram | 33 |
| J.A.North | run out | 9 |
| P.Moores + | c Fairbrother b Wasim Akram | 2 |
| A.C.S.Pigott | c & b DeFreitas | 29 |
| I.D.K.Salisbury | b Austin | 10 |
| R.A.Bunting | not out | 2 |
| E.S.H.Giddins | b DeFreitas | 0 |
| Extras | (b 3,lb 9,w 4) | 16 |
| TOTAL | (44.3 overs) | 207 |

| SUSSEX | O | M | R | W | | FALL OF WICKETS | | |
|---|---|---|---|---|---|---|---|---|
| | | | | | | | LAN | SUS |
| Pigott | 11 | 0 | 71 | 0 | 1st | | 84 | 64 |
| Giddins | 8 | 2 | 46 | 1 | 2nd | | 252 | 68 |
| North | 9 | 0 | 80 | 2 | 3rd | | 317 | 91 |
| Salisbury | 11 | 2 | 33 | 1 | 4th | | 321 | 138 |
| Bunting | 6 | 0 | 41 | 0 | 5th | | | 153 |
| Greenfield | 10 | 0 | 54 | 0 | 6th | | | 156 |
| | | | | | 7th | | | 170 |
| LANCASHIRE | O | M | R | W | 8th | | | 205 |
| Allott | 8 | 2 | 29 | 0 | 9th | | | 207 |
| DeFreitas | 7.3 | 1 | 36 | 2 | 10th | | | 207 |
| Austin | 9 | 0 | 62 | 1 | | | | |
| Wasim Akram | 9 | 3 | 18 | 4 | | | | |
| Yates | 11 | 0 | 50 | 2 | | | | |

## GLAMORGAN vs. YORKSHIRE
at Cardiff on 7th May 1991
Toss : Glamorgan. Umpires : B.Hassan and R.Julian
Yorkshire won by 8 wickets. Glamorgan 0 pts, Yorks 2 pts
Man of the match: M.D.Moxon

**GLAMORGAN**

|  | | |
|---|---|---|
| A.R.Butcher * | c Sidebottom b Hartley | 127 |
| H.Morris | b Fletcher | 36 |
| R.J.Shastri | c Blakey b Fletcher | 7 |
| M.P.Maynard | c Fletcher b Batty | 19 |
| G.C.Holmes | not out | 35 |
| I.Smith | b Jarvis | 1 |
| M.L.Roberts + | not out | 1 |
| S.J.Dennis | | |
| S.L.Watkin | | |
| S.R.Barwick | | |
| M.Frost | | |
| Extras | (lb 6,w 3) | 9 |
| TOTAL | (55 overs)(for 5 wkts) | 235 |

**YORKSHIRE**

|  | | |
|---|---|---|
| M.D.Moxon * | not out | 141 |
| A.A.Metcalfe | c Barwick b Shastri | 84 |
| D.Byas | lbw b Watkin | 7 |
| R.J.Blakey + | not out | 1 |
| P.E.Robinson | | |
| S.A.Kellett | | |
| P.J.Hartley | | |
| P.W.Jarvis | | |
| A.Sidebottom | | |
| S.D.Fletcher | | |
| J.D.Batty | | |
| Extras | (lb 4) | 4 |
| TOTAL | (49 overs)(for 2 wkts) | 237 |

| YORKSHIRE | O | M | R | W | | FALL OF WICKETS | | |
|---|---|---|---|---|---|---|---|---|
| | | | | | | | GLA | YOR |
| Jarvis | 11 | 0 | 57 | 1 | 1st | | 105 | 213 |
| Sidebottom | 11 | 2 | 22 | 0 | 2nd | | 117 | 225 |
| Hartley | 11 | 0 | 47 | 1 | 3rd | | 140 | |
| Batty | 11 | 1 | 34 | 1 | 4th | | 229 | |
| Fletcher | 11 | 0 | 69 | 2 | 5th | | 232 | |
| | | | | | 6th | | | |
| GLAMORGAN | O | M | R | W | 7th | | | |
| Frost | 9 | 2 | 44 | 0 | 8th | | | |
| Dennis | 11 | 1 | 49 | 0 | 9th | | | |
| Watkin | 11 | 0 | 51 | 1 | 10th | | | |
| Barwick | 8 | 0 | 41 | 0 | | | | |
| Shastri | 10 | 0 | 48 | 1 | | | | |

## SCOTLAND vs. KENT
at Glasgow on 7th May 1991
Toss : Scotland. Umpires : H.D.Bird and R.Palmer
Kent won by 130 runs. Scotland 0 pts, Kent 2 pts
Man of the match: N.R.Taylor

**KENT**

|  | | |
|---|---|---|
| N.R.Taylor | c Govan b Russell | 110 |
| M.R.Benson * | b Govan | 64 |
| T.R.Ward | c Philip b Russell | 29 |
| G.R.Cowdrey | st Haggo b Russell | 5 |
| C.S.Cowdrey | c Reifer b Russell | 11 |
| M.V.Fleming | c Henry b Cowan | 52 |
| R.M.Ellison | run out | 15 |
| V.J.Wells + | c Henry b Bee | 7 |
| M.A.Ealham | not out | 0 |
| T.A.Merrick | not out | 4 |
| A.P.Igglesden | | |
| Extras | (b 1,lb 10,w 11) | 22 |
| TOTAL | (55 overs)(for 8 wkts) | 319 |

**SCOTLAND**

|  | | |
|---|---|---|
| I.L.Philip | c Cowdrey C.S. b Igglesden | 2 |
| B.M.W.Patterson | c Wells b Igglesden | 23 |
| G.N.Reifer | lbw b Merrick | 9 |
| G.Salmond | c Merrick b Igglesden | 4 |
| A.B.Russell | c Cowdrey C.S. b Merrick | 0 |
| O.Henry * | c Wells b Ellison | 18 |
| J.W.Govan | c Ward b Ellison | 23 |
| D.J.Haggo + | c Ealham b Cowdrey C.S. | 25 |
| A.W.Bee | b Cowdrey C.S. | 35 |
| D.Cowan | b Fleming | 6 |
| J.D.Moir | not out | 2 |
| Extras | (b 4,lb 16,w 21,nb 1) | 42 |
| TOTAL | (47.3 overs) | 189 |

| SCOTLAND | O | M | R | W | | FALL OF WICKETS | | |
|---|---|---|---|---|---|---|---|---|
| | | | | | | | KEN | SCO |
| Moir | 10 | 3 | 57 | 0 | 1st | | 127 | 13 |
| Reifer | 3 | 0 | 16 | 0 | 2nd | | 210 | 45 |
| Bee | 7 | 0 | 47 | 1 | 3rd | | 217 | 51 |
| Govan | 11 | 0 | 63 | 1 | 4th | | 236 | 58 |
| Cowan | 6 | 0 | 33 | 1 | 5th | | 247 | 58 |
| Henry | 11 | 0 | 50 | 0 | 6th | | 296 | 104 |
| Russell | 7 | 0 | 42 | 4 | 7th | | 307 | 124 |
| | | | | | 8th | | 315 | 162 |
| KENT | O | M | R | W | 9th | | | 187 |
| Igglesden | 8 | 3 | 24 | 3 | 10th | | | 189 |
| Ealham | 8 | 1 | 32 | 0 | | | | |
| Merrick | 7 | 0 | 31 | 2 | | | | |
| Ellison | 11 | 1 | 42 | 2 | | | | |
| Fleming | 8.3 | 0 | 23 | 1 | | | | |
| Cowdrey C.S. | 5 | 1 | 17 | 2 | | | | |

## NOTTS vs. MINOR COUNTIES
at Trent Bridge on 7th May 1991
Toss : Min C'ties. Umpires : J.H.Hampshire and P.B.Wight
Notts won by 51 runs. Notts 2 pts, Minor Counties 0 pts
Man of the match: N.A.Folland

**NOTTS**

|  | | |
|---|---|---|
| B.C.Broad | c Brown b Arnold | 24 |
| D.W.Randall | b Thomas | 84 |
| R.T.Robinson * | c Folland b Taylor | 42 |
| P.Johnson | not out | 102 |
| M.A.Crawley | run out | 16 |
| F.D.Stephenson | c Greensword b Arnold | 1 |
| K.P.Evans | not out | 1 |
| B.N.French + | | |
| E.E.Hemmings | | |
| R.A.Pick | | |
| J.A.Afford | | |
| Extras | (lb 2,w 7) | 9 |
| TOTAL | (55 overs)(for 5 wkts) | 279 |

**MINOR COUNTIES**

|  | | |
|---|---|---|
| G.K.Brown | c Randall b Hemmings | 17 |
| M.J.Roberts | c Evans b Pick | 1 |
| N.A.Folland | not out | 100 |
| D.R.Turner | b Afford | 15 |
| S.G.Plumb | c Robinson b Crawley | 52 |
| D.R.Thomas | run out | 0 |
| A.R.Fothergill + | run out | 4 |
| I.E.Conn | not out | 23 |
| S.Greensword * | | |
| N.R.Taylor | | |
| K.A.Arnold | | |
| Extras | (lb 9,w 5,nb 2) | 16 |
| TOTAL | (55 overs)(for 6 wkts) | 228 |

| MIN. COUNTIES | O | M | R | W | | FALL OF WICKETS | | |
|---|---|---|---|---|---|---|---|---|
| | | | | | | | NOT | MIN |
| Taylor | 11 | 1 | 63 | 1 | 1st | | 39 | 21 |
| Arnold | 11 | 0 | 52 | 2 | 2nd | | 133 | 25 |
| Conn | 11 | 1 | 40 | 0 | 3rd | | 201 | 63 |
| Thomas | 11 | 1 | 61 | 1 | 4th | | 249 | 157 |
| Greensword | 5 | 0 | 28 | 0 | 5th | | 274 | 158 |
| Plumb | 6 | 0 | 33 | 0 | 6th | | | 169 |
| | | | | | 7th | | | |
| NOTTS | O | M | R | W | 8th | | | |
| Pick | 11 | 1 | 36 | 1 | 9th | | | |
| Stephenson | 4 | 3 | 3 | 0 | 10th | | | |
| Evans | 10 | 2 | 39 | 0 | | | | |
| Hemmings | 11 | 3 | 54 | 1 | | | | |
| Afford | 11 | 0 | 43 | 1 | | | | |
| Crawley | 8 | 0 | 44 | 1 | | | | |

## BENSON & HEDGES CUP
### FINAL LEAGUE TABLES

| | P | W | L | T | NR | Pts | Run Rate | Runs | Balls |
|---|---|---|---|---|---|---|---|---|---|
| **Group A** | | | | | | | | | |
| Worcestershire | 4 | 3 | 1 | 0 | 0 | 6 | 64.67 | 747 | 1155 |
| Northants | 4 | 3 | 1 | 0 | 0 | 6 | 63.57 | 796 | 1252 |
| Derbyshire | 4 | 2 | 2 | 0 | 0 | 4 | 71.06 | 938 | 1320 |
| Gloucs | 4 | 2 | 2 | 0 | 0 | 4 | 56.60 | 741 | 1309 |
| Combined U | 4 | 0 | 4 | 0 | 0 | 0 | 43.71 | 577 | 1320 |
| **Group B** | | | | | | | | | |
| Essex | 4 | 4 | 0 | 0 | 0 | 8 | 79.74 | 933 | 1170 |
| Warwickshire | 4 | 3 | 1 | 0 | 0 | 6 | 77.19 | 1019 | 1320 |
| Somerset | 4 | 1 | 3 | 0 | 0 | 2 | 68.55 | 898 | 1310 |
| Surrey | 4 | 1 | 3 | 0 | 0 | 2 | 65.90 | 870 | 1320 |
| Middlesex | 4 | 1 | 3 | 0 | 0 | 2 | 59.79 | 754 | 1261 |
| **Group C** | | | | | | | | | |
| Lancashire | 4 | 4 | 0 | 0 | 0 | 8 | 74.13 | 857 | 1156 |
| Kent | 4 | 3 | 1 | 0 | 0 | 6 | 76.25 | 1005 | 1318 |
| Sussex | 4 | 2 | 2 | 0 | 0 | 4 | 69.24 | 914 | 1320 |
| Leicestershire | 4 | 1 | 3 | 0 | 0 | 2 | 64.31 | 849 | 1320 |
| Scotland | 4 | 0 | 4 | 0 | 0 | 0 | 58.48 | 772 | 1320 |
| **Group D** | | | | | | | | | |
| Yorkshire | 4 | 3 | 1 | 0 | 0 | 6 | 70.17 | 894 | 1274 |
| Hampshire | 4 | 3 | 1 | 0 | 0 | 6 | 64.23 | 828 | 1289 |
| Notts | 4 | 2 | 2 | 0 | 0 | 4 | 76.14 | 1002 | 1316 |
| Glamorgan | 4 | 2 | 2 | 0 | 0 | 4 | 70.98 | 937 | 1320 |
| Minor Counties | 4 | 0 | 4 | 0 | 0 | 0 | 63.63 | 840 | 1320 |

# REFUGE ASSURANCE LEAGUE

## HAMPSHIRE vs. KENT
at Southampton on 12th May 1991
Toss : Kent. Umpires : D.J.Constant and B.J.Meyer
Hampshire won by 5 wickets. Hampshire 4 pts, Kent 0 pts

**KENT**

| | | |
|---|---|---|
| N.R.Taylor | lbw b James | 2 |
| M.R.Benson * | run out | 65 |
| T.R.Ward | c Udal b Aqib Javed | 2 |
| G.R.Cowdrey | c Udal b Bakker | 35 |
| C.S.Cowdrey | run out | 14 |
| M.V.Fleming | c Smith b Bakker | 19 |
| V.J.Wells + | c Terry b James | 8 |
| R.M.Ellison | not out | 24 |
| R.P.Davis | run out | 0 |
| T.A.Merrick | c Wood b Connor | 4 |
| A.P.Igglesden | not out | 1 |
| Extras | (lb 7,w 6) | 13 |
| TOTAL | (39 overs)(for 9 wkts) | 187 |

**HAMPSHIRE**

| | | |
|---|---|---|
| V.P.Terry | c & b Igglesden | 1 |
| C.L.Smith | c & b Davis | 40 |
| D.I.Gower | c Cowdrey C.S. b Igglesden | 3 |
| J.R.Wood | c Cowdrey C.S. b Merrick | 18 |
| M.C.J.Nicholas * | b Igglesden | 43 |
| K.D.James | not out | 58 |
| A.N Aymes + | not out | 15 |
| S.D.Udal | | |
| C.A.Connor | | |
| P.J.Bakker | | |
| Aqib Javed | | |
| Extras | (b 1,lb 9,w 3) | 13 |
| TOTAL | (38.4 overs)(for 5 wkts) | 191 |

| HAMPSHIRE | O | M | R | W | FALL OF WICKETS | | |
|---|---|---|---|---|---|---|---|
| | | | | | | KEN | HAM |
| James | 8 | 1 | 31 | 2 | 1st | 12 | 10 |
| Aqib Javed | 7 | 0 | 33 | 1 | 2nd | 27 | 16 |
| Bakker | 8 | 0 | 36 | 2 | 3rd | 105 | 48 |
| Connor | 8 | 0 | 33 | 1 | 4th | 121 | 76 |
| Udal | 8 | 0 | 47 | 0 | 5th | 133 | 146 |
| | | | | | 6th | 145 | |
| KENT | O | M | R | W | 7th | 171 | |
| Igglesden | 7.4 | 0 | 33 | 3 | 8th | 171 | |
| Ellison | 8 | 0 | 25 | 0 | 9th | 185 | |
| Merrick | 8 | 0 | 56 | 1 | 10th | | |
| Davis | 7 | 0 | 34 | 1 | | | |
| Fleming | 8 | 0 | 33 | 0 | | | |

## NOTTS vs. ESSEX
at Trent Bridge on 12th May 1991
Toss : Essex. Umpires : B.Dudleston and N.T.Plews
Notts won by 10 runs. Notts 4 pts, Essex 0 pts

**NOTTS**

| | | |
|---|---|---|
| B.C.Broad | run out | 14 |
| D.W.Randall | c Stephenson b Such | 19 |
| R.T.Robinson * | b Pringle | 25 |
| P.Johnson | b Gooch | 55 |
| M.A.Crawley | st Garnham b Such | 19 |
| M.Saxelby | c Pringle b Ilott | 20 |
| F.D.Stephenson | c Gooch b Pringle | 13 |
| B.N.French + | run out | 9 |
| K.P.Evans | c Prichard b Gooch | 3 |
| K.E.Cooper | not out | 4 |
| E.E.Hemmings | not out | 2 |
| Extras | (lb 5,w 4,nb 2) | 11 |
| TOTAL | (40 overs)(for 9 wkts) | 194 |

**ESSEX**

| | | |
|---|---|---|
| G.A.Gooch * | c French b Saxelby | 41 |
| J.P.Stephenson | c & b Hemmings | 29 |
| Salim Malik | c French b Hemmings | 6 |
| P.J.Prichard | c French b Saxelby | 15 |
| N.Hussain | b Johnson b Evans | 45 |
| D.R.Pringle | b Evans | 28 |
| N.Shahid | run out | 1 |
| M.A.Garnham + | b Stephenson | 4 |
| T.D.Topley | lbw b Stephenson | 1 |
| M.C.Ilott | b Stephenson | 0 |
| P.M.Such | not out | 2 |
| Extras | (lb 7,w 4,nb 1) | 12 |
| TOTAL | (38 overs) | 184 |

| ESSEX | O | M | R | W | FALL OF WICKETS | | |
|---|---|---|---|---|---|---|---|
| | | | | | | NOT | ESS |
| Ilott | 8 | 1 | 28 | 1 | 1st | 24 | 73 |
| Pringle | 8 | 0 | 45 | 2 | 2nd | 47 | 75 |
| Gooch | 8 | 0 | 36 | 2 | 3rd | 95 | 95 |
| Topley | 8 | 0 | 35 | 0 | 4th | 132 | 103 |
| Such | 8 | 0 | 45 | 2 | 5th | 153 | 167 |
| | | | | | 6th | 167 | 170 |
| NOTTS | O | M | R | W | 7th | 179 | 180 |
| Cooper | 8 | 0 | 33 | 0 | 8th | 187 | 180 |
| Stephenson | 7 | 0 | 33 | 3 | 9th | 187 | 181 |
| Saxelby | 8 | 0 | 28 | 2 | 10th | | 184 |
| Evans | 7 | 0 | 54 | 2 | | | |
| Hemmings | 8 | 0 | 29 | 2 | | | |

## SURREY vs. GLOUCS
at The Oval on 12th May 1991
Toss : Surrey. Umpires : H.D.Bird and R.Palmer
Gloucs won by 25 runs. Surrey 0 pts, Gloucs 4 pts

**GLOUCS**

| | | |
|---|---|---|
| R.J.Scott | b Bicknell M.P. | 2 |
| C.W.J.Athey | c Greig b Murphy | 79 |
| A.J.Wright * | b Murphy | 71 |
| M.W.Alleyne | b Waqar Younis | 37 |
| R.C.Russell + | b Murphy | 11 |
| P.W.Romaines | not out | 5 |
| J.W.Lloyds | | |
| D.R.Gilbert | | |
| S.N.Barnes | | |
| A.M.Babington | | |
| A.M.Smith | | |
| Extras | (b 1,lb 10,w 9) | 20 |
| TOTAL | (40 overs)(for 5 wkts) | 225 |

**SURREY**

| | | |
|---|---|---|
| D.J.Bicknell | run out | 36 |
| A.D.Brown | c Russell b Gilbert | 10 |
| A.J.Stewart + | c Russell b Alleyne | 9 |
| D.M.Ward | c Russell b Babington | 3 |
| G.P.Thorpe | c Russell b Barnes | 47 |
| I.A.Greig * | c Athey b Scott | 5 |
| J.D.Robinson | c Romaines b Babington | 50 |
| M.P.Bicknell | run out | 12 |
| J.Boiling | c Lloyds b Babington | 4 |
| Waqar Younis | c Wright b Gilbert | 8 |
| A.J.Murphy | not out | 1 |
| Extras | (lb 5,w 10) | 15 |
| TOTAL | (39.4 overs) | 200 |

| SURREY | O | M | R | W | FALL OF WICKETS | | |
|---|---|---|---|---|---|---|---|
| | | | | | | GLO | SUR |
| Bicknell M.P. | 8 | 1 | 41 | 1 | | | |
| Murphy | 8 | 1 | 45 | 3 | 1st | 6 | 24 |
| Robinson | 8 | 0 | 40 | 0 | 2nd | 145 | 43 |
| Boiling | 3 | 0 | 19 | 0 | 3rd | 194 | 50 |
| Waqar Younis | 8 | 1 | 43 | 1 | 4th | 213 | 76 |
| Greig | 3 | 0 | 16 | 0 | 5th | 225 | 91 |
| Thorpe | 2 | 0 | 10 | 0 | 6th | | 157 |
| | | | | | 7th | | 179 |
| GLOUCS | O | M | R | W | 8th | | 191 |
| Gilbert | 7.4 | 0 | 27 | 2 | 9th | | 191 |
| Barnes | 8 | 0 | 33 | 1 | 10th | | 200 |
| Smith | 0.3 | 0 | 3 | 0 | | | |
| Alleyne | 7.3 | 0 | 32 | 1 | | | |
| Babington | 8 | 0 | 39 | 3 | | | |
| Scott | 7 | 0 | 52 | 1 | | | |
| Athey | 1 | 0 | 9 | 0 | | | |

## NORTHANTS vs. LEICESTERSHIRE
at Northampton on 12th May 1991
Toss : Northants. Umpires : J.D.Bond and J.H.Hampshire
Northants won by 5 wickets. Northants 4 pts, Leics 0 pts

**LEICESTERSHIRE**

| | | |
|---|---|---|
| P.Whitticase + | c Ripley b Taylor | 0 |
| N.E.Briers * | b Penberthy | 48 |
| J.J.Whitaker | c Walker b Capel | 34 |
| P.Willey | run out | 27 |
| C.C.Lewis | c Ripley b Penberthy | 6 |
| L.Potter | c & b Thomas | 33 |
| B.F.Smith | run out | 16 |
| P.N.Hepworth | not out | 17 |
| C.Wilkinson | not out | 0 |
| J.N.Maguire | | |
| D.J.Millns | | |
| Extras | (lb 22,w 7) | 29 |
| TOTAL | (40 overs)(for 7 wkts) | 210 |

**NORTHANTS**

| | | |
|---|---|---|
| A.Fordham | lbw b Wilkinson | 40 |
| W.Larkins | c Briers b Millns | 5 |
| R.J.Bailey | c Lewis b Willey | 22 |
| D.J.Capel | not out | 77 |
| A.J.Lamb * | c Briers b Hepworth | 23 |
| R.G.Williams | c Millns b Wilkinson | 22 |
| A.L.Penberthy | not out | 8 |
| D.Ripley + | | |
| J.G.Thomas | | |
| J.P.Taylor | | |
| A.Walker | | |
| Extras | (lb 9,w 6,nb 2) | 17 |
| TOTAL | (39.3 overs)(for 5 wkts) | 214 |

| NORTHANTS | O | M | R | W | FALL OF WICKETS | | |
|---|---|---|---|---|---|---|---|
| | | | | | | LEI | NOR |
| Taylor | 8 | 1 | 32 | 1 | | | |
| Walker | 8 | 2 | 31 | 0 | 1st | 2 | 6 |
| Thomas | 6 | 0 | 42 | 1 | 2nd | 77 | 61 |
| Capel | 7 | 0 | 31 | 1 | 3rd | 119 | 90 |
| Williams | 6 | 0 | 32 | 0 | 4th | 129 | 129 |
| Penberthy | 5 | 0 | 20 | 2 | 5th | 133 | 144 |
| | | | | | 6th | 159 | |
| LEICS | O | M | R | W | 7th | 210 | |
| Lewis | 7.3 | 1 | 26 | 0 | 8th | | |
| Millns | 7 | 0 | 36 | 1 | 9th | | |
| Maguire | 8 | 0 | 48 | 0 | 10th | | |
| Wilkinson | 8 | 0 | 50 | 2 | | | |
| Willey | 4 | 0 | 19 | 1 | | | |
| Hepworth | 5 | 0 | 26 | 1 | | | |

## SOMERSET vs. GLAMORGAN
at Taunton on 12th May 1991
Toss : Glamorgan. Umpires : R.Julien and M.J.Kitchen
Somerset won by 35 runs. Somerset 4 pts, Glamorgan 0 pts

**SOMERSET**

| | | |
|---|---|---|
| S.J.Cook | lbw b Dennis | 10 |
| R.J.Bartlett | c Metson b Frost | 0 |
| C.J.Tavare * | c Metson b Frost | 46 |
| R.J.Harden | lbw b Croft | 40 |
| G.D.Rose | c Morris b Barwick | 59 |
| N.D.Burns + | not out | 52 |
| K.H.Macleay | lbw b Frost | 2 |
| R.P.Lefebvre | c Dennis b Barwick | 3 |
| P.M.Roebuck | | |
| N.A.Mallender | | |
| D.A.Graveney | | |
| Extras | (b 1,lb 6,w 6) | 13 |
| TOTAL | (40 overs)(for 7 wkts) | 225 |

**GLAMORGAN**

| | | |
|---|---|---|
| A.Dale | c & b Macleay | 24 |
| H.Morris * | b Graveney | 27 |
| M.P.Maynard | c Cook b Graveney | 19 |
| R.J.Shastri | c Tavare b Roebuck | 27 |
| G.C.Holmes | c Burns b Rose | 33 |
| I.Smith | not out | 34 |
| R.D.B.Croft | c Bartlett b Lefebvre | 9 |
| C.P.Metson + | c & b Lefebvre | 4 |
| S.J.Dennis | b Lefebvre | 3 |
| S.R.Barwick | not out | 1 |
| M.Frost | | |
| Extras | (b 2,lb 6,w 1) | 9 |
| TOTAL | (40 overs)(for 8 wkts) | 190 |

| GLAMORGAN | O | M | R | W | FALL OF WICKETS | | |
|---|---|---|---|---|---|---|---|
| | | | | | | SOM | GLA |
| Frost | 8 | 0 | 35 | 3 | | | |
| Dennis | 8 | 0 | 36 | 1 | 1st | 1 | 49 |
| Barwick | 8 | 0 | 46 | 2 | 2nd | 22 | 69 |
| Dale | 8 | 0 | 60 | 0 | 3rd | 100 | 82 |
| Shastri | 3 | 0 | 13 | 0 | 4th | 108 | 130 |
| Croft | 5 | 1 | 28 | 1 | 5th | 200 | 142 |
| | | | | | 6th | 214 | 164 |
| SOMERSET | O | M | R | W | 7th | 225 | 176 |
| Mallender | 7 | 1 | 29 | 0 | 8th | | 189 |
| Lefebvre | 8 | 1 | 30 | 3 | 9th | | |
| Rose | 6 | 0 | 43 | 1 | 10th | | |
| Macleay | 8 | 0 | 30 | 1 | | | |
| Graveney | 8 | 0 | 39 | 2 | | | |
| Roebuck | 3 | 0 | 11 | 1 | | | |

## SUSSEX vs. MIDDLESEX
at Hove on 12th May 1991
Toss : Sussex. Umpires : D.O.Oslear and K.E.Palmer
Middlesex won by 5 wickets. Sussex 0 pts, Middlesex 4 pts

**SUSSEX**

| | | |
|---|---|---|
| P.Moores + | b Emburey | 25 |
| J.W.Hall | c Fraser b Hughes | 34 |
| P.W.G.Parker * | lbw b Fraser | 33 |
| A.P.Wells | c Williams b Emburey | 10 |
| M.P.Speight | c Brown b Ramprakash | 15 |
| K.Greenfield | not out | 32 |
| A.C.S.Pigott | c Gatting b Ramprakash | 10 |
| I.D.K.Salisbury | not out | 2 |
| R.A.Bunting | | |
| E.S.H.Giddins | | |
| A.N.Jones | | |
| Extras | (lb 5,w 1,nb 4) | 10 |
| TOTAL | (40 overs)(for 6 wkts) | 171 |

**MIDDLESEX**

| | | |
|---|---|---|
| M.W.Gatting * | c Wells b Bunting | 25 |
| M.A.Roseberry | c Speight b Bunting | 21 |
| M.R.Ramprakash | not out | 62 |
| K.R.Brown | run out | 4 |
| M.Keech | b Bunting | 38 |
| P.R.Downton + | c Wells b Bunting | 3 |
| J.E.Emburey | not out | 2 |
| N.F.Williams | | |
| S.P.Hughes | | |
| A.R.C.Fraser | | |
| R.M.Ellcock | | |
| Extras | (b 1,lb 6,w 10) | 17 |
| TOTAL | (38.3 overs)(for 5 wkts) | 172 |

| MIDDLESEX | O | M | R | W | FALL OF WICKETS | | |
|---|---|---|---|---|---|---|---|
| | | | | | | SUS | MID |
| Williams | 4 | 0 | 18 | 0 | | | |
| Ellcock | 5 | 0 | 25 | 0 | 1st | 65 | 56 |
| Hughes | 8 | 1 | 39 | 1 | 2nd | 65 | 59 |
| Emburey | 8 | 2 | 18 | 2 | 3rd | 81 | 68 |
| Fraser | 8 | 0 | 34 | 1 | 4th | 104 | 152 |
| Ramprakash | 7 | 0 | 32 | 2 | 5th | 148 | 158 |
| | | | | | 6th | 161 | |
| SUSSEX | O | M | R | W | 7th | | |
| Jones | 4 | 0 | 23 | 0 | 8th | | |
| Pigott | 7 | 0 | 28 | 0 | 9th | | |
| Bunting | 7.3 | 0 | 35 | 4 | 10th | | |
| Giddins | 5 | 0 | 19 | 0 | | | |
| Salisbury | 8 | 0 | 23 | 0 | | | |
| Greenfield | 7 | 0 | 37 | 0 | | | |

# REFUGE ASSURANCE LEAGUE

## WORCESTERSHIRE vs. LANCASHIRE

at Worcester on 12th May 1991
Toss : Lancashire. Umpires : B.Hassan and P.B.Wight
Lancashire won by 6 wickets. Worcs 0 pts, Lancs 4 pts

### WORCESTERSHIRE

| | | |
|---|---|---|
| T.S.Curtis | lbw b DeFreitas | 2 |
| T.M.Moody | run out | 50 |
| G.A.Hick | c Hegg b DeFreitas | 5 |
| I.T.Botham | b Austin | 58 |
| D.B.D'Oliveira | c Hegg b Yates | 12 |
| P.A.Neale * | c Fairbrother b Wasim Akram | 39 |
| M.J.Weston | c Hegg b Yates | 4 |
| R.K.Illingworth | not out | 24 |
| P.J.Newport | not out | 11 |
| S.R.Lampitt | | |
| S.R.Bevins + | | |
| Extras | (lb 2,w 2) | 4 |
| TOTAL | (40 overs)(for 7 wkts) | 209 |

### LANCASHIRE

| | | |
|---|---|---|
| G.D.Mendis | c & b Illingworth | 31 |
| G.Fowler | b Illingworth | 27 |
| M.A.Atherton | b Hick | 6 |
| N.H.Fairbrother * | lbw b Hick | 46 |
| G.D.Lloyd | not out | 79 |
| Wasim Akram | not out | 7 |
| P.A.J.DeFreitas | | |
| W.K.Hegg + | | |
| G.Yates | | |
| I.D.Austin | | |
| P.J.W.Allott | | |
| Extras | (lb 14,w 1) | 15 |
| TOTAL | (39.2 overs)(for 4 wkts) | 211 |

| LANCASHIRE | O | M | R | W | FALL OF WICKETS | | |
|---|---|---|---|---|---|---|---|
| | | | | | | WOR | LAN |
| DeFreitas | 8 | 0 | 35 | 2 | 1st | 8 | 54 |
| Allott | 8 | 0 | 31 | 0 | 2nd | 20 | 67 |
| Yates | 8 | 1 | 45 | 2 | 3rd | 99 | 71 |
| Wasim Akram | 8 | 0 | 56 | 1 | 4th | 121 | 189 |
| Austin | 8 | 1 | 40 | 1 | 5th | 136 | |
| | | | | | 6th | 144 | |
| WORCS | O | M | R | W | 7th | 188 | |
| Weston | 8 | 0 | 30 | 0 | 8th | | |
| Newport | 5.2 | 0 | 32 | 0 | 9th | | |
| Illingworth | 8 | 1 | 26 | 2 | 10th | | |
| Hick | 8 | 0 | 42 | 2 | | | |
| Botham | 6 | 0 | 41 | 0 | | | |
| Lampitt | 4 | 0 | 26 | 0 | | | |

## YORKSHIRE vs. WARWICKSHIRE

at Headingley on 12th May 1991
Toss : Yorkshire. Umpires : J.C.Balderstone and R.A.White
Warwickshire won by 2 runs. Yorks 0 pts, Warwicks 4 pts

### WARWICKSHIRE

| | | |
|---|---|---|
| A.J.Moles | c Kellett b Jarvis | 67 |
| Asif Din | b Jarvis | 0 |
| T.A.Lloyd * | lbw b Carrick | 38 |
| P.A.Smith | c & b Fletcher | 75 |
| D.A.Reeve | c Kellett b Fletcher | 2 |
| D.P.Ostler | not out | 14 |
| R.G.Twose | b Fletcher | 1 |
| K.J.Piper + | not out | 1 |
| G.C.Small | | |
| A.R.K.Pierson | | |
| T.A.Munton | | |
| Extras | (b 2,lb 3,w 1) | 6 |
| TOTAL | (40 overs)(for 6 wkts) | 204 |

### YORKSHIRE

| | | |
|---|---|---|
| M.D.Moxon * | st Piper b Pierson | 39 |
| A.A.Metcalfe | c Lloyd b Small | 27 |
| R.J.Blakey + | c Asif Din b Smith | 51 |
| D.Byas | lbw b Smith | 23 |
| P.E.Robinson | c Small b Smith | 3 |
| S.A.Kellett | run out | 17 |
| P.Carrick | b Munton | 6 |
| P.W.Jarvis | run out | 9 |
| P.J.Hartley | not out | 0 |
| A.Sidebottom | not out | 1 |
| S.D.Fletcher | | |
| Extras | (b 1,lb 14,w 11) | 26 |
| TOTAL | (40 overs)(for 8 wkts) | 202 |

| YORKSHIRE | O | M | R | W | FALL OF WICKETS | | |
|---|---|---|---|---|---|---|---|
| | | | | | | WAR | YOR |
| Jarvis | 8 | 0 | 37 | 2 | 1st | 1 | 59 |
| Sidebottom | 8 | 0 | 22 | 0 | 2nd | 67 | 74 |
| Hartley | 6 | 0 | 41 | 0 | 3rd | 158 | 137 |
| Carrick | 8 | 0 | 38 | 1 | 4th | 163 | 148 |
| Fletcher | 8 | 0 | 47 | 3 | 5th | 201 | 180 |
| Moxon | 2 | 0 | 14 | 0 | 6th | 203 | 182 |
| | | | | | 7th | | 189 |
| WARWICKS | O | M | R | W | 8th | | 201 |
| Munton | 5 | 0 | 17 | 1 | 9th | | |
| Twose | 5 | 0 | 23 | 0 | 10th | | |
| Reeve | 8 | 0 | 40 | 0 | | | |
| Pierson | 8 | 1 | 35 | 1 | | | |
| Small | 7 | 0 | 29 | 1 | | | |
| Smith | 7 | 0 | 43 | 3 | | | |

Andy Moles, whose runs were vital in Warwickshire's narrow win over Yorkshire.

## HEADLINES

### Refuge Assurance League

### 12th May

• Nottinghamshire gained their fourth successive victory in the competition with a 10-run win over Essex at Chelmsford. Essex suffered their first defeat of the season in dramatic fashion, Franklyn Stephenson taking three wickets in six balls as they lost their last six wickets for 17 runs.

• Somerset made it three Sunday victories out of three by beating Glamorgan by 35 runs at Taunton, Graeme Rose and Neil Burns overcoming a mid-innings crisis with a fifth-wicket stand of 92.

• Middlesex regained their composure with a five-wicket win over Sussex to move into third place, largely thanks to Mark Ramprakash who hit an unbeaten 62 as well as taking two wickets.

• Although Tom Moody and Graeme Hick both passed the fifty mark, Worcestershire's total of 209 for seven was not enough to contain Lancashire at Worcester. Graham Lloyd saw the Lancastrians home to their sixth successive one-day victory with an unbeaten 79.

Paul Smith had an eventful afternoon at Headingley where Warwickshire beat Yorkshire by two runs. He hit a rapid 75 to build on foundations laid by Andy Moles and Andy Lloyd, claimed three wickets in the Yorkshire middle-order and was entrusted with the last over of the match when 12 runs were needed, but the home side's chance was lost with the run out of Paul Jarvis.

• Bill Athey and Tony Wright set Gloucestershire on the road to a 25-run victory over Surrey at The Oval with a second-wicket stand of 139. Andy Babington took three for 39 as Surrey were bowled out for 200.

• Kevan James, with two for 31 and 58 not out, was Hampshire's match-winner over Kent at Southampton, a five-wicket success being achieved with just two balls to spare.

• Northamptonshire's contest against Leicestershire at Northampton was also decided in the final over, an unbroken sixth-wicket stand of 70 between David Capel and Tony Penberthy carrying the visitors to victory with three balls in hand.

# BRITANNIC ASSURANCE CHAMPIONSHIP

## MIDDLESEX vs. SUSSEX
at Lord's on 9th, 10th, 11th May 1991
Toss : Sussex.  Umpires : D.O.Oslear and K.E.Palmer
Sussex won by 10 wickets.  Middlesex 4 pts (Bt: 2, Bw: 2), Sussex 24 pts (Bt: 4, Bw: 4)
100 overs scores :Sussex 317 for 6

### MIDDLESEX
| | | | | | |
|---|---|---|---|---|---|
| I.J.F.Hutchinson | c Moores b Pigott | 5 | (2) c Moores b Jones | | 3 |
| M.A.Roseberry | b Jones | 18 | (1) c Greenfield b Pigott | | 0 |
| M.W.Gatting * | c Salisbury b Pigott | 19 | b Pigott | | 4 |
| M.R.Ramprakash | c Moores b Giddins | 65 | c Greenfield b Pigott | | 119 |
| K.R.Brown | lbw b North | 30 | lbw b North | | 19 |
| P.R.Downton + | not out | 51 | c Greenfield b North | | 38 |
| J.E.Emburey | c Salisbury b Pigott | 14 | c Moores b Jones | | 17 |
| N.F.Williams | lbw b North | 0 | lbw b Pigott | | 28 |
| D.W.Headley | c Greenfield b Pigott | 2 | (10) c Moores b Jones | | 3 |
| P.C.R.Tufnell | b Pigott | 0 | (9) not out | | 8 |
| N.G.Cowans | b North | 5 | c Hall b Jones | | 2 |
| Extras | (b 1,lb 9,w 5,nb 3) | 18 | (b 3,lb 10,w 2) | | 15 |
| TOTAL | | 227 | | | 256 |

### SUSSEX
| | | | | |
|---|---|---|---|---|
| D.M.Smith | c Downton b Emburey | 90 | | |
| J.W.Hall | lbw b Headley | 18 | (1) not out | 18 |
| K.Greenfield | run out | 5 | | |
| A.P.Wells * | c Hutchinson b Headley | 120 | | |
| M.P.Speight | c Downton b Emburey | 5 | | |
| J.A.North | c Brown b Emburey | 0 | | |
| P.Moores + | c Gatting b Williams | 8 | (2) not out | 86 |
| A.C.S.Pigott | b Cowans | 65 | | |
| I.D.K.Salisbury | c Downton b Williams | 19 | | |
| A.N.Jones | b Williams | 6 | | |
| E.S.H.Giddins | not out | 14 | | |
| Extras | (b 2,lb 2,nb 22) | 26 | (lb 4,w 1) | 5 |
| TOTAL | | 376 | (for 0 wkts) | 109 |

| SUSSEX | O | M | R | W | O | M | R | W | FALL OF WICKETS | | | |
|---|---|---|---|---|---|---|---|---|---|---|---|---|
| | | | | | | | | | | MID | SUS | MID | SUS |
| Jones | 14 | 3 | 48 | 1 | 21.4 | 5 | 65 | 4 | 1st | 7 | 38 | 2 |
| Pigott | 19 | 7 | 37 | 5 | 21 | 5 | 52 | 4 | 2nd | 37 | 56 | 8 |
| Giddins | 14 | 1 | 43 | 1 | 16 | 2 | 49 | 0 | 3rd | 45 | 186 | 10 |
| North | 18.3 | 5 | 65 | 3 | 3 | 3 | 55 | 2 | 4th | 98 | 195 | 60 |
| Salisbury | 9 | 1 | 24 | 0 | 16 | 6 | 22 | 0 | 5th | 183 | 195 | 137 |
| | | | | | | | | | 6th | 212 | 209 | 194 |
| MIDDLESEX | O | M | R | W | O | M | R | W | 7th | 213 | 331 | 242 |
| Cowans | 25 | 11 | 86 | 1 | 6 | 1 | 25 | 0 | 8th | 218 | 337 | 243 |
| Williams | 29.3 | 4 | 91 | 3 | 6 | 1 | 20 | 0 | 9th | 218 | 346 | 254 |
| Headley | 25 | 2 | 96 | 2 | 3 | 0 | 19 | 0 | 10th | 227 | 376 | 256 |
| Emburey | 32 | 10 | 64 | 3 | 4 | 2 | 10 | 0 | | | | |
| Tufnell | 10 | 0 | 35 | 0 | 6.4 | 1 | 31 | 0 | | | | |

## YORKSHIRE vs. WARWICKSHIRE
at Headingley on 9th, 10th, 11th, 13th May 1991
Toss : Warwickshire.  Umpires : J.C.Balderstone and R.A.White
Warwickshire won by 30 runs.  Yorkshire 5 pts (Bt: 1, Bw: 4), Warwicks 23 pts (Bt: 3, Bw: 4)
100 overs scores : Warwickshire 251 for 9

### WARWICKSHIRE
| | | | | | |
|---|---|---|---|---|---|
| A.J.Moles | c Blakey b Hartley | 0 | lbw b Hartley | | 73 |
| J.D.Ratcliffe | c Robinson P.E. b Fletcher | 13 | lbw b Robinson M.A. | | 5 |
| T.A.Lloyd * | c Byas b Robinson M.A. | 56 | c Robinson P.E. b Pickles | | 15 |
| P.A.Smith | lbw b Fletcher | 38 | c Metcalfe b Pickles | | 0 |
| D.A.Reeve | c Kellett b Fletcher | 5 | lbw b Hartley | | 24 |
| D.P.Ostler | c Blakey b Hartley | 28 | c Moxon b Carrick | | 1 |
| K.J.Piper + | b Fletcher | 8 | lbw b Hartley | | 3 |
| P.A.Booth | run out | 10 | lbw b Fletcher | | 17 |
| G.C.Small | c Moxon b Hartley | 58 | not out | | 10 |
| T.A.Munton | b Moxon | 31 | c Byas b Carrick | | 2 |
| A.A.Donald | not out | 11 | lbw b Carrick | | 0 |
| Extras | (b 2,lb 2, w 2,nb 4) | 6 | (lb 4,w 2) | | 6 |
| TOTAL | | 268 | | | 156 |

### YORKSHIRE
| | | | | | |
|---|---|---|---|---|---|
| M.D.Moxon * | c Moles b Donald | 14 | c Lloyd b Donald | | 57 |
| A.A.Metcalfe | lbw b Munton | 52 | c Piper b Donald | | 1 |
| D.Byas | lbw b Reeve | 44 | lbw b Smith | | 7 |
| R.J.Blakey + | c Ratcliffe b Donald | 2 | lbw b Reeve | | 9 |
| P.E.Robinson | b Donald | 0 | lbw b Munton | | 33 |
| S.A.Kellett | lbw b Munton | 8 | b Donald | | 17 |
| C.S.Pickles | b Munton | 10 | lbw b Booth | | 1 |
| P.Carrick | not out | 13 | lbw b Donald | | 36 |
| P.J.Hartley | c Munton b Donald | 1 | c Reeve b Munton | | 21 |
| S.D.Fletcher | c Lloyd b Munton | 0 | lbw b Donald | | 5 |
| M.A.Robinson | lbw b Donald | 0 | not out | | 0 |
| Extras | (b 9,lb 4, w 3,nb 5) | 21 | (b 10,lb 17,w 6,nb 9) | | 42 |
| TOTAL | | 165 | | | 229 |

| YORKSHIRE | O | M | R | W | O | M | R | W | FALL OF WICKETS | | | |
|---|---|---|---|---|---|---|---|---|---|---|---|---|
| | | | | | | | | | | WAR | YOR | WAR | YOR |
| Hartley | 24.1 | 9 | 47 | 3 | 20 | 5 | 53 | 3 | 1st | 3 | 18 | 22 | 12 |
| Robinson M.A. | 18 | 6 | 40 | 1 | 18 | 4 | 42 | 1 | 2nd | 50 | 100 | 59 | 35 |
| Pickles | 18 | 2 | 59 | 0 | 4 | 1 | 8 | 2 | 3rd | 101 | 104 | 59 | 57 |
| Fletcher | 28 | 8 | 70 | 4 | 11 | 3 | 36 | 1 | 4th | 119 | 112 | 122 | 108 |
| Carrick | 9 | 1 | 31 | 0 | 17.5 | 10 | 13 | 3 | 5th | 122 | 123 | 123 | 151 |
| Moxon | 7 | 1 | 17 | 1 | | | | | 6th | 132 | 132 | 123 | 152 |
| | | | | | | | | | 7th | 161 | 148 | 134 | 173 |
| WARWICKS | O | M | R | W | O | M | R | W | 8th | 167 | 156 | 153 | 215 |
| Donald | 14.3 | 2 | 42 | 5 | 22 | 5 | 54 | 5 | 9th | 230 | 161 | 156 | 228 |
| Munton | 30 | 11 | 57 | 4 | 30.1 | 7 | 65 | 2 | 10th | 268 | 165 | 156 | 229 |
| Small | 13 | 4 | 27 | 0 | 13 | 4 | 26 | 0 | | | | |
| Smith | 10 | 3 | 20 | 0 | 10 | 2 | 26 | 1 | | | | |
| Reeve | 5 | 1 | 6 | 1 | 9 | 4 | 14 | 1 | | | | |
| Booth | | | | | 7 | 4 | 17 | 1 | | | | |

## NORTHANTS vs. ESSEX
at Northampton on 9th, 10th, 11th, 13th May 1991
Toss : Northants.  Umpires : J.D.Bond and J.H.Hampshire
Essex won by 8 wickets.  Northants 6 pts (Bt: 4, Bw: 2), Essex 23 pts (Bt: 4, Bw: 3)
100 overs scores : Northants 301 for 8, Essex 370 for 6

### NORTHANTS
| | | | | | |
|---|---|---|---|---|---|
| A.Fordham | c Garnham b Pringle | 90 | lbw b Pringle | | 47 |
| N.A.Felton | b Foster | 0 | c Garnham b Foster | | 5 |
| R.J.Bailey | lbw b Pringle | 57 | c Hussain b Childs | | 30 |
| A.J.Lamb * | lbw b Pringle | 24 | c Salim Malik b Childs | | 61 |
| D.J.Capel | c Foster b Pringle | 22 | c Garnham b Childs | | 0 |
| W.Larkins | b Pringle | 0 | c Salim Malik b Foster | | 27 |
| E.A.E.Baptiste | c Prichard b Topley | 28 | c Pringle b Foster | | 24 |
| D.Ripley + | c Garnham b Salim Malik | 30 | b Childs | | 15 |
| J.G.Thomas | c Foster b Salim Malik | 43 | c Hussain b Such | | 11 |
| N.G.B.Cook | not out | 12 | not out | | 6 |
| J.P.Taylor | not out | 5 | lbw b Such | | 0 |
| Extras | (b 1,lb 13,w 1,nb 2) | 17 | (b 2,lb 17,w 1,nb 2) | | 22 |
| TOTAL | | (for 9 wkts dec) 328 | | | 248 |

### ESSEX
| | | | | |
|---|---|---|---|---|
| G.A.Gooch * | c & b Baptiste | 45 | c Ripley b Taylor | 22 |
| J.P.Stephenson | c Taylor b Thomas | 11 | c Ripley b Thomas | 1 |
| P.J.Prichard | c Ripley b Thomas | 190 | | |
| Salim Malik | b Baptiste | 24 | not out | 37 |
| N.Hussain | c Ripley b Capel | 17 | | |
| M.A.Garnham + | c Ripley b Capel | 1 | | |
| D.R.Pringle | st Ripley b Bailey | 68 | (3) not out | 37 |
| N.A.Foster | c Ripley b Thomas | 63 | | |
| T.D.Topley | lbw b Thomas | 30 | | |
| J.H.Childs | lbw b Thomas | 0 | | |
| P.M.Such | not out | 2 | | |
| Extras | (b 10,lb 18) | 28 | (lb 1) | 1 |
| TOTAL | | 479 | (for 2 wkts) | 98 |

| ESSEX | O | M | R | W | O | M | R | W | FALL OF WICKETS | | | |
|---|---|---|---|---|---|---|---|---|---|---|---|---|
| | | | | | | | | | | NOR | ESS | NOR | ESS |
| Foster | 20 | 3 | 78 | 1 | 17 | 5 | 44 | 3 | 1st | 3 | 34 | 29 | 20 |
| Pringle | 29 | 6 | 70 | 5 | 15 | 3 | 51 | 1 | 2nd | 148 | 94 | 79 | 28 |
| Topley | 17 | 1 | 63 | 1 | 16 | 2 | 54 | 0 | 3rd | 163 | 142 | 111 | |
| Childs | 13 | 5 | 32 | 0 | 30 | 12 | 69 | 4 | 4th | 198 | 164 | 113 | |
| Gooch | 11 | 7 | 8 | 0 | | | | | 5th | 204 | 170 | 184 | |
| Such | 12 | 2 | 37 | 0 | 5 | 1 | 8 | 2 | 6th | 221 | 336 | 190 | |
| Salim Malik | 6 | 1 | 26 | 2 | 1 | 0 | 3 | 0 | 7th | 241 | 392 | 220 | |
| | | | | | | | | | 8th | 297 | 474 | 230 | |
| NORTHANTS | O | M | R | W | O | M | R | W | 9th | 319 | 474 | 248 | |
| Taylor | 34 | 8 | 101 | 0 | 8 | 1 | 43 | 1 | 10th | | 479 | 248 | |
| Thomas | 33.5 | 4 | 146 | 5 | 7 | 1 | 25 | 1 | | | | |
| Capel | 22 | 2 | 73 | 2 | 2 | 0 | 19 | 0 | | | | |
| Baptiste | 17 | 4 | 59 | 2 | | | | | | | | |
| Bailey | 19 | 1 | 72 | 1 | 1.1 | 0 | 10 | 0 | | | | |

## SURREY vs. KENT
at The Oval on 9th, 10th, 11th, 13th May 1991
Toss : Kent.  Umpires : H.D.Bird and R.Palmer
Kent won by an innings and 3 runs.  Surrey 3 pts (Bt: 1, Bw: 2), Kent 22 pts (Bt: 2, Bw: 4)
100 overs scores : Kent 231 for 5

### KENT
| | | |
|---|---|---|
| N.R.Taylor | lbw b Bicknell M.P. | 8 |
| M.R.Benson * | b Murphy | 96 |
| T.R.Ward | c Sargeant b Robson | 17 |
| G.R.Cowdrey | b Murphy | 58 |
| C.S.Cowdrey | c Medlycott b Murphy | 13 |
| R.M.Ellison | b Medlycott | 50 |
| R.P.Davis | c Thorpe b Bicknell M.P. | 36 |
| C.Penn | c Alikhan b Medlycott | 39 |
| G.J.Kersey + | not out | 27 |
| T.A.Merrick | c Sargeant b Medlycott | 36 |
| A.P.Igglesden | b Medlycott | 5 |
| Extras | (b 2,lb 27,w 1,nb 5) | 35 |
| TOTAL | | 420 |

### SURREY
| | | | | | |
|---|---|---|---|---|---|
| D.J.Bicknell | c Kersey b Merrick | 13 | c Kersey b Merrick | | 0 |
| R.I.Alikhan | c Ellison b Penn | 29 | b Davis | | 31 |
| A.J.Stewart | b Igglesden | 7 | b Ellison | | 12 |
| D.M.Ward | c Cowdrey G.R. b Ellison | 40 | c Cowdrey G.R. b Igglesden | | 23 |
| G.P.Thorpe | c Kersey b Penn | 6 | c Cowdrey G.R. b Penn | | 40 |
| I.A.Greig * | c Taylor b Igglesden | 25 | c Benson b Igglesden | | 44 |
| K.T.Medlycott | c Cowdrey C.S. b Penn | 4 | lbw b Penn | | 1 |
| N.F.Sargeant + | not out | 24 | not out | | 23 |
| M.P.Bicknell | c Penn b Merrick | 16 | lbw b Penn | | 12 |
| A.G.Robson | c Kersey b Igglesden | 0 | b Merrick | | 3 |
| A.J.Murphy | c Kersey b Penn | 11 | c Davis b Penn | | 18 |
| Extras | (b 8,lb 4, w 2,nb 6) | 20 | (b 4,lb 5,w 2,nb 4) | | 15 |
| TOTAL | | 195 | | | 222 |

| SURREY | O | M | R | W | O | M | R | W | FALL OF WICKETS | | | |
|---|---|---|---|---|---|---|---|---|---|---|---|---|
| | | | | | | | | | | KEN | SUR | SUR | KEN |
| Bicknell M.P. | 45 | 16 | 95 | 2 | | | | | 1st | 24 | 17 | 0 |
| Murphy | 46 | 20 | 98 | 3 | | | | | 2nd | 50 | 34 | 21 |
| Robson | 24 | 10 | 72 | 1 | | | | | 3rd | 191 | 83 | 48 |
| Medlycott | 38.3 | 13 | 103 | 4 | | | | | 4th | 206 | 103 | 107 |
| Greig | 10 | 3 | 23 | 0 | | | | | 5th | 211 | 104 | 113 |
| | | | | | | | | | 6th | 303 | 118 | 120 |
| KENT | O | M | R | W | O | M | R | W | 7th | 309 | 135 | 167 |
| Merrick | 21 | 7 | 51 | 2 | 23 | 7 | 59 | 2 | 8th | 352 | 165 | 191 |
| Igglesden | 26 | 5 | 59 | 3 | 21 | 10 | 31 | 2 | 9th | 406 | 166 | 199 |
| Penn | 17.1 | 2 | 48 | 4 | 22.4 | 4 | 50 | 4 | 10th | 420 | 195 | 222 |
| Ellison | 12 | 8 | 25 | 1 | 15 | 3 | 47 | 1 | | | | |
| Davis | | | | | 18 | 10 | 26 | 1 | | | | |

# BRITANNIC ASSURANCE CHAMPIONSHIP

## HEADLINES

### Britannic Assurance Championship

### 9th - 13th May

• The 1991 first-class season at last got fully under way almost a month after its official starting point, but it was worth the wait as seven of the eight four-day Championship matches finished in positive results with hardly a declaration in sight. The exponents of a full programme of four-day cricket found evidence aplenty to support their cause.

• The 1990 Championship table was turned upside down at Lord's where champions Middlesex were beaten inside three days by bottom-placed county Sussex whom they had defeated by an innings to claim the Championship title the previous September. Sussex owed their triumph to a splendid all-round effort from a largely inexperienced side. John North and Ed Giddins gave Tony Pigott and Adrian Jones good support in the seam bowling department, while 120 from stand-in captain Alan Wells ensured a healthy first innings lead of 149. Mark Ramprakash top-scored in each innings for Middlesex, but even his 119 in the second innings could not prevent a damaging 10-wicket defeat. Sussex's 24 points gave them an unlikely but well-deserved early lead at the top of the 1991 table.

• 1990 runners-up Essex fared rather better, defeating Northamptonshire by eight wickets at Northampton. Derek Pringle and John Childs showed they were both still formidable propositions with the ball, but it was Paul Prichard's 190, as the Essex batsmen took advantage of a weakened bowling attack, that put the visitors in command.

• Yorkshire's absorbing battle with Warwickshire at Headingley suggested that the batsmen may not have it all their own way this season as all 40 wickets were taken for just over 800 runs. Allan Donald, the South African retained by Warwickshire ahead of Tom Moody, was the main difference between the two sides, returning match figures of 10 for 96, as the visitors gained a 32-run victory.

• Surrey's first Championship match of the season at The Fosters Oval proved a severe disappointment, when Ian Greig's men lost to Kent by an innings and three runs. Mark Benson top-scored as most of the Kent side contributed effectively to a total of 420, then Chris Penn collected four wickets in each innings as Surrey's batting lacked any consistency.

• Leicestershire did well to extend their match with Nottinghamshire into the fourth day after they had collapsed to 93 for seven on the opening morning at Trent Bridge, Kevin Evans returning career-best bowling figures. Derek Randall's century helped the home side engineer a lead of 159, but Nigel Briers and James Whitaker responded with a third-wicket stand of 190 before the loss of their last eight wickets for 43 finally killed off Leicester's hopes of saving the game.

## NOTTS vs. LEICESTERSHIRE

at Trent Bridge on 9th, 10th, 11th, 13th May 1991
Toss : Leicestershire. Umpires : B.Dudleston and N.T.Plews
Notts won by 7 wickets. Notts 24 pts (Bt: 4, Bw: 4), Leicestershire 5 pts (Bt: 2, Bw: 3)
100 overs scores :Notts 316 for 7

### LEICESTERSHIRE

| | | | | |
|---|---|---|---|---|
| T.J.Boon | c French b Pick | 3 | b Stephenson | 2 |
| N.E.Briers * | b Stephenson | 22 | c Pollard b Stephenson | 160 |
| P.N.Hepworth | b Pick | 0 | c Robinson b Pick | 37 |
| J.J.Whitaker | c Johnson b Evans | 15 | c Pollard b Evans | 86 |
| L.Potter | c French b Evans | 6 | c Pick b Evans | 0 |
| P.Willey | c Afford b Evans | 24 | c Broad b Evans | 0 |
| P.Whitticase + | b Evans | 9 | c French b Stephenson | 0 |
| L.Tennant | c Pollard b Stephenson | 13 | lbw b Pick | 8 |
| C.Wilkinson | b Evans | 41 | b Evans | 16 |
| D.J.Millns | not out | 26 | not out | 0 |
| J.N.Maguire | lbw b Stephenson | 33 | c Randall b Pick | 0 |
| Extras | (b 2,lb 11,w 4,nb 11) | 28 | (b 6,lb 3,w 1,nb 6) | 16 |
| TOTAL | | 220 | | 325 |

### NOTTS

| | | | | |
|---|---|---|---|---|
| B.C.Broad | c Whitticase b Maguire | 67 | c Briers b Hepworth | 29 |
| P.Pollard | c Whitticase b Tennant | 45 | lbw b Millns | 0 |
| R.T.Robinson * | c Millns b Tennant | 13 | (4) not out | 68 |
| R.A.Pick | c Whitticase b Maguire | 0 | | |
| P.Johnson | c Whitticase b Wilkinson | 37 | not out | 57 |
| D.W.Randall | c Briers b Millns | 104 | | |
| K.P.Evans | c Hepworth b Tennant | 22 | | |
| F.D.Stephenson | c Whitticase b Wilkinson | 28 | | |
| B.N.French + | c Potter b Maguire | 9 | (3) run out | 1 |
| E.E.Hemmings | not out | 15 | | |
| J.A.Afford | c Wilkinson b Maguire | 13 | | |
| Extras | (b 2,lb 10,w 5,nb 9) | 26 | (lb 6,nb 6) | 12 |
| TOTAL | | 379 | (for 3 wkts) | 167 |

| NOTTS | O | M | R | W | O | M | R | W | FALL OF WICKETS | | | |
|---|---|---|---|---|---|---|---|---|---|---|---|---|
| | | | | | | | | | | LEI | NOT | LEI NOT |
| Stephenson | 20.4 | 6 | 52 | 3 | 27 | 11 | 33 | 3 | 1st | 3 | 103 | 14 1 |
| Pick | 19 | 5 | 75 | 2 | 22.1 | 2 | 89 | 3 | 2nd | 9 | 121 | 92 4 |
| Evans | 21 | 5 | 52 | 5 | 29 | 8 | 83 | 4 | 3rd | 42 | 128 | 282 43 |
| Hemmings | 6 | 1 | 20 | 0 | 25 | 6 | 56 | 0 | 4th | 53 | 132 | 282 |
| Afford | 3 | 1 | 8 | 0 | 23 | 6 | 55 | 0 | 5th | 60 | 198 | 300 |
| | | | | | | | | | 6th | 73 | 245 | 300 |
| LEICS | O | M | R | W | O | M | R | W | 7th | 95 | 296 | 302 |
| Millns | 31 | 6 | 86 | 1 | 11 | 3 | 23 | 1 | 8th | 153 | 332 | 319 |
| Maguire | 30.3 | 5 | 92 | 4 | 8 | 1 | 34 | 0 | 9th | 155 | 352 | 325 |
| Wilkinson | 22 | 5 | 80 | 2 | 2 | 0 | 17 | 0 | 10th | 220 | 379 | 325 |
| Willey | 7 | 1 | 15 | 0 | | | | | | | | |
| Tennant | 19 | 3 | 65 | 3 | 6 | 2 | 22 | 0 | | | | |
| Potter | 10 | 0 | 29 | 0 | 12 | 2 | 34 | 0 | | | | |
| Hepworth | | | | | 8 | 0 | 31 | 1 | | | | |

## SOMERSET vs. GLAMORGAN

at Taunton on 9th, 10th, 11th, 13th May 1991
Toss : Glamorgan. Umpires : R.Julian and M.J.Kitchen
Glamorgan won by 180 runs. Glamorgan 6 pts (Bt: 4, Bw: 2), Glamorgan 22 pts (Bt: 3, Bw: 3)
100 overs scores : Glamorgan 251 for 6, Somerset 325 for 7

### GLAMORGAN

| | | | | |
|---|---|---|---|---|
| A.R.Butcher * | lbw b Mallender | 12 | c Cook b Swallow | 65 |
| H.Morris | c Tavare b Graveney | 141 | c Rose b Graveney | 39 |
| R.J.Shastri | b Swallow | 37 | c Harden b Graveney | 68 |
| M.P.Maynard | c Lefebvre b Graveney | 85 | not out | 133 |
| G.C.Holmes | c Harden b Graveney | 2 | not out | 25 |
| I.Smith | lbw b Rose | 6 | | |
| R.D.B.Croft | c Harden b Graveney | 2 | | |
| C.P.Metson + | c Tavare b Rose | 24 | | |
| S.L.Watkin | not out | 25 | | |
| D.J.Foster | not out | 6 | | |
| M.Frost | | | | |
| Extras | (lb 6,w 5,nb 2) | 13 | (b 5,lb 7,nb 6) | 18 |
| TOTAL | (for 8 wkts dec) | 353 | (for 3 wkts dec) | 348 |

### SOMERSET

| | | | | |
|---|---|---|---|---|
| P.M.Roebuck | c Smith b Foster | 101 | c Butcher b Foster | 64 |
| S.J.Cook | c Metson b Foster | 15 | b Foster | 20 |
| R.J.Harden | b Foster | 73 | c Smith b Foster | 26 |
| C.J.Tavare * | c Metson b Frost | 8 | b Watkin | 9 |
| R.J.Bartlett | c Metson b Foster | 32 | lbw b Frost | 0 |
| N.D.Burns + | b Foster | 6 | c Croft b Frost | 0 |
| N.A.Mallender | c Metson b Watkin | 19 | (10) c Metson b Watkin | 4 |
| G.D.Rose | lbw b Frost | 24 | (7) c Smith b Watkin | 2 |
| R.P.Lefebvre | c Metson b Watkin | 39 | (8) c Metson b Watkin | 1 |
| I.G.Swallow | b Foster | 1 | (9) not out | 41 |
| D.A.Graveney | not out | 0 | c Metson b Watkin | 17 |
| Extras | (lb 8,w 1,nb 7) | 16 | (w 1,nb 2) | 3 |
| TOTAL | | 334 | | 187 |

| SOMERSET | O | M | R | W | O | M | R | W | FALL OF WICKETS | | | |
|---|---|---|---|---|---|---|---|---|---|---|---|---|
| | | | | | | | | | | GLA | SOM | GLA SOM |
| Mallender | 29 | 7 | 58 | 1 | 21 | 5 | 75 | 0 | 1st | 20 | 26 | 88 34 |
| Rose | 29 | 5 | 89 | 2 | 9 | 0 | 28 | 0 | 2nd | 94 | 155 | 131 85 |
| Lefebvre | 26 | 10 | 51 | 0 | 14 | 2 | 49 | 0 | 3rd | 235 | 189 | 278 104 |
| Graveney | 29 | 7 | 89 | 4 | 31 | 8 | 110 | 2 | 4th | 237 | 227 | 105 |
| Swallow | 17 | 5 | 47 | 1 | 13 | 1 | 62 | 1 | 5th | 244 | 246 | 105 |
| Roebuck | 7 | 2 | 13 | 0 | 7 | 1 | 12 | 0 | 6th | 250 | 284 | 114 |
| | | | | | | | | | 7th | 309 | 284 | 124 |
| GLAMORGAN | O | M | R | W | O | M | R | W | 8th | 330 | 333 | 124 |
| Foster | 28.2 | 3 | 84 | 6 | 21 | 6 | 63 | 3 | 9th | | 334 | 134 |
| Watkin | 32 | 5 | 120 | 2 | 20.3 | 5 | 63 | 5 | 10th | | 334 | 187 |
| Frost | 21 | 3 | 56 | 2 | 15 | 0 | 52 | 2 | | | | |
| Croft | 23 | 3 | 66 | 0 | 3 | 2 | 4 | 0 | | | | |
| Shastri | | | | | 1 | 0 | 5 | 0 | | | | |

# BRITANNIC ASSURANCE CHAMPIONSHIP

## GLOUCS vs. HAMPSHIRE

at Bristol on 9th, 10th, 11th, 13th May 1991
Toss : Gloucs. Umpires : D.J.Constant and B.J.Meyer
Gloucs won by 8 wickets. Gloucs 21 pts (Bt: 3, Bw: 2), Hampshire 6 pts (Bt: 3, Bw: 3)
100 overs scores : Hampshire 282 for 6, Gloucs 290 for 7

### HAMPSHIRE

|  | | | | |
|---|---|---|---|---|
| V.P.Terry | c Wright b Lawrence | 18 | c Russell b Lawrence | 5 |
| C.L.Smith | b Lawrence | 125 | b Babington | 24 |
| D.I.Gower | c Russell b Babington | 14 | c Wright b Lawrence | 3 |
| R.A.Smith | b Lawrence | 31 | lbw b Gilbert | 74 |
| M.C.J.Nicholas * | c Athey b Lawrence | 9 | c Lloyds b Lawrence | 31 |
| K.D.James | lbw b Lawrence | 3 | c Lloyds b Babington | 34 |
| A.N Aymes + | b Gilbert | 17 | lbw b Lawrence | 1 |
| R.J.Maru | c Russell b Lawrence | 61 | c Russell b Gilbert | 31 |
| C.A.Connor | b Gilbert | 1 | lbw b Gilbert | 4 |
| P.J.Bakker | b Gilbert | 0 | not out | 6 |
| Aqib Javed | not out | 4 | c Gilbert b Lawrence | 0 |
| Extras | (b 4,lb 7,w 2,nb 4) | 17 | (lb 1,nb 4) | 5 |
| TOTAL | | 300 | | 218 |

### GLOUCS

|  | | | | |
|---|---|---|---|---|
| G.D.Hodgson | lbw b James | 26 | c sub b Aqib Javed | 8 |
| R.J.Scott | b James | 29 | c Aymes b Aqib Javed | 0 |
| A.J.Wright * | c Aymes b James | 15 | not out | 61 |
| C.W.J.Athey | c Aymes b Maru | 9 | not out | 65 |
| M.W.Alleyne | c Aymes b Maru | 79 | | |
| J.W.Lloyds | c Terry b Aqib Javed | 48 | | |
| R.C.Russell + | b Maru | 111 | | |
| D.V.Lawrence | b Aqib Javed | 0 | | |
| D.R.Gilbert | b James | 20 | | |
| A.M.Smith | b Aqib Javed | 3 | | |
| A.M.Babington | not out | 0 | | |
| Extras | (b 3,lb 10,w 1,nb 6) | 20 | (b 4,lb 12,w 1,nb 8) | 25 |
| TOTAL | | 360 | (for 2 wkts) | 159 |

| GLOUCS | O | M | R | W | O | M | R | W |
|---|---|---|---|---|---|---|---|---|
| Gilbert | 24.4 | 5 | 57 | 3 | 32 | 11 | 51 | 3 |
| Lawrence | 25 | 4 | 77 | 6 | 27.1 | 6 | 52 | 5 |
| Babington | 19 | 1 | 70 | 1 | 25 | 8 | 53 | 2 |
| Smith | 21 | 7 | 50 | 0 | 10 | 3 | 22 | 0 |
| Lloyds | 9 | 2 | 15 | 0 | 21 | 8 | 39 | 0 |
| Scott | 4 | 1 | 17 | 0 | | | | |
| Athey | 3 | 0 | 3 | 0 | | | | |

**FALL OF WICKETS**

| | HAM | GLO | HAM | GLO |
|---|---|---|---|---|
| 1st | 41 | 58 | 22 | 5 |
| 2nd | 57 | 67 | 26 | 16 |
| 3rd | 117 | 82 | 57 | |
| 4th | 132 | 82 | 112 | |
| 5th | 137 | 168 | 147 | |
| 6th | 169 | 265 | 150 | |
| 7th | 295 | 268 | 202 | |
| 8th | 296 | 313 | 208 | |
| 9th | 296 | 328 | 213 | |
| 10th | 300 | 360 | 218 | |

| HAMPSHIRE | O | M | R | W | O | M | R | W |
|---|---|---|---|---|---|---|---|---|
| Aqib Javed | 29 | 4 | 95 | 3 | 12 | 3 | 16 | 2 |
| Connor | 26 | 6 | 70 | 0 | 8 | 1 | 41 | 0 |
| James | 23 | 6 | 72 | 4 | 9 | 4 | 24 | 0 |
| Maru | 37.5 | 14 | 95 | 3 | 8 | 1 | 30 | 0 |
| Nicholas | 5 | 1 | 15 | 0 | 3.5 | 1 | 12 | 0 |
| Bakker | | | | | 15 | 7 | 20 | 0 |

## WORCESTERSHIRE vs. LANCASHIRE

at Worcester on 9th, 10th, 11th, 13th May 1991
Toss : Worcestershire. Umpires : B.Hassan and P.B.Wight
Match drawn. Worcestershire 4 pts (Bt: 3, Bw: 1), Lancashire 6 pts (Bt: 4, Bw: 2)
100 overs scores : Worcestershire 291 for 6, Lancashire 330 for 4

### WORCESTERSHIRE

|  | | | | |
|---|---|---|---|---|
| T.S.Curtis | c Fairbrother b Watkinson | 15 | (2) c Fairbrother b DeFreitas | 15 |
| G.J.Lord | c Hegg b DeFreitas | 12 | (1) lbw b DeFreitas | 0 |
| G.A.Hick | lbw b DeFreitas | 57 | b DeFreitas | 0 |
| T.M.Moody | lbw b Watkinson | 0 | c Hegg b DeFreitas | 135 |
| P.A.Neale * | lbw b Allott | 4 | c Allott b DeFreitas | 11 |
| I.T.Botham | c Lloyd b Wasim Akram | 104 | c Lloyd b Wasim Akram | 9 |
| S.J.Rhodes + | lbw b Allott | 67 | c Hegg b Wasim Akram | 6 |
| R.K.Illingworth | c Hegg b Allott | 34 | not out | 56 |
| P.J.Newport | c Fairbrother b Allott | 5 | c sub b Wasim Akram | 3 |
| C.M.Tolley | not out | 18 | c Fairbrother b Wasim Akram | 18 |
| G.R.Dilley | c Atherton b DeFreitas | 0 | c Fairbrother b DeFreitas | 0 |
| Extras | (b 5,lb 6,nb 2) | 13 | (b 1,lb 8,w 3,nb 7) | 19 |
| TOTAL | | 329 | | 272 |

### LANCASHIRE

|  | | | | |
|---|---|---|---|---|
| G.D.Mendis | c Curtis b Dilley | 9 | c Moody b Newport | 14 |
| G.Fowler | lbw b Botham | 80 | run out | 1 |
| M.A.Atherton | c Neale b Botham | 110 | c Neale b Dilley | 0 |
| N.H.Fairbrother * | c Dilley b Tolley | 109 | (6) c Hick b Dilley | 10 |
| G.D.Lloyd | c sub b Dilley | 24 | (4) c Hick b Dilley | 1 |
| M.Watkinson | b Dilley | 12 | (8) b Newport | 6 |
| Wasim Akram | c Hick b Dilley | 17 | c Lord b Newport | 24 |
| P.A.J.DeFreitas | b Botham | 12 | (5) b Newport | 47 |
| W.K.Hegg + | c Moody b Dilley | 0 | not out | 27 |
| G.Yates | b Botham | 4 | lbw b Botham | 0 |
| P.J.W.Allott | not out | 3 | not out | 5 |
| Extras | (b 1,lb 10,w 1,nb 11) | 23 | (b 5,lb 5,nb 3) | 13 |
| TOTAL | | 403 | (for 9 wkts) | 148 |

| LANCASHIRE | O | M | R | W | O | M | R | W |
|---|---|---|---|---|---|---|---|---|
| Wasim Akram | 30 | 9 | 69 | 1 | 36 | 9 | 89 | 4 |
| DeFreitas | 30.4 | 10 | 91 | 3 | 31.5 | 6 | 88 | 6 |
| Watkinson | 11.4 | 6 | 22 | 2 | | | | |
| Allott | 28 | 9 | 56 | 4 | 15 | 1 | 62 | 0 |
| Yates | 23 | 3 | 80 | 0 | 5 | 1 | 24 | 0 |

**FALL OF WICKETS**

| | WOR | LAN | WOR | LAN |
|---|---|---|---|---|
| 1st | 24 | 40 | 3 | 21 |
| 2nd | 36 | 137 | 3 | 21 |
| 3rd | 36 | 326 | 45 | 21 |
| 4th | 44 | 326 | 91 | 36 |
| 5th | 150 | 341 | 108 | 74 |
| 6th | 221 | 375 | 122 | 88 |
| 7th | 291 | 396 | 227 | 98 |
| 8th | 297 | 396 | 230 | 125 |
| 9th | 329 | 396 | 270 | 125 |
| 10th | 329 | 403 | 272 | |

| WORCS | O | M | R | W | O | M | R | W |
|---|---|---|---|---|---|---|---|---|
| Dilley | 36 | 8 | 91 | 5 | 14.2 | 2 | 64 | 3 |
| Newport | 38 | 8 | 106 | 0 | 17 | 3 | 58 | 4 |
| Botham | 31.1 | 4 | 105 | 4 | 4 | 1 | 16 | 1 |
| Tolley | 12 | 0 | 45 | 1 | | | | |
| Illingworth | 16 | 3 | 45 | 0 | | | | |

## HEADLINES

### Britannic Assurance Championship

#### 9th - 13th May

- Glamorgan could be well pleased with the manner of their victory over Somerset at Taunton. They scored more than 700 runs, Hugh Morris and Matthew Maynard both hitting their first 100s of the season, and their three seam bowlers neatly divided the 20 wickets between themselves to secure victory by 180 runs. Darren Foster particularly enjoyed his return to his former county, returning career-best figures on his Championship début for Glamorgan.

- David Lawrence continued his aggressive start to the season in Gloucestershire's eight-wicket success over Hampshire at Bristol, claiming 11 wickets in the match to deny the best efforts of the Smith brothers, Chris hitting his fourth 100 in all cricket and Robin quickly finding his form after a hernia operation. Jack Russell warmed up for the West Indies with the third first-class 100 of his career and victory was sealed for the home side in fine style with an ubroken stand of 143 between Tony Wright and Bill Athey.

- Although the match was eventually drawn thanks to the intervention of the weather, Worcestershire's encounter with Lancashire at Worcester more than lived up to expectations, amounting in many ways to an unofficial Test trial. Ian Botham immediately took centre stage by hitting a 111-ball 100 as the home side recovered from 44 for four. Michael Atherton and Neil Fairbrother compiled contrasting centuries as Lancashire gained a first-innings lead of 74, and Phil DeFreitas pressed home their advantage with six second-innings wickets. Tom Moody duly scored his first first-class 100 for Worcestershire, and Richard Illingworth managed to stretch the lead to 198 and, with rain clouds threatening, Graham Dilley and Phil Newport finally turned the match in Worcestershire's favour, only for Warren Hegg and Paul Allott to survive long enough to secure an eventful draw, courtesy of a missed catch by Dilley.

- First-class débuts: E.S.H.Giddins (Sussex); G.J.Kersey (Kent); C.Wilkinson (Leicestershire).

# OTHER FIRST-CLASS MATCHES

## CAMBRIDGE U vs. DERBYSHIRE

at Fenner's on 9th, 10th, 11th May 1991
Toss : Cambridge U. Umpires : V.A.Holder and A.G.T.Whitehead
Match drawn

**DERBYSHIRE**

| | | | | | |
|---|---|---|---|---|---|
| P.D.Bowler | c Clitheroe b Hooper | 81 | c Arscott b Viljoen | | 31 |
| T.J.G.O'Gorman | b Johnson | 14 | (4) c Pearson b Lowrey | | 14 |
| J.E.Morris | c Arscott b Pearson | 131 | | | |
| M.Azharuddin | not out | 116 | (9) not out | | 20 |
| C.J.Adams | c Clitheroe b Arscott | 39 | (2) c Bush b Pearson | | 134 |
| B.Roberts | not out | 36 | (8) not out | | 44 |
| K.M.Krikken + | | | (3) c Thwaites b Pearson | | 11 |
| M.Jean-Jacques | | | (5) b Pearson | | 2 |
| O.H.Mortensen | | | (6) b Pearson | | 0 |
| A.E.Warner | | | (7) c Lowrey b Arscott | | 53 |
| K.J.Barnett * | | | | | |
| Extras | (b 6,lb 1,w 1,nb 6) | 14 | (b 5,lb 10,nb 1) | | 16 |
| TOTAL | (for 4 wkts dec) | 431 | (for 7 wkts dec) | | 325 |

**CAMBRIDGE UNIVERSITY**

| | | | | | |
|---|---|---|---|---|---|
| A.M.Hooper | c Roberts b Warner | 21 | not out | | 48 |
| R.I.Clitheroe + | lbw b Jean-Jacques | 36 | c Krikken b Adams | | 7 |
| J.P.Crawley * | c Barnett b Warner | 0 | | | |
| M.J.Lowrey | c Mortensen b Warner | 2 | (3) not out | | 4 |
| M.J.Morris | c Morris b Barnett | 17 | | | |
| G.E.Thwaites | c Krikken b Warner | 32 | | | |
| J.P.Arscott | c Azharuddin b Jean-Jacques | 74 | | | |
| S.W.Johnson | lbw b Barnett | 18 | | | |
| R.M.Pearson | lbw b Barnett | 21 | | | |
| D.J.Bush | c Krikken b Jean-Jacques | 13 | | | |
| J.N.Viljoen | not out | 1 | | | |
| Extras | (b 4,lb 11,nb 8) | 23 | (nb 1) | | 1 |
| TOTAL | | 258 | (for 1 wkt) | | 60 |

| CAMBRIDGE U | O | M | R | W | O | M | R | W |
|---|---|---|---|---|---|---|---|---|
| Johnson | 17 | 1 | 66 | 1 | 8 | 3 | 25 | 0 |
| Bush | 16 | 4 | 53 | 0 | 7 | 1 | 44 | 0 |
| Viljoen | 11 | 0 | 65 | 0 | 11 | 2 | 34 | 1 |
| Pearson | 32 | 7 | 92 | 1 | 27 | 2 | 84 | 4 |
| Arscott | 11 | 1 | 52 | 1 | 6 | 0 | 42 | 1 |
| Lowrey | 15 | 1 | 61 | 0 | 14 | 1 | 46 | 1 |
| Hooper | 5 | 1 | 35 | 1 | 5 | 2 | 15 | 0 |
| Morris | | | | | 3 | 1 | 15 | 0 |
| Crawley | | | | | 1 | 0 | 5 | 0 |

| DERBYSHIRE | O | M | R | W | O | M | R | W |
|---|---|---|---|---|---|---|---|---|
| Mortensen | 16 | 1 | 37 | 0 | 8 | 4 | 8 | 0 |
| Warner | 23 | 2 | 60 | 4 | | | | |
| Jean-Jacques | 17.5 | 6 | 34 | 3 | 10 | 2 | 25 | 0 |
| Barnett | 33 | 12 | 71 | 3 | | | | |
| Azharuddin | 23 | 9 | 41 | 0 | | | | |
| Adams | | | | | 7 | 2 | 11 | 1 |
| Bowler | | | | | 5 | 2 | 16 | 0 |

| FALL OF WICKETS | | | | |
|---|---|---|---|---|
| | DER | CAM | DER | CAM |
| 1st | 20 | 40 | 65 | 41 |
| 2nd | 228 | 40 | 165 | |
| 3rd | 230 | 44 | 192 | |
| 4th | 361 | 82 | 200 | |
| 5th | | 88 | 202 | |
| 6th | | 140 | 204 | |
| 7th | | 174 | 286 | |
| 8th | | 230 | | |
| 9th | | 252 | | |
| 10th | | 258 | | |

## CAMBRIDGE U vs. MIDDLESEX

at Fenner's on 15th, 16th, 17th May 1991
Toss : Middlesex. Umpires : B.J.Meyer and H.J.Rhodes
Match drawn

**MIDDLESEX**

| | | | | | |
|---|---|---|---|---|---|
| I.J.F.Hutchinson | b Arscott | 92 | | | |
| M.A.Roseberry | not out | 123 | | | |
| M.R.Ramprakash | b Pearson | 0 | | | |
| K.R.Brown | c Morris b Bush | 34 | (1) c Crawley b Pearson | | 28 |
| M.Keech | not out | 12 | (2) lbw b Jenkins | | 46 |
| P.Farbrace + | | | (3) c Johnson b Jenkins | | 9 |
| P.C.R.Tufnell | | | (4) not out | | 14 |
| J.E.Emburey * | | | (5) not out | | 1 |
| S.P.Hughes | | | | | |
| R.M.Ellcock | | | | | |
| N.G.Cowans | | | | | |
| Extras | (b 8,lb 4,w 6,nb 1) | 19 | (b 4,lb 2,nb 2) | | 8 |
| TOTAL | (for 3 wkts dec) | 280 | (for 3 wkts dec) | | 106 |

**CAMBRIDGE U**

| | | | | | |
|---|---|---|---|---|---|
| A.M.Hooper | c Emburey b Cowans | 2 | b Ellcock | | 0 |
| R.I.Clitheroe + | b Cowans | 6 | c Farbrace b Cowans | | 4 |
| J.P.Crawley | not out | 52 | c & b Tufnell | | 43 |
| M.J.Lowrey | c Roseberry b Cowans | 2 | (5) c Hutchinson b Tufnell | | 9 |
| M.J.Morris | c Hutchinson b Tufnell | 2 | (6) c Hutchinson b Emburey | | 0 |
| J.P.Arscott | c Farbrace b Tufnell | 2 | (7) c Emburey b Tufnell | | 1 |
| R.J.Turner * | not out | 69 | (4) c Ellcock b Emburey | | 38 |
| R.H.J.Jenkins | | | c Brown b Tufnell | | 10 |
| R.M.Pearson | | | not out | | 4 |
| S.W.Johnson | | | not out | | 4 |
| D.J.Bush | | | | | |
| Extras | (lb 2,nb 4) | 6 | (b 4,lb 2,nb 2) | | 8 |
| TOTAL | (for 5 wkts dec) | 139 | (for 8 wkts) | | 121 |

| CAMBRIDGE U | O | M | R | W | O | M | R | W |
|---|---|---|---|---|---|---|---|---|
| Johnson | 7 | 2 | 37 | 0 | 5 | 0 | 28 | 0 |
| Jenkins | 19 | 6 | 39 | 0 | 14 | 1 | 46 | 2 |
| Bush | 15.3 | 5 | 52 | 1 | | | | |
| Pearson | 20 | 2 | 56 | 1 | 6 | 2 | 10 | 1 |
| Hooper | 8 | 2 | 28 | 0 | 3 | 1 | 16 | 0 |
| Arscott | 3 | 0 | 32 | 1 | | | | |
| Lowrey | 10 | 0 | 24 | 0 | | | | |

| MIDDLESEX | O | M | R | W | O | M | R | W |
|---|---|---|---|---|---|---|---|---|
| Cowans | 8 | 4 | 10 | 3 | 5 | 3 | 19 | 1 |
| Ellcock | 7 | 3 | 11 | 0 | 5 | 3 | 4 | 1 |
| Tufnell | 13 | 6 | 13 | 2 | 21 | 14 | 14 | 4 |
| Hughes | 10 | 4 | 29 | 0 | 8 | 2 | 25 | 0 |
| Ramprakash | 2 | 0 | 11 | 0 | 9 | 2 | 36 | 0 |
| Keech | 3 | 0 | 20 | 0 | | | | |
| Roseberry | 5 | 0 | 27 | 0 | | | | |
| Brown | 2.5 | 1 | 16 | 0 | | | | |
| Emburey | | | | | 17 | 10 | 17 | 2 |

| FALL OF WICKETS | | | | |
|---|---|---|---|---|
| | MID | CAM | MID | CAM |
| 1st | 164 | 7 | 79 | 0 |
| 2nd | 165 | 12 | 79 | 4 |
| 3rd | 257 | 16 | 98 | 83 |
| 4th | | 20 | | 87 |
| 5th | | 38 | | 87 |
| 6th | | | | 90 |
| 7th | | | | 108 |
| 8th | | | | 113 |
| 9th | | | | |
| 10th | | | | |

## OXFORD U vs. GLOUCS

at The Parks on 15th, 16th, 17th (no play) May 1991
Toss : Oxford U. Umpires : D.J.Constant and D.Fawkner-Corbett
Match drawn

**GLOUCS**

| | | |
|---|---|---|
| G.D.Hodgson | c Montgomerie b MacDonald | 105 |
| R.J.Scott | c Sandiford b MacDonald | 49 |
| C.W.J.Athey | c Gupte b MacDonald | 127 |
| M.W.Alleyne | not out | 5 |
| S.N.Barnes | not out | 0 |
| A.J.Wright * | | |
| J.W.Lloyds | | |
| R.C.Russell + | | |
| E.T.Milburn | | |
| R.M.Bell | | |
| A.M.Babington | | |
| Extras | (b 3,lb 6,w 3,nb 2) | 14 |
| TOTAL | (for 3 wkts dec) | 300 |

**OXFORD U**

| | | |
|---|---|---|
| R.R.Montgomerie | lbw b Babington | 8 |
| R.E.Morris | lbw b Babington | 6 |
| C.Gupte | not out | 55 |
| G.Lovell | c Hodgson b Babington | 49 |
| G.J.Turner * | not out | 1 |
| D.Pfaff | | |
| D.Sandiford + | | |
| H.Davies | | |
| R.MacDonald | | |
| J.M.E.Oppenheimer | | |
| B.Wood | | |
| Extras | (lb 3) | 3 |
| TOTAL | (for 3 wkts) | 122 |

| OXFORD U | O | M | R | W | O | M | R | W |
|---|---|---|---|---|---|---|---|---|
| MacDonald | 23 | 8 | 66 | 3 | | | | |
| Wood | 13 | 1 | 53 | 0 | | | | |
| Turner | 27 | 12 | 36 | 0 | | | | |
| Oppenheimer | 19 | 5 | 33 | 0 | | | | |
| Davies | 22 | 3 | 70 | 0 | | | | |
| Gupte | 2 | 0 | 22 | 0 | | | | |
| Lovell | 6 | 0 | 11 | 0 | | | | |

| GLOUCS | O | M | R | W | O | M | R | W |
|---|---|---|---|---|---|---|---|---|
| Babington | 12.3 | 4 | 22 | 3 | | | | |
| Barnes | 12 | 4 | 23 | 0 | | | | |
| Bell | 5 | 2 | 9 | 0 | | | | |
| Milburn | 7 | 1 | 29 | 0 | | | | |
| Lloyds | 3 | 0 | 11 | 0 | | | | |
| Alleyne | 6 | 1 | 15 | 0 | | | | |
| Athey | 6 | 2 | 10 | 0 | | | | |

| FALL OF WICKETS | | | | |
|---|---|---|---|---|
| | GLO | OXF | GLO | OXF |
| 1st | 97 | 9 | | |
| 2nd | 277 | 18 | | |
| 3rd | 298 | 117 | | |
| 4th | | | | |
| 5th | | | | |
| 6th | | | | |
| 7th | | | | |
| 8th | | | | |
| 9th | | | | |
| 10th | | | | |

---

## HEADLINES

### Other first-class matches

#### 9th - 11th May

- Kim Barnett opted for extended batting practice rather than pressing for a Derbyshire victory over Cambridge University at Fenner's, but the match did produce centuries for Mohammad Azharuddin, his first for the county, Chris Adams, a new career best, and John Morris, while Cambridge's Jeremy Arscott hit his maiden first-class fifty.

- First-class début: J.N.Viljoen (Cambridge U).

#### 15th - 17th May

- Mike Roseberry made his first hundred of the season for Middlesex against Cambridge University at Fenner's, while John Crawley and Rob Turner virtually monopolised the scoring in both the University's innings, sharing stands of 101* and 79, before Phil Tufnell almost spun Middlesex to victory.

- At The Parks, Dean Hodgson and Bill Athey both hit centuries for Gloucestershire and Gupte made a maiden first-class fifty for Oxford University, before rain intervened on the second day.

- First-class début: M.Keech (Middlesex).

# TOUR MATCHES

## L OF NORFOLK XI vs. WEST INDIES

at Arundel Castle on 12th May 1991
Toss : L of Norfolk XI.  Umpires : A.A.Jones and K.J.Lyons
L of Norfolk XI won by 2 wickets

**WEST INDIES**

| | | |
|---|---|---|
| C.G.Greenidge | c Azharuddin b Donelan | 22 |
| P.V.Simmons | c Azharuddin b Donelan | 40 |
| R.B.Richardson | b Bainbridge | 5 |
| B.C.Lara | b Donelan | 15 |
| C.L.Hooper | c Krikken b Bainbridge | 1 |
| A.L.Logie | c & b Bainbridge | 61 |
| I.V.A.Richards * | c Azharuddin b Barnett | 17 |
| P.J.L.Dujon + | not out | 21 |
| H.A.G.Anthony | c Butcher b Mortensen | 4 |
| I.B.A.Allen | not out | 2 |
| B.P.Patterson | | |
| Extras | (b 1,lb 12,w 9,nb 1) | 23 |
| TOTAL | (50 overs)(for 8 wkts) | 211 |

**L OF NORFOLK XI**

| | | |
|---|---|---|
| K.J.Barnett | c Dujon b Patterson | 12 |
| B.R.Hardie | b Anthony | 18 |
| J.E.Morris | c Logie b Anthony | 98 |
| M.Azharuddin | c Logie b Hooper | 21 |
| R.O.Butcher | b Hooper | 0 |
| T.J.G.O'Gorman | b Allen | 13 |
| P.Bainbridge | c Hooper b Richards | 9 |
| K.M.Krikken + | not out | 7 |
| B.T.P.Donelan | c Dujon b Patterson | 1 |
| O.H.Mortensen | not out | 1 |
| J.K.Lever | | |
| Extras | (b 9,lb 12,w 10,nb 4) | 32 |
| TOTAL | (47.4 overs)(for 8 wkts) | 212 |

| D OF NORFOLK | O | M | R | W | | FALL OF WICKETS | |
|---|---|---|---|---|---|---|---|
| | | | | | | WI | LON |
| Mortensen | 10 | 1 | 32 | 1 | 1st | 33 | 33 |
| Lever | 10 | 3 | 33 | 0 | 2nd | 45 | 74 |
| Bainbridge | 10 | 1 | 36 | 3 | 3rd | 76 | 134 |
| Donelan | 10 | 1 | 41 | 3 | 4th | 77 | 134 |
| Barnett | 6 | 0 | 32 | 1 | 5th | 107 | 185 |
| Azharuddin | 4 | 0 | 24 | 0 | 6th | 174 | 195 |
| | | | | | 7th | 186 | 205 |
| WEST INDIES | O | M | R | W | 8th | 208 | 206 |
| Patterson | 8 | 2 | 23 | 2 | 9th | | |
| Allen | 10 | 1 | 41 | 1 | 10th | | |
| Anthony | 10 | 1 | 56 | 2 | | | |
| Simmons | 10 | 0 | 52 | 0 | | | |
| Hooper | 6 | 1 | 13 | 2 | | | |
| Richardson | 1 | 0 | 4 | 0 | | | |
| Richards | 2.4 | 0 | 5 | 1 | | | |

---

# HEADLINES

### Tour matches

### 12th May

• The West Indies tour opened in the traditional relaxed fashion at Arundel Castle, in complete contrast to the frenzied Antigua Recreation Ground where the West Indians had lost a Test match to Australia less than two weeks before. The visitors, in fact, lost again, by two wickets to Lavinia, Duchess of Norfolk's XI in front of 9,000 spectators who all enjoyed the warm Sussex sunshine, the idyllic surroundings and a reminder from Derbyshire's John Morris, with a handsome 98, of what a powerful striker of the ball he can be.

### 14th May

• The West Indians gained their first victory of their tour on their visit to Bristol. Tony Wright and Jerry Lloyds helped to take Gloucestershire's total to 206 for five, but the tourists were taken to victory by an innings of 101 from Desmond Haynes, quickly re-adapting to English conditions.

---

## GLOUCS vs. WEST INDIES

at Bristol on 14th May 1991
Toss : West Indies.  Umpires : H.D.Bird and D.R.Shepherd
West Indies won by 6 wickets

**GLOUCS**

| | | |
|---|---|---|
| R.J.Scott | c Hooper b Ambrose | 2 |
| C.W.J.Athey | b Marshall | 9 |
| A.J.Wright * | not out | 78 |
| M.W.Alleyne | b Hooper | 15 |
| R.C.Russell + | b Hooper | 21 |
| P.W.Romaines | b Hooper | 11 |
| J.W.Lloyds | not out | 45 |
| D.V.Lawrence | | |
| D.R.Gilbert | | |
| S.N.Barnes | | |
| A.M.Babington | | |
| Extras | (b 2,lb 13,w 7,nb 3) | 25 |
| TOTAL | (55 overs)(for 5 wkts) | 206 |

**WEST INDIES**

| | | |
|---|---|---|
| P.V.Simmons | c Russell b Babington | 2 |
| D.L.Haynes * | c Lloyds b Gilbert | 101 |
| R.B.Richardson | c Romaines b Alleyne | 25 |
| B.C.Lara | c Russell b Lawrence | 30 |
| C.L.Hooper | not out | 22 |
| A.L.Logie | not out | 12 |
| D.Williams + | | |
| M.D.Marshall | | |
| H.A.G.Anthony | | |
| C.E.L.Ambrose | | |
| I.B.A.Allen | | |
| Extras | (lb 8,w 7,nb 2) | 17 |
| TOTAL | (53 overs)(for 4 wkts) | 209 |

| WEST INDIES | O | M | R | W | | FALL OF WICKETS | |
|---|---|---|---|---|---|---|---|
| | | | | | | GLO | WI |
| Ambrose | 4 | 2 | 5 | 1 | 1st | 3 | 11 |
| Allen | 10 | 2 | 32 | 0 | 2nd | 28 | 82 |
| Marshall | 11 | 4 | 32 | 1 | 3rd | 65 | 155 |
| Anthony | 11 | 1 | 46 | 0 | 4th | 110 | 183 |
| Simmons | 8 | 0 | 40 | 0 | 5th | 132 | |
| Hooper | 11 | 1 | 36 | 3 | 6th | | |
| | | | | | 7th | | |
| GLOUCS | O | M | R | W | 8th | | |
| Gilbert | 11 | 0 | 36 | 1 | 9th | | |
| Babington | 11 | 4 | 26 | 1 | 10th | | |
| Lawrence | 11 | 2 | 47 | 1 | | | |
| Barnes | 9 | 0 | 26 | 0 | | | |
| Alleyne | 9 | 0 | 54 | 1 | | | |
| Lloyds | 2 | 0 | 12 | 0 | | | |

---

## WORCESTERSHIRE vs. WEST INDIES

at Worcester on 15th, 16th, 17th May 1991
Toss : West Indies.  Umpires : J.H.Hampshire and K.E.Palmer
Match drawn

**WEST INDIES**

| | | | | |
|---|---|---|---|---|
| C.G.Greenidge | c Lampitt b Botham | 26 | not out | 12 |
| P.V.Simmons | b Illingworth | 134 | not out | 24 |
| R.B.Richardson | c Moody b Botham | 6 | | |
| B.C.Lara | b Newport | 26 | | |
| I.V.A.Richards * | c Illingworth b Newport | 131 | | |
| C.L.Hooper | c Illingworth b Dilley | 42 | | |
| P.J.L.Dujon + | c Bevins b Dilley | 0 | | |
| H.A.G.Anthony | not out | 33 | | |
| I.B.A.Allen | | | | |
| C.A.Walsh | | | | |
| B.P.Patterson | | | | |
| Extras | (b 1,lb 4,nb 6) | 11 | | 0 |
| TOTAL | (for 7 wkts dec) | 409 | (for 0 wkts) | 36 |

**WORCESTERSHIRE**

| | | |
|---|---|---|
| T.S.Curtis | c Lara b Patterson | 30 |
| G.J.Lord | c Hooper b Patterson | 1 |
| G.A.Hick | b Allen | 11 |
| T.M.Moody | run out | 11 |
| P.A.Neale * | run out | 34 |
| I.T.Botham | c Allen b Anthony | 161 |
| P.J.Newport | c Greenidge b Patterson | 0 |
| S.R.Lampitt | c Allen b Walsh | 3 |
| R.K.Illingworth | b Walsh | 4 |
| S.R.Bevins | c Allen b Walsh | 6 |
| G.R.Dilley | not out | 0 |
| Extras | (b 2,lb 11,w 1,nb 13) | 27 |
| TOTAL | | 288 |

| WORCS | O | M | R | W | O | M | R | W | | FALL OF WICKETS | | |
|---|---|---|---|---|---|---|---|---|---|---|---|---|
| | | | | | | | | | | WI | WOR | WI WOR |
| Dilley | 21.2 | 4 | 68 | 2 | 3 | 2 | 3 | 0 | 1st | 54 | 15 | |
| Botham | 29 | 5 | 83 | 2 | | | | | 2nd | 75 | 40 | |
| Newport | 29 | 6 | 110 | 2 | 8 | 2 | 20 | 0 | 3rd | 139 | 50 | |
| Lampitt | 17 | 2 | 81 | 0 | 5 | 3 | 13 | 0 | 4th | 278 | 60 | |
| Illingworth | 18 | 4 | 62 | 1 | | | | | 5th | 341 | 196 | |
| | | | | | | | | | 6th | 346 | 222 | |
| WEST INDIES | O | M | R | W | O | M | R | W | 7th | 409 | 245 | |
| Patterson | 20 | 5 | 49 | 3 | | | | | 8th | | 272 | |
| Allen | 18 | 5 | 64 | 1 | | | | | 9th | | 288 | |
| Anthony | 13 | 1 | 63 | 1 | | | | | 10th | | 288 | |
| Walsh | 13.1 | 1 | 64 | 3 | | | | | | | | |
| Simmons | 5 | 1 | 35 | 0 | | | | | | | | |

---

# HEADLINES

### Tetley Bitter Challenge

### 15th - 17th May

• The West Indies' opening first-class fixture, their encounter with Worcestershire at Worcester, had promised much, with Ian Botham and Viv Richards in opposition, and Graeme Hick facing his first test of the summer from a four-pronged fast bowling attack. The match more than lived up to expectations. The West Indies captain lost no time in imposing his authority over long-suffering bowlers on his fifth full tour to England, hitting his 111th first-class century, well supported by Phil Simmons who made 134 to confirm his complete recovery from the head injury he suffered in 1988. Then attention turned to Hick and Botham, both of whom had just learnt of their selection for England's Texaco Trophy squad. Hick could muster only 11 in a searching examination from the West Indian fast bowlers before falling to newcomer Ian Allen, but Botham gave a batting display that brought back memories of his performances against Australia a decade earlier. He reached his first 100 against the West Indies in any form of cricket from only 83 balls, producing a succession of mighty drives and pulls, and his assault continued until he had made 161 out of 228. It was an innings that showed his determination still to prove himself against the world's most powerful Test opposition.

# REFUGE ASSURANCE LEAGUE

## LEICESTERSHIRE vs. YORKSHIRE

at Leicester on 19th May 1991
Toss : Yorkshire. Umpires : R.Julien and D.R.Shepherd
Leicestershire won by 7 runs. Leics 4 pts, Yorkshire 0 pts

### LEICESTERSHIRE

| | | |
|---|---|---|
| P.Whitticase + | lbw b Sidebottom | 24 |
| N.E.Briers * | c Sidebottom b Fletcher | 25 |
| J.J.Whitaker | b Gough | 31 |
| P.Willey | c Byas b Batty | 16 |
| C.C.Lewis | lbw b Hartley | 27 |
| L.Potter | not out | 40 |
| B.F.Smith | not out | 20 |
| P.N.Hepworth | | |
| C.Wilkinson | | |
| J.N.Maguire | | |
| D.J.Millns | | |
| Extras | (b 1,lb 14,w 5) | 20 |
| TOTAL | (40 overs)(for 5 wkts) | 203 |

### YORKSHIRE

| | | |
|---|---|---|
| M.D.Moxon * | b Maguire | 8 |
| A.A.Metcalfe | c Briers b Lewis | 5 |
| D.Byas | not out | 74 |
| P.E.Robinson | lbw b Millns | 2 |
| C.A.Chapman + | lbw b Wilkinson | 2 |
| A.Sidebottom | b Wilkinson | 10 |
| P.J.Hartley | c Whitticase b Maguire | 2 |
| D.Gough | not out | 72 |
| S.D.Fletcher | | |
| J.D.Batty | | |
| M.A.Robinson | | |
| Extras | (lb 9,w 11,nb 1) | 21 |
| TOTAL | (40 overs)(for 6 wkts) | 196 |

| YORKSHIRE | O | M | R | W | | FALL OF WICKETS | |
|---|---|---|---|---|---|---|---|
| | | | | | | LEI | YOR |
| Sidebottom | 8 | 0 | 25 | 1 | | | |
| Hartley | 8 | 1 | 43 | 1 | 1st | 46 | 14 |
| Fletcher | 7 | 0 | 34 | 1 | 2nd | 60 | 22 |
| Robinson M.A. | 5 | 0 | 20 | 0 | 3rd | 101 | 28 |
| Batty | 8 | 0 | 40 | 1 | 4th | 120 | 39 |
| Gough | 4 | 0 | 26 | 1 | 5th | 156 | 65 |
| | | | | | 6th | | 67 |
| LEICS | O | M | R | W | 7th | | |
| Lewis | 8 | 0 | 46 | 1 | 8th | | |
| Maguire | 8 | 0 | 46 | 2 | 9th | | |
| Millns | 8 | 1 | 38 | 1 | 10th | | |
| Wilkinson | 8 | 0 | 31 | 2 | | | |
| Willey | 8 | 1 | 26 | 0 | | | |

## NORTHANTS vs. WORCESTERSHIRE

at Northampton on 19th May 1991
Toss : Northants. Umpires : J.C.Balderstone and J.H.Harris
Worcs won by 27 runs. Northants 0 pts, Worcs 4 pts

### WORCESTERSHIRE

| | | |
|---|---|---|
| T.S.Curtis | run out | 49 |
| T.M.Moody | c Walker b Roberts | 100 |
| G.A.Hick | c Lamb b Walker | 47 |
| I.T.Botham | b Thomas | 10 |
| D.B.D'Oliveira | run out | 3 |
| P.A.Neale * | not out | 19 |
| M.J.Weston | not out | 1 |
| R.K.Illingworth | | |
| S.R.Lampitt | | |
| S.R.Bevins + | | |
| N.V.Radford | | |
| Extras | (lb 12,w 10) | 22 |
| TOTAL | (40 overs)(for 5 wkts) | 251 |

### NORTHANTS

| | | |
|---|---|---|
| A.Fordham | c Moody b Radford | 13 |
| N.A.Felton | c Neale b Lampitt | 65 |
| A.J.Lamb * | b Radford | 1 |
| D.J.Capel | c D'Oliveira b Radford | 12 |
| R.J.Bailey | c Curtis b Illingworth | 25 |
| A.L.Penberthy | not out | 41 |
| D.Ripley + | b Illingworth | 0 |
| J.G.Thomas | c Curtis b Illingworth | 34 |
| A.R.Roberts | c Curtis b Illingworth | 14 |
| A.Walker | b Illingworth | 6 |
| J.P.Taylor | b Botham | 5 |
| Extras | (lb 1,w 7) | 8 |
| TOTAL | (38.3 overs) | 224 |

| NORTHANTS | O | M | R | W | | FALL OF WICKETS | |
|---|---|---|---|---|---|---|---|
| | | | | | | WOR | NOR |
| Taylor | 7 | 0 | 48 | 0 | | | |
| Walker | 7 | 0 | 38 | 1 | 1st | 152 | 21 |
| Penberthy | 6 | 0 | 35 | 0 | 2nd | 176 | 36 |
| Capel | 5 | 0 | 46 | 0 | 3rd | 195 | 50 |
| Thomas | 8 | 0 | 36 | 1 | 4th | 200 | 113 |
| Roberts | 7 | 0 | 36 | 1 | 5th | 247 | 124 |
| | | | | | 6th | | 125 |
| WORCS | O | M | R | W | 7th | | 170 |
| Weston | 7 | 0 | 36 | 0 | 8th | | 203 |
| Radford | 7 | 0 | 31 | 3 | 9th | | 210 |
| Botham | 6.3 | 0 | 46 | 1 | 10th | | 224 |
| Lampitt | 8 | 0 | 44 | 1 | | | |
| Illingworth | 8 | 0 | 49 | 5 | | | |
| Hick | 2 | 0 | 17 | 0 | | | |

## SUSSEX vs. GLOUCS

at Hove on 19th May 1991
Toss : Gloucs. Umpires : H.D.Bird and R.C.Tolchard
Gloucs won by 62 runs. Sussex 0 pts, Gloucs 4 pts

### GLOUCS

| | | |
|---|---|---|
| C.W.J.Athey | b Jones | 3 |
| R.J.Scott | b Donelan | 44 |
| A.J.Wright * | b Salisbury | 20 |
| M.W.Alleyne | c Lenham b Jones | 59 |
| R.C.Russell + | c & b Jones | 42 |
| P.W.Romaines | c North b Pigott | 2 |
| J.W.Lloyds | c Donelan b Pigott | 7 |
| D.V.Lawrence | b Pigott | 0 |
| D.R.Gilbert | not out | 0 |
| A.M.Smith | not out | 1 |
| A.M.Babington | | |
| Extras | (lb 14,w 14,nb 1) | 29 |
| TOTAL | (40 overs)(for 8 wkts) | 207 |

### SUSSEX

| | | |
|---|---|---|
| D.M.Smith | c Athey b Alleyne | 40 |
| J.W.Hall | c Babington b Lawrence | 12 |
| N.J.Lenham | b Babington | 12 |
| A.P.Wells * | c Lloyds b Smith | 3 |
| K.Greenfield | c Wright b Smith | 5 |
| J.A.North | c Russell b Alleyne | 14 |
| P.Moores + | c Russell b Athey | 6 |
| A.C.S.Pigott | st Russell b Athey | 7 |
| I.D.K.Salisbury | c Smith b Babington | 14 |
| B.T.P.Donelan | b Smith | 19 |
| A.N.Jones | not out | 0 |
| Extras | (lb 9,w 3,nb 1) | 13 |
| TOTAL | (35.1 overs) | 145 |

| SUSSEX | O | M | R | W | | FALL OF WICKETS | |
|---|---|---|---|---|---|---|---|
| | | | | | | GLO | SUS |
| Jones | 8 | 2 | 25 | 3 | | | |
| Pigott | 8 | 0 | 40 | 3 | 1st | 22 | 32 |
| Donelan | 8 | 1 | 35 | 1 | 2nd | 75 | 45 |
| North | 7 | 0 | 44 | 0 | 3rd | 79 | 53 |
| Salisbury | 7 | 1 | 36 | 1 | 4th | 189 | 59 |
| Greenfield | 2 | 0 | 13 | 0 | 5th | 193 | 79 |
| | | | | | 6th | 198 | 95 |
| GLOUCS | O | M | R | W | 7th | 206 | 106 |
| Gilbert | 6 | 0 | 27 | 0 | 8th | 206 | 112 |
| Babington | 8 | 0 | 26 | 2 | 9th | | 136 |
| Lawrence | 8 | 0 | 30 | 1 | 10th | | 145 |
| Smith | 4.1 | 0 | 16 | 3 | | | |
| Alleyne | 5 | 0 | 19 | 2 | | | |
| Athey | 4 | 0 | 18 | 2 | | | |

West Indies wicketkeeper Jeffrey Dujon congratulates Ian Botham on his first century against the West Indies in any cricket.

# REFUGE ASSURANCE LEAGUE

## DERBYSHIRE vs. LANCASHIRE

at Derby on 19th May 1991
Toss : Derby. Umpires : K.J.Lyons and D.O.Oslear
Lancashire won by 63 runs. Derby 0 pts, Lancashire 4 pts

### LANCASHIRE

| | | |
|---|---|---|
| G.Fowler | b Malcolm | 59 |
| G.D.Mendis | c Bowler b Mortensen | 0 |
| M.A.Atherton | c Adams b Base | 48 |
| G.D.Lloyd | c Base b Malcolm | 26 |
| M.Watkinson | c Base b Jean-Jacques | 82 |
| Wasim Akram | c Barnett b Jean-Jacques | 18 |
| P.A.J.DeFreitas | not out | 14 |
| W.K.Hegg + | not out | 11 |
| D.P.Hughes * | | |
| I.D.Austin | | |
| P.J.W.Allott | | |
| Extras | (lb 7,w 5,nb 6) | 18 |
| TOTAL | (40 overs)(for 6 wkts) | 276 |

### DERBYSHIRE

| | | |
|---|---|---|
| K.J.Barnett * | c Mendis b DeFreitas | 15 |
| P.D.Bowler + | c Hughes b Austin | 51 |
| T.J.G.O'Gorman | c Atherton b Allott | 5 |
| M.Azharuddin | c Hughes b Allott | 2 |
| B.Roberts | b Watkinson | 8 |
| C.J.Adams | b Wasim Akram | 71 |
| A.E.Warner | b Austin | 16 |
| M.Jean-Jacques | b Austin | 23 |
| S.J.Base | b Austin | 1 |
| D.E.Malcolm | b Austin | 11 |
| O.H.Mortensen | not out | 1 |
| Extras | (lb 5,w 3,nb 1) | 9 |
| TOTAL | (39.3 overs) | 213 |

| DERBYSHIRE | O | M | R | W | FALL OF WICKETS | | |
|---|---|---|---|---|---|---|---|
| | | | | | | LAN | DER |
| Mortensen | 8 | 1 | 41 | 1 | | | |
| Base | 8 | 0 | 51 | 1 | 1st | 0 | 26 |
| Jean-Jacques | 8 | 1 | 56 | 2 | 2nd | 95 | 44 |
| Warner | 8 | 0 | 70 | 0 | 3rd | 118 | 49 |
| Malcolm | 8 | 0 | 51 | 2 | 4th | 208 | 66 |
| | | | | | 5th | 245 | 109 |
| LANCASHIRE | O | M | R | W | 6th | 251 | 135 |
| DeFreitas | 8 | 1 | 29 | 1 | 7th | | 199 |
| Allott | 8 | 1 | 45 | 2 | 8th | | 201 |
| Wasim Akram | 8 | 0 | 42 | 1 | 9th | | 202 |
| Watkinson | 8 | 1 | 36 | 1 | 10th | | 213 |
| Austin | 7.3 | 0 | 56 | 5 | | | |

## HAMPSHIRE vs. SOMERSET

at Bournemouth on 19th May 1991
Toss : Somerset. Umpires : D.J.Constant and K.E.Palmer
Somerset won by 7 wickets. Hants 0 pts, Somerset 4 pts

### HAMPSHIRE

| | | |
|---|---|---|
| V.P.Terry | lbw b Mallender | 6 |
| C.L.Smith | c Burns b Hayhurst | 47 |
| R.A.Smith | b Lefebvre | 1 |
| D.I.Gower | c Tavare b Macleay | 8 |
| M.C.J.Nicholas * | c Burns b Rose | 43 |
| K.D.James | c Cook b Mallender | 16 |
| A.N Aymes + | not out | 18 |
| S.D.Udal | not out | 4 |
| C.A.Connor | | |
| P.J.Bakker | | |
| Aqib Javed | | |
| Extras | (lb 2,w 4) | 6 |
| TOTAL | (40 overs)(for 6 wkts) | 149 |

### SOMERSET

| | | |
|---|---|---|
| S.J.Cook | c Aymes b Udal | 43 |
| R.J.Bartlett | c Aymes b James | 6 |
| C.J.Tavare * | not out | 75 |
| R.J.Harden | c Aymes b Aqib Javed | 5 |
| G.D.Rose | not out | 11 |
| A.N.Hayhurst | | |
| P.M.Roebuck | | |
| N.D.Burns + | | |
| K.H.Macleay | | |
| R.P.Lefebvre | | |
| N.A.Mallender | | |
| Extras | (lb 5,w 7,nb 1) | 13 |
| TOTAL | (39 overs)(for 3 wkts) | 153 |

| SOMERSET | O | M | R | W | FALL OF WICKETS | | |
|---|---|---|---|---|---|---|---|
| | | | | | | HAM | SOM |
| Mallender | 8 | 0 | 21 | 2 | | | |
| Lefebvre | 8 | 1 | 35 | 1 | 1st | 12 | 23 |
| Macleay | 8 | 1 | 16 | 1 | 2nd | 15 | 92 |
| Rose | 8 | 0 | 31 | 1 | 3rd | 45 | 102 |
| Hayhurst | 8 | 0 | 44 | 1 | 4th | 81 | |
| | | | | | 5th | 114 | |
| HAMPSHIRE | O | M | R | W | 6th | 137 | |
| Aqib Javed | 8 | 1 | 20 | 1 | 7th | | |
| Bakker | 8 | 1 | 21 | 0 | 8th | | |
| Connor | 8 | 0 | 31 | 0 | 9th | | |
| James | 7 | 0 | 43 | 1 | 10th | | |
| Udal | 8 | 0 | 33 | 1 | | | |

## HEADLINES

### Refuge Assurance League

### 19th May

• Somerset gained their fourth victory in four matches to join Nottinghamshire at the top of the Sunday League table by defeating Hampshire by seven wickets at Bournemouth. Hampshire were restricted to 149 for six in their 40 overs and an unbeaten 75 from Chris Tavare saw the visitors home to a comfortable victory.

• Warwickshire moved into third place following their 13-run victory over Glamorgan at Swansea. Career-best scores from both Andy Moles and Dominic Ostler carried the visitors to 211 for five, and, after reaching 170 for three, the home side were finally reduced to their fifth consecutive defeat by losing their next six wickets for 28.

• Lancashire were impressive winners of their encounter with 1990 champions Derbyshire at Derby. Graeme Fowler and Mike Atherton provided the foundation and Mike Watkinson, with a career-best 82, the final flourish in a total of 276 for five, then Ian Austin returned competition-best figures, and even Chris Adams's highest Sunday score could not prevent the home side's first Sunday defeat of the season.

• Tom Moody made his third century in four Refuge innings and Richard Illingworth took five wickets in Sunday League cricket for the second time in his career, as Worcestershire were comfortable 27-run victors over Northamptonshire at Northampton.

• The season's first tied match occurred at Folkestone where Kent and Essex both found it difficult to dominate some tidy bowling, the control of spinners Peter Such and Richard Davis being particularly impressive.

• There was a deceptively close encounter at Leicester where Leicestershire defeated Yorkshire by seven runs. The home side had dominated proceedings by reaching 203 for five in 40 overs and then reducing Yorkshire to a miserable 67 for six, but David Byas and Darren Gough first brought respectability then a hint of victory with an unbroken seventh-wicket stand of 129 as both made career-best scores.

• Gloucestershire overcame Sussex by 62 runs at Hove, Mark Alleyne and Jack Russell adding 110 for the fourth wicket and Mark Smith returning career-best figures of 3 for 16, as the home side's batting badly misfired.

## GLAMORGAN vs. WARWICKSHIRE

at Swansea on 19th May 1991
Toss : Glam. Umpires : A.G.T.Whitehead and P.B.Wight
Warwicks won by 13 runs. Glam 0 pts, Warwicks 4 pts

### WARWICKSHIRE

| | | |
|---|---|---|
| A.J.Moles | not out | 93 |
| Asif Din | c Shastri b Frost | 46 |
| S.J.Green | c Morris b Frost | 2 |
| P.A.Smith | c Metson b Barwick | 0 |
| D.A.Reeve * | c Metson b Frost | 2 |
| D.P.Ostler | c Dennis b Barwick | 55 |
| K.J.Piper + | not out | 0 |
| G.C.Small | | |
| A.R.K.Pierson | | |
| T.A.Munton | | |
| A.A.Donald | | |
| Extras | (lb 10,w 3) | 13 |
| TOTAL | (40 overs)(for 5 wkts) | 211 |

### GLAMORGAN

| | | |
|---|---|---|
| A.R.Butcher * | c Ostler b Munton | 0 |
| H.Morris | lbw b Small | 39 |
| R.J.Shastri | c Asif Din b Small | 32 |
| G.C.Holmes | c Piper b Reeve | 46 |
| I.Smith | b Reeve | 41 |
| A.Dale | b Smith | 3 |
| C.P.Metson + | not out | 12 |
| S.J.Dennis | run out | 6 |
| S.L.Watkin | b Smith | 0 |
| S.R.Barwick | b Smith | 0 |
| M.Frost | not out | 0 |
| Extras | (b 1,lb 8,w 8,nb 2) | 19 |
| TOTAL | (40 overs)(for 9 wkts) | 198 |

| GLAMORGAN | O | M | R | W | FALL OF WICKETS | | |
|---|---|---|---|---|---|---|---|
| | | | | | | WAR | GLA |
| Watkin | 8 | 0 | 27 | 0 | | | |
| Frost | 8 | 0 | 42 | 3 | 1st | 92 | 0 |
| Dale | 4 | 0 | 12 | 0 | 2nd | 100 | 64 |
| Dennis | 8 | 0 | 46 | 0 | 3rd | 100 | 79 |
| Shastri | 4 | 0 | 21 | 0 | 4th | 104 | 170 |
| Barwick | 8 | 0 | 53 | 2 | 5th | 209 | 175 |
| | | | | | 6th | | 177 |
| WARWICKS | O | M | R | W | 7th | | 196 |
| Munton | 8 | 1 | 15 | 1 | 8th | | 198 |
| Donald | 8 | 0 | 43 | 0 | 9th | | 198 |
| Reeve | 8 | 0 | 45 | 2 | 10th | | |
| Small | 8 | 1 | 33 | 2 | | | |
| Pierson | 1 | 0 | 11 | 0 | | | |
| Smith | 7 | 1 | 42 | 3 | | | |

## KENT vs. ESSEX

at Folkestone on 19th May 1991
Toss : Essex. Umpires : B.Dudleston and A.A.Jones
Match tied. Kent 2 pts, Essex 2 pts

### KENT

| | | |
|---|---|---|
| N.R.Taylor | lbw b Pringle | 4 |
| M.R.Benson * | c Stephenson b Topley | 43 |
| S.G.Hinks | c Pringle b Such | 25 |
| G.R.Cowdrey | c Gooch b Topley | 14 |
| N.J.Llong | st Garnham b Such | 5 |
| M.V.Fleming | b Gooch | 51 |
| S.A.Marsh + | b Andrew | 7 |
| R.M.Ellison | not out | 15 |
| R.P.Davis | not out | 8 |
| T.A.Merrick | | |
| A.P.Igglesden | | |
| Extras | (lb 6,w 5) | 11 |
| TOTAL | (40 overs)(for 7 wkts) | 183 |

### ESSEX

| | | |
|---|---|---|
| G.A.Gooch * | b Igglesden | 0 |
| J.P.Stephenson | b Ellison | 4 |
| Salim Malik | c Marsh b Merrick | 37 |
| P.J.Prichard | c Cowdrey b Fleming | 25 |
| N.Hussain | c Marsh b Igglesden | 48 |
| D.R.Pringle | run out | 9 |
| N.Shahid | c Marsh b Ellison | 27 |
| M.A.Garnham + | b Igglesden | 14 |
| T.D.Topley | not out | 3 |
| S.J.W.Andrew | not out | 6 |
| P.M.Such | | |
| Extras | (b 1,lb 8,w 1) | 10 |
| TOTAL | (40 overs)(for 8 wkts) | 183 |

| ESSEX | O | M | R | W | FALL OF WICKETS | | |
|---|---|---|---|---|---|---|---|
| | | | | | | KEN | ESS |
| Andrew | 8 | 1 | 30 | 1 | | | |
| Pringle | 8 | 1 | 41 | 1 | 1st | 11 | 0 |
| Gooch | 8 | 0 | 43 | 1 | 2nd | 54 | 22 |
| Such | 8 | 0 | 22 | 2 | 3rd | 76 | 62 |
| Topley | 8 | 0 | 41 | 2 | 4th | 86 | 80 |
| | | | | | 5th | 100 | 93 |
| KENT | O | M | R | W | 6th | 142 | 147 |
| Igglesden | 8 | 1 | 34 | 3 | 7th | 166 | 163 |
| Ellison | 8 | 0 | 37 | 2 | 8th | | 174 |
| Merrick | 8 | 0 | 39 | 1 | 9th | | |
| Fleming | 8 | 0 | 40 | 1 | 10th | | |
| Davis | 8 | 0 | 24 | 0 | | | |

# BRITANNIC ASSURANCE CHAMPIONSHIP

## KENT vs. ESSEX

at Folkestone on 16th, 17th, 18th, 20th May 1991
Toss : Kent.  Umpires : B.Dudleston and A.A.Jones
Match drawn.  Kent 5 pts (Bt: 4, Bw: 1), Essex 5 pts (Bt: 4, Bw: 1)
100 overs scores : Kent 307 for 4, Essex 301 for 4

### KENT

| | | | | | |
|---|---|---|---|---|---|
| N.R.Taylor | c Garnham b Pringle | 26 | (3) b Pringle | | 4 |
| M.R.Benson * | c Hussain b Topley | 88 | lbw b Foster | | 3 |
| T.R.Ward | lbw b Salim Malik | 141 | | | |
| G.R.Cowdrey | c Foster b Salim Malik | 32 | c Garnham b Such | | 36 |
| S.G.Hinks | c Salim Malik b Pringle | 6 | (1) b Such | | 40 |
| R.M.Ellison | lbw b Foster | 0 | (5) b Pringle | | 7 |
| S.A.Marsh + | b Topley | 18 | (6) run out | | 36 |
| R.P.Davis | b Gooch | 5 | (7) c Hussain b Foster | | 30 |
| C.Penn | not out | 2 | (8) not out | | 2 |
| T.A.Merrick | b Gooch | 8 | (9) not out | | 4 |
| A.P.Igglesden | b Topley | 1 | | | |
| Extras | (b 1,lb 7,w 3,nb 7) | 18 | (lb 6,w 2,nb 4) | | 12 |
| TOTAL | | 345 | (for 7 wkts) | | 174 |

### ESSEX

| | | |
|---|---|---|
| G.A.Gooch * | lbw b Merrick | 7 |
| J.P.Stephenson | c Marsh b Ellison | 45 |
| P.J.Prichard | run out | 53 |
| Salim Malik | c Cowdrey b Ellison | 173 |
| T.D.Topley | run out | 37 |
| N.Hussain | c Igglesden b Ellison | 72 |
| D.R.Pringle | lbw b Ellison | 5 |
| M.A.Garnham + | c Benson b Igglesden | 57 |
| N.A.Foster | c Hinks b Davis | 38 |
| J.H.Childs | b Merrick | 15 |
| P.M.Such | not out | 23 |
| Extras | (lb 12,nb 7) | 19 |
| TOTAL | | 544 |

| ESSEX | O | M | R | W | O | M | R | W |
|---|---|---|---|---|---|---|---|---|
| Foster | 26 | 4 | 98 | 1 | 24 | 7 | 57 | 2 |
| Pringle | 28 | 9 | 56 | 2 | 20 | 9 | 25 | 2 |
| Topley | 32 | 7 | 98 | 3 | 9 | 4 | 16 | 0 |
| Childs | 9 | 2 | 28 | 0 | 24 | 12 | 34 | 0 |
| Gooch | 12 | 5 | 21 | 2 | | | | |
| Such | 9 | 3 | 20 | 0 | 24 | 15 | 19 | 2 |
| Stephenson | 1 | 0 | 3 | 0 | | | | |
| Salim Malik | 3 | 0 | 13 | 2 | 10 | 3 | 17 | 0 |

| KENT | O | M | R | W | O | M | R | W |
|---|---|---|---|---|---|---|---|---|
| Merrick | 34 | 6 | 109 | 2 | | | | |
| Igglesden | 37 | 7 | 113 | 1 | | | | |
| Penn | 25 | 2 | 99 | 0 | | | | |
| Ellison | 42 | 8 | 125 | 4 | | | | |
| Davis | 21 | 5 | 86 | 1 | | | | |

#### FALL OF WICKETS

| | KEN | ESS | KEN | ESS |
|---|---|---|---|---|
| 1st | 58 | 12 | 5 | |
| 2nd | 242 | 78 | 11 | |
| 3rd | 296 | 169 | 77 | |
| 4th | 305 | 233 | 88 | |
| 5th | 307 | 383 | 104 | |
| 6th | 309 | 393 | 152 | |
| 7th | 334 | 419 | 165 | |
| 8th | 334 | 492 | | |
| 9th | 342 | 499 | | |
| 10th | 345 | 544 | | |

## GLAMORGAN vs. WARWICKSHIRE

at Swansea on 16th, 17th, 18th, 20th May 1991
Toss : Glamorgan.  Umpires : A.G.T.Whitehead and P.B.Wight
Warwicks won by 6 wickets.  Glamorgan 5 pts (Bt: 1, Bw: 4), Warwicks 23 pts (Bt: 3, Bw: 4)

### GLAMORGAN

| | | | | | |
|---|---|---|---|---|---|
| A.R.Butcher * | lbw b Donald | 8 | c sub b Booth | | 12 |
| H.Morris | lbw b Reeve | 11 | lbw b Donald | | 6 |
| S.P.James | c Piper b Small | 5 | b Donald | | 14 |
| R.J.Shastri | c Piper b Reeve | 5 | c Smith b Small | | 31 |
| G.C.Holmes | c Piper b Donald | 54 | lbw b Donald | | 1 |
| I.Smith | b Reeve | 28 | c Smith b Booth | | 29 |
| R.D.B.Croft | lbw b Munton | 10 | c sub b Munton | | 31 |
| C.P.Metson + | lbw b Donald | 28 | c Booth b Donald | | 57 |
| S.J.Dennis | c Piper b Donald | 0 | c Small b Booth | | 3 |
| S.L.Watkin | not out | 1 | not out | | 2 |
| D.J.Foster | c Munton b Donald | 0 | b Donald | | 0 |
| Extras | (b 1,lb 10,w 4,nb 8) | 23 | (b 5,lb 7,nb 5) | | 17 |
| TOTAL | | 173 | | | 203 |

### WARWICKSHIRE

| | | | | | |
|---|---|---|---|---|---|
| A.J.Moles | st Metson b Croft | 55 | c Morris b Croft | | 45 |
| Asif Din | c Butcher b Watkin | 15 | c James b Watkin | | 29 |
| P.A.Smith | c Metson b Watkin | 37 | (5) run out | | 6 |
| T.A.Lloyd * | c & b Croft | 29 | | | |
| D.A.Reeve | c Metson b Foster | 1 | | | |
| D.P.Ostler | b Croft | 10 | (4) not out | | 12 |
| K.J.Piper + | c Smith b Croft | 21 | (6) not out | | 5 |
| P.A.Booth | c Metson b Croft | 18 | | | |
| G.C.Small | c Holmes b Watkin | 31 | | | |
| T.A.Munton | c Smith b Foster | 6 | (3) c Morris b Shastri | | 6 |
| A.A.Donald | not out | 2 | | | |
| Extras | (lb 19,w 3,nb 9) | 31 | (b 4,lb 6,nb 8) | | 18 |
| TOTAL | | 256 | (for 4 wkts) | | 121 |

| WARWICKSHIRE | O | M | R | W | O | M | R | W |
|---|---|---|---|---|---|---|---|---|
| Donald | 17.5 | 5 | 38 | 5 | 14.4 | 2 | 36 | 5 |
| Munton | 24 | 8 | 43 | 1 | 22 | 9 | 41 | 1 |
| Small | 17 | 4 | 35 | 1 | 15 | 6 | 34 | 1 |
| Reeve | 24 | 11 | 30 | 3 | | | | |
| Smith | 6 | 0 | 16 | 0 | 2 | 0 | 9 | 0 |
| Booth | | | | | 27 | 5 | 71 | 3 |

| GLAMORGAN | O | M | R | W | O | M | R | W |
|---|---|---|---|---|---|---|---|---|
| Foster | 19 | 2 | 73 | 2 | 2 | 0 | 17 | 0 |
| Watkin | 19.4 | 7 | 53 | 3 | 14 | 3 | 31 | 1 |
| Dennis | 12 | 1 | 49 | 0 | | | | |
| Croft | 24 | 5 | 62 | 5 | 16.2 | 4 | 38 | 1 |
| Shastri | | | | | 12 | 3 | 25 | 1 |

#### FALL OF WICKETS

| | GLA | WAR | GLA | WAR |
|---|---|---|---|---|
| 1st | 20 | 27 | 13 | 54 |
| 2nd | 29 | 82 | 29 | 80 |
| 3rd | 33 | 135 | 53 | 100 |
| 4th | 42 | 157 | 55 | 106 |
| 5th | 80 | 167 | 84 | |
| 6th | 108 | 171 | 116 | |
| 7th | 154 | 205 | 187 | |
| 8th | 158 | 215 | 200 | |
| 9th | 173 | 241 | 203 | |
| 10th | 173 | 256 | 203 | |

## NORTHANTS vs. LEICESTERSHIRE

at Northampton on 16th, 17th, 18th, 20th May 1991
Toss : Northants.  Umpires : J.C.Balderstone and J.H.Harris
Match drawn.  Northants 5 pts (Bt: 1, Bw: 4), Leicestershire 2 pts (Bt: 2, Bw: 0)

### LEICESTERSHIRE

| | | | | | |
|---|---|---|---|---|---|
| T.J.Boon | c Cook b Thomas | 49 | lbw b Taylor | | 20 |
| N.E.Briers * | b Thomas | 8 | c Cook b Taylor | | 2 |
| P.N.Hepworth | lbw b Williams | 15 | lbw b Taylor | | 23 |
| J.J.Whitaker | c Capel b Thomas | 33 | b Taylor | | 99 |
| L.Potter | c Ripley b Taylor | 10 | c Bailey b Taylor | | 22 |
| P.Willey | c Fordham b Thomas | 0 | c Penberthy b Capel | | 26 |
| C.C.Lewis | lbw b Thomas | 12 | not out | | 8 |
| P.Whitticase + | c Felton b Taylor | 73 | | | |
| L.Tennant | c Larkins b Taylor | 12 | | | |
| D.J.Millns | c Ripley b Williams | 14 | | | |
| J.N.Maguire | not out | 0 | | | |
| Extras | (b 5,lb 8,nb 1) | 14 | (lb 4,nb 1) | | 5 |
| TOTAL | | 240 | (for 6 wkts dec) | | 205 |

### NORTHANTS

| | | | | | |
|---|---|---|---|---|---|
| A.Fordham | lbw b Lewis | 1 | c Willey b Millns | | 42 |
| W.Larkins | retired hurt | 39 | | | |
| R.J.Bailey * | c Millns b Lewis | 7 | c Briers b Maguire | | 32 |
| N.A.Felton | not out | 31 | (2) c Whitaker b Millns | | 25 |
| D.J.Capel | not out | 58 | (4) c Whitaker b Maguire | | 10 |
| A.L.Penberthy | | | (5) lbw b Maguire | | 0 |
| D.Ripley + | | | (6) c Whitticase b Potter | | 20 |
| J.G.Thomas | | | (7) not out | | 36 |
| J.P.Taylor | | | (8) c Willey b Potter | | 3 |
| N.G.B.Cook | | | (9) c Whitticase b Maguire | | 0 |
| R.G.Williams | | | (10) not out | | 4 |
| Extras | (lb 2,nb 13) | 15 | (b 4,lb 5,w 1,nb 11) | | 21 |
| TOTAL | | 151 | (for 8 wkts) | | 193 |

| NORTHANTS | O | M | R | W | O | M | R | W |
|---|---|---|---|---|---|---|---|---|
| Thomas | 26.4 | 6 | 62 | 5 | 9 | 1 | 44 | 0 |
| Taylor | 31 | 5 | 72 | 3 | 14.4 | 2 | 42 | 5 |
| Penberthy | 4.2 | 1 | 10 | 0 | 10 | 1 | 43 | 0 |
| Cook | 10 | 1 | 28 | 0 | 2 | 1 | 2 | 0 |
| Williams | 12.4 | 3 | 29 | 2 | 0.2 | 0 | 3 | 0 |
| Capel | 9 | 2 | 26 | 0 | 12 | 5 | 28 | 1 |
| Bailey | | | | | 10.4 | 0 | 39 | 0 |

| LEICS | O | M | R | W | O | M | R | W |
|---|---|---|---|---|---|---|---|---|
| Lewis | 8 | 1 | 38 | 2 | 16 | 3 | 41 | 0 |
| Millns | 10 | 1 | 45 | 0 | 12 | 1 | 45 | 2 |
| Maguire | 10 | 1 | 42 | 0 | 21 | 4 | 69 | 4 |
| Tennant | 2 | 0 | 24 | 0 | 4 | 1 | 9 | 0 |
| Willey | | | | | 1 | 0 | 4 | 0 |
| Potter | | | | | 9 | 8 | 14 | 2 |
| Hepworth | | | | | 1 | 0 | 2 | 0 |

#### FALL OF WICKETS

| | LEI | NOR | LEI | NOR |
|---|---|---|---|---|
| 1st | 27 | 2 | 14 | 71 |
| 2nd | 52 | 14 | 42 | 90 |
| 3rd | 112 | | 63 | 100 |
| 4th | 119 | | 123 | 100 |
| 5th | 119 | | 194 | 127 |
| 6th | 135 | | 205 | 166 |
| 7th | 153 | | | 186 |
| 8th | 175 | | | 187 |
| 9th | 240 | | | |
| 10th | 240 | | | |

## SUSSEX vs. HAMPSHIRE

at Hove on 16th, 17th, 18th, 20th May 1991
Toss : Sussex.  Umpires : H.D.Bird and R.C.Tolchard
Match drawn.  Sussex 4 pts (Bt: 4, Bw: 0), Hampshire 7 pts (Bt: 4, Bw: 3)
100 overs scores : Hampshire 344 for 1

### HAMPSHIRE

| | | | | | |
|---|---|---|---|---|---|
| V.P.Terry | c & b North | 171 | c sub b Salisbury | | 55 |
| C.L.Smith | c Salisbury b Pigott | 145 | lbw b Giddins | | 101 |
| R.A.Smith | c Jones b North | 68 | c Hall b Salisbury | | 16 |
| D.I.Gower | c Moores b Salisbury | 15 | not out | | 13 |
| M.C.J.Nicholas * | b Salisbury | 23 | not out | | 6 |
| K.D.James | not out | 17 | | | |
| A.N Aymes + | | | | | |
| R.J.Maru | | | | | |
| C.A.Connor | | | | | |
| P.J.Bakker | | | | | |
| Aqib Javed | | | | | |
| Extras | (lb 20,w 2) | 22 | (b 7,lb 4,nb 1) | | 12 |
| TOTAL | | 461 | (for 3 wkts dec) | | 203 |

### SUSSEX

| | | | | | |
|---|---|---|---|---|---|
| D.M.Smith | c Aymes b Bakker | 82 | c Terry b Bakker | | 5 |
| J.W.Hall | lbw b Bakker | 65 | c Connor b Maru | | 40 |
| N.J.Lenham | b Connor | 35 | c Aymes b Bakker | | 8 |
| A.P.Wells * | c Smith R.A. b Maru | 49 | not out | | 83 |
| K.Greenfield | c Terry b Connor | 1 | c Maru b Connor | | 0 |
| J.A.North | not out | 63 | b Maru | | 22 |
| P.Moores + | b James | 16 | | | |
| A.C.S.Pigott | c Maru b James | 0 | (7) not out | | 13 |
| I.D.K.Salisbury | not out | 10 | | | |
| A.N.Jones | | | | | |
| E.S.H.Giddins | | | | | |
| Extras | (b 2,lb 13,w 2,nb 12) | 29 | (lb 7,w 1,nb 3) | | 11 |
| TOTAL | | 350 | (for 5 wkts) | | 182 |

| SUSSEX | O | M | R | W | O | M | R | W |
|---|---|---|---|---|---|---|---|---|
| Jones | 21 | 3 | 64 | 0 | 12.5 | 3 | 42 | 0 |
| Giddins | 19 | 3 | 65 | 0 | 7.2 | 0 | 29 | 1 |
| North | 22 | 2 | 114 | 2 | 10 | 0 | 39 | 0 |
| Pigott | 25 | 5 | 77 | 1 | 9 | 2 | 36 | 0 |
| Salisbury | 37.4 | 9 | 107 | 2 | 14.1 | 4 | 46 | 2 |
| Lenham | 5 | 0 | 14 | 0 | | | | |

| HAMPSHIRE | O | M | R | W | O | M | R | W |
|---|---|---|---|---|---|---|---|---|
| Aqib Javed | 20 | 1 | 79 | 0 | 8 | 1 | 17 | 0 |
| Bakker | 21 | 7 | 52 | 2 | 13 | 1 | 32 | 2 |
| Connor | 19 | 2 | 88 | 2 | 12 | 1 | 49 | 1 |
| James | 23 | 5 | 61 | 2 | 3 | 0 | 19 | 0 |
| Nicholas | 8 | 0 | 40 | 0 | 2 | 1 | 5 | 0 |
| Maru | 8 | 1 | 15 | 1 | 17 | 6 | 53 | 2 |

#### FALL OF WICKETS

| | HAM | SUS | HAM | SUS |
|---|---|---|---|---|
| 1st | 274 | 157 | 129 | 5 |
| 2nd | 384 | 168 | 167 | 17 |
| 3rd | 417 | 239 | 193 | 94 |
| 4th | 421 | 242 | | 116 |
| 5th | 461 | 267 | | 157 |
| 6th | | 297 | | |
| 7th | | 297 | | |
| 8th | | | | |
| 9th | | | | |
| 10th | | | | |

# BRITANNIC ASSURANCE CHAMPIONSHIP

## LANCASHIRE vs. DERBYSHIRE

at Old Trafford on 16th (no play), 17th, 18th, 20th May 1991
Toss : Lancashire.  Umpires : R.Julian and K.J.Lyons
Match drawn.  Lancashire 4 pts (Bt: 1, Bw: 3), Derby 8 pts (Bt: 4, Bw: 4)

### LANCASHIRE

| | | | | |
|---|---|---|---|---|
| G.D.Mendis | c Base b Malcolm | 7 | c Adams b Mortensen | 1 |
| G.Fowler | b Malcolm | 10 | not out | 103 |
| N.J.Speak | c Bowler b Mortensen | 0 | c Krikken b Malcolm | 3 |
| M.A.Atherton | b Mortensen | 16 | not out | 62 |
| G.D.Lloyd | c Barnett b Malcolm | 20 | | |
| Wasim Akram | b Base | 15 | | |
| P.A.J.DeFreitas | c & b Mortensen | 26 | | |
| W.K.Hegg + | c O'Gorman b Mortensen | 13 | | |
| G.Yates | not out | 19 | | |
| I.D.Austin | b Warner | 12 | | |
| P.J.W.Allott * | c Krikken b Warner | 9 | | |
| Extras | (b 1,lb 10,w 1,nb 2) | 14 | (lb 6,nb 1) | 7 |
| TOTAL | | 161 | (for 2 wkts) | 176 |

### DERBYSHIRE

| | | |
|---|---|---|
| K.J.Barnett * | c Fowler b DeFreitas | 15 |
| P.D.Bowler | c Hegg b DeFreitas | 1 |
| T.J.G.O'Gorman | b Yates | 148 |
| M.Azharuddin | c Speak b Allott | 53 |
| C.J.Adams | b Yates | 18 |
| K.M.Krikken + | lbw b Wasim Akram | 10 |
| J.E.Morris | c Atherton b Allott | 53 |
| A.E.Warner | b Yates | 0 |
| S.J.Base | not out | 15 |
| D.E.Malcolm | | |
| O.H.Mortensen | | |
| Extras | (b 1,lb 7,w 2,nb 14) | 24 |
| TOTAL | (for 8 wkts dec) | 337 |

| DERBYSHIRE | O | M | R | W | O | M | R | W |
|---|---|---|---|---|---|---|---|---|
| Mortensen | 23 | 5 | 46 | 4 | 9 | 4 | 19 | 1 |
| Malcolm | 16 | 2 | 47 | 3 | 12 | 3 | 38 | 1 |
| Base | 10 | 2 | 37 | 1 | 10 | 0 | 28 | 0 |
| Warner | 3.5 | 0 | 20 | 2 | 10 | 2 | 28 | 0 |
| Barnett | | | | | 11 | 2 | 28 | 0 |
| Azharuddin | | | | | 8 | 1 | 29 | 0 |

| LANCASHIRE | O | M | R | W | O | M | R | W |
|---|---|---|---|---|---|---|---|---|
| Wasim Akram | 22 | 3 | 90 | 1 | | | | |
| DeFreitas | 16 | 2 | 74 | 2 | | | | |
| Austin | 4 | 0 | 36 | 0 | | | | |
| Allott | 15 | 0 | 60 | 2 | | | | |
| Yates | 18.2 | 2 | 69 | 3 | | | | |

| FALL OF WICKETS | | | | |
|---|---|---|---|---|
| | LAN | DER | LAN | DER |
| 1st | 11 | 10 | 6 | |
| 2nd | 12 | 25 | 9 | |
| 3rd | 26 | 133 | | |
| 4th | 58 | 162 | | |
| 5th | 74 | 201 | | |
| 6th | 88 | 317 | | |
| 7th | 109 | 318 | | |
| 8th | 125 | 337 | | |
| 9th | 143 | | | |
| 10th | 161 | | | |

## YORKSHIRE vs. NOTTS

at Headingley on 16th (no play), 17th, 18th, 20th May 1991
Toss : Notts.  Umpires : J.D.Bond and B.Leadbeater
Match drawn.  Yorkshire 5 pts (Bt: 3, Bw: 2), Notts 6 pts (Bt: 2, Bw: 4)

### YORKSHIRE

| | | | | |
|---|---|---|---|---|
| M.D.Moxon * | b Stephenson | 2 | c French b Hemmings | 36 |
| A.A.Metcalfe | lbw b Stephenson | 22 | lbw b Pick | 28 |
| D.Byas | lbw b Stephenson | 4 | lbw b Hemmings | 23 |
| R.J.Blakey | lbw b Pick | 11 | c Pollard b Evans | 1 |
| P.E.Robinson | c French b Hemmings | 57 | not out | 53 |
| S.A.Kellett | lbw b Hemmings | 41 | c Pollard b Hemmings | 0 |
| P.Carrick | c Broad b Pick | 47 | not out | 20 |
| P.W.Jarvis | b Hemmings | 31 | | |
| P.J.Hartley | c French b Stephenson | 24 | | |
| S.D.Fletcher | c Hemmings b Pick | 1 | | |
| M.A.Robinson | not out | 0 | | |
| Extras | (lb 10,w 6,nb 4) | 20 | (b 1,lb 15,w 1,nb 9) | 26 |
| TOTAL | | 260 | (for 5 wkts dec) | 187 |

### NOTTS

| | | | | |
|---|---|---|---|---|
| B.C.Broad | lbw b Hartley | 86 | c Blakey b Jarvis | 48 |
| P.Pollard | c Kellett b Hartley | 2 | lbw b Robinson M.A. | 40 |
| R.T.Robinson * | c Robinson P.E. b Fletcher | 25 | (4) c Kellett b Robinson M.A. | 2 |
| P.Johnson | lbw b Hartley | 31 | (3) c Byas b Carrick | 7 |
| D.W.Randall | not out | 37 | b Carrick | 7 |
| M.Saxelby | c Carrick | 17 | lbw b Jarvis | 16 |
| K.P.Evans | not out | | not out | 3 |
| F.D.Stephenson | | | not out | 24 |
| B.N.French + | | | | |
| E.E.Hemmings | | | | |
| R.A.Pick | | | | |
| Extras | (lb 7,nb 1) | 8 | (b 2,w 1,nb 1) | 4 |
| TOTAL | (for 5 wkts dec) | 213 | (for 6 wkts) | 151 |

| NOTTS | O | M | R | W | O | M | R | W |
|---|---|---|---|---|---|---|---|---|
| Stephenson | 24 | 3 | 84 | 4 | 15 | 5 | 50 | 0 |
| Pick | 25.3 | 5 | 76 | 3 | 15 | 2 | 38 | 1 |
| Evans | 20 | 4 | 44 | 0 | 13 | 3 | 24 | 1 |
| Hemmings | 10 | 2 | 37 | 3 | 22 | 6 | 59 | 3 |
| Saxelby | 6 | 4 | 9 | 0 | | | | |

| YORKSHIRE | O | M | R | W | O | M | R | W |
|---|---|---|---|---|---|---|---|---|
| Jarvis | 15 | 3 | 37 | 0 | 15 | 6 | 49 | 2 |
| Hartley | 14 | 2 | 46 | 3 | 6 | 0 | 27 | 0 |
| Robinson M.A. | 17 | 3 | 42 | 0 | 9 | 0 | 30 | 2 |
| Carrick | 15 | 6 | 28 | 1 | 15 | 7 | 28 | 2 |
| Fletcher | 15 | 2 | 53 | 1 | 3 | 0 | 15 | 0 |

| FALL OF WICKETS | | | | |
|---|---|---|---|---|
| | YOR | NOT | YOR | NOT |
| 1st | 3 | 12 | 55 | 69 |
| 2nd | 17 | 97 | 89 | 82 |
| 3rd | 40 | 143 | 96 | 91 |
| 4th | 59 | 146 | 118 | 108 |
| 5th | 137 | 186 | 120 | 108 |
| 6th | 148 | | | 126 |
| 7th | 212 | | | |
| 8th | 254 | | | |
| 9th | 260 | | | |
| 10th | 260 | | | |

## HEADLINES

### Britannic Assurance Championship

#### 16th - 20th May

• Warwickshire were the only winners, the other five matches not yielding positive results, and so installed themselves at the top of the Championship table. Their second victory of the season, over Glamorgan at Swansea, was achieved thanks to another outstanding performance from Allan Donald, who returned match figures of 10 for 74, as he took five wickets in both innings for the second match in succession. Glamorgan's young off-spinner Robert Croft returned career-best figures of 5 for 62 but Andy Moles top-scored in each innings to see Warwickshire to a six-wicket victory,

• Essex lost their chance of victory over Kent at Folkestone when they could not bowl out the home side on the final day, having established a first innings lead of 199. Kent had lost their last eight first-innings wickets for 49 after Trevor Ward and Mark Benson appeared to put them on the path to an imposing total, while the Essex lower-order built on a career best 173 from Salim Malik to such effect that they reached 544. The loss of two early wickets on the last morning put Kent on to the defensive but their resistance could not be broken.

• Leicestershire finished tantalisingly close to victory over an injury-hit Northamptonshire at Northampton. Wayne Larkins had retired hurt in the first innings and Richard Williams was able to bat only in the final stages, but the visitors could not quite finish the job after they had asked Northants to make 295 to win. Better news for the home side was the career-best bowling performance from Jonathan Taylor, the least heralded but currently most effective of their new signings.

• Sussex's match with Hampshire at Hove was full of runs, particularly for the visiting side's openers. Chris Smith and Paul Terry shared partnerships of 274 and 129, Smith beginning to resemble a run machine with 100s in each innings to take his season's run-aggregate in all cricket past the 1,000 mark. Sussex's openers David Smith and Jamie Hall responded with a stand of 157 in their first innings and John North completed his maiden first-class fifty, but a victory target of 315 to remain Championship front-runners proved beyond Sussex.

• After the opening day had been lost, Derbyshire were quick to take the initiative over Lancashire at Old Trafford, Devon Malcolm and Ole Mortensen proving an awkward combination after Paul Allott had chosen to bat first. Tim O'Gorman then scored a career best 148 as the visitors raced to a lead of 166, but Graeme Fowler and Mike Atherton calmly played out for a draw with an unbroken stand of 167.

• Yorkshire's contest against Nottinghamshire at Headingley also began a day late, but despite two declarations the match never quite recovered as neither batsmen nor bowlers could take the ascendancy. After being asked to make 235 to win, Notts could manage only 151 for six.

| TOUR MATCH | OTHER FIRST-CLASS MATCH |
|---|---|

## MIDDLESEX vs. WEST INDIES

at Lord's on 18th, 19th, 20th May 1991
Toss : Middlesex. Umpires : M.J.Kitchen and R.Palmer
West Indies won by 6 wickets

**MIDDLESEX**

| | | | | |
|---|---|---|---|---|
| I.J.F.Hutchinson | c Williams b Anthony | 37 | c Richards b Patterson | 20 |
| M.A.Roseberry | c Hooper b Patterson | 45 | lbw b Walsh | 23 |
| M.W.Gatting * | c Anthony b Patterson | 8 | (9) b Walsh | 5 |
| M.R.Ramprakash | c Anthony b Patterson | 38 | (3) c Richardson b Walsh | 21 |
| K.R.Brown | c Richards b Patterson | 2 | (4) lbw b Simmons | 7 |
| P.R.Downton + | b Walsh | 23 | (5) c Williams b Anthony | 21 |
| J.E.Emburey | c Logie b Anthony | 29 | (6) b Simmons | 10 |
| N.F.Williams | run out | 5 | (7) b Hooper | 21 |
| P.C.R.Tufnell | not out | 14 | (8) c Patterson b Anthony | 26 |
| S.P.Hughes | c Williams b Patterson | 5 | not out | 3 |
| N.G.Cowans | b Walsh | 35 | b Walsh | 1 |
| Extras | (lb 13,nb 21) | 34 | (b 4,lb 7,nb 8) | 19 |
| TOTAL | | 275 | | 177 |

**WEST INDIES**

| | | | | |
|---|---|---|---|---|
| C.G.Greenidge | c & b Williams | 26 | b Cowans | 8 |
| P.V.Simmons | c Roseberry b Emburey | 136 | c Downton b Williams | 5 |
| R.B.Richardson | c Downton b Cowans | 7 | not out | 10 |
| C.L.Hooper | c Gatting b Hutchinson | 42 | c Brown b Cowans | 16 |
| A.L.Logie | c & b Emburey | 60 | c Emburey b Williams | 1 |
| M.D.Marshall | c sub b Hughes | 19 | | |
| D.Williams + | c Brown b Williams | 35 | | |
| I.V.A.Richards * | c sub b Cowans | 28 | (6) not out | 28 |
| H.A.G.Anthony | b Cowans | 11 | | |
| C.A.Walsh | not out | 0 | | |
| B.P.Patterson | | | | |
| Extras | (b 5,lb 6,nb 9) | 20 | (lb 4) | 4 |
| TOTAL | (for 9 wkts dec) | 384 | (for 4 wkts) | 72 |

| WEST INDIES | O | M | R | W | O | M | R | W |
|---|---|---|---|---|---|---|---|---|
| Patterson | 20 | 4 | 88 | 5 | 13 | 4 | 29 | 1 |
| Marshall | 11 | 1 | 31 | 0 | 6 | 1 | 17 | 0 |
| Anthony | 14 | 2 | 59 | 2 | 12 | 4 | 35 | 2 |
| Walsh | 15.5 | 3 | 63 | 2 | 15.1 | 4 | 39 | 4 |
| Simmons | 4 | 1 | 21 | 0 | 11 | 3 | 34 | 2 |
| Hooper | | | | | 4 | 2 | 12 | 1 |

| MIDDLESEX | O | M | R | W | O | M | R | W |
|---|---|---|---|---|---|---|---|---|
| Cowans | 21.5 | 11 | 37 | 3 | 6 | 0 | 26 | 2 |
| Williams | 24 | 7 | 82 | 2 | 5.3 | 1 | 42 | 2 |
| Hughes | 19 | 5 | 64 | 1 | | | | |
| Emburey | 22.4 | 4 | 84 | 2 | | | | |
| Tufnell | 21 | 3 | 67 | 0 | | | | |
| Gatting | 2.2 | 1 | 9 | 0 | | | | |
| Hutchinson | 6 | 0 | 18 | 1 | | | | |
| Ramprakash | 2 | 0 | 12 | 0 | | | | |

**FALL OF WICKETS**

| | MID | WI | MID | WI |
|---|---|---|---|---|
| 1st | 93 | 88 | 35 | 8 |
| 2nd | 101 | 111 | 74 | 14 |
| 3rd | 102 | 210 | 81 | 35 |
| 4th | 108 | 234 | 81 | 36 |
| 5th | 147 | 285 | 96 | |
| 6th | 189 | 318 | 133 | |
| 7th | 210 | 362 | 155 | |
| 8th | 222 | 382 | 160 | |
| 9th | 227 | 384 | 175 | |
| 10th | 275 | | 177 | |

## CAMBRIDGE U vs. SURREY

at Fenner's on 18th, 20th, 21st May 1991
Toss : Surrey. Umpires : H.J.Rhodes and D.R.Shepherd
Surrey won by 38 runs

**SURREY**

| | | | | |
|---|---|---|---|---|
| D.J.Bicknell | c Arscott b Pyman | 82 | | |
| R.I.Alikhan | c Crawley b Pyman | 92 | | |
| D.M.Ward | c Pyman b Lowrey | 66 | (7) not out | 2 |
| G.P.Thorpe | not out | 1 | (2) lbw b Bush | 1 |
| I.A.Greig * | c Crawley b Lowrey | 0 | (1) c Thwaites b Cotton | 17 |
| K.T.Medlycott | c Arscott b Lowrey | 2 | (4) c Turner b Pearson | 109 |
| M.A.Feltham | not out | 0 | (5) c Turner b Pearson | 48 |
| N.F.Sargeant + | | | (3) b Pyman | 29 |
| C.K.Bullen | | | (6) not out | 37 |
| J.Boiling | | | | |
| Waqar Younis | | | | |
| Extras | (b 3,lb 7,w 2) | 12 | (b 5,lb 2,w 1,nb 1) | 9 |
| TOTAL | (for 5 wkts dec) | 255 | (for 5 wkts dec) | 252 |

**CAMBRIDGE U**

| | | | | |
|---|---|---|---|---|
| A.M.Hooper | c Sargeant b Thorpe | 47 | c Alikhan b Medlycott | 125 |
| R.I.Clitheroe | c Bullen b Greig | 34 | lbw b Medlycott | 6 |
| J.P.Crawley | st Sargeant b Boiling | 69 | c Ward b Bullen | 56 |
| R.J.Turner *+ | c Bullen b Medlycott | 35 | c Boiling b Bullen | 3 |
| M.J.Lowrey | c Feltham b Medlycott | 2 | c Bullen b Medlycott | 21 |
| G.E.Thwaites | b Medlycott | 7 | st Sargeant b Bullen | 4 |
| J.P.Arscott | lbw b Medlycott | 1 | (8) c Bullen b Medlycott | 3 |
| R.A.Pyman | c Sargeant b Boiling | 6 | (9) c sub b Medlycott | 0 |
| R.M.Pearson | st Sargeant b Boiling | 3 | (7) c sub b Bullen | 1 |
| D.J.Bush | c Waqar Younis b Medlycott | 11 | not out | 2 |
| D.C.Cotton | not out | 0 | c Sargeant b Medlycott | 0 |
| Extras | (b 9,lb 7,nb 4) | 20 | (b 7,lb 2,w 1,nb 3) | 13 |
| TOTAL | | 235 | | 234 |

| CAMBRIDGE U | O | M | R | W | O | M | R | W |
|---|---|---|---|---|---|---|---|---|
| Bush | 8 | 1 | 38 | 0 | 6 | 2 | 14 | 1 |
| Cotton | 13 | 4 | 42 | 0 | 8 | 0 | 43 | 1 |
| Pearson | 20 | 7 | 46 | 0 | 19 | 2 | 73 | 2 |
| Pyman | 28 | 9 | 74 | 2 | 13 | 2 | 52 | 1 |
| Lowrey | 18 | 6 | 31 | 3 | 15 | 3 | 63 | 0 |
| Hooper | 5 | 0 | 14 | 0 | | | | |

| SURREY | O | M | R | W | O | M | R | W |
|---|---|---|---|---|---|---|---|---|
| Waqar Younis | 9 | 3 | 28 | 0 | 2.5 | 0 | 5 | 0 |
| Feltham | 13 | 1 | 57 | 0 | 8 | 0 | 22 | 0 |
| Thorpe | 10 | 3 | 37 | 1 | | | | |
| Greig | 7 | 2 | 22 | 1 | 4.1 | 1 | 6 | 0 |
| Medlycott | 25 | 11 | 36 | 5 | 26.5 | 6 | 98 | 6 |
| Boiling | 18.2 | 4 | 39 | 3 | 14 | 3 | 46 | 0 |
| Bullen | | | | | 17 | 2 | 48 | 4 |

**FALL OF WICKETS**

| | SUR | CAM | SUR | CAM |
|---|---|---|---|---|
| 1st | 125 | 77 | 20 | 37 |
| 2nd | 246 | 93 | 20 | 146 |
| 3rd | 252 | 165 | 94 | 162 |
| 4th | 252 | 173 | 172 | 195 |
| 5th | 254 | 195 | 230 | 202 |
| 6th | | 199 | | 222 |
| 7th | | 216 | | 229 |
| 8th | | 217 | | 230 |
| 9th | | 232 | | 234 |
| 10th | | 235 | | 234 |

# HEADLINES

### Tetley Bitter Challenge

### 18th - 20th May

• The West Indians' encounter with county champions Middlesex at Lord's, for long periods a tense battle of attrition, finally exploded into life on the last afternoon, as the home side's second innings resistance was finally broken and, after the loss of four wickets for 36, Viv Richards brought his side victory with an avalanche of boundaries. The earlier proceedings had been marked by a tidy opening for Middlesex from Ian Hutchinson and Mike Roseberry, a hostile riposte from Patrick Patterson and a second successive century from Phil Simmons, as the touring side gained their last preparation for the Texaco Trophy matches.

# HEADLINES

### Other first-class match

### 18th - 21st May

• Cambridge University's spirited attempt for victory over Surrey at Fenner's was finally ended by Keith Medlycott who confirmed his return to form with match figures of 11 for 134, as well as scoring a second innings 100, as the visitors gained victory by 38 runs. But the students could take much heart from their batting performances, John Crawley adding another pair of accomplished half-centuries to his season's aggregate, and Anthony Hooper making his maiden first-class 100 as Cambridge chased a target of 273.

# BRITANNIC ASSURANCE CHAMPIONSHIP

## GLAMORGAN vs. NORTHANTS

at Cardiff on 22nd, 23rd, 24th May 1991
Toss : Glamorgan. Umpires : J.D.Bond and A.A.Jones
Match drawn. Glamorgan 7 pts (Bt: 3, Bw: 4), Northants 3 pts (Bt: 1, Bw: 2)
100 overs scores : Glamorgan 258 for 6

GLAMORGAN
| | | | | | |
|---|---|---|---|---|---|
| A.R.Butcher * | lbw b Taylor | 2 | c Capel b Penberthy | | 96 |
| H.Morris | run out | 132 | not out | | 88 |
| S.P.James | lbw b Penberthy | 15 | not out | | 11 |
| R.J.Shastri | lbw b Bailey | 50 | | | |
| G.C.Holmes | c Thomas b Penberthy | 21 | | | |
| I.Smith | run out | 13 | | | |
| R.D.B.Croft | b Bailey | 16 | | | |
| C.P.Metson + | lbw b Bailey | 24 | | | |
| S.L.Watkin | not out | 5 | | | |
| S.Bastien | not out | 0 | | | |
| D.J.Foster | | | | | |
| Extras | (b 5,lb 15,w 1) | 21 | (b 2,lb 5,nb 1) | | 8 |
| TOTAL | (for 8 wkts dec) | 299 | (for 1 wkt dec) | | 203 |

NORTHANTS
| | | | | | |
|---|---|---|---|---|---|
| A.Fordham | c Metson b Watkin | 13 | lbw b Watkin | | 3 |
| N.A.Felton | b Bastien | 13 | b Watkin | | 3 |
| R.J.Bailey * | c Butcher b Bastien | 5 | c Metson b Foster | | 61 |
| D.J.Capel | b Foster | 41 | b Croft | | 56 |
| K.M.Curran | lbw b Watkin | 0 | c James b Watkin | | 11 |
| A.L.Penberthy | c Metson b Bastien | 7 | b Watkin | | 2 |
| J.G.Thomas | lbw b Foster | 2 | c Metson b Watkin | | 0 |
| D.Ripley + | c Metson b Bastien | 49 | not out | | 32 |
| W.M.Noon | c Metson b Bastien | 10 | lbw b Watkin | | 0 |
| A.R.Roberts | not out | 17 | not out | | 13 |
| J.P.Taylor | b Watkin | 2 | | | |
| Extras | (b 6,lb 14,w 1,nb 7) | 28 | (b 9,lb 3,w 1,nb 5) | | 18 |
| TOTAL | | 187 | (for 8 wkts) | | 199 |

| NORTHANTS | O | M | R | W | O | M | R | W |
|---|---|---|---|---|---|---|---|---|
| Taylor | 14 | 2 | 37 | 1 | 14 | 2 | 49 | 0 |
| Thomas | 21 | 3 | 61 | 0 | 9 | 0 | 44 | 0 |
| Penberthy | 17 | 5 | 37 | 2 | 12 | 0 | 49 | 1 |
| Capel | 22 | 8 | 27 | 0 | 7 | 2 | 21 | 0 |
| Roberts | 16 | 2 | 56 | 0 | | | | |
| Bailey | 23 | 5 | 61 | 3 | 6 | 0 | 33 | 0 |

| GLAMORGAN | O | M | R | W | O | M | R | W |
|---|---|---|---|---|---|---|---|---|
| Watkin | 20.4 | 6 | 30 | 3 | 25.5 | 6 | 55 | 6 |
| Foster | 21 | 5 | 53 | 2 | 11 | 2 | 23 | 1 |
| Bastien | 22 | 8 | 39 | 5 | 24 | 7 | 66 | 0 |
| Croft | 13 | 3 | 35 | 0 | 12 | 5 | 25 | 1 |
| Smith | 4 | 0 | 10 | 0 | 2 | 1 | 2 | 0 |
| Shastri | | | | | 3 | 0 | 16 | 0 |
| Butcher | | | | | 1 | 1 | 0 | 0 |

FALL OF WICKETS
| | GLA | NOR | GLA | NOR |
|---|---|---|---|---|
| 1st | 6 | 17 | 149 | 6 |
| 2nd | 18 | 24 | | 7 |
| 3rd | 158 | 61 | | 101 |
| 4th | 219 | 69 | | 129 |
| 5th | 247 | 83 | | 143 |
| 6th | 253 | 96 | | 143 |
| 7th | 286 | 105 | | 164 |
| 8th | 299 | 129 | | 170 |
| 9th | | 184 | | |
| 10th | | 187 | | |

## SURREY vs. LANCASHIRE

at The Oval on 22nd, 23rd, 24th May 1991
Toss : Lancashire. Umpires : R.Palmer and A.G.T.Whitehead
Surrey won by 8 wickets. Surrey 24 pts (Bt: 4, Bw: 4), Lancashire 6 pts (Bt: 3, Bw: 3)
100 overs scores :Surrey 316 for 7

LANCASHIRE
| | | | | | |
|---|---|---|---|---|---|
| G.D.Mendis | c Alikhan b Waqar Younis | 15 | (2) b Waqar Younis | | 8 |
| G.Fowler | b Feltham | 113 | (1) c Stewart b Waqar Younis | | 5 |
| G.D.Lloyd | c Sargeant b Feltham | 0 | (5) b Waqar Younis | | 20 |
| N.J.Speak | c Boiling b Waqar Younis | 6 | c Sargeant b Waqar Younis | | 6 |
| M.Watkinson | b Waqar Younis | 55 | (6) not out | | 114 |
| Wasim Akram | c & b Boiling | 19 | (7) c Alikhan b Feltham | | 3 |
| W.K.Hegg + | c Sargeant b Medlycott | 27 | (8) c Bicknell D.J. b Waqar | | |
| I.D.Austin | b Waqar Younis | 6 | (3) Stewart b Bicknell M.P. | | 0 |
| D.P.Hughes * | not out | 20 | c Stewart b Waqar Younis | | 5 |
| G.Yates | b Waqar Younis | 0 | b Medlycott | | 12 |
| P.J.W.Allott | c Waqar Younis b Feltham | 3 | c Alikhan b Bicknell M.P. | | 0 |
| Extras | (b 1,lb 11,nb 5) | 17 | (b 12,lb 8,w 1,nb 2) | | 23 |
| TOTAL | | 254 | | | 233 |

SURREY
| | | | | | |
|---|---|---|---|---|---|
| D.J.Bicknell | lbw b Allott | 7 | c Hegg b Watkinson | | 4 |
| R.I.Alikhan | c Hughes b Yates | 67 | c Speak b Yates | | 26 |
| A.J.Stewart | c Hughes b Watkinson | 62 | not out | | 67 |
| D.M.Ward | c Speak b Yates | 43 | not out | | 17 |
| I.A.Greig * | c Hegg b Wasim Akram | 21 | | | |
| K.T.Medlycott | c Mendis b Watkinson | 66 | | | |
| M.A.Feltham | b Yates | 20 | | | |
| N.F.Sargeant + | b Austin | 10 | | | |
| M.P.Bicknell | c Lloyd b Hughes | 30 | | | |
| J.Boiling | lbw b Watkinson | 1 | | | |
| Waqar Younis | not out | 9 | | | |
| Extras | (b 5,lb 4,nb 16) | 25 | (b 3,lb 3,w 1,nb 6) | | 13 |
| TOTAL | | 361 | (for 2 wkts) | | 127 |

| SURREY | O | M | R | W | O | M | R | W |
|---|---|---|---|---|---|---|---|---|
| Bicknell M.P. | 16 | 2 | 45 | 0 | 17.2 | 8 | 58 | 2 |
| Waqar Younis | 19 | 3 | 57 | 5 | 25 | 9 | 65 | 6 |
| Feltham | 16.3 | 0 | 64 | 3 | 13 | 2 | 58 | 1 |
| Greig | 7 | 2 | 13 | 0 | | | | |
| Medlycott | 9 | 2 | 19 | 1 | 7 | 3 | 17 | 1 |
| Boiling | 13 | 2 | 44 | 1 | 6 | 0 | 15 | 0 |

| LANCASHIRE | O | M | R | W | O | M | R | W |
|---|---|---|---|---|---|---|---|---|
| Wasim Akram | 29 | 9 | 84 | 1 | 9 | 1 | 37 | 0 |
| Allott | 13 | 5 | 35 | 1 | | | | |
| Watkinson | 25 | 4 | 82 | 3 | 6 | 0 | 37 | 1 |
| Austin | 13 | 2 | 40 | 1 | 4 | 0 | 20 | 0 |
| Yates | 25 | 6 | 95 | 3 | 6.3 | 0 | 27 | 1 |
| Hughes | 8 | 3 | 16 | 1 | | | | |

FALL OF WICKETS
| | LAN | SUR | LAN | SUR |
|---|---|---|---|---|
| 1st | 27 | 24 | 6 | 13 |
| 2nd | 33 | 122 | 7 | 94 |
| 3rd | 44 | 167 | 19 | |
| 4th | 135 | 203 | 22 | |
| 5th | 165 | 220 | 56 | |
| 6th | 212 | 265 | 65 | |
| 7th | 228 | 293 | 150 | |
| 8th | 242 | 325 | 176 | |
| 9th | 243 | 327 | 206 | |
| 10th | 254 | 361 | 233 | |

## YORKSHIRE vs. GLOUCS

at Sheffield on 22nd, 23rd, 24th May 1991
Toss : Yorkshire. Umpires : R.C.Tolchard and P.B.Wight
Match drawn. Yorkshire 4 pts (Bt: 3, Bw: 1), Gloucs 4 pts (Bt: 3, Bw: 1)
100 overs scores : Yorkshire 278 for 4, Gloucs 250 for 4

YORKSHIRE
| | | | | | |
|---|---|---|---|---|---|
| M.D.Moxon * | c Wright b Athey | 65 | st Williams b Lloyds | | 55 |
| A.A.Metcalfe | b Smith | 15 | c Alleyne b Lloyds | | 47 |
| D.Byas | c Hodgson b Alleyne | 87 | | | |
| R.J.Blakey + | lbw b Babington | 55 | | | |
| P.E.Robinson | c Gilbert b Babington | 31 | (3) not out | | 6 |
| S.A.Kellett | lbw b Gilbert | 26 | | | |
| P.W.Jarvis | not out | 37 | | | |
| D.Gough | c Babington b Gilbert | 26 | | | |
| P.J.Hartley | | | | | |
| J.D.Batty | | | | | |
| M.A.Robinson | | | | | |
| Extras | (b 14,lb 13,w 1,nb 18) | 46 | (lb 9,nb 2) | | 11 |
| TOTAL | (for 7 wkts dec) | 388 | (for 2 wkts dec) | | 119 |

GLOUCS
| | | | | | |
|---|---|---|---|---|---|
| G.D.Hodgson | c Blakey b Batty | 54 | b Batty | | 20 |
| R.J.Scott | c Gough b Jarvis | 17 | c & b Robinson M.A. | | 14 |
| A.J.Wright * | not out | 100 | lbw b Batty | | 0 |
| C.W.J.Athey | lbw b Gough | 12 | c Kellett b Batty | | 0 |
| M.W.Alleyne | c Byas b Batty | 40 | not out | | 55 |
| J.J.E.Hardy | not out | 21 | not out | | 32 |
| J.W.Lloyds | | | | | |
| R.C.J.Williams + | | | | | |
| D.R.Gilbert | | | | | |
| A.M.Smith | | | | | |
| A.M.Babington | | | | | |
| Extras | (b 20,lb 5,w 2,nb 2) | 29 | (b 2,lb 1,w 1,nb 1) | | 5 |
| TOTAL | (for 4 wkts dec) | 273 | (for 4 wkts) | | 126 |

| GLOUCS | O | M | R | W | O | M | R | W |
|---|---|---|---|---|---|---|---|---|
| Gilbert | 30 | 6 | 80 | 2 | 6 | 0 | 18 | 0 |
| Babington | 39 | 3 | 121 | 2 | 9 | 3 | 23 | 0 |
| Smith | 19 | 2 | 55 | 1 | 2 | 0 | 19 | 0 |
| Lloyds | 20 | 6 | 48 | 0 | 8 | 0 | 32 | 2 |
| Alleyne | 12 | 0 | 39 | 1 | 2 | 0 | 18 | 0 |
| Athey | 7 | 1 | 18 | 1 | | | | |

| YORKSHIRE | O | M | R | W | O | M | R | W |
|---|---|---|---|---|---|---|---|---|
| Hartley | 14.4 | 3 | 45 | 0 | 7 | 1 | 18 | 0 |
| Jarvis | 14 | 4 | 25 | 1 | | | | |
| Gough | 23 | 6 | 54 | 1 | 9 | 2 | 28 | 0 |
| Batty | 37 | 8 | 95 | 2 | 18 | 5 | 44 | 3 |
| Robinson M.A. | 12 | 2 | 24 | 0 | 10 | 3 | 19 | 1 |
| Robinson P.E. | 2 | 0 | 5 | 0 | 3 | 1 | 14 | 0 |

FALL OF WICKETS
| | YOR | GLO | YOR | GLO |
|---|---|---|---|---|
| 1st | 23 | 35 | 100 | 32 |
| 2nd | 144 | 124 | 119 | 34 |
| 3rd | 240 | 144 | | 34 |
| 4th | 272 | 223 | | 44 |
| 5th | 297 | | | |
| 6th | 326 | | | |
| 7th | 388 | | | |
| 8th | | | | |
| 9th | | | | |
| 10th | | | | |

## NOTTS vs. KENT

at Trent Bridge on 22nd, 23rd, 24th May 1991
Toss : Notts. Umpires : H.D.Bird and R.A.White
Match drawn. Notts 7 pts (Bt: 4, Bw: 3), Kent 5 pts (Bt: 3, Bw: 2)
100 overs scores :Kent 276 for 8

NOTTS
| | | | | | |
|---|---|---|---|---|---|
| B.C.Broad | c Marsh b Merrick | 166 | c Marsh b Merrick | | 0 |
| P.Pollard | c Marsh b Igglesden | 16 | c Fleming b Ellison | | 48 |
| R.T.Robinson * | c Marsh b Penn | 85 | c Marsh b Merrick | | 16 |
| D.W.Randall | c Taylor b Ellison | 12 | (5) not out | | 64 |
| P.Johnson | not out | 38 | (4) c Merrick b Penn | | 65 |
| F.D.Stephenson | c Penn b Ellison | 1 | c Taylor b Penn | | 2 |
| B.N.French + | c Taylor b Fleming | 12 | run out | | 1 |
| E.E.Hemmings | | | c Llong b Penn | | 8 |
| R.A.Pick | | | not out | | 11 |
| K.E.Cooper | | | | | |
| J.A.Afford | | | | | |
| Extras | (lb 9,w 3,nb 3) | 15 | (lb 1,w 1,nb 1) | | 3 |
| TOTAL | (for 6 wkts dec) | 345 | (for 7 wkts dec) | | 218 |

KENT
| | | | | | |
|---|---|---|---|---|---|
| S.G.Hinks | not out | 61 | | | |
| M.R.Benson * | lbw b Pick | 0 | (1) c sub b Pick | | 6 |
| C.Penn | c sub b Cooper | 13 | (8) not out | | 8 |
| N.R.Taylor | c Broad b Afford | 45 | (2) b Pick | | 0 |
| G.R.Cowdrey | not out | 109 | (3) c French b Afford | | 36 |
| M.V.Fleming | c Pollard b Hemmings | 40 | (4) c Hemmings b Afford | | 27 |
| N.J.Llong | c French b Hemmings | 4 | (5) not out | | 42 |
| R.M.Ellison | run out | 5 | (7) c Randall b Afford | | 13 |
| S.A.Marsh + | lbw b Hemmings | 10 | (6) st French b Afford | | 11 |
| T.A.Merrick | c Broad b Hemmings | 4 | | | |
| A.P.Igglesden | | | | | |
| Extras | (b 4,lb 2,w 1,nb 6) | 13 | (b 4,lb 2,nb 6) | | 12 |
| TOTAL | (for 8 wkts dec) | 300 | (for 6 wkts) | | 155 |

| KENT | O | M | R | W | O | M | R | W |
|---|---|---|---|---|---|---|---|---|
| Merrick | 19 | 1 | 78 | 1 | 17 | 3 | 67 | 2 |
| Igglesden | 18 | 5 | 60 | 1 | 11 | 1 | 48 | 0 |
| Ellison | 24 | 8 | 85 | 2 | 5 | 0 | 22 | 1 |
| Penn | 17 | 1 | 63 | 1 | 13 | 0 | 64 | 3 |
| Fleming | 17.2 | 5 | 38 | 1 | | | | |
| Llong | 3 | 1 | 12 | 0 | 2 | 0 | 16 | 0 |

| NOTTS | O | M | R | W | O | M | R | W |
|---|---|---|---|---|---|---|---|---|
| Stephenson | 16.2 | 4 | 44 | 0 | 12 | 3 | 26 | 0 |
| Pick | 19 | 5 | 44 | 1 | 11.3 | 1 | 48 | 2 |
| Hemmings | 29 | 9 | 70 | 4 | 16 | 6 | 31 | 0 |
| Cooper | 17 | 3 | 54 | 1 | | | | |
| Afford | 25 | 6 | 82 | 1 | 19 | 8 | 44 | 4 |

FALL OF WICKETS
| | NOT | KEN | NOT | KEN |
|---|---|---|---|---|
| 1st | 36 | 3 | 0 | 1 |
| 2nd | 250 | 30 | 46 | 12 |
| 3rd | 289 | 144 | 126 | 70 |
| 4th | 303 | 215 | 132 | 89 |
| 5th | 304 | 215 | 146 | 113 |
| 6th | 345 | 223 | 149 | 138 |
| 7th | | 240 | 180 | |
| 8th | | 276 | | |
| 9th | | | | |
| 10th | | | | |

# BRITANNIC ASSURANCE CHAMPIONSHIP

## HEADLINES

**Britannic Assurance Championship**

**22nd - 24th May**

• With their nine-wicket victory over Warwickshire at Chelmsford, Essex moved above the Midlands side to the top of the Championship table. Essex's bowling attack proved too strong for the visitors, Neil Foster leading the way with first innings figures of five for 80. Dominic Ostler's unbeaten 94 was a career-best score, but only Paul Smith offered support. Essex battled to a first innings lead of 70 and, after again breaching Warwickshire's defences on the last afternoon, needed only 12.4 overs to reach their target of 93.

• Surrey were the only other winners, defeating Lancashire by eight wickets at The Oval. Waqar Younis, restored to full fitness, was the decisive force, returning match figures of 11 for 122. Graeme Fowler and Mike Watkinson both hit centuries but Waqar was more than a match for the rest of the Lancashire batsmen. In contrast, Surrey's first innings total of 361, bringing with it a lead of 107, showed the virtue of a consistent batting performance.

• Glamorgan dominated their match with Northamptonshire at Cardiff, but were denied victory by a stubborn ninth-wicket stand between David Ripley and Andy Roberts. Otherwise the visitors' performance was largely undistinguished, and it was Glamorgan's Hugh Morris, Steve Bastien and Steve Watkin who shared the individual honours.

• Somerset finished on the brink of victory over Derbyshire at Derby after forcing the home side to follow on 151 behind. Andy Hayhurst and Richard Harden had both completed centuries and the four Somerset seamers shared the Derbyshire first innings wickets. Peter Bowler and John Morris led a second innings revival, but David Graveney and Peter Roebuck eventually claimed eight wickets between them in 71 overs of flight and guile. Somerset needed 157 runs in 22 overs, a task which proved just beyond them.

• Chris Broad showed he was looking to improve on his 1990 run-aggregate with 166 in Nottinghamshire's first innings total of 345 for six against Kent at Trent Bridge. Graham Cowdrey responded with his first hundred of the season, but on the last day Kent could make little of a target of 264, finishing on 155 for six.

• There was little to set the pulse racing at Sheffield where Yorkshire and Gloucestershire could manage only the tamest of draws. Tony Wright reached an unbeaten 100 before declaring 115 behind, but his gesture proved fruitless as the visitors lost their first four second innings wickets for 44 in pursuit of a target of 235.

---

### DERBYSHIRE vs. SOMERSET

at Derby on 22nd, 23rd, 24th May 1991
Toss : Somerset. Umpires : B.Dudleston and D.R.Shepherd
Match drawn. Derby 4 pts (Bt: 2, Bw: 2), Somerset 7 pts (Bt: 3, Bw: 4)
100 overs scores : Somerset 285 for 5

**SOMERSET**

| Batsman | Dismissal | Runs | 2nd Innings | Runs |
|---|---|---|---|---|
| S.J.Cook | c Krikken b Mortensen | 10 | b Mortensen | 7 |
| P.M.Roebuck | c Krikken b Warner | 0 | (9) not out | 8 |
| A.N.Hayhurst | b Azharuddin | 116 | (2) b Mortensen | 12 |
| C.J.Tavare * | c Krikken b Jean-Jacques | 13 | (3) c Krikken b Mortensen | 26 |
| R.J.Harden | c O'Gorman b Folley | 134 | (4) c Adams b Jean-Jacques | 23 |
| N.D.Burns + | lbw b Barnett | 0 | (8) not out | 7 |
| K.H.Macleay | not out | 26 | (6) b Mortensen | 11 |
| G.D.Rose | run out | 37 | (5) run out | 32 |
| R.P.Lefebvre | not out | 12 | (7) c Azharuddin b J-Jacques | 8 |
| D.A.Graveney | | | | |
| N.A.Mallender | | | | |
| Extras | (b 4,lb 6,nb 15) | 25 | (lb 10) | 10 |
| TOTAL | (for 7 wkts dec) | 373 | (for 7 wkts) | 144 |

**DERBYSHIRE**

| Batsman | Dismissal | Runs | 2nd Innings | Runs |
|---|---|---|---|---|
| P.D.Bowler | lbw b Macleay | 13 | c Harden b Graveney | 59 |
| J.E.Morris | c Tavare b Macleay | 43 | c Lefebvre b Graveney | 91 |
| T.J.G.O'Gorman | c Tavare b Lefebvre | 23 | lbw b Roebuck | 7 |
| M.Azharuddin | b Lefebvre | 10 | (5) b Roebuck | 37 |
| C.J.Adams | c Lefebvre b Rose | 15 | (6) c Burns b Graveney | 37 |
| K.J.Barnett * | c Rose b Lefebvre | 1 | (7) c Lefebvre b Rose | 21 |
| K.M.Krikken + | not out | 46 | (8) not out | 30 |
| A.E.Warner | lbw b Mallender | 31 | (10) b Roebuck | 1 |
| I.Folley | lbw b Mallender | 0 | (4) c Tavare b Mallender | 3 |
| M.Jean-Jacques | b Macleay | 28 | (9) c Tavare b Graveney | 2 |
| O.H.Mortensen | c Burns b Mallender | 1 | c Harden b Graveney | 1 |
| Extras | (lb 5,nb 6) | 11 | (b 11,lb 3,nb 4) | 18 |
| TOTAL | | 222 | | 307 |

| DERBYSHIRE | O | M | R | W | O | M | R | W |
|---|---|---|---|---|---|---|---|---|
| Mortensen | 21 | 8 | 36 | 1 | 11 | 0 | 47 | 4 |
| Warner | 20 | 0 | 68 | 1 | | | | |
| Jean-Jacques | 18 | 1 | 62 | 1 | 10.5 | 0 | 87 | 2 |
| Folley | 26 | 2 | 107 | 1 | | | | |
| Barnett | 22 | 2 | 54 | 1 | | | | |
| Azharuddin | 13 | 2 | 36 | 1 | | | | |

| SOMERSET | O | M | R | W | O | M | R | W |
|---|---|---|---|---|---|---|---|---|
| Mallender | 17.3 | 3 | 52 | 3 | 16 | 4 | 37 | 1 |
| Rose | 11 | 1 | 43 | 1 | 17 | 6 | 44 | 1 |
| Macleay | 12 | 2 | 40 | 3 | 16 | 4 | 60 | 0 |
| Lefebvre | 15 | 5 | 51 | 3 | 14 | 3 | 42 | 0 |
| Graveney | 11 | 3 | 31 | 0 | 44.3 | 21 | 68 | 5 |
| Hayhurst | | | | | 4 | 2 | 5 | 0 |
| Roebuck | | | | | 27 | 12 | 37 | 3 |

**FALL OF WICKETS**

| | SOM | DER | DER | SOM |
|---|---|---|---|---|
| 1st | 8 | 62 | 110 | 12 |
| 2nd | 20 | 65 | 123 | 27 |
| 3rd | 65 | 90 | 131 | 68 |
| 4th | 252 | 105 | 198 | 73 |
| 5th | 253 | 107 | 210 | 107 |
| 6th | 306 | 113 | 249 | 127 |
| 7th | 358 | 156 | 285 | 127 |
| 8th | | 156 | 293 | |
| 9th | | 221 | 294 | |
| 10th | | 222 | 307 | |

---

### ESSEX vs. WARWICKSHIRE

at Chelmsford on 22nd, 23rd, 24th May 1991
Toss : Essex. Umpires : D.O.Oslear and N.T.Plews
Essex won by 9 wickets. Essex 23 pts (Bt: 3, Bw: 4), Warwickshire 5 pts (Bt: 2, Bw: 3)
100 overs scores : Warwickshire 235 for 9, Essex 288 for 7

**WARWICKSHIRE**

| Batsman | Dismissal | Runs | 2nd Innings | Runs |
|---|---|---|---|---|
| A.J.Moles | lbw b Foster | 23 | c Garnham b Foster | 6 |
| Asif Din | c Hussain b Andrew | 10 | c Hussain b Foster | 20 |
| T.A.Lloyd * | b Foster | 10 | (4) c Garnham b Andrew | 22 |
| P.A.Smith | c Lewis b Foster | 43 | (5) lbw b Topley | 2 |
| D.A.Reeve | b Foster | 4 | (6) b Andrew | 20 |
| D.P.Ostler | not out | 94 | (7) c Garnham b Andrew | 7 |
| K.J.Piper + | run out | 4 | (8) c Garnham b Andrew | 11 |
| G.C.Small | c Shahid b Childs | 1 | (9) c Garnham b Foster | 11 |
| T.A.Munton | c Salim Malik b Foster | 14 | (3) c Garnham b Topley | 10 |
| A.R.K.Pierson | lbw b Topley | 1 | not out | 14 |
| A.A.Donald | run out | 12 | run out | 4 |
| Extras | (lb 6,nb 15) | 21 | (b 4,lb 11,w 5,nb 15) | 35 |
| TOTAL | | 237 | | 162 |

**ESSEX**

| Batsman | Dismissal | Runs | 2nd Innings | Runs |
|---|---|---|---|---|
| J.P.Stephenson | c Piper b Munton | 79 | not out | 40 |
| N.Shahid | c & b Donald | 11 | | |
| P.J.Prichard | c Piper b Donald | 5 | (2) c Piper b Small | 26 |
| Salim Malik | c & b Munton | 21 | | |
| N.Hussain | b Reeve | 55 | | |
| J.J.B.Lewis | lbw b Pierson | 48 | | |
| M.A.Garnham + | not out | 46 | not out | 12 |
| N.A.Foster * | c Asif Din b Pierson | 2 | | |
| T.D.Topley | c Piper b Donald | 4 | | |
| S.J.W.Andrew | c Reeve b Pierson | 7 | | |
| J.H.Childs | | | | |
| Extras | (b 8,lb 13,w 1,nb 7) | 29 | (b 10,lb 2,w 3) | 15 |
| TOTAL | (for 9 wkts dec) | 307 | (for 1 wkt) | 93 |

| ESSEX | O | M | R | W | O | M | R | W |
|---|---|---|---|---|---|---|---|---|
| Foster | 28 | 3 | 80 | 5 | 26.4 | 8 | 49 | 3 |
| Andrew | 23 | 5 | 47 | 1 | 21 | 9 | 38 | 4 |
| Topley | 19 | 6 | 60 | 1 | 23 | 6 | 60 | 2 |
| Childs | 26 | 15 | 35 | 1 | | | | |
| Salim Malik | 2 | 0 | 3 | 0 | | | | |
| Stephenson | 3.1 | 0 | 6 | 0 | | | | |

| WARWICKS | O | M | R | W | O | M | R | W |
|---|---|---|---|---|---|---|---|---|
| Donald | 19 | 3 | 52 | 3 | 6 | 0 | 27 | 0 |
| Munton | 24 | 6 | 75 | 2 | | | | |
| Small | 17 | 5 | 34 | 0 | 6 | 0 | 41 | 1 |
| Reeve | 25 | 6 | 58 | 1 | 0.4 | 0 | 13 | 0 |
| Pierson | 14 | 1 | 45 | 3 | | | | |
| Smith | 8 | 0 | 22 | 0 | | | | |

**FALL OF WICKETS**

| | WAR | ESS | WAR | ESS |
|---|---|---|---|---|
| 1st | 22 | 34 | 8 | 44 |
| 2nd | 49 | 41 | 47 | |
| 3rd | 52 | 66 | 57 | |
| 4th | 58 | 142 | 65 | |
| 5th | 142 | 210 | 98 | |
| 6th | 146 | 281 | 110 | |
| 7th | 164 | 287 | 111 | |
| 8th | 193 | 300 | 125 | |
| 9th | 199 | 307 | 151 | |
| 10th | 237 | | 162 | |

| BRITANNIC ASS. CHAMPIONSHIP | OTHER FIRST-CLASS MATCH |
|---|---|

## SUSSEX vs. MIDDLESEX

at Hove on 22nd, 23rd, 24th May 1991
Toss : Sussex.  Umpires : B.Hassan and J.W.Holder
Match drawn.  Sussex 5 pts (Bt: 4, Bw: 1), Middlesex 5 pts (Bt: 4, Bw: 1)

**SUSSEX**

| | | | | |
|---|---|---|---|---|
| D.M.Smith | not out | 126 | (7) run out | 28 |
| J.W.Hall | b Cowans | 3 | lbw b Tufnell | 41 |
| N.J.Lenham | c Brown b Williams | 11 | (1) st Downton b Embury | 32 |
| A.P.Wells * | c Downton b Cowans | 137 | c & b Embury | 2 |
| M.P.Speight | c Cowans b Embury | 40 | (3) c Hutchinson b Embury | 0 |
| A.I.C.Dodemaide | | | (5) c Roseberry b Embury | 3 |
| P.Moores + | | | (6) c Roseberry b Embury | 9 |
| A.C.S.Pigott | | | c Tufnell b Embury | 6 |
| I.D.K.Salisbury | | | c Brown b Embury | 5 |
| B.T.P.Donelan | | | not out | 27 |
| R.A.Bunting | | | c Brown b Tufnell | 39 |
| Extras | (b 5,lb 7,w 1,nb 10) | 23 | (lb 6,nb 5) | 11 |
| TOTAL | (for 4 wkts dec) | 340 | | 203 |

**MIDDLESEX**

| | | | | |
|---|---|---|---|---|
| I.J.F.Hutchinson | lbw b Bunting | 125 | lbw b Dodemaide | 46 |
| M.A.Roseberry | c Wells b Dodemaide | 25 | c Dodemaide b Bunting | 47 |
| M.W.Gatting * | not out | 117 | run out | 31 |
| K.R.Brown | lbw b Pigott | 28 | lbw b Bunting | 3 |
| M.Keech | not out | 0 | st Moores b Salisbury | 27 |
| P.R.Downton + | | | not out | 24 |
| N.G.Cowans | | | b Donelan | 0 |
| J.E.Embury | | | not out | 5 |
| N.F.Williams | | | | |
| P.C.R.Tufnell | | | | |
| R.M.Ellcock | | | | |
| Extras | (b 2,nb 3) | 5 | (b 2,lb 2,w 1,nb 3) | 8 |
| TOTAL | (for 3 wkts dec) | 300 | (for 6 wkts) | 191 |

| MIDDLESEX | O | M | R | W | O | M | R | W |
|---|---|---|---|---|---|---|---|---|
| Ellcock | 9 | 3 | 28 | 0 | 9 | 1 | 29 | 0 |
| Cowans | 13 | 3 | 39 | 2 | 4 | 1 | 8 | 0 |
| Williams | 18 | 4 | 65 | 1 | 5 | 0 | 20 | 0 |
| Embury | 25 | 7 | 76 | 1 | 37 | 11 | 71 | 7 |
| Tufnell | 30 | 8 | 111 | 0 | 30 | 9 | 69 | 2 |
| Hutchinson | 4 | 0 | 9 | 0 | | | | |
| Keech | | | | | 1 | 1 | 0 | 0 |

**FALL OF WICKETS**

| | SUS | MID | SUS | MID |
|---|---|---|---|---|
| 1st | 8 | 67 | 67 | 73 |
| 2nd | 35 | 242 | 67 | 128 |
| 3rd | 252 | 298 | 73 | 133 |
| 4th | 340 | | 77 | 133 |
| 5th | | | 87 | 180 |
| 6th | | | 107 | 181 |
| 7th | | | 122 | |
| 8th | | | 132 | |
| 9th | | | 139 | |
| 10th | | | 203 | |

| SUSSEX | O | M | R | W | O | M | R | W |
|---|---|---|---|---|---|---|---|---|
| Pigott | 23 | 11 | 48 | 1 | 4 | 1 | 11 | 0 |
| Dodemaide | 19 | 3 | 63 | 1 | 9 | 1 | 30 | 1 |
| Bunting | 18 | 2 | 60 | 1 | 8 | 0 | 34 | 2 |
| Salisbury | 12 | 1 | 62 | 0 | 12 | 1 | 62 | 1 |
| Donelan | 16.1 | 5 | 54 | 0 | 12 | 1 | 50 | 1 |
| Lenham | 3 | 0 | 11 | 0 | | | | |

## CAMBRIDGE U vs. LEICESTERSHIRE

at Fenner's on 22nd, 23rd, 24th May 1991
Toss : Cambridge U.  Umpires : D.Fawkner-Corbett and B.Leadbeater
Match drawn

**CAMBRIDGE U**

| | | | | |
|---|---|---|---|---|
| A.M.Hooper | c Boon b Tennant | 10 | c Briers b Potter | 92 |
| R.I.Clitheroe | b Wilkinson | 35 | c Whitticase b Tennant | 0 |
| J.P.Crawley | c Whitticase b Maguire | 7 | lbw b Tennant | 0 |
| M.J.Morris | c Hepworth b Tennant | 60 | b Tennant | 22 |
| R.J.Turner *+ | c Boon b Potter | 10 | c Briers b Wilkinson | 4 |
| M.J.Lowrey | c Potter b Wilkinson | 32 | c Potter b Gidley | 30 |
| G.W.Jones | c Potter b Tennant | 0 | not out | 13 |
| R.A.Pyman | c Briers b Tennant | 6 | not out | 8 |
| R.M.Pearson | st Whitticase b Hepworth | 13 | | |
| D.J.Bush | not out | 24 | | |
| N.C.W.Fenton | not out | 7 | | |
| Extras | (b 5,lb 11,w 2,nb 6) | 24 | (b 3,lb 1,nb 13) | 17 |
| TOTAL | (for 9 wkts dec) | 228 | (for 6 wkts) | 186 |

**LEICESTERSHIRE**

| | | |
|---|---|---|
| T.J.Boon | c Bush b Pyman | 108 |
| N.E.Briers * | c Turner b Bush | 50 |
| P.N.Hepworth | b Lowrey | 115 |
| J.J.Whitaker | c & b Lowrey | 47 |
| L.Potter | not out | 73 |
| B.F.Smith | not out | 47 |
| M.I.Gidley | | |
| P.Whitticase + | | |
| C.Wilkinson | | |
| L.Tennant | | |
| J.N.Maguire | | |
| Extras | (b 3,lb 9) | 12 |
| TOTAL | (for 4 wkts dec) | 452 |

| LEICESTERSHIRE | O | M | R | W | O | M | R | W |
|---|---|---|---|---|---|---|---|---|
| Tennant | 22 | 7 | 54 | 4 | 8 | 1 | 43 | 3 |
| Maguire | 17 | 4 | 38 | 1 | 7 | 1 | 47 | 0 |
| Wilkinson | 15 | 5 | 26 | 2 | 7 | 3 | 9 | 1 |
| Smith | 5 | 1 | 20 | 0 | 1 | 1 | 0 | 0 |
| Potter | 13 | 4 | 27 | 1 | 15 | 6 | 27 | 1 |
| Hepworth | 13 | 0 | 36 | 1 | 4 | 0 | 23 | 0 |
| Gidley | 4 | 1 | 11 | 0 | 19 | 10 | 33 | 1 |

**FALL OF WICKETS**

| | CAM | LEI | CAM | LEI |
|---|---|---|---|---|
| 1st | 21 | 91 | 10 | |
| 2nd | 40 | 232 | 10 | |
| 3rd | 74 | 295 | 78 | |
| 4th | 96 | 358 | 95 | |
| 5th | 157 | | 147 | |
| 6th | 157 | | 177 | |
| 7th | 172 | | | |
| 8th | 189 | | | |
| 9th | 218 | | | |
| 10th | | | | |

| CAMBRIDGE U | O | M | R | W | O | M | R | W |
|---|---|---|---|---|---|---|---|---|
| Fenton | 25 | 5 | 95 | 0 | | | | |
| Pyman | 24 | 4 | 90 | 1 | | | | |
| Pearson | 28 | 6 | 103 | 0 | | | | |
| Bush | 11 | 0 | 49 | 1 | | | | |
| Lowrey | 14 | 1 | 62 | 2 | | | | |
| Hooper | 5 | 0 | 32 | 0 | | | | |
| Crawley | 1 | 0 | 9 | 0 | | | | |

# HEADLINES

### Britannic Assurance Championship

### 22nd - 24th May

• Middlesex were hoping to avenge their surprise defeat by Sussex earlier in the month when they visited Hove. The first two days' cricket were dominated by the batsmen, David Smith, Alan Wells, Ian Hutchinson and Mike Gatting all hitting centuries. Middlesex looked to have taken control when they reduced the home side to 139 for nine in their second innings, John Emburey claiming seven wickets, but Brad Donelan and Rodney Bunting added 64 determined runs for the last wicket. Middlesex could not approach the required run-rate and Paul Downton, having announced his retirement because of continuing difficulties with his eyesight, could only play out for the draw.

# HEADLINES

### Other first-class match

### 22nd - 24th May

• Peter Hepworth hit his maiden first-class 100 at Fenner's in Leicestershire's 452 for 4 declared against Cambridge University. Faced with a deficit of 224 the students battled hard for a draw, achieved thanks to 92 from Anthony Hooper, dismissed eight short of his second 100 in a week.

# TEXACO TROPHY

## ENGLAND vs. WEST INDIES

at Edgbaston on 23rd, 24th May 1991
Toss : England.  Umpires : J.H.Hampshire and M.J.Kitchen
England won by 1 wicket
Man of the match: M.A.Atherton

### WEST INDIES

| | | |
|---|---|---|
| C.G.Greenidge | c Russell b Botham | 23 |
| P.V.Simmons | c Gooch b Lewis | 4 |
| R.B.Richardson | c Illingworth b Botham | 3 |
| I.V.A.Richards * | c Fairbrother b Gooch | 30 |
| C.L.Hooper | c Russell b Botham | 10 |
| A.L.Logie | c DeFreitas b Botham | 18 |
| P.J.L.Dujon + | c Lewis b Illingworth | 5 |
| M.D.Marshall | c Lewis b DeFreitas | 17 |
| C.E.L.Ambrose | not out | 21 |
| C.A.Walsh | not out | 29 |
| B.P.Patterson | | |
| Extras | (b 1,lb 5,w 6,nb 1) | 13 |
| TOTAL | (55 overs)(for 8 wkts) | 173 |

### ENGLAND

| | | |
|---|---|---|
| G.A.Gooch * | lbw b Ambrose | 0 |
| M.A.Atherton | not out | 69 |
| G.A.Hick | c Richardson b Marshall | 14 |
| A.J.Lamb | b Hooper | 18 |
| N.H.Fairbrother | c Dujon b Hooper | 4 |
| I.T.Botham | lbw b Walsh | 8 |
| D.R.Pringle | c Richardson b Walsh | 1 |
| R.C.Russell + | c Dujon b Patterson | 1 |
| P.A.J.DeFreitas | c Richardson b Marshall | 8 |
| C.C.Lewis | c Richardson b Patterson | 0 |
| R.K.Illingworth | not out | 9 |
| Extras | (lb 9,w 18,nb 16) | 43 |
| TOTAL | (49.4 overs)(for 9 wkts) | 175 |

| ENGLAND | O | M | R | W | FALL OF WICKETS | | |
|---|---|---|---|---|---|---|---|
| | | | | | | WI | ENG |
| DeFreitas | 11 | 3 | 22 | 1 | 1st | 8 | 1 |
| Lewis | 11 | 3 | 41 | 1 | 2nd | 16 | 41 |
| Pringle | 7 | 0 | 22 | 0 | 3rd | 48 | 80 |
| Botham | 11 | 2 | 45 | 4 | 4th | 78 | 87 |
| Gooch | 5 | 0 | 17 | 1 | 5th | 84 | 123 |
| Illingworth | 10 | 1 | 20 | 1 | 6th | 98 | 126 |
| | | | | | 7th | 103 | 134 |
| WEST INDIES | O | M | R | W | 8th | 121 | 147 |
| Ambrose | 11 | 2 | 34 | 1 | 9th | | 152 |
| Patterson | 11 | 2 | 38 | 2 | 10th | | |
| Marshall | 11 | 1 | 32 | 2 | | | |
| Walsh | 11 | 0 | 34 | 2 | | | |
| Simmons | 3 | 0 | 10 | 0 | | | |
| Hooper | 2.4 | 0 | 18 | 2 | | | |

## HEADLINES

### 1st match - Edgbaston

• England gained victory over West Indies in the opening match of the Texaco Trophy series only thanks to a last-wicket stand of 23 between Mike Atherton and Richard Illingworth. Ian Botham's return to the international stage had begun in theatrical style, as he took a wicket with his second ball. West Indies were restricted to 173 for eight, but any illusions that victory would be a formality for England were shattered when Curtly Ambrose removed Graham Gooch in his first over.  Graeme Hick had to endure a torrid baptism on his long-awaited England début before giving Richie Richardson the first of four slip catches.  Bad light ended the day's proceedings with England on 107 for four.  On the second morning all was going well for England until Botham pulled a hamstring attempting a quick single and was lbw to Courtney Walsh's next ball.  Batsmen came and went, but Atherton played with great composure and a nail-biting victory was achieved with 5.2 overs to spare.

• One-Day International débuts:
G.A.Hick and R.K.Illingworth

## ENGLAND vs. WEST INDIES

at Old Trafford on 25th May 1991
Toss : West Indies.  Umpires : H.D.Bird and D.R.Shepherd
England won by 9 runs
Man of the match: A.J.Lamb

### ENGLAND

| | | |
|---|---|---|
| G.A.Gooch * | b Hooper | 54 |
| M.A.Atherton | c sub b Ambrose | 74 |
| G.A.Hick | b Ambrose | 29 |
| A.J.Lamb | c Dujon b Patterson | 62 |
| N.H.Fairbrother | not out | 5 |
| M.R.Ramprakash | not out | 6 |
| D.R.Pringle | | |
| R.C.Russell + | | |
| C.C.Lewis | | |
| P.A.J.DeFreitas | | |
| R.K.Illingworth | | |
| Extras | (b 4,lb 16,w 14,nb 6) | 40 |
| TOTAL | (55 overs)(for 4 wkts) | 270 |

### WEST INDIES

| | | |
|---|---|---|
| P.V.Simmons | run out | 28 |
| P.J.L.Dujon + | c DeFreitas b Lewis | 21 |
| R.B.Richardson | c Russell b Gooch | 13 |
| C.L.Hooper | c sub b Lewis | 48 |
| I.V.A.Richards * | lbw b Lewis | 78 |
| A.L.Logie | c Illingworth b Pringle | 24 |
| M.D.Marshall | c & b Pringle | 22 |
| C.G.Greenidge | run out | 4 |
| C.E.L.Ambrose | not out | 5 |
| C.A.Walsh | not out | 1 |
| B.P.Patterson | | |
| Extras | (lb 4,w 10,nb 3) | 17 |
| TOTAL | (55 overs)(for 8 wkts) | 261 |

| WEST INDIES | O | M | R | W | FALL OF WICKETS | | |
|---|---|---|---|---|---|---|---|
| | | | | | | ENG | WI |
| Ambrose | 11 | 3 | 36 | 2 | 1st | 156 | 34 |
| Patterson | 10 | 1 | 39 | 1 | 2nd | 156 | 61 |
| Walsh | 11 | 0 | 56 | 0 | 3rd | 258 | 69 |
| Marshall | 10 | 0 | 45 | 0 | 4th | 260 | 190 |
| Simmons | 4 | 0 | 30 | 0 | 5th | | 208 |
| Hooper | 9 | 0 | 44 | 1 | 6th | | 250 |
| | | | | | 7th | | 250 |
| ENGLAND | O | M | R | W | 8th | | 256 |
| DeFreitas | 11 | 3 | 50 | 0 | 9th | | |
| Lewis | 11 | 0 | 62 | 3 | 10th | | |
| Pringle | 11 | 2 | 52 | 2 | | | |
| Illingworth | 11 | 1 | 42 | 0 | | | |
| Gooch | 11 | 1 | 51 | 1 | | | |

## HEADLINES

### 2nd match - Old Trafford

• England's nine-run victory brought them the Texaco Trophy and they won in impressive fashion, after compiling their highest score in One-Day Internationals against West Indies. Graham Gooch and Michael Atherton, again improving his best score, launched the innings with a stand of 156, and Graeme Hick and man of the match Allan Lamb added extra impetus with a third-wicket partnership of 102. Although Gordon Greenidge had injured himself while fielding a West Indies victory was still very much on the cards while Carl Hooper and Viv Richards were adding 121 for the fourth wicket, but Chris Lewis and Derek Pringle both claimed wickets at important moments and England held on to achieve their fifth successive one-day victory over West Indies in this country.

• One-Day International début:
M.R.Ramprakash

## ENGLAND vs. WEST INDIES

at Lord's on 27th May 1991
Toss : England.  Umpires : M.J.Kitchen and D.R.Shepherd
England won by 7 wickets
Man of the match: N.H.Fairbrother

### WEST INDIES

| | | |
|---|---|---|
| P.V.Simmons | c Russell b DeFreitas | 5 |
| P.J.L.Dujon + | b Lawrence | 0 |
| R.B.Richardson | c DeFreitas b Illingworth | 41 |
| B.C.Lara | c & b Illingworth | 23 |
| I.V.A.Richards * | c Illingworth b DeFreitas | 37 |
| A.L.Logie | c & b Gooch | 82 |
| C.L.Hooper | c Fairbrother b Lawrence | 26 |
| M.D.Marshall | c DeFreitas b Lawrence | 13 |
| C.E.L.Ambrose | not out | 6 |
| C.A.Walsh | lbw b Lawrence | 0 |
| B.P.Patterson | not out | 2 |
| Extras | (b 1,lb 9,w 14,nb 5) | 29 |
| TOTAL | (55 overs)(for 9 wkts) | 264 |

### ENGLAND

| | | |
|---|---|---|
| G.A.Gooch * | run out | 11 |
| M.A.Atherton | c Dujon b Marshall | 25 |
| G.A.Hick | not out | 86 |
| N.H.Fairbrother | c Richards b Patterson | 113 |
| M.R.Ramprakash | not out | 0 |
| D.A.Reeve | | |
| D.R.Pringle | | |
| R.C.Russell + | | |
| P.A.J.DeFreitas | | |
| R.K.Illingworth | | |
| D.V.Lawrence | | |
| Extras | (b 4,lb 12,w 10,nb 4) | 30 |
| TOTAL | (46.1 overs)(for 3 wkts) | 265 |

| ENGLAND | O | M | R | W | FALL OF WICKETS | | |
|---|---|---|---|---|---|---|---|
| | | | | | | WI | ENG |
| Lawrence | 11 | 1 | 67 | 4 | 1st | 8 | 28 |
| DeFreitas | 11 | 1 | 26 | 2 | 2nd | 8 | 48 |
| Reeve | 11 | 1 | 43 | 0 | 3rd | 71 | 261 |
| Illingworth | 11 | 1 | 53 | 2 | 4th | 91 | |
| Pringle | 9 | 0 | 56 | 0 | 5th | 164 | |
| Gooch | 2 | 0 | 9 | 1 | 6th | 227 | |
| | | | | | 7th | 241 | |
| WEST INDIES | O | M | R | W | 8th | 258 | |
| Ambrose | 8 | 0 | 31 | 0 | 9th | 258 | |
| Patterson | 10 | 0 | 62 | 1 | 10th | | |
| Marshall | 11 | 1 | 49 | 1 | | | |
| Walsh | 11 | 1 | 50 | 0 | | | |
| Hooper | 4.1 | 0 | 36 | 0 | | | |
| Simmons | 2 | 0 | 21 | 0 | | | |

## HEADLINES

### 3rd match - Lord's

• England gained their second successive 3–0 whitewash of West Indies in the Texaco Trophy with a crushing seven-wicket victory with almost nine overs to spare. West Indies lost both openers with only eight runs on the board, but Richie Richardson and Gus Logie led an entertaining counter-attack. David Lawrence was at times expensive but demolished the tail to finish with four for 67 keeping the England target to 265. Graham Gooch and Mike Atherton could not repeat their Old Trafford performance, but it gave Graeme Hick and Neil Fairbrother the opportunity to prove themselves in a sparkling third-wicket stand of 213 made in only 30 overs: Fairbrother was at his inventive best, as he reached his first 100 for England; Hick was the perfect foil, less flamboyant but quick to punish the bad ball, as he showed he could come to terms with the pressures of a big occasion.

• One-Day International débuts:
D.V.Lawrence and D.A.Reeve.

# REFUGE ASSURANCE LEAGUE

## KENT vs. DERBYSHIRE

at Canterbury on 26th May 1991
Toss : Derby.  Umpires : J.W.Holder and N.T.Plews
Kent won by 6 runs.  Kent 4 pts, Derby 0 pts

### KENT

| | | |
|---|---|---|
| M.V.Fleming | c Jean-Jacques b Malcolm | 35 |
| M.R.Benson * | c Roberts b Base | 24 |
| N.R.Taylor | b Base | 56 |
| G.R.Cowdrey | c Bowler b Mortensen | 17 |
| T.R.Ward | c Bowler b Malcolm | 14 |
| C.S.Cowdrey | c Adams b Barnett | 45 |
| S.A.Marsh + | c Base b Barnett | 0 |
| R.M.Ellison | not out | 8 |
| M.J.McCague | not out | 5 |
| R.P.Davis | | |
| A.P.Igglesden | | |
| Extras | (b 1,lb 7,w 2) | 10 |
| TOTAL | (40 overs)(for 7 wkts) | 214 |

### DERBYSHIRE

| | | |
|---|---|---|
| K.J.Barnett * | c & b Davis | 16 |
| P.D.Bowler + | lbw b Fleming | 25 |
| J.E.Morris | c Ward b Davis | 11 |
| M.Azharuddin | c sub b McCague | 73 |
| B.Roberts | c Cowdrey C.S. b Ellison | 15 |
| T.J.G.O'Gorman | c Benson b Ellison | 41 |
| C.J.Adams | c Marsh b McCague | 8 |
| M.Jean-Jacques | b McCague | 0 |
| D.E.Malcolm | not out | 4 |
| S.J.Base | c Benson b McCague | 3 |
| O.H.Mortensen | | |
| Extras | (lb 6,w 5,nb 1) | 12 |
| TOTAL | (40 overs)(for 9 wkts) | 208 |

| DERBYSHIRE | O | M | R | W | FALL OF WICKETS | | |
|---|---|---|---|---|---|---|---|
| Jean-Jacques | 8 | 0 | 55 | 0 | | KEN | DER |
| Mortensen | 8 | 0 | 42 | 1 | 1st | 47 | 38 |
| Malcolm | 8 | 1 | 34 | 2 | 2nd | 69 | 50 |
| Base | 8 | 1 | 35 | 2 | 3rd | 109 | 68 |
| Barnett | 8 | 0 | 40 | 2 | 4th | 131 | 95 |
| | | | | | 5th | 195 | 174 |
| KENT | O | M | R | W | 6th | 198 | 199 |
| Igglesden | 8 | 0 | 32 | 0 | 7th | 202 | 199 |
| Ellison | 8 | 0 | 46 | 2 | 8th | | 202 |
| McCague | 8 | 0 | 51 | 4 | 9th | | 208 |
| Davis | 8 | 1 | 29 | 2 | 10th | | |
| Fleming | 8 | 1 | 44 | 1 | | | |

## SOMERSET vs. MIDDLESEX

at Taunton on 26th May 1991
Toss : Middlesex.  Umpires : J.H.Harris and B.J.Meyer
Middlesex won by 7 wickets.  Somerset 0 pts, Middx 4 pts

### SOMERSET

| | | |
|---|---|---|
| S.J.Cook | b Hughes | 1 |
| A.N.Hayhurst | c Williams b Emburey | 19 |
| C.J.Tavare * | c Gatting b Hughes | 65 |
| R.J.Harden | run out | 35 |
| G.D.Rose | c Farbrace b Williams | 0 |
| R.J.Bartlett | c Farbrace b Emburey | 6 |
| N.D.Burns + | st Farbrace b Emburey | 8 |
| K.H.Macleay | st Farbrace b Emburey | 19 |
| R.P.Lefebvre | c Weekes b Emburey | 11 |
| P.M.Roebuck | run out | 2 |
| N.A.Mallender | not out | 6 |
| Extras | (lb 14,w 3,nb 3) | 20 |
| TOTAL | (40 overs) | 192 |

### MIDDLESEX

| | | |
|---|---|---|
| I.J.F.Hutchinson | c Lefebvre b Macleay | 20 |
| M.A.Roseberry | c Macleay b Roebuck | 30 |
| M.W.Gatting * | not out | 65 |
| K.R.Brown | c Burns b Hayhurst | 18 |
| M.Keech | not out | 49 |
| J.E.Emburey | | |
| P.Farbrace + | | |
| P.N.Weekes | | |
| N.F.Williams | | |
| S.P.Hughes | | |
| N.G.Cowans | | |
| Extras | (b 1,lb 9,w 3) | 13 |
| TOTAL | (38 overs)(for 3 wkts) | 195 |

| MIDDLESEX | O | M | R | W | FALL OF WICKETS | | |
|---|---|---|---|---|---|---|---|
| Hughes | 8 | 0 | 42 | 2 | | SOM | MID |
| Cowans | 8 | 0 | 31 | 0 | 1st | 3 | 31 |
| Williams | 8 | 0 | 40 | 1 | 2nd | 62 | 70 |
| Weekes | 8 | 0 | 42 | 0 | 3rd | 122 | 108 |
| Emburey | 8 | 0 | 23 | 5 | 4th | 124 | |
| | | | | | 5th | 137 | |
| SOMERSET | O | M | R | W | 6th | 142 | |
| Mallender | 8 | 0 | 36 | 0 | 7th | 154 | |
| Lefebvre | 7 | 1 | 39 | 0 | 8th | 182 | |
| Rose | 4 | 0 | 18 | 0 | 9th | 182 | |
| Macleay | 8 | 0 | 28 | 1 | 10th | 192 | |
| Roebuck | 7 | 0 | 47 | 1 | | | |
| Hayhurst | 4 | 0 | 17 | 1 | | | |

## WARWICKSHIRE vs. WORCS

at Edgbaston on 26th May 1991
Toss : Warwicks.  Umpires : J.C.Balderstone & B.Dudleston
Match tied.  Warwickshire 2 pts, Worcestershire 2 pts

### WARWICKSHIRE

| | | |
|---|---|---|
| A.J.Moles | b Radford | 39 |
| Asif Din | b Dilley | 11 |
| T.A.Lloyd * | lbw b Stemp | 34 |
| P.A.Smith | c Stemp b Newport | 16 |
| D.P.Ostler | c Newport b Dilley | 48 |
| R.G.Twose | not out | 26 |
| K.J.Piper + | not out | 15 |
| G.C.Small | | |
| A.R.K.Pierson | | |
| T.A.Munton | | |
| A.A.Donald | | |
| Extras | (lb 6,w 8) | 14 |
| TOTAL | (40 overs)(for 5 wkts) | 203 |

### WORCESTERSHIRE

| | | |
|---|---|---|
| T.S.Curtis * | c Lloyd b Donald | 67 |
| T.M.Moody | b Smith | 45 |
| M.J.Weston | c Twose b Smith | 51 |
| D.B.D'Oliveira | c Donald b Pierson | 4 |
| D.A.Leatherdale | c Piper b Munton | 12 |
| S.J.Rhodes + | run out | 1 |
| P.J.Newport | c Asif Din b Munton | 0 |
| S.R.Lampitt | not out | 0 |
| N.V.Radford | not out | 1 |
| R.D.Stemp | | |
| G.R.Dilley | | |
| Extras | (b 2,lb 7,w 12,nb 1) | 22 |
| TOTAL | (40 overs)(for 7 wkts) | 203 |

| WORCS | O | M | R | W | FALL OF WICKETS | | |
|---|---|---|---|---|---|---|---|
| Dilley | 8 | 0 | 48 | 2 | | WAR | WOR |
| Weston | 6 | 0 | 28 | 0 | 1st | 16 | 92 |
| Radford | 8 | 1 | 42 | 1 | 2nd | 89 | 158 |
| Stemp | 7 | 0 | 22 | 1 | 3rd | 89 | 162 |
| Newport | 5 | 0 | 25 | 1 | 4th | 135 | 200 |
| Lampitt | 6 | 0 | 32 | 0 | 5th | 174 | 201 |
| | | | | | 6th | | 201 |
| WARWICKS | O | M | R | W | 7th | | 201 |
| Munton | 8 | 2 | 20 | 2 | 8th | | |
| Donald | 8 | 0 | 43 | 1 | 9th | | |
| Twose | 1 | 0 | 9 | 0 | 10th | | |
| Pierson | 7 | 0 | 45 | 1 | | | |
| Small | 8 | 0 | 32 | 0 | | | |
| Smith | 8 | 0 | 45 | 2 | | | |

## LEICESTERSHIRE vs. NOTTS

at Leicester on 26th May 1991
Toss : Notts.  Umpires : G.I.Burgess and R.Julian
Notts won by 5 wickets.  Leicestershire 0 pts, Notts 4 pts

### LEICESTERSHIRE

| | | |
|---|---|---|
| T.J.Boon | c French b Saxelby | 50 |
| N.E.Briers * | lbw b Saxelby | 19 |
| J.J.Whitaker | b Saxelby | 10 |
| P.Willey | c French b Saxelby | 42 |
| L.Potter | not out | 42 |
| B.F.Smith | lbw b Hemmings | 2 |
| P.Whitticase + | c French b Crawley | 0 |
| P.N.Hepworth | b Hemmings | 0 |
| C.Wilkinson | c Robinson b Crawley | 6 |
| D.J.Millns | not out | 20 |
| J.N.Maguire | | |
| Extras | (lb 6,w 6,nb 1) | 13 |
| TOTAL | (40 overs)(for 8 wkts) | 170 |

### NOTTS

| | | |
|---|---|---|
| B.C.Broad | lbw b Maguire | 3 |
| D.W.Randall | not out | 83 |
| R.T.Robinson * | c Whitticase b Millns | 8 |
| P.Johnson | b Hepworth | 46 |
| M.A.Crawley | c Whitticase b Wilkinson | 6 |
| M.Saxelby | c Millns b Hepworth | 12 |
| B.N.French + | not out | 16 |
| F.D.Stephenson | | |
| K.P.Evans | | |
| E.E.Hemmings | | |
| R.A.Pick | | |
| Extras | (b 2,lb 3,w 3,nb 2) | 10 |
| TOTAL | (36.3 overs)(for 5 wkts) | 174 |

| NOTTS | O | M | R | W | FALL OF WICKETS | | |
|---|---|---|---|---|---|---|---|
| Pick | 5 | 0 | 20 | 0 | | LEI | NOT |
| Stephenson | 7 | 1 | 30 | 0 | 1st | 57 | 12 |
| Saxelby | 8 | 0 | 29 | 4 | 2nd | 74 | 34 |
| Evans | 7 | 0 | 51 | 0 | 3rd | 98 | 126 |
| Hemmings | 8 | 0 | 21 | 2 | 4th | 105 | 136 |
| Crawley | 5 | 0 | 13 | 2 | 5th | 108 | 143 |
| | | | | | 6th | 109 | |
| LEICS | O | M | R | W | 7th | 110 | |
| Maguire | 6 | 0 | 30 | 1 | 8th | 117 | |
| Millns | 8 | 1 | 30 | 1 | 9th | | |
| Wilkinson | 6.3 | 1 | 27 | 1 | 10th | | |
| Willey | 4 | 0 | 17 | 0 | | | |
| Smith | 3 | 0 | 15 | 0 | | | |
| Potter | 3 | 0 | 17 | 0 | | | |
| Hepworth | 6 | 1 | 33 | 2 | | | |

## SURREY vs. ESSEX

at The Oval on 26th May 1991
Toss : Surrey.  Umpires : B.Hassan and A.G.T.Whitehead
Surrey won by 7 wickets.  Surrey 4 pts, Essex 0 pts

### ESSEX

| | | |
|---|---|---|
| P.J.Prichard | b Murphy | 4 |
| J.P.Stephenson | b Waqar Younis | 64 |
| Salim Malik | c Sargeant b Feltham | 12 |
| N.Hussain | c Medlycott b Robinson | 22 |
| N.Shahid | c Lynch b Murphy | 16 |
| K.A.Butler | lbw b Waqar Younis | 1 |
| N.A.Foster * | not out | 27 |
| D.E.East + | run out | 2 |
| T.D.Topley | b Waqar Younis | 3 |
| S.J.W.Andrew | c Ward b Murphy | 8 |
| P.M.Such | not out | 1 |
| Extras | (lb 6,w 6,nb 1) | 13 |
| TOTAL | (40 overs)(for 9 wkts) | 173 |

### SURREY

| | | |
|---|---|---|
| M.A.Lynch | c Salim Malik b Andrew | 85 |
| A.D.Brown | c Prichard b Foster | 45 |
| D.M.Ward | c Butler b Topley | 5 |
| G.P.Thorpe | not out | 29 |
| J.D.Robinson | not out | 2 |
| K.T.Medlycott * | | |
| M.A.Feltham | | |
| N.F.Sargeant + | | |
| C.K.Bullen | | |
| A.J.Murphy | | |
| Waqar Younis | | |
| Extras | (lb 6,w 2) | 8 |
| TOTAL | (38.2 overs)(for 3 wkts) | 174 |

| SURREY | O | M | R | W | FALL OF WICKETS | | |
|---|---|---|---|---|---|---|---|
| Feltham | 8 | 0 | 22 | 1 | | ESS | SUR |
| Murphy | 8 | 0 | 28 | 3 | 1st | 10 | 97 |
| Robinson | 8 | 1 | 28 | 1 | 2nd | 31 | 103 |
| Bullen | 6 | 0 | 45 | 0 | 3rd | 77 | 167 |
| Thorpe | 2 | 0 | 17 | 0 | 4th | 121 | |
| Waqar Younis | 8 | 1 | 27 | 3 | 5th | 126 | |
| | | | | | 6th | 139 | |
| ESSEX | O | M | R | W | 7th | 144 | |
| Andrew | 8 | 1 | 44 | 1 | 8th | 148 | |
| Foster | 6 | 0 | 22 | 1 | 9th | 162 | |
| Topley | 8 | 1 | 28 | 1 | 10th | | |
| Such | 8 | 1 | 46 | 0 | | | |
| Stephenson | 4 | 0 | 16 | 0 | | | |
| Salim Malik | 4.2 | 1 | 12 | 0 | | | |

## YORKSHIRE vs. NORTHANTS

at Headingley on 26th May 1991
Toss : Yorkshire.  Umpires : R.C.Tolchard and P.B.Wight
Yorkshire won by 3 wickets.  Yorks 4 pts, Northants 0 pts

### NORTHANTS

| | | |
|---|---|---|
| A.Fordham | c & b Batty | 76 |
| N.A.Felton | c Batty b Robinson M.A. | 9 |
| R.J.Bailey * | lbw b Fletcher | 1 |
| D.J.Capel | run out | 30 |
| K.M.Curran | c Moxon b Batty | 8 |
| A.L.Penberthy | c Hartley b Moxon | 6 |
| J.G.Thomas | not out | 30 |
| D.Ripley + | c Blakey b Robinson M.A. | 10 |
| W.M.Noon | not out | 1 |
| A.R.Roberts | | |
| A.Walker | | |
| Extras | (b 1,lb 7,w 9,nb 2) | 19 |
| TOTAL | (40 overs)(for 7 wkts) | 197 |

### YORKSHIRE

| | | |
|---|---|---|
| M.D.Moxon * | c Ripley b Penberthy | 31 |
| A.A.Metcalfe | c Ripley b Curran | 33 |
| R.J.Blakey + | not out | 71 |
| D.Byas | b Capel | 27 |
| P.E.Robinson | lbw b Capel | 2 |
| D.Gough | c Penberthy b Walker | 13 |
| C.A.Chapman | b Thomas | 1 |
| P.J.Hartley | run out | 5 |
| J.D.Batty | not out | 2 |
| S.D.Fletcher | | |
| M.A.Robinson | | |
| Extras | (b 2,lb 4,w 7) | 13 |
| TOTAL | (39.4 overs)(for 7 wkts) | 198 |

| YORKSHIRE | O | M | R | W | FALL OF WICKETS | | |
|---|---|---|---|---|---|---|---|
| Robinson M.A. | 7 | 0 | 24 | 2 | | NOR | YOR |
| Gough | 3 | 0 | 21 | 0 | 1st | 33 | 47 |
| Fletcher | 6 | 0 | 31 | 1 | 2nd | 36 | 81 |
| Hartley | 8 | 0 | 47 | 0 | 3rd | 131 | 146 |
| Batty | 8 | 2 | 32 | 2 | 4th | 134 | 158 |
| Moxon | 8 | 0 | 34 | 1 | 5th | 141 | 177 |
| | | | | | 6th | 159 | 181 |
| NORTHANTS | O | M | R | W | 7th | 186 | 195 |
| Thomas | 8 | 0 | 37 | 1 | 8th | | |
| Walker | 7.4 | 2 | 27 | 1 | 9th | | |
| Capel | 8 | 0 | 29 | 2 | 10th | | |
| Penberthy | 8 | 2 | 43 | 1 | | | |
| Roberts | 2 | 0 | 15 | 0 | | | |
| Curran | 6 | 0 | 41 | 1 | | | |

# REFUGE ASSURANCE LEAGUE

## GLAMORGAN vs. SUSSEX

at Swansea on 26th May 1991
Toss : Glamorgan. Umpires : J.D.Bond and A.A.Jones
Sussex won by 113 runs. Glamorgan 0 pts, Sussex 4 pts

### SUSSEX

| | | |
|---|---|---|
| N.J.Lenham | c Holmes b Watkin | 13 |
| K.Greenfield | c Holmes b Dale | 38 |
| P.W.G.Parker * | lbw b Dale | 32 |
| A.P.Wells | c Barwick b Smith | 5 |
| M.P.Speight | c Maynard b Frost | 47 |
| A.I.C.Dodemaide | c Shastri b Smith | 9 |
| P.Moores + | run out | 34 |
| A.C.S.Pigott | lbw b Watkin | 2 |
| I.D.K.Salisbury | b Frost | 4 |
| R.A.Bunting | not out | 2 |
| A.N.Jones | c Dale b Barwick | 2 |
| Extras | (b 1,lb 7,w 8,nb 1) | 17 |
| TOTAL | (37.5 overs) | 205 |

### GLAMORGAN

| | | |
|---|---|---|
| A.R.Butcher * | c Moores b Pigott | 9 |
| H.Morris | c & b Pigott | 24 |
| M.P.Maynard | run out | 0 |
| R.J.Shastri | c Parker b Pigott | 14 |
| G.C.Holmes | c Moores b Bunting | 5 |
| I.Smith | c Parker b Bunting | 8 |
| A.Dale | c Jones b Salisbury | 17 |
| C.P.Metson + | run out | 2 |
| S.L.Watkin | b Salisbury | 0 |
| S.R.Barwick | b Salisbury | 2 |
| M.Frost | not out | 0 |
| Extras | (lb 3,w 8) | 11 |
| TOTAL | (30.1 overs) | 92 |

| GLAMORGAN | O | M | R | W | | FALL OF WICKETS | | |
|---|---|---|---|---|---|---|---|---|
| Watkin | 8 | 0 | 44 | 2 | | | SUS | GLA |
| Frost | 7 | 0 | 46 | 2 | 1st | 30 | 5 |
| Barwick | 6.5 | 0 | 35 | 1 | 2nd | 77 | 24 |
| Dale | 8 | 0 | 37 | 2 | 3rd | 96 | 29 |
| Smith | 8 | 0 | 35 | 2 | 4th | 97 | 33 |
| | | | | | 5th | 117 | 47 |
| SUSSEX | O | M | R | W | 6th | 187 | 54 |
| Jones | 5 | 2 | 11 | 0 | 7th | 193 | 73 |
| Dodemaide | 5 | 0 | 10 | 0 | 8th | 200 | 80 |
| Pigott | 8 | 0 | 26 | 3 | 9th | 200 | 92 |
| Bunting | 8 | 0 | 32 | 2 | 10th | 205 | 92 |
| Salisbury | 4.1 | 0 | 10 | 3 | | | |

## GLOUCS vs. HAMPSHIRE

at Swindon on 26th May 1991
Toss : Hampshire. Umpires : D.J.Constant and K.E.Palmer
Gloucs won by 26 runs. Gloucs 4 pts, Hampshire 0 pts

### GLOUCS

| | | |
|---|---|---|
| R.J.Scott | lbw b Udal | 77 |
| C.W.J.Athey | c Smith b Bakker | 85 |
| A.J.Wright * | not out | 60 |
| M.W.Alleyne | not out | 37 |
| J.J.E.Hardy | | |
| P.W.Romaines | | |
| J.W.Lloyds | | |
| R.C.J.Williams + | | |
| D.R.Gilbert | | |
| A.M.Smith | | |
| A.M.Babington | | |
| Extras | (b 4,lb 8,w 10) | 22 |
| TOTAL | (40 overs)(for 2 wkts) | 281 |

### HAMPSHIRE

| | | |
|---|---|---|
| V.P.Terry | b Smith | 123 |
| T.C.Middleton | b Smith | 36 |
| R.A.Smith | c & b Lloyds | 16 |
| D.I.Gower | c Alleyne b Lloyds | 2 |
| M.C.J.Nicholas * | b Gilbert | 45 |
| K.D.James | c Athey b Smith | 8 |
| J.R.Ayling | not out | 9 |
| A.N Aymes + | not out | 4 |
| S.D.Udal | | |
| P.J.Bakker | | |
| Aqib Javed | | |
| Extras | (lb 7,w 5) | 12 |
| TOTAL | (40 overs)(for 6 wkts) | 255 |

| HAMPSHIRE | O | M | R | W | | FALL OF WICKETS | | |
|---|---|---|---|---|---|---|---|---|
| James | 4 | 0 | 25 | 0 | | | GLO | HAM |
| Aqib Javed | 8 | 0 | 51 | 0 | 1st | 130 | 62 |
| Bakker | 8 | 0 | 45 | 1 | 2nd | 208 | 88 |
| Ayling | 7 | 0 | 49 | 0 | 3rd | | 99 |
| Nicholas | 5 | 0 | 42 | 0 | 4th | | 219 |
| Udal | 8 | 0 | 57 | 1 | 5th | | 238 |
| | | | | | 6th | | 240 |
| GLOUCS | O | M | R | W | 7th | | |
| Gilbert | 8 | 0 | 51 | 1 | 8th | | |
| Babington | 8 | 0 | 50 | 0 | 9th | | |
| Athey | 5 | 0 | 28 | 0 | 10th | | |
| Smith | 8 | 0 | 47 | 3 | | | |
| Lloyds | 7 | 0 | 47 | 2 | | | |
| Alleyne | 4 | 0 | 25 | 0 | | | |

### Refuge Assurance League Table as at 26th May 1991

| | | P | W | L | T | NR | Away Wins | Pts | Run Rate |
|---|---|---|---|---|---|---|---|---|---|
| 1 | Notts (4) | 5 | 5 | 0 | 0 | 0 | 3 | 20 | 85.77 |
| 2 | Somerset (8) | 5 | 4 | 1 | 0 | 0 | 2 | 16 | 80.46 |
| 3 | Warwickshire (14) | 6 | 3 | 1 | 1 | 1 | 2 | 16 | 82.05 |
| 4 | Middlesex (3) | 5 | 3 | 1 | 0 | 1 | 3 | 14 | 88.07 |
| 5 | Worcestershire (10) | 5 | 3 | 1 | 1 | 0 | 2 | 14 | 100.43 |
| 6 | Lancashire (2) | 4 | 3 | 1 | 0 | 0 | 2 | 12 | 94.11 |
| 7 | Gloucs (9) | 5 | 3 | 2 | 0 | 0 | 2 | 12 | 89.19 |
| 8 | Northants (17) | 6 | 2 | 3 | 0 | 1 | 1 | 10 | 87.45 |
| 9 | Leicestershire (16) | 6 | 2 | 3 | 0 | 1 | 0 | 10 | 82.40 |
| 10 | Surrey (7) | 4 | 2 | 2 | 0 | 0 | 1 | 8 | 83.72 |
| 11 | Derbyshire (1) | 4 | 2 | 2 | 0 | 0 | 1 | 8 | 82.54 |
| 12 | Hampshire (5) | 5 | 2 | 3 | 0 | 0 | 0 | 8 | 80.77 |
| 13 | Kent (11) | 5 | 1 | 2 | 1 | 1 | 0 | 8 | 86.41 |
| 14 | Essex (12) | 5 | 1 | 2 | 1 | 1 | 0 | 8 | 75.24 |
| 15 | Sussex (13) | 5 | 1 | 4 | 0 | 0 | 1 | 4 | 76.62 |
| 16 | Yorkshire (6) | 5 | 1 | 4 | 0 | 0 | 0 | 4 | 74.91 |
| 17 | Glamorgan (15) | 6 | 0 | 6 | 0 | 0 | 0 | 0 | 75.20 |

## HEADLINES

### Refuge Assurance League

### 26th May

• Nottinghamshire gained a four-point lead at the top of the table with their fifth successive Sunday victory, achieved at the expense of Leicestershire at Leicester. Mark Saxelby returned career-best bowling figures as the home side were limited to 170 for eight, and Derek Randall's 83 not out ensured a solid five-wicket success.

• Somerset's unbeaten run was ended by Middlesex at Taunton, a total of 192 never looking enough to bring the home side their fifth victory of the season. John Emburey claimed his best Sunday League figures and Mike Gatting and Matthew Keech saw Middlesex to a seven-wicket win with an unbeaten stand of 87.

• Warwickshire and Worcestershire tied their match at Edgbaston. A largely uneventful game came to life in its last over, bowled by Tim Munton, with the visitors needing just four to win. Victory was snatched away from Worcestershire by the loss of three wickets without a run being scored, and only a scampered bye off the last ball salvaged a tie.

• Swindon played host to a match full of runs between Gloucestershire and Hampshire, an opening stand of 130 between Richard Scott and Bill Athey providing the base for Gloucestershire's total of 281 for two, and even Paul Terry's fifth Sunday League 100 could not prevent a 26-run defeat for the visitors.

• Derbyshire's defence of their title suffered another setback at Canterbury where they were beaten by six runs by a Kent side growing in confidence. A useful all-round batting performance brought the home side to 214 for seven and four wickets for Australian newcomer Mike McCague left the visitors short of their target.

• Glamorgan's miserable start to their Sunday League campaign continued as they were bowled out for 92 by Sussex at Swansea. Ian Salisbury's figures of three for 10 were his best in the competition in Sussex's first Sunday win of the season.

• Surrey gained their first Sunday success with a comfortable seven-wicket win over Essex at The Oval, Waqar Younis and Tony Murphy each taking three wickets and Monte Lynch contributing a rapid 85 in Surrey's reply.

• Yorkshire also broke their duck with a three-wicket win over Northants, achieved with two balls to spare thanks to an unbeaten 71 from Richard Blakey, after Mark Robinson and Jeremy Batty had restricted Northants to 197 for seven.

# BRITANNIC ASSURANCE CHAMPIONSHIP

## GLAMORGAN vs. SUSSEX
at Cardiff on 25th, 27th, 28th May 1991
Toss : Sussex.  Umpires : J.D.Bond and A.A.Jones
Match drawn.  Glamorgan 7 pts (Bt: 4, Bw: 3), Sussex 3 pts (Bt: 3, Bw: 0)
100 overs scores : Sussex 257 for 8, Glamorgan 321 for 2

### SUSSEX
| | | | | | |
|---|---|---|---|---|---|
| D.M.Smith | b Frost | 61 | lbw b Frost | | 0 |
| J.W.Hall | c Metson b Watkin | 3 | c Metson b Frost | | 7 |
| N.J.Lenham | c Morris b Croft | 21 | (4) b Bastien | | 11 |
| A.P.Wells | b Croft | 0 | (5) not out | | 153 |
| P.W.G.Parker * | b Bastien | 95 | (6) lbw b Croft | | 9 |
| A.I.C.Dodemaide | c Metson b Smith | 12 | (7) not out | | 100 |
| P.Moores + | b Frost | 28 | | | |
| I.D.K.Salisbury | lbw b Frost | 0 | | | |
| B.T.P.Donelan | b Bastien | 17 | (3) b Watkin | | 22 |
| R.A.Bunting | not out | 2 | | | |
| A.N.Jones | c Shastri b Watkin | 3 | | | |
| Extras | (b 3,lb 14,w 2,nb 2) | 21 | (b 1,lb 5,nb 4) | | 10 |
| TOTAL | | 263 | (for 5 wkts) | | 312 |

### GLAMORGAN
| | | |
|---|---|---|
| A.R.Butcher * | c Smith b Salisbury | 52 |
| H.Morris | not out | 156 |
| R.J.Shastri | b Bunting | 26 |
| M.P.Maynard | c Moores b Jones | 127 |
| G.C.Holmes | lbw b Jones | 0 |
| I.Smith | not out | 12 |
| R.D.B.Croft | | |
| C.P.Metson + | | |
| S.L.Watkin | | |
| S.Bastien | | |
| M.Frost | | |
| Extras | (b 11,lb 6,w 1,nb 4) | 22 |
| TOTAL | (for 4 wkts dec) | 395 |

| GLAMORGAN | O | M | R | W | O | M | R | W | FALL OF WICKETS | | | |
|---|---|---|---|---|---|---|---|---|---|---|---|---|
| | | | | | | | | | | SUS | GLA | SUS | GLA |
| Watkin | 20 | 2 | 52 | 2 | 21 | 5 | 59 | 1 | | | | |
| Frost | 20 | 4 | 45 | 3 | 23 | 3 | 75 | 2 | 1st | 12 | 102 | 1 |
| Bastien | 24 | 9 | 49 | 2 | 23 | 11 | 40 | 1 | 2nd | 71 | 170 | 26 |
| Croft | 34 | 12 | 93 | 2 | 25 | 3 | 103 | 1 | 3rd | 71 | 372 | 32 |
| Smith | 5 | 3 | 7 | 1 | 7.1 | 1 | 28 | 0 | 4th | 114 | 376 | 53 |
| Butcher | | | | | 1 | 0 | 1 | 0 | 5th | 154 | | 90 |
| | | | | | | | | | 6th | 205 | | |
| SUSSEX | O | M | R | W | O | M | R | W | 7th | 205 | | |
| Dodemaide | 21 | 4 | 57 | 0 | | | | | 8th | 257 | | |
| Jones | 24 | 2 | 92 | 2 | | | | | 9th | 258 | | |
| Salisbury | 30 | 9 | 85 | 1 | | | | | 10th | 263 | | |
| Donelan | 23 | 3 | 78 | 0 | | | | | | | | |
| Bunting | 16 | 2 | 66 | 1 | | | | | | | | |

## HAMPSHIRE vs. SURREY
at Bournemouth on 25th, 27th, 28th May 1991
Toss : Surrey.  Umpires : B.Hassan and A.G.T.Whitehead
Surrey won by 1 wicket.  Hampshire 7 pts (Bt: 3, Bw: 4), Surrey 22 pts (Bt: 2, Bw: 4)

### HAMPSHIRE
| | | | | | |
|---|---|---|---|---|---|
| V.P.Terry | c Sargeant b Waqar Younis | 8 | c Sargeant b Waqar Younis | | 17 |
| C.L.Smith | c Ward b Waqar Younis | 55 | c Sargeant b Waqar Younis | | 47 |
| M.C.J.Nicholas * | c Sargeant b Waqar Younis | 14 | lbw b Waqar Younis | | 14 |
| R.A.Smith | c Lynch b Thorpe | 33 | c Medlycott b Waqar Younis | | 29 |
| D.I.Gower | b Murphy | 29 | (6) lbw b Waqar Younis | | 3 |
| K.D.James | c Sargeant b Waqar Younis | 29 | (7) not out | | 39 |
| A.N Aymes + | b Greig | 53 | (8) not out | | 23 |
| R.J.Maru | b Waqar Younis | 36 | (5) c Lynch b Murphy | | 23 |
| C.A.Connor | c sub b Murphy | 12 | | | |
| P.J.Bakker | b Waqar Younis | 0 | | | |
| Aqib Javed | not out | 1 | | | |
| Extras | (b 6,lb 17,w 1,nb 1) | 25 | (b 2,lb 8,w 3,nb 1) | | 14 |
| TOTAL | | 281 | (for 6 wkts dec) | | 209 |

### SURREY
| | | | | | |
|---|---|---|---|---|---|
| D.J.Bicknell | b Connor | 48 | b Bakker | | 0 |
| R.I.Alikhan | b Bakker | 13 | c Smith R.A. b Aqib Javed | | 53 |
| D.M.Ward | c Maru b James | 22 | lbw b Bakker | | 18 |
| M.A.Lynch | c Smith R.A. b Connor | 0 | c Nicholas b Connor | | 30 |
| G.P.Thorpe | b Connor | 25 | c Gower b Maru | | 58 |
| K.T.Medlycott | c Smith R.A. b James | 45 | (7) b Connor | | 0 |
| I.A.Greig * | c Smith R.A. b Connor | 45 | (6) c & b Connor | | 61 |
| N.F.Sargeant + | lbw b Aqib Javed | 4 | c & b Maru | | 0 |
| M.P.Bicknell | b Aqib Javed | 18 | c Smith C.L. b Maru | | 0 |
| Waqar Younis | not out | 16 | not out | | 4 |
| A.J.Murphy | c Terry b Aqib Javed | 9 | not out | | 1 |
| Extras | (b 5,lb 16,nb 10) | 31 | (b 3,lb 8,w 1,nb 2) | | 14 |
| TOTAL | | 235 | (for 9 wkts) | | 256 |

| SURREY | O | M | R | W | O | M | R | W | FALL OF WICKETS | | | |
|---|---|---|---|---|---|---|---|---|---|---|---|---|
| | | | | | | | | | | HAM | SUR | HAM | SUR |
| Waqar Younis | 19 | 5 | 66 | 6 | 30 | 5 | 70 | 5 | 1st | 8 | 57 | 56 | 0 |
| Bicknell M.P. | 15 | 10 | 23 | 0 | | | | | 2nd | 8 | 81 | 85 | 32 |
| Murphy | 25.4 | 8 | 56 | 2 | 41.5 | 12 | 103 | 1 | 3rd | 85 | 86 | 90 | 102 |
| Greig | 22.3 | 4 | 47 | 1 | 13 | 2 | 26 | 0 | 4th | 110 | 95 | 136 | 115 |
| Thorpe | 9 | 1 | 38 | 1 | | | | | 5th | 141 | 166 | 140 | 226 |
| Medlycott | 8.3 | 3 | 28 | 0 | | | | | 6th | 211 | 175 | 144 | 226 |
| | | | | | | | | | 7th | 258 | 175 | | 243 |
| HAMPSHIRE | O | M | R | W | O | M | R | W | 8th | 279 | 196 | | 243 |
| Aqib Javed | 20.4 | 1 | 72 | 3 | 17 | 3 | 73 | 1 | 9th | 279 | 197 | | 254 |
| Bakker | 18 | 4 | 48 | 1 | 13 | 1 | 56 | 2 | 10th | 281 | 235 | | |
| Maru | 2 | 1 | 1 | 0 | 14 | 2 | 65 | 3 | | | | | |
| Connor | 16 | 2 | 49 | 4 | 12 | 1 | 41 | 3 | | | | | |
| James | 15 | 4 | 44 | 2 | 4 | 0 | 10 | 0 | | | | | |

## KENT vs. DERBYSHIRE
at Canterbury on 25th, 27th, 28th May 1991
Toss : Kent.  Umpires : J.W.Holder and N.T.Plews
Kent won by 208 runs.  Kent 22 pts (Bt: 2, Bw: 4), Derby 6 pts (Bt: 2, Bw: 4)

### KENT
| | | | | | |
|---|---|---|---|---|---|
| N.R.Taylor | b Jean-Jacques | 24 | c O'Gorman b Base | | 146 |
| M.R.Benson * | lbw b Malcolm | 14 | c Base b Malcolm | | 160 |
| G.R.Cowdrey | c Adams b Jean-Jacques | 8 | not out | | 37 |
| M.V.Fleming | lbw b Base | 33 | hit wicket b Malcolm | | 10 |
| N.J.Llong | c Krikken b Base | 11 | not out | | 1 |
| R.M.Ellison | c Azharuddin b Base | 16 | | | |
| S.A.Marsh + | b Base | 3 | | | |
| R.P.Davis | c Adams b Jean-Jacques | 27 | | | |
| C.Penn | c Barnett b Malcolm | 19 | | | |
| T.A.Merrick | not out | 13 | | | |
| A.P.Igglesden | c Adams b Jean-Jacques | 1 | | | |
| Extras | (b 4,lb 10,w 2,nb 20) | 36 | (lb 5,w 3,nb 10) | | 18 |
| TOTAL | | 205 | (for 3 wkts dec) | | 372 |

### DERBYSHIRE
| | | | | | |
|---|---|---|---|---|---|
| K.J.Barnett * | c Cowdrey b Merrick | 85 | c Igglesden b Merrick | | 0 |
| P.D.Bowler | run out | 14 | b Merrick | | 24 |
| J.E.Morris | b Merrick | 10 | c Llong b Penn | | 17 |
| M.Azharuddin | c Ellison b Penn | 12 | b Penn | | 47 |
| I.Folley | c Marsh b Penn | 0 | (9) not out | | 17 |
| T.J.G.O'Gorman | b Merrick | 36 | (5) c Davis b Penn | | 7 |
| C.J.Adams | c Merrick b Davis | 26 | b Davis | | 11 |
| K.M.Krikken + | c Marsh b Merrick | 1 | (6) c & b Davis | | 18 |
| M.Jean-Jacques | b Davis | 0 | (8) lbw b Merrick | | 3 |
| S.J.Base | not out | 19 | st Marsh b Davis | | 0 |
| D.E.Malcolm | c Marsh b Davis | 2 | c Davis b Igglesden | | 18 |
| Extras | (b 1,lb 3,nb 6) | 10 | (b 1,nb 4) | | 5 |
| TOTAL | | 202 | | | 167 |

| DERBYSHIRE | O | M | R | W | O | M | R | W | FALL OF WICKETS | | | |
|---|---|---|---|---|---|---|---|---|---|---|---|---|
| | | | | | | | | | | KEN | DER | KEN | DER |
| Malcolm | 23 | 3 | 54 | 2 | 21.5 | 2 | 87 | 2 | 1st | 37 | 14 | 300 | 0 |
| Jean-Jacques | 18.5 | 5 | 54 | 4 | 9 | 1 | 54 | 0 | 2nd | 47 | 34 | 328 | 27 |
| Base | 16 | 4 | 43 | 4 | 21 | 2 | 109 | 1 | 3rd | 49 | 87 | 370 | 78 |
| Folley | 20 | 4 | 40 | 0 | 20 | 2 | 70 | 0 | 4th | 82 | 87 | | 94 |
| Barnett | | | | | 10 | 1 | 47 | 0 | 5th | 109 | 151 | | 103 |
| | | | | | | | | | 6th | 121 | 151 | | 122 |
| KENT | O | M | R | W | O | M | R | W | 7th | 126 | 153 | | 127 |
| Merrick | 18 | 3 | 55 | 4 | 13 | 2 | 60 | 3 | 8th | 181 | 162 | | 147 |
| Igglesden | 9 | 0 | 50 | 0 | 6.5 | 0 | 22 | 1 | 9th | 198 | 195 | | 147 |
| Ellison | 3 | 0 | 17 | 0 | | | | | 10th | 205 | 202 | | 167 |
| Penn | 12 | 0 | 48 | 2 | 12 | 1 | 31 | 3 | | | | | |
| Davis | 17.1 | 1 | 28 | 3 | 17 | 4 | 53 | 3 | | | | | |

## LEICESTERSHIRE vs. NOTTS
at Leicester on 25th, 27th, 28th May 1991
Toss : Notts.  Umpires : G.I.Burgess and R.Julian
Match drawn.  Leicestershire 5 pts (Bt: 3, Bw: 2), Notts 8 pts (Bt: 4, Bw: 4)

### LEICESTERSHIRE
| | | | | | |
|---|---|---|---|---|---|
| T.J.Boon | c Evans b Afford | 30 | run out | | 5 |
| N.E.Briers * | c Pick b Evans | 14 | b Stephenson | | 21 |
| P.N.Hepworth | b Evans | 21 | (4) c Johnson b Afford | | 56 |
| J.J.Whitaker | c French b Pick | 65 | (5) c French b Evans | | 14 |
| L.Potter | lbw b Evans | 44 | (6) lbw b Afford | | 64 |
| B.F.Smith | c Randall b Pick | 43 | (7) c French b Pick | | 43 |
| P.Willey | c Afford b Pick | 2 | (8) lbw b Afford | | 6 |
| P.Whitticase + | c Evans b Afford | 4 | (9) lbw b Pick | | 1 |
| L.Tennant | b Pick | 12 | (10) not out | | 8 |
| D.J.Millns | not out | 2 | (3) c Robinson b Stephenson | | 5 |
| J.N.Maguire | b Pick | 0 | b Stephenson | | 0 |
| Extras | (b 8,lb 19,w 1,nb 8) | 36 | (lb 8,nb 9) | | 17 |
| TOTAL | | 270 | | | 235 |

### NOTTS
| | | | | | |
|---|---|---|---|---|---|
| B.C.Broad | c Briers b Maguire | 51 | c & b Maguire | | 91 |
| P.Pollard | retired hurt/ill | 14 | b Maguire | | 33 |
| R.T.Robinson * | c & b Maguire | 101 | (5) c Briers b Millns | | 1 |
| P.Johnson | c Hepworth b Tennant | 24 | (3) c Potter b Maguire | | 20 |
| D.W.Randall | c Whitticase b Potter | 45 | (4) b Millns | | 35 |
| M.Saxelby | c & b Hepworth | 44 | (8) not out | | 3 |
| K.P.Evans | not out | 6 | | | |
| F.D.Stephenson | not out | 16 | (7) not out | | 3 |
| B.N.French + | | | (6) c Whitticase b Millns | | 0 |
| R.A.Pick | | | | | |
| J.A.Afford | | | | | |
| Extras | (lb 1,nb 5) | 6 | (b 1,lb 5,w 1,nb 1) | | 8 |
| TOTAL | (for 5 wkts dec) | 300 | (for 6 wkts) | | 194 |

| NOTTS | O | M | R | W | O | M | R | W | FALL OF WICKETS | | | |
|---|---|---|---|---|---|---|---|---|---|---|---|---|
| | | | | | | | | | | LEI | NOT | LEI | NOT |
| Stephenson | 17 | 8 | 33 | 0 | 19.5 | 4 | 53 | 3 | 1st | 32 | 72 | 9 | 68 |
| Pick | 23.4 | 6 | 66 | 5 | 20 | 0 | 66 | 2 | 2nd | 75 | 115 | 14 | 98 |
| Evans | 19 | 4 | 72 | 3 | 15 | 3 | 42 | 1 | 3rd | 85 | 187 | 39 | 164 |
| Afford | 30 | 17 | 48 | 2 | 13 | 5 | 46 | 3 | 4th | 192 | 278 | 74 | 177 |
| Saxelby | 5 | 1 | 24 | 0 | 4 | 0 | 20 | 0 | 5th | 225 | 278 | 139 | 177 |
| | | | | | | | | | 6th | 237 | | 193 | 187 |
| LEICS | O | M | R | W | O | M | R | W | 7th | 248 | | 219 | |
| Millns | 17 | 4 | 69 | 0 | 16 | 1 | 70 | 3 | 8th | 266 | | 223 | |
| Maguire | 28.5 | 3 | 105 | 2 | 20 | 0 | 90 | 3 | 9th | 267 | | 225 | |
| Tennant | 7 | 0 | 40 | 1 | | | | | 10th | 270 | | 235 | |
| Willey | 11 | 2 | 40 | 0 | 4 | 0 | 28 | 0 | | | | | |
| Potter | 18 | 7 | 37 | 1 | | | | | | | | | |
| Hepworth | 1 | 0 | 8 | 1 | | | | | | | | | |

# BRITANNIC ASSURANCE CHAMPIONSHIP

## HEADLINES

### Britannic Assurance Championship

### 25th - 28th May

- Warwickshire returned to the top of the Championship table with their two-day destruction of Gloucestershire. Andy Moles hit the county's first first-class 100 of the season to bring maximum batting points, then their fast bowlers gave the visitors a torrid time. Paul Smith collected nine wickets on the second day, his first innings figures of five for 28 being a new career best, and Allan Donald claimed five wickets in an innings for the fifth time in less than a month as Gloucestershire were asked to follow on. Even Bill Athey's 120 and a ninth-wicket stand of 104 with Mark Smith could not prevent a demoralising nine-wicket defeat.

- Kent moved into second place with their 208-run success over Derbyshire. In a match in which runs were otherwise hard to come by, the county record opening stand by Neil Taylor and Mark Benson was a remarkable effort. Starting Kent's second innings with a lead of just three runs the openers changed the course of the game with a partnership of 300 to break a record that had stood since 1938.

- Surrey gained their second successive Championship win in dramatic fashion as they beat Hampshire by one wicket at Bournemouth. Waqar Younis took his tally of wickets in the last two matches to 22 with figures of 11 for 136 as only Chris Smith and Adrian Aymes could pass 50 for Hampshire. Surrey looked to be coasting to victory on 226 for four with Graham Thorpe and Ian Greig in control but the loss of five wickets for 28 runs brought many palpitations to the visiting camp before victory was secured.

- Middlesex again found their first victory elusive when they visited Somerset. They forged a potentially match-winning lead of 203 thanks to four wickets apiece from Ricky Ellcock and Neil Williams and a batting effort led by Mike Gatting, who shared century stands with Keith Brown and Matthew Keech, the latter hitting his maiden first-class fifty; but Jimmy Cook and Peter Roebuck put Somerset well on the way to safety with an opening partnership of 145.

- Glamorgan were also unable to make the most of a healthy first innings lead against Sussex at Cardiff. Hugh Morris, scoring his third 100 of the season, and Matthew Maynard, scoring his second, added 202 for the third wicket to give the home side an lead of 132, but Sussex were rescued from 90 for five by 100s from Alan Wells, another consistent early-season run-scorer, and Tony Dodemaide, who shared an unbroken sixth-wicket stand of 222.

- Nottinghamshire would have been disappointed not to have forced victory over Leicestershire after twice bowling out the home side and finishing 12 short of their target of 206 in 40 overs, despite 91 from Chris Broad. David Millns and John Maguire bowled with great stamina to deny them.

- Northamptonshire had another narrow escape on their visit to Yorkshire at Headingley, forced to bat out for a draw with eight second innings wickets down after being asked to make 266 for victory. Martyn Moxon became the first Yorkshire batsman to pass the 100 mark, while Phil Carrick showed he was still a useful peformer with four for 25 as Northants's hopes of victory soon evaporated.

## SOMERSET vs. MIDDLESEX

at Taunton on 25th, 27th, 28th May 1991
Toss : Somerset.  Umpires : J.H.Harris and B.J.Meyer
Match drawn.  Somerset 4 pts (Bt: 2, Bw: 2), Middlesex 8 pts (Bt: 4, Bw: 4)
100 overs scores : Middlesex 318 for 5

### SOMERSET

| | | | | | |
|---|---|---|---|---|---|
| S.J.Cook | c Farbrace b Ellcock | 45 | c Farbrace b Emburey | 89 |
| P.M.Roebuck | not out | 91 | c Brown b Tufnell | 49 |
| A.N.Hayhurst | c Emburey b Ellcock | 0 | lbw b Ellcock | 26 |
| C.J.Tavare * | c Farbrace b Williams | 22 | c Hutchinson b Emburey | 18 |
| R.J.Harden | c Farbrace b Williams | 0 | not out | 58 |
| N.D.Burns + | c Farbrace b Ellcock | 6 | c Farbrace b Ellcock | 0 |
| K.H.Macleay | c Brown b Tufnell | 19 | not out | 9 |
| G.D.Rose | c Emburey b Tufnell | 17 | | |
| N.A.Mallender | c Farbrace b Williams | 6 | | |
| H.R.J.Trump | c Keech b Ellcock | 5 | | |
| D.A.Graveney | c Hutchinson b Williams | 1 | | |
| Extras | (b 4,w 1,nb 7) | 12 | (b 4,lb 5,w 1,nb 10) | 20 |
| TOTAL | | 224 | (for 5 wkts) | 269 |

### MIDDLESEX

| | | |
|---|---|---|
| I.J.F.Hutchinson | c Burns b Mallender | 2 |
| M.A.Roseberry | c Graveney b Rose | 7 |
| M.W.Gatting * | lbw b Roebuck | 180 |
| K.R.Brown | c Hayhurst b Mallender | 53 |
| M.Keech | run out | 51 |
| J.E.Emburey | lbw b Trump | 17 |
| N.F.Williams | lbw b Mallender | 41 |
| P.Farbrace + | b Trump | 6 |
| P.C.R.Tufnell | c Hayhurst b Graveney | 9 |
| R.M.Ellcock | not out | 26 |
| N.G.Cowans | c Rose b Macleay | 20 |
| Extras | (b 1,lb 7,w 1,nb 6) | 15 |
| TOTAL | | 427 |

| MIDDLESEX | O | M | R | W | O | M | R | W |
|---|---|---|---|---|---|---|---|---|
| Ellcock | 14 | 1 | 60 | 4 | 11 | 1 | 50 | 2 |
| Cowans | 14 | 2 | 47 | 0 | 10 | 0 | 32 | 0 |
| Williams | 20.2 | 5 | 46 | 4 | 1 | 0 | 2 | 0 |
| Emburey | 18 | 5 | 32 | 0 | 49 | 22 | 66 | 2 |
| Tufnell | 22 | 8 | 35 | 2 | 48 | 13 | 108 | 1 |
| Roseberry | | | | | 2 | 1 | 2 | 0 |
| Keech | | | | | 1 | 1 | 0 | 0 |

| SOMERSET | O | M | R | W | O | M | R | W |
|---|---|---|---|---|---|---|---|---|
| Mallender | 21 | 2 | 82 | 3 | | | | |
| Rose | 5 | 1 | 14 | 1 | | | | |
| Hayhurst | 12 | 3 | 34 | 0 | | | | |
| Macleay | 19.2 | 3 | 54 | 1 | | | | |
| Trump | 26 | 2 | 113 | 2 | | | | |
| Graveney | 34 | 4 | 111 | 1 | | | | |
| Roebuck | 6 | 2 | 11 | 1 | | | | |

| FALL OF WICKETS | SOM | MID | SOM | MID |
|---|---|---|---|---|
| 1st | 64 | 3 | 145 | |
| 2nd | 64 | 11 | 156 | |
| 3rd | 123 | 142 | 187 | |
| 4th | 123 | 304 | 227 | |
| 5th | 135 | 305 | 231 | |
| 6th | 161 | 338 | | |
| 7th | 183 | 344 | | |
| 8th | 201 | 361 | | |
| 9th | 223 | 404 | | |
| 10th | 224 | 427 | | |

## WARWICKSHIRE vs. GLOUCS

at Edgbaston on 25th, 27th May 1991
Toss : Gloucs.  Umpires : J.C.Balderstone and B.Dudleston
Warwickshire won by 9 wickets.  Warwicks 24 pts (Bt: 4, Bw: 4), Gloucs 4 pts (Bt: 0, Bw: 4)

### WARWICKSHIRE

| | | | | | |
|---|---|---|---|---|---|
| A.J.Moles | b Alleyne | 133 | (2) not out | 2 |
| Asif Din | b Babington | 0 | (1) b Smith | 4 |
| T.A.Lloyd * | c Williams b Smith | 38 | | |
| P.A.Smith | lbw b Smith | 1 | | |
| D.P.Ostler | b Smith | 42 | (3) not out | 6 |
| R.G.Twose | c Alleyne b Lloyds | 41 | | |
| K.J.Piper + | b Athey | 29 | | |
| P.A.Booth | run out | 4 | | |
| G.C.Small | c & b Alleyne | 3 | | |
| T.A.Munton | c Scott b Alleyne | 3 | | |
| A.A.Donald | not out | 2 | | |
| Extras | (b 1,lb 16,w 2,nb 3) | 22 | (lb 3,nb 2) | 5 |
| TOTAL | | 318 | (for 1 wkt) | 17 |

### GLOUCS

| | | | | | |
|---|---|---|---|---|---|
| G.D.Hodgson | c Donald b Smith | 27 | c Piper b Donald | 16 |
| R.J.Scott | c Booth b Small | 0 | lbw b Smith | 0 |
| R.C.J.Williams + | c Munton b Small | 8 | (8) b Donald | 0 |
| A.J.Wright * | b Munton | 24 | (3) c Piper b Smith | 2 |
| C.W.J.Athey | c Piper b Donald | 6 | (4) c Piper b Smith | 120 |
| M.W.Alleyne | c Piper b Small | 23 | (5) c Piper b Donald | 0 |
| J.J.E.Hardy | lbw b Smith | 0 | (6) lbw b Donald | 0 |
| J.W.Lloyds | not out | 22 | (7) lbw b Donald | 0 |
| D.R.Gilbert | c Asif Din b Smith | 7 | c Booth b Munton | 19 |
| A.M.Smith | c Piper b Smith | 0 | lbw b Smith | 22 |
| A.M.Babington | c Lloyd b Smith | 8 | not out | 1 |
| Extras | (lb 7,nb 2) | 9 | (lb 16,nb 4) | 20 |
| TOTAL | | 134 | | 200 |

| GLOUCS | O | M | R | W | O | M | R | W |
|---|---|---|---|---|---|---|---|---|
| Gilbert | 19 | 5 | 64 | 0 | | | | |
| Babington | 18 | 4 | 47 | 1 | 4 | 0 | 11 | 0 |
| Smith | 27 | 5 | 71 | 3 | 3.4 | 1 | 3 | 1 |
| Athey | 9 | 0 | 29 | 1 | | | | |
| Lloyds | 15 | 0 | 55 | 1 | | | | |
| Alleyne | 9.2 | 1 | 35 | 3 | | | | |

| WARWICKS | O | M | R | W | O | M | R | W |
|---|---|---|---|---|---|---|---|---|
| Donald | 13 | 6 | 27 | 1 | 10 | 3 | 33 | 5 |
| Small | 15 | 5 | 46 | 3 | 10 | 2 | 34 | 0 |
| Smith | 12.4 | 3 | 28 | 5 | 8.3 | 2 | 28 | 4 |
| Munton | 10 | 3 | 25 | 1 | 14 | 3 | 51 | 1 |
| Lloyd | 2 | 2 | 0 | 0 | | | | |
| Booth | 2 | 1 | 1 | 0 | 9 | 0 | 38 | 0 |

| FALL OF WICKETS | WAR | GLO | GLO | WAR |
|---|---|---|---|---|
| 1st | 0 | 4 | 4 | 6 |
| 2nd | 82 | 12 | 8 | |
| 3rd | 92 | 64 | 47 | |
| 4th | 171 | 66 | 49 | |
| 5th | 250 | 85 | 49 | |
| 6th | 306 | 96 | 50 | |
| 7th | 310 | 96 | 50 | |
| 8th | 313 | 121 | 75 | |
| 9th | 313 | 122 | 179 | |
| 10th | 318 | 134 | 200 | |

## BRITANNIC ASS. CHAMPIONSHIP

### YORKSHIRE vs. NORTHANTS

at Headingley on 25th, 27th, 28th May 1991
Toss : Yorkshire.  Umpires : R.C.Tolchard and P.B.Wight
Match drawn.  Yorkshire 4 pts (Bt: 3, Bw: 1), Northants 6 pts (Bt: 2, Bw: 4)
100 overs scores : Yorkshire 272 for 9

**YORKSHIRE**

| | | | | | |
|---|---|---|---|---|---|
| M.D.Moxon * | c Ripley b Curran | 108 | b Capel | | 42 |
| A.A.Metcalfe | c Ripley b Capel | 27 | b Roberts | | 53 |
| D.Byas | b Penberthy | 5 | not out | | 40 |
| R.J.Blakey + | c Curran b Hughes | 3 | | | |
| P.E.Robinson | lbw b Capel | 5 | (4) lbw b Curran | | 21 |
| S.A.Kellett | lbw b Bailey | 53 | (5) c Thomas b Curran | | 5 |
| P.Carrick | lbw b Thomas | 23 | (6) not out | | 31 |
| P.J.Hartley | b Thomas | 0 | | | |
| J.D.Batty | c Curran b Thomas | 31 | | | |
| S.D.Fletcher | lbw b Capel | 2 | | | |
| M.A.Robinson | not out | 1 | | | |
| Extras | (b 1,lb 16,w 2) | 19 | (b 3,lb 4) | | 7 |
| TOTAL | | 277 | (for 4 wkts dec) | | 199 |

**NORTHANTS**

| | | | | | |
|---|---|---|---|---|---|
| A.Fordham | c Metcalfe b Fletcher | 33 | b Hartley | | 33 |
| N.A.Felton | c Batty b Moxon | 43 | c Metcalfe b Carrick | | 32 |
| R.J.Bailey * | b Fletcher | 50 | c Blakey b Robinson M.A. | | 6 |
| D.J.Capel | not out | 69 | lbw b Carrick | | 9 |
| K.M.Curran | c Moxon b Batty | 1 | not out | | 28 |
| A.L.Penberthy | not out | 2 | c Robinson P.E. b Carrick | | 4 |
| D.Ripley + | | | (8) b Hartley | | 8 |
| J.G.Thomas | | | (7) c Kellett b Carrick | | 0 |
| W.M.Noon | | | b Hartley | | 0 |
| A.R.Roberts | | | not out | | 9 |
| J.G.Hughes | | | | | |
| Extras | (lb 7,w 1,nb 5) | 13 | (lb 5,nb 4) | | 9 |
| TOTAL | (for 4 wkts dec) | 211 | (for 8 wkts) | | 138 |

| NORTHANTS | O | M | R | W | O | M | R | W | | FALL OF WICKETS | | | |
|---|---|---|---|---|---|---|---|---|---|---|---|---|---|
| | | | | | | | | | | YOR | NOR | YOR | NOR |
| Thomas | 21.1 | 3 | 48 | 3 | 6 | 0 | 9 | 0 | 1st | 68 | 68 | 92 | 49 |
| Penberthy | 15 | 3 | 54 | 1 | 7 | 0 | 32 | 0 | 2nd | 87 | 100 | 100 | 68 |
| Roberts | 17 | 4 | 36 | 0 | 6 | 0 | 45 | 1 | 3rd | 101 | 195 | 139 | 82 |
| Capel | 21 | 5 | 45 | 3 | 8 | 0 | 32 | 1 | 4th | 124 | 198 | 151 | 89 |
| Curran | 11 | 3 | 24 | 1 | 6.5 | 1 | 41 | 2 | 5th | 169 | | | 101 |
| Hughes | 12 | 1 | 43 | 1 | | | | | 6th | 210 | | | 101 |
| Bailey | 4 | 0 | 10 | 1 | 7 | 1 | 33 | 0 | 7th | 210 | | | 124 |
| | | | | | | | | | 8th | 256 | | | 124 |
| YORKSHIRE | O | M | R | W | O | M | R | W | 9th | 267 | | | |
| Fletcher | 19.3 | 3 | 41 | 2 | 5 | 0 | 28 | 0 | 10th | 277 | | | |
| Hartley | 16 | 5 | 35 | 0 | 16.5 | 5 | 34 | 3 | | | | | |
| Carrick | 18 | 5 | 36 | 0 | 19 | 9 | 25 | 4 | | | | | |
| Robinson M.A. | 12 | 2 | 29 | 0 | 9 | 2 | 28 | 1 | | | | | |
| Moxon | 4 | 1 | 10 | 1 | | | | | | | | | |
| Batty | 16 | 2 | 53 | 1 | 10 | 4 | 18 | 0 | | | | | |

### Britannic Assurance League Table
### as at 28th May 1991

| | | P | W | L | D | T | Bt | Bl | Pts |
|---|---|---|---|---|---|---|---|---|---|
| 1 | Warwickshire (5) | 5 | 3 | 1 | 1 | 0 | 13 | 16 | 77 |
| 2 | Kent (16) | 5 | 2 | 0 | 3 | 0 | 15 | 12 | 59 |
| 3 | Essex (2) | 4 | 2 | 0 | 2 | 0 | 13 | 12 | 57 |
| 4 | Surrey (9) | 4 | 2 | 1 | 1 | 0 | 10 | 11 | 53 |
| 5 | Notts (13) | 4 | 1 | 0 | 3 | 0 | 14 | 15 | 45 |
| 6 | Sussex (17) | 5 | 1 | 0 | 4 | 0 | 19 | 9 | 44 |
| 7 | Glamorgan (8) | 5 | 1 | 1 | 3 | 0 | 12 | 14 | 42 |
| 8 | Gloucs (13) | 4 | 1 | 1 | 2 | 0 | 10 | 8 | 34 |
| 9 | Northants (11) | 5 | 0 | 1 | 4 | 0 | 12 | 12 | 24 |
| 10 | Lancashire (6) | 4 | 0 | 1 | 3 | 0 | 12 | 11 | 23 |
| 11 | Somerset (15) | 4 | 0 | 1 | 3 | 0 | 11 | 10 | 21 |
| | Yorkshire (10) | 5 | 0 | 1 | 4 | 0 | 12 | 9 | 21 |
| | Hampshire (3) | 4 | 0 | 2 | 2 | 0 | 10 | 11 | 21 |
| 14 | Derbyshire (12) | 4 | 0 | 1 | 3 | 0 | 8 | 11 | 19 |
| 15 | Middlesex (1) | 4 | 0 | 1 | 3 | 0 | 10 | 8 | 18 |
| 16 | Leicestershire (7) | 4 | 0 | 1 | 3 | 0 | 7 | 9 | 16 |
| 17 | Worcestershire (4) | 2 | 0 | 0 | 2 | 0 | 6 | 3 | 9 |

## OTHER FIRST-CLASS MATCH

### OXFORD U vs. WORCESTERSHIRE

at The Parks on 25th, 27th, 28th May 1991
Toss : Oxford U.  Umpires : R.Palmer and R.A.White
Worcestershire won by an innings and 122 runs

**OXFORD U**

| | | | | | |
|---|---|---|---|---|---|
| R.R.Montgomerie | lbw b Newport | 0 | c Bevins b Newport | | 10 |
| J.Morris | c Leatherdale b Newport | 15 | (3) b Moody | | 28 |
| C.Gupte | c Moody b Newport | 0 | (2) b Lampitt | | 15 |
| G.Lovell | c Bevins b Newport | 8 | c Moody b Lampitt | | 7 |
| G.J.Turner * | b Lampitt | 24 | c Moody b Lampitt | | 99 |
| D.Pfaff | c Bevins b Stemp | 46 | run out | | 11 |
| M.J.Russell | lbw b Lampitt | 0 | b Curtis | | 25 |
| D.Sandiford + | b Stemp | 1 | c Leatherdale b Lampitt | | 0 |
| H.Davies | not out | 6 | c Weston b Lampitt | | 38 |
| R.MacDonald | b Lampitt | 8 | not out | | 3 |
| B.Wood | b Lampitt | 0 | c Bevins b Lampitt | | 0 |
| Extras | (b 5,lb 4,nb 2) | 11 | (b 7,lb 1,w 1,nb 4) | | 13 |
| TOTAL | | 119 | | | 249 |

**WORCESTERSHIRE**

| | | | |
|---|---|---|---|
| T.S.Curtis * | st Sandiford b Davies | | 67 |
| G.J.Lord | c Morris b MacDonald | | 21 |
| T.M.Moody | c Pfaff b Turner | | 20 |
| D.B.D'Oliveira | c Lovell b Turner | | 237 |
| M.J.Weston | c Montgomerie b Davies | | 1 |
| D.A.Leatherdale | c Lovell b Wood | | 94 |
| P.J.Newport | c Sandiford b MacDonald | | 13 |
| S.R.Lampitt | lbw b Wood | | 23 |
| C.M.Tolley | not out | | 7 |
| S.R.Bevins + | | | |
| R.D.Stemp | | | |
| Extras | (b 1,lb 4,w 1,nb 1) | | 7 |
| TOTAL | (for 8 wkts dec) | | 490 |

| WORCS | O | M | R | W | O | M | R | W |
|---|---|---|---|---|---|---|---|---|
| Newport | 11 | 3 | 27 | 4 | 21 | 7 | 43 | 1 |
| Tolley | 6 | 2 | 10 | 0 | 9 | 3 | 18 | 0 |
| Weston | 7 | 1 | 25 | 0 | | | | |
| Lampitt | 10 | 0 | 39 | 4 | 27 | 2 | 85 | 5 |
| Stemp | 7 | 1 | 9 | 2 | 24 | 12 | 34 | 0 |
| D'Oliveira | | | | | 11 | 5 | 19 | 0 |
| Moody | | | | | 15 | 7 | 19 | 1 |
| Leatherdale | | | | | 2 | 0 | 6 | 0 |
| Curtis | | | | | 7 | 1 | 17 | 2 |

| OXFORD U | O | M | R | W | O | M | R | W |
|---|---|---|---|---|---|---|---|---|
| MacDonald | 30 | 8 | 103 | 2 | | | | |
| Wood | 19.5 | 3 | 79 | 2 | | | | |
| Turner | 23 | 2 | 106 | 2 | | | | |
| Davies | 30 | 5 | 144 | 2 | | | | |
| Lovell | 7 | 0 | 53 | 0 | | | | |

| FALL OF WICKETS | | | |
|---|---|---|---|
| | OXF | WOR | OXF |
| WOR | | | |
| 1st | 0 | 40 | 15 |
| 2nd | 1 | 66 | 38 |
| 3rd | 18 | 163 | 53 |
| 4th | 28 | 177 | 88 |
| 5th | 93 | 420 | 115 |
| 6th | 93 | 460 | 174 |
| 7th | 100 | 460 | 176 |
| 8th | 106 | 490 | 225 |
| 9th | 119 | | 249 |
| 10th | 119 | | 249 |

### HEADLINES

**Other first-class match**

**25th - 27th May**

• Worcestershire ended Oxford University's long unbeaten record in first-class cricket that stretched back almost two years with victory by an innings and 22 runs at The Parks. Damian D'Oliveira hit a career best 237 as the visitors raced to a lead of 371, but the students fought bravely in their second innings, Graeme Turner being unfortunate to be dismissed one short of a maiden first-class 100, one of Stuart Lampitt's nine wickets in the match.

• First-class debut: J.Morris (Oxford U).

# TOUR MATCH

## SOMERSET vs. WEST INDIES
at Taunton on 29th, 30th, 31st May 1991
Toss : West Indies. Umpires : B.Hassan and K.E.Palmer
Match drawn

### WEST INDIES

|  | | | | | | |
|---|---|---|---|---|---|---|
| P.V.Simmons | b Graveney | 10 | (2) lbw b Caddick | 51 | | |
| D.L.Haynes * | c Roebuck b Caddick | 1 | (1) retired hurt/ill | 16 | | |
| R.B.Richardson | c Cook b Caddick | 7 | not out | 91 | | |
| B.C.Lara | c & b Trump | 93 | c Cook b Graveney | 50 | | |
| C.L.Hooper | lbw b Hayhurst | 123 | not out | 48 | | |
| A.L.Logie | c Harden b Trump | 48 | | | | |
| M.D.Marshall | c Harden b Hayhurst | 14 | | | | |
| D.Williams + | not out | 14 | | | | |
| C.E.L.Ambrose | not out | 16 | | | | |
| H.A.G.Anthony | | | | | | |
| I.B.A.Allen | | | | | | |
| Extras | (lb 13,nb 3) | 16 | (lb 2,w 2,nb 3) | 7 | | |
| TOTAL | (for 7 wkts dec) | 342 | (for 2 wkts dec) | 263 | | |

### SOMERSET

|  | | | | | |
|---|---|---|---|---|---|
| S.J.Cook | not out | 162 | c Williams b Ambrose | 14 |
| P.M.Roebuck | c Lara b Ambrose | 10 | b Allen | 3 |
| A.N.Hayhurst | lbw b Marshall | 22 | b Ambrose | 5 |
| C.J.Tavare * | lbw b Ambrose | 10 | not out | 109 |
| R.J.Harden | c Williams b Marshall | 7 | c Williams b Marshall | 6 |
| N.D.Burns + | c Hooper b Anthony | 0 | b Hooper | 14 |
| K.H.Macleay | b Simmons | 15 | c Richardson b Allen | 14 |
| R.P.Lefebvre | b Hooper | 5 | (11) not out | 0 |
| H.R.J.Trump | not out | 20 | (8) c Allen b Hooper | 9 |
| A.R.Caddick | | | (9) lbw b Hooper | 0 |
| D.A.Graveney | | | (10) lbw b Anthony | 8 |
| Extras | (b 2,lb 1,nb 16) | 19 | (b 5,lb 1,nb 10) | 16 |
| TOTAL | (for 7 wkts dec) | 270 | (for 9 wkts) | 198 |

### SOMERSET

| Bowler | O | M | R | W | O | M | R | W |
|---|---|---|---|---|---|---|---|---|
| Caddick | 20 | 2 | 85 | 2 | 12 | 0 | 68 | 1 |
| Lefebvre | 12 | 3 | 27 | 0 | | | | |
| Hayhurst | 10 | 2 | 42 | 2 | 4 | 0 | 23 | 0 |
| Macleay | 11 | 3 | 32 | 0 | 7 | 0 | 33 | 0 |
| Graveney | 21 | 3 | 68 | 1 | 14 | 2 | 51 | 1 |
| Trump | 20 | 2 | 69 | 2 | 14 | 0 | 86 | 0 |
| Roebuck | 2 | 1 | 6 | 0 | | | | |

### WEST INDIES

| Bowler | O | M | R | W | O | M | R | W |
|---|---|---|---|---|---|---|---|---|
| Ambrose | 18 | 7 | 35 | 2 | 18 | 7 | 35 | 2 |
| Allen | 15.4 | 1 | 71 | 0 | 12 | 1 | 61 | 2 |
| Marshall | 15 | 4 | 35 | 2 | 8 | 0 | 35 | 1 |
| Anthony | 16 | 0 | 72 | 1 | 9 | 5 | 34 | 1 |
| Hooper | 16 | 1 | 38 | 1 | 19 | 7 | 27 | 3 |
| Simmons | 7 | 1 | 16 | 1 | | | | |

### FALL OF WICKETS

| | WI | SOM | WI | SOM |
|---|---|---|---|---|
| 1st | 7 | 45 | 95 | 16 |
| 2nd | 21 | 94 | 178 | 20 |
| 3rd | 71 | 141 | | 26 |
| 4th | 158 | 159 | | 46 |
| 5th | 265 | 160 | | 109 |
| 6th | 298 | 199 | | 131 |
| 7th | 313 | 214 | | 140 |
| 8th | | | | 156 |
| 9th | | | | 192 |
| 10th | | | | |

## HEADLINES

### Tetley Bitter Challenge

### 29th - 31st May

• West Indies were denied victory over Somerset at Taunton when Brian Lara dropped last man Roland Lefebvre in the final over of the match. Competition for places in the Test middle-order was hotting up as Carl Hooper scored his first century in England, Lara 93 and 50, and Richie Richardson 91 not out before West Indies left the home side 336 to win. Not such goood news for the tourists was the reccurrence of Desmond Haynes's back trouble which could have left them without either of their premier opening batsmen in the First Test. For Somerset, Jimmy Cook relished his first opportunity to play against the official West Indian side, hitting his first 100 of the season, and Chris Tavare's unbeaten 109 deserved to bring his side to safety, which, with Lara's assistance, it did.

• First-class début: A.R.Caddick (Somerset).

## LEADING FIRST-CLASS AVERAGES

BATTING AVERAGES Qualifying requirements : 4 completed innings

| Name | Matches | Inns | NO | Runs | HS | Avge | 100s | 50s |
|---|---|---|---|---|---|---|---|---|
| H.Morris | 6 | 10 | 3 | 643 | 156 * | 91.85 | 3 | 1 |
| A.P.Wells | 5 | 8 | 2 | 547 | 153 * | 91.16 | 3 | 1 |
| C.L.Smith | 5 | 8 | 0 | 716 | 200 | 89.50 | 4 | 1 |
| M.R.Benson | 5 | 8 | 0 | 624 | 257 | 78.00 | 2 | 2 |
| P.V.Simmons | 3 | 6 | 1 | 360 | 136 | 72.00 | 2 | 1 |
| C.L.Hooper | 3 | 5 | 1 | 271 | 123 | 67.75 | 1 | - |
| B.C.Broad | 4 | 8 | 0 | 538 | 166 | 67.25 | 1 | 4 |
| M.A.Atherton | 4 | 6 | 1 | 336 | 138 | 67.20 | 2 | 1 |
| M.W.Gatting | 5 | 8 | 2 | 389 | 180 | 64.83 | 2 | - |
| D.M.Smith | 5 | 8 | 1 | 445 | 126 * | 63.57 | 1 | 4 |
| P.Johnson | 5 | 9 | 3 | 376 | 97 * | 62.66 | - | 3 |
| T.M.Moody | 4 | 5 | 1 | 248 | 135 | 62.00 | 1 | 1 |
| D.W.Randall | 4 | 7 | 2 | 304 | 104 | 60.80 | 1 | 1 |
| J.P.Stephenson | 5 | 8 | 2 | 361 | 85 | 60.16 | - | 3 |
| M.Azharuddin | 5 | 7 | 2 | 295 | 116 * | 59.00 | 1 | 1 |
| N.H.Fairbrother | 4 | 6 | 1 | 293 | 121 | 58.60 | 2 | - |
| J.E.Morris | 5 | 6 | 0 | 345 | 131 | 57.50 | 1 | 2 |
| C.W.J.Athey | 5 | 8 | 1 | 395 | 127 | 56.42 | 2 | 2 |
| G.Fowler | 5 | 9 | 1 | 435 | 113 | 54.37 | 2 | 2 |
| G.R.Cowdrey | 5 | 8 | 2 | 316 | 109 * | 52.66 | 1 | 1 |

BOWLING AVERAGES
Qualifying requirements : 10 wickets taken

| Name | Overs | Mdns | Runs | Wkts | Avge | Best | 5wI | 10wM |
|---|---|---|---|---|---|---|---|---|
| A.A.Donald | 134 | 28 | 367 | 29 | 12.65 | 5-33 | 5 | 2 |
| Waqar Younis | 104.5 | 25 | 291 | 22 | 13.22 | 6-65 | 4 | 2 |
| P.Carrick | 93.5 | 38 | 161 | 10 | 16.10 | 4-25 | - | - |
| D.V.Lawrence | 64.1 | 11 | 179 | 11 | 16.27 | 6-77 | 2 | 1 |
| P.A.Smith | 67.1 | 11 | 189 | 11 | 17.18 | 5-28 | 1 | - |
| K.T.Medlycott | 114.5 | 38 | 301 | 17 | 17.70 | 6-98 | 2 | 1 |
| A.C.S.Pigott | 122 | 37 | 297 | 14 | 21.21 | 5-37 | 1 | - |
| D.R.Pringle | 137 | 41 | 298 | 14 | 21.28 | 5-70 | 1 | - |
| G.R.Dilley | 74.4 | 16 | 226 | 10 | 22.60 | 5-91 | 1 | - |
| K.P.Evans | 117 | 27 | 317 | 14 | 22.64 | 5-52 | 1 | - |
| M.Frost | 106 | 17 | 273 | 12 | 22.75 | 3-29 | - | - |
| N.A.Foster | 190.4 | 43 | 528 | 23 | 22.95 | 5-80 | 1 | - |
| O.H.Mortensen | 110 | 28 | 255 | 11 | 23.18 | 4-46 | - | - |
| S.L.Watkin | 217.4 | 48 | 580 | 25 | 23.20 | 6-55 | 2 | - |
| L.Tennant | 68 | 14 | 257 | 11 | 23.36 | 4-54 | - | - |
| S.Bastien | 107 | 40 | 234 | 10 | 23.40 | 5-39 | 1 | - |
| P.A.J.DeFreitas | 129.3 | 33 | 379 | 16 | 23.68 | 6-88 | 1 | - |
| C.Penn | 121.5 | 10 | 409 | 17 | 24.05 | 4-48 | - | - |
| D.J.Foster | 115.2 | 19 | 374 | 15 | 24.93 | 6-84 | 1 | - |
| P.J.Hartley | 119.4 | 31 | 305 | 12 | 25.41 | 3-34 | - | - |

# BENSON & HEDGES CUP – QUARTER-FINALS

## ESSEX vs. HAMPSHIRE

at Chelmsford on 29th May 1991
Toss : Hampshire. Umpires : M.J.Kitchen and R.A.White
Essex won by 32 runs
Man of the match: T.D.Topley

**ESSEX**

| | | |
|---|---|---|
| G.A.Gooch * | lbw b James | 29 |
| J.P.Stephenson | run out | 38 |
| P.J.Prichard | b Connor | 2 |
| Salim Malik | c Smith R.A. b Aqib Javed | 38 |
| N.Hussain | c Aymes b Bakker | 17 |
| D.R.Pringle | c Aymes b Udal | 3 |
| N.Shahid | st Aymes b Udal | 42 |
| M.A.Garnham + | b Udal | 11 |
| N.A.Foster | b Aqib Javed | 5 |
| T.D.Topley | not out | 6 |
| P.M.Such | b Connor | 4 |
| Extras | (lb 8,w 16,nb 3) | 28 |
| TOTAL | (55 overs) | 223 |

**HAMPSHIRE**

| | | |
|---|---|---|
| V.P.Terry | c & b Topley | 10 |
| C.L.Smith | b Foster | 71 |
| D.I.Gower | lbw b Gooch | 18 |
| R.A.Smith | c Garnham b Topley | 35 |
| M.C.J.Nicholas * | not out | 22 |
| K.D.James | c Gooch b Topley | 2 |
| A.N Aymes + | c Garnham b Topley | 2 |
| S.D.Udal | b Pringle | 9 |
| C.A.Connor | run out | 0 |
| P.J.Bakker | c Stephenson b Pringle | 4 |
| Aqib Javed | b Gooch | 3 |
| Extras | (lb 8,w 2,nb 5) | 15 |
| TOTAL | (53.5 overs) | 191 |

| HAMPSHIRE | O | M | R | W | FALL OF WICKETS | | |
|---|---|---|---|---|---|---|---|
| | | | | | | ESS | HAM |
| Bakker | 11 | 0 | 34 | 1 | | | |
| Aqib Javed | 11 | 1 | 49 | 2 | 1st | 56 | 27 |
| Connor | 11 | 1 | 45 | 2 | 2nd | 60 | 72 |
| James | 11 | 0 | 45 | 1 | 3rd | 110 | 142 |
| Udal | 11 | 1 | 41 | 3 | 4th | 132 | 146 |
| | | | | | 5th | 135 | 153 |
| ESSEX | O | M | R | W | 6th | 175 | 156 |
| Foster | 11 | 3 | 24 | 1 | 7th | 204 | 176 |
| Pringle | 10 | 2 | 36 | 2 | 8th | 205 | 176 |
| Topley | 11 | 3 | 41 | 4 | 9th | 214 | 183 |
| Gooch | 10.5 | 1 | 42 | 2 | 10th | 223 | 191 |
| Such | 11 | 1 | 40 | 0 | | | |

## LANCASHIRE vs. NORTHANTS

at Old Trafford on 29th May 1991
Toss : Lancashire. Umpires : H.D.Bird and N.T.Plews
Lancashire won by 7 wickets
Man of the match: G.D.Mendis

**NORTHANTS**

| | | |
|---|---|---|
| A.Fordham | c Fairbrother b Allott | 19 |
| N.A.Felton | run out | 44 |
| R.J.Bailey | b Austin | 75 |
| A.J.Lamb * | c Fowler b Allott | 48 |
| D.J.Capel | c Hughes b Watkinson | 19 |
| K.M.Curran | b Wasim Akram | 0 |
| A.L.Penberthy | b Wasim Akram | 3 |
| J.G.Thomas | c DeFreitas b Wasim Akram | 9 |
| D.Ripley + | not out | 6 |
| A.Walker | not out | 0 |
| N.G.B.Cook | | |
| Extras | (b 3,lb 8,w 7,nb 5) | 23 |
| TOTAL | (55 overs)(for 8 wkts) | 246 |

**LANCASHIRE**

| | | |
|---|---|---|
| G.D.Mendis | not out | 125 |
| G.Fowler | c Ripley b Thomas | 9 |
| M.A.Atherton | c Cook b Walker | 56 |
| N.H.Fairbrother | c Lamb b Thomas | 13 |
| M.Watkinson | not out | 32 |
| Wasim Akram | | |
| P.A.J.DeFreitas | | |
| W.K.Hegg + | | |
| D.P.Hughes * | | |
| I.D.Austin | | |
| P.J.W.Allott | | |
| Extras | (lb 4,w 7,nb 1) | 12 |
| TOTAL | (52.4 overs)(for 3 wkts) | 247 |

| LANCASHIRE | O | M | R | W | FALL OF WICKETS | | |
|---|---|---|---|---|---|---|---|
| | | | | | | NOR | LAN |
| DeFreitas | 11 | 0 | 54 | 0 | 1st | 40 | 28 |
| Allott | 11 | 0 | 38 | 2 | 2nd | 101 | 170 |
| Wasim Akram | 11 | 0 | 57 | 3 | 3rd | 182 | 192 |
| Watkinson | 11 | 1 | 46 | 1 | 4th | 219 | |
| Austin | 11 | 0 | 40 | 1 | 5th | 219 | |
| | | | | | 6th | 227 | |
| NORTHANTS | O | M | R | W | 7th | 229 | |
| Thomas | 11 | 0 | 54 | 2 | 8th | 244 | |
| Walker | 9 | 1 | 33 | 1 | 9th | | |
| Capel | 10.4 | 1 | 52 | 0 | 10th | | |
| Cook | 11 | 0 | 40 | 0 | | | |
| Curran | 3 | 0 | 21 | 0 | | | |
| Penberthy | 8 | 0 | 43 | 0 | | | |

# HEADLINES

**Benson & Hedges Cup
Quarter-Finals**

**29th May**

• The four group winners all made good use of home advantage to reach the semi-finals on a day when excitement levels largely matched the continuing cheerless weather.

• On paper, the closest match came at Worcester where Kent came within 27 runs of Worcestershire's massive 308 for five. But despite the visitors' brave efforts, led by Mark Benson and Neil Taylor, the result was virtually a foregone conclusion once Tom Moody had scored his fifth one-day 100 of the season and Graeme Hick had scored 34 from his last nine balls to finish on 84 not out.

• At Old Trafford, Lancashire had 14 balls to spare as they eased to a seven-wicket victory over Northamptonshire, thanks to a career best 125 not out from Gehan Mendis, who added 142 for the second wicket with Michael Atherton. Rob Bailey and Allan Lamb had seen Northants through to a total of 246 for eight, but the visitors never looked likely to contain the champions' powerful batting line-up.

• When Essex managed only 223 against Hampshire at Chelmsford and the Smith brothers had taken the visitors' score to 142 for two the prospects of a home victory looked decidedly remote, but the dismissal of both batsmen in rapid succession was the prelude to a woeful collapse that saw Hampshire's last eight wickets crumple for 49 runs. Essex were victorious by the surprisingly comfortable margin of 32 runs.

• Warwickshire had already beaten Yorkshire twice at Headingley in the past month, and stood at the top of the County Championship, so it was unexpected that they should be defeated by as wide a margin as 122 runs. The home side's batsmen were able to accelerate after lunch, following a watchful beginning against a formidable bowling attack, but when Warwickshire attempted to increase their run-rate against Martyn Moxon and Phil Carrick they came completely unstuck. Both finished with their best figures in the competition, Moxon returning his best analysis for Yorkshire in any form of cricket.

## WORCESTERSHIRE vs. KENT

at Worcester on 29th May 1991
Toss : Worcestershire. Umpires : J.D.Bond and J.H.Harris
Worcestershire won by 27 runs
Man of the match: T.M.Moody

**WORCESTERSHIRE**

| | | |
|---|---|---|
| T.S.Curtis | c Marsh b Igglesden | 53 |
| T.M.Moody | lbw b Fleming | 100 |
| G.A.Hick | not out | 84 |
| D.B.D'Oliveira | run out | 2 |
| P.A.Neale * | c Cowdrey C.S. b Igglesden | 47 |
| S.J.Rhodes + | b Merrick | 8 |
| R.K.Illingworth | not out | 1 |
| P.J.Newport | | |
| S.R.Lampitt | | |
| N.V.Radford | | |
| G.R.Dilley | | |
| Extras | (b 1,lb 7,w 5) | 13 |
| TOTAL | (55 overs)(for 5 wkts) | 308 |

**KENT**

| | | |
|---|---|---|
| M.V.Fleming | c Hick b Radford | 22 |
| M.R.Benson * | st Rhodes b Illingworth | 56 |
| C.S.Cowdrey | b Illingworth | 25 |
| N.R.Taylor | not out | 89 |
| T.R.Ward | c Neale b Newport | 10 |
| G.R.Cowdrey | b Dilley | 8 |
| S.A.Marsh + | c Curtis b Radford | 24 |
| R.M.Ellison | run out | 6 |
| R.P.Davis | c Neale b Lampitt | 1 |
| T.A.Merrick | c Neale b Lampitt | 0 |
| A.P.Igglesden | not out | 26 |
| Extras | (lb 5,w 8,nb 1) | 14 |
| TOTAL | (55 overs)(for 9 wkts) | 281 |

| KENT | O | M | R | W | FALL OF WICKETS | | |
|---|---|---|---|---|---|---|---|
| | | | | | | WOR | KEN |
| Merrick | 11 | 0 | 59 | 1 | | | |
| Igglesden | 11 | 1 | 85 | 2 | 1st | 138 | 47 |
| Ellison | 11 | 0 | 49 | 0 | 2nd | 168 | 110 |
| Davis | 11 | 1 | 62 | 0 | 3rd | 178 | 113 |
| Fleming | 11 | 0 | 45 | 1 | 4th | 263 | 137 |
| | | | | | 5th | 307 | 159 |
| WORCS | O | M | R | W | 6th | | 215 |
| Dilley | 11 | 0 | 72 | 1 | 7th | | 229 |
| Radford | 11 | 1 | 57 | 2 | 8th | | 231 |
| Illingworth | 11 | 1 | 50 | 2 | 9th | | 231 |
| Lampitt | 11 | 0 | 59 | 2 | 10th | | |
| Newport | 11 | 1 | 38 | 1 | | | |

## YORKSHIRE vs. WARWICKSHIRE

at Headingley on 29th May 1991
Toss : Warwicks. Umpires : J.C.Balderstone and B.J.Meyer
Yorkshire won by 122 runs
Man of the match: M.D.Moxon

**YORKSHIRE**

| | | |
|---|---|---|
| M.D.Moxon * | b Smith | 30 |
| A.A.Metcalfe | c Piper b Donald | 3 |
| S.A.Kellett | b Donald | 44 |
| D.Byas | c Reeve b Munton | 58 |
| R.J.Blakey + | b Donald | 15 |
| P.E.Robinson | b Munton | 29 |
| P.W.Jarvis | not out | 12 |
| P.J.Hartley | not out | 1 |
| P.Carrick | | |
| A.Sidebottom | | |
| S.D.Fletcher | | |
| Extras | (b 4,lb 20,w 15,nb 2) | 41 |
| TOTAL | (55 overs)(for 6 wkts) | 233 |

**WARWICKSHIRE**

| | | |
|---|---|---|
| A.J.Moles | c Blakey b Hartley | 10 |
| Asif Din | c Piper b Fletcher | 23 |
| T.A.Lloyd * | c Moxon b Carrick | 24 |
| P.A.Smith | c & b Moxon | 3 |
| D.A.Reeve | c Blakey b Moxon | 0 |
| D.P.Ostler | lbw b Moxon | 8 |
| K.J.Piper + | c & b Moxon | 11 |
| G.C.Small | lbw b Carrick | 2 |
| T.A.Munton | c Hartley b Carrick | 10 |
| A.A.Donald | c Carrick b Moxon | 0 |
| A.R.K.Pierson | not out | 3 |
| Extras | (lb 6,w 9,nb 2) | 17 |
| TOTAL | (42 overs) | 111 |

| WARWICKSHIRE | O | M | R | W | FALL OF WICKETS | | |
|---|---|---|---|---|---|---|---|
| | | | | | | YOR | WAR |
| Munton | 11 | 3 | 37 | 2 | | | |
| Donald | 11 | 1 | 46 | 3 | 1st | 7 | 24 |
| Small | 11 | 1 | 43 | 0 | 2nd | 63 | 44 |
| Reeve | 11 | 0 | 35 | 0 | 3rd | 104 | 59 |
| Smith | 9 | 2 | 41 | 1 | 4th | 157 | 59 |
| Pierson | 2 | 0 | 7 | 0 | 5th | 194 | 75 |
| | | | | | 6th | 224 | 96 |
| YORKSHIRE | O | M | R | W | 7th | | 96 |
| Sidebottom | 9 | 4 | 11 | 0 | 8th | | 101 |
| Jarvis | 5 | 0 | 11 | 0 | 9th | | 106 |
| Hartley | 6 | 2 | 19 | 1 | 10th | | 111 |
| Fletcher | 4 | 1 | 11 | 1 | | | |
| Carrick | 10 | 1 | 22 | 3 | | | |
| Moxon | 8 | 0 | 31 | 5 | | | |

# REFUGE ASSURANCE LEAGUE

## DERBYSHIRE vs. YORKSHIRE

at Chesterfield on 2nd June 1991
Toss : Yorkshire. Umpires : M.J.Kitchen and N.T.Plews
Yorkshire won by 3 wickets. Derby 0 pts, Yorkshire 4 pts

### DERBYSHIRE

| | | |
|---|---|---|
| K.J.Barnett * | c Blakey b Hartley | 9 |
| P.D.Bowler + | c Robinson P.E. b Hartley | 30 |
| J.E.Morris | c Pickles b Hartley | 0 |
| M.Azharuddin | not out | 29 |
| B.Roberts | c Pickles b Fletcher | 9 |
| A.E.Warner | run out | 23 |
| T.J.G.O'Gorman | | |
| C.J.Adams | | |
| S.J.Base | | |
| D.E.Malcolm | | |
| D.G.Cork | | |
| Extras | (lb 4,w 1) | 5 |
| TOTAL | (10 overs)(for 5 wkts) | 105 |

### YORKSHIRE

| | | |
|---|---|---|
| M.D.Moxon * | c & b Warner | 20 |
| A.A.Metcalfe | c O'Gorman b Roberts | 0 |
| R.J.Blakey + | c Malcolm b Cork | 7 |
| D.Byas | c & b Malcolm | 14 |
| P.E.Robinson | not out | 57 |
| C.S.Pickles | run out | 0 |
| D.Gough | run out | 0 |
| P.J.Hartley | run out | 0 |
| S.A.Kellett | not out | 0 |
| S.D.Fletcher | | |
| M.A.Robinson | | |
| Extras | (b 1,lb 2,w 5) | 8 |
| TOTAL | (9.5 overs)(for 7 wkts) | 106 |

| YORKSHIRE | O | M | R | W | FALL OF WICKETS | | |
|---|---|---|---|---|---|---|---|
| | | | | | | DER | YOR |
| Robinson M.A. | 2 | 0 | 33 | 0 | | | |
| Pickles | 2 | 0 | 25 | 0 | 1st | 28 | 2 |
| Hartley | 2 | 0 | 6 | 3 | 2nd | 28 | 16 |
| Gough | 2 | 0 | 20 | 0 | 3rd | 50 | 34 |
| Fletcher | 2 | 0 | 17 | 1 | 4th | 80 | 72 |
| | | | | | 5th | 105 | 72 |
| DERBYSHIRE | O | M | R | W | 6th | | 82 |
| Roberts | 2 | 0 | 27 | 1 | 7th | | 92 |
| Cork | 2 | 0 | 15 | 1 | 8th | | |
| Base | 2 | 0 | 15 | 0 | 9th | | |
| Warner | 1.5 | 0 | 27 | 1 | 10th | | |
| Malcolm | 2 | 0 | 19 | 1 | | | |

## LANCASHIRE vs. SUSSEX

at Old Trafford on 2nd June 1991
Toss : Sussex. Umpires : J.C.Balderstone and J.D.Bond
Lancashire won by 53 runs. Lancashire 4 pts, Sussex 0 pts

### LANCASHIRE

| | | |
|---|---|---|
| G.Fowler | b Jones | 22 |
| G.D.Lloyd | c Moores b Pigott | 22 |
| N.H.Fairbrother | c Wells C.M. b Bunting | 12 |
| M.Watkinson | c Salisbury b Jones | 83 |
| Wasim Akram | c Jones b Wells C.M. | 14 |
| P.A.J.DeFreitas | c Speight b Jones | 19 |
| M.A.Atherton | not out | 1 |
| W.K.Hegg + | | |
| D.P.Hughes * | | |
| I.D.Austin | | |
| P.J.W.Allott | | |
| Extras | (b 1,lb 1,w 1) | 3 |
| TOTAL | (18 overs)(for 6 wkts) | 176 |

### SUSSEX

| | | |
|---|---|---|
| K.Greenfield | run out | 6 |
| P.W.G.Parker * | c Fairbrother b Watkinson | 28 |
| A.P.Wells | c Hughes b DeFreitas | 1 |
| M.P.Speight | c Watkinson b DeFreitas | 39 |
| N.J.Lenham | not out | 24 |
| C.M.Wells | b Austin | 3 |
| P.Moores + | c Watkinson b DeFreitas | 4 |
| A.C.S.Pigott | c Austin b Watkinson | 5 |
| I.D.K.Salisbury | c Wasim Akram b Watkinson | 0 |
| R.A.Bunting | run out | 0 |
| A.N.Jones | not out | 6 |
| Extras | (lb 3,w 4) | 7 |
| TOTAL | (18 overs)(for 9 wkts) | 123 |

| SUSSEX | O | M | R | W | FALL OF WICKETS | | |
|---|---|---|---|---|---|---|---|
| | | | | | | LAN | SUS |
| Wells C.M. | 3 | 0 | 31 | 1 | 1st | 33 | 17 |
| Jones | 4 | 0 | 39 | 3 | 2nd | 49 | 20 |
| Bunting | 4 | 0 | 43 | 1 | 3rd | 75 | 68 |
| Pigott | 4 | 0 | 21 | 1 | 4th | 139 | 81 |
| Salisbury | 2 | 0 | 24 | 0 | 5th | 174 | 86 |
| Greenfield | 1 | 0 | 16 | 0 | 6th | 176 | 91 |
| LANCASHIRE | O | M | R | W | 7th | | 105 |
| Allott | 3 | 0 | 23 | 0 | 8th | | 106 |
| DeFreitas | 4 | 0 | 28 | 3 | 9th | | 107 |
| Wasim Akram | 4 | 0 | 22 | 0 | 10th | | |
| Watkinson | 3 | 0 | 27 | 3 | | | |
| Austin | 4 | 0 | 20 | 1 | | | |

## NORTHANTS vs. HAMPSHIRE

at Northampton on 2nd June 1991
Toss : Hampshire. Umpires : K.J.Lyons and R.A.White
Northants won by 99 runs. Northants 4 pts, Hants 0 pts

### NORTHANTS

| | | |
|---|---|---|
| A.Fordham | c Connor b Udal | 41 |
| N.A.Felton | b Bakker | 69 |
| A.J.Lamb * | c Nicholas b Ayling | 61 |
| D.J.Capel | not out | 30 |
| R.J.Bailey | b Udal | 47 |
| K.M.Curran | not out | 2 |
| A.L.Penberthy | | |
| D.Ripley + | | |
| J.G.Thomas | | |
| A.R.Roberts | | |
| A.Walker | | |
| Extras | (b 4,lb 14,w 11,nb 1) | 30 |
| TOTAL | (36 overs)(for 4 wkts) | 280 |

### HAMPSHIRE

| | | |
|---|---|---|
| V.P.Terry | c Lamb b Thomas | 14 |
| T.C.Middleton | c Fordham b Curran | 56 |
| R.A.Smith | c Roberts b Thomas | 2 |
| M.C.J.Nicholas * | b Walker | 1 |
| C.L.Smith | b Penberthy | 19 |
| J.R.Ayling | c Fordham b Curran | 4 |
| A.N.Aymes + | not out | 33 |
| S.D.Udal | c Fordham b Roberts | 13 |
| C.A.Connor | c Capel b Roberts | 18 |
| P.J.Bakker | b Roberts | 4 |
| Aqib Javed | not out | 1 |
| Extras | (b 4,lb 6,w 6) | 16 |
| TOTAL | (36 overs)(for 9 wkts) | 181 |

| HAMPSHIRE | O | M | R | W | FALL OF WICKETS | | |
|---|---|---|---|---|---|---|---|
| | | | | | | NOR | HAM |
| Bakker | 8 | 0 | 53 | 1 | 1st | 101 | 22 |
| Aqib Javed | 7 | 0 | 50 | 0 | 2nd | 166 | 28 |
| Connor | 8 | 0 | 60 | 0 | 3rd | 203 | 32 |
| Ayling | 7 | 0 | 52 | 1 | 4th | 278 | 70 |
| Udal | 6 | 0 | 47 | 2 | 5th | | 87 |
| NORTHANTS | O | M | R | W | 6th | | 108 |
| Walker | 7 | 0 | 24 | 1 | 7th | | 140 |
| Thomas | 5 | 0 | 20 | 2 | 8th | | 170 |
| Curran | 7 | 0 | 30 | 2 | 9th | | 180 |
| Penberthy | 8 | 0 | 45 | 1 | 10th | | |
| Roberts | 6 | 0 | 26 | 3 | | | |
| Bailey | 3 | 0 | 26 | 0 | | | |

## GLAMORGAN vs. ESSEX

at Pontypridd on 2nd June 1991
Toss : Essex. Umpires : J.W.Holder and R.Palmer
No result. Glamorgan 2 pts, Essex 2 pts

### GLAMORGAN

| | | |
|---|---|---|
| A.R.Butcher * | c Prichard b Andrew | 14 |
| H.Morris | c Garnham b Andrew | 3 |
| M.P.Maynard | b Andrew | 6 |
| R.J.Shastri | c Gooch b Stephenson | 22 |
| I.Smith | c Garnham b Topley | 8 |
| A.Dale | run out | 2 |
| J.Derrick | b Pringle | 25 |
| C.P.Metson + | not out | 6 |
| S.L.Watkin | | |
| S.R.Barwick | | |
| S.Bastien | | |
| Extras | (lb 5,w 7,nb 1) | 13 |
| TOTAL | (27.3 overs)(for 7 wkts) | 99 |

### ESSEX

| | | |
|---|---|---|
| G.A.Gooch * | | |
| J.P.Stephenson | | |
| P.J.Prichard | | |
| N.Hussain | | |
| N.Shahid | | |
| D.R.Pringle | | |
| M.A.Garnham + | | |
| N.A.Foster | | |
| T.D.Topley | | |
| S.J.W.Andrew | | |
| P.M.Such | | |
| Extras | | |
| TOTAL | | |

| ESSEX | O | M | R | W | FALL OF WICKETS | | |
|---|---|---|---|---|---|---|---|
| | | | | | | GLA | ESS |
| Andrew | 8 | 1 | 33 | 3 | 1st | 16 | |
| Pringle | 5.3 | 0 | 26 | 1 | 2nd | 27 | |
| Gooch | 5 | 1 | 11 | 0 | 3rd | 29 | |
| Topley | 6 | 1 | 16 | 1 | 4th | 52 | |
| Stephenson | 3 | 1 | 8 | 1 | 5th | 66 | |
| GLAMORGAN | O | M | R | W | 6th | 66 | |
| | | | | | 7th | 99 | |
| | | | | | 8th | | |
| | | | | | 9th | | |
| | | | | | 10th | | |

## MIDDLESEX vs. KENT

at Southgate on 2nd June 1991
Toss : Kent. Umpires : B.Dudleston and P.B.Wight
Kent won by 21 runs. Middlesex 0 pts, Kent 4 pts

### KENT

| | | |
|---|---|---|
| M.V.Fleming | c Roseberry b Ellcock | 2 |
| M.R.Benson * | c Farbrace b Fraser | 78 |
| N.R.Taylor | c Ramprakash b Emburey | 66 |
| T.R.Ward | c Williams b Emburey | 55 |
| G.R.Cowdrey | c Farbrace b Cowans | 9 |
| C.S.Cowdrey | not out | 38 |
| S.A.Marsh + | c Farbrace b Williams | 2 |
| M.A.Ealham | not out | 6 |
| R.P.Davis | | |
| T.A.Merrick | | |
| A.P.Igglesden | | |
| Extras | (b 8,lb 12) | 20 |
| TOTAL | (40 overs)(for 6 wkts) | 276 |

### MIDDLESEX

| | | |
|---|---|---|
| M.W.Gatting * | run out | 15 |
| M.A.Roseberry | c Marsh b Fleming | 79 |
| M.R.Ramprakash | lbw b Igglesden | 47 |
| K.R.Brown | c Fleming b Merrick | 34 |
| M.Keech | lbw b Igglesden | 4 |
| J.E.Emburey | c Cowdrey G.R. b Ealham | 5 |
| N.F.Williams | run out | 27 |
| P.Farbrace + | b Ealham | 6 |
| N.G.Cowans | b Fleming | 1 |
| R.M.Ellcock | not out | 8 |
| A.R.C.Fraser | not out | 8 |
| Extras | (lb 15,w 5,nb 1) | 21 |
| TOTAL | (40 overs)(for 9 wkts) | 255 |

| MIDDLESEX | O | M | R | W | FALL OF WICKETS | | |
|---|---|---|---|---|---|---|---|
| | | | | | | KEN | MID |
| Ellcock | 6 | 0 | 33 | 1 | 1st | 2 | 43 |
| Cowans | 8 | 1 | 49 | 1 | 2nd | 137 | 126 |
| Williams | 6 | 0 | 55 | 1 | 3rd | 178 | 188 |
| Fraser | 8 | 0 | 44 | 1 | 4th | 214 | 196 |
| Emburey | 8 | 0 | 48 | 2 | 5th | 235 | 199 |
| Ramprakash | 4 | 0 | 27 | 0 | 6th | 256 | 203 |
| KENT | O | M | R | W | 7th | | 230 |
| Igglesden | 8 | 1 | 37 | 2 | 8th | | 235 |
| Merrick | 8 | 0 | 41 | 1 | 9th | | 242 |
| Davis | 8 | 0 | 48 | 0 | 10th | | |
| Ealham | 8 | 0 | 56 | 2 | | | |
| Fleming | 8 | 0 | 58 | 2 | | | |

## WARWICKSHIRE vs. SOMERSET

at Edgbaston on 2nd June 1991
Toss : Warwicks. Umpires : J.H.Hampshire and A.A.Jones
No result. Warwickshire 2 pts, Somerset 2 pts

### SOMERSET

| | | |
|---|---|---|
| S.J.Cook | b Reeve | 67 |
| R.J.Bartlett | run out | 7 |
| C.J.Tavare * | c Benjamin b Smith P.A. | 59 |
| G.D.Rose | c Benjamin b Smith P.A. | 2 |
| R.J.Harden | c Benjamin b Smith P.A. | 13 |
| N.D.Burns + | c & b Smith P.A. | 2 |
| A.N.Hayhurst | not out | 12 |
| R.P.Lefebvre | b Small | 4 |
| K.H.Macleay | not out | 1 |
| N.A.Mallender | | |
| D.A.Graveney | | |
| Extras | (lb 6,w 3) | 9 |
| TOTAL | (32 overs)(for 7 wkts) | 176 |

### WARWICKSHIRE

| | | |
|---|---|---|
| R.G.Twose | | |
| A.J.Moles | | |
| T.A.Lloyd * | | |
| P.A.Smith | | |
| D.P.Ostler | | |
| D.A.Reeve | | |
| K.J.Piper + | | |
| N.M.K.Smith | | |
| G.C.Small | | |
| J.E.Benjamin | | |
| A.A.Donald | | |
| Extras | | |
| TOTAL | | |

| WARWICKS | O | M | R | W | FALL OF WICKETS | | |
|---|---|---|---|---|---|---|---|
| | | | | | | SOM | WAR |
| Donald | 8 | 1 | 21 | 0 | 1st | 28 | |
| Benjamin | 7 | 0 | 29 | 0 | 2nd | 124 | |
| Reeve | 8 | 0 | 60 | 1 | 3rd | 127 | |
| Small | 6 | 0 | 39 | 1 | 4th | 149 | |
| Smith P.A. | 3 | 0 | 21 | 4 | 5th | 153 | |
| SOMERSET | O | M | R | W | 6th | 167 | |
| | | | | | 7th | 173 | |
| | | | | | 8th | | |
| | | | | | 9th | | |
| | | | | | 10th | | |

# REFUGE ASSURANCE LEAGUE

## WORCESTERSHIRE vs. SURREY

at Worcester on 2nd June 1991
Toss : Surrey.  Umpires : G.I.Burgess and B.Leadbeater
No result.  Worcestershire 2 pts, Surrey 2 pts

**WORCESTERSHIRE**

| | | |
|---|---|---|
| T.S.Curtis | c Lynch b Murphy | 65 |
| T.M.Moody | c Lynch b Murphy | 62 |
| M.J.Weston | c Greig b Waqar Younis | 27 |
| D.B.D'Oliveira | not out | 28 |
| P.A.Neale * | c sub b Feltham | 5 |
| D.A.Leatherdale | not out | 0 |
| S.J.Rhodes + | | |
| P.J.Newport | | |
| R.K.Illingworth | | |
| S.R.Lampitt | | |
| N.V.Radford | | |
| Extras | (lb 5,w 5,nb 2) | 12 |
| TOTAL | (31 overs)(for 4 wkts) | 199 |

**SURREY**

| | | |
|---|---|---|
| M.A.Lynch | not out | 18 |
| M.A.Feltham | not out | 23 |
| A.J.Stewart + | | |
| D.M.Ward | | |
| A.D.Brown | | |
| G.P.Thorpe | | |
| I.A.Greig * | | |
| J.D.Robinson | | |
| C.K.Bullen | | |
| Waqar Younis | | |
| A.J.Murphy | | |
| Extras | (lb 2,w 1,nb 1) | 4 |
| TOTAL | (8 overs)(for 0 wkts) | 45 |

| SURREY | O | M | R | W |
|---|---|---|---|---|
| Feltham | 8 | 1 | 51 | 1 |
| Murphy | 8 | 0 | 58 | 2 |
| Waqar Younis | 8 | 0 | 36 | 1 |
| Robinson | 5 | 0 | 33 | 0 |
| Greig | 2 | 0 | 16 | 0 |

| WORCS | O | M | R | W |
|---|---|---|---|---|
| Weston | 4 | 0 | 16 | 0 |
| Newport | 4 | 0 | 27 | 0 |

| FALL OF WICKETS | WOR | SUR |
|---|---|---|
| 1st | 116 | |
| 2nd | 156 | |
| 3rd | 173 | |
| 4th | 187 | |
| 5th | | |
| 6th | | |
| 7th | | |
| 8th | | |
| 9th | | |
| 10th | | |

Tom Moody was in prolific form for Worcestershire in the Refuge Assurance League.

---

## HEADLINES

### Refuge Assurance League

### 2nd June

• Bad weather affected all but one of the day's matches, three not being completed, including Warwickshire's game with Somerset at Edgbaston. The winners could have joined Nottinghamshire at the top of the table, but after the home side had restricted Somerset to 176 for seven in 32 overs, Paul Smith claiming his best Sunday figures, rain brought an early abandonment.

• Another century partnership between Tim Curtis and Tom Moody was to no avail at Worcester, where Worcestershire's contest against Surrey was also brought to a premature end, while Glamorgan gained their first points of the season when their match against Essex at Pontypridd met the same fate.

• A 10-over match replaced the original game at Chesterfield, and Yorkshire were grateful for the second chance as they beat Derbyshire by three wickets thanks to a last-over assault from Phil Robinson as he completed a thrilling unbeaten 57.

• Although they faced only 18 overs, Lancashire's batsmen rattled up 176 for six against an unfortunate Sussex attack at Old Trafford, Mike Watkinson hitting a career-best 83 and following up with three wickets in his three overs as the home side managed a 53-run victory.

• Middlesex's long-awaited (almost 150 years) return to Southgate was rewarded with a full-length match, a feast of runs, but defeat by 21 runs by Kent who reached 276 for six in their 40 overs, Neil Taylor and Mark Benson adding 135 for the second wicket. Although Middlesex reached 188 for two, their later batsmen found the rate required too formidable a proposition.

• Northamptonshire needed only 36 overs to amass 280 for four at Northampton, the first five in their batting order all making healthy contributions, but Hampshire could do no better than 181 for nine, leg-spinner Andy Roberts making the most of an ideal opportunity by taking three for 26 in Northants' 99-run victory.

# BRITANNIC ASSURANCE CHAMPIONSHIP

## GLOUCS vs. ESSEX
at Bristol on 31st May, 1st June 1991
Toss : Essex. Umpires : J.W.Holder and R.Palmer
Essex won by an innings and 124 runs. Gloucs 3 pts (Bt: 0, Bw: 3), Essex 24 pts (Bt: 4, Bw: 4)
100 overs scores :Essex 412 for 7

### GLOUCS

| | | | | |
|---|---|---|---|---|
| G.D.Hodgson | b Foster | 3 | c Hussain b Childs | 40 |
| R.J.Scott | lbw b Andrew | 13 | lbw b Foster | 15 |
| A.J.Wright * | c Salim Malik b Pringle | 22 | c Topley b Andrew | - 8 |
| C.W.J.Athey | c Salim Malik b Pringle | 10 | lbw b Andrew | 4 |
| M.W.Alleyne | b Topley | 17 | c Garnham b Foster | 46 |
| R.C.Russell + | c Hussain b Topley | 26 | c Foster b Andrew | 3 |
| J.W.Lloyds | c Garnham b Andrew | 4 | c Garnham b Foster | 56 |
| D.V.Lawrence | c Garnham b Andrew | 3 | c sub b Foster | 10 |
| A.M.Smith | lbw b Topley | 9 | b Foster | 4 |
| J.M.De La Pena | not out | 1 | b Topley | 0 |
| A.M.Babington | c Garnham b Topley | 0 | not out | 0 |
| Extras | (b 1,lb 2,nb 7) | 10 | (w 1,nb 4) | 5 |
| TOTAL | | 118 | | 191 |

### ESSEX

| | | |
|---|---|---|
| G.A.Gooch * | b Lawrence | 1 |
| J.P.Stephenson | c Lloyds b Smith | 38 |
| P.J.Prichard | c Russell b De La Pena | 10 |
| N.Hussain | c Russell b Lawrence | 67 |
| M.A.Garnham + | b Babington | 14 |
| D.R.Pringle | lbw b Lawrence | 24 |
| Salim Malik | c Wright b Lawrence | 163 |
| N.A.Foster | run out | 39 |
| T.D.Topley | not out | 50 |
| S.J.W.Andrew | | |
| J.H.Childs | | |
| Extras | (lb 13,nb 14) | 27 |
| TOTAL | (for 8 wkts dec) | 433 |

| ESSEX | O | M | R | W | O | M | R | W |
|---|---|---|---|---|---|---|---|---|
| Foster | 13 | 9 | 13 | 1 | 16 | 4 | 54 | 5 |
| Andrew | 15 | 2 | 51 | 3 | 14 | 2 | 51 | 3 |
| Topley | 10.4 | 0 | 34 | 4 | 7.2 | 1 | 35 | 1 |
| Pringle | 9 | 2 | 17 | 2 | 5 | 3 | 4 | 0 |
| Childs | | | | | 9 | 2 | 47 | 1 |

| GLOUCS | O | M | R | W | O | M | R | W |
|---|---|---|---|---|---|---|---|---|
| Lawrence | 27.2 | 4 | 111 | 4 | | | | |
| Babington | 28 | 3 | 101 | 1 | | | | |
| Smith | 21 | 2 | 68 | 1 | | | | |
| De La Pena | 12 | 0 | 69 | 1 | | | | |
| Alleyne | 4 | 0 | 21 | 0 | | | | |
| Lloyds | 7 | 1 | 35 | 0 | | | | |
| Athey | 3 | 0 | 15 | 0 | | | | |

| FALL OF WICKETS | GLO | ESS | GLO | ESS |
|---|---|---|---|---|
| 1st | 16 | 4 | 35 | |
| 2nd | 21 | 53 | 51 | |
| 3rd | 43 | 60 | 55 | |
| 4th | 66 | 92 | 75 | |
| 5th | 77 | 152 | 84 | |
| 6th | 84 | 174 | 159 | |
| 7th | 90 | 309 | 171 | |
| 8th | 113 | 433 | 177 | |
| 9th | 118 | | 191 | |
| 10th | 118 | | 191 | |

## NORTHANTS vs. DERBYSHIRE
at Northampton on 31st May, 1st, 3rd June 1991
Toss : Derby. Umpires : K.J.Lyons and R.A.White
Match drawn. Northants 6 pts (Bt: 2, Bw: 4), Derby 5 pts (Bt: 1, Bw: 4)

### NORTHANTS

| | | | | |
|---|---|---|---|---|
| A.Fordham | c Krikken b Malcolm | 4 | c Base b Malcolm | 105 |
| N.A.Felton | c Krikken b Mortensen | 15 | c Krikken b Mortensen | 37 |
| R.J.Bailey | c Azharuddin b Mortensen | 7 | c Barnett b Malcolm | 56 |
| A.J.Lamb * | c Adams b Mortensen | 8 | (5) c Base b Malcolm | 9 |
| D.J.Capel | c Azharuddin b Jean-Jacques | 70 | (6) c & b Mortensen | 13 |
| K.M.Curran | c Adams b Mortensen | 6 | (7) run out | 9 |
| A.L.Penberthy | c Krikken b Mortensen | 0 | (8) not out | 1 |
| J.G.Thomas | b Malcolm | 64 | (4) c Mortensen b Malcolm | 9 |
| D.Ripley + | not out | 53 | not out | 0 |
| A.Walker | c O'Gorman b Malcolm | 8 | | |
| N.G.B.Cook | c Krikken b Malcolm | 4 | | |
| Extras | (lb 8,w 1) | 9 | (lb 8,w 1,nb 1) | 10 |
| TOTAL | | 248 | (for 7 wkts dec) | 249 |

### DERBYSHIRE

| | | | | |
|---|---|---|---|---|
| K.J.Barnett * | c Lamb b Thomas | 11 | c Fordham b Cook | 122 |
| P.D.Bowler | c Ripley b Thomas | 0 | c Ripley b Walker | 28 |
| J.E.Morris | c Walker b Curran | 87 | c Lamb b Curran | 4 |
| M.Azharuddin | lbw b Walker | 2 | b Cook | 55 |
| T.J.G.O'Gorman | c Ripley b Thomas | 4 | c Ripley b Capel | 14 |
| C.J.Adams | lbw b Capel | 18 | c Lamb b Cook | 2 |
| K.M.Krikken + | c Felton b Curran | 37 | st Ripley b Cook | 46 |
| M.Jean-Jacques | c Cook b Thomas | 0 | (10) not out | 0 |
| S.J.Base | c Ripley b Curran | 8 | c Walker b Curran | 2 |
| D.E.Malcolm | b Curran | 6 | (8) c Penberthy b Curran | 5 |
| O.H.Mortensen | not out | 1 | not out | 0 |
| Extras | (b 4,lb 10,w 1) | 15 | (b 3,lb 9) | 12 |
| TOTAL | | 189 | (for 9 wkts) | 290 |

| DERBYSHIRE | O | M | R | W | O | M | R | W |
|---|---|---|---|---|---|---|---|---|
| Malcolm | 23.5 | 2 | 76 | 4 | 23.5 | 3 | 99 | 4 |
| Mortensen | 21 | 5 | 57 | 5 | 24 | 6 | 59 | 2 |
| Base | 22 | 2 | 57 | 0 | 12 | 3 | 34 | 0 |
| Jean-Jacques | 18 | 5 | 50 | 1 | 11 | 1 | 49 | 0 |

| NORTHANTS | O | M | R | W | O | M | R | W |
|---|---|---|---|---|---|---|---|---|
| Thomas | 17 | 3 | 62 | 4 | 8 | 0 | 44 | 0 |
| Walker | 13 | 2 | 42 | 1 | 13 | 4 | 27 | 1 |
| Capel | 8 | 2 | 30 | 1 | 13 | 1 | 47 | 1 |
| Curran | 13.1 | 1 | 39 | 4 | 19 | 3 | 68 | 3 |
| Penberthy | 1 | 0 | 2 | 0 | 6 | 1 | 18 | 0 |
| Cook | | | | | 21 | 3 | 74 | 4 |

| FALL OF WICKETS | NOR | DER | NOR | DER |
|---|---|---|---|---|
| 1st | 14 | 1 | 79 | 60 |
| 2nd | 23 | 20 | 180 | 67 |
| 3rd | 28 | 27 | 194 | 160 |
| 4th | 39 | 42 | 216 | 189 |
| 5th | 77 | 95 | 235 | 196 |
| 6th | 83 | 154 | 245 | 271 |
| 7th | 147 | 157 | 247 | 281 |
| 8th | 200 | 170 | | 288 |
| 9th | 226 | 176 | | 290 |
| 10th | 248 | 189 | | |

## WARWICKSHIRE vs. YORKSHIRE
at Edgbaston on 31st May, 1st, 3rd June 1991
Toss : Yorkshire. Umpires : J.H.Hampshire and A.A.Jones
Warwickshire won by 39 runs. Warwicks 24 pts (Bt: 4, Bw: 4), Yorkshire 5 pts (Bt: 2, Bw: 3)
100 overs scores : Warwickshire 309 for 8

### WARWICKSHIRE

| | | | | |
|---|---|---|---|---|
| A.J.Moles | b Fletcher | 17 | b Carrick | 73 |
| J.D.Ratcliffe | c Byas b Robinson M.A. | 68 | c Robinson P.E. b Carrick | 44 |
| T.A.Lloyd * | c Byas b Fletcher | 2 | not out | 13 |
| D.P.Ostler | c Blakey b Fletcher | 77 | c Metcalfe b Carrick | 7 |
| P.A.Smith | c Byas b Gough | 11 | not out | 9 |
| D.A.Reeve | not out | 99 | | |
| K.J.Piper + | c Kellett b Fletcher | 19 | | |
| P.A.Booth | b Hartley | 7 | | |
| G.C.Small | lbw b Hartley | 0 | | |
| T.A.Munton | b Fletcher | 28 | | |
| A.A.Donald | b Fletcher | 0 | | |
| Extras | (b 4,lb 14,w 2,nb 6) | 26 | (b 4,lb 12,w 2,nb 6) | 24 |
| TOTAL | | 354 | (for 3 wkts dec) | 170 |

### YORKSHIRE

| | | | | |
|---|---|---|---|---|
| M.D.Moxon * | c Moles b Booth | 37 | c Ratcliffe b Munton | 27 |
| A.A.Metcalfe | c Donald b Booth | 44 | c Piper b Munton | 26 |
| D.Byas | c Small b Reeve | 33 | b Donald | 49 |
| R.J.Blakey + | c Reeve b Smith | 5 | b Munton | 0 |
| P.E.Robinson | b Small | 16 | c Moles b Munton | 93 |
| S.A.Kellett | c Piper b Donald | 30 | c Ratcliffe b Reeve | 0 |
| P.Carrick | b Small | 0 | c Small b Smith | 8 |
| D.Gough | b Donald | 24 | c Booth b Munton | 25 |
| P.J.Hartley | c Piper b Donald | 0 | not out | 14 |
| S.D.Fletcher | not out | 4 | c Ratcliffe b Donald | 8 |
| M.A.Robinson | b Donald | 0 | c Donald b Munton | 0 |
| Extras | (b 6,lb 14,w 2,nb 2) | 24 | (lb 14,nb 4) | 18 |
| TOTAL | | 217 | | 268 |

| YORKSHIRE | O | M | R | W | O | M | R | W |
|---|---|---|---|---|---|---|---|---|
| Hartley | 23 | 3 | 82 | 2 | 9 | 1 | 36 | 0 |
| Robinson M.A. | 28 | 6 | 70 | 1 | 9 | 0 | 35 | 0 |
| Fletcher | 27 | 6 | 70 | 6 | 4 | 0 | 27 | 0 |
| Gough | 20 | 3 | 85 | 1 | 6 | 1 | 24 | 0 |
| Carrick | 9 | 2 | 22 | 0 | 10 | 1 | 32 | 3 |
| Byas | 2 | 0 | 7 | 0 | | | | |

| WARWICKS | O | M | R | W | O | M | R | W |
|---|---|---|---|---|---|---|---|---|
| Donald | 12.3 | 4 | 28 | 4 | 13.3 | 3 | 47 | 2 |
| Small | 19 | 8 | 34 | 2 | 12 | 2 | 33 | 0 |
| Smith | 13 | 6 | 29 | 1 | 9 | 0 | 37 | 1 |
| Reeve | 17 | 5 | 44 | 1 | 7 | 1 | 22 | 1 |
| Booth | 19 | 5 | 62 | 2 | 12 | 0 | 62 | 0 |
| Munton | | | | | 21 | 3 | 53 | 6 |

| FALL OF WICKETS | WAR | YOR | WAR | YOR |
|---|---|---|---|---|
| 1st | 37 | 89 | 118 | 47 |
| 2nd | 48 | 94 | 139 | 74 |
| 3rd | 132 | 111 | 147 | 74 |
| 4th | 178 | 141 | | 160 |
| 5th | 199 | 150 | | 165 |
| 6th | 237 | 150 | | 179 |
| 7th | 257 | 201 | | 236 |
| 8th | 257 | 201 | | 257 |
| 9th | 354 | 217 | | 260 |
| 10th | 354 | 217 | | 268 |

## HEADLINES

### Britannic Assurance Championship

### 31st May - 3rd June

• Warwickshire maintained their lead over Essex with a maximum points victory at Edgbaston, completing the Championship double over Yorkshire. Dermot Reeve, with an unbeaten 99, ensured that good work from Jason Ratcliffe and Dominic Ostler was not wasted, as the home side reached 354; four wickets for Allan Donald brought a first innings lead of 137 but it was Tim Munton, with six for 53, who secured victory by 38 runs as Yorkshire chased a target of 308.

• Essex needed only two days to demolish Gloucestershire at Bristol by an innings and 124 runs. The home side were first despatched for 118 in 47.4 overs, then could only watch as an Essex score of 174 for six was converted to 433 for eight thanks to a superb 163 form Salim Malik, supported in century stands by Neil Foster and Don Topley. Foster's five for 54 in the Gloucester second innings made certain of a swift conclusion.

59

# BRITANNIC ASSURANCE CHAMPIONSHIP

## MIDDLESEX vs. KENT
at Lord's on 31st May, 1st, 3rd June 1991
Toss : Middlesex. Umpires : B.Dudleston and P.B.Wight
Match drawn. Middlesex 5 pts (Bt: 1, Bw: 4), Kent 5 pts (Bt: 1, Bw: 4)

**KENT**

| | | | | | |
|---|---|---|---|---|---|
| N.R.Taylor | c Gatting b Taylor | 46 | c Hutchinson b Emburey | 64 |
| M.R.Benson * | run out | 9 | c Fraser b Taylor | 1 |
| T.R.Ward | c Emburey b Taylor | 12 | lbw b Taylor | 4 |
| G.R.Cowdrey | c Farbrace b Fraser | 25 | lbw b Taylor | 20 |
| C.S.Cowdrey | lbw b Fraser | 6 | c Gatting b Fraser | 38 |
| R.M.Ellison | c Farbrace b Fraser | 7 | c Brown b Emburey | 0 |
| S.A.Marsh + | c Gatting b Taylor | 6 | not out | 108 |
| R.P.Davis | c Farbrace b Hughes | 10 | lbw b Williams | 5 |
| C.Penn | not out | 6 | | |
| M.J.McCague | c Hutchinson b Hughes | 11 | (9) not out | 21 |
| T.A.Merrick | c Farbrace b Fraser | 4 | | |
| Extras | (b 8,lb 4,nb 6) | 18 | (b 3,lb 12,nb 9) | 24 |
| TOTAL | | 160 | (for 7 wkts dec) | 345 |

**MIDDLESEX**

| | | | | | |
|---|---|---|---|---|---|
| I.J.F.Hutchinson | c Marsh b Penn | 22 | c Marsh b Ellison | 1 |
| M.A.Roseberry | c Marsh b Merrick | 2 | b Ellison | 16 |
| M.W.Gatting * | c Marsh b McCague | 34 | b Ellison | 32 |
| M.R.Ramprakash | c Marsh b Ellison | 1 | c Cowdrey G.R. b Ellison | 0 |
| K.R.Brown | not out | 47 | not out | 76 |
| J.E.Emburey | c Taylor b Ellison | 5 | b Ellison | 13 |
| N.F.Williams | c Marsh b Ellison | 0 | c Ellison b McCague | 8 |
| P.Farbrace + | c Marsh b Merrick | 0 | not out | 7 |
| C.W.Taylor | c Marsh b Merrick | 21 | | |
| A.R.C.Fraser | c Marsh b Ellison | 12 | | |
| S.P.Hughes | c sub b Davis | 1 | | |
| Extras | (b 8,lb 4,nb 6) | 18 | (lb 6,w 3,nb 2) | 11 |
| TOTAL | | 163 | (for 6 wkts) | 164 |

| MIDDLESEX | O | M | R | W | O | M | R | W |
|---|---|---|---|---|---|---|---|---|
| Hughes | 12 | 2 | 46 | 2 | 24 | 4 | 95 | 0 |
| Fraser | 15.5 | 9 | 24 | 4 | 15 | 1 | 47 | 1 |
| Williams | 13 | 3 | 39 | 0 | 27 | 3 | 66 | 1 |
| Taylor | 13 | 4 | 35 | 3 | 20 | 4 | 61 | 3 |
| Emburey | 1 | 0 | 4 | 0 | 29 | 7 | 60 | 2 |
| Hutchinson | | | | | 1 | 0 | 1 | 0 |

| KENT | O | M | R | W | O | M | R | W |
|---|---|---|---|---|---|---|---|---|
| McCague | 9.1 | 4 | 51 | 1 | 7 | 0 | 18 | 1 |
| Merrick | 18 | 4 | 61 | 3 | 15.3 | 3 | 38 | 0 |
| Davis | 3.4 | 0 | 11 | 1 | 13 | 4 | 25 | 0 |
| Penn | 5 | 0 | 19 | 1 | | | | |
| Ellison | 23 | 9 | 39 | 4 | 27 | 3 | 77 | 5 |

| FALL OF WICKETS | KEN | MID | KEN | MID |
|---|---|---|---|---|
| 1st | 15 | 10 | 9 | 7 |
| 2nd | 24 | 46 | 23 | 36 |
| 3rd | 76 | 69 | 81 | 36 |
| 4th | 87 | 79 | 118 | 89 |
| 5th | 95 | 92 | 137 | 128 |
| 6th | 111 | 92 | 282 | 143 |
| 7th | 133 | 93 | 305 | |
| 8th | 135 | 129 | | |
| 9th | 152 | 148 | | |
| 10th | 160 | 163 | | |

## LANCASHIRE vs. SUSSEX
at Old Trafford on 31st May, 1st, 3rd June 1991
Toss : Lancashire. Umpires : J.C.Balderstone and J.D.Bond
Lancashire won by 7 wickets. Lancashire 24 pts (Bt: 4, Bw: 4), Sussex 5 pts (Bt: 2, Bw: 3)
100 overs scores :Lancashire 339 for 7

**SUSSEX**

| | | | | | |
|---|---|---|---|---|---|
| D.M.Smith | c Atherton b Watkinson | 40 | (7) b Wasim Akram | 2 |
| J.W.Hall | lbw b Wasim Akram | 4 | b Watkinson | 92 |
| N.J.Lenham | b Wasim Akram | 0 | (1) c Hegg b DeFreitas | 18 |
| A.P.Wells | c Hughes b Watkinson | 6 | (5) b Watkinson | 40 |
| P.W.G.Parker * | lbw b DeFreitas | 11 | (3) c Mendis b Yates | 17 |
| A.I.C.Dodemaide | lbw b Yates | 20 | (8) c Hegg b Wasim Akram | 0 |
| P.Moores + | c Watkinson b Wasim Akram | 33 | (6) lbw b Watkinson | 51 |
| A.C.S.Pigott | b Wasim Akram | 1 | (9) c Yates b Watkinson | 4 |
| I.D.K.Salisbury | b Yates | 17 | (4) c Fairbrother b Wasim Akram | 17 |
| R.A.Bunting | not out | 51 | not out | 14 |
| A.N.Jones | c Wasim Akram b DeFreitas | 28 | b Wasim Akram | 1 |
| Extras | (b 5,lb 3,w 3,nb 4) | 15 | (b 18,lb 4,w 5,nb 7) | 34 |
| TOTAL | | 209 | | 290 |

**LANCASHIRE**

| | | | | | |
|---|---|---|---|---|---|
| G.D.Mendis | b Dodemaide | 13 | b Jones | 39 |
| G.Fowler | c Smith b Pigott | 32 | b Salisbury | 36 |
| M.A.Atherton | c Moores b Jones | 39 | | |
| N.H.Fairbrother | c Moores b Bunting | 22 | not out | 7 |
| W.K.Hegg + | b Pigott | 86 | | |
| G.D.Lloyd | lbw b Jones | 45 | (3) c Moores b Salisbury | 8 |
| M.Watkinson | lbw b Salisbury | 41 | (5) not out | 2 |
| Wasim Akram | c Moores b Bunting | 37 | | |
| P.A.J.DeFreitas | b Bunting | 60 | | |
| D.P.Hughes * | b Bunting | 1 | | |
| G.Yates | not out | 1 | | |
| Extras | (b 3,lb 16,w 5) | 24 | (b 1,lb 6) | 7 |
| TOTAL | | 401 | (for 3 wkts) | 99 |

| LANCASHIRE | O | M | R | W | O | M | R | W |
|---|---|---|---|---|---|---|---|---|
| Wasim Akram | 26 | 6 | 76 | 4 | 38.4 | 11 | 86 | 4 |
| DeFreitas | 12.2 | 5 | 21 | 2 | 18 | 6 | 42 | 1 |
| Watkinson | 18 | 3 | 64 | 2 | 30 | 6 | 95 | 4 |
| Yates | 12 | 1 | 40 | 2 | 24 | 5 | 45 | 1 |

| SUSSEX | O | M | R | W | O | M | R | W |
|---|---|---|---|---|---|---|---|---|
| Jones | 26 | 4 | 86 | 2 | 10 | 0 | 38 | 1 |
| Dodemaide | 5.2 | 1 | 21 | 1 | | | | |
| Bunting | 19.2 | 3 | 99 | 4 | 1 | 0 | 1 | 0 |
| Pigott | 23 | 3 | 88 | 2 | 6 | 0 | 38 | 0 |
| Salisbury | 36 | 11 | 88 | 1 | 4.5 | 1 | 15 | 2 |

| FALL OF WICKETS | SUS | LAN | SUS | LAN |
|---|---|---|---|---|
| 1st | 15 | 13 | 41 | 74 |
| 2nd | 15 | 67 | 86 | 80 |
| 3rd | 32 | 110 | 127 | 97 |
| 4th | 65 | 127 | 187 | |
| 5th | 73 | 225 | 217 | |
| 6th | 125 | 284 | 254 | |
| 7th | 125 | 306 | 254 | |
| 8th | 126 | 398 | 265 | |
| 9th | 135 | 398 | 278 | |
| 10th | 209 | 401 | 290 | |

## NOTTS vs. HAMPSHIRE
at Trent Bridge on 31st May, 1st, 3rd June 1991
Toss : Notts. Umpires : M.J.Kitchen and N.T.Plews
Match drawn. Notts 4 pts (Bt: 3, Bw: 1), Hampshire 6 pts (Bt: 3, Bw: 3)
100 overs scores : Notts 275 for 7

**NOTTS**

| | | | | | |
|---|---|---|---|---|---|
| B.C.Broad | c Gower b Aqib Javed | 5 | b James | 59 |
| P.Pollard | c Bakker b Aqib Javed | 100 | c Aymes b Aqib Javed | 0 |
| R.T.Robinson * | c Gower b Aqib Javed | 48 | not out | 95 |
| P.Johnson | b Connor | 16 | lbw b James | 0 |
| D.W.Randall | c Aymes b Aqib Javed | 13 | not out | 48 |
| K.P.Evans | lbw b Aqib Javed | 16 | | |
| F.D.Stephenson | c Aymes b Maru | 22 | | |
| B.N.French + | b Bakker | 21 | | |
| E.E.Hemmings | b Aqib Javed | 25 | | |
| R.A.Pick | b Bakker | 4 | | |
| J.A.Afford | not out | 0 | | |
| Extras | (b 6,lb 8,w 1,nb 4) | 19 | (b 1,lb 2,w 7,nb 9) | 19 |
| TOTAL | | 289 | (for 3 wkts dec) | 221 |

**HAMPSHIRE**

| | | | | | |
|---|---|---|---|---|---|
| T.C.Middleton | lbw b Pick | 26 | st French b Hemmings | 63 |
| C.L.Smith | b Stephenson | 22 | c French b Stephenson | 0 |
| M.C.J.Nicholas * | not out | 107 | b Hemmings | 29 |
| R.A.Smith | c Pollard b Evans | 46 | b Evans | 60 |
| D.I.Gower | c Johnson b Stephenson | 10 | c Evans b Stephenson | 44 |
| K.D.James | not out | 21 | not out | 2 |
| A.N Aymes + | | | | |
| R.J.Maru | | | | |
| C.A.Connor | | | | |
| P.J.Bakker | | | | |
| Aqib Javed | | | | |
| Extras | (lb 9,nb 10) | 19 | (b 1,lb 14,w 1,nb 4) | 20 |
| TOTAL | (for 4 wkts dec) | 251 | (for 5 wkts) | 218 |

| HAMPSHIRE | O | M | R | W | O | M | R | W |
|---|---|---|---|---|---|---|---|---|
| Bakker | 21.1 | 10 | 42 | 2 | 8 | 2 | 23 | 0 |
| Aqib Javed | 30 | 6 | 91 | 6 | 8 | 1 | 32 | 1 |
| Connor | 20 | 5 | 62 | 1 | | | | |
| James | 10 | 4 | 28 | 0 | 12 | 2 | 27 | 2 |
| Maru | 24 | 7 | 52 | 1 | 17 | 4 | 58 | 0 |
| Nicholas | | | | | 10 | 0 | 47 | 0 |
| Smith C.L. | | | | | 10 | 0 | 31 | 0 |

| NOTTS | O | M | R | W | O | M | R | W |
|---|---|---|---|---|---|---|---|---|
| Stephenson | 17 | 6 | 23 | 2 | 12 | 1 | 57 | 2 |
| Pick | 13 | 2 | 43 | 1 | | | | |
| Evans | 12 | 4 | 21 | 1 | 13.2 | 2 | 36 | 1 |
| Hemmings | 25 | 5 | 75 | 0 | 16 | 2 | 59 | 2 |
| Afford | 16.5 | 2 | 80 | 0 | 9 | 0 | 51 | 0 |

| FALL OF WICKETS | NOT | HAM | NOT | HAM |
|---|---|---|---|---|
| 1st | 5 | 40 | 2 | 1 |
| 2nd | 127 | 81 | 116 | 67 |
| 3rd | 162 | 151 | 118 | 136 |
| 4th | 181 | 175 | | 212 |
| 5th | 194 | | | 218 |
| 6th | 237 | | | |
| 7th | 275 | | | |
| 8th | 275 | | | |
| 9th | 285 | | | |
| 10th | 289 | | | |

## WORCESTERSHIRE vs. GLAMORGAN
at Worcester on 31st May, 1st, 3rd June 1991
Toss : Worcestershire. Umpires : G.I.Burgess and B.Leadbeater
Match drawn. Worcestershire 6 pts (Bt: 2, Bw: 4), Glamorgan 5 pts (Bt: 1, Bw: 4)

**WORCESTERSHIRE**

| | | | | | |
|---|---|---|---|---|---|
| T.S.Curtis | lbw b Frost | 70 | lbw b Watkin | 14 |
| G.J.Lord | c Metson b Frost | 0 | lbw b Croft | 8 |
| G.A.Hick | c Watkin b Smith | 50 | c Morris b Frost | 0 |
| T.M.Moody | c Butcher b Watkin | 0 | lbw b Watkin | 118 |
| P.A.Neale * | b Bastien | 12 | lbw b Frost | 7 |
| S.J.Rhodes + | lbw b Watkin | 5 | not out | 66 |
| R.K.Illingworth | b Frost | 26 | lbw b Frost | 13 |
| P.J.Newport | c Frost b Watkin | 16 | not out | 2 |
| S.R.Lampitt | c Smith b Watkin | 19 | | |
| N.V.Radford | c Watkin b Frost | 0 | | |
| G.R.Dilley | not out | 0 | | |
| Extras | (lb 6,nb 1) | 7 | (b 2,lb 8,nb 2) | 12 |
| TOTAL | | 205 | (for 6 wkts dec) | 240 |

**GLAMORGAN**

| | | | | | |
|---|---|---|---|---|---|
| A.R.Butcher * | lbw b Dilley | 17 | lbw b Dilley | 5 |
| H.Morris | b Radford | 8 | not out | 74 |
| R.J.Shastri | not out | 84 | c Hick b Lampitt | 28 |
| C.P.Metson + | c Rhodes b Radford | 8 | | |
| M.P.Maynard | c Illingworth b Dilley | 5 | (4) not out | 33 |
| G.C.Holmes | lbw b Lampitt | 15 | | |
| I.Smith | c Curtis b Newport | 14 | | |
| R.D.B.Croft | c Moody b Lampitt | 3 | | |
| S.L.Watkin | c Moody b Lampitt | 10 | | |
| S.Bastien | c Curtis b Dilley | 1 | | |
| M.Frost | c Moody b Dilley | 0 | | |
| Extras | (b 4,lb 3,nb 6) | 13 | (lb 7,nb 7) | 14 |
| TOTAL | | 178 | (for 2 wkts) | 154 |

| GLAMORGAN | O | M | R | W | O | M | R | W |
|---|---|---|---|---|---|---|---|---|
| Watkin | 24 | 10 | 40 | 4 | 25 | 8 | 61 | 2 |
| Frost | 29.5 | 10 | 67 | 4 | 24 | 4 | 87 | 3 |
| Bastien | 26 | 6 | 51 | 1 | 28 | 6 | 71 | 0 |
| Smith | 12 | 1 | 41 | 1 | | | | |
| Croft | | | | | 5 | 0 | 11 | 1 |

| WORCS | O | M | R | W | O | M | R | W |
|---|---|---|---|---|---|---|---|---|
| Dilley | 19.3 | 2 | 60 | 4 | 10 | 1 | 31 | 1 |
| Radford | 10 | 1 | 42 | 2 | 12 | 1 | 45 | 0 |
| Lampitt | 20 | 5 | 37 | 2 | 11 | 3 | 38 | 1 |
| Newport | 11 | 2 | 32 | 2 | 9.3 | 1 | 31 | 0 |
| Illingworth | | | | | 1 | 0 | 2 | 0 |

| FALL OF WICKETS | WOR | GLA | WOR | GLA |
|---|---|---|---|---|
| 1st | 6 | 22 | 19 | 11 |
| 2nd | 87 | 28 | 20 | 71 |
| 3rd | 90 | 42 | 39 | |
| 4th | 110 | 47 | 57 | |
| 5th | 123 | 99 | 194 | |
| 6th | 165 | 130 | 236 | |
| 7th | 168 | 138 | | |
| 8th | 199 | 161 | | |
| 9th | 205 | 176 | | |
| 10th | 205 | 178 | | |

## BRITANNIC ASS. CHAMPIONSHIP

## TOUR MATCH

# HEADLINES

### Britannic Assurance Championship

### 31st May - 3rd June

• Lancashire were the only other winners, gaining their first Championship success of the summer at the expense of Sussex, by seven wickets at Old Trafford. Wasim Akram broke through Sussex resistance with four wickets in each innings, and Lancashire also showed the depth of talent in their batting line up, as seven men passed thirty, Warren Hegg and Phil DeFreitas making the largest contributions.

• Northamptonshire and Derbyshire played out a closely contested draw at Northampton, the visitors finishing 19 short of victory with their last pair at the crease. Both sides' first innings were dominated by penetrative seam bowling, first from Devon Malcolm and Ole Mortensen, then from Greg Thomas and Kevin Curran, but batting became progressively easier, Alan Fordham hitting his second 100 of the season to leave Derbyshire 80 overs to score 309. Kim Barnett's 122 had seemed to put his side on the way to success, but in the game's last moments it was Northants who were pressing for victory.

• At Worcester, after two days' cricket when the fast bowlers had again been firmly in control, the batsmen gained the initiative on the last day to such an extent that Glamorgan were well on their way to victory over Worcestershire when the weather closed in. Tom Moody had made his third 100 in successive first-class matches against Glamorgan, before the declaration leaving the visitors a target of 267, and Hugh Morris and Matthew Maynard, both high in the national averages, batted with assurance to carry the score to 154 for two.

• Steve Marsh took the honours in Middlesex's drawn match with Kent at Lord's with a feat unique in cricket history. The Kent wicket-keeper first equalled a world record by claiming eight catches in the Middlesex first innings, then created a new entry in cricket's record books by scoring 108 not out to take his side out of danger. Angus Fraser had given Middlesex the early advantage with figures of four for 24 on his brief return to first-class cricket, but Richard Ellison backed up Marsh's performance with nine wickets in the match.

• Hampshire looked to have a chance of victory over Nottinghamshire at Trent Bridge when Robin Smith and David Gower were going well as they chased a target of 260, but their dismissals ensured the match was drawn. Paul Pollard and Aqib Javed battled for the honours in the Notts first innings, Pollard making his first 100 of the season, Aqib returning career-best figures, then Mark Nicholas also reached 100 for the first time in 1991 before his declaration 38 behind.

• First-class début: J.M.De La Pena (Gloucestershire).

## LEICESTERSHIRE vs. WEST INDIES

at Leicester on 1st, 2nd, 3rd June 1991
Toss : Leicestershire. Umpires : B.J.Meyer and A.G.T.Whitehead
West Indies won by 6 wickets

### LEICESTERSHIRE

| | | | | | |
|---|---|---|---|---|---|
| N.E.Briers * | c Allen b Anthony | 68 | c Anthony b Allen | | 9 |
| T.J.Boon | c Dujon b Patterson | 15 | lbw b Anthony | | 5 |
| P.N.Hepworth | c Logie b Simmons | 68 | c Dujon b Anthony | | 21 |
| D.R.Martyn | c Richardson b Allen | 35 | not out | | 60 |
| L.Potter | c Anthony b Richards | 53 | lbw b Anthony | | 2 |
| B.F.Smith | c Simmons b Walsh | 13 | not out | | 29 |
| C.C.Lewis | c Lara b Anthony | 72 | | | |
| P.A.Nixon + | not out | 9 | | | |
| M.I.Gidley | not out | 0 | | | |
| D.J.Millns | | | | | |
| J.N.Maguire | | | | | |
| Extras | (b 1,lb 8,w 7,nb 6) | 22 | (lb 9,w 1) | | 10 |
| TOTAL | (for 7 wkts dec) | 355 | (for 4 wkts dec) | | 136 |

### WEST INDIES

| | | | | | |
|---|---|---|---|---|---|
| P.V.Simmons | c Nixon b Maguire | 42 | c Boon b Lewis | | 0 |
| C.B.Lambert | b Maguire | 4 | c Hepworth b Maguire | | 51 |
| R.B.Richardson | lbw b Maguire | 63 | not out | | 135 |
| B.C.Lara | c Nixon b Maguire | 3 | c Gidley b Maguire | | 26 |
| A.L.Logie | c & b Lewis | 32 | b Lewis | | 10 |
| I.V.A.Richards * | b Maguire | 45 | not out | | 39 |
| P.J.L.Dujon + | not out | 9 | | | |
| H.A.G.Anthony | c Potter b Millns | 9 | | | |
| I.B.A.Allen | not out | 0 | | | |
| C.A.Walsh | | | | | |
| B.P.Patterson | | | | | |
| Extras | (lb 1,nb 8) | 9 | (lb 12,nb 4) | | 16 |
| TOTAL | (for 7 wkts dec) | 216 | (for 4 wkts) | | 277 |

| WEST INDIES | O | M | R | W | | O | M | R | W |
|---|---|---|---|---|---|---|---|---|---|
| Patterson | 20 | 4 | 75 | 1 | | 11 | 7 | 15 | 0 |
| Allen | 16 | 3 | 65 | 1 | | 11 | 3 | 46 | 1 |
| Anthony | 13 | 1 | 69 | 2 | | 8 | 3 | 28 | 3 |
| Walsh | 19 | 5 | 60 | 1 | | 8 | 5 | 18 | 0 |
| Simmons | 9 | 3 | 45 | 1 | | 2 | 0 | 6 | 0 |
| Richards | 9 | 3 | 32 | 1 | | | | | |
| Lara | | | | | | 2 | 0 | 14 | 0 |

| LEICS | O | M | R | W | | O | M | R | W |
|---|---|---|---|---|---|---|---|---|---|
| Lewis | 19 | 5 | 60 | 1 | | 15 | 0 | 63 | 2 |
| Maguire | 17 | 3 | 44 | 5 | | 14.1 | 0 | 86 | 2 |
| Millns | 13.3 | 1 | 64 | 1 | | 14 | 1 | 78 | 0 |
| Potter | 11 | 2 | 47 | 0 | | | | | |
| Gidley | | | | | | 5 | 0 | 38 | 0 |

| FALL OF WICKETS | | | | |
|---|---|---|---|---|
| | LEI | WI | LEI | WI |
| 1st | 27 | 7 | 14 | 0 |
| 2nd | 105 | 100 | 27 | 121 |
| 3rd | 158 | 117 | 46 | 166 |
| 4th | 253 | 122 | 48 | 183 |
| 5th | 253 | 179 | | |
| 6th | 317 | 207 | | |
| 7th | 352 | 216 | | |
| 8th | | | | |
| 9th | | | | |
| 10th | | | | |

# HEADLINES

### Tetley Bitter Challenge

### 1st - 3rd June

• West Indies warmed up for the First Test with a six-wicket victory over Leicestershire at Leicester. The home side gave an impressive account of themselves on the first two days, a consistent batting effort bringing them to 355 for seven, and John Maguire proving a difficult proposition with ball, but the match was taken away from them on the last afternoon by a wonderful 135 not out from Richie Richardson, at last passing the 100-mark on his third tour to England.

# BRITANNIC ASSURANCE CHAMPIONSHIP

## KENT vs. WARWICKSHIRE

at Tunbridge Wells on 4th, 5th, 6th June 1991
Toss : Kent. Umpires : D.J.Constant and B.Hassan
Match drawn. Kent 8 pts (Bt: 4, Bw: 4), Warwickshire 4 pts (Bt: 0, Bw: 4)
100 overs scores : Kent 351 for 9

### KENT

| | | |
|---|---|---|
| N.R.Taylor | b Donald | 4 |
| M.R.Benson * | run out | 105 |
| T.R.Ward | lbw b Small | 5 |
| G.R.Cowdrey | lbw b Reeve | 114 |
| M.V.Fleming | c Ratcliffe b Reeve | 42 |
| R.M.Ellison | c Piper b Reeve | 0 |
| S.A.Marsh + | b Reeve | 0 |
| R.P.Davis | c Piper b Reeve | 9 |
| M.J.McCague | c Piper b Smith | 18 |
| T.A.Merrick | not out | 25 |
| A.P.Igglesden | c Lloyd b Reeve | 10 |
| Extras | (b 4,lb 15,nb 1) | 20 |
| TOTAL | | 352 |

### WARWICKSHIRE

| | | | | |
|---|---|---|---|---|
| A.J.Moles | c Marsh b Merrick | 3 | lbw b Igglesden | 48 |
| J.D.Ratcliffe | c Davis b Ellison | 13 | c Igglesden b McCague | 33 |
| T.A.Lloyd * | run out | 34 | c Davis b Igglesden | 97 |
| D.P.Ostler | lbw b Ellison | 7 | not out | 120 |
| P.A.Smith | lbw b Ellison | 7 | c Davis b Igglesden | 2 |
| D.A.Reeve | c Fleming b Ellison | 7 | not out | 66 |
| K.J.Piper + | lbw b Ellison | 0 | | |
| P.A.Booth | lbw b Ellison | 0 | | |
| G.C.Small | c McCague b Ellison | 5 | | |
| T.A.Munton | b Merrick | 6 | | |
| A.A.Donald | not out | 0 | | |
| Extras | (w 1) | 1 | (b 2,lb 10,w 9,nb 2) | 23 |
| TOTAL | | 83 | (for 4 wkts) | 389 |

| WARWICKS | O | M | R | W | O | M | R | W |
|---|---|---|---|---|---|---|---|---|
| Donald | 9 | 1 | 22 | 1 | | | | |
| Small | 22 | 3 | 68 | 1 | | | | |
| Reeve | 26.4 | 9 | 73 | 6 | | | | |
| Munton | 20 | 3 | 66 | 0 | | | | |
| Booth | 11 | 0 | 60 | 0 | | | | |
| Smith | 11 | 2 | 38 | 1 | | | | |
| Moles | 1 | 0 | 6 | 0 | | | | |

| KENT | O | M | R | W | O | M | R | W |
|---|---|---|---|---|---|---|---|---|
| Merrick | 13.1 | 5 | 14 | 2 | 15 | 4 | 42 | 0 |
| Igglesden | 6 | 3 | 13 | 0 | 29 | 6 | 69 | 3 |
| Ellison | 14 | 3 | 33 | 7 | 24 | 5 | 72 | 0 |
| McCague | 7 | 1 | 23 | 0 | 22 | 3 | 51 | 1 |
| Davis | | | | | 30 | 11 | 86 | 0 |
| Fleming | | | | | 9 | 1 | 27 | 0 |
| Marsh | | | | | 5 | 0 | 28 | 0 |
| Benson | | | | | 1 | 0 | 2 | 0 |

| FALL OF WICKETS | | | | |
|---|---|---|---|---|
| | KEN | WAR | WAR | KEN |
| 1st | 4 | 4 | 48 | |
| 2nd | 9 | 23 | 178 | |
| 3rd | 178 | 35 | 203 | |
| 4th | 265 | 65 | 209 | |
| 5th | 269 | 65 | | |
| 6th | 269 | 65 | | |
| 7th | 293 | 71 | | |
| 8th | 313 | 76 | | |
| 9th | 319 | 83 | | |
| 10th | 352 | 83 | | |

## HAMPSHIRE vs. LANCASHIRE

at Basingstoke on 4th, 5th, 6th June 1991
Toss : Lancashire. Umpires : B.Dudleston and R.Julian
Lancashire won by 128 runs. Hampshire 4 pts (Bt: 0, Bw: 4), Lancashire 20 pts (Bt: 4, Bw: 0)

### LANCASHIRE

| | | | | |
|---|---|---|---|---|
| G.D.Mendis | c Maru b Aqib Javed | 13 | (2) not out | 39 |
| G.Fowler | c Terry b Aqib Javed | 57 | (1) not out | 40 |
| G.D.Lloyd | lbw b James | 8 | | |
| N.H.Fairbrother | c Gower b James | 25 | | |
| M.Watkinson | lbw b Bakker | 6 | | |
| Wasim Akram | c James b Bakker | 122 | | |
| W.K.Hegg + | c & b Maru | 69 | | |
| I.D.Austin | b Bakker | 2 | | |
| G.Yates | run out | 15 | | |
| D.P.Hughes * | c Nicholas b Bakker | 4 | | |
| P.J.Martin | not out | 1 | | |
| Extras | (lb 3,nb 7) | 10 | (lb 1,nb 3) | 4 |
| TOTAL | | 332 | (for 0 wkts dec) | 83 |

### HAMPSHIRE

| | | | | |
|---|---|---|---|---|
| T.C.Middleton | not out | 25 | c Hegg b Wasim Akram | 16 |
| C.L.Smith | c Hegg b Watkinson | 22 | c Martin b Wasim Akram | 51 |
| M.C.J.Nicholas * | not out | 14 | (6) lbw b Wasim Akram | 19 |
| A.N Aymes + | | | (3) run out | 33 |
| V.P.Terry | | | (4) b Martin | 52 |
| D.I.Gower | | | (5) c Fairbrother b Austin | 14 |
| K.D.James | | | b Watkinson | 14 |
| R.J.Maru | | | not out | 5 |
| C.A.Connor | | | b Wasim Akram | 0 |
| P.J.Bakker | | | lbw b Wasim Akram | 0 |
| Aqib Javed | | | b Wasim Akram | 0 |
| Extras | (b 2,nb 3) | 5 | (b 8,lb 4,nb 5) | 17 |
| TOTAL | (for 1 wkt dec) | 66 | | 221 |

| HAMPSHIRE | O | M | R | W | O | M | R | W |
|---|---|---|---|---|---|---|---|---|
| Bakker | 21.2 | 7 | 66 | 4 | | | | |
| Aqib Javed | 18 | 4 | 67 | 2 | | | | |
| Connor | 11 | 1 | 56 | 0 | 9 | 1 | 40 | 0 |
| James | 14 | 3 | 50 | 2 | 7 | 1 | 18 | 0 |
| Maru | 27 | 8 | 69 | 1 | 5 | 2 | 8 | 0 |
| Nicholas | 5 | 0 | 21 | 0 | 3 | 0 | 13 | 0 |
| Smith | | | | | 1 | 0 | 3 | 0 |

| LANCASHIRE | O | M | R | W | O | M | R | W |
|---|---|---|---|---|---|---|---|---|
| Wasim Akram | 8 | 4 | 10 | 0 | 20.4 | 3 | 48 | 5 |
| Martin | 7 | 1 | 20 | 0 | 19 | 5 | 60 | 1 |
| Austin | 8 | 2 | 23 | 0 | 11 | 4 | 26 | 1 |
| Watkinson | 7 | 3 | 11 | 1 | 16 | 3 | 48 | 2 |
| Yates | | | | | 6 | 1 | 27 | 0 |

| FALL OF WICKETS | | | | |
|---|---|---|---|---|
| | LAN | HAM | LAN | HAM |
| 1st | 35 | 36 | | 55 |
| 2nd | 56 | | | 83 |
| 3rd | 90 | | | 149 |
| 4th | 106 | | | 171 |
| 5th | 115 | | | 179 |
| 6th | 250 | | | 212 |
| 7th | 277 | | | 217 |
| 8th | 325 | | | 221 |
| 9th | 331 | | | 221 |
| 10th | 332 | | | 221 |

## GLAMORGAN vs. SOMERSET

at Swansea on 4th, 5th (no play), 6th June 1991
Toss : Somerset. Umpires : J.W.Holder and K.E.Palmer
Match drawn. Glamorgan 1 pt (Bt: 0, Bw: 1), Somerset 4 pts (Bt: 4, Bw: 0)
100 overs scores : Somerset 370 for 4

### SOMERSET

| | | |
|---|---|---|
| S.J.Cook | b Frost | 152 |
| P.M.Roebuck | c Butcher b Frost | 7 |
| A.N.Hayhurst | c Metson b Barwick | 1 |
| C.J.Tavare * | c Maynard b Barwick | 162 |
| R.J.Harden | c Cann b Croft | 15 |
| N.D.Burns + | not out | 62 |
| K.H.Macleay | not out | 8 |
| G.D.Rose | | |
| H.R.J.Trump | | |
| N.A.Mallender | | |
| D.A.Graveney | | |
| Extras | (b 4,lb 5,w 1,nb 5) | 15 |
| TOTAL | (for 5 wkts dec) | 422 |

### GLAMORGAN

| | | | | |
|---|---|---|---|---|
| I.Smith | not out | 33 | (6) run out | 11 |
| C.P.Metson + | not out | 21 | (7) c Tavare b Rose | 0 |
| A.R.Butcher * | | | (1) c Mallender b Macleay | 102 |
| H.Morris | | | (2) lbw b Macleay | 84 |
| R.J.Shastri | | | (3) c Tavare b Mallender | 8 |
| M.P.Maynard | | | (4) c Tavare b Rose | 39 |
| M.J.Cann | | | (5) not out | 29 |
| R.D.B.Croft | | | not out | 4 |
| S.Bastien | | | | |
| S.R.Barwick | | | | |
| M.Frost | | | | |
| Extras | (b 1,lb 2) | 3 | (b 2,lb 10,w 1,nb 14) | 27 |
| TOTAL | (for 0 wkts dec) | 57 | (for 6 wkts) | 304 |

| GLAMORGAN | O | M | R | W | O | M | R | W |
|---|---|---|---|---|---|---|---|---|
| Frost | 16 | 0 | 81 | 2 | | | | |
| Bastien | 25 | 2 | 113 | 0 | | | | |
| Barwick | 30 | 5 | 85 | 2 | | | | |
| Smith | 3 | 1 | 7 | 0 | | | | |
| Croft | 28 | 6 | 90 | 1 | | | | |
| Cann | 8 | 0 | 37 | 0 | | | | |

| SOMERSET | O | M | R | W | O | M | R | W |
|---|---|---|---|---|---|---|---|---|
| Harden | 4.5 | 0 | 28 | 0 | | | | |
| Cook | 4 | 0 | 26 | 0 | | | | |
| Mallender | | | | | 14 | 3 | 42 | 1 |
| Rose | | | | | 11 | 1 | 31 | 2 |
| Hayhurst | | | | | 13 | 2 | 49 | 0 |
| Macleay | | | | | 17 | 0 | 71 | 2 |
| Trump | | | | | 9 | 3 | 24 | 0 |
| Graveney | | | | | 18 | 4 | 53 | 0 |
| Roebuck | | | | | 7 | 0 | 22 | 0 |

| FALL OF WICKETS | | | | |
|---|---|---|---|---|
| | SOM | GLA | SOM | GLA |
| 1st | 40 | | | 183 |
| 2nd | 41 | | | 209 |
| 3rd | 283 | | | 230 |
| 4th | 303 | | | 279 |
| 5th | 372 | | | 298 |
| 6th | | | | 298 |
| 7th | | | | |
| 8th | | | | |
| 9th | | | | |
| 10th | | | | |

## ESSEX vs. LEICESTERSHIRE

at Ilford on 4th, 5th, 6th June 1991
Toss : Essex. Umpires : D.O.Oslear and A.G.T.Whitehead
Match drawn. Essex 8 pts (Bt: 4, Bw: 4), Leicestershire 7 pts (Bt: 3, Bw: 4)

### ESSEX

| | | | | |
|---|---|---|---|---|
| J.P.Stephenson | lbw b Millns | 24 | lbw b Maguire | 16 |
| N.Shahid | c Whitticase b Maguire | 4 | c Boon b Millns | 4 |
| P.J.Prichard | c Potter b Maguire | 10 | c & b Potter | 50 |
| Salim Malik | run out | 215 | c Hepworth b Potter | 74 |
| N.Hussain | b Maguire | 9 | not out | 38 |
| M.A.Garnham + | b Smith | 63 | not out | 12 |
| N.A.Foster * | c Whitticase b Maguire | 8 | | |
| T.D.Topley | c & b Millns | 2 | | |
| S.J.W.Andrew | b Maguire | 1 | | |
| J.H.Childs | lbw b Maguire | 0 | | |
| P.M.Such | not out | 0 | | |
| Extras | (lb 7,w 1,nb 15) | 23 | (b 1,nb 8) | 9 |
| TOTAL | | 355 | (for 4 wkts dec) | 203 |

### LEICESTERSHIRE

| | | | | |
|---|---|---|---|---|
| T.J.Boon | c Shahid b Topley | 66 | c Shahid b Topley | 42 |
| N.E.Briers * | c Garnham b Topley | 23 | b Andrew | 23 |
| P.N.Hepworth | lbw b Foster | 12 | lbw b Topley | 7 |
| J.J.Whitaker | lbw b Foster | 0 | c Shahid b Andrew | 12 |
| L.Potter | c Garnham b Andrew | 85 | c Foster b Childs | 37 |
| B.F.Smith | lbw b Childs | 20 | not out | 41 |
| P.Willey | c Shahid b Topley | 11 | not out | 3 |
| P.Whitticase + | c Garnham b Andrew | 21 | | |
| D.J.Millns | not out | 23 | | |
| C.Wilkinson | lbw b Topley | 0 | | |
| J.N.Maguire | c Shahid b Topley | 21 | | |
| Extras | (lb 2,nb 12) | 14 | (b 1,lb 2,w 1,nb 4) | 8 |
| TOTAL | | 296 | (for 5 wkts) | 173 |

| LEICESTERSHIRE | O | M | R | W | O | M | R | W |
|---|---|---|---|---|---|---|---|---|
| Millns | 18 | 2 | 73 | 2 | 10 | 0 | 49 | 1 |
| Maguire | 29.5 | 8 | 85 | 6 | 21 | 4 | 72 | 1 |
| Wilkinson | 17 | 1 | 96 | 0 | 2 | 0 | 18 | 0 |
| Potter | 21 | 1 | 66 | 0 | 13 | 0 | 63 | 2 |
| Willey | 5 | 1 | 23 | 0 | | | | |
| Smith | 1 | 0 | 5 | 1 | | | | |

| ESSEX | O | M | R | W | O | M | R | W |
|---|---|---|---|---|---|---|---|---|
| Foster | 24 | 9 | 42 | 2 | 13 | 2 | 53 | 0 |
| Andrew | 17 | 2 | 63 | 2 | 12 | 3 | 55 | 2 |
| Such | 12 | 2 | 55 | 0 | 4 | 1 | 8 | 0 |
| Topley | 18 | 3 | 58 | 5 | 11 | 3 | 33 | 2 |
| Childs | 26 | 6 | 76 | 1 | 7.3 | 1 | 21 | 1 |

| FALL OF WICKETS | | | | |
|---|---|---|---|---|
| | ESS | LEI | ESS | LEI |
| 1st | 0 | 54 | 14 | 59 |
| 2nd | 21 | 85 | 26 | 70 |
| 3rd | 103 | 85 | 127 | 89 |
| 4th | 117 | 126 | 178 | 94 |
| 5th | 286 | 195 | | 162 |
| 6th | 323 | 216 | | |
| 7th | 336 | 242 | | |
| 8th | 347 | 270 | | |
| 9th | 347 | 270 | | |
| 10th | 355 | 296 | | |

# BRITANNIC ASSURANCE CHAMPIONSHIP

## HEADLINES

### Britannic Assurance Championship

### 4th - 6th June

• The Championship table was little altered as continuous interruptions for rain and bad light around the country made positive results difficult to achieve.

• Lancashire began to catch the early pacesetters with their second consecutive victory, overcoming the almost total loss of the second day to beat Hampshire by 128 runs. Again they owed much to Wasim Akram who followed a flamboyant 122 in their first innings with five wickets for 48 as the home side went for a target of 350.

• Northamptonshire, although missing half their first-choice side, were the only other winners, gaining their first success of the season at the expense of Worcestershire, who had taken charge of the early proceedings, reaching 327 for seven declared. The weather's intervention made two further declarations necessary to keep the game alive. Northamptonshire reached a target of 271 at less than four an over thanks to an opening stand of 106 from Alan Fordham and Nigel Felton, and an unbeaten 95 from Rob Bailey.

• Warwickshire's batsmen went from one extreme to another against Kent, following the worst batting display of the season so far with their best. Kent dominated the first two days thanks to 100s from Mark Benson and Graham Cowdrey, and a career-best seven for 33 from Richard Ellison, gaining a first-innings lead of 269. The leaders rallied strongly to save the game with a maiden first-class 100 from Dominic Ostler in an unbroken fifth-wicket stand of 180 with Dermot Reeve.

• Essex could reduce Warwickshire's lead by only four points as their game with Leicestershire at Ilford also finished in a draw. Salim Malik dominated the opening day with a glittering career-best 215 as the home side reached 355, but Essex could gain a first innings advantage of only 59, and after Neil Foster's declaration, Leicestershire's batsmen gave stubborn resistance when a target of 263 proved out of range.

• At Swansea, Glamorgan made a splendid effort to make the 366 runs they required for victory after the loss of the second day had forced Somerset to forfeit their second innings. An opening partnership of 184 from Alan Butcher and Hugh Morris took them past the halfway mark, but the regular loss of wickets put their target out of reach. The opening day had seen a fourth-wicket partnership of 242 from Jimmy Cook and Chris Tavare as Somerset reached 422 for five declared.

• A match of differing character at Bristol also suffered the loss of the second day, and with it Middlesex lost their best chance of victory over Gloucestershire. The visitors owed everything to a sterling 114 from Ian Hutchinson to lift them past 200 in their first innings. A career-best six for 34 from Phil Tufnell, looking to recover his Test place, gave them a lead of 77, but with time fast running out, the champions could manage only a solitary second-innings wicket.

• First-class début: M.B. Loye (Northants).

## GLOUCS vs. MIDDLESEX

at Bristol on 4th, 5th (no play), 6th June 1991
Toss : Middlesex. Umpires : B.J.Meyer and R.Palmer
Match drawn. Gloucs 4 pts (Bt: 0, Bw: 4), Middlesex 6 pts (Bt: 2, Bw: 4)

### MIDDLESEX

| | | | | | |
|---|---|---|---|---|---|
| I.J.F.Hutchinson | c Babington b Scott | 114 | c Scott b Lawrence | | 0 |
| M.A.Roseberry | c Hodgson b Babington | 17 | c Babington b Gilbert | | 7 |
| M.W.Gatting * | c Athey b Gilbert | 15 | not out | | 68 |
| K.R.Brown | b Gilbert | 3 | c Williams b Gilbert | | 2 |
| M.Keech | b Lawrence | 8 | c Williams b Lawrence | | 2 |
| J.E.Emburey | c Williams b Lawrence | 6 | run out | | 74 |
| P.Farbrace + | b Babington | 5 | not out | | 0 |
| A.R.C.Fraser | b Gilbert | 0 | | | |
| P.C.R.Tufnell | c Williams b Babington | 4 | | | |
| C.W.Taylor | c Williams b Lawrence | 11 | | | |
| N.G.Cowans | not out | 0 | | | |
| Extras | (lb 15,w 1,nb 10) | 26 | (b 1,lb 12,w 1,nb 5) | | 19 |
| TOTAL | | 209 | (for 5 wkts dec) | | 172 |

### GLOUCS

| | | | | | |
|---|---|---|---|---|---|
| G.D.Hodgson | lbw b Emburey | 16 | not out | | 15 |
| R.J.Scott | b Emburey | 14 | c Fraser b Taylor | | 0 |
| A.J.Wright * | lbw b Fraser | 9 | not out | | 35 |
| C.W.J.Athey | c Hutchinson b Emburey | 19 | | | |
| M.W.Alleyne | st Farbrace b Tufnell | 25 | | | |
| R.C.J.Williams + | c Brown b Tufnell | 0 | | | |
| J.J.E.Hardy | c Brown b Tufnell | 15 | | | |
| J.W.Lloyds | c & b Tufnell | 2 | | | |
| D.V.Lawrence | b Tufnell | 8 | | | |
| D.R.Gilbert | c Taylor b Tufnell | 14 | | | |
| A.M.Babington | not out | 1 | | | |
| Extras | (lb 8) | 8 | (b 4,lb 3,w 1) | | 8 |
| TOTAL | | 131 | (for 1 wkt) | | 58 |

| GLOUCS | O | M | R | W | O | M | R | W |
|---|---|---|---|---|---|---|---|---|
| Lawrence | 17.2 | 4 | 44 | 3 | 9 | 0 | 35 | 2 |
| Babington | 21 | 4 | 56 | 3 | 6 | 1 | 32 | 0 |
| Gilbert | 21 | 2 | 49 | 3 | 10 | 4 | 22 | 2 |
| Athey | 3 | 0 | 8 | 0 | | | | |
| Scott | 9 | 1 | 29 | 1 | 7 | 0 | 14 | 0 |
| Lloyds | 4 | 1 | 8 | 0 | 7 | 0 | 26 | 0 |
| Alleyne | | | | | 4 | 0 | 30 | 0 |

| MIDDLESEX | O | M | R | W | O | M | R | W |
|---|---|---|---|---|---|---|---|---|
| Taylor | 6 | 1 | 15 | 0 | 3 | 2 | 1 | 1 |
| Cowans | 4 | 1 | 10 | 0 | | | | |
| Emburey | 27 | 7 | 50 | 3 | 11 | 4 | 11 | 0 |
| Fraser | 5 | 0 | 14 | 1 | 4 | 2 | 6 | 0 |
| Tufnell | 14.3 | 3 | 34 | 6 | 13 | 2 | 19 | 0 |
| Keech | | | | | 7 | 4 | 9 | 0 |
| Roseberry | | | | | 2 | 0 | 5 | 0 |

FALL OF WICKETS

| | MID | GLO | MID | GLO |
|---|---|---|---|---|
| 1st | 56 | 29 | 0 | 1 |
| 2nd | 77 | 30 | 10 | |
| 3rd | 85 | 44 | 19 | |
| 4th | 112 | 73 | 26 | |
| 5th | 125 | 82 | 171 | |
| 6th | 142 | 87 | | |
| 7th | 148 | 89 | | |
| 8th | 157 | 101 | | |
| 9th | 209 | 118 | | |
| 10th | 209 | 131 | | |

## NORTHANTS vs. WORCESTERSHIRE

at Northampton on 4th, 5th, 6th June 1991
Toss : Northants. Umpires : K.J.Lyons and R.A.White
Northants won by 6 wickets. Northants 20 pts (Bt: 1, Bw: 3), Worcs 4 pts (Bt: 3, Bw: 1)
100 overs scores : Worcestershire 278 for 7

### WORCESTERSHIRE

| | | | | | |
|---|---|---|---|---|---|
| T.S.Curtis | c Ripley b Curran | 52 | c Loye b Cook | | 30 |
| G.J.Lord | c Curran b Walker | 55 | c Ripley b Curran | | 38 |
| T.M.Moody | c Fordham b Curran | 71 | not out | | 14 |
| D.B.D'Oliveira | c Ripley b Penberthy | 33 | run out | | 0 |
| P.A.Neale * | c Roberts b Penberthy | 7 | not out | | 4 |
| M.J.Weston | b Penberthy | 9 | | | |
| S.J.Rhodes + | not out | 56 | | | |
| P.J.Newport | c Roberts b Curran | 15 | | | |
| S.R.Lampitt | not out | 18 | | | |
| N.V.Radford | | | | | |
| R.D.Stemp | | | | | |
| Extras | (b 1,lb 9,w 1) | 11 | (b 1,lb 1,w 5) | | 7 |
| TOTAL | (for 7 wkts dec) | 327 | (for 3 wkts dec) | | 93 |

### NORTHANTS

| | | | | | |
|---|---|---|---|---|---|
| A.Fordham | c Rhodes b Radford | 13 | c Rhodes b Lampitt | | 60 |
| N.A.Felton | lbw b Newport | 40 | c & b Newport | | 47 |
| R.J.Bailey * | c Moody b Radford | 50 | not out | | 95 |
| D.J.Capel | b Newport | 16 | c Rhodes b Weston | | 1 |
| K.M.Curran | not out | 17 | c Radford b Lampitt | | 32 |
| M.B.Loye | not out | 3 | | | |
| D.Ripley + | | | (6) not out | | 27 |
| A.L.Penberthy | | | | | |
| A.R.Roberts | | | | | |
| A.Walker | | | | | |
| N.G.B.Cook | | | | | |
| Extras | (lb 7,nb 4) | 11 | (lb 6,nb 3) | | 9 |
| TOTAL | (for 4 wkts dec) | 150 | (for 4 wkts) | | 271 |

| NORTHANTS | O | M | R | W | O | M | R | W |
|---|---|---|---|---|---|---|---|---|
| Walker | 20 | 4 | 62 | 1 | 6 | 2 | 20 | 0 |
| Penberthy | 30 | 7 | 97 | 3 | 6 | 0 | 27 | 0 |
| Curran | 22 | 11 | 45 | 3 | 4 | 2 | 4 | 1 |
| Capel | 5 | 1 | 17 | 0 | | | | |
| Cook | 15 | 4 | 53 | 0 | 5 | 0 | 26 | 1 |
| Roberts | 16 | 5 | 43 | 0 | | | | |
| Fordham | | | | | 1 | 0 | 14 | 0 |

| WORCS | O | M | R | W | O | M | R | W |
|---|---|---|---|---|---|---|---|---|
| Radford | 12.1 | 1 | 61 | 2 | 12 | 0 | 53 | 0 |
| Newport | 18 | 3 | 49 | 2 | 20.2 | 1 | 77 | 1 |
| Lampitt | 13 | 2 | 33 | 0 | 19 | 1 | 74 | 2 |
| Stemp | | | | | 12 | 3 | 34 | 0 |
| Weston | | | | | 5 | 1 | 27 | 1 |

FALL OF WICKETS

| | WOR | NOR | WOR | NOR |
|---|---|---|---|---|
| 1st | 92 | 41 | 74 | 106 |
| 2nd | 154 | 81 | 74 | 128 |
| 3rd | 193 | 123 | 75 | 129 |
| 4th | 222 | 141 | | 199 |
| 5th | 223 | | | |
| 6th | 236 | | | |
| 7th | 263 | | | |
| 8th | | | | |
| 9th | | | | |
| 10th | | | | |

# BRITANNIC ASS. CHAMPIONSHIP

# OTHER FIRST-CLASS MATCH

Darren Bicknell took 200 runs off Nottinghamshire at The Oval.

## OXFORD U vs. YORKSHIRE

at The Parks on 4th, 5th, 6th June 1991
Toss : Yorkshire.  Umpires : N.T.Plews and G.A.Stickley
Match drawn

### YORKSHIRE

| | | | | | |
|---|---|---|---|---|---|
| A.A.Metcalfe * | c Pfaff b Wood | 27 | lbw b Davies | | 62 |
| S.A.Kellett | lbw b Wood | 20 | c Lovell b Gupte | | 63 |
| D.Byas | c & b Morris R.E. | 101 | (4) not out | | 0 |
| R.J.Blakey + | b Morris R.E. | 196 | | | |
| P.E.Robinson | not out | 35 | (3) c Montgomerie b Davies | | 22 |
| A.P.Grayson | not out | 18 | | | |
| D.Gough | | | | | |
| J.D.Batty | | | | | |
| M.Broadhurst | | | | | |
| S.D.Fletcher | | | | | |
| M.A.Robinson | | | | | |
| Extras | (lb 3,w 4,nb 1) | 8 | (b 5,lb 2,nb 4) | | 11 |
| TOTAL | (for 4 wkts dec) | 405 | (for 3 wkts) | | 158 |

### OXFORD U

| | | |
|---|---|---|
| R.R.Montgomerie | c Byas b Batty | 54 |
| R.E.Morris | c Blakey b Broadhurst | 2 |
| D.Sandiford + | b Broadhurst | 83 |
| C.Gupte | c Blakey b Gough | 48 |
| G.Lovell | lbw b Broadhurst | 2 |
| G.J.Turner * | c & b Grayson | 10 |
| D.Pfaff | not out | 40 |
| J.Morris | b Gough | 0 |
| H.Davies | lbw b Batty | 1 |
| B.Wood | st Blakey b Batty | 6 |
| R.MacDonald | not out | 1 |
| Extras | (b 6,lb 1,nb 13) | 20 |
| TOTAL | (for 9 wkts dec) | 267 |

| OXFORD U | O | M | R | W | O | M | R | W |
|---|---|---|---|---|---|---|---|---|
| MacDonald | 14 | 4 | 48 | 0 | | | | |
| Wood | 27 | 5 | 85 | 2 | 11 | 2 | 37 | 0 |
| Turner | 22 | 3 | 91 | 0 | 8 | 1 | 16 | 0 |
| Davies | 12 | 2 | 68 | 0 | 14 | 2 | 46 | 2 |
| Lovell | 7 | 1 | 28 | 0 | | | | |
| Morris R.E. | 17 | 3 | 82 | 2 | 3 | 0 | 19 | 0 |
| Gupte | | | | | 8.1 | 1 | 33 | 1 |

| YORKSHIRE | O | M | R | W | O | M | R | W |
|---|---|---|---|---|---|---|---|---|
| Fletcher | 8 | 0 | 27 | 0 | | | | |
| Broadhurst | 19 | 5 | 61 | 3 | | | | |
| Gough | 18 | 3 | 55 | 2 | | | | |
| Batty | 27 | 8 | 63 | 3 | | | | |
| Robinson M.A. | 14 | 2 | 44 | 0 | | | | |
| Grayson | 7 | 4 | 3 | 1 | | | | |
| Byas | 7 | 2 | 7 | 0 | | | | |

| FALL OF WICKETS | YOR | OXF | YOR | OXF |
|---|---|---|---|---|
| 1st | 42 | 9 | 115 | |
| 2nd | 49 | 93 | 158 | |
| 3rd | 318 | 171 | 158 | |
| 4th | 363 | 175 | | |
| 5th | | 198 | | |
| 6th | | 241 | | |
| 7th | | 245 | | |
| 8th | | 246 | | |
| 9th | | 266 | | |
| 10th | | | | |

## SURREY vs. NOTTS

at The Oval on 4th, 5th, 6th June 1991
Toss : Notts.  Umpires : G.I.Burgess and J.H.Harris
Match drawn.  Surrey 4 pts (Bt: 4, Bw: 0), Notts 4 pts (Bt: 3, Bw: 1)

### SURREY

| | | | | |
|---|---|---|---|---|
| D.J.Bicknell | c Stephenson b Hemmings | 125 | c Scott b Hemmings | 81 |
| R.I.Alikhan | c Scott b Evans | 69 | not out | 96 |
| A.J.Stewart | c Scott b Evans | 30 | not out | 37 |
| D.M.Ward | not out | 52 | | |
| G.P.Thorpe | not out | 19 | | |
| I.A.Greig * | | | | |
| K.T.Medlycott | | | | |
| M.A.Feltham | | | | |
| N.F.Sargeant + | | | | |
| Waqar Younis | | | | |
| A.J.Murphy | | | | |
| Extras | (lb 5,w 1,nb 1) | 7 | (lb 7) | 7 |
| TOTAL | (for 3 wkts dec) | 302 | (for 1 wkt dec) | 221 |

### NOTTS

| | | | | |
|---|---|---|---|---|
| B.C.Broad | not out | 137 | | |
| P.Pollard | b Feltham | 62 | c Sargeant b Waqar Younis | 1 |
| M.A.Crawley | lbw b Medlycott | 22 | (1) not out | 20 |
| P.Johnson | not out | 8 | | |
| R.T.Robinson * | | | (3) not out | 6 |
| D.W.Randall | | | | |
| K.P.Evans | | | | |
| F.D.Stephenson | | | | |
| C.W.Scott + | | | | |
| M.Saxelby | | | | |
| E.E.Hemmings | | | | |
| Extras | (b 4,lb 1,w 6,nb 10) | 21 | (nb 6) | 6 |
| TOTAL | (for 2 wkts dec) | 250 | (for 1 wkt) | 33 |

| NOTTS | O | M | R | W | O | M | R | W |
|---|---|---|---|---|---|---|---|---|
| Stephenson | 18 | 4 | 51 | 0 | 6 | 2 | 8 | 0 |
| Evans | 26 | 5 | 71 | 2 | 13 | 2 | 34 | 0 |
| Saxelby | 9.2 | 2 | 49 | 0 | 16 | 1 | 96 | 0 |
| Hemmings | 37 | 8 | 109 | 1 | 21 | 9 | 29 | 1 |
| Crawley | 7 | 2 | 17 | 0 | 21 | 6 | 47 | 0 |

| FALL OF WICKETS | SUR | NOT | SUR | NOT |
|---|---|---|---|---|
| 1st | 161 | 154 | 124 | 15 |
| 2nd | 203 | 227 | | |
| 3rd | 233 | | | |
| 4th | | | | |
| 5th | | | | |
| 6th | | | | |
| 7th | | | | |
| 8th | | | | |
| 9th | | | | |
| 10th | | | | |

| SURREY | O | M | R | W | O | M | R | W |
|---|---|---|---|---|---|---|---|---|
| Waqar Younis | 17 | 4 | 54 | 0 | 3.3 | 0 | 12 | 1 |
| Murphy | 19.3 | 5 | 56 | 0 | 3 | 0 | 21 | 0 |
| Feltham | 15 | 1 | 42 | 1 | | | | |
| Medlycott | 34 | 6 | 84 | 1 | | | | |
| Greig | 3 | 1 | 9 | 0 | | | | |

---

# HEADLINES

### Britannic Assurance Championship

#### 4th - 6th June

• Surrey's match with Nottinghamshire at The Oval degenerated into a no-contest as regular breaks in play conspired with a pitch completely in the batsmen's favour. Bowlers only managed to claim seven wickets in three days and Surrey were never able to leave their visitors a realistic target. Darren Bicknell and Chris Broad both took advantage to compile comfortable centuries.

#### Other first-class match

#### 4th - 6th June

• Yorkshire's visit to The Parks allowed Richard Blakey to rediscover his best batting form with 196 as he added 271 for the third wicket with David Byas, while 16-year-old Mark Broadhurst took three wickets on his first-class début. Oxford's David Sandiford compiled a career-best 83 as the students batted their way to safety.

• First-class début: M. Broadhurst (Yorkshire).

# REFUGE ASSURANCE LEAGUE

## DERBYSHIRE vs. SURREY
at Chesterfield on 9th June 1991
Toss : Derby. Umpires : J.H.Hampshire and B.J.Meyer
Surrey won on faster scoring rate. Derby 0 pts, Surrey 4 pts

**SURREY**

| | | |
|---|---|---|
| D.J.Bicknell | b Cork | 68 |
| M.A.Lynch | c Bowler b Base | 10 |
| A.J.Stewart + | b Base | 60 |
| D.M.Ward | b Warner | 15 |
| G.P.Thorpe | c Bowler b Cork | 1 |
| I.A.Greig * | b Cork | 24 |
| J.D.Robinson | c Cork b Goldsmith | 17 |
| M.A.Feltham | c Cork b Goldsmith | 19 |
| C.K.Bullen | not out | 0 |
| Waqar Younis | b Goldsmith | 0 |
| A.J.Murphy | not out | 0 |
| Extras | (lb 5,w 4) | 9 |
| TOTAL | (40 overs)(for 9 wkts) | 223 |

**DERBYSHIRE**

| | | |
|---|---|---|
| K.J.Barnett * | c Stewart b Murphy | 11 |
| P.D.Bowler + | not out | 47 |
| T.J.G.O'Gorman | not out | 49 |
| M.Azharuddin | | |
| C.J.Adams | | |
| S.C.Goldsmith | | |
| A.E.Warner | | |
| F.A.Griffith | | |
| I.Folley | | |
| D.G.Cork | | |
| S.J.Base | | |
| Extras | (lb 4,w 9) | 13 |
| TOTAL | (23 overs)(for 1 wkt) | 120 |

| DERBYSHIRE | O | M | R | W | FALL OF WICKETS | | |
|---|---|---|---|---|---|---|---|
| | | | | | | SUR | DER |
| Warner | 8 | 0 | 52 | 1 | | | |
| Base | 8 | 0 | 21 | 2 | 1st | 25 | 25 |
| Cork | 8 | 0 | 45 | 3 | 2nd | 144 | |
| Goldsmith | 8 | 0 | 48 | 3 | 3rd | 144 | |
| Folley | 4 | 0 | 28 | 0 | 4th | 146 | |
| Griffith | 4 | 0 | 24 | 0 | 5th | 182 | |
| | | | | | 6th | 188 | |
| SURREY | O | M | R | W | 7th | 220 | |
| Feltham | 7 | 0 | 33 | 0 | 8th | 222 | |
| Murphy | 6 | 0 | 35 | 1 | 9th | 222 | |
| Robinson | 2 | 0 | 9 | 0 | 10th | | |
| Greig | 4 | 0 | 16 | 0 | | | |
| Waqar Younis | 4 | 0 | 23 | 0 | | | |

## ESSEX vs. WORCESTERSHIRE
at Ilford on 9th June 1991
Toss : Worcs. Umpires : D.O.Oslear and A.G.T.Whitehead
Essex won by 34 runs. Essex 4 pts, Worcestershire 0 pts

**ESSEX**

| | | |
|---|---|---|
| J.P.Stephenson | c Weston b Botham | 67 |
| A.C.Seymour | lbw b Weston | 20 |
| Salim Malik | c Newport b Radford | 89 |
| P.J.Prichard | c Botham b Radford | 36 |
| N.Hussain | not out | 22 |
| M.A.Garnham + | b Botham | 1 |
| N.A.Foster * | run out | 5 |
| N.Shahid | | |
| T.D.Topley | | |
| S.J.W.Andrew | | |
| P.M.Such | | |
| Extras | (lb 5,w 4,nb 1) | 10 |
| TOTAL | (40 overs)(for 6 wkts) | 250 |

**WORCESTERSHIRE**

| | | |
|---|---|---|
| T.S.Curtis | c Topley b Stephenson | 46 |
| T.M.Moody | b Foster | 0 |
| M.J.Weston | c Hussain b Andrew | 4 |
| D.B.D'Oliveira | c Salim Malik b Topley | 25 |
| I.T.Botham | c Shahid b Andrew | 33 |
| P.A.Neale * | c Salim Malik b Foster | 39 |
| S.J.Rhodes + | c Salim Malik b Stephenson | 0 |
| N.V.Radford | b Stephenson | 5 |
| S.R.Lampitt | c Stephenson b Foster | 4 |
| R.K.Illingworth | not out | 25 |
| P.J.Newport | not out | 3 |
| Extras | (b 5,lb 18,w 4,nb 5) | 32 |
| TOTAL | (40 overs)(for 9 wkts) | 216 |

| WORCS | O | M | R | W | FALL OF WICKETS | | |
|---|---|---|---|---|---|---|---|
| | | | | | | ESS | WOR |
| Weston | 8 | 0 | 37 | 1 | | | |
| Newport | 4 | 0 | 28 | 0 | 1st | 47 | 1 |
| Lampitt | 5 | 0 | 29 | 0 | 2nd | 151 | 11 |
| Radford | 8 | 0 | 67 | 2 | 3rd | 193 | 58 |
| Illingworth | 8 | 0 | 45 | 0 | 4th | 232 | 117 |
| Botham | 7 | 1 | 39 | 2 | 5th | 233 | 149 |
| | | | | | 6th | 250 | 150 |
| ESSEX | O | M | R | W | 7th | | 158 |
| Foster | 8 | 0 | 28 | 3 | 8th | | 175 |
| Andrew | 8 | 0 | 45 | 2 | 9th | | 205 |
| Such | 8 | 1 | 38 | 0 | 10th | | |
| Topley | 8 | 0 | 65 | 1 | | | |
| Stephenson | 8 | 0 | 17 | 3 | | | |

## HEADLINES

### Refuge Assurance League

### 9th June

• Nottinghamshire continued to build a healthy advantage at the top of the Sunday League with their sixth win in six matches, overcoming their nearest challengers Somerset at Trent Bridge by four runs, again showing that they could defend a relatively modest score.

• Champions Derbyshire could not halt their slide down the table, losing on faster run-rate to Surrey at Chesterfield when rain brought an end to their innings after 23 overs, and Lancashire's title aspirations were also hindered by the weather, rain intervening after 8.2 overs of their innings as they chased a reduced target of 120 in 20 overs to beat Glamorgan at Old Trafford.

• Essex dealt a blow to Worcestershire's prospects with a 34-run victory at Ilford, John Stephenson and Salim Malik who hit a Sunday-best 89, helping the home side to a total of 250 for six with their second-wicket stand of 104. Stephenson also weighed in with a career-best three for 17 as Worcestershire could not challenge a testing target.

• Sussex beat Hampshire by 14 runs even after collapsing to 59 for six, from which predicament they were rescued by a career-best 78 not out from Keith Greenfield. Hampshire, by contrast, reached 94 for one before collapsing to 158 all out, Tony Pigott collecting five wickets.

• Leicestershire beat Middlesex by a more convincing margin of 73 runs at Uxbridge, their bowlers restricting the home side to just 129 for nine in their 40 overs.

• Gloucestershire and Northamptonshire must have come close to contesting the shortest match ever recorded when their day's cricket at Moreton in Marsh was abandoned after a single ball had been bowled by Northants's Alan Walker.

## GLOUCS vs. NORTHANTS
at Moreton in Marsh on 9th June 1991
Toss : Northants. Umpires : R.Palmer and A.A.Jones
No result. Gloucs 2 pts, Northants 2 pts

**GLOUCS**

| | | |
|---|---|---|
| R.J.Scott | not out | 0 |
| C.W.J.Athey + | not out | 0 |
| A.J.Wright * | | |
| M.W.Alleyne | | |
| J.W.Lloyds | | |
| P.W.Romaines | | |
| D.V.Lawrence | | |
| D.R.Gilbert | | |
| A.M.Smith | | |
| A.M.Babington | | |
| T.Hancock | | |
| Extras | | 0 |
| TOTAL | (0.1 overs)(for 0 wkts) | 0 |

**NORTHANTS**

| | |
|---|---|
| A.Fordham | |
| N.A.Felton | |
| R.J.Bailey * | |
| D.J.Capel | |
| K.M.Curran | |
| R.G.Williams | |
| A.L.Penberthy | |
| J.G.Thomas | |
| D.Ripley + | |
| A.Walker | |
| N.G.B.Cook | |
| Extras | |
| TOTAL | |

| NORTHANTS | O | M | R | W | FALL OF WICKETS | | |
|---|---|---|---|---|---|---|---|
| | | | | | | GLO | NOR |
| Walker | 0.1 | 0 | 0 | 0 | | | |
| | | | | | 1st | | |
| GLOUCS | O | M | R | W | 2nd | | |
| | | | | | 3rd | | |
| | | | | | 4th | | |
| | | | | | 5th | | |
| | | | | | 6th | | |
| | | | | | 7th | | |
| | | | | | 8th | | |
| | | | | | 9th | | |
| | | | | | 10th | | |

## HAMPSHIRE vs. SUSSEX
at Basingstoke on 9th June 1991
Toss : Hampshire. Umpires : B.Dudleston and R.Julian
Sussex won by 14 runs. Hampshire 0 pts, Sussex 4 pts

**SUSSEX**

| | | |
|---|---|---|
| N.J.Lenham | b Connor | 9 |
| P.W.G.Parker * | c Terry b Connor | 1 |
| A.P.Wells | c Gower b Aqib Javed | 1 |
| M.P.Speight | c Udal b Aqib Javed | 7 |
| K.Greenfield | not out | 78 |
| C.M.Wells | c & b Ayling | 16 |
| A.I.C.Dodemaide | lbw b Ayling | 0 |
| P.Moores + | b Udal | 33 |
| A.C.S.Pigott | c Gower b Connor | 4 |
| I.D.K.Salisbury | c Gower b Connor | 2 |
| A.N.Jones | not out | 3 |
| Extras | (b 3,lb 10,w 4,nb 1) | 18 |
| TOTAL | (40 overs)(for 9 wkts) | 172 |

**HAMPSHIRE**

| | | |
|---|---|---|
| V.P.Terry | lbw b Pigott | 42 |
| T.C.Middleton | c Speight b Jones | 8 |
| J.R.Wood | c Jones b Pigott | 39 |
| D.I.Gower | c Wells A.P. b Pigott | 0 |
| M.C.J.Nicholas * | c Wells A.P. b Pigott | 23 |
| J.R.Ayling | c & b Salisbury | 7 |
| A.N Aymes + | lbw b Jones | 5 |
| T.M.Tremlett | c Pigott b Salisbury | 8 |
| S.D.Udal | c Moores b Pigott | 3 |
| C.A.Connor | b Pigott | 2 |
| Aqib Javed | not out | 4 |
| Extras | (lb 10,w 6,nb 1) | 17 |
| TOTAL | (39.1 overs) | 158 |

| HAMPSHIRE | O | M | R | W | FALL OF WICKETS | | |
|---|---|---|---|---|---|---|---|
| | | | | | | SUS | HAM |
| Connor | 8 | 0 | 29 | 4 | | | |
| Aqib Javed | 8 | 2 | 16 | 2 | 1st | 7 | 31 |
| Tremlett | 8 | 0 | 33 | 0 | 2nd | 8 | 94 |
| Ayling | 8 | 1 | 41 | 2 | 3rd | 18 | 97 |
| Udal | 8 | 0 | 40 | 1 | 4th | 18 | 108 |
| | | | | | 5th | 59 | 132 |
| SUSSEX | O | M | R | W | 6th | 59 | 138 |
| Dodemaide | 8 | 0 | 20 | 0 | 7th | 138 | 143 |
| Jones | 8 | 0 | 33 | 3 | 8th | 150 | 151 |
| Wells C.M. | 8 | 0 | 32 | 0 | 9th | 159 | 151 |
| Pigott | 7.1 | 1 | 30 | 5 | 10th | | 158 |
| Salisbury | 8 | 1 | 33 | 2 | | | |

# REFUGE ASSURANCE LEAGUE

## LANCASHIRE vs. GLAMORGAN
at Old Trafford on 9th June 1991
Toss : Lancashire.  Umpires : N.T.Plews and R.A.White
No result.  Lancashire 2 pts, Glamorgan 2 pts

GLAMORGAN
| | | |
|---|---|---|
| H.Morris * | b Austin | 66 |
| M.P.Maynard | lbw b Wasim Akram | 19 |
| G.C.Holmes | not out | 50 |
| I.Smith | b Austin | 23 |
| M.J.Cann | b Wasim Akram | 2 |
| J.Derrick | not out | 4 |
| A.Dale | | |
| C.P.Metson + | | |
| S.J.Dennis | | |
| S.R.Barwick | | |
| M.Frost | | |
| Extras | (lb 7,w 2,nb 1) | 10 |
| TOTAL | (27 overs)(for 4 wkts) | 174 |

LANCASHIRE
| | | |
|---|---|---|
| G.D.Mendis | c sub b Derrick | 11 |
| G.Fowler | not out | 38 |
| G.D.Lloyd | not out | 4 |
| N.H.Fairbrother | | |
| M.Watkinson | | |
| Wasim Akram | | |
| W.K.Hegg + | | |
| D.P.Hughes * | | |
| I.D.Austin | | |
| P.J.W.Allott | | |
| P.J.Martin | | |
| Extras | | 0 |
| TOTAL | (8.2 overs)(for 1 wkt) | 53 |

| LANCASHIRE | O | M | R | W |
|---|---|---|---|---|
| Martin | 4 | 0 | 19 | 0 |
| Allott | 6 | 1 | 26 | 0 |
| Wasim Akram | 7 | 0 | 46 | 2 |
| Watkinson | 5 | 0 | 43 | 0 |
| Austin | 5 | 0 | 33 | 2 |

| GLAMORGAN | O | M | R | W |
|---|---|---|---|---|
| Dennis | 2 | 0 | 13 | 0 |
| Frost | 2 | 0 | 9 | 0 |
| Derrick | 2.2 | 0 | 17 | 1 |
| Barwick | 2 | .0 | 14 | 0 |

| FALL OF WICKETS | GLA | LAN |
|---|---|---|
| 1st | 40 | 40 |
| 2nd | 124 | |
| 3rd | 163 | |
| 4th | 167 | |
| 5th | | |
| 6th | | |
| 7th | | |
| 8th | | |
| 9th | | |
| 10th | | |

## MIDDLESEX vs. LEICESTERSHIRE
at Uxbridge on 9th June 1991
Toss : Middlesex.  Umpires : M.J.Kitchen and R.C.Tolchard
Leicestershire won by 73 runs.  Middlesex 0 pts, Leics 4 pts

LEICESTERSHIRE
| | | |
|---|---|---|
| T.J.Boon * | lbw b Cowans | 4 |
| N.E.Briers * | run out | 44 |
| P.N.Hepworth | b Hughes | 1 |
| C.C.Lewis | st Farbrace b Weekes | 10 |
| B.F.Smith | c Gatting b Embury | 33 |
| J.D.R.Benson | run out | 42 |
| P.Willey | c Embury b Hutchinson | 10 |
| P.Whitticase + | b Embury | 1 |
| D.J.Millns | c Farbrace b Hughes | 5 |
| C.Wilkinson | not out | 35 |
| J.N.Maguire | not out | 0 |
| Extras | (lb 9,w 6,nb 2) | 17 |
| TOTAL | (40 overs)(for 9 wkts) | 202 |

MIDDLESEX
| | | |
|---|---|---|
| I.J.F.Hutchinson | lbw b Lewis | 0 |
| M.A.Roseberry | b Maguire | 1 |
| M.W.Gatting * | lbw b Millns | 16 |
| K.R.Brown | c Hepworth b Benson | 40 |
| M.Keech | run out | 20 |
| P.N.Weekes | lbw b Maguire | 20 |
| J.E.Embury | b Willey | 2 |
| N.F.Williams | c Millns b Benson | 1 |
| P.Farbrace + | not out | 14 |
| S.P.Hughes | c Wilkinson b Lewis | 4 |
| N.G.Cowans | not out | 0 |
| Extras | (lb 6,w 3,nb 2) | 11 |
| TOTAL | (40 overs)(for 9 wkts) | 129 |

| MIDDLESEX | O | M | R | W |
|---|---|---|---|---|
| Cowans | 8 | 0 | 30 | 1 |
| Hughes | 8 | 0 | 29 | 2 |
| Williams | 6 | 0 | 40 | 0 |
| Weekes | 8 | 0 | 45 | 1 |
| Embury | 8 | 0 | 39 | 2 |
| Hutchinson | 2 | 0 | 10 | 1 |

| LEICS | O | M | R | W |
|---|---|---|---|---|
| Lewis | 6 | 1 | 14 | 2 |
| Maguire | 8 | 2 | 16 | 2 |
| Millns | 6 | 0 | 27 | 1 |
| Wilkinson | 4 | 0 | 18 | 0 |
| Willey | 8 | 0 | 22 | 1 |
| Benson | 8 | 0 | 26 | 2 |

| FALL OF WICKETS | LEI | MID |
|---|---|---|
| 1st | 10 | 0 |
| 2nd | 17 | 2 |
| 3rd | 41 | 39 |
| 4th | 98 | 82 |
| 5th | 118 | 87 |
| 6th | 153 | 91 |
| 7th | 156 | 100 |
| 8th | 157 | 119 |
| 9th | 191 | 128 |
| 10th | | |

## NOTTS vs. SOMERSET
at Trent Bridge on 9th June 1991
Toss : Somerset.  Umpires : K.J.Lyons and R.Palmer
Notts won by 4 runs.  Notts 4 pts, Somerset 0 pts

NOTTS
| | | |
|---|---|---|
| B.C.Broad | c Harden b Trump | 41 |
| D.W.Randall | lbw b Hayhurst | 39 |
| P.Johnson | c Burns b Macleay | 31 |
| R.T.Robinson * | run out | 15 |
| M.A.Crawley | c & b Macleay | 9 |
| M.Saxelby | lbw b Lefebvre | 27 |
| F.D.Stephenson | c Tavare b Macleay | 0 |
| B.N.French + | not out | 5 |
| K.P.Evans | | |
| E.E.Hemmings | | |
| K.E.Cooper | | |
| Extras | (lb 8,w 5) | 13 |
| TOTAL | (40 overs)(for 7 wkts) | 180 |

SOMERSET
| | | |
|---|---|---|
| S.J.Cook | lbw b Stephenson | 2 |
| R.J.Bartlett | c Broad b Cooper | 19 |
| C.J.Tavare * | c Randall b Evans | 16 |
| R.J.Harden | not out | 79 |
| N.D.Burns + | c Broad b Saxelby | 9 |
| K.H.Macleay | c & b Hemmings | 2 |
| A.N.Hayhurst | c French b Saxelby | 27 |
| R.P.Lefebvre | run out | 4 |
| N.A.Mallender | not out | 5 |
| H.R.J.Trump | | |
| D.A.Graveney | | |
| Extras | (lb 10,w 3) | 13 |
| TOTAL | (40 overs)(for 7 wkts) | 176 |

| SOMERSET | O | M | R | W |
|---|---|---|---|---|
| Mallender | 8 | 0 | 41 | 0 |
| Lefebvre | 7 | 0 | 25 | 1 |
| Hayhurst | 6 | 0 | 33 | 1 |
| Macleay | 8 | 0 | 31 | 3 |
| Graveney | 5 | 0 | 20 | 0 |
| Trump | 6 | 0 | 22 | 1 |

| NOTTS | O | M | R | W |
|---|---|---|---|---|
| Cooper | 8 | 0 | 20 | 1 |
| Stephenson | 8 | 1 | 26 | 1 |
| Evans | 8 | 0 | 40 | 1 |
| Hemmings | 8 | 1 | 33 | 1 |
| Saxelby | 6 | 0 | 31 | 2 |
| Crawley | 2 | 0 | 16 | 0 |

| FALL OF WICKETS | NOT | SOM |
|---|---|---|
| 1st | 80 | 8 |
| 2nd | 99 | 36 |
| 3rd | 129 | 49 |
| 4th | 139 | 76 |
| 5th | 153 | 88 |
| 6th | 153 | 156 |
| 7th | 180 | 167 |
| 8th | | |
| 9th | | |
| 10th | | |

An unhappy beginning for Graeme Hick, caught by Dujon off Walsh for 6 in his first Test innings.

# CORNHILL TEST MATCH

## HEADLINES

### England v West Indies
### First Cornhill Test Match

### Headingley: 6th - 10th June

• The 100th Test match played between England and West Indies provided England with their first victory over West Indies on home soil since the Headingley Test of 1969 when Ray Illingworth's team won by 30 runs. England's 1991 victory was a personal triumph for Graham Gooch who became the fifth Englishman to carry his bat in a Test match with his heroic second innings 154*, but every member of the team played his part.

• England's first innings was reminiscent of many batting performances in the 24 matches played since their last home success against West Indies, every batsman struggling against the four fast bowlers, but the first hint of a dramatic change in fortunes came on the second afternoon when Mark Ramprakash, in the space of a few minutes, first held a brilliant diving catch at cover point to dismiss Phil Simmons and then with a devastating pick up and throw ran out Carl Hooper. Even an innings of 73 from Viv Richards that mixed caution with brutal strokeplay could not wrest the advantage from England and a priceless first innings lead of 25 was gained. Phil DeFreitas and Derek Pringle both took their 50th Test wickets during the innings, DeFreitas returning his best figures against West Indies.

• Curtly Ambrose made England work exceptionally hard to build a winning lead, twice taking two wickets with successive balls as he claimed the first six second innings wickets, but Gooch remained massively secure and shared crucial restorative partnerships of 78 with Mark Ramprakash, who batted with great courage in each innings of his début Test, and 98 with Derek Pringle, who won over his staunchest Headingley critics with his performance. When Devon Malcolm was last out England's lead had reached 277 and Gooch had become the first Englishman to carry his bat in Test cricket since Geoff Boycott was marooned on 99 against Australia at Perth in 1979-80 and the second after Len Hutton (against West Indies in 1950) to do so in England. Gooch's 154* was his 14th Test 100, and his highest score against West Indies, and his innings had given his team the opportunity to stage a repeat of their unexpected victory at Kingston in 1990.

• DeFreitas gave them the best possible start by removing Simmons first ball, and wickets fell on the last day with a regularity that soon convinced the doubters that an English victory could only be prevented by the weather which had interrupted play on each of the five days. Steve Watkin made the most telling breakthrough by dismissing Hooper, Richards and Logie in his first three overs, DeFreitas finished with match figures of eight for 93, a fine reward for his best Test performance, but it was left to Malcolm to collect the last wicket, Courtney Walsh caught by at square cover by a tumbling Michael Atherton.

• West Indies had reverted to their old failings, batting like millionaires, rather than preserving their wickets like misers, but England deserved their success for an all-round team effort, following the shining example set by Graham Gooch.

• Test débuts: G.A.Hick, M.R.Ramprakash, S.L.Watkin (England).

• Man of the match: G.A.Gooch.

## ENGLAND vs. WEST INDIES

at Headingley on 6th, 7th, 8th, 9th, 10th June 1991
Toss : West Indies.  Umpires : H.D.Bird and D.R.Shepherd
England won by 115 runs

### ENGLAND

| Batsman | Dismissal | R | Dismissal | R |
|---|---|---|---|---|
| G.A.Gooch * | c Dujon b Marshall | 34 | not out | 154 |
| M.A.Atherton | b Patterson | 2 | c Dujon b Ambrose | 6 |
| G.A.Hick | c Dujon b Walsh | 6 | b Ambrose | 6 |
| A.J.Lamb | c Hooper b Marshall | 11 | c Hooper b Ambrose | 0 |
| M.R.Ramprakash | c Hooper b Marshall | 27 | c Dujon b Ambrose | 27 |
| R.A.Smith | run out | 54 | lbw b Ambrose | 0 |
| R.C.Russell + | lbw b Patterson | 5 | c Dujon b Ambrose | 4 |
| D.R.Pringle | c Logie b Patterson | 16 | c Dujon b Marshall | 27 |
| P.A.J.DeFreitas | c Simmons b Ambrose | 15 | lbw b Walsh | 3 |
| S.L.Watkin | b Ambrose | 2 | c Hooper b Marshall | 0 |
| D.E.Malcolm | not out | 5 | b Marshall | 4 |
| Extras | (lb 5,w 2,nb 14) | 21 | (b 4,lb 9,w 1,nb 7) | 21 |
| TOTAL | | 198 | | 252 |

### WEST INDIES

| Batsman | Dismissal | R | Dismissal | R |
|---|---|---|---|---|
| P.V.Simmons | c Ramprakash b DeFreitas | 38 | b DeFreitas | 0 |
| D.L.Haynes | c Russell b Watkin | 7 | c Smith b Pringle | 19 |
| R.B.Richardson | run out | 29 | c Lamb b DeFreitas | 68 |
| C.L.Hooper | run out | 0 | c Lamb b Watkin | 5 |
| I.V.A.Richards * | c Lamb b Pringle | 73 | c Gooch b Watkin | 3 |
| A.L.Logie | c Lamb b DeFreitas | 6 | c Gooch b Watkin | 3 |
| P.J.L.Dujon + | c Ramprakash b Watkin | 6 | lbw b DeFreitas | 33 |
| M.D.Marshall | c Hick b Pringle | 0 | lbw b Pringle | 1 |
| C.E.L.Ambrose | c Hick b DeFreitas | 0 | c Pringle b DeFreitas | 14 |
| C.A.Walsh | c Gooch b DeFreitas | 3 | c Atherton b Malcolm | 9 |
| B.P.Patterson | not out | 5 | not out | 0 |
| Extras | (lb 1,nb 5) | 6 | (lb 1,nb 6) | 7 |
| TOTAL | | 173 | | 162 |

| WEST INDIES | O | M | R | W | O | M | R | W |
|---|---|---|---|---|---|---|---|---|
| Ambrose | 26 | 8 | 49 | 2 | 28 | 6 | 52 | 6 |
| Patterson | 26.2 | 8 | 67 | 3 | 15 | 1 | 52 | 0 |
| Walsh | 14 | 7 | 31 | 1 | 30 | 5 | 61 | 1 |
| Marshall | 13 | 4 | 46 | 3 | 25 | 4 | 58 | 3 |
| Hooper | | | | | 4 | 1 | 11 | 0 |
| Richards | | | | | 4 | 1 | 5 | 0 |

| ENGLAND | O | M | R | W | O | M | R | W |
|---|---|---|---|---|---|---|---|---|
| Malcolm | 14 | 0 | 69 | 0 | 6.4 | 0 | 26 | 1 |
| DeFreitas | 17.1 | 5 | 34 | 4 | 21 | 4 | 59 | 4 |
| Watkin | 14 | 2 | 55 | 2 | 7 | 0 | 38 | 3 |
| Pringle | 9 | 3 | 14 | 2 | 22 | 6 | 38 | 2 |

### FALL OF WICKETS

| | ENG | WI | ENG | WI |
|---|---|---|---|---|
| 1st | 13 | 36 | 22 | 0 |
| 2nd | 45 | 54 | 38 | 61 |
| 3rd | 45 | 58 | 38 | 77 |
| 4th | 64 | 102 | 116 | 85 |
| 5th | 129 | 139 | 116 | 88 |
| 6th | 149 | 156 | 124 | 136 |
| 7th | 154 | 160 | 222 | 137 |
| 8th | 177 | 165 | 236 | 139 |
| 9th | 181 | 167 | 238 | 162 |
| 10th | 198 | 173 | 252 | 162 |

Graham Gooch dispatches Courtney Walsh to the boundary during his match-winning innings.

# BRITANNIC ASSURANCE CHAMPIONSHIP

## HEADLINES

### Britannic Assurance Championship

### 7th - 10th June

- Derbyshire and Gloucestershire were the only winners and both counties remained in the lower half of the Championship table. Derbyshire's victory, a 108-run defeat of Glamorgan at Chesterfield, was their first of the season and was achieved largely thanks to career-best bowling performances from Kim Barnett and Dominic Cork as Glamorgan collapsed from 105 for nought to 192 all out in their second innings. John Morris had also played his part by scoring a rapid 122 not out to allow Barnett to delcare exactly 300 ahead.

- Gloucestershire, recently beaten in two days by both Warwickshire and Essex, would have been relieved to gain their six-wicket success over Hampshire at Southampton. Both captains were forced to forfeit an innings in a bid to gain a result and with the top three in Gloucestershire's order all passing fifty that result was rarely in doubt.

- Kent and Sussex showed a refreshingly positive approach at Tunbridge Wells, refusing the umpires' offer to end their match early in appalling light. Ian Salisbury almost spun Sussex to victory with five second innings wickets as Kent found 224 in 40 overs a taxing proposition. The visitors had held the initiative for most of the match, following a third wicket stand of 235 between Neil Lenham, who improved his career-best score, and Alan Wells, who hit his fourth 100 of the season.

- Although John Emburey (4 for 59) and Phil Tufnell (6 for 82) shared all ten wickets in Leicestershire's second innings, Middlesex did not have sufficient time to press for victory at Uxbridge. Ben Smith had earlier completed his maiden first-class fifty and David Millns a career-best 44 in Leicester's first innings and Mike Roseberry hit his first Championship 100 of the summer in Middlesex's reply.

- Rain at Edgbaston and Warwickshire's attempt to improve their over-rate combined to provide a dismal end to their match with Somerset, Andy Lloyd and Andy Moles bowling 21 maidens in 24 overs as the visitors blocked out in their second innings. Simon Green, making his highest first-class score, and Dermot Reeve added 152 for the fifth wicket to take Warwickshire's first innings total to 359, but Somerset's batsmen were equally comfortable, once Allan Donald had suffered a stomach muscle strain.

- Worcestershire were always in control of their match against Essex at Ilford, but repeated delays for rain made victory impossible. Stuart Lampitt contributed a career-best 58 not out at number 10 to take the visitors to 350 in their first innings, then helped Neal Radford and Phil Newport to bowl Essex out for 255. Tom Moody made his highest score in county cricket before the declaration, but, although Essex lost four second innings wickets, a draw was never in doubt.

### ESSEX vs. WORCESTERSHIRE

at Ilford on 7th, 8th, 10th June 1991
Toss : Worcestershire.  Umpires : D.O.Oslear and A.G.T.Whitehead
Match drawn.  Essex 6 pts (Bt: 3, Bw: 3), Worcestershire 7 pts (Bt: 3, Bw: 4)
100 overs scores : Worcestershire 293 for 8

WORCESTERSHIRE

| | | | | |
|---|---|---:|---|---:|
| T.S.Curtis | lbw b Foster | 2 | not out | 68 |
| G.J.Lord | c Stephenson b Topley | 85 | c Prichard b Foster | 0 |
| T.M.Moody | b Andrew | 10 | not out | 181 |
| D.B.D'Oliveira | c Andrew b Topley | 25 | | |
| P.A.Neale * | b Foster | 28 | | |
| M.J.Weston | c Garnham b Topley | 5 | | |
| S.J.Rhodes + | b Childs | 64 | | |
| R.K.Illingworth | b Salim Malik | 19 | | |
| P.J.Newport | c Hussain b Foster | 12 | | |
| S.R.Lampitt | not out | 58 | | |
| N.V.Radford | not out | 7 | | |
| Extras | (b 6,lb 7,w 5,nb 17) | 35 | (lb 3,nb 13) | 16 |
| TOTAL | (for 9 wkts dec) | 350 | (for 1 wkt dec) | 265 |

ESSEX

| | | | | |
|---|---|---:|---|---:|
| J.P.Stephenson | lbw b Radford | 0 | b Radford | 4 |
| A.C.Seymour | c D'Oliveira b Lampitt | 67 | lbw b Radford | 3 |
| P.J.Prichard | c Rhodes b Newport | 9 | (6) not out | 0 |
| Salim Malik | c Moody b Radford | 37 | | |
| N.Hussain | c Moody b Radford | 8 | | |
| N.Shahid | c D'Oliveira b Lampitt | 15 | (3) not out | 22 |
| M.A.Garnham + | lbw b Radford | 68 | | |
| N.A.Foster * | c Moody b Newport | 32 | (5) c D'Oliveira b Illingworth | 6 |
| T.D.Topley | lbw b Radford | 3 | (4) c Rhodes b Radford | 7 |
| S.J.W.Andrew | b Radford | 0 | | |
| J.H.Childs | not out | 2 | (lb 2) | 2 |
| Extras | (b 4,lb 4,w 1,nb 5) | 14 | (for 4 wkts) | 44 |
| TOTAL | | 255 | | |

| ESSEX | O | M | R | W | O | M | R | W | FALL OF WICKETS | | | | |
|---|---|---|---|---|---|---|---|---|---|---|---|---|---|
| | | | | | | | | | | WOR | ESS | WOR | ESS |
| Andrew | 28 | 4 | 86 | 1 | 5 | 0 | 32 | 0 | 1st | 3 | 0 | 1 | 4 |
| Foster | 36.4 | 8 | 102 | 3 | 6 | 2 | 27 | 1 | 2nd | 19 | 11 | | 7 |
| Topley | 21 | 4 | 77 | 3 | 11 | 1 | 44 | 0 | 3rd | 92 | 69 | | 15 |
| Childs | 16 | 6 | 44 | 1 | 13 | 3 | 33 | 0 | 4th | 141 | 95 | | 44 |
| Stephenson | 4 | 2 | 9 | 0 | 4 | 0 | 27 | 0 | 5th | 149 | 142 | | |
| Salim Malik | 4 | 1 | 19 | 1 | 2 | 0 | 11 | 0 | 6th | 182 | 145 | | |
| Prichard | | | | | 5 | 0 | 52 | 0 | 7th | 229 | 215 | | |
| Seymour | | | | | 4 | 0 | 27 | 0 | 8th | 248 | 234 | | |
| Hussain | | | | | 3 | 0 | 9 | 0 | 9th | 331 | 246 | | |
| | | | | | | | | | 10th | | 255 | | |

| WORCS | O | M | R | W | O | M | R | W |
|---|---|---|---|---|---|---|---|---|
| Radford | 21.2 | 4 | 76 | 6 | 7 | 1 | 19 | 3 |
| Newport | 24 | 2 | 76 | 2 | 4 | 1 | 16 | 0 |
| Illingworth | 23 | 5 | 51 | 0 | 7 | 6 | 11 | 1 |
| Lampitt | 14 | 3 | 44 | 2 | 4 | 1 | 6 | 0 |

### DERBYSHIRE vs. GLAMORGAN

at Chesterfield on 7th, 8th, 10th June 1991
Toss : Derby.  Umpires : J.H.Hampshire and B.J.Meyer
Derby won by 108 runs.  Derby 23 pts (Bt: 3, Bw: 4), Glamorgan 5 pts (Bt: 1, Bw: 4)

DERBYSHIRE

| | | | | |
|---|---|---:|---|---:|
| K.J.Barnett * | c Metson b Barwick | 38 | c Morris b Barwick | 63 |
| P.D.Bowler | c Metson b Frost | 38 | c & b Foster | 15 |
| J.E.Morris | c Metson b Barwick | 0 | not out | 122 |
| M.Azharuddin | c Metson b Frost | 43 | c Foster b Smith | 9 |
| T.J.G.O'Gorman | c Metson b Frost | 15 | (6) not out | 2 |
| C.J.Adams | c Smith b Barwick | 13 | | |
| K.M.Krikken + | c Metson b Foster | 40 | | |
| D.G.Cork | not out | 34 | | |
| A.E.Warner | c Morris b Foster | 19 | (5) run out | 3 |
| S.J.Base | c Metson b Barwick | 0 | | |
| O.H.Mortensen | c Morris b Frost | 7 | | |
| Extras | (lb 1,nb 11) | 12 | (lb 6,nb 5) | 11 |
| TOTAL | | 259 | (for 4 wkts dec) | 225 |

GLAMORGAN

| | | | | |
|---|---|---:|---|---:|
| A.R.Butcher * | c Cork b Base | 32 | c Bowler b Cork | 71 |
| H.Morris | c Base b Warner | 50 | b Warner | 51 |
| M.P.Maynard | c Krikken b Warner | 8 | (4) lbw b Cork | 8 |
| R.J.Shastri | c Krikken b Warner | 2 | (8) c Morris b Barnett | 1 |
| I.Smith | c Krikken b Base | 4 | b Barnett | 7 |
| A.Dale | c Krikken b Warner | 12 | (3) c O'Gorman b Barnett | 13 |
| R.D.B.Croft | c O'Gorman b Mortensen | 0 | (6) c Krikken b Cork | 5 |
| C.P.Metson + | c Adams b Cork | 34 | (7) b Barnett | 7 |
| S.R.Barwick | b Mortensen | 13 | c Adams b Barnett | 0 |
| D.J.Foster | c Bowler b Mortensen | 0 | not out | 13 |
| M.Frost | not out | 8 | c Morris b Barnett | 0 |
| Extras | (lb 9,w 1,nb 11) | 21 | (b 6,w 3,nb 7) | 16 |
| TOTAL | | 184 | | 192 |

| GLAMORGAN | O | M | R | W | O | M | R | W | FALL OF WICKETS | | | | |
|---|---|---|---|---|---|---|---|---|---|---|---|---|---|
| | | | | | | | | | | DER | GLA | DER | GLA |
| Frost | 16 | 2 | 84 | 4 | 11 | 1 | 72 | 0 | 1st | 80 | 75 | 49 | 105 |
| Foster | 15 | 0 | 102 | 2 | 6 | 0 | 27 | 1 | 2nd | 80 | 85 | 148 | 133 |
| Barwick | 22 | 5 | 61 | 4 | 13 | 0 | 53 | 1 | 3rd | 80 | 95 | 193 | 145 |
| Dale | 3 | 0 | 11 | 0 | 6 | 2 | 30 | 0 | 4th | 96 | 105 | 199 | 158 |
| Smith | | | | | 3 | 0 | 37 | 1 | 5th | 123 | 127 | | 161 |
| | | | | | | | | | 6th | 180 | 127 | | 169 |
| DERBYSHIRE | O | M | R | W | O | M | R | W | 7th | 210 | 127 | | 177 |
| Mortensen | 21 | 7 | 40 | 3 | 4 | 1 | 9 | 0 | 8th | 231 | 172 | | 178 |
| Cork | 11.3 | 1 | 37 | 1 | 24 | 7 | 59 | 3 | 9th | 241 | 172 | | 183 |
| Base | 15 | 0 | 56 | 2 | 16 | 2 | 54 | 0 | 10th | 259 | 184 | | 192 |
| Warner | 24 | 10 | 42 | 4 | 13 | 3 | 36 | 1 | | | | | |
| Barnett | | | | | 19.1 | 7 | 28 | 6 | | | | | |

# BRITANNIC ASSURANCE CHAMPIONSHIP

## WARWICKSHIRE vs. SOMERSET

at Edgbaston on 7th, 8th, 10th June 1991
Toss : Somerset.  Umpires : K.J.Lyons and R.Palmer
Match drawn.  Warwickshire 5 pts (Bt: 4, Bw: 1), Somerset 3 pts (Bt: 2, Bw: 1)
100 overs scores : Warwickshire 316 for 4

### WARWICKSHIRE

| | | | | | |
|---|---|---|---|---|---|
| A.J.Moles | c Burns b Macleay | 16 | c Harden b Mallender | 16 |
| J.D.Ratcliffe | c Bartlett b Hayhurst | 29 | c Burns b Lefebvre | 0 |
| T.A.Lloyd * | c Hayhurst b Graveney | 62 | not out | 53 |
| D.P.Ostler | c Burns b Graveney | 59 | b Macleay | 40 |
| D.A.Reeve | c Macleay b Graveney | 82 | not out | 3 |
| S.J.Green | not out | 77 | | |
| R.G.Twose | not out | 1 | | |
| K.J.Piper + | | | | |
| G.C.Small | | | | |
| T.A.Munton | | | | |
| A.A.Donald | | | | |
| Extras | (b 10,lb 15,w 6,nb 2) | 33 | (lb 7,nb 2) | 9 |
| TOTAL | (for 5 wkts dec) | 359 | (for 3 wkts dec) | 121 |

### SOMERSET

| | | | | | |
|---|---|---|---|---|---|
| S.J.Cook | not out | 94 | run out | 8 |
| P.M.Roebuck | c Piper b Munton | 60 | not out | 20 |
| A.N.Hayhurst | c Piper b Reeve | 18 | b Small | 8 |
| R.J.Harden | lbw b Twose | 20 | | |
| R.J.Bartlett | not out | 0 | | |
| C.J.Tavare * | | | (4) not out | 13 |
| N.D.Burns + | | | | |
| K.H.Macleay | | | | |
| R.P.Lefebvre | | | | |
| N.A.Mallender | | | | |
| D.A.Graveney | | | | |
| Extras | (b 5,lb 12,nb 1) | 18 | (b 1) | 1 |
| TOTAL | (for 3 wkts dec) | 210 | (for 2 wkts) | 50 |

| SOMERSET | O | M | R | W | O | M | R | W | FALL OF WICKETS | | | |
|---|---|---|---|---|---|---|---|---|---|---|---|---|
| | | | | | | | | | | WAR | SOM | WAR | SOM |
| Mallender | 16 | 4 | 29 | 0 | 6 | 0 | 40 | 1 | 1st | 41 | 140 | 5 | 15 |
| Lefebvre | 26 | 5 | 57 | 0 | 4 | 0 | 26 | 1 | 2nd | 59 | 167 | 26 | 36 |
| Macleay | 27 | 3 | 67 | 1 | 3 | 0 | 22 | 1 | 3rd | 172 | 206 | 116 | |
| Hayhurst | 14 | 3 | 67 | 1 | 5 | 0 | 26 | 0 | 4th | 205 | | | |
| Graveney | 23 | 1 | 114 | 3 | | | | | 5th | 357 | | | |
| WARWICKS | O | M | R | W | O | M | R | W | 6th | | | | |
| Donald | 8 | 3 | 20 | 0 | | | | | 7th | | | | |
| Small | 10 | 2 | 27 | 0 | 6 | 0 | 26 | 1 | 8th | | | | |
| Munton | 22 | 5 | 52 | 1 | 5 | 0 | 13 | 0 | 9th | | | | |
| Reeve | 22.3 | 5 | 67 | 1 | 2 | 2 | 0 | 0 | 10th | | | | |
| Twose | 9 | 0 | 27 | 1 | | | | | | | | | |
| Lloyd | | | | | 11 | 11 | 0 | 0 | | | | | |
| Moles | | | | | 13 | 10 | 10 | 0 | | | | | |

## KENT vs. SUSSEX

at Tunbridge Wells on 7th, 8th, 10th June 1991
Toss : Kent.  Umpires : D.J.Constant and B.Hassan
Match drawn.  Kent 4 pts (Bt: 2, Bw: 2), Sussex 8 pts (Bt: 4, Bw: 4)

### SUSSEX

| | | | | | |
|---|---|---|---|---|---|
| D.M.Smith | c Davis b Igglesden | 48 | b McCague | 17 |
| J.W.Hall | c Marsh b Igglesden | 5 | c Davis b McCague | 11 |
| N.J.Lenham | c Fleming b Igglesden | 137 | lbw b Igglesden | 1 |
| A.P.Wells | c Benson b Igglesden | 107 | c Davis b Igglesden | 0 |
| P.W.G.Parker * | c Fleming b Davis | 20 | c Marsh b McCague | 8 |
| C.M.Wells | c Taylor b Davis | 3 | not out | 30 |
| P.Moores + | not out | 1 | | |
| A.I.C.Dodemaide | | | (7) not out | 37 |
| A.C.S.Pigott | | | | |
| I.D.K.Salisbury | | | | |
| A.N.Jones | | | | |
| Extras | (b 4,lb 4) | 8 | (lb 10) | 10 |
| TOTAL | (for 6 wkts dec) | 329 | (for 5 wkts dec) | 114 |

### KENT

| | | | | | |
|---|---|---|---|---|---|
| N.R.Taylor | c Moores b Pigott | 52 | c Parker b Wells C.M. | 58 |
| M.R.Benson * | c Lenham b Dodemaide | 4 | c Smith b Jones | 8 |
| T.R.Ward | b Wells C.M. | 13 | c Parker b Jones | 2 |
| G.R.Cowdrey | c Pigott b Jones | 16 | c Hall b Salisbury | 41 |
| M.V.Fleming | c Dodemaide b Jones | 0 | c Moores b Salisbury | 4 |
| R.M.Ellison | c Moores b Pigott | 4 | (7) not out | 23 |
| S.A.Marsh + | b Pigott | 50 | (6) c Smith b Salisbury | 26 |
| R.P.Davis | c Moores b Dodemaide | 44 | c Lenham b Salisbury | 6 |
| M.J.McCague | c Wells A.P. b Pigott | 2 | (10) not out | 0 |
| T.A.Merrick | b Wells C.M. | 10 | (9) lbw b Salisbury | 1 |
| A.P.Igglesden | not out | 16 | | |
| Extras | (lb 7,w 2) | 9 | (lb 7,w 4) | 11 |
| TOTAL | | 220 | (for 8 wkts) | 180 |

| KENT | O | M | R | W | O | M | R | W | FALL OF WICKETS | | | |
|---|---|---|---|---|---|---|---|---|---|---|---|---|
| | | | | | | | | | | SUS | KEN | SUS | KEN |
| Merrick | 8 | 0 | 36 | 0 | | | | | 1st | 26 | 8 | 33 | 29 |
| Igglesden | 24 | 4 | 68 | 4 | 14 | 5 | 22 | 2 | 2nd | 70 | 38 | 34 | 31 |
| Ellison | 20 | 5 | 72 | 0 | | | | | 3rd | 305 | 84 | 34 | 106 |
| McCague | 10 | 1 | 44 | 0 | 13 | 1 | 38 | 3 | 4th | 312 | 84 | 40 | 121 |
| Fleming | 18 | 7 | 39 | 0 | | | | | 5th | 328 | 91 | 51 | 126 |
| Davis | 19.3 | 3 | 62 | 2 | | | | | 6th | 329 | 92 | | 165 |
| Benson | | | | | 4 | 0 | 18 | 0 | 7th | | 168 | | 176 |
| Taylor | | | | | 3 | 0 | 26 | 0 | 8th | | 170 | | 179 |
| SUSSEX | O | M | R | W | O | M | R | W | 9th | | 186 | | |
| Jones | 17 | 1 | 41 | 2 | 9 | 0 | 56 | 2 | 10th | | 220 | | |
| Dodemaide | 14.3 | 6 | 25 | 2 | 8 | 1 | 27 | 0 | | | | | |
| Pigott | 22 | 5 | 75 | 4 | 5 | 0 | 25 | 0 | | | | | |
| Wells C.M. | 23 | 7 | 48 | 2 | 7 | 0 | 25 | 1 | | | | | |
| Salisbury | 12 | 5 | 24 | 0 | 10.5 | 1 | 40 | 5 | | | | | |

## MIDDLESEX vs. LEICESTERSHIRE

at Uxbridge on 7th, 8th, 10th June 1991
Toss : Middlesex.  Umpires : M.J.Kitchen and R.C.Tolchard
Match drawn.  Middlesex 7 pts (Bt: 3, Bw: 4), Leicestershire 5 pts (Bt: 3, Bw: 2)

### LEICESTERSHIRE

| | | | | | |
|---|---|---|---|---|---|
| T.J.Boon | c Farbrace b Ellcock | 11 | c Roseberry b Tufnell | 33 |
| N.E.Briers * | b Taylor | 0 | c Brown b Emburey | 50 |
| P.N.Hepworth | c Emburey b Williams | 32 | b Emburey | 8 |
| J.J.Whitaker | c Emburey b Williams | 35 | (7) b Tufnell | 16 |
| L.Potter | c Hutchinson b Emburey | 41 | (4) c & b Emburey | 2 |
| B.F.Smith | c Brown b Tufnell | 54 | (5) st Farbrace b Tufnell | 17 |
| P.Willey | not out | 42 | (6) st Farbrace b Tufnell | 26 |
| P.Whitticase + | c Williams b Taylor | 9 | c Farbrace b Tufnell | 0 |
| D.J.Millns | c Roseberry b Tufnell | 44 | b Tufnell | 10 |
| C.Wilkinson | c Brown b Williams | 0 | c Hutchinson b Emburey | 8 |
| J.N.Maguire | c Gatting b Williams | 2 | not out | 1 |
| Extras | (b 1,lb 5,w 5,nb 10) | 21 | (b 6,lb 7,w 3,nb 5) | 21 |
| TOTAL | | 291 | | 192 |

### MIDDLESEX

| | | | | | |
|---|---|---|---|---|---|
| I.J.F.Hutchinson | c Whitticase b Maguire | 12 | not out | 29 |
| M.A.Roseberry | not out | 119 | not out | 44 |
| M.W.Gatting * | c Willey b Wilkinson | 6 | | |
| K.R.Brown | lbw b Millns | 30 | | |
| M.Keech | c Millns b Willey | 16 | | |
| J.E.Emburey | lbw b Millns | 24 | | |
| N.F.Williams | not out | 19 | | |
| P.Farbrace + | | | | |
| C.W.Taylor | | | | |
| P.C.R.Tufnell | | | | |
| R.M.Ellcock | | | | |
| Extras | (b 6,lb 3,nb 17) | 26 | (lb 1,nb 2) | 3 |
| TOTAL | (for 5 wkts dec) | 252 | (for 0 wkts) | 76 |

| MIDDLESEX | O | M | R | W | O | M | R | W | FALL OF WICKETS | | | |
|---|---|---|---|---|---|---|---|---|---|---|---|---|
| | | | | | | | | | | LEI | MID | LEI | MID |
| Ellcock | 7 | 3 | 22 | 1 | | | | | 1st | 6 | 52 | 70 | |
| Taylor | 16 | 1 | 84 | 2 | | | | | 2nd | 18 | 64 | 99 | |
| Williams | 22.4 | 3 | 79 | 4 | 11 | 1 | 31 | 0 | 3rd | 72 | 106 | 100 | |
| Emburey | 14 | 3 | 43 | 1 | 37.5 | 17 | 59 | 4 | 4th | 99 | 146 | 103 | |
| Tufnell | 22 | 5 | 57 | 2 | 36 | 6 | 82 | 6 | 5th | 149 | 200 | 144 | |
| Keech | | | | | 2 | 0 | 7 | 0 | 6th | 209 | | 159 | |
| LEICS | O | M | R | W | O | M | R | W | 7th | 224 | | 160 | |
| Millns | 21 | 1 | 95 | 2 | 7 | 1 | 18 | 0 | 8th | 285 | | 179 | |
| Maguire | 29 | 8 | 70 | 1 | 4 | 0 | 15 | 0 | 9th | 285 | | 186 | |
| Wilkinson | 25 | 8 | 41 | 1 | 2 | 0 | 10 | 0 | 10th | 291 | | 192 | |
| Willey | 17.4 | 6 | 37 | 1 | 6 | 1 | 11 | 0 | | | | | |
| Hepworth | | | | | 4 | 1 | 20 | 0 | | | | | |
| Smith | | | | | 1 | 0 | 1 | 0 | | | | | |

## HAMPSHIRE vs. GLOUCS

at Southampton on 7th, 8th, 10th June 1991
Toss : Gloucs.  Umpires : B.Dudleston and R.Julian
Gloucs won by 6 wickets.  Hampshire 3 pts (Bt: 3, Bw: 0), Gloucs 19 pts (Bt: 0, Bw: 3)

### HAMPSHIRE

| | | | |
|---|---|---|---|
| T.C.Middleton | c Wright b Lawrence | 27 |
| C.L.Smith * | c Williams b Gilbert | 61 |
| K.D.James | c Babington b Smith | 14 |
| V.P.Terry | lbw b Babington | 19 |
| D.I.Gower | c Lloyds b Gilbert | 28 |
| R.M.F.Cox | c Hodgson b Babington | 15 |
| A.N Aymes + | not out | 38 |
| R.J.Maru | c Williams b Smith | 20 |
| K.J.Shine | lbw b Smith | 0 |
| P.J.Bakker | not out | 7 |
| Aqib Javed | | |
| Extras | (b 5,lb 19,nb 4) | 28 |
| TOTAL | (for 8 wkts dec) | 256 |

### GLOUCS

| | | | |
|---|---|---|---|
| G.D.Hodgson | run out | 89 |
| J.J.E.Hardy | b Shine | 52 |
| J.W.Lloyds | run out | 67 |
| A.J.Wright * | c Aymes b Maru | 17 |
| C.W.J.Athey | not out | 10 |
| M.W.Alleyne | not out | 3 |
| R.C.J.Williams + | | |
| D.V.Lawrence | | |
| D.R.Gilbert | | |
| A.M.Smith | | |
| A.M.Babington | | |
| Extras | (b 6,lb 5,w 1,nb 7) | 19 |
| TOTAL | (for 4 wkts) | 257 |

| GLOUCS | O | M | R | W | O | M | R | W | FALL OF WICKETS | | | |
|---|---|---|---|---|---|---|---|---|---|---|---|---|
| | | | | | | | | | | HAM | GLO | HAM | GLO |
| Gilbert | 17 | 5 | 46 | 2 | | | | | 1st | 85 | | | 99 |
| Lawrence | 17 | 5 | 38 | 1 | | | | | 2nd | 104 | | | 199 |
| Smith | 23 | 8 | 54 | 3 | | | | | 3rd | 131 | | | 235 |
| Babington | 18 | 1 | 69 | 2 | | | | | 4th | 145 | | | 249 |
| Lloyds | 10 | 3 | 25 | 0 | | | | | 5th | 172 | | | |
| HAMPSHIRE | O | M | R | W | O | M | R | W | 6th | 190 | | | |
| Aqib Javed | | | | | 10 | 0 | 47 | 0 | 7th | 241 | | | |
| Shine | | | | | 13 | 0 | 67 | 1 | 8th | 241 | | | |
| Bakker | | | | | 9 | 2 | 54 | 0 | 9th | | | | |
| Maru | | | | | 12.3 | 0 | 48 | 1 | 10th | | | | |
| James | | | | | 5 | 0 | 30 | 0 | | | | | |

## OTHER FIRST-CLASS

## BENSON & HEDGES CUP – SEMI-FINALS

### HEADLINES

**Other first-class match**

**7th - 10th June**

• Trevor Jesty made his first 100 for Lancashire to help his county to a five-wicket victory over Oxford University at the Parks. Graeme Turner finally achieved his maiden first-class 100 in Oxford's first innings before a series of declarations set up an exciting last afternoon.

• First-class débuts: T.M.Orrell, M. Sharp and M. Ward (Lancashire)

---

**ESSEX vs. WORCESTERSHIRE**

at Chelmsford on 12th June 1991
Toss : Worcs. Umpires : D.J.Constant and B.Leadbeater
Worcestershire won by 9 wickets
Man of the match: I.T.Botham

**ESSEX**

| | | |
|---|---|---|
| G.A.Gooch * | c Rhodes b Dilley | 12 |
| J.P.Stephenson | c Rhodes b Lampitt | 13 |
| P.J.Prichard | c Rhodes b Botham | 18 |
| Salim Malik | c Neale b Dilley | 2 |
| N.Hussain | c Rhodes b Radford | 26 |
| D.R.Pringle | run out | 4 |
| N.Shahid | c & b Radford | 1 |
| M.A.Garnham + | lbw b Botham | 2 |
| N.A.Foster | b Radford | 16 |
| T.D.Topley | b Botham | 1 |
| P.M.Such | not out | 1 |
| Extras | (lb 4,w 2,nb 2) | 8 |
| TOTAL | (34.5 overs) | 104 |

**WORCESTERSHIRE**

| | | |
|---|---|---|
| T.S.Curtis | run out | 27 |
| T.M.Moody | not out | 72 |
| G.A.Hick | not out | 4 |
| I.T.Botham | | |
| D.B.D'Oliveira | | |
| P.A.Neale * | | |
| S.J.Rhodes + | | |
| R.K.Illingworth | | |
| S.R.Lampitt | | |
| N.V.Radford | | |
| G.R.Dilley | | |
| Extras | (lb 2,w 3,nb 2) | 7 |
| TOTAL | (31.1 overs)(for 1 wkt) | 110 |

| WORCS | O | M | R | W |
|---|---|---|---|---|
| Dilley | 8 | 1 | 17 | 2 |
| Lampitt | 6 | 1 | 31 | 1 |
| Botham | 11 | 6 | 11 | 3 |
| Radford | 9.5 | 2 | 41 | 3 |

| ESSEX | O | M | R | W |
|---|---|---|---|---|
| Foster | 7 | 0 | 14 | 0 |
| Pringle | 7 | 1 | 16 | 0 |
| Topley | 8 | 1 | 26 | 0 |
| Gooch | 5.1 | 0 | 27 | 0 |
| Such | 4 | 0 | 25 | 0 |

**FALL OF WICKETS**

| | ESS | WOR |
|---|---|---|
| 1st | 26 | 100 |
| 2nd | 27 | |
| 3rd | 43 | |
| 4th | 56 | |
| 5th | 71 | |
| 6th | 74 | |
| 7th | 85 | |
| 8th | 85 | |
| 9th | 89 | |
| 10th | 104 | |

---

**LANCASHIRE vs. YORKSHIRE**

at Old Trafford on 12th June 1991
Toss : Yorks. Umpires : K.J.Lyons and A.G.T.Whitehead
Lancashire won by 68 runs
Man of the match: A.A.Metcalfe

**LANCASHIRE**

| | | |
|---|---|---|
| G.D.Mendis | b Carrick | 75 |
| G.Fowler | c Blakey b Carrick | 58 |
| M.A.Atherton | c Moxon b Fletcher | 24 |
| N.H.Fairbrother | c Blakey b Gough | 40 |
| M.Watkinson | c Blakey b Robinson M.A. | 12 |
| Wasim Akram | c Fletcher b Robinson M.A. | 6 |
| P.A.J.DeFreitas | c Carrick b Fletcher | 12 |
| W.K.Hegg + | b Gough | 0 |
| I.D.Austin | b Fletcher | 22 |
| D.P.Hughes * | not out | 1 |
| P.J.W.Allott | b Fletcher | 0 |
| Extras | (lb 11,w 4,nb 3) | 18 |
| TOTAL | (54 overs) | 268 |

**YORKSHIRE**

| | | |
|---|---|---|
| M.D.Moxon * | c Hegg b DeFreitas | 15 |
| A.A.Metcalfe | b Watkinson | 114 |
| S.A.Kellett | run out | 2 |
| D.Byas | c Allott b Wasim Akram | 0 |
| R.J.Blakey + | b Watkinson | 38 |
| P.E.Robinson | b Watkinson | 9 |
| P.Carrick | b DeFreitas | 7 |
| D.Gough | c Allott b DeFreitas | 1 |
| P.J.Hartley | b Watkinson | 0 |
| S.D.Fletcher | b Watkinson | 1 |
| M.A.Robinson | not out | 1 |
| Extras | (b 1,lb 2,w 7,nb 2) | 12 |
| TOTAL | (49.4 overs) | 200 |

| YORKSHIRE | O | M | R | W |
|---|---|---|---|---|
| Hartley | 11 | 0 | 56 | 0 |
| Robinson M.A. | 9 | 1 | 43 | 2 |
| Gough | 8 | 0 | 41 | 2 |
| Fletcher | 10 | 0 | 51 | 4 |
| Carrick | 11 | 0 | 36 | 2 |
| Moxon | 5 | 0 | 30 | 0 |

| LANCASHIRE | O | M | R | W |
|---|---|---|---|---|
| DeFreitas | 11 | 0 | 34 | 3 |
| Allott | 11 | 1 | 46 | 0 |
| Austin | 9 | 0 | 36 | 0 |
| Wasim Akram | 8 | 0 | 32 | 1 |
| Watkinson | 10.4 | 0 | 49 | 5 |

**FALL OF WICKETS**

| | LAN | YOR |
|---|---|---|
| 1st | 125 | 22 |
| 2nd | 163 | 49 |
| 3rd | 179 | 53 |
| 4th | 210 | 162 |
| 5th | 224 | 182 |
| 6th | 234 | 193 |
| 7th | 234 | 198 |
| 8th | 266 | 198 |
| 9th | 268 | 199 |
| 10th | 268 | 200 |

---

**OXFORD U vs. LANCASHIRE**

at The Parks on 7th, 8th, 10th June 1991
Toss : Oxford U. Umpires : A.A.Jones and K.E.Palmer
Lancashire won by 5 wickets

**OXFORD U**

| | | | | | |
|---|---|---|---|---|---|
| R.R.Montgomery | c Titchard b Yates | 24 | c Speak b Martin | | 3 |
| R.E.Morris | lbw b Sharp | 15 | not out | | 50 |
| C.Gupte | run out | 23 | c Martin b Yates | | 43 |
| G.Lovell | lbw b Martin | 1 | not out | | 16 |
| D.Sandiford + | b Fitton | 0 | | | |
| G.J.Turner * | not out | 101 | | | |
| D.Pfaff | c Stanworth b Martin | 20 | | | |
| H.Davies | c Yates b Fitton | 4 | | | |
| P.S.Gerrans | not out | 17 | | | |
| J.M.E.Oppenheimer | | | | | |
| B.Wood | | | | | |
| Extras | (b 4,lb 3,nb 10) | 17 | (lb 1) | | 1 |
| TOTAL | (for 7 wkts dec) | 222 | (for 2 wkts dec) | | 113 |

**LANCASHIRE**

| | | | | | |
|---|---|---|---|---|---|
| N.J.Speak | not out | 30 | c Sandiford b Oppenheimer | | 8 |
| T.M.Orrell | b Wood | 5 | lbw b Oppenheimer | | 16 |
| S.P.Titchard | run out | 39 | b Gerrans | | 43 |
| T.E.Jesty | not out | 4 | not out | | 122 |
| G.Yates | | | c Sandiford b Turner | | 12 |
| J.D.Fitton | | | c Montgomerie b Wood | | 16 |
| R.Irani | | | not out | | 31 |
| J.Stanworth *+ | | | | | |
| P.J.Martin | | | | | |
| M.Sharp | | | | | |
| M.Ward | | | | | |
| Extras | (b 1,lb 1,nb 1) | 3 | (b 2,lb 3,w 1,nb 1) | | 7 |
| TOTAL | (for 2 wkts dec) | 81 | (for 5 wkts) | | 255 |

| LANCASHIRE | O | M | R | W | O | M | R | W |
|---|---|---|---|---|---|---|---|---|
| Martin | 24 | 6 | 47 | 2 | 8 | 2 | 14 | 1 |
| Sharp | 15 | 7 | 21 | 1 | | | | |
| Irani | 19 | 3 | 50 | 0 | 13.2 | 2 | 32 | 0 |
| Yates | 22 | 6 | 55 | 1 | 14 | 5 | 26 | 1 |
| Fitton | 19 | 6 | 42 | 2 | 10 | 1 | 34 | 0 |
| Ward | | | | | 2 | 0 | 6 | 0 |

| OXFORD U | O | M | R | W | O | M | R | W |
|---|---|---|---|---|---|---|---|---|
| Oppenheimer | 10 | 1 | 35 | 0 | 15 | 1 | 85 | 2 |
| Wood | 6 | 0 | 23 | 1 | 12 | 2 | 52 | 1 |
| Gerrans | 7 | 2 | 21 | 0 | 15.3 | 2 | 52 | 1 |
| Turner | | | | | 13 | 2 | 61 | 1 |

**FALL OF WICKETS**

| | OXF | LAN | OXF | LAN |
|---|---|---|---|---|
| 1st | 28 | 6 | 8 | 11 |
| 2nd | 50 | 72 | 84 | 46 |
| 3rd | 51 | | | 86 |
| 4th | 54 | | | 125 |
| 5th | 110 | | | 159 |
| 6th | 159 | | | |
| 7th | 182 | | | |
| 8th | | | | |
| 9th | | | | |
| 10th | | | | |

---

### HEADLINES

**Benson & Hedges Cup**
**Semi-Finals**

**12th June**

• Worcestershire and Lancashire ensured that the 1991 Benson & Hedges Cup Final would see a repeat performance of last year's final with their convincing victories over Essex and Yorkshire respectively.

• Worcestershire's victory at Chelmsford was unexpectedly emphatic. Essex, invited to bat by Phil Neale in awkward batting conditions, were soon in trouble against the Worcestershire seamers. Their main tormentor was a half-fit Ian Botham who bowled his 11 overs for 11 runs and claimed three wickets. Essex only passed the 100-mark with a last-wicket stand of 15. Needing only 105 to win, Worcestershire's place in the final was never in doubt, and once Tom Moody got going the capacity crowd was guaranteed an early away day.

• Lancashire reached Lord's with a 68-run win over Yorkshire at Old Trafford, the visitors never being able to get back on level terms once Gehan Mendis and Graeme Fowler had started with an opening stand of 125. Although Lancashire would have been disappointed to be bowled out within their 55 overs, Mike Watkinson returned career-best figures to restrict Yorkshire to 200, despite Ashley Metcalfe's first B & H century.

# TILCON TROPHY

# REFUGE ASS. LEAGUE

## DURHAM vs. LEICESTERSHIRE
at Harrogate on 11th June 1991
Toss : Leicestershire.  Umpires : J.D.Bond and G.I.Burgess
No result

**DURHAM**

| | | |
|---|---|---|
| G.Cook * | run out | 43 |
| S.J.Weeks | c & b Maguire | 4 |
| N.G.Nicholson | c Willey b Lewis | 16 |
| Ijaz Ahmed | c Benson b Wilkinson | 20 |
| P.Bainbridge | not out | 48 |
| D.A.Blenkiron | not out | 20 |
| P.W.Henderson | | |
| J.Wood | | |
| A.R.Fothergill + | | |
| P.A.W.Heseltine | | |
| A.C.Day | | |
| Extras | (lb 8,w 4) | 12 |
| TOTAL | (33 overs)(for 4 wkts) | 163 |

**LEICESTERSHIRE**

| | | |
|---|---|---|
| T.J.Boon | b Bainbridge | 10 |
| N.E.Briers * | c Blenkiron b Wood | 2 |
| B.F.Smith | not out | 2 |
| L.Potter | not out | 0 |
| J.D.R.Benson | | |
| C.C.Lewis | | |
| P.Willey | | |
| P.Whitticase + | | |
| D.J.Millns | | |
| C.Wilkinson | | |
| J.N.Maguire | | |
| Extras | (lb 1,w 1) | 2 |
| TOTAL | (6.1 overs)(for 2 wkts) | 16 |

| LEICS | O | M | R | W | FALL OF WICKETS | | |
|---|---|---|---|---|---|---|---|
| Lewis | 7 | 1 | 17 | 1 | | DUR | LEI |
| Maguire | 7 | 0 | 27 | 1 | 1st | 10 | 5 |
| Millns | 5 | 0 | 32 | 0 | 2nd | 60 | 15 |
| Wilkinson | 7 | 1 | 37 | 1 | 3rd | 74 | |
| Willey | 5 | 0 | 32 | 0 | 4th | 109 | |
| Benson | 2 | 0 | 10 | 0 | 5th | | |
| | | | | | 6th | | |
| DURHAM | O | M | R | W | 7th | | |
| Wood | 3.1 | 0 | 10 | 1 | 8th | | |
| Bainbridge | 3 | 1 | 5 | 1 | 9th | | |
| | | | | | 10th | | |

## SURREY vs. WARWICKSHIRE
at Harrogate on 12th June 1991
Toss : Warwickshire.  Umpires : J.D.Bond and G.I.Burgess
Surrey won by 1 run

**SURREY**

| | | |
|---|---|---|
| D.J.Bicknell | lbw b Small | 8 |
| R.I.Alikhan | c Munton b Small | 7 |
| M.A.Lynch | c Burns b Small | 2 |
| D.M.Ward | b Munton | 16 |
| G.P.Thorpe | c Green b Booth | 44 |
| A.J.Stewart *+ | lbw b Lloyd | 61 |
| J.D.Robinson | c Green b Lloyd | 3 |
| K.T.Medlycott | lbw b Lloyd | 5 |
| M.A.Feltham | not out | 32 |
| J.Boiling | not out | 11 |
| A.J.Murphy | | |
| Extras | (b 4,lb 12,w 13,nb 3) | 32 |
| TOTAL | (55 overs)(for 8 wkts) | 221 |

**WARWICKSHIRE**

| | | |
|---|---|---|
| J.D.Ratcliffe | b Robinson | 42 |
| R.G.Twose | lbw b Robinson | 16 |
| S.J.Green | c Stewart b Robinson | 0 |
| D.P.Ostler | b Robinson | 0 |
| D.A.Reeve | st Stewart b Medlycott | 48 |
| M.Burns + | run out | 27 |
| T.A.Lloyd * | c Ward b Murphy | 46 |
| G.C.Small | c Boiling b Feltham | 15 |
| P.A.Booth | b Feltham | 0 |
| T.A.Munton | not out | 13 |
| G.Smith | not out | 1 |
| Extras | (lb 4,w 8) | 12 |
| TOTAL | (55 overs)(for 9 wkts) | 220 |

| WARWICKS | O | M | R | W | FALL OF WICKETS | | |
|---|---|---|---|---|---|---|---|
| Small | 7 | 1 | 16 | 3 | | SUR | WAR |
| Smith | 9 | 0 | 24 | 0 | 1st | 11 | 53 |
| Reeve | 9 | 2 | 29 | 0 | 2nd | 17 | 53 |
| Munton | 7 | 0 | 41 | 1 | 3rd | 20 | 61 |
| Booth | 11 | 1 | 43 | 1 | 4th | 55 | 67 |
| Lloyd | 11 | 0 | 47 | 3 | 5th | 156 | 129 |
| Twose | 1 | 0 | 5 | 0 | 6th | 159 | 155 |
| | | | | | 7th | 165 | 193 |
| SURREY | O | M | R | W | 8th | 166 | 193 |
| Feltham | 11 | 2 | 33 | 2 | 9th | | 218 |
| Murphy | 10 | 1 | 48 | 1 | 10th | | |
| Thorpe | 2 | 0 | 17 | 0 | | | |
| Robinson | 11 | 1 | 28 | 4 | | | |
| Boiling | 11 | 0 | 35 | 0 | | | |
| Medlycott | 10 | 1 | 55 | 1 | | | |

## DERBYSHIRE vs. SOMERSET
at Derby on 16th June 1991
Toss : Derby.  Umpires : A.A.Jones and R.A.White
Somerset won by 46 runs.  Derby 0 pts, Somerset 4 pts

**SOMERSET**

| | | |
|---|---|---|
| S.J.Cook | c Bowler b Griffith | 32 |
| P.M.Roebuck | run out | 45 |
| C.J.Tavare * | c Barnett b Griffith | 3 |
| R.J.Harden | b Malcolm | 4 |
| G.D.Rose | c Warner b Griffith | 17 |
| N.D.Burns + | c Azharuddin b Warner | 32 |
| K.H.Macleay | b Malcolm | 9 |
| R.P.Lefebvre | run out | 13 |
| A.N.Hayhurst | not out | 18 |
| N.A.Mallender | b Base | 0 |
| D.A.Graveney | not out | 2 |
| Extras | (lb 10,w 12,nb 1) | 23 |
| TOTAL | (40 overs)(for 9 wkts) | 198 |

**DERBYSHIRE**

| | | |
|---|---|---|
| K.J.Barnett * | c Lefebvre b Hayhurst | 17 |
| P.D.Bowler + | b Lefebvre | 9 |
| J.E.Morris | c Roebuck b Macleay | 27 |
| M.Azharuddin | c Burns b Graveney | 20 |
| T.J.G.O'Gorman | b Roebuck | 31 |
| C.J.Adams | st Burns b Roebuck | 9 |
| F.A.Griffith | c Cook b Roebuck | 6 |
| D.G.Cork | run out | 7 |
| A.E.Warner | b Roebuck | 12 |
| D.E.Malcolm | not out | 3 |
| S.J.Base | c Tavare b Roebuck | 0 |
| Extras | (lb 9,w 2) | 11 |
| TOTAL | (35.4 overs) | 152 |

| DERBYSHIRE | O | M | R | W | FALL OF WICKETS | | |
|---|---|---|---|---|---|---|---|
| Warner | 8 | 0 | 34 | 1 | | SOM | DER |
| Cork | 8 | 1 | 30 | 0 | 1st | 61 | 21 |
| Base | 8 | 0 | 46 | 1 | 2nd | 69 | 31 |
| Griffith | 8 | 0 | 37 | 3 | 3rd | 94 | 66 |
| Malcolm | 8 | 0 | 41 | 2 | 4th | 103 | 82 |
| | | | | | 5th | 140 | 113 |
| SOMERSET | O | M | R | W | 6th | 161 | 129 |
| Mallender | 4 | 0 | 13 | 0 | 7th | 165 | 130 |
| Lefebvre | 6 | 0 | 28 | 1 | 8th | 191 | 139 |
| Hayhurst | 5 | 0 | 23 | 1 | 9th | 193 | 152 |
| Macleay | 8 | 0 | 31 | 1 | 10th | | 152 |
| Graveney | 8 | 0 | 37 | 2 | | | |
| Roebuck | 4.4 | 0 | 11 | 4 | | | |

## SURREY vs. DURHAM
at Harrogate on 13th June 1991
Toss : Durham.  Umpires : G.I.Burgess and J.D.Bond
Surrey won by 78 runs

**SURREY**

| | | |
|---|---|---|
| D.J.Bicknell | not out | 149 |
| J.D.Robinson | c Cook G. b Brown | 0 |
| A.J.Stewart + | c Briers b Wood | 0 |
| M.A.Lynch | b Wood | 1 |
| D.M.Ward | c Bainbridge b Brown | 51 |
| G.P.Thorpe | b Day | 21 |
| I.A.Greig * | not out | 3 |
| K.T.Medlycott | | |
| M.A.Feltham | | |
| J.Boiling | | |
| M.P.Bicknell | | |
| Extras | (b 8,lb 6,w 3) | 17 |
| TOTAL | (32 overs)(for 5 wkts) | 242 |

**DURHAM**

| | | |
|---|---|---|
| G.Cook * | c Lynch b Ward | 102 |
| S.J.Weeks | b Feltham | 1 |
| N.G.Nicholson | c Stewart b Bicknell M.P. | 0 |
| D.A.Blenkiron | b Bicknell M.P. | 6 |
| P.Bainbridge | st Stewart b Medlycott | 7 |
| M.P.Briers | run out | 1 |
| A.R.Fothergill + | c & b Boiling | 13 |
| J.Wood | b Boiling | 2 |
| P.A.W.Heseltine | c Boiling b Robinson | 2 |
| S.J.Brown | not out | 10 |
| A.C.Day | | |
| Extras | (b 6,lb 5,w 9) | 20 |
| TOTAL | (32 overs)(for 9 wkts) | 164 |

| DURHAM | O | M | R | W | FALL OF WICKETS | | |
|---|---|---|---|---|---|---|---|
| Brown | 7 | 1 | 53 | 2 | | SUR | DUR |
| Wood | 6 | 1 | 28 | 2 | 1st | 12 | 4 |
| Bainbridge | 6 | 0 | 44 | 0 | 2nd | 13 | 9 |
| Day | 6 | 0 | 46 | 1 | 3rd | 23 | 20 |
| Heseltine | 7 | 0 | 57 | 0 | 4th | 178 | 42 |
| | | | | | 5th | 236 | 44 |
| SURREY | O | M | R | W | 6th | | 68 |
| Bicknell M.P. | 6 | 0 | 24 | 2 | 7th | | 78 |
| Feltham | 4 | 1 | 9 | 1 | 8th | | 95 |
| Medlycott | 7 | 0 | 29 | 1 | 9th | | 164 |
| Boiling | 7 | 1 | 29 | 2 | 10th | | |
| Robinson | 4 | 0 | 31 | 1 | | | |
| Bicknell D.J. | 3 | 0 | 23 | 0 | | | |
| Ward | 1 | 0 | 8 | 1 | | | |

## ESSEX vs. HAMPSHIRE
at Chelmsford on 16th June 1991
Toss : Hampshire.  Umpires : B.Hassan and M.J.Kitchen
No result.  Essex 2 pts, Hampshire 2 pts

**ESSEX**

| | | |
|---|---|---|
| G.A.Gooch * | run out | 50 |
| J.P.Stephenson | c Connor b Ayling | 38 |
| P.J.Prichard | c Aqib Javed b Tremlett | 34 |
| N.Hussain | c Ayling b Udal | 10 |
| D.R.Pringle | b Connor | 17 |
| N.Shahid | not out | 17 |
| M.A.Garnham + | not out | 0 |
| A.C.Seymour | | |
| T.D.Topley | | |
| S.J.W.Andrew | | |
| P.M.Such | | |
| Extras | (b 3,lb 5,w 5,nb 1) | 14 |
| TOTAL | (33.3 overs)(for 5 wkts) | 180 |

**HAMPSHIRE**

| | |
|---|---|
| V.P.Terry | |
| J.R.Wood | |
| R.A.Smith | |
| D.I.Gower | |
| M.C.J.Nicholas * | |
| J.R.Ayling | |
| A.N Aymes + | |
| S.D.Udal | |
| T.M.Tremlett | |
| C.A.Connor | |
| Aqib Javed | |
| Extras | |
| TOTAL | |

| HAMPSHIRE | O | M | R | W | FALL OF WICKETS | | |
|---|---|---|---|---|---|---|---|
| Connor | 6.3 | 0 | 31 | 1 | | ESS | HAM |
| Aqib Javed | 7 | 0 | 41 | 0 | 1st | 69 | |
| Tremlett | 8 | 0 | 30 | 1 | 2nd | 116 | |
| Ayling | 4 | 0 | 29 | 1 | 3rd | 142 | |
| Udal | 8 | 1 | 41 | 1 | 4th | 145 | |
| | | | | | 5th | 180 | |
| ESSEX | O | M | R | W | 6th | | |
| | | | | | 7th | | |
| | | | | | 8th | | |
| | | | | | 9th | | |
| | | | | | 10th | | |

# HEADLINES

**Tilcon Trophy**

**11th - 13th June**

• Surrey could be pleased with their long trip up to Harrogate as they claimed the 1991 Tilcon Trophy, by defeating Warwickshire by one run and Durham by 78 runs. Durham had reached the final by winning a bowling competition after their match against Leicestershire had been abandoned, but they found Surrey's Darren Bicknell in inspired form. In an innings restricted to 32 overs he made an unbeaten 149, the highest score in the history of the Tilcon Trophy, adding 155 with David Ward. Geoff Cook, captaining Durham as they prepare for first-class status, also reached his 100, but his team fell well short of a stiff target.

# REFUGE ASSURANCE LEAGUE

## GLAMORGAN vs. MIDDLESEX

at Cardiff on 16th June 1991
Toss : Middlesex. Umpires : D.J.Constant and K.J.Lyons
Glamorgan won by 54 runs. Glam 4 pts, Middlesex 0 pts

**GLAMORGAN**

| | | |
|---|---|---|
| M.P.Maynard | b Williams | 25 |
| H.Morris * | c Gatting b Cowans | 75 |
| G.C.Holmes | st Farbrace b Weekes | 15 |
| R.J.Shastri | run out | 4 |
| I.Smith | lbw b Cowans | 22 |
| A.Dale | not out | 25 |
| J.Derrick | run out | 5 |
| C.P.Metson + | b Hughes | 7 |
| S.L.Watkin | c Weekes b Embury | 2 |
| S.R.Barwick | not out | 3 |
| M.Frost | | |
| Extras | (lb 14,w 1) | 15 |
| TOTAL | (40 overs)(for 8 wkts) | 198 |

**MIDDLESEX**

| | | |
|---|---|---|
| I.J.F.Hutchinson | c Maynard b Derrick | 42 |
| M.A.Roseberry | lbw b Watkin | 6 |
| M.W.Gatting * | b Watkin | 8 |
| M.R.Ramprakash | c Maynard b Derrick | 18 |
| K.R.Brown | c Holmes b Derrick | 16 |
| P.N.Weekes | lbw b Derrick | 1 |
| J.E.Emburey | not out | 20 |
| N.G.Cowans | c Smith b Dale | 4 |
| N.F.Williams | c Smith b Dale | 11 |
| P.Farbrace + | b Watkin | 3 |
| S.P.Hughes | lbw b Barwick | 4 |
| Extras | (b 1,lb 10) | 11 |
| TOTAL | (35.2 overs) | 144 |

| MIDDLESEX | O | M | R | W | FALL OF WICKETS | | |
|---|---|---|---|---|---|---|---|
| | | | | | | GLA | MID |
| Cowans | 8 | 0 | 44 | 2 | | | |
| Williams | 7 | 0 | 32 | 1 | 1st | 52 | 23 |
| Weekes | 8 | 0 | 40 | 1 | 2nd | 75 | 53 |
| Hughes | 8 | 2 | 23 | 1 | 3rd | 86 | 68 |
| Emburey | 8 | 1 | 33 | 1 | 4th | 133 | 85 |
| Ramprakash | 1 | 0 | 12 | 0 | 5th | 158 | 91 |
| | | | | | 6th | 169 | 108 |
| GLAMORGAN | O | M | R | W | 7th | 179 | 112 |
| Watkin | 8 | 0 | 34 | 3 | 8th | 182 | 129 |
| Frost | 6 | 0 | 20 | 0 | 9th | | 135 |
| Barwick | 5.2 | 0 | 18 | 1 | 10th | | 144 |
| Derrick | 8 | 0 | 25 | 4 | | | |
| Dale | 8 | 0 | 36 | 2 | | | |

## GLOUCS vs. NOTTS

at Gloucester on 16th June 1991
Toss : Notts. Umpires : B.Leadbeater and N.T.Plews
Notts won on faster scoring rate. Gloucs 0 pts, Notts 4 pts

**GLOUCS**

| | | |
|---|---|---|
| R.J.Scott | lbw b Cooper | 1 |
| C.W.J.Athey | b Crawley | 44 |
| J.W.Lloyds | c Evans b Saxelby | 15 |
| A.J.Wright * | b Evans | 4 |
| M.W.Alleyne | c Saxelby b Stephenson | 37 |
| J.J.E.Hardy | b Stephenson | 42 |
| R.C.Russell + | not out | 7 |
| D.V.Lawrence | not out | 9 |
| D.R.Gilbert | | |
| A.M.Smith | | |
| A.M.Babington | | |
| Extras | (lb 4,w 2,nb 1) | 7 |
| TOTAL | (37 overs)(for 6 wkts) | 166 |

**NOTTS**

| | | |
|---|---|---|
| B.C.Broad | run out | 36 |
| D.W.Randall | c & b Lawrence | 27 |
| R.T.Robinson * | not out | 24 |
| P.Johnson | not out | 52 |
| M.A.Crawley | | |
| M.Saxelby | | |
| F.D.Stephenson | | |
| B.N.French + | | |
| K.P.Evans | | |
| E.E.Hemmings | | |
| K.E.Cooper | | |
| Extras | (lb 3,w 7) | 10 |
| TOTAL | (30.1 overs)(for 2 wkts) | 149 |

| NOTTS | O | M | R | W | FALL OF WICKETS | | |
|---|---|---|---|---|---|---|---|
| | | | | | | GLO | NOT |
| Cooper | 8 | 1 | 30 | 1 | 1st | 4 | 64 |
| Stephenson | 6 | 0 | 25 | 2 | 2nd | 31 | 71 |
| Saxelby | 4 | 0 | 18 | 1 | 3rd | 52 | |
| Evans | 6 | 1 | 34 | 1 | 4th | 83 | |
| Hemmings | 8 | 0 | 39 | 0 | 5th | 135 | |
| Crawley | 5 | 0 | 16 | 1 | 6th | 151 | |
| GLOUCS | O | M | R | W | 7th | | |
| Gilbert | 8 | 0 | 39 | 0 | 8th | | |
| Babington | 7 | 0 | 38 | 0 | 9th | | |
| Smith | 6.1 | 1 | 29 | 0 | 10th | | |
| Lawrence | 8 | 0 | 35 | 1 | | | |
| Lloyds | 1 | 0 | 5 | 0 | | | |

## HEADLINES

### Refuge Assurance League

### 16th June

• Nottinghamshire's stay at the head of the Refuge table showed no sign of coming to an early end, as they gained their seventh successive victory at the expense of Gloucestershire at Gloucester, the visitors easily bettering their hosts' modest run-rate thanks to Paul Johnson's unbeaten 52.

• Lancashire emerged as the main challengers following their four-wicket dismissal of Warwickshire at Edgbaston. Dermot Reeve had led a revival from 45 for four with his first Sunday 100, as he and Paul Smith added 143 for the fifth wicket, but Wasim Akram and Phil DeFreitas stole the match from the home side with a punishing sixth-wicket stand of 80.

• Derbyshire's defence of their title went from bad to worse, as they were beaten by Somerset, still maintaining an impressive Sunday record, by 46 runs at Derby. Peter Roebuck gave an immaculate all-round performance, top-scoring with 45 and returning career-best bowling figures.

• Glamorgan gained their first win of the season by defeating Middlesex by 54 runs at Cardiff, John Derrick and Steve Watkin sharing seven wickets as the visitors were bowled out for 144.

• Leicestershire fared even worse at the hands of Surrey at Leicester, when they were despatched for just 83, Tony Murphy and Ian Greig each taking three wickets as the visitors were surprisingly able to convert their own modest total of 134 for nine into a 51-run victory.

• Run-making proved an easier proposition at Scarborough where Richard Blakey made his highest Sunday League score in Yorkshire's total of 241 for six, before Jeremy Batty returned career-best figures of four for 33 to send Kent to defeat by 67 runs.

• The day's other two matches did not even reach the half-way mark, Essex and Hampshire sharing the points at Chelmsford, Sussex and Worcestershire doing the same at Hove, where the home side had looked on the way to a formidable total with Martin Speight just reaching his maiden Sunday 100 before the weather's intervention.

## LEICESTERSHIRE vs. SURREY

at Leicester on 16th June 1991
Toss : Leicestershire. Umpires : J.W.Holder and R.Julien
Surrey won by 51 runs. Leicestershire 0 pts, Surrey 4 pts

**SURREY**

| | | |
|---|---|---|
| D.J.Bicknell | b Maguire | 1 |
| M.A.Lynch | b Maguire | 1 |
| A.J.Stewart + | c Lewis b Wilkinson | 13 |
| D.M.Ward | c Smith b Willey | 19 |
| G.P.Thorpe | b Willey | 28 |
| I.A.Greig * | lbw b Willey | 2 |
| J.D.Robinson | lbw b Lewis | 22 |
| M.A.Feltham | c & b Willey | 11 |
| C.K.Bullen | not out | 16 |
| Waqar Younis | c Briers b Lewis | 1 |
| A.J.Murphy | not out | 5 |
| Extras | (b 2,lb 4,w 8,nb 1) | 15 |
| TOTAL | (40 overs)(for 9 wkts) | 134 |

**LEICESTERSHIRE**

| | | |
|---|---|---|
| J.J.Whitaker | c Bicknell b Murphy | 19 |
| N.E.Briers * | lbw b Murphy | 3 |
| B.F.Smith | c Bullen b Murphy | 12 |
| L.Potter | c Bicknell b Robinson | 9 |
| C.C.Lewis | run out | 7 |
| J.D.R.Benson | b Waqar Younis | 0 |
| P.Willey | c Stewart b Greig | 17 |
| P.Whitticase + | lbw b Greig | 2 |
| D.J.Millns | c Ward b Feltham | 7 |
| C.Wilkinson | not out | 0 |
| J.N.Maguire | c Waqar Younis b Greig | 0 |
| Extras | (lb 5,w 2) | 7 |
| TOTAL | (31.5 overs) | 83 |

| LEICS | O | M | R | W | FALL OF WICKETS | | |
|---|---|---|---|---|---|---|---|
| | | | | | | SUR | LEI |
| Lewis | 8 | 1 | 14 | 2 | 1st | 1 | 12 |
| Maguire | 8 | 3 | 20 | 2 | 2nd | 3 | 29 |
| Millns | 4 | 0 | 18 | 0 | 3rd | 23 | 38 |
| Wilkinson | 5 | 0 | 25 | 1 | 4th | 65 | 46 |
| Willey | 8 | 1 | 17 | 4 | 5th | 68 | 47 |
| Benson | 7 | 0 | 34 | 0 | 6th | 78 | 67 |
| SURREY | O | M | R | W | 7th | 99 | 70 |
| Feltham | 7 | 1 | 23 | 1 | 8th | 116 | 83 |
| Murphy | 6 | 2 | 15 | 3 | 9th | 120 | 83 |
| Waqar Younis | 6 | 2 | 10 | 1 | 10th | | 83 |
| Robinson | 8 | 1 | 20 | 1 | | | |
| Greig | 4.5 | 0 | 10 | 3 | | | |

## SUSSEX vs. WORCESTERSHIRE

at Hove on 16th June 1991
Toss : Worcestershire. Umpires : H.D.Bird and J.H.Harris
No result. Sussex 2 pts, Worcestershire 2 pts

**SUSSEX**

| | | |
|---|---|---|
| N.J.Lenham | b Radford | 8 |
| P.W.G.Parker * | b Weston | 14 |
| A.P.Wells | c Neale b Hick | 58 |
| M.P.Speight | not out | 106 |
| K.Greenfield | not out | 4 |
| C.M.Wells | | |
| A.I.C.Dodemaide | | |
| A.C.S.Pigott | | |
| P.Moores + | | |
| I.D.K.Salisbury | | |
| A.N.Jones | | |
| Extras | (lb 8,w 2,nb 2) | 12 |
| TOTAL | (30.2 overs)(for 3 wkts) | 202 |

**WORCESTERSHIRE**

| |
|---|
| T.S.Curtis |
| T.M.Moody |
| G.A.Hick |
| M.J.Weston |
| D.B.D'Oliveira |
| P.A.Neale * |
| S.J.Rhodes + |
| P.J.Newport |
| R.K.Illingworth |
| S.R.Lampitt |
| N.V.Radford |
| Extras |
| TOTAL |

| WORCS | O | M | R | W | FALL OF WICKETS | | |
|---|---|---|---|---|---|---|---|
| | | | | | | SUS | WOR |
| Radford | 5 | 0 | 11 | 1 | 1st | 1 | |
| Weston | 8 | 0 | 33 | 1 | 2nd | 24 | |
| Newport | 8 | 0 | 70 | 0 | 3rd | 176 | |
| Illingworth | 4 | 0 | 40 | 0 | 4th | | |
| Lampitt | 4 | 0 | 35 | 0 | 5th | | |
| Hick | 1.2 | 0 | 5 | 1 | 6th | | |
| SUSSEX | O | M | R | W | 7th | | |
| | | | | | 8th | | |
| | | | | | 9th | | |
| | | | | | 10th | | |

# REFUGE ASSURANCE LEAGUE

## WARWICKSHIRE vs. LANCASHIRE

at Edgbaston on 16th June 1991
Toss : Lancs. Umpires : D.R.Shepherd and R.C.Tolchard
Lancashire won by 4 wickets. Warwicks 0 pts, Lancs 4 pts

### WARWICKSHIRE

| | | |
|---|---|---|
| A.J.Moles | c Atherton b DeFreitas | 7 |
| T.A.Lloyd * | c Fowler b DeFreitas | 16 |
| S.J.Green | c Hegg b Watkinson | 5 |
| D.P.Ostler | c Lloyd b DeFreitas | 7 |
| D.A.Reeve | c Fairbrother b Austin | 100 |
| P.A.Smith | c Atherton b Austin | 49 |
| N.M.K.Smith | not out | 4 |
| K.J.Piper + | | |
| G.C.Small | | |
| J.E.Benjamin | | |
| T.A.Munton | | |
| Extras | (b 2,lb 7,w 8,nb 1) | 18 |
| TOTAL | (40 overs)(for 6 wkts) | 206 |

### LANCASHIRE

| | | |
|---|---|---|
| G.Fowler | b Smith P.A. | 26 |
| M.A.Atherton | c Piper b Benjamin | 0 |
| G.D.Lloyd | b Small | 50 |
| N.H.Fairbrother | c Smith N.M.K. b Small | 20 |
| M.Watkinson | c Small b Reeve | 7 |
| Wasim Akram | run out | 38 |
| P.A.J.DeFreitas | not out | 41 |
| W.K.Hegg + | not out | 2 |
| D.P.Hughes * | | |
| I.D.Austin | | |
| P.J.W.Allott | | |
| Extras | (lb 12,w 7,nb 4) | 23 |
| TOTAL | (38.3 overs)(for 6 wkts) | 207 |

| LANCASHIRE | O | M | R | W | | FALL OF WICKETS | |
|---|---|---|---|---|---|---|---|
| | | | | | | WAR | LAN |
| DeFreitas | 8 | 1 | 27 | 3 | | | |
| Allott | 2 | 0 | 13 | 0 | 1st | 24 | 1 |
| Watkinson | 8 | 0 | 37 | 1 | 2nd | 30 | 64 |
| Wasim Akram | 8 | 0 | 51 | 0 | 3rd | 30 | 107 |
| Hughes | 6 | 0 | 33 | 0 | 4th | 45 | 119 |
| Austin | 8 | 1 | 36 | 2 | 5th | 188 | 121 |
| | | | | | 6th | 206 | 201 |
| WARWICKS | O | M | R | W | 7th | | |
| Benjamin | 8 | 0 | 26 | 1 | 8th | | |
| Munton | 7 | 0 | 20 | 0 | 9th | | |
| Reeve | 8 | 1 | 38 | 1 | 10th | | |
| Smith P.A. | 7.3 | 0 | 51 | 1 | | | |
| Small | 8 | 0 | 60 | 2 | | | |

## YORKSHIRE vs. KENT

at Scarborough on 16th June 1991
Toss : Kent. Umpires : J.D.Bond and G.I.Burgess
Yorkshire won by 67 runs. Yorkshire 4 pts, Kent 0 pts

### YORKSHIRE

| | | |
|---|---|---|
| M.D.Moxon * | retired hurt/ill | 3 |
| A.A.Metcalfe | run out | 20 |
| R.J.Blakey + | not out | 130 |
| D.Byas | c Cowdrey b Ellison | 45 |
| P.E.Robinson | c Benson b Davis | 11 |
| C.White | lbw b McCague | 3 |
| C.S.Pickles | c Ward b Davis | 0 |
| D.Gough | c Benson b Davis | 0 |
| J.D.Batty | not out | 13 |
| M.Broadhurst | | |
| S.D.Fletcher | | |
| Extras | (lb 7,w 9) | 16 |
| TOTAL | (40 overs)(for 6 wkts) | 241 |

### KENT

| | | |
|---|---|---|
| S.A.Marsh + | c Blakey b Fletcher | 3 |
| M.R.Benson * | c Robinson b Batty | 23 |
| N.R.Taylor | c sub b Batty | 41 |
| T.R.Ward | c Gough b Batty | 16 |
| G.R.Cowdrey | c Blakey b Pickles | 2 |
| N.J.Llong | c Blakey b Batty | 23 |
| M.J.McCague | b Fletcher | 13 |
| R.M.Ellison | b Pickles | 14 |
| R.P.Davis | lbw b Gough | 25 |
| T.A.Merrick | not out | 0 |
| A.P.Igglesden | b Gough | 0 |
| Extras | (b 1,lb 7,w 6) | 14 |
| TOTAL | (35.2 overs) | 174 |

| KENT | O | M | R | W | | FALL OF WICKETS | |
|---|---|---|---|---|---|---|---|
| | | | | | | YOR | KEN |
| Igglesden | 8 | 0 | 31 | 0 | | | |
| Ellison | 8 | 1 | 60 | 1 | 1st | 52 | 4 |
| Merrick | 8 | 0 | 48 | 0 | 2nd | 168 | 62 |
| Davis | 8 | 1 | 42 | 3 | 3rd | 187 | 82 |
| McCague | 8 | 0 | 53 | 1 | 4th | 192 | 88 |
| | | | | | 5th | 197 | 110 |
| YORKSHIRE | O | M | R | W | 6th | 198 | 130 |
| Broadhurst | 8 | 0 | 27 | 0 | 7th | | 130 |
| Fletcher | 6 | 0 | 23 | 2 | 8th | | 174 |
| Gough | 7.2 | 0 | 32 | 2 | 9th | | 174 |
| Batty | 8 | 0 | 33 | 4 | 10th | | 174 |
| Pickles | 6 | 0 | 51 | 2 | | | |

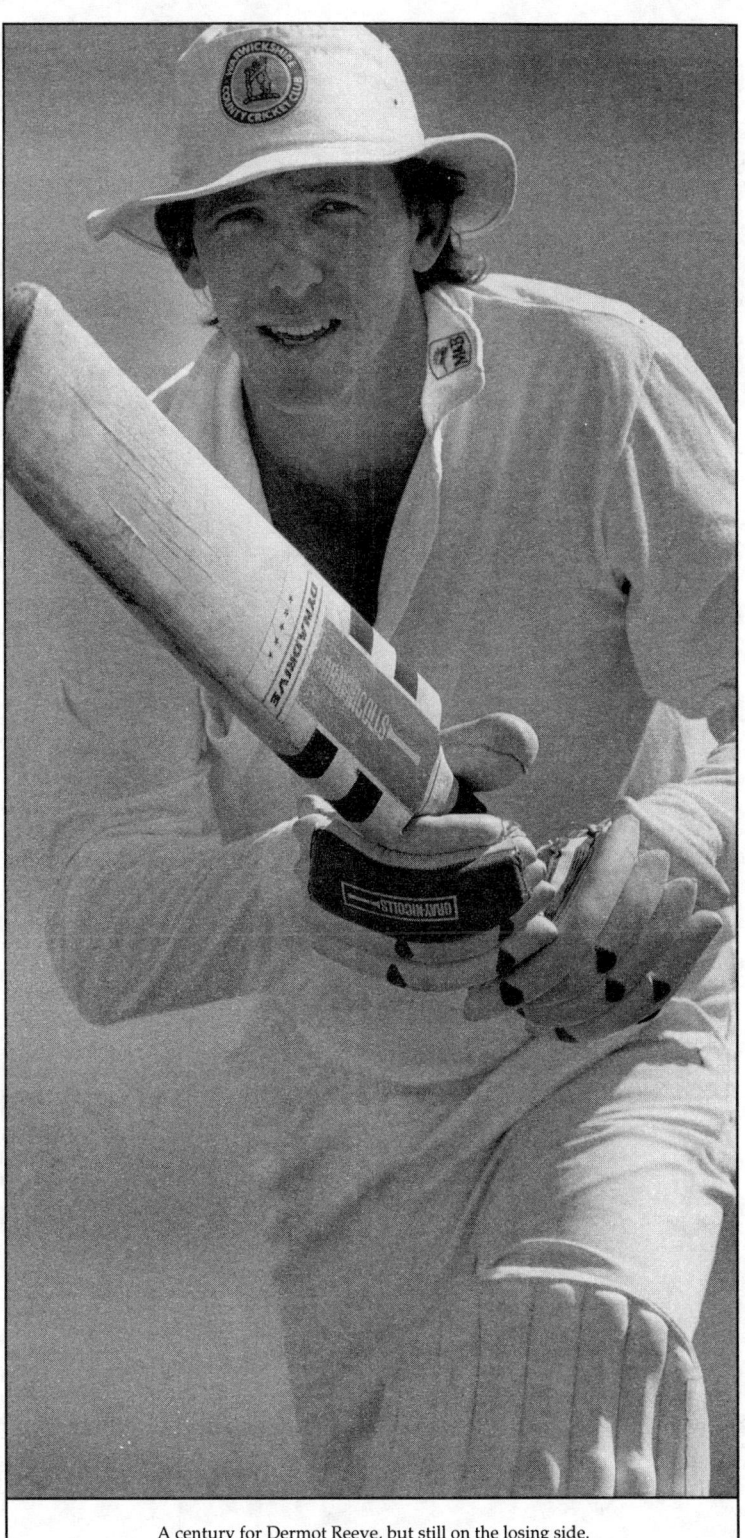

A century for Dermot Reeve, but still on the losing side.

| TOUR MATCHES | BRITANNIC ASS. CHAMPIONSHIP |
|---|---|

## DERBYSHIRE vs. WEST INDIES

at Derby on 12th, 13th, 14th June 1991
Toss : West Indies. Umpires : B.J.Meyer and R.A.White
Match drawn

### WEST INDIES

| Batsman | 1st innings | R | 2nd innings | R |
|---|---|---|---|---|
| C.B.Lambert | lbw b Base | 5 | lbw b Cork | 4 |
| D.L.Haynes * | lbw b Base | 31 | b Warner | 0 |
| R.B.Richardson | c Warner b Folley | 114 | (6) not out | 48 |
| B.C.Lara | lbw b Base | 1 | (3) lbw b Cork | 20 |
| C.L.Hooper | c Cork b Base | 82 | not out | 95 |
| A.L.Logie | not out | 3 | (4) b Warner | 9 |
| M.D.Marshall | | | | |
| D.Williams + | | | | |
| H.A.G.Anthony | | | | |
| C.E.L.Ambrose | | | | |
| I.B.A.Allen | | | | |
| Extras | (lb 10,w 3,nb 12) | 25 | (b 1,lb 10,nb 12) | 23 |
| TOTAL | (for 5 wkts dec) | 261 | (for 4 wkts dec) | 199 |

### DERBYSHIRE

| Batsman | 1st innings | R | 2nd innings | R |
|---|---|---|---|---|
| K.J.Barnett * | b Allen | 1 | not out | 12 |
| P.D.Bowler | c Lambert b Marshall | 13 | c Lambert b Allen | 63 |
| T.J.G.O'Gorman | b Ambrose | 4 | c Haynes b Hooper | 23 |
| M.Azharuddin | c Ambrose b Hooper | 72 | b Anthony | 35 |
| C.J.Adams | b Anthony | 55 | run out | 3 |
| F.A.Griffith | b Anthony | 6 | (7) st Williams b Hooper | 4 |
| K.M.Krikken + | c Richardson b Hooper | 6 | (8) run out | 3 |
| D.G.Cork | not out | 11 | (9) c Williams b Hooper | 4 |
| A.E.Warner | b Hooper | 7 | (6) st Williams b Hooper | 9 |
| I.Folley | | | b Marshall | 0 |
| S.J.Base | | | not out | 9 |
| Extras | (b 5,lb 16,nb 8) | 29 | (lb 15,nb 5) | 20 |
| TOTAL | (for 8 wkts dec) | 204 | (for 9 wkts) | 185 |

| DERBYSHIRE | O | M | R | W | O | M | R | W |
|---|---|---|---|---|---|---|---|---|
| Base | 22.4 | 7 | 44 | 4 | 9 | 1 | 19 | 0 |
| Warner | 17 | 3 | 52 | 0 | 10 | 2 | 26 | 2 |
| Folley | 11 | 2 | 67 | 1 | 10 | 0 | 52 | 0 |
| Griffith | 10 | 3 | 39 | 0 | 6 | 1 | 28 | 0 |
| Cork | 16 | 3 | 49 | 0 | 10 | 2 | 27 | 2 |
| Bowler | | | | | 5 | 0 | 36 | 0 |

| WEST INDIES | O | M | R | W | O | M | R | W |
|---|---|---|---|---|---|---|---|---|
| Ambrose | 11 | 3 | 26 | 1 | 7 | 2 | 18 | 0 |
| Allen | 11 | 3 | 35 | 1 | 8 | 0 | 37 | 1 |
| Anthony | 13 | 0 | 45 | 2 | 9 | 0 | 42 | 1 |
| Marshall | 8 | 1 | 27 | 1 | 9 | 2 | 22 | 1 |
| Hooper | 22.2 | 7 | 50 | 3 | 16 | 4 | 49 | 4 |
| Lara | | | | | 1 | 0 | 2 | 0 |

| FALL OF WICKETS | WI | DER | WI | DER |
|---|---|---|---|---|
| 1st | 23 | 5 | 0 | 70 |
| 2nd | 82 | 10 | 14 | 139 |
| 3rd | 84 | 51 | 33 | 153 |
| 4th | 248 | 135 | 48 | 156 |
| 5th | 261 | 171 | | 161 |
| 6th | | 181 | | 165 |
| 7th | | 182 | | 172 |
| 8th | | 204 | | 173 |
| 9th | | | | 185 |
| 10th | | | | |

## NORTHANTS vs. WEST INDIES

at Northampton on 15th (no play), 16th, 17th June 1991
Toss : West Indies. Umpires : J.C.Balderstone and B.Dudleston
Match drawn

### WEST INDIES

| Batsman | Dismissal | R |
|---|---|---|
| P.V.Simmons | c Cook b Curran | 29 |
| D.L.Haynes | c Ripley b Curran | 60 |
| B.C.Lara | c Cook b Baptiste | 4 |
| A.L.Logie | lbw b Curran | 19 |
| P.J.L.Dujon + | c Cook b Thomas | 82 |
| I.V.A.Richards * | c Lamb b Thomas | 47 |
| C.L.Hooper | not out | 49 |
| H.A.G.Anthony | b Cook | 6 |
| I.B.A.Allen | lbw b Cook | 8 |
| C.A.Walsh | | |
| B.P.Patterson | | |
| Extras | (b 1,lb 4,nb 1) | 6 |
| TOTAL | (for 8 wkts dec) | 310 |

### NORTHANTS

| Batsman | Dismissal | R |
|---|---|---|
| A.Fordham | not out | 34 |
| N.A.Felton | b Anthony | 20 |
| R.J.Bailey | not out | 1 |
| A.J.Lamb * | | |
| D.J.Capel | | |
| K.M.Curran | | |
| E.A.E.Baptiste | | |
| J.G.Thomas | | |
| D.Ripley + | | |
| J.P.Taylor | | |
| N.G.B.Cook | | |
| Extras | (b 2,lb 4,w 1,nb 6) | 13 |
| TOTAL | (for 1 wkt dec) | 68 |

| NORTHANTS | O | M | R | W | O | M | R | W |
|---|---|---|---|---|---|---|---|---|
| Thomas | 15 | 1 | 87 | 2 | | | | |
| Taylor | 10 | 2 | 36 | 0 | | | | |
| Cook | 16.2 | 1 | 74 | 2 | | | | |
| Baptiste | 12 | 5 | 25 | 1 | | | | |
| Curran | 16 | 4 | 60 | 3 | | | | |
| Capel | 6 | 0 | 23 | 0 | | | | |

| WEST INDIES | O | M | R | W | O | M | R | W |
|---|---|---|---|---|---|---|---|---|
| Patterson | 0.2 | 0 | 2 | 0 | | | | |
| Walsh | 7.4 | 1 | 13 | 0 | | | | |
| Allen | 7 | 0 | 27 | 0 | | | | |
| Lara | 3 | 1 | 9 | 0 | | | | |
| Anthony | 2 | 1 | 11 | 1 | | | | |

| FALL OF WICKETS | WI | NOR | WI | NOR |
|---|---|---|---|---|
| 1st | 74 | 66 | | |
| 2nd | 95 | | | |
| 3rd | 95 | | | |
| 4th | 136 | | | |
| 5th | 232 | | | |
| 6th | 269 | | | |
| 7th | 284 | | | |
| 8th | 310 | | | |
| 9th | | | | |
| 10th | | | | |

## GLAMORGAN vs. MIDDLESEX

at Cardiff on 14th, 15th, 17th June 1991
Toss : Glamorgan. Umpires : D.J.Constant and K.J.Lyons
Glamorgan won by 129 runs. Glamorgan 19 pts (Bt: 3, Bw: 0), Middlesex 3 pts (Bt: 0, Bw: 3)
100 overs scores : Glamorgan 272 for 7

### GLAMORGAN

| Batsman | 1st innings | R | 2nd innings | R |
|---|---|---|---|---|
| A.R.Butcher * | c Roseberry b Cowans | 31 | c Sylvester b Brown | 57 |
| H.Morris | c Emburey b Tufnell | 48 | b Tufnell | 15 |
| R.J.Shastri | c Emburey b Cowans | 33 | not out | 25 |
| M.P.Maynard | c Farbrace b Tufnell | 0 | not out | 9 |
| P.A.Cottey | c Williams b Cowans | 24 | | |
| A.Dale | c Farbrace b Cowans | 34 | | |
| R.D.B.Croft | c Emburey b Williams | 50 | | |
| C.P.Metson + | b Tufnell | 49 | | |
| S.L.Watkin | not out | 13 | | |
| S.R.Barwick | | | | |
| M.Frost | | | | |
| Extras | (b 5,lb 7,w 1,nb 18) | 31 | (b 5,lb 1,nb 1) | 7 |
| TOTAL | (for 8 wkts dec) | 313 | (for 2 wkts dec) | 113 |

### MIDDLESEX

| Batsman | 1st innings | R | 2nd innings | R |
|---|---|---|---|---|
| I.J.F.Hutchinson | c Metson b Frost | 9 | c Metson b Frost | 5 |
| M.A.Roseberry | not out | 40 | lbw b Barwick | 37 |
| M.W.Gatting * | b Watkin | 13 | not out | 96 |
| M.R.Ramprakash | not out | 16 | c Metson b Barwick | 0 |
| K.R.Brown | | | c Butcher b Frost | 10 |
| J.E.Emburey | | | lbw b Frost | 47 |
| N.F.Williams | | | c Cottey b Frost | 0 |
| P.Farbrace + | | | run out | 0 |
| P.C.R.Tufnell | | | c Maynard b Barwick | 6 |
| N.G.Cowans | | | b Barwick | 0 |
| S.A.Sylvester | | | c Metson b Watkin | 0 |
| Extras | (lb 7,nb 1) | 8 | (b 1,lb 8,nb 1) | 10 |
| TOTAL | (for 2 wkts dec) | 86 | | 211 |

| MIDDLESEX | O | M | R | W | O | M | R | W |
|---|---|---|---|---|---|---|---|---|
| Williams | 26 | 6 | 79 | 1 | | | | |
| Sylvester | 15 | 2 | 80 | 0 | 5 | 0 | 18 | 0 |
| Cowans | 19 | 8 | 42 | 4 | 4 | 0 | 16 | 0 |
| Tufnell | 36.3 | 13 | 76 | 3 | 7 | 0 | 25 | 1 |
| Emburey | 10 | 2 | 24 | 0 | 5 | 0 | 31 | 0 |
| Brown | | | | | 3 | 0 | 17 | 1 |

| GLAMORGAN | O | M | R | W | O | M | R | W |
|---|---|---|---|---|---|---|---|---|
| Watkin | 13 | 4 | 35 | 1 | 25.5 | 3 | 82 | 1 |
| Barwick | 12 | 6 | 20 | 0 | 24 | 8 | 49 | 4 |
| Frost | 9 | 3 | 24 | 1 | 21 | 6 | 53 | 4 |
| Dale | | | | | 4 | 1 | 6 | 0 |
| Croft | | | | | 6 | 2 | 10 | 0 |

| FALL OF WICKETS | GLA | MID | GLA | MID |
|---|---|---|---|---|
| 1st | 51 | 30 | 64 | 15 |
| 2nd | 101 | 52 | 92 | 62 |
| 3rd | 101 | | | 62 |
| 4th | 145 | | | 82 |
| 5th | 150 | | | 156 |
| 6th | 227 | | | 158 |
| 7th | 269 | | | 181 |
| 8th | 313 | | | 198 |
| 9th | | | | 198 |
| 10th | | | | 211 |

# HEADLINES

### Tetley Bitter Challenge

#### 12th - 14th June

• For the second time in three matches against the counties, West Indies were denied victory with the last batting pair at the crease. Simon Base and Kim Barnett, returning after retiring hurt with a back injury, ensured that Derbyshire escaped with a draw, after being asked to make 257 in 50 overs in their second innings. Richie Richardson had again shown he was beginning to enjoy English conditions with his second 100 of the tour, and he was well supported by Carl Hooper, who also collected seven wickets with his off-spinners.

#### 15th - 17th June

• The West Indies's visit to Northampton was reduced to little more than a few hours' batting practice as all of the first and most of the second day were conceded to the weather. Desmond Haynes and Jeff Dujon both made their highest scores of the tour so far, but, in Northants's brief innings, Pat Patterson only managed to deliver two balls before injuring himself.

# BRITANNIC ASSURANCE CHAMPIONSHIP

## GLOUCS vs. NOTTS

at Gloucester on 14th, 15th (no play), 17th June 1991
Toss : Gloucs. Umpires : B.Leadbeater and N.T.Plews
Match drawn. Gloucs 3 pts (Bt: 2, Bw: 1), Notts 4 pts (Bt: 0, Bw: 4)

### GLOUCS

| | | | | |
|---|---|---|---|---|
| G.D.Hodgson | c Crawley b Stephenson | 11 | (2) b Afford | 57 |
| J.J.E.Hardy | lbw b Pick | 10 | (1) c Johnson b Afford | 31 |
| A.J.Wright * | c French b Pick | 34 | not out | 45 |
| C.W.J.Athey | c French b Afford | 63 | | |
| M.W.Alleyne | lbw b Stephenson | 1 | | |
| J.W.Lloyds | c Pollard b Crawley | 18 | (4) not out | 3 |
| R.C.Russell + | b Afford | 5 | | |
| D.V.Lawrence | b Pick | 41 | | |
| D.R.Gilbert | c Afford b Pick | 8 | | |
| A.M.Smith | c Evans b Stephenson | 2 | | |
| A.M.Babington | not out | 0 | | |
| Extras | (lb 3,w 1,nb 4) | 8 | (lb 3,nb 4) | 7 |
| TOTAL | | 201 | (for 2 wkts dec) | 143 |

### NOTTS

| | | | | |
|---|---|---|---|---|
| B.C.Broad | lbw b Gilbert | 19 | lbw b Babington | 16 |
| P.Pollard | lbw b Lawrence | 3 | lbw b Lawrence | 0 |
| R.T.Robinson * | b Gilbert | 28 | c Wright b Lawrence | 0 |
| P.Johnson | c Russell b Gilbert | 0 | lbw b Gilbert | 6 |
| D.W.Randall | not out | 9 | not out | 85 |
| K.P.Evans | not out | 2 | | |
| M.A.Crawley | | | (6) not out | 49 |
| F.D.Stephenson | | | | |
| B.N.French + | | | | |
| R.A.Pick | | | | |
| J.A.Afford | | | | |
| Extras | (nb 3) | 3 | (lb 4,nb 5) | 9 |
| TOTAL | (for 4 wkts dec) | 64 | (for 4 wkts) | 165 |

| NOTTS | O | M | R | W | O | M | R | W | FALL OF WICKETS | | | |
|---|---|---|---|---|---|---|---|---|---|---|---|---|
| | | | | | | | | | | GLO | NOT | GLO | NOT |
| Pick | 20.4 | 4 | 61 | 4 | 6 | 1 | 22 | 0 | | | | |
| Stephenson | 19 | 6 | 51 | 3 | 6 | 4 | 10 | 0 | 1st | 21 | 5 | 56 | 0 |
| Evans | 10 | 0 | 39 | 0 | 7 | 0 | 35 | 0 | 2nd | 25 | 45 | 121 | 0 |
| Afford | 13 | 6 | 32 | 2 | 12 | 0 | 48 | 2 | 3rd | 105 | 45 | | 14 |
| Crawley | 4 | 1 | 15 | 1 | 4 | 0 | 25 | 0 | 4th | 108 | 62 | | 35 |
| | | | | | | | | | 5th | 143 | | | |
| GLOUCS | O | M | R | W | O | M | R | W | 6th | 143 | | | |
| Lawrence | 7 | 1 | 18 | 1 | 10 | 0 | 37 | 2 | 7th | 148 | | | |
| Gilbert | 11 | 4 | 18 | 3 | 9.4 | 1 | 20 | 1 | 8th | 170 | | | |
| Babington | 3 | 0 | 13 | 0 | 4.2 | 3 | 5 | 1 | 9th | 177 | | | |
| Lloyds | 6 | 1 | 15 | 0 | 11 | 0 | 62 | 0 | 10th | 201 | | | |
| Smith | | | | | 8 | 0 | 30 | 0 | | | | | |
| Athey | | | | | 2 | 0 | 7 | 0 | | | | | |

## LEICESTERSHIRE vs. SURREY

at Leicester on 14th, 15th (no play), 17th June 1991
Toss : Surrey. Umpires : J.W.Holder and R.Julian
Match drawn. Leicestershire 2 pts (Bt: 2, Bw: 0), Surrey 4 pts (Bt: 0, Bw: 4)

### LEICESTERSHIRE

| | | | | |
|---|---|---|---|---|
| T.J.Boon | b Waqar Younis | 9 | b Medlycott | 13 |
| N.E.Briers * | c Stewart b Murphy | 31 | c Sargeant b Medlycott | 30 |
| P.N.Hepworth | c Sargeant b Waqar Younis | 0 | b Murphy | 30 |
| J.J.Whitaker | b Waqar Younis | 44 | not out | 43 |
| L.Potter | c Bicknell b Waqar Younis | 10 | not out | 14 |
| B.F.Smith | c Sargeant b Feltham | 24 | | |
| C.C.Lewis | st Sargeant b Medlycott | 46 | | |
| P.Willey | c Sargeant b Feltham | 18 | | |
| P.Whitticase + | not out | 32 | | |
| D.J.Millns | b Waqar Younis | 3 | | |
| J.N.Maguire | c & b Feltham | 5 | | |
| Extras | (lb 6,nb 4) | 10 | (lb 3) | 3 |
| TOTAL | | 232 | (for 3 wkts dec) | 133 |

### SURREY

| | | | | |
|---|---|---|---|---|
| D.J.Bicknell | c Hepworth b Millns | 38 | b Lewis | 86 |
| R.I.Alikhan | not out | 28 | c Hepworth b Millns | 35 |
| A.J.Stewart | not out | 17 | c Whitticase b Potter | 13 |
| D.M.Ward | | | c Smith b Maguire | 60 |
| G.P.Thorpe | | | c Whitticase b Millns | 24 |
| I.A.Greig * | | | not out | 27 |
| K.T.Medlycott | | | b Lewis | 3 |
| M.A.Feltham | | | c Potter b Lewis | 2 |
| N.F.Sargeant + | | | c Briers b Lewis | 0 |
| Waqar Younis | | | not out | 2 |
| A.J.Murphy | | | | |
| Extras | (lb 7) | 7 | (b 1,lb 5,w 1,nb 2) | 9 |
| TOTAL | (for 1 wkt dec) | 90 | (for 8 wkts) | 261 |

| SURREY | O | M | R | W | O | M | R | W | FALL OF WICKETS | | | |
|---|---|---|---|---|---|---|---|---|---|---|---|---|
| | | | | | | | | | | LEI | SUR | LEI | SUR |
| Waqar Younis | 16 | 3 | 57 | 5 | 3 | 0 | 9 | 0 | 1st | 30 | 60 | 27 | 71 |
| Murphy | 21 | 6 | 67 | 1 | 17.5 | 1 | 53 | 1 | 2nd | 36 | | 66 | 96 |
| Feltham | 27 | 5 | 91 | 3 | 6 | 0 | 22 | 0 | 3rd | 63 | | 112 | 181 |
| Medlycott | 6 | 2 | 11 | 1 | 20 | 6 | 46 | 2 | 4th | 100 | | | 224 |
| | | | | | | | | | 5th | 107 | | | 226 |
| LEICESTERSHIRE | O | M | R | W | O | M | R | W | 6th | 165 | | | 245 |
| Lewis | 9 | 3 | 17 | 0 | 14 | 3 | 45 | 4 | 7th | 183 | | | 255 |
| Maguire | 9 | 3 | 22 | 0 | 12 | 2 | 45 | 1 | 8th | 207 | | | 255 |
| Willey | 11 | 5 | 19 | 0 | 14 | 2 | 50 | 0 | 9th | 227 | | | |
| Millns | 10 | 4 | 25 | 1 | 5 | 0 | 43 | 2 | 10th | 232 | | | |
| Potter | 1 | 1 | 0 | 0 | 17 | 1 | 72 | 1 | | | | | |

## HEADLINES

### Britannic Assurance Championship

### 14th - 17th June

• Another round of Championship matches was badly affected by miserable weather, with Glamorgan the only side to gain victory, defeating Middlesex by 129 runs at Cardiff. The champions' disappointing start to the season continued as they never looked like approaching a victory target of 341, Mike Gatting, unbeaten on 96, gaining little support from his colleagues. Hugh Morris's 63 runs in the match were not enough to take him past the 1,000 mark in first-class cricket; he needed a further 27 to become the first batsman to reach four figures.

• Although the second day was completely lost Leicestershire and Surrey at least managed an entertaining last day at Leicester. Surrey were left 276 for victory in 62 overs and finished 15 short with two wickets in hand, Chris Lewis's four wickets forcing the visitors to give up their chase. Waqar Younis had earlier taken five wickets in an innings for the fifth time this season.

• Graeme Hick made his first century of the 1991 season in Worcestershire's first innings total of 410 for five wickets, finding an easy-paced Hove pitch and a friendly Sussex bowling attack much to his taste, as he reached 186, after 10 first-class innings in which his highest score had been 58. After two declarations on the third morning, the visitors looked set for their first Championship win of the season when they claimed the first five Sussex second innings wickets for 70, but Paul Parker and Tony Dodemaide remained to frustrate their hopes of moving up the table.

• Nottinghamshire's visit to Gloucester was not a memorable one as rain washed out Saturday's play and regularly interrupted on the last day as the visitors attempted to score 281 for victory. Gloucestershire briefly scented a second successive win when they reduced Notts to 35 for four, but Derek Randall and Mark Crawley then added 130 in an unbroken fifth wicket stand.

• Yorkshire's contest with Kent at Harrogate did not get beyond the opening day, Martyn Moxon and Matthew Fleming competing for the individual honours with 90 and three for 28 respectively.

First-class début: S.A. Sylvester (Middlesex).

# BRITANNIC ASSURANCE CHAMPIONSHIP

## SUSSEX vs. WORCESTERSHIRE

at Hove on 14th, 15th, 17th June 1991
Toss : Sussex. Umpires : H.D.Bird and J.H.Harris
Match drawn. Sussex 1 pt (Bt: 0, Bw: 1), Worcestershire 4 pts (Bt: 4, Bw: 0)
100 overs scores : Worcestershire 373 for 4

### WORCESTERSHIRE

| | | | | |
|---|---|---|---|---|
| T.S.Curtis | c Dodemaide b Salisbury | 24 | not out | 33 |
| S.J.Rhodes + | b Pigott | 77 | c Hall b Wells A.P. | 10 |
| G.A.Hick | b Dodemaide | 186 | not out | 28 |
| T.M.Moody | c Moores b Dodemaide | 73 | | |
| P.A.Neale * | b Pigott | 28 | | |
| D.B.D'Oliveira | not out | 12 | | |
| R.K.Illingworth | not out | 1 | | |
| P.J.Newport | | | | |
| S.R.Lampitt | | | | |
| N.V.Radford | | | | |
| G.R.Dilley | | | | |
| Extras | (lb 3,nb 6) | 9 | (b 1,lb 4) | 5 |
| TOTAL | (for 5 wkts dec) | 410 | (for 1 wkt dec) | 76 |

### SUSSEX

| | | | | |
|---|---|---|---|---|
| D.M.Smith | not out | 67 | c Rhodes b Dilley | 5 |
| J.W.Hall | lbw b Illingworth | 55 | c Rhodes b Radford | 7 |
| N.J.Lenham | not out | 4 | c Hick b Newport | 21 |
| A.P.Wells | | | c Moody b Newport | 20 |
| P.W.G.Parker * | | | not out | 56 |
| C.M.Wells | | | lbw b Newport | 0 |
| A.I.C.Dodemaide | | | not out | 35 |
| P.Moores + | | | | |
| A.C.S.Pigott | | | | |
| I.D.K.Salisbury | | | | |
| A.N.Jones | | | | |
| Extras | (b 2,lb 1,nb 2) | 5 | (lb 3,nb 9) | 12 |
| TOTAL | (for 1 wkt dec) | 131 | (for 5 wkts) | 156 |

| SUSSEX | O | M | R | W | O | M | R | W | FALL OF WICKETS | | | | |
|---|---|---|---|---|---|---|---|---|---|---|---|---|---|
| | | | | | | | | | | WOR | SUS | WOR | SUS |
| Jones | 18 | 4 | 48 | 0 | | | | | | | | | |
| Dodemaide | 21 | 7 | 45 | 2 | | | | | 1st | 46 | 124 | 19 | 8 |
| Wells C.M. | 17 | 3 | 77 | 0 | | | | | 2nd | 200 | | | 30 |
| Pigott | 20 | 5 | 69 | 2 | | | | | 3rd | 364 | | | 44 |
| Salisbury | 35 | 5 | 168 | 1 | | | | | 4th | 373 | | | 70 |
| Wells A.P. | | | | | 5 | 1 | 21 | 1 | 5th | 409 | | | 70 |
| Lenham | | | | | 8 | 0 | 25 | 0 | 6th | | | | |
| Parker | | | | | 2 | 0 | 10 | 0 | 7th | | | | |
| Smith | | | | | 2 | 0 | 15 | 0 | 8th | | | | |
| | | | | | | | | | 9th | | | | |
| WORCS | O | M | R | W | O | M | R | W | 10th | | | | |
| Dilley | 12 | 4 | 32 | 0 | 12 | 2 | 25 | 1 | | | | | |
| Radford | 9 | 3 | 22 | 0 | 14 | 5 | 32 | 1 | | | | | |
| Lampitt | 6 | 1 | 24 | 0 | 12 | 3 | 31 | 0 | | | | | |
| Illingworth | 12 | 5 | 32 | 1 | 16 | 8 | 21 | 0 | | | | | |
| Newport | 5 | 0 | 18 | 0 | 18 | 7 | 32 | 3 | | | | | |
| Hick | | | | | 3 | 1 | 8 | 0 | | | | | |
| Moody | | | | | 2 | 1 | 4 | 0 | | | | | |
| D'Oliveira | | | | | 1 | 1 | 0 | 0 | | | | | |

## YORKSHIRE vs. KENT

at Harrogate on 14th, 15th (no play), 17th (no play) June 1991
Toss : Yorkshire. Umpires : J.D.Bond and G.I.Burgess
Match drawn. Yorkshire 1 pt (Bt: 1, Bw: 0), Kent 2 pts (Bt: 0, Bw: 2)

### YORKSHIRE

| | | |
|---|---|---|
| M.D.Moxon * | b Fleming | 90 |
| A.A.Metcalfe | c Penn b McCague | 10 |
| D.Byas | c Taylor b Ellison | 36 |
| R.J.Blakey + | not out | 30 |
| P.E.Robinson | lbw b Fleming | 0 |
| S.A.Kellett | c Marsh b Fleming | 5 |
| P.Carrick | not out | 12 |
| D.Gough | | |
| C.S.Pickles | | |
| J.D.Batty | | |
| S.D.Fletcher | | |
| Extras | (b 2,lb 7,w 2,nb 2) | 13 |
| TOTAL | (for 5 wkts) | 196 |

### KENT

N.R.Taylor
M.R.Benson *
T.R.Ward
G.R.Cowdrey
M.V.Fleming
R.M.Ellison
S.A.Marsh +
R.P.Davis
M.J.McCague
C.Penn
A.P.Igglesden
Extras
TOTAL

| KENT | O | M | R | W | O | M | R | W | FALL OF WICKETS | | | |
|---|---|---|---|---|---|---|---|---|---|---|---|---|
| | | | | | | | | | | YOR | KEN | YOR | KEN |
| Igglesden | 14 | 4 | 33 | 0 | | | | | 1st | 18 | | | |
| McCague | 22 | 6 | 55 | 1 | | | | | 2nd | 105 | | | |
| Davis | 3 | 2 | 6 | 0 | | | | | 3rd | 158 | | | |
| Ellison | 12 | 2 | 51 | 1 | | | | | 4th | 158 | | | |
| Penn | 7 | 2 | 14 | 0 | | | | | 5th | 169 | | | |
| Fleming | 15 | 7 | 28 | 3 | | | | | 6th | | | | |
| | | | | | | | | | 7th | | | | |
| YORKSHIRE | O | M | R | W | O | M | R | W | 8th | | | | |
| | | | | | | | | | 9th | | | | |
| | | | | | | | | | 10th | | | | |

## HEADLINES

### Britannic Assurance Championship

### 18th - 20th June

• After another round of matches where results could often only be achieved by declaration and forfeiture thanks to more disruption from dispiriting June weather, Warwickshire stretched their lead to an impressive 34 points with their fifth victory in nine games, over Sussex by 98 runs at Coventry. After Andy Lloyd had forfeited Warwickshire's second innings to leave the visitors two sessions to make 256, Allan Donald, with his sixth five-wicket haul of the summer, well supported by Gladstone Small, with his best return of the season so far, made victory a formality as Sussex were dismissed for 157.

• Lancashire moved into third place with their 115-run win over Leicestershire at Leicester, a victory that they owed entirely to their bowlers after the home side had dominated for most ot the match. But two Lancashire batting collapses (125 for eight and 57 for six respectively) were made irrelevant by the constant interruptions and Leicestershire could not come to terms with a target of 274 on the final afternoon, Wasim Akram claiming five for 61.

• Derbyshire's victory over Gloucestershire at Gloucester was, however, fully merited, after they had bowled the home side out twice. Mohammad Azharuddin had put Derbyshire in the driving seat with his first Championship 100, sharing a fourth-wicket stand of 211 with Tim O'Gorman, and their bowlers took full advantage. Gloucestershire were forced to follow on 226 behind on first innings, and even 101 from Bill Athey and a stand of 104 for the eighth wicket with Richard Williams could not prevent defeat by six wickets.

• Worcestershire gained their first Championship win of the season in the most dramatic style, their one-wicket victory over Nottinghamshire at Worcester only being achieved with a last wicket stand of 24 between Stuart Lampitt and Richard Stemp. Chris Broad hit his third 100 of the season in Notts's first innings 313 for seven declared, but was more than matched by Tom Moody who just failed to score 100s in both innings. His second innings dismissal looked to have ended the home side's hopes of victory but the lower-order batsmen had other ideas and even five wickets for Franklyn Stephenson could not stop them.

• First-class débuts: G.R. Haynes (Worcestershire); E. McCray (Derbyshire); M.J.Gerrard and R.C.Williams (Gloucestershire).

# BRITANNIC ASSURANCE CHAMPIONSHIP

## GLOUCS vs. DERBYSHIRE

at Gloucester on 18th, 19th, 20th June 1991
Toss : Gloucs. Umpires : B.Leadbeater and N.T.Plews
Derby won by 6 wickets. Gloucs 3 pts (Bt: 1, Bw: 2), Derby 24 pts (Bt: 4, Bw: 4)
100 overs scores : Derby 306 for 6

### DERBYSHIRE

| | | | | | |
|---|---|---|---|---|---|
| P.D.Bowler | c Lloyds b Gilbert | 0 | b Smith | 24 |
| C.J.Adams | b Smith | 0 | b Smith | 6 |
| J.E.Morris | c Williams R.C.J. b Gerrard | 30 | run out | 0 |
| M.Azharuddin | st Williams R.C.J. b Lloyds | 154 | not out | 31 |
| T.J.G.O'Gorman | c Athey b Williams R.C. | 73 | st Williams R.C.J. b Smith | 3 |
| K.J.Barnett * | b Smith | 20 | | |
| K.M.Krikken + | c Alleyne b Lloyds | 23 | (6) not out | 1 |
| E.J.McCray | b Smith | 37 | | |
| D.G.Cork | not out | 27 | | |
| A.E.Warner | | | | |
| O.H.Mortensen | | | | |
| Extras | (lb 8,w 3,nb 6) | 17 | (lb 2,nb 1) | 3 |
| TOTAL | (for 8 wkts dec) | 381 | (for 4 wkts) | 68 |

### GLOUCS

| | | | | | |
|---|---|---|---|---|---|
| J.J.E.Hardy | c Barnett b Warner | 0 | (2) lbw b Mortensen | 13 |
| R.C.J.Williams + | c Azharuddin b Warner | 8 | (9) not out | 55 |
| A.J.Wright * | c Adams b Warner | 13 | c Krikken b Cork | 20 |
| C.W.J.Athey | c Krikken b Mortensen | 11 | b Cork | 101 |
| M.W.Alleyne | c Adams b Cork | 18 | c & b Mortensen | 4 |
| J.W.Lloyds | c McCray b Barnett | 69 | c Krikken b Mortensen | 7 |
| R.C.Williams | lbw b Cork | 0 | (8) c Bowler b Barnett | 13 |
| G.D.Hodgson | b Barnett | 12 | (1) lbw b Mortensen | 22 |
| D.R.Gilbert | c Krikken b Barnett | 13 | (7) lbw b Cork | 15 |
| A.M.Smith | lbw b Cork | 0 | lbw b Barnett | 15 |
| M.J.Gerrard | not out | 3 | b Warner | 0 |
| Extras | (lb 1,nb 7) | 8 | (b 5,lb 12,nb 11) | 28 |
| TOTAL | | 155 | | 293 |

| GLOUCS | O | M | R | W | O | M | R | W | FALL OF WICKETS | | | | |
|---|---|---|---|---|---|---|---|---|---|---|---|---|---|
| | | | | | | | | | | DER | GLO | GLO | DER |
| Gilbert | 24 | 3 | 84 | 1 | 8 | 1 | 31 | 0 | 1st | 0 | 7 | 20 | 25 |
| Smith | 19.5 | 3 | 71 | 3 | 9.4 | 1 | 21 | 3 | 2nd | 0 | 14 | 52 | 25 |
| Gerrard | 13 | 4 | 46 | 1 | 2 | 0 | 14 | 0 | 3rd | 55 | 33 | 63 | 50 |
| Williams R.C. | 26 | 4 | 81 | 1 | | | | | 4th | 266 | 33 | 71 | 59 |
| Lloyds | 32 | 11 | 81 | 2 | | | | | 5th | 266 | 69 | 86 | |
| Athey | 4 | 1 | 10 | 0 | | | | | 6th | 298 | 69 | 120 | |
| | | | | | | | | | 7th | 328 | 109 | 154 | |
| DERBYSHIRE | O | M | R | W | O | M | R | W | 8th | 381 | 151 | 258 | |
| Mortensen | 17 | 6 | 28 | 1 | 25 | 3 | 66 | 4 | 9th | | 151 | 291 | |
| Warner | 15 | 2 | 35 | 3 | 15.4 | 3 | 53 | 1 | 10th | | 155 | 293 | |
| McCray | 15 | 5 | 41 | 0 | 10 | 5 | 12 | 0 | | | | | |
| Cork | 11 | 1 | 36 | 3 | 25 | 1 | 101 | 3 | | | | | |
| Barnett | 9.3 | 2 | 14 | 3 | 24 | 8 | 36 | 2 | | | | | |
| Bowler | | | | | 3 | 1 | 8 | 0 | | | | | |

## WORCESTERSHIRE vs. NOTTS

at Worcester on 18th, 19th, 20th June 1991
Toss : Notts. Umpires : D.J.Constant and M.J.Kitchen
Worcestershire won by 1 wicket. Worcs 20 pts (Bt: 2, Bw: 2), Notts 6 pts (Bt: 4, Bw: 2)
100 overs scores : Notts 305 for 6

### NOTTS

| | | | | | |
|---|---|---|---|---|---|
| B.C.Broad | c & b Dilley | 162 | c Rhodes b Lampitt | 8 |
| P.Pollard | c Moody b Lampitt | 18 | c Moody b Neale | 13 |
| R.T.Robinson * | lbw b Lampitt | 12 | not out | 89 |
| P.Johnson | c Rhodes b Lampitt | 22 | retired hurt/ill | 34 |
| D.W.Randall | c Rhodes b Radford | 9 | not out | 42 |
| M.A.Crawley | run out | 11 | | |
| K.P.Evans | not out | 56 | | |
| F.D.Stephenson | c Moody b Dilley | 11 | | |
| B.N.French + | | | | |
| R.A.Pick | | | | |
| J.A.Afford | | | | |
| Extras | (lb 3,w 2,nb 7) | 12 | (lb 9,w 2) | 11 |
| TOTAL | (for 7 wkts dec) | 313 | (for 2 wkts dec) | 197 |

### WORCESTERSHIRE

| | | | | | |
|---|---|---|---|---|---|
| T.S.Curtis | b Stephenson | 0 | c Afford b Stephenson | 0 |
| S.J.Rhodes + | c French b Pick | 0 | c Crawley b Stephenson | 17 |
| T.M.Moody | c Broad b Robinson | 107 | c Randall b Evans | 96 |
| D.B.D'Oliveira | c & b Stephenson | 26 | c French b Pick | 25 |
| P.A.Neale * | not out | 46 | c French b Afford | 18 |
| S.R.Lampitt | c Crawley b Johnson | 1 | not out | 50 |
| G.R.Haynes | not out | 13 | b Stephenson | 16 |
| P.J.Newport | | | c Crawley b Stephenson | 48 |
| N.V.Radford | | | lbw b Stephenson | 2 |
| G.R.Dilley | | | c & b Afford | 2 |
| R.D.Stemp | | | not out | 15 |
| Extras | (b 2,lb 2,w 1,nb 2) | 7 | (b 4,lb 10,nb 8) | 22 |
| TOTAL | (for 5 wkts dec) | 200 | (for 9 wkts) | 311 |

| WORCS | O | M | R | W | O | M | R | W | FALL OF WICKETS | | | | |
|---|---|---|---|---|---|---|---|---|---|---|---|---|---|
| | | | | | | | | | | NOT | WOR | NOT | WOR |
| Dilley | 19.2 | 1 | 46 | 2 | 4 | 0 | 12 | 0 | 1st | 45 | 0 | 14 | 0 |
| Radford | 13 | 5 | 20 | 1 | | | | | 2nd | 69 | 0 | 27 | 56 |
| Lampitt | 29 | 6 | 97 | 3 | 4 | 0 | 14 | 1 | 3rd | 121 | 72 | | 108 |
| Newport | 25 | 5 | 79 | 0 | | | | | 4th | 142 | 148 | | 164 |
| Stemp | 4 | 0 | 13 | 0 | | | | | 5th | 187 | 149 | | 166 |
| Haynes | 12 | 1 | 55 | 0 | 6 | 0 | 27 | 0 | 6th | 289 | | | 198 |
| Neale | | | | | 16.5 | 1 | 81 | 1 | 7th | 313 | | | 275 |
| Curtis | | | | | 12 | 0 | 50 | 0 | 8th | | | | 278 |
| Moody | | | | | 2 | 1 | 4 | 0 | 9th | | | | 287 |
| NOTTS | O | M | R | W | O | M | R | W | 10th | | | | |
| Stephenson | 12 | 4 | 16 | 2 | 25 | 2 | 74 | 5 | | | | | |
| Pick | 8 | 0 | 36 | 1 | 18 | 2 | 60 | 1 | | | | | |
| Evans | 8 | 0 | 37 | 0 | 14 | 0 | 69 | 1 | | | | | |
| Afford | 6 | 1 | 38 | 0 | 28.1 | 8 | 94 | 2 | | | | | |
| Crawley | 4 | 1 | 13 | 0 | | | | | | | | | |
| Robinson | 5 | 0 | 30 | 1 | | | | | | | | | |
| Johnson | 4.2 | 1 | 26 | 1 | | | | | | | | | |

## LEICESTERSHIRE vs. LANCASHIRE

at Leicester on 18th, 19th, 20th June 1991
Toss : Leicestershire. Umpires : J.W.Holder and R.Julian
Lancashire won by 115 runs. Leicse 4 pts (Bt: 0, Bw: 4), Lancs 18 pts (Bt: 2, Bw: 0)

### LANCASHIRE

| | | | | | |
|---|---|---|---|---|---|
| G.D.Mendis | b Millns | 37 | c & b Maguire | 26 |
| G.Fowler | run out | 23 | c Lewis b Millns | 5 |
| G.D.Lloyd | lbw b Lewis | 0 | c Potter b Maguire | 13 |
| N.H.Fairbrother | lbw b Lewis | 0 | b Millns | 7 |
| N.J.Speak | c Whitticase b Lewis | 26 | lbw b Maguire | 0 |
| W.K.Hegg + | c Briers b Lewis | 23 | (8) not out | 4 |
| M.Watkinson | c Hepworth b Millns | 12 | (6) c Whitaker b Millns | 6 |
| Wasim Akram | c Potter b Lewis | 0 | (7) not out | 20 |
| I.D.Austin | c Potter b Willey | 43 | | |
| D.P.Hughes * | c Briers b Willey | 51 | | |
| P.J.Martin | not out | 2 | | |
| Extras | (lb 1,w 1,nb 7) | 9 | | 0 |
| TOTAL | | 226 | (for 6 wkts dec) | 81 |

### LEICESTERSHIRE

| | | | | | |
|---|---|---|---|---|---|
| T.J.Boon | c Fairbrother b Wasim Akram | 7 | c Fairbrother b Wasim Akram | 0 |
| N.E.Briers * | not out | 21 | c Fairbrother b Martin | 7 |
| P.N.Hepworth | not out | 0 | c Fairbrother b Wasim Akram | 25 |
| J.J.Whitaker | | | c Martin b Austin | 28 |
| L.Potter | | | c Hughes b Wasim Akram | 10 |
| B.F.Smith | | | c Speak b Watkinson | 13 |
| C.C.Lewis | | | lbw b Wasim Akram | 9 |
| P.Willey | | | c Mendis b Watkinson | 0 |
| P.Whitticase + | | | not out | 51 |
| D.J.Millns | | | b Wasim Akram | 3 |
| J.N.Maguire | | | b Watkinson | 5 |
| Extras | (lb 4,nb 2) | 6 | (b 3,lb 2,nb 2) | 7 |
| TOTAL | (for 1 wkt dec) | 34 | | 158 |

| LEICS | O | M | R | W | O | M | R | W | FALL OF WICKETS | | | |
|---|---|---|---|---|---|---|---|---|---|---|---|---|
| | | | | | | | | | | LAN | LEI | LAN | LEI |
| Lewis | 27 | 8 | 60 | 5 | 5 | 3 | 3 | 0 | 1st | 35 | 21 | 24 | 6 |
| Millns | 25 | 3 | 99 | 2 | 14.3 | 4 | 45 | 3 | 2nd | 39 | | 32 | 8 |
| Maguire | 15 | 2 | 51 | 0 | 9 | 5 | 13 | 3 | 3rd | 39 | | 51 | 58 |
| Willey | 4 | 0 | 15 | 2 | | | | | 4th | 83 | | 51 | 64 |
| Smith | | | | | 1 | 0 | 20 | 0 | 5th | 87 | | 53 | 85 |
| | | | | | | | | | 6th | 121 | | 57 | 95 |
| LANCASHIRE | O | M | R | W | O | M | R | W | 7th | 125 | | | 95 |
| Wasim Akram | 6.2 | 3 | 7 | 1 | 26 | 8 | 61 | 5 | 8th | 125 | | | 103 |
| Martin | 6 | 1 | 23 | 0 | 14 | 4 | 17 | 1 | 9th | 213 | | | 119 |
| Watkinson | | | | | 22.3 | 9 | 47 | 3 | 10th | 226 | | | 158 |
| Austin | | | | | 9 | 1 | 28 | 1 | | | | | |

## WARWICKSHIRE vs. SUSSEX

at Coventry on 18th, 19th, 20th June 1991
Toss : Sussex. Umpires : G.I.Burgess and J.H.Hampshire
Warwickshire won by 98 runs. Warwicks 19 pts (Bt: 3, Bw: 0), Sussex 4 pts (Bt: 0, Bw: 4)

### WARWICKSHIRE

| | | | |
|---|---|---|---|
| A.J.Moles | b Wells C.M. | 28 |
| J.D.Ratcliffe | run out | 10 |
| T.A.Lloyd * | c Parker b Wells C.M. | 83 |
| D.P.Ostler | b Wells C.M. | 9 |
| D.A.Reeve | b Dodemaide | 56 |
| P.A.Smith | lbw b Dodemaide | 11 |
| K.J.Piper + | b Jones | 41 |
| G.C.Small | c Dodemaide b Pigott | 25 |
| P.A.Booth | c Moores b Jones | 2 |
| T.A.Munton | not out | 5 |
| A.A.Donald | b Jones | 4 |
| Extras | (lb 9) | 9 |
| TOTAL | | 283 |

### SUSSEX

| | | | | | |
|---|---|---|---|---|---|
| D.M.Smith | not out | 7 | b Donald | 0 |
| J.W.Hall | b Donald | 0 | c Piper b Donald | 17 |
| N.J.Lenham | not out | 16 | c Piper b Small | 20 |
| A.P.Wells | | | c Piper b Small | 11 |
| P.W.G.Parker * | | | b Donald | 23 |
| C.M.Wells | | | c Piper b Reeve | 24 |
| A.I.C.Dodemaide | | | c Munton b Donald | 27 |
| P.Moores + | | | c Donald b Small | 14 |
| A.C.S.Pigott | | | c Piper b Donald | 2 |
| I.D.K.Salisbury | | | b Small | 0 |
| A.N.Jones | | | not out | 4 |
| Extras | (b 4,lb 1) | 5 | (b 9,lb 3,w 1,nb 2) | 15 |
| TOTAL | (for 1 wkt dec) | 28 | | 157 |

| SUSSEX | O | M | R | W | O | M | R | W | FALL OF WICKETS | | |
|---|---|---|---|---|---|---|---|---|---|---|---|
| | | | | | | | | | | WAR | SUS | WAR | SUS |
| Jones | 21 | 2 | 97 | 3 | | | | | 1st | 27 | 5 | | 0 |
| Dodemaide | 22 | 4 | 60 | 2 | | | | | 2nd | 99 | | | 21 |
| Pigott | 21 | 4 | 75 | 1 | | | | | 3rd | 111 | | | 41 |
| Wells C.M. | 13 | 3 | 42 | 3 | | | | | 4th | 154 | | | 52 |
| | | | | | | | | | 5th | 187 | | | 85 |
| WARWICKS | O | M | R | W | O | M | R | W | 6th | 224 | | | 103 |
| Donald | 4 | 1 | 8 | 1 | 15 | 3 | 48 | 5 | 7th | 268 | | | 129 |
| Small | 5 | 2 | 7 | 0 | 11.3 | 3 | 36 | 4 | 8th | 274 | | | 137 |
| Smith | 4 | 2 | 6 | 0 | 5 | 1 | 15 | 0 | 9th | 276 | | | 150 |
| Reeve | 2 | 1 | 2 | 0 | 6 | 3 | 10 | 1 | 10th | 283 | | | 157 |
| Munton | | | | | 10 | 2 | 36 | 0 | | | | | |

| BRITANNIC ASS. CHAMPIONSHIP | OTHER FIRST-CLASS MATCHES |
|---|---|

## SOMERSET vs. HAMPSHIRE

at Bath on 18th, 19th, 20th June 1991
Toss : Hampshire.  Umpires : D.R.Shepherd and A.G.T.Whitehead
Match drawn.  Somerset 4 pts (Bt: 2, Bw: 2), Hampshire 2 pts (Bt: 2, Bw: 0)
100 overs scores : Hampshire 211 for 5

### HAMPSHIRE

| | | | | |
|---|---|---|---|---|
| T.C.Middleton | c Burns b Lefebvre | 35 | b Trump | 102 |
| C.L.Smith | b Lefebvre | 2 | c Burns b Macleay | 65 |
| M.C.J.Nicholas * | b Macleay | 23 | c Cook b Trump | 28 |
| V.P.Terry | c Trump b Hayhurst | 43 | not out | 10 |
| D.I.Gower | c Harden b Graveney | 69 | not out | 18 |
| K.D.James | not out | 75 | | |
| A.N.Aymes + | c Burns b Mallender | 3 | | |
| R.J.Maru | b Mallender | 2 | | |
| I.J.Turner | lbw b Mallender | 0 | | |
| P.J.Bakker | lbw b Mallender | 5 | | |
| Aqib Javed | not out | 15 | | |
| Extras | (lb 8,nb 11) | 19 | (b 1,lb 1,nb 1) | 3 |
| TOTAL | (for 9 wkts dec) | 291 | (for 3 wkts dec) | 226 |

### SOMERSET

| | | | | |
|---|---|---|---|---|
| S.J.Cook | not out | 107 | b Bakker | 17 |
| P.M.Roebuck | lbw b Aqib Javed | 4 | b Aqib Javed | 12 |
| A.N.Hayhurst | b Aqib Javed | 32 | c Terry b James | 12 |
| C.J.Tavare * | not out | 49 | c Aymes b Turner | 27 |
| R.J.Harden | | | c Middleton b Maru | 13 |
| N.D.Burns + | | | c Aymes b Aqib Javed | 49 |
| K.H.Macleay | | | c Aymes b Nicholas | 8 |
| R.P.Lefebvre | | | b Nicholas | 4 |
| N.A.Mallender | | | b Nicholas | 0 |
| H.R.J.Trump | | | not out | 0 |
| D.A.Graveney | | | not out | 0 |
| Extras | (lb 1,nb 7) | 8 | (lb 7,nb 11) | 18 |
| TOTAL | (for 2 wkts dec) | 200 | (for 9 wkts) | 160 |

| SOMERSET | O | M | R | W | O | M | R | W |
|---|---|---|---|---|---|---|---|---|
| Mallender | 30 | 10 | 68 | 4 | 5 | 2 | 11 | 0 |
| Lefebvre | 31 | 8 | 66 | 2 | 4 | 1 | 12 | 0 |
| Graveney | 21 | 5 | 49 | 1 | 23 | 4 | 70 | 0 |
| Macleay | 16 | 5 | 30 | 1 | 10 | 3 | 17 | 1 |
| Trump | 16 | 3 | 40 | 0 | 13 | 1 | 69 | 2 |
| Hayhurst | 9 | 1 | 30 | 1 | 10 | 1 | 45 | 0 |

| HAMPSHIRE | O | M | R | W | O | M | R | W |
|---|---|---|---|---|---|---|---|---|
| Aqib Javed | 12 | 1 | 39 | 2 | 13 | 2 | 50 | 2 |
| Bakker | 11 | 2 | 35 | 0 | 6 | 0 | 17 | 1 |
| Turner | 15.5 | 0 | 47 | 0 | 12 | 6 | 17 | 1 |
| James | 9 | 3 | 18 | 0 | 6 | 0 | 21 | 1 |
| Maru | 15 | 1 | 60 | 0 | 19 | 9 | 22 | 1 |
| Smith | | | | | 3 | 2 | 1 | 0 |
| Nicholas | | | | | 9 | 3 | 25 | 3 |

| FALL OF WICKETS | HAM | SOM | HAM | SOM |
|---|---|---|---|---|
| 1st | 7 | 8 | 114 | 26 |
| 2nd | 44 | 87 | 196 | 30 |
| 3rd | 88 | | 200 | 48 |
| 4th | 145 | | | 79 |
| 5th | 210 | | | 93 |
| 6th | 221 | | | 121 |
| 7th | 223 | | | 134 |
| 8th | 223 | | | 152 |
| 9th | 239 | | | 159 |
| 10th | | | | |

---

## HEADLINES

### Britannic Assurance Championship

#### 18th - 20th June

- At Bath, Somerset would have begun their quest for 318 in 68 overs with high hopes of their first victory of the season, after Jimmy Cook had made his third 100 in four matches in their first innings, but it was visitors Hampshire who came closest to beating their duck. Somerset's last pair, Harvey Trump and David Graveney, were forced to hang on for a draw after Mark Nicholas had taken three late wickets. David Gower, putting an appalling run of scores behind him, had earlier passed 50 for the first time in the summer.

#### Other first-class matches

- Although Hugh Morris could manage only 10 in his first innings against Cambridge University at Fenner's he gratefully took advantage of a second chance to become the first batsman to complete 1,000 runs in first-class cricket as he captained Glamorgan to a 181-run success.

- Kent gained a first-innings lead of 212 over Oxford University but could not convert it into victory as Oxford resisted for more than 90 overs in their second innings. Trevor Ward's 122 was his second century of the season.

- First-class début: C. Jones (Oxford University).

---

## CAMBRIDGE U vs. GLAMORGAN

at Fenner's on 18th, 19th, 20th June 1991
Toss : Cambridge U.  Umpires : V.A.Holder and P.B.Wight
Glamorgan won by 181 runs

### GLAMORGAN

| | | | | |
|---|---|---|---|---|
| M.P.Maynard | b Jenkins | 21 | (2) b Waller | 1 |
| H.Morris * | c Turner b Johnson | 10 | (1) c Pearson b Hooper | 33 |
| R.J.Shastri | not out | 52 | | |
| I.Smith | c Jenkins b Waller | 47 | c Turner b Waller | 2 |
| P.A.Cottey | not out | 2 | (3) c Turner b Waller | 21 |
| A.Dale | | | (5) not out | 45 |
| R.D.B.Croft | | | (6) c Turner b Jenkins | 14 |
| J.Derrick | | | (7) not out | 12 |
| M.L.Roberts + | | | | |
| S.J.Dennis | | | | |
| S.Bastien | | | | |
| Extras | (b 5,lb 3,nb 1) | 9 | (b 4,w 3,nb 4) | 11 |
| TOTAL | (for 3 wkts dec) | 141 | (for 5 wkts dec) | 139 |

### CAMBRIDGE U

| | | | | |
|---|---|---|---|---|
| A.M.Hooper | | | c Shastri b Bastien | 14 |
| R.I.Clitheroe | | | c Maynard b Shastri | 31 |
| J.P.Crawley | | | c Dale b Croft | 22 |
| R.J.Turner *+ | | | c Derrick b Bastien | 2 |
| M.J.Morris | | | lbw b Croft | 20 |
| M.J.Lowrey | | | c Croft b Bastien | 4 |
| J.P.Arscott | | | st Roberts b Shastri | 5 |
| R.M.Pearson | | | c Roberts b Shastri | 1 |
| R.H.J.Jenkins | | | lbw b Croft | 0 |
| S.W.Johnson | | | st Roberts b Shastri | 0 |
| R.B.Waller | | | not out | 0 |
| Extras | | | | 0 |
| TOTAL | | | | 99 |

| CAMBRIDGE U | O | M | R | W | O | M | R | W |
|---|---|---|---|---|---|---|---|---|
| Johnson | 9 | 1 | 34 | 1 | | | | |
| Jenkins | 15 | 3 | 55 | 1 | 9 | 0 | 47 | 1 |
| Pearson | 11 | 5 | 35 | 0 | 8 | 1 | 27 | 0 |
| Waller | 4.3 | 2 | 9 | 1 | 11 | 4 | 31 | 3 |
| Hooper | | | | | 8 | 0 | 30 | 1 |

| GLAMORGAN | O | M | R | W | O | M | R | W |
|---|---|---|---|---|---|---|---|---|
| Bastien | | | | | 13 | 5 | 37 | 3 |
| Dennis | | | | | 7 | 1 | 18 | 0 |
| Shastri | | | | | 19 | 8 | 20 | 4 |
| Derrick | | | | | 7 | 3 | 16 | 0 |
| Croft | | | | | 6 | 2 | 8 | 3 |

| FALL OF WICKETS | GLA | CAM | GLA | CAM |
|---|---|---|---|---|
| 1st | 20 | | 2 | 20 |
| 2nd | | | 40 | 56 |
| 3rd | 128 | | 51 | 68 |
| 4th | | | 77 | 73 |
| 5th | | | 104 | 79 |
| 6th | | | | 96 |
| 7th | | | | 98 |
| 8th | | | | 99 |
| 9th | | | | 99 |
| 10th | | | | 99 |

---

## OXFORD U vs. KENT

at The Parks on 18th, 19th, 20th June 1991
Toss : Kent.  Umpires : D.Fawkner-Corbett and J.H.Harris
Match drawn

### KENT

| | | | | |
|---|---|---|---|---|
| T.R.Ward | c Warley b Wood | 122 | | |
| M.V.Fleming | c Morris R.E. b Oppenheimer | 60 | | |
| N.J.Llong | c & b Oppenheimer | 9 | | |
| V.J.Wells | c Morris J. b Russell | 58 | | |
| S.A.Marsh * | b Russell | 57 | | |
| M.C.Dobson | not out | 13 | (1) c Sandiford b Wood | 50 |
| D.J.M.Kelleher | b Russell | 10 | (3) not out | 29 |
| R.P.Davis | lbw b Russell | 8 | | |
| M.A.Ealham | not out | 2 | (2) c Morris J. b Oppenheimer | 37 |
| G.J.Kersey + | | | | |
| T.N.Wren | | | | |
| Extras | (b 2,lb 1,nb 2) | 5 | (b 1,lb 8,w 4) | 13 |
| TOTAL | (for 7 wkts dec) | 344 | (for 2 wkts dec) | 129 |

### OXFORD U

| | | | | |
|---|---|---|---|---|
| R.E.Morris * | c Llong b Kelleher | 2 | c Kersey b Wells | 37 |
| M.J.Russell | c Davis b Kelleher | 23 | b Wells | 30 |
| S.Warley | lbw b Ealham | 11 | c Marsh b Davis | 1 |
| G.Lovell | c Dobson b Kelleher | 17 | c Kersey b Wren | 29 |
| J.Morris | b Wren | 19 | b Wells | 1 |
| C.Jones | lbw b Ealham | 4 | b Fleming | 23 |
| P.S.Gerrans | b Wells | 14 | b Fleming | 4 |
| D.Sandiford + | b Wren | 28 | not out | 35 |
| H.Davies | b Davis | 0 | not out | 12 |
| J.M.E.Oppenheimer | not out | 0 | | |
| B.Wood | b Wren | 0 | | |
| Extras | (lb 3,w 1,nb 10) | 14 | (b 1,lb 4,w 1,nb 10) | 16 |
| TOTAL | | 132 | (for 7 wkts) | 188 |

| OXFORD U | O | M | R | W | O | M | R | W |
|---|---|---|---|---|---|---|---|---|
| Oppenheimer | 10 | 1 | 51 | 2 | 11 | 2 | 47 | 1 |
| Wood | 23 | 4 | 77 | 1 | 13 | 2 | 60 | 1 |
| Gerrans | 17 | 2 | 84 | 0 | 2 | 0 | 13 | 0 |
| Davies | 12 | 2 | 70 | 0 | | | | |
| Morris R.E. | 4 | 0 | 28 | 0 | | | | |
| Russell | 8 | 2 | 31 | 4 | | | | |

| KENT | O | M | R | W | O | M | R | W |
|---|---|---|---|---|---|---|---|---|
| Wren | 7.3 | 2 | 14 | 3 | 12 | 1 | 34 | 1 |
| Kelleher | 16 | 3 | 25 | 3 | 10 | 2 | 22 | 0 |
| Ealham | 10 | 2 | 38 | 2 | 10 | 2 | 42 | 0 |
| Wells | 10 | 3 | 24 | 1 | 12.4 | 5 | 21 | 3 |
| Davis | 11 | 2 | 31 | 1 | 20 | 12 | 22 | 1 |
| Fleming | | | | | 13 | 2 | 25 | 2 |
| Dobson | | | | | 8 | 1 | 17 | 0 |

| FALL OF WICKETS | KEN | OXF | KEN | OXF |
|---|---|---|---|---|
| 1st | 96 | 7 | 57 | 75 |
| 2nd | 152 | 40 | 129 | 76 |
| 3rd | 215 | 58 | | 77 |
| 4th | 285 | 63 | | 83 |
| 5th | 314 | 68 | | 131 |
| 6th | 325 | 89 | | 138 |
| 7th | 341 | 131 | | 139 |
| 8th | | 132 | | |
| 9th | | 132 | | |
| 10th | | 132 | | |

# REFUGE ASSURANCE LEAGUE

## LANCASHIRE vs. KENT
at Old Trafford on 23rd June 1991
Toss : Lancashire. Umpires : D.O.Oslear and P.B.Wight
Lancashire won by 6 wickets. Lancashire 4 pts, Kent 0 pts

### KENT
| | | |
|---|---|---|
| M.V.Fleming | c Watkinson b Wasim Akram | 44 |
| M.R.Benson * | b Martin | 1 |
| N.R.Taylor | c Hegg b Watkinson | 10 |
| T.R.Ward | not out | 62 |
| G.R.Cowdrey | b Wasim Akram | 10 |
| C.S.Cowdrey | c Hegg b Austin | 11 |
| S.A.Marsh + | not out | 4 |
| R.M.Ellison | | |
| M.J.McCague | | |
| C.Penn | | |
| A.P.Igglesden | | |
| Extras | (b 1,lb 11,w 6,nb 2) | 20 |
| TOTAL | (23 overs)(for 5 wkts) | 162 |

### LANCASHIRE
| | | |
|---|---|---|
| G.D.Mendis | c & b Fleming | 44 |
| G.Fowler | c Penn b Igglesden | 46 |
| G.D.Lloyd | run out | 18 |
| N.H.Fairbrother | not out | 31 |
| M.Watkinson | c Fleming b Penn | 6 |
| Wasim Akram | not out | 16 |
| W.K.Hegg + | | |
| I.D.Austin | | |
| G.Yates | | |
| D.P.Hughes * | | |
| P.J.Martin | | |
| Extras | (lb 1,w 2,nb 1) | 4 |
| TOTAL | (22.2 overs)(for 4 wkts) | 165 |

| LANCASHIRE | O | M | R | W | FALL OF WICKETS | | |
|---|---|---|---|---|---|---|---|
| | | | | | | KEN | LAN |
| Watkinson | 6 | 0 | 34 | 1 | 1st | 7 | 91 |
| Martin | 4 | 0 | 20 | 1 | 2nd | 36 | 95 |
| Wasim Akram | 6 | 0 | 40 | 2 | 3rd | 105 | 118 |
| Yates | 2 | 0 | 18 | 0 | 4th | 127 | 129 |
| Austin | 5 | 0 | 38 | 1 | 5th | 153 | |
| KENT | O | M | R | W | 6th | | |
| Igglesden | 5.2 | 0 | 34 | 1 | 7th | | |
| McCague | 6 | 0 | 43 | 0 | 8th | | |
| Penn | 6 | 0 | 56 | 1 | 9th | | |
| Fleming | 5 | 0 | 31 | 1 | 10th | | |

## NOTTS vs. MIDDLESEX
at Trent Bridge on 23rd June 1991
Toss : Middlesex. Umpires : J.D.Bond and M.J.Kitchen
Middlesex won by 7 wickets. Notts 0 pts, Middlesex 4 pts

### NOTTS
| | | |
|---|---|---|
| B.C.Broad | c Roseberry b Cowans | 0 |
| D.W.Randall | c Williams b Emburey | 37 |
| R.T.Robinson * | c Gatting b Weekes | 23 |
| P.Johnson | c Hutchinson b Williams | 9 |
| M.A.Crawley | b Weekes | 0 |
| M.Saxelby | st Farbrace b Emburey | 22 |
| F.D.Stephenson | c Weekes b Cowans | 27 |
| K.P.Evans | b Emburey | 6 |
| B.N.French + | not out | 17 |
| E.E.Hemmings | c Keech b Emburey | 0 |
| K.E.Cooper | not out | 0 |
| Extras | (b 1,lb 11,w 6,nb 1) | 19 |
| TOTAL | (36 overs)(for 9 wkts) | 160 |

### MIDDLESEX
| | | |
|---|---|---|
| M.A.Roseberry | lbw b Stephenson | 3 |
| I.J.F.Hutchinson | lbw b Stephenson | 25 |
| M.W.Gatting * | c Robinson b Stephenson | 61 |
| K.R.Brown | not out | 47 |
| M.Keech | not out | 14 |
| P.N.Weekes | | |
| J.E.Emburey | | |
| N.F.Williams | | |
| P.Farbrace + | | |
| S.P.Hughes | | |
| N.G.Cowans | | |
| Extras | (lb 5,w 5,nb 1) | 11 |
| TOTAL | (33 overs)(for 3 wkts) | 161 |

| MIDDLESEX | O | M | R | W | FALL OF WICKETS | | |
|---|---|---|---|---|---|---|---|
| | | | | | | NOT | MID |
| Cowans | 7 | 1 | 30 | 2 | 1st | 0 | 19 |
| Hughes | 7 | 0 | 35 | 0 | 2nd | 51 | 31 |
| Weekes | 7 | 1 | 20 | 2 | 3rd | 69 | 126 |
| Williams | 7 | 1 | 25 | 1 | 4th | 69 | |
| Emburey | 8 | 1 | 38 | 4 | 5th | 83 | |
| NOTTS | O | M | R | W | 6th | 128 | |
| Cooper | 5 | 0 | 38 | 0 | 7th | 134 | |
| Stephenson | 8 | 0 | 20 | 3 | 8th | 151 | |
| Evans | 7 | 0 | 26 | 0 | 9th | 153 | |
| Hemmings | 7 | 0 | 30 | 0 | 10th | | |
| Saxelby | 2 | 0 | 21 | 0 | | | |
| Crawley | 4 | 0 | 21 | 0 | | | |

## HEADLINES

### Refuge Assurance League

### 23rd June

• Only half the day's programme survived, but two of the matches that were played could have had deep significance on deciding the eventual league winners.

• Nottinghamshire, winners of all their first seven fixtures, suffered their first defeat at the hands of Middlesex at Trent Bridge. The leaders could only manage 160 for nine in their 36 overs, John Emburey taking his aggregate of Sunday wickets in 1991 to 20 with four for 38, and Middlesex had three overs in hand when they reached their target thanks to 61 from Mike Gatting and an unbeaten 47 from Keith Brown.

• Lancashire, only beaten once themselves so far in the season, drew within two points of Notts thanks to a six-wicket victory over Kent at Old Trafford. The visitors would have been pleased with their total of 162 for five in 23 overs against any other opposition, but Lancashire were put on their way to victory by an opening stand of 91 between Gehan Mendis and Graeme Fowler.

• The day's other winners were Yorkshire who beat Worcestershire by four wickets at Sheffield after restricting the visitors to 146 for nine in 40 overs. The matches at Bath, Horsham and Edgbaston were abandoned without a ball being bowled.

## YORKSHIRE vs. WORCESTERSHIRE
at Sheffield on 23rd June 1991
Toss : Yorkshire. Umpires : J.H.Hampshire and J.W.Holder
Yorkshire won by 4 wickets. Yorkshire 4 pts, Worcs 0 pts

### WORCESTERSHIRE
| | | |
|---|---|---|
| T.S.Curtis | lbw b Hartley | 8 |
| T.M.Moody | c Gough b Carrick | 19 |
| M.J.Weston | c Robinson b Batty | 13 |
| D.B.D'Oliveira | b Pickles | 27 |
| N.V.Radford | c Batty b Fletcher | 12 |
| P.A.Neale * | lbw b Fletcher | 2 |
| D.A.Leatherdale | c Robinson b Fletcher | 15 |
| S.J.Rhodes + | lbw b Pickles | 0 |
| S.R.Lampitt | c Blakey b Pickles | 1 |
| R.K.Illingworth | not out | 17 |
| P.J.Newport | not out | 17 |
| Extras | (lb 3,w 11,nb 1) | 15 |
| TOTAL | (40 overs)(for 9 wkts) | 146 |

### YORKSHIRE
| | | |
|---|---|---|
| A.A.Metcalfe * | c Leatherdale b Radford | 0 |
| D.Byas | c Illingworth b Newport | 54 |
| R.J.Blakey + | lbw b Weston | 3 |
| P.E.Robinson | c Radford b Illingworth | 10 |
| P.J.Hartley | b Lampitt | 11 |
| C.White | c Illingworth b Lampitt | 9 |
| C.S.Pickles | not out | 30 |
| P.Carrick | not out | 17 |
| D.Gough | | |
| J.D.Batty | | |
| S.D.Fletcher | | |
| Extras | (lb 9,w 6) | 15 |
| TOTAL | (39.1 overs)(for 6 wkts) | 149 |

| YORKSHIRE | O | M | R | W | FALL OF WICKETS | | |
|---|---|---|---|---|---|---|---|
| | | | | | | WOR | YOR |
| Hartley | 7 | 1 | 28 | 1 | 1st | 22 | 0 |
| Gough | 8 | 0 | 29 | 0 | 2nd | 38 | 15 |
| Carrick | 8 | 0 | 15 | 1 | 3rd | 46 | 53 |
| Batty | 8 | 2 | 33 | 1 | 4th | 76 | 76 |
| Fletcher | 6 | 1 | 26 | 3 | 5th | 81 | 90 |
| Pickles | 3 | 0 | 12 | 3 | 6th | 99 | 100 |
| WORCS | O | M | R | W | 7th | 100 | |
| Radford | 8 | 0 | 33 | 1 | 8th | 102 | |
| Weston | 7.1 | 1 | 21 | 1 | 9th | 123 | |
| Newport | 8 | 0 | 29 | 1 | 10th | | |
| Illingworth | 8 | 0 | 30 | 1 | | | |
| Lampitt | 8 | 1 | 27 | 2 | | | |

## SOMERSET vs. GLOUCS
at Bath on 23rd June 1991
Match abandoned. Somerset 2 pts, Gloucs 2 pts

## REFUGE ASS. LEAGUE

## CORNHILL TEST MATCH

**SUSSEX vs. ESSEX**
at Horsham on 23rd June 1991
Match abandoned. Sussex 2 pts, Essex 2 pts

**WARWICKSHIRE vs. SURREY**
at Edgbaston on 23rd June 1991
Match abandoned. Warwickshire 2 pts, Surrey 2 pts

Robin Smith acknowledges the applause for his century which spearheaded the England counter-attack.

# CORNHILL TEST MATCH

## ENGLAND vs. WEST INDIES

at Lord's on 20th, 21st, 22nd, 23rd (np), 24th June
Toss : West Indies. Umpires : B.J.Meyer and K.E.Palmer
Match drawn

**WEST INDIES**

| | | | | | |
|---|---|--:|---|---|--:|
| P.V.Simmons | c Lamb b Hick | 33 | lbw b DeFreitas | | 2 |
| D.L.Haynes | c Russell b Pringle | 60 | not out | | 4 |
| R.B.Richardson | c DeFreitas b Hick | 57 | c Hick b Malcolm | | 1 |
| C.L.Hooper | c Lamb b Pringle | 111 | not out | | 1 |
| I.V.A.Richards * | lbw b DeFreitas | 63 | | | |
| A.L.Logie | b DeFreitas | 5 | | | |
| P.J.L.Dujon + | c Lamb b Pringle | 20 | | | |
| M.D.Marshall | lbw b Pringle | 25 | | | |
| C.E.L.Ambrose | c & b Malcolm | 5 | | | |
| C.A.Walsh | c Atherton b Pringle | 10 | | | |
| I.B.A.Allen | not out | 1 | | | |
| Extras | (b 3,lb 7,nb 19) | 29 | (lb 2,nb 2) | | 4 |
| TOTAL | | 419 | (for 2 wkts) | | 12 |

**ENGLAND**

| | | |
|---|---|--:|
| G.A.Gooch * | b Walsh | 37 |
| M.A.Atherton | b Ambrose | 5 |
| G.A.Hick | c Richardson b Ambrose | 0 |
| A.J.Lamb | c Haynes b Marshall | 1 |
| M.R.Ramprakash | c Richards b Allen | 24 |
| R.A.Smith | not out | 148 |
| R.C.Russell + | c Dujon b Hooper | 46 |
| D.R.Pringle | c Simmons b Allen | 35 |
| P.A.J.DeFreitas | c Dujon b Marshall | 29 |
| S.L.Watkin | b Ambrose | 6 |
| D.E.Malcolm | b Ambrose | 0 |
| Extras | (lb 1,nb 22) | 23 |
| TOTAL | | 354 |

| ENGLAND | O | M | R | W | O | M | R | W |
|---|--:|--:|--:|--:|--:|--:|--:|--:|
| DeFreitas | 31 | 6 | 93 | 2 | 3 | 2 | 1 | 1 |
| Malcolm | 19 | 3 | 76 | 1 | 2.5 | 0 | 9 | 1 |
| Watkin | 15 | 2 | 60 | 0 | | | | |
| Pringle | 35.1 | 6 | 100 | 5 | | | | |
| Hick | 18 | 4 | 77 | 2 | | | | |
| Gooch | 2 | 0 | 3 | 0 | | | | |

| WEST INDIES | O | M | R | W | O | M | R | W |
|---|--:|--:|--:|--:|--:|--:|--:|--:|
| Ambrose | 34 | 10 | 87 | 4 | | | | |
| Marshall | 30 | 4 | 78 | 2 | | | | |
| Walsh | 26 | 4 | 90 | 1 | | | | |
| Allen | 23 | 2 | 88 | 2 | | | | |
| Hooper | 5 | 2 | 10 | 1 | | | | |

**FALL OF WICKETS**

| | WI | ENG | WI | ENG |
|---|--:|--:|--:|--:|
| 1st | 90 | 5 | 9 | |
| 2nd | 102 | 6 | 10 | |
| 3rd | 198 | 16 | | |
| 4th | 322 | 60 | | |
| 5th | 332 | 84 | | |
| 6th | 366 | 180 | | |
| 7th | 382 | 269 | | |
| 8th | 402 | 316 | | |
| 9th | 410 | 353 | | |
| 10th | 419 | 354 | | |

West Indies century-maker Carl Hooper also enjoys the special atmosphere at Lord's.

# HEADLINES

### England v West Indies
### Second Cornhill Test Match

#### Lord's: 20th -24th June

• When England were 84 for five in reply to West Indies' first innings total of 419, it appeared that the tourists would quickly re-impose their authority over their hosts, but England's triumphant recovery at Lord's, gloriously orchestrated by Robin Smith, may prove as critical in determining the outcome of the series as their victory at Headingley.

• The first day could not have gone better for the visitors: after winning the toss, all their top five batsmen made valuable contributions to a close of play total of 317 for three; Phil Simmons and Desmond Haynes provided an untroubled opening stand of 90, Richie Richardson continued his improving relationship with English wickets with a bright and breezy 57, then, after tea, Carl Hooper and Viv Richards provided a century stand at better than a run a minute that threatened to carry West Indies to an impregnable score.

• Day two was in complete contrast: after a delayed start, the bowlers of both sides were in such control that 12 wickets were claimed for 212 runs. Although Hooper reached an accomplished first 100 against England and the third of his Test career, West Indies' last seven wickets accumulated only 102 more runs, Derek Pringle taking five wickets in a Test innings for the third time. England were soon in trouble, losing their first three wickets for 16, as numbers two, three and four in the batting order took their combined run-total for the series to 37 for nine, and although Graham Gooch and Mark Ramprakash steadied the innings, both were back in the pavilion before the close.

• At the start of play on Saturday few people in the capacity crowd could have been confident that England could score the 110 runs still needed to avoid the follow on, and their final total of 354 was completely beyond all expectations, as Robin Smith became the second England batsman to play the innings of his life in successive Test matches, his undefeated 148 matching Gooch's Headingley masterpiece in every respect. The last five wickets added 270, as Jack Russell, Derek Pringle, Phil DeFreitas and Steve Watkin all gave sterling support to Smith who grew in confidence with every stroke he played. Most memorable of his 20 fours were the square cuts which rocketed to the boundary with brutal power, as Smith reached his fifth Test 100 and surpassed his previous highest Test score.

• West Indies had to be satisfied with a lead of just 65, and any thoughts of a series-levelling victory were abandoned with the loss of Sunday's play to torrential rain. Instead the visitors were very much on the defensive when they lost two wickets in the 25 minutes play possible on the final morning before proceedings were brought to a close.

• Test débuts: I.B.A. Allen (West Indies)

• Man of the match: R.A. Smith

# BRITANNIC ASSURANCE CHAMPIONSHIP

## GLAMORGAN vs. LEICESTERSHIRE

at Neath on 21st, 22nd, 23rd (no play) June 1991
Toss : Glamorgan.  Umpires : G.I.Burgess and D.R.Shepherd
Match drawn.  Glamorgan 3 pts (Bt: 3, Bw: 0), Leicestershire 2 pts (Bt: 0, Bw: 2)
100 overs scores : Glamorgan 256 for 6

**GLAMORGAN**

| | | |
|---|---|---|
| A.R.Butcher * | c Boon b Maguire | 15 |
| H.Morris | c Whitticase b Wilkinson | 35 |
| R.J.Shastri | c Briers b Wilkinson | 107 |
| M.P.Maynard | c & b Wilkinson | 61 |
| P.A.Cottey | c sub b Lewis | 7 |
| A.Dale | c Whitticase b Wilkinson | 15 |
| R.D.B.Croft | lbw b Maguire | 25 |
| C.P.Metson + | c Briers b Potter | 14 |
| S.Bastien | not out | 22 |
| S.R.Barwick | not out | 24 |
| M.Frost | | |
| Extras | (lb 4,w 2,nb 6) | 12 |
| TOTAL | (for 8 wkts dec) | 337 |

**LEICESTERSHIRE**

| | | |
|---|---|---|
| T.J.Boon | not out | 18 |
| N.E.Briers * | b Frost | 4 |
| P.N.Hepworth | b Bastien | 21 |
| J.J.Whitaker | not out | 2 |
| L.Potter | | |
| B.F.Smith | | |
| C.C.Lewis | | |
| P.Whitticase + | | |
| D.J.Millns | | |
| C.Wilkinson | | |
| J.N.Maguire | | |
| Extras | (nb 1) | 1 |
| TOTAL | (for 2 wkts) | 46 |

| LEICS | O | M | R | W | O | M | R | W | FALL OF WICKETS | | | | |
|---|---|---|---|---|---|---|---|---|---|---|---|---|---|
| | | | | | | | | | | GLA | LEI | GLA | LEI |
| Lewis | 33 | 8 | 90 | 1 | | | | | 1st | 36 | 12 | | |
| Maguire | 35 | 11 | 77 | 2 | | | | | 2nd | 79 | 39 | | |
| Millns | 8 | 1 | 14 | 0 | | | | | 3rd | 156 | | | |
| Wilkinson | 31 | 9 | 106 | 4 | | | | | 4th | 168 | | | |
| Potter | 13 | 1 | 46 | 1 | | | | | 5th | 195 | | | |
| | | | | | | | | | 6th | 252 | | | |
| GLAMORGAN | O | M | R | W | O | M | R | W | 7th | 281 | | | |
| Frost | 10 | 4 | 20 | 1 | | | | | 8th | 307 | | | |
| Barwick | 6 | 3 | 9 | 0 | | | | | 9th | | | | |
| Bastien | 8 | 2 | 17 | 1 | | | | | 10th | | | | |
| Croft | 1 | 1 | 0 | 0 | | | | | | | | | |

## NORTHANTS vs. HAMPSHIRE

at Northampton on 21st, 22nd, 23rd June 1991
Toss : Hampshire.  Umpires : B.Hassan and B.Leadbeater
Match drawn.  Northants 5 pts (Bt: 3, Bw: 2), Hampshire 6 pts (Bt: 2, Bw: 4)

**NORTHANTS**

| | | | | |
|---|---|---|---|---|
| A.Fordham | c Gower b Aqib Javed | 13 | not out | 40 |
| N.A.Felton | b Aqib Javed | 1 | not out | 38 |
| R.J.Bailey * | c Terry b Aqib Javed | 37 | | |
| D.J.Capel | c Smith b Maru | 71 | | |
| K.M.Curran | c Maru b Shine | 31 | | |
| E.A.E.Baptiste | run out | 60 | | |
| J.G.Thomas | b Maru | 8 | | |
| D.Ripley + | b Aqib Javed | 13 | | |
| A.L.Penberthy | c Maru b Aqib Javed | 3 | | |
| J.P.Taylor | b Maru | 3 | | |
| N.G.B.Cook | not out | 1 | | |
| Extras | (lb 4,w 4,nb 12) | 20 | (lb 4,nb 1) | 5 |
| TOTAL | | 261 | (for 0 wkts) | 83 |

**HAMPSHIRE**

| | | |
|---|---|---|
| T.C.Middleton | c Thomas b Baptiste | 25 |
| C.L.Smith | c Ripley b Baptiste | 85 |
| M.C.J.Nicholas * | c Ripley b Taylor | 1 |
| V.P.Terry | c Bailey b Penberthy | 22 |
| D.I.Gower | run out | 22 |
| K.D.James | b Baptiste | 18 |
| A.N Aymes + | not out | 10 |
| R.J.Maru | not out | 0 |
| K.J.Shine | | |
| P.J.Bakker | | |
| Aqib Javed | | |
| Extras | (b 1,lb 16,nb 3) | 20 |
| TOTAL | (for 6 wkts dec) | 203 |

| HAMPSHIRE | O | M | R | W | O | M | R | W | FALL OF WICKETS | | | | |
|---|---|---|---|---|---|---|---|---|---|---|---|---|---|
| | | | | | | | | | | NOR | HAM | NOR | HAM |
| Aqib Javed | 20 | 4 | 49 | 5 | 7 | 0 | 27 | 0 | 1st | 2 | 85 | | |
| Bakker | 15 | 4 | 35 | 0 | 6 | 0 | 20 | 0 | 2nd | 35 | 86 | | |
| Shine | 10 | 0 | 66 | 1 | 5 | 3 | 13 | 0 | 3rd | 89 | 142 | | |
| James | 12 | 1 | 59 | 0 | | | | | 4th | 141 | 171 | | |
| Maru | 16.5 | 5 | 48 | 3 | 6 | 1 | 19 | 0 | 5th | 201 | 172 | | |
| | | | | | | | | | 6th | 211 | 199 | | |
| NORTHANTS | O | M | R | W | O | M | R | W | 7th | 248 | | | |
| Thomas | 13 | 4 | 37 | 0 | | | | | 8th | 249 | | | |
| Taylor | 13 | 4 | 27 | 1 | | | | | 9th | 259 | | | |
| Curran | 13 | 3 | 36 | 0 | | | | | 10th | 261 | | | |
| Baptiste | 18 | 5 | 49 | 3 | | | | | | | | | |
| Penberthy | 10.2 | 0 | 37 | 1 | | | | | | | | | |

## DERBYSHIRE vs. SURREY

at Derby on 21st, 22nd, 24th June 1991
Toss : Derby.  Umpires : D.J.Constant and R.Julian
Derby won by 3 wickets.  Derby 20 pts (Bt: 0, Bw: 4), Surrey 1 pt (Bt: 0, Bw: 1)

**SURREY**

| | | | | |
|---|---|---|---|---|
| D.J.Bicknell | c O'Gorman b Mortensen | 9 | lbw b Goldsmith | 5 |
| R.I.Alikhan | c Cork b Base | 3 | lbw b Adams | 15 |
| A.J.Stewart | lbw b Mortensen | 5 | retired hurt/ill | 10 |
| D.M.Ward | run out | 26 | not out | 94 |
| G.P.Thorpe | c O'Gorman b Base | 3 | c Bowler b Griffith | 1 |
| I.A.Greig * | lbw b Cork | 5 | c Goldsmith b O'Gorman | 27 |
| K.T.Medlycott | c Bowler b Griffith | 18 | | |
| N.F.Sargeant + | c Cork b Base | 4 | | |
| M.P.Bicknell | not out | 34 | (7) not out | 24 |
| Waqar Younis | c Morris b Mortensen | 17 | | |
| A.J.Murphy | b Mortensen | 7 | | |
| Extras | (lb 3,w 1,nb 2) | 6 | (b 2,lb 6) | 8 |
| TOTAL | | 137 | (for 4 wkts dec) | 184 |

**DERBYSHIRE**

| | | | | |
|---|---|---|---|---|
| P.D.Bowler | not out | 30 | lbw b Bicknell M.P. | 27 |
| J.E.Morris * | lbw b Waqar Younis | 14 | b Waqar Younis | 12 |
| T.J.G.O'Gorman | b Waqar Younis | 2 | b Bicknell M.P. | 38 |
| M.Azharuddin | b Waqar Younis | 26 | lbw b Waqar Younis | 63 |
| C.J.Adams | not out | 0 | lbw b Medlycott | 11 |
| S.C.Goldsmith | | | not out | 73 |
| K.M.Krikken + | | | lbw b Medlycott | 13 |
| F.A.Griffith | | | b Waqar Younis | 1 |
| D.G.Cork | | | not out | 0 |
| S.J.Base | | | | |
| O.H.Mortensen | | | | |
| Extras | (b 4,lb 4) | 8 | (b 1,lb 3) | 4 |
| TOTAL | (for 3 wkts dec) | 80 | (for 7 wkts) | 242 |

| DERBYSHIRE | O | M | R | W | O | M | R | W | FALL OF WICKETS | | | | |
|---|---|---|---|---|---|---|---|---|---|---|---|---|---|
| | | | | | | | | | | SUR | DER | SUR | DER |
| Mortensen | 13.5 | 3 | 43 | 4 | | | | | 1st | 6 | 23 | 10 | 26 |
| Base | 15 | 0 | 60 | 3 | | | | | 2nd | 11 | 26 | 44 | 57 |
| Cork | 9 | 2 | 15 | 1 | | | | | 3rd | 22 | 73 | 51 | 92 |
| Griffith | 7 | 0 | 16 | 1 | 8 | 2 | 42 | 1 | 4th | 32 | | 117 | 115 |
| Goldsmith | | | | | 11 | 3 | 41 | 1 | 5th | 53 | | | 171 |
| Adams | | | | | 6 | 0 | 19 | 1 | 6th | 68 | | | 234 |
| Bowler | | | | | 9 | 2 | 27 | 0 | 7th | 75 | | | 241 |
| Morris | | | | | 2 | 0 | 30 | 0 | 8th | 82 | | | |
| O'Gorman | | | | | 3 | 0 | 17 | 1 | 9th | 115 | | | |
| | | | | | | | | | 10th | 137 | | | |
| SURREY | O | M | R | W | O | M | R | W | | | | | |
| Waqar Younis | 7 | 2 | 11 | 2 | 13.2 | 1 | 66 | 3 | | | | | |
| Bicknell M.P. | 8 | 0 | 32 | 0 | 11 | 3 | 35 | 2 | | | | | |
| Murphy | 8.5 | 1 | 29 | 1 | 6 | 0 | 35 | 0 | | | | | |
| Medlycott | | | | | 11 | 0 | 102 | 2 | | | | | |

## LANCASHIRE vs. KENT

at Old Trafford on 21st, 22nd, 24th June 1991
Toss : Kent.  Umpires : D.O.Oslear and P.B.Wight
Lancashire won by 59 runs.  Lancashire 20 pts (Bt: 4, Bw: 0), Kent 4 pts (Bt: 0, Bw: 4)
100 overs scores : Lancashire 319 for 9

**LANCASHIRE**

| | | |
|---|---|---|
| G.D.Mendis | c Fleming b Igglesden | 5 |
| G.Fowler | c Marsh b Igglesden | 27 |
| G.D.Lloyd | b Igglesden | 32 |
| N.H.Fairbrother | c Ward b Merrick | 24 |
| N.J.Speak | c Davis b Merrick | 24 |
| M.Watkinson | c Ward b Merrick | 52 |
| Wasim Akram | c Ward b Ellison | 42 |
| W.K.Hegg + | c Ellison b Penn | 45 |
| I.D.Austin | c & b Penn | 7 |
| D.P.Hughes * | not out | 25 |
| P.J.Martin | not out | 21 |
| Extras | (lb 12,nb 4) | 16 |
| TOTAL | (for 9 wkts dec) | 320 |

**KENT**

| | | |
|---|---|---|
| T.R.Ward | | c Speak b Martin | 37 |
| M.R.Benson * | | c Watkinson b Wasim Akram | 52 |
| N.R.Taylor | | c Lloyd b Wasim Akram | 33 |
| G.R.Cowdrey | | c Hegg b Wasim Akram | 2 |
| M.V.Fleming | | c Fairbrother b Wasim Akram | 64 |
| S.A.Marsh + | | c Hegg b Austin | 3 |
| R.P.Davis | | c Hegg b Wasim Akram | 19 |
| C.Penn | | c Lloyd b Austin | 12 |
| R.M.Ellison | | not out | 19 |
| T.A.Merrick | | c Austin b Wasim Akram | 4 |
| A.P.Igglesden | | b Austin | 1 |
| Extras | | (lb 2,w 2,nb 11) | 15 |
| TOTAL | | | 261 |

| KENT | O | M | R | W | O | M | R | W | FALL OF WICKETS | | | | |
|---|---|---|---|---|---|---|---|---|---|---|---|---|---|
| | | | | | | | | | | LAN | KEN | LAN | KEN |
| Merrick | 23 | 6 | 88 | 3 | | | | | 1st | 11 | | | 49 |
| Igglesden | 25 | 3 | 75 | 3 | | | | | 2nd | 70 | | | 123 |
| Ellison | 15 | 4 | 47 | 1 | | | | | 3rd | 79 | | | 125 |
| Penn | 21 | 6 | 62 | 2 | | | | | 4th | 103 | | | 153 |
| Davis | 1 | 0 | 4 | 0 | | | | | 5th | 153 | | | 158 |
| Ward | 8 | 3 | 6 | 0 | | | | | 6th | 186 | | | 224 |
| Benson | 8 | 0 | 24 | 0 | | | | | 7th | 253 | | | 224 |
| | | | | | | | | | 8th | 270 | | | 245 |
| LANCASHIRE | O | M | R | W | O | M | R | W | 9th | 280 | | | 255 |
| Wasim Akram | | | | | 29 | 7 | 86 | 6 | 10th | | | | 261 |
| Martin | | | | | 22 | 4 | 79 | 1 | | | | | |
| Watkinson | | | | | 14 | 4 | 36 | 0 | | | | | |
| Austin | | | | | 20.4 | 4 | 58 | 3 | | | | | |

# BRITANNIC ASSURANCE CHAMPIONSHIP

## HEADLINES

**Britannic Assurance Championship**

**21st - 24th June**

• Although the dismal June weather showed no sign of improving, Lancashire were still able to achieve a fourth successive victory to take them into second place in the Championship table. A positive conclusion to their match with Kent at Old Trafford was only possible by means of two forfeitures which left the visitors the last day to score 321, and again Wasim Akram proved the decisive force, claiming six wickets for 86, as Kent's brave effort fell 59 short.

• After forfeiting their second innings at Trent Bridge, Warwickshire left Nottinghamshire the last day to score 298 for victory, but for once the visitors' fast bowlers could not produce a match-winning performance with the ball, and Nottinghamshire batted out for a draw on 172 for five, rain already having taken their target out of reach.

• Essex's campaign suffered badly at the hands of the weather, a promising position over Sussex at Horsham coming to nothing as the last day was completely washed out. Neil Foster had earlier hit his second 100 in first-class cricket and Alistair Fraser reached his maiden fifty on his first-class début for Essex, as the visitors managed maximum batting points.

• Derbyshire lifted themselves into fourth place with a three-wicket win over Surrey at Derby, first bowling out the visitors for a paltry 137, then, after a pair of declarations, reaching a target of 242 in 41 overs, Steve Goldsmith leading the way with 73 not out in his first Championship appearance of the season.

• Three declarations in Yorkshire's match with Middlesex at Sheffield looked to have given the two counties an equal chance of gaining their first Championship success, Middlesex being asked to make 277 in what became 69 overs. The visitors still had hopes of victory until Mike Gatting's dismissal for 82, but last pair Simon Hughes and Phil Tufnell had to stave off defeat after Peter Hartley had taken five for 32.

• The last day of the Bath Festival was washed out, to complete a bad week for county finances, Somerset also losing the chance to press home their advantage over Gloucestershire, gained thanks to figures of six for 43 from Neil Mallender and a career-best 172 not out from Andy Hayhurst.

• Leicestershire's visit to Glamorgan's outpost at Neath also proved a disappointment, the whole of Sunday's final day being lost to the weather, leaving Ravi Shastri's first 100 of the season as the only notable performance.

• Northamptonshire's match against Hampshire at Northampton also finished on Sunday, but the last day's play barely got underway before the game was abandoned as a draw. Eldine Baptiste hit his first half-century for Northants and also claimed three wickets, while Hampshire's Aqib Javed also enhanced his reputation with five for 49 in the home side's first innings.

## NOTTS vs. WARWICKSHIRE

at Trent Bridge on 21st, 22nd, 24th June 1991
Toss : Notts. Umpires : J.D.Bond and M.J.Kitchen
Match drawn. Notts 3 pts (Bt: 0, Bw: 3), Warwickshire 3 pts (Bt: 3, Bw: 0)
100 overs scores : Warwickshire 253 for 7

**WARWICKSHIRE**

| | | |
|---|---|---|
| A.J.Moles | c Crawley b Evans | 57 |
| J.D.Ratcliffe | lbw b Crawley | 47 |
| K.J.Piper + | c Johnson b Crawley | 55 |
| T.A.Lloyd * | run out | 4 |
| D.P.Ostler | lbw b Afford | 14 |
| D.A.Reeve | not out | 70 |
| P.A.Smith | st French b Afford | 7 |
| G.C.Small | b Afford | 4 |
| P.A.Booth | lbw b Afford | 12 |
| T.A.Munton | c Robinson b Pick | 25 |
| A.A.Donald | b Crawley | 5 |
| Extras | (b 2,lb 25,nb 7) | 34 |
| TOTAL | | 334 |

**NOTTS**

| | | | | | |
|---|---|---|---|---|---|
| B.C.Broad | not out | 28 | c Piper b Small | 8 |
| P.Pollard | not out | 8 | b Booth | 38 |
| R.T.Robinson * | | | b Booth | 39 |
| P.Johnson | | | c Munton b Donald | 12 |
| D.W.Randall | | | c Piper b Booth | 21 |
| M.A.Crawley | | | not out | 22 |
| K.P.Evans | | | not out | 17 |
| F.D.Stephenson | | | | |
| B.N.French + | | | | |
| R.A.Pick | | | | |
| J.A.Afford | | | | |
| Extras | (nb 1) | 1 | (lb 8,w 4,nb 3) | 15 |
| TOTAL | (for 0 wkts dec) | 37 | (for 5 wkts) | 172 |

| NOTTS | O | M | R | W | O | M | R | W |
|---|---|---|---|---|---|---|---|---|
| Stephenson | 7 | 3 | 17 | 0 | | | | |
| Pick | 30 | 5 | 77 | 1 | | | | |
| Afford | 29 | 6 | 65 | 4 | | | | |
| Evans | 29 | 7 | 91 | 1 | | | | |
| Crawley | 23.2 | 7 | 57 | 3 | | | | |

| WARWICKS | O | M | R | W | O | M | R | W |
|---|---|---|---|---|---|---|---|---|
| Donald | 2 | 1 | 1 | 0 | 17 | 5 | 31 | 1 |
| Munton | 6 | 2 | 12 | 0 | 12 | 5 | 26 | 0 |
| Smith | 6 | 2 | 10 | 0 | 9 | 3 | 20 | 0 |
| Booth | 2 | 0 | 8 | 0 | 23 | 7 | 47 | 3 |
| Lloyd | 1 | 0 | 6 | 0 | | | | |
| Small | | | | | 9 | 3 | 14 | 1 |
| Reeve | | | | | 9 | 3 | 21 | 0 |
| Moles | | | | | 1 | 0 | 5 | 0 |

**FALL OF WICKETS**

| | WAR | NOT | WAR | NOT |
|---|---|---|---|---|
| 1st | 99 | | | 17 |
| 2nd | 171 | | | 74 |
| 3rd | 177 | | | 88 |
| 4th | 184 | | | 112 |
| 5th | 210 | | | 123 |
| 6th | 232 | | | |
| 7th | 236 | | | |
| 8th | 258 | | | |
| 9th | 319 | | | |
| 10th | 334 | | | |

## SOMERSET vs. GLOUCS

at Bath on 21st, 22nd, 24th (no play) June 1991
Toss : Gloucs. Umpires : R.C.Tolchard and A.G.T.Whitehead
Match drawn. Somerset 6 pts (Bt: 2, Bw: 4), Gloucs 3 pts (Bt: 1, Bw: 2)
100 overs scores :Somerset 215 for 5

**GLOUCS**

| | | |
|---|---|---|
| G.D.Hodgson | lbw b Macleay | 30 |
| J.J.E.Hardy | lbw b Mallender | 9 |
| A.J.Wright * | c Burns b Mallender | 0 |
| C.W.J.Athey | lbw b Mallender | 10 |
| M.W.Alleyne | b Mallender | 47 |
| J.W.Lloyds | c Graveney b Macleay | 2 |
| R.J.Scott | not out | 34 |
| R.C.J.Williams + | b Trump | 8 |
| D.V.Lawrence | c Tavare b Trump | 19 |
| D.R.Gilbert | c Burns b Mallender | 7 |
| A.M.Smith | lbw b Mallender | 0 |
| Extras | (lb 8,w 2,nb 7) | 17 |
| TOTAL | | 183 |

**SOMERSET**

| | | |
|---|---|---|
| S.J.Cook | c Athey b Lawrence | 0 |
| P.M.Roebuck | lbw b Smith | 15 |
| A.N.Hayhurst | not out | 172 |
| C.J.Tavare * | lbw b Lawrence | 4 |
| R.J.Harden | c Williams b Scott | 49 |
| K.H.Macleay | b Lloyds | 5 |
| N.D.Burns + | c Williams b Lawrence | 39 |
| R.P.Lefebvre | not out | 5 |
| H.R.J.Trump | | |
| N.A.Mallender | | |
| D.A.Graveney | | |
| Extras | (b 4,lb 10,w 2,nb 6) | 22 |
| TOTAL | (for 6 wkts) | 311 |

| SOMERSET | O | M | R | W | O | M | R | W |
|---|---|---|---|---|---|---|---|---|
| Mallender | 17 | 2 | 43 | 6 | | | | |
| Lefebvre | 15 | 3 | 52 | 0 | | | | |
| Macleay | 20 | 5 | 48 | 2 | | | | |
| Hayhurst | 9 | 5 | 11 | 0 | | | | |
| Graveney | 3 | 1 | 6 | 0 | | | | |
| Trump | 8 | 2 | 15 | 2 | | | | |

| GLOUCS | O | M | R | W | O | M | R | W |
|---|---|---|---|---|---|---|---|---|
| Lawrence | 23 | 5 | 69 | 3 | | | | |
| Gilbert | 10 | 2 | 27 | 0 | | | | |
| Smith | 28 | 9 | 53 | 1 | | | | |
| Scott | 27 | 10 | 67 | 1 | | | | |
| Athey | 5 | 0 | 12 | 0 | | | | |
| Lloyds | 27 | 5 | 69 | 1 | | | | |

**FALL OF WICKETS**

| | GLO | SOM | GLO | SOM |
|---|---|---|---|---|
| 1st | 18 | 2 | | |
| 2nd | 18 | 54 | | |
| 3rd | 39 | 73 | | |
| 4th | 94 | 179 | | |
| 5th | 106 | 193 | | |
| 6th | 113 | 294 | | |
| 7th | 135 | | | |
| 8th | 171 | | | |
| 9th | 183 | | | |
| 10th | 183 | | | |

| BRITANNIC ASS. CHAMPIONSHIP | OTHER FIRST-CLASS MATCH |
|---|---|

## SUSSEX vs. ESSEX

at Horsham on 21st, 22nd, 24th (no play) June 1991
Toss : Sussex.  Umpires : H.D.Bird and A.A.Jones
Match drawn.  Sussex 4 pts (Bt: 1, Bw: 3), Essex 7 pts (Bt: 4, Bw: 3)

### ESSEX

| | | |
|---|---|---|
| J.P.Stephenson | c Parker b Jones | 2 |
| A.C.Seymour | lbw b Jones | 9 |
| P.J.Prichard | c Lenham b Wells C.M. | 13 |
| Salim Malik | c Wells A.P. b Pigott | 40 |
| N.Hussain | c Moores b Dodemaide | 20 |
| N.Shahid | c Moores b Pigott | 0 |
| M.A.Garnham + | b Dodemaide | 41 |
| N.A.Foster * | not out | 107 |
| A.G.J.Fraser | not out | 52 |
| S.J.W.Andrew | | |
| J.H.Childs | | |
| Extras | (lb 10,w 2,nb 7) | 19 |
| TOTAL | (for 7 wkts dec) | 303 |

### SUSSEX

| | | |
|---|---|---|
| N.J.Lenham | c Foster b Childs | 60 |
| J.W.Hall | c Stephenson b Andrew | 9 |
| P.W.G.Parker * | b Andrew | 2 |
| A.P.Wells | lbw b Foster | 26 |
| M.P.Speight | c Childs b Foster | 6 |
| C.M.Wells | c Garnham b Childs | 7 |
| A.I.C.Dodemaide | not out | 27 |
| P.Moores + | b Childs | 10 |
| A.C.S.Pigott | c Seymour b Childs | 26 |
| I.D.K.Salisbury | not out | 0 |
| A.N.Jones | | |
| Extras | (lb 1,nb 2) | 3 |
| TOTAL | (for 8 wkts) | 176 |

| SUSSEX | O | M | R | W | O | M | R | W | FALL OF WICKETS | | | | |
|---|---|---|---|---|---|---|---|---|---|---|---|---|---|
| | | | | | | | | | | ESS | SUS | ESS | SUS |
| Jones | 18 | 0 | 110 | 2 | | | | | 1st | 6 | 42 | | |
| Dodemaide | 21.3 | 7 | 43 | 2 | | | | | 2nd | 17 | 48 | | |
| Wells C.M. | 15 | 5 | 37 | 1 | | | | | 3rd | 43 | 99 | | |
| Pigott | 16 | 3 | 61 | 2 | | | | | 4th | 73 | 99 | | |
| Salisbury | 12 | 4 | 42 | 0 | | | | | 5th | 73 | 112 | | |
| | | | | | | | | | 6th | 109 | 112 | | |
| ESSEX | O | M | R | W | O | M | R | W | 7th | 173 | 131 | | |
| Foster | 19 | 4 | 39 | 2 | | | | | 8th | | 175 | | |
| Andrew | 16 | 5 | 44 | 2 | | | | | 9th | | | | |
| Fraser | 5 | 0 | 13 | 0 | | | | | 10th | | | | |
| Stephenson | 3 | 0 | 16 | 0 | | | | | | | | | |
| Childs | 25 | 9 | 63 | 4 | | | | | | | | | |

## YORKSHIRE vs. MIDDLESEX

at Sheffield on 21st, 22nd, 24th June 1991
Toss : Middlesex.  Umpires : J.H.Hampshire and J.W.Holder
Match drawn.  Yorkshire 4 pts (Bt: 3, Bw: 1), Middlesex 2 pts (Bt: 0, Bw: 2)

### YORKSHIRE

| | | | | | |
|---|---|---|---|---|---|
| S.A.Kellett | c Brown b Williams | 13 | b Tufnell | | 18 |
| A.A.Metcalfe * | lbw b Cowans | 61 | c & b Hughes | | 3 |
| D.Byas | lbw b Tufnell | 49 | c Roseberry b Emburey | | 2 |
| R.J.Blakey + | c Hutchinson b Hughes | 44 | (5) b Emburey | | 21 |
| P.E.Robinson | c Farbrace b Hughes | 33 | (6) lbw b Tufnell | | 0 |
| C.S.Pickles | not out | 22 | (7) lbw b Emburey | | 51 |
| P.Carrick | not out | 13 | (8) not out | | 12 |
| J.D.Batty | | | (4) c Farbrace b Williams | | 10 |
| D.Gough | | | not out | | 2 |
| P.J.Hartley | | | | | |
| S.D.Fletcher | | | | | |
| Extras | (lb 7,nb 8) | 15 | (b 4,lb 5,nb 2) | | 11 |
| TOTAL | (for 5 wkts dec) | 250 | (for 7 wkts dec) | | 130 |

### MIDDLESEX

| | | | | | |
|---|---|---|---|---|---|
| I.J.F.Hutchinson | c Blakey b Pickles | 21 | c Blakey b Hartley | | 0 |
| M.A.Roseberry | c Fletcher b Gough | 12 | c Byas b Pickles | | 29 |
| K.R.Brown | run out | 0 | (4) lbw b Hartley | | 30 |
| M.Keech | c & b Batty | 30 | (5) b Batty | | 9 |
| P.Farbrace + | not out | 36 | (9) c Blakey b Hartley | | 11 |
| N.F.Williams | not out | 0 | (7) c Kellett b Carrick | | 5 |
| M.W.Gatting * | | | (3) b Hartley | | 82 |
| J.E.Emburey | | | (6) lbw b Hartley | | 1 |
| N.G.Cowans | | | (8) c Blakey b Carrick | | 5 |
| S.P.Hughes | | | not out | | 0 |
| P.C.R.Tufnell | | | not out | | 1 |
| Extras | (lb 2,nb 3) | 5 | (lb 2,nb 2) | | 4 |
| TOTAL | (for 4 wkts dec) | 104 | (for 9 wkts) | | 177 |

| MIDDLESEX | O | M | R | W | O | M | R | W | FALL OF WICKETS | | | | |
|---|---|---|---|---|---|---|---|---|---|---|---|---|---|
| | | | | | | | | | | YOR | MID | YOR | MID |
| Williams | 18 | 3 | 53 | 1 | 9 | 1 | 23 | 1 | 1st | 30 | 32 | 4 | 0 |
| Cowans | 16 | 5 | 30 | 1 | 5 | 2 | 3 | 0 | 2nd | 133 | 37 | 16 | 63 |
| Emburey | 23 | 7 | 54 | 0 | 13 | 2 | 35 | 3 | 3rd | 133 | 38 | 30 | 136 |
| Tufnell | 26.5 | 9 | 62 | 1 | 20 | 6 | 59 | 2 | 4th | 207 | 104 | 39 | 146 |
| Hughes | 14 | 3 | 44 | 2 | 5 | 4 | 1 | 1 | 5th | 212 | | 41 | 148 |
| | | | | | | | | | 6th | | | 73 | 160 |
| YORKSHIRE | O | M | R | W | O | M | R | W | 7th | | | 128 | 160 |
| Hartley | 8 | 1 | 27 | 0 | 18 | 8 | 32 | 5 | 8th | | | | 176 |
| Gough | 7 | 4 | 13 | 1 | 6 | 0 | 26 | 0 | 9th | | | | 176 |
| Fletcher | 4 | 1 | 12 | 0 | 14 | 3 | 32 | 0 | 10th | | | | |
| Pickles | 5 | 0 | 18 | 1 | 10 | 4 | 24 | 1 | | | | | |
| Carrick | 7 | 3 | 19 | 0 | 12 | 7 | 32 | 2 | | | | | |
| Batty | 6 | 3 | 13 | 1 | 9 | 2 | 29 | 1 | | | | | |

## IRELAND vs. SCOTLAND

at Dublin on 22nd, 23rd, 24th June 1991
Toss : Scotland.  Umpires : L.Hogan and R.McClancy
Ireland won by 95 runs

### IRELAND

| | | | | | |
|---|---|---|---|---|---|
| S.J.S.Warke * | b Cowan | 32 | lbw b Cowan | | 78 |
| M.F.Cohen | c Salmond b Goram | 4 | b Goram | | 44 |
| M.P.Rea | c Govan b Duthie | 27 | c & b Cowan | | 12 |
| D.A.Lewis | run out | 14 | st Haggo b Henry | | 44 |
| T.J.T.Patterson | not out | 73 | c Swan b Cowan | | 3 |
| G.D.Harrison | b Cowan | 77 | c Duthie b Govan | | 21 |
| S.G.Smyth | c Philip b Duthie | 14 | not out | | 7 |
| N.E.Thompson | not out | 21 | run out | | 0 |
| C.Hoey | | | not out | | 1 |
| K.Bailey + | | | | | |
| A.N.Nelson | | | | | |
| Extras | (b 9,lb 6,w 3,nb 4) | 22 | (lb 21,w 1,nb 1) | | 23 |
| TOTAL | (for 6 wkts dec) | 284 | (for 7 wkts dec) | | 233 |

### SCOTLAND

| | | | | | |
|---|---|---|---|---|---|
| I.L.Philip | not out | 116 | c & b Nelson | | 7 |
| B.M.W.Patterson | run out | 108 | c Bailey b Nelson | | 6 |
| R.G.Swan | | | lbw b Nelson | | 15 |
| G.Salmond | | | c Harrison b Lewis | | 66 |
| A.B.Russell | | | run out | | 16 |
| A.L.Goram | | | st Bailey b Harrison | | 5 |
| O.Henry * | | | b Hoey | | 22 |
| D.J.Haggo + | | | lbw b Nelson | | 25 |
| J.W.Govan | | | lbw b Hoey | | 1 |
| P.G.Duthie | | | b Hoey | | 0 |
| D.Cowan | | | not out | | 2 |
| Extras | (b 5,lb 3,w 1,nb 3) | 12 | (b 14,lb 6,nb 1) | | 21 |
| TOTAL | (for 1 wkt dec) | 236 | | | 186 |

| SCOTLAND | O | M | R | W | O | M | R | W | FALL OF WICKETS | | | | |
|---|---|---|---|---|---|---|---|---|---|---|---|---|---|
| | | | | | | | | | | IRE | SCO | IRE | SCO |
| Cowan | 31 | 8 | 92 | 2 | 22 | 5 | 41 | 3 | 1st | 26 | 236 | 115 | 7 |
| Duthie | 30 | 9 | 80 | 2 | 17 | 6 | 35 | 0 | 2nd | 56 | | 140 | 16 |
| Goram | 7 | 1 | 16 | 1 | 16 | 5 | 46 | 1 | 3rd | 84 | | 147 | 40 |
| Henry | 21 | 7 | 42 | 0 | 20 | 6 | 43 | 1 | 4th | 89 | | 157 | 102 |
| Govan | 11 | 2 | 29 | 0 | 13 | 3 | 47 | 1 | 5th | 230 | | 216 | 104 |
| Russell | 5 | 2 | 10 | 0 | | | | | 6th | 255 | | 230 | 128 |
| | | | | | | | | | 7th | | | 230 | 156 |
| IRELAND | O | M | R | W | O | M | R | W | 8th | | | | 176 |
| Nelson | 13 | 2 | 49 | 0 | 14 | 4 | 30 | 4 | 9th | | | | 180 |
| Thompson | 11.3 | 1 | 52 | 0 | 18 | 5 | 15 | 0 | 10th | | | | 186 |
| Harrison | 18 | 5 | 50 | 0 | 8 | 1 | 43 | 1 | | | | | |
| Hoey | 12 | 1 | 47 | 0 | 13.2 | 6 | 38 | 3 | | | | | |
| Lewis | 6 | 0 | 23 | 0 | 10 | 1 | 40 | 1 | | | | | |
| Smyth | 1 | 0 | 7 | 0 | | | | | | | | | |

# HEADLINES

### Other first-class match

### 22nd - 24th June

• Ireland gained their first victory over Scotland for six years with their 95-run victory at Dublin, bowling out the Scots in their second innings for 186 with 10 balls to spare. The visitors would have hoped to have fared better as their openers, Iain Philip and Bruce Patterson, had shared an opening stand 236 in the first innings.

# NATWEST TROPHY – 1st ROUND

## BEDFORDSHIRE vs. WORCS

at Bedford on 26th June 1991
Toss : Worcestershire. Umpires : K.J.Lyons and T.C.Wilson
Worcestershire won by 8 wickets
Man of the match: N.V.Radford

### BEDFORDSHIRE

| | | |
|---|---|---|
| M.R.Gouldstone | lbw b Radford | 2 |
| P.D.B.Hoare | c Moody b Dilley | 0 |
| R.Swann | lbw b Radford | 7 |
| N.G.Folland | b Radford | 10 |
| R.Ashton | c Hick b Radford | 1 |
| S.D.L.Davis | b Radford | 14 |
| A.Dean | b Radford | 0 |
| J.R.Wake * | c D'Oliveira b Radford | 2 |
| P.D.Thomas | c & b Illingworth | 4 |
| B.C.Banks | not out | 12 |
| G.D.Sandford + | lbw b Lampitt | 0 |
| Extras | (b 1,lb 7,w 5,nb 1) | 14 |
| TOTAL | (30 overs) | 66 |

### WORCESTERSHIRE

| | | |
|---|---|---|
| T.M.Moody | not out | 42 |
| S.J.Rhodes + | c Wake b Dean | 10 |
| G.A.Hick | b Dean | 0 |
| D.B.D'Oliveira | not out | 10 |
| T.S.Curtis | | |
| P.A.Neale * | | |
| S.R.Lampitt | | |
| R.K.Illingworth | | |
| P.J.Newport | | |
| N.V.Radford | | |
| G.R.Dilley | | |
| Extras | (lb 4,w 2,nb 1) | 7 |
| TOTAL | (12.5 overs)(for 2 wkts) | 69 |

| WORCS | O | M | R | W | FALL OF WICKETS | | |
|---|---|---|---|---|---|---|---|
| | | | | | | BED | WOR |
| Dilley | 6 | 2 | 12 | 1 | | | |
| Radford | 12 | 4 | 19 | 7 | 1st | 4 | 45 |
| Hick | 5 | 2 | 11 | 0 | 2nd | 10 | 53 |
| Illingworth | 4 | 1 | 12 | 1 | 3rd | 14 | |
| Lampitt | 3 | 1 | 4 | 1 | 4th | 22 | |
| | | | | | 5th | 30 | |
| BEDFORDSHIRE | O | M | R | W | 6th | 30 | |
| Banks | 2 | 0 | 8 | 0 | 7th | 45 | |
| Ashton | 2 | 0 | 25 | 0 | 8th | 46 | |
| Dean | 4.5 | 0 | 20 | 2 | 9th | 65 | |
| Swann | 4 | 0 | 12 | 0 | 10th | 66 | |

## DURHAM vs. GLAMORGAN

at Darlington on 26th June 1991
Toss : Durham. Umpires : B.Hassan and D.O.Oslear
Glamorgan won by 40 runs
Man of the match: M.P.Maynard

### GLAMORGAN

| | | |
|---|---|---|
| A.R.Butcher * | c Fothergill b Brown | 17 |
| H.Morris | not out | 126 |
| R.J.Shastri | c Fothergill b Heseltine | 26 |
| M.P.Maynard | not out | 151 |
| I.Smith | | |
| A.Dale | | |
| J.Derrick | | |
| C.P.Metson + | | |
| S.L.Watkin | | |
| S.R.Barwick | | |
| M.Frost | | |
| Extras | (b 3,lb 11,w 11) | 25 |
| TOTAL | (60 overs)(for 2 wkts) | 345 |

### DURHAM

| | | |
|---|---|---|
| G.Cook * | c Smith b Frost | 13 |
| J.D.Glendenen | c Frost b Watkin | 109 |
| P.Burn | c Morris b Watkin | 2 |
| Ijaz Ahmed | lbw b Barwick | 10 |
| P.Bainbridge | run out | 27 |
| D.A.Blenkiron | c Frost b Derrick | 56 |
| A.S.Patel | c Dale b Smith | 25 |
| A.R.Fothergill + | c Shastri b Smith | 24 |
| J.Wood | b Smith | 1 |
| S.J.Brown | not out | 7 |
| P.A.W.Heseltine | not out | 5 |
| Extras | (lb 13,w 8,nb 5) | 26 |
| TOTAL | (60 overs)(for 9 wkts) | 305 |

| DURHAM | O | M | R | W | FALL OF WICKETS | | |
|---|---|---|---|---|---|---|---|
| | | | | | | GLA | DUR |
| Brown | 12 | 1 | 73 | 1 | | | |
| Wood | 10 | 0 | 82 | 0 | 1st | 27 | 17 |
| Bainbridge | 12 | 0 | 42 | 0 | 2nd | 86 | 24 |
| Ijaz Ahmed | 11 | 0 | 79 | 0 | 3rd | | 47 |
| Heseltine | 12 | 1 | 37 | 1 | 4th | | 119 |
| Patel | 3 | 0 | 18 | 0 | 5th | | 222 |
| | | | | | 6th | | 249 |
| GLAMORGAN | O | M | R | W | 7th | | 276 |
| Watkin | 12 | 1 | 41 | 2 | 8th | | 292 |
| Frost | 12 | 2 | 45 | 1 | 9th | | 294 |
| Barwick | 9 | 0 | 51 | 1 | 10th | | |
| Derrick | 12 | 0 | 59 | 1 | | | |
| Dale | 6 | 0 | 36 | 0 | | | |
| Smith | 9 | 0 | 60 | 3 | | | |

## BERKSHIRE vs. HAMPSHIRE

at Reading on 26th (no play), 27th June 1991
Toss : Hampshire. Umpires : D.Dennis and P.B.Wight
Hampshire won by 10 wickets
Man of the match: S.D.Udal

### BERKSHIRE

| | | |
|---|---|---|
| G.E.Loveday | lbw b Connor | 14 |
| M.G.Lickley | c Smith C.L. b Aqib Javed | 13 |
| G.T.Headley | b Udal | 12 |
| D.J.M.Mercer | c Aqib Javed b Udal | 11 |
| M.L.Simmons * | not out | 9 |
| P.J.Oxley | run out | 18 |
| D.Shaw | not out | 1 |
| M.G.Stear | | |
| M.E.Stevens + | | |
| P.J.Lewington | | |
| J.H.Jones | | |
| Extras | (b 1,lb 5,w 4,nb 2) | 12 |
| TOTAL | (22 overs)(for 5 wkts) | 90 |

### HAMPSHIRE

| | | |
|---|---|---|
| V.P.Terry | not out | 42 |
| R.A.Smith | not out | 43 |
| M.C.J.Nicholas * | | |
| C.L.Smith | | |
| D.I.Gower | | |
| K.D.James | | |
| A.N Aymes + | | |
| S.D.Udal | | |
| C.A.Connor | | |
| P.J.Bakker | | |
| Aqib Javed | | |
| Extras | (b 1,lb 1,w 5,nb 1) | 8 |
| TOTAL | (20.2 overs)(for 0 wkts) | 93 |

| HAMPSHIRE | O | M | R | W | FALL OF WICKETS | | |
|---|---|---|---|---|---|---|---|
| | | | | | | BER | HAM |
| Bakker | 4 | 1 | 15 | 0 | | | |
| Aqib Javed | 5 | 1 | 21 | 1 | 1st | 18 | |
| James | 2 | 0 | 14 | 0 | 2nd | 42 | |
| Connor | 4 | 0 | 11 | 1 | 3rd | 48 | |
| Udal | 5 | 0 | 14 | 2 | 4th | 61 | |
| Nicholas | 2 | 0 | 9 | 0 | 5th | 88 | |
| | | | | | 6th | | |
| BERKSHIRE | O | M | R | W | 7th | | |
| Jones | 3 | 0 | 9 | 0 | 8th | | |
| Stear | 3 | 0 | 11 | 0 | 9th | | |
| Headley | 4 | 0 | 19 | 0 | 10th | | |
| Lewington | 5 | 0 | 26 | 0 | | | |
| Shaw | 3.2 | 0 | 17 | 0 | | | |
| Lickley | 2 | 0 | 9 | 0 | | | |

## DEVON vs. ESSEX

at Exmouth on 26th June 1991
Toss : Essex. Umpires : A.A.Jones and G.A.Stickley
Essex won by 8 wickets
Man of the match: N.A.Folland

### DEVON

| | | |
|---|---|---|
| J.H.Edwards * | lbw b Foster | 0 |
| K.G.Rice | c Salim Malik b Such | 15 |
| N.A.Folland | lbw b Gooch | 55 |
| A.J.Pugh | lbw b Such | 0 |
| R.I.Dawson | c Garnham b Pringle | 13 |
| K.Donohue | c Garnham b Pringle | 4 |
| T.W.Ward | lbw b Pringle | 1 |
| J.K.Tierney | c Hussain b Topley | 26 |
| C.S.Pritchard + | lbw b Childs | 0 |
| M.J.Record | not out | 8 |
| M.C.Woodman | c Salim Malik b Childs | 8 |
| Extras | (b 1,lb 8,w 5,nb 5) | 19 |
| TOTAL | (57.4 overs) | 149 |

### ESSEX

| | | |
|---|---|---|
| G.A.Gooch * | c Folland b Donohue | 57 |
| J.P.Stephenson | c Folland b Donohue | 57 |
| P.J.Prichard | not out | 27 |
| Salim Malik | not out | 6 |
| N.Hussain | | |
| D.R.Pringle | | |
| M.A.Garnham + | | |
| N.A.Foster | | |
| T.D.Topley | | |
| J.H.Childs | | |
| P.M.Such | | |
| Extras | (lb 2,nb 1) | 3 |
| TOTAL | (44.4 overs)(for 2 wkts) | 150 |

| ESSEX | O | M | R | W | FALL OF WICKETS | | |
|---|---|---|---|---|---|---|---|
| | | | | | | DEV | ESS |
| Foster | 8 | 4 | 17 | 1 | | | |
| Pringle | 10 | 2 | 21 | 3 | 1st | 0 | 108 |
| Such | 12 | 1 | 29 | 2 | 2nd | 48 | 119 |
| Childs | 11.4 | 4 | 43 | 2 | 3rd | 49 | |
| Topley | 11 | 3 | 21 | 1 | 4th | 92 | |
| Gooch | 5 | 1 | 9 | 1 | 5th | 94 | |
| | | | | | 6th | 99 | |
| DEVON | O | M | R | W | 7th | 99 | |
| Donohue | 12 | 3 | 34 | 2 | 8th | 128 | |
| Woodman | 10 | 4 | 24 | 0 | 9th | 128 | |
| Ward | 10.4 | 4 | 35 | 0 | 10th | 149 | |
| Record | 6 | 0 | 32 | 0 | | | |
| Tierney | 6 | 0 | 23 | 0 | | | |

## GLOUCS vs. NORFOLK

at Bristol on 26th, 27th June 1991
Toss : Norfolk. Umpires : D.J.Halfyard and R.Julian
Gloucs won by 153 runs
Man of the match: D.V.Lawrence

### GLOUCS

| | | |
|---|---|---|
| G.D.Hodgson | b Belmont | 7 |
| J.J.E.Hardy | run out | 70 |
| A.J.Wright * | c Stamp b Plumb | 56 |
| C.W.J.Athey | not out | 47 |
| M.W.Alleyne | run out | 3 |
| J.W.Lloyds | b Ellis | 4 |
| R.J.Scott | c Stamp b Ellis | 11 |
| R.C.Russell + | c Ellis b Thomas | 23 |
| D.V.Lawrence | not out | 2 |
| A.M.Smith | | |
| A.M.Babington | | |
| Extras | (b 1,lb 10,w 3) | 14 |
| TOTAL | (60 overs)(for 7 wkts) | 237 |

### NORFOLK

| | | |
|---|---|---|
| C.J.Rogers | b Lawrence | 2 |
| D.R.Thomas * | b Lawrence | 2 |
| D.M.Stamp | c Russell b Scott | 6 |
| R.J.Finney | c Hodgson b Scott | 27 |
| S.G.Plumb | c Russell b Smith | 11 |
| S.B.Dixon | b Lawrence | 0 |
| R.J.Belmont | hit wicket b Lawrence | 9 |
| D.G.Savage | lbw b Scott | 4 |
| R.Kingshott | not out | 1 |
| D.E.Mattocks + | b Lawrence | 1 |
| M.T.Ellis | st Russell b Scott | 0 |
| Extras | (b 2,lb 9,w 3,nb 7) | 21 |
| TOTAL | (33.2 overs) | 84 |

| NORFOLK | O | M | R | W | FALL OF WICKETS | | |
|---|---|---|---|---|---|---|---|
| | | | | | | GLO | NFK |
| Ellis | 12 | 4 | 33 | 2 | | | |
| Belmont | 12 | 2 | 53 | 1 | 1st | 15 | 4 |
| Thomas | 12 | 0 | 58 | 1 | 2nd | 133 | 14 |
| Kingshott | 12 | 0 | 46 | 0 | 3rd | 152 | 47 |
| Plumb | 12 | 0 | 36 | 1 | 4th | 158 | 61 |
| | | | | | 5th | 165 | 62 |
| GLOUCS | O | M | R | W | 6th | 183 | 67 |
| Lawrence | 9 | 0 | 17 | 5 | 7th | 234 | 77 |
| Babington | 6 | 0 | 17 | 0 | 8th | | 77 |
| Scott | 10.2 | 3 | 22 | 4 | 9th | | 78 |
| Smith | 6 | 1 | 14 | 1 | 10th | | 84 |
| Lloyds | 2 | 0 | 3 | 0 | | | |

## DORSET vs. LANCASHIRE

at Bournemouth on 26th June 1991
Toss : Lancashire. Umpires : M.A.Johnson and R.Palmer
Lancashire won by 5 wickets
Man of the match: N.H.Fairbrother

### DORSET

| | | |
|---|---|---|
| G.S.Calway | c Hegg b Martin | 12 |
| J.A.Claughton | b Austin | 29 |
| J.M.H.Gr'hm-Brown | c Hughes b Watkinson | 18 |
| J.R.Hall | c DeFreitas b Martin | 14 |
| G.D.Reynolds + | run out | 22 |
| V.B.Lewis * | c Hughes b Watkinson | 4 |
| R.A.Pyman | c Hughes b Wasim Akram | 1 |
| S.Sawney | c Mendis b Wasim Akram | 8 |
| A.Willows | c Hegg b Wasim Akram | 14 |
| N.R.Taylor | run out | 10 |
| J.H.Shackleton | not out | 0 |
| Extras | (lb 8,w 6,nb 1) | 15 |
| TOTAL | (59.3 overs) | 147 |

### LANCASHIRE

| | | |
|---|---|---|
| G.Fowler | c Calway b Taylor | 9 |
| G.D.Mendis | b Taylor | 5 |
| M.A.Atherton | run out | 38 |
| N.H.Fairbrother | c Claughton b Calway | 68 |
| M.Watkinson | c Lewis b Hall | 5 |
| Wasim Akram | not out | 11 |
| P.A.J.DeFreitas | not out | 6 |
| W.K.Hegg + | | |
| D.P.Hughes * | | |
| I.D.Austin | | |
| P.J.Martin | | |
| Extras | (lb 4,w 3,nb 2) | 9 |
| TOTAL | (52.2 overs)(for 5 wkts) | 151 |

| LANCASHIRE | O | M | R | W | FALL OF WICKETS | | |
|---|---|---|---|---|---|---|---|
| | | | | | | DOR | LAN |
| DeFreitas | 12 | 3 | 24 | 0 | | | |
| Martin | 12 | 2 | 19 | 2 | 1st | 25 | 7 |
| Austin | 12 | 1 | 46 | 1 | 2nd | 63 | 20 |
| Wasim Akram | 11.3 | 2 | 40 | 3 | 3rd | 67 | 103 |
| Watkinson | 12 | 7 | 10 | 2 | 4th | 105 | 114 |
| | | | | | 5th | 110 | 143 |
| DORSET | O | M | R | W | 6th | 111 | |
| Shackleton | 12 | 5 | 16 | 0 | 7th | 113 | |
| Taylor | 12 | 2 | 25 | 2 | 8th | 134 | |
| Calway | 10 | 3 | 34 | 1 | 9th | 147 | |
| Pyman | 12 | 2 | 41 | 0 | 10th | 147 | |
| Hall | 4 | 0 | 16 | 1 | | | |
| Sawney | 2.2 | 0 | 15 | 0 | | | |

# NATWEST TROPHY – 1st ROUND

## HEADLINES

### NatWest Trophy
### 1st Round

#### 26th - 27th June

• A waterlogged Bishop's Stortford ground was the scene of the one upset in the opening round of the NatWest Trophy, Hertfordshire winning through at Derbyshire's expense. When no play was possible on either of the two allocated days the match was decided by a bowling competition, Hertfordshire achieving two hits to Derbyshire's one, as each side had 10 deliveries at an undefended set of stumps.

• Surrey almost suffered a similar fate at The Oval, where their match with Oxfordshire, although started twice, could not be completed, but the home side overcame the minor county by three hits to two in an indoor bowling competition to reach the second round.

• The only match to be played between two first-class counties was quickly decided in Warwickshire's favour as Allan Donald destroyed Yorkshire's frontline batting with figures of four for 16 at Edgbaston. The visitors could only reach 123 which posed few problems for Warwickshire.

• Neal Radford returned the best figures of the round, a career-best seven for 19, as Worcestershire made up for lost time when their contest at Bedford eventually got under way. The visitors needed less than 11 overs to overcome Bedfordshire's modest total of 66.

• Gloucestershire's David Lawrence was another bowler in destructive mood, claiming five for 17 against Norfolk at Bristol, his best figures in the competition as his prolific wicket-taking in all forms of cricket showed no signs of letting up.

• Alan Igglesden also returned his best figures in the NatWest Trophy as Kent defeated Cambridgeshire by six wickets at Canterbury, but Ajaz Akhtar stole the honours for the visitors by dismissing all four Kent batsmen in the space of 16 runs.

## IRELAND vs. MIDDLESEX

at Dublin on 26th, 27th June 1991
Toss : Ireland.  Umpires : J.C.Balderstone and D.R.Shepherd
Middlesex won by 45 runs
Man of the match: D.A.Lewis

### MIDDLESEX

| | | |
|---|---|---|
| I.J.F.Hutchinson | c Patterson b Thompson | 23 |
| M.A.Roseberry | c Harrison b McCrum | 6 |
| M.W.Gatting * | c Patterson b Lewis | 65 |
| M.R.Ramprakash | c Warke b Lewis | 32 |
| K.R.Brown | c Rea b McCrum | 49 |
| J.E.Emburey | b Nelson | 1 |
| N.G.Cowans | lbw b Lewis | 0 |
| P.N.Weekes | lbw b Lewis | 7 |
| P.Farbrace + | not out | 13 |
| N.F.Williams | c Cohen b McCrum | 6 |
| S.P.Hughes | not out | 0 |
| Extras | (lb 9,w 5) | 14 |
| TOTAL | (60 overs)(for 9 wkts) | 216 |

### IRELAND

| | | |
|---|---|---|
| S.J.S.Warke * | c Hutchinson b Cowans | 3 |
| M.F.Cohen | run out | 26 |
| M.P.Rea | c Farbrace b Williams | 3 |
| D.A.Lewis | c Roseberry b Weekes | 25 |
| T.J.T.Patterson | c Hutchinson b Hughes | 5 |
| G.D.Harrison | c Williams b Ramprakash | 9 |
| N.E.Thompson | c Cowans b Hughes | 14 |
| C.Hoey | not out | 26 |
| K.Bailey + | b Ramprakash | 0 |
| P.McCrum | st Farbrace b Gatting | 16 |
| A.N.Nelson | not out | 8 |
| Extras | (b 5,lb 10,w 19,nb 2) | 36 |
| TOTAL | (60 overs)(for 9 wkts) | 171 |

| IRELAND | O | M | R | W | FALL OF WICKETS | | |
|---|---|---|---|---|---|---|---|
| | | | | | | MID | IRE |
| McCrum | 10 | 1 | 31 | 3 | 1st | 12 | 12 |
| Nelson | 11 | 3 | 39 | 1 | 2nd | 44 | 21 |
| Thompson | 12 | 3 | 30 | 1 | 3rd | 122 | 73 |
| Hoey | 12 | 3 | 33 | 0 | 4th | 160 | 73 |
| Harrison | 5 | 0 | 27 | 0 | 5th | 165 | 85 |
| Lewis | 10 | 0 | 47 | 4 | 6th | 166 | 114 |
| | | | | | 7th | 184 | 115 |
| MIDDLESEX | O | M | R | W | 8th | 196 | 116 |
| Cowans | 6 | 1 | 10 | 1 | 9th | 212 | 163 |
| Williams | 6 | 2 | 11 | 1 | 10th | | |
| Weekes | 12 | 1 | 30 | 1 | | | |
| Emburey | 12 | 7 | 13 | 0 | | | |
| Ramprakash | 7 | 1 | 15 | 2 | | | |
| Hughes | 11 | 2 | 24 | 2 | | | |
| Hutchinson | 2 | 0 | 17 | 0 | | | |
| Roseberry | 2 | 0 | 20 | 0 | | | |
| Brown | 1 | 0 | 8 | 0 | | | |
| Gatting | 1 | 0 | 8 | 1 | | | |

## SURREY vs. OXFORDSHIRE

at The Oval on 26th, 27th June 1991
Surrey won 3–2 in a bowling competition

## NOTTS vs. LINCOLNSHIRE

at Trent Bridge on 26th June 1991
Toss : Lincs.  Umpires : H.D.Bird and D.Fawkner-Corbett
Notts won by 134 runs
Man of the match: M.A.Crawley

### NOTTS

| | | |
|---|---|---|
| B.C.Broad | b McKeown | 14 |
| D.W.Randall | c & b Storer | 25 |
| R.T.Robinson * | c Fell b McKeown | 124 |
| P.Johnson | b McKeown | 48 |
| M.A.Crawley | not out | 74 |
| M.Saxelby | not out | 6 |
| F.D.Stephenson + | | |
| B.N.French | | |
| E.E.Hemmings | | |
| R.A.Pick | | |
| J.A.Afford | | |
| Extras | (lb 9,w 6) | 15 |
| TOTAL | (60 overs)(for 4 wkts) | 306 |

### LINCOLNSHIRE

| | | |
|---|---|---|
| P.J.Heseltine | c French b Stephenson | 2 |
| D.B.Storer | c Robinson b Crawley | 28 |
| S.N.Warman | b Crawley | 28 |
| J.D.Love * | c French b Crawley | 24 |
| M.A.Fell | c French b Saxelby | 39 |
| N.J.C.Gandon | lbw b Crawley | 0 |
| A.C.Jelfs | b Hemmings | 25 |
| D.A.Christmas | c & b Saxelby | 4 |
| P.D.McKeown | not out | 1 |
| N.P.Dobbs + | not out | 0 |
| D.Marshall | | |
| Extras | (lb 6,w 15) | 21 |
| TOTAL | (50.4 overs)(for 8 wkts) | 172 |

| LINCS | O | M | R | W | FALL OF WICKETS | | |
|---|---|---|---|---|---|---|---|
| | | | | | | NOT | LIN |
| McKeown | 12 | 0 | 52 | 3 | 1st | 20 | 2 |
| Christmas | 12 | 2 | 80 | 0 | 2nd | 64 | 59 |
| Jelfs | 9 | 1 | 51 | 0 | 3rd | 138 | 78 |
| Storer | 5 | 0 | 17 | 1 | 4th | 284 | 105 |
| Marshall | 12 | 0 | 48 | 0 | 5th | | 105 |
| Fell | 10 | 0 | 49 | 0 | 6th | | 157 |
| | | | | | 7th | | 168 |
| NOTTS | O | M | R | W | 8th | | 172 |
| Stephenson | 5 | 0 | 10 | 1 | 9th | | |
| Pick | 6 | 2 | 10 | 0 | 10th | | |
| Hemmings | 9 | 1 | 40 | 1 | | | |
| Saxelby | 6.4 | 0 | 42 | 2 | | | |
| Crawley | 12 | 1 | 26 | 4 | | | |
| Afford | 12 | 2 | 38 | 0 | | | |

## SOMERSET vs. BUCKS

at Bath on 26th June 1991
Toss : Bucks.  Umpires : R.C.Tolchard and R.A.White
Somerset won by 6 wickets
Man of the match: P.M.Roebuck

### BUCKS

| | | |
|---|---|---|
| A.R.Harwood | c Graveney b Mallender | 4 |
| M.J.Roberts | c Harden b Hayhurst | 21 |
| T.J.A.Scriven | lbw b Mallender | 0 |
| S.Burrow | c Lefebvre b Macleay | 12 |
| B.S.Percy | c Burns b Lefebvre | 13 |
| N.G.Hames * | b Graveney | 11 |
| G.R.Black | b Macleay | 11 |
| T.G.Roshier | c Roebuck b Mallender | 32 |
| T.J.Barry | not out | 30 |
| D.J.Goldsmith + | not out | 2 |
| C.D.Booden | | |
| Extras | (b 9,lb 10,w 3,nb 1) | 23 |
| TOTAL | (60 overs)(for 8 wkts) | 159 |

### SOMERSET

| | | |
|---|---|---|
| S.J.Cook | b Roshier | 35 |
| P.M.Roebuck | not out | 63 |
| A.N.Hayhurst | c Hames b Burrow | 5 |
| C.J.Tavare * | c Black b Scriven | 25 |
| R.J.Harden | b Percy | 20 |
| N.D.Burns + | not out | 5 |
| G.D.Rose | | |
| K.H.Macleay | | |
| R.P.Lefebvre | | |
| N.A.Mallender | | |
| D.A.Graveney | | |
| Extras | (b 1,lb 3,w 4) | 8 |
| TOTAL | (48.4 overs)(for 4 wkts) | 161 |

| SOMERSET | O | M | R | W | FALL OF WICKETS | | |
|---|---|---|---|---|---|---|---|
| | | | | | | BUC | SOM |
| Mallender | 12 | 4 | 23 | 3 | 1st | 7 | 52 |
| Lefebvre | 12 | 5 | 30 | 1 | 2nd | 7 | 70 |
| Macleay | 12 | 0 | 35 | 2 | 3rd | 41 | 113 |
| Hayhurst | 12 | 2 | 28 | 1 | 4th | 47 | 149 |
| Graveney | 12 | 4 | 24 | 1 | 5th | 66 | |
| | | | | | 6th | 86 | |
| BUCKS | O | M | R | W | 7th | 103 | |
| Roshier | 12 | 1 | 40 | 1 | 8th | 153 | |
| Black | 7 | 0 | 30 | 0 | 9th | | |
| Burrow | 9 | 2 | 18 | 1 | 10th | | |
| Booden | 9.4 | 2 | 35 | 0 | | | |
| Scriven | 8 | 1 | 32 | 1 | | | |
| Percy | 3 | 2 | 2 | 1 | | | |

# NATWEST TROPHY – 1st ROUND

## HERTFORDSHIRE vs. DERBYSHIRE
at Bishop's Stortford on 26th, 27th June 1991
Hertfordshire won 2–1 in a bowling competition

## LEICESTERSHIRE vs. SHROPSHIRE
at Leicester on 26th June 1991
Toss : Leics. Umpires : B.Leadbeater and H.J.Rhodes
Leicestershire won by 7 wickets
Man of the match: T.J.Boon

### SHROPSHIRE

| | | |
|---|---|---|
| J.Foster * | c Whitticase b Wilkinson | 10 |
| J.B.R.Jones | c Lewis b Millns | 1 |
| J.Abrahams | run out | 53 |
| T.Parton | c Boon b Lewis | 17 |
| A.N.Johnson | c Lewis b Wilkinson | 20 |
| J.R.Weaver + | c Whitticase b Wilkinson | 6 |
| A.B.Byram | b Millns | 0 |
| P.B.Wormwald | b Lewis | 9 |
| A.S.Barnard | not out | 17 |
| A.P.Pridgeon | b Lewis | 4 |
| G.Edmunds | not out | 3 |
| Extras | (lb 5,w 6,nb 1) | 12 |
| TOTAL | (60 overs)(for 9 wkts) | 152 |

### LEICESTERSHIRE

| | | |
|---|---|---|
| T.J.Boon | not out | 76 |
| N.E.Briers * | run out | 9 |
| J.J.Whitaker | c Abrahams b Wormwald | 39 |
| P.Willey | c Abrahams b Byram | 6 |
| L.Potter | not out | 25 |
| C.C.Lewis | | |
| B.F.Smith | | |
| P.Whitticase + | | |
| D.J.Millns | | |
| C.Wilkinson | | |
| J.N.Maguire | | |
| Extras | (lb 1) | 1 |
| TOTAL | (56.5 overs)(for 3 wkts) | 156 |

| LEICS | O | M | R | W | FALL OF WICKETS | |
|---|---|---|---|---|---|---|
| | | | | | SHR | LEI |
| Lewis | 12 | 2 | 28 | 3 | | |
| Millns | 12 | 4 | 27 | 2 | 1st 2 | 12 |
| Maguire | 12 | 0 | 49 | 0 | 2nd 38 | 84 |
| Wilkinson | 12 | 5 | 16 | 3 | 3rd 84 | 95 |
| Willey | 12 | 3 | 27 | 0 | 4th 89 | |
| | | | | | 5th 117 | |
| SHROPSHIRE | O | M | R | W | 6th 117 | |
| Pridgeon | 10.5 | 7 | 21 | 0 | 7th 120 | |
| Barnard | 12 | 5 | 26 | 0 | 8th 132 | |
| Edmunds | 12 | 0 | 40 | 0 | 9th 142 | |
| Abrahams | 8 | 0 | 25 | 0 | 10th | |
| Wormwald | 8 | 1 | 18 | 1 | | |
| Byram | 6 | 0 | 25 | 1 | | |

## KENT vs. CAMBRIDGESHIRE
at Canterbury on 26th June 1991
Toss : Kent. Umpires : P.Adams and D.J.Constant
Kent won by 6 wickets
Man of the match: Ajaz Akhtar

### CAMBRIDGESHIRE

| | | |
|---|---|---|
| R.A.Milne | c Marsh b Igglesden | 0 |
| N.T.Gadsby * | b Merrick | 15 |
| R.P.Merriman | c Igglesden b Penn | 0 |
| N.J.Adams | c & b Davis | 44 |
| N.P.Norman | b Merrick | 2 |
| A.M.Cade | c & b Merrick | 0 |
| Ajaz Akhtar | lbw b Fleming | 2 |
| S.Turner | c Cowdrey C.S. b Igglesden | 7 |
| M.W.C.Olley + | not out | 20 |
| M.G.Stephenson | lbw b Igglesden | 2 |
| K.O.Thomas | c Marsh b Igglesden | 2 |
| Extras | (lb 9,w 4) | 13 |
| TOTAL | (44.2 overs) | 107 |

### KENT

| | | |
|---|---|---|
| T.R.Ward | c Stephenson b Ajaz Akhtar | 20 |
| M.R.Benson * | b Ajaz Akhtar | 21 |
| N.R.Taylor | c Olley b Ajaz Akhtar | 2 |
| G.R.Cowdrey | not out | 25 |
| C.S.Cowdrey | b Ajaz Akhtar | 0 |
| M.V.Fleming | not out | 35 |
| S.A.Marsh + | | |
| R.P.Davis | | |
| C.Penn | | |
| T.A.Merrick | | |
| A.P.Igglesden | | |
| Extras | (lb 4,w 3,nb 1) | 8 |
| TOTAL | (35.4 overs)(for 4 wkts) | 111 |

| KENT | O | M | R | W | FALL OF WICKETS | |
|---|---|---|---|---|---|---|
| | | | | | CMB | KEN |
| Penn | 9 | 4 | 14 | 1 | | |
| Igglesden | 9.2 | 1 | 29 | 4 | 1st 2 | 43 |
| Merrick | 12 | 3 | 27 | 3 | 2nd 3 | 46 |
| Davis | 9 | 2 | 22 | 1 | 3rd 36 | 55 |
| Fleming | 5 | 1 | 6 | 1 | 4th 44 | 59 |
| | | | | | 5th 58 | |
| CAMBS | O | M | R | W | 6th 76 | |
| Thomas | 4 | 0 | 22 | 0 | 7th 76 | |
| Turner | 12 | 3 | 23 | 0 | 8th 93 | |
| Ajaz Akhtar | 12 | 6 | 28 | 4 | 9th 101 | |
| Stephenson | 5.4 | 4 | 19 | 0 | 10th 107 | |
| Adams | 2 | 0 | 15 | 0 | | |

## SCOTLAND vs. SUSSEX
at Edinburgh on 26th June 1991
Toss : Scotland. Umpires : G.I.Burgess and B.Dudleston
Sussex won by 72 runs
Man of the match: N.J.Lenham

### SUSSEX

| | | |
|---|---|---|
| N.J.Lenham | b Goram | 66 |
| D.M.Smith | lbw b Duthie | 40 |
| M.P.Speight | c Haggo b Reifer | 20 |
| P.W.G.Parker * | c Henry b Goram | 12 |
| C.M.Wells | c Goram b Henry | 0 |
| A.P.Wells | st Haggo b Duthie | 8 |
| A.C.S.Pigott | c Haggo b Russell | 7 |
| A.I.C.Dodemaide | not out | 32 |
| P.Moores + | c Philip b Moir | 26 |
| I.D.K.Salisbury | st Haggo b Russell | 4 |
| A.N.Jones | not out | 0 |
| Extras | (b 3,lb 3,w 6,nb 4) | 16 |
| TOTAL | (60 overs)(for 9 wkts) | 231 |

### SCOTLAND

| | | |
|---|---|---|
| I.L.Philip | lbw b Dodemaide | 9 |
| B.M.W.Patterson | lbw b Dodemaide | 4 |
| G.N.Reifer | lbw b Wells C.M. | 13 |
| R.G.Swan | b Wells C.M. | 45 |
| G.Salmond | lbw b Lenham | 1 |
| O.Henry * | b Lenham | 12 |
| A.B.Russell | b Salisbury | 0 |
| A.L.Goram | c Parker b Wells C.M. | 21 |
| P.G.Duthie | c Moores b Pigott | 19 |
| D.J.Haggo + | c Parker b Pigott | 1 |
| J.D.Moir | not out | 11 |
| Extras | (lb 15,w 8) | 23 |
| TOTAL | (54.5 overs) | 159 |

| SCOTLAND | O | M | R | W | FALL OF WICKETS | |
|---|---|---|---|---|---|---|
| | | | | | SUS | SCO |
| Moir | 11 | 1 | 47 | 1 | | |
| Reifer | 8 | 0 | 40 | 1 | 1st 78 | 12 |
| Duthie | 12 | 2 | 42 | 2 | 2nd 126 | 28 |
| Goram | 12 | 1 | 42 | 2 | 3rd 142 | 49 |
| Henry | 12 | 2 | 34 | 1 | 4th 154 | 52 |
| Russell | 5 | 0 | 20 | 2 | 5th 156 | 68 |
| | | | | | 6th 163 | 71 |
| SUSSEX | O | M | R | W | 7th 170 | 108 |
| Jones | 5 | 0 | 30 | 0 | 8th 211 | 114 |
| Dodemaide | 10 | 3 | 12 | 2 | 9th 219 | 131 |
| Pigott | 7.5 | 1 | 25 | 2 | 10th | 159 |
| Lenham | 11 | 1 | 25 | 2 | | |
| Wells C.M. | 12 | 3 | 16 | 3 | | |
| Salisbury | 9 | 0 | 36 | 1 | | |

| NATWEST TROPHY – 1st ROUND | TOUR MATCHES |
|---|---|

## STAFFORDSHIRE vs. NORTHANTS

at Stone on 26th June 1991
Toss : Staffs.  Umpires : J.H.Hampshire and V.A.Holder
Northants won by 152 runs
Man of the match: R.J.Bailey

**NORTHANTS**

| | | |
|---|---|---|
| A.Fordham | b Newman | 56 |
| N.A.Felton | c Dean b Hackett | 11 |
| R.J.Bailey | c Cartledge b Hackett | 145 |
| A.J.Lamb * | run out | 31 |
| D.J.Capel | b Hackett | 1 |
| K.M.Curran | not out | 3 |
| E.A.E.Baptiste | not out | 0 |
| D.Ripley + | | |
| J.P.Taylor | | |
| N.G.B.Cook | | |
| A.Walker | | |
| Extras | (lb 7,w 6) | 13 |
| TOTAL | (60 overs)(for 5 wkts) | 260 |

**STAFFORDSHIRE**

| | | |
|---|---|---|
| S.J.Dean | c Cook b Taylor | 0 |
| D.Cartledge | b Walker | 4 |
| J.P.Addison | b Taylor | 11 |
| D.A.Banks | b Baptiste | 3 |
| N.J.Archer * | c Ripley b Baptiste | 14 |
| A.J.Dutton | lbw b Baptiste | 12 |
| P.G.Newman | b Cook | 28 |
| M.I.Humphries + | lbw b Baptiste | 0 |
| R.A.Spiers | not out | 13 |
| G.D.Williams | c Cook b Bailey | 7 |
| N.Hackett | lbw b Fordham | 0 |
| Extras | (b 4,lb 7,w 5) | 16 |
| TOTAL | (43.3 overs) | 108 |

| STAFFS | O | M | R | W | FALL OF WICKETS | NOR | STA |
|---|---|---|---|---|---|---|---|
| Newman | 12 | 3 | 29 | 1 | | | |
| Hackett | 12 | 0 | 45 | 3 | 1st | 26 | 0 |
| Williams | 12 | 0 | 41 | 0 | 2nd | 130 | 15 |
| Dutton | 12 | 0 | 54 | 0 | 3rd | 234 | 17 |
| Spiers | 10 | 1 | 65 | 0 | 4th | 246 | 31 |
| Addison | 2 | 0 | 19 | 0 | 5th | 259 | 54 |
| | | | | | 6th | | 59 |
| NORTHANTS | O | M | R | W | 7th | | 61 |
| Taylor | 8 | 0 | 11 | 2 | 8th | | 87 |
| Walker | 8 | 2 | 18 | 1 | 9th | | 104 |
| Baptiste | 12 | 1 | 27 | 4 | 10th | | 108 |
| Cook | 12 | 0 | 35 | 1 | | | |
| Bailey | 2 | 0 | 3 | 1 | | | |
| Fordham | 1.3 | 0 | 3 | 1 | | | |

## WARWICKSHIRE vs. YORKSHIRE

at Edgbaston on 26th June 1991
Toss : Yorkshire.  Umpires : M.J.Kitchen and N.T.Plews
Warwickshire won by 7 wickets
Man of the match: A.A.Donald

**YORKSHIRE**

| | | |
|---|---|---|
| M.D.Moxon * | lbw b Donald | 2 |
| A.A.Metcalfe | c Reeve b Munton | 8 |
| D.Byas | b Donald | 2 |
| R.J.Blakey + | b Donald | 0 |
| P.E.Robinson | c Reeve b Small | 40 |
| C.S.Pickles | b Donald | 12 |
| P.Carrick | c Munton b Small | 12 |
| D.Gough | b Smith | 2 |
| P.J.Hartley | not out | 6 |
| J.D.Batty | c Piper b Small | 4 |
| S.D.Fletcher | c Piper b Reeve | 9 |
| Extras | (lb 9,w 14,nb 3) | 26 |
| TOTAL | (45.1 overs) | 123 |

**WARWICKSHIRE**

| | | |
|---|---|---|
| A.J.Moles | c Pickles b Batty | 30 |
| J.D.Ratcliffe | run out | 26 |
| D.P.Ostler | not out | 34 |
| D.A.Reeve | c Moxon b Pickles | 7 |
| P.A.Smith | not out | 2 |
| T.A.Lloyd * | | |
| K.J.Piper + | | |
| G.C.Small | | |
| P.A.Booth | | |
| T.A.Munton | | |
| A.A.Donald | | |
| Extras | (b 2,lb 5,w 7,nb 11) | 25 |
| TOTAL | (43.3 overs)(for 3 wkts) | 124 |

| WARWICKS | O | M | R | W | FALL OF WICKETS | YOR | WAR |
|---|---|---|---|---|---|---|---|
| Donald | 9 | 2 | 16 | 4 | | | |
| Small | 12 | 5 | 28 | 3 | 1st | 5 | 65 |
| Munton | 8 | 1 | 21 | 1 | 2nd | 16 | 96 |
| Reeve | 6.1 | 0 | 17 | 1 | 3rd | 16 | 110 |
| Smith | 10 | 1 | 32 | 1 | 4th | 42 | |
| | | | | | 5th | 83 | |
| YORKSHIRE | O | M | R | W | 6th | 88 | |
| Hartley | 8 | 1 | 19 | 0 | 7th | 102 | |
| Fletcher | 5 | 0 | 15 | 0 | 8th | 102 | |
| Pickles | 10.3 | 2 | 30 | 1 | 9th | 107 | |
| Gough | 8 | 2 | 18 | 0 | 10th | 123 | |
| Carrick | 6 | 1 | 18 | 0 | | | |
| Batty | 6 | 2 | 17 | 1 | | | |

## LEAGUE CC XI vs. WEST INDIES

at Trowbridge on 28th June 1991
Toss : West Indies.  Umpires : M.Lovell and J.Stokes
West Indies won by 9 wickets

**LEAGUE CC XI**

| | | |
|---|---|---|
| G.I.Foley | b Simmons | 36 |
| D.J.Lampitt | c Logie b Simmons | 22 |
| M.J.Ingham | not out | 48 |
| N.J.Heaton * | st Williams b Lara | 44 |
| R.A.Harper | c Hooper b Richards | 18 |
| S.C.Wundke | not out | 2 |
| J.Macauley | | |
| K.W.McLeod | | |
| K.Ecclesharf | | |
| V.de C.Walcott | | |
| B.L.Holmes | | |
| Extras | (lb 9,w 5,nb 10) | 24 |
| TOTAL | (55 overs)(for 4 wkts) | 194 |

**WEST INDIES**

| | | |
|---|---|---|
| P.V.Simmons | c Lampitt b Holmes | 70 |
| C.B.Lambert | not out | 101 |
| R.B.Richardson | not out | 11 |
| B.C.Lara | | |
| C.L.Hooper | | |
| I.V.A.Richards * | | |
| A.L.Logie | | |
| M.D.Marshall | | |
| D.Williams + | | |
| H.A.G.Anthony | | |
| I.B.A.Allen | | |
| Extras | (b 1,lb 6,w 1,nb 5) | 13 |
| TOTAL | (31 overs)(for 1 wkt) | 195 |

| WEST INDIES | O | M | R | W | FALL OF WICKETS | LCC | WI |
|---|---|---|---|---|---|---|---|
| Marshall | 5 | 0 | 15 | 0 | | | |
| Allen | 5 | 1 | 7 | 0 | 1st | 62 | 162 |
| Anthony | 5 | 0 | 17 | 0 | 2nd | 74 | |
| Simmons | 11 | 0 | 44 | 2 | 3rd | 156 | |
| Hooper | 11 | 4 | 22 | 0 | 4th | 191 | |
| Lara | 11 | 0 | 53 | 1 | 5th | | |
| Richards | 7 | 0 | 27 | 1 | 6th | | |
| | | | | | 7th | | |
| LEAGUE CC XI | O | M | R | W | 8th | | |
| McLeod | 5 | 0 | 32 | 0 | 9th | | |
| Walcott | 3 | 0 | 19 | 0 | 10th | | |
| Harper | 5 | 0 | 27 | 0 | | | |
| Ecclesharf | 3 | 0 | 33 | 0 | | | |
| Wundke | 8 | 0 | 42 | 0 | | | |
| Holmes | 7 | 0 | 35 | 1 | | | |

## COMBINED U vs. WEST INDIES

at The Parks on 26th, 27th June 1991
Toss : West Indies.  Umpires : J.D.Bond and J.W.Holder
Match drawn

**WEST INDIES**

| | | | | | |
|---|---|---|---|---|---|
| P.V.Simmons | b Gerrans | 28 | (2) c Crawley b Turner G.J. | | 81 |
| C.B.Lambert | c Crawley b Pearson | 49 | (1) lbw b Oppenheimer | | 14 |
| A.L.Logie | c & b Gerrans | 18 | c Turner R.J. b Jenkins | | 73 |
| B.C.Lara | b Pearson | 1 | b Pearson | | 110 |
| P.J.L.Dujon | run out | 31 | | | |
| D.L.Haynes * | lbw b Gerrans | 1 | (5) st Turner R.J. b Turner G.J. | | 46 |
| M.D.Marshall | b Gerrans | 12 | | | |
| D.Williams + | lbw b Jenkins | 17 | (6) c Gerrans b Turner G.J. | | 14 |
| H.A.G.Anthony | not out | 50 | (7) not out | | 21 |
| I.B.A.Allen | lbw b Jenkins | 8 | (8) not out | | 0 |
| C.A.Walsh | b Oppenheimer | 3 | | | |
| Extras | (b 1,lb 10,w 2,nb 11) | 24 | (b 2,lb 9,w 3,nb 6) | | 20 |
| TOTAL | | 242 | (for 6 wkts dec) | | 379 |

**COMBINED U**

| | | |
|---|---|---|
| A.M.Hooper | c Simmons b Anthony | 18 |
| R.E.Morris | c Simmons b Allen | 1 |
| J.P.Crawley | b Walsh | 9 |
| G.J.Turner * | lbw b Marshall | 3 |
| R.J.Turner + | retired hurt/ill | 19 |
| D.Pfaff | lbw b Anthony | 24 |
| M.J.Lowrey | lbw b Walsh | 22 |
| P.S.Gerrans | c sub b Marshall | 31 |
| R.M.Pearson | not out | 14 |
| R.H.J.Jenkins | st Williams b Lara | 18 |
| J.M.E.Oppenheimer | not out | 1 |
| Extras | (lb 3,nb 12) | 15 |
| TOTAL | (for 8 wkts dec) | 175 |

| COMBINED U | O | M | R | W | O | M | R | W | FALL OF WICKETS | | | |
|---|---|---|---|---|---|---|---|---|---|---|---|---|
| | | | | | | | | | | WI | COM | WI COM |
| Jenkins | 14 | 2 | 48 | 2 | 13 | 2 | 76 | 1 | 1st | 73 | 20 | 22 |
| Oppenheimer | 8.5 | 1 | 36 | 1 | 9 | 1 | 62 | 1 | 2nd | 101 | 20 | 151 |
| Gerrans | 16 | 3 | 45 | 4 | 11 | 2 | 59 | 0 | 3rd | 101 | 35 | 206 |
| Pearson | 24 | 5 | 85 | 2 | 13 | 1 | 80 | 1 | 4th | 103 | 36 | 327 |
| Turner G.J. | 3 | 1 | 17 | 0 | 19 | 0 | 91 | 3 | 5th | 104 | 76 | 345 |
| | | | | | | | | | 6th | 118 | 125 | 377 |
| WEST INDIES | O | M | R | W | O | M | R | W | 7th | 161 | 143 | |
| Allen | 13 | 3 | 38 | 1 | | | | | 8th | 192 | 171 | |
| Anthony | 15 | 2 | 50 | 2 | | | | | 9th | 210 | | |
| Walsh | 12 | 7 | 28 | 2 | | | | | 10th | 242 | | |
| Marshall | 9 | 2 | 31 | 2 | | | | | | | | |
| Simmons | 2 | 0 | 11 | 0 | | | | | | | | |
| Lara | 1 | 0 | 14 | 1 | | | | | | | | |

# HEADLINES

## Tour matches

### 26th - 28th June

• The West Indians preferred extended batting practice in their two-day match against the Combined Universities at The Parks to any attempt to gain victory, Brian Lara making his first 100 of the tour, while Clayton Lambert did likewise in the nine-wicket victory over the League Cricket Conference XI at Trowbridge.

# REFUGE ASSURANCE LEAGUE

## KENT vs. GLOUCESTERSHIRE

at Canterbury on 30th June 1991
Toss : Gloucs. Umpires : J.C.Balderstone and D.R.Shepherd
Kent won by 67 runs. Kent 4 pts, Gloucs 0 pts

### KENT

| | | |
|---|---|---|
| M.V.Fleming | c Babington b Gerrard | 13 |
| M.R.Benson * | run out | 7 |
| N.R.Taylor | c Russell b Alleyne | 39 |
| T.R.Ward | c Russell b Babington | 0 |
| G.R.Cowdrey | b Smith | 80 |
| C.S.Cowdrey | b Smith | 22 |
| S.A.Marsh + | not out | 24 |
| R.P.Davis | not out | 2 |
| M.J.McCague | | |
| T.A.Merrick | | |
| A.P.Igglesden | | |
| Extras | (b 1,lb 13,w 9) | 23 |
| TOTAL | (40 overs)(for 6 wkts) | 210 |

### GLOUCESTERSHIRE

| | | |
|---|---|---|
| R.J.Scott | run out | 58 |
| C.W.J.Athey | c Ward b Davis | 18 |
| A.J.Wright * | c Benson b McCague | 24 |
| J.J.E.Hardy | b McCague | 1 |
| M.W.Alleyne | c Cowdrey G.R. b Igglesden | 1 |
| R.C.Russell + | c Cowdrey C.S. b Merrick | 22 |
| J.W.Lloyds | b Igglesden | 4 |
| T.Hancock | b McCague | 0 |
| M.J.Gerrard | run out | 7 |
| A.M.Smith | not out | 0 |
| A.M.Babington | absent hurt/ill | |
| Extras | (lb 8) | 8 |
| TOTAL | (35.2 overs) | 143 |

| GLOUCS | O | M | R | W | FALL OF WICKETS | | |
|---|---|---|---|---|---|---|---|
| | | | | | | KEN | GLO |
| Gerrard | 8 | 0 | 52 | 1 | 1st | 22 | 41 |
| Babington | 4 | 0 | 15 | 1 | 2nd | 24 | 102 |
| Smith | 8 | 1 | 35 | 2 | 3rd | 26 | 104 |
| Scott | 8 | 1 | 24 | 0 | 4th | 105 | 105 |
| Alleyne | 8 | 0 | 46 | 1 | 5th | 147 | 105 |
| Athey | 4 | 0 | 24 | 0 | 6th | 186 | 115 |
| KENT | O | M | R | W | 7th | | 118 |
| McCague | 8 | 0 | 39 | 3 | 8th | | 142 |
| Igglesden | 8 | 1 | 18 | 2 | 9th | | 143 |
| Davis | 8 | 0 | 37 | 1 | 10th | | |
| Merrick | 5.2 | 1 | 16 | 1 | | | |
| Fleming | 6 | 0 | 25 | 0 | | | |

## ESSEX vs. DERBYSHIRE

at Chelmsford on 30th June 1991
Toss : Derbyshire. Umpires : G.I.Burgess and D.J.Constant
Essex won by 11 runs. Essex 4 pts, Derbyshire 0 pts

### ESSEX

| | | |
|---|---|---|
| G.A.Gooch * | lbw b Base | 56 |
| J.P.Stephenson | c Krikken b Malcolm | 27 |
| Salim Malik | c Krikken b Malcolm | 36 |
| P.J.Prichard | c Mortensen b Malcolm | 40 |
| N.Hussain | b Warner | 15 |
| D.R.Pringle | c Goldsmith b Warner | 4 |
| N.Shahid | b Warner | 6 |
| M.A.Garnham + | not out | 1 |
| T.D.Topley | run out | 1 |
| S.J.W.Andrew | run out | 0 |
| P.M.Such | | |
| Extras | (b 1,lb 6,w 7,nb 2) | 16 |
| TOTAL | (40 overs)(for 9 wkts) | 202 |

### DERBYSHIRE

| | | |
|---|---|---|
| P.D.Bowler | run out | 30 |
| C.J.Adams | c Garnham b Andrew | 0 |
| J.E.Morris * | c Prichard b Such | 46 |
| M.Azharuddin | c Salim Malik b Such | 23 |
| T.J.G.O'Gorman | b Such | 3 |
| S.C.Goldsmith | c Hussain b Such | 4 |
| K.M.Krikken + | not out | 44 |
| A.E.Warner | run out | 12 |
| S.J.Base | lbw b Topley | 1 |
| D.E.Malcolm | c Stephenson b Pringle | 18 |
| O.H.Mortensen | not out | 3 |
| Extras | (lb 4,w 3) | 7 |
| TOTAL | (40 overs)(for 9 wkts) | 191 |

| DERBYSHIRE | O | M | R | W | FALL OF WICKETS | | |
|---|---|---|---|---|---|---|---|
| | | | | | | ESS | DER |
| Mortensen | 8 | 1 | 22 | 0 | 1st | 81 | 2 |
| Warner | 8 | 0 | 38 | 3 | 2nd | 97 | 61 |
| Base | 8 | 0 | 46 | 1 | 3rd | 171 | 87 |
| Goldsmith | 8 | 0 | 46 | 0 | 4th | 171 | 98 |
| Malcolm | 8 | 1 | 43 | 3 | 5th | 185 | 106 |
| ESSEX | O | M | R | W | 6th | 199 | 111 |
| Andrew | 8 | 0 | 43 | 1 | 7th | 201 | 136 |
| Pringle | 8 | 0 | 49 | 1 | 8th | 202 | 141 |
| Topley | 8 | 1 | 29 | 1 | 9th | 202 | 186 |
| Gooch | 8 | 0 | 36 | 0 | 10th | | |
| Such | 8 | 0 | 30 | 4 | | | |

## NORTHANTS vs. SOMERSET

at Luton on 30th June 1991
Toss : Northants. Umpires : J.H.Harris and R.A.White
Northants won by 4 wickets. Northants 4 pts, Som 0 pts

### SOMERSET

| | | |
|---|---|---|
| S.J.Cook | c Bailey b Walker | 5 |
| P.M.Roebuck | b Walker | 0 |
| C.J.Tavare * | c Ripley b Curran | 23 |
| R.J.Harden | run out | 1 |
| A.N.Hayhurst | run out | 2 |
| N.D.Burns + | c Bailey b Curran | 24 |
| G.D.Rose | b Curran | 2 |
| R.P.Lefebvre | c Taylor b Capel | 24 |
| K.H.Macleay | not out | 12 |
| N.A.Mallender | not out | 13 |
| D.A.Graveney | | |
| Extras | (lb 4,w 16) | 20 |
| TOTAL | (40 overs)(for 8 wkts) | 126 |

### NORTHANTS

| | | |
|---|---|---|
| A.Fordham | lbw b Roebuck | 67 |
| N.A.Felton | b Mallender | 10 |
| D.J.Capel | lbw b Macleay | 1 |
| R.J.Bailey | c Hayhurst b Graveney | 19 |
| A.J.Lamb * | b Roebuck | 3 |
| K.M.Curran | b Roebuck | 3 |
| E.A.E.Baptiste | not out | 10 |
| D.Ripley + | not out | 6 |
| J.P.Taylor | | |
| N.G.B.Cook | | |
| A.Walker | | |
| Extras | (b 1,lb 6,w 2,nb 1) | 10 |
| TOTAL | (37.2 overs)(for 6 wkts) | 129 |

| NORTHANTS | O | M | R | W | FALL OF WICKETS | | |
|---|---|---|---|---|---|---|---|
| | | | | | | SOM | NOR |
| Taylor | 8 | 1 | 22 | 0 | 1st | 5 | 36 |
| Walker | 8 | 2 | 7 | 2 | 2nd | 6 | 45 |
| Baptiste | 8 | 0 | 43 | 0 | 3rd | 11 | 100 |
| Curran | 8 | 1 | 24 | 3 | 4th | 22 | 103 |
| Capel | 8 | 0 | 26 | 1 | 5th | 68 | 109 |
| SOMERSET | O | M | R | W | 6th | 70 | 118 |
| Mallender | 8 | 0 | 31 | 1 | 7th | 81 | |
| Lefebvre | 5 | 0 | 25 | 0 | 8th | 103 | |
| Macleay | 8 | 0 | 24 | 1 | 9th | | |
| Graveney | 8 | 1 | 23 | 1 | 10th | | |
| Roebuck | 8 | 2 | 15 | 3 | | | |
| Hayhurst | 0.2 | 0 | 4 | 0 | | | |

## SURREY vs. NOTTS

at The Oval on 30th June 1991
Toss : Notts. Umpires : H.D.Bird and B.Leadbeater
Notts won on faster scoring rate. Surrey 0 pts, Notts 4 pts

### SURREY

| | | |
|---|---|---|
| D.J.Bicknell | run out | 64 |
| M.A.Lynch | c Johnson b Hemmings | 33 |
| A.J.Stewart + | lbw b Stephenson | 1 |
| D.M.Ward | c & b Crawley | 4 |
| G.P.Thorpe | c Crawley b Evans | 34 |
| J.D.Robinson | b Evans | 6 |
| I.A.Greig * | c & b Crawley | 3 |
| M.A.Feltham | not out | 14 |
| M.P.Bicknell | c Robinson b Stephenson | 11 |
| Waqar Younis | run out | 0 |
| A.J.Murphy | | |
| Extras | (lb 7,w 6,nb 2) | 15 |
| TOTAL | (40 overs)(for 9 wkts) | 185 |

### NOTTS

| | | |
|---|---|---|
| B.C.Broad | not out | 79 |
| D.W.Randall | b Waqar Younis | 67 |
| P.Johnson | lbw b Waqar Younis | 0 |
| R.T.Robinson * | not out | 3 |
| M.A.Crawley | | |
| M.Saxelby | | |
| F.D.Stephenson | | |
| K.P.Evans | | |
| B.N.French + | | |
| E.E.Hemmings | | |
| R.A.Pick | | |
| Extras | (lb 7,w 6) | 13 |
| TOTAL | (32 overs)(for 2 wkts) | 162 |

| NOTTS | O | M | R | W | FALL OF WICKETS | | |
|---|---|---|---|---|---|---|---|
| | | | | | | SUR | NOT |
| Pick | 6 | 0 | 24 | 0 | 1st | 98 | 154 |
| Stephenson | 8 | 1 | 27 | 2 | 2nd | 100 | 154 |
| Evans | 8 | 0 | 43 | 2 | 3rd | 111 | |
| Saxelby | 4 | 0 | 28 | 0 | 4th | 116 | |
| Hemmings | 8 | 0 | 36 | 1 | 5th | 139 | |
| Crawley | 6 | 1 | 20 | 2 | 6th | 150 | |
| SURREY | O | M | R | W | 7th | 161 | |
| Murphy | 8 | 0 | 26 | 0 | 8th | 185 | |
| Bicknell M.P. | 8 | 0 | 39 | 0 | 9th | 185 | |
| Feltham | 6 | 0 | 43 | 0 | 10th | | |
| Waqar Younis | 8 | 0 | 33 | 2 | | | |
| Robinson | 2 | 0 | 14 | 0 | | | |

# REFUGE ASSURANCE LEAGUE

## WORCESTERSHIRE vs. LEICS

at Worcester on 30th June 1991
Toss : Leics. Umpires : J.H.Hampshire and K.J.Lyons
Worcestershire won by 7 wickets. Worcs 4 pts, Leics 0 pts

**LEICESTERSHIRE**

| | | |
|---|---|---|
| J.J.Whitaker | c Lampitt b Radford | 63 |
| N.E.Briers * | st Rhodes b Illingworth | 29 |
| P.A.Nixon + | b Illingworth | 17 |
| C.C.Lewis | c D'Oliveira b Newport | 28 |
| B.F.Smith | not out | 30 |
| L.Potter | not out | 31 |
| P.Willey | | |
| J.D.R.Benson | | |
| D.J.Millns | | |
| C.Wilkinson | | |
| J.N.Maguire | | |
| Extras | (lb 4,w 1) | 5 |
| TOTAL | (40 overs)(for 4 wkts) | 203 |

**WORCESTERSHIRE**

| | | |
|---|---|---|
| T.S.Curtis | not out | 88 |
| T.M.Moody | b Lewis | 9 |
| G.A.Hick | c Whitaker b Maguire | 84 |
| D.B.D'Oliveira | c & b Benson | 1 |
| P.A.Neale * | not out | 18 |
| S.J.Rhodes + | | |
| R.K.Illingworth | | |
| S.R.Lampitt | | |
| P.J.Newport | | |
| C.M.Tolley | | |
| N.V.Radford | | |
| Extras | (lb 6,w 1) | 7 |
| TOTAL | (38.2 overs)(for 3 wkts) | 207 |

| WORCS | O | M | R | W | FALL OF WICKETS | | |
|---|---|---|---|---|---|---|---|
| | | | | | | LEI | WOR |
| Radford | 8 | 0 | 48 | 1 | | | |
| Tolley | 5 | 0 | 41 | 0 | 1st | 65 | 13 |
| Lampitt | 8 | 0 | 35 | 0 | 2nd | 91 | 170 |
| Illingworth | 8 | 1 | 19 | 2 | 3rd | 137 | 173 |
| Newport | 8 | 0 | 37 | 1 | 4th | 148 | |
| Hick | 3 | 0 | 19 | 0 | 5th | | |
| | | | | | 6th | | |
| LEICS | O | M | R | W | 7th | | |
| Lewis | 7.2 | 1 | 37 | 1 | 8th | | |
| Maguire | 8 | 0 | 28 | 1 | 9th | | |
| Millns | 4 | 0 | 28 | 0 | 10th | | |
| Benson | 8 | 0 | 38 | 1 | | | |
| Wilkinson | 7 | 0 | 46 | 0 | | | |
| Willey | 4 | 0 | 24 | 0 | | | |

## YORKSHIRE vs. GLAMORGAN

at Headingley on 30th June 1991
Toss : Glamorgan. Umpires : B.Hassan and J.W.Holder
Yorkshire won by 95 runs. Yorks 4 pts, Glamorgan 0 pts

**YORKSHIRE**

| | | |
|---|---|---|
| M.D.Moxon * | c Frost b Dale | 52 |
| A.A.Metcalfe | lbw b Watkin | 96 |
| R.J.Blakey + | c Dale b Frost | 47 |
| D.Byas | c Dale b Frost | 14 |
| P.E.Robinson | not out | 21 |
| C.S.Pickles | not out | 8 |
| P.Carrick | | |
| D.Gough | | |
| P.J.Hartley | | |
| J.D.Batty | | |
| S.D.Fletcher | | |
| Extras | (lb 8,w 6,nb 1) | 15 |
| TOTAL | (40 overs)(for 4 wkts) | 253 |

**GLAMORGAN**

| | | |
|---|---|---|
| M.P.Maynard | c Blakey b Carrick | 44 |
| H.Morris * | c Blakey b Gough | 20 |
| G.C.Holmes | c Batty b Carrick | 6 |
| R.J.Shastri | c Fletcher b Carrick | 4 |
| I.Smith | c Robinson b Carrick | 23 |
| A.Dale | not out | 20 |
| J.Derrick | c Fletcher b Carrick | 5 |
| S.L.Watkin | b Fletcher | 14 |
| S.R.Barwick | b Hartley | 8 |
| C.P.Metson + | | |
| M.Frost | | |
| Extras | (b 3,lb 7,w 4) | 14 |
| TOTAL | (40 overs)(for 8 wkts) | 158 |

| GLAMORGAN | O | M | R | W | FALL OF WICKETS | | |
|---|---|---|---|---|---|---|---|
| | | | | | | YOR | GLA |
| Frost | 8 | 0 | 53 | 2 | | | |
| Watkin | 8 | 0 | 40 | 1 | 1st | 116 | 49 |
| Derrick | 4 | 0 | 37 | 0 | 2nd | 207 | 77 |
| Barwick | 7 | 0 | 47 | 0 | 3rd | 214 | 78 |
| Dale | 8 | 0 | 43 | 1 | 4th | 224 | 89 |
| Smith | 5 | 0 | 25 | 0 | 5th | | 112 |
| | | | | | 6th | | 123 |
| YORKSHIRE | O | M | R | W | 7th | | 147 |
| Fletcher | 7 | 0 | 31 | 1 | 8th | | 158 |
| Hartley | 8 | 0 | 24 | 1 | 9th | | |
| Gough | 5 | 0 | 26 | 1 | 10th | | |
| Pickles | 4 | 0 | 11 | 0 | | | |
| Carrick | 8 | 1 | 22 | 5 | | | |
| Batty | 8 | 0 | 34 | 0 | | | |

### Refuge Assurance League Table as at 30th June 1991

| | | P | W | L | T | NR | Away | Pts | Run Rate |
|---|---|---|---|---|---|---|---|---|---|
| 1 | Notts (4) | 9 | 8 | 1 | 0 | 0 | 5 | 32 | 82.75 |
| 2 | Lancashire (2) | 8 | 6 | 1 | 0 | 1 | 3 | 26 | 101.49 |
| 3 | Somerset (8) | 10 | 5 | 3 | 0 | 2 | 3 | 24 | 77.55 |
| 4 | Worcestershire (10) | 10 | 4 | 3 | 1 | 2 | 2 | 22 | 93.95 |
| 5 | Essex (12) | 10 | 3 | 2 | 1 | 4 | 0 | 22 | 82.70 |
| 6 | Yorkshire (6) | 9 | 5 | 4 | 0 | 0 | 1 | 20 | 83.52 |
| 7 | Surrey (7) | 9 | 4 | 3 | 0 | 2 | 3 | 20 | 80.44 |
| 8 | Northants (17) | 9 | 4 | 3 | 0 | 2 | 1 | 20 | 88.95 |
| 9 | Warwickshire (14) | 9 | 3 | 2 | 1 | 3 | 2 | 20 | 82.77 |
| 10 | Middlesex (3) | 9 | 4 | 4 | 0 | 1 | 4 | 18 | 81.63 |
| 11 | Gloucs (9) | 9 | 3 | 4 | 0 | 2 | 2 | 16 | 82.92 |
| 12 | Kent (11) | 9 | 3 | 4 | 1 | 1 | 1 | 16 | 90.88 |
| 13 | Leicestershire (16) | 9 | 3 | 5 | 0 | 1 | 1 | 14 | 76.55 |
| 14 | Sussex (13) | 9 | 2 | 5 | 0 | 2 | 2 | 12 | 82.51 |
| 15 | Hampshire (5) | 8 | 2 | 5 | 0 | 1 | 0 | 10 | 78.98 |
| 16 | Derbyshire (1) | 8 | 2 | 6 | 0 | 0 | 1 | 8 | 83.06 |
| 17 | Glamorgan (15) | 10 | 1 | 7 | 0 | 2 | 0 | 8 | 76.19 |

Five wickets for Phil Carrick at Headingley.

# BRITANNIC ASSURANCE CHAMPIONSHIP

## WORCESTERSHIRE vs. LEICESTERSHIRE

at Worcester on 28th, 29th June, 1st July 1991
Toss : Worcs.  Umpires : J.H.Hampshire and K.J.Lyons
Match drawn.  Worcestershire 4 pts (Bt: 2, Bw: 2), Leicestershire 5 pts (Bt: 3, Bw: 2)
100 overs scores : Leicestershire 278 for 5

### LEICESTERSHIRE

| | | | | |
|---|---|---|---|---|
| T.J.Boon | c Neale b Newport | 76 | lbw b Radford | 38 |
| N.E.Briers * | c Rhodes b Lampitt | 29 | lbw b Botham | 104 |
| P.N.Hepworth | c Rhodes b Newport | 19 | | |
| J.J.Whitaker | c Curtis b Newport | 10 | (3) lbw b Botham | 23 |
| L.Potter | c Rhodes b Lampitt | 15 | (4) not out | 16 |
| B.F.Smith | c Lampitt b Newport | 71 | (5) not out | 8 |
| C.C.Lewis | lbw b Botham | 68 | | |
| P.Willey | not out | 0 | | |
| P.A.Nixon + | | | | |
| C.Wilkinson | | | | |
| J.N.Maguire | | | | |
| Extras | (b 3,lb 9,nb 5) | 17 | (lb 13,nb 2) | 15 |
| TOTAL | (for 7 wkts dec) | 305 | (for 3 wkts dec) | 204 |

### WORCESTERSHIRE

| | | | | |
|---|---|---|---|---|
| T.S.Curtis | c Nixon b Maguire | 0 | lbw b Lewis | 47 |
| G.J.Lord | c Potter b Willey | 43 | b Maguire | 64 |
| G.A.Hick | lbw b Maguire | 0 | b Lewis | 24 |
| T.M.Moody | c Willey b Lewis | 25 | c Wilkinson b Lewis | 13 |
| P.A.Neale * | not out | 69 | (6) not out | 0 |
| I.T.Botham | lbw b Lewis | 8 | (5) not out | 3 |
| S.J.Rhodes + | lbw b Lewis | 36 | | |
| R.K.Illingworth | not out | 17 | | |
| S.R.Lampitt | | | | |
| P.J.Newport | | | | |
| N.V.Radford | | | | |
| Extras | (lb 2) | 2 | (b 4,lb 7) | 11 |
| TOTAL | (for 6 wkts dec) | 200 | (for 4 wkts) | 162 |

| WORCS | O | M | R | W | O | M | R | W |
|---|---|---|---|---|---|---|---|---|
| Radford | 17 | 5 | 48 | 0 | 19 | 6 | 55 | 1 |
| Newport | 18.2 | 2 | 70 | 4 | 20 | 6 | 48 | 0 |
| Botham | 17 | 4 | 59 | 1 | 7 | 2 | 26 | 2 |
| Lampitt | 19 | 5 | 42 | 2 | 16 | 0 | 40 | 0 |
| Illingworth | 30 | 14 | 64 | 0 | 4 | 1 | 10 | 0 |
| Hick | 2 | 0 | 10 | 0 | | | | |
| Neale | | | | | 1 | 0 | 5 | 0 |
| Moody | | | | | 0.4 | 0 | 7 | 0 |

| LEICS | O | M | R | W | O | M | R | W |
|---|---|---|---|---|---|---|---|---|
| Lewis | 25 | 10 | 40 | 3 | 19 | 4 | 39 | 3 |
| Maguire | 24 | 7 | 61 | 2 | 20 | 2 | 65 | 1 |
| Wilkinson | 16 | 7 | 49 | 0 | 5 | 1 | 33 | 0 |
| Willey | 8 | 2 | 19 | 1 | 3 | 0 | 14 | 0 |
| Potter | 9 | 3 | 29 | 0 | | | | |

| FALL OF WICKETS | | | | |
|---|---|---|---|---|
| | LEI | WOR | LEI | WOR |
| 1st | 69 | 7 | 119 | 90 |
| 2nd | 124 | 7 | 173 | 134 |
| 3rd | 144 | 68 | 188 | 154 |
| 4th | 145 | 70 | | 161 |
| 5th | 199 | 82 | | |
| 6th | 301 | 164 | | |
| 7th | 305 | | | |
| 8th | | | | |
| 9th | | | | |
| 10th | | | | |

## SURREY vs. SOMERSET

at The Oval on 28th (no play), 29th June, 1st July 1991
Toss : Surrey.  Umpires : H.D.Bird and B.Leadbeater
Match drawn.  Surrey 3 pts (Bt: 0, Bw: 3), Somerset 4 pts (Bt: 4, Bw: 0)
100 overs scores : Somerset 313 for 7

### SOMERSET

| | | |
|---|---|---|
| S.J.Cook | b Murphy | 41 |
| P.M.Roebuck | c Thorpe b Waqar Younis | 47 |
| A.N.Hayhurst | c Thorpe b Bicknell M.P. | 9 |
| C.J.Tavare * | c Bicknell M.P. b Murphy | 18 |
| R.J.Harden | b Bicknell M.P. | 13 |
| N.D.Burns + | c Sargeant b Bicknell M.P. | 39 |
| K.H.Macleay | c Ward b Medlycott | 57 |
| R.P.Lefebvre | c Murphy b Medlycott | 93 |
| N.A.Mallender | not out | 12 |
| D.A.Graveney | not out | 0 |
| A.P.van Troost | | |
| Extras | (b 2,lb 11,w 1,nb 13) | 27 |
| TOTAL | (for 8 wkts dec) | 356 |

### SURREY

| | | |
|---|---|---|
| D.J.Bicknell | b van Troost | 15 |
| R.I.Alikhan | c Burns b Mallender | 6 |
| A.J.Stewart | c Harden b Mallender | 3 |
| D.M.Ward | c sub b Graveney | 71 |
| G.P.Thorpe | c Graveney b Macleay | 2 |
| I.A.Greig * | c Roebuck b Macleay | 0 |
| K.T.Medlycott | c Lefebvre b Graveney | 52 |
| N.F.Sargeant + | not out | 16 |
| M.P.Bicknell | not out | 1 |
| Waqar Younis | | |
| A.J.Murphy | | |
| Extras | (b 1,lb 2,w 1,nb 2) | 6 |
| TOTAL | (for 7 wkts) | 172 |

| SURREY | O | M | R | W | O | M | R | W |
|---|---|---|---|---|---|---|---|---|
| Waqar Younis | 21 | 1 | 86 | 1 | | | | |
| Bicknell M.P. | 28 | 2 | 56 | 3 | | | | |
| Murphy | 27 | 4 | 84 | 2 | | | | |
| Greig | 9 | 3 | 20 | 0 | | | | |
| Medlycott | 25 | 2 | 97 | 2 | | | | |

| SOMERSET | O | M | R | W | O | M | R | W |
|---|---|---|---|---|---|---|---|---|
| Mallender | | | | | 11 | 2 | 44 | 2 |
| van Troost | | | | | 12.4 | 0 | 55 | 1 |
| Graveney | | | | | 17 | 4 | 30 | 2 |
| Macleay | | | | | 11 | 2 | 25 | 2 |
| Lefebvre | | | | | 2 | 0 | 8 | 0 |
| Roebuck | | | | | 3 | 1 | 7 | 0 |

| FALL OF WICKETS | | | | |
|---|---|---|---|---|
| | SOM | SUR | SOM | SUR |
| 1st | 60 | | | 21 |
| 2nd | 79 | | | 25 |
| 3rd | 121 | | | 27 |
| 4th | 123 | | | 37 |
| 5th | 152 | | | 37 |
| 6th | 210 | | | 135 |
| 7th | 291 | | | 161 |
| 8th | 356 | | | |
| 9th | | | | |
| 10th | | | | |

## HEADLINES

### Britannic Assurance Championship

### 28th June - 1st July

• Warwickshire's leading position in the Championship table looked decidedly vulnerable after their heavy 173-run defeat by fourth-placed Derbyshire at Edgbaston. Mohammad Azharuddin led a wristy counter-attack against the home side's bowlers with such success that Warwickshire needed to score 310 for victory in the fourth innings, a task which always looked beyond their batsmen. Devon Malcolm boosted his confidence with his best figures of the season, as Derbyshire gained their third successive victory.

• Essex returned to winning ways to reclaim second place with a convincing 113-run success over champions Middlesex at Lord's. The first three innings had been marked by centuries from Paul Prichard, Mike Gatting and Graham Gooch respectively, but the home side's batsmen could not come to terms with  a target of 250.

• Gloucestershire defeated Northamptonshire by three wickets after an evenly balanced contest at Luton. The irrepressible David Lawrence recorded his best figures of the season to bowl out Northants for 188, but the home side still gained a lead of 21 and, after Jerry Lloyds had claimed all six wickets in Northants' second innings, Allan Lamb left the visitors needing the highest score of the match to win. This they achieved with an unbroken eighth-wicket stand of 59 between Jack Russell and Lawrence, despite a career-best four for 63 from leg-spinner Andy Roberts.

• At Liverpool, Lancashire could not add to their string of victories, as they were denied by a formidable batting display from their opponents, Glamorgan. Alan Butcher hit 100s in each innings and he was given excellent support by Ravi Shastri and Matthew Maynard, but Neil Fairbrother, with a first innings 100, was the only Lancashire batsman to respond.

• Surrey escaped with a draw against Somerset at The Oval after being reduced to 37 for five as they attempted a victory target of 357 after both sides had forfeited an innings, rain having claimed the first day's play. Roland Lefebvre made a career best 93 to bring Somerset's first innings total to a healthy 356 for eight.

• Worcestershire and Leicestershire were also content to draw at Worcester, as the home side finished at 162 for four, after being set a target of 310 for victory. Ben Smith, with a career best 71, and Chris Lewis, who also took six wickets in the match, enlivened the opening day for Leicestershire with a sixth-wicket stand of 102, but Worcestershire's batting never looked like succeeding in a last afternoon run-chase.

• First-class début: A.P. van Troost (Somerset).

# BRITANNIC ASSURANCE CHAMPIONSHIP

## MIDDLESEX vs. ESSEX

at Lord's on 28th, 29th June, 1st July 1991
Toss : Essex. Umpires : J.C.Balderstone and D.R.Shepherd
Essex won by 113 runs. Middlesex 5 pts (Bt: 3, Bw: 2), Essex 20 pts (Bt: 4, Bw: 0)

**ESSEX**

| | | | | | |
|---|---|---|---|---|---|
| G.A.Gooch * | c Farbrace b Williams | 47 | c Roseberry b Farbrace | 106 |
| J.P.Stephenson | c Farbrace b Cowans | 2 | c Hughes b Tufnell | 38 |
| P.J.Prichard | c Hutchinson b Cowans | 129 | b Tufnell | 0 |
| Salim Malik | c Emburey b Tufnell | 8 | (5) not out | 12 |
| N.Hussain | c & b Tufnell | 0 | | |
| M.A.Garnham + | not out | 91 | | |
| D.R.Pringle | not out | 0 | | |
| J.H.Childs | | | (4) not out | 41 |
| N.A.Foster | | | | |
| S.J.W.Andrew | | | | |
| P.M.Such | | | | |
| Extras | (b 4,lb 10,nb 12) | 26 | (lb 3,w 1) | 4 |
| TOTAL | (for 5 wkts dec) | 303 | (for 3 wkts dec) | 201 |

**MIDDLESEX**

| | | | | | |
|---|---|---|---|---|---|
| I.J.F.Hutchinson | c Gooch b Foster | 4 | c Salim Malik b Foster | 3 |
| M.A.Roseberry | lbw b Stephenson | 24 | lbw b Foster | 19 |
| M.W.Gatting * | not out | 138 | (8) not out | 11 |
| M.R.Ramprakash | not out | 70 | (3) lbw b Foster | 12 |
| K.R.Brown | | | (4) c Foster b Pringle | 23 |
| J.E.Emburey | | | (5) lbw b Pringle | 46 |
| P.Farbrace + | | | (6) c Garnham b Foster | 4 |
| N.F.Williams | | | (7) c Garnham b Pringle | 0 |
| S.P.Hughes | | | c Hussain b Andrew | 2 |
| P.C.R.Tufnell | | | c Garnham b Andrew | 4 |
| N.G.Cowans | | | c & b Andrew | 0 |
| Extras | (b 4,lb 6,nb 8) | 18 | (lb 6,nb 7) | 13 |
| TOTAL | (for 2 wkts dec) | 254 | | 137 |

| MIDDLESEX | O | M | R | W | O | M | R | W | FALL OF WICKETS | | | | |
|---|---|---|---|---|---|---|---|---|---|---|---|---|---|
| | | | | | | | | | | ESS | MID | ESS | MID |
| Cowans | 23 | 6 | 61 | 2 | 7 | 2 | 29 | 0 | 1st | 7 | 14 | 84 | 11 |
| Williams | 28.4 | 7 | 89 | 1 | 3.1 | 2 | 4 | 0 | 2nd | 88 | 91 | 84 | 38 |
| Hughes | 12 | 1 | 71 | 0 | 3.5 | 0 | 13 | 0 | 3rd | 113 | | 185 | 45 |
| Emburey | 8 | 0 | 33 | 0 | 9 | 2 | 50 | 0 | 4th | 117 | | | 107 |
| Tufnell | 14 | 5 | 35 | 2 | 6 | 2 | 16 | 2 | 5th | 291 | | | 114 |
| Hutchinson | | | | | 1 | 0 | 1 | 0 | 6th | | | | 114 |
| Roseberry | | | | | 2 | 0 | 21 | 0 | 7th | | | | 122 |
| Farbrace | | | | | 4.1 | 0 | 64 | 1 | 8th | | | | 131 |
| | | | | | | | | | 9th | | | | 136 |
| ESSEX | O | M | R | W | O | M | R | W | 10th | | | | 137 |
| Foster | 14.2 | 1 | 62 | 1 | 16 | 6 | 36 | 4 | | | | | |
| Andrew | 18 | 6 | 71 | 0 | 14 | 4 | 30 | 3 | | | | | |
| Pringle | 13 | 2 | 44 | 0 | 14 | 5 | 38 | 3 | | | | | |
| Stephenson | 6 | 2 | 16 | 1 | | | | | | | | | |
| Such | 5 | 0 | 22 | 0 | | | | | | | | | |
| Childs | 5 | 0 | 29 | 0 | 8 | 2 | 27 | 0 | | | | | |

## LANCASHIRE vs. GLAMORGAN

at Liverpool on 28th, 29th, 1st July 1991
Toss : Lancashire. Umpires : J.D.Bond and N.T.Plews
Match drawn. Lancashire 4 pts (Bt: 3, Bw: 1), Glamorgan 6 pts (Bt: 4, Bw: 2)
100 overs scores : Glamorgan 392 for 3

**GLAMORGAN**

| | | | | | |
|---|---|---|---|---|---|
| A.R.Butcher * | c & b Yates | 129 | c Watkinson b DeFreitas | 104 |
| H.Morris | lbw b Watkinson | 35 | c Hegg b DeFreitas | 28 |
| R.J.Shastri | not out | 133 | not out | 58 |
| M.P.Maynard | c Atherton b Austin | 89 | not out | 43 |
| P.A.Cottey | not out | 2 | | |
| A.Dale | | | | |
| R.D.B.Croft | | | | |
| C.P.Metson + | | | | |
| S.L.Watkin | | | | |
| S.R.Barwick | | | | |
| S.Bastien | | | | |
| Extras | (lb 1,nb 4) | 5 | (lb 4) | 4 |
| TOTAL | (for 3 wkts dec) | 393 | (for 2 wkts dec) | 237 |

**LANCASHIRE**

| | | | | | |
|---|---|---|---|---|---|
| G.D.Mendis | c Bastien b Watkin | 15 | not out | 18 |
| G.Fowler | c Metson b Bastien | 4 | | |
| W.K.Hegg + | c Dale b Watkin | 6 | (5) not out | 11 |
| M.A.Atherton | c Metson b Croft | 43 | | |
| N.H.Fairbrother * | not out | 107 | | |
| N.J.Speak | b Dale | 38 | (2) c Metson b Watkin | 17 |
| M.Watkinson | not out | 20 | (3) b Watkin | 21 |
| P.A.J.DeFreitas | | | (4) c Croft b Bastien | 12 |
| G.Yates | | | | |
| I.D.Austin | | | | |
| P.J.Martin | | | | |
| Extras | (lb 10,w 1,nb 8) | 19 | (nb 1) | 1 |
| TOTAL | (for 5 wkts dec) | 252 | (for 3 wkts) | 80 |

| LANCASHIRE | O | M | R | W | O | M | R | W | FALL OF WICKETS | | | | |
|---|---|---|---|---|---|---|---|---|---|---|---|---|---|
| | | | | | | | | | | GLA | LAN | GLA | LAN |
| DeFreitas | 18 | 3 | 71 | 0 | 23 | 1 | 78 | 2 | 1st | 70 | 9 | 59 | 20 |
| Martin | 16 | 2 | 55 | 0 | 16 | 1 | 57 | 0 | 2nd | 327 | 16 | 176 | 50 |
| Watkinson | 20 | 1 | 84 | 1 | 1 | 0 | 8 | 0 | 3rd | 383 | 38 | | 63 |
| Yates | 24 | 1 | 109 | 1 | 13 | 1 | 66 | 0 | 4th | | 118 | | |
| Austin | 23 | 2 | 73 | 1 | 7 | 0 | 24 | 0 | 5th | | 212 | | |
| | | | | | | | | | 6th | | | | |
| GLAMORGAN | O | M | R | W | O | M | R | W | 7th | | | | |
| Watkin | 18 | 3 | 71 | 2 | 9 | 0 | 40 | 2 | 8th | | | | |
| Bastien | 16 | 5 | 55 | 1 | 8 | 0 | 40 | 1 | 9th | | | | |
| Barwick | 16 | 3 | 45 | 0 | | | | | 10th | | | | |
| Croft | 22 | 8 | 34 | 1 | | | | | | | | | |
| Shastri | 3 | 0 | 11 | 0 | | | | | | | | | |
| Dale | 4.1 | 1 | 26 | 1 | | | | | | | | | |

## NORTHANTS vs. GLOUCS

at Luton on 28th, 29th June, 1st July 1991
Toss : Gloucs. Umpires : J.H.Harris and R.A.White
Gloucs won by 3 wickets. Northants 5 pts (Bt: 1, Bw: 4), Gloucs 21 pts (Bt: 1, Bw: 4)

**NORTHANTS**

| | | | | | |
|---|---|---|---|---|---|
| A.Fordham | lbw b Lawrence | 1 | c Alleyne b Lloyds | 24 |
| N.A.Felton | lbw b Lawrence | 0 | c & b Lloyds | 4 |
| R.J.Bailey | lbw b Smith | 57 | c Lawrence b Lloyds | 30 |
| A.J.Lamb * | c Russell b Lawrence | 3 | b Lloyds | 51 |
| D.J.Capel | b Lawrence | 5 | c sub b Lloyds | 5 |
| K.M.Curran | c Russell b Lawrence | 5 | not out | 22 |
| E.A.E.Baptiste | c Russell b Gilbert | 51 | c Scott b Lloyds | 44 |
| D.Ripley + | c Alleyne b Lawrence | 34 | not out | 8 |
| A.R.Roberts | not out | 18 | | |
| N.G.B.Cook | b Lloyds | 6 | | |
| J.P.Taylor | c Russell b Lloyds | 0 | | |
| Extras | (lb 2,w 1,nb 5) | 8 | (b 3,lb 5,nb 3) | 11 |
| TOTAL | | 188 | (for 6 wkts dec) | 199 |

**GLOUCS**

| | | | | | |
|---|---|---|---|---|---|
| G.D.Hodgson | lbw b Taylor | 1 | lbw b Cook | 60 |
| J.J.E.Hardy | lbw b Curran | 0 | (6) c & b Roberts | 12 |
| A.J.Wright * | b Baptiste | 14 | c Curran b Roberts | 20 |
| C.W.J.Athey | c Capel b Taylor | 33 | c Fordham b Roberts | 17 |
| J.W.Lloyds | c Taylor b Curran | 26 | (7) c Ripley b Baptiste | 1 |
| M.W.Alleyne | b Curran | 22 | (5) c Lamb b Roberts | 0 |
| R.J.Scott | c Curran b Capel | 17 | (2) c & b Baptiste | 50 |
| R.C.Russell + | not out | 34 | not out | 20 |
| D.V.Lawrence | c Baptiste b Cook | 2 | not out | 36 |
| A.M.Smith | c Ripley b Capel | 1 | | |
| D.R.Gilbert | c Ripley b Taylor | 3 | | |
| Extras | (lb 11,w 3) | 14 | (b 1,lb 6) | 7 |
| TOTAL | | 167 | (for 7 wkts) | 223 |

| GLOUCS | O | M | R | W | O | M | R | W | FALL OF WICKETS | | | | |
|---|---|---|---|---|---|---|---|---|---|---|---|---|---|
| | | | | | | | | | | NOR | GLO | NOR | GLO |
| Lawrence | 27.2 | 8 | 67 | 6 | 2 | 2 | 0 | 0 | 1st | 1 | 1 | 11 | 90 |
| Gilbert | 15.4 | 3 | 43 | 1 | | | | | 2nd | 4 | 7 | 50 | 127 |
| Smith | 14 | 3 | 41 | 1 | 2 | 0 | 8 | 0 | 3rd | 12 | 37 | 109 | 139 |
| Lloyds | 17 | 6 | 35 | 2 | 21 | 4 | 94 | 6 | 4th | 22 | 74 | 114 | 144 |
| Scott | 2 | 2 | 0 | 0 | 9 | 1 | 50 | 0 | 5th | 32 | 95 | 123 | 162 |
| Athey | | | | | 12 | 6 | 29 | 0 | 6th | 99 | 125 | 181 | 163 |
| Russell | | | | | 0.3 | 0 | 10 | 0 | 7th | 141 | 127 | | 164 |
| | | | | | | | | | 8th | 172 | 145 | | |
| NORTHANTS | O | M | R | W | O | M | R | W | 9th | 180 | 146 | | |
| Taylor | 18.5 | 7 | 31 | 3 | 5 | 1 | 37 | 0 | 10th | 188 | 167 | | |
| Curran | 17 | 9 | 23 | 3 | 7 | 3 | 16 | 0 | | | | | |
| Cook | 19 | 4 | 34 | 1 | 14 | 0 | 42 | 1 | | | | | |
| Baptiste | 15 | 5 | 34 | 1 | 17 | 2 | 58 | 2 | | | | | |
| Capel | 9 | 2 | 34 | 2 | | | | | | | | | |
| Roberts | | | | | 24 | 8 | 63 | 4 | | | | | |

## WARWICKSHIRE vs. DERBYSHIRE

at Edgbaston on 28th, 29th June, 1st July 1991
Toss : Warwickshire. Umpires : B.J.Meyer and K.E.Palmer
Derby won by 173 runs. Warwickshire 7 pts (Bt: 3, Bw: 4), Derby 23 pts (Bt: 3, Bw: 4)

**DERBYSHIRE**

| | | | | | |
|---|---|---|---|---|---|
| K.J.Barnett * | lbw b Munton | 12 | c Reeve b Donald | 0 |
| P.D.Bowler | c Munton b Small | 40 | run out | 2 |
| J.E.Morris | c Donald b Munton | 24 | run out | 99 |
| M.Azharuddin | c Piper b Munton | 100 | (6) c Small b Booth | 73 |
| T.J.G.O'Gorman | c Munton b Small | 5 | (4) lbw b Donald | 37 |
| S.C.Goldsmith | b Small | 49 | (5) lbw b Reeve | 19 |
| K.M.Krikken + | b Reeve | 13 | lbw b Munton | 14 |
| D.G.Cork | lbw b Munton | 0 | c Piper b Munton | 13 |
| A.E.Warner | c Piper b Munton | 0 | not out | 13 |
| D.E.Malcolm | b Small | 15 | | |
| O.H.Mortensen | not out | 0 | | |
| Extras | (nb 2) | 2 | (b 9,lb 5,w 9,nb 6) | 29 |
| TOTAL | | 260 | (for 8 wkts dec) | 299 |

**WARWICKSHIRE**

| | | | | | |
|---|---|---|---|---|---|
| A.J.Moles | c Krikken b Warner | 40 | c Krikken b Malcolm | 1 |
| J.D.Ratcliffe | c O'Gorman b Cork | 15 | c Azharuddin b Malcolm | 3 |
| T.A.Lloyd * | c Bowler b Mortensen | 20 | c Krikken b Mortensen | 16 |
| D.P.Ostler | lbw b Mortensen | 9 | c O'Gorman b Mortensen | 0 |
| K.J.Piper + | c Krikken b Cork | 9 | (7) lbw b Cork | 1 |
| D.A.Reeve | b Goldsmith | 66 | (5) c Barnett b Malcolm | 66 |
| P.A.Smith | lbw b Mortensen | 5 | (6) c Morris b Warner | 13 |
| G.C.Small | c Krikken b Malcolm | 19 | lbw b Barnett | 7 |
| P.A.Booth | run out | 29 | (10) c Azharuddin b Malcolm | 5 |
| T.A.Munton | lbw b Goldsmith | 3 | (9) c Bowler b Malcolm | 5 |
| A.A.Donald | not out | 0 | not out | 0 |
| Extras | (lb 11,w 1,nb 23) | 35 | (b 4,lb 14,nb 6) | 24 |
| TOTAL | | 250 | | 136 |

| WARWICKS | O | M | R | W | O | M | R | W | FALL OF WICKETS | | | | |
|---|---|---|---|---|---|---|---|---|---|---|---|---|---|
| | | | | | | | | | | DER | WAR | DER | WAR |
| Donald | 10 | 0 | 53 | 0 | 16 | 4 | 51 | 2 | 1st | 18 | 35 | 0 | 2 |
| Small | 17.2 | 4 | 36 | 4 | 14 | 2 | 51 | 0 | 2nd | 56 | 69 | 3 | 21 |
| Munton | 21 | 3 | 77 | 5 | 13.5 | 1 | 60 | 2 | 3rd | 112 | 84 | 91 | 21 |
| Reeve | 20 | 3 | 55 | 1 | 15 | 3 | 25 | 1 | 4th | 130 | 100 | 175 | 29 |
| Booth | 1 | 1 | 0 | 0 | 24 | 6 | 81 | 1 | 5th | 208 | 134 | 199 | 72 |
| Smith | 5 | 0 | 39 | 0 | 4 | 0 | 17 | 0 | 6th | 242 | 146 | 245 | 75 |
| | | | | | | | | | 7th | 243 | 214 | 279 | 124 |
| DERBYSHIRE | O | M | R | W | O | M | R | W | 8th | 245 | 220 | 299 | 136 |
| Malcolm | 27 | 8 | 86 | 1 | 13 | 2 | 45 | 5 | 9th | 249 | 240 | | 136 |
| Warner | 20 | 5 | 35 | 1 | 8 | 4 | 13 | 1 | 10th | 260 | 250 | | 136 |
| Cork | 22 | 1 | 64 | 2 | 7 | 1 | 20 | 1 | | | | | |
| Mortensen | 20 | 7 | 36 | 3 | 6 | 0 | 33 | 2 | | | | | |
| Goldsmith | 6 | 1 | 18 | 2 | | | | | | | | | |
| Barnett | | | | | 5.3 | 3 | 7 | 1 | | | | | |

# OTHER FIRST-CLASS MATCH

## SUSSEX vs. CAMBRIDGE U

at Hove on 29th, 30th (np) June, 1st (np) July 1991
Toss : Sussex. Umpires : R.Palmer and G.A.Stickley
Match drawn

**SUSSEX**

| | | |
|---|---|---|
| K.Greenfield * | not out | 127 |
| J.W.Hall | b Jenkins | 1 |
| M.P.Speight + | b Lowrey | 149 |
| C.M.Wells | not out | 52 |
| R.Hanley | | |
| J.A.North | | |
| I.D.K.Salisbury | | |
| B.T.P.Donelan | | |
| R.A.Bunting | | |
| A.N.Jones | | |
| P.W.Threlfall | | |
| Extras | (b 2,lb 6,nb 3) | 11 |
| TOTAL | (for 2 wkts dec) | 340 |

**CAMBRIDGE U**

| | | |
|---|---|---|
| A.M.Hooper | c Bunting b Jones | 6 |
| R.I.Clitheroe | not out | 8 |
| R.H.J.Jenkins | b Threlfall | 3 |
| J.P.Crawley | c Speight b Threlfall | 0 |
| R.J.Turner *+ | not out | 0 |
| M.J.Morris | | |
| M.J.Lowrey | | |
| J.P.Arscott | | |
| R.M.Pearson | | |
| D.J.Bush | | |
| R.B.Waller | | |
| Extras | (nb 2) | 2 |
| TOTAL | (for 3 wkts) | 19 |

| CAMBRIDGE U | O | M | R | W | O | M | R | W |
|---|---|---|---|---|---|---|---|---|
| Jenkins | 18 | 3 | 71 | 1 | | | | |
| Bush | 13 | 0 | 59 | 0 | | | | |
| Waller | 21 | 4 | 92 | 0 | | | | |
| Pearson | 13 | 1 | 35 | 0 | | | | |
| Lowrey | 17 | 1 | 58 | 1 | | | | |
| Hooper | 4 | 0 | 17 | 0 | | | | |

| SUSSEX | O | M | R | W | O | M | R | W |
|---|---|---|---|---|---|---|---|---|
| Jones | 5 | 1 | 9 | 1 | | | | |
| Threlfall | 4 | 1 | 10 | 2 | | | | |

**FALL OF WICKETS**

| | SUS | CAM | SUS | CAM |
|---|---|---|---|---|
| 1st | 3 | 15 | | |
| 2nd | 240 | 18 | | |
| 3rd | | 19 | | |
| 4th | | | | |
| 5th | | | | |
| 6th | | | | |
| 7th | | | | |
| 8th | | | | |
| 9th | | | | |
| 10th | | | | |

## HEADLINES

### Other first-class match

### 29th June - 1st July

• Play was only possible on the opening day at Hove, Sussex totally dominating proceedings at Cambridge University's expense. The home side amassed 340 for two declared, Keith Greenfield and Martin Speight both recording career-best scores as they shared a second-wicket stand of 237. Sussex then claimed three wickets in the first nine overs of the University's innings.

### Britannic Assurance League Table
### as at 1st July 1991

| | | P | W | L | D | T | Bt | Bl | Pts |
|---|---|---|---|---|---|---|---|---|---|
| 1 | Warwickshire (5) | 11 | 5 | 2 | 4 | 0 | 30 | 29 | 139 |
| 2 | Essex (2) | 9 | 4 | 0 | 5 | 0 | 32 | 26 | 122 |
| 3 | Derbyshire (12) | 9 | 4 | 1 | 4 | 0 | 19 | 31 | 114 |
| 4 | Lancashire (6) | 9 | 4 | 1 | 4 | 0 | 29 | 16 | 109 |
| 5 | Gloucs (13) | 11 | 3 | 3 | 5 | 0 | 15 | 27 | 90 |
| 6 | Kent (16) | 10 | 2 | 1 | 7 | 0 | 22 | 28 | 82 |
| 7 | Glamorgan (8) | 11 | 2 | 2 | 7 | 0 | 24 | 25 | 81 |
| 8 | Sussex (17) | 10 | 1 | 2 | 7 | 0 | 26 | 24 | 66 |
| | Notts (13) | 9 | 1 | 1 | 7 | 0 | 24 | 26 | 66 |
| 10 | Surrey (9) | 8 | 2 | 2 | 4 | 0 | 14 | 19 | 65 |
| 11 | Northants (11) | 9 | 1 | 2 | 6 | 0 | 19 | 25 | 60 |
| 12 | Worcestershire (4) | 8 | 1 | 1 | 6 | 0 | 22 | 16 | 54 |
| 13 | Middlesex (1) | 10 | 0 | 3 | 7 | 0 | 19 | 27 | 46 |
| 14 | Somerset (15) | 9 | 0 | 1 | 8 | 0 | 25 | 17 | 42 |
| | Hampshire (3) | 9 | 0 | 4 | 5 | 0 | 20 | 22 | 42 |
| 16 | Leicestershire (7) | 10 | 0 | 2 | 8 | 0 | 18 | 23 | 41 |
| 17 | Yorkshire (10) | 8 | 0 | 2 | 6 | 0 | 18 | 13 | 31 |

## LEADING FIRST-CLASS AVERAGES
### as at 1st July 1991

**BATTING AVERAGES - Including fielding**
Qualifying requirements : 6 completed innings

| Name | Matches | Inns | NO | Runs | HS | Avge | 100s | 50s |
|---|---|---|---|---|---|---|---|---|
| C.L.Hooper | 8 | 13 | 4 | 810 | 196 | 90.00 | 3 | 2 |
| M.A.Garnham | 10 | 10 | 4 | 495 | 102 * | 82.50 | 1 | 4 |
| M.W.Gatting | 11 | 18 | 6 | 884 | 180 | 73.66 | 3 | 3 |
| T.M.Moody | 10 | 16 | 3 | 956 | 181 * | 73.53 | 4 | 4 |
| Salim Malik | 10 | 15 | 2 | 902 | 215 | 69.38 | 3 | 1 |
| I.V.A.Richards | 7 | 10 | 3 | 472 | 131 | 67.42 | 1 | 2 |
| R.B.Richardson | 8 | 14 | 4 | 669 | 135 * | 66.90 | 2 | 4 |
| D.W.Randall | 9 | 14 | 6 | 531 | 104 | 66.37 | 1 | 2 |
| B.C.Broad | 9 | 17 | 2 | 980 | 166 | 65.33 | 3 | 5 |
| S.J.Cook | 10 | 16 | 3 | 838 | 162 * | 64.46 | 3 | 3 |
| C.L.Smith | 10 | 16 | 0 | 1024 | 200 | 64.00 | 4 | 5 |
| R.A.Smith | 7 | 12 | 2 | 621 | 148 * | 62.10 | 1 | 5 |
| G.A.Gooch | 8 | 11 | 2 | 557 | 154 * | 61.88 | 3 | - |
| H.Morris | 13 | 22 | 4 | 1114 | 156 * | 61.88 | 3 | 5 |
| P.J.Prichard | 10 | 15 | 5 | 599 | 190 | 59.90 | 2 | 3 |

**BOWLING AVERAGES**
Qualifying requirements : 20 wickets taken

| Name | Overs | Mdns | Runs | Wkts | Avge | Best | 5wI | 10wM |
|---|---|---|---|---|---|---|---|---|
| A.A.Donald | 241 | 53 | 676 | 45 | 15.02 | 5-33 | 6 | 2 |
| Waqar Younis | 185.4 | 36 | 586 | 34 | 17.23 | 6-65 | 5 | 2 |
| O.H.Mortensen | 261.5 | 66 | 626 | 35 | 17.88 | 5-57 | 1 | - |
| C.E.L.Ambrose | 173 | 55 | 394 | 22 | 17.90 | 6-52 | 1 | - |
| D.V.Lawrence | 204.1 | 40 | 598 | 33 | 18.12 | 6-67 | 3 | 1 |
| K.M.Curran | 139 | 45 | 372 | 20 | 18.60 | 4-39 | - | - |
| D.R.Pringle | 244.1 | 68 | 553 | 28 | 19.75 | 5-70 | 2 | - |
| C.C.Lewis | 216 | 55 | 539 | 26 | 20.73 | 5-35 | 2 | - |
| N.A.Foster | 348.4 | 88 | 956 | 42 | 22.76 | 5-54 | 2 | - |
| Wasim Akram | 294.4 | 76 | 776 | 33 | 23.51 | 6-86 | 3 | - |
| P.A.J.DeFreitas | 273 | 65 | 778 | 32 | 24.31 | 6-88 | 1 | - |
| M.Frost | 242.5 | 47 | 763 | 31 | 24.61 | 4-55 | - | - |
| C.Penn | 154.5 | 18 | 504 | 20 | 25.20 | 4-48 | - | - |
| F.D.Stephenson | 273.5 | 76 | 682 | 27 | 25.25 | 5-74 | 1 | - |
| S.L.Watkin | 368.3 | 80 | 1062 | 42 | 25.28 | 6-55 | 2 | - |

| TOUR MATCH | BRITANNIC ASS. CHAMPIONSHIP |
|---|---|

## HAMPSHIRE vs. WEST INDIES
at Southampton on 29th, 30th June, 1st July 1991
Toss : Hampshire. Umpires : B.Dudleston and R.Julian
Match drawn

**HAMPSHIRE**

| | | | | |
|---|---|---|---|---|
| V.P.Terry | c Anthony b Patterson | 12 | (2) c Dujon b Ambrose | 2 |
| T.C.Middleton | c Richardson b Walsh | 20 | (1) not out | 76 |
| M.C.J.Nicholas * | c Simmons b Hooper | 37 | not out | 59 |
| R.A.Smith | retired hurt | 62 | | |
| D.I.Gower | b Hooper | 10 | | |
| K.D.James | not out | 11 | | |
| A.N Aymes + | c Hooper b Walsh | 5 | | |
| R.J.Maru | c Haynes b Ambrose | 23 | | |
| S.D.Udal | c Hooper b Ambrose | 0 | | |
| C.A.Connor | c Dujon b Ambrose | 0 | | |
| K.J.Shine | c sub b Ambrose | 12 | | |
| Extras | (b 4,lb 4,nb 4) | 10 | (lb 7,w 4,nb 4) | 15 |
| TOTAL | | 202 | (for 1 wkt) | 152 |

**WEST INDIES**

| | | |
|---|---|---|
| P.V.Simmons | c Nicholas b Shine | 0 |
| D.L.Haynes | b Connor | 44 |
| R.B.Richardson | c Aymes b James | 33 |
| B.C.Lara | b Udal | 75 |
| C.L.Hooper | c Maru b Udal | 196 |
| P.J.L.Dujon + | c Aymes b Connor | 68 |
| I.V.A.Richards * | not out | 15 |
| H.A.G.Anthony | | |
| C.E.L.Ambrose | | |
| C.A.Walsh | | |
| B.P.Patterson | | |
| Extras | (b 3,lb 5,w 1,nb 9) | 18 |
| TOTAL | (for 6 wkts dec) | 449 |

| WEST INDIES | O | M | R | W | O | M | R | W |
|---|---|---|---|---|---|---|---|---|
| Ambrose | 19 | 7 | 70 | 4 | 12 | 5 | 22 | 1 |
| Patterson | 7 | 2 | 19 | 1 | | | | |
| Walsh | 18 | 7 | 41 | 2 | 13 | 3 | 22 | 0 |
| Anthony | 10 | 2 | 30 | 0 | 14 | 1 | 57 | 0 |
| Hooper | 24 | 10 | 36 | 2 | 12 | 1 | 28 | 0 |
| Richards | | | | | 4 | 1 | 13 | 0 |
| Simmons | | | | | 2 | 0 | 3 | 0 |

| HAMPSHIRE | O | M | R | W | O | M | R | W |
|---|---|---|---|---|---|---|---|---|
| Shine | 27 | 4 | 104 | 1 | | | | |
| Connor | 28 | 2 | 100 | 2 | | | | |
| James | 19 | 2 | 77 | 1 | | | | |
| Udal | 22 | 3 | 117 | 2 | | | | |
| Maru | 8 | 2 | 43 | 0 | | | | |

| FALL OF WICKETS | HAM | WI HAM | WI |
|---|---|---|---|
| 1st | 21 | 7 | 9 |
| 2nd | 42 | 67 | |
| 3rd | 144 | 102 | |
| 4th | 151 | 212 | |
| 5th | 158 | 396 | |
| 6th | 186 | 449 | |
| 7th | 186 | | |
| 8th | 190 | | |
| 9th | 202 | | |
| 10th | | | |

---

## HEADLINES

### Tetley Bitter Challenge

### 29th June - 1st July

• Robin Smith and Carl Hooper took over where they had left off at Lord's on the West Indians' visit to play Hampshire at Southampton. Smith contributed a swashbuckling 62 before retiring with a hand injury and the elegant and increasingly composed Hooper his third 100 of the tour and a new career-best, before falling four short of his double-century. Tony Middleton and Paul Terry played out time with a second-wicket stand of 143.

---

## ESSEX vs. HAMPSHIRE
at Chelmsford on 2nd, 3rd, 4th July 1991
Toss : Hampshire. Umpires : H.D.Bird and R.Julian
Match drawn. Essex 5 pts (Bt: 1, Bw: 4), Hampshire 4 pts (Bt: 2, Bw: 2)

**HAMPSHIRE**

| | | | | |
|---|---|---|---|---|
| T.C.Middleton | c Garnham b Topley | 31 | lbw b Andrew | 3 |
| C.L.Smith | c Hussain b Childs | 44 | c sub b Salim Malik | 93 |
| M.C.J.Nicholas * | c Topley b Foster | 1 | (4) c Topley b Foster | 0 |
| V.P.Terry | lbw b Foster | 14 | (5) c Garnham b Topley | 12 |
| D.I.Gower | c Salim Malik b Foster | 23 | (6) retired hurt | 52 |
| K.D.James | lbw b Topley | 51 | (7) c Salim Malik b Prichard | 45 |
| A.N Aymes + | c Prichard b Andrew | 17 | (8) not out | 20 |
| R.J.Maru | c Andrew b Foster | 14 | (3) c Garnham b Foster | 0 |
| C.A.Connor | b Topley | 5 | | |
| K.J.Shine | c Stephenson b Foster | 0 | | |
| Aqib Javed | not out | 0 | | |
| Extras | (lb 8,nb 12) | 20 | (lb 1,nb 5) | 6 |
| TOTAL | | 220 | (for 6 wkts dec) | 231 |

**ESSEX**

| | | | | |
|---|---|---|---|---|
| J.P.Stephenson | c Aymes b Aqib Javed | 17 | b Aqib Javed | 5 |
| A.C.Seymour | run out | 50 | c Maru b James | 23 |
| P.J.Prichard | c Shine b James | 3 | (4) c Aymes b Connor | 38 |
| Salim Malik | c Maru b Connor | 12 | (3) c Smith b Aqib Javed | 66 |
| N.Hussain | not out | 29 | c Middleton b Shine | 52 |
| M.A.Garnham + | b Shine | 8 | c Terry b Aqib Javed | 14 |
| N.A.Foster * | not out | 12 | c & b Maru | 10 |
| A.G.J.Fraser | | | b Shine | 23 |
| T.D.Topley | | | not out | 33 |
| J.H.Childs | | | c Terry b Shine | 3 |
| S.J.W.Andrew | | | not out | 6 |
| Extras | (b 1,lb 3,w 2,nb 15) | 21 | (b 9,lb 4,w 1,nb 2) | 16 |
| TOTAL | (for 5 wkts dec) | 152 | (for 9 wkts) | 289 |

| ESSEX | O | M | R | W | O | M | R | W |
|---|---|---|---|---|---|---|---|---|
| Foster | 23 | 8 | 45 | 5 | 13 | 3 | 38 | 2 |
| Andrew | 17 | 4 | 41 | 1 | 3 | 1 | 8 | 1 |
| Topley | 18.1 | 3 | 59 | 3 | 11 | 4 | 38 | 1 |
| Childs | 17 | 7 | 34 | 1 | 9 | 2 | 37 | 0 |
| Fraser | 14 | 5 | 31 | 0 | | | | |
| Stephenson | 2 | 1 | 2 | 0 | | | | |
| Salim Malik | | | | | 8 | 0 | 42 | 1 |
| Garnham | | | | | 4 | 0 | 39 | 0 |
| Prichard | | | | | 3.3 | 0 | 28 | 1 |

| HAMPSHIRE | O | M | R | W | O | M | R | W |
|---|---|---|---|---|---|---|---|---|
| Aqib Javed | 12.2 | 0 | 54 | 1 | 17 | 3 | 64 | 3 |
| Shine | 9 | 3 | 34 | 1 | 12 | 0 | 68 | 3 |
| James | 12 | 4 | 36 | 1 | 5 | 0 | 20 | 1 |
| Connor | 9 | 3 | 24 | 1 | 5 | 0 | 23 | 1 |
| Maru | | | | | 18 | 0 | 101 | 1 |

| FALL OF WICKETS | HAM | ESS HAM | ESS |
|---|---|---|---|
| 1st | 82 | 36 | 9 | 26 |
| 2nd | 84 | 60 | 12 | 45 |
| 3rd | 89 | 80 | 12 | 117 |
| 4th | 119 | 127 | 41 | 178 |
| 5th | 125 | 140 | 159 | 198 |
| 6th | 166 | | 231 | 213 |
| 7th | 207 | | | 237 |
| 8th | 220 | | | 252 |
| 9th | 220 | | | 268 |
| 10th | 220 | | | |

## WARWICKSHIRE vs. MIDDLESEX
at Edgbaston on 2nd, 3rd, 4th July 1991
Toss : Warwickshire. Umpires : B.J.Meyer and K.E.Palmer
Warwickshire won by 93 runs. Warwicks 22 pts (Bt: 2, Bw: 4), Middlesex 6 pts (Bt: 2, Bw: 4)

**WARWICKSHIRE**

| | | | | |
|---|---|---|---|---|
| A.J.Moles | c Brown b Cowans | 38 | c Cowans b Williams | 27 |
| J.D.Ratcliffe | c Farbrace b Taylor | 5 | c Emburey b Taylor | 94 |
| T.A.Lloyd * | c Farbrace b Taylor | 14 | c Roseberry b Tufnell | 82 |
| D.P.Ostler | b Emburey | 17 | not out | 48 |
| Asif Din | c Brown b Williams | 11 | c Pooley b Taylor | 3 |
| P.A.Smith | c Roseberry b Cowans | 68 | lbw b Taylor | 0 |
| K.J.Piper + | c Brown b Cowans | 4 | | |
| G.C.Small | c Brown b Williams | 24 | (7) not out | 3 |
| P.A.Booth | b Williams | 14 | | |
| T.A.Munton | not out | 8 | | |
| A.A.Donald | b Cowans | 4 | | |
| Extras | (b 3,lb 3,w 5,nb 12) | 23 | (lb 13,w 2,nb 2) | 17 |
| TOTAL | | 230 | (for 5 wkts dec) | 274 |

**MIDDLESEX**

| | | | | |
|---|---|---|---|---|
| I.J.F.Hutchinson | c Piper b Munton | 5 | lbw b Small | 30 |
| M.A.Roseberry | c Ostler b Munton | 27 | lbw b Munton | 15 |
| K.R.Brown | c Donald b Munton | 12 | (4) b Donald | 47 |
| J.C.Pooley | c Booth b Small | 18 | (3) c Asif Din b Munton | 2 |
| M.Keech | lbw b Munton | 26 | c Ratcliffe b Donald | 11 |
| J.E.Emburey * | lbw b Munton | 0 | c Asif Din b Small | 13 |
| P.Farbrace + | b Munton | 24 | not out | 11 |
| N.F.Williams | c Moles b Munton | 77 | c Lloyd b Booth | 3 |
| C.W.Taylor | c Ostler b Booth | 4 | c Ostler b Small | 12 |
| P.C.R.Tufnell | c Ostler b Munton | 0 | lbw b Munton | 2 |
| N.G.Cowans | not out | 3 | b Donald | 4 |
| Extras | (b 12,lb 25,nb 4) | 41 | (b 11,lb 7,nb 6) | 24 |
| TOTAL | | 237 | | 174 |

| MIDDLESEX | O | M | R | W | O | M | R | W |
|---|---|---|---|---|---|---|---|---|
| Cowans | 18 | 5 | 44 | 4 | 18 | 2 | 59 | 0 |
| Taylor | 17 | 3 | 44 | 2 | 12 | 1 | 43 | 3 |
| Williams | 25 | 4 | 73 | 3 | 7 | 0 | 42 | 1 |
| Tufnell | 14 | 4 | 26 | 0 | 17 | 3 | 61 | 1 |
| Emburey | 21 | 8 | 37 | 1 | 13 | 0 | 56 | 0 |

| WARWICKS | O | M | R | W | O | M | R | W |
|---|---|---|---|---|---|---|---|---|
| Donald | 15 | 4 | 43 | 0 | 16.2 | 1 | 46 | 3 |
| Small | 21 | 8 | 47 | 1 | 15 | 5 | 23 | 3 |
| Munton | 30.2 | 14 | 89 | 8 | 22 | 4 | 38 | 3 |
| Smith | 2 | 1 | 6 | 0 | | | | |
| Booth | 4 | 0 | 15 | 1 | 15 | 2 | 49 | 1 |

| FALL OF WICKETS | WAR | MID WAR | MID |
|---|---|---|---|
| 1st | 14 | 25 | 54 | 49 |
| 2nd | 36 | 56 | 189 | 50 |
| 3rd | 63 | 57 | 248 | 55 |
| 4th | 87 | 106 | 254 | 88 |
| 5th | 98 | 110 | 267 | 120 |
| 6th | 106 | 133 | | 146 |
| 7th | 166 | 157 | | 157 |
| 8th | 194 | 201 | | 164 |
| 9th | 219 | 208 | | 170 |
| 10th | 230 | 237 | | 174 |

# BRITANNIC ASSURANCE CHAMPIONSHIP

## KENT vs. NORTHANTS
at Maidstone on 2nd, 3rd, 4th July 1991
Toss : Northants. Umpires : G.I.Burgess and R.Palmer
Kent won by 120 runs. Kent 17 pts (Bt: 1, Bw: 0), Northants 4 pts (Bt: 0, Bw: 4)

### KENT

| Batsman | Dismissal | Runs | Dismissal | Runs |
|---|---|---|---|---|
| T.R.Ward | c Ripley b Baptiste | 31 | c Bailey b Cook | 18 |
| S.G.Hinks | c Curran b Thomas | 1 | c Curran b Taylor | 7 |
| N.R.Taylor | b Baptiste | 18 | (4) c Capel b Taylor | 26 |
| G.R.Cowdrey | lbw b Baptiste | 2 | (5) not out | 36 |
| M.R.Benson * | not out | 50 | (6) c Taylor b Cook | 1 |
| M.V.Fleming | c Ripley b Baptiste | 3 | (7) not out | 15 |
| S.A.Marsh + | b Baptiste | 14 | | |
| C.Penn | lbw b Thomas | 1 | | |
| M.J.McCague | c Cook b Baptiste | 10 | (3) b Taylor | 7 |
| T.A.Merrick | b Cook | 18 | | |
| A.P.Igglesden | lbw b Cook | 0 | | |
| Extras | (lb 8,w 2) | 10 | (lb 3,w 1,nb 1) | 5 |
| TOTAL | | 158 | (for 5 wkts dec) | 115 |

### NORTHANTS

| Batsman | Dismissal | Runs |
|---|---|---|
| A.Fordham | c Hinks b Penn | 38 |
| N.A.Felton | b Igglesden | 0 |
| R.J.Bailey * | c Marsh b Igglesden | 1 |
| A.R.Roberts | lbw b Penn | 11 |
| K.M.Curran | b Penn | 15 |
| E.A.E.Baptiste | c Fleming b Penn | 2 |
| D.J.Capel | c Taylor b Igglesden | 56 |
| J.G.Thomas | c Merrick b Igglesden | 10 |
| D.Ripley + | c Marsh b Igglesden | 7 |
| N.G.B.Cook | c Taylor b Penn | 2 |
| J.P.Taylor | not out | 0 |
| Extras | (b 4,lb 5,nb 2) | 11 |
| TOTAL | | 153 |

| NORTHANTS | O | M | R | W | O | M | R | W |
|---|---|---|---|---|---|---|---|---|
| Thomas | 11 | 3 | 35 | 2 | 11 | 1 | 38 | 0 |
| Taylor | 10 | 0 | 28 | 0 | 18 | 3 | 45 | 3 |
| Baptiste | 26 | 5 | 57 | 6 | | | | |
| Curran | 12 | 2 | 26 | 0 | | | | |
| Cook | 1 | 0 | 4 | 2 | 8 | 2 | 29 | 2 |
| Roberts | | | | | 1 | 1 | 0 | 0 |

| KENT | O | M | R | W | O | M | R | W |
|---|---|---|---|---|---|---|---|---|
| Merrick | | | | | 13 | 3 | 39 | 0 |
| Igglesden | | | | | 17 | 8 | 36 | 5 |
| Penn | | | | | 12 | 2 | 43 | 5 |
| McCague | | | | | 7 | 1 | 26 | 0 |

| FALL OF WICKETS | KEN | NOR | KEN | NOR |
|---|---|---|---|---|
| 1st | 19 | | 23 | 2 |
| 2nd | 44 | | 32 | 4 |
| 3rd | 48 | | 38 | 31 |
| 4th | 73 | | 84 | 60 |
| 5th | 81 | | 85 | 70 |
| 6th | 108 | | | 72 |
| 7th | 111 | | | 111 |
| 8th | 126 | | | 142 |
| 9th | 158 | | | 147 |
| 10th | 158 | | | 153 |

## LEICESTERSHIRE vs. GLOUCESTERSHIRE
at Hinckley on 2nd, 3rd (no play), 4th July 1991
Toss : Gloucs. Umpires : A.A.Jones and N.T.Plews
Gloucs won by 36 runs. Leicestershire 1 pt (Bt: 0, Bw: 1), Gloucs 19 pts (Bt: 3, Bw: 0)
100 overs scores : Gloucs 250 for 4

### GLOUCESTERSHIRE

| Batsman | Dismissal | Runs |
|---|---|---|
| G.D.Hodgson | c Hepworth b Lewis | 7 |
| R.J.Scott | run out | 51 |
| A.J.Wright * | st Nixon b Potter | 63 |
| C.W.J.Athey | lbw b Maguire | 52 |
| M.W.Alleyne | c Nixon b Willey | 55 |
| J.J.E.Hardy | b Hepworth | 35 |
| J.W.Lloyds | not out | 6 |
| R.C.J.Williams + | not out | 5 |
| A.M.Smith | | |
| J.M.De La Pena | | |
| M.J.Gerrard | | |
| Extras | (b 5,lb 13,w 1,nb 14) | 33 |
| TOTAL | (for 6 wkts dec) | 307 |

### LEICESTERSHIRE

| Batsman | Dismissal | Runs |
|---|---|---|
| T.J.Boon | c Lloyds b Smith | 2 |
| N.E.Briers * | c Lloyds b De La Pena | 14 |
| P.N.Hepworth | c Lloyds b Scott | 35 |
| J.J.Whitaker | b Scott | 30 |
| L.Potter | c Wright b Lloyds | 1 |
| B.F.Smith | c Hodgson b Lloyds | 29 |
| C.C.Lewis | c sub b Smith | 73 |
| P.Willey | c Williams b De La Pena | 6 |
| P.A.Nixon + | b Smith | 31 |
| C.Wilkinson | c Wright b Smith | 10 |
| J.N.Maguire | not out | 2 |
| Extras | (b 5,lb 3,w 4,nb 26) | 38 |
| TOTAL | | 271 |

| LEICS | O | M | R | W | O | M | R | W |
|---|---|---|---|---|---|---|---|---|
| Lewis | 15 | 3 | 36 | 1 | | | | |
| Maguire | 24 | 5 | 75 | 1 | | | | |
| Wilkinson | 19 | 4 | 41 | 0 | | | | |
| Willey | 37 | 10 | 87 | 1 | | | | |
| Potter | 18 | 8 | 31 | 1 | | | | |
| Hepworth | 9 | 5 | 19 | 1 | | | | |

| GLOUCS | O | M | R | W | O | M | R | W |
|---|---|---|---|---|---|---|---|---|
| Smith | | | | | 17.1 | 3 | 41 | 4 |
| De La Pena | | | | | 13 | 0 | 69 | 2 |
| Gerrard | | | | | 8 | 0 | 24 | 0 |
| Lloyds | | | | | 35 | 9 | 93 | 2 |
| Scott | | | | | 15 | 1 | 36 | 2 |

| FALL OF WICKETS | GLO | LEI | GLO | LEI |
|---|---|---|---|---|
| 1st | 25 | | | 8 |
| 2nd | 133 | | | 59 |
| 3rd | 155 | | | 91 |
| 4th | 231 | | | 100 |
| 5th | 272 | | | 102 |
| 6th | 300 | | | 147 |
| 7th | | | | 162 |
| 8th | | | | 252 |
| 9th | | | | 262 |
| 10th | | | | |

## HEADLINES

### Britannic Assurance Championship

### 2nd - 4th July

• Warwickshire maintained their advantage at the top of the table with their 93-run victory over 1990 champions Middlesex at Edgbaston. Tim Munton returned career-best figures, also the best of the season so far, in Middlesex's first innings, and then combined with Allan Donald and Gladstone Small to make the visitors' victory target of 268 a distant prospect, as Warwickshire's fast bowling attack again took the honours in their sixth success in 12 Championship matches.

• Essex made a valiant effort to keep the pressure on the leaders with their pursuit of 300 for victory over Hampshire at Chelmsford, but despite half-centuries from Salim Malik and Nasser Hussain the second-placed side had to be content with a draw, finishing 11 runs short with one wicket standing. Neil Foster had earlier ensured maximum bowling points for Essex with figures of five for 45. Chris Smith responded with 93 when Hampshire lost their first four second innings wickets for 41.

• Batsmen struggled throughout at Maidstone where Kent defeated Northants by 120 runs, even after being dismissed for 158 in their first innings, Eldine Baptiste taking six for 57 against his former county. The visitors forfeited their first innings to keep the match alive, but could not come to terms with the bowling of Alan Igglesden or Chris Penn who claimed five wickets apiece as Northants attempted a target of 274.

• Gloucestershire enjoyed their visit to Hinckley, gaining victory over Leicestershire by 26 runs after both sides had forfeited an innings. The visitors passed 300 thanks to a consistent batting effort then bowled out their opponents as Mark Smith continued to impress in his first season of county cricket with four wickets for 41.

# BRITANNIC ASSURANCE CHAMPIONSHIP

## HEADLINES

### Britannic Assurance Championship

### 2nd - 4th July

• Somerset claimed their first Championship victory of the season at Lancashire's expense at Taunton in a match dominated by the batsmen. Neil Fairbrother scored 100s in each innings for Lancashire and Jimmy Cook, in familiar heavy-scoring vein, replied with 131 and then 61 as he set the home side well on their way towards a target of 294 in 60 overs with an opening stand of 104 with Peter Roebuck.

• Yorkshire also broke their duck with a 115-run win over Worcestershire at Headingley, the visitors losing their first five wickets to the new ball for 24 and the remainder to Phil Carrick who finished with figures of five for 13. Richard Stemp had earlier returned career-best figures as Yorkshire reached 291 for eight before both sides forfeited an innings.

• Sussex entertained Surrey at the Arundel Castle ground but denied the visitors victory with a determined last-day rearguard action after they had conceded a first innings lead of 177, Darren Bicknell top-scoring for Surrey with 126.

• While the bowlers had taken charge of the early stages of Glamorgan's contest with Nottinghamshire at Cardiff, the batsmen took over as the visitors engineered an eight-wicket victory. With Glamorgan faced with a deficit of 67, Matthew Maynard dominated their second innings with the first double century of his career, but the home side's hopes of success were quickly dashed as Derek Randall and Paul Johnson carried Notts to their target with a third-wicket stand of 175.

---

## SOMERSET vs. LANCASHIRE

at Taunton on 2nd, 3rd, 4th July 1991
Toss : Lancashire.  Umpires : D.J.Constant and B.Dudleston
Somerset won by 4 wickets.  Somerset 22 pts (Bt: 3, Bw: 3), Lancashire 5 pts (Bt: 4, Bw: 1)

### LANCASHIRE

| | | | | |
|---|---|---|---|---|
| G.D.Mendis | c & b Trump | 31 | b Lefebvre | 1 |
| G.Fowler | c & b Macleay | 14 | lbw b Mallender | 0 |
| N.J.Speak | c Harden b Macleay | 56 | c Graveney b Lefebvre | 49 |
| N.H.Fairbrother | c Macleay b Roebuck | 109 | not out | 102 |
| S.P.Titchard | c Burns b Lefebvre | 53 | b Lefebvre | 0 |
| M.Watkinson | c Harden b Trump | 13 | (7) c Graveney b Harden | 30 |
| Wasim Akram | b Trump | 39 | (8) lbw b Harden | 2 |
| W.K.Hegg + | not out | 0 | (6) c Burns b Macleay | 17 |
| G.Yates | lbw b Lefebvre | 0 | not out | 27 |
| D.P.Hughes * | | | | |
| P.J.Martin | | | | |
| Extras | (b 4,lb 1,w 2,nb 4) | 11 | (b 4,lb 1,nb 2) | 7 |
| TOTAL | (for 8 wkts dec) | 326 | (for 7 wkts dec) | 235 |

### SOMERSET

| | | | | |
|---|---|---|---|---|
| S.J.Cook | c Speak b Watkinson | 131 | st Hegg b Hughes | 61 |
| A.N.Hayhurst | c Titchard b Martin | 29 | (8) not out | 22 |
| P.M.Roebuck | c Hegg b Hughes | 46 | (2) c Titchard b Yates | 52 |
| R.J.Harden | not out | 29 | c Titchard b Yates | 12 |
| N.D.Burns + | not out | 27 | c Fairbrother b Watkinson | 25 |
| C.J.Tavare * | | | (3) run out | 50 |
| K.H.Macleay | | | (6) c & b Yates | 36 |
| R.P.Lefebvre | | | (7) not out | 23 |
| N.A.Mallender | | | | |
| H.R.J.Trump | | | | |
| D.A.Graveney | | | | |
| Extras | (lb 4,w 1,nb 1) | 6 | (b 6,lb 5,w 1,nb 1) | 13 |
| TOTAL | (for 3 wkts dec) | 268 | (for 6 wkts) | 294 |

| SOMERSET | O | M | R | W | O | M | R | W |
|---|---|---|---|---|---|---|---|---|
| Mallender | 15 | 3 | 42 | 0 | 3 | 0 | 6 | 1 |
| Lefebvre | 13.2 | 3 | 48 | 2 | 16 | 1 | 54 | 3 |
| Macleay | 18 | 5 | 42 | 2 | 17 | 5 | 39 | 1 |
| Hayhurst | 8 | 0 | 39 | 0 | 2 | 2 | 0 | 0 |
| Trump | 15 | 2 | 47 | 3 | 28 | 8 | 45 | 0 |
| Graveney | 16 | 4 | 61 | 0 | | | | |
| Roebuck | 13 | 1 | 42 | 1 | 11 | 3 | 16 | 0 |
| Harden | | | | | 13 | 0 | 70 | 2 |

| LANCASHIRE | O | M | R | W | O | M | R | W |
|---|---|---|---|---|---|---|---|---|
| Wasim Akram | 3 | 1 | 7 | 0 | | | | |
| Martin | 13 | 0 | 42 | 1 | 7 | 2 | 25 | 0 |
| Watkinson | 21 | 3 | 70 | 1 | 11 | 0 | 85 | 1 |
| Yates | 26 | 8 | 59 | 0 | 23.4 | 3 | 83 | 3 |
| Hughes | 32 | 3 | 86 | 1 | 19 | 4 | 90 | 1 |

| FALL OF WICKETS | LAN | SOM | LAN | SOM |
|---|---|---|---|---|
| 1st | 24 | 86 | 1 | 104 |
| 2nd | 66 | 206 | 2 | 124 |
| 3rd | 177 | 216 | 76 | 144 |
| 4th | 233 | | 82 | 197 |
| 5th | 276 | | 129 | 238 |
| 6th | 326 | | 180 | 248 |
| 7th | 326 | | 182 | |
| 8th | 326 | | | |
| 9th | | | | |
| 10th | | | | |

---

## SUSSEX vs. SURREY

at Arundel on 2nd, 3rd, 4th July 1991
Toss : Surrey.  Umpires : J.H.Harris and D.R.Shepherd
Match drawn.  Sussex 3 pts (Bt: 2, Bw: 1), Surrey 7 pts (Bt: 3, Bw: 4)
100 overs scores :Surrey 279 for 4

### SUSSEX

| | | | | |
|---|---|---|---|---|
| N.J.Lenham | b Bicknell M.P. | 15 | b Waqar Younis | 5 |
| D.M.Smith | b Greig | 29 | c Greig b Medlycott | 46 |
| P.W.G.Parker | lbw b Waqar Younis | 26 | c Sergeant b Waqar Younis | 4 |
| A.P.Wells | c Stewart b Bicknell M.P. | 20 | b Medlycott | 77 |
| M.P.Speight | c Stewart b Greig | 42 | c Sergeant b Bicknell M.P. | 15 |
| C.M.Wells | c Stewart b Greig | 4 | c Alikhan b Medlycott | 1 |
| A.I.C.Dodemaide | c Sergeant b Murphy | 1 | b Waqar Younis | 2 |
| P.Moores + | b Waqar Younis | 8 | lbw b Greig | 14 |
| A.C.S.Pigott | lbw b Waqar Younis | 26 | not out | 12 |
| I.D.K.Salisbury | c Sergeant b Bicknell M.P. | 17 | b Medlycott | 4 |
| A.N.Jones | not out | 14 | not out | 0 |
| Extras | (b 2,lb 8,nb 4) | 14 | (b 8,lb 7,w 2,nb 6) | 23 |
| TOTAL | | 216 | (for 9 wkts) | 203 |

### SURREY

| | | |
|---|---|---|
| D.J.Bicknell | c Salisbury b Jones | 126 |
| R.I.Alikhan | lbw b Dodemaide | 58 |
| A.J.Stewart | c Moores b Salisbury | 71 |
| D.M.Ward | c Moores b Jones | 7 |
| G.P.Thorpe | not out | 56 |
| I.A.Greig * | lbw b Dodemaide | 27 |
| K.T.Medlycott | c Wells C.M. b Dodemaide | 20 |
| N.F.Sergeant + | st Moores b Salisbury | 4 |
| M.P.Bicknell | not out | 7 |
| Waqar Younis | | |
| A.J.Murphy | | |
| Extras | (b 3,lb 10,w 3,nb 1) | 17 |
| TOTAL | (for 7 wkts dec) | 393 |

| SURREY | O | M | R | W | O | M | R | W |
|---|---|---|---|---|---|---|---|---|
| Waqar Younis | 23 | 2 | 69 | 3 | 19 | 2 | 42 | 3 |
| Bicknell M.P. | 24.3 | 9 | 57 | 3 | 19 | 6 | 30 | 1 |
| Murphy | 20 | 3 | 50 | 1 | 11 | 2 | 34 | 0 |
| Greig | 12 | 3 | 30 | 3 | 10 | 1 | 23 | 1 |
| Medlycott | | | | | 38 | 14 | 56 | 4 |
| Stewart | | | | | 1 | 0 | 3 | 0 |

| SUSSEX | O | M | R | W | O | M | R | W |
|---|---|---|---|---|---|---|---|---|
| Dodemaide | 35 | 7 | 108 | 3 | | | | |
| Jones | 29 | 2 | 94 | 2 | | | | |
| Pigott | 21 | 4 | 77 | 0 | | | | |
| Wells C.M. | 16 | 7 | 39 | 0 | | | | |
| Lenham | 3 | 1 | 10 | 0 | | | | |
| Salisbury | 24 | 10 | 52 | 2 | | | | |

| FALL OF WICKETS | SUS | SUR | SUS | SUR |
|---|---|---|---|---|
| 1st | 15 | 147 | 12 | |
| 2nd | 71 | 233 | 22 | |
| 3rd | 71 | 242 | 94 | |
| 4th | 133 | 278 | 116 | |
| 5th | 144 | 337 | 134 | |
| 6th | 145 | 363 | 143 | |
| 7th | 151 | 369 | 186 | |
| 8th | 162 | | 190 | |
| 9th | 200 | | 198 | |
| 10th | 216 | | | |

| BRITANNIC ASS. CHAMPIONSHIP | VARSITY MATCH |
|---|---|

## GLAMORGAN vs. NOTTS

at Cardiff on 2nd, 3rd, 4th July 1991
Toss : Glamorgan.  Umpires : D.O.Oslear and R.C.Tolchard
Notts won by 8 wickets.  Glamorgan 5 pts (Bt: 1, Bw: 4), Notts 22 pts (Bt: 2, Bw: 4)

**GLAMORGAN**

| | | | | |
|---|---|---|---|---|
| A.R.Butcher * | b Stephenson | 37 | c Afford b Stephenson | 1 |
| S.P.James | lbw b Pick | 1 | lbw b Pick | 42 |
| R.J.Shastri | lbw b Pick | 0 | c Stephenson b Afford | 7 |
| M.P.Maynard | c Pick b Stephenson | 2 | c Hemmings b Crawley | 204 |
| P.A.Cottey | lbw b Pick | 46 | c Pollard b Crawley | 55 |
| A.Dale | st French b Afford | 25 | b Afford | 13 |
| R.D.B.Croft | c Pollard b Stephenson | 0 | not out | 1 |
| C.P.Metson + | run out | 4 | | |
| S.L.Watkin | b Stephenson | 15 | | |
| S.R.Barwick | c French b Afford | 0 | | |
| M.Frost | not out | 2 | | |
| Extras | (lb 5,w 4,nb 10) | 19 | (b 4,lb 6,nb 7) | 17 |
| TOTAL | | 151 | (for 6 wkts dec) | 340 |

**NOTTS**

| | | | | |
|---|---|---|---|---|
| B.C.Broad | c & b Croft | 34 | c Barwick b Frost | 36 |
| P.Pollard | c Cottey b Frost | 26 | lbw b Barwick | 33 |
| R.T.Robinson * | not out | 91 | | |
| P.Johnson | run out | 8 | not out | 77 |
| D.W.Randall | lbw b Watkin | 20 | (3) not out | 112 |
| M.A.Crawley | c Cottey b Watkin | 5 | | |
| F.D.Stephenson | b Barwick | 22 | | |
| B.N.French + | b Barwick | 3 | | |
| E.E.Hemmings | b Watkin | 4 | | |
| R.A.Pick | c Metson b Watkin | 0 | | |
| J.A.Afford | lbw b Watkin | 0 | | |
| Extras | (nb 5) | 5 | (b 4,lb 7,w 1,nb 6) | 18 |
| TOTAL | | 218 | (for 2 wkts) | 276 |

| NOTTS | O | M | R | W | O | M | R | W | FALL OF WICKETS | | | |
|---|---|---|---|---|---|---|---|---|---|---|---|---|
| | | | | | | | | | | GLA | NOT | GLA | NOT |
| Pick | 18 | 4 | 54 | 3 | 17 | 6 | 60 | 1 | 1st | 8 | 57 | 3 | 38 |
| Stephenson | 13.3 | 3 | 40 | 4 | 16 | 4 | 66 | 1 | 2nd | 8 | 68 | 15 | 101 |
| Hemmings | 11 | 5 | 19 | 0 | 14 | 2 | 65 | 0 | 3rd | 24 | 84 | 167 | |
| Crawley | 3 | 0 | 13 | 0 | 18.3 | 3 | 72 | 2 | 4th | 49 | 126 | 301 | |
| Afford | 13 | 6 | 20 | 2 | 27 | 9 | 67 | 2 | 5th | 114 | 134 | 332 | |
| | | | | | | | | | 6th | 117 | 195 | 340 | |
| GLAMORGAN | O | M | R | W | O | M | R | W | 7th | 127 | 204 | | |
| Watkin | 22.5 | 3 | 59 | 5 | 12 | 0 | 47 | 0 | 8th | 132 | 218 | | |
| Frost | 15 | 0 | 58 | 1 | 9 | 0 | 59 | 1 | 9th | 133 | 218 | | |
| Croft | 41 | 11 | 89 | 1 | 15 | 1 | 65 | 0 | 10th | 151 | 218 | | |
| Barwick | 14 | 8 | 12 | 2 | 15 | 3 | 67 | 1 | | | | | |
| Shastri | | | | | 8 | 0 | 27 | 0 | | | | | |

## CAMBRIDGE U vs. OXFORD U

at Lord's on 2nd, 3rd, 4th July 1991
Toss : Cambridge U.  Umpires : J.C.Balderstone and K.J.Lyons
Match drawn

**CAMBRIDGE U**

| | | | | |
|---|---|---|---|---|
| A.M.Hooper | c Lovell b Gerrans | 89 | b Wood | 4 |
| R.I.Clitheroe | c Lovell b Wood | 6 | c Sandiford b Gerrans | 0 |
| J.P.Crawley | b Wood | 66 | not out | 59 |
| R.J.Turner *+ | lbw b Oppenheimer | 27 | lbw b Wood | 0 |
| M.J.Morris | c Lovell b Gerrans | 6 | b Oppenheimer | 27 |
| M.J.Lowrey | c Morris b Turner | 25 | lbw b MacDonald | 0 |
| J.P.Arscott | c Pfaff b Turner | 14 | run out | 10 |
| R.M.Pearson | c Montgomerie b Turner | 0 | c Sandiford b Gerrans | 10 |
| R.H.J.Jenkins | c Sandiford b MacDonald | 9 | not out | 17 |
| S.W.Johnson | c Gupte b MacDonald | 7 | | |
| R.B.Waller | not out | 6 | | |
| Extras | (b 1,lb 11,w 1,nb 11) | 24 | (lb 5,w 3,nb 11) | 19 |
| TOTAL | | 279 | (for 7 wkts dec) | 146 |

**OXFORD U**

| | | | | |
|---|---|---|---|---|
| R.R.Montgomerie | not out | 50 | not out | 53 |
| R.E.Morris | c Arscott b Waller | 71 | c Arscott b Jenkins | 18 |
| G.Lovell | not out | 15 | not out | 30 |
| G.J.Turner * | | | | |
| D.Pfaff | | | | |
| C.Gupte | | | | |
| D.Sandiford + | | | | |
| P.S.Gerrans | | | | |
| R.MacDonald | | | | |
| J.M.E.Oppenheimer | | | | |
| B.Wood | | | | |
| Extras | (b 6,lb 2,nb 1) | 9 | (b 3,lb 2,w 1,nb 1) | 7 |
| TOTAL | (for 1 wkt dec) | 145 | (for 1 wkt) | 108 |

| OXFORD U | O | M | R | W | O | M | R | W | FALL OF WICKETS | | | |
|---|---|---|---|---|---|---|---|---|---|---|---|---|
| | | | | | | | | | | CAM | OXF | CAM | OXF |
| MacDonald | 24.2 | 6 | 73 | 2 | 8 | 3 | 16 | 1 | 1st | 12 | 125 | 5 | 30 |
| Wood | 21 | 7 | 41 | 2 | 7 | 2 | 24 | 2 | 2nd | 172 | | 10 | |
| Turner | 8 | 2 | 32 | 3 | 8 | 1 | 25 | 0 | 3rd | 182 | | 20 | |
| Gerrans | 23 | 5 | 73 | 2 | 13 | 1 | 65 | 2 | 4th | 198 | | 72 | |
| Oppenheimer | 19 | 4 | 48 | 1 | 4 | 2 | 11 | 1 | 5th | 228 | | 81 | |
| | | | | | | | | | 6th | 253 | | 111 | |
| CAMBRIDGE U | O | M | R | W | O | M | R | W | 7th | 253 | | 126 | |
| Johnson | 12 | 2 | 47 | 0 | 3 | 0 | 25 | 0 | 8th | 256 | | | |
| Jenkins | 10 | 2 | 29 | 0 | 8 | 0 | 25 | 1 | 9th | 267 | | | |
| Waller | 9.5 | 2 | 33 | 1 | 4 | 0 | 16 | 0 | 10th | 279 | | | |
| Pearson | 8 | 1 | 28 | 0 | 11 | 2 | 24 | 0 | | | | | |
| Arscott | | | | | 1 | 0 | 13 | 0 | | | | | |

## YORKSHIRE vs. WORCESTERSHIRE

at Headingley on 2nd, 3rd, 4th July 1991
Toss : Yorkshire.  Umpires : B.Hassan and J.W.Holder
Yorkshire won by 115 runs.  Yorkshire 19 pts (Bt: 3, Bw: 0), Worcs 3 pts (Bt: 0, Bw: 3)

**YORKSHIRE**

| | | |
|---|---|---|
| M.D.Moxon * | b Newport | 26 |
| A.A.Metcalfe | lbw b Newport | 13 |
| D.Byas | lbw b Lampitt | 37 |
| R.J.Blakey + | c D'Oliveira b Stemp | 79 |
| P.E.Robinson | c Botham b Stemp | 57 |
| S.A.Kellett | not out | 36 |
| C.S.Pickles | lbw b Newport | 4 |
| P.Carrick | st Rhodes b Stemp | 13 |
| D.Gough | c D'Oliveira b Stemp | 2 |
| P.J.Hartley | not out | 0 |
| S.D.Fletcher | | |
| Extras | (b 8,nb 16) | 24 |
| TOTAL | (for 8 wkts dec) | 291 |

**WORCESTERSHIRE**

| | | |
|---|---|---|
| T.S.Curtis | c & b Fletcher | 1 |
| G.J.Lord | lbw b Hartley | 0 |
| T.M.Moody | c Byas b Hartley | 6 |
| D.B.D'Oliveira | c Blakey b Fletcher | 7 |
| P.A.Neale * | lbw b Hartley | 10 |
| I.T.Botham | c Fletcher b Carrick | 57 |
| S.J.Rhodes + | c Pickles b Carrick | 4 |
| S.R.Lampitt | c Moxon b Carrick | 28 |
| P.J.Newport | c Byas b Carrick | 44 |
| G.R.Dilley | not out | 1 |
| R.D.Stemp | b Carrick | 0 |
| Extras | (b 8,lb 10) | 18 |
| TOTAL | | 176 |

| WORCS | O | M | R | W | O | M | R | W | FALL OF WICKETS | | |
|---|---|---|---|---|---|---|---|---|---|---|---|
| | | | | | | | | | | YOR | WOR | YOR | WOR |
| Dilley | 23 | 2 | 61 | 0 | | | | | 1st | 41 | 1 |
| Lampitt | 20 | 5 | 57 | 1 | | | | | 2nd | 42 | 1 |
| Newport | 25 | 5 | 76 | 3 | | | | | 3rd | 138 | 7 |
| Botham | 7 | 0 | 27 | 0 | | | | | 4th | 223 | 20 |
| Stemp | 21 | 3 | 62 | 4 | | | | | 5th | 243 | 24 |
| | | | | | | | | | 6th | 248 | 92 |
| YORKSHIRE | O | M | R | W | O | M | R | W | 7th | 277 | 96 |
| Hartley | | | | | 16 | 4 | 70 | 3 | 8th | 279 | 171 |
| Fletcher | | | | | 16 | 5 | 36 | 2 | 9th | | 176 |
| Carrick | | | | | 8.5 | 5 | 13 | 5 | 10th | | 176 |
| Gough | | | | | 10 | 7 | 14 | 0 | | | |
| Pickles | | | | | 5 | 0 | 25 | 0 | | | |

---

# HEADLINES

## The Varsity Match

### 2nd - 4th July 1991

The Varsity Match, as so often in recent seasons, was badly affected by the weather, although batsmen from both sides were still able to parade their talents at the home of cricket. Anthony Hooper and John Crawley impressed for Cambridge, sharing a second-wicket stand of 160 in their first innings, while Richard Montgomerie and Russell Morris responded with an opening stand of 125, but on the final day Oxford could make little progress towards a second innings target of 281.

# REFUGE ASSURANCE LEAGUE

## SOMERSET vs. LANCASHIRE

at Taunton on 5th July 1991
Toss : Lancashire. Umpires : D.O.Oslear and R.C.Tolchard
Lancashire won by 8 wickets. Somerset 0 pts, Lancs 4 pts

### SOMERSET

| | | |
|---|---|---|
| S.J.Cook | b Austin | 53 |
| P.M.Roebuck | c Hegg b Wasim Akram | 20 |
| C.J.Tavare * | run out | 57 |
| R.J.Harden | c Hegg b Watkinson | 25 |
| N.J.Pringle | c Allott b Wasim Akram | 7 |
| N.D.Burns + | c & b Austin | 6 |
| R.P.Lefebvre | run out | 2 |
| K.H.Macleay | b Austin | 1 |
| A.N.Hayhurst | not out | 2 |
| H.R.J.Trump | not out | 2 |
| J.C.Hallett | | |
| Extras | (b 2,lb 9,w 4,nb 6) | 21 |
| TOTAL | (40 overs)(for 8 wkts) | 196 |

### LANCASHIRE

| | | |
|---|---|---|
| G.D.Mendis | c Tavare b Hallett | 79 |
| G.Fowler | c Hallett b Macleay | 20 |
| G.D.Lloyd | not out | 78 |
| N.H.Fairbrother * | not out | 12 |
| M.Watkinson | | |
| Wasim Akram | | |
| N.J.Speak | | |
| W.K.Hegg + | | |
| I.D.Austin | | |
| P.J.W.Allott | | |
| P.J.Martin | | |
| Extras | (lb 4,w 2,nb 2) | 8 |
| TOTAL | (37 overs)(for 2 wkts) | 197 |

| LANCASHIRE | O | M | R | W | FALL OF WICKETS | | |
|---|---|---|---|---|---|---|---|
| | | | | | | SOM | LAN |
| Allott | 8 | 0 | 41 | 0 | | | |
| Martin | 8 | 1 | 32 | 0 | 1st | 53 | 38 |
| Wasim Akram | 8 | 0 | 30 | 2 | 2nd | 104 | 155 |
| Watkinson | 8 | 0 | 42 | 1 | 3rd | 170 | |
| Austin | 8 | 0 | 40 | 3 | 4th | 173 | |
| | | | | | 5th | 185 | |
| SOMERSET | O | M | R | W | 6th | 187 | |
| Lefebvre | 7 | 0 | 35 | 0 | 7th | 192 | |
| Hallett | 7 | 0 | 33 | 1 | 8th | 192 | |
| Macleay | 7 | 0 | 25 | 1 | 9th | | |
| Roebuck | 4 | 0 | 26 | 0 | 10th | | |
| Trump | 8 | 0 | 59 | 0 | | | |
| Hayhurst | 4 | 0 | 15 | 0 | | | |

## MIDDLESEX vs. YORKSHIRE

at Lord's on 7th July 1991
Toss : Middlesex. Umpires : R.Julian and B.J.Meyer
Yorkshire won by 7 wickets. Middlesex 0 pts, Yorks 4 pts

### MIDDLESEX

| | | |
|---|---|---|
| M.W.Gatting * | c Blakey b Fletcher | 14 |
| M.A.Roseberry | not out | 106 |
| K.R.Brown | c Robinson b Pickles | 6 |
| M.Keech | c Moxon b Gough | 5 |
| I.J.F.Hutchinson | run out | 17 |
| J.E.Emburey | c Metcalfe b Fletcher | 15 |
| P.N.Weekes | not out | 32 |
| P.Farbrace + | | |
| N.F.Williams | | |
| C.W.Taylor | | |
| N.G.Cowans | | |
| Extras | (lb 8,w 7) | 15 |
| TOTAL | (40 overs)(for 5 wkts) | 210 |

### YORKSHIRE

| | | |
|---|---|---|
| M.D.Moxon * | b Emburey | 64 |
| A.A.Metcalfe | c Taylor b Emburey | 116 |
| R.J.Blakey + | c Hutchinson b Emburey | 2 |
| D.Byas | not out | 6 |
| P.E.Robinson | not out | 3 |
| C.S.Pickles | | |
| P.Carrick | | |
| P.J.Hartley | | |
| D.Gough | | |
| J.D.Batty | | |
| S.D.Fletcher | | |
| Extras | (b 2,lb 13,w 2,nb 3) | 20 |
| TOTAL | (39.2 overs)(for 3 wkts) | 211 |

| YORKSHIRE | O | M | R | W | FALL OF WICKETS | | |
|---|---|---|---|---|---|---|---|
| | | | | | | MID | YOR |
| Hartley | 8 | 0 | 46 | 0 | | | |
| Fletcher | 8 | 0 | 43 | 2 | 1st | 23 | 167 |
| Gough | 8 | 0 | 35 | 1 | 2nd | 50 | 172 |
| Pickles | 4 | 0 | 13 | 1 | 3rd | 65 | 204 |
| Carrick | 8 | 0 | 38 | 0 | 4th | 91 | |
| Batty | 4 | 0 | 27 | 0 | 5th | 126 | |
| | | | | | 6th | | |
| MIDDLESEX | O | M | R | W | 7th | | |
| Williams | 8 | 0 | 47 | 0 | 8th | | |
| Taylor | 8 | 0 | 37 | 0 | 9th | | |
| Emburey | 8 | 0 | 34 | 3 | 10th | | |
| Cowans | 8 | 0 | 42 | 0 | | | |
| Weekes | 7.2 | 0 | 36 | 0 | | | |

---

## HEADLINES

### Refuge Assurance League

### 5th July

• With their Sunday League match against Somerset re-arranged to a Friday because of the following weekend's B & H final, Lancashire were able to cut Nottinghamshire's lead to two points after a comfortable eight-wicket victory at Taunton. The home side's middle order could not captilalise on a sound start, then Gehan Mendis and Graham Lloyd added 117 for the second wicket as a target of 197 was passed with three overs to spare.

### 7th July

• Lancashire's second victory in three days and their eighth in succession took them to the top of the table. Their five-wicket win at Leicester was virtually a carbon copy of their previous match: again needing 197 to win their batsmen had one over to spare when victory was secured.

• With Nottinghamshire not playing, other counties were also able to make up ground. Worcestershire's challenge was sustained thanks to a victory on faster scoring rate over Hampshire, Tim Curtis and Tom Moody providing yet another century partnership after the unstoppable Chris Smith had contributed 114 in the home side's total of 255 for five.

• Essex moved closer to the leaders thanks to their six-wicket success over Wawickshire at Chelmsford, John Stephenson following career-best bowling figures of four for 17 with an innings of 60 as he and Salim Malik added 115 for the second wicket.

• Kent beat Glamorgan by eight wickets thanks to a second-wicket partnership of 147 between Mark Benson and Neil Taylor as the visitors' 204 for three was easily passed.

• There were two century-makers in Middlesex's seven-wicket defeat by Yorkshire at Lord's. Mike Roseberry batted through the home side's innings for his first Sunday 100, then Ashley Metcalfe improved his career-best score as he added 167 for the first wicket with Martyn Moxon.

---

## ESSEX vs. WARWICKSHIRE

at Chelmsford on 7th July 1991
Toss : Essex. Umpires : J.C.Balderstone and R.A.White
Essex won by 6 wickets. Essex 4 pts, Warwickshire 0 pts

### WARWICKSHIRE

| | | |
|---|---|---|
| A.J.Moles | run out | 53 |
| Asif Din | c Garnham b Stephenson | 45 |
| T.A.Lloyd * | lbw b Stephenson | 1 |
| D.A.Reeve | st Garnham b Stephenson | 2 |
| D.P.Ostler | run out | 4 |
| P.A.Smith | c & b Salim Malik | 3 |
| N.M.K.Smith | not out | 38 |
| P.C.L.Holloway + | lbw b Stephenson | 8 |
| J.E.Benjamin | not out | 12 |
| T.A.Munton | | |
| A.A.Donald | | |
| Extras | (b 6,lb 7,w 3,nb 2) | 18 |
| TOTAL | (40 overs)(for 7 wkts) | 184 |

### ESSEX

| | | |
|---|---|---|
| M.A.Garnham + | b Donald | 8 |
| J.P.Stephenson | c Moles b Donald | 60 |
| Salim Malik | b Benjamin | 64 |
| P.J.Prichard | lbw b Smith P.A. | 5 |
| N.Hussain | not out | 17 |
| N.A.Foster * | not out | 16 |
| N.Shahid | | |
| K.A.Butler | | |
| A.G.J.Fraser | | |
| T.D.Topley | | |
| P.M.Such | | |
| Extras | (b 1,lb 6,w 6,nb 4) | 17 |
| TOTAL | (37 overs)(for 4 wkts) | 187 |

| ESSEX | O | M | R | W | FALL OF WICKETS | | |
|---|---|---|---|---|---|---|---|
| | | | | | | WAR | ESS |
| Foster | 6 | 1 | 19 | 0 | | | |
| Topley | 6 | 0 | 44 | 0 | 1st | 106 | 18 |
| Fraser | 6 | 0 | 33 | 0 | 2nd | 107 | 133 |
| Such | 6 | 0 | 33 | 0 | 3rd | 111 | 142 |
| Stephenson | 8 | 0 | 17 | 4 | 4th | 112 | 154 |
| Salim Malik | 8 | 0 | 25 | 1 | 5th | 117 | |
| | | | | | 6th | 123 | |
| WARWICKS | O | M | R | W | 7th | 138 | |
| Donald | 8 | 0 | 30 | 2 | 8th | | |
| Munton | 8 | 0 | 34 | 0 | 9th | | |
| Benjamin | 7 | 0 | 41 | 1 | 10th | | |
| Reeve | 3 | 0 | 24 | 0 | | | |
| Smith N.M.K. | 7 | 0 | 27 | 0 | | | |
| Smith P.A. | 4 | 0 | 24 | 1 | | | |

## HAMPSHIRE vs. WORCESTERSHIRE

at Southampton on 7th July 1991
Toss : Worcs. Umpires : K.J.Lyons and D.R.Shepherd
Worcs won on faster scoring rate. Hants 0 pts, Worcs 4 pts

### HAMPSHIRE

| | | |
|---|---|---|
| M.C.J.Nicholas * | c Rhodes b Weston | 2 |
| C.L.Smith | c & b Newport | 114 |
| D.I.Gower | c Radford b Newport | 16 |
| J.R.Wood | c Lampitt b Radford | 54 |
| V.P.Terry | not out | 42 |
| K.D.James | c D'Oliveira b Lampitt | 3 |
| J.R.Ayling | not out | 14 |
| R.J.Parks + | | |
| S.D.Udal | | |
| C.A.Connor | | |
| Aqib Javed | | |
| Extras | (lb 8,w 1,nb 1) | 10 |
| TOTAL | (40 overs)(for 5 wkts) | 255 |

### WORCESTERSHIRE

| | | |
|---|---|---|
| T.S.Curtis | c Nicholas b Aqib Javed | 76 |
| T.M.Moody | c James b Udal | 66 |
| D.B.D'Oliveira | b Aqib Javed | 36 |
| I.T.Botham | c Gower b Aqib Javed | 7 |
| P.A.Neale * | not out | 12 |
| M.J.Weston | not out | 0 |
| S.J.Rhodes + | | |
| S.R.Lampitt | | |
| P.J.Newport | | |
| N.V.Radford | | |
| R.D.Stemp | | |
| Extras | (lb 4,w 8) | 12 |
| TOTAL | (31.4 overs)(for 4 wkts) | 205 |

| WORCS | O | M | R | W | FALL OF WICKETS | | |
|---|---|---|---|---|---|---|---|
| | | | | | | HAM | WOR |
| Radford | 8 | 1 | 37 | 1 | | | |
| Weston | 4 | 0 | 21 | 1 | 1st | 4 | 126 |
| Newport | 7 | 0 | 53 | 2 | 2nd | 64 | 177 |
| Lampitt | 8 | 0 | 52 | 1 | 3rd | 178 | 189 |
| Stemp | 5 | 0 | 33 | 0 | 4th | 204 | 196 |
| Botham | 8 | 0 | 51 | 0 | 5th | 213 | |
| | | | | | 6th | | |
| HAMPSHIRE | O | M | R | W | 7th | | |
| Aqib Javed | 8 | 0 | 50 | 3 | 8th | | |
| James | 2 | 0 | 14 | 0 | 9th | | |
| Connor | 8 | 0 | 46 | 0 | 10th | | |
| Udal | 8 | 0 | 47 | 1 | | | |
| Ayling | 5.4 | 0 | 44 | 0 | | | |

# REFUGE ASSURANCE LEAGUE

## KENT vs. GLAMORGAN

at Maidstone on 7th July 1991
Toss : Kent.  Umpires : G.I.Burgess and R.Palmer
Kent won by 8 wickets.  Kent 4 pts, Glamorgan 0 pts

### GLAMORGAN

| | | |
|---|---|---|
| M.P.Maynard | c Benson b Igglesden | 23 |
| H.Morris | b Fleming | 32 |
| R.J.Shastri | not out | 90 |
| A.R.Butcher * | c & b Fleming | 30 |
| P.A.Cottey | not out | 18 |
| A.Dale | | |
| R.D.B.Croft | | |
| C.P.Metson + | | |
| S.L.Watkin | | |
| S.R.Barwick | | |
| S.Bastien | | |
| Extras | (lb 4,w 7) | 11 |
| TOTAL | (40 overs)(for 3 wkts) | 204 |

### KENT

| | | |
|---|---|---|
| M.V.Fleming | c Morris b Bastien | 2 |
| M.R.Benson * | c Morris b Bastien | 84 |
| N.R.Taylor | not out | 82 |
| T.R.Ward | not out | 33 |
| G.R.Cowdrey | | |
| C.S.Cowdrey | | |
| S.A.Marsh + | | |
| R.P.Davis | | |
| M.J.McCague | | |
| T.A.Merrick | | |
| A.P.Igglesden | | |
| Extras | (lb 5,w 2) | 7 |
| TOTAL | (37 overs)(for 2 wkts) | 208 |

| KENT | O | M | R | W | FALL OF WICKETS | | |
|---|---|---|---|---|---|---|---|
| | | | | | | GLA | KEN |
| McCague | 8 | 0 | 42 | 0 | | | |
| Igglesden | 8 | 0 | 38 | 1 | 1st | 34 | 3 |
| Davis | 8 | 1 | 46 | 0 | 2nd | 102 | 150 |
| Merrick | 8 | 1 | 29 | 0 | 3rd | 170 | |
| Fleming | 8 | 0 | 45 | 2 | 4th | | |
| | | | | | 5th | | |
| GLAMORGAN | O | M | R | W | 6th | | |
| Watkin | 8 | 0 | 48 | 0 | 7th | | |
| Bastien | 8 | 0 | 42 | 2 | 8th | | |
| Croft | 8 | 1 | 34 | 0 | 9th | | |
| Shastri | 6 | 0 | 35 | 0 | 10th | | |
| Barwick | 5 | 0 | 26 | 0 | | | |
| Dale | 2 | 0 | 18 | 0 | | | |

## LEICESTERSHIRE vs. LANCASHIRE

at Leicester on 7th July 1991
Toss : Lancashire.  Umpires : A.A.Jones and N.T.Plews
Lancashire won by 5 wickets.  Leics 0 pts, Lancs 4 pts

### LEICESTERSHIRE

| | | |
|---|---|---|
| J.J.Whitaker | run out | 88 |
| N.E.Briers * | c Speak b Martin | 8 |
| C.C.Lewis | b Martin | 9 |
| B.F.Smith | lbw b Watkinson | 26 |
| L.Potter | c Hegg b Watkinson | 1 |
| J.D.R.Benson | c Speak b Allott | 29 |
| P.Whitticase * | not out | 14 |
| P.Willey | not out | 12 |
| C.Wilkinson | | |
| D.J.Millns | | |
| J.N.Maguire | | |
| Extras | (lb 7,w 1,nb 1) | 9 |
| TOTAL | (40 overs)(for 6 wkts) | 196 |

### LANCASHIRE

| | | |
|---|---|---|
| G.D.Mendis | c Whitaker b Maguire | 13 |
| G.Fowler | c Potter b Benson | 49 |
| G.D.Lloyd | b Willey | 33 |
| N.H.Fairbrother * | c Wilkinson b Benson | 18 |
| N.J.Speak | not out | 27 |
| M.Watkinson | c Millns b Maguire | 31 |
| Wasim Akram | not out | 8 |
| W.K.Hegg + | | |
| I.D.Austin | | |
| P.J.W.Allott | | |
| P.J.Martin | | |
| Extras | (lb 11,w 7) | 18 |
| TOTAL | (39 overs)(for 5 wkts) | 197 |

| LANCASHIRE | O | M | R | W | FALL OF WICKETS | | |
|---|---|---|---|---|---|---|---|
| | | | | | | LEI | LAN |
| Allott | 8 | 0 | 31 | 1 | | | |
| Martin | 8 | 0 | 38 | 2 | 1st | 12 | 30 |
| Wasim Akram | 8 | 0 | 40 | 0 | 2nd | 38 | 88 |
| Watkinson | 8 | 0 | 33 | 2 | 3rd | 98 | 118 |
| Austin | 8 | 0 | 47 | 0 | 4th | 100 | 136 |
| | | | | | 5th | 161 | 186 |
| LEICESTERSHIRE | O | M | R | W | 6th | 179 | |
| Lewis | 8 | 0 | 33 | 0 | 7th | | |
| Maguire | 8 | 0 | 33 | 2 | 8th | | |
| Millns | 4 | 0 | 21 | 0 | 9th | | |
| Wilkinson | 4 | 0 | 19 | 0 | 10th | | |
| Willey | 8 | 0 | 30 | 1 | | | |
| Benson | 7 | 0 | 50 | 2 | | | |

## HEADLINES

### Refuge Assurance League

#### 7th July

Although Monte Lynch and Graham Thorpe both passed 50, Surrey could not overcome Northamptonshire's total of 181 at Tring, the home side gaining a narrow 15-run victory.

Derbyshire still could not return to winning ways against Sussex at Derby, falling by just five runs after the visitors had reached 231 for five in their 40 overs. Kim Barnett led a spirited Derbyshire revival from 104 for five but could not save the champions from another defeat.

#### 9th July

Derbyshire's run of defeats continued two days later as they were beaten by eight wickets in a re-arranged match at Worcester. Neal Radford, Ian Botham , and Richard Stemp all claimed three wickets to restrict Derbyshire to 169 for nine, then Tim Curtis's unbeaten 63 saw Worcestershire to victory with 7.3 overs to spare.

## NORTHANTS vs. SURREY

at Tring on 7th July 1991
Toss : Northants.  Umpires : K.E.Palmer and P.B.Wight
Northants won by 15 runs.  Northants 4 pts, Surrey 0 pts

### NORTHANTS

| | | |
|---|---|---|
| A.Fordham | c Stewart b Waqar Younis | 49 |
| N.A.Felton | c Stewart b Murphy | 4 |
| D.J.Capel | c Medlycott b Robinson | 16 |
| R.J.Bailey * | c Ward b Boiling | 33 |
| K.M.Curran | c Lynch b Murphy | 13 |
| E.A.E.Baptiste | lbw b Waqar Younis | 1 |
| R.G.Williams | c Stewart b Waqar Younis | 0 |
| D.Ripley + | b Boiling | 13 |
| A.Walker | c & b Bicknell M.P. | 4 |
| N.G.B.Cook | not out | 17 |
| J.P.Taylor | run out | 16 |
| Extras | (lb 9,w 4,nb 2) | 15 |
| TOTAL | (39.1 overs) | 181 |

### SURREY

| | | |
|---|---|---|
| D.J.Bicknell | b Taylor | 0 |
| M.A.Lynch | c Baptiste b Williams | 55 |
| A.J.Stewart *+ | lbw b Taylor | 1 |
| D.M.Ward | b Walker | 3 |
| G.P.Thorpe | c & b Capel | 50 |
| J.D.Robinson | c Walker b Capel | 11 |
| K.T.Medlycott | run out | 9 |
| M.P.Bicknell | not out | 20 |
| Waqar Younis | b Baptiste | 1 |
| J.Boiling | not out | 3 |
| A.J.Murphy | | |
| Extras | (b 1,lb 5,w 7) | 13 |
| TOTAL | (40 overs)(for 8 wkts) | 166 |

| SURREY | O | M | R | W | FALL OF WICKETS | | |
|---|---|---|---|---|---|---|---|
| | | | | | | NOR | SUR |
| Bicknell M.P. | 8 | 0 | 28 | 1 | | | |
| Murphy | 8 | 2 | 26 | 2 | 1st | 22 | 3 |
| Robinson | 5.1 | 0 | 26 | 1 | 2nd | 46 | 12 |
| Thorpe | 2 | 0 | 14 | 0 | 3rd | 98 | 17 |
| Boiling | 8 | 0 | 41 | 2 | 4th | 113 | 103 |
| Waqar Younis | 8 | 1 | 37 | 3 | 5th | 115 | 125 |
| | | | | | 6th | 115 | 136 |
| NORTHANTS | O | M | R | W | 7th | 134 | 152 |
| Walker | 8 | 1 | 14 | 1 | 8th | 145 | 156 |
| Taylor | 7 | 2 | 18 | 2 | 9th | 145 | |
| Curran | 4 | 0 | 21 | 0 | 10th | 181 | |
| Baptiste | 7 | 1 | 25 | 1 | | | |
| Cook | 4 | 0 | 25 | 0 | | | |
| Williams | 5 | 0 | 28 | 1 | | | |
| Capel | 5 | 0 | 29 | 2 | | | |

## DERBYSHIRE vs. SUSSEX

at Derby on 7th July 1991
Toss : Sussex.  Umpires : J.W.Holder and B.Leadbeater
Sussex won by 5 runs.  Derbyshire 0 pts, Sussex 4 pts

### SUSSEX

| | | |
|---|---|---|
| N.J.Lenham | run out | 11 |
| P.W.G.Parker * | b Goldsmith | 27 |
| D.M.Smith | c Adams b Base | 78 |
| M.P.Speight | c & b Goldsmith | 3 |
| K.Greenfield | c Goldsmith b Barnett | 53 |
| C.M.Wells | not out | 34 |
| A.C.S.Pigott | not out | 4 |
| A.I.C.Dodemaide | | |
| P.Moores + | | |
| I.D.K.Salisbury | | |
| A.N.Jones | | |
| Extras | (lb 13,w 8) | 21 |
| TOTAL | (40 overs)(for 5 wkts) | 231 |

### DERBYSHIRE

| | | |
|---|---|---|
| P.D.Bowler | lbw b Pigott | 26 |
| C.J.Adams | run out | 44 |
| J.E.Morris | c & b Pigott | 6 |
| M.Azharuddin | b Jones | 3 |
| T.J.G.O'Gorman | b Jones | 3 |
| S.C.Goldsmith | b Lenham | 42 |
| K.J.Barnett * | not out | 60 |
| A.E.Warner | b Pigott | 8 |
| F.A.Griffith | not out | 12 |
| K.M.Krikken + | | |
| S.J.Base | | |
| Extras | (b 2,lb 12,w 7,nb 1) | 22 |
| TOTAL | (40 overs)(for 7 wkts) | 226 |

| DERBYSHIRE | O | M | R | W | FALL OF WICKETS | | |
|---|---|---|---|---|---|---|---|
| | | | | | | SUS | DER |
| Base | 8 | 0 | 42 | 1 | | | |
| Warner | 8 | 0 | 56 | 0 | 1st | 28 | 40 |
| Goldsmith | 8 | 1 | 33 | 2 | 2nd | 66 | 52 |
| Griffith | 8 | 0 | 49 | 0 | 3rd | 75 | 64 |
| Barnett | 8 | 0 | 38 | 1 | 4th | 182 | 70 |
| | | | | | 5th | 220 | 104 |
| SUSSEX | O | M | R | W | 6th | | 185 |
| Dodemaide | 8 | 0 | 25 | 0 | 7th | | 205 |
| Wells | 8 | 0 | 35 | 0 | 8th | | |
| Jones | 8 | 0 | 55 | 2 | 9th | | |
| Pigott | 8 | 0 | 44 | 3 | 10th | | |
| Salisbury | 6 | 0 | 34 | 0 | | | |
| Lenham | 2 | 0 | 19 | 1 | | | |

## WORCS vs. DERBYSHIRE

at Worcester on 9th July 1991
Toss : Worcestershire.  Umpires : R.Julian and R.Palmer
Worcs won by 8 wickets.  Worcs 4 pts, Derbyshire 0 pts

### DERBYSHIRE

| | | |
|---|---|---|
| P.D.Bowler | b Radford | 9 |
| C.J.Adams | c Newport b Botham | 36 |
| J.E.Morris | c & b Stemp | 51 |
| F.A.Griffith | lbw b Botham | 9 |
| T.J.G.O'Gorman | st Rhodes b Stemp | 4 |
| S.C.Goldsmith | b Stemp | 4 |
| K.J.Barnett * | not out | 16 |
| K.M.Krikken + | b Botham | 0 |
| A.E.Warner | c Newport b Radford | 21 |
| S.J.Base | b Radford | 0 |
| D.E.Malcolm | not out | 2 |
| Extras | (b 2,lb 8,w 3,nb 4) | 17 |
| TOTAL | (40 overs)(for 9 wkts) | 169 |

### WORCESTERSHIRE

| | | |
|---|---|---|
| T.S.Curtis | not out | 63 |
| T.M.Moody | c Krikken b Warner | 1 |
| D.B.D'Oliveira | c O'Gorman b Malcolm | 54 |
| I.T.Botham | not out | 36 |
| P.A.Neale * | | |
| M.J.Weston | | |
| S.J.Rhodes + | | |
| S.R.Lampitt | | |
| P.J.Newport | | |
| N.V.Radford | | |
| R.D.Stemp | | |
| Extras | (b 4,lb 10,w 2,nb 1) | 17 |
| TOTAL | (32.3 overs)(for 2 wkts) | 171 |

| WORCS | O | M | R | W | FALL OF WICKETS | | |
|---|---|---|---|---|---|---|---|
| | | | | | | DER | WOR |
| Radford | 7 | 0 | 16 | 3 | | | |
| Weston | 5 | 0 | 24 | 0 | 1st | 16 | 2 |
| Newport | 5 | 0 | 23 | 0 | 2nd | 91 | 100 |
| Lampitt | 7 | 0 | 57 | 0 | 3rd | 117 | |
| Botham | 8 | 1 | 21 | 3 | 4th | 119 | |
| Stemp | 8 | 1 | 18 | 3 | 5th | 125 | |
| | | | | | 6th | 128 | |
| DERBYSHIRE | O | M | R | W | 7th | 129 | |
| Base | 8 | 1 | 28 | 0 | 8th | 162 | |
| Warner | 5 | 0 | 10 | 1 | 9th | 163 | |
| Malcolm | 8 | 0 | 57 | 1 | 10th | | |
| Goldsmith | 8 | 1 | 33 | 0 | | | |
| Griffith | 3 | 0 | 22 | 0 | | | |
| Morris | 0.3 | 0 | 7 | 0 | | | |

# BRITANNIC ASSURANCE CHAMPIONSHIP

## DERBYSHIRE vs. SUSSEX

at Derby on 5th, 6th, 8th July 1991
Toss : Sussex. Umpires : J.W.Holder and B.Leadbeater
Match drawn. Derbyshire 6 pts (Bt: 2, Bw: 4), Sussex 7 pts (Bt: 3, Bw: 4)

### SUSSEX

| | | | | | |
|---|---|---|---|---|---|
| N.J.Lenham | c Cork b Base | 48 | c Krikken b Cork | | 13 |
| D.M.Smith | c Krikken b Malcolm | 43 | lbw b Malcolm | | 16 |
| J.W.Hall | lbw b Cork | 2 | (4) b Cork | | 8 |
| P.W.G.Parker * | c Base b Warner | 7 | (5) c Azharuddin b Cork | | 20 |
| M.P.Speight | c Barnett b Malcolm | 60 | (6) c O'Gorman b Cork | | 56 |
| C.M.Wells | c Cork | 38 | (7) not out | | 14 |
| A.I.C.Dodemaide | c Barnett b Malcolm | 2 | (8) not out | | 9 |
| P.Moores + | c Azharuddin b Goldsmith | 19 | | | |
| A.C.S.Pigott | not out | 29 | | | |
| I.D.K.Salisbury | c Krikken b Cork | 9 | (3) b Goldsmith | | 34 |
| A.N.Jones | c Warner b Cork | 6 | | | |
| Extras | (b 1,lb 9,w 3,nb 13) | 26 | (lb 5,w 2,nb 6) | | 13 |
| TOTAL | | 289 | (for 6 wkts dec) | | 183 |

### DERBYSHIRE

| | | | | | |
|---|---|---|---|---|---|
| K.J.Barnett * | c Moores b Pigott | 8 | c Moores b Jones | | 3 |
| P.D.Bowler | c Lenham b Wells | 38 | lbw b Dodemaide | | 7 |
| T.J.G.O'Gorman | b Wells | 32 | (5) c Moores b Salisbury | | 19 |
| M.Azharuddin | c Moores b Jones | 1 | c Parker b Salisbury | | 59 |
| J.E.Morris | c Salisbury b Wells | 76 | (3) c Pigott b Jones | | 14 |
| S.C.Goldsmith | lbw b Jones | 35 | lbw b Salisbury | | 6 |
| K.M.Krikken + | c & b Wells | 18 | not out | | 27 |
| D.G.Cork | lbw b Wells | 13 | not out | | 6 |
| A.E.Warner | c Hall b Wells | 6 | | | |
| S.J.Base | not out | 0 | | | |
| D.E.Malcolm | c Salisbury b Wells | 0 | | | |
| Extras | (w 1,nb 2) | 3 | (lb 1,w 1,nb 1) | | 3 |
| TOTAL | | 230 | (for 6 wkts) | | 144 |

| DERBYSHIRE | O | M | R | W | O | M | R | W |
|---|---|---|---|---|---|---|---|---|
| Malcolm | 20 | 3 | 79 | 3 | 10 | 3 | 29 | 1 |
| Base | 17 | 1 | 58 | 1 | 15 | 2 | 34 | 0 |
| Cork | 20.1 | 2 | 66 | 4 | 11 | 2 | 25 | 4 |
| Warner | 16 | 5 | 32 | 1 | | | | |
| Barnett | 2 | 0 | 9 | 0 | 1 | 0 | 3 | 0 |
| Goldsmith | 15 | 6 | 35 | 1 | 7 | 0 | 41 | 1 |
| Bowler | | | | | 4 | 0 | 46 | 0 |

| SUSSEX | O | M | R | W | O | M | R | W |
|---|---|---|---|---|---|---|---|---|
| Jones | 15 | 2 | 67 | 2 | 8 | 1 | 36 | 2 |
| Dodemaide | 16 | 3 | 59 | 0 | 6 | 0 | 21 | 1 |
| Pigott | 21 | 2 | 62 | 1 | 7.5 | 0 | 36 | 0 |
| Wells | 20.4 | 8 | 42 | 7 | 8 | 2 | 33 | 0 |
| Salisbury | | | | | 6 | 1 | 17 | 3 |

| FALL OF WICKETS | | | | |
|---|---|---|---|---|
| | SUS | DER | SUS | DER |
| 1st | 69 | 10 | 30 | 8 |
| 2nd | 76 | 79 | 42 | 20 |
| 3rd | 93 | 80 | 57 | 28 |
| 4th | 157 | 84 | 88 | 86 |
| 5th | 195 | 171 | 136 | 98 |
| 6th | 197 | 202 | 166 | 116 |
| 7th | 242 | 220 | | |
| 8th | 254 | 226 | | |
| 9th | 279 | 230 | | |
| 10th | 289 | 230 | | |

## LEICESTERSHIRE vs. NORTHANTS

at Leicester on 5th, 6th, 8th July 1991
Toss : Northants. Umpires : A.A.Jones and N.T.Plews
Match drawn. Leicestershire 3 pts (Bt: 0, Bw: 3), Northants 8 pts (Bt: 4, Bw: 4)

### NORTHANTS

| | | |
|---|---|---|
| A.Fordham | lbw b Maguire | 116 |
| N.A.Felton | c Nixon b Maguire | 28 |
| R.J.Bailey * | b Maguire | 0 |
| D.J.Capel | c Nixon b Maguire | 7 |
| K.M.Curran | b Millns | 67 |
| E.A.E.Baptiste | c Nixon b Millns | 40 |
| J.G.Thomas | not out | 22 |
| D.Ripley + | c Nixon b Millns | 0 |
| A.R.Roberts | not out | 6 |
| N.G.B.Cook | | |
| J.P.Taylor | | |
| Extras | (b 2,lb 6,w 2,nb 4) | 14 |
| TOTAL | (for 7 wkts dec) | 300 |

### LEICESTERSHIRE

| | | | | | |
|---|---|---|---|---|---|
| T.J.Boon | c Cook b Thomas | 0 | c Capel b Thomas | | 5 |
| N.E.Briers * | not out | 60 | c Capel b Curran | | 133 |
| D.J.Millns | c Felton b Taylor | 0 | (9) not out | | 31 |
| J.J.Whitaker | c Baptiste b Taylor | 0 | (3) b Roberts | | 74 |
| L.Potter | c Ripley b Thomas | 4 | (4) c Bailey b Roberts | | 0 |
| C.C.Lewis | c Felton b Thomas | 8 | (5) lbw b Baptiste | | 3 |
| B.F.Smith | lbw b Cook | 12 | c Ripley b Curran | | 47 |
| P.Willey | c Ripley b Baptiste | 9 | not out | | 19 |
| P.A.Nixon | c Ripley b Baptiste | 5 | (6) lbw b Bailey | | 9 |
| C.Wilkinson | lbw b Cook | 0 | | | |
| J.N.Maguire | c Bailey b Baptiste | 4 | | | |
| Extras | (lb 1,w 1,nb 4) | 6 | (b 4,lb 10,nb 6) | | 20 |
| TOTAL | | 108 | (for 7 wkts dec) | | 341 |

| LEICS | O | M | R | W | O | M | R | W |
|---|---|---|---|---|---|---|---|---|
| Millns | 19 | 4 | 70 | 3 | | | | |
| Maguire | 23 | 5 | 57 | 4 | | | | |
| Wilkinson | 13 | 3 | 33 | 0 | | | | |
| Willey | 29 | 6 | 79 | 0 | | | | |
| Potter | 15 | 1 | 53 | 0 | | | | |

| NORTHANTS | O | M | R | W | O | M | R | W |
|---|---|---|---|---|---|---|---|---|
| Taylor | 11 | 0 | 37 | 2 | 11 | 1 | 54 | 0 |
| Thomas | 9 | 4 | 21 | 3 | 24 | 1 | 64 | 1 |
| Baptiste | 10.3 | 4 | 37 | 3 | 30 | 9 | 66 | 1 |
| Cook | 9 | 3 | 12 | 2 | 21 | 9 | 33 | 0 |
| Curran | | | | | 13 | 4 | 38 | 2 |
| Roberts | | | | | 24 | 10 | 42 | 2 |
| Capel | | | | | 8 | 3 | 21 | 0 |
| Bailey | | | | | 4 | 2 | 9 | 1 |

| FALL OF WICKETS | | | | |
|---|---|---|---|---|
| | NOR | LEI | LEI | NOR |
| 1st | 64 | 6 | 12 | |
| 2nd | 64 | 14 | 148 | |
| 3rd | 74 | 14 | 150 | |
| 4th | 221 | 19 | 163 | |
| 5th | 248 | 41 | 177 | |
| 6th | 277 | 61 | 284 | |
| 7th | 277 | 94 | 289 | |
| 8th | | 100 | | |
| 9th | | 101 | | |
| 10th | | 108 | | |

## HAMPSHIRE vs. YORKSHIRE

at Southampton on 5th, 6th, 8th (no play) July 1991
Toss : Hampshire. Umpires : K.J.Lyons and D.R.Shepherd
Match drawn. Hampshire 7 pts (Bt: 4, Bw: 3), Yorkshire 4 pts (Bt: 2, Bw: 2)
100 overs scores : Hampshire 359 for 6, Yorkshire 246 for 7

### HAMPSHIRE

| | | | | | |
|---|---|---|---|---|---|
| V.P.Terry | c Robinson b Fletcher | 13 | not out | | 6 |
| C.L.Smith | c Robinson b Hartley | 112 | not out | | 2 |
| M.C.J.Nicholas * | c Moxon b Hartley | 16 | | | |
| D.I.Gower | c Carrick b Hartley | 49 | | | |
| J.R.Wood | lbw b Hartley | 0 | | | |
| K.D.James | not out | 134 | | | |
| A.N Aymes + | c Hartley b Carrick | 34 | | | |
| R.J.Maru | b Gough | 36 | | | |
| I.J.Turner | | | | | |
| K.J.Shine | | | | | |
| Aqib Javed | | | | | |
| Extras | (b 7,lb 12,w 2,nb 2) | 23 | | | 0 |
| TOTAL | (for 7 wkts dec) | 417 | (for 0 wkts) | | 8 |

### YORKSHIRE

| | | |
|---|---|---|
| M.D.Moxon * | c Aymes b Aqib Javed | 68 |
| A.A.Metcalfe | c Aymes b James | 6 |
| D.Byas | c & b Turner | 27 |
| R.J.Blakey + | c Maru b Aqib Javed | 4 |
| P.E.Robinson | c Aymes b Maru | 25 |
| S.A.Kellett | not out | 56 |
| P.Carrick | c Aymes b Maru | 6 |
| D.Gough | c Maru b Turner | 32 |
| P.J.Hartley | b Turner | 26 |
| J.D.Batty | not out | 0 |
| S.D.Fletcher | | |
| Extras | (b 1,lb 5,w 2,nb 10) | 18 |
| TOTAL | (for 8 wkts dec) | 268 |

| YORKSHIRE | O | M | R | W | O | M | R | W |
|---|---|---|---|---|---|---|---|---|
| Hartley | 21 | 4 | 82 | 4 | 3 | 1 | 3 | 0 |
| Fletcher | 20 | 5 | 57 | 1 | 2 | 1 | 5 | 0 |
| Carrick | 34 | 6 | 109 | 1 | | | | |
| Gough | 18 | 0 | 86 | 1 | | | | |
| Batty | 17 | 1 | 64 | 0 | | | | |

| HAMPSHIRE | O | M | R | W | O | M | R | W |
|---|---|---|---|---|---|---|---|---|
| Shine | 11 | 2 | 41 | 0 | | | | |
| Aqib Javed | 20.1 | 4 | 55 | 2 | | | | |
| Maru | 34 | 9 | 79 | 2 | | | | |
| James | 8 | 1 | 20 | 1 | | | | |
| Turner | 32 | 9 | 67 | 3 | | | | |
| Smith | 1 | 1 | 0 | 0 | | | | |

| FALL OF WICKETS | | | | |
|---|---|---|---|---|
| | HAM | YOR | HAM | YOR |
| 1st | 29 | 47 | | |
| 2nd | 82 | 109 | | |
| 3rd | 194 | 118 | | |
| 4th | 194 | 122 | | |
| 5th | 195 | 159 | | |
| 6th | 314 | 173 | | |
| 7th | 417 | 229 | | |
| 8th | | 265 | | |
| 9th | | | | |
| 10th | | | | |

Alan Fordham, a century against Leicestershire.

# BRITANNIC ASSURANCE CHAMPIONSHIP

## KENT vs. GLAMORGAN

at Maidstone on 5th, 6th, 8th July 1991
Toss : Kent.  Umpires : G.I.Burgess and K.E.Palmer
Match drawn.  Kent 8 pts (Bt: 4, Bw: 4), Glamorgan 6 pts (Bt: 2, Bw: 4)

### KENT

| | | | | |
|---|---|---|---|---|
| T.R.Ward | c Butcher b Bastien | 110 | c Metson b Frost | 109 |
| S.G.Hinks | c Croft b Watkin | 5 | not out | 55 |
| N.R.Taylor | b Bastien | 77 | | |
| G.R.Cowdrey | not out | 55 | | |
| M.R.Benson * | c Metson b Croft | 5 | | |
| M.V.Fleming | c Metson b Bastien | 4 | (3) not out | 1 |
| S.A.Marsh + | c Maynard b Croft | 0 | | |
| C.Penn | c Shastri b Frost | 21 | | |
| M.J.McCague | run out | 28 | | |
| T.A.Merrick | lbw b Watkin | 5 | | |
| A.P.Igglesden | b Croft | 2 | | |
| Extras | (lb 8,nb 14) | 22 | (lb 5,w 1,nb 4) | 10 |
| TOTAL | | 334 | (for 1 wkt dec) | 175 |

### GLAMORGAN

| | | | | |
|---|---|---|---|---|
| A.R.Butcher * | c Fleming b Igglesden | 12 | c Hinks b Penn | 13 |
| H.Morris | c Marsh b McCague | 40 | c Marsh b Merrick | 11 |
| C.P.Metson + | b Fleming | 84 | | |
| R.J.Shastri | c Penn b McCague | 4 | | |
| M.P.Maynard | b Penn | 59 | (4) c Fleming b Merrick | 16 |
| P.A.Cottey | c Fleming b Penn | 4 | (3) c Marsh b Merrick | 16 |
| A.Dale | c Marsh b McCague | 9 | (5) not out | 23 |
| R.D.B.Croft | b Fleming | 1 | (6) not out | 15 |
| S.L.Watkin | not out | 7 | | |
| S.Bastien | run out | 1 | | |
| M.Frost | lbw b Fleming | 0 | | |
| Extras | (b 2,lb 8,w 4,nb 6) | 20 | (w 2,nb 7) | 9 |
| TOTAL | | 241 | (for 4 wkts) | 103 |

| GLAMORGAN | O | M | R | W | O | M | R | W |
|---|---|---|---|---|---|---|---|---|
| Watkin | 16 | 2 | 76 | 2 | 19 | 1 | 63 | 0 |
| Frost | 15 | 2 | 65 | 1 | 7.2 | 0 | 52 | 1 |
| Bastien | 25 | 7 | 73 | 3 | 6 | 1 | 27 | 0 |
| Croft | 39.4 | 8 | 97 | 3 | 12 | 3 | 26 | 0 |
| Dale | 3 | 0 | 15 | 0 | | | | |
| Shastri | | | | | 4 | 2 | 2 | 0 |

| KENT | O | M | R | W | O | M | R | W |
|---|---|---|---|---|---|---|---|---|
| Merrick | 11 | 1 | 39 | 0 | 12 | 3 | 26 | 3 |
| Igglesden | 16 | 3 | 64 | 1 | 5 | 0 | 23 | 0 |
| Penn | 16 | 4 | 46 | 2 | 11 | 0 | 49 | 1 |
| McCague | 14 | 1 | 36 | 3 | 1.2 | 0 | 5 | 0 |
| Ward | 1 | 0 | 6 | 0 | | | | |
| Fleming | 18.1 | 5 | 40 | 3 | | | | |

| FALL OF WICKETS | KEN | GLA | KEN | GLA |
|---|---|---|---|---|
| 1st | 13 | 16 | 167 | 16 |
| 2nd | 197 | 73 | | 32 |
| 3rd | 209 | 83 | | 42 |
| 4th | 222 | 181 | | 72 |
| 5th | 227 | 209 | | |
| 6th | 228 | 216 | | |
| 7th | 255 | 222 | | |
| 8th | 310 | 236 | | |
| 9th | 327 | 241 | | |
| 10th | 334 | 241 | | |

## SURREY vs. ESSEX

at The Oval on 5th, 6th, 8th July 1991
Toss : Essex.  Umpires : R.Julian and B.J.Meyer
Surrey won by 5 wickets.  Surrey 21 pts (Bt: 3, Bw: 2), Essex 7 pts (Bt: 4, Bw: 3)
100 overs scores :Surrey 279 for 8

### ESSEX

| | | | | |
|---|---|---|---|---|
| J.P.Stephenson | c Sargeant b Bicknell M.P. | 0 | (2) c Ward b Murphy | 18 |
| A.C.Seymour | c Sargeant b Bicknell M.P. | 5 | (9) not out | 10 |
| P.J.Prichard | b Bicknell M.P. | 3 | (4) c Thorpe b Bicknell M.P. | 14 |
| Salim Malik | not out | 185 | (5) not out | 59 |
| N.Hussain | b Murphy | 128 | (6) c Sargeant b Murphy | 36 |
| N.Shahid | lbw b Murphy | 0 | (8) run out | 12 |
| M.A.Garnham + | not out | 2 | (1) b Murphy | 6 |
| N.A.Foster * | | | (7) b Murphy | 0 |
| T.D.Topley | | | (3) b Murphy | 17 |
| J.H.Childs | | | | |
| P.M.Such | | | | |
| Extras | (b 7,lb 7,nb 1) | 15 | (lb 9,w 4) | 13 |
| TOTAL | (for 5 wkts dec) | 338 | (for 7 wkts) | 185 |

### SURREY

| | | | | |
|---|---|---|---|---|
| D.J.Bicknell | c Garnham b Foster | 0 | lbw b Such | 54 |
| R.I.Alikhan | b Topley | 20 | c Prichard b Childs | 8 |
| N.F.Sargeant + | lbw b Foster | 14 | | |
| A.J.Stewart | c Seymour b Childs | 33 | (3) not out | 83 |
| D.M.Ward | c Prichard b Childs | 98 | (4) lbw b Such | 54 |
| G.P.Thorpe | b Such | 28 | (5) b Childs | 2 |
| I.A.Greig * | lbw b Childs | 20 | (6) c Salim Malik b Childs | 9 |
| K.T.Medlycott | c Prichard b Such | 20 | (7) not out | 0 |
| M.A.Feltham | b Childs | 28 | | |
| M.P.Bicknell | c Hussain b Childs | 23 | | |
| A.J.Murphy | not out | 1 | | |
| Extras | (b 3,lb 11) | 14 | (b 8,lb 12) | 20 |
| TOTAL | | 299 | (for 5 wkts) | 230 |

| SURREY | O | M | R | W | O | M | R | W |
|---|---|---|---|---|---|---|---|---|
| Bicknell M.P. | 17 | 3 | 53 | 3 | 16 | 2 | 53 | 1 |
| Murphy | 18 | 5 | 52 | 2 | 19 | 2 | 63 | 5 |
| Feltham | 18 | 3 | 69 | 0 | | | | |
| Medlycott | 30 | 5 | 89 | 0 | 10 | 3 | 40 | 0 |
| Greig | 11 | 1 | 43 | 0 | | | | |
| Thorpe | 5 | 0 | 18 | 0 | 3 | 0 | 20 | 0 |

| ESSEX | O | M | R | W | O | M | R | W |
|---|---|---|---|---|---|---|---|---|
| Foster | 18 | 6 | 52 | 2 | 4 | 0 | 17 | 0 |
| Topley | 12 | 2 | 34 | 1 | 4 | 0 | 14 | 0 |
| Childs | 43.1 | 12 | 112 | 5 | 25.5 | 7 | 85 | 3 |
| Such | 34 | 8 | 87 | 2 | 24 | 5 | 91 | 2 |
| Salim Malik | | | | | 1 | 0 | 3 | 0 |

| FALL OF WICKETS | ESS | SUR | ESS | SUR |
|---|---|---|---|---|
| 1st | 0 | 4 | 11 | 30 |
| 2nd | 8 | 28 | 34 | 89 |
| 3rd | 9 | 44 | 50 | 185 |
| 4th | 323 | 83 | 87 | 188 |
| 5th | 323 | 174 | 145 | 218 |
| 6th | | 202 | 145 | |
| 7th | | 241 | 160 | |
| 8th | | 249 | | |
| 9th | | 298 | | |
| 10th | | 299 | | |

## HEADLINES

### Britannic Assurance Championship

#### 5th - 8th July

• Surrey were the only winners of the round, gaining their third victory of the season after Essex had looked to their spinners for success on the final afternoon at The Oval. Salim Malik and Nasser Hussain shared a record fourth-wicket partnership of 314 full of wristy elegance to transform Essex's first innings. David Ward's 98 allowed the visitors a lead of only 39, then Alec Stewart saw Surrey home with an unbeaten 83, to inflict on Essex their first Championship defeat of the summer.

• Derbyshire's run of success came to an end when they were held by Sussex at Derby. Dominic Cork improved his career-best bowling performance in both innings, while Colin Wells also recorded a personal best with figures of seven for 42 as Sussex gained a first innings lead of 59. Needing 247 for victory, the home side were under pressure from the leg-spin of Ian Salisbury when bad light closed in.

• Chris Smith compiled his fifth 100 of the season and Kevan James his first as Hampshire reached 417 for seven declared against Yorkshire at Southampton. The visitors were just able to avoid the follow-on, but Hampshire were prevented from pursuing their first victory of the season by the loss of the last day's play.

• Kent's Trevor Ward hit centuries in both innings in his county's drawn match with Glamorgan at Maidstone. The visitors were asked to make 259 for victory but had reached only 103 for four at close of play.

• Leicestershire's captain Nigel Briers almost singlehandedly prevented a Northamptonshire victory at Leicester: first, he carried his bat for 60 not out in a dismal Leicester first innings of 108, then made 133 as his side batted to much greater effect when they followed on. Earlier Alan Fordham had made his third century of the season in Northants' innings.

# CORNHILL TEST MATCH

## ENGLAND vs. WEST INDIES

at Trent Bridge on 4th, 5th, 6th, 8th, 9th July 1991
Toss : England. Umpires : J.H.Hampshire and M.J.Kitchen
West Indies won by 9 wickets

### ENGLAND

| | | | | |
|---|---|---|---|---|
| G.A.Gooch * | lbw b Marshall | 68 | b Ambrose | 13 |
| M.A.Atherton | lbw b Ambrose | 32 | b Marshall | 4 |
| G.A.Hick | c Dujon b Ambrose | 43 | c Dujon b Ambrose | 0 |
| A.J.Lamb | lbw b Ambrose | 13 | lbw b Marshall | 29 |
| M.R.Ramprakash | b Ambrose | 13 | c Dujon b Ambrose | 21 |
| R.A.Smith | not out | 64 | c Richards b Walsh | 15 |
| R.C.Russell + | c Logie b Allen | 3 | b Walsh | 3 |
| D.R.Pringle | c sub b Allen | 0 | c Simmons b Walsh | 3 |
| P.A.J.DeFreitas | b Walsh | 8 | not out | 55 |
| R.K.Illingworth | c Hooper b Ambrose | 13 | c Simmons b Walsh | 13 |
| D.V.Lawrence | c Allen b Marshall | 4 | c Hooper b Allen | 34 |
| Extras | (lb 17,w 1,nb 21) | 39 | (lb 14,w 3,nb 4) | 21 |
| TOTAL | | 300 | | 211 |

### WEST INDIES

| | | | | |
|---|---|---|---|---|
| P.V.Simmons | b Illingworth | 12 | c Russell b Lawrence | 1 |
| D.L.Haynes | c Smith b Lawrence | 18 | not out | 57 |
| R.B.Richardson | b Lawrence | 43 | not out | 52 |
| C.L.Hooper | c Russell b DeFreitas | 11 | | |
| I.V.A.Richards * | b Illingworth | 80 | | |
| A.L.Logie | c Ramprakash b DeFreitas | 78 | | |
| P.J.L.Dujon + | c Hick b Pringle | 19 | | |
| M.D.Marshall | c Illingworth b DeFreitas | 67 | | |
| C.E.L.Ambrose | b Illingworth | 17 | | |
| C.A.Walsh | lbw b Pringle | 12 | | |
| I.B.A.Allen | not out | 4 | | |
| Extras | (b 2,lb 13,w 1,nb 20) | 36 | (nb 5) | 5 |
| TOTAL | | 397 | (for 1 wkt) | 115 |

| WEST INDIES | O | M | R | W | O | M | R | W |
|---|---|---|---|---|---|---|---|---|
| Ambrose | 34 | 7 | 74 | 5 | 27 | 7 | 61 | 3 |
| Marshall | 21.5 | 6 | 54 | 2 | 21 | 6 | 49 | 2 |
| Walsh | 24 | 4 | 75 | 1 | 24 | 7 | 64 | 4 |
| Allen | 17 | 0 | 69 | 2 | 7 | 2 | 23 | 1 |
| Hooper | 6 | 4 | 10 | 0 | | | | |
| Richards | 1 | 0 | 1 | 0 | | | | |

| ENGLAND | O | M | R | W | O | M | R | W |
|---|---|---|---|---|---|---|---|---|
| DeFreitas | 31.1 | 9 | 67 | 3 | 11 | 3 | 29 | 0 |
| Lawrence | 24 | 2 | 116 | 2 | 12.2 | 0 | 61 | 1 |
| Illingworth | 33 | 8 | 110 | 3 | 2 | 0 | 5 | 0 |
| Pringle | 25 | 6 | 71 | 2 | 7 | 2 | 20 | 0 |
| Hick | 5 | 0 | 18 | 0 | | | | |

### FALL OF WICKETS

| | ENG | WI | ENG | WI |
|---|---|---|---|---|
| 1st | 108 | 32 | 4 | 1 |
| 2nd | 113 | 32 | 8 | |
| 3rd | 138 | 45 | 25 | |
| 4th | 186 | 118 | 67 | |
| 5th | 192 | 239 | 100 | |
| 6th | 212 | 272 | 106 | |
| 7th | 217 | 324 | 106 | |
| 8th | 228 | 358 | 115 | |
| 9th | 270 | 392 | 153 | |
| 10th | 300 | 397 | 211 | |

Viv Richards waits for the umpire's decision – which was that he had been bowled by Richard Illingworth.

West Indies celebrate the early departure of Graham Gooch in England's second innings.

| CORNHILL TEST MATCH | TOUR MATCH |
|---|---|

## CORNHILL TEST MATCH

# HEADLINES

### Third Cornhill Test Match
### England v West Indies

### Trent Bridge: 4th - 9th July

• West Indies showed that they were still very much a force in world cricket by levelling the series at one match apiece. They re-asserted their familiar superiority over England with a nine-wicket win completed just before lunch on the fifth day, Desmond Haynes and Richie Richardson bringing the visitors to victory with an unbroken second-wicket stand of 114.

• England retained the upper hand only for the first session of the match, Graham Gooch and Michael Atherton carrying them to lunch on 106 for no wicket, but in conditions very much in favour of the batting side England then lost eight wickets for 120 runs, although Graeme Hick, without looking at home, reached 43. Only Robin Smith's unbeaten 64 carried the home side to 300 as Curtly Ambrose claimed five wickets.

• West Indies' reply did not get off to the smoothest of starts, Richard Illingworth dismissing Phil Simmons with his first ball in Test cricket, as the first three wickets were claimed for 45. Viv Richards was at his most disciplined and shared a fifth-wicket stand of 121 with Gus Logie before becoming Illingworth's second victim, but a healthy lead of 97 was only forthcoming after Malcolm Marshall's flamboyant 67 was well supported by the tailenders.

• The final session of Saturday's play turned the match decisively in West Indies' favour, Ambrose and Marshall claiming the first three wickets of England's second innings, and the rest of the middle order was clinically despatched on the fourth day to leave England only 18 runs ahead with two wickets left. But there was a sting in the tail as the last two wickets added 96 runs, Phil DeFreitas hitting the first fifty of his Test career, Illingworth giving sound support and David Lawrence surpassing himself with an ebullient 34.

• Although Lawrence then dismissed Phil Simmons in his first over West Indies found their target of 115 for victory an undemanding one, leaving England needing to regroup their resources if they were to continue to compete in the series. The home side had been able to exploit West Indies weaknesses in each of the first three Tests, but with the series now level vulnerabilities in both England's batting and bowling needed radical attention if the series was to be saved.

Test début: R.K.Illingworth (England)
Man of the Match: C.E.L.Ambrose

## TOUR MATCH

**MINER COUNTIES vs. WEST INDIES**

MINOR COUNTIES vs. WEST INDIES

at Darlington on 10th, 11th July 1991
Toss : West Indies.  Umpires : G.A.Stickley and T.G.Wilson
Match drawn

WEST INDIES

| | | | | |
|---|---|---|---|---|
| P.V.Simmons | c Roberts b Greensword | 33 | not out | 78 |
| C.B.Lambert | b Evans | 50 | c Love b Taylor | 23 |
| R.B.Richardson | st Fothergill b Evans | 29 | c Fothergill b Arnold | 0 |
| B.C.Lara | c Greensword b Arnold | 82 | b Arnold | 13 |
| C.L.Hooper | c Arnold b Plumb | 21 | not out | 41 |
| D.Williams + | run out | 3 | | |
| H.A.G.Anthony | not out | 63 | | |
| I.B.A.Allen | b Taylor | 1 | | |
| I.V.A.Richards * | c Dean b Taylor | 4 | | |
| C.A.Walsh | not out | 9 | | |
| B.P.Patterson | | | | |
| Extras | (lb 2,w 1,nb 2) | 5 | (b 4,lb 4) | 8 |
| TOTAL | (for 8 wkts dec) | 300 | (for 3 wkts) | 163 |

MINOR COUNTIES

| | | |
|---|---|---|
| G.K.Brown | c Williams b Patterson | 10 |
| M.J.Roberts | c Richards b Anthony | 63 |
| N.A.Folland | c Lambert b Allen | 6 |
| J.D.Love | b Allen | 2 |
| S.J.Dean | b Patterson | 6 |
| S.G.Plumb | c Williams b Anthony | 5 |
| S.Greensword * | c Williams b Anthony | 10 |
| A.R.Fothergill + | c Richards b Anthony | 7 |
| R.A.Evans | not out | 50 |
| K.A.Arnold | c Williams b Anthony | 9 |
| N.R.Taylor | not out | 52 |
| Extras | (b 5,lb 2,w 7,nb 22) | 36 |
| TOTAL | (for 9 wkts dec) | 256 |

| MIN. COUNTIES | O | M | R | W | O | M | R | W |
|---|---|---|---|---|---|---|---|---|
| Taylor | 18 | 5 | 59 | 2 | 8 | 2 | 43 | 1 |
| Arnold | 19.5 | 1 | 69 | 1 | 10 | 1 | 48 | 2 |
| Greensword | 21 | 7 | 53 | 1 | | | | |
| Evans | 24 | 7 | 67 | 2 | 4 | 1 | 17 | 0 |
| Plumb | 12 | 2 | 50 | 1 | 5 | 1 | 22 | 0 |
| Brown | | | | | 3 | 1 | 15 | 0 |
| Love | | | | | 3 | 0 | 10 | 0 |

| WEST INDIES | O | M | R | W | O | M | R | W |
|---|---|---|---|---|---|---|---|---|
| Patterson | 10 | 2 | 49 | 2 | | | | |
| Allen | 11 | 0 | 32 | 2 | | | | |
| Anthony | 17 | 4 | 45 | 5 | | | | |
| Lara | 22.2 | 1 | 104 | 0 | | | | |
| Hooper | 8 | 2 | 15 | 0 | | | | |
| Richards | 2 | 1 | 4 | 0 | | | | |

| FALL OF WICKETS | WI | MIN | WI | MIN |
|---|---|---|---|---|
| 1st | 87 | 14 | 34 | |
| 2nd | 87 | 34 | 39 | |
| 3rd | 139 | 38 | 55 | |
| 4th | 204 | 68 | | |
| 5th | 219 | 87 | | |
| 6th | 223 | 111 | | |
| 7th | 235 | 121 | | |
| 8th | 282 | 134 | | |
| 9th | | 155 | | |
| 10th | | | | |

# HEADLINES

### Tour matches

### 10th - 15th July

• West Indies enjoyed a relaxing few days away from the cricket spotlight with matches against Minor Counties, Ireland and Wales played respectively at Darlington, Downpatrick and Brecon (see also page 108). A determined last-wicket partnership of 101 between Rupert Evans and Neil Taylor, who both passed 50 in representative cricket for the first time helped Minor Counties to an honourable draw, and, even though the tourists amassed 321 for four declared with Clayton Lambert and Gus Logie both hitting 100s, neither could they break down Ireland's defences. Wales, however, were defeated by 204 runs in a 55-over match, West Indies' batsmen peppering the boundaries on their way to 362 for six.

# NATWEST TROPHY – 2nd ROUND

## GLOUCESTERSHIRE vs. NOTTS

at Bristol on 11th, 12th July 1991
Toss : Notts. Umpires : J.W.Holder and N.T.Plews
Notts won by 3 wickets
Man of the match: C.W.J.Athey

### GLOUCESTERSHIRE

| | | |
|---|---|---|
| J.J.E.Hardy | b Hemmings | 23 |
| R.J.Scott | c French b Pick | 0 |
| A.J.Wright * | c French b Afford | 11 |
| C.W.J.Athey | c French b Pick | 76 |
| M.W.Alleyne | c & b Pick | 45 |
| R.C.Russell + | c French b Stephenson | 25 |
| J.W.Lloyds | not out | 13 |
| D.V.Lawrence | not out | 5 |
| D.R.Gilbert | | |
| A.M.Smith | | |
| M.J.Gerrard | | |
| Extras | (b 1,lb 12,w 8,nb 2) | 23 |
| TOTAL | (60 overs)(for 6 wkts) | 221 |

### NOTTS

| | | |
|---|---|---|
| B.C.Broad | c Russell b Gilbert | 38 |
| D.W.Randall | c Russell b Scott | 46 |
| R.T.Robinson * | c Lloyds b Scott | 48 |
| P.Johnson | c Russell b Lawrence | 18 |
| M.A.Crawley | not out | 35 |
| F.D.Stephenson | lbw b Lawrence | 1 |
| K.P.Evans | c Lloyds b Smith | 2 |
| B.N.French + | c & b Gilbert | 1 |
| E.E.Hemmings | not out | 17 |
| R.A.Pick | | |
| J.A.Afford | | |
| Extras | (b 1,lb 5,w 7,nb 3) | 16 |
| TOTAL | (60 overs)(for 7 wkts) | 222 |

| NOTTS | O | M | R | W | FALL OF WICKETS | | |
|---|---|---|---|---|---|---|---|
| | | | | | | GLO | NOT |
| Stephenson | 12 | 0 | 46 | 1 | 1st | 14 | 83 |
| Pick | 12 | 1 | 41 | 3 | 2nd | 37 | 104 |
| Evans | 12 | 2 | 51 | 0 | 3rd | 50 | 137 |
| Hemmings | 12 | 2 | 27 | 1 | 4th | 172 | 180 |
| Afford | 11 | 3 | 40 | 1 | 5th | 179 | 183 |
| Crawley | 1 | 0 | 3 | 0 | 6th | 212 | 187 |
| GLOUCS | O | M | R | W | 7th | | 192 |
| Gilbert | 12 | 0 | 41 | 2 | 8th | | |
| Smith | 10 | 1 | 49 | 1 | 9th | | |
| Gerrard | 2 | 0 | 10 | 0 | 10th | | |
| Lawrence | 12 | 3 | 48 | 2 | | | |
| Lloyds | 12 | 1 | 36 | 0 | | | |
| Scott | 12 | 0 | 32 | 2 | | | |

## NORTHANTS vs. LEICESTERSHIRE

at Northampton on 11th July 1991
Toss : Northants. Umpires : H.D.Bird and K.J.Lyons
Northants won by 9 wickets
Man of the match: A.Fordham

### LEICESTERSHIRE

| | | |
|---|---|---|
| T.J.Boon | run out | 14 |
| N.E.Briers * | c Ripley b Baptiste | 29 |
| J.J.Whitaker | not out | 94 |
| C.C.Lewis | c Felton b Baptiste | 6 |
| L.Potter | b Taylor | 57 |
| B.F.Smith | c Williams b Taylor | 6 |
| P.Willey | b Baptiste | 28 |
| P.Whitticase + | | |
| D.J.Millns | | |
| C.Wilkinson | | |
| J.N.Maguire | | |
| Extras | (b 1,lb 13,w 6,nb 1) | 21 |
| TOTAL | (60 overs)(for 6 wkts) | 255 |

### NORTHANTS

| | | |
|---|---|---|
| A.Fordham | not out | 132 |
| N.A.Felton | b Potter | 54 |
| R.J.Bailey | not out | 48 |
| A.J.Lamb * | | |
| D.J.Capel | | |
| K.M.Curran | | |
| R.G.Williams | | |
| E.A.E.Baptiste | | |
| D.Ripley + | | |
| A.Walker | | |
| J.P.Taylor | | |
| Extras | (b 4,lb 11,w 8,nb 2) | 25 |
| TOTAL | (46.5 overs)(for 1 wkt) | 259 |

| NORTHANTS | O | M | R | W | FALL OF WICKETS | | |
|---|---|---|---|---|---|---|---|
| | | | | | | LEI | NOR |
| Walker | 10 | 0 | 40 | 0 | 1st | 49 | 162 |
| Taylor | 10 | 1 | 50 | 2 | 2nd | 55 | |
| Baptiste | 11 | 3 | 45 | 3 | 3rd | 73 | |
| Curran | 12 | 1 | 58 | 0 | 4th | 194 | |
| Williams | 12 | 2 | 24 | 0 | 5th | 208 | |
| Capel | 5 | 0 | 24 | 0 | 6th | 255 | |
| LEICESTERSHIRE | O | M | R | W | 7th | | |
| Lewis | 9 | 0 | 32 | 0 | 8th | | |
| Millns | 9 | 0 | 60 | 0 | 9th | | |
| Maguire | 11 | 1 | 45 | 0 | 10th | | |
| Willey | 7 | 0 | 29 | 0 | | | |
| Wilkinson | 4.5 | 0 | 46 | 0 | | | |
| Potter | 6 | 1 | 32 | 1 | | | |

## SURREY vs. KENT

at The Oval on 11th July 1991
Toss : Kent. Umpires : K.E.Palmer and R.C.Tolchard
Surrey won by 7 wickets
Man of the match: J.D.Robinson

### KENT

| | | |
|---|---|---|
| T.R.Ward | b Waqar Younis | 55 |
| M.R.Benson * | c Boiling b Murphy | 14 |
| N.R.Taylor | c Stewart b Robinson | 44 |
| G.R.Cowdrey | lbw b Waqar Younis | 0 |
| S.G.Hinks | b Boiling | 34 |
| M.V.Fleming | b Robinson | 21 |
| S.A.Marsh + | c Stewart b Feltham | 15 |
| R.P.Davis | lbw b Robinson | 2 |
| C.Penn | not out | 20 |
| M.J.McCague | not out | 9 |
| T.A.Merrick | lbw b Waqar Younis | 0 |
| Extras | (b 1,lb 21,w 7,nb 2) | 31 |
| TOTAL | (57.2 overs) | 245 |

### SURREY

| | | |
|---|---|---|
| D.J.Bicknell | c Merrick b Davis | 27 |
| M.A.Lynch | run out | 48 |
| A.J.Stewart *+ | not out | 76 |
| D.M.Ward | c Marsh b Penn | 55 |
| G.P.Thorpe | not out | 20 |
| J.D.Robinson | | |
| M.A.Feltham | | |
| M.P.Bicknell | | |
| J.Boiling | | |
| Waqar Younis | | |
| A.J.Murphy | | |
| Extras | (lb 9,w 7,nb 7) | 23 |
| TOTAL | (47.2 overs)(for 3 wkts) | 249 |

| SURREY | O | M | R | W | FALL OF WICKETS | | |
|---|---|---|---|---|---|---|---|
| | | | | | | KEN | SUR |
| Waqar Younis | 10.2 | 2 | 51 | 3 | 1st | 33 | 58 |
| Bicknell M.P. | 3.5 | 1 | 9 | 0 | 2nd | 100 | 106 |
| Murphy | 9 | 2 | 27 | 1 | 3rd | 100 | 191 |
| Thorpe | 0.1 | 0 | 0 | 0 | 4th | 147 | |
| Feltham | 10 | 1 | 46 | 1 | 5th | 163 | |
| Boiling | 12 | 1 | 44 | 1 | 6th | 188 | |
| Robinson | 12 | 2 | 46 | 3 | 7th | 192 | |
| KENT | O | M | R | W | 8th | 208 | |
| Merrick | 9 | 1 | 47 | 0 | 9th | 244 | |
| McCague | 7 | 0 | 47 | 0 | 10th | 245 | |
| Davis | 11 | 2 | 34 | 1 | | | |
| Penn | 9 | 0 | 55 | 1 | | | |
| Fleming | 7.2 | 0 | 39 | 0 | | | |
| Cowdrey | 4 | 0 | 19 | 0 | | | |

## HAMPSHIRE vs. LANCASHIRE

at Southampton on 11th, 12th July 1991
Toss : Hampshire. Umpires : B.Hassan and D.R.Shepherd
Hampshire won by 8 wickets
Man of the match: R.A.Smith

### LANCASHIRE

| | | |
|---|---|---|
| G.D.Mendis | lbw b Udal | 50 |
| G.Fowler | b Udal | 71 |
| G.D.Lloyd | c Aymes b Connor | 39 |
| N.H.Fairbrother | c Udal b Connor | 24 |
| M.Watkinson | c Aqib Javed b Udal | 7 |
| Wasim Akram | c Connor b Ayling | 29 |
| P.A.J.DeFreitas | c Terry b Connor | 11 |
| W.K.Hegg + | run out | 7 |
| I.D.Austin | c Maru b Aqib Javed | 2 |
| D.P.Hughes * | not out | 5 |
| P.J.W.Allott | c Ayling b Connor | 2 |
| Extras | (lb 6,w 6,nb 2) | 14 |
| TOTAL | (59.1 overs) | 261 |

### HAMPSHIRE

| | | |
|---|---|---|
| V.P.Terry | c Hegg b Watkinson | 47 |
| C.L.Smith | c Hegg b Wasim Akram | 66 |
| R.A.Smith | not out | 79 |
| D.I.Gower | not out | 54 |
| M.C.J.Nicholas * | | |
| J.R.Ayling | | |
| A.N Aymes + | | |
| S.D.Udal | | |
| R.J.Maru | | |
| Aqib Javed | | |
| C.A.Connor | | |
| Extras | (lb 4,w 9,nb 3) | 16 |
| TOTAL | (53.5 overs)(for 2 wkts) | 262 |

| HAMPSHIRE | O | M | R | W | FALL OF WICKETS | | |
|---|---|---|---|---|---|---|---|
| | | | | | | LAN | HAM |
| Aqib Javed | 12 | 0 | 53 | 1 | 1st | 111 | 87 |
| Connor | 11.1 | 0 | 61 | 4 | 2nd | 138 | 133 |
| Maru | 12 | 2 | 37 | 0 | 3rd | 190 | |
| Ayling | 12 | 0 | 57 | 1 | 4th | 199 | |
| Udal | 12 | 0 | 47 | 3 | 5th | 205 | |
| LANCASHIRE | O | M | R | W | 6th | 232 | |
| Allott | 12 | 3 | 48 | 0 | 7th | 247 | |
| DeFreitas | 10 | 2 | 38 | 0 | 8th | 254 | |
| Wasim Akram | 12 | 0 | 46 | 1 | 9th | 258 | |
| Austin | 9 | 0 | 59 | 0 | 10th | 261 | |
| Watkinson | 10 | 0 | 62 | 1 | | | |
| Hughes | 0.5 | 0 | 5 | 0 | | | |

## SOMERSET vs. MIDDLESEX

at Taunton on 11th, 12th July 1991
Toss : Somerset. Umpires : A.A.Jones and R.Julian
Somerset won by 10 runs
Man of the match: M.W.Gatting

### SOMERSET

| | | |
|---|---|---|
| S.J.Cook | b Cowans | 7 |
| P.M.Roebuck | c Brown b Tufnell | 31 |
| A.N.Hayhurst | c Roseberry b Emburey | 58 |
| C.J.Tavare * | b Cowans | 59 |
| R.J.Harden | c Gatting b Cowans | 39 |
| K.H.Macleay | not out | 25 |
| R.P.Lefebvre | c Gatting b Cowans | 13 |
| N.D.Burns + | b Emburey | 5 |
| D.Beal | run out | 0 |
| H.R.J.Trump | run out | 1 |
| D.A.Graveney | | |
| Extras | (lb 6,w 1,nb 7) | 14 |
| TOTAL | (60 overs)(for 9 wkts) | 252 |

### MIDDLESEX

| | | |
|---|---|---|
| I.J.F.Hutchinson | lbw b Graveney | 17 |
| M.A.Roseberry | run out | 44 |
| M.W.Gatting * | b Lefebvre | 85 |
| M.R.Ramprakash | lbw b Hayhurst | 25 |
| K.R.Brown | b Macleay | 8 |
| J.E.Emburey | run out | 2 |
| P.Farbrace + | run out | 7 |
| N.F.Williams | c Macleay b Lefebvre | 3 |
| D.W.Headley | not out | 11 |
| P.C.R.Tufnell | c & b Roebuck | 8 |
| N.G.Cowans | b Hayhurst | 10 |
| Extras | (b 2,lb 15,w 5) | 22 |
| TOTAL | (59.3 overs) | 242 |

| MIDDLESEX | O | M | R | W | FALL OF WICKETS | | |
|---|---|---|---|---|---|---|---|
| | | | | | | SOM | MID |
| Cowans | 12 | 0 | 51 | 4 | 1st | 10 | 46 |
| Williams | 6 | 0 | 32 | 0 | 2nd | 84 | 97 |
| Tufnell | 12 | 2 | 29 | 1 | 3rd | 124 | 141 |
| Headley | 12 | 1 | 51 | 0 | 4th | 196 | 177 |
| Emburey | 12 | 0 | 52 | 2 | 5th | 238 | 182 |
| Ramprakash | 6 | 0 | 31 | 0 | 6th | 238 | 195 |
| SOMERSET | O | M | R | W | 7th | 243 | 209 |
| Lefebvre | 12 | 1 | 32 | 2 | 8th | 243 | 215 |
| Beal | 2 | 0 | 12 | 0 | 9th | 252 | 230 |
| Macleay | 12 | 1 | 32 | 1 | 10th | | 242 |
| Hayhurst | 11.3 | 1 | 49 | 2 | | | |
| Graveney | 7 | 1 | 24 | 1 | | | |
| Trump | 6 | 0 | 33 | 0 | | | |
| Roebuck | 9 | 0 | 43 | 1 | | | |

## SUSSEX vs. ESSEX

at Hove on 11th July 1991
Toss : Sussex. Umpires : D.J.Constant and P.B.Wight
Essex won by 4 wickets
Man of the match: G.A.Gooch

### SUSSEX

| | | |
|---|---|---|
| N.J.Lenham | c Prichard b Such | 19 |
| D.M.Smith | c Salim Malik b Topley | 62 |
| M.P.Speight | run out | 48 |
| A.P.Wells | c Shahid b Foster | 40 |
| P.W.G.Parker * | c & b Pringle | 17 |
| C.M.Wells | c Salim Malik b Pringle | 11 |
| A.I.C.Dodemaide | not out | 27 |
| P.Moores + | c Hussain b Topley | 4 |
| A.C.S.Pigott | b Topley | 0 |
| I.D.K.Salisbury | not out | 14 |
| A.N.Jones | | |
| Extras | (lb 3,w 3,nb 6) | 12 |
| TOTAL | (60 overs)(for 8 wkts) | 254 |

### ESSEX

| | | |
|---|---|---|
| G.A.Gooch * | c Dodemaide b Lenham | 95 |
| J.P.Stephenson | b Jones | 1 |
| P.J.Prichard | c Moores b Jones | 0 |
| Salim Malik | b Wells C.M. | 23 |
| N.Hussain | c Smith b Pigott | 97 |
| D.R.Pringle | b Salisbury | 2 |
| M.A.Garnham + | not out | 12 |
| N.A.Foster | not out | 10 |
| N.Shahid | | |
| T.D.Topley | | |
| P.M.Such | | |
| Extras | (lb 3,w 11,nb 1) | 15 |
| TOTAL | (58 overs)(for 6 wkts) | 255 |

| ESSEX | O | M | R | W | FALL OF WICKETS | | |
|---|---|---|---|---|---|---|---|
| | | | | | | SUS | ESS |
| Foster | 12 | 0 | 53 | 1 | 1st | 76 | 19 |
| Pringle | 12 | 1 | 54 | 2 | 2nd | 97 | 27 |
| Such | 12 | 0 | 36 | 1 | 3rd | 177 | 70 |
| Topley | 12 | 1 | 38 | 3 | 4th | 183 | 212 |
| Salim Malik | 6 | 0 | 34 | 0 | 5th | 204 | 219 |
| Stephenson | 1 | 0 | 8 | 0 | 6th | 213 | 238 |
| Gooch | 5 | 0 | 28 | 0 | 7th | 224 | |
| SUSSEX | O | M | R | W | 8th | 224 | |
| Jones | 7 | 0 | 46 | 2 | 9th | | |
| Dodemaide | 11 | 0 | 52 | 0 | 10th | | |
| Pigott | 12 | 0 | 40 | 1 | | | |
| Wells C.M. | 9 | 0 | 39 | 1 | | | |
| Salisbury | 12 | 1 | 40 | 1 | | | |
| Lenham | 7 | 0 | 35 | 1 | | | |

# NATWEST TROPHY – 2nd ROUND

## HEADLINES

### NatWest Trophy

### 2nd Round

### 11th - 12th July

• Lancashire, defending NatWest champions, unbeaten in knockout cricket for almost two years and undefeated in their last 16 one-day games in all competitions, were decisively beaten by eight wickets by Hampshire at Southampton, the home side winning at a canter with 6.1 overs in hand. Gehan Mendis and Graeme Fowler had given Lancashire the perfect start with an opening stand of 111, but their last eight wickets fell for 71, Cardgian Connor and Sean Udal both recording competition best figures. Paul Terry and Chris Smith opened with a stand of 87, then as the match extended into a second day Robin Smith and David Gower saw Hampshire home with a third-wicket partnership of 129.

• Worcestershire were also unexpectedly heavily defeated at Worcester by Glamorgan who first bowled and fielded admirably to restrict their hosts to 223 for nine in 60 overs, then coasted to a seven-wicket victory thanks to a career-best 86 from Adrian Dale and a hard-hitting 78 not out from Matthew Maynard.

• Essex were grateful to a fourth-wicket stand of 142 between Graham Gooch and Nasser Hussain, who hit a career-best 97, for taking them to a four-wicket win over Sussex at Hove, after the home side had reached 254 for eight in their 60 overs.

• Gloucestershire's contest with Nottinghamshire at Bristol was seriously interrupted on both days and not decided until the last available ball of Notts' innings. Needing 222 to win, the visitors were in control at 180 for three, then lost four wickets for 12 runs, before being taken into the quarter-finals by Mark Crawley and Eddie Hemmings who calmly added 30 for the eighth wicket.

• At Leicester, James Whitaker's unbeaten 94 lifted Leicestershire to a total of 255 for six in their 60 overs against Northamptonshire but it proved no match for the first three in the visitors' batting line up. Alan Fordham hit a competition best 132 not out and was well supported by Nigel Felton and Rob Bailey as Northants raced to a nine-wicket victory.

• Middlesex's last hopes of a trophy in 1991 disappeared with their 10-run defeat by Somerset at Taunton when the visitors found a target of 253 too much for them despite 85 from Mike Gatting.

• At The Oval, Surrey overcame the early loss of Martin Bicknell to bowl out Kent for 245, seventh bowler Jonathan Robinson claiming a career-best three for 46, then Alec Stewart contributed an unbeaten 76 to seal a seven-wicket victory.

• Hertfordshire found Warwickshire stern opponents at Edgbaston, managing only 135 for seven in their 60 overs despite the assistance of 40 extras, before Andy Moles and Jason Ratcliffe secured a ten-wicket win with a stand of 138.

## WARWICKS vs. HERTFORDSHIRE

at Edgbaston on 11th July 1991
Toss : Hertfordshire.  Umpires : J.D.Bond and D.O.Oslear
Warwickshire won by 10 wickets
Man of the match: J.D.Ratcliffe

**HERTFORDSHIRE**

| | | |
|---|---|---|
| J.D.Carr | run out | 14 |
| N.P.G.Wright | c Piper b Small | 6 |
| B.G.Evans | c Munton b Reeve | 7 |
| M.F.Voss | c & b Smith | 2 |
| N.R.C.Maclaurin | c Piper b Donald | 3 |
| A.Needham | lbw b Smith | 4 |
| D.C.G.Ligertwood + | not out | 37 |
| D.M.Smith | b Reeve | 15 |
| W.G.Merry | not out | 7 |
| D.Surridge * | | |
| G.A.R.Harris | | |
| Extras | (lb 5,w 33,nb 2) | 40 |
| TOTAL | (60 overs)(for 7 wkts) | 135 |

**WARWICKSHIRE**

| | | |
|---|---|---|
| A.J.Moles | not out | 62 |
| J.D.Ratcliffe | not out | 68 |
| T.A.Lloyd * | | |
| D.P.Ostler | | |
| D.A.Reeve | | |
| P.A.Smith | | |
| Asif Din | | |
| K.J.Piper + | | |
| G.C.Small | | |
| T.A.Munton | | |
| A.A.Donald | | |
| Extras | (lb 6,w 2) | 8 |
| TOTAL | (36.4 overs)(for 0 wkts) | 138 |

| WARWICKS | O | M | R | W | FALL OF WICKETS | | |
|---|---|---|---|---|---|---|---|
| | | | | | | HER | WAR |
| Donald | 12 | 1 | 40 | 1 | | | |
| Small | 12 | 4 | 25 | 1 | 1st | 20 | |
| Munton | 12 | 2 | 22 | 0 | 2nd | 33 | |
| Reeve | 12 | 5 | 19 | 2 | 3rd | 35 | |
| Smith | 12 | 2 | 24 | 2 | 4th | 38 | |
| | | | | | 5th | 43 | |
| HERTS | O | M | R | W | 6th | 56 | |
| Harris | 4 | 1 | 17 | 0 | 7th | 113 | |
| Surridge | 4 | 1 | 15 | 0 | 8th | | |
| Needham | 12 | 4 | 25 | 0 | 9th | | |
| Merry | 5 | 1 | 18 | 0 | 10th | | |
| Carr | 6 | 0 | 13 | 0 | | | |
| Smith | 3 | 0 | 15 | 0 | | | |
| Maclaurin | 2 | 0 | 20 | 0 | | | |
| Wright | 0.4 | 0 | 9 | 0 | | | |

## WORCS vs. GLAMORGAN

at Worcester on 11th, 12th July 1991
Toss : Worcestershire.  Umpires : G.I.Burgess and B.J.Meyer
Glamorgan won by 7 wickets
Man of the match: A.Dale

**WORCESTERSHIRE**

| | | |
|---|---|---|
| T.S.Curtis | run out | 34 |
| T.M.Moody | c Metson b Barwick | 37 |
| G.A.Hick | c Dale b Croft | 10 |
| D.B.D'Oliveira | c Frost b Dale | 13 |
| P.A.Neale * | b Croft | 8 |
| I.T.Botham | c Butcher b Barwick | 27 |
| S.J.Rhodes + | c Butcher b Frost | 41 |
| R.K.Illingworth | run out | 10 |
| S.R.Lampitt | run out | 7 |
| N.V.Radford | not out | 15 |
| G.R.Dilley | not out | 7 |
| Extras | (b 1,lb 8,w 5) | 14 |
| TOTAL | (60 overs)(for 9 wkts) | 223 |

**GLAMORGAN**

| | | |
|---|---|---|
| A.R.Butcher * | c & b Dilley | 0 |
| H.Morris | c & b Illingworth | 40 |
| A.Dale | c Botham b Lampitt | 86 |
| M.P.Maynard | not out | 78 |
| P.A.Cottey | not out | 3 |
| I.Smith | | |
| R.D.B.Croft | | |
| C.P.Metson + | | |
| S.L.Watkin | | |
| S.R.Barwick | | |
| M.Frost | | |
| Extras | (lb 7,w 6,nb 4) | 17 |
| TOTAL | (53.4 overs)(for 3 wkts) | 224 |

| GLAMORGAN | O | M | R | W | FALL OF WICKETS | | |
|---|---|---|---|---|---|---|---|
| | | | | | | WOR | GLA |
| Watkin | 12 | 1 | 35 | 0 | | | |
| Frost | 12 | 0 | 58 | 1 | 1st | 56 | 8 |
| Barwick | 12 | 0 | 51 | 2 | 2nd | 88 | 116 |
| Dale | 12 | 1 | 42 | 1 | 3rd | 91 | 208 |
| Croft | 12 | 0 | 28 | 2 | 4th | 107 | |
| | | | | | 5th | 115 | |
| WORCS | O | M | R | W | 6th | 153 | |
| Dilley | 12 | 1 | 35 | 1 | 7th | 166 | |
| Radford | 10 | 0 | 35 | 0 | 8th | 181 | |
| Botham | 10 | 0 | 39 | 0 | 9th | 203 | |
| Lampitt | 9.4 | 0 | 61 | 1 | 10th | | |
| Illingworth | 12 | 1 | 47 | 1 | | | |

## BENSON & HEDGES CUP FINAL

## TOUR MATCHES

### LANCASHIRE vs. WORCS

at Lord's on 13th, 14th July 1991
Toss : Lancashire.  Umpires : J.W.Holder and D.R.Shepherd
Worcestershire won by 65 runs
Man of the match: G.A.Hick

**WORCESTERSHIRE**

| | | |
|---|---|---|
| T.S.Curtis | b DeFreitas | 4 |
| T.M.Moody | b Allott | 12 |
| G.A.Hick | c & b Allott | 88 |
| D.B.D'Oliveira | c DeFreitas b Wasim Akram | 25 |
| I.T.Botham | c Fowler b Watkinson | 19 |
| P.A.Neale * | c Watkinson b Austin | 4 |
| S.J.Rhodes + | c Allott b Wasim Akram | 13 |
| R.K.Illingworth | not out | 17 |
| P.J.Newport | c DeFreitas b Wasim Akram | 2 |
| N.V.Radford | not out | 25 |
| G.R.Dilley | | |
| Extras | (lb 8,w 15,nb 4) | 27 |
| TOTAL | (55 overs)(for 8 wkts) | 236 |

**LANCASHIRE**

| | | |
|---|---|---|
| G.D.Mendis | b Radford | 14 |
| G.Fowler | c Hick b Radford | 54 |
| M.A.Atherton | c Rhodes b Radford | 5 |
| N.H.Fairbrother * | run out | 1 |
| G.D.Lloyd | c Hick b Botham | 10 |
| M.Watkinson | c Hick b Dilley | 13 |
| Wasim Akram | run out | 14 |
| P.A.J.DeFreitas | c Neale b Newport | 19 |
| W.K.Hegg + | not out | 13 |
| I.D.Austin | c Illingworth b Newport | 7 |
| P.J.W.Allott | c Neale b Dilley | 10 |
| Extras | (lb 5,w 4,nb 2) | 11 |
| TOTAL | (47.2 overs) | 171 |

| LANCASHIRE | O | M | R | W | FALL OF WICKETS | | |
|---|---|---|---|---|---|---|---|
| | | | | | | WOR | LAN |
| DeFreitas | 11 | 1 | 38 | 1 | | | |
| Allott | 11 | 3 | 26 | 2 | 1st | 4 | 24 |
| Watkinson | 11 | 0 | 54 | 1 | 2nd | 38 | 31 |
| Wasim Akram | 11 | 1 | 58 | 3 | 3rd | 97 | 32 |
| Austin | 11 | 0 | 52 | 1 | 4th | 166 | 64 |
| | | | | | 5th | 172 | 92 |
| WORCS | O | M | R | W | 6th | 175 | 111 |
| Dilley | 8.2 | 2 | 19 | 2 | 7th | 195 | 134 |
| Radford | 9 | 1 | 48 | 3 | 8th | 203 | 140 |
| Botham | 8 | 1 | 23 | 1 | 9th | | 158 |
| Newport | 11 | 1 | 38 | 2 | 10th | | 171 |
| Illingworth | 11 | 0 | 38 | 0 | | | |

### IRELAND vs. WEST INDIES

at Downpatrick on 13th July 1991
Toss : W. Indies.  Umpires : H.Henderson & M.A.C.Moore
Match drawn

**WEST INDIES**

| | | |
|---|---|---|
| P.V.Simmons | c Thompson b Hoey | 50 |
| C.B.Lambert | c Jackson b Lewis | 105 |
| B.C.Lara | c Cohen b Hoey | 4 |
| A.L.Logie | run out | 118 |
| C.L.Hooper | not out | 26 |
| D.L.Haynes * | not out | 14 |
| D.Williams + | | |
| H.A.G.Anthony | | |
| C.A.Walsh | | |
| I.B.A.Allen | | |
| B.P.Patterson | | |
| Extras | (b 1,lb 2,nb 1) | 4 |
| TOTAL | (for 4 wkts dec) | 321 |

**IRELAND**

| | | |
|---|---|---|
| S.J.S.Warke * | b Hooper | 44 |
| M.F.Cohen | c Simmons b Hooper | 17 |
| S.G.Smyth | c Williams b Anthony | 18 |
| D.A.Lewis | not out | 41 |
| T.J.T.Patterson | run out | 8 |
| D.A.Vincent | c Lara b Haynes | 16 |
| G.D.Harrison | not out | 2 |
| N.E.Thompson | | |
| P.B.Jackson + | | |
| C.Hoey | | |
| A.N.Nelson | | |
| Extras | (b 8,lb 6,w 2,nb 3) | 19 |
| TOTAL | (for 5 wkts) | 165 |

| IRELAND | O | M | R | W | FALL OF WICKETS | | |
|---|---|---|---|---|---|---|---|
| | | | | | | WI | IRE |
| Nelson | 14 | 2 | 73 | 0 | 1st | 94 | 33 |
| Thompson | 12 | 1 | 74 | 0 | 2nd | 98 | 88 |
| Hoey | 12 | 1 | 63 | 2 | 3rd | 279 | 92 |
| Lewis | 15 | 2 | 78 | 1 | 4th | 287 | 115 |
| Harrison | 7 | 0 | 30 | 0 | 5th | | 156 |
| WEST INDIES | O | M | R | W | 6th | | |
| Patterson | 5 | 0 | 14 | 0 | 7th | | |
| Allen | 7 | 1 | 17 | 0 | 8th | | |
| Hooper | 17 | 6 | 52 | 2 | 9th | | |
| Walsh | 6 | 2 | 13 | 0 | 10th | | |
| Anthony | 8 | 3 | 28 | 1 | | | |
| Haynes | 3 | 0 | 14 | 1 | | | |
| Lara | 3 | 0 | 13 | 0 | | | |

### WALES vs. WEST INDIES

at Brecon on 15th July 1991
Toss : West Indies.  Umpires : S.W.Kuhlmann and J.Waite
West Indies won by 204 runs

**WEST INDIES**

| | | |
|---|---|---|
| P.V.Simmons | c Bishop b Smith | 64 |
| R.B.Richardson | c Shaw b Griffiths | 22 |
| B.C.Lara | st Shaw b Watkins | 82 |
| I.V.A.Richards * | c Griffiths b Edwards | 68 |
| C.L.Hooper | st Shaw b Edwards | 88 |
| P.J.L.Dujon + | c Shaw b Griffiths | 19 |
| A.L.Logie | not out | 2 |
| M.D.Marshall | | |
| H.A.G.Anthony | | |
| I.B.A.Allen | | |
| B.P.Patterson | | |
| Extras | (b 4,lb 8,w 5) | 17 |
| TOTAL | (55 overs)(for 6 wkts) | 362 |

**WALES**

| | | |
|---|---|---|
| S.G.Watkins | c Dujon b Patterson | 3 |
| T.C.Hughes | b Patterson | 3 |
| A.W.Harris | c Logie b Lara | 4 |
| J.Bishop | c Richards b Hooper | 50 |
| N.G.Roberts | c Richards b Patterson | 16 |
| A.C.Puddle * | c Marshall b Lara | 16 |
| B.J.Lloyd | st sub b Richards | 23 |
| W.G.Edwards | not out | 19 |
| A.Smith | c Richardson b Logie | 1 |
| A.D.Shaw + | c sub b Richards | 0 |
| A.D.Griffiths | not out | 8 |
| Extras | (b 4,lb 2,w 5,nb 4) | 15 |
| TOTAL | (55 overs)(for 9 wkts) | 158 |

| WALES | O | M | R | W | FALL OF WICKETS | | |
|---|---|---|---|---|---|---|---|
| | | | | | | WI | WAL |
| Edwards | 11 | 0 | 61 | 2 | 1st | 52 | 6 |
| Griffiths | 11 | 1 | 51 | 2 | 2nd | 137 | 9 |
| Lloyd | 11 | 0 | 59 | 0 | 3rd | 196 | 29 |
| Smith | 11 | 1 | 57 | 1 | 4th | 299 | 60 |
| Watkins | 8 | 0 | 74 | 1 | 5th | 352 | 92 |
| Roberts | 3 | 0 | 48 | 0 | 6th | 362 | 104 |
| WEST INDIES | O | M | R | W | 7th | | 144 |
| Patterson | 7 | 2 | 17 | 3 | 8th | | 146 |
| Allen | 7 | 3 | 6 | 0 | 9th | | 149 |
| Lara | 11 | 4 | 29 | 2 | 10th | | |
| Anthony | 6 | 1 | 19 | 0 | | | |
| Richards | 10 | 0 | 34 | 2 | | | |
| Hooper | 11 | 2 | 27 | 1 | | | |
| Logie | 3 | 0 | 20 | 1 | | | |

A Lord's victory at last for Phil Neale, with Man of the Match Graeme Hick.

# REFUGE ASSURANCE LEAGUE

## KENT vs. LEICESTERSHIRE

at Canterbury on 14th July 1991
Toss : Kent. Umpires : B.Dudleston and M.J.Kitchen
Kent won by 3 wickets. Kent 4 pts, Leicestershire 0 pts

### LEICESTERSHIRE

| | | |
|---|---|---|
| J.J.Whitaker | c Cowdrey b Davis | 48 |
| N.E.Briers * | run out | 16 |
| B.F.Smith | c & b Davis | 21 |
| C.C.Lewis | b Davis | 8 |
| L.Potter | c Ward b Merrick | 19 |
| J.D.R.Benson | c Marsh b Fleming | 2 |
| P.Willey | b McCague | 31 |
| M.I.Gidley | c & b McCague | 2 |
| P.Whitticase + | c Davis b Fleming | 9 |
| D.J.Millns | b Fleming | 13 |
| J.N.Maguire | not out | 0 |
| Extras | (lb 8,w 5,nb 2) | 15 |
| TOTAL | (39.4 overs) | 184 |

### KENT

| | | |
|---|---|---|
| M.V.Fleming | c Potter b Lewis | 5 |
| M.R.Benson * | c Smith b Benson | 12 |
| N.R.Taylor | lbw b Lewis | 0 |
| T.R.Ward | c Potter b Benson | 15 |
| G.R.Cowdrey | lbw b Willey | 17 |
| S.G.Hinks | c & b Benson | 35 |
| S.A.Marsh + | c Whitticase b Lewis | 59 |
| R.P.Davis | not out | 11 |
| M.J.McCague | not out | 17 |
| T.A.Merrick | | |
| A.P.Igglesden | | |
| Extras | (lb 5,w 8,nb 1) | 14 |
| TOTAL | (39.3 overs)(for 7 wkts) | 185 |

| KENT | O | M | R | W | | FALL OF WICKETS | |
|---|---|---|---|---|---|---|---|
| | | | | | | LEI | KEN |
| Igglesden | 8 | 1 | 27 | 0 | 1st | 36 | 12 |
| Merrick | 8 | 0 | 38 | 1 | 2nd | 75 | 12 |
| McCague | 8 | 0 | 37 | 2 | 3rd | 91 | 40 |
| Fleming | 7.4 | 0 | 41 | 3 | 4th | 104 | 46 |
| Davis | 8 | 0 | 33 | 3 | 5th | 107 | 76 |
| | | | | | 6th | 153 | 131 |
| LEICESTERSHIRE | O | M | R | W | 7th | 159 | 163 |
| Lewis | 8 | 2 | 25 | 3 | 8th | 159 | |
| Maguire | 7.3 | 0 | 30 | 0 | 9th | 180 | |
| Millns | 8 | 0 | 41 | 0 | 10th | 184 | |
| Benson | 7 | 0 | 39 | 3 | | | |
| Willey | 5 | 0 | 25 | 1 | | | |
| Potter | 4 | 0 | 20 | 0 | | | |

## NOTTS vs. HAMPSHIRE

at Trent Bridge on 14th July 1991
Toss : Notts. Umpires : J.H.Hampshire and D.O.Oslear
Notts won by 3 wickets. Notts 4 pts, Hampshire 0 pts

### HAMPSHIRE

| | | |
|---|---|---|
| V.P.Terry | c Saxelby b Hemmings | 61 |
| R.A.Smith | b Pick | 9 |
| J.R.Wood | b Pick | 11 |
| M.C.J.Nicholas * | c Hemmings b Evans | 32 |
| K.D.James | not out | 28 |
| J.R.Ayling | run out | 34 |
| A.N Aymes + | run out | 8 |
| S.D.Udal | | |
| R.J.Maru | | |
| C.A.Connor | | |
| Aqib Javed | | |
| Extras | (b 1,lb 10,w 7,nb 5) | 23 |
| TOTAL | (40 overs)(for 6 wkts) | 206 |

### NOTTS

| | | |
|---|---|---|
| B.C.Broad | c Aymes b Connor | 12 |
| D.W.Randall | c Smith b Udal | 83 |
| R.T.Robinson * | b Maru | 7 |
| P.Johnson | b Udal | 31 |
| M.A.Crawley | c Terry b Ayling | 6 |
| M.Saxelby | run out | 24 |
| F.D.Stephenson | run out | 21 |
| B.N.French + | not out | 1 |
| K.P.Evans | not out | 4 |
| E.E.Hemmings | | |
| R.A.Pick | | |
| Extras | (b 4,lb 9,w 7,nb 1) | 21 |
| TOTAL | (40 overs)(for 7 wkts) | 210 |

| NOTTS | O | M | R | W | | FALL OF WICKETS | |
|---|---|---|---|---|---|---|---|
| | | | | | | HAM | NOT |
| Stephenson | 8 | 1 | 32 | 0 | 1st | 23 | 22 |
| Pick | 8 | 1 | 27 | 2 | 2nd | 45 | 35 |
| Evans | 8 | 0 | 52 | 1 | 3rd | 131 | 122 |
| Crawley | 8 | 0 | 49 | 0 | 4th | 132 | 146 |
| Hemmings | 8 | 0 | 35 | 1 | 5th | 194 | 160 |
| | | | | | 6th | 206 | 204 |
| HAMPSHIRE | O | M | R | W | 7th | | 206 |
| Connor | 7 | 0 | 40 | 1 | 8th | | |
| Aqib Javed | 8 | 0 | 43 | 0 | 9th | | |
| Ayling | 7 | 1 | 34 | 1 | 10th | | |
| Maru | 8 | 1 | 27 | 1 | | | |
| Udal | 8 | 1 | 42 | 2 | | | |
| James | 2 | 0 | 11 | 0 | | | |

## HEADLINES

### Refuge Assurance League

### 14th July

• Notts returned to the top of the table with their success over Hampshire, Kevin Evans hitting four off the last ball of their 40th over to secure victory.

• Kent were indebted to Steve Marsh's best Sunday score to take them past Leicestershire's total of 184 at Canterbury and secure a three-wicket win with just three balls to spare.

• Surrey's victory over Sussex was much more clearcut, Alec Stewart and David Ward adding 120 for the third wicket to take the home side to an eight-wicket success.

• Warwickshire's margin of victory over Middlesex was even more convincing, Asif Din's third Sunday League 100 bringing his side home with nine wickets in hand.

• David Lawrence performed with the bat as well as the ball in Gloucestershire's defeat of Yorkshire by 10 runs. After an unbeaten 38 he then claimed four wickets for 27.

## SURREY vs. SUSSEX

at The Oval on 14th July 1991
Toss : Sussex. Umpires : J.H.Harris and P.B.Wight
Surrey won by 8 wickets. Surrey 4 pts, Sussex 0 pts

### SUSSEX

| | | |
|---|---|---|
| N.J.Lenham | c Stewart b Feltham | 11 |
| P.W.G.Parker * | c Thorpe b Robinson | 60 |
| D.M.Smith | st Stewart b Boiling | 19 |
| M.P.Speight | c Ward b Boiling | 9 |
| K.Greenfield | run out | 22 |
| C.M.Wells | c Feltham b Murphy | 10 |
| A.I.C.Dodemaide | not out | 17 |
| P.Moores + | c Stewart b Murphy | 2 |
| A.C.S.Pigott | c Stewart b Feltham | 14 |
| I.D.K.Salisbury | b Feltham | 8 |
| A.N.Jones | not out | 0 |
| Extras | (b 1,lb 10,w 4,nb 3) | 18 |
| TOTAL | (40 overs)(for 9 wkts) | 190 |

### SURREY

| | | |
|---|---|---|
| D.J.Bicknell | c Smith b Lenham | 40 |
| M.A.Lynch | c Smith b Dodemaide | 6 |
| A.J.Stewart + | not out | 84 |
| D.M.Ward | not out | 51 |
| G.P.Thorpe | | |
| I.A.Greig * | | |
| J.D.Robinson | | |
| M.A.Feltham | | |
| J.Boiling | | |
| Waqar Younis | | |
| A.J.Murphy | | |
| Extras | (lb 4,w 9) | 13 |
| TOTAL | (38.5 overs)(for 2 wkts) | 194 |

| SURREY | O | M | R | W | | FALL OF WICKETS | |
|---|---|---|---|---|---|---|---|
| | | | | | | SUS | SUR |
| Feltham | 8 | 0 | 44 | 3 | 1st | 27 | 7 |
| Murphy | 8 | 1 | 36 | 2 | 2nd | 66 | 74 |
| Robinson | 8 | 0 | 39 | 1 | 3rd | 95 | |
| Boiling | 8 | 0 | 24 | 2 | 4th | 134 | |
| Waqar Younis | 8 | 1 | 36 | 0 | 5th | 137 | |
| | | | | | 6th | 151 | |
| SUSSEX | O | M | R | W | 7th | 154 | |
| Dodemaide | 7 | 1 | 32 | 1 | 8th | 174 | |
| Wells | 7 | 0 | 26 | 0 | 9th | 189 | |
| Pigott | 7.5 | 0 | 43 | 0 | 10th | | |
| Salisbury | 8 | 0 | 52 | 0 | | | |
| Lenham | 2 | 0 | 12 | 1 | | | |
| Jones | 7 | 1 | 25 | 0 | | | |

## YORKSHIRE vs. GLOUCS

at Scarborough on 14th July 1991
Toss : Gloucs. Umpires : J.D.Bond and R.A.White
Gloucs won by 10 runs. Yorkshire 0 pts, Gloucs 4 pts

### GLOUCESTERSHIRE

| | | |
|---|---|---|
| R.J.Scott | c Byas b Gough | 31 |
| C.W.J.Athey | b Fletcher | 3 |
| A.J.Wright * | c Robinson b Batty | 41 |
| R.C.Russell + | c Fletcher b Pickles | 29 |
| M.W.Alleyne | b Pickles | 4 |
| J.J.E.Hardy | b Pickles | 10 |
| J.W.Lloyds | not out | 42 |
| D.V.Lawrence | not out | 38 |
| D.R.Gilbert | | |
| A.M.Smith | | |
| M.C.J.Ball | | |
| Extras | (lb 8,w 2,nb 1) | 11 |
| TOTAL | (40 overs)(for 6 wkts) | 209 |

### YORKSHIRE

| | | |
|---|---|---|
| M.D.Moxon * | c Ball b Lawrence | 6 |
| A.A.Metcalfe | c Russell b Lawrence | 11 |
| R.J.Blakey | lbw b Lawrence | 43 |
| D.Byas + | c Russell b Smith | 19 |
| P.E.Robinson | b Alleyne | 64 |
| C.S.Pickles | c Gilbert b Lawrence | 7 |
| P.Carrick | c Lloyds b Smith | 25 |
| D.Gough | b Smith | 7 |
| P.J.Hartley | c Hardy b Scott | 1 |
| J.D.Batty | b Scott | 0 |
| S.D.Fletcher | not out | 3 |
| Extras | (lb 3,w 6,nb 4) | 13 |
| TOTAL | (39.5 overs) | 199 |

| YORKSHIRE | O | M | R | W | | FALL OF WICKETS | |
|---|---|---|---|---|---|---|---|
| | | | | | | GLO | YOR |
| Hartley | 7 | 1 | 33 | 0 | 1st | 14 | 21 |
| Fletcher | 6 | 0 | 42 | 1 | 2nd | 60 | 22 |
| Carrick | 8 | 0 | 23 | 0 | 3rd | 104 | 56 |
| Gough | 7 | 1 | 35 | 1 | 4th | 112 | 119 |
| Batty | 6 | 0 | 38 | 1 | 5th | 121 | 130 |
| Pickles | 6 | 0 | 30 | 3 | 6th | 149 | 184 |
| | | | | | 7th | | 192 |
| GLOUCS | O | M | R | W | 8th | | 194 |
| Lawrence | 8 | 1 | 27 | 4 | 9th | | 195 |
| Gilbert | 8 | 0 | 41 | 0 | 10th | | 199 |
| Smith | 7.5 | 0 | 41 | 3 | | | |
| Lloyds | 4 | 0 | 23 | 0 | | | |
| Scott | 4 | 0 | 26 | 2 | | | |
| Alleyne | 8 | 0 | 38 | 1 | | | |

## WARWICKSHIRE vs. MIDDLESEX

at Edgbaston on 14th July 1991
Toss : Middlesex. Umpires : G.I.Burgess and N.T.Plews
Warwicks won by 9 wickets. Warwicks 4 pts, Middx 0 pts

### MIDDLESEX

| | | |
|---|---|---|
| M.W.Gatting * | lbw b Smith P.A. | 33 |
| M.A.Roseberry | c Lloyd b Smith P.A. | 17 |
| M.R.Ramprakash | st Piper b Smith N.M.K. | 11 |
| K.R.Brown | c Smith N.M.K. b Smith P.A. | 52 |
| M.Keech | b Donald | 4 |
| P.N.Weekes | run out | 16 |
| J.E.Emburey | not out | 33 |
| P.Farbrace + | c Benjamin b Donald | 4 |
| N.F.Williams | not out | 7 |
| D.W.Headley | | |
| N.G.Cowans | | |
| Extras | (b 1,lb 10,w 3,nb 2) | 16 |
| TOTAL | (40 overs)(for 7 wkts) | 193 |

### WARWICKSHIRE

| | | |
|---|---|---|
| A.J.Moles | c Roseberry b Williams | 38 |
| Asif Din | not out | 101 |
| T.A.Lloyd * | not out | 44 |
| D.P.Ostler | | |
| D.A.Reeve | | |
| P.A.Smith | | |
| N.M.K.Smith | | |
| K.J.Piper + | | |
| J.E.Benjamin | | |
| T.A.Munton | | |
| A.A.Donald | | |
| Extras | (lb 5,w 2,nb 4) | 11 |
| TOTAL | (36.2 overs)(for 1 wkt) | 194 |

| WARWICKS | O | M | R | W | | FALL OF WICKETS | |
|---|---|---|---|---|---|---|---|
| | | | | | | MID | WAR |
| Benjamin | 4 | 0 | 29 | 0 | 1st | 51 | 87 |
| Munton | 8 | 1 | 33 | 0 | 2nd | 56 | |
| Smith P.A. | 8 | 0 | 33 | 3 | 3rd | 91 | |
| Donald | 8 | 0 | 44 | 2 | 4th | 98 | |
| Reeve | 8 | 1 | 32 | 0 | 5th | 135 | |
| Smith N.M.K. | 4 | 0 | 11 | 1 | 6th | 165 | |
| | | | | | 7th | 177 | |
| MIDDLESEX | O | M | R | W | 8th | | |
| Headley | 8 | 0 | 28 | 0 | 9th | | |
| Cowans | 8 | 0 | 31 | 0 | 10th | | |
| Weekes | 8 | 0 | 50 | 0 | | | |
| Williams | 6 | 0 | 34 | 1 | | | |
| Emburey | 6 | 0 | 44 | 0 | | | |
| Brown | 0.2 | 0 | 2 | 0 | | | |

# BRITANNIC ASSURANCE CHAMPIONSHIP

## ESSEX vs. KENT

at Southend on 16th, 17th, 18th July 1991
Toss : Essex.  Umpires : J.D.Bond and K.E.Palmer
Kent won by 112 runs.  Essex 6 pts (Bt: 3, Bw: 3), Kent 20 pts (Bt: 4, Bw: 0)
100 overs scores : Kent 303 for 8

**KENT**

| | | | | | |
|---|---|---|---|---|---|
| T.R.Ward | c Gooch b Pringle | 53 | not out | | 88 |
| M.R.Benson * | lbw b Foster | 0 | not out | | 92 |
| N.R.Taylor | lbw b Topley | 50 | | | |
| G.R.Cowdrey | c Hussain b Andrew | 67 | | | |
| S.G.Hinks | c Hussain b Andrew | 8 | | | |
| M.V.Fleming | c Topley b Andrew | 4 | | | |
| S.A.Marsh + | c Garnham b Andrew | 83 | | | |
| R.P.Davis | c Garnham b Childs | 7 | | | |
| C.Penn | b Childs | 52 | | | |
| M.J.McCague | b Pringle | 16 | | | |
| A.P.Igglesden | not out | 12 | | | |
| Extras | (b 6,lb 8,w 1,nb 13) | 28 | (lb 1,nb 2) | | 3 |
| TOTAL | | 380 | (for 0 wkts dec) | | 183 |

**ESSEX**

| | | | | | |
|---|---|---|---|---|---|
| G.A.Gooch * | lbw b Igglesden | 0 | c Marsh b Fleming | | 27 |
| J.P.Stephenson | not out | 113 | c Taylor b Igglesden | | 19 |
| P.J.Prichard | c Ward b Davis | 122 | c Marsh b Fleming | | 14 |
| Salim Malik | not out | 8 | c Benson b Penn | | 51 |
| N.Hussain | | | lbw b Igglesden | | 0 |
| M.A.Garnham + | | | c Marsh b Igglesden | | 16 |
| D.R.Pringle | | | c Benson b Davis | | 27 |
| T.D.Topley | | | run out | | 5 |
| N.A.Foster | | | c Ward b Davis | | 33 |
| S.J.W.Andrew | | | b Igglesden | | 1 |
| J.H.Childs | | | not out | | 0 |
| Extras | (lb 3,w 1,nb 4) | 8 | (b 1,lb 5,nb 1) | | 7 |
| TOTAL | (for 2 wkts dec) | 251 | | | 200 |

**ESSEX**

| | O | M | R | W | O | M | R | W |
|---|---|---|---|---|---|---|---|---|
| Foster | 17 | 2 | 58 | 1 | | | | |
| Andrew | 28 | 5 | 104 | 4 | 3 | 1 | 7 | 0 |
| Pringle | 27 | 7 | 74 | 2 | 3 | 1 | 4 | 0 |
| Topley | 22 | 5 | 64 | 1 | | | | |
| Childs | 19.3 | 5 | 66 | 2 | 5 | 2 | 4 | 0 |
| Salim Malik | | | | | 4 | 1 | 8 | 0 |
| Gooch | | | | | 5.1 | 0 | 81 | 0 |
| Prichard | | | | | 5 | 0 | 78 | 0 |

**KENT**

| | O | M | R | W | O | M | R | W |
|---|---|---|---|---|---|---|---|---|
| McCague | 11 | 1 | 47 | 0 | 3 | 0 | 25 | 0 |
| Igglesden | 15 | 4 | 35 | 1 | 13.3 | 1 | 36 | 4 |
| Davis | 28 | 5 | 97 | 1 | 9 | 0 | 70 | 2 |
| Penn | 8 | 1 | 36 | 0 | 6 | 1 | 18 | 1 |
| Fleming | 11.3 | 1 | 27 | 0 | 8 | 0 | 45 | 2 |
| Cowdrey | 2 | 1 | 6 | 0 | | | | |

**FALL OF WICKETS**

| | KEN | ESS | KEN | ESS |
|---|---|---|---|---|
| 1st | 1 | 17 | | 44 |
| 2nd | 86 | 233 | | 61 |
| 3rd | 139 | | | 67 |
| 4th | 171 | | | 75 |
| 5th | 175 | | | 101 |
| 6th | 267 | | | 156 |
| 7th | 294 | | | 160 |
| 8th | 294 | | | 193 |
| 9th | 358 | | | 200 |
| 10th | 380 | | | 200 |

## HAMPSHIRE vs. WORCESTERSHIRE

at Portsmouth on 16th, 17th, 18th July 1991
Toss : Worcestershire.  Umpires : J.H.Harris and A.G.T.Whitehead
Match drawn.  Hampshire 8 pts (Bt: 4, Bw: 4), Worcestershire 4 pts (Bt: 1, Bw: 3)
100 overs scores : Hampshire 379 for 7

**HAMPSHIRE**

| | | |
|---|---|---|
| V.P.Terry | c Rhodes b Dilley | 87 |
| C.L.Smith | b Dilley | 87 |
| M.C.J.Nicholas * | c Hick b Newport | 9 |
| D.I.Gower | c sub b Hick | 77 |
| K.D.James | c Moody b Botham | 84 |
| J.R.Ayling | c Rhodes b Dilley | 3 |
| A.N.Aymes + | run out | 10 |
| R.J.Maru | c Rhodes b Botham | 27 |
| C.A.Connor | c Newport b Botham | 18 |
| K.J.Shine | b Illingworth | 1 |
| Aqib Javed | not out | 1 |
| Extras | (lb 7,w 2,nb 6) | 15 |
| TOTAL | | 419 |

**WORCESTERSHIRE**

| | | | | | |
|---|---|---|---|---|---|
| T.S.Curtis | c Maru b Shine | 53 | c Gower b Shine | | 6 |
| G.J.Lord | c Aymes b Aqib Javed | 2 | c Nicholas b Aqib Javed | | 0 |
| R.K.Illingworth | b Aqib Javed | 0 | | | |
| G.A.Hick | b Connor | 15 | (3) c Terry b Shine | | 141 |
| T.M.Moody | c Terry b Shine | 10 | (4) c Maru b Ayling | | 25 |
| P.A.Neale * | c Maru b Ayling | 15 | (5) c Gower b Shine | | 49 |
| I.T.Botham | c Terry b Shine | 26 | (6) c Aymes b Shine | | 42 |
| S.J.Rhodes + | c Maru b Shine | 0 | not out | | 46 |
| P.J.Newport | c sub b Connor | 12 | | | |
| N.V.Radford | not out | 6 | | | |
| G.R.Dilley | b Shine | 0 | (7) not out | | 15 |
| Extras | (lb 1,w 2,nb 22) | 25 | (lb 11,w 1,nb 24) | | 36 |
| TOTAL | | 164 | (for 6 wkts) | | 360 |

**WORCS**

| | O | M | R | W | O | M | R | W |
|---|---|---|---|---|---|---|---|---|
| Dilley | 21 | 7 | 50 | 3 | | | | |
| Radford | 16 | 1 | 72 | 0 | | | | |
| Botham | 11.5 | 2 | 51 | 3 | | | | |
| Newport | 10 | 0 | 60 | 1 | | | | |
| Illingworth | 26 | 2 | 94 | 1 | | | | |
| Hick | 19 | 2 | 85 | 1 | | | | |

**HAMPSHIRE**

| | O | M | R | W | O | M | R | W |
|---|---|---|---|---|---|---|---|---|
| Aqib Javed | 13 | 1 | 37 | 2 | 16 | 2 | 69 | 1 |
| Maru | 1 | 0 | 4 | 0 | 21 | 7 | 44 | 0 |
| Shine | 11.5 | 2 | 43 | 5 | 17 | 2 | 91 | 4 |
| Connor | 14 | 3 | 46 | 2 | 8 | 0 | 39 | 0 |
| James | 4 | 1 | 5 | 0 | 11 | 1 | 54 | 0 |
| Ayling | 5 | 2 | 28 | 1 | 15 | 2 | 52 | 1 |

**FALL OF WICKETS**

| | HAM | WOR | WOR | HAM |
|---|---|---|---|---|
| 1st | 172 | 9 | 5 | |
| 2nd | 179 | 12 | 8 | |
| 3rd | 212 | 47 | 84 | |
| 4th | 289 | 74 | 227 | |
| 5th | 309 | 102 | 270 | |
| 6th | 360 | 138 | 291 | |
| 7th | 376 | 138 | | |
| 8th | 404 | 144 | | |
| 9th | 413 | 164 | | |
| 10th | 419 | 164 | | |

# BRITANNIC ASSURANCE CHAMPIONSHIP

## MIDDLESEX vs. NORTHANTS

at Uxbridge on 16th, 17th, 18th (no play) July 1991
Toss : Northants. Umpires : J.C.Balderstone and R.C.Tolchard
Match drawn. Middlesex 7 pts (Bt: 4, Bw: 3), Northants 5 pts (Bt: 3, Bw: 2)
100 overs scores : Northants 284 for 8

### NORTHANTS

| | | | | | |
|---|---|---|---|---|---|
| A.Fordham | c Pooley b Cowans | 85 | c Emburey b Tufnell | 4 |
| N.A.Felton | c Farbrace b Ramprakash | 55 | c Brown b Tufnell | 6 |
| R.J.Bailey | c Farbrace b Cowans | 51 | not out | 20 |
| A.J.Lamb * | st Farbrace b Tufnell | 1 | not out | 12 |
| D.J.Capel | c Farbrace b Tufnell | 36 | | |
| K.M.Curran | lbw b Emburey | 32 | | |
| E.A.E.Baptiste | c & b Tufnell | 3 | | |
| R.G.Williams | b Tufnell | 0 | | |
| D.Ripley + | not out | 43 | | |
| A.R.Roberts | c Tufnell b Emburey | 10 | | |
| N.G.B.Cook | b Cowans | 14 | | |
| Extras | (b 1,lb 11,nb 6) | 18 | (nb 1) | 1 |
| TOTAL | | 348 | (for 2 wkts) | 43 |

### MIDDLESEX

| | | | |
|---|---|---|---|
| M.A.Roseberry | lbw b Cook | 47 |
| J.C.Pooley | c Ripley b Cook | 20 |
| M.R.Ramprakash | c Felton b Cook | 25 |
| K.R.Brown | c Ripley b Baptiste | 53 |
| M.Keech | c Baptiste b Williams | 31 |
| M.W.Gatting * | not out | 100 |
| J.E.Emburey | not out | 16 |
| P.Farbrace + | | |
| D.W.Headley | | |
| P.C.R.Tufnell | | |
| N.G.Cowans | | |
| Extras | (b 5,lb 5,nb 1) | 11 |
| TOTAL | (for 5 wkts dec) | 303 |

| MIDDLESEX | O | M | R | W | O | M | R | W | FALL OF WICKETS | | | |
|---|---|---|---|---|---|---|---|---|---|---|---|---|
| | | | | | | | | | | NOR | MID | NOR | MID |
| Cowans | 19.2 | 5 | 57 | 3 | 1 | 0 | 1 | 0 | | | | |
| Headley | 15 | 2 | 74 | 0 | | | | | 1st | 128 | 49 | 10 |
| Emburey | 49 | 14 | 110 | 2 | 7 | 1 | 21 | 0 | 2nd | 167 | 89 | 21 |
| Tufnell | 39 | 8 | 95 | 4 | 7 | 2 | 21 | 2 | 3rd | 174 | 102 | |
| Ramprakash | 1 | 1 | 0 | 1 | | | | | 4th | 222 | 163 | |
| | | | | | | | | | 5th | 256 | 214 | |
| NORTHANTS | O | M | R | W | O | M | R | W | 6th | 276 | | |
| Capel | 5 | 0 | 19 | 0 | | | | | 7th | 280 | | |
| Curran | 6 | 0 | 21 | 0 | | | | | 8th | 280 | | |
| Cook | 30 | 4 | 120 | 3 | | | | | 9th | 308 | | |
| Baptiste | 19 | 4 | 43 | 1 | | | | | 10th | 348 | | |
| Roberts | 6 | 2 | 26 | 0 | | | | | | | | |
| Williams | 16.4 | 1 | 64 | 1 | | | | | | | | |

## NOTTS vs. LANCASHIRE

at Trent Bridge on 16th, 17th, 18th July 1991
Toss : Notts. Umpires : D.J.Constant and D.R.Shepherd
Notts won by an innings and 34 runs. Notts 24 pts (Bt: 4, Bw: 4), Lancs 5 pts (Bt: 1, Bw: 4)

### NOTTS

| | | |
|---|---|---|
| B.C.Broad | c Titchard b Wasim Akram | 12 |
| P.Pollard | b DeFreitas | 145 |
| R.T.Robinson * | c Hegg b Wasim Akram | 2 |
| P.Johnson | c Hegg b Wasim Akram | 71 |
| D.W.Randall | run out | 120 |
| M.A.Crawley | c Hegg b Watkinson | 0 |
| F.D.Stephenson | lbw b Watkinson | 0 |
| B.N.French + | c Watkinson b Wasim Akram | 26 |
| E.E.Hemmings | b Wasim Akram | 0 |
| R.A.Pick | not out | 20 |
| J.A.Afford | run out | 1 |
| Extras | (b 14,lb 8,nb 7) | 29 |
| TOTAL | | 426 |

### LANCASHIRE

| | | | | | |
|---|---|---|---|---|---|
| G.D.Mendis | c Robinson b Stephenson | 29 | b Pick | 50 |
| G.Fowler | c French b Stephenson | 22 | run out | 34 |
| N.J.Speak | c sub b Pick | 0 | c Robinson b Afford | 38 |
| N.H.Fairbrother | c Pollard b Hemmings | 54 | b Hemmings | 10 |
| S.P.Titchard | c Pollard b Afford | 46 | b Hemmings | 23 |
| M.Watkinson | c French b Afford | 18 | b Hemmings | 0 |
| Wasim Akram | c Afford b Hemmings | 1 | c Robinson b Afford | 18 |
| P.A.J.DeFreitas | b Hemmings | 8 | b Hemmings | 3 |
| W.K.Hegg + | st French b Afford | 0 | c Randall b Hemmings | 1 |
| D.P.Hughes * | not out | 1 | b Hemmings | 4 |
| G.Yates | c French b Afford | 1 | not out | 0 |
| Extras | (b 6,lb 4,w 1,nb 2) | 13 | (b 7,lb 7,nb 4) | 18 |
| TOTAL | | 193 | | 199 |

| LANCASHIRE | O | M | R | W | O | M | R | W | FALL OF WICKETS | | | |
|---|---|---|---|---|---|---|---|---|---|---|---|---|
| | | | | | | | | | | NOT | LAN | LAN | NOT |
| Wasim Akram | 29 | 5 | 117 | 5 | | | | | 1st | 33 | 46 | 63 |
| DeFreitas | 13 | 4 | 55 | 1 | | | | | 2nd | 61 | 53 | 133 |
| Watkinson | 12 | 2 | 67 | 2 | | | | | 3rd | 220 | 55 | 144 |
| Yates | 34.4 | 6 | 137 | 0 | | | | | 4th | 265 | 152 | 144 |
| Hughes | 9 | 3 | 28 | 0 | | | | | 5th | 266 | 168 | 144 |
| | | | | | | | | | 6th | 266 | 169 | 185 |
| NOTTS | O | M | R | W | O | M | R | W | 7th | 341 | 179 | 191 |
| Stephenson | 18 | 4 | 56 | 2 | 9 | 2 | 32 | 0 | 8th | 341 | 184 | 193 |
| Pick | 14 | 4 | 31 | 1 | 13 | 4 | 44 | 1 | 9th | 425 | 191 | 194 |
| Hemmings | 29 | 13 | 50 | 3 | 35.2 | 20 | 46 | 6 | 10th | 426 | 193 | 199 |
| Afford | 15.3 | 2 | 46 | 4 | 40 | 18 | 62 | 2 | | | | |
| Crawley | | | | | 4 | 3 | 1 | 0 | | | | |

## SURREY vs. GLOUCESTERSHIRE

at Guildford on 16th, 17th, 18th July 1991
Toss : Gloucs. Umpires : D.O.Oslear and R.A.White
Surrey won by 2 wickets. Surrey 22 pts (Bt: 3, Bw: 3), Gloucs 4 pts (Bt: 3, Bw: 1)
100 overs scores : Gloucs 251 for 8

### GLOUCESTERSHIRE

| | | | | | |
|---|---|---|---|---|---|
| G.D.Hodgson | b Waqar Younis | 34 | c Alikhan b Ward | 21 |
| R.J.Scott | b Waqar Younis | 63 | c Medlycott b Ward | 47 |
| A.J.Wright * | not out | 101 | c Ward b Sargeant | 29 |
| C.W.J.Athey | b Medlycott | 19 | not out | 62 |
| M.W.Alleyne | b Murphy | 1 | not out | 37 |
| R.C.Russell + | b Waqar Younis | 0 | | |
| J.W.Lloyds | lbw b Waqar Younis | 10 | | |
| D.V.Lawrence | b Waqar Younis | 19 | | |
| D.R.Gilbert | b Waqar Younis | 15 | | |
| M.C.J.Ball | b Waqar Younis | 28 | | |
| A.M.Smith | | | | |
| Extras | (b 9,lb 4,nb 1) | 14 | (lb 1) | 1 |
| TOTAL | (for 9 wkts dec) | 304 | (for 3 wkts dec) | 197 |

### SURREY

| | | | | | |
|---|---|---|---|---|---|
| D.J.Bicknell | c Russell b Lloyds | 95 | c Russell b Lawrence | 10 |
| R.I.Alikhan | lbw b Lawrence | 4 | c Russell b Smith | 70 |
| A.J.Stewart | b Lloyds | 109 | run out | 1 |
| D.M.Ward | not out | 40 | c Russell b Smith | 80 |
| G.P.Thorpe | not out | 0 | c Russell b Smith | 33 |
| J.D.Robinson | | | b Lawrence | 20 |
| I.A.Greig * | | | not out | 23 |
| K.T.Medlycott | | | c Athey b Lawrence | 0 |
| N.F.Sargeant + | | | c Russell b Smith | 1 |
| Waqar Younis | | | not out | 2 |
| A.J.Murphy | | | | |
| Extras | (lb 1,nb 1) | 2 | (b 3,lb 6,nb 3) | 12 |
| TOTAL | (for 3 wkts dec) | 250 | (for 8 wkts) | 252 |

| SURREY | O | M | R | W | O | M | R | W | FALL OF WICKETS | | | |
|---|---|---|---|---|---|---|---|---|---|---|---|---|
| | | | | | | | | | | GLO | SUR | GLO | SUR |
| Waqar Younis | 31.5 | 6 | 87 | 7 | 4 | 0 | 15 | 0 | 1st | 105 | 8 | 34 | 22 |
| Murphy | 35 | 4 | 108 | 1 | 6 | 3 | 14 | 0 | 2nd | 108 | 182 | 91 | 25 |
| Robinson | 7 | 1 | 19 | 0 | | | | | 3rd | 117 | 245 | 126 | 168 |
| Greig | 16.5 | 5 | 25 | 0 | | | | | 4th | 118 | | | 175 |
| Thorpe | 2 | 0 | 5 | 0 | | | | | 5th | 130 | | | 223 |
| Medlycott | 16 | 4 | 47 | 1 | 2 | 0 | 4 | 0 | 6th | 160 | | | 235 |
| Ward | | | | | 7.5 | 0 | 66 | 2 | 7th | 190 | | | 242 |
| Sargeant | | | | | 5 | 0 | 88 | 1 | 8th | 246 | | | 245 |
| Stewart | | | | | 2 | 0 | 9 | 0 | 9th | 304 | | | |
| | | | | | | | | | 10th | | | | |
| GLOUCS | O | M | R | W | O | M | R | W | | | | |
| Lawrence | 10 | 1 | 42 | 1 | 12.4 | 1 | 51 | 3 | | | | |
| Gilbert | 16 | 4 | 64 | 0 | 11 | 1 | 60 | 0 | | | | |
| Ball | 4 | 1 | 16 | 0 | | | | | | | | |
| Lloyds | 27.2 | 8 | 67 | 2 | 11 | 1 | 58 | 0 | | | | |
| Smith | 7 | 0 | 30 | 0 | 15 | 0 | 70 | 4 | | | | |
| Scott | 7 | 1 | 22 | 0 | 1 | 0 | 4 | 0 | | | | |
| Athey | 3 | 0 | 8 | 0 | | | | | | | | |

Eddie Hemmings, whose six wickets in Surrey's second innings secured an innings win for Nottinghamshire.

| BRITANNIC ASS. CHAMPIONSHIP | TOUR MATCH |
|---|---|

## SUSSEX vs. SOMERSET

at Hove on 16th, 17th, 18th July 1991
Toss : Sussex. Umpires : B.Hassan and K.J.Lyons
Match drawn. Sussex 8 pts (Bt: 4, Bw: 4), Somerset 5 pts (Bt: 4, Bw: 1)
100 overs scores : Somerset 304 for 9, Sussex 388 for 4

**SOMERSET**

| | | | | | |
|---|---|---|---|---|---|
| S.J.Cook | c Lenham b Dodemaide | 30 | c Moores b Lenham | 66 |
| P.M.Roebuck | c Moores b Jones | 22 | c Smith b Salisbury | 55 |
| A.N.Hayhurst | lbw b Dodemaide | 12 | c & b Lenham | 0 |
| C.J.Tavare * | c Parker b Dodemaide | 134 | | |
| R.J.Harden | run out | 34 | (4) not out | 27 |
| K.H.Macleay | b Dodemaide | 20 | (5) not out | 2 |
| N.D.Burns + | run out | 6 | | |
| R.P.Lefebvre | b Salisbury | 14 | | |
| D.Beal | lbw b Salisbury | 1 | | |
| H.R.J.Trump | not out | 30 | | |
| D.A.Graveney | not out | 7 | | |
| Extras | (lb 12,nb 2) | 14 | (lb 11,nb 3) | 14 |
| TOTAL | (for 9 wkts dec) | 324 | (for 3 wkts) | 164 |

**SUSSEX**

| | | |
|---|---|---|
| N.J.Lenham | c Cook b Macleay | 106 |
| D.M.Smith | c Burns b Hayhurst | 38 |
| P.W.G.Parker * | c Burns b Macleay | 7 |
| A.P.Wells | b Roebuck | 159 |
| M.P.Speight | c Harden b Hayhurst | 67 |
| C.M.Wells | c Roebuck b Macleay | 12 |
| A.I.C.Dodemaide | not out | 27 |
| P.Moores + | not out | 17 |
| A.C.S.Pigott | | |
| I.D.K.Salisbury | | |
| A.N.Jones | | |
| Extras | (lb 9,nb 4) | 13 |
| TOTAL | (for 6 wkts dec) | 446 |

| SUSSEX | O | M | R | W | O | M | R | W |
|---|---|---|---|---|---|---|---|---|
| Jones | 17 | 2 | 73 | 1 | 12 | 0 | 66 | 0 |
| Dodemaide | 28 | 6 | 90 | 4 | 8 | 1 | 46 | 0 |
| Pigott | 14 | 4 | 50 | 0 | | | | |
| Wells C.M. | 20 | 6 | 56 | 0 | 6 | 1 | 14 | 0 |
| Salisbury | 25 | 12 | 43 | 2 | 16 | 7 | 22 | 1 |
| Lenham | | | | | 6 | 4 | 5 | 2 |

| SOMERSET | O | M | R | W | O | M | R | W |
|---|---|---|---|---|---|---|---|---|
| Beal | 21 | 0 | 97 | 0 | | | | |
| Lefebvre | 19 | 2 | 55 | 0 | | | | |
| Macleay | 23 | 3 | 83 | 3 | | | | |
| Hayhurst | 12 | 2 | 67 | 2 | | | | |
| Graveney | 14 | 4 | 38 | 0 | | | | |
| Trump | 15 | 0 | 58 | 0 | | | | |
| Roebuck | 6 | 0 | 39 | 1 | | | | |

| FALL OF WICKETS | | | | |
|---|---|---|---|---|
| | SOM | SUS | SOM | SUS |
| 1st | 49 | 75 | 121 | |
| 2nd | 65 | 86 | 125 | |
| 3rd | 88 | 248 | 139 | |
| 4th | 195 | 375 | | |
| 5th | 251 | 394 | | |
| 6th | 264 | 404 | | |
| 7th | 273 | | | |
| 8th | 274 | | | |
| 9th | 293 | | | |
| 10th | | | | |

## YORKSHIRE vs. DERBYSHIRE

at Scarborough on 16th, 17th, 18th July 1991
Toss : Derbyshire. Umpires : H.D.Bird and J.H.Hampshire
Match drawn. Yorkshire 8 pts (Bt: 4, Bw: 4), Derbyshire 5 pts (Bt: 2, Bw: 3)
100 overs scores : Yorkshire 318 for 7

**YORKSHIRE**

| | | |
|---|---|---|
| M.D.Moxon * | c O'Gorman b Mortensen | 44 |
| A.A.Metcalfe | lbw b Malcolm | 8 |
| D.Byas | lbw b Goldsmith | 135 |
| R.J.Blakey + | b Goldsmith | 90 |
| P.E.Robinson | c Cork b Sladdin | 2 |
| S.A.Kellett | b Malcolm | 36 |
| P.Carrick | c Barnett b Goldsmith | 2 |
| D.Gough | b Sladdin | 1 |
| P.J.Hartley | not out | 50 |
| J.D.Batty | not out | 27 |
| S.D.Fletcher | | |
| Extras | (b 8,lb 11,w 1,nb 3) | 23 |
| TOTAL | (for 8 wkts dec) | 418 |

**DERBYSHIRE**

| | | | | | |
|---|---|---|---|---|---|
| K.J.Barnett * | b Hartley | 33 | c Blakey b Carrick | 22 |
| P.D.Bowler | run out | 73 | c Moxon b Carrick | 48 |
| J.E.Morris | c Metcalfe b Carrick | 25 | c Moxon b Carrick | 59 |
| M.Azharuddin | c Metcalfe b Gough | 1 | c Moxon b Carrick | 0 |
| T.J.G.O'Gorman | c Kellett b Batty | 0 | c Robinson b Batty | 0 |
| S.C.Goldsmith | c Blakey b Batty | 37 | c Robinson b Batty | 4 |
| K.M.Krikken + | c Byas b Batty | 13 | not out | 16 |
| D.G.Cork | c Blakey b Hartley | 26 | c Moxon b Batty | 8 |
| R.W.Sladdin | c Byas b Carrick | 7 | not out | 8 |
| D.E.Malcolm | not out | 6 | | |
| O.H.Mortensen | lbw b Fletcher | 0 | | |
| Extras | (b 9,lb 9,nb 3) | 21 | (b 4,lb 3,w 4) | 11 |
| TOTAL | | 242 | (for 7 wkts) | 176 |

| DERBYSHIRE | O | M | R | W | O | M | R | W |
|---|---|---|---|---|---|---|---|---|
| Malcolm | 23 | 5 | 86 | 2 | | | | |
| Cork | 19 | 3 | 52 | 0 | | | | |
| Mortensen | 21 | 5 | 86 | 1 | | | | |
| Sladdin | 34 | 11 | 112 | 2 | | | | |
| Barnett | 4 | 1 | 21 | 0 | | | | |
| Goldsmith | 17 | 7 | 42 | 3 | | | | |

| FALL OF WICKETS | | | | |
|---|---|---|---|---|
| | YOR | DER | YOR | DER |
| 1st | 13 | 54 | | 48 |
| 2nd | 128 | 101 | | 105 |
| 3rd | 278 | 102 | | 105 |
| 4th | 293 | 115 | | 106 |
| 5th | 293 | 154 | | 138 |
| 6th | 305 | 191 | | 138 |
| 7th | 318 | 196 | | 165 |
| 8th | 373 | 224 | | |
| 9th | | 239 | | |
| 10th | | 242 | | |

| YORKSHIRE | O | M | R | W | O | M | R | W |
|---|---|---|---|---|---|---|---|---|
| Hartley | 22 | 6 | 72 | 2 | 9 | 3 | 14 | 0 |
| Fletcher | 12.4 | 2 | 33 | 1 | 6 | 2 | 20 | 0 |
| Carrick | 30 | 14 | 50 | 2 | 43 | 28 | 48 | 4 |
| Gough | 7 | 1 | 25 | 1 | 4 | 0 | 17 | 0 |
| Batty | 22 | 10 | 44 | 3 | 35.2 | 14 | 70 | 3 |

## GLAMORGAN vs. WEST INDIES

at Swansea on 16th, 17th, 18th July 1991
Toss : Glamorgan. Umpires : J.W.Holder and D.Fawkner-Corbett
Match drawn

**GLAMORGAN**

| | | | | | |
|---|---|---|---|---|---|
| S.P.James | c Williams b Patterson | 8 | c Richardson b Ambrose | 24 |
| H.Morris | c Lara b Ambrose | 0 | c Williams b Ambrose | 0 |
| A.Dale | c Richardson b Ambrose | 62 | (4) not out | 51 |
| M.P.Maynard | c Williams b Marshall | 8 | (5) not out | 7 |
| P.A.Cottey | c Richardson b Marshall | 8 | | |
| A.R.Butcher * | b Anthony | 94 | | |
| R.D.B.Croft | c Williams b Ambrose | 0 | | |
| C.P.Metson + | c & b Hooper | 27 | (3) b Ambrose | 5 |
| S.L.Watkin | c Williams b Ambrose | 5 | | |
| S.R.Barwick | c Williams b Ambrose | 0 | | |
| M.Frost | not out | 0 | | |
| Extras | (lb 6,w 2,nb 32) | 40 | (b 8,lb 3,w 1,nb 3) | 15 |
| TOTAL | | 252 | (for 3 wkts) | 102 |

**WEST INDIES**

| | | |
|---|---|---|
| C.B.Lambert | lbw b Barwick | 99 |
| D.L.Haynes * | b Watkin | 45 |
| R.B.Richardson | st Metson b Croft | 109 |
| C.L.Hooper | c Croft b Barwick | 80 |
| A.L.Logie | b Dale | 8 |
| B.C.Lara | c Maynard b Frost | 6 |
| D.Williams + | c Maynard b Dale | 6 |
| M.D.Marshall | not out | 46 |
| H.A.G.Anthony | not out | 4 |
| C.E.L.Ambrose | | |
| B.P.Patterson | | |
| Extras | (lb 6,w 2,nb 5) | 13 |
| TOTAL | (for 7 wkts dec) | 416 |

| WEST INDIES | O | M | R | W | O | M | R | W |
|---|---|---|---|---|---|---|---|---|
| Ambrose | 22.1 | 6 | 56 | 5 | 12 | 6 | 14 | 3 |
| Patterson | 19 | 5 | 61 | 1 | 13 | 7 | 14 | 0 |
| Marshall | 10 | 2 | 34 | 2 | | | | |
| Anthony | 15 | 3 | 59 | 1 | 9.2 | 2 | 30 | 0 |
| Hooper | 17 | 4 | 36 | 1 | 10 | 2 | 22 | 0 |
| Lara | | | | | 2 | 0 | 11 | 0 |

| GLAMORGAN | O | M | R | W | O | M | R | W |
|---|---|---|---|---|---|---|---|---|
| Watkin | 23 | 7 | 86 | 1 | | | | |
| Frost | 19 | 1 | 111 | 1 | | | | |
| Croft | 37 | 8 | 116 | 1 | | | | |
| Barwick | 21 | 7 | 41 | 2 | | | | |
| Dale | 14 | 2 | 56 | 2 | | | | |

| FALL OF WICKETS | | | | |
|---|---|---|---|---|
| | GLA | WI | GLA | WI |
| 1st | 1 | 92 | | 1 |
| 2nd | 16 | 208 | | 14 |
| 3rd | 38 | 221 | | 87 |
| 4th | 60 | 280 | | |
| 5th | 186 | 297 | | |
| 6th | 191 | 323 | | |
| 7th | 217 | 408 | | |
| 8th | 243 | | | |
| 9th | 252 | | | |
| 10th | 252 | | | |

# HEADLINES

**Tetley Bitter Challenge**

**16th - 18th July**

• Curtly Ambrose was in destructive form in the West Indies' drawn match with Glamorgan at Swansea, returning match figures of eight for 70 and dismissing Hugh Morris, looking to impress the England committee, without scoring in both innings. 99 from Clayton Lambert and Richie Richardson's third 100 of the tour helped the visitors to a lead of 164, but Adrian Dale's second fifty of the game carried Glamorgan to safety.

# REFUGE ASSURANCE LEAGUE

## WORCS vs. GLAMORGAN

at Worcester on 21st July 1991
Toss : Worcs. Umpires : M.J.Kitchen and B.Leadbeater
Worcs won by 7 wickets. Worcs 4 pts, Glamorgan 0 pts

### GLAMORGAN

| | | |
|---|---|---|
| M.P.Maynard | c D'Oliveira b Newport | 15 |
| H.Morris | c Curtis b Radford | 16 |
| R.J.Shastri | c D'Oliveira b Illingworth | 22 |
| A.Dale | c Radford b Stemp | 56 |
| I.Smith | c Radford b Newport | 24 |
| A.R.Butcher * | not out | 51 |
| P.A.Cottey | not out | 26 |
| R.D.B.Croft | | |
| C.P.Metson + | | |
| S.Bastien | | |
| S.R.Barwick | | |
| Extras | (lb 14,w 6) | 20 |
| TOTAL | (40 overs)(for 5 wkts) | 230 |

### WORCESTERSHIRE

| | | |
|---|---|---|
| T.S.Curtis * | c Maynard b Croft | 55 |
| T.M.Moody | c Shastri b Croft | 58 |
| G.A.Hick | not out | 34 |
| D.B.D'Oliveira | c Smith b Shastri | 45 |
| I.T.Botham | not out | 24 |
| M.J.Weston | | |
| S.J.Rhodes + | | |
| R.K.Illingworth | | |
| P.J.Newport | | |
| N.V.Radford | | |
| R.D.Stemp | | |
| Extras | (lb 13,w 5) | 18 |
| TOTAL | (39.1 overs)(for 3 wkts) | 234 |

| WORCS | O | M | R | W | FALL OF WICKETS | | |
|---|---|---|---|---|---|---|---|
| | | | | | | GLA | WOR |
| Weston | 8 | 2 | 17 | 0 | | | |
| Newport | 8 | 0 | 43 | 2 | 1st | 20 | 111 |
| Radford | 6 | 0 | 37 | 1 | 2nd | 54 | 130 |
| Illingworth | 8 | 0 | 38 | 1 | 3rd | 74 | 186 |
| Botham | 8 | 0 | 65 | 0 | 4th | 117 | |
| Stemp | 2 | 0 | 16 | 1 | 5th | 168 | |
| | | | | | 6th | | |
| GLAMORGAN | O | M | R | W | 7th | | |
| Barwick | 7 | 0 | 44 | 0 | 8th | | |
| Bastien | 6 | 0 | 37 | 0 | 9th | | |
| Dale | 5 | 0 | 27 | 0 | 10th | | |
| Croft | 8 | 0 | 36 | 2 | | | |
| Smith | 6 | 0 | 42 | 0 | | | |
| Shastri | 6 | 0 | 29 | 1 | | | |
| Maynard | 1 | 0 | 2 | 0 | | | |
| Butcher | 0.1 | 0 | 4 | 0 | | | |

## ESSEX vs. SOMERSET

at Southend on 21st July 1991
Toss : Somerset. Umpires : J.D.Bond and K.E.Palmer
Essex won by 30 runs. Essex 4 pts, Somerset 0 pts

### ESSEX

| | | |
|---|---|---|
| G.A.Gooch * | c Burns b Lefebvre | 107 |
| J.P.Stephenson | c Lefebvre b Hallett | 10 |
| Salim Malik | c & b Trump | 41 |
| P.J.Prichard | lbw b Lefebvre | 22 |
| N.Hussain | not out | 33 |
| D.R.Pringle | not out | 27 |
| N.Shahid | | |
| M.A.Garnham + | | |
| T.D.Topley | | |
| S.J.W.Andrew | | |
| P.M.Such | | |
| Extras | (lb 6,w 1) | 7 |
| TOTAL | (40 overs)(for 4 wkts) | 247 |

### SOMERSET

| | | |
|---|---|---|
| S.J.Cook | c Shahid b Topley | 93 |
| P.M.Roebuck | c Hussain b Such | 41 |
| C.J.Tavare * | b Stephenson | 34 |
| R.J.Harden | b Topley | 13 |
| R.P.Lefebvre | lbw b Topley | 0 |
| N.J.Pringle | c Prichard b Stephenson | 1 |
| K.H.Macleay | not out | 10 |
| N.D.Burns + | not out | 10 |
| A.N.Hayhurst | | |
| H.R.J.Trump | | |
| J.C.Hallett | | |
| Extras | (lb 9,w 5,nb 1) | 15 |
| TOTAL | (40 overs)(for 6 wkts) | 217 |

| SOMERSET | O | M | R | W | FALL OF WICKETS | | |
|---|---|---|---|---|---|---|---|
| | | | | | | ESS | SOM |
| Lefebvre | 8 | 0 | 40 | 2 | 1st | 30 | 92 |
| Hallett | 5 | 0 | 22 | 1 | 2nd | 126 | 152 |
| Macleay | 8 | 0 | 67 | 0 | 3rd | 182 | 180 |
| Trump | 8 | 0 | 39 | 1 | 4th | 187 | 180 |
| Roebuck | 7 | 0 | 38 | 0 | 5th | | 183 |
| Hayhurst | 4 | 0 | 35 | 0 | 6th | | 202 |
| ESSEX | O | M | R | W | 7th | | |
| Andrew | 4 | 0 | 38 | 0 | 8th | | |
| Pringle | 6 | 0 | 29 | 0 | 9th | | |
| Topley | 8 | 0 | 36 | 3 | 10th | | |
| Such | 8 | 0 | 32 | 1 | | | |
| Gooch | 6 | 0 | 24 | 0 | | | |
| Stephenson | 8 | 0 | 49 | 2 | | | |

## HAMPSHIRE vs. WARWICKSHIRE

at Portsmouth on 21st July 1991
Toss : Warwicks. Umpires : J.H.Harris & A.G.T.Whitehead
Warwicks won by 5 wickets. Hants 0 pts, Warwicks 4 pts

### HAMPSHIRE

| | | |
|---|---|---|
| V.P.Terry | c Smith N.M.K. b Small | 27 |
| C.L.Smith | b Munton | 2 |
| J.R.Wood | c Piper b Reeve | 19 |
| M.C.J.Nicholas * | lbw b Reeve | 4 |
| K.D.James | c Munton b Smith P.A. | 21 |
| J.R.Ayling | st Piper b Smith N.M.K. | 37 |
| A.N Aymes + | not out | 14 |
| R.J.Maru | c Moles b Smith N.M.K. | 17 |
| T.M.Tremlett | not out | 5 |
| S.D.Udal | | |
| C.A.Connor | | |
| Extras | (lb 2,w 5) | 7 |
| TOTAL | (40 overs)(for 7 wkts) | 153 |

### WARWICKSHIRE

| | | |
|---|---|---|
| A.J.Moles | c Aymes b James | 13 |
| Asif Din | c Maru b Ayling | 30 |
| P.A.Smith | c Aymes b Ayling | 10 |
| D.P.Ostler | c Aymes b Ayling | 4 |
| D.A.Reeve | not out | 44 |
| T.A.Lloyd * | c Maru b Tremlett | 24 |
| N.M.K.Smith | not out | 8 |
| K.J.Piper + | | |
| G.C.Small | | |
| J.E.Benjamin | | |
| T.A.Munton | | |
| Extras | (lb 6,w 10,nb 5) | 21 |
| TOTAL | (37.1 overs)(for 5 wkts) | 154 |

| WARWICKS | O | M | R | W | FALL OF WICKETS | | |
|---|---|---|---|---|---|---|---|
| | | | | | | HAM | WAR |
| Munton | 7 | 0 | 21 | 1 | 1st | 7 | 51 |
| Benjamin | 4 | 0 | 17 | 0 | 2nd | 47 | 61 |
| Reeve | 6 | 0 | 27 | 2 | 3rd | 53 | 66 |
| Small | 7 | 1 | 33 | 1 | 4th | 65 | 71 |
| Smith P.A. | 8 | 0 | 29 | 1 | 5th | 107 | 137 |
| Smith N.M.K. | 8 | 0 | 24 | 2 | 6th | 119 | |
| HAMPSHIRE | O | M | R | W | 7th | 141 | |
| Connor | 6 | 0 | 20 | 0 | 8th | | |
| Tremlett | 6.1 | 0 | 27 | 1 | 9th | | |
| Udal | 7 | 0 | 23 | 0 | 10th | | |
| Ayling | 8 | 0 | 25 | 3 | | | |
| James | 8 | 0 | 38 | 1 | | | |
| Maru | 2 | 0 | 15 | 0 | | | |

## SUSSEX vs. LEICESTERSHIRE

at Hove on 21st July 1991
Toss : Sussex. Umpires : B.Hassan and K.J.Lyons
Sussex won by 14 runs. Sussex 4 pts, Leicestershire 0 pts

### SUSSEX

| | | |
|---|---|---|
| N.J.Lenham | c Nixon b Lewis | 10 |
| P.W.G.Parker * | b Lewis | 104 |
| A.P.Wells | c Maguire b Hepworth | 36 |
| M.P.Speight | lbw b Maguire | 4 |
| K.Greenfield | c Nixon b Maguire | 13 |
| C.M.Wells | c Nixon b Hepworth | 7 |
| A.I.C.Dodemaide | c Lewis b Benson | 18 |
| P.Moores + | not out | 4 |
| A.C.S.Pigott | not out | 1 |
| I.D.K.Salisbury | | |
| A.N.Jones | | |
| Extras | (b 1,lb 2,w 3) | 6 |
| TOTAL | (40 overs)(for 7 wkts) | 203 |

### LEICESTERSHIRE

| | | |
|---|---|---|
| J.J.Whitaker | c Moores b Jones | 17 |
| N.E.Briers * | c Moores b Jones | 20 |
| B.F.Smith | c Moores b Jones | 0 |
| L.Potter | c Parker b Pigott | 59 |
| C.C.Lewis | run out | 36 |
| J.D.R.Benson | run out | 23 |
| P.N.Hepworth | b Pigott | 2 |
| P.A.Nixon + | lbw b Jones | 5 |
| D.J.Millns | not out | 10 |
| L.Tennant | c Speight b Jones | 0 |
| J.N.Maguire | not out | 0 |
| Extras | (lb 9,w 7,nb 1) | 17 |
| TOTAL | (40 overs)(for 9 wkts) | 189 |

| LEICS | O | M | R | W | FALL OF WICKETS | | |
|---|---|---|---|---|---|---|---|
| | | | | | | SUS | LEI |
| Millns | 6 | 0 | 24 | 0 | | | |
| Lewis | 8 | 1 | 33 | 2 | 1st | 19 | 40 |
| Benson | 7 | 0 | 40 | 1 | 2nd | 80 | 40 |
| Tennant | 3 | 0 | 26 | 0 | 3rd | 96 | 46 |
| Maguire | 8 | 0 | 34 | 2 | 4th | 139 | 113 |
| Hepworth | 8 | 0 | 43 | 2 | 5th | 151 | 169 |
| | | | | | 6th | 192 | 170 |
| SUSSEX | O | M | R | W | 7th | 199 | 173 |
| Wells C.M. | 8 | 0 | 36 | 0 | 8th | | 188 |
| Dodemaide | 8 | 2 | 19 | 0 | 9th | | 188 |
| Pigott | 8 | 1 | 35 | 2 | 10th | | |
| Jones | 8 | 0 | 32 | 5 | | | |
| Salisbury | 5 | 0 | 34 | 0 | | | |
| Lenham | 3 | 0 | 24 | 0 | | | |

## GLOUCS vs. DERBYSHIRE

at Cheltenham on 21st July 1991
Toss : Derbyshire. Umpires : G.I.Burgess and P.B.Wight
Derbyshire won by 94 runs. Gloucs 0 pts, Derbyshire 4 pts

### DERBYSHIRE

| | | |
|---|---|---|
| P.D.Bowler | b Lawrence | 8 |
| C.J.Adams | c Russell b Gilbert | 67 |
| J.E.Morris | c Russell b Scott | 21 |
| M.Azharuddin | c Russell b Alleyne | 26 |
| T.J.G.O'Gorman | c Ball b Lawrence | 16 |
| S.C.Goldsmith | not out | 67 |
| A.E.Warner | c Ball b Lawrence | 8 |
| K.J.Barnett * | not out | 36 |
| K.M.Krikken + | | |
| D.G.Cork | | |
| S.J.Base | | |
| Extras | (lb 3,w 3) | 6 |
| TOTAL | (40 overs)(for 6 wkts) | 255 |

### GLOUCESTERSHIRE

| | | |
|---|---|---|
| R.J.Scott | c Krikken b Base | 17 |
| C.W.J.Athey | c O'Gorman b Cork | 9 |
| R.C.Russell + | c Krikken b Cork | 7 |
| A.J.Wright * | c Krikken b Warner | 19 |
| M.W.Alleyne | c O'Gorman b Warner | 17 |
| J.J.E.Hardy | c sub b Bowler | 54 |
| J.W.Lloyds | c Adams b Barnett | 0 |
| D.V.Lawrence | c Morris b Base | 13 |
| M.C.J.Ball | c Barnett b Bowler | 5 |
| D.R.Gilbert | c Azharuddin b Bowler | 7 |
| A.M.Smith | not out | 2 |
| Extras | (lb 3,w 8) | 11 |
| TOTAL | (35.2 overs) | 161 |

| GLOUCS | O | M | R | W | FALL OF WICKETS | | |
|---|---|---|---|---|---|---|---|
| | | | | | | DER | GLO |
| Lawrence | 7 | 0 | 51 | 3 | | | |
| Gilbert | 8 | 0 | 49 | 1 | 1st | 26 | 27 |
| Smith | 6 | 0 | 47 | 0 | 2nd | 63 | 33 |
| Scott | 7 | 0 | 48 | 1 | 3rd | 120 | 35 |
| Ball | 8 | 0 | 35 | 0 | 4th | 127 | 56 |
| Alleyne | 4 | 0 | 22 | 1 | 5th | 150 | 85 |
| | | | | | 6th | 161 | 88 |
| DERBYSHIRE | O | M | R | W | 7th | | 110 |
| Cork | 6 | 0 | 27 | 2 | 8th | | 142 |
| Base | 8 | 0 | 37 | 2 | 9th | | 155 |
| Warner | 8 | 0 | 36 | 2 | 10th | | 161 |
| Barnett | 8 | 0 | 27 | 1 | | | |
| Bowler | 5.2 | 0 | 31 | 3 | | | |

## MIDDLESEX vs. LANCASHIRE

at Lord's on 21st July 1991
Toss : Lancs. Umpires : J.C.Balderstone & R.C.Tolchard
Lancashire won by 2 wickets. Middlesex 0 pts, Lancs 4 pts

### MIDDLESEX

| | | |
|---|---|---|
| M.A.Roseberry | c Hegg b Austin | 42 |
| M.W.Gatting * | c Lloyd b DeFreitas | 7 |
| M.R.Ramprakash | c Hegg b Wasim Akram | 6 |
| K.R.Brown | c Atherton b Watkinson | 1 |
| M.Keech | c Fairbrother b Austin | 16 |
| P.N.Weekes | not out | 26 |
| J.E.Emburey | lbw b Austin | 2 |
| P.Farbrace + | not out | 26 |
| D.W.Headley | | |
| N.F.Williams | | |
| N.G.Cowans | | |
| Extras | (lb 4,w 10,nb 3) | 17 |
| TOTAL | (38 overs)(for 6 wkts) | 143 |

### LANCASHIRE

| | | |
|---|---|---|
| G.Fowler | run out | 1 |
| M.A.Atherton | lbw b Cowans | 1 |
| G.D.Lloyd | lbw b Cowans | 5 |
| N.H.Fairbrother | c Emburey b Cowans | 0 |
| M.Watkinson | c Farbrace b Cowans | 2 |
| Wasim Akram | c Roseberry b Cowans | 10 |
| P.A.J.DeFreitas | lbw b Cowans | 0 |
| W.K.Hegg | not out | 47 |
| I.D.Austin | run out | 48 |
| D.P.Hughes * | not out | 4 |
| P.J.W.Allott | | |
| Extras | (b 8,lb 10,w 10,nb 1) | 29 |
| TOTAL | (37.5 overs)(for 8 wkts) | 147 |

| LANCASHIRE | O | M | R | W | FALL OF WICKETS | | |
|---|---|---|---|---|---|---|---|
| | | | | | | MID | LAN |
| DeFreitas | 8 | 0 | 25 | 1 | | | |
| Allott | 8 | 2 | 21 | 0 | 1st | 21 | 1 |
| Wasim Akram | 7 | 0 | 30 | 1 | 2nd | 45 | 2 |
| Watkinson | 8 | 0 | 21 | 1 | 3rd | 49 | 2 |
| Austin | 7 | 0 | 42 | 3 | 4th | 82 | 4 |
| | | | | | 5th | 92 | 22 |
| MIDDLESEX | O | M | R | W | 6th | 95 | 22 |
| Cowans | 8 | 2 | 9 | 6 | 7th | | 36 |
| Williams | 8 | 0 | 23 | 0 | 8th | | 141 |
| Headley | 6 | 0 | 29 | 0 | 9th | | |
| Emburey | 8 | 0 | 28 | 0 | 10th | | |
| Gatting | 5.5 | 0 | 32 | 0 | | | |
| Weekes | 2 | 0 | 8 | 0 | | | |

# REFUGE ASSURANCE LEAGUE

## NORTHANTS vs. NOTTS
at Wellingborough School on 21st July 1991
Toss : Notts. Umpires : H.D.Bird and B.J.Meyer
Northants won by 5 runs. Northants 4 pts, Notts 0 pts

### NORTHANTS
| | | |
|---|---|---|
| A.Fordham | c French b Stephenson | 8 |
| N.A.Felton | run out | 37 |
| W.Larkins | c Pollard b Evans | 63 |
| A.J.Lamb * | c French b Stephenson | 2 |
| D.J.Capel | b Stephenson | 28 |
| K.M.Curran | c Johnson b Pick | 26 |
| E.A.E.Baptiste | lbw b Stephenson | 5 |
| R.G.Williams | b Stephenson | 10 |
| W.M.Noon + | b Evans | 4 |
| A.Walker | b Evans | 2 |
| J.P.Taylor | not out | 1 |
| Extras | (lb 9,w 6,nb 1) | 16 |
| TOTAL | (40 overs) | 202 |

### NOTTS
| | | |
|---|---|---|
| P.Pollard | c Noon b Taylor | 6 |
| D.W.Randall | b Williams | 48 |
| P.Johnson | c Felton b Walker | 0 |
| R.T.Robinson * | b Capel | 35 |
| M.Saxelby | b Williams | 2 |
| F.D.Stephenson | b Baptiste | 19 |
| M.Newell | c Felton b Curran | 12 |
| K.P.Evans | b Curran | 8 |
| B.N.French + | c Lamb b Walker | 26 |
| E.E.Hemmings | b Taylor | 17 |
| R.A.Pick | not out | 2 |
| Extras | (lb 18,w 4) | 22 |
| TOTAL | (40 overs) | 197 |

| NOTTS | O | M | R | W | FALL OF WICKETS | | |
|---|---|---|---|---|---|---|---|
| | | | | | | NOR | NOT |
| Stephenson | 8 | 0 | 31 | 5 | | | |
| Pick | 8 | 0 | 37 | 1 | 1st | 12 | 19 |
| Saxelby | 8 | 1 | 46 | 0 | 2nd | 104 | 21 |
| Hemmings | 8 | 0 | 38 | 0 | 3rd | 109 | 84 |
| Evans | 8 | 1 | 41 | 3 | 4th | 120 | 93 |
| | | | | | 5th | 166 | 106 |
| NORTHANTS | O | M | R | W | 6th | 184 | 136 |
| Walker | 8 | 0 | 24 | 2 | 7th | 185 | 141 |
| Taylor | 7 | 0 | 45 | 2 | 8th | 199 | 155 |
| Curran | 7 | 0 | 28 | 2 | 9th | 199 | 191 |
| Baptiste | 8 | 0 | 37 | 1 | 10th | 202 | 197 |
| Capel | 5 | 0 | 23 | 1 | | | |
| Williams | 5 | 0 | 22 | 2 | | | |

## SURREY vs. YORKSHIRE
at The Oval on 21st July 1991
Toss : Yorkshire. Umpires : D.O.Oslear and R.A.White
Yorkshire won by 8 wickets. Surrey 0 pts, Yorkshire 4 pts

### SURREY
| | | |
|---|---|---|
| D.J.Bicknell | lbw b Robinson M.A. | 7 |
| M.A.Lynch | b Grayson | 97 |
| A.J.Stewart + | c Blakey b Hartley | 5 |
| D.M.Ward | c Blakey b Robinson M.A. | 56 |
| G.P.Thorpe | c Moxon b Fletcher | 4 |
| I.A.Greig * | b Robinson M.A. | 15 |
| J.D.Robinson | b Robinson M.A. | 16 |
| M.A.Feltham | not out | 12 |
| J.Boiling | run out | 1 |
| Waqar Younis | not out | 0 |
| A.J.Murphy | | |
| Extras | (lb 4,w 7,nb 3) | 14 |
| TOTAL | (40 overs)(for 8 wkts) | 227 |

### YORKSHIRE
| | | |
|---|---|---|
| M.D.Moxon * | not out | 129 |
| A.A.Metcalfe | c Feltham b Boiling | 31 |
| R.J.Blakey + | c Stewart b Waqar Younis | 24 |
| D.Byas | not out | 28 |
| P.E.Robinson | | |
| C.S.Pickles | | |
| A.P.Grayson | | |
| P.J.Hartley | | |
| J.D.Batty | | |
| S.D.Fletcher | | |
| M.A.Robinson | | |
| Extras | (lb 11,w 5) | 16 |
| TOTAL | (36.1 overs)(for 2 wkts) | 228 |

| YORKSHIRE | O | M | R | W | FALL OF WICKETS | | |
|---|---|---|---|---|---|---|---|
| | | | | | | SUR | YOR |
| Hartley | 8 | 0 | 25 | 1 | | | |
| Robinson M.A. | 8 | 1 | 33 | 4 | 1st | 9 | 89 |
| Pickles | 8 | 0 | 48 | 0 | 2nd | 23 | 161 |
| Fletcher | 8 | 0 | 51 | 1 | 3rd | 179 | |
| Batty | 3 | 0 | 34 | 0 | 4th | 179 | |
| Grayson | 5 | 0 | 32 | 1 | 5th | 185 | |
| | | | | | 6th | 205 | |
| SURREY | O | M | R | W | 7th | 224 | |
| Murphy | 7 | 0 | 46 | 0 | 8th | 226 | |
| Feltham | 6.1 | 0 | 41 | 0 | 9th | | |
| Robinson | 5 | 0 | 26 | 0 | 10th | | |
| Waqar Younis | 8 | 0 | 34 | 1 | | | |
| Boiling | 8 | 0 | 54 | 1 | | | |
| Greig | 2 | 0 | 16 | 0 | | | |

# HEADLINES

### Refuge Assurance League

### 21st July

• Lancashire put their recent setbacks behind them to take over from Nottinghamshire as Sunday League leaders, but only after the most eventful of victories over Middlesex at Lord's. The visitors' bowlers had given a workmanlike performance to limit Middlesex to 143 for six in their 40 overs, but Norman Cowans wrought havoc with their early batting as the scoreboard first read four for four then 36 for seven. Lancashire were eventually rescued by a determined rearguard action from Warren Hegg and Ian Austin who shared an eighth-wicket stand of 105 to secure victory by two wickets.

• Meanwhile Nottinghamshire who could have built up a useful cushion of six points had results been reversed fell two points behind by losing to Northamptonshire by five runs at Wellingborough School, the home side putting the embarrassment of their two-day Championship defeat behind them. Franklyn Stephenson's career-best five for 31 could not prevent Notts' second Sunday defeat of the season.

• Several other teams all with hopes of at least qualifying for the Refuge Cup also took advantage of Notts' defeat to move nearer to the front-runners. Graham Gooch's eleventh Sunday 100 helped Essex to a healthy 247 for four and victory by 30 runs over Somerset at Southend.

• Worcestershire beat Glamorgan by seven wickets at Worcester, Tim Curtis and Tom Moody setting them on their way to success with a stand of 111 as Glamorgan's total of 230 for five was overcome with the minimum of effort, the home side gaining compensation for their NatWest Trophy defeat.

• Martyn Moxon led Yorkshire to an impressive eight-wicket victory over fellow hopefuls Surrey at The Oval with an unbeaten 129, his highest score in the Sunday League. Mark Robinson had earlier improved his best bowling figures with a return of four for 33 after a second-wicket partnership of 156 between Monte Lynch and David Ward had threatened to take Surrey out of range.

• Warwickshire's chances of a top four finish were also improved by their five-wicket victory over Hampshire at Portsmouth. Dermot Reeve's unbeaten 44 was the highest score of a largely featureless contest.

• Derbyshire ended their disappointing run of results in convincing fashion with victory by 94 runs over Gloucestershire at Cheltenham. Peter Bowler took a break from keeping wicket to claim three wickets for 31 as the home side could not approach their target of 256.

• Sussex were the day's other winners, Paul Parker's 104 and Adrian Jones's five wickets for 32 proving too much for Leicestershire at Hove.

# BRITANNIC ASSURANCE CHAMPIONSHIP

## ESSEX vs. SOMERSET

at Southend on 19th, 20th, 22nd July 1991
Toss : Somerset. Umpires : J.D.Bond and K.E.Palmer
Essex won by 136 runs. Essex 22 pts (Bt: 4, Bw: 2), Somerset 4 pts (Bt: 3, Bw: 1)
100 overs scores : Essex 331 for 3, Somerset 266 for 5

### ESSEX

| | | | | |
|---|---|---|---|---|
| G.A.Gooch * | c & b Hallett | 79 | c Harden b Hayhurst | 97 |
| J.P.Stephenson | run out | 70 | c Trump b Beal | 11 |
| P.J.Prichard | b Hallett | 0 | lbw b Macleay | 8 |
| Salim Malik | c Tavare b Lefebvre | 102 | not out | 35 |
| N.Hussain | c Hallett b Macleay | 88 | not out | 0 |
| M.A.Garnham + | b Macleay | 14 | | |
| D.R.Pringle | not out | 25 | | |
| T.D.Topley | not out | 16 | | |
| S.J.W.Andrew | | | | |
| J.H.Childs | | | | |
| P.M.Such | | | | |
| Extras | (b 1,lb 12,w 2,nb 4) | 19 | (b 2,lb 1,nb 2) | 5 |
| TOTAL | (for 6 wkts dec) | 413 | (for 3 wkts dec) | 156 |

### SOMERSET

| | | | | |
|---|---|---|---|---|
| S.J.Cook | not out | 193 | c Prichard b Childs | 21 |
| P.M.Roebuck | c Garnham b Childs | 38 | b Andrew | 11 |
| A.N.Hayhurst | c Garnham b Childs | 11 | (5) c Gooch b Such | 0 |
| C.J.Tavare * | c Hussain b Such | 0 | (3) b Stephenson | 20 |
| R.J.Harden | lbw b Such | 20 | (4) b Such | 45 |
| K.H.Macleay | c Topley b Childs | 6 | c Salim Malik b Such | 7 |
| N.D.Burns + | not out | 13 | b Childs | 4 |
| R.P.Lefebvre | | | c Hussain b Childs | 0 |
| D.Beal | | | lbw b Childs | 0 |
| H.R.J.Trump | | | not out | 0 |
| J.C.Hallett | | | b Childs | 4 |
| Extras | (lb 4,w 1,nb 22) | 27 | (b 3,lb 3,nb 7) | 13 |
| TOTAL | (for 5 wkts dec) | 308 | | 125 |

| SOMERSET | O | M | R | W | O | M | R | W |
|---|---|---|---|---|---|---|---|---|
| Hallett | 20 | 2 | 52 | 2 | 6 | 0 | 36 | 0 |
| Beal | 15 | 1 | 75 | 0 | 8 | 2 | 37 | 1 |
| Macleay | 22 | 4 | 72 | 2 | 7 | 1 | 32 | 1 |
| Lefebvre | 17 | 1 | 72 | 1 | 5 | 0 | 30 | 0 |
| Trump | 29 | 1 | 102 | 0 | 1.1 | 0 | 9 | 0 |
| Roebuck | 8 | 0 | 25 | 0 | | | | |
| Hayhurst | 1 | 0 | 2 | 0 | 1 | 0 | 9 | 1 |

| ESSEX | O | M | R | W | O | M | R | W |
|---|---|---|---|---|---|---|---|---|
| Andrew | 13 | 0 | 65 | 0 | 5 | 1 | 11 | 1 |
| Pringle | 18 | 2 | 55 | 0 | 9 | 1 | 40 | 0 |
| Childs | 39 | 16 | 66 | 3 | 17.4 | 8 | 20 | 5 |
| Topley | 5 | 0 | 26 | 0 | 2 | 0 | 17 | 0 |
| Such | 26 | 7 | 46 | 2 | 15 | 7 | 23 | 3 |
| Salim Malik | 13 | 1 | 46 | 0 | | | | |
| Stephenson | | | | | 4 | 2 | 8 | 1 |

| FALL OF WICKETS | ESS | SOM | ESS | SOM |
|---|---|---|---|---|
| 1st | 140 | 128 | 64 | 24 |
| 2nd | 146 | 169 | 99 | 37 |
| 3rd | 171 | 174 | 149 | 92 |
| 4th | 351 | 216 | | 95 |
| 5th | 357 | 262 | | 112 |
| 6th | 380 | | | 121 |
| 7th | | | | 121 |
| 8th | | | | 121 |
| 9th | | | | 121 |
| 10th | | | | 125 |

## HAMPSHIRE vs. WARWICKSHIRE

at Portsmouth on 19th, 20th, 22nd July 1991
Toss : Hampshire. Umpires : J.H.Harris and A.G.T.Whitehead
Warwicks won by 3 wickets. Hampshire 7 pts (Bt: 3, Bw: 4), Warwicks 21 pts (Bt: 1, Bw: 4)

### HAMPSHIRE

| | | | | |
|---|---|---|---|---|
| V.P.Terry | lbw b Reeve | 124 | c Ratcliffe b Munton | 18 |
| M.C.J.Nicholas * | lbw b Small | 0 | c Piper b Donald | 5 |
| K.D.James | c Reeve b Munton | 7 | c Piper b Reeve | 19 |
| R.A.Smith | c Asif Din b Munton | 19 | (7) c Piper b Reeve | 0 |
| D.I.Gower | c Piper b Donald | 43 | (4) c Moles b Donald | 18 |
| J.R.Ayling | not out | 42 | c Donald b Reeve | 16 |
| A.N Aymes + | c & b Reeve | 7 | (5) c Ostler b Small | 35 |
| R.J.Maru | c Ratcliffe b Reeve | 2 | c Ostler b Reeve | 6 |
| C.A.Connor | c Ratcliffe b Reeve | 4 | run out | 17 |
| K.J.Shine | c Piper b Small | 1 | b Donald | 0 |
| Aqib Javed | c Ostler b Small | 0 | not out | 2 |
| Extras | (b 1,lb 6,w 4,nb 5) | 16 | (b 16,lb 9,w 12,nb 3) | 40 |
| TOTAL | | 265 | | 176 |

### WARWICKSHIRE

| | | | | |
|---|---|---|---|---|
| A.J.Moles | b Shine | 1 | c Maru b James | 15 |
| J.D.Ratcliffe | lbw b Aqib Javed | 52 | c Gower b Shine | 77 |
| T.A.Lloyd * | lbw b Aqib Javed | 11 | c Nicholas b Connor | 10 |
| D.P.Ostler | lbw b Aqib Javed | 20 | c Aymes b Ayling | 12 |
| D.A.Reeve | c Terry b James | 3 | lbw b Ayling | 14 |
| Asif Din | c Terry b Ayling | 19 | c James b Ayling | 13 |
| P.A.Smith | c Maru b James | 7 | c Aymes b Shine | 27 |
| K.J.Piper + | c Aymes b Ayling | 6 | not out | 31 |
| G.C.Small | c Aymes b Ayling | 17 | not out | 12 |
| T.A.Munton | c Maru b Shine | 14 | | |
| A.A.Donald | not out | 8 | | |
| Extras | (b 1,lb 15,nb 17) | 33 | (b 4,lb 4,w 6,nb 16) | 40 |
| TOTAL | | 191 | (for 7 wkts) | 251 |

| WARWICKS | O | M | R | W | O | M | R | W |
|---|---|---|---|---|---|---|---|---|
| Donald | 13.5 | 1 | 41 | 1 | 15.4 | 4 | 32 | 3 |
| Small | 17.1 | 4 | 45 | 3 | 16 | 3 | 50 | 1 |
| Munton | 22 | 3 | 80 | 2 | 8 | 1 | 28 | 1 |
| Reeve | 22 | 7 | 46 | 4 | 15 | 5 | 27 | 4 |
| Smith | 8 | 0 | 38 | 0 | 2 | 0 | 14 | 0 |
| Asif Din | 3 | 1 | 8 | 0 | | | | |

| HAMPSHIRE | O | M | R | W | O | M | R | W |
|---|---|---|---|---|---|---|---|---|
| Aqib Javed | 13 | 5 | 18 | 3 | 6 | 2 | 23 | 0 |
| Shine | 16 | 1 | 63 | 2 | 22 | 3 | 68 | 2 |
| Connor | 9 | 3 | 32 | 0 | 18 | 1 | 59 | 1 |
| James | 12 | 3 | 39 | 2 | 10.5 | 1 | 33 | 1 |
| Ayling | 10.1 | 2 | 23 | 3 | 20 | 4 | 47 | 3 |
| Maru | | | | | 4 | 3 | 3 | 0 |

| FALL OF WICKETS | HAM | WAR | HAM | WAR |
|---|---|---|---|---|
| 1st | 2 | 17 | 25 | 68 |
| 2nd | 21 | 29 | 41 | 115 |
| 3rd | 67 | 97 | 78 | 129 |
| 4th | 128 | 101 | 80 | 141 |
| 5th | 254 | 110 | 127 | 152 |
| 6th | 256 | 134 | 144 | 175 |
| 7th | 258 | 145 | 144 | 219 |
| 8th | 263 | 159 | 166 | |
| 9th | 263 | 183 | 167 | |
| 10th | 265 | 191 | 176 | |

## GLOUCESTERSHIRE vs. GLAMORGAN

at Cheltenham on 19th, 20th, 22nd July 1991
Toss : Gloucs. Umpires : G.I.Burgess and P.B.Wight
Match drawn. Gloucs 4 pts (Bt: 0, Bw: 4), Glamorgan 6 pts (Bt: 2, Bw: 4)

### GLAMORGAN

| | | | | |
|---|---|---|---|---|
| A.R.Butcher | c Hodgson b Lawrence | 0 | b Gilbert | 12 |
| H.Morris * | lbw b Lawrence | 6 | c Russell b Alleyne | 84 |
| A.Dale | c Scott b Lawrence | 4 | c Russell b Lawrence | 0 |
| M.P.Maynard | c Russell b Lloyds | 129 | c Athey b Lawrence | 126 |
| R.J.Shastri | c Wright b Smith | 22 | c Hodgson b Smith | 4 |
| P.A.Cottey | lbw b Smith | 0 | not out | 37 |
| R.D.B.Croft | run out | 44 | c Russell b Alleyne | 0 |
| C.P.Metson + | c Lawrence b Lloyds | 5 | b Gilbert | 16 |
| S.L.Watkin | c Russell b Lawrence | 15 | not out | 5 |
| S.R.Barwick | c Russell b Lloyds | 12 | | |
| M.Frost | not out | 0 | | |
| Extras | (lb 6,w 3,nb 1) | 10 | (lb 7,w 2,nb 1) | 10 |
| TOTAL | | 247 | (for 7 wkts dec) | 294 |

### GLOUCESTERSHIRE

| | | | | |
|---|---|---|---|---|
| G.D.Hodgson | c Shastri b Frost | 29 | c Metson b Frost | 0 |
| R.J.Scott | lbw b Frost | 0 | c Maynard b Frost | 122 |
| A.J.Wright * | lbw b Watkin | 0 | c Metson b Watkin | 4 |
| C.W.J.Athey | c Maynard b Croft | 21 | c Cottey b Barwick | 37 |
| M.W.Alleyne | c Dale b Frost | 2 | (6) c Metson b Frost | 4 |
| P.W.Romaines | c Dale b Watkin | 28 | (5) c Metson b Frost | 0 |
| R.C.Russell + | c Metson b Watkin | 21 | not out | 79 |
| J.W.Lloyds | c Cottey b Watkin | 24 | c Metson b Frost | 61 |
| D.V.Lawrence | c Metson b Frost | 6 | c Maynard b Frost | 0 |
| A.M.Smith | c Morris b Watkin | 1 | (11) not out | 0 |
| D.R.Gilbert | not out | 2 | (10) lbw b Frost | 17 |
| Extras | (b 2,lb 4) | 6 | (b 7,lb 9,w 3,nb 3) | 22 |
| TOTAL | | 140 | (for 9 wkts) | 346 |

| GLOUCS | O | M | R | W | O | M | R | W |
|---|---|---|---|---|---|---|---|---|
| Lawrence | 18 | 3 | 62 | 4 | 12 | 2 | 38 | 2 |
| Gilbert | 14 | 5 | 37 | 0 | 16 | 2 | 45 | 2 |
| Smith | 15 | 2 | 56 | 2 | 15 | 1 | 71 | 1 |
| Scott | 4 | 0 | 32 | 0 | 2 | 0 | 19 | 0 |
| Lloyds | 9 | 4 | 27 | 3 | 13 | 3 | 56 | 0 |
| Alleyne | 6 | 0 | 27 | 0 | 11.3 | 0 | 48 | 2 |
| Athey | | | | | 2 | 0 | 10 | 0 |

| GLAMORGAN | O | M | R | W | O | M | R | W |
|---|---|---|---|---|---|---|---|---|
| Watkin | 17.4 | 3 | 49 | 5 | 35 | 9 | 89 | 1 |
| Frost | 15 | 4 | 44 | 4 | 29 | 7 | 99 | 7 |
| Barwick | 8 | 4 | 9 | 0 | 36 | 10 | 67 | 1 |
| Dale | 3 | 0 | 9 | 0 | | | | |
| Croft | 8 | 3 | 23 | 1 | 24 | 10 | 45 | 0 |
| Shastri | | | | | 16 | 5 | 30 | 0 |

| FALL OF WICKETS | GLA | GLO | GLA | GLO |
|---|---|---|---|---|
| 1st | 0 | 4 | 26 | 1 |
| 2nd | 10 | 7 | 31 | 1 |
| 3rd | 13 | 52 | 204 | 100 |
| 4th | 57 | 52 | 213 | 117 |
| 5th | 57 | 61 | 242 | 123 |
| 6th | 203 | 91 | 243 | 197 |
| 7th | 213 | 108 | 283 | 307 |
| 8th | 233 | 114 | | 307 |
| 9th | 245 | 127 | | 346 |
| 10th | 247 | 140 | | |

## MIDDLESEX vs. LANCASHIRE

at Uxbridge on 19th, 20th, 22nd July 1991
Toss : Middlesex. Umpires : J.C.Balderstone and R.C.Tolchard
Lancashire won by 6 wickets. Middlesex 5 pts (Bt: 3, Bw: 2), Lancashire 22 pts (Bt: 2, Bw: 4)
100 overs scores :Lancashire 227 for 5

### MIDDLESEX

| | | | | |
|---|---|---|---|---|
| M.A.Roseberry | lbw b Wasim Akram | 63 | run out | 65 |
| J.C.Pooley | c Watkinson b Wasim Akram | 5 | c Yates b Martin | 5 |
| M.R.Ramprakash | c Fairbrother b Martin | 5 | lbw b Watkinson | 56 |
| K.R.Brown | c Hegg b Martin | 2 | lbw b Wasim Akram | 16 |
| M.Keech | b Wasim Akram | 35 | lbw b Wasim Akram | 0 |
| M.W.Gatting * | b Yates | 41 | lbw b Wasim Akram | 3 |
| J.E.Emburey | b Wasim Akram | 4 | b Wasim Akram | 27 |
| P.Farbrace + | c Mendis b Hughes | 42 | lbw b Wasim Akram | 19 |
| N.F.Williams | lbw b Wasim Akram | 0 | not out | 5 |
| P.C.R.Tufnell | not out | 24 | c Atherton b Watkinson | 1 |
| N.G.Cowans | c Wasim Akram b Hughes | 6 | b Wasim Akram | 0 |
| Extras | (b 7,lb 7,nb 9) | 23 | (b 1,lb 10,nb 12) | 23 |
| TOTAL | | 250 | | 220 |

### LANCASHIRE

| | | | | |
|---|---|---|---|---|
| G.D.Mendis | lbw b Cowans | 43 | (2) b Cowans | 2 |
| G.Fowler | b Cowans | 2 | (1) b Cowans | 34 |
| M.A.Atherton | c Farbrace b Tufnell | 91 | c Pooley b Tufnell | 35 |
| N.H.Fairbrother | c Pooley b Cowans | 53 | | |
| N.J.Speak | lbw b Williams | 11 | (4) not out | 25 |
| M.Watkinson | c Cowans b Emburey | 35 | (5) c Farbrace b Emburey | 21 |
| Wasim Akram | st Farbrace b Tufnell | 63 | (6) not out | 15 |
| W.K.Hegg + | c Gatting b Emburey | 5 | | |
| G.Yates | not out | 0 | | |
| D.P.Hughes * | b Emburey | 0 | | |
| P.J.Martin | lbw b Emburey | 0 | | |
| Extras | (b 14,lb 5,w 1,nb 6) | 26 | (b 9,lb 2,w 1,nb 1) | 13 |
| TOTAL | | 329 | (for 4 wkts) | 145 |

| LANCASHIRE | O | M | R | W | O | M | R | W |
|---|---|---|---|---|---|---|---|---|
| Wasim Akram | 22 | 4 | 63 | 5 | 17.2 | 3 | 66 | 6 |
| Martin | 22 | 5 | 65 | 2 | 15 | 4 | 43 | 1 |
| Watkinson | 9 | 0 | 41 | 0 | 14 | 3 | 40 | 2 |
| Yates | 20 | 6 | 60 | 1 | 11 | 0 | 42 | 0 |
| Hughes | 3.2 | 1 | 7 | 2 | 14 | 7 | 18 | 0 |

| MIDDLESEX | O | M | R | W | O | M | R | W |
|---|---|---|---|---|---|---|---|---|
| Williams | 22 | 3 | 60 | 1 | 4 | 0 | 18 | 0 |
| Cowans | 24 | 7 | 51 | 3 | 10 | 1 | 35 | 2 |
| Tufnell | 44 | 16 | 94 | 2 | 8 | 1 | 32 | 1 |
| Emburey | 39.2 | 11 | 96 | 4 | 11.1 | 0 | 49 | 1 |
| Ramprakash | 1 | 0 | 9 | 0 | | | | |

| FALL OF WICKETS | MID | LAN | MID | LAN |
|---|---|---|---|---|
| 1st | 7 | 18 | 43 | 8 |
| 2nd | 15 | 68 | 88 | 74 |
| 3rd | 19 | 197 | 132 | 100 |
| 4th | 79 | 215 | 132 | 129 |
| 5th | 136 | 215 | 144 | |
| 6th | 151 | 303 | 176 | |
| 7th | 174 | 329 | 207 | |
| 8th | 176 | 329 | 214 | |
| 9th | 244 | 329 | 219 | |
| 10th | 250 | 329 | 220 | |

# BRITANNIC ASSURANCE CHAMPIONSHIP

## HEADLINES

### Britannic Assurance Championship

### 19th - 22nd July

• Although Warwickshire gained their seventh victory of the summer after a tension-filled final day at Portsmouth to remain 20 points clear at the top of the table, their leading rivals were also successful, each displaying their credentials as Championship contenders by bowling out the opposition rather than relying on declaration cricket.

• Warwickshire's seam bowling had been responsible for most of the county's successes in Championship cricket in 1991, and the five-man attack again played its part against Hampshire, Dermot Reeve returning the most impressive figures with eight wickets for 73. The visitors' batting had been much less convincing, and after conceding a first innings lead of 74 to Hampshire, Warwickshire needed to make 251 for victory. Jason Ratcliffe saw them off to a secure start but an eighth-wicket stand of 32 between Keith Piper and Gladstone Small was still required before Midlands nerves were calmed.

• Essex remained in second place with their 136-run victory over Somerset at Southend. The first two days were dominated by the batsmen. Salim Malik hit his fifth first-class 100 of the season as Essex reached 413 for six declared, but Jimmy Cook responded with an unbeaten 193, also his fifth 100, to limit the home side's advantage to 105. After an early declaration from Graham Gooch who just missed out on a century before lunch, the Essex spinners proved a daunting propostion. John Childs and Peter Such shared eight wickets for 43 in 32.4 overs as Somerset were dismissed for just 125 in their second innings.

• Lancashire returned to winning ways at Uxbridge with a six-wicket win over Middlesex which owed a great deal to the efforts of Wasim Akram who returned match figures of 11 for 129. Michael Atherton proved his fitness with 91 as the visitors gained a lead of 79, and an eventual target of 142 proved well within reach as the Lancastrians reclaimed third place.

• Surrey kept up their challenge by gaining their third successive win in a week at Guildford, by one wicket after Yorkshire had victory within their grasp. Waqar Younis's eight wickets took his tally past 50 in first-class cricket, but it was his batting contribution that finally secured victory, sharing a ninth wicket stand of 52 with Keith Medlycott when Surrey had looked certain to fall short of their target.

## NORTHANTS vs. NOTTS

at Wellingborough School on 19th, 20th, 22nd July 1991
Toss : Notts. Umpires : H.D.Bird and B.J.Meyer
Notts won by an innings and 1 run. Northants 7 pts (Bt: 3, Bw: 4), Notts 24 pts (Bt: 4, Bw: 4)
100 overs scores :Notts 311 for 9

### NORTHANTS

| | | | | | |
|---|---|---|---|---|---|
| A.Fordham | b Stephenson | 12 | lbw b Pick | 9 |
| N.A.Felton | c Pollard b Pick | 0 | c sub b Pick | 1 |
| R.J.Bailey | c Robinson b Pick | 57 | b Stephenson | 2 |
| A.J.Lamb * | lbw b Evans | 33 | c Pick b Stephenson | 2 |
| D.J.Capel | c Johnson b Evans | 0 | c French b Pick | 0 |
| K.M.Curran | b Stephenson | 18 | not out | 20 |
| E.A.E.Baptiste | b Stephenson | 80 | b Stephenson | 3 |
| R.G.Williams | b Stephenson | 12 | c Evans b Pick | 0 |
| D.Ripley + | b Pick | 8 | (10) b Stephenson | 6 |
| N.G.B.Cook | not out | 15 | (9) b Stephenson | 4 |
| J.P.Taylor | lbw b Stephenson | 4 | b Pick | 2 |
| Extras | (b 1,lb 12,nb 1) | 14 | (b 14,lb 5) | 19 |
| TOTAL | | 253 | | 68 |

### NOTTS

| | | |
|---|---|---|
| P.Pollard | c Cook b Capel | 52 |
| M.A.Crawley | not out | 17 |
| R.T.Robinson * | lbw b Taylor | 43 |
| P.Johnson | b Cook | 81 |
| D.W.Randall | lbw b Curran | 45 |
| K.P.Evans | c & b Curran | 1 |
| B.N.French + | b Curran | 2 |
| F.D.Stephenson | c Ripley b Curran | 1 |
| E.E.Hemmings | b Cook | 10 |
| R.A.Pick | c Bailey b Taylor | 46 |
| J.A.Afford | lbw b Curran | 0 |
| Extras | (b 6,lb 16,w 1,nb 1) | 24 |
| TOTAL | | 322 |

| NOTTS | O | M | R | W | O | M | R | W |
|---|---|---|---|---|---|---|---|---|
| Stephenson | 22.4 | 7 | 61 | 5 | 12 | 2 | 27 | 5 |
| Pick | 24 | 6 | 74 | 3 | 8.5 | 2 | 17 | 5 |
| Evans | 21 | 5 | 65 | 2 | 3 | 1 | 5 | 0 |
| Afford | 8 | 2 | 19 | 0 | | | | |
| Crawley | 8 | 3 | 15 | 0 | | | | |
| Hemmings | 3 | 0 | 6 | 0 | | | | |

| NORTHANTS | O | M | R | W | O | M | R | W |
|---|---|---|---|---|---|---|---|---|
| Taylor | 19.5 | 2 | 68 | 2 | | | | |
| Baptiste | 29 | 4 | 81 | 0 | | | | |
| Cook | 20 | 6 | 51 | 2 | | | | |
| Williams | 1 | 0 | 6 | 0 | | | | |
| Capel | 13 | 4 | 34 | 1 | | | | |
| Curran | 24 | 6 | 60 | 5 | | | | |

### FALL OF WICKETS

| | NOR | NOT | NOR | NOT |
|---|---|---|---|---|
| 1st | 12 | 87 | 9 | |
| 2nd | 12 | 127 | 12 | |
| 3rd | 56 | 213 | 12 | |
| 4th | 60 | 215 | 14 | |
| 5th | 90 | 217 | 14 | |
| 6th | 155 | 227 | 19 | |
| 7th | 181 | 250 | 20 | |
| 8th | 219 | 266 | 39 | |
| 9th | 249 | 267 | 57 | |
| 10th | 253 | 322 | 68 | |

## SURREY vs. YORKSHIRE

at Guildford on 19th, 20th, 22nd July 1991
Toss : Surrey. Umpires : D.O.Oslear and R.A.White
Surrey won by 1 wicket. Surrey 22 pts (Bt: 3, Bw: 3), Yorkshire 2 pts (Bt: 2, Bw: 0)
100 overs scores : Yorkshire 217 for 7

### YORKSHIRE

| | | | | | |
|---|---|---|---|---|---|
| M.D.Moxon * | c Alikhan b Medlycott | 73 | b Waqar Younis | 68 |
| A.A.Metcalfe | c Medlycott b Feltham | 6 | b Murphy | 2 |
| D.Byas | c Bicknell b Feltham | 33 | lbw b Waqar Younis | 0 |
| R.J.Blakey + | b Waqar Younis | 11 | c Alikhan b Medlycott | 17 |
| P.E.Robinson | b Feltham | 74 | c & b Medlycott | 17 |
| S.A.Kellett | b Waqar Younis | 6 | (7) lbw b Waqar Younis | 13 |
| C.S.Pickles | b Murphy | 1 | (8) c Bicknell b Waqar Younis | 2 |
| P.Carrick | c Bicknell b Medlycott | 18 | (10) b Waqar Younis | 7 |
| P.J.Hartley | not out | 35 | b Waqar Younis | 0 |
| J.D.Batty | b Murphy | 4 | (6) c Feltham b Murphy | 12 |
| S.D.Fletcher | c Alikhan b Feltham | 6 | not out | 9 |
| Extras | (b 1,lb 9,nb 12) | 22 | (b 2,lb 2,nb 2) | 6 |
| TOTAL | | 289 | | 153 |

### SURREY

| | | | | | |
|---|---|---|---|---|---|
| D.J.Bicknell | c Robinson b Carrick | 80 | c Robinson b Hartley | 11 |
| R.I.Alikhan | c Pickles b Batty | 86 | c Byas b Carrick | 21 |
| A.J.Stewart * | not out | 53 | c & b Batty | 36 |
| D.M.Ward | not out | 18 | c Blakey b Fletcher | 3 |
| G.P.Thorpe | | | c Carrick b Batty | 22 |
| M.A.Lynch | | | c Moxon b Carrick | 13 |
| K.T.Medlycott | | | not out | 30 |
| M.A.Feltham | | | run out | 6 |
| N.F.Sargeant + | | | c Kellett b Batty | 3 |
| Waqar Younis | | | c Batty b Carrick | 31 |
| A.J.Murphy | | | not out | 2 |
| Extras | (lb 4,w 2,nb 7) | 13 | (b 6,lb 6,w 1,nb 2) | 15 |
| TOTAL | (for 2 wkts dec) | 250 | (for 9 wkts) | 193 |

| SURREY | O | M | R | W | O | M | R | W |
|---|---|---|---|---|---|---|---|---|
| Waqar Younis | 28 | 8 | 54 | 2 | 22.3 | 3 | 40 | 6 |
| Murphy | 28 | 6 | 66 | 2 | 11 | 1 | 30 | 2 |
| Feltham | 34.2 | 10 | 64 | 4 | 6 | 1 | 20 | 0 |
| Thorpe | 8 | 4 | 8 | 0 | | | | |
| Medlycott | 24 | 5 | 87 | 2 | 17 | 2 | 59 | 2 |

| YORKSHIRE | O | M | R | W | O | M | R | W |
|---|---|---|---|---|---|---|---|---|
| Hartley | 13 | 4 | 56 | 0 | 9 | 1 | 33 | 1 |
| Fletcher | 10 | 0 | 44 | 0 | 9 | 3 | 31 | 1 |
| Pickles | 10 | 1 | 35 | 0 | 2 | 0 | 13 | 0 |
| Carrick | 25 | 5 | 44 | 1 | 22.4 | 5 | 56 | 3 |
| Batty | 16.4 | 0 | 67 | 1 | 15 | 2 | 48 | 3 |

### FALL OF WICKETS

| | YOR | SUR | YOR | SUR |
|---|---|---|---|---|
| 1st | 17 | 150 | 6 | 35 |
| 2nd | 106 | 228 | 9 | 49 |
| 3rd | 135 | | 38 | 68 |
| 4th | 135 | | 57 | 94 |
| 5th | 164 | | 106 | 115 |
| 6th | 170 | | 133 | 123 |
| 7th | 208 | | 135 | 130 |
| 8th | 255 | | 136 | 139 |
| 9th | 268 | | 136 | 191 |
| 10th | 289 | | 153 | |

# BRITANNIC ASSURANCE CHAMPIONSHIP

## WORCESTERSHIRE vs. DERBYSHIRE

at Kidderminster on 19th, 20th, 22nd July 1991
Toss : Derbyshire.  Umpires : M.J.Kitchen and B.Leadbeater
Match drawn.  Worcestershire 5 pts (Bt: 2, Bw: 3), Derbyshire 8 pts (Bt: 4, Bw: 4)
100 overs scores : Derbyshire 362 for 7

### DERBYSHIRE

| | | | | |
|---|---|---|---|---|
| K.J.Barnett * | lbw b Botham | 80 | | |
| P.D.Bowler | c Hick b Lampitt | 2 | (3) not out | 2 |
| J.E.Morris | b Illingworth | 97 | | |
| M.Azharuddin | c Rhodes b Newport | 25 | | |
| T.J.G.O'Gorman | c Radford b Illingworth | 78 | | |
| S.C.Goldsmith | c & b Illingworth | 10 | | |
| K.M.Krikken + | c Lampitt b Newport | 32 | | |
| D.G.Cork | st Rhodes b Illingworth | 15 | (1) not out | 15 |
| A.E.Warner | c Botham b Illingworth | 15 | | |
| D.E.Malcolm | c Rhodes b Radford | 0 | (2) c Radford b Illingworth | 4 |
| O.H.Mortensen | not out | 0 | | |
| Extras | (lb 9,w 1,nb 8) | 18 | | 0 |
| TOTAL | | 372 | (for 1 wkt) | 21 |

### WORCESTERSHIRE

| | | | | |
|---|---|---|---|---|
| T.S.Curtis | lbw b Cork | 32 | lbw b Mortensen | 14 |
| G.J.Lord | c Krikken b Malcolm | 3 | b Mortensen | 17 |
| G.A.Hick | c Krikken b Cork | 24 | run out | 3 |
| T.M.Moody | c O'Gorman b Warner | 51 | c O'Gorman b Goldsmith | 29 |
| P.A.Neale * | b Cork | 0 | c Bowler b Mortensen | 42 |
| I.T.Botham | c Cork b Warner | 5 | (7) b Mortensen | 17 |
| S.J.Rhodes + | c Krikken b Warner | 15 | (8) c Morris b Mortensen | 90 |
| R.K.Illingworth | c Warner b Malcolm | 31 | (6) c Azharuddin b Mortensen | 21 |
| S.R.Lampitt | not out | 17 | b Cork | 93 |
| P.J.Newport | c Krikken b Mortensen | 6 | not out | 18 |
| N.V.Radford | lbw b Malcolm | 19 | c Bowler b Barnett | 45 |
| Extras | (lb 8,w 1,nb 6) | 15 | (b 4,lb 15,w 3,nb 13) | 35 |
| TOTAL | | 218 | | 424 |

| WORCS | O | M | R | W | O | M | R | W | | FALL OF WICKETS | | | |
|---|---|---|---|---|---|---|---|---|---|---|---|---|---|
| | | | | | | | | | | DER | WOR | WOR | DER |
| Radford | 18 | 5 | 61 | 1 | | | | | 1st | 9 | 9 | 36 | 9 |
| Lampitt | 13 | 1 | 82 | 1 | | | | | 2nd | 122 | 48 | 37 | |
| Newport | 19 | 3 | 80 | 2 | | | | | 3rd | 180 | 93 | 56 | |
| Botham | 22 | 3 | 76 | 1 | | | | | 4th | 222 | 93 | 85 | |
| Illingworth | 33.3 | 10 | 64 | 5 | 5 | 3 | 7 | 1 | 5th | 263 | 120 | 143 | |
| Curtis | | | | | 4 | 1 | 14 | 0 | 6th | 327 | 126 | 150 | |
| | | | | | | | | | 7th | 339 | 172 | 163 | |
| DERBYSHIRE | O | M | R | W | O | M | R | W | 8th | 362 | 178 | 347 | |
| Malcolm | 16.3 | 3 | 57 | 3 | 26 | 3 | 90 | 0 | 9th | 362 | 197 | 361 | |
| Mortensen | 17 | 8 | 29 | 1 | 31 | 9 | 101 | 6 | 10th | 372 | 218 | 424 | |
| Cork | 14 | 1 | 49 | 3 | 24 | 5 | 84 | 1 | | | | | |
| Warner | 20 | 2 | 75 | 3 | 20 | 6 | 40 | 0 | | | | | |
| Goldsmith | | | | | 8 | 1 | 23 | 1 | | | | | |
| Barnett | | | | | 15.2 | 2 | 46 | 1 | | | | | |
| Bowler | | | | | 5 | 0 | 21 | 0 | | | | | |

## SUSSEX vs. LEICESTERSHIRE

at Hove on 19th, 20th, 22nd July 1991
Toss : Sussex.  Umpires : B.Hassan and K.J.Lyons
Sussex won by 5 runs.  Sussex 23 pts (Bt: 4, Bw: 3), Leicestershire 4 pts (Bt: 3, Bw: 1)
100 overs scores : Sussex 322 for 4, Leicestershire 264 for 8

### SUSSEX

| | | | | |
|---|---|---|---|---|
| N.J.Lenham | b Maguire | 193 | c Benson b Lewis | 4 |
| D.M.Smith | c Benson b Lewis | 3 | c sub b Hepworth | 50 |
| P.W.G.Parker * | c Willey b Lewis | 33 | c Lewis b Hepworth | 55 |
| A.P.Wells | c Benson b Lewis | 12 | not out | 33 |
| M.P.Speight | c Smith b Maguire | 64 | b Potter | 18 |
| C.M.Wells | not out | 31 | not out | 14 |
| A.I.C.Dodemaide | not out | 12 | | |
| P.Moores + | | | | |
| I.D.K.Salisbury | | | | |
| B.T.P.Donelan | | | | |
| A.N.Jones | | | | |
| Extras | (lb 6) | 6 | (lb 5) | 5 |
| TOTAL | (for 5 wkts dec) | 354 | (for 4 wkts dec) | 179 |

### LEICESTERSHIRE

| | | | | |
|---|---|---|---|---|
| P.N.Hepworth | c Lenham b Jones | 7 | lbw b Salisbury | 56 |
| N.E.Briers * | lbw b Salisbury | 29 | st Moores b Salisbury | 41 |
| J.J.Whitaker | c Smith b Jones | 0 | b Donelan | 5 |
| L.Potter | c Wells A.P. b Donelan | 89 | b Donelan | 0 |
| B.F.Smith | b Donelan | 17 | c Dodemaide b Donelan | 19 |
| J.D.R.Benson | b Salisbury | 45 | b Donelan | 62 |
| C.C.Lewis | c Parker b Salisbury | 15 | c sub b Donelan | 21 |
| P.Willey | not out | 14 | c & b Salisbury | 11 |
| P.Whitticase + | c Speight b Dodemaide | 29 | c Smith b Salisbury | 5 |
| L.Tennant | not out | 23 | b Donelan | 7 |
| J.N.Maguire | | | not out | 11 |
| Extras | (b 4,lb 7,nb 7) | 18 | (lb 1,w 3) | 4 |
| TOTAL | (for 8 wkts dec) | 286 | | 242 |

| LEICS | O | M | R | W | O | M | R | W | | FALL OF WICKETS | | | |
|---|---|---|---|---|---|---|---|---|---|---|---|---|---|
| | | | | | | | | | | SUS | LEI | SUS | LEI |
| Lewis | 35 | 5 | 106 | 3 | 8.5 | 3 | 24 | 1 | 1st | 9 | 13 | 6 | 94 |
| Maguire | 35 | 10 | 85 | 2 | 9 | 2 | 40 | 0 | 2nd | 74 | 16 | 110 | 103 |
| Tennant | 10 | 3 | 54 | 0 | | | | | 3rd | 100 | 78 | 119 | 105 |
| Potter | 17 | 5 | 51 | 0 | 11 | 1 | 48 | 1 | 4th | 269 | 111 | 148 | 105 |
| Benson | 10 | 2 | 40 | 0 | | | | | 5th | 342 | 184 | | 149 |
| Hepworth | 2 | 0 | 12 | 0 | 12 | 2 | 62 | 2 | 6th | | 213 | | 192 |
| | | | | | | | | | 7th | | 219 | | 206 |
| SUSSEX | O | M | R | W | O | M | R | W | 8th | | 255 | | 224 |
| Jones | 9 | 2 | 20 | 2 | 5 | 2 | 23 | 0 | 9th | | | | 228 |
| Dodemaide | 14 | 3 | 29 | 1 | 8 | 0 | 34 | 0 | 10th | | | | 242 |
| Salisbury | 45 | 8 | 130 | 3 | 27 | 4 | 92 | 4 | | | | | |
| Donelan | 39 | 14 | 96 | 2 | 27.5 | 1 | 92 | 6 | | | | | |

## HEADLINES

### Britannic Assurance Championship

### 19th - 22nd July

• Nottinghamshire also recorded their third consecutive victory by defeating Northamptonshire by an innings and one run with a day to spare at Wellingborough School. A last-wicket stand of 55 between Andy Pick and Mark Crawley had given the visitors a first innings lead of 69 but this proved one too many for Northants who were dismissed for the season's lowest total, Franklyn Stephenson completing match figures of 10 for 88.

• Sussex gained their second win of the season by five runs at Hove after young spinners Ian Salisbury and Brad Donelan shared all 10 wickets in Leicestershire's second innings. Neil Lenham recorded a career-best 193 in Sussex's first innings, but it was the last afternoon's play which really caught the attention as the visitors attempted a target of 248 in 68 overs. An opening stand of 94 put them on course before the two spinners began to work their way through Leicester's batting. The last man was removed with one ball to spare as Donelan finished with a career-best six for 92.

• Glamorgan looked certain to record victory over Gloucestershire at Cheltenham after reducing the home side to 123 for five as they chased an improbable 402 for victory, but despite career-best figures from Mark Frost Gloucestershire survived thanks to a century from Richard Scott and five hours' determined resistance from Jack Russell who shared a seventh-wicket stand of 110 with Jeremy Lloyds. Matthew Maynard had earlier scored spectacular 100s in both Glamorgan innings.

• Worcestershire were forced to follow on for the second time in a week, this time by Derbyshire at Kidderminster, but they again escaped with a draw by reaching 424 in their second innings thanks to an eighth-wicket partnership of 184 between Steven Rhodes and Stuart Lampitt who hit a career best 93. Richard Illingworth at last had a productive bowl in Derbyshire's first innings, but it was the visitors' seam bowlers that placed Worcestershire under severe pressure.

115

| TOUR MATCH | BRITANNIC ASS. CHAMPIONSHIP |
|---|---|

## KENT vs. WEST INDIES

at Canterbury on 20th, 21st, 22nd July 1991
Toss : West Indies.  Umpires : D.J.Constant and M.J.Harris
West Indies won by 4 runs

**WEST INDIES**

| | | | | | |
|---|---|---|---|---|---|
| P.V.Simmons | c Ellison b Davis | 77 | c & b Merrick | 107 |
| D.L.Haynes | c Igglesden b Merrick | 4 | c Marsh b Igglesden | 4 |
| B.C.Lara | lbw b Ellison | 19 | b Davis | 18 |
| A.L.Logie | c Marsh b Igglesden | 70 | c Ellison b Merrick | 26 |
| I.V.A.Richards * | c Marsh b Fleming | 29 | c Marsh b Davis | 56 |
| C.L.Hooper | not out | 61 | not out | 54 |
| P.J.L.Dujon + | c Ward b Ellison | 22 | | |
| H.A.G.Anthony | b Fleming | 7 | (7) not out | 6 |
| I.B.A.Allen | not out | 3 | | |
| C.A.Walsh | | | | |
| B.P.Patterson | | | | |
| Extras | (lb 4,nb 14) | 18 | (lb 4,w 2,nb 1) | 7 |
| TOTAL | (for 7 wkts dec) | 310 | (for 5 wkts dec) | 278 |

**KENT**

| | | | | | |
|---|---|---|---|---|---|
| T.R.Ward | c Lara b Patterson | 0 | c sub b Patterson | 2 |
| S.G.Hinks | c Lara b Patterson | 8 | c Richards b Hooper | 31 |
| N.R.Taylor | not out | 138 | c Richards b Allen | 21 |
| G.R.Cowdrey | c Patterson b Anthony | 7 | c Lara b Patterson | 104 |
| M.V.Fleming | c Allen b Walsh | 7 | b Walsh | 116 |
| S.A.Marsh *+ | b Patterson | 22 | run out | 8 |
| R.M.Ellison | c Simmons b Allen | 14 | b Anthony | 4 |
| R.P.Davis | c Hooper b Patterson | 27 | (9) b Anthony | 10 |
| C.Penn | c Lara b Anthony | 9 | (8) c Lara b Anthony | 3 |
| T.A.Merrick | | | c Logie b Patterson | 6 |
| A.P.Igglesden | | | not out | 1 |
| Extras | (b 1,lb 8,w 1,nb 5) | 15 | (b 9,lb 18,w 3,nb 1) | 31 |
| TOTAL | (for 8 wkts dec) | 247 | | 337 |

| KENT | O | M | R | W | O | M | R | W | | FALL OF WICKETS | | | |
|---|---|---|---|---|---|---|---|---|---|---|---|---|---|
| | | | | | | | | | | | WI | KEN | WI | KEN |
| Merrick | 12 | 1 | 48 | 1 | 10 | 0 | 51 | 2 | 1st | 20 | 0 | 29 | 6 |
| Igglesden | 14 | 6 | 20 | 1 | 8 | 2 | 43 | 1 | 2nd | 79 | 30 | 106 | 46 |
| Ellison | 18 | 2 | 55 | 2 | 9 | 1 | 50 | 0 | 3rd | 147 | 45 | 145 | 80 |
| Penn | 10 | 2 | 46 | 0 | 12 | 1 | 61 | 0 | 4th | 207 | 56 | 174 | 272 |
| Davis | 16 | 1 | 87 | 1 | 11 | 1 | 69 | 2 | 5th | 213 | 125 | 263 | 293 |
| Fleming | 17 | 3 | 50 | 2 | | | | | 6th | 270 | 150 | | 301 |
| | | | | | | | | | 7th | 281 | 220 | | 311 |
| WEST INDIES | O | M | R | W | O | M | R | W | 8th | | 247 | | 327 |
| Patterson | 20 | 4 | 70 | 4 | 9.4 | 2 | 57 | 3 | 9th | | | | 331 |
| Allen | 19 | 5 | 57 | 1 | 8 | 2 | 24 | 1 | 10th | | | | 337 |
| Anthony | 14.1 | 2 | 47 | 2 | 13 | 0 | 65 | 3 | | | | | |
| Walsh | 12 | 1 | 45 | 1 | 16 | 3 | 57 | 1 | | | | | |
| Hooper | 10 | 1 | 19 | 0 | 14 | 2 | 64 | 1 | | | | | |
| Richards | | | | | 9 | 1 | 43 | 0 | | | | | |

## HEADLINES

### Tetley Bitter Challenge

#### 20th - 22nd July

• Kent came within one boundary of becoming the first English county to beat the West Indies since 1976 after they had made a valiant effort to reach a target of 342 in 70 overs at Canterbury. Graham Cowdrey and Matthew Fleming both hit 100s and shared a fourth-wicket stand of 192 but on Fleming's dismissal wickets began to fall regularly and last man Tony Merrick was caught at mid on with two balls of the last over remaining. Even before this compelling finale the match had produced plenty of entertainment, Phil Simmons and Carl Hooper taking the honours for the tourists, and Neil Taylor holding Kent's first innings together with an unbeaten 138. Despite their eventual defeat Kent had competed on level terms with the West Indies to give England much-needed encouragement with the Test series about to enter its decisive final stages.

## DERBYSHIRE vs. HAMPSHIRE

at Chesterfield on 23rd, 25th July 1991
Toss : Hampshire.  Umpires : D.O.Oslear and K.E.Palmer
Hampshire won by 94 runs.  Derbyshire 4 pts (Bt: 0, Bw: 4), Hampshire 19 pts (Bt: 3, Bw: 0)

**HAMPSHIRE**

| | | | | | |
|---|---|---|---|---|---|
| T.C.Middleton | run out | 3 | c Krikken b Goldsmith | 11 |
| C.L.Smith | c Krikken b Malcolm | 114 | not out | 16 |
| K.D.James | lbw b Mortensen | 101 | c Barnett b Sladdin | 1 |
| D.I.Gower | hit wicket b Malcolm | 3 | not out | 0 |
| M.C.J.Nicholas * | c Azharuddin b Mortensen | 2 | | |
| J.R.Ayling | run out | 1 | | |
| A.N Aymes + | c Cork b Mortensen | 5 | | |
| R.J.Maru | b Cork | 4 | | |
| I.J.Turner | not out | 6 | | |
| C.A.Connor | c Bowler b Cork | 0 | | |
| K.J.Shine | c Azharuddin b Mortensen | 0 | | |
| Extras | (lb 5,nb 14) | 19 | (nb 1) | 1 |
| TOTAL | | 258 | (for 2 wkts dec) | 29 |

**DERBYSHIRE**

| | | | |
|---|---|---|---|
| K.J.Barnett * | retired hurt | 74 |
| P.D.Bowler | c Aymes b Connor | 0 |
| J.E.Morris | b Maru | 35 |
| M.Azharuddin | c Middleton b Maru | 0 |
| T.J.G.O'Gorman | c Aymes b Turner | 42 |
| S.C.Goldsmith | c sub b Turner | 10 |
| K.M.Krikken + | c Middleton b Turner | 1 |
| D.G.Cork | b James | 0 |
| D.E.Malcolm | c Nicholas b Turner | 5 |
| R.W.Sladdin | lbw b James | 4 |
| O.H.Mortensen | not out | 0 |
| Extras | (b 7,lb 4,w 2,nb 9) | 22 |
| TOTAL | | 193 |

| DERBYSHIRE | O | M | R | W | O | M | R | W | | FALL OF WICKETS | | |
|---|---|---|---|---|---|---|---|---|---|---|---|---|
| | | | | | | | | | | HAM | DER | HAM | DER |
| Malcolm | 22 | 2 | 84 | 2 | | | | | 1st | 17 | | 28 | 16 |
| Mortensen | 28.2 | 6 | 50 | 4 | | | | | 2nd | 219 | | 29 | 88 |
| Cork | 26 | 6 | 53 | 2 | | | | | 3rd | 235 | | | 88 |
| Goldsmith | 6 | 1 | 22 | 0 | 7.4 | 0 | 11 | 1 | 4th | 235 | | | 177 |
| Sladdin | 13 | 2 | 44 | 0 | 8 | 3 | 18 | 1 | 5th | 238 | | | 179 |
| | | | | | | | | | 6th | 239 | | | 181 |
| HAMPSHIRE | O | M | R | W | O | M | R | W | 7th | 245 | | | 182 |
| Shine | 4 | 0 | 34 | 0 | | | | | 8th | 256 | | | 193 |
| Connor | 7 | 1 | 22 | 1 | | | | | 9th | 257 | | | 193 |
| Ayling | 10 | 1 | 38 | 0 | | | | | 10th | 258 | | | |
| Maru | 22 | 10 | 48 | 2 | | | | | | | | | |
| Turner | 16 | 10 | 28 | 4 | | | | | | | | | |
| James | 6 | 1 | 12 | 2 | | | | | | | | | |

## GLAMORGAN vs. ESSEX

at Cardiff on 23rd, 24th, 25th July 1991
Toss : Glamorgan.  Umpires : J.C.Balderstone and A.A.Jones
Glamorgan won by 4 wickets.  Glamorgan 16 pts (Bt: 0, Bw: 0), Essex 3 pts (Bt: 3, Bw: 0)

**ESSEX**

| | | |
|---|---|---|
| A.C.Seymour | b Croft | 157 |
| J.P.Stephenson | b Frost | 76 |
| P.J.Prichard * | not out | 22 |
| N.Hussain | not out | 6 |
| Salim Malik | | |
| N.Shahid | | |
| M.A.Garnham + | | |
| A.G.J.Fraser | | |
| T.D.Topley | | |
| J.H.Childs | | |
| S.J.W.Andrew | | |
| Extras | (lb 5,w 1,nb 3) | 9 |
| TOTAL | (for 2 wkts dec) | 270 |

**GLAMORGAN**

| | | |
|---|---|---|
| A.R.Butcher * | hit wicket b Stephenson | 61 |
| S.P.James | c Topley b Stephenson | 16 |
| A.Dale | c Hussain b Andrew | 9 |
| M.P.Maynard | c & b Childs | 38 |
| R.J.Shastri | not out | 70 |
| P.A.Cottey | b Childs | 20 |
| R.D.B.Croft | c Salim Malik b Andrew | 10 |
| C.P.Metson + | not out | 19 |
| S.L.Watkin | | |
| S.Bastien | | |
| M.Frost | | |
| Extras | (b 6,lb 5,w 1,nb 16) | 28 |
| TOTAL | (for 6 wkts) | 271 |

| GLAMORGAN | O | M | R | W | O | M | R | W | | FALL OF WICKETS | | |
|---|---|---|---|---|---|---|---|---|---|---|---|---|
| | | | | | | | | | | ESS | GLA | ESS | GLA |
| Watkin | 23 | 3 | 75 | 0 | | | | | 1st | 206 | | | 90 |
| Frost | 17 | 1 | 58 | 1 | | | | | 2nd | 258 | | | 94 |
| Bastien | 22 | 6 | 63 | 0 | | | | | 3rd | | | | 143 |
| Croft | 10.1 | 2 | 23 | 1 | | | | | 4th | | | | 150 |
| Dale | 10 | 1 | 46 | 0 | | | | | 5th | | | | 199 |
| | | | | | | | | | 6th | | | | 224 |
| ESSEX | O | M | R | W | O | M | R | W | 7th | | | | |
| Andrew | | | | | 22.3 | 3 | 90 | 2 | 8th | | | | |
| Topley | | | | | 17 | 1 | 50 | 0 | 9th | | | | |
| Stephenson | | | | | 9 | 2 | 50 | 2 | 10th | | | | |
| Childs | | | | | 18 | 5 | 70 | 2 | | | | | |

# BRITANNIC ASSURANCE CHAMPIONSHIP

## GLOUCESTERSHIRE vs. SUSSEX

at Cheltenham on 23rd, 24th, 25th July 1991
Toss : Sussex. Umpires : G.I.Burgess and P.B.Wight
Match drawn. Gloucs 3 pts (Bt: 3, Bw: 0), Sussex 4 pts (Bt: 0, Bw: 4)

### GLOUCESTERSHIRE

| | | |
|---|---|---|
| G.D.Hodgson | b Dodemaide | 46 |
| R.J.Scott | c Speight b Dodemaide | 18 |
| A.J.Wright * | c Moores b Jones | 70 |
| C.W.J.Athey | c Lenham b Dodemaide | 10 |
| M.W.Alleyne | b Jones | 0 |
| P.W.Romaines | c Moores b Jones | 4 |
| J.W.Lloyds | c Speight b Dodemaide | 8 |
| R.C.J.Williams + | c Smith b Dodemaide | 5 |
| D.R.Gilbert | not out | 28 |
| A.M.Babington | c Lenham b Jones | 58 |
| M.J.Gerrard | c Moores b Jones | 2 |
| Extras | (lb 19,w 1,nb 14) | 34 |
| TOTAL | | 283 |

### SUSSEX

| | | |
|---|---|---|
| N.J.Lenham | c Alleyne b Gilbert | 46 |
| P.Moores + | c Scott b Babington | 6 |
| P.W.G.Parker * | c Babington b Gerrard | 13 |
| A.P.Wells | c Hodgson b Gerrard | 7 |
| M.P.Speight | c Wright b Gilbert | 26 |
| A.I.C.Dodemaide | lbw b Gilbert | 0 |
| A.C.S.Pigott | b Lloyds | 1 |
| D.M.Smith | not out | 65 |
| B.T.P.Donelan | not out | 28 |
| I.D.K.Salisbury | | |
| A.N.Jones | | |
| Extras | (b 1,lb 3,w 1,nb 2) | 7 |
| TOTAL | (for 7 wkts) | 199 |

| SUSSEX | O | M | R | W | O | M | R | W | FALL OF WICKETS | | | |
|---|---|---|---|---|---|---|---|---|---|---|---|---|
| | | | | | | | | | | GLO | SUS GLO | SUS |
| Jones | 23 | 3 | 84 | 5 | | | | | 1st | 25 | | 14 |
| Dodemaide | 33 | 3 | 130 | 5 | | | | | 2nd | 142 | | 40 |
| Pigott | 7 | 3 | 13 | 0 | | | | | 3rd | 165 | | 51 |
| Lenham | 4 | 0 | 14 | 0 | | | | | 4th | 170 | | 97 |
| Salisbury | 2 | 0 | 8 | 0 | | | | | 5th | 170 | | 98 |
| Donelan | 10 | 5 | 15 | 0 | | | | | 6th | 178 | | 98 |
| | | | | | | | | | 7th | 190 | | 111 |
| GLOUCS | O | M | R | W | O | M | R | W | 8th | 190 | | |
| Gilbert | | | | | 28.4 | 5 | 78 | 3 | 9th | 268 | | |
| Babington | | | | | 17 | 3 | 66 | 1 | 10th | 283 | | |
| Gerrard | | | | | 10 | 2 | 25 | 2 | | | | |
| Lloyds | | | | | 14 | 6 | 26 | 1 | | | | |

## LANCASHIRE vs. WARWICKSHIRE

at Old Trafford on 23rd, 24th, 25th July 1991
Toss : Warwickshire. Umpires : R.Palmer and N.T.Plews
Match drawn. Lancashire 7 pts (Bt: 4, Bw: 3), Warwickshire 3 pts (Bt: 3, Bw: 0)
100 overs scores : Warwickshire 296 for 9

### WARWICKSHIRE

| | | | | |
|---|---|---|---|---|
| A.J.Moles | lbw b Martin | 9 | | |
| J.D.Ratcliffe | c Allott b Martin | 0 | (1) not out | 51 |
| Asif Din | c Titchard b Watkinson | 100 | | |
| D.P.Ostler | lbw b Martin | 9 | (2) c Stanworth b Watkinson | 32 |
| D.A.Reeve * | b Wasim Akram | 88 | (3) not out | 12 |
| P.A.Smith | b Yates | 24 | | |
| P.C.L.Holloway + | not out | 26 | | |
| G.C.Small | c Mendis b Yates | 0 | | |
| T.A.Munton | c Martin b Watkinson | 3 | | |
| A.A.Donald | st Stanworth b Watkinson | 1 | | |
| A.R.K.Pierson | not out | 3 | | |
| Extras | (b 3,lb 4,nb 26) | 33 | (b 4,nb 2) | 6 |
| TOTAL | (for 9 wkts dec) | 296 | (for 1 wkt) | 101 |

### LANCASHIRE

| | | |
|---|---|---|
| G.D.Mendis | c Ratcliffe b Pierson | 119 |
| G.D.Lloyd | c Holloway b Asif Din | 96 |
| S.P.Titchard | not out | 15 |
| N.H.Fairbrother * | not out | 6 |
| G.Fowler | | |
| M.Watkinson | | |
| Wasim Akram | | |
| G.Yates | | |
| P.J.W.Allott | | |
| P.J.Martin | | |
| J.Stanworth + | | |
| Extras | (lb 10,nb 4) | 14 |
| TOTAL | (for 2 wkts dec) | 250 |

| LANCASHIRE | O | M | R | W | O | M | R | W | FALL OF WICKETS | | | |
|---|---|---|---|---|---|---|---|---|---|---|---|---|
| | | | | | | | | | | WAR | LAN WAR | LAN |
| Wasim Akram | 24.5 | 4 | 86 | 1 | | | | | 1st | 4 | 214 | 66 |
| Martin | 20 | 9 | 40 | 3 | | | | | 2nd | 16 | 243 | |
| Allott | 17.1 | 7 | 45 | 0 | | | | | 3rd | 35 | | |
| Watkinson | 19 | 2 | 58 | 3 | 18 | 4 | 61 | 1 | 4th | 215 | | |
| Yates | 19 | 5 | 60 | 2 | 18 | 9 | 36 | 0 | 5th | 251 | | |
| | | | | | | | | | 6th | 258 | | |
| WARWICKS | O | M | R | W | O | M | R | W | 7th | 263 | | |
| Donald | 14 | 1 | 50 | 0 | | | | | 8th | 285 | | |
| Small | 8 | 2 | 18 | 0 | | | | | 9th | 292 | | |
| Reeve | 12 | 2 | 29 | 0 | | | | | 10th | | | |
| Munton | 14 | 4 | 34 | 0 | | | | | | | | |
| Pierson | 16 | 0 | 67 | 1 | | | | | | | | |
| Asif Din | 17 | 6 | 42 | 1 | | | | | | | | |

# BRITANNIC ASSURANCE CHAMPIONSHIP

## NORTHANTS vs. SOMERSET

at Northampton on 23rd, 24th, 25th July 1991
Toss : Northants. Umpires : H.D.Bird and B.J.Meyer
Match drawn. Northants 0 pts (Bt: 0, Bw: 0), Somerset 5 pts (Bt: 4, Bw: 1)
100 overs scores : Somerset 309 for 2

### SOMERSET

| | | | | | |
|---|---|---|---|---|---|
| S.J.Cook | not out | | 210 | | |
| P.M.Roebuck | c Ripley b Baptiste | | 32 | | |
| A.N.Hayhurst | b Cook | | 29 | (1) c Curran b Fordham | 23 |
| C.J.Tavare * | not out | | 65 | | |
| R.J.Harden | | | | (2) not out | 59 |
| K.H.Macleay | | | | (4) not out | 21 |
| N.D.Burns + | | | | (3) run out | 11 |
| R.P.Lefebvre | | | | | |
| J.C.Hallett | | | | | |
| A.P.van Troost | | | | | |
| D.A.Graveney | | | | | |
| Extras | (lb 6,w 4,nb 2) | | 12 | (lb 1,w 2,nb 1) | 4 |
| TOTAL | (for 2 wkts dec) | | 348 | (for 2 wkts dec) | 118 |

### NORTHANTS

| | | | | | |
|---|---|---|---|---|---|
| A.Fordham | b Lefebvre | | 73 | c Burns b Graveney | 84 |
| N.A.Felton | c & b Hallett | | 4 | b Hallett | 2 |
| R.J.Bailey * | c van Troost b Harden | | 40 | st Burns b Graveney | 117 |
| W.Larkins | not out | | 4 | c Hayhurst b Graveney | 19 |
| D.J.Capel | b Lefebvre | | 15 | c sub b Hayhurst | 0 |
| K.M.Curran | | | | run out | 60 |
| E.A.E.Baptiste | | | | run out | 18 |
| R.G.Williams | | | | b van Troost | 3 |
| J.G.Thomas | | | | not out | 1 |
| D.Ripley + | | | | b van Troost | 0 |
| N.G.B.Cook | | | | not out | 0 |
| Extras | (w 1) | | 1 | (b 3,lb 11,w 2,nb 1) | 17 |
| TOTAL | (for 4 wkts dec) | | 137 | (for 9 wkts) | 321 |

| NORTHANTS | O | M | R | W | O | M | R | W | FALL OF WICKETS | | | | |
|---|---|---|---|---|---|---|---|---|---|---|---|---|---|
| | | | | | | | | | | SOM | NOR | SOM | NOR |
| Thomas | 22 | 2 | 89 | 0 | | | | | 1st | 135 | 22 | 36 | 10 |
| Baptiste | 26 | 3 | 99 | 1 | 3 | 1 | 4 | 0 | 2nd | 230 | 103 | 57 | 148 |
| Capel | 17 | 3 | 41 | 0 | | | | | 3rd | | 119 | | 208 |
| Curran | 10 | 1 | 39 | 0 | 3 | 2 | 5 | 0 | 4th | | 137 | | 209 |
| Cook | 16 | 6 | 42 | 1 | | | | | 5th | | | | 259 |
| Williams | 17 | 7 | 32 | 0 | | | | | 6th | | | | 307 |
| Fordham | | | | | 6 | 0 | 42 | 1 | 7th | | | | 317 |
| Felton | | | | | 6 | 0 | 66 | 0 | 8th | | | | 320 |
| | | | | | | | | | 9th | | | | 321 |
| | | | | | | | | | 10th | | | | |

| SOMERSET | O | M | R | W | O | M | R | W |
|---|---|---|---|---|---|---|---|---|
| Hallett | 8 | 4 | 14 | 1 | 9 | 4 | 20 | 1 |
| van Troost | 9 | 2 | 24 | 0 | 12 | 1 | 52 | 2 |
| Hayhurst | 6 | 1 | 25 | 0 | 12 | 1 | 33 | 1 |
| Lefebvre | 10.4 | 3 | 39 | 2 | 18 | 4 | 58 | 0 |
| Graveney | 6 | 1 | 22 | 0 | 28 | 1 | 111 | 3 |
| Harden | 3 | 0 | 13 | 1 | | | | |
| Macleay | | | | | 7 | 1 | 33 | 0 |

David Byas, who shared an important partnership with Phil Carrick against Nottinghamshire.

## NOTTS vs. YORKSHIRE

at Worksop on 23rd, 24th, 25th July 1991
Toss : Yorkshire. Umpires : J.H.Hampshire and R.A.White
Yorkshire won by 111 runs. Notts 4 pts (Bt: 0, Bw: 4), Yorkshire 20 pts (Bt: 4, Bw: 0)
100 overs scores : Yorkshire 313

### YORKSHIRE

| | | | | | |
|---|---|---|---|---|---|
| M.D.Moxon * | c French b Stephenson | | 0 | not out | 25 |
| A.A.Metcalfe | c Robinson b Pick | | 29 | not out | 20 |
| D.Byas | c Robinson b Evans | | 153 | | |
| R.J.Blakey + | c French b Evans | | 19 | | |
| P.E.Robinson | c Randall b Stephenson | | 3 | | |
| S.A.Kellett | c Pollard b Stephenson | | 9 | | |
| P.Carrick | c French b Evans | | 63 | | |
| P.J.Hartley | not out | | 7 | | |
| J.D.Batty | c Pick b Evans | | 3 | | |
| S.D.Fletcher | lbw b Hemmings | | 2 | | |
| M.A.Robinson | lbw b Hemmings | | 0 | | |
| Extras | (lb 17,nb 8) | | 25 | (lb 5) | 5 |
| TOTAL | | | 313 | (for 0 wkts dec) | 50 |

### NOTTS

| | | | | | |
|---|---|---|---|---|---|
| B.C.Broad | not out | | 24 | c Metcalfe b Batty | 54 |
| P.Pollard | c Blakey b Robinson M.A. | | 8 | b Hartley | 35 |
| R.T.Robinson * | not out | | 0 | (4) run out | 0 |
| P.Johnson | | | | (5) c Robinson P.E. b Batty | 13 |
| D.W.Randall | | | | (3) c Carrick b Batty | 65 |
| K.P.Evans | | | | c Blakey b Batty | 6 |
| F.D.Stephenson | | | | c Metcalfe b Carrick | 10 |
| B.N.French + | | | | c Kellett b Batty | 11 |
| E.E.Hemmings | | | | c Robinson P.E. b Batty | 13 |
| R.A.Pick | | | | c Robinson P.E. b Carrick | 4 |
| J.A.Afford | | | | not out | 0 |
| Extras | | | 0 | (lb 2,nb 7) | 9 |
| TOTAL | (for 1 wkt dec) | | 32 | | 220 |

| NOTTS | O | M | R | W | O | M | R | W | FALL OF WICKETS | | | | |
|---|---|---|---|---|---|---|---|---|---|---|---|---|---|
| | | | | | | | | | | YOR | NOT | YOR | NOT |
| Stephenson | 19 | 3 | 57 | 3 | 4 | 0 | 19 | 0 | 1st | 0 | 24 | | 73 |
| Pick | 20 | 4 | 50 | 1 | 5 | 1 | 17 | 0 | 2nd | 54 | | | 92 |
| Evans | 18 | 4 | 56 | 4 | 2 | 1 | 9 | 0 | 3rd | 118 | | | 92 |
| Hemmings | 35 | 10 | 102 | 2 | | | | | 4th | 142 | | | 127 |
| Afford | 8 | 2 | 31 | 0 | | | | | 5th | 156 | | | 143 |
| | | | | | | | | | 6th | 289 | | | 154 |
| YORKSHIRE | O | M | R | W | O | M | R | W | 7th | 304 | | | 199 |
| Hartley | 5 | 1 | 15 | 0 | 18 | 1 | 75 | 1 | 8th | 310 | | | 215 |
| Robinson M.A. | 4.5 | 1 | 17 | 1 | 11 | 0 | 42 | 0 | 9th | 313 | | | 220 |
| Fletcher | | | | | 3 | 0 | 16 | 0 | 10th | 313 | | | 220 |
| Carrick | | | | | 15 | 6 | 37 | 2 | | | | | |
| Batty | | | | | 23.5 | 11 | 48 | 6 | | | | | |

## WORCESTERSHIRE vs. KENT

at Worcester on 23rd, 24th, 25th (no play) July 1991
Toss : Worcestershire. Umpires : M.J.Kitchen and B.Leadbeater
Match drawn. Worcestershire 0 pts (Bt: 0, Bw: 0), Kent 0 pts (Bt: 0, Bw: 0)

### WORCESTERSHIRE

| | | | |
|---|---|---|---|
| T.S.Curtis | c Hinks b Merrick | | 27 |
| P.Bent | c Marsh b Merrick | | 0 |
| T.M.Moody | not out | | 30 |
| D.B.D'Oliveira | not out | | 3 |
| P.A.Neale * | | | |
| G.R.Haynes | | | |
| S.J.Rhodes + | | | |
| S.R.Lampitt | | | |
| P.J.Newport | | | |
| G.R.Dilley | | | |
| R.D.Stemp | | | |
| Extras | (lb 4) | | 4 |
| TOTAL | (for 2 wkts) | | 64 |

### KENT

T.R.Ward
M.R.Benson *
N.R.Taylor
G.R.Cowdrey
S.G.Hinks
M.V.Fleming
S.A.Marsh +
R.P.Davis
C.Penn
T.A.Merrick
A.P.Igglesden
Extras
TOTAL

| KENT | O | M | R | W | O | M | R | W | FALL OF WICKETS | | | | |
|---|---|---|---|---|---|---|---|---|---|---|---|---|---|
| | | | | | | | | | | WOR | KEN | WOR | KEN |
| Merrick | 10 | 2 | 35 | 2 | | | | | 1st | 5 | | | |
| Igglesden | 6 | 0 | 11 | 0 | | | | | 2nd | 58 | | | |
| Penn | 4 | 1 | 14 | 0 | | | | | 3rd | | | | |
| | | | | | | | | | 4th | | | | |
| WORCS | O | M | R | W | O | M | R | W | 5th | | | | |
| | | | | | | | | | 6th | | | | |
| | | | | | | | | | 7th | | | | |
| | | | | | | | | | 8th | | | | |
| | | | | | | | | | 9th | | | | |
| | | | | | | | | | 10th | | | | |

# CORNHILL TEST MATCH

## ENGLAND vs. WEST INDIES

at Edgbaston on 25th, 26th, 27th, 28th July 1991
Toss : West Indies.  Umpires : B.Dudleston and D.R.Shepherd
West Indies won by 7 wickets

**ENGLAND**

| | | | | | |
|---|---|---|---|---|---|
| G.A.Gooch * | b Marshall | 45 | b Patterson | | 40 |
| H.Morris | c Dujon b Patterson | 3 | lbw b Patterson | | 1 |
| M.A.Atherton | lbw b Walsh | 16 | c Hooper b Patterson | | 1 |
| G.A.Hick | c Richards b Ambrose | 19 | b Ambrose | | 1 |
| A.J.Lamb | lbw b Marshall | 9 | c Dujon b Walsh | | 25 |
| M.R.Ramprakash | c Logie b Walsh | 29 | c Dujon b Marshall | | 25 |
| R.C.Russell + | c Richardson b Ambrose | 12 | c Dujon b Patterson | | 0 |
| D.R.Pringle | b Ambrose | 2 | c Logie b Marshall | | 45 |
| P.A.J.DeFreitas | c Richardson b Marshall | 10 | b Patterson | | 7 |
| C.C.Lewis | lbw b Marshall | 13 | c sub b Ambrose | | 65 |
| R.K.Illingworth | not out | 0 | not out | | 5 |
| Extras | (b 4,lb 3,nb 23) | 30 | (b 5,lb 21,nb 14) | | 40 |
| TOTAL | | 188 | | | 255 |

**WEST INDIES**

| | | | | | |
|---|---|---|---|---|---|
| P.V.Simmons | c Hick b Lewis | 28 | lbw b DeFreitas | | 16 |
| D.L.Haynes | c Russell b DeFreitas | 32 | c Hick b DeFreitas | | 8 |
| R.B.Richardson | lbw b Lewis | 104 | c Hick b DeFreitas | | 0 |
| C.L.Hooper | b Illingworth | 31 | not out | | 55 |
| I.V.A.Richards * | c Lewis b Pringle | 22 | not out | | 73 |
| A.L.Logie | c Atherton b Lewis | 28 | | | |
| P.J.L.Dujon + | lbw b DeFreitas | 6 | | | |
| M.D.Marshall | not out | 6 | | | |
| C.E.L.Ambrose | c Hick b Lewis | 1 | | | |
| C.A.Walsh | c & b Lewis | 18 | | | |
| B.P.Patterson | b Lewis | 3 | | | |
| Extras | (lb 7,nb 6) | 13 | (lb 4,nb 1) | | 5 |
| TOTAL | | 292 | (for 3 wkts) | | 157 |

**WEST INDIES**

| | O | M | R | W | O | M | R | W |
|---|---|---|---|---|---|---|---|---|
| Ambrose | 23 | 6 | 64 | 3 | 33 | 16 | 42 | 2 |
| Patterson | 11 | 2 | 39 | 1 | 31 | 6 | 81 | 5 |
| Walsh | 21 | 6 | 43 | 2 | 7 | 1 | 20 | 1 |
| Marshall | 12.4 | 1 | 33 | 4 | 19.4 | 3 | 53 | 2 |
| Hooper | 3 | 2 | 2 | 0 | 12 | 3 | 26 | 0 |
| Simmons | | | | | 3 | 0 | 7 | 0 |

**ENGLAND**

| | O | M | R | W | O | M | R | W |
|---|---|---|---|---|---|---|---|---|
| DeFreitas | 25.3 | 9 | 40 | 2 | 13 | 2 | 54 | 3 |
| Lewis | 35 | 10 | 111 | 6 | 16 | 7 | 45 | 0 |
| Pringle | 23 | 9 | 48 | 1 | 7 | 1 | 31 | 0 |
| Illingworth | 17 | 2 | 75 | 1 | 4.4 | 0 | 23 | 0 |
| Gooch | 6 | 1 | 11 | 0 | | | | |
| Hick | 1 | 1 | 0 | 0 | | | | |

**FALL OF WICKETS**

| | ENG | WI | ENG | WI |
|---|---|---|---|---|
| 1st | 6 | 52 | 2 | 23 |
| 2nd | 53 | 93 | 4 | 23 |
| 3rd | 88 | 148 | 5 | 24 |
| 4th | 108 | 194 | 71 | |
| 5th | 129 | 257 | 94 | |
| 6th | 159 | 258 | 96 | |
| 7th | 163 | 266 | 127 | |
| 8th | 163 | 267 | 144 | |
| 9th | 184 | 285 | 236 | |
| 10th | 188 | 292 | 255 | |

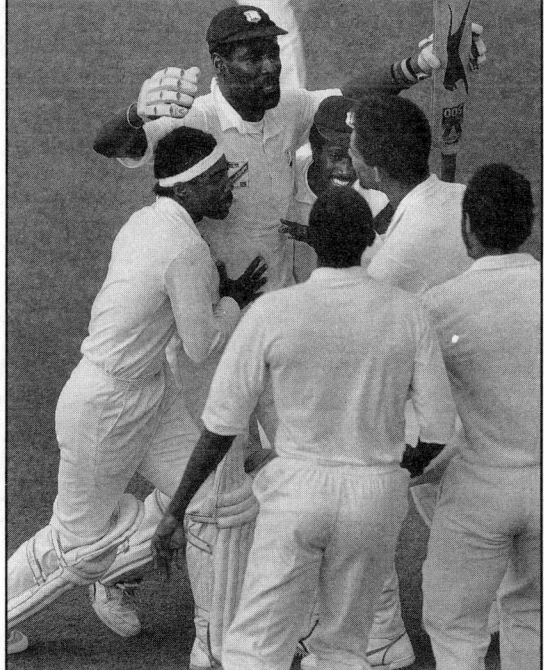

West Indies players greet Viv Richards after he and Carl Hooper
had completed a match-winning partnership.

## HEADLINES

### England v West Indies

### Fourth Cornhill Test Match

### 25th - 28th July: Edgbaston

• When Viv Richards nonchalantly came down the wicket to Richard Illingworth and cleared the straight boundary with a blow of extraordinary timing, West Indies claimed a seven-wicket victory over England to take a two-one lead in the series. Richards, ably supported by Carl Hooper, had orchestrated a rousing finale to a gripping Test match played on an unreliable pitch, reviving West Indies from 24 for three in their second innings with an unbroken stand of 133 to put an end to England's second courageous fight-back of the match, both inspired by Chris Lewis.

• The home side were outplayed for a large proportion of the match: they could muster only 188 in their first innings, Curtly Ambrose and Malcolm Marshall sharing seven wickets; then, once the new ball had been negotiated with a great deal of good fortune, the West Indies batsmen took control, Richie Richardson reaching his first Test 100 in England just before the close of the second day with his side comfortably placed for a big lead on 256 for four.

• England's fast bowlers enjoyed a dramatic change of fortune next morning, claiming the last six wickets for just 35, Lewis taking five for 16 on the way to Test-best figures of six for 111. West Indies' lead was unexpectedly restricted to 104, but any hopes of a home victory seemed to have evaporated when England, having first clawed their way back from five for three, were reduced to 144 for eight: a lead of 40 with two wickets in hand and a three-day defeat still a possibility.

• However, dependable Derek Pringle had taken anchor and proved the perfect foil for Lewis, now brimming with confidence, to play an array of stylish strokes to delight the Sunday crowd. Operating with the old ball the fast bowlers held no terrors and the West Indies were greatly relieved when Lewis was caught at cover for 65 bringing to an end a ninth-wicket stand of 92. Pringle's resistance, stretching to not far short of six hours, was eventually halted to leave the visitors a target of 152. Patrick Patterson, taking his turn as the main wicket-taker, recorded his best figures against England with five for 81.

• Phil DeFreitas's three quick wickets brought back memories of the famous Edgbaston Sunday 10 years before when Australia, attempting a similar target, collapsed to Ian Botham but Richards and Hooper, first intent only on defence, then unleashed a barrage of boundaries as the tension lifted, and saw their side home to a victory that ensured Richards would not lose a Test rubber in six and a half years as West Indies captain. England could look only to The Oval and a victory which could bring a share in the series

• Test début: H.Morris (England).

• Man of the match: R.B.Richardson (West Indies)

# REFUGE ASSURANCE LEAGUE

## DERBYSHIRE vs. NORTHANTS

at Derby on 28th July 1991
Toss : Derbyshire. Umpires : J.C.Balderstone and B.Hassan
Derbyshire won by 46 runs. Derbys 4 pts, Northants 0 pts

**DERBYSHIRE**

| | | |
|---|---|---|
| J.E.Morris * | c Walker b Curran | 40 |
| D.G.Cork | run out | 7 |
| T.J.G.O'Gorman | b Williams | 38 |
| M.Azharuddin | c Walker b Capel | 25 |
| S.C.Goldsmith | lbw b Williams | 5 |
| F.A.Griffith | b Taylor | 20 |
| E.McCray | c Curran b Taylor | 18 |
| A.E.Warner | not out | 16 |
| B.J.M.Maher + | not out | 0 |
| S.J.Base | | |
| O.H.Mortensen | | |
| Extras | (b 1,lb 10,w 4) | 15 |
| TOTAL | (40 overs)(for 7 wkts) | 184 |

**NORTHANTS**

| | | |
|---|---|---|
| A.Fordham | run out | 7 |
| N.A.Felton | c O'Gorman b Base | 4 |
| W.Larkins | lbw b Mortensen | 2 |
| D.J.Capel | c Base b McCray | 10 |
| R.J.Bailey * | c Maher b McCray | 22 |
| K.M.Curran | c Cork b Warner | 21 |
| E.A.E.Baptiste | st Maher b McCray | 9 |
| R.G.Williams | not out | 28 |
| D.Ripley + | c Morris b Base | 14 |
| A.Walker | c Azharuddin b Base | 5 |
| J.P.Taylor | c O'Gorman b Base | 0 |
| Extras | (lb 9,w 6,nb 1) | 16 |
| TOTAL | (36.5 overs) | 138 |

| NORTHANTS | O | M | R | W | | FALL OF WICKETS | |
|---|---|---|---|---|---|---|---|
| | | | | | | DER | NOR |
| Walker | 8 | 0 | 36 | 0 | | | |
| Taylor | 7 | 1 | 24 | 2 | 1st | 28 | 10 |
| Baptiste | 5 | 0 | 26 | 0 | 2nd | 59 | 15 |
| Curran | 7 | 1 | 32 | 1 | 3rd | 109 | 16 |
| Williams | 8 | 0 | 22 | 2 | 4th | 124 | 48 |
| Capel | 5 | 0 | 33 | 1 | 5th | 126 | 72 |
| | | | | | 6th | 155 | 86 |
| DERBYSHIRE | O | M | R | W | 7th | 178 | 90 |
| Base | 6.5 | 1 | 14 | 4 | 8th | | 124 |
| Mortensen | 8 | 1 | 19 | 1 | 9th | | 137 |
| Cork | 6 | 0 | 25 | 0 | 10th | | 138 |
| McCray | 8 | 0 | 38 | 3 | | | |
| Warner | 6 | 0 | 21 | 1 | | | |
| Goldsmith | 2 | 0 | 12 | 0 | | | |

## GLOUCESTERSHIRE vs. ESSEX

at Cheltenham on 28th July 1991
Toss : Essex. Umpires : J.D.Bond and D.J.Constant
Essex won by 4 wickets. Gloucs 0 pts, Essex 4 pts

**GLOUCESTERSHIRE**

| | | |
|---|---|---|
| R.J.Scott | b Topley | 11 |
| C.W.J.Athey * | lbw b Stephenson | 49 |
| A.J.Wright * | c Garnham b Fraser | 10 |
| M.W.Alleyne | c Seymour b Stephenson | 13 |
| T.Hancock | b Stephenson | 0 |
| J.W.Lloyds | c Fraser b Such | 12 |
| E.T.Milburn | c Prichard b Topley | 21 |
| M.C.J.Ball | run out | 1 |
| A.M.Babington | c Foster b Such | 11 |
| A.M.Smith | not out | 15 |
| M.J.Gerrard | c Shahid b Topley | 3 |
| Extras | (lb 6,w 3,nb 3) | 12 |
| TOTAL | (38.1 overs) | 158 |

**ESSEX**

| | | |
|---|---|---|
| A.C.Seymour | b Gerrard | 1 |
| J.P.Stephenson | c Athey b Babington | 0 |
| Salim Malik | lbw b Scott | 27 |
| P.J.Prichard | b Babington | 0 |
| N.Hussain | lbw b Alleyne | 44 |
| N.Shahid | c Athey b Alleyne | 36 |
| N.A.Foster * | not out | 29 |
| M.A.Garnham + | not out | 18 |
| A.G.J.Fraser | | |
| T.D.Topley | | |
| P.M.Such | | |
| Extras | (lb 1,w 1,nb 2) | 4 |
| TOTAL | (37.4 overs)(for 6 wkts) | 159 |

| ESSEX | O | M | R | W | | FALL OF WICKETS | |
|---|---|---|---|---|---|---|---|
| | | | | | | GLO | ESS |
| Foster | 7 | 0 | 24 | 0 | | | |
| Fraser | 8 | 0 | 21 | 1 | 1st | 22 | 1 |
| Topley | 7.1 | 1 | 35 | 3 | 2nd | 39 | 1 |
| Stephenson | 8 | 1 | 31 | 3 | 3rd | 79 | 2 |
| Such | 8 | 0 | 41 | 2 | 4th | 79 | 58 |
| | | | | | 5th | 100 | 109 |
| GLOUCS | O | M | R | W | 6th | 111 | 112 |
| Babington | 8 | 0 | 24 | 2 | 7th | 112 | |
| Gerrard | 8 | 1 | 42 | 1 | 8th | 127 | |
| Scott | 8 | 0 | 23 | 1 | 9th | 152 | |
| Smith | 3 | 0 | 23 | 0 | 10th | 158 | |
| Ball | 5 | 0 | 27 | 0 | | | |
| Alleyne | 5.4 | 0 | 19 | 2 | | | |

## HEADLINES

### Refuge Assurance League

### 28th July

• Lancashire remained two points clear of Nottinghamshire after both sides recorded victories that kept them well ahead of the chasing pack. Lancashire made surprisingly heavy weather of overcoming a moderate Hampshire total of 182 for five at Southampton, victors by two wickets thanks to Warren Hegg who came to the rescue for the second week in succession.

• Nottinghamshire remained on Lancashire's heels with a more comfortable six-wicket success over Sussex at Hove, Paul Pollard and Mark Saxelby sealing victory with a fifth-wicket stand of 51.

• Essex were the only side with a realistic chance of a place in the top four to gain victory, overcoming Gloucestershire at Cheltenham by four wickets after at one stage being in line for embarrassment on two for three.

• Kent kept their hopes of a late challenge alive by beating Somerset by 35 runs at Taunton, Matthew Fleming claiming career-best figures as the home side were dismissed for 185.

• Northamptonshire lost valuable ground by losing to Derbyshire at Derby by 46 runs, Simon Base (four for 14) and Ewan McCray (three for 38) both returning career bests as Northants collapsed to 138 all out.

• Surrey's slender hopes were ruined by a three-run defeat at the hands of Glamorgan at The Oval, although Surrey's Mark Butcher almost got the better of father Alan, Glamorgan's captain, as he hit an unbeaten 48 in a ninth-wicket stand of 58 on his senior début.

## HAMPSHIRE vs. LANCASHIRE

at Southampton on 28th July 1991
Toss : Lancashire. Umpires : G.I.Burgess and K.E.Palmer
Lancashire won by 2 wickets. Hampshire 0 pts, Lancs 4 pts

**HAMPSHIRE**

| | | |
|---|---|---|
| V.P.Terry | lbw b Watkinson | 1 |
| K.D.James | c Hegg b Watkinson | 10 |
| J.R.Wood | c Hegg b Allott | 10 |
| C.L.Smith | c Hegg b Austin | 60 |
| M.C.J.Nicholas * | not out | 65 |
| J.R.Ayling | c Mendis b Watkinson | 9 |
| A.N Aymes + | not out | 18 |
| S.D.Udal | | |
| R.J.Maru | | |
| C.A.Connor | | |
| K.J.Shine | | |
| Extras | (lb 5,w 2,nb 2) | 9 |
| TOTAL | (40 overs)(for 5 wkts) | 182 |

**LANCASHIRE**

| | | |
|---|---|---|
| G.D.Mendis | c Aymes b Shine | 5 |
| G.Fowler | c Smith b Maru | 38 |
| G.D.Lloyd | c Terry b Shine | 9 |
| N.H.Fairbrother * | c Aymes b Ayling | 37 |
| N.J.Speak | b Udal | 8 |
| M.Watkinson | b Connor | 25 |
| Wasim Akram | c Nicholas b Connor | 0 |
| W.K.Hegg + | not out | 42 |
| I.D.Austin | b Connor | 1 |
| P.J.W.Allott | not out | 10 |
| G.Yates | | |
| Extras | (lb 4,w 5,nb 1) | 10 |
| TOTAL | (38.2 overs)(for 8 wkts) | 185 |

| LANCASHIRE | O | M | R | W | | FALL OF WICKETS | |
|---|---|---|---|---|---|---|---|
| | | | | | | HAM | LAN |
| Watkinson | 8 | 0 | 34 | 3 | | | |
| Allott | 8 | 2 | 28 | 1 | 1st | 2 | 9 |
| Yates | 8 | 0 | 42 | 0 | 2nd | 19 | 27 |
| Wasim Akram | 8 | 0 | 35 | 0 | 3rd | 28 | 82 |
| Austin | 8 | 0 | 38 | 1 | 4th | 113 | 96 |
| | | | | | 5th | 137 | 125 |
| HAMPSHIRE | O | M | R | W | 6th | | 127 |
| Connor | 8 | 0 | 33 | 3 | 7th | | 133 |
| Shine | 7 | 0 | 35 | 2 | 8th | | 140 |
| Maru | 8 | 0 | 31 | 1 | 9th | | |
| Ayling | 7.2 | 0 | 52 | 1 | 10th | | |
| Udal | 8 | 1 | 30 | 1 | | | |

## SOMERSET vs. KENT

at Taunton on 28th July 1991
Toss : Kent. Umpires : J.H.Harris and R.Julian
Kent won by 35 runs. Somerset 0 pts, Kent 4 pts

**KENT**

| | | |
|---|---|---|
| T.R.Ward * | st Burns b Graveney | 56 |
| M.R.Benson * | c Tavare b Hallett | 8 |
| N.R.Taylor | st Burns b Graveney | 36 |
| S.G.Hinks | st Burns b Graveney | 11 |
| G.R.Cowdrey | b Lefebvre | 50 |
| M.V.Fleming | b Burns b Trump | 20 |
| S.A.Marsh + | lbw b Trump | 3 |
| R.P.Davis | c Roebuck b Lefebvre | 2 |
| M.J.McCague | b Lefebvre | 4 |
| T.A.Merrick | not out | 13 |
| A.P.Igglesden | not out | 3 |
| Extras | (lb 5,w 8,nb 1) | 14 |
| TOTAL | (40 overs)(for 9 wkts) | 220 |

**SOMERSET**

| | | |
|---|---|---|
| S.J.Cook | c Marsh b Merrick | 1 |
| P.M.Roebuck | c & b Fleming | 34 |
| C.J.Tavare * | b Fleming | 19 |
| R.J.Harden | b Fleming | 46 |
| M.Lathwell | st Marsh b Davis | 15 |
| N.D.Burns + | c Marsh b Davis | 5 |
| G.D.Rose | lbw b Igglesden | 0 |
| R.P.Lefebvre | c Ward b Fleming | 27 |
| H.R.J.Trump | b Igglesden | 19 |
| J.C.Hallett | c Cowdrey b Igglesden | 1 |
| D.A.Graveney | not out | 14 |
| Extras | (w 4) | 4 |
| TOTAL | (38.1 overs) | 185 |

| SOMERSET | O | M | R | W | | FALL OF WICKETS | |
|---|---|---|---|---|---|---|---|
| | | | | | | KEN | SOM |
| Hallett | 6 | 0 | 25 | 1 | | | |
| Lefebvre | 7 | 1 | 30 | 3 | 1st | 17 | 9 |
| Rose | 3 | 0 | 25 | 0 | 2nd | 107 | 48 |
| Graveney | 8 | 1 | 21 | 3 | 3rd | 114 | 82 |
| Trump | 8 | 0 | 58 | 2 | 4th | 121 | 107 |
| Roebuck | 8 | 0 | 56 | 0 | 5th | 163 | 115 |
| | | | | | 6th | 181 | 117 |
| KENT | O | M | R | W | 7th | 186 | 130 |
| Merrick | 8 | 0 | 33 | 1 | 8th | 203 | 163 |
| Igglesden | 8 | 0 | 38 | 3 | 9th | 208 | 165 |
| McCague | 7 | 0 | 42 | 0 | 10th | | 185 |
| Fleming | 7.1 | 0 | 45 | 4 | | | |
| Davis | 8 | 0 | 27 | 2 | | | |

| REFUGE ASSURANCE LEAGUE | TOUR MATCHES |
|---|---|

## SURREY vs. GLAMORGAN

at The Oval on 28th July 1991
Toss : Surrey. Umpires : J.H.Hampshire and M.J.Kitchen
Glamorgan won by 3 runs. Surrey 0 pts, Glamorgan 4 pts

### GLAMORGAN

| | | |
|---|---|---|
| M.P.Maynard | b Robinson | 51 |
| M.J.Cann | lbw b Feltham | 2 |
| A.Dale | c Feltham b Robinson | 23 |
| A.R.Butcher * | c Ward b Greig | 39 |
| P.A.Cottey | c Thorpe b Feltham | 47 |
| D.L.Hemp | lbw b Bullen | 7 |
| S.Kirnon | lbw b Bullen | 0 |
| R.D.B.Croft | c Bullen b Feltham | 19 |
| C.P.Metson + | not out | 18 |
| S.R.Barwick | c Lynch b Bullen | 3 |
| D.J.Foster | not out | 0 |
| Extras | (lb 7,w 8,nb 1) | 16 |
| TOTAL | (40 overs)(for 9 wkts) | 225 |

### SURREY

| | | |
|---|---|---|
| D.J.Bicknell | c Metson b Kirnon | 31 |
| M.A.Lynch | c Butcher b Barwick | 28 |
| A.J.Stewart + | c Foster b Dale | 3 |
| D.M.Ward | c Metson b Dale | 0 |
| G.P.Thorpe | c Croft b Kirnon | 58 |
| J.D.Robinson | c & b Croft | 8 |
| I.A.Greig * | b Barwick | 5 |
| M.A.Feltham | c Maynard b Croft | 7 |
| M.Butcher | not out | 48 |
| C.K.Bullen | not out | 22 |
| J.Boiling | | |
| Extras | (lb 5,w 7) | 12 |
| TOTAL | (40 overs)(for 8 wkts) | 222 |

| SURREY | O | M | R | W | FALL OF WICKETS | | |
|---|---|---|---|---|---|---|---|
| | | | | | | GLA | SUR |
| Feltham | 8 | 0 | 60 | 3 | | | |
| Butcher | 3 | 0 | 16 | 0 | 1st | 14 | 53 |
| Robinson | 8 | 0 | 32 | 2 | 2nd | 74 | 58 |
| Boiling | 8 | 0 | 51 | 0 | 3rd | 93 | 58 |
| Bullen | 8 | 0 | 38 | 3 | 4th | 150 | 79 |
| Greig | 5 | 0 | 21 | 1 | 5th | 182 | 97 |
| | | | | | 6th | 182 | 102 |
| GLAMORGAN | O | M | R | W | 7th | 189 | 121 |
| Foster | 8 | 0 | 39 | 0 | 8th | 206 | 164 |
| Kirnon | 8 | 0 | 48 | 2 | 9th | 221 | |
| Dale | 8 | 1 | 48 | 2 | 10th | | |
| Barwick | 8 | 0 | 44 | 2 | | | |
| Croft | 8 | 0 | 38 | 2 | | | |

## SUSSEX vs. NOTTS

at Hove on 28th July 1991
Toss : Notts. Umpires : A.G.T.Whitehead and P.B.Wight
Notts won by 6 wickets. Sussex 0 pts, Notts 4 pts

### SUSSEX

| | | |
|---|---|---|
| N.J.Lenham | c Randall b Saxelby | 21 |
| P.W.G.Parker * | c French b Stephenson | 4 |
| A.P.Wells | c & b Hemmings | 33 |
| M.P.Speight | c French b Evans | 44 |
| K.Greenfield | c French b Saxelby | 0 |
| C.M.Wells | c & b Stephenson | 28 |
| A.I.C.Dodemaide | not out | 31 |
| A.C.S.Pigott | b Evans | 2 |
| P.Moores + | not out | 7 |
| I.D.K.Salisbury | | |
| A.N.Jones | | |
| Extras | (lb 12,w 4,nb 2) | 18 |
| TOTAL | (40 overs)(for 7 wkts) | 188 |

### NOTTS

| | | |
|---|---|---|
| B.C.Broad | c Moores b Salisbury | 65 |
| D.W.Randall | b Jones | 22 |
| R.T.Robinson * | b Dodemaide | 10 |
| P.Johnson | lbw b Lenham | 20 |
| P.Pollard | not out | 30 |
| M.Saxelby | not out | 23 |
| F.D.Stephenson | | |
| K.P.Evans | | |
| B.N.French + | | |
| E.E.Hemmings | | |
| R.A.Pick | | |
| Extras | (lb 12,w 8,nb 2) | 22 |
| TOTAL | (38.5 overs)(for 4 wkts) | 192 |

| NOTTS | O | M | R | W | FALL OF WICKETS | | |
|---|---|---|---|---|---|---|---|
| | | | | | | SUS | NOT |
| Stephenson | 8 | 0 | 36 | 2 | | | |
| Pick | 8 | 1 | 30 | 0 | 1st | 2 | 53 |
| Saxelby | 8 | 0 | 26 | 2 | 2nd | 42 | 114 |
| Evans | 8 | 0 | 50 | 2 | 3rd | 79 | 136 |
| Hemmings | 8 | 0 | 34 | 1 | 4th | 82 | 141 |
| | | | | | 5th | 137 | |
| SUSSEX | O | M | R | W | 6th | 160 | |
| Wells C.M. | 7 | 0 | 23 | 0 | 7th | 168 | |
| Dodemaide | 8 | 0 | 35 | 1 | 8th | | |
| Pigott | 7.5 | 0 | 47 | 0 | 9th | | |
| Jones | 7 | 0 | 45 | 1 | 10th | | |
| Salisbury | 8 | 1 | 22 | 1 | | | |
| Lenham | 1 | 0 | 8 | 1 | | | |

## ENGLAND AM. XI vs. SRI LANKA

at Wolverhampton on 24th July 1991
Toss : England Am. XI. Umpires : T.Brown and R.Julian
Sri Lanka won on faster scoring rate

### ENGLAND AM. XI

| | | |
|---|---|---|
| S.J.Dean | c Kaluwitharana b Madurasinghe | 86 |
| S.N.V.Waterton + | c Jayasuriya b Gurusinha | 19 |
| J.Wright | c Jayasuriya b Muralitharan | 26 |
| R.J.Leiper | c Kuruppu b Madurasinghe | 22 |
| M.Hussain | b Muralitharan | 0 |
| P.J.Garner * | c Gurusinha b Jayasuriya | 0 |
| N.J.Archer | lbw b Madurasinghe | 4 |
| P.Roshier | b Jayasuriya | 1 |
| N.French | st Kaluwitharana b Jayasuriya | 4 |
| R.A.Evans | c & b Jayasuriya | 5 |
| K.A.Arnold | not out | 6 |
| Extras | (lb 7,w 2,nb 9) | 18 |
| TOTAL | (51.4 overs) | 191 |

### SRI LANKA

| | | |
|---|---|---|
| R.S.Mahanama | c Dean b Evans | 26 |
| U.C.Hathurusinghe | c Archer b Garner | 28 |
| A.P.Gurusinha * | c Dean b Garner | 9 |
| M.S.Atapattu | run out | 12 |
| K.I.W.Wijeguna' | c Leiper b Evans | 1 |
| S.T.Jayasuriya | not out | 57 |
| D.S.B.P.Kuruppu | not out | 11 |
| R.S.Kaluwitharana + | | |
| M.A.W.R.Madurasinghe | | |
| C.P.Ramanayake | | |
| M.Muralitharan | | |
| Extras | (lb 5,w 3,nb 1) | 9 |
| TOTAL | (37.3 overs)(for 5 wkts) | 153 |

| SRI LANKA | O | M | R | W | FALL OF WICKETS | | |
|---|---|---|---|---|---|---|---|
| | | | | | | AXI | SRI |
| Ramanayake | 7 | 1 | 23 | 0 | | | |
| Wijeguna' | 4 | 0 | 33 | 0 | 1st | 72 | 54 |
| Hathurusinghe | 3 | 0 | 10 | 0 | 2nd | 147 | 66 |
| Muralitharan | 11 | 0 | 30 | 2 | 3rd | 152 | 71 |
| Gurusinha | 5 | 1 | 23 | 1 | 4th | 153 | 74 |
| Jayasuriya | 10.4 | 1 | 39 | 4 | 5th | 154 | 107 |
| Madurasinghe | 11 | 3 | 26 | 3 | 6th | 167 | |
| | | | | | 7th | 168 | |
| ENG. AM. XI | O | M | R | W | 8th | 180 | |
| Arnold | 9 | 1 | 38 | 0 | 9th | 180 | |
| Roshier | 1.1 | 0 | 2 | 0 | 10th | 191 | |
| Archer | 0.5 | 0 | 5 | 0 | | | |
| French | 8 | 2 | 28 | 0 | | | |
| Hussain | 6.3 | 1 | 18 | 0 | | | |
| Wright | 3 | 0 | 9 | 0 | | | |
| Evans | 6 | 1 | 31 | 2 | | | |
| Garner | 3 | 0 | 17 | 2 | | | |

## DURHAM vs. SRI LANKA

at Chester-le-Street on 26th July 1991
Toss : Durham. Umpires : B.Hassan and N.T.Plews
Sri Lanka won by 72 runs

### SRI LANKA

| | | |
|---|---|---|
| R.S.Mahanama | c Cook b Briers | 67 |
| D.S.B.P.Kuruppu | lbw b Wood | 53 |
| A.P.Gurusinha | run out | 1 |
| P.A.De Silva * | c Glendenen b Briers | 5 |
| S.T.Jayasuriya | c Blenkiron b Bainbridge | 22 |
| R.S.Kaluwitharana + | run out | 2 |
| M.S.Atapattu | not out | 33 |
| R.J.Ratnayake | b Bainbridge | 10 |
| C.P.Ramanayake | run out | 9 |
| R.Madurasinghe | b Wood | 0 |
| S.D.Anurasiri | not out | 1 |
| Extras | (b 1,lb 9,w 5,nb 3) | 18 |
| TOTAL | (55 overs)(for 9 wkts) | 221 |

### DURHAM

| | | |
|---|---|---|
| G.K.Brown | c Kaluwitharana b Ratnayake | 3 |
| J.D.Glendenen | c De Silva b Ramanayake | 15 |
| P.Burn | c & b Anurasiri | 10 |
| P.Bainbridge | c Ramanayake b Jayasuriya | 62 |
| M.P.Briers | b Anurasiri | 12 |
| D.A.Blenkiron | c Jayasuriya b De Silva | 2 |
| G.Cook * | st Kaluwitharana b Jayasuriya | 20 |
| A.R.Fothergill + | run out | 2 |
| J.Wood | c Mahanama b Jayasuriya | 8 |
| I.E.Conn | run out | 1 |
| S.J.Brown | not out | 0 |
| Extras | (lb 2,w 3,nb 3) | 14 |
| TOTAL | (48.1 overs) | 149 |

| DURHAM | O | M | R | W | FALL OF WICKETS | | |
|---|---|---|---|---|---|---|---|
| | | | | | | SRI | DUR |
| Brown S.J. | 11 | 1 | 50 | 0 | | | |
| Wood | 11 | 3 | 31 | 2 | 1st | 123 | 8 |
| Conn | 11 | 1 | 36 | 0 | 2nd | 126 | 27 |
| Bainbridge | 11 | 1 | 47 | 2 | 3rd | 131 | 49 |
| Briers | 8 | 0 | 36 | 2 | 4th | 154 | 78 |
| Blenkiron | 3 | 0 | 11 | 0 | 5th | 163 | 94 |
| | | | | | 6th | 172 | 128 |
| SRI LANKA | O | M | R | W | 7th | 205 | 136 |
| Ratnayake | 5 | 0 | 12 | 1 | 8th | 220 | 138 |
| Ramanayake | 7 | 2 | 16 | 1 | 9th | 220 | 147 |
| Madurasinghe | 10.1 | 3 | 34 | 0 | 10th | | 149 |
| Gurusinha | 2 | 0 | 8 | 0 | | | |
| Anurasiri | 11 | 0 | 35 | 2 | | | |
| De Silva | 7 | 0 | 16 | 1 | | | |
| Jayasuriya | 6 | 0 | 26 | 3 | | | |

### Refuge Assurance League Table
### at 28th July 1991

| | | P | W | L | T | NR | Away wins | Pts | Run Rate |
|---|---|---|---|---|---|---|---|---|---|
| 1 | Lancashire (2) | 12 | 10 | 1 | 0 | 1 | 7 | 42 | 93.08 |
| 2 | Notts (4) | 12 | 10 | 2 | 0 | 0 | 6 | 40 | 83.08 |
| 3 | Worcestershire (10) | 13 | 7 | 3 | 1 | 2 | 3 | 34 | 94.98 |
| 4 | Essex (12) | 13 | 6 | 2 | 1 | 4 | 1 | 34 | 83.75 |
| 5 | Yorkshire (6) | 12 | 7 | 5 | 0 | 0 | 3 | 28 | 85.74 |
| 6 | Kent (11) | 12 | 6 | 4 | 1 | 1 | 2 | 28 | 89.99 |
| 7 | Northants (17) | 12 | 6 | 4 | 0 | 2 | 1 | 28 | 83.83 |
| 8 | Warwickshire (14) | 12 | 5 | 3 | 1 | 3 | 3 | 28 | 81.14 |
| 9 | Surrey (7) | 13 | 5 | 6 | 0 | 2 | 3 | 24 | 82.03 |
| 10 | Somerset (8) | 13 | 5 | 6 | 0 | 2 | 3 | 24 | 79.01 |
| 11 | Sussex (13) | 13 | 4 | 7 | 0 | 2 | 3 | 20 | 83.30 |
| 12 | Gloucestershire (9) | 12 | 4 | 6 | 0 | 2 | 3 | 20 | 80.01 |
| 13 | Middlesex (3) | 12 | 4 | 7 | 0 | 1 | 4 | 18 | 80.39 |
| 14 | Derbyshire (1) | 12 | 4 | 8 | 0 | 0 | 2 | 16 | 84.48 |
| 15 | Leicestershire (16) | 12 | 3 | 8 | 0 | 1 | 1 | 14 | 77.26 |
| 16 | Glamorgan (15) | 13 | 2 | 9 | 0 | 2 | 1 | 12 | 79.91 |
| 17 | Hampshire (5) | 12 | 2 | 9 | 0 | 1 | 0 | 10 | 80.43 |

# TOUR MATCH

# BRITANNIC ASS. CHAMPIONSHIP

## YORKSHIRE vs. SRI LANKA
at Headingley on 27th, 28th, 29th July 1991
Toss : Yorkshire. Umpires : H.D.Bird and A.A.Jones
Match drawn

**YORKSHIRE**

| | | | | | |
|---|---|---|---|---|---|
| S.A.Kellett | b Ratnayake | 82 | not out | | 109 |
| A.A.Metcalfe * | c Kuruppu b Madurasinghe | 26 | b Madurasinghe | | 35 |
| D.Byas | lbw b Anurasiri | 12 | not out | | 31 |
| R.J.Blakey + | c Mahanama b Anurasiri | 6 | | | |
| P.E.Robinson | c Ratnayake b Ramanayake | 100 | | | |
| A.P.Grayson | lbw b Ratnayake | 0 | | | |
| J.D.Batty | c & b Anurasiri | 51 | | | |
| A.Sidebottom | not out | 18 | | | |
| M.Broadhurst | b Ramanayake | 1 | | | |
| I.J.Houseman | | | | | |
| M.A.Robinson | | | | | |
| Extras | (b 2,lb 4,nb 12) | 18 | (lb 3,nb 6) | | 9 |
| TOTAL | (for 8 wkts dec) | 314 | (for 1 wkt dec) | | 184 |

**SRI LANKA**

| | | |
|---|---|---|
| R.S.Mahanama | c Blakey b Broadhurst | 0 |
| D.S.B.P.Kuruppu | lbw b Sidebottom | 19 |
| C.P.Ramanayake | c Blakey b Broadhurst | 25 |
| A.P.Gurusinha | c Blakey b Houseman | 98 |
| P.A.De Silva * | c Robinson P.E. b Batty | 18 |
| S.T.Jayasuriya | c Kellett b Robinson M.A. | 94 |
| M.S.Atapattu | c Kellett b Robinson M.A. | 41 |
| R.S.Kaluwitharana + | c Sidebottom b Broadhurst | 31 |
| R.J.Ratnayake | not out | 68 |
| M.A.W.R.Madurasinghe | not out | 17 |
| S.D.Anurasiri | | |
| Extras | (lb 5,w 2,nb 4) | 11 |
| TOTAL | (for 8 wkts dec) | 422 |

| SRI LANKA | O | M | R | W | O | M | R | W | FALL OF WICKETS | | | | |
|---|---|---|---|---|---|---|---|---|---|---|---|---|---|
| | | | | | | | | | | YOR | SRI | YOR | SRI |
| Ratnayake | 16 | 2 | 61 | 2 | 2 | 0 | 6 | 0 | 1st | 67 | 0 | 102 | |
| Ramanayake | 6 | 1 | 23 | 2 | 13 | 2 | 36 | 0 | 2nd | 88 | 32 | | |
| Anurasiri | 45 | 8 | 122 | 3 | 27 | 9 | 64 | 0 | 3rd | 108 | 62 | | |
| Madurasinghe | 24 | 5 | 67 | 1 | 23 | 4 | 75 | 1 | 4th | 168 | 94 | | |
| De Silva | 9 | 2 | 27 | 0 | | | | | 5th | 176 | 243 | | |
| Jayasuriya | 1 | 0 | 8 | 0 | | | | | 6th | 274 | 276 | | |
| | | | | | | | | | 7th | 310 | 335 | | |
| YORKSHIRE | O | M | R | W | O | M | R | W | 8th | 314 | 347 | | |
| Broadhurst | 19 | 2 | 69 | 3 | | | | | 9th | | | | |
| Robinson M.A. | 25 | 5 | 71 | 2 | | | | | 10th | | | | |
| Sidebottom | 11 | 4 | 26 | 1 | | | | | | | | | |
| Houseman | 21 | 4 | 52 | 1 | | | | | | | | | |
| Batty | 33 | 7 | 146 | 1 | | | | | | | | | |
| Grayson | 20 | 6 | 53 | 0 | | | | | | | | | |

## HEADLINES

### Tour matches

### 24th - 26th July

• The Sri Lankans began their tour with one-day victories over the England Amateur XI at Wolverhampton and Durham at Chester-le-Street.

### Tetley Bitter Challenge

### 27th - 29th July

• The opening first-class fixture of Sri Lanka's tour at Headingley became little more than an extended practice session for the visitors when they extended their first innings to 422 for eight, gaining a lead over Yorkshire of 108. The home side comfortably batted out for a draw. The most notable feature of the match was provided by Simon Kellett who scored his maiden first-class 100.

## GLOUCESTERSHIRE vs. WORCESTERSHIRE
at Cheltenham on 26th, 27th, 29th July 1991
Toss : Gloucs. Umpires : J.D.Bond and D.J.Constant
Worcestershire won by 108 runs. Gloucs 6 pts (Bt: 2, Bw: 4), Worcs 24 pts (Bt: 4, Bw: 4)
100 overs scores : Worcestershire 328 for 9

**WORCESTERSHIRE**

| | | | | | |
|---|---|---|---|---|---|
| T.S.Curtis | c Lloyds b Gilbert | 65 | c Wright b Gilbert | | 6 |
| P.Bent | c Williams b Gilbert | 9 | c Williams b Gilbert | | 42 |
| T.M.Moody | c Athey b Scott | 31 | c Romaines b Alleyne | | 80 |
| D.B.D'Oliveira | b Lawrence | 79 | c Lloyds b Gilbert | | 11 |
| P.A.Neale * | c Lloyds b Scott | 0 | (8) c Gerrard b Gilbert | | 6 |
| I.T.Botham | c Gilbert b Lloyds | 74 | b Lawrence | | 0 |
| S.J.Rhodes + | c Lloyds b Alleyne | 2 | c Wright b Lawrence | | 10 |
| S.R.Lampitt | b Lloyds | 12 | (9) b Lawrence | | 21 |
| P.J.Newport | c Athey b Lawrence | 48 | (10) not out | | 24 |
| G.R.Dilley | lbw b Gilbert | 0 | (5) b Lawrence | | 14 |
| R.D.Stemp | not out | 3 | not out | | 0 |
| Extras | (lb 8,w 1,nb 1) | 10 | (lb 8,nb 2) | | 10 |
| TOTAL | | 333 | (for 9 wkts dec) | | 224 |

**GLOUCESTERSHIRE**

| | | | | | |
|---|---|---|---|---|---|
| G.D.Hodgson | c Moody b Botham | 12 | c Moody b Lampitt | | 71 |
| R.J.Scott | b Dilley | 10 | c D'Oliveira b Dilley | | 6 |
| A.J.Wright * | c Botham b Dilley | 120 | c D'Oliveira b Dilley | | 52 |
| C.W.J.Athey | c Moody b Dilley | 2 | c Rhodes b Stemp | | 15 |
| M.W.Alleyne | b Lampitt | 44 | lbw b Dilley | | 5 |
| P.W.Romaines | c Moody b Dilley | 3 | c Dilley b Stemp | | 0 |
| J.W.Lloyds | b Lampitt | 19 | c Moody b Dilley | | 21 |
| R.C.J.Williams + | c Neale b Botham | 2 | (9) run out | | 0 |
| D.V.Lawrence | c Rhodes b Botham | 1 | (8) c Rhodes b Stemp | | 17 |
| D.R.Gilbert | c Neale b Newport | 17 | c Moody b Stemp | | 2 |
| M.J.Gerrard | not out | 0 | not out | | 0 |
| Extras | (lb 6,nb 5) | 11 | (b 1,lb 3,nb 15) | | 19 |
| TOTAL | | 241 | | | 208 |

| GLOUCS | O | M | R | W | O | M | R | W | FALL OF WICKETS | | | | |
|---|---|---|---|---|---|---|---|---|---|---|---|---|---|
| | | | | | | | | | | WOR | GLO | WOR | GLO |
| Lawrence | 19.1 | 2 | 60 | 2 | 16 | 1 | 80 | 4 | 1st | 30 | 21 | 7 | 12 |
| Gilbert | 24 | 7 | 72 | 3 | 21 | 6 | 59 | 4 | 2nd | 76 | 31 | 120 | 124 |
| Gerrard | 19 | 4 | 72 | 0 | 7 | 0 | 21 | 0 | 3rd | 168 | 47 | 140 | 149 |
| Scott | 17 | 4 | 39 | 2 | 4 | 0 | 16 | 0 | 4th | 177 | 111 | 160 | 159 |
| Lloyds | 14 | 4 | 48 | 2 | 5 | 1 | 25 | 0 | 5th | 211 | 140 | 160 | 161 |
| Alleyne | 9 | 1 | 34 | 1 | 6 | 2 | 15 | 1 | 6th | 227 | 169 | 166 | 186 |
| WORCS | O | M | R | W | O | M | R | W | 7th | 253 | 182 | 167 | 188 |
| Dilley | 15.3 | 7 | 45 | 4 | 16 | 1 | 39 | 4 | 8th | 294 | 192 | 181 | 199 |
| Newport | 14 | 4 | 44 | 1 | 7 | 2 | 24 | 0 | 9th | 303 | 236 | 216 | 208 |
| Botham | 21 | 3 | 74 | 3 | 6 | 1 | 21 | 0 | 10th | 333 | 241 | | 208 |
| Lampitt | 18 | 2 | 72 | 2 | 9 | 1 | 35 | 1 | | | | | |
| Stemp | | | | | 28 | 6 | 85 | 4 | | | | | |

## MIDDLESEX vs. NOTTS
at Lord's on 26th, 27th, 29th July 1991
Toss : Middlesex. Umpires : A.G.T.Whitehead and P.B.Wight
Notts won by 4 wickets. Middlesex 5 pts (Bt: 1, Bw: 4), Notts 22 pts (Bt: 2, Bw: 4)

**MIDDLESEX**

| | | | | | |
|---|---|---|---|---|---|
| M.A.Roseberry | c Pollard b Stephenson | 2 | c French b Stephenson | | 4 |
| J.C.Pooley | lbw b Stephenson | 11 | c Evans b Field-Buss | | 58 |
| M.W.Gatting * | lbw b Stephenson | 5 | not out | | 143 |
| K.R.Brown | c Pollard b Evans | 38 | c French b Pick | | 42 |
| M.Keech | c Broad b Stephenson | 32 | not out | | 58 |
| J.E.Emburey | c French b Pick | 34 | | | |
| P.Farbrace + | c Broad b Pick | 20 | | | |
| N.F.Williams | c Pollard b Hemmings | 9 | | | |
| D.W.Headley | not out | 19 | | | |
| P.C.R.Tufnell | c Robinson b Hemmings | 1 | | | |
| N.G.Cowans | b Evans | 9 | | | |
| Extras | (b 4,lb 3,nb 7) | 14 | (lb 17,nb 8) | | 25 |
| TOTAL | | 194 | (for 3 wkts dec) | | 330 |

**NOTTS**

| | | | | | |
|---|---|---|---|---|---|
| B.C.Broad | b Williams | 14 | c Brown b Williams | | 3 |
| P.Pollard | run out | 11 | c Headley b Emburey | | 42 |
| R.T.Robinson * | c Farbrace b Williams | 20 | b Cowans | | 62 |
| D.W.Randall | c Farbrace b Williams | 34 | c Brown b Emburey | | 8 |
| P.Johnson | c Williams b Headley | 34 | c Emburey b Headley | | 105 |
| K.P.Evans | c Farbrace b Williams | 0 | not out | | 28 |
| B.N.French + | not out | 58 | run out | | 2 |
| F.D.Stephenson | b Emburey | 14 | not out | | 11 |
| M.G.Field-Buss | c Farbrace b Cowans | 25 | | | |
| E.E.Hemmings | lbw b Williams | 5 | | | |
| R.A.Pick | c Gatting b Headley | 5 | | | |
| Extras | (lb 8,w 1,nb 14) | 23 | (b 7,lb 8,w 1,nb 7) | | 23 |
| TOTAL | | 243 | (for 6 wkts) | | 284 |

| NOTTS | O | M | R | W | O | M | R | W | FALL OF WICKETS | | | | |
|---|---|---|---|---|---|---|---|---|---|---|---|---|---|
| | | | | | | | | | | MID | NOT | MID | NOT |
| Stephenson | 20 | 2 | 59 | 4 | 22 | 5 | 71 | 1 | 1st | 2 | 17 | 12 | 7 |
| Pick | 19 | 4 | 54 | 2 | 17 | 3 | 76 | 1 | 2nd | 8 | 49 | 116 | 71 |
| Evans | 20.5 | 7 | 44 | 2 | 16.4 | 2 | 69 | 0 | 3rd | 44 | 49 | 209 | 101 |
| Hemmings | 16 | 4 | 30 | 2 | 4 | 2 | 24 | 0 | 4th | 85 | 121 | | 195 |
| Field-Buss | | | | | 18 | 3 | 73 | 1 | 5th | 113 | 126 | | 262 |
| | | | | | | | | | 6th | 144 | 126 | | 264 |
| MIDDLESEX | O | M | R | W | O | M | R | W | 7th | 163 | 151 | | |
| Cowans | 23 | 11 | 38 | 1 | 13 | 0 | 59 | 1 | 8th | 163 | 225 | | |
| Williams | 29 | 7 | 89 | 5 | 11 | 2 | 42 | 1 | 9th | 170 | 234 | | |
| Headley | 24.2 | 5 | 61 | 2 | 16.1 | 0 | 82 | 1 | 10th | 194 | 243 | | |
| Emburey | 12 | 6 | 22 | 1 | 25 | 6 | 86 | 2 | | | | | |
| Tufnell | 10 | 3 | 25 | 0 | | | | | | | | | |

# BRITANNIC ASSURANCE CHAMPIONSHIP

## LEICESTERSHIRE vs. WARWICKSHIRE

at Leicester on 26th, 27th, 28th July 1991
Toss : Leicestershire.  Umpires : B.J.Meyer and D.O.Oslear
Warwicks won by an inns & 44 runs. Leics 3 pts (Bt: 1, Bw: 2), Warwicks 24 pts (Bt: 4, Bw: 4)
100 overs scores :Warwickshire 321 for 5

### LEICESTERSHIRE

| Batsman | Dismissal 1 | Score | Dismissal 2 | Score |
|---|---|---|---|---|
| T.J.Boon | c Holloway b Donald | 18 | b Munton | 41 |
| N.E.Briers * | c Holloway b Munton | 33 | c Holloway b Small | 3 |
| P.N.Hepworth | run out | 15 | c Ostler b Donald | 32 |
| J.J.Whitaker | b Munton | 23 | b Donald | 12 |
| L.Potter | c Holloway b Small | 8 | (6) c Reeve b Small | 44 |
| J.D.R.Benson | c Lloyd b Munton | 11 | (7) c Moles b Munton | 8 |
| M.I.Gidley | c Asif Din b Munton | 10 | (8) c Ostler b Munton | 1 |
| P.Whitticase + | lbw b Munton | 2 | (5) b Donald | 17 |
| D.J.Millns | b Donald | 6 | not out | 24 |
| L.Tennant | not out | 11 | b Munton | 0 |
| J.N.Maguire | b Donald | 2 | c Pierson b Donald | 18 |
| Extras | (b 9,lb 5,w 1,nb 7) | 22 | (b 19,lb 21,w 1,nb 3) | 44 |
| TOTAL | | 161 | | 244 |

### WARWICKSHIRE

| Batsman | Dismissal | Score |
|---|---|---|
| A.J.Moles | c Hepworth b Millns | 5 |
| J.D.Ratcliffe | b Millns | 7 |
| T.A.Lloyd * | c Whitticase b Tennant | 20 |
| D.P.Ostler | c Briers b Millns | 65 |
| D.A.Reeve | c Whitticase b Potter | 67 |
| Asif Din | c Gidley b Maguire | 140 |
| P.C.L.Holloway + | not out | 89 |
| G.C.Small | st Whitticase b Gidley | 14 |
| A.R.K.Pierson | c Boon b Benson | 35 |
| A.A.Donald | not out | 1 |
| T.A.Munton | | |
| Extras | (lb 3,w 2,nb 1) | 6 |
| TOTAL | (for 8 wkts dec) | 449 |

| WARWICKS | O | M | R | W | O | M | R | W |
|---|---|---|---|---|---|---|---|---|
| Donald | 13 | 0 | 64 | 3 | 24 | 7 | 59 | 4 |
| Small | 13 | 4 | 34 | 1 | 16 | 3 | 52 | 2 |
| Reeve | 7 | 4 | 7 | 0 | 6 | 3 | 9 | 0 |
| Munton | 24 | 10 | 32 | 5 | 20 | 4 | 46 | 4 |
| Asif Din | 4 | 0 | 10 | 0 | | | | |
| Pierson | | | | | 15 | 4 | 38 | 0 |

| LEICS | O | M | R | W | O | M | R | W |
|---|---|---|---|---|---|---|---|---|
| Millns | 27 | 5 | 106 | 3 | | | | |
| Maguire | 24 | 6 | 85 | 1 | | | | |
| Tennant | 21 | 3 | 82 | 1 | | | | |
| Gidley | 23 | 1 | 79 | 1 | | | | |
| Benson | 7 | 3 | 18 | 1 | | | | |
| Potter | 16 | 3 | 58 | 1 | | | | |
| Hepworth | 3 | 0 | 18 | 0 | | | | |

| FALL OF WICKETS | LEI | WAR | LEI | WAR |
|---|---|---|---|---|
| 1st | 28 | 7 | 20 | |
| 2nd | 59 | 24 | 65 | |
| 3rd | 80 | 50 | 88 | |
| 4th | 111 | 133 | 114 | |
| 5th | 123 | 217 | 165 | |
| 6th | 127 | 354 | 184 | |
| 7th | 138 | 375 | 186 | |
| 8th | 146 | 445 | 192 | |
| 9th | 149 | | 192 | |
| 10th | 161 | | 244 | |

## SOMERSET vs. KENT

at Taunton on 26th, 27th, 29th July 1991
Toss : Kent.  Umpires : J.H.Harris and R.Julian
Match drawn.  Somerset 6 pts (Bt: 3, Bw: 3), Kent 4 pts (Bt: 3, Bw: 1)
100 overs scores : Kent 284 for 8, Somerset 272 for 4

### KENT

| Batsman | Dismissal 1 | Score | Dismissal 2 | Score |
|---|---|---|---|---|
| T.R.Ward | b Graveney | 31 | c Cook b van Troost | 0 |
| M.R.Benson * | c & b Graveney | 29 | b Trump | 76 |
| N.R.Taylor | b Graveney | 0 | lbw b Graveney | 23 |
| G.R.Cowdrey | b Graveney | 9 | lbw b van Troost | 0 |
| S.G.Hinks | c Burns b van Troost | 39 | c Cook b Graveney | 0 |
| M.V.Fleming | b Rose | 54 | run out | 59 |
| S.A.Marsh + | not out | 113 | not out | 28 |
| R.P.Davis | lbw b Graveney | 10 | (9) not out | 13 |
| M.M.Patel | c Pringle b Graveney | 0 | | |
| T.A.Merrick | lbw b Trump | 5 | (8) b Trump | 2 |
| A.P.Igglesden | c Tavare b Graveney | 15 | | |
| Extras | (b 3,lb 9,nb 2) | 14 | (b 4,lb 4,w 1,nb 2) | 11 |
| TOTAL | | 319 | (for 7 wkts dec) | 212 |

### SOMERSET

| Batsman | Dismissal 1 | Score | Dismissal 2 | Score |
|---|---|---|---|---|
| S.J.Cook | lbw b Patel | 126 | c Marsh b Igglesden | 10 |
| A.N.Hayhurst | lbw b Merrick | 1 | c Fleming b Merrick | 5 |
| R.J.Harden | b Merrick | 54 | b Merrick | 57 |
| C.J.Tavare * | c Cowdrey b Davis | 72 | run out | 100 |
| N.J.Pringle | st Marsh b Davis | 7 | b Patel | 17 |
| N.D.Burns + | c Taylor b Patel | 6 | b Igglesden | 27 |
| G.D.Rose | c & b Davis | 3 | b Igglesden | 0 |
| K.H.Macleay | not out | 2 | run out | 10 |
| H.R.J.Trump | | | not out | 1 |
| D.A.Graveney | | | c Patel b Igglesden | 4 |
| A.P.van Troost | | | not out | 0 |
| Extras | (b 8,lb 9) | 17 | (b 2,lb 9) | 11 |
| TOTAL | (for 7 wkts dec) | 288 | (for 9 wkts) | 242 |

| SOMERSET | O | M | R | W | O | M | R | W |
|---|---|---|---|---|---|---|---|---|
| van Troost | 16 | 3 | 41 | 1 | 11 | 1 | 25 | 2 |
| Rose | 11 | 1 | 52 | 1 | | | | |
| Macleay | 2.1 | 1 | 5 | 0 | | | | |
| Graveney | 41 | 10 | 105 | 7 | 23.4 | 4 | 88 | 2 |
| Trump | 38.5 | 9 | 87 | 1 | 22 | 5 | 91 | 2 |
| Hayhurst | 5 | 1 | 17 | 0 | | | | |

| KENT | O | M | R | W | O | M | R | W |
|---|---|---|---|---|---|---|---|---|
| Merrick | 14 | 2 | 60 | 2 | 16 | 2 | 73 | 2 |
| Igglesden | 13 | 1 | 51 | 0 | 10 | 0 | 45 | 4 |
| Patel | 34 | 7 | 75 | 2 | 19 | 1 | 61 | 1 |
| Davis | 38.5 | 15 | 67 | 3 | 13 | 2 | 52 | 0 |
| Fleming | 8 | 0 | 18 | 0 | | | | |

| FALL OF WICKETS | KEN | SOM | KEN | SOM |
|---|---|---|---|---|
| 1st | 54 | 5 | 1 | 15 |
| 2nd | 56 | 131 | 45 | 15 |
| 3rd | 63 | 238 | 46 | 121 |
| 4th | 83 | 255 | 47 | 158 |
| 5th | 134 | 282 | 138 | 210 |
| 6th | 195 | 282 | 174 | 210 |
| 7th | 251 | 288 | 180 | 233 |
| 8th | 275 | | | 233 |
| 9th | 284 | | | 241 |
| 10th | 319 | | | |

## HEADLINES

### Britannic Assurance Championship

### 26th - 29th July

- Warwickshire, now long-term Championship pacemakers, gave clear notice that they would have to be regarded as potential champions with their emphatic defeat of Leicestershire at Hinckley by an innings and 44 runs. It was their eighth success of the summer, three more than any of their competitiors, and streched their lead to a comforting 44 points. Allan Donald and Tim Munton were the pick of the seam attack, returning match figures of nine for 78 and seven for 123 respectively, and the occasionally vulnerable batting line-up gave one of their most convincing displays, Asif Din hitting his second 100 in successive innings and Piran Holloway a career-best 89 not out.

- Nottinghamshire remained in the chasing pack with their fifth victory of the season at the expense of Middlesex at Lord's, owing their success to a last innings run-chase. Mike Gatting's unbeaten 143 in Middlesex's second innings allowed him to declare with a lead of 281, but Notts reached their target in 65.1 overs thanks to Paul Johnson's first century of the season.

- Worcestershire gained their second win of the year with a 108-run victory over Gloucestershire at Cheltenham, after working hard for their runs against David Lawrence and Dave Gilbert and bowling the home side out twice. Graham Dilley returned match figures of eight for 84 and Richard Stemp claimed four for 85 as Gloucestershire declined from 124 for one to 208 all out in their second innings.

- Surrey and Glamorgan made good use of an ideal surface at The Oval. Matthew Maynard hit the fastest 100 of the season, his sixth in first-class cricket in 1991, to allow the visitors to declare with a lead of 319. Surrey made a fine effort to reach their target, Graham Thorpe completing his first 100 of the year, but finished on 288 for eight.

- Bat and ball were also finely balanced at Taunton, where Somerset and Kent played out the most exciting of draws. Needing 244 for victory in 58 overs the home side were finally denied victory when Alan Igglesden dismissed David Graveney with the final ball of the day to leave Somerset on 242 for nine at the close. Graveney had earlier recorded his best bowling figures for his new county, but could not get the better of Steve Marsh who hit an unbeaten 113 to carry Kent's first innings to 319. Not even 100s from both Jimmy Cook and Chris Tavare could bring Somerset victory.

# BRITANNIC ASSURANCE CHAMPIONSHIP

## SURREY vs. GLAMORGAN

at The Oval on 26th, 27th, 29th July 1991
Toss : Glamorgan.  Umpires : J.H.Hampshire and M.J.Kitchen
Match drawn.  Surrey 6 pts (Bt: 3, Bw: 3), Glamorgan 7 pts (Bt: 4, Bw: 3)
100 overs scores : Glamorgan 321 for 8

### GLAMORGAN

| | | | | | |
|---|---|---|---|---|---|
| A.R.Butcher * | c Sargeant b Murphy | 15 | st Sargeant b Medlycott | | 68 |
| S.P.James | run out | 70 | lbw b Feltham | | 24 |
| A.Dale | b Waqar Younis | 89 | c Sargeant b Greig | | 20 |
| M.P.Maynard | c sub b Feltham | 75 | not out | | 103 |
| R.J.Shastri | b Waqar Younis | 38 | | | |
| P.A.Cottey | lbw b Waqar Younis | 1 | (5) st Sargeant b Medlycott | | 17 |
| R.D.B.Croft | c Stewart b Medlycott | 10 | (6) not out | | 11 |
| C.P.Metson + | lbw b Medlycott | 5 | | | |
| S.L.Watkin | b Waqar Younis | 3 | | | |
| S.Bastien | not out | 0 | | | |
| S.R.Barwick | | | | | |
| Extras | (b 8,lb 4,w 1,nb 2) | 15 | (lb 2,nb 3) | | 5 |
| TOTAL | (for 9 wkts dec) | 321 | (for 4 wkts dec) | | 248 |

### SURREY

| | | | | | |
|---|---|---|---|---|---|
| D.J.Bicknell | c Cottey b Watkin | 0 | c Cottey b Dale | | 18 |
| R.I.Alikhan | c Croft b Barwick | 40 | b Shastri | | 25 |
| N.F.Sargeant + | lbw b Dale | 32 | (10) not out | | 3 |
| A.J.Stewart | c Cottey b Barwick | 34 | (3) run out | | 29 |
| D.M.Ward | b Barwick | 5 | (4) lbw b Barwick | | 71 |
| G.P.Thorpe | not out | 74 | (5) not out | | 106 |
| I.A.Greig * | c Metson b Barwick | 4 | (6) lbw b Barwick | | 0 |
| K.T.Medlycott | b Bastien | 5 | (7) b Shastri | | 28 |
| M.A.Feltham | not out | 38 | (8) c Shastri b Barwick | | 3 |
| Waqar Younis | | | (9) c James b Shastri | | 0 |
| A.J.Murphy | | | | | |
| Extras | (b 4,lb 10,nb 4) | 18 | (b 2,lb 3) | | 5 |
| TOTAL | (for 7 wkts dec) | 250 | (for 8 wkts) | | 288 |

| SURREY | O | M | R | W | O | M | R | W | FALL OF WICKETS | | | | |
|---|---|---|---|---|---|---|---|---|---|---|---|---|---|
| | | | | | | | | | | GLA | SUR | GLA | SUR |
| Waqar Younis | 26 | 6 | 75 | 4 | | | | | 1st | 23 | 0 | 87 | 29 |
| Murphy | 10 | 2 | 33 | 1 | | | | | 2nd | 177 | 63 | 97 | 70 |
| Feltham | 25 | 5 | 58 | 1 | 20 | 2 | 77 | 1 | 3rd | 212 | 106 | 146 | 76 |
| Greig | 13 | 2 | 38 | 0 | 9 | 0 | 49 | 1 | 4th | 275 | 114 | 207 | 211 |
| Medlycott | 26.1 | 2 | 105 | 2 | 24 | 7 | 100 | 2 | 5th | 292 | 121 | | 217 |
| Thorpe | | | | | 1 | 0 | 10 | 0 | 6th | 303 | 145 | | 270 |
| Stewart | | | | | 2 | 0 | 10 | 0 | 7th | 308 | 158 | | 279 |
| | | | | | | | | | 8th | 321 | | | 279 |
| GLAMORGAN | O | M | R | W | O | M | R | W | 9th | 321 | | | |
| Watkin | 10 | 4 | 14 | 1 | | | | | 10th | | | | |
| Bastien | 23.2 | 6 | 74 | 1 | | | | | | | | | |
| Barwick | 23 | 8 | 46 | 4 | 17.5 | 1 | 75 | 3 | | | | | |
| Dale | 19 | 6 | 63 | 1 | 5 | 0 | 19 | 1 | | | | | |
| Croft | 20 | 6 | 39 | 0 | 23 | 2 | 111 | 0 | | | | | |
| Shastri | | | | | 23 | 2 | 78 | 3 | | | | | |

## Britannic Assurance Championship Table at 29th July 1991

| | | P | W | L | D | T | Bt | Bl | Pts |
|---|---|---|---|---|---|---|---|---|---|
| 1 | Warwickshire (5) | 15 | 8 | 2 | 5 | 0 | 40 | 41 | 209 |
| 2 | Essex  (2) | 14 | 5 | 3 | 6 | 0 | 47 | 38 | 165 |
| 3 | Notts  (13) | 14 | 5 | 2 | 7 | 0 | 36 | 46 | 162 |
| 4 | Lancashire (6) | 13 | 5 | 3 | 5 | 0 | 39 | 29 | 148 |
| 5 | Surrey  (9) | 13 | 5 | 2 | 6 | 0 | 29 | 34 | 143 |
| 6 | Derbyshire (12) | 13 | 4 | 2 | 7 | 0 | 27 | 46 | 137 |
| 7 | Kent  (16) | 15 | 4 | 1 | 10 | 0 | 34 | 33 | 131 |
| 8 | Gloucs (13) | 16 | 4 | 5 | 7 | 0 | 26 | 36 | 126 |
| 9 | Glamorgan (8) | 16 | 3 | 3 | 10 | 0 | 33 | 40 | 121 |
| 10 | Sussex (17) | 15 | 2 | 2 | 11 | 0 | 39 | 40 | 111 |
| 11 | Worcestershire (4) | 13 | 2 | 2 | 9 | 0 | 29 | 29 | 90 |
| 12 | Hampshire (3) | 14 | 1 | 5 | 8 | 0 | 36 | 35 | 87 |
| 13 | Yorkshire (10) | 13 | 2 | 3 | 8 | 0 | 33 | 19 | 84 |
| 14 | Northants (11) | 14 | 1 | 4 | 9 | 0 | 29 | 39 | 84 |
| | Somerset (15) | 14 | 1 | 2 | 11 | 0 | 42 | 26 | 84 |
| 16 | Middlesex (1) | 14 | 0 | 6 | 8 | 0 | 29 | 40 | 69 |
| 17 | Leicestershire (7) | 14 | 0 | 5 | 9 | 0 | 22 | 30 | 52 |

## LEADING FIRST-CLASS AVERAGES
### as at  29th July 1991

BATTING AVERAGES - Including fielding
Qualifying requirements : 6 completed innings

| Name | Matches | Inns | NO | Runs | HS | Avge | 100s | 50s |
|---|---|---|---|---|---|---|---|---|
| C.L.Hooper | 12 | 19 | 7 | 1102 | 196 | 91.83 | 3 | 6 |
| S.J.Cook | 15 | 25 | 5 | 1686 | 210 * | 84.30 | 7 | 5 |
| Salim Malik | 15 | 23 | 6 | 1420 | 215 | 83.52 | 5 | 4 |
| M.W.Gatting | 14 | 23 | 8 | 1176 | 180 | 78.40 | 5 | 3 |
| C.L.Smith | 14 | 23 | 2 | 1492 | 200 | 71.04 | 6 | 7 |
| M.P.Maynard | 17 | 27 | 6 | 1470 | 204 | 70.00 | 6 | 5 |
| R.B.Richardson | 11 | 19 | 5 | 977 | 135 * | 69.78 | 4 | 5 |
| D.W.Randall | 14 | 21 | 7 | 935 | 120 | 66.78 | 3 | 3 |
| I.V.A.Richards | 10 | 15 | 4 | 732 | 131 | 66.54 | 1 | 5 |
| T.M.Moody | 15 | 24 | 4 | 1218 | 181 * | 60.90 | 4 | 6 |
| A.P.Wells | 14 | 21 | 3 | 1065 | 159 | 59.16 | 5 | 2 |
| N.H.Fairbrother | 13 | 19 | 5 | 819 | 121 | 58.50 | 5 | 2 |
| G.J.Turner | 8 | 8 | 2 | 349 | 101 * | 58.16 | 1 | 2 |
| M.R.Benson | 15 | 21 | 2 | 1056 | 257 | 55.57 | 3 | 6 |
| R.A.Smith | 9 | 16 | 3 | 719 | 148 * | 55.30 | 1 | 6 |

BOWLING AVERAGES
Qualifying requirements : 20 wickets taken

| Name | Overs | Mdns | Runs | Wkts | Avge | Best | 5wI | 10wM |
|---|---|---|---|---|---|---|---|---|
| C.E.L.Ambrose | 324.1 | 103 | 705 | 43 | 16.39 | 6-52 | 3 | - |
| Waqar Younis | 340 | 63 | 968 | 59 | 16.40 | 7-87 | 7 | 2 |
| A.A.Donald | 352.5 | 71 | 1011 | 59 | 17.13 | 5-33 | 6 | 2 |
| P.Carrick | 310.2 | 120 | 623 | 33 | 18.87 | 5-13 | 1 | - |
| O.H.Mortensen | 359.1 | 94 | 892 | 47 | 18.97 | 6-101 | 2 | - |
| K.M.Curran | 207 | 60 | 561 | 27 | 20.77 | 5-60 | 1 | - |
| D.V.Lawrence | 328.2 | 52 | 1108 | 52 | 21.30 | 6-67 | 3 | 1 |
| G.R.Dilley | 227 | 43 | 627 | 29 | 21.62 | 5-91 | 1 | - |
| D.A.Reeve | 271.5 | 84 | 600 | 27 | 22.22 | 6-73 | 1 | - |
| Wasim Akram | 390.5 | 93 | 1115 | 50 | 22.30 | 6-66 | 6 | 1 |
| N.A.Foster | 423.4 | 107 | 1166 | 52 | 22.42 | 5-45 | 3 | - |
| F.D.Stephenson | 430 | 108 | 1170 | 52 | 22.50 | 5-27 | 3 | 1 |
| M.D.Marshall | 210.1 | 39 | 572 | 25 | 22.88 | 4-33 | - | - |
| C.C.Lewis | 325.5 | 83 | 861 | 37 | 23.27 | 6-111 | 3 | - |
| T.A.Munton | 476.3 | 121 | 1250 | 51 | 24.51 | 8-89 | 4 | 1 |

# NATWEST TROPHY – QUARTER-FINALS

## HAMPSHIRE vs. NOTTS

at Southampton on 31st July 1991
Toss : Hampshire. Umpires : J.C.Balderstone and R.Palmer
Hampshire won by 7 wickets
Man of the match: C.L.Smith

### NOTTS

| | | |
|---|---|---|
| B.C.Broad | lbw b Maru | 31 |
| D.W.Randall | b Aqib Javed | 95 |
| R.T.Robinson * | c Aymes b Aqib Javed | 25 |
| P.Johnson | c Maru b Connor | 0 |
| P.Pollard | lbw b Connor | 6 |
| M.Saxelby | b Ayling | 36 |
| K.P.Evans | c Aymes b Aqib Javed | 20 |
| F.D.Stephenson | c Nicholas b Aqib Javed | 7 |
| B.N.French + | c Terry b Connor | 7 |
| E.E.Hemmings | not out | 5 |
| R.A.Pick | not out | 0 |
| Extras | (lb 8,w 11,nb 1) | 20 |
| TOTAL | (60 overs)(for 9 wkts) | 252 |

### HAMPSHIRE

| | | |
|---|---|---|
| V.P.Terry | run out | 26 |
| C.L.Smith | not out | 105 |
| R.A.Smith | b Pick | 67 |
| D.I.Gower | c Evans b Saxelby | 19 |
| M.C.J.Nicholas * | not out | 24 |
| J.R.Ayling | | |
| A.N Aymes + | | |
| R.J.Maru | | |
| S.D.Udal | | |
| C.A.Connor | | |
| Aqib Javed | | |
| Extras | (lb 3,w 8,nb 1) | 12 |
| TOTAL | (59 overs)(for 3 wkts) | 253 |

| HAMPSHIRE | O | M | R | W | FALL OF WICKETS | | |
|---|---|---|---|---|---|---|---|
| | | | | | | NOT | HAM |
| Aqib Javed | 12 | 0 | 51 | 4 | | | |
| Connor | 12 | 0 | 42 | 3 | 1st | 64 | 41 |
| Ayling | 12 | 0 | 55 | 1 | 2nd | 129 | 155 |
| Maru | 12 | 0 | 42 | 1 | 3rd | 140 | 205 |
| Udal | 12 | 0 | 54 | 0 | 4th | 157 | |
| | | | | | 5th | 198 | |
| NOTTS | O | M | R | W | 6th | 218 | |
| Stephenson | 12 | 0 | 43 | 0 | 7th | 230 | |
| Pick | 12 | 1 | 60 | 1 | 8th | 238 | |
| Evans | 11 | 1 | 31 | 0 | 9th | 247 | |
| Saxelby | 12 | 1 | 48 | 1 | 10th | | |
| Hemmings | 12 | 0 | 68 | 0 | | | |

## NORTHANTS vs. GLAMORGAN

at Northampton on 31st July 1991
Toss : Glamorgan. Umpires : J.D.Bond and J.W.Holder
Northants won by 26 runs
Man of the match: A.Fordham

### NORTHANTS

| | | |
|---|---|---|
| A.Fordham | c Watkin b Shastri | 71 |
| W.Larkins | lbw b Watkin | 8 |
| R.J.Bailey | c Shastri b Barwick | 55 |
| A.J.Lamb * | b Shastri | 29 |
| D.J.Capel | c Metson b Barwick | 0 |
| K.M.Curran | not out | 36 |
| E.A.E.Baptiste | c Metson b Watkin | 17 |
| R.G.Williams | run out | 6 |
| D.Ripley + | not out | 10 |
| A.Walker | | |
| J.P.Taylor | | |
| Extras | (b 1,lb 13,w 7,nb 1) | 22 |
| TOTAL | (60 overs)(for 7 wkts) | 254 |

### GLAMORGAN

| | | |
|---|---|---|
| A.R.Butcher * | c Williams b Baptiste | 70 |
| H.Morris | c & b Baptiste | 37 |
| A.Dale | run out | 15 |
| M.P.Maynard | run out | 27 |
| R.J.Shastri | run out | 25 |
| P.A.Cottey | c & b Taylor | 10 |
| R.D.B.Croft | c Lamb b Curran | 13 |
| C.P.Metson | b Walker | 9 |
| S.L.Watkin | not out | 5 |
| S.R.Barwick | lbw b Taylor | 3 |
| M.Frost | b Walker | 3 |
| Extras | (lb 2,w 6,nb 3) | 11 |
| TOTAL | (60 overs) | 228 |

| GLAMORGAN | O | M | R | W | FALL OF WICKETS | | |
|---|---|---|---|---|---|---|---|
| | | | | | | NOR | GLA |
| Watkin | 12 | 0 | 40 | 2 | 1st | 1 | 85 |
| Frost | 7 | 0 | 34 | 0 | 2nd | 127 | 117 |
| Barwick | 12 | 0 | 51 | 2 | 3rd | 171 | 151 |
| Dale | 11 | 1 | 37 | 0 | 4th | 171 | 156 |
| Croft | 5 | 0 | 18 | 0 | 5th | 183 | 170 |
| Shastri | 12 | 0 | 60 | 2 | 6th | 221 | 194 |
| NORTHANTS | O | M | R | W | 7th | 233 | 216 |
| Taylor | 12 | 2 | 34 | 2 | 8th | | 217 |
| Walker | 12 | 1 | 39 | 2 | 9th | | 221 |
| Baptiste | 12 | 0 | 51 | 2 | 10th | | 228 |
| Curran | 12 | 0 | 61 | 1 | | | |
| Williams | 12 | 1 | 41 | 0 | | | |

# HEADLINES

### NatWest Trophy
### Quarter-Finals

### 31st July

• Home advantage proved decisive as all four quarter-final ties were won by sides playing on their own grounds.

• Most impressive winners were Hampshire who overcame Nottinghamshire by seven wickets at Southampton. Aqib Javed improved his best figures in the competition to restrict Notts to 252 for nine in their 60 overs after Derek Randall had appeared to put them on course for a much larger score, then Chris Smith hit his seventh NatWest 100 to guide his side through to their third semi-final in successive years.

• Glamorgan looked to have a fine chance of reaching the semi-finals when their total stood at 151 for two in reply to Northamptonshire's 254 for seven at Northampton, but the visitors lost their last eight wickets for 77 as they suffered a 26-run defeat.

• Surrey, at one stage 143 for five, battled hard to reach 253 against Essex at The Oval, then bowled themselves into the semi-finals by dismissing the visitors for 222 in 56.1 overs, Waqar Younis again proving a devastating force with four wickets for 37.

• The individual peformance of the round came from Somerset's Andy Hayhurst against Warwickshire at Edgbaston: he claimed five wickets in the closing stages of Warwickshire's innings to finish with his best figures in the competition, then scored 91 not out, another career best, in Somerset's reply when his eighth-wicket stand of 67 with Roland Lefebvre almost brought Somerset an improbable victory. Warwickshire just held on to a five-run win when Hayhurst failed to hit the last ball of the match for six.

## WARWICKSHIRE vs. SOMERSET

at Edgbaston on 31st July 1991
Toss : Somerset. Umpires : K.J.Lyons and B.J.Meyer
Warwickshire won by 5 runs
Man of the match: A.N.Hayhurst

### WARWICKSHIRE

| | | |
|---|---|---|
| A.J.Moles | c Tavare b Lefebvre | 13 |
| Asif Din | c Tavare b Lefebvre | 17 |
| T.A.Lloyd * | c Burns b Hayhurst | 78 |
| D.P.Ostler | c Tavare b Graveney | 10 |
| D.A.Reeve | run out | 25 |
| N.M.K.Smith | b Hayhurst | 38 |
| P.A.Smith | b Hayhurst | 26 |
| P.C.L.Holloway + | lbw b Hayhurst | 2 |
| G.C.Small | c & b Hayhurst | 3 |
| T.A.Munton | lbw b Lefebvre | 1 |
| A.A.Donald | not out | 2 |
| Extras | (lb 8,w 3,nb 3) | 14 |
| TOTAL | (60 overs) | 229 |

### SOMERSET

| | | |
|---|---|---|
| S.J.Cook | c Holloway b Small | 14 |
| P.M.Roebuck | c Reeve b Small | 5 |
| R.J.Harden | c Holloway b Munton | 10 |
| C.J.Tavare * | st Holloway b Smith N.M.K. | 43 |
| A.N.Hayhurst | not out | 91 |
| M.Lathwell | c Moles b Munton | 16 |
| N.D.Burns + | c Reeve b Donald | 1 |
| G.D.Rose | run out | 3 |
| R.P.Lefebvre | not out | 21 |
| J.C.Hallett | | |
| D.A.Graveney | | |
| Extras | (b 1,lb 5,w 12,nb 2) | 20 |
| TOTAL | (60 overs)(for 7 wkts) | 224 |

| SOMERSET | O | M | R | W | FALL OF WICKETS | | |
|---|---|---|---|---|---|---|---|
| | | | | | | WAR | SOM |
| Rose | 7 | 0 | 40 | 0 | 1st | 33 | 21 |
| Hallett | 12 | 1 | 31 | 0 | 2nd | 34 | 35 |
| Lefebvre | 12 | 1 | 27 | 3 | 3rd | 72 | 41 |
| Hayhurst | 12 | 1 | 60 | 5 | 4th | 131 | 113 |
| Graveney | 12 | 0 | 44 | 1 | 5th | 191 | 137 |
| Roebuck | 5 | 0 | 19 | 0 | 6th | 200 | 151 |
| WARWICKSHIRE | O | M | R | W | 7th | 208 | 157 |
| Donald | 12 | 1 | 35 | 1 | 8th | 212 | |
| Small | 12 | 2 | 26 | 2 | 9th | 219 | |
| Munton | 12 | 3 | 42 | 2 | 10th | 229 | |
| Reeve | 12 | 1 | 54 | 0 | | | |
| Smith P.A. | 7 | 0 | 41 | 0 | | | |
| Smith N.M.K. | 5 | 0 | 20 | 1 | | | |

## SURREY vs. ESSEX

at The Oval on 31st July 1991
Toss : Essex. Umpires : J.H.Hampshire and R.A.White
Surrey won by 31 runs
Man of the match: Waqar Younis

### SURREY

| | | |
|---|---|---|
| D.J.Bicknell | lbw b Topley | 28 |
| J.D.Robinson | b Such | 47 |
| A.J.Stewart + | b Gooch | 35 |
| D.M.Ward | c & b Foster | 62 |
| G.P.Thorpe | c Garnham b Gooch | 2 |
| M.A.Lynch | lbw b Such | 6 |
| I.A.Greig * | c Hussain b Topley | 20 |
| M.P.Bicknell | c Seymour b Pringle | 4 |
| Waqar Younis | c Hussain b Foster | 26 |
| J.Boiling | lbw b Pringle | 7 |
| A.J.Murphy | not out | 0 |
| Extras | (b 1,lb 4,w 9,nb 2) | 16 |
| TOTAL | (59.5 overs) | 253 |

### ESSEX

| | | |
|---|---|---|
| G.A.Gooch * | c Stewart b Waqar Younis | 50 |
| J.P.Stephenson | c Lynch b Bicknell M.P. | 59 |
| P.J.Prichard | c Boiling b Bicknell M.P. | 11 |
| Salim Malik | run out | 26 |
| N.Hussain | b Murphy | 17 |
| D.R.Pringle | lbw b Waqar Younis | 19 |
| N.A.Foster | c Lynch b Robinson | 9 |
| M.A.Garnham + | c Stewart b Waqar Younis | 9 |
| A.C.Seymour | lbw b Waqar Younis | 0 |
| T.D.Topley | run out | 7 |
| P.M.Such | not out | 0 |
| Extras | (lb 11,w 4) | 15 |
| TOTAL | (56.1 overs) | 222 |

| ESSEX | O | M | R | W | FALL OF WICKETS | | |
|---|---|---|---|---|---|---|---|
| | | | | | | SUR | ESS |
| Foster | 11.5 | 2 | 57 | 2 | 1st | 55 | 92 |
| Pringle | 12 | 0 | 52 | 2 | 2nd | 118 | 121 |
| Topley | 11 | 2 | 44 | 2 | 3rd | 118 | 132 |
| Stephenson | 5 | 0 | 28 | 0 | 4th | 121 | 172 |
| Such | 12 | 1 | 37 | 2 | 5th | 143 | 175 |
| Gooch | 8 | 2 | 30 | 2 | 6th | 193 | 185 |
| SURREY | O | M | R | W | 7th | 209 | 198 |
| Bicknell M.P. | 12 | 0 | 49 | 2 | 8th | 222 | 198 |
| Waqar Younis | 10.1 | 1 | 37 | 4 | 9th | 243 | 222 |
| Murphy | 10 | 3 | 30 | 1 | 10th | 253 | 222 |
| Robinson | 12 | 1 | 48 | 1 | | | |
| Boiling | 12 | 0 | 47 | 0 | | | |

# TOUR MATCHES

## WORCESTERSHIRE vs. SRI LANKA

at Worcester on 30th, 31st July, 1st August 1991
Toss : Sri Lanka.  Umpires : D.J.Constant and R.C.Tolchard
Worcestershire won by an innings and 24 runs

### SRI LANKA

| | | | | | |
|---|---|---|---|---|---|
| D.S.B.P.Kuruppu | c Illingworth b Newport | 9 | c Curtis b Newport | 4 |
| U.C.Hathurusinghe | c Tolley b Newport | 0 | c Rhodes b Tolley | 0 |
| A.P.Gurusinha | lbw b Tolley | 44 | c Rhodes b Tolley | 0 |
| P.A.De Silva * | b Tolley | 26 | c Rhodes b Newport | 16 |
| S.T.Jayasuriya | c Rhodes b Lampitt | 20 | c Moody b Illingworth | 78 |
| M.S.Atapattu | st Rhodes b Tolley | 2 | lbw b Tolley | 2 |
| R.S.Kaluwitharana + | lbw b Lampitt | 0 | c Haynes b Illingworth | 34 |
| C.P.Ramanayake | c Moody b Newport | 8 | lbw b Illingworth | 4 |
| K.I.W.Wijeguna' | lbw b Illingworth | 26 | not out | 6 |
| F.S.Ahangama | c Moody b Tolley | 7 | c Haynes b Illingworth | 0 |
| M.Muralitharan | not out | 22 | c Rhodes b Illingworth | 0 |
| Extras | (lb 4,nb 13) | 17 | (b 1,lb 6,nb 3) | 10 |
| TOTAL | | 181 | | 154 |

### WORCESTERSHIRE

| | | |
|---|---|---|
| T.S.Curtis * | c Gurusinha b Ahangama | 1 |
| P.Bent | b Ramanayake | 3 |
| T.M.Moody | b Wijegunawardene | 86 |
| D.B.D'Oliveira | lbw b Wijegunawardene | 14 |
| D.A.Leatherdale | c Kaluwitharana b Wijeguna' | 66 |
| G.R.Haynes | run out | 16 |
| S.J.Rhodes + | c Muralitharan b Wijeguna' | 35 |
| S.R.Lampitt | not out | 50 |
| R.K.Illingworth | not out | 47 |
| P.J.Newport | | |
| C.M.Tolley | | |
| Extras | (lb 16,nb 25) | 41 |
| TOTAL | (for 7 wkts dec) | 359 |

| WORCS | O | M | R | W | O | M | R | W | | FALL OF WICKETS | | | |
|---|---|---|---|---|---|---|---|---|---|---|---|---|---|
| | | | | | | | | | | | SRI | WOR | SRI | WOR |
| Newport | 20 | 3 | 51 | 3 | 14 | 2 | 49 | 2 | 1st | 1 | 2 | 0 | |
| Tolley | 29 | 8 | 69 | 4 | 12 | 5 | 24 | 3 | 2nd | 41 | 15 | 4 | |
| Lampitt | 15 | 3 | 50 | 2 | 7 | 0 | 17 | 0 | 3rd | 82 | 80 | 6 | |
| Illingworth | 3.4 | 0 | 7 | 1 | 20.1 | 7 | 43 | 5 | 4th | 107 | 124 | 30 | |
| D'Oliveira | | | | | 9 | 4 | 11 | 0 | 5th | 115 | 170 | 53 | |
| Moody | | | | | 3 | 1 | 3 | 0 | 6th | 115 | 217 | 131 | |
| | | | | | | | | | 7th | 115 | 248 | 137 | |
| SRI LANKA | O | M | R | W | O | M | R | W | 8th | 133 | | 148 | |
| Ramanayake | 22 | 4 | 84 | 1 | | | | | 9th | 147 | | 154 | |
| Ahangama | 17 | 6 | 41 | 1 | | | | | 10th | 181 | | 154 | |
| Wijeguna' | 19 | 2 | 112 | 4 | | | | | | | | | |
| Muralitharan | 31 | 2 | 98 | 0 | | | | | | | | | |
| Gurusinha | 2 | 0 | 8 | 0 | | | | | | | | | |

## GLOUCESTERSHIRE vs. WEST INDIES

at Bristol on 31st July, 1st, 2nd August 1991
Toss : West Indies.  Umpires : J.H.Harris and D.O.Oslear
Match drawn

### WEST INDIES

| | | | | | |
|---|---|---|---|---|---|
| P.V.Simmons | c Russell b Gilbert | 26 | lbw b Babington | 72 |
| D.L.Haynes * | c Athey b Lloyds | 151 | | |
| R.B.Richardson | st Russell b Scott | 119 | (6) st Alleyne b Russell | 48 |
| C.B.Lambert | not out | 30 | (2) c Wright b Gilbert | 8 |
| A.L.Logie | lbw b Babington | 27 | | |
| D.Williams + | | | (3) lbw b Babington | 4 |
| C.L.Hooper | | | (4) not out | 111 |
| M.D.Marshall | | | (5) c Hancock b Smith | 1 |
| H.A.G.Anthony | | | | |
| I.B.A.Allen | | | | |
| B.P.Patterson | | | | |
| Extras | (lb 3,nb 12) | 15 | (lb 8,nb 9) | 17 |
| TOTAL | (for 4 wkts dec) | 368 | (for 5 wkts dec) | 261 |

### GLOUCESTERSHIRE

| | | | | | |
|---|---|---|---|---|---|
| G.D.Hodgson | retired hurt | 6 | | |
| R.J.Scott | c Williams b Marshall | 9 | (1) c Simmons b Hooper | 19 |
| A.J.Wright * | c Williams b Anthony | 12 | (2) c Williams b Hooper | 60 |
| C.W.J.Athey | st Williams b Hooper | 35 | (3) retired hurt/ill | 4 |
| M.W.Alleyne | c & b Hooper | 68 | (4) c Allen b Hooper | 26 |
| T.Hancock | c Williams b Allen | 1 | (5) not out | 7 |
| R.C.Russell + | c Patterson b Hooper | 35 | (6) run out | 2 |
| J.W.Lloyds | not out | 71 | (7) not out | 3 |
| D.R.Gilbert | not out | 6 | | |
| A.M.Babington | | | | |
| A.M.Smith | | | | |
| Extras | (lb 9,w 1,nb 18) | 28 | (lb 8,nb 3) | 11 |
| TOTAL | (for 6 wkts dec) | 271 | (for 4 wkts) | 132 |

| GLOUCS | O | M | R | W | O | M | R | W | | FALL OF WICKETS | | | |
|---|---|---|---|---|---|---|---|---|---|---|---|---|---|
| | | | | | | | | | | | WI | GLO | WI | GLO |
| Gilbert | 11 | 0 | 56 | 1 | 10 | 1 | 38 | 1 | 1st | 56 | 11 | 21 | 54 |
| Babington | 13.4 | 0 | 65 | 1 | 15 | 1 | 68 | 2 | 2nd | 296 | 47 | 26 | 117 |
| Smith | 13 | 2 | 46 | 0 | 13 | 2 | 69 | 1 | 3rd | 314 | 107 | 146 | 119 |
| Scott | 14 | 1 | 48 | 1 | | | | | 4th | 368 | 116 | 149 | 123 |
| Lloyds | 21 | 1 | 112 | 1 | 7 | 0 | 34 | 0 | 5th | | 167 | 261 | |
| Alleyne | 9 | 1 | 38 | 0 | 11 | 2 | 40 | 0 | 6th | | 242 | | |
| Russell | | | | | 0.5 | 0 | 4 | 1 | 7th | | | | |
| | | | | | | | | | 8th | | | | |
| WEST INDIES | O | M | R | W | O | M | R | W | 9th | | | | |
| Patterson | 11 | 2 | 28 | 0 | 6 | 2 | 16 | 0 | 10th | | | | |
| Allen | 19 | 3 | 55 | 1 | 7 | 2 | 14 | 0 | | | | | |
| Marshall | 16 | 2 | 57 | 1 | 6 | 2 | 6 | 0 | | | | | |
| Hooper | 24.4 | 6 | 55 | 3 | 23 | 5 | 43 | 3 | | | | | |
| Anthony | 17 | 0 | 67 | 1 | 5 | 0 | 27 | 0 | | | | | |
| Richardson | | | | | 5 | 2 | 6 | 0 | | | | | |
| Simmons | | | | | 8 | 3 | 12 | 0 | | | | | |
| Lambert | | | | | 1 | 1 | 0 | 0 | | | | | |

# HEADLINES

### Tetley Bitter Challenge

#### 30th July - 1st August

- The Sri Lankans suffered the first defeat of their tour when they were beaten by an innings and 24 runs by Worcestershire at Worcester. After Sri Lanka struggled against Worcester's seam attack to be bowled out for 181, the home side were taken to a lead of 178 by an unbroken eighth-wicket stand of 111 from Stuart Lampitt and Richard Illingworth. Then Illingworth, with five for 43, made certain of a convincing victory.

# HEADLINES

### Tetley Bitter Challenge

#### 31st July - 2nd August

- West Indies, entering the final stages of their tour, made little effort to convert their superiority over Gloucestershire into victory at Bristol. Desmond Haynes made his highest score of the summer, sharing a second-wicket partnership of 240 with Richie Richardson who hit his fifth century of the tour, while Carl Hooper followed with his fourth 100 in the second innings, also taking three wickets in each innings as the fast bowlers were sparingly used.

First-class début: T.Hancock
(Gloucestershire)

| JESMOND FESTIVAL | REFUGE ASSURANCE LEAGUE |
| --- | --- |

## ENGLAND XI vs. REST OF WORLD

at Jesmond on 31st July 1991
Toss : Rest of World. Umpires : S.Levinson and G.McLean
England XI won by 5 wickets

### REST OF WORLD

| | | |
| --- | --- | --- |
| Mudassar Nazar | c Blakey b Salisbury | 31 |
| S.V.Manjrekar | c Blakey b Allott | 100 |
| S.R.Tendulkar | c Salisbury b Emburey | 54 |
| M.Azharuddin * | c Moxon b Emburey | 6 |
| Ijaz Ahmed | b Allott | 46 |
| J.C.Adams + | not out | 14 |
| Wasim Akram | b Allott | 7 |
| P.R.Sleep | not out | 12 |
| A.I.C.Dodemaide | | |
| P.R.Reiffel | | |
| I.R.Bishop | | |
| Extras | (b 4,lb 2,w 1,nb 6) | 13 |
| TOTAL | (55 overs)(for 6 wkts) | 283 |

### ENGLAND XI

| | | |
| --- | --- | --- |
| K.J.Barnett | b Dodemaide | 49 |
| M.D.Moxon | c Ijaz Ahmed b Wasim Akram | 5 |
| M.A.Atherton | b Sleep | 31 |
| N.H.Fairbrother | c Azharuddin b Dodemaide | 21 |
| J.E.Morris | c Adams b Reiffel | 42 |
| C.C.Lewis | not out | 89 |
| R.J.Blakey + | not out | 21 |
| J.E.Emburey * | | |
| P.J.W.Allott | | |
| I.D.K.Salisbury | | |
| D.E.Malcolm | | |
| Extras | (lb 16,w 5,nb 8) | 29 |
| TOTAL | (45.1 overs)(for 5 wkts) | 287 |

| ENGLAND XI | O | M | R | W | FALL OF WICKETS | | |
| --- | --- | --- | --- | --- | --- | --- | --- |
| | | | | | | ROW | EXI |
| Malcolm | 11 | 0 | 61 | 0 | 1st | 72 | 26 |
| Lewis | 11 | 1 | 40 | 0 | 2nd | 166 | 92 |
| Salisbury | 11 | 1 | 72 | 1 | 3rd | 190 | 103 |
| Allott | 11 | 2 | 47 | 3 | 4th | 247 | 116 |
| Emburey | 11 | 1 | 57 | 2 | 5th | 250 | 172 |
| | | | | | 6th | 258 | |
| REST OF W. | O | M | R | W | 7th | | |
| Bishop | 8 | 0 | 60 | 0 | 8th | | |
| Wasim Akram | 8.1 | 2 | 21 | 1 | 9th | | |
| Dodemaide | 9 | 1 | 66 | 2 | 10th | | |
| Reiffel | 9 | 0 | 59 | 1 | | | |
| Sleep | 11 | 1 | 65 | 1 | | | |

## ENGLAND XI vs. REST OF WORLD

at Jesmond on 1st August 1991
Toss : England XI. Umpires : S.Levinson and G.McLean
Rest of World won by 4 wickets

### ENGLAND XI

| | | |
| --- | --- | --- |
| K.J.Barnett | b Dodemaide | 26 |
| M.D.Moxon | st Adams b Sleep | 40 |
| M.A.Atherton | b Reiffel | 41 |
| N.H.Fairbrother | c Adams b Reiffel | 0 |
| J.E.Morris | b Wasim Akram | 107 |
| C.C.Lewis | c Azharuddin b Bishop | 12 |
| R.J.Blakey + | c Dodemaide b Reiffel | 25 |
| J.E.Emburey * | b Bishop | 5 |
| P.J.W.Allott | run out | 0 |
| I.D.K.Salisbury | b Bishop | 5 |
| D.E.Malcolm | not out | 0 |
| Extras | (b 8,lb 5,w 3,nb 7) | 23 |
| TOTAL | (53.2 overs) | 284 |

### REST OF WORLD

| | | |
| --- | --- | --- |
| S.V.Manjrekar | c Blakey b Malcolm | 14 |
| Mudassar Nazar | c Blakey b Malcolm | 12 |
| Wasim Akram | c Morris b Lewis | 6 |
| S.R.Tendulkar | c Emburey b Malcolm | 102 |
| M.Azharuddin * | c Allott b Lewis | 56 |
| Ijaz Ahmed | c Fairbrother b Salisbury | 39 |
| J.C.Adams + | not out | 28 |
| A.I.C.Dodemaide | not out | 6 |
| P.R.Sleep | | |
| P.R.Reiffel | | |
| I.R.Bishop | | |
| Extras | (b 4,lb 7,w 10,nb 2) | 23 |
| TOTAL | (42 overs)(for 6 wkts) | 286 |

| REST OF W. | O | M | R | W | FALL OF WICKETS | | |
| --- | --- | --- | --- | --- | --- | --- | --- |
| | | | | | | EXI | ROW |
| Bishop | 10.2 | 0 | 38 | 3 | 1st | 62 | 24 |
| Wasim Akram | 10 | 2 | 49 | 1 | 2nd | 88 | 34 |
| Sleep | 11 | 0 | 48 | 1 | 3rd | 93 | 45 |
| Dodemaide | 11 | 2 | 60 | 1 | 4th | 154 | 198 |
| Reiffel | 9 | 0 | 61 | 3 | 5th | 186 | 219 |
| Mudassar | 2 | 0 | 15 | 0 | 6th | 251 | 270 |
| ENGLAND XI | O | M | R | W | 7th | 259 | |
| Malcolm | 9 | 0 | 61 | 3 | 8th | 260 | |
| Lewis | 11 | 0 | 52 | 2 | 9th | 283 | |
| Allott | 6 | 0 | 39 | 0 | 10th | 284 | |
| Salisbury | 8 | 0 | 75 | 1 | | | |
| Emburey | 8 | 1 | 48 | 0 | | | |

# HEADLINES

### Jesmond Festival

### 31st July - 1st August

• Jesmond again proved an ideal stage for some of the most exciting players in the world of cricket to give two richly entertaining displays as an England XI and a Rest of the World XI won one match apiece.

### Refuge Assurance League

### 4th August

• The two leading sides in the League both lost with the result that Lancashire remained two points clear of Nottinghamshire, but now only four points ahead of Worcestershire in third place who outplayed Notts at Worcester by eight wickets thanks to a second-wicket stand of 187 between Tim Curtis and Graeme Hick.

• Lancashire could not take advantage of Notts's third defeat of the season, their long run of Sunday success being ended by Yorkshire. Phil Carrick collected four for 28 to restrict Lancashire to 196 for nine, then the first four Yorkshire batsmen all weighed in to bring a comfortable victory with two overs to spare.

• Northants and Warwickshire remained in sixth and seventh places with their wins over Sussex and Derbyshire respectively. At Eastbourne, Sussex's total of 170 for eight proved inadequate and Northants won by five wickets with 2.4 overs to spare, while at Edgbaston, Dermot Reeve's four for 18 gave Warwicks victory by 32 runs.

• Surrey beat Kent by six wickets at Canterbury, the unstoppable Waqar Younis removing the heart of the home side's batting with a spell of four for 21.

• At last Middlesex gained some success in front of their home crowd at Lord's, defeating bottom of the table Hampshire by seven wickets. Paul Weekes claimed his best Sunday figures and later Mark Ramprakash and Mike Gatting added 116 for the second wicket.

• James Whitaker's 85 helped Leicestershire to beat Somerset by seven wickets at Weston, while Glamorgan gave their best Sunday performance of the season in beating Gloucestershire by 100 runs.

## GLAMORGAN vs. GLOUCS

at Swansea on 4th August 1991
Toss : Glamorgan. Umpires : J.C.Balderstone & J.H.Harris
Glamorgan won by 100 runs. Glam 4 pts, Gloucs 0 pts

### GLAMORGAN

| | | |
| --- | --- | --- |
| M.P.Maynard | c Russell b Alleyne | 81 |
| S.P.James | c Russell b Gerrard | 23 |
| R.J.Shastri | run out | 6 |
| A.Dale | b Lawrence | 32 |
| P.A.Cottey | b Babington | 33 |
| A.R.Butcher * | b Lawrence | 20 |
| R.D.B.Croft | run out | 1 |
| C.P.Metson + | c Milburn b Babington | 7 |
| S.L.Watkin | c Athey b Babington | 6 |
| S.R.Barwick | not out | 1 |
| D.J.Foster | b Babington | 0 |
| Extras | (b 1,lb 16,w 5,nb 4) | 26 |
| TOTAL | (40 overs) | 236 |

### GLOUCESTERSHIRE

| | | |
| --- | --- | --- |
| R.J.Scott | c Cottey b Foster | 2 |
| C.W.J.Athey | c Metson b Watkin | 3 |
| R.C.Russell + | b Dale | 40 |
| A.J.Wright * | c Dale b Croft | 23 |
| M.W.Alleyne | b Croft | 8 |
| J.W.Lloyds | c James b Dale | 20 |
| E.T.Milburn | run out | 13 |
| D.V.Lawrence | c Maynard b Dale | 13 |
| A.M.Babington | c Maynard b Shastri | 4 |
| M.C.J.Ball | not out | 2 |
| M.J.Gerrard | b Foster | 4 |
| Extras | (lb 2,w 2) | 4 |
| TOTAL | (35 overs) | 136 |

| GLOUCS | O | M | R | W | FALL OF WICKETS | | |
| --- | --- | --- | --- | --- | --- | --- | --- |
| | | | | | | GLA | GLO |
| Lawrence | 8 | 0 | 48 | 2 | 1st | 71 | 3 |
| Babington | 8 | 0 | 53 | 4 | 2nd | 100 | 6 |
| Gerrard | 8 | 2 | 35 | 1 | 3rd | 128 | 63 |
| Scott | 8 | 0 | 29 | 0 | 4th | 180 | 79 |
| Alleyne | 7 | 0 | 44 | 1 | 5th | 219 | 83 |
| Ball | 1 | 0 | 10 | 0 | 6th | 220 | 113 |
| GLAMORGAN | O | M | R | W | 7th | 222 | 114 |
| Watkin | 5 | 2 | 11 | 1 | 8th | 233 | 127 |
| Foster | 6 | 0 | 16 | 2 | 9th | 235 | 132 |
| Barwick | 4 | 0 | 18 | 0 | 10th | 236 | 136 |
| Croft | 8 | 0 | 30 | 2 | | | |
| Dale | 8 | 0 | 44 | 3 | | | |
| Shastri | 4 | 1 | 15 | 1 | | | |

## KENT vs. SURREY

at Canterbury on 4th August 1991
Toss : Surrey. Umpires : R.Julian and K.J.Lyons
Surrey won by 6 wickets. Kent 0 pts, Surrey 4 pts

### KENT

| | | |
| --- | --- | --- |
| T.R.Ward | c Bicknell D.J. b Robinson | 27 |
| M.R.Benson * | b Robson | 14 |
| N.R.Taylor | c Stewart b Waqar Younis | 29 |
| S.G.Hinks | b Waqar Younis | 18 |
| G.R.Cowdrey | lbw b Waqar Younis | 36 |
| M.V.Fleming | c Robinson b Robson | 15 |
| S.A.Marsh + | not out | 28 |
| M.A.Ealham | lbw b Waqar Younis | 2 |
| R.P.Davis | b Bicknell M.P. | 0 |
| T.A.Merrick | not out | 2 |
| A.P.Igglesden | | |
| Extras | (lb 8,w 4) | 12 |
| TOTAL | (39 overs)(for 8 wkts) | 183 |

### SURREY

| | | |
| --- | --- | --- |
| D.J.Bicknell | b Ealham | 13 |
| G.P.Thorpe | c Marsh b Fleming | 54 |
| A.J.Stewart + | c Taylor b Ealham | 64 |
| D.M.Ward | c Igglesden b Fleming | 22 |
| M.A.Lynch | not out | 17 |
| J.D.Robinson | not out | 7 |
| I.A.Greig * | | |
| M.P.Bicknell | | |
| J.Boiling | | |
| Waqar Younis | | |
| A.G.Robson | | |
| Extras | (lb 4,w 5) | 9 |
| TOTAL | (38.4 overs)(for 4 wkts) | 186 |

| SURREY | O | M | R | W | FALL OF WICKETS | | |
| --- | --- | --- | --- | --- | --- | --- | --- |
| | | | | | | KEN | SUR |
| Bicknell M.P. | 8 | 0 | 34 | 1 | 1st | 36 | 29 |
| Robson | 8 | 0 | 40 | 2 | 2nd | 48 | 125 |
| Robinson | 8 | 1 | 26 | 1 | 3rd | 86 | 144 |
| Boiling | 6 | 0 | 33 | 0 | 4th | 106 | 169 |
| Waqar Younis | 7 | 1 | 21 | 4 | 5th | 144 | |
| Greig | 2 | 0 | 21 | 0 | 6th | 158 | |
| KENT | O | M | R | W | 7th | 176 | |
| Igglesden | 8 | 0 | 32 | 0 | 8th | 179 | |
| Merrick | 7 | 0 | 47 | 0 | 9th | | |
| Ealham | 8 | 0 | 25 | 2 | 10th | | |
| Davis | 8 | 2 | 41 | 0 | | | |
| Fleming | 7.4 | 0 | 37 | 2 | | | |

# REFUGE ASSURANCE LEAGUE

## LANCASHIRE vs. YORKSHIRE
at Old Trafford on 4th August 1991
Toss : Yorkshire.  Umpires : A.A.Jones & A.G.T.Whitehead
Yorkshire won by 5 wickets.  Lancs 0 pts, Yorkshire 4 pts

### LANCASHIRE
| | | |
|---|---|---|
| G.D.Mendis | c Moxon b Carrick | 39 |
| G.Fowler | c Metcalfe b Carrick | 39 |
| G.D.Lloyd | c & b Carrick | 21 |
| N.H.Fairbrother * | c Blakey b Pickles | 39 |
| M.Watkinson | c Hartley b Carrick | 4 |
| Wasim Akram | c Blakey b Pickles | 1 |
| M.A.Atherton | c & b Pickles | 11 |
| P.A.J.DeFreitas | c Pickles b Hartley | 5 |
| W.K.Hegg + | not out | 27 |
| I.D.Austin | lbw b Robinson M.A. | 3 |
| P.J.W.Allott | not out | 1 |
| Extras | (b 1,lb 5) | 6 |
| TOTAL | (40 overs)(for 9 wkts) | 196 |

### YORKSHIRE
| | | |
|---|---|---|
| M.D.Moxon * | c DeFreitas b Austin | 76 |
| A.A.Metcalfe | b Austin | 41 |
| R.J.Blakey + | c Fairbrother b Watkinson | 32 |
| D.Byas | not out | 31 |
| P.E.Robinson | b Austin | 9 |
| S.A.Kellett | c Hegg b Austin | 0 |
| C.S.Pickles | not out | 1 |
| P.Carrick | | |
| P.J.Hartley | | |
| J.D.Batty | | |
| M.A.Robinson | | |
| Extras | (b 1,lb 3,w 1,nb 2) | 7 |
| TOTAL | (38 overs)(for 5 wkts) | 197 |

| YORKSHIRE | O | M | R | W | FALL OF WICKETS | | |
|---|---|---|---|---|---|---|---|
| | | | | | | LAN | YOR |
| Hartley | 8 | 0 | 29 | 1 | | | |
| Robinson M.A. | 8 | 1 | 48 | 1 | 1st | 76 | 78 |
| Pickles | 8 | 0 | 49 | 3 | 2nd | 89 | 138 |
| Batty | 8 | 0 | 36 | 0 | 3rd | 116 | 166 |
| Carrick | 8 | 0 | 28 | 4 | 4th | 122 | 196 |
| | | | | | 5th | 126 | 196 |
| LANCASHIRE | O | M | R | W | 6th | 146 | |
| DeFreitas | 8 | 0 | 33 | 0 | 7th | 153 | |
| Allott | 8 | 0 | 37 | 0 | 8th | 176 | |
| Wasim Akram | 7 | 0 | 32 | 0 | 9th | 185 | |
| Watkinson | 8 | 0 | 51 | 1 | 10th | | |
| Austin | 7 | 0 | 40 | 4 | | | |

## NOTTS vs. WORCESTERSHIRE
at Trent Bridge on 4th August 1991
Toss : Worcestershire.  Umpires : B.Dudleston & R.A.White
Worcestershire won by 8 wickets.  Notts 0 pts, Worcs 4 pts

### NOTTS
| | | |
|---|---|---|
| B.C.Broad | lbw b Newport | 11 |
| D.W.Randall | c & b Illingworth | 50 |
| R.T.Robinson * | c & b Radford | 8 |
| P.Johnson | c Hick b Illingworth | 18 |
| P.Pollard | lbw b Lampitt | 73 |
| M.Saxelby | run out | 12 |
| F.D.Stephenson | not out | 18 |
| B.N.French + | not out | 4 |
| K.P.Evans | | |
| E.E.Hemmings | | |
| R.A.Pick | | |
| Extras | (lb 10,w 4,nb 1) | 15 |
| TOTAL | (40 overs)(for 6 wkts) | 209 |

### WORCESTERSHIRE
| | | |
|---|---|---|
| T.S.Curtis * | not out | 66 |
| T.M.Moody | c French b Pick | 0 |
| G.A.Hick | b Stephenson | 109 |
| D.B.D'Oliveira | not out | 16 |
| I.T.Botham | | |
| M.J.Weston | | |
| S.J.Rhodes + | | |
| R.K.Illingworth | | |
| S.R.Lampitt | | |
| P.J.Newport | | |
| N.V.Radford | | |
| Extras | (lb 9,w 10,nb 1) | 20 |
| TOTAL | (39.1 overs)(for 2 wkts) | 211 |

| WORCS | O | M | R | W | FALL OF WICKETS | | |
|---|---|---|---|---|---|---|---|
| | | | | | | NOT | WOR |
| Weston | 8 | 0 | 22 | 0 | | | |
| Newport | 8 | 0 | 38 | 1 | 1st | 22 | 1 |
| Radford | 4 | 0 | 25 | 1 | 2nd | 32 | 188 |
| Illingworth | 8 | 1 | 30 | 2 | 3rd | 70 | |
| Botham | 6 | 0 | 38 | 0 | 4th | 125 | |
| Lampitt | 6 | 0 | 46 | 1 | 5th | 146 | |
| | | | | | 6th | 209 | |
| NOTTS | O | M | R | W | 7th | | |
| Pick | 8 | 0 | 34 | 1 | 8th | | |
| Stephenson | 8 | 2 | 26 | 1 | 9th | | |
| Saxelby | 8 | 1 | 47 | 0 | 10th | | |
| Evans | 8 | 0 | 35 | 0 | | | |
| Hemmings | 7.1 | 0 | 60 | 0 | | | |

## SUSSEX vs. NORTHANTS
at Eastbourne on 4th August 1991
Toss : Sussex.  Umpires : R.Palmer and D.R.Shepherd
Northants won by 5 wickets.  Sussex 0 pts, Northants 4 pts

### SUSSEX
| | | |
|---|---|---|
| K.Greenfield | c Larkins b Williams | 57 |
| P.W.G.Parker * | c Felton b Taylor | 1 |
| A.P.Wells | c Williams b Curran | 38 |
| M.P.Speight | c Walker b Williams | 2 |
| C.M.Wells | not out | 24 |
| J.A.North | b Taylor | 18 |
| A.I.C.Dodemaide | c Felton b Walker | 8 |
| A.C.S.Pigott | b Baptiste | 0 |
| P.Moores + | b Baptiste | 0 |
| I.D.K.Salisbury | not out | 6 |
| A.N.Jones | | |
| Extras | (lb 10,w 6) | 16 |
| TOTAL | (40 overs)(for 8 wkts) | 170 |

### NORTHANTS
| | | |
|---|---|---|
| A.Fordham | st Moores b Salisbury | 20 |
| N.A.Felton | c Parker b Dodemaide | 5 |
| W.Larkins | c Moores b Jones | 43 |
| A.J.Lamb * | c Moores b Dodemaide | 35 |
| D.J.Capel | b Salisbury | 22 |
| K.M.Curran | not out | 25 |
| E.A.E.Baptiste | not out | 14 |
| R.G.Williams | | |
| D.Ripley + | | |
| A.Walker | | |
| J.P.Taylor | | |
| Extras | (lb 7,w 3) | 10 |
| TOTAL | (37.2 overs)(for 5 wkts) | 174 |

| NORTHANTS | O | M | R | W | FALL OF WICKETS | | |
|---|---|---|---|---|---|---|---|
| | | | | | | SUS | NOR |
| Taylor | 6 | 1 | 25 | 2 | | | |
| Walker | 8 | 1 | 26 | 1 | 1st | 17 | 8 |
| Capel | 5 | 0 | 23 | 0 | 2nd | 103 | 60 |
| Baptiste | 8 | 1 | 25 | 2 | 3rd | 108 | 94 |
| Williams | 8 | 0 | 32 | 2 | 4th | 111 | 130 |
| Curran | 5 | 0 | 29 | 1 | 5th | 142 | 148 |
| | | | | | 6th | 154 | |
| SUSSEX | O | M | R | W | 7th | 154 | |
| Wells C.M. | 7 | 0 | 22 | 0 | 8th | 158 | |
| Dodemaide | 8 | 1 | 22 | 2 | 9th | | |
| Greenfield | 7 | 0 | 29 | 0 | 10th | | |
| Salisbury | 8 | 0 | 43 | 2 | | | |
| Jones | 3.2 | 0 | 28 | 1 | | | |
| Pigott | 4 | 0 | 23 | 0 | | | |

## MIDDLESEX vs. HAMPSHIRE
at Lord's on 4th August 1991
Toss : Middlesex.  Umpires : B.Leadbeater and K.E.Palmer
Middlesex won by 7 wickets.  Middlesex 4 pts, Hants 0 pts

### HAMPSHIRE
| | | |
|---|---|---|
| V.P.Terry | c Roseberry b Emburey | 34 |
| R.A.Smith | c Farbrace b Taylor | 14 |
| J.R.Wood | b Emburey | 17 |
| M.C.J.Nicholas * | not out | 50 |
| K.D.James | st Farbrace b Weekes | 9 |
| J.R.Ayling | b Weekes | 4 |
| R.J.Parks + | c Taylor b Weekes | 6 |
| R.J.Maru | | |
| S.D.Udal | | |
| C.A.Connor | | |
| K.J.Shine | | |
| Extras | (b 2,lb 6,w 10) | 18 |
| TOTAL | (40 overs)(for 6 wkts) | 152 |

### MIDDLESEX
| | | |
|---|---|---|
| M.A.Roseberry | b Connor | 5 |
| M.W.Gatting * | c James b Connor | 58 |
| M.R.Ramprakash | c Parks b Shine | 68 |
| K.R.Brown | not out | 14 |
| M.Keech | not out | 5 |
| P.N.Weekes | | |
| J.E.Emburey | | |
| P.Farbrace + | | |
| D.W.Headley | | |
| C.W.Taylor | | |
| N.G.Cowans | | |
| Extras | (lb 1,w 4,nb 4) | 9 |
| TOTAL | (33.5 overs)(for 3 wkts) | 154 |

| MIDDLESEX | O | M | R | W | FALL OF WICKETS | | |
|---|---|---|---|---|---|---|---|
| | | | | | | HAM | MID |
| Cowans | 8 | 0 | 39 | 0 | | | |
| Headley | 6 | 0 | 16 | 0 | 1st | 37 | 12 |
| Taylor | 4 | 0 | 14 | 1 | 2nd | 67 | 128 |
| Gatting | 8 | 0 | 27 | 0 | 3rd | 76 | 145 |
| Emburey | 8 | 1 | 21 | 2 | 4th | 116 | |
| Weekes | 6 | 0 | 27 | 3 | 5th | 132 | |
| | | | | | 6th | 152 | |
| HAMPSHIRE | O | M | R | W | 7th | | |
| Connor | 8 | 0 | 30 | 2 | 8th | | |
| Shine | 7 | 0 | 22 | 1 | 9th | | |
| Ayling | 7 | 0 | 37 | 0 | 10th | | |
| Udal | 4.5 | 0 | 29 | 0 | | | |
| Maru | 3 | 0 | 19 | 0 | | | |
| James | 4 | 0 | 16 | 0 | | | |

## SOMERSET vs. LEICESTERSHIRE
at Weston-Super-Mare on 4th August 1991
Toss : Leicestershire.  Umpires : B.Hassan and B.J.Meyer
Leicestershire won by 7 wickets.  Somerset 0 pts, Leics 4 pts

### SOMERSET
| | | |
|---|---|---|
| S.J.Cook | lbw b Mullally | 2 |
| P.M.Roebuck | c Whitticase b Lewis | 10 |
| C.J.Tavare * | c Benson b Wilkinson | 41 |
| R.J.Harden | c Whitticase b Mullally | 4 |
| M.Lathwell | c Briers b Benson | 20 |
| A.N.Hayhurst | c Mullally b Maguire | 35 |
| N.D.Burns + | not out | 51 |
| G.D.Rose | not out | 0 |
| R.P.Lefebvre | | |
| H.R.J.Trump | | |
| J.C.Hallett | | |
| Extras | (lb 9,nb 1) | 10 |
| TOTAL | (40 overs)(for 6 wkts) | 173 |

### LEICESTERSHIRE
| | | |
|---|---|---|
| J.J.Whitaker | c Lathwell b Roebuck | 85 |
| N.E.Briers * | st Burns b Roebuck | 26 |
| B.F.Smith | b Rose | 22 |
| C.C.Lewis | not out | 18 |
| L.Potter | not out | 13 |
| J.D.R.Benson | | |
| P.N.Hepworth | | |
| P.Whitticase + | | |
| C.Wilkinson | | |
| A.D.Mullally | | |
| J.N.Maguire | | |
| Extras | (b 1,lb 8,w 3) | 12 |
| TOTAL | (39.1 overs)(for 3 wkts) | 176 |

| LEICS | O | M | R | W | FALL OF WICKETS | | |
|---|---|---|---|---|---|---|---|
| | | | | | | SOM | LEI |
| Lewis | 8 | 1 | 31 | 1 | | | |
| Mullally | 8 | 1 | 19 | 2 | 1st | 9 | 93 |
| Maguire | 8 | 1 | 42 | 1 | 2nd | 23 | 141 |
| Benson | 8 | 0 | 37 | 1 | 3rd | 38 | 150 |
| Wilkinson | 8 | 0 | 35 | 1 | 4th | 84 | |
| | | | | | 5th | 84 | |
| SOMERSET | O | M | R | W | 6th | 170 | |
| Lefebvre | 8 | 0 | 24 | 0 | 7th | | |
| Hallett | 6 | 0 | 29 | 0 | 8th | | |
| Rose | 5.1 | 0 | 33 | 1 | 9th | | |
| Lathwell | 4 | 0 | 19 | 0 | 10th | | |
| Trump | 8 | 1 | 30 | 0 | | | |
| Roebuck | 8 | 1 | 32 | 2 | | | |

## WARWICKSHIRE vs. DERBYSHIRE
at Edgbaston on 4th August 1991
Toss : Warwickshire.  Umpires : J.W.Holder & R.C.Tolchard
Warwicks won by 32 runs.  Warwicks 4 pts, Derbys 0 pts

### WARWICKSHIRE
| | | |
|---|---|---|
| A.J.Moles | lbw b Cork | 44 |
| J.D.Ratcliffe | lbw b Mortensen | 1 |
| T.A.Lloyd * | c Base b McCray | 45 |
| D.P.Ostler | not out | 62 |
| D.A.Reeve | b Cork | 38 |
| N.M.K.Smith | not out | 14 |
| R.G.Twose | | |
| P.C.L.Holloway + | | |
| J.E.Benjamin | | |
| T.A.Munton | | |
| D.Brown | | |
| Extras | (lb 16,w 4,nb 1) | 21 |
| TOTAL | (40 overs)(for 4 wkts) | 225 |

### DERBYSHIRE
| | | |
|---|---|---|
| K.J.Barnett * | b Benjamin | 10 |
| C.J.Adams | c Holloway b Reeve | 35 |
| J.E.Morris | c Lloyd b Benjamin | 17 |
| T.J.G.O'Gorman | c & b Reeve | 32 |
| M.Azharuddin | lbw b Brown | 24 |
| S.C.Goldsmith | lbw b Benjamin | 10 |
| S.J.Base | b Smith | 12 |
| D.G.Cork | c Moles b Reeve | 30 |
| E.McCray | b Munton | 1 |
| B.J.M.Maher + | c Benjamin b Reeve | 4 |
| O.H.Mortensen | not out | 1 |
| Extras | (lb 11,w 6) | 17 |
| TOTAL | (37.4 overs) | 193 |

| DERBYSHIRE | O | M | R | W | FALL OF WICKETS | | |
|---|---|---|---|---|---|---|---|
| | | | | | | WAR | DER |
| Base | 8 | 0 | 38 | 0 | | | |
| Mortensen | 8 | 1 | 41 | 1 | 1st | 2 | 13 |
| McCray | 8 | 0 | 37 | 1 | 2nd | 76 | 38 |
| Cork | 8 | 0 | 38 | 2 | 3rd | 121 | 93 |
| Goldsmith | 8 | 1 | 55 | 0 | 4th | 210 | 122 |
| | | | | | 5th | | 140 |
| WARWICKS | O | M | R | W | 6th | | 142 |
| Brown | 6 | 0 | 35 | 1 | 7th | | 182 |
| Benjamin | 8 | 0 | 33 | 3 | 8th | | 183 |
| Munton | 7 | 0 | 29 | 1 | 9th | | 191 |
| Smith | 8 | 0 | 50 | 1 | 10th | | 193 |
| Reeve | 6.4 | 0 | 18 | 4 | | | |
| Twose | 2 | 0 | 17 | 0 | | | |

# BRITANNIC ASSURANCE CHAMPIONSHIP

## KENT vs. SURREY
at Canterbury on 2nd, 3rd, 5th August 1991
Toss : Kent. Umpires : R.Julian and K.J.Lyons
Match drawn. Kent 8 pts (Bt: 4, Bw: 4), Surrey 5 pts (Bt: 1, Bw: 4)

### KENT
| | | | | |
|---|---|---:|---|---:|
| T.R.Ward | b Waqar Younis | 6 | c Bicknell b Murphy | 26 |
| M.R.Benson * | b Medlycott | 142 | | |
| N.R.Taylor | c Stewart b Waqar Younis | 5 | c Greig b Medlycott | 35 |
| G.R.Cowdrey | c Sargeant b Feltham | 40 | b Feltham | 15 |
| S.G.Hinks | lbw b Feltham | 5 | (2) c Bicknell b Murphy | 9 |
| M.V.Fleming | c Greig b Waqar Younis | 113 | (5) c Murphy b Medlycott | 3 |
| S.A.Marsh + | not out | 20 | (6) b Waqar Younis | 3 |
| R.M.Ellison | b Waqar Younis | 0 | (7) not out | 5 |
| C.Penn | b Waqar Younis | 0 | (8) lbw b Waqar Younis | 0 |
| T.A.Merrick | b Waqar Younis | 4 | (9) not out | 4 |
| A.P.Igglesden | c Greig b Medlycott | 5 | | |
| Extras | (b 8,lb 8,w 2) | 18 | (lb 3) | 3 |
| TOTAL | | 358 | (for 7 wkts) | 103 |

### SURREY
| | | | | |
|---|---|---:|---|---:|
| D.J.Bicknell | c Fleming b Ellison | 41 | c & b Ellison | 151 |
| R.I.Alikhan | c Hinks b Fleming | 30 | b Penn | 20 |
| A.J.Stewart | c Marsh b Ellison | 10 | lbw b Ellison | 32 |
| D.M.Ward | c Marsh b Penn | 53 | (5) c sub b Merrick | 35 |
| G.P.Thorpe | b Igglesden | 7 | (6) c Cowdrey b Igglesden | 25 |
| I.A.Greig * | not out | 8 | (7) b Ellison | 22 |
| K.T.Medlycott | c Taylor b Penn | 4 | (8) b Igglesden | 24 |
| M.A.Feltham | run out | 0 | (9) not out | 10 |
| N.F.Sargeant + | b Igglesden | 0 | (4) c Cowdrey b Ward | 34 |
| Waqar Younis | c Cowdrey b Penn | 8 | c Hinks b Merrick | 9 |
| A.J.Murphy | b Penn | 7 | b Merrick | 0 |
| Extras | (b 2,lb 1,w 1,nb 6) | 10 | (lb 8,w 1,nb 14) | 23 |
| TOTAL | | 178 | | 385 |

| SURREY | O | M | R | W | O | M | R | W | FALL OF WICKETS | | | | |
|---|---|---|---|---|---|---|---|---|---|---|---|---|---|
| | | | | | | | | | | KEN | SUR | SUR | KEN |
| Waqar Younis | 29 | 3 | 72 | 6 | 12 | 7 | 26 | 2 | 1st | 8 | 65 | 48 | 10 |
| Murphy | 11 | 4 | 35 | 0 | 7 | 1 | 41 | 2 | 2nd | 22 | 75 | 138 | 62 |
| Feltham | 26 | 11 | 64 | 2 | 4 | 0 | 15 | 1 | 3rd | 129 | 120 | 249 | 87 |
| Medlycott | 21.4 | 1 | 119 | 2 | 8.5 | 4 | 18 | 2 | 4th | 137 | 148 | 253 | 90 |
| Greig | 3 | 0 | 11 | 0 | | | | | 5th | 315 | 149 | 306 | 94 |
| Stewart | 2 | 0 | 12 | 0 | | | | | 6th | 327 | 154 | 325 | 94 |
| Thorpe | 4 | 0 | 29 | 0 | | | | | 7th | 327 | 157 | 346 | 94 |
| KENT | O | M | R | W | O | M | R | W | 8th | 327 | 157 | 372 | |
| Merrick | 12 | 4 | 33 | 0 | 25.3 | 3 | 86 | 3 | 9th | 333 | 166 | 385 | |
| Igglesden | 16 | 2 | 51 | 2 | 26 | 6 | 81 | 2 | 10th | 358 | 178 | 385 | |
| Penn | 15 | 4 | 36 | 4 | 26 | 9 | 70 | 1 | | | | | |
| Ellison | 7 | 0 | 43 | 2 | 35 | 9 | 102 | 3 | | | | | |
| Fleming | 3 | 0 | 12 | 1 | 11 | 7 | 18 | 0 | | | | | |
| Ward | | | | | 7 | 1 | 20 | 1 | | | | | |

## LANCASHIRE vs. YORKSHIRE
at Old Trafford on 2nd, 3rd, 5th August 1991
Toss : Lancashire. Umpires : A.A.Jones and A.G.T.Whitehead
Match drawn. Lancashire 7 pts (Bt: 3, Bw: 4), Yorkshire 7 pts (Bt: 4, Bw: 3)

### YORKSHIRE
| | | | | |
|---|---|---:|---|---:|
| M.D.Moxon * | c Hegg b Wasim Akram | 0 | c Atherton b DeFreitas | 30 |
| A.A.Metcalfe | c Wasim Akram b DeFreitas | 30 | not out | 113 |
| D.Byas | c Atherton b Wasim Akram | 0 | run out | 26 |
| R.J.Blakey + | c Fairbrother b DeFreitas | 9 | c Yates b Lloyd | 7 |
| P.E.Robinson | b Martin | 58 | c Hegg b Fowler | 44 |
| S.A.Kellett | b Watkinson | 81 | not out | 1 |
| C.S.Pickles | c Martin b Wasim Akram | 50 | | |
| P.Carrick | c Watkinson b Yates | 26 | | |
| D.Gough | b Wasim Akram | 9 | | |
| P.J.Hartley | not out | 6 | | |
| M.A.Robinson | b Wasim Akram | 4 | | |
| Extras | (b 2,lb 8,w 6,nb 29) | 45 | (b 7,lb 7,w 1,nb 2) | 17 |
| TOTAL | | 318 | (for 4 wkts dec) | 238 |

### LANCASHIRE
| | | | | |
|---|---|---:|---|---:|
| G.D.Mendis | lbw b Robinson M.A. | 10 | not out | 59 |
| G.Fowler | c Byas b Robinson M.A. | 9 | c Moxon b Hartley | 4 |
| W.K.Hegg + | c Blakey b Hartley | 19 | | |
| M.A.Atherton | not out | 114 | (3) not out | 37 |
| N.H.Fairbrother * | c Gough b Robinson M.A. | 32 | | |
| G.D.Lloyd | c Blakey b Carrick | 31 | | |
| M.Watkinson | b Carrick | 21 | | |
| Wasim Akram | c Robinson M.A. b Carrick | 14 | | |
| P.A.J.DeFreitas | b Carrick | 5 | | |
| G.Yates | not out | 10 | | |
| P.J.Martin | | | | |
| Extras | (b 3,lb 2,nb 6) | 11 | (b 2,lb 2,w 1) | 5 |
| TOTAL | | (for 8 wkts dec) 276 | (for 1 wkt) | 105 |

| LANCASHIRE | O | M | R | W | O | M | R | W | FALL OF WICKETS | | | | |
|---|---|---|---|---|---|---|---|---|---|---|---|---|---|
| | | | | | | | | | | YOR | LAN | YOR | LAN |
| Wasim Akram | 22.2 | 1 | 91 | 5 | 5 | 2 | 9 | 0 | 1st | 0 | 18 | 49 | 29 |
| DeFreitas | 19 | 2 | 66 | 2 | 9.3 | 2 | 23 | 1 | 2nd | 1 | 21 | 107 | |
| Martin | 18 | 5 | 41 | 1 | 1 | 0 | 1 | 0 | 3rd | 16 | 52 | 132 | |
| Watkinson | 27 | 1 | 93 | 1 | 2.3 | 1 | 5 | 0 | 4th | 93 | 109 | 229 | |
| Yates | 11 | 3 | 17 | 1 | 19 | 0 | 88 | 0 | 5th | 139 | 175 | | |
| Fowler | | | | | 7 | 0 | 41 | 1 | 6th | 241 | 218 | | |
| Lloyd | | | | | 10 | 0 | 57 | 1 | 7th | 286 | 239 | | |
| YORKSHIRE | O | M | R | W | O | M | R | W | 8th | 306 | 253 | | |
| Hartley | 17 | 2 | 72 | 1 | 9 | 2 | 28 | 1 | 9th | 306 | | | |
| Robinson M.A. | 14 | 4 | 43 | 3 | 5 | 0 | 34 | 0 | 10th | 318 | | | |
| Gough | 13 | 2 | 51 | 0 | 4 | 0 | 23 | 0 | | | | | |
| Carrick | 30 | 11 | 75 | 4 | 5 | 1 | 12 | 0 | | | | | |
| Pickles | 9 | 0 | 30 | 0 | 2 | 0 | 4 | 0 | | | | | |

## WORCESTERSHIRE vs. WARWICKSHIRE
at Worcester on 2nd, 3rd, 5th August 1991
Toss : Worcestershire. Umpires : J.W.Holder and R.C.Tolchard
Worcs won by an inns & 33 runs. Worcs 23 pts (Bt: 4, Bw: 3), Warwicks 6 pts (Bt: 3, Bw: 3)
100 overs scores :Warwickshire 271 for 8

### WORCESTERSHIRE
| | | | |
|---|---|---:|
| T.S.Curtis * | c Ostler b Donald | 10 |
| T.M.Moody | c Asif Din b Reeve | 210 |
| G.A.Hick | b Donald | 4 |
| D.B.D'Oliveira | run out | 10 |
| S.J.Rhodes + | c Ostler b Reeve | 48 |
| I.T.Botham | c Donald b Asif Din | 81 |
| S.R.Lampitt | lbw b Reeve | 0 |
| R.K.Illingworth | c Holloway b Munton | 21 |
| P.J.Newport | not out | 26 |
| N.V.Radford | not out | 10 |
| G.R.Dilley | | |
| Extras | (b 10,lb 11,w 5,nb 8) | 34 |
| TOTAL | (for 8 wkts dec) | 454 |

### WARWICKSHIRE
| | | | | |
|---|---|---:|---|---:|
| A.J.Moles | b Dilley | 9 | lbw b Dilley | 21 |
| J.D.Ratcliffe | b Newport | 48 | c Hick b Botham | 28 |
| Asif Din | c Moody b Radford | 0 | (6) b Botham | 3 |
| D.P.Ostler | b Newport | 55 | b Botham | 0 |
| D.A.Reeve | st Rhodes b Illingworth | 97 | b Dilley | 0 |
| T.A.Lloyd * | c D'Oliveira b Newport | 0 | (3) lbw b Botham | 1 |
| P.C.L.Holloway + | c Botham b Radford | 16 | c Rhodes b Botham | 41 |
| G.C.Small | lbw b Botham | 6 | c D'Oliveira b Botham | 13 |
| T.A.Munton | c Botham b Dilley | 12 | lbw b Botham | 0 |
| A.A.Donald | c Rhodes b Dilley | 18 | b Newport | 12 |
| A.R.K.Pierson | not out | 2 | not out | 0 |
| Extras | (b 1,lb 13,w 1,nb 20) | 35 | (lb 2,w 1,nb 1) | 4 |
| TOTAL | | 298 | | 123 |

| WARWICKS | O | M | R | W | O | M | R | W | FALL OF WICKETS | | | | |
|---|---|---|---|---|---|---|---|---|---|---|---|---|---|
| | | | | | | | | | | WOR | WAR | WAR | WOR |
| Donald | 17 | 3 | 90 | 2 | | | | | 1st | 17 | 17 | 46 | |
| Small | 18 | 3 | 72 | 0 | | | | | 2nd | 25 | 48 | 51 | |
| Reeve | 21 | 3 | 67 | 3 | | | | | 3rd | 46 | 78 | 51 | |
| Munton | 23 | 4 | 87 | 1 | | | | | 4th | 190 | 194 | 52 | |
| Pierson | 13 | 1 | 80 | 0 | | | | | 5th | 376 | 194 | 52 | |
| Asif Din | 6 | 0 | 37 | 1 | | | | | 6th | 376 | 228 | 67 | |
| WORCS | O | M | R | W | O | M | R | W | 7th | 414 | 240 | 93 | |
| Dilley | 27.2 | 7 | 56 | 3 | 12 | 3 | 23 | 2 | 8th | 431 | 266 | 95 | |
| Radford | 20 | 4 | 55 | 2 | 6 | 0 | 18 | 0 | 9th | | 292 | 119 | |
| Illingworth | 14 | 2 | 32 | 1 | | | | | 10th | | 298 | 123 | |
| Botham | 20 | 5 | 43 | 1 | 18 | 5 | 54 | 7 | | | | | |
| Newport | 21 | 2 | 59 | 3 | 5.2 | 1 | 26 | 1 | | | | | |
| Lampitt | 9 | 0 | 38 | 0 | | | | | | | | | |
| D'Oliveira | 1 | 0 | 1 | 0 | | | | | | | | | |

## SUSSEX vs. NORTHANTS
at Eastbourne on 2nd, 3rd, 5th August 1991
Toss : Sussex. Umpires : R.Palmer and D.R.Shepherd
Match drawn. Sussex 7 pts (Bt: 3, Bw: 4), Northants 3 pts (Bt: 1, Bw: 2)
100 overs scores : Sussex 254 for 5

### SUSSEX
| | | | | |
|---|---|---:|---|---:|
| N.J.Lenham | c Penberthy b Baptiste | 75 | b Taylor | 6 |
| D.M.Smith | c & b Baptiste | 67 | lbw b Baptiste | 39 |
| P.W.G.Parker * | b Baptiste | 6 | c & b Baptiste | 18 |
| A.P.Wells | lbw b Baptiste | 0 | c Taylor b Baptiste | 11 |
| M.P.Speight | c Penberthy b Cook | 89 | b Penberthy | 22 |
| C.M.Wells | c Lamb b Curran | 12 | not out | 20 |
| A.I.C.Dodemaide | b Cook | 28 | c Ripley b Baptiste | 1 |
| P.Moores + | b Cook | 7 | run out | 5 |
| B.T.P.Donelan | not out | 17 | b Curran | 2 |
| I.D.K.Salisbury | not out | 10 | c Larkins b Curran | 0 |
| A.N.Jones | | | not out | 7 |
| Extras | (b 2,lb 4) | 6 | (lb 6) | 6 |
| TOTAL | (for 8 wkts dec) | 317 | (for 9 wkts dec) | 137 |

### NORTHANTS
| | | | | |
|---|---|---:|---|---:|
| A.Fordham | b Jones | 0 | b Dodemaide | 14 |
| N.A.Stanley | b Dodemaide | 6 | (3) c & b Dodemaide | 36 |
| W.Larkins | b Wells C.M. | 34 | (2) c & b Dodemaide | 45 |
| A.J.Lamb * | c Wells A.P. b Salisbury | 13 | c Salisbury b Donelan | 32 |
| K.M.Curran | c Smith b Jones | 24 | b Salisbury | 34 |
| A.L.Penberthy | b Jones | 26 | (8) c Moores b Donelan | 8 |
| E.A.E.Baptiste | b Salisbury | 8 | (6) c Donelan b Salisbury | 14 |
| D.Ripley + | b Donelan | 22 | (9) not out | 11 |
| R.G.Williams | b Donelan | 22 | (7) st Moores b Salisbury | 35 |
| N.G.B.Cook | c Wells A.P. b Salisbury | 10 | | |
| J.P.Taylor | not out | 3 | (10) not out | 0 |
| Extras | (b 11,lb 5,nb 9) | 25 | (b 1,lb 10,nb 3) | 14 |
| TOTAL | | 193 | (for 8 wkts) | 243 |

| NORTHANTS | O | M | R | W | O | M | R | W | FALL OF WICKETS | | | | |
|---|---|---|---|---|---|---|---|---|---|---|---|---|---|
| | | | | | | | | | | SUS | NOR | SUS | NOR |
| Taylor | 9 | 1 | 37 | 0 | 11 | 1 | 33 | 1 | 1st | 142 | 0 | 8 | 24 |
| Baptiste | 30 | 8 | 79 | 4 | 19 | 2 | 64 | 4 | 2nd | 145 | 21 | 64 | 77 |
| Penberthy | 9 | 2 | 22 | 0 | 4 | 0 | 9 | 1 | 3rd | 145 | 59 | 69 | 110 |
| Cook | 31 | 7 | 74 | 3 | 3 | 2 | 1 | 0 | 4th | 166 | 61 | 90 | 158 |
| Curran | 14 | 5 | 33 | 1 | 4 | 1 | 19 | 2 | 5th | 212 | 108 | 103 | 182 |
| Williams | 26 | 4 | 66 | 0 | 3 | 1 | 5 | 0 | 6th | 266 | 126 | 104 | 210 |
| SUSSEX | O | M | R | W | O | M | R | W | 7th | 285 | 126 | 116 | 221 |
| Jones | 12 | 3 | 36 | 3 | 4 | 0 | 19 | 0 | 8th | 290 | 162 | 126 | 242 |
| Dodemaide | 23 | 4 | 52 | 1 | 20 | 7 | 45 | 3 | 9th | | 179 | 126 | |
| Salisbury | 21 | 6 | 35 | 3 | 15.5 | 0 | 66 | 3 | 10th | | 193 | | |
| Wells C.M. | 9 | 2 | 19 | 1 | 6 | 1 | 22 | 0 | | | | | |
| Donelan | 19.3 | 8 | 35 | 2 | 26 | 0 | 80 | 2 | | | | | |

# BRITANNIC ASSURANCE CHAMPIONSHIP

## HEADLINES

### Britannic Assurance Championship

### 2nd - 5th August

• Two outstanding individual performances from Tom Moody and Ian Botham brought Worcestershire victory over neighbours Warwickshire by an innings and 33 runs at Worcester. Moody gave Warwickshire followers a reminder of the quality of his batting by hitting a career-best 210 off his former county as Worcestershire reached 454 for eight, then, after the visitors had just failed in their quest to avoid the follow-on, they were hurried to defeat by the best figures of Botham's 18-year career in county cricket – recorded the day after his recall to the England team for the Oval Test. The only consolation for the leaders was that, despite their third defeat of the season, they had actually increased their advantage to 50 points.

• Hampshire were the only other side to win, defeating Middlesex by five wickets at Lord's. Phil Tufnell had made his Test selection a formality by taking a career-best seven for 116 in Hampshire's first innings, but could not prevent the visitors claiming a lead of 32; nor could the Middlesex slow-left-armer, even with four more wickets, stop David Gower, with 80 not out, his highest score of the season, steering Hampshire to their second successive Championship victory.

• Surrey, looking to close the gap on the leaders, were outplayed for long periods by Kent at Canterbury. Centuries for Mark Benson and Matthew Fleming, who shared a fifth-wicket stand of 178 carried Kent's first innings to 358, then Surrey's last eight wickets fell for 58 to concede a lead of 180. Darren Bicknell's 151 took the visitors to safety and when Kent lost five wickets for seven runs in the final overs of the match, a remarkable victory became a possibility, if only briefly.

• A positive conclusion to the Roses match at Old Trafford never looked likely, even after the first two days had produced much competitive cricket. Yorkshire could be pleased with their revival to 318 all out after losing their first three wickets for 16, then Michael Atherton and Phil Carrick enjoyed an intriguing battle in Lancashire's reply. Atherton completed his third 100 of the season and Carrick claimed his 1,000th victim of his first-class career when he bowled Phil DeFreitas. Although Ashley Metcalfe took advantage of some declaration bowling as he also passed the 100-mark, the weather's intervention soon placed Lancashire's target out of range.

• Run-scoring was never easy in Somerset's drawn match with Leicestershire at Weston-super-Mare, and will be remembered fondly only by off-spinner Harvey Trump who recorded career-best figures in Leicestershire's first innings.

• Northamptonshire finished 19 runs short of victory over Sussex at Eastbourne with two wickets in hand after they had staged an impressive revival on the final day, having conceded a first innings lead of 124.

## SOMERSET vs. LEICESTERSHIRE

at Weston-Super-Mare on 2nd, 3rd, 5th August 1991
Toss : Leicestershire. Umpires : B.Hassan and B.J.Meyer
Match drawn. Somerset 5 pts (Bt: 2, Bw: 3), Leicestershire 5 pts (Bt: 2, Bw: 3)
100 overs scores : Leicestershire 234 for 8, Somerset 205 for 7

**LEICESTERSHIRE**

| | | | | | |
|---|---|---|---|---|---|
| T.J.Boon * | c Roebuck b Trump | 61 | lbw b Roebuck | | 40 |
| N.E.Briers * | c Trump b Rose | 2 | c & b Graveney | | 46 |
| P.N.Hepworth | b Graveney | 30 | c Harden b Graveney | | 4 |
| J.J.Whitaker | b Trump | 5 | b Roebuck | | 16 |
| L.Potter | b Trump | 22 | not out | | 43 |
| J.D.R.Benson | lbw b Hallett | 49 | st Burns b Roebuck | | 14 |
| C.C.Lewis | c Cook b Trump | 7 | b Swallow | | 43 |
| M.I.Gidley | lbw b Trump | 1 | (9) not out | | 4 |
| P.Whitticase + | c Harden b Trump | 52 | (8) c Hayhurst b Swallow | | 9 |
| D.J.Millns | lbw b Rose | 23 | | | |
| J.N.Maguire | not out | 0 | | | |
| Extras | (b 4,lb 2,w 1,nb 4) | 11 | (b 4,lb 7,nb 2) | | 13 |
| TOTAL | | 263 | (for 7 wkts dec) | | 232 |

**SOMERSET**

| | | | | | |
|---|---|---|---|---|---|
| S.J.Cook | c Whitticase b Lewis | 10 | c Whitticase b Lewis | | 0 |
| P.M.Roebuck | c Millns b Lewis | 4 | b Potter | | 14 |
| H.R.J.Trump | lbw b Rose | 0 | | | |
| R.J.Harden | c Hepworth b Millns | 64 | | | |
| A.N.Hayhurst | st Whitticase b Potter | 71 | (3) not out | | 26 |
| C.J.Tavare * | c Whitticase b Potter | 17 | (4) not out | | 20 |
| N.D.Burns + | not out | 29 | | | |
| G.D.Rose | c Whitaker b Millns | 14 | | | |
| I.G.Swallow | not out | 13 | | | |
| J.C.Hallett | | | | | |
| D.A.Graveney | | | | | |
| Extras | (lb 3,w 1) | 4 | (w 1) | | 1 |
| TOTAL | (for 7 wkts dec) | 226 | (for 2 wkts) | | 61 |

| SOMERSET | O | M | R | W | O | M | R | W | FALL OF WICKETS |
|---|---|---|---|---|---|---|---|---|---|
| | | | | | | | | | LEI | SOM | LEI | SOM |
| Rose | 16 | 6 | 24 | 2 | 3 | 0 | 7 | 0 | 1st | 3 | 5 | 83 | 0 |
| Hallett | 13 | 5 | 29 | 1 | 2 | 0 | 6 | 0 | 2nd | 77 | 6 | 90 | 27 |
| Trump | 33 | 7 | 107 | 6 | 18 | 3 | 82 | 0 | 3rd | 92 | 29 | 107 | |
| Hayhurst | 5 | 0 | 17 | 0 | | | | | 4th | 119 | 123 | 118 | |
| Graveney | 25 | 9 | 39 | 1 | 20 | 5 | 71 | 2 | 5th | 134 | 164 | 134 | |
| Swallow | 17 | 3 | 41 | 0 | 9 | 2 | 45 | 2 | 6th | 146 | 181 | 208 | |
| Roebuck | | | | | 8 | 4 | 10 | 3 | 7th | 162 | 204 | 222 | |
| LEICS | O | M | R | W | O | M | R | W | 8th | 210 | | | |
| Lewis | 14 | 6 | 22 | 3 | 4 | 2 | 10 | 1 | 9th | 259 | | | |
| Maguire | 23 | 5 | 62 | 0 | 4 | 2 | 5 | 0 | 10th | 263 | | | |
| Millns | 19 | 6 | 43 | 2 | 2 | 1 | 4 | 0 | | | | | |
| Gidley | 18 | 8 | 33 | 0 | 9 | 4 | 15 | 0 | | | | | |
| Potter | 31 | 11 | 52 | 2 | 9 | 5 | 13 | 1 | | | | | |
| Hepworth | 2 | 0 | 11 | 0 | 3 | 1 | 5 | 0 | | | | | |
| Boon | | | | | 5 | 3 | 9 | 0 | | | | | |

## MIDDLESEX vs. HAMPSHIRE

at Lord's on 2nd, 3rd, 5th August 1991
Toss : Hampshire. Umpires : B.Leadbeater and K.E.Palmer
Hampshire won by 5 wickets. Middlesex 6 pts (Bt: 3, Bw: 3), Hampshire 23 pts (Bt: 3, Bw: 4)
100 overs scores :Hampshire 260 for 7

**MIDDLESEX**

| | | | | | |
|---|---|---|---|---|---|
| M.A.Roseberry | c Middleton b James | 47 | c Terry b Connor | | 38 |
| J.C.Pooley | b Shine | 4 | c Aymes b Connor | | 27 |
| M.W.Gatting * | b Shine | 0 | (4) b Smith | | 85 |
| M.R.Ramprakash | c Gower b James | 79 | (5) not out | | 28 |
| K.R.Brown | c James b Connor | 53 | (6) not out | | 6 |
| M.Keech | c Shine b James | 0 | | | |
| P.Farbrace + | c Middleton b Connor | 1 | | | |
| D.W.Headley | c Aymes b James | 26 | (3) st Aymes b Middleton | | 76 |
| C.W.Taylor | c Maru b Ayling | 11 | | | |
| P.C.R.Tufnell | c Maru b Ayling | 17 | | | |
| N.G.Cowans | not out | 4 | | | |
| Extras | (b 3,lb 5,nb 9) | 17 | (lb 7,w 3,nb 4) | | 14 |
| TOTAL | | 259 | (for 4 wkts dec) | | 274 |

**HAMPSHIRE**

| | | | | | |
|---|---|---|---|---|---|
| T.C.Middleton | c Gatting b Tufnell | 23 | c Farbrace b Tufnell | | 32 |
| V.P.Terry | c Farbrace b Tufnell | 25 | c Farbrace b Tufnell | | 39 |
| K.D.James | c Brown b Tufnell | 36 | (6) c Taylor b Headley | | 7 |
| R.A.Smith | st Farbrace b Tufnell | 55 | c Ramprakash b Tufnell | | 57 |
| D.I.Gower | c Headley b Tufnell | 40 | (3) not out | | 80 |
| M.C.J.Nicholas * | c Gatting b Tufnell | 4 | (5) b Tufnell | | 0 |
| J.R.Ayling | c Roseberry b Taylor | 58 | not out | | 10 |
| A.N Aymes + | b Cowans | 31 | | | |
| R.J.Maru | c Farbrace b Taylor | 0 | | | |
| C.A.Connor | b Tufnell | 7 | | | |
| K.J.Shine | not out | 4 | | | |
| Extras | (b 1,lb 5,w 1,nb 1) | 8 | (b 8,lb 9,w 2,nb 2) | | 21 |
| TOTAL | | 291 | (for 5 wkts) | | 246 |

| HAMPSHIRE | O | M | R | W | O | M | R | W | FALL OF WICKETS |
|---|---|---|---|---|---|---|---|---|---|
| | | | | | | | | | MID | HAM | MID | HAM |
| Shine | 15 | 3 | 70 | 2 | 11 | 0 | 48 | 0 | 1st | 6 | 58 | 53 |
| Connor | 18 | 3 | 61 | 2 | 11 | 1 | 61 | 2 | 2nd | 6 | 73 | 76 | 114 |
| Ayling | 20.2 | 6 | 52 | 2 | 2 | 0 | 8 | 0 | 3rd | 103 | 99 | 205 | 211 |
| Maru | 15 | 3 | 36 | 0 | 17 | 5 | 42 | 0 | 4th | 178 | 173 | 255 | 211 |
| James | 13 | 0 | 32 | 4 | 8 | 3 | 17 | 0 | 5th | 178 | 187 | | 234 |
| Smith | | | | | 9 | 1 | 55 | 1 | 6th | 190 | 192 | | |
| Middleton | | | | | 8 | 2 | 36 | 1 | 7th | 209 | 260 | | |
| MIDDLESEX | O | M | R | W | O | M | R | W | 8th | 225 | 260 | | |
| Cowans | 20 | 7 | 43 | 1 | 10 | 2 | 47 | 0 | 9th | 255 | 275 | | |
| Headley | 18 | 3 | 45 | 0 | 14 | 0 | 50 | 1 | 10th | 259 | 291 | | |
| Taylor | 26 | 9 | 65 | 2 | 6 | 1 | 20 | 0 | | | | | |
| Tufnell | 48 | 13 | 116 | 7 | 24.4 | 1 | 112 | 4 | | | | | |
| Ramprakash | 3 | 0 | 16 | 0 | | | | | | | | | |

# TOUR MATCHES

## DERBYSHIRE vs. SRI LANKA
at Derby on 2nd, 3rd, 5th August 1991
Toss : Derbyshire.  Umpires : H.D.Bird and J.D.Bond
Match drawn

**DERBYSHIRE**

| | | |
|---|---|---|
| K.J.Barnett * | c Tillekaratne b Wijeguna' | 68 |
| A.M.Brown | c Kuruppu b Ramanayake | 3 |
| C.J.Adams | c Mahanama b Wijeguna' | 24 |
| T.J.G.O'Gorman | c De Silva b Ramanayake | 1 |
| S.C.Goldsmith | b Wijegunawardene | 127 |
| D.G.Cork | c Tillekaratne b Ratnayake | 13 |
| E.McCray | lbw b Ramanayake | 31 |
| B.J.M.Maher + | b Ratnayake | 5 |
| A.E.Warner | c Atapattu b Wijeguna' | 52 |
| S.J.Base | c Mahanama b Anurasiri | 6 |
| R.W.Sladdin | not out | 0 |
| Extras | (lb 15,w 4,nb 9) | 28 |
| TOTAL | | 358 |

**SRI LANKA**

| | | |
|---|---|---|
| R.S.Mahanama | lbw b Base | 14 |
| D.S.B.P.Kuruppu | c Barnett b Sladdin | 76 |
| A.P.Gurusinha | b Goldsmith | 46 |
| U.C.Hathurusinghe | not out | 74 |
| C.P.Ramanayake | not out | 41 |
| P.A.De Silva * | | |
| H.P.Tillekaratne + | | |
| M.S.Atapattu | | |
| R.J.Ratnayake | | |
| K.I.W.Wijegunawardene | | |
| S.D.Anurasiri | | |
| Extras | (lb 8,nb 8) | 16 |
| TOTAL | (for 3 wkts) | 267 |

| SRI LANKA | O | M | R | W | O | M | R | W |
|---|---|---|---|---|---|---|---|---|
| Ratnayake' | 32 | 3 | 94 | 2 | | | | |
| Ramanayake | 24 | 6 | 84 | 3 | | | | |
| Wijeguna' | 31.3 | 9 | 97 | 4 | | | | |
| Anurasiri | 35 | 14 | 62 | 1 | | | | |
| Gurusinha | 3 | 2 | 6 | 0 | | | | |

| DERBYSHIRE | O | M | R | W | O | M | R | W |
|---|---|---|---|---|---|---|---|---|
| Base | 16 | 3 | 33 | 1 | | | | |
| Warner | 6 | 2 | 11 | 0 | | | | |
| Sladdin | 53 | 25 | 84 | 1 | | | | |
| Cork | 11 | 3 | 34 | 0 | | | | |
| Goldsmith | 13 | 4 | 31 | 1 | | | | |
| McCray | 17 | 6 | 34 | 0 | | | | |
| Barnett | 16 | 2 | 32 | 0 | | | | |

**FALL OF WICKETS**

| | DER | SRI | DER | SRI |
|---|---|---|---|---|
| 1st | 12 | 28 | | |
| 2nd | 55 | 92 | | |
| 3rd | 63 | 166 | | |
| 4th | 116 | | | |
| 5th | 141 | | | |
| 6th | 260 | | | |
| 7th | 272 | | | |
| 8th | 323 | | | |
| 9th | 354 | | | |
| 10th | 358 | | | |

## GLOUCESTERSHIRE vs. SRI LANKA
at Bristol on 6th, 7th August 1991
Toss : Gloucs.  Umpires : B.Leadbeater and G.A.Stickley
Gloucs won by 8 wickets

**SRI LANKA**

| | | | | |
|---|---|---|---|---|
| R.S.Mahanama | c Hancock b Gerrard | 26 | c Russell b Gilbert | 0 |
| D.S.B.P.Kuruppu | c Russell b Gilbert | 17 | c Athey b Gilbert | 10 |
| H.P.Tillekaratne | c Ball b Gerrard | 9 | (6) c Athey b Gerrard | 0 |
| U.C.Hathurusinghe | b Gerrard | 0 | c Wright b Gerrard | 11 |
| S.T.Jayasuriya | lbw b Gilbert | 3 | c Alleyne b Gerrard | 30 |
| A.P.Gurusinha * | c Ball b Gerrard | 0 | (3) b Ball | 36 |
| R.S.Kaluwitharana + | run out | 8 | lbw b Gerrard | 0 |
| R.J.Ratnayake | b Gilbert | 27 | c Hunt b Gerrard | 29 |
| R.Madurasinghe | c Russell b Babington | 4 | not out | 6 |
| F.S.Ahangama | not out | 0 | c Alleyne b Gilbert | 0 |
| M.Muralitharan | c Ball b Gilbert | 0 | c Wright b Gerrard | 5 |
| Extras | (lb 3) | 3 | (lb 4,nb 3) | 7 |
| TOTAL | | 97 | | 134 |

**GLOUCESTERSHIRE**

| | | | | |
|---|---|---|---|---|
| R.J.Scott | c Hathurusinghe b Gurusinha | 8 | | |
| A.J.Hunt | c Tillekaratne b Ratnayake | 3 | c Mahanama b Ratnayake | 12 |
| A.J.Wright * | lbw b Ratnayake | 47 | | |
| C.W.J.Athey | c Kuruppu b Ratnayake | 6 | | |
| M.W.Alleyne | c Tillekaratne b Ahangama | 91 | (4) not out | 10 |
| T.Hancock | c Tillekaratne b Ahangama | 1 | (3) c & b Ratnayake | 1 |
| R.C.Russell + | lbw b Ratnayake | 2 | (1) not out | 22 |
| M.C.J.Ball | c Madurasinghe b Gurusinha | 1 | | |
| D.R.Gilbert | c Kaluwitharana b Mad'singhe | 5 | | |
| A.M.Babington | b Ratnayake | 0 | | |
| M.J.Gerrard | not out | 0 | | |
| Extras | (b 4,lb 6,w 2,nb 11) | 23 | (lb 1,nb 2) | 3 |
| TOTAL | | 187 | (for 2 wkts) | 48 |

| GLOUCS | O | M | R | W | O | M | R | W |
|---|---|---|---|---|---|---|---|---|
| Gilbert | 12.3 | 1 | 53 | 4 | 13 | 4 | 23 | 3 |
| Babington | 10 | 4 | 15 | 1 | 4 | 0 | 17 | 0 |
| Gerrard | 10 | 2 | 20 | 4 | 15.1 | 2 | 40 | 6 |
| Ball | 1 | 0 | 6 | 0 | 7 | 2 | 29 | 1 |
| Scott | | | | | 10 | 1 | 21 | 0 |

| SRI LANKA | O | M | R | W | O | M | R | W |
|---|---|---|---|---|---|---|---|---|
| Ratnayake | 26.3 | 2 | 97 | 6 | 8 | 0 | 29 | 2 |
| Ahangama | 22 | 8 | 51 | 1 | 6 | 3 | 12 | 0 |
| Gurusinha | 11 | 3 | 16 | 2 | | | | |
| Madurasinghe | 2 | 0 | 13 | 1 | | | | |
| Hathurusinghe | | | | | 1.3 | 0 | 6 | 0 |

**FALL OF WICKETS**

| | SRI | GLO | SRI | GLO |
|---|---|---|---|---|
| 1st | 44 | 6 | 0 | 35 |
| 2nd | 46 | 40 | 33 | 37 |
| 3rd | 52 | 51 | 58 | |
| 4th | 57 | 89 | 78 | |
| 5th | 57 | 90 | 84 | |
| 6th | 59 | 117 | 94 | |
| 7th | 69 | 120 | 105 | |
| 8th | 97 | 154 | 127 | |
| 9th | 97 | 158 | 127 | |
| 10th | 97 | 187 | 134 | |

## ESSEX vs. WEST INDIES
at Chelmsford on 3rd, 4th, 5th August 1991
Toss : West Indies.  Umpires : G.I.Burgess and N.T.Plews
Match drawn

**WEST INDIES**

| | | | | | |
|---|---|---|---|---|---|
| P.V.Simmons | lbw b Pringle | 51 | (6) c Gooch b Andrew | 40 |
| C.B.Lambert | c & b Such | 116 | (5) not out | 82 |
| P.J.L.Dujon | not out | 142 | (7) not out | 27 |
| D.Williams + | c Andrew b Pringle | 24 | | |
| H.A.G.Anthony | c Childs b Andrew | 0 | | |
| D.L.Haynes | not out | 23 | (1) c Hussain b Such | 19 |
| R.B.Richardson | | | (2) c Such b Andrew | 5 |
| I.V.A.Richards * | | | (3) lbw b Pringle | 23 |
| C.L.Hooper | | | (4) c Stephenson b Such | 12 |
| C.E.L.Ambrose | | | | |
| I.B.A.Allen | | | | |
| Extras | (lb 6,nb 5) | 11 | (b 2,lb 2,nb 5) | 9 |
| TOTAL | (for 4 wkts dec) | 367 | (for 5 wkts dec) | 217 |

**ESSEX**

| | | | | | |
|---|---|---|---|---|---|
| A.C.Seymour | c Williams b Richards | 74 | c Hooper b Ambrose | 5 |
| J.P.Stephenson | c Simmons b Ambrose | 0 | c & b Anthony | 33 |
| P.J.Prichard | c Williams b Anthony | 5 | c Hooper b Allen | 13 |
| Salim Malik | b Simmons | 9 | | |
| N.Hussain | c Williams b Simmons | 28 | (4) c Williams b Anthony | 41 |
| G.A.Gooch * | c Williams b Ambrose | 66 | not out | 25 |
| M.A.Garnham + | c Anthony b Hooper | 12 | (5) not out | 8 |
| D.R.Pringle | not out | 31 | | |
| S.J.W.Andrew | c Simmons b Ambrose | 0 | | |
| J.H.Childs | c Richards b Hooper | 1 | | |
| P.M.Such | b Ambrose | 4 | | |
| Extras | (lb 4,w 1,nb 14) | 19 | (lb 4,nb 7) | 11 |
| TOTAL | | 249 | (for 4 wkts) | 136 |

| ESSEX | O | M | R | W | O | M | R | W |
|---|---|---|---|---|---|---|---|---|
| Andrew | 19 | 1 | 90 | 1 | 14 | 1 | 51 | 2 |
| Pringle | 16 | 4 | 48 | 2 | 11 | 2 | 29 | 1 |
| Gooch | 13 | 4 | 46 | 0 | | | | |
| Childs | 19 | 8 | 64 | 0 | 15 | 5 | 51 | 0 |
| Stephenson | 10 | 2 | 37 | 0 | 6 | 0 | 26 | 0 |
| Such | 28 | 8 | 76 | 1 | 14 | 3 | 56 | 2 |

| WEST INDIES | O | M | R | W | O | M | R | W |
|---|---|---|---|---|---|---|---|---|
| Ambrose | 14.5 | 6 | 29 | 4 | 7 | 5 | 4 | 1 |
| Allen | 10 | 1 | 27 | 0 | 9 | 2 | 48 | 1 |
| Simmons | 23 | 4 | 84 | 2 | | | | |
| Anthony | 10 | 1 | 23 | 1 | 7 | 2 | 15 | 2 |
| Richards | 13 | 3 | 49 | 1 | 7 | 0 | 18 | 0 |
| Hooper | 12 | 1 | 33 | 2 | 17 | 2 | 47 | 0 |

**FALL OF WICKETS**

| | WI | ESS | WI | ESS |
|---|---|---|---|---|
| 1st | 93 | 4 | 15 | 8 |
| 2nd | 225 | 34 | 47 | 24 |
| 3rd | 296 | 45 | 59 | 89 |
| 4th | 299 | 106 | 60 | 106 |
| 5th | | 153 | 151 | |
| 6th | | 192 | | |
| 7th | | 231 | | |
| 8th | | 231 | | |
| 9th | | 234 | | |
| 10th | | 249 | | |

## HEADLINES

### Tetley Bitter Challenge

### 2nd - 5th August

• The Sri Lankans' visit to Derby was not a memorable one, their match against Derbyshire not developing beyond the first two innings, but at least Steve Goldsmith made the most of the home side's extended batting time to record his maiden first-class century.

### 3rd - 5th August

• The West Indies' county programme ended with an air of anti-climax at Chelmsford, a re-arranged first innings batting order and a delayed second innings declaration showing that batting practice rather than match-winning was the tourists' prime concern. Clayton Lambert and Jeff Dujon both made their highest scores of the tour in West Indies' first innings.

### 6th - 7th August

• Gloucestershire needed less than two days to beat Sri Lanka by eight wickets at Bristol. Martin Gerrard bettered his career best in each innings to return match figures of 10 for 60 as the tourists' batsmen were not able to come to terms with a lively pitch.

# BRITANNIC ASSURANCE CHAMPIONSHIP

## KENT vs. HAMPSHIRE

at Canterbury on 6th, 7th, 8th August 1991
Toss : Kent. Umpires : J.C.Balderstone and K.J.Lyons
Match drawn. Kent 7 pts (Bt: 3, Bw: 4), Hampshire 6 pts (Bt: 2, Bw: 4)

### KENT

| | | | | | |
|---|---|---|---|---|---|
| T.R.Ward | c Aymes b Shine | 65 | c Nicholas b Connor | | 50 |
| V.J.Wells | c Middleton b Shine | 1 | c Ayling b James | | 28 |
| N.R.Taylor | b Connor | 24 | not out | | 59 |
| G.R.Cowdrey | c Terry b Shine | 16 | b James | | 12 |
| M.V.Fleming | lbw b Ayling | 12 | b Middleton | | 23 |
| S.A.Marsh *+ | c Gower b Ayling | 73 | (6) st Aymes b Middleton | | 2 |
| R.M.Ellison | not out | 61 | (7) not out | | 19 |
| R.P.Davis | c Gower b Connor | 27 | | | |
| C.Penn | run out | 3 | | | |
| T.A.Merrick | lbw b Connor | 0 | | | |
| A.P.Igglesden | run out | 1 | | | |
| Extras | (lb 1,w 1,nb 5) | 7 | (b 1,lb 8,nb 1) | | 10 |
| TOTAL | | 290 | (for 5 wkts dec) | | 203 |

### HAMPSHIRE

| | | | | | |
|---|---|---|---|---|---|
| V.P.Terry | c Davis b Ellison | 26 | b Merrick | | 7 |
| C.L.Smith | c Marsh b Merrick | 10 | (5) c Taylor b Davis | | 2 |
| R.J.Maru | c Fleming b Igglesden | 10 | (9) not out | | 21 |
| T.C.Middleton | st Marsh b Davis | 66 | (2) c Marsh b Davis | | 26 |
| D.I.Gower | c Marsh b Merrick | 36 | (4) c Ward b Davis | | 40 |
| K.D.James | b Merrick | 7 | (3) c Marsh b Penn | | 15 |
| M.C.J.Nicholas * | lbw b Fleming | 33 | (6) run out | | 15 |
| J.R.Ayling | c Marsh b Fleming | 19 | (7) c Wells b Ellison | | 17 |
| A.N Aymes + | c Marsh b Merrick | 8 | (8) not out | | 48 |
| C.A.Connor | b Davis | 7 | | | |
| K.J.Shine | not out | 2 | | | |
| Extras | (b 5,lb 3,w 2,nb 7) | 17 | (lb 1,nb 4) | | 5 |
| TOTAL | | 241 | (for 7 wkts) | | 196 |

| HAMPSHIRE | O | M | R | W | O | M | R | W |
|---|---|---|---|---|---|---|---|---|
| Shine | 18 | 3 | 75 | 3 | 6 | 1 | 23 | 0 |
| Connor | 22 | 5 | 57 | 3 | 10 | 1 | 39 | 1 |
| James | 13 | 2 | 35 | 0 | 12 | 0 | 44 | 2 |
| Ayling | 22 | 1 | 64 | 2 | 3 | 2 | 1 | 0 |
| Maru | 24.3 | 6 | 58 | 0 | | | | |
| Nicholas | | | | | 4 | 0 | 18 | 0 |
| Smith | | | | | 4 | 0 | 28 | 0 |
| Middleton | | | | | 4 | 0 | 41 | 2 |

| FALL OF WICKETS | | | | |
|---|---|---|---|---|
| | KEN | HAM | KEN | HAM |
| 1st | 10 | 17 | 74 | 10 |
| 2nd | 76 | 36 | 86 | 43 |
| 3rd | 104 | 69 | 108 | 55 |
| 4th | 121 | 121 | 154 | 77 |
| 5th | 121 | 137 | 164 | 92 |
| 6th | 236 | 187 | | 116 |
| 7th | 282 | 215 | | 131 |
| 8th | 287 | 221 | | |
| 9th | 287 | 238 | | |
| 10th | 290 | 241 | | |

| KENT | O | M | R | W | O | M | R | W |
|---|---|---|---|---|---|---|---|---|
| Merrick | 22.5 | 2 | 67 | 4 | 17 | 2 | 54 | 1 |
| Igglesden | 17 | 3 | 43 | 1 | 6 | 1 | 10 | 0 |
| Ellison | 16 | 0 | 47 | 1 | 4 | 0 | 13 | 1 |
| Penn | 13 | 2 | 33 | 0 | 8 | 0 | 32 | 1 |
| Davis | 10 | 4 | 25 | 2 | 15.4 | 4 | 62 | 3 |
| Fleming | 8 | 0 | 18 | 2 | 9 | 2 | 24 | 0 |

## DERBYSHIRE vs. ESSEX

at Derby on 6th, 7th, 8th August 1991
Toss : Essex. Umpires : R.A.White and P.B.Wight
Derbyshire won by 199 runs. Derbyshire 21 pts (Bt: 1, Bw: 4), Essex 4 pts (Bt: 0, Bw: 4)

### DERBYSHIRE

| | | | | | |
|---|---|---|---|---|---|
| K.J.Barnett * | b Foster | 16 | b Stephenson | | 91 |
| P.D.Bowler | c Knight b Andrew | 6 | c Salim Malik b Andrew | | 56 |
| J.E.Morris | c Garnham b Topley | 35 | c Salim Malik b Andrew | | 36 |
| T.J.G.O'Gorman | b Topley | 25 | c Prichard b Stephenson | | 28 |
| S.C.Goldsmith | c Garnham b Andrew | 3 | not out | | 60 |
| C.J.Adams | c & b Topley | 37 | (7) c Garnham b Andrew | | 17 |
| K.M.Krikken + | lbw b Foster | 9 | (8) run out | | 3 |
| D.G.Cork | c Garnham b Topley | 3 | | | |
| S.J.Base | c Childs b Topley | 11 | (6) c Hussain b Stephenson | | 3 |
| D.E.Malcolm | c Seymour b Foster | 10 | | | |
| O.H.Mortensen | not out | 2 | | | |
| Extras | (lb 11,w 2,nb 10) | 23 | (b 4,lb 3,w 4,nb 13) | | 24 |
| TOTAL | | 180 | (for 7 wkts dec) | | 318 |

### ESSEX

| | | | | | |
|---|---|---|---|---|---|
| A.C.Seymour | c Barnett b Cork | 22 | c Barnett b Cork | | 0 |
| J.P.Stephenson | lbw b Cork | 14 | c Krikken b Base | | 35 |
| P.J.Prichard | c Adams b Mortensen | 20 | c O'Gorman b Mortensen | | 11 |
| Salim Malik | c Krikken b Cork | 15 | c O'Gorman b Base | | 27 |
| N.Hussain | lbw b Mortensen | 0 | c Goldsmith b Base | | 12 |
| N.V.Knight | b Cork | 4 | c Krikken b Malcolm | | 24 |
| M.A.Garnham + | b Cork | 15 | b Malcolm | | 0 |
| N.A.Foster * | c Base b Cork | 19 | (9) c Krikken b Malcolm | | 24 |
| T.D.Topley | c Krikken b Cork | 11 | (8) lbw b Cork | | 9 |
| S.J.W.Andrew | c Base b Cork | 0 | not out | | 2 |
| J.H.Childs | not out | 1 | b Malcolm | | 19 |
| Extras | (nb 3) | 3 | (lb 2,w 2,nb 8) | | 12 |
| TOTAL | | 124 | | | 175 |

| ESSEX | O | M | R | W | O | M | R | W |
|---|---|---|---|---|---|---|---|---|
| Foster | 14 | 2 | 57 | 3 | 9 | 1 | 41 | 0 |
| Andrew | 14 | 4 | 33 | 2 | 17.3 | 2 | 71 | 3 |
| Topley | 17.2 | 1 | 79 | 5 | 14 | 0 | 65 | 0 |
| Childs | | | | | 17 | 6 | 48 | 0 |
| Stephenson | | | | | 23 | 2 | 86 | 3 |

| FALL OF WICKETS | | | | |
|---|---|---|---|---|
| | DER | ESS | DER | ESS |
| 1st | 18 | 37 | 145 | 3 |
| 2nd | 35 | 46 | 193 | 16 |
| 3rd | 81 | 74 | 203 | 54 |
| 4th | 95 | 74 | 262 | 91 |
| 5th | 112 | 75 | 275 | 94 |
| 6th | 150 | 79 | 308 | 103 |
| 7th | 150 | 107 | 318 | 119 |
| 8th | 154 | 117 | | 154 |
| 9th | 173 | 117 | | 154 |
| 10th | 180 | 124 | | 175 |

| DERBYSHIRE | O | M | R | W | O | M | R | W |
|---|---|---|---|---|---|---|---|---|
| Malcolm | 4 | 0 | 18 | 0 | 14.2 | 1 | 84 | 4 |
| Mortensen | 20 | 3 | 53 | 2 | 8 | 2 | 30 | 1 |
| Cork | 16.1 | 2 | 53 | 8 | 8 | 2 | 25 | 2 |
| Base | | | | | 14 | 3 | 34 | 3 |

## WARWICKSHIRE vs. SURREY

at Edgbaston on 6th, 7th, 8th August 1991
Toss : Warwickshire. Umpires : B.Dudleston and R.C.Tolchard
Surrey won by 67 runs. Warwickshire 5 pts (Bt: 1, Bw: 4), Surrey 22 pts (Bt: 2, Bw: 4)

### SURREY

| | | | | | |
|---|---|---|---|---|---|
| D.J.Bicknell | c Munton b Small | 18 | not out | | 75 |
| R.I.Alikhan | c Piper b Munton | 9 | c Ostler b Benjamin | | 0 |
| M.A.Lynch | lbw b Reeve | 10 | c Ostler b Small | | 1 |
| D.M.Ward | lbw b Reeve | 11 | c Munton b Small | | 14 |
| G.P.Thorpe | b Reeve | 6 | lbw b Benjamin | | 17 |
| I.A.Greig * | lbw b Munton | 22 | b Smith | | 52 |
| M.A.Feltham | not out | 69 | not out | | 14 |
| N.F.Sargeant + | c Ostler b Munton | 7 | | | |
| M.P.Bicknell | c Munton b Benjamin | 11 | | | |
| Waqar Younis | b Benjamin | 22 | | | |
| A.J.Murphy | b Reeve | 0 | | | |
| Extras | (b 1,lb 11,w 1,nb 8) | 21 | (b 2,lb 11,w 6,nb 3) | | 22 |
| TOTAL | | 206 | (for 5 wkts dec) | | 195 |

### WARWICKSHIRE

| | | | | | |
|---|---|---|---|---|---|
| A.J.Moles | b Feltham | 59 | b Feltham | | 37 |
| J.D.Ratcliffe | b Waqar Younis | 1 | b Waqar Younis | | 9 |
| T.A.Lloyd * | c Sargeant b Waqar Younis | 15 | lbw b Bicknell M.P. | | 17 |
| D.P.Ostler | b Murphy | 27 | run out | | 25 |
| Asif Din | b Feltham | 5 | (6) b Feltham | | 2 |
| D.A.Reeve | lbw b Waqar Younis | 25 | (5) c Sargeant b Feltham | | 7 |
| N.M.K.Smith | b Waqar Younis | 5 | not out | | 40 |
| K.J.Piper + | lbw b Waqar Younis | 5 | c Lynch b Waqar Younis | | 2 |
| G.C.Small | c Bicknell M.P. b Feltham | 8 | b Waqar Younis | | 6 |
| J.E.Benjamin | c & b Feltham | 1 | (11) c Lynch b Bicknell M.P. | | 11 |
| T.A.Munton | not out | 1 | (10) b Waqar Younis | | 4 |
| Extras | (b 2,lb 7,w 3,nb 3) | 15 | (lb 3,nb 4) | | 7 |
| TOTAL | | 167 | | | 167 |

| WARWICKS | O | M | R | W | O | M | R | W |
|---|---|---|---|---|---|---|---|---|
| Small | 14 | 4 | 38 | 1 | 19 | 7 | 26 | 2 |
| Benjamin | 22 | 3 | 62 | 2 | 19 | 4 | 64 | 2 |
| Munton | 19 | 8 | 40 | 3 | 17 | 7 | 46 | 0 |
| Reeve | 28 | 9 | 54 | 4 | 4 | 1 | 23 | 0 |
| Smith | | | | | 3 | 2 | 3 | 1 |
| Lloyd | | | | | 2 | 0 | 20 | 0 |

| FALL OF WICKETS | | | | |
|---|---|---|---|---|
| | SUR | WAR | SUR | WAR |
| 1st | 27 | 3 | 2 | 17 |
| 2nd | 33 | 35 | 7 | 63 |
| 3rd | 49 | 96 | 32 | 63 |
| 4th | 50 | 109 | 89 | 97 |
| 5th | 78 | 134 | 172 | 97 |
| 6th | 110 | 139 | | 107 |
| 7th | 118 | 151 | | 117 |
| 8th | 146 | 161 | | 137 |
| 9th | 186 | 166 | | 145 |
| 10th | 206 | 167 | | 167 |

| SURREY | O | M | R | W | O | M | R | W |
|---|---|---|---|---|---|---|---|---|
| Waqar Younis | 22 | 4 | 47 | 5 | 18 | 5 | 50 | 4 |
| Bicknell M.P. | 14 | 4 | 38 | 0 | 15.1 | 3 | 56 | 2 |
| Murphy | 14 | 4 | 32 | 1 | 7 | 2 | 30 | 0 |
| Feltham | 14 | 1 | 41 | 4 | 11 | 2 | 28 | 3 |

## SUSSEX vs. NOTTS

at Eastbourne on 6th, 7th, 8th August 1991
Toss : Notts. Umpires : R.Palmer and D.R.Shepherd
Match drawn. Sussex 3 pts (Bt: 2, Bw: 1), Notts 8 pts (Bt: 4, Bw: 4)
100 overs scores : Notts 335 for 4, Sussex 235 for 9

### NOTTS

| | | | | | |
|---|---|---|---|---|---|
| B.C.Broad | c Salisbury b Dodemaide | 158 | | | |
| P.Pollard | c Moores b Pigott | 13 | | | |
| R.T.Robinson * | b Jones | 95 | | | |
| D.W.Randall | b Salisbury | 26 | | | |
| P.Johnson | b Dodemaide | 52 | | | |
| K.P.Evans | c Moores b Pigott | 37 | | | |
| F.D.Stephenson | not out | 0 | | | |
| B.N.French + | c Moores b Dodemaide | 10 | | | |
| E.E.Hemmings | | | | | |
| R.A.Pick | | | | | |
| J.A.Afford | | | | | |
| Extras | (lb 10,nb 2) | 12 | | | |
| TOTAL | (for 7 wkts dec) | 403 | | | |

### SUSSEX

| | | | | | |
|---|---|---|---|---|---|
| N.J.Lenham | c Robinson b Stephenson | 85 | c Robinson b Afford | | 26 |
| D.M.Smith | b Stephenson | 10 | c Randall b Afford | | 46 |
| P.W.G.Parker * | b Hemmings | 24 | c Randall b Afford | | 2 |
| A.P.Wells | c Pollard b Hemmings | 6 | run out | | 73 |
| M.P.Speight | c French b Afford | 10 | not out | | 37 |
| A.I.C.Dodemaide | lbw b Afford | 2 | not out | | 0 |
| P.Moores + | c Pollard b Hemmings | 12 | | | |
| A.C.S.Pigott | c & b Afford | 12 | | | |
| B.T.P.Donelan | st French b Afford | 32 | | | |
| I.D.K.Salisbury | not out | 19 | | | |
| A.N.Jones | c French b Stephenson | 9 | | | |
| Extras | (b 7,lb 9,nb 4) | 20 | (lb 8,nb 1) | | 9 |
| TOTAL | | 241 | (for 4 wkts) | | 193 |

| SUSSEX | O | M | R | W | O | M | R | W |
|---|---|---|---|---|---|---|---|---|
| Jones | 13 | 2 | 32 | 1 | | | | |
| Dodemaide | 25 | 5 | 71 | 3 | | | | |
| Pigott | 24 | 5 | 66 | 2 | | | | |
| Salisbury | 32 | 1 | 118 | 1 | | | | |
| Donelan | 28 | 3 | 106 | 0 | | | | |

| FALL OF WICKETS | | | | |
|---|---|---|---|---|
| | NOT | SUS | SUS | NOT |
| 1st | 34 | 24 | 58 | |
| 2nd | 226 | 86 | 66 | |
| 3rd | 269 | 96 | 91 | |
| 4th | 321 | 111 | 193 | |
| 5th | 393 | 121 | | |
| 6th | 393 | 134 | | |
| 7th | 403 | 147 | | |
| 8th | | 193 | | |
| 9th | | 212 | | |
| 10th | | 241 | | |

| NOTTS | O | M | R | W | O | M | R | W |
|---|---|---|---|---|---|---|---|---|
| Stephenson | 16.3 | 5 | 26 | 3 | 11 | 0 | 29 | 0 |
| Pick | 6 | 1 | 20 | 0 | 6 | 2 | 17 | 0 |
| Evans | 8 | 2 | 22 | 0 | 7 | 2 | 12 | 0 |
| Hemmings | 35 | 12 | 88 | 3 | 34 | 10 | 77 | 0 |
| Afford | 37 | 15 | 69 | 4 | 35 | 17 | 50 | 3 |

# BRITANNIC ASSURANCE CHAMPIONSHIP

## LEICESTERSHIRE vs. YORKSHIRE

at Leicester on 6th, 7th, 8th August 1991
Toss : Yorkshire.  Umpires : J.D.Bond and D.O.Oslear
Match drawn.  Leicestershire 5 pts (Bt: 4, Bw: 1), Yorkshire 0 pts (Bt: 0, Bw: 0)
100 overs scores : Leicestershire 300 for 2

### LEICESTERSHIRE

| | | | | |
|---|---|---|---|---|
| T.J.Boon | c Kellett b Robinson M.A. | 102 | not out | 29 |
| N.E.Briers * | c Blakey b Hartley | 114 | not out | 51 |
| J.J.Whitaker | not out | 31 | | |
| P.N.Hepworth | not out | 40 | | |
| L.Potter | | | | |
| J.D.R.Benson | | | | |
| P.Whitticase + | | | | |
| D.J.Millns | | | | |
| C.Wilkinson | | | | |
| A.D.Mullally | | | | |
| J.N.Maguire | | | | |
| Extras | (lb 6,nb 7) | 13 | (lb 3,nb 3) | 6 |
| TOTAL | (for 2 wkts dec) | 300 | (for 0 wkts dec) | 86 |

### YORKSHIRE

| | | | | |
|---|---|---|---|---|
| M.D.Moxon * | c Whitticase b Mullally | 22 | c Hepworth b Millns | 12 |
| A.A.Metcalfe | c Potter b Millns | 0 | lbw b Millns | 2 |
| D.Byas | not out | 32 | not out | 122 |
| R.J.Blakey + | c Whitaker b Maguire | 8 | c Whitaker b Millns | 2 |
| P.E.Robinson | not out | 7 | c Briers b Millns | 9 |
| S.A.Kellett | | | b Millns | 3 |
| C.S.Pickles | | | c Potter b Millns | 0 |
| P.Carrick | | | c Benson b Hepworth | 61 |
| P.J.Hartley | | | b Hepworth | 2 |
| J.D.Batty | | | not out | 4 |
| M.A.Robinson | | | | |
| Extras | (lb 3,nb 2) | 5 | (b 1,lb 7,w 4,nb 5) | 17 |
| TOTAL | (for 3 wkts dec) | 74 | (for 8 wkts) | 234 |

| YORKSHIRE | O | M | R | W | O | M | R | W |
|---|---|---|---|---|---|---|---|---|
| Hartley | 24 | 3 | 78 | 1 | 3 | 1 | 7 | 0 |
| Robinson M.A. | 24 | 6 | 59 | 1 | 4 | 1 | 11 | 0 |
| Pickles | 13 | 2 | 45 | 0 | 2 | 0 | 9 | 0 |
| Carrick | 22 | 3 | 58 | 0 | | | | |
| Batty | 17 | 4 | 54 | 0 | | | | |
| Kellett | | | | | 2 | 0 | 3 | 0 |
| Robinson P.E. | | | | | 5 | 0 | 30 | 0 |
| Metcalfe | | | | | 3 | 0 | 23 | 0 |

| LEICS | O | M | R | W | O | M | R | W |
|---|---|---|---|---|---|---|---|---|
| Millns | 9 | 1 | 33 | 1 | 22 | 6 | 59 | 6 |
| Mullally | 10.4 | 1 | 35 | 1 | 9 | 2 | 20 | 0 |
| Maguire | 3 | 1 | 3 | 1 | 14 | 2 | 53 | 0 |
| Wilkinson | | | | | 12 | 3 | 35 | 0 |
| Potter | | | | | 7 | 1 | 20 | 0 |
| Benson | | | | | 4 | 1 | 9 | 0 |
| Hepworth | | | | | 11 | 3 | 29 | 2 |
| Boon | | | | | 1 | 0 | 1 | 0 |

### FALL OF WICKETS

| | LEI | YOR | LEI | YOR |
|---|---|---|---|---|
| 1st | 219 | 7 | | 7 |
| 2nd | 234 | 38 | | 19 |
| 3rd | | 64 | | 21 |
| 4th | | | | 49 |
| 5th | | | | 53 |
| 6th | | | | 53 |
| 7th | | | | 208 |
| 8th | | | | 214 |
| 9th | | | | |
| 10th | | | | |

## LANCASHIRE vs. NORTHANTS

at Lytham on 6th, 7th, 8th August 1991
Toss : Northants.  Umpires : A.A.Jones and A.G.T.Whitehead
Northants won by 53 runs.  Lancashire 2 pts (Bt: 0, Bw: 2), Northants 21 pts (Bt: 4, Bw: 1)
100 overs scores : Northants 409 for 6

### NORTHANTS

| | | |
|---|---|---|
| A.Fordham | c Allott b Martin | 10 |
| W.Larkins | lbw b Allott | 10 |
| N.A.Stanley | b Austin | 132 |
| A.J.Lamb * | c Hegg b Martin | 125 |
| A.L.Penberthy | c & b Yates | 38 |
| K.M.Curran | not out | 89 |
| E.A.E.Baptiste | st Hegg b Fitton | 14 |
| D.Ripley + | not out | 6 |
| A.R.Roberts | | |
| N.G.B.Cook | | |
| J.P.Taylor | | |
| Extras | (b 13,lb 8,w 5) | 26 |
| TOTAL | (for 6 wkts dec) | 450 |

### LANCASHIRE

| | | | | |
|---|---|---|---|---|
| G.D.Mendis | b Taylor | 4 | c Ripley b Cook | 19 |
| G.Fowler | lbw b Lamb | 24 | c Lamb b Curran | 24 |
| G.D.Lloyd | lbw b Lamb | 28 | c Fordham b Roberts | 79 |
| G.Yates | not out | 28 | (9) c Curran b Roberts | 0 |
| N.H.Fairbrother * | not out | 13 | (4) c Ripley b Taylor | 38 |
| N.J.Speak | | | (5) b Roberts | 13 |
| W.K.Hegg + | | | (6) c Baptiste b Curran | 37 |
| I.D.Austin | | | (7) c Curran b Roberts | 0 |
| J.D.Fitton | | | (8) c Fordham b Roberts | 60 |
| P.J.W.Allott | | | b Roberts | 6 |
| P.J.Martin | | | not out | 5 |
| Extras | (b 1,lb 1,nb 1) | 3 | (b 5,lb 8,nb 3) | 16 |
| TOTAL | (for 3 wkts dec) | 100 | | 297 |

| LANCASHIRE | O | M | R | W | O | M | R | W |
|---|---|---|---|---|---|---|---|---|
| Martin | 24 | 2 | 87 | 2 | | | | |
| Allott | 21 | 3 | 84 | 1 | | | | |
| Austin | 20 | 4 | 63 | 1 | | | | |
| Yates | 25 | 4 | 89 | 1 | | | | |
| Fitton | 22 | 1 | 106 | 1 | | | | |

| NORTHANTS | O | M | R | W | O | M | R | W |
|---|---|---|---|---|---|---|---|---|
| Taylor | 8 | 0 | 33 | 1 | 17 | 5 | 54 | 1 |
| Baptiste | 7 | 1 | 15 | 0 | 11 | 4 | 30 | 0 |
| Cook | 2 | 0 | 3 | 0 | 22 | 8 | 79 | 1 |
| Roberts | 2 | 2 | 0 | 0 | 23.3 | 7 | 72 | 6 |
| Lamb | 3.4 | 0 | 29 | 2 | | | | |
| Fordham | 4 | 0 | 18 | 0 | | | | |
| Curran | | | | | 15 | 3 | 49 | 2 |

### FALL OF WICKETS

| | NOR | LAN | NOR | LAN |
|---|---|---|---|---|
| 1st | 18 | 4 | | 37 |
| 2nd | 20 | 55 | | 47 |
| 3rd | 256 | 74 | | 141 |
| 4th | 286 | | | 178 |
| 5th | 382 | | | 185 |
| 6th | 409 | | | 193 |
| 7th | | | | 269 |
| 8th | | | | 281 |
| 9th | | | | 286 |
| 10th | | | | 297 |

## HEADLINES

### Britannic Assurance Championship

#### 6th - 8th August

• Warwickshire's Championship aspirations suffered another setback  when they fell to their second successive defeat, losing to Surrey by 67 runs at Edgbaston. Although the leaders retained their 50-point advantage, Surrey's 22 points lifted them into second place and marked them out as genuine title contenders. Warwickshire could not take full advantage from taking early wickets in both Surrey innings, and their batting again looked decidedly fragile, Waqar Younis's deadly combination of pace and direction that had now brought him 76 wickets in 13 matches proving too much.

• Neither Essex nor Nottinghamshire could take advantage of Warwickshire's difficulties. At Derby, Essex were undermined by a magnificent piece of fast bowling from Derbyshire's Dominic Cork, who claimed eight for 53, the best figures of the season, to celebrate his 20th birthday in the best possible manner, as Essex collapsed to 124 all out to concede a first innings deficit of 56. They could make little of their eventual target of 375 and were defeated by the crushing margin of 199 runs

• Chris Broad scored his fourth 100 of the season in Notts's first innings total of 403 for seven declared against Sussex at Eastbourne and seven wickets for spinners Eddie Hemmings and Andy Afford enabled Tim Robinson to enforce the follow-on. But a fourth-wicket stand of 102 between Alan Wells and Martin Speight took the home side to safety.

• Leg-spinner Andy Roberts claimed a career-best six for 72 to spin Northamptonshire to a 53-run victory over Lancashire at Lytham as the home side chased a target of 351. Northants had earlier extended their first innings to 450 for six, Neil Stanley hitting hs maiden first-class 100 and Allan Lamb his first of the season during a third-wicket partnership of 236.

• At Canterbury, Kent left Hampshire to score 252 in 50 overs for victory but the visitors were grateful to an unbroken eighth-wicket stand of 65 between Adrian Aymes and Raj Maru for holding on to the draw.

• Yorkshire, asked to score 313 in 80 overs by Leicestershire at Leicester, survived with a draw even after David Millns had taken their first six second-innings wickets with only 53 on the board. David Byas, compiling his fourth 100 of the summer, added 155 for the seventh wicket with Phil Carrick. Earlier Tim Boon and Nigel Briers had opened with a stand of 219 as Leicester reached 300 for two in their first innings.

• First-class début: N.V.Knight (Essex).

# BRITANNIC ASSURANCE CHAMPIONSHIP

## SOMERSET vs. WORCESTERSHIRE

at Weston-Super-Mare on 6th, 7th, 8th August 1991
Toss : Somerset.  Umpires : B.Hassan and B.J.Meyer
Match drawn.  Somerset 6 pts (Bt: 4, Bw: 2), Worcestershire 5 pts (Bt: 3, Bw: 2)
100 overs scores : Somerset 310 for 6

### SOMERSET

| | | | | |
|---|---|---|---|---|
| S.J.Cook | c Moody b Lampitt | 37 | c Rhodes b Illingworth | 38 |
| P.M.Roebuck | lbw b Newport | 11 | b Radford | 6 |
| A.N.Hayhurst | lbw b Radford | 40 | lbw b Stemp | 13 |
| C.J.Tavare * | c D'Oliveira b Lampitt | 10 | st Rhodes b Stemp | 11 |
| R.J.Harden | c Hick b Radford | 0 | not out | 74 |
| N.D.Burns + | c Hick b Stemp | 96 | run out | 0 |
| G.D.Rose | lbw b Newport | 12 | not out | 24 |
| R.P.Lefebvre | st Rhodes b Illingworth | 100 | | |
| H.R.J.Trump | not out | 12 | | |
| J.C.Hallett | | | | |
| D.A.Graveney | | | | |
| Extras | (b 3,lb 7,w 1,nb 11) | 22 | (lb 4,nb 4) | 8 |
| TOTAL | (for 8 wkts dec) | 340 | (for 5 wkts dec) | 174 |

### WORCESTERSHIRE

| | | | | |
|---|---|---|---|---|
| T.S.Curtis * | c Cook b Rose | 7 | lbw b Trump | 55 |
| P.Bent | lbw b Hayhurst | 39 | st Burns b Graveney | 65 |
| G.A.Hick | b Rose | 10 | c Harden b Trump | 24 |
| T.M.Moody | c Burns b Graveney | 77 | lbw b Trump | 12 |
| D.B.D'Oliveira | c Tavare b Graveney | 1 | st Burns b Trump | 9 |
| S.J.Rhodes + | not out | 53 | c Tavare b Graveney | 26 |
| R.K.Illingworth | run out | 24 | (8) st Burns b Trump | 9 |
| N.V.Radford | not out | 32 | (7) b Trump | 0 |
| S.R.Lampitt | | | st Burns b Graveney | 7 |
| P.J.Newport | | | not out | 8 |
| R.D.Stemp | | | not out | 0 |
| Extras | (b 1,lb 3,nb 3) | 7 | (lb 16,nb 1) | 17 |
| TOTAL | (for 6 wkts dec) | 250 | (for 9 wkts) | 232 |

| WORCS | O | M | R | W | O | M | R | W |
|---|---|---|---|---|---|---|---|---|
| Radford | 28 | 4 | 105 | 2 | 5 | 0 | 25 | 1 |
| Newport | 30 | 3 | 90 | 2 | 6 | 2 | 25 | 0 |
| Lampitt | 22 | 2 | 70 | 2 | 3 | 0 | 8 | 0 |
| Illingworth | 19 | 7 | 37 | 1 | 6 | 2 | 7 | 1 |
| Hick | 1 | 1 | 0 | 0 | | | | |
| Stemp | 10.1 | 2 | 28 | 1 | 7 | 0 | 23 | 2 |
| D'Oliveira | | | | | 5 | 3 | 10 | 0 |
| Moody | | | | | 3 | 1 | 6 | 0 |
| Curtis | | | | | 5 | 1 | 31 | 0 |
| Bent | | | | | 3 | 1 | 5 | 0 |
| Rhodes | | | | | 1 | 0 | 30 | 0 |

| FALL OF WICKETS | | | | |
|---|---|---|---|---|
| | SOM | WOR | SOM | WOR |
| 1st | 25 | 26 | 27 | 110 |
| 2nd | 83 | 46 | 60 | 149 |
| 3rd | 97 | 101 | 68 | 171 |
| 4th | 98 | 118 | 82 | 176 |
| 5th | 113 | 155 | 86 | 191 |
| 6th | 158 | 192 | | 191 |
| 7th | 322 | | | 215 |
| 8th | 340 | | | 219 |
| 9th | | | | 232 |
| 10th | | | | |

| SOMERSET | O | M | R | W | O | M | R | W |
|---|---|---|---|---|---|---|---|---|
| Rose | 14 | 2 | 58 | 2 | 6 | 2 | 15 | 0 |
| Hallett | 11 | 2 | 36 | 0 | 9 | 1 | 34 | 0 |
| Lefebvre | 5 | 3 | 11 | 0 | | | | |
| Graveney | 21 | 3 | 54 | 2 | 29 | 5 | 87 | 3 |
| Hayhurst | 7 | 1 | 18 | 1 | 4 | 1 | 15 | 0 |
| Trump | 19 | 2 | 69 | 0 | 16 | 2 | 48 | 6 |
| Roebuck | | | | | 5 | 1 | 17 | 0 |

Roland Lefebvre, a maiden first-class century against Worcestershire.

## HEADLINES

### Britannic Assurance Championship

#### 6th - 8th August

• Somerset were unlucky not to gain victory over Worcestershire at Weston, the last pair holding out until the close. Harvey Trump again improved his best bowling performance as the visitors collapsed from 110 for no wicket. Somerset had been revived on the first day by a seventh-wicket stand of 164 between Neil Burns and Roland Lefebvre who completed his maiden first-class 100.

# REFUGE ASSURANCE LEAGUE

## GLAMORGAN vs. HAMPSHIRE
at Ebbw Vale on 11th August 1991
Toss : Glamorgan. Umpires : D.J.Constant & R.C.Tolchard
Glamorgan won by 6 runs. Glamorgan 4 pts, Hants 0 pts

### GLAMORGAN
| | | |
|---|---|---|
| M.P.Maynard | b Connor | 2 |
| S.P.James | b Shine | 11 |
| A.Dale | b Connor | 7 |
| R.J.Shastri | c Aymes b Ayling | 36 |
| P.A.Cottey | not out | 92 |
| A.R.Butcher * | b Udal | 6 |
| R.D.B.Croft | lbw b Udal | 0 |
| C.P.Metson + | c Maru b Connor | 20 |
| S.L.Watkin | lbw b Udal | 2 |
| S.R.Barwick | not out | 5 |
| D.J.Foster | | |
| Extras | (b 1,lb 8,w 7) | 16 |
| TOTAL | (36 overs)(for 8 wkts) | 197 |

### HAMPSHIRE
| | | |
|---|---|---|
| T.C.Middleton | c Croft b Shastri | 32 |
| V.P.Terry | lbw b Croft | 24 |
| R.M.F.Cox | b Shastri | 2 |
| M.C.J.Nicholas * | c Maynard b Dale | 29 |
| K.D.James | st Metson b Shastri | 8 |
| J.R.Ayling | c Metson b Watkin | 13 |
| A.N Aymes + | c Dale b Watkin | 8 |
| R.J.Maru | not out | 33 |
| S.D.Udal | c Butcher b Dale | 23 |
| C.A.Connor | c Maynard b Foster | 8 |
| K.J.Shine | not out | 2 |
| Extras | (lb 4,w 5) | 9 |
| TOTAL | (36 overs)(for 9 wkts) | 191 |

| HAMPSHIRE | O | M | R | W | FALL OF WICKETS | | |
|---|---|---|---|---|---|---|---|
| | | | | | | GLA | HAM |
| Connor | 7 | 0 | 36 | 3 | | | |
| Shine | 8 | 0 | 17 | 1 | 1st | 4 | 58 |
| Ayling | 7 | 0 | 53 | 1 | 2nd | 19 | 61 |
| James | 6 | 1 | 30 | 0 | 3rd | 39 | 63 |
| Udal | 6 | 0 | 40 | 3 | 4th | 80 | 77 |
| Maru | 2 | 0 | 12 | 0 | 5th | 103 | 114 |
| | | | | | 6th | 103 | 118 |
| GLAMORGAN | O | M | R | W | 7th | 187 | 141 |
| Watkin | 7 | 0 | 37 | 2 | 8th | 191 | 176 |
| Foster | 5 | 0 | 27 | 1 | 9th | | 188 |
| Shastri | 8 | 0 | 26 | 3 | 10th | | |
| Barwick | 3 | 0 | 29 | 0 | | | |
| Croft | 7 | 0 | 30 | 1 | | | |
| Dale | 6 | 0 | 38 | 2 | | | |

## GLOUCESTERSHIRE vs. LANCS
at Bristol on 11th August 1991
Toss : Lancashire. Umpires : B.Hassan and D.R.Shepherd
Lancashire won by 8 wickets. Gloucs 0 pts, Lancs 4 pts

### GLOUCESTERSHIRE
| | | |
|---|---|---|
| C.W.J.Athey | lbw b Allott | 5 |
| R.C.Russell + | run out | 12 |
| A.J.Wright * | c & b Watkinson | 33 |
| M.W.Alleyne | c Wasim Akram b Watkinson | 11 |
| J.J.E.Hardy | b Austin | 20 |
| J.W.Lloyds | c Lloyd b Wasim Akram | 5 |
| E.T.Milburn | b Austin | 0 |
| A.M.Babington | b Austin | 0 |
| M.C.J.Ball | c Hegg b Austin | 2 |
| A.M.Smith | run out | 4 |
| M.J.Gerrard | not out | 3 |
| Extras | (lb 4,w 5) | 13 |
| TOTAL | (29 overs) | 108 |

### LANCASHIRE
| | | |
|---|---|---|
| G.D.Mendis | c Hardy b Smith | 23 |
| G.Fowler | b Alleyne | 15 |
| G.D.Lloyd | not out | 25 |
| N.H.Fairbrother * | not out | 43 |
| M.Watkinson | | |
| N.J.Speak | | |
| Wasim Akram | | |
| W.K.Hegg + | | |
| I.D.Austin | | |
| P.J.W.Allott | | |
| P.J.Martin | | |
| Extras | (lb 3,w 2,nb 1) | 6 |
| TOTAL | (22.5 overs)(for 2 wkts) | 112 |

| LANCASHIRE | O | M | R | W | FALL OF WICKETS | | |
|---|---|---|---|---|---|---|---|
| | | | | | | GLO | LAN |
| Allott | 6 | 0 | 17 | 1 | | | |
| Wasim Akram | 8 | 0 | 25 | 1 | 1st | 18 | 35 |
| Martin | 7 | 0 | 28 | 0 | 2nd | 22 | 43 |
| Watkinson | 4 | 0 | 20 | 2 | 3rd | 65 | |
| Austin | 4 | 0 | 10 | 4 | 4th | 72 | |
| | | | | | 5th | 93 | |
| GLOUCS | O | M | R | W | 6th | 98 | |
| Babington | 7 | 0 | 41 | 0 | 7th | 98 | |
| Gerrard | 5 | 0 | 35 | 0 | 8th | 100 | |
| Smith | 4 | 0 | 10 | 1 | 9th | 101 | |
| Alleyne | 4 | 1 | 7 | 1 | 10th | 108 | |
| Ball | 2.5 | 0 | 16 | 0 | | | |

## LEICESTERSHIRE vs. WARWICKS
at Leicester on 11th August 1991
Toss : Warwickshire. Umpires : J.D.Bond and D.O.Oslear
Warwickshire won by 2 runs. Leics 0 pts, Warwicks 4 pts

### WARWICKSHIRE
| | | |
|---|---|---|
| A.J.Moles | c Maguire b Parsons | 1 |
| Asif Din | lbw b Parsons | 0 |
| T.A.Lloyd * | c Whitaker b Benson | 39 |
| D.P.Ostler | b Millns | 2 |
| D.A.Reeve | b Millns | 2 |
| P.A.Smith | c Wilkinson b Benson | 38 |
| N.M.K.Smith | b Wilkinson | 15 |
| P.C.L.Holloway + | not out | 25 |
| G.C.Small | b Maguire | 0 |
| J.E.Benjamin | c Potter b Benson | 0 |
| T.A.Munton | not out | 0 |
| Extras | (lb 14,w 14,nb 1) | 29 |
| TOTAL | (31 overs)(for 9 wkts) | 151 |

### LEICESTERSHIRE
| | | |
|---|---|---|
| J.J.Whitaker | b Smith N.M.K. | 29 |
| N.E.Briers * | c Holloway b Small | 40 |
| T.J.Boon | c Moles b Reeve | 11 |
| B.F.Smith | not out | 21 |
| L.Potter | b Small | 15 |
| J.D.R.Benson | run out | 3 |
| P.Whitticase + | not out | 16 |
| G.J.Parsons | | |
| C.Wilkinson | | |
| D.J.Millns | | |
| J.N.Maguire | | |
| Extras | (lb 7,w 6,nb 1) | 14 |
| TOTAL | (31 overs)(for 5 wkts) | 149 |

| LEICS | O | M | R | W | FALL OF WICKETS | | |
|---|---|---|---|---|---|---|---|
| | | | | | | WAR | LEI |
| Millns | 6 | 0 | 20 | 2 | | | |
| Parsons | 5 | 0 | 28 | 2 | 1st | 1 | 49 |
| Maguire | 6 | 0 | 20 | 1 | 2nd | 2 | 76 |
| Wilkinson | 8 | 0 | 32 | 1 | 3rd | 9 | 100 |
| Benson | 6 | 0 | 37 | 3 | 4th | 19 | 121 |
| | | | | | 5th | 79 | 126 |
| WARWICKS | O | M | R | W | 6th | 104 | |
| Munton | 6 | 0 | 27 | 0 | 7th | 128 | |
| Benjamin | 4 | 0 | 25 | 0 | 8th | 140 | |
| Reeve | 7 | 0 | 24 | 1 | 9th | 145 | |
| Smith N.M.K. | 6 | 0 | 27 | 1 | 10th | | |
| Small | 5 | 0 | 25 | 2 | | | |
| Smith P.A. | 3 | 0 | 14 | 0 | | | |

## MIDDLESEX vs. DERBYSHIRE
at Lord's on 11th August 1991
Toss : Derbyshire. Umpires : R.Palmer and R.A.White
Middx won on faster scoring rate. Middx 4 pts, Derby 0 pts

### MIDDLESEX
| | | |
|---|---|---|
| M.A.Roseberry | st Krikken b Goldsmith | 63 |
| J.C.Pooley | c Mortensen b Goldsmith | 109 |
| M.W.Gatting * | run out | 22 |
| K.R.Brown | lbw b Mortensen | 2 |
| M.Keech | c Krikken b Malcolm | 2 |
| P.N.Weekes | c Cork b Mortensen | 13 |
| J.E.Emburey | run out | 7 |
| P.Farbrace + | lbw b Mortensen | 0 |
| N.F.Williams | not out | 2 |
| D.W.Headley | c Krikken b Base | 4 |
| N.G.Cowans | not out | 5 |
| Extras | (lb 8,w 5) | 13 |
| TOTAL | (39 overs)(for 9 wkts) | 242 |

### DERBYSHIRE
| | | |
|---|---|---|
| P.D.Bowler | b Gatting | 37 |
| C.J.Adams | c Roseberry b Williams | 20 |
| T.J.G.O'Gorman | c Weekes b Gatting | 12 |
| D.E.Malcolm | b Emburey | 0 |
| M.Azharuddin | not out | 37 |
| K.J.Barnett * | not out | 22 |
| S.C.Goldsmith | | |
| K.M.Krikken + | | |
| D.G.Cork | | |
| S.J.Base | | |
| O.H.Mortensen | | |
| Extras | (lb 4,w 5) | 9 |
| TOTAL | (30 overs)(for 4 wkts) | 137 |

| DERBYSHIRE | O | M | R | W | FALL OF WICKETS | | |
|---|---|---|---|---|---|---|---|
| | | | | | | MID | DER |
| Base | 8 | 0 | 39 | 1 | | | |
| Mortensen | 8 | 0 | 29 | 3 | 1st | 167 | 50 |
| Cork | 8 | 0 | 56 | 0 | 2nd | 184 | 70 |
| Malcolm | 8 | 0 | 65 | 1 | 3rd | 187 | 74 |
| Goldsmith | 7 | 0 | 45 | 2 | 4th | 192 | 76 |
| | | | | | 5th | 222 | |
| MIDDLESEX | O | M | R | W | 6th | 223 | |
| Cowans | 5 | 0 | 18 | 0 | 7th | 225 | |
| Williams | 8 | 0 | 24 | 1 | 8th | 231 | |
| Emburey | 6 | 0 | 39 | 1 | 9th | 236 | |
| Gatting | 7 | 0 | 34 | 2 | 10th | | |
| Headley | 4 | 0 | 18 | 0 | | | |

## HEADLINES

**Refuge Assurance League**

**11th August**

• Both Lancashire and Nottinghamshire returned to winning ways, Lancashire remaining two points ahead of their closest rivals with two rounds of matches to be played.

• Ian Austin's four wickets were decisive as Lancashire bowled out Gloucestershire for 108 at Bristol in a match reduced to 29 overs-a-side on their way to an eight-wicket win, while Notts owed their four-wicket victory over Kent at Trent Bridge to 76 from Chris Broad and an unbeaten 56 from Paul Pollard.

• Yorkshire moved into fourth place after beating Sussex by 77 runs at Middlesbrough, Martyn Moxon, and Ashley Metcalfe sharing an opening partnership of 171 as the home side made their highest total in Sunday League cricket. Phil Carrick again made the most his Indian summer with five more wickets.

• Northamptonshire remained level on points with Yorkshire with their 62-run victory over Essex at Northampton. Alan Fordham and Wayne Larkins opened with a stand of 155 as Northants reached 277 for seven, a total which proved well out of reach for the visitors who lost valuable ground in the competition for Refuge Cup places.

• Warwickshire's fourth successive Sunday victory kept them in contention for a place in the top four, just holding on to defeat Leicestershire by two runs at Leicester in a 31-over match.

• At the foot of the table, Glamorgan's improved Sunday form continued at Hampshire's expense at Ebbw Vale, the home side victorious by six runs after Tony Cottey had made a career-best 92 not out.

• Jason Pooley hit his first Sunday League century as he and Mike Roseberry shared an opening stand of 167 to lay the foundations for Middlesex's victory by faster scoring rate over Derbyshire at Lord's.

# REFUGE ASSURANCE LEAGUE

## NORTHANTS vs. ESSEX

at Northampton on 11th August 1991
Toss : Northants. Umpires : G.I.Burgess and B.Leadbeater
Northants won by 62 runs. Northants 4 pts, Essex 0 pts

### NORTHANTS

| | | |
|---|---|---|
| A.Fordham | c Such b Topley | 73 |
| W.Larkins | c Stephenson b Pringle | 108 |
| A.J.Lamb * | b Such | 36 |
| D.J.Capel | c Knight b Pringle | 23 |
| R.J.Bailey | b Topley | 2 |
| K.M.Curran | c Prichard b Foster | 19 |
| E.A.E.Baptiste | c Stephenson b Pringle | 3 |
| D.Ripley + | not out | 0 |
| R.G.Williams | | |
| A.Walker | | |
| J.P.Taylor | | |
| Extras | (lb 11,w 1,nb 1) | 13 |
| TOTAL | (40 overs)(for 7 wkts) | 277 |

### ESSEX

| | | |
|---|---|---|
| J.P.Stephenson | b Taylor | 12 |
| A.C.Seymour | b Taylor | 0 |
| Salim Malik | c sub b Capel | 58 |
| P.J.Prichard | c Williams b Curran | 13 |
| N.Hussain | c Ripley b Capel | 0 |
| D.R.Pringle * | c Ripley b Capel | 6 |
| N.A.Foster | run out | 57 |
| M.A.Garnham + | lbw b Williams | 9 |
| N.V.Knight | not out | 31 |
| T.D.Topley | b Walker | 4 |
| P.M.Such | not out | 1 |
| Extras | (b 4,lb 16,w 3,nb 1) | 24 |
| TOTAL | (40 overs)(for 9 wkts) | 215 |

| ESSEX | O | M | R | W | FALL OF WICKETS | | |
|---|---|---|---|---|---|---|---|
| | | | | | | NOR | ESS |
| Foster | 8 | 0 | 45 | 1 | 1st | 155 | 1 |
| Pringle | 8 | 0 | 43 | 3 | 2nd | 228 | 22 |
| Stephenson | 2 | 0 | 20 | 0 | 3rd | 228 | 60 |
| Topley | 8 | 0 | 57 | 2 | 4th | 231 | 80 |
| Such | 8 | 1 | 67 | 1 | 5th | 270 | 82 |
| Salim Malik | 6 | 0 | 34 | 0 | 6th | 277 | 111 |
| | | | | | 7th | 277 | 145 |
| NORTHANTS | O | M | R | W | 8th | | 190 |
| Taylor | 8 | 0 | 33 | 2 | 9th | | 214 |
| Walker | 8 | 0 | 30 | 1 | 10th | | |
| Baptiste | 8 | 2 | 30 | 0 | | | |
| Curran | 3 | 0 | 7 | 1 | | | |
| Capel | 6 | 0 | 30 | 3 | | | |
| Williams | 7 | 0 | 65 | 1 | | | |

## NOTTS vs. KENT

at Trent Bridge on 11th August 1991
Toss : Kent. Umpires : J.H.Harris and K.E.Palmer
Notts won by 4 wickets. Notts 4 pts, Kent 0 pts

### KENT

| | | |
|---|---|---|
| T.R.Ward | c Hemmings b Saxelby | 15 |
| S.G.Hinks | b Stephenson | 10 |
| N.R.Taylor | c Stephenson b Saxelby | 38 |
| G.R.Cowdrey | c Randall b Evans | 26 |
| M.V.Fleming | c Pollard b Saxelby | 9 |
| M.A.Ealham | b Pick | 18 |
| S.A.Marsh *+ | b Stephenson | 56 |
| R.M.Ellison | not out | 29 |
| M.J.McCague | b Stephenson | 0 |
| R.P.Davis | not out | 7 |
| T.A.Merrick | | |
| Extras | (lb 2,w 5,nb 2) | 9 |
| TOTAL | (40 overs)(for 8 wkts) | 217 |

### NOTTS

| | | |
|---|---|---|
| B.C.Broad | b Ealham | 76 |
| D.W.Randall | lbw b Ellison | 16 |
| R.T.Robinson * | c Hinks b Ellison | 30 |
| P.Johnson | b Ealham | 3 |
| P.Pollard | not out | 56 |
| M.Saxelby | lbw b Ealham | 1 |
| B.N.French + | c Ellison b McCague | 12 |
| F.D.Stephenson | not out | 15 |
| K.P.Evans | | |
| E.E.Hemmings | | |
| R.A.Pick | | |
| Extras | (lb 6,w 1,nb 2) | 9 |
| TOTAL | (39 overs)(for 6 wkts) | 218 |

| NOTTS | O | M | R | W | FALL OF WICKETS | | |
|---|---|---|---|---|---|---|---|
| | | | | | | KEN | NOT |
| Pick | 8 | 0 | 32 | 1 | 1st | 18 | 51 |
| Stephenson | 8 | 0 | 48 | 3 | 2nd | 40 | 108 |
| Hemmings | 8 | 0 | 46 | 0 | 3rd | 78 | 114 |
| Saxelby | 8 | 0 | 40 | 3 | 4th | 94 | 156 |
| Evans | 8 | 0 | 49 | 1 | 5th | 104 | 160 |
| | | | | | 6th | 137 | 194 |
| KENT | O | M | R | W | 7th | 196 | |
| McCague | 6 | 0 | 42 | 1 | 8th | 196 | |
| Merrick | 7 | 0 | 36 | 0 | 9th | | |
| Davis | 5 | 0 | 33 | 0 | 10th | | |
| Ellison | 8 | 0 | 29 | 2 | | | |
| Fleming | 5 | 0 | 36 | 0 | | | |
| Ealham | 8 | 0 | 36 | 3 | | | |

## YORKSHIRE vs. SUSSEX

at Middlesbrough on 11th August 1991
Toss : Sussex. Umpires : B.Dudleston & A.G.T.Whitehead
Yorkshire won by 77 runs. Yorkshire 4 pts, Sussex 0 pts

### YORKSHIRE

| | | |
|---|---|---|
| M.D.Moxon * | c Dodemaide b North | 112 |
| A.A.Metcalfe | c North b Pigott | 68 |
| R.J.Blakey + | c Speight b North | 26 |
| D.Byas | c Lenham b Dodemaide | 16 |
| P.E.Robinson | c Moores b Dodemaide | 13 |
| S.A.Kellett | c North b Pigott | 13 |
| C.S.Pickles | c & b Pigott | 1 |
| D.Gough | b North | 7 |
| P.J.Hartley | not out | 5 |
| P.Carrick | not out | 1 |
| M.A.Robinson | | |
| Extras | (lb 7,w 4,nb 1) | 12 |
| TOTAL | (40 overs)(for 8 wkts) | 274 |

### SUSSEX

| | | |
|---|---|---|
| N.J.Lenham | c Robinson M.A. b Carrick | 64 |
| K.Greenfield | c Metcalfe b Robinson M.A. | 2 |
| A.P.Wells * | run out | 30 |
| M.P.Speight | c Blakey b Carrick | 19 |
| C.M.Wells | c Gough b Carrick | 6 |
| J.A.North | c Pickles b Carrick | 6 |
| A.I.C.Dodemaide | lbw b Hartley | 7 |
| P.Moores + | b Gough | 15 |
| A.C.S.Pigott | st Blakey b Carrick | 4 |
| I.D.K.Salisbury | c Pickles b Hartley | 23 |
| A.N.Jones | not out | 7 |
| Extras | (b 2,lb 8,w 3,nb 1) | 14 |
| TOTAL | (36.2 overs) | 197 |

| SUSSEX | O | M | R | W | FALL OF WICKETS | | |
|---|---|---|---|---|---|---|---|
| | | | | | | YOR | SUS |
| Wells C.M. | 5 | 0 | 23 | 0 | 1st | 171 | 9 |
| Dodemaide | 8 | 0 | 48 | 2 | 2nd | 216 | 67 |
| Jones | 2 | 0 | 21 | 0 | 3rd | 216 | 99 |
| North | 6 | 0 | 38 | 3 | 4th | 243 | 107 |
| Salisbury | 7 | 0 | 50 | 0 | 5th | 258 | 129 |
| Pigott | 8 | 0 | 57 | 3 | 6th | 260 | 131 |
| Greenfield | 4 | 0 | 30 | 0 | 7th | 261 | 141 |
| | | | | | 8th | 270 | 156 |
| YORKSHIRE | O | M | R | W | 9th | | 178 |
| Hartley | 6.2 | 0 | 16 | 2 | 10th | | 197 |
| Robinson M.A. | 6 | 0 | 27 | 1 | | | |
| Gough | 8 | 0 | 47 | 1 | | | |
| Pickles | 8 | 0 | 57 | 0 | | | |
| Carrick | 8 | 0 | 40 | 5 | | | |

Martyn Moxon (right) and Paul Pollard (far right), who were both in the runs in the Refuge League.

# CORNHILL TEST MATCH

## ENGLAND vs. WEST INDIES

at The Oval on 8th, 9th, 10th, 11th, 12th August 1991
Toss : England.  Umpires : J.W.Holder and M.J.Kitchen
England won by 5 wickets

### ENGLAND

| Batsman | Dismissal | Runs | Dismissal (2nd) | Runs |
|---|---|---|---|---|
| G.A.Gooch * | lbw b Ambrose | 60 | lbw b Marshall | 29 |
| H.Morris | c Lambert b Ambrose | 44 | c Dujon b Patterson | 2 |
| M.A.Atherton | c Hooper b Walsh | 0 | c Hooper b Patterson | 13 |
| R.A.Smith | lbw b Marshall | 109 | c Patterson b Walsh | 26 |
| M.R.Ramprakash | c Lambert b Hooper | 25 | lbw b Lambert | 19 |
| A.J.Stewart + | c Richardson b Patterson | 31 | not out | 38 |
| I.T.Botham | hit wicket b Ambrose | 31 | not out | 4 |
| C.C.Lewis | not out | 47 | | |
| P.A.J.DeFreitas | c Dujon b Walsh | 7 | | |
| D.V.Lawrence | c Richards b Walsh | 9 | | |
| P.C.R.Tufnell | c Haynes b Patterson | 2 | | |
| Extras | (b 8,lb 10,w 1,nb 35) | 54 | (b 4,w 1,nb 10) | 15 |
| TOTAL | | 419 | (for 5 wkts) | 146 |

### WEST INDIES

| Batsman | Dismissal | Runs | Dismissal (2nd) | Runs |
|---|---|---|---|---|
| P.V.Simmons | lbw b Lawrence | 15 | c Lewis b Botham | 36 |
| D.L.Haynes | not out | 75 | lbw b Lawrence | 43 |
| R.B.Richardson | c Stewart b Botham | 20 | (4) c Gooch b Lawrence | 121 |
| C.L.Hooper | c Stewart b DeFreitas | 3 | (5) c Gooch b Tufnell | 54 |
| C.B.Lambert | c Ramprakash b Tufnell | 39 | (3) lbw b Botham | 14 |
| P.J.L.Dujon + | lbw b Lawrence | 0 | (7) c Stewart b Lawrence | 5 |
| M.D.Marshall | c Botham b Tufnell | 0 | (8) b DeFreitas | 17 |
| I.V.A.Richards * | c Stewart b Tufnell | 2 | (6) c Morris b Lawrence | 60 |
| C.E.L.Ambrose | c Botham b Tufnell | 0 | lbw b DeFreitas | 0 |
| C.A.Walsh | c Gooch b Tufnell | 0 | lbw b Lawrence | 14 |
| B.P.Patterson | c Botham b Tufnell | 2 | not out | 1 |
| Extras | (lb 9,nb 11) | 20 | (b 7,lb 5,w 2,nb 6) | 20 |
| TOTAL | | 176 | | 385 |

### WEST INDIES

| Bowler | O | M | R | W | O | M | R | W |
|---|---|---|---|---|---|---|---|---|
| Ambrose | 36 | 8 | 83 | 3 | 8 | 0 | 48 | 0 |
| Patterson | 25.1 | 3 | 87 | 2 | 9 | 0 | 63 | 2 |
| Walsh | 32 | 5 | 91 | 3 | 9 | 3 | 18 | 1 |
| Marshall | 24 | 5 | 62 | 1 | 5 | 3 | 9 | 1 |
| Hooper | 34 | 1 | 78 | 1 | | | | |
| Lambert | | | | | 0.4 | 0 | 4 | 1 |

### ENGLAND

| Bowler | O | M | R | W | O | M | R | W |
|---|---|---|---|---|---|---|---|---|
| DeFreitas | 13 | 6 | 38 | 1 | 20 | 9 | 42 | 2 |
| Lawrence | 16 | 1 | 67 | 2 | 25.5 | 4 | 106 | 5 |
| Tufnell | 14.3 | 3 | 25 | 6 | 46 | 6 | 150 | 1 |
| Botham | 11 | 4 | 27 | 1 | 16 | 4 | 40 | 2 |
| Lewis | 3 | 1 | 10 | 0 | 25 | 12 | 35 | 0 |

### FALL OF WICKETS

| | ENG | WI | WI | ENG |
|---|---|---|---|---|
| 1st | 112 | 52 | 53 | 3 |
| 2nd | 114 | 95 | 71 | 40 |
| 3rd | 120 | 98 | 125 | 80 |
| 4th | 188 | 158 | 208 | 80 |
| 5th | 263 | 160 | 305 | 142 |
| 6th | 336 | 161 | 311 | |
| 7th | 351 | 172 | 356 | |
| 8th | 386 | 172 | 356 | |
| 9th | 411 | 172 | 378 | |
| 10th | 419 | 176 | 385 | |

Ian Botham celebrates the fall of a West Indies wicket
on his return to Test cricket.

## HEADLINES

### England v West Indies
### Fifth Cornhill Test Match

### The Oval: 8th - 12th August

• The most competitive Test series played in England in the last two decades ended as it had begun with a hard-earned victory for the home side, as England's 'high-risk' selection paid full dividends and gained England's first drawn series with West Indies since 1973-74.  After losing seven series to West Indies with only one victory in 33 Test matches, a rubber drawn by two matches apiece was a great achievement for Graham Gooch's side.

• England's positive approach was apparent from the first morning when Gooch won the toss and decided to bat: he and Hugh Morris courageously repelled a frightening onslaught from the West Indian fast bowlers and posted England's best start of the series with a stand of 112.  After three wickets had fallen for eight runs, Robin Smith, given determined support by Mark Ramprakash, and the recalled Alec Stewart and Ian Botham, reached his Test 100 and his second of the series.  Chris Lewis added 47 not out to give England their best total against West Indies since 1976.

• West Indies reached 90 for one so confidently by the close of the second day that the procession of wickets next day was astonishing.  West Indies were running smoothly on 158 for three when Phil Tufnell was brought on.  With his first ball, he induced a suicidal stroke from Clayton Lambert, and either side of lunch collected six wickets for four runs in 27 deliveries.  Desmond Haynes carried his bat for the second time in his Test career as seven wickets raised only 18 runs and West Indies were asked to follow on by England for the first time in 22 years, 243 behind.

• The visitors did their best to atone for their first innings performance, Richie Richardson playing one of the most restrained innings of his Test career: he was last out having completed his 14th 100 in Test cricket and his fourth against England, but his marathon effort was overshadowed by the flamboyant strokeplay of Carl Hooper and an emotional final Test innings from Viv Richards.  After reaching the half-century mark, as he had done in each Test of the series, Richards looked ready to unleash a final salvo, but at 60 a lofted drive off David Lawrence was caught by Morris to close an illustrious career and give England a great chance of victory.

• West Indies led by 113 when rain and bad light brought an early end to the fourth day's play.  The opening over of the last swung the match back into England's favour, Phil DeFreitas removing Marshall and Ambrose in the space of four balls.  Lawrence took the last two wickets to leave England 143 for victory.

• Gooch and Smith made a positive start but both were dismissed in successive overs to leave the score on 80 for four.  Ramprakash and Stewart steadied English nerves with a stand of 62 before Ramprakash's dismissal brought in Botham with the scores level: with one blow the match was won and England had deservedly levelled the series.

• Test début: C.B.Lambert (West Indies)

• Man ot the match: R.A.Smith (England); Men of the series: G.A.Gooch (England); C.E.L.Ambrose (West Indies).

# BRITANNIC ASSURANCE CHAMPIONSHIP

## GLAMORGAN vs. HAMPSHIRE
at Swansea on 9th, 10th (no play), 12th August 1991
Toss : Glamorgan.  Umpires : D.J.Constant and R.C.Tolchard
Hampshire won by 172 runs.  Glamorgan 4 pts (Bt: 0, Bw: 4), Hampshire 18 pts (Bt: 2, Bw: 0)

### HAMPSHIRE
| | | | | |
|---|---|---|---|---|
| T.C.Middleton | c Maynard b Barwick | 20 | | |
| C.L.Smith | c James b Foster | 0 | not out | 49 |
| K.D.James | c Shastri b Watkin | 32 | | |
| D.I.Gower | c Dale b Foster | 47 | | |
| M.C.J.Nicholas * | c Metson b Watkin | 4 | (1) not out | 50 |
| R.M.F.Cox | b Frost | 26 | | |
| A.N Aymes + | c Butcher b Watkin | 13 | | |
| T.M.Tremlett | c Metson b Frost | 2 | | |
| I.J.Turner | not out | 39 | | |
| C.A.Connor | lbw b Frost | 12 | | |
| K.J.Shine | not out | 0 | | |
| Extras | (b 9,lb 9,nb 3) | 21 | (nb 1) | 1 |
| TOTAL | (for 9 wkts dec) | 216 | (for 0 wkts dec) | 100 |

### GLAMORGAN
| | | |
|---|---|---|
| A.R.Butcher * | c Connor b Shine | 1 |
| S.P.James | lbw b Tremlett | 20 |
| A.Dale | c Aymes b James | 18 |
| M.P.Maynard | c Middleton b James | 4 |
| R.J.Shastri | not out | 44 |
| R.D.B.Croft | c Turner b Shine | 16 |
| C.P.Metson + | c Aymes b Connor | 10 |
| S.L.Watkin | c Aymes b Shine | 5 |
| D.J.Foster | c Cox b Shine | 0 |
| M.Frost | b Shine | 6 |
| S.R.Barwick | c Aymes b James | 3 |
| Extras | (b 4,lb 1,w 4,nb 8) | 17 |
| TOTAL | | 144 |

| GLAMORGAN | O | M | R | W | O | M | R | W | FALL OF WICKETS | | | | |
|---|---|---|---|---|---|---|---|---|---|---|---|---|---|
| | | | | | | | | | | HAM | GLA | HAM | GLA |
| Watkin | 24 | 11 | 57 | 3 | | | | | 1st | | | | 2 |
| Foster | 12.3 | 5 | 39 | 2 | | | | | 2nd | | 57 | | 39 |
| Frost | 15 | 2 | 56 | 3 | | | | | 3rd | | 75 | | 55 |
| Barwick | 16 | 3 | 46 | 1 | | | | | 4th | | 80 | | 57 |
| Dale | | | | | 6 | 2 | 17 | 0 | 5th | | 136 | | 84 |
| Croft | | | | | 10 | 1 | 49 | 0 | 6th | | 144 | | 105 |
| Maynard | | | | | 4.5 | 0 | 34 | 0 | 7th | | 146 | | 118 |
| | | | | | | | | | 8th | | 181 | | 118 |
| HAMPSHIRE | O | M | R | W | O | M | R | W | 9th | | 215 | | 128 |
| Shine | 16 | 1 | 58 | 5 | | | | | 10th | | | | 144 |
| Connor | 12 | 5 | 15 | 1 | | | | | | | | | |
| Tremlett | 10 | 3 | 39 | 1 | | | | | | | | | |
| James | 13 | 5 | 27 | 3 | | | | | | | | | |

## GLOUCESTERSHIRE vs. LANCASHIRE
at Bristol on 9th, 10th, 12th August 1991
Toss : Lancashire.  Umpires : B.Hassan and D.R.Shepherd
Gloucs won by an innings and 98 runs.  Gloucs 24 pts (Bt: 4, Bw: 4), Lancs 1 pt (Bt: 1, Bw: 0)
100 overs scores :Gloucs 322 for 2

### LANCASHIRE
| | | | | |
|---|---|---|---|---|
| G.D.Mendis | c Wright b Gilbert | 18 | c Lloyds b Gilbert | 44 |
| G.Fowler | c & b Ball | 23 | run out | 4 |
| G.D.Lloyd | c Russell b Babington | 20 | c Russell b Babington | 8 |
| N.J.Speak | b Ball | 29 | c Russell b Ball | 16 |
| S.P.Titchard | c & b Ball | 20 | (7) c Hancock b Gerrard | 20 |
| M.Watkinson | c Lloyds b Gilbert | 9 | (5) c Alleyne b Ball | 0 |
| Wasim Akram | c Ball b Babington | 7 | (8) b Gilbert | 13 |
| W.K.Hegg + | c Russell b Babington | 13 | (6) c Hancock b Ball | 16 |
| G.Yates | c Ball b Babington | 3 | not out | 15 |
| P.J.W.Allott * | c Athey b Ball | 4 | c Gerrard b Babington | 26 |
| P.J.Martin | not out | 1 | c Alleyne b Ball | 0 |
| Extras | (lb 4) | 4 | (lb 3) | 3 |
| TOTAL | | 151 | | 165 |

### GLOUCESTERSHIRE
| | | |
|---|---|---|
| C.W.J.Athey | b Martin | 127 |
| R.C.Russell + | c Titchard b Wasim Akram | 15 |
| A.J.Wright * | c Hegg b Watkinson | 85 |
| M.W.Alleyne | c sub b Martin | 90 |
| J.J.E.Hardy | c sub b Martin | 12 |
| J.W.Lloyds | c Watkinson b Martin | 12 |
| T.Hancock | not out | 17 |
| M.C.J.Ball | c sub b Watkinson | 8 |
| A.M.Babington | c Hegg b Watkinson | 22 |
| D.R.Gilbert | | |
| M.J.Gerrard | | |
| Extras | (b 6,lb 12,nb 8) | 26 |
| TOTAL | (for 8 wkts dec) | 414 |

| GLOUCS | O | M | R | W | O | M | R | W | FALL OF WICKETS | | | | |
|---|---|---|---|---|---|---|---|---|---|---|---|---|---|
| | | | | | | | | | | LAN | GLO | LAN | GLO |
| Gilbert | 14 | 2 | 46 | 2 | 22 | 6 | 44 | 2 | 1st | 22 | 31 | 14 | |
| Babington | 19 | 5 | 33 | 4 | 13 | 2 | 40 | 2 | 2nd | 49 | 186 | 47 | |
| Gerrard | 9 | 2 | 19 | 0 | 7 | 0 | 21 | 1 | 3rd | 90 | 322 | 75 | |
| Alleyne | 7 | 3 | 9 | 0 | | | | | 4th | 99 | 352 | 75 | |
| Ball | 16.3 | 4 | 40 | 4 | 23.1 | 6 | 55 | 4 | 5th | 110 | 356 | 80 | |
| Lloyds | | | | | 2 | 0 | 2 | 0 | 6th | 130 | 365 | 96 | |
| | | | | | | | | | 7th | 130 | 381 | 116 | |
| LANCASHIRE | O | M | R | W | O | M | R | W | 8th | 146 | 414 | 131 | |
| Wasim Akram | 11.2 | 3 | 36 | 1 | | | | | 9th | 149 | | 165 | |
| Martin | 34.4 | 11 | 97 | 4 | | | | | 10th | 151 | | 165 | |
| Allott | 23 | 8 | 39 | 0 | | | | | | | | | |
| Yates | 25 | 2 | 84 | 0 | | | | | | | | | |
| Watkinson | 30 | 3 | 140 | 3 | | | | | | | | | |

## LEICESTERSHIRE vs. KENT
at Leicester on 9th, 10th, 12th August 1991
Toss : Leicestershire.  Umpires : J.D.Bond and D.O.Oslear
Leicestershire won by 5 wickets.  Leicestershire 23 pts (Bt: 3, Bw: 4), Kent 3 pts (Bt: 0, Bw: 3)
100 overs scores : Leicestershire 281 for 7

### LEICESTERSHIRE
| | | | | |
|---|---|---|---|---|
| T.J.Boon | c Marsh b Merrick | 63 | c & b Davis | 47 |
| N.E.Briers * | c Marsh b McCague | 29 | st Marsh b Davis | 66 |
| P.N.Hepworth | c Marsh b McCague | 8 | | |
| J.J.Whitaker | c Marsh b McCague | 36 | (3) c Cowdrey b Davis | 70 |
| L.Potter | c Ellison b Patel | 61 | (4) c Fleming b Davis | 37 |
| J.D.R.Benson | b Davis | 31 | (5) lbw b Patel | 5 |
| B.F.Smith | lbw b Patel | 27 | (6) not out | 19 |
| P.Whitticase + | not out | 2 | | |
| D.J.Millns | c Marsh b McCague | 11 | (7) not out | 6 |
| C.Wilkinson | c Marsh b McCague | 0 | | |
| J.N.Maguire | b McCague | 0 | | |
| Extras | (lb 4,nb 10) | 14 | (lb 1,w 1,nb 2) | 4 |
| TOTAL | | 282 | (for 5 wkts) | 254 |

### KENT
| | | | | |
|---|---|---|---|---|
| T.R.Ward | lbw b Maguire | 1 | c Briers b Wilkinson | 41 |
| R.P.Davis | c Potter b Millns | 6 | | |
| V.J.Wells | b Maguire | 0 | | |
| N.R.Taylor | lbw b Maguire | 18 | (2) c Millns b Potter | 150 |
| G.R.Cowdrey | lbw b Millns | 4 | (3) c Hepworth b Wilkinson | 90 |
| M.V.Fleming | c Benson b Maguire | 0 | (4) c Whitaker b Boon | 58 |
| S.A.Marsh *+ | b Maguire | 1 | (5) not out | 39 |
| R.M.Ellison | c Hepworth b Maguire | 13 | (6) not out | 7 |
| M.J.McCague | c Millns b Potter | 29 | | |
| M.M.Patel | c Smith b Maguire | 43 | | |
| T.A.Merrick | not out | 6 | | |
| Extras | (b 1,lb 6,w 1,nb 1) | 9 | (lb 10,w 3,nb 5) | 18 |
| TOTAL | | 130 | (for 4 wkts dec) | 403 |

| KENT | O | M | R | W | O | M | R | W | FALL OF WICKETS | | | | |
|---|---|---|---|---|---|---|---|---|---|---|---|---|---|
| | | | | | | | | | | LEI | KEN | KEN | LEI |
| Merrick | 21 | 4 | 43 | 1 | 7 | 0 | 32 | 0 | 1st | 69 | 1 | 70 | 111 |
| McCague | 26 | 4 | 88 | 6 | 1 | 0 | 4 | 0 | 2nd | 87 | 1 | 287 | 120 |
| Ellison | 19 | 2 | 53 | 0 | 9 | 1 | 37 | 0 | 3rd | 132 | 27 | 302 | 212 |
| Davis | 25 | 6 | 70 | 1 | 19.3 | 2 | 81 | 4 | 4th | 145 | 33 | 376 | 222 |
| Patel | 3 | 2 | 4 | 2 | 23 | 2 | 93 | 1 | 5th | 218 | 34 | | 240 |
| Fleming | 7 | 0 | 20 | 0 | | | | | 6th | 269 | 34 | | |
| Ward | | | | | 1 | 0 | 6 | 0 | 7th | 269 | 35 | | |
| | | | | | | | | | 8th | 282 | 57 | | |
| LEICESTERSHIRE | O | M | R | W | O | M | R | W | 9th | 282 | 107 | | |
| Millns | 19 | 7 | 27 | 2 | 15 | 1 | 61 | 0 | 10th | 282 | 130 | | |
| Maguire | 18.2 | 6 | 57 | 7 | 19 | 2 | 85 | 0 | | | | | |
| Wilkinson | 5 | 1 | 23 | 0 | 18 | 2 | 52 | 2 | | | | | |
| Potter | 5 | 2 | 16 | 1 | 37 | 9 | 90 | 1 | | | | | |
| Benson | | | | | 5.1 | 1 | 22 | 0 | | | | | |
| Hepworth | | | | | 5 | 0 | 13 | 0 | | | | | |
| Smith | | | | | 4 | 0 | 45 | 0 | | | | | |
| Boon | | | | | 4 | 0 | 11 | 1 | | | | | |
| Whitaker | | | | | 1 | 0 | 14 | 0 | | | | | |

John Maguire, Leicestershire's Australian fast bowler, who took seven wickets in Kent's first innings.

# BRITANNIC ASSURANCE CHAMPIONSHIP

## HEADLINES

### Britannic Assurance Championship

### 9th - 12th August

• Essex's Championship hopes were put back on course as they returned to second place after their three-wicket victory over Nottinghamshire, only one point behind them at the start of the match, at Trent Bridge. The visitors were made to struggle all the way for their success, only reducing Notts's first innings advantage to 75 thanks to 50 from Don Topley. After Neil Foster completed match figures of nine for 114 Essex's victory target was 291 and it needed composed contributions from both Salim Malik and Nasser Hussain and 42 from Nick Knight in only his second first-class match to bring them home.

• Once Warwickshire's batsmen had amassed 460 for eight declared against Northants at Northampton, the leaders were hopeful of a return to winning ways, but victory for Andy Lloyd's men was put out of reach once Andy Roberts and Nick Cook had avoided the follow-on with a last-wicket stand of 85. Warwickshire's lead was thus trimmed to 37 points.

• Gloucestershire gained their second innings victory of the week at Bristol by defeating a Lancashire side fast sliding out of Championship contention by an innings and 98 runs. Martin Ball collected match figures of eight 95 as Gehan Mendis was the only Lancashire batsman to pass 30 in either innings. The home side reached 414 for eight as Bill Athey hit his fourth 100 of the season.

• Middlesex gained their first Championship success of the summer in memorable style in beating Debyshire by two runs at Lord's. Mike Gatting contributed 215 not out and Jason Pooley a career-best 88 to their first innings of 454 for three declared, then Alex Barnett, on his second first-class appearance, claimed the last wicket with the the the visitors only three short of victory.

• Sussex were well rewarded for their marathon trip up to Middlesbrough, beating Yorkshire by an innings and 24 runs thanks to nine wickets from Adrian Jones and a career best 253 not out from Alan Wells.

• Leicestershire defeated Kent by five wickets at Leicester but only after a fine revival from the visitors after they had been forced to follow on 152 behind. Neil Taylor and Graham Cowdrey added 217 for the second wicket before Kent declared at 403 for four, but Leicestershire reached their target of 252 in 60 overs. Australians Martin McCague and John Maguire had earlier both recorded their best figures in English cricket.

• Kevin Shine's five for 58 helped Hampshire to victory by 172 runs over Glamorgan at Swansea, the loss of the second day very much aiding the visitors' cause.

## MIDDLESEX vs. DERBYSHIRE

at Lord's on 9th, 10th, 12th August 1991
Toss : Middlesex. Umpires : R.Palmer and R.A.White
Middlesex won by 2 runs. Middlesex 22 pts (Bt: 4, Bw: 2), Derbyshire 3 pts (Bt: 3, Bw: 0)
100 overs scores : Middlesex 412 for 2, Derbyshire 261 for 6

### MIDDLESEX

| | | | | | |
|---|---|---|---|---|---|
| M.A.Roseberry | lbw b Base | 28 | b Goldsmith | | 15 |
| J.C.Pooley | c & b Cork | 88 | b Mortensen | | 29 |
| M.W.Gatting * | not out | 215 | (6) retired hurt/ill | | 2 |
| K.R.Brown | c Azharuddin b Cork | 96 | (3) c Azharuddin b Goldsmith | | 25 |
| M.Keech | | | (4) b Goldsmith | | 0 |
| P.Farbrace + | | | (5) st Krikken b Base | | 50 |
| N.G.Cowans | | | not out | | 16 |
| A.A.Barnett | | | not out | | 1 |
| J.E.Emburey | | | | | |
| D.W.Headley | | | | | |
| C.W.Taylor | | | | | |
| Extras | (b 1,lb 16,w 2,nb 8) | 27 | (b 2,lb 3,w 1,nb 2) | | 8 |
| TOTAL | (for 3 wkts dec) | 454 | (for 5 wkts dec) | | 146 |

### DERBYSHIRE

| | | | | | |
|---|---|---|---|---|---|
| K.J.Barnett * | c Brown b Cowans | 4 | c Brown b Cowans | | 13 |
| P.D.Bowler | c Gatting b Emburey | 63 | run out | | 89 |
| T.J.G.O'Gorman | c Farbrace b Taylor | 16 | c Roseberry b Emburey | | 38 |
| M.Azharuddin | c Emburey b Barnett | 110 | c Keech b Emburey | | 72 |
| S.C.Goldsmith | b Barnett | 1 | (6) c Roseberry b Barnett | | 6 |
| K.M.Krikken + | not out | 40 | (7) c Brown b Barnett | | 27 |
| D.G.Cork | lbw b Barnett | 18 | (8) st Farbrace b Barnett | | 11 |
| J.E.Morris | not out | 45 | (11) c Roseberry b Barnett | | 0 |
| D.E.Malcolm | | | (5) b Emburey | | 4 |
| S.J.Base | | | (9) c & b Emburey | | 0 |
| O.H.Mortensen | | | (10) not out | | 7 |
| Extras | (b 8,lb 6,nb 4) | 18 | (b 5,lb 5,nb 6) | | 16 |
| TOTAL | (for 6 wkts dec) | 315 | | | 283 |

| DERBYSHIRE | O | M | R | W | O | M | R | W |
|---|---|---|---|---|---|---|---|---|
| Malcolm | 18 | 0 | 95 | 0 | | | | |
| Mortensen | 20 | 2 | 50 | 0 | 7 | 2 | 12 | 1 |
| Base | 21 | 1 | 80 | 1 | 5 | 2 | 11 | 1 |
| Cork | 16.4 | 2 | 61 | 2 | 8 | 2 | 25 | 0 |
| Goldsmith | 24 | 1 | 102 | 0 | 16.2 | 0 | 62 | 3 |
| Barnett | 10 | 0 | 49 | 0 | | | | |
| Bowler | | | | | 2 | 0 | 31 | 0 |

| MIDDLESEX | O | M | R | W | O | M | R | W |
|---|---|---|---|---|---|---|---|---|
| Cowans | 12 | 3 | 35 | 1 | 10 | 4 | 35 | 1 |
| Taylor | 8 | 1 | 55 | 1 | | | | |
| Headley | 12 | 2 | 42 | 0 | 6 | 1 | 23 | 0 |
| Emburey | 39 | 19 | 52 | 1 | 26 | 1 | 96 | 4 |
| Barnett | 46 | 13 | 117 | 3 | 23.4 | 2 | 119 | 4 |

| FALL OF WICKETS | MID | DER | MID | DER |
|---|---|---|---|---|
| 1st | 58 | 10 | 30 | 36 |
| 2nd | 196 | 37 | 75 | 110 |
| 3rd | 454 | 175 | 75 | 213 |
| 4th | | 178 | 75 | 219 |
| 5th | | 218 | 136 | 236 |
| 6th | | 246 | | 241 |
| 7th | | | | 260 |
| 8th | | | | 261 |
| 9th | | | | 283 |
| 10th | | | | 283 |

## NOTTS vs. ESSEX

at Trent Bridge on 9th, 10th, 12th August 1991
Toss : Notts. Umpires : J.H.Harris and K.E.Palmer
Essex won by 3 wickets. Notts 7 pts (Bt: 3, Bw: 4), Essex 22 pts (Bt: 2, Bw: 4)

### NOTTS

| | | | | | |
|---|---|---|---|---|---|
| B.C.Broad | c Salim Malik b Topley | 36 | b Foster | | 10 |
| P.Pollard | lbw b Foster | 56 | c Garnham b Foster | | 16 |
| R.T.Robinson * | b Topley | 6 | c Garnham b Foster | | 0 |
| D.W.Randall | c Hussain b Childs | 6 | c Garnham b Foster | | 44 |
| P.Johnson | c Andrew b Childs | 124 | c Salim Malik b Foster | | 0 |
| K.P.Evans | lbw b Foster | 32 | c Foster b Childs | | 22 |
| F.D.Stephenson | lbw b Foster | 0 | b Stephenson | | 58 |
| B.N.French + | c Garnham b Foster | 2 | c Seymour b Stephenson | | 35 |
| E.E.Hemmings | c Topley b Andrew | 2 | b Topley | | 1 |
| R.A.Pick | b Topley | 14 | not out | | 5 |
| J.A.Afford | not out | 4 | c Seymour b Stephenson | | 3 |
| Extras | (lb 2,w 2,nb 8) | 12 | (b 2,lb 3,w 2,nb 14) | | 21 |
| TOTAL | | 294 | | | 215 |

### ESSEX

| | | | | | |
|---|---|---|---|---|---|
| A.C.Seymour | run out | 13 | (2) c Stephenson b Evans | | 19 |
| J.P.Stephenson | c French b Evans | 4 | (1) c French b Evans | | 14 |
| P.J.Prichard | c Robinson b Evans | 25 | lbw b Evans | | 38 |
| Salim Malik | b Evans | 18 | b Pick | | 74 |
| N.Hussain | c French b Evans | 13 | st French b Afford | | 64 |
| N.V.Knight | c French b Hemmings | 31 | c French b Stephenson | | 42 |
| M.A.Garnham + | c Robinson b Evans | 6 | c Johnson b Stephenson | | 9 |
| N.A.Foster * | c Robinson b Stephenson | 12 | not out | | 15 |
| T.D.Topley | b Stephenson | 50 | not out | | 0 |
| S.J.W.Andrew | run out | 13 | | | |
| J.H.Childs | not out | 13 | | | |
| Extras | (b 3,lb 8,w 1,nb 9) | 21 | (b 4,lb 10,nb 4) | | 18 |
| TOTAL | | 219 | (for 7 wkts) | | 293 |

| ESSEX | O | M | R | W | O | M | R | W |
|---|---|---|---|---|---|---|---|---|
| Foster | 19 | 1 | 58 | 4 | 23 | 2 | 56 | 5 |
| Andrew | 14 | 0 | 65 | 1 | 13 | 4 | 37 | 0 |
| Topley | 22 | 4 | 92 | 3 | 19 | 2 | 72 | 1 |
| Childs | 22.5 | 1 | 77 | 2 | 8 | 1 | 25 | 1 |
| Stephenson | | | | | 5.2 | 0 | 20 | 3 |

| NOTTS | O | M | R | W | O | M | R | W |
|---|---|---|---|---|---|---|---|---|
| Stephenson | 22.2 | 7 | 46 | 2 | 19.2 | 0 | 90 | 2 |
| Pick | 28 | 5 | 62 | 0 | 12 | 2 | 40 | 1 |
| Hemmings | 5 | 1 | 16 | 1 | 13 | 1 | 54 | 0 |
| Evans | 24 | 5 | 66 | 5 | 12 | 2 | 51 | 3 |
| Afford | 8 | 3 | 18 | 0 | 11 | 1 | 44 | 1 |

| FALL OF WICKETS | NOT | ESS | NOT | ESS |
|---|---|---|---|---|
| 1st | 66 | 39 | 23 | 28 |
| 2nd | 95 | 47 | 24 | 51 |
| 3rd | 102 | 48 | 36 | 122 |
| 4th | 110 | 79 | 36 | 182 |
| 5th | 200 | 80 | 73 | 258 |
| 6th | 200 | 95 | 123 | 273 |
| 7th | 209 | 112 | 202 | 285 |
| 8th | 221 | 155 | 205 | |
| 9th | 274 | 195 | 207 | |
| 10th | 294 | 219 | 215 | |

| BRITANNIC ASS. CHAMPIONSHIP | TOUR MATCH |
|---|---|

## NORTHANTS vs. WARWICKSHIRE

at Northampton on 9th, 10th, 12th August 1991
Toss : Northants. Umpires : G.I.Burgess and B.Leadbeater
Match drawn. Northants 6 pts (Bt: 4, Bw: 2), Warwickshire 8 pts (Bt: 4, Bw: 4)
100 overs scores : Warwickshire 324 for 6, Northants 323 for 9

### WARWICKSHIRE

| | | | | |
|---|---|---|---|---|
| A.J.Moles | c Larkins b Curran | 71 | not out | 57 |
| J.D.Ratcliffe | c Stanley b Capel | 21 | lbw b Capel | 12 |
| T.A.Lloyd * | c Lamb b Curran | 26 | | |
| D.P.Ostler | b Curran | 1 | (3) b Roberts | 65 |
| D.A.Reeve | b Baptiste | 65 | | |
| Asif Din | b Cook | 92 | (4) not out | 17 |
| N.M.K.Smith | c Penberthy b Capel | 70 | | |
| P.C.L.Holloway + | not out | 74 | | |
| J.E.Benjamin | lbw b Capel | 0 | | |
| T.A.Munton | not out | 17 | | |
| A.A.Donald | | | | |
| Extras | (b 6,lb 13,w 3,nb 1) | 23 | (b 5,lb 3) | 8 |
| TOTAL | (for 8 wkts dec) | 460 | (for 2 wkts dec) | 159 |

### NORTHANTS

| | | | | |
|---|---|---|---|---|
| A.Fordham | c Ostler b Donald | 66 | not out | 44 |
| W.Larkins | b Benjamin | 3 | not out | 28 |
| N.A.Stanley | c Holloway b Munton | 62 | | |
| A.J.Lamb * | c Benjamin b Smith | 35 | | |
| D.J.Capel | b Munton | 0 | | |
| A.L.Penberthy | c Moles b Munton | 52 | | |
| K.M.Curran | b Reeve | 9 | | |
| E.A.E.Baptiste | lbw b Donald | 21 | | |
| D.Ripley + | c & b Munton | 5 | | |
| A.R.Roberts | not out | 36 | | |
| N.G.B.Cook | c Asif Din b Benjamin | 29 | | |
| Extras | (b 14,lb 22,w 1,nb 19) | 56 | (w 1) | 1 |
| TOTAL | | 374 | (for 0 wkts) | 73 |

| NORTHANTS | O | M | R | W | O | M | R | W |
|---|---|---|---|---|---|---|---|---|
| Capel | 24 | 0 | 109 | 3 | 5 | 0 | 21 | 1 |
| Baptiste | 30 | 2 | 118 | 1 | 5 | 0 | 12 | 0 |
| Penberthy | 5 | 1 | 16 | 0 | 10 | 3 | 21 | 0 |
| Curran | 27 | 8 | 57 | 3 | | | | |
| Roberts | 6 | 1 | 49 | 0 | 20 | 5 | 44 | 1 |
| Cook | 29 | 5 | 92 | 1 | 9 | 3 | 31 | 0 |
| Stanley | | | | | 9 | 2 | 16 | 0 |
| Larkins | | | | | 6 | 4 | 2 | 0 |
| Fordham | | | | | 2 | 0 | 4 | 0 |

| WARWICKSHIRE | O | M | R | W | O | M | R | W |
|---|---|---|---|---|---|---|---|---|
| Donald | 26 | 3 | 82 | 2 | | | | |
| Benjamin | 21.4 | 4 | 66 | 2 | | | | |
| Munton | 30 | 7 | 85 | 4 | | | | |
| Smith | 14 | 3 | 50 | 1 | 5 | 3 | 2 | 0 |
| Reeve | 17 | 5 | 55 | 1 | | | | |
| Moles | | | | | 10 | 1 | 30 | 0 |
| Asif Din | | | | | 9 | 1 | 20 | 0 |
| Ratcliffe | | | | | 3 | 1 | 14 | 0 |
| Ostler | | | | | 2 | 1 | 7 | 0 |

| FALL OF WICKETS | | | | |
|---|---|---|---|---|
| | WAR | NOR | WAR | NOR |
| 1st | 55 | 4 | 19 | |
| 2nd | 119 | 121 | 126 | |
| 3rd | 124 | 161 | | |
| 4th | 125 | 161 | | |
| 5th | 259 | 216 | | |
| 6th | 300 | 233 | | |
| 7th | 408 | 278 | | |
| 8th | 413 | 278 | | |

## YORKSHIRE vs. SUSSEX

at Middlesbrough on 9th, 10th, 12th August 1991
Toss : Yorkshire. Umpires : B.Dudleston and A.G.T.Whitehead
Sussex won by an innings and 24 runs. Yorks 5 pts (Bt: 2, Bw: 3), Sussex 24 pts (Bt: 4, Bw: 4)
100 overs scores :Sussex 309 for 7

### YORKSHIRE

| | | | | |
|---|---|---|---|---|
| M.D.Moxon * | lbw b Jones | 33 | c sub b Jones | 0 |
| A.A.Metcalfe | c Moores b Dodemaide | 1 | c & b Donelan | 36 |
| D.Byas | c Moores b Jones | 8 | c Moores b Donelan | 46 |
| S.A.Kellett | c sub b Jones | 66 | b Jones | 8 |
| P.E.Robinson | c Speight b Jones | 8 | lbw b Salisbury | 10 |
| R.J.Blakey + | c Moores b Wells C.M. | 33 | run out | 0 |
| C.S.Pickles | c Salisbury b Dodemaide | 48 | c Moores b Dodemaide | 33 |
| P.Carrick | c Moores b Jones | 2 | c Salisbury b Donelan | 14 |
| P.J.Hartley | c Moores b Dodemaide | 17 | c Moores b Jones | 10 |
| J.D.Batty | c Smith b Dodemaide | 5 | not out | 1 |
| M.A.Robinson | not out | 1 | lbw b Jones | 0 |
| Extras | (b 4,lb 8,nb 7) | 19 | (b 2,lb 9,nb 2) | 13 |
| TOTAL | | 241 | | 171 |

### SUSSEX

| | | |
|---|---|---|
| N.J.Lenham | c Blakey b Hartley | 0 |
| P.Moores + | c Robinson P.E. b Robinson M.A. | 9 |
| D.M.Smith | b Robinson M.A. | 11 |
| A.P.Wells * | not out | 253 |
| M.P.Speight | c Robinson P.E. b Hartley | 7 |
| C.M.Wells | c Kellett b Carrick | 42 |
| A.I.C.Dodemaide | c Robinson P.E. b Carrick | 11 |
| J.W.Hall | c Moxon b Carrick | 28 |
| B.T.P.Donelan | run out | 59 |
| I.D.K.Salisbury | st Blakey b Carrick | 3 |
| A.N.Jones | c Kellett b Carrick | 1 |
| Extras | (b 1,lb 6,w 1,nb 4) | 12 |
| TOTAL | | 436 |

| SUSSEX | O | M | R | W | O | M | R | W |
|---|---|---|---|---|---|---|---|---|
| Jones | 18 | 3 | 46 | 5 | 12.5 | 2 | 41 | 4 |
| Dodemaide | 24 | 2 | 67 | 4 | 21 | 8 | 36 | 1 |
| Wells C.M. | 11 | 2 | 30 | 1 | 4 | 1 | 4 | 0 |
| Donelan | 13 | 4 | 32 | 0 | 27 | 15 | 43 | 3 |
| Salisbury | 19 | 5 | 54 | 0 | 12 | 4 | 36 | 1 |

| YORKSHIRE | O | M | R | W | O | M | R | W |
|---|---|---|---|---|---|---|---|---|
| Hartley | 30 | 3 | 128 | 2 | | | | |
| Robinson M.A. | 29 | 3 | 118 | 2 | | | | |
| Pickles | 14 | 3 | 51 | 0 | | | | |
| Carrick | 40 | 10 | 103 | 5 | | | | |
| Batty | 8 | 2 | 29 | 0 | | | | |

| FALL OF WICKETS | | | | |
|---|---|---|---|---|
| | YOR | SUS | YOR | SUS |
| 1st | 8 | 0 | 0 | |
| 2nd | 27 | 20 | 76 | |
| 3rd | 82 | 33 | 90 | |
| 4th | 95 | 40 | 100 | |
| 5th | 161 | 124 | 100 | |
| 6th | 191 | 144 | 121 | |
| 7th | 203 | 225 | 146 | |
| 8th | 229 | 403 | 170 | |
| 9th | 240 | 434 | 171 | |
| 10th | 241 | 436 | 171 | |

## SOMERSET vs. SRI LANKA

at Taunton on 10th, 11th, 12th August 1991
Toss : Sri Lanka. Umpires : J.H.Hampshire and P.B.Wight
Sri Lanka won by 8 wickets

### SOMERSET

| | | | | |
|---|---|---|---|---|
| S.J.Cook * | not out | 209 | | |
| G.T.J.Townsend | c Hathurusinghe b Wijeguna' | 53 | | |
| N.J.Pringle | c De Silva b Madurasinghe | 1 | (2) c Mahanama b Wijeguna' | 20 |
| R.J.Harden | not out | 100 | | |
| G.White | | | (1) c Atapattu b Mad'singhe | 42 |
| M.Lathwell | | | (3) c sub b Wijegunawardene | 16 |
| R.J.Turner + | | | (4) not out | 18 |
| G.D.Rose | | | (5) not out | 23 |
| H.R.J.Trump | | | | |
| A.R.Caddick | | | | |
| D.Beal | | | | |
| Extras | (lb 2,nb 12) | 14 | (b 1,lb 5,nb 1) | 7 |
| TOTAL | (for 2 wkts dec) | 377 | (for 3 wkts dec) | 126 |

### SRI LANKA

| | | | | |
|---|---|---|---|---|
| D.S.B.P.Kuruppu | c Turner b Caddick | 86 | c Townsend b Lathwell | 77 |
| U.C.Hathurusinghe | b Rose | 19 | c Turner b Beal | 67 |
| C.P.Ramanayake | c Turner b White | 38 | | |
| M.S.Atapattu | not out | 33 | | |
| P.A.De Silva * | c Beal b Trump | 21 | (3) not out | 57 |
| R.S.Mahanama | lbw b Caddick | 0 | | |
| S.T.Jayasuriya | b Beal | 33 | (4) not out | 37 |
| R.Madurasinghe | c Caddick b Rose | 1 | | |
| K.I.W.Wijeguna' | c Cook b Trump | 10 | | |
| H.P.Tillekaratne + | | | | |
| F.S.Ahangama | | | | |
| Extras | (b 1,lb 10,nb 3) | 14 | (b 5,lb 4,nb 2) | 11 |
| TOTAL | (for 8 wkts dec) | 255 | (for 2 wkts) | 249 |

| SRI LANKA | O | M | R | W | O | M | R | W |
|---|---|---|---|---|---|---|---|---|
| Ramanayake | 14 | 3 | 65 | 0 | 7 | 0 | 24 | 0 |
| Ahangama | 14 | 3 | 59 | 0 | 5 | 0 | 26 | 0 |
| Wijeguna' | 20 | 1 | 109 | 1 | 10 | 1 | 35 | 2 |
| Hathurusinghe | 8 | 0 | 43 | 0 | | | | |
| Madurasinghe | 23 | 4 | 64 | 1 | 10 | 2 | 33 | 1 |
| Jayasuriya | 4.5 | 0 | 35 | 0 | 1 | 0 | 2 | 0 |

| SOMERSET | O | M | R | W | O | M | R | W |
|---|---|---|---|---|---|---|---|---|
| Caddick | 21 | 8 | 40 | 2 | 11.5 | 3 | 58 | 0 |
| Beal | 20 | 2 | 64 | 1 | 7 | 1 | 47 | 1 |
| Trump | 20.5 | 6 | 54 | 2 | 12 | 1 | 78 | 0 |
| Rose | 10 | 2 | 41 | 2 | 6 | 0 | 28 | 0 |
| Lathwell | 6 | 3 | 15 | 0 | 5 | 0 | 29 | 1 |
| White | 6 | 1 | 30 | 1 | | | | |

| FALL OF WICKETS | | | | |
|---|---|---|---|---|
| | SOM | SRI | SOM | SRI |
| 1st | 158 | 59 | 39 | 135 |
| 2nd | 169 | 150 | 81 | 166 |
| 3rd | | 150 | 86 | |
| 4th | | 179 | | |
| 5th | | 179 | | |
| 6th | | 219 | | |
| 7th | | 240 | | |
| 8th | | 255 | | |
| 9th | | | | |
| 10th | | | | |

# HEADLINES

## Tetley Bitter Challenge

### 10th - 12th August

- Even though their bowlers only managed to claim five wickets in the match, the Sri Lankans were relieved to gain their first first-class victory of the tour over Somerset by eight wickets at Taunton. Jimmy Cook coasted to his second undefeated double-century of the season in Somerset's first innings, but the tourists showed off the quality of their batting in reaching their target of 249 in only 42 overs.

- First-class débuts: M.Lathwell and G.White (Somerset).

## NATWEST TROPHY – SEMI-FINALS | ONE-DAY INTERNATIONALS

### SURREY vs. NORTHANTS
at The Oval on 14th, 15th August 1991
Toss : Surrey.  Umpires : B.Dudleston and J.H.Harris
Surrey won by 7 runs
Man of the match: Waqar Younis

**SURREY**

| | | |
|---|---|---|
| D.J.Bicknell | run out | 21 |
| J.D.Robinson | c Ripley b Taylor | 0 |
| A.J.Stewart + | c Larkins b Williams | 34 |
| D.M.Ward | b Capel | 4 |
| G.P.Thorpe | c Larkins b Taylor | 23 |
| M.A.Lynch | lbw b Capel | 2 |
| I.A.Greig * | lbw b Williams | 8 |
| M.P.Bicknell | not out | 66 |
| J.Boiling | c Williams b Capel | 22 |
| Waqar Younis | b Walker | 4 |
| A.J.Murphy | not out | 1 |
| Extras | (b 4,lb 6,w 13) | 23 |
| TOTAL | (60 overs)(for 9 wkts) | 208 |

**NORTHANTS**

| | | |
|---|---|---|
| A.Fordham | b Boiling | 29 |
| W.Larkins | c Thorpe b Boiling | 31 |
| R.J.Bailey | c Stewart b Waqar Younis | 5 |
| A.J.Lamb * | c Boiling b Bicknell M.P. | 24 |
| D.J.Capel | lbw b Waqar Younis | 6 |
| K.M.Curran | c Lynch b Waqar Younis | 38 |
| E.A.E.Baptiste | b Waqar Younis | 34 |
| R.G.Williams | b Waqar Younis | 1 |
| D.Ripley + | b Bicknell M.P. | 3 |
| A.Walker | run out | 11 |
| J.P.Taylor | not out | 3 |
| Extras | (lb 6,w 9,nb 1) | 16 |
| TOTAL | (59.2 overs) | 201 |

| NORTHANTS | O | M | R | W | FALL OF WICKETS | | |
|---|---|---|---|---|---|---|---|
| | | | | | | SUR | NOR |
| Walker | 12 | 3 | 32 | 1 | | 8 | 68 |
| Taylor | 12 | 3 | 37 | 2 | 1st | 8 | 68 |
| Curran | 8 | 2 | 21 | 0 | 2nd | 56 | 73 |
| Baptiste | 7 | 0 | 48 | 0 | 3rd | 70 | 78 |
| Capel | 9 | 0 | 26 | 3 | 4th | 70 | 91 |
| Williams | 12 | 1 | 34 | 2 | 5th | 72 | 113 |
| | | | | | 6th | 91 | 164 |
| SURREY | O | M | R | W | 7th | 124 | 166 |
| Waqar Younis | 12 | 2 | 40 | 5 | 8th | 186 | 174 |
| Bicknell M.P. | 12 | 0 | 45 | 2 | 9th | 194 | 187 |
| Murphy | 9.2 | 0 | 45 | 0 | 10th | | 201 |
| Robinson | 4 | 1 | 15 | 0 | | | |
| Boiling | 12 | 2 | 22 | 2 | | | |
| Lynch | 10 | 1 | 28 | 0 | | | |

### WARWICKSHIRE vs. HAMPSHIRE
at Edgbaston on 14th August 1991
Toss : Warwicks.  Umpires : B.Leadbeater & A.G.T.Whitehead
Hampshire won by 9 wickets
Man of the match: V.P.Terry

**WARWICKSHIRE**

| | | |
|---|---|---|
| A.J.Moles | c Terry b Connor | 4 |
| Asif Din | c Aymes b Maru | 44 |
| T.A.Lloyd * | st Aymes b Udal | 18 |
| D.P.Ostler | c Terry b James | 3 |
| D.A.Reeve | not out | 57 |
| N.M.K.Smith | c Udal b Maru | 0 |
| P.A.Smith | c Aymes b Connor | 14 |
| K.J.Piper + | c & b Connor | 1 |
| G.C.Small | c Aymes b Connor | 2 |
| T.A.Munton | b Aqib Javed | 5 |
| A.A.Donald | c Nicholas b Aqib Javed | 1 |
| Extras | (b 1,lb 8,w 6,nb 8) | 23 |
| TOTAL | (58.5 overs) | 172 |

**HAMPSHIRE**

| | | |
|---|---|---|
| V.P.Terry | not out | 62 |
| C.L.Smith | c Reeve b Smith N.M.K. | 23 |
| R.A.Smith | not out | 64 |
| D.I.Gower | | |
| M.C.J.Nicholas * | | |
| K.D.James | | |
| A.N Aymes + | | |
| S.D.Udal | | |
| R.J.Maru | | |
| C.A.Connor | | |
| Aqib Javed | | |
| Extras | (b 6,lb 11,w 5,nb 2) | 24 |
| TOTAL | (50 overs)(for 1 wkt) | 173 |

| HAMPSHIRE | O | M | R | W | FALL OF WICKETS | | |
|---|---|---|---|---|---|---|---|
| | | | | | | WAR | HAM |
| Aqib Javed | 11.5 | 1 | 34 | 2 | 1st | 17 | 63 |
| Connor | 12 | 2 | 29 | 4 | 2nd | 66 | |
| James | 11 | 0 | 50 | 1 | 3rd | 77 | |
| Udal | 12 | 3 | 30 | 1 | 4th | 94 | |
| Maru | 12 | 5 | 20 | 2 | 5th | 96 | |
| | | | | | 6th | 124 | |
| WARWICKS | O | M | R | W | 7th | 128 | |
| Donald | 9 | 0 | 41 | 0 | 8th | 134 | |
| Small | 9 | 2 | 32 | 0 | 9th | 170 | |
| Munton | 9 | 1 | 26 | 0 | | | |
| Reeve | 5.4 | 1 | 11 | 0 | | | |
| Smith N.M.K. | 8 | 1 | 17 | 1 | | | |
| Asif Din | 3 | 0 | 10 | 0 | | | |
| Smith P.A. | 6.2 | 0 | 19 | 0 | | | |

---

## HEADLINES

### NatWest Trophy
### Semi-finals

### 14th-15th August

• Hampshire reached the NatWest final for the first time with a decisive nine-wicket victory over Warwickshire at Edgbaston. The home side could not break the stranglehold imposed by spinners Raj Maru and Sean Udal, and Cardigan Connor claimed his best figures in the competition as Warwickshire slumped from 66 for one to 134 for eight and only Dermot Reeve's unbeaten 57 carried Warwickshire's final total to 172. Although Chris Smith was dismissed for 23 in his final innings for Hampshire before departing for Western Australia, brother Robin joined Paul Terry in a stand of 110 as Hampshire raced to victory with 10 overs to spare.

• Surrey finally defeated Northamptonshire by seven runs in the other semi-final at The Oval, after the two sides resumed battle on Thursday morning with the visitors needing a further 22 in six overs with two wickets left after bad light had prevented a conclusion the previous evening. Waqar Younis, already with four wickets to his name, forced Kevin Curran to edge to slip from his first ball of the day, and the efforts of the last pair were in vain. Surrey had only reached 208 for nine thanks to a career best 66* from Martin Bicknell, then supported the fearsome spearhead of their bowling attack with some outstanding fielding to make Northants's task a formidable one.

### England A v Sri Lanka

### One-Day Internationals

### 14th - 15th August

• England A were comfortable winners of the first of two matches against the Sri Lankans at Old Trafford thanks to 49 from Martyn Moxon and 66 from Neil Fairbrother and tidy performances from their spin bowlers; but their 63-run victory was reversed the following day as Anurasiri claimed four for 35 with his slow left-arm to restrict England A to 212 for six and the tourists reached their target with three wickets in hand.

---

### ENGLAND A vs. SRI LANKA
at Old Trafford on 14th August 1991
Toss : England A.  Umpires : J.H.Hampshire & D.O.Oslear
England A won by 63 runs

**ENGLAND A**

| | | |
|---|---|---|
| M.D.Moxon * | run out | 49 |
| T.R.Ward | b Ratnayake | 5 |
| G.A.Hick | c Tillekaratne b Ramanayake | 5 |
| N.H.Fairbrother | c & b Madurasinghe | 66 |
| P.Johnson | st Tillekaratne b Jayasuriya | 32 |
| M.Watkinson | not out | 25 |
| S.A.Marsh + | not out | 26 |
| R.K.Illingworth | | |
| D.G.Cork | | |
| R.A.Pick | | |
| P.M.Such | | |
| Extras | (b 9,lb 17,w 6,nb 3) | 35 |
| TOTAL | (55 overs)(for 5 wkts) | 243 |

**SRI LANKA**

| | | |
|---|---|---|
| R.S.Mahanama | lbw b Watkinson | 73 |
| D.S.B.P.Kuruppu | run out | 3 |
| A.P.Gurusinha | c Moxon b Illingworth | 12 |
| P.A.De Silva | c & b Madurasinghe | 10 |
| S.T.Jayasuriya | c Marsh b Illingworth | 4 |
| M.S.Atapattu | c & b Such | 7 |
| H.P.Tillekaratne + | c Illingworth b Hick | 3 |
| R.J.Ratnayake | c Fairbrother b Such | 0 |
| C.P.Ramanayake | c Ward b Hick | 3 |
| K.I.W.Wijeguna' | c Moxon b Pick | 27 |
| R.Madurasinghe | not out | 5 |
| Extras | (lb 17,w 12,nb 4) | 33 |
| TOTAL | (55 overs) | 180 |

| SRI LANKA | O | M | R | W | FALL OF WICKETS | | |
|---|---|---|---|---|---|---|---|
| | | | | | | ENA | SRI |
| Ramanayake | 8 | 3 | 22 | 1 | | | |
| Ratnayake | 10 | 2 | 28 | 1 | 1st | 16 | 15 |
| Wijegunawardene | 7 | 0 | 39 | 0 | 2nd | 35 | 36 |
| Gurusinha | 8 | 0 | 44 | 0 | 3rd | 121 | 46 |
| Madurasinghe | 11 | 0 | 41 | 1 | 4th | 177 | 53 |
| Jayasuriya | 11 | 0 | 43 | 1 | 5th | 191 | 66 |
| | | | | | 6th | | 83 |
| ENGLAND A | O | M | R | W | 7th | | 95 |
| Pick | 11 | 2 | 23 | 1 | 8th | | 99 |
| Cork | 10 | 2 | 41 | 0 | 9th | | 152 |
| Illingworth | 11 | 0 | 31 | 2 | 10th | | 180 |
| Watkinson | 6 | 0 | 21 | 2 | | | |
| Such | 11 | 1 | 29 | 2 | | | |
| Hick | 6 | 1 | 18 | 2 | | | |

### ENGLAND A vs. SRI LANKA
at Old Trafford on 15th August 1991
Toss : England A.  Umpires : G.I.Burgess and R.Palmer
Sri Lanka won by 3 wickets

**ENGLAND A**

| | | |
|---|---|---|
| T.R.Ward | c Madurasinghe b Anurasiri | 78 |
| M.D.Moxon * | st Tillekaratne b Anurasiri | 32 |
| G.A.Hick | b Ratnayake | 1 |
| N.Hussain | c Tillekaratne b Anurasiri | 22 |
| P.Johnson | c & b Jayasuriya | 22 |
| M.Watkinson | c Kuruppu b Anurasiri | 2 |
| S.A.Marsh + | not out | 28 |
| R.K.Illingworth | not out | 10 |
| R.A.Pick | | |
| P.J.Martin | | |
| P.M.Such | | |
| Extras | (b 4,lb 5,w 3,nb 5) | 17 |
| TOTAL | (55 overs)(for 6 wkts) | 212 |

**SRI LANKA**

| | | |
|---|---|---|
| U.C.Hathurusinghe | c Illingworth b Such | 33 |
| D.S.B.P.Kuruppu | c Moxon b Pick | 0 |
| A.P.Gurusinha * | c Marsh b Martin | 10 |
| R.S.Mahanama | run out | 44 |
| S.T.Jayasuriya | c Johnson b Watkinson | 35 |
| M.S.Atapattu | not out | 41 |
| H.P.Tillekaratne + | c Moxon b Hick | 5 |
| C.P.Ramanayake | run out | 2 |
| R.J.Ratnayake | not out | 26 |
| R.Madurasinghe | | |
| S.D.Anurasiri | | |
| Extras | (lb 6,w 7,nb 4) | 17 |
| TOTAL | (52.5 overs)(for 7 wkts) | 213 |

| SRI LANKA | O | M | R | W | FALL OF WICKETS | | |
|---|---|---|---|---|---|---|---|
| | | | | | | ENA | SRI |
| Ramanayake | 8 | 1 | 31 | 0 | | | |
| Ratnayake | 5 | 1 | 10 | 1 | 1st | 66 | 1 |
| Gurusinha | 2 | 0 | 11 | 0 | 2nd | 72 | 17 |
| Anurasiri | 11 | 0 | 35 | 4 | 3rd | 121 | 74 |
| Madurasinghe | 11 | 0 | 49 | 0 | 4th | 168 | 129 |
| Jayasuriya | 11 | 0 | 40 | 1 | 5th | 173 | 136 |
| Tillekaratne | 7 | 0 | 27 | 0 | 6th | 175 | 156 |
| | | | | | 7th | | 160 |
| ENGLAND A | O | M | R | W | 8th | | |
| Pick | 6.5 | 0 | 31 | 1 | 9th | | |
| Martin | 6 | 1 | 18 | 1 | 10th | | |
| Watkinson | 11 | 2 | 35 | 1 | | | |
| Such | 11 | 1 | 49 | 1 | | | |
| Illingworth | 11 | 0 | 36 | 0 | | | |
| Hick | 7 | 0 | 38 | 1 | | | |

# REFUGE ASSURANCE LEAGUE

## HEADLINES

### Refuge Assurance League

### 18th August

• Nottinghamshire, who had led the league table for the first half of the summer, returned to the top with their two-wicket victory over Yorkshire at Scarborough. Michael Field-Buss, in his first Sunday match of the year, played a crucial part, taking two for 22 in his eight overs as Yorkshire were restricted to 187 for seven, then supporting Kevin Evans as the last nine runs were achieved.

• Lancashire dropped to second place after their 21-run defeat by Surrey at Old Trafford. After Graham Thorpe's first Sunday 100 carried the visitors' total to 228 for five, Lancashire could not afford a disappointing batting effort, and victory was out of reach once Neil Fairbrother had been run out for 62.

• Northamptonshire moved into third place by beating Kent by two runs at Canterbury, just holding on after an eighth-wicket stand of 67 between Steve Marsh and Richard Davis had brought Kent back into contention.

• Warwickshire's nine-wicket victory over Gloucestershire at Edgbaston, their fifth in succession on Sundays, carried them into fourth place in the table and would have helped restore flagging morale. Tim Munton's five for 28 and a second-wicket stand of 102 between Asif Din and Andy Lloyd brought the most decisive of wins.

• Worcestershire dropped out of the first four by losing to Somerset by 18 runs at Worcester, Jimmy Cook batting through the visitors's innings for 129 not out, his seventh Sunday League 100.

• Essex remained in contention for a place in the Refuge Cup after beating Middlesex by 95 runs at Colchester, the visitors' last seven wickets falling for 44.

• Derbyshire, playing beyond the county boundaries at Checkley in Staffordshire, made the day's highest total on the way to victory over Glamorgan by 29 runs, despite 101 from Matthew Maynard. Ewan McCray improved his best figures with four for 49.

• Leicestershire's four-wicket win over Hampshire at Bournemouth ensured that the NatWest finalists would finish bottom of the Refuge League.

---

## DERBYSHIRE vs. GLAMORGAN

at Checkley on 18th August 1991
Toss : Glamorgan.  Umpires : D.J.Constant and J.H.Harris
Derbyshire won by 29 runs.  Derbyshire 4 pts, Glam 0 pts

### DERBYSHIRE

| | | |
|---|---|---:|
| P.D.Bowler | st Metson b Shastri | 39 |
| C.J.Adams | run out | 0 |
| T.J.G.O'Gorman | lbw b Frost | 11 |
| M.Azharuddin | c Frost b Watkin | 36 |
| A.E.Warner | c Dale b Watkin | 51 |
| S.C.Goldsmith | b Foster | 31 |
| K.J.Barnett * | c Metson b Dale | 14 |
| K.M.Krikken + | lbw b Foster | 8 |
| D.G.Cork | lbw b Frost | 28 |
| E.McCray | c Metson b Foster | 1 |
| O.H.Mortensen | not out | 7 |
| Extras | (lb 15,w 9,nb 1) | 25 |
| TOTAL | (39 overs) | 251 |

### GLAMORGAN

| | | |
|---|---|---:|
| M.P.Maynard | st Krikken b McCray | 101 |
| H.Morris | b Mortensen | 21 |
| A.Dale | c Krikken b Cork | 4 |
| R.J.Shastri | b Cork | 16 |
| P.A.Cottey | c O'Gorman b McCray | 14 |
| A.R.Butcher * | st Krikken b McCray | 6 |
| R.D.B.Croft | lbw b McCray | 0 |
| C.P.Metson + | c Goldsmith b Mortensen | 20 |
| S.L.Watkin | not out | 31 |
| M.Frost | run out | 2 |
| D.J.Foster | not out | 2 |
| Extras | (lb 4,nb 1) | 5 |
| TOTAL | (40 overs)(for 9 wkts) | 222 |

| GLAMORGAN | O | M | R | W | | FALL OF WICKETS | |
|---|---|---|---|---|---|---|---|
| | | | | | | DER | GLA |
| Frost | 7 | 1 | 39 | 2 | 1st | 1 | 47 |
| Foster | 7 | 0 | 30 | 3 | 2nd | 29 | 81 |
| Croft | 8 | 0 | 33 | 0 | 3rd | 79 | 123 |
| Watkin | 8 | 0 | 50 | 2 | 4th | 149 | 157 |
| Shastri | 4 | 0 | 33 | 1 | 5th | 167 | 161 |
| Dale | 5 | 0 | 51 | 1 | 6th | 195 | 161 |
| DERBYSHIRE | O | M | R | W | 7th | 212 | 176 |
| McCray | 8 | 0 | 49 | 4 | 8th | 230 | 197 |
| Mortensen | 8 | 1 | 36 | 2 | 9th | 239 | 209 |
| Goldsmith | 8 | 0 | 62 | 0 | 10th | 251 | |
| Warner | 8 | 0 | 51 | 0 | | | |
| Cork | 8 | 2 | 20 | 2 | | | |

---

## ESSEX vs. MIDDLESEX

at Colchester on 18th August 1991
Toss : Essex.  Umpires : R.Julian and R.C.Tolchard
Essex won by 95 runs.  Essex 4 pts, Middlesex 0 pts

### ESSEX

| | | |
|---|---|---:|
| G.A.Gooch * | b Weekes | 45 |
| J.P.Stephenson | c Ramprakash b Embury | 44 |
| Salim Malik | c Taylor b Cowans | 33 |
| P.J.Prichard | not out | 54 |
| N.Hussain | c Farbrace b Cowans | 0 |
| D.R.Pringle | c sub b Cowans | 34 |
| N.A.Foster | not out | 14 |
| M.A.Garnham + | | |
| T.D.Topley | | |
| J.H.Childs | | |
| P.M.Such | | |
| Extras | (lb 11,w 4) | 15 |
| TOTAL | (40 overs)(for 5 wkts) | 239 |

### MIDDLESEX

| | | |
|---|---|---:|
| M.A.Roseberry | c Garnham b Pringle | 2 |
| J.C.Pooley | c Pringle b Foster | 12 |
| M.W.Gatting * | lbw b Topley | 8 |
| M.R.Ramprakash | b Topley | 59 |
| K.R.Brown | c Topley b Such | 33 |
| P.N.Weekes | run out | 0 |
| J.E.Emburey | c Hussain b Childs | 8 |
| P.Farbrace + | run out | 5 |
| D.W.Headley | not out | 6 |
| C.W.Taylor | lbw b Childs | 3 |
| N.G.Cowans | b Topley | 4 |
| Extras | (lb 4) | 4 |
| TOTAL | (33.4 overs) | 144 |

| MIDDLESEX | O | M | R | W | | FALL OF WICKETS | |
|---|---|---|---|---|---|---|---|
| | | | | | | ESS | MID |
| Taylor | 4 | 0 | 32 | 0 | | | |
| Cowans | 8 | 2 | 35 | 3 | 1st | 96 | 2 |
| Headley | 8 | 0 | 56 | 0 | 2nd | 103 | 18 |
| Emburey | 8 | 1 | 37 | 1 | 3rd | 150 | 31 |
| Weekes | 8 | 0 | 42 | 1 | 4th | 150 | 100 |
| Gatting | 4 | 0 | 26 | 0 | 5th | 223 | 101 |
| | | | | | 6th | | 116 |
| ESSEX | O | M | R | W | 7th | | 130 |
| Pringle | 4 | 0 | 6 | 1 | 8th | | 132 |
| Foster | 6 | 0 | 23 | 1 | 9th | | 135 |
| Topley | 7.4 | 0 | 36 | 3 | 10th | | 144 |
| Such | 8 | 0 | 40 | 1 | | | |
| Childs | 8 | 0 | 35 | 2 | | | |

# REFUGE ASSURANCE LEAGUE

## HAMPSHIRE vs. LEICESTERSHIRE

at Bournemouth on 18th August 1991
Toss : Leicestershire.  Umpires : N.T.Plews and R.A.White
Leics won by 4 wickets.  Hampshire 0 pts, Leics 4 pts

### HAMPSHIRE

| | | |
|---|---|---|
| V.P.Terry | lbw b Maguire | 20 |
| T.C.Middleton | run out | 8 |
| R.A.Smith | b Maguire | 75 |
| M.C.J.Nicholas * | c Whitaker b Millns | 56 |
| K.D.James | b Maguire | 2 |
| J.R.Ayling | b Lewis | 17 |
| R.J.Parks + | b Millns | 8 |
| R.J.Maru | not out | 3 |
| S.D.Udal | not out | 1 |
| Aqib Javed | | |
| K.J.Shine | | |
| Extras | (lb 4,w 1) | 5 |
| TOTAL | (40 overs)(for 7 wkts) | 195 |

### LEICESTERSHIRE

| | | |
|---|---|---|
| J.J.Whitaker | c Udal b Shine | 1 |
| N.E.Briers * | c Ayling b James | 42 |
| T.J.Boon | c Nicholas b Ayling | 68 |
| C.C.Lewis | c James b Ayling | 16 |
| L.Potter | run out | 2 |
| J.D.R.Benson | not out | 23 |
| P.Whitticase + | c Terry b Udal | 17 |
| M.I.Gidley | not out | 12 |
| D.J.Millns | | |
| C.Wilkinson | | |
| J.N.Maguire | | |
| Extras | (lb 4,w 12,nb 1) | 17 |
| TOTAL | (39.3 overs)(for 6 wkts) | 198 |

| LEICESTERSHIRE | O | M | R | W | FALL OF WICKETS | | |
|---|---|---|---|---|---|---|---|
| | | | | | | HAM | LEI |
| Millns | 8 | 0 | 33 | 2 | 1st | 14 | 8 |
| Lewis | 8 | 0 | 28 | 1 | 2nd | 56 | 110 |
| Wilkinson | 8 | 0 | 32 | 0 | 3rd | 154 | 138 |
| Maguire | 8 | 1 | 44 | 3 | 4th | 156 | 144 |
| Benson | 4 | 0 | 21 | 0 | 5th | 180 | 146 |
| Gidley | 4 | 0 | 33 | 0 | 6th | 191 | 178 |
| | | | | | 7th | 193 | |
| HAMPSHIRE | O | M | R | W | 8th | | |
| Aqib Javed | 8 | 0 | 36 | 0 | 9th | | |
| Shine | 5 | 0 | 28 | 1 | 10th | | |
| Ayling | 7 | 0 | 29 | 2 | | | |
| Udal | 7.3 | 0 | 46 | 1 | | | |
| Maru | 8 | 0 | 32 | 0 | | | |
| James | 4 | 0 | 23 | 1 | | | |

## LANCASHIRE vs. SURREY

at Old Trafford on 18th August 1991
Toss : Lancashire.  Umpires : A.A.Jones and B.J.Meyer
Surrey won by 21 runs.  Lancashire 0 pts, Surrey 4 pts

### SURREY

| | | |
|---|---|---|
| G.P.Thorpe | not out | 115 |
| A.D.Brown | c Mendis b Watkinson | 44 |
| A.J.Stewart + | b Allott | 16 |
| D.M.Ward | c Hegg b Wasim Akram | 3 |
| M.A.Lynch | c Hegg b Wasim Akram | 37 |
| J.D.Robinson | run out | 0 |
| I.A.Greig * | not out | 0 |
| M.P.Bicknell | | |
| J.Boiling | | |
| A.J.Murphy | | |
| A.G.Robson | | |
| Extras | (b 3,lb 3,w 6,nb 1) | 13 |
| TOTAL | (40 overs)(for 5 wkts) | 228 |

### LANCASHIRE

| | | |
|---|---|---|
| G.D.Mendis | b Bicknell | 0 |
| G.Fowler | c Greig b Robson | 12 |
| M.A.Atherton | b Murphy | 34 |
| G.D.Lloyd | run out | 11 |
| N.H.Fairbrother * | run out | 62 |
| M.Watkinson | c Greig b Boiling | 9 |
| Wasim Akram | b Robson | 38 |
| P.A.J.DeFreitas | b Bicknell | 11 |
| W.K.Hegg + | c Lynch b Bicknell | 7 |
| I.D.Austin | not out | 10 |
| P.J.W.Allott | not out | 3 |
| Extras | (b 1,lb 4,w 4,nb 1) | 10 |
| TOTAL | (40 overs)(for 9 wkts) | 207 |

| LANCASHIRE | O | M | R | W | FALL OF WICKETS | | |
|---|---|---|---|---|---|---|---|
| | | | | | | SUR | LAN |
| Allott | 8 | 0 | 37 | 1 | 1st | 76 | 1 |
| DeFreitas | 8 | 0 | 51 | 0 | 2nd | 119 | 29 |
| Watkinson | 8 | 0 | 48 | 1 | 3rd | 130 | 55 |
| Wasim Akram | 8 | 0 | 49 | 2 | 4th | 223 | 85 |
| Austin | 8 | 0 | 37 | 0 | 5th | 223 | 98 |
| | | | | | 6th | | 173 |
| SURREY | O | M | R | W | 7th | | 179 |
| Bicknell | 8 | 0 | 36 | 3 | 8th | | 193 |
| Robson | 8 | 0 | 46 | 2 | 9th | | 194 |
| Robinson | 8 | 0 | 41 | 0 | 10th | | |
| Boiling | 8 | 0 | 34 | 1 | | | |
| Murphy | 8 | 0 | 45 | 1 | | | |

## WORCESTERSHIRE vs. SOMERSET

at Worcester on 18th August 1991
Toss : Somerset.  Umpires : B.Dudleston and D.O.Oslear
Somerset won by 18 runs.  Worcs 0 pts, Somerset 4 pts

### SOMERSET

| | | |
|---|---|---|
| S.J.Cook | not out | 129 |
| G.T.J.Townsend | c Curtis b Newport | 27 |
| R.J.Harden | c & b Botham | 31 |
| C.J.Tavare + | b Botham | 24 |
| G.D.Rose | run out | 14 |
| A.N.Hayhurst | not out | 7 |
| N.D.Burns + | | |
| H.R.J.Trump | | |
| J.C.Hallett | | |
| D.A.Graveney | | |
| D.Beal | | |
| Extras | (w 1,nb 2) | 3 |
| TOTAL | (40 overs)(for 4 wkts) | 235 |

### WORCESTERSHIRE

| | | |
|---|---|---|
| T.S.Curtis * | b Trump | 16 |
| T.M.Moody | c Burns b Hayhurst | 91 |
| G.A.Hick | c Beal b Trump | 11 |
| D.B.D'Oliveira | c & b Graveney | 23 |
| I.T.Botham | c Trump b Hayhurst | 17 |
| S.J.Rhodes + | c Burns b Hayhurst | 0 |
| M.J.Weston | not out | 30 |
| N.V.Radford | not out | 20 |
| R.K.Illingworth | | |
| S.R.Lampitt | | |
| P.J.Newport | | |
| Extras | (lb 6,w 3) | 9 |
| TOTAL | (40 overs)(for 6 wkts) | 217 |

| WORCS | O | M | R | W | FALL OF WICKETS | | |
|---|---|---|---|---|---|---|---|
| | | | | | | SOM | WOR |
| Weston | 4 | 0 | 22 | 0 | 1st | 73 | 40 |
| Radford | 8 | 0 | 63 | 0 | 2nd | 133 | 58 |
| Newport | 8 | 1 | 18 | 1 | 3rd | 196 | 104 |
| Illingworth | 8 | 0 | 45 | 0 | 4th | 215 | 147 |
| Lampitt | 4 | 0 | 29 | 0 | 5th | | 147 |
| Botham | 8 | 0 | 58 | 2 | 6th | | 185 |
| | | | | | 7th | | |
| SOMERSET | O | M | R | W | 8th | | |
| Rose | 8 | 0 | 49 | 0 | 9th | | |
| Hallett | 8 | 0 | 57 | 0 | 10th | | |
| Trump | 8 | 0 | 31 | 2 | | | |
| Hayhurst | 8 | 0 | 38 | 3 | | | |
| Graveney | 8 | 0 | 36 | 1 | | | |

## KENT vs. NORTHANTS

at Canterbury on 18th August 1991
Toss : Kent.  Umpires : J.C.Balderstone and B.Hassan
Northants won by 2 runs.  Kent 0 pts, Northants 4 pts

### NORTHANTS

| | | |
|---|---|---|
| A.Fordham | run out | 30 |
| W.Larkins | c & b Davis | 56 |
| A.J.Lamb * | c Cowdrey b Igglesden | 30 |
| R.J.Bailey | c Cowdrey b Igglesden | 23 |
| K.M.Curran | not out | 35 |
| D.J.Capel | c Ellison b Fleming | 3 |
| E.A.E.Baptiste | not out | 15 |
| A.L.Penberthy | | |
| R.G.Williams | | |
| D.Ripley + | | |
| A.Walker | | |
| Extras | (lb 5,w 5) | 10 |
| TOTAL | (40 overs)(for 5 wkts) | 202 |

### KENT

| | | |
|---|---|---|
| T.R.Ward | run out | 9 |
| M.R.Benson * | b Curran | 45 |
| N.R.Taylor | b Walker | 2 |
| M.A.Ealham | lbw b Capel | 3 |
| G.R.Cowdrey | lbw b Capel | 13 |
| M.V.Fleming | lbw b Williams | 18 |
| S.A.Marsh + | b Baptiste | 52 |
| R.M.Ellison | run out | 0 |
| R.P.Davis | not out | 40 |
| T.A.Merrick | not out | 3 |
| A.P.Igglesden | | |
| Extras | (b 2,lb 11,w 2) | 15 |
| TOTAL | (40 overs)(for 8 wkts) | 200 |

| KENT | O | M | R | W | FALL OF WICKETS | | |
|---|---|---|---|---|---|---|---|
| | | | | | | NOR | KEN |
| Igglesden | 8 | 0 | 27 | 2 | 1st | 88 | 29 |
| Ellison | 4 | 0 | 28 | 0 | 2nd | 95 | 33 |
| Merrick | 6 | 0 | 42 | 0 | 3rd | 143 | 51 |
| Davis | 8 | 0 | 28 | 1 | 4th | 152 | 69 |
| Ealham | 6 | 0 | 26 | 0 | 5th | 161 | 81 |
| Fleming | 8 | 0 | 46 | 1 | 6th | | 111 |
| | | | | | 7th | | 116 |
| NORTHANTS | O | M | R | W | 8th | | 183 |
| Walker | 8 | 0 | 27 | 1 | 9th | | |
| Baptiste | 8 | 1 | 20 | 1 | 10th | | |
| Capel | 6 | 0 | 24 | 2 | | | |
| Curran | 8 | 0 | 49 | 1 | | | |
| Williams | 6 | 0 | 46 | 1 | | | |
| Penberthy | 4 | 0 | 21 | 0 | | | |

## WARWICKSHIRE vs. GLOUCS

at Edgbaston on 18th August 1991
Toss : Gloucs.  Umpires : J.H.Hampshire and P.B.Wight
Warwicks won by 9 wickets.  Warwicks 4 pts, Gloucs 0 pts

### GLOUCESTERSHIRE

| | | |
|---|---|---|
| R.J.Scott | lbw b Munton | 1 |
| M.W.Alleyne | b Munton | 17 |
| A.J.Wright * | c Donald b Benjamin | 56 |
| C.W.J.Athey | c Reeve b Benjamin | 2 |
| R.C.Russell + | c Piper b Donald | 28 |
| J.J.E.Hardy | lbw b Smith P.A. | 13 |
| T.Hancock | b Munton | 20 |
| M.C.J.Ball | b Munton | 4 |
| D.R.Gilbert | b Munton | 0 |
| A.M.Babington | not out | 6 |
| A.M.Smith | not out | 5 |
| Extras | (lb 18,w 7) | 25 |
| TOTAL | (40 overs)(for 9 wkts) | 177 |

### WARWICKSHIRE

| | | |
|---|---|---|
| A.J.Moles | b Scott | 26 |
| Asif Din | not out | 81 |
| T.A.Lloyd * | not out | 56 |
| D.P.Ostler | | |
| D.A.Reeve | | |
| N.M.K.Smith | | |
| P.A.Smith | | |
| K.J.Piper | | |
| J.E.Benjamin | | |
| T.A.Munton | | |
| A.A.Donald | | |
| Extras | (lb 6,w 7,nb 2) | 15 |
| TOTAL | (37.5 overs)(for 1 wkt) | 178 |

| WARWICKS | O | M | R | W | FALL OF WICKETS | | |
|---|---|---|---|---|---|---|---|
| | | | | | | GLO | WAR |
| Donald | 8 | 0 | 35 | 1 | 1st | 5 | 76 |
| Munton | 8 | 0 | 28 | 5 | 2nd | 39 | |
| Benjamin | 8 | 0 | 36 | 2 | 3rd | 42 | |
| Smith P.A. | 8 | 0 | 27 | 1 | 4th | 113 | |
| Smith N.M.K. | 8 | 0 | 33 | 0 | 5th | 131 | |
| | | | | | 6th | 144 | |
| GLOUCS | O | M | R | W | 7th | 165 | |
| Gilbert | 8 | 1 | 35 | 0 | 8th | 165 | |
| Babington | 8 | 1 | 25 | 0 | 9th | 166 | |
| Ball | 8 | 0 | 27 | 0 | 10th | | |
| Smith | 5 | 0 | 39 | 0 | | | |
| Scott | 6 | 0 | 29 | 1 | | | |
| Alleyne | 2.5 | 0 | 17 | 0 | | | |

## YORKSHIRE vs. NOTTS

at Scarborough on 18th August 1991
Toss : Notts.  Umpires : K.E.Palmer and R.Palmer
Notts won by 2 wickets.  Yorkshire 0 pts, Notts 4 pts

### YORKSHIRE

| | | |
|---|---|---|
| S.A.Kellett | run out | 26 |
| A.A.Metcalfe * | b Evans | 33 |
| R.J.Blakey + | c French b Field-Buss | 11 |
| D.Byas | c Broad b Field-Buss | 9 |
| P.E.Robinson | run out | 32 |
| C.White | b Stephenson | 37 |
| C.S.Pickles | not out | 15 |
| P.Carrick | c & b Pick | 2 |
| P.J.Hartley | | |
| J.D.Batty | | |
| M.A.Robinson | | |
| Extras | (lb 14,w 8) | 22 |
| TOTAL | (40 overs)(for 7 wkts) | 187 |

### NOTTS

| | | |
|---|---|---|
| B.C.Broad | c Batty b Hartley | 15 |
| D.W.Randall | c Robinson P.E. b Batty | 10 |
| R.T.Robinson * | c Blakey b Batty | 23 |
| P.Johnson | run out | 0 |
| P.Pollard | c White b Robinson M.A. | 53 |
| M.Saxelby | c Byas b Pickles | 55 |
| F.D.Stephenson | c Blakey b Robinson M.A. | 0 |
| B.N.French + | c Blakey b Pickles | 8 |
| K.P.Evans | not out | 12 |
| M.G.Field-Buss | not out | 0 |
| R.A.Pick | | |
| Extras | (lb 10,w 2) | 12 |
| TOTAL | (39.5 overs)(for 8 wkts) | 188 |

| NOTTS | O | M | R | W | FALL OF WICKETS | | |
|---|---|---|---|---|---|---|---|
| | | | | | | YOR | NOT |
| Pick | 8 | 0 | 35 | 1 | 1st | 60 | 23 |
| Stephenson | 8 | 0 | 39 | 1 | 2nd | 65 | 32 |
| Saxelby | 8 | 0 | 30 | 0 | 3rd | 83 | 32 |
| Evans | 8 | 0 | 47 | 1 | 4th | 84 | 70 |
| Field-Buss | 8 | 1 | 22 | 2 | 5th | 160 | 167 |
| | | | | | 6th | 178 | 168 |
| YORKSHIRE | O | M | R | W | 7th | 187 | 171 |
| Robinson M.A. | 7.5 | 0 | 46 | 2 | 8th | | 179 |
| Hartley | 8 | 0 | 42 | 1 | 9th | | |
| Carrick | 8 | 1 | 24 | 0 | 10th | | |
| Batty | 8 | 0 | 31 | 2 | | | |
| Pickles | 8 | 0 | 35 | 2 | | | |

# BRITANNIC ASSURANCE CHAMPIONSHIP

## NOTTS vs. SOMERSET

at Trent Bridge on 16th, 17th, 19th August 1991
Toss : Somerset. Umpires : J.H.Hampshire and P.B.Wight
Match drawn. Notts 5 pts (Bt: 4, Bw: 1), Somerset 6 pts (Bt: 4, Bw: 2)
100 overs scores : Somerset 323 for 4

**SOMERSET**

|  | | | | |
|---|---|---|---|---|
| S.J.Cook | c Pick b Stephenson | 43 | lbw b Pick | 2 |
| G.T.J.Townsend | b Stephenson | 20 | c French b Pick | 1 |
| A.N.Hayhurst | c Stephenson b Afford | 33 | not out | 100 |
| C.J.Tavare * | c Johnson b Evans | 47 | lbw b Evans | 50 |
| R.J.Harden | c French b Stephenson | 101 | b Johnson | 38 |
| N.D.Burns + | b Evans | 108 | not out | 19 |
| G.D.Rose | c French b Stephenson | 31 | | |
| I.G.Swallow | not out | 8 | | |
| H.R.J.Trump | c Robinson b Evans | 1 | | |
| D.A.Graveney | | | | |
| J.C.Hallett | | | | |
| Extras | (b 1,lb 5,nb 8) | 14 | (b 1,lb 3,nb 1) | 5 |
| TOTAL | (for 8 wkts dec) | 406 | (for 4 wkts dec) | 215 |

**NOTTS**

|  | | | | |
|---|---|---|---|---|
| B.C.Broad | b Graveney | 37 | c Swallow b Hallett | 131 |
| P.Pollard | lbw b Trump | 63 | c Rose b Graveney | 25 |
| R.T.Robinson * | c & b Trump | 49 | lbw b Hayhurst | 44 |
| D.W.Randall | c Swallow b Hayhurst | 13 | (5) not out | 73 |
| P.Johnson | not out | 71 | (4) run out | 19 |
| K.P.Evans | c Hallett b Swallow | 14 | (8) b Hallett | 7 |
| F.D.Stephenson | b Graveney | 44 | (6) run out | 9 |
| B.N.French + | not out | 0 | (7) lbw b Trump | 0 |
| E.E.Hemmings | | | not out | 0 |
| R.A.Pick | | | | |
| J.A.Afford | | | | |
| Extras | (b 2,lb 1,w 2,nb 4) | 9 | (b 1,lb 5,w 1,nb 2) | 9 |
| TOTAL | (for 6 wkts dec) | 300 | (for 7 wkts) | 317 |

| NOTTS | O | M | R | W | O | M | R | W |
|---|---|---|---|---|---|---|---|---|
| Stephenson | 28 | 6 | 73 | 4 | 7 | 2 | 23 | 0 |
| Pick | 16 | 1 | 79 | 0 | 8 | 2 | 24 | 2 |
| Evans | 37.1 | 10 | 105 | 3 | 6 | 1 | 24 | 1 |
| Hemmings | 24 | 6 | 81 | 0 | | | | |
| Afford | 21 | 8 | 62 | 1 | 13 | 3 | 64 | 0 |
| Johnson | | | | | 8 | 0 | 36 | 1 |
| Pollard | | | | | 3.5 | 0 | 29 | 0 |
| French | | | | | 1 | 0 | 11 | 0 |

| SOMERSET | O | M | R | W | O | M | R | W |
|---|---|---|---|---|---|---|---|---|
| Rose | 14 | 2 | 51 | 0 | 5 | 0 | 28 | 0 |
| Hallett | 12 | 1 | 44 | 0 | 9 | 0 | 50 | 2 |
| Hayhurst | 14 | 2 | 48 | 1 | 8 | 0 | 37 | 1 |
| Graveney | 13 | 1 | 46 | 2 | 15 | 0 | 60 | 1 |
| Trump | 16 | 2 | 41 | 2 | 18 | 2 | 87 | 1 |
| Swallow | 12.1 | 1 | 67 | 1 | 11 | 1 | 49 | 0 |

**FALL OF WICKETS**

| | SOM | NOT | SOM | NOT |
|---|---|---|---|---|
| 1st | 54 | 60 | 3 | 54 |
| 2nd | 65 | 153 | 4 | 132 |
| 3rd | 149 | 158 | 92 | 158 |
| 4th | 149 | 158 | 156 | 259 |
| 5th | 327 | 226 | | 286 |
| 6th | 381 | 299 | | 286 |
| 7th | 404 | | | 311 |
| 8th | 406 | | | |
| 9th | | | | |
| 10th | | | | |

## ESSEX vs. NORTHANTS

at Colchester on 16th, 17th, 19th August 1991
Toss : Essex. Umpires : R.Julian and R.C.Tolchard
Essex won by an inns and 12 runs. Essex 24 pts (Bt: 4, Bw: 4), Northants 3 pts (Bt: 1, Bw: 2)
100 overs scores : Essex 358 for 6

**ESSEX**

|  | | |
|---|---|---|
| G.A.Gooch * | c Capel b Roberts | 173 |
| J.P.Stephenson | c Roberts b Capel | 0 |
| P.J.Prichard | b Capel | 2 |
| Salim Malik | c Bailey b Capel | 0 |
| N.Hussain | c Lamb b Williams | 141 |
| M.A.Garnham + | b Curran | 16 |
| D.R.Pringle | c Lamb b Roberts | 5 |
| N.A.Foster | not out | 41 |
| T.D.Topley | c Williams b Bailey | 7 |
| J.H.Childs | not out | 7 |
| P.M.Such | | |
| Extras | (b 1,lb 10) | 11 |
| TOTAL | (for 8 wkts dec) | 403 |

**NORTHANTS**

|  | | | | |
|---|---|---|---|---|
| A.J.Lamb * | c Stephenson b Topley | 9 | c Garnham b Pringle | 4 |
| A.Fordham | c Garnham b Childs | 29 | c Topley b Pringle | 18 |
| R.J.Bailey | c Prichard b Such | 21 | c Hussain b Salim Malik | 56 |
| N.A.Stanley | c Prichard b Childs | 0 | b Such | 23 |
| D.J.Capel | c Prichard b Such | 0 | c Salim Malik b Childs | 0 |
| K.M.Curran | c Hussain b Childs | 11 | c Prichard b Such | 8 |
| E.A.E.Baptiste | c Childs | 42 | lbw b Salim Malik | 28 |
| R.G.Williams | c Stephenson b Such | 19 | c Hussain b Such | 17 |
| D.Ripley + | b Childs | 17 | c Garnham b Salim Malik | 15 |
| A.R.Roberts | not out | 12 | not out | 17 |
| N.G.B.Cook | lbw b Childs | 0 | c Salim Malik b Childs | 11 |
| Extras | (b 4,lb 6,nb 2) | 12 | (b 15,lb 4,nb 3) | 22 |
| TOTAL | | 172 | | 219 |

| NORTHANTS | O | M | R | W | O | M | R | W |
|---|---|---|---|---|---|---|---|---|
| Capel | 14 | 3 | 40 | 3 | | | | |
| Baptiste | 23 | 7 | 61 | 0 | | | | |
| Curran | 16 | 2 | 44 | 1 | | | | |
| Cook | 18.1 | 2 | 65 | 0 | | | | |
| Williams | 10.5 | 1 | 51 | 1 | | | | |
| Roberts | 21 | 0 | 107 | 2 | | | | |
| Bailey | 7 | 1 | 24 | 1 | | | | |

| ESSEX | O | M | R | W | O | M | R | W |
|---|---|---|---|---|---|---|---|---|
| Foster | 8 | 3 | 21 | 0 | 7 | 3 | 17 | 0 |
| Pringle | 10 | 3 | 14 | 0 | 7 | 1 | 26 | 2 |
| Topley | 7 | 2 | 20 | 1 | | | | |
| Childs | 20.1 | 6 | 61 | 6 | 23.3 | 5 | 77 | 2 |
| Such | 19 | 4 | 46 | 3 | 16 | 4 | 54 | 3 |
| Salim Malik | | | | | 8 | 2 | 26 | 3 |

**FALL OF WICKETS**

| | ESS | NOR | NOR |
|---|---|---|---|
| 1st | 15 | 28 | 16 |
| 2nd | 21 | 51 | 31 |
| 3rd | 21 | 51 | 76 |
| 4th | 308 | 54 | 77 |
| 5th | 333 | 67 | 110 |
| 6th | 347 | 81 | 151 |
| 7th | 368 | 141 | 158 |
| 8th | 385 | 141 | 185 |
| 9th | | 172 | 190 |
| 10th | | 172 | 219 |

## DERBYSHIRE vs. LANCASHIRE

at Derby on 16th, 17th, 19th August 1991
Toss : Lancashire. Umpires : D.J.Constant and J.H.Harris
Derbyshire won by 5 wickets. Derbyshire 23 pts (Bt: 4, Bw: 3), Lancashire 5 pts (Bt: 4, Bw: 1)

**LANCASHIRE**

|  | | | | |
|---|---|---|---|---|
| G.D.Mendis | c Azharuddin b Mortensen | 65 | b Cork | 12 |
| N.J.Speak | lbw b Base | 32 | c & b Sladdin | 39 |
| M.A.Atherton | c O'Gorman b Sladdin | 14 | b Base | 32 |
| N.H.Fairbrother * | c Krikken b Mortensen | 33 | c Base b Adams | 72 |
| G.D.Lloyd | st Krikken b Sladdin | 85 | lbw b Adams | 4 |
| M.Watkinson | c Barnett b Goldsmith | 25 | lbw b Adams | 3 |
| P.A.J.DeFreitas | st Krikken b Goldsmith | 35 | c Sladdin b Bowler | 17 |
| W.K.Hegg + | c Azharuddin b Sladdin | 30 | not out | 37 |
| G.Yates | not out | 4 | b Adams | 7 |
| P.J.Martin | | | not out | 6 |
| P.J.W.Allott | | | | |
| Extras | (b 4,lb 6,nb 14) | 24 | (b 2,lb 11,nb 1) | 14 |
| TOTAL | (for 8 wkts dec) | 347 | (for 8 wkts dec) | 243 |

**DERBYSHIRE**

|  | | | | |
|---|---|---|---|---|
| K.J.Barnett * | b DeFreitas | 5 | c Yates b Allott | 52 |
| P.D.Bowler | not out | 104 | lbw b Allott | 62 |
| S.J.Base | c Hegg b Allott | 22 | | |
| T.J.G.O'Gorman | b DeFreitas | 2 | (3) c Hegg b Martin | 24 |
| M.Azharuddin | not out | 160 | (4) run out | 67 |
| S.C.Goldsmith | | | (5) c Allott b Martin | 20 |
| C.J.Adams | | | (6) not out | 29 |
| K.M.Krikken + | | | (7) not out | 17 |
| D.G.Cork | | | | |
| R.W.Sladdin | | | | |
| O.H.Mortensen | | | | |
| Extras | (lb 3,w 1,nb 3) | 7 | (b 10,lb 8,w 2) | 20 |
| TOTAL | (for 3 wkts dec) | 300 | (for 5 wkts) | 291 |

| DERBYSHIRE | O | M | R | W | O | M | R | W |
|---|---|---|---|---|---|---|---|---|
| Mortensen | 18 | 4 | 48 | 2 | 12 | 2 | 35 | 0 |
| Cork | 20 | 2 | 59 | 0 | 6 | 1 | 31 | 1 |
| Base | 20 | 2 | 97 | 1 | 10 | 2 | 24 | 1 |
| Sladdin | 27.3 | 6 | 93 | 3 | 15 | 7 | 23 | 1 |
| Goldsmith | 13 | 2 | 40 | 2 | | | | |
| Adams | | | | | 6.4 | 1 | 29 | 4 |
| O'Gorman | | | | | 12 | 0 | 42 | 0 |
| Bowler | | | | | 7 | 1 | 46 | 1 |

| LANCASHIRE | O | M | R | W | O | M | R | W |
|---|---|---|---|---|---|---|---|---|
| DeFreitas | 22 | 8 | 62 | 2 | 17 | 3 | 58 | 0 |
| Martin | 22.3 | 5 | 78 | 0 | 17 | 2 | 102 | 2 |
| Allott | 15 | 3 | 39 | 1 | 18 | 6 | 39 | 2 |
| Watkinson | 11 | 1 | 46 | 0 | 5 | 1 | 21 | 0 |
| Yates | 16 | 2 | 72 | 0 | 8 | 0 | 53 | 0 |

**FALL OF WICKETS**

| | LAN | DER | LAN | DER |
|---|---|---|---|---|
| 1st | 64 | 6 | 12 | 110 |
| 2nd | 118 | 51 | 73 | 118 |
| 3rd | 158 | 60 | 115 | 177 |
| 4th | 163 | | 126 | 237 |
| 5th | 217 | | 144 | 239 |
| 6th | 286 | | 180 | |
| 7th | 336 | | 219 | |
| 8th | 347 | | 227 | |
| 9th | | | | |
| 10th | | | | |

## WORCESTERSHIRE vs. SURREY

at Worcester on 16th, 17th, 19th August 1991
Toss : Surrey. Umpires : B.Dudleston and D.O.Oslear
Worcestershire won by 3 wickets. Worcs 24 pts (Bt: 4, Bw: 4), Surrey 5 pts (Bt: 1, Bw: 4)
100 overs scores : Worcestershire 401 for 9

**SURREY**

|  | | | | |
|---|---|---|---|---|
| D.J.Bicknell | c D'Oliveira b Lampitt | 35 | lbw b Dilley | 79 |
| R.I.Alikhan | c Rhodes b Botham | 30 | b Newport | 0 |
| A.J.Stewart | c Curtis b Dilley | 9 | c D'Oliveira b Lampitt | 57 |
| D.M.Ward | lbw b Botham | 14 | (5) c Botham b Lampitt | 1 |
| G.P.Thorpe | lbw b Illingworth | 22 | (6) c Curtis b Lampitt | 30 |
| I.A.Greig * | not out | 38 | (7) c Rhodes b Lampitt | 72 |
| K.T.Medlycott | c D'Oliveira b Illingworth | 4 | (8) c D'Oliveira b Lampitt | 57 |
| N.F.Sargeant + | c D'Oliveira b Botham | 3 | (4) c Moody b Dilley | 11 |
| M.P.Bicknell | c Lampitt b Botham | 0 | b Botham | 10 |
| Waqar Younis | c D'Oliveira b Illingworth | 15 | c Newport b Lampitt | 7 |
| A.J.Murphy | c Curtis b Medlycott | 1 | not out | 2 |
| Extras | (lb 3,w 2,nb 9) | 14 | (b 12,lb 10,nb 12) | 34 |
| TOTAL | | 185 | | 360 |

**WORCESTERSHIRE**

|  | | | | |
|---|---|---|---|---|
| T.S.Curtis * | c Sargeant b Waqar Younis | 98 | c Stewart b Bicknell M.P. | 8 |
| P.Bent | b Waqar Younis | 5 | c Sargeant b Bicknell M.P. | 0 |
| G.A.Hick | b Waqar Younis | 145 | c Greig b Medlycott | 85 |
| T.M.Moody | c Murphy b Bicknell M.P. | 37 | b Waqar Younis | 17 |
| D.B.D'Oliveira | b Waqar Younis | 0 | b Waqar Younis | 1 |
| S.J.Rhodes + | c Sargeant b Bicknell M.P. | 12 | (7) not out | 23 |
| I.T.Botham | c Thorpe b Medlycott | 61 | (6) b Waqar Younis | 0 |
| R.K.Illingworth | lbw b Bicknell M.P. | 9 | c Sargeant b Medlycott | 0 |
| S.R.Lampitt | b Bicknell M.P. | 3 | not out | 5 |
| P.J.Newport | not out | 2 | | |
| G.R.Dilley | not out | 5 | | |
| Extras | (b 1,lb 20,w 2,nb 1) | 24 | (lb 5,nb 1) | 6 |
| TOTAL | (for 9 wkts dec) | 401 | (for 7 wkts) | 145 |

| WORCS | O | M | R | W | O | M | R | W |
|---|---|---|---|---|---|---|---|---|
| Dilley | 14 | 4 | 30 | 1 | 25 | 5 | 87 | 2 |
| Newport | 12 | 4 | 30 | 0 | 19 | 4 | 64 | 1 |
| Lampitt | 9 | 3 | 25 | 1 | 18.4 | 3 | 70 | 5 |
| Botham | 20.5 | 4 | 67 | 5 | 15 | 3 | 43 | 1 |
| Illingworth | 13 | 5 | 30 | 3 | 26 | 8 | 39 | 1 |
| Hick | | | | | 10 | 1 | 30 | 0 |
| D'Oliveira | | | | | 4 | 2 | 8 | 0 |

| SURREY | O | M | R | W | O | M | R | W |
|---|---|---|---|---|---|---|---|---|
| Waqar Younis | 24 | 5 | 78 | 4 | 14 | 3 | 56 | 3 |
| Bicknell M.P. | 33 | 5 | 104 | 4 | 4 | 1 | 30 | 2 |
| Murphy | 18 | 3 | 91 | 0 | | | | |
| Greig | 4 | 1 | 12 | 0 | | | | |
| Medlycott | 21 | 3 | 95 | 1 | 9.1 | 0 | 54 | 2 |

**FALL OF WICKETS**

| | SUR | WOR | SUR | WOR |
|---|---|---|---|---|
| 1st | 59 | 15 | 14 | 8 |
| 2nd | 79 | 247 | 124 | 25 |
| 3rd | 91 | 266 | 147 | 82 |
| 4th | 123 | 303 | 153 | 90 |
| 5th | 123 | 303 | 172 | 92 |
| 6th | 131 | 352 | 229 | 137 |
| 7th | 142 | 382 | 351 | 137 |
| 8th | 142 | 394 | 351 | |
| 9th | 169 | 396 | 351 | |
| 10th | 185 | | 360 | |

# BRITANNIC ASSURANCE CHAMPIONSHIP

## HEADLINES

### Britannic Assurance Championship

### 16th - 19th August

• Essex, still with one match in hand, reduced Warwickshire's lead to 13 points after their victory by an innings and 12 runs over Northamptonshire at Colchester. The home side reached 403 for eight thanks to a fourth-wicket stand of 287 between Graham Gooch, who recorded his fourth 100 of the summer, and Nasser Hussain, who hit his second, then spinners John Childs, who returned figures of six for 61 in Northants' first innings, Peter Such and Salim Malik proved too much for the visitors as 19 wickets fell on the second day. The ease with which Essex's seventh win of the season was achieved backed claims that they were the strongest all-round side in the country.

• Other sides retaining an interest in the 1991 Championship enjoyed mixed fortunes. Derbyshire overcame Lancashire by five wickets at Derby, reaching a target of 291 in 65 overs. Mohammad Azharuddin had earlier dominated Derbyshire's first innings with an unbeaten 160, his fifth 100 of the summer, made out of a stand of 240 for the fourth wicket with Peter Bowler who completed his first 100 of the year.

• Surrey's title challenge suffered when they lost by three wickets to Worcestershire at Worcester. Ian Botham's five for 67 skittled them out for 185 and the home side established a first innings lead of 216 thanks to Graeme Hick, who put his recent problems behind him with 145. Surrey made a better effort of their second innings, first Darren Bicknell and Alec Stewart, then Ian Greig and Keith Medlycott sharing century partnerships as their total reached 360, leaving Worcestershire with a potentially tricky 145 for victory. Seven wickets were lost but Hick's 85 saw Worcestershire to the brink of success.

• At Trent Bridge, Nottinghamshire faced an imposing target for victory over Somerset to revive their Championship ambitions. Asked to make 322 in 67 overs, Notts finished just five runs short thanks to 131 from Chris Broad, his fifth 100 of the season. Somerset had taken control of the match by reaching 406 for eight in their first innings after 100s from both Richard Harden and Neil Burns.

• Hampshire gained their fourth win in five matches with their two-wicket success over Leicestershire at Bournemouth. In the visitors' first innings both Justin Benson and Phil Whitticase reached maiden first-class 100s as they added 219 for the seventh wicket.

• Rain on the last day condemned Yorkshire's match with Glamorgan at Headingley to stalemate. Openers Ashley Metcalfe, who hit his second 100 of the summer, and Hugh Morris, who equalled his career best, had taken the batting honours on the first two days before the Glamorgan spinners claimed three wickets apiece as Yorkshire slumped to 99 for eight in their second innings.

## HAMPSHIRE vs. LEICESTERSHIRE

at Bournemouth on 16th, 17th, 19th August 1991
Toss : Leicestershire.  Umpires : N.T.Plews and R.A.White
Hampshire won by 2 wickets.  Hampshire 21 pts (Bt: 3, Bw: 2), Leics 6 pts (Bt: 4, Bw: 2)
100 overs scores : Leicestershire 394 for 6, Hampshire 256 for 6

**LEICESTERSHIRE**

| | | | | |
|---|---|---|---|---|
| T.J.Boon | run out | 53 | c Nicholas b Shine | 12 |
| N.E.Briers * | c Aymes b Aqib Javed | 8 | not out | 80 |
| P.N.Hepworth | c Middleton b James | 4 | not out | 43 |
| J.J.Whitaker | c Aymes b Turner | 10 | | |
| L.Potter | lbw b James | 14 | | |
| J.D.R.Benson | not out | 133 | | |
| C.C.Lewis | c Middleton b Turner | 34 | | |
| P.Whitticase + | not out | 114 | | |
| D.J.Millns | | | | |
| C.Wilkinson | | | | |
| J.N.Maguire | | | | |
| Extras | (b 8,lb 3,nb 13) | 24 | (b 7,lb 3,nb 5) | 15 |
| TOTAL | (for 6 wkts dec) | 394 | (for 1 wkt dec) | 150 |

**HAMPSHIRE**

| | | | | |
|---|---|---|---|---|
| T.C.Middleton | c Benson b Lewis | 22 | (2) lbw b Lewis | 20 |
| V.P.Terry | lbw b Millns | 10 | (1) lbw b Maguire | 79 |
| I.J.Turner | c Whitticase b Millns | 1 | (9) not out | 1 |
| K.D.James | c Wilkinson b Maguire | 45 | (6) c Whitaker b Millns | 72 |
| R.A.Smith | c Wilkinson b Potter | 61 | (4) c Wilkinson b Potter | 39 |
| D.I.Gower | c Lewis b Potter | 11 | (3) c Potter b Millns | 16 |
| M.C.J.Nicholas * | not out | 73 | (5) b Maguire | 9 |
| A.N Aymes + | not out | 32 | (7) run out | 29 |
| C.A.Connor | | | (8) run out | 1 |
| K.J.Shine | | | not out | 8 |
| Aqib Javed | | | | |
| Extras | (w 2,nb 5) | 7 | (b 3,lb 4,w 1,nb 3) | 11 |
| TOTAL | (for 6 wkts dec) | 262 | (for 8 wkts) | 285 |

| HAMPSHIRE | O | M | R | W | O | M | R | W |
|---|---|---|---|---|---|---|---|---|
| Aqib Javed | 16 | 2 | 72 | 1 | 11 | 3 | 22 | 0 |
| Connor | 17 | 4 | 62 | 0 | 9 | 0 | 34 | 0 |
| Shine | 15 | 2 | 66 | 0 | 11 | 1 | 46 | 1 |
| James | 17 | 4 | 56 | 2 | 3 | 1 | 6 | 0 |
| Turner | 25 | 7 | 69 | 2 | 13 | 3 | 32 | 0 |
| Nicholas | 6 | 0 | 36 | 0 | | | | |
| Smith | 4 | 1 | 22 | 0 | | | | |

| LEICS | O | M | R | W | O | M | R | W |
|---|---|---|---|---|---|---|---|---|
| Lewis | 20 | 7 | 42 | 1 | 16.5 | 1 | 72 | 1 |
| Millns | 19 | 6 | 48 | 3 | 11 | 1 | 65 | 2 |
| Maguire | 27 | 7 | 52 | 1 | 19 | 3 | 65 | 2 |
| Wilkinson | 13 | 1 | 51 | 0 | | | | |
| Potter | 19 | 1 | 59 | 2 | 14 | 2 | 56 | 1 |
| Hepworth | 3 | 2 | 1 | 0 | 5 | 1 | 20 | 0 |
| Benson | 2 | 0 | 9 | 0 | | | | |

**FALL OF WICKETS**

| | LEI | HAM | LEI | HAM |
|---|---|---|---|---|
| 1st | 14 | 12 | 23 | 59 |
| 2nd | 31 | 18 | | 83 |
| 3rd | 65 | 41 | | 156 |
| 4th | 97 | 130 | | 166 |
| 5th | 97 | 150 | | 187 |
| 6th | 175 | 178 | | 272 |
| 7th | | | | 275 |
| 8th | | | | 277 |
| 9th | | | | |
| 10th | | | | |

## YORKSHIRE vs. GLAMORGAN

at Headingley on 16th, 17th, 19th August 1991
Toss : Yorkshire.  Umpires : K.E.Palmer and R.Palmer
Match drawn.  Yorkshire 5 pts (Bt: 4, Bw: 1), Glamorgan 5 pts (Bt: 4, Bw: 1)
100 overs scores : Yorkshire 307 for 4, Glamorgan 303 for 4

**YORKSHIRE**

| | | | | |
|---|---|---|---|---|
| M.D.Moxon * | c Shastri b Watkin | 80 | (8) b Shastri | 0 |
| A.A.Metcalfe | lbw b Foster | 123 | lbw b Frost | 26 |
| D.Byas | c Metson b Frost | 32 | c Shastri b Croft | 20 |
| S.A.Kellett | b Croft | 34 | (1) b Foster | 16 |
| P.E.Robinson | b Watkin | 51 | (4) c & b Croft | 8 |
| R.J.Blakey + | c Dale b Croft | 3 | (5) c Dale b Shastri | 3 |
| C.S.Pickles | c Butcher b Watkin | 28 | (6) not out | 34 |
| P.Carrick | c Butcher b Shastri | 9 | (7) c Cottey b Shastri | 1 |
| P.J.Hartley | not out | 8 | c Metson b Croft | 6 |
| J.D.Batty | not out | 4 | not out | 19 |
| M.A.Robinson | | | | |
| Extras | (lb 15,nb 14) | 29 | (b 4,lb 3,nb 3) | 10 |
| TOTAL | (for 8 wkts dec) | 401 | (for 8 wkts dec) | 143 |

**GLAMORGAN**

| | | | | |
|---|---|---|---|---|
| A.R.Butcher * | b Batty | 79 | not out | 7 |
| H.Morris | not out | 156 | not out | 2 |
| A.Dale | b Batty | 0 | | |
| M.P.Maynard | c Blakey b Batty | 21 | | |
| R.J.Shastri | c Byas b Batty | 41 | | |
| P.A.Cottey | not out | 9 | | |
| R.D.B.Croft | | | | |
| C.P.Metson + | | | | |
| S.L.Watkin | | | | |
| M.Frost | | | | |
| D.J.Foster | | | | |
| Extras | (b 12,lb 4,nb 5) | 21 | | 0 |
| TOTAL | (for 4 wkts dec) | 327 | (for 0 wkts) | 9 |

| GLAMORGAN | O | M | R | W | O | M | R | W |
|---|---|---|---|---|---|---|---|---|
| Watkin | 18.4 | 2 | 64 | 3 | 10 | 1 | 34 | 0 |
| Frost | 16 | 3 | 55 | 1 | 5 | 0 | 12 | 1 |
| Shastri | 38 | 5 | 111 | 1 | 14 | 7 | 18 | 3 |
| Foster | 20 | 7 | 48 | 1 | 6 | 1 | 27 | 1 |
| Croft | 37 | 5 | 108 | 2 | 19 | 3 | 45 | 3 |

| YORKSHIRE | O | M | R | W | O | M | R | W |
|---|---|---|---|---|---|---|---|---|
| Robinson M.A. | 16 | 6 | 42 | 0 | 2.2 | 2 | 1 | 0 |
| Hartley | 12 | 4 | 26 | 0 | 3 | 0 | 8 | 0 |
| Carrick | 35 | 9 | 97 | 0 | | | | |
| Pickles | 9 | 2 | 28 | 0 | | | | |
| Batty | 35 | 4 | 118 | 4 | | | | |

**FALL OF WICKETS**

| | YOR | GLA | YOR | GLA |
|---|---|---|---|---|
| 1st | 156 | 164 | 10 | |
| 2nd | 245 | 164 | 57 | |
| 3rd | 277 | 194 | 73 | |
| 4th | 305 | 262 | 75 | |
| 5th | 315 | | 77 | |
| 6th | 358 | | 88 | |
| 7th | 380 | | 88 | |
| 8th | 396 | | 99 | |
| 9th | | | | |
| 10th | | | | |

## TOUR MATCH

## BRITANNIC ASS. CHAMPIONSHIP

### SUSSEX vs. SRI LANKA
at Hove on 17th, 18th, 19th August 1991
Toss : Sri Lanka.  Umpires : M.J.Harris and K.J.Lyons
Match drawn

**SUSSEX**

| Batsman | Dismissal | R | Dismissal 2 | R2 |
|---|---|---|---|---|
| N.J.Lenham | c Gurusinha b Ramanayake | 61 | lbw b Ramanayake | 2 |
| D.M.Smith | lbw b Ramanayake | 8 | (3) not out | 100 |
| K.Greenfield | c Mahanama b Wijeguna' | 7 | (2) run out | 104 |
| A.P.Wells * | c Tillekaratne b Wijeguna' | 0 | not out | 7 |
| M.P.Speight | lbw b Hathurusinghe | 33 | | |
| C.M.Wells | c Tillekaratne b Hathurusinghe | 0 | | |
| J.A.North | c Tillekaratne b Wijeguna' | 41 | | |
| P.Moores + | c Tillekaratne b Wijeguna' | 102 | | |
| A.C.S.Pigott | c Muralitharan b Ramanayake | 29 | | |
| I.D.K.Salisbury | not out | 9 | | |
| A.N.Jones | not out | 9 | | |
| Extras | (b 3,lb 12,w 5,nb 11) | 31 | (lb 4,nb 7) | 11 |
| TOTAL | (for 9 wkts dec) | 330 | (for 2 wkts dec) | 224 |

**SRI LANKA**

| Batsman | Dismissal | R | Dismissal 2 | R2 |
|---|---|---|---|---|
| D.S.B.P.Kuruppu | lbw b North | 6 | lbw b North | 59 |
| U.C.Hathurusinghe | run out | 18 | b North | 31 |
| A.P.Gurusinha * | c Moores b Jones | 29 | c Wells C.M. b North | 1 |
| H.P.Tillekaratne + | lbw b Salisbury | 30 | (6) not out | 80 |
| R.S.Mahanama | c Moores b North | 24 | (4) lbw b Jones | 65 |
| S.T.Jayasuriya | not out | 100 | (7) lbw b Pigott | 10 |
| M.S.Atapattu | not out | 52 | (5) c Moores b North | 2 |
| C.P.Ramanayake | | | (9) run out | 2 |
| K.I.W.Wijeguna' | | | (8) run out | 0 |
| S.D.Anurasiri | | | not out | 0 |
| M.Muralitharan | | | | |
| Extras | (b 4,lb 7,w 2,nb 8) | 21 | (lb 5) | 5 |
| TOTAL | (for 5 wkts dec) | 280 | (for 8 wkts) | 255 |

| SRI LANKA | O | M | R | W | O | M | R | W |
|---|---|---|---|---|---|---|---|---|
| Ramanayake | 22 | 4 | 83 | 3 | 14 | 2 | 34 | 1 |
| Wijeguna' | 24 | 3 | 111 | 4 | 8 | 3 | 24 | 0 |
| Gurusinha | 2 | 0 | 11 | 0 | | | | |
| Hathurusinghe | 12 | 4 | 18 | 2 | 1 | 0 | 3 | 0 |
| Muralitharan | 19 | 4 | 43 | 0 | 20.1 | 2 | 69 | 0 |
| Anurasiri | 23 | 3 | 45 | 0 | 25 | 7 | 87 | 0 |
| Jayasuriya | 3 | 1 | 4 | 0 | 2 | 1 | 3 | 0 |

| SUSSEX | O | M | R | W | O | M | R | W |
|---|---|---|---|---|---|---|---|---|
| Jones | 11 | 4 | 30 | 1 | 9 | 1 | 50 | 1 |
| Pigott | 16 | 5 | 61 | 0 | 12.5 | 1 | 48 | 1 |
| North | 15.3 | 5 | 43 | 2 | 12 | 1 | 47 | 4 |
| Wells C.M. | 14 | 2 | 46 | 0 | | | | |
| Salisbury | 19 | 3 | 89 | 1 | 14 | 1 | 75 | 0 |
| Greenfield | | | | | 6 | 0 | 30 | 0 |

| FALL OF WICKETS | SUS | SRI | SUS | SRI |
|---|---|---|---|---|
| 1st | 24 | 22 | 2 | 81 |
| 2nd | 31 | 45 | 196 | 92 |
| 3rd | 31 | 75 | | 97 |
| 4th | 86 | 122 | | 109 |
| 5th | 98 | 140 | | 228 |
| 6th | 127 | | | 249 |
| 7th | 202 | | | 252 |
| 8th | 305 | | | 254 |
| 9th | 313 | | | |
| 10th | | | | |

---

### HEADLINES

**Tetley Bitter Challenge**

**17th - 19th August**

• Sri Lanka finished 20 runs short of victory over Sussex at Hove with two wickets in hand, having gained some encouragement from their performance in their final match before the Lord's Test. Seam bowlers Ramanayake and Wijegunawardene reduced Sussex to 127 for six in their first innings before Peter Moores led a revival, while Sanath Jayasuriya became the first Sri Lankan to reach three figures, and Marvin Atapattu, Roshan Mahanama and Hashan Tillekeratne also made their highest scores of the tour so far.

---

### DERBYSHIRE vs. LEICESTERSHIRE
at Derby on 20th, 21st August 1991
Toss : Leicestershire.  Umpires : D.J.Constant and J.H.Harris
Leics won by an innings and 131 runs.  Derbys 3 pts (Bt: 0, Bw: 3), Leics 23 pts (Bt: 3, Bw: 4)
100 overs scores :Leicestershire 291 for 7

**DERBYSHIRE**

| Batsman | Dismissal | R | Dismissal 2 | R2 |
|---|---|---|---|---|
| K.J.Barnett * | b Millns | 20 | c Whitticase b Wilkinson | 26 |
| P.D.Bowler | b Millns | 0 | c Whitticase b Maguire | 5 |
| T.J.G.O'Gorman | c Potter b Millns | 6 | c Whitticase b Millns | 13 |
| C.J.Adams | c Whitticase b Wilkinson | 44 | lbw b Millns | 0 |
| M.Azharuddin | c Whitticase b Millns | 3 | lbw b Maguire | 26 |
| S.C.Goldsmith | lbw b Millns | 0 | run out | 20 |
| K.M.Krikken + | lbw b Millns | 0 | c Boon b Wilkinson | 24 |
| D.G.Cork | c Whitticase b Millns | 25 | b Wilkinson | 8 |
| A.E.Warner | b Millns | 10 | c Whitticase b Wilkinson | 8 |
| D.E.Malcolm | not out | 5 | c Whitticase b Millns | 4 |
| O.H.Mortensen | b Millns | 0 | not out | 0 |
| Extras | (lb 3,nb 1) | 4 | (lb 1,w 3,nb 6) | 10 |
| TOTAL | | 117 | | 144 |

**LEICESTERSHIRE**

| Batsman | Dismissal | R |
|---|---|---|
| T.J.Boon | c Azharuddin b Warner | 35 |
| N.E.Briers * | b Malcolm | 0 |
| P.N.Hepworth | b Cork | 18 |
| J.J.Whitaker | c O'Gorman b Mortensen | 47 |
| L.Potter | b Malcolm | 25 |
| B.F.Smith | c Adams b Cork | 51 |
| P.Whitticase + | b Warner | 93 |
| J.D.R.Benson | c Adams b Cork | 19 |
| D.J.Millns | c Krikken b Goldsmith | 17 |
| C.Wilkinson | not out | 31 |
| J.N.Maguire | c O'Gorman b Barnett | 26 |
| Extras | (b 5,lb 17,w 3,nb 5) | 30 |
| TOTAL | | 392 |

| LEICS | O | M | R | W | O | M | R | W |
|---|---|---|---|---|---|---|---|---|
| Millns | 18.3 | 4 | 37 | 9 | 13 | 0 | 54 | 3 |
| Maguire | 13 | 2 | 37 | 0 | 12 | 3 | 30 | 2 |
| Wilkinson | 9 | 1 | 34 | 1 | 14 | 0 | 59 | 4 |
| Potter | 1 | 0 | 1 | 0 | | | | |
| Benson | 1 | 0 | 5 | 0 | | | | |

| DERBYSHIRE | O | M | R | W | O | M | R | W |
|---|---|---|---|---|---|---|---|---|
| Malcolm | 32 | 5 | 117 | 2 | | | | |
| Mortensen | 28 | 8 | 59 | 1 | | | | |
| Cork | 25 | 8 | 62 | 3 | | | | |
| Warner | 29 | 3 | 99 | 2 | | | | |
| Goldsmith | 9 | 1 | 31 | 1 | | | | |
| Barnett | 1.4 | 0 | 2 | 1 | | | | |

| FALL OF WICKETS | DER | LEI | DER | LEI |
|---|---|---|---|---|
| 1st | 1 | 3 | 19 | |
| 2nd | 24 | 49 | 45 | |
| 3rd | 39 | 67 | 93 | |
| 4th | 43 | 125 | 47 | |
| 5th | 45 | 151 | 91 | |
| 6th | 57 | 234 | 100 | |
| 7th | 99 | 284 | 119 | |
| 8th | 109 | 314 | 131 | |
| 9th | 113 | 341 | 136 | |
| 10th | 117 | 392 | 144 | |

---

### ESSEX vs. YORKSHIRE
at Colchester on 20th, 21st, 22nd August 1991
Toss : Yorkshire.  Umpires : R.Julian and R.C.Tolchard
Yorkshire won by 3 runs.  Essex 5 pts (Bt: 4, Bw: 1), Yorkshire 21 pts (Bt: 4, Bw: 1)
100 overs scores : Yorkshire 312 for 4

**YORKSHIRE**

| Batsman | Dismissal | R | Dismissal 2 | R2 |
|---|---|---|---|---|
| M.D.Moxon * | c Garnham b Foster | 200 | c & b Topley | 66 |
| A.A.Metcalfe | c Garnham b Foster | 22 | c Seymour b Topley | 4 |
| D.Byas | c Garnham b Such | 25 | c Seymour b Topley | 7 |
| S.A.Kellett | c Garnham b Salim Malik | 58 | lbw b Childs | 41 |
| P.E.Robinson | lbw b Salim Malik | 0 | not out | 35 |
| R.J.Blakey + | c Knight b Topley | 56 | not out | 4 |
| C.S.Pickles | lbw b Topley | 0 | | |
| P.Carrick | c Knight b Stephenson | 28 | | |
| P.J.Hartley | not out | 33 | | |
| J.D.Batty | c Prichard b Stephenson | 5 | | |
| M.A.Robinson | | | | |
| Extras | (lb 9,w 2,nb 8) | 19 | (b 8,lb 5,nb 2) | 15 |
| TOTAL | (for 9 wkts dec) | 446 | (for 4 wkts dec) | 172 |

**ESSEX**

| Batsman | Dismissal | R | Dismissal 2 | R2 |
|---|---|---|---|---|
| A.C.Seymour | c Kellett b Carrick | 27 | c Moxon b Hartley | 9 |
| J.P.Stephenson | c Metcalfe b Robinson M.A. | 116 | lbw b Batty | 97 |
| P.J.Prichard | c Byas b Robinson M.A. | 128 | b Robinson M.A. | 8 |
| Salim Malik | not out | 11 | c Kellett b Batty | 56 |
| N.Hussain | not out | 1 | st Blakey b Carrick | 5 |
| N.V.Knight | | | c Metcalfe b Carrick | 60 |
| M.A.Garnham + | | | c Robinson M.A. b Carrick | 68 |
| N.A.Foster * | | | b Batty | 4 |
| T.D.Topley | | | c sub b Batty | 3 |
| J.H.Childs | | | c Batty b Carrick | 1 |
| P.M.Such | | | not out | 0 |
| Extras | (lb 16,nb 1) | 17 | (b 2,lb 2) | 4 |
| TOTAL | (for 3 wkts dec) | 300 | | 315 |

| ESSEX | O | M | R | W | O | M | R | W |
|---|---|---|---|---|---|---|---|---|
| Foster | 30 | 7 | 97 | 2 | 11 | 2 | 46 | 0 |
| Topley | 21 | 3 | 86 | 2 | 16 | 3 | 47 | 3 |
| Stephenson | 5.1 | 1 | 19 | 2 | 2 | 0 | 24 | 0 |
| Childs | 36 | 11 | 86 | 0 | 10 | 1 | 42 | 1 |
| Such | 14 | 1 | 52 | 1 | | | | |
| Salim Malik | 23 | 0 | 97 | 2 | | | | |

| YORKSHIRE | O | M | R | W | O | M | R | W |
|---|---|---|---|---|---|---|---|---|
| Robinson M.A. | 17 | 7 | 36 | 2 | 11 | 1 | 62 | 1 |
| Hartley | 10 | 1 | 34 | 0 | 6 | 0 | 52 | 1 |
| Carrick | 32 | 12 | 89 | 1 | 25.2 | 1 | 92 | 4 |
| Batty | 22 | 4 | 104 | 0 | 21 | 0 | 86 | 4 |
| Pickles | 6 | 1 | 21 | 0 | 4 | 0 | 19 | 0 |

| FALL OF WICKETS | YOR | ESS | YOR | ESS |
|---|---|---|---|---|
| 1st | 50 | 34 | 6 | 12 |
| 2nd | 90 | 280 | 20 | 31 |
| 3rd | 255 | 289 | 100 | 102 |
| 4th | 262 | | 162 | 107 |
| 5th | 364 | | | 205 |
| 6th | 365 | | | 293 |
| 7th | 380 | | | 303 |
| 8th | 436 | | | 311 |
| 9th | 446 | | | 314 |
| 10th | | | | 315 |

# BRITANNIC ASSURANCE CHAMPIONSHIP

## WARWICKSHIRE vs. GLAMORGAN

at Edgbaston on 20th, 21st, 22nd August 1991
Toss : Warwickshire. Umpires : J.C.Balderstone and B.Leadbeater
Match drawn. Warwickshire 6 pts (Bt: 4, Bw: 2), Glamorgan 7 pts (Bt: 4, Bw: 3)

### WARWICKSHIRE

| | | | | |
|---|---|---:|---|---:|
| A.J.Moles | c Metson b Dale | 65 | c Metson b Watkin | 10 |
| P.A.Smith | c Shastri b Dale | 50 | b Frost | 16 |
| T.A.Lloyd * | b Shastri | 86 | (8) c Butcher b Shastri | 0 |
| D.P.Ostler | c James b Shastri | 35 | b Shastri | 56 |
| D.A.Reeve | c Croft b Shastri | 40 | not out | 55 |
| Asif Din | c Dale b Watkin | 45 | (3) c Maynard b Shastri | 27 |
| N.M.K.Smith | c James b Shastri | 6 | (6) lbw b Shastri | 17 |
| P.C.L.Holloway + | not out | 4 | (7) b Shastri | 0 |
| G.C.Small | c Metson b Watkin | 4 | not out | 45 |
| T.A.Munton | | | | |
| A.A.Donald | | | | |
| Extras | (b 2,lb 19,nb 2) | 23 | (b 6,lb 12,nb 2) | 20 |
| TOTAL | (for 8 wkts dec) | 358 | (for 7 wkts dec) | 246 |

### GLAMORGAN

| | | | | |
|---|---|---:|---|---:|
| A.R.Butcher * | b Donald | 61 | b Small | 1 |
| S.P.James | c Moles b Munton | 4 | not out | 11 |
| C.P.Metson + | lbw b Donald | 47 | | |
| A.Dale | b Smith P.A. | 99 | (3) lbw b Small | 0 |
| M.P.Maynard | lbw b Smith N.M.K. | 24 | (4) c Ostler b Small | 0 |
| R.J.Shastri | not out | 80 | (5) not out | 39 |
| P.A.Cottey | not out | 2 | | |
| R.D.B.Croft | | | | |
| S.L.Watkin | | | | |
| M.Frost | | | | |
| S.Bastien | | | | |
| Extras | (b 10,lb 7,w 4,nb 8) | 29 | (b 1,lb 1,w 1) | 3 |
| TOTAL | (for 5 wkts dec) | 346 | (for 3 wkts) | 54 |

| GLAMORGAN | O | M | R | W | O | M | R | W |
|---|---:|---:|---:|---:|---:|---:|---:|---:|
| Watkin | 14.5 | 3 | 68 | 2 | 18 | 5 | 46 | 1 |
| Frost | 12 | 3 | 35 | 0 | 12 | 0 | 75 | 1 |
| Bastien | 20 | 6 | 61 | 0 | 9 | 3 | 18 | 0 |
| Dale | 15 | 3 | 43 | 2 | | | | |
| Croft | 17 | 6 | 57 | 0 | 6 | 2 | 18 | 0 |
| Shastri | 17 | 2 | 73 | 4 | 22 | 8 | 71 | 5 |

| WARWICKS | O | M | R | W | O | M | R | W |
|---|---:|---:|---:|---:|---:|---:|---:|---:|
| Donald | 23 | 3 | 68 | 2 | 1 | 0 | 2 | 0 |
| Small | 15 | 7 | 25 | 0 | 9 | 2 | 24 | 3 |
| Munton | 16.1 | 6 | 38 | 1 | 7 | 4 | 18 | 0 |
| Smith N.M.K. | 21 | 8 | 68 | 1 | 1 | 1 | 0 | 0 |
| Smith P.A. | 12 | 3 | 55 | 1 | | | | |
| Asif Din | 12 | 1 | 75 | 0 | 1 | 0 | 8 | 0 |

| FALL OF WICKETS | | | | |
|---|---:|---:|---:|---:|
| | WAR | GLA | WAR | GLA |
| 1st | 85 | 24 | 21 | 2 |
| 2nd | 207 | 118 | 38 | 2 |
| 3rd | 223 | 134 | 106 | 2 |
| 4th | 259 | 185 | 125 | |
| 5th | 338 | 323 | 149 | |
| 6th | 344 | | 155 | |
| 7th | 354 | | 155 | |
| 8th | 358 | | | |
| 9th | | | | |
| 10th | | | | |

## SURREY vs. MIDDLESEX

at The Oval on 20th, 21st, 22nd August 1991
Toss : Surrey. Umpires : G.I.Burgess and A.A.Jones
Match drawn. Surrey 7 pts (Bt: 3, Bw: 4), Middlesex 5 pts (Bt: 3, Bw: 2)
100 overs scores : Surrey 267 for 5

### SURREY

| | | | | |
|---|---|---:|---|---:|
| D.J.Bicknell | b Barnett | 33 | b Cowans | 22 |
| N.F.Sargeant + | c Weekes b Barnett | 37 | b Headley | 19 |
| G.P.Thorpe | c Emburey b Barnett | 0 | c Roseberry b Emburey | 40 |
| D.M.Ward | c Brown b Emburey | 9 | c Roseberry b Emburey | 43 |
| M.A.Lynch | not out | 141 | lbw b Emburey | 0 |
| I.A.Greig * | c & b Weekes | 9 | c Gatting b Headley | 4 |
| K.T.Medlycott | c Pooley b Headley | 59 | b Weekes | 40 |
| M.P.Bicknell | c Roseberry b Headley | 24 | c Keech b Headley | 1 |
| Waqar Younis | c Keech b Cowans | 4 | b Headley | 0 |
| J.Boiling | b Headley | 0 | c Roseberry b Weekes | 16 |
| A.J.Murphy | not out | 2 | not out | 7 |
| Extras | (b 8,lb 6,w 4,nb 5) | 23 | (b 4,lb 7,nb 5) | 16 |
| TOTAL | (for 9 wkts dec) | 341 | | 208 |

### MIDDLESEX

| | | | | |
|---|---|---:|---|---:|
| M.A.Roseberry | lbw b Waqar Younis | 2 | c & b Medlycott | 51 |
| J.C.Pooley | b Boiling | 20 | lbw b Murphy | 1 |
| M.W.Gatting * | c Boiling b Medlycott | 50 | not out | 40 |
| K.R.Brown | c Sargeant b Waqar Younis | 30 | not out | 8 |
| M.Keech | c Sargeant b Bicknell M.P. | 18 | | |
| P.N.Weekes | st Sargeant b Boiling | 86 | | |
| J.E.Emburey | c Waqar Younis b Medlycott | 59 | | |
| P.Farbrace + | b Waqar Younis | 3 | | |
| D.W.Headley | c Sargeant b Waqar Younis | 4 | | |
| N.G.Cowans | b Waqar Younis | 0 | | |
| A.A.Barnett | not out | 11 | | |
| Extras | (b 4,lb 7,w 1,nb 2) | 14 | (b 1) | 1 |
| TOTAL | | 297 | (for 2 wkts) | 101 |

| MIDDLESEX | O | M | R | W | O | M | R | W |
|---|---:|---:|---:|---:|---:|---:|---:|---:|
| Headley | 18 | 2 | 65 | 3 | 21 | 3 | 69 | 4 |
| Cowans | 19 | 3 | 65 | 1 | 12 | 1 | 27 | 1 |
| Emburey | 31 | 4 | 79 | 1 | 21 | 0 | 78 | 3 |
| Barnett | 36 | 7 | 88 | 3 | 2 | 1 | 5 | 0 |
| Weekes | 10 | 4 | 30 | 1 | 5.4 | 1 | 18 | 2 |

| SURREY | O | M | R | W | O | M | R | W |
|---|---:|---:|---:|---:|---:|---:|---:|---:|
| Waqar Younis | 24 | 6 | 61 | 5 | 3.3 | 1 | 8 | 0 |
| Bicknell M.P. | 20 | 4 | 56 | 1 | 6 | 0 | 25 | 0 |
| Murphy | 9 | 3 | 21 | 0 | 4 | 2 | 2 | 1 |
| Boiling | 23.5 | 6 | 58 | 2 | 11 | 3 | 41 | 0 |
| Medlycott | 20 | 3 | 90 | 2 | 9 | 3 | 24 | 1 |

| FALL OF WICKETS | | | | |
|---|---:|---:|---:|---:|
| | SUR | MID | SUR | MID |
| 1st | 72 | 6 | 41 | 10 |
| 2nd | 72 | 38 | 59 | 85 |
| 3rd | 85 | 96 | 125 | |
| 4th | 95 | 123 | 130 | |
| 5th | 129 | 131 | 135 | |
| 6th | 283 | 262 | 148 | |
| 7th | 319 | 266 | 159 | |
| 8th | 325 | 276 | 159 | |
| 9th | 334 | 284 | 191 | |
| 10th | | 297 | 208 | |

## HEADLINES

### Britannic Assurance Championship

#### 20th - 23rd August

• Essex missed a golden opportunity to take over as Championship leaders when they lost to Yorkshire at Colchester by three runs after losing their last five second innings wickets for just 22. Martyn Moxon's double century had enabled the visiotrs to reach 446 for nine in their first innings, but John Stephenson and Paul Prichard had replied with a second-wicket stand of 246 as Essex gained maximum batting points. Essex were left a formidable 319 for victory, and had looked to be on their way back to the top of table when they reached 293 with only five wickets down, before the Yorkshire spinners' success in the match's final overs brought their side a dramatic victory.

• Warwickshire's match against Glamorgan at Edgbaston had already been abandoned as a draw, rain preventing the home side from pressing for their ninth win of the season which had become a possiblity when Gladstone Small claimed the first three wickets in the Glamorgan second innings in the space of one over. Earlier batsmen had been in control as both sides comfortably passed 300 to collect maximum batting points. Glamorgan's Adrian Dale missed his maiden first-class 100 by one run. Warwickshire had now gone four matches without a victory, but Essex's defeat meant that they had actually increased their lead at the top of the Championship table to seven points.

• Derbyshire remained in third place despite suffering a disastrous two-day defeat at Derby where a remarkable bowling performance from David Millns set Leicestershire on the way to victory by an innings and 131 runs. Millns returned career-best figures of nine for 37, also improving the season's best return, as the home side could reach only 117 in their first innings. Leicestershire established a lead of 275 thanks to 93 from Phil Whitticase and their seam bowlers needed only 39 overs to complete an emphatic victory, Millns finishing with match figures of 12 for 91.

• Surrey were not able to make up any leeway on the leading sides, as their match against Middlesex at The Oval finished in a draw. Monte Lynch made his first 100 of the summer and the remarkable Waqar Younis collected five wickets in an innings for the 10th time in 1991, as Surrey gained a first-innings lead of 44, but the rain's intervention on the final afternoon made a draw the inevitable result.

# BRITANNIC ASSURANCE CHAMPIONSHIP

## HAMPSHIRE vs. SUSSEX

at Bournemouth on 20th, 21st, 22nd August 1991
Toss : Hampshire.  Umpires : N.T.Plews and R.A.White
Match drawn.  Hampshire 7 pts (Bt: 3, Bw: 4), Sussex 4 pts (Bt: 1, Bw: 3)
100 overs scores : Hampshire 258 for 7

### HAMPSHIRE

| | | | | | |
|---|---|--:|---|---|--:|
| T.C.Middleton | c Speight b Jones | 6 | c Moores b Pigott | | 36 |
| V.P.Terry | c Greenfield b Jones | 4 | c Greenfield b Pigott | | 42 |
| K.D.James | c Smith b Donelan | 68 | not out | | 50 |
| D.I.Gower | c Lenham b Dodemaide | 51 | b North | | 58 |
| M.C.J.Nicholas * | c Pigott b Dodemaide | 55 | not out | | 10 |
| J.R.Ayling | c Moores b Pigott | 13 | | | |
| A.N Aymes + | lbw b North | 15 | | | |
| R.J.Maru | c Greenfield b Donelan | 34 | | | |
| I.J.Turner | b Jones | 6 | | | |
| K.J.Shine | not out | 16 | | | |
| Aqib Javed | not out | 0 | | | |
| Extras | (b 5,lb 4,w 1,nb 19) | 29 | (lb 6,w 2,nb 2) | | 10 |
| TOTAL | (for 9 wkts dec) | 297 | (for 3 wkts dec) | | 206 |

### SUSSEX

| | | | | | |
|---|---|--:|---|---|--:|
| N.J.Lenham | c Terry b Aqib Javed | 8 | c Turner b Shine | | 1 |
| D.M.Smith | c Middleton b Aqib Javed | 10 | not out | | 16 |
| K.Greenfield | c Terry b Ayling | 22 | lbw b Aqib Javed | | 0 |
| A.P.Wells * | c Aymes b Aqib Javed | 76 | not out | | 18 |
| M.P.Speight | c Terry b Maru | 8 | | | |
| J.A.North | c Maru b Turner | 22 | | | |
| A.I.C.Dodemaide | c Terry b Aqib Javed | 12 | | | |
| P.Moores + | run out | 1 | | | |
| A.C.S.Pigott | c Ayling b Turner | 10 | | | |
| B.T.P.Donelan | not out | 7 | | | |
| A.N.Jones | b Aqib Javed | 7 | | | |
| Extras | (lb 9,nb 6) | 15 | (lb 2) | | 2 |
| TOTAL | | 198 | (for 2 wkts) | | 37 |

| SUSSEX | O | M | R | W | O | M | R | W | | FALL OF WICKETS | | | |
|---|--:|--:|--:|--:|--:|--:|--:|--:|---|---|--:|--:|--:|
| Jones | 18 | 6 | 46 | 3 | 10 | 1 | 37 | 0 | | | HAM | SUS | HAM | SUS |
| Dodemaide | 28 | 4 | 71 | 2 | 14 | 1 | 47 | 0 | 1st | 7 | 13 | 76 | 3 |
| Pigott | 15 | 3 | 34 | 1 | 18 | 5 | 51 | 2 | 2nd | 10 | 26 | 83 | 6 |
| North | 20 | 6 | 55 | 1 | 4 | 0 | 18 | 1 | 3rd | 120 | 69 | 185 | |
| Donelan | 29 | 10 | 82 | 2 | 18 | 2 | 47 | 0 | 4th | 150 | 104 | | |
| | | | | | | | | | 5th | 184 | 147 | | |
| HAMPSHIRE | O | M | R | W | O | M | R | W | 6th | 222 | 165 | | |
| Aqib Javed | 15 | 4 | 47 | 5 | 8 | 4 | 11 | 1 | 7th | 253 | 166 | | |
| Shine | 5 | 0 | 32 | 0 | 7 | 2 | 19 | 1 | 8th | 274 | 175 | | |
| James | 6 | 2 | 12 | 0 | | | | | 9th | 297 | 187 | | |
| Ayling | 9 | 2 | 27 | 1 | | | | | 10th | | 198 | | |
| Maru | 20 | 8 | 38 | 1 | 2 | 0 | 2 | 0 | | | | | |
| Turner | 22 | 9 | 33 | 2 | 4 | 1 | 3 | 0 | | | | | |

## KENT vs. GLOUCESTERSHIRE

at Canterbury on 20th, 21st, 22nd August 1991
Toss : Gloucs.  Umpires : B.Hassan and K.J.Lyons
Kent won by 1 wicket.  Kent 20 pts (Bt: 0, Bw: 4), Gloucs 5 pts (Bt: 1, Bw: 4)

### GLOUCESTERSHIRE

| | | | | | |
|---|---|--:|---|---|--:|
| G.D.Hodgson | c Marsh b Patel | 60 | b Merrick | | 26 |
| R.J.Scott | b Merrick | 17 | c Marsh b Penn | | 30 |
| A.J.Wright * | c Cowdrey b Merrick | 47 | c Marsh b Davis | | 45 |
| C.W.J.Athey | c Marsh b Igglesden | 22 | lbw b Igglesden | | 13 |
| M.W.Alleyne | c Ward b Penn | 0 | lbw b Igglesden | | 0 |
| J.W.Lloyds | b Patel | 8 | not out | | 67 |
| R.C.J.Williams + | b Patel | 0 | c Penn b Igglesden | | 4 |
| M.C.J.Ball | c Marsh b Igglesden | 15 | b Patel | | 11 |
| D.R.Gilbert | not out | 4 | not out | | 22 |
| A.M.Babington | c Cowdrey b Igglesden | 0 | | | |
| M.J.Gerrard | b Igglesden | 0 | | | |
| Extras | (b 3,lb 2,nb 4) | 9 | (b 5,lb 4,nb 6) | | 15 |
| TOTAL | | 182 | (for 7 wkts dec) | | 233 |

### KENT

| | | | | | |
|---|---|--:|---|---|--:|
| T.R.Ward | c Williams b Gilbert | 0 | c & b Ball | | 48 |
| M.R.Benson * | c Williams b Babington | 6 | b Gilbert | | 2 |
| N.R.Taylor | not out | 17 | c Wright b Ball | | 109 |
| G.R.Cowdrey | b Gilbert | 6 | lbw b Babington | | 12 |
| M.V.Fleming | lbw b Gilbert | 0 | c Williams b Babington | | 0 |
| S.A.Marsh + | c Athey b Gilbert | 30 | c Williams b Gerrard | | 36 |
| R.P.Davis | lbw b Gilbert | 0 | not out | | 37 |
| C.Penn | c Athey b Gilbert | 16 | b Ball | | 35 |
| M.M.Patel | b Gilbert | 4 | b Ball | | 3 |
| T.A.Merrick | lbw b Gilbert | 12 | c Athey b Ball | | 18 |
| A.P.Igglesden | c Gilbert b Ball | 13 | not out | | 0 |
| Extras | (lb 2,nb 1) | 3 | (b 2,lb 4,nb 3) | | 9 |
| TOTAL | | 107 | (for 9 wkts) | | 309 |

| KENT | O | M | R | W | O | M | R | W | | FALL OF WICKETS | | | |
|---|--:|--:|--:|--:|--:|--:|--:|--:|---|---|--:|--:|--:|
| Merrick | 16 | 5 | 41 | 2 | 20 | 4 | 85 | 1 | | | GLO | KEN | GLO | KEN |
| Igglesden | 15.3 | 2 | 46 | 4 | 19 | 1 | 47 | 3 | 1st | 23 | 0 | 49 | 11 |
| Penn | 18 | 3 | 41 | 1 | 6 | 1 | 10 | 1 | 2nd | 124 | 12 | 91 | 117 |
| Davis | 9 | 2 | 16 | 0 | 26 | 6 | 57 | 1 | 3rd | 136 | 12 | 117 | 152 |
| Patel | 22 | 9 | 33 | 3 | 12 | 3 | 25 | 1 | 4th | 142 | 21 | 119 | 152 |
| | | | | | | | | | 5th | 153 | 21 | 121 | 198 |
| GLOUCS | O | M | R | W | O | M | R | W | 6th | 153 | 56 | 148 | 217 |
| Gilbert | 22 | 7 | 55 | 8 | 21.2 | 3 | 50 | 1 | 7th | 171 | 60 | 177 | 276 |
| Babington | 10 | 2 | 25 | 1 | 24 | 6 | 68 | 2 | 8th | 182 | 75 | | 286 |
| Ball | 17.5 | 7 | 25 | 1 | 42 | 5 | 128 | 5 | 9th | 182 | 80 | | 308 |
| Gerrard | | | | | 13 | 2 | 35 | 1 | 10th | 182 | 107 | | |
| Scott | | | | | 4 | 0 | 22 | 0 | | | | | |

## LANCASHIRE vs. WORCESTERSHIRE

at Blackpool on 20th, 21st, 22nd August 1991
Toss : Worcestershire.  Umpires : B.Dudleston and J.W.Holder
Match drawn.  Lancashire 5 pts (Bt: 2, Bw: 3), Worcestershire 6 pts (Bt: 2, Bw: 4)
100 overs scores : Worcestershire 222 for 8

### WORCESTERSHIRE

| | | | | | |
|---|---|--:|---|---|--:|
| T.S.Curtis * | c & b Austin | 32 | c Austin b Fitton | | 120 |
| P.Bent | lbw b Martin | 3 | not out | | 100 |
| G.A.Hick | c Hegg b Watkinson | 12 | not out | | 15 |
| T.M.Moody | c Mendis b Martin | 1 | | | |
| D.B.D'Oliveira | b Yates | 30 | | | |
| S.R.Lampitt | b Martin | 25 | | | |
| S.J.Rhodes + | lbw b Martin | 48 | | | |
| R.K.Illingworth | run out | 29 | | | |
| C.M.Tolley | b Yates | 36 | | | |
| P.J.Newport | not out | 22 | | | |
| N.V.Radford | b Austin | 11 | | | |
| Extras | (lb 9,nb 3) | 12 | (lb 10,w 5,nb 1) | | 16 |
| TOTAL | | 261 | (for 1 wkt dec) | | 251 |

### LANCASHIRE

| | | | | | |
|---|---|--:|---|---|--:|
| G.D.Mendis | lbw b Tolley | 47 | c D'Oliveira b Tolley | | 47 |
| G.Fowler | c D'Oliveira b Tolley | 12 | c Curtis b Radford | | 19 |
| N.J.Speak | b Lampitt | 10 | c Rhodes b Illingworth | | 45 |
| N.H.Fairbrother * | lbw b Illingworth | 44 | b Moody b Tolley | | 0 |
| G.D.Lloyd | c Moody b Illingworth | 19 | b Illingworth | | 58 |
| M.Watkinson | c Moody b Illingworth | 0 | run out | | 51 |
| W.K.Hegg + | b D'Oliveira | 10 | (8) not out | | 21 |
| J.D.Fitton | c Bent b Hick | 1 | (9) not out | | 9 |
| I.D.Austin | lbw b Illingworth | 43 | (7) run out | | 0 |
| G.Yates | not out | 29 | | | |
| P.J.Martin | c Hick b Illingworth | 17 | | | |
| Extras | (lb 7,w 1,nb 1) | 9 | (b 4,lb 5,w 1,nb 1) | | 11 |
| TOTAL | | 241 | (for 7 wkts) | | 261 |

| LANCASHIRE | O | M | R | W | O | M | R | W | | FALL OF WICKETS | | | |
|---|--:|--:|--:|--:|--:|--:|--:|--:|---|---|--:|--:|--:|
| Martin | 20 | 7 | 30 | 4 | 9 | 4 | 14 | 0 | | | WOR | LAN | WOR | LAN |
| Watkinson | 24 | 4 | 81 | 1 | 17 | 4 | 48 | 0 | 1st | 7 | 42 | 225 | 25 |
| Austin | 19.3 | 4 | 39 | 2 | 6 | 0 | 38 | 0 | 2nd | 20 | 75 | | 101 |
| Yates | 27 | 10 | 39 | 2 | 19 | 4 | 67 | 0 | 3rd | 27 | 81 | | 101 |
| Fitton | 25 | 11 | 63 | 0 | 16.5 | 1 | 74 | 1 | 4th | 56 | 123 | | 124 |
| | | | | | | | | | 5th | 107 | 129 | | 206 |
| WORCS | O | M | R | W | O | M | R | W | 6th | 113 | 140 | | 209 |
| Newport | 6 | 0 | 32 | 0 | 7 | 1 | 19 | 0 | 7th | 160 | 143 | | 243 |
| Radford | 12 | 5 | 21 | 0 | 6 | 2 | 24 | 1 | 8th | 215 | 186 | | |
| Tolley | 15 | 6 | 30 | 2 | 7 | 0 | 27 | 2 | 9th | 238 | 199 | | |
| Lampitt | 14 | 4 | 33 | 1 | 5 | 1 | 21 | 0 | 10th | 261 | 241 | | |
| Illingworth | 21.1 | 6 | 49 | 5 | 19 | 3 | 82 | 2 | | | | | |
| Hick | 7 | 1 | 33 | 1 | 6 | 1 | 47 | 0 | | | | | |
| D'Oliveira | 9 | 1 | 36 | 1 | 6 | 0 | 32 | 0 | | | | | |

---

# HEADLINES

## Britannic Assurance Championship

### 20th - 23rd August

• Kent beat Gloucestershire by nine wickets in an eventful match at Canterbury. The visitors gained a first innings lead of 75 when Kent were dismissed for 107, Dave Gilbert returning career-best figures, and left the home side to make 309 for victory on the last day. Neil Taylor made his fourth 100 of the season, but, after Martin Ball had claimed five wickets in an innings for the first time, it was left to Richard Davis to see Kent home by the narrowest of margins.

• Lancashire were left stranded 11 runs short of victory over Worcestershire, when the Blackpool weather finally brought the players back to the pavilion. Bowlers had been in charge on the first two days, Peter Martin recording his best figures for Lancashire and Richard Illingworth taking five for 49 to give Worcestershire a lead of 20, but then Tim Curtis and Paul Bent hit 100s as they shared an opening stand of 225 before the declaration.

• Rain also had the final word at Bournemouth where Hampshire drew with Sussex. Aqib Javed took five wickets in an innings for the third time in his Hampshire career to give his side a first-innings lead of 99 and Sussex's victory target of 306 had looked a distant one when they lost their first two second-innings wickets for only six.

# REFUGE ASSURANCE LEAGUE

## LANCASHIRE vs. ESSEX

at Old Trafford on 25th August 1991
Toss : Lancashire. Umpires : B.Dudleston and J.W.Holder
Lancashire won by 5 wickets. Lancashire 4 pts, Essex 0 pts

### ESSEX

| | | |
|---|---|---|
| A.C.Seymour | run out | 25 |
| J.P.Stephenson | c Speak b Allott | 12 |
| N.Hussain | c Hegg b Allott | 0 |
| J.J.B.Lewis | c Hegg b Watkinson | 19 |
| N.V.Knight | lbw b Wasim Akram | 0 |
| D.R.Pringle * | not out | 51 |
| M.A.Garnham + | c & b Watkinson | 12 |
| T.D.Topley | not out | 38 |
| S.J.W.Andrew | | |
| J.H.Childs | | |
| G.Lovell | | |
| Extras | (lb 5,w 3,nb 4) | 12 |
| TOTAL | (40 overs)(for 6 wkts) | 169 |

### LANCASHIRE

| | | |
|---|---|---|
| G.D.Mendis | c Stephenson b Topley | 24 |
| G.Fowler | lbw b Childs | 41 |
| G.D.Lloyd | b Pringle | 23 |
| N.H.Fairbrother * | c Knight b Topley | 52 |
| N.J.Speak | lbw b Topley | 0 |
| M.Watkinson | c Knight b Topley | 3 |
| Wasim Akram | not out | 11 |
| W.K.Hegg + | | |
| I.D.Austin | | |
| P.J.W.Allott | | |
| P.J.Martin | | |
| Extras | (lb 10,w 6,nb 1) | 17 |
| TOTAL | (39.1 overs)(for 5 wkts) | 171 |

| LANCASHIRE | O | M | R | W | FALL OF WICKETS | | |
|---|---|---|---|---|---|---|---|
| | | | | | | ESS | LAN |
| Allott | 8 | 0 | 30 | 2 | 1st | 32 | 73 |
| Martin | 8 | 0 | 37 | 0 | 2nd | 32 | 83 |
| Wasim Akram | 8 | 0 | 35 | 1 | 3rd | 50 | 139 |
| Watkinson | 8 | 0 | 34 | 2 | 4th | 57 | 140 |
| Austin | 8 | 1 | 28 | 0 | 5th | 63 | 146 |
| | | | | | 6th | 91 | |
| ESSEX | O | M | R | W | 7th | | |
| Andrew | 5 | 0 | 20 | 0 | 8th | | |
| Pringle | 7.1 | 0 | 34 | 1 | 9th | | |
| Stephenson | 6 | 0 | 17 | 0 | 10th | | |
| Topley | 7 | 1 | 29 | 3 | | | |
| Childs | 8 | 1 | 27 | 1 | | | |
| Lovell | 6 | 0 | 34 | 0 | | | |

## LEICESTERSHIRE vs. GLOUCS

at Leicester on 25th August 1991
Toss : Leicestershire. Umpires : D.J.Constant & K.E.Palmer
Gloucs won by 12 runs. Leicestershire 0 pts, Gloucs 4 pts

### GLOUCESTERSHIRE

| | | |
|---|---|---|
| M.W.Alleyne | not out | 76 |
| R.J.Scott | c Whitaker b Hepworth | 56 |
| A.J.Wright * | c Whitticase b Wilkinson | 29 |
| C.W.J.Athey | c Parsons b Maguire | 25 |
| J.J.E.Hardy | not out | 11 |
| T.Hancock | | |
| R.C.J.Williams + | | |
| M.C.J.Ball | | |
| D.R.Gilbert | | |
| A.M.Babington | | |
| A.M.Smith | | |
| Extras | (b 1,lb 7,w 10,nb 3) | 21 |
| TOTAL | (40 overs)(for 3 wkts) | 218 |

### LEICESTERSHIRE

| | | |
|---|---|---|
| J.J.Whitaker | c Athey b Scott | 30 |
| N.E.Briers * | b Smith | 0 |
| T.J.Boon | c Smith b Babington | 18 |
| B.F.Smith | lbw b Gilbert | 23 |
| L.Potter | c Smith b Gilbert | 53 |
| P.Whitticase + | c Hancock b Scott | 17 |
| P.N.Hepworth | run out | 31 |
| D.J.Millns | c Athey b Smith | 4 |
| G.J.Parsons | c Babington b Smith | 9 |
| C.Wilkinson | not out | 12 |
| J.N.Maguire | not out | 0 |
| Extras | (lb 5,w 3,nb 1) | 9 |
| TOTAL | (40 overs)(for 9 wkts) | 206 |

| LEICS | O | M | R | W | FALL OF WICKETS | | |
|---|---|---|---|---|---|---|---|
| | | | | | | GLO | LEI |
| Millns | 8 | 0 | 36 | 0 | 1st | 108 | 6 |
| Parsons | 8 | 0 | 23 | 0 | 2nd | 148 | 38 |
| Wilkinson | 8 | 0 | 55 | 1 | 3rd | 198 | 71 |
| Maguire | 8 | 0 | 58 | 1 | 4th | | 80 |
| Hepworth | 8 | 0 | 38 | 1 | 5th | | 111 |
| | | | | | 6th | | 178 |
| GLOUCS | O | M | R | W | 7th | | 181 |
| Smith | 8 | 0 | 52 | 3 | 8th | | 185 |
| Babington | 8 | 2 | 34 | 1 | 9th | | 206 |
| Gilbert | 8 | 0 | 37 | 2 | 10th | | |
| Ball | 8 | 0 | 40 | 0 | | | |
| Scott | 8 | 1 | 38 | 2 | | | |

## NORTHANTS vs. WARWICKS

at Northampton on 25th August 1991
Toss : Northants. Umpires : B.Leadbeater and K.J.Lyons
Northants won by 8 runs. Northants 4 pts, Warwicks 0 pts

### NORTHANTS

| | | |
|---|---|---|
| A.Fordham | c & b Benjamin | 16 |
| W.Larkins | b Smith N.M.K. | 66 |
| A.J.Lamb * | c Moles b Benjamin | 4 |
| R.J.Bailey | not out | 78 |
| E.A.E.Baptiste | c Moles b Smith N.M.K. | 10 |
| K.M.Curran | c Small b Smith N.M.K. | 10 |
| D.J.Capel | not out | 14 |
| A.L.Penberthy | | |
| R.G.Williams | | |
| W.M.Noon + | | |
| A.Walker | | |
| Extras | (b 5,lb 6,w 9) | 20 |
| TOTAL | (40 overs)(for 5 wkts) | 218 |

### WARWICKSHIRE

| | | |
|---|---|---|
| A.J.Moles | b Walker | 4 |
| Asif Din | c Noon b Baptiste | 7 |
| T.A.Lloyd * | c Curran b Williams | 24 |
| D.P.Ostler | st Noon b Williams | 26 |
| D.A.Reeve | b Curran | 43 |
| P.A.Smith | c Noon b Capel | 2 |
| N.M.K.Smith | c Capel b Penberthy | 39 |
| P.C.L.Holloway + | not out | 34 |
| G.C.Small | b Curran | 3 |
| J.E.Benjamin | run out | 2 |
| T.A.Munton | not out | 10 |
| Extras | (lb 11,w 5) | 16 |
| TOTAL | (40 overs)(for 9 wkts) | 210 |

| WARWICKS | O | M | R | W | FALL OF WICKETS | | |
|---|---|---|---|---|---|---|---|
| | | | | | | NOR | WAR |
| Munton | 8 | 1 | 38 | 0 | 1st | 36 | 10 |
| Benjamin | 8 | 0 | 26 | 2 | 2nd | 50 | 20 |
| Small | 6 | 1 | 26 | 0 | 3rd | 122 | 41 |
| Reeve | 5.3 | 0 | 26 | 0 | 4th | 138 | 74 |
| Smith P.A. | 6 | 0 | 39 | 0 | 5th | 169 | 80 |
| Smith N.M.K. | 6.3 | 0 | 52 | 3 | 6th | | 152 |
| NORTHANTS | O | M | R | W | 7th | | 158 |
| Walker | 7 | 0 | 24 | 1 | 8th | | 176 |
| Baptiste | 8 | 0 | 36 | 1 | 9th | | 190 |
| Williams | 8 | 0 | 42 | 2 | 10th | | |
| Capel | 8 | 1 | 40 | 1 | | | |
| Curran | 8 | 0 | 56 | 2 | | | |
| Penberthy | 1 | 0 | 1 | 1 | | | |

## SOMERSET vs. YORKSHIRE

at Taunton on 25th August 1991
Toss : Somerset. Umpires : J.C.Balderstone and N.T.Plews
Somerset won by 46 runs. Somerset 4 pts, Yorkshire 0 pts

### SOMERSET

| | | |
|---|---|---|
| S.J.Cook | c & b Carrick | 44 |
| G.T.J.Townsend | c Moxon b Carrick | 27 |
| R.J.Harden | c Robinson P.E. b Carrick | 29 |
| C.J.Tavare * | not out | 65 |
| G.D.Rose | c & b Batty | 3 |
| A.N.Hayhurst | c Gough b Robinson M.A. | 14 |
| N.D.Burns + | not out | 25 |
| H.R.J.Trump | | |
| J.C.Hallett | | |
| D.A.Graveney | | |
| D.Beal | | |
| Extras | (b 6,lb 3,w 7,nb 1) | 17 |
| TOTAL | (40 overs)(for 5 wkts) | 224 |

### YORKSHIRE

| | | |
|---|---|---|
| M.D.Moxon * | b Rose | 0 |
| A.A.Metcalfe | c Townsend b Trump | 49 |
| R.J.Blakey + | c Burns b Rose | 1 |
| D.Byas | run out | 2 |
| P.E.Robinson | run out | 39 |
| S.A.Kellett | b Hallett | 10 |
| C.S.Pickles | b Graveney | 16 |
| P.Carrick | not out | 18 |
| D.Gough | c Trump b Hallett | 6 |
| J.D.Batty | b Hayhurst | 12 |
| M.A.Robinson | b Hayhurst | 2 |
| Extras | (b 3,lb 13,w 7) | 23 |
| TOTAL | (37.1 overs) | 178 |

| YORKSHIRE | O | M | R | W | FALL OF WICKETS | | |
|---|---|---|---|---|---|---|---|
| | | | | | | SOM | YOR |
| Robinson M.A. | 7 | 0 | 48 | 1 | 1st | 77 | 0 |
| Gough | 8 | 0 | 45 | 0 | 2nd | 88 | 12 |
| Pickles | 6 | 0 | 30 | 0 | 3rd | 136 | 17 |
| Kellett | 3 | 0 | 16 | 0 | 4th | 148 | 102 |
| Carrick | 8 | 0 | 38 | 3 | 5th | 178 | 107 |
| Batty | 8 | 0 | 38 | 1 | 6th | | 132 |
| SOMERSET | O | M | R | W | 7th | | 137 |
| Rose | 7 | 0 | 21 | 2 | 8th | | 149 |
| Hallett | 8 | 0 | 32 | 2 | 9th | | 172 |
| Hayhurst | 6.1 | 0 | 27 | 2 | 10th | | 178 |
| Graveney | 8 | 0 | 44 | 1 | | | |
| Trump | 8 | 0 | 38 | 1 | | | |

## HEADLINES

### Refuge Assurance League

### 25th August

• Nottinghamshire won the Sunday League for the first time when they defeated Derbyshire by nine wickets at Trent Bridge. After the visitors had been restricted to 176 for nine in their 40 overs Chris Broad and Derek Randall shared an opening stand of 134 and Notts reached their target with 13 balls to spare.

• Lancashire, runners-up in 1990, again finished in second place following their comfortable five-wicket victory over a below-par Essex at Old Trafford.

• Northamptonshire won the play-off for third place with Warwickshire by eight runs at Northampton. Rob Bailey's unbeaten 78 carried the hosts to 218 for five, but the visitors were under pressure once they had lost their first five wickets for 80. Northants's victory ensured their first appearance in the Refuge Cup, but Warwickshire just missed out, falling to fifth place.

• Worcestershire claimed fourth place with an emphatic defeat of Middlesex at Worcester by 103 runs, Tom Moody ending his Sunday League campaign with his fourth century of the summer, to give him a record Sunday aggregate of 917 runs.

• Hampshire defeated their NatWest Final opponents Surrey by three wickets at The Oval, taking advantage of the absence of Waqar Younis to gain victory with two balls to spare.

• Sussex finished their Sunday season with a four-wicket win over Kent, Tony Pigott and John North both claiming three wickets as Kent were restricted to 171 for nine.

• Somerset defeated Yorkshire by 46 runs at Taunton, after making 224 for five in their 40 overs, Jimmy Cook completing 2,000 runs in the Sunday League at the end of his third season and Chris Tavare hitting an unbeaten 65.

• Richard Scott and Mark Alleyne shared an opening stand of 108 as Gloucestershire reached 218 for three against Leicestershire at Leicester on their way to victory by 12 runs.

# REFUGE ASSURANCE LEAGUE

## NOTTS vs. DERBYSHIRE
at Trent Bridge on 25th August 1991
Toss : Notts. Umpires : M.J.Kitchen and P.B.Wight
Notts won by 9 wickets. Notts 4 pts, Derbyshire 0 pts

### DERBYSHIRE
| | | |
|---|---|---:|
| K.J.Barnett * | c Robinson b Stephenson | 6 |
| C.J.Adams | c Johnson b Field-Buss | 47 |
| T.J.G.O'Gorman | b Field-Buss | 16 |
| M.Azharuddin | b Saxelby | 53 |
| S.C.Goldsmith | run out | 2 |
| K.M.Krikken + | run out | 15 |
| D.G.Cork | run out | 11 |
| E.McCray | c French b Pick | 2 |
| I.Folley | not out | 6 |
| S.J.Base | c Randall b Stephenson | 4 |
| O.H.Mortensen | not out | 1 |
| Extras | (lb 7,w 5,nb 1) | 13 |
| TOTAL | (40 overs)(for 9 wkts) | 176 |

### NOTTS
| | | |
|---|---|---:|
| B.C.Broad | not out | 73 |
| D.W.Randall | c Mortensen b Cork | 67 |
| R.T.Robinson * | not out | 25 |
| P.Johnson | | |
| P.Pollard | | |
| M.Saxelby | | |
| K.P.Evans | | |
| F.D.Stephenson | | |
| B.N.French + | | |
| R.A.Pick | | |
| M.G.Field-Buss | | |
| Extras | (lb 7,w 8) | 15 |
| TOTAL | (37.5 overs)(for 1 wkt) | 180 |

| NOTTS | O | M | R | W | FALL OF WICKETS | | |
|---|---|---|---|---|---|---|---|
| | | | | | | DER | NOT |
| Stephenson | 8 | 4 | 13 | 2 | 1st | 12 | 134 |
| Pick | 8 | 0 | 34 | 1 | 2nd | 55 | |
| Saxelby | 8 | 0 | 38 | 1 | 3rd | 106 | |
| Evans | 8 | 0 | 41 | 0 | 4th | 110 | |
| Field-Buss | 8 | 0 | 43 | 2 | 5th | 146 | |
| | | | | | 6th | 149 | |
| DERBYSHIRE | O | M | R | W | 7th | 160 | |
| Mortensen | 8 | 0 | 24 | 0 | 8th | 164 | |
| Base | 6 | 0 | 30 | 0 | 9th | 171 | |
| Cork | 8 | 0 | 35 | 1 | 10th | | |
| McCray | 8 | 0 | 42 | 0 | | | |
| Folley | 4 | 0 | 26 | 0 | | | |
| Goldsmith | 3 | 0 | 11 | 0 | | | |
| Azharuddin | 0.5 | 0 | 5 | 0 | | | |

## SURREY vs. HAMPSHIRE
at The Oval on 25th August 1991
Toss : Hampshire. Umpires : G.I.Burgess and R.A.White
Hampshire won by 3 wickets. Surrey 0 pts, Hants 4 pts

### SURREY
| | | |
|---|---|---:|
| G.P.Thorpe | c Cox b Aqib Javed | 1 |
| A.D.Brown | b Connor | 16 |
| D.M.Ward | st Aymes b Udal | 29 |
| M.A.Lynch | c Ayling b Maru | 32 |
| J.D.Robinson | c Maru b James | 33 |
| I.A.Greig * | c Aymes b Ayling | 10 |
| M.A.Feltham | run out | 7 |
| N.F.Sargeant + | not out | 13 |
| J.Boiling | not out | 12 |
| A.G.Robson | | |
| A.J.Murphy | | |
| Extras | (lb 5,w 8,nb 1) | 14 |
| TOTAL | (40 overs)(for 7 wkts) | 167 |

### HAMPSHIRE
| | | |
|---|---|---:|
| R.M.F.Cox | b Robinson | 13 |
| V.P.Terry | b Robson | 8 |
| J.R.Wood | b Murphy | 3 |
| J.R.Ayling | c Murphy b Robinson | 56 |
| A.N Aymes + | b Robson | 29 |
| K.D.James | c Robinson b Boiling | 1 |
| M.C.J.Nicholas * | not out | 24 |
| R.J.Maru | b Robson | 10 |
| S.D.Udal | not out | 16 |
| C.A.Connor | | |
| Aqib Javed | | |
| Extras | (lb 2,w 8,nb 1) | 11 |
| TOTAL | (39.4 overs)(for 7 wkts) | 171 |

| HAMPSHIRE | O | M | R | W | FALL OF WICKETS | | |
|---|---|---|---|---|---|---|---|
| | | | | | | SUR | HAM |
| Connor | 6 | 1 | 19 | 1 | | | |
| Aqib Javed | 8 | 0 | 36 | 1 | 1st | 9 | 16 |
| Ayling | 8 | 0 | 34 | 1 | 2nd | 21 | 19 |
| James | 5 | 0 | 20 | 1 | 3rd | 75 | 57 |
| Udal | 8 | 1 | 19 | 1 | 4th | 98 | 116 |
| Maru | 5 | 0 | 34 | 1 | 5th | 118 | 118 |
| | | | | | 6th | 118 | 138 |
| SURREY | O | M | R | W | 7th | 142 | 140 |
| Murphy | 8 | 0 | 32 | 1 | 8th | | |
| Robson | 8 | 0 | 42 | 3 | 9th | | |
| Feltham | 7 | 0 | 20 | 0 | 10th | | |
| Robinson | 8 | 0 | 34 | 2 | | | |
| Boiling | 8 | 0 | 35 | 1 | | | |
| Lynch | 0.4 | 0 | 6 | 0 | | | |

## SUSSEX vs. KENT
at Hove on 25th August 1991
Toss : Sussex. Umpires : J.H.Harris and D.R.Shepherd
Sussex won by 4 wickets. Sussex 4 pts, Kent 0 pts

### KENT
| | | |
|---|---|---:|
| T.R.Ward | c & b Pigott | 3 |
| M.R.Benson * | c Moores b Dodemaide | 6 |
| J.I.Longley | c Greenfield b Pigott | 1 |
| G.R.Cowdrey | lbw b North | 18 |
| M.A.Ealham | c Hanley b North | 17 |
| M.V.Fleming | c Dodemaide b Pigott | 77 |
| S.A.Marsh + | c & b North | 4 |
| N.J.Llong | run out | 8 |
| R.P.Davis | run out | 6 |
| A.P.Igglesden | not out | 13 |
| T.N.Wren | not out | 0 |
| Extras | (lb 4,w 7,nb 7) | 18 |
| TOTAL | (40 overs)(for 9 wkts) | 171 |

### SUSSEX
| | | |
|---|---|---:|
| N.J.Lenham | b Igglesden | 86 |
| K.Greenfield | b Davis | 26 |
| A.P.Wells * | c Longley b Davis | 28 |
| R.Hanley | c & b Igglesden | 2 |
| J.A.North | c Cowdrey b Wren | 6 |
| A.I.C.Dodemaide | not out | 6 |
| P.Moores + | run out | 11 |
| A.C.S.Pigott | not out | 1 |
| B.T.P.Donelan | | |
| I.D.K.Salisbury | | |
| A.N.Jones | | |
| Extras | (lb 4,w 2) | 6 |
| TOTAL | (40 overs)(for 6 wkts) | 172 |

| SUSSEX | O | M | R | W | FALL OF WICKETS | | |
|---|---|---|---|---|---|---|---|
| | | | | | | KEN | SUS |
| Pigott | 8 | 0 | 26 | 3 | 1st | 9 | 56 |
| Dodemaide | 8 | 1 | 29 | 1 | 2nd | 11 | 139 |
| North | 8 | 1 | 29 | 3 | 3rd | 13 | 144 |
| Jones | 7 | 0 | 49 | 0 | 4th | 40 | 153 |
| Salisbury | 2 | 0 | 11 | 0 | 5th | 56 | 155 |
| Donelan | 7 | 0 | 23 | 0 | 6th | 77 | 169 |
| | | | | | 7th | 96 | |
| KENT | O | M | R | W | 8th | 115 | |
| Igglesden | 8 | 2 | 21 | 2 | 9th | 168 | |
| Wren | 5 | 0 | 33 | 1 | 10th | | |
| Ealham | 8 | 0 | 35 | 0 | | | |
| Davis | 8 | 0 | 23 | 2 | | | |
| Fleming | 8 | 0 | 39 | 0 | | | |
| Llong | 3 | 0 | 17 | 0 | | | |

## WORCS vs. MIDDLESEX
at Worcester on 25th August 1991
Toss : Middlesex. Umpires : A.A.Jones and D.O.Oslear
Worcs won by 103 runs. Worcs 4 pts, Middlesex 0 pts

### WORCESTERSHIRE
| | | |
|---|---|---:|
| T.S.Curtis * | b Weekes | 37 |
| T.M.Moody | not out | 128 |
| G.A.Hick | c Weekes b Emburey | 65 |
| D.B.D'Oliveira | c & b Williams | 11 |
| M.J.Weston | c Brown b Headley | 0 |
| S.J.Rhodes + | not out | 11 |
| S.R.Lampitt | | |
| R.K.Illingworth | | |
| C.M.Tolley | | |
| P.J.Newport | | |
| G.R.Dilley | | |
| Extras | (b 1,lb 2,w 1,nb 1) | 5 |
| TOTAL | (40 overs)(for 4 wkts) | 257 |

### MIDDLESEX
| | | |
|---|---|---:|
| M.A.Roseberry | b Weston | 6 |
| J.C.Pooley | c Moody b Weston | 22 |
| M.W.Gatting * | not out | 60 |
| P.N.Weekes | b Lampitt | 4 |
| K.R.Brown | c Tolley b Lampitt | 3 |
| M.Keech | c Rhodes b Lampitt | 7 |
| J.E.Emburey | st Rhodes b Hick | 32 |
| P.Farbrace + | not out | 9 |
| N.F.Williams | | |
| D.W.Headley | | |
| N.G.Cowans | | |
| Extras | (lb 7,w 3,nb 1) | 11 |
| TOTAL | (40 overs)(for 6 wkts) | 154 |

| MIDDLESEX | O | M | R | W | FALL OF WICKETS | | |
|---|---|---|---|---|---|---|---|
| | | | | | | WOR | MID |
| Cowans | 8 | 1 | 34 | 0 | 1st | 79 | 15 |
| Williams | 8 | 0 | 44 | 1 | 2nd | 207 | 40 |
| Emburey | 8 | 0 | 43 | 1 | 3rd | 228 | 59 |
| Weekes | 8 | 1 | 63 | 1 | 4th | 239 | 67 |
| Headley | 8 | 0 | 70 | 1 | 5th | | 81 |
| | | | | | 6th | | 135 |
| WORCS | O | M | R | W | 7th | | |
| Weston | 8 | 0 | 27 | 2 | 8th | | |
| Dilley | 4 | 0 | 24 | 0 | 9th | | |
| Lampitt | 8 | 0 | 23 | 3 | 10th | | |
| Newport | 6 | 0 | 24 | 0 | | | |
| Tolley | 3 | 0 | 11 | 0 | | | |
| Illingworth | 6 | 0 | 18 | 0 | | | |
| Hick | 5 | 0 | 20 | 1 | | | |

### Refuge Assurance League
### Final Table

| | | P | W | L | T | NR | Away Wins | Pts | Run Rate | Runs | Balls |
|---|---|---|---|---|---|---|---|---|---|---|---|
| 1 | Notts (4) | 16 | 13 | 3 | 0 | 0 | 7 | 52 | 83.47 | 3040 | 3642 |
| 2 | Lancashire (2) | 16 | 12 | 3 | 0 | 1 | 8 | 50 | 89.78 | 2908 | 3239 |
| 3 | Northants (17) | 16 | 10 | 4 | 0 | 2 | 3 | 44 | 86.26 | 2826 | 3276 |
| 4 | Worcestershire (10) | 16 | 9 | 4 | 1 | 2 | 4 | 42 | 95.16 | 3206 | 3369 |
| 5 | Warwickshire (14) | 16 | 8 | 4 | 1 | 3 | 4 | 40 | 82.53 | 2339 | 2834 |
| 6 | Essex (12) | 16 | 7 | 4 | 1 | 4 | 1 | 38 | 84.41 | 2541 | 3010 |
| 7 | Yorkshire (6) | 16 | 9 | 7 | 0 | 0 | 4 | 36 | 86.38 | 3116 | 3607 |
| 8 | Surrey (7) | 16 | 7 | 7 | 0 | 2 | 5 | 32 | 81.94 | 2764 | 3373 |
| 9 | Somerset (8) | 16 | 7 | 7 | 0 | 2 | 4 | 32 | 80.85 | 2771 | 3427 |
| 10 | Kent (11) | 16 | 6 | 8 | 1 | 1 | 2 | 28 | 87.46 | 3020 | 3453 |
| 11 | Middlesex (3) | 16 | 6 | 9 | 0 | 1 | 4 | 26 | 79.15 | 2756 | 3482 |
| 12 | Gloucestershire (9) | 16 | 5 | 9 | 0 | 2 | 4 | 24 | 77.68 | 2541 | 3271 |
| 13 | Sussex (13) | 16 | 5 | 9 | 0 | 2 | 3 | 24 | 81.42 | 2625 | 3224 |
| 14 | Leicestershire (16) | 16 | 5 | 10 | 0 | 1 | 3 | 22 | 78.29 | 2676 | 3418 |
| 15 | Derbyshire (1) | 16 | 5 | 11 | 0 | 0 | 2 | 20 | 84.38 | 2930 | 3472 |
| 16 | Glamorgan (15) | 16 | 4 | 10 | 0 | 2 | 1 | 20 | 82.61 | 3026 | 3663 |
| 17 | Hampshire (5) | 16 | 3 | 12 | 0 | 1 | 1 | 14 | 79.24 | 2802 | 3536 |

# BRITANNIC ASSURANCE CHAMPIONSHIP

## NORTHANTS vs. SURREY

at Northampton on 23rd, 24th, 26th August 1991
Toss : Northants.  Umpires : B.Leadbeater and K.J.Lyons
Northants won by 138 runs. Northants 21 pts (Bt: 4, Bw: 1), Surrey 4 pts (Bt: 1, Bw: 3)
100 overs scores : Northants 322 for 7

### NORTHANTS

|  | | | | | |
|---|---|---|---|---|---|
| R.R.Montgomerie | lbw b Bicknell M.P. | 2 | | lbw b Alikhan | 7 |
| A.Fordham | c Sargeant b Murphy | 28 | | b Alikhan | 25 |
| R.J.Bailey | b Murphy | 4 | | not out | 37 |
| A.J.Lamb * | run out | 194 | | | |
| N.A.Stanley | lbw b Robinson | 18 | (4) | c Murphy b Bicknell D.J. | 16 |
| D.J.Capel | c Sargeant b Bicknell M.P. | 1 | | | |
| A.R.Roberts | c Sargeant b Feltham | 11 | | | |
| K.M.Curran | b Bicknell M.P. | 52 | (6) | not out | 6 |
| E.A.E.Baptiste | not out | 63 | | | |
| A.L.Penberthy | c Ward b Medlycott | 0 | | | |
| W.M.Noon + | not out | 8 | (5) | c Sargeant b Bicknell D.J. | 14 |
| Extras | (lb 18,nb 2) | 20 | | | 0 |
| TOTAL | (for 9 wkts dec) | 401 | | (for 4 wkts dec) | 105 |

### SURREY

|  | | | | |
|---|---|---|---|---|
| D.J.Bicknell | c Baptiste b Penberthy | 40 | c Penberthy b Capel | 4 |
| R.I.Alikhan | c Montgomerie b Penberthy | 37 | c Montgomerie b Baptiste | 1 |
| G.P.Thorpe | not out | 51 | not out | 116 |
| D.M.Ward | c Roberts b Penberthy | 5 | c Noon b Curran | 28 |
| M.A.Lynch | b Roberts | 14 | lbw b Curran | 1 |
| J.D.Robinson | not out | 0 | lbw b Bailey | 22 |
| K.T.Medlycott * | | | c Stanley b Curran | 4 |
| M.A.Feltham | | | b Bailey | 16 |
| N.F.Sargeant + | | | c Noon b Roberts | 5 |
| M.P.Bicknell | | | c & b Roberts | 0 |
| A.J.Murphy | | | c Fordham b Bailey | 0 |
| Extras | (b 1,lb 2) | 3 | (b 11,lb 9,w 1) | 21 |
| TOTAL | (for 4 wkts dec) | 150 | | 218 |

| SURREY | O | M | R | W | O | M | R | W |
|---|---|---|---|---|---|---|---|---|
| Bicknell M.P. | 33 | 8 | 92 | 3 | | | | |
| Murphy | 27 | 4 | 103 | 2 | | | | |
| Feltham | 27.1 | 5 | 68 | 1 | | | | |
| Robinson | 13 | 1 | 58 | 1 | | | | |
| Medlycott | 13 | 1 | 62 | 1 | | | | |
| Bicknell D.J. | | | | | 5.3 | 0 | 62 | 2 |
| Alikhan | | | | | 5 | 0 | 43 | 2 |

| NORTHANTS | O | M | R | W | O | M | R | W |
|---|---|---|---|---|---|---|---|---|
| Curran | 6 | 0 | 37 | 0 | 11 | 5 | 26 | 3 |
| Capel | 7 | 0 | 29 | 0 | 11 | 4 | 26 | 1 |
| Penberthy | 8 | 0 | 37 | 3 | 4 | 1 | 4 | 0 |
| Roberts | 8 | 0 | 41 | 1 | 25 | 9 | 73 | 2 |
| Bailey | 1.1 | 0 | 3 | 0 | 12.3 | 2 | 44 | 3 |
| Baptiste | | | | | 11 | 4 | 22 | 1 |
| Stanley | | | | | 1 | 0 | 3 | 0 |

| FALL OF WICKETS | NOR | SUR | NOR | SUR |
|---|---|---|---|---|
| 1st | 10 | 72 | 9 | 10 |
| 2nd | 15 | 85 | 44 | 16 |
| 3rd | 61 | 98 | 63 | 56 |
| 4th | 102 | 149 | 99 | 58 |
| 5th | 109 | | | 126 |
| 6th | 147 | | | 136 |
| 7th | 282 | | | 186 |
| 8th | 377 | | | 213 |
| 9th | 381 | | | 217 |
| 10th | | | | 218 |

## LANCASHIRE vs. ESSEX

at Old Trafford on 23rd, 24th, 26th August 1991
Toss : Lancashire.  Umpires : B.Dudleston and J.W.Holder
Essex won by 8 wickets. Lancashire 3 pts (Bt: 2, Bw: 1), Essex 21 pts (Bt: 1, Bw: 4)

### LANCASHIRE

|  | | | | | |
|---|---|---|---|---|---|
| G.D.Mendis | c Garnham b Pringle | 49 | (4) | not out | 30 |
| G.Fowler | c Topley b Foster | 43 | (1) | b Such | 26 |
| N.J.Speak | b Foster | 15 | (2) | lbw b Pringle | 2 |
| N.H.Fairbrother * | c Garnham b Topley | 1 | | | |
| G.D.Lloyd | c Childs b Foster | 3 | | | |
| M.Watkinson | b Foster | 20 | | | |
| W.K.Hegg + | c & b Foster | 30 | | | |
| J.D.Fitton | c Stephenson b Foster | 36 | | | |
| I.D.Austin | not out | 25 | | | |
| G.Yates | c Salim Malik b Foster | 6 | (3) | not out | 100 |
| P.J.Martin | c Topley b Foster | 0 | | | |
| Extras | (lb 7,w 1,nb 10) | 18 | | (b 8,lb 1,nb 6) | 15 |
| TOTAL | | 246 | | (for 2 wkts dec) | 173 |

### ESSEX

|  | | | | |
|---|---|---|---|---|
| A.C.Seymour | c Fairbrother b Watkinson | 28 | c Hegg b Watkinson | 12 |
| J.P.Stephenson | lbw b Martin | 5 | c Watkinson b Fitton | 85 |
| N.V.Knight | c Hegg b Fitton | 37 | not out | 101 |
| Salim Malik | retired hurt/ill | 11 | not out | 70 |
| N.Hussain | not out | 65 | | |
| M.A.Garnham + | not out | 0 | | |
| D.R.Pringle | | | | |
| N.A.Foster * | | | | |
| T.D.Topley | | | | |
| J.H.Childs | | | | |
| P.M.Such | | | | |
| Extras | (lb 3,nb 1) | 4 | (b 1,lb 3,nb 1) | 5 |
| TOTAL | (for 3 wkts dec) | 150 | (for 2 wkts) | 273 |

| ESSEX | O | M | R | W | O | M | R | W |
|---|---|---|---|---|---|---|---|---|
| Foster | 34.4 | 9 | 99 | 8 | 10 | 4 | 16 | 0 |
| Pringle | 22 | 9 | 44 | 1 | 11 | 2 | 24 | 1 |
| Topley | 14 | 5 | 60 | 1 | 5 | 1 | 27 | 0 |
| Childs | 6 | 0 | 25 | 0 | 5 | 2 | 10 | 0 |
| Salim Malik | 2 | 0 | 11 | 0 | | | | |
| Such | | | | | 9 | 3 | 14 | 1 |
| Hussain | | | | | 5.3 | 0 | 41 | 0 |
| Knight | | | | | 5 | 0 | 32 | 0 |

| FALL OF WICKETS | LAN | ESS | LAN | ESS |
|---|---|---|---|---|
| 1st | 71 | 17 | 2 | 13 |
| 2nd | 106 | 49 | 77 | 153 |
| 3rd | 106 | | 149 | |
| 4th | 123 | | | |
| 5th | 139 | | | |
| 6th | 206 | | | |
| 7th | 209 | | | |
| 8th | 213 | | | |
| 9th | 238 | | | |
| 10th | 246 | | | |

| LANCASHIRE | O | M | R | W | O | M | R | W |
|---|---|---|---|---|---|---|---|---|
| Martin | 13 | 4 | 47 | 1 | 11 | 2 | 34 | 0 |
| Watkinson | 16 | 5 | 49 | 1 | 15 | 1 | 65 | 1 |
| Austin | 11 | 4 | 24 | 0 | 19.3 | 3 | 80 | 0 |
| Yates | 5.3 | 1 | 20 | 0 | 9 | 2 | 48 | 0 |
| Fitton | 3 | 0 | 7 | 1 | 12 | 2 | 42 | 1 |

# HEADLINES

## Britannic Assurance Championship

### 23rd - 26th August

• Essex finally ended Warwickshire's three-month reign as County Championship leaders thanks to their eight-wicket victory over a weakened Lancashire side at Old Trafford. Neil Foster had quickly made up for lost time on the first day by taking a career-best eight for 99 in Lancashire's first innings and then by declaring 96 behind. After Gary Yates had hit his second 100 in first-class cricket, Neil Fairbrother set the visitors a target of 270 in 66 overs, a generous gesture with a place at the top of the Championship table the prize. Essex made no mistake, coasting home thanks to a miden first-class 100 by Nick Knight, who shared century stands with John Stephenson and Salim Malik, to establish a seven-point advantage over Warwickshire.

• Derbyshire continued a highly erratic season by beating local rivals Nottinghamshire by four wickets at Trent Bridge to consolidate their hold on third place. The two sides scored 300 apiece in their first innings, Derbyshire taking the individual honours through Richard Sladdin and Mohammad Azharuddin, then evergreen Derek Randall hit his fourth 100 of the season to take Notts past 300 in their second innings. With 78 overs to score 303, Derbyshire were set on their way by Peter Bowler who shared century partnerships with Kim Barnett and Azharuddin, but had only one ball to spare when they gained their seventh victory of the season.

• Northamptonshire easily overcame Surrey at Northampton by 138 runs after Allan Lamb's 194 had restored the home side from 147 for six to 401 for nine. Two declarations left Surrey needing to socre 357 to further their Championship aspirations, but only Graham Thorpe, with an unbeaten 100 was up to the task.

• Yorkshire could not take advantage of an opening stand of 148 between Martyn Moxon and Ashley Metcalfe to press for victory over Somerset at Taunton, losing six wickets for 52 as they attempted to reach a target of 311. Graham Rose recorded his maiden first-class 100 in Somerset's first innings.

• Worcestershire's contest with Middlesex at Worcester also finished in a draw, Mike Gatting hitting his seventh 100 of the season to take his side to safety after Worcestershire had gained a first-innings lead of 97, Tom Moody dominating their innings with 135, his sixth 100 of the summer.

# BRITANNIC ASSURANCE CHAMPIONSHIP

## NOTTS vs. DERBYSHIRE

at Trent Bridge on 23rd, 24th, 26th August 1991
Toss : Notts.  Umpires : M.J.Kitchen and P.B.Wight
Derbyshire won by 4 wickets.  Notts 5 pts (Bt: 4, Bw: 1), Derbyshire 23 pts (Bt: 4, Bw: 3)

### NOTTS

| | | | | |
|---|---|---|---|---|
| B.C.Broad | c Krikken b Mortensen | 36 | c Krikken b Mortensen | 5 |
| P.Pollard | b Mortensen | 7 | b Warner | 2 |
| R.T.Robinson * | c Krikken b Sladdin | 53 | c Folley b Sladdin | 67 |
| D.W.Randall | b Sladdin | 76 | not out | 143 |
| P.Johnson | c Azharuddin b Sladdin | 58 | c Sladdin b Goldsmith | 33 |
| M.Saxelby | c Barnett b Warner | 9 | c Barnett b Sladdin | 28 |
| F.D.Stephenson | c & b Folley | 24 | not out | 10 |
| B.N.French + | not out | 9 | | |
| M.G.Field-Buss | b Sladdin | 16 | | |
| R.A.Pick | not out | 0 | | |
| J.A.Afford | | | | |
| Extras | (b 3,lb 7,nb 2) | 12 | (b 5,lb 3,w 1,nb 5) | 14 |
| TOTAL | (for 8 wkts dec) | 300 | (for 5 wkts dec) | 302 |

### DERBYSHIRE

| | | | | |
|---|---|---|---|---|
| K.J.Barnett * | c Randall b Stephenson | 32 | c Field-Buss b Afford | 65 |
| P.D.Bowler | b Pick | 10 | c & b Pick | 99 |
| J.E.Morris | c Broad b Stephenson | 63 | c French b Afford | 0 |
| M.Azharuddin | c Broad b Stephenson | 129 | b Stephenson | 72 |
| T.J.G.O'Gorman | not out | 51 | c & b Afford | 0 |
| S.C.Goldsmith | | | not out | 29 |
| A.E.Warner | | | b Stephenson | 5 |
| K.M.Krikken + | | | not out | 5 |
| R.W.Sladdin | | | | |
| I.Folley | | | | |
| O.H.Mortensen | | | | |
| Extras | (b 2,lb 8,w 2,nb 3) | 15 | (b 5,lb 20,nb 3) | 28 |
| TOTAL | (for 3 wkts dec) | 300 | (for 6 wkts) | 303 |

| DERBYSHIRE | O | M | R | W | O | M | R | W | FALL OF WICKETS | | | | |
|---|---|---|---|---|---|---|---|---|---|---|---|---|---|
| | | | | | | | | | | NOT | DER | NOT | DER |
| Mortensen | 23 | 3 | 63 | 2 | 11 | 2 | 34 | 1 | 1st | 23 | 22 | 6 | 103 |
| Warner | 13 | 4 | 49 | 1 | 11 | 2 | 32 | 1 | 2nd | 48 | 110 | 13 | 103 |
| Sladdin | 42.3 | 10 | 118 | 4 | 25 | 1 | 118 | 2 | 3rd | 174 | 117 | 146 | 217 |
| Folley | 21 | 3 | 60 | 1 | 19 | 1 | 73 | 0 | 4th | 177 | | 210 | 222 |
| Goldsmith | | | | | 7 | 0 | 37 | 1 | 5th | 204 | | 288 | 275 |
| | | | | | | | | | 6th | 253 | | | 282 |
| NOTTS | O | M | R | W | O | M | R | W | 7th | 273 | | | |
| Stephenson | 10 | 0 | 44 | 2 | 17 | 1 | 62 | 2 | 8th | 296 | | | |
| Pick | 12 | 2 | 41 | 1 | 11.5 | 1 | 50 | 1 | 9th | | | | |
| Saxelby | 11 | 1 | 54 | 0 | 3 | 1 | 3 | 0 | 10th | | | | |
| Afford | 23 | 4 | 96 | 0 | 26 | 4 | 104 | 3 | | | | | |
| Field-Buss | 14 | 1 | 55 | 0 | 21 | 7 | 59 | 0 | | | | | |

## SOMERSET vs. YORKSHIRE

at Taunton on 23rd, 24th, 26th August 1991
Toss : Yorkshire.  Umpires : J.C.Balderstone and N.T.Plews
Match drawn.  Somerset 6 pts (Bt: 4, Bw: 2), Yorkshire 6 pts (Bt: 2, Bw: 4)

### SOMERSET

| | | | | |
|---|---|---|---|---|
| S.J.Cook | lbw b Gough | 79 | not out | 85 |
| P.M.Roebuck | c Blakey b Pickles | 31 | c Byas b Robinson M.A. | 2 |
| A.N.Hayhurst | lbw b Robinson M.A. | 21 | retired hurt | 9 |
| C.J.Tavare * | c Metcalfe b Carrick | 27 | c Batty b Pickles | 18 |
| R.J.Harden | lbw b Carrick | 13 | not out | 24 |
| R.J.Bartlett | c Blakey b Carrick | 71 | | |
| N.D.Burns + | b Carrick | 0 | | |
| G.D.Rose | not out | 105 | | |
| H.R.J.Trump | lbw b Gough | 0 | | |
| D.A.Graveney | b Gough | 7 | | |
| J.C.Hallett | not out | 1 | | |
| Extras | (b 4,lb 12,nb 7) | 23 | (b 3,lb 3,w 1,nb 6) | 13 |
| TOTAL | (for 9 wkts dec) | 378 | (for 2 wkts dec) | 151 |

### YORKSHIRE

| | | | | |
|---|---|---|---|---|
| M.D.Moxon * | c Tavare b Rose | 34 | c Tavare b Graveney | 91 |
| A.A.Metcalfe | lbw b Rose | 6 | c Burns b Graveney | 62 |
| D.Byas | c Cook b Trump | 79 | not out | 27 |
| S.A.Kellett | c Burns b Graveney | 67 | c & b Graveney | 1 |
| P.E.Robinson | not out | 22 | run out | 4 |
| R.J.Blakey + | c & b Trump | 7 | b Trump | 1 |
| C.S.Pickles | not out | 0 | c Harden b Trump | 0 |
| P.Carrick | | | not out | 11 |
| D.Gough | | | | |
| J.D.Batty | | | | |
| M.A.Robinson | | | | |
| Extras | (lb 2,w 1,nb 1) | 4 | (b 3,lb 3,nb 3) | 9 |
| TOTAL | (for 5 wkts dec) | 219 | (for 6 wkts) | 206 |

| YORKSHIRE | O | M | R | W | O | M | R | W | FALL OF WICKETS | | | | |
|---|---|---|---|---|---|---|---|---|---|---|---|---|---|
| | | | | | | | | | | SOM | YOR | SOM | YOR |
| Robinson M.A. | 16 | 2 | 77 | 1 | 10 | 1 | 40 | 1 | 1st | 66 | 33 | 20 | 148 |
| Gough | 27 | 6 | 99 | 3 | 8 | 1 | 25 | 0 | 2nd | 124 | 42 | 86 | 161 |
| Pickles | 17 | 3 | 43 | 1 | 8 | 0 | 36 | 1 | 3rd | 147 | 190 | | 165 |
| Kellett | 2 | 0 | 4 | 0 | | | | | 4th | 169 | 195 | | 174 |
| Carrick | 30.3 | 5 | 111 | 4 | 8 | 1 | 24 | 0 | 5th | 208 | 208 | | 183 |
| Batty | 6 | 1 | 28 | 0 | 3 | 0 | 20 | 0 | 6th | 212 | | | 190 |
| SOMERSET | O | M | R | W | O | M | R | W | 7th | 295 | | | |
| Hallett | 13 | 3 | 42 | 0 | 6 | 1 | 26 | 0 | 8th | 296 | | | |
| Hayhurst | 10 | 1 | 35 | 0 | 3 | 0 | 10 | 0 | 9th | 358 | | | |
| Graveney | 26 | 9 | 58 | 1 | 22 | 4 | 61 | 3 | 10th | | | | |
| Rose | 13 | 3 | 29 | 2 | 5 | 0 | 28 | 0 | | | | | |
| Trump | 24 | 7 | 53 | 2 | 24 | 5 | 71 | 2 | | | | | |
| Roebuck | | | | | 3 | 2 | 4 | 0 | | | | | |

## WORCESTERSHIRE vs. MIDDLESEX

at Worcester on 23rd, 24th, 26th August 1991
Toss : Middlesex.  Umpires : A.A.Jones and D.O.Oslear
Match drawn.  Worcestershire 7 pts (Bt: 3, Bw: 4), Middlesex 5 pts (Bt: 1, Bw: 4)

### MIDDLESEX

| | | | | |
|---|---|---|---|---|
| M.A.Roseberry | c Rhodes b Lampitt | 36 | c Moody b Newport | 15 |
| J.C.Pooley | c Rhodes b Newport | 8 | lbw b Radford | 28 |
| M.W.Gatting * | b Lampitt | 9 | b Hick | 120 |
| K.R.Brown | c Moody b Radford | 26 | c Moody b Newport | 1 |
| M.Keech | c Bent b Tolley | 1 | (6) b Radford | 4 |
| P.N.Weekes | not out | 57 | (5) c Rhodes b Radford | 48 |
| J.E.Emburey | c Rhodes b Radford | 4 | not out | 55 |
| P.Farbrace + | c Curtis b Tolley | 18 | lbw b Newport | 11 |
| N.F.Williams | b Tolley | 15 | run out | 0 |
| D.W.Headley | c Rhodes b Lampitt | 0 | b Newport | 0 |
| N.G.Cowans | c Rhodes b Lampitt | 0 | not out | 2 |
| Extras | (b 6,lb 1,nb 8) | 15 | (b 3,lb 11,w 2,nb 4) | 20 |
| TOTAL | | 189 | (for 9 wkts) | 304 |

### WORCESTERSHIRE

| | | |
|---|---|---|
| T.S.Curtis * | b Weekes | 22 |
| P.Bent | b Cowans | 1 |
| R.K.Illingworth | c Farbrace b Williams | 16 |
| G.A.Hick | c Gatting b Emburey | 30 |
| T.M.Moody | c Pooley b Headley | 135 |
| D.B.D'Oliveira | c Headley b Weekes | 10 |
| S.J.Rhodes + | lbw b Emburey | 0 |
| S.R.Lampitt | c & b Weekes | 35 |
| C.M.Tolley | c Farbrace b Headley | 14 |
| P.J.Newport | c Williams b Headley | 4 |
| N.V.Radford | not out | 0 |
| Extras | (lb 12,w 1,nb 6) | 19 |
| TOTAL | | 286 |

| WORCS | O | M | R | W | O | M | R | W | FALL OF WICKETS | | | |
|---|---|---|---|---|---|---|---|---|---|---|---|---|
| | | | | | | | | | | MID | WOR | MID | WOR |
| Newport | 14 | 3 | 35 | 1 | 27 | 11 | 51 | 4 | 1st | 13 | 3 | 51 | |
| Radford | 13 | 2 | 45 | 2 | 14 | 2 | 46 | 3 | 2nd | 38 | 25 | 53 | |
| Tolley | 19 | 4 | 40 | 3 | 7 | 1 | 37 | 0 | 3rd | 64 | 71 | 64 | |
| Lampitt | 15.5 | 2 | 53 | 4 | | | | | 4th | 67 | 93 | 173 | |
| Illingworth | 1 | 0 | 9 | 0 | 39 | 10 | 90 | 0 | 5th | 112 | 111 | 179 | |
| Hick | | | | | 14 | 4 | 33 | 1 | 6th | 128 | 114 | 243 | |
| D'Oliveira | | | | | 5 | 0 | 29 | 0 | 7th | 156 | 240 | 277 | |
| Moody | | | | | 1 | 0 | 4 | 0 | 8th | 184 | 281 | 278 | |
| MIDDLESEX | O | M | R | W | O | M | R | W | 9th | 189 | 281 | 280 | |
| Cowans | 11 | 2 | 23 | 1 | | | | | 10th | 189 | 286 | | |
| Headley | 24.5 | 6 | 67 | 3 | | | | | | | | | |
| Williams | 12 | 3 | 36 | 1 | | | | | | | | | |
| Gatting | 4 | 0 | 15 | 0 | | | | | | | | | |
| Emburey | 28 | 4 | 76 | 2 | | | | | | | | | |
| Weekes | 19 | 5 | 57 | 3 | | | | | | | | | |

Mohammad Azharuddin who enjoyed a prolific first season
with Derbyshire.

# CORNHILL TEST MATCH

## HEADLINES

**Cornhill Test Match
England v Sri Lanka**

**Lord's: 22nd - 27th August**

• England gained their third Test victory in four matches against Sri Lanka, and their third success of the season, with victory by 137 runs to end a highly satisfying summer of international cricket. Sri Lanka quickly showed that they were worthy opponents by dismissing England for 282 in their first innings, their attack proving an effective mixture of seam, swing and spin. England were grateful to a maiden Test 100 from Alec Stewart for avoiding complete embarrassment, as the other batsmen failed to adjust to the gentler pace of the Sri Lankan bowling. Rumesh Ratnayake took five wickets in an innings for the fifth time in his Test career.

• When Aravinda De Silva delighted the second day crowd, who had endured long delays for rain, with an unbeaten 42 from 30 balls, to take his side to 75 for two by the close, the visitors even had visions of their first overseas Test victory, but following his dismissal in the first over of Saturday's play Sri Lanka's innings fell away, with only Ratnayake passing 50, as England gained a lead of 58. Phil DeFreitas gained full reward for his consistent bowling throughout the summer by returning his best Test figures.

• Graham Gooch then made sure that England took control of the match with his 15th Test 100 and the highest score by an England batsman against Sri Lanka, sharing century stands with Stewart and Robin Smith. Gooch also became the fifth Englishman to complete 7,000 runs in Test cricket, joining Hammond, Cowdrey, Boycott and Gower as England built a lead of 422 before their declaration.

• Sri Lanka had four full sessions to make the runs, but although 10 out of 11 batsmen reached double figures, none could play the major innings the visitors needed if they were to approach a possible world record match-winning score, Jayasuriya top-scoring with a Test-best 66. Phil Tufnell again played an important part in England's victory by claiming five wickets in a Test innings for the third time in only his sixth match as Sri Lanka's resistance was finally broken moments after tea on the final afternoon of a memorable summer in which England had done much to re-establish themselves as a leading force in Test cricket.

• Test début: K.I.W.Wijegunawardene (Sri Lanka)

• Man of the match: G.A.Gooch (England).

## ENGLAND vs. SRI LANKA

at Lord's on 22nd, 23rd, 24th, 26th, 27th August 1991
Toss : England.  Umpires : H.D.Bird and J.H.Hampshire
England won by 137 runs

**ENGLAND**

| Batsman | First Innings | | Second Innings | |
|---|---|---|---|---|
| G.A.Gooch * | c & b Ramanayake | 38 | b Anurasiri | 174 |
| H.Morris | lbw b Ratnayake | 42 | c Mahanama b Anurasiri | 23 |
| A.J.Stewart | not out | 113 | c De Silva b Anurasiri | 43 |
| R.A.Smith | c Tillekaratne b Ratnayake | 4 | not out | 63 |
| M.R.Ramprakash | c Mahanama b Hathurusinghe | 0 | | |
| I.T.Botham | c Mahanama b Ramanayake | 22 | | |
| C.C.Lewis | c De Silva b Anurasiri | 11 | | |
| R.C.Russell + | b Anurasiri | 17 | (5) not out | 12 |
| P.A.J.DeFreitas | b Ratnayake | 1 | | |
| D.V.Lawrence | c & b Ratnayake | 3 | | |
| P.C.R.Tufnell | lbw b Ratnayake | 0 | | |
| Extras | (b 9,lb 8,nb 14) | 31 | (b 15,lb 23,w 1,nb 10) | 49 |
| TOTAL | | 282 | (for 3 wkts dec) | 364 |

**SRI LANKA**

| Batsman | First Innings | | Second Innings | |
|---|---|---|---|---|
| D.S.B.P.Kuruppu | b DeFreitas | 5 | lbw b Lewis | 21 |
| U.C.Hathurusinghe | c Tufnell b DeFreitas | 66 | c Morris b Tufnell | 25 |
| A.P.Gurusinha | lbw b DeFreitas | 4 | b Tufnell | 34 |
| P.A.De Silva * | c Lewis b DeFreitas | 42 | c Russell b Lawrence | 18 |
| R.S.Mahanama | c Russell b Botham | 2 | c Botham b Tufnell | 15 |
| S.T.Jayasuriya | c Smith b Lewis | 11 | c Russell b Lewis | 66 |
| H.P.Tillekaratne + | c Morris b Lawrence | 20 | b Tufnell | 16 |
| R.J.Ratnayake | b DeFreitas | 52 | c sub b Lawrence | 17 |
| C.P.Ramanayake | lbw b DeFreitas | 0 | not out | 34 |
| K.I.W.Wijeguna' | not out | 6 | c Botham b DeFreitas | 4 |
| S.D.Anurasiri | b Lawrence | 1 | lbw b Tufnell | 16 |
| Extras | (lb 15) | 15 | (b 1,lb 16,nb 2) | 19 |
| TOTAL | | 224 | | 285 |

| SRI LANKA | O | M | R | W | O | M | R | W |
|---|---|---|---|---|---|---|---|---|
| Ratnayake | 27 | 4 | 69 | 5 | 26 | 4 | 91 | 0 |
| Ramanayake | 24 | 5 | 75 | 2 | 20 | 2 | 86 | 0 |
| Wijeguna' | 10 | 1 | 36 | 0 | 2 | 0 | 13 | 0 |
| Hathurusinghe | 17 | 6 | 40 | 1 | | | | |
| Anurasiri | 17 | 4 | 45 | 2 | 36.1 | 8 | 135 | 3 |
| Jayasuriya | | | | | 1 | 0 | 1 | 0 |

| ENGLAND | O | M | R | W | O | M | R | W |
|---|---|---|---|---|---|---|---|---|
| DeFreitas | 26 | 8 | 70 | 7 | 22 | 8 | 45 | 1 |
| Lawrence | 15.1 | 3 | 61 | 2 | 23 | 7 | 83 | 2 |
| Lewis | 10 | 5 | 29 | 0 | 18 | 4 | 31 | 2 |
| Botham | 10 | 3 | 26 | 1 | 6 | 2 | 15 | 0 |
| Tufnell | 7 | 2 | 23 | 0 | 34.3 | 14 | 94 | 5 |

**FALL OF WICKETS**

| | ENG | SRI | ENG | SRI |
|---|---|---|---|---|
| 1st | 70 | 12 | 78 | 50 |
| 2nd | 114 | 22 | 217 | 50 |
| 3rd | 119 | 75 | 322 | 111 |
| 4th | 120 | 86 | | 119 |
| 5th | 160 | 105 | | 159 |
| 6th | 183 | 139 | | 212 |
| 7th | 246 | 213 | | 212 |
| 8th | 258 | 213 | | 241 |
| 9th | 276 | 220 | | 253 |
| 10th | 282 | 224 | | 285 |

Alec Stewart, whose maiden Test century gave some respectability to England's first innings.

# BRITANNIC ASSURANCE CHAMPIONSHIP

## GLAMORGAN vs. GLOUCESTERSHIRE

at Abergavenny on 28th, 29th, 30th, 31st August 1991
Toss : Glamorgan. Umpires : K.E.Palmer and A.G.T.Whitehead
Glamorgan won by 9 wickets. Glamorgan 23 pts (Bt: 4, Bw: 3), Gloucs 4 pts (Bt: 3, Bw: 1)
100 overs scores : Glamorgan 331 for 4, Gloucs 298 for 8

### GLAMORGAN

| | | | | |
|---|---|---|---|---|
| A.R.Butcher * | c & b Gilbert | 147 | c Russell b Babington | 20 |
| H.Morris | c Russell b Lawrence | 85 | not out | 50 |
| A.Dale | run out | 140 | not out | 80 |
| M.P.Maynard | c & b Babington | 2 | | |
| R.J.Shastri | lbw b Babington | 0 | | |
| S.P.James | b Ball | 66 | | |
| R.D.B.Croft | c Russell b Scott | 14 | | |
| C.P.Metson + | not out | 26 | | |
| S.L.Watkin | run out | 4 | | |
| S.Bastien | st Russell b Ball | 2 | | |
| M.Frost | | | | |
| Extras | (b 4,lb 10,nb 14) | 28 | (b 1,lb 1,nb 1) | 3 |
| TOTAL | (for 9 wkts dec) | 514 | (for 1 wkt) | 153 |

### GLOUCESTERSHIRE

| | | | | |
|---|---|---|---|---|
| G.D.Hodgson | c Metson b Croft | 38 | lbw b Watkin | 4 |
| R.J.Scott | lbw b Bastien | 21 | (3) c Metson b Dale | 10 |
| A.J.Wright * | c James b Shastri | 89 | (4) c Maynard b Frost | 83 |
| C.W.J.Athey | c Morris b Shastri | 2 | (5) lbw b Dale | 0 |
| M.W.Alleyne | c Metson b Frost | 40 | (6) c Butcher b Shastri | 33 |
| R.C.Russell + | run out | 15 | (7) st Metson b Croft | 39 |
| J.W.Lloyds | c & b Croft | 50 | (2) c Metson b Shastri | 12 |
| M.C.J.Ball | c Morris b Shastri | 0 | c Maynard b Shastri | 23 |
| D.V.Lawrence | c Metson b Frost | 66 | b Watkin | 44 |
| D.R.Gilbert | b Shastri | 2 | (11) not out | 16 |
| A.M.Babington | not out | 14 | (10) c Butcher b Frost | 24 |
| Extras | (lb 8,nb 12) | 20 | (b 4,lb 10,nb 7) | 21 |
| TOTAL | | 357 | | 309 |

| GLOUCS | O | M | R | W | O | M | R | W |
|---|---|---|---|---|---|---|---|---|
| Lawrence | 21 | 2 | 63 | 1 | 5 | 0 | 23 | 0 |
| Gilbert | 23 | 2 | 85 | 1 | 9 | 1 | 31 | 0 |
| Babington | 32 | 3 | 120 | 2 | 4 | 0 | 13 | 1 |
| Ball | 36.3 | 7 | 109 | 2 | 7 | 1 | 29 | 0 |
| Scott | 19 | 4 | 59 | 1 | | | | |
| Lloyds | 8 | 0 | 28 | 0 | 7 | 2 | 24 | 0 |
| Alleyne | 12 | 4 | 33 | 0 | | | | |
| Athey | 2 | 0 | 3 | 0 | 5 | 0 | 27 | 0 |
| Wright | | | | | 0.3 | 0 | 4 | 0 |

| GLAMORGAN | O | M | R | W | O | M | R | W |
|---|---|---|---|---|---|---|---|---|
| Watkin | 24 | 7 | 51 | 0 | 16 | 3 | 73 | 2 |
| Frost | 21 | 5 | 82 | 2 | 11.4 | 3 | 30 | 2 |
| Bastien | 17 | 4 | 76 | 1 | 3 | 0 | 13 | 0 |
| Croft | 23.1 | 4 | 66 | 2 | 31 | 9 | 73 | 1 |
| Shastri | 38 | 13 | 74 | 4 | 42 | 20 | 73 | 3 |
| Dale | | | | | 7 | 2 | 33 | 2 |

| FALL OF WICKETS | | | | |
|---|---|---|---|---|
| | GLA | GLO | GLO | GLA |
| 1st | 197 | 51 | 17 | 30 |
| 2nd | 254 | 69 | 17 | |
| 3rd | 256 | 72 | 46 | |
| 4th | 256 | 148 | 46 | |
| 5th | 428 | 216 | 106 | |
| 6th | 477 | 221 | 178 | |
| 7th | 478 | 223 | 211 | |
| 8th | 494 | 296 | 268 | |
| 9th | 514 | 309 | 268 | |
| 10th | | 357 | 309 | |

## WARWICKSHIRE vs. WORCESTERSHIRE

at Edgbaston on 28th, 29th, 30th August 1991
Toss : Worcestershire. Umpires : R.Julian and P.B.Wight
Warwickshire won by 4 wickets. Warwicks 20 pts (Bt: 0, Bw: 4), Worcs 5 pts (Bt: 1, Bw: 4)

### WORCESTERSHIRE

| | | | | |
|---|---|---|---|---|
| T.S.Curtis * | lbw b Munton | 11 | c Munton b Reeve | 77 |
| P.Bent | c Holloway b Small | 1 | b Munton | 20 |
| G.A.Hick | lbw b Small | 0 | c & b Donald | 13 |
| T.M.Moody | b Munton | 91 | c Ratcliffe b Donald | 3 |
| D.B.D'Oliveira | c Reeve b Munton | 1 | c Lloyd b Small | 1 |
| S.J.Rhodes + | lbw b Munton | 4 | b Benjamin | 7 |
| I.T.Botham | b Munton | 24 | b Munton | 17 |
| R.K.Illingworth | c Ostler b Munton | 3 | c Ratcliffe b Munton | 4 |
| C.M.Tolley | c Lloyd b Munton | 7 | c Holloway b Reeve | 1 |
| P.J.Newport | c Lloyd b Small | 12 | not out | 0 |
| N.V.Radford | not out | 0 | lbw b Reeve | 0 |
| Extras | (b 5,lb 3,nb 5) | 13 | (b 9,lb 7,w 7,nb 4) | 27 |
| TOTAL | | 166 | | 170 |

### WARWICKSHIRE

| | | | | |
|---|---|---|---|---|
| A.J.Moles | c Rhodes b Botham | 26 | c Rhodes b Newport | 56 |
| J.D.Ratcliffe | b Botham | 22 | c & b Tolley | 25 |
| T.A.Lloyd * | lbw b Tolley | 7 | (4) c Illingworth b Newport | 13 |
| D.P.Ostler | c D'Oliveira b Botham | 7 | (5) b Newport | 41 |
| D.A.Reeve | c Radford b Botham | 13 | (6) st Rhodes b Illingworth | 29 |
| Asif Din | c Hick b Radford | 26 | (3) lbw b Radford | 23 |
| P.C.L.Holloway + | c Rhodes b Radford | 6 | not out | 7 |
| G.C.Small | c Bent b Newport | 0 | not out | 4 |
| T.A.Munton | not out | 5 | | |
| J.E.Benjamin | lbw b Newport | 0 | | |
| A.A.Donald | b Newport | 0 | | |
| Extras | (b 2,lb 7,nb 5) | 14 | (b 1,lb 13,nb 2) | 16 |
| TOTAL | | 126 | (for 6 wkts) | 214 |

| WARWICKS | O | M | R | W | O | M | R | W |
|---|---|---|---|---|---|---|---|---|
| Donald | 13 | 1 | 51 | 0 | 10 | 0 | 27 | 2 |
| Small | 11 | 4 | 20 | 3 | 15 | 2 | 45 | 1 |
| Munton | 18.3 | 2 | 59 | 7 | 19 | 6 | 32 | 3 |
| Benjamin | 6 | 0 | 28 | 0 | 8 | 0 | 37 | 1 |
| Reeve | | | | | 5 | 3 | 13 | 3 |

| FALL OF WICKETS | | | | |
|---|---|---|---|---|
| | WOR | WAR | WOR | WAR |
| 1st | 6 | 41 | 49 | 60 |
| 2nd | 6 | 50 | 70 | 106 |
| 3rd | 39 | 64 | 83 | 112 |
| 4th | 39 | 65 | 85 | 127 |
| 5th | 45 | 90 | 118 | 197 |
| 6th | 83 | 119 | 156 | 203 |
| 7th | 89 | 119 | 168 | |
| 8th | 145 | 124 | 169 | |
| 9th | 166 | 126 | 170 | |
| 10th | 166 | 126 | 170 | |

| WORCS | O | M | R | W | O | M | R | W |
|---|---|---|---|---|---|---|---|---|
| Radford | 14 | 9 | 14 | 2 | 20 | 4 | 54 | 1 |
| Newport | 15.4 | 3 | 36 | 3 | 19 | 1 | 51 | 3 |
| Botham | 17 | 2 | 50 | 4 | 27 | 8 | 52 | 0 |
| Tolley | 10 | 3 | 14 | 1 | 7 | 2 | 21 | 1 |
| Illingworth | 1 | 0 | 3 | 0 | 9 | 4 | 22 | 1 |

## HAMPSHIRE vs. SOMERSET

at Southampton on 28th, 29th, 30th, 31st August 1991
Toss : Somerset. Umpires : A.A.Jones and D.R.Shepherd
Hampshire won by 2 wickets. Hampshire 21 pts (Bt: 4, Bw: 1), Somerset 6 pts (Bt: 4, Bw: 2)
100 overs scores : Somerset 320 for 4, Hampshire 314 for 5

### SOMERSET

| | | | | |
|---|---|---|---|---|
| S.J.Cook | c Aymes b James | 197 | retired hurt/ill | 115 |
| G.T.J.Townsend | c James b Shine | 29 | c Smith b Turner | 18 |
| R.J.Harden | c Aymes b Maru | 0 | c Gower b Maru | 62 |
| C.J.Tavare * | c Middleton b Shine | 66 | not out | 15 |
| I.Fletcher | c Aymes b Aqib Javed | 56 | not out | 2 |
| N.D.Burns + | not out | 61 | | |
| G.D.Rose | c Smith b Turner | 20 | | |
| R.P.Lefebvre | run out | 12 | | |
| H.R.J.Trump | not out | 16 | | |
| A.P.van Troost | | | | |
| D.A.Graveney | | | | |
| Extras | (b 4,lb 6,nb 13) | 23 | (b 4,lb 3,nb 8) | 15 |
| TOTAL | (for 7 wkts dec) | 480 | (for 2 wkts dec) | 227 |

### HAMPSHIRE

| | | | | |
|---|---|---|---|---|
| V.P.Terry | c Burns b Trump | 86 | c & b Trump | 31 |
| T.C.Middleton | c Townsend b Trump | 24 | b Trump | 49 |
| K.D.James | c Tavare b Trump | 25 | c & b Graveney | 10 |
| R.A.Smith | st Burns b Trump | 81 | c Graveney b Lefebvre | 107 |
| D.I.Gower | c Cook b Trump | 73 | c Burns b Graveney | 15 |
| M.C.J.Nicholas * | not out | 27 | not out | 90 |
| A.N Aymes + | c Townsend b Trump | 13 | b Graveney | 33 |
| R.J.Maru | c Cook b Rose | 1 | b Graveney | 3 |
| I.J.Turner | c Burns b Rose | 0 | run out | 3 |
| K.J.Shine | not out | 0 | not out | 16 |
| Aqib Javed | | | | |
| Extras | (lb 3,nb 5) | 8 | (lb 8,w 4,nb 1) | 13 |
| TOTAL | (for 8 wkts dec) | 338 | (for 8 wkts) | 370 |

| HAMPSHIRE | O | M | R | W | O | M | R | W |
|---|---|---|---|---|---|---|---|---|
| Aqib Javed | 24 | 1 | 102 | 1 | 11 | 2 | 54 | 0 |
| Shine | 22 | 2 | 91 | 2 | 8 | 2 | 17 | 0 |
| James | 28 | 6 | 67 | 1 | 7 | 2 | 17 | 0 |
| Turner | 34 | 6 | 114 | 1 | 23 | 7 | 70 | 1 |
| Maru | 40 | 17 | 78 | 1 | 20 | 3 | 62 | 1 |
| Nicholas | 4 | 0 | 18 | 0 | | | | |

| FALL OF WICKETS | | | | |
|---|---|---|---|---|
| | SOM | HAM | SOM | HAM |
| 1st | 91 | 47 | 74 | 75 |
| 2nd | 105 | 99 | 199 | 94 |
| 3rd | 267 | 201 | | 98 |
| 4th | 320 | 253 | | 160 |
| 5th | 380 | 314 | | 243 |
| 6th | 428 | 336 | | 316 |
| 7th | 447 | 338 | | 326 |
| 8th | | 338 | | 333 |
| 9th | | | | |
| 10th | | | | |

| SOMERSET | O | M | R | W | O | M | R | W |
|---|---|---|---|---|---|---|---|---|
| van Troost | 18 | 5 | 42 | 0 | 8 | 0 | 28 | 0 |
| Rose | 20 | 3 | 78 | 2 | 11 | 0 | 32 | 0 |
| Lefebvre | 23 | 5 | 52 | 0 | 12 | 1 | 29 | 1 |
| Trump | 43 | 11 | 121 | 6 | 33 | 3 | 132 | 2 |
| Harden | 3 | 0 | 11 | 0 | | | | |
| Graveney | 7 | 1 | 31 | 0 | 30.1 | 3 | 141 | 4 |

## SURREY vs. SUSSEX

at The Oval on 28th, 29th, 30th August 1991
Toss : Sussex. Umpires : N.T.Plews and R.C.Tolchard
Surrey won by an inns and 128 runs. Surrey 24 pts (Bt: 4, Bw: 4), Sussex 3 pts (Bt: 1, Bw: 2)
100 overs scores : Surrey 357 for 6

### SURREY

| | | |
|---|---|---|
| D.J.Bicknell | b North | 36 |
| R.I.Alikhan | c Moores b Pigott | 11 |
| G.P.Thorpe | b Dodemaide | 177 |
| D.M.Ward | lbw b Donelan | 44 |
| A.J.Stewart + | c Smith b Donelan | 47 |
| M.A.Lynch | lbw b Donelan | 0 |
| I.A.Greig * | c Moores b Dodemaide | 25 |
| K.T.Medlycott | c Wells b Pigott | 4 |
| M.A.Feltham | c Lenham b Dodemaide | 37 |
| M.P.Bicknell | b North | 26 |
| Waqar Younis | not out | 3 |
| Extras | (b 9,lb 9,w 3,nb 14) | 35 |
| TOTAL | | 445 |

### SUSSEX

| | | | | |
|---|---|---|---|---|
| N.J.Lenham | retired hurt/ill | 2 | absent hurt/ill | |
| D.M.Smith | c Bicknell D.J. b Bicknell M.P. | 10 | c Lynch b Bicknell M.P. | 0 |
| K.Greenfield | c Thorpe b Feltham | 21 | c Bicknell D.J. b Bicknell M.P. | 8 |
| A.P.Wells * | c sub b Feltham | 28 | (6) c Stewart b Bicknell M.P. | 3 |
| R.Hanley | c Lynch b Feltham | 19 | (7) c Stewart b Bicknell M.P. | 0 |
| J.A.North | b Waqar Younis | 0 | (8) lbw b Bicknell M.P. | 0 |
| A.I.C.Dodemaide | c Waqar Younis b Bicknell M.P. | 23 | (9) run out | 48 |
| P.Moores + | lbw b Waqar Younis | 54 | (1) c Ward b Bicknell M.P. | 7 |
| A.C.S.Pigott | c Stewart b Waqar Younis | 0 | (10) not out | 18 |
| B.T.P.Donelan | c Stewart b Waqar Younis | 4 | (4) b Feltham | 36 |
| A.N.Jones | not out | 4 | (5) b Bicknell M.P. | 19 |
| Extras | (b 6,nb 4) | 10 | (b 2,lb 1) | 3 |
| TOTAL | | 175 | | 142 |

| SUSSEX | O | M | R | W | O | M | R | W |
|---|---|---|---|---|---|---|---|---|
| Jones | 21 | 1 | 83 | 0 | | | | |
| Dodemaide | 32.3 | 6 | 104 | 3 | | | | |
| North | 23 | 4 | 107 | 2 | | | | |
| Pigott | 21 | 4 | 69 | 2 | | | | |
| Donelan | 30 | 9 | 64 | 3 | | | | |

| FALL OF WICKETS | | | | |
|---|---|---|---|---|
| | SUR | SUS | SUS | SUR |
| 1st | 54 | 23 | 7 | |
| 2nd | 54 | 39 | 15 | |
| 3rd | 200 | 72 | 26 | |
| 4th | 340 | 73 | 58 | |
| 5th | 340 | 89 | 72 | |
| 6th | 353 | 167 | 74 | |
| 7th | 374 | 167 | 74 | |
| 8th | 374 | 171 | 85 | |
| 9th | 440 | 175 | 142 | |
| 10th | 445 | | | |

| SURREY | O | M | R | W | O | M | R | W |
|---|---|---|---|---|---|---|---|---|
| Waqar Younis | 17 | 2 | 52 | 4 | 15 | 2 | 51 | 0 |
| Bicknell M.P. | 14.1 | 5 | 35 | 2 | 23 | 5 | 52 | 7 |
| Feltham | 16 | 2 | 63 | 3 | 11 | 1 | 36 | 1 |
| Thorpe | 2 | 0 | 11 | 0 | | | | |
| Medlycott | 5 | 1 | 8 | 0 | 1 | 1 | 0 | 0 |

# BRITANNIC ASSURANCE CHAMPIONSHIP

## KENT vs. MIDDLESEX
at Canterbury on 28th, 29th, 30th, 31st August 1991
Toss : Middlesex. Umpires : B.Hassan and R.Palmer
Kent won by 208 runs. Kent 21 pts (Bt: 3, Bw: 2), Middlesex 7 pts (Bt: 3, Bw: 4)
100 overs scores :Middlesex 290 for 5

### KENT
| | | | | | |
|---|---|---|---|---|---|
| T.R.Ward | c Farbrace b Cowans | 51 | not out | | 235 |
| M.R.Benson * | lbw b Headley | 8 | c Pooley b Tufnell | | 20 |
| N.R.Taylor | c Farbrace b Headley | 17 | c sub b Williams | | 101 |
| G.R.Cowdrey | c Farbrace b Headley | 38 | c Farbrace b Tufnell | | 46 |
| M.V.Fleming | b Headley | 30 | not out | | 23 |
| S.A.Marsh + | c Emburey b Williams | 5 | | | |
| M.A.Ealham | c Farbrace b Williams | 34 | | | |
| R.M.Ellison | b Headley | 33 | | | |
| R.P.Davis | not out | 15 | | | |
| C.Penn | lbw b Williams | 0 | | | |
| A.P.Igglesden | c Headley b Emburey | 11 | | | |
| Extras | (b 5,lb 4,nb 7) | 16 | (b 8,lb 8,nb 9) | | 25 |
| TOTAL | | 258 | (for 3 wkts dec) | | 450 |

### MIDDLESEX
| | | | | | |
|---|---|---|---|---|---|
| M.A.Roseberry | c Ellison b Penn | 18 | c Ellison b Ealham | | 5 |
| J.C.Pooley | c Marsh b Igglesden | 11 | c Marsh b Ellison | | 14 |
| P.Farbrace + | lbw b Penn | 0 | (6) lbw b Ellison | | 0 |
| M.R.Ramprakash | lbw b Ellison | 87 | (3) c sub b Ellison | | 5 |
| P.N.Weekes | c Davis b Ellison | 4 | (4) c Marsh b Ealham | | 2 |
| J.E.Emburey | lbw b Ealham | 20 | (5) c Marsh b Ellison | | 11 |
| M.W.Gatting * | c Davis b Ealham | 174 | c Ealham b Penn | | 9 |
| N.F.Williams | lbw b Penn | 1 | c Ward b Penn | | 5 |
| D.W.Headley | b Penn | 26 | b Penn | | 14 |
| P.C.R.Tufnell | not out | 31 | c Marsh b Penn | | 4 |
| N.G.Cowans | lbw b Penn | 5 | not out | | 23 |
| Extras | (b 1,lb 12,nb 14) | 27 | (lb 1,nb 3) | | 4 |
| TOTAL | | 404 | | | 96 |

| MIDDLESEX | O | M | R | W | O | M | R | W | FALL OF WICKETS | | | | |
|---|---|---|---|---|---|---|---|---|---|---|---|---|---|
| | | | | | | | | | | KEN | MID | KEN | MID |
| Cowans | 15 | 3 | 42 | 1 | 22 | 3 | 78 | 0 | 1st | 24 | 27 | 39 | 19 |
| Williams | 23 | 5 | 52 | 3 | 22 | 0 | 87 | 1 | 2nd | 64 | 28 | 265 | 21 |
| Headley | 24 | 5 | 100 | 5 | 19 | 1 | 112 | 0 | 3rd | 108 | 33 | 399 | 28 |
| Tufnell | 16 | 6 | 31 | 0 | 30 | 9 | 70 | 2 | 4th | 145 | 39 | | 28 |
| Gatting | 8 | 4 | 13 | 0 | | | | | 5th | 162 | 87 | | 30 |
| Emburey | 6.5 | 1 | 11 | 1 | 21 | 4 | 53 | 0 | 6th | 162 | 306 | | 45 |
| Weekes | | | | | 12 | 1 | 34 | 0 | 7th | 231 | 311 | | 53 |
| KENT | O | M | R | W | O | M | R | W | 8th | 232 | 342 | | 61 |
| Igglesden | 5.1 | 1 | 12 | 1 | | | | | 9th | 232 | 393 | | 71 |
| Penn | 39.5 | 11 | 105 | 5 | 11 | 3 | 44 | 4 | 10th | 258 | 404 | | 96 |
| Ealham | 18.5 | 4 | 47 | 2 | 8 | 3 | 11 | 2 | | | | | |
| Ellison | 35 | 9 | 88 | 2 | 18 | 5 | 40 | 4 | | | | | |
| Fleming | 17 | 3 | 65 | 0 | | | | | | | | | |
| Davis | 17 | 1 | 74 | 0 | | | | | | | | | |

## LANCASHIRE vs. NOTTS
at Old Trafford on 28th, 29th, 30th, 31st August 1991
Toss : Lancashire. Umpires : J.D.Bond and R.A.White
Notts won by 3 wickets. Lancashire 6 pts (Bt: 2, Bw: 4), Notts 22 pts (Bt: 2, Bw: 4)
100 overs scores : Lancashire 243 for 9

### LANCASHIRE
| | | | | | |
|---|---|---|---|---|---|
| G.D.Mendis | b Pick | 7 | b Stephenson | | 0 |
| N.J.Speak | b Pick | 9 | c French b Pick | | 11 |
| G.D.Lloyd | b Saxelby | 25 | b Stephenson b Hemmings | | 22 |
| N.H.Fairbrother * | c Randall b Pick | 0 | c Robinson b Hemmings | | 12 |
| S.P.Titchard | b French b Pick | 135 | c French b Pick | | 77 |
| M.Watkinson | c French b Afford | 20 | c Johnson b Afford | | 27 |
| P.A.J.DeFreitas | c Pollard b Afford | 2 | b Hemmings | | 16 |
| W.K.Hegg + | c French b Hemmings | 33 | c Randall b Hemmings | | 40 |
| J.D.Fitton | c Robinson b Afford | 7 | lbw b Pick | | 1 |
| G.Yates | c Johnson b Afford | 0 | not out | | 11 |
| I.D.Austin | not out | 61 | lbw b Hemmings | | 2 |
| Extras | (b 6,lb 12,nb 9) | 27 | (b 11,lb 8,w 1,nb 5) | | 25 |
| TOTAL | | 326 | | | 244 |

### NOTTS
| | | | | | |
|---|---|---|---|---|---|
| B.C.Broad | c Fairbrother b Fitton | 54 | lbw b DeFreitas | | 10 |
| P.Pollard | c Austin b Yates | 43 | lbw b Austin | | 12 |
| R.T.Robinson * | lbw b DeFreitas | 44 | not out | | 59 |
| D.W.Randall | c Speak b Watkinson | 0 | b Watkinson | | 39 |
| P.Johnson | c Lloyd b Yates | 11 | lbw b DeFreitas | | 114 |
| M.Saxelby | c Lloyd b Watkinson | 5 | (7) lbw b DeFreitas | | 1 |
| F.D.Stephenson | b DeFreitas | 24 | (8) b DeFreitas | | 6 |
| B.N.French + | b DeFreitas | 6 | (6) c Hegg b DeFreitas | | 65 |
| E.E.Hemmings | b Watkinson | 6 | not out | | 29 |
| R.A.Pick | c Lloyd b Watkinson | 1 | | | |
| J.A.Afford | not out | 0 | | | |
| Extras | (b 4,lb 10,nb 4) | 18 | (b 8,lb 15,nb 1) | | 24 |
| TOTAL | | 212 | (for 7 wkts) | | 359 |

| NOTTS | O | M | R | W | O | M | R | W | FALL OF WICKETS | | | | |
|---|---|---|---|---|---|---|---|---|---|---|---|---|---|
| | | | | | | | | | | LAN | NOT | LAN | NOT |
| Stephenson | 23 | 4 | 62 | 0 | 12 | 0 | 55 | 1 | 1st | 11 | 102 | 2 | 12 |
| Pick | 22.3 | 3 | 75 | 4 | 11 | 1 | 37 | 3 | 2nd | 26 | 124 | 21 | 35 |
| Saxelby | 5 | 2 | 17 | 1 | | | | | 3rd | 33 | 133 | 54 | 101 |
| Afford | 36 | 11 | 78 | 4 | 20 | 5 | 58 | 1 | 4th | 67 | 154 | 54 | 259 |
| Hemmings | 37 | 16 | 76 | 1 | 23.1 | 3 | 75 | 5 | 5th | 111 | 173 | 93 | 278 |
| | | | | | | | | | 6th | 135 | 173 | 120 | 280 |
| LANCASHIRE | O | M | R | W | O | M | R | W | 7th | 178 | 199 | 218 | 296 |
| DeFreitas | 25 | 8 | 44 | 3 | 38 | 12 | 71 | 5 | 8th | 193 | 208 | 223 | |
| Watkinson | 23.1 | 7 | 55 | 4 | 49.3 | 11 | 165 | 1 | 9th | 193 | 211 | 239 | |
| Austin | 4 | 1 | 15 | 0 | 9 | 3 | 21 | 1 | 10th | 326 | 212 | 244 | |
| Fitton | 17 | 3 | 37 | 1 | 10 | 0 | 39 | 0 | | | | | |
| Yates | 25 | 5 | 47 | 2 | 9 | 0 | 40 | 0 | | | | | |

## LEICESTERSHIRE vs. DERBYSHIRE
at Leicester on 28th, 29th, 30th, 31st August 1991
Toss : Derbyshire. Umpires : J.C.Balderstone and G.I.Burgess
Derbyshire won by 195 runs. Leicestershire 6 pts (Bt: 2, Bw: 4), Derbys 23 pts (Bt: 3, Bw: 4)
100 overs scores : Derbyshire 274 for 9

### DERBYSHIRE
| | | | | | |
|---|---|---|---|---|---|
| K.J.Barnett * | c Whitaker b Millns | 1 | (6) c Potter b Hepworth | | 36 |
| P.D.Bowler | lbw b Wilkinson | 104 | (1) c Potter b Wilkinson | | 26 |
| J.E.Morris | c Briers b Maguire | 37 | (2) b Maguire | | 17 |
| M.Azharuddin | c Whitticase b Maguire | 0 | c Maguire b Parsons | | 212 |
| T.J.G.O'Gorman | c Whitaker b Maguire | 0 | (3) c Whitticase b Wilkinson | | 33 |
| S.C.Goldsmith | c Whitticase b Maguire | 0 | (5) c Boon b Potter | | 9 |
| K.M.Krikken + | c Whitticase b Parsons | 9 | c Boon b Gidley | | 65 |
| D.G.Cork | c Whitaker b Wilkinson | 28 | not out | | 22 |
| A.E.Warner | c Hepworth b Parsons | 46 | c Millns b Hepworth | | 6 |
| S.J.Base | b Maguire | 36 | c Wilkinson b Gidley | | 8 |
| R.W.Sladdin | not out | 4 | | | |
| Extras | (b 4,lb 5) | 9 | (b 1,lb 6,w 1,nb 5) | | 13 |
| TOTAL | | 274 | (for 9 wkts dec) | | 447 |

### LEICESTERSHIRE
| | | | | | |
|---|---|---|---|---|---|
| T.J.Boon | c Krikken b Cork | 0 | c Krikken b Warner | | 40 |
| N.E.Briers * | c Azharuddin b Warner | 10 | c Barnett b Cork | | 3 |
| G.J.Parsons | lbw b Cork | 0 | (8) not out | | 10 |
| P.N.Hepworth | c Barnett b Base | 22 | (3) c Barnett b Warner | | 7 |
| J.J.Whitaker | c Krikken b Warner | 12 | (4) c Azharuddin b Sladdin | | 85 |
| L.Potter | lbw b Barnett | 24 | (5) c Morris b Sladdin | | 64 |
| P.Whitticase + | c Krikken b Base | 0 | (6) c Azharuddin b Bowler | | 33 |
| M.I.Gidley | c Barnett b Sladdin | 80 | (7) c Azharuddin b Bowler | | 0 |
| D.J.Millns | c & b Maguire | 12 | b Bowler | | 0 |
| C.Wilkinson | c Base b Barnett | 6 | c Base b Sladdin | | 22 |
| J.N.Maguire | not out | 44 | run out | | 20 |
| Extras | (b 4,lb 11,nb 10) | 25 | (w 1,nb 6) | | 7 |
| TOTAL | | 235 | | | 291 |

| LEICS | O | M | R | W | O | M | R | W | FALL OF WICKETS | | | | |
|---|---|---|---|---|---|---|---|---|---|---|---|---|---|
| | | | | | | | | | | DER | LEI | DER | LEI |
| Millns | 24 | 5 | 63 | 1 | 15 | 1 | 68 | 0 | 1st | 2 | 0 | 39 | 11 |
| Maguire | 23.2 | 4 | 67 | 5 | 20 | 5 | 62 | 1 | 2nd | 58 | 0 | 51 | 23 |
| Wilkinson | 26 | 5 | 59 | 2 | 20 | 2 | 81 | 2 | 3rd | 58 | 28 | 152 | 84 |
| Parsons | 16 | 5 | 44 | 2 | 10 | 1 | 45 | 1 | 4th | 60 | 43 | 175 | 173 |
| Potter | 11 | 2 | 32 | 0 | 20 | 3 | 69 | 1 | 5th | 60 | 53 | 288 | 237 |
| Gidley | | | | | 11.4 | 0 | 58 | 2 | 6th | 79 | 53 | 396 | 237 |
| Hepworth | | | | | 8 | 1 | 57 | 2 | 7th | 127 | 111 | 421 | 237 |
| DERBYSHIRE | O | M | R | W | O | M | R | W | 8th | 206 | 130 | 439 | 237 |
| Cork | 18 | 3 | 38 | 2 | 20 | 3 | 74 | 1 | 9th | 251 | 139 | 447 | 263 |
| Warner | 21 | 5 | 76 | 2 | 17 | 5 | 55 | 2 | 10th | 274 | 235 | | 291 |
| Base | 15 | 7 | 28 | 2 | 22 | 7 | 54 | 0 | | | | | |
| Barnett | 27 | 5 | 49 | 2 | | | | | | | | | |
| Sladdin | 17.1 | 4 | 29 | 2 | 30.4 | 11 | 60 | 3 | | | | | |
| Goldsmith | | | | | 4 | 1 | 7 | 0 | | | | | |
| Bowler | | | | | 11 | 2 | 41 | 3 | | | | | |

## NORTHANTS vs. YORKSHIRE
at Northampton on 28th, 29th, 30th, 31st August 1991
Toss : Northants. Umpires : B.Dudleston and J.H.Harris
Northants won by 9 wickets. Northants 22 pts (Bt: 4, Bw: 2), Yorkshire 3 pts (Bt: 1, Bw: 1)
100 overs scores : Yorkshire 229 for 6, Northants 396 for 4

### YORKSHIRE
| | | | | | |
|---|---|---|---|---|---|
| M.D.Moxon * | lbw b Baptiste | 12 | b Baptiste | | 55 |
| A.A.Metcalfe | lbw b Baptiste | 66 | lbw b Baptiste | | 42 |
| D.Byas | c Roberts b Penberthy | 8 | b Roberts | | 38 |
| S.A.Kellett | run out | 36 | c & b Bailey | | 3 |
| P.E.Robinson | lbw b Roberts | 30 | c Lamb b Baptiste | | 34 |
| R.J.Blakey + | b Roberts | 19 | (7) c Noon b Baptiste | | 20 |
| P.Carrick | lbw b Capel | 67 | (6) not out | | 29 |
| D.Gough | c Noon b Curran | 22 | (6) c Stanley b Baptiste | | 72 |
| P.J.Hartley | not out | 19 | c Stanley b Roberts | | 4 |
| S.D.Fletcher | c Fordham b Curran | 5 | c Bailey b Baptiste | | 5 |
| M.A.Robinson | b Capel | 3 | b Baptiste | | 0 |
| Extras | (b 4,lb 20,nb 4) | 28 | (b 5,lb 15,nb 3) | | 23 |
| TOTAL | | 315 | | | 325 |

### NORTHANTS
| | | | | | |
|---|---|---|---|---|---|
| A.Fordham | c Fletcher b Hartley | 165 | c Hartley b Robinson M.A. | | 44 |
| W.Larkins | c Blakey b Hartley | 5 | not out | | 62 |
| R.J.Bailey | c Robinson P.E. b Fletcher | 12 | not out | | 31 |
| A.J.Lamb * | c Blakey b Hartley | 109 | | | |
| N.A.Stanley | lbw b Hartley | 34 | | | |
| D.J.Capel | c Blakey b Hartley | 66 | | | |
| K.M.Curran | c Robinson M.A. b Gough | 2 | | | |
| E.A.E.Baptiste | lbw b Hartley | 5 | | | |
| A.L.Penberthy | c Fletcher b Carrick | 41 | | | |
| A.R.Roberts | c Moxon b Robinson M.A. | 9 | | | |
| W.M.Noon + | not out | 10 | | | |
| Extras | (b 4,lb 23,w 2,nb 10) | 39 | (lb 6,nb 1) | | 7 |
| TOTAL | | 497 | (for 1 wkt) | | 144 |

| NORTHANTS | O | M | R | W | O | M | R | W | FALL OF WICKETS | | | | |
|---|---|---|---|---|---|---|---|---|---|---|---|---|---|
| | | | | | | | | | | YOR | NOR | YOR | NOR |
| Capel | 38.1 | 10 | 99 | 2 | 15 | 4 | 46 | 0 | 1st | 51 | 5 | 98 | 79 |
| Curran | 25 | 9 | 51 | 2 | 16 | 4 | 55 | 0 | 2nd | 66 | 43 | 99 | |
| Baptiste | 31 | 12 | 64 | 1 | 32 | 5 | 95 | 7 | 3rd | 130 | 216 | 102 | |
| Penberthy | 5 | 1 | 16 | 1 | | | | | 4th | 148 | 302 | 187 | |
| Roberts | 20 | 6 | 40 | 2 | 29 | 4 | 90 | 2 | 5th | 188 | 402 | 187 | |
| Bailey | 7 | 0 | 21 | 0 | 8 | 4 | 19 | 1 | 6th | 211 | 427 | 237 | |
| YORKSHIRE | O | M | R | W | O | M | R | W | 7th | 284 | 429 | 298 | |
| Hartley | 38 | 6 | 151 | 6 | 4 | 0 | 27 | 0 | 8th | 284 | 433 | 312 | |
| Gough | 30 | 7 | 87 | 1 | 4 | 0 | 19 | 0 | 9th | 303 | 452 | 325 | |
| Fletcher | 11 | 0 | 78 | 1 | 10 | 1 | 34 | 0 | 10th | 315 | 497 | 325 | |
| Robinson M.A. | 27 | 6 | 58 | 1 | 7 | 0 | 27 | 1 | | | | | |
| Carrick | 31.4 | 6 | 96 | 1 | 8.4 | 1 | 21 | 0 | | | | | |

# BRITANNIC ASSURANCE CHAMPIONSHIP

## HEADLINES

### Britannic Assurance Championship

### 28th - 31st August

• The County Championship moved into its decisive final stage with the return of four-day cricket. All eight matches produced positive results and, with Essex not playing, Warwickshire moved back to the top of the table after a tension-filled victory over Worcestershire on an Edgbaston pitch that aroused plenty of controversy but did not bring the ultimate penalty of a 25-point deduction.

• Seventeen wickets fell on the opening day as bowlers of both sides gained extravagent movement from an unreliable surface: Tim Munton claimed seven wickets as Worcestershire were dismissed for 166 in less than 50 overs, but Warwickshire's cause looked bleak when their batsmen could muster only 126 and the visitors, under the watchful eye of Tim Curtis, looked to be heading towards a winning lead. Although Worcestershire's last five second innings wickets were captured for only 14 runs, the home side's batsmen still needed to make the highest total of the match to gain victory. With the county's Championship hopes firmly on the line all made an effective contribution, Andy Moles top-scoring with 56, then Dominic Ostler and Dermot Reeve sharing the biggest partnership of the match. Victory, and a 13-point lead over Essex, was finally achieved with four wickets in hand and almost half the available playing time unused.

• Derbyshire remained in close contention, in third place only 21 points behind Warwickshire with a game in hand, after their convincing 195-run victory over Leicestershire at Leicester. The first two days were highly competitive, a marathon century from Peter Bowler restoring the visitors' fortunes from a precarious 79 for six, then a last-wicket stand of 96 between Martin Gidley who made a career best 80 and John Maguire reduced Leicestershire's deficit to 39, but a dazzling double century from Mohammad Azharuddin completely changed the complexion of the match. Kim Barnett was able to declare 476 ahead with plenty of time for his bowlers to press for victory, and spinners Richard Sladdin and Peter Bowler proved the match-winners, taking four wickets without a run being scored.

• Although Surrey defeated Sussex by an innings and 128 runs at The Oval with a day to spare they stayed in a distant fourth place. Graham Thorpe's career-best 177 formed the basis of the home side's 445 as he dominated century stands with David Ward and Alec Stewart before Sussex's batting floundered first against Waqar Younis, then as they followed on 270 adrift, against Martin Bickell who claimed a Championship-best of seven for 52.

• Nottinghamshire also remained in the hunt for a place in the top five with a three-wicket win over Lancashire at Old Trafford. The home side built a useful first innings advantage of 114 thanks to a maiden first-class 100 from Stephen Titchard, who shared a last-wicket stand of 133 with Ian Austin, and a disappointing batting effort from Notts in which an opening stand of 102 was followed by all 10 wickets falling for 110. The visitors fought their way back into the match as Eddie Hemmings claimed five wickets in Lancashire's second innings, but they still required 359, the highest score of the match, to win. Paul Johnson, given solid support by Bruce French, hit his third 100 of the summer, but victory was finally achieved by an eighth-wicket stand of 63 from Hemmings and Tim Robinson.

• Kent staged an impressive comeback to defeat Middlesex by 208 runs at Canterbury after being 146 runs behind on first innings. Dean Headley claimed five wickets for the second time in his début season as the home side were dismissed for 258, then Mike Gatting, batting at number seven, once again came to his side's aid with his eighth 100 of the season, adding 219 for the sixth-wicket with Mark Ramprakash as Middlesex reached 404. Trevor Ward and Neil Taylor trumped that effort with a second-wicket partnership of 226, Ward completing the first double century of his career before Kent's declaration 314 ahead. The match came to a sudden end, Middlesex manging only 96 in their second innings, Chris Penn and Richard Ellison sharing eight wickets.

• Hampshire's contest with Somerset at Southampton was full of runs from beginning to end when Hampshire gained victory by two wickets with 11 balls to spare. Jimmy Cook's pair of 100s brought his tally for the season to 10, equalling Bill Alley's Somerset record, and also giving him an outside chance of becoming the first batsman since Alley to make 3,000 first-class runs in an English season. But despite Cook's third season of heavy scoring Somerset are finding it difficult to win matches and so it proved again, although Harvey Trump again impressed with six first innings wickets. Hampshire were set on the way to success by Robin Smith's first Championship 100 of the summer, and guided home by Mark Nicholas's unbeaten 90.

• Glamorgan beat Gloucestershire by nine wickets with an encouraging all-round effort at Abergavenny. The home side passed the 500-mark after an opening stand of 197 from Alan Butcher and Hugh Morris and a maiden first-class 100 from Adrian Dale. Gloucestershire were dismissed for 357, just failing to avoid the follow-on, and though they also reached 300 in their second innigs, Glamorgan needed only 153 for victory, which they achieved with Dale well on the way to another 100.

• Northamptonshire defeated Yorkshire in similar fashion at Northampton, the visitors making more than 300 in each innings, yet ending the match thoroughly outplayed. No Yorkshireman could play a major innings, Phil Carrick and Darren Gough proving more effective than the specialist batsmen, but for Northants Alan Fordham made his fourth 100 of the summer and Allan Lamb his third as the home side's lead stretched to 182. Eldine Baptiste's seven for 95, his best figures for the county, ensured that Northants needed only 144 for victory, and they lost only one wicket in reaching that target.

• First-class début: I.Fletcher (Somerset).

# SCARBOROUGH FESTIVAL

## WORLD XI vs. WEST INDIES XI

at Scarborough on 28th, 29th, 30th August 1991
Toss : West Indies XI.  Umpires : B.Leadbeater and D.O.Oslear
Match drawn

### WEST INDIES XI

| Batsman | Dismissal | Runs | Dismissal 2 | Runs 2 |
|---|---|---|---|---|
| P.V.Simmons | c Javed Miandad b Wasson | 24 | c sub b Kapil Dev | 22 |
| C.B.Lambert | c Madan Lal b Maninder | 80 | c Morrison b Kapil Dev | 19 |
| R.B.Richardson | c Mudassar b Morrison | 15 | c Wasson b Maninder | 98 |
| B.C.Lara | lbw b Morrison | 2 | (6) st Sleep b Maninder | 1 |
| R.Staples | b Maninder | 40 | (4) c Kapil Dev b Wasson | 56 |
| C.L.Hooper | not out | 164 | (8) c Morrison b Wasson | 55 |
| C.G.Greenidge * | c & b Madan Lal | 14 | not out | 55 |
| R.A.Harper | not out | 63 | (9) not out | 24 |
| D.Williams + | | | (5) c Sleep b Wasson | 19 |
| M.D.Marshall | | | | |
| I.R.Bishop | | | | |
| Extras | (b 2,lb 11,w 1,nb 7) | 21 | (b 2,lb 3,nb 8) | 13 |
| TOTAL | (for 6 wkts dec) | 423 | (for 7 wkts dec) | 362 |

### WORLD XI

| Batsman | Dismissal | Runs | Dismissal 2 | Runs 2 |
|---|---|---|---|---|
| Mudassar Nazar* | c Hooper b Marshall | 3 | | |
| S.V.Manjrekar | c Williams b Bishop | 45 | (1) not out | 154 |
| S.R.Tendulkar | c Simmons b Hooper | 61 | c Richardson b Simmons | 14 |
| Javed Miandad | c Greenidge b Hooper | 88 | c sub b Lambert | 22 |
| P.R.Sleep + | c Staples b Harper | 37 | c Greenidge b Lambert | 13 |
| Kapil Dev | c Lambert b Marshall | 22 | (7) not out | 5 |
| Madan Lal | c Simmons b Hooper | 9 | (6) c Richardson b Greenidge | 16 |
| W.W.Davis | not out | 54 | | |
| A.Wasson | b Bishop | 23 | (2) c sub b Simmons | 10 |
| Maninder Singh | c Simmons b Hooper | 0 | | |
| D.K.Morrison | c Staples b Hooper | 1 | | |
| Extras | (b 13,lb 13,w 1,nb 5) | 32 | (b 7,lb 7,w 2,nb 5) | 21 |
| TOTAL | | 375 | (for 5 wkts) | 255 |

| WORLD XI | O | M | R | W | O | M | R | W |
|---|---|---|---|---|---|---|---|---|
| Davis | 14 | 5 | 32 | 0 | 6 | 0 | 47 | 0 |
| Wasson | 22 | 3 | 106 | 1 | 27 | 1 | 114 | 3 |
| Morrison | 14 | 2 | 82 | 2 | 3 | 0 | 31 | 0 |
| Maninder | 20 | 2 | 122 | 2 | 24 | 3 | 86 | 2 |
| Kapil Dev | 6 | 0 | 23 | 0 | 7 | 0 | 42 | 2 |
| Madan Lal | 6 | 0 | 25 | 1 | 3 | 0 | 22 | 0 |
| Tendulkar | 2 | 0 | 20 | 0 | 2 | 0 | 15 | 0 |

| W. INDIES XI | O | M | R | W | O | M | R | W |
|---|---|---|---|---|---|---|---|---|
| Marshall | 21 | 6 | 76 | 2 | | | | |
| Simmons | 13 | 3 | 44 | 0 | 13 | 4 | 39 | 2 |
| Hooper | 16.2 | 1 | 94 | 5 | 15 | 2 | 47 | 0 |
| Bishop | 17 | 3 | 58 | 2 | | | | |
| Harper | 17 | 1 | 77 | 1 | | | | |
| Staples | | | | | 8 | 1 | 56 | 0 |
| Lambert | | | | | 10 | 2 | 33 | 2 |
| Lara | | | | | 3 | 0 | 23 | 0 |
| Richardson | | | | | 5 | 0 | 36 | 0 |
| Greenidge | | | | | 2 | 0 | 7 | 1 |

### FALL OF WICKETS

| | WIN | WXI | WIN | WXI |
|---|---|---|---|---|
| 1st | 49 | 4 | 30 | 34 |
| 2nd | 84 | 74 | 62 | 89 |
| 3rd | 95 | 146 | 182 | 145 |
| 4th | 152 | 230 | 206 | 169 |
| 5th | 188 | 276 | 207 | 250 |
| 6th | 232 | 292 | 230 | |
| 7th | | 292 | 319 | |
| 8th | | 349 | | |
| 9th | | 360 | | |
| 10th | | 375 | | |

## HEADLINES

### Scarborough Festival

### 28th - 30th August

• A good selection of the West Indian touring side regathered to contest a high-scoring draw with a World XI at Scarborough. Carl Hooper, hitting his fifth 100 of the summer and taking five wickets in an innings for the first time, impressed with both bat and ball, while Sanjay Manjrekar made an unbeaten 154 as the World XI attempted an unlikely 411 for victory.

### Britannic Assurance Championship Table at 1st September 1991

| | | P | W | L | D | T | Bt | Bl | Pts |
|---|---|---|---|---|---|---|---|---|---|
| 1 | Warwickshire (5) | 20 | 9 | 4 | 7 | 0 | 52 | 58 | 254 |
| 2 | Essex (2) | 19 | 8 | 5 | 6 | 0 | 58 | 55 | 241 |
| 3 | Derbyshire (12) | 19 | 8 | 4 | 7 | 0 | 42 | 63 | 233 |
| 4 | Surrey (9) | 19 | 7 | 4 | 8 | 0 | 41 | 57 | 210 |
| 5 | Notts (13) | 19 | 6 | 4 | 9 | 0 | 53 | 60 | 209 |
| 6 | Kent (16) | 20 | 6 | 2 | 12 | 0 | 44 | 50 | 190 |
| 7 | Hampshire (3) | 20 | 5 | 5 | 10 | 0 | 53 | 50 | 183 |
| 8 | Lancashire (6) | 20 | 5 | 8 | 7 | 0 | 53 | 44 | 177 |
| 9 | Worcestershire (4) | 19 | 4 | 3 | 12 | 0 | 46 | 50 | 160 |
| | Glamorgan (8) | 20 | 4 | 4 | 12 | 0 | 45 | 51 | 160 |
| | Northants (11) | 20 | 4 | 5 | 11 | 0 | 47 | 49 | 160 |
| 12 | Gloucs (13) | 19 | 5 | 7 | 7 | 0 | 34 | 45 | 159 |
| 13 | Sussex (17) | 20 | 3 | 3 | 14 | 0 | 50 | 54 | 152 |
| 14 | Yorkshire (10) | 20 | 3 | 5 | 12 | 0 | 51 | 32 | 131 |
| 15 | Leicestershire (7) | 20 | 2 | 7 | 11 | 0 | 40 | 48 | 120 |
| 16 | Middlesex (1) | 19 | 1 | 8 | 10 | 0 | 43 | 55 | 114 |
| 17 | Somerset (15) | 19 | 1 | 3 | 15 | 0 | 60 | 37 | 113 |

## LEADING FIRST-CLASS AVERAGES
### as at 1st September 1991

BATTING AVERAGES - Including fielding
Qualifying requirements : 6 completed innings

| Name | Matches | Inns | NO | Runs | HS | Avge | 100s | 50s |
|---|---|---|---|---|---|---|---|---|
| C.L.Hooper | 16 | 25 | 9 | 1501 | 196 | 93.81 | 5 | 8 |
| S.J.Cook | 21 | 36 | 8 | 2501 | 210 * | 89.32 | 10 | 7 |
| M.W.Gatting | 19 | 33 | 11 | 1880 | 215 * | 85.45 | 8 | 5 |
| Salim Malik | 21 | 33 | 9 | 1711 | 215 | 71.29 | 5 | 7 |
| R.B.Richardson | 15 | 26 | 5 | 1403 | 135 * | 66.81 | 6 | 6 |
| G.A.Gooch | 16 | 26 | 3 | 1491 | 174 | 64.82 | 5 | 5 |
| C.L.Smith | 16 | 27 | 3 | 1553 | 200 | 64.70 | 6 | 7 |
| D.W.Randall | 19 | 30 | 9 | 1355 | 143 * | 64.52 | 4 | 5 |
| M.Azharuddin | 20 | 35 | 5 | 1895 | 212 | 63.16 | 7 | 9 |
| T.M.Moody | 22 | 34 | 4 | 1887 | 210 | 62.90 | 6 | 9 |
| R.A.Smith | 14 | 26 | 4 | 1321 | 148 * | 60.04 | 3 | 11 |
| A.P.Wells | 20 | 32 | 6 | 1540 | 253 * | 59.23 | 6 | 4 |
| M.P.Maynard | 21 | 32 | 6 | 1521 | 204 | 58.50 | 6 | 5 |
| I.V.A.Richards | 12 | 18 | 4 | 817 | 131 | 58.35 | 1 | 6 |
| G.J.Turner | 8 | 8 | 2 | 349 | 101 * | 58.16 | 1 | 2 |

BOWLING AVERAGES
Qualifying requirements : 20 wickets taken

| Name | Overs | Mdns | Runs | Wkts | Avge | Best | 5wI | 10wM |
|---|---|---|---|---|---|---|---|---|
| Waqar Younis | 518.3 | 101 | 1469 | 92 | 15.96 | 7-87 | 10 | 2 |
| C.E.L.Ambrose | 390 | 122 | 869 | 51 | 17.03 | 6-52 | 3 | - |
| A.A.Donald | 442.5 | 81 | 1331 | 67 | 19.86 | 5-33 | 6 | 2 |
| D.A.Reeve | 346.5 | 105 | 812 | 38 | 21.36 | 6-73 | 1 | - |
| G.R.Dilley | 305.2 | 62 | 823 | 37 | 22.24 | 5-91 | 1 | - |
| Wasim Akram | 429.3 | 99 | 1251 | 56 | 22.33 | 6-66 | 7 | 1 |
| O.H.Mortensen | 506.1 | 122 | 1276 | 57 | 22.38 | 6-101 | 2 | - |
| N.A.Foster | 589.2 | 141 | 1674 | 74 | 22.62 | 8-99 | 5 | - |
| K.M.Curran | 341 | 97 | 932 | 41 | 22.73 | 5-60 | 1 | - |
| R.J.Shastri | 262 | 75 | 640 | 28 | 22.85 | 5-71 | 1 | - |
| D.V.Lawrence | 434.2 | 69 | 1511 | 64 | 23.60 | 6-67 | 4 | 1 |
| T.A.Munton | 626.1 | 165 | 1655 | 70 | 23.64 | 8-89 | 5 | 2 |
| P.A.J.DeFreitas | 578.1 | 158 | 1542 | 65 | 23.72 | 7-70 | 3 | - |
| D.G.Cork | 398.3 | 66 | 1199 | 49 | 24.46 | 8-53 | 1 | 1 |
| M.D.Marshall | 282.1 | 57 | 782 | 30 | 26.06 | 4-33 | - | - |

# REFUGE ASSURANCE CUP – SEMI-FINALS

## LANCASHIRE vs. NORTHANTS

at Old Trafford on 1st September 1991
Toss : Lancashire.  Umpires : D.J.Constant and B.J.Meyer
Lancashire won by 4 wickets

### NORTHANTS

| | | |
|---|---|---|
| A.Fordham | c & b Austin | 54 |
| W.Larkins | run out | 20 |
| A.J.Lamb * | c Hegg b Watkinson | 2 |
| R.J.Bailey | st Hegg b Fitton | 9 |
| D.J.Capel | c Fairbrother b Watkinson | 21 |
| K.M.Curran | not out | 61 |
| E.A.E.Baptiste | lbw b Allott | 0 |
| R.G.Williams | not out | 13 |
| A.R.Roberts | | |
| W.M.Noon + | | |
| A.Walker | | |
| Extras | (lb 4,w 1) | 5 |
| TOTAL | (40 overs)(for 6 wkts) | 185 |

### LANCASHIRE

| | | |
|---|---|---|
| G.D.Mendis | run out | 23 |
| N.J.Speak | not out | 94 |
| G.D.Lloyd | lbw b Capel | 10 |
| N.H.Fairbrother * | c Larkins b Roberts | 6 |
| S.P.Titchard | run out | 13 |
| I.D.Austin | c Williams b Curran | 17 |
| M.Watkinson | c Lamb b Roberts | 0 |
| J.D.Fitton | not out | 14 |
| P.A.J.DeFreitas | | |
| W.K.Hegg + | | |
| P.J.W.Allott | | |
| Extras | (lb 7,w 2) | 9 |
| TOTAL | (39.1 overs)(for 6 wkts) | 186 |

| LANCASHIRE | O | M | R | W | FALL OF WICKETS | | |
|---|---|---|---|---|---|---|---|
| | | | | | | NOR | LAN |
| DeFreitas | 8 | 0 | 30 | 0 | | | |
| Allott | 8 | 0 | 27 | 1 | 1st | 50 | 59 |
| Watkinson | 8 | 0 | 47 | 2 | 2nd | 58 | 84 |
| Fitton | 8 | 0 | 31 | 1 | 3rd | 87 | 94 |
| Austin | 8 | 0 | 46 | 1 | 4th | 89 | 126 |
| | | | | | 5th | 150 | 149 |
| NORTHANTS | O | M | R | W | 6th | 151 | 155 |
| Walker | 6 | 0 | 27 | 0 | 7th | | |
| Baptiste | 6 | 0 | 25 | 0 | 8th | | |
| Curran | 6.1 | 0 | 30 | 1 | 9th | | |
| Williams | 8 | 0 | 22 | 0 | 10th | | |
| Capel | 6 | 0 | 23 | 1 | | | |
| Roberts | 6 | 0 | 41 | 2 | | | |
| Bailey | 1 | 0 | 11 | 0 | | | |

## HEADLINES

### Refuge Assurance Cup
### Semi-Finals

### 1st September

• Worcestershire and Lancashire made sure that they would meet in a cup final for the third time in two seasons with their semi-final victories over Nottinghamshire and Northamptonshire.

• At Trent Bridge, the Refuge League champions were spun to defeat by Graeme Hick who claimed a career-best five for 35 to gain victory by 14 runs after Notts had been well placed on 112 for one. Worcestershire's cause had earlier been revived by a seventh-wicket stand of 77 in eight overs by Steven Rhodes and Richard Illingworth.

• At Old Trafford league runners-up Lancashire overcame third-placed Northants by four wickets with five balls to spare, Nick Speak batting through Lancashire's innings for his highest score in 40-over cricket.

## NOTTS vs. WORCESTERSHIRE

at Trent Bridge on 1st September 1991
Toss : Notts.  Umpires : R.Palmer and N.T.Plews
Worcestershire won by 14 runs

### WORCESTERSHIRE

| | | |
|---|---|---|
| T.S.Curtis * | b Saxelby | 16 |
| T.M.Moody | lbw b Stephenson | 9 |
| G.A.Hick | c & b Saxelby | 33 |
| D.B.D'Oliveira | c Saxelby b Pick | 28 |
| I.T.Botham | c Stephenson b Field-Buss | 23 |
| M.J.Weston | c French b Pick | 18 |
| S.J.Rhodes + | not out | 47 |
| R.K.Illingworth | lbw b Stephenson | 24 |
| C.M.Tolley | | |
| P.J.Newport | | |
| N.V.Radford | | |
| Extras | (b 1,lb 18,w 8) | 27 |
| TOTAL | (40 overs)(for 7 wkts) | 225 |

### NOTTS

| | | |
|---|---|---|
| B.C.Broad | c Moody b Weston | 12 |
| D.W.Randall | st Rhodes b Hick | 45 |
| P.Pollard | c Botham b Hick | 50 |
| P.Johnson * | c Curtis b Hick | 3 |
| M.A.Crawley | not out | 47 |
| M.Saxelby | b Hick | 1 |
| F.D.Stephenson | c Curtis b Hick | 0 |
| B.N.French + | c & b Tolley | 31 |
| E.E.Hemmings | run out | 9 |
| M.G.Field-Buss | not out | 0 |
| R.A.Pick | | |
| Extras | (b 2,lb 9,w 2) | 13 |
| TOTAL | (40 overs)(for 8 wkts) | 211 |

| NOTTS | O | M | R | W | FALL OF WICKETS | | |
|---|---|---|---|---|---|---|---|
| | | | | | | WOR | NOT |
| Stephenson | 8 | 0 | 39 | 2 | 1st | 24 | 28 |
| Pick | 8 | 0 | 35 | 2 | 2nd | 60 | 112 |
| Saxelby | 8 | 0 | 41 | 2 | 3rd | 82 | 118 |
| Hemmings | 4 | 1 | 13 | 0 | 4th | 116 | 123 |
| Field-Buss | 8 | 0 | 42 | 1 | 5th | 143 | 133 |
| Crawley | 4 | 0 | 36 | 0 | 6th | 148 | 133 |
| WORCS | O | M | R | W | 7th | 225 | 195 |
| Weston | 6 | 0 | 28 | 1 | 8th | | 208 |
| Radford | 7 | 0 | 36 | 0 | 9th | | |
| Illingworth | 8 | 0 | 26 | 0 | 10th | | |
| Newport | 8 | 0 | 52 | 0 | | | |
| Hick | 8 | 1 | 35 | 5 | | | |
| Tolley | 3 | 0 | 23 | 1 | | | |

Nick Speak (right) and Graeme Hick (far right) both made major contributions, with bat and ball respectively, to their team's semi-final victories.

# BRITANNIC ASSURANCE CHAMPIONSHIP

## GLOUCESTERSHIRE vs. NORTHANTS

at Bristol on 3rd, 4th, 5th, 6th September 1991
Toss : Northants. Umpires : K.J.Lyons and D.R.Shepherd
Northants won by 5 wickets. Gloucs 7 pts (Bt: 3, Bw: 4), Northants 22 pts (Bt: 4, Bw: 2)
100 overs scores : Gloucs 279 for 5

### GLOUCESTERSHIRE

| | | | | | |
|---|---|---|---|---|---|
| G.D.Hodgson | b Walker | 15 | b Capel | 1 | |
| R.J.Scott | c Noon b Walker | 11 | b Curran | 8 | |
| A.J.Wright * | c Larkins b Capel | 42 | run out | 52 | |
| C.W.J.Athey | c Roberts b Capel | 54 | c Capel b Curran | 86 | |
| M.W.Alleyne | c Lamb b Walker | 165 | c Lamb b Roberts | 0 | |
| R.C.Russell + | lbw b Baptiste | 12 | b Roberts | 0 | |
| J.W.Lloyds | c Larkins b Capel | 59 | c Noon b Baptiste | 13 | |
| M.C.J.Ball | c Stanley b Capel | 8 | c Noon b Roberts | 12 | |
| D.V.Lawrence | b Curran | 24 | b Curran | 4 | |
| D.R.Gilbert | not out | 7 | b Curran | 2 | |
| A.M.Babington | c Curran b Baptiste | 17 | not out | 4 | |
| Extras | (b 3,lb 12,w 1,nb 6) | 22 | (b 2,lb 3) | 5 | |
| TOTAL | | 436 | | 187 | |

### NORTHANTS

| | | | | | |
|---|---|---|---|---|---|
| A.Fordham | c Athey b Lawrence | 96 | c & b Scott | 90 | |
| R.J.Bailey | b Babington | 9 | st Russell b Lloyds | 28 | |
| A.J.Lamb * | lbw b Babington | 16 | c Russell b Lloyds | 82 | |
| N.A.Stanley | lbw b Gilbert | 27 | c Russell b Lawrence | 30 | |
| D.J.Capel | c Athey b Ball | 1 | c Athey b Lawrence | 43 | |
| K.M.Curran | c Babington b Ball | 11 | not out | 19 | |
| E.A.E.Baptiste | lbw b Lawrence | 29 | | | |
| A.R.Roberts | c Lloyds b Lawrence | 48 | | | |
| W.M.Noon + | c Russell b Lloyds | 36 | | | |
| A.Walker | c Lloyds b Lawrence | 13 | | | |
| W.Larkins | not out | 0 | (7) not out | 4 | |
| Extras | (b 4,lb 11,nb 10) | 25 | (b 3,lb 10,nb 6) | 19 | |
| TOTAL | | 311 | (for 5 wkts) | 315 | |

| NORTHANTS | O | M | R | W | O | M | R | W |
|---|---|---|---|---|---|---|---|---|
| Capel | 30 | 8 | 83 | 4 | 8 | 2 | 20 | 1 |
| Curran | 32 | 3 | 115 | 1 | 20.1 | 1 | 52 | 4 |
| Walker | 26 | 5 | 84 | 3 | 10 | 1 | 26 | 0 |
| Baptiste | 31.5 | 11 | 67 | 2 | 13 | 2 | 36 | 1 |
| Roberts | 11 | 3 | 41 | 0 | 19 | 3 | 48 | 3 |
| Bailey | 8 | 0 | 31 | 0 | | | | |

| GLOUCS | O | M | R | W | O | M | R | W |
|---|---|---|---|---|---|---|---|---|
| Lawrence | 24 | 4 | 64 | 4 | 14.5 | 1 | 65 | 2 |
| Gilbert | 16 | 4 | 48 | 1 | 17 | 3 | 45 | 0 |
| Babington | 13 | 3 | 59 | 2 | 19 | 5 | 32 | 0 |
| Ball | 21 | 3 | 95 | 2 | 10 | 0 | 50 | 0 |
| Scott | 5 | 0 | 10 | 0 | 3 | 0 | 15 | 1 |
| Lloyds | 12 | 4 | 20 | 1 | 27 | 6 | 86 | 2 |
| Alleyne | | | | | 4 | 1 | 9 | 0 |

### FALL OF WICKETS

| | GLO | NOR | GLO | NOR |
|---|---|---|---|---|
| 1st | 27 | 32 | 9 | 62 |
| 2nd | 30 | 60 | 9 | 189 |
| 3rd | 123 | 99 | 103 | 211 |
| 4th | 134 | 104 | 113 | 281 |
| 5th | 153 | 122 | 115 | 289 |
| 6th | 334 | 183 | 148 | |
| 7th | 352 | 210 | 173 | |
| 8th | 387 | 287 | 179 | |
| 9th | 417 | 310 | 182 | |
| 10th | 436 | 311 | 187 | |

## ESSEX vs. DERBYSHIRE

at Chelmsford on 3rd, 4th, 5th, 6th September 1991
Toss : Derbyshire. Umpires : B.Dudleston and B.Hassan
Essex won by an innings and 72 runs. Essex 23 pts (Bt: 3, Bw: 4), Derbys 4 pts (Bt: 2, Bw: 2)
100 overs scores :Essex 250 for 5

### DERBYSHIRE

| | | | | | |
|---|---|---|---|---|---|
| K.J.Barnett * | c Hussain b Childs | 99 | b Foster | 0 | |
| P.D.Bowler | run out | 1 | c Pringle b Foster | 9 | |
| J.E.Morris | c Knight b Foster | 0 | b Childs | 42 | |
| M.Azharuddin | c Hussain b Gooch | 13 | c Hussain b Childs | 12 | |
| T.J.G.O'Gorman | c Prichard b Gooch | 7 | c Hussain b Childs | 16 | |
| S.C.Goldsmith | lbw b Childs | 18 | c Salim Malik b Childs | 37 | |
| K.M.Krikken + | lbw b Foster | 19 | c Garnham b Salim Malik | 56 | |
| D.G.Cork | c Knight b Foster | 30 | c Garnham b Childs | 0 | |
| A.E.Warner | c Prichard b Salim Malik | 25 | c Foster b Childs | 28 | |
| R.W.Sladdin | not out | 8 | lbw b Salim Malik | 18 | |
| O.H.Mortensen | c & b Salim Malik | 0 | not out | 5 | |
| Extras | (lb 6,nb 5) | 11 | (b 3,lb 5,nb 9) | 17 | |
| TOTAL | | 231 | | 240 | |

### ESSEX

| | | | |
|---|---|---|---|
| G.A.Gooch * | c Morris b Cork | 44 | |
| J.P.Stephenson | lbw b Mortensen | 14 | |
| P.J.Prichard | b Sladdin | 27 | |
| Salim Malik | c & b Sladdin | 165 | |
| N.Hussain | c Barnett b Sladdin | 35 | |
| N.V.Knight | b Sladdin | 28 | |
| M.A.Garnham + | b Sladdin | 117 | |
| D.R.Pringle | not out | 78 | |
| N.A.Foster | c O'Gorman b Azharuddin | 6 | |
| J.H.Childs | | | |
| P.M.Such | | | |
| Extras | (b 11,lb 14,nb 4) | 29 | |
| TOTAL | (for 8 wkts dec) | 543 | |

| ESSEX | O | M | R | W | O | M | R | W |
|---|---|---|---|---|---|---|---|---|
| Foster | 24 | 6 | 69 | 3 | 15 | 5 | 39 | 2 |
| Pringle | 14 | 2 | 44 | 0 | 5 | 1 | 20 | 0 |
| Gooch | 7 | 3 | 16 | 2 | | | | |
| Childs | 25 | 11 | 45 | 2 | 34 | 12 | 68 | 6 |
| Such | 19 | 3 | 30 | 0 | 18 | 5 | 57 | 0 |
| Salim Malik | 5.5 | 0 | 21 | 2 | 10.3 | 0 | 48 | 2 |

| DERBYSHIRE | O | M | R | W | O | M | R | W |
|---|---|---|---|---|---|---|---|---|
| Mortensen | 36 | 13 | 73 | 1 | | | | |
| Cork | 21 | 6 | 44 | 1 | | | | |
| Warner | 27 | 3 | 87 | 0 | | | | |
| Sladdin | 68 | 13 | 186 | 5 | | | | |
| Bowler | 28 | 6 | 93 | 0 | | | | |
| Azharuddin | 10.4 | 2 | 35 | 1 | | | | |

### FALL OF WICKETS

| | DER | ESS | DER | ESS |
|---|---|---|---|---|
| 1st | 10 | 53 | 0 | |
| 2nd | 10 | 80 | 26 | |
| 3rd | 39 | 116 | 56 | |
| 4th | 47 | 180 | 82 | |
| 5th | 94 | 248 | 122 | |
| 6th | 143 | 367 | 131 | |
| 7th | 179 | 536 | 141 | |
| 8th | 200 | 543 | 193 | |
| 9th | 231 | | 233 | |
| 10th | 231 | | 240 | |

## NOTTS vs. MIDDLESEX

at Trent Bridge on 3rd, 4th, 5th, 6th September 1991
Toss : Middlesex. Umpires : H.D.Bird and J.H.Hampshire
Middlesex won by 248 runs. Notts 4 pts (Bt: 3, Bw: 1), Middlesex 22 pts (Bt: 3, Bw: 3)
100 overs scores : Middlesex 298 for 4, Notts 275 for 7

### MIDDLESEX

| | | | | | |
|---|---|---|---|---|---|
| M.A.Roseberry | b Pick | 9 | c Crawley b Afford | 56 | |
| J.C.Pooley | c French b Pick | 2 | st French b Hemmings | 36 | |
| M.R.Ramprakash | c Randall b Hemmings | 110 | not out | 83 | |
| M.W.Gatting * | c Afford b Pick | 91 | lbw b Hemmings | 14 | |
| K.R.Brown | not out | 143 | b Hemmings | 3 | |
| P.N.Weekes | c French b Pick | 31 | c French b Afford | 10 | |
| J.E.Emburey | run out | 21 | lbw b Afford | 7 | |
| N.F.Williams | b Afford | 7 | | | |
| P.Farbrace + | c Johnson b Hemmings | 3 | | | |
| P.C.R.Tufnell | c Crawley b Afford | 6 | | | |
| N.G.Cowans | b Pick | 19 | (8) not out | 9 | |
| Extras | (b 5,lb 5,nb 3) | 13 | (b 5,lb 15,nb 3) | 23 | |
| TOTAL | | 455 | (for 6 wkts dec) | 241 | |

### NOTTS

| | | | | | |
|---|---|---|---|---|---|
| B.C.Broad | b Tufnell | 45 | c Tufnell b Emburey | 4 | |
| P.Pollard | b Emburey | 26 | b Tufnell | 18 | |
| R.T.Robinson * | st Farbrace b Tufnell | 34 | c Brown b Emburey | 20 | |
| D.W.Randall | c Weekes b Emburey | 121 | b Emburey | 25 | |
| P.Johnson | c Tufnell b Williams | 52 | b Tufnell | 0 | |
| M.A.Crawley | b Williams | 0 | c Brown b Emburey | 0 | |
| F.D.Stephenson | c Cowans b Tufnell | 0 | not out | 19 | |
| B.N.French + | c Brown b Emburey | 3 | b Tufnell | 0 | |
| E.E.Hemmings | not out | 23 | b Tufnell | 2 | |
| R.A.Pick | c Pooley b Emburey | 14 | b Tufnell | 1 | |
| J.A.Afford | c Ramprakash b Tufnell | 12 | run out | 0 | |
| Extras | (lb 10,nb 6) | 16 | (lb 13) | 13 | |
| TOTAL | | 346 | | 102 | |

| NOTTS | O | M | R | W | O | M | R | W |
|---|---|---|---|---|---|---|---|---|
| Stephenson | 27 | 7 | 50 | 0 | 7 | 1 | 18 | 0 |
| Pick | 31 | 7 | 86 | 5 | 5 | 1 | 19 | 0 |
| Crawley | 17 | 2 | 64 | 0 | | | | |
| Hemmings | 40 | 3 | 144 | 2 | 27 | 2 | 98 | 3 |
| Afford | 38 | 5 | 101 | 2 | 26 | 7 | 86 | 3 |

| MIDDLESEX | O | M | R | W | O | M | R | W |
|---|---|---|---|---|---|---|---|---|
| Williams | 17 | 3 | 47 | 2 | 3 | 1 | 4 | 0 |
| Cowans | 11 | 0 | 38 | 0 | 6 | 3 | 13 | 0 |
| Emburey | 36 | 3 | 90 | 4 | 21 | 9 | 38 | 4 |
| Tufnell | 46.3 | 13 | 137 | 4 | 18.3 | 4 | 30 | 5 |
| Weekes | 5 | 1 | 24 | 0 | 1 | 0 | 4 | 0 |

### FALL OF WICKETS

| | MID | NOT | MID | NOT |
|---|---|---|---|---|
| 1st | 4 | 45 | 85 | 21 |
| 2nd | 40 | 102 | 119 | 27 |
| 3rd | 196 | 145 | 144 | 75 |
| 4th | 244 | 247 | 156 | 78 |
| 5th | 327 | 253 | 183 | 78 |
| 6th | 369 | 254 | 217 | 78 |
| 7th | 404 | 271 | | 84 |
| 8th | 407 | 311 | | 88 |
| 9th | 426 | 332 | | 98 |
| 10th | 455 | 346 | | 102 |

## SURREY vs. HAMPSHIRE

at The Oval on 3rd, 4th, 5th September 1991
Toss : Hampshire. Umpires : J.H.Harris and R.C.Tolchard
Surrey won by 171 runs. Surrey 23 pts (Bt: 3, Bw: 4), Hampshire 4 pts (Bt: 0, Bw: 4)

### SURREY

| | | | | | |
|---|---|---|---|---|---|
| D.J.Bicknell | b Aqib Javed | 136 | c Terry b Aqib Javed | 54 | |
| R.I.Alikhan | lbw b James | 11 | lbw b James | 11 | |
| G.P.Thorpe | c Smith b Ayling | 0 | c Terry b Aqib Javed | 8 | |
| D.M.Ward | c Aymes b Ayling | 0 | c Terry b Ayling | 1 | |
| A.J.Stewart + | c Smith b Maru | 8 | lbw b Aqib Javed | 0 | |
| M.A.Lynch | c Terry b Shine | 51 | b Shine | 3 | |
| I.A.Greig * | c Middleton b Ayling | 5 | c Maru b Shine | 11 | |
| K.T.Medlycott | c Smith b Maru | 0 | c James b Shine | 25 | |
| M.A.Feltham | c Smith b Maru | 20 | c Aymes b Ayling | 24 | |
| Waqar Younis | not out | 14 | not out | 27 | |
| A.J.Murphy | b Maru | 0 | c Maru b Ayling | 0 | |
| Extras | (b 9,lb 2,w 2,nb 13) | 26 | (b 10,lb 3,w 1,nb 9) | 23 | |
| TOTAL | | 258 | | 187 | |

### HAMPSHIRE

| | | | | | |
|---|---|---|---|---|---|
| V.P.Terry | c Bicknell b Waqar Younis | 30 | c Lynch b Waqar Younis | 2 | |
| T.C.Middleton | c Lynch b Waqar Younis | 6 | b Murphy | 3 | |
| K.D.James | lbw b Waqar Younis | 1 | not out | 42 | |
| R.A.Smith | b Feltham | 12 | c Stewart b Greig | 21 | |
| D.I.Gower | lbw b Waqar Younis | 7 | c Stewart b Waqar Younis | 3 | |
| M.C.J.Nicholas * | c Lynch b Feltham | 4 | (7) retired hurt | 13 | |
| J.R.Ayling | b Waqar Younis | 34 | (8) b Waqar Younis | 23 | |
| A.N.Aymes + | c Stewart b Feltham | 9 | (9) c Greig b Waqar Younis | 4 | |
| R.J.Maru | c Stewart b Feltham | 3 | (6) c Ward b Feltham | 4 | |
| K.J.Shine | b Waqar Younis | 1 | b Waqar Younis | 25 | |
| Aqib Javed | not out | 0 | b Waqar Younis | 2 | |
| Extras | (b 4,lb 1,nb 3) | 8 | (b 5,lb 3,nb 3) | 11 | |
| TOTAL | | 119 | | 155 | |

| HAMPSHIRE | O | M | R | W | O | M | R | W |
|---|---|---|---|---|---|---|---|---|
| Shine | 14 | 2 | 65 | 1 | 10 | 1 | 52 | 3 |
| Aqib Javed | 22 | 5 | 51 | 1 | 23 | 6 | 50 | 3 |
| James | 11 | 2 | 37 | 1 | 8 | 3 | 22 | 1 |
| Ayling | 13 | 2 | 47 | 4 | 17.4 | 5 | 43 | 3 |
| Maru | 20 | 7 | 47 | 3 | 3 | 1 | 7 | 0 |

| SURREY | O | M | R | W | O | M | R | W |
|---|---|---|---|---|---|---|---|---|
| Waqar Younis | 13.2 | 2 | 45 | 6 | 16.4 | 3 | 47 | 6 |
| Murphy | 9 | 0 | 30 | 0 | 18 | 2 | 67 | 1 |
| Feltham | 12 | 2 | 36 | 4 | 6 | 1 | 11 | 1 |
| Greig | | | | | 4 | 1 | 4 | 1 |
| Medlycott | | | | | 4 | 2 | 5 | 0 |
| Lynch | | | | | 3 | 0 | 13 | 0 |

### FALL OF WICKETS

| | SUR | HAM | SUR | HAM |
|---|---|---|---|---|
| 1st | 30 | 27 | 51 | 3 |
| 2nd | 48 | 33 | 77 | 18 |
| 3rd | 48 | 49 | 92 | 52 |
| 4th | 79 | 56 | 92 | 66 |
| 5th | 177 | 60 | 92 | 66 |
| 6th | 198 | 68 | 107 | 111 |
| 7th | 199 | 86 | 113 | 115 |
| 8th | 257 | 117 | 147 | 149 |
| 9th | 257 | 119 | 187 | 155 |
| 10th | 258 | 119 | 187 | |

# BRITANNIC ASSURANCE CHAMPIONSHIP

## HEADLINES

Britannic Assurance Championship

3rd - 6th September

• Essex re-assumed pole position in the battle for the 1991 County Championship by defeating Derbyshire, who would have moved to the top of the table themselves had they repeated their recent victory over Essex, by an innings and 72 runs at Chelmsford to achieve a 10-point advantage over Warwickshire with two rounds of matches remaining. Neil Foster played the leading role as Derbyshire were dismissed for 231 in their first innings. Salim Malik made a highly-disciplined 165, his sixth 100 of a rewarding first summer in county cricket, to ensure that Essex would enjoy a useful advantage, then Mike Garnham, with a career best 117, and Derek Pringle added 169 for the seventh wicket to carry that lead to a daunting 312. Richard Sladdin was rewarded for his perseverance with career-best figures of five for 186 in 68 overs. John Childs came close to wrapping up victory with a day to spare, but the Derbyshire tail-enders made the home side wait until the fourth morning. Two more Essex victories and the title would certainly be returning to Chelmsford.

• Surrey maintained their hopes of an impressive finish to Ian Greig's last season as county captain and gained a psychological advantage for the NatWest final by overwhelming Hampshire by 171 runs at The Oval in a match were all 40 wickets fell in little over two days. Darren Bicknell top-scored in both innings for Surrey, but the decisive force was again provided by Waqar Younis who claimed match figures of 12 for 92, the third time he had taken 10 or more in 1991, taking his 100th wicket of the season in the process, and ruining Mark Nicholas' hopes of leading Hampshire at Lord's by badly damaging his left hand.

• Nottinghamshire could not keep the pressure on the leading counties, losing by 248 runs to Middlesex at Trent Bridge. Mark Ramprakash and Keith Brown took the batting honours to help Middlesex to a healthy first-innings score and, despite Derek Randall's fifth 100 of one of his most profitable seasons, the visitors gained an advantage of 109 thanks to four wickets apiece from John Emburey and Phil Tufnell. With the ball turning appreciably Nottinghamshire's fourth innings target was always likely to be difficult, and attempting to score 351 on the last day proved completely beyond them, the last eight wickets collapsing for 27, the spinners snaring nine more victims.

• Worcestershire took full advantage of a marathon batting effort against Somerset at Taunton: they kept their hosts in the field under a boiling sun for 175 overs until they had reached 575 for eight, then the season's highest total, Tim Curtis batting 10 hours for a career-best 248 and David Leatherdale making a dashing maiden first-class 100 as the pair added 256 for the third-wicket. Somerset's first innings never recovered from the shock of losing Jimmy Cook to the first ball and mustered only 83, and although they made a brave effort second time around the home side's batsmen could not reel in a deficit of 492, and Worcestershire won by an innings and 142 runs with a day to spare.

• At Bristol, Gloucestershire did not make the most of their first innings lead of 115, achieved thanks to Mark Alleyne's highest score of the season and more competitive fast bowling from David Lawrence, and allowed Northamptonshire to claim a five-wicket victoy. The home side could manage no more than 187 in their second innings, leaving Northants more than a day to make 313 to win, a target towards which they made steady progress with Alan Fordham and Allan Lamb both contributing effectively.

• The first three days of the Roses match had gone largely according to expectations with the batsmen of both sides enjoying an easy-paced wicket: David Byas and Phil Robinson, who hit a career best 189, shared a third-wicket stand of 233 to put Yorkshire on the way to a score of 501 for six, then Gehan Mendis and Nick Speak opening with a stand of 180 and John Crawley reaching 50 in his first Championship innings saw Lancashire to 403 for seven. But, after Martyn Moxon had declared 342 ahead, having first completed his third 100 of the year, the game suddenly dramatically came to life. Darren Gough and Phil Carrick shared eight wickets to reduce Lancashire to a miserable 129 for eight, but Ian Austin counter-attacked with such vigour that he made his maiden first-class 100, and the fastest of the season, in 61 balls – the last two wickets adding 165. Yorkshire were greatly relieved when they finally claimed the last wicket and victory by 48 runs.

• The last match of the round to be completed, all seven of which again produced positive results, was a remarkable affair, even an aggregate of 1578 and a collection of 37 wickets not being enough to seperate Sussex and Kent at Hove, Sussex managing the highest score in the history of cricket to tie a first-class match, Tony Pigott the last man out caught at slip off Minal Patel. Neil Taylor, coming to the end of the season in prolific fashion, made a century and double century in a match for the second time, as Kent reached 381 in their first inngs, then stretched their overall lead to 436. Sussex, who had been bowled out for 353 in their first innings, Mark Ealham claiming a career best five for 39, were given a perfect start in their second by Paul Parker, hitting his first 100 of the season, and Jamie Hall, and looked to be coasting to victory with Alan Wells, having completed his seventh 100 of the summer, fully in command. Despite the efforts of Tony Merrick, on his way to his best figures for Kent, Sussex still had four wickets in hand with only nine runs needed, but the last few runs of an epic encounter proved the most difficult: when Patel got the better of Pigott, Sussex's great effort finished, agonisingly, one run short.

# BRITANNIC ASSURANCE CHAMPIONSHIP

## SUSSEX vs. KENT

at Hove on 3rd, 4th, 5th, 6th September 1991
Toss : Kent. Umpires : M.J.Kitchen and R.A.White
Match tied. Sussex 16 pts (Bt: 4, Bw: 4), Kent 14 pts (Bt: 4, Bw: 2)
100 overs scores : Kent 381 for 9, Sussex 310 for 6

### KENT

| Batsman | | Runs | | Runs |
|---|---|---|---|---|
| T.R.Ward | c Greenfield b Salisbury | 51 | c Donelan b Dodemaide | 38 |
| M.R.Benson * | c Moores b Dodemaide | 48 | c Moores b Dodemaide | 5 |
| N.R.Taylor | lbw b Dodemaide | 111 | not out | 203 |
| G.R.Cowdrey | c Greenfield b Dodemaide | 4 | run out | 78 |
| M.V.Fleming | c Hall b Pigott | 69 | c Pigott b Salisbury | 20 |
| S.A.Marsh + | c Greenfield b Salisbury | 19 | lbw b Dodemaide | 0 |
| M.A.Ealham | st Moores b Donelan | 26 | b Dodemaide | 0 |
| R.M.Ellison | not out | 17 | c Moores b Salisbury | 1 |
| R.P.Davis | lbw b Salisbury | 0 | not out | 29 |
| T.A.Merrick | c Greenfield b Salisbury | 6 | | |
| M.M.Patel | lbw b Pigott | 8 | | |
| Extras | (b 2,lb 6,w 1,nb 13) | 22 | (b 4,lb 16,w 3,nb 11) | 34 |
| TOTAL | | 381 | (for 7 wkts dec) | 408 |

### SUSSEX

| Batsman | | Runs | | Runs |
|---|---|---|---|---|
| P.Moores + | b Merrick | 8 | (7) lbw b Merrick | 0 |
| J.W.Hall | c Cowdrey b Ealham | 41 | b Merrick | 52 |
| B.T.P.Donelan | b Davis | 61 | (9) run out | 2 |
| K.Greenfield | c Davis b Ealham | 22 | (3) c Cowdrey b Merrick | 0 |
| A.P.Wells | c Fleming b Patel | 74 | (4) b Merrick | 162 |
| P.W.G.Parker * | c Marsh b Ealham | 2 | (1) lbw b Merrick | 111 |
| C.M.Wells | b Merrick | 76 | (5) lbw b Merrick | 34 |
| A.I.C.Dodemaide | not out | 23 | (6) c Benson b Patel | 25 |
| A.C.S.Pigott | b Ealham | 5 | (8) c Cowdrey b Patel | 26 |
| I.D.K.Salisbury | b Ealham | 0 | (11) not out | 1 |
| A.N.Jones | b Ellison | 8 | (10) b Merrick | 1 |
| Extras | (b 6,lb 5,w 6,nb 16) | 33 | (lb 12,w 1,nb 9) | 22 |
| TOTAL | | 353 | | 436 |

| SUSSEX | O | M | R | W | O | M | R | W |
|---|---|---|---|---|---|---|---|---|
| Jones | 9 | 0 | 57 | 0 | 10 | 1 | 64 | 0 |
| Dodemaide | 24 | 4 | 64 | 3 | 22 | 3 | 87 | 4 |
| Pigott | 14.4 | 0 | 56 | 2 | 13 | 3 | 44 | 0 |
| Wells C.M. | 12 | 3 | 43 | 0 | 7 | 1 | 30 | 0 |
| Donelan | 14 | 3 | 52 | 1 | 21 | 4 | 61 | 0 |
| Salisbury | 27 | 6 | 101 | 4 | 21 | 3 | 102 | 2 |

| KENT | O | M | R | W | O | M | R | W |
|---|---|---|---|---|---|---|---|---|
| Merrick | 24 | 8 | 81 | 2 | 27 | 1 | 99 | 7 |
| Ellison | 22.5 | 8 | 68 | 1 | 15 | 0 | 59 | 0 |
| Fleming | 15 | 3 | 51 | 0 | 2 | 0 | 9 | 0 |
| Davis | 25 | 5 | 72 | 1 | 32 | 5 | 109 | 0 |
| Ealham | 21 | 6 | 39 | 5 | 16 | 1 | 80 | 0 |
| Patel | 10 | 2 | 31 | 1 | 23.2 | 3 | 68 | 2 |

**FALL OF WICKETS**

| | KEN | SUS | KEN | SUS |
|---|---|---|---|---|
| 1st | 91 | 8 | 30 | 146 |
| 2nd | 123 | 103 | 53 | 146 |
| 3rd | 139 | 143 | 259 | 254 |
| 4th | 277 | 147 | 288 | 371 |
| 5th | 309 | 165 | 309 | 378 |
| 6th | 321 | 255 | 309 | 378 |
| 7th | 348 | 331 | 310 | 428 |
| 8th | 349 | 340 | | 430 |
| 9th | 356 | 342 | | 434 |
| 10th | 381 | 353 | | 436 |

## WORCESTERSHIRE vs. SOMERSET

at Worcester on 3rd, 4th, 5th September 1991
Toss : Somerset. Umpires : J.W.Holder and R.Julian
Worcs won by an inns and 142 runs. Worcs 24 pts (Bt: 4, Bw: 4), Somerset 1 pt (Bt: 0, Bw: 1)
100 overs scores : Worcestershire 337 for 3

### WORCESTERSHIRE

| Batsman | | Runs |
|---|---|---|
| T.S.Curtis * | c Burns b Hallett | 248 |
| W.P.C.Weston | c Burns b Mallender | 5 |
| G.A.Hick | lbw b Mallender | 11 |
| D.A.Leatherdale | b Mallender | 157 |
| S.J.Rhodes + | c Burns b Mallender | 58 |
| S.R.Lampitt | b Mallender | 4 |
| G.R.Haynes | c Burns b Hallett | 6 |
| R.K.Illingworth | c Burns b Hallett | 36 |
| C.M.Tolley | not out | 24 |
| P.J.Newport | not out | 1 |
| N.V.Radford | | |
| Extras | (lb 15,w 1,nb 9) | 25 |
| TOTAL | (for 8 wkts dec) | 575 |

### SOMERSET

| Batsman | | Runs | | Runs |
|---|---|---|---|---|
| S.J.Cook | b Radford | 0 | lbw b Lampitt | 50 |
| N.D.Burns + | c Hick b Newport | 11 | lbw b Lampitt | 88 |
| R.J.Harden | lbw b Radford | 3 | c Rhodes b Lampitt | 8 |
| C.J.Tavare * | not out | 39 | c Curtis b Lampitt | 59 |
| M.Lathwell | lbw b Radford | 4 | c Hick b Newport | 43 |
| G.D.Rose | c Leatherdale b Radford | 4 | c Hick b Lampitt | 58 |
| N.A.Mallender | lbw b Radford | 6 | c Tolley b Newport | 14 |
| H.R.J.Trump | lbw b Radford | 2 | run out | 0 |
| D.A.Graveney | c Rhodes b Newport | 1 | (10) not out | 0 |
| J.C.Hallett | c Rhodes b Radford | 11 | (9) c Curtis b Radford | 4 |
| A.N.Hayhurst | absent hurt | | absent hurt | |
| Extras | (nb 2) | 2 | (b 5,lb 8,w 3,nb 10) | 26 |
| TOTAL | | 83 | | 350 |

| SOMERSET | O | M | R | W | O | M | R | W |
|---|---|---|---|---|---|---|---|---|
| Mallender | 32 | 7 | 80 | 5 | | | | |
| Rose | 23 | 5 | 55 | 0 | | | | |
| Hallett | 36.3 | 6 | 154 | 3 | | | | |
| Hayhurst | 14.3 | 1 | 56 | 0 | | | | |
| Lathwell | 17 | 6 | 55 | 0 | | | | |
| Trump | 25 | 1 | 75 | 0 | | | | |
| Graveney | 27 | 7 | 85 | 0 | | | | |

| WORCS | O | M | R | W | O | M | R | W |
|---|---|---|---|---|---|---|---|---|
| Radford | 15.4 | 3 | 43 | 7 | 24 | 6 | 85 | 1 |
| Newport | 15 | 3 | 40 | 2 | 26 | 9 | 67 | 2 |
| Illingworth | | | | | 28 | 11 | 46 | 0 |
| Lampitt | | | | | 20.1 | 4 | 78 | 5 |
| Hick | | | | | 17.4 | 5 | 42 | 0 |
| Tolley | | | | | 8 | 2 | 19 | 0 |
| Haynes | | | | | 1.2 | 1 | 0 | 0 |

**FALL OF WICKETS**

| | WOR | SOM | SOM | WOR |
|---|---|---|---|---|
| 1st | 7 | 0 | 101 | |
| 2nd | 25 | 8 | 114 | |
| 3rd | 281 | 22 | 211 | |
| 4th | 388 | 29 | 225 | |
| 5th | 399 | 37 | 280 | |
| 6th | 416 | 57 | 326 | |
| 7th | 516 | 59 | 326 | |
| 8th | 561 | 68 | 344 | |
| 9th | | 83 | 350 | |
| 10th | | | | |

## YORKSHIRE vs. LANCASHIRE

at Scarborough on 3rd, 4th, 5th, 6th September 1991
Toss : Yorkshire. Umpires : B.J.Meyer and D.O.Oslear
Yorkshire won by 48 runs. Yorkshire 21 pts (Bt: 4, Bw: 1), Lancashire 5 pts (Bt: 4, Bw: 1)
100 overs scores : Yorkshire 309 for 4, Lancashire 305 for 4

### YORKSHIRE

| Batsman | | Runs | | Runs |
|---|---|---|---|---|
| M.D.Moxon * | c Hegg b DeFreitas | 4 | c Titchard b Watkinson | 115 |
| A.A.Metcalfe | c Crawley b DeFreitas | 2 | lbw b DeFreitas | 2 |
| D.Byas | c Lloyd b Martin | 120 | c Crawley b Watkinson | 21 |
| S.A.Kellett | c Hegg b Martin | 7 | c Mendis b Fitton | 5 |
| P.E.Robinson | lbw b Martin | 189 | not out | 79 |
| R.J.Blakey + | c Crawley b Watkinson | 59 | st Hegg b Watkinson | 1 |
| P.Carrick | not out | 36 | lbw b Watkinson | 3 |
| D.Gough | not out | 60 | not out | 5 |
| P.J.Hartley | | | | |
| J.D.Batty | | | | |
| M.A.Robinson | | | | |
| Extras | (lb 17,w 1,nb 6) | 24 | (lb 11,nb 2) | 13 |
| TOTAL | (for 6 wkts dec) | 501 | (for 6 wkts dec) | 244 |

### LANCASHIRE

| Batsman | | Runs | | Runs |
|---|---|---|---|---|
| G.D.Mendis | c Blakey b Robinson M.A. | 114 | lbw b Gough | 6 |
| N.J.Speak | lbw b Hartley | 73 | lbw b Gough | 11 |
| J.P.Crawley | lbw b Hartley | 52 | c Gough b Carrick | 13 |
| J.D.Fitton | c Byas b Hartley | 33 | (9) st Blakey b Batty | 34 |
| G.D.Lloyd | b Gough | 51 | (4) lbw b Gough | 3 |
| S.P.Titchard | b Hartley | 35 | (5) lbw b Carrick | 22 |
| M.Watkinson * | lbw b Hartley | 0 | (6) c Blakey b Gough | 17 |
| P.A.J.DeFreitas | not out | 24 | (7) c Metcalfe b Carrick | 50 |
| I.D.Austin | not out | 3 | (10) not out | 101 |
| W.K.Hegg + | | | (8) c Blakey b Gough | 2 |
| P.J.Martin | | | c Moxon b Hartley | 29 |
| Extras | (lb 10,nb 8) | 18 | (lb 4,nb 2) | 6 |
| TOTAL | (for 7 wkts dec) | 403 | | 294 |

| LANCASHIRE | O | M | R | W | O | M | R | W |
|---|---|---|---|---|---|---|---|---|
| DeFreitas | 30 | 5 | 104 | 2 | 6 | 3 | 7 | 1 |
| Martin | 32 | 11 | 71 | 3 | 5 | 1 | 8 | 0 |
| Austin | 30 | 6 | 97 | 0 | 6 | 1 | 20 | 0 |
| Watkinson | 37 | 7 | 117 | 1 | 23 | 1 | 85 | 4 |
| Fitton | 21.5 | 3 | 95 | 0 | 29.3 | 3 | 113 | 1 |

| YORKSHIRE | O | M | R | W | O | M | R | W |
|---|---|---|---|---|---|---|---|---|
| Hartley | 27 | 2 | 100 | 5 | 12.5 | 1 | 36 | 1 |
| Gough | 17 | 3 | 79 | 1 | 18 | 6 | 41 | 5 |
| Robinson M.A. | 31 | 8 | 84 | 1 | | | | |
| Carrick | 32 | 15 | 52 | 0 | 23 | 3 | 184 | 3 |
| Batty | 17.5 | 2 | 78 | 0 | 7 | 1 | 29 | 1 |

**FALL OF WICKETS**

| | YOR | LAN | YOR | LAN |
|---|---|---|---|---|
| 1st | 4 | 180 | 12 | 18 |
| 2nd | 7 | 211 | 50 | 19 |
| 3rd | 18 | 273 | 79 | 23 |
| 4th | 251 | 288 | 224 | 48 |
| 5th | 381 | 356 | 231 | 67 |
| 6th | 426 | 356 | 237 | 95 |
| 7th | | 383 | | 99 |
| 8th | | | | 129 |
| 9th | | | | 212 |
| 10th | | | | 294 |

Jamie Hall, who with Alan Wells laid the foundation for Sussex's brave challenge in their second innings.

# NATWEST TROPHY FINAL

## HAMPSHIRE vs. SURREY

at Lord's on 7th September 1990
Toss : Hampshire.  Umpires : M.J.Kitchen and K.E.Palmer
Hampshire won by 4 wickets
Man of the match: R.A.Smith

### SURREY

| | | |
|---|---|---:|
| D.J.Bicknell | b Ayling | 13 |
| J.D.Robinson | not out | 3 |
| A.J.Stewart + | b Ayling | 61 |
| G.P.Thorpe | c James b Connor | 93 |
| D.M.Ward | c Maru b Connor | 43 |
| M.A.Lynch | c Ayling b Connor | 10 |
| I.A.Greig * | not out | 7 |
| M.P.Bicknell | | |
| J.Boiling | | |
| Waqar Younis | | |
| A.J.Murphy | | |
| Extras | (b 2,lb 4,w 3,nb 1) | 10 |
| TOTAL | (60 overs)(for 5 wkts) | 240 |

### HAMPSHIRE

| | | |
|---|---|---:|
| V.P.Terry | run out | 32 |
| T.C.Middleton | b Murphy | 78 |
| R.A.Smith | run out | 78 |
| D.I.Gower * | lbw b Waqar Younis | 9 |
| K.D.James | c Stewart b Bicknell M.P. | 0 |
| J.R.Ayling | not out | 18 |
| A.N Aymes + | run out | 2 |
| R.J.Maru | not out | 1 |
| S.D.Udal | | |
| C.A.Connor | | |
| Aqib Javed | | |
| Extras | (lb 17,w 5,nb 3) | 25 |
| TOTAL | (59.4 overs)(for 6 wkts) | 243 |

| HAMPSHIRE | O | M | R | W | FALL OF WICKETS | | |
|---|---|---|---|---|---|---|---|
| Aqib Javed | 12 | 2 | 54 | 0 | | SUR | HAM |
| Connor | 12 | 4 | 39 | 3 | 1st | 25 | 90 |
| Ayling | 12 | 0 | 39 | 2 | 2nd | 139 | 160 |
| James | 9 | 3 | 33 | 0 | 3rd | 203 | 192 |
| Maru | 6 | 0 | 23 | 0 | 4th | 222 | 193 |
| Udal | 9 | 0 | 46 | 0 | 5th | 233 | 231 |
| | | | | | 6th | | 238 |
| SURREY | O | M | R | W | 7th | | |
| Waqar Younis | 12 | 0 | 43 | 1 | 8th | | |
| Bicknell M.P. | 11.4 | 1 | 32 | 1 | 9th | | |
| Murphy | 12 | 0 | 56 | 1 | 10th | | |
| Robinson | 12 | 0 | 43 | 0 | | | |
| Boiling | 12 | 1 | 52 | 0 | | | |

## HEADLINES

### NatWest Trophy Final

### 7th September

• The 11th NatWest Trophy final proved to be one of the very best, the result of an absorbing contest remaining in doubt until the winning runs had been scored by Jonathan Ayling, who had replaced the unfortunate, injured Mark Nicholas, to bring Hampshire victory over Surrey with two balls to spare.

• David Gower, captaining Hampshire for the first time, gave his side the initial advantage by winning the toss and asking Surrey to bat. Although they survived the awkward opening overs for the loss only of Jonathan Robinson, hit in the face by Aqib Javed, the run-rate barely crept above two runs an over in the first half of the Surrey innings. Alec Stewart and Graham Thorpe, who shared a second-wicket stand of 114, both accelerated as they grew in confidence, Thorpe particularly impressive as he made his highest score in the competition, but it was David Ward, whose 43 was full of aggression and improvisation, who made sure Surrey built the impetus to reach 240.

• Hampshire were well aware of the threat that Waqar Younis posed, but they survived the first onslaught as openers Paul Terry and Tony Middleton were still together at the tea interval. The first of three run outs ended Terry's innings, but Middleton, passing 50 in his first NatWest match, and Robin Smith, quickly into his stride, survived a taxing second burst from Younis. Hampshire were very much in the driving seat, only two wickets down and well ahead of Surrey's run-rate at a similar stage, when the game moved into the decisive final 10 overs.

• Younis returned for his final spell, and when Gower and Kevan James perished in successive overs, Surrey suddenly saw their chance. Smith again batted in imperious fashion, but Ayling struggled to lay bat to ball, and Hampshire were falling behind when he suddenly flat-batted Tony Murphy for six over square-point as the 58th over of the innings crucially cost 14. When Smith and Aymes were both run out, Hampshire still needed two runs for victory with three balls to come, but Ayling held his nerve and pulled Martin Bicknell for four to give Hampshire their first Gillette Cup or NatWest Trophy success.

Cup-final fever as Alec Stewart appeals for the run-out of Paul Terry.

# SCARBOROUGH FESTIVAL/OTHER ONE-DAY MATCHES

## ESSEX vs. DURHAM
at Scarborough on 31st August 1991
Toss : Durham.  Umpires : B.Leadbeater and D.O.Oslear
Essex won by 154 runs

ESSEX
| | | |
|---|---|---|
| G.A.Gooch | c Fothergill b Brown S.J. | 0 |
| J.P.Stephenson | c & b Henderson | 107 |
| P.J.Prichard * | b Brown S.J. | 1 |
| Salim Malik | c Glendenen b Lovell | 108 |
| N.Hussain | not out | 81 |
| N.V.Knight | b Brown S.J. | 12 |
| M.A.Garnham | not out | 5 |
| D.E.East + | | |
| T.D.Topley | | |
| P.M.Such | | |
| S.J.W.Andrew | | |
| Extras | (lb 4,w 3,nb 2) | 9 |
| TOTAL | (50 overs)(for 5 wkts) | 323 |

DURHAM
| | | |
|---|---|---|
| J.D.Glendenen | c Knight b Andrew | 0 |
| S.Hutton | run out | 0 |
| G.K.Brown | c East b Andrew | 7 |
| D.J.Lovell | c East b Gooch | 32 |
| G.Cook * | not out | 48 |
| D.A.Blenkiron | c Prichard b Andrew | 0 |
| P.W.Henderson | run out | 1 |
| A.R.Fothergill + | lbw b Such | 1 |
| J.Wood | c Knight b Such | 30 |
| I.E.Conn | c East b Andrew | 18 |
| S.J.Brown | c East b Stephenson | 5 |
| Extras | (lb 7,w 21,nb 4) | 32 |
| TOTAL | (40.2 overs) | 169 |

| DURHAM | O | M | R | W | FALL OF WICKETS | | |
|---|---|---|---|---|---|---|---|
| | | | | | | ESS | DUR |
| Wood | 10 | 1 | 66 | 0 | 1st | 1 | 8 |
| Brown S.J. | 10 | 1 | 29 | 3 | 2nd | 3 | 17 |
| Lovell | 10 | 0 | 72 | 1 | 3rd | 185 | 32 |
| Conn | 10 | 1 | 80 | 0 | 4th | 278 | 34 |
| Henderson | 10 | 0 | 72 | 1 | 5th | 303 | 74 |
| | | | | | 6th | | 83 |
| ESSEX | O | M | R | W | 7th | | 89 |
| Andrew | 10 | 0 | 41 | 4 | 8th | | 127 |
| Topley | 6 | 1 | 15 | 0 | 9th | | 167 |
| Gooch | 8 | 0 | 34 | 1 | 10th | | |
| Such | 10 | 1 | 33 | 2 | | | |
| Stephenson | 6.2 | 0 | 39 | 1 | | | |

## YORKSHIRE vs. ESSEX
at Scarborough on 2nd September 1991
Toss : Yorkshire.  Umpires : B.Leadbeater and D.O.Oslear
Yorkshire won by 5 wickets

ESSEX
| | | |
|---|---|---|
| G.A.Gooch | c Blakey b Gough | 22 |
| J.P.Stephenson | c Blakey b Gough | 57 |
| P.J.Prichard * | b Batty | 42 |
| N.Hussain | c Moxon b Batty | 16 |
| N.V.Knight | c Robinson P.E. b Batty | 0 |
| M.A.Garnham | not out | 61 |
| D.E.East + | lbw b Pickles | 6 |
| T.D.Topley | run out | 18 |
| P.M.Such | not out | 0 |
| W.G.Lovell | | |
| S.J.W.Andrew | | |
| Extras | (lb 9,w 7,nb 4) | 20 |
| TOTAL | (50 overs)(for 7 wkts) | 242 |

YORKSHIRE
| | | |
|---|---|---|
| M.D.Moxon * | c Gooch b Lovell | 32 |
| A.A.Metcalfe | c Garnham b Topley | 21 |
| R.J.Blakey + | c East b Such | 42 |
| D.Byas | run out | 64 |
| P.E.Robinson | c Such b Stephenson | 41 |
| S.A.Kellett | not out | 10 |
| C.S.Pickles | not out | 10 |
| P.J.Hartley | | |
| D.Gough | | |
| J.D.Batty | | |
| M.A.Robinson | | |
| Extras | (b 4,lb 13,w 5,nb 1) | 23 |
| TOTAL | (49 overs)(for 5 wkts) | 243 |

| YORKSHIRE | O | M | R | W | FALL OF WICKETS | | |
|---|---|---|---|---|---|---|---|
| | | | | | | ESS | YOR |
| Hartley | 8 | 0 | 50 | 0 | 1st | 38 | 34 |
| Robinson M.A. | 10 | 1 | 21 | 0 | 2nd | 105 | 79 |
| Gough | 10 | 0 | 46 | 2 | 3rd | 151 | 141 |
| Pickles | 10 | 1 | 57 | 1 | 4th | 152 | 217 |
| Batty | 10 | 2 | 35 | 3 | 5th | 154 | 217 |
| Kellett | 2 | 0 | 24 | 0 | 6th | 174 | |
| | | | | | 7th | 236 | |
| ESSEX | O | M | R | W | 8th | | |
| Topley | 7 | 2 | 24 | 1 | 9th | | |
| Andrew | 8 | 0 | 47 | 0 | 10th | | |
| Lovell | 9 | 0 | 38 | 1 | | | |
| Gooch | 5 | 0 | 21 | 0 | | | |
| Such | 10 | 0 | 53 | 1 | | | |
| Stephenson | 10 | 0 | 43 | 1 | | | |

## YORKSHIRE vs. YORKSHIREMEN
at Scarborough on 7th September 1991
Toss : Yorkshire.  Umpires :
Yorkshiremen won by 3 wickets

YORKSHIRE
| | | |
|---|---|---|
| M.D.Moxon * | b Leatherdale | 34 |
| A.A.Metcalfe | c Athey b Illingworth | 67 |
| R.J.Blakey + | c Rhodes b Illingworth | 13 |
| D.Byas | c Illingworth b Athey | 23 |
| P.E.Robinson | c Mallender b Dennis | 24 |
| S.A.Kellett | not out | 26 |
| D.Gough | b Athey | 11 |
| P.J.Hartley | b Athey | 7 |
| J.D.Batty | not out | 10 |
| P.W.Jarvis | | |
| S.D.Fletcher | | |
| Extras | (lb 4,w 4) | 8 |
| TOTAL | (50 overs)(for 7 wkts) | 223 |

YORKSHIREMEN
| | | |
|---|---|---|
| T.J.Boon | b Jarvis | 7 |
| C.W.J.Athey | lbw b Hartley | 76 |
| J.J.Whitaker | c Batty b Gough | 24 |
| D.A.Leatherdale | c Metcalfe b Batty | 13 |
| G.Cook * | c Moxon b Gough | 25 |
| S.J.Rhodes + | run out | 56 |
| P.N.Hepworth | c Blakey b Fletcher | 1 |
| R.K.Illingworth | not out | 7 |
| I.G.Swallow | not out | 2 |
| N.A.Mallender | | |
| S.J.Dennis | | |
| Extras | (b 5,lb 6,w 2) | 13 |
| TOTAL | (50 overs)(for 7 wkts) | 224 |

| YORKS'MEN | O | M | R | W | FALL OF WICKETS | | |
|---|---|---|---|---|---|---|---|
| | | | | | | YOR | YMN |
| Mallender | 8 | 1 | 16 | 0 | 1st | 93 | 10 |
| Dennis | 9 | 0 | 49 | 1 | 2nd | 105 | 81 |
| Swallow | 8 | 0 | 47 | 0 | 3rd | 143 | 111 |
| Leatherdale | 10 | 0 | 35 | 1 | 4th | 145 | 136 |
| Illingworth | 8 | 0 | 49 | 2 | 5th | 184 | 184 |
| Athey | 7 | 0 | 23 | 3 | 6th | 191 | 191 |
| | | | | | 7th | 201 | 222 |
| YORKSHIRE | O | M | R | W | 8th | | |
| Jarvis | 10 | 1 | 33 | 1 | 9th | | |
| Hartley | 10 | 1 | 32 | 1 | 10th | | |
| Batty | 10 | 0 | 60 | 1 | | | |
| Gough | 10 | 0 | 34 | 2 | | | |
| Fletcher | 10 | 0 | 54 | 1 | | | |

## YORKSHIRE vs. DERBYSHIRE
at Scarborough on 1st September 1991
Toss : Yorkshire.  Umpires : B.Leadbeater and D.O.Oslear
Yorkshire won by 4 wickets

DERBYSHIRE
| | | |
|---|---|---|
| P.D.Bowler | lbw b Sidebottom | 6 |
| C.J.Adams | b Pickles | 30 |
| J.E.Morris | b Carrick | 16 |
| T.J.G.O'Gorman | b Hartley | 93 |
| S.C.Goldsmith | run out | 21 |
| K.M.Krikken + | b Pickles | 26 |
| S.J.Base | not out | 17 |
| D.G.Cork | c Robinson b Pickles | 8 |
| K.J.Barnett * | b Pickles | 10 |
| E.McCray | c Metcalfe b Pickles | 0 |
| R.W.Sladdin | not out | 1 |
| Extras | (w 5,nb 4) | 9 |
| TOTAL | (50 overs)(for 9 wkts) | 237 |

YORKSHIRE
| | | |
|---|---|---|
| M.D.Moxon * | c Barnett b Sladdin | 63 |
| A.A.Metcalfe | c Barnett b Sladdin | 61 |
| R.J.Blakey + | c Krikken b Cork | 31 |
| D.Byas | st Krikken b Bowler | 35 |
| P.E.Robinson | c Adams b Base | 5 |
| S.A.Kellett | b Base | 13 |
| C.S.Pickles | not out | 10 |
| P.Carrick | not out | 9 |
| P.J.Hartley | | |
| A.Sidebottom | | |
| J.D.Batty | | |
| Extras | (lb 6,w 5,nb 3) | 14 |
| TOTAL | (49.1 overs)(for 6 wkts) | 241 |

| YORKSHIRE | O | M | R | W | FALL OF WICKETS | | |
|---|---|---|---|---|---|---|---|
| | | | | | | DER | YOR |
| Sidebottom | 5 | 0 | 26 | 1 | 1st | 12 | 110 |
| Hartley | 9 | 0 | 45 | 1 | 2nd | 54 | 143 |
| Carrick | 10 | 1 | 39 | 1 | 3rd | 60 | 184 |
| Pickles | 10 | 1 | 50 | 5 | 4th | 137 | 202 |
| Batty | 10 | 0 | 55 | 0 | 5th | 194 | 215 |
| Kellett | 6 | 1 | 22 | 0 | 6th | 210 | 225 |
| | | | | | 7th | 219 | |
| DERBYSHIRE | O | M | R | W | 8th | 230 | |
| Cork | 10 | 0 | 43 | 1 | 9th | 230 | |
| Base | 9.1 | 1 | 40 | 2 | 10th | | |
| Goldsmith | 7 | 0 | 53 | 0 | | | |
| Sladdin | 10 | 0 | 45 | 2 | | | |
| McCray | 10 | 1 | 42 | 0 | | | |
| Bowler | 3 | 1 | 12 | 1 | | | |

## HEADLINES

### Scarborough Festival

### 31st August - 8th September

- The Festival continued with a four-team 50-over knockout competition involving Yorkshire, Essex, Derbyshire and Durham. The host county emerged victorious with wins over Derbyshire by four wickets and Essex by five wickets. Essex had earlier overwhelmed Durham by 154 runs, John Stephenson and Salim Malik both hitting 100s. However, the following weekend Yorkshire were defeated both by the Yorkshiremen, by three wickets, and by a World XI, by 34 runs.

## YORKSHIRE vs. WORLD XI
at Scarborough on 8th September 1991
Toss : World XI.  Umpires :
World XI won by 34 runs

WORLD XI
| | | |
|---|---|---|
| B.C.Broad * | c Blakey b Gough | 15 |
| J.E.Morris | c Moxon b Jarvis | 5 |
| C.L.Hooper | c Blakey b Carrick | 30 |
| D.W.Randall | c Robinson P.E. b Carrick | 24 |
| G.E.Bradburn | c Carrick b Gough | 51 |
| S.J.Rhodes + | b Gough | 55 |
| E.E.Hemmings | not out | 21 |
| P.J.Newport | not out | 5 |
| I.R.Bishop | | |
| W.W.Davis | | |
| Maninder Singh | | |
| Extras | (b 4,lb 4,w 7) | 15 |
| TOTAL | (50 overs)(for 6 wkts) | 221 |

YORKSHIRE
| | | |
|---|---|---|
| M.D.Moxon * | c Rhodes b Newport | 18 |
| A.A.Metcalfe | lbw b Hemmings | 42 |
| D.Byas | c Davis b Hooper | 59 |
| R.J.Blakey + | c & b Maninder | 17 |
| P.E.Robinson | c & b Bishop | 15 |
| S.A.Kellett | run out | 9 |
| P.Carrick | b Hooper | 5 |
| D.Gough | b Newport | 0 |
| J.D.Batty | lbw b Hooper | 5 |
| P.W.Jarvis | not out | 1 |
| M.A.Robinson | b Newport | 1 |
| Extras | (lb 6,w 9) | 15 |
| TOTAL | (45 overs) | 187 |

| YORKSHIRE | O | M | R | W | FALL OF WICKETS | | |
|---|---|---|---|---|---|---|---|
| | | | | | | WXI | YOR |
| Gough | 9 | 2 | 33 | 3 | 1st | 8 | 48 |
| Jarvis | 10 | 2 | 46 | 1 | 2nd | 37 | 86 |
| Carrick | 10 | 2 | 36 | 2 | 3rd | 67 | 125 |
| Robinson M.A. | 5 | 0 | 14 | 0 | 4th | 102 | 157 |
| Batty | 10 | 0 | 49 | 0 | 5th | 182 | 171 |
| Kellett | 6 | 0 | 35 | 0 | 6th | 199 | 179 |
| | | | | | 7th | | 180 |
| WORLD XI | O | M | R | W | 8th | | 185 |
| Bishop | 8 | 0 | 33 | 1 | 9th | | 185 |
| Davis | 8 | 2 | 27 | 0 | 10th | | 187 |
| Newport | 9 | 1 | 39 | 3 | | | |
| Hemmings | 10 | 0 | 45 | 1 | | | |
| Maninder | 6 | 0 | 25 | 1 | | | |
| Hooper | 4 | 0 | 12 | 3 | | | |

# SEEBOARD TROPHY

## SUSSEX vs. KENT

at Hove on 7th September 1991
Toss : Kent.  Umpires :R.C.Tolchard and R.A.White
Sussex won by 1 wicket

### KENT

| | | |
|---|---|---|
| T.R.Ward | run out | 2 |
| M.A.Ealham | run out | 12 |
| J.I.Longley | run out | 40 |
| N.J.Llong | c & b Bunting | 3 |
| G.R.Cowdrey | c Moores b Pigott | 25 |
| M.V.Fleming | c Pigott b Salisbury | 8 |
| S.A.Marsh + | b Pigott | 3 |
| M.R.Benson * | b Salisbury | 1 |
| R.P.Davis | c Donelan b Greenfield | 7 |
| R.M.Ellison | not out | 0 |
| M.M.Patel | b Donelan | 1 |
| Extras | (b 2,lb 4,w 6,nb 3) | 15 |
| TOTAL | (34.2 overs) | 117 |

### SUSSEX

| | | |
|---|---|---|
| P.W.G.Parker * | c Benson b Patel | 1 |
| J.W.Hall | c Davis b Ealham | 2 |
| K.Greenfield | b Ealham | 5 |
| C.M.Wells | lbw b Ealham | 3 |
| P.Moores + | b Llong | 25 |
| A.I.C.Dodemaide | b Davis | 12 |
| A.P.Wells | c Marsh b Davis | 2 |
| A.C.S.Pigott | run out | 0 |
| B.T.P.Donelan | not out | 45 |
| I.D.K.Salisbury | c Cowdrey b Fleming | 15 |
| R.A.Bunting | not out | 2 |
| Extras | (lb 6,w 2,nb 1) | 9 |
| TOTAL | (46.4 overs)(for 9 wkts) | 121 |

| SUSSEX | O | M | R | W | FALL OF WICKETS | | |
|---|---|---|---|---|---|---|---|
| | | | | | | KEN | SUS |
| Dodemaide | 5 | 0 | 12 | 0 | 1st | 14 | 1 |
| Bunting | 6 | 0 | 20 | 1 | 2nd | 16 | 10 |
| Pigott | 7 | 0 | 18 | 2 | 3rd | 30 | 11 |
| Salisbury | 10 | 1 | 45 | 2 | 4th | 75 | 16 |
| Donelan | 5.2 | 1 | 14 | 1 | 5th | 83 | 51 |
| Greenfield | 1 | 0 | 2 | 1 | 6th | 88 | 53 |
| KENT | O | M | R | W | 7th | 99 | 53 |
| Ealham | 10 | 1 | 32 | 3 | 8th | 114 | 62 |
| Patel | 10 | 5 | 13 | 1 | 9th | 114 | 115 |
| Llong | 10 | 1 | 23 | 1 | 10th | 117 | |
| Davis | 10 | 5 | 13 | 2 | | | |
| Fleming | 5 | 0 | 27 | 1 | | | |
| Ellison | 1.4 | 0 | 7 | 0 | | | |

## GLOUCESTERSHIRE vs. SOMERSET

at Hove on 8th September 1990
Toss : Gloucs.  Umpires :R.C.Tolchard and R.A.White
Gloucs won by 27 runs

### GLOUCESTERSHIRE

| | | |
|---|---|---|
| R.J.Scott | c Cook b Mallender | 12 |
| M.W.Alleyne | b Trump | 77 |
| A.J.Wright * | c Mallender b Trump | 57 |
| J.W.Lloyds | b Lefebvre | 26 |
| R.I.Dawson | st Burns b Trump | 4 |
| R.C.Russell + | run out | 15 |
| T.Hancock | c & b Lefebvre | 23 |
| R.C.Williams | b Lefebvre | 6 |
| M.C.J.Ball | not out | 4 |
| A.M.Babington | c Bartlett b Macleay | 6 |
| M.J.Gerrard | run out | 0 |
| Extras | (lb 8,w 3,nb 5) | 16 |
| TOTAL | (49 overs) | 246 |

### SOMERSET

| | | |
|---|---|---|
| S.J.Cook * | b Babington | 0 |
| G.T.J.Townsend | c Lloyds b Babington | 4 |
| R.J.Harden | run out | 31 |
| R.J.Bartlett | c Williams b Lloyds | 67 |
| K.H.Macleay | c Russell b Gerrard | 29 |
| N.D.Burns + | c Ball b Babington | 29 |
| R.P.Lefebvre | run out | 2 |
| N.A.Mallender | b Gerrard | 6 |
| H.R.J.Trump | not out | 18 |
| D.Beal | run out | 4 |
| J.C.Hallett | not out | 3 |
| Extras | (lb 13,w 6,nb 7) | 26 |
| TOTAL | (50 overs)(for 9 wkts) | 219 |

| SOMERSET | O | M | R | W | FALL OF WICKETS | | |
|---|---|---|---|---|---|---|---|
| | | | | | | GLO | SOM |
| Mallender | 6 | 2 | 17 | 1 | | | |
| Beal | 8 | 0 | 43 | 0 | 1st | 18 | 2 |
| Lefebvre | 7 | 0 | 31 | 3 | 2nd | 150 | 5 |
| Hallett | 10 | 0 | 59 | 0 | 3rd | 160 | 53 |
| Trump | 10 | 0 | 41 | 3 | 4th | 166 | 124 |
| Macleay | 9 | 0 | 47 | 1 | 5th | 197 | 164 |
| | | | | | 6th | 220 | 167 |
| GLOUCS | O | M | R | W | 7th | 233 | 189 |
| Babington | 10 | 3 | 36 | 3 | 8th | 238 | 190 |
| Gerrard | 9 | 0 | 18 | 2 | 9th | 245 | 210 |
| Ball | 7 | 0 | 38 | 0 | 10th | 246 | |
| Williams | 6 | 1 | 19 | 0 | | | |
| Lloyds | 10 | 0 | 46 | 1 | | | |
| Scott | 4 | 0 | 24 | 0 | | | |
| Alleyne | 4 | 0 | 25 | 0 | | | |

---

# HEADLINES

### Seeboard Trophy

### 7th - 9th September

• Hove's four-team tournament is also becoming a regular feature in the end of season fixture list, and once again it was the home county who triumphed: Sussex first defeated Kent by one wicket after needing only 118 for victory, then overcame Gloucestershire, who had beaten Somerset by 27 runs, by virtue of a faster scoring rate earlier in their innings after scores had finished level.

---

## SUSSEX vs. GLOUCESTERSHIRE

at Hove on 9th September 1991
Toss : Gloucs.  Umpires : R.C.Tolchard and R.A.White
Sussex won on faster scoring rate

### GLOUCESTERSHIRE

| | | |
|---|---|---|
| M.W.Alleyne | c Moores b Bunting | 1 |
| R.J.Scott | c Pigott b Bunting | 1 |
| R.C.Russell + | c Hall b Dodemaide | 74 |
| T.Hancock | st Moores b Salisbury | 59 |
| R.I.Dawson | st Moores b Greenfield | 34 |
| J.W.Lloyds | run out | 15 |
| A.J.Wright * | b Pigott | 3 |
| R.C.Williams | run out | 16 |
| A.M.Smith | run out | 1 |
| A.M.Babington | not out | 1 |
| M.J.Gerrard | | |
| Extras | (b 1,lb 3,w 7,nb 5) | 16 |
| TOTAL | (50 overs)(for 9 wkts) | 221 |

### SUSSEX

| | | |
|---|---|---|
| J.W.Hall | c Russell b Smith | 24 |
| P.W.G.Parker * | b Smith | 15 |
| K.Greenfield | b Gerrard | 26 |
| A.P.Wells | run out | 13 |
| C.M.Wells | run out | 15 |
| P.Moores + | c Gerrard b Smith | 66 |
| A.I.C.Dodemaide | c Alleyne b Williams | 1 |
| A.C.S.Pigott | lbw b Williams | 0 |
| B.T.P.Donelan | b Lloyds | 24 |
| I.D.K.Salisbury | not out | 6 |
| R.A.Bunting | not out | 0 |
| Extras | (b 1,lb 11,w 8,nb 11) | 31 |
| TOTAL | (50 overs)(for 9 wkts) | 221 |

| SUSSEX | O | M | R | W | FALL OF WICKETS | | |
|---|---|---|---|---|---|---|---|
| | | | | | | GLO | SUS |
| Dodemaide | 10 | 0 | 30 | 1 | 1st | 3 | 47 |
| Bunting | 6 | 0 | 20 | 2 | 2nd | 4 | 54 |
| Donelan | 10 | 0 | 41 | 0 | 3rd | 108 | 85 |
| Pigott | 10 | 1 | 50 | 1 | 4th | 166 | 112 |
| Salisbury | 7 | 0 | 32 | 1 | 5th | 195 | 118 |
| Greenfield | 7 | 0 | 44 | 1 | 6th | 200 | 119 |
| GLOUCS | O | M | R | W | 7th | 208 | 119 |
| Babington | 10 | 0 | 31 | 0 | 8th | 219 | 205 |
| Gerrard | 9 | 0 | 38 | 1 | 9th | 221 | 219 |
| Smith | 10 | 0 | 38 | 3 | 10th | | |
| Lloyds | 10 | 1 | 46 | 1 | | | |
| Williams | 6 | 0 | 29 | 2 | | | |
| Alleyne | 5 | 0 | 27 | 0 | | | |

Jack Russell, batting at No 3 and top-scorer against Sussex in the final of the Seeboard Trophy.

# BRITANNIC ASSURANCE CHAMPIONSHIP

## GLOUCESTERSHIRE vs. SOMERSET

at Bristol on 10th, 11th, 12th September 1991
Toss : Gloucs. Umpires : A.A.Jones and B.J.Meyer
Somerset won by 9 wickets. Gloucs 5 pts (Bt: 3, Bw: 2), Somerset 23 pts (Bt: 3, Bw: 4)
100 overs scores :Somerset 263 for 5

### GLOUCESTERSHIRE

| | | | | | |
|---|---|---|---|---|---|
| G.D.Hodgson | c Burns b Macleay | 29 | c Burns b Mallender | | 6 |
| C.W.J.Athey | c Rose b Macleay | 90 | not out | | 77 |
| A.J.Wright * | lbw b Mallender | 16 | c Rose b Mallender | | 11 |
| M.W.Alleyne | lbw b Hallett | 47 | c & b Trump | | 4 |
| J.W.Lloyds | c Cook b Rose | 3 | lbw b Lefebvre | | 23 |
| T.Hancock | c Tavare b Mallender | 12 | c Burns b Lefebvre | | 0 |
| R.C.Russell + | run out | 0 | c Macleay b Trump | | 8 |
| D.V.Lawrence | c Tavare b Hallett | 30 | c & b Trump | | 0 |
| D.R.Gilbert | c Bartlett b Rose | 28 | c Harden b Trump | | 0 |
| A.M.Babington | c Burns b Lefebvre | 1 | b Mallender | | 0 |
| M.J.Gerrard | not out | 2 | c Harden b Trump | | 42 |
| Extras | (lb 9,nb 7) | 16 | (lb 2,nb 13) | | 15 |
| TOTAL | | 274 | | | 186 |

### SOMERSET

| | | | | | |
|---|---|---|---|---|---|
| S.J.Cook | c Wright b Lawrence | 21 | lbw b Babington | | 16 |
| N.D.Burns + | c Russell b Gilbert | 37 | not out | | 6 |
| R.J.Harden | c Hancock b Babington | 1 | not out | | 1 |
| C.J.Tavare * | lbw b Lawrence | 183 | | | |
| R.J.Bartlett | c Alleyne b Lloyds | 1 | | | |
| K.H.Macleay | b Gilbert | 31 | | | |
| G.D.Rose | c Hancock b Lloyds | 106 | | | |
| R.P.Lefebvre | c Russell b Lawrence | 13 | | | |
| N.A.Mallender | not out | 13 | | | |
| H.R.J.Trump | c Hancock b Lloyds | 0 | | | |
| J.C.Hallett | c Russell b Gilbert | 15 | | | |
| Extras | (lb 14,w 1,nb 5) | 20 | | | 0 |
| TOTAL | | 441 | (for 1 wkt) | | 23 |

| SOMERSET | O | M | R | W | O | M | R | W | | FALL OF WICKETS | | | |
|---|---|---|---|---|---|---|---|---|---|---|---|---|---|
| | | | | | | | | | | | GLO | SOM | GLO | SOM |
| Mallender | 20 | 6 | 44 | 2 | 16 | 2 | 60 | 3 | 1st | 87 | 41 | 15 | 17 |
| Hallett | 19 | 2 | 71 | 2 | 5 | 0 | 23 | 0 | 2nd | 133 | 42 | 53 | |
| Lefebvre | 21 | 4 | 64 | 1 | 7 | 1 | 20 | 2 | 3rd | 173 | 80 | 68 | |
| Rose | 20 | 5 | 46 | 2 | 7 | 1 | 17 | 0 | 4th | 178 | 93 | 111 | |
| Macleay | 12 | 4 | 28 | 2 | | | | | 5th | 202 | 174 | 111 | |
| Trump | 7 | 4 | 12 | 0 | 22.3 | 5 | 64 | 5 | 6th | 202 | 381 | 128 | |
| | | | | | | | | | 7th | 242 | 401 | 128 | |
| GLOUCS | O | M | R | W | O | M | R | W | 8th | 245 | 411 | 128 | |
| Lawrence | 31 | 4 | 106 | 3 | | | | | 9th | 248 | 412 | 130 | |
| Gilbert | 25.1 | 5 | 78 | 3 | | | | | 10th | 274 | 441 | 186 | |
| Babington | 24 | 0 | 55 | 1 | 2 | 0 | 9 | 1 | | | | | |
| Gerrard | 16 | 1 | 64 | 0 | 2.4 | 1 | 14 | 0 | | | | | |
| Lloyds | 46 | 12 | 106 | 3 | | | | | | | | | |
| Alleyne | 8 | 3 | 18 | 0 | | | | | | | | | |

## MIDDLESEX vs. SURREY

at Lord's on 10th, 11th, 12th, 13th September 1991
Toss : Middlesex. Umpires : D.R.Shepherd and R.A.White
Middlesex won by 60 runs. Middlesex 22 pts (Bt: 2, Bw: 4), Surrey 6 pts (Bt: 2, Bw: 4)

### MIDDLESEX

| | | | | | |
|---|---|---|---|---|---|
| M.A.Roseberry | b Waqar Younis | 53 | b Waqar Younis | | 62 |
| D.W.Headley | run out | 2 | c Thorpe b Bicknell M.P. | | 7 |
| M.R.Ramprakash | lbw b Bicknell M.P. | 85 | c Sargeant b Feltham | | 12 |
| M.W.Gatting * | b Waqar Younis | 8 | b Waqar Younis | | 29 |
| K.R.Brown | b Waqar Younis | 34 | c Sargeant b Waqar Younis | | 5 |
| P.N.Weekes | c Greig b Boiling | 0 | c Sargeant b Bicknell M.P. | | 6 |
| J.E.Emburey | c Lynch b Bicknell M.P. | 6 | c Thorpe b Waqar Younis | | 2 |
| N.F.Williams | c Lynch b Bicknell M.P. | 18 | lbw b Kendrick | | 26 |
| P.Farbrace + | lbw b Waqar Younis | 0 | b Kendrick | | 26 |
| P.C.R.Tufnell | b Waqar Younis | 1 | b Bicknell M.P. | | 1 |
| N.G.Cowans | not out | 6 | not out | | 0 |
| Extras | (lb 8,nb 3) | 11 | (b 5,lb 6) | | 11 |
| TOTAL | | 224 | | | 187 |

### SURREY

| | | | | | |
|---|---|---|---|---|---|
| D.J.Bicknell | c Emburey b Williams | 41 | lbw b Williams | | 6 |
| N.F.Sargeant + | lbw b Williams | 2 | b Tufnell | | 19 |
| G.P.Thorpe | c & b Emburey | 117 | b Cowans | | 4 |
| D.M.Ward | b Williams | 0 | b Emburey | | 23 |
| M.A.Lynch | run out | 0 | b Emburey | | 12 |
| I.A.Greig * | lbw b Tufnell | 24 | (7) c Emburey b Tufnell | | 4 |
| M.A.Feltham | c sub b Emburey | 25 | (8) b Emburey | | 15 |
| M.P.Bicknell | b Emburey | 5 | (9) c Brown b Tufnell | | 1 |
| N.M.Kendrick | not out | 4 | (6) c Brown b Tufnell | | 11 |
| Waqar Younis | b Emburey | 0 | b Tufnell | | 0 |
| J.Boiling | c Brown b Tufnell | 3 | not out | | 0 |
| Extras | (lb 8,nb 4) | 12 | (b 2,lb 15,nb 4) | | 21 |
| TOTAL | | 235 | | | 116 |

| SURREY | O | M | R | W | O | M | R | W | | FALL OF WICKETS | | | |
|---|---|---|---|---|---|---|---|---|---|---|---|---|---|
| | | | | | | | | | | MID | SUR | MID | SUR |
| Waqar Younis | 17.3 | 3 | 53 | 5 | 16 | 3 | 42 | 4 | 1st | 6 | 13 | 10 | 16 |
| Bicknell M.P. | 20 | 4 | 62 | 3 | 21.4 | 7 | 33 | 3 | 2nd | 123 | 90 | 37 | 25 |
| Feltham | 14 | 2 | 48 | 0 | 6 | 0 | 21 | 1 | 3rd | 151 | 90 | 101 | 43 |
| Kendrick | 11 | 3 | 34 | 0 | 18 | 4 | 54 | 2 | 4th | 157 | 99 | 107 | 69 |
| Boiling | 12 | 3 | 19 | 1 | 13 | 5 | 26 | 0 | 5th | 163 | 161 | 126 | 79 |
| | | | | | | | | | 6th | 190 | 201 | 128 | 94 |
| MIDDLESEX | O | M | R | W | O | M | R | W | 7th | 208 | 219 | 129 | 109 |
| Williams | 21 | 7 | 52 | 3 | 13 | 4 | 25 | 1 | 8th | 208 | 224 | 174 | 113 |
| Cowans | 11 | 5 | 28 | 0 | 6 | 2 | 10 | 1 | 9th | 218 | 224 | 187 | 113 |
| Headley | 19 | 4 | 70 | 0 | 2 | 0 | 6 | 0 | 10th | 224 | 235 | 187 | 116 |
| Emburey | 26 | 8 | 25 | 4 | 23.4 | 8 | 41 | 2 | | | | | |
| Tufnell | 21.3 | 5 | 52 | 2 | 19 | 11 | 17 | 5 | | | | | |

## GLAMORGAN vs. WORCESTERSHIRE

at Cardiff on 10th, 11th, 12th, 13th September 1991
Toss : Worcestershire. Umpires : R.Palmer and A.G.T.Whitehead
Worcs won by 10 wickets. Glamorgan 3 pts (Bt: 1, Bw: 2), Worcs 23 pts (Bt: 3, Bw: 4)
100 overs scores : Worcestershire 257 for 6

### WORCESTERSHIRE

| | | | | | |
|---|---|---|---|---|---|
| T.S.Curtis * | not out | 186 | | | |
| C.M.Tolley | b Frost | 15 | not out | | 4 |
| G.A.Hick | c Metson b Frost | 4 | | | |
| D.A.Leatherdale | c Metson b Barwick | 24 | | | |
| D.B.D'Oliveira | c Morris b Barwick | 2 | | | |
| S.J.Rhodes + | c Metson b Frost | 19 | (1) not out | | 33 |
| S.R.Lampitt | b Barwick | 31 | | | |
| R.K.Illingworth | c Morris b Shastri | 44 | | | |
| P.J.Newport | c Metson b Shastri | 0 | | | |
| N.V.Radford | c Maynard b Croft | 20 | | | |
| R.D.Stemp | c Metson b Shastri | 3 | | | |
| Extras | (b 1,lb 9,w 3,nb 21) | 34 | (nb 1) | | 1 |
| TOTAL | | 382 | (for 0 wkts) | | 38 |

### GLAMORGAN

| | | | | | |
|---|---|---|---|---|---|
| A.R.Butcher * | c Rhodes b Lampitt | 61 | c Rhodes b Hick | | 93 |
| H.Morris | c D'Oliveira b Newport | 2 | c Rhodes b Lampitt | | 7 |
| A.Dale | c Rhodes b Radford | 12 | c Rhodes b Stemp | | 46 |
| M.P.Maynard | b Radford | 0 | c Illingworth b Hick | | 21 |
| R.J.Shastri | b Tolley | 10 | c Curtis b Stemp | | 3 |
| S.P.James | not out | 47 | b Stemp | | 30 |
| R.D.B.Croft | lbw b Newport | 9 | b Hick | | 4 |
| C.P.Metson + | c Curtis b Newport | 0 | b Stemp | | 10 |
| S.R.Barwick | b Radford | 2 | c Newport b Hick | | 5 |
| D.J.Foster | b Radford | 0 | (11) c Lampitt b Hick | | 12 |
| M.Frost | b Newport | 0 | (10) not out | | 2 |
| Extras | (b 10,lb 5,w 2,nb 7) | 24 | (b 4,lb 4,w 4,nb 8) | | 20 |
| TOTAL | | 167 | | | 251 |

| GLAMORGAN | O | M | R | W | O | M | R | W | | FALL OF WICKETS | | | |
|---|---|---|---|---|---|---|---|---|---|---|---|---|---|
| | | | | | | | | | | WOR | GLA | GLA | WOR |
| Frost | 29 | 4 | 72 | 3 | 3 | 1 | 6 | 0 | 1st | 25 | 5 | 22 | |
| Foster | 22 | 0 | 99 | 0 | | | | | 2nd | 29 | 31 | 125 | |
| Barwick | 33 | 7 | 68 | 3 | 2 | 1 | 2 | 0 | 3rd | 90 | 31 | 166 | |
| Dale | 8 | 3 | 24 | 0 | | | | | 4th | 97 | 79 | 167 | |
| Shastri | 42 | 13 | 63 | 3 | 3.5 | 0 | 21 | 0 | 5th | 135 | 120 | 187 | |
| Croft | 22 | 6 | 46 | 1 | 3 | 1 | 9 | 0 | 6th | 210 | 143 | 212 | |
| | | | | | | | | | 7th | 322 | 153 | 224 | |
| WORCS | O | M | R | W | O | M | R | W | 8th | 324 | 160 | 231 | |
| Radford | 18 | 8 | 29 | 4 | 3 | 0 | 16 | 0 | 9th | 379 | 160 | 238 | |
| Newport | 22 | 3 | 44 | 4 | 9 | 1 | 27 | 0 | 10th | 382 | 167 | 251 | |
| Tolley | 13 | 3 | 29 | 1 | 7 | 0 | 30 | 0 | | | | | |
| Lampitt | 5 | 0 | 36 | 1 | 10 | 0 | 39 | 1 | | | | | |
| Illingworth | 9 | 4 | 8 | 0 | 8 | 1 | 15 | 0 | | | | | |
| Stemp | 5 | 2 | 6 | 0 | 37 | 11 | 74 | 4 | | | | | |
| Hick | | | | | 29 | 11 | 42 | 5 | | | | | |

## WARWICKSHIRE vs. NORTHANTS

at Edgbaston on 10th, 11th, 12th, 13th September 1991
Toss : Warwickshire. Umpires : H.D.Bird and G.I.Burgess
Warwicks won by 3 wickets. Warwicks 22 pts (Bt: 3, Bw: 3), Northants 7 pts (Bt: 4, Bw: 3)
100 overs scores : Northants 348 for 7, Warwickshire 270 for 7

### NORTHANTS

| | | | | | |
|---|---|---|---|---|---|
| A.Fordham | c Piper b Donald | 6 | c Munton b Donald | | 16 |
| W.Larkins | b Munton | 75 | c Moles b Donald | | 10 |
| R.J.Bailey | b Donald | 49 | c Piper b Small | | 4 |
| A.J.Lamb * | b Donald | 74 | b Donald | | 22 |
| N.A.Stanley | b Smith | 32 | c Asif Din b Reeve | | 54 |
| D.J.Capel | b Smith | 2 | b Small | | 3 |
| K.M.Curran | c Piper b Small | 71 | b Donald | | 39 |
| E.A.E.Baptiste | lbw b Smith | 12 | b Donald | | 0 |
| A.R.Roberts | not out | 20 | c Ratcliffe b Reeve | | 7 |
| W.M.Noon + | c Lloyd b Reeve | 5 | lbw b Donald | | 13 |
| A.Walker | c Piper b Reeve | 6 | not out | | 8 |
| Extras | (b 9,lb 7,nb 7) | 23 | (b 16,lb 1,w 1,nb 2) | | 20 |
| TOTAL | | 375 | | | 196 |

### WARWICKSHIRE

| | | | | | |
|---|---|---|---|---|---|
| A.J.Moles | lbw b Baptiste | 18 | b Capel | | 8 |
| J.D.Ratcliffe | c Larkins b Baptiste | 6 | c Noon b Roberts | | 70 |
| T.A.Lloyd * | c Capel b Curran | 53 | c Noon b Baptiste | | 61 |
| D.P.Ostler | b Baptiste | 68 | c Noon b Baptiste | | 13 |
| D.A.Reeve | c Noon b Baptiste | 24 | b Roberts | | 64 |
| Asif Din | b Curran | 6 | c Bailey b Roberts | | 15 |
| N.M.K.Smith | not out | 50 | run out | | 18 |
| K.J.Piper + | c Lamb b Baptiste | 1 | not out | | 23 |
| G.C.Small | not out | 31 | | | 7 |
| T.A.Munton | | | | | |
| A.A.Donald | | | | | |
| Extras | (b 5,lb 14) | 19 | (b 7,lb 10) | | 17 |
| TOTAL | (7 wkts dec) | 276 | (for 7 wkts) | | 296 |

| WARWICKS | O | M | R | W | O | M | R | W | | FALL OF WICKETS | | | |
|---|---|---|---|---|---|---|---|---|---|---|---|---|---|
| | | | | | | | | | | NOR | WAR | NOR | WAR |
| Donald | 15.4 | 2 | 55 | 3 | 20.4 | 2 | 69 | 6 | 1st | 14 | 19 | 16 | 38 |
| Small | 23 | 3 | 83 | 1 | 15 | 1 | 69 | 2 | 2nd | 114 | 36 | 28 | 144 |
| Munton | 29 | 9 | 99 | 1 | | | | | 3rd | 141 | 104 | 56 | 144 |
| Reeve | 28.2 | 7 | 72 | 2 | 8 | 3 | 10 | 2 | 4th | 207 | 173 | 57 | 159 |
| Smith | 19 | 4 | 50 | 3 | 9 | 3 | 31 | 0 | 5th | 211 | 186 | 64 | 210 |
| | | | | | | | | | 6th | 288 | 196 | 139 | 242 |
| NORTHANTS | O | M | R | W | O | M | R | W | 7th | 325 | 209 | 139 | 270 |
| Curran | 33.1 | 8 | 78 | 2 | 10 | 1 | 27 | 0 | 8th | 350 | | 170 | |
| Capel | 19 | 6 | 49 | 0 | 21 | 5 | 63 | 1 | 9th | 363 | | 182 | |
| Baptiste | 34 | 8 | 95 | 5 | 29 | 5 | 73 | 2 | 10th | 375 | | 196 | |
| Walker | 15 | 2 | 35 | 0 | | | | | | | | | |
| Roberts | | | | | 37.2 | 0 | 116 | 3 | | | | | |

# BRITANNIC ASSURANCE CHAMPIONSHIP

## DERBYSHIRE vs. NOTTS
at Derby on 10th, 11th, 12th, 13th September 1991
Toss : Derbyshire. Umpires : J.W.Holder and D.O.Oslear
Match drawn. Derbyshire 3 pts (Bt: 2, Bw: 1), Notts 8 pts (Bt: 4, Bw: 4)
100 overs scores : Notts 316 for 3

### NOTTS
| | | | | |
|---|---|---|---|---|
| B.C.Broad | c Azharuddin b Cork | 14 | c Krikken b Base | 4 |
| P.Pollard | c Barnett b Bowler | 123 | not out | 35 |
| R.T.Robinson * | b Base | 145 | not out | 31 |
| P.Johnson | c Barnett b Bowler | 0 | | |
| D.W.Randall | c Krikken b Cork | 27 | | |
| M.A.Crawley | lbw b Base | 4 | | |
| M.Saxelby | lbw b Base | 13 | | |
| F.D.Stephenson | c Base b Cork | 45 | | |
| B.N.French + | c O'Gorman b Base | 3 | | |
| V.J.P.Broadley | lbw b Cork | 6 | | |
| R.A.Pick | not out | 3 | | |
| Extras | (b 8,lb 32,w 1,nb 24) | 65 | (lb 1,nb 6) | 7 |
| TOTAL | | 448 | (for 1 wkt) | 77 |

### DERBYSHIRE
| | | | | |
|---|---|---|---|---|
| K.J.Barnett * | c Broad b Stephenson | 19 | c Randall b Crawley | 217 |
| P.D.Bowler | c French b Saxelby | 65 | c French b Stephenson | 45 |
| J.E.Morris | c Randall b Crawley | 39 | run out | 28 |
| M.Azharuddin | c French b Saxelby | 9 | c Crawley b Broadley | 87 |
| T.J.G.O'Gorman | not out | 34 | not out | 108 |
| S.C.Goldsmith | lbw b Saxelby | 0 | b Pollard | 6 |
| K.M.Krikken + | c French b Pick | 3 | c Crawley b French | 1 |
| D.G.Cork | c Randall b Pick | 0 | c Pollard b Randall | 44 |
| A.E.Warner | lbw b Crawley | 7 | not out | 8 |
| S.J.Base | c & b Crawley | 1 | | |
| O.H.Mortensen | b Stephenson | 8 | | |
| Extras | (b 8,lb 2,nb 10) | 20 | (b 4,lb 11,w 2,nb 11) | 28 |
| TOTAL | | 205 | (for 7 wkts dec) | 572 |

| DERBYSHIRE | O | M | R | W | O | M | R | W |
|---|---|---|---|---|---|---|---|---|
| Mortensen | 11 | 6 | 21 | 0 | 6 | 2 | 14 | 0 |
| Base | 32 | 2 | 128 | 4 | 10 | 1 | 35 | 1 |
| Warner | 18 | 9 | 23 | 0 | 3 | 2 | 4 | 0 |
| Cork | 34 | 9 | 91 | 4 | 3 | 0 | 12 | 0 |
| Goldsmith | 15 | 2 | 39 | 0 | | | | |
| Bowler | 21 | 5 | 58 | 2 | | | | |
| Azharuddin | 13 | 2 | 48 | 0 | 5 | 1 | 11 | 0 |

| NOTTS | O | M | R | W | O | M | R | W |
|---|---|---|---|---|---|---|---|---|
| Pick | 15 | 3 | 53 | 2 | 19 | 2 | 69 | 0 |
| Stephenson | 19.5 | 1 | 61 | 2 | 34 | 7 | 112 | 1 |
| Broadley | 6 | 1 | 19 | 0 | 26 | 5 | 92 | 1 |
| Saxelby | 13 | 1 | 41 | 3 | 25 | 4 | 110 | 0 |
| Crawley | 13 | 7 | 21 | 3 | 35 | 15 | 63 | 1 |
| Pollard | | | | | 20 | 8 | 46 | 1 |
| French | | | | | 13 | 4 | 37 | 1 |
| Randall | | | | | 4 | 0 | 19 | 1 |
| Robinson | | | | | 3 | 0 | 9 | 0 |

### FALL OF WICKETS
| | NOT | DER | DER | NOT |
|---|---|---|---|---|
| 1st | 36 | 41 | 130 | 5 |
| 2nd | 301 | 117 | 180 | |
| 3rd | 301 | 144 | 354 | |
| 4th | 350 | 151 | 437 | |
| 5th | 364 | 151 | 452 | |
| 6th | 379 | 154 | 463 | |
| 7th | 410 | 154 | 549 | |
| 8th | 424 | 179 | | |
| 9th | 435 | 193 | | |
| 10th | 448 | 205 | | |

## LEICESTERSHIRE vs. ESSEX
at Leicester on 10th, 11th, 12th, 13th September 1991
Toss : Essex. Umpires : M.J.Kitchen and K.E.Palmer
Essex won by 9 wickets. Leicestershire 5 pts (Bt: 4, Bw: 1), Essex 24 pts (Bt: 4, Bw: 4)
100 overs scores : Leicestershire 349 for 9, Essex 403 for 4

### LEICESTERSHIRE
| | | | | |
|---|---|---|---|---|
| T.J.Boon | c Prichard b Foster | 12 | c Hussain b Childs | 15 |
| N.E.Briers * | c Gooch b Foster | 3 | c Garnham b Foster | 22 |
| J.J.Whitaker | c sub b Topley | 105 | c Prichard b Childs | 83 |
| J.D.R.Benson | c Gooch b Foster | 0 | c Hussain b Childs | 16 |
| L.Potter | lbw b Foster | 0 | c Gooch b Pringle | 45 |
| P.N.Hepworth | b Foster | 115 | lbw b Such | 17 |
| C.C.Lewis | c Gooch b Topley | 49 | c Hussain b Foster | 17 |
| M.I.Gidley | run out | 6 | c Such b Childs | 5 |
| P.Whitticase + | c Childs b Pringle | 10 | not out | 21 |
| D.J.Millns | c Foster b Topley | 28 | c Hussain b Such | 0 |
| J.N.Maguire | not out | 9 | lbw b Foster | 16 |
| Extras | (lb 6,w 1,nb 9) | 16 | (b 16,lb 11,nb 6) | 33 |
| TOTAL | | 353 | | 290 |

### ESSEX
| | | | | |
|---|---|---|---|---|
| G.A.Gooch * | lbw b Lewis | 68 | not out | 18 |
| J.P.Stephenson | c Whitaker b Maguire | 113 | b Hepworth | 5 |
| P.J.Prichard | c Benson b Lewis | 9 | not out | 2 |
| Salim Malik | lbw b Lewis | 16 | | |
| N.Hussain | b Maguire | 196 | | |
| M.A.Garnham + | c Hepworth b Potter | 123 | | |
| D.R.Pringle | not out | 45 | | |
| N.A.Foster | c Gidley b Potter | 3 | | |
| T.D.Topley | c Gidley b Potter | 7 | | |
| J.H.Childs | c Benson b Maguire | 9 | | |
| P.M.Such | b Potter | 2 | | |
| Extras | (b 8,lb 15,w 5,nb 2) | 30 | (b 2,lb 1) | 3 |
| TOTAL | | 621 | (for 1 wkt) | 28 |

| ESSEX | O | M | R | W | O | M | R | W |
|---|---|---|---|---|---|---|---|---|
| Foster | 27 | 7 | 86 | 5 | 22.5 | 3 | 71 | 3 |
| Pringle | 25.4 | 5 | 78 | 1 | 14 | 5 | 22 | 1 |
| Topley | 18 | 1 | 91 | 3 | 3 | 0 | 6 | 0 |
| Gooch | 7 | 2 | 29 | 0 | | | | |
| Childs | 15 | 7 | 24 | 0 | 39 | 16 | 82 | 4 |
| Such | 10 | 1 | 21 | 0 | 15 | 3 | 53 | 2 |
| Salim Malik | 3 | 1 | 18 | 0 | 5 | 0 | 29 | 0 |
| Stephenson | 1 | 1 | 0 | 0 | | | | |

| LEICS | O | M | R | W | O | M | R | W |
|---|---|---|---|---|---|---|---|---|
| Millns | 17 | 1 | 96 | 0 | | | | |
| Lewis | 35 | 6 | 101 | 3 | | | | |
| Maguire | 41 | 5 | 157 | 3 | | | | |
| Potter | 31.5 | 5 | 116 | 4 | 4.3 | 2 | 13 | 0 |
| Gidley | 18 | 5 | 56 | 0 | | | | |
| Hepworth | 6 | 0 | 30 | 0 | 4 | 1 | 12 | 1 |
| Benson | 6 | 0 | 42 | 0 | | | | |

### FALL OF WICKETS
| | LEI | ESS | LEI | ESS |
|---|---|---|---|---|
| 1st | 5 | 189 | 38 | 14 |
| 2nd | 18 | 209 | 54 | |
| 3rd | 27 | 223 | 92 | |
| 4th | 27 | 232 | 204 | |
| 5th | 231 | 548 | 208 | |
| 6th | 271 | 560 | 226 | |
| 7th | 299 | 567 | 239 | |
| 8th | 304 | 586 | 254 | |
| 9th | 337 | 614 | 254 | |
| 10th | 353 | 621 | 290 | |

Nasser Hussain (right) and Mike Garnham (far right), who shared a record-breaking fifth-wicket partnership for Essex.

# BRITANNIC ASSURANCE CHAMPIONSHIP

## HEADLINES

### Britannic Assurance Championship

### 10th - 13th September

• Events at Leicester and Edgbaston kept the cricket-scribes fully occupied as Essex and Warwickshire continued their quest for the Britannic Assurance Championship. When Essex completed their 10th victory of the season by defeating Leicestershire by nine wickets shortly after lunch on the fourth day, Graham Gooch's side were on the verge of claiming the 1991 title, but Warwickshire, gamely keeping up their chase, finally claimed their 10th success, a three-wicket win over Northamptonshire, with just four balls to spare to ensure the title race would go the full distance.

• Although James Whitaker and Peter Hepworth's fourth-wicket partnership of 204 transformed Leicestershire's first innings from a disastrous 27 for four, Essex's bowlers had captured maximum bowling points by the end of the first day; nor did the home's side's 353 prevent Essex from establishing a lead of 268, such was the quality of the visitors' batting. John Stephenson, the first of three century-makers, dominated an opening stand of 189 with Gooch, and after a mini-collapse, Essex took complete control thanks to a record fifth-wicket partnership of 316 between Nasser Hussain, dismissed just four short of his double-century, and Mike Garnham, who again improved his career best. Essex's final total, 621 all out, was the best of the season and provided the perfect platform for victory. Leicestershire, still with a chance of survival at 203 for three at the end of the third day, were quickly dismantled on the last morning by the mixture of seam and spin that served Essex well all season; victory was easily achieved but Gooch's men had to wait for the result from Edgbaston before the Championship could be claimed.

• Warwickshire did not make the best of starts against Northamptonshire. The visitors reached 375 in their first innings, bad light cut the second day's play almost by half, and the home side were only taken past the follow-on mark by an unbeaten eighth-wicket stand of 67; but Andy Lloyd's decision to declare 99 behind paid full dividend, as Northants' first five second-innings wickets were captured in the opening 14 overs. Allan Donald, Warwickshire's trump card, fighting pain from his back, finished with five for 69 in a marathon 20-over opening spell, and returned to claim the last wicket of the innings with the fourth ball of the final day. Warwickshire needed 296 form 98 overs to keep their Championship hopes alive, and characteristically runs were evenly shared: Jason Ratcliffe added 106 for the second-wicket with Lloyd and the most consistent contributor of them all, Dermot Reeve, saw the county to within 26 of their target; but, in a tension-filled finale, victory was never certain until the the final over brought the winning runs.

• Competition for the minor placings behind the two leading counties remained strong: Derbyshire's contest with rivals Nottinghamshire at Derby ended in stalemate, but only after the home side had been forced to follow on 243 behind. Paul Pollard and Tim Robinson added 265 for the second wicket in the Notts first innings, but Kim Barnett's 217 saw Derbyshire on the way to safety and a second innings total of 572 for seven. Derbyshire remained in third place, Notts in fifth.

• Victory for Surrey over Middlesex would have carried them above Derbyshire, but they were spun to a 60-run defeat by John Emburey and Phil Tufnell, to stay in fourth place. Nine wickets for Waqar Younis and a century for Graham Thorpe were not enough to save Surrey, who lost their last seven second innings wickets for 47, after needing 177 for victory.

• Worcestershire moved into sixth place with a nine-wicket win over Glamorgan at Cardiff, which owed much to the powers of concentration of their newly-appointed captain, Tim Curtis, who carried his bat for 186 in the visitors' first innings. Glamorgan's batsmen were undermined first by Neal Radford and Phil Newport then, as they followed on, by Richard Stemp and Graeme Hick.

• Somerset's second victory of the season, by nine wickets over Gloucestershire at Bristol, lifted them off the bottom of the Championship table. They gained a first innings advantage of 167 thanks to a sixth-wicket stand of 207 between Chris Tavare and Graham Rose, and were spun to success by off-spinner Harvey Trump who claimed five wickets in an innings for the fourth time in the 1991 season.

• First-class début: V.J.P.Broadley (Notts)

| REFUGE ASSURANCE CUP FINAL | OTHER MATCHES |
|---|---|

## LANCASHIRE vs. WORCESTERSHIRE ▬

at Old Trafford on 15th September 1991
Toss : Lancashire.  Umpires : H.D.Bird and J.H.Hampshire
Worcestershire won by 7 runs

### WORCESTERSHIRE

| T.S.Curtis * | run out | | 31 |
|---|---|---|---|
| S.J.Rhodes + | c Allott b Watkinson | | 105 |
| G.A.Hick | c Lloyd b Fitton | | 37 |
| D.A.Leatherdale | run out | | 0 |
| I.T.Botham | not out | | 21 |
| D.B.D'Oliveira | b Fitton | | 1 |
| M.J.Weston | not out | | 14 |
| R.K.Illingworth | | | |
| C.M.Tolley | | | |
| P.J.Newport | | | |
| N.V.Radford | | | |
| Extras | (b 2,lb 16,w 6,nb 2) | | 26 |
| TOTAL | (40 overs)(for 5 wkts) | | 235 |

### LANCASHIRE

| G.D.Mendis | c Curtis b Weston | 18 |
|---|---|---|
| G.Fowler | c Radford b Illingworth | 51 |
| P.A.J.DeFreitas | c Hick b Weston | 2 |
| G.D.Lloyd | lbw b Botham | 32 |
| N.H.Fairbrother * | c Newport b Tolley | 30 |
| N.J.Speak | b Radford | 26 |
| M.Watkinson | c Newport b Radford | 34 |
| I.D.Austin | b Radford | 0 |
| W.K.Hegg + | lbw b Radford | 9 |
| J.D.Fitton | c Illingworth b Radford | 8 |
| P.J.W.Allott | not out | 5 |
| Extras | (lb 8,w 5) | 13 |
| TOTAL | (40 overs) | 228 |

| LANCASHIRE | O | M | R | W | | FALL OF WICKETS | | |
|---|---|---|---|---|---|---|---|---|
| DeFreitas | 8 | 2 | 42 | 0 | | | WOR | LAN |
| Allott | 8 | 2 | 17 | 0 | 1st | | 114 | 30 |
| Watkinson | 8 | 0 | 44 | 1 | 2nd | | 190 | 38 |
| Fitton | 8 | 0 | 67 | 2 | 3rd | | 190 | 104 |
| Austin | 8 | 0 | 47 | 0 | 4th | | 194 | 111 |
| | | | | | 5th | | 197 | 165 |
| WORCS | O | M | R | W | 6th | | | 188 |
| Weston | 8 | 0 | 25 | 2 | 7th | | | 188 |
| Radford | 8 | 1 | 42 | 5 | 8th | | | 212 |
| Newport | 6 | 0 | 30 | 0 | 9th | | | 213 |
| Botham | 8 | 0 | 53 | 1 | 10th | | | 228 |
| Illingworth | 7 | 0 | 38 | 1 | | | | |
| Tolley | 3 | 0 | 32 | 1 | | | | |

## HEADLINES

### Refuge Assurance Cup

### Final

### 15th September

### Lancashire v Worcestershire

• The last match under the sponsorship of Refuge Assurance saw Worcestershire gain their second cup final success of the summer over Lancashire. The Old Trafford crowd watched Steven Rhodes hit his first one-day 100 as Worcestershire reached 235 for five in their 40 overs, then saw Neal Radford claim five wickets as the home side were bowled out for 228, giving Worcestershire victory by seven runs.

## DURHAM vs. VICTORIA ▬

at Durham University on 16th September 1991
Toss : Victoria.  Umpires : A.Stobart and A.G.T.Whitehead
Durham won on faster scoring rate

### VICTORIA

| W.N.Phillips | b Brown G.K. | 72 |
|---|---|---|
| W.G.Ayres | c & b Cooper | 50 |
| D.M.Jones | c Wood b Brown G.K. | 29 |
| D.S.Lehmann | not out | 55 |
| S.P.O'Donnell * | not out | 14 |
| G.R.Parker | | |
| M.G.Hughes | | |
| D.S.Berry + | | |
| P.J.Smith | | |
| D.W.Fleming | | |
| P.W.Jackson | | |
| Extras | (b 1,lb 6,w 4,nb 1) | 12 |
| TOTAL | (43 overs)(for 3 wkts) | 232 |

### DURHAM

| S.Hutton | c O'Donnell b Jackson | 55 |
|---|---|---|
| J.D.Glendenen | not out | 69 |
| G.K.Brown | c Berry b Jackson | 2 |
| P.Bainbridge | not out | 6 |
| M.P.Briers | | |
| D.A.Blenkiron | | |
| G.Cook * | | |
| S.J.Cooper | | |
| A.R.Fothergill + | | |
| J.Wood | | |
| S.J.Brown | | |
| Extras | (b 4,lb 11,w 2,nb 8) | 25 |
| TOTAL | (26.1 overs)(for 2 wkts) | 157 |

| DURHAM | O | M | R | W | | FALL OF WICKETS | | |
|---|---|---|---|---|---|---|---|---|
| Brown S.J. | 7 | 0 | 26 | 0 | | | VIC | DUR |
| Bainbridge | 6 | 2 | 27 | 0 | 1st | | 104 | 126 |
| Wood | 10 | 0 | 71 | 0 | 2nd | | 145 | 132 |
| Cooper | 10 | 0 | 39 | 1 | 3rd | | 192 | |
| Brown G.K. | 10 | 0 | 62 | 2 | 4th | | | |
| | | | | | 5th | | | |
| VICTORIA | O | M | R | W | 6th | | | |
| Hughes | 5 | 0 | 23 | 0 | 7th | | | |
| Fleming | 6 | 0 | 24 | 0 | 8th | | | |
| O'Donnell | 4 | 0 | 37 | 0 | 9th | | | |
| Jackson | 7 | 3 | 29 | 2 | 10th | | | |
| Smith | 4.1 | 0 | 29 | 0 | | | | |

## HEADLINES

### Other matches

### 16th - 19th September

Durham gained valuable experience of three-day cricket in their non-first-class match against the Sheffield Shield champions Victoria at Durham University. Dean Jones delighted the crowd by hitting 144 against his future team-mates, and Ramshaw, Lehmann and Parker also scored centuries for Victoria, but the Durham batsmen were not overawed, reaching 354 for three declared in their first innings thanks to a double century from John Glendenen, a consistent scorer throughout the season, and they emerged with a creditable draw after spinner Paul Jackson had claimed six second-innings wickets. Durham had earlier defeated Victoria in a rain-interrupted one-day match on faster scoring rate.

## DURHAM vs. VICTORIA ▬

at Durham University on 17th, 18th, 19th September 1991
Toss : Victoria.  Umpires : J.Stobart and A.G.T.Whitehead
Match drawn

### VICTORIA

| W.N.Phillips | lbw b Bainbridge | 9 | c Cook b Wood | 50 |
|---|---|---|---|---|
| D.J.Ramshaw + | c Brown G.K. b Bainbridge | 110 | c Cook b Cooper | 49 |
| D.M.Jones | c Scott b Wood | 144 | (5) not out | 1 |
| D.S.Lehmann | c Brown G.K. b Cooper | 56 | not out | 137 |
| S.P.O'Donnell * | b Brown S.J. | 60 | | |
| G.R.Parker | not out | 0 | (3) st Scott b Bainbridge | 104 |
| W.G.Ayres | | | | |
| M.G.Hughes | | | | |
| D.W.Fleming | | | | |
| P.W.Jackson | | | | |
| J.A.Sutherland | | | | |
| Extras | (b 4,lb 14,w 1,nb 4) | 23 | (b 2,lb 2,nb 5) | 9 |
| TOTAL | (for 5 wkts dec) | 402 | (for 3 wkts dec) | 350 |

### DURHAM

| G.K.Brown | lbw b Hughes | 49 | c Phillips b Hughes | 5 |
|---|---|---|---|---|
| J.D.Glendenen | not out | 200 | st Ramshaw b Jackson | 28 |
| D.J.Lovell | b Jackson | 33 | c Hughes b Fleming | 7 |
| P.Bainbridge | c Ayres b Jackson | 21 | c Ramshaw b Jackson | 44 |
| M.P.Briers | not out | 34 | c Ayres b Jackson | 12 |
| D.A.Blenkiron | | | st Ramshaw b Jackson | 11 |
| C.W.Scott + | | | not out | 17 |
| G.Cook * | | | c Fleming b Jackson | 8 |
| S.J.Cooper | | | lbw b Jackson | 0 |
| J.Wood | | | not out | 21 |
| S.J.Brown | | | | |
| Extras | (b 2,lb 7,w 1,nb 7) | 17 | (b 6,lb 7,nb 6) | 19 |
| TOTAL | (for 3 wkts dec) | 354 | (for 8 wkts) | 172 |

| DURHAM | O | M | R | W | O | M | R | W | | FALL OF WICKETS | | | |
|---|---|---|---|---|---|---|---|---|---|---|---|---|---|
| Brown S.J. | 17 | 6 | 48 | 1 | 13 | 1 | 55 | 0 | | | VIC | DUR | VIC | DUR |
| Wood | 15 | 1 | 70 | 1 | 15 | 0 | 70 | 1 | 1st | | 26 | 122 | 80 | 25 |
| Bainbridge | 21 | 7 | 83 | 2 | 8 | 2 | 43 | 1 | 2nd | | 259 | 210 | 124 | 39 |
| Cooper | 11.2 | 2 | 67 | 1 | 25 | 3 | 112 | 1 | 3rd | | 287 | 258 | 323 | 89 |
| Briers | 13 | 1 | 89 | 0 | 8 | 0 | 34 | 0 | 4th | | 402 | | | 112 |
| Lovell | 6 | 0 | 27 | 0 | | | | | 5th | | 402 | | | 117 |
| Blenkiron | | | | | 8 | 0 | 32 | 0 | 6th | | | | | 133 |
| | | | | | | | | | 7th | | | | | 145 |
| VICTORIA | O | M | R | W | O | M | R | W | 8th | | | | | 148 |
| Hughes | 15 | 2 | 68 | 1 | 10 | 0 | 34 | 1 | 9th | | | | | |
| Fleming | 16.1 | 0 | 57 | 0 | 11 | 2 | 30 | 1 | 10th | | | | | |
| O'Donnell | 14 | 1 | 66 | 0 | 7 | 3 | 14 | 0 | | | | | | |
| Sutherland | 13 | 2 | 54 | 0 | 10 | 4 | 19 | 0 | | | | | | |
| Jackson | 24 | 4 | 100 | 2 | 25 | 10 | 53 | 6 | | | | | | |
| Jones | | | | | 9 | 4 | 9 | 0 | | | | | | |

# BRITANNIC ASSURANCE CHAMPIONSHIP

## ESSEX vs. MIDDLESEX

at Chelmsford on 17th, 18th, 19th September 1991
Toss : Essex. Umpires : B.Hassan and N.T.Plews
Essex won by an innings and 208 runs. Essex 24 pts (Bt: 4, Bw: 4), Middx 1 pt (Bt: 0, Bw: 1)
100 overs scores :Essex 440 for 4

### MIDDLESEX

| | | | | | |
|---|---|---|---|---|---|
| M.A.Roseberry | b Pringle | 2 | c Gooch b Pringle | 99 |
| M.Keech | hit wicket b Foster | 3 | c Garnham b Foster | 0 |
| M.W.Gatting * | lbw b Pringle | 0 | c Gooch b Foster | 35 |
| M.R.Ramprakash | c Pringle b Foster | 0 | b Foster | 19 |
| K.R.Brown | c Gooch b Foster | 4 | c Hussain b Pringle | 59 |
| P.N.Weekes | run out | 5 | b Andrew | 0 |
| J.E.Emburey | lbw b Pringle | 1 | lbw b Topley | 37 |
| N.F.Williams | c Hussain b Andrew | 23 | c Topley b Foster | 6 |
| D.W.Headley | c Garnham b Foster | 1 | (10) c Salim Malik b Foster | 22 |
| P.Farbrace + | not out | 12 | (9) c Topley b Foster | 8 |
| N.G.Cowans | c Hussain b Andrew | 0 | not out | 8 |
| Extras | | 0 | (lb 5,w 9) | 14 |
| TOTAL | | 51 | | 307 |

### ESSEX

| | | |
|---|---|---|
| G.A.Gooch * | c Weekes b Williams | 259 |
| J.P.Stephenson | lbw b Headley | 18 |
| P.J.Prichard | lbw b Williams | 11 |
| Salim Malik | c Brown b Headley | 80 |
| N.Hussain | c Farbrace b Cowans | 57 |
| N.V.Knight | c Farbrace b Weekes | 61 |
| M.A.Garnham + | not out | 24 |
| D.R.Pringle | not out | 14 |
| N.A.Foster | | |
| T.D.Topley | | |
| S.J.W.Andrew | | |
| Extras | (b 14,lb 11,w 2,nb 15) | 42 |
| TOTAL | (for 6 wkts dec) | 566 |

| ESSEX | O | M | R | W | O | M | R | W | FALL OF WICKETS | | | |
|---|---|---|---|---|---|---|---|---|---|---|---|---|
| | | | | | | | | | | MID | ESS | MID | ESS |
| Foster | 11 | 6 | 18 | 4 | 30.4 | 4 | 104 | 6 | | | | | |
| Pringle | 12 | 3 | 25 | 3 | 20 | 8 | 38 | 2 | 1st | 5 | 37 | 5 | |
| Andrew | 1.3 | 0 | 8 | 2 | 13 | 1 | 48 | 1 | 2nd | 5 | 74 | 63 | |
| Topley | | | | | 19 | 5 | 70 | 1 | 3rd | 5 | 256 | 91 | |
| Stephenson | | | | | 5 | 1 | 10 | 0 | 4th | 15 | 395 | 213 | |
| Salim Malik | | | | | 7 | 0 | 32 | 0 | 5th | 12 | 494 | 222 | |
| | | | | | | | | | 6th | 15 | 539 | 225 | |
| MIDDLESEX | O | M | R | W | O | M | R | W | 7th | 15 | | 262 | |
| Williams | 30 | 7 | 140 | 2 | | | | | 8th | 26 | | 268 | |
| Cowans | 26 | 7 | 70 | 1 | | | | | 9th | 51 | | 278 | |
| Headley | 30 | 3 | 153 | 2 | | | | | 10th | 51 | | 307 | |
| Gatting | 16 | 0 | 62 | 0 | | | | | | | | | |
| Emburey | 14 | 0 | 87 | 0 | | | | | | | | | |
| Weekes | 4 | 0 | 21 | 1 | | | | | | | | | |
| Roseberry | 3 | 0 | 8 | 0 | | | | | | | | | |

## DERBYSHIRE vs. YORKSHIRE

at Chesterfield on 17th, 18th, 19th, 20th September 1991
Toss : Derbyshire. Umpires : K.J.Lyons and D.O.Oslear
Derbyshire won by 40 runs. Derbyshire 18 pts (Bt: 0, Bw: 2), Yorkshire 7 pts (Bt: 3, Bw: 4)
100 overs scores : Yorkshire 271 for 5

### DERBYSHIRE

| | | | | | |
|---|---|---|---|---|---|
| K.J.Barnett * | c Blakey b Jarvis | 2 | c Byas b Jarvis | 12 |
| P.D.Bowler | c Byas b Hartley | 0 | c Moxon b Carrick | 54 |
| J.E.Morris | c Batty b Gough | 13 | c Moxon b Jarvis | 0 |
| C.J.Adams | b Jarvis | 40 | st Blakey b Carrick | 112 |
| T.J.G.O'Gorman | c Blakey b Carrick | 0 | (6) c Hartley b Batty | 74 |
| S.C.Goldsmith | lbw b Carrick | 1 | (7) b Jarvis | 30 |
| K.M.Krikken + | c Blakey b Jarvis | 0 | (8) c Robinson b Batty | 0 |
| D.G.Cork | not out | 40 | (9) b Batty | 9 |
| A.E.Warner | c Kellett b Hartley | 25 | (10) not out | 33 |
| S.J.Base | c Blakey b Jarvis | 7 | (11) c Kellett b Carrick | 4 |
| R.W.Sladdin | lbw b Hartley | 7 | (5) lbw b Batty | 12 |
| Extras | (lb 4,w 1,nb 4) | 9 | (b 12,lb 15,nb 7) | 34 |
| TOTAL | | 144 | | 374 |

### YORKSHIRE

| | | | | | |
|---|---|---|---|---|---|
| M.D.Moxon * | c & b Warner | 50 | c Krikken b Base | 13 |
| A.A.Metcalfe | c Bowler b Cork | 28 | c Krikken b Warner | 4 |
| D.Byas | lbw b Fork | 6 | b Base | 0 |
| S.A.Kellett | not out | 125 | c Bowler b Sladdin | 26 |
| P.E.Robinson | c Krikken b Warner | 12 | c Bowler b Base | 0 |
| R.J.Blakey + | c Base b Cork | 7 | run out | 2 |
| P.Carrick | run out | 50 | c Barnett b Base | 1 |
| D.Gough | c Barnett b Bowler | 0 | c Base b Sladdin | 27 |
| P.J.Hartley | c Sladdin b Bowler | 5 | not out | 34 |
| P.W.Jarvis | b Bowler | 2 | b Warner | 22 |
| J.D.Batty | b Warner | 12 | c Adams b Sladdin | 14 |
| Extras | (lb 9,nb 22) | 31 | (b 2,lb 4,nb 1) | 7 |
| TOTAL | | 328 | | 150 |

| YORKSHIRE | O | M | R | W | O | M | R | W | FALL OF WICKETS | | | |
|---|---|---|---|---|---|---|---|---|---|---|---|---|
| | | | | | | | | | | DER | YOR | DER | YOR |
| Jarvis | 16 | 4 | 28 | 4 | 29 | 8 | 71 | 3 | 1st | 2 | 53 | 32 | 11 |
| Hartley | 14 | 3 | 45 | 2 | 19 | 3 | 57 | 0 | 2nd | 2 | 70 | 32 | 12 |
| Gough | 9 | 2 | 31 | 1 | 12 | 1 | 53 | 0 | 3rd | 42 | 138 | 123 | 19 |
| Carrick | 22.2 | 11 | 36 | 3 | 45.3 | 22 | 75 | 3 | 4th | 55 | 164 | 165 | 19 |
| Batty | | | | | 37 | 11 | 91 | 4 | 5th | 61 | 199 | 246 | 30 |
| | | | | | | | | | 6th | 61 | 301 | 315 | 36 |
| DERBYSHIRE | O | M | R | W | O | M | R | W | 7th | 61 | 301 | 321 | 75 |
| Cork | 25 | 2 | 83 | 3 | 13 | 1 | 31 | 0 | 8th | 113 | 309 | 325 | 84 |
| Base | 22 | 2 | 65 | 0 | 17 | 6 | 34 | 4 | 9th | 131 | 315 | 359 | 131 |
| Warner | 27.1 | 8 | 52 | 3 | 4 | 4 | 52 | 2 | 10th | 144 | 328 | 374 | 150 |
| Sladdin | 22 | 4 | 53 | 0 | 13 | 4 | 27 | 3 | | | | | |
| Goldsmith | 8 | 2 | 25 | 0 | | | | | | | | | |
| Bowler | 14 | 1 | 41 | 3 | | | | | | | | | |

## HAMPSHIRE vs. GLAMORGAN

at Southampton on 17th, 18th, 19th, 20th September 1991
Toss : Hampshire. Umpires : R.Palmer and P.B.Wight
Glamorgan won by 7 wickets. Hampshire 6 pts (Bt: 4, Bw: 2), Glam 24 pts (Bt: 4, Bw: 4)
100 overs scores :Glamorgan 354 for 5

### HAMPSHIRE

| | | | | | |
|---|---|---|---|---|---|
| V.P.Terry | c Metson b Frost | 81 | b Croft | 70 |
| T.C.Middleton | c Morris b Watkin | 8 | b Watkin | 43 |
| K.D.James | c Maynard b Croft | 49 | b Foster | 43 |
| R.A.Smith | b Croft | 14 | b Croft | 29 |
| D.I.Gower * | c James b Foster | 59 | b Croft | 38 |
| J.R.Ayling | c Maynard b Watkin | 5 | c Croft b Watkin | 28 |
| A.N Aymes + | c Maynard b Watkin | 46 | b Croft | 0 |
| R.J.Maru | c Metson b Frost | 19 | c & b Foster | 1 |
| I.J.Turner | lbw b Frost | 3 | not out | 28 |
| C.A.Connor | run out | 30 | b Frost | 30 |
| K.J.Shine | not out | 3 | b Watkin | 3 |
| Extras | (lb 3,w 1,nb 9) | 13 | (lb 8,nb 2) | 10 |
| TOTAL | | 330 | | 323 |

### GLAMORGAN

| | | | | | |
|---|---|---|---|---|---|
| S.P.James | c Smith b James | 31 | (2) c James b Maru | 22 |
| H.Morris | c Smith b Maru | 131 | | |
| A.Dale | c & b Maru | 3 | not out | 47 |
| M.P.Maynard | c Maru b Connor | 243 | c James b Smith | 18 |
| A.R.Butcher * | c Aymes b Connor | 1 | (1) b Smith | 58 |
| D.L.Hemp | b Maru | 8 | (5) not out | 4 |
| R.D.B.Croft | c & b James | 35 | | |
| C.P.Metson + | lbw b Maru | 19 | | |
| S.L.Watkin | c Aymes b Connor | 0 | | |
| M.Frost | c Ayling b Maru | 1 | | |
| D.J.Foster | not out | 4 | | |
| Extras | (b 1,lb 11,w 1,nb 15) | 28 | (w 1,nb 2) | 3 |
| TOTAL | | 504 | (for 3 wkts) | 152 |

| GLAMORGAN | O | M | R | W | O | M | R | W | FALL OF WICKETS | | | |
|---|---|---|---|---|---|---|---|---|---|---|---|---|
| | | | | | | | | | | HAM | GLA | HAM | GLA |
| Frost | 22.3 | 4 | 89 | 3 | 17 | 3 | 47 | 1 | 1st | 22 | 108 | 118 | 50 |
| Watkin | 26 | 5 | 70 | 3 | 30.2 | 6 | 92 | 3 | 2nd | 140 | 134 | 120 | 110 |
| Foster | 13 | 0 | 62 | 1 | 14 | 3 | 36 | 2 | 3rd | 153 | 227 | 153 | 144 |
| Dale | 5 | 0 | 17 | 0 | 8 | 1 | 21 | 0 | 4th | 185 | 242 | 224 | |
| Croft | 22 | 2 | 89 | 2 | 43 | 9 | 119 | 4 | 5th | 196 | 265 | 234 | |
| | | | | | | | | | 6th | 236 | 419 | 235 | |
| HAMPSHIRE | O | M | R | W | O | M | R | W | 7th | 288 | 489 | 236 | |
| Shine | 24 | 8 | 84 | 0 | 4 | 0 | 16 | 0 | 8th | 293 | 489 | 271 | |
| Connor | 24 | 7 | 49 | 3 | 5 | 1 | 9 | 0 | 9th | 315 | 499 | 320 | |
| Ayling | 11 | 3 | 44 | 0 | 5 | 1 | 17 | 0 | 10th | 330 | 504 | 323 | |
| Turner | 24 | 3 | 109 | 0 | 18 | 4 | 48 | 0 | | | | | |
| James | 17 | 5 | 78 | 2 | 3 | 0 | 10 | 0 | | | | | |
| Maru | 38.3 | 7 | 128 | 5 | 10 | 3 | 28 | 1 | | | | | |
| Smith | | | | | 5 | 1 | 20 | 2 | | | | | |
| Gower | | | | | 0.1 | 0 | 4 | 0 | | | | | |

## KENT vs. LEICESTERSHIRE

at Canterbury on 17th, 18th, 19th, 20th September 1991
Toss : Leicestershire. Umpires : G.I.Burgess and B.Dudleston
Leicestershire won by 90 runs. Kent 5 pts (Bt: 2, Bw: 3), Leicestershire 22 pts (Bt: 2, Bw: 4)
100 overs scores : Leicestershire 244 for 8

### LEICESTERSHIRE

| | | | | | |
|---|---|---|---|---|---|
| T.J.Boon | c Benson b Ellison | 10 | c Ealham b Davis | 50 |
| N.E.Briers * | c Ward b Ellison | 0 | b Penn | 20 |
| J.J.Whitaker | b Penn | 15 | c & b Davis | 58 |
| B.F.Smith | lbw b Ealham | 6 | (7) c Marsh b Ealham | 24 |
| L.Potter | c Davis b Ellison | 4 | (4) c & b Davis | 42 |
| P.N.Hepworth | c Benson b Penn | 97 | (5) run out | 30 |
| P.Whitticase + | c Ealham b Penn | 27 | (6) c Davis b Ealham | 9 |
| G.J.Parsons | c Patel b Penn | 63 | (6) c Marsh b Ealham | 5 |
| D.J.Millns | not out | 20 | b Ealham | 3 |
| C.Wilkinson | c Llong b Penn | 2 | not out | 2 |
| J.N.Maguire | c Davis b Ellison | 17 | b Ealham | 1 |
| Extras | (b 2,lb 9,w 1,nb 12) | 24 | (b 2,lb 9,nb 4) | 15 |
| TOTAL | | 281 | | 259 |

### KENT

| | | | | | |
|---|---|---|---|---|---|
| T.R.Ward | c Boon b Millns | 38 | c Whitaker b Wilkinson | 13 |
| M.R.Benson * | b Millns | 8 | c Whitticase b Maguire | 34 |
| N.R.Taylor | c & b Maguire | 59 | c & b Maguire | 32 |
| M.V.Fleming | c Potter b Maguire | 19 | c Millns b Hepworth | 4 |
| N.J.Llong | b Maguire | 0 | c Boon b Maguire | 0 |
| S.A.Marsh + | c Hepworth b Millns | 69 | b Potter | 17 |
| M.A.Ealham | c Hepworth b Maguire | 0 | c Whitticase b Potter | 36 |
| R.M.Ellison | b Millns | 13 | (11) c Maguire b Hepworth | 23 |
| R.P.Davis | lbw b Millns | 0 | (8) c Whitticase b Potter | 7 |
| C.Penn | c Whitaker b Wilkinson | 2 | (9) lbw b Maguire | 27 |
| M.M.Patel | not out | 0 | (10) not out | 18 |
| Extras | (lb 8,nb 5) | 13 | (b 8,lb 5,w 1,nb 4) | 18 |
| TOTAL | | 221 | | 229 |

| KENT | O | M | R | W | O | M | R | W | FALL OF WICKETS | | | |
|---|---|---|---|---|---|---|---|---|---|---|---|---|
| | | | | | | | | | | LEI | KEN | LEI | KEN |
| Penn | 39 | 13 | 90 | 5 | 20 | 6 | 45 | 1 | 1st | 1 | 9 | 72 | 28 |
| Ellison | 31.2 | 3 | 93 | 4 | 9 | 4 | 20 | 0 | 2nd | 28 | 93 | 87 | 79 |
| Ealham | 11 | 1 | 32 | 1 | 23.2 | 5 | 65 | 5 | 3rd | 28 | 125 | 156 | 92 |
| Patel | 16 | 8 | 13 | 0 | 16 | 2 | 65 | 0 | 4th | 31 | 125 | 193 | 92 |
| Davis | 15 | 7 | 28 | 0 | 29 | 13 | 58 | 3 | 5th | 38 | 140 | 209 | 92 |
| Fleming | 5 | 0 | 14 | 0 | 2 | 0 | 5 | 0 | 6th | 109 | 142 | 242 | 124 |
| | | | | | | | | | 7th | 229 | 172 | 248 | 132 |
| LEICS | O | M | R | W | O | M | R | W | 8th | 243 | 186 | 252 | 183 |
| Millns | 21.5 | 7 | 65 | 5 | 18 | 3 | 61 | 0 | 9th | 247 | 189 | 257 | 185 |
| Wilkinson | 15 | 2 | 43 | 1 | 7 | 1 | 13 | 1 | 10th | 281 | 221 | 259 | 229 |
| Maguire | 16 | 6 | 39 | 4 | 17 | 3 | 59 | 3 | | | | | |
| Parsons | 14 | 4 | 27 | 0 | | | | | | | | | |
| Hepworth | 3 | 1 | 3 | 0 | 12.2 | 2 | 51 | 3 | | | | | |
| Potter | 11 | 4 | 36 | 0 | 15 | 3 | 32 | 3 | | | | | |

# BRITANNIC ASSURANCE CHAMPIONSHIP

## LANCASHIRE vs. SURREY

at Old Trafford on 17th, 18th, 19th, 20th September 1991
Toss : Lancashire.  Umpires : J.W.Holder and B.Leadbeater
Lancashire won by 1 wicket.  Lancashire 23 pts (Bt: 3, Bw: 4), Surrey 2 pts (Bt: 1, Bw: 1)
100 overs scores : Lancashire 252 for 4

### LANCASHIRE

| Batsman | Dismissal | R | Dismissal 2 | R2 |
|---|---|---|---|---|
| G.D.Mendis | c Ward b Robinson | 19 | b Murphy | 26 |
| N.J.Speak | c & b Boiling | 153 | c Stewart b Murphy | 12 |
| J.P.Crawley | lbw b Boiling | 130 | lbw b Kendrick | 35 |
| G.D.Lloyd | st Sargeant b Kendrick | 2 | (5) c & b Kendrick | 15 |
| S.P.Titchard | b Kendrick | 1 | (4) c Stewart b Kendrick | 17 |
| M.Watkinson * | lbw b Boiling | 21 | c Bicknell M.P. b Kendrick | 5 |
| P.A.J.DeFreitas | c Boiling b Kendrick | 8 | lbw b Kendrick | 0 |
| W.K.Hegg + | c & b Boiling | 97 | not out | 36 |
| I.D.Austin | lbw b Kendrick | 3 | b Boiling | 7 |
| J.D.Fitton | c Ward b Kendrick | 5 | run out | 15 |
| P.J.Martin | not out | 0 | not out | 3 |
| Extras | (b 8,lb 7,w 4,nb 5) | 24 | (b 4,lb 5,nb 1) | 10 |
| TOTAL | | 463 | (for 9 wkts) | 181 |

### SURREY

| Batsman | Dismissal | R | Dismissal 2 | R2 |
|---|---|---|---|---|
| D.J.Bicknell | b Martin | 18 | c Hegg b DeFreitas | 3 |
| J.D.Robinson | c Lloyd b Watkinson | 79 | b Fitton | 50 |
| G.P.Thorpe | c Hegg b Martin | 11 | b Martin | 34 |
| A.J.Stewart * | c Hegg b DeFreitas | 14 | b Watkinson | 28 |
| D.M.Ward | c Hegg b DeFreitas | 0 | b Martin | 151 |
| M.A.Lynch | c Hegg b Martin | 30 | run out | 25 |
| N.F.Sargeant + | lbw b Watkinson | 10 | lbw b Fitton | 49 |
| M.P.Bicknell | c Crawley b Watkinson | 0 | b Austin | 63 |
| N.M.Kendrick | c Crawley b Martin | 17 | c Crawley b DeFreitas | 24 |
| J.Boiling | lbw b Watkinson | 1 | c Crawley b DeFreitas | 1 |
| A.J.Murphy | not out | 0 | not out | 1 |
| Extras | (b 5,lb 6,nb 8) | 19 | (b 2,lb 10,w 1,nb 2) | 15 |
| TOTAL | | 199 | | 444 |

| SURREY | O | M | R | W | O | M | R | W |
|---|---|---|---|---|---|---|---|---|
| Bicknell M.P. | 22 | 4 | 72 | 0 | 4 | 0 | 20 | 0 |
| Murphy | 14 | 2 | 65 | 0 | 9 | 1 | 38 | 2 |
| Robinson | 6 | 1 | 18 | 1 | | | | |
| Boiling | 53.2 | 17 | 157 | 4 | 17 | 1 | 60 | 1 |
| Kendrick | 53 | 16 | 120 | 5 | 23 | 3 | 54 | 5 |
| Lynch | 6 | 1 | 16 | 0 | | | | |

| LANCASHIRE | O | M | R | W | O | M | R | W |
|---|---|---|---|---|---|---|---|---|
| DeFreitas | 16 | 6 | 45 | 2 | 27 | 1 | 82 | 3 |
| Martin | 21.3 | 4 | 57 | 4 | 19 | 3 | 69 | 2 |
| Austin | 2 | 0 | 15 | 0 | 10.4 | 1 | 47 | 1 |
| Fitton | 7 | 1 | 26 | 0 | 23 | 5 | 89 | 2 |
| Watkinson | 18 | 4 | 45 | 4 | 30 | 3 | 145 | 1 |

### FALL OF WICKETS

| | LAN | SUR | SUR | LAN |
|---|---|---|---|---|
| 1st | 32 | 79 | 14 | 14 |
| 2nd | 243 | 95 | 77 | 61 |
| 3rd | 246 | 111 | 98 | 92 |
| 4th | 252 | 111 | 151 | 103 |
| 5th | 283 | 171 | 199 | 115 |
| 6th | 294 | 171 | 312 | 115 |
| 7th | 408 | 174 | 380 | 130 |
| 8th | 423 | 191 | 428 | 139 |
| 9th | 463 | 193 | 434 | 170 |
| 10th | 463 | 199 | 444 | |

## SOMERSET vs. WARWICKSHIRE

at Taunton on 17th, 18th, 19th, 20th September 1991
Toss : Warwickshire.  Umpires : D.R.Shepherd and R.C.Tolchard
Warwickshire won by 5 runs.  Somerset 6 pts (Bt: 3, Bw: 3), Warwicks 23 pts (Bt: 3, Bw: 4)
100 overs scores : Warwickshire 281 for 7

### WARWICKSHIRE

| Batsman | Dismissal | R | Dismissal 2 | R2 |
|---|---|---|---|---|
| A.J.Moles | c Bartlett b Graveney | 26 | c Trump b Rose | 1 |
| J.D.Ratcliffe | c Macleay b Mallender | 61 | c Rose b Trump | 84 |
| T.A.Lloyd * | c Trump b Graveney | 69 | c Cook b Graveney | 18 |
| D.P.Ostler | c Tavare b Trump | 79 | b Rose | 58 |
| D.A.Reeve | lbw b Mallender | 11 | c Lefebvre b Rose | 57 |
| Asif Din | b Mallender | 11 | b Mallender | 34 |
| N.M.K.Smith | lbw b Mallender | 2 | b Mallender | 1 |
| K.J.Piper + | c Burns b Mallender | 35 | b Rose | 30 |
| P.A.Booth | c Rose b Trump | 62 | c Cook b Graveney | 0 |
| T.A.Munton | not out | 5 | not out | 12 |
| A.A.Donald | b Mallender | 4 | not out | 8 |
| Extras | (lb 4,nb 6) | 10 | (b 2,lb 14,w 1,nb 1) | 18 |
| TOTAL | | 376 | (for 9 wkts dec) | 321 |

### SOMERSET

| Batsman | Dismissal | R | Dismissal 2 | R2 |
|---|---|---|---|---|
| S.J.Cook | c Piper b Booth | 127 | c Ratcliffe b Booth | 40 |
| N.D.Burns + | b Donald | 5 | b Donald | 0 |
| R.J.Harden | b Booth | 5 | c Reeve b Smith | 68 |
| C.J.Tavare * | lbw b Munton | 0 | b Booth | 85 |
| R.J.Bartlett | lbw b Reeve | 38 | c Ostler b Reeve | 35 |
| K.H.Macleay | c Ostler b Donald | 63 | c Piper b Reeve | 47 |
| G.D.Rose | c Ostler b Donald | 10 | c Piper b Munton | 55 |
| R.P.Lefebvre | b Donald | 6 | c Ratcliffe b Smith | 15 |
| N.A.Mallender | b Donald | 6 | not out | 13 |
| H.R.J.Trump | b Donald | 8 | b Booth | 4 |
| D.A.Graveney | not out | 2 | b Booth | 8 |
| Extras | (b 4,lb 8,nb 7) | 19 | (b 14,lb 13,nb 6) | 33 |
| TOTAL | | 289 | | 403 |

| SOMERSET | O | M | R | W | O | M | R | W |
|---|---|---|---|---|---|---|---|---|
| Mallender | 28.2 | 7 | 68 | 6 | 16 | 4 | 55 | 2 |
| Rose | 18 | 2 | 70 | 0 | 20 | 3 | 77 | 4 |
| Trump | 32 | 10 | 95 | 2 | 19 | 2 | 69 | 1 |
| Graveney | 26 | 6 | 73 | 2 | 24 | 3 | 79 | 2 |
| Lefebvre | 12 | 4 | 27 | 0 | 8 | 0 | 25 | 0 |
| Macleay | 7 | 0 | 39 | 0 | | | | |

| WARWICKS | O | M | R | W | O | M | R | W |
|---|---|---|---|---|---|---|---|---|
| Donald | 20.2 | 2 | 84 | 6 | 23 | 4 | 95 | 1 |
| Munton | 20 | 5 | 52 | 1 | 18 | 5 | 57 | 1 |
| Booth | 27 | 6 | 76 | 2 | 43.1 | 10 | 103 | 4 |
| Smith | 11 | 2 | 38 | 0 | 28 | 6 | 79 | 2 |
| Reeve | 6 | 1 | 27 | 1 | 13 | 1 | 36 | 2 |
| Asif Din | | | | | 1 | 0 | 6 | 0 |

### FALL OF WICKETS

| | WAR | SOM | WAR | SOM |
|---|---|---|---|---|
| 1st | 74 | 18 | 11 | 3 |
| 2nd | 95 | 46 | 46 | 89 |
| 3rd | 225 | 51 | 161 | 132 |
| 4th | 249 | 117 | 175 | 224 |
| 5th | 255 | 243 | 241 | 290 |
| 6th | 257 | 251 | 243 | 320 |
| 7th | 270 | 257 | 278 | 362 |
| 8th | 362 | 275 | 285 | 382 |
| 9th | 365 | 280 | 309 | 387 |
| 10th | 376 | 289 | | 403 |

## NOTTS vs. WORCESTERSHIRE

at Trent Bridge on 17th, 18th, 19th September 1991
Toss : Notts.  Umpires : J.C.Balderstone and J.D.Bond
Notts won by an innings and 70 runs.  Notts 24 pts (Bt: 4, Bw: 4), Worcs 2 pts (Bt: 1, Bw: 1)
100 overs scores : Notts 308 for 4

### NOTTS

| Batsman | Dismissal | R |
|---|---|---|
| B.C.Broad | lbw b Newport | 38 |
| P.Pollard | c Leatherdale b Lampitt | 10 |
| R.T.Robinson * | c Rhodes b Lampitt | 180 |
| D.W.Randall | lbw b Lampitt | 39 |
| P.Johnson | b Illingworth | 57 |
| M.A.Crawley | c Rhodes b Radford | 10 |
| F.D.Stephenson | c D'Oliveira b Lampitt | 19 |
| B.N.French + | not out | 36 |
| E.E.Hemmings | c & b Lampitt | 0 |
| R.A.Pick | lbw b Illingworth | 14 |
| J.A.Afford | b Newport | 9 |
| Extras | (b 2,lb 7,w 2,nb 5) | 16 |
| TOTAL | | 428 |

### WORCESTERSHIRE

| Batsman | Dismissal | R | Dismissal 2 | R2 |
|---|---|---|---|---|
| T.S.Curtis * | lbw b Stephenson | 31 | lbw b Hemmings | 27 |
| W.P.C.Weston | lbw b Stephenson | 8 | c French b Pick | 15 |
| G.A.Hick | c & b Crawley | 17 | c Crawley b Afford | 63 |
| D.A.Leatherdale | run out | 31 | b Hemmings | 7 |
| D.B.D'Oliveira | lbw b Hemmings | 33 | c & b Hemmings | 17 |
| S.J.Rhodes + | c French b Afford | 5 | c Johnson b Afford | 0 |
| S.R.Lampitt | c French b Afford | 17 | lbw b Afford | 3 |
| R.K.Illingworth | c Crawley b Stephenson | 20 | not out | 9 |
| P.J.Newport | lbw b Stephenson | 8 | run out | 4 |
| N.V.Radford | b Stephenson | 1 | c Crawley b Stephenson | 4 |
| R.D.Stemp | not out | 1 | b Stephenson | 8 |
| Extras | (b 3,lb 6,nb 3) | 12 | (lb 9,w 1,nb 7) | 17 |
| TOTAL | | 184 | | 174 |

| WORCS | O | M | R | W | O | M | R | W |
|---|---|---|---|---|---|---|---|---|
| Radford | 27 | 3 | 83 | 1 | | | | |
| Newport | 29.3 | 7 | 83 | 2 | | | | |
| Lampitt | 30 | 6 | 86 | 5 | | | | |
| Illingworth | 30 | 8 | 71 | 2 | | | | |
| Stemp | 17 | 3 | 57 | 0 | | | | |
| Hick | 9 | 0 | 39 | 0 | | | | |

| NOTTS | O | M | R | W | O | M | R | W |
|---|---|---|---|---|---|---|---|---|
| Pick | 5 | 1 | 16 | 0 | 8 | 1 | 19 | 1 |
| Stephenson | 19.3 | 4 | 63 | 5 | 15.4 | 5 | 26 | 2 |
| Crawley | 11 | 1 | 24 | 1 | 4 | 2 | 16 | 0 |
| Afford | 25 | 14 | 28 | 2 | 13 | 5 | 23 | 3 |
| Hemmings | 20 | 3 | 44 | 1 | 26 | 4 | 81 | 3 |

### FALL OF WICKETS

| | NOT | WOR | WOR | NOT |
|---|---|---|---|---|
| 1st | 42 | 30 | 31 | |
| 2nd | 60 | 59 | 74 | |
| 3rd | 155 | 59 | 91 | |
| 4th | 277 | 118 | 113 | |
| 5th | 312 | 126 | 114 | |
| 6th | 355 | 138 | 142 | |
| 7th | 377 | 166 | 155 | |
| 8th | 381 | 182 | 160 | |
| 9th | 417 | 183 | 164 | |
| 10th | 428 | 184 | 174 | |

## SUSSEX vs. GLOUCESTERSHIRE

at Hove on 17th, 18th, 19th, 20th September 1991
Toss : Sussex.  Umpires : J.H.Harris and M.J.Kitchen
Sussex won by 139 runs.  Sussex 21 pts (Bt: 3, Bw: 2), Gloucs 4 pts (Bt: 2, Bw: 2)
100 overs scores : Sussex 276 for 5, Gloucs 229 for 6

### SUSSEX

| Batsman | Dismissal | R | Dismissal 2 | R2 |
|---|---|---|---|---|
| P.W.G.Parker * | c Lloyds b Babington | 3 | b Lloyds | 24 |
| J.W.Hall | lbw b Babington | 25 | c Wright b Lloyds | 17 |
| K.Greenfield | b Scott | 64 | c Lloyds b Gilbert | 13 |
| A.P.Wells | lbw b Scott | 7 | c Lloyds b Gilbert | 1 |
| C.M.Wells | b Alleyne | 64 | c Russell b Lloyds | 25 |
| A.I.C.Dodemaide | lbw b Gilbert | 72 | b Scott | 22 |
| P.Moores + | lbw b Scott | 69 | b Scott | 51 |
| B.T.P.Donelan | c & b Lawrence | 9 | not out | 30 |
| A.C.S.Pigott | c Lloyds b Alleyne | 30 | c Lawrence b Scott | 0 |
| I.D.K.Salisbury | not out | 0 | not out | 31 |
| A.N.Jones | c sub b Alleyne | 1 | | |
| Extras | (lb 15,w 1,nb 11) | 27 | (b 3,lb 7,nb 5) | 15 |
| TOTAL | | 371 | (for 8 wkts dec) | 229 |

### GLOUCESTERSHIRE

| Batsman | Dismissal | R | Dismissal 2 | R2 |
|---|---|---|---|---|
| G.D.Hodgson | b Jones | 3 | b Donelan | 16 |
| C.W.J.Athey | not out | 103 | c Moores b Dodemaide | 12 |
| A.J.Wright * | b Wells C.M. | 31 | not out | 68 |
| R.J.Scott | b Donelan | 8 | c Parker b Salisbury | 11 |
| M.W.Alleyne | c Hall b Donelan | 0 | b Donelan | 12 |
| J.W.Lloyds | b Donelan | 4 | c Greenfield b Donelan | 0 |
| T.Hancock | b Wells C.M. | 51 | c Moores b Salisbury | 3 |
| R.C.Russell + | c Greenfield b Donelan | 11 | b Donelan | 1 |
| D.V.Lawrence | b Jones | 22 | b Donelan | 8 |
| D.R.Gilbert | lbw b Jones | 0 | b Donelan | 8 |
| A.M.Babington | b Dodemaide | 2 | c Pigott b Dodemaide | 11 |
| Extras | (b 9,lb 8,w 1,nb 34) | 52 | (b 4,lb 7,nb 13) | 24 |
| TOTAL | | 287 | | 174 |

| GLOUCS | O | M | R | W | O | M | R | W |
|---|---|---|---|---|---|---|---|---|
| Lawrence | 11 | 1 | 44 | 1 | | | | |
| Babington | 22 | 0 | 83 | 2 | 15 | 6 | 41 | 0 |
| Gilbert | 32 | 8 | 73 | 1 | 17 | 6 | 37 | 2 |
| Lloyds | 22 | 5 | 60 | 0 | 33 | 8 | 98 | 3 |
| Scott | 25 | 8 | 51 | 3 | 15 | 5 | 43 | 3 |
| Alleyne | 23.2 | 8 | 45 | 3 | | | | |

| SUSSEX | O | M | R | W | O | M | R | W |
|---|---|---|---|---|---|---|---|---|
| Jones | 19 | 1 | 68 | 3 | 12 | 5 | 22 | 0 |
| Dodemaide | 18.5 | 4 | 34 | 1 | 13.2 | 5 | 17 | 2 |
| Pigott | 4 | 2 | 7 | 0 | | | | |
| Wells C.M. | 22 | 8 | 37 | 2 | | | | |
| Donelan | 30 | 8 | 74 | 4 | 27 | 13 | 62 | 6 |
| Salisbury | 24 | 8 | 50 | 0 | 24 | 4 | 62 | 2 |

### FALL OF WICKETS

| | SUS | GLO | SUS | GLO |
|---|---|---|---|---|
| 1st | 6 | 5 | 40 | 30 |
| 2nd | 94 | 85 | 53 | 31 |
| 3rd | 104 | 96 | 58 | 65 |
| 4th | 104 | 96 | 79 | 88 |
| 5th | 218 | 112 | 91 | 88 |
| 6th | 287 | 218 | 162 | 100 |
| 7th | 315 | 241 | 173 | 101 |
| 8th | 370 | 278 | 177 | 118 |
| 9th | 370 | 278 | | 143 |
| 10th | 371 | 287 | | 174 |

# BRITANNIC ASSURANCE CHAMPIONSHIP

## HEADLINES

### Britannic Assurance Championship

### 17th - 20th September

• The 1991 Britannic Assurance Championship was effectively decided by a remarkable first day's play at Chelmsford, which must rank as one of the most one-sided in the history of the County Championship, Essex dismissing Middlesex for 51, the season's lowest total, and themselves reaching 385 for three. Neil Foster and Derek Pringle had reduced the 1990 champions to 26 for eight by the end of the first hour, and the innings was over before the 25th over was completed, but doubts about the pitch were soon dispelled by Graham Gooch who reached his ninth first-class 200 just before the close. His final score, 259, was the highest of the season and helped Essex to a lead of 515. Although the visitors recovered a little self-esteem in their second innings, Foster completed match figures of 10 for 122 to give Essex victory by an innings and 208 runs with a day and a half to spare, and their first Championship success since 1986.

• Although quickly aware of the inevitability of Essex's victory to put the title out of their reach, Warwickshire recorded their 11th win of the season by beating Somerset by five runs at Taunton, to complete their most successful Championship campaign for 20 years. Somerset's Jimmy Cook took the individual honours in his last match for the county, hitting his 11th 100 of the season, a new county record, and his 28th in three seasons of county cricket; his final aggregate of 2755 runs was the best since the reduction in the county programme in 1969, and only six short of Bill Alley's Somerset record. Warwickshire gained a first innings lead of 87 thanks largely to Allan Donald, but it was spinners, Paul Booth and Neil Smith, who finally prevented Somerset from reaching a target of 409.

• Derbyshire claimed third place after coming from behind to defeat Yorkshire by 40 runs at Chesterfield. Paul Jarvis put the visitors firmly in control as Derbyshire collapsed to 61 for seven and a career-best 125 not out from Simon Kellett gave them a lead of 184, but Chris Adams's second 100 of the season helped Derbyshire's second innings reach 374, and Yorkshire's pursuit of a target of 191 was doomed once they had lost their first six wickets for 36.

• Nottinghamshire finished fourth by beating Worcestershire by an innings and 70 runs at Trent Bridge. Tim Robinson's 180 carried the home side to a first innings total of 428, and after Franklyn Stephenson had claimed five for 63 on his farewell appearance for Notts, Worcestershire were forced to follow on 244 behind. The visitors' batsmen fared even worse in their second effort, Stephenson building on good work by the spinners by capturing the last two wickets to end his four years with Notts on a high note.

• Surrey had to be satisfied with fifth place after just failing to beat Lancashire at Old Trafford after following on 264 behind. Nick Speak, hitting a career best 153, and John Crawley, a maiden first-class 100, shared a second-wicket association of 211, and Surrey

spinners Neil Kendrick and James Boiling both returned career-best bowling figures in Lancashire's first innings. Surrey's batsmen, ineffecitve in their first attempt, fought back strongly in their second, David Ward making his highest score of the season and Neil Sargeant and Martin Bicknell both reaching career-best scores. When Lancashire's second innings stood at 139 for eight, needing 181 for victory, Surrey had assumed control. Although Kendrick improved on his first innings performance to collect 10 wickets in the match, Warren Hegg steered Lancs to a nail-biting one-wicket victory.

• Glamorgan's victory over Hampshire at Southampton was much more straightforward. The home side's first innings total of 330 proved insufficient when Hugh Morris and Matthew Maynard both hit 100s, Maynard compiling a career best 243 as Glamorgan pressed on past 500. Although Hampshire's batsmen again managed more than 300, Glamorgan's target of 150 presented few problems and a seven-wicket win was quickly achieved.

• Gloucestershire suffered their fifth consecutive Championship defeat when they lost to Sussex by 139 runs at Hove. Four batsman passed 50, as Sussex reached 371 in their first innings, and although Bill Athey and Tony Wright held firm, Gloucestershire's batting was undermined by the off-spin of Brad Donelan who claimed 10 wickets in a match for the first time.

• Leicestershire avoided finishing in last place, claimed instead by Somerset, after beating Kent by 90 runs at Canterbury. David Millns and John Maguire bowled the visitors to a first inngs lead of 60, then a target of 320 proved too much for Kent.

First-class début: D.L.Hemp (Glamorgan)

### Britannic Assurance Championship
### Final Table

|    |                      | P  | W  | L  | D  | T | Bt | Bl | Pts |
|----|----------------------|----|----|----|----|---|----|----|-----|
| 1  | Essex (2)            | 22 | 11 | 5  | 6  | 0 | 69 | 67 | 312 |
| 2  | Warwickshire (5)     | 22 | 11 | 4  | 7  | 0 | 58 | 65 | 299 |
| 3  | Derbyshire (12)      | 22 | 9  | 5  | 8  | 0 | 46 | 68 | 258 |
| 4  | Notts (13)           | 22 | 7  | 5  | 10 | 0 | 64 | 69 | 245 |
| 5  | Surrey (9)           | 22 | 8  | 6  | 8  | 0 | 47 | 64 | 241 |
| 6  | Worcestershire (4)   | 22 | 6  | 4  | 12 | 0 | 54 | 59 | 209 |
|    | Kent (16)            | 22 | 6  | 3  | 12 | 1 | 50 | 55 | 209 |
| 8  | Lancashire (6)       | 22 | 6  | 9  | 7  | 0 | 60 | 49 | 205 |
| 9  | Hampshire (3)        | 22 | 5  | 7  | 10 | 0 | 57 | 56 | 193 |
| 10 | Northants (11)       | 22 | 5  | 6  | 11 | 0 | 55 | 54 | 189 |
| 11 | Sussex (17)          | 22 | 4  | 3  | 14 | 1 | 57 | 60 | 189 |
| 12 | Glamorgan (8)        | 22 | 5  | 5  | 12 | 0 | 50 | 57 | 187 |
| 13 | Gloucestershire (13) | 22 | 5  | 10 | 7  | 0 | 42 | 53 | 175 |
| 14 | Yorkshire (10)       | 22 | 4  | 6  | 12 | 0 | 58 | 37 | 159 |
| 15 | Middlesex (1)        | 22 | 3  | 9  | 10 | 0 | 48 | 63 | 159 |
| 16 | Leicestershire (7)   | 22 | 3  | 8  | 11 | 0 | 46 | 53 | 147 |
| 17 | Somerset (15)        | 22 | 2  | 5  | 15 | 0 | 66 | 45 | 143 |

# BRITANNIC ASSURANCE CHALLENGE

## ESSEX vs. VICTORIA
at Chelmsford on 22nd September 1991
Toss : Victoria. Umpires : D.J.Constant and A.A.Jones
Victoria won by 59 runs
Man of the match: S.P.O'Donnell

### VICTORIA
| | | |
|---|---|---|
| D.J.Ramshaw | b Pringle | 71 |
| W.N.Phillips | run out | 23 |
| D.M.Jones | not out | 86 |
| D.S.Lehmann | c Andrew b Pringle | 5 |
| S.P.O'Donnell * | not out | 71 |
| G.R.Parker | | |
| A.I.C.Dodemaide | | |
| M.G.Hughes | | |
| D.S.Berry + | | |
| D.W.Fleming | | |
| P.W.Jackson | | |
| Extras | (b 1,lb 11,w 3,nb 3) | 18 |
| TOTAL | (50 overs)(for 3 wkts) | 274 |

### ESSEX
| | | |
|---|---|---|
| G.A.Gooch * | c Berry b Hughes | 0 |
| J.P.Stephenson | b Jackson | 49 |
| P.J.Prichard | c Lehmann b Hughes | 12 |
| N.Hussain | c Berry b Dodemaide | 36 |
| D.R.Pringle | c Lehmann b Hughes | 51 |
| N.V.Knight | b Jackson | 10 |
| M.A.Garnham + | c & b Fleming | 23 |
| J.J.B.Lewis | b Fleming | 0 |
| T.D.Topley | b Hughes | 17 |
| S.J.W.Andrew | not out | 4 |
| P.M.Such | b Hughes | 0 |
| Extras | (b 1,lb 6,w 2,nb 1) | 13 |
| TOTAL | (48.5 overs) | 215 |

| ESSEX | O | M | R | W | FALL OF WICKETS | | |
|---|---|---|---|---|---|---|---|
| | | | | | | VIC | ESS |
| Andrew | 10 | 0 | 74 | 0 | | | |
| Pringle | 10 | 0 | 50 | 2 | 1st | 56 | 0 |
| Topley | 10 | 0 | 46 | 0 | 2nd | 148 | 44 |
| Such | 10 | 1 | 41 | 0 | 3rd | 154 | 102 |
| Gooch | 8 | 0 | 36 | 0 | 4th | | 108 |
| Stephenson | 2 | 0 | 15 | 0 | 5th | | 130 |
| | | | | | 6th | | 163 |
| VICTORIA | O | M | R | W | 7th | | 163 |
| Hughes | 9.5 | 1 | 41 | 5 | 8th | | 205 |
| Fleming | 10 | 0 | 40 | 2 | 9th | | 213 |
| Dodemaide | 10 | 0 | 40 | 1 | 10th | | 215 |
| O'Donnell | 9 | 0 | 39 | 0 | | | |
| Jackson | 10 | 0 | 45 | 2 | | | |

## ESSEX vs. VICTORIA
at Chelmsford on 23rd, 24th, 25th, 26th September 1991
Toss : Essex. Umpires : R.Julian and K.E.Palmer
Match drawn

### ESSEX
| | | |
|---|---|---|
| G.A.Gooch * | c Berry b Fleming | 31 |
| J.P.Stephenson | b Dodemaide | 54 |
| P.J.Prichard | lbw b O'Donnell | 2 |
| N.Hussain | c & b Dodemaide | 5 |
| N.V.Knight | run out | 53 |
| J.J.B.Lewis | b Jackson | 25 |
| M.A.Garnham + | lbw b Fleming | 33 |
| D.R.Pringle | lbw b Hughes | 68 |
| N.A.Foster | st Berry b Jackson | 37 |
| J.H.Childs | not out | 8 |
| P.M.Such | | |
| Extras | (b 10,lb 9,w 4,nb 4) | 27 |
| TOTAL | (for 9 wkts dec) | 343 |

### VICTORIA
| | | | | | |
|---|---|---|---|---|---|
| D.J.Ramshaw | lbw b Childs | 11 | c Garnham b Foster | 0 |
| W.N.Phillips | c Pringle b Foster | 2 | lbw b Stephenson | 11 |
| D.M.Jones | c Gooch b Childs | 25 | c Hussain b Such | 9 |
| D.S.Lehmann | c Hussain b Such | 15 | lbw b Childs | 8 |
| S.P.O'Donnell * | c Prichard b Such | 12 | b Childs | 5 |
| G.R.Parker | b Childs | 0 | lbw b Childs | 1 |
| A.I.C.Dodemaide | lbw b Foster | 21 | b Such | 0 |
| M.G.Hughes | not out | 60 | not out | 12 |
| D.S.Berry + | c Prichard b Childs | 1 | lbw b Such | 4 |
| D.W.Fleming | c Garnham b Foster | 8 | | |
| P.W.Jackson | c Gooch b Foster | 4 | | |
| Extras | (lb 9) | 9 | (b 3,lb 3) | 6 |
| TOTAL | | 168 | (for 8 wkts) | 56 |

| VICTORIA | O | M | R | W | O | M | R | W | FALL OF WICKETS | | | |
|---|---|---|---|---|---|---|---|---|---|---|---|---|
| | | | | | | | | | | ESS | VIC | VIC | ESS |
| Hughes | 30.3 | 7 | 85 | 1 | | | | | | | | |
| Fleming | 25 | 5 | 88 | 2 | | | | | 1st | 61 | 3 | 8 |
| O'Donnell | 13 | 6 | 47 | 1 | | | | | 2nd | 80 | 39 | 14 |
| Dodemaide | 24 | 6 | 54 | 2 | | | | | 3rd | 96 | 48 | 29 |
| Jackson | 18 | 11 | 50 | 2 | | | | | 4th | 103 | 70 | 33 |
| | | | | | | | | | 5th | 159 | 71 | 37 |
| ESSEX | O | M | R | W | O | M | R | W | 6th | 206 | 71 | 40 |
| Foster | 33.3 | 12 | 63 | 4 | 4 | 1 | 14 | 1 | 7th | 217 | 136 | 40 |
| Pringle | 3 | 3 | 0 | 0 | | | | | 8th | 277 | 137 | 56 |
| Childs | 43 | 15 | 71 | 4 | 7 | 2 | 19 | 3 | 9th | 343 | 158 | |
| Such | 17 | 7 | 25 | 2 | 6.1 | 2 | 7 | 3 | 10th | | 168 | |
| Stephenson | | | | | 4 | 1 | 10 | 1 | | | | |

---

## HEADLINES

### Britannic Assurance Challenge

### Essex v Victoria

### 21st - 25th September

The 1991 Britannic Assurance Championship winners Essex and the 1990-91 Sheffield Shield winners Victoria contested the inaugural Britannic Assurance Challenge at Chelmsford to bring to an end a marathon English season that lasted almost five and a half months.

Victoria took the honours in the one-day match: Dean Jones and Simon O'Donnell carried their total to an impressive 274 for three in 50 overs with a belligerent fourth wicket partnership of 121 in 13 overs, and Merv Hughes dismissed Graham Gooch for nought and finished with figures of five for 41 as Essex were bowled out for 215, 59 runs adrift.

The Autumnal rains, arriving a week too soon for Essex followers, deprived the county champions of a convincing victory over their Australian counterparts in the four-day match: Victoria, having been forced to follow on, were languishing at 56 for eight when the Chelmsford outfield was flooded by torrential rain in the middle of the final afternoon. After Essex had reached 343 for nine, Derek Pringle top-scoring with 68, Neil Foster took a starring role with the ball, claiming his 100th first-class wicket as the Victorians were dismissed for 168, but it was the Essex spinners John Childs and Peter Such who undermined the visitors' second innings, taking three wickets apiece, and the Australian domestic champions were only saved from an embarrassing defeat by the English weather. Essex, although denied £12.,000 in prize money, had again shown their strength in depth as worthy winners of the County Championship.

# THE
# AVERAGES

# CORNHILL TEST MATCHES

## ENGLAND v WEST INDIES

### ENGLAND

#### BATTING AVERAGES - Including fielding

| Name | Matches | Inns | NO | Runs | HS | Avge | 100s | 50s | Ct | St |
|---|---|---|---|---|---|---|---|---|---|---|
| R.A.Smith | 4 | 7 | 2 | 416 | 148 * | 83.20 | 2 | 2 | 2 | - |
| A.J.Stewart | 1 | 2 | 1 | 69 | 38 * | 69.00 | - | - | 4 | - |
| C.C.Lewis | 2 | 3 | 1 | 125 | 65 | 62.50 | - | 1 | 3 | - |
| G.A.Gooch | 5 | 9 | 1 | 480 | 154 * | 60.00 | 1 | 2 | 6 | - |
| I.T.Botham | 1 | 2 | 1 | 35 | 31 | 35.00 | - | - | 3 | - |
| M.R.Ramprakash | 5 | 9 | 0 | 210 | 29 | 23.33 | - | - | 4 | - |
| P.A.J.DeFreitas | 5 | 8 | 1 | 134 | 55 * | 19.14 | - | 1 | 1 | - |
| D.R.Pringle | 4 | 7 | 0 | 128 | 45 | 18.28 | - | - | 1 | - |
| D.V.Lawrence | 2 | 3 | 0 | 47 | 34 | 15.66 | - | - | - | - |
| R.K.Illingworth | 2 | 4 | 2 | 31 | 13 | 15.50 | - | - | 1 | - |
| A.J.Lamb | 4 | 7 | 0 | 88 | 29 | 12.57 | - | - | 7 | - |
| H.Morris | 2 | 4 | 0 | 50 | 44 | 12.50 | - | - | 1 | - |
| G.A.Hick | 4 | 7 | 0 | 75 | 43 | 10.71 | - | - | 8 | - |
| R.C.Russell | 4 | 7 | 0 | 73 | 46 | 10.42 | - | - | 5 | - |
| M.A.Atherton | 5 | 9 | 0 | 79 | 32 | 8.77 | - | - | 3 | - |
| D.E.Malcolm | 2 | 3 | 1 | 9 | 5 * | 4.50 | - | - | 1 | - |
| S.L.Watkin | 2 | 3 | 0 | 8 | 6 | 2.66 | - | - | - | - |
| P.C.R.Tufnell | 1 | 1 | 0 | 2 | 2 | 2.00 | - | - | - | - |

#### BOWLING AVERAGES

| Name | Overs | Mdns | Runs | Wkts | Avge | Best | 5wI | 10wM |
|---|---|---|---|---|---|---|---|---|
| P.A.J.DeFreitas | 185.5 | 55 | 457 | 22 | 20.77 | 4-34 | - | - |
| I.T.Botham | 27 | 8 | 67 | 3 | 22.33 | 2-40 | - | - |
| P.C.R.Tufnell | 60.3 | 9 | 175 | 7 | 25.00 | 6-25 | 1 | - |
| D.R.Pringle | 128.1 | 33 | 322 | 12 | 26.83 | 5-100 | 1 | - |
| S.L.Watkin | 36 | 4 | 153 | 5 | 30.60 | 3-38 | - | - |
| C.C.Lewis | 79 | 30 | 201 | 6 | 33.50 | 6-111 | 1 | - |
| D.V.Lawrence | 78.1 | 7 | 350 | 10 | 35.00 | 5-106 | 1 | - |
| G.A.Hick | 24 | 5 | 95 | 2 | 47.50 | 2-77 | - | - |
| R.K.Illingworth | 56.4 | 10 | 213 | 4 | 53.25 | 3-110 | - | - |
| D.E.Malcolm | 42.3 | 3 | 180 | 3 | 60.00 | 1-9 | - | - |
| G.A.Gooch | 8 | 1 | 14 | 0 | - | - | - | - |

### WEST INDIES

#### BATTING AVERAGES - Including fielding

| Name | Matches | Inns | NO | Runs | HS | Avge | 100s | 50s | Ct | St |
|---|---|---|---|---|---|---|---|---|---|---|
| R.B.Richardson | 5 | 10 | 1 | 495 | 121 | 55.00 | 2 | 3 | 4 | - |
| I.V.A.Richards | 5 | 8 | 1 | 376 | 80 | 53.71 | - | 5 | 4 | - |
| D.L.Haynes | 5 | 10 | 3 | 323 | 75 * | 46.14 | - | 3 | 2 | - |
| C.L.Hooper | 5 | 9 | 2 | 271 | 111 | 38.71 | 1 | 2 | 9 | - |
| C.B.Lambert | 1 | 2 | 0 | 53 | 39 | 26.50 | - | - | 2 | - |
| A.L.Logie | 4 | 5 | 0 | 120 | 78 | 24.00 | - | 1 | 4 | - |
| M.D.Marshall | 5 | 7 | 1 | 116 | 67 | 19.33 | - | 1 | - | - |
| P.V.Simmons | 5 | 10 | 0 | 181 | 38 | 18.10 | - | - | 4 | - |
| P.J.L.Dujon | 5 | 7 | 0 | 89 | 33 | 12.71 | - | - | 17 | - |
| C.A.Walsh | 5 | 7 | 0 | 66 | 18 | 9.42 | - | - | - | - |
| B.P.Patterson | 3 | 5 | 3 | 11 | 5 * | 5.50 | - | - | 1 | - |
| C.E.L.Ambrose | 5 | 7 | 0 | 37 | 17 | 5.28 | - | - | - | - |
| I.B.A.Allen | 2 | 2 | 2 | 5 | 4 * | - | - | - | 1 | - |

#### BOWLING AVERAGES

| Name | Overs | Mdns | Runs | Wkts | Avge | Best | 5wI | 10wM |
|---|---|---|---|---|---|---|---|---|
| C.B.Lambert | 0.4 | 0 | 4 | 1 | 4.00 | 1-4 | - | - |
| C.E.L.Ambrose | 249 | 68 | 560 | 28 | 20.00 | 6-52 | 2 | - |
| M.D.Marshall | 172.1 | 36 | 442 | 20 | 22.10 | 4-33 | - | - |
| B.P.Patterson | 117.3 | 20 | 389 | 13 | 29.92 | 5-81 | 1 | - |
| C.A.Walsh | 187 | 42 | 493 | 15 | 32.86 | 4-64 | - | - |
| I.B.A.Allen | 47 | 4 | 180 | 5 | 36.00 | 2-69 | - | - |
| C.L.Hooper | 64 | 13 | 137 | 2 | 68.50 | 1-10 | - | - |
| I.V.A.Richards | 5 | 1 | 6 | 0 | - | - | - | - |
| P.V.Simmons | 3 | 0 | 7 | 0 | - | - | - | - |

## ALL TEST MATCHES

### ENGLAND

#### BATTING AVERAGES - Including fielding

| Name | Matches | Inns | NO | Runs | HS | Avge | 100s | 50s | Ct | St |
|---|---|---|---|---|---|---|---|---|---|---|
| A.J.Stewart | 2 | 4 | 2 | 225 | 113 * | 112.50 | 1 | - | 4 | - |
| R.A.Smith | 5 | 9 | 3 | 483 | 148 * | 80.50 | 2 | 3 | 3 | - |
| G.A.Gooch | 6 | 11 | 1 | 692 | 174 | 69.20 | 2 | 2 | 6 | - |
| C.C.Lewis | 3 | 4 | 1 | 136 | 65 | 45.33 | - | 1 | 4 | - |
| I.T.Botham | 2 | 3 | 1 | 57 | 31 | 28.50 | - | - | 5 | - |
| M.R.Ramprakash | 6 | 10 | 0 | 210 | 29 | 21.00 | - | - | 4 | - |
| H.Morris | 3 | 6 | 0 | 115 | 44 | 19.16 | - | - | 3 | - |
| D.R.Pringle | 4 | 7 | 0 | 128 | 45 | 18.28 | - | - | 1 | - |
| P.A.J.DeFreitas | 6 | 9 | 1 | 135 | 55 * | 16.87 | - | 1 | 1 | - |
| R.K.Illingworth | 2 | 4 | 2 | 31 | 13 | 15.50 | - | - | 1 | - |
| R.C.Russell | 5 | 9 | 1 | 102 | 46 | 12.75 | - | - | 8 | - |
| A.J.Lamb | 4 | 7 | 0 | 88 | 29 | 12.57 | - | - | 7 | - |
| D.V.Lawrence | 3 | 4 | 0 | 50 | 34 | 12.50 | - | - | - | - |
| G.A.Hick | 4 | 7 | 0 | 75 | 43 | 10.71 | - | - | 8 | - |
| M.A.Atherton | 5 | 9 | 0 | 79 | 32 | 8.77 | - | - | 3 | - |
| D.E.Malcolm | 2 | 3 | 1 | 9 | 5 * | 4.50 | - | - | 1 | - |
| S.L.Watkin | 2 | 3 | 0 | 8 | 6 | 2.66 | - | - | - | - |
| P.C.R.Tufnell | 2 | 2 | 0 | 2 | 2 | 1.00 | - | - | 1 | - |

#### BOWLING AVERAGES

| Name | Overs | Mdns | Runs | Wkts | Avge | Best | 5wI | 10wM |
|---|---|---|---|---|---|---|---|---|
| P.A.J.DeFreitas | 233.5 | 71 | 572 | 30 | 19.06 | 7-70 | 1 | - |
| P.C.R.Tufnell | 102 | 25 | 292 | 12 | 24.33 | 6-25 | 2 | - |
| D.R.Pringle | 128.1 | 33 | 322 | 12 | 26.83 | 5-100 | 1 | - |
| I.T.Botham | 43 | 13 | 108 | 4 | 27.00 | 2-40 | - | - |
| S.L.Watkin | 36 | 4 | 153 | 5 | 30.60 | 3-38 | - | - |
| C.C.Lewis | 107 | 39 | 261 | 8 | 32.62 | 6-111 | 1 | - |
| D.V.Lawrence | 116.2 | 17 | 494 | 14 | 35.28 | 5-106 | 1 | - |
| G.A.Hick | 24 | 5 | 95 | 2 | 47.50 | 2-77 | - | - |
| R.K.Illingworth | 56.4 | 10 | 213 | 4 | 53.25 | 3-110 | - | - |
| D.E.Malcolm | 42.3 | 3 | 180 | 3 | 60.00 | 1-9 | - | - |
| G.A.Gooch | 8 | 1 | 14 | 0 | - | - | - | - |

# TEXACO TROPHY

## ENGLAND v WEST INDIES

### ENGLAND

**BATTING AVERAGES - Including fielding**

| Name | Matches | Inns | NO | Runs | HS | Avge | 100s | 50s | Ct | St |
|---|---|---|---|---|---|---|---|---|---|---|
| M.A.Atherton | 3 | 3 | 1 | 168 | 74 | 84.00 | - | 2 | - | - |
| G.A.Hick | 3 | 3 | 1 | 129 | 86 * | 64.50 | - | 1 | - | - |
| N.H.Fairbrother | 3 | 3 | 1 | 122 | 113 | 61.00 | 1 | - | 2 | - |
| A.J.Lamb | 2 | 2 | 0 | 80 | 62 | 40.00 | - | 1 | - | - |
| G.A.Gooch | 3 | 3 | 0 | 65 | 54 | 21.66 | - | 1 | 2 | - |
| I.T.Botham | 1 | 1 | 0 | 8 | 8 | 8.00 | - | - | - | - |
| P.A.J.DeFreitas | 3 | 1 | 0 | 8 | 8 | 8.00 | - | - | 4 | - |
| D.R.Pringle | 3 | 1 | 0 | 1 | 1 | 1.00 | - | - | 1 | - |
| R.C.Russell | 3 | 1 | 0 | 1 | 1 | 1.00 | - | - | 4 | - |
| C.C.Lewis | 2 | 1 | 0 | 0 | 0 | 0.00 | - | - | 2 | - |
| R.K.Illingworth | 3 | 1 | 1 | 9 | 9 * | - | - | - | 4 | - |
| M.R.Ramprakash | 2 | 2 | 2 | 6 | 6 * | - | - | - | - | - |
| D.V.Lawrence | 1 | 0 | 0 | 0 | 0 | - | - | - | - | - |
| D.A.Reeve | 1 | 0 | 0 | 0 | 0 | - | - | - | - | - |

**BOWLING AVERAGES**

| Name | Overs | Mdns | Runs | Wkts | Avge | Best | 5wI |
|---|---|---|---|---|---|---|---|
| I.T.Botham | 11 | 2 | 45 | 4 | 11.25 | 4-45 | - |
| D.V.Lawrence | 11 | 1 | 67 | 4 | 16.75 | 4-67 | - |
| G.A.Gooch | 18 | 1 | 77 | 3 | 25.66 | 1-9 | - |
| C.C.Lewis | 22 | 3 | 103 | 4 | 25.75 | 3-62 | - |
| P.A.J.DeFreitas | 33 | 7 | 98 | 3 | 32.66 | 2-26 | - |
| R.K.Illingworth | 32 | 3 | 115 | 3 | 38.33 | 2-53 | - |
| D.R.Pringle | 27 | 2 | 130 | 2 | 65.00 | 2-52 | - |
| D.A.Reeve | 11 | 1 | 43 | 0 | - | - | - |

### WEST INDIES

**BATTING AVERAGES - Including fielding**

| Name | Matches | Inns | NO | Runs | HS | Avge | 100s | 50s | Ct | St |
|---|---|---|---|---|---|---|---|---|---|---|
| I.V.A.Richards | 3 | 3 | 0 | 145 | 78 | 48.33 | - | 1 | 1 | - |
| A.L.Logie | 3 | 3 | 0 | 124 | 82 | 41.33 | - | 1 | - | - |
| C.A.Walsh | 3 | 3 | 2 | 30 | 29 * | 30.00 | - | - | - | - |
| C.L.Hooper | 3 | 3 | 0 | 84 | 48 | 28.00 | - | - | - | - |
| B.C.Lara | 1 | 1 | 0 | 23 | 23 | 23.00 | - | - | - | - |
| R.B.Richardson | 3 | 3 | 0 | 57 | 41 | 19.00 | - | - | 4 | - |
| M.D.Marshall | 3 | 3 | 0 | 52 | 22 | 17.33 | - | - | - | - |
| C.G.Greenidge | 2 | 2 | 0 | 27 | 23 | 13.50 | - | - | - | - |
| P.V.Simmons | 3 | 3 | 0 | 37 | 28 | 12.33 | - | - | - | - |
| P.J.L.Dujon | 3 | 3 | 0 | 26 | 21 | 8.66 | - | - | 4 | - |
| C.E.L.Ambrose | 3 | 3 | 3 | 32 | 21 * | - | - | - | - | - |
| B.P.Patterson | 3 | 1 | 1 | 2 | 2 * | - | - | - | - | - |

**BOWLING AVERAGES**

| Name | Overs | Mdns | Runs | Wkts | Avge | Best | 5wI |
|---|---|---|---|---|---|---|---|
| C.L.Hooper | 15.5 | 0 | 98 | 3 | 32.66 | 2-18 | - |
| C.E.L.Ambrose | 30 | 5 | 101 | 3 | 33.66 | 2-36 | - |
| B.P.Patterson | 31 | 3 | 139 | 4 | 34.75 | 2-38 | - |
| M.D.Marshall | 32 | 2 | 126 | 3 | 42.00 | 2-32 | - |
| C.A.Walsh | 33 | 1 | 140 | 2 | 70.00 | 2-34 | - |
| P.V.Simmons | 9 | 0 | 61 | 0 | - | - | - |

# TOURISTS – ALL FIRST-CLASS MATCHES

## WEST INDIES

### BATTING AVERAGES - Including fielding

| Name | Matches | Inns | NO | Runs | HS | Avge | 100s | 50s | Ct | St |
|---|---|---|---|---|---|---|---|---|---|---|
| C.L.Hooper | 15 | 23 | 8 | 1282 | 196 | 85.46 | 4 | 7 | 19 | - |
| R.B.Richardson | 14 | 24 | 5 | 1290 | 135* | 67.89 | 6 | 5 | 12 | - |
| I.V.A.Richards | 12 | 18 | 4 | 817 | 131 | 58.35 | 1 | 6 | 9 | - |
| C.B.Lambert | 6 | 11 | 2 | 452 | 116 | 50.22 | 1 | 3 | 4 | - |
| D.L.Haynes | 13 | 22 | 5 | 721 | 151 | 42.41 | 1 | 4 | 4 | - |
| P.J.L.Dujon | 11 | 14 | 3 | 439 | 142* | 39.90 | 1 | 2 | 21 | - |
| P.V.Simmons | 14 | 26 | 1 | 985 | 136 | 39.40 | 3 | 4 | 10 | - |
| B.C.Lara | 8 | 12 | 0 | 341 | 93 | 28.41 | - | 3 | 9 | - |
| A.L.Logie | 12 | 17 | 1 | 433 | 78 | 27.06 | - | 3 | 7 | - |
| C.G.Greenidge | 2 | 4 | 1 | 72 | 26 | 24.00 | - | - | 1 | - |
| M.D.Marshall | 10 | 11 | 2 | 196 | 67 | 21.77 | - | 1 | - | - |
| D.Williams | 6 | 5 | 1 | 83 | 35 | 20.75 | - | - | 22 | 3 |
| I.B.A.Allen | 10 | 5 | 4 | 16 | 8 | 16.00 | - | - | 8 | - |
| H.A.G.Anthony | 11 | 8 | 3 | 76 | 33* | 15.20 | - | - | 7 | - |
| C.A.Walsh | 11 | 8 | 1 | 66 | 18 | 9.42 | - | - | - | - |
| C.E.L.Ambrose | 10 | 8 | 1 | 53 | 17 | 7.57 | - | - | 1 | - |
| B.P.Patterson | 11 | 5 | 3 | 11 | 5* | 5.50 | - | - | 4 | - |

### BOWLING AVERAGES

| Name | Overs | Mdns | Runs | Wkts | Avge | Best | 5wI | 10wM |
|---|---|---|---|---|---|---|---|---|
| C.B.Lambert | 1.4 | 1 | 4 | 1 | 4.00 | 1-4 | - | - |
| C.E.L.Ambrose | 390 | 122 | 869 | 51 | 17.03 | 6-52 | 3 | - |
| M.D.Marshall | 261.1 | 51 | 706 | 28 | 25.21 | 4-33 | - | - |
| C.L.Hooper | 305 | 68 | 696 | 26 | 26.76 | 4-49 | - | - |
| B.P.Patterson | 287.3 | 68 | 912 | 32 | 28.50 | 5-81 | 2 | - |
| C.A.Walsh | 324.5 | 75 | 915 | 29 | 31.55 | 4-39 | - | - |
| H.A.G.Anthony | 223.3 | 30 | 878 | 26 | 33.76 | 3-28 | - | - |
| P.V.Simmons | 74 | 16 | 263 | 6 | 43.83 | 2-34 | - | - |
| I.B.A.Allen | 217.4 | 35 | 811 | 16 | 50.68 | 2-61 | - | - |
| I.V.A.Richards | 47 | 9 | 161 | 2 | 80.50 | 1-32 | - | - |
| R.B.Richardson | 5 | 2 | 6 | 0 | - | - | - | - |
| B.C.Lara | 8 | 1 | 36 | 0 | - | - | - | - |

## SRI LANKA

### BATTING AVERAGES - Including fielding

| Name | Matches | Inns | NO | Runs | HS | Avge | 100s | 50s | Ct | St |
|---|---|---|---|---|---|---|---|---|---|---|
| S.T.Jayasuriya | 6 | 11 | 2 | 482 | 100* | 53.55 | 1 | 3 | - | - |
| R.J.Ratnayake | 4 | 5 | 1 | 193 | 68* | 48.25 | - | 2 | 3 | - |
| P.A.De Silva | 5 | 7 | 1 | 198 | 57* | 33.00 | - | 1 | 4 | - |
| M.S.Atapattu | 5 | 6 | 2 | 132 | 52* | 33.00 | - | 1 | 2 | - |
| D.S.B.P.Kuruppu | 7 | 12 | 0 | 389 | 86 | 32.41 | - | 4 | 3 | - |
| U.C.Hathurusinghe | 6 | 11 | 1 | 311 | 74* | 31.10 | - | 3 | 2 | - |
| H.P.Tillekaratne | 5 | 6 | 1 | 155 | 80* | 31.00 | - | 1 | 9 | - |
| A.P.Gurusinha | 6 | 10 | 0 | 292 | 98 | 29.20 | - | 1 | 2 | - |
| C.P.Ramanayake | 6 | 8 | 2 | 152 | 41* | 25.33 | - | - | 1 | - |
| R.S.Mahanama | 6 | 9 | 0 | 146 | 65 | 16.22 | - | 1 | 9 | - |
| R.S.Kaluwitharana | 3 | 5 | 0 | 73 | 34 | 14.60 | - | - | 2 | - |
| M.A.W.R.Madurasinghe | 3 | 4 | 2 | 28 | 17* | 14.00 | - | - | 1 | - |
| K.I.W.Wijegunawardene | 5 | 6 | 2 | 52 | 26 | 13.00 | - | - | - | - |
| M.Muralitharan | 3 | 4 | 1 | 27 | 22* | 9.00 | - | - | 2 | - |
| S.D.Anurasiri | 4 | 3 | 1 | 17 | 16 | 8.50 | - | - | 1 | - |
| F.S.Ahangama | 3 | 4 | 1 | 7 | 7 | 2.33 | - | - | - | - |

### BOWLING AVERAGES

| Name | Overs | Mdns | Runs | Wkts | Avge | Best | 5wI | 10wM |
|---|---|---|---|---|---|---|---|---|
| A.P.Gurusinha | 18 | 5 | 41 | 2 | 20.50 | 2-16 | - | - |
| R.J.Ratnayake | 137.3 | 15 | 447 | 17 | 26.29 | 6-97 | 2 | - |
| K.I.W.Wijegunaw'dene | 124.3 | 14 | 537 | 15 | 35.80 | 4-97 | - | - |
| U.C.Hathurusinghe | 39.3 | 10 | 110 | 3 | 36.66 | 2-18 | - | - |
| C.P.Ramanayake | 166 | 29 | 594 | 12 | 49.50 | 3-83 | - | - |
| M.A.W.R.Madurasinghe | 82 | 15 | 252 | 5 | 50.40 | 1-13 | - | - |
| S.D.Anurasiri | 208.1 | 53 | 560 | 9 | 62.22 | 3-122 | - | - |
| F.S.Ahangama | 64 | 20 | 189 | 2 | 94.50 | 1-41 | - | - |
| P.A.De Silva | 9 | 2 | 27 | 0 | - | - | - | - |
| S.T.Jayasuriya | 12.5 | 2 | 53 | 0 | - | - | - | - |
| M.Muralitharan | 70.1 | 8 | 210 | 0 | - | - | - | - |

# DERBYSHIRE

## BRITANNIC ASS. CHAMPIONSHIP

**BATTING AVERAGES - Including fielding**

| Name | Matches | Inns | NO | Runs | HS | Avge | 100s | 50s | Ct | St |
|---|---|---|---|---|---|---|---|---|---|---|
| M.Azharuddin | 20 | 35 | 3 | 1773 | 212 | 55.40 | 6 | 9 | 23 | - |
| J.E.Morris | 20 | 35 | 2 | 1267 | 122* | 38.39 | 1 | 8 | 7 | - |
| K.J.Barnett | 21 | 36 | 1 | 1318 | 217 | 37.65 | 2 | 8 | 23 | - |
| E.McCray | 1 | 1 | 0 | 37 | 37 | 37.00 | - | - | 1 | - |
| P.D.Bowler | 22 | 40 | 3 | 1270 | 104* | 34.32 | 2 | 9 | 15 | - |
| T.J.G.O'Gorman | 22 | 39 | 4 | 1060 | 148 | 30.28 | 2 | 4 | 21 | - |
| C.J.Adams | 12 | 19 | 2 | 436 | 112 | 25.64 | 1 | - | 15 | - |
| K.M.Krikken | 22 | 35 | 8 | 677 | 65 | 25.07 | - | 2 | 55 | 3 |
| S.C.Goldsmith | 15 | 25 | 3 | 483 | 73* | 21.95 | - | 2 | 2 | - |
| D.G.Cork | 16 | 25 | 7 | 395 | 44 | 21.94 | - | - | 8 | - |
| A.E.Warner | 14 | 20 | 3 | 289 | 46 | 17.00 | - | - | 3 | - |
| R.W.Sladdin | 7 | 8 | 3 | 68 | 18 | 13.60 | - | - | 6 | - |
| S.J.Base | 13 | 16 | 3 | 136 | 36 | 10.46 | - | - | 14 | - |
| D.E.Malcolm | 11 | 14 | 2 | 84 | 18 | 7.00 | - | - | - | - |
| I.Folley | 3 | 4 | 1 | 20 | 17* | 6.66 | - | - | 2 | - |
| M.Jean-Jacques | 4 | 6 | 1 | 33 | 28 | 6.60 | - | - | - | - |
| O.H.Mortensen | 18 | 16 | 9 | 32 | 8 | 4.57 | - | - | 4 | - |
| F.A.Griffith | 1 | 1 | 0 | 1 | 1 | 1.00 | - | - | - | - |

**BOWLING AVERAGES**

| Name | Overs | Mdns | Runs | Wkts | Avge | Best | 5wI | 10wM |
|---|---|---|---|---|---|---|---|---|
| C.J.Adams | 12.4 | 1 | 48 | 5 | 9.60 | 4-29 | - | - |
| O.H.Mortensen | 535.1 | 138 | 1339 | 58 | 23.08 | 6-101 | 2 | - |
| K.J.Barnett | 162.1 | 33 | 393 | 17 | 23.11 | 6-28 | 1 | - |
| D.G.Cork | 457.3 | 76 | 1350 | 55 | 24.54 | 8-53 | 1 | 1 |
| F.A.Griffith | 15 | 2 | 58 | 2 | 29.00 | 1-16 | - | - |
| D.E.Malcolm | 346.2 | 50 | 1271 | 39 | 32.59 | 5-45 | 1 | - |
| S.C.Goldsmith | 174 | 28 | 576 | 17 | 33.88 | 3-42 | - | - |
| R.W.Sladdin | 315.5 | 76 | 881 | 26 | 33.88 | 5-186 | 1 | - |
| A.E.Warner | 390.4 | 92 | 1066 | 31 | 34.38 | 4-42 | - | - |
| S.J.Base | 386 | 58 | 1248 | 31 | 40.25 | 4-34 | - | - |
| P.D.Bowler | 104 | 18 | 412 | 9 | 45.77 | 3-41 | - | - |
| M.Jean-Jacques | 113.4 | 18 | 437 | 9 | 48.55 | 4-54 | - | - |
| T.J.G.O'Gorman | 15 | 0 | 59 | 1 | 59.00 | 1-17 | - | - |
| M.Azharuddin | 63.4 | 9 | 211 | 3 | 70.33 | 1-35 | - | - |
| I.Folley | 106 | 12 | 350 | 2 | 175.00 | 1-60 | - | - |
| J.E.Morris | 2 | 0 | 30 | 0 | - | - | - | - |
| E.McCray | 25 | 10 | 53 | 0 | - | - | - | - |

## BENSON & HEDGES CUP

**BATTING AVERAGES - Including fielding**

| Name | Matches | Inns | NO | Runs | HS | Avge | 100s | 50s | Ct | St |
|---|---|---|---|---|---|---|---|---|---|---|
| K.J.Barnett | 4 | 4 | 0 | 256 | 102 | 64.00 | 1 | 2 | 3 | - |
| M.Azharuddin | 4 | 4 | 1 | 125 | 44* | 41.66 | - | - | 4 | - |
| T.J.G.O'Gorman | 4 | 3 | 1 | 78 | 49 | 39.00 | - | - | 1 | - |
| P.D.Bowler | 4 | 4 | 0 | 141 | 100 | 35.25 | 1 | - | 6 | - |
| B.Roberts | 4 | 3 | 0 | 75 | 49 | 25.00 | - | - | 2 | - |
| J.E.Morris | 4 | 4 | 0 | 89 | 71 | 22.25 | - | 1 | 1 | - |
| A.E.Warner | 4 | 4 | 2 | 39 | 35* | 19.50 | - | - | - | - |
| D.E.Malcolm | 4 | 3 | 0 | 37 | 15 | 12.33 | - | - | - | - |
| C.J.Adams | 4 | 3 | 1 | 18 | 16* | 9.00 | - | - | 1 | - |
| O.H.Mortensen | 4 | 2 | 1 | 6 | 4* | 6.00 | - | - | - | - |
| S.J.Base | 4 | 2 | 0 | 8 | 7 | 4.00 | - | - | - | - |

**BOWLING AVERAGES**

| Name | Overs | Mdns | Runs | Wkts | Avge | Best | 5wI |
|---|---|---|---|---|---|---|---|
| O.H.Mortensen | 40 | 10 | 115 | 6 | 19.16 | 2-16 | - |
| D.E.Malcolm | 39 | 3 | 151 | 5 | 30.20 | 2-14 | - |
| K.J.Barnett | 29 | 4 | 97 | 3 | 32.33 | 1-28 | - |
| A.E.Warner | 37.3 | 6 | 130 | 4 | 32.50 | 2-57 | - |
| B.Roberts | 13 | 1 | 69 | 2 | 34.50 | 1-11 | - |
| S.J.Base | 36 | 4 | 134 | 3 | 44.66 | 2-40 | - |
| M.Azharuddin | 16 | 0 | 58 | 1 | 58.00 | 1-17 | - |
| T.J.G.O'Gorman | 1 | 0 | 1 | 0 | - | - | - |
| C.J.Adams | 1 | 0 | 3 | 0 | - | - | - |
| J.E.Morris | 4 | 0 | 14 | 0 | - | - | - |

## REFUGE ASSURANCE LEAGUE

**BATTING AVERAGES - Including fielding**

| Name | Matches | Inns | NO | Runs | HS | Avge | 100s | 50s | Ct | St |
|---|---|---|---|---|---|---|---|---|---|---|
| C.J.Adams | 15 | 13 | 2 | 375 | 71 | 34.09 | - | 2 | 4 | - |
| P.D.Bowler | 13 | 13 | 1 | 396 | 77 | 33.00 | - | 2 | 8 | - |
| M.Azharuddin | 15 | 14 | 2 | 371 | 73 | 30.91 | - | 2 | 6 | - |
| K.J.Barnett | 14 | 14 | 4 | 289 | 60* | 28.90 | - | 1 | 6 | - |
| J.E.Morris | 11 | 11 | 0 | 277 | 51 | 25.18 | - | 1 | 2 | - |
| A.E.Warner | 11 | 10 | 2 | 189 | 51 | 23.62 | - | 1 | 4 | - |
| S.C.Goldsmith | 10 | 8 | 1 | 165 | 67* | 23.57 | - | 1 | 4 | - |
| T.J.G.O'Gorman | 16 | 15 | 2 | 293 | 49* | 22.53 | - | - | 7 | - |
| K.M.Krikken | 7 | 4 | 1 | 67 | 44* | 22.33 | - | - | 9 | 3 |
| D.G.Cork | 9 | 5 | 0 | 83 | 30 | 16.60 | - | - | 4 | - |
| F.A.Griffith | 5 | 4 | 1 | 47 | 20 | 15.66 | - | - | - | - |
| D.E.Malcolm | 9 | 6 | 3 | 38 | 18 | 12.66 | - | - | 2 | - |
| M.Jean-Jacques | 3 | 2 | 0 | 23 | 23 | 11.50 | - | - | 1 | - |
| B.Roberts | 5 | 5 | 0 | 44 | 15 | 8.80 | - | - | 1 | - |
| E.McCray | 4 | 4 | 0 | 22 | 18 | 5.50 | - | - | - | - |
| B.J.M.Maher | 2 | 2 | 1 | 4 | 4 | 4.00 | - | - | 2 | - |
| S.J.Base | 15 | 7 | 0 | 21 | 12 | 3.00 | - | - | 5 | - |
| O.H.Mortensen | 10 | 5 | 5 | 13 | 7* | - | - | - | 3 | - |
| I.Folley | 2 | 1 | 1 | 6 | 6* | - | - | - | - | - |

**BOWLING AVERAGES**

| Name | Overs | Mdns | Runs | Wkts | Avge | Best | 5wI |
|---|---|---|---|---|---|---|---|
| P.D.Bowler | 5.2 | 0 | 31 | 3 | 10.33 | 3-31 | - |
| E.McCray | 32 | 0 | 166 | 8 | 20.75 | 4-49 | - |
| D.E.Malcolm | 66 | 2 | 384 | 15 | 25.60 | 3-43 | - |
| K.J.Barnett | 24 | 0 | 105 | 4 | 26.25 | 2-40 | - |
| S.J.Base | 104.5 | 4 | 474 | 18 | 26.33 | 4-14 | - |
| O.H.Mortensen | 80 | 7 | 317 | 12 | 26.41 | 3-29 | - |
| D.G.Cork | 62 | 3 | 291 | 11 | 26.45 | 3-45 | - |
| B.Roberts | 10 | 1 | 61 | 2 | 30.50 | 1-27 | - |
| A.E.Warner | 76.5 | 2 | 429 | 12 | 35.75 | 3-38 | - |
| F.A.Griffith | 23 | 0 | 132 | 3 | 44.00 | 3-37 | - |
| S.C.Goldsmith | 60 | 3 | 345 | 7 | 49.28 | 3-48 | - |
| M.Jean-Jacques | 18 | 1 | 124 | 2 | 62.00 | 2-56 | - |
| M.Azharuddin | 0.5 | 0 | 5 | 0 | - | - | - |
| J.E.Morris | 0.3 | 0 | 7 | 0 | - | - | - |
| I.Folley | 8 | 0 | 54 | 0 | - | - | - |

## NATWEST TROPHY

Derbyshire were eliminated in the first round after a bowling competition.

# ESSEX

## BRITANNIC ASS. CHAMPIONSHIP

### BATTING AVERAGES - Including fielding

| Name | Matches | Inns | NO | Runs | HS | Avge | 100s | 50s | Ct | St |
|---|---|---|---|---|---|---|---|---|---|---|
| Salim Malik | 22 | 33 | 9 | 1891 | 215 | 78.79 | 6 | 8 | 22 | - |
| A.G.J.Fraser | 3 | 2 | 1 | 75 | 52* | 75.00 | - | 1 | - | - |
| G.A.Gooch | 11 | 16 | 1 | 996 | 259 | 66.40 | 3 | 3 | 11 | - |
| D.R.Pringle | 12 | 11 | 6 | 328 | 78* | 65.60 | - | 2 | 4 | - |
| N.Hussain | 22 | 29 | 7 | 1233 | 196 | 56.04 | 3 | 8 | 34 | - |
| N.V.Knight | 6 | 9 | 1 | 388 | 101* | 48.50 | 1 | 2 | 5 | - |
| J.J.B.Lewis | 1 | 1 | 0 | 48 | 48 | 48.00 | - | - | 1 | - |
| M.A.Garnham | 22 | 25 | 6 | 831 | 123 | 43.73 | 2 | 5 | 58 | - |
| P.J.Prichard | 21 | 33 | 5 | 1031 | 190 | 36.82 | 4 | 2 | 17 | - |
| J.P.Stephenson | 22 | 36 | 2 | 1234 | 116 | 36.29 | 3 | 6 | 6 | - |
| A.C.Seymour | 9 | 16 | 1 | 454 | 157 | 30.26 | 1 | 2 | 7 | - |
| N.A.Foster | 20 | 20 | 4 | 474 | 107* | 29.62 | 1 | 1 | 11 | - |
| P.M.Such | 11 | 5 | 4 | 27 | 23* | 27.00 | - | - | 1 | - |
| T.D.Topley | 19 | 19 | 4 | 320 | 50* | 21.33 | - | 2 | 14 | - |
| J.H.Childs | 20 | 13 | 6 | 111 | 41* | 15.85 | - | - | 5 | - |
| N.Shahid | 7 | 8 | 1 | 64 | 22* | 9.14 | - | - | 6 | - |
| S.J.W.Andrew | 14 | 8 | 2 | 30 | 13 | 5.00 | - | - | 4 | - |

### BOWLING AVERAGES

| Name | Overs | Mdns | Runs | Wkts | Avge | Best | 5wI | 10wM |
|---|---|---|---|---|---|---|---|---|
| N.A.Foster | 693.5 | 163 | 2000 | 91 | 21.97 | 8-99 | 7 | 1 |
| J.P.Stephenson | 77.4 | 14 | 296 | 12 | 24.66 | 3-20 | - | - |
| J.H.Childs | 667.1 | 218 | 1702 | 58 | 29.34 | 6-61 | 4 | - |
| D.R.Pringle | 359.4 | 95 | 887 | 30 | 29.56 | 5-70 | 1 | - |
| S.J.W.Andrew | 366.3 | 72 | 1211 | 40 | 30.27 | 4-38 | - | - |
| Salim Malik | 118.2 | 10 | 473 | 15 | 31.53 | 3-26 | - | - |
| P.M.Such | 290 | 75 | 743 | 23 | 32.30 | 3-23 | - | - |
| T.D.Topley | 484.3 | 83 | 1720 | 53 | 32.45 | 5-58 | 3 | - |
| G.A.Gooch | 42.1 | 17 | 155 | 4 | 38.75 | 2-16 | - | - |
| P.J.Prichard | 13.3 | 0 | 158 | 1 | 158.00 | 1-28 | - | - |
| A.C.Seymour | 4 | 0 | 27 | 0 | - | - | - | - |
| N.V.Knight | 5 | 0 | 32 | 0 | - | - | - | - |
| M.A.Garnham | 4 | 0 | 39 | 0 | - | - | - | - |
| A.G.J.Fraser | 19 | 5 | 44 | 0 | - | - | - | - |
| N.Hussain | 8.3 | 0 | 50 | 0 | - | - | - | - |

## BENSON & HEDGES CUP

### BATTING AVERAGES - Including fielding

| Name | Matches | Inns | NO | Runs | HS | Avge | 100s | 50s | Ct | St |
|---|---|---|---|---|---|---|---|---|---|---|
| J.P.Stephenson | 6 | 6 | 0 | 349 | 142 | 58.16 | 1 | 2 | 4 | - |
| Salim Malik | 6 | 6 | 2 | 217 | 90* | 54.25 | - | 2 | 1 | - |
| G.A.Gooch | 6 | 6 | 0 | 202 | 72 | 33.66 | - | 1 | 3 | - |
| N.A.Foster | 6 | 3 | 1 | 60 | 39* | 30.00 | - | - | - | - |
| D.R.Pringle | 6 | 5 | 2 | 77 | 36* | 25.66 | - | - | 1 | - |
| P.J.Prichard | 6 | 6 | 1 | 111 | 38 | 22.20 | - | - | 3 | - |
| N.Shahid | 6 | 4 | 0 | 51 | 42 | 12.75 | - | - | 1 | - |
| N.Hussain | 6 | 5 | 1 | 46 | 26 | 11.50 | - | - | 2 | - |
| M.A.Garnham | 6 | 4 | 1 | 27 | 11 | 9.00 | - | - | 7 | 1 |
| T.D.Topley | 3 | 2 | 1 | 7 | 6* | 7.00 | - | - | 1 | - |
| P.M.Such | 6 | 2 | 1 | 5 | 4 | 5.00 | - | - | 1 | - |
| M.C.Ilott | 3 | 0 | 0 | 0 | 0 | | | | | |

### BOWLING AVERAGES

| Name | Overs | Mdns | Runs | Wkts | Avge | Best | 5wI |
|---|---|---|---|---|---|---|---|
| Salim Malik | 2 | 0 | 7 | 1 | 7.00 | 1-7 | - |
| D.R.Pringle | 56.2 | 6 | 191 | 12 | 15.91 | 5-51 | 1 |
| M.C.Ilott | 31 | 6 | 101 | 5 | 20.20 | 3-34 | - |
| N.A.Foster | 61 | 8 | 185 | 7 | 26.42 | 2-28 | - |
| T.D.Topley | 28 | 4 | 124 | 4 | 31.00 | 4-41 | - |
| G.A.Gooch | 56 | 2 | 235 | 7 | 33.57 | 2-19 | - |
| J.P.Stephenson | 11 | 0 | 57 | 1 | 57.00 | 1-17 | - |
| P.M.Such | 58 | 4 | 232 | 4 | 58.00 | 2-52 | - |

## REFUGE ASSURANCE LEAGUE

### BATTING AVERAGES - Including fielding

| Name | Matches | Inns | NO | Runs | HS | Avge | 100s | 50s | Ct | St |
|---|---|---|---|---|---|---|---|---|---|---|
| N.A.Foster | 7 | 6 | 4 | 148 | 57 | 74.00 | - | 1 | 1 | - |
| G.A.Gooch | 8 | 7 | 1 | 358 | 107 | 59.66 | 1 | 3 | 3 | - |
| Salim Malik | 11 | 11 | 1 | 451 | 89 | 45.10 | - | 3 | 6 | - |
| N.V.Knight | 2 | 2 | 1 | 31 | 31* | 31.00 | - | - | 2 | - |
| J.P.Stephenson | 14 | 13 | 0 | 399 | 67 | 30.69 | - | 3 | 7 | - |
| D.R.Pringle | 10 | 8 | 2 | 176 | 51* | 29.33 | - | 1 | 3 | - |
| N.Hussain | 14 | 12 | 3 | 256 | 48 | 28.44 | - | - | 4 | - |
| P.J.Prichard | 13 | 11 | 1 | 248 | 54* | 24.80 | - | 1 | 7 | - |
| N.Shahid | 11 | 6 | 1 | 103 | 36 | 20.60 | - | - | 3 | - |
| J.J.B.Lewis | 1 | 1 | 0 | 19 | 19 | 19.00 | - | - | - | - |
| T.D.Topley | 14 | 6 | 2 | 50 | 38* | 12.50 | - | - | 2 | - |
| A.C.Seymour | 5 | 4 | 0 | 46 | 25 | 11.50 | - | - | 1 | - |
| M.A.Garnham | 13 | 9 | 3 | 67 | 18* | 11.16 | - | - | 10 | 3 |
| S.J.W.Andrew | 8 | 3 | 1 | 14 | 8 | 7.00 | - | - | - | - |
| D.E.East | 1 | 1 | 0 | 2 | 2 | 2.00 | - | - | - | - |
| K.A.Butler | 2 | 1 | 0 | 1 | 1 | 1.00 | - | - | 1 | - |
| M.C.Ilott | 2 | 1 | 0 | 0 | 0 | 0.00 | - | - | 1 | - |
| P.M.Such | 13 | 3 | 3 | 4 | 2* | | - | - | 2 | - |
| J.H.Childs | 2 | 0 | 0 | 0 | 0 | | - | - | - | - |
| A.G.J.Fraser | 2 | 0 | 0 | 0 | 0 | | - | - | 1 | - |
| G.Lovell | 1 | 0 | 0 | 0 | 0 | | - | - | - | - |

### BOWLING AVERAGES

| Name | Overs | Mdns | Runs | Wkts | Avge | Best | 5wI |
|---|---|---|---|---|---|---|---|
| J.P.Stephenson | 51 | 2 | 194 | 13 | 14.92 | 4-17 | - |
| M.C.Ilott | 14 | 1 | 54 | 3 | 18.00 | 2-26 | - |
| J.H.Childs | 16 | 1 | 62 | 3 | 20.66 | 2-35 | - |
| T.D.Topley | 95.5 | 5 | 469 | 20 | 23.45 | 3-29 | - |
| D.R.Pringle | 62.4 | 2 | 301 | 12 | 25.08 | 3-43 | - |
| N.A.Foster | 41 | 1 | 161 | 6 | 26.83 | 3-28 | - |
| G.A.Gooch | 43 | 2 | 175 | 6 | 29.16 | 3-25 | - |
| S.J.W.Andrew | 49 | 3 | 253 | 8 | 31.62 | 3-33 | - |
| P.M.Such | 86 | 3 | 423 | 13 | 32.53 | 4-30 | - |
| A.G.J.Fraser | 14 | 0 | 54 | 1 | 54.00 | 1-21 | - |
| Salim Malik | 18.2 | 1 | 71 | 1 | 71.00 | 1-25 | - |
| G.Lovell | 6 | 0 | 34 | 0 | - | - | - |

## NATWEST TROPHY

### BATTING AVERAGES - Including fielding

| Name | Matches | Inns | NO | Runs | HS | Avge | 100s | 50s | Ct | St |
|---|---|---|---|---|---|---|---|---|---|---|
| G.A.Gooch | 3 | 3 | 0 | 202 | 95 | 67.33 | - | 3 | - | - |
| N.Hussain | 3 | 2 | 0 | 114 | 97 | 57.00 | - | 1 | 4 | - |
| J.P.Stephenson | 3 | 3 | 0 | 117 | 59 | 39.00 | - | 2 | - | - |
| Salim Malik | 3 | 3 | 1 | 55 | 26 | 27.50 | - | - | 4 | - |
| M.A.Garnham | 3 | 2 | 1 | 21 | 12* | 21.00 | - | - | 3 | - |
| N.A.Foster | 3 | 2 | 1 | 19 | 10* | 19.00 | - | - | 1 | - |
| P.J.Prichard | 3 | 3 | 1 | 38 | 27* | 19.00 | - | - | 1 | - |
| D.R.Pringle | 3 | 2 | 0 | 21 | 19 | 10.50 | - | - | 1 | - |
| T.D.Topley | 3 | 1 | 0 | 7 | 7 | 7.00 | - | - | - | - |
| A.C.Seymour | 1 | 1 | 0 | 0 | 0 | 0.00 | - | - | 1 | - |
| J.H.Childs | 1 | 0 | 0 | 0 | 0 | | - | - | - | - |
| N.Shahid | 1 | 0 | 0 | 0 | 0 | | - | - | 1 | - |
| P.M.Such | 3 | 1 | 1 | 0 | 0* | | | | | |

### BOWLING AVERAGES

| Name | Overs | Mdns | Runs | Wkts | Avge | Best | 5wI |
|---|---|---|---|---|---|---|---|
| T.D.Topley | 34 | 6 | 103 | 6 | 17.16 | 3-38 | - |
| D.R.Pringle | 34 | 3 | 127 | 7 | 18.14 | 3-21 | - |
| P.M.Such | 36 | 2 | 102 | 5 | 20.40 | 2-29 | - |
| J.H.Childs | 11.4 | 4 | 43 | 2 | 21.50 | 2-43 | - |
| G.A.Gooch | 18 | 3 | 67 | 3 | 22.33 | 2-30 | - |
| N.A.Foster | 31.5 | 6 | 127 | 4 | 31.75 | 2-57 | - |
| Salim Malik | 6 | 0 | 34 | 0 | - | - | - |
| J.P.Stephenson | 6 | 0 | 36 | 0 | - | - | - |

# GLAMORGAN

## BRITANNIC ASS. CHAMPIONSHIP

### BATTING AVERAGES - Including fielding

| Name | Matches | Inns | NO | Runs | HS | Avge | 100s | 50s | Ct | St |
|------|---------|------|-----|------|-----|------|------|-----|-----|-----|
| H.Morris | 17 | 30 | 7 | 1601 | 156* | 69.60 | 5 | 8 | 13 | - |
| M.P.Maynard | 20 | 32 | 5 | 1766 | 243 | 65.40 | 7 | 5 | 14 | - |
| R.J.Shastri | 21 | 31 | 8 | 1056 | 133* | 45.91 | 2 | 6 | 8 | - |
| A.R.Butcher | 21 | 37 | 1 | 1558 | 147 | 43.27 | 4 | 12 | 13 | - |
| A.Dale | 15 | 23 | 3 | 711 | 140 | 35.55 | 1 | 3 | 7 | - |
| S.P.James | 10 | 17 | 3 | 429 | 70 | 30.64 | - | 2 | 8 | - |
| C.P.Metson | 22 | 24 | 3 | 511 | 84 | 24.33 | - | 2 | 67 | 2 |
| P.A.Cottey | 11 | 16 | 5 | 259 | 55 | 23.54 | - | 1 | 9 | - |
| I.Smith | 8 | 11 | 2 | 196 | 39 | 21.77 | - | - | 7 | - |
| G.C.Holmes | 6 | 8 | 1 | 136 | 54 | 19.42 | - | 1 | 1 | - |
| S.L.Watkin | 18 | 15 | 8 | 123 | 25* | 17.57 | - | - | 2 | - |
| R.D.B.Croft | 22 | 25 | 4 | 331 | 50 | 15.76 | - | 1 | 10 | - |
| D.L.Hemp | 1 | 2 | 1 | 12 | 8 | 12.00 | - | - | - | - |
| S.Bastien | 11 | 6 | 3 | 26 | 22* | 8.66 | - | - | 1 | - |
| S.R.Barwick | 11 | 9 | 1 | 64 | 24* | 8.00 | - | - | 1 | - |
| D.J.Foster | 8 | 9 | 3 | 35 | 13* | 5.83 | - | - | 3 | - |
| M.Frost | 18 | 11 | 4 | 19 | 8* | 2.71 | - | - | 1 | - |
| S.J.Dennis | 1 | 2 | 0 | 3 | 3 | 1.50 | - | - | - | - |
| M.J.Cann | 1 | 1 | 1 | 29 | 29* | - | - | - | 1 | - |

### BOWLING AVERAGES

| Name | Overs | Mdns | Runs | Wkts | Avge | Best | 5wI | 10wM |
|------|-------|------|------|------|------|------|-----|------|
| R.J.Shastri | 288.5 | 80 | 704 | 27 | 26.07 | 5-71 | 1 | - |
| S.R.Barwick | 296.5 | 79 | 726 | 26 | 27.92 | 4-46 | - | - |
| S.L.Watkin | 639.5 | 137 | 1848 | 66 | 28.00 | 6-55 | 4 | - |
| M.Frost | 497.2 | 84 | 1728 | 61 | 28.32 | 7-99 | 1 | 1 |
| D.J.Foster | 210.5 | 34 | 753 | 24 | 31.37 | 6-84 | 1 | - |
| I.Smith | 36.1 | 7 | 132 | 3 | 44.00 | 1-7 | - | - |
| R.D.B.Croft | 646.2 | 151 | 1777 | 34 | 52.26 | 5-62 | 1 | - |
| A.Dale | 106.1 | 22 | 380 | 7 | 54.28 | 2-33 | - | - |
| S.Bastien | 329.2 | 89 | 946 | 17 | 55.64 | 5-39 | 1 | - |
| A.R.Butcher | 2 | 1 | 1 | 0 | - | - | - | - |
| M.P.Maynard | 4.5 | 0 | 34 | 0 | - | - | - | - |
| M.J.Cann | 8 | 0 | 37 | 0 | - | - | - | - |
| S.J.Dennis | 12 | 1 | 49 | 0 | - | - | - | - |

## BENSON & HEDGES CUP

### BATTING AVERAGES - Including fielding

| Name | Matches | Inns | NO | Runs | HS | Avge | 100s | 50s | Ct | St |
|------|---------|------|-----|------|-----|------|------|-----|-----|-----|
| R.J.Shastri | 3 | 3 | 1 | 161 | 138* | 80.50 | 1 | - | 1 | - |
| A.R.Butcher | 4 | 4 | 0 | 279 | 127 | 69.75 | 1 | 2 | 1 | - |
| G.C.Holmes | 4 | 4 | 1 | 92 | 35* | 30.66 | - | - | - | - |
| S.J.Dennis | 3 | 2 | 0 | 55 | 50 | 27.50 | - | 1 | - | - |
| M.P.Maynard | 4 | 4 | 0 | 94 | 62 | 23.50 | - | 1 | 2 | - |
| I.Smith | 4 | 4 | 0 | 90 | 51 | 22.50 | - | 1 | 1 | - |
| A.Dale | 1 | 1 | 0 | 19 | 19 | 19.00 | - | - | - | - |
| S.L.Watkin | 4 | 3 | 1 | 25 | 15 | 12.50 | - | - | - | - |
| H.Morris | 4 | 4 | 0 | 43 | 36 | 10.75 | - | - | - | - |
| M.L.Roberts | 3 | 3 | 1 | 2 | 1* | 1.00 | - | - | 2 | - |
| R.D.B.Croft | 1 | 1 | 0 | 0 | 0 | 0.00 | - | - | - | - |
| M.Frost | 4 | 2 | 1 | 0 | 0* | 0.00 | - | - | - | - |
| C.P.Metson | 1 | 1 | 0 | 0 | 0 | 0.00 | - | - | - | - |
| S.R.Barwick | 4 | 2 | 2 | 5 | 4* | - | - | - | 3 | - |

### BOWLING AVERAGES

| Name | Overs | Mdns | Runs | Wkts | Avge | Best | 5wI |
|------|-------|------|------|------|------|------|-----|
| R.D.B.Croft | 9 | 0 | 49 | 2 | 24.50 | 2-49 | - |
| M.Frost | 40 | 6 | 177 | 5 | 35.40 | 3-38 | - |
| S.L.Watkin | 44 | 7 | 190 | 5 | 38.00 | 3-28 | - |
| S.R.Barwick | 39 | 4 | 175 | 4 | 43.75 | 2-61 | - |
| R.J.Shastri | 32 | 1 | 124 | 2 | 62.00 | 1-40 | - |
| I.Smith | 10 | 0 | 69 | 1 | 69.00 | 1-51 | - |
| A.R.Butcher | 3 | 0 | 16 | 0 | - | - | - |
| A.Dale | 4 | 0 | 30 | 0 | - | - | - |
| S.J.Dennis | 33 | 3 | 119 | 0 | - | - | - |

## REFUGE ASSURANCE LEAGUE

### BATTING AVERAGES - Including fielding

| Name | Matches | Inns | NO | Runs | HS | Avge | 100s | 50s | Ct | St |
|------|---------|------|-----|------|-----|------|------|-----|-----|-----|
| P.A.Cottey | 7 | 7 | 3 | 233 | 92* | 58.25 | - | 1 | 1 | - |
| G.C.Holmes | 9 | 8 | 2 | 240 | 72 | 40.00 | - | 2 | 3 | - |
| H.Morris | 13 | 13 | 0 | 433 | 75 | 33.30 | - | 3 | 6 | - |
| A.R.Butcher | 11 | 11 | 1 | 329 | 77 | 32.90 | - | 3 | 3 | - |
| M.P.Maynard | 15 | 15 | 1 | 458 | 101 | 32.71 | 1 | 3 | 9 | - |
| R.J.Shastri | 13 | 13 | 2 | 342 | 90* | 31.09 | - | 2 | 3 | - |
| I.Smith | 11 | 11 | 3 | 244 | 41 | 30.50 | - | - | 3 | - |
| A.Dale | 14 | 11 | 2 | 213 | 56 | 23.66 | - | 1 | 6 | - |
| S.P.James | 2 | 2 | 0 | 34 | 23 | 17.00 | - | - | 1 | - |
| C.P.Metson | 15 | 10 | 4 | 97 | 20 | 16.16 | - | - | 12 | 2 |
| J.Derrick | 4 | 4 | 1 | 39 | 25 | 13.00 | - | - | - | - |
| S.L.Watkin | 12 | 7 | 1 | 55 | 31* | 9.16 | - | - | 1 | - |
| D.L.Hemp | 1 | 1 | 0 | 7 | 7 | 7.00 | - | - | - | - |
| R.D.B.Croft | 10 | 6 | 0 | 35 | 19 | 5.83 | - | - | 3 | - |
| S.R.Barwick | 15 | 8 | 4 | 23 | 8 | 5.75 | - | - | 3 | - |
| S.J.Dennis | 3 | 2 | 0 | 9 | 6 | 4.50 | - | - | 2 | - |
| M.J.Cann | 2 | 2 | 0 | 4 | 2 | 2.00 | - | - | - | - |
| D.J.Foster | 4 | 3 | 2 | 2 | 2* | 2.00 | - | - | 1 | - |
| M.Frost | 10 | 3 | 2 | 2 | 2 | 2.00 | - | - | 3 | - |
| S.Kirnon | 1 | 1 | 0 | 0 | 0 | 0.00 | - | - | - | - |
| S.Bastien | 3 | 0 | 0 | 0 | 0 | - | - | - | - | - |
| M.L.Roberts | 1 | 0 | 0 | 0 | 0 | - | - | - | 1 | - |

### BOWLING AVERAGES

| Name | Overs | Mdns | Runs | Wkts | Avge | Best | 5wI |
|------|-------|------|------|------|------|------|-----|
| J.Derrick | 14.2 | 0 | 79 | 5 | 15.80 | 4-25 | - |
| D.J.Foster | 26 | 0 | 112 | 6 | 18.66 | 3-30 | - |
| S.L.Watkin | 83 | 4 | 382 | 16 | 23.87 | 3-30 | - |
| S.Kirnon | 8 | 0 | 48 | 2 | 24.00 | 2-48 | - |
| M.Frost | 70 | 2 | 357 | 14 | 25.50 | 3-35 | - |
| A.Dale | 72 | 1 | 430 | 13 | 33.07 | 3-44 | - |
| R.D.B.Croft | 69 | 2 | 333 | 10 | 33.30 | 2-30 | - |
| R.J.Shastri | 51 | 1 | 241 | 7 | 34.42 | 3-26 | - |
| S.R.Barwick | 81.1 | 0 | 441 | 12 | 36.75 | 3-30 | - |
| S.Bastien | 14 | 0 | 79 | 2 | 39.50 | 2-42 | - |
| I.Smith | 28 | 0 | 158 | 4 | 39.50 | 2-35 | - |
| S.J.Dennis | 18 | 0 | 95 | 1 | 95.00 | 1-36 | - |
| M.P.Maynard | 1 | 0 | 2 | 0 | - | - | - |
| G.C.Holmes | 1.5 | 0 | 24 | 0 | - | - | - |
| A.R.Butcher | 5.1 | 0 | 36 | 0 | - | - | - |

## NATWEST TROPHY

### BATTING AVERAGES - Including fielding

| Name | Matches | Inns | NO | Runs | HS | Avge | 100s | 50s | Ct | St |
|------|---------|------|-----|------|-----|------|------|-----|-----|-----|
| M.P.Maynard | 3 | 3 | 2 | 256 | 151* | 256.00 | 1 | 1 | - | - |
| H.Morris | 3 | 3 | 1 | 203 | 126* | 101.50 | 1 | - | 1 | - |
| A.Dale | 3 | 2 | 0 | 101 | 86 | 50.50 | - | 1 | 2 | - |
| A.R.Butcher | 3 | 3 | 0 | 87 | 70 | 29.00 | - | 1 | 2 | - |
| R.J.Shastri | 2 | 2 | 0 | 51 | 26 | 25.50 | - | - | 2 | - |
| P.A.Cottey | 2 | 2 | 1 | 13 | 10 | 13.00 | - | - | - | - |
| R.D.B.Croft | 2 | 1 | 0 | 13 | 13 | 13.00 | - | - | - | - |
| C.P.Metson | 3 | 1 | 0 | 9 | 9 | 9.00 | - | - | 3 | - |
| S.R.Barwick | 3 | 1 | 0 | 3 | 3 | 3.00 | - | - | - | - |
| M.Frost | 3 | 1 | 0 | 3 | 3 | 3.00 | - | - | 3 | - |
| S.L.Watkin | 3 | 1 | 1 | 5 | 5* | - | - | - | 1 | - |
| J.Derrick | 1 | 0 | 0 | 0 | 0 | - | - | - | - | - |
| I.Smith | 2 | 0 | 0 | 0 | 0 | - | - | - | 1 | - |

### BOWLING AVERAGES

| Name | Overs | Mdns | Runs | Wkts | Avge | Best | 5wI |
|------|-------|------|------|------|------|------|-----|
| I.Smith | 9 | 0 | 60 | 3 | 20.00 | 3-60 | - |
| R.D.B.Croft | 17 | 0 | 46 | 2 | 23.00 | 2-28 | - |
| S.L.Watkin | 36 | 2 | 116 | 4 | 29.00 | 2-40 | - |
| R.J.Shastri | 12 | 0 | 60 | 2 | 30.00 | 2-60 | - |
| S.R.Barwick | 33 | 0 | 153 | 5 | 30.60 | 2-51 | - |
| J.Derrick | 12 | 0 | 59 | 1 | 59.00 | 1-59 | - |
| M.Frost | 31 | 2 | 137 | 2 | 68.50 | 1-45 | - |
| A.Dale | 30 | 2 | 115 | 1 | 115.00 | 1-42 | - |

# GLOUCESTERSHIRE

## BRITANNIC ASS. CHAMPIONSHIP

### BATTING AVERAGES - Including fielding

| Name | Matches | Inns | NO | Runs | HS | Avge | 100s | 50s | Ct | St |
|---|---|---|---|---|---|---|---|---|---|---|
| A.J.Wright | 22 | 38 | 6 | 1477 | 120 | 46.15 | 3 | 9 | 16 | - |
| C.W.J.Athey | 22 | 36 | 5 | 1350 | 127 | 43.54 | 4 | 9 | 15 | - |
| R.C.Russell | 12 | 19 | 3 | 464 | 111 | 29.00 | 1 | 2 | 37 | 2 |
| M.W.Alleyne | 22 | 35 | 3 | 921 | 165 | 28.78 | 1 | 4 | 10 | - |
| G.D.Hodgson | 21 | 37 | 1 | 990 | 89 | 27.50 | - | 7 | 7 | - |
| R.J.Scott | 17 | 30 | 1 | 763 | 127 | 26.31 | 2 | 3 | 6 | - |
| J.W.Lloyds | 22 | 33 | 4 | 729 | 69 | 25.13 | - | 7 | 21 | - |
| T.Hancock | 3 | 5 | 1 | 83 | 51 | 20.75 | - | 1 | 5 | - |
| J.J.E.Hardy | 10 | 15 | 2 | 242 | 52 | 18.61 | - | 1 | - | - |
| D.V.Lawrence | 15 | 22 | 1 | 383 | 66 | 18.23 | - | 1 | 4 | - |
| A.M.Babington | 15 | 19 | 7 | 176 | 58 | 14.66 | - | 1 | 7 | - |
| D.R.Gilbert | 20 | 26 | 6 | 292 | 28* | 14.60 | - | - | 5 | - |
| M.C.J.Ball | 5 | 8 | 0 | 105 | 28 | 13.12 | - | - | 5 | - |
| M.J.Gerrard | 7 | 8 | 4 | 49 | 42 | 12.25 | - | - | 2 | - |
| R.C.J.Williams | 10 | 12 | 2 | 95 | 55* | 9.50 | - | 1 | 18 | 3 |
| P.W.Romaines | 3 | 5 | 0 | 35 | 28 | 7.00 | - | - | 1 | - |
| R.C.Williams | 1 | 2 | 0 | 13 | 13 | 6.50 | - | - | - | - |
| A.M.Smith | 13 | 13 | 2 | 60 | 22 | 5.45 | - | - | - | - |
| J.M.De La Pena | 2 | 2 | 1 | 1 | 1* | 1.00 | - | - | - | - |

### BOWLING AVERAGES

| Name | Overs | Mdns | Runs | Wkts | Avge | Best | 5wI | 10wM |
|---|---|---|---|---|---|---|---|---|
| D.V.Lawrence | 398.5 | 62 | 1296 | 60 | 21.60 | 6-67 | 3 | 1 |
| M.C.J.Ball | 178 | 34 | 547 | 18 | 30.38 | 5-128 | 1 | - |
| D.R.Gilbert | 602.2 | 131 | 1695 | 55 | 30.81 | 8-55 | 1 | - |
| A.M.Smith | 284.2 | 51 | 868 | 28 | 31.00 | 4-41 | - | - |
| M.W.Alleyne | 118.1 | 23 | 381 | 11 | 34.63 | 3-35 | - | - |
| A.M.Babington | 428.2 | 70 | 1300 | 35 | 37.14 | 4-33 | - | - |
| R.J.Scott | 175 | 38 | 545 | 14 | 38.92 | 3-43 | - | - |
| J.W.Lloyds | 510.2 | 121 | 1493 | 33 | 45.24 | 6-94 | 1 | - |
| J.M.De La Pena | 25 | 0 | 138 | 3 | 46.00 | 2-69 | - | - |
| M.J.Gerrard | 106.4 | 16 | 355 | 5 | 71.00 | 2-25 | - | - |
| R.C.Williams | 26 | 4 | 81 | 1 | 81.00 | 1-81 | - | - |
| C.W.J.Athey | 60 | 8 | 179 | 2 | 89.50 | 1-18 | - | - |
| A.J.Wright | 0.3 | 0 | 4 | 0 | - | - | - | - |
| R.C.Russell | 0.3 | 0 | 10 | 0 | - | - | - | - |

## BENSON & HEDGES CUP

### BATTING AVERAGES - Including fielding

| Name | Matches | Inns | NO | Runs | HS | Avge | 100s | 50s | Ct | St |
|---|---|---|---|---|---|---|---|---|---|---|
| A.J.Wright | 4 | 4 | 0 | 175 | 81 | 43.75 | - | 1 | - | - |
| C.W.J.Athey | 4 | 4 | 1 | 108 | 81 | 36.00 | - | 1 | 2 | - |
| R.C.Russell | 4 | 4 | 1 | 85 | 51 | 28.33 | - | 1 | 4 | - |
| D.V.Lawrence | 4 | 3 | 1 | 51 | 23 | 25.50 | - | - | - | - |
| R.J.Scott | 4 | 4 | 0 | 99 | 46 | 24.75 | - | - | - | - |
| P.W.Romaines | 1 | 1 | 0 | 22 | 22 | 22.00 | - | - | 1 | - |
| J.W.Lloyds | 3 | 2 | 0 | 43 | 24 | 21.50 | - | - | 2 | - |
| A.M.Smith | 4 | 3 | 2 | 12 | 8 | 12.00 | - | - | 1 | - |
| D.R.Gilbert | 4 | 3 | 0 | 25 | 16 | 8.33 | - | - | - | - |
| A.M.Babington | 4 | 3 | 1 | 13 | 8 | 6.50 | - | - | 1 | - |
| G.D.Hodgson | 3 | 3 | 0 | 19 | 9 | 6.33 | - | - | 1 | - |
| J.J.E.Hardy | 1 | 1 | 0 | 6 | 6 | 6.00 | - | - | - | - |
| M.W.Alleyne | 4 | 3 | 0 | 7 | 6 | 2.33 | - | - | 2 | - |

### BOWLING AVERAGES

| Name | Overs | Mdns | Runs | Wkts | Avge | Best | 5wI |
|---|---|---|---|---|---|---|---|
| J.W.Lloyds | 9 | 2 | 14 | 3 | 4.66 | 3-14 | - |
| D.V.Lawrence | 44 | 7 | 137 | 13 | 10.53 | 6-20 | 1 |
| A.M.Babington | 40 | 9 | 111 | 3 | 37.00 | 2-49 | - |
| D.R.Gilbert | 44 | 5 | 138 | 3 | 46.00 | 1-31 | - |
| A.M.Smith | 33 | 2 | 95 | 2 | 47.50 | 1-30 | - |
| M.W.Alleyne | 15 | 0 | 67 | 1 | 67.00 | 1-24 | - |
| R.J.Scott | 16.5 | 0 | 81 | 1 | 81.00 | 1-42 | - |

## REFUGE ASSURANCE LEAGUE

### BATTING AVERAGES - Including fielding

| Name | Matches | Inns | NO | Runs | HS | Avge | 100s | 50s | Ct | St |
|---|---|---|---|---|---|---|---|---|---|---|
| M.W.Alleyne | 15 | 14 | 2 | 409 | 76* | 34.08 | - | 2 | 1 | - |
| A.J.Wright | 15 | 14 | 1 | 414 | 71 | 31.84 | - | 3 | 3 | - |
| R.J.Scott | 14 | 14 | 1 | 376 | 77 | 28.92 | - | 3 | - | - |
| A.M.Smith | 13 | 7 | 6 | 27 | 15* | 27.00 | - | - | 3 | - |
| C.W.J.Athey | 15 | 15 | 1 | 352 | 85 | 25.14 | - | 2 | 8 | - |
| J.J.E.Hardy | 9 | 8 | 1 | 171 | 54 | 24.42 | - | 1 | 2 | - |
| P.W.Romaines | 6 | 4 | 2 | 47 | 27* | 23.50 | - | - | 1 | - |
| R.C.Russell | 11 | 11 | 1 | 214 | 42 | 21.40 | - | - | 15 | 1 |
| D.V.Lawrence | 8 | 7 | 2 | 82 | 38* | 16.40 | - | 1 | - | - |
| J.W.Lloyds | 12 | 9 | 1 | 116 | 42* | 14.50 | - | 4 | - | - |
| E.T.Milburn | 3 | 3 | 0 | 34 | 21 | 11.33 | - | - | 1 | - |
| A.M.Babington | 13 | 5 | 1 | 27 | 11 | 6.75 | - | 3 | - | - |
| T.Hancock | 5 | 3 | 0 | 20 | 20 | 6.66 | - | - | 1 | - |
| D.R.Gilbert | 11 | 5 | 2 | 17 | 10* | 5.66 | - | 1 | - | - |
| M.J.Gerrard | 4 | 4 | 1 | 17 | 7 | 5.66 | - | - | - | - |
| M.C.J.Ball | 8 | 5 | 1 | 14 | 5 | 3.50 | - | - | 3 | - |
| S.N.Barnes | 1 | 0 | 0 | 0 | 0 | - | - | - | - | - |
| R.C.J.Williams | 2 | 0 | 0 | 0 | 0 | - | - | - | - | - |

### BOWLING AVERAGES

| Name | Overs | Mdns | Runs | Wkts | Avge | Best | 5wI |
|---|---|---|---|---|---|---|---|
| A.M.Smith | 66.4 | 2 | 378 | 15 | 25.20 | 3-16 | - |
| D.V.Lawrence | 55 | 1 | 285 | 11 | 25.90 | 4-27 | - |
| A.M.Babington | 88.4 | 3 | 426 | 14 | 30.42 | 4-53 | - |
| S.N.Barnes | 8 | 0 | 33 | 1 | 33.00 | 1-33 | - |
| M.W.Alleyne | 65 | 1 | 344 | 10 | 34.40 | 2-19 | - |
| J.W.Lloyds | 12 | 0 | 75 | 2 | 37.50 | 2-47 | - |
| R.J.Scott | 62 | 2 | 303 | 8 | 37.87 | 2-26 | - |
| C.W.J.Athey | 14 | 0 | 79 | 2 | 39.50 | 2-18 | - |
| M.J.Gerrard | 29 | 3 | 164 | 3 | 54.66 | 1-35 | - |
| D.R.Gilbert | 77.4 | 1 | 391 | 6 | 65.16 | 2-27 | - |
| M.C.J.Ball | 34.5 | 0 | 174 | 0 | - | - | - |

## NATWEST TROPHY

### BATTING AVERAGES - Including fielding

| Name | Matches | Inns | NO | Runs | HS | Avge | 100s | 50s | Ct | St |
|---|---|---|---|---|---|---|---|---|---|---|
| C.W.J.Athey | 2 | 2 | 1 | 123 | 76 | 123.00 | - | 1 | - | - |
| J.J.E.Hardy | 2 | 2 | 0 | 93 | 70 | 46.50 | - | 1 | - | - |
| A.J.Wright | 2 | 2 | 0 | 67 | 56 | 33.50 | - | 1 | - | - |
| M.W.Alleyne | 2 | 2 | 0 | 48 | 45 | 24.00 | - | - | - | - |
| R.C.Russell | 2 | 2 | 0 | 48 | 25 | 24.00 | - | - | 5 | 1 |
| J.W.Lloyds | 2 | 2 | 1 | 17 | 13* | 17.00 | - | - | 2 | - |
| G.D.Hodgson | 1 | 1 | 0 | 7 | 7 | 7.00 | - | - | 1 | - |
| R.J.Scott | 2 | 2 | 0 | 11 | 11 | 5.50 | - | - | - | - |
| D.V.Lawrence | 2 | 2 | 2 | 7 | 5* | - | - | - | - | - |
| A.M.Babington | 1 | 0 | 0 | 0 | 0 | - | - | - | - | - |
| D.R.Gilbert | 1 | 0 | 0 | 0 | 0 | - | - | - | 1 | - |
| A.M.Smith | 2 | 0 | 0 | 0 | 0 | - | - | - | - | - |
| M.J.Gerrard | 1 | 0 | 0 | 0 | 0 | - | - | - | - | - |

### BOWLING AVERAGES

| Name | Overs | Mdns | Runs | Wkts | Avge | Best | 5wI |
|---|---|---|---|---|---|---|---|
| R.J.Scott | 22.2 | 3 | 54 | 6 | 9.00 | 4-22 | - |
| D.V.Lawrence | 21 | 3 | 65 | 7 | 9.28 | 5-17 | 1 |
| D.R.Gilbert | 12 | 0 | 41 | 2 | 20.50 | 2-41 | - |
| A.M.Smith | 16 | 2 | 63 | 2 | 31.50 | 1-14 | - |
| M.J.Gerrard | 2 | 0 | 10 | 0 | - | - | - |
| A.M.Babington | 6 | 0 | 17 | 0 | - | - | - |
| J.W.Lloyds | 14 | 1 | 39 | 0 | - | - | - |

# HAMPSHIRE

## BRITANNIC ASS. CHAMPIONSHIP

### BATTING AVERAGES - Including fielding

| Name | Matches | Inns | NO | Runs | HS | Avge | 100s | 50s | Ct | St |
|------|---------|------|----|------|-----|------|------|-----|----|----|
| C.L.Smith | 15 | 26 | 3 | 1353 | 145 | 58.82 | 5 | 7 | 3 | - |
| K.D.James | 22 | 35 | 9 | 1216 | 134 * | 46.76 | 2 | 6 | 8 | - |
| R.A.Smith | 10 | 20 | 0 | 852 | 107 | 42.60 | 1 | 7 | 12 | - |
| V.P.Terry | 18 | 32 | 2 | 1226 | 171 | 40.86 | 2 | 7 | 23 | - |
| D.I.Gower | 22 | 37 | 5 | 1132 | 80 * | 35.37 | - | 8 | 13 | - |
| M.C.J.Nicholas | 20 | 34 | 9 | 723 | 107 * | 28.92 | 1 | 4 | 8 | - |
| T.C.Middleton | 16 | 28 | 1 | 766 | 102 | 28.37 | 1 | 2 | 14 | - |
| A.N Aymes | 22 | 28 | 6 | 587 | 53 | 26.68 | - | 1 | 45 | 2 |
| J.R.Ayling | 9 | 13 | 2 | 269 | 58 | 24.45 | - | 1 | 3 | - |
| R.M.F.Cox | 2 | 2 | 0 | 41 | 26 | 20.50 | - | - | 1 | - |
| R.J.Maru | 20 | 25 | 3 | 369 | 61 | 16.77 | - | 1 | 29 | - |
| I.J.Turner | 8 | 10 | 4 | 87 | 39 * | 14.50 | - | - | 3 | - |
| J.R.Wood | 2 | 2 | 0 | 25 | 25 | 12.50 | - | - | - | - |
| C.A.Connor | 14 | 15 | 0 | 148 | 30 | 9.86 | - | - | 3 | - |
| K.J.Shine | 15 | 17 | 8 | 80 | 25 | 8.88 | - | - | 2 | - |
| Aqib Javed | 17 | 12 | 8 | 25 | 15 * | 6.25 | - | - | - | - |
| P.J.Bakker | 9 | 6 | 2 | 17 | 6 * | 4.25 | - | - | 2 | - |
| T.M.Tremlett | 1 | 1 | 0 | 2 | 2 | 2.00 | - | - | - | - |

### BOWLING AVERAGES

| Name | Overs | Mdns | Runs | Wkts | Avge | Best | 5wI | 10wM |
|------|-------|------|------|------|------|------|-----|------|
| T.C.Middleton | 12 | 2 | 77 | 3 | 25.66 | 2-41 | - | - |
| J.R.Ayling | 185.5 | 36 | 555 | 21 | 26.42 | 4-47 | - | - |
| Aqib Javed | 485.1 | 81 | 1586 | 53 | 29.92 | 6-91 | 3 | - |
| R.A.Smith | 18 | 3 | 97 | 3 | 32.33 | 2-20 | - | - |
| K.D.James | 396.5 | 85 | 1219 | 37 | 32.94 | 4-32 | - | - |
| P.J.Bakker | 209.3 | 52 | 595 | 18 | 33.05 | 4-66 | - | - |
| K.J.Shine | 316.5 | 44 | 1350 | 37 | 36.48 | 5-43 | 2 | - |
| C.A.Connor | 331 | 58 | 1128 | 29 | 38.89 | 4-49 | - | - |
| T.M.Tremlett | 10 | 3 | 39 | 1 | 39.00 | 1-39 | - | - |
| R.J.Maru | 570.1 | 159 | 1534 | 34 | 45.11 | 5-128 | 1 | - |
| I.J.Turner | 238.5 | 65 | 637 | 14 | 45.50 | 4-28 | - | - |
| M.C.J.Nicholas | 67.5 | 6 | 288 | 4 | 72.00 | 3-25 | - | - |
| D.I.Gower | 0.1 | 0 | 4 | 0 | - | - | - | - |
| J.R.Wood | 6 | 0 | 17 | 0 | - | - | - | - |
| C.L.Smith | 19 | 3 | 63 | 0 | - | - | - | - |

## BENSON & HEDGES CUP

### BATTING AVERAGES - Including fielding

| Name | Matches | Inns | NO | Runs | HS | Avge | 100s | 50s | Ct | St |
|------|---------|------|----|------|-----|------|------|-----|----|----|
| C.L.Smith | 5 | 5 | 2 | 413 | 142 | 137.66 | 2 | 2 | 1 | - |
| M.C.J.Nicholas | 5 | 4 | 2 | 87 | 50 | 43.50 | - | 1 | - | - |
| T.C.Middleton | 4 | 4 | 0 | 156 | 60 | 39.00 | - | 2 | 3 | - |
| R.A.Smith | 1 | 1 | 0 | 35 | 35 | 35.00 | - | - | 1 | - |
| J.R.Wood | 4 | 4 | 1 | 90 | 70 * | 30.00 | - | 1 | 3 | - |
| D.I.Gower | 5 | 5 | 0 | 97 | 63 | 19.40 | - | 1 | 1 | - |
| J.R.Ayling | 4 | 3 | 2 | 10 | 5 * | 10.00 | - | - | 2 | - |
| V.P.Terry | 1 | 1 | 0 | 10 | 10 | 10.00 | - | - | - | - |
| A.N Aymes | 5 | 2 | 0 | 12 | 10 | 6.00 | - | - | 4 | 4 |
| P.J.Bakker | 4 | 2 | 0 | 11 | 7 | 5.50 | - | - | 1 | - |
| S.D.Udal | 5 | 2 | 0 | 10 | 9 | 5.00 | - | - | 2 | - |
| Aqib Javed | 5 | 2 | 1 | 3 | 3 | 3.00 | - | - | - | - |
| K.D.James | 2 | 1 | 0 | 2 | 2 | 2.00 | - | - | - | - |
| C.A.Connor | 5 | 2 | 0 | 3 | 3 | 1.50 | - | - | 3 | - |

### BOWLING AVERAGES

| Name | Overs | Mdns | Runs | Wkts | Avge | Best | 5wI |
|------|-------|------|------|------|------|------|-----|
| M.C.J.Nicholas | 4 | 0 | 27 | 2 | 13.50 | 2-27 | - |
| S.D.Udal | 55 | 9 | 189 | 9 | 21.00 | 3-41 | - |
| Aqib Javed | 53 | 6 | 208 | 9 | 23.11 | 3-43 | - |
| C.A.Connor | 55 | 4 | 272 | 10 | 27.20 | 3-54 | - |
| P.J.Bakker | 44 | 6 | 146 | 4 | 36.50 | 2-37 | - |
| J.R.Ayling | 42 | 0 | 186 | 4 | 46.50 | 2-56 | - |
| K.D.James | 22 | 0 | 100 | 1 | 100.00 | 1-45 | - |

## REFUGE ASSURANCE LEAGUE

### BATTING AVERAGES - Including fielding

| Name | Matches | Inns | NO | Runs | HS | Avge | 100s | 50s | Ct | St |
|------|---------|------|----|------|-----|------|------|-----|----|----|
| C.L.Smith | 8 | 8 | 0 | 397 | 114 | 49.62 | 1 | 2 | 3 | - |
| A.N Aymes | 13 | 11 | 7 | 169 | 33 * | 42.25 | - | - | 13 | 3 |
| M.C.J.Nicholas | 16 | 15 | 4 | 462 | 65 * | 42.00 | - | 3 | 4 | - |
| R.J.Maru | 7 | 4 | 2 | 63 | 33 * | 31.50 | - | - | 4 | - |
| V.P.Terry | 15 | 14 | 1 | 408 | 123 | 31.38 | 1 | 1 | 5 | - |
| T.C.Middleton | 6 | 6 | 0 | 162 | 56 | 27.00 | - | 1 | - | - |
| J.R.Ayling | 13 | 12 | 3 | 206 | 56 | 22.88 | - | 1 | 4 | - |
| J.R.Wood | 11 | 10 | 0 | 204 | 54 | 20.40 | - | 1 | 2 | - |
| R.A.Smith | 7 | 6 | 0 | 117 | 75 | 19.50 | - | 1 | 2 | - |
| K.D.James | 13 | 12 | 2 | 176 | 58 * | 17.60 | - | 1 | 3 | - |
| S.D.Udal | 16 | 7 | 3 | 66 | 23 | 16.50 | - | - | 4 | - |
| D.I.Gower | 8 | 7 | 0 | 111 | 45 | 15.85 | - | - | 4 | - |
| T.M.Tremlett | 3 | 2 | 1 | 13 | 8 | 13.00 | - | - | - | - |
| C.A.Connor | 14 | 4 | 1 | 28 | 18 | 9.33 | - | - | 2 | - |
| R.M.F.Cox | 2 | 2 | 0 | 15 | 13 | 7.50 | - | - | 1 | - |
| R.J.Parks | 3 | 2 | 0 | 14 | 8 | 7.00 | - | - | 1 | - |
| P.J.Bakker | 5 | 1 | 0 | 4 | 4 | 4.00 | - | - | - | - |
| Aqib Javed | 12 | 2 | 2 | 5 | 4 * | - | - | - | 1 | - |
| K.J.Shine | 4 | 1 | 1 | 2 | 2 * | - | - | - | - | - |

### BOWLING AVERAGES

| Name | Overs | Mdns | Runs | Wkts | Avge | Best | 5wI |
|------|-------|------|------|------|------|------|-----|
| K.J.Shine | 27 | 0 | 102 | 5 | 20.40 | 2-35 | - |
| C.A.Connor | 103.3 | 1 | 481 | 18 | 26.72 | 4-29 | - |
| K.D.James | 66 | 3 | 304 | 11 | 27.63 | 3-24 | - |
| S.D.Udal | 119.2 | 6 | 594 | 17 | 34.94 | 3-40 | - |
| J.R.Ayling | 91 | 2 | 512 | 14 | 36.57 | 3-25 | - |
| Aqib Javed | 92.1 | 4 | 423 | 10 | 42.30 | 3-50 | - |
| T.M.Tremlett | 22.1 | 0 | 90 | 2 | 45.00 | 1-27 | - |
| P.J.Bakker | 40 | 2 | 186 | 4 | 46.50 | 2-36 | - |
| R.J.Maru | 36 | 1 | 170 | 3 | 56.66 | 1-27 | - |
| M.C.J.Nicholas | 5 | 0 | 42 | 0 | - | - | - |

## NATWEST TROPHY

### BATTING AVERAGES - Including fielding

| Name | Matches | Inns | NO | Runs | HS | Avge | 100s | 50s | Ct | St |
|------|---------|------|----|------|-----|------|------|-----|----|----|
| R.A.Smith | 5 | 5 | 3 | 331 | 79 * | 165.50 | - | 4 | - | - |
| C.L.Smith | 4 | 3 | 1 | 194 | 105 * | 97.00 | 1 | 1 | 1 | - |
| T.C.Middleton | 1 | 1 | 0 | 78 | 78 | 78.00 | - | 1 | - | - |
| V.P.Terry | 5 | 5 | 2 | 209 | 62 * | 69.66 | - | 1 | 4 | - |
| D.I.Gower | 5 | 3 | 1 | 82 | 54 * | 41.00 | - | 1 | - | - |
| A.N Aymes | 5 | 1 | 0 | 2 | 2 | 2.00 | - | - | 6 | 1 |
| K.D.James | 3 | 1 | 0 | 0 | 0 | 0.00 | - | - | 1 | - |
| M.C.J.Nicholas | 4 | 1 | 1 | 24 | 24 * | - | - | - | 2 | - |
| J.R.Ayling | 3 | 1 | 1 | 18 | 18 * | - | - | - | 2 | - |
| R.J.Maru | 4 | 1 | 1 | 1 | 1 * | - | - | - | 3 | - |
| P.J.Bakker | 1 | 0 | 0 | 0 | 0 | - | - | - | - | - |
| C.A.Connor | 5 | 0 | 0 | 0 | 0 | - | - | - | 2 | - |
| S.D.Udal | 5 | 0 | 0 | 0 | 0 | - | - | - | 2 | - |
| Aqib Javed | 5 | 0 | 0 | 0 | 0 | - | - | - | 2 | - |

### BOWLING AVERAGES

| Name | Overs | Mdns | Runs | Wkts | Avge | Best | 5wI |
|------|-------|------|------|------|------|------|-----|
| C.A.Connor | 51.1 | 6 | 182 | 15 | 12.13 | 4-29 | - |
| Aqib Javed | 52.5 | 4 | 213 | 8 | 26.62 | 4-51 | - |
| S.D.Udal | 50 | 3 | 191 | 6 | 31.83 | 3-47 | - |
| J.R.Ayling | 36 | 0 | 151 | 4 | 37.75 | 2-39 | - |
| R.J.Maru | 42 | 7 | 122 | 3 | 40.66 | 2-20 | - |
| K.D.James | 22 | 3 | 97 | 1 | 97.00 | 1-50 | - |
| M.C.J.Nicholas | 2 | 0 | 9 | 0 | - | - | - |
| P.J.Bakker | 4 | 1 | 15 | 0 | - | - | - |

# KENT

## BRITANNIC ASS. CHAMPIONSHIP

### BATTING AVERAGES - Including fielding

| Name | Matches | Inns | NO | Runs | HS | Avge | 100s | 50s | Ct | St |
|------|---------|------|----|----|----|----|----|----|----|----|
| N.R.Taylor | 22 | 34 | 3 | 1647 | 203* | 53.12 | 6 | 7 | 14 | - |
| M.R.Benson | 20 | 30 | 2 | 1329 | 257 | 47.46 | 4 | 6 | 9 | - |
| T.R.Ward | 20 | 31 | 2 | 1369 | 235* | 47.20 | 4 | 6 | 9 | - |
| C.S.Cowdrey | 3 | 4 | 0 | 154 | 97 | 38.50 | - | 1 | 1 | - |
| G.R.Cowdrey | 21 | 32 | 4 | 1064 | 114 | 38.00 | 2 | 5 | 17 | - |
| S.A.Marsh | 21 | 29 | 5 | 823 | 113* | 34.29 | 2 | 4 | 61 | 4 |
| M.V.Fleming | 18 | 29 | 3 | 734 | 113 | 28.23 | 1 | 5 | 14 | - |
| S.G.Hinks | 8 | 12 | 2 | 236 | 61* | 23.60 | - | 2 | 6 | - |
| R.M.Ellison | 16 | 24 | 7 | 397 | 61* | 23.35 | - | 3 | 8 | - |
| M.A.Ealham | 3 | 5 | 0 | 96 | 36 | 19.20 | - | - | 3 | - |
| C.Penn | 17 | 20 | 4 | 299 | 52 | 18.68 | - | 1 | 6 | - |
| R.P.Davis | 18 | 23 | 4 | 338 | 44 | 17.78 | - | - | 22 | - |
| M.J.McCague | 8 | 10 | 2 | 142 | 29 | 17.75 | - | - | 1 | - |
| M.M.Patel | 5 | 7 | 2 | 76 | 43 | 15.20 | - | - | 2 | - |
| N.J.Llong | 3 | 6 | 2 | 54 | 42* | 13.50 | - | - | 3 | - |
| T.A.Merrick | 18 | 22 | 6 | 198 | 36 | 12.37 | - | - | 3 | - |
| V.J.Wells | 2 | 3 | 0 | 29 | 28 | 9.66 | - | - | 1 | - |
| A.P.Igglesden | 18 | 16 | 3 | 100 | 16* | 7.69 | - | - | 3 | - |
| G.J.Kersey | 1 | 1 | 1 | 27 | 27* | - | - | - | 5 | - |

### BOWLING AVERAGES

| Name | Overs | Mdns | Runs | Wkts | Avge | Best | 5wI | 10wM |
|------|-------|------|------|------|------|------|-----|------|
| M.A.Ealham | 98.1 | 20 | 274 | 15 | 18.26 | 5-39 | 2 | - |
| C.Penn | 407.4 | 79 | 1216 | 52 | 23.38 | 5-43 | 3 | - |
| A.P.Igglesden | 449 | 86 | 1288 | 48 | 26.83 | 5-36 | 1 | - |
| T.A.Merrick | 517 | 100 | 1688 | 58 | 29.10 | 7-99 | 1 | - |
| M.J.McCague | 153.3 | 23 | 481 | 16 | 30.06 | 6-88 | 1 | - |
| R.M.Ellison | 457.1 | 99 | 1375 | 45 | 30.55 | 7-33 | 2 | - |
| M.M.Patel | 183.2 | 43 | 458 | 13 | 35.23 | 3-33 | - | - |
| T.R.Ward | 17 | 4 | 40 | 1 | 40.00 | 1-20 | - | - |
| R.P.Davis | 455.2 | 117 | 1325 | 32 | 41.40 | 4-81 | - | - |
| M.V.Fleming | 184 | 41 | 498 | 12 | 41.50 | 3-28 | - | - |
| G.R.Cowdrey | 2 | 1 | 6 | 0 | - | - | - | - |
| N.R.Taylor | 3 | 0 | 26 | 0 | - | - | - | - |
| N.J.Llong | 5 | 1 | 28 | 0 | - | - | - | - |
| S.A.Marsh | 5 | 0 | 28 | 0 | - | - | - | - |
| M.R.Benson | 13 | 0 | 44 | 0 | - | - | - | - |

## BENSON & HEDGES CUP

### BATTING AVERAGES - Including fielding

| Name | Matches | Inns | NO | Runs | HS | Avge | 100s | 50s | Ct | St |
|------|---------|------|----|----|----|----|----|----|----|----|
| S.A.Marsh | 3 | 3 | 1 | 118 | 71 | 59.00 | - | 1 | 5 | - |
| N.R.Taylor | 5 | 5 | 1 | 230 | 110 | 57.50 | 1 | 1 | 2 | - |
| M.R.Benson | 5 | 5 | 0 | 228 | 76 | 45.60 | - | 3 | - | - |
| T.R.Ward | 5 | 5 | 0 | 165 | 87 | 33.00 | - | 1 | 2 | - |
| A.P.Igglesden | 5 | 2 | 1 | 29 | 26* | 29.00 | - | - | 1 | - |
| G.R.Cowdrey | 5 | 5 | 1 | 111 | 70* | 27.75 | - | 1 | 1 | - |
| T.A.Merrick | 5 | 3 | 2 | 26 | 22* | 26.00 | - | - | 1 | - |
| C.S.Cowdrey | 5 | 5 | 1 | 97 | 57* | 24.25 | - | 1 | 4 | - |
| M.V.Fleming | 5 | 5 | 0 | 90 | 52 | 18.00 | - | 1 | - | - |
| V.J.Wells | 2 | 2 | 0 | 32 | 25 | 16.00 | - | - | 2 | - |
| M.J.McCague | 2 | 1 | 0 | 12 | 12 | 12.00 | - | - | - | - |
| R.M.Ellison | 5 | 4 | 1 | 34 | 15 | 11.33 | - | - | 1 | - |
| R.P.Davis | 1 | 1 | 0 | 1 | 1 | 1.00 | - | - | - | - |
| M.A.Ealham | 2 | 1 | 1 | 0 | 0* | - | - | - | 2 | - |

### BOWLING AVERAGES

| Name | Overs | Mdns | Runs | Wkts | Avge | Best | 5wI |
|------|-------|------|------|------|------|------|-----|
| C.S.Cowdrey | 5 | 1 | 17 | 2 | 8.50 | 2-17 | - |
| M.J.McCague | 18 | 2 | 85 | 4 | 21.25 | 2-32 | - |
| A.P.Igglesden | 50.5 | 7 | 224 | 10 | 22.40 | 3-24 | - |
| M.V.Fleming | 44 | 0 | 170 | 5 | 34.00 | 2-52 | - |
| T.A.Merrick | 50 | 2 | 207 | 6 | 34.50 | 2-31 | - |
| R.M.Ellison | 52 | 7 | 199 | 5 | 39.80 | 2-19 | - |
| M.A.Ealham | 19 | 1 | 78 | 1 | 78.00 | 1-46 | - |
| R.P.Davis | 11 | 1 | 62 | 0 | - | - | - |

## REFUGE ASSURANCE LEAGUE

### BATTING AVERAGES - Including fielding

| Name | Matches | Inns | NO | Runs | HS | Avge | 100s | 50s | Ct | St |
|------|---------|------|----|----|----|----|----|----|----|----|
| R.M.Ellison | 8 | 7 | 5 | 102 | 29* | 51.00 | - | - | 2 | - |
| N.R.Taylor | 14 | 14 | 1 | 467 | 82* | 35.92 | - | 4 | 1 | - |
| C.S.Cowdrey | 7 | 6 | 1 | 154 | 45 | 30.80 | - | - | 4 | - |
| M.R.Benson | 14 | 14 | 0 | 422 | 84 | 30.14 | - | 3 | 6 | - |
| T.R.Ward | 14 | 14 | 2 | 347 | 62* | 28.91 | - | 3 | 5 | - |
| S.A.Marsh | 14 | 13 | 3 | 269 | 59 | 26.90 | - | 3 | 9 | 1 |
| M.V.Fleming | 14 | 14 | 0 | 336 | 77 | 24.00 | - | 2 | 5 | - |
| G.R.Cowdrey | 15 | 14 | 0 | 327 | 80 | 23.35 | - | 2 | 9 | - |
| S.G.Hinks | 5 | 5 | 0 | 99 | 35 | 19.80 | - | - | 1 | - |
| R.P.Davis | 14 | 11 | 5 | 108 | 40* | 18.00 | - | - | 7 | - |
| M.J.McCague | 8 | 5 | 2 | 39 | 17* | 13.00 | - | - | 1 | - |
| N.J.Llong | 3 | 3 | 0 | 36 | 23 | 12.00 | - | - | - | - |
| M.A.Ealham | 5 | 5 | 1 | 46 | 18 | 11.50 | - | - | - | - |
| T.A.Merrick | 12 | 6 | 4 | 23 | 13* | 11.50 | - | - | - | - |
| A.P.Igglesden | 14 | 5 | 3 | 18 | 13* | 9.00 | - | - | 3 | - |
| V.J.Wells | 1 | 1 | 0 | 8 | 8 | 8.00 | - | - | - | - |
| J.I.Longley | 1 | 1 | 0 | 1 | 1 | 1.00 | - | - | 1 | - |
| C.Penn | 1 | 0 | 0 | 0 | 0 | - | - | - | 1 | - |
| T.N.Wren | 1 | 1 | 1 | 0 | 0* | - | - | - | - | - |

### BOWLING AVERAGES

| Name | Overs | Mdns | Runs | Wkts | Avge | Best | 5wI |
|------|-------|------|------|------|------|------|-----|
| A.P.Igglesden | 109 | 6 | 461 | 23 | 20.04 | 4-59 | - |
| M.A.Ealham | 38 | 0 | 178 | 7 | 25.42 | 3-36 | - |
| M.J.McCague | 59 | 0 | 349 | 11 | 31.72 | 4-51 | - |
| R.P.Davis | 105 | 5 | 485 | 15 | 32.33 | 3-33 | - |
| T.N.Wren | 5 | 0 | 33 | 1 | 33.00 | 1-33 | - |
| M.V.Fleming | 102.3 | 1 | 576 | 17 | 33.88 | 4-45 | - |
| R.M.Ellison | 52 | 1 | 272 | 7 | 38.85 | 2-29 | - |
| C.Penn | 6 | 0 | 56 | 1 | 56.00 | 1-56 | - |
| T.A.Merrick | 89.2 | 3 | 463 | 6 | 77.16 | 1-16 | - |
| N.J.Llong | 3 | 0 | 17 | 0 | - | - | - |
| C.S.Cowdrey | 3 | 0 | 37 | 0 | - | - | - |

## NATWEST TROPHY

### BATTING AVERAGES - Including fielding

| Name | Matches | Inns | NO | Runs | HS | Avge | 100s | 50s | Ct | St |
|------|---------|------|----|----|----|----|----|----|----|----|
| M.V.Fleming | 2 | 2 | 1 | 56 | 35* | 56.00 | - | - | - | - |
| T.R.Ward | 2 | 2 | 0 | 75 | 55 | 37.50 | - | 1 | - | - |
| S.G.Hinks | 1 | 1 | 0 | 34 | 34 | 34.00 | - | - | - | - |
| G.R.Cowdrey | 2 | 2 | 1 | 25 | 25* | 25.00 | - | - | - | - |
| N.R.Taylor | 2 | 2 | 0 | 46 | 44 | 23.00 | - | - | - | - |
| M.R.Benson | 2 | 2 | 0 | 35 | 21 | 17.50 | - | - | - | - |
| S.A.Marsh | 2 | 1 | 0 | 15 | 15 | 15.00 | - | - | 3 | - |
| M.J.McCague | 1 | 1 | 0 | 9 | 9 | 9.00 | - | - | - | - |
| R.P.Davis | 2 | 1 | 0 | 2 | 2 | 2.00 | - | - | 1 | - |
| C.S.Cowdrey | 1 | 1 | 0 | 0 | 0 | 0.00 | - | - | 1 | - |
| T.A.Merrick | 2 | 1 | 0 | 0 | 0 | 0.00 | - | - | 2 | - |
| C.Penn | 2 | 1 | 1 | 20 | 20* | - | - | - | - | - |
| A.P.Igglesden | 1 | 0 | 0 | 0 | 0 | - | - | - | 1 | - |

### BOWLING AVERAGES

| Name | Overs | Mdns | Runs | Wkts | Avge | Best | 5wI |
|------|-------|------|------|------|------|------|-----|
| A.P.Igglesden | 9.2 | 1 | 29 | 4 | 7.25 | 4-29 | - |
| T.A.Merrick | 21 | 4 | 74 | 3 | 24.66 | 3-27 | - |
| R.P.Davis | 20 | 4 | 56 | 2 | 28.00 | 1-22 | - |
| C.Penn | 18 | 4 | 69 | 2 | 34.50 | 1-14 | - |
| M.V.Fleming | 12.2 | 1 | 44 | 1 | 44.00 | 1-6 | - |
| G.R.Cowdrey | 4 | 0 | 19 | 0 | - | - | - |
| M.J.McCague | 7 | 0 | 47 | 0 | - | - | - |

# LANCASHIRE

## BRITANNIC ASS. CHAMPIONSHIP

### BATTING AVERAGES - Including fielding

| Name | Matches | Inns | NO | Runs | HS | Avge | 100s | 50s | Ct | St |
|---|---|---|---|---|---|---|---|---|---|---|
| M.A.Atherton | 8 | 13 | 3 | 603 | 114 * | 60.30 | 2 | 2 | 7 | - |
| J.P.Crawley | 2 | 4 | 0 | 230 | 130 | 57.50 | 1 | 1 | 7 | - |
| N.H.Fairbrother | 17 | 26 | 5 | 1011 | 121 | 48.14 | 5 | 3 | 18 | - |
| S.P.Titchard | 7 | 13 | 1 | 464 | 135 | 38.66 | 1 | 2 | 7 | - |
| G.D.Mendis | 22 | 41 | 4 | 1223 | 119 | 33.05 | 3 | 3 | 7 | - |
| W.K.Hegg | 21 | 31 | 7 | 758 | 97 | 31.58 | - | 3 | 39 | 3 |
| G.Fowler | 18 | 31 | 2 | 865 | 113 | 29.82 | 2 | 2 | 1 | - |
| N.J.Speak | 17 | 31 | 2 | 806 | 153 | 27.79 | 1 | 2 | 7 | - |
| Wasim Akram | 14 | 19 | 2 | 471 | 122 | 27.70 | 1 | 1 | 5 | - |
| I.D.Austin | 12 | 16 | 4 | 315 | 101 * | 26.25 | 1 | 1 | 4 | - |
| G.D.Lloyd | 17 | 28 | 0 | 720 | 96 | 25.71 | - | 5 | 10 | - |
| G.Yates | 18 | 24 | 12 | 292 | 100 * | 24.33 | 1 | - | 7 | - |
| M.Watkinson | 20 | 33 | 3 | 713 | 114 * | 23.76 | 1 | 3 | 8 | - |
| J.D.Fitton | 6 | 10 | 1 | 201 | 60 | 22.33 | - | 1 | - | - |
| P.A.J.DeFreitas | 11 | 16 | 1 | 325 | 60 | 21.66 | - | 2 | - | - |
| D.P.Hughes | 8 | 9 | 3 | 111 | 51 | 18.50 | - | 1 | 4 | - |
| P.J.Martin | 15 | 13 | 8 | 85 | 29 | 17.00 | - | - | 4 | - |
| P.J.W.Allott | 8 | 8 | 2 | 63 | 26 | 10.50 | - | - | 4 | - |
| J.Stanworth | 1 | 0 | 0 | 0 | 0 | - | - | - | 1 | 1 |

### BOWLING AVERAGES

| Name | Overs | Mdns | Runs | Wkts | Avge | Best | 5wI | 10wM |
|---|---|---|---|---|---|---|---|---|
| N.J.Speak | 0.1 | 0 | 0 | 1 | 0.00 | 1-0 | - | - |
| Wasim Akram | 429.3 | 99 | 1251 | 56 | 22.33 | 6-66 | 7 | 1 |
| P.A.J.DeFreitas | 394.2 | 95 | 1127 | 39 | 28.89 | 6-88 | 2 | - |
| P.J.Martin | 422.4 | 99 | 1262 | 33 | 38.24 | 4-30 | - | - |
| P.J.W.Allott | 173.1 | 43 | 489 | 12 | 40.75 | 4-56 | - | - |
| G.Fowler | 7 | 0 | 41 | 1 | 41.00 | 1-41 | - | - |
| M.Watkinson | 603.2 | 107 | 2116 | 51 | 41.49 | 4-45 | - | - |
| D.P.Hughes | 85.2 | 21 | 245 | 5 | 49.00 | 2-7 | - | - |
| G.D.Lloyd | 10 | 0 | 57 | 1 | 57.00 | 1-57 | - | - |
| I.D.Austin | 237.2 | 42 | 787 | 12 | 65.58 | 3-58 | - | - |
| G.Yates | 529.4 | 97 | 1770 | 26 | 68.07 | 3-47 | - | - |
| J.D.Fitton | 187.1 | 30 | 691 | 8 | 86.37 | 2-89 | - | - |

## BENSON & HEDGES CUP

### BATTING AVERAGES - Including fielding

| Name | Matches | Inns | NO | Runs | HS | Avge | 100s | 50s | Ct | St |
|---|---|---|---|---|---|---|---|---|---|---|
| G.D.Mendis | 7 | 7 | 1 | 366 | 125 * | 61.00 | 1 | 2 | 4 | - |
| M.Watkinson | 5 | 5 | 3 | 94 | 32 * | 47.00 | - | - | 1 | - |
| G.Fowler | 7 | 7 | 0 | 320 | 136 | 45.71 | 1 | 2 | 2 | - |
| N.H.Fairbrother | 7 | 7 | 2 | 225 | 53 * | 45.00 | - | 2 | 5 | - |
| M.A.Atherton | 7 | 7 | 0 | 282 | 91 | 40.28 | - | 3 | 3 | - |
| Wasim Akram | 6 | 4 | 2 | 71 | 45 * | 35.50 | - | - | - | - |
| G.D.Lloyd | 3 | 3 | 2 | 17 | 10 | 17.00 | - | - | - | - |
| P.A.J.DeFreitas | 7 | 2 | 0 | 31 | 19 | 15.50 | - | - | 5 | - |
| I.D.Austin | 7 | 2 | 0 | 29 | 22 | 14.50 | - | - | 1 | - |
| W.K.Hegg | 7 | 2 | 1 | 13 | 13 * | 13.00 | - | - | 6 | - |
| P.J.W.Allott | 7 | 2 | 0 | 10 | 10 | 5.00 | - | - | 5 | - |
| D.P.Hughes | 2 | 1 | 1 | 1 | 1 * | - | - | - | 1 | - |
| J.D.Fitton | 1 | 0 | 0 | 0 | 0 | - | - | - | - | - |
| N.J.Speak | 1 | 0 | 0 | 0 | 0 | - | - | - | - | - |
| G.Yates | 3 | 0 | 0 | 0 | 0 | - | - | - | 1 | - |

### BOWLING AVERAGES

| Name | Overs | Mdns | Runs | Wkts | Avge | Best | 5wI |
|---|---|---|---|---|---|---|---|
| P.A.J.DeFreitas | 73.1 | 13 | 235 | 14 | 16.78 | 4-15 | - |
| P.J.W.Allott | 74 | 17 | 200 | 11 | 18.18 | 4-23 | - |
| M.Watkinson | 54.4 | 4 | 221 | 12 | 18.41 | 5-49 | 1 |
| Wasim Akram | 61 | 5 | 246 | 11 | 22.36 | 4-18 | - |
| G.Yates | 22 | 3 | 85 | 2 | 42.50 | 2-50 | - |
| J.D.Fitton | 11 | 0 | 47 | 1 | 47.00 | 1-47 | - |
| I.D.Austin | 72 | 2 | 319 | 6 | 53.16 | 2-50 | - |

## REFUGE ASSURANCE LEAGUE

### BATTING AVERAGES - Including fielding

| Name | Matches | Inns | NO | Runs | HS | Avge | 100s | 50s | Ct | St |
|---|---|---|---|---|---|---|---|---|---|---|
| N.J.Speak | 7 | 5 | 2 | 155 | 94 * | 51.66 | - | 1 | 3 | - |
| W.K.Hegg | 18 | 8 | 5 | 152 | 47 * | 50.66 | - | - | 22 | 1 |
| N.H.Fairbrother | 17 | 16 | 5 | 451 | 62 | 41.00 | - | 2 | 6 | - |
| G.D.Lloyd | 18 | 18 | 4 | 519 | 79 * | 37.07 | - | 4 | 4 | - |
| G.Fowler | 17 | 17 | 1 | 572 | 59 | 35.75 | - | 3 | 2 | - |
| G.D.Mendis | 14 | 14 | 0 | 344 | 79 | 24.57 | - | 1 | 3 | - |
| M.Watkinson | 17 | 14 | 0 | 315 | 83 | 22.50 | - | 2 | 5 | - |
| J.D.Fitton | 2 | 2 | 1 | 22 | 14 * | 22.00 | - | - | - | - |
| M.A.Atherton | 9 | 9 | 1 | 171 | 48 | 21.37 | - | - | 5 | - |
| Wasim Akram | 16 | 13 | 4 | 179 | 38 | 19.88 | - | - | 2 | - |
| P.A.J.DeFreitas | 11 | 9 | 3 | 105 | 41 * | 17.50 | - | - | 1 | - |
| I.D.Austin | 18 | 7 | 2 | 83 | 48 | 16.60 | - | - | 3 | - |
| S.P.Titchard | 1 | 1 | 0 | 13 | 13 | 13.00 | - | - | - | - |
| P.J.W.Allott | 17 | 5 | 5 | 20 | 10 * | - | - | - | 2 | - |
| D.P.Hughes | 6 | 1 | 1 | 4 | 4 * | - | - | - | 3 | - |
| P.J.Martin | 6 | 0 | 0 | 0 | 0 | - | - | - | - | - |
| G.Yates | 4 | 0 | 0 | 0 | 0 | - | - | - | - | - |

### BOWLING AVERAGES

| Name | Overs | Mdns | Runs | Wkts | Avge | Best | 5wI |
|---|---|---|---|---|---|---|---|
| I.D.Austin | 124.3 | 3 | 660 | 29 | 22.75 | 5-56 | 1 |
| M.Watkinson | 122 | 1 | 644 | 22 | 29.27 | 3-27 | - |
| P.A.J.DeFreitas | 84 | 5 | 369 | 12 | 30.75 | 3-27 | - |
| J.D.Fitton | 16 | 0 | 98 | 3 | 32.66 | 2-67 | - |
| P.J.W.Allott | 121 | 8 | 481 | 11 | 43.72 | 2-30 | - |
| Wasim Akram | 117.5 | 1 | 620 | 13 | 47.69 | 2-30 | - |
| P.J.Martin | 39 | 1 | 174 | 3 | 58.00 | 2-38 | - |
| G.Yates | 20 | 1 | 125 | 2 | 62.50 | 2-45 | - |
| D.P.Hughes | 6 | 0 | 33 | 0 | - | - | - |

## NATWEST TROPHY

### BATTING AVERAGES - Including fielding

| Name | Matches | Inns | NO | Runs | HS | Avge | 100s | 50s | Ct | St |
|---|---|---|---|---|---|---|---|---|---|---|
| N.H.Fairbrother | 2 | 2 | 0 | 92 | 68 | 46.00 | - | 1 | - | - |
| G.Fowler | 2 | 2 | 0 | 80 | 71 | 40.00 | - | 1 | - | - |
| Wasim Akram | 2 | 2 | 1 | 40 | 29 | 40.00 | - | - | - | - |
| G.D.Lloyd | 1 | 1 | 0 | 39 | 39 | 39.00 | - | - | - | - |
| M.A.Atherton | 1 | 1 | 0 | 38 | 38 | 38.00 | - | - | - | - |
| G.D.Mendis | 2 | 2 | 0 | 55 | 50 | 27.50 | - | 1 | 1 | - |
| P.A.J.DeFreitas | 2 | 2 | 1 | 17 | 11 | 17.00 | - | - | 1 | - |
| W.K.Hegg | 2 | 1 | 0 | 7 | 7 | 7.00 | - | - | 4 | - |
| M.Watkinson | 2 | 2 | 0 | 12 | 7 | 6.00 | - | - | - | - |
| P.J.W.Allott | 1 | 1 | 0 | 2 | 2 | 2.00 | - | - | - | - |
| I.D.Austin | 2 | 1 | 0 | 2 | 2 | 2.00 | - | - | - | - |
| D.P.Hughes | 2 | 1 | 1 | 5 | 5 * | - | - | - | 3 | - |
| P.J.Martin | 1 | 0 | 0 | 0 | 0 | - | - | - | - | - |

### BOWLING AVERAGES

| Name | Overs | Mdns | Runs | Wkts | Avge | Best | 5wI |
|---|---|---|---|---|---|---|---|
| P.J.Martin | 12 | 2 | 19 | 2 | 9.50 | 2-19 | - |
| Wasim Akram | 23.3 | 2 | 86 | 4 | 21.50 | 3-40 | - |
| M.Watkinson | 22 | 7 | 72 | 3 | 24.00 | 2-10 | - |
| I.D.Austin | 21 | 1 | 105 | 1 | 105.00 | 1-46 | - |
| D.P.Hughes | 0.5 | 0 | 5 | 0 | - | - | - |
| P.J.W.Allott | 12 | 3 | 48 | 0 | - | - | - |
| P.A.J.DeFreitas | 22 | 5 | 62 | 0 | - | - | - |

# LEICESTERSHIRE

## BRITANNIC ASS. CHAMPIONSHIP

### BATTING AVERAGES - Including fielding

| Name | Matches | Inns | NO | Runs | HS | Avge | 100s | 50s | Ct | St |
|---|---|---|---|---|---|---|---|---|---|---|
| N.E.Briers | 22 | 40 | 5 | 1358 | 160 | 38.80 | 4 | 5 | 15 | - |
| J.J.Whitaker | 22 | 36 | 3 | 1242 | 105 | 37.63 | 1 | 8 | 14 | - |
| J.D.R.Benson | 9 | 12 | 1 | 393 | 133* | 35.72 | 1 | 1 | 9 | - |
| B.F.Smith | 13 | 20 | 3 | 585 | 71 | 34.41 | - | 3 | 3 | - |
| P.Whitticase | 19 | 25 | 5 | 620 | 114* | 31.00 | 1 | 4 | 42 | 2 |
| T.J.Boon | 20 | 37 | 2 | 1057 | 102 | 30.20 | 1 | 6 | 8 | - |
| P.N.Hepworth | 21 | 35 | 4 | 915 | 115 | 29.51 | 1 | 3 | 17 | - |
| C.C.Lewis | 12 | 15 | 1 | 413 | 73 | 29.50 | - | 2 | 4 | - |
| L.Potter | 22 | 34 | 3 | 899 | 89 | 29.00 | - | 5 | 17 | - |
| G.J.Parsons | 2 | 4 | 1 | 78 | 63 | 26.00 | - | 1 | - | - |
| D.J.Millns | 19 | 24 | 8 | 306 | 44 | 19.12 | - | - | 9 | - |
| P.Willey | 12 | 18 | 5 | 217 | 42* | 16.69 | - | - | 6 | - |
| L.Tennant | 5 | 9 | 3 | 94 | 23* | 15.66 | - | - | - | - |
| M.I.Gidley | 4 | 8 | 1 | 107 | 80 | 15.28 | - | 1 | 3 | - |
| P.A.Nixon | 3 | 3 | 0 | 45 | 31 | 15.00 | - | - | 6 | 1 |
| J.N.Maguire | 22 | 24 | 7 | 237 | 44* | 13.94 | - | - | 7 | - |
| C.Wilkinson | 13 | 13 | 2 | 138 | 41 | 12.54 | - | - | 7 | - |
| A.D.Mullally | 2 | 0 | 0 | 0 | 0 | - | - | - | - | - |

### BOWLING AVERAGES

| Name | Overs | Mdns | Runs | Wkts | Avge | Best | 5wI | 10wM |
|---|---|---|---|---|---|---|---|---|
| T.J.Boon | 10 | 3 | 21 | 1 | 21.00 | 1-11 | - | - |
| C.C.Lewis | 330.4 | 83 | 829 | 37 | 22.40 | 5-35 | 2 | - |
| D.J.Millns | 522.4 | 93 | 1815 | 62 | 29.27 | 9-37 | 3 | 1 |
| P.N.Hepworth | 102.2 | 20 | 404 | 13 | 31.07 | 3-51 | - | - |
| J.N.Maguire | 730.5 | 160 | 2222 | 69 | 32.20 | 7-57 | 3 | - |
| G.J.Parsons | 40 | 10 | 116 | 3 | 38.66 | 2-44 | - | - |
| L.Potter | 418.2 | 93 | 1237 | 26 | 47.57 | 4-116 | - | - |
| C.Wilkinson | 293 | 56 | 974 | 20 | 48.70 | 4-59 | - | - |
| L.Tennant | 69 | 12 | 296 | 5 | 59.20 | 3-65 | - | - |
| B.F.Smith | 7 | 0 | 71 | 1 | 71.00 | 1-5 | - | - |
| M.I.Gidley | 79.4 | 18 | 241 | 3 | 80.33 | 2-58 | - | - |
| P.Willey | 157.4 | 36 | 441 | 5 | 88.20 | 2-15 | - | - |
| A.D.Mullally | 37.4 | 10 | 99 | 1 | 99.00 | 1-35 | - | - |
| J.D.R.Benson | 35.1 | 7 | 145 | 1 | 145.00 | 1-18 | - | - |
| J.J.Whitaker | 1 | 0 | 14 | 0 | - | - | - | - |

## BENSON & HEDGES CUP

### BATTING AVERAGES - Including fielding

| Name | Matches | Inns | NO | Runs | HS | Avge | 100s | 50s | Ct | St |
|---|---|---|---|---|---|---|---|---|---|---|
| T.J.Boon | 3 | 2 | 0 | 119 | 103 | 59.50 | 1 | - | 1 | - |
| J.J.Whitaker | 4 | 4 | 0 | 187 | 100 | 46.75 | 1 | 1 | - | - |
| P.Whitticase | 4 | 3 | 1 | 67 | 34* | 33.50 | - | - | 1 | 1 |
| N.E.Briers | 4 | 4 | 0 | 103 | 46 | 25.75 | - | - | 4 | - |
| L.Potter | 4 | 4 | 1 | 65 | 54 | 21.66 | - | 1 | 1 | - |
| P.N.Hepworth | 3 | 2 | 0 | 42 | 33 | 21.00 | - | - | 1 | - |
| J.D.R.Benson | 3 | 3 | 1 | 36 | 27 | 18.00 | - | - | - | - |
| P.Willey | 4 | 4 | 0 | 69 | 36 | 17.25 | - | - | - | - |
| J.N.Maguire | 4 | 3 | 0 | 37 | 35 | 12.33 | - | - | 1 | - |
| C.C.Lewis | 2 | 2 | 0 | 13 | 8 | 6.50 | - | - | - | - |
| A.D.Mullally | 3 | 2 | 0 | 6 | 5 | 3.00 | - | - | - | - |
| C.Wilkinson | 3 | 2 | 2 | 28 | 19* | - | - | - | 2 | - |
| D.J.Millns | 3 | 1 | 1 | 11 | 11* | - | - | - | 1 | - |

### BOWLING AVERAGES

| Name | Overs | Mdns | Runs | Wkts | Avge | Best | 5wI |
|---|---|---|---|---|---|---|---|
| P.N.Hepworth | 20 | 2 | 83 | 5 | 16.60 | 4-39 | - |
| C.C.Lewis | 22 | 0 | 115 | 3 | 38.33 | 3-62 | - |
| J.D.R.Benson | 7 | 0 | 39 | 1 | 39.00 | 1-10 | - |
| C.Wilkinson | 31 | 3 | 130 | 3 | 43.33 | 3-46 | - |
| P.Willey | 36.5 | 4 | 111 | 2 | 55.50 | 1-29 | - |
| J.N.Maguire | 37 | 7 | 154 | 2 | 77.00 | 1-27 | - |
| D.J.Millns | 23 | 3 | 101 | 1 | 101.00 | 1-25 | - |
| A.D.Mullally | 33 | 2 | 134 | 1 | 134.00 | 1-45 | - |
| L.Potter | 9 | 0 | 42 | 0 | - | - | - |

## REFUGE ASSURANCE LEAGUE

### BATTING AVERAGES - Including fielding

| Name | Matches | Inns | NO | Runs | HS | Avge | 100s | 50s | Ct | St |
|---|---|---|---|---|---|---|---|---|---|---|
| C.Wilkinson | 13 | 6 | 5 | 52 | 35* | 52.00 | - | - | 3 | - |
| J.J.Whitaker | 14 | 14 | 0 | 550 | 88 | 39.28 | - | 4 | 6 | - |
| L.Potter | 14 | 14 | 4 | 374 | 59 | 37.40 | - | 2 | 4 | - |
| T.J.Boon | 6 | 6 | 0 | 173 | 68 | 28.83 | - | 2 | - | - |
| B.F.Smith | 12 | 12 | 3 | 226 | 33 | 25.11 | - | - | 2 | - |
| N.E.Briers | 15 | 15 | 0 | 352 | 48 | 23.46 | - | - | 5 | - |
| J.D.R.Benson | 11 | 9 | 2 | 136 | 42 | 19.42 | - | - | 5 | - |
| P.Willey | 10 | 9 | 1 | 153 | 31 | 19.12 | - | - | 2 | - |
| C.C.Lewis | 12 | 12 | 1 | 174 | 36 | 15.81 | - | - | 4 | - |
| D.J.Millns | 12 | 6 | 2 | 59 | 20* | 14.75 | - | - | 4 | - |
| M.I.Gidley | 2 | 2 | 1 | 14 | 12* | 14.00 | - | - | - | - |
| P.Whitticase | 13 | 12 | 3 | 108 | 24 | 12.00 | - | - | 7 | - |
| P.N.Hepworth | 8 | 6 | 1 | 56 | 31 | 11.20 | - | - | 1 | - |
| P.A.Nixon | 2 | 2 | 0 | 22 | 17 | 11.00 | - | - | 3 | - |
| G.J.Parsons | 2 | 1 | 0 | 9 | 9 | 9.00 | - | - | 1 | - |
| J.N.Maguire | 15 | 6 | 5 | 2 | 2* | 2.00 | - | - | 3 | - |
| L.Tennant | 2 | 1 | 0 | 0 | 0 | 0.00 | - | - | - | - |
| A.D.Mullally | 2 | 0 | 0 | 0 | 0 | - | - | - | 2 | - |

### BOWLING AVERAGES

| Name | Overs | Mdns | Runs | Wkts | Avge | Best | 5wI |
|---|---|---|---|---|---|---|---|
| A.D.Mullally | 16 | 1 | 50 | 4 | 12.50 | 2-19 | - |
| C.C.Lewis | 91.2 | 10 | 341 | 15 | 22.73 | 3-25 | - |
| P.N.Hepworth | 27 | 1 | 140 | 6 | 23.33 | 2-33 | - |
| J.N.Maguire | 113.3 | 7 | 505 | 21 | 24.04 | 3-31 | - |
| J.D.R.Benson | 67 | 0 | 354 | 14 | 25.28 | 3-37 | - |
| G.J.Parsons | 13 | 0 | 51 | 2 | 25.50 | 2-28 | - |
| P.Willey | 60 | 2 | 238 | 8 | 29.75 | 4-17 | - |
| C.Wilkinson | 88.3 | 1 | 437 | 10 | 43.70 | 2-31 | - |
| D.J.Millns | 77 | 2 | 352 | 8 | 44.00 | 2-20 | - |
| L.Potter | 11 | 0 | 74 | 1 | 74.00 | 1-37 | - |
| B.F.Smith | 3 | 0 | 15 | 0 | - | - | - |
| M.I.Gidley | 4 | 0 | 33 | 0 | - | - | - |
| L.Tennant | 9 | 0 | 56 | 0 | - | - | - |

## NATWEST TROPHY

### BATTING AVERAGES - Including fielding

| Name | Matches | Inns | NO | Runs | HS | Avge | 100s | 50s | Ct | St |
|---|---|---|---|---|---|---|---|---|---|---|
| J.J.Whitaker | 2 | 2 | 1 | 133 | 94* | 133.00 | - | 1 | - | - |
| T.J.Boon | 2 | 2 | 1 | 90 | 76* | 90.00 | - | 1 | 1 | - |
| L.Potter | 2 | 2 | 1 | 82 | 57 | 82.00 | - | 1 | - | - |
| N.E.Briers | 2 | 2 | 0 | 38 | 29 | 19.00 | - | - | - | - |
| P.Willey | 2 | 2 | 0 | 34 | 28 | 17.00 | - | - | - | - |
| C.C.Lewis | 2 | 1 | 0 | 6 | 6 | 6.00 | - | - | 2 | - |
| B.F.Smith | 2 | 1 | 0 | 6 | 6 | 6.00 | - | - | - | - |
| D.J.Millns | 2 | 0 | 0 | 0 | 0 | - | - | - | - | - |
| P.Whitticase | 2 | 0 | 0 | 0 | 0 | - | - | - | 2 | - |
| C.Wilkinson | 2 | 0 | 0 | 0 | 0 | - | - | - | - | - |
| J.N.Maguire | 2 | 0 | 0 | 0 | 0 | - | - | - | - | - |

### BOWLING AVERAGES

| Name | Overs | Mdns | Runs | Wkts | Avge | Best | 5wI |
|---|---|---|---|---|---|---|---|
| C.C.Lewis | 21 | 2 | 60 | 3 | 20.00 | 3-28 | - |
| C.Wilkinson | 16.5 | 5 | 62 | 3 | 20.66 | 3-16 | - |
| L.Potter | 6 | 1 | 32 | 1 | 32.00 | 1-32 | - |
| D.J.Millns | 21 | 4 | 87 | 2 | 43.50 | 2-27 | - |
| P.Willey | 19 | 3 | 56 | 0 | - | - | - |
| J.N.Maguire | 23 | 1 | 94 | 0 | - | - | - |

# MIDDLESEX

## BRITANNIC ASS. CHAMPIONSHIP

### BATTING AVERAGES - Including fielding

| Name | Matches | Inns | NO | Runs | HS | Avge | 100s | 50s | Ct | St |
|---|---|---|---|---|---|---|---|---|---|---|
| P.R.Downton | 3 | 3 | 2 | 113 | 51 * | 113.00 | - | 1 | 8 | 1 |
| M.W.Gatting | 21 | 37 | 11 | 2044 | 215 * | 78.61 | 8 | 6 | 13 | - |
| M.R.Ramprakash | 12 | 22 | 4 | 877 | 119 | 48.72 | 2 | 7 | 2 | - |
| K.R.Brown | 21 | 36 | 6 | 1069 | 143 * | 35.63 | 1 | 6 | 33 | - |
| M.A.Roseberry | 21 | 40 | 3 | 1222 | 119 * | 33.02 | 1 | 7 | 17 | - |
| P.N.Weekes | 6 | 11 | 1 | 249 | 86 | 24.90 | - | 2 | 5 | - |
| I.J.F.Hutchinson | 11 | 20 | 1 | 437 | 125 | 23.00 | 2 | - | 11 | - |
| J.E.Emburey | 21 | 29 | 3 | 586 | 74 | 22.53 | - | 3 | 21 | - |
| J.C.Pooley | 11 | 20 | 0 | 390 | 88 | 19.50 | - | 2 | 8 | - |
| M.Keech | 14 | 22 | 2 | 362 | 58 * | 18.10 | - | 2 | 4 | - |
| D.W.Headley | 11 | 14 | 1 | 202 | 76 | 15.53 | - | 1 | 4 | - |
| P.Farbrace | 19 | 26 | 5 | 317 | 50 | 15.09 | - | 1 | 44 | 8 |
| N.F.Williams | 16 | 24 | 3 | 296 | 77 | 14.09 | - | 1 | 4 | - |
| C.W.Taylor | 7 | 5 | 0 | 59 | 21 | 11.80 | - | - | 2 | - |
| N.G.Cowans | 20 | 26 | 10 | 146 | 23 * | 9.12 | - | - | 5 | - |
| P.C.R.Tufnell | 17 | 18 | 4 | 120 | 37 * | 8.57 | - | - | 7 | - |
| A.R.C.Fraser | 2 | 2 | 0 | 12 | 12 | 6.00 | - | - | 2 | - |
| S.P.Hughes | 3 | 3 | 1 | 3 | 2 | 1.50 | - | - | 2 | - |
| S.A.Sylvester | 1 | 1 | 0 | 0 | 0 | 0.00 | - | - | 1 | - |
| R.M.Ellcock | 3 | 1 | 1 | 26 | 26 * | - | - | - | - | - |
| A.A.Barnett | 2 | 2 | 2 | 12 | 11 * | - | - | - | - | - |

### BOWLING AVERAGES

| Name | Overs | Mdns | Runs | Wkts | Avge | Best | 5wI | 10wM |
|---|---|---|---|---|---|---|---|---|
| A.R.C.Fraser | 39.5 | 12 | 91 | 6 | 15.16 | 4-24 | - | - |
| K.R.Brown | 3 | 0 | 17 | 1 | 17.00 | 1-17 | - | - |
| M.R.Ramprakash | 5 | 1 | 25 | 1 | 25.00 | 1-0 | - | - |
| P.C.R.Tufnell | 733.4 | 199 | 1818 | 70 | 25.97 | 7-116 | 5 | 1 |
| C.W.Taylor | 147 | 29 | 480 | 18 | 26.66 | 3-35 | - | - |
| P.N.Weekes | 56.4 | 12 | 188 | 7 | 26.85 | 3-57 | - | - |
| R.M.Ellcock | 50 | 9 | 189 | 7 | 27.00 | 4-60 | - | - |
| J.E.Emburey | 855.5 | 228 | 2031 | 64 | 31.73 | 7-71 | 1 | - |
| A.A.Barnett | 107.4 | 23 | 329 | 10 | 32.90 | 4-119 | - | - |
| N.F.Williams | 477.2 | 89 | 1474 | 41 | 35.95 | 5-89 | 1 | - |
| N.G.Cowans | 485.2 | 120 | 1370 | 34 | 40.29 | 4-42 | - | - |
| D.W.Headley | 309.2 | 44 | 1180 | 28 | 42.14 | 5-46 | 2 | - |
| S.P.Hughes | 70.5 | 14 | 270 | 5 | 54.00 | 2-44 | - | - |
| P.Farbrace | 4.1 | 0 | 64 | 1 | 64.00 | 1-64 | - | - |
| I.J.F.Hutchinson | 6 | 0 | 11 | 0 | - | - | - | - |
| M.Keech | 11 | 6 | 16 | 0 | - | - | - | - |
| M.A.Roseberry | 9 | 1 | 36 | 0 | - | - | - | - |
| M.W.Gatting | 28 | 4 | 90 | 0 | - | - | - | - |
| S.A.Sylvester | 20 | 2 | 98 | 0 | - | - | - | - |

## BENSON & HEDGES CUP

### BATTING AVERAGES - Including fielding

| Name | Matches | Inns | NO | Runs | HS | Avge | 100s | 50s | Ct | St |
|---|---|---|---|---|---|---|---|---|---|---|
| P.R.Downton | 4 | 3 | 1 | 134 | 58 | 67.00 | - | 1 | 7 | 1 |
| M.W.Gatting | 4 | 4 | 0 | 169 | 112 | 42.25 | 1 | - | 1 | - |
| M.Keech | 2 | 2 | 0 | 84 | 47 | 42.00 | - | - | 1 | - |
| M.R.Ramprakash | 4 | 4 | 1 | 120 | 78 * | 40.00 | - | 1 | 3 | - |
| K.R.Brown | 4 | 4 | 1 | 57 | 25 | 19.00 | - | - | 1 | - |
| J.E.Emburey | 4 | 3 | 0 | 38 | 23 | 12.66 | - | - | 3 | - |
| D.W.Headley | 4 | 3 | 0 | 30 | 26 | 10.00 | - | - | 1 | - |
| P.C.R.Tufnell | 4 | 3 | 1 | 19 | 18 | 9.50 | - | - | 1 | - |
| I.J.F.Hutchinson | 1 | 1 | 0 | 8 | 8 | 8.00 | - | - | - | - |
| N.G.Cowans | 3 | 2 | 1 | 5 | 5 | 5.00 | - | - | - | - |
| J.C.Pooley | 3 | 3 | 0 | 11 | 8 | 3.66 | - | - | - | - |
| N.F.Williams | 4 | 3 | 0 | 10 | 6 | 3.33 | - | - | - | - |
| R.M.Ellcock | 1 | 1 | 0 | 0 | 0 | 0.00 | - | - | - | - |
| P.N.Weekes | 1 | 1 | 0 | 0 | 0 | 0.00 | - | - | 1 | - |
| M.A.Roseberry | 1 | 0 | 0 | 0 | 0 | - | - | - | - | - |

### BOWLING AVERAGES

| Name | Overs | Mdns | Runs | Wkts | Avge | Best | 5wI |
|---|---|---|---|---|---|---|---|
| N.G.Cowans | 33 | 2 | 130 | 8 | 16.25 | 3-39 | - |
| J.E.Emburey | 44 | 3 | 167 | 9 | 18.55 | 5-37 | 1 |
| N.F.Williams | 44 | 8 | 123 | 5 | 24.60 | 2-19 | - |
| P.C.R.Tufnell | 39 | 0 | 187 | 4 | 46.75 | 3-50 | - |
| R.M.Ellcock | 10 | 0 | 55 | 1 | 55.00 | 1-55 | - |
| D.W.Headley | 42.1 | 4 | 180 | 3 | 60.00 | 1-34 | - |

## REFUGE ASSURANCE LEAGUE

### BATTING AVERAGES - Including fielding

| Name | Matches | Inns | NO | Runs | HS | Avge | 100s | 50s | Ct | St |
|---|---|---|---|---|---|---|---|---|---|---|
| M.R.Ramprakash | 8 | 8 | 2 | 382 | 111 * | 63.66 | 1 | 3 | 3 | - |
| J.C.Pooley | 4 | 4 | 0 | 185 | 109 | 46.25 | 1 | - | - | - |
| M.W.Gatting | 15 | 15 | 2 | 525 | 111 | 40.38 | 1 | 4 | 5 | - |
| K.R.Brown | 15 | 15 | 4 | 359 | 81 * | 32.63 | - | 2 | 4 | - |
| M.A.Roseberry | 14 | 14 | 1 | 383 | 106 * | 29.46 | 1 | 2 | 7 | - |
| M.Keech | 12 | 12 | 3 | 195 | 49 * | 21.66 | - | - | 2 | - |
| I.J.F.Hutchinson | 5 | 5 | 0 | 104 | 42 | 20.80 | - | - | 2 | - |
| J.E.Emburey | 15 | 11 | 4 | 142 | 33 * | 20.28 | - | - | 2 | - |
| P.N.Weekes | 13 | 9 | 2 | 115 | 32 * | 16.42 | - | - | 6 | - |
| N.F.Williams | 12 | 5 | 2 | 48 | 27 | 16.00 | - | - | 6 | - |
| P.Farbrace | 12 | 8 | 3 | 67 | 26 * | 13.40 | - | - | 9 | 6 |
| D.W.Headley | 8 | 2 | 1 | 10 | 6 * | 10.00 | - | - | - | - |
| N.G.Cowans | 13 | 5 | 2 | 14 | 5 * | 4.66 | - | - | - | - |
| P.R.Downton | 3 | 2 | 0 | 8 | 5 | 4.00 | - | - | 1 | 2 |
| S.P.Hughes | 6 | 2 | 0 | 8 | 4 | 4.00 | - | - | - | - |
| C.W.Taylor | 5 | 1 | 0 | 3 | 3 | 3.00 | - | - | 4 | - |
| R.M.Ellcock | 2 | 1 | 1 | 8 | 8 * | - | - | - | - | - |
| A.R.C.Fraser | 2 | 1 | 1 | 8 | 8 * | - | - | - | 1 | - |
| P.C.R.Tufnell | 1 | 0 | 0 | 0 | 0 | - | - | - | - | - |

### BOWLING AVERAGES

| Name | Overs | Mdns | Runs | Wkts | Avge | Best | 5wI |
|---|---|---|---|---|---|---|---|
| P.C.R.Tufnell | 8 | 0 | 28 | 3 | 9.33 | 3-28 | - |
| I.J.F.Hutchinson | 2 | 0 | 10 | 1 | 10.00 | 1-10 | - |
| J.E.Emburey | 114 | 6 | 528 | 28 | 18.85 | 5-23 | 1 |
| N.G.Cowans | 98.5 | 7 | 425 | 18 | 23.61 | 6-9 | 1 |
| S.P.Hughes | 47 | 3 | 214 | 8 | 26.75 | 2-29 | - |
| M.R.Ramprakash | 12 | 0 | 71 | 2 | 35.50 | 2-32 | - |
| A.R.C.Fraser | 16 | 0 | 78 | 2 | 39.00 | 1-34 | - |
| P.N.Weekes | 70.2 | 2 | 373 | 9 | 41.44 | 3-27 | - |
| N.F.Williams | 83 | 2 | 408 | 8 | 51.00 | 1-24 | - |
| C.W.Taylor | 27.2 | 0 | 153 | 3 | 51.00 | 1-14 | - |
| R.M.Ellcock | 11 | 0 | 58 | 1 | 58.00 | 1-33 | - |
| M.W.Gatting | 24.5 | 0 | 119 | 2 | 59.50 | 2-34 | - |
| D.W.Headley | 56 | 0 | 296 | 1 | 296.00 | 1-70 | - |
| K.R.Brown | 0.2 | 0 | 2 | 0 | - | - | - |

## NATWEST TROPHY

### BATTING AVERAGES - Including fielding

| Name | Matches | Inns | NO | Runs | HS | Avge | 100s | 50s | Ct | St |
|---|---|---|---|---|---|---|---|---|---|---|
| M.W.Gatting | 2 | 2 | 0 | 150 | 85 | 75.00 | - | 2 | 2 | - |
| K.R.Brown | 2 | 2 | 0 | 57 | 49 | 28.50 | - | - | 1 | - |
| M.R.Ramprakash | 2 | 2 | 0 | 57 | 32 | 28.50 | - | - | - | - |
| M.A.Roseberry | 2 | 2 | 0 | 50 | 44 | 25.00 | - | - | 2 | - |
| P.Farbrace | 2 | 2 | 1 | 20 | 13 * | 20.00 | - | - | 1 | 1 |
| I.J.F.Hutchinson | 2 | 2 | 0 | 40 | 23 | 20.00 | - | - | 2 | - |
| P.C.R.Tufnell | 1 | 1 | 0 | 8 | 8 | 8.00 | - | - | - | - |
| P.N.Weekes | 1 | 1 | 0 | 7 | 7 | 7.00 | - | - | - | - |
| N.G.Cowans | 2 | 2 | 0 | 10 | 10 | 5.00 | - | - | 1 | - |
| N.F.Williams | 2 | 2 | 0 | 9 | 6 | 4.50 | - | - | 1 | - |
| J.E.Emburey | 2 | 2 | 0 | 3 | 2 | 1.50 | - | - | - | - |
| D.W.Headley | 1 | 1 | 1 | 11 | 11 * | - | - | - | - | - |
| S.P.Hughes | 1 | 1 | 1 | 0 | 0 * | - | - | - | - | - |

### BOWLING AVERAGES

| Name | Overs | Mdns | Runs | Wkts | Avge | Best | 5wI |
|---|---|---|---|---|---|---|---|
| M.W.Gatting | 1 | 0 | 8 | 1 | 8.00 | 1-8 | - |
| S.P.Hughes | 11 | 2 | 24 | 2 | 12.00 | 2-24 | - |
| N.G.Cowans | 18 | 1 | 61 | 5 | 12.20 | 4-51 | - |
| M.R.Ramprakash | 13 | 1 | 46 | 2 | 23.00 | 2-15 | - |
| P.C.R.Tufnell | 12 | 2 | 29 | 1 | 29.00 | 1-29 | - |
| P.N.Weekes | 12 | 1 | 30 | 1 | 30.00 | 1-30 | - |
| J.E.Emburey | 24 | 7 | 65 | 2 | 32.50 | 2-52 | - |
| N.F.Williams | 12 | 2 | 43 | 1 | 43.00 | 1-11 | - |
| K.R.Brown | 1 | 0 | 8 | 0 | - | - | - |
| I.J.F.Hutchinson | 2 | 0 | 17 | 0 | - | - | - |
| M.A.Roseberry | 2 | 0 | 20 | 0 | - | - | - |
| D.W.Headley | 12 | 0 | 51 | 0 | - | - | - |

# NORTHAMPTONSHIRE

## BRITANNIC ASSURANCE

### BATTING AVERAGES - Including fielding

| Name | Matches | Inns | NO | Runs | HS | Avge | 100s | 50s | Ct | St |
|---|---|---|---|---|---|---|---|---|---|---|
| A.J.Lamb | 14 | 23 | 2 | 993 | 194 | 47.28 | 3 | 5 | 13 | - |
| A.Fordham | 22 | 40 | 2 | 1725 | 165 | 45.39 | 4 | 8 | 8 | - |
| A.R.Roberts | 14 | 15 | 9 | 244 | 48 | 40.66 | - | - | 7 | - |
| R.J.Bailey | 19 | 34 | 4 | 1202 | 117 | 40.06 | 1 | 11 | 10 | - |
| W.Larkins | 9 | 16 | 6 | 365 | 75 | 36.50 | - | 2 | 6 | - |
| N.A.Stanley | 8 | 13 | 0 | 470 | 132 | 36.15 | 1 | 2 | 5 | - |
| K.M.Curran | 19 | 30 | 7 | 749 | 89* | 32.56 | - | 5 | 12 | - |
| E.A.E.Baptiste | 17 | 22 | 1 | 589 | 80 | 28.04 | - | 4 | 9 | - |
| D.Ripley | 18 | 24 | 8 | 429 | 53* | 26.81 | - | 1 | 37 | 2 |
| D.J.Capel | 20 | 32 | 2 | 692 | 71 | 23.06 | - | 7 | 9 | - |
| J.G.Thomas | 10 | 12 | 3 | 206 | 64 | 22.88 | - | 1 | 3 | - |
| N.A.Felton | 14 | 25 | 2 | 439 | 55 | 19.08 | - | 1 | 5 | - |
| R.G.Williams | 7 | 10 | 2 | 123 | 35 | 15.37 | - | - | 1 | - |
| A.L.Penberthy | 11 | 14 | 2 | 184 | 52 | 15.33 | - | 1 | 6 | - |
| W.M.Noon | 6 | 9 | 2 | 96 | 36 | 13.71 | - | - | 11 | - |
| A.Walker | 4 | 4 | 1 | 35 | 13 | 11.66 | - | - | 2 | - |
| N.G.B.Cook | 16 | 15 | 5 | 114 | 29 | 11.40 | - | - | 6 | - |
| R.R.Montgomerie | 1 | 2 | 0 | 9 | 7 | 4.50 | - | - | 2 | - |
| J.P.Taylor | 11 | 11 | 4 | 22 | 5* | 3.14 | - | - | 4 | - |
| M.B.Loye | 1 | 1 | 1 | 3 | 3* | - | - | - | 1 | - |
| J.G.Hughes | 1 | 0 | 0 | 0 | 0 | - | - | - | - | - |

### BOWLING AVERAGES

| Name | Overs | Mdns | Runs | Wkts | Avge | Best | 5wI | 10wM |
|---|---|---|---|---|---|---|---|---|
| A.J.Lamb | 3.4 | 0 | 29 | 2 | 14.50 | 2-29 | - | - |
| K.M.Curran | 410.2 | 101 | 1128 | 45 | 25.06 | 5-60 | 1 | - |
| E.A.E.Baptiste | 517.2 | 117 | 1418 | 49 | 28.93 | 7-95 | 3 | - |
| J.P.Taylor | 267.2 | 45 | 828 | 24 | 34.50 | 5-42 | 1 | - |
| J.G.Thomas | 248.4 | 34 | 829 | 24 | 34.54 | 5-62 | 2 | - |
| A.R.Roberts | 331.5 | 72 | 1032 | 29 | 35.58 | 6-72 | 1 | - |
| R.J.Bailey | 118.3 | 16 | 409 | 11 | 37.18 | 3-44 | - | - |
| N.G.B.Cook | 305.1 | 70 | 895 | 24 | 37.29 | 4-74 | - | - |
| D.J.Capel | 374.1 | 81 | 1099 | 28 | 39.25 | 4-83 | - | - |
| A.L.Penberthy | 163.4 | 26 | 531 | 13 | 40.84 | 3-37 | - | - |
| J.G.Hughes | 12 | 1 | 43 | 1 | 43.00 | 1-43 | - | - |
| A.Walker | 103 | 20 | 296 | 6 | 49.33 | 3-84 | - | - |
| R.G.Williams | 87.3 | 17 | 256 | 4 | 64.00 | 2-29 | - | - |
| A.Fordham | 13 | 0 | 78 | 1 | 78.00 | 1-42 | - | - |
| W.Larkins | 6 | 4 | 2 | 0 | - | - | - | - |
| N.A.Stanley | 10 | 2 | 19 | 0 | - | - | - | - |
| N.A.Felton | 6 | 0 | 66 | 0 | - | - | - | - |

## BENSON & HEDGES CUP

### BATTING AVERAGES - Including fielding

| Name | Matches | Inns | NO | Runs | HS | Avge | 100s | 50s | Ct | St |
|---|---|---|---|---|---|---|---|---|---|---|
| R.G.Williams | 4 | 4 | 2 | 96 | 29 | 48.00 | - | - | 1 | - |
| D.Ripley | 5 | 3 | 2 | 47 | 36* | 47.00 | - | - | 7 | 1 |
| A.Fordham | 5 | 5 | 1 | 183 | 93* | 45.75 | - | 2 | 1 | - |
| R.J.Bailey | 5 | 5 | 0 | 184 | 75 | 36.80 | - | 2 | 1 | - |
| A.J.Lamb | 5 | 5 | 0 | 150 | 48 | 30.00 | - | - | 2 | - |
| N.A.Felton | 5 | 5 | 0 | 119 | 44 | 23.80 | - | - | 2 | - |
| D.J.Capel | 5 | 5 | 0 | 102 | 42 | 20.40 | - | - | - | - |
| E.A.E.Baptiste | 4 | 3 | 1 | 28 | 15* | 14.00 | - | - | - | - |
| K.M.Curran | 2 | 2 | 0 | 26 | 26 | 13.00 | - | - | - | - |
| J.G.Thomas | 5 | 4 | 1 | 19 | 9 | 6.33 | - | - | - | - |
| A.L.Penberthy | 2 | 1 | 0 | 3 | 3 | 3.00 | - | - | - | - |
| N.G.B.Cook | 3 | 2 | 0 | 1 | 1 | 0.50 | - | - | 1 | - |
| J.P.Taylor | 4 | 2 | 2 | 2 | 1* | - | - | - | 1 | - |
| A.Walker | 1 | 1 | 1 | 0 | 0* | - | - | - | - | - |

### BOWLING AVERAGES

| Name | Overs | Mdns | Runs | Wkts | Avge | Best | 5wI |
|---|---|---|---|---|---|---|---|
| J.G.Thomas | 49.3 | 5 | 173 | 9 | 19.22 | 5-29 | 1 |
| J.P.Taylor | 42 | 9 | 106 | 4 | 26.50 | 2-30 | - |
| D.J.Capel | 40.4 | 3 | 147 | 5 | 29.40 | 4-37 | - |
| A.L.Penberthy | 17 | 3 | 65 | 2 | 32.50 | 2-22 | - |
| A.Walker | 9 | 1 | 33 | 1 | 33.00 | 1-33 | - |
| R.G.Williams | 33 | 2 | 109 | 2 | 54.50 | 1-31 | - |
| N.G.B.Cook | 26 | 2 | 77 | 1 | 77.00 | 1-21 | - |
| E.A.E.Baptiste | 31.1 | 5 | 118 | 1 | 118.00 | 1-30 | - |
| K.M.Curran | 6 | 0 | 36 | 0 | - | - | - |

## REFUGE ASSURANCE

### BATTING AVERAGES - Including fielding

| Name | Matches | Inns | NO | Runs | HS | Avge | 100s | 50s | Ct | St |
|---|---|---|---|---|---|---|---|---|---|---|
| A.L.Penberthy | 8 | 3 | 2 | 69 | 41* | 69.00 | - | - | 2 | - |
| R.G.Williams | 12 | 7 | 4 | 141 | 66* | 47.00 | - | 1 | 3 | - |
| W.Larkins | 8 | 8 | 0 | 363 | 108 | 45.37 | 1 | 3 | 2 | - |
| J.G.Thomas | 7 | 3 | 1 | 69 | 34 | 34.50 | - | - | 2 | - |
| A.Fordham | 16 | 15 | 0 | 509 | 76 | 33.93 | - | 4 | 3 | - |
| R.J.Bailey | 14 | 13 | 1 | 388 | 99 | 32.33 | - | 2 | 3 | - |
| D.J.Capel | 16 | 15 | 3 | 360 | 77* | 30.00 | - | 2 | 3 | - |
| K.M.Curran | 13 | 12 | 4 | 236 | 61* | 29.50 | - | 1 | 2 | - |
| N.A.Felton | 9 | 8 | 0 | 203 | 69 | 25.37 | - | 2 | 4 | - |
| N.G.B.Cook | 5 | 2 | 1 | 23 | 17* | 23.00 | - | - | 1 | - |
| A.J.Lamb | 12 | 12 | 0 | 212 | 61 | 17.66 | - | 1 | 5 | - |
| A.R.Roberts | 4 | 1 | 0 | 14 | 14 | 14.00 | - | - | 1 | - |
| W.M.Noon | 4 | 2 | 1 | 12 | 8* | 12.00 | - | - | 3 | 1 |
| E.A.E.Baptiste | 11 | 11 | 4 | 83 | 15* | 11.85 | - | - | 2 | - |
| D.Ripley | 13 | 7 | 2 | 57 | 14 | 11.40 | - | - | 8 | - |
| J.P.Taylor | 10 | 5 | 2 | 24 | 16 | 8.00 | - | - | 1 | - |
| A.Walker | 14 | 4 | 0 | 17 | 6 | 4.25 | - | - | 6 | - |

### BOWLING AVERAGES

| Name | Overs | Mdns | Runs | Wkts | Avge | Best | 5wI |
|---|---|---|---|---|---|---|---|
| A.R.Roberts | 21 | 0 | 118 | 6 | 19.66 | 3-26 | - |
| J.P.Taylor | 74 | 7 | 301 | 15 | 20.06 | 2-18 | - |
| D.J.Capel | 80 | 1 | 400 | 17 | 23.52 | 3-30 | - |
| K.M.Curran | 77.1 | 2 | 384 | 16 | 24.00 | 3-24 | - |
| A.Walker | 98.5 | 8 | 335 | 12 | 27.91 | 2-7 | - |
| R.G.Williams | 70 | 0 | 360 | 12 | 30.00 | 2-22 | - |
| A.L.Penberthy | 32 | 2 | 165 | 5 | 33.00 | 2-20 | - |
| J.G.Thomas | 39 | 0 | 209 | 6 | 34.83 | 2-20 | - |
| E.A.E.Baptiste | 81.1 | 5 | 340 | 6 | 56.66 | 2-25 | - |
| R.J.Bailey | 4 | 0 | 37 | 0 | - | - | - |
| N.G.B.Cook | 17 | 0 | 80 | 0 | - | - | - |

## NATWEST TROPHY

### BATTING AVERAGES - Including fielding

| Name | Matches | Inns | NO | Runs | HS | Avge | 100s | 50s | Ct | St |
|---|---|---|---|---|---|---|---|---|---|---|
| A.Fordham | 4 | 4 | 1 | 288 | 132* | 96.00 | 1 | 2 | - | - |
| R.J.Bailey | 4 | 4 | 1 | 253 | 145 | 84.33 | 1 | 1 | - | - |
| K.M.Curran | 4 | 3 | 2 | 77 | 38 | 77.00 | - | - | - | - |
| N.A.Felton | 2 | 2 | 0 | 65 | 54 | 32.50 | - | 1 | 1 | - |
| A.J.Lamb | 4 | 3 | 0 | 84 | 31 | 28.00 | - | - | 1 | - |
| E.A.E.Baptiste | 4 | 3 | 1 | 51 | 34 | 25.50 | - | - | 1 | - |
| W.Larkins | 2 | 2 | 0 | 39 | 31 | 19.50 | - | - | 2 | - |
| D.Ripley | 4 | 2 | 1 | 13 | 10* | 13.00 | - | - | 3 | - |
| A.Walker | 4 | 1 | 0 | 11 | 11 | 11.00 | - | - | - | - |
| R.G.Williams | 3 | 2 | 0 | 7 | 6 | 3.50 | - | - | 3 | - |
| D.J.Capel | 4 | 3 | 0 | 7 | 6 | 2.33 | - | - | - | - |
| J.P.Taylor | 4 | 1 | 1 | 3 | 3* | - | - | - | 1 | - |
| N.G.B.Cook | 1 | 0 | 0 | 0 | 0 | - | - | - | 2 | - |

### BOWLING AVERAGES

| Name | Overs | Mdns | Runs | Wkts | Avge | Best | 5wI |
|---|---|---|---|---|---|---|---|
| R.J.Bailey | 2 | 0 | 3 | 1 | 3.00 | 1-3 | - |
| A.Fordham | 1.3 | 0 | 3 | 1 | 3.00 | 1-3 | - |
| J.P.Taylor | 42 | 6 | 132 | 8 | 16.50 | 2-11 | - |
| D.J.Capel | 14 | 0 | 50 | 3 | 16.66 | 3-26 | - |
| E.A.E.Baptiste | 42 | 4 | 171 | 9 | 19.00 | 4-27 | - |
| A.Walker | 42 | 6 | 129 | 4 | 32.25 | 2-39 | - |
| N.G.B.Cook | 12 | 0 | 35 | 1 | 35.00 | 1-35 | - |
| R.G.Williams | 36 | 4 | 99 | 2 | 49.50 | 2-34 | - |
| K.M.Curran | 32 | 3 | 140 | 1 | 140.00 | 1-61 | - |

# NOTTINGHAMSHIRE

## BRITANNIC ASS. CHAMPIONSHIP

### BATTING AVERAGES - Including fielding

| Name | Matches | Inns | NO | Runs | HS | Avge | 100s | 50s | Ct | St |
|---|---|---|---|---|---|---|---|---|---|---|
| D.W.Randall | 22 | 34 | 9 | 1567 | 143* | 62.68 | 5 | 5 | 15 | - |
| R.T.Robinson | 22 | 37 | 8 | 1673 | 180 | 57.69 | 3 | 10 | 18 | - |
| B.C.Broad | 21 | 38 | 3 | 1739 | 166 | 49.68 | 5 | 7 | 9 | - |
| P.Johnson | 22 | 36 | 6 | 1357 | 124 | 45.23 | 3 | 10 | 12 | - |
| P.Pollard | 22 | 40 | 3 | 1235 | 145 | 33.37 | 3 | 4 | 21 | - |
| K.P.Evans | 14 | 17 | 7 | 276 | 56* | 27.60 | - | 1 | 6 | - |
| F.D.Stephenson | 22 | 27 | 7 | 423 | 58 | 21.15 | - | 1 | 6 | - |
| M.G.Field-Buss | 2 | 2 | 0 | 41 | 25 | 20.50 | - | - | 1 | - |
| M.A.Crawley | 10 | 12 | 4 | 160 | 49* | 20.00 | - | - | 14 | - |
| M.Saxelby | 6 | 9 | 1 | 136 | 44 | 17.00 | - | - | - | - |
| B.N.French | 21 | 24 | 4 | 315 | 65 | 15.75 | - | 2 | 54 | 8 |
| R.A.Pick | 21 | 16 | 5 | 142 | 46 | 12.90 | - | - | 7 | - |
| E.E.Hemmings | 16 | 16 | 4 | 143 | 29* | 11.91 | - | - | 4 | - |
| V.J.P.Broadley | 1 | 1 | 0 | 6 | 6 | 6.00 | - | - | - | - |
| J.A.Afford | 18 | 12 | 4 | 42 | 13 | 5.25 | - | - | 10 | - |
| K.E.Cooper | 1 | 0 | 0 | 0 | 0 | - | - | - | - | - |
| C.W.Scott | 1 | 0 | 0 | 0 | 0 | - | - | - | 3 | - |

### BOWLING AVERAGES

| Name | Overs | Mdns | Runs | Wkts | Avge | Best | 5wI | 10wM |
|---|---|---|---|---|---|---|---|---|
| D.W.Randall | 4 | 0 | 19 | 1 | 19.00 | 1-19 | - | - |
| F.D.Stephenson | 719.1 | 158 | 2010 | 78 | 25.76 | 5-27 | 4 | 1 |
| R.A.Pick | 623.4 | 113 | 1985 | 65 | 30.53 | 5-17 | 3 | - |
| P.Johnson | 12.2 | 1 | 62 | 2 | 31.00 | 1-26 | - | - |
| J.A.Afford | 670.3 | 207 | 1817 | 57 | 31.87 | 4-44 | - | - |
| K.P.Evans | 425 | 89 | 1278 | 40 | 31.95 | 5-52 | 2 | - |
| E.E.Hemmings | 638.3 | 171 | 1721 | 46 | 37.41 | 6-46 | 2 | - |
| R.T.Robinson | 8 | 0 | 39 | 1 | 39.00 | 1-30 | - | - |
| M.A.Crawley | 176.5 | 53 | 463 | 11 | 42.09 | 3-21 | - | - |
| B.N.French | 14 | 4 | 48 | 1 | 48.00 | 1-37 | - | - |
| K.E.Cooper | 17 | 3 | 54 | 1 | 54.00 | 1-54 | - | - |
| P.Pollard | 23.5 | 8 | 75 | 1 | 75.00 | 1-46 | - | - |
| M.Saxelby | 97.2 | 17 | 423 | 4 | 105.75 | 3-41 | - | - |
| V.J.P.Broadley | 32 | 6 | 111 | 1 | 111.00 | 1-92 | - | - |
| M.G.Field-Buss | 53 | 11 | 187 | 1 | 187.00 | 1-73 | - | - |

## BENSON & HEDGES CUP

### BATTING AVERAGES - Including fielding

| Name | Matches | Inns | NO | Runs | HS | Avge | 100s | 50s | Ct | St |
|---|---|---|---|---|---|---|---|---|---|---|
| R.T.Robinson | 4 | 4 | 0 | 239 | 116 | 59.75 | 1 | 1 | 1 | - |
| P.Johnson | 4 | 4 | 1 | 144 | 102* | 48.00 | 1 | - | 1 | - |
| D.W.Randall | 4 | 4 | 0 | 189 | 86 | 47.25 | - | 2 | 5 | - |
| B.C.Broad | 4 | 4 | 1 | 140 | 108* | 46.66 | 1 | - | - | - |
| M.A.Crawley | 3 | 3 | 1 | 74 | 58 | 37.00 | - | 1 | - | - |
| M.Saxelby | 3 | 2 | 0 | 37 | 32 | 18.50 | - | - | - | - |
| M.Newell | 1 | 1 | 0 | 18 | 18 | 18.00 | - | - | - | - |
| F.D.Stephenson | 4 | 3 | 1 | 19 | 14 | 9.50 | - | - | 1 | - |
| E.E.Hemmings | 4 | 1 | 0 | 9 | 9 | 9.00 | - | - | - | - |
| K.E.Cooper | 3 | 1 | 0 | 0 | 0 | 0.00 | - | - | - | - |
| B.N.French | 4 | 1 | 1 | 37 | 37* | - | - | - | 3 | - |
| R.A.Pick | 2 | 1 | 1 | 25 | 25* | - | - | - | - | - |
| K.P.Evans | 3 | 2 | 2 | 6 | 5* | - | - | - | 1 | - |
| J.A.Afford | 1 | 0 | 0 | 0 | 0 | - | - | - | - | - |

### BOWLING AVERAGES

| Name | Overs | Mdns | Runs | Wkts | Avge | Best | 5wI |
|---|---|---|---|---|---|---|---|
| F.D.Stephenson | 37 | 9 | 135 | 7 | 19.28 | 5-30 | 1 |
| K.P.Evans | 32 | 2 | 132 | 6 | 22.00 | 4-43 | - |
| J.A.Afford | 11 | 0 | 43 | 1 | 43.00 | 1-43 | - |
| R.A.Pick | 22 | 1 | 97 | 2 | 48.50 | 1-36 | - |
| E.E.Hemmings | 44 | 4 | 201 | 4 | 50.25 | 2-49 | - |
| K.E.Cooper | 31 | 5 | 103 | 2 | 51.50 | 1-27 | - |
| M.A.Crawley | 17 | 0 | 82 | 1 | 82.00 | 1-44 | - |
| M.Saxelby | 26 | 1 | 118 | 1 | 118.00 | 1-36 | - |

## REFUGE ASSURANCE LEAGUE

### BATTING AVERAGES - Including fielding

| Name | Matches | Inns | NO | Runs | HS | Avge | 100s | 50s | Ct | St |
|---|---|---|---|---|---|---|---|---|---|---|
| P.Pollard | 7 | 6 | 2 | 268 | 73 | 67.00 | - | 4 | 2 | - |
| B.C.Broad | 16 | 16 | 3 | 647 | 108 | 49.76 | 2 | 4 | 6 | - |
| D.W.Randall | 17 | 17 | 1 | 718 | 83* | 44.87 | - | 5 | 4 | - |
| B.N.French | 17 | 11 | 6 | 137 | 31 | 27.40 | - | - | 17 | 1 |
| P.Johnson | 17 | 15 | 1 | 370 | 80 | 26.42 | - | 3 | 6 | - |
| R.T.Robinson | 16 | 16 | 4 | 278 | 35 | 23.16 | - | - | 6 | - |
| F.D.Stephenson | 17 | 11 | 3 | 164 | 36* | 20.50 | - | - | 3 | - |
| M.A.Crawley | 11 | 8 | 2 | 121 | 47* | 20.16 | - | - | 3 | - |
| M.Saxelby | 17 | 13 | 1 | 208 | 55 | 17.33 | - | 1 | 4 | - |
| K.P.Evans | 16 | 6 | 3 | 47 | 14* | 15.66 | - | - | 1 | - |
| M.Newell | 1 | 1 | 0 | 12 | 12 | 12.00 | - | - | - | - |
| E.E.Hemmings | 15 | 4 | 1 | 28 | 17 | 9.33 | - | - | 7 | - |
| K.E.Cooper | 7 | 2 | 2 | 4 | 4* | - | - | - | - | - |
| R.A.Pick | 10 | 1 | 1 | 2 | 2* | - | - | - | 1 | - |
| M.G.Field-Buss | 3 | 2 | 2 | 0 | 0* | - | - | - | - | - |

### BOWLING AVERAGES

| Name | Overs | Mdns | Runs | Wkts | Avge | Best | 5wI |
|---|---|---|---|---|---|---|---|
| F.D.Stephenson | 129.2 | 11 | 525 | 32 | 16.40 | 5-31 | 1 |
| M.G.Field-Buss | 24 | 1 | 107 | 5 | 21.40 | 2-22 | - |
| M.Saxelby | 108 | 3 | 516 | 18 | 28.66 | 4-29 | - |
| M.A.Crawley | 46 | 1 | 232 | 8 | 29.00 | 2-13 | - |
| R.A.Pick | 75 | 2 | 308 | 9 | 34.22 | 2-27 | - |
| E.E.Hemmings | 112.1 | 4 | 488 | 14 | 34.85 | 4-26 | - |
| K.P.Evans | 118 | 2 | 679 | 18 | 37.72 | 3-41 | - |
| K.E.Cooper | 50 | 3 | 200 | 3 | 66.66 | 1-20 | - |

## NATWEST TROPHY

### BATTING AVERAGES - Including fielding

| Name | Matches | Inns | NO | Runs | HS | Avge | 100s | 50s | Ct | St |
|---|---|---|---|---|---|---|---|---|---|---|
| R.T.Robinson | 3 | 3 | 0 | 197 | 124 | 65.66 | 1 | - | 1 | - |
| D.W.Randall | 3 | 3 | 0 | 166 | 95 | 55.33 | - | 1 | - | - |
| M.Saxelby | 2 | 2 | 1 | 42 | 36 | 42.00 | - | - | 1 | - |
| B.C.Broad | 3 | 3 | 0 | 83 | 38 | 27.66 | - | - | - | - |
| P.Johnson | 3 | 3 | 0 | 66 | 48 | 22.00 | - | - | - | - |
| K.P.Evans | 2 | 2 | 0 | 22 | 20 | 11.00 | - | - | 1 | - |
| P.Pollard | 1 | 1 | 0 | 6 | 6 | 6.00 | - | - | - | - |
| B.N.French | 3 | 2 | 0 | 8 | 7 | 4.00 | - | - | 7 | - |
| F.D.Stephenson | 3 | 2 | 0 | 8 | 7 | 4.00 | - | - | - | - |
| M.A.Crawley | 2 | 2 | 2 | 109 | 74* | - | - | 1 | - | - |
| E.E.Hemmings | 3 | 2 | 2 | 22 | 17* | - | - | - | - | - |
| J.A.Afford | 2 | 0 | 0 | 0 | 0 | - | - | - | - | - |
| R.A.Pick | 3 | 1 | 1 | 0 | 0* | - | - | - | 1 | - |

### BOWLING AVERAGES

| Name | Overs | Mdns | Runs | Wkts | Avge | Best | 5wI |
|---|---|---|---|---|---|---|---|
| M.A.Crawley | 13 | 1 | 29 | 4 | 7.25 | 4-26 | - |
| R.A.Pick | 30 | 4 | 111 | 4 | 27.75 | 3-41 | - |
| M.Saxelby | 18.4 | 1 | 90 | 3 | 30.00 | 2-42 | - |
| F.D.Stephenson | 29 | 0 | 99 | 2 | 49.50 | 1-10 | - |
| E.E.Hemmings | 33 | 3 | 135 | 2 | 67.50 | 1-27 | - |
| J.A.Afford | 23 | 5 | 78 | 1 | 78.00 | 1-40 | - |
| K.P.Evans | 23 | 3 | 82 | 0 | - | - | - |

# SOMERSET

## BRITANNIC ASS. CHAMPIONSHIP

### BATTING AVERAGES - Including fielding

| Name | Matches | Inns | NO | Runs | HS | Avge | 100s | 50s | Ct | St |
|---|---|---|---|---|---|---|---|---|---|---|
| S.J.Cook | 22 | 39 | 6 | 2370 | 210* | 71.81 | 9 | 8 | 13 | - |
| I.Fletcher | 1 | 2 | 1 | 58 | 56 | 58.00 | - | 1 | - | - |
| C.J.Tavare | 22 | 35 | 6 | 1482 | 183 | 51.10 | 4 | 7 | 20 | - |
| R.J.Harden | 22 | 36 | 7 | 1242 | 134 | 42.82 | 2 | 9 | 19 | - |
| A.N.Hayhurst | 18 | 30 | 5 | 883 | 172* | 35.32 | 3 | 1 | 5 | - |
| P.M.Roebuck | 16 | 27 | 3 | 820 | 101 | 34.16 | 1 | 5 | 3 | - |
| I.G.Swallow | 4 | 5 | 3 | 67 | 41* | 33.50 | - | - | 3 | - |
| G.D.Rose | 14 | 19 | 2 | 567 | 106 | 33.35 | 2 | 2 | 8 | - |
| N.D.Burns | 22 | 32 | 8 | 794 | 108 | 33.08 | 1 | 4 | 35 | 8 |
| K.H.Macleay | 14 | 19 | 6 | 388 | 63 | 29.84 | - | 2 | 5 | - |
| R.J.Bartlett | 5 | 7 | 1 | 177 | 71 | 29.50 | - | 1 | 3 | - |
| R.P.Lefebvre | 15 | 16 | 3 | 361 | 100 | 27.76 | 1 | 1 | 6 | - |
| M.Lathwell | 1 | 2 | 0 | 47 | 43 | 23.50 | - | - | - | - |
| G.T.J.Townsend | 2 | 4 | 0 | 68 | 29 | 17.00 | - | - | 2 | - |
| N.A.Mallender | 13 | 11 | 3 | 108 | 19 | 13.50 | - | - | 1 | - |
| N.J.Pringle | 1 | 2 | 0 | 24 | 17 | 12.00 | - | - | 1 | - |
| H.R.J.Trump | 16 | 15 | 6 | 79 | 30* | 8.77 | - | - | 11 | - |
| J.C.Hallett | 8 | 5 | 1 | 35 | 15 | 8.75 | - | - | 4 | - |
| D.A.Graveney | 20 | 13 | 7 | 51 | 17 | 8.50 | - | - | 10 | - |
| D.Beal | 2 | 2 | 0 | 1 | 1 | 0.50 | - | - | - | - |
| A.P.van Troost | 4 | 1 | 1 | 0 | 0* | - | - | - | 1 | - |

### BOWLING AVERAGES

| Name | Overs | Mdns | Runs | Wkts | Avge | Best | 5wI | 10wM |
|---|---|---|---|---|---|---|---|---|
| N.A.Mallender | 349.5 | 76 | 969 | 42 | 23.07 | 6-43 | 3 | - |
| K.H.Macleay | 266.3 | 51 | 807 | 25 | 32.28 | 3-40 | - | - |
| P.M.Roebuck | 128 | 32 | 309 | 9 | 34.33 | 3-10 | - | - |
| D.A.Graveney | 673.2 | 147 | 2041 | 53 | 38.50 | 7-105 | 2 | - |
| H.R.J.Trump | 570.3 | 102 | 1826 | 47 | 38.85 | 6-48 | 4 | - |
| R.J.Harden | 23.5 | 0 | 122 | 3 | 40.66 | 2-70 | - | - |
| G.D.Rose | 307 | 51 | 1006 | 23 | 43.73 | 4-77 | - | - |
| I.G.Swallow | 100.1 | 16 | 354 | 8 | 44.25 | 3-43 | - | - |
| A.P.van Troost | 86.4 | 12 | 267 | 6 | 44.50 | 2-25 | - | - |
| J.C.Hallett | 178.3 | 31 | 637 | 12 | 53.08 | 3-154 | - | - |
| R.P.Lefebvre | 353 | 71 | 1048 | 18 | 58.22 | 3-51 | - | - |
| A.N.Hayhurst | 191.3 | 30 | 715 | 9 | 79.44 | 2-67 | - | - |
| D.Beal | 44 | 3 | 209 | 1 | 209.00 | 1-37 | - | - |
| S.J.Cook | 4 | 0 | 26 | 0 | - | - | - | - |
| M.Lathwell | 17 | 6 | 55 | 0 | - | - | - | - |

## BENSON & HEDGES CUP

### BATTING AVERAGES - Including fielding

| Name | Matches | Inns | NO | Runs | HS | Avge | 100s | 50s | Ct | St |
|---|---|---|---|---|---|---|---|---|---|---|
| S.J.Cook | 4 | 4 | 0 | 213 | 76 | 53.25 | - | 2 | 1 | - |
| A.N.Hayhurst | 2 | 2 | 0 | 102 | 70 | 51.00 | - | 1 | 1 | - |
| N.D.Burns | 4 | 4 | 1 | 110 | 43* | 36.66 | - | - | 1 | 1 |
| C.J.Tavare | 4 | 4 | 0 | 139 | 53 | 34.75 | - | 1 | 2 | - |
| R.P.Lefebvre | 4 | 4 | 2 | 51 | 23* | 25.50 | - | - | 1 | - |
| P.M.Roebuck | 4 | 4 | 0 | 74 | 61 | 18.50 | - | 1 | - | - |
| M.W.Cleal | 2 | 1 | 0 | 18 | 18 | 18.00 | - | - | - | - |
| R.J.Bartlett | 2 | 2 | 0 | 28 | 14 | 14.00 | - | - | 1 | - |
| G.D.Rose | 4 | 4 | 0 | 37 | 23 | 9.25 | - | - | - | - |
| R.J.Harden | 4 | 4 | 0 | 26 | 21 | 6.50 | - | - | - | - |
| I.G.Swallow | 3 | 2 | 0 | 5 | 3 | 2.50 | - | - | 1 | - |
| N.A.Mallender | 4 | 3 | 1 | 4 | 2* | 2.00 | - | - | 1 | - |
| D.Beal | 2 | 2 | 1 | 1 | 1 | 1.00 | - | - | - | - |
| D.A.Graveney | 1 | 1 | 1 | 3 | 3* | - | - | - | - | - |

### BOWLING AVERAGES

| Name | Overs | Mdns | Runs | Wkts | Avge | Best | 5wI |
|---|---|---|---|---|---|---|---|
| R.P.Lefebvre | 38 | 6 | 150 | 4 | 37.50 | 3-44 | - |
| D.Beal | 16 | 1 | 114 | 3 | 38.00 | 2-63 | - |
| I.G.Swallow | 24 | 1 | 111 | 2 | 55.50 | 1-31 | - |
| G.D.Rose | 38.5 | 2 | 172 | 3 | 57.33 | 2-48 | - |
| N.A.Mallender | 41 | 3 | 181 | 3 | 60.33 | 1-35 | - |
| A.N.Hayhurst | 5.1 | 0 | 18 | 0 | - | - | - |
| D.A.Graveney | 7 | 0 | 33 | 0 | - | - | - |
| M.W.Cleal | 10 | 0 | 55 | 0 | - | - | - |
| P.M.Roebuck | 13 | 0 | 63 | 0 | - | - | - |

## REFUGE ASSURANCE LEAGUE

### BATTING AVERAGES - Including fielding

| Name | Matches | Inns | NO | Runs | HS | Avge | 100s | 50s | Ct | St |
|---|---|---|---|---|---|---|---|---|---|---|
| C.J.Tavare | 15 | 15 | 2 | 542 | 75* | 41.69 | - | 5 | 7 | - |
| S.J.Cook | 15 | 15 | 1 | 546 | 129* | 39.00 | 1 | 3 | 4 | - |
| A.N.Hayhurst | 13 | 11 | 5 | 163 | 35 | 27.16 | - | - | 2 | - |
| G.T.J.Townsend | 2 | 2 | 0 | 54 | 27 | 27.00 | - | - | 1 | - |
| N.D.Burns | 15 | 13 | 4 | 235 | 52* | 26.11 | - | 2 | 12 | 6 |
| R.J.Harden | 15 | 15 | 1 | 342 | 79* | 24.42 | - | 1 | 1 | - |
| P.M.Roebuck | 9 | 7 | 0 | 152 | 45 | 21.71 | - | - | 2 | - |
| H.R.J.Trump | 7 | 2 | 1 | 21 | 19 | 21.00 | - | - | 3 | - |
| M.Lathwell | 2 | 2 | 0 | 35 | 20 | 17.50 | - | - | 1 | - |
| G.D.Rose | 12 | 12 | 2 | 160 | 59 | 16.00 | - | 2 | 2 | - |
| R.J.Bartlett | 7 | 7 | 0 | 98 | 34 | 14.00 | - | - | 1 | - |
| N.A.Mallender | 9 | 5 | 3 | 24 | 13* | 12.00 | - | - | - | - |
| K.H.Macleay | 9 | 8 | 3 | 56 | 19 | 11.20 | - | - | 3 | - |
| R.P.Lefebvre | 13 | 11 | 1 | 107 | 27 | 10.70 | - | - | 4 | - |
| N.J.Pringle | 2 | 2 | 0 | 8 | 7 | 4.00 | - | - | - | - |
| J.C.Hallett | 6 | 1 | 0 | 1 | 1 | 1.00 | - | - | 1 | - |
| D.A.Graveney | 10 | 3 | 3 | 20 | 14* | - | - | - | 1 | - |
| I.G.Swallow | 1 | 1 | 1 | 4 | 4* | - | - | - | 1 | - |
| D.Beal | 3 | 0 | 0 | 0 | 0 | - | - | - | 1 | - |

### BOWLING AVERAGES

| Name | Overs | Mdns | Runs | Wkts | Avge | Best | 5wI |
|---|---|---|---|---|---|---|---|
| D.Beal | 8 | 0 | 40 | 2 | 20.00 | 2-40 | - |
| P.M.Roebuck | 49.4 | 3 | 236 | 11 | 21.45 | 4-11 | - |
| D.A.Graveney | 60 | 2 | 253 | 11 | 23.00 | 3-21 | - |
| R.P.Lefebvre | 87 | 5 | 367 | 15 | 24.46 | 3-29 | - |
| K.H.Macleay | 63 | 1 | 252 | 9 | 28.00 | 3-31 | - |
| G.D.Rose | 54.1 | 0 | 290 | 9 | 32.22 | 2-21 | - |
| A.N.Hayhurst | 61.3 | 0 | 308 | 9 | 34.22 | 3-38 | - |
| H.R.J.Trump | 54 | 1 | 277 | 7 | 39.57 | 2-31 | - |
| J.C.Hallett | 40 | 0 | 198 | 5 | 39.60 | 2-32 | - |
| N.A.Mallender | 59 | 1 | 246 | 3 | 82.00 | 2-21 | - |
| I.G.Swallow | 3 | 0 | 16 | 0 | - | - | - |
| M.Lathwell | 4 | 0 | 19 | 0 | - | - | - |

## NATWEST TROPHY

### BATTING AVERAGES - Including fielding

| Name | Matches | Inns | NO | Runs | HS | Avge | 100s | 50s | Ct | St |
|---|---|---|---|---|---|---|---|---|---|---|
| A.N.Hayhurst | 3 | 3 | 1 | 154 | 91* | 77.00 | - | 2 | 1 | - |
| P.M.Roebuck | 3 | 3 | 1 | 99 | 63* | 49.50 | - | 1 | 2 | - |
| C.J.Tavare | 3 | 3 | 0 | 127 | 59 | 42.33 | - | 1 | 3 | - |
| R.P.Lefebvre | 3 | 2 | 1 | 34 | 21* | 34.00 | - | - | 1 | - |
| R.J.Harden | 3 | 3 | 0 | 69 | 39 | 23.00 | - | - | 1 | - |
| S.J.Cook | 3 | 3 | 0 | 56 | 35 | 18.66 | - | - | - | - |
| M.Lathwell | 1 | 1 | 0 | 16 | 16 | 16.00 | - | - | - | - |
| N.D.Burns | 3 | 3 | 1 | 11 | 5* | 5.50 | - | - | 2 | - |
| G.D.Rose | 2 | 1 | 0 | 3 | 3 | 3.00 | - | - | - | - |
| H.R.J.Trump | 1 | 1 | 0 | 1 | 1 | 1.00 | - | - | - | - |
| D.Beal | 1 | 1 | 0 | 0 | 0 | 0.00 | - | - | - | - |
| K.H.Macleay | 2 | 1 | 1 | 25 | 25* | - | - | - | 1 | - |
| D.A.Graveney | 3 | 0 | 0 | 0 | 0 | - | - | - | 1 | - |
| N.A.Mallender | 1 | 0 | 0 | 0 | 0 | - | - | - | - | - |
| J.C.Hallett | 1 | 0 | 0 | 0 | 0 | - | - | - | - | - |

### BOWLING AVERAGES

| Name | Overs | Mdns | Runs | Wkts | Avge | Best | 5wI |
|---|---|---|---|---|---|---|---|
| N.A.Mallender | 12 | 4 | 23 | 3 | 7.66 | 3-23 | - |
| R.P.Lefebvre | 36 | 7 | 89 | 6 | 14.83 | 3-27 | - |
| A.N.Hayhurst | 35.3 | 4 | 137 | 8 | 17.12 | 5-60 | 1 |
| K.H.Macleay | 24 | 1 | 67 | 3 | 22.33 | 2-35 | - |
| D.A.Graveney | 31 | 5 | 92 | 3 | 30.66 | 1-24 | - |
| P.M.Roebuck | 14 | 0 | 62 | 1 | 62.00 | 1-43 | - |
| D.Beal | 2 | 0 | 12 | 0 | - | - | - |
| J.C.Hallett | 12 | 1 | 31 | 0 | - | - | - |
| H.R.J.Trump | 6 | 0 | 33 | 0 | - | - | - |
| G.D.Rose | 7 | 0 | 40 | 0 | - | - | - |

# SURREY

## BRITANNIC ASS. CHAMPIONSHIP

### BATTING AVERAGES - Including fielding

| Name | Matches | Inns | NO | Runs | HS | Avge | 100s | 50s | Ct | St |
|---|---|---|---|---|---|---|---|---|---|---|
| D.J.Bicknell | 22 | 40 | 2 | 1762 | 151 | 46.36 | 5 | 8 | 10 | - |
| G.P.Thorpe | 21 | 35 | 7 | 1164 | 177 | 41.57 | 4 | 4 | 8 | - |
| D.M.Ward | 22 | 38 | 5 | 1304 | 151 | 39.51 | 1 | 9 | 9 | - |
| A.J.Stewart | 17 | 30 | 6 | 936 | 109 | 39.00 | 1 | 6 | 20 | - |
| J.D.Robinson | 4 | 6 | 1 | 186 | 79 | 37.20 | - | 2 | - | - |
| R.I.Alikhan | 18 | 33 | 2 | 963 | 96 * | 31.06 | - | 7 | 9 | - |
| M.A.Feltham | 12 | 16 | 4 | 327 | 69 * | 27.25 | - | 1 | 3 | - |
| I.A.Greig | 19 | 29 | 4 | 593 | 72 | 23.72 | - | 3 | 7 | - |
| K.T.Medlycott | 18 | 25 | 2 | 513 | 66 | 22.30 | - | 4 | 6 | - |
| M.A.Lynch | 10 | 17 | 1 | 342 | 141 * | 21.37 | 1 | 1 | 13 | - |
| N.M.Kendrick | 2 | 4 | 1 | 58 | 24 | 19.33 | - | - | 1 | - |
| M.P.Bicknell | 15 | 22 | 4 | 312 | 63 | 17.33 | - | 1 | 3 | - |
| N.F.Sargeant | 20 | 27 | 4 | 362 | 49 | 15.73 | - | - | 43 | 5 |
| Waqar Younis | 17 | 20 | 8 | 177 | 31 | 14.75 | - | - | 3 | - |
| A.J.Murphy | 19 | 20 | 8 | 71 | 18 | 5.91 | - | - | 4 | - |
| J.Boiling | 4 | 7 | 1 | 22 | 16 | 3.66 | - | - | 6 | - |
| A.G.Robson | 2 | 3 | 0 | 3 | 3 | 1.00 | - | - | - | - |

### BOWLING AVERAGES

| Name | Overs | Mdns | Runs | Wkts | Avge | Best | 5wI | 10wM |
|---|---|---|---|---|---|---|---|---|
| Waqar Younis | 570.1 | 109 | 1623 | 113 | 14.36 | 7-87 | 13 | 3 |
| R.I.Alikhan | 5 | 0 | 43 | 2 | 21.50 | 2-43 | - | - |
| N.M.Kendrick | 105 | 26 | 262 | 12 | 21.83 | 5-54 | 2 | 1 |
| M.P.Bicknell | 470.5 | 118 | 1256 | 45 | 27.91 | 7-52 | 1 | - |
| M.A.Feltham | 328 | 56 | 996 | 35 | 28.45 | 4-36 | - | - |
| D.J.Bicknell | 5.3 | 0 | 62 | 2 | 31.00 | 2-62 | - | - |
| D.M.Ward | 7.5 | 0 | 66 | 2 | 33.00 | 2-66 | - | - |
| K.T.Medlycott | 458.5 | 98 | 1569 | 38 | 41.28 | 4-56 | - | - |
| I.A.Greig | 154.2 | 31 | 398 | 9 | 44.22 | 3-30 | - | - |
| J.Boiling | 149.1 | 37 | 420 | 9 | 46.66 | 4-157 | - | - |
| A.J.Murphy | 546.4 | 118 | 1667 | 35 | 47.62 | 5-63 | 1 | - |
| J.D.Robinson | 28 | 3 | 110 | 2 | 55.00 | 1-18 | - | - |
| N.F.Sargeant | 5 | 0 | 88 | 1 | 88.00 | 1-88 | - | - |
| A.G.Robson | 39 | 14 | 103 | 1 | 103.00 | 1-72 | - | - |
| G.P.Thorpe | 39 | 5 | 157 | 1 | 157.00 | 1-38 | - | - |
| M.A.Lynch | 9 | 1 | 29 | 0 | | - | - | - |
| A.J.Stewart | 7 | 0 | 34 | 0 | | - | - | - |

## BENSON & HEDGES CUP

### BATTING AVERAGES - Including fielding

| Name | Matches | Inns | NO | Runs | HS | Avge | 100s | 50s | Ct | St |
|---|---|---|---|---|---|---|---|---|---|---|
| A.J.Stewart | 4 | 4 | 1 | 195 | 110 * | 65.00 | 1 | 1 | 3 | - |
| A.D.Brown | 1 | 1 | 0 | 37 | 37 | 37.00 | - | - | - | - |
| D.M.Ward | 4 | 4 | 0 | 120 | 46 | 30.00 | - | - | - | - |
| G.P.Thorpe | 4 | 4 | 0 | 112 | 41 | 28.00 | - | - | 1 | - |
| D.J.Bicknell | 4 | 4 | 0 | 108 | 53 | 27.00 | - | 1 | 1 | - |
| J.D.Robinson | 3 | 3 | 0 | 77 | 38 | 25.66 | - | - | 2 | - |
| I.A.Greig | 4 | 4 | 0 | 93 | 47 | 23.25 | - | - | 2 | - |
| J.Boiling | 2 | 2 | 1 | 10 | 7 | 10.00 | - | - | - | - |
| M.A.Lynch | 2 | 2 | 0 | 20 | 20 | 10.00 | - | - | - | - |
| C.K.Bullen | 2 | 2 | 0 | 16 | 16 | 8.00 | - | - | 2 | - |
| Waqar Younis | 4 | 3 | 2 | 8 | 5 * | 8.00 | - | - | 1 | - |
| M.P.Bicknell | 4 | 3 | 0 | 17 | 7 | 5.66 | - | - | - | - |
| M.A.Feltham | 2 | 2 | 0 | 6 | 4 | 3.00 | - | - | 1 | - |
| A.J.Murphy | 4 | 2 | 1 | 1 | 1 | 1.00 | - | - | - | - |

### BOWLING AVERAGES

| Name | Overs | Mdns | Runs | Wkts | Avge | Best | 5wI |
|---|---|---|---|---|---|---|---|
| I.A.Greig | 9.2 | 0 | 26 | 2 | 13.00 | 2-26 | - |
| J.D.Robinson | 19.2 | 3 | 60 | 3 | 20.00 | 2-31 | - |
| M.P.Bicknell | 41 | 2 | 158 | 5 | 31.60 | 3-28 | - |
| M.A.Feltham | 21.2 | 1 | 103 | 3 | 34.33 | 2-45 | - |
| Waqar Younis | 35.4 | 2 | 140 | 4 | 35.00 | 3-29 | - |
| A.J.Murphy | 41 | 4 | 151 | 4 | 37.75 | 2-23 | - |
| J.Boiling | 20 | 0 | 81 | 2 | 40.50 | 1-38 | - |
| C.K.Bullen | 13 | 0 | 58 | 1 | 58.00 | 1-29 | - |
| G.P.Thorpe | 8 | 0 | 35 | 0 | | - | - |

## REFUGE ASSURANCE

### BATTING AVERAGES - Including fielding

| Name | Matches | Inns | NO | Runs | HS | Avge | 100s | 50s | Ct | St |
|---|---|---|---|---|---|---|---|---|---|---|
| G.P.Thorpe | 15 | 13 | 2 | 431 | 115 * | 39.18 | 1 | 3 | 2 | - |
| M.A.Lynch | 14 | 14 | 2 | 433 | 97 | 36.08 | - | 3 | 6 | - |
| A.J.Stewart | 13 | 12 | 1 | 341 | 84 * | 31.00 | - | 4 | 13 | 1 |
| D.J.Bicknell | 9 | 9 | 0 | 260 | 68 | 28.88 | - | 2 | 3 | - |
| J.D.Robinson | 15 | 13 | 3 | 253 | 55 * | 25.30 | - | 2 | 4 | - |
| M.P.Bicknell | 7 | 4 | 2 | 50 | 20 * | 25.00 | - | - | 2 | - |
| M.A.Feltham | 9 | 7 | 3 | 93 | 23 * | 23.25 | - | - | 3 | - |
| A.D.Brown | 7 | 6 | 0 | 133 | 45 | 22.16 | - | - | - | - |
| D.M.Ward | 15 | 14 | 1 | 268 | 56 | 20.61 | - | 3 | 6 | - |
| I.A.Greig | 13 | 10 | 2 | 162 | 68 * | 20.25 | - | 1 | 4 | - |
| J.Boiling | 9 | 4 | 2 | 20 | 12 * | 10.00 | - | - | - | - |
| K.T.Medlycott | 2 | 1 | 0 | 9 | 9 | 9.00 | - | - | 2 | - |
| Waqar Younis | 12 | 6 | 1 | 10 | 8 | 2.00 | - | - | 2 | - |
| M.A.Butcher | 1 | 1 | 1 | 48 | 48 * | | - | - | - | - |
| C.K.Bullen | 6 | 4 | 4 | 40 | 22 * | | - | - | 2 | - |
| N.F.Sargeant | 2 | 1 | 1 | 13 | 13 * | | - | - | 1 | - |
| A.J.Murphy | 13 | 3 | 3 | 6 | 5 * | | - | - | 1 | - |
| A.G.Robson | 3 | 0 | 0 | 0 | 0 | | - | - | - | - |

### BOWLING AVERAGES

| Name | Overs | Mdns | Runs | Wkts | Avge | Best | 5wI |
|---|---|---|---|---|---|---|---|
| Waqar Younis | 88.4 | 8 | 371 | 21 | 17.66 | 4-21 | - |
| A.G.Robson | 24 | 0 | 128 | 7 | 18.28 | 3-42 | - |
| I.A.Greig | 29.5 | 0 | 146 | 6 | 24.33 | 3-10 | - |
| A.J.Murphy | 97 | 7 | 444 | 18 | 24.66 | 3-15 | - |
| G.P.Thorpe | 12 | 0 | 78 | 3 | 26.00 | 3-21 | - |
| C.K.Bullen | 14 | 0 | 83 | 3 | 27.66 | 3-38 | - |
| M.P.Bicknell | 51 | 1 | 239 | 7 | 34.14 | 3-36 | - |
| M.A.Feltham | 65.1 | 2 | 337 | 9 | 37.44 | 3-44 | - |
| J.Boiling | 60 | 0 | 312 | 8 | 39.00 | 2-24 | - |
| J.D.Robinson | 88.1 | 3 | 402 | 9 | 44.66 | 2-32 | - |
| M.A.Lynch | 0.4 | 0 | 6 | 0 | | - | - |
| M.A.Butcher | 3 | 0 | 16 | 0 | | - | - |

## NATWEST TROPHY

### BATTING AVERAGES - Including fielding

| Name | Matches | Inns | NO | Runs | HS | Avge | 100s | 50s | Ct | St |
|---|---|---|---|---|---|---|---|---|---|---|
| M.P.Bicknell | 4 | 2 | 1 | 70 | 66 * | 70.00 | - | 1 | - | - |
| A.J.Stewart | 4 | 4 | 1 | 206 | 76 * | 68.66 | - | 2 | 6 | - |
| G.P.Thorpe | 4 | 4 | 1 | 138 | 93 | 46.00 | - | 1 | 1 | - |
| D.M.Ward | 4 | 4 | 0 | 164 | 62 | 41.00 | - | 2 | - | - |
| J.D.Robinson | 4 | 3 | 1 | 50 | 47 | 25.00 | - | - | - | - |
| D.J.Bicknell | 4 | 4 | 0 | 89 | 28 | 22.25 | - | - | - | - |
| I.A.Greig | 3 | 3 | 1 | 35 | 20 | 17.50 | - | - | - | - |
| M.A.Lynch | 4 | 4 | 0 | 66 | 48 | 16.50 | - | - | 3 | - |
| Waqar Younis | 4 | 2 | 0 | 30 | 26 | 15.00 | - | - | - | - |
| J.Boiling | 4 | 2 | 0 | 29 | 22 | 14.50 | - | - | 3 | - |
| A.J.Murphy | 4 | 2 | 2 | 1 | 1 * | | - | - | - | - |
| M.A.Feltham | 1 | 0 | 0 | 0 | 0 | | - | - | - | - |

### BOWLING AVERAGES

| Name | Overs | Mdns | Runs | Wkts | Avge | Best | 5wI |
|---|---|---|---|---|---|---|---|
| Waqar Younis | 44.3 | 5 | 171 | 13 | 13.15 | 5-40 | 1 |
| M.P.Bicknell | 39.3 | 2 | 135 | 5 | 27.00 | 2-45 | - |
| J.D.Robinson | 40 | 4 | 152 | 4 | 38.00 | 3-46 | - |
| M.A.Feltham | 10 | 1 | 46 | 1 | 46.00 | 1-46 | - |
| A.J.Murphy | 40.2 | 5 | 158 | 3 | 52.66 | 1-27 | - |
| J.Boiling | 48 | 4 | 165 | 3 | 55.00 | 2-22 | - |
| G.P.Thorpe | 0.1 | 0 | 0 | 0 | | - | - |
| M.A.Lynch | 10 | 1 | 28 | 0 | | - | - |

# SUSSEX

## BRITANNIC ASS. CHAMPIONSHIP

### BATTING AVERAGES - Including fielding

| Name | Matches | Inns | NO | Runs | HS | Avge | 100s | 50s | Ct | St |
|---|---|---|---|---|---|---|---|---|---|---|
| R.A.Bunting | 3 | 4 | 3 | 106 | 51 * | 106.00 | - | 1 | - | - |
| A.P.Wells | 21 | 34 | 5 | 1777 | 253 * | 61.27 | 7 | 5 | 7 | - |
| D.M.Smith | 19 | 33 | 5 | 1130 | 126 * | 40.35 | 1 | 8 | 14 | - |
| N.J.Lenham | 18 | 31 | 3 | 1028 | 193 | 36.71 | 3 | 3 | 11 | - |
| B.T.P.Donelan | 12 | 15 | 5 | 353 | 61 | 35.30 | - | 2 | 3 | - |
| M.P.Speight | 12 | 18 | 1 | 572 | 89 | 33.64 | - | 5 | 5 | - |
| C.M.Wells | 12 | 19 | 5 | 451 | 76 | 32.21 | - | 2 | 2 | - |
| A.I.C.Dodemaide | 19 | 28 | 9 | 581 | 100 * | 30.57 | 1 | 1 | 7 | - |
| J.W.Hall | 14 | 25 | 2 | 685 | 117 * | 29.78 | 1 | 4 | 8 | - |
| P.Moores | 22 | 27 | 3 | 612 | 86 * | 25.50 | - | 6 | 53 | 5 |
| P.W.G.Parker | 16 | 26 | 1 | 607 | 111 | 24.28 | 1 | 3 | 8 | - |
| J.A.North | 5 | 7 | 1 | 122 | 63 * | 20.33 | - | 1 | 1 | - |
| A.C.S.Pigott | 18 | 21 | 5 | 291 | 65 | 18.18 | - | 1 | 5 | - |
| K.Greenfield | 7 | 11 | 0 | 156 | 64 | 14.18 | - | 1 | 15 | - |
| I.D.K.Salisbury | 20 | 20 | 7 | 179 | 34 | 13.76 | - | - | 12 | - |
| A.N.Jones | 21 | 17 | 5 | 119 | 28 | 9.91 | - | - | 1 | - |
| R.Hanley | 1 | 2 | 0 | 19 | 19 | 9.50 | - | - | - | - |
| E.S.H.Giddins | 2 | 1 | 1 | 14 | 14 * | - | - | - | - | - |

### BOWLING AVERAGES

| Name | Overs | Mdns | Runs | Wkts | Avge | Best | 5wI | 10wM |
|---|---|---|---|---|---|---|---|---|
| A.P.Wells | 5 | 1 | 21 | 1 | 21.00 | 1-21 | - | - |
| A.I.C.Dodemaide | 555 | 110 | 1583 | 52 | 30.44 | 5-130 | 1 | - |
| R.A.Bunting | 62.2 | 7 | 260 | 8 | 32.50 | 4-99 | - | - |
| C.M.Wells | 216.4 | 60 | 598 | 18 | 33.22 | 7-42 | 1 | - |
| B.T.P.Donelan | 426.3 | 112 | 1162 | 34 | 34.17 | 6-62 | 2 | 1 |
| A.N.Jones | 502.2 | 68 | 1829 | 53 | 34.50 | 5-46 | 2 | - |
| J.A.North | 129 | 20 | 507 | 14 | 36.21 | 3-54 | - | - |
| A.C.S.Pigott | 415.3 | 92 | 1293 | 35 | 36.94 | 5-37 | 1 | - |
| I.D.K.Salisbury | 605.2 | 144 | 1837 | 47 | 39.08 | 5-40 | 1 | - |
| N.J.Lenham | 29 | 5 | 79 | 2 | 39.50 | 2-5 | - | - |
| E.S.H.Giddins | 56.2 | 6 | 186 | 2 | 93.00 | 1-29 | - | - |
| P.W.G.Parker | 2 | 0 | 10 | 0 | - | - | - | - |
| D.M.Smith | 2 | 0 | 15 | 0 | - | - | - | - |

## BENSON & HEDGES CUP

### BATTING AVERAGES - Including fielding

| Name | Matches | Inns | NO | Runs | HS | Avge | 100s | 50s | Ct | St |
|---|---|---|---|---|---|---|---|---|---|---|
| D.M.Smith | 4 | 4 | 0 | 209 | 102 | 52.25 | 1 | 1 | 2 | - |
| P.W.G.Parker | 3 | 3 | 0 | 123 | 87 | 41.00 | - | 1 | - | - |
| J.W.Hall | 4 | 4 | 0 | 150 | 71 | 37.50 | - | 1 | - | - |
| K.Greenfield | 2 | 2 | 1 | 33 | 33 | 33.00 | - | - | 3 | - |
| A.P.Wells | 4 | 4 | 1 | 96 | 66 | 32.00 | - | 1 | 1 | - |
| I.D.K.Salisbury | 4 | 3 | 1 | 32 | 17 * | 16.00 | - | - | 2 | - |
| A.C.S.Pigott | 4 | 3 | 0 | 47 | 29 | 15.66 | - | - | 3 | - |
| J.A.North | 4 | 3 | 0 | 44 | 22 | 14.66 | - | - | - | - |
| M.P.Speight | 3 | 3 | 0 | 42 | 35 | 14.00 | - | - | - | - |
| P.Moores | 4 | 3 | 0 | 31 | 20 | 10.33 | - | - | 6 | - |
| E.S.H.Giddins | 1 | 1 | 0 | 0 | 0 | 0.00 | - | - | - | - |
| B.T.P.Donelan | 1 | 1 | 1 | 8 | 8 * | - | - | - | - | - |
| R.A.Bunting | 2 | 2 | 2 | 3 | 2 * | - | - | - | 1 | - |
| A.I.C.Dodemaide | 1 | 0 | 0 | 0 | 0 | - | - | - | - | - |
| A.N.Jones | 3 | 1 | 1 | 0 | 0 * | - | - | - | - | - |

### BOWLING AVERAGES

| Name | Overs | Mdns | Runs | Wkts | Avge | Best | 5wI |
|---|---|---|---|---|---|---|---|
| A.N.Jones | 30.4 | 4 | 117 | 7 | 16.71 | 3-33 | - |
| A.I.C.Dodemaide | 7 | 3 | 17 | 1 | 17.00 | 1-17 | - |
| I.D.K.Salisbury | 41 | 3 | 149 | 6 | 24.83 | 3-40 | - |
| A.C.S.Pigott | 41.4 | 4 | 175 | 5 | 35.00 | 3-29 | - |
| E.S.H.Giddins | 8 | 2 | 46 | 1 | 46.00 | 1-46 | - |
| J.A.North | 41 | 1 | 208 | 4 | 52.00 | 2-80 | - |
| R.A.Bunting | 17 | 1 | 75 | 1 | 75.00 | 1-34 | - |
| K.Greenfield | 18 | 0 | 89 | 1 | 89.00 | 1-35 | - |
| B.T.P.Donelan | 11 | 0 | 54 | 0 | - | - | - |

## REFUGE ASSURANCE LEAGUE

### BATTING AVERAGES - Including fielding

| Name | Matches | Inns | NO | Runs | HS | Avge | 100s | 50s | Ct | St |
|---|---|---|---|---|---|---|---|---|---|---|
| D.M.Smith | 5 | 5 | 0 | 208 | 78 | 41.60 | - | 1 | 3 | - |
| J.W.Hall | 3 | 3 | 0 | 96 | 50 | 32.00 | - | 1 | - | - |
| K.Greenfield | 15 | 14 | 3 | 341 | 78 * | 31.00 | - | 3 | 1 | - |
| M.P.Speight | 11 | 11 | 1 | 295 | 106 * | 29.50 | 1 | - | 5 | - |
| P.W.G.Parker | 11 | 11 | 0 | 307 | 104 | 27.90 | 1 | 1 | 5 | - |
| N.J.Lenham | 12 | 12 | 1 | 272 | 86 | 24.72 | - | 2 | 2 | - |
| A.P.Wells | 13 | 13 | 0 | 289 | 58 | 22.23 | - | 1 | 4 | - |
| C.M.Wells | 9 | 8 | 2 | 128 | 34 * | 21.33 | - | - | 1 | - |
| I.J.Gould | 1 | 1 | 0 | 21 | 21 | 21.00 | - | - | - | - |
| A.I.C.Dodemaide | 11 | 8 | 3 | 96 | 31 * | 19.20 | - | - | 3 | - |
| B.T.P.Donelan | 2 | 1 | 0 | 19 | 19 | 19.00 | - | - | 1 | - |
| A.N.Jones | 15 | 7 | 6 | 18 | 7 * | 18.00 | - | - | 5 | - |
| P.Moores | 14 | 12 | 2 | 153 | 34 | 15.30 | - | - | 15 | 1 |
| J.A.North | 6 | 6 | 1 | 50 | 18 | 10.00 | - | - | 5 | - |
| I.D.K.Salisbury | 15 | 9 | 2 | 61 | 23 | 8.71 | - | - | 2 | - |
| A.C.S.Pigott | 15 | 14 | 3 | 73 | 14 | 6.63 | - | - | 5 | - |
| R.A.Bunting | 4 | 3 | 2 | 3 | 2 * | 3.00 | - | - | - | - |
| R.Hanley | 1 | 1 | 0 | 2 | 2 | 2.00 | - | - | 1 | - |
| E.S.H.Giddins | 2 | 0 | 0 | 0 | 0 | - | - | - | - | - |

### BOWLING AVERAGES

| Name | Overs | Mdns | Runs | Wkts | Avge | Best | 5wI |
|---|---|---|---|---|---|---|---|
| A.C.S.Pigott | 95.5 | 2 | 461 | 27 | 17.07 | 5-30 | 1 |
| R.A.Bunting | 24.3 | 0 | 137 | 8 | 17.12 | 4-35 | - |
| J.A.North | 27 | 1 | 162 | 8 | 20.25 | 3-29 | - |
| A.N.Jones | 81.2 | 5 | 448 | 22 | 20.36 | 5-32 | 1 |
| N.J.Lenham | 8 | 0 | 63 | 3 | 21.00 | 1-8 | - |
| A.I.C.Dodemaide | 70 | 5 | 260 | 7 | 37.14 | 2-22 | - |
| I.D.K.Salisbury | 82.1 | 4 | 399 | 10 | 39.90 | 3-10 | - |
| B.T.P.Donelan | 15 | 1 | 58 | 1 | 58.00 | 1-35 | - |
| C.M.Wells | 53 | 0 | 228 | 1 | 228.00 | 1-31 | - |
| E.S.H.Giddins | 7 | 0 | 38 | 0 | - | - | - |
| K.Greenfield | 25.3 | 0 | 154 | 0 | - | - | - |

## NATWEST TROPHY

### BATTING AVERAGES - Including fielding

| Name | Matches | Inns | NO | Runs | HS | Avge | 100s | 50s | Ct | St |
|---|---|---|---|---|---|---|---|---|---|---|
| D.M.Smith | 2 | 2 | 0 | 102 | 62 | 51.00 | - | 1 | 1 | - |
| N.J.Lenham | 2 | 2 | 0 | 85 | 66 | 42.50 | - | 1 | - | - |
| M.P.Speight | 2 | 2 | 0 | 68 | 48 | 34.00 | - | - | - | - |
| A.P.Wells | 2 | 2 | 0 | 48 | 40 | 24.00 | - | - | - | - |
| I.D.K.Salisbury | 2 | 2 | 1 | 18 | 14 * | 18.00 | - | - | - | - |
| P.Moores | 2 | 2 | 0 | 30 | 26 | 15.00 | - | - | 2 | - |
| P.W.G.Parker | 2 | 2 | 0 | 29 | 17 | 14.50 | - | - | 2 | - |
| C.M.Wells | 2 | 2 | 0 | 11 | 11 | 5.50 | - | - | - | - |
| A.C.S.Pigott | 2 | 2 | 0 | 7 | 7 | 3.50 | - | - | - | - |
| A.I.C.Dodemaide | 2 | 2 | 2 | 59 | 32 * | - | - | - | 1 | - |
| A.N.Jones | 2 | 1 | 1 | 0 | 0 * | - | - | - | - | - |

### BOWLING AVERAGES

| Name | Overs | Mdns | Runs | Wkts | Avge | Best | 5wI |
|---|---|---|---|---|---|---|---|
| C.M.Wells | 21 | 3 | 55 | 4 | 13.75 | 3-16 | - |
| N.J.Lenham | 18 | 1 | 60 | 3 | 20.00 | 2-25 | - |
| A.C.S.Pigott | 19.5 | 1 | 65 | 3 | 21.66 | 2-25 | - |
| A.I.C.Dodemaide | 21 | 3 | 64 | 2 | 32.00 | 2-12 | - |
| A.N.Jones | 12 | 0 | 76 | 2 | 38.00 | 2-46 | - |
| I.D.K.Salisbury | 21 | 1 | 76 | 2 | 38.00 | 1-36 | - |

# WARWICKSHIRE

## BRITANNIC ASS. CHAMPIONSHIP

### BATTING AVERAGES - Including fielding

| Name | Matches | Inns | NO | Runs | HS | Avge | 100s | 50s | Ct | St |
|---|---|---|---|---|---|---|---|---|---|---|
| P.C.L.Holloway | 6 | 9 | 5 | 263 | 89* | 65.75 | - | 2 | 9 | - |
| D.A.Reeve | 20 | 33 | 7 | 1260 | 99* | 48.46 | - | 14 | 9 | - |
| R.G.Twose | 2 | 2 | 1 | 42 | 41 | 42.00 | - | - | - | - |
| D.P.Ostler | 22 | 40 | 5 | 1284 | 120* | 36.68 | 1 | 10 | 21 | - |
| A.J.Moles | 22 | 39 | 2 | 1246 | 133 | 33.67 | 1 | 10 | 10 | - |
| T.A.Lloyd | 21 | 35 | 2 | 1076 | 97 | 32.60 | - | 10 | 10 | - |
| J.D.Ratcliffe | 17 | 31 | 1 | 953 | 94 | 31.76 | - | 8 | 15 | - |
| N.M.K.Smith | 5 | 9 | 2 | 209 | 70 | 29.85 | - | 2 | - | - |
| A.R.K.Pierson | 5 | 6 | 4 | 55 | 35 | 27.50 | - | - | 1 | - |
| Asif Din | 15 | 27 | 1 | 685 | 140 | 26.34 | 2 | 1 | 9 | - |
| P.A.Smith | 14 | 23 | 1 | 411 | 68 | 18.68 | - | 2 | 2 | - |
| K.J.Piper | 16 | 23 | 3 | 349 | 55 | 17.45 | - | 1 | 48 | - |
| G.C.Small | 20 | 29 | 7 | 370 | 58 | 16.81 | - | 1 | 5 | - |
| P.A.Booth | 10 | 13 | 0 | 175 | 62 | 13.46 | - | 1 | 5 | - |
| T.A.Munton | 22 | 25 | 8 | 226 | 31 | 13.29 | - | - | 14 | - |
| A.A.Donald | 21 | 21 | 9 | 96 | 18 | 8.00 | - | - | 10 | - |
| J.E.Benjamin | 3 | 4 | 0 | 12 | 11 | 3.00 | - | - | 1 | - |
| S.J.Green | 1 | 1 | 1 | 77 | 77* | - | - | 1 | - | - |

### BOWLING AVERAGES

| Name | Overs | Mdns | Runs | Wkts | Avge | Best | 5wI | 10wM |
|---|---|---|---|---|---|---|---|---|
| A.A.Donald | 522.3 | 91 | 1634 | 83 | 19.68 | 6-69 | 8 | 2 |
| D.A.Reeve | 402.1 | 117 | 957 | 45 | 21.26 | 6-73 | 1 | - |
| T.A.Munton | 662 | 177 | 1795 | 71 | 25.28 | 8-89 | 5 | 2 |
| R.G.Twose | 9 | 0 | 27 | 1 | 27.00 | 1-27 | - | - |
| G.C.Small | 498 | 126 | 1347 | 45 | 29.93 | 4-36 | - | - |
| P.A.Smith | 157.1 | 31 | 513 | 15 | 34.20 | 5-28 | 1 | - |
| J.E.Benjamin | 76.4 | 11 | 257 | 7 | 36.71 | 2-62 | - | - |
| P.A.Booth | 226.1 | 47 | 690 | 18 | 38.33 | 4-103 | - | - |
| N.M.K.Smith | 111 | 32 | 321 | 8 | 40.12 | 3-50 | - | - |
| A.J.Moles | 33 | 13 | 65 | 1 | 65.00 | 1-14 | - | - |
| A.R.K.Pierson | 73 | 11 | 279 | 4 | 69.75 | 3-45 | - | - |
| Asif Din | 53 | 9 | 206 | 2 | 103.00 | 1-37 | - | - |
| D.P.Ostler | 2 | 1 | 7 | 0 | - | - | - | - |
| J.D.Ratcliffe | 3 | 1 | 14 | 0 | - | - | - | - |
| T.A.Lloyd | 16 | 13 | 26 | 0 | - | - | - | - |

## BENSON & HEDGES CUP

### BATTING AVERAGES - Including fielding

| Name | Matches | Inns | NO | Runs | HS | Avge | 100s | 50s | Ct | St |
|---|---|---|---|---|---|---|---|---|---|---|
| Asif Din | 4 | 4 | 0 | 291 | 137 | 72.75 | 1 | 1 | - | - |
| A.J.Moles | 5 | 5 | 0 | 166 | 65 | 33.20 | - | 2 | 4 | - |
| T.A.Lloyd | 5 | 5 | 0 | 154 | 58 | 30.80 | - | 1 | 3 | - |
| J.D.Ratcliffe | 1 | 1 | 0 | 29 | 29 | 29.00 | - | - | - | - |
| D.A.Reeve | 5 | 5 | 0 | 124 | 80 | 24.80 | - | 1 | 3 | - |
| N.M.K.Smith | 1 | 1 | 0 | 23 | 23 | 23.00 | - | - | - | - |
| D.P.Ostler | 5 | 5 | 0 | 100 | 45 | 20.00 | - | - | 2 | - |
| K.J.Piper | 4 | 4 | 2 | 35 | 11* | 17.50 | - | - | 5 | - |
| P.A.Booth | 3 | 2 | 1 | 15 | 11 | 15.00 | - | - | 3 | - |
| P.A.Smith | 5 | 5 | 0 | 62 | 34 | 12.40 | - | - | 1 | - |
| T.A.Munton | 5 | 3 | 1 | 18 | 10 | 9.00 | - | - | 1 | - |
| A.A.Donald | 5 | 3 | 2 | 8 | 6* | 8.00 | - | - | 1 | - |
| R.G.Twose | 1 | 1 | 0 | 5 | 5 | 5.00 | - | - | - | - |
| M.Burns | 1 | 1 | 0 | 3 | 3 | 3.00 | - | - | - | - |
| G.C.Small | 4 | 3 | 0 | 5 | 2 | 1.66 | - | - | 1 | - |
| A.R.K.Pierson | 1 | 1 | 1 | 3 | 3* | - | - | - | - | - |

### BOWLING AVERAGES

| Name | Overs | Mdns | Runs | Wkts | Avge | Best | 5wI |
|---|---|---|---|---|---|---|---|
| A.J.Moles | 4 | 1 | 19 | 1 | 19.00 | 1-19 | - |
| T.A.Munton | 51.4 | 5 | 187 | 9 | 20.77 | 4-35 | - |
| D.A.Reeve | 51.5 | 0 | 233 | 10 | 23.30 | 4-43 | - |
| A.A.Donald | 49 | 2 | 266 | 11 | 24.18 | 4-55 | - |
| P.A.Smith | 28 | 3 | 108 | 4 | 27.00 | 3-28 | - |
| P.A.Booth | 13 | 0 | 81 | 1 | 81.00 | 1-35 | - |
| G.C.Small | 44 | 2 | 193 | 1 | 193.00 | 1-55 | - |
| A.R.K.Pierson | 2 | 0 | 7 | 0 | - | - | - |
| N.M.K.Smith | 4 | 0 | 32 | 0 | - | - | - |

## REFUGE ASSURANCE LEAGUE

### BATTING AVERAGES - Including fielding

| Name | Matches | Inns | NO | Runs | HS | Avge | 100s | 50s | Ct | St |
|---|---|---|---|---|---|---|---|---|---|---|
| P.C.L.Holloway | 5 | 3 | 2 | 67 | 34* | 67.00 | - | - | 2 | - |
| T.A.Lloyd | 13 | 12 | 3 | 373 | 56* | 41.44 | - | 1 | 4 | - |
| Asif Din | 11 | 11 | 2 | 330 | 101* | 36.66 | 1 | 1 | 3 | - |
| A.J.Moles | 13 | 12 | 1 | 385 | 93* | 35.00 | - | 3 | 6 | - |
| N.M.K.Smith | 11 | 8 | 4 | 127 | 39 | 31.75 | - | - | 4 | - |
| D.A.Reeve | 13 | 10 | 1 | 260 | 100 | 28.88 | 1 | - | 2 | - |
| D.P.Ostler | 14 | 11 | 2 | 253 | 62* | 28.11 | - | 2 | 2 | - |
| R.G.Twose | 5 | 3 | 2 | 27 | 26* | 27.00 | - | - | 2 | - |
| P.A.Smith | 13 | 10 | 0 | 252 | 55 | 25.20 | - | 1 | 2 | - |
| K.J.Piper | 9 | 4 | 3 | 17 | 15* | 17.00 | - | - | 7 | 3 |
| J.E.Benjamin | 9 | 3 | 1 | 14 | 12* | 7.00 | - | - | 6 | - |
| A.A.Donald | 8 | 1 | 0 | 7 | 7 | 7.00 | - | - | 3 | - |
| S.J.Green | 2 | 2 | 0 | 7 | 5 | 3.50 | - | - | - | - |
| G.C.Small | 10 | 3 | 0 | 4 | 3 | 1.33 | - | - | 3 | - |
| J.D.Ratcliffe | 1 | 1 | 0 | 1 | 1 | 1.00 | - | - | - | - |
| T.A.Munton | 13 | 3 | 3 | 13 | 10* | - | - | - | 2 | - |
| A.R.K.Pierson | 3 | 0 | 0 | 0 | 0 | - | - | - | - | - |
| D.Brown | 1 | 0 | 0 | 0 | 0 | - | - | - | - | - |

### BOWLING AVERAGES

| Name | Overs | Mdns | Runs | Wkts | Avge | Best | 5wI |
|---|---|---|---|---|---|---|---|
| P.A.Smith | 77.3 | 1 | 404 | 21 | 19.23 | 4-21 | - |
| T.A.Munton | 90 | 6 | 333 | 13 | 25.61 | 5-28 | 1 |
| N.M.K.Smith | 53.3 | 0 | 268 | 10 | 26.80 | 3-52 | - |
| J.E.Benjamin | 58 | 0 | 262 | 9 | 29.11 | 3-33 | - |
| D.A.Reeve | 70.1 | 2 | 352 | 11 | 32.00 | 4-18 | - |
| G.C.Small | 65 | 3 | 322 | 10 | 32.20 | 2-25 | - |
| A.A.Donald | 58 | 1 | 264 | 8 | 33.00 | 2-7 | - |
| D.Brown | 6 | 0 | 35 | 1 | 35.00 | 1-35 | - |
| A.R.K.Pierson | 16 | 1 | 91 | 2 | 45.50 | 1-35 | - |
| A.J.Moles | 4 | 0 | 24 | 0 | - | - | - |
| R.G.Twose | 8 | 0 | 49 | 0 | - | - | - |

## NATWEST TROPHY

### BATTING AVERAGES - Including fielding

| Name | Matches | Inns | NO | Runs | HS | Avge | 100s | 50s | Ct | St |
|---|---|---|---|---|---|---|---|---|---|---|
| J.D.Ratcliffe | 2 | 2 | 1 | 94 | 68* | 94.00 | - | 1 | - | - |
| T.A.Lloyd | 4 | 2 | 0 | 96 | 78 | 48.00 | - | 1 | - | - |
| D.A.Reeve | 4 | 3 | 1 | 89 | 57* | 44.50 | - | 1 | 5 | - |
| A.J.Moles | 4 | 4 | 1 | 109 | 62* | 36.33 | - | 1 | 1 | - |
| Asif Din | 3 | 2 | 0 | 61 | 44 | 30.50 | - | - | - | - |
| D.P.Ostler | 4 | 3 | 1 | 47 | 34* | 23.50 | - | - | - | - |
| P.A.Smith | 4 | 3 | 1 | 42 | 26 | 21.00 | - | - | 1 | - |
| N.M.K.Smith | 2 | 2 | 0 | 38 | 38 | 19.00 | - | - | - | - |
| A.A.Donald | 4 | 2 | 1 | 3 | 2* | 3.00 | - | - | - | - |
| T.A.Munton | 4 | 2 | 0 | 6 | 5 | 3.00 | - | - | 2 | - |
| G.C.Small | 4 | 2 | 0 | 5 | 3 | 2.50 | - | - | - | - |
| P.C.L.Holloway | 1 | 1 | 0 | 2 | 2 | 2.00 | - | - | 2 | 1 |
| K.J.Piper | 3 | 1 | 0 | 1 | 1 | 1.00 | - | - | 4 | - |
| P.A.Booth | 1 | 0 | 0 | 0 | 0 | - | - | - | - | - |

### BOWLING AVERAGES

| Name | Overs | Mdns | Runs | Wkts | Avge | Best | 5wI |
|---|---|---|---|---|---|---|---|
| G.C.Small | 45 | 13 | 111 | 6 | 18.50 | 3-28 | - |
| N.M.K.Smith | 13 | 1 | 37 | 2 | 18.50 | 1-17 | - |
| A.A.Donald | 42 | 4 | 132 | 6 | 22.00 | 4-16 | - |
| D.A.Reeve | 35.5 | 7 | 101 | 3 | 33.66 | 2-19 | - |
| T.A.Munton | 41 | 7 | 111 | 3 | 37.00 | 2-42 | - |
| P.A.Smith | 35.2 | 3 | 116 | 3 | 38.66 | 2-24 | - |
| Asif Din | 3 | 0 | 10 | 0 | - | - | - |

# WORCESTERSHIRE

## BRITANNIC ASS. CHAMPIONSHIP

### BATTING AVERAGES - Including fielding

| Name | Matches | Inns | NO | Runs | HS | Avge | 100s | 50s | Ct | St |
|---|---|---|---|---|---|---|---|---|---|---|
| T.M.Moody | 19 | 31 | 4 | 1770 | 210 | 65.55 | 6 | 8 | 30 | - |
| D.A.Leatherdale | 3 | 4 | 0 | 219 | 157 | 54.75 | 1 | - | 2 | - |
| T.S.Curtis | 22 | 37 | 3 | 1555 | 248 | 45.73 | 3 | 8 | 14 | - |
| G.A.Hick | 16 | 27 | 2 | 975 | 186 | 39.00 | 3 | 4 | 16 | - |
| I.T.Botham | 10 | 17 | 2 | 567 | 104 | 37.80 | 1 | 4 | 7 | - |
| S.J.Rhodes | 22 | 32 | 6 | 907 | 90 | 34.88 | - | 8 | 48 | 7 |
| S.R.Lampitt | 19 | 20 | 5 | 447 | 93 | 29.80 | - | 3 | 5 | - |
| P.Bent | 7 | 12 | 1 | 285 | 100* | 25.90 | 1 | 1 | 3 | - |
| P.A.Neale | 13 | 20 | 4 | 385 | 69* | 24.06 | - | 1 | 5 | - |
| R.K.Illingworth | 17 | 23 | 4 | 442 | 56* | 23.26 | - | 1 | 4 | - |
| C.M.Tolley | 6 | 9 | 3 | 137 | 36 | 22.83 | - | - | 2 | - |
| P.J.Newport | 22 | 24 | 9 | 340 | 48 | 22.66 | - | - | 4 | - |
| G.J.Lord | 9 | 16 | 0 | 356 | 85 | 22.25 | - | 3 | 2 | - |
| G.R.Haynes | 3 | 3 | 1 | 35 | 16 | 17.50 | - | - | - | - |
| D.B.D'Oliveira | 15 | 22 | 2 | 335 | 79 | 16.75 | - | 1 | 21 | - |
| N.V.Radford | 17 | 16 | 6 | 157 | 45 | 15.70 | - | - | 4 | - |
| R.D.Stemp | 8 | 8 | 5 | 30 | 15* | 10.00 | - | - | - | - |
| W.P.C.Weston | 2 | 3 | 0 | 28 | 15 | 9.33 | - | - | - | - |
| M.J.Weston | 2 | 2 | 0 | 14 | 9 | 7.00 | - | - | - | - |
| G.R.Dilley | 10 | 10 | 4 | 37 | 15* | 6.16 | - | - | 3 | - |

### BOWLING AVERAGES

| Name | Overs | Mdns | Runs | Wkts | Avge | Best | 5wI | 10wM |
|---|---|---|---|---|---|---|---|---|
| G.R.Dilley | 281 | 56 | 752 | 35 | 21.48 | 5-91 | 1 | - |
| I.T.Botham | 279.1 | 55 | 886 | 38 | 23.31 | 7-54 | 3 | - |
| R.D.Stemp | 141.1 | 30 | 382 | 15 | 25.46 | 4-62 | - | - |
| C.M.Tolley | 105 | 21 | 292 | 11 | 26.54 | 3-40 | - | - |
| M.J.Weston | 5 | 1 | 27 | 1 | 27.00 | 1-27 | - | - |
| N.V.Radford | 434.1 | 92 | 1363 | 46 | 29.63 | 7-43 | 2 | - |
| S.R.Lampitt | 422.4 | 74 | 1358 | 45 | 30.17 | 5-70 | 3 | - |
| P.J.Newport | 609.4 | 115 | 1840 | 54 | 34.07 | 4-44 | - | - |
| R.K.Illingworth | 430.4 | 132 | 971 | 26 | 37.34 | 5-49 | 2 | - |
| G.A.Hick | 123.4 | 29 | 379 | 8 | 47.37 | 5-42 | 1 | - |
| P.A.Neale | 17.5 | 1 | 86 | 1 | 86.00 | 1-81 | - | - |
| D.B.D'Oliveira | 31 | 7 | 116 | 1 | 116.00 | 1-36 | - | - |
| P.Bent | 3 | 1 | 5 | 0 | - | - | - | - |
| T.M.Moody | 8.4 | 3 | 25 | 0 | - | - | - | - |
| S.J.Rhodes | 1 | 0 | 30 | 0 | - | - | - | - |
| G.R.Haynes | 19.2 | 2 | 82 | 0 | - | - | - | - |
| T.S.Curtis | 21 | 2 | 95 | 0 | - | - | - | - |

## BENSON & HEDGES CUP

### BATTING AVERAGES - Including fielding

| Name | Matches | Inns | NO | Runs | HS | Avge | 100s | 50s | Ct | St |
|---|---|---|---|---|---|---|---|---|---|---|
| P.A.Neale | 7 | 5 | 3 | 159 | 52* | 79.50 | - | 1 | 6 | - |
| T.M.Moody | 7 | 7 | 2 | 382 | 110* | 76.40 | 2 | 2 | 2 | - |
| G.A.Hick | 7 | 7 | 2 | 297 | 88 | 59.40 | - | 4 | 8 | - |
| I.T.Botham | 6 | 5 | 3 | 88 | 35* | 44.00 | - | - | 1 | - |
| M.J.Weston | 1 | 1 | 0 | 30 | 30 | 30.00 | - | - | - | - |
| T.S.Curtis | 7 | 7 | 0 | 163 | 53 | 23.28 | - | 1 | 3 | - |
| S.J.Rhodes | 7 | 3 | 1 | 34 | 13* | 17.00 | - | - | 10 | 1 |
| D.B.D'Oliveira | 7 | 6 | 0 | 79 | 25 | 13.16 | - | - | 3 | - |
| P.J.Newport | 6 | 1 | 0 | 2 | 2 | 2.00 | - | - | 4 | - |
| N.V.Radford | 6 | 1 | 1 | 25 | 25* | - | - | - | 2 | - |
| R.K.Illingworth | 6 | 2 | 2 | 18 | 17* | - | - | - | 2 | - |
| G.R.Dilley | 5 | 0 | 0 | 0 | 0 | - | - | - | - | - |
| S.R.Lampitt | 5 | 0 | 0 | 0 | 0 | - | - | - | 1 | - |

### BOWLING AVERAGES

| Name | Overs | Mdns | Runs | Wkts | Avge | Best | 5wI |
|---|---|---|---|---|---|---|---|
| T.M.Moody | 6 | 0 | 22 | 2 | 11.00 | 2-22 | - |
| N.V.Radford | 61.5 | 13 | 244 | 16 | 15.25 | 3-22 | - |
| G.R.Dilley | 49.2 | 4 | 200 | 11 | 18.18 | 4-35 | - |
| S.R.Lampitt | 48.1 | 4 | 211 | 11 | 19.18 | 4-46 | - |
| I.T.Botham | 63 | 14 | 174 | 8 | 21.75 | 3-11 | - |
| P.J.Newport | 66 | 5 | 242 | 7 | 34.57 | 2-36 | - |
| M.J.Weston | 11 | 0 | 41 | 1 | 41.00 | 1-41 | - |
| R.K.Illingworth | 49 | 2 | 189 | 2 | 94.50 | 2-50 | - |

## REFUGE ASSURANCE

### BATTING AVERAGES - Including fielding

| Name | Matches | Inns | NO | Runs | HS | Avge | 100s | 50s | Ct | St |
|---|---|---|---|---|---|---|---|---|---|---|
| R.K.Illingworth | 15 | 4 | 3 | 90 | 25* | 90.00 | - | - | 6 | - |
| T.M.Moody | 17 | 16 | 2 | 926 | 160 | 66.14 | 4 | 5 | 3 | - |
| T.S.Curtis | 18 | 17 | 4 | 816 | 88* | 62.76 | - | 9 | 10 | - |
| G.A.Hick | 12 | 10 | 1 | 433 | 109 | 48.11 | 1 | 2 | 3 | - |
| I.T.Botham | 12 | 10 | 3 | 249 | 58 | 35.57 | - | 1 | 3 | - |
| P.A.Neale | 11 | 8 | 4 | 139 | 39 | 34.75 | - | - | 3 | - |
| S.J.Rhodes | 16 | 7 | 2 | 164 | 105 | 32.80 | 1 | - | 3 | 4 |
| P.J.Newport | 16 | 4 | 3 | 31 | 17* | 31.00 | - | - | 7 | - |
| D.B.D'Oliveira | 18 | 16 | 3 | 319 | 54 | 24.53 | - | 1 | 7 | - |
| M.J.Weston | 17 | 11 | 4 | 162 | 51 | 23.14 | - | 1 | 4 | - |
| N.V.Radford | 16 | 4 | 2 | 38 | 20* | 19.00 | - | - | 7 | - |
| D.A.Leatherdale | 4 | 4 | 1 | 27 | 15 | 9.00 | - | - | 1 | - |
| S.R.Lampitt | 14 | 3 | 1 | 5 | 4 | 2.50 | - | - | 2 | - |
| S.R.Bevins | 2 | 0 | 0 | 0 | 0 | - | - | - | - | - |
| G.R.Dilley | 2 | 0 | 0 | 0 | 0 | - | - | - | - | - |
| C.M.Tolley | 4 | 0 | 0 | 0 | 0 | - | - | - | 2 | - |
| R.D.Stemp | 4 | 0 | 0 | 0 | 0 | - | - | - | 2 | - |

### BOWLING AVERAGES

| Name | Overs | Mdns | Runs | Wkts | Avge | Best | 5wI |
|---|---|---|---|---|---|---|---|
| G.A.Hick | 27.2 | 1 | 138 | 9 | 15.33 | 5-35 | 1 |
| R.D.Stemp | 22 | 1 | 89 | 5 | 17.80 | 3-18 | - |
| N.V.Radford | 108 | 3 | 571 | 25 | 22.84 | 5-42 | 1 |
| R.K.Illingworth | 100 | 4 | 473 | 16 | 29.56 | 5-49 | 1 |
| G.R.Dilley | 12 | 0 | 72 | 2 | 36.00 | 2-48 | - |
| T.M.Moody | 5 | 0 | 38 | 1 | 38.00 | 1-38 | - |
| I.T.Botham | 80.3 | 2 | 493 | 12 | 41.08 | 3-21 | - |
| M.J.Weston | 113.1 | 4 | 437 | 10 | 43.70 | 2-25 | - |
| S.R.Lampitt | 84 | 1 | 477 | 10 | 47.70 | 3-23 | - |
| C.M.Tolley | 14 | 0 | 107 | 2 | 53.50 | 1-23 | - |
| P.J.Newport | 106.2 | 1 | 576 | 10 | 57.60 | 2-43 | - |

## NATWEST TROPHY

### BATTING AVERAGES - Including fielding

| Name | Matches | Inns | NO | Runs | HS | Avge | 100s | 50s | Ct | St |
|---|---|---|---|---|---|---|---|---|---|---|
| T.M.Moody | 2 | 2 | 1 | 79 | 42* | 79.00 | - | - | 1 | - |
| T.S.Curtis | 2 | 1 | 0 | 34 | 34 | 34.00 | - | - | - | - |
| I.T.Botham | 1 | 1 | 0 | 27 | 27 | 27.00 | - | - | 1 | - |
| S.J.Rhodes | 2 | 2 | 0 | 51 | 41 | 25.50 | - | - | - | - |
| D.B.D'Oliveira | 2 | 2 | 1 | 23 | 13 | 23.00 | - | - | 1 | - |
| R.K.Illingworth | 2 | 1 | 0 | 10 | 10 | 10.00 | - | - | 2 | - |
| P.A.Neale | 2 | 1 | 0 | 8 | 8 | 8.00 | - | - | - | - |
| S.R.Lampitt | 2 | 1 | 0 | 7 | 7 | 7.00 | - | - | - | - |
| G.A.Hick | 2 | 2 | 0 | 10 | 10 | 5.00 | - | - | 1 | - |
| N.V.Radford | 2 | 1 | 1 | 15 | 15* | - | - | - | - | - |
| G.R.Dilley | 2 | 1 | 1 | 7 | 7* | - | - | - | 1 | - |
| P.J.Newport | 1 | 0 | 0 | 0 | 0 | - | - | - | - | - |

### BOWLING AVERAGES

| Name | Overs | Mdns | Runs | Wkts | Avge | Best | 5wI |
|---|---|---|---|---|---|---|---|
| N.V.Radford | 22 | 4 | 54 | 7 | 7.71 | 7-19 | 1 |
| G.R.Dilley | 18 | 3 | 47 | 2 | 23.50 | 1-12 | - |
| R.K.Illingworth | 16 | 2 | 59 | 2 | 29.50 | 1-12 | - |
| S.R.Lampitt | 12.4 | 1 | 65 | 2 | 32.50 | 1-4 | - |
| G.A.Hick | 5 | 2 | 11 | 0 | - | - | - |
| I.T.Botham | 10 | 0 | 39 | 0 | - | - | - |

# YORKSHIRE

## BRITANNIC ASS. CHAMPIONSHIP

### BATTING AVERAGES - Including fielding

| Name | Matches | Inns | NO | Runs | HS | Avge | 100s | 50s | Ct | St |
|---|---|---|---|---|---|---|---|---|---|---|
| M.D.Moxon | 21 | 37 | 1 | 1669 | 200 | 46.36 | 3 | 12 | 17 | - |
| D.Byas | 22 | 37 | 4 | 1413 | 153 | 42.81 | 4 | 2 | 20 | - |
| P.W.Jarvis | 4 | 5 | 2 | 114 | 37* | 38.00 | - | - | - | - |
| P.E.Robinson | 22 | 38 | 6 | 1136 | 189 | 35.50 | 1 | 8 | 19 | - |
| S.A.Kellett | 22 | 36 | 4 | 992 | 125* | 31.00 | 1 | 6 | 17 | - |
| P.Carrick | 21 | 32 | 9 | 662 | 67 | 28.78 | - | 4 | 3 | - |
| A.A.Metcalfe | 22 | 39 | 2 | 1060 | 123 | 28.64 | 2 | 5 | 12 | - |
| D.Gough | 12 | 14 | 3 | 307 | 72 | 27.90 | - | 2 | 3 | - |
| P.J.Hartley | 20 | 24 | 10 | 322 | 50* | 23.00 | - | 1 | 3 | - |
| C.S.Pickles | 11 | 16 | 3 | 284 | 51 | 21.84 | - | 2 | 2 | - |
| R.J.Blakey | 22 | 36 | 2 | 739 | 97 | 21.73 | - | 6 | 35 | 4 |
| J.D.Batty | 16 | 16 | 6 | 151 | 31 | 15.10 | - | - | 7 | - |
| S.D.Fletcher | 12 | 11 | 2 | 48 | 9* | 5.33 | - | - | 5 | - |
| M.A.Robinson | 15 | 13 | 4 | 17 | 8 | 1.88 | - | - | 4 | - |

### BOWLING AVERAGES

| Name | Overs | Mdns | Runs | Wkts | Avge | Best | 5wI | 10wM |
|---|---|---|---|---|---|---|---|---|
| M.D.Moxon | 11 | 2 | 27 | 2 | 13.50 | 1-10 | - | - |
| P.W.Jarvis | 95 | 26 | 235 | 12 | 19.58 | 4-28 | - | - |
| P.Carrick | 701.2 | 231 | 1748 | 61 | 28.65 | 5-13 | 2 | - |
| J.D.Batty | 399.4 | 91 | 1230 | 37 | 33.24 | 6-48 | 1 | - |
| P.J.Hartley | 522.3 | 100 | 1751 | 50 | 35.02 | 6-151 | 3 | - |
| S.D.Fletcher | 230.1 | 45 | 738 | 20 | 36.90 | 6-70 | 1 | - |
| M.A.Robinson | 377.1 | 78 | 1126 | 23 | 48.95 | 3-43 | - | - |
| D.Gough | 252 | 52 | 890 | 16 | 55.62 | 5-41 | 1 | - |
| C.S.Pickles | 138 | 19 | 468 | 6 | 78.00 | 2-8 | - | - |
| D.Byas | 2 | 0 | 7 | 0 | - | - | - | - |
| S.A.Kellett | 4 | 0 | 7 | 0 | - | - | - | - |
| A.A.Metcalfe | 3 | 0 | 23 | 0 | - | - | - | - |
| P.E.Robinson | 10 | 1 | 49 | 0 | - | - | - | - |

## BENSON & HEDGES CUP

### BATTING AVERAGES - Including fielding

| Name | Matches | Inns | NO | Runs | HS | Avge | 100s | 50s | Ct | St |
|---|---|---|---|---|---|---|---|---|---|---|
| M.D.Moxon | 6 | 6 | 1 | 370 | 141* | 74.00 | 1 | 2 | 5 | - |
| A.A.Metcalfe | 6 | 6 | 1 | 350 | 114 | 70.00 | 1 | 2 | 1 | - |
| D.Byas | 6 | 6 | 0 | 207 | 92 | 34.50 | - | 2 | - | - |
| S.A.Kellett | 5 | 3 | 1 | 46 | 44 | 23.00 | - | - | - | - |
| P.E.Robinson | 6 | 5 | 1 | 92 | 43 | 23.00 | - | - | 3 | - |
| R.J.Blakey | 6 | 6 | 1 | 113 | 39 | 22.60 | - | - | 11 | - |
| P.W.Jarvis | 5 | 3 | 2 | 15 | 12* | 15.00 | - | - | - | - |
| P.J.Hartley | 5 | 4 | 1 | 15 | 13 | 5.00 | - | - | 1 | - |
| P.Carrick | 3 | 2 | 0 | 9 | 7 | 4.50 | - | - | 2 | - |
| S.D.Fletcher | 6 | 2 | 1 | 3 | 2* | 3.00 | - | - | 4 | - |
| D.Gough | 1 | 1 | 0 | 1 | 1 | 1.00 | - | - | - | - |
| K.Sharp | 1 | 1 | 0 | 0 | 0 | 0.00 | - | - | - | - |
| M.A.Robinson | 3 | 1 | 1 | 1 | 1* | - | - | - | - | - |
| J.D.Batty | 3 | 0 | 0 | 0 | 0 | - | - | - | - | - |
| C.S.Pickles | 1 | 0 | 0 | 0 | 0 | - | - | - | - | - |
| A.Sidebottom | 3 | 0 | 0 | 0 | 0 | - | - | - | 1 | - |

### BOWLING AVERAGES

| Name | Overs | Mdns | Runs | Wkts | Avge | Best | 5wI |
|---|---|---|---|---|---|---|---|
| M.D.Moxon | 13 | 0 | 61 | 5 | 12.20 | 5-31 | 1 |
| A.Sidebottom | 31 | 11 | 52 | 4 | 13.00 | 4-19 | - |
| D.Gough | 8 | 0 | 41 | 2 | 20.50 | 2-41 | - |
| P.Carrick | 32 | 1 | 106 | 5 | 21.20 | 3-22 | - |
| P.W.Jarvis | 44.2 | 9 | 142 | 6 | 23.66 | 2-13 | - |
| C.S.Pickles | 11 | 0 | 49 | 2 | 24.50 | 2-49 | - |
| S.D.Fletcher | 49.2 | 6 | 208 | 8 | 26.00 | 4-51 | - |
| M.A.Robinson | 31 | 3 | 128 | 4 | 32.00 | 2-43 | - |
| P.J.Hartley | 46 | 5 | 185 | 5 | 37.00 | 2-7 | - |
| J.D.Batty | 22 | 3 | 75 | 1 | 75.00 | 1-34 | - |

## REFUGE ASSURANCE LEAGUE

### BATTING AVERAGES - Including fielding

| Name | Matches | Inns | NO | Runs | HS | Avge | 100s | 50s | Ct | St |
|---|---|---|---|---|---|---|---|---|---|---|
| M.D.Moxon | 14 | 14 | 2 | 561 | 129* | 46.75 | 2 | 3 | 6 | - |
| K.Sharp | 2 | 2 | 0 | 78 | 41 | 39.00 | - | - | 1 | - |
| R.J.Blakey | 15 | 15 | 2 | 490 | 130* | 37.69 | 1 | 2 | 18 | 1 |
| A.A.Metcalfe | 16 | 16 | 0 | 540 | 116 | 33.75 | 1 | 2 | 3 | - |
| D.Byas | 16 | 16 | 4 | 369 | 74* | 30.75 | - | 2 | 3 | - |
| P.Carrick | 10 | 7 | 4 | 89 | 25 | 29.66 | - | - | 2 | - |
| P.E.Robinson | 16 | 15 | 3 | 301 | 64 | 25.08 | - | 2 | 9 | - |
| D.Gough | 10 | 7 | 1 | 105 | 72* | 17.50 | - | 1 | 4 | - |
| C.White | 3 | 3 | 0 | 49 | 37 | 16.33 | - | - | 1 | - |
| C.S.Pickles | 11 | 9 | 4 | 78 | 30* | 15.60 | - | - | 6 | - |
| S.D.Fletcher | 12 | 3 | 2 | 15 | 11* | 15.00 | - | - | 6 | - |
| J.D.Batty | 11 | 4 | 2 | 27 | 13* | 13.50 | - | - | 6 | - |
| S.A.Kellett | 6 | 6 | 1 | 66 | 26 | 13.20 | - | - | 2 | - |
| A.Sidebottom | 4 | 4 | 2 | 24 | 10 | 12.00 | - | - | 1 | - |
| P.W.Jarvis | 3 | 3 | 0 | 18 | 9 | 6.00 | - | - | - | - |
| P.J.Hartley | 13 | 8 | 2 | 32 | 11 | 5.33 | - | - | 2 | - |
| M.A.Robinson | 10 | 2 | 1 | 4 | 2* | 4.00 | - | - | 1 | - |
| C.A.Chapman | 2 | 2 | 0 | 3 | 2 | 1.50 | - | - | - | - |
| A.P.Grayson | 1 | 0 | 0 | 0 | 0 | - | - | - | - | - |
| M.Broadhurst | 1 | 0 | 0 | 0 | 0 | - | - | - | - | - |

### BOWLING AVERAGES

| Name | Overs | Mdns | Runs | Wkts | Avge | Best | 5wI |
|---|---|---|---|---|---|---|---|
| P.Carrick | 74 | 2 | 276 | 19 | 14.52 | 5-22 | 2 |
| S.D.Fletcher | 80 | 2 | 426 | 18 | 23.66 | 3-26 | - |
| C.S.Pickles | 63 | 0 | 361 | 14 | 25.78 | 3-12 | - |
| J.D.Batty | 77 | 4 | 376 | 12 | 31.33 | 4-33 | - |
| M.A.Robinson | 64.5 | 3 | 349 | 11 | 31.72 | 4-33 | - |
| P.J.Hartley | 92.2 | 3 | 416 | 13 | 32.00 | 3-6 | - |
| A.P.Grayson | 5 | 0 | 32 | 1 | 32.00 | 1-32 | - |
| D.Gough | 60.2 | 1 | 316 | 7 | 45.14 | 2-32 | - |
| P.W.Jarvis | 23 | 3 | 103 | 2 | 51.50 | 2-37 | - |
| M.D.Moxon | 11.3 | 0 | 55 | 1 | 55.00 | 1-34 | - |
| A.Sidebottom | 32 | 0 | 115 | 2 | 57.50 | 1-25 | - |
| S.A.Kellett | 3 | 0 | 16 | 0 | - | - | - |
| M.Broadhurst | 8 | 0 | 27 | 0 | - | - | - |

## NATWEST TROPHY

### BATTING AVERAGES - Including fielding

| Name | Matches | Inns | NO | Runs | HS | Avge | 100s | 50s | Ct | St |
|---|---|---|---|---|---|---|---|---|---|---|
| P.E.Robinson | 1 | 1 | 0 | 40 | 40 | 40.00 | - | - | - | - |
| P.Carrick | 1 | 1 | 0 | 12 | 12 | 12.00 | - | - | - | - |
| C.S.Pickles | 1 | 1 | 0 | 12 | 12 | 12.00 | - | - | 1 | - |
| S.D.Fletcher | 1 | 1 | 0 | 9 | 9 | 9.00 | - | - | - | - |
| A.A.Metcalfe | 1 | 1 | 0 | 8 | 8 | 8.00 | - | - | - | - |
| J.D.Batty | 1 | 1 | 0 | 4 | 4 | 4.00 | - | - | - | - |
| D.Byas | 1 | 1 | 0 | 2 | 2 | 2.00 | - | - | - | - |
| D.Gough | 1 | 1 | 0 | 2 | 2 | 2.00 | - | - | - | - |
| M.D.Moxon | 1 | 1 | 0 | 2 | 2 | 2.00 | - | - | 1 | - |
| R.J.Blakey | 1 | 1 | 0 | 0 | 0 | 0.00 | - | - | - | - |
| P.J.Hartley | 1 | 1 | 1 | 6 | 6* | - | - | - | - | - |

### BOWLING AVERAGES

| Name | Overs | Mdns | Runs | Wkts | Avge | Best | 5wI |
|---|---|---|---|---|---|---|---|
| J.D.Batty | 6 | 2 | 17 | 1 | 17.00 | 1-17 | - |
| C.S.Pickles | 10.3 | 2 | 30 | 1 | 30.00 | 1-30 | - |
| S.D.Fletcher | 5 | 0 | 15 | 0 | - | - | - |
| P.Carrick | 6 | 1 | 18 | 0 | - | - | - |
| D.Gough | 8 | 2 | 18 | 0 | - | - | - |
| P.J.Hartley | 8 | 1 | 19 | 0 | - | - | - |

| OXFORD UNIVERSITY | CAMBRIDGE UNIVERSITY |
|---|---|

## ALL FIRST-CLASS

### BATTING AVERAGES - Including fielding

| Name | Matches | Inns | NO | Runs | HS | Avge | 100s | 50s | Ct | St |
|---|---|---|---|---|---|---|---|---|---|---|
| G.J.Turner | 8 | 8 | 2 | 349 | 101* | 58.16 | 1 | 2 | 1 | - |
| D.Pfaff | 8 | 7 | 2 | 231 | 50 | 46.20 | - | 1 | 3 | - |
| R.R.Montgomerie | 8 | 11 | 2 | 300 | 88 | 33.33 | - | 4 | 7 | - |
| C.Gupte | 8 | 9 | 1 | 200 | 55* | 25.00 | - | 1 | 2 | - |
| G.Lovell | 9 | 13 | 3 | 250 | 49 | 25.00 | - | - | 6 | - |
| D.Sandiford | 9 | 9 | 1 | 189 | 83 | 23.62 | - | 1 | 11 | 1 |
| R.E.Morris | 8 | 11 | 1 | 236 | 71 | 23.60 | - | 2 | 3 | - |
| P.S.Gerrans | 3 | 3 | 1 | 35 | 17* | 17.50 | - | - | - | - |
| M.J.Russell | 3 | 6 | 0 | 91 | 30 | 15.16 | - | - | - | - |
| R.MacDonald | 7 | 6 | 3 | 41 | 20 | 13.66 | - | - | - | - |
| C.Jones | 1 | 2 | 0 | 27 | 23 | 13.50 | - | - | - | - |
| H.Davies | 7 | 9 | 3 | 80 | 38 | 13.33 | - | - | - | - |
| J.Morris | 3 | 5 | 0 | 63 | 28 | 12.60 | - | - | 3 | - |
| S.Warley | 2 | 3 | 0 | 15 | 11 | 5.00 | - | - | 1 | - |
| B.Wood | 9 | 6 | 1 | 8 | 6 | 1.60 | - | - | - | - |
| D.A.Hagan | 1 | 0 | 0 | 0 | 0 | - | - | - | - | - |
| J.M.E.Oppenheimer | 5 | 1 | 1 | 0 | 0* | - | - | - | 1 | - |

### BOWLING AVERAGES

| Name | Overs | Mdns | Runs | Wkts | Avge | Best | 5wI | 10wM |
|---|---|---|---|---|---|---|---|---|
| M.J.Russell | 8 | 2 | 31 | 4 | 7.75 | 4-31 | - | - |
| C.Gupte | 24.1 | 3 | 120 | 3 | 40.00 | 2-41 | - | - |
| R.MacDonald | 157 | 48 | 457 | 10 | 45.70 | 3-66 | - | - |
| J.M.E.Oppenheimer | 107 | 18 | 385 | 8 | 48.12 | 2-51 | - | - |
| B.Wood | 187.5 | 34 | 665 | 12 | 55.41 | 2-24 | - | - |
| P.S.Gerrans | 77.3 | 12 | 308 | 5 | 61.60 | 2-65 | - | - |
| G.J.Turner | 169 | 36 | 564 | 9 | 62.66 | 3-32 | - | - |
| R.E.Morris | 24 | 3 | 129 | 2 | 64.50 | 2-82 | - | - |
| H.Davies | 107.1 | 16 | 476 | 4 | 119.00 | 2-46 | - | - |
| G.Lovell | 32 | 3 | 141 | 1 | 141.00 | 1-13 | - | - |
| D.Pfaff | 2 | 0 | 6 | 0 | - | - | - | - |

## ALL FIRST-CLASS

### BATTING AVERAGES - Including fielding

| Name | Matches | Inns | NO | Runs | HS | Avge | 100s | 50s | Ct | St |
|---|---|---|---|---|---|---|---|---|---|---|
| J.P.Crawley | 10 | 16 | 2 | 619 | 83 | 44.21 | - | 7 | 6 | - |
| A.M.Hooper | 7 | 12 | 1 | 458 | 125 | 41.63 | 1 | 2 | - | - |
| R.J.Turner | 8 | 12 | 3 | 231 | 69* | 25.66 | - | 1 | 9 | 1 |
| R.J.Lyons | 1 | 2 | 0 | 38 | 20 | 19.00 | - | - | - | - |
| S.W.Johnson | 7 | 8 | 3 | 85 | 20 | 17.00 | - | - | 3 | - |
| M.J.Lowrey | 10 | 16 | 2 | 234 | 51 | 16.71 | - | 1 | 2 | - |
| R.I.Clitheroe | 10 | 17 | 2 | 228 | 36 | 15.20 | - | - | 3 | - |
| J.P.Arscott | 9 | 12 | 1 | 157 | 74 | 14.27 | - | 1 | 7 | - |
| G.E.Thwaites | 3 | 5 | 0 | 68 | 32 | 13.60 | - | - | 2 | - |
| M.J.Morris | 9 | 13 | 0 | 171 | 60 | 13.15 | - | 1 | 2 | - |
| R.B.Waller | 5 | 4 | 3 | 12 | 6* | 12.00 | - | - | 1 | - |
| D.J.Bush | 7 | 7 | 2 | 58 | 24* | 11.60 | - | - | 3 | - |
| R.H.J.Jenkins | 6 | 8 | 1 | 64 | 20 | 9.14 | - | - | 2 | - |
| R.A.Pyman | 2 | 4 | 1 | 20 | 8* | 6.66 | - | - | 1 | - |
| R.M.Pearson | 10 | 12 | 1 | 70 | 21 | 6.36 | - | - | 2 | - |
| G.W.Jones | 3 | 5 | 1 | 19 | 13* | 4.75 | - | - | - | - |
| D.C.Cotton | 1 | 2 | 1 | 0 | 0* | 0.00 | - | - | - | - |
| N.C.W.Fenton | 1 | 1 | 1 | 7 | 7* | - | - | - | - | - |
| J.N.Viljoen | 1 | 1 | 1 | 1 | 1* | - | - | - | - | - |

### BOWLING AVERAGES

| Name | Overs | Mdns | Runs | Wkts | Avge | Best | 5wI | 10wM |
|---|---|---|---|---|---|---|---|---|
| R.J.Lyons | 4 | 0 | 26 | 1 | 26.00 | 1-26 | - | - |
| J.P.Arscott | 48 | 4 | 252 | 7 | 36.00 | 1-17 | - | - |
| R.B.Waller | 85.2 | 16 | 363 | 7 | 51.85 | 3-31 | - | - |
| R.A.Pyman | 65 | 15 | 216 | 4 | 54.00 | 2-74 | - | - |
| M.J.Lowrey | 136 | 17 | 496 | 9 | 55.11 | 3-31 | - | - |
| R.M.Pearson | 332 | 59 | 1098 | 15 | 73.20 | 4-84 | - | - |
| R.H.J.Jenkins | 150 | 20 | 514 | 7 | 73.42 | 2-46 | - | - |
| D.C.Cotton | 21 | 4 | 85 | 1 | 85.00 | 1-43 | - | - |
| D.J.Bush | 131.3 | 22 | 540 | 6 | 90.00 | 1-14 | - | - |
| A.M.Hooper | 43 | 6 | 187 | 2 | 93.50 | 1-30 | - | - |
| J.N.Viljoen | 22 | 2 | 99 | 1 | 99.00 | 1-34 | - | - |
| S.W.Johnson | 131.1 | 17 | 608 | 3 | 202.66 | 1-34 | - | - |
| J.P.Crawley | 2 | 0 | 14 | 0 | - | - | - | - |
| M.J.Morris | 3 | 1 | 15 | 0 | - | - | - | - |
| N.C.W.Fenton | 25 | 5 | 95 | 0 | - | - | - | - |

# COMBINED UNIVERSITIES, SCOTLAND, MINOR COUNTIES, DURHAM

## BENSON & HEDGES CUP

### MINOR COUNTIES

#### BATTING AVERAGES - Including fielding

| Name | Matches | Inns | NO | Runs | HS | Avge | 100s | 50s | Ct | St |
|---|---|---|---|---|---|---|---|---|---|---|
| J.D.Love | 3 | 3 | 1 | 236 | 81 | 118.00 | - | 3 | - | - |
| N.A.Folland | 4 | 4 | 1 | 199 | 100* | 66.33 | 1 | 1 | 2 | - |
| S.G.Plumb | 4 | 4 | 1 | 98 | 52 | 32.66 | - | 1 | - | - |
| G.K.Brown | 4 | 4 | 0 | 107 | 82 | 26.75 | - | 1 | 2 | - |
| D.R.Turner | 1 | 1 | 0 | 15 | 15 | 15.00 | - | - | - | - |
| M.J.Roberts | 4 | 4 | 0 | 51 | 40 | 12.75 | - | - | 2 | - |
| R.A.Evans | 3 | 2 | 1 | 10 | 5* | 10.00 | - | - | - | - |
| A.R.Fothergill | 4 | 4 | 1 | 24 | 15* | 8.00 | - | - | 2 | - |
| S.Greensword | 4 | 1 | 0 | 3 | 3 | 3.00 | - | - | 1 | - |
| D.R.Thomas | 2 | 2 | 0 | 6 | 6 | 3.00 | - | - | - | - |
| I.E.Conn | 1 | 1 | 1 | 23 | 23* | - | - | - | - | - |
| N.R.Taylor | 4 | 1 | 1 | 1 | 1* | - | - | - | - | - |
| K.A.Arnold | 1 | 0 | 0 | 0 | 0 | - | - | - | - | - |
| C.R.Green | 2 | 1 | 1 | 0 | 0* | - | - | - | - | - |
| A.J.Mack | 3 | 0 | 0 | 0 | 0 | - | - | - | 1 | - |

#### BOWLING AVERAGES

| Name | Overs | Mdns | Runs | Wkts | Avge | Best | 5wI |
|---|---|---|---|---|---|---|---|
| S.Greensword | 38 | 8 | 115 | 5 | 23.00 | 2-21 | - |
| K.A.Arnold | 11 | 0 | 52 | 2 | 26.00 | 2-52 | - |
| C.R.Green | 20.5 | 0 | 90 | 2 | 45.00 | 2-55 | - |
| N.R.Taylor | 41.2 | 10 | 173 | 3 | 57.66 | 2-33 | - |
| D.R.Thomas | 22 | 1 | 110 | 1 | 110.00 | 1-61 | - |
| I.E.Conn | 11 | 1 | 40 | 0 | - | - | - |
| S.G.Plumb | 9 | 0 | 51 | 0 | - | - | - |
| R.A.Evans | 30 | 1 | 119 | 0 | - | - | - |
| A.J.Mack | 30 | 6 | 129 | 0 | - | - | - |

## BENSON & HEDGES CUP

### COMBINED U

#### BATTING AVERAGES - Including fielding

| Name | Matches | Inns | NO | Runs | HS | Avge | 100s | 50s | Ct | St |
|---|---|---|---|---|---|---|---|---|---|---|
| G.J.Turner | 4 | 4 | 2 | 170 | 80* | 85.00 | - | 2 | - | - |
| R.MacDonald | 4 | 3 | 2 | 18 | 12* | 18.00 | - | - | - | - |
| J.I.Longley | 4 | 4 | 0 | 63 | 47 | 15.75 | - | - | 1 | - |
| N.V.Knight | 4 | 4 | 0 | 62 | 36 | 15.50 | - | - | 5 | - |
| P.C.L.Holloway | 4 | 4 | 0 | 59 | 27 | 14.75 | - | - | 4 | - |
| J.P.Crawley | 4 | 4 | 0 | 58 | 40 | 14.50 | - | - | 1 | - |
| A.R.Hansford | 4 | 2 | 1 | 13 | 13* | 13.00 | - | - | - | - |
| R.E.Morris | 4 | 4 | 0 | 44 | 19 | 11.00 | - | - | - | - |
| R.H.J.Jenkins | 4 | 2 | 1 | 9 | 9 | 9.00 | - | - | 2 | - |
| I.Fletcher | 1 | 1 | 0 | 9 | 9 | 9.00 | - | - | 1 | - |
| P.J.Rendell | 2 | 2 | 0 | 8 | 8 | 4.00 | - | - | 1 | - |
| J.C.Hallett | 4 | 2 | 0 | 5 | 5 | 2.50 | - | - | 1 | - |
| R.M.Pearson | 1 | 0 | 0 | 0 | 0 | - | - | - | - | - |

#### BOWLING AVERAGES

| Name | Overs | Mdns | Runs | Wkts | Avge | Best | 5wI |
|---|---|---|---|---|---|---|---|
| J.C.Hallett | 43.1 | 0 | 149 | 6 | 24.83 | 3-36 | - |
| R.MacDonald | 36 | 1 | 216 | 8 | 27.00 | 6-36 | 1 |
| G.J.Turner | 30.4 | 4 | 120 | 3 | 40.00 | 2-18 | - |
| P.J.Rendell | 6 | 0 | 55 | 1 | 55.00 | 1-55 | - |
| A.R.Hansford | 32.5 | 3 | 125 | 1 | 125.00 | 1-55 | - |
| R.H.J.Jenkins | 26 | 1 | 141 | 1 | 141.00 | 1-58 | - |
| N.V.Knight | 1 | 0 | 4 | 0 | - | - | - |
| R.M.Pearson | 6 | 0 | 24 | 0 | - | - | - |

## BENSON & HEDGES CUP

### SCOTLAND

#### BATTING AVERAGES - Including fielding

| Name | Matches | Inns | NO | Runs | HS | Avge | 100s | 50s | Ct | St |
|---|---|---|---|---|---|---|---|---|---|---|
| R.G.Swan | 1 | 1 | 0 | 55 | 55 | 55.00 | - | 1 | - | - |
| G.N.Reifer | 4 | 4 | 0 | 141 | 76 | 35.25 | - | 1 | 3 | - |
| D.J.Haggo | 4 | 4 | 2 | 58 | 25 | 29.00 | - | - | 2 | 3 |
| O.Henry | 4 | 4 | 0 | 80 | 32 | 20.00 | - | - | 2 | - |
| A.B.Russell | 4 | 4 | 0 | 78 | 45 | 19.50 | - | - | 2 | - |
| A.W.Bee | 4 | 4 | 1 | 52 | 35 | 17.33 | - | - | - | - |
| J.W.Govan | 4 | 4 | 0 | 60 | 23 | 15.00 | - | - | 2 | - |
| G.Salmond | 3 | 3 | 0 | 34 | 24 | 11.33 | - | - | - | - |
| I.L.Philip | 4 | 4 | 0 | 39 | 35 | 9.75 | - | - | 2 | - |
| B.M.W.Patterson | 4 | 4 | 0 | 37 | 23 | 9.25 | - | - | - | - |
| D.Cowan | 4 | 3 | 1 | 9 | 6 | 4.50 | - | - | 1 | - |
| J.D.Moir | 4 | 2 | 2 | 8 | 6* | - | - | - | - | - |

#### BOWLING AVERAGES

| Name | Overs | Mdns | Runs | Wkts | Avge | Best | 5wI |
|---|---|---|---|---|---|---|---|
| A.B.Russell | 7 | 0 | 42 | 4 | 10.50 | 4-42 | - |
| A.W.Bee | 26 | 0 | 134 | 6 | 22.33 | 4-31 | - |
| D.Cowan | 28 | 1 | 157 | 5 | 31.40 | 2-47 | - |
| J.D.Moir | 40 | 11 | 146 | 2 | 73.00 | 2-47 | - |
| J.W.Govan | 42 | 4 | 191 | 2 | 95.50 | 1-26 | - |
| G.N.Reifer | 29.2 | 4 | 109 | 1 | 109.00 | 1-36 | - |
| O.Henry | 39 | 2 | 143 | 1 | 143.00 | 1-31 | - |

## ALL ONE-DAY

### DURHAM

#### BATTING AVERAGES - Including fielding

| Name | Matches | Inns | NO | Runs | HS | Avge | 100s | 50s | Ct | St |
|---|---|---|---|---|---|---|---|---|---|---|
| J.D.Glendenen | 4 | 4 | 1 | 193 | 109 | 64.33 | 1 | 1 | 2 | - |
| G.Cook | 6 | 5 | 1 | 226 | 102 | 56.50 | 1 | - | 2 | - |
| P.Bainbridge | 5 | 5 | 2 | 150 | 62 | 50.00 | - | 1 | 1 | - |
| D.J.Lovell | 1 | 1 | 0 | 32 | 32 | 32.00 | - | - | - | - |
| S.Hutton | 2 | 2 | 0 | 55 | 55 | 27.50 | - | 1 | - | - |
| A.S.Patel | 1 | 1 | 0 | 25 | 25 | 25.00 | - | - | - | - |
| D.A.Blenkiron | 6 | 5 | 1 | 84 | 56 | 21.00 | - | 1 | 2 | - |
| S.J.Brown | 5 | 4 | 3 | 17 | 10* | 17.00 | - | - | - | - |
| Ijaz Ahmed | 2 | 2 | 0 | 30 | 20 | 15.00 | - | - | - | - |
| J.Wood | 6 | 4 | 0 | 41 | 30 | 10.25 | - | - | 1 | - |
| A.R.Fothergill | 6 | 4 | 0 | 40 | 24 | 10.00 | - | - | 3 | - |
| I.E.Conn | 2 | 2 | 0 | 19 | 18 | 9.50 | - | - | - | - |
| N.G.Nicholson | 2 | 2 | 0 | 16 | 16 | 8.00 | - | - | - | - |
| P.A.W.Heseltine | 3 | 2 | 1 | 7 | 5* | 7.00 | - | - | - | - |
| M.P.Briers | 3 | 2 | 0 | 13 | 12 | 6.50 | - | - | 1 | - |
| P.Burn | 2 | 2 | 0 | 12 | 10 | 6.00 | - | - | - | - |
| G.K.Brown | 3 | 3 | 0 | 12 | 7 | 4.00 | - | - | - | - |
| S.J.Weeks | 2 | 2 | 0 | 5 | 4 | 2.50 | - | - | - | - |
| P.W.Henderson | 2 | 1 | 0 | 1 | 1 | 1.00 | - | - | 1 | - |
| A.C.Day | 2 | 0 | 0 | 0 | 0 | - | - | - | - | - |
| S.J.Cooper | 1 | 0 | 0 | 0 | 0 | - | - | - | 1 | - |

#### BOWLING AVERAGES

| Name | Overs | Mdns | Runs | Wkts | Avge | Best | 5wI |
|---|---|---|---|---|---|---|---|
| M.P.Briers | 8 | 0 | 36 | 2 | 18.00 | 2-36 | - |
| G.K.Brown | 10 | 0 | 62 | 2 | 31.00 | 2-62 | - |
| S.J.Brown | 47 | 4 | 231 | 6 | 38.50 | 3-29 | - |
| S.J.Cooper | 10 | 0 | 39 | 1 | 39.00 | 1-39 | - |
| A.C.Day | 6 | 0 | 46 | 1 | 46.00 | 1-46 | - |
| P.Bainbridge | 38 | 4 | 165 | 3 | 55.00 | 2-47 | - |
| J.Wood | 50.1 | 5 | 288 | 5 | 57.60 | 2-28 | - |
| P.W.Henderson | 10 | 0 | 72 | 1 | 72.00 | 1-72 | - |
| D.J.Lovell | 10 | 0 | 72 | 1 | 72.00 | 1-72 | - |
| P.A.W.Heseltine | 19 | 1 | 94 | 1 | 94.00 | 1-37 | - |
| D.A.Blenkiron | 3 | 0 | 11 | 0 | - | - | - |
| A.S.Patel | 3 | 0 | 18 | 0 | - | - | - |
| Ijaz Ahmed | 11 | 0 | 79 | 0 | - | - | - |
| I.E.Conn | 21 | 2 | 116 | 0 | - | - | - |

# BRITANNIC ASSURANCE CHAMPIONSHIP

## BATTING AVERAGES - Including fielding
**Qualifying requirements : 6 completed innings**

| Name | Matches | Inns | NO | Runs | HS | Avge | 100s | 50s | Ct | St |
|---|---|---|---|---|---|---|---|---|---|---|
| Salim Malik | 22 | 33 | 9 | 1891 | 215 | 78.79 | 6 | 8 | 22 | - |
| M.W.Gatting | 21 | 37 | 11 | 2044 | 215* | 78.61 | 8 | 6 | 13 | - |
| S.J.Cook | 22 | 39 | 6 | 2370 | 210* | 71.81 | 9 | 8 | 13 | - |
| H.Morris | 17 | 30 | 7 | 1601 | 156* | 69.60 | 5 | 8 | 13 | - |
| G.A.Gooch | 11 | 16 | 1 | 996 | 259 | 66.40 | 3 | 3 | 11 | - |
| T.M.Moody | 19 | 31 | 4 | 1770 | 210 | 65.55 | 6 | 8 | 30 | - |
| M.P.Maynard | 20 | 32 | 5 | 1766 | 243 | 65.40 | 7 | 5 | 14 | - |
| D.W.Randall | 22 | 34 | 9 | 1567 | 143* | 62.68 | 5 | 5 | 15 | - |
| A.P.Wells | 21 | 34 | 5 | 1777 | 253* | 61.27 | 7 | 5 | 7 | - |
| M.A.Atherton | 8 | 13 | 3 | 603 | 114* | 60.30 | 2 | 2 | 7 | - |
| C.L.Smith | 15 | 26 | 3 | 1353 | 145 | 58.82 | 5 | 7 | 3 | - |
| R.T.Robinson | 22 | 37 | 8 | 1673 | 180 | 57.69 | 3 | 10 | 18 | - |
| N.Hussain | 22 | 29 | 7 | 1233 | 196 | 56.04 | 3 | 8 | 34 | - |
| M.Azharuddin | 20 | 35 | 3 | 1773 | 212 | 55.40 | 6 | 9 | 23 | - |
| N.R.Taylor | 22 | 34 | 3 | 1647 | 203* | 53.12 | 6 | 7 | 14 | - |
| C.J.Tavare | 22 | 35 | 6 | 1482 | 183 | 51.10 | 4 | 7 | 20 | - |
| B.C.Broad | 21 | 38 | 3 | 1739 | 166 | 49.68 | 5 | 7 | 9 | - |
| M.R.Ramprakash | 12 | 22 | 4 | 877 | 119 | 48.72 | 2 | 7 | 2 | - |
| N.V.Knight | 6 | 9 | 1 | 388 | 101* | 48.50 | 1 | 2 | 5 | - |
| D.A.Reeve | 20 | 33 | 7 | 1260 | 99* | 48.46 | - | 14 | 9 | - |
| N.H.Fairbrother | 17 | 26 | 5 | 1011 | 121 | 48.14 | 5 | 3 | 18 | - |
| M.R.Benson | 20 | 30 | 2 | 1329 | 257 | 47.46 | 4 | 6 | 9 | - |
| A.J.Lamb | 14 | 23 | 2 | 993 | 194 | 47.28 | 3 | 5 | 13 | - |
| T.R.Ward | 20 | 31 | 2 | 1369 | 235* | 47.20 | 4 | 6 | 9 | - |
| K.D.James | 22 | 35 | 9 | 1216 | 134* | 46.76 | 2 | 6 | 8 | - |
| D.J.Bicknell | 22 | 40 | 2 | 1762 | 151 | 46.36 | 5 | 8 | 10 | - |
| M.D.Moxon | 21 | 37 | 1 | 1669 | 200 | 46.36 | 3 | 12 | 17 | - |
| A.J.Wright | 22 | 38 | 6 | 1477 | 120 | 46.15 | 3 | 9 | 16 | - |
| R.J.Shastri | 21 | 31 | 8 | 1056 | 133* | 45.91 | 2 | 6 | 8 | - |
| T.S.Curtis | 22 | 37 | 3 | 1555 | 248 | 45.73 | 3 | 8 | 14 | - |
| A.Fordham | 22 | 40 | 2 | 1725 | 165 | 45.39 | 4 | 8 | 8 | - |
| P.Johnson | 22 | 36 | 6 | 1357 | 124 | 45.23 | 3 | 10 | 12 | - |
| M.A.Garnham | 22 | 25 | 6 | 831 | 123 | 43.73 | 2 | 5 | 58 | - |
| C.W.J.Athey | 22 | 36 | 5 | 1350 | 127 | 43.54 | 4 | 9 | 15 | - |
| A.R.Butcher | 21 | 37 | 1 | 1558 | 147 | 43.27 | 4 | 12 | 13 | - |
| R.J.Harden | 22 | 36 | 7 | 1242 | 134 | 42.82 | 2 | 9 | 19 | - |
| D.Byas | 22 | 37 | 4 | 1413 | 153 | 42.81 | 4 | 2 | 20 | - |
| R.A.Smith | 10 | 20 | 0 | 852 | 107 | 42.60 | 1 | 7 | 12 | - |
| G.P.Thorpe | 21 | 35 | 7 | 1164 | 177 | 41.57 | 4 | 4 | 8 | - |
| V.P.Terry | 18 | 32 | 2 | 1226 | 171 | 40.86 | 2 | 7 | 23 | - |
| A.R.Roberts | 14 | 15 | 9 | 244 | 48 | 40.66 | - | - | 7 | - |
| D.M.Smith | 19 | 33 | 5 | 1130 | 126* | 40.35 | 1 | 8 | 14 | - |
| R.J.Bailey | 19 | 34 | 4 | 1202 | 117 | 40.06 | 1 | 11 | 10 | - |
| D.M.Ward | 22 | 38 | 5 | 1304 | 151 | 39.51 | 1 | 9 | 9 | - |
| G.A.Hick | 16 | 27 | 2 | 975 | 186 | 39.00 | 3 | 4 | 16 | - |
| A.J.Stewart | 17 | 30 | 6 | 936 | 109 | 39.00 | 1 | 6 | 20 | - |
| N.E.Briers | 22 | 40 | 5 | 1358 | 160 | 38.80 | 4 | 5 | 15 | - |
| S.P.Titchard | 7 | 13 | 1 | 464 | 135 | 38.66 | 1 | 2 | 7 | - |
| J.E.Morris | 20 | 35 | 2 | 1267 | 122* | 38.39 | 1 | 8 | 14 | - |
| G.R.Cowdrey | 21 | 32 | 4 | 1064 | 114 | 38.00 | 2 | 5 | 17 | - |
| I.T.Botham | 10 | 17 | 2 | 567 | 104 | 37.80 | 1 | 4 | 7 | - |
| K.J.Barnett | 21 | 36 | 1 | 1318 | 217 | 37.65 | 2 | 8 | 23 | - |
| J.J.Whitaker | 22 | 36 | 3 | 1242 | 105 | 37.63 | 1 | 8 | 14 | - |
| P.J.Prichard | 21 | 33 | 5 | 1031 | 190 | 36.82 | 4 | 2 | 17 | - |
| N.J.Lenham | 18 | 31 | 3 | 1028 | 193 | 36.71 | 3 | 3 | 11 | - |
| D.P.Ostler | 22 | 40 | 5 | 1284 | 120* | 36.68 | 1 | 10 | 21 | - |
| W.Larkins | 9 | 16 | 6 | 365 | 75 | 36.50 | - | 2 | 6 | - |
| J.P.Stephenson | 22 | 36 | 2 | 1234 | 116 | 36.29 | 3 | 6 | 6 | - |
| N.A.Stanley | 8 | 13 | 0 | 470 | 132 | 36.15 | 1 | 2 | 5 | - |
| J.D.R.Benson | 9 | 12 | 1 | 393 | 133* | 35.72 | 1 | 1 | 9 | - |
| K.R.Brown | 21 | 36 | 6 | 1069 | 143* | 35.63 | 1 | 6 | 33 | - |
| A.Dale | 15 | 23 | 3 | 711 | 140 | 35.55 | 1 | 3 | 7 | - |
| P.E.Robinson | 22 | 38 | 6 | 1136 | 189 | 35.50 | 1 | 8 | 19 | - |
| D.I.Gower | 22 | 37 | 5 | 1132 | 80* | 35.37 | - | 8 | 13 | - |
| A.N.Hayhurst | 18 | 30 | 5 | 883 | 172* | 35.32 | 3 | 1 | 5 | - |
| B.T.P.Donelan | 12 | 15 | 5 | 353 | 61 | 35.30 | - | 2 | 3 | - |
| S.J.Rhodes | 22 | 32 | 6 | 907 | 90 | 34.88 | - | 8 | 48 | 7 |
| B.F.Smith | 13 | 20 | 3 | 585 | 71 | 34.41 | - | 3 | 3 | - |
| P.D.Bowler | 22 | 40 | 3 | 1270 | 104* | 34.32 | 2 | 9 | 15 | - |
| S.A.Marsh | 21 | 29 | 5 | 823 | 113* | 34.29 | 2 | 4 | 61 | 4 |
| P.M.Roebuck | 16 | 27 | 3 | 820 | 101 | 34.16 | 1 | 5 | 3 | - |
| A.J.Moles | 22 | 39 | 2 | 1246 | 133 | 33.67 | 1 | 10 | 10 | - |
| M.P.Speight | 12 | 18 | 1 | 572 | 89 | 33.64 | - | 5 | 5 | - |
| P.Pollard | 22 | 40 | 3 | 1235 | 145 | 33.37 | 3 | 4 | 21 | - |
| G.D.Rose | 14 | 19 | 2 | 567 | 106 | 33.35 | 2 | 2 | 8 | - |
| N.D.Burns | 22 | 32 | 8 | 794 | 108 | 33.08 | 1 | 4 | 35 | 8 |
| G.D.Mendis | 22 | 41 | 4 | 1223 | 119 | 33.05 | 3 | 3 | 7 | - |
| M.A.Roseberry | 21 | 40 | 3 | 1222 | 119* | 33.02 | 1 | 7 | 17 | - |
| T.A.Lloyd | 21 | 35 | 2 | 1076 | 97 | 32.60 | - | 10 | 10 | - |
| K.M.Curran | 19 | 30 | 7 | 749 | 89* | 32.56 | - | 5 | 12 | - |
| C.M.Wells | 12 | 19 | 5 | 451 | 76 | 32.21 | - | 2 | 2 | - |
| J.D.Ratcliffe | 17 | 31 | 1 | 953 | 94 | 31.76 | - | 8 | 15 | - |
| W.K.Hegg | 21 | 31 | 7 | 758 | 97 | 31.58 | - | 3 | 39 | 3 |
| R.I.Alikhan | 18 | 33 | 2 | 963 | 96* | 31.06 | - | 7 | 9 | - |
| S.A.Kellett | 22 | 36 | 4 | 992 | 125* | 31.00 | 1 | 6 | 17 | - |
| P.Whitticase | 19 | 25 | 5 | 620 | 114* | 31.00 | 1 | 4 | 42 | 2 |
| S.P.James | 10 | 17 | 3 | 429 | 70 | 30.64 | - | 2 | 8 | - |
| A.I.C.Dodemaide | 19 | 28 | 9 | 581 | 100* | 30.57 | 1 | 1 | 7 | - |
| T.J.G.O'Gorman | 22 | 39 | 4 | 1060 | 148 | 30.28 | 2 | 4 | 21 | - |
| A.C.Seymour | 9 | 16 | 1 | 454 | 157 | 30.26 | 1 | 2 | 7 | - |
| T.J.Boon | 20 | 37 | 2 | 1057 | 102 | 30.20 | 1 | 6 | 8 | - |
| N.M.K.Smith | 5 | 9 | 2 | 209 | 70 | 29.85 | - | 2 | - | - |
| K.H.Macleay | 14 | 19 | 6 | 388 | 63 | 29.84 | - | 2 | 5 | - |
| G.Fowler | 18 | 31 | 2 | 865 | 113 | 29.82 | 2 | 2 | 1 | - |
| S.R.Lampitt | 19 | 20 | 5 | 447 | 93 | 29.80 | - | 3 | 5 | - |
| J.W.Hall | 14 | 25 | 2 | 685 | 117* | 29.78 | 1 | 4 | 8 | - |
| N.A.Foster | 20 | 20 | 4 | 474 | 107* | 29.62 | 1 | 1 | 11 | - |
| P.N.Hepworth | 21 | 35 | 4 | 915 | 115 | 29.51 | 1 | 3 | 17 | - |
| R.J.Bartlett | 5 | 7 | 1 | 177 | 71 | 29.50 | - | 1 | 3 | - |
| C.C.Lewis | 12 | 15 | 1 | 413 | 73 | 29.50 | - | 2 | 4 | - |
| L.Potter | 22 | 34 | 3 | 899 | 89 | 29.00 | - | 5 | 17 | - |
| R.C.Russell | 12 | 19 | 3 | 464 | 111 | 29.00 | 1 | 2 | 37 | 2 |
| M.C.J.Nicholas | 20 | 34 | 9 | 723 | 107* | 28.92 | 1 | 4 | 8 | - |
| P.Carrick | 21 | 32 | 9 | 662 | 67 | 28.78 | - | 4 | 3 | - |
| M.W.Alleyne | 22 | 35 | 3 | 921 | 165 | 28.78 | 1 | 4 | 10 | - |
| A.A.Metcalfe | 22 | 39 | 2 | 1060 | 123 | 28.64 | 2 | 5 | 12 | - |
| T.C.Middleton | 16 | 28 | 1 | 766 | 102 | 28.37 | 1 | 2 | 14 | - |
| M.V.Fleming | 18 | 29 | 3 | 734 | 113 | 28.23 | 1 | 5 | 14 | - |
| E.A.E.Baptiste | 17 | 22 | 1 | 589 | 80 | 28.04 | - | 4 | 9 | - |
| D.Gough | 12 | 14 | 3 | 307 | 72 | 27.90 | - | 2 | 3 | - |
| N.J.Speak | 17 | 31 | 2 | 806 | 153 | 27.79 | 1 | 2 | 7 | - |
| R.P.Lefebvre | 15 | 16 | 3 | 361 | 100 | 27.76 | 1 | 1 | 6 | - |
| Wasim Akram | 14 | 19 | 2 | 471 | 122 | 27.70 | 1 | 1 | 5 | - |
| K.P.Evans | 14 | 17 | 7 | 276 | 56* | 27.60 | - | 1 | 6 | - |
| G.D.Hodgson | 21 | 37 | 1 | 990 | 89 | 27.50 | - | 7 | 7 | - |
| M.A.Feltham | 12 | 16 | 4 | 327 | 69* | 27.25 | - | 1 | 3 | - |
| D.Ripley | 18 | 24 | 8 | 429 | 53* | 26.81 | - | 1 | 37 | 2 |
| A.N.Aymes | 22 | 28 | 6 | 587 | 53 | 26.68 | - | 1 | 45 | 2 |
| Asif Din | 15 | 27 | 1 | 685 | 140 | 26.34 | 2 | 1 | 9 | - |
| R.J.Scott | 17 | 30 | 1 | 763 | 127 | 26.31 | 2 | 3 | 6 | - |
| I.D.Austin | 12 | 16 | 4 | 315 | 101* | 26.25 | 1 | 1 | 4 | - |
| P.Bent | 7 | 12 | 1 | 285 | 100* | 25.90 | 1 | 1 | 3 | - |
| G.D.Lloyd | 17 | 28 | 0 | 720 | 96 | 25.71 | - | 5 | 10 | - |
| C.J.Adams | 12 | 19 | 2 | 436 | 112 | 25.64 | 1 | - | 15 | - |
| P.Moores | 22 | 27 | 3 | 612 | 86* | 25.50 | - | 6 | 53 | 5 |
| J.W.Lloyds | 22 | 33 | 4 | 729 | 69 | 25.13 | - | 7 | 21 | - |
| K.M.Krikken | 22 | 35 | 8 | 677 | 65 | 25.07 | - | 2 | 55 | 3 |
| P.N.Weekes | 6 | 11 | 1 | 249 | 86 | 24.90 | - | 2 | 5 | - |
| J.R.Ayling | 9 | 13 | 2 | 269 | 58 | 24.45 | - | 1 | 3 | - |
| C.P.Metson | 22 | 24 | 3 | 511 | 84 | 24.33 | - | 2 | 67 | 2 |
| G.Yates | 18 | 24 | 12 | 292 | 100* | 24.33 | 1 | - | 7 | - |
| P.W.G.Parker | 16 | 26 | 1 | 607 | 111 | 24.28 | 1 | 3 | 8 | - |
| P.A.Neale | 13 | 20 | 4 | 385 | 69* | 24.06 | - | 1 | 5 | - |
| M.Watkinson | 20 | 33 | 3 | 713 | 114* | 23.76 | 1 | 3 | 8 | - |
| I.A.Greig | 19 | 29 | 4 | 593 | 72 | 23.72 | - | 3 | 7 | - |
| S.G.Hinks | 8 | 12 | 2 | 236 | 61* | 23.60 | - | 2 | 6 | - |
| P.A.Cottey | 11 | 16 | 5 | 259 | 55 | 23.54 | - | 1 | 9 | - |
| R.M.Ellison | 16 | 24 | 7 | 397 | 61* | 23.35 | - | 3 | 8 | - |
| R.K.Illingworth | 17 | 23 | 4 | 442 | 56* | 23.26 | - | 1 | 4 | - |
| D.J.Capel | 20 | 32 | 2 | 692 | 71 | 23.06 | - | 7 | 9 | - |
| P.J.Hartley | 20 | 24 | 10 | 322 | 50* | 23.00 | - | 2 | 3 | - |
| I.J.F.Hutchinson | 11 | 20 | 1 | 437 | 125 | 23.00 | 2 | - | 11 | - |
| J.G.Thomas | 10 | 12 | 3 | 206 | 64 | 22.88 | - | 1 | 3 | - |
| C.M.Tolley | 6 | 9 | 3 | 137 | 36 | 22.83 | - | - | 2 | - |
| P.J.Newport | 22 | 24 | 9 | 340 | 48 | 22.66 | - | - | 4 | - |
| J.E.Emburey | 21 | 29 | 3 | 586 | 74 | 22.53 | - | 3 | 21 | - |
| J.D.Fitton | 6 | 10 | 1 | 201 | 60 | 22.33 | - | 1 | - | - |

# BRITANNIC ASSURANCE CHAMPIONSHIP

| Name | Matches | Inns | NO | Runs | HS | Avge | 100s | 50s | Ct | St |
|---|---|---|---|---|---|---|---|---|---|---|
| K.T.Medlycott | 18 | 25 | 2 | 513 | 66 | 22.30 | - | 4 | 6 | - |
| G.J.Lord | 9 | 16 | 0 | 356 | 85 | 22.25 | - | 3 | 2 | - |
| S.C.Goldsmith | 15 | 25 | 3 | 483 | 73* | 21.95 | - | 2 | 2 | - |
| D.G.Cork | 16 | 25 | 7 | 395 | 44 | 21.94 | - | - | 8 | - |
| C.S.Pickles | 11 | 16 | 3 | 284 | 51 | 21.84 | - | 2 | 2 | - |
| I.Smith | 8 | 11 | 2 | 196 | 39 | 21.77 | - | - | 7 | - |
| R.J.Blakey | 22 | 36 | 2 | 739 | 97 | 21.73 | - | 6 | 35 | 4 |
| P.A.J.DeFreitas | 11 | 16 | 1 | 325 | 60 | 21.66 | - | 2 | 1 | - |
| M.A.Lynch | 10 | 17 | 1 | 342 | 141* | 21.37 | 1 | 1 | 13 | - |
| T.D.Topley | 19 | 19 | 4 | 320 | 50* | 21.33 | - | 2 | 14 | - |
| F.D.Stephenson | 22 | 27 | 7 | 423 | 58 | 21.15 | - | 1 | 6 | - |
| J.A.North | 5 | 7 | 1 | 122 | 63* | 20.33 | - | 1 | 1 | - |
| M.A.Crawley | 10 | 12 | 4 | 160 | 49* | 20.00 | - | - | 14 | - |
| J.C.Pooley | 11 | 20 | 0 | 390 | 88 | 19.50 | - | 2 | 8 | - |
| G.C.Holmes | 6 | 8 | 1 | 136 | 54 | 19.42 | - | 1 | 1 | - |
| D.J.Millns | 19 | 24 | 8 | 306 | 44 | 19.12 | - | - | 9 | - |
| N.A.Felton | 14 | 25 | 2 | 439 | 55 | 19.08 | - | 1 | 5 | - |
| C.Penn | 17 | 20 | 4 | 299 | 52 | 18.68 | - | 1 | 6 | - |
| P.A.Smith | 14 | 23 | 1 | 411 | 68 | 18.68 | - | 2 | 2 | - |
| J.J.E.Hardy | 10 | 15 | 2 | 242 | 52 | 18.61 | - | 1 | - | - |
| D.P.Hughes | 8 | 9 | 3 | 111 | 51 | 18.50 | - | 1 | 4 | - |
| D.V.Lawrence | 15 | 22 | 1 | 383 | 66 | 18.23 | - | 1 | 4 | - |
| A.C.S.Pigott | 18 | 21 | 5 | 291 | 65 | 18.18 | - | 1 | 5 | - |
| M.Keech | 14 | 22 | 2 | 362 | 58* | 18.10 | - | 2 | 4 | - |
| R.P.Davis | 18 | 23 | 4 | 338 | 44 | 17.78 | - | - | 22 | - |
| M.J.McCague | 8 | 10 | 2 | 142 | 29 | 17.75 | - | - | 1 | - |
| S.L.Watkin | 18 | 15 | 8 | 123 | 25* | 17.57 | - | - | 2 | - |
| K.J.Piper | 16 | 23 | 3 | 349 | 55 | 17.45 | - | 1 | 48 | - |
| M.P.Bicknell | 15 | 22 | 4 | 312 | 63 | 17.33 | - | 1 | 3 | - |
| M.Saxelby | 6 | 9 | 1 | 136 | 44 | 17.00 | - | - | - | - |
| A.E.Warner | 14 | 20 | 3 | 289 | 46 | 17.00 | - | - | 3 | - |
| G.C.Small | 20 | 29 | 7 | 370 | 58 | 16.81 | - | 1 | 5 | - |
| R.J.Maru | 20 | 25 | 3 | 369 | 61 | 16.77 | - | 1 | 29 | - |
| D.B.D'Oliveira | 15 | 22 | 2 | 335 | 79 | 16.75 | - | 1 | 21 | - |
| P.Willey | 12 | 18 | 5 | 217 | 42* | 16.69 | - | - | 6 | - |
| J.H.Childs | 20 | 13 | 6 | 111 | 41* | 15.85 | - | - | 5 | - |
| R.D.B.Croft | 22 | 25 | 4 | 331 | 50 | 15.76 | - | 1 | 10 | - |
| B.N.French | 21 | 24 | 4 | 315 | 65 | 15.75 | - | 2 | 54 | 8 |
| N.F.Sargeant | 20 | 27 | 4 | 362 | 49 | 15.73 | - | - | 43 | 5 |
| N.V.Radford | 17 | 16 | 6 | 157 | 45 | 15.70 | - | - | 4 | - |
| L.Tennant | 5 | 9 | 3 | 94 | 23* | 15.66 | - | - | - | - |
| D.W.Headley | 11 | 14 | 1 | 202 | 76 | 15.53 | - | 1 | 4 | - |
| R.G.Williams | 7 | 10 | 2 | 123 | 35 | 15.37 | - | - | 1 | - |
| A.L.Penberthy | 11 | 14 | 2 | 184 | 52 | 15.33 | - | 1 | 6 | - |
| M.I.Gidley | 4 | 8 | 1 | 107 | 80 | 15.28 | - | 1 | 3 | - |
| J.D.Batty | 16 | 16 | 6 | 151 | 31 | 15.10 | - | - | 7 | - |
| P.Farbrace | 19 | 26 | 5 | 317 | 50 | 15.09 | - | 1 | 44 | 8 |
| Waqar Younis | 17 | 20 | 8 | 177 | 31 | 14.75 | - | - | 3 | - |
| A.M.Babington | 15 | 19 | 7 | 176 | 58 | 14.66 | - | 1 | 7 | - |
| D.R.Gilbert | 20 | 26 | 6 | 292 | 28* | 14.60 | - | - | 5 | - |
| I.J.Turner | 8 | 10 | 4 | 87 | 39* | 14.50 | - | - | 3 | - |
| K.Greenfield | 7 | 11 | 0 | 156 | 64 | 14.18 | - | 1 | 15 | - |
| N.F.Williams | 16 | 24 | 3 | 296 | 77 | 14.09 | - | 1 | 4 | - |
| J.N.Maguire | 22 | 24 | 7 | 237 | 44* | 13.94 | - | - | 7 | - |
| I.D.K.Salisbury | 20 | 20 | 7 | 179 | 34 | 13.76 | - | - | 12 | - |
| W.M.Noon | 6 | 9 | 2 | 96 | 36 | 13.71 | - | - | 11 | - |
| N.A.Mallender | 13 | 11 | 3 | 108 | 19 | 13.50 | - | - | 1 | - |
| P.A.Booth | 10 | 13 | 0 | 175 | 62 | 13.46 | - | 1 | 5 | - |
| T.A.Munton | 22 | 25 | 8 | 226 | 31 | 13.29 | - | - | 14 | - |
| M.C.J.Ball | 5 | 8 | 0 | 105 | 28 | 13.12 | - | - | 5 | - |
| R.A.Pick | 21 | 16 | 5 | 142 | 46 | 12.90 | - | - | 7 | - |
| C.Wilkinson | 13 | 13 | 2 | 138 | 41 | 12.54 | - | - | 7 | - |
| T.A.Merrick | 18 | 22 | 6 | 198 | 36 | 12.37 | - | - | 3 | - |
| E.E.Hemmings | 16 | 16 | 4 | 143 | 29* | 11.91 | - | - | 4 | - |
| N.G.B.Cook | 16 | 15 | 5 | 114 | 29 | 11.40 | - | - | 6 | - |
| P.J.W.Allott | 8 | 8 | 2 | 63 | 26 | 10.50 | - | - | 4 | - |
| S.J.Base | 13 | 16 | 3 | 136 | 36 | 10.46 | - | - | 14 | - |
| A.N.Jones | 21 | 17 | 5 | 119 | 28 | 9.91 | - | - | 1 | - |
| C.A.Connor | 14 | 15 | 0 | 148 | 30 | 9.86 | - | - | 3 | - |
| R.C.J.Williams | 10 | 12 | 2 | 95 | 55* | 9.50 | - | 1 | 18 | 3 |
| N.Shahid | 7 | 8 | 1 | 64 | 22* | 9.14 | - | - | 6 | - |
| N.G.Cowans | 20 | 26 | 10 | 146 | 23* | 9.12 | - | - | 5 | - |
| K.J.Shine | 15 | 17 | 8 | 80 | 25 | 8.88 | - | - | 2 | - |
| H.R.J.Trump | 16 | 15 | 6 | 79 | 30* | 8.77 | - | - | 11 | - |
| P.C.R.Tufnell | 17 | 18 | 4 | 120 | 31* | 8.57 | - | - | 7 | - |
| D.A.Graveney | 20 | 13 | 7 | 51 | 17 | 8.50 | - | - | 10 | - |
| S.R.Barwick | 11 | 9 | 1 | 64 | 24* | 8.00 | - | - | 1 | - |
| A.A.Donald | 21 | 21 | 9 | 96 | 18 | 8.00 | - | - | 10 | - |
| A.P.Igglesden | 18 | 16 | 3 | 100 | 16* | 7.69 | - | - | 3 | - |
| D.E.Malcolm | 11 | 14 | 2 | 84 | 18 | 7.00 | - | - | - | - |
| G.R.Dilley | 10 | 10 | 4 | 37 | 15* | 6.16 | - | - | 3 | - |
| A.J.Murphy | 19 | 20 | 8 | 71 | 18 | 5.91 | - | - | 4 | - |
| D.J.Foster | 8 | 9 | 3 | 35 | 13* | 5.83 | - | - | 3 | - |
| A.M.Smith | 13 | 13 | 2 | 60 | 22 | 5.45 | - | - | - | - |
| S.D.Fletcher | 12 | 11 | 2 | 48 | 9* | 5.33 | - | - | 5 | - |
| J.A.Afford | 18 | 12 | 4 | 42 | 13 | 5.25 | - | - | 10 | - |
| S.J.W.Andrew | 14 | 8 | 2 | 30 | 13 | 5.00 | - | - | 4 | - |
| O.H.Mortensen | 18 | 16 | 9 | 32 | 8 | 4.57 | - | - | 4 | - |
| J.Boiling | 4 | 7 | 1 | 22 | 16 | 3.66 | - | - | 6 | - |
| J.P.Taylor | 11 | 11 | 4 | 22 | 5* | 3.14 | - | - | 4 | - |
| M.Frost | 18 | 11 | 4 | 19 | 8* | 2.71 | - | - | 1 | - |
| M.A.Robinson | 15 | 13 | 4 | 17 | 8 | 1.88 | - | - | 4 | - |

# BRITANNIC ASSURANCE CHAMPIONSHIP

## BOWLING AVERAGES
### Qualifying requirements : 10 wickets taken

| Name | Overs | Mdns | Runs | Wkts | Avge | Best | 5wI | 10wM |
|---|---|---|---|---|---|---|---|---|
| Waqar Younis | 570.1 | 109 | 1623 | 113 | 14.36 | 7-87 | 13 | 3 |
| M.A.Ealham | 98.1 | 20 | 274 | 15 | 18.26 | 5-39 | 2 | - |
| P.W.Jarvis | 95 | 26 | 235 | 12 | 19.58 | 4-28 | - | - |
| A.A.Donald | 522.3 | 91 | 1634 | 83 | 19.68 | 6-69 | 8 | 2 |
| D.A.Reeve | 402.1 | 117 | 957 | 45 | 21.26 | 6-73 | 1 | - |
| G.R.Dilley | 281 | 56 | 752 | 35 | 21.48 | 5-91 | 1 | - |
| D.V.Lawrence | 398.5 | 62 | 1296 | 60 | 21.60 | 6-67 | 3 | 1 |
| N.M.Kendrick | 105 | 26 | 262 | 12 | 21.83 | 5-54 | 2 | 1 |
| N.A.Foster | 693.5 | 163 | 2000 | 91 | 21.97 | 8-99 | 7 | 1 |
| Wasim Akram | 429.3 | 99 | 1251 | 56 | 22.33 | 6-66 | 7 | 1 |
| C.C.Lewis | 330.4 | 83 | 829 | 37 | 22.40 | 5-35 | 2 | - |
| N.A.Mallender | 349.5 | 76 | 969 | 42 | 23.07 | 6-43 | 3 | - |
| O.H.Mortensen | 535.1 | 138 | 1339 | 58 | 23.08 | 6-101 | 2 | - |
| K.J.Barnett | 162.1 | 33 | 393 | 17 | 23.11 | 6-28 | 1 | - |
| I.T.Botham | 279.1 | 55 | 886 | 38 | 23.31 | 7-54 | 1 | - |
| C.Penn | 407.4 | 79 | 1216 | 52 | 23.38 | 5-43 | 3 | - |
| D.G.Cork | 457.3 | 76 | 1350 | 55 | 24.54 | 8-53 | 1 | 1 |
| J.P.Stephenson | 77.4 | 14 | 296 | 12 | 24.66 | 3-20 | - | - |
| K.M.Curran | 410.2 | 101 | 1128 | 45 | 25.06 | 5-60 | 1 | - |
| T.A.Munton | 662 | 177 | 1795 | 71 | 25.28 | 8-89 | 5 | 2 |
| R.D.Stemp | 141.1 | 30 | 382 | 15 | 25.46 | 4-62 | - | - |
| F.D.Stephenson | 719.1 | 158 | 2010 | 78 | 25.76 | 5-27 | 4 | 1 |
| P.C.R.Tufnell | 733.4 | 199 | 1818 | 70 | 25.97 | 7-116 | 5 | 1 |
| R.J.Shastri | 288.5 | 80 | 704 | 27 | 26.07 | 5-71 | 1 | - |
| J.R.Ayling | 185.5 | 36 | 555 | 21 | 26.42 | 4-47 | - | - |
| C.M.Tolley | 105 | 21 | 292 | 11 | 26.54 | 3-40 | - | - |
| C.W.Taylor | 147 | 29 | 480 | 18 | 26.66 | 3-35 | - | - |
| A.P.Igglesden | 449 | 86 | 1288 | 48 | 26.83 | 5-36 | 1 | - |
| M.P.Bicknell | 470.5 | 118 | 1256 | 45 | 27.91 | 7-52 | 1 | - |
| S.R.Barwick | 296.5 | 79 | 726 | 26 | 27.92 | 4-46 | - | - |
| S.L.Watkin | 639.5 | 137 | 1848 | 66 | 28.00 | 6-55 | 4 | - |
| M.Frost | 497.2 | 84 | 1728 | 61 | 28.32 | 7-99 | 1 | 1 |
| M.A.Feltham | 327.5 | 56 | 996 | 35 | 28.45 | 4-36 | - | - |
| P.Carrick | 701.2 | 231 | 1748 | 61 | 28.65 | 5-13 | 2 | - |
| P.A.J.DeFreitas | 394.2 | 95 | 1127 | 39 | 28.89 | 6-88 | 2 | - |
| E.A.E.Baptiste | 517.2 | 117 | 1418 | 49 | 28.93 | 7-95 | 3 | - |
| T.A.Merrick | 517 | 100 | 1688 | 58 | 29.10 | 7-99 | 1 | - |
| D.J.Millns | 522.4 | 93 | 1815 | 62 | 29.27 | 9-37 | 3 | 1 |
| J.H.Childs | 667.1 | 218 | 1702 | 58 | 29.34 | 6-61 | 4 | - |
| D.R.Pringle | 359.4 | 95 | 887 | 30 | 29.56 | 5-70 | 1 | - |
| N.V.Radford | 434.1 | 92 | 1363 | 46 | 29.63 | 7-43 | 2 | - |
| Aqib Javed | 485.1 | 81 | 1586 | 53 | 29.92 | 6-91 | 3 | - |
| G.C.Small | 498 | 126 | 1347 | 45 | 29.93 | 4-36 | - | - |
| M.J.McCague | 153.3 | 23 | 481 | 16 | 30.06 | 6-88 | 1 | - |
| S.R.Lampitt | 422.4 | 74 | 1358 | 45 | 30.17 | 5-70 | 3 | - |
| S.J.W.Andrew | 366.3 | 72 | 1211 | 40 | 30.27 | 4-38 | - | - |
| M.C.J.Ball | 178 | 34 | 547 | 18 | 30.38 | 5-128 | 1 | - |
| A.I.C.Dodemaide | 555 | 110 | 1583 | 52 | 30.44 | 5-130 | 1 | - |
| R.A.Pick | 623.4 | 113 | 1985 | 65 | 30.53 | 5-17 | 3 | - |
| R.M.Ellison | 457.1 | 99 | 1375 | 45 | 30.55 | 7-33 | 2 | - |
| D.R.Gilbert | 602.2 | 131 | 1695 | 55 | 30.81 | 8-55 | 1 | - |
| A.M.Smith | 284.2 | 51 | 868 | 28 | 31.00 | 4-41 | - | - |
| P.N.Hepworth | 102.2 | 20 | 404 | 13 | 31.07 | 3-51 | - | - |
| D.J.Foster | 210.5 | 34 | 753 | 24 | 31.37 | 6-84 | 1 | - |
| Salim Malik | 118.2 | 10 | 473 | 15 | 31.53 | 3-26 | - | - |
| J.E.Emburey | 855.5 | 228 | 2031 | 64 | 31.73 | 7-71 | 1 | - |
| J.A.Afford | 670.3 | 207 | 1817 | 57 | 31.87 | 4-44 | - | - |
| K.P.Evans | 425 | 89 | 1278 | 40 | 31.95 | 5-52 | 2 | - |
| J.N.Maguire | 730.5 | 160 | 2222 | 69 | 32.20 | 7-57 | 3 | - |
| K.H.Macleay | 266.3 | 51 | 807 | 25 | 32.28 | 3-40 | - | - |
| P.M.Such | 290 | 75 | 743 | 23 | 32.30 | 3-23 | - | - |
| T.D.Topley | 484.3 | 83 | 1720 | 53 | 32.45 | 5-58 | 3 | - |
| D.E.Malcolm | 346.2 | 50 | 1271 | 39 | 32.59 | 5-45 | 1 | - |
| A.A.Barnett | 107.4 | 23 | 329 | 10 | 32.90 | 4-119 | - | - |
| K.D.James | 396.5 | 85 | 1219 | 37 | 32.94 | 4-32 | - | - |
| P.J.Bakker | 209.3 | 52 | 595 | 18 | 33.05 | 4-66 | - | - |
| C.M.Wells | 216.4 | 60 | 598 | 18 | 33.22 | 7-42 | 1 | - |
| J.D.Batty | 399.4 | 91 | 1230 | 37 | 33.24 | 6-48 | 1 | - |
| S.C.Goldsmith | 174 | 28 | 576 | 17 | 33.88 | 3-42 | - | - |
| R.W.Sladdin | 315.5 | 76 | 881 | 26 | 33.88 | 5-186 | 1 | - |
| P.J.Newport | 609.4 | 115 | 1840 | 54 | 34.07 | 4-44 | - | - |
| B.T.P.Donelan | 426.3 | 112 | 1162 | 34 | 34.17 | 6-62 | 2 | 1 |
| P.A.Smith | 157.1 | 31 | 513 | 15 | 34.20 | 5-28 | 1 | - |
| A.E.Warner | 390.4 | 92 | 1066 | 31 | 34.38 | 4-42 | - | - |
| J.P.Taylor | 267.2 | 45 | 828 | 24 | 34.50 | 5-42 | 1 | - |
| A.N.Jones | 502.2 | 68 | 1829 | 53 | 34.50 | 5-46 | 2 | - |
| J.G.Thomas | 248.4 | 34 | 829 | 24 | 34.54 | 5-62 | 2 | - |
| M.W.Alleyne | 118.1 | 23 | 381 | 11 | 34.63 | 3-35 | - | - |
| P.J.Hartley | 522.3 | 100 | 1751 | 50 | 35.02 | 6-151 | 3 | - |
| M.M.Patel | 183.2 | 43 | 458 | 13 | 35.23 | 3-33 | - | - |
| A.R.Roberts | 331.5 | 72 | 1032 | 29 | 35.58 | 6-72 | 1 | - |
| N.F.Williams | 477.2 | 89 | 1474 | 41 | 35.95 | 5-89 | 1 | - |
| J.A.North | 129 | 20 | 507 | 14 | 36.21 | 3-54 | - | - |
| K.J.Shine | 316.5 | 44 | 1350 | 37 | 36.48 | 5-43 | 2 | - |
| S.D.Fletcher | 230.1 | 45 | 738 | 20 | 36.90 | 6-70 | 1 | - |
| A.C.S.Pigott | 415.3 | 92 | 1293 | 35 | 36.94 | 5-37 | 2 | - |
| A.M.Babington | 428.2 | 70 | 1300 | 35 | 37.14 | 4-33 | - | - |
| R.J.Bailey | 118.3 | 16 | 409 | 11 | 37.18 | 3-44 | - | - |
| N.G.B.Cook | 305.1 | 70 | 895 | 24 | 37.29 | 4-74 | - | - |
| R.K.Illingworth | 430.4 | 132 | 971 | 26 | 37.34 | 5-49 | 2 | - |
| E.E.Hemmings | 638.3 | 171 | 1721 | 46 | 37.41 | 6-46 | 2 | - |
| P.J.Martin | 422.4 | 99 | 1262 | 33 | 38.24 | 4-30 | - | - |
| P.A.Booth | 226.1 | 47 | 690 | 18 | 38.33 | 4-103 | - | - |
| D.A.Graveney | 673.2 | 147 | 2041 | 53 | 38.50 | 7-105 | 2 | - |
| H.R.J.Trump | 570.3 | 102 | 1826 | 47 | 38.85 | 6-48 | 4 | - |
| C.A.Connor | 331 | 58 | 1128 | 29 | 38.89 | 4-49 | - | - |
| R.J.Scott | 175 | 38 | 545 | 14 | 38.92 | 3-43 | - | - |
| I.D.K.Salisbury | 605.2 | 144 | 1837 | 47 | 39.08 | 5-40 | 1 | - |
| D.J.Capel | 373.1 | 82 | 1099 | 28 | 39.25 | 4-83 | - | - |
| S.J.Base | 386 | 58 | 1248 | 31 | 40.25 | 4-34 | - | - |
| N.G.Cowans | 485.2 | 120 | 1370 | 34 | 40.29 | 4-42 | - | - |
| P.J.W.Allott | 173.1 | 43 | 489 | 12 | 40.75 | 4-56 | - | - |
| A.L.Penberthy | 163.4 | 26 | 531 | 13 | 40.84 | 3-37 | - | - |
| K.T.Medlycott | 458.5 | 98 | 1569 | 38 | 41.28 | 4-56 | - | - |
| R.P.Davis | 455.2 | 117 | 1325 | 32 | 41.40 | 4-81 | - | - |
| M.Watkinson | 603.2 | 107 | 2116 | 51 | 41.49 | 4-45 | - | - |
| M.V.Fleming | 184 | 41 | 498 | 12 | 41.50 | 3-28 | - | - |
| M.A.Crawley | 176.5 | 53 | 463 | 11 | 42.09 | 3-21 | - | - |
| D.W.Headley | 309.2 | 44 | 1180 | 28 | 42.14 | 5-46 | 2 | - |
| G.D.Rose | 307 | 51 | 1006 | 23 | 43.73 | 4-77 | - | - |
| R.J.Maru | 570.1 | 159 | 1534 | 34 | 45.11 | 5-128 | 1 | - |
| J.W.Lloyds | 510.2 | 121 | 1493 | 33 | 45.24 | 6-94 | 1 | - |
| I.J.Turner | 238.5 | 65 | 637 | 14 | 45.50 | 4-28 | - | - |
| L.Potter | 418.2 | 93 | 1237 | 26 | 47.57 | 4-116 | - | - |
| A.J.Murphy | 546.4 | 118 | 1667 | 35 | 47.62 | 5-63 | 1 | - |
| C.Wilkinson | 293 | 56 | 974 | 20 | 48.70 | 4-59 | - | - |
| M.A.Robinson | 377.1 | 78 | 1126 | 23 | 48.95 | 3-43 | - | - |
| R.D.B.Croft | 646.2 | 151 | 1777 | 34 | 52.26 | 5-62 | 1 | - |
| J.C.Hallett | 178.3 | 31 | 637 | 12 | 53.08 | 3-154 | - | - |
| D.Gough | 252 | 52 | 890 | 16 | 55.62 | 5-41 | 1 | - |
| S.Bastien | 329.2 | 89 | 946 | 17 | 55.64 | 5-39 | 1 | - |
| R.P.Lefebvre | 353 | 71 | 1048 | 18 | 58.22 | 3-51 | - | - |
| I.D.Austin | 237.2 | 42 | 787 | 12 | 65.58 | 3-58 | - | - |
| G.Yates | 529.4 | 97 | 1770 | 26 | 68.07 | 3-47 | - | - |

# ALL FIRST-CLASS MATCHES

## BATTING AVERAGES - Including fielding
### Qualifying requirements : 6 completed innings

| Name | Matches | Inns | NO | Runs | HS | Avge | 100s | 50s | Ct | St |
|---|---|---|---|---|---|---|---|---|---|---|
| C.L.Hooper | 16 | 25 | 9 | 1501 | 196 | 93.81 | 5 | 8 | 20 | - |
| S.J.Cook | 24 | 42 | 8 | 2755 | 210* | 81.02 | 11 | 8 | 16 | - |
| M.W.Gatting | 22 | 39 | 11 | 2057 | 215* | 73.46 | 8 | 6 | 14 | - |
| Salim Malik | 24 | 36 | 9 | 1972 | 215 | 73.03 | 6 | 8 | 25 | - |
| G.A.Gooch | 20 | 31 | 4 | 1911 | 259 | 70.77 | 6 | 6 | 22 | - |
| R.B.Richardson | 15 | 26 | 5 | 1403 | 135* | 66.81 | 6 | 6 | 14 | - |
| C.L.Smith | 16 | 27 | 3 | 1553 | 200 | 64.70 | 6 | 7 | 4 | - |
| D.A.Leatherdale | 5 | 6 | 0 | 379 | 157 | 63.16 | 1 | 2 | 4 | - |
| T.M.Moody | 22 | 34 | 4 | 1887 | 210 | 62.90 | 6 | 9 | 37 | - |
| D.W.Randall | 22 | 34 | 9 | 1567 | 143* | 62.68 | 5 | 5 | 15 | - |
| M.P.Maynard | 23 | 36 | 6 | 1803 | 243 | 60.10 | 7 | 5 | 18 | - |
| A.P.Wells | 22 | 36 | 6 | 1784 | 253* | 59.46 | 7 | 5 | 7 | - |
| M.Azharuddin | 22 | 39 | 5 | 2016 | 212 | 59.29 | 7 | 10 | 24 | - |
| I.V.A.Richards | 12 | 18 | 4 | 817 | 131 | 58.35 | 1 | 6 | 9 | - |
| G.J.Turner | 8 | 8 | 2 | 349 | 101* | 58.16 | 1 | 2 | 1 | - |
| R.T.Robinson | 22 | 37 | 8 | 1673 | 180 | 57.69 | 3 | 10 | 18 | - |
| N.R.Taylor | 23 | 36 | 4 | 1806 | 203* | 56.43 | 7 | 7 | 14 | - |
| N.Hussain | 25 | 33 | 8 | 1354 | 196 | 54.16 | 3 | 8 | 38 | - |
| R.A.Smith | 16 | 30 | 4 | 1397 | 148* | 53.73 | 3 | 11 | 15 | - |
| S.T.Jayasuriya | 6 | 11 | 2 | 482 | 100* | 53.55 | 1 | 3 | - | - |
| C.J.Tavare | 23 | 37 | 7 | 1601 | 183 | 53.36 | 5 | 7 | 20 | - |
| H.Morris | 23 | 41 | 7 | 1803 | 156* | 53.02 | 5 | 8 | 17 | - |
| C.B.Lambert | 7 | 13 | 2 | 551 | 116 | 50.09 | 1 | 4 | 5 | - |
| B.C.Broad | 21 | 38 | 3 | 1739 | 166 | 49.68 | 5 | 7 | 9 | - |
| N.V.Knight | 7 | 10 | 1 | 441 | 101* | 49.00 | 1 | 3 | 5 | - |
| P.Johnson | 23 | 37 | 7 | 1454 | 124 | 48.46 | 3 | 11 | 12 | - |
| D.A.Reeve | 20 | 33 | 7 | 1260 | 99* | 48.46 | - | 14 | 19 | - |
| R.J.Shastri | 22 | 32 | 9 | 1108 | 133* | 48.17 | 2 | 7 | 9 | - |
| M.R.Benson | 20 | 30 | 2 | 1329 | 257 | 47.46 | 4 | 6 | 9 | - |
| D.J.Bicknell | 24 | 42 | 2 | 1888 | 151 | 47.20 | 5 | 9 | 11 | - |
| K.D.James | 24 | 37 | 10 | 1274 | 134* | 47.18 | 2 | 6 | 9 | - |
| A.Fordham | 24 | 42 | 3 | 1840 | 165 | 47.17 | 4 | 9 | 8 | - |
| J.P.Crawley | 12 | 20 | 2 | 849 | 130 | 47.16 | 1 | 8 | 13 | - |
| M.A.Garnham | 25 | 29 | 8 | 986 | 123 | 46.95 | 3 | 5 | 62 | - |
| T.R.Ward | 22 | 34 | 2 | 1493 | 235* | 46.65 | 5 | 6 | 10 | - |
| M.D.Moxon | 21 | 37 | 1 | 1669 | 200 | 46.36 | 3 | 12 | 17 | - |
| N.H.Fairbrother | 19 | 29 | 6 | 1064 | 121 | 46.26 | 5 | 3 | 19 | - |
| A.J.Wright | 25 | 41 | 6 | 1596 | 120 | 45.60 | 3 | 10 | 19 | - |
| A.R.Butcher | 23 | 39 | 2 | 1677 | 147 | 45.32 | 4 | 13 | 13 | - |
| C.W.J.Athey | 25 | 40 | 6 | 1522 | 127 | 44.76 | 5 | 9 | 18 | - |
| T.S.Curtis | 25 | 40 | 3 | 1653 | 248 | 44.67 | 3 | 9 | 15 | - |
| A.J.Stewart | 19 | 34 | 8 | 1161 | 113* | 44.65 | 2 | 6 | 24 | - |
| D.Byas | 24 | 41 | 6 | 1557 | 153 | 44.48 | 5 | 2 | 21 | - |
| R.J.Harden | 24 | 39 | 8 | 1355 | 134 | 43.71 | 3 | 9 | 21 | - |
| I.T.Botham | 13 | 21 | 3 | 785 | 161 | 43.61 | 2 | 4 | 12 | - |
| D.R.Pringle | 19 | 21 | 7 | 607 | 78* | 43.35 | - | 4 | 9 | - |
| D.M.Smith | 20 | 35 | 6 | 1238 | 126* | 42.69 | 3 | 8 | 14 | - |
| D.L.Haynes | 13 | 22 | 5 | 721 | 151 | 42.41 | 1 | 4 | 4 | - |
| A.M.Hooper | 7 | 12 | 1 | 458 | 125 | 41.63 | 1 | 2 | - | - |
| G.P.Thorpe | 23 | 38 | 9 | 1203 | 177 | 41.48 | 4 | 4 | 8 | - |
| A.Dale | 17 | 26 | 5 | 869 | 140 | 41.38 | 1 | 5 | 8 | - |
| J.E.Morris | 21 | 36 | 2 | 1398 | 131 | 41.11 | 2 | 8 | 8 | - |
| M.A.Atherton | 14 | 23 | 3 | 820 | 138 | 41.00 | 3 | 2 | 10 | - |
| A.R.Roberts | 14 | 15 | 9 | 244 | 48 | 40.66 | - | - | 7 | - |
| D.M.Ward | 23 | 40 | 6 | 1372 | 151 | 40.35 | 1 | 10 | 10 | - |
| P.J.L.Dujon | 11 | 14 | 3 | 439 | 142* | 39.90 | 1 | 2 | 21 | - |
| M.P.Speight | 14 | 20 | 1 | 754 | 149 | 39.68 | 1 | 5 | 6 | - |
| R.J.Bailey | 21 | 36 | 5 | 1224 | 117 | 39.48 | 1 | 11 | 10 | - |
| G.R.Cowdrey | 22 | 34 | 4 | 1175 | 114 | 39.16 | 3 | 5 | 17 | - |
| N.E.Briers | 24 | 43 | 5 | 1485 | 160 | 39.07 | 4 | 7 | 18 | - |
| S.P.Titchard | 8 | 15 | 1 | 546 | 135 | 39.00 | 1 | 2 | 8 | - |
| V.P.Terry | 20 | 35 | 3 | 1244 | 171 | 38.87 | 2 | 7 | 24 | - |
| A.J.Lamb | 19 | 30 | 2 | 1081 | 194 | 38.60 | 3 | 5 | 21 | - |
| P.V.Simmons | 15 | 28 | 1 | 1031 | 136 | 38.18 | 3 | 4 | 13 | - |
| P.E.Robinson | 24 | 41 | 7 | 1293 | 189 | 38.02 | 2 | 8 | 20 | - |
| J.J.Whitaker | 23 | 37 | 3 | 1289 | 105 | 37.91 | 1 | 8 | 14 | - |
| K.J.Barnett | 24 | 39 | 2 | 1399 | 217 | 37.81 | 2 | 9 | 25 | - |
| M.A.Roseberry | 24 | 44 | 4 | 1511 | 133 | 37.77 | 2 | 8 | 20 | - |
| B.F.Smith | 15 | 23 | 5 | 674 | 71 | 37.44 | - | 3 | 3 | - |
| J.P.Stephenson | 25 | 41 | 3 | 1421 | 116 | 37.39 | 3 | 8 | 7 | - |
| M.R.Ramprakash | 21 | 36 | 4 | 1174 | 119 | 36.68 | 2 | 7 | 6 | - |
| D.P.Ostler | 22 | 40 | 5 | 1284 | 120* | 36.68 | 1 | 10 | 21 | - |
| G.D.Mendis | 23 | 43 | 5 | 1394 | 127* | 36.68 | 4 | 3 | 8 | - |
| W.Larkins | 9 | 16 | 6 | 365 | 75 | 36.50 | - | 2 | 6 | - |
| N.J.Lenham | 19 | 33 | 3 | 1091 | 193 | 36.36 | 3 | 4 | 11 | - |
| P.J.Prichard | 24 | 38 | 7 | 1124 | 190 | 36.25 | 4 | 3 | 19 | - |
| S.A.Kellett | 24 | 40 | 5 | 1266 | 125* | 36.17 | 2 | 8 | 19 | - |
| N.A.Stanley | 8 | 13 | 0 | 470 | 132 | 36.15 | 1 | 2 | 5 | - |
| J.D.R.Benson | 9 | 12 | 1 | 393 | 133* | 35.72 | 1 | 1 | 9 | - |
| P.D.Bowler | 24 | 44 | 3 | 1458 | 104* | 35.56 | 2 | 11 | 15 | - |
| B.T.P.Donelan | 13 | 15 | 5 | 353 | 61 | 35.30 | - | 2 | 3 | - |
| S.J.Rhodes | 24 | 33 | 6 | 942 | 90 | 34.88 | - | 8 | 54 | 8 |
| G.D.Rose | 15 | 20 | 3 | 590 | 106 | 34.70 | 2 | 2 | 8 | - |
| D.I.Gower | 23 | 38 | 5 | 1142 | 80* | 34.60 | - | 8 | 13 | - |
| K.M.Curran | 21 | 31 | 7 | 828 | 89* | 34.50 | - | 6 | 12 | - |
| C.C.Lewis | 16 | 20 | 2 | 621 | 73 | 34.50 | - | 4 | 9 | - |
| K.R.Brown | 24 | 41 | 6 | 1184 | 143* | 33.82 | 1 | 6 | 36 | - |
| A.N.Hayhurst | 19 | 32 | 5 | 910 | 172* | 33.70 | 3 | 1 | 5 | - |
| S.A.Marsh | 23 | 32 | 5 | 910 | 113* | 33.70 | 2 | 5 | 66 | 4 |
| A.J.Moles | 22 | 39 | 2 | 1246 | 133 | 33.67 | 1 | 10 | 10 | - |
| C.M.Wells | 14 | 21 | 6 | 503 | 76 | 33.53 | - | 3 | 3 | - |
| P.Pollard | 23 | 41 | 3 | 1255 | 145 | 33.02 | 3 | 4 | 21 | - |
| P.A.De Silva | 5 | 7 | 1 | 198 | 57* | 33.00 | - | 1 | 4 | - |
| R.I.Alikhan | 19 | 34 | 2 | 1055 | 96* | 32.96 | - | 8 | 10 | - |
| P.N.Hepworth | 23 | 38 | 4 | 1119 | 115 | 32.91 | 2 | 4 | 19 | - |
| G.A.Hick | 22 | 36 | 2 | 1119 | 186 | 32.91 | 3 | 5 | 25 | - |
| W.K.Hegg | 22 | 32 | 8 | 784 | 97 | 32.66 | - | 3 | 43 | 3 |
| T.A.Lloyd | 21 | 35 | 2 | 1076 | 97 | 32.60 | - | 10 | 10 | - |
| D.S.B.P.Kuruppu | 7 | 12 | 0 | 389 | 86 | 32.41 | - | 4 | 3 | - |
| P.M.Roebuck | 17 | 29 | 3 | 833 | 101 | 32.03 | 1 | 5 | 4 | - |
| M.W.Alleyne | 25 | 40 | 5 | 1121 | 165 | 32.02 | 1 | 6 | 12 | 1 |
| J.D.Ratcliffe | 17 | 31 | 1 | 953 | 94 | 31.76 | - | 8 | 15 | - |
| M.V.Fleming | 20 | 32 | 3 | 917 | 116 | 31.62 | 2 | 6 | 14 | - |
| C.J.Adams | 15 | 24 | 2 | 691 | 134 | 31.40 | 2 | 1 | 15 | - |
| A.C.Seymour | 10 | 18 | 1 | 533 | 157 | 31.35 | 1 | 3 | 7 | - |
| T.J.Boon | 22 | 40 | 2 | 1185 | 108 | 31.18 | 2 | 6 | 11 | - |
| L.Potter | 24 | 37 | 4 | 1027 | 89 | 31.12 | - | 7 | 21 | - |
| U.C.Hathurusinghe | 6 | 11 | 1 | 311 | 74* | 31.10 | - | 3 | 2 | - |
| N.D.Burns | 23 | 34 | 8 | 808 | 108 | 31.07 | 1 | 4 | 35 | 8 |
| P.Whitticase | 20 | 25 | 5 | 620 | 114* | 31.00 | 1 | 4 | 44 | 3 |
| S.R.Lampitt | 22 | 23 | 6 | 523 | 93 | 30.76 | - | 4 | 6 | - |
| G.Fowler | 19 | 33 | 2 | 953 | 113 | 30.74 | 2 | 3 | 2 | - |
| M.C.J.Nicholas | 22 | 37 | 10 | 826 | 107* | 30.59 | 1 | 5 | 10 | - |
| K.Greenfield | 9 | 14 | 1 | 394 | 127* | 30.30 | 2 | 1 | 15 | - |
| M.A.Crawley | 11 | 13 | 4 | 272 | 112 | 30.22 | 1 | - | 14 | - |
| N.M.K.Smith | 5 | 9 | 2 | 209 | 70 | 29.85 | - | 2 | - | - |
| T.C.Middleton | 18 | 31 | 2 | 864 | 102 | 29.79 | 1 | 3 | 15 | - |
| G.D.Hodgson | 23 | 39 | 2 | 1101 | 105 | 29.75 | 1 | 7 | 8 | - |
| A.A.Metcalfe | 24 | 43 | 2 | 1210 | 123 | 29.51 | 2 | 6 | 12 | - |
| R.J.Bartlett | 5 | 7 | 1 | 177 | 71 | 29.50 | - | 1 | 3 | - |
| A.P.Gurusinha | 6 | 10 | 0 | 292 | 98 | 29.20 | - | 1 | 2 | - |
| D.Ripley | 20 | 25 | 9 | 467 | 53* | 29.18 | - | 1 | 41 | 2 |
| J.R.Ayling | 10 | 14 | 3 | 321 | 58 | 29.18 | - | 2 | 3 | - |
| M.A.Feltham | 13 | 18 | 5 | 375 | 69* | 28.84 | - | 1 | 4 | - |
| S.P.James | 11 | 19 | 3 | 461 | 70 | 28.81 | - | 2 | 8 | - |
| P.Carrick | 21 | 32 | 9 | 662 | 67 | 28.78 | - | 4 | 3 | - |
| A.I.C.Dodemaide | 20 | 30 | 9 | 602 | 100* | 28.66 | 1 | 1 | 8 | - |
| J.W.Hall | 15 | 26 | 2 | 686 | 117* | 28.58 | 1 | 4 | 8 | - |
| P.Moores | 23 | 28 | 3 | 714 | 102 | 28.56 | 1 | 6 | 56 | 5 |
| I.J.F.Hutchinson | 14 | 24 | 1 | 656 | 125 | 28.52 | 2 | 2 | 14 | - |
| N.A.Foster | 22 | 22 | 4 | 513 | 107* | 28.50 | 1 | 1 | 11 | - |
| N.J.Speak | 18 | 33 | 3 | 844 | 153 | 28.13 | 1 | 2 | 8 | - |
| R.R.Montgomerie | 9 | 13 | 2 | 309 | 88 | 28.09 | - | 4 | 9 | - |
| E.A.E.Baptiste | 18 | 22 | 1 | 589 | 80 | 28.04 | - | 4 | 9 | - |
| A.N.Aymes | 24 | 30 | 7 | 644 | 53 | 28.00 | - | 2 | 51 | 2 |
| R.G.Williams | 8 | 11 | 3 | 224 | 101* | 28.00 | 1 | - | 1 | - |
| D.Gough | 13 | 14 | 3 | 307 | 72 | 27.90 | - | 2 | 3 | - |
| T.J.G.O'Gorman | 25 | 44 | 4 | 1116 | 148 | 27.90 | 2 | 4 | 21 | - |
| K.H.Macleay | 15 | 21 | 6 | 417 | 63 | 27.80 | - | 2 | 5 | - |
| Wasim Akram | 14 | 19 | 2 | 471 | 122 | 27.70 | 1 | 1 | 5 | - |
| J.W.Lloyds | 24 | 35 | 6 | 803 | 71* | 27.69 | - | 8 | 21 | - |
| R.J.Turner | 9 | 13 | 4 | 249 | 69* | 27.66 | - | 1 | 12 | 1 |
| G.D.Lloyd | 18 | 30 | 0 | 829 | 96 | 27.63 | - | 6 | 11 | - |
| A.L.Logie | 12 | 17 | 1 | 433 | 78 | 27.06 | - | 3 | 7 | - |
| D.B.D'Oliveira | 17 | 24 | 2 | 586 | 237 | 26.63 | 1 | 1 | 21 | - |
| S.C.Goldsmith | 16 | 26 | 3 | 610 | 127 | 26.52 | 1 | 2 | 2 | - |
| Asif Din | 15 | 27 | 1 | 685 | 140 | 26.34 | 2 | 1 | 9 | - |

# ALL FIRST-CLASS MATCHES

| Name | Matches | Inns | NO | Runs | HS | Avge | 100s | 50s | Ct | St |
|---|---|---|---|---|---|---|---|---|---|---|
| K.P.Evans | 15 | 18 | 7 | 289 | 56* | 26.27 | - | 1 | 6 | - |
| I.D.Austin | 12 | 16 | 4 | 315 | 101* | 26.25 | 1 | 1 | 4 | - |
| R.P.Lefebvre | 16 | 18 | 4 | 366 | 100 | 26.14 | 1 | 1 | 6 | - |
| R.J.Blakey | 24 | 38 | 2 | 941 | 196 | 26.13 | 1 | 6 | 40 | 5 |
| R.J.Scott | 20 | 34 | 1 | 848 | 127 | 25.69 | 2 | 3 | 6 | - |
| D.J.Capel | 22 | 33 | 2 | 792 | 100 | 25.54 | 1 | 7 | 9 | - |
| C.P.Ramanayake | 6 | 8 | 2 | 152 | 41* | 25.33 | - | - | 1 | - |
| C.Gupte | 8 | 9 | 1 | 200 | 55* | 25.00 | - | 1 | 2 | - |
| G.Lovell | 9 | 13 | 3 | 250 | 49 | 25.00 | - | - | 6 | - |
| K.T.Medlycott | 19 | 27 | 2 | 624 | 109 | 24.96 | 1 | 4 | 6 | - |
| P.N.Weekes | 6 | 11 | 1 | 249 | 86 | 24.90 | - | 2 | 5 | - |
| P.A.Neale | 14 | 21 | 4 | 419 | 69* | 24.64 | - | 1 | 5 | - |
| B.C.Lara | 9 | 14 | 0 | 344 | 93 | 24.57 | - | 3 | 9 | - |
| M.Watkinson | 21 | 35 | 4 | 758 | 114* | 24.45 | 1 | 3 | 8 | - |
| P.W.G.Parker | 16 | 26 | 1 | 607 | 111 | 24.28 | 1 | 3 | 8 | - |
| G.Yates | 20 | 26 | 13 | 315 | 100* | 24.23 | 1 | - | 8 | - |
| P.Bent | 8 | 13 | 1 | 288 | 100* | 24.00 | 1 | 1 | 3 | - |
| C.M.Tolley | 8 | 10 | 4 | 144 | 36 | 24.00 | - | - | 3 | - |
| R.K.Illingworth | 22 | 29 | 7 | 524 | 56* | 23.81 | - | 1 | 8 | - |
| D.Sandiford | 9 | 9 | 1 | 189 | 83 | 23.62 | - | 1 | 11 | 1 |
| C.P.Metson | 24 | 26 | 3 | 543 | 84 | 23.60 | - | 2 | 73 | 3 |
| R.E.Morris | 8 | 11 | 1 | 236 | 71 | 23.60 | - | 2 | 3 | - |
| J.A.North | 7 | 8 | 1 | 163 | 63* | 23.28 | - | 1 | 1 | - |
| K.M.Krikken | 24 | 38 | 8 | 697 | 65 | 23.23 | - | 2 | 58 | 3 |
| R.C.Russell | 20 | 32 | 5 | 627 | 111 | 23.22 | 1 | 2 | 49 | 3 |
| P.A.Cottey | 14 | 20 | 7 | 299 | 55 | 23.00 | - | 1 | 9 | - |
| P.J.Hartley | 20 | 24 | 10 | 322 | 50* | 23.00 | - | 1 | 3 | - |
| S.G.Hinks | 9 | 14 | 2 | 275 | 61* | 22.91 | - | 2 | 6 | - |
| J.G.Thomas | 12 | 12 | 3 | 206 | 64 | 22.88 | - | 1 | 3 | - |
| I.A.Greig | 20 | 31 | 4 | 610 | 72 | 22.59 | - | 3 | 7 | - |
| M.A.Ealham | 4 | 7 | 1 | 135 | 37 | 22.50 | - | - | 3 | - |
| I.Smith | 10 | 13 | 2 | 245 | 47 | 22.27 | - | - | 7 | - |
| C.S.Pickles | 11 | 16 | 3 | 284 | 51 | 21.84 | - | 2 | 2 | - |
| R.M.Ellison | 17 | 26 | 7 | 415 | 61* | 21.84 | - | 3 | 10 | - |
| M.D.Marshall | 11 | 11 | 2 | 196 | 67 | 21.77 | - | 1 | - | - |
| J.E.Emburey | 24 | 33 | 4 | 630 | 74 | 21.72 | - | 3 | 25 | - |
| J.D.Fitton | 8 | 11 | 1 | 217 | 60 | 21.70 | - | 1 | - | - |
| M.A.Lynch | 10 | 17 | 1 | 342 | 141* | 21.37 | 1 | 1 | 13 | - |
| T.D.Topley | 20 | 19 | 4 | 320 | 50* | 21.33 | - | 2 | 15 | - |
| F.D.Stephenson | 22 | 27 | 7 | 423 | 58 | 21.15 | - | 1 | 6 | - |
| D.G.Cork | 18 | 28 | 8 | 423 | 44 | 21.15 | - | - | 9 | - |
| G.J.Lord | 11 | 18 | 0 | 378 | 85 | 21.00 | - | 3 | 2 | - |
| P.A.J.DeFreitas | 18 | 26 | 2 | 499 | 60 | 20.79 | - | 3 | 2 | - |
| P.J.Newport | 25 | 26 | 9 | 353 | 48 | 20.76 | - | - | 4 | - |
| M.Keech | 15 | 24 | 3 | 420 | 58* | 20.00 | - | 2 | 4 | - |
| N.A.Felton | 16 | 28 | 3 | 497 | 55 | 19.88 | - | 1 | 5 | - |
| A.E.Warner | 17 | 24 | 3 | 410 | 53 | 19.52 | - | 2 | 4 | - |
| G.C.Holmes | 7 | 8 | 1 | 136 | 54 | 19.42 | - | 1 | 1 | - |
| J.C.Pooley | 12 | 21 | 0 | 407 | 88 | 19.38 | - | 2 | 8 | - |
| D.J.Millns | 20 | 24 | 8 | 306 | 44 | 19.12 | - | - | 9 | - |
| A.C.S.Pigott | 19 | 22 | 5 | 320 | 65 | 18.82 | - | 1 | 5 | - |
| P.A.Smith | 14 | 23 | 1 | 411 | 68 | 18.68 | - | 2 | 2 | - |
| J.J.E.Hardy | 10 | 15 | 2 | 242 | 52 | 18.61 | - | 1 | - | - |
| D.P.Hughes | 8 | 9 | 3 | 111 | 51 | 18.50 | - | 1 | 4 | - |
| N.Shahid | 8 | 9 | 1 | 147 | 83 | 18.37 | - | 1 | 7 | - |
| J.D.Batty | 18 | 17 | 6 | 202 | 51 | 18.36 | - | 1 | 7 | - |
| M.J.McCague | 8 | 10 | 2 | 142 | 29 | 17.75 | - | - | 1 | - |
| K.J.Piper | 16 | 23 | 3 | 349 | 55 | 17.45 | - | 1 | 48 | - |
| R.P.Davis | 20 | 26 | 4 | 383 | 44 | 17.40 | - | - | 23 | - |
| M.P.Bicknell | 15 | 22 | 4 | 312 | 63 | 17.33 | - | 1 | 3 | - |
| D.V.Lawrence | 18 | 26 | 1 | 433 | 66 | 17.32 | - | 1 | 4 | - |
| C.Penn | 18 | 22 | 4 | 311 | 52 | 17.27 | - | 1 | 6 | - |
| R.J.Maru | 22 | 26 | 3 | 392 | 61 | 17.04 | - | 1 | 31 | - |
| G.C.Small | 20 | 29 | 7 | 370 | 58 | 16.81 | - | 1 | 5 | - |
| M.J.Lowrey | 10 | 16 | 2 | 234 | 51 | 16.71 | - | 1 | 2 | - |
| P.Willey | 12 | 18 | 5 | 217 | 42* | 16.69 | - | - | 6 | - |
| M.Saxelby | 7 | 10 | 1 | 149 | 44 | 16.55 | - | - | - | - |
| N.F.Sargeant | 21 | 28 | 4 | 391 | 49 | 16.29 | - | - | 46 | 8 |
| R.S.Mahanama | 6 | 9 | 0 | 146 | 65 | 16.22 | - | 1 | 9 | - |
| B.N.French | 21 | 24 | 4 | 315 | 65 | 15.75 | - | 2 | 54 | 8 |
| N.V.Radford | 17 | 16 | 6 | 157 | 45 | 15.70 | - | - | 4 | - |
| L.Tennant | 6 | 9 | 3 | 94 | 23* | 15.66 | - | - | - | - |
| A.L.Penberthy | 12 | 15 | 3 | 186 | 52 | 15.50 | - | 1 | 6 | - |
| M.I.Gidley | 6 | 9 | 2 | 107 | 80 | 15.28 | - | 1 | 4 | - |
| R.I.Clitheroe | 10 | 17 | 2 | 228 | 36 | 15.20 | - | - | 3 | - |

| Name | Matches | Inns | NO | Runs | HS | Avge | 100s | 50s | Ct | St |
|---|---|---|---|---|---|---|---|---|---|---|
| M.J.Russell | 3 | 6 | 0 | 91 | 30 | 15.16 | - | - | - | - |
| J.H.Childs | 22 | 15 | 7 | 120 | 41* | 15.00 | - | - | 6 | - |
| R.D.B.Croft | 25 | 27 | 4 | 345 | 50 | 15.00 | - | 1 | 12 | - |
| P.Farbrace | 20 | 27 | 5 | 326 | 50 | 14.81 | - | 1 | 46 | 8 |
| Waqar Younis | 18 | 20 | 8 | 177 | 31 | 14.75 | - | - | 4 | - |
| N.F.Williams | 18 | 27 | 3 | 351 | 77 | 14.62 | - | 1 | 5 | - |
| I.J.Turner | 8 | 10 | 4 | 87 | 39* | 14.50 | - | - | 3 | - |
| I.D.K.Salisbury | 22 | 21 | 8 | 188 | 34 | 14.46 | - | - | 12 | - |
| D.R.Gilbert | 22 | 28 | 7 | 303 | 28* | 14.42 | - | - | 5 | - |
| D.W.Headley | 12 | 15 | 1 | 202 | 76 | 14.42 | - | 1 | 5 | - |
| J.P.Arscott | 9 | 12 | 1 | 157 | 74 | 14.27 | - | 1 | 7 | - |
| J.N.Maguire | 24 | 24 | 7 | 237 | 44* | 13.94 | - | - | 7 | - |
| W.M.Noon | 6 | 9 | 2 | 96 | 36 | 13.71 | - | - | 11 | - |
| A.M.Babington | 18 | 20 | 7 | 176 | 58 | 13.53 | - | 1 | 7 | - |
| N.A.Mallender | 13 | 11 | 3 | 108 | 19 | 13.50 | - | - | 1 | - |
| P.A.Booth | 10 | 13 | 0 | 175 | 62 | 13.46 | - | 1 | 5 | - |
| H.Davies | 7 | 9 | 3 | 80 | 38 | 13.33 | - | - | - | - |
| T.A.Munton | 23 | 25 | 8 | 226 | 31 | 13.29 | - | - | 14 | - |
| T.Hancock | 5 | 9 | 2 | 93 | 51 | 13.28 | - | 1 | 7 | - |
| M.J.Morris | 9 | 13 | 0 | 171 | 60 | 13.15 | - | 1 | 2 | - |
| R.A.Pick | 23 | 16 | 5 | 142 | 46 | 12.90 | - | - | 7 | - |
| C.Wilkinson | 14 | 13 | 2 | 138 | 41 | 12.54 | - | - | 7 | - |
| S.L.Watkin | 22 | 19 | 8 | 136 | 25* | 12.36 | - | - | 2 | - |
| T.A.Merrick | 19 | 23 | 6 | 204 | 36 | 12.00 | - | - | 4 | - |
| E.E.Hemmings | 16 | 16 | 4 | 143 | 29* | 11.91 | - | - | 4 | - |
| M.C.J.Ball | 6 | 9 | 0 | 106 | 28 | 11.77 | - | - | 8 | - |
| P.C.R.Tufnell | 22 | 24 | 6 | 210 | 34 | 11.66 | - | - | 9 | - |
| N.G.B.Cook | 18 | 15 | 5 | 114 | 29 | 11.40 | - | - | 10 | - |
| H.R.J.Trump | 18 | 17 | 7 | 108 | 30* | 10.80 | - | - | 12 | - |
| S.J.Base | 15 | 18 | 4 | 151 | 36 | 10.78 | - | - | 14 | - |
| A.N.Jones | 23 | 18 | 6 | 128 | 28 | 10.66 | - | - | 1 | - |
| P.J.W.Allott | 9 | 8 | 2 | 63 | 26 | 10.50 | - | - | 6 | - |
| N.G.Cowans | 23 | 29 | 11 | 186 | 35 | 10.33 | - | - | 5 | - |
| R.C.J.Williams | 10 | 12 | 2 | 95 | 55* | 9.50 | - | 1 | 18 | 3 |
| C.A.Walsh | 11 | 8 | 1 | 66 | 18 | 9.42 | - | - | - | - |
| C.A.Connor | 16 | 16 | 0 | 148 | 30 | 9.25 | - | - | 3 | - |
| K.J.Shine | 16 | 18 | 8 | 92 | 25 | 9.20 | - | - | 2 | - |
| R.H.J.Jenkins | 6 | 8 | 1 | 64 | 20 | 9.14 | - | - | 2 | - |
| D.A.Graveney | 21 | 14 | 7 | 59 | 17 | 8.42 | - | - | 10 | - |
| A.A.Donald | 21 | 21 | 9 | 96 | 18 | 8.00 | - | - | 10 | - |
| A.P.Igglesden | 19 | 17 | 4 | 101 | 16* | 7.76 | - | - | 4 | - |
| C.E.L.Ambrose | 10 | 8 | 1 | 53 | 17 | 7.57 | - | - | 1 | - |
| S.R.Barwick | 12 | 10 | 1 | 64 | 24* | 7.11 | - | - | 1 | - |
| D.E.Malcolm | 13 | 17 | 3 | 93 | 18 | 6.64 | - | - | 1 | - |
| R.M.Pearson | 10 | 12 | 1 | 70 | 21 | 6.36 | - | - | 2 | - |
| G.R.Dilley | 11 | 11 | 5 | 37 | 15* | 6.16 | - | - | 3 | - |
| A.J.Murphy | 19 | 20 | 8 | 71 | 18 | 5.91 | - | - | 4 | - |
| D.J.Foster | 9 | 9 | 3 | 35 | 13* | 5.83 | - | - | 3 | - |
| M.Jean-Jacques | 5 | 7 | 1 | 35 | 28 | 5.83 | - | - | - | - |
| A.M.Smith | 14 | 13 | 2 | 60 | 22 | 5.45 | - | - | - | - |
| S.D.Fletcher | 13 | 11 | 2 | 48 | 9* | 5.33 | - | - | 5 | - |
| J.A.Afford | 19 | 12 | 4 | 42 | 13 | 5.25 | - | - | 10 | - |
| S.J.W.Andrew | 15 | 9 | 2 | 30 | 13 | 4.28 | - | - | 5 | - |
| O.H.Mortensen | 19 | 17 | 9 | 32 | 8 | 4.00 | - | - | 5 | - |
| J.Boiling | 5 | 7 | 1 | 22 | 16 | 3.66 | - | - | 7 | - |
| J.P.Taylor | 13 | 11 | 4 | 22 | 5* | 3.14 | - | - | 4 | - |
| M.Frost | 20 | 12 | 5 | 19 | 8* | 2.71 | - | - | 1 | - |
| M.A.Robinson | 17 | 13 | 4 | 17 | 17 | 1.88 | - | - | 4 | - |

# ALL FIRST-CLASS MATCHES

## BOWLING AVERAGES
### Qualifying requirements : 10 wickets taken

| Name | Overs | Mdns | Runs | Wkts | Avge | Best | 5wI | 10wM |
|---|---|---|---|---|---|---|---|---|
| Waqar Younis | 582 | 112 | 1656 | 113 | 14.65 | 7-87 | 13 | 3 |
| C.E.L.Ambrose | 390 | 122 | 869 | 51 | 17.03 | 6-52 | 3 | - |
| P.W.Jarvis | 95 | 26 | 235 | 12 | 19.58 | 4-28 | - | - |
| A.A.Donald | 522.3 | 91 | 1634 | 83 | 19.68 | 6-69 | 8 | 2 |
| M.A.Ealham | 118.1 | 24 | 354 | 17 | 20.82 | 5-39 | 2 | - |
| N.A.Foster | 757.2 | 185 | 2138 | 102 | 20.96 | 8-99 | 7 | 1 |
| D.A.Reeve | 402.1 | 117 | 957 | 45 | 21.26 | 6-73 | 1 | - |
| N.M.Kendrick | 105 | 26 | 262 | 12 | 21.83 | 5-54 | 2 | 1 |
| G.R.Dilley | 305.2 | 62 | 823 | 37 | 22.24 | 5-91 | 1 | - |
| Wasim Akram | 429.3 | 99 | 1251 | 56 | 22.33 | 6-66 | 7 | 1 |
| C.M.Tolley | 161 | 39 | 413 | 18 | 22.94 | 4-69 | - | - |
| N.A.Mallender | 349.5 | 76 | 969 | 42 | 23.07 | 6-43 | 3 | - |
| R.J.Shastri | 307.5 | 88 | 724 | 31 | 23.35 | 5-71 | 1 | - |
| J.P.Stephenson | 106.4 | 19 | 399 | 17 | 23.47 | 4-30 | - | - |
| J.R.Ayling | 211.1 | 49 | 595 | 25 | 23.80 | 4-47 | - | - |
| O.H.Mortensen | 559.1 | 143 | 1384 | 58 | 23.86 | 6-101 | 2 | - |
| D.V.Lawrence | 515.1 | 79 | 1790 | 74 | 24.18 | 6-67 | 4 | 1 |
| P.A.J.DeFreitas | 657.1 | 173 | 1780 | 73 | 24.38 | 7-70 | 3 | - |
| I.T.Botham | 351.1 | 73 | 1077 | 44 | 24.47 | 7-54 | 3 | - |
| K.J.Barnett | 211.1 | 47 | 496 | 20 | 24.80 | 6-28 | 1 | - |
| R.D.Stemp | 172.1 | 43 | 425 | 17 | 25.00 | 4-62 | - | - |
| K.M.Curran | 436.2 | 110 | 1204 | 48 | 25.08 | 5-60 | 1 | - |
| P.C.R.Tufnell | 903.4 | 254 | 2219 | 88 | 25.21 | 7-116 | 7 | 1 |
| C.C.Lewis | 471.4 | 127 | 1213 | 48 | 25.27 | 6-111 | 3 | - |
| C.Penn | 429.4 | 82 | 1323 | 52 | 25.44 | 5-43 | 3 | - |
| T.A.Munton | 693.1 | 184 | 1863 | 73 | 25.52 | 8-89 | 5 | 2 |
| D.G.Cork | 494.3 | 84 | 1460 | 57 | 25.61 | 8-53 | 1 | 1 |
| F.D.Stephenson | 719.1 | 158 | 2010 | 78 | 25.76 | 5-27 | 4 | 1 |
| M.D.Marshall | 282.1 | 57 | 782 | 30 | 26.06 | 4-33 | - | - |
| R.J.Ratnayake | 137.3 | 15 | 447 | 17 | 26.29 | 6-97 | 2 | - |
| C.W.Taylor | 147 | 29 | 480 | 18 | 26.66 | 3-35 | - | - |
| C.L.Hooper | 336.2 | 71 | 837 | 31 | 27.00 | 5-94 | 1 | - |
| A.P.Igglesden | 471 | 94 | 1351 | 50 | 27.02 | 5-36 | 1 | - |
| S.R.Barwick | 317.5 | 86 | 767 | 28 | 27.39 | 4-46 | - | - |
| P.M.Such | 370.1 | 101 | 933 | 34 | 27.44 | 3-7 | - | - |
| M.J.Gerrard | 131.5 | 20 | 415 | 15 | 27.66 | 6-40 | 1 | 1 |
| D.R.Pringle | 533.5 | 145 | 1308 | 47 | 27.83 | 5-70 | 2 | - |
| M.P.Bicknell | 470.5 | 118 | 1256 | 45 | 27.91 | 7-52 | 1 | - |
| B.P.Patterson | 287.3 | 68 | 912 | 32 | 28.50 | 5-81 | 2 | - |
| P.Carrick | 701.2 | 231 | 1748 | 61 | 28.65 | 5-13 | 2 | - |
| M.Frost | 533.2 | 90 | 1868 | 65 | 28.73 | 7-99 | 1 | 1 |
| E.A.E.Baptiste | 529.2 | 122 | 1443 | 50 | 28.86 | 7-95 | 3 | - |
| D.R.Gilbert | 648.5 | 137 | 1865 | 64 | 29.14 | 8-55 | 1 | - |
| T.A.Merrick | 539 | 101 | 1787 | 61 | 29.29 | 7-99 | 1 | - |
| J.H.Childs | 751.1 | 248 | 1907 | 65 | 29.33 | 6-61 | 4 | - |
| S.R.Lampitt | 503.4 | 84 | 1643 | 56 | 29.33 | 5-70 | 4 | - |
| S.L.Watkin | 728.5 | 155 | 2175 | 74 | 29.39 | 6-55 | 4 | - |
| N.V.Radford | 434.1 | 92 | 1363 | 46 | 29.63 | 7-43 | 2 | - |
| J.A.North | 156.3 | 26 | 597 | 20 | 29.85 | 4-47 | - | - |
| G.C.Small | 498 | 126 | 1347 | 45 | 29.93 | 4-36 | - | - |
| M.J.McCague | 153.3 | 23 | 481 | 16 | 30.06 | 6-88 | 1 | - |
| A.I.C.Dodemaide | 579 | 116 | 1637 | 54 | 30.31 | 5-130 | 1 | - |
| M.C.J.Ball | 186 | 36 | 582 | 19 | 30.63 | 5-128 | 1 | - |
| M.A.Feltham | 349.5 | 57 | 1075 | 35 | 30.71 | 4-36 | - | - |
| R.A.Pick | 650.4 | 117 | 2080 | 67 | 31.04 | 5-17 | 3 | - |
| D.J.Millns | 550.1 | 95 | 1957 | 63 | 31.06 | 9-37 | 3 | 1 |
| Aqib Javed | 510.1 | 84 | 1656 | 53 | 31.24 | 6-91 | 3 | - |
| S.J.W.Andrew | 399.3 | 74 | 1352 | 43 | 31.44 | 4-38 | - | - |
| R.M.Ellison | 484.1 | 102 | 1480 | 47 | 31.48 | 7-33 | 2 | - |
| Salim Malik | 118.2 | 10 | 473 | 15 | 31.53 | 3-26 | - | - |
| C.A.Walsh | 324.5 | 75 | 915 | 29 | 31.55 | 4-39 | - | - |
| J.N.Maguire | 786 | 168 | 2437 | 77 | 31.64 | 7-57 | 4 | - |
| J.A.Afford | 670.3 | 207 | 1817 | 57 | 31.87 | 4-44 | - | - |
| J.E.Emburey | 906.3 | 246 | 2170 | 68 | 31.91 | 7-71 | 1 | - |
| K.P.Evans | 425 | 89 | 1278 | 40 | 31.95 | 5-52 | 2 | - |
| T.D.Topley | 498.3 | 86 | 1767 | 55 | 32.12 | 5-58 | 3 | - |
| P.J.Newport | 712.4 | 138 | 2140 | 66 | 32.42 | 4-27 | - | - |
| D.J.Foster | 223.5 | 35 | 814 | 25 | 32.56 | 6-84 | 1 | - |
| P.J.Bakker | 239.3 | 65 | 655 | 20 | 32.75 | 4-66 | - | - |
| L.Tennant | 99 | 20 | 393 | 12 | 32.75 | 4-54 | - | - |
| A.E.Warner | 446.4 | 101 | 1215 | 37 | 32.83 | 4-42 | - | - |
| A.A.Barnett | 107.4 | 23 | 329 | 10 | 32.90 | 4-119 | - | - |
| K.D.James | 442.5 | 99 | 1354 | 41 | 33.02 | 4-32 | - | - |
| P.N.Hepworth | 119.2 | 20 | 463 | 14 | 33.07 | 3-51 | - | - |
| J.G.Thomas | 278.4 | 40 | 937 | 28 | 33.46 | 5-62 | 2 | - |
| S.C.Goldsmith | 187 | 32 | 607 | 18 | 33.72 | 3-42 | - | - |
| H.A.G.Anthony | 223.3 | 30 | 878 | 26 | 33.76 | 3-28 | - | - |
| A.M.Smith | 310.2 | 55 | 983 | 29 | 33.89 | 4-41 | - | - |
| J.P.Taylor | 295.2 | 50 | 920 | 27 | 34.07 | 5-42 | 1 | - |
| N.G.Cowans | 542.1 | 144 | 1500 | 44 | 34.09 | 4-42 | - | - |
| B.T.P.Donelan | 426.3 | 112 | 1162 | 34 | 34.17 | 6-62 | 2 | 1 |
| P.A.Smith | 157.1 | 31 | 513 | 15 | 34.20 | 5-28 | 1 | - |
| A.N.Jones | 527.2 | 74 | 1918 | 56 | 34.25 | 5-46 | 2 | - |
| D.E.Malcolm | 388.5 | 53 | 1451 | 42 | 34.54 | 5-45 | 1 | - |
| K.T.Medlycott | 510.4 | 115 | 1703 | 49 | 34.75 | 6-98 | 2 | 1 |
| K.H.Macleay | 284.3 | 54 | 872 | 25 | 34.88 | 3-40 | - | - |
| P.J.Hartley | 522.3 | 100 | 1751 | 50 | 35.02 | 6-151 | 3 | - |
| J.D.Batty | 459.4 | 106 | 1439 | 41 | 35.09 | 6-48 | 1 | - |
| M.M.Patel | 183.2 | 43 | 458 | 13 | 35.23 | 3-33 | - | - |
| R.K.Illingworth | 551.1 | 155 | 1342 | 38 | 35.31 | 5-43 | 3 | - |
| A.M.Babington | 483.3 | 79 | 1487 | 42 | 35.40 | 4-33 | - | - |
| N.F.Williams | 524.5 | 99 | 1668 | 47 | 35.48 | 5-89 | 1 | - |
| N.G.B.Cook | 336.3 | 79 | 994 | 28 | 35.50 | 4-74 | - | - |
| A.R.Roberts | 331.5 | 72 | 1032 | 29 | 35.58 | 6-72 | 1 | - |
| R.W.Sladdin | 368.5 | 101 | 965 | 27 | 35.74 | 5-186 | 1 | - |
| C.M.Wells | 230.4 | 62 | 644 | 18 | 35.77 | 7-42 | 1 | - |
| K.I.Wijegunawardene | 124.3 | 14 | 537 | 15 | 35.80 | 4-97 | - | - |
| M.V.Fleming | 214 | 46 | 573 | 16 | 35.81 | 3-28 | - | - |
| P.J.Martin | 454.4 | 107 | 1323 | 36 | 36.75 | 4-30 | - | - |
| P.J.W.Allott | 192.1 | 49 | 516 | 14 | 36.85 | 4-56 | - | - |
| A.L.Penberthy | 174.2 | 29 | 555 | 15 | 37.00 | 3-37 | - | - |
| S.J.Base | 433.4 | 69 | 1344 | 36 | 37.33 | 4-34 | - | - |
| E.E.Hemmings | 638.3 | 171 | 1721 | 46 | 37.41 | 6-46 | 2 | - |
| R.J.Bailey | 122.3 | 16 | 419 | 11 | 38.09 | 3-44 | - | - |
| S.D.Fletcher | 238.1 | 45 | 765 | 20 | 38.25 | 6-70 | 1 | - |
| K.J.Shine | 343.5 | 48 | 1454 | 38 | 38.26 | 5-43 | 2 | - |
| P.A.Booth | 226.1 | 47 | 690 | 18 | 38.33 | 4-103 | - | - |
| C.A.Connor | 390 | 69 | 1306 | 34 | 38.41 | 4-49 | - | - |
| A.C.S.Pigott | 444.2 | 98 | 1402 | 36 | 38.94 | 5-37 | 1 | - |
| D.A.Graveney | 708.2 | 152 | 2160 | 55 | 39.27 | 7-105 | 2 | - |
| D.J.Capel | 383.1 | 83 | 1127 | 28 | 40.25 | 4-83 | - | - |
| R.J.Scott | 199 | 40 | 614 | 15 | 40.93 | 3-43 | - | - |
| M.Watkinson | 629.2 | 116 | 2173 | 53 | 41.00 | 4-45 | - | - |
| R.J.Maru | 625.1 | 178 | 1641 | 40 | 41.02 | 5-128 | 1 | - |
| M.Jean-Jacques | 141.3 | 26 | 496 | 12 | 41.33 | 4-54 | - | - |
| R.P.Davis | 513.2 | 133 | 1531 | 37 | 41.37 | 4-81 | - | - |
| H.R.J.Trump | 637.2 | 111 | 2113 | 51 | 41.43 | 6-48 | 4 | - |
| I.D.K.Salisbury | 638.2 | 148 | 2001 | 48 | 41.68 | 5-40 | 1 | - |
| J.Boiling | 181.3 | 44 | 505 | 12 | 42.08 | 4-157 | - | - |
| M.A.Crawley | 176.5 | 53 | 463 | 11 | 42.09 | 3-21 | - | - |
| I.A.Greig | 165.3 | 34 | 426 | 10 | 42.60 | 3-30 | - | - |
| G.D.Rose | 323 | 53 | 1075 | 25 | 43.00 | 4-77 | - | - |
| M.W.Alleyne | 144.1 | 27 | 474 | 11 | 43.09 | 3-35 | - | - |
| D.W.Headley | 329.3 | 51 | 1258 | 29 | 43.37 | 5-46 | 2 | - |
| C.Wilkinson | 315 | 64 | 1009 | 23 | 43.87 | 4-59 | - | - |
| I.J.Turner | 238.5 | 65 | 637 | 14 | 45.50 | 4-28 | - | - |
| R.MacDonald | 157 | 48 | 457 | 10 | 45.70 | 3-66 | - | - |
| S.Bastien | 356.2 | 99 | 1023 | 22 | 46.50 | 5-39 | 1 | - |
| A.J.Murphy | 546.4 | 118 | 1667 | 35 | 47.62 | 5-63 | 1 | - |
| L.Potter | 457.2 | 105 | 1338 | 28 | 47.78 | 4-116 | - | - |
| J.W.Lloyds | 541.2 | 122 | 1650 | 34 | 48.52 | 6-94 | 1 | - |
| G.A.Hick | 151.4 | 34 | 492 | 10 | 49.20 | 5-42 | 1 | - |
| C.P.Ramanayake | 166 | 29 | 594 | 12 | 49.50 | 3-83 | - | - |
| M.A.Robinson | 416.1 | 85 | 1241 | 25 | 49.64 | 3-43 | - | - |
| I.B.A.Allen | 217.4 | 35 | 811 | 16 | 50.68 | 2-61 | - | - |
| R.D.B.Croft | 704.2 | 168 | 1930 | 38 | 50.78 | 5-62 | 1 | - |
| D.Gough | 270 | 55 | 945 | 18 | 52.50 | 5-41 | 1 | - |
| J.C.Hallett | 178.3 | 31 | 637 | 12 | 53.08 | 3-154 | - | - |
| B.Wood | 187.5 | 34 | 665 | 12 | 55.41 | 2-24 | - | - |
| R.P.Lefebvre | 365 | 74 | 1075 | 18 | 59.72 | 3-51 | - | - |
| G.Yates | 591 | 117 | 1914 | 31 | 61.74 | 3-39 | - | - |
| I.D.Austin | 237.2 | 42 | 787 | 12 | 65.58 | 3-58 | - | - |
| J.D.Fitton | 237.1 | 39 | 829 | 12 | 69.08 | 2-42 | - | - |
| A.N.Hayhurst | 205.3 | 32 | 780 | 11 | 70.90 | 2-42 | - | - |
| R.M.Pearson | 332 | 59 | 1098 | 15 | 73.20 | 4-84 | - | - |

# REFUGE ASSURANCE LEAGUE AND CUP

## BATTING AVERAGES - Including fielding
Qualifying requirements : 2 completed innings

| Name | Matches | Inns | NO | Runs | HS | Avge | 100s | 50s | Ct | St |
|---|---|---|---|---|---|---|---|---|---|---|
| N.A.Foster | 7 | 6 | 4 | 148 | 57 | 74.00 | - | 1 | 1 | - |
| P.Pollard | 7 | 6 | 2 | 268 | 73 | 67.00 | - | 4 | 2 | - |
| T.M.Moody | 17 | 16 | 2 | 926 | 160 | 66.14 | 4 | 5 | 3 | - |
| M.R.Ramprakash | 8 | 8 | 2 | 382 | 111* | 63.66 | 1 | 3 | 3 | - |
| T.S.Curtis | 18 | 17 | 4 | 816 | 88* | 62.76 | - | 9 | 10 | - |
| G.A.Gooch | 8 | 7 | 1 | 358 | 107 | 59.66 | 1 | 3 | 3 | - |
| P.A.Cottey | 7 | 7 | 3 | 233 | 92* | 58.25 | - | 1 | 1 | - |
| N.J.Speak | 7 | 5 | 2 | 155 | 94* | 51.66 | - | 1 | 3 | - |
| R.M.Ellison | 8 | 7 | 5 | 102 | 29* | 51.00 | - | - | 2 | - |
| W.K.Hegg | 18 | 8 | 5 | 152 | 47* | 50.66 | - | - | 22 | 1 |
| B.C.Broad | 16 | 16 | 3 | 647 | 108 | 49.76 | 2 | 4 | 6 | - |
| C.L.Smith | 8 | 8 | 0 | 397 | 114 | 49.62 | 1 | 2 | 3 | - |
| G.A.Hick | 12 | 10 | 1 | 433 | 109 | 48.11 | 1 | 2 | 3 | - |
| R.G.Williams | 12 | 7 | 4 | 141 | 66* | 47.00 | - | 1 | 3 | - |
| M.D.Moxon | 14 | 14 | 2 | 561 | 129* | 46.75 | 2 | 3 | 6 | - |
| J.C.Pooley | 4 | 4 | 0 | 185 | 109 | 46.25 | 1 | - | - | - |
| W.Larkins | 8 | 8 | 0 | 363 | 108 | 45.37 | 1 | 3 | 2 | - |
| Salim Malik | 11 | 11 | 1 | 451 | 89 | 45.10 | - | 3 | 6 | - |
| D.W.Randall | 17 | 17 | 1 | 718 | 83* | 44.87 | - | 5 | 4 | - |
| A.N Aymes | 13 | 11 | 7 | 169 | 33* | 42.25 | - | - | 13 | 3 |
| M.C.J.Nicholas | 16 | 15 | 4 | 462 | 65* | 42.00 | - | 3 | 4 | - |
| C.J.Tavare | 15 | 15 | 2 | 542 | 75* | 41.69 | - | 5 | 7 | - |
| D.M.Smith | 5 | 5 | 0 | 208 | 78 | 41.60 | - | 1 | 3 | - |
| T.A.Lloyd | 13 | 12 | 3 | 373 | 56* | 41.44 | - | 1 | 4 | - |
| N.H.Fairbrother | 17 | 16 | 5 | 451 | 62 | 41.00 | - | 2 | 6 | - |
| M.W.Gatting | 15 | 15 | 2 | 525 | 111 | 40.38 | 1 | 4 | 5 | - |
| G.C.Holmes | 9 | 8 | 2 | 240 | 72 | 40.00 | - | 2 | 3 | - |
| J.J.Whitaker | 14 | 14 | 0 | 550 | 88 | 39.28 | - | 4 | 6 | - |
| G.P.Thorpe | 15 | 13 | 2 | 431 | 115* | 39.18 | 1 | 3 | 2 | - |
| S.J.Cook | 15 | 15 | 1 | 546 | 129* | 39.00 | 1 | 3 | 4 | - |
| K.Sharp | 2 | 2 | 0 | 78 | 41 | 39.00 | - | - | 1 | - |
| R.J.Blakey | 15 | 15 | 2 | 490 | 130* | 37.69 | 1 | 2 | 18 | 1 |
| L.Potter | 14 | 14 | 4 | 374 | 59 | 37.40 | - | 2 | 4 | - |
| G.D.Lloyd | 18 | 18 | 4 | 519 | 79* | 37.07 | - | 4 | 4 | - |
| Asif Din | 11 | 11 | 2 | 330 | 101* | 36.66 | 1 | 1 | 3 | - |
| M.A.Lynch | 14 | 14 | 2 | 433 | 97 | 36.08 | - | 3 | 6 | - |
| N.R.Taylor | 14 | 14 | 1 | 467 | 82* | 35.92 | - | 4 | 1 | - |
| G.Fowler | 17 | 17 | 1 | 572 | 59 | 35.75 | - | 3 | 2 | - |
| I.T.Botham | 12 | 10 | 3 | 249 | 58 | 35.57 | - | 1 | 3 | - |
| A.J.Moles | 13 | 12 | 1 | 385 | 93* | 35.00 | - | 3 | 6 | - |
| P.A.Neale | 11 | 8 | 4 | 139 | 39 | 34.75 | - | - | 3 | - |
| J.G.Thomas | 7 | 3 | 1 | 69 | 34 | 34.50 | - | - | 2 | - |
| C.J.Adams | 15 | 13 | 2 | 375 | 71 | 34.09 | - | 2 | 4 | - |
| M.W.Alleyne | 15 | 14 | 2 | 409 | 76* | 34.08 | - | 2 | 1 | - |
| A.Fordham | 16 | 15 | 0 | 509 | 76 | 33.93 | - | 4 | 3 | - |
| A.A.Metcalfe | 16 | 16 | 0 | 540 | 116 | 33.75 | 1 | 2 | 3 | - |
| H.Morris | 13 | 13 | 0 | 433 | 75 | 33.30 | - | 3 | 6 | - |
| P.D.Bowler | 13 | 13 | 1 | 396 | 75 | 33.00 | - | 2 | 8 | - |
| A.R.Butcher | 11 | 11 | 1 | 329 | 77 | 32.90 | - | 3 | 3 | - |
| S.J.Rhodes | 16 | 7 | 2 | 164 | 105 | 32.80 | 1 | - | 3 | 4 |
| M.P.Maynard | 15 | 15 | 1 | 458 | 101 | 32.71 | 1 | 3 | 9 | - |
| K.R.Brown | 15 | 15 | 4 | 359 | 81* | 32.63 | - | 2 | 4 | - |
| R.J.Bailey | 14 | 13 | 1 | 388 | 99 | 32.33 | - | 2 | 3 | - |
| J.W.Hall | 3 | 3 | 0 | 96 | 50 | 32.00 | - | 1 | - | - |
| A.J.Wright | 15 | 14 | 1 | 414 | 71 | 31.84 | - | 3 | 3 | - |
| N.M.K.Smith | 11 | 8 | 4 | 127 | 39 | 31.75 | - | - | 4 | - |
| R.J.Maru | 7 | 4 | 2 | 63 | 33* | 31.50 | - | - | 4 | - |
| V.P.Terry | 15 | 14 | 1 | 408 | 123 | 31.38 | 1 | 1 | 5 | - |
| R.J.Shastri | 13 | 13 | 2 | 342 | 90* | 31.09 | - | 2 | 3 | - |
| K.Greenfield | 15 | 14 | 3 | 341 | 78* | 31.00 | - | 3 | 1 | - |
| A.J.Stewart | 13 | 12 | 1 | 341 | 84* | 31.00 | - | 4 | 13 | 1 |
| M.Azharuddin | 15 | 14 | 2 | 371 | 73 | 30.91 | - | 2 | 6 | - |
| C.S.Cowdrey | 7 | 6 | 1 | 154 | 45 | 30.80 | - | - | 4 | - |
| D.Byas | 16 | 16 | 4 | 369 | 74* | 30.75 | - | 2 | 3 | - |
| J.P.Stephenson | 14 | 13 | 0 | 399 | 67 | 30.69 | - | 3 | 7 | - |
| I.Smith | 11 | 11 | 3 | 244 | 41 | 30.50 | - | - | 3 | - |
| M.R.Benson | 14 | 14 | 0 | 422 | 84 | 30.14 | - | 3 | 6 | - |
| D.J.Capel | 16 | 15 | 3 | 360 | 77* | 30.00 | - | 2 | 3 | - |
| P.Carrick | 10 | 7 | 4 | 89 | 25 | 29.66 | - | - | 2 | - |
| K.M.Curran | 13 | 12 | 4 | 236 | 61* | 29.50 | - | 1 | 2 | - |
| M.P.Speight | 11 | 11 | 1 | 295 | 106* | 29.50 | 1 | - | 5 | - |
| M.A.Roseberry | 14 | 14 | 1 | 383 | 106* | 29.46 | 1 | 2 | 7 | - |
| D.R.Pringle | 10 | 8 | 2 | 176 | 51* | 29.33 | - | 1 | 3 | - |
| R.J.Scott | 14 | 14 | 1 | 376 | 77 | 28.92 | - | 3 | - | - |
| T.R.Ward | 14 | 14 | 2 | 347 | 62* | 28.91 | - | 3 | 5 | - |
| K.J.Barnett | 14 | 14 | 4 | 289 | 60* | 28.90 | - | 1 | 6 | - |
| D.J.Bicknell | 9 | 9 | 0 | 260 | 68 | 28.88 | - | 2 | 3 | - |
| D.A.Reeve | 13 | 10 | 1 | 260 | 100 | 28.88 | 1 | - | 2 | - |
| T.J.Boon | 6 | 6 | 0 | 173 | 68 | 28.83 | - | 2 | - | - |
| N.Hussain | 14 | 12 | 3 | 256 | 68 | 28.44 | - | - | 4 | - |
| D.P.Ostler | 14 | 11 | 2 | 253 | 62* | 28.11 | - | 2 | 2 | - |
| P.W.G.Parker | 11 | 11 | 0 | 307 | 104 | 27.90 | 1 | 1 | 5 | - |
| B.N.French | 17 | 11 | 6 | 137 | 31 | 27.40 | - | - | 17 | 1 |
| A.N.Hayhurst | 13 | 11 | 5 | 163 | 35 | 27.16 | - | - | 2 | - |
| T.C.Middleton | 6 | 6 | 0 | 162 | 56 | 27.00 | - | 1 | - | - |
| G.T.J.Townsend | 2 | 2 | 0 | 54 | 27 | 27.00 | - | - | 1 | - |
| S.A.Marsh | 14 | 13 | 3 | 269 | 59 | 26.90 | - | 3 | 9 | 1 |
| P.Johnson | 17 | 15 | 1 | 370 | 80 | 26.42 | - | 3 | 6 | - |
| N.D.Burns | 15 | 13 | 4 | 235 | 52* | 26.11 | - | 2 | 12 | 6 |
| N.A.Felton | 9 | 8 | 0 | 203 | 69 | 25.37 | - | 2 | 4 | - |
| J.D.Robinson | 15 | 13 | 3 | 253 | 55* | 25.30 | - | 2 | 4 | - |
| P.A.Smith | 13 | 10 | 0 | 252 | 75 | 25.20 | - | 1 | 2 | - |
| J.E.Morris | 11 | 11 | 0 | 277 | 51 | 25.18 | - | 1 | 2 | - |
| C.W.J.Athey | 15 | 15 | 1 | 352 | 85 | 25.14 | - | 2 | 8 | - |
| B.F.Smith | 12 | 12 | 3 | 226 | 33 | 25.11 | - | - | 2 | - |
| P.E.Robinson | 16 | 15 | 3 | 301 | 64 | 25.08 | - | 2 | 9 | - |
| M.P.Bicknell | 7 | 4 | 2 | 50 | 20* | 25.00 | - | - | 2 | - |
| P.J.Prichard | 13 | 11 | 1 | 248 | 54* | 24.80 | - | 1 | 7 | - |
| N.J.Lenham | 12 | 12 | 1 | 272 | 86 | 24.72 | - | 2 | 2 | - |
| G.D.Mendis | 14 | 14 | 0 | 344 | 79 | 24.57 | - | 1 | 3 | - |
| D.B.D'Oliveira | 18 | 16 | 3 | 319 | 54 | 24.53 | - | 1 | 7 | - |
| R.J.Harden | 15 | 15 | 1 | 342 | 79* | 24.42 | - | 1 | 1 | - |
| J.J.E.Hardy | 9 | 8 | 1 | 171 | 54 | 24.42 | - | 1 | 2 | - |
| M.V.Fleming | 14 | 14 | 0 | 336 | 77 | 24.00 | - | 2 | 5 | - |
| A.Dale | 14 | 11 | 2 | 213 | 56 | 23.66 | - | 1 | 6 | - |
| A.E.Warner | 11 | 10 | 2 | 189 | 51 | 23.62 | - | 1 | 4 | - |
| S.C.Goldsmith | 10 | 8 | 1 | 165 | 67* | 23.57 | - | 1 | 4 | - |
| P.W.Romaines | 6 | 4 | 2 | 47 | 27* | 23.50 | - | - | 1 | - |
| N.E.Briers | 15 | 15 | 0 | 352 | 48 | 23.46 | - | - | 5 | - |
| G.R.Cowdrey | 15 | 14 | 0 | 327 | 80 | 23.35 | - | 2 | 9 | - |
| M.A.Feltham | 9 | 7 | 3 | 93 | 23* | 23.25 | - | - | 3 | - |
| R.T.Robinson | 16 | 16 | 4 | 278 | 35 | 23.16 | - | - | 6 | - |
| M.J.Weston | 17 | 11 | 4 | 162 | 51 | 23.14 | - | 1 | 4 | - |
| J.R.Ayling | 13 | 12 | 3 | 206 | 56 | 22.88 | - | 1 | 4 | - |
| T.J.G.O'Gorman | 16 | 15 | 2 | 293 | 49* | 22.53 | - | - | 7 | - |
| M.Watkinson | 17 | 14 | 0 | 315 | 83 | 22.50 | - | 2 | 5 | - |
| K.M.Krikken | 7 | 4 | 1 | 67 | 44* | 22.33 | - | - | 9 | 3 |
| A.P.Wells | 13 | 13 | 0 | 289 | 58 | 22.23 | - | 1 | 4 | - |
| A.D.Brown | 7 | 6 | 0 | 133 | 45 | 22.16 | - | - | 3 | - |
| P.M.Roebuck | 9 | 7 | 0 | 152 | 45 | 21.71 | - | - | 2 | - |
| M.Keech | 12 | 13 | 3 | 195 | 49* | 21.66 | - | - | 2 | - |
| R.C.Russell | 11 | 11 | 1 | 214 | 42 | 21.40 | - | - | 15 | 1 |
| M.A.Atherton | 9 | 9 | 1 | 171 | 48 | 21.37 | - | - | 5 | - |
| C.M.Wells | 9 | 8 | 2 | 128 | 34* | 21.33 | - | - | 1 | - |
| I.J.F.Hutchinson | 5 | 5 | 0 | 104 | 42 | 20.80 | - | - | 2 | - |
| D.M.Ward | 15 | 14 | 1 | 268 | 56 | 20.61 | - | 3 | 6 | - |
| N.Shahid | 11 | 6 | 1 | 103 | 36 | 20.60 | - | - | 3 | - |
| F.D.Stephenson | 17 | 11 | 3 | 164 | 36* | 20.50 | - | - | 3 | - |
| J.R.Wood | 11 | 10 | 0 | 204 | 54 | 20.40 | - | 1 | 2 | - |
| J.E.Emburey | 15 | 11 | 4 | 142 | 33* | 20.28 | - | - | 2 | - |
| I.A.Greig | 13 | 10 | 2 | 162 | 68* | 20.25 | - | 1 | 4 | - |
| M.A.Crawley | 11 | 8 | 2 | 121 | 47* | 20.16 | - | - | 3 | - |
| Wasim Akram | 16 | 13 | 4 | 179 | 38 | 19.88 | - | - | 2 | - |
| S.G.Hinks | 5 | 5 | 0 | 99 | 35 | 19.80 | - | - | 1 | - |
| R.A.Smith | 7 | 6 | 0 | 117 | 75 | 19.50 | - | 1 | 2 | - |
| J.D.R.Benson | 11 | 9 | 2 | 136 | 42 | 19.42 | - | - | 5 | - |
| A.I.C.Dodemaide | 11 | 8 | 3 | 96 | 31* | 19.20 | - | - | 3 | - |
| P.Willey | 10 | 9 | 1 | 153 | 31 | 19.12 | - | - | 7 | - |
| N.V.Radford | 16 | 4 | 2 | 38 | 20* | 19.00 | - | - | 7 | - |
| R.P.Davis | 14 | 11 | 5 | 108 | 40* | 18.00 | - | - | 7 | - |
| A.J.Lamb | 12 | 12 | 0 | 212 | 61 | 17.66 | - | 1 | 5 | - |
| K.D.James | 13 | 12 | 2 | 176 | 58* | 17.60 | - | 1 | 3 | - |
| P.A.J.DeFreitas | 11 | 9 | 3 | 105 | 41* | 17.50 | - | - | 4 | - |
| D.Gough | 10 | 7 | 1 | 105 | 72* | 17.50 | - | 1 | 4 | - |
| M.Lathwell | 2 | 2 | 0 | 35 | 20 | 17.50 | - | - | 1 | - |
| M.Saxelby | 17 | 13 | 1 | 208 | 55 | 17.33 | - | 1 | 4 | - |
| S.P.James | 2 | 2 | 0 | 34 | 23 | 17.00 | - | - | 1 | - |

# REFUGE ASSURANCE LEAGUE AND CUP

| Name | Matches | Inns | NO | Runs | HS | Avge | 100s | 50s | Ct | St |
|---|---|---|---|---|---|---|---|---|---|---|
| I.D.Austin | 18 | 7 | 2 | 83 | 48 | 16.60 | - | - | 3 | - |
| D.G.Cork | 9 | 5 | 0 | 83 | 30 | 16.60 | - | - | 4 | - |
| S.D.Udal | 16 | 7 | 3 | 66 | 23 | 16.50 | - | - | 4 | - |
| P.N.Weekes | 13 | 9 | 2 | 115 | 32* | 16.42 | - | - | 6 | - |
| D.V.Lawrence | 8 | 7 | 2 | 82 | 38* | 16.40 | - | - | 1 | - |
| C.White | 3 | 3 | 0 | 49 | 37 | 16.33 | - | - | 1 | - |
| C.P.Metson | 15 | 10 | 4 | 97 | 20 | 16.16 | - | - | 12 | 2 |
| G.D.Rose | 12 | 12 | 2 | 160 | 59 | 16.00 | - | 2 | 2 | - |
| N.F.Williams | 12 | 5 | 2 | 48 | 27 | 16.00 | - | - | 6 | - |
| D.I.Gower | 8 | 7 | 0 | 111 | 45 | 15.85 | - | - | 4 | - |
| C.C.Lewis | 12 | 12 | 1 | 174 | 36 | 15.81 | - | - | 4 | - |
| K.P.Evans | 16 | 6 | 3 | 47 | 14* | 15.66 | - | - | 1 | - |
| F.A.Griffith | 5 | 4 | 1 | 47 | 20 | 15.66 | - | - | - | - |
| C.S.Pickles | 11 | 9 | 4 | 78 | 30* | 15.60 | - | - | 6 | - |
| P.Moores | 14 | 12 | 2 | 153 | 34 | 15.30 | - | - | 15 | 1 |
| D.J.Millns | 12 | 6 | 2 | 59 | 20* | 14.75 | - | - | 4 | - |
| J.W.Lloyds | 12 | 9 | 1 | 116 | 42* | 14.50 | - | - | 4 | - |
| R.J.Bartlett | 7 | 7 | 0 | 98 | 34 | 14.00 | - | - | 1 | - |
| J.D.Batty | 11 | 4 | 2 | 27 | 13* | 13.50 | - | - | 6 | - |
| P.Farbrace | 12 | 8 | 3 | 67 | 26* | 13.40 | - | - | 9 | 6 |
| S.A.Kellett | 6 | 6 | 1 | 66 | 26 | 13.20 | - | - | 2 | - |
| J.Derrick | 4 | 4 | 1 | 39 | 25 | 13.00 | - | - | - | - |
| M.J.McCague | 8 | 5 | 2 | 39 | 17* | 13.00 | - | - | 1 | - |
| D.E.Malcolm | 9 | 6 | 3 | 38 | 18 | 12.66 | - | - | 2 | - |
| T.D.Topley | 14 | 6 | 2 | 50 | 38* | 12.50 | - | - | 2 | - |
| N.J.Llong | 3 | 3 | 0 | 36 | 23 | 12.00 | - | - | - | - |
| N.A.Mallender | 9 | 5 | 3 | 24 | 13* | 12.00 | - | - | - | - |
| A.Sidebottom | 4 | 4 | 2 | 24 | 10 | 12.00 | - | - | 1 | - |
| P.Whitticase | 13 | 12 | 3 | 108 | 24 | 12.00 | - | - | 7 | - |
| E.A.E.Baptiste | 11 | 11 | 4 | 83 | 15* | 11.85 | - | - | 2 | - |
| M.A.Ealham | 5 | 5 | 1 | 46 | 18 | 11.50 | - | - | - | - |
| M.Jean-Jacques | 3 | 2 | 0 | 23 | 23 | 11.50 | - | - | 1 | - |
| T.A.Merrick | 12 | 6 | 4 | 23 | 13* | 11.50 | - | - | - | - |
| A.C.Seymour | 5 | 4 | 0 | 46 | 25 | 11.50 | - | - | 1 | - |
| D.Ripley | 13 | 7 | 2 | 57 | 14 | 11.40 | - | - | 8 | - |
| E.T.Milburn | 3 | 3 | 0 | 34 | 21 | 11.33 | - | - | 1 | - |
| P.N.Hepworth | 8 | 6 | 1 | 56 | 31 | 11.20 | - | - | 1 | - |
| K.H.Macleay | 9 | 8 | 3 | 56 | 19 | 11.20 | - | - | 3 | - |
| M.A.Garnham | 13 | 9 | 3 | 67 | 18* | 11.16 | - | - | 10 | 3 |
| P.A.Nixon | 2 | 2 | 0 | 22 | 17 | 11.00 | - | - | 3 | - |
| R.P.Lefebvre | 13 | 11 | 1 | 107 | 27 | 10.70 | - | - | 4 | - |
| J.Boiling | 9 | 4 | 2 | 20 | 12* | 10.00 | - | - | - | - |
| J.A.North | 6 | 6 | 1 | 50 | 18 | 10.00 | - | - | 5 | - |
| C.A.Connor | 14 | 4 | 1 | 28 | 18 | 9.33 | - | - | 2 | - |
| E.E.Hemmings | 15 | 4 | 1 | 28 | 17 | 9.33 | - | - | 7 | - |
| S.L.Watkin | 12 | 7 | 1 | 55 | 31* | 9.16 | - | - | 1 | - |
| A.P.Igglesden | 14 | 5 | 3 | 18 | 13* | 9.00 | - | - | 3 | - |
| D.A.Leatherdale | 4 | 4 | 1 | 27 | 15 | 9.00 | - | - | 1 | - |
| B.Roberts | 5 | 5 | 0 | 44 | 15 | 8.80 | - | - | 1 | - |
| I.D.K.Salisbury | 15 | 9 | 2 | 61 | 23 | 8.71 | - | - | 2 | - |
| J.P.Taylor | 10 | 5 | 2 | 24 | 16 | 8.00 | - | - | 1 | - |
| R.M.F.Cox | 2 | 2 | 0 | 15 | 13 | 7.50 | - | - | 1 | - |
| S.J.W.Andrew | 8 | 3 | 1 | 14 | 8 | 7.00 | - | - | - | - |
| J.E.Benjamin | 9 | 3 | 1 | 14 | 12* | 7.00 | - | - | 6 | - |
| R.J.Parks | 3 | 2 | 0 | 14 | 8 | 7.00 | - | - | 1 | - |
| A.M.Babington | 13 | 5 | 1 | 27 | 11 | 6.75 | - | - | 3 | - |
| T.Hancock | 5 | 3 | 0 | 20 | 20 | 6.66 | - | - | 1 | - |
| A.C.S.Pigott | 15 | 14 | 3 | 73 | 14 | 6.63 | - | - | 5 | - |
| P.W.Jarvis | 3 | 3 | 0 | 18 | 9 | 6.00 | - | - | - | - |
| R.D.B.Croft | 10 | 6 | 0 | 35 | 19 | 5.83 | - | - | 3 | - |
| S.R.Barwick | 15 | 8 | 4 | 23 | 8 | 5.75 | - | - | 3 | - |
| D.R.Gilbert | 11 | 5 | 2 | 17 | 10* | 5.66 | - | - | 1 | - |
| M.J.Gerrard | 4 | 4 | 1 | 17 | 7 | 5.66 | - | - | - | - |
| E.McCray | 4 | 4 | 0 | 22 | 18 | 5.50 | - | - | - | - |
| P.J.Hartley | 13 | 8 | 2 | 32 | 11 | 5.33 | - | - | 2 | - |
| N.G.Cowans | 13 | 5 | 2 | 14 | 5* | 4.66 | - | - | - | - |
| S.J.Dennis | 3 | 2 | 0 | 9 | 6 | 4.50 | - | - | 2 | - |
| A.Walker | 14 | 4 | 0 | 17 | 6 | 4.25 | - | - | 6 | - |
| P.R.Downton | 3 | 2 | 0 | 8 | 5 | 4.00 | - | - | 1 | 2 |
| S.P.Hughes | 6 | 2 | 0 | 8 | 4 | 4.00 | - | - | - | - |
| N.J.Pringle | 2 | 2 | 0 | 8 | 7 | 4.00 | - | - | - | - |
| M.C.J.Ball | 8 | 5 | 1 | 14 | 5 | 3.50 | - | - | 3 | - |
| S.J.Green | 2 | 2 | 0 | 7 | 5 | 3.50 | - | - | - | - |
| S.J.Base | 15 | 7 | 0 | 21 | 12 | 3.00 | - | - | 5 | - |
| S.R.Lampitt | 14 | 3 | 1 | 5 | 4 | 2.50 | - | - | 2 | - |
| M.J.Cann | 2 | 2 | 0 | 4 | 2 | 2.00 | - | - | - | - |
| Waqar Younis | 12 | 6 | 1 | 10 | 8 | 2.00 | - | - | 2 | - |
| C.A.Chapman | 2 | 2 | 0 | 3 | 2 | 1.50 | - | - | - | - |
| G.C.Small | 10 | 3 | 0 | 4 | 3 | 1.33 | - | - | 3 | - |

# REFUGE ASSURANCE LEAGUE AND CUP

## BOWLING AVERAGES
**Qualifying requirements : 4 wickets taken**

| Name | Overs | Mdns | Runs | Wkts | Avge | Best | 5wI |
|------|------|------|------|------|------|------|-----|
| A.D.Mullally | 16 | 1 | 50 | 4 | 12.50 | 2-19 | - |
| P.Carrick | 74 | 2 | 276 | 19 | 14.52 | 5-22 | 2 |
| J.P.Stephenson | 51 | 2 | 194 | 13 | 14.92 | 4-17 | - |
| G.A.Hick | 27.2 | 1 | 138 | 9 | 15.33 | 5-35 | 1 |
| J.Derrick | 14.2 | 0 | 79 | 5 | 15.80 | 4-25 | - |
| F.D.Stephenson | 129.2 | 11 | 525 | 32 | 16.40 | 5-31 | 1 |
| A.C.S.Pigott | 95.5 | 2 | 461 | 27 | 17.07 | 5-30 | 1 |
| R.A.Bunting | 24.3 | 0 | 137 | 8 | 17.12 | 4-35 | - |
| Waqar Younis | 88.4 | 8 | 371 | 21 | 17.66 | 4-21 | - |
| R.D.Stemp | 22 | 1 | 89 | 5 | 17.80 | 3-18 | - |
| A.G.Robson | 24 | 0 | 128 | 7 | 18.28 | 3-42 | - |
| D.J.Foster | 26 | 0 | 112 | 6 | 18.66 | 3-30 | - |
| J.E.Emburey | 114 | 6 | 528 | 28 | 18.85 | 5-23 | 1 |
| P.A.Smith | 77.3 | 1 | 404 | 21 | 19.23 | 4-21 | - |
| A.R.Roberts | 21 | 0 | 118 | 6 | 19.66 | 3-26 | - |
| A.P.Igglesden | 109 | 6 | 461 | 23 | 20.04 | 4-59 | - |
| J.P.Taylor | 74 | 7 | 301 | 15 | 20.06 | 2-18 | - |
| J.A.North | 27 | 1 | 162 | 8 | 20.25 | 3-29 | - |
| A.N.Jones | 81.2 | 5 | 448 | 22 | 20.36 | 5-32 | 1 |
| K.J.Shine | 27 | 0 | 102 | 5 | 20.40 | 2-35 | - |
| E.McCray | 32 | 0 | 166 | 8 | 20.75 | 4-49 | - |
| M.G.Field-Buss | 24 | 1 | 107 | 5 | 21.40 | 2-22 | - |
| P.M.Roebuck | 49.4 | 3 | 236 | 11 | 21.45 | 4-11 | - |
| C.C.Lewis | 91.2 | 10 | 341 | 15 | 22.73 | 3-25 | - |
| I.D.Austin | 124.3 | 3 | 660 | 29 | 22.75 | 5-56 | 1 |
| N.V.Radford | 108 | 3 | 571 | 25 | 22.84 | 5-42 | 1 |
| D.A.Graveney | 60 | 2 | 253 | 11 | 23.00 | 3-21 | - |
| P.N.Hepworth | 27 | 1 | 140 | 6 | 23.33 | 2-33 | - |
| T.D.Topley | 95.5 | 5 | 469 | 20 | 23.45 | 3-29 | - |
| D.J.Capel | 80 | 1 | 400 | 17 | 23.52 | 3-30 | - |
| N.G.Cowans | 98.5 | 7 | 425 | 18 | 23.61 | 6-9 | 1 |
| S.D.Fletcher | 80 | 2 | 426 | 18 | 23.66 | 3-26 | - |
| S.L.Watkin | 83 | 4 | 382 | 16 | 23.87 | 3-30 | - |
| K.M.Curran | 77.1 | 2 | 384 | 16 | 24.00 | 3-24 | - |
| J.N.Maguire | 113.3 | 7 | 505 | 21 | 24.04 | 3-31 | - |
| I.A.Greig | 29.5 | 0 | 146 | 6 | 24.33 | 3-10 | - |
| R.P.Lefebvre | 87 | 5 | 367 | 15 | 24.46 | 3-29 | - |
| A.J.Murphy | 97 | 7 | 444 | 18 | 24.66 | 3-15 | - |
| D.R.Pringle | 62.4 | 2 | 301 | 12 | 25.08 | 3-43 | - |
| A.M.Smith | 66.4 | 2 | 378 | 15 | 25.20 | 3-16 | - |
| J.D.R.Benson | 67 | 0 | 354 | 14 | 25.28 | 3-37 | - |
| M.A.Ealham | 38 | 0 | 178 | 7 | 25.42 | 3-36 | - |
| M.Frost | 70 | 2 | 357 | 14 | 25.50 | 3-35 | - |
| D.E.Malcolm | 66 | 2 | 384 | 15 | 25.60 | 3-43 | - |
| T.A.Munton | 90 | 6 | 333 | 13 | 25.61 | 5-28 | 1 |
| C.S.Pickles | 63 | 0 | 361 | 14 | 25.78 | 3-12 | - |
| D.V.Lawrence | 55 | 1 | 285 | 11 | 25.90 | 4-27 | - |
| K.J.Barnett | 24 | 0 | 105 | 4 | 26.25 | 2-40 | - |
| S.J.Base | 104.5 | 4 | 474 | 18 | 26.33 | 4-14 | - |
| O.H.Mortensen | 80 | 7 | 317 | 12 | 26.41 | 3-29 | - |
| D.G.Cork | 62 | 3 | 291 | 11 | 26.45 | 3-45 | - |
| C.A.Connor | 103.3 | 1 | 481 | 18 | 26.72 | 4-29 | - |
| S.P.Hughes | 47 | 3 | 214 | 8 | 26.75 | 2-29 | - |
| N.M.K.Smith | 53.3 | 0 | 268 | 10 | 26.80 | 3-52 | - |
| N.A.Foster | 41 | 1 | 161 | 6 | 26.83 | 3-28 | - |
| K.D.James | 66 | 3 | 304 | 11 | 27.63 | 3-24 | - |
| A.Walker | 98.5 | 8 | 335 | 12 | 27.91 | 2-7 | - |
| K.H.Macleay | 63 | 1 | 252 | 9 | 28.00 | 3-31 | - |
| M.Saxelby | 108 | 3 | 516 | 18 | 28.66 | 4-29 | - |
| M.A.Crawley | 46 | 1 | 232 | 8 | 29.00 | 2-13 | - |
| J.E.Benjamin | 58 | 0 | 262 | 9 | 29.11 | 3-33 | - |
| G.A.Gooch | 43 | 2 | 175 | 6 | 29.16 | 3-25 | - |
| M.Watkinson | 122 | 1 | 644 | 22 | 29.27 | 3-27 | - |
| R.K.Illingworth | 100 | 4 | 473 | 16 | 29.56 | 5-49 | 1 |
| P.Willey | 60 | 2 | 238 | 8 | 29.75 | 4-17 | - |
| R.G.Williams | 70 | 0 | 360 | 12 | 30.00 | 2-22 | - |
| A.M.Babington | 88.4 | 3 | 426 | 14 | 30.42 | 4-53 | - |
| P.A.J.DeFreitas | 84 | 5 | 369 | 12 | 30.75 | 3-27 | - |
| J.D.Batty | 77 | 4 | 376 | 12 | 31.33 | 4-33 | - |
| S.J.W.Andrew | 49 | 3 | 253 | 8 | 31.62 | 3-33 | - |
| M.A.Robinson | 64.5 | 3 | 349 | 11 | 31.72 | 4-33 | - |
| M.J.McCague | 59 | 0 | 349 | 11 | 31.72 | 4-51 | - |
| P.J.Hartley | 92.2 | 3 | 416 | 13 | 32.00 | 3-6 | - |
| D.A.Reeve | 70.1 | 2 | 352 | 11 | 32.00 | 4-18 | - |
| G.C.Small | 65 | 3 | 322 | 10 | 32.20 | 2-25 | - |
| G.D.Rose | 54.1 | 0 | 290 | 9 | 32.22 | 2-21 | - |
| R.P.Davis | 105 | 5 | 485 | 15 | 32.33 | 3-33 | - |
| P.M.Such | 86 | 3 | 423 | 13 | 32.53 | 4-30 | - |
| A.A.Donald | 58 | 1 | 264 | 8 | 33.00 | 2-7 | - |
| A.L.Penberthy | 32 | 2 | 165 | 5 | 33.00 | 2-20 | - |
| A.Dale | 72 | 1 | 430 | 13 | 33.07 | 3-44 | - |
| R.D.B.Croft | 69 | 2 | 333 | 10 | 33.30 | 2-30 | - |
| M.V.Fleming | 102.3 | 1 | 576 | 17 | 33.88 | 4-45 | - |
| M.P.Bicknell | 51 | 1 | 239 | 7 | 34.14 | 3-36 | - |
| A.N.Hayhurst | 61.3 | 0 | 308 | 9 | 34.22 | 3-38 | - |
| R.A.Pick | 75 | 2 | 308 | 9 | 34.22 | 2-27 | - |
| M.W.Alleyne | 65 | 1 | 344 | 10 | 34.40 | 2-19 | - |
| R.J.Shastri | 51 | 1 | 241 | 7 | 34.42 | 3-26 | - |
| J.G.Thomas | 39 | 0 | 209 | 6 | 34.83 | 2-20 | - |
| E.E.Hemmings | 112.1 | 4 | 488 | 14 | 34.85 | 4-26 | - |
| S.D.Udal | 119.2 | 6 | 594 | 17 | 34.94 | 3-40 | - |
| A.E.Warner | 76.5 | 2 | 429 | 12 | 35.75 | 3-38 | - |
| J.R.Ayling | 91 | 2 | 512 | 14 | 36.57 | 3-25 | - |
| S.R.Barwick | 81.1 | 0 | 441 | 12 | 36.75 | 3-30 | - |
| A.I.C.Dodemaide | 70 | 5 | 260 | 7 | 37.14 | 2-22 | - |
| M.A.Feltham | 65.1 | 2 | 337 | 9 | 37.44 | 3-44 | - |
| K.P.Evans | 118 | 2 | 679 | 18 | 37.72 | 3-41 | - |
| R.J.Scott | 62 | 2 | 303 | 8 | 37.87 | 2-26 | - |
| R.M.Ellison | 52 | 1 | 272 | 7 | 38.85 | 2-29 | - |
| J.Boiling | 60 | 0 | 312 | 8 | 39.00 | 2-24 | - |
| I.Smith | 28 | 0 | 158 | 4 | 39.50 | 2-35 | - |
| H.R.J.Trump | 54 | 1 | 277 | 7 | 39.57 | 2-31 | - |
| J.C.Hallett | 40 | 0 | 198 | 5 | 39.60 | 2-32 | - |
| I.D.K.Salisbury | 82.1 | 4 | 399 | 10 | 39.90 | 3-10 | - |
| I.T.Botham | 80.3 | 2 | 493 | 12 | 41.08 | 3-21 | - |
| P.N.Weekes | 70.2 | 2 | 373 | 9 | 41.44 | 3-27 | - |
| Aqib Javed | 92.1 | 4 | 423 | 10 | 42.30 | 3-50 | - |
| M.J.Weston | 113.1 | 4 | 437 | 10 | 43.70 | 2-25 | - |
| C.Wilkinson | 88.3 | 1 | 437 | 10 | 43.70 | 2-31 | - |
| P.J.W.Allott | 121 | 8 | 481 | 11 | 43.72 | 2-30 | - |
| D.J.Millns | 77 | 2 | 352 | 8 | 44.00 | 2-20 | - |
| J.D.Robinson | 88.1 | 3 | 402 | 9 | 44.66 | 2-32 | - |
| D.Gough | 60.2 | 1 | 316 | 7 | 45.14 | 2-32 | - |
| P.J.Bakker | 40 | 2 | 186 | 4 | 46.50 | 2-36 | - |
| Wasim Akram | 117.5 | 1 | 620 | 13 | 47.69 | 2-30 | - |
| S.R.Lampitt | 84 | 1 | 477 | 10 | 47.70 | 3-23 | - |
| S.C.Goldsmith | 60 | 3 | 345 | 7 | 49.28 | 3-48 | - |
| N.F.Williams | 83 | 2 | 408 | 8 | 51.00 | 1-24 | - |
| E.A.E.Baptiste | 81.1 | 5 | 340 | 6 | 56.66 | 2-25 | - |
| P.J.Newport | 106.2 | 1 | 576 | 10 | 57.60 | 2-43 | - |
| D.R.Gilbert | 77.4 | 1 | 391 | 6 | 65.16 | 2-27 | - |
| T.A.Merrick | 89.2 | 3 | 463 | 6 | 77.16 | 1-16 | - |

# NATWEST TROPHY

## BATTING AVERAGES - Including fielding
**Qualifying requirements : 1 completed innings**

| Name | Matches | Inns | NO | Runs | HS | Avge | 100s | 50s | Ct | St |
|---|---|---|---|---|---|---|---|---|---|---|
| M.P.Maynard | 3 | 3 | 2 | 256 | 151* | 256.00 | 1 | 1 | - | - |
| R.A.Smith | 5 | 5 | 3 | 331 | 79* | 165.50 | - | 4 | - | - |
| J.J.Whitaker | 2 | 2 | 1 | 133 | 94* | 133.00 | - | 1 | - | - |
| C.W.J.Athey | 2 | 2 | 1 | 123 | 76 | 123.00 | - | 1 | - | - |
| J.D.Glendenen | 1 | 1 | 0 | 109 | 109 | 109.00 | 1 | - | - | - |
| H.Morris | 3 | 3 | 1 | 203 | 126* | 101.50 | 1 | - | 1 | - |
| C.L.Smith | 4 | 3 | 1 | 194 | 105* | 97.00 | 1 | 1 | 1 | - |
| A.Fordham | 4 | 4 | 1 | 288 | 132* | 96.00 | 1 | 2 | - | - |
| J.D.Ratcliffe | 2 | 2 | 1 | 94 | 68* | 94.00 | - | 1 | - | - |
| T.J.Boon | 2 | 2 | 1 | 90 | 76* | 90.00 | - | 1 | 1 | - |
| R.J.Bailey | 4 | 4 | 1 | 253 | 145 | 84.33 | 1 | 1 | - | - |
| L.Potter | 2 | 2 | 1 | 82 | 57 | 82.00 | - | 1 | - | - |
| T.M.Moody | 2 | 2 | 1 | 79 | 42* | 79.00 | - | - | 1 | - |
| T.C.Middleton | 1 | 1 | 0 | 78 | 78 | 78.00 | - | 1 | - | - |
| K.M.Curran | 4 | 3 | 2 | 77 | 38 | 77.00 | - | - | - | - |
| A.N.Hayhurst | 3 | 3 | 1 | 154 | 91* | 77.00 | - | 2 | 1 | - |
| M.W.Gatting | 2 | 2 | 0 | 150 | 85 | 75.00 | - | 2 | 2 | - |
| M.P.Bicknell | 4 | 2 | 1 | 70 | 66* | 70.00 | - | 1 | - | - |
| V.P.Terry | 5 | 5 | 2 | 209 | 62* | 69.66 | - | 1 | 4 | - |
| A.J.Stewart | 4 | 4 | 1 | 206 | 76* | 68.66 | - | 2 | 6 | - |
| G.A.Gooch | 3 | 3 | 0 | 202 | 95 | 67.33 | - | 3 | - | - |
| R.T.Robinson | 3 | 3 | 0 | 197 | 124 | 65.66 | 1 | - | 1 | - |
| N.Hussain | 3 | 2 | 0 | 114 | 97 | 57.00 | - | 1 | 4 | - |
| M.V.Fleming | 2 | 2 | 1 | 56 | 35* | 56.00 | - | - | - | - |
| D.A.Blenkiron | 1 | 1 | 0 | 56 | 56 | 56.00 | - | 1 | - | - |
| D.W.Randall | 3 | 3 | 0 | 166 | 95 | 55.33 | - | 1 | - | - |
| N.A.Folland | 1 | 1 | 0 | 55 | 55 | 55.00 | - | 1 | 2 | - |
| J.Abrahams | 1 | 1 | 0 | 53 | 53 | 53.00 | - | 1 | 2 | - |
| D.M.Smith | 2 | 2 | 0 | 102 | 62 | 51.00 | - | 1 | 1 | - |
| A.Dale | 3 | 2 | 0 | 101 | 86 | 50.50 | - | 1 | 2 | - |
| P.M.Roebuck | 3 | 3 | 1 | 99 | 63* | 49.50 | - | 1 | 2 | - |
| T.A.Lloyd | 4 | 2 | 0 | 96 | 78 | 48.00 | - | 1 | - | - |
| J.J.E.Hardy | 2 | 2 | 0 | 93 | 70 | 46.50 | - | 1 | - | - |
| N.H.Fairbrother | 2 | 2 | 0 | 92 | 68 | 46.00 | - | 1 | - | - |
| G.P.Thorpe | 4 | 4 | 1 | 138 | 93 | 46.00 | - | 1 | 1 | - |
| R.G.Swan | 1 | 1 | 0 | 45 | 45 | 45.00 | - | - | - | - |
| D.A.Reeve | 4 | 3 | 1 | 89 | 57* | 44.50 | - | 1 | 5 | - |
| N.J.Adams | 1 | 1 | 0 | 44 | 44 | 44.00 | - | - | - | - |
| N.J.Lenham | 2 | 2 | 0 | 85 | 66 | 42.50 | - | 1 | - | - |
| C.J.Tavare | 3 | 3 | 0 | 127 | 59 | 42.33 | - | 1 | 3 | - |
| M.Saxelby | 2 | 2 | 1 | 42 | 36 | 42.00 | - | - | 1 | - |
| D.I.Gower | 5 | 3 | 1 | 82 | 54* | 41.00 | - | 1 | - | - |
| D.M.Ward | 4 | 4 | 0 | 164 | 62 | 41.00 | - | 2 | - | - |
| G.Fowler | 2 | 2 | 0 | 80 | 71 | 40.00 | - | 1 | - | - |
| P.E.Robinson | 1 | 1 | 0 | 40 | 40 | 40.00 | - | - | - | - |
| Wasim Akram | 2 | 2 | 1 | 40 | 29 | 40.00 | - | - | - | - |
| G.D.Lloyd | 1 | 1 | 0 | 39 | 39 | 39.00 | - | - | - | - |
| J.P.Stephenson | 3 | 3 | 0 | 117 | 59 | 39.00 | - | 2 | - | - |
| M.A.Fell | 1 | 1 | 0 | 39 | 39 | 39.00 | - | - | - | - |
| M.A.Atherton | 1 | 1 | 0 | 38 | 38 | 38.00 | - | - | - | - |
| T.R.Ward | 2 | 2 | 0 | 75 | 55 | 37.50 | - | 1 | - | - |
| A.J.Moles | 4 | 4 | 1 | 109 | 62* | 36.33 | - | 1 | 1 | - |
| T.S.Curtis | 2 | 1 | 0 | 34 | 34 | 34.00 | - | - | - | - |
| S.G.Hinks | 1 | 1 | 0 | 34 | 34 | 34.00 | - | - | - | - |
| M.P.Speight | 2 | 2 | 0 | 68 | 48 | 34.00 | - | - | - | - |
| R.P.Lefebvre | 3 | 2 | 1 | 34 | 21* | 34.00 | - | - | 1 | - |
| A.J.Wright | 2 | 2 | 0 | 67 | 56 | 33.50 | - | 1 | - | - |
| N.A.Felton | 2 | 2 | 0 | 65 | 54 | 32.50 | - | 1 | 1 | - |
| T.G.Roshier | 1 | 1 | 0 | 32 | 32 | 32.00 | - | - | - | - |
| Asif Din | 3 | 2 | 0 | 61 | 44 | 30.50 | - | - | - | - |
| A.R.Butcher | 3 | 3 | 0 | 87 | 70 | 29.00 | - | 1 | 2 | - |
| J.A.Claughton | 1 | 1 | 0 | 29 | 29 | 29.00 | - | - | - | - |
| K.R.Brown | 2 | 2 | 0 | 57 | 49 | 28.50 | - | - | 1 | - |
| M.R.Ramprakash | 2 | 2 | 0 | 57 | 32 | 28.50 | - | - | - | - |
| A.J.Lamb | 4 | 3 | 0 | 84 | 31 | 28.00 | - | - | 1 | - |
| P.G.Newman | 1 | 1 | 0 | 28 | 28 | 28.00 | - | - | - | - |
| D.B.Storer | 1 | 1 | 0 | 28 | 28 | 28.00 | - | - | 1 | - |
| S.N.Warman | 1 | 1 | 0 | 28 | 28 | 28.00 | - | - | - | - |
| B.C.Broad | 3 | 3 | 0 | 83 | 38 | 27.66 | - | - | - | - |
| G.D.Mendis | 2 | 2 | 0 | 55 | 50 | 27.50 | - | 1 | 1 | - |
| Salim Malik | 3 | 3 | 1 | 55 | 26 | 27.50 | - | - | 4 | - |
| P.Bainbridge | 1 | 1 | 0 | 27 | 27 | 27.00 | - | - | - | - |
| I.T.Botham | 1 | 1 | 0 | 27 | 27 | 27.00 | - | - | 1 | - |
| R.J.Finney | 1 | 1 | 0 | 27 | 27 | 27.00 | - | - | - | - |
| M.F.Cohen | 1 | 1 | 0 | 26 | 26 | 26.00 | - | - | 1 | - |
| J.K.Tierney | 1 | 1 | 0 | 26 | 26 | 26.00 | - | - | - | - |
| S.J.Rhodes | 2 | 2 | 0 | 51 | 41 | 25.50 | - | - | - | - |
| R.J.Shastri | 2 | 2 | 0 | 51 | 26 | 25.50 | - | - | 2 | - |
| E.A.E.Baptiste | 4 | 3 | 1 | 51 | 34 | 25.50 | - | - | 1 | - |
| G.R.Cowdrey | 2 | 2 | 1 | 25 | 25* | 25.00 | - | - | - | - |
| J.D.Robinson | 4 | 3 | 1 | 50 | 47 | 25.00 | - | - | - | - |
| M.A.Roseberry | 2 | 2 | 0 | 50 | 44 | 25.00 | - | - | 2 | - |
| D.A.Lewis | 1 | 1 | 0 | 25 | 25 | 25.00 | - | - | - | - |
| A.S.Patel | 1 | 1 | 0 | 25 | 25 | 25.00 | - | - | - | - |
| A.C.Jelfs | 1 | 1 | 0 | 25 | 25 | 25.00 | - | - | - | - |
| M.W.Alleyne | 2 | 2 | 0 | 48 | 45 | 24.00 | - | - | - | - |
| J.D.Love | 1 | 1 | 0 | 24 | 24 | 24.00 | - | - | - | - |
| R.C.Russell | 2 | 2 | 0 | 48 | 25 | 24.00 | - | - | 5 | 1 |
| A.P.Wells | 2 | 2 | 0 | 48 | 40 | 24.00 | - | - | - | - |
| A.R.Fothergill | 1 | 1 | 0 | 24 | 24 | 24.00 | - | - | 2 | - |
| D.P.Ostler | 4 | 3 | 1 | 47 | 34* | 23.50 | - | - | - | - |
| D.B.D'Oliveira | 2 | 2 | 1 | 23 | 13 | 23.00 | - | - | 1 | - |
| R.J.Harden | 3 | 3 | 0 | 69 | 39 | 23.00 | - | - | 1 | - |
| N.R.Taylor | 2 | 2 | 0 | 46 | 44 | 23.00 | - | - | - | - |
| D.J.Bicknell | 4 | 4 | 0 | 89 | 28 | 22.25 | - | - | - | - |
| P.Johnson | 3 | 3 | 0 | 66 | 48 | 22.00 | - | - | - | - |
| G.D.Reynolds | 1 | 1 | 0 | 22 | 22 | 22.00 | - | - | - | - |
| M.A.Garnham | 3 | 2 | 1 | 21 | 12* | 21.00 | - | - | 3 | - |
| P.A.Smith | 4 | 3 | 1 | 42 | 26 | 21.00 | - | - | 1 | - |
| A.L.Goram | 1 | 1 | 0 | 21 | 21 | 21.00 | - | - | - | - |
| M.J.Roberts | 1 | 1 | 0 | 21 | 21 | 21.00 | - | - | - | - |
| P.Farbrace | 2 | 2 | 1 | 20 | 13* | 20.00 | - | - | 1 | 1 |
| I.J.F.Hutchinson | 2 | 2 | 0 | 40 | 23 | 20.00 | - | - | 2 | - |
| A.N.Johnson | 1 | 1 | 0 | 20 | 20 | 20.00 | - | - | - | - |
| W.Larkins | 2 | 2 | 0 | 39 | 31 | 19.50 | - | - | 2 | - |
| N.E.Briers | 2 | 2 | 0 | 38 | 29 | 19.00 | - | - | - | - |
| N.A.Foster | 3 | 2 | 1 | 19 | 10* | 19.00 | - | - | 1 | - |
| P.J.Prichard | 3 | 3 | 1 | 38 | 27* | 19.00 | - | - | 1 | - |
| N.M.K.Smith | 2 | 2 | 0 | 38 | 38 | 19.00 | - | - | - | - |
| P.G.Duthie | 1 | 1 | 0 | 19 | 19 | 19.00 | - | - | - | - |
| S.J.Cook | 3 | 3 | 0 | 56 | 35 | 18.66 | - | - | - | - |
| I.D.K.Salisbury | 2 | 2 | 1 | 18 | 14* | 18.00 | - | - | - | - |
| P.J.Oxley | 1 | 1 | 0 | 18 | 18 | 18.00 | - | - | - | - |
| J.M.H.Graham-Brown | 1 | 1 | 0 | 18 | 18 | 18.00 | - | - | - | - |
| M.R.Benson | 2 | 2 | 0 | 35 | 21 | 17.50 | - | - | - | - |
| I.A.Greig | 3 | 3 | 1 | 35 | 20 | 17.50 | - | - | - | - |
| P.A.J.DeFreitas | 2 | 2 | 1 | 17 | 11 | 17.00 | - | - | 1 | - |
| J.W.Lloyds | 2 | 2 | 1 | 17 | 13* | 17.00 | - | - | 2 | - |
| P.Willey | 2 | 2 | 0 | 34 | 28 | 17.00 | - | - | - | - |
| T.Parton | 1 | 1 | 0 | 17 | 17 | 17.00 | - | - | - | - |
| M.A.Lynch | 4 | 4 | 0 | 66 | 48 | 16.50 | - | - | 3 | - |
| P.McCrum | 1 | 1 | 0 | 16 | 16 | 16.00 | - | - | - | - |
| M.Lathwell | 1 | 1 | 0 | 16 | 16 | 16.00 | - | - | - | - |
| S.A.Marsh | 2 | 1 | 0 | 15 | 15 | 15.00 | - | - | 3 | - |
| P.Moores | 2 | 2 | 0 | 30 | 26 | 15.00 | - | - | 2 | - |
| N.T.Gadsby | 1 | 1 | 0 | 15 | 15 | 15.00 | - | - | - | - |
| K.G.Rice | 1 | 1 | 0 | 15 | 15 | 15.00 | - | - | - | - |
| D.M.Smith | 1 | 1 | 0 | 15 | 15 | 15.00 | - | - | - | - |
| Waqar Younis | 4 | 2 | 0 | 30 | 26 | 15.00 | - | - | - | - |
| J.Boiling | 4 | 2 | 0 | 29 | 22 | 14.50 | - | - | 3 | - |
| P.W.G.Parker | 2 | 2 | 0 | 29 | 17 | 14.50 | - | - | 2 | - |
| J.D.Carr | 1 | 1 | 0 | 14 | 14 | 14.00 | - | - | - | - |
| N.J.Archer | 1 | 1 | 0 | 14 | 14 | 14.00 | - | - | - | - |
| J.R.Hall | 1 | 1 | 0 | 14 | 14 | 14.00 | - | - | - | - |
| G.E.Loveday | 1 | 1 | 0 | 14 | 14 | 14.00 | - | - | - | - |
| N.E.Thompson | 1 | 1 | 0 | 14 | 14 | 14.00 | - | - | - | - |
| S.D.L.Davis | 1 | 1 | 0 | 14 | 14 | 14.00 | - | - | - | - |
| A.Willows | 1 | 1 | 0 | 14 | 14 | 14.00 | - | - | - | - |
| G.Cook | 1 | 1 | 0 | 13 | 13 | 13.00 | - | - | - | - |
| P.A.Cottey | 2 | 2 | 1 | 13 | 10 | 13.00 | - | - | - | - |
| R.D.B.Croft | 2 | 1 | 0 | 13 | 13 | 13.00 | - | - | - | - |
| D.Ripley | 4 | 2 | 1 | 13 | 10* | 13.00 | - | - | 3 | - |
| M.G.Lickley | 1 | 1 | 0 | 13 | 13 | 13.00 | - | - | - | - |
| R.I.Dawson | 1 | 1 | 0 | 13 | 13 | 13.00 | - | - | - | - |
| B.S.Percy | 1 | 1 | 0 | 13 | 13 | 13.00 | - | - | - | - |
| G.N.Reifer | 1 | 1 | 0 | 13 | 13 | 13.00 | - | - | - | - |
| P.Carrick | 1 | 1 | 0 | 12 | 12 | 12.00 | - | - | - | - |

# NATWEST TROPHY

| Name | Matches | Inns | NO | Runs | HS | Avge | 100s | 50s | Ct | St |
|---|---|---|---|---|---|---|---|---|---|---|
| C.S.Pickles | 1 | 1 | 0 | 12 | 12 | 12.00 | - | - | 1 | - |
| S.Burrow | 1 | 1 | 0 | 12 | 12 | 12.00 | - | - | - | - |
| G.S.Calway | 1 | 1 | 0 | 12 | 12 | 12.00 | - | - | 1 | - |
| A.J.Dutton | 1 | 1 | 0 | 12 | 12 | 12.00 | - | - | - | - |
| O.Henry | 1 | 1 | 0 | 12 | 12 | 12.00 | - | - | 1 | - |
| G.T.Headley | 1 | 1 | 0 | 12 | 12 | 12.00 | - | - | - | - |
| K.P.Evans | 2 | 2 | 0 | 22 | 20 | 11.00 | - | - | 1 | - |
| A.Walker | 4 | 1 | 0 | 11 | 11 | 11.00 | - | - | - | - |
| J.P.Addison | 1 | 1 | 0 | 11 | 11 | 11.00 | - | - | - | - |
| G.R.Black | 1 | 1 | 0 | 11 | 11 | 11.00 | - | - | 1 | - |
| D.J.M.Mercer | 1 | 1 | 0 | 11 | 11 | 11.00 | - | - | - | - |
| S.G.Plumb | 1 | 1 | 0 | 11 | 11 | 11.00 | - | - | - | - |
| N.G.Hames | 1 | 1 | 0 | 11 | 11 | 11.00 | - | - | 1 | - |
| D.R.Pringle | 3 | 2 | 0 | 21 | 19 | 10.50 | - | - | 1 | - |
| R.K.Illingworth | 2 | 1 | 0 | 10 | 10 | 10.00 | - | - | 2 | - |
| J.Foster | 1 | 1 | 0 | 10 | 10 | 10.00 | - | - | - | - |
| N.R.Taylor | 1 | 1 | 0 | 10 | 10 | 10.00 | - | - | - | - |
| Ijaz Ahmed | 1 | 1 | 0 | 10 | 10 | 10.00 | - | - | - | - |
| N.G.Folland | 1 | 1 | 0 | 10 | 10 | 10.00 | - | - | - | - |
| S.D.Fletcher | 1 | 1 | 0 | 9 | 9 | 9.00 | - | - | - | - |
| C.P.Metson | 3 | 1 | 0 | 9 | 9 | 9.00 | - | - | 3 | - |
| G.D.Harrison | 1 | 1 | 0 | 9 | 9 | 9.00 | - | - | 1 | - |
| I.L.Philip | 1 | 1 | 0 | 9 | 9 | 9.00 | - | - | 1 | - |
| P.B.Wormwald | 1 | 1 | 0 | 9 | 9 | 9.00 | - | - | - | - |
| M.J.McCague | 1 | 1 | 0 | 9 | 9 | 9.00 | - | - | - | - |
| R.J.Belmont | 1 | 1 | 0 | 9 | 9 | 9.00 | - | - | - | - |
| A.A.Metcalfe | 1 | 1 | 0 | 8 | 8 | 8.00 | - | - | - | - |
| P.A.Neale | 2 | 1 | 0 | 8 | 8 | 8.00 | - | - | - | - |
| P.C.R.Tufnell | 1 | 1 | 0 | 8 | 8 | 8.00 | - | - | - | - |
| S.Sawney | 1 | 1 | 0 | 8 | 8 | 8.00 | - | - | - | - |
| M.C.Woodman | 1 | 1 | 0 | 8 | 8 | 8.00 | - | - | - | - |
| W.K.Hegg | 2 | 1 | 0 | 7 | 7 | 7.00 | - | - | 4 | - |
| G.D.Hodgson | 1 | 1 | 0 | 7 | 7 | 7.00 | - | - | 1 | - |
| S.R.Lampitt | 2 | 1 | 0 | 7 | 7 | 7.00 | - | - | - | - |
| T.D.Topley | 3 | 1 | 0 | 7 | 7 | 7.00 | - | - | - | - |
| S.Turner | 1 | 1 | 0 | 7 | 7 | 7.00 | - | - | - | - |
| P.N.Weekes | 1 | 1 | 0 | 7 | 7 | 7.00 | - | - | - | - |
| B.G.Evans | 1 | 1 | 0 | 7 | 7 | 7.00 | - | - | - | - |
| R.Swann | 1 | 1 | 0 | 7 | 7 | 7.00 | - | - | - | - |
| G.D.Williams | 1 | 1 | 0 | 7 | 7 | 7.00 | - | - | - | - |
| C.C.Lewis | 2 | 1 | 0 | 6 | 6 | 6.00 | - | - | 2 | - |
| P.Pollard | 1 | 1 | 0 | 6 | 6 | 6.00 | - | - | - | - |
| M.Watkinson | 2 | 2 | 0 | 12 | 7 | 6.00 | - | - | - | - |
| N.P.G.Wright | 1 | 1 | 0 | 6 | 6 | 6.00 | - | - | - | - |
| B.F.Smith | 2 | 1 | 0 | 6 | 6 | 6.00 | - | - | - | - |
| J.R.Weaver | 1 | 1 | 0 | 6 | 6 | 6.00 | - | - | - | - |
| D.M.Stamp | 1 | 1 | 0 | 6 | 6 | 6.00 | - | - | 2 | - |
| N.D.Burns | 3 | 3 | 1 | 11 | 5* | 5.50 | - | - | 2 | - |
| R.J.Scott | 2 | 2 | 0 | 11 | 11 | 5.50 | - | - | - | - |
| C.M.Wells | 2 | 2 | 0 | 11 | 11 | 5.50 | - | - | - | - |
| N.G.Cowans | 2 | 2 | 0 | 10 | 10 | 5.00 | - | - | 1 | - |
| G.A.Hick | 2 | 2 | 0 | 10 | 10 | 5.00 | - | - | 1 | - |
| T.J.T.Patterson | 1 | 1 | 0 | 5 | 5 | 5.00 | - | - | 2 | - |
| N.F.Williams | 2 | 2 | 0 | 9 | 6 | 4.50 | - | - | 1 | - |
| J.D.Batty | 1 | 1 | 0 | 4 | 4 | 4.00 | - | - | - | - |
| B.N.French | 3 | 2 | 0 | 8 | 7 | 4.00 | - | - | 7 | - |
| A.P.Pridgeon | 1 | 1 | 0 | 4 | 4 | 4.00 | - | - | - | - |
| F.D.Stephenson | 3 | 2 | 0 | 8 | 7 | 4.00 | - | - | - | - |
| D.Cartledge | 1 | 1 | 0 | 4 | 4 | 4.00 | - | - | 1 | - |
| A.R.Harwood | 1 | 1 | 0 | 4 | 4 | 4.00 | - | - | - | - |
| A.Needham | 1 | 1 | 0 | 4 | 4 | 4.00 | - | - | - | - |
| B.M.W.Patterson | 1 | 1 | 0 | 4 | 4 | 4.00 | - | - | - | - |
| K.Donohue | 1 | 1 | 0 | 4 | 4 | 4.00 | - | - | - | - |
| V.B.Lewis | 1 | 1 | 0 | 4 | 4 | 4.00 | - | - | 1 | - |
| P.D.Thomas | 1 | 1 | 0 | 4 | 4 | 4.00 | - | - | - | - |
| D.A.Christmas | 1 | 1 | 0 | 4 | 4 | 4.00 | - | - | - | - |
| A.C.S.Pigott | 2 | 2 | 0 | 7 | 7 | 3.50 | - | - | - | - |
| R.G.Williams | 3 | 2 | 0 | 7 | 6 | 3.50 | - | - | 3 | - |
| D.A.Banks | 1 | 1 | 0 | 3 | 3 | 3.00 | - | - | - | - |
| S.R.Barwick | 3 | 1 | 0 | 3 | 3 | 3.00 | - | - | - | - |
| A.A.Donald | 4 | 2 | 1 | 3 | 2* | 3.00 | - | - | - | - |
| M.Frost | 3 | 1 | 0 | 3 | 3 | 3.00 | - | - | 3 | - |
| T.A.Munton | 4 | 2 | 0 | 6 | 5 | 3.00 | - | - | 2 | - |
| G.D.Rose | 2 | 1 | 0 | 3 | 3 | 3.00 | - | - | - | - |
| N.R.C.Maclaurin | 1 | 1 | 0 | 3 | 3 | 3.00 | - | - | - | - |

| Name | Matches | Inns | NO | Runs | HS | Avge | 100s | 50s | Ct | St |
|---|---|---|---|---|---|---|---|---|---|---|
| S.J.S.Warke | 1 | 1 | 0 | 3 | 3 | 3.00 | - | - | 1 | - |
| M.P.Rea | 1 | 1 | 0 | 3 | 3 | 3.00 | - | - | 1 | - |
| G.C.Small | 4 | 2 | 0 | 5 | 3 | 2.50 | - | - | - | - |
| D.J.Capel | 4 | 3 | 0 | 7 | 6 | 2.33 | - | - | - | - |
| P.J.W.Allott | 1 | 1 | 0 | 2 | 2 | 2.00 | - | - | - | - |
| I.D.Austin | 2 | 1 | 0 | 2 | 2 | 2.00 | - | - | - | - |
| A.N Aymes | 5 | 1 | 0 | 2 | 2 | 2.00 | - | - | 6 | 1 |
| D.Byas | 1 | 1 | 0 | 2 | 2 | 2.00 | - | - | - | - |
| R.P.Davis | 2 | 1 | 0 | 2 | 2 | 2.00 | - | - | 1 | - |
| D.Gough | 1 | 1 | 0 | 2 | 2 | 2.00 | - | - | - | - |
| M.R.Gouldstone | 1 | 1 | 0 | 2 | 2 | 2.00 | - | - | - | - |
| P.C.L.Holloway | 1 | 1 | 0 | 2 | 2 | 2.00 | - | - | 2 | 1 |
| M.D.Moxon | 1 | 1 | 0 | 2 | 2 | 2.00 | - | - | 1 | - |
| P.Burn | 1 | 1 | 0 | 2 | 2 | 2.00 | - | - | - | - |
| P.J.Heseltine | 1 | 1 | 0 | 2 | 2 | 2.00 | - | - | - | - |
| N.P.Norman | 1 | 1 | 0 | 2 | 2 | 2.00 | - | - | - | - |
| M.G.Stephenson | 1 | 1 | 0 | 2 | 2 | 2.00 | - | - | 1 | - |
| D.R.Thomas | 1 | 1 | 0 | 2 | 2 | 2.00 | - | - | - | - |
| K.O.Thomas | 1 | 1 | 0 | 2 | 2 | 2.00 | - | - | - | - |
| Ajaz Akhtar | 1 | 1 | 0 | 2 | 2 | 2.00 | - | - | - | - |
| J.R.Wake | 1 | 1 | 0 | 2 | 2 | 2.00 | - | - | 1 | - |
| C.J.Rogers | 1 | 1 | 0 | 2 | 2 | 2.00 | - | - | - | - |
| M.F.Voss | 1 | 1 | 0 | 2 | 2 | 2.00 | - | - | - | - |
| J.E.Emburey | 2 | 2 | 0 | 3 | 2 | 1.50 | - | - | - | - |
| K.J.Piper | 3 | 1 | 0 | 1 | 1 | 1.00 | - | - | 4 | - |
| R.A.Pyman | 1 | 1 | 0 | 1 | 1 | 1.00 | - | - | - | - |
| H.R.J.Trump | 1 | 1 | 0 | 1 | 1 | 1.00 | - | - | - | - |
| D.J.Haggo | 1 | 1 | 0 | 1 | 1 | 1.00 | - | - | 2 | 2 |
| J.B.R.Jones | 1 | 1 | 0 | 1 | 1 | 1.00 | - | - | - | - |
| D.E.Mattocks | 1 | 1 | 0 | 1 | 1 | 1.00 | - | - | - | - |
| G.Salmond | 1 | 1 | 0 | 1 | 1 | 1.00 | - | - | - | - |
| J.Wood | 1 | 1 | 0 | 1 | 1 | 1.00 | - | - | - | - |
| T.W.Ward | 1 | 1 | 0 | 1 | 1 | 1.00 | - | - | - | - |
| R.Ashton | 1 | 1 | 0 | 1 | 1 | 1.00 | - | - | - | - |
| D.G.Savage | 1 | 1 | 0 | 1 | 1 | 1.00 | - | - | - | - |
| R.J.Blakey | 1 | 1 | 0 | 0 | 0 | 0.00 | - | - | - | - |
| C.S.Cowdrey | 1 | 1 | 0 | 0 | 0 | 0.00 | - | - | 1 | - |
| K.D.James | 3 | 1 | 0 | 0 | 0 | 0.00 | - | - | 1 | - |
| T.A.Merrick | 2 | 1 | 0 | 0 | 0 | 0.00 | - | - | 2 | - |
| T.J.A.Scriven | 1 | 1 | 0 | 0 | 0 | 0.00 | - | - | - | - |
| A.C.Seymour | 1 | 1 | 0 | 0 | 0 | 0.00 | - | - | 1 | - |
| S.J.Dean | 1 | 1 | 0 | 0 | 0 | 0.00 | - | - | 1 | - |
| J.H.Edwards | 1 | 1 | 0 | 0 | 0 | 0.00 | - | - | - | - |
| A.B.Russell | 1 | 1 | 0 | 0 | 0 | 0.00 | - | - | - | - |
| A.J.Pugh | 1 | 1 | 0 | 0 | 0 | 0.00 | - | - | - | - |
| R.P.Merriman | 1 | 1 | 0 | 0 | 0 | 0.00 | - | - | - | - |
| A.B.Byram | 1 | 1 | 0 | 0 | 0 | 0.00 | - | - | - | - |
| M.I.Humphries | 1 | 1 | 0 | 0 | 0 | 0.00 | - | - | - | - |
| S.B.Dixon | 1 | 1 | 0 | 0 | 0 | 0.00 | - | - | - | - |
| M.T.Ellis | 1 | 1 | 0 | 0 | 0 | 0.00 | - | - | 1 | - |
| N.J.C.Gandon | 1 | 1 | 0 | 0 | 0 | 0.00 | - | - | - | - |
| D.Beal | 1 | 1 | 0 | 0 | 0 | 0.00 | - | - | - | - |
| K.Bailey | 1 | 1 | 0 | 0 | 0 | 0.00 | - | - | - | - |
| R.A.Milne | 1 | 1 | 0 | 0 | 0 | 0.00 | - | - | - | - |
| A.M.Cade | 1 | 1 | 0 | 0 | 0 | 0.00 | - | - | - | - |
| C.S.Pritchard | 1 | 1 | 0 | 0 | 0 | 0.00 | - | - | - | - |
| P.D.B.Hoare | 1 | 1 | 0 | 0 | 0 | 0.00 | - | - | - | - |
| A.Dean | 1 | 1 | 0 | 0 | 0 | 0.00 | - | - | - | - |
| G.D.Sandford | 1 | 1 | 0 | 0 | 0 | 0.00 | - | - | - | - |
| N.Hackett | 1 | 1 | 0 | 0 | 0 | 0.00 | - | - | - | - |

# NATWEST TROPHY

## BOWLING AVERAGES
**Qualifying requirements : 1 wickets taken**

| Name | Overs | Mdns | Runs | Wkts | Avge | Best | 5wI |
|---|---|---|---|---|---|---|---|
| B.S.Percy | 3 | 2 | 2 | 1 | 2.00 | 1-2 | - |
| R.J.Bailey | 2 | 0 | 3 | 1 | 3.00 | 1-3 | - |
| A.Fordham | 1.3 | 0 | 3 | 1 | 3.00 | 1-3 | - |
| Ajaz Akhtar | 12 | 6 | 28 | 4 | 7.00 | 4-28 | - |
| M.A.Crawley | 13 | 1 | 29 | 4 | 7.25 | 4-26 | - |
| A.P.Igglesden | 9.2 | 1 | 29 | 4 | 7.25 | 4-29 | - |
| N.A.Mallender | 12 | 4 | 23 | 3 | 7.66 | 3-23 | - |
| N.V.Radford | 22 | 4 | 54 | 7 | 7.71 | 7-19 | 1 |
| M.W.Gatting | 1 | 0 | 8 | 1 | 8.00 | 1-8 | - |
| R.J.Scott | 22.2 | 3 | 54 | 6 | 9.00 | 4-22 | - |
| D.V.Lawrence | 21 | 3 | 65 | 7 | 9.28 | 5-17 | 1 |
| P.J.Martin | 12 | 2 | 19 | 2 | 9.50 | 2-19 | - |
| A.B.Russell | 5 | 0 | 20 | 2 | 10.00 | 2-20 | - |
| A.Dean | 4.5 | 0 | 20 | 2 | 10.00 | 2-20 | - |
| P.McCrum | 10 | 1 | 31 | 3 | 10.33 | 3-31 | - |
| D.A.Lewis | 10 | 0 | 47 | 4 | 11.75 | 4-47 | - |
| S.P.Hughes | 11 | 2 | 24 | 2 | 12.00 | 2-24 | - |
| C.A.Connor | 51.1 | 6 | 182 | 15 | 12.13 | 4-29 | - |
| N.G.Cowans | 18 | 1 | 61 | 5 | 12.20 | 4-51 | - |
| N.R.Taylor | 12 | 2 | 25 | 2 | 12.50 | 2-25 | - |
| Waqar Younis | 44.3 | 5 | 171 | 13 | 13.15 | 5-40 | 1 |
| C.M.Wells | 21 | 3 | 55 | 4 | 13.75 | 3-16 | - |
| R.P.Lefebvre | 36 | 7 | 89 | 6 | 14.83 | 3-27 | - |
| N.Hackett | 12 | 0 | 45 | 3 | 15.00 | 3-45 | - |
| J.R.Hall | 4 | 0 | 16 | 1 | 16.00 | 1-16 | - |
| J.P.Taylor | 42 | 6 | 132 | 8 | 16.50 | 2-11 | - |
| M.T.Ellis | 12 | 4 | 33 | 2 | 16.50 | 2-33 | - |
| D.J.Capel | 14 | 0 | 50 | 3 | 16.66 | 3-26 | - |
| J.D.Batty | 6 | 2 | 17 | 1 | 17.00 | 1-17 | - |
| K.Donohue | 12 | 3 | 34 | 2 | 17.00 | 2-34 | - |
| D.B.Storer | 5 | 0 | 17 | 1 | 17.00 | 1-17 | - |
| A.N.Hayhurst | 35.3 | 4 | 137 | 8 | 17.12 | 5-60 | 1 |
| T.D.Topley | 34 | 6 | 103 | 6 | 17.16 | 3-38 | - |
| P.D.McKeown | 12 | 0 | 52 | 3 | 17.33 | 3-52 | - |
| S.Burrow | 9 | 2 | 18 | 1 | 18.00 | 1-18 | - |
| P.B.Wormwald | 8 | 1 | 18 | 1 | 18.00 | 1-18 | - |
| D.R.Pringle | 34 | 3 | 127 | 7 | 18.14 | 3-21 | - |
| G.C.Small | 45 | 13 | 111 | 6 | 18.50 | 3-28 | - |
| N.M.K.Smith | 13 | 1 | 37 | 2 | 18.50 | 1-17 | - |
| E.A.E.Baptiste | 42 | 4 | 171 | 9 | 19.00 | 4-27 | - |
| N.J.Lenham | 18 | 1 | 60 | 3 | 20.00 | 2-25 | - |
| C.C.Lewis | 21 | 2 | 60 | 3 | 20.00 | 3-28 | - |
| I.Smith | 9 | 0 | 60 | 3 | 20.00 | 3-60 | - |
| P.M.Such | 36 | 2 | 102 | 5 | 20.40 | 2-29 | - |
| D.R.Gilbert | 12 | 0 | 41 | 2 | 20.50 | 2-41 | - |
| C.Wilkinson | 16.5 | 5 | 62 | 3 | 20.66 | 3-16 | - |
| P.G.Duthie | 12 | 2 | 42 | 2 | 21.00 | 2-42 | - |
| A.L.Goram | 12 | 1 | 42 | 2 | 21.00 | 2-42 | - |
| J.H.Childs | 11.4 | 4 | 43 | 2 | 21.50 | 2-43 | - |
| Wasim Akram | 23.3 | 2 | 86 | 4 | 21.50 | 3-40 | - |
| A.C.S.Pigott | 19.5 | 1 | 65 | 3 | 21.66 | 2-25 | - |
| A.A.Donald | 42 | 4 | 132 | 6 | 22.00 | 4-16 | - |
| G.A.Gooch | 18 | 3 | 67 | 3 | 22.33 | 2-30 | - |
| K.H.Macleay | 24 | 1 | 67 | 3 | 22.33 | 2-35 | - |
| R.D.B.Croft | 17 | 0 | 46 | 2 | 23.00 | 2-28 | - |
| M.R.Ramprakash | 13 | 1 | 46 | 2 | 23.00 | 2-15 | - |
| G.R.Dilley | 18 | 3 | 47 | 2 | 23.50 | 1-12 | - |
| M.Watkinson | 22 | 7 | 72 | 3 | 24.00 | 2-10 | - |
| T.A.Merrick | 21 | 4 | 74 | 3 | 24.66 | 3-27 | - |
| A.B.Byram | 6 | 0 | 25 | 1 | 25.00 | 1-25 | - |
| Aqib Javed | 52.5 | 4 | 213 | 8 | 26.62 | 4-51 | - |
| M.P.Bicknell | 39.3 | 2 | 135 | 5 | 27.00 | 2-45 | - |
| R.A.Pick | 30 | 4 | 111 | 4 | 27.75 | 3-41 | - |
| R.P.Davis | 20 | 4 | 56 | 2 | 28.00 | 1-22 | - |
| P.G.Newman | 12 | 3 | 29 | 1 | 29.00 | 1-29 | - |
| P.C.R.Tufnell | 12 | 2 | 29 | 1 | 29.00 | 1-29 | - |
| S.L.Watkin | 36 | 2 | 116 | 4 | 29.00 | 2-40 | - |
| R.K.Illingworth | 16 | 2 | 59 | 2 | 29.50 | 1-12 | - |
| C.S.Pickles | 10.3 | 2 | 30 | 1 | 30.00 | 1-30 | - |
| M.Saxelby | 18.4 | 1 | 90 | 3 | 30.00 | 2-42 | - |
| R.J.Shastri | 12 | 0 | 60 | 2 | 30.00 | 2-60 | - |
| N.E.Thompson | 12 | 3 | 30 | 1 | 30.00 | 1-30 | - |
| P.N.Weekes | 12 | 1 | 30 | 1 | 30.00 | 1-30 | - |
| S.R.Barwick | 33 | 0 | 153 | 5 | 30.60 | 2-51 | - |
| D.A.Graveney | 31 | 5 | 92 | 3 | 30.66 | 1-24 | - |
| A.M.Smith | 16 | 2 | 63 | 2 | 31.50 | 1-14 | - |
| N.A.Foster | 31.5 | 6 | 127 | 4 | 31.75 | 2-57 | - |
| S.D.Udal | 50 | 3 | 191 | 6 | 31.83 | 3-47 | - |
| A.I.C.Dodemaide | 21 | 3 | 64 | 2 | 32.00 | 2-12 | - |
| L.Potter | 6 | 1 | 32 | 1 | 32.00 | 1-32 | - |
| T.J.A.Scriven | 8 | 1 | 32 | 1 | 32.00 | 1-32 | - |
| A.Walker | 42 | 6 | 129 | 4 | 32.25 | 2-39 | - |
| J.E.Emburey | 24 | 7 | 65 | 2 | 32.50 | 2-52 | - |
| S.R.Lampitt | 12.4 | 1 | 65 | 2 | 32.50 | 1-4 | - |
| D.A.Reeve | 35.5 | 7 | 101 | 3 | 33.66 | 2-19 | - |
| G.S.Calway | 10 | 3 | 34 | 1 | 34.00 | 1-34 | - |
| O.Henry | 12 | 2 | 34 | 1 | 34.00 | 1-34 | - |
| C.Penn | 18 | 4 | 69 | 2 | 34.50 | 1-14 | - |
| N.G.B.Cook | 12 | 0 | 35 | 1 | 35.00 | 1-35 | - |
| S.G.Plumb | 12 | 0 | 36 | 1 | 36.00 | 1-36 | - |
| T.A.Munton | 41 | 7 | 111 | 3 | 37.00 | 2-42 | - |
| P.A.W.Heseltine | 12 | 1 | 37 | 1 | 37.00 | 1-37 | - |
| J.R.Ayling | 36 | 0 | 151 | 4 | 37.75 | 2-39 | - |
| A.N.Jones | 12 | 0 | 76 | 2 | 38.00 | 2-46 | - |
| J.D.Robinson | 40 | 4 | 152 | 4 | 38.00 | 3-46 | - |
| I.D.K.Salisbury | 21 | 1 | 76 | 2 | 38.00 | 1-36 | - |
| P.A.Smith | 35.2 | 3 | 116 | 3 | 38.66 | 2-24 | - |
| A.N.Nelson | 11 | 3 | 39 | 1 | 39.00 | 1-39 | - |
| G.N.Reifer | 8 | 0 | 40 | 1 | 40.00 | 1-40 | - |
| T.G.Roshier | 12 | 1 | 40 | 1 | 40.00 | 1-40 | - |
| R.J.Maru | 42 | 7 | 122 | 3 | 40.66 | 2-20 | - |
| N.F.Williams | 12 | 2 | 43 | 1 | 43.00 | 1-11 | - |
| D.J.Millns | 21 | 4 | 87 | 2 | 43.50 | 2-27 | - |
| M.V.Fleming | 12.2 | 1 | 44 | 1 | 44.00 | 1-6 | - |
| M.A.Feltham | 10 | 1 | 46 | 1 | 46.00 | 1-46 | - |
| J.D.Moir | 11 | 1 | 47 | 1 | 47.00 | 1-47 | - |
| F.D.Stephenson | 29 | 0 | 99 | 2 | 49.50 | 1-10 | - |
| R.G.Williams | 36 | 4 | 99 | 2 | 49.50 | 2-34 | - |
| A.J.Murphy | 40.2 | 5 | 158 | 3 | 52.66 | 1-27 | - |
| R.J.Belmont | 12 | 2 | 53 | 1 | 53.00 | 1-53 | - |
| J.Boiling | 48 | 4 | 165 | 3 | 55.00 | 2-22 | - |
| D.R.Thomas | 12 | 0 | 58 | 1 | 58.00 | 1-58 | - |
| J.Derrick | 12 | 0 | 59 | 1 | 59.00 | 1-59 | - |
| P.M.Roebuck | 14 | 0 | 62 | 1 | 62.00 | 1-43 | - |
| E.E.Hemmings | 33 | 3 | 135 | 2 | 67.50 | 1-27 | - |
| M.Frost | 31 | 2 | 137 | 2 | 68.50 | 1-45 | - |
| S.J.Brown | 12 | 1 | 73 | 1 | 73.00 | 1-73 | - |
| J.A.Afford | 23 | 5 | 78 | 1 | 78.00 | 1-40 | - |
| K.D.James | 22 | 3 | 97 | 1 | 97.00 | 1-50 | - |
| I.D.Austin | 21 | 1 | 105 | 1 | 105.00 | 1-46 | - |
| A.Dale | 30 | 2 | 115 | 1 | 115.00 | 1-42 | - |
| K.M.Curran | 32 | 3 | 140 | 1 | 140.00 | 1-61 | - |

# BENSON & HEDGES CUP

## BATTING AVERAGES - Including fielding
### Qualifying requirements : 1 completed innings

| Name | Matches | Inns | NO | Runs | HS | Avge | 100s | 50s | Ct | St |
|---|---|---|---|---|---|---|---|---|---|---|
| C.L.Smith | 5 | 5 | 2 | 413 | 142 | 137.66 | 2 | 2 | 1 | - |
| J.D.Love | 3 | 3 | 1 | 236 | 81 | 118.00 | - | 3 | - | - |
| G.J.Turner | 4 | 4 | 2 | 170 | 80* | 85.00 | - | 2 | - | - |
| R.J.Shastri | 3 | 3 | 1 | 161 | 138* | 80.50 | 1 | - | 1 | - |
| P.A.Neale | 7 | 5 | 3 | 159 | 52* | 79.50 | - | 1 | 6 | - |
| T.M.Moody | 7 | 7 | 2 | 382 | 110* | 76.40 | 2 | 2 | 2 | - |
| M.D.Moxon | 6 | 6 | 1 | 370 | 141* | 74.00 | 1 | 2 | 5 | - |
| Asif Din | 4 | 4 | 0 | 291 | 137 | 72.75 | 1 | 1 | - | - |
| A.A.Metcalfe | 6 | 6 | 1 | 350 | 114 | 70.00 | 1 | 2 | 1 | - |
| A.R.Butcher | 4 | 4 | 0 | 279 | 127 | 69.75 | 1 | 2 | 1 | - |
| P.R.Downton | 4 | 3 | 1 | 134 | 58 | 67.00 | - | 1 | 7 | 1 |
| N.A.Folland | 4 | 4 | 1 | 199 | 100* | 66.33 | 1 | 1 | 2 | - |
| A.J.Stewart | 4 | 4 | 1 | 195 | 110* | 65.00 | 1 | 1 | 3 | - |
| K.J.Barnett | 4 | 4 | 0 | 256 | 102 | 64.00 | 1 | 2 | 3 | - |
| G.D.Mendis | 7 | 7 | 1 | 366 | 125* | 61.00 | 1 | 2 | 4 | - |
| R.T.Robinson | 4 | 4 | 0 | 239 | 116 | 59.75 | 1 | 1 | 1 | - |
| T.J.Boon | 3 | 2 | 0 | 119 | 103 | 59.50 | 1 | - | 1 | - |
| G.A.Hick | 7 | 7 | 2 | 297 | 88 | 59.40 | - | 4 | 8 | - |
| S.A.Marsh | 3 | 3 | 1 | 118 | 71 | 59.00 | - | 1 | 5 | - |
| J.P.Stephenson | 6 | 6 | 0 | 349 | 142 | 58.16 | 1 | 2 | 4 | - |
| N.R.Taylor | 5 | 5 | 1 | 230 | 110 | 57.50 | 1 | 1 | 2 | - |
| R.G.Swan | 1 | 1 | 0 | 55 | 55 | 55.00 | - | 1 | - | - |
| Salim Malik | 6 | 6 | 2 | 217 | 90* | 54.25 | - | 2 | 1 | - |
| S.J.Cook | 4 | 4 | 0 | 213 | 76 | 53.25 | - | 2 | 1 | - |
| D.M.Smith | 4 | 4 | 0 | 209 | 102 | 52.25 | 1 | 1 | 2 | - |
| A.N.Hayhurst | 2 | 2 | 0 | 102 | 70 | 51.00 | - | 1 | 1 | - |
| P.Johnson | 4 | 4 | 1 | 144 | 102* | 48.00 | 1 | - | 1 | - |
| R.G.Williams | 4 | 4 | 2 | 96 | 29 | 48.00 | - | - | 1 | - |
| D.W.Randall | 4 | 4 | 0 | 189 | 86 | 47.25 | - | 2 | 5 | - |
| D.Ripley | 5 | 3 | 2 | 47 | 36* | 47.00 | - | - | 7 | 1 |
| M.Watkinson | 5 | 5 | 3 | 94 | 32* | 47.00 | - | - | 1 | - |
| J.J.Whitaker | 4 | 4 | 0 | 187 | 100 | 46.75 | 1 | 1 | - | - |
| B.C.Broad | 4 | 4 | 1 | 140 | 108* | 46.66 | 1 | - | - | - |
| A.Fordham | 5 | 5 | 1 | 183 | 93* | 45.75 | - | 2 | 1 | - |
| G.Fowler | 7 | 7 | 0 | 320 | 136 | 45.71 | 1 | 2 | 2 | - |
| M.R.Benson | 5 | 5 | 0 | 228 | 76 | 45.60 | - | 3 | - | - |
| N.H.Fairbrother | 7 | 7 | 2 | 225 | 53* | 45.00 | - | 2 | 5 | - |
| I.T.Botham | 6 | 5 | 3 | 88 | 35* | 44.00 | - | - | 1 | - |
| A.J.Wright | 4 | 4 | 0 | 175 | 81 | 43.75 | - | 1 | - | - |
| M.C.J.Nicholas | 5 | 4 | 2 | 87 | 50 | 43.50 | - | 1 | - | - |
| M.W.Gatting | 4 | 4 | 0 | 169 | 112 | 42.25 | 1 | - | 1 | - |
| M.Keech | 2 | 2 | 0 | 84 | 47 | 42.00 | - | - | - | - |
| M.Azharuddin | 4 | 4 | 1 | 125 | 44* | 41.66 | - | - | 4 | - |
| P.W.G.Parker | 3 | 3 | 0 | 123 | 87 | 41.00 | - | 1 | 1 | - |
| M.A.Atherton | 7 | 7 | 0 | 282 | 91 | 40.28 | - | 3 | 3 | - |
| M.R.Ramprakash | 4 | 4 | 1 | 120 | 78* | 40.00 | - | 1 | 3 | - |
| T.C.Middleton | 4 | 4 | 0 | 156 | 60 | 39.00 | - | 2 | 3 | - |
| T.J.G.O'Gorman | 4 | 3 | 1 | 78 | 49 | 39.00 | - | - | 1 | - |
| J.W.Hall | 4 | 4 | 0 | 150 | 71 | 37.50 | - | 1 | - | - |
| M.A.Crawley | 3 | 3 | 1 | 74 | 58 | 37.00 | - | 1 | - | - |
| A.D.Brown | 1 | 1 | 0 | 37 | 37 | 37.00 | - | - | - | - |
| R.J.Bailey | 5 | 5 | 0 | 184 | 75 | 36.80 | - | 2 | 1 | - |
| N.D.Burns | 4 | 4 | 1 | 110 | 43* | 36.66 | - | - | 1 | 1 |
| C.W.J.Athey | 4 | 4 | 1 | 108 | 81 | 36.00 | - | 1 | 2 | - |
| Wasim Akram | 6 | 4 | 2 | 71 | 45* | 35.50 | - | - | - | - |
| P.D.Bowler | 4 | 4 | 0 | 141 | 100 | 35.25 | 1 | - | 6 | - |
| G.N.Reifer | 4 | 4 | 0 | 141 | 76 | 35.25 | - | 1 | 3 | - |
| R.A.Smith | 1 | 1 | 0 | 35 | 35 | 35.00 | - | - | 1 | - |
| C.J.Tavare | 4 | 4 | 0 | 139 | 53 | 34.75 | - | 1 | 2 | - |
| D.Byas | 6 | 6 | 0 | 207 | 92 | 34.50 | - | 2 | - | - |
| G.A.Gooch | 6 | 6 | 0 | 202 | 72 | 33.66 | - | 1 | 3 | - |
| P.Whitticase | 4 | 3 | 1 | 67 | 34* | 33.50 | - | - | 1 | 1 |
| A.J.Moles | 5 | 5 | 0 | 166 | 65 | 33.20 | - | 2 | 4 | - |
| K.Greenfield | 2 | 2 | 1 | 33 | 33 | 33.00 | - | - | 3 | - |
| T.R.Ward | 5 | 5 | 0 | 165 | 87 | 33.00 | - | 1 | 2 | - |
| S.G.Plumb | 4 | 4 | 0 | 98 | 52 | 32.66 | - | 1 | - | - |
| A.P.Wells | 4 | 4 | 1 | 96 | 66 | 32.00 | - | 1 | 1 | - |
| T.A.Lloyd | 5 | 5 | 0 | 154 | 58 | 30.80 | - | 1 | 3 | - |
| G.C.Holmes | 4 | 4 | 1 | 92 | 35* | 30.66 | - | - | 1 | - |
| N.A.Foster | 6 | 3 | 1 | 60 | 39* | 30.00 | - | - | - | - |
| A.J.Lamb | 5 | 5 | 0 | 150 | 48 | 30.00 | - | - | 2 | - |
| D.M.Ward | 4 | 4 | 0 | 120 | 46 | 30.00 | - | - | - | - |
| M.J.Weston | 1 | 1 | 0 | 30 | 30 | 30.00 | - | - | - | - |
| J.R.Wood | 4 | 4 | 1 | 90 | 70* | 30.00 | - | 1 | 3 | - |
| A.P.Igglesden | 5 | 2 | 1 | 29 | 26* | 29.00 | - | - | 1 | - |
| J.D.Ratcliffe | 1 | 1 | 0 | 29 | 29 | 29.00 | - | - | - | - |
| D.J.Haggo | 4 | 4 | 2 | 58 | 25 | 29.00 | - | - | 2 | 3 |
| R.C.Russell | 4 | 4 | 1 | 85 | 51 | 28.33 | - | 1 | 4 | - |
| G.P.Thorpe | 4 | 4 | 0 | 112 | 41 | 28.00 | - | - | 1 | - |
| G.R.Cowdrey | 5 | 5 | 1 | 111 | 70* | 27.75 | - | 1 | 1 | - |
| S.J.Dennis | 3 | 2 | 0 | 55 | 50 | 27.50 | - | 1 | - | - |
| D.J.Bicknell | 4 | 4 | 0 | 108 | 53 | 27.00 | - | 1 | 1 | - |
| G.K.Brown | 4 | 4 | 0 | 107 | 82 | 26.75 | - | 1 | 2 | - |
| T.A.Merrick | 5 | 3 | 2 | 26 | 22* | 26.00 | - | - | 1 | - |
| N.E.Briers | 4 | 4 | 0 | 103 | 46 | 25.75 | - | - | 4 | - |
| D.R.Pringle | 6 | 5 | 2 | 77 | 36* | 25.66 | - | - | 1 | - |
| J.D.Robinson | 3 | 3 | 0 | 77 | 38 | 25.66 | - | - | 2 | - |
| D.V.Lawrence | 4 | 3 | 1 | 51 | 23 | 25.50 | - | - | - | - |
| R.P.Lefebvre | 4 | 4 | 2 | 51 | 23* | 25.50 | - | - | 1 | - |
| B.Roberts | 4 | 3 | 0 | 75 | 49 | 25.00 | - | - | 2 | - |
| D.A.Reeve | 5 | 5 | 0 | 124 | 80 | 24.80 | - | 1 | 3 | - |
| R.J.Scott | 4 | 4 | 0 | 99 | 46 | 24.75 | - | - | - | - |
| C.S.Cowdrey | 5 | 5 | 1 | 97 | 57* | 24.25 | - | 1 | 4 | - |
| N.A.Felton | 5 | 5 | 0 | 119 | 44 | 23.80 | - | - | 2 | - |
| M.P.Maynard | 4 | 4 | 0 | 94 | 62 | 23.50 | - | 1 | 2 | - |
| T.S.Curtis | 7 | 7 | 0 | 163 | 53 | 23.28 | - | 1 | 3 | - |
| I.A.Greig | 4 | 4 | 0 | 93 | 47 | 23.25 | - | - | 2 | - |
| S.A.Kellett | 5 | 3 | 1 | 46 | 44 | 23.00 | - | - | - | - |
| P.E.Robinson | 6 | 5 | 1 | 92 | 43 | 23.00 | - | - | 3 | - |
| N.M.K.Smith | 1 | 1 | 0 | 23 | 23 | 23.00 | - | - | - | - |
| R.J.Blakey | 6 | 6 | 1 | 113 | 39 | 22.60 | - | - | 11 | - |
| I.Smith | 4 | 4 | 0 | 90 | 51 | 22.50 | - | 1 | 1 | - |
| J.E.Morris | 4 | 4 | 0 | 89 | 71 | 22.25 | - | 1 | 1 | - |
| P.J.Prichard | 6 | 6 | 1 | 111 | 38 | 22.20 | - | - | 3 | - |
| P.W.Romaines | 1 | 1 | 0 | 22 | 22 | 22.00 | - | - | 1 | - |
| L.Potter | 4 | 4 | 1 | 65 | 54 | 21.66 | - | 1 | 1 | - |
| J.W.Lloyds | 3 | 2 | 0 | 43 | 24 | 21.50 | - | - | 2 | - |
| P.N.Hepworth | 3 | 2 | 0 | 42 | 33 | 21.00 | - | - | 1 | - |
| D.J.Capel | 5 | 5 | 0 | 102 | 42 | 20.40 | - | - | 2 | - |
| O.Henry | 4 | 4 | 0 | 80 | 32 | 20.00 | - | - | 2 | - |
| D.P.Ostler | 5 | 5 | 0 | 100 | 45 | 20.00 | - | - | 2 | - |
| A.E.Warner | 4 | 4 | 2 | 39 | 35* | 19.50 | - | - | - | - |
| A.B.Russell | 4 | 4 | 0 | 78 | 45 | 19.50 | - | - | 2 | - |
| D.I.Gower | 5 | 5 | 0 | 97 | 63 | 19.40 | - | 1 | 1 | - |
| K.R.Brown | 4 | 4 | 1 | 57 | 25 | 19.00 | - | - | 1 | - |
| A.Dale | 1 | 1 | 0 | 19 | 19 | 19.00 | - | - | - | - |
| P.M.Roebuck | 4 | 4 | 0 | 74 | 61 | 18.50 | - | 1 | - | - |
| M.Saxelby | 3 | 2 | 0 | 37 | 32 | 18.50 | - | - | - | - |
| J.D.R.Benson | 3 | 3 | 1 | 36 | 27 | 18.00 | - | - | - | - |
| M.W.Cleal | 2 | 1 | 0 | 18 | 18 | 18.00 | - | - | - | - |
| M.V.Fleming | 5 | 5 | 0 | 90 | 52 | 18.00 | - | 1 | - | - |
| M.Newell | 1 | 1 | 0 | 18 | 18 | 18.00 | - | - | - | - |
| R.MacDonald | 4 | 3 | 2 | 18 | 12* | 18.00 | - | - | - | - |
| K.J.Piper | 4 | 4 | 2 | 35 | 11* | 17.50 | - | - | 5 | - |
| A.W.Bee | 4 | 4 | 1 | 52 | 35 | 17.33 | - | - | - | - |
| P.Willey | 4 | 4 | 0 | 69 | 36 | 17.25 | - | - | - | - |
| G.D.Lloyd | 3 | 3 | 2 | 17 | 10 | 17.00 | - | - | - | - |
| S.J.Rhodes | 7 | 3 | 1 | 34 | 13* | 17.00 | - | - | 10 | 1 |
| I.D.K.Salisbury | 4 | 3 | 1 | 32 | 17* | 16.00 | - | - | 2 | - |
| V.J.Wells | 2 | 2 | 0 | 32 | 25 | 16.00 | - | - | 2 | - |
| J.I.Longley | 4 | 4 | 0 | 63 | 47 | 15.75 | - | - | 1 | - |
| A.C.S.Pigott | 4 | 3 | 0 | 47 | 29 | 15.66 | - | - | 3 | - |
| P.A.J.DeFreitas | 7 | 2 | 0 | 31 | 19 | 15.50 | - | - | 5 | - |
| N.V.Knight | 4 | 4 | 0 | 62 | 36 | 15.50 | - | - | 1 | - |
| P.A.Booth | 3 | 2 | 1 | 15 | 11 | 15.00 | - | - | 3 | - |
| J.W.Govan | 4 | 4 | 0 | 60 | 23 | 15.00 | - | - | 2 | - |
| P.W.Jarvis | 5 | 3 | 2 | 15 | 12* | 15.00 | - | - | 1 | - |
| D.R.Turner | 1 | 1 | 0 | 15 | 15 | 15.00 | - | - | - | - |
| P.C.L.Holloway | 4 | 4 | 0 | 59 | 27 | 14.75 | - | - | 4 | - |
| J.A.North | 4 | 3 | 0 | 44 | 22 | 14.66 | - | - | - | - |
| I.D.Austin | 7 | 2 | 0 | 29 | 22 | 14.50 | - | - | 1 | - |
| J.P.Crawley | 4 | 4 | 0 | 58 | 40 | 14.50 | - | - | 1 | - |
| R.J.Bartlett | 2 | 2 | 0 | 28 | 14 | 14.00 | - | - | - | - |
| M.P.Speight | 3 | 3 | 0 | 42 | 35 | 14.00 | - | - | - | - |
| E.A.E.Baptiste | 4 | 3 | 1 | 28 | 15* | 14.00 | - | - | 1 | - |
| D.B.D'Oliveira | 7 | 6 | 0 | 79 | 25 | 13.16 | - | - | 3 | - |
| K.M.Curran | 2 | 2 | 0 | 26 | 26 | 13.00 | - | - | - | - |

# BENSON & HEDGES CUP

| Name | Matches | Inns | NO | Runs | HS | Avge | 100s | 50s | Ct | St |
|---|---|---|---|---|---|---|---|---|---|---|
| A.R.Hansford | 4 | 2 | 1 | 13 | 13* | 13.00 | - | - | - | - |
| W.K.Hegg | 7 | 2 | 1 | 13 | 13* | 13.00 | - | - | 6 | - |
| N.Shahid | 6 | 4 | 0 | 51 | 42 | 12.75 | - | - | 1 | - |
| M.J.Roberts | 4 | 4 | 0 | 51 | 40 | 12.75 | - | - | 2 | - |
| J.E.Emburey | 4 | 3 | 0 | 38 | 23 | 12.66 | - | - | 3 | - |
| S.L.Watkin | 4 | 3 | 1 | 25 | 15 | 12.50 | - | - | - | - |
| P.A.Smith | 5 | 5 | 0 | 62 | 34 | 12.40 | - | - | 1 | - |
| D.E.Malcolm | 4 | 3 | 0 | 37 | 15 | 12.33 | - | - | - | - |
| J.N.Maguire | 4 | 3 | 0 | 37 | 35 | 12.33 | - | - | 1 | - |
| A.M.Smith | 4 | 3 | 2 | 12 | 8 | 12.00 | - | - | 1 | - |
| M.J.McCague | 2 | 1 | 0 | 12 | 12 | 12.00 | - | - | - | - |
| N.Hussain | 6 | 5 | 1 | 46 | 26 | 11.50 | - | - | 2 | - |
| R.M.Ellison | 5 | 4 | 1 | 34 | 15 | 11.33 | - | - | 1 | - |
| G.Salmond | 3 | 3 | 0 | 34 | 24 | 11.33 | - | - | - | - |
| R.E.Morris | 4 | 4 | 0 | 44 | 19 | 11.00 | - | - | - | - |
| H.Morris | 4 | 4 | 0 | 43 | 36 | 10.75 | - | - | - | - |
| P.Moores | 4 | 3 | 0 | 31 | 20 | 10.33 | - | - | 6 | - |
| J.R.Ayling | 4 | 3 | 2 | 10 | 5* | 10.00 | - | - | 2 | - |
| J.Boiling | 2 | 2 | 1 | 10 | 7 | 10.00 | - | - | - | - |
| M.A.Lynch | 2 | 2 | 0 | 20 | 20 | 10.00 | - | - | - | - |
| V.P.Terry | 1 | 1 | 0 | 10 | 10 | 10.00 | - | - | - | - |
| R.A.Evans | 3 | 2 | 1 | 10 | 5* | 10.00 | - | - | - | - |
| D.W.Headley | 4 | 3 | 0 | 30 | 26 | 10.00 | - | - | 1 | - |
| I.L.Philip | 4 | 4 | 0 | 39 | 35 | 9.75 | - | - | 2 | - |
| F.D.Stephenson | 4 | 3 | 1 | 19 | 14 | 9.50 | - | - | 1 | - |
| P.C.R.Tufnell | 4 | 3 | 1 | 19 | 18 | 9.50 | - | - | 1 | - |
| G.D.Rose | 4 | 4 | 0 | 37 | 23 | 9.25 | - | - | - | - |
| B.M.W.Patterson | 4 | 4 | 0 | 37 | 23 | 9.25 | - | - | - | - |
| C.J.Adams | 4 | 3 | 1 | 18 | 16* | 9.00 | - | - | 1 | - |
| M.A.Garnham | 6 | 4 | 1 | 27 | 11 | 9.00 | - | - | 7 | 1 |
| E.E.Hemmings | 4 | 1 | 0 | 9 | 9 | 9.00 | - | - | - | - |
| T.A.Munton | 5 | 3 | 1 | 18 | 10 | 9.00 | - | - | 1 | - |
| R.H.J.Jenkins | 4 | 2 | 1 | 9 | 9 | 9.00 | - | - | 2 | - |
| I.Fletcher | 1 | 1 | 0 | 9 | 9 | 9.00 | - | - | 1 | - |
| D.R.Gilbert | 4 | 3 | 0 | 25 | 16 | 8.33 | - | - | - | - |
| C.K.Bullen | 2 | 2 | 0 | 16 | 16 | 8.00 | - | - | 2 | - |
| A.A.Donald | 5 | 3 | 2 | 8 | 6* | 8.00 | - | - | 1 | - |
| I.J.F.Hutchinson | 1 | 1 | 0 | 8 | 8 | 8.00 | - | - | - | - |
| A.R.Fothergill | 4 | 4 | 1 | 24 | 15* | 8.00 | - | - | 2 | - |
| Waqar Younis | 4 | 3 | 2 | 8 | 5* | 8.00 | - | - | 1 | - |
| T.D.Topley | 3 | 2 | 1 | 7 | 6* | 7.00 | - | - | 1 | - |
| A.M.Babington | 4 | 3 | 1 | 13 | 8 | 6.50 | - | - | 1 | - |
| R.J.Harden | 4 | 4 | 0 | 26 | 21 | 6.50 | - | - | - | - |
| C.C.Lewis | 2 | 2 | 0 | 13 | 8 | 6.50 | - | - | - | - |
| G.D.Hodgson | 3 | 3 | 0 | 19 | 9 | 6.33 | - | - | 1 | - |
| J.G.Thomas | 5 | 4 | 1 | 19 | 9 | 6.33 | - | - | - | - |
| A.N Aymes | 5 | 2 | 0 | 12 | 10 | 6.00 | - | - | 4 | 4 |
| J.J.E.Hardy | 1 | 1 | 0 | 6 | 6 | 6.00 | - | - | - | - |
| O.H.Mortensen | 4 | 2 | 1 | 6 | 4* | 6.00 | - | - | - | - |
| M.P.Bicknell | 4 | 3 | 0 | 17 | 7 | 5.66 | - | - | - | - |
| P.J.Bakker | 4 | 2 | 0 | 11 | 7 | 5.50 | - | - | 1 | - |
| P.J.W.Allott | 7 | 2 | 0 | 10 | 10 | 5.00 | - | - | 5 | - |
| N.G.Cowans | 3 | 2 | 1 | 5 | 5 | 5.00 | - | - | 1 | - |
| P.J.Hartley | 5 | 4 | 1 | 15 | 13 | 5.00 | - | - | 1 | - |
| P.M.Such | 6 | 2 | 1 | 5 | 4 | 5.00 | - | - | 1 | - |
| R.G.Twose | 1 | 1 | 0 | 5 | 5 | 5.00 | - | - | - | - |
| S.D.Udal | 5 | 2 | 0 | 10 | 9 | 5.00 | - | - | 2 | - |
| P.Carrick | 3 | 2 | 0 | 9 | 7 | 4.50 | - | - | 2 | - |
| D.Cowan | 4 | 3 | 1 | 9 | 6 | 4.50 | - | - | 1 | - |
| S.J.Base | 4 | 2 | 0 | 8 | 7 | 4.00 | - | - | - | - |
| P.J.Rendell | 2 | 2 | 0 | 8 | 8 | 4.00 | - | - | 1 | - |
| J.C.Pooley | 3 | 3 | 0 | 11 | 8 | 3.66 | - | - | - | - |
| N.F.Williams | 4 | 3 | 0 | 10 | 6 | 3.33 | - | - | 1 | - |
| M.A.Feltham | 2 | 2 | 0 | 6 | 4 | 3.00 | - | - | 1 | - |
| S.D.Fletcher | 6 | 2 | 1 | 3 | 2* | 3.00 | - | - | 4 | - |
| A.L.Penberthy | 2 | 1 | 0 | 3 | 3 | 3.00 | - | - | - | - |
| S.Greensword | 4 | 1 | 0 | 3 | 3 | 3.00 | - | - | 1 | - |
| A.D.Mullally | 3 | 2 | 0 | 6 | 5 | 3.00 | - | - | - | - |
| D.R.Thomas | 2 | 2 | 0 | 6 | 6 | 3.00 | - | - | - | - |
| Aqib Javed | 5 | 2 | 1 | 3 | 3 | 3.00 | - | - | - | - |
| M.Burns | 1 | 1 | 0 | 3 | 3 | 3.00 | - | - | - | - |
| I.G.Swallow | 3 | 2 | 0 | 5 | 5 | 2.50 | - | - | 1 | - |
| J.C.Hallett | 4 | 2 | 0 | 5 | 5 | 2.50 | - | - | 1 | - |
| M.W.Alleyne | 4 | 3 | 0 | 7 | 6 | 2.33 | - | - | 2 | - |
| K.D.James | 2 | 1 | 0 | 2 | 2 | 2.00 | - | - | - | - |
| N.A.Mallender | 4 | 3 | 1 | 4 | 2* | 2.00 | - | - | 1 | - |
| P.J.Newport | 6 | 1 | 0 | 2 | 2 | 2.00 | - | - | 4 | - |
| G.C.Small | 4 | 3 | 0 | 5 | 2 | 1.66 | - | - | 1 | - |
| C.A.Connor | 5 | 2 | 0 | 3 | 3 | 1.50 | - | - | 3 | - |
| R.P.Davis | 1 | 1 | 0 | 1 | 1 | 1.00 | - | - | - | - |
| D.Gough | 1 | 1 | 0 | 1 | 1 | 1.00 | - | - | - | - |
| A.J.Murphy | 4 | 2 | 1 | 1 | 1 | 1.00 | - | - | - | - |
| M.L.Roberts | 3 | 3 | 1 | 2 | 1* | 1.00 | - | - | 2 | - |
| D.Beal | 2 | 2 | 1 | 1 | 1 | 1.00 | - | - | - | - |
| N.G.B.Cook | 3 | 2 | 0 | 1 | 1 | 0.50 | - | - | 1 | - |
| K.E.Cooper | 3 | 1 | 0 | 0 | 0 | 0.00 | - | - | - | - |
| R.D.B.Croft | 1 | 1 | 0 | 0 | 0 | 0.00 | - | - | - | - |
| R.M.Ellcock | 1 | 1 | 0 | 0 | 0 | 0.00 | - | - | - | - |
| M.Frost | 4 | 2 | 1 | 0 | 0* | 0.00 | - | - | - | - |
| C.P.Metson | 1 | 1 | 0 | 0 | 0 | 0.00 | - | - | - | - |
| K.Sharp | 1 | 1 | 0 | 0 | 0 | 0.00 | - | - | - | - |
| P.N.Weekes | 1 | 1 | 0 | 0 | 0 | 0.00 | - | - | 1 | - |
| E.S.H.Giddins | 1 | 1 | 0 | 0 | 0 | 0.00 | - | - | - | - |

# BENSON & HEDGES CUP

## BOWLING AVERAGES
**Qualifying requirements : 1 wickets taken**

| Name | Overs | Mdns | Runs | Wkts | Avge | Best | 5wI |
|---|---|---|---|---|---|---|---|
| J.W.Lloyds | 9 | 2 | 14 | 3 | 4.66 | 3-14 | - |
| Salim Malik | 2 | 0 | 7 | 1 | 7.00 | 1-7 | - |
| C.S.Cowdrey | 5 | 1 | 17 | 2 | 8.50 | 2-17 | - |
| A.B.Russell | 7 | 0 | 42 | 4 | 10.50 | 4-42 | - |
| D.V.Lawrence | 44 | 7 | 137 | 13 | 10.53 | 6-20 | 1 |
| T.M.Moody | 6 | 0 | 22 | 2 | 11.00 | 2-22 | - |
| M.D.Moxon | 13 | 0 | 61 | 5 | 12.20 | 5-31 | 1 |
| I.A.Greig | 9.2 | 0 | 26 | 2 | 13.00 | 2-26 | - |
| A.Sidebottom | 31 | 11 | 52 | 4 | 13.00 | 4-19 | - |
| M.C.J.Nicholas | 4 | 0 | 27 | 2 | 13.50 | 2-27 | - |
| N.V.Radford | 61.5 | 13 | 244 | 16 | 15.25 | 3-22 | - |
| D.R.Pringle | 56.2 | 6 | 191 | 12 | 15.91 | 5-51 | 1 |
| N.G.Cowans | 33 | 2 | 130 | 8 | 16.25 | 3-39 | - |
| P.N.Hepworth | 20 | 2 | 83 | 5 | 16.60 | 4-39 | - |
| A.N.Jones | 30.4 | 4 | 117 | 7 | 16.71 | 3-33 | - |
| P.A.J.DeFreitas | 73.1 | 13 | 235 | 14 | 16.78 | 4-15 | - |
| A.I.C.Dodemaide | 7 | 3 | 17 | 1 | 17.00 | 1-17 | - |
| P.J.W.Allott | 74 | 17 | 200 | 11 | 18.18 | 4-23 | - |
| G.R.Dilley | 49.2 | 4 | 200 | 11 | 18.18 | 4-35 | - |
| M.Watkinson | 54.4 | 4 | 221 | 12 | 18.41 | 5-49 | 1 |
| J.E.Emburey | 44 | 3 | 167 | 9 | 18.55 | 5-37 | 1 |
| A.J.Moles | 4 | 1 | 19 | 1 | 19.00 | 1-19 | - |
| O.H.Mortensen | 40 | 10 | 115 | 6 | 19.16 | 2-16 | - |
| S.R.Lampitt | 48.1 | 4 | 211 | 11 | 19.18 | 4-44 | - |
| J.G.Thomas | 49.3 | 5 | 173 | 9 | 19.22 | 5-29 | 1 |
| F.D.Stephenson | 37 | 9 | 135 | 7 | 19.28 | 5-30 | 1 |
| J.D.Robinson | 19.2 | 3 | 60 | 3 | 20.00 | 2-31 | - |
| M.C.Ilott | 31 | 6 | 101 | 5 | 20.20 | 3-34 | - |
| D.Gough | 8 | 0 | 41 | 2 | 20.50 | 2-41 | - |
| T.A.Munton | 51.4 | 5 | 187 | 9 | 20.77 | 4-35 | - |
| S.D.Udal | 55 | 9 | 189 | 9 | 21.00 | 3-41 | - |
| P.Carrick | 32 | 1 | 106 | 5 | 21.20 | 3-22 | - |
| M.J.McCague | 18 | 2 | 85 | 4 | 21.25 | 2-32 | - |
| I.T.Botham | 63 | 14 | 174 | 8 | 21.75 | 3-11 | - |
| K.P.Evans | 32 | 2 | 132 | 6 | 22.00 | 4-43 | - |
| A.W.Bee | 26 | 0 | 134 | 6 | 22.33 | 4-31 | - |
| Wasim Akram | 61 | 5 | 246 | 11 | 22.36 | 4-18 | - |
| A.P.Igglesden | 50.5 | 7 | 224 | 10 | 22.40 | 3-24 | - |
| S.Greensword | 38 | 8 | 115 | 5 | 23.00 | 2-21 | - |
| Aqib Javed | 53 | 6 | 208 | 9 | 23.11 | 3-43 | - |
| D.A.Reeve | 51.5 | 0 | 233 | 10 | 23.30 | 4-43 | - |
| P.W.Jarvis | 44.2 | 9 | 142 | 6 | 23.66 | 2-13 | - |
| A.A.Donald | 49 | 2 | 266 | 11 | 24.18 | 4-55 | - |
| R.D.B.Croft | 9 | 0 | 49 | 2 | 24.50 | 2-49 | - |
| C.S.Pickles | 11 | 0 | 49 | 2 | 24.50 | 2-49 | - |
| N.F.Williams | 44 | 8 | 123 | 5 | 24.60 | 2-19 | - |
| I.D.K.Salisbury | 41 | 3 | 149 | 6 | 24.83 | 3-40 | - |
| J.C.Hallett | 43.1 | 0 | 149 | 6 | 24.83 | 3-36 | - |
| S.D.Fletcher | 49.2 | 6 | 208 | 8 | 26.00 | 4-51 | - |
| K.A.Arnold | 11 | 0 | 52 | 2 | 26.00 | 2-52 | - |
| N.A.Foster | 61 | 8 | 185 | 7 | 26.42 | 2-28 | - |
| J.P.Taylor | 42 | 9 | 106 | 4 | 26.50 | 2-30 | - |
| P.A.Smith | 28 | 3 | 108 | 4 | 27.00 | 3-28 | - |
| R.MacDonald | 36 | 1 | 216 | 8 | 27.00 | 6-33 | 1 |
| C.A.Connor | 55 | 4 | 272 | 10 | 27.20 | 3-54 | - |
| D.J.Capel | 40.4 | 3 | 147 | 5 | 29.40 | 4-37 | - |
| D.E.Malcolm | 39 | 3 | 151 | 5 | 30.20 | 2-14 | - |
| T.D.Topley | 28 | 4 | 124 | 4 | 31.00 | 4-41 | - |
| D.Cowan | 28 | 1 | 157 | 5 | 31.40 | 2-47 | - |
| M.P.Bicknell | 41 | 2 | 158 | 5 | 31.60 | 3-28 | - |
| M.A.Robinson | 31 | 3 | 128 | 4 | 32.00 | 2-43 | - |
| K.J.Barnett | 29 | 4 | 97 | 3 | 32.33 | 1-28 | - |
| A.L.Penberthy | 17 | 3 | 65 | 2 | 32.50 | 2-22 | - |
| A.E.Warner | 37.3 | 6 | 130 | 4 | 32.50 | 2-57 | - |
| A.Walker | 9 | 1 | 33 | 1 | 33.00 | 1-33 | - |
| G.A.Gooch | 56 | 2 | 235 | 7 | 33.57 | 2-19 | - |
| M.V.Fleming | 44 | 0 | 170 | 5 | 34.00 | 2-52 | - |
| M.A.Feltham | 21.2 | 1 | 103 | 3 | 34.33 | 2-45 | - |
| T.A.Merrick | 50 | 2 | 207 | 6 | 34.50 | 2-31 | - |
| B.Roberts | 13 | 1 | 69 | 2 | 34.50 | 1-11 | - |
| P.J.Newport | 66 | 5 | 242 | 7 | 34.57 | 2-36 | - |
| A.C.S.Pigott | 41.4 | 4 | 175 | 5 | 35.00 | 3-29 | - |

| Name | Overs | Mdns | Runs | Wkts | Avge | Best | 5wI |
|---|---|---|---|---|---|---|---|
| Waqar Younis | 35.4 | 2 | 140 | 4 | 35.00 | 3-29 | - |
| M.Frost | 40 | 6 | 177 | 5 | 35.40 | 3-38 | - |
| P.J.Bakker | 44 | 6 | 146 | 4 | 36.50 | 2-37 | - |
| A.M.Babington | 40 | 9 | 111 | 3 | 37.00 | 2-49 | - |
| P.J.Hartley | 46 | 5 | 185 | 5 | 37.00 | 2-7 | - |
| R.P.Lefebvre | 38 | 6 | 150 | 4 | 37.50 | 3-44 | - |
| A.J.Murphy | 41 | 4 | 151 | 4 | 37.75 | 2-23 | - |
| S.L.Watkin | 44 | 7 | 190 | 5 | 38.00 | 3-28 | - |
| D.Beal | 16 | 1 | 114 | 3 | 38.00 | 2-63 | - |
| C.C.Lewis | 22 | 0 | 115 | 3 | 38.33 | 3-62 | - |
| J.D.R.Benson | 7 | 0 | 39 | 1 | 39.00 | 1-10 | - |
| R.M.Ellison | 52 | 7 | 199 | 5 | 39.80 | 2-19 | - |
| G.J.Turner | 30.4 | 4 | 120 | 3 | 40.00 | 2-18 | - |
| J.Boiling | 20 | 0 | 81 | 2 | 40.50 | 1-38 | - |
| M.J.Weston | 11 | 0 | 41 | 1 | 41.00 | 1-41 | - |
| G.Yates | 22 | 3 | 85 | 2 | 42.50 | 2-50 | - |
| J.A.Afford | 11 | 0 | 43 | 1 | 43.00 | 1-43 | - |
| C.Wilkinson | 31 | 3 | 130 | 3 | 43.33 | 3-46 | - |
| S.R.Barwick | 39 | 4 | 175 | 4 | 43.75 | 2-61 | - |
| S.J.Base | 36 | 4 | 134 | 3 | 44.66 | 2-40 | - |
| C.R.Green | 20.5 | 0 | 90 | 2 | 45.00 | 2-55 | - |
| D.R.Gilbert | 44 | 5 | 138 | 3 | 46.00 | 1-31 | - |
| E.S.H.Giddins | 8 | 2 | 46 | 1 | 46.00 | 1-46 | - |
| J.R.Ayling | 42 | 0 | 186 | 4 | 46.50 | 2-56 | - |
| P.C.R.Tufnell | 39 | 0 | 187 | 4 | 46.75 | 3-50 | - |
| J.D.Fitton | 11 | 0 | 47 | 1 | 47.00 | 1-47 | - |
| A.M.Smith | 33 | 2 | 95 | 2 | 47.50 | 1-30 | - |
| R.A.Pick | 22 | 1 | 97 | 2 | 48.50 | 1-36 | - |
| E.E.Hemmings | 44 | 4 | 201 | 4 | 50.25 | 2-49 | - |
| K.E.Cooper | 31 | 5 | 103 | 2 | 51.50 | 1-27 | - |
| J.A.North | 41 | 1 | 208 | 4 | 52.00 | 2-80 | - |
| I.D.Austin | 72 | 2 | 319 | 6 | 53.16 | 2-50 | - |
| R.G.Williams | 33 | 2 | 109 | 2 | 54.50 | 1-31 | - |
| R.M.Ellcock | 10 | 0 | 55 | 1 | 55.00 | 1-55 | - |
| P.J.Rendell | 6 | 0 | 55 | 1 | 55.00 | 1-55 | - |
| I.G.Swallow | 24 | 1 | 111 | 2 | 55.50 | 1-31 | - |
| P.Willey | 36.5 | 4 | 111 | 2 | 55.50 | 1-29 | - |
| J.P.Stephenson | 11 | 0 | 57 | 1 | 57.00 | 1-17 | - |
| G.D.Rose | 38.5 | 2 | 172 | 3 | 57.33 | 2-48 | - |
| N.R.Taylor | 41.2 | 10 | 173 | 3 | 57.66 | 2-33 | - |
| C.K.Bullen | 13 | 0 | 58 | 1 | 58.00 | 1-29 | - |
| P.M.Such | 58 | 4 | 232 | 4 | 58.00 | 2-52 | - |
| M.Azharuddin | 16 | 0 | 58 | 1 | 58.00 | 1-17 | - |
| D.W.Headley | 42.1 | 4 | 180 | 3 | 60.00 | 1-34 | - |
| N.A.Mallender | 41 | 3 | 181 | 3 | 60.33 | 1-35 | - |
| R.J.Shastri | 32 | 1 | 124 | 2 | 62.00 | 1-40 | - |
| M.W.Alleyne | 15 | 0 | 67 | 1 | 67.00 | 1-24 | - |
| I.Smith | 10 | 0 | 69 | 1 | 69.00 | 1-51 | - |
| J.D.Moir | 40 | 11 | 146 | 2 | 73.00 | 2-47 | - |
| J.D.Batty | 22 | 3 | 75 | 1 | 75.00 | 1-34 | - |
| R.A.Bunting | 17 | 1 | 75 | 1 | 75.00 | 1-34 | - |
| N.G.B.Cook | 26 | 2 | 77 | 1 | 77.00 | 1-21 | - |
| J.N.Maguire | 37 | 7 | 154 | 2 | 77.00 | 1-27 | - |
| M.A.Ealham | 19 | 1 | 78 | 1 | 78.00 | 1-46 | - |
| P.A.Booth | 13 | 0 | 81 | 1 | 81.00 | 1-35 | - |
| R.J.Scott | 16.5 | 0 | 81 | 1 | 81.00 | 1-42 | - |
| M.A.Crawley | 17 | 0 | 82 | 1 | 82.00 | 1-44 | - |
| K.Greenfield | 18 | 0 | 89 | 1 | 89.00 | 1-35 | - |
| R.K.Illingworth | 49 | 2 | 189 | 2 | 94.50 | 2-50 | - |
| J.W.Govan | 42 | 4 | 191 | 2 | 95.50 | 1-26 | - |
| K.D.James | 22 | 0 | 100 | 1 | 100.00 | 1-45 | - |
| D.J.Millns | 23 | 3 | 101 | 1 | 101.00 | 1-25 | - |
| G.N.Reifer | 29.2 | 4 | 109 | 1 | 109.00 | 1-36 | - |
| D.R.Thomas | 22 | 1 | 110 | 1 | 110.00 | 1-61 | - |
| M.Saxelby | 26 | 1 | 118 | 1 | 118.00 | 1-36 | - |
| E.A.E.Baptiste | 31.1 | 5 | 118 | 1 | 118.00 | 1-30 | - |
| A.R.Hansford | 32.5 | 3 | 125 | 1 | 125.00 | 1-55 | - |
| A.D.Mullally | 33 | 2 | 134 | 1 | 134.00 | 1-45 | - |
| R.H.J.Jenkins | 26 | 1 | 141 | 1 | 141.00 | 1-58 | - |
| O.Henry | 39 | 2 | 143 | 1 | 143.00 | 1-31 | - |
| G.C.Small | 44 | 2 | 193 | 1 | 193.00 | 1-55 | - |

# ALL ONE-DAY MATCHES

## BATTING AVERAGES - Including fielding
### Qualifying requirements : 6 completed innings

| Name | Matches | Inns | NO | Runs | HS | Avge | 100s | 50s | Ct | St |
|---|---|---|---|---|---|---|---|---|---|---|
| C.L.Smith | 17 | 16 | 3 | 1004 | 142 | 77.23 | 4 | 5 | 5 | - |
| T.M.Moody | 26 | 25 | 5 | 1387 | 160 | 69.35 | 6 | 7 | 6 | - |
| R.A.Smith | 13 | 12 | 3 | 483 | 79* | 53.66 | - | 5 | 3 | - |
| M.R.Ramprakash | 16 | 16 | 5 | 565 | 111* | 51.36 | 1 | 4 | 6 | - |
| Salim Malik | 21 | 21 | 4 | 831 | 108 | 48.88 | 1 | 5 | 11 | - |
| T.S.Curtis | 27 | 25 | 4 | 1013 | 88* | 48.23 | - | 10 | 13 | - |
| D.M.Smith | 11 | 11 | 0 | 519 | 102 | 47.18 | 1 | 3 | 6 | - |
| M.D.Moxon | 29 | 29 | 3 | 1206 | 141* | 46.38 | 3 | 6 | 20 | - |
| D.W.Randall | 25 | 25 | 1 | 1097 | 95 | 45.70 | - | 8 | 9 | - |
| Asif Din | 18 | 17 | 2 | 682 | 137 | 45.46 | 2 | 2 | 3 | - |
| J.J.Whitaker | 21 | 21 | 1 | 894 | 100 | 44.70 | 1 | 6 | 6 | - |
| A.Fordham | 25 | 24 | 2 | 980 | 132* | 44.54 | 1 | 8 | 4 | - |
| M.W.Gatting | 21 | 21 | 2 | 844 | 112 | 44.42 | 2 | 6 | 8 | - |
| B.C.Broad | 24 | 24 | 4 | 885 | 108* | 44.25 | 3 | 4 | 6 | - |
| M.C.J.Nicholas | 25 | 20 | 7 | 573 | 65* | 44.07 | - | 4 | 6 | - |
| G.A.Hick | 26 | 24 | 4 | 875 | 109 | 43.75 | 1 | 7 | 12 | - |
| P.A.Neale | 20 | 14 | 7 | 306 | 52* | 43.71 | - | 1 | 9 | - |
| J.P.Stephenson | 26 | 25 | 0 | 1078 | 142 | 43.12 | 2 | 8 | 11 | - |
| M.P.Maynard | 22 | 22 | 3 | 808 | 151* | 42.52 | 2 | 5 | 11 | - |
| N.H.Fairbrother | 32 | 31 | 8 | 977 | 113 | 42.47 | 1 | 6 | 15 | - |
| A.J.Stewart | 23 | 22 | 3 | 803 | 110* | 42.26 | 1 | 8 | 24 | 3 |
| A.N.Hayhurst | 18 | 16 | 6 | 419 | 91* | 41.90 | - | 3 | 4 | - |
| A.A.Metcalfe | 27 | 27 | 1 | 1089 | 116 | 41.88 | 2 | 6 | 6 | - |
| C.L.Hooper | 9 | 8 | 2 | 251 | 88 | 41.83 | - | 1 | 3 | - |
| R.J.Bailey | 23 | 22 | 2 | 825 | 145 | 41.25 | 1 | 5 | 4 | - |
| A.R.Butcher | 18 | 18 | 1 | 695 | 127 | 40.88 | 1 | 6 | 6 | - |
| G.A.Gooch | 23 | 22 | 1 | 849 | 107 | 40.42 | 1 | 8 | 9 | - |
| C.J.Tavare | 22 | 22 | 2 | 808 | 75* | 40.40 | - | 7 | 12 | - |
| W.Larkins | 10 | 10 | 0 | 402 | 108 | 40.20 | 1 | 3 | 4 | - |
| T.A.Lloyd | 23 | 20 | 3 | 669 | 78 | 39.35 | - | 3 | 7 | - |
| N.R.Taylor | 21 | 21 | 2 | 743 | 110 | 39.10 | 1 | 5 | 3 | - |
| G.Fowler | 26 | 26 | 1 | 972 | 136 | 38.88 | 1 | 6 | 4 | - |
| M.A.Crawley | 16 | 13 | 5 | 304 | 74* | 38.00 | - | 2 | 3 | - |
| A.J.Wright | 24 | 23 | 2 | 794 | 81 | 37.81 | - | 7 | 3 | - |
| R.T.Robinson | 23 | 23 | 4 | 714 | 124 | 37.57 | 2 | 1 | 8 | - |
| G.P.Thorpe | 25 | 23 | 3 | 746 | 115* | 37.30 | 1 | 4 | 4 | - |
| L.Potter | 21 | 21 | 7 | 521 | 79* | 37.21 | - | 4 | 5 | - |
| S.J.Cook | 23 | 23 | 1 | 815 | 129* | 37.04 | 1 | 5 | 6 | - |
| R.J.Shastri | 18 | 18 | 3 | 554 | 138* | 36.93 | 1 | 2 | 6 | - |
| G.C.Holmes | 13 | 12 | 3 | 332 | 72 | 36.88 | 1 | 2 | 3 | - |
| V.P.Terry | 21 | 20 | 3 | 627 | 123 | 36.88 | 1 | 2 | 9 | - |
| M.A.Atherton | 22 | 22 | 2 | 731 | 91 | 36.55 | - | 5 | 8 | - |
| T.J.Boon | 13 | 12 | 1 | 399 | 103 | 36.27 | 1 | 3 | 2 | - |
| T.C.Middleton | 11 | 11 | 0 | 396 | 78 | 36.00 | - | 4 | 3 | - |
| G.D.Lloyd | 22 | 22 | 6 | 575 | 79* | 35.93 | - | 4 | 4 | - |
| H.Morris | 20 | 20 | 1 | 679 | 126* | 35.73 | 1 | 3 | 7 | - |
| K.J.Barnett | 22 | 22 | 4 | 642 | 102 | 35.66 | 1 | 3 | 11 | - |
| R.G.Williams | 19 | 13 | 6 | 244 | 66* | 34.85 | - | 1 | 7 | - |
| G.D.Mendis | 23 | 23 | 1 | 765 | 125* | 34.77 | 1 | 4 | 8 | - |
| A.J.Moles | 22 | 21 | 2 | 660 | 93* | 34.73 | - | 6 | 11 | - |
| D.J.Bicknell | 19 | 19 | 1 | 614 | 149* | 34.11 | 1 | 3 | 4 | - |
| I.T.Botham | 20 | 17 | 6 | 372 | 58 | 33.81 | - | 1 | 5 | - |
| C.W.J.Athey | 23 | 23 | 3 | 668 | 85 | 33.40 | - | 5 | 11 | - |
| D.Byas | 27 | 27 | 4 | 759 | 92 | 33.00 | - | 6 | 3 | - |
| P.V.Simmons | 8 | 8 | 0 | 263 | 70 | 32.87 | - | 3 | 1 | - |
| S.A.Marsh | 22 | 20 | 6 | 459 | 71 | 32.78 | - | 4 | 21 | 1 |
| S.J.Rhodes | 27 | 14 | 3 | 360 | 105 | 32.72 | 1 | 2 | 15 | 5 |
| M.Azharuddin | 22 | 21 | 3 | 579 | 73 | 32.16 | - | 3 | 15 | - |
| P.D.Bowler | 18 | 18 | 1 | 543 | 100 | 31.94 | 1 | 2 | 14 | - |
| N.Hussain | 27 | 23 | 5 | 571 | 97 | 31.72 | - | 2 | 10 | - |
| J.E.Morris | 20 | 20 | 0 | 634 | 107 | 31.70 | 1 | 3 | 4 | - |
| R.J.Blakey | 28 | 28 | 4 | 752 | 130* | 31.33 | 1 | 2 | 38 | 1 |
| M.R.Benson | 22 | 22 | 0 | 686 | 84 | 31.18 | - | 6 | 7 | - |
| K.M.Curran | 19 | 17 | 6 | 339 | 61* | 30.81 | - | 1 | 2 | - |
| D.A.Reeve | 24 | 19 | 2 | 521 | 100 | 30.64 | 1 | 2 | 10 | - |
| T.R.Ward | 24 | 24 | 2 | 672 | 87 | 30.54 | - | 6 | 8 | - |
| J.W.Hall | 9 | 9 | 0 | 272 | 71 | 30.22 | - | 2 | 1 | - |
| C.J.Adams | 20 | 17 | 3 | 423 | 71 | 30.21 | - | 2 | 6 | - |
| K.R.Brown | 21 | 21 | 5 | 473 | 81* | 29.56 | - | 2 | 6 | - |
| K.Greenfield | 19 | 18 | 4 | 405 | 78* | 28.92 | - | 3 | 4 | - |
| M.A.Roseberry | 17 | 16 | 1 | 433 | 106* | 28.86 | 1 | 2 | 9 | - |
| P.Johnson | 26 | 24 | 2 | 634 | 102* | 28.81 | 1 | 3 | 8 | - |
| T.J.G.O'Gorman | 22 | 20 | 3 | 477 | 93 | 28.05 | - | 1 | 8 | - |
| J.C.Pooley | 7 | 7 | 0 | 196 | 109 | 28.00 | 1 | - | - | - |
| M.W.Alleyne | 24 | 22 | 2 | 557 | 77 | 27.85 | - | 3 | 4 | - |
| I.Smith | 17 | 15 | 3 | 334 | 51 | 27.83 | - | 1 | 5 | - |
| A.Dale | 18 | 14 | 2 | 333 | 86 | 27.75 | - | 2 | 8 | - |
| N.J.Lenham | 14 | 14 | 1 | 357 | 86 | 27.46 | - | 3 | 2 | - |
| J.J.E.Hardy | 12 | 11 | 1 | 270 | 70 | 27.00 | - | 2 | 2 | - |
| M.P.Speight | 16 | 16 | 1 | 405 | 106* | 27.00 | 1 | - | 5 | - |
| D.M.Ward | 25 | 24 | 1 | 619 | 62 | 26.91 | - | 6 | 7 | - |
| N.M.K.Smith | 14 | 11 | 4 | 188 | 39 | 26.85 | - | - | 4 | - |
| P.W.G.Parker | 18 | 18 | 0 | 475 | 104 | 26.38 | 1 | 2 | 8 | - |
| A.N Aymes | 23 | 14 | 7 | 183 | 33* | 26.14 | - | - | 23 | 8 |
| M.A.Lynch | 22 | 22 | 2 | 522 | 97 | 26.10 | - | 3 | 10 | - |
| B.N.French | 24 | 14 | 7 | 182 | 37* | 26.00 | - | - | 27 | 1 |
| N.A.Felton | 16 | 15 | 0 | 387 | 69 | 25.80 | - | 3 | 7 | - |
| N.D.Burns | 23 | 21 | 6 | 385 | 52* | 25.66 | - | 2 | 15 | 8 |
| M.Keech | 14 | 14 | 3 | 279 | 49* | 25.36 | - | - | 3 | - |
| C.S.Cowdrey | 13 | 12 | 2 | 251 | 57* | 25.10 | - | 1 | 9 | - |
| D.R.Pringle | 23 | 17 | 4 | 326 | 51* | 25.07 | - | 2 | 6 | - |
| P.M.Roebuck | 16 | 14 | 1 | 325 | 63* | 25.00 | - | 2 | 4 | - |
| A.I.C.Dodemaide | 19 | 13 | 6 | 174 | 32* | 24.85 | - | - | 5 | - |
| P.E.Robinson | 27 | 25 | 4 | 518 | 64 | 24.66 | - | 2 | 15 | - |
| G.R.Cowdrey | 23 | 22 | 2 | 488 | 80 | 24.40 | - | 3 | 11 | - |
| A.D.Brown | 8 | 7 | 0 | 170 | 45 | 24.28 | - | - | - | - |
| R.C.Russell | 23 | 21 | 2 | 458 | 74 | 24.10 | - | 2 | 32 | 2 |
| M.J.Weston | 18 | 12 | 4 | 192 | 51 | 24.00 | - | 1 | 4 | - |
| A.J.Lamb | 23 | 22 | 0 | 526 | 62 | 23.90 | - | 2 | 8 | - |
| M.Watkinson | 26 | 23 | 4 | 448 | 83 | 23.57 | - | 2 | 6 | - |
| D.P.Ostler | 24 | 20 | 3 | 400 | 62* | 23.52 | - | 2 | 4 | - |
| D.J.Capel | 25 | 23 | 3 | 469 | 77* | 23.45 | - | 2 | 3 | - |
| J.R.Ayling | 20 | 16 | 6 | 234 | 56 | 23.40 | - | 1 | 8 | - |
| B.F.Smith | 15 | 14 | 4 | 234 | 33 | 23.40 | - | - | 2 | - |
| M.V.Fleming | 22 | 22 | 1 | 490 | 77 | 23.33 | - | 3 | 5 | - |
| S.C.Goldsmith | 11 | 9 | 1 | 186 | 67* | 23.25 | - | 1 | 4 | - |
| M.P.Bicknell | 16 | 9 | 3 | 137 | 66* | 22.83 | - | 1 | 2 | - |
| A.E.Warner | 15 | 14 | 4 | 228 | 51 | 22.80 | - | 1 | 4 | - |
| R.J.Scott | 23 | 23 | 1 | 501 | 77 | 22.77 | - | 3 | - | - |
| J.R.Wood | 15 | 14 | 1 | 294 | 70* | 22.61 | - | 2 | 5 | - |
| P.J.Prichard | 25 | 23 | 3 | 452 | 54* | 22.60 | - | 1 | 12 | - |
| J.D.Robinson | 24 | 21 | 4 | 383 | 55* | 22.52 | - | 2 | 6 | - |
| N.E.Briers | 22 | 22 | 0 | 495 | 48 | 22.50 | - | - | 9 | - |
| A.P.Wells | 21 | 21 | 1 | 448 | 66 | 22.40 | - | 2 | 5 | - |
| S.G.Hinks | 6 | 6 | 0 | 133 | 35 | 22.16 | - | - | 1 | - |
| M.A.Feltham | 14 | 10 | 4 | 131 | 32* | 21.83 | - | - | 4 | - |
| Wasim Akram | 26 | 21 | 7 | 303 | 45* | 21.64 | - | - | 2 | - |
| P.C.L.Holloway | 10 | 8 | 2 | 128 | 34* | 21.33 | - | - | 8 | 1 |
| R.J.Harden | 23 | 23 | 1 | 468 | 79* | 21.27 | - | 1 | 2 | - |
| D.B.D'Oliveira | 27 | 24 | 4 | 421 | 54 | 21.05 | - | 1 | 11 | - |
| P.A.Smith | 22 | 18 | 1 | 356 | 75 | 20.94 | - | 1 | 4 | - |
| I.A.Greig | 21 | 18 | 4 | 293 | 68* | 20.92 | - | 1 | 6 | - |
| D.I.Gower | 18 | 15 | 1 | 290 | 63 | 20.71 | - | 2 | 5 | - |
| J.W.Lloyds | 20 | 16 | 3 | 262 | 45* | 20.15 | - | - | 10 | - |
| D.V.Lawrence | 16 | 12 | 5 | 140 | 38* | 20.00 | - | - | 1 | - |
| R.B.Richardson | 7 | 7 | 1 | 120 | 41 | 20.00 | - | - | 5 | - |
| R.J.Bartlett | 10 | 10 | 0 | 193 | 67 | 19.30 | - | 1 | 3 | - |
| M.Saxelby | 22 | 17 | 2 | 287 | 55 | 19.13 | - | 1 | 5 | - |
| J.D.R.Benson | 15 | 12 | 3 | 172 | 42 | 19.11 | - | - | 6 | - |
| I.J.F.Hutchinson | 8 | 8 | 0 | 152 | 42 | 19.00 | - | - | 4 | - |
| S.A.Kellett | 15 | 13 | 4 | 170 | 44 | 18.88 | - | - | 2 | - |
| M.A.Garnham | 25 | 18 | 7 | 204 | 61* | 18.54 | - | 1 | 21 | 4 |
| C.C.Lewis | 21 | 18 | 2 | 294 | 89* | 18.37 | - | 1 | 8 | - |
| C.S.Pickles | 15 | 12 | 6 | 110 | 30* | 18.33 | - | - | 7 | - |
| K.H.Macleay | 12 | 10 | 4 | 110 | 29 | 18.33 | - | - | 4 | - |
| P.Willey | 17 | 15 | 1 | 256 | 36 | 18.28 | - | - | 3 | - |
| P.Moores | 22 | 19 | 2 | 305 | 62 | 17.94 | - | 1 | 25 | 3 |
| P.Carrick | 16 | 12 | 5 | 124 | 25 | 17.71 | - | - | 5 | - |
| J.I.Longley | 6 | 6 | 0 | 104 | 47 | 17.33 | - | - | 2 | - |
| N.Shahid | 18 | 10 | 1 | 154 | 42 | 17.11 | - | - | 3 | - |
| G.K.Brown | 7 | 7 | 0 | 119 | 82 | 17.00 | - | 1 | 2 | - |
| D.Ripley | 22 | 12 | 5 | 117 | 36* | 16.71 | - | - | 18 | 1 |
| P.A.J.DeFreitas | 23 | 14 | 4 | 161 | 41* | 16.10 | - | - | 11 | - |
| F.D.Stephenson | 24 | 16 | 4 | 191 | 36* | 15.91 | - | - | 4 | - |
| P.Whitticase | 20 | 15 | 4 | 175 | 34* | 15.90 | - | - | 10 | 1 |
| C.M.Wells | 13 | 12 | 2 | 157 | 34* | 15.70 | - | - | 1 | - |
| D.G.Cork | 11 | 6 | 0 | 91 | 30 | 15.16 | - | - | 4 | - |

# ALL ONE-DAY MATCHES

| Name | Matches | Inns | NO | Runs | HS | Avge | 100s | 50s | Ct | St |
|------|---------|------|-----|------|------|------|------|-----|-----|-----|
| B.Roberts | 9 | 8 | 0 | 119 | 49 | 14.87 | - | - | 3 | - |
| K.D.James | 18 | 14 | 2 | 178 | 58 * | 14.83 | - | 1 | 4 | - |
| E.A.E.Baptiste | 19 | 17 | 6 | 162 | 34 | 14.72 | - | - | 3 | - |
| P.Farbrace | 14 | 10 | 4 | 87 | 26 * | 14.50 | - | - | 10 | 7 |
| J.E.Emburey | 23 | 17 | 4 | 188 | 33 * | 14.46 | - | - | 6 | - |
| N.V.Knight | 9 | 9 | 1 | 115 | 36 | 14.37 | - | - | 9 | - |
| I.D.Austin | 27 | 10 | 2 | 114 | 48 | 14.25 | - | - | 4 | - |
| R.P.Lefebvre | 21 | 18 | 4 | 194 | 27 | 13.85 | - | - | 7 | - |
| P.N.Weekes | 15 | 11 | 2 | 122 | 32 * | 13.55 | - | - | 7 | - |
| G.D.Rose | 18 | 17 | 2 | 200 | 59 | 13.33 | - | 2 | 2 | - |
| C.P.Metson | 19 | 12 | 4 | 106 | 20 | 13.25 | - | - | 15 | 2 |
| R.P.Davis | 18 | 14 | 5 | 118 | 40 * | 13.11 | - | - | 9 | - |
| S.D.Udal | 26 | 9 | 3 | 76 | 23 | 12.66 | - | - | 8 | - |
| D.E.Malcolm | 15 | 10 | 4 | 75 | 18 | 12.50 | - | - | 2 | - |
| P.N.Hepworth | 12 | 9 | 1 | 99 | 33 | 12.37 | - | - | 2 | - |
| T.D.Topley | 23 | 11 | 3 | 99 | 38 * | 12.37 | - | - | 3 | - |
| D.Gough | 15 | 11 | 1 | 119 | 72 * | 11.90 | - | 1 | 4 | - |
| J.A.North | 10 | 9 | 1 | 94 | 22 | 11.75 | - | - | 5 | - |
| I.D.K.Salisbury | 25 | 17 | 5 | 137 | 23 | 11.41 | - | - | 5 | - |
| S.L.Watkin | 19 | 11 | 3 | 85 | 31 * | 10.62 | - | - | 2 | - |
| A.R.Fothergill | 10 | 8 | 1 | 64 | 24 | 9.14 | - | - | 5 | - |
| N.F.Williams | 18 | 10 | 2 | 67 | 27 | 8.37 | - | - | 8 | - |
| A.C.S.Pigott | 23 | 21 | 3 | 127 | 29 | 7.05 | - | - | 10 | - |
| D.R.Gilbert | 17 | 8 | 2 | 42 | 16 | 7.00 | - | - | 2 | - |
| A.M.Babington | 21 | 10 | 3 | 47 | 11 | 6.71 | - | - | 4 | - |
| R.D.B.Croft | 13 | 8 | 0 | 48 | 19 | 6.00 | - | - | 3 | - |
| P.J.Hartley | 22 | 14 | 4 | 60 | 13 | 6.00 | - | - | 3 | - |
| Waqar Younis | 20 | 11 | 3 | 48 | 26 | 6.00 | - | - | 3 | - |
| S.J.Base | 20 | 10 | 1 | 46 | 17 * | 5.11 | - | - | 5 | - |
| N.G.Cowans | 18 | 9 | 3 | 29 | 10 | 4.83 | - | - | 2 | - |
| G.C.Small | 19 | 9 | 0 | 29 | 15 | 3.22 | - | - | 4 | - |

# ALL ONE-DAY MATCHES

## BOWLING AVERAGES
**Qualifying requirements : 10 wickets taken**

| Name | Overs | Mdns | Runs | Wkts | Avge | Best | 5wI |
|---|---|---|---|---|---|---|---|
| D.V.Lawrence | 142 | 14 | 601 | 36 | 16.69 | 6-20 | 2 |
| G.A.Hick | 45.2 | 4 | 205 | 12 | 17.08 | 5-35 | 1 |
| P.Carrick | 132 | 7 | 475 | 27 | 17.59 | 5-22 | 2 |
| Waqar Younis | 168.5 | 15 | 682 | 38 | 17.94 | 5-40 | 1 |
| N.V.Radford | 191.5 | 20 | 869 | 48 | 18.10 | 7-19 | 2 |
| F.D.Stephenson | 195.2 | 20 | 759 | 41 | 18.51 | 5-30 | 2 |
| C.L.Hooper | 75.5 | 14 | 260 | 14 | 18.57 | 3-12 | - |
| A.P.Igglesden | 169.1 | 14 | 714 | 37 | 19.29 | 4-29 | - |
| N.G.Cowans | 149.5 | 10 | 616 | 31 | 19.87 | 6-9 | 1 |
| J.P.Taylor | 158 | 22 | 539 | 27 | 19.96 | 2-11 | - |
| A.C.S.Pigott | 174.2 | 8 | 769 | 38 | 20.23 | 5-30 | 1 |
| P.N.Hepworth | 47 | 3 | 223 | 11 | 20.27 | 4-39 | - |
| A.N.Jones | 124 | 9 | 641 | 31 | 20.67 | 5-32 | 1 |
| R.A.Bunting | 53.3 | 1 | 252 | 12 | 21.00 | 4-35 | - |
| J.E.Emburey | 201 | 18 | 865 | 41 | 21.09 | 5-23 | 2 |
| G.R.Dilley | 79.2 | 7 | 319 | 15 | 21.26 | 4-35 | - |
| C.A.Connor | 209.4 | 11 | 935 | 43 | 21.74 | 4-29 | - |
| P.A.Smith | 140.5 | 7 | 628 | 28 | 22.42 | 4-21 | - |
| R.P.Lefebvre | 168 | 18 | 637 | 28 | 22.75 | 3-27 | - |
| D.R.Pringle | 190 | 13 | 799 | 35 | 22.82 | 5-51 | 1 |
| C.S.Pickles | 104.3 | 4 | 547 | 23 | 23.78 | 5-50 | 1 |
| S.P.Hughes | 58 | 5 | 238 | 10 | 23.80 | 2-24 | - |
| D.J.Capel | 134.4 | 4 | 597 | 25 | 23.88 | 4-37 | - |
| J.P.Stephenson | 86.2 | 2 | 384 | 16 | 24.00 | 4-17 | - |
| O.H.Mortensen | 130 | 18 | 464 | 19 | 24.42 | 3-29 | - |
| M.Watkinson | 215.4 | 14 | 993 | 40 | 24.82 | 5-49 | 1 |
| T.D.Topley | 180.5 | 18 | 781 | 31 | 25.19 | 4-41 | - |
| J.G.Thomas | 88.3 | 5 | 382 | 15 | 25.46 | 5-29 | 1 |
| T.A.Munton | 189.4 | 18 | 672 | 26 | 25.84 | 5-28 | 1 |
| C.C.Lewis | 185.2 | 17 | 728 | 28 | 26.00 | 3-25 | - |
| S.D.Fletcher | 144.2 | 8 | 703 | 27 | 26.03 | 4-51 | - |
| A.M.Smith | 125.4 | 6 | 574 | 22 | 26.09 | 3-16 | - |
| M.A.Ealham | 67 | 2 | 288 | 11 | 26.18 | 3-32 | - |
| P.A.J.DeFreitas | 212.1 | 30 | 764 | 29 | 26.34 | 4-15 | - |
| M.A.Crawley | 76 | 2 | 343 | 13 | 26.38 | 4-26 | - |
| A.A.Donald | 149 | 7 | 662 | 25 | 26.48 | 4-16 | - |
| J.D.R.Benson | 76 | 0 | 403 | 15 | 26.86 | 3-37 | - |
| D.A.Graveney | 98 | 7 | 378 | 14 | 27.00 | 3-21 | - |
| A.N.Hayhurst | 102.1 | 4 | 463 | 17 | 27.23 | 5-60 | 1 |
| S.L.Watkin | 163 | 13 | 688 | 25 | 27.52 | 3-28 | - |
| N.A.Foster | 133.5 | 15 | 473 | 17 | 27.82 | 3-28 | - |
| N.M.K.Smith | 70.3 | 1 | 337 | 12 | 28.08 | 3-52 | - |
| K.H.Macleay | 96 | 2 | 366 | 13 | 28.15 | 3-31 | - |
| S.J.Base | 150 | 9 | 648 | 23 | 28.17 | 4-14 | - |
| D.E.Malcolm | 125 | 5 | 657 | 23 | 28.56 | 3-43 | - |
| A.Walker | 149.5 | 15 | 497 | 17 | 29.23 | 2-7 | - |
| M.P.Bicknell | 137.3 | 5 | 556 | 19 | 29.26 | 3-28 | - |
| P.M.Roebuck | 76.4 | 3 | 361 | 12 | 30.08 | 4-11 | - |
| I.D.Austin | 217.3 | 6 | 1084 | 36 | 30.11 | 5-56 | 1 |
| S.D.Udal | 224.2 | 18 | 974 | 32 | 30.43 | 3-40 | - |
| D.Gough | 105.2 | 5 | 488 | 16 | 30.50 | 3-33 | - |
| R.D.B.Croft | 95 | 2 | 428 | 14 | 30.57 | 2-28 | - |
| R.J.Scott | 105.1 | 5 | 462 | 15 | 30.80 | 4-22 | - |
| A.J.Murphy | 188.2 | 17 | 801 | 26 | 30.80 | 3-15 | - |
| A.M.Babington | 165.4 | 19 | 647 | 21 | 30.81 | 4-53 | - |
| J.A.North | 68 | 2 | 370 | 12 | 30.83 | 3-29 | - |
| D.G.Cork | 82 | 5 | 375 | 12 | 31.25 | 3-45 | - |
| Aqib Javed | 198 | 14 | 844 | 27 | 31.25 | 4-51 | - |
| I.T.Botham | 164.3 | 18 | 751 | 24 | 31.29 | 4-45 | - |
| D.A.Reeve | 177.5 | 12 | 758 | 24 | 31.58 | 4-18 | - |
| M.Frost | 141 | 10 | 671 | 21 | 31.95 | 3-35 | - |
| J.D.Robinson | 162.3 | 11 | 673 | 21 | 32.04 | 4-28 | - |
| M.J.McCague | 84 | 2 | 481 | 15 | 32.06 | 4-51 | - |
| G.C.Small | 161 | 19 | 642 | 20 | 32.10 | 3-16 | - |
| G.A.Gooch | 156 | 8 | 645 | 20 | 32.25 | 3-35 | - |
| P.W.Jarvis | 87.2 | 15 | 324 | 10 | 32.40 | 2-13 | - |
| R.P.Davis | 146 | 15 | 616 | 19 | 32.42 | 3-33 | - |
| J.N.Maguire | 180.3 | 15 | 780 | 24 | 32.50 | 3-31 | - |
| P.J.W.Allott | 224 | 30 | 815 | 25 | 32.60 | 4-23 | - |
| S.R.Lampitt | 144.5 | 6 | 753 | 23 | 32.73 | 4-46 | - |
| M.Saxelby | 152.4 | 5 | 724 | 22 | 32.90 | 4-29 | - |
| K.M.Curran | 115.1 | 5 | 560 | 17 | 32.94 | 3-24 | - |
| M.A.Feltham | 111.3 | 7 | 528 | 16 | 33.00 | 3-44 | - |
| R.A.Pick | 144.5 | 9 | 570 | 17 | 33.52 | 3-41 | - |
| M.V.Fleming | 163.5 | 2 | 817 | 24 | 34.04 | 4-45 | - |
| Wasim Akram | 220.3 | 12 | 1022 | 30 | 34.06 | 4-18 | - |
| M.A.Robinson | 110.5 | 7 | 512 | 15 | 34.13 | 4-33 | - |
| P.M.Such | 232 | 13 | 962 | 28 | 34.35 | 4-30 | - |
| S.J.W.Andrew | 77 | 3 | 415 | 12 | 34.58 | 4-41 | - |
| A.E.Warner | 114.2 | 8 | 559 | 16 | 34.93 | 3-38 | - |
| H.R.J.Trump | 70 | 1 | 351 | 10 | 35.10 | 3-41 | - |
| R.K.Illingworth | 227 | 11 | 952 | 27 | 35.25 | 5-49 | 1 |
| R.G.Williams | 139 | 6 | 568 | 16 | 35.50 | 2-22 | - |
| A.I.C.Dodemaide | 143 | 14 | 549 | 15 | 36.60 | 2-12 | - |
| S.R.Barwick | 153.1 | 4 | 769 | 21 | 36.61 | 3-30 | - |
| I.D.K.Salisbury | 180.1 | 10 | 848 | 23 | 36.87 | 3-10 | - |
| J.D.Batty | 145 | 11 | 667 | 18 | 37.05 | 4-33 | - |
| K.P.Evans | 173 | 7 | 893 | 24 | 37.20 | 4-43 | - |
| P.J.Hartley | 173.2 | 10 | 747 | 20 | 37.35 | 3-6 | - |
| K.D.James | 110 | 6 | 501 | 13 | 38.53 | 3-24 | - |
| J.R.Ayling | 169 | 2 | 849 | 22 | 38.59 | 3-25 | - |
| R.J.Shastri | 95 | 2 | 425 | 11 | 38.63 | 3-26 | - |
| C.Wilkinson | 143.2 | 10 | 666 | 17 | 39.17 | 3-16 | - |
| E.A.E.Baptiste | 154.2 | 14 | 629 | 16 | 39.31 | 4-27 | - |
| J.C.Hallett | 105.1 | 1 | 437 | 11 | 39.72 | 3-36 | - |
| R.M.Ellison | 105.4 | 8 | 478 | 12 | 39.83 | 2-19 | - |
| P.N.Weekes | 82.2 | 3 | 403 | 10 | 40.30 | 3-27 | - |
| N.F.Williams | 139 | 12 | 574 | 14 | 41.00 | 2-19 | - |
| A.Dale | 106 | 3 | 575 | 14 | 41.07 | 3-44 | - |
| E.E.Hemmings | 199.1 | 11 | 869 | 21 | 41.38 | 4-26 | - |
| J.Boiling | 146 | 5 | 622 | 15 | 41.46 | 2-22 | - |
| G.D.Rose | 100 | 2 | 502 | 12 | 41.83 | 2-21 | - |
| P.J.Newport | 181.2 | 7 | 857 | 20 | 42.85 | 3-39 | - |
| M.W.Alleyne | 98 | 1 | 517 | 12 | 43.08 | 2-19 | - |
| M.J.Weston | 124.1 | 4 | 478 | 11 | 43.45 | 2-25 | - |
| P.Willey | 120.5 | 9 | 437 | 10 | 43.70 | 4-17 | - |
| N.A.Mallender | 126 | 11 | 483 | 10 | 48.30 | 3-23 | - |
| T.A.Merrick | 160.2 | 9 | 744 | 15 | 49.60 | 3-27 | - |
| D.R.Gilbert | 144.4 | 6 | 606 | 12 | 50.50 | 2-27 | - |
| D.J.Millns | 126 | 9 | 572 | 11 | 52.00 | 2-20 | - |

# BEST
# PERFORMANCES
# AND
# HIGHEST
# AGGREGATES

# CORNHILL TEST MATCHES

## BATTING
### 50 Best Individual Scores

| Name | Score | For | Against | Venue | Date |
|------|-------|-----|---------|-------|------|
| G.A.Gooch | 174 | England | S Lanka | Lord's | 22/08/91 |
| G.A.Gooch | 154* | England | W Indies | Headingley | 06/06/91 |
| R.A.Smith | 148* | England | W Indies | Lord's | 20/06/91 |
| R.B.Richardson | 121 | W Indies | England | The Oval | 08/08/91 |
| A.J.Stewart | 113* | England | S Lanka | Lord's | 22/08/91 |
| C.L.Hooper | 111 | W Indies | England | Lord's | 20/06/91 |
| R.A.Smith | 109 | England | W Indies | The Oval | 08/08/91 |
| R.B.Richardson | 104 | W Indies | England | Edgbaston | 25/07/91 |
| I.V.A.Richards | 80 | W Indies | England | Trent Bridge | 04/07/91 |
| A.L.Logie | 78 | W Indies | England | Trent Bridge | 04/07/91 |
| D.L.Haynes | 75* | W Indies | England | The Oval | 08/08/91 |
| I.V.A.Richards | 73* | W Indies | England | Edgbaston | 25/07/91 |
| I.V.A.Richards | 73 | W Indies | England | Headingley | 06/06/91 |
| R.B.Richardson | 68 | W Indies | England | Headingley | 06/06/91 |
| G.A.Gooch | 68 | England | W Indies | Trent Bridge | 04/07/91 |
| M.D.Marshall | 67 | W Indies | England | Trent Bridge | 04/07/91 |
| U.C.Hath'singhe | 66 | S Lanka | England | Lord's | 22/08/91 |
| S.T.Jayasuriya | 66 | S Lanka | England | Lord's | 22/08/91 |
| C.C.Lewis | 65 | England | WIndies | Edgbaston | 25/07/91 |
| R.A.Smith | 64* | England | W Indies | Trent Bridge | 04/07/91 |
| R.A.Smith | 63* | England | S Lanka | Lord's | 22/08/91 |
| I.V.A.Richards | 63 | W Indies | England | Lord's | 20/06/91 |
| D.L.Haynes | 60 | W Indies | England | Lord's | 20/06/91 |
| G.A.Gooch | 60 | England | W Indies | The Oval | 08/08/91 |
| I.V.A.Richards | 60 | W Indies | England | The Oval | 08/08/91 |
| D.L.Haynes | 57* | W Indies | England | Trent Bridge | 04/07/91 |
| R.B.Richardson | 57 | W Indies | England | Lord's | 20/06/91 |
| P.A.J.DeFreitas | 55* | England | W Indies | Trent Bridge | 04/07/91 |
| C.L.Hooper | 55* | W Indies | England | Edgbaston | 25/07/91 |
| R.A.Smith | 54 | England | W Indies | Headingley | 06/06/91 |
| C.L.Hooper | 54 | W Indies | England | The Oval | 08/08/91 |
| R.B.Richardson | 52* | W Indies | England | Trent Bridge | 04/07/91 |
| R.J.Ratnayake | 52 | S Lanka | England | Lord's | 22/08/91 |
| C.C.Lewis | 47* | England | W Indies | The Oval | 08/08/91 |
| R.C.Russell | 46 | England | W Indies | Lord's | 20/06/91 |
| G.A.Gooch | 45 | England | W Indies | Edgbaston | 25/07/91 |
| D.R.Pringle | 45 | England | W Indies | Edgbaston | 25/07/91 |
| H.Morris | 44 | England | W Indies | The Oval | 08/08/91 |
| G.A.Hick | 43 | England | W Indies | Trent Bridge | 04/07/91 |
| R.B.Richardson | 43 | W Indies | England | Trent Bridge | 04/07/91 |
| D.L.Haynes | 43 | W Indies | England | The Oval | 08/08/91 |
| A.J.Stewart | 43 | England | S Lanka | Lord's | 22/08/91 |
| H.Morris | 42 | England | S Lanka | Lord's | 22/08/91 |
| P.A.De Silva | 42 | S Lanka | England | Lord's | 22/08/91 |
| G.A.Gooch | 40 | England | W Indies | Edgbaston | 25/07/91 |
| C.B.Lambert | 39 | W Indies | England | The Oval | 08/08/91 |
| A.J.Stewart | 38* | England | W Indies | The Oval | 08/08/91 |
| P.V.Simmons | 38 | W Indies | England | Headingley | 06/06/91 |
| G.A.Gooch | 38 | England | S Lanka | Lord's | 22/08/91 |
| G.A.Gooch | 37 | England | W Indies | Lord's | 20/06/91 |

## BOWLING
### 50 Best Innings Bowling Figures

| Name | Figures | For | Against | Venue | Date |
|------|---------|-----|---------|-------|------|
| P.A.J.DeFreitas | 7-70 | England | S Lanka | Lord's | 22/08/91 |
| P.C.R.Tufnell | 6-25 | England | W Indies | The Oval | 08/08/91 |
| C.E.L.Ambrose | 6-52 | W Indies | England | Headingley | 06/06/91 |
| C.C.Lewis | 6-111 | England | W Indies | Edgbaston | 25/07/91 |
| R.J.Ratnayake | 5-69 | S Lanka | England | Lord's | 22/08/91 |
| C.E.L.Ambrose | 5-74 | W Indies | England | Trent Bridge | 04/07/91 |
| B.P.Patterson | 5-81 | W Indies | England | Edgbaston | 25/07/91 |
| P.C.R.Tufnell | 5-94 | England | S Lanka | Lord's | 22/08/91 |
| D.R.Pringle | 5-100 | England | W Indies | Lord's | 20/06/91 |
| D.V.Lawrence | 5-106 | England | W Indies | The Oval | 08/08/91 |
| M.D.Marshall | 4-33 | W Indies | England | Edgbaston | 25/07/91 |
| P.A.J.DeFreitas | 4-34 | England | W Indies | Headingley | 06/06/91 |
| P.A.J.DeFreitas | 4-59 | England | W Indies | Headingley | 06/06/91 |
| C.A.Walsh | 4-64 | W Indies | England | Trent Bridge | 04/07/91 |
| C.E.L.Ambrose | 4-87 | W Indies | England | Lord's | 20/06/91 |
| S.L.Watkin | 3-38 | England | W Indies | Headingley | 06/06/91 |
| M.D.Marshall | 3-46 | W Indies | England | Headingley | 06/06/91 |
| P.A.J.DeFreitas | 3-54 | England | W Indies | Edgbaston | 25/07/91 |
| M.D.Marshall | 3-58 | W Indies | England | Headingley | 06/06/91 |
| C.E.L.Ambrose | 3-61 | W Indies | England | Trent Bridge | 04/07/91 |
| C.E.L.Ambrose | 3-64 | W Indies | England | Edgbaston | 25/07/91 |
| B.P.Patterson | 3-67 | W Indies | England | Headingley | 06/06/91 |
| P.A.J.DeFreitas | 3-67 | England | W Indies | Trent Bridge | 04/07/91 |
| C.E.L.Ambrose | 3-83 | W Indies | England | The Oval | 08/08/91 |
| C.A.Walsh | 3-91 | W Indies | England | The Oval | 08/08/91 |
| R.K.Illingworth | 3-110 | England | W Indies | Trent Bridge | 04/07/91 |
| S.D.Anurasiri | 3-135 | S Lanka | England | Lord's | 22/08/91 |
| D.R.Pringle | 2-14 | England | W Indies | Headingley | 06/06/91 |
| C.C.Lewis | 2-31 | England | S Lanka | Lord's | 22/08/91 |
| D.R.Pringle | 2-38 | England | W Indies | Headingley | 06/06/91 |
| P.A.J.DeFreitas | 2-40 | England | W Indies | Edgbaston | 25/07/91 |
| I.T.Botham | 2-40 | England | W Indies | The Oval | 08/08/91 |
| C.E.L.Ambrose | 2-42 | W Indies | England | Edgbaston | 25/07/91 |
| P.A.J.DeFreitas | 2-42 | England | W Indies | The Oval | 08/08/91 |
| C.A.Walsh | 2-43 | W Indies | England | Edgbaston | 25/07/91 |
| S.D.Anurasiri | 2-45 | S Lanka | England | Lord's | 22/08/91 |
| C.E.L.Ambrose | 2-49 | W Indies | England | Headingley | 06/06/91 |
| M.D.Marshall | 2-49 | W Indies | England | Trent Bridge | 04/07/91 |
| M.D.Marshall | 2-53 | W Indies | England | Edgbaston | 25/07/91 |
| M.D.Marshall | 2-54 | W Indies | England | Trent Bridge | 04/07/91 |
| S.L.Watkin | 2-55 | England | W Indies | Headingley | 06/06/91 |
| D.V.Lawrence | 2-61 | England | S Lanka | Lord's | 22/08/91 |
| B.P.Patterson | 2-63 | W Indies | England | The Oval | 08/08/91 |
| D.V.Lawrence | 2-67 | England | W Indies | The Oval | 08/08/91 |
| I.B.A.Allen | 2-69 | W Indies | England | Trent Bridge | 04/07/91 |
| D.R.Pringle | 2-71 | England | W Indies | Trent Bridge | 04/07/91 |
| C.P.Ramanayake | 2-75 | S Lanka | England | Lord's | 22/08/91 |
| G.A.Hick | 2-77 | England | W Indies | Lord's | 20/06/91 |
| M.D.Marshall | 2-78 | W Indies | England | Lord's | 20/06/91 |
| D.V.Lawrence | 2-83 | England | S Lanka | Lord's | 22/08/91 |

### 20 Best Match Bowling Figures

| Name | Figures | For | Against | Venue | Date |
|------|---------|-----|---------|-------|------|
| P.A.J.DeFreitas | 8-93 | England | W Indies | Headingley | 06/06/91 |
| C.E.L.Ambrose | 8-101 | W Indies | England | Headingley | 06/06/91 |
| P.A.J.DeFreitas | 8-115 | England | S Lanka | Lord's | 22/08/91 |
| C.E.L.Ambrose | 8-135 | W Indies | England | Trent Bridge | 04/07/91 |
| D.V.Lawrence | 7-173 | England | W Indies | The Oval | 08/08/91 |
| P.C.R.Tufnell | 7-175 | England | W Indies | The Oval | 08/08/91 |
| M.D.Marshall | 6-86 | W Indies | England | Edgbaston | 25/07/91 |
| M.D.Marshall | 6-104 | W Indies | England | Headingley | 06/06/91 |
| B.P.Patterson | 6-120 | W Indies | England | Edgbaston | 25/07/91 |
| C.C.Lewis | 6-156 | England | W Indies | Edgbaston | 25/07/91 |
| S.L.Watkin | 5-93 | England | W Indies | Headingley | 06/06/91 |
| P.A.J.DeFreitas | 5-94 | England | W Indies | Edgbaston | 25/07/91 |
| D.R.Pringle | 5-100 | England | W Indies | Lord's | 20/06/91 |
| C.E.L.Ambrose | 5-106 | W Indies | England | Edgbaston | 25/07/91 |
| P.C.R.Tufnell | 5-117 | England | S Lanka | Lord's | 22/08/91 |
| C.A.Walsh | 5-139 | W Indies | England | Trent Bridge | 04/07/91 |
| R.J.Ratnayake | 5-160 | S Lanka | England | Lord's | 22/08/91 |
| S.D.Anurasiri | 5-180 | S Lanka | England | Lord's | 22/08/91 |
| D.R.Pringle | 4-52 | England | W Indies | Headingley | 06/06/91 |
| C.E.L.Ambrose | 4-87 | W Indies | England | Lord's | 20/06/91 |

# BRITANNIC ASURANCE CHAMPIONSHIP

## BATTING
### 250 Best Individual Scores

| Name | Score | For | Against | Venue | Date |
|------|-------|-----|---------|-------|------|
| G.A.Gooch | 259 | Essex | Middx | Chelmsford | 17/09/91 |
| M.R.Benson | 257 | Kent | Hants | Southampton | 27/04/91 |
| A.P.Wells | 253 * | Sussex | Yorks | Midd'brough | 09/08/91 |
| T.S.Curtis | 248 | Worcs | Som | Worcester | 03/09/91 |
| M.P.Maynard | 243 | Glam | Hants | Southampton | 17/09/91 |
| T.R.Ward | 235 * | Kent | Middx | Canterbury | 28/08/91 |
| K.J.Barnett | 217 | Derby | Notts | Derby | 10/09/91 |
| M.W.Gatting | 215 * | Middx | Derby | Lord's | 09/08/91 |
| Salim Malik | 215 | Essex | Leics | Ilford | 04/06/91 |
| M.Azharuddin | 212 | Derby | Leics | Leicester | 28/08/91 |
| S.J.Cook | 210 * | Som | N'hants | Northampton | 23/07/91 |
| T.M.Moody | 210 | Worcs | W'wicks | Worcester | 02/08/91 |
| M.P.Maynard | 204 | Glam | Notts | Cardiff | 02/07/91 |
| N.R.Taylor | 203 * | Kent | Sussex | Hove | 03/09/91 |
| M.D.Moxon | 200 | Yorks | Essex | Colchester | 20/08/91 |
| S.J.Cook | 197 | Som | Hants | Southampton | 28/08/91 |
| N.Hussain | 196 | Essex | Leics | Leicester | 10/09/91 |
| A.J.Lamb | 194 | N'hants | Surrey | Northampton | 23/08/91 |
| S.J.Cook | 193 * | Som | Essex | Southend | 19/07/91 |
| N.J.Lenham | 193 | Sussex | Leics | Hove | 19/07/91 |
| P.J.Prichard | 190 | Essex | N'hants | Northampton | 09/05/91 |
| P.E.Robinson | 189 | Yorks | Lancs | Scarborough | 03/09/91 |
| T.S.Curtis | 186 * | Worcs | Glam | Cardiff | 10/09/91 |
| G.A.Hick | 186 | Worcs | Sussex | Hove | 14/06/91 |
| Salim Malik | 185 * | Essex | Surrey | The Oval | 05/07/91 |
| C.J.Tavare | 183 | Som | Glos | Bristol | 10/09/91 |
| T.M.Moody | 181 * | Worcs | Essex | Ilford | 07/06/91 |
| M.W.Gatting | 180 | Middx | Som | Taunton | 25/05/91 |
| R.T.Robinson | 180 | Notts | Worcs | Trent Bridge | 17/09/91 |
| G.P.Thorpe | 177 | Surrey | Sussex | The Oval | 28/08/91 |
| M.W.Gatting | 174 | Middx | Kent | Canterbury | 28/08/91 |
| Salim Malik | 173 | Essex | Kent | Folkestone | 16/05/91 |
| G.A.Gooch | 173 | Essex | N'hants | Colchester | 16/08/91 |
| A.N.Hayhurst | 172 * | Som | Glos | Bath | 21/06/91 |
| V.P.Terry | 171 | Hants | Sussex | Hove | 16/05/91 |
| B.C.Broad | 166 | Notts | Kent | Trent Bridge | 22/05/91 |
| A.Fordham | 165 | N'hants | Yorks | Northampton | 28/08/91 |
| Salim Malik | 165 | Essex | Derby | Chelmsford | 03/09/91 |
| M.W.Alleyne | 165 | Glos | N'hants | Bristol | 03/09/91 |
| Salim Malik | 163 | Essex | Glos | Bristol | 31/05/91 |
| C.J.Tavare | 162 | Som | Glam | Swansea | 04/06/91 |
| B.C.Broad | 162 | Notts | Worcs | Worcester | 18/06/91 |
| A.P.Wells | 162 | Sussex | Kent | Hove | 03/09/91 |
| M.Azharuddin | 160 * | Derby | Lancs | Derby | 16/08/91 |
| N.E.Briers | 160 | Leics | Notts | Trent Bridge | 09/05/91 |
| M.R.Benson | 160 | Kent | Derby | Canterbury | 25/05/91 |
| A.P.Wells | 159 | Sussex | Som | Hove | 16/07/91 |
| B.C.Broad | 158 | Notts | Sussex | Eastbourne | 06/08/91 |
| A.C.Seymour | 157 | Essex | Glam | Cardiff | 23/07/91 |
| D.A.Leatherdale | 157 | Worcs | Som | Worcester | 03/09/91 |
| H.Morris | 156 * | Glam | Sussex | Cardiff | 25/05/91 |
| H.Morris | 156 * | Glam | Yorks | Headingley | 16/08/91 |
| M.Azharuddin | 154 | Derby | Glos | Gloucester | 18/06/91 |
| A.P.Wells | 153 * | Sussex | Glam | Cardiff | 25/05/91 |
| D.Byas | 153 | Yorks | Notts | Worksop | 23/07/91 |
| N.J.Speak | 153 | Lancs | Surrey | Old Trafford | 17/09/91 |
| S.J.Cook | 152 | Som | Glam | Swansea | 04/06/91 |
| D.J.Bicknell | 151 | Surrey | Kent | Canterbury | 02/08/91 |
| D.M.Ward | 151 | Surrey | Lancs | Old Trafford | 17/09/91 |
| N.R.Taylor | 150 | Kent | Leics | Leicester | 09/08/91 |
| T.J.G.O'Gorman | 148 | Derby | Lancs | Old Trafford | 16/05/91 |
| A.R.Butcher | 147 | Glam | Glos | Abergavenny | 28/08/91 |
| N.R.Taylor | 146 | Kent | Derby | Canterbury | 25/05/91 |
| D.J.Bicknell | 145 * | Surrey | Essex | Chelmsford | 27/04/91 |
| C.L.Smith | 145 | Ham | Sussex | Hove | 16/05/91 |
| P.Pollard | 145 | Notts | Lancs | Trent Bridge | 16/07/91 |
| G.A.Hick | 145 | Worcs | Surrey | Worcester | 16/07/91 |
| R.T.Robinson | 145 | Notts | Derby | Derby | 10/09/91 |
| M.W.Gatting | 143 * | Middx | Notts | Lord's | 26/07/91 |
| D.W.Randall | 143 * | Notts | Derby | Trent Bridge | 23/08/91 |
| K.R.Brown | 143 * | Middx | Notts | Trent Bridge | 03/09/91 |
| M.R.Benson | 142 | Kent | Surrey | Canterbury | 02/08/91 |
| M.A.Lynch | 141 * | Surrey | Middx | The Oval | 20/08/91 |
| H.Morris | 141 | Glam | Som | Taunton | 09/05/91 |
| T.R.Ward | 141 | Kent | Essex | Folkestone | 16/05/91 |
| G.A.Hick | 141 | Worcs | Hants | Portsmouth | 16/07/91 |
| N.Hussain | 141 | Essex | N'hants | Colchester | 16/08/91 |
| Asif Din | 140 | W'wicks | Leics | Leicester | 26/07/91 |
| A.Dale | 140 | Glam | Glos | Abergavenny | 28/08/91 |
| M.W.Gatting | 138 * | Middx | Essex | Lord's | 28/06/91 |
| B.C.Broad | 137 * | Notts | Surrey | The Oval | 04/06/91 |
| A.P.Wells | 137 | Sussex | Middx | Hove | 22/05/91 |
| N.J.Lenham | 137 | Sussex | Kent | Tunbridge W | 07/06/91 |
| D.J.Bicknell | 136 | Surrey | Hants | The Oval | 03/09/91 |
| T.M.Moody | 135 | Worcs | Lancs | Worcester | 09/05/91 |
| D.Byas | 135 | Yorks | Derby | Scarborough | 16/07/91 |
| T.M.Moody | 135 | Worcs | Middx | Worcester | 23/08/91 |
| S.P.Titchard | 135 | Lancs | Notts | Old Trafford | 28/08/91 |
| K.D.James | 134 * | Hants | Yorks | Southampton | 05/07/91 |
| R.J.Harden | 134 | Som | Derby | Derby | 22/05/91 |
| C.J.Tavare | 134 | Som | Sussex | Hove | 16/07/91 |
| M.P.Maynard | 133 * | Glam | Som | Taunton | 09/05/91 |
| R.J.Shastri | 133 * | Glam | Lancs | Liverpool | 28/06/91 |
| J.D.R.Benson | 133 * | Leics | Hants | Bournemouth | 16/08/91 |
| A.J.Moles | 133 | W'wicks | Glos | Edgbaston | 25/05/91 |
| N.E.Briers | 133 | Leics | N'hants | Leicester | 05/07/91 |
| H.Morris | 132 | Glam | N'hants | Cardiff | 22/05/91 |
| N.A.Stanley | 132 | N'hants | Lancs | Lytham | 06/08/91 |
| A.Fordham | 131 | N'hants | Derby | Derby | 27/04/91 |
| S.J.Cook | 131 | Som | Lancs | Taunton | 02/07/91 |
| B.C.Broad | 131 | Notts | Som | Trent Bridge | 16/08/91 |
| H.Morris | 131 | Glam | Hants | Southampton | 17/09/91 |
| J.P.Crawley | 130 | Lancs | Surrey | Old Trafford | 17/09/91 |
| M.Azharuddin | 129 * | Derby | Notts | Trent Bridge | 23/08/91 |
| A.R.Butcher | 129 | Glam | Lancs | Liverpool | 28/06/91 |
| P.J.Prichard | 129 | Essex | Middx | Lord's | 28/06/91 |
| M.P.Maynard | 129 | Glam | Glos | Cheltenham | 19/07/91 |
| N.Hussain | 128 | Essex | Surrey | The Oval | 05/07/91 |
| P.J.Prichard | 128 | Essex | Yorks | Colchester | 20/08/91 |
| R.J.Scott | 127 | Glos | Worcs | Worcester | 27/04/91 |
| M.P.Maynard | 127 | Glam | Sussex | Cardiff | 25/05/91 |
| C.W.J.Athey | 127 | Glos | Lancs | Bristol | 09/08/91 |
| S.J.Cook | 127 | Som | W'wicks | Taunton | 17/09/91 |
| D.M.Smith | 126 * | Sussex | Middx | Hove | 22/05/91 |
| D.J.Bicknell | 126 | Surrey | Sussex | Arundel | 02/07/91 |
| M.P.Maynard | 126 | Glam | Glos | Cheltenham | 19/07/91 |
| S.J.Cook | 126 | Som | Kent | Taunton | 26/07/91 |
| S.A.Kellett | 125 * | York | Derby | Chesterfield | 17/09/91 |
| C.L.Smith | 125 | Hants | Glos | Bristol | 09/05/91 |
| I.J.F.Hutchinson | 125 | Middx | Sussex | Hove | 22/05/91 |
| D.J.Bicknell | 125 | Surrey | Notts | The Oval | 04/06/91 |
| A.J.Lamb | 125 | N'hants | Lancs | Lytham | 06/08/91 |
| V.P.Terry | 124 | Ham | W'wicks | Portsmouth | 19/07/91 |
| P.Johnson | 124 | Notts | Essex | Trent Bridge | 09/08/91 |
| A.A.Metcalfe | 123 | York | Glam | Headingley | 16/08/91 |
| P.Pollard | 123 | Notts | Derby | Derby | 10/09/91 |
| M.A.Garnham | 123 | Essex | Leics | Leicester | 10/09/91 |
| J.E.Morris | 122 * | Derby | Glam | Chesterfield | 07/06/91 |
| D.Byas | 122 * | Yorks | Leics | Leicester | 06/08/91 |
| K.J.Barnett | 122 | Derby | N'hants | Northampton | 31/05/91 |
| Wasim Akram | 122 | Lancs | Hants | Basingstoke | 04/06/91 |
| P.J.Prichard | 122 | Essex | Kent | Southend | 16/07/91 |
| R.J.Scott | 122 | Glos | Glam | Cheltenham | 19/07/91 |
| N.H.Fairbrother | 121 | Lancs | W'wicks | Edgbaston | 27/04/91 |
| D.W.Randall | 121 | Notts | Middx | Trent Bridge | 03/09/91 |
| D.P.Ostler | 120 * | W'wicks | Kent | Tunbridge W | 04/06/91 |
| A.P.Wells | 120 | Sussex | Middx | Lord's | 09/05/91 |
| C.W.J.Athey | 120 | Glos | W'wicks | Edgbaston | 25/05/91 |
| D.W.Randall | 120 | Notts | Lancs | Trent Bridge | 16/07/91 |
| A.J.Wright | 120 | Glos | Worcs | Cheltenham | 26/07/91 |
| T.S.Curtis | 120 | Worcs | Lancs | Blackpool | 20/08/91 |
| M.W.Gatting | 120 | Middx | Worcs | Worcester | 23/08/91 |
| D.Byas | 120 | Yorks | Lancs | Scarborough | 03/09/91 |
| M.A.Roseberry | 119 * | Middx | Leics | Uxbridge | 07/06/91 |
| M.R.Ramprakash | 119 | Middx | Sussex | Lord's | 09/05/91 |
| G.D.Mendis | 119 | Lancs | W'wicks | Old Trafford | 23/07/91 |
| T.M.Moody | 118 | Worcs | Glam | Worcester | 31/05/91 |

# BRITANNIC ASURANCE CHAMPIONSHIP

| Name | Score | For | Against | Venue | Date |
|---|---|---|---|---|---|
| J.W.Hall | 117* | Sussex | Som | Taunton | 27/04/91 |
| M.W.Gatting | 117* | Middx | Sussex | Hove | 22/05/91 |
| R.J.Bailey | 117 | N'hants | Som | Northampton | 23/07/91 |
| M.A.Garnham | 117 | Essex | Derby | Chelmsford | 03/09/91 |
| G.P.Thorpe | 117 | Surrey | Middx | Lord's | 10/09/91 |
| G.P.Thorpe | 116* | Surrey | N'hants | Northampton | 23/08/91 |
| A.N.Hayhurst | 116 | Som | Derby | Derby | 22/05/91 |
| A.Fordham | 116 | N'hants | Leics | Leicester | 05/07/91 |
| J.P.Stephenson | 116 | Essex | Yorks | Colchester | 20/08/91 |
| S.J.Cook | 115* | Som | Hants | Southampton | 28/08/91 |
| M.D.Moxon | 115 | Yorks | Lancs | Scarborough | 03/09/91 |
| P.N.Hepworth | 115 | Leics | Essex | Leicester | 10/09/91 |
| M.Watkinson | 114* | Lancs | Surrey | The Oval | 22/05/91 |
| M.A.Atherton | 114* | Lancs | Yorks | Old Trafford | 02/08/91 |
| P.Whitticase | 114* | Leics | Hants | Bournemouth | 16/08/91 |
| G.R.Cowdrey | 114 | Kent | W'wicks | Tunbridge W | 04/06/91 |
| I.J.F.Hutchinson | 114 | Middx | Glos | Bristol | 04/06/91 |
| C.L.Smith | 114 | Hants | Derby | Chesterfield | 23/07/91 |
| N.E.Briers | 114 | Leics | Yorks | Leicester | 06/08/91 |
| P.Johnson | 114 | Notts | Lancs | Old Trafford | 28/08/91 |
| G.D.Mendis | 114 | Lancs | Yorks | Scarborough | 03/09/91 |
| J.P.Stephenson | 113* | Essex | Kent | Southend | 16/07/91 |
| S.A.Marsh | 113* | Kent | Som | Taunton | 26/07/91 |
| A.A.Metcalfe | 113* | Yorks | Lancs | Old Trafford | 02/08/91 |
| G.D.Mendis | 113 | Lancs | W'wicks | Edgbaston | 27/04/91 |
| G.Fowler | 113 | Lancs | Surrey | The Oval | 22/05/91 |
| M.V.Fleming | 113 | Kent | Surrey | Canterbury | 02/08/91 |
| J.P.Stephenson | 113 | Essex | Leics | Leicester | 10/09/91 |
| D.W.Randall | 112* | Notts | Glam | Cardiff | 02/07/91 |
| C.L.Smith | 112 | Hants | Yorks | Southampton | 05/07/91 |
| C.J.Adams | 112 | Derby | Yorks | Chesterfield | 17/09/91 |
| R.C.Russell | 111 | Glos | Hants | Bristol | 09/05/91 |
| P.W.G.Parker | 111 | Sussex | Kent | Hove | 03/09/91 |
| N.R.Taylor | 111 | Kent | Sussex | Hove | 03/09/91 |
| M.A.Atherton | 110 | Lancs | Worcs | Worcester | 09/05/91 |
| T.R.Ward | 110 | Kent | Glam | Maidstone | 05/07/91 |
| M.Azharuddin | 110 | Derby | Middx | Lord's | 09/08/91 |
| M.R.Ramprakash | 110 | Middx | Notts | Trent Bridge | 03/09/91 |
| G.R.Cowdrey | 109* | Kent | Notts | Trent Bridge | 22/05/91 |
| N.H.Fairbrother | 109 | Lancs | Worcs | Worcester | 09/05/91 |
| N.H.Fairbrother | 109 | Lancs | Som | Taunton | 02/07/91 |
| T.R.Ward | 109 | Kent | Glam | Maidstone | 05/07/91 |
| A.J.Stewart | 109 | Surrey | Glos | Guildford | 16/07/91 |
| N.R.Taylor | 109 | Kent | Glos | Canterbury | 20/08/91 |
| A.J.Lamb | 109 | N'hants | Yorks | Northampton | 28/08/91 |
| S.A.Marsh | 108* | Kent | Middx | Lord's | 31/05/91 |
| T.J.G.O'Gorman | 108* | Derby | Notts | Derby | 10/09/91 |
| M.D.Moxon | 108 | Yorks | N'hants | Headingley | 25/05/91 |
| N.D.Burns | 108 | Som | Notts | Trent Bridge | 16/08/91 |
| M.C.J.Nicholas | 107* | Hants | Notts | Trent Bridge | 31/05/91 |
| S.J.Cook | 107* | Som | Hants | Bath | 18/06/91 |
| N.A.Foster | 107* | Essex | Sussex | Horsham | 21/06/91 |
| N.H.Fairbrother | 107* | Lancs | Glam | Liverpool | 28/06/91 |
| A.P.Wells | 107 | Sussex | Kent | Tunbridge W | 07/06/91 |
| T.M.Moody | 107 | Worcs | Notts | Worcester | 18/06/91 |
| R.J.Shastri | 107 | Glam | Leics | Neath | 21/06/91 |
| R.A.Smith | 107 | Hants | Som | Southampton | 28/08/91 |
| G.P.Thorpe | 106* | Surrey | Glam | The Oval | 26/07/91 |
| G.A.Gooch | 106 | Essex | Middx | Lord's | 28/06/91 |
| N.J.Lenham | 106 | Sussex | Som | Hove | 16/07/91 |
| G.D.Rose | 106 | Som | Glos | Bristol | 10/09/91 |
| G.D.Rose | 105* | Som | Yorks | Taunton | 23/08/91 |
| A.Fordham | 105 | N'hants | Derby | Northampton | 31/05/91 |
| M.R.Benson | 105 | Kent | W'wicks | Tunbridge W | 04/06/91 |
| P.Johnson | 105 | Notts | Middx | Lord's | 26/07/91 |
| J.J.Whitaker | 105 | Leics | Essex | Leicester | 10/09/91 |
| P.D.Bowler | 104* | Derby | Lancs | Derby | 16/08/91 |
| D.W.Randall | 104 | Notts | Leics | Trent Bridge | 09/05/91 |
| I.T.Botham | 104 | Worcs | Lancs | Worcester | 09/05/91 |
| A.R.Butcher | 104 | Glam | Lancs | Liverpool | 28/06/91 |
| N.E.Briers | 104 | Leics | Worcs | Worcester | 28/06/91 |
| P.D.Bowler | 104 | Derby | Leics | Leicester | 28/08/91 |
| G.Fowler | 103* | Lancs | Derby | Old Trafford | 16/05/91 |
| M.P.Maynard | 103* | Glam | Surrey | The Oval | 26/07/91 |
| C.W.J.Athey | 103* | Glos | Sussex | Hove | 17/09/91 |
| N.H.Fairbrother | 102* | Lancs | Som | Taunton | 02/07/91 |
| A.R.Butcher | 102 | Glam | Som | Swansea | 04/06/91 |
| T.C.Middleton | 102 | Hants | Som | Bath | 18/06/91 |
| Salim Malik | 102 | Essex | Som | Southend | 19/07/91 |
| T.J.Boon | 102 | Leics | Yorks | Leicester | 06/08/91 |
| A.J.Wright | 101* | Glos | Surrey | Guildford | 16/07/91 |
| N.V.Knight | 101* | Essex | Lancs | Old Trafford | 23/08/91 |
| I.D.Austin | 101* | Lancs | Yorks | Scarborough | 03/09/91 |
| P.M.Roebuck | 101 | Som | Glam | Taunton | 09/05/91 |
| C.L.Smith | 101 | Hants | Sussex | Hove | 16/05/91 |
| R.T.Robinson | 101 | Notts | Leics | Leicester | 25/05/91 |
| C.W.J.Athey | 101 | Glos | Derby | Gloucester | 18/06/91 |
| K.D.James | 101 | Hants | Derby | Chesterfield | 23/07/91 |
| R.J.Harden | 101 | Som | Notts | Trent Bridge | 16/08/91 |
| N.R.Taylor | 101 | Kent | Middx | Canterbury | 28/08/91 |
| A.J.Wright | 100* | Glos | Yorks | Sheffield | 22/05/91 |
| A.I.C.Dodemaide | 100* | Sussex | Glam | Cardiff | 25/05/91 |
| M.W.Gatting | 100* | Middx | N'hants | Uxbridge | 16/07/91 |
| A.N.Hayhurst | 100* | Som | Notts | Trent Bridge | 16/08/91 |
| P.Bent | 100* | Worcs | Lancs | Blackpool | 20/08/91 |
| G.Yates | 100* | Lancs | Essex | Old Trafford | 23/08/91 |
| P.Pollard | 100 | Notts | Hants | Trent Bridge | 31/05/91 |
| M.Azharuddin | 100 | Derby | W'wicks | Edgbaston | 28/06/91 |
| Asif Din | 100 | W'wicks | Lancs | Old Trafford | 23/07/91 |
| C.J.Tavare | 100 | Som | Kent | Taunton | 26/07/91 |
| R.P.Lefebvre | 100 | Som | Worcs | Weston | 06/08/91 |
| D.A.Reeve | 99* | W'wicks | Yorks | Edgbaston | 31/05/91 |
| J.J.Whitaker | 99 | Leics | N'hants | Northampton | 16/05/91 |
| J.E.Morris | 99 | Derby | W'wicks | Edgbaston | 28/06/91 |
| A.Dale | 99 | Glam | W'wicks | Edgbaston | 28/06/91 |
| P.D.Bowler | 99 | Derby | Notts | Trent Bridge | 23/08/91 |
| K.J.Barnett | 99 | Derby | Essex | Chelmsford | 03/09/91 |
| M.A.Roseberry | 99 | Middx | Essex | Chelmsford | 17/09/91 |

# BRITANNIC ASURANCE CHAMPIONSHIP

## BOWLING
### 250 Best Innings Bowling Figures

| Name | Figures | For | Against | Venue | Date |
|---|---|---|---|---|---|
| D.J.Millns | 9-37 | Leics | Derby | Derby | 20/08/91 |
| D.G.Cork | 8-53 | Derby | Essex | Derby | 06/08/91 |
| D.R.Gilbert | 8-55 | Glos | Kent | Canterbury | 20/08/91 |
| T.A.Munton | 8-89 | W'wicks | Middx | Edgbaston | 02/07/91 |
| N.A.Foster | 8-99 | Essex | Lancs | Old Trafford | 23/08/91 |
| R.M.Ellison | 7-33 | Kent | W'wicks | Tunbridge W | 04/06/91 |
| C.M.Wells | 7-42 | Sussex | Derby | Derby | 05/07/91 |
| N.V.Radford | 7-43 | Worcs | Som | Worcester | 03/09/91 |
| M.P.Bicknell | 7-52 | Surrey | Sussex | The Oval | 28/08/91 |
| I.T.Botham | 7-54 | Worcs | W'wicks | Worcester | 02/08/91 |
| J.N.Maguire | 7-57 | Leics | Kent | Leicester | 09/08/91 |
| T.A.Munton | 7-59 | W'wicks | Worcs | Edgbaston | 28/08/91 |
| J.E.Emburey | 7-71 | Middx | Sussex | Hove | 22/05/91 |
| Waqar Younis | 7-87 | Surrey | Glos | Guildford | 16/07/91 |
| E.A.E.Baptiste | 7-95 | N'hants | Yorks | Northampton | 28/08/91 |
| M.Frost | 7-99 | Glam | Glos | Cheltenham | 19/07/91 |
| T.A.Merrick | 7-99 | Kent | Sussex | Hove | 03/09/91 |
| D.A.Graveney | 7-105 | Som | Kent | Taunton | 26/07/91 |
| P.C.R.Tufnell | 7-116 | Middx | Hants | Lord's | 02/08/91 |
| K.J.Barnett | 6-28 | Derby | Glam | Chesterfield | 07/06/91 |
| P.C.R.Tufnell | 6-34 | Middx | Glos | Bristol | 04/06/91 |
| Waqar Younis | 6-40 | Surrey | Yorks | Guildford | 19/07/91 |
| N.A.Mallender | 6-43 | Som | Glos | Bath | 21/06/91 |
| Waqar Younis | 6-45 | Surrey | Hants | The Oval | 03/09/91 |
| E.E.Hemmings | 6-46 | Notts | Lancs | Trent Bridge | 16/07/91 |
| Waqar Younis | 6-47 | Surrey | Hants | The Oval | 03/09/91 |
| J.D.Batty | 6-48 | Yorks | Notts | Worksop | 23/07/91 |
| H.R.J.Trump | 6-48 | Som | Worcs | Weston | 06/08/91 |
| T.A.Munton | 6-53 | W'wicks | Yorks | Edgbaston | 31/05/91 |
| S.L.Watkin | 6-55 | Glam | N'hants | Cardiff | 22/05/91 |
| E.A.E.Baptiste | 6-57 | N'hants | Kent | Maidstone | 02/07/91 |
| D.J.Millns | 6-59 | Leics | Yorks | Leicester | 06/08/91 |
| J.H.Childs | 6-61 | Essex | N'hants | Colchester | 16/08/91 |
| B.T.P.Donelan | 6-62 | Sussex | Glos | Hove | 17/09/91 |
| Waqar Younis | 6-65 | Surrey | Lancs | The Oval | 22/05/91 |
| Waqar Younis | 6-66 | Surrey | Hants | Bournemouth | 25/05/91 |
| Wasim Akram | 6-66 | Lancs | Middx | Uxbridge | 19/07/91 |
| D.V.Lawrence | 6-67 | Glos | N'hants | Luton | 28/06/91 |
| J.H.Childs | 6-68 | Essex | Derby | Chelmsford | 03/09/91 |
| N.A.Mallender | 6-68 | Som | W'wicks | Taunton | 17/09/91 |
| A.A.Donald | 6-69 | W'wicks | N'hants | Edgbaston | 10/09/91 |
| S.D.Fletcher | 6-70 | Yorks | W'wicks | Edgbaston | 31/05/91 |
| Waqar Younis | 6-72 | Surrey | Kent | Canterbury | 02/08/91 |
| A.R.Roberts | 6-72 | N'hants | Lancs | Lytham | 06/08/91 |
| D.A.Reeve | 6-73 | W'wicks | Kent | Tunbridge W | 04/06/91 |
| N.V.Radford | 6-76 | Worcs | Essex | Ilford | 07/06/91 |
| D.V.Lawrence | 6-77 | Glos | Hants | Bristol | 09/05/91 |
| P.C.R.Tufnell | 6-82 | Middx | Leics | Uxbridge | 07/06/91 |
| D.J.Foster | 6-84 | Glam | Som | Taunton | 09/05/91 |
| A.A.Donald | 6-84 | W'wicks | Som | Taunton | 17/09/91 |
| J.N.Maguire | 6-85 | Leics | Essex | Ilford | 04/06/91 |
| Wasim Akram | 6-86 | Lancs | Kent | Old Trafford | 21/06/91 |
| P.A.J.DeFreitas | 6-88 | Lancs | Worcs | Worcester | 09/05/91 |
| M.J.McCague | 6-88 | Kent | Leics | Leicester | 09/08/91 |
| Aqib Javed | 6-91 | Hants | Notts | Trent Bridge | 31/05/91 |
| B.T.P.Donelan | 6-92 | Sussex | Leics | Hove | 19/07/91 |
| J.W.Lloyds | 6-94 | Glos | N'hants | Luton | 28/06/91 |
| O.H.Mortensen | 6-101 | Derby | Worcs | Kidd'minster | 19/07/91 |
| N.A.Foster | 6-104 | Essex | Middx | Chelmsford | 17/09/91 |
| H.R.J.Trump | 6-107 | Som | Leics | Weston | 02/08/91 |
| H.R.J.Trump | 6-121 | Som | Hants | Southampton | 28/08/91 |
| P.J.Hartley | 6-151 | Yorks | N'hants | Northampton | 28/08/91 |
| P.Carrick | 5-13 | Yorks | Worcs | Headingley | 02/07/91 |
| R.A.Pick | 5-17 | Notts | N'hants | Well'borough | 19/07/91 |
| P.C.R.Tufnell | 5-17 | Middx | Surrey | Lord's | 10/09/91 |
| J.H.Childs | 5-20 | Essex | Som | Southend | 19/07/91 |
| F.D.Stephenson | 5-27 | Notts | N'hants | Well'borough | 19/07/91 |
| P.A.Smith | 5-28 | W'wicks | Glos | Edgbaston | 25/05/91 |
| P.C.R.Tufnell | 5-30 | Middx | Notts | Trent Bridge | 03/09/91 |
| P.J.Hartley | 5-32 | Yorks | Middx | Sheffield | 21/06/91 |
| T.A.Munton | 5-32 | W'wicks | Leics | Leicester | 26/07/91 |
| A.A.Donald | 5-33 | W'wicks | Glos | Edgbaston | 25/05/91 |

| Name | Figures | For | Against | Venue | Date |
|---|---|---|---|---|---|
| C.C.Lewis | 5-35 | Leics | Glam | Leicester | 27/04/91 |
| A.A.Donald | 5-36 | W'wicks | Glam | Swansea | 16/05/91 |
| A.P.Igglesden | 5-36 | Kent | N'hants | Maidstone | 02/07/91 |
| A.C.S.Pigott | 5-37 | Sssex | Middx | Lord's | 09/05/91 |
| A.A.Donald | 5-38 | W'wicks | Glam | Swansea | 16/05/91 |
| S.Bastien | 5-39 | Glam | N'hants | Cardiff | 22/05/91 |
| M.A.Ealham | 5-39 | Kent | Sussex | Hove | 03/09/91 |
| I.D.K.Salisbury | 5-40 | Sussex | Kent | Tunbridge W | 07/06/91 |
| D.Gough | 5-41 | Yorks | Lancs | Scarborough | 03/09/91 |
| A.A.Donald | 5-42 | W'wicks | Yorks | Headingley | 09/05/91 |
| J.P.Taylor | 5-42 | N'hants | Leics | Northampton | 16/05/91 |
| G.A.Hick | 5-42 | Worcs | Glam | Cardiff | 10/09/91 |
| C.Penn | 5-43 | Kent | N'hants | Maidstone | 02/07/91 |
| K.J.Shine | 5-43 | Hants | Worcs | Portsmouth | 16/07/91 |
| D.E.Malcolm | 5-45 | Derby | W'wicks | Edgbaston | 28/06/91 |
| N.A.Foster | 5-45 | Essex | Hants | Chelmsford | 02/07/91 |
| D.W.Headley | 5-46 | Middx | Yorks | Lord's | 27/04/91 |
| A.N.Jones | 5-46 | Sussex | Yorks | Midd'brough | 09/08/91 |
| Waqar Younis | 5-47 | Surrey | W'wicks | Edgbaston | 06/08/91 |
| Aqib Javed | 5-47 | Hants | Sussex | Bournemouth | 20/08/91 |
| Wasim Akram | 5-48 | Lancs | Hants | Basingstoke | 04/06/91 |
| A.A.Donald | 5-48 | W'wicks | Sussex | Coventry | 18/06/91 |
| Aqib Javed | 5-49 | Hants | N'hants | Northampton | 21/06/91 |
| S.L.Watkin | 5-49 | Glam | Glos | Cheltenham | 19/07/91 |
| R.K.Illingworth | 5-49 | Worcs | Lancs | Blackpool | 20/08/91 |
| K.P.Evans | 5-52 | Notts | Leics | Trent Bridge | 09/05/91 |
| D.V.Lawrence | 5-52 | Glos | Hants | Bristol | 09/05/91 |
| Waqar Younis | 5-53 | Surrey | Middx | Lord's | 10/09/91 |
| A.A.Donald | 5-54 | W'wicks | Yorks | Headingley | 09/05/91 |
| N.A.Foster | 5-54 | Essex | Glos | Bristol | 31/05/91 |
| N.M.Kendrick | 5-54 | Surrey | Lancs | Old Trafford | 17/09/91 |
| N.A.Foster | 5-56 | Essex | Notts | Trent Bridge | 09/08/91 |
| Waqar Younis | 5-57 | Surrey | Lancs | The Oval | 22/05/91 |
| O.H.Mortensen | 5-57 | Derby | Notts | Northampton | 31/05/91 |
| Waqar Younis | 5-57 | Surrey | Leics | Leicester | 14/06/91 |
| T.D.Topley | 5-58 | Essex | Leics | Ilford | 04/06/91 |
| K.J.Shine | 5-58 | Hants | Glam | Swansea | 09/08/91 |
| S.L.Watkin | 5-59 | Glam | Notts | Cardiff | 02/07/91 |
| C.C.Lewis | 5-60 | Leics | Lancs | Leicester | 18/06/91 |
| K.M.Curran | 5-60 | N'hants | Notts | Well'borough | 19/07/91 |
| Wasim Akram | 5-61 | Lancs | Leics | Leicester | 18/06/91 |
| F.D.Stephenson | 5-61 | Notts | N'hants | Well'borough | 19/07/91 |
| Waqar Younis | 5-61 | Surrey | Middx | The Oval | 20/08/91 |
| R.D.B.Croft | 5-62 | Glam | W'wicks | Swansea | 16/05/91 |
| J.G.Thomas | 5-62 | N'hants | Leics | Northampton | 16/05/91 |
| S.L.Watkin | 5-63 | Glam | Som | Taunton | 09/05/91 |
| A.J.Murphy | 5-63 | Surrey | Essex | The Oval | 05/07/91 |
| Wasim Akram | 5-63 | Lancs | Middx | Uxbridge | 19/07/91 |
| F.D.Stephenson | 5-63 | Notts | Worcs | Trent Bridge | 17/09/91 |
| R.K.Illingworth | 5-64 | Worcs | Derby | Kidd'minster | 19/07/91 |
| H.R.J.Trump | 5-64 | Som | Glos | Bristol | 10/09/91 |
| M.A.Ealham | 5-65 | Kent | Leics | Canterbury | 17/09/91 |
| D.J.Millns | 5-65 | Leics | Kent | Canterbury | 17/09/91 |
| R.A.Pick | 5-66 | Notts | Leics | Leicester | 25/05/91 |
| K.P.Evans | 5-66 | Notts | Essex | Trent Bridge | 09/08/91 |
| I.T.Botham | 5-67 | Worcs | Surrey | Worcester | 16/08/91 |
| J.N.Maguire | 5-67 | Leics | Derby | Leicester | 28/08/91 |
| D.A.Graveney | 5-68 | Som | Derby | Derby | 22/05/91 |
| D.R.Pringle | 5-70 | Essex | N'hants | Northampton | 09/05/91 |
| Waqar Younis | 5-70 | Surrey | Hants | Bournemouth | 25/05/91 |
| S.R.Lampitt | 5-70 | Worcs | Surrey | Worcester | 16/08/91 |
| T.D.Topley | 5-71 | Essex | Surrey | Chelmsford | 27/04/91 |
| R.J.Shastri | 5-71 | Glam | W'wicks | Edgbaston | 20/08/91 |
| P.A.J.DeFreitas | 5-71 | Lancs | Notts | Old Trafford | 28/08/91 |
| F.D.Stephenson | 5-74 | Notts | Worcs | Worcester | 18/06/91 |
| R.M.Ellison | 5-77 | Kent | Middx | Lord's | 31/05/91 |
| T.A.Munton | 5-77 | W'wicks | Derby | Edgbaston | 28/06/91 |
| S.R.Lampitt | 5-78 | Worcs | Som | Worcester | 03/09/91 |
| T.D.Topley | 5-79 | Essex | Derby | Derby | 06/08/91 |
| N.A.Foster | 5-80 | Essex | W'wicks | Chelmsford | 22/05/91 |
| N.A.Mallender | 5-80 | Som | Worcs | Worcester | 03/09/91 |
| A.N.Jones | 5-84 | Sussex | Glos | Cheltenham | 23/07/91 |
| R.A.Pick | 5-86 | Notts | Middx | Trent Bridge | 03/09/91 |
| N.A.Foster | 5-86 | Essex | Leics | Leicester | 10/09/91 |
| S.R.Lampitt | 5-86 | Worcs | Notts | Trent Bridge | 17/09/91 |

# BRITANNIC ASURANCE CHAMPIONSHIP

| Name | Figures | For | Against | Venue | Date |
|---|---|---|---|---|---|
| N.F.Williams | 5-89 | Middx | Notts | Lord's | 26/07/91 |
| C.Penn | 5-90 | Kent | Leics | Canterbury | 17/09/91 |
| G.R.Dilley | 5-91 | Worcs | Lancs | Worcester | 09/05/91 |
| Wasim Akram | 5-91 | Lancs | Yorks | Old Trafford | 02/08/91 |
| E.A.E.Baptiste | 5-95 | N'hants | W'wicks | Edgbaston | 10/09/91 |
| D.W.Headley | 5-100 | Middx | Kent | Canterbury | 28/08/91 |
| P.J.Hartley | 5-100 | Yorks | Lancs | Scarborough | 03/09/91 |
| P.Carrick | 5-103 | Yorks | Sussex | Midd'brough | 09/08/91 |
| C.Penn | 5-105 | Kent | Middx | Canterbury | 28/08/91 |
| J.H.Childs | 5-112 | Essex | Surrey | The Oval | 05/07/91 |
| Wasim Akram | 5-117 | Lancs | Notts | Trent Bridge | 16/07/91 |
| N.M.Kendrick | 5-120 | Surrey | Lancs | Old Trafford | 17/09/91 |
| I.T.Botham | 5-125 | Worcs | Glos | Worcester | 27/04/91 |
| M.C.J.Ball | 5-128 | Glos | Kent | Canterbury | 20/08/91 |
| R.J.Maru | 5-128 | Hants | Glam | Southampton | 17/09/91 |
| A.I.C.Dodemaide | 5-130 | Sussex | Glos | Cheltenham | 23/07/91 |
| J.G.Thomas | 5-146 | N'hants | Essex | Northampton | 09/05/91 |
| R.W.Sladdin | 5-186 | Derby | Essex | Chelmsford | 03/09/91 |
| N.A.Foster | 4-18 | Essex | Middx | Chelmsford | 17/09/91 |
| A.R.C.Fraser | 4-24 | Middx | Kent | Lord's | 31/05/91 |
| P.Carrick | 4-25 | Yorks | N'hants | Headingley | 25/05/91 |
| D.G.Cork | 4-25 | Derby | Sussex | Derby | 05/07/91 |
| J.E.Emburey | 4-25 | Middx | Surrey | Lord's | 10/09/91 |
| D.A.Reeve | 4-27 | W'wicks | Hants | Portsmouth | 19/07/91 |
| P.A.Smith | 4-28 | W'wicks | Glos | Edgbaston | 25/05/91 |
| A.A.Donald | 4-28 | W'wicks | Yorks | Edgbaston | 31/05/91 |
| I.J.Turner | 4-28 | Hants | Derby | Chesterfield | 23/07/91 |
| P.W.Jarvis | 4-28 | Yorks | Derby | Chesterfield | 17/09/91 |
| C.J.Adams | 4-29 | Derby | Lancs | Derby | 16/08/91 |
| N.V.Radford | 4-29 | Worcs | Glam | Cardiff | 10/09/91 |
| P.J.Martin | 4-30 | Lancs | Worcs | Blackpool | 20/08/91 |
| K.D.James | 4-32 | Hants | Middx | Lord's | 02/08/91 |
| A.M.Babington | 4-33 | Glos | Lancs | Bristol | 09/08/91 |
| T.D.Topley | 4-34 | Essex | Glos | Bristol | 31/05/91 |
| S.J.Base | 4-34 | Derby | Yorks | Chesterfield | 17/09/91 |
| G.C.Small | 4-36 | W'wicks | Sussex | Coventry | 18/06/91 |
| N.A.Foster | 4-36 | Essex | Middx | Lord's | 28/06/91 |
| G.C.Small | 4-36 | W'wicks | Derby | Edgbaston | 28/06/91 |
| A.P.Igglesden | 4-36 | Kent | Essex | Southend | 16/07/91 |
| C.Penn | 4-36 | Kent | Surrey | Canterbury | 02/08/91 |
| M.A.Feltham | 4-36 | Surrey | Hants | The Oval | 03/09/91 |
| T.A.Merrick | 4-37 | Kent | Hants | Southampton | 27/04/91 |
| S.J.W.Andrew | 4-38 | EssexSS | W'wicks | Chelmsford | 22/05/91 |
| J.E.Emburey | 4-38 | Middx | Notts | Trent Bridge | 03/09/91 |
| K.M.Curran | 4-39 | N'hants | Derby | Northampton | 31/05/91 |
| R.M.Ellison | 4-39 | Kent | Middx | Lord's | 31/05/91 |
| G.R.Dilley | 4-39 | Worcs | Glos | Cheltenham | 26/07/91 |
| J.N.Maguire | 4-39 | Leics | Kent | Canterbury | 17/09/91 |
| S.L.Watkin | 4-40 | Glam | Worcs | Worcester | 31/05/91 |
| F.D.Stephenson | 4-40 | Notts | Glam | Cardiff | 02/07/91 |
| M.C.J.Ball | 4-40 | Glos | Lancs | Bristol | 09/08/91 |
| R.M.Ellison | 4-40 | Kent | Middx | Canterbury | 28/08/91 |
| A.M.Smith | 4-41 | Glos | Leics | Hinckley | 02/07/91 |
| M.A.Feltham | 4-41 | Surrey | W'wicks | Edgbaston | 06/08/91 |
| A.N.Jones | 4-41 | Sussex | Yorks | Midd'brough | 09/08/91 |
| A.E.Warner | 4-42 | Derby | Glam | Chesterfield | 07/06/91 |
| N.G.Cowans | 4-42 | Middx | Glam | Cardiff | 14/06/91 |
| Waqar Younis | 4-42 | Surrey | Middx | Lord's | 10/09/91 |
| S.J.Base | 4-43 | Derby | Kent | Canterbury | 25/05/91 |
| O.H.Mortensen | 4-43 | Derby | Surrey | Derby | 21/06/91 |
| J.A.Afford | 4-44 | Notts | Kent | Trent Bridge | 22/05/91 |
| N.G.Cowans | 4-44 | Middx | W'wicks | Edgbaston | 02/07/91 |
| M.Frost | 4-44 | Glam | Glos | Cheltenham | 19/07/91 |
| C.Penn | 4-44 | Kent | Middx | Canterbury | 28/08/91 |
| P.J.Newport | 4-44 | Worcs | Glam | Cardiff | 10/09/91 |
| C.C.Lewis | 4-45 | Leics | Surrey | Leicester | 14/06/91 |
| G.R.Dilley | 4-45 | Worcs | Glos | Cheltenham | 26/07/91 |
| A.P.Igglesden | 4-45 | Kent | Som | Taunton | 26/07/91 |
| M.Watkinson | 4-45 | Lancs | Surrey | Old Trafford | 17/09/91 |
| O.H.Mortensen | 4-46 | Derby | Lancs | Old Trafford | 16/05/91 |
| N.F.Williams | 4-46 | Middx | Som | Taunton | 25/05/91 |
| J.A.Afford | 4-46 | Notts | Lancs | Trent Bridge | 16/07/91 |
| D.A.Reeve | 4-46 | W'wicks | Hants | Portsmouth | 19/07/91 |
| T.A.Munton | 4-46 | W'wicks | Leics | Leicester | 26/07/91 |
| S.R.Barwick | 4-46 | Glam | Surrey | The Oval | 26/07/91 |
| A.P.Igglesden | 4-46 | Kent | Glos | Canterbury | 20/08/91 |
| O.H.Mortensen | 4-47 | Derby | Som | Derby | 22/05/91 |
| J.R.Ayling | 4-47 | Hants | Surrey | The Oval | 03/09/91 |
| C.Penn | 4-48 | Kent | Surrey | The Oval | 09/05/91 |
| P.Carrick | 4-48 | Yorks | Derby | Scarborough | 16/07/91 |
| C.A.Connor | 4-49 | Hants | Surrey | Bournemouth | 25/05/91 |
| S.R.Barwick | 4-49 | Glam | Middx | Cardiff | 14/06/91 |
| C.Penn | 4-50 | Kent | Surrey | The Oval | 09/05/91 |
| O.H.Mortensen | 4-50 | Derby | Hants | Chesterfield | 23/07/91 |
| Waqar Younis | 4-50 | Surrey | W'wicks | Edgbaston | 06/08/91 |
| I.T.Botham | 4-50 | Worcs | W'wicks | Edgbaston | 28/08/91 |
| P.J.Newport | 4-51 | Worcs | Middx | Worcester | 23/08/91 |
| A.C.S.Pigott | 4-52 | Sussex | Middx | Lord's | 09/05/91 |
| Waqar Younis | 4-52 | Surrey | Sussex | The Oval | 28/08/91 |
| K.M.Curran | 4-52 | N'hants | Glos | Bristol | 03/09/91 |
| S.R.Lampitt | 4-53 | Worcs | Middx | Worcester | 23/08/91 |
| M.Jean-Jacques | 4-54 | Derby | Kent | Canterbury | 25/05/91 |
| D.A.Reeve | 4-54 | W'wicks | Surrey | Edgbaston | 06/08/91 |
| T.A.Merrick | 4-55 | Kent | Derby | Canterbury | 25/05/91 |
| M.Frost | 4-55 | Glam | Middx | Cardiff | 14/06/91 |
| M.C.J.Ball | 4-55 | Glos | Lancs | Bristol | 09/08/91 |
| M.Watkinson | 4-55 | Lancs | Notts | Old Trafford | 28/08/91 |
| P.J.W.Allott | 4-56 | Lancs | Worcs | Worcester | 09/05/91 |
| K.T.Medlycott | 4-56 | Surrey | Sussex | Arundel | 02/07/91 |
| K.P.Evans | 4-56 | Notts | Yorks | Worksop | 23/07/91 |
| T.A.Munton | 4-57 | W'wicks | Yorks | Headingley | 09/05/91 |
| J.N.Maguire | 4-57 | Leics | N'hants | Leicester | 05/07/91 |

# BRITANNIC ASURANCE CHAMPIONSHIP

## BOWLING
### 100 Best Match Bowling Figures

| Name | Figures | For | Against | Venue | Date |
|---|---|---|---|---|---|
| D.J.Millns | 12-91 | Leics | Derby | Derby | 20/08/91 |
| Waqar Younis | 12-92 | Surrey | Hants | The Oval | 03/09/91 |
| Waqar Younis | 11-122 | Surrey | Lancs | The Oval | 22/05/91 |
| T.A.Munton | 11-127 | W'icks | Middx | Edgbaston | 02/07/91 |
| D.V.Lawrence | 11-129 | Glos | Hants | Bristol | 09/05/91 |
| Wasim Akram | 11-129 | Lancs | Middx | Uxbridge | 19/07/91 |
| Waqar Younis | 11-136 | Surrey | Hants | Bournemouth | 25/05/91 |
| M.Frost | 11-143 | Glam | Glos | Cheltenham | 19/07/91 |
| P.C.R.Tufnell | 11-228 | Middx | Hants | Lord's | 02/08/91 |
| A.A.Donald | 10-74 | W'icks | Glam | Swansea | 16/05/91 |
| D.G.Cork | 10-78 | Derby | Essex | Derby | 06/08/91 |
| F.D.Stephenson | 10-88 | Notts | N'hants | Well'borough | 19/07/91 |
| T.A.Munton | 10-91 | W'icks | Worcs | Edgbaston | 28/08/91 |
| A.A.Donald | 10-96 | W'icks | Yorks | Headingley | 09/05/91 |
| N.A.Foster | 10-122 | Essex | Middx | Chelmsford | 17/09/91 |
| B.T.P.Donelan | 10-136 | Sussex | Glos | Hove | 17/09/91 |
| N.M.Kendrick | 10-174 | Surrey | Lancs | Old Trafford | 17/09/91 |
| P.A.Smith | 9-56 | W'icks | Glos | Edgbaston | 25/05/91 |
| T.A.Munton | 9-78 | W'icks | Leics | Leicester | 26/07/91 |
| S.L.Watkin | 9-85 | Glam | N'hants | Cardiff | 22/05/91 |
| A.N.Jones | 9-87 | Sussex | Yorks | Midd'brough | 09/08/91 |
| M.P.Bicknell | 9-87 | Surrey | Sussex | The Oval | 28/08/91 |
| A.C.S.Pigott | 9-89 | Sussex | Middx | Lord's | 09/05/91 |
| N.V.Radford | 9-95 | Worcs | Essex | Ilford | 07/06/91 |
| Waqar Younis | 9-95 | Surrey | Middx | Lord's | 10/09/91 |
| E.E.Hemmings | 9-96 | Notts | Lancs | Trent Bridge | 16/07/91 |
| Waqar Younis | 9-97 | Surrey | W'wicks | Edgbaston | 06/08/91 |
| D.R.Gilbert | 9-105 | Glos | Kent | Canterbury | 20/08/91 |
| N.A.Foster | 9-114 | Essex | Notts | Trent Bridge | 09/08/91 |
| R.M.Ellison | 9-116 | Kent | Middx | Lord's | 31/05/91 |
| A.A.Donald | 9-124 | W'wicks | N'hants | Edgbaston | 10/09/91 |
| K.J.Shine | 9-134 | Hants | Worcs | Portsmouth | 16/07/91 |
| K.P.Evans | 9-135 | Notts | Leics | Trent Bridge | 09/05/91 |
| R.J.Shastri | 9-144 | Glam | W'wicks | Edgbaston | 20/08/91 |
| D.J.Foster | 9-147 | Glam | Som | Taunton | 09/05/91 |
| C.Penn | 9-149 | Kent | Middx | Canterbury | 28/08/91 |
| E.A.E.Baptiste | 9-159 | N'hants | Yorks | Northampton | 28/08/91 |
| P.C.R.Tufnell | 9-167 | Middx | Notts | Trent Bridge | 03/09/91 |
| P.A.J.DeFreitas | 9-179 | Lancs | Worcs | Worcester | 09/05/91 |
| T.A.Merrick | 9-180 | Kent | Sussex | Hove | 03/09/91 |
| D.A.Graveney | 9-193 | Som | Kent | Taunton | 26/07/91 |
| D.A.Reeve | 8-73 | W'wicks | Hants | Portsmouth | 19/07/91 |
| G.R.Dilley | 8-84 | Worcs | Glos | Cheltenham | 26/07/91 |
| J.H.Childs | 8-86 | Essex | Som | Southend | 19/07/91 |
| D.G.Cork | 8-91 | Derby | Sussex | Derby | 05/07/91 |
| R.A.Pick | 8-91 | Notts | N'hants | Well'borough | 19/07/91 |
| Waqar Younis | 8-94 | Surrey | Yorks | Guildford | 19/07/91 |
| M.C.J.Ball | 8-95 | Glos | Lancs | Bristol | 09/08/91 |
| I.T.Botham | 8-97 | Worcs | W'wicks | Worcester | 02/08/91 |
| C.Penn | 8-98 | Kent | Surrey | The Oval | 09/05/91 |
| Waqar Younis | 8-98 | Surrey | Kent | Canterbury | 02/08/91 |
| J.H.Childs | 8-113 | Essex | Derby | Chelmsford | 03/09/91 |
| J.P.Taylor | 8-114 | N'hants | Leics | Northampton | 16/05/91 |
| N.A.Foster | 8-115 | Essex | Lancs | Old Trafford | 23/08/91 |
| P.A.J.DeFreitas | 8-115 | Lancs | Notts | Old Trafford | 28/08/91 |
| K.P.Evans | 8-117 | Notts | Essex | Trent Bridge | 09/08/91 |
| N.A.Mallender | 8-123 | Som | W'wicks | Taunton | 17/09/91 |
| J.E.Emburey | 8-128 | Middx | Notts | Trent Bridge | 03/09/91 |
| N.V.Radford | 8-128 | Worcs | Som | Worcester | 03/09/91 |
| N.A.Foster | 8-129 | Essex | W'wicks | Chelmsford | 22/05/91 |
| J.W.Lloyds | 8-129 | Glos | N'hants | Luton | 28/06/91 |
| J.H.Childs | 8-138 | Essex | N'hants | Colchester | 16/08/91 |
| P.C.R.Tufnell | 8-139 | Middx | Leics | Uxbridge | 07/06/91 |
| E.A.E.Baptiste | 8-143 | N'hants | Sussex | Eastbourne | 02/08/91 |
| J.E.Emburey | 8-147 | Middx | Sussex | Hove | 22/05/91 |
| G.R.Dilley | 8-155 | Worcs | Lancs | Worcester | 09/05/91 |
| N.A.Foster | 8-157 | Essex | Leics | Leicester | 10/09/91 |
| Wasim Akram | 8-162 | Lancs | Sussex | Old Trafford | 31/05/91 |
| D.E.Malcolm | 8-175 | Derby | N'hants | Northampton | 31/05/91 |
| B.T.P.Donelan | 8-188 | Sussex | Leics | Hove | 19/07/91 |
| J.H.Childs | 8-197 | Essex | Surrey | The Oval | 05/07/91 |
| H.R.J.Trump | 8-253 | Som | Hants | Southampton | 28/08/91 |

| Name | Figures | For | Against | Venue | Date |
|---|---|---|---|---|---|
| M.A.Feltham | 7-69 | Surrey | W'wicks | Edgbaston | 06/08/91 |
| P.C.R.Tufnell | 7-69 | Middx | Surrey | Lord's | 10/09/91 |
| C.M.Wells | 7-75 | Sussex | Derby | Derby | 05/07/91 |
| N.A.Foster | 7-83 | Essex | Hants | Chelmsford | 02/07/91 |
| F.D.Stephenson | 7-89 | Notts | Worcs | Trent Bridge | 17/09/91 |
| C.A.Connor | 7-90 | Hants | Surrey | Bournemouth | 25/05/91 |
| F.D.Stephenson | 7-90 | Notts | Worcs | Worcester | 18/06/91 |
| J.R.Ayling | 7-90 | Hants | Surrey | The Oval | 03/09/91 |
| T.D.Topley | 7-91 | Essex | Leics | Ilford | 04/06/91 |
| D.J.Millns | 7-92 | Leics | Yorks | Leicester | 06/08/91 |
| A.P.Igglesden | 7-93 | Kent | Glos | Canterbury | 20/08/91 |
| J.N.Maguire | 7-98 | Leics | Kent | Canterbury | 17/09/91 |
| P.W.Jarvis | 7-99 | Yorks | Derby | Chesterfield | 17/09/91 |
| Waqar Younis | 7-102 | Surrey | Glos | Guildford | 16/07/91 |
| R.M.Ellison | 7-105 | Kent | W'wicks | Tunbridge W | 04/06/91 |
| K.M.Curran | 7-107 | N'hants | Derby | Northampton | 31/05/91 |
| R.A.Pick | 7-112 | Notts | Lancs | Old Trafford | 28/08/91 |
| T.A.Merrick | 7-115 | Kent | Derby | Canterbury | 25/05/91 |
| A.J.Murphy | 7-115 | Surrey | Essex | The Oval | 05/07/91 |
| O.H.Mortensen | 7-116 | Derby | N'hants | Northampton | 31/05/91 |
| J.A.Afford | 7-119 | Notts | Sussex | Eastbourne | 06/08/91 |
| S.R.Barwick | 7-121 | Glam | Surrey | The Oval | 26/07/91 |
| Aqib Javed | 7-123 | Hants | Notts | Trent Bridge | 31/05/91 |
| A.A.Donald | 7-123 | W'wicks | Leics | Leicester | 26/07/91 |
| O.H.Mortensen | 7-130 | Derby | Worcs | Kidd'minster | 19/07/91 |
| D.R.Gilbert | 7-131 | Glos | Worcs | Cheltenham | 26/07/91 |
| R.K.Illingworth | 7-131 | Worcs | Lancs | Blackpool | 20/08/91 |
| R.A.Pick | 7-132 | Notts | Leics | Leicester | 25/05/91 |

# ALL FIRST-CLASS MATCHES

## BATTING
### 250 Best Individual Scores

| Name | Score | For | Against | Venue | Date |
|---|---|---|---|---|---|
| G.A.Gooch | 259 | Essex | Middx | Chelmsford | 17/09/91 |
| M.R.Benson | 257 | Kent | Hants | Southampton | 27/04/91 |
| A.P.Wells | 253* | Sussex | Yorks | Midd'brough | 09/08/91 |
| T.S.Curtis | 248 | Worcs | Som | Worcester | 03/09/91 |
| M.P.Maynard | 243 | Glam | Hants | Southampton | 17/09/91 |
| D.B.D'Oliveira | 237 | Worcs | Oxford U | The Parks | 25/05/91 |
| T.R.Ward | 235* | Kent | Middx | Canterbury | 28/08/91 |
| K.J.Barnett | 217 | Derby | Notts | Derby | 10/09/91 |
| M.W.Gatting | 215* | Middx | Derby | Lord's | 09/08/91 |
| Salim Malik | 215 | Essex | Leics | Ilford | 04/06/91 |
| M.Azharuddin | 212 | Derby | Leics | Leicester | 28/08/91 |
| S.J.Cook | 210* | Som | N'hants | Northampton | 23/07/91 |
| T.M.Moody | 210 | Worcs | W'wicks | Worcester | 02/08/91 |
| S.J.Cook | 209* | Som | S Lanka | Taunton | 10/08/91 |
| M.P.Maynard | 204 | Glam | Notts | Cardiff | 02/07/91 |
| N.R.Taylor | 203* | Kent | Sussex | Hove | 03/09/91 |
| C.L.Smith | 200 | Hants | Oxford U | The Parks | 13/04/91 |
| M.D.Moxon | 200 | Yorks | Essex | Colchester | 20/08/91 |
| S.J.Cook | 197 | Som | Hants | Southampton | 28/08/91 |
| R.J.Blakey | 196 | Yorks | Oxford U | The Parks | 04/06/91 |
| C.L.Hooper | 196 | W Indies | Hants | Southampton | 29/06/91 |
| N.Hussain | 196 | Essex | Leics | Leicester | 10/09/91 |
| A.J.Lamb | 194 | N'hants | Surrey | Northampton | 23/08/91 |
| S.J.Cook | 193* | Som | Essex | Southend | 19/07/91 |
| N.J.Lenham | 193 | Sussex | Leics | Hove | 19/07/91 |
| P.J.Prichard | 190 | Essex | N'hants | Northampton | 09/05/91 |
| P.E.Robinson | 189 | Yorks | Lancs | Scarborough | 03/09/91 |
| T.S.Curtis | 186* | Worcs | Glam | Cardiff | 10/09/91 |
| G.A.Hick | 186 | Worcs | Sussex | Hove | 14/06/91 |
| Salim Malik | 185* | Esex | Surrey | The Oval | 05/07/91 |
| C.J.Tavare | 183 | Som | Glos | Bristol | 10/09/91 |
| T.M.Moody | 181* | Worcs | Essex | Ilford | 07/06/91 |
| M.W.Gatting | 180 | Middx | Som | Taunton | 25/05/91 |
| R.T.Robinson | 180 | Notts | Worcs | Trent Bridge | 17/09/91 |
| G.P.Thorpe | 177 | Surrey | Sussex | The Oval | 28/08/91 |
| G.A.Gooch | 174 | England | S Lanka | Lord's | 22/08/91 |
| M.W.Gatting | 174 | Middx | Kent | Canterbury | 28/08/91 |
| Salim Malik | 173 | Essex | Kent | Folkestone | 16/05/91 |
| G.A.Gooch | 173 | Essex | N'hants | Colchester | 16/08/91 |
| A.N.Hayhurst | 172* | Som | Glos | Bath | 21/06/91 |
| V.P.Terry | 171 | Hants | Sussex | Hove | 16/05/91 |
| B.C.Broad | 166 | Notts | Kent | Trent Bridge | 22/05/91 |
| A.Fordham | 165 | N'hants | Yorks | Northampton | 28/08/91 |
| Salim Malik | 165 | Essex | Derby | Chelmsford | 03/09/91 |
| M.W.Alleyne | 165 | Glos | N'hants | Bristol | 03/09/91 |
| C.L.Hooper | 164* | W Indies | World XI | Scarborough | 28/08/91 |
| Salim Malik | 163 | Essex | Glos | Bristol | 31/05/91 |
| S.J.Cook | 162* | Som | WIndies | Taunton | 29/05/91 |
| C.J.Tavare | 162 | Som | Glam | Swansea | 04/06/91 |
| B.C.Broad | 162 | Notts | Worcs | Worcester | 18/06/91 |
| A.P.Wells | 162 | Sussex | Kent | Hove | 03/09/91 |
| I.T.Botham | 161 | Worcs | W Indies | Worcester | 15/05/91 |
| M.Azharuddin | 160* | Derby | Lancs | Derby | 16/08/91 |
| N.E.Briers | 160 | Leics | Notts | Trent Bridge | 09/05/91 |
| M.R.Benson | 160 | Kent | Derby | Canterbury | 25/05/91 |
| A.P.Wells | 159 | Sussex | Som | Hove | 16/07/91 |
| B.C.Broad | 158 | Notts | Sussex | Eastbourne | 06/08/91 |
| A.C.Seymour | 157 | Essex | Glam | Cardiff | 23/07/91 |
| D.A.Leatherdale | 157 | Worcs | Som | Worcester | 03/09/91 |
| H.Morris | 156* | Glam | Sussex | Cardiff | 25/05/91 |
| H.Morris | 156* | Glam | Yorks | Headingley | 16/08/91 |
| G.A.Gooch | 154* | England | W Indies | Headingley | 06/06/91 |
| S.V.Manjrekar | 154* | World XI | W Indies | Scarborough | 28/08/91 |
| M.Azharuddin | 154 | Derby | Glos | Gloucester | 18/06/91 |
| A.P.Wells | 153* | Sussex | Glam | Cardiff | 25/05/91 |
| D.Byas | 153 | Yorks | Notts | Worksop | 23/07/91 |
| N.J.Speak | 153 | Lancs | Surrey | Old Trafford | 17/09/91 |
| S.J.Cook | 152 | Som | Glam | Swansea | 04/06/91 |
| D.L.Haynes | 151 | W Indies | Glos | Bristol | 31/07/91 |
| D.J.Bicknell | 151 | Surrey | Kent | Canterbury | 02/08/91 |
| D.M.Ward | 151 | Surrey | Lancs | Old Trafford | 17/09/91 |
| N.R.Taylor | 150 | Kent | Leics | Leicester | 09/08/91 |
| M.P.Speight | 149 | Sussex | Camb U | Hove | 29/06/91 |
| R.A.Smith | 148* | England | W Indies | Lord's | 20/06/91 |
| T.J.G.O'Gorman | 148 | Derby | Lancs | Old Trafford | 16/05/91 |
| A.R.Butcher | 147 | Glam | Glos | Abergavenny | 28/08/91 |
| N.R.Taylor | 146 | Kent | Derby | Canterbury | 25/05/91 |
| D.J.Bicknell | 145* | Surrey | Essex | Chelmsford | 27/04/91 |
| C.L.Smith | 145 | Hants | Sussex | Hove | 16/05/91 |
| P.Pollard | 145 | Notts | Lancs | Trent Bridge | 16/07/91 |
| G.A.Hick | 145 | Worcs | Surrey | Worcester | 16/08/91 |
| R.T.Robinson | 145 | Notts | Derby | Derby | 10/09/91 |
| M.W.Gatting | 143* | Middx | Notts | Lord's | 26/07/91 |
| D.W.Randall | 143* | Notts | Derby | Trent Bridge | 23/08/91 |
| K.R.Brown | 143* | Middx | Notts | Trent Bridge | 03/09/91 |
| P.J.L.Dujon | 142* | W Indies | Essex | Chelmsford | 03/08/91 |
| M.R.Benson | 142 | Kent | Surrey | Canterbury | 02/08/91 |
| M.A.Lynch | 141* | Surrey | Middx | The Oval | 20/08/91 |
| H.Morris | 141 | Glam | Som | Taunton | 09/05/91 |
| T.R.Ward | 141 | Kent | Essex | Folkestone | 16/05/91 |
| G.A.Hick | 141 | Worcs | Hants | Portsmouth | 16/07/91 |
| N.Hussain | 141 | Essex | N'hants | Colchester | 16/08/91 |
| Asif Din | 140 | W'wicks | Leics | Leicester | 26/07/91 |
| A.Dale | 140 | Glam | Glos | Abergavenny | 28/08/91 |
| M.W.Gatting | 138* | Middx | Essex | Lord's | 28/06/91 |
| N.R.Taylor | 138* | Kent | W Indies | Canterbury | 20/07/91 |
| M.A.Atherton | 138 | Lancs | Camb U | Fenner's | 13/04/91 |
| B.C.Broad | 137* | Notts | Surrey | The Oval | 04/06/91 |
| A.P.Wells | 137 | Sussex | Middx | Hove | 22/05/91 |
| N.J.Lenham | 137 | Sussex | Kent | Tunbridge W | 07/06/91 |
| P.V.Simmons | 136 | W Indies | Middx | Lord's | 18/05/91 |
| D.J.Bicknell | 136 | Surrey | Hants | The Oval | 03/09/91 |
| R.B.Richardson | 135* | W Indies | Leics | Leicester | 01/06/91 |
| T.M.Moody | 135 | Worcs | Lancs | Worcester | 09/05/91 |
| D.Byas | 135 | Yorks | Derby | Scarborough | 16/07/91 |
| T.M.Moody | 135 | Worcs | Middx | Worcester | 23/08/91 |
| S.P.Titchard | 135 | Lancs | Notts | Old Trafford | 28/08/91 |
| K.D.James | 134* | Hants | Yorks | Southampton | 05/07/91 |
| C.J.Adams | 134 | Derby | Camb U | Fenner's | 09/05/91 |
| P.V.Simmons | 134 | W Indies | Worcs | Worcester | 15/05/91 |
| R.J.Harden | 134 | Som | Derby | Derby | 22/05/91 |
| C.J.Tavare | 134 | Som | Sussex | Hove | 16/07/91 |
| M.P.Maynard | 133* | Glam | Som | Taunton | 09/05/91 |
| R.J.Shastri | 133* | Glam | Lancs | Liverpool | 28/06/91 |
| J.D.R.Benson | 133* | Leics | Hants | Bournemouth | 16/08/91 |
| A.J.Moles | 133 | W'wicks | Glos | Edgbaston | 25/05/91 |
| N.E.Briers | 133 | Leics | N'hants | Leicester | 05/07/91 |
| H.Morris | 132 | Glam | N'hants | Cardiff | 22/05/91 |
| N.A.Stanley | 132 | N'hants | Lancs | Lytham | 06/08/91 |
| A.Fordham | 131 | N'hants | Derby | Derby | 27/04/91 |
| J.E.Morris | 131 | Derby | Camb U | Fenner's | 09/05/91 |
| I.V.A.Richards | 131 | W Indies | Worcs | Worcester | 15/05/91 |
| S.J.Cook | 131 | Som | Lancs | Taunton | 02/07/91 |
| B.C.Broad | 131 | Notts | Som | Trent Bridge | 16/08/91 |
| H.Morris | 131 | Glam | Hants | Southampton | 17/09/91 |
| J.P.Crawley | 130 | Lancs | Surrey | Old Trafford | 17/09/91 |
| M.Azharuddin | 129* | Derby | Notts | Trent Bridge | 23/08/91 |
| A.R.Butcher | 129 | Glam | Lancs | Liverpool | 28/06/91 |
| P.J.Prichard | 129 | Essex | Middx | Lord's | 28/06/91 |
| M.P.Maynard | 129 | Glam | Glos | Cheltenham | 19/07/91 |
| N.Hussain | 128 | Essex | Surrey | The Oval | 05/07/91 |
| P.J.Prichard | 128 | Essex | Yorks | Colchester | 20/08/91 |
| G.D.Mendis | 127* | Lancs | Camb U | Fenner's | 13/04/91 |
| K.Greenfield | 127* | Sussex | Camb U | Hove | 29/06/91 |
| R.J.Scott | 127 | Glos | Worcs | Worcester | 27/04/91 |
| C.W.J.Athey | 127 | Glos | Oxford U | The Parks | 15/06/91 |
| M.P.Maynard | 127 | Glam | Sussex | Cardiff | 25/05/91 |
| S.C.Goldsmith | 127 | Derby | S Lanka | Derby | 02/08/91 |
| C.W.J.Athey | 127 | Glos | Lancs | Bristol | 09/08/91 |
| S.J.Cook | 127 | Som | W'wicks | Taunton | 17/09/91 |
| D.M.Smith | 126* | Sussex | Middx | Hove | 22/05/91 |
| D.J.Bicknell | 126 | Surrey | Sussex | Arundel | 02/07/91 |
| M.P.Maynard | 126 | Glam | Glos | Cheltenham | 19/07/91 |
| S.J.Cook | 126 | Som | Kent | Taunton | 26/07/91 |
| S.A.Kellett | 125* | Yorks | Derby | Chesterfield | 17/09/91 |
| C.L.Smith | 125 | Hants | Glos | Bristol | 09/05/91 |
| A.M.Hooper | 125 | Camb U | Surrey | Fenner's | 18/05/91 |

# ALL FIRST-CLASS MATCHES

| Name | Score | For | Against | Venue | Date |
|---|---|---|---|---|---|
| I.J.F.Hutchinson | 125 | Middx | Sussex | Hove | 22/05/91 |
| D.J.Bicknell | 125 | Surrey | Notts | The Oval | 04/06/91 |
| A.J.Lamb | 125 | N'hants | Lancs | Lytham | 06/08/91 |
| V.P.Terry | 124 | Hants | W'wicks | Portsmouth | 19/07/91 |
| P.Johnson | 124 | Notts | Essex | Trent Bridge | 09/08/91 |
| M.A.Roseberry | 123* | Middx | Camb U | Fenner's | 15/05/91 |
| C.L.Hooper | 123 | W Indies | Som | Taunton | 29/05/91 |
| A.A.Metcalfe | 123 | Yorks | Glam | Headingley | 16/08/91 |
| P.Pollard | 123 | Notts | Derby | Derby | 10/09/91 |
| M.A.Garnham | 123 | Essex | Leics | Leicester | 10/09/91 |
| J.E.Morris | 122* | Derby | Glam | Chesterfield | 07/06/91 |
| T.E.Jesty | 122* | Lancs | Oxford U | The Parks | 07/06/91 |
| D.Byas | 122* | Yorks | Leics | Leicester | 06/08/91 |
| K.J.Barnett | 122 | Derby | N'hants | Northampton | 31/05/91 |
| Wasim Akram | 122 | Lancs | Hants | Basingstoke | 04/06/91 |
| T.R.Ward | 122 | Kent | Oxford U | The Parks | 18/06/91 |
| P.J.Prichard | 122 | Essex | Kent | Southend | 16/07/91 |
| R.J.Scott | 122 | Glos | Glam | Cheltenham | 19/07/91 |
| N.H.Fairbrother | 121 | Lancs | W'wicks | Edgbaston | 27/04/91 |
| R.B.Richardson | 121 | W Indies | England | The Oval | 08/08/91 |
| D.W.Randall | 121 | Notts | Middx | Trent Bridge | 03/09/91 |
| D.P.Ostler | 120* | W'wicks | Kent | Tunbridge W | 04/06/91 |
| A.P.Wells | 120 | Sussex | Middx | Lord's | 09/05/91 |
| C.W.J.Athey | 120 | Glos | W'wicks | Edgbaston | 25/05/91 |
| D.W.Randall | 120 | Notts | Lancs | Trent Bridge | 16/07/91 |
| A.J.Wright | 120 | Glos | Worcs | Cheltenham | 26/07/91 |
| T.S.Curtis | 120 | Worcs | Lancs | Blackpool | 20/08/91 |
| M.W.Gatting | 120 | Middx | Worcs | Worcester | 23/08/91 |
| D.Byas | 120 | Yorks | Lancs | Scarborough | 03/09/91 |
| M.A.Roseberry | 119* | Middx | Leics | Uxbridge | 07/06/91 |
| M.R.Ramprakash | 119 | Middx | Sussex | Lord's | 09/05/91 |
| G.D.Mendis | 119 | Lancs | W'wicks | Old Trafford | 23/07/91 |
| R.B.Richardson | 119 | WI | Glos | Bristol | 31/07/91 |
| T.M.Moody | 118 | Worcs | Glam | Worcester | 31/05/91 |
| J.W.Hall | 117* | Sussex | Som | Taunton | 27/04/91 |
| M.W.Gatting | 117* | Middx | Sussex | Hove | 22/05/91 |
| R.J.Bailey | 117 | N'hants | Som | Northampton | 23/07/91 |
| M.A.Garnham | 117 | Essex | Derby | Chelmsford | 03/09/91 |
| G.P.Thorpe | 117 | Surrey | Middx | Lord's | 10/09/91 |
| M.Azharuddin | 116* | Derby | Camb U | Fenner's | 09/05/91 |
| I.L.Philip | 116* | Scotland | Ireland | Dublin | 22/06/91 |
| G.P.Thorpe | 116* | Surrey | N'hants | Northampton | 23/08/91 |
| A.N.Hayhurst | 116 | Som | Derby | Derby | 22/05/91 |
| A.Fordham | 116 | N'hants | Leics | Leicester | 05/07/91 |
| M.V.Fleming | 116 | Kent | W Indies | Canterbury | 20/07/91 |
| C.B.Lambert | 116 | W Indies | Essex | Chelmsford | 03/08/91 |
| J.P.Stephenson | 116 | Essex | Yorks | Colchester | 20/08/91 |
| S.J.Cook | 115* | Som | Hants | Southampton | 28/08/91 |
| P.N.Hepworth | 115 | Leics | Camb U | Fenner's | 22/05/91 |
| M.D.Moxon | 115 | Yorks | Lancs | Scarborough | 03/09/91 |
| P.N.Hepworth | 115 | Leics | Essex | Leicester | 10/09/91 |
| M.Watkinson | 114* | Lancs | Surrey | The Oval | 22/05/91 |
| M.A.Atherton | 114* | Lancs | Yorks | Old Trafford | 02/08/91 |
| P.Whitticase | 114* | Leics | Hants | Bournemouth | 16/08/91 |
| G.R.Cowdrey | 114 | Kent | W'wicks | Tunbridge W | 04/06/91 |
| I.J.F.Hutchinson | 114 | Middx | Glos | Bristol | 04/06/91 |
| R.B.Richardson | 114 | W Indies | Derby | Derby | 12/06/91 |
| C.L.Smith | 114 | Hants | Derby | Chesterfield | 23/07/91 |
| N.E.Briers | 114 | Leics | Yorks | Leicester | 06/08/91 |
| P.Johnson | 114 | Notts | Lancs | Old Trafford | 28/08/91 |
| G.D.Mendis | 114 | Lancs | Yorks | Scarborough | 03/09/91 |
| J.P.Stephenson | 113* | Essex | Kent | Southend | 16/07/91 |
| S.A.Marsh | 113* | Kent | Som | Taunton | 26/07/91 |
| A.A.Metcalfe | 113* | Yorks | Lancs | Old Trafford | 02/08/91 |
| A.J.Stewart | 113* | England | S Lanka | Lord's | 22/08/91 |
| G.D.Mendis | 113 | Lancs | W'wicks | Edgbaston | 27/04/91 |
| G.Fowler | 113 | Lancs | Surrey | The Oval | 22/05/91 |
| M.V.Fleming | 113 | Kent | Surrey | Canterbury | 02/08/91 |
| J.P.Stephenson | 113 | Essex | Leics | Leicester | 10/09/91 |
| D.W.Randall | 112* | Notts | Glam | Cardiff | 02/07/91 |
| M.A.Crawley | 112 | Notts | Oxford U | The Parks | 27/04/91 |
| C.L.Smith | 112 | Hants | Yorks | Southampton | 05/07/91 |
| C.J.Adams | 112 | Derby | Yorks | Chesterfield | 17/09/91 |
| C.L.Hooper | 111* | W Indies | Glos | Bristol | 31/07/91 |
| R.C.Russell | 111 | Glos | Hants | Bristol | 09/05/91 |
| C.L.Hooper | 111 | W Indies | England | Lord's | 20/06/91 |
| P.W.G.Parker | 111 | Sussex | Kent | Hove | 03/09/91 |
| N.R.Taylor | 111 | Kent | Sussex | Hove | 03/09/91 |
| M.A.Atherton | 110 | Lancs | Worcs | Worcester | 09/05/91 |
| T.R.Ward | 110 | Kent | Glam | Maidstone | 05/07/91 |
| M.Azharuddin | 110 | Derby | Middx | Lord's | 09/08/91 |
| M.R.Ramprakash | 110 | Middx | Notts | Trent Bridge | 03/09/91 |
| G.R.Cowdrey | 109* | Kent | Notts | Trent Bridge | 22/05/91 |
| C.J.Tavare | 109* | Som | W Indies | Taunton | 29/05/91 |
| S.A.Kellett | 109* | Yorks | S Lanka | Headingley | 27/07/91 |
| N.H.Fairbrother | 109 | Lancs | Worcs | Worcester | 09/05/91 |
| K.T.Medlycott | 109 | Surrey | Camb U | Fenner's | 18/05/91 |
| N.H.Fairbrother | 109 | Lancs | Som | Taunton | 02/07/91 |
| T.R.Ward | 109 | Kent | Glam | Maidstone | 05/07/91 |
| A.J.Stewart | 109 | Surrey | Glos | Guildford | 16/07/91 |
| R.B.Richardson | 109 | W Indies | Glam | Swansea | 16/07/91 |
| R.A.Smith | 109 | England | W Indies | The Oval | 08/08/91 |
| N.R.Taylor | 109 | Kent | Glos | Canterbury | 20/08/91 |
| A.J.Lamb | 109 | N'hants | Yorks | Northampton | 28/08/91 |
| S.A.Marsh | 108* | Kent | Middx | Lord's | 31/05/91 |
| T.J.G.O'Gorman | 108* | Derby | Notts | Derby | 10/09/91 |
| T.J.Boon | 108 | Leics | Camb U | Fenner's | 22/05/91 |
| M.D.Moxon | 108 | Yorks | N'hants | Headingley | 25/05/91 |
| B.M.W.Patterson | 108 | Scotland | Ireland | Dublin | 22/06/91 |
| N.D.Burns | 108 | Som | Notts | Trent Bridge | 16/08/91 |
| M.C.J.Nicholas | 107* | Hants | Notts | Trent Bridge | 31/05/91 |
| S.J.Cook | 107* | Som | Hants | Bath | 18/06/91 |
| N.A.Foster | 107* | Essex | Sussex | Horsham | 21/06/91 |
| N.H.Fairbrother | 107* | Lancs | Glam | Liverpool | 28/06/91 |
| A.P.Wells | 107 | Sussex | Kent | Tunbridge W | 07/06/91 |
| T.M.Moody | 107 | Worcs | Notts | Worcester | 18/06/91 |
| R.J.Shastri | 107 | Glam | Leics | Neath | 21/06/91 |
| P.V.Simmons | 107 | W Indies | Kent | Canterbury | 20/07/91 |
| R.A.Smith | 107 | Hants | Som | Southampton | 28/08/91 |

# ALL FIRST-CLASS MATCHES

## BOWLING
### 250 Best Innings Bowling Figures

| Name | Figures | For | Against | Venue | Date |
|---|---|---|---|---|---|
| D.J.Millns | 9-37 | Leics | Derby | Derby | 20/08/91 |
| D.G.Cork | 8-53 | Derby | Essex | Derby | 06/08/91 |
| D.R.Gilbert | 8-55 | Glos | Kent | Canterbury | 20/08/91 |
| T.A.Munton | 8-89 | W'wicks | Middx | Edgbaston | 02/07/91 |
| N.A.Foster | 8-99 | Essex | Lancs | Old Trafford | 23/08/91 |
| R.M.Ellison | 7-33 | Kent | W'wicks | Tunbridge W | 04/06/91 |
| C.M.Wells | 7-42 | Sussex | Derby | Derby | 05/07/91 |
| N.V.Radford | 7-43 | Worcs | Som | Worcester | 03/09/91 |
| M.P.Bicknell | 7-52 | Surrey | Sussex | The Oval | 28/08/91 |
| I.T.Botham | 7-54 | Worcs | W'wicks | Worcester | 02/08/91 |
| J.N.Maguire | 7-57 | Leics | Kent | Leicester | 09/08/91 |
| T.A.Munton | 7-59 | W'wicks | Worcs | Edgbaston | 28/08/91 |
| P.A.J.DeFreitas | 7-70 | England | S Lanka | Lord's | 22/08/91 |
| J.E.Emburey | 7-71 | Middx | Sussex | Hove | 22/05/91 |
| Waqar Younis | 7-87 | Surrey | Glos | Guildford | 16/07/91 |
| E.A.E.Baptiste | 7-95 | N'hants | Yorks | Northampton | 28/08/91 |
| M.Frost | 7-99 | Glam | Glos | Cheltenham | 19/07/91 |
| T.A.Merrick | 7-99 | Kent | Sussex | Hove | 03/09/91 |
| D.A.Graveney | 7-105 | Som | Kent | Taunton | 26/07/91 |
| P.C.R.Tufnell | 7-116 | Middx | Hants | Lord's | 02/08/91 |
| P.C.R.Tufnell | 6-25 | England | W Indies | The Oval | 08/08/91 |
| K.J.Barnett | 6-28 | Derby | Glam | Chesterfield | 07/06/91 |
| P.C.R.Tufnell | 6-34 | Middx | Glos | Bristol | 04/06/91 |
| Waqar Younis | 6-40 | Surrey | Yorks | Guildford | 19/07/91 |
| M.J.Gerrard | 6-40 | Glos | S Lanka | Bristol | 06/08/91 |
| N.A.Mallender | 6-43 | Som | Glos | Bath | 21/06/91 |
| Waqar Younis | 6-45 | Surrey | Hants | The Oval | 03/09/91 |
| E.E.Hemmings | 6-46 | Notts | Lancs | Trent Bridge | 16/07/91 |
| Waqar Younis | 6-47 | Surrey | Hants | The Oval | 03/09/91 |
| J.D.Batty | 6-48 | Yorks | Notts | Worksop | 23/07/91 |
| H.R.J.Trump | 6-48 | Som | Worcs | Weston | 06/08/91 |
| C.E.L.Ambrose | 6-52 | W Indies | England | Headingley | 06/06/91 |
| T.A.Munton | 6-53 | W'wicks | Yorks | Edgbaston | 31/05/91 |
| S.L.Watkin | 6-55 | Glam | N'hants | Cardiff | 22/05/91 |
| E.A.E.Baptiste | 6-57 | N'hants | Kent | Maidstone | 02/07/91 |
| D.J.Millns | 6-59 | Leics | Yorks | Leicester | 06/08/91 |
| J.H.Childs | 6-61 | Essex | N'hants | Colchester | 16/08/91 |
| B.T.P.Donelan | 6-62 | Sussex | Glos | Hove | 17/09/91 |
| Waqar Younis | 6-65 | Surrey | Lancs | The Oval | 22/05/91 |
| Waqar Younis | 6-66 | Surrey | Hants | Bournemouth | 25/05/91 |
| Wasim Akram | 6-66 | Lancs | Middx | Uxbridge | 19/07/91 |
| D.V.Lawrence | 6-67 | Glos | N'hants | Luton | 28/06/91 |
| J.H.Childs | 6-68 | Essex | Derby | Chelmsford | 03/09/91 |
| N.A.Mallender | 6-68 | Som | W'wicks | Taunton | 17/09/91 |
| A.A.Donald | 6-69 | W'wicks | N'hants | Edgbaston | 10/09/91 |
| S.D.Fletcher | 6-70 | Yorks | W'wicks | Edgbaston | 31/05/91 |
| Waqar Younis | 6-72 | Surrey | Kent | Canterbury | 02/08/91 |
| A.R.Roberts | 6-72 | N'hants | Lancs | Lytham | 06/08/91 |
| D.A.Reeve | 6-73 | W'wicks | Kent | Tunbridge W | 04/06/91 |
| N.V.Radford | 6-76 | Worcs | Essex | Ilford | 07/06/91 |
| D.V.Lawrence | 6-77 | Glos | Hants | Bristol | 09/05/91 |
| P.C.R.Tufnell | 6-82 | Middx | Leics | Uxbridge | 07/06/91 |
| D.J.Foster | 6-84 | Glam | Som | Taunton | 09/05/91 |
| A.A.Donald | 6-84 | W'wicks | Som | Taunton | 17/09/91 |
| J.N.Maguire | 6-85 | Leics | Essex | Ilford | 04/06/91 |
| Wasim Akram | 6-86 | Lancs | Kent | Old Trafford | 21/06/91 |
| P.A.J.DeFreitas | 6-88 | Lancs | Worcs | Worcester | 09/05/91 |
| M.J.McCague | 6-88 | Kent | Leics | Leicester | 09/08/91 |
| Aqib Javed | 6-91 | Hants | Notts | Trent Bridge | 31/05/91 |
| B.T.P.Donelan | 6-92 | Sussex | Leics | Hove | 19/07/91 |
| J.W.Lloyds | 6-94 | Glos | N'hants | Luton | 28/06/91 |
| R.J.Ratnayake | 6-97 | S Lanka | Glos | Bristol | 06/08/91 |
| K.T.Medlycott | 6-98 | Surrey | Camb U | Fenner's | 18/05/91 |
| O.H.Mortensen | 6-101 | Derby | Worcs | Kidd'minster | 19/07/91 |
| N.A.Foster | 6-104 | Essex | Middx | Chelmsford | 17/09/91 |
| H.R.J.Trump | 6-107 | Som | Leics | Weston | 02/08/91 |
| C.C.Lewis | 6-111 | England | W Indies | Edgbaston | 25/07/91 |
| H.R.J.Trump | 6-121 | Som | Hants | Southampton | 28/08/91 |
| P.J.Hartley | 6-151 | Yorks | N'hants | Northampton | 28/08/91 |
| P.Carrick | 5-13 | Yorks | Worcs | Headingley | 02/07/91 |
| R.A.Pick | 5-17 | Notts | N'hants | Well'borough | 19/07/91 |
| P.C.R.Tufnell | 5-17 | Middx | Surrey | Lord's | 10/09/91 |
| J.H.Childs | 5-20 | Essex | Som | Southend | 19/07/91 |
| F.D.Stephenson | 5-27 | Notts | N'hants | Well'borough | 19/07/91 |
| P.A.Smith | 5-28 | W'wicks | Glos | Edgbaston | 25/05/91 |
| P.C.R.Tufnell | 5-30 | Middx | Notts | Trent Bridge | 03/09/91 |
| P.J.Hartley | 5-32 | Yorks | Middx | Sheffield | 21/06/91 |
| T.A.Munton | 5-32 | W'wicks | Leics | Leicester | 26/07/91 |
| A.A.Donald | 5-33 | W'wicks | Glos | Edgbaston | 25/05/91 |
| C.C.Lewis | 5-35 | Leics | Glam | Leicester | 27/04/91 |
| A.A.Donald | 5-36 | W'wicks | Glam | Swansea | 16/05/91 |
| K.T.Medlycott | 5-36 | Surrey | Camb U | Fenner's | 18/05/91 |
| A.P.Igglesden | 5-36 | Kent | N'hants | Maidstone | 02/07/91 |
| A.C.S.Pigott | 5-37 | Sussex | Middx | Lord's | 06/05/91 |
| A.A.Donald | 5-38 | W'wicks | Glam | Swansea | 16/05/91 |
| S.Bastien | 5-39 | Glam | N'hants | Cardiff | 22/05/91 |
| M.A.Ealham | 5-39 | Kent | Sussex | Hove | 03/09/91 |
| I.D.K.Salisbury | 5-40 | Sussex | Kent | Tunbridge W | 07/06/91 |
| D.Gough | 5-41 | Yorks | Lancs | Scarborough | 03/09/91 |
| A.A.Donald | 5-42 | W'wicks | Yorks | Headingley | 09/05/91 |
| J.P.Taylor | 5-42 | N'hants | Leics | Northampton | 16/05/91 |
| G.A.Hick | 5-42 | Worcs | Glam | Cardiff | 10/09/91 |
| C.Penn | 5-43 | Kent | N'hants | Maidstone | 02/07/91 |
| K.J.Shine | 5-43 | Hants | Worcs | Portsmouth | 16/07/91 |
| R.K.Illingworth | 5-43 | Worcs | S Lanka | Worcester | 30/07/91 |
| J.N.Maguire | 5-44 | Leics | W Indies | Leicester | 01/06/91 |
| D.E.Malcolm | 5-45 | Derby | W'wicks | Edgbaston | 28/06/91 |
| N.A.Foster | 5-45 | Essex | Hants | Chelmsford | 02/07/91 |
| D.W.Headley | 5-46 | Middx | Yorks | Lord's | 27/04/91 |
| A.N.Jones | 5-46 | Sussex | Yorks | Midd'brough | 09/08/91 |
| Waqar Younis | 5-47 | Surrey | W'wicks | Edgbaston | 06/08/91 |
| Aqib Javed | 5-47 | Hants | Sussex | Bournemouth | 20/08/91 |
| Wasim Akram | 5-48 | Lancs | Hants | Basingstoke | 04/06/91 |
| A.A.Donald | 5-48 | W'wicks | Sussex | Coventry | 18/06/91 |
| Aqib Javed | 5-49 | Hants | N'hants | Northampton | 21/06/91 |
| S.L.Watkin | 5-49 | Glam | Glos | Cheltenham | 19/07/91 |
| R.K.Illingworth | 5-49 | Worcs | Lancs | Blackpool | 20/08/91 |
| K.P.Evans | 5-52 | Notts | Leics | Trent Bridge | 09/05/91 |
| D.V.Lawrence | 5-52 | Glos | Hants | Bristol | 09/05/91 |
| Waqar Younis | 5-53 | Surrey | Middx | Lord's | 10/09/91 |
| A.A.Donald | 5-54 | W'wicks | Yorks | Headingley | 09/05/91 |
| N.A.Foster | 5-54 | Essex | Glos | Bristol | 31/05/91 |
| N.M.Kendrick | 5-54 | Surrey | Lancs | Old Trafford | 17/09/91 |
| C.E.L.Ambrose | 5-56 | W Indies | Glam | Swansea | 16/07/91 |
| N.A.Foster | 5-56 | Essex | Notts | Trent Bridge | 09/08/91 |
| Waqar Younis | 5-57 | Surrey | Lancs | The Oval | 22/05/91 |
| O.H.Mortensen | 5-57 | Derby | N'hants | Northampton | 31/05/91 |
| Waqar Younis | 5-57 | Surrey | Leics | Leicester | 14/06/91 |
| T.D.Topley | 5-58 | Essex | Leics | Ilford | 04/06/91 |
| K.J.Shine | 5-58 | Hants | Glam | Swansea | 09/08/91 |
| S.L.Watkin | 5-59 | Glam | Notts | Cardiff | 02/07/91 |
| C.C.Lewis | 5-60 | Leics | Lancs | Leicester | 18/06/91 |
| K.M.Curran | 5-60 | N'hants | Notts | Well'borough | 19/07/91 |
| Wasim Akram | 5-61 | Lancs | Leics | Leicester | 18/06/91 |
| F.D.Stephenson | 5-61 | Notts | N'hants | Well'borough | 19/07/91 |
| Waqar Younis | 5-61 | Surrey | Middx | The Oval | 20/08/91 |
| R.D.B.Croft | 5-62 | Glam | W'wicks | Swansea | 16/05/91 |
| J.G.Thomas | 5-62 | N'hants | Leics | Northampton | 16/05/91 |
| S.L.Watkin | 5-63 | Glam | Som | Taunton | 09/05/91 |
| A.J.Murphy | 5-63 | Surrey | Essex | The Oval | 05/05/91 |
| Wasim Akram | 5-63 | Lancs | Middx | Uxbridge | 19/07/91 |
| F.D.Stephenson | 5-63 | Notts | Worcs | Trent Bridge | 17/09/91 |
| R.K.Illingworth | 5-64 | Worcs | Derby | Kidd'minster | 19/07/91 |
| H.R.J.Trump | 5-64 | Som | Glos | Bristol | 10/09/91 |
| M.A.Ealham | 5-65 | Kent | Leics | Canterbury | 17/09/91 |
| D.J.Millns | 5-65 | Leics | Kent | Canterbury | 17/09/91 |
| R.A.Pick | 5-66 | Notts | Leics | Leicester | 25/05/91 |
| K.P.Evans | 5-66 | Notts | Essex | Trent Bridge | 09/08/91 |
| I.T.Botham | 5-67 | Worcs | Surrey | Worcester | 16/08/91 |
| J.N.Maguire | 5-67 | Leics | Derby | Leicester | 28/08/91 |
| D.A.Graveney | 5-68 | Som | Derby | Derby | 22/05/91 |
| R.J.Ratnayake | 5-69 | S Lanka | England | Lord's | 22/08/91 |
| D.R.Pringle | 5-70 | Essex | N'hants | Northampton | 09/05/91 |
| Waqar Younis | 5-70 | Surrey | Hants | Bournemouth | 25/05/91 |
| S.R.Lampitt | 5-70 | Worcs | Surrey | Worcester | 16/08/91 |
| T.D.Topley | 5-71 | Essex | Surrey | Chelmsford | 27/04/91 |
| R.J.Shastri | 5-71 | Glam | W'wicks | Edgbaston | 20/08/91 |

# ALL FIRST-CLASS MATCHES

| Name | Figures | For | Against | Venue | Date |
|---|---|---|---|---|---|
| P.A.J.DeFreitas | 5-71 | Lancs | Notts | Old Trafford | 28/08/91 |
| F.D.Stephenson | 5-74 | Notts | Worcs | Worcester | 18/06/91 |
| C.E.L.Ambrose | 5-74 | W Indies | England | Trent Bridge | 04/07/91 |
| E.E.Hemmings | 5-75 | Notts | Lancs | Old Trafford | 28/08/91 |
| R.M.Ellison | 5-77 | Kent | Middx | Lord's | 31/05/91 |
| T.A.Munton | 5-77 | W'wicks | Derby | Edgbaston | 28/06/91 |
| S.R.Lampitt | 5-78 | Worcs | Som | Worcester | 03/09/91 |
| T.D.Topley | 5-79 | Essex | Derby | Derby | 06/08/91 |
| N.A.Foster | 5-80 | Essex | W'wicks | Chelmsford | 22/05/91 |
| N.A.Mallender | 5-80 | Som | Worcs | Worcester | 03/09/91 |
| B.P.Patterson | 5-81 | W Indies | England | Edgbaston | 25/07/91 |
| A.N.Jones | 5-84 | Sussex | Glos | Cheltenham | 23/07/91 |
| S.R.Lampitt | 5-85 | Worcs | Oxford U | The Parks | 25/05/91 |
| R.A.Pick | 5-86 | Notts | Middx | Trent Bridge | 03/09/91 |
| N.A.Foster | 5-86 | Essex | Leics | Leicester | 10/09/91 |
| S.R.Lampitt | 5-86 | Worcs | Notts | Trent Bridge | 17/09/91 |
| B.P.Patterson | 5-88 | W Indies | Middx | Lord's | 18/05/91 |
| N.F.Williams | 5-89 | Middx | Notts | Lord's | 26/07/91 |
| C.Penn | 5-90 | Kent | Leics | Canterbury | 17/09/91 |
| G.R.Dilley | 5-91 | Worcs | Lancs | Worcester | 09/05/91 |
| Wasim Akram | 5-91 | Lancs | Yorks | Old Trafford | 02/08/91 |
| P.C.R.Tufnell | 5-94 | England | S Lanka | Lord's | 22/08/91 |
| C.L.Hooper | 5-94 | W Indies | World XI | Scarborough | 28/08/91 |
| E.A.E.Baptiste | 5-95 | N'hants | W'wicks | Edgbaston | 10/09/91 |
| D.R.Pringle | 5-100 | England | W Indies | Lord's | 20/06/91 |
| D.W.Headley | 5-100 | Middx | Kent | Canterbury | 28/08/91 |
| P.J.Hartley | 5-100 | Yorks | Lancs | Scarborough | 03/09/91 |
| P.Carrick | 5-103 | Yorks | Sussex | Midd'brough | 09/08/91 |
| C.Penn | 5-105 | Kent | Middx | Canterbury | 28/08/91 |
| D.V.Lawrence | 5-106 | England | W Indies | The Oval | 08/08/91 |
| J.H.Childs | 5-112 | Essex | Surrey | The Oval | 05/07/91 |
| Wasim Akram | 5-117 | Lancs | Notts | Trent Bridge | 16/07/91 |
| N.M.Kendrick | 5-120 | Surrey | Lancs | Old Trafford | 17/09/91 |
| I.T.Botham | 5-125 | Worcs | Glos | Worcester | 27/04/91 |
| M.C.J.Ball | 5-128 | Glos | Kent | Canterbury | 20/08/91 |
| R.J.Maru | 5-128 | Hants | Glam | Southampton | 17/09/91 |
| A.I.C.Dodemaide | 5-130 | Sussex | Glos | Cheltenham | 23/07/91 |
| J.G.Thomas | 5-146 | N'hants | Essex | Northampton | 09/05/91 |
| R.W.Sladdin | 5-186 | Derby | Essex | Chelmsford | 03/09/91 |
| P.C.R.Tufnell | 4-14 | Middx | Camb U | Fenner's | 15/05/91 |
| R.J.Maru | 4-17 | Hants | Oxford U | The Parks | 13/04/91 |
| N.A.Foster | 4-18 | Essex | Middx | Chelmsford | 17/09/91 |
| R.J.Shastri | 4-20 | Glam | Camb U | Fenner's | 18/06/91 |
| M.J.Gerrard | 4-20 | Glos | S Lanka | Bristol | 06/08/91 |
| A.R.C.Fraser | 4-24 | Middx | Kent | Lord's | 31/05/91 |
| P.Carrick | 4-25 | Yorks | N'hants | Headingley | 25/05/91 |
| D.G.Cork | 4-25 | Derby | Sussex | Derby | 05/07/91 |
| J.E.Emburey | 4-25 | Middx | Surrey | Lord's | 10/09/91 |
| P.J.Newport | 4-27 | Worcs | Oxford U | The Parks | 25/05/91 |
| D.A.Reeve | 4-27 | W'wicks | Hants | Portsmouth | 19/07/91 |
| P.A.Smith | 4-28 | W'wicks | Glos | Edgbaston | 25/05/91 |
| A.A.Donald | 4-28 | W'wicks | Yorks | Edgbaston | 31/05/91 |
| I.J.Turner | 4-28 | Hants | Derby | Chesterfield | 23/07/91 |
| P.W.Jarvis | 4-28 | Yorks | Derby | Chesterfield | 17/09/91 |
| N.A.Foster | 4-29 | Essex | Camb U | Fenner's | 19/04/91 |
| C.E.L.Ambrose | 4-29 | W Indies | Essex | Chelmsford | 03/08/91 |
| C.J.Adams | 4-29 | Derby | Lancs | Derby | 16/08/91 |
| N.V.Radford | 4-29 | Worcs | Glam | Cardiff | 10/09/91 |
| J.P.Stephenson | 4-30 | Essex | Camb U | Fenner's | 19/04/91 |
| A.N.Nelson | 4-30 | Ireland | Scotland | Dublin | 22/06/91 |
| P.J.Martin | 4-30 | Lancs | Worcs | Blackpool | 20/08/91 |
| M.J.Russell | 4-31 | Oxford U | Kent | The Parks | 18/06/91 |
| K.D.James | 4-32 | Hants | Middx | Lord's | 02/08/91 |
| M.D.Marshall | 4-33 | W Indies | England | Edgbaston | 25/07/91 |
| A.M.Babington | 4-33 | Glos | Lancs | Bristol | 09/08/91 |
| T.D.Topley | 4-34 | Essex | Glos | Bristol | 31/05/91 |
| P.A.J.DeFreitas | 4-34 | England | W Indies | Headingley | 06/06/91 |
| S.J.Base | 4-34 | Derby | Yorks | Chesterfield | 17/09/91 |
| G.C.Small | 4-36 | W'wicks | Sussex | Coventry | 18/06/91 |
| N.A.Foster | 4-36 | Essex | Middx | Lord's | 28/06/91 |
| G.C.Small | 4-36 | W'wicks | Derby | Edgbaston | 28/06/91 |
| A.P.Igglesden | 4-36 | Kent | Essex | Southend | 16/07/91 |
| C.Penn | 4-36 | Kent | Surrey | Canterbury | 02/08/91 |
| M.A.Feltham | 4-36 | Surrey | Hants | The Oval | 03/09/91 |
| T.A.Merrick | 4-37 | Kent | Hants | Southampton | 27/04/91 |
| S.J.W.Andrew | 4-38 | Essex | W'wicks | Chelmsford | 22/05/91 |
| J.E.Emburey | 4-38 | Middx | Notts | Trent Bridge | 03/09/91 |
| C.A.Walsh | 4-39 | W Indies | Middx | Lord's | 18/05/91 |
| S.R.Lampitt | 4-39 | Worcs | Oxford U | The Parks | 25/05/91 |
| K.M.Curran | 4-39 | N'hants | Derby | Northampton | 31/05/91 |
| R.M.Ellison | 4-39 | Kent | Middx | Lord's | 31/05/91 |
| G.R.Dilley | 4-39 | Worcs | Glos | Cheltenham | 26/07/91 |
| J.N.Maguire | 4-39 | Leics | Kent | Canterbury | 17/09/91 |
| S.L.Watkin | 4-40 | Glam | Worcs | Worcester | 31/05/91 |
| F.D.Stephenson | 4-40 | Notts | Glam | Cardiff | 02/07/91 |
| M.C.J.Ball | 4-40 | Glos | Lancs | Bristol | 09/08/91 |
| R.M.Ellison | 4-40 | Kent | Middx | Canterbury | 28/08/91 |
| A.M.Smith | 4-41 | Glos | Leics | Hinckley | 02/07/91 |
| M.A.Feltham | 4-41 | Surrey | W'wicks | Edgbaston | 06/08/91 |
| A.N.Jones | 4-41 | Sussex | Yorks | Midd'brough | 09/08/91 |
| A.E.Warner | 4-42 | Derby | Glam | Chesterfield | 07/06/91 |
| N.G.Cowans | 4-42 | Middx | Glam | Cardiff | 14/06/91 |
| Waqar Younis | 4-42 | Surrey | Middx | Lord's | 10/09/91 |
| S.J.Base | 4-43 | Derby | Kent | Canterbury | 25/05/91 |
| O.H.Mortensen | 4-43 | Derby | Surrey | Derby | 21/06/91 |
| J.A.Afford | 4-44 | Notts | Kent | Trent Bridge | 22/05/91 |
| S.J.Base | 4-44 | Derby | W Indies | Derby | 12/06/91 |
| N.G.Cowans | 4-44 | Middx | W'wicks | Edgbaston | 02/07/91 |
| M.Frost | 4-44 | Glam | Glos | Cheltenham | 19/07/91 |
| C.Penn | 4-44 | Kent | Middx | Canterbury | 28/08/91 |
| P.J.Newport | 4-44 | Worcs | Glam | Cardiff | 10/09/91 |
| C.C.Lewis | 4-45 | Leics | Surrey | Leicester | 14/06/91 |
| G.R.Dilley | 4-45 | Worcs | Glos | Cheltenham | 26/07/91 |

# ALL FIRST-CLASS MATCHES

## 100 Best Match Bowling Figures

| Name | Figures | For | Against | Venue | Date |
|---|---|---|---|---|---|
| D.J.Millns | 12-91 | Leics | Derby | Derby | 20/08/91 |
| Waqar Younis | 12-92 | Surrey | Hants | The Oval | 03/09/91 |
| Waqar Younis | 11-122 | Surrey | Lancs | The Oval | 22/05/91 |
| T.A.Munton | 11-127 | W'wicks | Middx | Edgbaston | 02/07/91 |
| D.V.Lawrence | 11-129 | Glos | Hants | Bristol | 09/05/91 |
| Wasim Akram | 11-129 | Lancs | Middx | Uxbridge | 19/07/91 |
| K.T.Medlycott | 11-134 | Surrey | Camb U | Fenner's | 18/05/91 |
| Waqar Younis | 11-136 | Surrey | Hants | Bournemouth | 25/05/91 |
| M.Frost | 11-143 | Glam | Glos | Cheltenham | 19/07/91 |
| P.C.R.Tufnell | 11-228 | Middx | Hants | Lord's | 02/08/91 |
| M.J.Gerrard | 10-60 | Glos | S Lanka | Bristol | 06/08/91 |
| A.A.Donald | 10-74 | W'wicks | Glam | Swansea | 16/05/91 |
| D.G.Cork | 10-78 | Derby | Essex | Derby | 06/08/91 |
| F.D.Stephenson | 10-88 | Notts | N'hants | Well'borough | 19/07/91 |
| T.A.Munton | 10-91 | W'wicks | Worcs | Edgbaston | 28/08/91 |
| A.A.Donald | 10-96 | W'wicks | Yorks | Headingley | 09/05/91 |
| N.A.Foster | 10-122 | Essex | Middx | Chelmsford | 17/09/91 |
| B.T.P.Donelan | 10-136 | Sussex | Glos | Hove | 17/09/91 |
| N.M.Kendrick | 10-174 | Surrey | Lancs | Old Trafford | 17/09/91 |
| P.A.Smith | 9-56 | W'wicks | Glos | Edgbaston | 25/05/91 |
| T.A.Munton | 9-78 | W'wicks | Leics | Leicester | 26/07/91 |
| S.L.Watkin | 9-85 | Glam | N'hants | Cardiff | 22/05/91 |
| A.N.Jones | 9-87 | Sussex | Yorks | Midd'brough | 09/08/91 |
| M.P.Bicknell | 9-87 | Surrey | Sussex | The Oval | 28/08/91 |
| A.C.S.Pigott | 9-89 | Sussex | Middx | Lord's | 09/05/91 |
| N.V.Radford | 9-95 | Worcs | Essex | Ilford | 07/06/91 |
| Waqar Younis | 9-95 | Surrey | Middx | Lord's | 10/09/91 |
| E.E.Hemmings | 9-96 | Notts | Lancs | Trent Bridge | 16/07/91 |
| Waqar Younis | 9-97 | Surrey | W'wicks | Edgbaston | 06/08/91 |
| D.R.Gilbert | 9-105 | Glos | Kent | Canterbury | 20/08/91 |
| N.A.Foster | 9-114 | Essex | Notts | Trent Bridge | 09/08/91 |
| R.M.Ellison | 9-116 | Kent | Middx | Lord's | 31/05/91 |
| S.R.Lampitt | 9-124 | Worcs | Oxford U | The Parks | 25/05/91 |
| A.A.Donald | 9-124 | W'wicks | N'hants | Edgbaston | 10/09/91 |
| K.J.Shine | 9-134 | Hants | Worcs | Portsmouth | 16/07/91 |
| K.P.Evans | 9-135 | Notts | Leics | Trent Bridge | 09/05/91 |
| R.J.Shastri | 9-144 | Glam | W'wicks | Edgbaston | 20/08/91 |
| D.J.Foster | 9-147 | Glam | Som | Taunton | 09/05/91 |
| C.Penn | 9-149 | Kent | Middx | Canterbury | 28/08/91 |
| E.A.E.Baptiste | 9-159 | N'hants | Yorks | Northampton | 28/08/91 |
| P.C.R.Tufnell | 9-167 | Middx | Notts | Trent Bridge | 03/09/91 |
| P.A.J.DeFreitas | 9-179 | Lancs | Worcs | Worcester | 09/05/91 |
| T.A.Merrick | 9-180 | Kent | Sussex | Hove | 03/09/91 |
| D.A.Graveney | 9-193 | Som | Kent | Taunton | 26/07/91 |
| C.E.L.Ambrose | 8-70 | W Indies | Glam | Swansea | 16/07/91 |
| D.A.Reeve | 8-73 | W'wicks | Hants | Portsmouth | 19/07/91 |
| G.R.Dilley | 8-84 | Worcs | Glos | Cheltenham | 26/07/91 |
| J.H.Childs | 8-86 | Essex | Som | Southend | 19/07/91 |
| D.G.Cork | 8-91 | Derby | Sussex | Derby | 05/07/91 |
| R.A.Pick | 8-91 | Notts | N'hants | Well'borough | 19/07/91 |
| P.A.J.DeFreitas | 8-93 | England | W Indies | Headingley | 06/06/91 |
| Waqar Younis | 8-94 | Surrey | Yorks | Guildford | 19/07/91 |
| M.C.J.Ball | 8-95 | Glos | Lancs | Bristol | 09/08/91 |
| I.T.Botham | 8-97 | Worcs | W'wicks | Worcester | 02/08/91 |
| C.Penn | 8-98 | Kent | Surrey | The Oval | 09/05/91 |
| Waqar Younis | 8-98 | Surrey | Kent | Canterbury | 02/08/91 |
| C.E.L.Ambrose | 8-101 | W Indies | England | Headingley | 06/06/91 |
| J.H.Childs | 8-113 | Essex | Derby | Chelmsford | 03/09/91 |
| J.P.Taylor | 8-114 | N'hants | Leics | Northampton | 16/05/91 |
| N.A.Foster | 8-115 | Essex | Lancs | Old Trafford | 23/08/91 |
| .A.J.DeFreitas | 8-115 | England | S Lanka | Lord's | 22/08/91 |
| P.A.J.DeFreitas | 8-115 | Lancs | Notts | Old Trafford | 28/08/91 |
| K.P.Evans | 8-117 | Notts | Essex | Trent Bridge | 09/08/91 |
| N.A.Mallender | 8-123 | Som | W'wicks | Taunton | 17/09/91 |
| R.J.Ratnayake | 8-126 | S Lanka | Glos | Bristol | 06/08/91 |
| J.E.Emburey | 8-128 | Middx | Notts | Trent Bridge | 03/09/91 |
| N.V.Radford | 8-128 | Worcs | Som | Worcester | 03/09/91 |
| N.A.Foster | 8-129 | Essex | W'wicks | Chelmsford | 22/05/91 |
| J.W.Lloyds | 8-129 | Glos | N'hants | Luton | 28/06/91 |
| C.E.L.Ambrose | 8-135 | W Indies | England | Trent Bridge | 04/07/91 |
| J.H.Childs | 8-138 | Essex | N'hants | Colchester | 16/08/91 |
| P.C.R.Tufnell | 8-139 | Middx | Leics | Uxbridge | 07/06/91 |
| E.A.E.Baptiste | 8-143 | N'hants | Sussex | Eastbourne | 02/08/91 |
| J.E.Emburey | 8-147 | Middx | Sussex | Hove | 22/05/91 |
| G.R.Dilley | 8-155 | Worcs | Lancs | Worcester | 09/05/91 |
| N.A.Foster | 8-157 | Essex | Leics | Leicester | 10/09/91 |
| Wasim Akram | 8-162 | Lancs | Sussex | Old Trafford | 31/05/91 |
| D.E.Malcolm | 8-175 | Derby | N'hants | Northampton | 31/05/91 |
| B.T.P.Donelan | 8-188 | Sussex | Leics | Hove | 19/07/91 |
| J.H.Childs | 8-197 | Essex | Surrey | The Oval | 05/07/91 |
| H.R.J.Trump | 8-253 | Som | Hants | Southampton | 28/08/91 |
| M.A.Feltham | 7-69 | Surrey | W'wicks | Edgbaston | 06/08/91 |
| P.C.R.Tufnell | 7-69 | Middx | Surrey | Lord's | 10/09/91 |
| C.M.Wells | 7-75 | Sussex | Derby | Derby | 05/07/91 |
| D.R.Gilbert | 7-76 | Glos | S Lanka | Bristol | 06/08/91 |
| N.A.Foster | 7-83 | Essex | Hants | Chelmsford | 02/07/91 |
| F.D.Stephenson | 7-89 | Notts | Worcs | Trent Bridge | 17/09/91 |
| C.A.Connor | 7-90 | Hants | Surrey | Bournemouth | 25/05/91 |
| F.D.Stephenson | 7-90 | Notts | Worcs | Worcester | 18/06/91 |
| J.R.Ayling | 7-90 | Hants | Surrey | The Oval | 03/09/91 |
| J.H.Childs | 7-90 | Essex | Victoria | Chelmsford | 23/09/91 |
| T.D.Topley | 7-91 | Essex | Leics | Ilford | 04/06/91 |
| D.J.Millns | 7-92 | Leics | Yorks | Leicester | 06/08/91 |
| C.M.Tolley | 7-93 | Worcs | S Lanka | Worcester | 30/07/91 |
| A.P.Igglesden | 7-93 | Kent | Glos | Canterbury | 20/08/91 |
| L.Tennant | 7-97 | Leics | Camb U | Fenner's | 22/05/91 |
| J.N.Maguire | 7-98 | Leics | Kent | Canterbury | 17/09/91 |
| C.L.Hooper | 7-99 | W Indies | Derby | Derby | 12/06/91 |
| P.W.Jarvis | 7-99 | Yorks | Derby | Chesterfield | 17/09/91 |
| Waqar Younis | 7-102 | Surrey | Glos | Guildford | 16/07/91 |

# TEXACO TROPHY

## BATTING
### 20 Best Individual Scores

| Name | Score | For | Against | Venue | Date |
|---|---|---|---|---|---|
| N.H.Fairbrother | 113 | England | W Indies | Lord's | 27/05/91 |
| G.A.Hick | 86* | England | W Indies | Lord's | 27/05/91 |
| A.L.Logie | 82 | W Indies | England | Lord's | 27/05/91 |
| I.V.A.Richards | 78 | W Indies | England | Old Trafford | 25/05/91 |
| M.A.Atherton | 74 | England | W Indies | Old Trafford | 25/05/91 |
| M.A.Atherton | 69* | England | W Indies | Edgbaston | 23/05/91 |
| A.J.Lamb | 62 | England | W Indies | Old Trafford | 25/05/91 |
| G.A.Gooch | 54 | England | W Indies | Old Trafford | 25/05/91 |
| C.L.Hooper | 48 | W Indies | England | Old Trafford | 25/05/91 |
| R.B.Richardson | 41 | W Indies | England | Lord's | 27/05/91 |
| I.V.A.Richards | 37 | W Indies | England | Lord's | 27/05/91 |
| I.V.A.Richards | 30 | W Indies | England | Edgbaston | 23/05/91 |
| C.A.Walsh | 29* | W Indies | England | Edgbaston | 23/05/91 |
| G.A.Hick | 29 | England | W Indies | Old Trafford | 25/05/91 |
| P.V.Simmons | 28 | W Indies | England | Old Trafford | 25/05/91 |
| C.L.Hooper | 26 | W Indies | England | Lord's | 27/05/91 |
| M.A.Atherton | 25 | England | W Indies | Lord's | 27/05/91 |
| A.L.Logie | 24 | W Indies | England | Old Trafford | 25/05/91 |
| C.G.Greenidge | 23 | W Indies | England | Edgbaston | 23/05/91 |
| B.C.Lara | 23 | W Indies | England | Lord's | 27/05/91 |

## BOWLING
### 20 Best Bowling Figures

| Name | Figures | For | Against | Venue | Date |
|---|---|---|---|---|---|
| I.T.Botham | 4-45 | England | W Indies | Edgbaston | 23/05/91 |
| D.V.Lawrence | 4-67 | England | W Indies | Lord's | 27/05/91 |
| C.C.Lewis | 3-62 | England | W Indies | Old Trafford | 25/05/91 |
| C.L.Hooper | 2-18 | W Indies | England | Edgbaston | 23/05/91 |
| P.A.J.DeFreitas | 2-26 | England | W Indies | Lord's | 27/05/91 |
| M.D.Marshall | 2-32 | W Indies | England | Edgbaston | 23/05/91 |
| C.A.Walsh | 2-34 | W Indies | England | Edgbaston | 23/05/91 |
| C.E.L.Ambrose | 2-36 | W Indies | England | Old Trafford | 25/05/91 |
| B.P.Patterson | 2-38 | W Indies | England | Edgbaston | 23/05/91 |
| D.R.Pringle | 2-52 | England | W Indies | Old Trafford | 25/05/91 |
| R.K.Illingworth | 2-53 | England | W Indies | Lord's | 27/05/91 |
| G.A.Gooch | 1-9 | England | W Indies | Lord's | 27/05/91 |
| G.A.Gooch | 1-17 | England | W Indies | Edgbaston | 23/05/91 |
| R.K.Illingworth | 1-20 | England | W Indies | Edgbaston | 23/05/91 |
| P.A.J.DeFreitas | 1-22 | England | W Indies | Edgbaston | 23/05/91 |
| C.E.L.Ambrose | 1-34 | W Indies | England | Edgbaston | 23/05/91 |
| B.P.Patterson | 1-39 | W Indies | England | Old Trafford | 25/05/91 |
| C.C.Lewis | 1-41 | England | W Indies | Edgbaston | 23/05/91 |
| C.L.Hooper | 1-44 | W Indies | England | Old Trafford | 25/05/91 |
| M.D.Marshall | 1-49 | W Indies | England | Lord's | 27/05/91 |

# REFUGE ASSURANCE LEAGUE AND CUP

## BATTING
### 100 Best Individual Scores

| Name | Score | For | Against | Venue | Date |
|---|---|---|---|---|---|
| T.M.Moody | 160 | Worcs | Kent | Worcester | 21/04/91 |
| R.J.Blakey | 130* | Yorks | KentN | Scarborough | 16/06/91 |
| M.D.Moxon | 129* | Yorks | Surrey | The Oval | 21/07/91 |
| S.J.Cook | 129* | Som | Worcs | Worcester | 18/08/91 |
| T.M.Moody | 128* | Worcs | Glos | Bristol | 05/05/91 |
| T.M.Moody | 128* | Worcs | Middx | Worcester | 25/08/91 |
| V.P.Terry | 123 | Hants | Glos | Swindon | 26/05/91 |
| A.A.Metcalfe | 116 | Yorks | Middx | Lord's | 07/07/91 |
| G.P.Thorpe | 115* | Surrey | Lancs | Old Trafford | 18/08/91 |
| C.L.Smith | 114 | Hants | Worcs | Southampton | 07/07/91 |
| M.D.Moxon | 112 | Yorks | Sussex | Midd'brough | 11/08/91 |
| M.R.Ramprakash | 111* | Middx | Glos | Bristol | 21/04/91 |
| M.W.Gatting | 111 | Middx | Glos | Bristol | 21/04/91 |
| G.A.Hick | 109 | Worcs | Notts | Trent Bridge | 04/08/91 |
| J.C.Pooley | 109 | Middx | Derby | Lord's | 11/08/91 |
| B.C.Broad | 108 | Notts | Glam | Cardiff | 05/05/91 |
| W.Larkins | 108 | N'hants | Essex | Peterborough | 11/08/91 |
| G.A.Gooch | 107 | Essex | Som | Southend | 21/07/91 |
| M.P.Speight | 106* | Sussex | Worcs | Hove | 16/06/91 |
| M.A.Roseberry | 106* | Middx | Yorks | Lord's | 07/07/91 |
| S.J.Rhodes | 105 | Worcs | Lancs | Old Trafford | 15/09/91 |
| P.W.G.Parker | 104 | Sussex | Leics | Hove | 21/07/91 |
| Asif Din | 101* | W'wicks | Middx | Edgbaston | 14/07/91 |
| M.P.Maynard | 101 | Glam | Derby | Checkley | 18/08/91 |
| B.C.Broad | 100* | Notts | Lancs | Old Trafford | 21/04/91 |
| T.M.Moody | 100 | Worcs | N'hants | Northampton | 19/05/91 |
| D.A.Reeve | 100 | W'wicks | Lancs | Edgbaston | 16/06/91 |
| R.J.Bailey | 99 | N'hants | Lancs | Old Trafford | 28/04/91 |
| M.A.Lynch | 97 | Surrey | Yorks | The Oval | 21/07/91 |
| A.A.Metcalfe | 96 | Yorks | Glam | Headingley | 30/06/91 |
| N.J.Speak | 94* | Lancs | N'hants | Old Trafford | 01/09/91 |
| A.J.Moles | 93* | W'wicks | Glam | Swansea | 19/05/91 |
| S.J.Cook | 93 | Som | Essex | Southend | 21/07/91 |
| P.A.Cottey | 92* | Glam | Hants | Ebbw Vale | 11/08/91 |
| T.M.Moody | 91 | Worcs | Som | Worcester | 18/08/91 |
| R.J.Shastri | 90* | Glam | Kent | Maidstone | 07/07/91 |
| Salim Malik | 89 | Essex | Worcs | Ilford | 09/06/91 |
| T.S.Curtis | 88* | Worcs | Leics | Worcester | 30/06/91 |
| J.J.Whitaker | 88 | Leics | Lancs | Leicester | 07/07/91 |
| C.L.Smith | 86 | Hants | Yorks | Southampton | 21/04/91 |
| N.J.Lenham | 86 | Sussex | Kent | Hove | 25/08/91 |
| C.W.J.Athey | 85 | Glos | Hants | Swindon | 26/05/91 |
| M.A.Lynch | 85 | Surrey | Essex | The Oval | 26/05/91 |
| J.J.Whitaker | 85 | Leics | Som | Weston | 04/08/91 |
| A.J.Stewart | 84* | Surrey | Sussex | The Oval | 14/07/91 |
| G.A.Hick | 84 | Worcs | Leics | Worcester | 30/06/91 |
| M.R.Benson | 84 | Kent | Glam | Maidstone | 07/07/91 |
| D.W.Randall | 83* | Notts | Leics | Leicester | 26/05/91 |
| M.Watkinson | 83 | Lancs | Sussex | Old Trafford | 02/06/91 |
| D.W.Randall | 83 | Notts | Hants | Trent Bridge | 14/07/91 |
| N.R.Taylor | 82* | Kent | Glam | Maidstone | 07/07/91 |
| M.Watkinson | 82 | Lancs | Derby | Derby | 19/05/91 |
| K.R.Brown | 81* | Middx | Surrey | Lord's | 28/04/91 |
| Asif Din | 81* | W'wicks | Glos | Edgbaston | 18/08/91 |
| M.P.Maynard | 81 | Glam | Glos | Swansea | 04/08/91 |
| P.Johnson | 80 | Notts | W'wicks | Trent Bridge | 28/04/91 |
| G.R.Cowdrey | 80 | Kent | Glos | Canterbury | 30/06/91 |
| G.D.Lloyd | 79* | Lancs | Worcs | Worcester | 12/05/91 |
| R.J.Harden | 79* | Som | Notts | Trent Bridge | 09/06/91 |
| B.C.Broad | 79* | Notts | Surrey | The Oval | 30/06/91 |
| C.W.J.Athey | 79 | Glos | Surrey | The Oval | 12/05/91 |
| M.A.Roseberry | 79 | Middx | Kent | Southgate | 02/06/91 |
| G.D.Mendis | 79 | Lancs | Som | Taunton | 05/07/91 |
| K.Greenfield | 78* | Sussex | Hants | Basingstoke | 09/06/91 |
| G.D.Lloyd | 78* | Lancs | Som | Taunton | 05/07/91 |
| R.J.Bailey | 78* | N'hants | W'wicks | Northampton | 25/08/91 |
| M.R.Benson | 78 | Kent | Middx | Southgate | 02/06/91 |
| D.M.Smith | 78 | Sussex | Derby | Derby | 07/07/91 |
| D.J.Capel | 77* | N'hants | Leics | Northampton | 12/05/91 |
| A.R.Butcher | 77 | Glam | N'hants | Cardiff | 21/04/91 |
| P.D.Bowler | 77 | Derby | Leics | Leicester | 21/04/91 |
| A.R.Butcher | 77 | Glam | Notts | Cardiff | 05/05/91 |
| R.J.Scott | 77 | Glos | Hants | Swindon | 26/05/91 |
| M.V.Fleming | 77 | Kent | Sussex | Hove | 25/08/91 |
| M.W.Alleyne | 76* | Glos | Leics | Leicester | 25/08/91 |
| A.Fordham | 76 | N'hants | Yorks | Headingley | 26/05/91 |
| T.S.Curtis | 76 | Worcs | Hants | Southampton | 07/07/91 |
| M.D.Moxon | 76 | Yorks | Lancs | Old Trafford | 04/08/91 |
| B.C.Broad | 76 | Notts | Kent | Trent Bridge | 11/08/91 |
| C.J.Tavare | 75* | Som | Hants | Bournemouth | 19/05/91 |
| P.A.Smith | 75 | W'wicks | Yorks | Headingley | 12/05/91 |
| H.Morris | 75 | Glam | Middx | Cardiff | 16/06/91 |
| R.A.Smith | 75 | Hants | Leics | Bournemouth | 18/08/91 |
| D.Byas | 74* | Yorks | Leics | Leicester | 19/05/91 |
| B.C.Broad | 73* | Notts | Derby | Trent Bridge | 25/08/91 |
| J.J.Whitaker | 73 | Leics | Glam | Leicester | 28/04/91 |
| M.Azharuddin | 73 | Derby | Kent | Canterbury | 26/05/91 |
| P.Pollard | 73 | Notts | Worcs | Trent Bridge | 04/08/91 |
| A.Fordham | 73 | N'hants | Essex | Peterborough | 11/08/91 |
| D.Gough | 72* | Yorks | Leics | Leicester | 19/05/91 |
| G.C.Holmes | 72 | Glam | Leics | Leicester | 28/04/91 |
| R.J.Blakey | 71* | Yorks | N'hants | Headingley | 26/05/91 |
| G.D.Lloyd | 71 | Lancs | N'hants | Old Trafford | 28/04/91 |
| A.J.Stewart | 71 | Surrey | Middx | Lord's | 28/04/91 |
| A.J.Wright | 71 | Glos | Surrey | The Oval | 12/05/91 |
| C.J.Adams | 71 | Derby | Lancs | Derby | 19/05/91 |
| T.S.Curtis | 70 | Worcs | Kent | Worcester | 21/04/91 |
| N.A.Felton | 69 | N'hants | Hants | Northampton | 02/06/91 |
| I.A.Greig | 68* | Surrey | Middx | Lord's | 28/04/91 |
| D.J.Bicknell | 68 | Surrey | Derby | Chesterfield | 09/06/91 |
| M.R.Ramprakash | 68 | Middx | Hants | Lord's | 04/08/91 |
| A.A.Metcalfe | 68 | Yorks | Sussex | Midd'brough | 11/08/91 |
| T.J.Boon | 68 | Leics | Hants | Bournemouth | 18/08/91 |

# REFUGE ASSURANCE LEAGUE AND CUP

## BOWLING
## 100 Best Bowling Figures

| Name | Figures | For | Against | Venue | Date |
|---|---|---|---|---|---|
| N.G.Cowans | 6-9 | Middx | Lancs | Lord's | 21/07/91 |
| P.Carrick | 5-22 | Yorks | Glam | Headingley | 30/06/91 |
| J.E.Emburey | 5-23 | Middx | Som | Taunton | 26/05/91 |
| T.A.Munton | 5-28 | W'wicks | Glos | Edgbaston | 18/08/91 |
| A.C.S.Pigott | 5-30 | Sussex | Hants | Basingstoke | 09/06/91 |
| F.D.Stephenson | 5-31 | Notts | N'hants | Well'borough | 21/07/91 |
| A.N.Jones | 5-32 | Sussex | Leics | Hove | 21/07/91 |
| G.A.Hick | 5-35 | Worcs | Notts | Trent Bridge | 01/09/91 |
| P.Carrick | 5-40 | Yorks | Sussex | Midd'brough | 11/08/91 |
| N.V.Radford | 5-42 | Worcs | Lancs | Old Trafford | 15/09/91 |
| R.K.Illingworth | 5-49 | Worcs | N'hants | Northampton | 19/05/91 |
| I.D.Austin | 5-56 | Lancs | Derby | Derby | 19/05/91 |
| I.D.Austin | 4-10 | Lancs | Glos | Bristol | 11/08/91 |
| P.M.Roebuck | 4-11 | Som | Derby | Derby | 16/06/91 |
| S.J.Base | 4-14 | Derby | N'hants | Derby | 28/07/91 |
| P.Willey | 4-17 | Leics | Surrey | Leicester | 16/06/91 |
| J.P.Stephenson | 4-17 | Essex | W'wicks | Chelmsford | 07/07/91 |
| D.A.Reeve | 4-18 | W'wicks | Derby | Edgbaston | 04/08/91 |
| P.A.Smith | 4-21 | W'wicks | Som | Edgbaston | 02/06/91 |
| Waqar Younis | 4-21 | Surrey | Kent | Canterbury | 04/08/91 |
| J.Derrick | 4-25 | Glam | Middx | Cardiff | 16/06/91 |
| E.E.Hemmings | 4-26 | Notts | W'wicks | Trent Bridge | 28/04/91 |
| D.V.Lawrence | 4-27 | Glos | Yorks | Scarborough | 14/07/91 |
| P.Carrick | 4-28 | Yorks | Lancs | Old Trafford | 04/08/91 |
| M.Saxelby | 4-29 | Notts | Leics | Leicester | 26/05/91 |
| C.A.Connor | 4-29 | Hants | Sussex | Basingstoke | 09/06/91 |
| Waqar Younis | 4-30 | Surrey | Som | The Oval | 21/04/91 |
| P.M.Such | 4-30 | Essex | Derby | Chelmsford | 30/06/91 |
| J.D.Batty | 4-33 | Yorks | Kent | Scarborough | 16/06/91 |
| M.A.Robinson | 4-33 | Yorks | Surrey | The Oval | 21/07/91 |
| R.A.Bunting | 4-35 | Sussex | Middx | Hove | 12/05/91 |
| J.E.Emburey | 4-38 | Middx | Notts | Trent Bridge | 23/06/91 |
| J.E.Emburey | 4-39 | Middx | Glos | Bristol | 21/04/91 |
| I.D.Austin | 4-40 | Lancs | Yorks | Old Trafford | 04/08/91 |
| M.V.Fleming | 4-45 | Kent | Som | Taunton | 28/07/91 |
| E.McCray | 4-49 | Derby | Glam | Checkley | 18/08/91 |
| M.J.McCague | 4-51 | Kent | Derby | Canterbury | 26/05/91 |
| A.M.Babington | 4-53 | Glos | Glam | Swansea | 04/08/91 |
| A.P.Igglesden | 4-59 | Kent | Worcs | Worcester | 21/04/91 |
| P.J.Hartley | 3-6 | Yorks | Derby | Chesterfield | 02/06/91 |
| I.D.K.Salisbury | 3-10 | Sussex | Glam | Swansea | 26/05/91 |
| I.A.Greig | 3-10 | Surrey | Leics | Leicester | 16/06/91 |
| A.C.S.Pigott | 3-11 | Sussex | W'wicks | Edgbaston | 21/04/91 |
| C.S.Pickles | 3-12 | Yorks | Worcs | Sheffield | 23/06/91 |
| A.J.Murphy | 3-15 | Surrey | Leics | Leicester | 16/06/91 |
| P.M.Roebuck | 3-15 | Som | N'hants | Luton | 30/06/91 |
| A.M.Smith | 3-16 | Glos | Sussex | Hove | 19/05/91 |
| N.V.Radford | 3-16 | Worcs | Derby | Worcester | 09/07/91 |
| F.D.Stephenson | 3-17 | Notts | W'wicks | Trent Bridge | 28/04/91 |
| J.P.Stephenson | 3-17 | Essex | Worcs | Ilford | 09/06/91 |
| R.D.Stemp | 3-18 | Worcs | Derby | Worcester | 09/07/91 |
| F.D.Stephenson | 3-20 | Notts | Middx | Trent Bridge | 23/06/91 |
| G.P.Thorpe | 3-21 | Surrey | Som | The Oval | 21/04/91 |
| I.T.Botham | 3-21 | Worcs | Derby | Worcester | 09/07/91 |
| D.A.Graveney | 3-21 | Som | Kent | Taunton | 28/07/91 |
| S.R.Lampitt | 3-23 | Worcs | Middx | Worcester | 25/08/91 |
| K.D.James | 3-24 | Hants | Yorks | Southampton | 21/04/91 |
| K.M.Curran | 3-24 | N'hants | Som | Luton | 30/06/91 |
| G.A.Gooch | 3-25 | Essex | Yorks | Chelmsford | 28/04/91 |
| A.N.Jones | 3-25 | Sussex | Glos | Hove | 19/05/91 |
| C.C.Lewis | 3-25 | Leics | Kent | Canterbury | 14/07/91 |
| J.R.Ayling | 3-25 | Hants | W'wicks | Portsmouth | 21/07/91 |
| A.C.S.Pigott | 3-26 | Sussex | Glam | Swansea | 26/05/91 |
| A.R.Roberts | 3-26 | N'hants | Hants | Northampton | 02/06/91 |
| S.D.Fletcher | 3-26 | Yorks | Worcs | Sheffield | 23/06/91 |
| R.J.Shastri | 3-26 | Glam | Hants | Ebbw Vale | 11/08/91 |
| A.C.S.Pigott | 3-26 | Sussex | Kent | Hove | 25/08/91 |
| Waqar Younis | 3-27 | Surrey | Essex | The Oval | 26/05/91 |
| M.Watkinson | 3-27 | Lancs | Surrey | Old Trafford | 02/06/91 |
| P.A.J.DeFreitas | 3-27 | Lancs | W'wicks | Edgbaston | 16/06/91 |
| P.N.Weekes | 3-27 | Middx | Hants | Lord's | 04/08/91 |
| P.C.R.Tufnell | 3-28 | Middx | Surrey | Lord's | 28/04/91 |
| A.J.Murphy | 3-28 | Surrey | Essex | The Oval | 26/05/91 |
| P.A.J.DeFreitas | 3-28 | Lancs | Sussex | Old Trafford | 02/06/91 |
| N.A.Foster | 3-28 | Essex | Worcs | Ilford | 09/06/91 |
| R.P.Lefebvre | 3-29 | Som | Sussex | Taunton | 28/04/91 |
| O.H.Mortensen | 3-29 | Derby | Middx | Lord's | 11/08/91 |
| T.D.Topley | 3-29 | Essex | Lancs | Old Trafford | 25/08/91 |
| J.A.North | 3-29 | Sussex | Kent | Hove | 25/08/91 |
| S.L.Watkin | 3-30 | Glam | N'hants | Cardiff | 21/04/91 |
| S.R.Barwick | 3-30 | Glam | N'hants | Cardiff | 21/04/91 |
| R.P.Lefebvre | 3-30 | Som | Glam | Taunton | 12/05/91 |
| C.S.Pickles | 3-30 | Yorks | Glos | Scarborough | 14/07/91 |
| R.P.Lefebvre | 3-30 | Som | Kent | Taunton | 28/07/91 |
| D.J.Capel | 3-30 | N'hants | Essex | Peterborough | 11/08/91 |
| D.J.Foster | 3-30 | Glam | Derby | Checkley | 18/08/91 |
| J.N.Maguire | 3-31 | Leics | Glam | Leicester | 28/04/91 |
| N.V.Radford | 3-31 | Worcs | N'hants | Northampton | 19/05/91 |
| K.H.Macleay | 3-31 | Som | Notts | Trent Bridge | 09/06/91 |
| P.D.Bowler | 3-31 | Derby | Glos | Cheltenham | 21/07/91 |
| J.P.Stephenson | 3-31 | Essex | Glos | Cheltenham | 28/07/91 |
| N.G.Cowans | 3-33 | Middx | Glos | Bristol | 21/04/91 |
| A.P.Igglesden | 3-33 | Kent | Hants | Southampton | 12/05/91 |
| F.D.Stephenson | 3-33 | Notts | Essex | Trent Bridge | 12/05/91 |
| S.J.W.Andrew | 3-33 | Essex | Glam | Pontypridd | 02/06/91 |
| A.N.Jones | 3-33 | Sussex | Hants | Basingstoke | 09/06/91 |
| R.P.Davis | 3-33 | Kent | Leics | Canterbury | 14/07/91 |
| P.A.Smith | 3-33 | W'wicks | Middx | Edgbaston | 14/07/91 |
| C.A.Connor | 3-33 | Hants | Lancs | Southampton | 28/07/91 |
| J.E.Benjamin | 3-33 | W'wicks | Derby | Edgbaston | 04/08/91 |

# BENSON & HEDGES CUP

## BATTING
### 100 Best Individual Scores

| Name | Score | For | Against | Venue | Date |
|------|-------|-----|---------|-------|------|
| J.P.Stephenson | 142 | Essex | W'wicks | Edgbaston | 25/04/91 |
| C.L.Smith | 142 | Hants | Glam | Southampton | 02/05/91 |
| M.D.Moxon | 141 * | Yorks | Glam | Cardiff | 07/05/91 |
| R.J.Shastri | 138 * | Glam | Min Co | Trowbridge | 23/04/91 |
| Asif Din | 137 | W'wicks | Som | Edgbaston | 02/05/91 |
| G.Fowler | 136 | Lancs | Sussex | Old Trafford | 07/05/91 |
| A.R.Butcher | 127 | Glam | Yorks | Cardiff | 07/05/91 |
| G.D.Mendis | 125 * | Lancs | N'hants | Old Trafford | 29/05/91 |
| C.L.Smith | 121 * | Hants | Notts | Southampton | 23/04/91 |
| R.T.Robinson | 116 | Notts | Glam | Cardiff | 04/05/91 |
| A.A.Metcalfe | 114 | Yorks | Lancs | Old Trafford | 16/06/91 |
| M.W.Gatting | 112 | Middx | Som | Taunton | 23/04/91 |
| T.M.Moody | 110 * | Worcs | Derby | Worcester | 04/05/91 |
| A.J.Stewart | 110 * | Surrey | Som | Taunton | 04/05/91 |
| N.R.Taylor | 110 | Kent | Scotland | Glasgow | 07/05/91 |
| B.C.Broad | 108 * | Notts | Yorks | Trent Bridge | 25/04/91 |
| T.J.Boon | 103 | Leics | Scotland | Leicester | 02/05/91 |
| P.Johnson | 102 * | Notts | Min Co | Trent Bridge | 07/05/91 |
| D.M.Smith | 102 | Sussex | Scotland | Hove | 04/05/91 |
| K.J.Barnett | 102 | Derby | Glos | Derby | 07/05/91 |
| N.A.Folland | 100 * | Min Co | Notts | Trent Bridge | 07/05/91 |
| J.J.Whitaker | 100 | Leics | Kent | Canterbury | 23/04/91 |
| P.D.Bowler | 100 | Derby | Comb U | The Parks | 25/04/91 |
| T.M.Moody | 100 | Worcs | Kent | Worcester | 29/05/91 |
| Asif Din | 97 | W'wicks | Middx | Lord's | 04/05/91 |
| M.D.Moxon | 95 | Yorks | Notts | Trent Bridge | 25/04/91 |
| A.Fordham | 93 * | N'hants | Comb U | Northampton | 04/05/91 |
| A.A.Metcalfe | 92 * | Yorks | Min Co | Headingley | 02/05/91 |
| D.Byas | 92 | Yorks | Hants | Headingley | 04/05/91 |
| M.A.Atherton | 91 | Lancs | Sussex | Old Trafford | 07/05/91 |
| Salim Malik | 90 * | Essex | Surrey | The Oval | 23/04/91 |
| N.R.Taylor | 89 * | Kent | Worcs | Worcester | 29/05/91 |
| G.A.Hick | 88 | Worcs | Lancs | Lord's | 13/07/91 |
| T.R.Ward | 87 | Kent | Leics | Canterbury | 23/04/91 |
| P.W.G.Parker | 87 | Sussex | Leics | Hove | 25/04/91 |
| D.W.Randall | 86 | Notts | Yorks | Trent Bridge | 25/04/91 |
| G.A.Hick | 84 * | Worcs | Kent | Worcester | 29/05/91 |
| J.J.Whitaker | 84 | Leics | Scotland | Leicester | 02/05/91 |
| A.A.Metcalfe | 84 | Yorks | Glam | Cardiff | 07/05/91 |
| D.W.Randall | 84 | Notts | Min Co | Trent Bridge | 07/05/91 |
| K.J.Barnett | 82 | Derby | Comb U | The Parks | 25/04/91 |
| G.K.Brown | 82 | Min Co | Hants | Trowbridge | 25/04/91 |
| J.D.Love | 81 | Min Co | Glam | Trowbridge | 23/04/91 |
| A.J.Wright | 81 | Glos | N'hants | Bristol | 02/05/91 |
| C.W.J.Athey | 81 | Glos | Derby | Derby | 07/05/91 |
| J.D.Love | 80 * | Min Co | Yorks | Headingley | 02/05/91 |
| G.J.Turner | 80 * | Comb U | N'hants | Northampton | 04/05/91 |
| D.A.Reeve | 80 | W'wicks | Essex | Edgbaston | 25/04/91 |
| M.R.Ramprakash | 78 * | Middx | Som | Taunton | 23/04/91 |
| C.L.Smith | 78 * | Hants | Min Co | Trowbridge | 25/04/91 |
| M.R.Benson | 76 | Kent | Leics | Canterbury | 23/04/91 |
| D.M.Smith | 76 | Sussex | Leics | Hove | 25/04/91 |
| S.J.Cook | 76 | Som | Surrey | Taunton | 04/05/91 |
| G.N.Reifer | 76 | Scotland | Sussex | Hove | 04/05/91 |
| J.D.Love | 75 | Min Co | Hants | Trowbridge | 25/04/91 |
| R.J.Bailey | 75 | N'hants | Lancs | Old Trafford | 29/05/91 |
| G.D.Mendis | 75 | Lancs | Yorks | Old Trafford | 16/06/91 |
| M.A.Atherton | 74 | Lancs | Leics | Leicester | 04/05/91 |
| J.P.Stephenson | 73 | Essex | Surrey | The Oval | 23/04/91 |
| T.M.Moody | 72 * | Worcs | Essex | Chelmsford | 12/06/91 |
| Salim Malik | 72 | Essex | W'wicks | Edgbaston | 25/04/91 |
| G.A.Gooch | 72 | Essex | Som | Chelmsford | 07/05/91 |
| J.E.Morris | 71 | Derby | Comb U | The Parks | 25/04/91 |
| S.A.Marsh | 71 | Kent | Lancs | Old Trafford | 25/04/91 |
| J.W.Hall | 71 | Sussex | Lancs | Old Trafford | 07/05/91 |
| C.L.Smith | 71 | Hants | Essex | Chelmsford | 29/05/91 |
| G.R.Cowdrey | 70 * | Kent | Leics | Canterbury | 23/04/91 |
| G.J.Turner | 70 * | Comb U | Derby | The Parks | 25/04/91 |
| J.R.Wood | 70 * | Hants | Min Co | Trowbridge | 25/04/91 |
| A.N.Hayhurst | 70 | Som | W'wicks | Edgbaston | 02/05/91 |
| A.R.Butcher | 70 | Glam | Hants | Southampton | 02/05/91 |
| A.Fordham | 70 | N'hants | Worcs | Northampton | 07/05/91 |

| Name | Score | For | Against | Venue | Date |
|------|-------|-----|---------|-------|------|
| A.P.Wells | 66 | Sussex | Kent | Canterbury | 02/05/91 |
| K.J.Barnett | 66 | Derby | Worcs | Worcester | 04/05/91 |
| A.J.Moles | 65 | W'wicks | Som | Edgbaston | 02/05/91 |
| M.D.Moxon | 65 | Yorks | Min Co | Headingley | 02/05/91 |
| M.R.Benson | 64 | Kent | Scotland | Glasgow | 07/05/91 |
| G.D.Mendis | 63 | Lancs | Scotland | Forfar | 23/04/91 |
| D.I.Gower | 63 | Hants | Glam | Southampton | 02/05/91 |
| M.P.Maynard | 62 | Glam | Notts | Cardiff | 04/05/91 |
| P.M.Roebuck | 61 | Som | Middx | Taunton | 23/04/91 |
| T.C.Middleton | 60 | Hants | Notts | Southampton | 23/04/91 |
| J.P.Stephenson | 60 | Essex | Som | Chelmsford | 07/05/91 |
| T.A.Lloyd | 58 | W'wicks | Essex | Edgbaston | 25/04/91 |
| P.R.Downton | 58 | Middx | Essex | Chelmsford | 02/05/91 |
| S.J.Cook | 58 | Som | W'wicks | Edgbaston | 02/05/91 |
| M.A.Crawley | 58 | Notts | Glam | Cardiff | 04/05/91 |
| D.Byas | 58 | Yorks | W'wicks | Headingley | 29/05/91 |
| G.Fowler | 58 | Lancs | Yorks | Old Trafford | 16/06/91 |
| C.S.Cowdrey | 57 * | Kent | Sussex | Canterbury | 02/05/91 |
| A.R.Butcher | 57 | Glam | Notts | Cardiff | 04/05/91 |
| G.A.Hick | 56 | Worcs | Glos | Worcester | 25/04/91 |
| M.A.Atherton | 56 | Lancs | N'hants | Old Trafford | 29/05/91 |
| M.R.Benson | 56 | Kent | Worcs | Worcester | 29/05/91 |
| A.J.Stewart | 55 | Surrey | Middx | Lord's | 25/04/91 |
| G.A.Hick | 55 | Worcs | Comb U | Fenner's | 02/05/91 |
| R.G.Swan | 55 | Scotland | Leics | Leicester | 02/05/91 |
| R.J.Bailey | 55 | N'hants | Worcs | Northampton | 07/05/91 |
| R.T.Robinson | 54 | Notts | Hants | Southampton | 23/04/91 |
| T.C.Middleton | 54 | Hants | Glam | Southampton | 02/05/91 |

# BENSON & HEDGES CUP

## BOWLING
### 100 Best Bowling Figures

| Name | Figures | For | Against | Venue | Date |
|---|---|---|---|---|---|
| D.V.Lawrence | 6-20 | Glos | Comb U | Bristol | 23/04/91 |
| R.MacDonald | 6-36 | Comb U | Glos | Bristol | 23/04/91 |
| J.G.Thomas | 5-29 | N'hants | Derby | Derby | 23/04/91 |
| F.D.Stephenson | 5-30 | Notts | Yorks | Trent Bridge | 25/04/91 |
| M.D.Moxon | 5-31 | Yorks | W'wicks | Headingley | 29/05/91 |
| J.E.Emburey | 5-37 | Middx | Som | Taunton | 23/04/91 |
| M.Watkinson | 5-49 | Lancs | Yorks | Old Trafford | 16/06/91 |
| D.R.Pringle | 5-51 | Essex | W'wicks | Edgbaston | 25/04/91 |
| P.A.J.DeFreitas | 4-15 | Lancs | Kent | Old Trafford | 25/04/91 |
| Wasim Akram | 4-18 | Lancs | Sussex | Old Trafford | 07/05/91 |
| A.Sidebottom | 4-19 | Yorks | Hants | Headingley | 04/05/91 |
| P.A.J.DeFreitas | 4-21 | Lancs | Scotland | Forfar | 23/04/91 |
| P.J.W.Allott | 4-23 | Lancs | Leics | Leicester | 04/05/91 |
| A.W.Bee | 4-31 | Scotland | Sussex | Hove | 04/05/91 |
| G.R.Dilley | 4-35 | Worcs | N'hants | Northampton | 07/05/91 |
| T.A.Munton | 4-35 | W'wicks | Surrey | The Oval | 07/05/91 |
| D.J.Capel | 4-37 | N'hants | Derby | Derby | 23/04/91 |
| P.N.Hepworth | 4-39 | Leics | Scotland | Leicester | 02/05/91 |
| T.D.Topley | 4-41 | Essex | Hants | Chelmsford | 29/05/91 |
| A.B.Russell | 4-42 | Scotland | Kent | Glasgow | 07/05/91 |
| K.P.Evans | 4-43 | Notts | Glam | Cardiff | 04/05/91 |
| D.A.Reeve | 4-43 | W'wicks | Surrey | The Oval | 07/05/91 |
| D.V.Lawrence | 4-44 | Glos | N'hants | Bristol | 02/05/91 |
| S.R.Lampitt | 4-46 | Worcs | Glos | Worcester | 25/04/91 |
| S.D.Fletcher | 4-51 | Yorks | Lancs | Old Trafford | 16/06/91 |
| A.A.Donald | 4-55 | W'wicks | Som | Edgbaston | 02/05/91 |
| I.T.Botham | 3-11 | Worcs | Essex | Chelmsford | 12/06/91 |
| J.W.Lloyds | 3-14 | Glos | Comb U | Bristol | 23/04/91 |
| P.J.W.Allott | 3-17 | Lancs | Kent | Old Trafford | 25/04/91 |
| N.V.Radford | 3-22 | Worcs | Comb U | Fenner's | 02/05/91 |
| P.Carrick | 3-22 | Yorks | W'wicks | Headingley | 29/05/91 |
| A.P.Igglesden | 3-24 | Kent | Scotland | Glasgow | 07/05/91 |
| S.L.Watkin | 3-28 | Glam | Min Co | Trowbridge | 23/04/91 |
| M.P.Bicknell | 3-28 | Surrey | Middx | Lord's | 25/04/91 |
| P.A.Smith | 3-28 | W'wicks | Middx | Lord's | 04/05/91 |
| A.C.S.Pigott | 3-29 | Sussex | Leics | Hove | 25/04/91 |
| Waqar Younis | 3-29 | Surrey | Som | Taunton | 04/05/91 |
| D.R.Pringle | 3-31 | Essex | Som | Chelmsford | 07/05/91 |
| A.P.Igglesden | 3-32 | Kent | Leics | Canterbury | 23/04/91 |
| A.N.Jones | 3-33 | Sussex | Leics | Hove | 25/04/91 |
| M.C.Ilott | 3-34 | Essex | Surrey | The Oval | 23/04/91 |
| P.A.J.DeFreitas | 3-34 | Lancs | Yorks | Old Trafford | 16/06/91 |
| J.C.Hallett | 3-36 | Comb U | Worcs | Fenner's | 02/05/91 |
| M.Frost | 3-38 | Glam | Notts | Cardiff | 04/05/91 |
| N.G.Cowans | 3-39 | Middx | W'wicks | Lord's | 04/05/91 |
| N.V.Radford | 3-40 | Worcs | Glos | Worcester | 25/04/91 |
| J.E.Emburey | 3-40 | Middx | Essex | Chelmsford | 02/05/91 |
| I.D.K.Salisbury | 3-40 | Sussex | Kent | Canterbury | 02/05/91 |
| S.D.Udal | 3-41 | Hants | Essex | Chelmsford | 29/05/91 |
| N.V.Radford | 3-41 | Worcs | Essex | Chelmsford | 12/06/91 |
| N.G.Cowans | 3-42 | Middx | Surrey | Lord's | 25/04/91 |
| M.Watkinson | 3-42 | Lancs | Kent | Old Trafford | 25/04/91 |
| Aqib Javed | 3-43 | Hants | Min Co | Trowbridge | 25/04/91 |
| D.A.Reeve | 3-43 | W'wicks | Som | Edgbaston | 02/05/91 |
| A.N.Jones | 3-43 | Sussex | Scotland | Hove | 04/05/91 |
| R.P.Lefebvre | 3-44 | Som | Surrey | Taunton | 04/05/91 |
| C.Wilkinson | 3-46 | Leics | Scotland | Leicester | 02/05/91 |
| S.R.Lampitt | 3-46 | Worcs | Derby | Worcester | 04/05/91 |
| I.T.Botham | 3-46 | Worcs | N'hants | Northampton | 07/05/91 |
| A.A.Donald | 3-46 | W'wicks | Yorks | Headingley | 29/05/91 |
| S.D.Udal | 3-48 | Hants | Notts | Southampton | 23/04/91 |
| D.A.Reeve | 3-48 | W'wicks | Middx | Lord's | 04/05/91 |
| N.V.Radford | 3-48 | Worcs | Lancs | Lord's | 13/07/91 |
| P.C.R.Tufnell | 3-50 | Middx | Surrey | Lord's | 25/04/91 |
| Aqib Javed | 3-51 | Hants | Yorks | Headingley | 04/05/91 |
| C.A.Connor | 3-54 | Hants | Glam | Southampton | 02/05/91 |
| Wasim Akram | 3-57 | Lancs | N'hants | Old Trafford | 29/05/91 |
| Wasim Akram | 3-58 | Lancs | Worcs | Lord's | 13/07/91 |
| C.C.Lewis | 3-62 | Leics | Kent | Canterbury | 23/04/91 |
| P.J.Hartley | 2-7 | Yorks | Hants | Headingley | 04/05/91 |
| P.W.Jarvis | 2-13 | Yorks | Hants | Headingley | 04/05/91 |
| D.E.Malcolm | 2-14 | Derby | Comb U | The Parks | 25/04/91 |
| O.H.Mortensen | 2-16 | Derby | N'hants | Derby | 23/04/91 |
| O.H.Mortensen | 2-16 | Derby | Comb U | The Parks | 25/04/91 |
| C.S.Cowdrey | 2-17 | Kent | Scotland | Glasgow | 07/05/91 |
| G.R.Dilley | 2-17 | Worcs | Essex | Chelmsford | 12/06/91 |
| G.J.Turner | 2-18 | Comb U | Glos | Bristol | 23/04/91 |
| N.F.Williams | 2-19 | Middx | Essex | Chelmsford | 02/05/91 |
| R.M.Ellison | 2-19 | Kent | Sussex | Canterbury | 02/05/91 |
| G.A.Gooch | 2-19 | Essex | Som | Chelmsford | 07/05/91 |
| G.R.Dilley | 2-19 | Worcs | Lancs | Lord's | 13/07/91 |
| S.Greensword | 2-21 | Min Co | Yorks | Headingley | 02/05/91 |
| T.M.Moody | 2-22 | Worcs | Glos | Worcester | 25/04/91 |
| A.L.Penberthy | 2-22 | N'hants | Comb U | Northampton | 04/05/91 |
| A.J.Murphy | 2-23 | Surrey | Middx | Lord's | 25/04/91 |
| I.A.Greig | 2-26 | Surrey | W'wicks | The Oval | 07/05/91 |
| P.J.W.Allott | 2-26 | Lancs | Worcs | Lord's | 13/07/91 |
| M.C.J.Nicholas | 2-27 | Hants | Glam | Southampton | 02/05/91 |
| P.W.Jarvis | 2-27 | Yorks | Min Co | Headingley | 02/05/91 |
| N.A.Foster | 2-28 | Essex | Middx | Chelmsford | 02/05/91 |
| M.Watkinson | 2-30 | Lancs | Scotland | Forfar | 23/04/91 |
| J.P.Taylor | 2-30 | N'hants | Worcs | Northampton | 07/05/91 |
| S.Greensword | 2-31 | Min Co | Glam | Trowbridge | 23/04/91 |
| J.D.Robinson | 2-31 | Surrey | Middx | Lord's | 25/04/91 |
| T.A.Merrick | 2-31 | Kent | Scotland | Glasgow | 07/05/91 |
| M.J.McCague | 2-32 | Kent | Lancs | Old Trafford | 25/04/91 |
| N.R.Taylor | 2-33 | Min Co | Glam | Trowbridge | 23/04/91 |
| S.D.Udal | 2-33 | Hants | Glam | Southampton | 02/05/91 |
| T.A.Merrick | 2-34 | Kent | Leics | Canterbury | 23/04/91 |
| D.V.Lawrence | 2-35 | Glos | Worcs | Worcester | 25/04/91 |

# NATWEST TROPHY

## BATTING
### 100 Best Individual Scores

| Name | Score | For | Against | Venue | Date |
|---|---|---|---|---|---|
| M.P.Maynard | 151 * | Glam | Durham | Darlington | 26/06/91 |
| R.J.Bailey | 145 | N'hants | Staffs | Stone | 26/06/91 |
| A.Fordham | 132 * | N'hants | Leics | Northampton | 11/07/91 |
| H.Morris | 126 * | Glam | Durham | Darlington | 26/06/91 |
| R.T.Robinson | 124 | Notts | Lincs | Trent Bridge | 26/06/91 |
| J.D.Glendenen | 109 | Durham | Glam | Darlington | 26/06/91 |
| C.L.Smith | 105 * | Hants | Notts | Southampton | 31/07/91 |
| N.Hussain | 97 | Essex | Sussex | Hove | 11/07/91 |
| G.A.Gooch | 95 | Essex | Sussex | Hove | 11/07/91 |
| D.W.Randall | 95 | Notts | Hants | Southampton | 31/07/91 |
| J.J.Whitaker | 94 * | Leics | N'hants | Northampton | 11/07/91 |
| G.P.Thorpe | 93 | Surrey | Hants | Lord's | 07/09/90 |
| A.N.Hayhurst | 91 * | Som | W'wicks | Edgbaston | 31/07/91 |
| A.Dale | 86 | Glam | Worcs | Worcester | 11/07/91 |
| M.W.Gatting | 85 | Middx | Som | Taunton | 11/07/91 |
| R.A.Smith | 79 * | Hants | Lancs | Southampton | 11/07/91 |
| M.P.Maynard | 78 * | Glam | Worcs | Worcester | 11/07/91 |
| T.A.Lloyd | 78 | W'wicks | Som | Edgbaston | 31/07/91 |
| T.C.Middleton | 78 | Hants | Surrey | Lord's | 07/09/90 |
| R.A.Smith | 78 | Hants | Surrey | Lord's | 07/09/90 |
| T.J.Boon | 76 * | Leics | Shrops | Leicester | 26/06/91 |
| A.J.Stewart | 76 * | Surrey | Kent | The Oval | 11/07/91 |
| C.W.J.Athey | 76 | Glos | Notts | Bristol | 11/07/91 |
| M.A.Crawley | 74 * | Notts | Lincs | Trent Bridge | 26/06/91 |
| G.Fowler | 71 | Lancs | Hants | Southampton | 11/07/91 |
| A.Fordham | 71 | N'hants | Glam | Northampton | 31/07/91 |
| J.J.E.Hardy | 70 | Glos | Norfolk | Bristol | 26/06/91 |
| A.R.Butcher | 70 | Glam | N'hants | Northampton | 31/07/91 |
| J.D.Ratcliffe | 68 * | W'wicks | Herts | Edgbaston | 11/07/91 |
| N.H.Fairbrother | 68 | Lancs | Dorset | Bournemouth | 26/06/91 |
| R.A.Smith | 67 | Hants | Notts | Southampton | 31/07/91 |
| M.P.Bicknell | 66 * | Surrey | N'hants | The Oval | 14/08/91 |
| N.J.Lenham | 66 | Sussex | Scotland | Edinburgh | 26/06/91 |
| C.L.Smith | 66 | Hants | Lancs | Southampton | 11/07/91 |
| M.W.Gatting | 65 | Middx | Ireland | Dublin | 26/06/91 |
| R.A.Smith | 64 * | Hants | W'wicks | Edgbaston | 14/08/91 |
| P.M.Roebuck | 63 * | Som | Bucks | Bath | 26/06/91 |
| A.J.Moles | 62 * | W'wicks | Herts | Edgbaston | 11/07/91 |
| V.P.Terry | 62 * | Hants | W'wicks | Edgbaston | 14/08/91 |
| D.M.Smith | 62 | Sussex | Essex | Hove | 11/07/91 |
| D.M.Ward | 62 | Surrey | Essex | The Oval | 31/07/91 |
| A.J.Stewart | 61 | Surrey | Hants | Lord's | 07/09/90 |
| C.J.Tavare | 59 | Som | Middx | Taunton | 11/07/91 |
| J.P.Stephenson | 59 | Essex | Surrey | The Oval | 31/07/91 |
| A.N.Hayhurst | 58 | Som | Middx | Taunton | 11/07/91 |
| D.A.Reeve | 57 * | W'wicks | Hants | Edgbaston | 14/08/91 |
| G.A.Gooch | 57 | Essex | Devon | Exmouth | 26/06/91 |
| J.P.Stephenson | 57 | Essex | Devon | Exmouth | 26/06/91 |
| L.Potter | 57 | Leics | N'hants | Northampton | 11/07/91 |
| D.A.Blenkiron | 56 | Durham | Glam | Darlington | 26/06/91 |
| A.J.Wright | 56 | Glos | Norfolk | Bristol | 26/06/91 |
| A.Fordham | 56 | N'hants | Staffs | Stone | 26/06/91 |
| N.A.Folland | 55 | Devon | Essex | Exmouth | 26/06/91 |
| D.M.Ward | 55 | Surrey | Kent | The Oval | 11/07/91 |
| T.R.Ward | 55 | Kent | Surrey | The Oval | 11/07/91 |
| R.J.Bailey | 55 | N'hants | Glam | Northampton | 31/07/91 |
| D.I.Gower | 54 * | Hants | Lancs | Southampton | 11/07/91 |
| N.A.Felton | 54 | N'hants | Leics | Northampton | 11/07/91 |
| J.Abrahams | 53 | Shrops | Leics | Leicester | 26/06/91 |
| G.D.Mendis | 50 | Lancs | Hants | Southampton | 11/07/91 |
| G.A.Gooch | 50 | Essex | Surrey | The Oval | 31/07/91 |
| K.R.Brown | 49 | Middx | Ireland | Dublin | 26/06/91 |
| R.J.Bailey | 48 * | N'hants | Leics | Northampton | 11/07/91 |
| P.Johnson | 48 | Notts | Lincs | Trent Bridge | 26/06/91 |
| R.T.Robinson | 48 | Notts | Glos | Bristol | 11/07/91 |
| M.A.Lynch | 48 | Surrey | Kent | The Oval | 11/07/91 |
| M.P.Speight | 48 | Sussex | Essex | Hove | 11/07/91 |
| C.W.J.Athey | 47 * | Glos | Norfolk | Bristol | 26/06/91 |
| V.P.Terry | 47 | Hants | Lancs | Southampton | 11/07/91 |
| J.D.Robinson | 47 | Surrey | Essex | The Oval | 31/07/91 |
| D.W.Randall | 46 | Notts | Glos | Bristol | 11/07/91 |
| R.G.Swan | 45 | Scotland | Sussex | Edinburgh | 26/06/91 |
| M.W.Alleyne | 45 | Glos | Notts | Bristol | 11/07/91 |
| N.J.Adams | 44 | Cambs | Kent | Canterbury | 26/06/91 |
| M.A.Roseberry | 44 | Middx | Som | Taunton | 11/07/91 |
| N.R.Taylor | 44 | Kent | Surrey | The Oval | 11/07/91 |
| Asif Din | 44 | W'wicks | Hants | Edgbaston | 14/08/91 |
| R.A.Smith | 43 * | Hants | Berks | Reading | 26/06/91 |
| C.J.Tavare | 43 | Som | W'wicks | Edgbaston | 31/07/91 |
| D.M.Ward | 43 | Surrey | Hants | Lord's | 07/09/90 |
| T.M.Moody | 42 * | Worcs | Beds | Bedford | 26/06/91 |
| V.P.Terry | 42 * | Hants | Berks | Reading | 26/06/91 |
| S.J.Rhodes | 41 | Worcs | Glam | Worcester | 11/07/91 |
| D.M.Smith | 40 | Sussex | Scotland | Edinburgh | 26/06/91 |
| P.E.Robinson | 40 | Yorks | W'wicks | Edgbaston | 26/06/91 |
| A.P.Wells | 40 | Sussex | Essex | Hove | 11/07/91 |
| H.Morris | 40 | Glam | Worcs | Worcester | 11/07/91 |
| J.J.Whitaker | 39 | Leics | Shrops | Leicester | 26/06/91 |
| M.A.Fell | 39 | Lincs | Notts | Trent Bridge | 26/06/91 |
| G.D.Lloyd | 39 | Lancs | Hants | Southampton | 11/07/91 |
| R.J.Harden | 39 | Som | Middx | Taunton | 11/07/91 |
| M.A.Atherton | 38 | Lancs | Dorset | Bournemouth | 26/06/91 |
| B.C.Broad | 38 | Notts | Glos | Bristol | 11/07/91 |
| N.M.K.Smith | 38 | W'wicks | Som | Edgbaston | 31/07/91 |
| K.M.Curran | 38 | N'hants | Surrey | The Oval | 14/08/91 |
| D.C.Ligertwood | 37 * | Herts | W'wicks | Edgbaston | 11/07/91 |
| T.M.Moody | 37 | Worcs | Glam | Worcester | 11/07/91 |
| H.Morris | 37 | Glam | N'hants | Northampton | 31/07/91 |
| K.M.Curran | 36 * | N'hants | Glam | Northampton | 31/07/91 |
| M.Saxelby | 36 | Notts | Hants | Southampton | 31/07/91 |

# NATWEST TROPHY

## BOWLING
## 100 Best Figures

| Name | Figures | For | Against | Venue | Date |
|---|---|---|---|---|---|
| N.V.Radford | 7-19 | Worcs | Beds | Bedford | 26/06/91 |
| D.V.Lawrence | 5-17 | Glos | Norfolk | Bristol | 26/06/91 |
| Waqar Younis | 5-40 | Surrey | N'hants | The Oval | 14/08/91 |
| A.N.Hayhurst | 5-60 | Som | W'wicks | Edgbaston | 31/07/91 |
| A.A.Donald | 4-16 | W'wicks | Yorks | Edgbaston | 26/06/91 |
| R.J.Scott | 4-22 | Glos | Norfolk | Bristol | 26/06/91 |
| M.A.Crawley | 4-26 | Notts | Lincs | Trent Bridge | 26/06/91 |
| E.A.E.Baptiste | 4-27 | N'hants | Staffs | Stone | 26/06/91 |
| Ajaz Akhtar | 4-28 | Cambs | Kent | Canterbury | 26/06/91 |
| A.P.Igglesden | 4-29 | Kent | Cambs | Canterbury | 26/06/91 |
| C.A.Connor | 4-29 | Hants | W'wicks | Edgbaston | 14/08/91 |
| Waqar Younis | 4-37 | Surrey | Essex | The Oval | 31/07/91 |
| D.A.Lewis | 4-47 | Ireland | Middx | Dublin | 26/06/91 |
| N.G.Cowans | 4-51 | Middx | Som | Taunton | 11/07/91 |
| Aqib Javed | 4-51 | Hants | Notts | Southampton | 31/07/91 |
| C.A.Connor | 4-61 | Hants | Lancs | Southampton | 11/07/91 |
| C.Wilkinson | 3-16 | Leics | Shrops | Leicester | 26/06/91 |
| C.M.Wells | 3-16 | Sussex | Scotland | Edinburgh | 26/06/91 |
| D.R.Pringle | 3-21 | Essex | Devon | Exmouth | 26/06/91 |
| N.A.Mallender | 3-23 | Som | Bucks | Bath | 26/06/91 |
| D.J.Capel | 3-26 | N'hants | Surrey | The Oval | 14/08/91 |
| T.A.Merrick | 3-27 | Kent | Cambs | Canterbury | 26/06/91 |
| R.P.Lefebvre | 3-27 | Som | W'wicks | Edgbaston | 31/07/91 |
| C.C.Lewis | 3-28 | Leics | Shrops | Leicester | 26/06/91 |
| G.C.Small | 3-28 | W'wicks | Yorks | Edgbaston | 26/06/91 |
| P.McCrum | 3-31 | Ireland | Middx | Dublin | 26/06/91 |
| T.D.Topley | 3-38 | Essex | Sussex | Hove | 11/07/91 |
| C.A.Connor | 3-39 | Hants | Surrey | Lord's | 07/09/90 |
| Wasim Akram | 3-40 | Lancs | Dorset | Bournemouth | 26/06/91 |
| R.A.Pick | 3-41 | Notts | Glos | Bristol | 11/07/91 |
| C.A.Connor | 3-42 | Hants | Notts | Southampton | 31/07/91 |
| N.Hackett | 3-45 | Staffs | N'hants | Stone | 26/06/91 |
| E.A.E.Baptiste | 3-45 | N'hants | Leics | Northampton | 11/07/91 |
| J.D.Robinson | 3-46 | Surrey | Kent | The Oval | 11/07/91 |
| S.D.Udal | 3-47 | Hants | Lancs | Southampton | 11/07/91 |
| Waqar Younis | 3-51 | Surrey | Kent | The Oval | 11/07/91 |
| P.D.McKeown | 3-52 | Lincs | Notts | Trent Bridge | 26/06/91 |
| I.Smith | 3-60 | Glam | Durham | Darlington | 26/06/91 |
| M.Watkinson | 2-10 | Lancs | Dorset | Bournemouth | 26/06/91 |
| J.P.Taylor | 2-11 | N'hants | Staffs | Stone | 26/06/91 |
| A.I.C.Dodemaide | 2-12 | Sussex | Scotland | Edinburgh | 26/06/91 |
| S.D.Udal | 2-14 | Hants | Berks | Reading | 26/06/91 |
| M.R.Ramprakash | 2-15 | Middx | Ireland | Dublin | 26/06/91 |
| P.J.Martin | 2-19 | Lancs | Dorset | Bournemouth | 26/06/91 |
| D.A.Reeve | 2-19 | W'wicks | Herts | Edgbaston | 11/07/91 |
| A.Dean | 2-20 | Beds | Worcs | Bedford | 26/06/91 |
| A.B.Russell | 2-20 | Scotland | Sussex | Edinburgh | 26/06/91 |
| R.J.Maru | 2-20 | Hants | W'wicks | Edgbaston | 14/08/91 |
| J.Boiling | 2-22 | Surrey | N'hants | The Oval | 14/08/91 |
| S.P.Hughes | 2-24 | Middx | Ireland | Dublin | 26/06/91 |
| P.A.Smith | 2-24 | W'wicks | Herts | Edgbaston | 11/07/91 |
| N.R.Taylor | 2-25 | Dorset | Lancs | Bournemouth | 26/06/91 |
| N.J.Lenham | 2-25 | Sussex | Scotland | Edinburgh | 26/06/91 |
| A.C.S.Pigott | 2-25 | Sussex | Scotland | Edinburgh | 26/06/91 |
| G.C.Small | 2-26 | W'wicks | Som | Edgbaston | 31/07/91 |
| D.J.Millns | 2-27 | Leics | Shrops | Leicester | 26/06/91 |
| R.D.B.Croft | 2-28 | Glam | Worcs | Worcester | 11/07/91 |
| P.M.Such | 2-29 | Essex | Devon | Exmouth | 26/06/91 |
| G.A.Gooch | 2-30 | Essex | Surrey | The Oval | 31/07/91 |
| R.J.Scott | 2-32 | Glos | Notts | Bristol | 11/07/91 |
| R.P.Lefebvre | 2-32 | Som | Middx | Taunton | 11/07/91 |
| M.T.Ellis | 2-33 | Norfolk | Glos | Bristol | 26/06/91 |
| K.Donohue | 2-34 | Devon | Essex | Exmouth | 26/06/91 |
| J.P.Taylor | 2-34 | N'hants | Glam | Northampton | 31/07/91 |
| R.G.Williams | 2-34 | N'hants | Surrey | The Oval | 14/08/91 |
| Aqib Javed | 2-34 | Hants | W'wicks | Edgbaston | 14/08/91 |
| K.H.Macleay | 2-35 | Som | Bucks | Bath | 26/06/91 |
| P.M.Such | 2-37 | Essex | Surrey | The Oval | 31/07/91 |
| J.P.Taylor | 2-37 | N'hants | Surrey | The Oval | 14/08/91 |
| A.Walker | 2-39 | N'hants | Glam | Northampton | 31/07/91 |
| J.R.Ayling | 2-39 | Hants | Surrey | Lord's | 07/09/90 |
| S.L.Watkin | 2-40 | Glam | N'hants | Northampton | 31/07/91 |
| S.L.Watkin | 2-41 | Glam | Durham | Darlington | 26/06/91 |
| D.R.Gilbert | 2-41 | Glos | Notts | Bristol | 11/07/91 |
| M.Saxelby | 2-42 | Notts | Lincs | Trent Bridge | 26/06/91 |
| A.L.Goram | 2-42 | Scotland | Sussex | Edinburgh | 26/06/91 |
| P.G.Duthie | 2-42 | Scotland | Sussex | Edinburgh | 26/06/91 |
| T.A.Munton | 2-42 | W'wicks | Som | Edgbaston | 31/07/91 |
| J.H.Childs | 2-43 | Essex | Devon | Exmouth | 26/06/91 |
| T.D.Topley | 2-44 | Essex | Surrey | The Oval | 31/07/91 |
| M.P.Bicknell | 2-45 | Surrey | N'hants | The Oval | 14/08/91 |
| A.N.Jones | 2-46 | Sussex | Essex | Hove | 11/07/91 |
| D.V.Lawrence | 2-48 | Glos | Notts | Bristol | 11/07/91 |
| A.N.Hayhurst | 2-49 | Somerset | Middx | Taunton | 11/07/91 |
| M.P.Bicknell | 2-49 | Surrey | Essex | The Oval | 31/07/91 |
| J.P.Taylor | 2-50 | Norfolk | Leics | Northampton | 11/07/91 |
| S.R.Barwick | 2-51 | Glam | Worcs | Worcester | 11/07/91 |
| E.A.E.Baptiste | 2-51 | N'hants | Glam | Northampton | 31/07/91 |
| S.R.Barwick | 2-51 | Glam | N'hants | Northampton | 31/07/91 |
| J.E.Emburey | 2-52 | Middx | Somerset | Taunton | 11/07/91 |
| D.R.Pringle | 2-52 | Essex | Surrey | The Oval | 31/07/91 |
| D.R.Pringle | 2-54 | Essex | Sussex | Hove | 11/07/91 |
| N.A.Foster | 2-57 | Essex | Surrey | The Oval | 31/07/91 |
| R.J.Shastri | 2-60 | Glam | N'hants | Northampton | 31/07/91 |
| B.S.Percy | 1-2 | Bucks | Somerset | Bath | 26/06/91 |
| A.Fordham | 1-3 | N'hants | Staffs | Stone | 26/06/91 |
| R.J.Bailey | 1-3 | N'hants | Staffs | Stone | 26/06/91 |
| S.R.Lampitt | 1-4 | Worcs | Beds | Bedford | 26/06/91 |
| M.V.Fleming | 1-6 | Kent | Cambs | Canterbury | 26/06/91 |
| M.W.Gatting | 1-8 | Middx | Ireland | Dublin | 26/06/91 |

# HIGHEST PARTNERSHIPS

## CORNHILL TEST MATCHES

| Wkt | Partnership | Batsmen | For | Against | Venue | Date |
|---|---|---|---|---|---|---|
| 1 | 112 | G.A.Gooch & H.Morris | England | West Indies | The Oval | 08/08/91 |
| 2 | 139 | G.A.Gooch & A.J.Stewart | England | Sri Lanka | Lord's | 22/08/91 |
| 3 | 105 | G.A.Gooch & R.A.Smith | England | Sri Lanka | Lord's | 22/08/91 |
| 4 | 133* | C.L.Hooper & I.V.A.Richards | West Indies | England | Edgbaston | 25/07/91 |
| 5 | 121 | I.V.A.Richards & A.L.Logie | West Indies | England | Trent Bridge | 04/07/91 |
| 6 | 96 | R.A.Smith & R.C.Russell | England | West Indies | Lord's | 20/06/91 |
| 7 | 98 | G.A.Gooch & D.R.Pringle | England | West Indies | Headingley | 06/06/91 |
| 8 | 47 | R.A.Smith & P.A.J.DeFreitas | England | West Indies | Lord's | 20/06/91 |
| 9 | 92 | D.R.Pringle & C.C.Lewis | England | West Indies | Edgbaston | 25/07/91 |
| 10 | 58 | P.A.J.DeFreitas & D.V.Lawrence | England | West Indies | Trent Bridge | 04/07/91 |

## BRITANNIC ASSURANCE CHAMPIONSHIP

| Wkt | Partnership | Batsmen | For | Against | Venue | Date |
|---|---|---|---|---|---|---|
| 1 | 300 | N.R.Taylor & M.R.Benson | Kent | Derby | Canterbury | 25/05/91 |
| 2 | 265 | P.Pollard & R.T.Robinson | Notts | Derby | Derby | 10/09/91 |
| 3 | 258 | M.W.Gatting & K.R.Brown | Middx | Derby | Lord's | 09/08/91 |
| 4 | 314 | Salim Malik & N.Hussain | Essex | Surrey | The Oval | 05/07/91 |
| 5 | 316 | N.Hussain & M.A.Garnham | Essex | Leics | Leicester | 10/09/91 |
| 6 | 222* | A.P.Wells & A.I.C.Dodemaide | Sussex | Glamorgan | Cardiff | 25/05/91 |
| 7 | 219* | J.D.R.Benson & P.Whitticase | Leics | Hants | Bournemouth | 16/08/91 |
| 8 | 184 | S.J.Rhodes & S.R.Lampitt | Worcs | Derby | Kidd'minster | 19/07/91 |
| 9 | 104 | C.W.J.Athey & A.M.Smith | Gloucs | Warwicks | Edgbaston | 25/05/91 |
| 10 | 133 | S.P.Titchard & I.D.Austin | Lancs | Notts | Old Trafford | 25/08/91 |

## ALL FIRST-CLASS

| Wkt | Partnership | Batsmen | For | Against | Venue | Date |
|---|---|---|---|---|---|---|
| 1 | 300 | N.R.Taylor & M.R.Benson | Kent | Derby | Canterbury | 25/05/91 |
| 2 | 265 | P.Pollard & R.T.Robinson | Notts | Derby | Derby | 10/09/91 |
| 3 | 269 | D.Byas & R.J.Blakey | Yorks | Oxford Univ | The Parks | 04/06/91 |
| 4 | 314 | Salim Malik & N.Hussain | Essex | Surrey | The Oval | 05/07/91 |
| 5 | 316 | N.Hussain & M.A.Garnham | Essex | Leics | Leicester | 10/09/91 |
| 6 | 222* | A.P.Wells & A.I.C.Dodemaide | Sussex | Glamorgan | Cardiff | 25/05/91 |
| 7 | 219* | J.D.R.Benson & P.Whitticase | Leics | Hants | Bournemouth | 16/08/91 |
| 8 | 184 | S.J.Rhodes & S.R.Lampitt | Worcs | Derby | Kidd'minster | 19/07/91 |
| 9 | 104 | C.W.J.Athey & A.M.Smith | Gloucs | Warwicks | Edgbaston | 25/05/91 |
| 10 | 133 | S.P.Titchard & I.D.Austin | Lancs | Notts | Old Trafford | 25/08/91 |

## TEXACO TROPHY

| Wkt | Partnership | Batsmen | For | Against | Venue | Date |
|---|---|---|---|---|---|---|
| 1 | 156 | G.A.Gooch & M.A.Atherton | England | West Indies | Old Trafford | 25/05/91 |
| 2 | 40 | M.A.Atherton & G.A.Hick | England | West Indies | Edgbaston | 23/05/91 |
| 3 | 213 | G.A.Hick & N.H.Fairbrother | England | West Indies | Lord's | 27/05/91 |
| 4 | 121 | C.L.Hooper & I.V.A.Richards | West Indies | England | Old Trafford | 25/05/91 |
| 5 | 73 | I.V.A.Richards & A.L.Logie | West Indies | England | Lord's | 27/05/91 |
| 6 | 63 | A.L.Logie & C.L.Hooper | West Indies | England | Lord's | 27/05/91 |
| 7 | 14 | A.L.Logie & M.D.Marshall | West Indies | England | Lord's | 27/05/91 |
| 8 | 18 | M.D.Marshall & C.E.L.Ambrose | West Indies | England | Edgbaston | 23/05/91 |
| 9 | 52* | C.E.L.Ambrose & C.A.Walsh | West Indies | England | Edgbaston | 23/05/91 |
| 10 | 23* | M.A.Atherton & R.K.Illingworth | England | West Indies | Edgbaston | 23/05/91 |

## REFUGE ASSURANCE LEAGUE

| Wkt | Partnership | Batsmen | For | Against | Venue | Date |
|---|---|---|---|---|---|---|
| 1 | 198 | T.S.Curtis & T.M.Moody | Worcs | Kent | Worcester | 21/04/91 |
| 2 | 194 | M.W.Gatting & M.R.Ramprakash | Middx | Gloucs | Bristol | 21/04/91 |
| 3 | 156 | M.A.Lynch & D.M.Ward | Surrey | Yorks | The Oval | 21/07/91 |
| 4 | 120 | V.P.Terry & M.C.J.Nicholas | Hants | Gloucs | Swindon | 26/05/91 |
| 5 | 143 | D.A.Reeve & P.A.Smith | Warwicks | Lancs | Edgbaston | 16/06/91 |
| 6 | 86 | A.N.Hayhurst & N.D.Burns | Somerset | Leics | Weston | 04/08/91 |
| 7 | 129* | D.Byas & D.Gough | Yorks | Leics | Leicester | 19/05/91 |
| 8 | 105 | W.K.Hegg & I.D.Austin | Lancs | Middx | Lord's | 21/07/91 |
| 9 | 58* | M.A.Butcher & C.K.Bullen | Surrey | Glamorgan | The Oval | 28/07/91 |
| 10 | 36 | N.G.B.Cook & J.P.Taylor | Northants | Surrey | Tring | 07/07/91 |

# HIGHEST PARTNERSHIPS

## BENSON & HEDGES CUP

| Wkt | Partnership | Batsmen | For | Against | Venue | Date |
|---|---|---|---|---|---|---|
| 1 | 213 | M.D.Moxon & A.A.Metcalfe | Yorks | Glamorgan | Cardiff | 07/05/91 |
| 2 | 198 | M.W.Gatting & M.R.Ramprakash | Middx | Somerset | Taunton | 23/04/91 |
| 3 | 180 | J.P.Stephenson & Salim Malik | Essex | Warwicks | Edgbaston | 25/04/91 |
| 4 | 147 | R.T.Robinson & M.A.Crawley | Notts | Glamorgan | Cardiff | 04/05/91 |
| 5 | 81 | R.J.Shastri & G.C.Holmes | Glamorgan | M Counties | Trowbridge | 23/04/91 |
| 6 | 90 | J.D.Robinson & D.J.Bicknell | Surrey | Warwicks | The Oval | 07/05/91 |
| 7 | 76 | I.Smith & S.J.Dennis | Glamorgan | Hants | Southampton | 02/05/91 |
| 8 | 69 * | D.R.Pringle & N.A.Foster | Essex | Middx | Chelmsford | 02/05/91 |
| 9 | 80 | S.A.Marsh & T.A.Merrick | Kent | Lancs | Old Trafford | 25/04/91 |
| 10 | 50 * | N.R.Taylor & A.P.Igglesden | Kent | Worcs | Worcester | 29/05/91 |

## NATWEST TROPHY

| Wkt | Partnership | Batsmen | For | Against | Venue | Date |
|---|---|---|---|---|---|---|
| 1 | 162 | A.Fordham & N.A.Felton | Northants | Leics | Northampton | 11/07/91 |
| 2 | 126 | A.Fordham & R.J.Bailey | Northants | Glamorgan | Northampton | 31/07/91 |
| 3 | 259 * | H.Morris & M.P.Maynard | Glamorgan | Durham | Darlington | 26/06/91 |
| 4 | 146 | R.T.Robinson & M.A.Crawley | Notts | Lincs | Trent Bridge | 26/06/91 |
| 5 | 103 | J.D.Glendenen & D.A.Blenkiron | Durham | Glamorgan | Darlington | 26/06/91 |
| 6 | 52 | M.A.Fell & A.C.Jelfs | Lincs | Notts | Trent Bridge | 26/06/91 |
| 7 | 57 | A.G.T.Ligertwood & D.M.Smith | Herts | Warwicks | Edgbaston | 11/07/91 |
| 8 | 67 * | A.N.Hayhurst & R.P.Lefebvre | Somerset | Warwicks | Edgbaston | 31/07/91 |
| 9 | 47 | C.Hoey & P.McCrum | Ireland | Middx | Dublin | 26/06/91 |
| 10 | 28 | P.G.Duthie & J.D.Moir | Scotland | Sussex | Edinburgh | 26/06/91 |

# DOUBLE-CENTURY PARTNERSHIPS

## ALL FIRST-CLASS

### 1st Wicket

| Partnership | Batsmen | For | Against | Venue | Date |
|---|---|---|---|---|---|
| 300 | N.R.Taylor & M.R.Benson | Kent | Derby | Canterbury | 25/05/91 |
| 274 | V.P.Terry & C.L.Smith | Hants | Sussex | Hove | 16/05/91 |
| 236 | I.L.Philip & B.M.W.Patterson | Scotland | Ireland | Dublin | 2/06/91 |
| 225 | T.S.Curtis & P.Bent | Worcs | Lancs | Blackpool | 20/08/91 |
| 219 | T.J.Boon & N.E.Briers | Leics | Yorks | Leicester | 06/08/91 |
| 214 | G.D.Mendis & G.D.Lloyd | Lancs | Warwicks | Old Trafford | 23/07/91 |
| 209 | G.A.Gooch & N.Shahid | Essex | Camb Univ | Fenner's | 19/04/91 |
| 206 | A.C.Seymour & J.P.Stephenson | Essex | Glamorgan | Cardiff | 23/07/91 |

### 2nd Wicket

| Partnership | Batsmen | For | Against | Venue | Date |
|---|---|---|---|---|---|
| 265 | P.Pollard & R.T.Robinson | Notts | Derby | Derby | 10/09/91 |
| 264 * | T.S.Curtis & T.M.Moody | Worcs | Essex | Ilford | 07/06/91 |
| 257 | A.R.Butcher & R.J.Shastri | Glamorgan | Lancs | Liverpool | 28/06/91 |
| 246 | J.P.Stephenson & P.J.Prichard | Essex | Yorks | Colchester | 20/08/91 |
| 240 | D.L.Haynes & R.B.Richardson | West Indies | Gloucs | Bristol | 31/07/91 |
| 237 | K.Greenfield & M.P.Speight | Sussex | Camb Univ | Hove | 29/06/91 |
| 232 | T.S.Curtis & G.A.Hick | Worcs | Surrey | Worcester | 16/08/91 |
| 226 | T.R.Ward & N.R.Taylor | Kent | Middx | Canterbury | 28/08/91 |
| 217 | N.R.Taylor & G.R.Cowdrey | Kent | Leics | Leicester | 09/08/91 |
| 216 | J.P.Stephenson & P.J.Prichard | Essex | Kent | Southend | 16/07/91 |
| 214 | B.C.Broad & R.T.Robinson | Notts | Kent | Trent Bridge | 22/05/91 |
| 211 | N.J.Speak & J.P.Crawley | Lancs | Surrey | Old Trafford | 17/09/91 |
| 208 | P.D.Bowler & J.E.Morris | Derby | Camb Univ | Fenner's | 09/05/91 |
| 202 | C.L.Smith & K.D.James | Hants | Derby | Chesterfield | 23/07/91 |

### 3rd Wicket

| Partnership | Batsmen | For | Against | Venue | Date |
|---|---|---|---|---|---|
| 269 | D.Byas & R.J.Blakey | Yorks | Oxford Univ | The Parks | 04/06/91 |
| 258 | M.W.Gatting & K.R.Brown | Middx | Derby | Lord's | 09/08/91 |
| 256 | T.S.Curtis & D.A.Leatherdale | Worcs | Somerset | Worcester | 03/09/91 |
| 242 | S.J.Cook & C.J.Tavare | Somerset | Glamorgan | Swansea | 04/06/91 |
| 236 | N.A.Stanley & A.J.Lamb | Northants | Lancs | Lytham | 06/08/91 |
| 235 | N.J.Lenham & A.P.Wells | Sussex | Kent | Tunbridge Wells | 07/06/91 |
| 217 | D.M.Smith & A.P.Wells | Sussex | Middx | Hove | 22/05/91 |
| 208 * | S.J.Cook & R.J.Harden | Somerset | Sri Lanka | Taunton | 10/08/91 |
| 206 | N.R.Taylor & G.R.Cowdrey | Kent | Sussex | Hove | 03/09/91 |
| 202 | H.Morris & M.P.Maynard | Glamorgan | Sussex | Cardiff | 25/05/91 |

### 4th Wicket

| Partnership | Batsmen | For | Against | Venue | Date |
|---|---|---|---|---|---|
| 314 | Salim Malik & N.Hussain | Essex | Surrey | The Oval | 05/07/91 |
| 287 | G.A.Gooch & N.Hussain | Essex | Northants | Colchester | 16/08/91 |
| 240 * | P.D.Bowler & M.Azharuddin | Derby | Lancs | Derby | 16/08/91 |
| 233 | D.Byas & P.E.Robinson | Yorks | Lancs | Scarborough | 03/09/91 |
| 224 | M.R.Benson & C.S.Cowdrey | Kent | Hants | Southampton | 27/04/91 |
| 211 | M.Azharuddin & T.J.G.O'Gorman | Derby | Gloucs | Gloucester | 18/06/91 |

### 5th Wicket

| Partnership | Batsmen | For | Against | Venue | Date |
|---|---|---|---|---|---|
| 316 | N.Hussain & M.A.Garnham | Essex | Leics | Leicester | 10/09/91 |
| 243 | D.B.D'Oliveira & D.A.Leatherdale | Worcs | Oxford Univ | The Parks | 25/05/91 |
| 204 | J.J.Whitaker & P.N.Hepworth | Leics | Essex | Leicester | 10/09/91 |

### 6th Wicket

| Partnership | Batsmen | For | Against | Venue | Date |
|---|---|---|---|---|---|
| 222 * | A.P.Wells & A.I.C.Dodemaide | Sussex | Glamorgan | Cardiff | 25/05/91 |
| 219 | M.R.Ramprakash & M.W.Gatting | Middx | Kent | Canterbury | 28/08/91 |
| 207 | C.J.Tavare & G.D.Rose | Somerset | Gloucs | Bristol | 10/09/91 |

### 7th Wicket

| Partnership | Batsmen | For | Against | Venue | Date |
|---|---|---|---|---|---|
| 219 * | J.D.R.Benson & P.Whitticase | Leics | Hants | Bournemouth | 16/08/91 |

# MOST RUNS

## CORNHILL TEST MATCHES
### Top 10

| Name | Runs Scored |
| --- | --- |
| G.A.Gooch | 692 |
| R.B.Richardson | 495 |
| R.A.Smith | 483 |
| I.V.A.Richards | 376 |
| D.L.Haynes | 323 |
| C.L.Hooper | 271 |
| A.J.Stewart | 225 |
| M.R.Ramprakash | 210 |
| P.V.Simmons | 181 |
| C.C.Lewis | 136 |

## BRITANNIC ASS. CHAMPIONSHIP
### Top 100

| Name | Runs Scored |
| --- | --- |
| S.J.Cook | 2370 |
| M.W.Gatting | 1044 |
| Salim Malik | 1891 |
| A.P.Wells | 1777 |
| M.Azharuddin | 1773 |
| T.M.Moody | 1770 |
| M.P.Maynard | 1766 |
| D.J.Bicknell | 1762 |
| B.C.Broad | 1739 |
| A.Fordham | 1725 |
| R.T.Robinson | 1673 |
| M.D.Moxon | 1669 |
| N.R.Taylor | 1647 |
| H.Morris | 1601 |
| D.W.Randall | 1567 |
| A.R.Butcher | 1558 |
| T.S.Curtis | 1555 |
| C.J.Tavare | 1482 |
| A.J.Wright | 1477 |
| D.Byas | 1413 |
| T.R.Ward | 1369 |
| N.E.Briers | 1358 |
| P.Johnson | 1357 |
| C.L.Smith | 1353 |
| C.W.J.Athey | 1350 |
| M.R.Benson | 1329 |
| K.J.Barnett | 1318 |
| D.M.Ward | 1304 |
| D.P.Ostler | 1284 |
| P.D.Bowler | 1270 |
| J.E.Morris | 1267 |
| D.A.Reeve | 1260 |
| A.J.Moles | 1246 |
| R.J.Harden | 1242 |
| J.J.Whitaker | 1242 |
| P.Pollard | 1235 |
| J.P.Stephenson | 1234 |
| N.Hussain | 1233 |
| V.P.Terry | 1226 |
| G.D.Mendis | 1223 |
| M.A.Roseberry | 1222 |
| K.D.James | 1216 |
| R.J.Bailey | 1202 |
| G.P.Thorpe | 1164 |
| P.E.Robinson | 1136 |
| D.I.Gower | 1132 |
| D.M.Smith | 1130 |
| T.A.Lloyd | 1076 |
| K.R.Brown | 1069 |
| G.R.Cowdrey | 1064 |
| A.A.Metcalfe | 1060 |
| T.J.G.O'Gorman | 1060 |
| T.J.Boon | 1057 |
| R.J.Shastri | 1056 |
| P.J.Prichard | 1031 |
| N.J.Lenham | 1028 |

| Name | Runs Scored |
| --- | --- |
| N.H.Fairbrother | 1011 |
| G.A.Gooch | 996 |
| A.J.Lamb | 993 |
| S.A.Kellett | 992 |
| G.D.Hodgson | 990 |
| G.A.Hick | 975 |
| R.I.Alikhan | 963 |
| J.D.Ratcliffe | 953 |
| A.J.Stewart | 936 |
| M.W.Alleyne | 921 |
| P.N.Hepworth | 915 |
| S.J.Rhodes | 907 |
| L.Potter | 899 |
| A.N.Hayhurst | 883 |
| M.R.Ramprakash | 877 |
| G.Fowler | 865 |
| R.A.Smith | 852 |
| M.A.Garnham | 831 |
| S.A.Marsh | 823 |
| P.M.Roebuck | 820 |
| N.J.Speak | 806 |
| N.D.Burns | 794 |
| T.C.Middleton | 766 |
| R.J.Scott | 763 |
| W.K.Hegg | 758 |
| K.M.Curran | 749 |
| R.J.Blakey | 739 |
| M.V.Fleming | 734 |
| J.W.Lloyds | 729 |
| M.C.J.Nicholas | 723 |
| G.D.Lloyd | 720 |
| M.Watkinson | 713 |
| A.Dale | 711 |
| D.J.Capel | 692 |
| Asif Din | 685 |
| J.W.Hall | 685 |
| K.M.Krikken | 677 |
| P.Carrick | 662 |
| P.Whitticase | 620 |
| P.Moores | 612 |
| P.W.G.Parker | 607 |
| M.A.Atherton | 603 |
| I.A.Greig | 593 |
| E.A.E.Baptiste | 589 |

## MOST CENTURIES IN THE BRITANNIC ASSURANCE CHAMPIONSHIP

| | |
| --- | --- |
| 9 | S.J.Cook |
| 8 | M.W.Gatting |
| 7 | M.P.Maynard |
| | A.P.Wells |
| 6 | T.M.Moody |
| | N.R.Taylor |
| | M.Azharuddin |
| | Salim Malik |
| 5 | D.J.Bicknell |
| | B.C.Broad |
| | N.H.Fairbrother |
| | H.Morris |
| | D.W.Randall |
| | C.L.Smith |
| 4 | C.W.J.Athey |
| | M.R.Benson |
| | N.E.Briers |
| | A.R.Butcher |
| | D.Byas |
| | A.Fordham |
| | P.J.Prichard |
| | C.J.Tavare |
| | G.P.Thorpe |
| | T.R.Ward |
| 3 | T.S.Curtis |
| | G.A.Gooch |
| 3 | A.N.Hayhurst |
| | G.A.Hick |
| | N.Hussain |
| | P.Johnson |
| | A.J.Lamb |
| | N.J.Lenham |
| | G.D.Mendis |
| | M.D.Moxon |
| | P.Pollard |
| | R.T.Robinson |
| | J.P.Stephenson |
| | A.J.Wright |

## ALL FIRST-CLASS MATCHES
### Top 100

| Name | Runs Scored |
| --- | --- |
| S.J.Cook | 2755 |
| M.W.Gatting | 2057 |
| M.Azharuddin | 2016 |
| Salim Malik | 1972 |
| G.A.Gooch | 1911 |
| D.J.Bicknell | 1888 |
| T.M.Moody | 1887 |
| A.Fordham | 1840 |
| N.R.Taylor | 1806 |
| M.P.Maynard | 1803 |
| H.Morris | 1803 |
| A.P.Wells | 1784 |
| B.C.Broad | 1739 |
| A.R.Butcher | 1677 |
| R.T.Robinson | 1673 |
| M.D.Moxon | 1669 |
| T.S.Curtis | 1653 |
| C.J.Tavare | 1601 |
| A.J.Wright | 1596 |
| D.W.Randall | 1567 |
| D.Byas | 1557 |
| C.L.Smith | 1553 |
| C.W.J.Athey | 1522 |
| M.A.Roseberry | 1511 |
| C.L.Hooper | 1501 |
| T.R.Ward | 1493 |
| N.E.Briers | 1485 |
| P.D.Bowler | 1458 |
| P.Johnson | 1454 |
| J.P.Stephenson | 1421 |
| R.B.Richardson | 1403 |
| K.J.Barnett | 1399 |
| J.E.Morris | 1398 |
| R.A.Smith | 1397 |
| G.D.Mendis | 1394 |
| D.M.Ward | 1372 |
| R.J.Harden | 1355 |
| N.Hussain | 1354 |
| M.R.Benson | 1329 |
| P.E.Robinson | 1293 |
| J.J.Whitaker | 1289 |
| D.P.Ostler | 1284 |
| K.D.James | 1274 |
| S.A.Kellett | 1266 |
| D.A.Reeve | 1260 |
| P.Pollard | 1255 |
| A.J.Moles | 1246 |
| V.P.Terry | 1244 |
| D.M.Smith | 1238 |
| R.J.Bailey | 1224 |
| A.A.Metcalfe | 1210 |
| G.P.Thorpe | 1203 |
| T.J.Boon | 1185 |
| K.R.Brown | 1184 |
| G.R.Cowdrey | 1175 |
| M.R.Ramprakash | 1174 |
| A.J.Stewart | 1161 |
| D.I.Gower | 1142 |

# MOST RUNS

| Name | Runs Scored |
|---|---|
| P.J.Prichard | 1124 |
| M.W.Alleyne | 1121 |
| P.N.Hepworth | 1119 |
| G.A.Hick | 1119 |
| T.J.G.O'Gorman | 1116 |
| R.J.Shastri | 1108 |
| G.D.Hodgson | 1101 |
| N.J.Lenham | 1091 |
| A.J.Lamb | 1081 |
| T.A.Lloyd | 1076 |
| N.H.Fairbrother | 1064 |
| R.I.Alikhan | 1055 |
| P.V.Simmons | 1031 |
| L.Potter | 1027 |
| M.A.Garnham | 986 |
| G.Fowler | 953 |
| J.D.Ratcliffe | 953 |
| S.J.Rhodes | 942 |
| R.J.Blakey | 941 |
| M.V.Fleming | 917 |
| A.N.Hayhurst | 910 |
| S.A.Marsh | 910 |
| A.Dale | 869 |
| T.C.Middleton | 864 |
| J.P.Crawley | 849 |
| R.J.Scott | 848 |
| N.J.Speak | 844 |
| P.M.Roebuck | 833 |
| G.D.Lloyd | 829 |
| K.M.Curran | 828 |
| M.C.J.Nicholas | 826 |
| M.A.Atherton | 820 |
| I.V.A.Richards | 817 |
| N.D.Burns | 808 |
| J.W.Lloyds | 803 |
| D.J.Capel | 792 |
| I.T.Botham | 785 |
| W.K.Hegg | 784 |
| M.Watkinson | 758 |
| M.P.Speight | 754 |
| D.L.Haynes | 721 |
| P.Moores | 714 |

## MOST FIRST-CLASS CENTURIES

| | |
|---|---|
| 11 | S.J.Cook |
| 8 | M.W.Gatting |
| 7 | M.P.Maynard |
| | N.R.Taylor |
| | A.P.Wells |
| | M.Azharuddin |
| 6 | G.A.Gooch |
| | T.M.Moody |
| | C.L.Smith |
| | R.B.Richardson |
| | Salim Malik |
| 5 | C.W.J.Athey |
| | D.J.Bicknell |
| | B.C.Broad |
| | D.Byas |
| | N.H.Fairbrother |
| | H.Morris |
| | D.W.Randall |
| | C.J.Tavare |
| | T.R.Ward |
| | C.L.Hooper |
| 4 | M.R.Benson |
| | N.E.Briers |
| | A.R.Butcher |
| | A.Fordham |
| | G.D.Mendis |
| | P.J.Prichard |
| | G.P.Thorpe |
| 3 | M.A.Atherton |
| 3 | G.R.Cowdrey |
| | T.S.Curtis |
| | M.A.Garnham |
| | R.J.Harden |
| | A.N.Hayhurst |
| | G.A.Hick |
| | N.Hussain |
| | P.Johnson |
| | A.J.Lamb |
| | N.J.Lenham |
| | M.D.Moxon |
| | P.Pollard |
| | R.T.Robinson |
| | R.A.Smith |
| | J.P.Stephenson |
| | A.J.Wright |
| | P.V.Simmons |

## TEXACO TROPHY
### Top 10

| Name | Runs Scored |
|---|---|
| M.A.Atherton | 168 |
| I.V.A.Richards | 145 |
| G.A.Hick | 129 |
| A.L.Logie | 124 |
| N.H.Fairbrother | 122 |
| C.L.Hooper | 84 |
| A.J.Lamb | 80 |
| G.A.Gooch | 65 |
| R.B.Richardson | 57 |
| M.D.Marshall | 52 |

## REFUGE ASSURANCE LEAGUE
### Top 50

| Name | Runs Scored |
|---|---|
| T.M.Moody | 926 |
| T.S.Curtis | 816 |
| D.W.Randall | 718 |
| B.C.Broad | 647 |
| G.Fowler | 572 |
| M.D.Moxon | 561 |
| J.J.Whitaker | 550 |
| S.J.Cook | 546 |
| C.J.Tavare | 542 |
| A.A.Metcalfe | 540 |
| M.W.Gatting | 525 |
| G.D.Lloyd | 519 |
| A.Fordham | 509 |
| R.J.Blakey | 490 |
| N.R.Taylor | 467 |
| M.C.J.Nicholas | 462 |
| M.P.Maynard | 458 |
| N.H.Fairbrother | 451 |
| Salim Malik | 451 |
| G.A.Hick | 433 |
| M.A.Lynch | 433 |
| H.Morris | 433 |
| G.P.Thorpe | 431 |
| M.R.Benson | 422 |
| A.J.Wright | 414 |
| M.W.Alleyne | 409 |
| V.P.Terry | 408 |
| J.P.Stephenson | 399 |
| C.L.Smith | 397 |
| P.D.Bowler | 396 |
| R.J.Bailey | 388 |
| A.J.Moles | 385 |
| M.A.Roseberry | 383 |
| M.R.Ramprakash | 382 |
| R.J.Scott | 376 |
| C.J.Adams | 375 |
| L.Potter | 374 |
| T.A.Lloyd | 373 |
| M.Azharuddin | 371 |
| P.Johnson | 370 |
| D.Byas | 369 |
| W.Larkins | 363 |
| D.J.Capel | 360 |
| K.R.Brown | 359 |
| G.A.Gooch | 358 |
| C.W.J.Athey | 352 |
| N.E.Briers | 352 |
| T.R.Ward | 347 |
| G.D.Mendis | 344 |
| R.J.Harden | 342 |

## BENSON & HEDGES CUP
### Top 20

| Name | Runs Scored |
|---|---|
| C.L.Smith | 413 |
| T.M.Moody | 382 |
| M.D.Moxon | 370 |
| G.D.Mendis | 366 |
| A.A.Metcalfe | 350 |
| J.P.Stephenson | 349 |
| G.Fowler | 320 |
| G.A.Hick | 197 |
| Asif Din | 191 |
| M.A.Atherton | 182 |
| A.R.Butcher | 179 |
| K.J.Barnett | 256 |
| R.T.Robinson | 239 |
| J.D.Love | 236 |
| N.R.Taylor | 230 |
| M.R.Benson | 228 |
| N.H.Fairbrother | 225 |
| Salim Malik | 217 |
| S.J.Cook | 213 |
| D.M.Smith | 209 |

## NATWEST TROPHY
### Top 20

| Name | Runs Scored |
|---|---|
| R.A.Smith | 331 |
| A.Fordham | 288 |
| M.P.Maynard | 256 |
| R.J.Bailey | 253 |
| V.P.Terry | 209 |
| A.J.Stewart | 206 |
| H.Morris | 203 |
| G.A.Gooch | 202 |
| R.T.Robinson | 197 |
| C.L.Smith | 194 |
| D.W.Randall | 166 |
| D.M.Ward | 164 |
| A.N.Hayhurst | 154 |
| M.W.Gatting | 150 |
| G.P.Thorpe | 138 |
| J.J.Whitaker | 133 |
| C.J.Tavare | 127 |
| C.W.J.Athey | 123 |
| J.P.Stephenson | 117 |
| N.Hussain | 114 |

## ALL ONE-DAY MATCHES
### Top 100

| Name | Runs Scored |
|---|---|
| T.M.Moody | 1387 |
| M.D.Moxon | 1206 |
| D.W.Randall | 1097 |
| A.A.Metcalfe | 1089 |

# MOST RUNS

| Name | Runs Scored |
|---|---|
| J.P.Stephenson | 1029 |
| T.S.Curtis | 1013 |
| C.L.Smith | 1004 |
| A.Fordham | 980 |
| N.H.Fairbrother | 977 |
| G.Fowler | 972 |
| J.J.Whitaker | 894 |
| B.C.Broad | 885 |
| G.A.Hick | 875 |
| G.A.Gooch | 849 |
| M.W.Gatting | 844 |
| Salim Malik | 831 |
| R.J.Bailey | 825 |
| S.J.Cook | 815 |
| M.P.Maynard | 808 |
| C.J.Tavare | 808 |
| A.J.Stewart | 803 |
| A.J.Wright | 794 |
| G.D.Mendis | 765 |
| D.Byas | 759 |
| R.J.Blakey | 752 |
| G.P.Thorpe | 746 |
| N.R.Taylor | 743 |
| M.A.Atherton | 731 |
| R.T.Robinson | 714 |
| A.R.Butcher | 695 |
| M.R.Benson | 686 |
| Asif Din | 682 |
| H.Morris | 679 |
| T.R.Ward | 672 |
| T.A.Lloyd | 669 |
| C.W.J.Athey | 668 |
| A.J.Moles | 660 |
| K.J.Barnett | 642 |
| P.Johnson | 634 |
| J.E.Morris | 634 |
| V.P.Terry | 627 |
| D.M.Ward | 619 |
| D.J.Bicknell | 614 |
| M.Azharuddin | 579 |
| G.D.Lloyd | 575 |
| M.C.J.Nicholas | 573 |
| M.R.Ramprakash | 565 |
| M.W.Alleyne | 557 |
| R.J.Shastri | 554 |
| P.D.Bowler | 543 |
| N.Hussain | 535 |
| A.J.Lamb | 526 |
| M.A.Lynch | 522 |
| L.Potter | 521 |
| D.A.Reeve | 521 |
| D.M.Smith | 519 |
| P.E.Robinson | 518 |
| R.J.Scott | 501 |
| N.E.Briers | 495 |
| M.V.Fleming | 490 |
| G.R.Cowdrey | 488 |
| R.A.Smith | 483 |
| T.J.G.O'Gorman | 477 |
| P.W.G.Parker | 475 |
| K.R.Brown | 473 |
| D.J.Capel | 469 |
| R.J.Harden | 468 |
| S.A.Marsh | 459 |
| R.C.Russell | 458 |
| M.Watkinson | 448 |
| A.P.Wells | 448 |
| P.J.Prichard | 440 |
| M.A.Roseberry | 433 |
| C.J.Adams | 423 |
| D.B.D'Oliveira | 421 |
| A.N.Hayhurst | 419 |
| K.Greenfield | 405 |
| M.P.Speight | 405 |
| W.Larkins | 402 |

| Name | Runs Scored |
|---|---|
| D.P.Ostler | 400 |
| T.J.Boon | 399 |
| T.C.Middleton | 396 |
| N.A.Felton | 387 |
| N.D.Burns | 385 |
| J.D.Robinson | 383 |
| I.T.Botham | 372 |
| S.J.Rhodes | 360 |
| N.J.Lenham | 357 |
| P.A.Smith | 356 |
| K.M.Curran | 339 |
| I.Smith | 334 |
| A.Dale | 333 |
| G.C.Holmes | 332 |
| P.M.Roebuck | 325 |
| A.L.Logie | 317 |
| P.A.Neale | 306 |
| P.Moores | 305 |
| M.A.Crawley | 304 |
| Wasim Akram | 303 |
| C.C.Lewis | 294 |

## ALL MATCHES (FIRST-CLASS AND ONE-DAY) Top 100

| Name | Runs Scored |
|---|---|
| S.J.Cook | 3570 |
| T.M.Moody | 3274 |
| M.W.Gatting | 2901 |
| M.D.Moxon | 2875 |
| A.Fordham | 2820 |
| Salim Malik | 2803 |
| G.A.Gooch | 2760 |
| T.S.Curtis | 2666 |
| D.W.Randall | 2664 |
| B.C.Broad | 2624 |
| M.P.Maynard | 2611 |
| M.Azharuddin | 2595 |
| C.L.Smith | 2557 |
| N.R.Taylor | 2549 |
| D.J.Bicknell | 2502 |
| H.Morris | 2482 |
| J.P.Stephenson | 2450 |
| C.J.Tavare | 2409 |
| A.J.Wright | 2390 |
| R.T.Robinson | 2387 |
| A.R.Butcher | 2372 |
| D.Byas | 2316 |
| A.A.Metcalfe | 2299 |
| A.P.Wells | 2232 |
| C.W.J.Athey | 2190 |
| J.J.Whitaker | 2183 |
| T.R.Ward | 2165 |
| G.D.Mendis | 2159 |
| P.Johnson | 2088 |
| R.J.Bailey | 2049 |
| K.J.Barnett | 2041 |
| N.H.Fairbrother | 2041 |
| J.E.Morris | 2032 |
| M.R.Benson | 2015 |
| P.D.Bowler | 2001 |
| G.A.Hick | 1994 |
| D.M.Ward | 1991 |
| N.E.Briers | 1980 |
| A.J.Stewart | 1964 |
| G.P.Thorpe | 1949 |
| M.A.Roseberry | 1944 |
| G.Fowler | 1925 |
| A.J.Moles | 1906 |
| N.Hussain | 1889 |
| R.A.Smith | 1880 |
| V.P.Terry | 1871 |
| R.J.Harden | 1823 |

| Name | Runs Scored |
|---|---|
| P.E.Robinson | 1811 |
| D.A.Reeve | 1781 |
| D.M.Smith | 1757 |
| C.L.Hooper | 1752 |
| T.A.Lloyd | 1745 |
| M.R.Ramprakash | 1739 |
| R.J.Blakey | 1693 |
| D.P.Ostler | 1684 |
| M.W.Alleyne | 1678 |
| G.R.Cowdrey | 1663 |
| R.J.Shastri | 1662 |
| K.R.Brown | 1657 |
| A.J.Lamb | 1607 |
| T.J.G.O'Gorman | 1593 |
| T.J.Boon | 1584 |
| P.J.Prichard | 1564 |
| M.A.Atherton | 1551 |
| L.Potter | 1548 |
| P.Pollard | 1529 |
| R.B.Richardson | 1523 |
| K.D.James | 1452 |
| N.J.Lenham | 1448 |
| S.A.Kellett | 1436 |
| D.I.Gower | 1432 |
| M.V.Fleming | 1407 |
| G.D.Lloyd | 1404 |
| M.C.J.Nicholas | 1399 |
| S.A.Marsh | 1369 |
| Asif Din | 1367 |
| R.J.Scott | 1349 |
| A.N.Hayhurst | 1329 |
| S.J.Rhodes | 1302 |
| P.V.Simmons | 1294 |
| D.J.Capel | 1261 |
| T.C.Middleton | 1260 |
| P.N.Hepworth | 1218 |
| M.Watkinson | 1206 |
| A.Dale | 1202 |
| N.D.Burns | 1193 |
| K.M.Curran | 1167 |
| M.A.Garnham | 1167 |
| M.P.Speight | 1159 |
| P.M.Roebuck | 1158 |
| I.T.Botham | 1157 |
| G.D.Hodgson | 1127 |
| J.D.Ratcliffe | 1119 |
| C.J.Adams | 1114 |
| R.C.Russell | 1085 |
| P.W.G.Parker | 1082 |
| J.W.Lloyds | 1065 |
| R.I.Alikhan | 1062 |
| I.V.A.Richards | 1047 |
| P.Moores | 1019 |

# MOST WICKETS

## CORNHILL TEST MATCHES
### 5 wickets or more

| Name | Wickets Taken |
|---|---|
| P.A.J.DeFreitas | 30 |
| C.E.L.Ambrose | 28 |
| M.D.Marshall | 20 |
| C.A.Walsh | 15 |
| D.V.Lawrence | 14 |
| B.P.Patterson | 13 |
| D.R.Pringle | 12 |
| P.C.R.Tufnell | 12 |
| C.C.Lewis | 8 |
| S.L.Watkin | 5 |
| I.B.A.Allen | 5 |

## BRITANNIC ASS. CHAMPIONSHIP
### 20 wickets or more

| Name | Wickets Taken |
|---|---|
| Waqar Younis | 113 |
| N.A.Foster | 91 |
| A.A.Donald | 83 |
| F.D.Stephenson | 78 |
| T.A.Munton | 71 |
| P.C.R.Tufnell | 70 |
| J.N.Maguire | 69 |
| S.L.Watkin | 66 |
| R.A.Pick | 65 |
| J.E.Emburey | 64 |
| D.J.Millns | 62 |
| P.Carrick | 61 |
| M.Frost | 61 |
| D.V.Lawrence | 60 |
| J.H.Childs | 58 |
| T.A.Merrick | 58 |
| O.H.Mortensen | 58 |
| J.A.Afford | 57 |
| Wasim Akram | 56 |
| D.G.Cork | 55 |
| D.R.Gilbert | 55 |
| P.J.Newport | 54 |
| D.A.Graveney | 53 |
| A.N.Jones | 53 |
| T.D.Topley | 53 |
| Aqib Javed | 53 |
| A.I.C.Dodemaide | 52 |
| C.Penn | 52 |
| M.Watkinson | 51 |
| P.J.Hartley | 50 |
| E.A.E.Baptiste | 49 |
| A.P.Igglesden | 48 |
| I.D.K.Salisbury | 47 |
| H.R.J.Trump | 47 |
| E.E.Hemmings | 46 |
| N.V.Radford | 46 |
| M.P.Bicknell | 45 |
| K.M.Curran | 45 |
| R.M.Ellison | 45 |
| S.R.Lampitt | 45 |
| D.A.Reeve | 45 |
| G.C.Small | 45 |
| N.A.Mallender | 42 |
| N.F.Williams | 41 |
| S.J.W.Andrew | 40 |
| K.P.Evans | 40 |
| P.A.J.DeFreitas | 39 |
| D.E.Malcolm | 39 |
| I.T.Botham | 38 |
| K.T.Medlycott | 38 |
| J.D.Batty | 37 |
| K.D.James | 37 |
| C.C.Lewis | 37 |
| K.J.Shine | 37 |
| A.M.Babington | 35 |

| Name | Wickets Taken |
|---|---|
| G.R.Dilley | 35 |
| M.A.Feltham | 35 |
| A.J.Murphy | 35 |
| A.C.S.Pigott | 35 |
| N.G.Cowans | 34 |
| R.D.B.Croft | 34 |
| B.T.P.Donelan | 34 |
| R.J.Maru | 34 |
| J.W.Lloyds | 33 |
| P.J.Martin | 33 |
| R.P.Davis | 32 |
| S.J.Base | 31 |
| A.E.Warner | 31 |
| D.R.Pringle | 30 |
| C.A.Connor | 29 |
| A.R.Roberts | 29 |
| D.J.Capel | 28 |
| D.W.Headley | 28 |
| A.M.Smith | 28 |
| R.J.Shastri | 27 |
| S.R.Barwick | 26 |
| R.K.Illingworth | 26 |
| L.Potter | 26 |
| G.Yates | 26 |
| R.W.Sladdin | 26 |
| K.H.Macleay | 25 |
| N.G.B.Cook | 24 |
| D.J.Foster | 24 |
| J.G.Thomas | 24 |
| J.P.Taylor | 24 |
| M.A.Robinson | 23 |
| G.D.Rose | 23 |
| P.M.Such | 23 |
| J.R.Ayling | 21 |
| S.D.Fletcher | 20 |
| C.Wilkinson | 20 |

## MOST FIVE WICKETS IN AN INNINGS IN THE BRITANNIC ASSURANCE CHAMPIONSHIP

| | |
|---|---|
| 13 | Waqar Younis |
| 8 | A.A.Donald |
| 7 | N.A.Foster |
| | Wasim Akram |
| 5 | T.A.Munton |
| | P.C.R.Tufnell |
| 4 | J.H.Childs |
| | F.D.Stephenson |
| | H.R.J.Trump |
| | S.L.Watkin |
| 3 | I.T.Botham |
| | P.J.Hartley |
| | S.R.Lampitt |
| | D.V.Lawrence |
| | N.A.Mallender |
| | D.J.Millns |
| | C.Penn |
| | R.A.Pick |
| | T.D.Topley |
| | Aqib Javed |
| | J.N.Maguire |
| | E.A.E.Baptiste |
| | P.Carrick |
| | P.A.J.DeFreitas |
| | B.T.P.Donelan |
| | M.A.Ealham |
| 2 | R.M.Ellison |
| | K.P.Evans |
| | D.A.Graveney |
| | E.E.Hemmings |
| | R.K.Illingworth |
| | A.N.Jones |
| | N.M.Kendrick |
| | C.C.Lewis |

| | |
|---|---|
| 2 | O.H.Mortensen |
| | N.V.Radford |
| | K.J.Shine |
| | J.G.Thomas |
| | D.W.Headley |

## ALL-FIRST CLASS
### 20 wickets or more

| Name | Wickets Taken |
|---|---|
| Waqar Younis | 113 |
| N.A.Foster | 102 |
| P.C.R.Tufnell | 88 |
| A.A.Donald | 83 |
| F.D.Stephenson | 78 |
| J.N.Maguire | 77 |
| D.V.Lawrence | 74 |
| S.L.Watkin | 74 |
| P.A.J.DeFreitas | 73 |
| T.A.Munton | 73 |
| J.E.Emburey | 68 |
| R.A.Pick | 67 |
| P.J.Newport | 66 |
| J.H.Childs | 65 |
| M.Frost | 65 |
| D.R.Gilbert | 64 |
| D.J.Millns | 63 |
| P.Carrick | 61 |
| T.A.Merrick | 61 |
| O.H.Mortensen | 58 |
| J.A.Afford | 57 |
| D.G.Cork | 57 |
| A.N.Jones | 56 |
| S.R.Lampitt | 56 |
| Wasim Akram | 56 |
| D.A.Graveney | 55 |
| T.D.Topley | 55 |
| A.I.C.Dodemaide | 54 |
| M.Watkinson | 53 |
| Aqib Javed | 53 |
| C.Penn | 52 |
| C.E.L.Ambrose | 51 |
| H.R.J.Trump | 51 |
| P.J.Hartley | 50 |
| A.P.Igglesden | 50 |
| E.A.E.Baptiste | 50 |
| K.T.Medlycott | 49 |
| K.M.Curran | 48 |
| C.C.Lewis | 48 |
| I.D.K.Salisbury | 48 |
| R.M.Ellison | 47 |
| D.R.Pringle | 47 |
| N.F.Williams | 47 |
| E.E.Hemmings | 46 |
| N.V.Radford | 46 |
| M.P.Bicknell | 45 |
| D.A.Reeve | 45 |
| G.C.Small | 45 |
| I.T.Botham | 44 |
| N.G.Cowans | 44 |
| S.J.W.Andrew | 43 |
| A.M.Babington | 42 |
| D.E.Malcolm | 42 |
| N.A.Mallender | 42 |
| J.D.Batty | 41 |
| K.D.James | 41 |
| K.P.Evans | 40 |
| R.J.Maru | 40 |
| R.D.B.Croft | 38 |
| R.K.Illingworth | 38 |
| K.J.Shine | 38 |
| R.P.Davis | 37 |
| G.R.Dilley | 37 |
| A.E.Warner | 37 |
| S.J.Base | 36 |

# MOST WICKETS

| Name | Wickets Taken |
|---|---|
| P.J.Martin | 36 |
| A.C.S.Pigott | 36 |
| M.A.Feltham | 35 |
| A.J.Murphy | 35 |
| C.A.Connor | 34 |
| B.T.P.Donelan | 34 |
| J.W.Lloyds | 34 |
| P.M.Such | 34 |
| B.P.Patterson | 32 |
| R.J.Shastri | 31 |
| G.Yates | 31 |
| C.L.Hooper | 31 |
| M.D.Marshall | 30 |
| A.R.Roberts | 29 |
| C.A.Walsh | 29 |
| D.W.Headley | 29 |
| A.M.Smith | 29 |
| S.R.Barwick | 28 |
| D.J.Capel | 28 |
| N.G.B.Cook | 28 |
| L.Potter | 28 |
| J.G.Thomas | 28 |
| J.P.Taylor | 27 |
| R.W.Sladdin | 27 |
| H.A.G.Anthony | 26 |
| J.R.Ayling | 25 |
| D.J.Foster | 25 |
| M.A.Robinson | 25 |
| G.D.Rose | 25 |
| K.H.Macleay | 25 |
| C.Wilkinson | 23 |
| S.Bastien | 22 |
| P.J.Bakker | 20 |
| K.J.Barnett | 20 |
| S.D.Fletcher | 20 |
| J.A.North | 20 |

## MOST FIVE WICKETS IN AN INNINGS IN ALL FIRST-CLASS CRICKET

| | |
|---|---|
| 13 | Waqar Younis |
| 8 | A.A.Donald |
| 7 | N.A.Foster |
| | P.C.R.Tufnell |
| | Wasim Akram |
| 5 | T.A.Munton |
| 4 | J.H.Childs |
| | S.R.Lampitt |
| | D.V.Lawrence |
| | F.D.Stephenson |
| | H.R.J.Trump |
| | S.L.Watkin |
| | J.N.Maguire |
| 3 | C.E.L.Ambrose |
| | I.T.Botham |
| | P.A.J.DeFreitas |
| | P.J.Hartley |
| | R.K.Illingworth |
| | C.C.Lewis |
| | N.A.Mallender |
| | D.J.Millns |
| | C.Penn |
| | R.A.Pick |
| | T.D.Topley |
| | Aqib Javed |
| | E.A.E.Baptiste |
| 2 | P.Carrick |
| | B.T.P.Donelan |
| | M.A.Ealham |
| | R.M.Ellison |
| | K.P.Evans |
| | D.A.Graveney |
| | E.E.Hemmings |
| | A.N.Jones |

| | |
|---|---|
| 2 | N.M.Kendrick |
| | K.T.Medlycott |
| | O.H.Mortensen |
| | B.P.Patterson |
| | D.R.Pringle |
| | N.V.Radford |
| | K.J.Shine |
| | J.G.Thomas |
| | D.W.Headley |
| | R.J.Ratnayake |

## TEXACO TROPHY
### 3 wickets or more

| Name | Wickets Taken |
|---|---|
| I.T.Botham | 4 |
| D.V.Lawrence | 4 |
| C.C.Lewis | 4 |
| B.P.Patterson | 4 |
| C.E.L.Ambrose | 3 |
| P.A.J.DeFreitas | 3 |
| G.A.Gooch | 3 |
| R.K.Illingworth | 3 |
| M.D.Marshall | 3 |
| C.L.Hooper | 3 |

## REFUGE ASSURANCE LEAGUE
### 12 wickets or more

| Name | Wickets Taken |
|---|---|
| F.D.Stephenson | 32 |
| I.D.Austin | 29 |
| J.E.Emburey | 28 |
| A.C.S.Pigott | 27 |
| N.V.Radford | 25 |
| A.P.Igglesden | 23 |
| A.N.Jones | 22 |
| M.Watkinson | 22 |
| P.A.Smith | 21 |
| Waqar Younis | 21 |
| J.N.Maguire | 21 |
| T.D.Topley | 20 |
| P.Carrick | 19 |
| S.J.Base | 18 |
| C.A.Connor | 18 |
| N.G.Cowans | 18 |
| K.P.Evans | 18 |
| S.D.Fletcher | 18 |
| A.J.Murphy | 18 |
| M.Saxelby | 18 |
| D.J.Capel | 17 |
| M.V.Fleming | 17 |
| S.D.Udal | 17 |
| K.M.Curran | 16 |
| R.K.Illingworth | 16 |
| S.L.Watkin | 16 |
| R.P.Davis | 15 |
| C.C.Lewis | 15 |
| D.E.Malcolm | 15 |
| J.P.Taylor | 15 |
| R.P.Lefebvre | 15 |
| A.M.Smith | 15 |
| J.R.Ayling | 14 |
| A.M.Babington | 14 |
| J.D.R.Benson | 14 |
| M.Frost | 14 |
| E.E.Hemmings | 14 |
| C.S.Pickles | 14 |
| A.Dale | 13 |
| P.J.Hartley | 13 |
| T.A.Munton | 13 |
| J.P.Stephenson | 13 |
| P.M.Such | 13 |
| Wasim Akram | 13 |

| Name | Wickets Taken |
|---|---|
| S.R.Barwick | 12 |
| J.D.Batty | 12 |
| I.T.Botham | 12 |
| P.A.J.DeFreitas | 12 |
| O.H.Mortensen | 12 |
| D.R.Pringle | 12 |
| A.Walker | 12 |
| A.E.Warner | 12 |
| R.G.Williams | 12 |

## BENSON AND HEDGES CUP
### 9 wickets or more

| Name | Wickets Taken |
|---|---|
| N.V.Radford | 16 |
| P.A.J.DeFreitas | 14 |
| D.V.Lawrence | 13 |
| D.R.Pringle | 12 |
| M.Watkinson | 12 |
| P.J.W.Allott | 11 |
| G.R.Dilley | 11 |
| A.A.Donald | 11 |
| S.R.Lampitt | 11 |
| Wasim Akram | 11 |
| C.A.Connor | 10 |
| A.P.Igglesden | 10 |
| D.A.Reeve | 10 |
| J.E.Emburey | 9 |
| T.A.Munton | 9 |
| J.G.Thomas | 9 |
| S.D.Udal | 9 |
| Aqib Javed | 9 |

## NATWEST TROPHY
### 5 wickets or more

| Name | Wickets Taken |
|---|---|
| C.A.Connor | 15 |
| Waqar Younis | 13 |
| E.A.E.Baptiste | 9 |
| A.N.Hayhurst | 8 |
| J.P.Taylor | 8 |
| Aqib Javed | 8 |
| D.V.Lawrence | 7 |
| D.R.Pringle | 7 |
| N.V.Radford | 7 |
| A.A.Donald | 6 |
| R.J.Scott | 6 |
| G.C.Small | 6 |
| T.D.Topley | 6 |
| S.D.Udal | 6 |
| R.P.Lefebvre | 6 |
| S.R.Barwick | 5 |
| M.P.Bicknell | 5 |
| N.G.Cowans | 5 |
| P.M.Such | 5 |

## ALL ONE-DAY MATCHES
### 12 wickets or more

| Name | Wickets Taken |
|---|---|
| N.V.Radford | 48 |
| C.A.Connor | 43 |
| J.E.Emburey | 41 |
| F.D.Stephenson | 41 |
| M.Watkinson | 40 |
| A.C.S.Pigott | 38 |
| Waqar Younis | 38 |
| A.P.Igglesden | 37 |
| I.D.Austin | 36 |
| D.V.Lawrence | 36 |
| D.R.Pringle | 33 |

# MOST WICKETS

| Name | Wickets Taken |
|---|---|
| S.D.Udal | 32 |
| N.G.Cowans | 31 |
| A.N.Jones | 31 |
| T.D.Topley | 31 |
| Wasim Akram | 30 |
| P.A.J.DeFreitas | 29 |
| C.C.Lewis | 28 |
| P.A.Smith | 28 |
| P.M.Such | 28 |
| R.P.Lefebvre | 28 |
| P.Carrick | 27 |
| S.D.Fletcher | 27 |
| R.K.Illingworth | 27 |
| J.P.Taylor | 27 |
| Aqib Javed | 27 |
| T.A.Munton | 26 |
| A.J.Murphy | 26 |
| P.J.W.Allott | 25 |
| D.J.Capel | 25 |
| A.A.Donald | 25 |
| S.L.Watkin | 25 |
| I.T.Botham | 24 |
| K.P.Evans | 24 |
| M.V.Fleming | 24 |
| D.A.Reeve | 24 |
| J.N.Maguire | 24 |
| S.J.Base | 23 |
| S.R.Lampitt | 23 |
| D.E.Malcolm | 23 |
| C.S.Pickles | 23 |
| I.D.K.Salisbury | 23 |
| J.R.Ayling | 22 |
| M.Saxelby | 22 |
| A.M.Smith | 22 |
| A.M.Babington | 21 |
| S.R.Barwick | 21 |
| M.Frost | 21 |
| E.E.Hemmings | 21 |
| J.D.Robinson | 21 |
| G.A.Gooch | 20 |
| P.J.Hartley | 20 |
| P.J.Newport | 20 |
| G.C.Small | 20 |
| M.P.Bicknell | 19 |
| R.P.Davis | 19 |
| O.H.Mortensen | 19 |
| J.D.Batty | 18 |
| K.M.Curran | 17 |
| N.A.Foster | 17 |
| A.N.Hayhurst | 17 |
| R.A.Pick | 17 |
| A.Walker | 17 |
| C.Wilkinson | 17 |
| M.A.Feltham | 16 |
| D.Gough | 16 |
| J.P.Stephenson | 16 |
| A.E.Warner | 16 |
| R.G.Williams | 16 |
| E.A.E.Baptiste | 16 |
| J.D.R.Benson | 15 |
| J.Boiling | 15 |
| G.R.Dilley | 15 |
| T.A.Merrick | 15 |
| M.A.Robinson | 15 |
| R.J.Scott | 15 |
| J.G.Thomas | 15 |
| M.J.McCague | 15 |
| R.D.B.Croft | 14 |
| A.Dale | 14 |
| A.I.C.Dodemaide | 14 |
| D.A.Graveney | 14 |
| N.F.Williams | 14 |
| C.L.Hooper | 14 |
| M.A.Crawley | 13 |
| K.D.James | 13 |

| Name | Wickets Taken |
|---|---|
| K.H.Macleay | 13 |
| M.W.Alleyne | 12 |
| S.J.W.Andrew | 12 |
| R.A.Bunting | 12 |
| R.M.Ellison | 12 |
| G.A.Hick | 12 |
| P.M.Roebuck | 12 |
| G.D.Rose | 12 |
| N.M.K.Smith | 12 |
| J.A.North | 12 |
| D.G.Cork | 12 |
| D.R.Gilbert | 12 |

## ALL MATCHES
## (FIRST-CLASS AND ONE-DAY)
## 25 wickets or more

| Name | Wickets Taken |
|---|---|
| Waqar Younis | 151 |
| F.D.Stephenson | 119 |
| N.A.Foster | 119 |
| D.V.Lawrence | 110 |
| J.E.Emburey | 109 |
| A.A.Donald | 108 |
| P.A.J.DeFreitas | 102 |
| J.N.Maguire | 101 |
| T.A.Munton | 99 |
| S.L.Watkin | 99 |
| P.C.R.Tufnell | 96 |
| N.V.Radford | 94 |
| M.Watkinson | 93 |
| P.Carrick | 88 |
| A.P.Igglesden | 87 |
| A.N.Jones | 87 |
| M.Frost | 86 |
| P.J.Newport | 86 |
| T.D.Topley | 86 |
| Wasim Akram | 86 |
| R.A.Pick | 84 |
| D.R.Pringle | 80 |
| Aqib Javed | 80 |
| S.R.Lampitt | 79 |
| C.A.Connor | 77 |
| O.H.Mortensen | 77 |
| C.C.Lewis | 76 |
| T.A.Merrick | 76 |
| D.R.Gilbert | 76 |
| N.G.Cowans | 75 |
| D.J.Millns | 74 |
| A.C.S.Pigott | 74 |
| I.D.K.Salisbury | 71 |
| J.H.Childs | 70 |
| P.J.Hartley | 70 |
| D.A.Graveney | 69 |
| D.A.Reeve | 69 |
| D.G.Cork | 69 |
| I.T.Botham | 68 |
| A.I.C.Dodemaide | 68 |
| E.E.Hemmings | 67 |
| E.A.E.Baptiste | 66 |
| K.M.Curran | 65 |
| R.K.Illingworth | 65 |
| D.E.Malcolm | 65 |
| G.C.Small | 65 |
| M.P.Bicknell | 64 |
| K.P.Evans | 64 |
| A.M.Babington | 63 |
| P.M.Such | 62 |
| A.J.Murphy | 61 |
| H.R.J.Trump | 61 |
| N.F.Williams | 61 |
| J.A.Afford | 59 |
| S.J.Base | 59 |
| J.D.Batty | 59 |

| Name | Wickets Taken |
|---|---|
| R.M.Ellison | 59 |
| R.P.Davis | 56 |
| C.E.L.Ambrose | 55 |
| S.J.W.Andrew | 55 |
| C.Penn | 55 |
| K.D.James | 54 |
| J.P.Taylor | 54 |
| D.J.Capel | 53 |
| A.E.Warner | 53 |
| R.D.B.Croft | 52 |
| G.R.Dilley | 52 |
| N.A.Mallender | 52 |
| M.A.Feltham | 51 |
| K.T.Medlycott | 51 |
| A.M.Smith | 51 |
| S.R.Barwick | 49 |
| I.D.Austin | 48 |
| J.R.Ayling | 47 |
| S.D.Fletcher | 47 |
| R.J.Maru | 46 |
| R.P.Lefebvre | 46 |
| C.L.Hooper | 45 |
| K.J.Shine | 43 |
| P.A.Smith | 43 |
| J.G.Thomas | 43 |
| P.J.Martin | 42 |
| R.J.Shastri | 42 |
| J.W.Lloyds | 41 |
| B.P.Patterson | 41 |
| M.V.Fleming | 40 |
| M.A.Robinson | 40 |
| C.Wilkinson | 40 |
| P.J.W.Allott | 39 |
| B.T.P.Donelan | 39 |
| K.H.Macleay | 38 |
| G.D.Rose | 37 |
| A.R.Roberts | 35 |
| G.Yates | 35 |
| D.Gough | 34 |
| M.D.Marshall | 34 |
| S.D.Udal | 34 |
| D.W.Headley | 33 |
| J.P.Stephenson | 32 |
| J.A.North | 32 |
| D.J.Foster | 31 |
| C.A.Walsh | 31 |
| M.J.McCague | 31 |
| N.G.B.Cook | 30 |
| L.Potter | 30 |
| R.J.Scott | 30 |
| C.S.Pickles | 29 |
| H.A.G.Anthony | 29 |
| R.W.Sladdin | 29 |
| P.J.Bakker | 28 |
| K.J.Barnett | 28 |
| M.A.Ealham | 28 |
| A.N.Hayhurst | 28 |
| J.Boiling | 27 |
| M.Saxelby | 26 |
| S.C.Goldsmith | 25 |
| P.N.Hepworth | 25 |

# MOST DISMISSALS

## CORNHILL TEST MATCHES
### 4 dismissals or more

| Name | Dismissals | |
|---|---|---|
| P.J.L.Dujon | 17 | |
| C.L.Hooper | 9 | |
| G.A.Hick | 8 | |
| R.C.Russell | 8 | |
| A.J.Lamb | 7 | |
| G.A.Gooch | 6 | |
| I.T.Botham | 5 | |
| C.C.Lewis | 4 | |
| M.R.Ramprakash | 4 | |
| I.V.A.Richards | 4 | |

## BRITANNIC ASS. CHAMPIONSHIP
### 10 dismissals or more

| Name | Dismissals | |
|---|---|---|
| C.P.Metson | 69 | (incl 2st) |
| S.A.Marsh | 65 | (incl 4st) |
| B.N.French | 62 | (incl 8st) |
| M.A.Garnham | 58 | |
| K.M.Krikken | 58 | (incl 3st) |
| P.Moores | 58 | (incl 5st) |
| S.J.Rhodes | 55 | (incl 7st) |
| P.Farbrace | 52 | (incl 8st) |
| K.J.Piper | 48 | |
| N.F.Sargeant | 48 | (incl 5st) |
| A.N Aymes | 47 | (incl 2st) |
| P.Whitticase | 44 | (incl 2st) |
| N.D.Burns | 43 | (incl 8st) |
| W.K.Hegg | 42 | (incl 3st) |
| R.J.Blakey | 39 | (incl 4st) |
| D.Ripley | 39 | (incl 2st) |
| R.C.Russell | 39 | (incl 2st) |
| N.Hussain | 34 | |
| K.R.Brown | 33 | |
| T.M.Moody | 30 | |
| R.J.Maru | 29 | |
| M.Azharuddin | 23 | |
| K.J.Barnett | 23 | |
| V.P.Terry | 23 | |
| R.P.Davis | 22 | |
| Salim Malik | 22 | |
| D.B.D'Oliveira | 21 | |
| J.E.Emburey | 21 | |
| J.W.Lloyds | 21 | |
| T.J.G.O'Gorman | 21 | |
| D.P.Ostler | 21 | |
| P.Pollard | 21 | |
| R.C.J.Williams | 21 | (incl 3st) |
| D.Byas | 20 | |
| A.J.Stewart | 20 | |
| C.J.Tavare | 20 | |
| R.J.Harden | 19 | |
| P.E.Robinson | 19 | |
| N.H.Fairbrother | 18 | |
| R.T.Robinson | 18 | |
| G.R.Cowdrey | 17 | |
| P.N.Hepworth | 17 | |
| S.A.Kellett | 17 | |
| M.D.Moxon | 17 | |
| L.Potter | 17 | |
| P.J.Prichard | 17 | |
| M.A.Roseberry | 17 | |
| G.A.Hick | 16 | |
| A.J.Wright | 16 | |
| C.J.Adams | 15 | |
| P.D.Bowler | 15 | |
| N.E.Briers | 15 | |
| K.Greenfield | 15 | |
| D.W.Randall | 15 | |
| J.D.Ratcliffe | 15 | |

| Name | Dismissals | |
|---|---|---|
| M.A.Crawley | 14 | |
| T.S.Curtis | 14 | |
| M.V.Fleming | 14 | |
| M.P.Maynard | 14 | |
| T.C.Middleton | 14 | |
| T.A.Munton | 14 | |
| D.M.Smith | 14 | |
| N.R.Taylor | 14 | |
| T.D.Topley | 14 | |
| J.J.Whitaker | 14 | |
| S.J.Base | 13 | |
| A.R.Butcher | 13 | |
| S.J.Cook | 13 | |
| M.W.Gatting | 13 | |
| D.I.Gower | 13 | |
| A.J.Lamb | 13 | |
| M.A.Lynch | 13 | |
| H.Morris | 13 | |
| K.M.Curran | 12 | |
| P.Johnson | 12 | |
| A.A.Metcalfe | 12 | |
| I.D.K.Salisbury | 12 | |
| R.A.Smith | 12 | |
| N.A.Foster | 11 | |
| G.A.Gooch | 11 | |
| I.J.F.Hutchinson | 11 | |
| N.J.Lenham | 11 | |
| W.M.Noon | 11 | |
| H.R.J.Trump | 11 | |
| J.A.Afford | 10 | |
| M.W.Alleyne | 10 | |
| R.J.Bailey | 10 | |
| D.J.Bicknell | 10 | |
| R.D.B.Croft | 10 | |
| A.A.Donald | 10 | |
| D.A.Graveney | 10 | |
| G.D.Lloyd | 10 | |
| T.A.Lloyd | 10 | |
| A.J.Moles | 10 | |

## ALL FIRST-CLASS MATCHES
### 12 dismissals or more

| Name | Dismissals | |
|---|---|---|
| C.P.Metson | 76 | (incl 3st) |
| S.A.Marsh | 70 | (incl 4st) |
| B.N.French | 62 | (incl 8st) |
| M.A.Garnham | 62 | |
| S.J.Rhodes | 62 | (incl 8st) |
| K.M.Krikken | 61 | (incl 3st) |
| P.Moores | 61 | (incl 5st) |
| P.Farbrace | 54 | (incl 8st) |
| N.F.Sargeant | 54 | (incl 8st) |
| A.N Aymes | 53 | (incl 2st) |
| R.C.Russell | 52 | (incl 3st) |
| K.J.Piper | 48 | |
| P.Whitticase | 47 | (incl 3st) |
| W.K.Hegg | 46 | (incl 3st) |
| R.J.Blakey | 45 | (incl 5st) |
| N.D.Burns | 43 | (incl 8st) |
| D.Ripley | 43 | (incl 2st) |
| N.Hussain | 38 | |
| T.M.Moody | 37 | |
| K.R.Brown | 36 | |
| R.J.Maru | 31 | |
| D.Williams | 26 | (incl 3st) |
| K.J.Barnett | 25 | |
| J.E.Emburey | 25 | |
| G.A.Hick | 25 | |
| Salim Malik | 25 | |
| A.J.Stewart | 24 | |
| V.P.Terry | 24 | |
| M.Azharuddin | 24 | |
| R.P.Davis | 23 | |

| Name | Dismissals | |
|---|---|---|
| G.A.Gooch | 22 | |
| D.Byas | 21 | |
| D.B.D'Oliveira | 21 | |
| R.J.Harden | 21 | |
| A.J.Lamb | 21 | |
| J.W.Lloyds | 21 | |
| T.J.G.O'Gorman | 21 | |
| P.Pollard | 21 | |
| L.Potter | 21 | |
| P.E.Robinson | 21 | |
| P.J.L.Dujon | 21 | |
| D.P.Ostler | 21 | |
| R.C.J.Williams | 21 | (incl 3st) |
| M.A.Roseberry | 20 | |
| C.J.Tavare | 20 | |
| C.L.Hooper | 20 | |
| N.H.Fairbrother | 19 | |
| P.N.Hepworth | 19 | |
| S.A.Kellett | 19 | |
| P.J.Prichard | 19 | |
| A.J.Wright | 19 | |
| C.W.J.Athey | 18 | |
| N.E.Briers | 18 | |
| M.P.Maynard | 18 | |
| R.T.Robinson | 18 | |
| G.R.Cowdrey | 17 | |
| H.Morris | 17 | |
| M.D.Moxon | 17 | |
| S.J.Cook | 16 | |
| C.J.Adams | 15 | |
| P.D.Bowler | 15 | |
| T.S.Curtis | 15 | |
| K.Greenfield | 15 | |
| T.C.Middleton | 15 | |
| D.W.Randall | 15 | |
| J.D.Ratcliffe | 15 | |
| R.A.Smith | 15 | |
| T.D.Topley | 15 | |
| M.V.Fleming | 14 | |
| M.W.Gatting | 14 | |
| I.J.F.Hutchinson | 14 | |
| T.A.Munton | 14 | |
| D.M.Smith | 14 | |
| N.R.Taylor | 14 | |
| J.J.Whitaker | 14 | |
| R.B.Richardson | 14 | |
| M.W.Alleyne | 13 | (incl 1st) |
| S.J.Base | 13 | |
| A.R.Butcher | 13 | |
| M.A.Crawley | 13 | |
| D.I.Gower | 13 | |
| P.Johnson | 13 | |
| M.A.Lynch | 13 | |
| R.J.Turner | 13 | (incl 1st) |
| P.V.Simmons | 13 | |
| J.P.Crawley | 13 | |
| I.T.Botham | 12 | |
| R.D.B.Croft | 12 | |
| K.M.Curran | 12 | |
| P.R.Downton | 12 | (incl 1st) |
| A.A.Metcalfe | 12 | |
| I.D.K.Salisbury | 12 | |
| H.R.J.Trump | 12 | |
| D.Sandiford | 12 | (incl 1st) |

## TEXACO TROPHY
### 2 or more dismissals

| Name | Dismissals |
|---|---|
| P.A.J.DeFreitas | 4 |
| R.K.Illingworth | 4 |
| R.C.Russell | 4 |
| P.J.L.Dujon | 4 |
| R.B.Richardson | 4 |

# MOST DISMISSALS

| Name | Dismissals |
|---|---|
| N.H.Fairbrother | 2 |
| G.A.Gooch | 2 |
| C.C.Lewis | 2 |

## REFUGE ASSURANCE LEAGUE
**9 dismissals or more**

| Name | Dismissals | |
|---|---|---|
| W.K.Hegg | 23 | (incl 1st) |
| R.J.Blakey | 19 | (incl 1st) |
| N.D.Burns | 18 | (incl 6st) |
| B.N.French | 18 | (incl 1st) |
| A.N Aymes | 16 | (incl 3st) |
| P.Moores | 16 | (incl 1st) |
| R.C.Russell | 16 | (incl 1st) |
| P.Farbrace | 15 | (incl 6st) |
| C.P.Metson | 14 | (incl 2st) |
| A.J.Stewart | 14 | (incl 1st) |
| M.A.Garnham | 13 | (incl 3st) |
| K.M.Krikken | 12 | (incl 3st) |
| T.S.Curtis | 10 | |
| S.A.Marsh | 10 | (incl 1st) |
| K.J.Piper | 10 | (incl 3st) |
| G.R.Cowdrey | 9 | |
| M.P.Maynard | 9 | |
| P.E.Robinson | 9 | |

## BENSON & HEDGES CUP
**5 dismissals or more**

| Name | Dismissals | |
|---|---|---|
| R.J.Blakey | 11 | |
| S.J.Rhodes | 11 | (incl 1st) |
| A.N Aymes | 8 | (incl 4st) |
| P.R.Downton | 8 | (incl 1st) |
| M.A.Garnham | 8 | (incl 1st) |
| G.A.Hick | 8 | |
| D.Ripley | 8 | (incl 1st) |
| P.D.Bowler | 6 | |
| W.K.Hegg | 6 | |
| P.Moores | 6 | |
| P.A.Neale | 6 | |
| P.J.W.Allott | 5 | |
| P.A.J.DeFreitas | 5 | |
| N.H.Fairbrother | 5 | |
| S.A.Marsh | 5 | |
| M.D.Moxon | 5 | |
| K.J.Piper | 5 | |
| D.W.Randall | 5 | |
| D.J.Haggo | 5 | (incl 3st) |
| N.V.Knight | 5 | |

## NATWEST TROPHY
**4 dismissals or more**

| Name | Dismissals | |
|---|---|---|
| A.N Aymes | 7 | (incl 1st) |
| B.N.French | 7 | |
| R.C.Russell | 6 | (incl 1st) |
| A.J.Stewart | 6 | |
| D.A.Reeve | 5 | |
| W.K.Hegg | 4 | |
| N.Hussain | 4 | |
| K.J.Piper | 4 | |
| V.P.Terry | 4 | |
| D.J.Haggo | 4 | (incl 2st) |
| Salim Malik | 4 | |

# PLAYER
# RECORDS

## EDITOR'S NOTE

The records that follow refer to all players who have appeared in any of the matches featured in the preceding pages. Under each player there is a sub-section for each of the competitions in which he appeared and also categories of Other First-Class and Other One-Day for those matches outside the major competitions. Where players have represented more than one team every attempt has been made to make it clear whom they were representing in each match listed. In the case of all those playing in Cornhill Test Matches, the Texaco Trophy or the Britannic Assurance Championship their country and/or county are listed against the player's name. All others listed are credited with the teams for which they played most regularly – naturally there are several who played for Oxford or Cambridge University and also represented Combined Universities in the Benson & Hedges Cup or against the tourists. Similarly there are those who appeared for Minor Counties as well as for their individual minor county in the NatWest Trophy. Sub-headings within the match listings have been introduced where it was felt appropriate to indicate the team represented and in a number of cases a further sub-head has been used to indicate that the listing has reverted to the original team.

# PLAYER RECORDS
A

## J.ABRAHAMS - *Shropshire*

| Opposition | Venue | Date | Batting | Fielding | Bowling |
|---|---|---|---|---|---|
| **NATWEST TROPHY** | | | | | |
| Leicestershire | Leicester | June 26 | 53 | 2Ct | 0-25 |

**BATTING AVERAGES - Including fielding**

| | Matches | Inns | NO | Runs | HS | Avge | 100s | 50s | Ct | St |
|---|---|---|---|---|---|---|---|---|---|---|
| NatWest Trophy | 1 | 1 | 0 | 53 | 53 | 53.00 | - | 1 | 2 | - |
| | | | | | | | | | | |
| ALL ONE-DAY | 1 | 1 | 0 | 53 | 53 | 53.00 | - | 1 | 2 | - |

**BOWLING AVERAGES**

| | Overs | Mdns | Runs | Wkts | Avge | Best | 5wI | 10wM |
|---|---|---|---|---|---|---|---|---|
| NatWest Trophy | 8 | 0 | 25 | 0 | - | - | - | |
| | | | | | | | | |
| ALL ONE-DAY | 8 | 0 | 25 | 0 | - | - | - | |

## C.J.ADAMS - *Derbyshire*

| Opposition | Venue | Date | Batting | Fielding | Bowling |
|---|---|---|---|---|---|
| **BRITANNIC ASSURANCE** | | | | | |
| Northants | Derby | April 27 | | | |
| Lancashire | Old Trafford | May 16 | 18 | 1Ct | |
| Somerset | Derby | May 22 | 15 & 37 | 1Ct | |
| Kent | Canterbury | May 25 | 26 & 11 | 3Ct | |
| Northants | Northampton | May 31 | 18 & 2 | 2Ct | |
| Glamorgan | Chesterfield | June 7 | 13 | 2Ct | |
| Gloucs | Gloucester | June 18 | 0 & 6 | 2Ct | |
| Surrey | Derby | June 21 | 0* & 11 | | 1-19 |
| Essex | Derby | Aug 6 | 37 & 17 | 1Ct | |
| Lancashire | Derby | Aug 16 | 29* | | 4-29 |
| Leicestershire | Derby | Aug 20 | 44 & 0 | 2Ct | |
| Yorkshire | Chesterfield | Sept 17 | 40 & 112 | 1Ct | |
| **OTHER FIRST-CLASS** | | | | | |
| Cambridge U | Fenner's | May 9 | 39 & 134 | | 1-11 |
| West Indies | Derby | June 12 | 55 & 3 | | |
| Sri Lanka | Derby | Aug 2 | 24 | | |
| **REFUGE ASSURANCE** | | | | | |
| Leicestershire | Leicester | April 21 | 4* | | |
| Hampshire | Derby | May 5 | 34* | | |
| Lancashire | Derby | May 19 | 71 | 1Ct | |
| Kent | Canterbury | May 26 | 8 | 1Ct | |
| Yorkshire | Chesterfield | June 2 | | | |
| Surrey | Chesterfield | June 9 | | | |
| Somerset | Derby | June 16 | 9 | | |
| Essex | Chelmsford | June 30 | 0 | | |
| Sussex | Derby | July 7 | 44 | 1Ct | |
| Worcestershire | Worcester | July 9 | 36 | | |
| Gloucs | Cheltenham | July 21 | 67 | 1Ct | |
| Warwickshire | Edgbaston | Aug 4 | 35 | | |
| Middlesex | Lord's | Aug 11 | 20 | | |
| Glamorgan | Checkley | Aug 18 | 0 | | |
| Notts | Trent Bridge | Aug 25 | 47 | | |
| **BENSON & HEDGES CUP** | | | | | |
| Northants | Derby | April 23 | 0 | | |
| Combined U | The Parks | April 25 | | 1Ct | 0-3 |
| Worcestershire | Worcester | May 4 | 16* | | |
| Gloucs | Derby | May 7 | 2 | | |
| **OTHER ONE-DAY** | | | | | |
| Yorkshire | Scarborough | Sept 1 | 30 | 1Ct | |

**BATTING AVERAGES - Including fielding**

| | Matches | Inns | NO | Runs | HS | Avge | 100s | 50s | Ct | St |
|---|---|---|---|---|---|---|---|---|---|---|
| Britannic Assurance | 12 | 19 | 2 | 436 | 112 | 25.64 | 1 | - | 15 | - |
| Other First-Class | 3 | 5 | 0 | 255 | 134 | 51.00 | 1 | 1 | - | - |
| | | | | | | | | | | |
| ALL FIRST-CLASS | 15 | 24 | 2 | 691 | 134 | 31.40 | 2 | 1 | 15 | - |
| | | | | | | | | | | |
| Refuge Assurance | 15 | 13 | 2 | 375 | 71 | 34.09 | - | 2 | 4 | - |
| Benson & Hedges Cup | 4 | 3 | 1 | 18 | 16* | 9.00 | - | - | 1 | - |
| Other One-Day | 1 | 1 | 0 | 30 | 30 | 30.00 | - | - | 1 | - |
| | | | | | | | | | | |
| ALL ONE-DAY | 20 | 17 | 3 | 423 | 71 | 30.21 | - | 2 | 6 | - |

## BOWLING AVERAGES (J.ABRAHAMS continued, right column)

| | Overs | Mdns | Runs | Wkts | Avge | Best | 5wI | 10wM |
|---|---|---|---|---|---|---|---|---|
| Britannic Assurance | 12.4 | 1 | 48 | 5 | 9.60 | 4-29 | - | - |
| Other First-Class | 7 | 2 | 11 | 1 | 11.00 | 1-11 | - | - |
| | | | | | | | | |
| ALL FIRST-CLASS | 19.4 | 3 | 59 | 6 | 9.83 | 4-29 | - | - |
| | | | | | | | | |
| Refuge Assurance | | | | | | | | |
| Benson & Hedges Cup | 1 | 0 | 3 | 0 | - | - | - | - |
| Other One-Day | | | | | | | | |
| | | | | | | | | |
| ALL ONE-DAY | 1 | 0 | 3 | 0 | - | - | - | - |

## J.C.ADAMS - *Rest of World*

| Opposition | Venue | Date | Batting | Fielding | Bowling |
|---|---|---|---|---|---|
| **OTHER ONE-DAY** | | | | | |
| England XI | Jesmond | July 31 | 14* | 1Ct | |
| England XI | Jesmond | Aug 1 | 28* | 1Ct,1St | |

**BATTING AVERAGES - Including fielding**

| | Matches | Inns | NO | Runs | HS | Avge | 100s | 50s | Ct | St |
|---|---|---|---|---|---|---|---|---|---|---|
| Other One-Day | 2 | 2 | 2 | 42 | 28* | - | - | - | 2 | 1 |
| | | | | | | | | | | |
| ALL ONE-DAY | 2 | 2 | 2 | 42 | 28* | - | - | - | 2 | 1 |

**BOWLING AVERAGES**
Did not bowl

## N.J.ADAMS - *Cambridgeshire*

| Opposition | Venue | Date | Batting | Fielding | Bowling |
|---|---|---|---|---|---|
| **NATWEST TROPHY** | | | | | |
| Kent | Canterbury | June 26 | 44 | | 0-15 |

**BATTING AVERAGES - Including fielding**

| | Matches | Inns | NO | Runs | HS | Avge | 100s | 50s | Ct | St |
|---|---|---|---|---|---|---|---|---|---|---|
| NatWest Trophy | 1 | 1 | 0 | 44 | 44 | 44.00 | - | - | - | - |
| | | | | | | | | | | |
| ALL ONE-DAY | 1 | 1 | 0 | 44 | 44 | 44.00 | - | - | - | - |

**BOWLING AVERAGES**

| | Overs | Mdns | Runs | Wkts | Avge | Best | 5wI | 10wM |
|---|---|---|---|---|---|---|---|---|
| NatWest Trophy | 2 | 0 | 15 | 0 | - | - | - | |
| | | | | | | | | |
| ALL ONE-DAY | 2 | 0 | 15 | 0 | - | - | - | |

## J.P.ADDISON - *Staffordshire*

| Opposition | Venue | Date | Batting | Fielding | Bowling |
|---|---|---|---|---|---|
| **NATWEST TROPHY** | | | | | |
| Northants | Stone | June 26 | 11 | | 0-19 |

**BATTING AVERAGES - Including fielding**

| | Matches | Inns | NO | Runs | HS | Avge | 100s | 50s | Ct | St |
|---|---|---|---|---|---|---|---|---|---|---|
| NatWest Trophy | 1 | 1 | 0 | 11 | 11 | 11.00 | - | - | - | - |
| | | | | | | | | | | |
| ALL ONE-DAY | 1 | 1 | 0 | 11 | 11 | 11.00 | - | - | - | - |

**BOWLING AVERAGES**

| | Overs | Mdns | Runs | Wkts | Avge | Best | 5wI | 10wM |
|---|---|---|---|---|---|---|---|---|
| NatWest Trophy | 2 | 0 | 19 | 0 | - | - | - | |
| | | | | | | | | |
| ALL ONE-DAY | 2 | 0 | 19 | 0 | - | - | - | |

# A PLAYER RECORDS

## J.A.AFFORD - *Nottinghamshire*

| Opposition | Venue | Date | Batting | Fielding | Bowling |
|---|---|---|---|---|---|
| **BRITANNIC ASSURANCE** | | | | | |
| Leicestershire | Trent Bridge | May 9 | 13 | 1Ct | 0-8 & 0-55 |
| Kent | Trent Bridge | May 22 | | | 1-82 & 4-44 |
| Leicestershire | Leicester | May 25 | | 1Ct | 2-48 & 3-46 |
| Hampshire | Trent Bridge | May 31 | 0 * | | 0-80 & 0-51 |
| Gloucs | Gloucester | June 14 | | 1Ct | 2-32 & 2-48 |
| Worcestershire | Worcester | June 18 | | 2Ct | 0-38 & 2-94 |
| Warwickshire | Trent Bridge | June 21 | | | 4-65 |
| Glamorgan | Cardiff | July 2 | 0 | 1Ct | 2-20 & 2-67 |
| Lancashire | Trent Bridge | July 16 | 1 | 1Ct | 4-46 & 2-62 |
| Northants | Well'borough | July 19 | 0 | | 0-19 |
| Yorkshire | Worksop | July 23 | | 0 * | 0-31 |
| Sussex | Eastbourne | Aug 6 | | 1Ct | 4-69 & 3-50 |
| Essex | Trent Bridge | Aug 9 | 4 * & | 3 | 0-18 & 1-44 |
| Somerset | Trent Bridge | Aug 16 | | | 1-62 & 0-64 |
| Derbyshire | Trent Bridge | Aug 23 | | 1Ct | 0-96 & 3-104 |
| Lancashire | Old Trafford | Aug 28 | 0 * | | 4-78 & 1-58 |
| Middlesex | Trent Bridge | Sept 3 | 12 & 0 | 1Ct | 2-101 & 3-86 |
| Worcestershire | Trent Bridge | Sept 17 | 9 | | 2-28 & 3-23 |
| **OTHER FIRST-CLASS** | | | | | |
| Oxford U | The Parks | April 27 | | | |
| **NATWEST TROPHY** | | | | | |
| Lincolnshire | Trent Bridge | June 26 | | | 0-38 |
| Gloucs | Bristol | July 11 | | | 1-40 |
| **BENSON & HEDGES CUP** | | | | | |
| Min Counties | Trent Bridge | May 7 | | | 1-43 |

**BATTING AVERAGES - Including fielding**

| | Matches | Inns | NO | Runs | HS | Avge | 100s | 50s | Ct | St |
|---|---|---|---|---|---|---|---|---|---|---|
| Britannic Assurance | 18 | 12 | 4 | 42 | 13 | 5.25 | - | - | 10 | - |
| Other First-Class | 1 | 0 | 0 | 0 | 0 | - | - | - | - | - |
| ALL FIRST-CLASS | 19 | 12 | 4 | 42 | 13 | 5.25 | - | - | 10 | - |
| NatWest Trophy | 2 | 0 | 0 | 0 | 0 | - | - | - | - | - |
| Benson & Hedges Cup | 1 | 0 | 0 | 0 | 0 | - | - | - | - | - |
| ALL ONE-DAY | 3 | 0 | 0 | 0 | 0 | - | - | - | - | - |

**BOWLING AVERAGES**

| | Overs | Mdns | Runs | Wkts | Avge | Best | 5wI | 10wM |
|---|---|---|---|---|---|---|---|---|
| Britannic Assurance | 670.3 | 207 | 1817 | 57 | 31.87 | 4-44 | - | - |
| Other First-Class | | | | | | | | |
| ALL FIRST-CLASS | 670.3 | 207 | 1817 | 57 | 31.87 | 4-44 | - | - |
| NatWest Trophy | 23 | 5 | 78 | 1 | 78.00 | 1-40 | - | |
| Benson & Hedges Cup | 11 | 0 | 43 | 1 | 43.00 | 1-43 | - | |
| ALL ONE-DAY | 34 | 5 | 121 | 2 | 60.50 | 1-40 | - | |

## F.S.AHANGAMA - *Sri Lanka*

| Opposition | Venue | Date | Batting | Fielding | Bowling |
|---|---|---|---|---|---|
| **OTHER FIRST-CLASS** | | | | | |
| Worcestershire | Worcester | July 30 | 7 & 0 | | 1-41 |
| Gloucs | Bristol | Aug 6 | 0 * & 0 | | 1-51 & 0-12 |
| Somerset | Taunton | Aug 10 | | | 0-59 & 0-26 |

**BATTING AVERAGES - Including fielding**

| | Matches | Inns | NO | Runs | HS | Avge | 100s | 50s | Ct | St |
|---|---|---|---|---|---|---|---|---|---|---|
| Other First-Class | 3 | 4 | 1 | 7 | 7 | 2.33 | - | - | - | - |
| ALL FIRST-CLASS | 3 | 4 | 1 | 7 | 7 | 2.33 | - | - | - | - |

**BOWLING AVERAGES**

| | Overs | Mdns | Runs | Wkts | Avge | Best | 5wI | 10wM |
|---|---|---|---|---|---|---|---|---|
| Other First-Class | 64 | 20 | 189 | 2 | 94.50 | 1-41 | - | - |
| ALL FIRST-CLASS | 64 | 20 | 189 | 2 | 94.50 | 1-41 | - | - |

## R.I.ALIKHAN - *Surrey*

| Opposition | Venue | Date | Batting | Fielding | Bowling |
|---|---|---|---|---|---|
| **BRITANNIC ASSURANCE** | | | | | |
| Kent | The Oval | May 9 | 29 & 31 | 1Ct | |
| Lancashire | The Oval | May 22 | 67 & 26 | 3Ct | |
| Hampshire | Bournemouth | May 25 | 13 & 53 | | |
| Notts | The Oval | June 4 | 69 & 96 * | | |
| Leicestershire | Leicester | June 14 | 28 * & 35 | | |
| Derbyshire | Derby | June 21 | 3 & 15 | | |
| Somerset | The Oval | June 28 | 6 | | |
| Sussex | Arundel | July 2 | 58 | 1Ct | |
| Essex | The Oval | July 5 | 20 & 8 | | |
| Gloucs | Guildford | July 16 | 4 & 70 | 1Ct | |
| Yorkshire | Guildford | July 19 | 86 & 21 | 3Ct | |
| Glamorgan | The Oval | July 26 | 40 & 25 | | |
| Kent | Canterbury | Aug 2 | 30 & 20 | | |
| Warwickshire | Edgbaston | Aug 6 | 9 & 0 | | |
| Worcestershire | Worcester | Aug 16 | 30 & 0 | | |
| Northants | Northampton | Aug 23 | 37 & 1 | | 2-43 |
| Sussex | The Oval | Aug 28 | 11 | | |
| Hampshire | The Oval | Sept 3 | 11 & 11 | | |
| **OTHER FIRST-CLASS** | | | | | |
| Cambridge U | Fenner's | May 18 | 92 | 1Ct | |
| **OTHER ONE-DAY** | | | | | |
| Warwickshire | Harrogate | June 12 | 7 | | |

**BATTING AVERAGES - Including fielding**

| | Matches | Inns | NO | Runs | HS | Avge | 100s | 50s | Ct | St |
|---|---|---|---|---|---|---|---|---|---|---|
| Britannic Assurance | 18 | 33 | 2 | 963 | 96 * | 31.06 | - | 7 | 9 | - |
| Other First-Class | 1 | 1 | 0 | 92 | 92 | 92.00 | - | 1 | 1 | - |
| ALL FIRST-CLASS | 19 | 34 | 2 | 1055 | 96 * | 32.96 | - | 8 | 10 | - |
| Other One-Day | 1 | 1 | 0 | 7 | 7 | 7.00 | - | - | - | - |
| ALL ONE-DAY | 1 | 1 | 0 | 7 | 7 | 7.00 | - | - | - | - |

**BOWLING AVERAGES**

| | Overs | Mdns | Runs | Wkts | Avge | Best | 5wI | 10wM |
|---|---|---|---|---|---|---|---|---|
| Britannic Assurance | 5 | 0 | 43 | 2 | 21.50 | 2-43 | - | - |
| Other First-Class | | | | | | | | |
| ALL FIRST-CLASS | 5 | 0 | 43 | 2 | 21.50 | 2-43 | - | - |
| Other One-Day | | | | | | | | |
| ALL ONE-DAY | | | | | | | | |

## AJAZ AKHTAR - *Cambridgeshire*

| Opposition | Venue | Date | Batting | Fielding | Bowling |
|---|---|---|---|---|---|
| **NATWEST TROPHY** | | | | | |
| Kent | Canterbury | June 26 | 2 | | 4-28 |

**BATTING AVERAGES - Including fielding**

| | Matches | Inns | NO | Runs | HS | Avge | 100s | 50s | Ct | St |
|---|---|---|---|---|---|---|---|---|---|---|
| NatWest Trophy | 1 | 1 | 0 | 2 | 2 | 2.00 | - | - | - | - |
| ALL ONE-DAY | 1 | 1 | 0 | 2 | 2 | 2.00 | - | - | - | - |

**BOWLING AVERAGES**

| | Overs | Mdns | Runs | Wkts | Avge | Best | 5wI | 10wM |
|---|---|---|---|---|---|---|---|---|
| NatWest Trophy | 12 | 6 | 28 | 4 | 7.00 | 4-28 | - | |
| ALL ONE-DAY | 12 | 6 | 28 | 4 | 7.00 | 4-28 | - | |

# PLAYER RECORDS

**A**

## I.B.A.ALLEN - *West Indies*

| Opposition | Venue | Date | Batting | Fielding | Bowling |
|---|---|---|---|---|---|
| **CORNHILL TEST MATCHES** | | | | | |
| England | Lord's | June 20 | 1 * | | 2-88 |
| England | Trent Bridge | July 4 | 4 * | 1Ct | 2-69 & 1-23 |
| **OTHER FIRST-CLASS** | | | | | |
| Worcestershire | Worcester | May 15 | | 3Ct | 1-64 |
| Somerset | Taunton | May 29 | | 1Ct | 0-71 & 2-61 |
| Leicestershire | Leicester | June 1 | 0 * | 1Ct | 1-65 & 1-46 |
| Derbyshire | Derby | June 12 | | | 1-35 & 1-37 |
| Northants | Northampton | June 15 | 8 | | 0-27 |
| Kent | Canterbury | July 20 | 3 * | 1Ct | 1-57 & 1-24 |
| Gloucs | Bristol | July 31 | | 1Ct | 1-55 & 0-14 |
| Essex | Chelmsford | Aug 3 | | | 0-27 & 1-48 |
| **OTHER ONE-DAY** | | | | | |
| D of Norfolk | Arundel | May 12 | 2 * | | 1-41 |
| Gloucs | Bristol | May 14 | | | 0-32 |
| League CC XI | Trowbridge | June 28 | | | 0-7 |
| Ireland | Downpatrick | July 13 | | | 0-17 |
| Wales | Brecon | July 15 | | | 0-6 |

**BATTING AVERAGES - Including fielding**

| | Matches | Inns | NO | Runs | HS | Avge | 100s | 50s | Ct | St |
|---|---|---|---|---|---|---|---|---|---|---|
| Cornhill Test Matches | 2 | 2 | 2 | 5 | 4 * | - | - | - | 1 | - |
| Other First-Class | 8 | 3 | 2 | 11 | 8 | 11.00 | - | - | 7 | - |
| ALL FIRST-CLASS | 10 | 5 | 4 | 16 | 8 | 16.00 | - | - | 8 | - |
| Other One-Day | 5 | 1 | 1 | 2 | 2 * | - | - | - | - | - |
| ALL ONE-DAY | 5 | 1 | 1 | 2 | 2 * | - | - | - | - | - |

**BOWLING AVERAGES**

| | Overs | Mdns | Runs | Wkts | Avge | Best | 5wI | 10wM |
|---|---|---|---|---|---|---|---|---|
| Cornhill Test Matches | 47 | 4 | 180 | 5 | 36.00 | 2-69 | - | - |
| Other First-Class | 170.4 | 31 | 631 | 11 | 57.36 | 2-61 | - | - |
| ALL FIRST-CLASS | 217.4 | 35 | 811 | 16 | 50.68 | 2-61 | - | - |
| Other One-Day | 39 | 8 | 103 | 1 | 103.00 | 1-41 | - | |
| ALL ONE-DAY | 39 | 8 | 103 | 1 | 103.00 | 1-41 | - | |

## M.W.ALLEYNE - *Gloucestershire*

| Opposition | Venue | Date | Batting | | Fielding | Bowling |
|---|---|---|---|---|---|---|
| **BRITANNIC ASSURANCE** | | | | | | |
| Worcestershire | Worcester | April 27 | 2 | | | |
| Hampshire | Bristol | May 9 | 79 | | | |
| Yorkshire | Sheffield | May 22 | 40 & | 55 * | 1Ct | 1-39 & 0-18 |
| Warwickshire | Edgbaston | May 25 | 23 & | 0 | 2Ct | 3-35 |
| Essex | Bristol | May 31 | 17 & | 46 | | 0-21 |
| Middlesex | Bristol | June 4 | 25 | | | 0-30 |
| Hampshire | Southampton | June 7 | | 3 * | | |
| Notts | Gloucester | June 14 | 1 | | | |
| Derbyshire | Gloucester | June 18 | 18 & | 4 | 1Ct | |
| Somerset | Bath | June 21 | 47 | | | |
| Northants | Luton | June 28 | 22 & | 0 | 2Ct | |
| Leicestershire | Hinckley | July 2 | 55 | | | |
| Surrey | Guildford | July 16 | 1 & | 37 * | | |
| Glamorgan | Cheltenham | July 19 | 2 & | 4 | | 0-27 & 2-48 |
| Sussex | Cheltenham | July 23 | 0 | | 1Ct | |
| Worcestershire | Cheltenham | July 26 | 44 & | 5 | | 1-34 & 1-15 |
| Lancashire | Bristol | Aug 9 | 90 | | 2Ct | 0-9 |
| Kent | Canterbury | Aug 20 | 0 & | 0 | | |
| Glamorgan | Abergavenny | Aug 28 | 40 & | 33 | | 0-33 |
| Northants | Bristol | Sept 3 | 165 & | 0 | | 0-9 |
| Somerset | Bristol | Sept 10 | 47 & | 4 | 1Ct | 0-18 |
| Sussex | Hove | Sept 17 | 0 & | 12 | | 3-45 |
| **OTHER FIRST-CLASS** | | | | | | |
| Oxford U | The Parks | June 15 | 5 * | | | 0-15 |
| West Indies | Bristol | July 31 | 68 & | 26 | 0Ct,1St | 0-38 & 0-40 |
| Sri Lanka | Bristol | Aug 6 | 91 & | 10 * | 2Ct | |

## REFUGE ASSURANCE

| Middlesex | Bristol | April 21 | 48 | | 0-42 |
|---|---|---|---|---|---|
| Worcestershire | Bristol | May 5 | 44 | | 0-33 |
| Surrey | The Oval | May 12 | 37 | | 1-32 |
| Sussex | Hove | May 19 | 59 | | 2-19 |
| Hampshire | Swindon | May 26 | 37 * | 1Ct | 0-25 |
| Northants | Moreton | June 9 | | | |
| Notts | Gloucester | June 16 | 37 | | |
| Kent | Canterbury | June 30 | 1 | | 1-46 |
| Yorkshire | Scarborough | July 14 | 4 | | 1-38 |
| Derbyshire | Cheltenham | July 21 | 17 | | 1-22 |
| Essex | Cheltenham | July 28 | 13 | | 2-19 |
| Glamorgan | Swansea | Aug 4 | 8 | | 1-44 |
| Lancashire | Bristol | Aug 11 | 11 | | 1-7 |
| Warwickshire | Edgbaston | Aug 18 | 17 | | 0-17 |
| Leicestershire | Leicester | Aug 25 | 76 * | | |

**NATWEST TROPHY**

| Norfolk | Bristol | June 26 | 3 | | |
|---|---|---|---|---|---|
| Notts | Bristol | July 11 | 45 | | |

**BENSON & HEDGES CUP**

| Combined U | Bristol | April 23 | 6 | 1Ct | |
|---|---|---|---|---|---|
| Worcestershire | Worcester | April 25 | 0 | | 0-19 |
| Northants | Bristol | May 2 | | 1Ct | 1-24 |
| Derbyshire | Derby | May 7 | 1 | | 0-24 |

**OTHER ONE-DAY**

| West Indies | Bristol | May 14 | 15 | | 1-54 |
|---|---|---|---|---|---|
| Somerset | Hove | Sept 8 | 77 | | 0-25 |
| Sussex | Hove | Sept 9 | 1 | 1Ct | 0-27 |

**BATTING AVERAGES - Including fielding**

| | Matches | Inns | NO | Runs | HS | Avge | 100s | 50s | Ct | St |
|---|---|---|---|---|---|---|---|---|---|---|
| Britannic Assurance | 22 | 35 | 3 | 921 | 165 | 28.78 | 1 | 4 | 10 | - |
| Other First-Class | 3 | 5 | 2 | 200 | 91 | 66.66 | - | 2 | 2 | 1 |
| ALL FIRST-CLASS | 25 | 40 | 5 | 1121 | 165 | 32.02 | 1 | 6 | 12 | 1 |
| Refuge Assurance | 15 | 14 | 2 | 409 | 76 * | 34.08 | - | 2 | 1 | - |
| NatWest Trophy | 2 | 2 | 0 | 48 | 45 | 24.00 | - | - | - | - |
| Benson & Hedges Cup | 4 | 3 | 0 | 7 | 6 | 2.33 | - | - | 2 | - |
| Other One-Day | 3 | 3 | 0 | 93 | 77 | 31.00 | - | 1 | 1 | - |
| ALL ONE-DAY | 24 | 22 | 2 | 557 | 77 | 27.85 | - | 3 | 4 | - |

**BOWLING AVERAGES**

| | Overs | Mdns | Runs | Wkts | Avge | Best | 5wI | 10wM |
|---|---|---|---|---|---|---|---|---|
| Britannic Assurance | 118.1 | 23 | 381 | 11 | 34.63 | 3-35 | - | - |
| Other First-Class | 26 | 4 | 93 | 0 | - | - | - | - |
| ALL FIRST-CLASS | 144.1 | 27 | 474 | 11 | 43.09 | 3-35 | - | - |
| Refuge Assurance | 65 | 1 | 344 | 10 | 34.40 | 2-19 | - | - |
| NatWest Trophy | | | | | | | | |
| Benson & Hedges Cup | 15 | 0 | 67 | 1 | 67.00 | 1-24 | - | - |
| Other One-Day | 18 | 0 | 106 | 1 | 106.00 | 1-54 | - | - |
| ALL ONE-DAY | 98 | 1 | 517 | 12 | 43.08 | 2-19 | - | - |

## P.J.W.ALLOTT - *Lancashire*

| Opposition | Venue | Date | Batting | | Fielding | Bowling |
|---|---|---|---|---|---|---|
| **BRITANNIC ASSURANCE** | | | | | | |
| Warwickshire | Edgbaston | April 27 | | | | 1-30 |
| Worcestershire | Worcester | May 9 | 3 * & | 5 * | 1Ct | 4-56 & 0-62 |
| Derbyshire | Old Trafford | May 16 | 9 | | | 2-60 |
| Surrey | The Oval | May 22 | 0 & | 10 | | 1-35 |
| Warwickshire | Old Trafford | July 23 | | | 1Ct | 0-45 |
| Northants | Lytham | Aug 6 | | 6 | 1Ct | 1-84 |
| Gloucs | Bristol | Aug 9 | 4 & | 26 | | 0-39 |
| Derbyshire | Derby | Aug 16 | | | 1Ct | 1-39 & 2-39 |
| **OTHER FIRST-CLASS** | | | | | | |
| Cambridge U | Fenner's | April 13 | | | 2Ct | 1-23 & 1-4 |
| **REFUGE ASSURANCE** | | | | | | |
| Notts | Old Trafford | April 21 | 1 * | | | 1-30 |
| Northants | Old Trafford | April 28 | | | | 1-27 |
| Worcestershire | Worcester | May 12 | | | | 0-31 |
| Derbyshire | Derby | May 19 | | | | 2-45 |

# A

# PLAYER RECORDS

| | | | | | |
|---|---|---|---|---|---|
| Sussex | Old Trafford | June 2 | | | 0-23 |
| Glamorgan | Old Trafford | June 9 | | | 0-26 |
| Warwickshire | Edgbaston | June 16 | | | 0-13 |
| Somerset | Taunton | July 5 | | 1Ct | 0-41 |
| Leicestershire | Leicester | July 7 | | | 1-31 |
| Middlesex | Lord's | July 21 | | | 0-21 |
| Hampshire | Southampton | July 28 | 10* | | 1-28 |
| Yorkshire | Old Trafford | Aug 4 | 1* | | 0-37 |
| Gloucs | Bristol | Aug 11 | | | 1-17 |
| Surrey | Old Trafford | Aug 18 | 3* | | 1-37 |
| Essex | Old Trafford | Aug 25 | | | 2-30 |
| Northants | Old Trafford | Sept 1 | | | 1-27 |
| Worcestershire | Old Trafford | Sept 15 | 5* | 1Ct | 0-17 |

**NATWEST TROPHY**

| | | | | | |
|---|---|---|---|---|---|
| Hampshire | Southampton | July 11 | 2 | | 0-48 |

**BENSON & HEDGES CUP**

| | | | | | |
|---|---|---|---|---|---|
| Scotland | Forfar | April 23 | | | 0-21 |
| Kent | Old Trafford | April 25 | | 1Ct | 3-17 |
| Leicestershire | Leicester | May 4 | | | 4-23 |
| Sussex | Old Trafford | May 7 | | | 0-29 |
| Northants | Old Trafford | May 29 | | | 2-38 |
| Yorkshire | Old Trafford | June 16 | 0 | 2Ct | 0-46 |
| Worcestershire | Lord's | July 13 | 10 | 2Ct | 2-26 |

**OTHER ONE-DAY**
For England XI

| | | | | | |
|---|---|---|---|---|---|
| Rest of World | Jesmond | July 31 | | | 3-47 |
| Rest of World | Jesmond | Aug 1 | 0 | 1Ct | 0-39 |

**BATTING AVERAGES - Including fielding**

| | Matches | Inns | NO | Runs | HS | Avge | 100s | 50s | Ct | St |
|---|---|---|---|---|---|---|---|---|---|---|
| Britannic Assurance | 8 | 8 | 2 | 63 | 26 | 10.50 | - | - | 4 | - |
| Other First-Class | 1 | 0 | 0 | 0 | 0 | - | - | - | 2 | - |
| ALL FIRST-CLASS | 9 | 8 | 2 | 63 | 26 | 10.50 | - | - | 6 | - |
| Refuge Assurance | 17 | 5 | 5 | 20 | 10* | - | - | - | 2 | - |
| NatWest Trophy | 1 | 1 | 0 | 2 | 2 | 2.00 | - | - | - | - |
| Benson & Hedges Cup | 7 | 2 | 0 | 10 | 10 | 5.00 | - | - | 5 | - |
| Other One-Day | 2 | 1 | 0 | 0 | 0 | 0.00 | - | - | 1 | - |
| ALL ONE-DAY | 27 | 9 | 5 | 32 | 10* | 8.00 | - | - | 8 | - |

**BOWLING AVERAGES**

| | Overs | Mdns | Runs | Wkts | Avge | Best | 5wI | 10wM |
|---|---|---|---|---|---|---|---|---|
| Britannic Assurance | 173.1 | 43 | 489 | 12 | 40.75 | 4-56 | - | - |
| Other First-Class | 19 | 6 | 27 | 2 | 13.50 | 1-4 | - | - |
| ALL FIRST-CLASS | 192.1 | 49 | 516 | 14 | 36.85 | 4-56 | - | - |
| Refuge Assurance | 121 | 8 | 481 | 11 | 43.72 | 2-30 | - | |
| NatWest Trophy | 12 | 3 | 48 | 0 | - | - | - | |
| Benson & Hedges Cup | 74 | 17 | 200 | 11 | 18.18 | 4-23 | - | |
| Other One-Day | 17 | 2 | 86 | 3 | 28.66 | 3-47 | - | |
| ALL ONE-DAY | 224 | 30 | 815 | 25 | 32.60 | 4-23 | - | |

# C.E.L.AMBROSE - West Indies

| Opposition | Venue | Date | Batting | Fielding | Bowling |
|---|---|---|---|---|---|
| **CORNHILL TEST MATCHES** | | | | | |
| England | Headingley | June 6 | 0 & 14 | | 2-49 & 6-52 |
| England | Lord's | June 20 | 5 | | 4-87 |
| England | Trent Bridge | July 4 | 17 | | 5-74 & 3-61 |
| England | Edgbaston | July 25 | 1 | | 3-64 & 2-42 |
| England | The Oval | Aug 8 | 0 & 0 | | 3-83 & 0-48 |
| **OTHER FIRST-CLASS** | | | | | |
| Somerset | Taunton | May 29 | 16* | | 2-35 & 2-35 |
| Derbyshire | Derby | June 12 | | 1Ct | 1-26 & 0-18 |
| Hampshire | Southampton | June 29 | | | 4-70 & 1-22 |
| Glamorgan | Swansea | July 16 | | | 5-56 & 3-14 |
| Essex | Chelmsford | Aug 3 | | | 4-29 & 1-4 |
| **TEXACO TROPHY** | | | | | |
| England | Edgbaston | May 23 | 21* | | 1-34 |
| England | Old Trafford | May 25 | 5* | | 2-36 |
| England | Lord's | May 27 | 6* | | 0-31 |

**OTHER ONE-DAY**

| | | | | | |
|---|---|---|---|---|---|
| Gloucs | Bristol | May 14 | | | 1-5 |

**BATTING AVERAGES - Including fielding**

| | Matches | Inns | NO | Runs | HS | Avge | 100s | 50s | Ct | St |
|---|---|---|---|---|---|---|---|---|---|---|
| Cornhill Test Matches | 5 | 7 | 0 | 37 | 17 | 5.28 | - | - | - | - |
| Other First-Class | 5 | 1 | 1 | 16 | 16* | - | - | - | 1 | - |
| ALL FIRST-CLASS | 10 | 8 | 1 | 53 | 17 | 7.57 | - | - | 1 | - |
| Texaco Trophy | 3 | 3 | 3 | 32 | 21* | - | - | - | - | - |
| Other One-Day | 1 | 0 | 0 | 0 | 0 | - | - | - | - | - |
| ALL ONE-DAY | 4 | 3 | 3 | 32 | 21* | - | - | - | - | - |

**BOWLING AVERAGES**

| | Overs | Mdns | Runs | Wkts | Avge | Best | 5wI | 10wM |
|---|---|---|---|---|---|---|---|---|
| Cornhill Test Matches | 249 | 68 | 560 | 28 | 20.00 | 6-52 | 2 | - |
| Other First-Class | 141 | 54 | 309 | 23 | 13.43 | 5-56 | 1 | - |
| ALL FIRST-CLASS | 390 | 122 | 869 | 51 | 17.03 | 6-52 | 3 | - |
| Texaco Trophy | 30 | 5 | 101 | 3 | 33.66 | 2-36 | - | |
| Other One-Day | 4 | 2 | 5 | 1 | 5.00 | 1-5 | - | |
| ALL ONE-DAY | 34 | 7 | 106 | 4 | 26.50 | 2-36 | - | |

# S.J.W.ANDREW - Essex

| Opposition | Venue | Date | Batting | Fielding | Bowling |
|---|---|---|---|---|---|
| **BRITANNIC ASSURANCE** | | | | | |
| Surrey | Chelmsford | April 27 | | | 1-55 |
| Warwickshire | Chelmsford | May 22 | 7 | | 1-47 & 4-38 |
| Gloucs | Bristol | May 31 | | | 3-51 & 3-51 |
| Leicestershire | Ilford | June 4 | 1 | | 2-63 & 2-55 |
| Worcestershire | Ilford | June 7 | 0 | | 1-86 & 0-32 |
| Sussex | Horsham | June 21 | | | 2-44 |
| Middlesex | Lord's | June 28 | | 1Ct | 0-71 & 3-30 |
| Hampshire | Chelmsford | July 2 | | 6* 1Ct | 1-41 & 1-8 |
| Kent | Southend | July 16 | | 1 | 4-104 & 0-7 |
| Somerset | Southend | July 19 | | | 0-65 & 1-11 |
| Glamorgan | Cardiff | July 23 | | | 2-90 |
| Derbyshire | Derby | Aug 6 | 0 & 2* | | 2-33 & 3-71 |
| Notts | Trent Bridge | Aug 9 | 13 | 1Ct | 1-65 & 0-37 |
| Middlesex | Chelmsford | Sept 17 | | | 2-8 & 1-48 |
| **OTHER FIRST-CLASS** | | | | | |
| West Indies | Chelmsford | Aug 3 | 0 | 1Ct | 1-90 & 2-51 |
| **REFUGE ASSURANCE** | | | | | |
| Kent | Folkestone | May 19 | 6* | | 1-30 |
| Surrey | The Oval | May 26 | 8 | | 1-44 |
| Glamorgan | Pontypridd | June 2 | | | 3-33 |
| Worcestershire | Ilford | June 9 | | | 2-45 |
| Hampshire | Chelmsford | June 16 | | | |
| Derbyshire | Chelmsford | June 30 | 0 | | 1-43 |
| Somerset | Southend | July 21 | | | 0-38 |
| Lancashire | Old Trafford | Aug 25 | | | 0-20 |
| **OTHER ONE-DAY** | | | | | |
| Durham | Scarborough | Aug 31 | | | 4-41 |
| Yorkshire | Scarborough | Sept 2 | | | 0-47 |
| Victoria | Chelmsford | Sept 22 | 4* | 1Ct | 0-74 |

**BATTING AVERAGES - Including fielding**

| | Matches | Inns | NO | Runs | HS | Avge | 100s | 50s | Ct | St |
|---|---|---|---|---|---|---|---|---|---|---|
| Britannic Assurance | 14 | 8 | 2 | 30 | 13 | 5.00 | - | - | 4 | - |
| Other First-Class | 1 | 1 | 0 | 0 | 0 | 0.00 | - | - | 1 | - |
| ALL FIRST-CLASS | 15 | 9 | 2 | 30 | 13 | 4.28 | - | - | 5 | - |
| Refuge Assurance | 8 | 3 | 1 | 14 | 8 | 7.00 | - | - | - | - |
| Other One-Day | 3 | 1 | 1 | 4 | 4* | - | - | - | 1 | - |
| ALL ONE-DAY | 11 | 4 | 2 | 18 | 8 | 9.00 | - | - | 1 | - |

# PLAYER RECORDS

# A

## BOWLING AVERAGES

|  | Overs | Mdns | Runs | Wkts | Avge | Best | 5wI | 10wM |
|---|---|---|---|---|---|---|---|---|
| Britannic Assurance | 366.3 | 72 | 1211 | 40 | 30.27 | 4-38 | - | - |
| Other First-Class | 33 | 2 | 141 | 3 | 47.00 | 2-51 | - | - |
| ALL FIRST-CLASS | 399.3 | 74 | 1352 | 43 | 31.44 | 4-38 | - | - |
| Refuge Assurance | 49 | 3 | 253 | 8 | 31.62 | 3-33 | - | |
| Other One-Day | 28 | 0 | 162 | 4 | 40.50 | 4-41 | - | |
| ALL ONE-DAY | 77 | 3 | 415 | 12 | 34.58 | 4-41 | - | |

## H.A.G.ANTHONY - *West Indies*

| Opposition | Venue | Date | Batting | Fielding | Bowling |
|---|---|---|---|---|---|
| **OTHER FIRST-CLASS** | | | | | |
| Worcestershire | Worcester | May 15 | 33* | | 1-63 |
| Middlesex | Lord's | May 18 | 11 | 2Ct | 2-59 & 2-35 |
| Somerset | Taunton | May 29 | | | 1-72 & 1-34 |
| Leicestershire | Leicester | June 1 | 9 | 2Ct | 2-69 & 3-28 |
| Derbyshire | Derby | June 12 | | | 2-45 & 1-42 |
| Northants | Northampton | June 15 | 6 | | 1-11 |
| Hampshire | Southampton | June 29 | | 1Ct | 0-30 & 0-57 |
| Glamorgan | Swansea | July 16 | 4* | | 1-59 & 0-30 |
| Kent | Canterbury | July 20 | 7 & 6* | | 2-47 & 3-65 |
| Gloucs | Bristol | July 31 | | | 1-67 & 0-27 |
| Essex | Chelmsford | Aug 3 | 0 | 2Ct | 1-23 & 2-15 |
| **OTHER ONE-DAY** | | | | | |
| D of Norfolk | Arundel | May 12 | 4 | | 2-56 |
| Gloucs | Bristol | May 14 | | | 0-46 |
| League CC XI | Trowbridge | June 28 | | | 0-17 |
| Ireland | Downpatrick | July 13 | | | 1-28 |
| Wales | Brecon | July 15 | | | 0-19 |

### BATTING AVERAGES - Including fielding

|  | Matches | Inns | NO | Runs | HS | Avge | 100s | 50s | Ct | St |
|---|---|---|---|---|---|---|---|---|---|---|
| Other First-Class | 11 | 8 | 3 | 76 | 33* | 15.20 | - | - | 7 | - |
| ALL FIRST-CLASS | 11 | 8 | 3 | 76 | 33* | 15.20 | - | - | 7 | - |
| Other One-Day | 5 | 1 | 0 | 4 | 4 | 4.00 | - | - | - | - |
| ALL ONE-DAY | 5 | 1 | 0 | 4 | 4 | 4.00 | - | - | - | - |

### BOWLING AVERAGES

|  | Overs | Mdns | Runs | Wkts | Avge | Best | 5wI | 10wM |
|---|---|---|---|---|---|---|---|---|
| Other First-Class | 223.3 | 30 | 878 | 26 | 33.76 | 3-28 | - | - |
| ALL FIRST-CLASS | 223.3 | 30 | 878 | 26 | 33.76 | 3-28 | - | - |
| Other One-Day | 40 | 6 | 166 | 3 | 55.33 | 2-56 | - | |
| ALL ONE-DAY | 40 | 6 | 166 | 3 | 55.33 | 2-56 | - | |

## S.D.ANURASIRI - *Sri Lanka*

| Opposition | Venue | Date | Batting | Fielding | Bowling |
|---|---|---|---|---|---|
| **CORNHILL TEST MATCHES** | | | | | |
| England | Lord's | Aug 22 | 1 & 16 | | 2-45 & 3-135 |
| **OTHER FIRST-CLASS** | | | | | |
| Yorkshire | Headingley | July 27 | | 1Ct | 3-122 & 0-64 |
| Derbyshire | Derby | Aug 2 | | | 1-62 |
| Sussex | Hove | Aug 17 | 0* | | 0-45 & 0-87 |
| **OTHER ONE-DAY** | | | | | |
| Durham | Chester-le-S | July 26 | 1* | 1Ct | 2-35 |
| England A | Old Trafford | Aug 15 | | | 4-35 |

### BATTING AVERAGES - Including fielding

|  | Matches | Inns | NO | Runs | HS | Avge | 100s | 50s | Ct | St |
|---|---|---|---|---|---|---|---|---|---|---|
| Cornhill Test Matches | 1 | 2 | 0 | 17 | 16 | 8.50 | - | - | - | - |
| Other First-Class | 3 | 1 | 1 | 0 | 0* | - | - | - | 1 | - |
| ALL FIRST-CLASS | 4 | 3 | 1 | 17 | 16 | 8.50 | - | - | 1 | - |
| Other One-Day | 2 | 1 | 1 | 1 | 1* | - | - | - | 1 | - |
| ALL ONE-DAY | 2 | 1 | 1 | 1 | 1* | - | - | - | 1 | - |

### BOWLING AVERAGES

|  | Overs | Mdns | Runs | Wkts | Avge | Best | 5wI | 10wM |
|---|---|---|---|---|---|---|---|---|
| Cornhill Test Matches | 53.1 | 12 | 180 | 5 | 36.00 | 3-135 | - | - |
| Other First-Class | 155 | 41 | 380 | 4 | 95.00 | 3-122 | - | - |
| ALL FIRST-CLASS | 208.1 | 53 | 560 | 9 | 62.22 | 3-122 | - | |
| Other One-Day | 22 | 0 | 70 | 6 | 11.66 | 4-35 | - | |
| ALL ONE-DAY | 22 | 0 | 70 | 6 | 11.66 | 4-35 | - | |

## AQIB JAVED - *Hampshire*

| Opposition | Venue | Date | Batting | Fielding | Bowling |
|---|---|---|---|---|---|
| **BRITANNIC ASSURANCE** | | | | | |
| Kent | Southampton | April 27 | | | 2-103 |
| Gloucs | Bristol | May 9 | 4* & 0 | | 3-95 & 2-16 |
| Sussex | Hove | May 16 | | | 0-79 & 0-17 |
| Surrey | Bournemouth | May 25 | 1* | | 3-72 & 1-73 |
| Notts | Trent Bridge | May 31 | | | 6-91 & 1-32 |
| Lancashire | Basingstoke | June 4 | 0 | | 2-67 |
| Gloucs | Southampton | June 7 | | | 0-47 |
| Somerset | Bath | June 18 | 15* | | 2-39 & 2-50 |
| Northants | Northampton | June 21 | | | 5-49 & 0-27 |
| Essex | Chelmsford | July 2 | 0* | | 1-54 & 3-64 |
| Yorkshire | Southampton | July 5 | | | 2-55 |
| Worcestershire | Portsmouth | July 16 | 1* | | 2-37 & 1-69 |
| Warwickshire | Portsmouth | July 19 | 0 & 2* | | 3-18 & 0-23 |
| Leicestershire | Bournemouth | Aug 16 | | | 1-72 & 0-22 |
| Sussex | Bournemouth | Aug 20 | 0* | | 5-47 & 1-11 |
| Somerset | Southampton | Aug 28 | | | 1-102 & 0-54 |
| Surrey | The Oval | Sept 3 | 0* & 2 | | 1-51 & 3-50 |
| **OTHER FIRST-CLASS** | | | | | |
| Oxford U | The Parks | April 13 | | | 0-27 & 0-43 |
| **REFUGE ASSURANCE** | | | | | |
| Yorkshire | Southampton | April 21 | | | 2-21 |
| Derbyshire | Derby | May 5 | | | 0-26 |
| Kent | Southampton | May 12 | | | 1-33 |
| Somerset | Bournemouth | May 19 | | | 1-20 |
| Gloucs | Swindon | May 26 | | | 0-51 |
| Northants | Northampton | June 2 | 1* | | 0-50 |
| Sussex | Basingstoke | June 9 | 4* | | 2-16 |
| Essex | Chelmsford | June 16 | | 1Ct | 0-41 |
| Worcestershire | Southampton | July 7 | | | 3-50 |
| Notts | Trent Bridge | July 14 | | | 0-43 |
| Leicestershire | Bournemouth | Aug 18 | | | 0-36 |
| Surrey | The Oval | Aug 25 | | | 1-36 |
| **NATWEST TROPHY** | | | | | |
| Berkshire | Reading | June 26 | | 1Ct | 1-21 |
| Lancashire | Southampton | July 11 | | 1Ct | 1-53 |
| Notts | Southampton | July 31 | | | 4-51 |
| Warwickshire | Edgbaston | Aug 14 | | | 2-34 |
| Surrey | Lord's | Sept 7 | | | 0-54 |
| **BENSON & HEDGES CUP** | | | | | |
| Notts | Southampton | April 23 | | | 1-35 |
| Min Counties | Trowbridge | April 25 | | | 3-43 |
| Glamorgan | Southampton | May 2 | | | 0-30 |
| Yorkshire | Headingley | May 4 | 0* | | 3-51 |
| Essex | Chelmsford | May 29 | 3 | | 2-49 |

### BATTING AVERAGES - Including fielding

|  | Matches | Inns | NO | Runs | HS | Avge | 100s | 50s | Ct | St |
|---|---|---|---|---|---|---|---|---|---|---|
| Britannic Assurance | 17 | 12 | 8 | 25 | 15* | 6.25 | - | - | - | - |
| Other First-Class | 1 | 0 | 0 | 0 | 0 | - | - | - | - | - |
| ALL FIRST-CLASS | 18 | 12 | 8 | 25 | 15* | 6.25 | - | - | - | - |
| Refuge Assurance | 12 | 2 | 2 | 5 | 4* | - | - | - | 1 | - |
| NatWest Trophy | 5 | 0 | 0 | 0 | 0 | - | - | - | 2 | - |
| Benson & Hedges Cup | 5 | 2 | 1 | 3 | 3 | 3.00 | - | - | - | - |
| ALL ONE-DAY | 22 | 4 | 3 | 8 | 4* | 8.00 | - | - | 3 | - |

## A — PLAYER RECORDS

### BOWLING AVERAGES

| | Overs | Mdns | Runs | Wkts | Avge | Best | 5wI | 10wM |
|---|---|---|---|---|---|---|---|---|
| Britannic Assurance | 485.1 | 81 | 1586 | 53 | 29.92 | 6-91 | 3 | - |
| Other First-Class | 25 | 3 | 70 | 0 | - | - | - | - |
| ALL FIRST-CLASS | 510.1 | 84 | 1656 | 53 | 31.24 | 6-91 | 3 | - |
| Refuge Assurance | 92.1 | 4 | 423 | 10 | 42.30 | 3-50 | - | |
| NatWest Trophy | 52.5 | 4 | 213 | 8 | 26.62 | 4-51 | - | |
| Benson & Hedges Cup | 53 | 6 | 208 | 9 | 23.11 | 3-43 | - | |
| ALL ONE-DAY | 198 | 14 | 844 | 27 | 31.25 | 4-51 | - | |

### N.J.ARCHER - *Staffordshire*

| Opposition | Venue | Date | Batting | Fielding | Bowling |
|---|---|---|---|---|---|
| **NATWEST TROPHY** | | | | | |
| Northants | Stone | June 26 | 14 | | |
| **OTHER ONE-DAY** | | | | | |
| For England Am. XI | | | | | |
| Sri Lanka | Wolv'hampton | July 24 | 4 | 1Ct | 0-5 |

### BATTING AVERAGES - Including fielding

| | Matches | Inns | NO | Runs | HS | Avge | 100s | 50s | Ct | St |
|---|---|---|---|---|---|---|---|---|---|---|
| NatWest Trophy | 1 | 1 | 0 | 14 | 14 | 14.00 | - | - | - | - |
| Other One-Day | 1 | 1 | 0 | 4 | 4 | 4.00 | - | - | 1 | - |
| ALL ONE-DAY | 2 | 2 | 0 | 18 | 14 | 9.00 | - | - | 1 | - |

### BOWLING AVERAGES

| | Overs | Mdns | Runs | Wkts | Avge | Best | 5wI | 10wM |
|---|---|---|---|---|---|---|---|---|
| NatWest Trophy | | | | | | | | |
| Other One-Day | 0.5 | 0 | 5 | 0 | - | - | - | |
| ALL ONE-DAY | 0.5 | 0 | 5 | 0 | - | - | - | |

### K.A.ARNOLD - *Minor Counties*

| Opposition | Venue | Date | Batting | Fielding | Bowling |
|---|---|---|---|---|---|
| **BENSON & HEDGES CUP** | | | | | |
| Notts | Trent Bridge | May 7 | | | 2-52 |
| **OTHER ONE-DAY** | | | | | |
| For England Am. XI | | | | | |
| Sri Lanka | Wolv'hampton | July 24 | 6* | | 0-38 |

### BATTING AVERAGES - Including fielding

| | Matches | Inns | NO | Runs | HS | Avge | 100s | 50s | Ct | St |
|---|---|---|---|---|---|---|---|---|---|---|
| Benson & Hedges Cup | 1 | 0 | 0 | 0 | 0 | - | - | - | - | - |
| Other One-Day | 1 | 1 | 1 | 6 | 6* | - | - | - | - | - |
| ALL ONE-DAY | 2 | 1 | 1 | 6 | 6* | - | - | - | - | - |

### BOWLING AVERAGES

| | Overs | Mdns | Runs | Wkts | Avge | Best | 5wI | 10wM |
|---|---|---|---|---|---|---|---|---|
| Benson & Hedges Cup | 11 | 0 | 52 | 2 | 26.00 | 2-52 | - | - |
| Other One-Day | 9 | 1 | 38 | 0 | - | - | - | |
| ALL ONE-DAY | 20 | 1 | 90 | 2 | 45.00 | 2-52 | - | - |

### J.P.ARSCOTT - *Cambridge University*

| Opposition | Venue | Date | Batting | | Fielding | Bowling |
|---|---|---|---|---|---|---|
| **OTHER FIRST-CLASS** | | | | | | |
| Lancashire | Fenner's | April 13 | 35* | | 1Ct | 1-44 & 0-5 |
| Northants | Fenner's | April 16 | 12 | | | 1-26 |
| Essex | Fenner's | April 19 | 0 & | 0 | | 1-17 & 1-21 |
| Derbyshire | Fenner's | May 9 | 74 | | 2Ct | 1-52 & 1-42 |
| Middlesex | Fenner's | May 15 | 2 & | 1 | | 1-32 |
| Surrey | Fenner's | May 18 | 1 & | 3 | 2Ct | |

| Glamorgan | Fenner's | June 18 | | 5 | | |
|---|---|---|---|---|---|---|
| Sussex | Hove | June 29 | | | | |
| Oxford U | Lord's | July 2 | 14 & | 10 | 2Ct | 0-13 |

### BATTING AVERAGES - Including fielding

| | Matches | Inns | NO | Runs | HS | Avge | 100s | 50s | Ct | St |
|---|---|---|---|---|---|---|---|---|---|---|
| Other First-Class | 9 | 12 | 1 | 157 | 74 | 14.27 | - | 1 | 7 | - |
| ALL FIRST-CLASS | 9 | 12 | 1 | 157 | 74 | 14.27 | - | 1 | 7 | - |

### BOWLING AVERAGES

| | Overs | Mdns | Runs | Wkts | Avge | Best | 5wI | 10wM |
|---|---|---|---|---|---|---|---|---|
| Other First-Class | 48 | 4 | 252 | 7 | 36.00 | 1-17 | - | - |
| ALL FIRST-CLASS | 48 | 4 | 252 | 7 | 36.00 | 1-17 | - | - |

### R.ASHTON - *Bedfordshire*

| Opposition | Venue | Date | Batting | Fielding | Bowling |
|---|---|---|---|---|---|
| **NATWEST TROPHY** | | | | | |
| Worcestershire | Bedford | June 26 | 1 | | 0-25 |

### BATTING AVERAGES - Including fielding

| | Matches | Inns | NO | Runs | HS | Avge | 100s | 50s | Ct | St |
|---|---|---|---|---|---|---|---|---|---|---|
| NatWest Trophy | 1 | 1 | 0 | 1 | 1 | 1.00 | - | - | - | - |
| ALL ONE-DAY | 1 | 1 | 0 | 1 | 1 | 1.00 | - | - | - | - |

### BOWLING AVERAGES

| | Overs | Mdns | Runs | Wkts | Avge | Best | 5wI | 10wM |
|---|---|---|---|---|---|---|---|---|
| NatWest Trophy | 2 | 0 | 25 | 0 | - | - | - | |
| ALL ONE-DAY | 2 | 0 | 25 | 0 | - | - | - | |

### ASIF DIN - *Warwickshire*

| Opposition | Venue | Date | Batting | | Fielding | Bowling |
|---|---|---|---|---|---|---|
| **BRITANNIC ASSURANCE** | | | | | | |
| Lancashire | Edgbaston | April 27 | 15 | | | |
| Glamorgan | Swansea | May 16 | 15 & | 29 | | |
| Essex | Chelmsford | May 22 | 10 & | 20 | 1Ct | |
| Gloucs | Edgbaston | May 25 | 0 & | 4 | 1Ct | |
| Middlesex | Edgbaston | July 2 | 11 & | 3 | 2Ct | |
| Hampshire | Portsmouth | July 19 | 19 & | 13 | 1Ct | 0-8 |
| Lancashire | Old Trafford | July 23 | 100 | | | 1-42 |
| Leicestershire | Leicester | July 26 | 140 | | | 0-10 |
| Worcestershire | Worcester | Aug 2 | 0 & | 3 | 1Ct | 1-37 |
| Surrey | Edgbaston | Aug 6 | 5 & | 2 | | |
| Northants | Northampton | Aug 9 | 92 & | 17* | 1Ct | 0-20 |
| Glamorgan | Edgbaston | Aug 20 | 45 & | 27 | | 0-75 & 0-8 |
| Worcestershire | Edgbaston | Aug 28 | 26 & | 23 | | |
| Northants | Edgbaston | Sept 10 | 6 & | 15 | 1Ct | |
| Somerset | Taunton | Sept 17 | 11 & | 34 | | 0-6 |
| **REFUGE ASSURANCE** | | | | | | |
| Sussex | Edgbaston | April 21 | 3 | | | |
| Notts | Trent Bridge | April 28 | 6 | | | |
| Yorkshire | Headingley | May 12 | 0 | | 1Ct | |
| Glamorgan | Swansea | May 19 | 46 | | 1Ct | |
| Worcestershire | Edgbaston | May 26 | 11 | | 1Ct | |
| Essex | Chelmsford | July 7 | 45 | | | |
| Middlesex | Edgbaston | July 14 | 101* | | | |
| Hampshire | Portsmouth | July 21 | 30 | | | |
| Leicestershire | Leicester | Aug 11 | 0 | | | |
| Gloucs | Edgbaston | Aug 18 | 81* | | | |
| Northants | Northampton | Aug 25 | 7 | | | |
| **NATWEST TROPHY** | | | | | | |
| Hertfordshire | Edgbaston | July 11 | | | | |
| Somerset | Edgbaston | July 31 | 17 | | | |
| Hampshire | Edgbaston | Aug 14 | 44 | | | 0-10 |
| **BENSON & HEDGES CUP** | | | | | | |
| Essex | Edgbaston | April 25 | 34 | | | |

# PLEAYER RECORDS

**A**

| Somerset | Edgbaston | May 2 | 137 |
| Middlesex | Lord's | May 4 | 97 |
| Yorkshire | Headingley | May 29 | 23 |

### BATTING AVERAGES - Including fielding

| | Matches | Inns | NO | Runs | HS | Avge | 100s | 50s | Ct | St |
|---|---|---|---|---|---|---|---|---|---|---|
| Britannic Assurance | 15 | 27 | 1 | 685 | 140 | 26.34 | 2 | 1 | 9 | - |
| ALL FIRST-CLASS | 15 | 27 | 1 | 685 | 140 | 26.34 | 2 | 1 | 9 | - |
| Refuge Assurance | 11 | 11 | 2 | 330 | 101 * | 36.66 | 1 | 1 | 3 | - |
| NatWest Trophy | 3 | 2 | 0 | 61 | 44 | 30.50 | - | - | - | - |
| Benson & Hedges Cup | 4 | 4 | 0 | 291 | 137 | 72.75 | 1 | 1 | - | - |
| ALL ONE-DAY | 18 | 17 | 2 | 682 | 137 | 45.46 | 2 | 2 | 3 | - |

### BOWLING AVERAGES

| | Overs | Mdns | Runs | Wkts | Avge | Best | 5wI | 10wM |
|---|---|---|---|---|---|---|---|---|
| Britannic Assurance | 53 | 9 | 206 | 2 | 103.00 | 1-37 | - | - |
| ALL FIRST-CLASS | 53 | 9 | 206 | 2 | 103.00 | 1-37 | - | - |
| Refuge Assurance | | | | | | | | |
| NatWest Trophy | 3 | 0 | 10 | 0 | - | - | - | |
| Benson & Hedges Cup | | | | | | | | |
| ALL ONE-DAY | 3 | 0 | 10 | 0 | - | - | - | |

## M.S.ATAPATTU - *Sri Lanka*

| Opposition | Venue | Date | Batting | Fielding | Bowling |
|---|---|---|---|---|---|

### OTHER FIRST-CLASS

| Yorkshire | Headingley | July 27 | 41 | | |
| Worcestershire | Worcester | July 30 | 2 & 2 | | |
| Derbyshire | Derby | Aug 2 | | 1Ct | |
| Somerset | Taunton | Aug 10 | 33 * | 1Ct | |
| Sussex | Hove | Aug 17 | 52 * & 2 | | |

### OTHER ONE-DAY

| England Am. | Wolv'hampton | July 24 | 12 | | |
| Durham | Chester-le-S | July 26 | 33 * | | |
| England A | Old Trafford | Aug 14 | 7 | | |
| England A | Old Trafford | Aug 15 | 41 * | | |

### BATTING AVERAGES - Including fielding

| | Matches | Inns | NO | Runs | HS | Avge | 100s | 50s | Ct | St |
|---|---|---|---|---|---|---|---|---|---|---|
| Other First-Class | 5 | 6 | 2 | 132 | 52 * | 33.00 | - | 1 | 2 | - |
| ALL FIRST-CLASS | 5 | 6 | 2 | 132 | 52 * | 33.00 | - | 1 | 2 | - |
| Other One-Day | 4 | 4 | 2 | 93 | 41 * | 46.50 | - | - | - | - |
| ALL ONE-DAY | 4 | 4 | 2 | 93 | 41 * | 46.50 | - | - | - | - |

### BOWLING AVERAGES
Did not bowl

## M.A.ATHERTON - *Lancashire & England*

| Opposition | Venue | Date | Batting | Fielding | Bowling |
|---|---|---|---|---|---|

### CORNHILL TEST MATCHES

| West Indies | Headingley | June 6 | 2 & 6 | 1Ct | |
| West Indies | Lord's | June 20 | 5 | 1Ct | |
| West Indies | Trent Bridge | July 4 | 32 & 4 | | |
| West Indies | Edgbaston | July 25 | 16 & 1 | 1Ct | |
| West Indies | The Oval | Aug 8 | 0 & 13 | | |

### BRITANNIC ASSURANCE

| Warwickshire | Edgbaston | April 27 | 10 | | |
| Worcestershire | Worcester | May 9 | 110 & 0 | 1Ct | |
| Derbyshire | Old Trafford | May 16 | 16 & 62 * | 1Ct | |
| Sussex | Old Trafford | May 31 | 39 | 1Ct | |
| Glamorgan | Liverpool | June 28 | 43 | 1Ct | |
| Middlesex | Uxbridge | July 19 | 91 & 35 | 1Ct | |
| Yorkshire | Old Trafford | Aug 2 | 114 * & 37 * | 2Ct | |
| Derbyshire | Derby | Aug 16 | 14 & 32 | | |

### OTHER FIRST-CLASS
Cambridge U Fenner's April 13 138

### TEXACO TROPHY

| West Indies | Edgbaston | May 23 | 69 * | |
| West Indies | Old Trafford | May 25 | 74 | |
| West Indies | Lord's | May 27 | 25 | |

### REFUGE ASSURANCE

| Notts | Old Trafford | April 21 | 45 | 1Ct |
| Northants | Old Trafford | April 28 | 25 | |
| Worcestershire | Worcester | May 12 | 6 | |
| Derbyshire | Derby | May 19 | 48 | 1Ct |
| Sussex | Old Trafford | June 2 | 1 * | |
| Warwickshire | Edgbaston | June 16 | 0 | 2Ct |
| Middlesex | Lord's | July 21 | 1 | 1Ct |
| Yorkshire | Old Trafford | Aug 4 | 11 | |
| Surrey | Old Trafford | Aug 18 | 34 | |

### NATWEST TROPHY
Dorset Bournemouth June 26 38

### BENSON & HEDGES CUP

| Scotland | Forfar | April 23 | 10 | 1Ct |
| Kent | Old Trafford | April 25 | 22 | |
| Leicestershire | Leicester | May 4 | 74 | |
| Sussex | Old Trafford | May 7 | 91 | 2Ct |
| Northants | Old Trafford | May 29 | 56 | |
| Yorkshire | Old Trafford | June 16 | 24 | |
| Worcestershire | Lord's | July 13 | 5 | |

### OTHER ONE-DAY
For England XI

| Rest of World | Jesmond | July 31 | 31 | |
| Rest of World | Jesmond | Aug 1 | 41 | |

### BATTING AVERAGES - Including fielding

| | Matches | Inns | NO | Runs | HS | Avge | 100s | 50s | Ct | St |
|---|---|---|---|---|---|---|---|---|---|---|
| Cornhill Test Matches | 5 | 9 | 0 | 79 | 32 | 8.77 | - | - | 3 | - |
| Britannic Assurance | 8 | 13 | 3 | 603 | 114 * | 60.30 | 2 | 2 | 7 | - |
| Other First-Class | 1 | 1 | 0 | 138 | 138 | 138.00 | 1 | - | - | - |
| ALL FIRST-CLASS | 14 | 23 | 3 | 820 | 138 | 41.00 | 3 | 2 | 10 | - |
| Texaco Trophy | 3 | 3 | 1 | 168 | 74 | 84.00 | - | 2 | - | - |
| Refuge Assurance | 9 | 9 | 1 | 171 | 48 | 21.37 | - | - | 5 | - |
| NatWest Trophy | 1 | 1 | 0 | 38 | 38 | 38.00 | - | - | - | - |
| Benson & Hedges Cup | 7 | 7 | 0 | 282 | 91 | 40.28 | - | 3 | 3 | - |
| Other One-Day | 2 | 2 | 0 | 72 | 41 | 36.00 | - | - | - | - |
| ALL ONE-DAY | 22 | 22 | 2 | 731 | 91 | 36.55 | - | 5 | 8 | - |

### BOWLING AVERAGES
Did not bowl

## C.W.J.ATHEY - *Gloucestershire*

| Opposition | Venue | Date | Batting | Fielding | Bowling |
|---|---|---|---|---|---|

### BRITANNIC ASSURANCE

| Worcestershire | Worcester | April 27 | 56 | | |
| Hampshire | Bristol | May 9 | 9 & 65 * | 1Ct | 0-3 |
| Yorkshire | Sheffield | May 22 | 12 & 0 | | 1-18 |
| Warwickshire | Edgbaston | May 25 | 6 & 120 | | 1-29 |
| Essex | Bristol | May 31 | 10 & 4 | | 0-15 |
| Middlesex | Bristol | June 4 | 19 | 1Ct | 0-8 |
| Hampshire | Southampton | June 7 | 10 * | | |
| Notts | Gloucester | June 14 | 63 | | 0-7 |
| Derbyshire | Gloucester | June 18 | 11 & 101 | 1Ct | 0-10 |
| Somerset | Bath | June 21 | 10 | 1Ct | 0-12 |
| Northants | Luton | June 28 | 33 & 17 | | 0-29 |
| Leicestershire | Hinckley | July 2 | 52 | | |
| Surrey | Guildford | July 16 | 19 & 62 * | 1Ct | 0-8 |
| Glamorgan | Cheltenham | July 19 | 21 & 37 | 1Ct | 0-10 |
| Sussex | Cheltenham | July 23 | 10 | | |
| Worcestershire | Cheltenham | July 26 | 2 & 15 | 2Ct | |
| Lancashire | Bristol | Aug 9 | 127 | 1Ct | |
| Kent | Canterbury | Aug 20 | 22 & 13 | 3Ct | |
| Glamorgan | Abergavenny | Aug 28 | 2 & 0 | | 0-3 & 0-27 |
| Northants | Bristol | Sept 3 | 54 & 86 | 3Ct | |
| Somerset | Bristol | Sept 10 | 90 & 77 * | | |
| Sussex | Hove | Sept 17 | 103 * & 12 | | |

## A — PLAYER RECORDS

### OTHER FIRST-CLASS

| Opposition | Venue | Date | Batting | Fielding | Bowling |
|---|---|---|---|---|---|
| Oxford U | The Parks | June 15 | 127 | | 0-10 |
| West Indies | Bristol | July 31 | 35 & 4* | 1Ct | |
| Sri Lanka | Bristol | Aug 6 | 6 | 2Ct | |

### REFUGE ASSURANCE

| Opposition | Venue | Date | Batting | Fielding | Bowling |
|---|---|---|---|---|---|
| Middlesex | Bristol | April 21 | 1 | | |
| Worcestershire | Bristol | May 5 | 26 | | |
| Surrey | The Oval | May 12 | 79 | 1Ct | 0-9 |
| Sussex | Hove | May 19 | 3 | 1Ct | 2-18 |
| Hampshire | Swindon | May 26 | 85 | 1Ct | 0-28 |
| Northants | Moreton | June 9 | 0* | | |
| Notts | Gloucester | June 16 | 44 | | |
| Kent | Canterbury | June 30 | 18 | | 0-24 |
| Yorkshire | Scarborough | July 14 | 3 | | |
| Derbyshire | Cheltenham | July 21 | 9 | | |
| Essex | Cheltenham | July 28 | 49 | 2Ct | |
| Glamorgan | Swansea | Aug 4 | 3 | 1Ct | |
| Lancashire | Bristol | Aug 11 | 5 | | |
| Warwickshire | Edgbaston | Aug 18 | 2 | | |
| Leicestershire | Leicester | Aug 25 | 25 | 2Ct | |

### NATWEST TROPHY

| Opposition | Venue | Date | Batting | Fielding | Bowling |
|---|---|---|---|---|---|
| Norfolk | Bristol | June 26 | 47* | | |
| Notts | Bristol | July 11 | 76 | | |

### BENSON & HEDGES CUP

| Opposition | Venue | Date | Batting | Fielding | Bowling |
|---|---|---|---|---|---|
| Combined U | Bristol | April 23 | 0 | | |
| Worcestershire | Worcester | April 25 | 5 | | |
| Northants | Bristol | May 2 | 22* | 2Ct | |
| Derbyshire | Derby | May 7 | 81 | | |

### OTHER ONE-DAY

| Opposition | Venue | Date | Batting | Fielding | Bowling |
|---|---|---|---|---|---|
| West Indies | Bristol | May 14 | 9 | | |
| For Yorkshiremen | | | | | |
| Yorkshire | Scarborough | Sept 7 | 76 | 1Ct | 3-23 |

### BATTING AVERAGES - Including fielding

| | Matches | Inns | NO | Runs | HS | Avge | 100s | 50s | Ct | St |
|---|---|---|---|---|---|---|---|---|---|---|
| Britannic Assurance | 22 | 36 | 5 | 1350 | 127 | 43.54 | 4 | 9 | 15 | - |
| Other First-Class | 3 | 4 | 1 | 172 | 127 | 57.33 | 1 | - | 3 | - |
| ALL FIRST-CLASS | 25 | 40 | 6 | 1522 | 127 | 44.76 | 5 | 9 | 18 | - |
| Refuge Assurance | 15 | 15 | 1 | 352 | 85 | 25.14 | - | 2 | 8 | - |
| NatWest Trophy | 2 | 2 | 1 | 123 | 76 | 123.00 | - | 1 | - | - |
| Benson & Hedges Cup | 4 | 4 | 1 | 108 | 81 | 36.00 | - | 1 | 2 | - |
| Other One-Day | 2 | 2 | 0 | 85 | 76 | 42.50 | - | 1 | 1 | - |
| ALL ONE-DAY | 23 | 23 | 3 | 668 | 85 | 33.40 | - | 5 | 11 | - |

### BOWLING AVERAGES

| | Overs | Mdns | Runs | Wkts | Avge | Best | 5wI | 10wM |
|---|---|---|---|---|---|---|---|---|
| Britannic Assurance | 60 | 8 | 179 | 2 | 89.50 | 1-18 | - | - |
| Other First-Class | 6 | 2 | 10 | 0 | - | - | - | - |
| ALL FIRST-CLASS | 66 | 10 | 189 | 2 | 94.50 | 1-18 | - | - |
| Refuge Assurance | 14 | 0 | 79 | 2 | 39.50 | 2-18 | - | |
| NatWest Trophy | | | | | | | | |
| Benson & Hedges Cup | | | | | | | | |
| Other One-Day | 7 | 0 | 23 | 3 | 7.66 | 3-23 | - | |
| ALL ONE-DAY | 21 | 0 | 102 | 5 | 20.40 | 3-23 | - | |

## I.D.AUSTIN - Lancashire

| Opposition | Venue | Date | Batting | Fielding | Bowling |
|---|---|---|---|---|---|
| **BRITANNIC ASSURANCE** | | | | | |
| Derbyshire | Old Trafford | May 16 | 12 | | 0-36 |
| Surrey | The Oval | May 22 | 6 & 0 | | 1-40 & 0-20 |
| Hampshire | Basingstoke | June 4 | 2 | | 0-23 & 1-26 |
| Leicestershire | Leicester | June 18 | 43 | | 1-28 |
| Kent | Old Trafford | June 21 | 7 | 1Ct | 3-58 |
| Glamorgan | Liverpool | June 28 | | | 1-73 & 0-24 |
| Northants | Lytham | Aug 6 | 0 | | 1-63 |
| Worcestershire | Blackpool | Aug 20 | 43 & 0 | 2Ct | 2-39 & 0-38 |
| Essex | Old Trafford | Aug 23 | 25* | | 0-24 & 0-80 |
| Notts | Old Trafford | Aug 28 | 61*& 2 | 1Ct | 0-15 & 1-21 |
| Yorkshire | Scarborough | Sept 3 | 3*& 101* | | 0-97 & 0-20 |
| Surrey | Old Trafford | Sept 17 | 3 & 7 | | 0-15 & 1-47 |

## REFUGE ASSURANCE

| Opposition | Venue | Date | Batting | Fielding | Bowling |
|---|---|---|---|---|---|
| Notts | Old Trafford | April 21 | 4* | | 0-30 |
| Northants | Old Trafford | April 28 | | | 1-32 |
| Worcestershire | Worcester | May 12 | | | 1-40 |
| Derbyshire | Derby | May 19 | | | 5-56 |
| Sussex | Old Trafford | June 2 | | 1Ct | 1-20 |
| Glamorgan | Old Trafford | June 9 | | | 2-33 |
| Warwickshire | Edgbaston | June 16 | | | 2-36 |
| Kent | Old Trafford | June 23 | | | 1-38 |
| Somerset | Taunton | July 5 | | 1Ct | 3-40 |
| Leicestershire | Leicester | July 7 | | | 0-47 |
| Middlesex | Lord's | July 21 | 48 | | 3-42 |
| Hampshire | Southampton | July 28 | 1 | | 1-38 |
| Yorkshire | Old Trafford | Aug 4 | 3 | | 4-40 |
| Gloucs | Bristol | Aug 11 | | | 4-10 |
| Surrey | Old Trafford | Aug 18 | 10* | | 0-37 |
| Essex | Old Trafford | Aug 25 | | | 0-28 |
| Northants | Old Trafford | Sept 1 | 17 | 1Ct | 1-46 |
| Worcestershire | Old Trafford | Sept 15 | 0 | | 0-47 |

### NATWEST TROPHY

| Opposition | Venue | Date | Batting | Fielding | Bowling |
|---|---|---|---|---|---|
| Dorset | Bournemouth | June 26 | | | 1-46 |
| Hampshire | Southampton | July 11 | 2 | | 0-59 |

### BENSON & HEDGES CUP

| Opposition | Venue | Date | Batting | Fielding | Bowling |
|---|---|---|---|---|---|
| Scotland | Forfar | April 23 | | | 2-50 |
| Kent | Old Trafford | April 25 | | | 0-38 |
| Leicestershire | Leicester | May 4 | | 1Ct | 1-41 |
| Sussex | Old Trafford | May 7 | | | 1-62 |
| Northants | Old Trafford | May 29 | | | 1-40 |
| Yorkshire | Old Trafford | June 16 | 22 | | 0-36 |
| Worcestershire | Lord's | July 13 | 7 | | 1-52 |

### BATTING AVERAGES - Including fielding

| | Matches | Inns | NO | Runs | HS | Avge | 100s | 50s | Ct | St |
|---|---|---|---|---|---|---|---|---|---|---|
| Britannic Assurance | 12 | 16 | 4 | 315 | 101* | 26.25 | 1 | 1 | 4 | - |
| ALL FIRST-CLASS | 12 | 16 | 4 | 315 | 101* | 26.25 | 1 | 1 | 4 | - |
| Refuge Assurance | 18 | 7 | 2 | 83 | 48 | 16.60 | - | - | 3 | - |
| NatWest Trophy | 2 | 1 | 0 | 2 | 2 | 2.00 | - | - | - | - |
| Benson & Hedges Cup | 7 | 2 | 0 | 29 | 22 | 14.50 | - | - | 1 | - |
| ALL ONE-DAY | 27 | 10 | 2 | 114 | 48 | 14.25 | - | - | 4 | - |

### BOWLING AVERAGES

| | Overs | Mdns | Runs | Wkts | Avge | Best | 5wI | 10wM |
|---|---|---|---|---|---|---|---|---|
| Britannic Assurance | 237.2 | 42 | 787 | 12 | 65.58 | 3-58 | - | - |
| ALL FIRST-CLASS | 237.2 | 42 | 787 | 12 | 65.58 | 3-58 | - | - |
| Refuge Assurance | 124.3 | 3 | 660 | 29 | 22.75 | 5-56 | 1 | |
| NatWest Trophy | 21 | 1 | 105 | 1 | 105.00 | 1-46 | - | |
| Benson & Hedges Cup | 72 | 2 | 319 | 6 | 53.16 | 2-50 | - | |
| ALL ONE-DAY | 217.3 | 6 | 1084 | 36 | 30.11 | 5-56 | 1 | |

## J.R.AYLING - Hampshire

| Opposition | Venue | Date | Batting | Fielding | Bowling |
|---|---|---|---|---|---|
| **BRITANNIC ASSURANCE** | | | | | |
| Kent | Southampton | April 27 | | | 1-64 |
| Worcestershire | Portsmouth | July 16 | 3 | | 1-28 & 1-52 |
| Warwickshire | Portsmouth | July 19 | 42*& 16 | | 3-23 & 3-47 |
| Derbyshire | Chesterfield | July 23 | 1 | | 0-38 |
| Middlesex | Lord's | Aug 2 | 58 & 10* | | 2-52 & 0-8 |
| Kent | Canterbury | Aug 6 | 19 & 17 | 1Ct | 2-64 & 0-1 |
| Sussex | Bournemouth | Aug 20 | 13 | 1Ct | 1-27 |
| Surrey | The Oval | Sept 3 | 34 & 23 | | 4-47 & 3-43 |
| Glamorgan | Southampton | Sept 17 | 5 & 28 | 1Ct | 0-44 & 0-17 |
| **OTHER FIRST-CLASS** | | | | | |
| Oxford U | The Parks | April 13 | 52* | | 3-16 & 1-24 |
| **REFUGE ASSURANCE** | | | | | |
| Yorkshire | Southampton | April 21 | 2* | | 1-33 |
| Gloucs | Swindon | May 26 | 9* | | 0-49 |
| Northants | Northampton | June 2 | 4 | | 1-52 |
| Sussex | Basingstoke | June 9 | 7 | 1Ct | 2-41 |
| Essex | Chelmsford | June 16 | | 1Ct | 1-29 |
| Worcestershire | Southampton | July 7 | 14* | | 0-44 |

# PLAYER RECORDS

**A**

| Notts | Trent Bridge | July 14 | 34 | | 1-34 |
|---|---|---|---|---|---|
| Warwickshire | Portsmouth | July 21 | 37 | | 3-25 |
| Lancashire | Southampton | July 28 | 9 | | 1-52 |
| Middlesex | Lord's | Aug 4 | 4 | | 0-37 |
| Glamorgan | Ebbw Vale | Aug 11 | 13 | | 1-53 |
| Leicestershire | Bournemouth | Aug 18 | 17 | 1Ct | 2-29 |
| Surrey | The Oval | Aug 25 | 56 | 1Ct | 1-34 |

### NATWEST TROPHY

| Lancashire | Southampton | July 11 | | 1Ct | 1-57 |
|---|---|---|---|---|---|
| Notts | Southampton | July 31 | | | 1-55 |
| Surrey | Lord's | Sept 7 | 18* | 1Ct | 2-39 |

### BENSON & HEDGES CUP

| Notts | Southampton | April 23 | 3* | | 2-56 |
|---|---|---|---|---|---|
| Min Counties | Trowbridge | April 25 | | | 0-28 |
| Glamorgan | Southampton | May 2 | 5* | | 1-51 |
| Yorkshire | Headingley | May 4 | 2 | 2Ct | 1-51 |

### BATTING AVERAGES - Including fielding

| | Matches | Inns | NO | Runs | HS | Avge | 100s | 50s | Ct | St |
|---|---|---|---|---|---|---|---|---|---|---|
| Britannic Assurance | 9 | 13 | 2 | 269 | 58 | 24.45 | - | 1 | 3 | - |
| Other First-Class | 1 | 1 | 1 | 52 | 52* | - | - | 1 | - | - |
| ALL FIRST-CLASS | 10 | 14 | 3 | 321 | 58 | 29.18 | - | 2 | 3 | - |
| Refuge Assurance | 13 | 12 | 3 | 206 | 56 | 22.88 | - | 1 | 4 | - |
| NatWest Trophy | 3 | 1 | 1 | 18 | 18* | - | - | - | 2 | - |
| Benson & Hedges Cup | 4 | 3 | 2 | 10 | 5* | 10.00 | - | - | 2 | - |
| ALL ONE-DAY | 20 | 16 | 6 | 234 | 56 | 23.40 | - | 1 | 8 | - |

### BOWLING AVERAGES

| | Overs | Mdns | Runs | Wkts | Avge | Best | 5wI | 10wM |
|---|---|---|---|---|---|---|---|---|
| Britannic Assurance | 185.5 | 36 | 555 | 21 | 26.42 | 4-47 | - | - |
| Other First-Class | 25.2 | 13 | 40 | 4 | 10.00 | 3-16 | - | - |
| ALL FIRST-CLASS | 211.1 | 49 | 595 | 25 | 23.80 | 4-47 | - | - |
| Refuge Assurance | 91 | 2 | 512 | 14 | 36.57 | 3-25 | - | |
| NatWest Trophy | 36 | 0 | 151 | 4 | 37.75 | 2-39 | - | |
| Benson & Hedges Cup | 42 | 0 | 186 | 4 | 46.50 | 2-56 | - | |
| ALL ONE-DAY | 169 | 2 | 849 | 22 | 38.59 | 3-25 | - | |

## A.N AYMES - *Hampshire*

| Opposition | Venue | Date | Batting | | | Fielding | Bowling |
|---|---|---|---|---|---|---|---|

### BRITANNIC ASSURANCE

| Kent | Southampton | April 27 | | | | 1Ct | |
|---|---|---|---|---|---|---|---|
| Gloucs | Bristol | May 9 | 17 | & | 1 | 4Ct | |
| Sussex | Hove | May 16 | | | | 2Ct | |
| Surrey | Bournemouth | May 25 | 53 | & | 23* | | |
| Notts | Trent Bridge | May 31 | | | | 3Ct | |
| Lancashire | Basingstoke | June 4 | | 33 | | | |
| Gloucs | Southampton | June 7 | 38* | | | 1Ct | |
| Somerset | Bath | June 18 | 3 | | | 3Ct | |
| Northants | Northampton | June 21 | 10* | | | | |
| Essex | Chelmsford | July 2 | 17 | & | 20* | 2Ct | |
| Yorkshire | Southampton | July 5 | 34 | | | 4Ct | |
| Worcestershire | Portsmouth | July 16 | 10 | | | 2Ct | |
| Warwickshire | Portsmouth | July 19 | 7 | & | 35 | 4Ct | |
| Derbyshire | Chesterfield | July 23 | 5 | | | 2Ct | |
| Middlesex | Lord's | Aug 2 | 31 | | | 2Ct,1St | |
| Kent | Canterbury | Aug 6 | 8 | & | 48* | 1Ct,1St | |
| Glamorgan | Swansea | Aug 9 | 13 | | | 4Ct | |
| Leicestershire | Bournemouth | Aug 16 | 32* | & | 29 | 2Ct | |
| Sussex | Bournemouth | Aug 20 | 15 | | | 1Ct | |
| Somerset | Southampton | Aug 28 | 13 | & | 33 | 3Ct | |
| Surrey | The Oval | Sept 3 | 9 | & | 4 | 2Ct | |
| Glamorgan | Southampton | Sept 17 | 46 | & | 0 | 2Ct | |

### OTHER FIRST-CLASS

| Oxford U | The Parks | April 13 | 52* | | | 4Ct | |
|---|---|---|---|---|---|---|---|
| West Indies | Southampton | June 29 | 5 | | | 2Ct | |

### REFUGE ASSURANCE

| Yorkshire | Southampton | April 21 | | | 2Ct,1St |
|---|---|---|---|---|---|
| Derbyshire | Derby | May 5 | 17* | | 0Ct,1St |
| Kent | Southampton | May 12 | 15* | | |
| Somerset | Bournemouth | May 19 | 18* | | 3Ct |

| Gloucs | Swindon | May 26 | 4* | |
|---|---|---|---|---|
| Northants | Northampton | June 2 | 33* | |
| Sussex | Basingstoke | June 9 | 5 | |
| Essex | Chelmsford | June 16 | | |
| Notts | Trent Bridge | July 14 | 8 | 1Ct |
| Warwickshire | Portsmouth | July 21 | 14* | 3Ct |
| Lancashire | Southampton | July 28 | 18* | 2Ct |
| Glamorgan | Ebbw Vale | Aug 11 | 8 | 1Ct |
| Surrey | The Oval | Aug 25 | 29 | 1Ct,1St |

### NATWEST TROPHY

| Berkshire | Reading | June 26 | | |
|---|---|---|---|---|
| Lancashire | Southampton | July 11 | | 1Ct |
| Notts | Southampton | July 31 | | 2Ct |
| Warwickshire | Edgbaston | Aug 14 | | 3Ct,1St |
| Surrey | Lord's | Sept 7 | 2 | |

### BENSON & HEDGES CUP

| Notts | Southampton | April 23 | | 0Ct,1St |
|---|---|---|---|---|
| Min Counties | Trowbridge | April 25 | | 0Ct,2St |
| Glamorgan | Southampton | May 2 | | 2Ct |
| Yorkshire | Headingley | May 4 | 10 | |
| Essex | Chelmsford | May 29 | 2 | 2Ct,1St |

### BATTING AVERAGES - Including fielding

| | Matches | Inns | NO | Runs | HS | Avge | 100s | 50s | Ct | St |
|---|---|---|---|---|---|---|---|---|---|---|
| Britannic Assurance | 22 | 28 | 6 | 587 | 53 | 26.68 | - | 1 | 45 | 2 |
| Other First-Class | 2 | 2 | 1 | 57 | 52* | 57.00 | - | 1 | 6 | - |
| ALL FIRST-CLASS | 24 | 30 | 7 | 644 | 53 | 28.00 | - | 2 | 51 | 2 |
| Refuge Assurance | 13 | 11 | 7 | 169 | 33* | 42.25 | - | - | 13 | 3 |
| NatWest Trophy | 5 | 1 | 0 | 2 | 2 | 2.00 | - | - | 6 | 1 |
| Benson & Hedges Cup | 5 | 2 | 0 | 12 | 10 | 6.00 | - | - | 4 | 4 |
| ALL ONE-DAY | 23 | 14 | 7 | 183 | 33* | 26.14 | - | - | 23 | 8 |

### BOWLING AVERAGES
Did not bowl

## W.G.AYRES - *Victoria*

| Opposition | Venue | Date | Batting | Fielding | Bowling |
|---|---|---|---|---|---|

### OTHER ONE-DAY

| Durham | Durham U. | Sept 16 | 50 | | |
|---|---|---|---|---|---|

### BATTING AVERAGES - Including fielding

| | Matches | Inns | NO | Runs | HS | Avge | 100s | 50s | Ct | St |
|---|---|---|---|---|---|---|---|---|---|---|
| Other One-Day | 1 | 1 | 0 | 50 | 50 | 50.00 | - | 1 | - | - |
| ALL ONE-DAY | 1 | 1 | 0 | 50 | 50 | 50.00 | - | 1 | - | - |

### BOWLING AVERAGES
Did not bowl

## M.AZHARUDDIN - *Derbyshire*

| Opposition | Venue | Date | Batting | | | Fielding | Bowling |
|---|---|---|---|---|---|---|---|

### BRITANNIC ASSURANCE

| Northants | Derby | April 27 | | | | | 1-52 |
|---|---|---|---|---|---|---|---|
| Lancashire | Old Trafford | May 16 | 53 | | | | 0-29 |
| Somerset | Derby | May 22 | 10 | & | 37 | 1Ct | 1-36 |
| Kent | Canterbury | May 25 | 12 | & | 47 | 1Ct | |
| Northants | Northampton | May 31 | 2 | & | 55 | 2Ct | |
| Glamorgan | Chesterfield | June 7 | 43 | & | 9 | | |
| Gloucs | Gloucester | June 18 | 154 | & | 31* | 1Ct | |
| Surrey | Derby | June 21 | 26 | & | 63 | | |
| Warwickshire | Edgbaston | June 28 | 100 | & | 73 | 2Ct | |
| Sussex | Derby | July 5 | 1 | & | 59 | 2Ct | |
| Yorkshire | Scarborough | July 16 | 1 | & | 0 | | |
| Worcestershire | Kidd'minster | July 19 | 25 | | | | |
| Hampshire | Chesterfield | July 23 | | | 0 | 2Ct | |
| Middlesex | Lord's | Aug 9 | 110 | & | 72 | 2Ct | |
| Lancashire | Derby | Aug 16 | 160* | & | 67 | 2Ct | |
| Leicestershire | Derby | Aug 20 | 3 | & | 26 | 1Ct | |
| Notts | Trent Bridge | Aug 23 | 129* | & | 72 | 1Ct | |

## A     PLAYER RECORDS

| Leicestershire | Leicester | Aug 28 | 0 & 212 | 4Ct | |
|---|---|---|---|---|---|
| Essex | Chelmsford | Sept 3 | 13 & 12 | | 1-35 |
| Notts | Derby | Sept 10 | 9 & 87 | 1Ct | 0-48 & 0-11 |

### OTHER FIRST-CLASS
| Cambridge U | Fenner's | May 9 | 116 * & 20 * | 1Ct | 0-41 |
|---|---|---|---|---|---|
| West Indies | Derby | June 12 | 72 & 35 | | |

### REFUGE ASSURANCE
| Leicestershire | Leicester | April 21 | 11 | 1Ct | |
|---|---|---|---|---|---|
| Hampshire | Derby | May 5 | 9 | 2Ct | |
| Lancashire | Derby | May 19 | 2 | | |
| Kent | Canterbury | May 26 | 73 | | |
| Yorkshire | Chesterfield | June 2 | 29 * | | |
| Surrey | Chesterfield | June 9 | | | |
| Somerset | Derby | June 16 | 20 | 1Ct | |
| Essex | Chelmsford | June 30 | 23 | | |
| Sussex | Derby | July 7 | 3 | | |
| Gloucs | Cheltenham | July 21 | 26 | 1Ct | |
| Northants | Derby | July 28 | 25 | 1Ct | |
| Warwickshire | Edgbaston | Aug 4 | 24 | | |
| Middlesex | Lord's | Aug 11 | 37 * | | |
| Glamorgan | Checkley | Aug 18 | 36 | | |
| Notts | Trent Bridge | Aug 25 | 53 | | 0-5 |

### BENSON & HEDGES CUP
| Northants | Derby | April 23 | 29 | 2Ct | |
|---|---|---|---|---|---|
| Combined U | The Parks | April 25 | 44 * | 1Ct | 0-29 |
| Worcestershire | Worcester | May 4 | 30 | | 0-12 |
| Gloucs | Derby | May 7 | 22 | 1Ct | 1-17 |

### OTHER ONE-DAY
For D of Norfolk
| West Indies | Arundel | May 12 | 21 | 3Ct | 0-24 |
|---|---|---|---|---|---|

For Rest of World
| England XI | Jesmond | July 31 | 6 | 1Ct | |
|---|---|---|---|---|---|
| England XI | Jesmond | Aug 1 | 56 | 1Ct | |

### BATTING AVERAGES - Including fielding
| | Matches | Inns | NO | Runs | HS | Avge | 100s | 50s | Ct | St |
|---|---|---|---|---|---|---|---|---|---|---|
| Britannic Assurance | 20 | 35 | 3 | 1773 | 212 | 55.40 | 6 | 9 | 23 | - |
| Other First-Class | 2 | 4 | 2 | 243 | 116 * | 121.50 | 1 | 1 | 1 | - |
| ALL FIRST-CLASS | 22 | 39 | 5 | 2016 | 212 | 59.29 | 7 | 10 | 24 | - |
| Refuge Assurance | 15 | 14 | 2 | 371 | 73 | 30.91 | - | 2 | 6 | - |
| Benson & Hedges Cup | 4 | 4 | 1 | 125 | 44 * | 41.66 | - | - | 4 | - |
| Other One-Day | 3 | 3 | 0 | 83 | 56 | 27.66 | - | 1 | 5 | - |
| ALL ONE-DAY | 22 | 21 | 3 | 579 | 73 | 32.16 | - | 3 | 15 | - |

### BOWLING AVERAGES
| | Overs | Mdns | Runs | Wkts | Avge | Best | 5wI | 10wM |
|---|---|---|---|---|---|---|---|---|
| Britannic Assurance | 63.4 | 9 | 211 | 3 | 70.33 | 1-35 | - | - |
| Other First-Class | 23 | 9 | 41 | 0 | - | - | - | - |
| ALL FIRST-CLASS | 86.4 | 18 | 252 | 3 | 84.00 | 1-35 | - | - |
| Refuge Assurance | 0.5 | 0 | 5 | 0 | - | - | - | |
| Benson & Hedges Cup | 16 | 0 | 58 | 1 | 58.00 | 1-17 | - | |
| Other One-Day | 4 | 0 | 24 | 0 | - | - | - | |
| ALL ONE-DAY | 20.5 | 0 | 87 | 1 | 87.00 | 1-17 | - | |

## A.M.BABINGTON - *Gloucestershire*

| Opposition | Venue | Date | Batting | | | Fielding | Bowling |
|---|---|---|---|---|---|---|---|
| **BRITANNIC ASSURANCE** | | | | | | | |
| Worcestershire | Worcester | April 27 | 13 | | | | 3-55 |
| Hampshire | Bristol | May 9 | 0 * | | | | 1-70 & 2-53 |
| Yorkshire | Sheffield | May 22 | | | | 1Ct | 2-121 & 0-23 |
| Warwickshire | Edgbaston | May 25 | 8 | & | 1 * | | 1-47 & 0-11 |
| Essex | Bristol | May 31 | 0 | & | 0 * | | 1-101 |
| Middlesex | Bristol | June 4 | 1 * | | | 2Ct | 3-56 & 0-32 |
| Hampshire | Southampton | June 7 | | | | 1Ct | 2-69 |
| Notts | Gloucester | June 14 | 0 * | | | | 0-13 & 1-5 |
| Sussex | Cheltenham | July 23 | 58 | | | 1Ct | 1-66 |
| Lancashire | Bristol | Aug 9 | 22 | | | | 4-33 & 2-40 |
| Kent | Canterbury | Aug 20 | 0 | | | | 1-25 & 2-68 |
| Glamorgan | Abergavenny | Aug 28 | 14 * & | 24 | | 1Ct | 2-120 & 1-13 |
| Northants | Bristol | Sept 3 | 17 & | 4 * | | 1Ct | 2-59 & 0-32 |
| Somerset | Bristol | Sept 10 | 1 | & | 0 | | 1-55 & 1-9 |
| Sussex | Hove | Sept 17 | 2 | & | 11 | | 2-83 & 0-41 |
| **OTHER FIRST-CLASS** | | | | | | | |
| Oxford U | The Parks | June 15 | | | | | 3-22 |
| West Indies | Bristol | July 31 | | | | | 1-65 & 2-68 |
| Sri Lanka | Bristol | Aug 6 | 0 | | | | 1-15 & 0-17 |
| **REFUGE ASSURANCE** | | | | | | | |
| Middlesex | Bristol | April 21 | 6 | | | | 1-33 |
| Worcestershire | Bristol | May 5 | | | | | 0-48 |
| Surrey | The Oval | May 12 | | | | | 3-39 |
| Sussex | Hove | May 19 | | | | 1Ct | 2-26 |
| Hampshire | Swindon | May 26 | | | | | 0-50 |
| Northants | Moreton | June 9 | | | | | |
| Notts | Gloucester | June 16 | | | | | 0-38 |
| Kent | Canterbury | June 30 | | | | 1Ct | 1-15 |
| Essex | Cheltenham | July 28 | 11 | | | | 2-24 |
| Glamorgan | Swansea | Aug 4 | 4 | | | | 4-53 |
| Lancashire | Bristol | Aug 11 | 0 | | | | 0-41 |
| Warwickshire | Edgbaston | Aug 18 | 6 * | | | | 0-25 |
| Leicestershire | Leicester | Aug 25 | | | | 1Ct | 1-34 |
| **NATWEST TROPHY** | | | | | | | |
| Norfolk | Bristol | June 26 | | | | | 0-17 |
| **BENSON & HEDGES CUP** | | | | | | | |
| Combined U | Bristol | April 23 | 1 * | | | | 0-11 |
| Worcestershire | Worcester | April 25 | 8 | | | | 0-27 |
| Northants | Bristol | May 2 | | | | 1Ct | 1-24 |
| Derbyshire | Derby | May 7 | 4 | | | | 2-49 |
| **OTHER ONE-DAY** | | | | | | | |
| West Indies | Bristol | May 14 | | | | | 1-26 |
| Somerset | Hove | Sept 8 | 6 | | | | 3-36 |
| Sussex | Hove | Sept 9 | 1 * | | | | 0-31 |

### BATTING AVERAGES - Including fielding

| | Matches | Inns | NO | Runs | HS | Avge | 100s | 50s | Ct | St |
|---|---|---|---|---|---|---|---|---|---|---|
| Britannic Assurance | 15 | 19 | 7 | 176 | 58 | 14.66 | - | 1 | 7 | - |
| Other First-Class | 3 | 1 | 0 | 0 | 0 | 0.00 | - | - | - | - |
| ALL FIRST-CLASS | 18 | 20 | 7 | 176 | 58 | 13.53 | - | 1 | 7 | - |
| Refuge Assurance | 13 | 5 | 1 | 27 | 11 | 6.75 | - | - | 3 | - |
| NatWest Trophy | 1 | 0 | 0 | 0 | 0 | - | - | - | - | - |
| Benson & Hedges Cup | 4 | 3 | 1 | 13 | 8 | 6.50 | - | - | 1 | - |
| Other One-Day | 3 | 2 | 1 | 7 | 6 | 7.00 | - | - | - | - |
| ALL ONE-DAY | 21 | 10 | 3 | 47 | 11 | 6.71 | - | - | 4 | - |

### BOWLING AVERAGES

| | Overs | Mdns | Runs | Wkts | Avge | Best | 5wI | 10wM |
|---|---|---|---|---|---|---|---|---|
| Britannic Assurance | 428.2 | 70 | 1300 | 35 | 37.14 | 4-33 | - | - |
| Other First-Class | 55.1 | 9 | 187 | 7 | 26.71 | 3-22 | - | - |
| ALL FIRST-CLASS | 483.3 | 79 | 1487 | 42 | 35.40 | 4-33 | - | - |
| Refuge Assurance | 88.4 | 3 | 426 | 14 | 30.42 | 4-53 | - | |
| NatWest Trophy | 6 | 0 | 17 | 0 | - | - | - | |
| Benson & Hedges Cup | 40 | 9 | 111 | 3 | 37.00 | 2-49 | - | |
| Other One-Day | 31 | 7 | 93 | 4 | 23.25 | 3-36 | - | |
| ALL ONE-DAY | 165.4 | 19 | 647 | 21 | 30.81 | 4-53 | - | |

## K.BAILEY - *Ireland*

| Opposition | Venue | Date | Batting | Fielding | Bowling |
|---|---|---|---|---|---|
| **OTHER FIRST-CLASS** | | | | | |
| For Ireland | | | | | |
| Scotland | Dublin | June 22 | | 1Ct,1St | |
| **NATWEST TROPHY** | | | | | |
| Middlesex | Dublin | June 26 | 0 | | |

### BATTING AVERAGES - Including fielding

| | Matches | Inns | NO | Runs | HS | Avge | 100s | 50s | Ct | St |
|---|---|---|---|---|---|---|---|---|---|---|
| Other First-Class | 1 | 0 | 0 | 0 | 0 | - | - | - | 1 | 1 |
| ALL FIRST-CLASS | 1 | 0 | 0 | 0 | 0 | - | - | - | 1 | 1 |
| NatWest Trophy | 1 | 1 | 0 | 0 | 0 | 0.00 | - | - | - | - |
| ALL ONE-DAY | 1 | 1 | 0 | 0 | 0 | 0.00 | - | - | - | - |

### BOWLING AVERAGES
Did not bowl

## R.J.BAILEY - *Northamptonshire*

| Opposition | Venue | Date | Batting | | | Fielding | Bowling |
|---|---|---|---|---|---|---|---|
| **BRITANNIC ASSURANCE** | | | | | | | |
| Derbyshire | Derby | April 27 | 83 | | | | |
| Essex | Northampton | May 9 | 57 | & | 30 | | 1-72 & 0-10 |
| Leicestershire | Northampton | May 16 | 7 | & | 32 | 1Ct | 0-39 |
| Glamorgan | Cardiff | May 22 | 5 | & | 61 | | 3-61 & 0-33 |
| Yorkshire | Headingley | May 25 | 50 | & | 6 | | 1-10 & 0-33 |
| Derbyshire | Northampton | May 31 | 7 | & | 56 | | |
| Worcestershire | Northampton | June 4 | 50 | & | 95 * | | |
| Hampshire | Northampton | June 21 | 37 | | | 1Ct | |
| Gloucs | Luton | June 28 | 57 | & | 30 | | |
| Kent | Maidstone | July 2 | | | 1 | 1Ct | |
| Leicestershire | Leicester | July 5 | 0 | | | 2Ct | 1-9 |
| Middlesex | Uxbridge | July 16 | 51 | & | 20 * | | |
| Notts | Well'borough | July 19 | 57 | & | 2 | 1Ct | |
| Somerset | Northampton | July 23 | 40 | & | 117 | | |
| Essex | Colchester | Aug 16 | 21 | & | 56 | 1Ct | 1-24 |
| Surrey | Northampton | Aug 23 | 4 | & | 37 * | | 0-3 & 3-44 |
| Yorkshire | Northampton | Aug 28 | 12 | & | 31 * | 2Ct | 0-21 & 1-19 |
| Gloucs | Bristol | Sept 3 | 9 | & | 28 | | 0-31 |
| Warwickshire | Edgbaston | Sept 10 | 49 | & | 4 | 1Ct | |
| **OTHER FIRST-CLASS** | | | | | | | |
| Cambridge U | Fenner's | April 16 | 21 | | | | 0-10 |
| West Indies | Northampton | June 15 | 1 * | | | | |
| **REFUGE ASSURANCE** | | | | | | | |
| Glamorgan | Cardiff | April 21 | 8 | | | | |
| Lancashire | Old Trafford | April 28 | 99 | | | 1Ct | |
| Leicestershire | Northampton | May 12 | 22 | | | | |
| Worcestershire | Northampton | May 19 | 25 | | | | |
| Yorkshire | Headingley | May 26 | 1 | | | | |
| Hampshire | Northampton | June 2 | 47 | | | | 0-26 |
| Gloucs | Moreton | June 9 | | | | | |
| Somerset | Luton | June 30 | 19 | | | 2Ct | |
| Surrey | Tring | July 7 | 33 | | | | |
| Derbyshire | Derby | July 28 | 22 | | | | |
| Essex | Northampton | Aug 11 | 2 | | | | |
| Kent | Canterbury | Aug 18 | 23 | | | | |
| Warwickshire | Northampton | Aug 25 | 78 * | | | | |
| Lancashire | Old Trafford | Sept 1 | 9 | | | | 0-11 |
| **NATWEST TROPHY** | | | | | | | |
| Staffordshire | Stone | June 26 | 145 | | | | 1-3 |
| Leicestershire | Northampton | July 11 | 48 * | | | | |
| Glamorgan | Northampton | July 31 | 55 | | | | |
| Surrey | The Oval | Aug 14 | 5 | | | | |
| **BENSON & HEDGES CUP** | | | | | | | |
| Derbyshire | Derby | April 23 | 38 | | | 1Ct | |
| Gloucs | Bristol | May 2 | 15 | | | | |
| Combined U | Northampton | May 4 | 1 | | | | |
| Worcestershire | Northampton | May 7 | 55 | | | | |

**B** # PLAYER RECORDS

| Lancashire | Old Trafford | May 29 | | 75 |
|---|---|---|---|---|

**BATTING AVERAGES - Including fielding**

| | Matches | Inns | NO | Runs | HS | Avge | 100s | 50s | Ct | St |
|---|---|---|---|---|---|---|---|---|---|---|
| Britannic Assurance | 19 | 34 | 4 | 1202 | 117 | 40.06 | 1 | 11 | 10 | - |
| Other First-Class | 2 | 2 | 1 | 22 | 21 | 22.00 | - | - | - | - |
| ALL FIRST-CLASS | 21 | 36 | 5 | 1224 | 117 | 39.48 | 1 | 11 | 10 | - |
| Refuge Assurance | 14 | 13 | 1 | 388 | 99 | 32.33 | - | 2 | 3 | - |
| NatWest Trophy | 4 | 4 | 1 | 253 | 145 | 84.33 | 1 | 1 | - | - |
| Benson & Hedges Cup | 5 | 5 | 0 | 184 | 75 | 36.80 | - | 2 | 1 | - |
| ALL ONE-DAY | 23 | 22 | 2 | 825 | 145 | 41.25 | 1 | 5 | 4 | - |

**BOWLING AVERAGES**

| | Overs | Mdns | Runs | Wkts | Avge | Best | 5wI | 10wM |
|---|---|---|---|---|---|---|---|---|
| Britannic Assurance | 118.3 | 16 | 409 | 11 | 37.18 | 3-44 | - | - |
| Other First-Class | 4 | 0 | 10 | 0 | - | - | - | - |
| ALL FIRST-CLASS | 122.3 | 16 | 419 | 11 | 38.09 | 3-44 | - | - |
| Refuge Assurance | 4 | 0 | 37 | 0 | - | - | - | - |
| NatWest Trophy | 2 | 0 | 3 | 1 | 3.00 | 1-3 | - | |
| Benson & Hedges Cup | | | | | | | | |
| ALL ONE-DAY | 6 | 0 | 40 | 1 | 40.00 | 1-3 | - | |

## P.BAINBRIDGE - *Durham*

| Opposition | Venue | Date | Batting | Fielding | Bowling |
|---|---|---|---|---|---|
| **NATWEST TROPHY** | | | | | |
| Glamorgan | Darlington | June 26 | 27 | | 0-42 |
| **OTHER ONE-DAY** | | | | | |
| For D of Norfolk | | | | | |
| West Indies | Arundel | May 12 | 9 | 1Ct | 3-36 |
| For Durham | | | | | |
| Leicestershire | Harrogate | June 11 | 48* | | 1-5 |
| Surrey | Harrogate | June 13 | 7 | 1Ct | 0-44 |
| Sri Lanka | Chester-le-S | July 26 | 62 | | 2-47 |
| Victoria | Durham U. | Sept 16 | 6* | | 0-27 |

**BATTING AVERAGES - Including fielding**

| | Matches | Inns | NO | Runs | HS | Avge | 100s | 50s | Ct | St |
|---|---|---|---|---|---|---|---|---|---|---|
| NatWest Trophy | 1 | 1 | 0 | 27 | 27 | 27.00 | - | - | - | - |
| Other One-Day | 5 | 5 | 2 | 132 | 62 | 44.00 | - | 1 | 2 | - |
| ALL ONE-DAY | 6 | 6 | 2 | 159 | 62 | 39.75 | - | 1 | 2 | - |

**BOWLING AVERAGES**

| | Overs | Mdns | Runs | Wkts | Avge | Best | 5wI | 10wM |
|---|---|---|---|---|---|---|---|---|
| NatWest Trophy | 12 | 0 | 42 | 0 | - | - | - | |
| Other One-Day | 36 | 5 | 159 | 6 | 26.50 | 3-36 | - | |
| ALL ONE-DAY | 48 | 5 | 201 | 6 | 33.50 | 3-36 | - | |

## P.J.BAKKER - *Hampshire*

| Opposition | Venue | Date | Batting | Fielding | Bowling |
|---|---|---|---|---|---|
| **BRITANNIC ASSURANCE** | | | | | |
| Kent | Southampton | April 27 | | 1Ct | 4-95 |
| Gloucs | Bristol | May 9 | 0 & 6* | | 0-20 |
| Sussex | Hove | May 16 | | | 2-52 & 2-32 |
| Surrey | Bournemouth | May 25 | 0 | | 1-48 & 2-56 |
| Notts | Trent Bridge | May 31 | | 1Ct | 2-42 & 0-23 |
| Lancashire | Basingstoke | June 4 | 0 | | 4-66 |
| Gloucs | Southampton | June 7 | 6* | | 0-54 |
| Somerset | Bath | June 18 | 5 | | 0-35 & 1-17 |
| Northants | Northampton | June 21 | | | 0-35 & 0-20 |
| **OTHER FIRST-CLASS** | | | | | |
| Oxford U | The Parks | April 13 | | | 0-18 & 2-42 |
| **REFUGE ASSURANCE** | | | | | |
| Derbyshire | Derby | May 5 | | | 0-31 |

| Kent | Southampton | May 12 | | | 2-36 |
|---|---|---|---|---|---|
| Somerset | Bournemouth | May 19 | | | 0-21 |
| Gloucs | Swindon | May 26 | | | 1-45 |
| Northants | Northampton | June 2 | | 4 | 1-53 |

**NATWEST TROPHY**

| Berkshire | Reading | June 26 | | | 0-15 |
|---|---|---|---|---|---|

**BENSON & HEDGES CUP**

| Min Counties | Trowbridge | April 25 | | | 1-21 |
|---|---|---|---|---|---|
| Glamorgan | Southampton | May 2 | | 1Ct | 2-37 |
| Yorkshire | Headingley | May 4 | | 7 | 0-54 |
| Essex | Chelmsford | May 29 | | 4 | 1-34 |

**BATTING AVERAGES - Including fielding**

| | Matches | Inns | NO | Runs | HS | Avge | 100s | 50s | Ct | St |
|---|---|---|---|---|---|---|---|---|---|---|
| Britannic Assurance | 9 | 6 | 2 | 17 | 6* | 4.25 | - | - | 2 | - |
| Other First-Class | 1 | 0 | 0 | 0 | 0 | - | - | - | - | - |
| ALL FIRST-CLASS | 10 | 6 | 2 | 17 | 6* | 4.25 | - | - | 2 | - |
| Refuge Assurance | 5 | 1 | 0 | 4 | 4 | 4.00 | - | - | - | - |
| NatWest Trophy | 1 | 0 | 0 | 0 | 0 | - | - | - | - | - |
| Benson & Hedges Cup | 4 | 2 | 0 | 11 | 7 | 5.50 | - | - | 1 | - |
| ALL ONE-DAY | 10 | 3 | 0 | 15 | 7 | 5.00 | - | - | 1 | - |

**BOWLING AVERAGES**

| | Overs | Mdns | Runs | Wkts | Avge | Best | 5wI | 10wM |
|---|---|---|---|---|---|---|---|---|
| Britannic Assurance | 209.3 | 52 | 595 | 18 | 33.05 | 4-66 | - | - |
| Other First-Class | 30 | 13 | 60 | 2 | 30.00 | 2-42 | - | - |
| ALL FIRST-CLASS | 239.3 | 65 | 655 | 20 | 32.75 | 4-66 | - | - |
| Refuge Assurance | 40 | 2 | 186 | 4 | 46.50 | 2-36 | - | |
| NatWest Trophy | 4 | 1 | 15 | 0 | - | - | - | |
| Benson & Hedges Cup | 44 | 6 | 146 | 4 | 36.50 | 2-37 | - | |
| ALL ONE-DAY | 88 | 9 | 347 | 8 | 43.37 | 2-36 | - | |

## M.C.J.BALL - *Gloucestershire*

| Opposition | Venue | Date | Batting | Fielding | Bowling |
|---|---|---|---|---|---|
| **BRITANNIC ASSURANCE** | | | | | |
| Surrey | Guildford | July 16 | 28 | | 0-16 |
| Lancashire | Bristol | Aug 9 | 8 | 4Ct | 4-40 & 4-55 |
| Kent | Canterbury | Aug 20 | 15 & 11 | 1Ct | 1-25 & 5-128 |
| Glamorgan | Abergavenny | Aug 28 | 0 & 23 | | 2-109 & 0-29 |
| Northants | Bristol | Sept 3 | 8 & 12 | | 2-95 & 0-50 |
| **OTHER FIRST-CLASS** | | | | | |
| Sri Lanka | Bristol | Aug 6 | 1 | 3Ct | 0-6 & 1-29 |
| **REFUGE ASSURANCE** | | | | | |
| Worcestershire | Bristol | May 5 | | | 0-19 |
| Yorkshire | Scarborough | July 14 | | 1Ct | |
| Derbyshire | Cheltenham | July 21 | 5 | 2Ct | 0-35 |
| Essex | Cheltenham | July 28 | 1 | | 0-27 |
| Glamorgan | Swansea | Aug 4 | 2* | | 0-10 |
| Lancashire | Bristol | Aug 11 | 2 | | 0-16 |
| Warwickshire | Edgbaston | Aug 18 | 4 | | 0-27 |
| Leicestershire | Leicester | Aug 25 | | | 0-40 |
| **OTHER ONE-DAY** | | | | | |
| Somerset | Hove | Sept 8 | 4* | 1Ct | 0-38 |

**BATTING AVERAGES - Including fielding**

| | Matches | Inns | NO | Runs | HS | Avge | 100s | 50s | Ct | St |
|---|---|---|---|---|---|---|---|---|---|---|
| Britannic Assurance | 5 | 8 | 0 | 105 | 28 | 13.12 | - | - | 5 | - |
| Other First-Class | 1 | 1 | 0 | 1 | 1 | 1.00 | - | - | 3 | - |
| ALL FIRST-CLASS | 6 | 9 | 0 | 106 | 28 | 11.77 | - | - | 8 | - |
| Refuge Assurance | 8 | 5 | 1 | 14 | 5 | 3.50 | - | - | 3 | - |
| Other One-Day | 1 | 1 | 1 | 4 | 4* | - | - | - | 1 | - |
| ALL ONE-DAY | 9 | 6 | 2 | 18 | 5 | 4.50 | - | - | 4 | - |

**BOWLING AVERAGES**

| | Overs | Mdns | Runs | Wkts | Avge | Best | 5wI | 10wM |
|---|---|---|---|---|---|---|---|---|
| Britannic Assurance | 178 | 34 | 547 | 18 | 30.38 | 5-128 | 1 | |

## PLEAYER RECORDS | B

| | | | | | | | |
|---|---|---|---|---|---|---|---|
| Other First-Class | 8 | 2 | 35 | 1 | 35.00 | 1-29 | - - |
| ALL FIRST-CLASS | 186 | 36 | 582 | 19 | 30.63 | 5-128 | 1 - |
| Refuge Assurance | 34.5 | 0 | 174 | 0 | - | - | - - |
| Other One-Day | 7 | 0 | 38 | 0 | - | - | - - |
| ALL ONE-DAY | 41.5 | 0 | 212 | 0 | - | - | - - |

---

# B.C.BANKS - *Bedfordshire*

| Opposition | Venue | Date | Batting | Fielding | Bowling |
|---|---|---|---|---|---|
| **NATWEST TROPHY** | | | | | |
| Worcestershire | Bedford | June 26 | 12* | | 0-8 |

**BATTING AVERAGES - Including fielding**

| | Matches | Inns | NO | Runs | HS | Avge | 100s | 50s | Ct | St |
|---|---|---|---|---|---|---|---|---|---|---|
| NatWest Trophy | 1 | 1 | 1 | 12 | 12* | - | - | - | - | - |
| ALL ONE-DAY | 1 | 1 | 1 | 12 | 12* | - | - | - | - | - |

**BOWLING AVERAGES**

| | Overs | Mdns | Runs | Wkts | Avge | Best | 5wI | 10wM |
|---|---|---|---|---|---|---|---|---|
| NatWest Trophy | 2 | 0 | 8 | 0 | - | - | - | - |
| ALL ONE-DAY | 2 | 0 | 8 | 0 | - | - | - | - |

---

# D.A.BANKS - *Staffordshire*

| Opposition | Venue | Date | Batting | Fielding | Bowling |
|---|---|---|---|---|---|
| **NATWEST TROPHY** | | | | | |
| Northants | Stone | June 26 | 3 | | |

**BATTING AVERAGES - Including fielding**

| | Matches | Inns | NO | Runs | HS | Avge | 100s | 50s | Ct | St |
|---|---|---|---|---|---|---|---|---|---|---|
| NatWest Trophy | 1 | 1 | 0 | 3 | 3 | 3.00 | - | - | - | - |
| ALL ONE-DAY | 1 | 1 | 0 | 3 | 3 | 3.00 | - | - | - | - |

**BOWLING AVERAGES**
Did not bowl

---

# E.A.E.BAPTISTE - *Northamptonshire*

| Opposition | Venue | Date | Batting | | Fielding | Bowling |
|---|---|---|---|---|---|---|
| **BRITANNIC ASSURANCE** | | | | | | |
| Derbyshire | Derby | April 27 | | | | |
| Essex | Northampton | May 9 | 28 & | 24 | 1Ct | 2-59 |
| Hampshire | Northampton | June 21 | 60 | | | 3-49 |
| Gloucs | Luton | June 28 | 51 & | 44 | 2Ct | 1-34 & 2-58 |
| Kent | Maidstone | July 2 | | 2 | | 6-57 |
| Leicestershire | Leicester | July 5 | 40 | | 1Ct | 3-37 & 1-66 |
| Middlesex | Uxbridge | July 16 | 3 | | 1Ct | 1-43 |
| Notts | Well'borough | July 19 | 80 & | 3 | | 0-81 |
| Somerset | Northampton | July 23 | | 18 | | 1-99 & 0-4 |
| Sussex | Eastbourne | Aug 2 | 8 & | 14 | 2Ct | 4-79 & 4-64 |
| Lancashire | Lytham | Aug 6 | 14 | | 1Ct | 0-15 & 0-30 |
| Warwickshire | Northampton | Aug 9 | 21 | | | 1-118 & 0-12 |
| Essex | Colchester | Aug 16 | 42 & | 28 | | 0-61 |
| Surrey | Northampton | Aug 23 | 63* | | 1Ct | 1-22 |
| Yorkshire | Northampton | Aug 28 | 5 | | | 2-64 & 7-95 |
| Gloucs | Bristol | Sept 3 | 29 | | | 2-67 & 1-36 |
| Warwickshire | Edgbaston | Sept 10 | 12 & | 0 | | 5-95 & 2-73 |
| **OTHER FIRST-CLASS** | | | | | | |
| West Indies | Northampton | June 15 | | | | 1-25 |
| **REFUGE ASSURANCE** | | | | | | |
| Glamorgan | Cardiff | April 21 | 11 | | 1Ct | 0-39 |
| Lancashire | Old Trafford | April 28 | 5* | | | 0-34 |
| Somerset | Luton | June 30 | 10* | | | 0-43 |

| Opposition | Venue | Date | Batting | Fielding | Bowling |
|---|---|---|---|---|---|
| Surrey | Tring | July 7 | 1 | 1Ct | 1-25 |
| Notts | Well'borough | July 21 | 5 | | 1-37 |
| Derbyshire | Derby | July 28 | 9 | | 0-26 |
| Sussex | Eastbourne | Aug 4 | 14* | | 2-25 |
| Essex | Northampton | Aug 11 | 3 | | 0-30 |
| Kent | Canterbury | Aug 18 | 15* | | 1-20 |
| Warwickshire | Northampton | Aug 25 | 10 | | 1-36 |
| Lancashire | Old Trafford | Sept 1 | 0 | | 0-25 |
| **NATWEST TROPHY** | | | | | |
| Staffordshire | Stone | June 26 | 0* | | 4-27 |
| Leicestershire | Northampton | July 11 | | | 3-45 |
| Glamorgan | Northampton | July 31 | 17 | 1Ct | 2-51 |
| Surrey | The Oval | Aug 14 | 34 | | 0-48 |
| **BENSON & HEDGES CUP** | | | | | |
| Derbyshire | Derby | April 23 | 15* | | 0-26 |
| Gloucs | Bristol | May 2 | 11 | | 0-38 |
| Combined U | Northampton | May 4 | | | 0-24 |
| Worcestershire | Northampton | May 7 | 2 | | 1-30 |

**BATTING AVERAGES - Including fielding**

| | Matches | Inns | NO | Runs | HS | Avge | 100s | 50s | Ct | St |
|---|---|---|---|---|---|---|---|---|---|---|
| Britannic Assurance | 17 | 22 | 1 | 589 | 80 | 28.04 | - | 4 | 9 | - |
| Other First-Class | 1 | 0 | 0 | 0 | 0 | | | | | |
| ALL FIRST-CLASS | 18 | 22 | 1 | 589 | 80 | 28.04 | - | 4 | 9 | - |
| Refuge Assurance | 11 | 11 | 4 | 83 | 15* | 11.85 | - | - | 2 | - |
| NatWest Trophy | 4 | 3 | 1 | 51 | 34 | 25.50 | - | - | 1 | - |
| Benson & Hedges Cup | 4 | 3 | 1 | 28 | 15* | 14.00 | - | - | - | - |
| ALL ONE-DAY | 19 | 17 | 6 | 162 | 34 | 14.72 | - | - | 3 | - |

**BOWLING AVERAGES**

| | Overs | Mdns | Runs | Wkts | Avge | Best | 5wI | 10wM |
|---|---|---|---|---|---|---|---|---|
| Britannic Assurance | 517.2 | 117 | 1418 | 49 | 28.93 | 7-95 | 3 | - |
| Other First-Class | 12 | 5 | 25 | 1 | 25.00 | 1-25 | - | - |
| ALL FIRST-CLASS | 529.2 | 122 | 1443 | 50 | 28.86 | 7-95 | 3 | - |
| Refuge Assurance | 81.1 | 5 | 340 | 6 | 56.66 | 2-25 | - | |
| NatWest Trophy | 42 | 4 | 171 | 9 | 19.00 | 4-27 | - | |
| Benson & Hedges Cup | 31.1 | 5 | 118 | 1 | 118.00 | 1-30 | - | |
| ALL ONE-DAY | 154.2 | 14 | 629 | 16 | 39.31 | 4-27 | - | |

---

# A.S.BARNARD - *Shropshire*

| Opposition | Venue | Date | Batting | Fielding | Bowling |
|---|---|---|---|---|---|
| **NATWEST TROPHY** | | | | | |
| Leicestershire | Leicester | June 26 | 17* | | 0-26 |

**BATTING AVERAGES - Including fielding**

| | Matches | Inns | NO | Runs | HS | Avge | 100s | 50s | Ct | St |
|---|---|---|---|---|---|---|---|---|---|---|
| NatWest Trophy | 1 | 1 | 1 | 17 | 17* | - | - | - | - | - |
| ALL ONE-DAY | 1 | 1 | 1 | 17 | 17* | - | - | - | - | - |

**BOWLING AVERAGES**

| | Overs | Mdns | Runs | Wkts | Avge | Best | 5wI | 10wM |
|---|---|---|---|---|---|---|---|---|
| NatWest Trophy | 12 | 5 | 26 | 0 | - | - | - | - |
| ALL ONE-DAY | 12 | 5 | 26 | 0 | - | - | - | - |

---

# S.N.BARNES - *Gloucestershire*

| Opposition | Venue | Date | Batting | Fielding | Bowling |
|---|---|---|---|---|---|
| **OTHER FIRST-CLASS** | | | | | |
| For Gloucestershire | | | | | |
| Oxford U | The Parks | June 15 | 0* | | 0-23 |
| **REFUGE ASSURANCE** | | | | | |
| Surrey | The Oval | May 12 | | | 1-33 |

| B | PLAYER RECORDS |
|---|---|

**OTHER ONE-DAY**

| | | | | |
|---|---|---|---|---|
| West Indies | Bristol | May 14 | | 0-26 |

**BATTING AVERAGES - Including fielding**

| | Matches | Inns | NO | Runs | HS | Avge | 100s | 50s | Ct | St |
|---|---|---|---|---|---|---|---|---|---|---|
| Other First-Class | 1 | 1 | 1 | 0 | 0* | - | - | - | - | - |
| ALL FIRST-CLASS | 1 | 1 | 1 | 0 | 0* | - | - | - | - | - |
| Refuge Assurance | 1 | 0 | 0 | 0 | 0 | - | - | - | - | - |
| Other One-Day | 1 | 0 | 0 | 0 | 0 | - | - | - | - | - |
| ALL ONE-DAY | 2 | 0 | 0 | 0 | 0 | - | - | - | - | - |

**BOWLING AVERAGES**

| | Overs | Mdns | Runs | Wkts | Avge | Best | 5wI | 10wM |
|---|---|---|---|---|---|---|---|---|
| Other First-Class | 12 | 4 | 23 | 0 | - | - | - | - |
| ALL FIRST-CLASS | 12 | 4 | 23 | 0 | - | - | - | - |
| Refuge Assurance | 8 | 0 | 33 | 1 | 33.00 | 1-33 | - | |
| Other One-Day | 9 | 0 | 26 | 0 | - | - | - | |
| ALL ONE-DAY | 17 | 0 | 59 | 1 | 59.00 | 1-33 | - | |

## A.A.BARNETT - *Middlesex*

| Opposition | Venue | Date | Batting | Fielding | Bowling |
|---|---|---|---|---|---|
| **BRITANNIC ASSURANCE** | | | | | |
| Derbyshire | Lord's | Aug 9 | 1* | | 3-117 & 4-119 |
| Surrey | The Oval | Aug 20 | 11* | | 3-88 & 0-5 |

**BATTING AVERAGES - Including fielding**

| | Matches | Inns | NO | Runs | HS | Avge | 100s | 50s | Ct | St |
|---|---|---|---|---|---|---|---|---|---|---|
| Britannic Assurance | 2 | 2 | 2 | 12 | 11* | - | - | - | - | - |
| ALL FIRST-CLASS | 2 | 2 | 2 | 12 | 11* | - | - | - | - | - |

**BOWLING AVERAGES**

| | Overs | Mdns | Runs | Wkts | Avge | Best | 5wI | 10wM |
|---|---|---|---|---|---|---|---|---|
| Britannic Assurance | 107.4 | 23 | 329 | 10 | 32.90 | 4-119 | - | - |
| ALL FIRST-CLASS | 107.4 | 23 | 329 | 10 | 32.90 | 4-119 | - | - |

## K.J.BARNETT - *Derbyshire*

| Opposition | Venue | Date | Batting | | | Fielding | Bowling |
|---|---|---|---|---|---|---|---|
| **BRITANNIC ASSURANCE** | | | | | | | |
| Northants | Derby | April 27 | | | | | |
| Lancashire | Old Trafford | May 16 | 15 | | | 1Ct | 0-28 |
| Somerset | Derby | May 22 | 1 | & | 21 | | 1-54 |
| Kent | Canterbury | May 25 | 85 | & | 0 | 1Ct | 0-47 |
| Northants | Northampton | May 31 | 11 | & | 122 | 1Ct | |
| Glamorgan | Chesterfield | June 7 | 38 | & | 63 | | 6-28 |
| Gloucs | Gloucester | June 18 | 20 | | | 1Ct | 3-14 & 2-36 |
| Warwickshire | Edgbaston | June 28 | 12 | & | 0 | 1Ct | 1-7 |
| Sussex | Derby | July 5 | 8 | & | 3 | 2Ct | 0-9 & 0-3 |
| Yorkshire | Scarborough | July 16 | 33 | & | 22 | 1Ct | 0-21 |
| Worcestershire | Kidd'minster | July 19 | 80 | | | | 1-46 |
| Hampshire | Chesterfield | July 23 | | | 74* | 1Ct | |
| Essex | Derby | Aug 6 | 16 | & | 91 | 2Ct | |
| Middlesex | Lord's | Aug 9 | 4 | & | 13 | | 0-49 |
| Lancashire | Derby | Aug 16 | 5 | & | 52 | 1Ct | |
| Leicestershire | Derby | Aug 20 | 20 | & | 26 | | 1-2 |
| Notts | Trent Bridge | Aug 23 | 32 | & | 65 | 2Ct | |
| Leicestershire | Leicester | Aug 28 | 1 | & | 36 | 4Ct | 2-49 |
| Essex | Chelmsford | Sept 3 | 99 | & | 0 | 1Ct | |
| Notts | Derby | Sept 10 | 19 | & | 217 | 2Ct | |
| Yorkshire | Chesterfield | Sept 17 | 2 | & | 12 | 2Ct | |
| **OTHER FIRST-CLASS** | | | | | | | |
| Cambridge U | Fenner's | May 9 | | | | 1Ct | 3-71 |
| West Indies | Derby | June 12 | 1 | & | 12* | | |
| Sri Lanka | Derby | Aug 2 | 68 | | | 1Ct | 0-32 |

**REFUGE ASSURANCE**

| | | | | | |
|---|---|---|---|---|---|
| Leicestershire | Leicester | April 21 | 46 | 3Ct | |
| Hampshire | Derby | May 5 | 11 | | |
| Lancashire | Derby | May 19 | 15 | 1Ct | |
| Kent | Canterbury | May 26 | 16 | | 2-40 |
| Yorkshire | Chesterfield | June 2 | 9 | | |
| Surrey | Chesterfield | June 9 | 11 | | |
| Somerset | Derby | June 16 | 17 | 1Ct | |
| Sussex | Derby | July 7 | 60* | | 1-38 |
| Worcestershire | Worcester | July 9 | 16* | | |
| Gloucs | Cheltenham | July 21 | 36* | 1Ct | 1-27 |
| Warwickshire | Edgbaston | Aug 4 | 10 | | |
| Middlesex | Lord's | Aug 11 | 22* | | |
| Glamorgan | Checkley | Aug 18 | 14 | | |
| Notts | Trent Bridge | Aug 25 | 6 | | |

**BENSON & HEDGES CUP**

| | | | | | |
|---|---|---|---|---|---|
| Northants | Derby | April 23 | 6 | 1Ct | 1-35 |
| Combined U | The Parks | April 25 | 82 | | 1-28 |
| Worcestershire | Worcester | May 4 | 66 | | |
| Gloucs | Derby | May 7 | 102 | 2Ct | 1-34 |

**OTHER ONE-DAY**

| For D of Norfolk | | | | | |
|---|---|---|---|---|---|
| West Indies | Arundel | May 12 | 12 | | 1-32 |
| For England XI | | | | | |
| Rest of World | Jesmond | July 31 | 49 | | |
| Rest of World | Jesmond | Aug 1 | 26 | | |
| For Derbyshire | | | | | |
| Yorkshire | Scarborough | Sept 1 | 10 | 2Ct | |

**BATTING AVERAGES - Including fielding**

| | Matches | Inns | NO | Runs | HS | Avge | 100s | 50s | Ct | St |
|---|---|---|---|---|---|---|---|---|---|---|
| Britannic Assurance | 21 | 36 | 1 | 1318 | 217 | 37.65 | 2 | 8 | 23 | - |
| Other First-Class | 3 | 3 | 1 | 81 | 68 | 40.50 | - | 1 | 2 | - |
| ALL FIRST-CLASS | 24 | 39 | 2 | 1399 | 217 | 37.81 | 2 | 9 | 25 | - |
| Refuge Assurance | 14 | 14 | 4 | 289 | 60* | 28.90 | - | 1 | 6 | - |
| Benson & Hedges Cup | 4 | 4 | 0 | 256 | 102 | 64.00 | 1 | 2 | 3 | - |
| Other One-Day | 4 | 4 | 0 | 97 | 49 | 24.25 | - | - | 2 | - |
| ALL ONE-DAY | 22 | 22 | 4 | 642 | 102 | 35.66 | 1 | 3 | 11 | - |

**BOWLING AVERAGES**

| | Overs | Mdns | Runs | Wkts | Avge | Best | 5wI | 10wM |
|---|---|---|---|---|---|---|---|---|
| Britannic Assurance | 162.1 | 33 | 393 | 17 | 23.11 | 6-28 | 1 | - |
| Other First-Class | 49 | 14 | 103 | 3 | 34.33 | 3-71 | - | - |
| ALL FIRST-CLASS | 211.1 | 47 | 496 | 20 | 24.80 | 6-28 | 1 | - |
| Refuge Assurance | 24 | 0 | 105 | 4 | 26.25 | 2-40 | - | |
| Benson & Hedges Cup | 29 | 4 | 97 | 3 | 32.33 | 1-28 | - | |
| Other One-Day | 6 | 0 | 32 | 1 | 32.00 | 1-32 | - | |
| ALL ONE-DAY | 59 | 4 | 234 | 8 | 29.25 | 2-40 | - | |

## T.J.BARRY - *Buckinghamshire*

| Opposition | Venue | Date | Batting | Fielding | Bowling |
|---|---|---|---|---|---|
| **NATWEST TROPHY** | | | | | |
| Somerset | Bath | June 26 | 30* | | |

**BATTING AVERAGES - Including fielding**

| | Matches | Inns | NO | Runs | HS | Avge | 100s | 50s | Ct | St |
|---|---|---|---|---|---|---|---|---|---|---|
| NatWest Trophy | 1 | 1 | 1 | 30 | 30* | - | - | - | - | - |
| ALL ONE-DAY | 1 | 1 | 1 | 30 | 30* | - | - | - | - | - |

**BOWLING AVERAGES**
Did not bowl

# PLAYER RECORDS | B

## R.J.BARTLETT - *Somerset*

| Opposition | Venue | Date | Batting | Fielding | Bowling |
|---|---|---|---|---|---|
| **BRITANNIC ASSURANCE** | | | | | |
| Glamorgan | Taunton | May 9 | 32 & 0 | | |
| Warwickshire | Edgbaston | June 7 | 0 * | 1Ct | |
| Yorkshire | Taunton | Aug 23 | 71 | | |
| Gloucs | Bristol | Sept 10 | 1 | 1Ct | |
| Warwickshire | Taunton | Sept 17 | 38 & 35 | 1Ct | |
| **REFUGE ASSURANCE** | | | | | |
| Surrey | The Oval | April 21 | 34 | | |
| Sussex | Taunton | April 28 | 26 | | |
| Glamorgan | Taunton | May 12 | 0 | 1Ct | |
| Hampshire | Bournemouth | May 19 | 6 | | |
| Middlesex | Taunton | May 26 | 6 | | |
| Warwickshire | Edgbaston | June 2 | 7 | | |
| Notts | Trent Bridge | June 9 | 19 | | |
| **BENSON & HEDGES CUP** | | | | | |
| Surrey | Taunton | May 4 | 14 | | |
| Essex | Chelmsford | May 7 | 14 | 1Ct | |
| **OTHER ONE-DAY** | | | | | |
| Gloucs | Hove | Sept 8 | 67 | 1Ct | |

### BATTING AVERAGES - Including fielding

| | Matches | Inns | NO | Runs | HS | Avge | 100s | 50s | Ct | St |
|---|---|---|---|---|---|---|---|---|---|---|
| Britannic Assurance | 5 | 7 | 1 | 177 | 71 | 29.50 | - | 1 | 3 | - |
| ALL FIRST-CLASS | 5 | 7 | 1 | 177 | 71 | 29.50 | - | 1 | 3 | - |
| Refuge Assurance | 7 | 7 | 0 | 98 | 34 | 14.00 | - | - | 1 | - |
| Benson & Hedges Cup | 2 | 2 | 0 | 28 | 14 | 14.00 | - | - | 1 | - |
| Other One-Day | 1 | 1 | 0 | 67 | 67 | 67.00 | - | 1 | 1 | - |
| ALL ONE-DAY | 10 | 10 | 0 | 193 | 67 | 19.30 | - | 1 | 3 | - |

### BOWLING AVERAGES
Did not bowl

## S.R.BARWICK - *Glamorgan*

| Opposition | Venue | Date | Batting | Fielding | Bowling |
|---|---|---|---|---|---|
| **BRITANNIC ASSURANCE** | | | | | |
| Leicestershire | Leicester | April 27 | 5 | | 0-12 |
| Somerset | Swansea | June 4 | | | 2-85 |
| Derbyshire | Chesterfield | June 7 | 13 & 0 | | 4-61 & 1-53 |
| Middlesex | Cardiff | June 14 | | | 0-20 & 4-49 |
| Leicestershire | Neath | June 21 | 24 * | | 0-9 |
| Lancashire | Liverpool | June 28 | | | 0-45 |
| Notts | Cardiff | July 2 | 0 | 1Ct | 2-12 & 1-67 |
| Gloucs | Cheltenham | July 19 | 12 | | 0-9 & 1-67 |
| Surrey | The Oval | July 26 | | | 4-46 & 3-75 |
| Hampshire | Swansea | Aug 9 | 3 | | 1-46 |
| Worcestershire | Cardiff | Sept 10 | 2 & 5 | | 3-68 & 0-2 |
| **OTHER FIRST-CLASS** | | | | | |
| West Indies | Swansea | July 16 | 0 | | 2-41 |
| **REFUGE ASSURANCE** | | | | | |
| Northants | Cardiff | April 21 | | 1Ct | 3-30 |
| Leicestershire | Leicester | April 28 | | 1Ct | 1-29 |
| Notts | Cardiff | May 5 | | | 0-8 |
| Somerset | Taunton | May 12 | 1 * | | 2-46 |
| Warwickshire | Swansea | May 19 | 0 | | 2-53 |
| Sussex | Swansea | May 26 | 2 | 1Ct | 1-35 |
| Essex | Pontypridd | June 2 | | | |
| Lancashire | Old Trafford | June 9 | | | 0-14 |
| Middlesex | Cardiff | June 16 | 3 * | | 1-18 |
| Yorkshire | Headingley | June 30 | 8 | | 0-47 |
| Kent | Maidstone | July 7 | | | 0-26 |
| Worcestershire | Worcester | July 21 | | | 0-44 |
| Surrey | The Oval | July 28 | 3 | | 2-44 |
| Gloucs | Swansea | Aug 4 | 1 * | | 0-18 |
| Hampshire | Ebbw Vale | Aug 11 | 5 * | | 0-29 |

## NATWEST TROPHY

| | | | | | |
|---|---|---|---|---|---|
| Durham | Darlington | June 26 | | | 1-51 |
| Worcestershire | Worcester | July 11 | | | 2-51 |
| Northants | Northampton | July 31 | 3 | | 2-51 |

### BENSON & HEDGES CUP

| | | | | | |
|---|---|---|---|---|---|
| Min Counties | Trowbridge | April 23 | | 1Ct | 1-31 |
| Hampshire | Southampton | May 2 | 1 * | | 2-61 |
| Notts | Cardiff | May 4 | 4 * | 1Ct | 1-42 |
| Yorkshire | Cardiff | May 7 | | 1Ct | 0-41 |

### BATTING AVERAGES - Including fielding

| | Matches | Inns | NO | Runs | HS | Avge | 100s | 50s | Ct | St |
|---|---|---|---|---|---|---|---|---|---|---|
| Britannic Assurance | 11 | 9 | 1 | 64 | 24 * | 8.00 | - | - | 1 | - |
| Other First-Class | 1 | 1 | 0 | 0 | 0 | 0.00 | - | - | - | - |
| ALL FIRST-CLASS | 12 | 10 | 1 | 64 | 24 * | 7.11 | - | - | 1 | - |
| Refuge Assurance | 15 | 8 | 4 | 23 | 8 | 5.75 | - | - | 3 | - |
| NatWest Trophy | 3 | 1 | 0 | 3 | 3 | 3.00 | - | - | - | - |
| Benson & Hedges Cup | 4 | 2 | 2 | 5 | 4 * | - | - | - | 3 | - |
| ALL ONE-DAY | 22 | 11 | 6 | 31 | 8 | 6.20 | - | - | 6 | - |

### BOWLING AVERAGES

| | Overs | Mdns | Runs | Wkts | Avge | Best | 5wI | 10wM |
|---|---|---|---|---|---|---|---|---|
| Britannic Assurance | 296.5 | 79 | 726 | 26 | 27.92 | 4-46 | - | - |
| Other First-Class | 21 | 7 | 41 | 2 | 20.50 | 2-41 | - | - |
| ALL FIRST-CLASS | 317.5 | 86 | 767 | 28 | 27.39 | 4-46 | - | - |
| Refuge Assurance | 81.1 | 0 | 441 | 12 | 36.75 | 3-30 | - | |
| NatWest Trophy | 33 | 0 | 153 | 5 | 30.60 | 2-51 | - | |
| Benson & Hedges Cup | 39 | 4 | 175 | 4 | 43.75 | 2-61 | - | |
| ALL ONE-DAY | 153.1 | 4 | 769 | 21 | 36.61 | 3-30 | | |

## S.J.BASE - *Derbyshire*

| Opposition | Venue | Date | Batting | Fielding | Bowling |
|---|---|---|---|---|---|
| **BRITANNIC ASSURANCE** | | | | | |
| Northants | Derby | April 27 | | | 1-88 |
| Lancashire | Old Trafford | May 16 | 15 * | 1Ct | 1-37 & 0-28 |
| Kent | Canterbury | May 25 | 19 * & 0 | 1Ct | 4-43 & 1-109 |
| Northants | Northampton | May 31 | 8 & 2 | 2Ct | 0-57 & 0-34 |
| Glamorgan | Chesterfield | June 7 | 0 | 1Ct | 2-56 & 0-54 |
| Surrey | Derby | June 21 | | | 3-60 |
| Sussex | Derby | July 5 | 0 * | 1Ct | 1-58 & 0-34 |
| Essex | Derby | Aug 6 | 11 & 3 | 2Ct | 3-34 |
| Middlesex | Lord's | Aug 9 | 0 | | 1-80 & 1-11 |
| Lancashire | Derby | Aug 16 | 22 | 1Ct | 1-97 & 1-24 |
| Leicestershire | Leicester | Aug 28 | 36 & 8 | 2Ct | 2-28 & 0-54 |
| Notts | Derby | Sept 10 | 1 | 1Ct | 4-128 & 1-35 |
| Yorkshire | Chesterfield | Sept 17 | 7 & 4 | 2Ct | 0-65 & 4-34 |
| **OTHER FIRST-CLASS** | | | | | |
| West Indies | Derby | June 12 | 9 * | | 4-44 & 0-19 |
| Sri Lanka | Derby | Aug 2 | 6 | | 1-33 |
| **REFUGE ASSURANCE** | | | | | |
| Leicestershire | Leicester | April 21 | | | 2-5 |
| Hampshire | Derby | May 5 | | | 1-27 |
| Lancashire | Derby | May 19 | 1 | 2Ct | 1-51 |
| Kent | Canterbury | May 26 | 3 | 1Ct | 2-35 |
| Yorkshire | Chesterfield | June 2 | | | 0-15 |
| Surrey | Chesterfield | June 9 | | | 2-21 |
| Somerset | Derby | June 16 | 0 | | 1-46 |
| Essex | Chelmsford | June 30 | 1 | | 1-46 |
| Sussex | Derby | July 7 | | | 1-42 |
| Worcestershire | Worcester | July 9 | 0 | | 0-28 |
| Gloucs | Cheltenham | July 21 | | | 2-37 |
| Northants | Derby | July 28 | | 1Ct | 4-14 |
| Warwickshire | Edgbaston | Aug 4 | 12 | 1Ct | 0-38 |
| Middlesex | Lord's | Aug 11 | | | 1-39 |
| Notts | Trent Bridge | Aug 25 | 4 | | 0-30 |
| **BENSON & HEDGES CUP** | | | | | |
| Northants | Derby | April 23 | 7 | | 2-40 |
| Combined U | The Parks | April 25 | | | 0-24 |
| Worcestershire | Worcester | May 4 | 1 | | 0-44 |
| Gloucs | Derby | May 7 | | | 1-26 |

## B   PLAYER RECORDS

### OTHER ONE-DAY

| | | | | | |
|---|---|---|---|---|---|
| Yorkshire | Scarborough | Sept 1 | 17* | | 2-41 |

### BATTING AVERAGES - Including fielding

| | Matches | Inns | NO | Runs | HS | Avge | 100s | 50s | Ct | St |
|---|---|---|---|---|---|---|---|---|---|---|
| Britannic Assurance | 13 | 16 | 3 | 136 | 36 | 10.46 | - | - | 14 | - |
| Other First-Class | 2 | 2 | 1 | 15 | 9* | 15.00 | - | - | - | - |
| ALL FIRST-CLASS | 15 | 18 | 4 | 151 | 36 | 10.78 | - | - | 14 | - |
| Refuge Assurance | 15 | 7 | 0 | 21 | 12 | 3.00 | - | - | 5 | - |
| Benson & Hedges Cup | 4 | 2 | 0 | 8 | 7 | 4.00 | - | - | - | - |
| Other One-Day | 1 | 1 | 1 | 17 | 17* | - | - | - | - | - |
| ALL ONE-DAY | 20 | 10 | 1 | 46 | 17* | 5.11 | - | - | 5 | - |

### BOWLING AVERAGES

| | Overs | Mdns | Runs | Wkts | Avge | Best | 5wI | 10wM |
|---|---|---|---|---|---|---|---|---|
| Britannic Assurance | 386 | 58 | 1248 | 31 | 40.25 | 4-34 | - | - |
| Other First-Class | 47.4 | 11 | 96 | 5 | 19.20 | 4-44 | - | - |
| ALL FIRST-CLASS | 433.4 | 69 | 1344 | 36 | 37.33 | 4-34 | - | - |
| Refuge Assurance | 104.5 | 4 | 474 | 18 | 26.33 | 4-14 | - | |
| Benson & Hedges Cup | 36 | 4 | 134 | 3 | 44.66 | 2-40 | - | |
| Other One-Day | 9.1 | 1 | 40 | 2 | 20.00 | 2-40 | - | |
| ALL ONE-DAY | 150 | 9 | 648 | 23 | 28.17 | 4-14 | - | |

## S.BASTIEN - *Glamorgan*

| Opposition | Venue | Date | Batting | Fielding | Bowling |
|---|---|---|---|---|---|
| **BRITANNIC ASSURANCE** | | | | | |
| Northants | Cardiff | May 22 | 0* | | 5-39 & 0-66 |
| Sussex | Cardiff | May 25 | | | 2-49 & 1-40 |
| Worcestershire | Worcester | May 31 | 1 | | 1-51 & 0-71 |
| Somerset | Swansea | June 4 | | | 0-113 |
| Leicestershire | Neath | June 21 | 22* | | 1-17 |
| Lancashire | Liverpool | June 28 | | 1Ct | 1-55 & 1-40 |
| Kent | Maidstone | July 5 | 1 | | 3-73 & 0-27 |
| Essex | Cardiff | July 23 | | | 0-63 |
| Surrey | The Oval | July 26 | 0* | | 1-74 |
| Warwickshire | Edgbaston | Aug 20 | | | 0-61 & 0-18 |
| Gloucs | Abergavenny | Aug 28 | 2 | | 1-76 & 0-13 |
| **OTHER FIRST-CLASS** | | | | | |
| Oxford U | The Parks | April 17 | | | 2-40 |
| Cambridge U | Fenner's | June 18 | | | 3-37 |
| **REFUGE ASSURANCE** | | | | | |
| Essex | Pontypridd | June 2 | | | |
| Kent | Maidstone | July 7 | | | 2-42 |
| Worcestershire | Worcester | July 21 | | | 0-37 |

### BATTING AVERAGES - Including fielding

| | Matches | Inns | NO | Runs | HS | Avge | 100s | 50s | Ct | St |
|---|---|---|---|---|---|---|---|---|---|---|
| Britannic Assurance | 11 | 6 | 3 | 26 | 22* | 8.66 | - | - | 1 | - |
| Other First-Class | 2 | 0 | 0 | 0 | 0 | - | - | - | - | - |
| ALL FIRST-CLASS | 13 | 6 | 3 | 26 | 22* | 8.66 | - | - | 1 | - |
| Refuge Assurance | 3 | 0 | 0 | 0 | 0 | - | | | | |
| ALL ONE-DAY | 3 | 0 | 0 | 0 | 0 | - | | | | |

### BOWLING AVERAGES

| | Overs | Mdns | Runs | Wkts | Avge | Best | 5wI | 10wM |
|---|---|---|---|---|---|---|---|---|
| Britannic Assurance | 329.2 | 89 | 946 | 17 | 55.64 | 5-39 | 1 | - |
| Other First-Class | 27 | 10 | 77 | 5 | 15.40 | 3-37 | - | - |
| ALL FIRST-CLASS | 356.2 | 99 | 1023 | 22 | 46.50 | 5-39 | 1 | - |
| Refuge Assurance | 14 | 0 | 79 | 2 | 39.50 | 2-42 | - | |
| ALL ONE-DAY | 14 | 0 | 79 | 2 | 39.50 | 2-42 | - | |

## J.D.BATTY - *Yorkshire*

| Opposition | Venue | Date | Batting | Fielding | Bowling |
|---|---|---|---|---|---|
| **BRITANNIC ASSURANCE** | | | | | |
| Middlesex | Lord's | April 27 | 0 | | |
| Gloucs | Sheffield | May 22 | | | 2-95 & 3-44 |
| Northants | Headingley | May 25 | 31 | 1Ct | 1-53 & 0-18 |
| Kent | Harrogate | June 14 | | | |
| Middlesex | Sheffield | June 21 | 10 | 1Ct | 1-13 & 1-29 |
| Hampshire | Southampton | July 5 | 0* | | 0-64 |
| Derbyshire | Scarborough | July 16 | 27* | | 3-44 & 3-70 |
| Surrey | Guildford | July 19 | 4 & 12 | 2Ct | 1-67 & 3-48 |
| Notts | Worksop | July 23 | 3 | | 6-48 |
| Leicestershire | Leicester | Aug 6 | 4* | | 0-54 |
| Sussex | Midd'brough | Aug 9 | 5 & 1* | | 0-29 |
| Glamorgan | Headingley | Aug 16 | 4* & 19* | | 4-118 |
| Essex | Colchester | Aug 20 | 5 | 1Ct | 0-104 & 4-86 |
| Somerset | Taunton | Aug 23 | | 1Ct | 0-28 & 0-20 |
| Lancashire | Scarborough | Sept 3 | | | 0-78 & 1-29 |
| Derbyshire | Chesterfield | Sept 17 | 12 & 14 | 1Ct | 4-91 |
| **OTHER FIRST-CLASS** | | | | | |
| Oxford U | The Parks | June 4 | | | 3-63 |
| Sri Lanka | Headingley | July 27 | 51 | | 1-146 |
| **REFUGE ASSURANCE** | | | | | |
| Leicestershire | Leicester | May 19 | | | 1-40 |
| Northants | Headingley | May 26 | 2* | 2Ct | 2-32 |
| Kent | Scarborough | June 16 | 13* | | 4-33 |
| Worcestershire | Sheffield | June 23 | | 1Ct | 1-33 |
| Glamorgan | Headingley | June 30 | | 1Ct | 0-34 |
| Middlesex | Lord's | July 7 | | | 0-27 |
| Gloucs | Scarborough | July 14 | 0 | | 1-38 |
| Surrey | The Oval | July 21 | | | 0-34 |
| Lancashire | Old Trafford | Aug 4 | | | 0-36 |
| Notts | Scarborough | Aug 18 | | 1Ct | 2-31 |
| Somerset | Taunton | Aug 25 | 12 | 1Ct | 1-38 |
| **NATWEST TROPHY** | | | | | |
| Warwickshire | Edgbaston | June 26 | 4 | | 1-17 |
| **BENSON & HEDGES CUP** | | | | | |
| Minor Counties | Headingley | May 2 | | | 0-41 |
| Hampshire | Headingley | May 4 | | | |
| Glamorgan | Cardiff | May 7 | | | 1-34 |
| **OTHER ONE-DAY** | | | | | |
| Derbyshire | Scarborough | Sept 1 | | | 0-55 |
| Essex | Scarburgh | Sept 2 | | | 3-35 |
| Yorkshiremen | Scarborough | Sept 7 | 10* | 1Ct | 1-60 |
| World XI | Scarborough | Sept 8 | 5 | | 0-49 |

### BATTING AVERAGES - Including fielding

| | Matches | Inns | NO | Runs | HS | Avge | 100s | 50s | Ct | St |
|---|---|---|---|---|---|---|---|---|---|---|
| Britannic Assurance | 16 | 16 | 6 | 151 | 31 | 15.10 | - | - | 7 | - |
| Other First-Class | 2 | 1 | 0 | 51 | 51 | 51.00 | - | 1 | - | - |
| ALL FIRST-CLASS | 18 | 17 | 6 | 202 | 51 | 18.36 | - | 1 | 7 | - |
| Refuge Assurance | 11 | 4 | 2 | 27 | 13* | 13.50 | - | - | 6 | - |
| NatWest Trophy | 1 | 1 | 0 | 4 | 4 | 4.00 | - | - | - | - |
| Benson & Hedges Cup | 3 | 0 | 0 | 0 | 0 | - | - | - | - | - |
| Other One-Day | 4 | 2 | 1 | 15 | 10* | 15.00 | - | - | 1 | - |
| ALL ONE-DAY | 19 | 7 | 3 | 46 | 13* | 11.50 | - | - | 7 | - |

### BOWLING AVERAGES

| | Overs | Mdns | Runs | Wkts | Avge | Best | 5wI | 10wM |
|---|---|---|---|---|---|---|---|---|
| Britannic Assurance | 399.4 | 91 | 1230 | 37 | 33.24 | 6-48 | 1 | - |
| Other First-Class | 60 | 15 | 209 | 4 | 52.25 | 3-63 | - | - |
| ALL FIRST-CLASS | 459.4 | 106 | 1439 | 41 | 35.09 | 6-48 | 1 | - |
| Refuge Assurance | 77 | 4 | 376 | 12 | 31.33 | 4-33 | - | |
| NatWest Trophy | 6 | 2 | 17 | 1 | 17.00 | 1-17 | - | |
| Benson & Hedges Cup | 22 | 3 | 75 | 1 | 75.00 | 1-34 | - | |
| Other One-Day | 40 | 2 | 199 | 4 | 49.75 | 3-35 | - | |
| ALL ONE-DAY | 145 | 11 | 667 | 18 | 37.05 | 4-33 | - | |

# PLEAYER RECORDS

# PLAYER RECORDS   B

## D.BEAL - *Somerset*

| Opposition | Venue | Date | Batting | Fielding | Bowling |
|---|---|---|---|---|---|
| **BRITANNIC ASSURANCE** | | | | | |
| Sussex | Hove | July 16 | 1 | | 0-97 |
| Essex | Southend | July 19 | | 0 | 0-75 & 1-37 |
| **OTHER FIRST-CLASS** | | | | | |
| Sri Lanka | Taunton | Aug 10 | | 1Ct | 1-64 & 1-47 |
| **REFUGE ASSURANCE** | | | | | |
| Surrey | The Oval | April 21 | | | 2-40 |
| Worcestershire | Worcester | Aug 18 | | 1Ct | |
| Yorkshire | Taunton | Aug 25 | | | |
| **NATWEST TROPHY** | | | | | |
| Middlesex | Taunton | July 11 | 0 | | 0-12 |
| **BENSON & HEDGES CUP** | | | | | |
| Middlesex | Taunton | April 23 | 1 | | 1-51 |
| Warwickshire | Edgbaston | May 2 | 0* | | 2-63 |
| **OTHER ONE-DAY** | | | | | |
| Gloucs | Hove | Sept 8 | 4 | | 0-43 |

### BATTING AVERAGES - Including fielding

| | Matches | Inns | NO | Runs | HS | Avge | 100s | 50s | Ct | St |
|---|---|---|---|---|---|---|---|---|---|---|
| Britannic Assurance | 2 | 2 | 0 | 1 | 1 | 0.50 | - | - | - | - |
| Other First-Class | 1 | 0 | 0 | 0 | 0 | - | - | - | 1 | - |
| ALL FIRST-CLASS | 3 | 2 | 0 | 1 | 1 | 0.50 | - | - | 1 | - |
| Refuge Assurance | 3 | 0 | 0 | 0 | 0 | - | - | - | 1 | - |
| NatWest Trophy | 1 | 1 | 0 | 0 | 0 | 0.00 | - | - | - | - |
| Benson & Hedges Cup | 2 | 2 | 1 | 1 | 1 | 1.00 | - | - | - | - |
| Other One-Day | 1 | 1 | 0 | 4 | 4 | 4.00 | - | - | - | - |
| ALL ONE-DAY | 7 | 4 | 1 | 5 | 4 | 1.66 | - | - | 1 | - |

### BOWLING AVERAGES

| | Overs | Mdns | Runs | Wkts | Avge | Best | 5wI | 10wM |
|---|---|---|---|---|---|---|---|---|
| Britannic Assurance | 44 | 3 | 209 | 1 | 209.00 | 1-37 | - | - |
| Other First-Class | 27 | 3 | 111 | 2 | 55.50 | 1-47 | - | - |
| ALL FIRST-CLASS | 71 | 6 | 320 | 3 | 106.66 | 1-37 | - | - |
| Refuge Assurance | 8 | 0 | 40 | 2 | 20.00 | 2-40 | - | |
| NatWest Trophy | 2 | 0 | 12 | 0 | - | - | - | |
| Benson & Hedges Cup | 16 | 1 | 114 | 3 | 38.00 | 2-63 | - | |
| Other One-Day | 8 | 0 | 43 | 0 | - | - | - | |
| ALL ONE-DAY | 34 | 1 | 209 | 5 | 41.80 | 2-40 | - | |

## A.W.BEE - *Scotland*

| Opposition | Venue | Date | Batting | Fielding | Bowling |
|---|---|---|---|---|---|
| **BENSON & HEDGES CUP** | | | | | |
| Lancashire | Forfar | April 23 | 13 | | 0-18 |
| Leicestershire | Leicester | May 2 | 3 | | 1-38 |
| Sussex | Hove | May 4 | 1* | | 4-31 |
| Kent | Glasgow | May 7 | 35 | | 1-47 |

### BATTING AVERAGES - Including fielding

| | Matches | Inns | NO | Runs | HS | Avge | 100s | 50s | Ct | St |
|---|---|---|---|---|---|---|---|---|---|---|
| Benson & Hedges Cup | 4 | 4 | 1 | 52 | 35 | 17.33 | - | - | - | - |
| ALL ONE-DAY | 4 | 4 | 1 | 52 | 35 | 17.33 | - | - | - | - |

### BOWLING AVERAGES

| | Overs | Mdns | Runs | Wkts | Avge | Best | 5wI | 10wM |
|---|---|---|---|---|---|---|---|---|
| Benson & Hedges Cup | 26 | 0 | 134 | 6 | 22.33 | 4-31 | - | |
| ALL ONE-DAY | 26 | 0 | 134 | 6 | 22.33 | 4-31 | - | |

## R.M.BELL - *Gloucestershire*

| Opposition | Venue | Date | Batting | Fielding | Bowling |
|---|---|---|---|---|---|
| **OTHER FIRST-CLASS** | | | | | |
| Oxford U | The Parks | June 15 | | | 0-9 |

### BATTING AVERAGES - Including fielding

| | Matches | Inns | NO | Runs | HS | Avge | 100s | 50s | Ct | St |
|---|---|---|---|---|---|---|---|---|---|---|
| Other First-Class | 1 | 0 | 0 | 0 | 0 | - | - | - | - | - |
| ALL FIRST-CLASS | 1 | 0 | 0 | 0 | 0 | - | - | - | - | - |

### BOWLING AVERAGES

| | Overs | Mdns | Runs | Wkts | Avge | Best | 5wI | 10wM |
|---|---|---|---|---|---|---|---|---|
| Other First-Class | 5 | 2 | 9 | 0 | - | - | - | - |
| ALL FIRST-CLASS | 5 | 2 | 9 | 0 | - | - | - | - |

## R.J.BELMONT - *Norfolk*

| Opposition | Venue | Date | Batting | Fielding | Bowling |
|---|---|---|---|---|---|
| **NATWEST TROPHY** | | | | | |
| Gloucs | Bristol | June 26 | 9 | | 1-53 |

### BATTING AVERAGES - Including fielding

| | Matches | Inns | NO | Runs | HS | Avge | 100s | 50s | Ct | St |
|---|---|---|---|---|---|---|---|---|---|---|
| NatWest Trophy | 1 | 1 | 0 | 9 | 9 | 9.00 | - | - | - | - |
| ALL ONE-DAY | 1 | 1 | 0 | 9 | 9 | 9.00 | - | - | - | - |

### BOWLING AVERAGES

| | Overs | Mdns | Runs | Wkts | Avge | Best | 5wI | 10wM |
|---|---|---|---|---|---|---|---|---|
| NatWest Trophy | 12 | 2 | 53 | 1 | 53.00 | 1-53 | - | |
| ALL ONE-DAY | 12 | 2 | 53 | 1 | 53.00 | 1-53 | - | |

## J.E.BENJAMIN - *Warwickshire*

| Opposition | Venue | Date | Batting | Fielding | Bowling |
|---|---|---|---|---|---|
| **BRITANNIC ASSURANCE** | | | | | |
| Surrey | Edgbaston | Aug 6 | 1 & 11 | | 2-62 & 2-64 |
| Northants | Northampton | Aug 9 | 0 | 1Ct | 2-66 |
| Worcestershire | Edgbaston | Aug 28 | 0 | | 0-28 & 1-37 |
| **REFUGE ASSURANCE** | | | | | |
| Somerset | Edgbaston | June 2 | | 3Ct | 0-29 |
| Lancashire | Edgbaston | June 16 | | | 1-26 |
| Essex | Chelmsford | July 7 | 12* | | 1-41 |
| Middlesex | Edgbaston | July 14 | | 1Ct | 0-29 |
| Hampshire | Portsmouth | July 21 | | | 0-17 |
| Derbyshire | Edgbaston | Aug 4 | | 1Ct | 3-33 |
| Leicestershire | Leicester | Aug 11 | 0 | | 0-25 |
| Gloucs | Edgbaston | Aug 18 | | | 2-36 |
| Northants | Northampton | Aug 25 | 2 | 1Ct | 2-26 |

### BATTING AVERAGES - Including fielding

| | Matches | Inns | NO | Runs | HS | Avge | 100s | 50s | Ct | St |
|---|---|---|---|---|---|---|---|---|---|---|
| Britannic Assurance | 3 | 4 | 0 | 12 | 11 | 3.00 | - | - | 1 | - |
| ALL FIRST-CLASS | 3 | 4 | 0 | 12 | 11 | 3.00 | - | - | 1 | - |
| Refuge Assurance | 9 | 3 | 1 | 14 | 12* | 7.00 | - | - | 6 | - |
| ALL ONE-DAY | 9 | 3 | 1 | 14 | 12* | 7.00 | - | - | 6 | - |

### BOWLING AVERAGES

| | Overs | Mdns | Runs | Wkts | Avge | Best | 5wI | 10wM |
|---|---|---|---|---|---|---|---|---|
| Britannic Assurance | 76.4 | 11 | 257 | 7 | 36.71 | 2-62 | - | - |
| ALL FIRST-CLASS | 76.4 | 11 | 257 | 7 | 36.71 | 2-62 | - | - |
| Refuge Assurance | 58 | 0 | 262 | 9 | 29.11 | 3-33 | - | |

## B      PLAYER RECORDS

| | | | | | | | |
|---|---|---|---|---|---|---|---|
| ALL ONE-DAY | 58 | 0 | 262 | 9 | 29.11 | 3-33 | - |

### J.D.R.BENSON - *Leicestershire*

| Opposition | Venue | Date | Batting | | | Fielding | Bowling |
|---|---|---|---|---|---|---|---|
| **BRITANNIC ASSURANCE** | | | | | | | |
| Glamorgan | Leicester | April 27 | | | | 1Ct | |
| Sussex | Hove | July 19 | 45 | & | 62 | 3Ct | 0-40 |
| Warwickshire | Leicester | July 26 | 11 | & | 8 | | 1-18 |
| Somerset | Weston | Aug 2 | 49 | & | 14 | | |
| Yorkshire | Leicester | Aug 6 | | | | 1Ct | 0-9 |
| Kent | Leicester | Aug 9 | 31 | & | 5 | 1Ct | 0-22 |
| Hampshire | Bournemouth | Aug 16 | 133* | | | 1Ct | 0-9 |
| Derbyshire | Derby | Aug 20 | 19 | | | | 0-5 |
| Essex | Leicester | Sept 10 | 0 | & | 16 | 2Ct | 0-42 |
| **REFUGE ASSURANCE** | | | | | | | |
| Derbyshire | Leicester | April 21 | 0 | | | | |
| Glamorgan | Leicester | April 28 | 14* | | | 2Ct | 1-32 |
| Middlesex | Uxbridge | June 9 | 42 | | | | 2-26 |
| Surrey | Leicester | June 16 | 0 | | | | 0-34 |
| Worcestershire | Worcester | June 30 | | | | 1Ct | 1-38 |
| Lancashire | Leicester | July 7 | 29 | | | | 2-50 |
| Kent | Canterbury | July 14 | 2 | | | 1Ct | 3-39 |
| Sussex | Hove | July 21 | 23 | | | | 1-40 |
| Somerset | Weston | Aug 4 | | | | 1Ct | 1-37 |
| Warwickshire | Leicester | Aug 11 | 3 | | | | 3-37 |
| Hampshire | Bournemouth | Aug 18 | 23* | | | | 0-21 |
| **BENSON & HEDGES CUP** | | | | | | | |
| Kent | Canterbury | April 23 | 27 | | | | 0-29 |
| Sussex | Hove | April 25 | 3 | | | | 1-10 |
| Scotland | Leicester | May 2 | 6* | | | | |
| **OTHER ONE-DAY** | | | | | | | |
| Durham | Harrogate | June 11 | | | | 1Ct | 0-10 |

**BATTING AVERAGES - Including fielding**

| | Matches | Inns | NO | Runs | HS | Avge | 100s | 50s | Ct | St |
|---|---|---|---|---|---|---|---|---|---|---|
| Britannic Assurance | 9 | 12 | 1 | 393 | 133* | 35.72 | 1 | 1 | 9 | - |
| ALL FIRST-CLASS | 9 | 12 | 1 | 393 | 133* | 35.72 | 1 | 1 | 9 | - |
| Refuge Assurance | 11 | 9 | 2 | 136 | 42 | 19.42 | - | - | 5 | - |
| Benson & Hedges Cup | 3 | 3 | 1 | 36 | 27 | 18.00 | - | - | - | - |
| Other One-Day | 1 | 0 | 0 | 0 | 0 | | - | - | 1 | - |
| ALL ONE-DAY | 15 | 12 | 3 | 172 | 42 | 19.11 | - | - | 6 | - |

**BOWLING AVERAGES**

| | Overs | Mdns | Runs | Wkts | Avge | Best | 5wI | 10wM |
|---|---|---|---|---|---|---|---|---|
| Britannic Assurance | 35.1 | 7 | 145 | 1 | 145.00 | 1-18 | - | - |
| ALL FIRST-CLASS | 35.1 | 7 | 145 | 1 | 145.00 | 1-18 | - | - |
| Refuge Assurance | 67 | 0 | 354 | 14 | 25.28 | 3-37 | - | |
| Benson & Hedges Cup | 7 | 0 | 39 | 1 | 39.00 | 1-10 | - | |
| Other One-Day | 2 | 0 | 10 | 0 | - | - | - | |
| ALL ONE-DAY | 76 | 0 | 403 | 15 | 26.86 | 3-37 | - | |

### M.R.BENSON - *Kent*

| Opposition | Venue | Date | Batting | | | Fielding | Bowling |
|---|---|---|---|---|---|---|---|
| **BRITANNIC ASSURANCE** | | | | | | | |
| Hampshire | Southampton | April 27 | 257 | | | 1Ct | |
| Surrey | The Oval | May 9 | 96 | | | 1Ct | |
| Essex | Folkestone | May 16 | 88 | & | 3 | 1Ct | |
| Notts | Trent Bridge | May 22 | 0 | & | 6 | | |
| Derbyshire | Canterbury | May 25 | 14 | & | 160 | | |
| Middlesex | Lord's | May 31 | 9 | & | 1 | | |
| Warwickshire | Tunbridge W | June 4 | 105 | | | | 0-2 |
| Sussex | Tunbridge W | June 7 | 4 | & | 8 | 1Ct | 0-18 |
| Yorkshire | Harrogate | June 14 | | | | | |
| Lancashire | Old Trafford | June 21 | 52 | | | | 0-24 |
| Northants | Maidstone | July 2 | 50*& | | 1 | | |
| Glamorgan | Maidstone | July 5 | 5 | | | | |
| Essex | Southend | July 16 | 0 | & | 92* | 2Ct | |
| Worcestershire | Worcester | July 23 | | | | | |
| Somerset | Taunton | July 26 | 29 | & | 76 | | |
| Surrey | Canterbury | Aug 2 | 142 | | | | |
| Gloucs | Canterbury | Aug 20 | 6 | & | 2 | | |
| Middlesex | Canterbury | Aug 28 | 8 | & | 20 | | |
| Sussex | Hove | Sept 3 | 48 | & | 5 | 1Ct | |
| Leicestershire | Canterbury | Sept 17 | 8 | & | 34 | 2Ct | |
| **REFUGE ASSURANCE** | | | | | | | |
| Worcestershire | Worcester | April 21 | 12 | | | | |
| Hampshire | Southampton | May 12 | 65 | | | | |
| Essex | Folkestone | May 19 | 43 | | | | |
| Derbyshire | Canterbury | May 26 | 24 | | | 2Ct | |
| Middlesex | Southgate | June 2 | 78 | | | | |
| Yorkshire | Scarborough | June 16 | 23 | | | 2Ct | |
| Lancashire | Old Trafford | June 23 | 1 | | | | |
| Gloucs | Canterbury | June 30 | 7 | | | 1Ct | |
| Glamorgan | Maidstone | July 7 | 84 | | | 1Ct | |
| Leicestershire | Canterbury | July 14 | 12 | | | | |
| Somerset | Taunton | July 28 | 8 | | | | |
| Surrey | Canterbury | Aug 4 | 14 | | | | |
| Northants | Canterbury | Aug 18 | 45 | | | | |
| Sussex | Hove | Aug 25 | 6 | | | | |
| **NATWEST TROPHY** | | | | | | | |
| Cambs | Canterbury | June 26 | 21 | | | | |
| Surrey | The Oval | July 11 | 14 | | | | |
| **BENSON & HEDGES CUP** | | | | | | | |
| Leicestershire | Canterbury | April 23 | 76 | | | | |
| Lancashire | Old Trafford | April 25 | 4 | | | | |
| Sussex | Canterbury | May 2 | 28 | | | | |
| Scotland | Glasgow | May 7 | 64 | | | | |
| Worcestershire | Worcester | May 29 | 56 | | | | |
| **OTHER ONE-DAY** | | | | | | | |
| Sussex | Hove | Sept 7 | 1 | | | 1Ct | |

**BATTING AVERAGES - Including fielding**

| | Matches | Inns | NO | Runs | HS | Avge | 100s | 50s | Ct | St |
|---|---|---|---|---|---|---|---|---|---|---|
| Britannic Assurance | 20 | 30 | 2 | 1329 | 257 | 47.46 | 4 | 6 | 9 | - |
| ALL FIRST-CLASS | 20 | 30 | 2 | 1329 | 257 | 47.46 | 4 | 6 | 9 | - |
| Refuge Assurance | 14 | 14 | 0 | 422 | 84 | 30.14 | - | 3 | 6 | - |
| NatWest Trophy | 2 | 2 | 0 | 35 | 21 | 17.50 | - | - | - | - |
| Benson & Hedges Cup | 5 | 5 | 0 | 228 | 76 | 45.60 | - | 3 | - | - |
| Other One-Day | 1 | 1 | 0 | 1 | 1 | 1.00 | - | - | 1 | - |
| ALL ONE-DAY | 22 | 22 | 0 | 686 | 84 | 31.18 | - | 6 | 7 | - |

**BOWLING AVERAGES**

| | Overs | Mdns | Runs | Wkts | Avge | Best | 5wI | 10wM |
|---|---|---|---|---|---|---|---|---|
| Britannic Assurance | 13 | 0 | 44 | 0 | - | - | - | - |
| ALL FIRST-CLASS | 13 | 0 | 44 | 0 | - | - | - | - |
| Refuge Assurance | | | | | | | | |
| NatWest Trophy | | | | | | | | |
| Benson & Hedges Cup | | | | | | | | |
| Other One-Day | | | | | | | | |
| ALL ONE-DAY | | | | | | | | |

### P.BENT - *Worcestershire*

| Opposition | Venue | Date | Batting | | | Fielding | Bowling |
|---|---|---|---|---|---|---|---|
| **BRITANNIC ASSURANCE** | | | | | | | |
| Kent | Worcester | July 23 | 0 | | | | |
| Gloucs | Cheltenham | July 26 | 9 | & | 42 | | |
| Somerset | Weston | Aug 6 | 39 | & | 65 | | 0-5 |
| Surrey | Worcester | Aug 16 | 5 | & | 0 | | |
| Lancashire | Blackpool | Aug 20 | 3 | & | 100* | 1Ct | |
| Middlesex | Worcester | Aug 23 | 1 | | | 1Ct | |
| Warwickshire | Edgbaston | Aug 28 | 1 | & | 20 | 1Ct | |
| **OTHER FIRST-CLASS** | | | | | | | |
| Sri Lanka | Worcester | July 30 | 3 | | | | |

# PLAYER RECORDS | B

## (continued)

### BATTING AVERAGES - Including fielding

| | Matches | Inns | NO | Runs | HS | Avge | 100s | 50s | Ct | St |
|---|---|---|---|---|---|---|---|---|---|---|
| Britannic Assurance | 7 | 12 | 1 | 285 | 100* | 25.90 | 1 | 1 | 3 | - |
| Other First-Class | 1 | 1 | 0 | 3 | 3 | 3.00 | - | - | - | - |
| ALL FIRST-CLASS | 8 | 13 | 1 | 288 | 100* | 24.00 | 1 | 1 | 3 | - |

### BOWLING AVERAGES

| | Overs | Mdns | Runs | Wkts | Avge | Best | 5wI | 10wM |
|---|---|---|---|---|---|---|---|---|
| Britannic Assurance | 3 | 1 | 5 | 0 | - | - | - | - |
| Other First-Class | | | | | | | | |
| ALL FIRST-CLASS | 3 | 1 | 5 | 0 | - | - | - | - |

## D.S.BERRY - *Victoria*

| Opposition | Venue | Date | Batting | | Fielding | Bowling |
|---|---|---|---|---|---|---|
| **OTHER FIRST-CLASS** | | | | | | |
| Essex | Chelmsford | Sept 23 | 1 & | 4 | 1Ct,1St | |
| **OTHER ONE-DAY** | | | | | | |
| Durham | Durham U. | Sept 16 | | | 1Ct | |
| Essex | Chelmsford | Sept 22 | | | 2Ct | |

### BATTING AVERAGES - Including fielding

| | Matches | Inns | NO | Runs | HS | Avge | 100s | 50s | Ct | St |
|---|---|---|---|---|---|---|---|---|---|---|
| Other First-Class | 1 | 2 | 0 | 5 | 4 | 2.50 | - | - | 1 | 1 |
| ALL FIRST-CLASS | 1 | 2 | 0 | 5 | 4 | 2.50 | - | - | 1 | 1 |
| Other One-Day | 2 | 0 | 0 | 0 | 0 | - | - | - | 3 | - |
| ALL ONE-DAY | 2 | 0 | 0 | 0 | 0 | - | - | - | 3 | - |

### BOWLING AVERAGES
Did not bowl

## S.R.BEVINS - *Worcestershire*

| Opposition | Venue | Date | Batting | Fielding | Bowling |
|---|---|---|---|---|---|
| **OTHER FIRST-CLASS** | | | | | |
| West Indies | Worcester | May 15 | 6 | 1Ct | |
| Oxford U | The Parks | May 25 | | 4Ct | |
| **REFUGE ASSURANCE** | | | | | |
| Lancashire | Worcester | May 12 | | | |
| Northants | Northampton | May 19 | | | |

### BATTING AVERAGES - Including fielding

| | Matches | Inns | NO | Runs | HS | Avge | 100s | 50s | Ct | St |
|---|---|---|---|---|---|---|---|---|---|---|
| Other First-Class | 2 | 1 | 0 | 6 | 6 | 6.00 | - | - | 5 | - |
| ALL FIRST-CLASS | 2 | 1 | 0 | 6 | 6 | 6.00 | - | - | 5 | - |
| Refuge Assurance | 2 | 0 | 0 | 0 | 0 | - | - | - | - | - |
| ALL ONE-DAY | 2 | 0 | 0 | 0 | 0 | - | - | - | - | - |

### BOWLING AVERAGES
Did not bowl

## D.J.BICKNELL - *Surrey*

| Opposition | Venue | Date | Batting | | Fielding | Bowling |
|---|---|---|---|---|---|---|
| **BRITANNIC ASSURANCE** | | | | | | |
| Essex | Chelmsford | April 27 | 145* | | | |
| Kent | The Oval | May 9 | 13 & | 0 | | |
| Lancashire | The Oval | May 22 | 7 & | 4 | 1Ct | |
| Hampshire | Bournemouth | May 25 | 48 & | 0 | | |
| Notts | The Oval | June 4 | 125 & | 81 | | |
| Leicestershire | Leicester | June 14 | 38 & | 86 | 1Ct | |
| Derbyshire | Derby | June 21 | 9 & | 5 | | |
| Somerset | The Oval | June 28 | 15 | | | |
| Sussex | Arundel | July 2 | 126 | | | |
| Essex | The Oval | July 5 | 0 & | 54 | | |
| Gloucs | Guildford | July 16 | 95 & | 10 | | |
| Yorkshire | Guildford | July 19 | 80 & | 11 | 3Ct | |
| Glamorgan | The Oval | July 26 | 0 & | 18 | | |
| Kent | Canterbury | Aug 2 | 41 & | 151 | 2Ct | |
| Warwickshire | Edgbaston | Aug 6 | 18 & | 75* | | |
| Worcestershire | Worcester | Aug 16 | 35 & | 79 | | |
| Middlesex | The Oval | Aug 20 | 33 & | 22 | | |
| Northants | Northampton | Aug 23 | 40 & | 4 | | 2-62 |
| Sussex | The Oval | Aug 28 | 36 | | 2Ct | |
| Hampshire | The Oval | Sept 3 | 136 & | 54 | 1Ct | |
| Middlesex | Lord's | Sept 10 | 41 & | 6 | | |
| Lancashire | Old Trafford | Sept 17 | 18 & | 3 | | |
| **OTHER FIRST-CLASS** | | | | | | |
| For MCC | | | | | | |
| Middlesex | Lord's | April 16 | 44 | | 1Ct | |
| For Surrey | | | | | | |
| Cambridge U | Fenner's | May 18 | 82 | | | |
| **REFUGE ASSURANCE** | | | | | | |
| Gloucs | The Oval | May 12 | 36 | | | |
| Derbyshire | Chesterfield | June 9 | 68 | | | |
| Leicestershire | Leicester | June 16 | 1 | | 2Ct | |
| Notts | The Oval | June 30 | 64 | | | |
| Northants | Tring | July 7 | 0 | | | |
| Sussex | The Oval | July 14 | 40 | | | |
| Yorkshire | The Oval | July 21 | 7 | | | |
| Glamorgan | The Oval | July 28 | 31 | | | |
| Kent | Canterbury | Aug 4 | 13 | | 1Ct | |
| **NATWEST TROPHY** | | | | | | |
| Kent | The Oval | July 11 | 27 | | | |
| Essex | The Oval | July 31 | 28 | | | |
| Northants | The Oval | Aug 14 | 21 | | | |
| Hampshire | Lord's | Sept 7 | 13 | | | |
| **BENSON & HEDGES CUP** | | | | | | |
| Essex | The Oval | April 23 | 43 | | | |
| Middlesex | Lord's | April 25 | 1 | | 1Ct | |
| Somerset | Taunton | May 4 | 11 | | | |
| Warwickshire | The Oval | May 7 | 53 | | | |
| **OTHER ONE-DAY** | | | | | | |
| Warwickshire | Harrogate | June 12 | 8 | | | |
| Durham | Harrogate | June 13 | 149* | | | 0-23 |

### BATTING AVERAGES - Including fielding

| | Matches | Inns | NO | Runs | HS | Avge | 100s | 50s | Ct | St |
|---|---|---|---|---|---|---|---|---|---|---|
| Britannic Assurance | 22 | 40 | 2 | 1762 | 151 | 46.36 | 5 | 8 | 10 | - |
| Other First-Class | 2 | 2 | 0 | 126 | 82 | 63.00 | - | 1 | 1 | - |
| ALL FIRST-CLASS | 24 | 42 | 2 | 1888 | 151 | 47.20 | 5 | 9 | 11 | - |
| Refuge Assurance | 9 | 9 | 0 | 260 | 68 | 28.88 | - | 2 | 3 | - |
| NatWest Trophy | 4 | 4 | 0 | 89 | 28 | 22.25 | - | - | - | - |
| Benson & Hedges Cup | 4 | 4 | 0 | 108 | 53 | 27.00 | - | 1 | 1 | - |
| Other One-Day | 2 | 2 | 1 | 157 | 149* | 157.00 | 1 | - | - | - |
| ALL ONE-DAY | 19 | 19 | 1 | 614 | 149* | 34.11 | 1 | 3 | 4 | - |

### BOWLING AVERAGES

| | Overs | Mdns | Runs | Wkts | Avge | Best | 5wI | 10wM |
|---|---|---|---|---|---|---|---|---|
| Britannic Assurance | 5.3 | 0 | 62 | 2 | 31.00 | 2-62 | - | - |
| Other First-Class | | | | | | | | |
| ALL FIRST-CLASS | 5.3 | 0 | 62 | 2 | 31.00 | 2-62 | - | - |
| Refuge Assurance | | | | | | | | |
| NatWest Trophy | | | | | | | | |
| Benson & Hedges Cup | | | | | | | | |
| Other One-Day | 3 | 0 | 23 | 0 | - | - | - | - |
| ALL ONE-DAY | 3 | 0 | 23 | 0 | - | - | - | - |

## B | PLAYER RECORDS

### M.P.BICKNELL - *Surrey*

| Opposition | Venue | Date | Batting | | | Fielding | Bowling |
|---|---|---|---|---|---|---|---|
| **BRITANNIC ASSURANCE** | | | | | | | |
| Essex | Chelmsford | April 27 | 6 | | | | 1-44 |
| Kent | The Oval | May 9 | 16 | & | 12 | | 2-95 |
| Lancashire | The Oval | May 22 | 30 | | | | 0-45 & 2-58 |
| Hampshire | Bournemouth | May 25 | 18 | & | 0 | | 0-23 |
| Derbyshire | Derby | June 21 | 34 * | & | 24 * | | 0-32 & 2-35 |
| Somerset | The Oval | June 28 | | | 1 * | 1Ct | 3-56 |
| Sussex | Arundel | July 2 | 7 * | | | | 3-57 & 1-30 |
| Essex | The Oval | July 5 | 23 | | | | 3-53 & 1-53 |
| Warwickshire | Edgbaston | Aug 6 | 11 | | | 1Ct | 0-38 & 2-56 |
| Worcestershire | Worcester | Aug 16 | 0 | & | 10 | | 4-104 & 2-30 |
| Middlesex | The Oval | Aug 20 | 24 | & | 1 | | 1-56 & 0-25 |
| Northants | Northampton | Aug 23 | | | 0 | | 3-92 |
| Sussex | The Oval | Aug 28 | 26 | | | | 2-35 & 7-52 |
| Middlesex | Lord's | Sept 10 | 5 | & | 1 | | 3-62 & 3-33 |
| Lancashire | Old Trafford | Sept 17 | 0 | & | 63 | 1Ct | 0-72 & 0-20 |
| **REFUGE ASSURANCE** | | | | | | | |
| Somerset | The Oval | April 21 | | | | | 0-24 |
| Middlesex | Lord's | April 28 | 7 * | | | 1Ct | 1-37 |
| Gloucs | The Oval | May 12 | 12 | | | | 1-41 |
| Notts | The Oval | June 30 | 11 | | | | 0-39 |
| Northants | Tring | July 7 | 20 * | | | 1Ct | 1-28 |
| Kent | Canterbury | Aug 4 | | | | | 1-34 |
| Lancashire | Old Trafford | Aug 18 | | | | | 3-36 |
| **NATWEST TROPHY** | | | | | | | |
| Kent | The Oval | July 11 | | | | | 0-9 |
| Essex | The Oval | July 31 | 4 | | | | 2-49 |
| Northants | The Oval | Aug 14 | 66 * | | | | 2-45 |
| Hampshire | Lord's | Sept 7 | | | | | 1-32 |
| **BENSON & HEDGES CUP** | | | | | | | |
| Essex | The Oval | April 23 | 6 | | | | 1-55 |
| Middlesex | Lord's | April 25 | 7 | | | | 3-28 |
| Somerset | Taunton | May 4 | | | | | 1-49 |
| Warwickshire | The Oval | May 7 | 4 | | | | 0-26 |
| **OTHER ONE-DAY** | | | | | | | |
| Durham | Harrogate | June 13 | | | | | 2-24 |

**BATTING AVERAGES - Including fielding**

| | Matches | Inns | NO | Runs | HS | Avge | 100s | 50s | Ct | St |
|---|---|---|---|---|---|---|---|---|---|---|
| Britannic Assurance | 15 | 22 | 4 | 312 | 63 | 17.33 | - | 1 | 3 | - |
| ALL FIRST-CLASS | 15 | 22 | 4 | 312 | 63 | 17.33 | - | 1 | 3 | - |
| Refuge Assurance | 7 | 4 | 2 | 50 | 20 * | 25.00 | - | - | 2 | - |
| NatWest Trophy | 4 | 2 | 1 | 70 | 66 * | 70.00 | - | 1 | - | - |
| Benson & Hedges Cup | 4 | 3 | 0 | 17 | 7 | 5.66 | - | - | - | - |
| Other One-Day | 1 | 0 | 0 | 0 | 0 | | - | - | - | - |
| ALL ONE-DAY | 16 | 9 | 3 | 137 | 66 * | 22.83 | - | 1 | 2 | - |

**BOWLING AVERAGES**

| | Overs | Mdns | Runs | Wkts | Avge | Best | 5wI | 10wM |
|---|---|---|---|---|---|---|---|---|
| Britannic Assurance | 470.5 | 118 | 1256 | 45 | 27.91 | 7-52 | 1 | - |
| ALL FIRST-CLASS | 470.5 | 118 | 1256 | 45 | 27.91 | 7-52 | 1 | - |
| Refuge Assurance | 51 | 1 | 239 | 7 | 34.14 | 3-36 | - | |
| NatWest Trophy | 39.3 | 2 | 135 | 5 | 27.00 | 2-45 | - | |
| Benson & Hedges Cup | 41 | 2 | 158 | 5 | 31.60 | 3-28 | - | |
| Other One-Day | 6 | 0 | 24 | 2 | 12.00 | 2-24 | - | |
| ALL ONE-DAY | 137.3 | 5 | 556 | 19 | 29.26 | 3-28 | - | |

### I.R.BISHOP - *World XI, Rest of World & West Indies XI*

| Opposition | Venue | Date | Batting | Fielding | Bowling |
|---|---|---|---|---|---|
| **OTHER FIRST-CLASS** | | | | | |
| For West Indies XI | | | | | |
| World XI | Scarborough | Aug 28 | | | 2-58 |

### OTHER ONE-DAY
For Rest of World

| | | | | | |
|---|---|---|---|---|---|
| England XI | Jesmond | July 31 | | | 0-60 |
| England XI | Jesmond | Aug 1 | | | 3-38 |
| For World XI | | | | | |
| Yorkshire | Scarborough | Sept 8 | | 1Ct | 1-33 |

**BATTING AVERAGES - Including fielding**

| | Matches | Inns | NO | Runs | HS | Avge | 100s | 50s | Ct | St |
|---|---|---|---|---|---|---|---|---|---|---|
| Other First-Class | 1 | 0 | 0 | 0 | 0 | - | - | - | - | - |
| ALL FIRST-CLASS | 1 | 0 | 0 | 0 | 0 | - | - | - | - | - |
| Other One-Day | 3 | 0 | 0 | 0 | 0 | - | - | - | 1 | - |
| ALL ONE-DAY | 3 | 0 | 0 | 0 | 0 | - | - | - | 1 | - |

**BOWLING AVERAGES**

| | Overs | Mdns | Runs | Wkts | Avge | Best | 5wI | 10wM |
|---|---|---|---|---|---|---|---|---|
| Other First-Class | 17 | 3 | 58 | 2 | 29.00 | 2-58 | - | - |
| ALL FIRST-CLASS | 17 | 3 | 58 | 2 | 29.00 | 2-58 | - | - |
| Other One-Day | 26.2 | 0 | 131 | 4 | 32.75 | 3-38 | - | |
| ALL ONE-DAY | 26.2 | 0 | 131 | 4 | 32.75 | 3-38 | - | |

### J.BISHOP - *Wales*

| Opposition | Venue | Date | Batting | Fielding | Bowling |
|---|---|---|---|---|---|
| **OTHER ONE-DAY** | | | | | |
| West Indies | Brecon | July 15 | 50 | 1Ct | |

**BATTING AVERAGES - Including fielding**

| | Matches | Inns | NO | Runs | HS | Avge | 100s | 50s | Ct | St |
|---|---|---|---|---|---|---|---|---|---|---|
| Other One-Day | 1 | 1 | 0 | 50 | 50 | 50.00 | - | 1 | 1 | - |
| ALL ONE-DAY | 1 | 1 | 0 | 50 | 50 | 50.00 | - | 1 | 1 | - |

**BOWLING AVERAGES**
Did not bowl

### G.R.BLACK - *Buckinghamshire*

| Opposition | Venue | Date | Batting | Fielding | Bowling |
|---|---|---|---|---|---|
| **NATWEST TROPHY** | | | | | |
| Somerset | Bath | June 26 | 11 | 1Ct | 0-30 |

**BATTING AVERAGES - Including fielding**

| | Matches | Inns | NO | Runs | HS | Avge | 100s | 50s | Ct | St |
|---|---|---|---|---|---|---|---|---|---|---|
| NatWest Trophy | 1 | 1 | 0 | 11 | 11 | 11.00 | - | - | 1 | - |
| ALL ONE-DAY | 1 | 1 | 0 | 11 | 11 | 11.00 | - | - | 1 | - |

**BOWLING AVERAGES**

| | Overs | Mdns | Runs | Wkts | Avge | Best | 5wI | 10wM |
|---|---|---|---|---|---|---|---|---|
| NatWest Trophy | 7 | 0 | 30 | 0 | | - | - | |
| ALL ONE-DAY | 7 | 0 | 30 | 0 | | - | - | |

### R.J.BLAKEY - *Yorkshire*

| Opposition | Venue | Date | Batting | | | Fielding | Bowling |
|---|---|---|---|---|---|---|---|
| **BRITANNIC ASSURANCE** | | | | | | | |
| Middlesex | Lord's | April 27 | 97 | | | 1Ct | |
| Warwickshire | Headingley | May 9 | 2 | & | 9 | 2Ct | |
| Notts | Headingley | May 16 | 11 | & | 1 | 1Ct | |
| Gloucs | Sheffield | May 22 | 55 | | | 1Ct | |
| Northants | Headingley | May 25 | 3 | | | 1Ct | |
| Warwickshire | Edgbaston | May 31 | 5 | & | 0 | 1Ct | |
| Kent | Harrogate | June 14 | 30 * | | | | |

# PLAYER RECORDS

**B**

| | | | | | | |
|---|---|---|---|---|---|---|
| Middlesex | Sheffield | June 21 | 44 | & | 21 | 4Ct |
| Worcestershire | Headingley | July 2 | 79 | | | 1Ct |
| Hampshire | Southampton | July 5 | 4 | | | |
| Derbyshire | Scarborough | July 16 | 90 | | | 3Ct |
| Surrey | Guildford | July 19 | 11 | & | 17 | 1Ct |
| Notts | Worksop | July 23 | 19 | | | 2Ct |
| Lancashire | Old Trafford | Aug 2 | 9 | & | 7 | 2Ct |
| Leicestershire | Leicester | Aug 6 | 8 | & | 2 | 1Ct |
| Sussex | Midd'brough | Aug 9 | 33 | & | 0 | 1Ct,1St |
| Glamorgan | Headingley | Aug 16 | 3 | & | 3 | 1Ct |
| Essex | Colchester | Aug 20 | 56 | & | 4 * | 0Ct,1St |
| Somerset | Taunton | Aug 23 | 7 | & | 1 | 2Ct |
| Northants | Northampton | Aug 28 | 19 | & | 20 | 3Ct |
| Lancashire | Scarborough | Sept 3 | 59 | & | 1 | 3Ct,1St |
| Derbyshire | Chesterfield | Sept 17 | 7 | & | 2 | 4Ct,1St |

### OTHER FIRST-CLASS

| | | | | | |
|---|---|---|---|---|---|
| Oxford U | The Parks | June 4 | 196 | | 2Ct,1St |
| Sri Lanka | Headingley | July 27 | 6 | | 3Ct |

### REFUGE ASSURANCE

| | | | | |
|---|---|---|---|---|
| Hampshire | Southampton | April 21 | 24 | |
| Essex | Chelmsford | April 28 | 18 | 1Ct |
| Warwickshire | Headingley | May 12 | 51 | |
| Northants | Headingley | May 26 | 71 * | 1Ct |
| Derbyshire | Chesterfield | June 2 | 7 | 1Ct |
| Kent | Scarborough | June 16 | 130 * | 3Ct |
| Worcestershire | Sheffield | June 23 | 3 | 1Ct |
| Glamorgan | Headingley | June 30 | 47 | 2Ct |
| Middlesex | Lord's | July 7 | 2 | 1Ct |
| Gloucs | Scarborough | July 14 | 43 | |
| Surrey | The Oval | July 21 | 24 | 2Ct |
| Lancashire | Old Trafford | Aug 4 | 32 | 2Ct |
| Sussex | Midd'brough | Aug 11 | 26 | 1Ct,1St |
| Notts | Scarborough | Aug 18 | 11 | 3Ct |
| Somerset | Taunton | Aug 25 | 1 | |

### NATWEST TROPHY

| | | | | |
|---|---|---|---|---|
| Warwickshire | Edgbaston | June 26 | 0 | |

### BENSON & HEDGES CUP

| | | | | |
|---|---|---|---|---|
| Notts | Trent Bridge | April 25 | 39 | 1Ct |
| Min Counties | Headingley | May 2 | 0 | 2Ct |
| Hampshire | Headingley | May 4 | 20 | 1Ct |
| Glamorgan | Cardiff | May 7 | 1 * | 1Ct |
| Warwickshire | Headingley | May 29 | 15 | 3Ct |
| Lancashire | Old Trafford | June 16 | 38 | 3Ct |

### OTHER ONE-DAY

For England XI

| | | | | |
|---|---|---|---|---|
| Rest of World | Jesmond | July 31 | 21 * | 2Ct |
| Rest of World | Jesmond | Aug 1 | 25 | 2Ct |

For Yorkshire

| | | | | |
|---|---|---|---|---|
| Derbyshire | Scarborough | Sept 1 | 31 | |
| Essex | Scarburgh | Sept 2 | 42 | 2Ct |
| Yorkshiremen | Scarborough | Sept 7 | 13 | 1Ct |
| World XI | Scarborough | Sept 8 | 17 | 2Ct |

### BATTING AVERAGES - Including fielding

| | Matches | Inns | NO | Runs | HS | Avge | 100s | 50s | Ct | St |
|---|---|---|---|---|---|---|---|---|---|---|
| Britannic Assurance | 22 | 36 | 2 | 739 | 97 | 21.73 | - | 6 | 35 | 4 |
| Other First-Class | 2 | 2 | 0 | 202 | 196 | 101.00 | 1 | - | 5 | 1 |
| ALL FIRST-CLASS | 24 | 38 | 2 | 941 | 196 | 26.13 | 1 | 6 | 40 | 5 |
| Refuge Assurance | 15 | 15 | 2 | 490 | 130 * | 37.69 | 1 | 2 | 18 | 1 |
| NatWest Trophy | 1 | 1 | 0 | 0 | 0 | 0.00 | - | - | - | - |
| Benson & Hedges Cup | 6 | 6 | 1 | 113 | 39 | 22.60 | - | - | 11 | - |
| Other One-Day | 6 | 6 | 1 | 149 | 42 | 29.80 | - | - | 9 | - |
| ALL ONE-DAY | 28 | 28 | 4 | 752 | 130 * | 31.33 | 1 | 2 | 38 | 1 |

### BOWLING AVERAGES

Did not bowl

---

# D.A.BLENKIRON - *Durham*

| Opposition | Venue | Date | Batting | Fielding | Bowling |
|---|---|---|---|---|---|

### NATWEST TROPHY

| | | | | |
|---|---|---|---|---|
| Glamorgan | Darlington | June 26 | 56 | |

---

### OTHER ONE-DAY

| | | | | | |
|---|---|---|---|---|---|
| Leicestershire | Harrogate | June 11 | 20 * | 1Ct | |
| Surrey | Harrogate | June 13 | 6 | | |
| Sri Lanka | Chester-le-S | July 26 | 2 | 1Ct | 0-11 |
| Essex | Scarborough | Aug 31 | 0 | | |
| Victoria | Durham U. | Sept 16 | | | |

### BATTING AVERAGES - Including fielding

| | Matches | Inns | NO | Runs | HS | Avge | 100s | 50s | Ct | St |
|---|---|---|---|---|---|---|---|---|---|---|
| NatWest Trophy | 1 | 1 | 0 | 56 | 56 | 56.00 | - | 1 | - | - |
| Other One-Day | 5 | 4 | 1 | 28 | 20 * | 9.33 | - | - | 2 | - |
| ALL ONE-DAY | 6 | 5 | 1 | 84 | 56 | 21.00 | - | 1 | 2 | - |

### BOWLING AVERAGES

| | Overs | Mdns | Runs | Wkts | Avge | Best | 5wI | 10wM |
|---|---|---|---|---|---|---|---|---|
| NatWest Trophy | | | | | | | | |
| Other One-Day | 3 | 0 | 11 | 0 | - | - | - | |
| ALL ONE-DAY | 3 | 0 | 11 | 0 | - | - | - | |

---

# J.BOILING - *Surrey*

| Opposition | Venue | Date | Batting | | | Fielding | Bowling |
|---|---|---|---|---|---|---|---|

### BRITANNIC ASSURANCE

| | | | | | | | |
|---|---|---|---|---|---|---|---|
| Lancashire | The Oval | May 22 | 1 | | | 2Ct | 1-44 & 0-15 |
| Middlesex | The Oval | Aug 20 | 0 | & | 16 | 1Ct | 2-58 & 0-41 |
| Middlesex | Lord's | Sept 10 | 3 | & | 0 * | | 1-19 & 0-26 |
| Lancashire | Old Trafford | Sept 17 | 1 | & | 1 | 3Ct | 4-157 & 1-60 |

### OTHER FIRST-CLASS

| | | | | | |
|---|---|---|---|---|---|
| Cambridge U | Fenner's | May 18 | | 1Ct | 3-39 & 0-46 |

### REFUGE ASSURANCE

| | | | | | |
|---|---|---|---|---|---|
| Middlesex | Lord's | April 28 | | | 1-21 |
| Gloucs | The Oval | May 12 | 4 | | 0-19 |
| Northants | Tring | July 7 | 3 * | | 2-41 |
| Sussex | The Oval | July 14 | | | 2-24 |
| Yorkshire | The Oval | July 21 | 1 | | 1-54 |
| Glamorgan | The Oval | July 28 | | | 0-51 |
| Kent | Canterbury | Aug 4 | | | 0-33 |
| Lancashire | Old Trafford | Aug 18 | | | 1-34 |
| Hampshire | The Oval | Aug 25 | 12 * | | 1-35 |

### NATWEST TROPHY

| | | | | | |
|---|---|---|---|---|---|
| Kent | The Oval | July 11 | | 1Ct | 1-44 |
| Essex | The Oval | July 31 | 7 | 1Ct | 0-47 |
| Northants | The Oval | Aug 14 | 22 | 1Ct | 2-22 |
| Hampshire | Lord's | Sept 7 | | | 0-52 |

### BENSON & HEDGES CUP

| | | | | | |
|---|---|---|---|---|---|
| Middlesex | Lord's | April 25 | 3 * | | 1-43 |
| Warwickshire | The Oval | May 7 | 7 | | 1-38 |

### OTHER ONE-DAY

| | | | | | |
|---|---|---|---|---|---|
| Warwickshire | Harrogate | June 12 | 11 * | 1Ct | 0-35 |
| Durham | Harrogate | June 13 | | 2Ct | 2-29 |

### BATTING AVERAGES - Including fielding

| | Matches | Inns | NO | Runs | HS | Avge | 100s | 50s | Ct | St |
|---|---|---|---|---|---|---|---|---|---|---|
| Britannic Assurance | 4 | 7 | 1 | 22 | 16 | 3.66 | - | - | 6 | - |
| Other First-Class | 1 | 0 | 0 | 0 | 0 | - | - | - | 1 | - |
| ALL FIRST-CLASS | 5 | 7 | 1 | 22 | 16 | 3.66 | - | - | 7 | - |
| Refuge Assurance | 9 | 4 | 2 | 20 | 12 * | 10.00 | - | - | - | - |
| NatWest Trophy | 4 | 2 | 0 | 29 | 22 | 14.50 | - | - | 3 | - |
| Benson & Hedges Cup | 2 | 2 | 1 | 10 | 7 | 10.00 | - | - | - | - |
| Other One-Day | 2 | 1 | 1 | 11 | 11 * | - | - | - | 3 | - |
| ALL ONE-DAY | 17 | 9 | 4 | 70 | 22 | 14.00 | - | - | 6 | - |

### BOWLING AVERAGES

| | Overs | Mdns | Runs | Wkts | Avge | Best | 5wI | 10wM |
|---|---|---|---|---|---|---|---|---|
| Britannic Assurance | 149.1 | 37 | 420 | 9 | 46.66 | 4-157 | - | - |
| Other First-Class | 32.2 | 7 | 85 | 3 | 28.33 | 3-39 | - | - |
| ALL FIRST-CLASS | 181.3 | 44 | 505 | 12 | 42.08 | 4-157 | - | - |
| Refuge Assurance | 60 | 0 | 312 | 8 | 39.00 | 2-24 | - | |
| NatWest Trophy | 48 | 4 | 165 | 3 | 55.00 | 2-22 | - | |

| B | PLAYER RECORDS |
|---|---|

| | | | | | | | |
|---|---|---|---|---|---|---|---|
| Benson & Hedges Cup | 20 | 0 | 81 | 2 | 40.50 | 1-38 | - |
| Other One-Day | 18 | 1 | 64 | 2 | 32.00 | 2-29 | - |
| ALL ONE-DAY | 146 | 5 | 622 | 15 | 41.46 | 2-22 | - |

## C.D.BOODEN - *Buckinghamshire*

| Opposition | Venue | Date | Batting | Fielding | Bowling |
|---|---|---|---|---|---|
| **NATWEST TROPHY** | | | | | |
| Somerset | Bath | June 26 | | | 0-35 |

**BATTING AVERAGES - Including fielding**

| | Matches | Inns | NO | Runs | HS | Avge | 100s | 50s | Ct | St |
|---|---|---|---|---|---|---|---|---|---|---|
| NatWest Trophy | 1 | 0 | 0 | 0 | 0 | - | - | - | - | - |
| ALL ONE-DAY | 1 | 0 | 0 | 0 | 0 | - | - | - | - | - |

**BOWLING AVERAGES**

| | Overs | Mdns | Runs | Wkts | Avge | Best | 5wI | 10wM |
|---|---|---|---|---|---|---|---|---|
| NatWest Trophy | 9.4 | 2 | 35 | 0 | - | - | - | - |
| ALL ONE-DAY | 9.4 | 2 | 35 | 0 | - | - | - | - |

## T.J.BOON - *Leicestershire*

| Opposition | Venue | Date | Batting | | | Fielding | Bowling |
|---|---|---|---|---|---|---|---|
| **BRITANNIC ASSURANCE** | | | | | | | |
| Notts | Trent Bridge | May 9 | 3 | & | 2 | | |
| Northants | Northampton | May 16 | 49 | & | 20 | | |
| Notts | Leicester | May 25 | 30 | & | 5 | | |
| Essex | Ilford | June 4 | 66 | & | 42 | 1Ct | |
| Middlesex | Uxbridge | June 7 | 11 | & | 33 | | |
| Surrey | Leicester | June 14 | 9 | & | 13 | | |
| Lancashire | Leicester | June 18 | 7 | & | 0 | | |
| Glamorgan | Neath | June 21 | 18* | | | 1Ct | |
| Worcestershire | Worcester | June 28 | 76 | & | 38 | | |
| Gloucs | Hinckley | July 2 | | | 2 | | |
| Northants | Leicester | July 5 | 0 | & | 5 | | |
| Warwickshire | Leicester | July 26 | 18 | & | 41 | 1Ct | |
| Somerset | Weston | Aug 2 | 61 | & | 40 | | 0-9 |
| Yorkshire | Leicester | Aug 6 | 102 | & | 29* | | 0-1 |
| Kent | Leicester | Aug 9 | 63 | & | 47 | | 1-11 |
| Hampshire | Bournemouth | Aug 16 | 53 | & | 12 | | |
| Derbyshire | Derby | Aug 20 | 35 | | | 1Ct | |
| Derbyshire | Leicester | Aug 28 | 0 | & | 40 | 2Ct | |
| Essex | Leicester | Sept 10 | 12 | & | 15 | | |
| Kent | Canterbury | Sept 17 | 10 | & | 50 | 2Ct | |
| **OTHER FIRST-CLASS** | | | | | | | |
| Cambridge U | Fenner's | May 22 | 108 | | | 2Ct | |
| West Indies | Leicester | June 1 | 15 | & | 5 | 1Ct | |
| **REFUGE ASSURANCE** | | | | | | | |
| Derbyshire | Leicester | April 21 | 22 | | | | |
| Notts | Leicester | May 26 | 50 | | | | |
| Middlesex | Uxbridge | June 9 | 4 | | | | |
| Warwickshire | Leicester | Aug 11 | 11 | | | | |
| Hampshire | Bournemouth | Aug 18 | 68 | | | | |
| Gloucs | Leicester | Aug 25 | 18 | | | | |
| **NATWEST TROPHY** | | | | | | | |
| Shropshire | Leicester | June 26 | 76* | | | 1Ct | |
| Northants | Northampton | July 11 | 14 | | | | |
| **BENSON & HEDGES CUP** | | | | | | | |
| Kent | Canterbury | April 23 | | | | | |
| Scotland | Leicester | May 2 | 103 | | | | |
| Lancashire | Leicester | May 4 | 16 | | | 1Ct | |
| **OTHER ONE-DAY** | | | | | | | |
| Durham For Yorkshiremen | Harrogate | June 11 | 10 | | | | |
| Yorkshire | Scarborough | Sept 7 | 7 | | | | |

**BATTING AVERAGES - Including fielding**

| | Matches | Inns | NO | Runs | HS | Avge | 100s | 50s | Ct | St |
|---|---|---|---|---|---|---|---|---|---|---|
| Britannic Assurance | 20 | 37 | 2 | 1057 | 102 | 30.20 | 1 | 6 | 8 | - |
| Other First-Class | 2 | 3 | 0 | 128 | 108 | 42.66 | 1 | - | 3 | - |
| ALL FIRST-CLASS | 22 | 40 | 2 | 1185 | 108 | 31.18 | 2 | 6 | 11 | - |
| Refuge Assurance | 6 | 6 | 0 | 173 | 68 | 28.83 | - | 2 | - | - |
| NatWest Trophy | 2 | 2 | 1 | 90 | 76* | 90.00 | - | 1 | 1 | - |
| Benson & Hedges Cup | 3 | 2 | 0 | 119 | 103 | 59.50 | 1 | - | 1 | - |
| Other One-Day | 2 | 2 | 0 | 17 | 10 | 8.50 | - | - | - | - |
| ALL ONE-DAY | 13 | 12 | 1 | 399 | 103 | 36.27 | 1 | 3 | 2 | - |

**BOWLING AVERAGES**

| | Overs | Mdns | Runs | Wkts | Avge | Best | 5wI | 10wM |
|---|---|---|---|---|---|---|---|---|
| Britannic Assurance | 10 | 3 | 21 | 1 | 21.00 | 1-11 | - | - |
| Other First-Class | | | | | | | | |
| ALL FIRST-CLASS | 10 | 3 | 21 | 1 | 21.00 | 1-11 | - | - |
| Refuge Assurance | | | | | | | | |
| NatWest Trophy | | | | | | | | |
| Benson & Hedges Cup | | | | | | | | |
| Other One-Day | | | | | | | | |
| ALL ONE-DAY | | | | | | | | |

## P.A.BOOTH - *Warwickshire*

| Opposition | Venue | Date | Batting | | | Fielding | Bowling |
|---|---|---|---|---|---|---|---|
| **BRITANNIC ASSURANCE** | | | | | | | |
| Yorkshire | Headingley | May 9 | 10 | & | 17 | | 1-17 |
| Glamorgan | Swansea | May 16 | 18 | | | 1Ct | 3-71 |
| Gloucs | Edgbaston | May 25 | 4 | | | 2Ct | 0-1 & 0-38 |
| Yorkshire | Edgbaston | May 31 | 7 | | | 1Ct | 2-62 & 0-62 |
| Kent | Tunbridge W | June 4 | 0 | | | | 0-60 |
| Sussex | Coventry | June 18 | 2 | | | | |
| Notts | Trent Bridge | June 21 | 12 | | | | 0-8 & 3-47 |
| Derbyshire | Edgbaston | June 28 | 29 | & | 0 | | 0-0 & 1-81 |
| Middlesex | Edgbaston | July 2 | 14 | | | 1Ct | 1-15 & 1-49 |
| Somerset | Taunton | Sept 17 | 62 | & | 0 | | 2-76 & 4-103 |
| **NATWEST TROPHY** | | | | | | | |
| Yorkshire | Edgbaston | June 26 | | | | | |
| **BENSON & HEDGES CUP** | | | | | | | |
| Somerset | Edgbaston | May 2 | | | | | 1-35 |
| Middlesex | Lord's | May 4 | 11 | | | | |
| Surrey | The Oval | May 7 | 4* | | | 3Ct | 0-46 |
| **OTHER ONE-DAY** | | | | | | | |
| Surrey | Harrogate | June 12 | 0 | | | | 1-43 |

**BATTING AVERAGES - Including fielding**

| | Matches | Inns | NO | Runs | HS | Avge | 100s | 50s | Ct | St |
|---|---|---|---|---|---|---|---|---|---|---|
| Britannic Assurance | 10 | 13 | 0 | 175 | 62 | 13.46 | - | 1 | 5 | - |
| ALL FIRST-CLASS | 10 | 13 | 0 | 175 | 62 | 13.46 | - | 1 | 5 | - |
| NatWest Trophy | 1 | 0 | 0 | 0 | 0 | - | - | - | - | - |
| Benson & Hedges Cup | 3 | 2 | 1 | 15 | 11 | 15.00 | - | - | 3 | - |
| Other One-Day | 1 | 1 | 0 | 0 | 0 | 0.00 | - | - | - | - |
| ALL ONE-DAY | 5 | 3 | 1 | 15 | 11 | 7.50 | - | - | 3 | - |

**BOWLING AVERAGES**

| | Overs | Mdns | Runs | Wkts | Avge | Best | 5wI | 10wM |
|---|---|---|---|---|---|---|---|---|
| Britannic Assurance | 226.1 | 47 | 690 | 18 | 38.33 | 4-103 | - | - |
| ALL FIRST-CLASS | 226.1 | 47 | 690 | 18 | 38.33 | 4-103 | - | - |
| NatWest Trophy | | | | | | | | |
| Benson & Hedges Cup | 13 | 0 | 81 | 1 | 81.00 | 1-35 | - | |
| Other One-Day | 11 | 1 | 43 | 1 | 43.00 | 1-43 | - | |
| ALL ONE-DAY | 24 | 1 | 124 | 2 | 62.00 | 1-35 | - | - |

# PLANER RECORDS... 

## I.T.BOTHAM - *Worcestershire & England*

| Opposition | Venue | Date | Batting | | | Fielding | Bowling |
|---|---|---|---|---|---|---|---|
| **CORNHILL TEST MATCHES** | | | | | | | |
| West Indies | The Oval | Aug 8 | 31 & | 4 * | | 3Ct | 1-27 & 2-40 |
| Sri Lanka | Lord's | Aug 22 | 22 | | | 2Ct | 1-26 & 0-15 |
| **BRITANNIC ASSURANCE** | | | | | | | |
| Gloucs | Worcester | April 27 | 39 * | | | 1Ct | 5-125 |
| Lancashire | Worcester | May 9 | 104 & | 9 | | | 4-105 & 1-16 |
| Leicestershire | Worcester | June 28 | 8 & | 3 * | | | 1-59 & 2-26 |
| Yorkshire | Headingley | July 2 | | 57 | | 1Ct | 0-27 |
| Hampshire | Portsmouth | July 16 | 26 & | 42 | | | 3-51 |
| Derbyshire | Kidd'minster | July 19 | 5 & | 17 | | 1Ct | 1-76 |
| Gloucs | Cheltenham | July 26 | 74 & | 0 | | 1Ct | 3-74 & 0-21 |
| Warwickshire | Worcester | Aug 2 | 81 | | | 2Ct | 1-43 & 7-54 |
| Surrey | Worcester | Aug 16 | 61 & | 0 | | 1Ct | 5-67 & 1-40 |
| Warwickshire | Edgbaston | Aug 28 | 24 & | 17 | | | 4-50 & 0-52 |
| **OTHER FIRST-CLASS** | | | | | | | |
| West Indies | Worcester | May 15 | 161 | | | | 2-83 |
| **TEXACO TROPHY** | | | | | | | |
| West Indies | Edgbaston | May 23 | 8 | | | | 4-45 |
| **REFUGE ASSURANCE** | | | | | | | |
| Kent | Worcester | April 21 | 20 | | | | 3-34 |
| Gloucs | Bristol | May 5 | | | | | 0-47 |
| Lancashire | Worcester | May 12 | 58 | | | | 0-41 |
| Northants | Northampton | May 19 | 10 | | | | 1-46 |
| Essex | Ilford | June 9 | 33 | | | 1Ct | 2-39 |
| Hampshire | Southampton | July 7 | 7 | | | | 0-51 |
| Derbyshire | Worcester | July 9 | 36 * | | | | 3-21 |
| Glamorgan | Worcester | July 21 | 24 * | | | | 0-65 |
| Notts | Trent Bridge | Aug 4 | | | | | 0-38 |
| Somerset | Worcester | Aug 18 | 17 | | | 1Ct | 2-58 |
| Notts | Trent Bridge | Sept 1 | 23 | | | 1Ct | |
| Lancashire | Old Trafford | Sept 15 | 21 * | | | | 1-53 |
| **NATWEST TROPHY** | | | | | | | |
| Glamorgan | Worcester | July 11 | 27 | | | 1Ct | 0-39 |
| **BENSON & HEDGES CUP** | | | | | | | |
| Gloucs | Worcester | April 25 | 18 * | | | | 0-28 |
| Combined U | Fenner's | May 2 | 16 * | | | 1Ct | 1-26 |
| Derbyshire | Worcester | May 4 | 35 * | | | | 0-40 |
| Northants | Northampton | May 7 | 0 | | | | 3-46 |
| Essex | Chelmsford | June 12 | | | | | 3-11 |
| Lancashire | Lord's | July 13 | 19 | | | | 1-23 |

### BATTING AVERAGES - Including fielding

| | Matches | Inns | NO | Runs | HS | Avge | 100s | 50s | Ct | St |
|---|---|---|---|---|---|---|---|---|---|---|
| Cornhill Test Matches | 2 | 3 | 1 | 57 | 31 | 28.50 | - | - | 5 | - |
| Britannic Assurance | 10 | 17 | 2 | 567 | 104 | 37.80 | 1 | 4 | 7 | - |
| Other First-Class | 1 | 1 | 0 | 161 | 161 | 161.00 | 1 | - | - | - |
| ALL FIRST-CLASS | 13 | 21 | 3 | 785 | 161 | 43.61 | 2 | 4 | 12 | - |
| Texaco Trophy | 1 | 1 | 0 | 8 | 8 | 8.00 | - | - | - | - |
| Refuge Assurance | 12 | 10 | 3 | 249 | 58 | 35.57 | - | 1 | 3 | - |
| NatWest Trophy | 1 | 1 | 0 | 27 | 27 | 27.00 | - | - | 1 | - |
| Benson & Hedges Cup | 6 | 5 | 3 | 88 | 35 * | 44.00 | - | - | 1 | - |
| ALL ONE-DAY | 20 | 17 | 6 | 372 | 58 | 33.81 | - | 1 | 5 | - |

### BOWLING AVERAGES

| | Overs | Mdns | Runs | Wkts | Avge | Best | 5wI | 10wM |
|---|---|---|---|---|---|---|---|---|
| Cornhill Test Matches | 43 | 13 | 108 | 4 | 27.00 | 2-40 | - | - |
| Britannic Assurance | 279.1 | 55 | 886 | 38 | 23.31 | 7-54 | 3 | - |
| Other First-Class | 29 | 5 | 83 | 2 | 41.50 | 2-83 | - | - |
| ALL FIRST-CLASS | 351.1 | 73 | 1077 | 44 | 24.47 | 7-54 | 3 | - |
| Texaco Trophy | 11 | 2 | 45 | 4 | 11.25 | 4-45 | - | |
| Refuge Assurance | 80.3 | 2 | 493 | 12 | 41.08 | 3-21 | - | |
| NatWest Trophy | 10 | 0 | 39 | 0 | - | - | - | |
| Benson & Hedges Cup | 63 | 14 | 174 | 8 | 21.75 | 3-11 | - | |
| ALL ONE-DAY | 164.3 | 18 | 751 | 24 | 31.29 | 4-45 | - | |

## P.D.BOWLER - *Derbyshire*

| Opposition | Venue | Date | Batting | | | Fielding | Bowling |
|---|---|---|---|---|---|---|---|
| **BRITANNIC ASSURANCE** | | | | | | | |
| Northants | Derby | April 27 | | | | 1Ct | |
| Lancashire | Old Trafford | May 16 | 1 | | | 1Ct | |
| Somerset | Derby | May 22 | 13 & | 59 | | | |
| Kent | Canterbury | May 25 | 1 & | 24 | | | |
| Northants | Northampton | May 31 | 0 & | 28 | | | |
| Glamorgan | Chesterfield | June 7 | 38 & | 15 | | 2Ct | |
| Gloucs | Gloucester | June 18 | 0 & | 24 | | 1Ct | 0-8 |
| Surrey | Derby | June 21 | 30 * & | 27 | | 2Ct | 0-27 |
| Warwickshire | Edgbaston | June 28 | 40 & | 2 | | 2Ct | |
| Sussex | Derby | July 5 | 38 & | 7 | | | 0-46 |
| Yorkshire | Scarborough | July 16 | 73 & | 48 | | | |
| Worcestershire | Kidd'minster | July 19 | 2 & | 2 * | | 2Ct | 0-21 |
| Hampshire | Chesterfield | July 23 | | 0 | | 1Ct | |
| Essex | Derby | Aug 6 | 6 & | 56 | | | |
| Middlesex | Lord's | Aug 9 | 63 & | 89 | | | 0-31 |
| Lancashire | Derby | Aug 16 | 104 * & | 62 | | | 1-46 |
| Leicestershire | Derby | Aug 20 | 0 & | 5 | | | |
| Notts | Trent Bridge | Aug 23 | 10 & | 99 | | | |
| Leicestershire | Leicester | Aug 28 | 104 & | 26 | | | 3-41 |
| Essex | Chelmsford | Sept 3 | 1 & | 9 | | | 0-93 |
| Notts | Derby | Sept 10 | 65 & | 45 | | | 2-58 |
| Yorkshire | Chesterfield | Sept 17 | 0 & | 54 | | 3Ct | 3-41 |
| **OTHER FIRST-CLASS** | | | | | | | |
| Cambridge U | Fenner's | May 9 | 81 & | 31 | | | 0-16 |
| West Indies | Derby | June 12 | 13 & | 63 | | | 0-36 |
| **REFUGE ASSURANCE** | | | | | | | |
| Leicestershire | Leicester | April 21 | 77 | | | 1Ct | |
| Hampshire | Derby | May 5 | 8 | | | 1Ct | |
| Lancashire | Derby | May 19 | 51 | | | 1Ct | |
| Kent | Canterbury | May 26 | 25 | | | 2Ct | |
| Yorkshire | Chesterfield | June 2 | 30 | | | | |
| Surrey | Chesterfield | June 9 | 47 * | | | 2Ct | |
| Somerset | Derby | June 16 | 9 | | | 1Ct | |
| Essex | Chelmsford | June 30 | 30 | | | | |
| Sussex | Derby | July 7 | 26 | | | | |
| Worcestershire | Worcester | July 9 | 9 | | | | |
| Gloucs | Cheltenham | July 21 | 8 | | | | 3-31 |
| Middlesex | Lord's | Aug 11 | 37 | | | | |
| Glamorgan | Checkley | Aug 18 | 39 | | | | |
| **BENSON & HEDGES CUP** | | | | | | | |
| Northants | Derby | April 23 | 5 | | | 1Ct | |
| Combined U | The Parks | April 25 | 100 | | | 2Ct | |
| Worcestershire | Worcester | May 4 | 29 | | | 1Ct | |
| Gloucs | Derby | May 7 | 7 | | | 2Ct | |
| **OTHER ONE-DAY** | | | | | | | |
| Yorkshire | Scarborough | Sept 1 | 6 | | | | 1-12 |

### BATTING AVERAGES - Including fielding

| | Matches | Inns | NO | Runs | HS | Avge | 100s | 50s | Ct | St |
|---|---|---|---|---|---|---|---|---|---|---|
| Britannic Assurance | 22 | 40 | 3 | 1270 | 104 * | 34.32 | 2 | 9 | 15 | - |
| Other First-Class | 2 | 4 | 0 | 188 | 81 | 47.00 | - | 2 | - | - |
| ALL FIRST-CLASS | 24 | 44 | 3 | 1458 | 104 * | 35.56 | 2 | 11 | 15 | - |
| Refuge Assurance | 13 | 13 | 1 | 396 | 77 | 33.00 | - | 2 | 8 | - |
| Benson & Hedges Cup | 4 | 4 | 0 | 141 | 100 | 35.25 | 1 | - | 6 | - |
| Other One-Day | 1 | 1 | 0 | 6 | 6 | 6.00 | - | - | - | - |
| ALL ONE-DAY | 18 | 18 | 1 | 543 | 100 | 31.94 | 1 | 2 | 14 | - |

### BOWLING AVERAGES

| | Overs | Mdns | Runs | Wkts | Avge | Best | 5wI | 10wM |
|---|---|---|---|---|---|---|---|---|
| Britannic Assurance | 104 | 18 | 412 | 9 | 45.77 | 3-41 | - | - |
| Other First-Class | 10 | 2 | 52 | 0 | - | - | - | - |
| ALL FIRST-CLASS | 114 | 20 | 464 | 9 | 51.55 | 3-41 | - | - |
| Refuge Assurance | 5.2 | 0 | 31 | 3 | 10.33 | 3-31 | - | |
| Benson & Hedges Cup | | | | | | | | |
| Other One-Day | 3 | 1 | 12 | 1 | 12.00 | 1-12 | | |
| ALL ONE-DAY | 8.2 | 1 | 43 | 4 | 10.75 | 3-31 | - | |

# B          PLAYER RECORDS

## G.E.BRADBURN - *World XI*

| Opposition | Venue | Date | Batting | Fielding | Bowling |
|---|---|---|---|---|---|
| **OTHER ONE-DAY** | | | | | |
| Yorkshire | Scarborough | Sept 8 | 51 | | |

**BATTING AVERAGES - Including fielding**

| | Matches | Inns | NO | Runs | HS | Avge | 100s | 50s | Ct | St |
|---|---|---|---|---|---|---|---|---|---|---|
| Other One-Day | 1 | 1 | 0 | 51 | 51 | 51.00 | - | 1 | - | - |
| ALL ONE-DAY | 1 | 1 | 0 | 51 | 51 | 51.00 | - | 1 | - | - |

**BOWLING AVERAGES**
Did not bowl

## M.P.BRIERS - *Durham*

| Opposition | Venue | Date | Batting | Fielding | Bowling |
|---|---|---|---|---|---|
| **OTHER ONE-DAY** | | | | | |
| Surrey | Harrogate | June 13 | 1 | 1Ct | |
| Sri Lanka | Chester-le-S | July 26 | 12 | | 2-36 |
| Victoria | Durham U. | Sept 16 | | | |

**BATTING AVERAGES - Including fielding**

| | Matches | Inns | NO | Runs | HS | Avge | 100s | 50s | Ct | St |
|---|---|---|---|---|---|---|---|---|---|---|
| Other One-Day | 3 | 2 | 0 | 13 | 12 | 6.50 | - | - | 1 | - |
| ALL ONE-DAY | 3 | 2 | 0 | 13 | 12 | 6.50 | - | - | 1 | - |

**BOWLING AVERAGES**

| | Overs | Mdns | Runs | Wkts | Avge | Best | 5wI | 10wM |
|---|---|---|---|---|---|---|---|---|
| Other One-Day | 8 | 0 | 36 | 2 | 18.00 | 2-36 | - | |
| ALL ONE-DAY | 8 | 0 | 36 | 2 | 18.00 | 2-36 | - | |

## N.E.BRIERS - *Leicestershire*

| Opposition | Venue | Date | Batting | | | Fielding | Bowling |
|---|---|---|---|---|---|---|---|
| **BRITANNIC ASSURANCE** | | | | | | | |
| Glamorgan | Leicester | April 27 | 42 * | | | 1Ct | |
| Notts | Trent Bridge | May 9 | 22 | & | 160 | 2Ct | |
| Northants | Northampton | May 16 | 8 | & | 2 | 1Ct | |
| Notts | Leicester | May 25 | 14 | & | 21 | 2Ct | |
| Essex | Ilford | June 4 | 23 | & | 23 | | |
| Middlesex | Uxbridge | June 7 | 0 | & | 50 | | |
| Surrey | Leicester | June 14 | 31 | & | 30 | 1Ct | |
| Lancashire | Leicester | June 18 | 21 * | & | 7 | 2Ct | |
| Glamorgan | Neath | June 21 | 4 | | | 2Ct | |
| Worcestershire | Worcester | June 28 | 29 | & | 104 | | |
| Gloucs | Hinckley | July 2 | | | 14 | | |
| Northants | Leicester | July 5 | 60 * | & | 133 | | |
| Sussex | Hove | July 19 | 29 | & | 41 | | |
| Warwickshire | Leicester | July 26 | 33 | & | 3 | 1Ct | |
| Somerset | Weston | Aug 2 | 2 | & | 46 | | |
| Yorkshire | Leicester | Aug 6 | 114 | & | 51 * | 1Ct | |
| Kent | Leicester | Aug 9 | 29 | & | 66 | 1Ct | |
| Hampshire | Bournemouth | Aug 16 | 8 | & | 80 * | | |
| Derbyshire | Derby | Aug 20 | 0 | | | | |
| Derbyshire | Leicester | Aug 28 | 10 | & | 3 | 1Ct | |
| Essex | Leicester | Sept 10 | 3 | & | 22 | | |
| Kent | Canterbury | Sept 17 | 0 | & | 20 | | |
| **OTHER FIRST-CLASS** | | | | | | | |
| Cambridge U | Fenner's | May 22 | 50 | | | 3Ct | |
| West Indies | Leicester | June 1 | 68 | & | 9 | | |
| **REFUGE ASSURANCE** | | | | | | | |
| Derbyshire | Leicester | April 21 | 21 | | | | |
| Glamorgan | Leicester | April 28 | 11 | | | | |
| Northants | Northampton | May 12 | 48 | | | 2Ct | |
| Yorkshire | Leicester | May 19 | 25 | | | 1Ct | |
| Notts | Leicester | May 26 | 19 | | | | |
| Middlesex | Uxbridge | June 9 | 44 | | | | |

(continued)

| Opposition | Venue | Date | Batting | Fielding |
|---|---|---|---|---|
| Surrey | Leicester | June 16 | 3 | 1Ct |
| Worcestershire | Worcester | June 30 | 29 | |
| Lancashire | Leicester | July 7 | 8 | |
| Kent | Canterbury | July 14 | 16 | |
| Sussex | Hove | July 21 | 20 | |
| Somerset | Weston | Aug 4 | 26 | 1Ct |
| Warwickshire | Leicester | Aug 11 | 40 | |
| Hampshire | Bournemouth | Aug 18 | 42 | |
| Gloucs | Leicester | Aug 25 | 0 | |
| **NATWEST TROPHY** | | | | |
| Shropshire | Leicester | June 26 | 9 | |
| Northants | Northampton | July 11 | 29 | |
| **BENSON & HEDGES CUP** | | | | |
| Kent | Canterbury | April 23 | 12 | 1Ct |
| Sussex | Hove | April 25 | 46 | 1Ct |
| Scotland | Leicester | May 2 | 36 | 1Ct |
| Lancashire | Leicester | May 4 | 9 | 1Ct |
| **OTHER ONE-DAY** | | | | |
| Durham | Harrogate | June 11 | 2 | |

**BATTING AVERAGES - Including fielding**

| | Matches | Inns | NO | Runs | HS | Avge | 100s | 50s | Ct | St |
|---|---|---|---|---|---|---|---|---|---|---|
| Britannic Assurance | 22 | 40 | 5 | 1358 | 160 | 38.80 | 4 | 5 | 15 | - |
| Other First-Class | 2 | 3 | 0 | 127 | 68 | 42.33 | - | 2 | 3 | - |
| ALL FIRST-CLASS | 24 | 43 | 5 | 1485 | 160 | 39.07 | 4 | 7 | 18 | - |
| Refuge Assurance | 15 | 15 | 0 | 352 | 48 | 23.46 | - | - | 5 | - |
| NatWest Trophy | 2 | 2 | 0 | 38 | 29 | 19.00 | - | - | - | - |
| Benson & Hedges Cup | 4 | 4 | 0 | 103 | 46 | 25.75 | - | - | 4 | - |
| Other One-Day | 1 | 1 | 0 | 2 | 2 | 2.00 | - | - | - | - |
| ALL ONE-DAY | 22 | 22 | 0 | 495 | 48 | 22.50 | - | - | 9 | - |

**BOWLING AVERAGES**
Did not bowl

## B.C.BROAD - *Nottinghamshire*

| Opposition | Venue | Date | Batting | | | Fielding | Bowling |
|---|---|---|---|---|---|---|---|
| **BRITANNIC ASSURANCE** | | | | | | | |
| Leicestershire | Trent Bridge | May 9 | 67 | & | 29 | 1Ct | |
| Yorkshire | Headingley | May 16 | 86 | & | 48 | 1Ct | |
| Kent | Trent Bridge | May 22 | 166 | & | 0 | 2Ct | |
| Leicestershire | Leicester | May 25 | 51 | & | 91 | | |
| Hampshire | Trent Bridge | May 31 | 5 | & | 59 | | |
| Surrey | The Oval | June 4 | 137 * | | | | |
| Gloucs | Gloucester | June 11 | 19 | & | 16 | | |
| Worcestershire | Worcester | June 18 | 162 | & | 8 | 1Ct | |
| Warwickshire | Trent Bridge | June 21 | 28 * | & | 8 | | |
| Glamorgan | Cardiff | July 2 | 34 | & | 36 | | |
| Lancashire | Trent Bridge | July 16 | 12 | | | | |
| Yorkshire | Worksop | July 23 | 24 * | & | 54 | | |
| Middlesex | Lord's | July 26 | 14 | & | 3 | 2Ct | |
| Sussex | Eastbourne | Aug 6 | 158 | | | | |
| Essex | Trent Bridge | Aug 9 | 36 | & | 10 | | |
| Somerset | Trent Bridge | Aug 16 | 37 | & | 131 | | |
| Derbyshire | Trent Bridge | Aug 23 | 36 | & | 5 | 1Ct | |
| Lancashire | Old Trafford | Aug 28 | 54 | & | 10 | | |
| Middlesex | Trent Bridge | Sept 3 | 45 | & | 4 | | |
| Derbyshire | Derby | Sept 10 | 14 | & | 4 | 1Ct | |
| Worcestershire | Trent Bridge | Sept 17 | 38 | | | | |
| **REFUGE ASSURANCE** | | | | | | | |
| Lancashire | Old Trafford | April 21 | 100 * | | | 1Ct | |
| Warwickshire | Trent Bridge | April 28 | 2 | | | 2Ct | |
| Glamorgan | Cardiff | May 5 | 108 | | | | |
| Essex | Trent Bridge | May 12 | 14 | | | | |
| Leicestershire | Leicester | May 26 | 3 | | | | |
| Somerset | Trent Bridge | June 9 | 41 | | | 2Ct | |
| Gloucs | Gloucester | June 16 | 36 | | | | |
| Middlesex | Trent Bridge | June 23 | 0 | | | | |
| Surrey | The Oval | June 30 | 79 * | | | | |
| Hampshire | Trent Bridge | July 14 | 12 | | | | |
| Sussex | Hove | July 28 | 65 | | | | |
| Worcestershire | Trent Bridge | Aug 4 | 11 | | | | |
| Kent | Trent Bridge | Aug 11 | 76 | | | | |
| Yorkshire | Scarborough | Aug 18 | 15 | | | 1Ct | |

# PLAYER RECORDS

| | | | |
|---|---|---|---|
| Derbyshire | Trent Bridge | Aug 25 | 73 * |
| Worcestershire | Trent Bridge | Sept 1 | 12 |

### NATWEST TROPHY
| | | | |
|---|---|---|---|
| Lincolnshire | Trent Bridge | June 26 | 14 |
| Gloucs | Bristol | July 11 | 38 |
| Hampshire | Southampton | July 31 | 31 |

### BENSON & HEDGES CUP
| | | | |
|---|---|---|---|
| Hampshire | Southampton | April 23 | 8 |
| Yorkshire | Trent Bridge | April 25 | 108 * |
| Glamorgan | Cardiff | May 4 | 0 |
| Min Counties | Trent Bridge | May 7 | 24 |

### OTHER ONE-DAY
For World XI
| | | | |
|---|---|---|---|
| Yorkshire | Scarborough | Sept 8 | 15 |

### BATTING AVERAGES - Including fielding
| | Matches | Inns | NO | Runs | HS | Avge | 100s | 50s | Ct | St |
|---|---|---|---|---|---|---|---|---|---|---|
| Britannic Assurance | 21 | 38 | 3 | 1739 | 166 | 49.68 | 5 | 7 | 9 | - |
| ALL FIRST-CLASS | 21 | 38 | 3 | 1739 | 166 | 49.68 | 5 | 7 | 9 | - |
| Refuge Assurance | 16 | 16 | 3 | 647 | 108 | 49.76 | 2 | 4 | 6 | - |
| NatWest Trophy | 3 | 3 | 0 | 83 | 38 | 27.66 | - | - | - | - |
| Benson & Hedges Cup | 4 | 4 | 1 | 140 | 108 * | 46.66 | 1 | - | - | - |
| Other One-Day | 1 | 1 | 0 | 15 | 15 | 15.00 | - | - | - | - |
| ALL ONE-DAY | 24 | 24 | 4 | 885 | 108 * | 44.25 | 3 | 4 | 6 | - |

### BOWLING AVERAGES
Did not bowl

## M.BROADHURST - *Yorkshire*

| Opposition | Venue | Date | Batting | Fielding | Bowling |
|---|---|---|---|---|---|
| **OTHER FIRST-CLASS** | | | | | |
| Oxford U | The Parks | June 4 | | | 3-61 |
| Sri Lanka | Headingley | July 27 | 1 | | 3-69 |
| **REFUGE ASSURANCE** | | | | | |
| Kent | Scarborough | June 16 | | | 0-27 |

### BATTING AVERAGES - Including fielding
| | Matches | Inns | NO | Runs | HS | Avge | 100s | 50s | Ct | St |
|---|---|---|---|---|---|---|---|---|---|---|
| Other First-Class | 2 | 1 | 0 | 1 | 1 | 1.00 | - | - | - | - |
| ALL FIRST-CLASS | 2 | 1 | 0 | 1 | 1 | 1.00 | - | - | - | - |
| Refuge Assurance | 1 | 0 | 0 | 0 | 0 | | - | - | - | - |
| ALL ONE-DAY | 1 | 0 | 0 | 0 | 0 | | - | - | - | - |

### BOWLING AVERAGES
| | Overs | Mdns | Runs | Wkts | Avge | Best | 5wI | 10wM |
|---|---|---|---|---|---|---|---|---|
| Other First-Class | 38 | 7 | 130 | 6 | 21.66 | 3-61 | - | - |
| ALL FIRST-CLASS | 38 | 7 | 130 | 6 | 21.66 | 3-61 | - | - |
| Refuge Assurance | 8 | 0 | 27 | 0 | | - | - | - |
| ALL ONE-DAY | 8 | 0 | 27 | 0 | | - | - | - |

## V.J.P.BROADLEY - *Nottinghamshire*

| Opposition | Venue | Date | Batting | Fielding | Bowling |
|---|---|---|---|---|---|
| **BRITANNIC ASSURANCE** | | | | | |
| Derbyshire | Derby | Sept 10 | 6 | | 0-19 & 1-92 |

### BATTING AVERAGES - Including fielding
| | Matches | Inns | NO | Runs | HS | Avge | 100s | 50s | Ct | St |
|---|---|---|---|---|---|---|---|---|---|---|
| Britannic Assurance | 1 | 1 | 0 | 6 | 6 | 6.00 | - | - | - | - |
| ALL FIRST-CLASS | 1 | 1 | 0 | 6 | 6 | 6.00 | - | - | - | - |

### BOWLING AVERAGES
| | Overs | Mdns | Runs | Wkts | Avge | Best | 5wI | 10wM |
|---|---|---|---|---|---|---|---|---|
| Britannic Assurance | 32 | 6 | 111 | 1 | 111.00 | 1-92 | - | - |
| ALL FIRST-CLASS | 32 | 6 | 111 | 1 | 111.00 | 1-92 | - | - |

## A.D.BROWN - *Surrey*

| Opposition | Venue | Date | Batting | Fielding | Bowling |
|---|---|---|---|---|---|
| **REFUGE ASSURANCE** | | | | | |
| Somerset | The Oval | April 21 | 3 | | |
| Middlesex | Lord's | April 28 | 15 | | |
| Gloucs | The Oval | May 12 | 10 | | |
| Essex | The Oval | May 26 | 45 | | |
| Worcestershire | Worcester | June 2 | | | |
| Lancashire | Old Trafford | Aug 18 | 44 | | |
| Hampshire | The Oval | Aug 25 | 16 | | |
| **BENSON & HEDGES CUP** | | | | | |
| Warwickshire | The Oval | May 7 | 37 | | |

### BATTING AVERAGES - Including fielding
| | Matches | Inns | NO | Runs | HS | Avge | 100s | 50s | Ct | St |
|---|---|---|---|---|---|---|---|---|---|---|
| Refuge Assurance | 7 | 6 | 0 | 133 | 45 | 22.16 | - | - | - | - |
| Benson & Hedges Cup | 1 | 1 | 0 | 37 | 37 | 37.00 | - | - | - | - |
| ALL ONE-DAY | 8 | 7 | 0 | 170 | 45 | 24.28 | - | - | - | - |

### BOWLING AVERAGES
Did not bowl

## A.M.BROWN - *Derbyshire*

| Opposition | Venue | Date | Batting | Fielding | Bowling |
|---|---|---|---|---|---|
| **OTHER FIRST-CLASS** | | | | | |
| Sri Lanka | Derby | Aug 2 | 3 | | |

### BATTING AVERAGES - Including fielding
| | Matches | Inns | NO | Runs | HS | Avge | 100s | 50s | Ct | St |
|---|---|---|---|---|---|---|---|---|---|---|
| Other First-Class | 1 | 1 | 0 | 3 | 3 | 3.00 | - | - | - | - |
| ALL FIRST-CLASS | 1 | 1 | 0 | 3 | 3 | 3.00 | - | - | - | - |

### BOWLING AVERAGES
Did not bowl

## D.BROWN - *Warwickshire*

| Opposition | Venue | Date | Batting | Fielding | Bowling |
|---|---|---|---|---|---|
| **REFUGE ASSURANCE** | | | | | |
| Derbyshire | Edgbaston | Aug 4 | | | 1-35 |

### BATTING AVERAGES - Including fielding
| | Matches | Inns | NO | Runs | HS | Avge | 100s | 50s | Ct | St |
|---|---|---|---|---|---|---|---|---|---|---|
| Refuge Assurance | 1 | 0 | 0 | 0 | 0 | | - | - | - | - |
| ALL ONE-DAY | 1 | 0 | 0 | 0 | 0 | | - | - | - | - |

### BOWLING AVERAGES
| | Overs | Mdns | Runs | Wkts | Avge | Best | 5wI | 10wM |
|---|---|---|---|---|---|---|---|---|
| Refuge Assurance | 6 | 0 | 35 | 1 | 35.00 | 1-35 | - | |
| ALL ONE-DAY | 6 | 0 | 35 | 1 | 35.00 | 1-35 | - | |

| B | PLAYER RECORDS |
|---|---|

## G.K.BROWN - *Minor Counties & Durham*

| Opposition | Venue | Date | Batting | Fielding | Bowling |
|---|---|---|---|---|---|
| **BENSON & HEDGES CUP** | | | | | |
| Glamorgan | Trowbridge | April 23 | 2 | 1Ct | |
| Hampshire | Trowbridge | April 25 | 82 | | |
| Yorkshire | Headingley | May 2 | 6 | | |
| Notts | Trent Bridge | May 7 | 17 | 1Ct | |

| | | | | |
|---|---|---|---|---|
| **OTHER ONE-DAY** | | | | |
| For Durham | | | | |
| Sri Lanka | Chester-le-S | July 26 | 3 | |
| Essex | Scarborough | Aug 31 | 7 | |
| Victoria | Durham U. | Sept 16 | 2 | 2-62 |

### BATTING AVERAGES - Including fielding

| | Matches | Inns | NO | Runs | HS | Avge | 100s | 50s | Ct | St |
|---|---|---|---|---|---|---|---|---|---|---|
| Benson & Hedges Cup | 4 | 4 | 0 | 107 | 82 | 26.75 | - | 1 | 2 | - |
| Other One-Day | 3 | 3 | 0 | 12 | 7 | 4.00 | - | - | - | - |
| ALL ONE-DAY | 7 | 7 | 0 | 119 | 82 | 17.00 | - | 1 | 2 | - |

### BOWLING AVERAGES

| | Overs | Mdns | Runs | Wkts | Avge | Best | 5wI | 10wM |
|---|---|---|---|---|---|---|---|---|
| Benson & Hedges Cup | | | | | | | | |
| Other One-Day | 10 | 0 | 62 | 2 | 31.00 | 2-62 | - | |
| ALL ONE-DAY | 10 | 0 | 62 | 2 | 31.00 | 2-62 | - | |

## K.R.BROWN - *Middlesex*

| Opposition | Venue | Date | Batting | | | Fielding | Bowling |
|---|---|---|---|---|---|---|---|
| **BRITANNIC ASSURANCE** | | | | | | | |
| Yorkshire | Lord's | April 27 | 12 * | | | 1Ct | |
| Sussex | Lord's | May 9 | 30 | & | 19 | 1Ct | |
| Sussex | Hove | May 22 | 28 | & | 3 | 3Ct | |
| Somerset | Taunton | May 25 | 53 | | | 2Ct | |
| Kent | Lord's | May 31 | 47 * | & | 76 * | 1Ct | |
| Gloucs | Bristol | June 4 | 3 | & | 2 | 2Ct | |
| Leicestershire | Uxbridge | June 7 | 30 | | | 3Ct | |
| Glamorgan | Cardiff | June 14 | | | 10 | | 1-17 |
| Yorkshire | Sheffield | June 21 | 0 | & | 30 | 1Ct | |
| Essex | Lord's | June 28 | | | 23 | | |
| Warwickshire | Edgbaston | July 2 | 12 | & | 47 | 4Ct | |
| Northants | Uxbridge | July 16 | 53 | | | 1Ct | |
| Lancashire | Uxbridge | July 19 | 2 | & | 16 | | |
| Notts | Lord's | July 26 | 38 | & | 42 | 2Ct | |
| Hampshire | Lord's | Aug 2 | 53 | & | 6 * | 1Ct | |
| Derbyshire | Lord's | Aug 9 | 96 | & | 25 | 3Ct | |
| Surrey | The Oval | Aug 20 | 30 | & | 8 * | 1Ct | |
| Worcestershire | Worcester | Aug 23 | 26 | & | 1 | | |
| Notts | Trent Bridge | Sept 3 | 143 * | & | 3 | 3Ct | |
| Surrey | Lord's | Sept 10 | 34 | & | 5 | 3Ct | |
| Essex | Chelmsford | Sept 17 | 4 | & | 59 | 1Ct | |

| | | | | | | | |
|---|---|---|---|---|---|---|---|
| **OTHER FIRST-CLASS** | | | | | | | |
| MCC | Lord's | April 16 | 44 | | | | |
| Cambridge U | Fenner's | May 15 | 34 | & | 28 | 1Ct | 0-16 |
| West Indies | Lord's | May 18 | 2 | & | 7 | 2Ct | |

| | | | | | |
|---|---|---|---|---|---|
| **REFUGE ASSURANCE** | | | | | |
| Gloucs | Bristol | April 21 | 8 * | | |
| Surrey | Lord's | April 28 | 81 * | 2Ct | |
| Sussex | Hove | May 12 | 4 | 1Ct | |
| Somerset | Taunton | May 26 | 18 | | |
| Kent | Southgate | June 2 | 34 | | |
| Leicestershire | Uxbridge | June 9 | 40 | | |
| Glamorgan | Cardiff | June 16 | 16 | | |
| Notts | Trent Bridge | June 23 | 47 * | | |
| Yorkshire | Lord's | July 7 | 6 | | |
| Warwickshire | Edgbaston | July 14 | 52 | | 0-2 |
| Lancashire | Lord's | July 21 | 1 | | |
| Hampshire | Lord's | Aug 4 | 14 * | | |
| Derbyshire | Lord's | Aug 11 | 2 | | |
| Essex | Colchester | Aug 18 | 33 | | |
| Worcestershire | Worcester | Aug 25 | 3 | 1Ct | |

---

### NATWEST TROPHY

| | | | | | |
|---|---|---|---|---|---|
| Ireland | Dublin | June 26 | 49 | | 0-8 |
| Somerset | Taunton | July 11 | 8 | 1Ct | |

### BENSON & HEDGES CUP

| | | | | |
|---|---|---|---|---|
| Somerset | Taunton | April 23 | 0 * | |
| Surrey | Lord's | April 25 | 25 | 1Ct |
| Essex | Chelmsford | May 2 | 20 | |
| Warwickshire | Lord's | May 4 | 12 | |

### BATTING AVERAGES - Including fielding

| | Matches | Inns | NO | Runs | HS | Avge | 100s | 50s | Ct | St |
|---|---|---|---|---|---|---|---|---|---|---|
| Britannic Assurance | 21 | 36 | 6 | 1069 | 143 * | 35.63 | 1 | 6 | 33 | - |
| Other First-Class | 3 | 5 | 0 | 115 | 44 | 23.00 | - | - | 3 | - |
| ALL FIRST-CLASS | 24 | 41 | 6 | 1184 | 143 * | 33.82 | 1 | 6 | 36 | - |
| Refuge Assurance | 15 | 15 | 4 | 359 | 81 * | 32.63 | - | 2 | 4 | - |
| NatWest Trophy | 2 | 2 | 0 | 57 | 49 | 28.50 | - | - | 1 | - |
| Benson & Hedges Cup | 4 | 4 | 1 | 57 | 25 | 19.00 | - | - | 1 | - |
| ALL ONE-DAY | 21 | 21 | 5 | 473 | 81 * | 29.56 | - | 2 | 6 | - |

### BOWLING AVERAGES

| | Overs | Mdns | Runs | Wkts | Avge | Best | 5wI | 10wM |
|---|---|---|---|---|---|---|---|---|
| Britannic Assurance | 3 | 0 | 17 | 1 | 17.00 | 1-17 | - | - |
| Other First-Class | 2.5 | 1 | 16 | 0 | - | - | - | - |
| ALL FIRST-CLASS | 5.5 | 1 | 33 | 1 | 33.00 | 1-17 | - | - |
| Refuge Assurance | 0.2 | 0 | 2 | 0 | - | - | - | - |
| NatWest Trophy | 1 | 0 | 8 | 0 | - | - | - | - |
| Benson & Hedges Cup | | | | | | | | |
| ALL ONE-DAY | 1.2 | 0 | 10 | 0 | - | - | - | - |

## S.J.BROWN - *Durham*

| Opposition | Venue | Date | Batting | Fielding | Bowling |
|---|---|---|---|---|---|
| **NATWEST TROPHY** | | | | | |
| Glamorgan | Darlington | June 26 | 7 * | | 1-73 |

| | | | | | |
|---|---|---|---|---|---|
| **OTHER ONE-DAY** | | | | | |
| Surrey | Harrogate | June 13 | 10 * | | 2-53 |
| Sri Lanka | Chester-le-S | July 26 | 0 * | | 0-50 |
| Essex | Scarborough | Aug 31 | 0 | | 3-29 |
| Victoria | Durham U. | Sept 16 | | | 0-26 |

### BATTING AVERAGES - Including fielding

| | Matches | Inns | NO | Runs | HS | Avge | 100s | 50s | Ct | St |
|---|---|---|---|---|---|---|---|---|---|---|
| NatWest Trophy | 1 | 1 | 1 | 7 | 7 * | - | - | - | - | - |
| Other One-Day | 4 | 3 | 2 | 10 | 10 * | 10.00 | - | - | - | - |
| ALL ONE-DAY | 5 | 4 | 3 | 17 | 10 * | 17.00 | - | - | - | - |

### BOWLING AVERAGES

| | Overs | Mdns | Runs | Wkts | Avge | Best | 5wI | 10wM |
|---|---|---|---|---|---|---|---|---|
| NatWest Trophy | 12 | 1 | 73 | 1 | 73.00 | 1-73 | - | |
| Other One-Day | 35 | 3 | 158 | 5 | 31.60 | 3-29 | | |
| ALL ONE-DAY | 47 | 4 | 231 | 6 | 38.50 | 3-29 | - | |

## C.K.BULLEN - *Surrey*

| Opposition | Venue | Date | Batting | Fielding | Bowling |
|---|---|---|---|---|---|
| **OTHER FIRST-CLASS** | | | | | |
| Cambridge U | Fenner's | May 18 | 37 * | 4Ct | 4-48 |
| **REFUGE ASSURANCE** | | | | | |
| Somerset | The Oval | April 21 | 2 * | | |
| Essex | The Oval | May 26 | | | 0-45 |
| Worcestershire | Worcester | June 2 | | | |
| Derbyshire | Chesterfield | June 9 | 0 * | | |
| Leicestershire | Leicester | June 16 | 16 * | 1Ct | |
| Glamorgan | The Oval | July 28 | 22 * | 1Ct | 3-38 |

# PLAYER RECORDS | B

## BENSON & HEDGES CUP

| | | | | | |
|---|---|---|---|---|---|
| Essex | The Oval | April 23 | 16 | 1Ct | 1-29 |
| Somerset | Taunton | May 4 | 0 | 1Ct | 0-29 |

### BATTING AVERAGES - Including fielding

| | Matches | Inns | NO | Runs | HS | Avge | 100s | 50s | Ct | St |
|---|---|---|---|---|---|---|---|---|---|---|
| Other First-Class | 1 | 1 | 1 | 37 | 37* | - | - | - | 4 | - |
| ALL FIRST-CLASS | 1 | 1 | 1 | 37 | 37* | - | - | - | 4 | - |
| Refuge Assurance | 6 | 4 | 4 | 40 | 22* | - | - | - | 2 | - |
| Benson & Hedges Cup | 2 | 2 | 0 | 16 | 16 | 8.00 | - | - | 2 | - |
| ALL ONE-DAY | 8 | 6 | 4 | 56 | 22* | 28.00 | - | - | 4 | - |

### BOWLING AVERAGES

| | Overs | Mdns | Runs | Wkts | Avge | Best | 5wI | 10wM |
|---|---|---|---|---|---|---|---|---|
| Other First-Class | 17 | 2 | 48 | 4 | 12.00 | 4-48 | - | - |
| ALL FIRST-CLASS | 17 | 2 | 48 | 4 | 12.00 | 4-48 | - | - |
| Refuge Assurance | 14 | 0 | 83 | 3 | 27.66 | 3-38 | - | |
| Benson & Hedges Cup | 13 | 0 | 58 | 1 | 58.00 | 1-29 | - | |
| ALL ONE-DAY | 27 | 0 | 141 | 4 | 35.25 | 3-38 | - | |

## R.A.BUNTING - Sussex

| Opposition | Venue | Date | Batting | Fielding | Bowling |
|---|---|---|---|---|---|
| **BRITANNIC ASSURANCE** | | | | | |
| Middlesex | Hove | May 22 | | 39 | 1-60 & 2-34 |
| Glamorgan | Cardiff | May 25 | 2* | | 1-66 |
| Lancashire | Old Trafford | May 31 | 51* & 14* | | 4-99 & 0-1 |
| **OTHER FIRST-CLASS** | | | | | |
| Cambridge U | Hove | June 29 | | 1Ct | |
| **REFUGE ASSURANCE** | | | | | |
| Somerset | Taunton | April 28 | 1* | | 1-27 |
| Middlesex | Hove | May 12 | | | 4-35 |
| Glamorgan | Swansea | May 26 | 2* | | 2-32 |
| Lancashire | Old Trafford | June 2 | 0 | | 1-43 |
| **BENSON & HEDGES CUP** | | | | | |
| Scotland | Hove | May 4 | 1* | | 1-34 |
| Lancashire | Old Trafford | May 7 | 2* | 1Ct | 0-41 |
| **OTHER ONE-DAY** | | | | | |
| Kent | Hove | Sept 7 | 2* | 1Ct | 1-20 |
| Gloucs | Hove | Sept 9 | 0* | | 2-20 |

### BATTING AVERAGES - Including fielding

| | Matches | Inns | NO | Runs | HS | Avge | 100s | 50s | Ct | St |
|---|---|---|---|---|---|---|---|---|---|---|
| Britannic Assurance | 3 | 4 | 3 | 106 | 51* | 106.00 | - | 1 | - | - |
| Other First-Class | 1 | 0 | 0 | 0 | 0 | - | - | - | 1 | - |
| ALL FIRST-CLASS | 4 | 4 | 3 | 106 | 51* | 106.00 | - | 1 | 1 | - |
| Refuge Assurance | 4 | 3 | 2 | 3 | 2* | 3.00 | - | - | - | - |
| Benson & Hedges Cup | 2 | 2 | 2 | 3 | 2* | - | - | - | 1 | - |
| Other One-Day | 2 | 2 | 2 | 2 | 2* | - | - | - | 1 | - |
| ALL ONE-DAY | 8 | 7 | 6 | 8 | 2* | 8.00 | - | - | 2 | - |

### BOWLING AVERAGES

| | Overs | Mdns | Runs | Wkts | Avge | Best | 5wI | 10wM |
|---|---|---|---|---|---|---|---|---|
| Britannic Assurance | 62.2 | 7 | 260 | 8 | 32.50 | 4-99 | - | - |
| Other First-Class | | | | | | | | |
| ALL FIRST-CLASS | 62.2 | 7 | 260 | 8 | 32.50 | 4-99 | - | |
| Refuge Assurance | 24.3 | 0 | 137 | 8 | 17.12 | 4-35 | - | |
| Benson & Hedges Cup | 17 | 1 | 75 | 1 | 75.00 | 1-34 | - | |
| Other One-Day | 12 | 0 | 40 | 3 | 13.33 | 2-20 | - | |
| ALL ONE-DAY | 53.3 | 1 | 252 | 12 | 21.00 | 4-35 | - | |

## P.BURN - Durham

| Opposition | Venue | Date | Batting | Fielding | Bowling |
|---|---|---|---|---|---|
| **NATWEST TROPHY** | | | | | |
| Glamorgan | Darlington | June 26 | 2 | | |
| **OTHER ONE-DAY** | | | | | |
| Sri Lanka | Chester-le-S | July 26 | 10 | | |

### BATTING AVERAGES - Including fielding

| | Matches | Inns | NO | Runs | HS | Avge | 100s | 50s | Ct | St |
|---|---|---|---|---|---|---|---|---|---|---|
| NatWest Trophy | 1 | 1 | 0 | 2 | 2 | 2.00 | - | - | - | - |
| Other One-Day | 1 | 1 | 0 | 10 | 10 | 10.00 | - | - | - | - |
| ALL ONE-DAY | 2 | 2 | 0 | 12 | 10 | 6.00 | - | - | - | - |

### BOWLING AVERAGES
Did not bowl

## M.BURNS - Warwickshire

| Opposition | Venue | Date | Batting | Fielding | Bowling |
|---|---|---|---|---|---|
| **BENSON & HEDGES CUP** | | | | | |
| Essex | Edgbaston | April 25 | 3 | | |
| **OTHER ONE-DAY** | | | | | |
| Surrey | Harrogate | June 12 | 27 | 1Ct | |

### BATTING AVERAGES - Including fielding

| | Matches | Inns | NO | Runs | HS | Avge | 100s | 50s | Ct | St |
|---|---|---|---|---|---|---|---|---|---|---|
| Benson & Hedges Cup | 1 | 1 | 0 | 3 | 3 | 3.00 | - | - | - | - |
| Other One-Day | 1 | 1 | 0 | 27 | 27 | 27.00 | - | - | 1 | - |
| ALL ONE-DAY | 2 | 2 | 0 | 30 | 27 | 15.00 | - | - | 1 | - |

### BOWLING AVERAGES
Did not bowl

## N.D.BURNS - Somerset

| Opposition | Venue | Date | Batting | Fielding | Bowling |
|---|---|---|---|---|---|
| **BRITANNIC ASSURANCE** | | | | | |
| Sussex | Taunton | April 27 | 7 | | 0Ct,1St |
| Glamorgan | Taunton | May 9 | 6 & 0 | | |
| Derbyshire | Derby | May 22 | 0 & 7* | | 2Ct |
| Middlesex | Taunton | May 25 | 6 & 0 | | 1Ct |
| Glamorgan | Swansea | June 4 | 62* | | |
| Warwickshire | Edgbaston | June 7 | | | 3Ct |
| Hampshire | Bath | June 18 | | 49 | 3Ct |
| Gloucs | Bath | June 21 | 39 | | 2Ct |
| Surrey | The Oval | June 28 | 39 | | 1Ct |
| Lancashire | Taunton | July 2 | 27* & | 25 | 2Ct |
| Sussex | Hove | July 16 | 6 | | 2Ct |
| Essex | Southend | July 19 | 13* & | 4 | |
| Northants | Northampton | July 23 | | 11 | 1Ct,1St |
| Kent | Taunton | July 26 | 6 & | 27 | 2Ct |
| Leicestershire | Weston | Aug 2 | 29* | | 0Ct,1St |
| Worcestershire | Weston | Aug 6 | 96 & | 0 | 1Ct,4St |
| Notts | Trent Bridge | Aug 16 | 108 & | 19* | |
| Yorkshire | Taunton | Aug 23 | 0 | | 2Ct |
| Hampshire | Southampton | Aug 28 | 61* | | 3Ct,1St |
| Worcestershire | Worcester | Sept 3 | 11 & | 88 | 5Ct |
| Gloucs | Bristol | Sept 10 | 37 & | 6* | 4Ct |
| Warwickshire | Taunton | Sept 17 | 5 & | 0 | 1Ct |
| **OTHER FIRST-CLASS** | | | | | |
| West Indies | Taunton | May 29 | 0 & 14 | | |
| **REFUGE ASSURANCE** | | | | | |
| Surrey | The Oval | April 21 | 5 | | 2Ct |
| Sussex | Taunton | April 28 | 6 | | |
| Glamorgan | Taunton | May 12 | 52* | | 1Ct |
| Hampshire | Bournemouth | May 19 | | | 2Ct |

# PLAYER RECORDS

| | | | | |
|---|---|---|---|---|
| Middlesex | Taunton | May 26 | 8 | 1Ct |
| Warwickshire | Edgbaston | June 2 | 2 | |
| Notts | Trent Bridge | June 9 | 9 | 1Ct |
| Derbyshire | Derby | June 16 | 32 | 1Ct,1St |
| Northants | Luton | June 30 | 24 | |
| Lancashire | Taunton | July 5 | 6 | |
| Essex | Southend | July 21 | 10 * | 1Ct |
| Kent | Taunton | July 28 | 5 | 0Ct,4St |
| Leicestershire | Weston | Aug 4 | 51 * | 0Ct,1St |
| Worcestershire | Worcester | Aug 18 | | 2Ct |
| Yorkshire | Taunton | Aug 25 | 25 * | 1Ct |

**NATWEST TROPHY**

| | | | | |
|---|---|---|---|---|
| Bucks | Bath | June 26 | 5 * | 1Ct |
| Middlesex | Taunton | July 11 | 5 | |
| Warwickshire | Edgbaston | July 31 | 1 | 1Ct |

**BENSON & HEDGES CUP**

| | | | | |
|---|---|---|---|---|
| Middlesex | Taunton | April 23 | 37 | |
| Warwickshire | Edgbaston | May 2 | 21 | 0Ct,1St |
| Surrey | Taunton | May 4 | 43 * | |
| Essex | Chelmsford | May 7 | 9 | 1Ct |

**OTHER ONE-DAY**

| | | | | |
|---|---|---|---|---|
| Gloucs | Hove | Sept 8 | 29 | 0Ct,1St |

**BATTING AVERAGES - Including fielding**

| | Matches | Inns | NO | Runs | HS | Avge | 100s | 50s | Ct | St |
|---|---|---|---|---|---|---|---|---|---|---|
| Britannic Assurance | 22 | 32 | 8 | 794 | 108 | 33.08 | 1 | 4 | 35 | 8 |
| Other First-Class | 1 | 2 | 0 | 14 | 14 | 7.00 | - | - | - | - |
| ALL FIRST-CLASS | 23 | 34 | 8 | 808 | 108 | 31.07 | 1 | 4 | 35 | 8 |
| Refuge Assurance | 15 | 13 | 4 | 235 | 52 * | 26.11 | - | 2 | 12 | 6 |
| NatWest Trophy | 3 | 3 | 1 | 11 | 5 * | 5.50 | - | - | 2 | - |
| Benson & Hedges Cup | 4 | 4 | 1 | 110 | 43 * | 36.66 | - | - | 1 | 1 |
| Other One-Day | 1 | 1 | 0 | 29 | 29 | 29.00 | - | - | - | 1 |
| ALL ONE-DAY | 23 | 21 | 6 | 385 | 52 * | 25.66 | - | 2 | 15 | 8 |

**BOWLING AVERAGES**
Did not bowl

## S.BURROW - *Buckinghamshire*

| Opposition | Venue | Date | Batting | Fielding | Bowling |
|---|---|---|---|---|---|
| **NATWEST TROPHY** | | | | | |
| Somerset | Bath | June 26 | 12 | | 1-18 |

**BATTING AVERAGES - Including fielding**

| | Matches | Inns | NO | Runs | HS | Avge | 100s | 50s | Ct | St |
|---|---|---|---|---|---|---|---|---|---|---|
| NatWest Trophy | 1 | 1 | 0 | 12 | 12 | 12.00 | - | - | - | - |
| ALL ONE-DAY | 1 | 1 | 0 | 12 | 12 | 12.00 | - | - | - | - |

**BOWLING AVERAGES**

| | Overs | Mdns | Runs | Wkts | Avge | Best | 5wI | 10wM |
|---|---|---|---|---|---|---|---|---|
| NatWest Trophy | 9 | 2 | 18 | 1 | 18.00 | 1-18 | - | |
| ALL ONE-DAY | 9 | 2 | 18 | 1 | 18.00 | 1-18 | - | |

## D.J.BUSH - *Cambridge University*

| Opposition | Venue | Date | Batting | Fielding | Bowling |
|---|---|---|---|---|---|
| **OTHER FIRST-CLASS** | | | | | |
| Lancashire | Fenner's | April 13 | 5 | 1Ct | 1-78 & 1-45 |
| Essex | Fenner's | April 19 | 0 & 3 | | 0-42 & 1-66 |
| Derbyshire | Fenner's | May 9 | 13 | 1Ct | 0-53 & 0-44 |
| Middlesex | Fenner's | May 15 | | | 1-52 |
| Surrey | Fenner's | May 18 | 11 & 2 * | | 0-38 & 1-14 |
| Leicestershire | Fenner's | May 22 | 24 * | 1Ct | 1-49 |
| Sussex | Hove | June 29 | | | 0-59 |

**BATTING AVERAGES - Including fielding**

| | Matches | Inns | NO | Runs | HS | Avge | 100s | 50s | Ct | St |
|---|---|---|---|---|---|---|---|---|---|---|
| Other First-Class | 7 | 7 | 2 | 58 | 24 * | 11.60 | - | - | 3 | - |
| ALL FIRST-CLASS | 7 | 7 | 2 | 58 | 24 * | 11.60 | - | - | 3 | - |

**BOWLING AVERAGES**

| | Overs | Mdns | Runs | Wkts | Avge | Best | 5wI | 10wM |
|---|---|---|---|---|---|---|---|---|
| Other First-Class | 131.3 | 22 | 540 | 6 | 90.00 | 1-14 | - | - |
| ALL FIRST-CLASS | 131.3 | 22 | 540 | 6 | 90.00 | 1-14 | - | - |

## A.R.BUTCHER - *Glamorgan*

| Opposition | Venue | Date | Batting | | | Fielding | Bowling |
|---|---|---|---|---|---|---|---|
| **BRITANNIC ASSURANCE** | | | | | | | |
| Somerset | Taunton | May 9 | 12 | & | 65 | 1Ct | |
| Warwickshire | Swansea | May 16 | 8 | & | 12 | 1Ct | |
| Northants | Cardiff | May 22 | 2 | & | 96 | 1Ct | 0-0 |
| Sussex | Cardiff | May 25 | 52 | | | | 0-1 |
| Worcestershire | Worcester | May 31 | 17 | & | 5 | 1Ct | |
| Somerset | Swansea | June 4 | | | 102 | 1Ct | |
| Derbyshire | Chesterfield | June 7 | 32 | & | 71 | | |
| Middlesex | Cardiff | June 14 | 31 | & | 57 | 1Ct | |
| Leicestershire | Neath | June 21 | 15 | | | | |
| Lancashire | Liverpool | June 28 | 129 | & | 104 | | |
| Notts | Cardiff | July 2 | 37 | & | 1 | | |
| Kent | Maidstone | July 5 | 12 | & | 13 | 1Ct | |
| Gloucs | Cheltenham | July 19 | 0 | & | 12 | | |
| Essex | Cardiff | July 23 | | | 61 | | |
| Surrey | The Oval | July 26 | 15 | & | 68 | | |
| Hampshire | Swansea | Aug 9 | | | 1 | 1Ct | |
| Yorkshire | Headingley | Aug 16 | 79 | & | 7 * | 2Ct | |
| Warwickshire | Edgbaston | Aug 20 | 61 | & | 1 | 1Ct | |
| Gloucs | Abergavenny | Aug 28 | 147 | & | 20 | 2Ct | |
| Worcestershire | Cardiff | Sept 10 | 61 | & | 93 | | |
| Hampshire | Southampton | Sept 17 | 1 | & | 58 | | |

**OTHER FIRST-CLASS**

| | | | | | | | |
|---|---|---|---|---|---|---|---|
| Oxford U | The Parks | April 17 | 25 * | | | | |
| West Indies | Swansea | July 16 | 94 | | | | |

**REFUGE ASSURANCE**

| | | | | | |
|---|---|---|---|---|---|
| Northants | Cardiff | April 21 | 77 | 1Ct | |
| Notts | Cardiff | May 5 | 77 | | 0-32 |
| Warwickshire | Swansea | May 19 | 0 | | |
| Sussex | Swansea | May 26 | 9 | | |
| Essex | Pontypridd | June 2 | 14 | | |
| Kent | Maidstone | July 7 | 30 | | |
| Worcestershire | Worcester | July 21 | 51 * | | 0-4 |
| Surrey | The Oval | July 28 | 39 | 1Ct | |
| Gloucs | Swansea | Aug 4 | 20 | | |
| Hampshire | Ebbw Vale | Aug 11 | 6 | 1Ct | |
| Derbyshire | Checkley | Aug 18 | 6 | | |

**NATWEST TROPHY**

| | | | | | |
|---|---|---|---|---|---|
| Durham | Darlington | June 26 | 17 | | |
| Worcestershire | Worcester | July 11 | 0 | 2Ct | |
| Northants | Northampton | July 31 | 70 | | |

**BENSON & HEDGES CUP**

| | | | | | |
|---|---|---|---|---|---|
| Min Counties | Trowbridge | April 23 | 25 | 1Ct | |
| Hampshire | Southampton | May 2 | 70 | | |
| Notts | Cardiff | May 4 | 57 | | 0-16 |
| Yorkshire | Cardiff | May 7 | 127 | | |

**BATTING AVERAGES - Including fielding**

| | Matches | Inns | NO | Runs | HS | Avge | 100s | 50s | Ct | St |
|---|---|---|---|---|---|---|---|---|---|---|
| Britannic Assurance | 21 | 37 | 1 | 1558 | 147 | 43.27 | 4 | 12 | 13 | - |
| Other First-Class | 2 | 2 | 1 | 119 | 94 | 119.00 | - | 1 | - | - |
| ALL FIRST-CLASS | 23 | 39 | 2 | 1677 | 147 | 45.32 | 4 | 13 | 13 | - |
| Refuge Assurance | 11 | 11 | 1 | 329 | 77 | 32.90 | - | 3 | 3 | - |
| NatWest Trophy | 3 | 3 | 0 | 87 | 70 | 29.00 | - | 1 | 2 | - |
| Benson & Hedges Cup | 4 | 4 | 0 | 279 | 127 | 69.75 | 1 | 2 | 1 | - |
| ALL ONE-DAY | 18 | 18 | 1 | 695 | 127 | 40.88 | 1 | 6 | 6 | - |

**BOWLING AVERAGES**

| | Overs | Mdns | Runs | Wkts | Avge | Best | 5wI | 10wM |
|---|---|---|---|---|---|---|---|---|
| Britannic Assurance | 2 | 1 | 1 | 0 | - | - | - | - |
| Other First-Class | | | | | | | | |

# PLAYER RECORDS

| | | | | | | | |
|---|---|---|---|---|---|---|---|
| ALL FIRST-CLASS | 2 | 1 | 1 | 0 | - | - | - | - |
| Refuge Assurance | 5.1 | 0 | 36 | 0 | - | - | - |
| NatWest Trophy | | | | | | | |
| Benson & Hedges Cup | 3 | 0 | 16 | 0 | - | - | - |
| ALL ONE-DAY | 8.1 | 0 | 52 | 0 | - | - | - |

## M.A.BUTCHER - *Surrey*

| Opposition | Venue | Date | Batting | Fielding | Bowling |
|---|---|---|---|---|---|
| **REFUGE ASSURANCE** | | | | | |
| Glamorgan | The Oval | July 28 | 48* | | 0-16 |

**BATTING AVERAGES - Including fielding**

| | Matches | Inns | NO | Runs | HS | Avge | 100s | 50s | Ct | St |
|---|---|---|---|---|---|---|---|---|---|---|
| Refuge Assurance | 1 | 1 | 1 | 48 | 48* | - | - | - | - | - |
| ALL ONE-DAY | 1 | 1 | 1 | 48 | 48* | - | - | - | - | - |

**BOWLING AVERAGES**

| | Overs | Mdns | Runs | Wkts | Avge | Best | 5wI | 10wM |
|---|---|---|---|---|---|---|---|---|
| Refuge Assurance | 3 | 0 | 16 | 0 | - | - | - | - |
| ALL ONE-DAY | 3 | 0 | 16 | 0 | - | - | - | - |

## R.O.BUTCHER - *Duchess of Norfolk's XI*

| Opposition | Venue | Date | Batting | Fielding | Bowling |
|---|---|---|---|---|---|
| **OTHER ONE-DAY** | | | | | |
| West Indies | Arundel | May 12 | 0 | 1Ct | |

**BATTING AVERAGES - Including fielding**

| | Matches | Inns | NO | Runs | HS | Avge | 100s | 50s | Ct | St |
|---|---|---|---|---|---|---|---|---|---|---|
| Other One-Day | 1 | 1 | 0 | 0 | 0 | 0.00 | - | - | 1 | - |
| ALL ONE-DAY | 1 | 1 | 0 | 0 | 0 | 0.00 | - | - | 1 | - |

**BOWLING AVERAGES**
Did not bowl

## K.A.BUTLER - *Essex*

| Opposition | Venue | Date | Batting | Fielding | Bowling |
|---|---|---|---|---|---|
| **REFUGE ASSURANCE** | | | | | |
| Surrey | The Oval | May 26 | 1 | 1Ct | |
| Warwickshire | Chelmsford | July 7 | | | |

**BATTING AVERAGES - Including fielding**

| | Matches | Inns | NO | Runs | HS | Avge | 100s | 50s | Ct | St |
|---|---|---|---|---|---|---|---|---|---|---|
| Refuge Assurance | 2 | 1 | 0 | 1 | 1 | 1.00 | - | - | 1 | - |
| ALL ONE-DAY | 2 | 1 | 0 | 1 | 1 | 1.00 | - | - | 1 | - |

**BOWLING AVERAGES**
Did not bowl

## D.BYAS - *Yorkshire*

| Opposition | Venue | Date | Batting | | | Fielding | Bowling |
|---|---|---|---|---|---|---|---|
| **BRITANNIC ASSURANCE** | | | | | | | |
| Middlesex | Lord's | April 27 | 32 | | | | |
| Warwickshire | Headingley | May 9 | 44 | & | 7 | 2Ct | |
| Notts | Headingley | May 16 | 4 | & | 23 | 1Ct | |
| Gloucs | Sheffield | May 22 | 87 | | | 1Ct | |
| Northants | Headingley | May 25 | 5 | & | 40* | | |
| Warwickshire | Edgbaston | May 31 | 33 | & | 49 | 3Ct | 0-7 |
| Kent | Harrogate | June 14 | 36 | | | | |
| Middlesex | Sheffield | June 21 | 49 | & | 2 | 1Ct | |
| Worcestershire | Headingley | July 2 | 37 | | | 2Ct | |
| Hampshire | Southampton | July 5 | 27 | | | | |
| Derbyshire | Scarborough | July 16 | 135 | | | 2Ct | |
| Surrey | Guildford | July 19 | 33 | & | 0 | 1Ct | |
| Notts | Worksop | July 23 | 153 | | | | |
| Lancashire | Old Trafford | Aug 2 | 0 | & | 26 | 1Ct | |
| Leicestershire | Leicester | Aug 6 | 32* | & | 122* | | |
| Sussex | Midd'brough | Aug 9 | 8 | & | 46 | | |
| Glamorgan | Headingley | Aug 16 | 32 | & | 20 | 1Ct | |
| Essex | Colchester | Aug 20 | 25 | & | 7 | 1Ct | |
| Somerset | Taunton | Aug 23 | 79 | & | 27* | 1Ct | |
| Northants | Northampton | Aug 28 | 8 | & | 38 | | |
| Lancashire | Scarborough | Sept 3 | 120 | & | 21 | 1Ct | |
| Derbyshire | Chesterfield | Sept 17 | 6 | & | 0 | 2Ct | |
| **OTHER FIRST-CLASS** | | | | | | | |
| Oxford U | The Parks | June 4 | 101 | & | 0* | 1Ct | 0-7 |
| Sri Lanka | Headingley | July 27 | 12 | & | 31* | | |
| **REFUGE ASSURANCE** | | | | | | | |
| Hampshire | Southampton | April 21 | 2 | | | | |
| Essex | Chelmsford | April 28 | 5 | | | | |
| Warwickshire | Headingley | May 12 | 23 | | | | |
| Leicestershire | Leicester | May 19 | 74* | | | 1Ct | |
| Northants | Headingley | May 26 | 27 | | | | |
| Derbyshire | Chesterfield | June 2 | 14 | | | | |
| Kent | Scarborough | June 16 | 45 | | | | |
| Worcestershire | Sheffield | June 23 | 54 | | | | |
| Glamorgan | Headingley | June 30 | 14 | | | | |
| Middlesex | Lord's | July 7 | 6* | | | | |
| Gloucs | Scarborough | July 14 | 19 | | | 1Ct | |
| Surrey | The Oval | July 21 | 28* | | | | |
| Lancashire | Old Trafford | Aug 4 | 31* | | | | |
| Sussex | Midd'brough | Aug 11 | 16 | | | | |
| Notts | Scarborough | Aug 18 | 9 | | | 1Ct | |
| Somerset | Taunton | Aug 25 | 2 | | | | |
| **NATWEST TROPHY** | | | | | | | |
| Warwickshire | Edgbaston | June 26 | 2 | | | | |
| **BENSON & HEDGES CUP** | | | | | | | |
| Notts | Trent Bridge | April 25 | 47 | | | | |
| Min Counties | Headingley | May 2 | 3 | | | | |
| Hampshire | Headingley | May 4 | 92 | | | | |
| Glamorgan | Cardiff | May 7 | 7 | | | | |
| Warwickshire | Headingley | May 29 | 58 | | | | |
| Lancashire | Old Trafford | June 16 | 0 | | | | |
| **OTHER ONE-DAY** | | | | | | | |
| Derbyshire | Scarborough | Sept 1 | 35 | | | | |
| Essex | Scarborough | Sept 2 | 64 | | | | |
| Yorkshiremen | Scarborough | Sept 7 | 23 | | | | |
| World XI | Scarborough | Sept 8 | 59 | | | | |

**BATTING AVERAGES - Including fielding**

| | Matches | Inns | NO | Runs | HS | Avge | 100s | 50s | Ct | St |
|---|---|---|---|---|---|---|---|---|---|---|
| Britannic Assurance | 22 | 37 | 4 | 1413 | 153 | 42.81 | 4 | 2 | 20 | - |
| Other First-Class | 2 | 4 | 2 | 144 | 101 | 72.00 | 1 | - | 1 | - |
| ALL FIRST-CLASS | 24 | 41 | 6 | 1557 | 153 | 44.48 | 5 | 2 | 21 | - |
| Refuge Assurance | 16 | 16 | 4 | 369 | 74* | 30.75 | - | 2 | 3 | - |
| NatWest Trophy | 1 | 1 | 0 | 2 | 2 | 2.00 | - | - | - | - |
| Benson & Hedges Cup | 6 | 6 | 0 | 207 | 92 | 34.50 | - | 2 | - | - |
| Other One-Day | 4 | 4 | 0 | 181 | 64 | 45.25 | - | 2 | - | - |
| ALL ONE-DAY | 27 | 27 | 4 | 759 | 92 | 33.00 | - | 6 | 3 | - |

**BOWLING AVERAGES**

| | Overs | Mdns | Runs | Wkts | Avge | Best | 5wI | 10wM |
|---|---|---|---|---|---|---|---|---|
| Britannic Assurance | 2 | 0 | 7 | 0 | - | - | - | - |
| Other First-Class | 7 | 2 | 7 | 0 | - | - | - | - |
| ALL FIRST-CLASS | 9 | 2 | 14 | 0 | - | - | - | - |
| Refuge Assurance | | | | | | | | |
| NatWest Trophy | | | | | | | | |
| Benson & Hedges Cup | | | | | | | | |
| Other One-Day | | | | | | | | |
| ALL ONE-DAY | | | | | | | | |

## A.B.BYRAM - *Shropshire*

| Opposition | Venue | Date | Batting | Fielding | Bowling |
|---|---|---|---|---|---|
| **NATWEST TROPHY** | | | | | |
| Leicestershire | Leicester | June 26 | 0 | | 1-25 |

**BATTING AVERAGES - Including fielding**

| | Matches | Inns | NO | Runs | HS | Avge | 100s | 50s | Ct | St |
|---|---|---|---|---|---|---|---|---|---|---|
| NatWest Trophy | 1 | 1 | 0 | 0 | 0 | 0.00 | - | - | - | - |
| ALL ONE-DAY | 1 | 1 | 0 | 0 | 0 | 0.00 | - | - | - | - |

**BOWLING AVERAGES**

| | Overs | Mdns | Runs | Wkts | Avge | Best | 5wI | 10wM |
|---|---|---|---|---|---|---|---|---|
| NatWest Trophy | 6 | 0 | 25 | 1 | 25.00 | 1-25 | - | |
| ALL ONE-DAY | 6 | 0 | 25 | 1 | 25.00 | 1-25 | - | |

# PLAYER RECORDS     C

## A.R.CADDICK - *Somerset*

| Opposition | Venue | Date | Batting | Fielding | Bowling |
|---|---|---|---|---|---|
| **OTHER FIRST-CLASS** | | | | | |
| West Indies | Taunton | May 29 | 0 | | 2-85 & 1-68 |
| Sri Lanka | Taunton | Aug 10 | | 1Ct | 2-40 & 0-58 |

**BATTING AVERAGES - Including fielding**

| | Matches | Inns | NO | Runs | HS | Avge | 100s | 50s | Ct | St |
|---|---|---|---|---|---|---|---|---|---|---|
| Other First-Class | 2 | 1 | 0 | 0 | 0 | 0.00 | - | - | 1 | - |
| ALL FIRST-CLASS | 2 | 1 | 0 | 0 | 0 | 0.00 | - | - | 1 | - |

**BOWLING AVERAGES**

| | Overs | Mdns | Runs | Wkts | Avge | Best | 5wI | 10wM |
|---|---|---|---|---|---|---|---|---|
| Other First-Class | 64.5 | 13 | 251 | 5 | 50.20 | 2-40 | - | - |
| ALL FIRST-CLASS | 64.5 | 13 | 251 | 5 | 50.20 | 2-40 | - | - |

## A.M.CADE - *Cambridgeshire*

| Opposition | Venue | Date | Batting | Fielding | Bowling |
|---|---|---|---|---|---|
| **NATWEST TROPHY** | | | | | |
| Kent | Canterbury | June 26 | 0 | | |

**BATTING AVERAGES - Including fielding**

| | Matches | Inns | NO | Runs | HS | Avge | 100s | 50s | Ct | St |
|---|---|---|---|---|---|---|---|---|---|---|
| NatWest Trophy | 1 | 1 | 0 | 0 | 0 | 0.00 | - | - | - | - |
| ALL ONE-DAY | 1 | 1 | 0 | 0 | 0 | 0.00 | - | - | - | - |

**BOWLING AVERAGES**
Did not bowl

## G.S.CALWAY - *Dorset*

| Opposition | Venue | Date | Batting | Fielding | Bowling |
|---|---|---|---|---|---|
| **NATWEST TROPHY** | | | | | |
| Lancashire | Bournemouth | June 26 | 12 | 1Ct | 1-34 |

**BATTING AVERAGES - Including fielding**

| | Matches | Inns | NO | Runs | HS | Avge | 100s | 50s | Ct | St |
|---|---|---|---|---|---|---|---|---|---|---|
| NatWest Trophy | 1 | 1 | 0 | 12 | 12 | 12.00 | - | - | 1 | - |
| ALL ONE-DAY | 1 | 1 | 0 | 12 | 12 | 12.00 | - | - | 1 | - |

**BOWLING AVERAGES**

| | Overs | Mdns | Runs | Wkts | Avge | Best | 5wI | 10wM |
|---|---|---|---|---|---|---|---|---|
| NatWest Trophy | 10 | 3 | 34 | 1 | 34.00 | 1-34 | - | |
| ALL ONE-DAY | 10 | 3 | 34 | 1 | 34.00 | 1-34 | - | |

## M.J.CANN - *Glamorgan*

| Opposition | Venue | Date | Batting | Fielding | Bowling |
|---|---|---|---|---|---|
| **BRITANNIC ASSURANCE** | | | | | |
| Somerset | Swansea | June 4 | 29* | 1Ct | 0-37 |
| **REFUGE ASSURANCE** | | | | | |
| Lancashire | Old Trafford | June 9 | 2 | | |
| Surrey | The Oval | July 28 | 2 | | |

**BATTING AVERAGES - Including fielding**

| | Matches | Inns | NO | Runs | HS | Avge | 100s | 50s | Ct | St |
|---|---|---|---|---|---|---|---|---|---|---|
| Britannic Assurance | 1 | 1 | 1 | 29 | 29* | - | - | - | 1 | - |
| ALL FIRST-CLASS | 1 | 1 | 1 | 29 | 29* | - | - | - | 1 | - |

| Refuge Assurance | 2 | 2 | 0 | 4 | 2 | 2.00 | - | - | - | - |
| ALL ONE-DAY | 2 | 2 | 0 | 4 | 2 | 2.00 | - | - | - | - |

**BOWLING AVERAGES**

| | Overs | Mdns | Runs | Wkts | Avge | Best | 5wI | 10wM |
|---|---|---|---|---|---|---|---|---|
| Britannic Assurance | 8 | 0 | 37 | 0 | - | - | - | - |
| ALL FIRST-CLASS | 8 | 0 | 37 | 0 | - | - | - | - |

Refuge Assurance

ALL ONE-DAY

## D.J.CAPEL - *Northamptonshire*

| Opposition | Venue | Date | Batting | Fielding | Bowling |
|---|---|---|---|---|---|
| **BRITANNIC ASSURANCE** | | | | | |
| Derbyshire | Derby | April 27 | 16 | | |
| Essex | Northampton | May 9 | 22 & 0 | | 2-73 & 0-19 |
| Leicestershire | Northampton | May 16 | 58* & 10 | 1Ct | 0-26 & 1-28 |
| Glamorgan | Cardiff | May 22 | 41 & 56 | 1Ct | 0-27 & 0-21 |
| Yorkshire | Headingley | May 25 | 69* & 9 | | 3-45 & 1-32 |
| Derbyshire | Northampton | May 31 | 70 & 13 | | 1-30 & 1-47 |
| Worcestershire | Northampton | June 4 | 16 & 1 | | 0-17 |
| Hampshire | Northampton | June 21 | 71 | | |
| Gloucs | Luton | June 28 | 5 & 5 | 1Ct | 2-34 |
| Kent | Maidstone | July 2 | 56 | | |
| Leicestershire | Leicester | July 5 | 7 | 2Ct | 0-21 |
| Middlesex | Uxbridge | July 16 | 36 | | 0-19 |
| Notts | Well'borough | July 19 | 0 & 0 | | 1-34 |
| Somerset | Northampton | July 23 | 15 & 0 | | 0-41 |
| Warwickshire | Northampton | Aug 9 | 0 | | 3-109 & 1-21 |
| Essex | Colchester | Aug 16 | 0 & 0 | 1Ct | 3-40 |
| Surrey | Northampton | Aug 23 | 1 | | 0-29 & 1-26 |
| Yorkshire | Northampton | Aug 28 | 66 | | 2-99 & 0-46 |
| Gloucs | Bristol | Sept 3 | 1 & 43 | 1Ct | 4-83 & 1-20 |
| Warwickshire | Edgbaston | Sept 10 | 2 & 3 | 1Ct | 0-49 & 1-63 |
| **OTHER FIRST-CLASS** | | | | | |
| Cambridge U | Fenner's | April 16 | 100 | | 0-5 |
| West Indies | Northampton | June 15 | | | 0-23 |
| **REFUGE ASSURANCE** | | | | | |
| Glamorgan | Cardiff | April 21 | 20 | | |
| Lancashire | Old Trafford | April 28 | 53 | | 2-43 |
| Leicestershire | Northampton | May 12 | 77* | | 1-31 |
| Worcestershire | Northampton | May 19 | 12 | | 0-46 |
| Yorkshire | Headingley | May 26 | 30 | | 2-29 |
| Hampshire | Northampton | June 2 | 30* | 1Ct | |
| Gloucs | Moreton | June 9 | | | |
| Somerset | Luton | June 30 | 1 | | 1-26 |
| Surrey | Tring | July 7 | 16 | 1Ct | 2-29 |
| Notts | Well'borough | July 21 | 28 | | 1-23 |
| Derbyshire | Derby | July 28 | 10 | | 1-33 |
| Sussex | Eastbourne | Aug 4 | 22 | | 0-23 |
| Essex | Northampton | Aug 11 | 23 | | 3-30 |
| Kent | Canterbury | Aug 18 | 3 | | 2-24 |
| Warwickshire | Northampton | Aug 25 | 14* | 1Ct | 1-40 |
| Lancashire | Old Trafford | Sept 1 | 21 | | 1-23 |
| **NATWEST TROPHY** | | | | | |
| Staffordshire | Stone | June 26 | 1 | | |
| Leicestershire | Northampton | July 11 | | | 0-24 |
| Glamorgan | Northampton | July 31 | 0 | | |
| Surrey | The Oval | Aug 14 | 6 | | 3-26 |
| **BENSON & HEDGES CUP** | | | | | |
| Derbyshire | Derby | April 23 | 3 | | 4-37 |
| Gloucs | Bristol | May 2 | 42 | | 0-29 |
| Combined U | Northampton | May 4 | 11 | | 0-20 |
| Worcestershire | Northampton | May 7 | 27 | | 1-9 |
| Lancashire | Old Trafford | May 29 | 19 | | 0-52 |

**BATTING AVERAGES - Including fielding**

| | Matches | Inns | NO | Runs | HS | Avge | 100s | 50s | Ct | St |
|---|---|---|---|---|---|---|---|---|---|---|
| Britannic Assurance | 20 | 32 | 2 | 692 | 71 | 23.06 | - | 7 | 9 | - |
| Other First-Class | 2 | 1 | 0 | 100 | 100 | 100.00 | 1 | - | - | - |
| ALL FIRST-CLASS | 22 | 33 | 2 | 792 | 100 | 25.54 | 1 | 7 | 9 | - |

# C

# PLAYER RECORDS

| | | | | | | | | | |
|---|---|---|---|---|---|---|---|---|---|
| Refuge Assurance | 16 | 15 | 3 | 360 | 77* | 30.00 | - | 2 | 3 | - |
| NatWest Trophy | 4 | 3 | 0 | 7 | 6 | 2.33 | - | - | - | - |
| Benson & Hedges Cup | 5 | 5 | 0 | 102 | 42 | 20.40 | - | - | - | - |
| | | | | | | | | | |
| ALL ONE-DAY | 25 | 23 | 3 | 469 | 77* | 23.45 | - | 2 | 3 | - |

**BOWLING AVERAGES**

| | Overs | Mdns | Runs | Wkts | Avge | Best | 5wI | 10wM |
|---|---|---|---|---|---|---|---|---|
| Britannic Assurance | 373.1 | 82 | 1099 | 28 | 39.25 | 4-83 | - | - |
| Other First-Class | 10 | 1 | 28 | 0 | - | - | - | - |
| | | | | | | | | |
| ALL FIRST-CLASS | 383.1 | 83 | 1127 | 28 | 40.25 | 4-83 | - | - |
| | | | | | | | | |
| Refuge Assurance | 80 | 1 | 400 | 17 | 23.52 | 3-30 | - | |
| NatWest Trophy | 14 | 0 | 50 | 3 | 16.66 | 3-26 | - | |
| Benson & Hedges Cup | 40.4 | 3 | 147 | 5 | 29.40 | 4-37 | - | |
| | | | | | | | | |
| ALL ONE-DAY | 134.4 | 4 | 597 | 25 | 23.88 | 4-37 | - | |

## J.D.CARR - *Hertfordshire*

| Opposition | Venue | Date | Batting | Fielding | Bowling |
|---|---|---|---|---|---|
| **NATWEST TROPHY** | | | | | |
| Warwickshire | Edgbaston | July 11 | 14 | | 0-13 |

**BATTING AVERAGES - Including fielding**

| | Matches | Inns | NO | Runs | HS | Avge | 100s | 50s | Ct | St |
|---|---|---|---|---|---|---|---|---|---|---|
| NatWest Trophy | 1 | 1 | 0 | 14 | 14 | 14.00 | - | - | - | - |
| | | | | | | | | | | |
| ALL ONE-DAY | 1 | 1 | 0 | 14 | 14 | 14.00 | - | - | - | - |

**BOWLING AVERAGES**

| | Overs | Mdns | Runs | Wkts | Avge | Best | 5wI | 10wM |
|---|---|---|---|---|---|---|---|---|
| NatWest Trophy | 6 | 0 | 13 | 0 | - | - | - | - |
| | | | | | | | | |
| ALL ONE-DAY | 6 | 0 | 13 | 0 | - | - | - | - |

## P.CARRICK - *Yorkshire*

| Opposition | Venue | Date | Batting | | Fielding | Bowling |
|---|---|---|---|---|---|---|
| **BRITANNIC ASSURANCE** | | | | | | |
| Middlesex | Lord's | April 27 | 0 | | | |
| Warwickshire | Headingley | May 9 | 13* & | 36 | | 0-31 & 3-13 |
| Notts | Headingley | May 16 | 47 & | 20* | | 1-28 & 2-28 |
| Northants | Headingley | May 25 | 23 & | 31* | | 0-36 & 4-25 |
| Warwickshire | Edgbaston | May 31 | 0 & | 8 | | 0-22 & 3-32 |
| Kent | Harrogate | June 14 | 12* | | | |
| Middlesex | Sheffield | June 21 | 13* & | 12* | | 0-19 & 2-32 |
| Worcestershire | Headingley | July 2 | 13 | | | 5-13 |
| Hampshire | Southampton | July 5 | 6 | | 1Ct | 1-109 |
| Derbyshire | Scarborough | July 16 | 2 | | | 2-50 & 4-48 |
| Surrey | Guildford | July 19 | 18 & | 7 | 1Ct | 1-44 & 3-56 |
| Notts | Worksop | July 23 | 63 | | 1Ct | 2-37 |
| Lancashire | Old Trafford | Aug 2 | 26 | | | 4-75 & 0-12 |
| Leicestershire | Leicester | Aug 6 | | 61 | | 0-58 |
| Sussex | Midd'brough | Aug 9 | 2 & | 14 | | 5-103 |
| Glamorgan | Headingley | Aug 16 | 9 & | 1 | | 0-97 |
| Essex | Colchester | Aug 20 | 28 | | | 1-89 & 4-92 |
| Somerset | Taunton | Aug 23 | | 11* | | 4-111 & 0-24 |
| Northants | Northampton | Aug 28 | 67 & | 29* | | 1-96 & 0-21 |
| Lancashire | Scarborough | Sept 3 | 36* & | 3 | | 0-52 & 3-184 |
| Derbyshire | Chesterfield | Sept 17 | 50 & | 1 | | 3-36 & 3-75 |
| **REFUGE ASSURANCE** | | | | | | |
| Essex | Chelmsford | April 28 | 20* | | | 0-10 |
| Warwickshire | Headingley | May 12 | 6 | | | 1-38 |
| Worcestershire | Sheffield | June 23 | 17* | | | 1-15 |
| Glamorgan | Headingley | June 30 | | | | 5-22 |
| Middlesex | Lord's | July 7 | | | | 0-38 |
| Gloucs | Scarborough | July 14 | 25 | | | 0-23 |
| Lancashire | Old Trafford | Aug 4 | | | 1Ct | 4-28 |
| Sussex | Midd'brough | Aug 11 | 1* | | | 5-40 |
| Notts | Scarborough | Aug 18 | 2 | | | 0-24 |
| Somerset | Taunton | Aug 25 | 18* | | 1Ct | 3-38 |

| | | | | | | | | | |
|---|---|---|---|---|---|---|---|---|---|
| **NATWEST TROPHY** | | | | | | | | | |
| Warwickshire | Edgbaston | June 26 | 12 | | | | | 0-18 | |

**BENSON & HEDGES CUP**

| | | | | | | |
|---|---|---|---|---|---|---|
| Notts | Trent Bridge | April 25 | 2 | | | 0-48 |
| Warwickshire | Headingley | May 29 | | | 1Ct | 3-22 |
| Lancashire | Old Trafford | June 16 | 7 | | 1Ct | 2-36 |

**OTHER ONE-DAY**

| | | | | | | |
|---|---|---|---|---|---|---|
| Derbyshire | Scarborough | Sept 1 | 9* | | | 1-39 |
| World XI | Scarborough | Sept 8 | 5 | | 1Ct | 2-36 |

**BATTING AVERAGES - Including fielding**

| | Matches | Inns | NO | Runs | HS | Avge | 100s | 50s | Ct | St |
|---|---|---|---|---|---|---|---|---|---|---|
| Britannic Assurance | 21 | 32 | 9 | 662 | 67 | 28.78 | - | 4 | 3 | - |
| | | | | | | | | | | |
| ALL FIRST-CLASS | 21 | 32 | 9 | 662 | 67 | 28.78 | - | 4 | 3 | - |
| | | | | | | | | | | |
| Refuge Assurance | 10 | 7 | 4 | 89 | 25 | 29.66 | - | - | 2 | - |
| NatWest Trophy | 1 | 1 | 0 | 12 | 12 | 12.00 | - | - | - | - |
| Benson & Hedges Cup | 3 | 2 | 0 | 9 | 7 | 4.50 | - | - | 2 | - |
| Other One-Day | 2 | 2 | 1 | 14 | 9* | 14.00 | - | - | 1 | - |
| | | | | | | | | | | |
| ALL ONE-DAY | 16 | 12 | 5 | 124 | 25 | 17.71 | - | - | 5 | - |

**BOWLING AVERAGES**

| | Overs | Mdns | Runs | Wkts | Avge | Best | 5wI | 10wM |
|---|---|---|---|---|---|---|---|---|
| Britannic Assurance | 701.2 | 231 | 1748 | 61 | 28.65 | 5-13 | 2 | - |
| | | | | | | | | |
| ALL FIRST-CLASS | 701.2 | 231 | 1748 | 61 | 28.65 | 5-13 | 2 | - |
| | | | | | | | | |
| Refuge Assurance | 74 | 2 | 276 | 19 | 14.52 | 5-22 | 2 | |
| NatWest Trophy | 6 | 1 | 18 | 0 | - | - | - | |
| Benson & Hedges Cup | 32 | 1 | 106 | 5 | 21.20 | 3-22 | - | |
| Other One-Day | 20 | 3 | 75 | 3 | 25.00 | 2-36 | - | |
| | | | | | | | | |
| ALL ONE-DAY | 132 | 7 | 475 | 27 | 17.59 | 5-22 | 2 | |

## D.CARTLEDGE - *Staffordshire*

| Opposition | Venue | Date | Batting | Fielding | Bowling |
|---|---|---|---|---|---|
| **NATWEST TROPHY** | | | | | |
| Northants | Stone | June 26 | 4 | 1Ct | |

**BATTING AVERAGES - Including fielding**

| | Matches | Inns | NO | Runs | HS | Avge | 100s | 50s | Ct | St |
|---|---|---|---|---|---|---|---|---|---|---|
| NatWest Trophy | 1 | 1 | 0 | 4 | 4 | 4.00 | - | - | 1 | - |
| | | | | | | | | | | |
| ALL ONE-DAY | 1 | 1 | 0 | 4 | 4 | 4.00 | - | - | 1 | - |

**BOWLING AVERAGES**
Did not bowl

## C.A.CHAPMAN - *Yorkshire*

| Opposition | Venue | Date | Batting | Fielding | Bowling |
|---|---|---|---|---|---|
| **REFUGE ASSURANCE** | | | | | |
| Leicestershire | Leicester | May 19 | 2 | | |
| Northants | Headingley | May 26 | 1 | | |

**BATTING AVERAGES - Including fielding**

| | Matches | Inns | NO | Runs | HS | Avge | 100s | 50s | Ct | St |
|---|---|---|---|---|---|---|---|---|---|---|
| Refuge Assurance | 2 | 2 | 0 | 3 | 2 | 1.50 | - | - | - | - |
| | | | | | | | | | | |
| ALL ONE-DAY | 2 | 2 | 0 | 3 | 2 | 1.50 | - | - | - | - |

**BOWLING AVERAGES**
Did not bowl

## PLAYER RECORDS

C

## J.H.CHILDS - *Essex*

| Opposition | Venue | Date | Batting | Fielding | Bowling |
|---|---|---|---|---|---|
| **BRITANNIC ASSURANCE** | | | | | |
| Northants | Northampton | May 9 | 0 | | 0-32 & 4-69 |
| Kent | Folkestone | May 16 | 15 | | 0-28 & 0-34 |
| Warwickshire | Chelmsford | May 22 | | | 1-35 |
| Gloucs | Bristol | May 31 | | | 1-47 |
| Leicestershire | Ilford | June 4 | 0 | | 1-76 & 1-21 |
| Worcestershire | Ilford | June 7 | 2 * | | 1-44 & 0-33 |
| Sussex | Horsham | June 21 | | 1Ct | 4-63 |
| Middlesex | Lord's | June 28 | 41 * | | 0-29 & 0-27 |
| Hampshire | Chelmsford | July 2 | 3 | | 1-34 & 0-37 |
| Surrey | The Oval | July 5 | | | 5-112 & 3-85 |
| Kent | Southend | July 16 | 0 * | | 2-66 & 0-4 |
| Somerset | Southend | July 19 | | | 3-66 & 5-20 |
| Glamorgan | Cardiff | July 23 | | 1Ct | 2-70 |
| Derbyshire | Derby | Aug 6 | 1 * & 19 | 1Ct | 0-48 |
| Notts | Trent Bridge | Aug 9 | 13 * | | 2-77 & 1-25 |
| Northants | Colchester | Aug 16 | 7 * | | 6-61 & 2-77 |
| Yorkshire | Colchester | Aug 20 | | 1 | 0-86 & 1-42 |
| Lancashire | Old Trafford | Aug 23 | | 1Ct | 0-25 & 0-10 |
| Derbyshire | Chelmsford | Sept 3 | | | 2-45 & 6-68 |
| Leicestershire | Leicester | Sept 10 | 9 | 1Ct | 0-24 & 4-82 |
| **OTHER FIRST-CLASS** | | | | | |
| West Indies | Chelmsford | Aug 3 | 1 | 1Ct | 0-64 & 0-51 |
| Victoria | Chelmsford | Sept 23 | 8 * | | 4-71 & 3-19 |
| **REFUGE ASSURANCE** | | | | | |
| Middlesex | Colchester | Aug 18 | | | 2-35 |
| Lancashire | Old Trafford | Aug 25 | | | 1-27 |
| **NATWEST TROPHY** | | | | | |
| Devon | Exmouth | June 26 | | | 2-43 |

**BATTING AVERAGES - Including fielding**

| | Matches | Inns | NO | Runs | HS | Avge | 100s | 50s | Ct | St |
|---|---|---|---|---|---|---|---|---|---|---|
| Britannic Assurance | 20 | 13 | 6 | 111 | 41 * | 15.85 | - | - | 5 | - |
| Other First-Class | 2 | 2 | 1 | 9 | 8 * | 9.00 | - | - | 1 | - |
| **ALL FIRST-CLASS** | 22 | 15 | 7 | 120 | 41 * | 15.00 | - | - | 6 | - |
| Refuge Assurance | 2 | 0 | 0 | 0 | 0 | - | - | - | - | - |
| NatWest Trophy | 1 | 0 | 0 | 0 | 0 | - | - | - | - | - |
| **ALL ONE-DAY** | 3 | 0 | 0 | 0 | 0 | - | - | - | - | - |

**BOWLING AVERAGES**

| | Overs | Mdns | Runs | Wkts | Avge | Best | 5wI | 10wM |
|---|---|---|---|---|---|---|---|---|
| Britannic Assurance | 667.1 | 218 | 1702 | 58 | 29.34 | 6-61 | 4 | - |
| Other First-Class | 84 | 30 | 205 | 7 | 29.28 | 4-71 | - | - |
| **ALL FIRST-CLASS** | 751.1 | 248 | 1907 | 65 | 29.33 | 6-61 | 4 | - |
| Refuge Assurance | 16 | 1 | 62 | 3 | 20.66 | 2-35 | - | |
| NatWest Trophy | 11.4 | 4 | 43 | 2 | 21.50 | 2-43 | - | |
| **ALL ONE-DAY** | 27.4 | 5 | 105 | 5 | 21.00 | 2-35 | - | |

## D.A.CHRISTMAS - *Lincolnshire*

| Opposition | Venue | Date | Batting | Fielding | Bowling |
|---|---|---|---|---|---|
| **NATWEST TROPHY** | | | | | |
| Notts | Trent Bridge | June 26 | 4 | | 0-80 |

**BATTING AVERAGES - Including fielding**

| | Matches | Inns | NO | Runs | HS | Avge | 100s | 50s | Ct | St |
|---|---|---|---|---|---|---|---|---|---|---|
| NatWest Trophy | 1 | 1 | 0 | 4 | 4 | 4.00 | - | - | - | - |
| **ALL ONE-DAY** | 1 | 1 | 0 | 4 | 4 | 4.00 | - | - | - | - |

**BOWLING AVERAGES**

| | Overs | Mdns | Runs | Wkts | Avge | Best | 5wI | 10wM |
|---|---|---|---|---|---|---|---|---|
| NatWest Trophy | 12 | 2 | 80 | 0 | - | - | - | - |
| **ALL ONE-DAY** | 12 | 2 | 80 | 0 | - | - | - | - |

## J.A.CLAUGHTON - *Dorset*

| Opposition | Venue | Date | Batting | Fielding | Bowling |
|---|---|---|---|---|---|
| **NATWEST TROPHY** | | | | | |
| Lancashire | Bournemouth | June 26 | 29 | 1Ct | |

**BATTING AVERAGES - Including fielding**

| | Matches | Inns | NO | Runs | HS | Avge | 100s | 50s | Ct | St |
|---|---|---|---|---|---|---|---|---|---|---|
| NatWest Trophy | 1 | 1 | 0 | 29 | 29 | 29.00 | - | - | 1 | - |
| **ALL ONE-DAY** | 1 | 1 | 0 | 29 | 29 | 29.00 | - | - | 1 | - |

**BOWLING AVERAGES**
Did not bowl

## M.W.CLEAL - *Somerset*

| Opposition | Venue | Date | Batting | Fielding | Bowling |
|---|---|---|---|---|---|
| **BENSON & HEDGES CUP** | | | | | |
| Surrey | Taunton | May 4 | | | 0-21 |
| Essex | Chelmsford | May 7 | 18 | | 0-34 |

**BATTING AVERAGES - Including fielding**

| | Matches | Inns | NO | Runs | HS | Avge | 100s | 50s | Ct | St |
|---|---|---|---|---|---|---|---|---|---|---|
| Benson & Hedges Cup | 2 | 1 | 0 | 18 | 18 | 18.00 | - | - | - | - |
| **ALL ONE-DAY** | 2 | 1 | 0 | 18 | 18 | 18.00 | - | - | - | - |

**BOWLING AVERAGES**

| | Overs | Mdns | Runs | Wkts | Avge | Best | 5wI | 10wM |
|---|---|---|---|---|---|---|---|---|
| Benson & Hedges Cup | 10 | 0 | 55 | 0 | - | - | - | |
| **ALL ONE-DAY** | 10 | 0 | 55 | 0 | - | - | - | |

## R.I.CLITHEROE - *Cambridge University*

| Opposition | Venue | Date | Batting | Fielding | Bowling |
|---|---|---|---|---|---|
| **OTHER FIRST-CLASS** | | | | | |
| Lancashire | Fenner's | April 13 | 8 & 22 * | | |
| Northants | Fenner's | April 16 | 8 | 1Ct | |
| Essex | Fenner's | April 19 | 13 & 4 | | |
| Derbyshire | Fenner's | May 9 | 36 & 7 | 2Ct | |
| Middlesex | Fenner's | May 15 | 6 & 4 | | |
| Surrey | Fenner's | May 18 | 34 & 6 | | |
| Leicestershire | Fenner's | May 22 | 35 & 0 | | |
| Glamorgan | Fenner's | June 18 | 31 | | |
| Sussex | Hove | June 29 | 8 * | | |
| Oxford U | Lord's | July 2 | 6 & 0 | | |

**BATTING AVERAGES - Including fielding**

| | Matches | Inns | NO | Runs | HS | Avge | 100s | 50s | Ct | St |
|---|---|---|---|---|---|---|---|---|---|---|
| Other First-Class | 10 | 17 | 2 | 228 | 36 | 15.20 | - | - | 3 | - |
| **ALL FIRST-CLASS** | 10 | 17 | 2 | 228 | 36 | 15.20 | - | - | 3 | - |

**BOWLING AVERAGES**
Did not bowl

## M.F.COHEN - *Ireland*

| Opposition | Venue | Date | Batting | Fielding | Bowling |
|---|---|---|---|---|---|
| **OTHER FIRST-CLASS** | | | | | |
| Scotland | Dublin | June 22 | 4 & 44 | | |
| **NATWEST TROPHY** | | | | | |
| Middlesex | Dublin | June 26 | 26 | 1Ct | |

# C — PLAYER RECORDS

## OTHER ONE-DAY

| | | | Batting | Fielding | Bowling |
|---|---|---|---|---|---|
| West Indies | Downpatrick | July 13 | 17 | 1Ct | |

### BATTING AVERAGES - Including fielding

| | Matches | Inns | NO | Runs | HS | Avge | 100s | 50s | Ct | St |
|---|---|---|---|---|---|---|---|---|---|---|---|
| Other First-Class | 1 | 2 | 0 | 48 | 44 | 24.00 | - | - | - | - |
| ALL FIRST-CLASS | 1 | 2 | 0 | 48 | 44 | 24.00 | - | - | - | - |
| NatWest Trophy | 1 | 1 | 0 | 26 | 26 | 26.00 | - | - | 1 | - |
| Other One-Day | 1 | 1 | 0 | 17 | 17 | 17.00 | - | - | 1 | - |
| ALL ONE-DAY | 2 | 2 | 0 | 43 | 26 | 21.50 | - | - | 2 | - |

### BOWLING AVERAGES
Did not bowl

## I.E.CONN - *Minor Counties & Durham*

| Opposition | Venue | Date | Batting | Fielding | Bowling |
|---|---|---|---|---|---|
| **BENSON & HEDGES CUP** | | | | | |
| Notts | Trent Bridge | May 7 | 23* | | 0-40 |
| **OTHER ONE-DAY** | | | | | |
| For Durham | | | | | |
| Sri Lanka | Chester-le-S | July 26 | 1 | | 0-36 |
| Essex | Scarborough | Aug 31 | 18 | | 0-80 |

### BATTING AVERAGES - Including fielding

| | Matches | Inns | NO | Runs | HS | Avge | 100s | 50s | Ct | St |
|---|---|---|---|---|---|---|---|---|---|---|---|
| Benson & Hedges Cup | 1 | 1 | 1 | 23 | 23* | - | - | - | - | - |
| Other One-Day | 2 | 2 | 0 | 19 | 18 | 9.50 | - | - | - | - |
| ALL ONE-DAY | 3 | 3 | 1 | 42 | 23* | 21.00 | - | - | - | - |

### BOWLING AVERAGES

| | Overs | Mdns | Runs | Wkts | Avge | Best | 5wI | 10wM |
|---|---|---|---|---|---|---|---|---|
| Benson & Hedges Cup | 11 | 1 | 40 | 0 | - | - | - | - |
| Other One-Day | 21 | 2 | 116 | 0 | - | - | - | - |
| ALL ONE-DAY | 32 | 3 | 156 | 0 | - | - | - | - |

## C.A.CONNOR - *Hampshire*

| Opposition | Venue | Date | Batting | | | Fielding | Bowling |
|---|---|---|---|---|---|---|---|
| **BRITANNIC ASSURANCE** | | | | | | | |
| Gloucs | Bristol | May 9 | 1 | & | 4 | | 0-70 & 0-41 |
| Sussex | Hove | May 16 | | | | 1Ct | 2-88 & 1-49 |
| Surrey | Bournemouth | May 25 | 12 | | | 1Ct | 4-49 & 3-41 |
| Notts | Trent Bridge | May 31 | | | | | 1-62 |
| Lancashire | Basingstoke | June 4 | | | 0 | | 0-56 & 0-40 |
| Essex | Chelmsford | July 2 | 5 | | | | 1-24 & 1-23 |
| Worcestershire | Portsmouth | July 16 | 18 | | | | 2-46 & 0-39 |
| Warwickshire | Portsmouth | July 19 | 4 | & | 17 | | 0-32 & 1-59 |
| Derbyshire | Chesterfield | July 23 | 0 | | | | 1-22 |
| Middlesex | Lord's | Aug 2 | 7 | | | | 2-61 & 2-61 |
| Kent | Canterbury | Aug 6 | 7 | | | | 3-57 & 1-39 |
| Glamorgan | Swansea | Aug 9 | 12 | | | 1Ct | 1-15 |
| Leicestershire | Bournemouth | Aug 16 | | | 1 | | 0-62 & 0-34 |
| Glamorgan | Southampton | Sept 17 | 30 | & | 30 | | 3-49 & 0-9 |
| **OTHER FIRST-CLASS** | | | | | | | |
| Oxford U | The Parks | April 13 | | | | | 1-40 & 2-38 |
| West Indies | Southampton | June 29 | 0 | | | | 2-100 |
| **REFUGE ASSURANCE** | | | | | | | |
| Yorkshire | Southampton | April 21 | | | | | 1-25 |
| Derbyshire | Derby | May 5 | 0* | | | | 1-48 |
| Kent | Southampton | May 12 | | | | | 1-33 |
| Somerset | Bournemouth | May 19 | | | | | 0-31 |
| Northants | Northampton | June 2 | 18 | | | 1Ct | 0-60 |
| Sussex | Basingstoke | June 9 | 2 | | | | 4-29 |
| Essex | Chelmsford | June 16 | | | | 1Ct | 1-31 |
| Worcestershire | Southampton | July 7 | | | | | 0-46 |
| Notts | Trent Bridge | July 14 | | | | | 1-40 |
| Warwickshire | Portsmouth | July 21 | | | | | 0-20 |

| | | | | Fielding | Bowling |
|---|---|---|---|---|---|
| Lancashire | Southampton | July 28 | | | 3-33 |
| Middlesex | Lord's | Aug 4 | | | 2-30 |
| Glamorgan | Ebbw Vale | Aug 11 | | 8 | 3-36 |
| Surrey | The Oval | Aug 25 | | | 1-19 |
| **NATWEST TROPHY** | | | | | |
| Berkshire | Reading | June 26 | | | 1-11 |
| Lancashire | Southampton | July 11 | | 1Ct | 4-61 |
| Notts | Southampton | July 31 | | | 3-42 |
| Warwickshire | Edgbaston | Aug 14 | | 1Ct | 4-29 |
| Surrey | Lord's | Sept 7 | | | 3-39 |
| **BENSON & HEDGES CUP** | | | | | |
| Notts | Southampton | April 23 | | 3Ct | 2-50 |
| Min Counties | Trowbridge | April 25 | | | 1-64 |
| Glamorgan | Southampton | May 2 | | | 3-54 |
| Yorkshire | Headingley | May 4 | | 3 | 2-59 |
| Essex | Chelmsford | May 29 | | 0 | 2-45 |

### BATTING AVERAGES - Including fielding

| | Matches | Inns | NO | Runs | HS | Avge | 100s | 50s | Ct | St |
|---|---|---|---|---|---|---|---|---|---|---|---|
| Britannic Assurance | 14 | 15 | 0 | 148 | 30 | 9.86 | - | - | 3 | - |
| Other First-Class | 2 | 1 | 0 | 0 | 0 | 0.00 | - | - | - | - |
| ALL FIRST-CLASS | 16 | 16 | 0 | 148 | 30 | 9.25 | - | - | 3 | - |
| Refuge Assurance | 14 | 4 | 1 | 28 | 18 | 9.33 | - | - | 2 | - |
| NatWest Trophy | 5 | 0 | 0 | 0 | 0 | - | - | - | 2 | - |
| Benson & Hedges Cup | 5 | 2 | 0 | 3 | 3 | 1.50 | - | - | 3 | - |
| ALL ONE-DAY | 24 | 6 | 1 | 31 | 18 | 6.20 | - | - | 7 | - |

### BOWLING AVERAGES

| | Overs | Mdns | Runs | Wkts | Avge | Best | 5wI | 10wM |
|---|---|---|---|---|---|---|---|---|
| Britannic Assurance | 331 | 58 | 1128 | 29 | 38.89 | 4-49 | - | - |
| Other First-Class | 59 | 11 | 178 | 5 | 35.60 | 2-38 | - | - |
| ALL FIRST-CLASS | 390 | 69 | 1306 | 34 | 38.41 | 4-49 | - | - |
| Refuge Assurance | 103.3 | 1 | 481 | 18 | 26.72 | 4-29 | - | - |
| NatWest Trophy | 51.1 | 6 | 182 | 15 | 12.13 | 4-29 | - | - |
| Benson & Hedges Cup | 55 | 4 | 272 | 10 | 27.20 | 3-54 | - | - |
| ALL ONE-DAY | 209.4 | 11 | 935 | 43 | 21.74 | 4-29 | - | - |

## G.COOK - *Durham*

| Opposition | Venue | Date | Batting | Fielding | Bowling |
|---|---|---|---|---|---|
| **NATWEST TROPHY** | | | | | |
| Glamorgan | Darlington | June 26 | 13 | | |
| **OTHER ONE-DAY** | | | | | |
| Leicestershire | Harrogate | June 11 | 43 | | |
| Surrey | Harrogate | June 13 | 102 | 1Ct | |
| Sri Lanka | Chester-le-S | July 26 | 20 | 1Ct | |
| Essex | Scarborough | Aug 31 | 48* | | |
| For Yorkshiremen | | | | | |
| Yorkshire | Scarborough | Sept 7 | 25 | | |
| For Durham | | | | | |
| Victoria | Durham U. | Sept 16 | | | |

### BATTING AVERAGES - Including fielding

| | Matches | Inns | NO | Runs | HS | Avge | 100s | 50s | Ct | St |
|---|---|---|---|---|---|---|---|---|---|---|---|
| NatWest Trophy | 1 | 1 | 0 | 13 | 13 | 13.00 | - | - | - | - |
| Other One-Day | 6 | 5 | 1 | 238 | 102 | 59.50 | 1 | - | 2 | - |
| ALL ONE-DAY | 7 | 6 | 1 | 251 | 102 | 50.20 | 1 | - | 2 | - |

### BOWLING AVERAGES
Did not bowl

## N.G.B.COOK - *Northamptonshire*

| Opposition | Venue | Date | Batting | Fielding | Bowling |
|---|---|---|---|---|---|
| **BRITANNIC ASSURANCE** | | | | | |
| Derbyshire | Derby | April 27 | | | |

# PLAYER RECORDS — C

| Opposition | Venue | Date | Batting | Fielding | Bowling |
|---|---|---|---|---|---|
| Essex | Northampton | May 9 | 12*& 6* | | |
| Leicestershire | Northampton | May 16 | 0 | 2Ct | 0-28 & 0-2 |
| Derbyshire | Northampton | May 31 | 4 | 1Ct | 4-74 |
| Worcestershire | Northampton | June 4 | | | 0-53 & 1-26 |
| Hampshire | Northampton | June 21 | 1* | | |
| Gloucs | Luton | June 28 | 6 | | 1-34 & 1-42 |
| Kent | Maidstone | July 2 | 2 | 1Ct | 2-4 & 2-29 |
| Leicestershire | Leicester | July 5 | | 1Ct | 2-12 & 0-33 |
| Middlesex | Uxbridge | July 16 | 14 | | 3-120 |
| Notts | Well'borough | July 19 | 15*& 4 | 1Ct | 2-51 |
| Somerset | Northampton | July 23 | 0* | | 1-42 |
| Sussex | Eastbourne | Aug 2 | 10 | | 3-74 & 0-1 |
| Lancashire | Lytham | Aug 6 | | | 0-3 & 1-79 |
| Warwickshire | Northampton | Aug 9 | 29 | | 1-92 & 0-31 |
| Essex | Colchester | Aug 16 | 0 & 11 | | 0-65 |

**OTHER FIRST-CLASS**

| | | | | | |
|---|---|---|---|---|---|
| Cambridge U | Fenner's | April 16 | | 1Ct | 2-25 |
| West Indies | | June 15 | | 3Ct | 2-74 |

**REFUGE ASSURANCE**

| | | | | | |
|---|---|---|---|---|---|
| Glamorgan | Cardiff | April 21 | 6 | | 0-19 |
| Lancashire | Old Trafford | April 28 | | 1Ct | 0-36 |
| Gloucs | Moreton | June 9 | | | |
| Somerset | Luton | June 30 | | | |
| Surrey | Tring | July 7 | 17* | | 0-25 |

**NATWEST TROPHY**

| | | | | | |
|---|---|---|---|---|---|
| Staffordshire | Stone | June 26 | | 2Ct | 1-35 |

**BENSON & HEDGES CUP**

| | | | | | |
|---|---|---|---|---|---|
| Gloucs | Bristol | May 2 | 1 | | 0-16 |
| Worcestershire | Northampton | May 7 | 0 | | 1-21 |
| Lancashire | Old Trafford | May 29 | | 1Ct | 0-40 |

**BATTING AVERAGES - Including fielding**

| | Matches | Inns | NO | Runs | HS | Avge | 100s | 50s | Ct | St |
|---|---|---|---|---|---|---|---|---|---|---|
| Britannic Assurance | 16 | 15 | 5 | 114 | 29 | 11.40 | - | - | 6 | - |
| Other First-Class | 2 | 0 | 0 | 0 | 0 | - | - | - | 4 | - |
| ALL FIRST-CLASS | 18 | 15 | 5 | 114 | 29 | 11.40 | - | - | 10 | - |
| Refuge Assurance | 5 | 2 | 1 | 23 | 17* | 23.00 | - | - | 1 | - |
| NatWest Trophy | 1 | 0 | 0 | 0 | 0 | - | - | - | 2 | - |
| Benson & Hedges Cup | 3 | 2 | 0 | 1 | 1 | 0.50 | - | - | 1 | - |
| ALL ONE-DAY | 9 | 4 | 1 | 24 | 17* | 8.00 | - | - | 4 | - |

**BOWLING AVERAGES**

| | Overs | Mdns | Runs | Wkts | Avge | Best | 5wI | 10wM |
|---|---|---|---|---|---|---|---|---|
| Britannic Assurance | 305.1 | 70 | 895 | 24 | 37.29 | 4-74 | - | - |
| Other First-Class | 31.2 | 9 | 99 | 4 | 24.75 | 2-25 | - | - |
| ALL FIRST-CLASS | 336.3 | 79 | 994 | 28 | 35.50 | 4-74 | - | - |
| Refuge Assurance | 17 | 0 | 80 | 0 | - | - | - | |
| NatWest Trophy | 12 | 0 | 35 | 1 | 35.00 | 1-35 | - | |
| Benson & Hedges Cup | 26 | 2 | 77 | 1 | 77.00 | 1-21 | - | |
| ALL ONE-DAY | 55 | 2 | 192 | 2 | 96.00 | 1-21 | - | |

# S.J.COOK - Somerset

| Opposition | Venue | Date | Batting | Fielding | Bowling |
|---|---|---|---|---|---|
| **BRITANNIC ASSURANCE** | | | | | |
| Sussex | Taunton | April 27 | 57 | | |
| Glamorgan | Taunton | May 9 | 15 & 20 | 1Ct | |
| Derbyshire | Derby | May 22 | 10 & 7 | | |
| Middlesex | Taunton | May 25 | 45 & 89 | | |
| Glamorgan | Swansea | June 4 | 152 | | 0-26 |
| Warwickshire | Edgbaston | June 7 | 94*& 8 | | |
| Hampshire | Bath | June 18 | 107*& 17 | 1Ct | |
| Gloucs | Bath | June 21 | 0 | | |
| Surrey | The Oval | June 28 | 41 | | |
| Lancashire | Taunton | July 2 | 131 & 61 | | |
| Sussex | Hove | July 16 | 30 & 66 | 1Ct | |
| Essex | Southend | July 19 | 193*& 21 | | |
| Northants | Northampton | July 23 | 210* | | |
| Kent | Taunton | July 26 | 126 & 10 | 2Ct | |
| Leicestershire | Weston | Aug 2 | 10 & 0 | 1Ct | |
| Worcestershire | Weston | Aug 6 | 37 & 38 | 1Ct | |
| Notts | Trent Bridge | Aug 16 | 43 & 2 | | |
| Yorkshire | Taunton | Aug 23 | 79 & 85* | 1Ct | |
| Hampshire | Southampton | Aug 28 | 197 & 115* | 2Ct | |
| Worcestershire | Worcester | Sept 3 | 0 & 50 | | |
| Gloucs | Bristol | Sept 10 | 21 & 16 | 1Ct | |
| Warwickshire | Taunton | Sept 17 | 127 & 40 | 2Ct | |

**OTHER FIRST-CLASS**

| | | | | | |
|---|---|---|---|---|---|
| West Indies | Taunton | May 29 | 162*& 14 | 2Ct | |
| Sri Lanka | Taunton | Aug 10 | 209* | 1Ct | |

**REFUGE ASSURANCE**

| | | | | | |
|---|---|---|---|---|---|
| Surrey | The Oval | April 21 | 31 | | |
| Sussex | Taunton | April 28 | 33 | 1Ct | |
| Glamorgan | Taunton | May 12 | 10 | 1Ct | |
| Hampshire | Bournemouth | May 19 | 43 | 1Ct | |
| Middlesex | Taunton | May 26 | 1 | | |
| Warwickshire | Edgbaston | June 2 | 67 | | |
| Notts | Trent Bridge | June 9 | 2 | | |
| Derbyshire | Derby | June 16 | 32 | 1Ct | |
| Northants | Luton | June 30 | 5 | | |
| Lancashire | Taunton | July 5 | 53 | | |
| Essex | Southend | July 21 | 93 | | |
| Kent | Taunton | July 28 | 1 | | |
| Leicestershire | Weston | Aug 4 | 2 | | |
| Worcestershire | Worcester | Aug 18 | 129* | | |
| Yorkshire | Taunton | Aug 25 | 44 | | |

**NATWEST TROPHY**

| | | | | | |
|---|---|---|---|---|---|
| Bucks | Bath | June 26 | 35 | | |
| Middlesex | Taunton | July 11 | 7 | | |
| Warwickshire | Edgbaston | July 31 | 14 | | |

**BENSON & HEDGES CUP**

| | | | | | |
|---|---|---|---|---|---|
| Middlesex | Taunton | April 23 | 41 | | |
| Warwickshire | Edgbaston | May 2 | 58 | 1Ct | |
| Surrey | Taunton | May 4 | 76 | | |
| Essex | Chelmsford | May 7 | 38 | | |

**OTHER ONE-DAY**

| | | | | | |
|---|---|---|---|---|---|
| Gloucs | Hove | Sept 8 | 0 | 1Ct | |

**BATTING AVERAGES - Including fielding**

| | Matches | Inns | NO | Runs | HS | Avge | 100s | 50s | Ct | St |
|---|---|---|---|---|---|---|---|---|---|---|
| Britannic Assurance | 22 | 39 | 6 | 2370 | 210* | 71.81 | 9 | 8 | 13 | - |
| Other First-Class | 2 | 3 | 2 | 385 | 209* | 385.00 | 2 | - | 3 | - |
| ALL FIRST-CLASS | 24 | 42 | 8 | 2755 | 210* | 81.02 | 11 | 8 | 16 | - |
| Refuge Assurance | 15 | 15 | 1 | 546 | 129* | 39.00 | 1 | 3 | 4 | - |
| NatWest Trophy | 3 | 3 | 0 | 56 | 35 | 18.66 | - | - | - | - |
| Benson & Hedges Cup | 4 | 4 | 0 | 213 | 76 | 53.25 | - | 2 | 1 | - |
| Other One-Day | 1 | 1 | 0 | 0 | 0 | 0.00 | - | - | 1 | - |
| ALL ONE-DAY | 23 | 23 | 1 | 815 | 129* | 37.04 | 1 | 5 | 6 | - |

**BOWLING AVERAGES**

| | Overs | Mdns | Runs | Wkts | Avge | Best | 5wI | 10wM |
|---|---|---|---|---|---|---|---|---|
| Britannic Assurance | 4 | 0 | 26 | 0 | - | - | - | - |
| Other First-Class | | | | | | | | |
| ALL FIRST-CLASS | 4 | 0 | 26 | 0 | - | - | - | - |
| Refuge Assurance | | | | | | | | |
| NatWest Trophy | | | | | | | | |
| Benson & Hedges Cup | | | | | | | | |
| Other One-Day | | | | | | | | |
| ALL ONE-DAY | | | | | | | | |

# K.E.COOPER - Nottinghamshire

| Opposition | Venue | Date | Batting | Fielding | Bowling |
|---|---|---|---|---|---|
| **BRITANNIC ASSURANCE** | | | | | |
| Kent | Trent Bridge | May 22 | | | 1-54 |
| **REFUGE ASSURANCE** | | | | | |
| Lancashire | Old Trafford | April 21 | | | 0-19 |
| Warwickshire | Trent Bridge | April 28 | | | 1-20 |
| Glamorgan | Cardiff | May 5 | | | 0-40 |
| Essex | Trent Bridge | May 12 | 4* | | 0-33 |

# C

# PLAYER RECORDS

| | | | | | |
|---|---|---|---|---|---|
| Somerset | Trent Bridge | June 9 | | | 1-20 |
| Gloucs | Gloucester | June 16 | | | 1-30 |
| Middlesex | Trent Bridge | June 23 | 0* | | 0-38 |

**BENSON & HEDGES CUP**

| | | | | | |
|---|---|---|---|---|---|
| Hampshire | Southampton | April 23 | 0 | | 1-42 |
| Yorkshire | Trent Bridge | April 25 | | | 1-27 |
| Glamorgan | Cardiff | May 4 | | | 0-34 |

**BATTING AVERAGES - Including fielding**

| | Matches | Inns | NO | Runs | HS | Avge | 100s | 50s | Ct | St |
|---|---|---|---|---|---|---|---|---|---|---|
| Britannic Assurance | 1 | 0 | 0 | 0 | 0 | - | - | - | - | - |
| ALL FIRST-CLASS | 1 | 0 | 0 | 0 | 0 | - | - | - | - | - |
| Refuge Assurance | 7 | 2 | 2 | 4 | 4* | - | - | - | - | - |
| Benson & Hedges Cup | 3 | 1 | 0 | 0 | 0 | 0.00 | - | - | - | - |
| ALL ONE-DAY | 10 | 3 | 2 | 4 | 4* | 4.00 | - | - | - | - |

**BOWLING AVERAGES**

| | Overs | Mdns | Runs | Wkts | Avge | Best | 5wI | 10wM |
|---|---|---|---|---|---|---|---|---|
| Britannic Assurance | 17 | 3 | 54 | 1 | 54.00 | 1-54 | - | - |
| ALL FIRST-CLASS | 17 | 3 | 54 | 1 | 54.00 | 1-54 | - | - |
| Refuge Assurance | 50 | 3 | 200 | 3 | 66.66 | 1-20 | - | |
| Benson & Hedges Cup | 31 | 5 | 103 | 2 | 51.50 | 1-27 | - | |
| ALL ONE-DAY | 81 | 8 | 303 | 5 | 60.60 | 1-20 | - | |

## S.J.COOPER - Durham

| Opposition | Venue | Date | Batting | Fielding | Bowling |
|---|---|---|---|---|---|
| **OTHER ONE-DAY** | | | | | |
| Victoria | Durham U. | Sept 16 | | 1Ct | 1-39 |

**BATTING AVERAGES - Including fielding**

| | Matches | Inns | NO | Runs | HS | Avge | 100s | 50s | Ct | St |
|---|---|---|---|---|---|---|---|---|---|---|
| Other One-Day | 1 | 0 | 0 | 0 | 0 | - | - | - | 1 | - |
| ALL ONE-DAY | 1 | 0 | 0 | 0 | 0 | - | - | - | 1 | - |

**BOWLING AVERAGES**

| | Overs | Mdns | Runs | Wkts | Avge | Best | 5wI | 10wM |
|---|---|---|---|---|---|---|---|---|
| Other One-Day | 10 | 0 | 39 | 1 | 39.00 | 1-39 | - | |
| ALL ONE-DAY | 10 | 0 | 39 | 1 | 39.00 | 1-39 | - | |

## D.G.CORK - Derbyshire

| Opposition | Venue | Date | Batting | | Fielding | Bowling |
|---|---|---|---|---|---|---|
| **BRITANNIC ASSURANCE** | | | | | | |
| Glamorgan | Chesterfield | June 7 | 34* | | 1Ct | 1-37 & 3-59 |
| Gloucs | Gloucester | June 18 | 27* | | | 3-36 & 3-101 |
| Surrey | Derby | June 21 | 0* | | 2Ct | 1-15 |
| Warwickshire | Edgbaston | June 28 | 0 & | 13 | | 2-64 & 1-20 |
| Sussex | Derby | July 5 | 13 & | 6* | 1Ct | 4-66 & 4-25 |
| Yorkshire | Scarborough | July 16 | 26 & | 8 | 1Ct | 0-52 |
| Worcestershire | Kidd'minster | July 19 | 15 & | 15* | 1Ct | 3-49 & 1-84 |
| Hampshire | Chesterfield | July 23 | 0 | | 1Ct | 2-53 |
| Essex | Derby | Aug 6 | 3 | | | 8-53 & 2-25 |
| Middlesex | Lord's | Aug 9 | 18 & | 11 | 1Ct | 2-61 & 0-25 |
| Lancashire | Derby | Aug 16 | | | | 0-59 & 1-31 |
| Leicestershire | Derby | Aug 20 | 25 & | 8 | | 3-62 |
| Leicestershire | Leicester | Aug 28 | 28 & | 22* | | 2-38 & 1-74 |
| Essex | Chelmsford | Sept 3 | 30 & | 0 | | 1-44 |
| Notts | Derby | Sept 10 | 0 & | 44 | | 4-91 & 0-12 |
| Yorkshire | Chesterfield | Sept 17 | 40* & | 9 | | 3-83 & 0-31 |
| **OTHER FIRST-CLASS** | | | | | | |
| West Indies | Derby | June 12 | 11* & | 4 | 1Ct | 0-49 & 2-27 |
| Sri Lanka | Derby | Aug 2 | 13 | | | 0-34 |
| **REFUGE ASSURANCE** | | | | | | |
| Yorkshire | Chesterfield | June 2 | | | | 1-15 |

| | | | | | |
|---|---|---|---|---|---|
| Surrey | Chesterfield | June 9 | | 2Ct | 3-45 |
| Somerset | Derby | June 16 | 7 | | 0-30 |
| Gloucs | Cheltenham | July 21 | | | 2-27 |
| Northants | Derby | July 28 | 7 | 1Ct | 0-25 |
| Warwickshire | Edgbaston | Aug 4 | 30 | | 2-38 |
| Middlesex | Lord's | Aug 11 | | 1Ct | 0-56 |
| Glamorgan | Checkley | Aug 18 | 28 | | 2-20 |
| Notts | Trent Bridge | Aug 25 | 11 | | 1-35 |

**OTHER ONE-DAY**
For England A

| | | | | | |
|---|---|---|---|---|---|
| Sri Lanka | Old Trafford | Aug 14 | | | 0-41 |

For Derbyshire

| | | | | | |
|---|---|---|---|---|---|
| Yorkshire | Scarborough | Sept 1 | 8 | | 1-43 |

**BATTING AVERAGES - Including fielding**

| | Matches | Inns | NO | Runs | HS | Avge | 100s | 50s | Ct | St |
|---|---|---|---|---|---|---|---|---|---|---|
| Britannic Assurance | 16 | 25 | 7 | 395 | 44 | 21.94 | - | - | 8 | - |
| Other First-Class | 2 | 3 | 1 | 28 | 13 | 14.00 | - | - | 1 | - |
| ALL FIRST-CLASS | 18 | 28 | 8 | 423 | 44 | 21.15 | - | - | 9 | - |
| Refuge Assurance | 9 | 5 | 0 | 83 | 30 | 16.60 | - | - | 4 | - |
| Other One-Day | 2 | 1 | 0 | 8 | 8 | 8.00 | - | - | - | - |
| ALL ONE-DAY | 11 | 6 | 0 | 91 | 30 | 15.16 | - | - | 4 | - |

**BOWLING AVERAGES**

| | Overs | Mdns | Runs | Wkts | Avge | Best | 5wI | 10wM |
|---|---|---|---|---|---|---|---|---|
| Britannic Assurance | 457.3 | 76 | 1350 | 55 | 24.54 | 8-53 | 1 | 1 |
| Other First-Class | 37 | 8 | 110 | 2 | 55.00 | 2-27 | - | - |
| ALL FIRST-CLASS | 494.3 | 84 | 1460 | 57 | 25.61 | 8-53 | 1 | 1 |
| Refuge Assurance | 62 | 3 | 291 | 11 | 26.45 | 3-45 | - | |
| Other One-Day | 20 | 2 | 84 | 1 | 84.00 | 1-43 | - | |
| ALL ONE-DAY | 82 | 5 | 375 | 12 | 31.25 | 3-45 | - | |

## P.A.COTTEY - Glamorgan

| Opposition | Venue | Date | Batting | | Fielding | Bowling |
|---|---|---|---|---|---|---|
| **BRITANNIC ASSURANCE** | | | | | | |
| Leicestershire | Leicester | April 27 | 3 & | 16* | | |
| Middlesex | Cardiff | June 14 | 24 | | 1Ct | |
| Leicestershire | Neath | June 21 | 7 | | | |
| Lancashire | Liverpool | June 28 | 2* | | | |
| Notts | Cardiff | July 2 | 46 & | 55 | 2Ct | |
| Kent | Maidstone | July 5 | 4 & | 16 | | |
| Gloucs | Cheltenham | July 19 | 0 & | 37* | 2Ct | |
| Essex | Cardiff | July 23 | 20 | | | |
| Surrey | The Oval | July 26 | 1 & | 17 | 3Ct | |
| Yorkshire | Headingley | Aug 16 | 9* | | 1Ct | |
| Warwickshire | Edgbaston | Aug 20 | 2* | | | |
| **OTHER FIRST-CLASS** | | | | | | |
| Oxford U | The Parks | April 17 | 9* | | | |
| Cambridge U | Fenner's | June 18 | 2* & | 21 | | |
| West Indies | Swansea | July 16 | 8 | | | |
| **REFUGE ASSURANCE** | | | | | | |
| Leicestershire | Leicester | April 28 | 3 | | | |
| Kent | Maidstone | July 7 | 18* | | | |
| Worcestershire | Worcester | July 21 | 26* | | | |
| Surrey | The Oval | July 28 | 47 | | | |
| Gloucs | Swansea | Aug 4 | 33 | | 1Ct | |
| Hampshire | Ebbw Vale | Aug 11 | 92* | | | |
| Derbyshire | Checkley | Aug 18 | 14 | | | |
| **NATWEST TROPHY** | | | | | | |
| Worcestershire | Worcester | July 11 | 3* | | | |
| Northants | Northampton | July 31 | 10 | | | |

**BATTING AVERAGES - Including fielding**

| | Matches | Inns | NO | Runs | HS | Avge | 100s | 50s | Ct | St |
|---|---|---|---|---|---|---|---|---|---|---|
| Britannic Assurance | 11 | 16 | 5 | 259 | 55 | 23.54 | - | 1 | 9 | - |
| Other First-Class | 3 | 4 | 2 | 40 | 21 | 20.00 | - | - | - | - |
| ALL FIRST-CLASS | 14 | 20 | 7 | 299 | 55 | 23.00 | - | 1 | 9 | - |
| Refuge Assurance | 7 | 7 | 3 | 233 | 92* | 58.25 | - | 1 | 1 | - |

# PLAYER RECORDS     C

| | | | | | | | | | |
|---|---|---|---|---|---|---|---|---|---|
| NatWest Trophy | 2 | 2 | 1 | 13 | 10 | 13.00 | - | - | - |
| ALL ONE-DAY | 9 | 9 | 4 | 246 | 92* | 49.20 | - | 1 | 1 | - |

**BOWLING AVERAGES**
Did not bowl

## D.C.COTTON - *Cambridge University*

| Opposition | Venue | Date | Batting | Fielding | Bowling |
|---|---|---|---|---|---|
| **OTHER FIRST-CLASS** | | | | | |
| Surrey | Fenner's | May 18 | 0* & 0 | | 0-42 & 1-43 |

**BATTING AVERAGES - Including fielding**

| | Matches | Inns | NO | Runs | HS | Avge | 100s | 50s | Ct | St |
|---|---|---|---|---|---|---|---|---|---|---|
| Other First-Class | 1 | 2 | 1 | 0 | 0* | 0.00 | - | - | - | - |
| ALL FIRST-CLASS | 1 | 2 | 1 | 0 | 0* | 0.00 | - | - | - | - |

**BOWLING AVERAGES**

| | Overs | Mdns | Runs | Wkts | Avge | Best | 5wI | 10wM |
|---|---|---|---|---|---|---|---|---|
| Other First-Class | 21 | 4 | 85 | 1 | 85.00 | 1-43 | - | - |
| ALL FIRST-CLASS | 21 | 4 | 85 | 1 | 85.00 | 1-43 | - | - |

## D.COWAN - *Scotland*

| Opposition | Venue | Date | Batting | Fielding | Bowling |
|---|---|---|---|---|---|
| **OTHER FIRST-CLASS** | | | | | |
| Ireland | Dublin | June 22 | 2* | 1Ct | 2-92 & 3-41 |
| **BENSON & HEDGES CUP** | | | | | |
| Lancashire | Forfar | April 23 | 3* | | 2-47 |
| Leicestershire | Leicester | May 2 | 0 | | 2-54 |
| Sussex | Hove | May 4 | | 1Ct | 0-23 |
| Kent | Glasgow | May 7 | 6 | | 1-33 |

**BATTING AVERAGES - Including fielding**

| | Matches | Inns | NO | Runs | HS | Avge | 100s | 50s | Ct | St |
|---|---|---|---|---|---|---|---|---|---|---|
| Other First-Class | 1 | 1 | 1 | 2 | 2* | - | - | - | 1 | - |
| ALL FIRST-CLASS | 1 | 1 | 1 | 2 | 2* | - | - | - | 1 | - |
| Benson & Hedges Cup | 4 | 3 | 1 | 9 | 6 | 4.50 | - | - | 1 | - |
| ALL ONE-DAY | 4 | 3 | 1 | 9 | 6 | 4.50 | - | - | 1 | - |

**BOWLING AVERAGES**

| | Overs | Mdns | Runs | Wkts | Avge | Best | 5wI | 10wM |
|---|---|---|---|---|---|---|---|---|
| Other First-Class | 53 | 13 | 133 | 5 | 26.60 | 3-41 | - | - |
| ALL FIRST-CLASS | 53 | 13 | 133 | 5 | 26.60 | 3-41 | - | - |
| Benson & Hedges Cup | 28 | 1 | 157 | 5 | 31.40 | 2-47 | - | |
| ALL ONE-DAY | 28 | 1 | 157 | 5 | 31.40 | 2-47 | - | |

## N.G.COWANS - *Middlesex*

| Opposition | Venue | Date | Batting | Fielding | Bowling |
|---|---|---|---|---|---|
| **BRITANNIC ASSURANCE** | | | | | |
| Yorkshire | Lord's | April 27 | | 1Ct | 1-44 |
| Sussex | Lord's | May 9 | 5 & 2 | | 1-86 & 0-25 |
| Sussex | Hove | May 22 | 0 | 1Ct | 2-39 & 0-8 |
| Somerset | Taunton | May 25 | 20 | | 0-47 & 0-32 |
| Gloucs | Bristol | June 4 | 0* | | 0-10 |
| Glamorgan | Cardiff | June 14 | 0 | | 4-42 & 0-16 |
| Yorkshire | Sheffield | June 21 | 5 | | 1-30 & 0-3 |
| Essex | Lord's | June 28 | 0 | | 2-61 & 0-29 |
| Warwickshire | Edgbaston | July 2 | 3*& 4 | 1Ct | 4-44 & 0-59 |

| Opposition | Venue | Date | Batting | Fielding | Bowling |
|---|---|---|---|---|---|
| Northants | Uxbridge | July 16 | | | 3-57 & 0-1 |
| Lancashire | Uxbridge | July 19 | 6 & 0 | 1Ct | 3-51 & 2-35 |
| Notts | Lord's | July 26 | 9 | | 1-38 & 1-59 |
| Hampshire | Lord's | Aug 2 | 4* | | 1-43 & 0-47 |
| Derbyshire | Lord's | Aug 9 | 16* | | 1-35 & 1-35 |
| Surrey | The Oval | Aug 20 | 0 | | 1-65 & 1-27 |
| Worcestershire | Worcester | Aug 23 | 0 & 2* | | 1-23 |
| Kent | Canterbury | Aug 28 | 5 & 23* | | 1-42 & 0-78 |
| Notts | Trent Bridge | Sept 3 | 19 & 9* | 1Ct | 0-38 & 0-13 |
| Surrey | Lord's | Sept 10 | 6*& 0* | | 0-28 & 1-10 |
| Essex | Chelmsford | Sept 17 | 0 & 8* | | 1-70 |
| **OTHER FIRST-CLASS** | | | | | |
| MCC | Lord's | April 16 | 4* | | 1-38 |
| Cambridge U | Fenner's | May 15 | | | 3-10 & 1-19 |
| West Indies | Lord's | May 18 | 35 & 1 | | 3-37 & 2-26 |
| **REFUGE ASSURANCE** | | | | | |
| Gloucs | Bristol | April 21 | | | 3-33 |
| Somerset | Taunton | May 26 | | | 0-31 |
| Kent | Southgate | June 2 | 1 | | 1-49 |
| Leicestershire | Uxbridge | June 9 | 0* | | 1-30 |
| Glamorgan | Cardiff | June 16 | 4 | | 2-44 |
| Notts | Trent Bridge | June 23 | | | 2-30 |
| Yorkshire | Lord's | July 7 | | | 0-42 |
| Warwickshire | Edgbaston | July 14 | | | 0-31 |
| Lancashire | Lord's | July 21 | | | 6-9 |
| Hampshire | Lord's | Aug 4 | | | 0-39 |
| Derbyshire | Lord's | Aug 11 | 5* | | 0-18 |
| Essex | Colchester | Aug 18 | 4 | | 3-35 |
| Worcestershire | Worcester | Aug 25 | | | 0-34 |
| **NATWEST TROPHY** | | | | | |
| Ireland | Dublin | June 26 | 0 | 1Ct | 1-10 |
| Somerset | Taunton | July 11 | 10 | | 4-51 |
| **BENSON & HEDGES CUP** | | | | | |
| Somerset | Taunton | April 23 | | 1Ct | 2-49 |
| Surrey | Lord's | April 25 | 5 | | 3-42 |
| Warwickshire | Lord's | May 4 | 0* | | 3-39 |

**BATTING AVERAGES - Including fielding**

| | Matches | Inns | NO | Runs | HS | Avge | 100s | 50s | Ct | St |
|---|---|---|---|---|---|---|---|---|---|---|
| Britannic Assurance | 20 | 26 | 10 | 146 | 23* | 9.12 | - | - | 5 | - |
| Other First-Class | 3 | 3 | 1 | 40 | 35 | 20.00 | - | - | - | - |
| ALL FIRST-CLASS | 23 | 29 | 11 | 186 | 35 | 10.33 | - | - | 5 | - |
| Refuge Assurance | 13 | 5 | 2 | 14 | 5* | 4.66 | - | - | - | - |
| NatWest Trophy | 2 | 2 | 0 | 10 | 10 | 5.00 | - | - | 1 | - |
| Benson & Hedges Cup | 3 | 2 | 1 | 5 | 5 | 5.00 | - | - | 1 | - |
| ALL ONE-DAY | 18 | 9 | 3 | 29 | 10 | 4.83 | - | - | 2 | - |

**BOWLING AVERAGES**

| | Overs | Mdns | Runs | Wkts | Avge | Best | 5wI | 10wM |
|---|---|---|---|---|---|---|---|---|
| Britannic Assurance | 485.2 | 120 | 1370 | 34 | 40.29 | 4-42 | - | - |
| Other First-Class | 56.5 | 24 | 130 | 10 | 13.00 | 3-10 | - | - |
| ALL FIRST-CLASS | 542.1 | 144 | 1500 | 44 | 34.09 | 4-42 | - | - |
| Refuge Assurance | 98.5 | 7 | 425 | 18 | 23.61 | 6-9 | 1 | |
| NatWest Trophy | 18 | 1 | 61 | 5 | 12.20 | 4-51 | - | |
| Benson & Hedges Cup | 33 | 2 | 130 | 8 | 16.25 | 3-39 | - | |
| ALL ONE-DAY | 149.5 | 10 | 616 | 31 | 19.87 | 6-9 | 1 | |

## C.S.COWDREY - *Kent*

| Opposition | Venue | Date | Batting | Fielding | Bowling |
|---|---|---|---|---|---|
| **BRITANNIC ASSURANCE** | | | | | |
| Hampshire | Southampton | April 27 | 97 | | |
| Surrey | The Oval | May 9 | 13 | 1Ct | |
| Middlesex | Lord's | May 31 | 6 & 38 | | |
| **REFUGE ASSURANCE** | | | | | |
| Worcestershire | Worcester | April 21 | 24 | | 0-37 |
| Hampshire | Southampton | May 12 | 14 | 2Ct | |
| Derbyshire | Canterbury | May 26 | 45 | 1Ct | |
| Middlesex | Southgate | June 2 | 38* | | |
| Lancashire | Old Trafford | June 23 | 11 | | |

# C PLAYER RECORDS

| | | | | | |
|---|---|---|---|---|---|
| Gloucs | Canterbury | June 30 | 22 | 1Ct | |
| Glamorgan | Maidstone | July 7 | | | |

**NATWEST TROPHY**

| | | | | |
|---|---|---|---|---|
| Cambs | Canterbury | June 26 | 0 | 1Ct |

**BENSON & HEDGES CUP**

| | | | | | |
|---|---|---|---|---|---|
| Leicestershire | Canterbury | April 23 | 4 | 1Ct | |
| Lancashire | Old Trafford | April 25 | 0 | | |
| Sussex | Canterbury | May 2 | 57 * | | |
| Scotland | Glasgow | May 7 | 11 | 2Ct | 2-17 |
| Worcestershire | Worcester | May 29 | 25 | 1Ct | |

**BATTING AVERAGES - Including fielding**

| | Matches | Inns | NO | Runs | HS | Avge | 100s | 50s | Ct | St |
|---|---|---|---|---|---|---|---|---|---|---|
| Britannic Assurance | 3 | 4 | 0 | 154 | 97 | 38.50 | - | 1 | 1 | - |
| ALL FIRST-CLASS | 3 | 4 | 0 | 154 | 97 | 38.50 | - | 1 | 1 | - |
| Refuge Assurance | 7 | 6 | 1 | 154 | 45 | 30.80 | - | - | 4 | - |
| NatWest Trophy | 1 | 1 | 0 | 0 | 0 | 0.00 | - | - | 1 | - |
| Benson & Hedges Cup | 5 | 5 | 1 | 97 | 57 * | 24.25 | - | 1 | 4 | - |
| ALL ONE-DAY | 13 | 12 | 2 | 251 | 57 * | 25.10 | - | 1 | 9 | - |

**BOWLING AVERAGES**

| | Overs | Mdns | Runs | Wkts | Avge | Best | 5wI | 10wM |
|---|---|---|---|---|---|---|---|---|
| Britannic Assurance | | | | | | | | |
| ALL FIRST-CLASS | | | | | | | | |
| Refuge Assurance | 3 | 0 | 37 | 0 | - | - | - | |
| NatWest Trophy | | | | | | | | |
| Benson & Hedges Cup | 5 | 1 | 17 | 2 | 8.50 | 2-17 | - | |
| ALL ONE-DAY | 8 | 1 | 54 | 2 | 27.00 | 2-17 | - | |

## G.R.COWDREY - *Kent*

| Opposition | Venue | Date | Batting | | | Fielding | Bowling |
|---|---|---|---|---|---|---|---|
| **BRITANNIC ASSURANCE** | | | | | | | |
| Hampshire | Southampton | April 27 | 0 | | | 1Ct | |
| Surrey | The Oval | May 9 | 58 | | | 3Ct | |
| Essex | Folkestone | May 16 | 32 | & | 36 | 1Ct | |
| Notts | Trent Bridge | May 22 | 109 * | & | 36 | | |
| Derbyshire | Canterbury | May 25 | 8 | & | 37 * | 1Ct | |
| Middlesex | Lord's | May 31 | 25 | & | 20 | 1Ct | |
| Warwickshire | Tunbridge W | June 4 | 114 | | | | |
| Sussex | Tunbridge W | June 7 | 16 | & | 41 | | |
| Yorkshire | Harrogate | June 14 | | | | | |
| Lancashire | Old Trafford | June 21 | | | 2 | | |
| Northants | Maidstone | July 2 | 2 | & | 36 * | | |
| Glamorgan | Maidstone | July 5 | 55 * | | | | |
| Essex | Southend | July 16 | 67 | | | | 0-6 |
| Worcestershire | Worcester | July 23 | | | | | |
| Somerset | Taunton | July 26 | 9 | & | 0 | 1Ct | |
| Surrey | Canterbury | Aug 2 | 40 | & | 15 | 3Ct | |
| Hampshire | Canterbury | Aug 6 | 16 | & | 12 | | |
| Leicestershire | Leicester | Aug 9 | 4 | & | 90 | 1Ct | |
| Gloucs | Canterbury | Aug 20 | 6 | & | 12 | 2Ct | |
| Middlesex | Canterbury | Aug 28 | 38 | & | 46 | | |
| Sussex | Hove | Sept 3 | 4 | & | 78 | 3Ct | |
| **OTHER FIRST-CLASS** | | | | | | | |
| West Indies | Canterbury | July 20 | 7 | & | 104 | | |
| **REFUGE ASSURANCE** | | | | | | | |
| Worcestershire | Worcester | April 21 | 0 | | | | |
| Hampshire | Southampton | May 12 | 35 | | | | |
| Essex | Folkestone | May 19 | 14 | | | 1Ct | |
| Derbyshire | Canterbury | May 26 | 17 | | | | |
| Middlesex | Southgate | June 2 | 9 | | | 1Ct | |
| Yorkshire | Scarborough | June 16 | 2 | | | 1Ct | |
| Lancashire | Old Trafford | June 23 | 10 | | | | |
| Gloucs | Canterbury | June 30 | 80 | | | 1Ct | |
| Glamorgan | Maidstone | July 7 | | | | | |
| Leicestershire | Canterbury | July 14 | 17 | | | 1Ct | |
| Somerset | Taunton | July 28 | 50 | | | 1Ct | |
| Surrey | Canterbury | Aug 4 | 36 | | | | |
| Notts | Trent Bridge | Aug 11 | 26 | | | | |
| Northants | Canterbury | Aug 18 | 13 | | | 2Ct | |

| | | | | | |
|---|---|---|---|---|---|
| Sussex | Hove | Aug 25 | 18 | 1Ct | |

**NATWEST TROPHY**

| | | | | | |
|---|---|---|---|---|---|
| Cambs | Canterbury | June 26 | 25 * | | |
| Surrey | The Oval | July 11 | 0 | | 0-19 |

**BENSON & HEDGES CUP**

| | | | | | |
|---|---|---|---|---|---|
| Leicestershire | Canterbury | April 23 | 70 * | 1Ct | |
| Lancashire | Old Trafford | April 25 | 10 | | |
| Sussex | Canterbury | May 2 | 18 | | |
| Scotland | Glasgow | May 7 | 5 | | |
| Worcestershire | Worcester | May 29 | 8 | | |

**OTHER ONE-DAY**

| | | | | |
|---|---|---|---|---|
| Sussex | Hove | Sept 7 | 25 | 1Ct |

**BATTING AVERAGES - Including fielding**

| | Matches | Inns | NO | Runs | HS | Avge | 100s | 50s | Ct | St |
|---|---|---|---|---|---|---|---|---|---|---|
| Britannic Assurance | 21 | 32 | 4 | 1064 | 114 | 38.00 | 2 | 5 | 17 | - |
| Other First-Class | 1 | 2 | 0 | 111 | 104 | 55.50 | 1 | - | - | - |
| ALL FIRST-CLASS | 22 | 34 | 4 | 1175 | 114 | 39.16 | 3 | 5 | 17 | - |
| Refuge Assurance | 15 | 14 | 0 | 327 | 80 | 23.35 | - | 2 | 9 | - |
| NatWest Trophy | 2 | 2 | 1 | 25 | 25 * | 25.00 | - | - | - | - |
| Benson & Hedges Cup | 5 | 5 | 1 | 111 | 70 * | 27.75 | - | 1 | 1 | - |
| Other One-Day | 1 | 1 | 0 | 25 | 25 | 25.00 | - | - | 1 | - |
| ALL ONE-DAY | 23 | 22 | 2 | 488 | 80 | 24.40 | - | 3 | 11 | - |

**BOWLING AVERAGES**

| | Overs | Mdns | Runs | Wkts | Avge | Best | 5wI | 10wM |
|---|---|---|---|---|---|---|---|---|
| Britannic Assurance | 2 | 1 | 6 | 0 | - | - | - | - |
| Other First-Class | | | | | | | | |
| ALL FIRST-CLASS | 2 | 1 | 6 | 0 | - | - | - | - |
| Refuge Assurance | | | | | | | | |
| NatWest Trophy | 4 | 0 | 19 | 0 | - | - | - | - |
| Benson & Hedges Cup | | | | | | | | |
| Other One-Day | | | | | | | | |
| ALL ONE-DAY | 4 | 0 | 19 | 0 | - | - | - | - |

## R.M.F.COX - *Hampshire*

| Opposition | Venue | Date | Batting | Fielding | Bowling |
|---|---|---|---|---|---|
| **BRITANNIC ASSURANCE** | | | | | |
| Gloucs | Southampton | June 7 | 15 | | |
| Glamorgan | Swansea | Aug 9 | 26 | 1Ct | |
| **REFUGE ASSURANCE** | | | | | |
| Glamorgan | Ebbw Vale | Aug 11 | 2 | | |
| Surrey | The Oval | Aug 25 | 13 | 1Ct | |

**BATTING AVERAGES - Including fielding**

| | Matches | Inns | NO | Runs | HS | Avge | 100s | 50s | Ct | St |
|---|---|---|---|---|---|---|---|---|---|---|
| Britannic Assurance | 2 | 2 | 0 | 41 | 26 | 20.50 | - | - | 1 | - |
| ALL FIRST-CLASS | 2 | 2 | 0 | 41 | 26 | 20.50 | - | - | 1 | - |
| Refuge Assurance | 2 | 2 | 0 | 15 | 13 | 7.50 | - | - | 1 | - |
| ALL ONE-DAY | 2 | 2 | 0 | 15 | 13 | 7.50 | - | - | 1 | - |

**BOWLING AVERAGES**
Did not bowl

## J.P.CRAWLEY - *Lancashire, Cambridge University & Combined Universities*

| Opposition | Venue | Date | Batting | | | Fielding | Bowling |
|---|---|---|---|---|---|---|---|
| **BRITANNIC ASSURANCE** | | | | | | | |
| Yorkshire | Scarborough | Sept 3 | 52 | & | 13 | 3Ct | |
| Surrey | Old Trafford | Sept 17 | 130 | & | 35 | 4Ct | |

# PLAYER RECORDS

## OTHER FIRST-CLASS
### For Cambridge U

| | | | | | | |
|---|---|---|---|---|---|---|
| Lancashire | Fenner's | April 13 | 83 & 30 | 1Ct | | |
| Northants | Fenner's | April 16 | 39 | 2Ct | | |
| Essex | Fenner's | April 19 | 39 & 54 | | | |
| Derbyshire | Fenner's | May 9 | 0 | | 0-5 | |
| Middlesex | Fenner's | May 15 | 52 * & 43 | 1Ct | | |
| Surrey | Fenner's | May 18 | 69 & 56 | 2Ct | | |
| Leicestershire | Fenner's | May 22 | 7 & 0 | | 0-9 | |
| Glamorgan | Fenner's | June 18 | 22 | | | |
| Sussex | Hove | June 29 | 0 | | | |
| Oxford U | Lord's | July 2 | 66 & 59 * | | | |

## BENSON & HEDGES CUP
### For Combined Universities

| | | | | |
|---|---|---|---|---|
| Gloucs | Bristol | April 23 | 0 | 1Ct |
| Derbyshire | The Parks | April 25 | 18 | |
| Worcestershire | Fenner's | May 2 | 0 | |
| Northants | Northampton | May 4 | 40 | |

## BATTING AVERAGES - Including fielding

| | Matches | Inns | NO | Runs | HS | Avge | 100s | 50s | Ct | St |
|---|---|---|---|---|---|---|---|---|---|---|
| Britannic Assurance | 2 | 4 | 0 | 230 | 130 | 57.50 | 1 | 1 | 7 | - |
| Other First-Class | 10 | 16 | 2 | 619 | 83 | 44.21 | - | 7 | 6 | - |
| ALL FIRST-CLASS | 12 | 20 | 2 | 849 | 130 | 47.16 | 1 | 8 | 13 | - |
| Benson & Hedges Cup | 4 | 4 | 0 | 58 | 40 | 14.50 | - | - | 1 | - |
| ALL ONE-DAY | 4 | 4 | 0 | 58 | 40 | 14.50 | - | - | 1 | - |

## BOWLING AVERAGES

| | Overs | Mdns | Runs | Wkts | Avge | Best | 5wI | 10wM |
|---|---|---|---|---|---|---|---|---|
| Britannic Assurance | | | | | | | | |
| Other First-Class | 2 | 0 | 14 | 0 | - | - | - | - |
| ALL FIRST-CLASS | 2 | 0 | 14 | 0 | - | - | - | - |
| Benson & Hedges Cup | | | | | | | | |
| ALL ONE-DAY | | | | | | | | |

# M.A.CRAWLEY - Nottinghamshire

| Opposition | Venue | Date | Batting | Fielding | Bowling |
|---|---|---|---|---|---|
| **BRITANNIC ASSURANCE** | | | | | |
| Surrey | The Oval | June 4 | 22 & 20 * | | 0-17 & 0-47 |
| Gloucs | Gloucester | June 14 | | 49 * | 1Ct | 1-15 & 0-25 |
| Worcestershire | Worcester | June 18 | 11 | 3Ct | 0-13 |
| Warwickshire | Trent Bridge | June 21 | 22 * | 1Ct | 3-57 |
| Glamorgan | Cardiff | July 2 | 5 | | 0-13 & 2-72 |
| Lancashire | Trent Bridge | July 16 | 0 | | 0-1 |
| Northants | Well'borough | July 19 | 17 * | | 0-15 |
| Middlesex | Trent Bridge | Sept 3 | 0 & 0 | 2Ct | 0-64 |
| Derbyshire | Derby | Sept 10 | 4 | 3Ct | 3-21 & 1-63 |
| Worcestershire | Trent Bridge | Sept 17 | 10 | 4Ct | 1-24 & 0-16 |
| **OTHER FIRST-CLASS** | | | | | |
| Oxford U | The Parks | April 27 | 112 | | |
| **REFUGE ASSURANCE** | | | | | |
| Lancashire | Old Trafford | April 21 | | | 1-20 |
| Warwickshire | Trent Bridge | April 28 | 29 | | 2-25 |
| Glamorgan | Cardiff | May 5 | 5 * | | 0-16 |
| Essex | Trent Bridge | May 12 | 19 | | |
| Leicestershire | Leicester | May 26 | 6 | | 2-13 |
| Somerset | Trent Bridge | June 9 | 9 | | 0-16 |
| Gloucs | Gloucester | June 16 | | | 1-16 |
| Middlesex | Trent Bridge | June 23 | 0 | | 0-21 |
| Surrey | The Oval | June 30 | | 3Ct | 2-20 |
| Hampshire | Trent Bridge | July 14 | 6 | | 0-49 |
| Worcestershire | Trent Bridge | Sept 1 | 47 * | | 0-36 |
| **NATWEST TROPHY** | | | | | |
| Lincolnshire | Trent Bridge | June 26 | 74 * | | 4-26 |
| Gloucs | Bristol | July 11 | 35 * | | 0-3 |
| **BENSON & HEDGES CUP** | | | | | |
| Yorkshire | Trent Bridge | April 25 | 0 * | | 0-22 |
| Glamorgan | Cardiff | May 4 | 58 | | 0-16 |
| Min Counties | Trent Bridge | May 7 | 16 | | 1-44 |

## BATTING AVERAGES - Including fielding

| | Matches | Inns | NO | Runs | HS | Avge | 100s | 50s | Ct | St |
|---|---|---|---|---|---|---|---|---|---|---|
| Britannic Assurance | 10 | 12 | 4 | 160 | 49 * | 20.00 | - | - | 14 | - |
| Other First-Class | 1 | 1 | 0 | 112 | 112 | 112.00 | 1 | - | - | - |
| ALL FIRST-CLASS | 11 | 13 | 4 | 272 | 112 | 30.22 | 1 | - | 14 | - |
| Refuge Assurance | 11 | 8 | 2 | 121 | 47 * | 20.16 | - | - | 3 | - |
| NatWest Trophy | 2 | 2 | 2 | 109 | 74 * | - | - | 1 | - | - |
| Benson & Hedges Cup | 3 | 3 | 1 | 74 | 58 | 37.00 | - | 1 | - | - |
| ALL ONE-DAY | 16 | 13 | 5 | 304 | 74 * | 38.00 | - | 2 | 3 | - |

## BOWLING AVERAGES

| | Overs | Mdns | Runs | Wkts | Avge | Best | 5wI | 10wM |
|---|---|---|---|---|---|---|---|---|
| Britannic Assurance | 176.5 | 53 | 463 | 11 | 42.09 | 3-21 | - | - |
| Other First-Class | | | | | | | | |
| ALL FIRST-CLASS | 176.5 | 53 | 463 | 11 | 42.09 | 3-21 | - | - |
| Refuge Assurance | 46 | 1 | 232 | 8 | 29.00 | 2-13 | - | |
| NatWest Trophy | 13 | 1 | 29 | 4 | 7.25 | 4-26 | - | |
| Benson & Hedges Cup | 17 | 0 | 82 | 1 | 82.00 | 1-44 | - | |
| ALL ONE-DAY | 76 | 2 | 343 | 13 | 26.38 | 4-26 | - | |

# R.D.B.CROFT - Glamorgan

| Opposition | Venue | Date | Batting | Fielding | Bowling |
|---|---|---|---|---|---|
| **BRITANNIC ASSURANCE** | | | | | |
| Leicestershire | Leicester | April 27 | 15 | | 0-9 |
| Somerset | Taunton | May 9 | 2 | 1Ct | 0-66 & 0-4 |
| Warwickshire | Swansea | May 16 | 10 & 31 | 1Ct | 5-62 & 1-38 |
| Northants | Cardiff | May 22 | 16 | | 0-35 & 1-25 |
| Sussex | Cardiff | May 25 | | | 2-93 & 1-103 |
| Worcestershire | Worcester | May 31 | 3 | | 1-11 |
| Somerset | Swansea | June 4 | | 4 * | 1-90 |
| Derbyshire | Chesterfield | June 7 | 0 & 5 | | |
| Middlesex | Cardiff | June 14 | 50 | | 0-10 |
| Leicestershire | Neath | June 21 | 25 | | 0-0 |
| Lancashire | Liverpool | June 28 | | 1Ct | 1-34 |
| Notts | Cardiff | July 2 | 0 & 1 * | 1Ct | 1-89 & 0-65 |
| Kent | Maidstone | July 5 | 1 & 15 * | 1Ct | 3-97 & 0-26 |
| Gloucs | Cheltenham | July 19 | 44 & 0 | | 1-23 & 0-45 |
| Essex | Cardiff | July 23 | | 10 | 1-23 |
| Surrey | The Oval | July 26 | 10 & 11 * | 1Ct | 0-39 & 0-111 |
| Hampshire | Swansea | Aug 9 | 16 | | 0-49 |
| Yorkshire | Headingley | Aug 16 | | 1Ct | 2-108 & 3-45 |
| Warwickshire | Edgbaston | Aug 20 | | 1Ct | 0-57 & 0-18 |
| Gloucs | Abergavenny | Aug 28 | 14 | 1Ct | 2-66 & 1-73 |
| Worcestershire | Cardiff | Sept 10 | 9 & 4 | | 1-46 & 0-9 |
| Hampshire | Southampton | Sept 17 | 35 | 1Ct | 2-89 & 4-119 |
| **OTHER FIRST-CLASS** | | | | | |
| Oxford U | The Parks | April 17 | | | 0-29 |
| Cambridge U | Fenner's | June 18 | | 14 | 1Ct | 3-8 |
| West Indies | Swansea | July 16 | 0 | 1Ct | 1-116 |
| **REFUGE ASSURANCE** | | | | | |
| Northants | Cardiff | April 21 | | | 0-16 |
| Leicestershire | Leicester | April 28 | 6 | | 1-49 |
| Notts | Cardiff | May 5 | | | 1-39 |
| Somerset | Taunton | May 12 | 9 | | 1-28 |
| Kent | Maidstone | July 7 | | | 0-34 |
| Worcestershire | Worcester | July 21 | | | 2-36 |
| Surrey | The Oval | July 28 | 19 | 2Ct | 2-38 |
| Gloucs | Swansea | Aug 4 | 1 | | 2-30 |
| Hampshire | Ebbw Vale | Aug 11 | 0 | 1Ct | 1-30 |
| Derbyshire | Checkley | Aug 18 | 0 | | 0-33 |
| **NATWEST TROPHY** | | | | | |
| Worcestershire | Worcester | July 11 | | | 2-28 |
| Northants | Northampton | July 31 | 13 | | 0-18 |
| **BENSON & HEDGES CUP** | | | | | |
| Min Counties | Trowbridge | April 23 | 0 | | 2-49 |

## BATTING AVERAGES - Including fielding

| | Matches | Inns | NO | Runs | HS | Avge | 100s | 50s | Ct | St |
|---|---|---|---|---|---|---|---|---|---|---|
| Britannic Assurance | 22 | 25 | 4 | 331 | 50 | 15.76 | - | 1 | 10 | - |
| Other First-Class | 3 | 2 | 0 | 14 | 14 | 7.00 | - | - | 2 | - |

# C | PLAYER RECORDS

| | | | | | | | | | |
|---|---|---|---|---|---|---|---|---|---|
| ALL FIRST-CLASS | 25 | 27 | 4 | 345 | 50 | 15.00 | - | 1 | 12 | - |

| | | | | | | | | | | |
|---|---|---|---|---|---|---|---|---|---|---|
| Refuge Assurance | 10 | 6 | 0 | 35 | 19 | 5.83 | - | - | 3 | - |
| NatWest Trophy | 2 | 1 | 0 | 13 | 13 | 13.00 | - | - | - | - |
| Benson & Hedges Cup | 1 | 1 | 0 | 0 | 0 | 0.00 | - | - | - | - |
| | | | | | | | | | | |
| ALL ONE-DAY | 13 | 8 | 0 | 48 | 19 | 6.00 | - | - | 3 | - |

## BOWLING AVERAGES

| | Overs | Mdns | Runs | Wkts | Avge | Best | 5wI | 10wM |
|---|---|---|---|---|---|---|---|---|
| Britannic Assurance | 646.2 | 151 | 1777 | 34 | 52.26 | 5-62 | 1 | - |
| Other First-Class | 58 | 17 | 153 | 4 | 38.25 | 3-8 | - | - |
| | | | | | | | | |
| ALL FIRST-CLASS | 704.2 | 168 | 1930 | 38 | 50.78 | 5-62 | 1 | - |
| | | | | | | | | |
| Refuge Assurance | 69 | 2 | 333 | 10 | 33.30 | 2-30 | - | |
| NatWest Trophy | 17 | 0 | 46 | 2 | 23.00 | 2-28 | - | |
| Benson & Hedges Cup | 9 | 0 | 49 | 2 | 24.50 | 2-49 | - | |
| | | | | | | | | |
| ALL ONE-DAY | 95 | 2 | 428 | 14 | 30.57 | 2-28 | - | |

## K.M.CURRAN - *Northamptonshire*

| Opposition | Venue | Date | Batting | Fielding | Bowling |
|---|---|---|---|---|---|
| **BRITANNIC ASSURANCE** | | | | | |
| Glamorgan | Cardiff | May 22 | 0 & 11 | | |
| Yorkshire | Headingley | May 25 | 1 & 28* | 2Ct | 1-24 & 2-41 |
| Derbyshire | Northampton | May 31 | 6 & 9 | | 4-39 & 3-68 |
| Worcestershire | Northampton | June 4 | 17* & 32 | 1Ct | 3-45 & 1-4 |
| Hampshire | Northampton | June 21 | 31 | | 0-36 |
| Gloucs | Luton | June 28 | 5 & 22* | 2Ct | 3-23 & 0-16 |
| Kent | Maidstone | July 2 | 15 | 2Ct | 0-26 |
| Leicestershire | Leicester | July 5 | 67 | | 2-38 |
| Middlesex | Uxbridge | July 16 | 32 | | 0-21 |
| Notts | Well'borough | July 19 | 18 & 20* | 1Ct | 5-60 |
| Somerset | Northampton | July 23 | 60 | 1Ct | 0-39 & 0-5 |
| Sussex | Eastbourne | Aug 2 | 24 & 34 | | 1-33 & 2-19 |
| Lancashire | Lytham | Aug 6 | 89* | 2Ct | 2-49 |
| Warwickshire | Northampton | Aug 9 | 9 | | 3-57 |
| Essex | Colchester | Aug 16 | 11 & 8 | | 1-44 |
| Surrey | Northampton | Aug 23 | 52 & 6* | | 0-37 & 3-26 |
| Yorkshire | Northampton | Aug 28 | 2 | | 2-51 & 0-55 |
| Gloucs | Bristol | Sept 3 | 11 & 19* | 1Ct | 1-115 & 4-52 |
| Warwickshire | Edgbaston | Sept 10 | 71 & 39 | | 2-78 & 0-27 |
| **OTHER FIRST-CLASS** | | | | | |
| Cambridge U | Fenner's | April 16 | 79 | | 0-16 |
| West Indies | Northampton | June 15 | | | 3-60 |
| **REFUGE ASSURANCE** | | | | | |
| Glamorgan | Cardiff | April 21 | 13 | | 1-37 |
| Yorkshire | Headingley | May 26 | 8 | | 1-41 |
| Hampshire | Northampton | June 2 | 2* | | 2-30 |
| Gloucs | Moreton | June 9 | | | |
| Somerset | Luton | June 30 | 3 | | 3-24 |
| Surrey | Tring | July 7 | 13 | | 0-21 |
| Notts | Well'borough | July 21 | 26 | | 2-28 |
| Derbyshire | Derby | July 28 | 21 | 1Ct | 1-32 |
| Sussex | Eastbourne | Aug 4 | 25* | | 1-29 |
| Essex | Northampton | Aug 11 | 19 | | 1-7 |
| Kent | Canterbury | Aug 18 | 35* | | 1-49 |
| Warwickshire | Northampton | Aug 25 | 10 | 1Ct | 2-56 |
| Lancashire | Old Trafford | Sept 1 | 61* | | 1-30 |
| **NATWEST TROPHY** | | | | | |
| Staffordshire | Stone | June 26 | 3* | | |
| Leicestershire | Northampton | July 11 | | | 0-58 |
| Glamorgan | Northampton | July 31 | 36* | | 1-61 |
| Surrey | The Oval | Aug 14 | 38 | | 0-21 |
| **BENSON & HEDGES CUP** | | | | | |
| Derbyshire | Derby | April 23 | 26 | | 0-15 |
| Lancashire | Old Trafford | May 29 | 0 | | 0-21 |

### BATTING AVERAGES - Including fielding

| | Matches | Inns | NO | Runs | HS | Avge | 100s | 50s | Ct | St |
|---|---|---|---|---|---|---|---|---|---|---|
| Britannic Assurance | 19 | 30 | 7 | 749 | 89* | 32.56 | - | 5 | 12 | - |
| Other First-Class | 2 | 1 | 0 | 79 | 79 | 79.00 | - | 1 | - | - |
| | | | | | | | | | | |
| ALL FIRST-CLASS | 21 | 31 | 7 | 828 | 89* | 34.50 | - | 6 | 12 | - |

| | | | | | | | | | | |
|---|---|---|---|---|---|---|---|---|---|---|
| Refuge Assurance | 13 | 12 | 4 | 236 | 61* | 29.50 | - | 1 | 2 | - |
| NatWest Trophy | 4 | 3 | 2 | 77 | 38 | 77.00 | - | - | - | - |
| Benson & Hedges Cup | 2 | 2 | 0 | 26 | 26 | 13.00 | - | - | - | - |
| | | | | | | | | | | |
| ALL ONE-DAY | 19 | 17 | 6 | 339 | 61* | 30.81 | - | 1 | 2 | - |

## BOWLING AVERAGES

| | Overs | Mdns | Runs | Wkts | Avge | Best | 5wI | 10wM |
|---|---|---|---|---|---|---|---|---|
| Britannic Assurance | 410.2 | 101 | 1128 | 45 | 25.06 | 5-60 | 1 | - |
| Other First-Class | 26 | 9 | 76 | 3 | 25.33 | 3-60 | - | - |
| | | | | | | | | |
| ALL FIRST-CLASS | 436.2 | 110 | 1204 | 48 | 25.08 | 5-60 | 1 | - |
| | | | | | | | | |
| Refuge Assurance | 77.1 | 2 | 384 | 16 | 24.00 | 3-24 | - | |
| NatWest Trophy | 32 | 3 | 140 | 1 | 140.00 | 1-61 | - | |
| Benson & Hedges Cup | 6 | 0 | 36 | 0 | - | - | - | |
| | | | | | | | | |
| ALL ONE-DAY | 115.1 | 5 | 560 | 17 | 32.94 | 3-24 | - | |

## T.S.CURTIS - *Worcestershire*

| Opposition | Venue | Date | Batting | Fielding | Bowling |
|---|---|---|---|---|---|
| **BRITANNIC ASSURANCE** | | | | | |
| Gloucs | Worcester | April 27 | 49 | 1Ct | |
| Lancashire | Worcester | May 9 | 15 & 15 | 1Ct | |
| Glamorgan | Worcester | May 31 | 70 & 14 | 2Ct | |
| Northants | Northampton | June 4 | 52 & 30 | | |
| Essex | Ilford | June 7 | 2 & 68* | | |
| Sussex | Hove | June 14 | 24 & 33* | | |
| Notts | Worcester | June 18 | 0 & 0 | | 0-50 |
| Leicestershire | Worcester | June 28 | 0 & 47 | 1Ct | |
| Yorkshire | Headingley | July 2 | 1 | | |
| Hampshire | Portsmouth | July 16 | 53 & 6 | | |
| Derbyshire | Kidd'minster | July 19 | 32 & 14 | | 0-14 |
| Kent | Worcester | July 23 | 27 | | |
| Gloucs | Cheltenham | July 26 | 65 & 6 | | |
| Warwickshire | Worcester | Aug 2 | 10 | | |
| Somerset | Weston | Aug 6 | 7 & 55 | | 0-31 |
| Surrey | Worcester | Aug 16 | 98 & 8 | 3Ct | |
| Lancashire | Blackpool | Aug 20 | 32 & 120 | 1Ct | |
| Middlesex | Worcester | Aug 23 | 22 | 1Ct | |
| Warwickshire | Edgbaston | Aug 28 | 11 & 77 | | |
| Somerset | Worcester | Sept 3 | 248 | 2Ct | |
| Glamorgan | Cardiff | Sept 10 | 186* | 2Ct | |
| Notts | Trent Bridge | Sept 17 | 31 & 27 | | |
| **OTHER FIRST-CLASS** | | | | | |
| West Indies | Worcester | May 15 | 30 | | |
| Oxford U | The Parks | May 25 | 67 | | 2-17 |
| Sri Lanka | Worcester | July 30 | 1 | 1Ct | |
| **REFUGE ASSURANCE** | | | | | |
| Kent | Worcester | April 21 | 70 | 1Ct | |
| Gloucs | Bristol | May 5 | 61* | 1Ct | |
| Lancashire | Worcester | May 12 | 2 | | |
| Northants | Northampton | May 19 | 49 | 3Ct | |
| Warwickshire | Edgbaston | May 26 | 67 | | |
| Surrey | Worcester | June 2 | 65 | | |
| Essex | Ilford | June 9 | 46 | | |
| Sussex | Hove | June 16 | | | |
| Yorkshire | Sheffield | June 23 | 8 | | |
| Leicestershire | Worcester | June 30 | 88* | | |
| Hampshire | Southampton | July 7 | 76 | | |
| Derbyshire | Worcester | July 9 | 63* | | |
| Glamorgan | Worcester | July 21 | 55 | 1Ct | |
| Notts | Trent Bridge | Aug 4 | 66* | | |
| Somerset | Worcester | Aug 18 | 16 | 1Ct | |
| Middlesex | Worcester | Aug 25 | 37 | | |
| Notts | Trent Bridge | Sept 1 | 16 | 2Ct | |
| Lancashire | Old Trafford | Sept 15 | 31 | 1Ct | |
| **NATWEST TROPHY** | | | | | |
| Bedfordshire | Bedford | June 26 | | | |
| Glamorgan | Worcester | July 11 | 34 | | |
| **BENSON & HEDGES CUP** | | | | | |
| Gloucs | Worcester | April 25 | 36 | 2Ct | |
| Combined U | Fenner's | May 2 | 2 | | |
| Derbyshire | Worcester | May 4 | 30 | | |
| Northants | Northampton | May 7 | 11 | | |
| Kent | Worcester | May 29 | 53 | 1Ct | |

# PLAYER RECORDS

| | | | |
|---|---|---|---|
| Essex | Chelmsford | June 12 | 27 |
| Lancashire | Lord's | July 13 | 4 |

## BATTING AVERAGES - Including fielding

| | Matches | Inns | NO | Runs | HS | Avge | 100s | 50s | Ct | St |
|---|---|---|---|---|---|---|---|---|---|---|
| Britannic Assurance | 22 | 37 | 3 | 1555 | 248 | 45.73 | 3 | 8 | 14 | - |
| Other First-Class | 3 | 3 | 0 | 98 | 67 | 32.66 | - | 1 | 1 | - |
| | | | | | | | | | | |
| ALL FIRST-CLASS | 25 | 40 | 3 | 1653 | 248 | 44.67 | 3 | 9 | 15 | - |
| | | | | | | | | | | |
| Refuge Assurance | 18 | 17 | 4 | 816 | 88 * | 62.76 | - | 9 | 10 | - |
| NatWest Trophy | 2 | 1 | 0 | 34 | 34 | 34.00 | - | - | - | - |
| Benson & Hedges Cup | 7 | 7 | 0 | 163 | 53 | 23.28 | - | 1 | 3 | - |
| | | | | | | | | | | |
| ALL ONE-DAY | 27 | 25 | 4 | 1013 | 88 * | 48.23 | - | 10 | 13 | - |

## BOWLING AVERAGES

| | Overs | Mdns | Runs | Wkts | Avge | Best | 5wI | 10wM |
|---|---|---|---|---|---|---|---|---|
| Britannic Assurance | 21 | 2 | 95 | 0 | - | - | - | - |
| Other First-Class | 7 | 1 | 17 | 2 | 8.50 | 2-17 | - | - |
| | | | | | | | | |
| ALL FIRST-CLASS | 28 | 3 | 112 | 2 | 56.00 | 2-17 | - | - |

Refuge Assurance
NatWest Trophy
Benson & Hedges Cup

ALL ONE-DAY

# D PLAYER RECORDS

## D.B.D'OLIVEIRA - *Worcestershire*

| Opposition | Venue | Date | Batting | | | Fielding | Bowling |
|---|---|---|---|---|---|---|---|
| **BRITANNIC ASSURANCE** | | | | | | | |
| Northants | Northampton | June 4 | 33 | & | 0 | | |
| Essex | Ilford | June 7 | 25 | | | 3Ct | |
| Sussex | Hove | June 14 | 12* | | | | 0-0 |
| Notts | Worcester | June 18 | 26 | & | 25 | | |
| Yorkshire | Headingley | July 2 | | | 7 | 2Ct | |
| Kent | Worcester | July 23 | 3* | | | | |
| Gloucs | Cheltenham | July 26 | 79 | & | 11 | 2Ct | |
| Warwickshire | Worcester | Aug 2 | 10 | | | 2Ct | 0-1 |
| Somerset | Weston | Aug 6 | 1 | & | 9 | 1Ct | 0-10 |
| Surrey | Worcester | Aug 16 | 0 | & | 1 | 6Ct | 0-8 |
| Lancashire | Blackpool | Aug 20 | 30 | | | 2Ct | 1-36 & 0-32 |
| Middlesex | Worcester | Aug 23 | 10 | | | | 0-29 |
| Warwickshire | Edgbaston | Aug 28 | 0 | & | 1 | 1Ct | |
| Glamorgan | Cardiff | Sept 10 | 2 | | | 1Ct | |
| Notts | Trent Bridge | Sept 17 | 33 | & | 17 | 1Ct | |
| **OTHER FIRST-CLASS** | | | | | | | |
| Oxford U | The Parks | May 25 | 237 | | | | 0-19 |
| Sri Lanka | Worcester | July 30 | 14 | | | | 0-11 |
| **REFUGE ASSURANCE** | | | | | | | |
| Kent | Worcester | April 21 | 9* | | | 1Ct | |
| Gloucs | Bristol | May 5 | | | | 1Ct | |
| Lancashire | Worcester | May 12 | 12 | | | | |
| Northants | Northampton | May 19 | 3 | | | 1Ct | |
| Warwickshire | Edgbaston | May 26 | 4 | | | | |
| Surrey | Worcester | June 2 | 28* | | | | |
| Essex | Ilford | June 9 | 25 | | | | |
| Sussex | Hove | June 16 | | | | | |
| Yorkshire | Sheffield | June 23 | 27 | | | | |
| Leicestershire | Worcester | June 30 | 1 | | | 1Ct | |
| Hampshire | Southampton | July 7 | 32 | | | 1Ct | |
| Derbyshire | Worcester | July 9 | 54 | | | | |
| Glamorgan | Worcester | July 21 | 45 | | | 2Ct | |
| Notts | Trent Bridge | Aug 4 | 16* | | | | |
| Somerset | Worcester | Aug 18 | 23 | | | | |
| Middlesex | Worcester | Aug 25 | 11 | | | | |
| Notts | Trent Bridge | Sept 1 | 28 | | | | |
| Lancashire | Old Trafford | Sept 15 | 1 | | | | |
| **NATWEST TROPHY** | | | | | | | |
| Bedfordshire | Bedford | June 26 | 10* | | | 1Ct | |
| Glamorgan | Worcester | July 11 | 13 | | | | |
| **BENSON & HEDGES CUP** | | | | | | | |
| Gloucs | Worcester | April 25 | 6 | | | 1Ct | |
| Combined U | Fenner's | May 2 | 8 | | | 2Ct | |
| Derbyshire | Worcester | May 4 | 17 | | | | |
| Northants | Northampton | May 7 | 21 | | | | |
| Kent | Worcester | May 29 | 2 | | | | |
| Essex | Chelmsford | June 12 | | | | | |
| Lancashire | Lord's | July 13 | 25 | | | | |

### BATTING AVERAGES - Including fielding

| | Matches | Inns | NO | Runs | HS | Avge | 100s | 50s | Ct | St |
|---|---|---|---|---|---|---|---|---|---|---|
| Britannic Assurance | 15 | 22 | 2 | 335 | 79 | 16.75 | - | 1 | 21 | - |
| Other First-Class | 2 | 2 | 0 | 251 | 237 | 125.50 | 1 | - | - | - |
| ALL FIRST-CLASS | 17 | 24 | 2 | 586 | 237 | 26.63 | 1 | 1 | 21 | - |
| Refuge Assurance | 18 | 16 | 3 | 319 | 54 | 24.53 | - | 1 | 7 | - |
| NatWest Trophy | 2 | 2 | 1 | 23 | 13 | 23.00 | - | - | 1 | - |
| Benson & Hedges Cup | 7 | 6 | 0 | 79 | 25 | 13.16 | - | - | 3 | - |
| ALL ONE-DAY | 27 | 24 | 4 | 421 | 54 | 21.05 | - | 1 | 11 | - |

### BOWLING AVERAGES

| | Overs | Mdns | Runs | Wkts | Avge | Best | 5wI | 10wM |
|---|---|---|---|---|---|---|---|---|
| Britannic Assurance | 31 | 7 | 116 | 1 | 116.00 | 1-36 | - | - |
| Other First-Class | 20 | 9 | 30 | 0 | - | - | - | - |
| ALL FIRST-CLASS | 51 | 16 | 146 | 1 | 146.00 | 1-36 | - | - |
| Refuge Assurance | | | | | | | | |
| NatWest Trophy | | | | | | | | |
| Benson & Hedges Cup | | | | | | | | |
| ALL ONE-DAY | | | | | | | | |

## A.DALE - *Glamorgan*

| Opposition | Venue | Date | Batting | | | Fielding | Bowling |
|---|---|---|---|---|---|---|---|
| **BRITANNIC ASSURANCE** | | | | | | | |
| Derbyshire | Chesterfield | June 7 | 12 | & | 13 | | 0-11 & 0-30 |
| Middlesex | Cardiff | June 14 | 34 | | | | 0-6 |
| Leicestershire | Neath | June 21 | 15 | | | | |
| Lancashire | Liverpool | June 28 | | | | 1Ct | 1-26 |
| Notts | Cardiff | July 2 | 25 | & | 13 | | |
| Kent | Maidstone | July 5 | 9 | & | 23* | | 0-15 |
| Gloucs | Cheltenham | July 19 | 4 | & | 0 | 2Ct | 0-9 |
| Essex | Cardiff | July 23 | | | 9 | | 0-46 |
| Surrey | The Oval | July 26 | 89 | & | 20 | | 1-63 & 1-19 |
| Hampshire | Swansea | Aug 9 | | | 18 | 1Ct | 0-17 |
| Yorkshire | Headingley | Aug 16 | 0 | | | 2Ct | |
| Warwickshire | Edgbaston | Aug 20 | 99 | & | 0 | 1Ct | 2-43 |
| Gloucs | Abergavenny | Aug 28 | 140 | & | 80* | | 2-33 |
| Worcestershire | Cardiff | Sept 10 | 12 | & | 46 | | 0-24 |
| Hampshire | Southampton | Sept 17 | 3 | & | 47* | | 0-17 & 0-21 |
| **OTHER FIRST-CLASS** | | | | | | | |
| Cambridge U | Fenner's | June 18 | | | 45* | 1Ct | |
| West Indies | Swansea | July 16 | 62 | & | 51* | | 2-56 |
| **REFUGE ASSURANCE** | | | | | | | |
| Notts | Cardiff | May 5 | | | | | 0-16 |
| Somerset | Taunton | May 12 | 24 | | | | 0-60 |
| Warwickshire | Swansea | May 19 | 3 | | | | 0-12 |
| Sussex | Swansea | May 26 | 17 | | | 1Ct | 2-37 |
| Essex | Pontypridd | June 2 | 2 | | | | |
| Lancashire | Old Trafford | June 9 | | | | | |
| Middlesex | Cardiff | June 16 | 25* | | | | 2-36 |
| Yorkshire | Headingley | June 30 | 20* | | | 2Ct | 1-43 |
| Kent | Maidstone | July 7 | | | | | 0-18 |
| Worcestershire | Worcester | July 21 | 56 | | | | 0-27 |
| Surrey | The Oval | July 28 | 23 | | | | 2-48 |
| Gloucs | Swansea | Aug 4 | 32 | | | 1Ct | 3-44 |
| Hampshire | Ebbw Vale | Aug 11 | 7 | | | 1Ct | 2-38 |
| Derbyshire | Checkley | Aug 18 | 4 | | | 1Ct | 1-51 |
| **NATWEST TROPHY** | | | | | | | |
| Durham | Darlington | June 26 | | | | 1Ct | 0-36 |
| Worcestershire | Worcester | July 11 | 86 | | | 1Ct | 1-42 |
| Northants | Northampton | July 31 | 15 | | | | 0-37 |
| **BENSON & HEDGES CUP** | | | | | | | |
| Hampshire | Southampton | May 2 | 19 | | | | 0-30 |

### BATTING AVERAGES - Including fielding

| | Matches | Inns | NO | Runs | HS | Avge | 100s | 50s | Ct | St |
|---|---|---|---|---|---|---|---|---|---|---|
| Britannic Assurance | 15 | 23 | 3 | 711 | 140 | 35.55 | 1 | 3 | 7 | - |
| Other First-Class | 2 | 3 | 2 | 158 | 62 | 158.00 | - | 2 | 1 | - |
| ALL FIRST-CLASS | 17 | 26 | 5 | 869 | 140 | 41.38 | 1 | 5 | 8 | - |
| Refuge Assurance | 14 | 11 | 2 | 213 | 56 | 23.66 | - | 1 | 6 | - |
| NatWest Trophy | 3 | 2 | 0 | 101 | 86 | 50.50 | - | 1 | 2 | - |
| Benson & Hedges Cup | 1 | 1 | 0 | 19 | 19 | 19.00 | - | - | - | - |
| ALL ONE-DAY | 18 | 14 | 2 | 333 | 86 | 27.75 | - | 2 | 8 | - |

### BOWLING AVERAGES

| | Overs | Mdns | Runs | Wkts | Avge | Best | 5wI | 10wM |
|---|---|---|---|---|---|---|---|---|
| Britannic Assurance | 106.1 | 22 | 380 | 7 | 54.28 | 2-33 | - | - |
| Other First-Class | 14 | 2 | 56 | 2 | 28.00 | 2-56 | - | - |
| ALL FIRST-CLASS | 120.1 | 24 | 436 | 9 | 48.44 | 2-33 | - | - |
| Refuge Assurance | 72 | 1 | 430 | 13 | 33.07 | 3-44 | - | - |
| NatWest Trophy | 30 | 2 | 115 | 1 | 115.00 | 1-42 | - | - |
| Benson & Hedges Cup | 4 | 0 | 30 | 0 | - | - | - | - |
| ALL ONE-DAY | 106 | 3 | 575 | 14 | 41.07 | 3-44 | - | - |

# PLAYER RECORDS

**D**

## H.DAVIES - *Oxford University*

| Opposition | Venue | Date | Batting | Fielding | Bowling |
|---|---|---|---|---|---|
| **OTHER FIRST-CLASS** | | | | | |
| Hampshire | The Parks | April 13 | 0 & 19 * | | 0-78 |
| Glamorgan | The Parks | April 17 | 0 | | |
| Gloucs | The Parks | June 15 | | | 0-70 |
| Worcestershire | The Parks | May 25 | 6 * & 38 | | 2-144 |
| Yorkshire | The Parks | June 4 | 1 | | 0-68 & 2-46 |
| Lancashire | The Parks | June 7 | 4 | | |
| Kent | The Parks | June 18 | 0 & 12 * | | 0-70 |

### BATTING AVERAGES - Including fielding

| | Matches | Inns | NO | Runs | HS | Avge | 100s | 50s | Ct | St |
|---|---|---|---|---|---|---|---|---|---|---|
| Other First-Class | 7 | 9 | 3 | 80 | 38 | 13.33 | - | - | - | - |
| ALL FIRST-CLASS | 7 | 9 | 3 | 80 | 38 | 13.33 | - | - | - | - |

### BOWLING AVERAGES

| | Overs | Mdns | Runs | Wkts | Avge | Best | 5wI | 10wM |
|---|---|---|---|---|---|---|---|---|
| Other First-Class | 107.1 | 16 | 476 | 4 | 119.00 | 2-46 | - | - |
| ALL FIRST-CLASS | 107.1 | 16 | 476 | 4 | 119.00 | 2-46 | - | - |

## R.P.DAVIS - *Kent*

| Opposition | Venue | Date | Batting | Fielding | Bowling |
|---|---|---|---|---|---|
| **BRITANNIC ASSURANCE** | | | | | |
| Hampshire | Southampton | April 27 | 0 | | |
| Surrey | The Oval | May 9 | 36 | 1Ct | 1-26 |
| Essex | Folkestone | May 16 | 5 & 30 | | 1-86 |
| Derbyshire | Canterbury | May 25 | 27 | 3Ct | 3-28 & 3-53 |
| Middlesex | Lord's | May 31 | 6 & 5 | | 1-11 & 0-25 |
| Warwickshire | Tunbridge W | June 4 | 9 | 3Ct | 0-86 |
| Sussex | Tunbridge W | June 7 | 44 & 6 | 3Ct | 2-62 |
| Yorkshire | Harrogate | June 14 | | | 0-6 |
| Lancashire | Old Trafford | June 21 | 19 | 1Ct | 0-4 |
| Essex | Southend | July 16 | 7 | | 1-97 & 2-70 |
| Worcestershire | Worcester | July 23 | | | |
| Somerset | Taunton | July 26 | 10 & 13 * | 1Ct | 3-67 & 0-52 |
| Hampshire | Canterbury | Aug 6 | 27 | 1Ct | 2-25 & 3-62 |
| Leicestershire | Leicester | Aug 9 | 6 | 1Ct | 1-70 & 4-81 |
| Gloucs | Canterbury | Aug 20 | 0 & 37 * | | 0-16 & 1-57 |
| Middlesex | Canterbury | Aug 28 | 15 * | 2Ct | 0-74 |
| Sussex | Hove | Sept 3 | 0 & 29 * | 1Ct | 1-72 & 0-109 |
| Leicestershire | Canterbury | Sept 17 | 0 & 7 | 5Ct | 0-28 & 3-58 |
| **OTHER FIRST-CLASS** | | | | | |
| Oxford U | The Parks | June 18 | 8 | 1Ct | 1-28 & 1-22 |
| West Indies | Canterbury | July 20 | 27 & 10 | | 1-87 & 2-69 |
| **REFUGE ASSURANCE** | | | | | |
| Worcestershire | Worcester | April 21 | 7 | 2Ct | 0-40 |
| Hampshire | Southampton | May 12 | 0 | 1Ct | 1-34 |
| Essex | Folkestone | May 19 | 8 * | | 0-24 |
| Derbyshire | Canterbury | May 26 | | 1Ct | 2-29 |
| Middlesex | Southgate | June 2 | | | 0-48 |
| Yorkshire | Scarborough | June 16 | 25 | | 3-42 |
| Gloucs | Canterbury | June 30 | 2 * | | 1-37 |
| Glamorgan | Maidstone | July 7 | | | 0-46 |
| Leicestershire | Canterbury | July 14 | 11 * | 2Ct | 3-33 |
| Somerset | Taunton | July 28 | 2 | | 2-27 |
| Surrey | Canterbury | Aug 4 | 0 | | 0-41 |
| Notts | Trent Bridge | Aug 11 | 7 * | | 0-33 |
| Northants | Canterbury | Aug 18 | 40 * | 1Ct | 1-28 |
| Sussex | Hove | Aug 25 | 6 | | 2-23 |
| **NATWEST TROPHY** | | | | | |
| Cambs | Canterbury | June 26 | | 1Ct | 1-22 |
| Surrey | The Oval | July 11 | 2 | | 1-34 |
| **BENSON & HEDGES CUP** | | | | | |
| Worcestershire | Worcester | May 29 | 1 | | 0-62 |
| **OTHER ONE-DAY** | | | | | |
| Sussex | Hove | Sept 7 | 7 | 1Ct | 2-13 |

### BATTING AVERAGES - Including fielding

| | Matches | Inns | NO | Runs | HS | Avge | 100s | 50s | Ct | St |
|---|---|---|---|---|---|---|---|---|---|---|
| Britannic Assurance | 18 | 23 | 4 | 338 | 44 | 17.78 | - | - | 22 | - |
| Other First-Class | 2 | 3 | 0 | 45 | 27 | 15.00 | - | - | 1 | - |
| ALL FIRST-CLASS | 20 | 26 | 4 | 383 | 44 | 17.40 | - | - | 23 | - |
| Refuge Assurance | 14 | 11 | 5 | 108 | 40 * | 18.00 | - | - | 7 | - |
| NatWest Trophy | 2 | 1 | 0 | 2 | 2 | 2.00 | - | - | 1 | - |
| Benson & Hedges Cup | 1 | 1 | 0 | 1 | 1 | 1.00 | - | - | - | - |
| Other One-Day | 1 | 1 | 0 | 7 | 7 | 7.00 | - | - | 1 | - |
| ALL ONE-DAY | 18 | 14 | 5 | 118 | 40 * | 13.11 | - | - | 9 | - |

### BOWLING AVERAGES

| | Overs | Mdns | Runs | Wkts | Avge | Best | 5wI | 10wM |
|---|---|---|---|---|---|---|---|---|
| Britannic Assurance | 455.2 | 117 | 1325 | 32 | 41.40 | 4-81 | - | - |
| Other First-Class | 58 | 16 | 206 | 5 | 41.20 | 2-69 | - | - |
| ALL FIRST-CLASS | 513.2 | 133 | 1531 | 37 | 41.37 | 4-81 | - | - |
| Refuge Assurance | 105 | 5 | 485 | 15 | 32.33 | 3-33 | - | |
| NatWest Trophy | 20 | 4 | 56 | 2 | 28.00 | 1-22 | - | |
| Benson & Hedges Cup | 11 | 1 | 62 | 0 | - | - | - | |
| Other One-Day | 10 | 5 | 13 | 2 | 6.50 | 2-13 | - | |
| ALL ONE-DAY | 146 | 15 | 616 | 19 | 32.42 | 3-33 | - | |

## S.D.L.DAVIS - *Bedfordshire*

| Opposition | Venue | Date | Batting | Fielding | Bowling |
|---|---|---|---|---|---|
| **NATWEST TROPHY** | | | | | |
| Worcestershire | Bedford | June 26 | 14 | | |

### BATTING AVERAGES - Including fielding

| | Matches | Inns | NO | Runs | HS | Avge | 100s | 50s | Ct | St |
|---|---|---|---|---|---|---|---|---|---|---|
| NatWest Trophy | 1 | 1 | 0 | 14 | 14 | 14.00 | - | - | - | - |
| ALL ONE-DAY | 1 | 1 | 0 | 14 | 14 | 14.00 | - | - | - | - |

### BOWLING AVERAGES
Did not bowl

## W.W.DAVIS - *World XI*

| Opposition | Venue | Date | Batting | Fielding | Bowling |
|---|---|---|---|---|---|
| **OTHER FIRST-CLASS** | | | | | |
| West Indies XI | Scarborough | Aug 28 | 54 * | | 0-32 & 0-47 |
| **OTHER ONE-DAY** | | | | | |
| Yorkshire | Scarborough | Sept 8 | | 1Ct | 0-27 |

### BATTING AVERAGES - Including fielding

| | Matches | Inns | NO | Runs | HS | Avge | 100s | 50s | Ct | St |
|---|---|---|---|---|---|---|---|---|---|---|
| Other First-Class | 1 | 1 | 1 | 54 | 54 * | - | - | 1 | - | - |
| ALL FIRST-CLASS | 1 | 1 | 1 | 54 | 54 * | - | - | 1 | - | - |
| Other One-Day | 1 | 0 | 0 | 0 | 0 | - | - | - | 1 | - |
| ALL ONE-DAY | 1 | 0 | 0 | 0 | 0 | - | - | - | 1 | - |

### BOWLING AVERAGES

| | Overs | Mdns | Runs | Wkts | Avge | Best | 5wI | 10wM |
|---|---|---|---|---|---|---|---|---|
| Other First-Class | 20 | 5 | 79 | 0 | - | - | - | - |
| ALL FIRST-CLASS | 20 | 5 | 79 | 0 | - | - | - | - |
| Other One-Day | 8 | 2 | 27 | 0 | - | | | |
| ALL ONE-DAY | 8 | 2 | 27 | 0 | - | | | |

| D | PLAYER RECORDS |
|---|---|

## R.I.DAWSON - *Devon & Gloucestershire*

| Opposition | Venue | Date | Batting | Fielding | Bowling |
|---|---|---|---|---|---|
| **NATWEST TROPHY** | | | | | |
| Essex | Exmouth | June 26 | 13 | | |
| **OTHER ONE-DAY** | | | | | |
| For Gloucestershire | | | | | |
| Somerset | Hove | Sept 8 | 4 | | |
| Sussex | Hove | Sept 9 | 34 | | |

**BATTING AVERAGES - Including fielding**

| | Matches | Inns | NO | Runs | HS | Avge | 100s | 50s | Ct | St |
|---|---|---|---|---|---|---|---|---|---|---|
| NatWest Trophy | 1 | 1 | 0 | 13 | 13 | 13.00 | - | - | - | - |
| Other One-Day | 2 | 2 | 0 | 38 | 34 | 19.00 | - | - | - | - |
| ALL ONE-DAY | 3 | 3 | 0 | 51 | 34 | 17.00 | - | - | - | - |

**BOWLING AVERAGES**
Did not bowl

## A.C.DAY - *Durham*

| Opposition | Venue | Date | Batting | Fielding | Bowling |
|---|---|---|---|---|---|
| **OTHER ONE-DAY** | | | | | |
| Leicestershire | Harrogate | June 11 | | | |
| Surrey | Harrogate | June 13 | | | 1-46 |

**BATTING AVERAGES - Including fielding**

| | Matches | Inns | NO | Runs | HS | Avge | 100s | 50s | Ct | St |
|---|---|---|---|---|---|---|---|---|---|---|
| Other One-Day | 2 | 0 | 0 | 0 | 0 | - | - | - | - | - |
| ALL ONE-DAY | 2 | 0 | 0 | 0 | 0 | - | - | - | - | - |

**BOWLING AVERAGES**

| | Overs | Mdns | Runs | Wkts | Avge | Best | 5wI | 10wM |
|---|---|---|---|---|---|---|---|---|
| Other One-Day | 6 | 0 | 46 | 1 | 46.00 | 1-46 | - | |
| ALL ONE-DAY | 6 | 0 | 46 | 1 | 46.00 | 1-46 | - | |

## J.M.DE LA PENA - *Gloucestershire*

| Opposition | Venue | Date | Batting | Fielding | Bowling |
|---|---|---|---|---|---|
| **BRITANNIC ASSURANCE** | | | | | |
| Essex | Bristol | May 31 | 1 * & 0 | | 1-69 |
| Leicestershire | Hinckley | July 2 | | | 2-69 |

**BATTING AVERAGES - Including fielding**

| | Matches | Inns | NO | Runs | HS | Avge | 100s | 50s | Ct | St |
|---|---|---|---|---|---|---|---|---|---|---|
| Britannic Assurance | 2 | 2 | 1 | 1 | 1* | 1.00 | - | - | - | - |
| ALL FIRST-CLASS | 2 | 2 | 1 | 1 | 1* | 1.00 | - | - | - | - |

**BOWLING AVERAGES**

| | Overs | Mdns | Runs | Wkts | Avge | Best | 5wI | 10wM |
|---|---|---|---|---|---|---|---|---|
| Britannic Assurance | 25 | 0 | 138 | 3 | 46.00 | 2-69 | - | - |
| ALL FIRST-CLASS | 25 | 0 | 138 | 3 | 46.00 | 2-69 | - | - |

## P.A.DE SILVA - *Sri Lanka*

| Opposition | Venue | Date | Batting | Fielding | Bowling |
|---|---|---|---|---|---|
| **CORNHILL TEST MATCHES** | | | | | |
| England | Lord's | Aug 22 | 42 & 18 | 2Ct | |
| **OTHER FIRST-CLASS** | | | | | |
| Yorkshire | Headingley | July 27 | 18 | | 0-27 |

| Worcestershire | Worcester | July 30 | 26 & 16 | | |
| Derbyshire | Derby | Aug 2 | | 1Ct | |
| Somerset | Taunton | Aug 10 | 21 & 57 * | 1Ct | |
| **OTHER ONE-DAY** | | | | | |
| Durham | Chester-le-S | July 26 | 5 | 1Ct | 1-16 |
| England A | Old Trafford | Aug 14 | 10 | | |

**BATTING AVERAGES - Including fielding**

| | Matches | Inns | NO | Runs | HS | Avge | 100s | 50s | Ct | St |
|---|---|---|---|---|---|---|---|---|---|---|
| Cornhill Test Matches | 1 | 2 | 0 | 60 | 42 | 30.00 | - | - | 2 | - |
| Other First-Class | 4 | 5 | 1 | 138 | 57* | 34.50 | - | 1 | 2 | - |
| ALL FIRST-CLASS | 5 | 7 | 1 | 198 | 57* | 33.00 | - | 1 | 4 | - |
| Other One-Day | 2 | 2 | 0 | 15 | 10 | 7.50 | - | - | 1 | - |
| ALL ONE-DAY | 2 | 2 | 0 | 15 | 10 | 7.50 | - | - | 1 | - |

**BOWLING AVERAGES**

| | Overs | Mdns | Runs | Wkts | Avge | Best | 5wI | 10wM |
|---|---|---|---|---|---|---|---|---|
| Cornhill Test Matches | | | | | | | | |
| Other First-Class | 9 | 2 | 27 | 0 | - | - | - | - |
| ALL FIRST-CLASS | 9 | 2 | 27 | 0 | - | - | - | - |
| Other One-Day | 7 | 0 | 16 | 1 | 16.00 | 1-16 | | |
| ALL ONE-DAY | 7 | 0 | 16 | 1 | 16.00 | 1-16 | | |

## A.DEAN - *Bedfordshire*

| Opposition | Venue | Date | Batting | Fielding | Bowling |
|---|---|---|---|---|---|
| **NATWEST TROPHY** | | | | | |
| Worcestershire | Bedford | June 26 | 0 | | 2-20 |

**BATTING AVERAGES - Including fielding**

| | Matches | Inns | NO | Runs | HS | Avge | 100s | 50s | Ct | St |
|---|---|---|---|---|---|---|---|---|---|---|
| NatWest Trophy | 1 | 1 | 0 | 0 | 0 | 0.00 | - | - | - | - |
| ALL ONE-DAY | 1 | 1 | 0 | 0 | 0 | 0.00 | - | - | - | - |

**BOWLING AVERAGES**

| | Overs | Mdns | Runs | Wkts | Avge | Best | 5wI | 10wM |
|---|---|---|---|---|---|---|---|---|
| NatWest Trophy | 4.5 | 0 | 20 | 2 | 10.00 | 2-20 | - | |
| ALL ONE-DAY | 4.5 | 0 | 20 | 2 | 10.00 | 2-20 | - | |

## S.J.DEAN - *Staffordshire*

| Opposition | Venue | Date | Batting | Fielding | Bowling |
|---|---|---|---|---|---|
| **NATWEST TROPHY** | | | | | |
| Northants | Stone | June 26 | 0 | 1Ct | |
| **OTHER ONE-DAY** | | | | | |
| For England Am. XI | | | | | |
| Sri Lanka | Wolv'hampton | July 24 | 86 | 2Ct | |

**BATTING AVERAGES - Including fielding**

| | Matches | Inns | NO | Runs | HS | Avge | 100s | 50s | Ct | St |
|---|---|---|---|---|---|---|---|---|---|---|
| NatWest Trophy | 1 | 1 | 0 | 0 | 0 | 0.00 | - | - | 1 | - |
| Other One-Day | 1 | 1 | 0 | 86 | 86 | 86.00 | - | 1 | 2 | - |
| ALL ONE-DAY | 2 | 2 | 0 | 86 | 86 | 43.00 | - | 1 | 3 | - |

**BOWLING AVERAGES**
Did not bowl

# PLACES RECORDS

## P.A.J.DEFREITAS - *Lancashire & England*

| Opposition | Venue | Date | Batting | | | Fielding | Bowling |
|---|---|---|---|---|---|---|---|
| **CORNHILL TEST MATCHES** | | | | | | | |
| West Indies | Headingley | June 6 | 15 | & | 3 | | 4-34 & 4-59 |
| West Indies | Lord's | June 20 | 29 | | | 1Ct | 2-93 & 1-1 |
| West Indies | Trent Bridge | July 4 | 8 | & | 55 * | | 3-67 & 0-29 |
| West Indies | Edgbaston | July 25 | 10 | & | 7 | | 2-40 & 3-54 |
| West Indies | The Oval | Aug 8 | 7 | | | | 1-38 & 2-42 |
| Sri Lanka | Lord's | Aug 22 | 1 | | | | 7-70 & 1-45 |
| **BRITANNIC ASSURANCE** | | | | | | | |
| Warwickshire | Edgbaston | April 27 | | | | | 1-45 |
| Worcestershire | Worcester | May 9 | 12 | & | 47 | | 3-91 & 6-88 |
| Derbyshire | Old Trafford | May 16 | 26 | | | | 2-74 |
| Sussex | Old Trafford | May 31 | 60 | | | | 2-21 & 1-42 |
| Glamorgan | Liverpool | June 28 | | | 12 | | 0-71 & 2-78 |
| Notts | Trent Bridge | July 16 | 8 | & | 3 | | 1-55 |
| Yorkshire | Old Trafford | Aug 2 | 5 | | | | 2-66 & 1-23 |
| Derbyshire | Derby | Aug 16 | 35 | & | 17 | | 2-62 & 0-58 |
| Notts | Old Trafford | Aug 28 | 2 | & | 16 | | 3-44 & 5-71 |
| Yorkshire | Scarborough | Sept 3 | 24 * | & | 50 | | 2-104 & 1-7 |
| Surrey | Old Trafford | Sept 17 | 8 | & | 0 | | 2-45 & 3-82 |
| **OTHER FIRST-CLASS** | | | | | | | |
| Cambridge U | Fenner's | April 13 | 39 | | | 1Ct | 3-62 & 1-19 |
| **TEXACO TROPHY** | | | | | | | |
| West Indies | Edgbaston | May 23 | 8 | | | 1Ct | 1-22 |
| West Indies | Old Trafford | May 25 | | | | 1Ct | 0-50 |
| West Indies | Lord's | May 27 | | | | 2Ct | 2-26 |
| **REFUGE ASSURANCE** | | | | | | | |
| Notts | Old Trafford | April 21 | 7 | | | | 0-30 |
| Northants | Old Trafford | April 28 | 6 * | | | | 2-39 |
| Worcestershire | Worcester | May 12 | | | | | 2-35 |
| Derbyshire | Derby | May 19 | 14 * | | | | 1-29 |
| Sussex | Old Trafford | June 2 | 19 | | | | 3-28 |
| Warwickshire | Edgbaston | June 16 | 41 * | | | | 3-27 |
| Middlesex | Lord's | July 21 | 0 | | | | 1-25 |
| Yorkshire | Old Trafford | Aug 4 | 5 | | | 1Ct | 0-33 |
| Surrey | Old Trafford | Aug 18 | 11 | | | | 0-51 |
| Northants | Old Trafford | Sept 1 | | | | | 0-30 |
| Worcestershire | Old Trafford | Sept 15 | 2 | | | | 0-42 |
| **NATWEST TROPHY** | | | | | | | |
| Dorset | Bournemouth | June 26 | 6 * | | | 1Ct | 0-24 |
| Hampshire | Southampton | July 11 | 11 | | | | 0-38 |
| **BENSON & HEDGES CUP** | | | | | | | |
| Scotland | Forfar | April 23 | | | | | 4-21 |
| Kent | Old Trafford | April 25 | | | | 1Ct | 4-15 |
| Leicestershire | Leicester | May 4 | | | | | 0-37 |
| Sussex | Old Trafford | May 7 | | | | 1Ct | 2-36 |
| Northants | Old Trafford | May 29 | | | | 1Ct | 0-54 |
| Yorkshire | Old Trafford | June 16 | 12 | | | | 3-34 |
| Worcestershire | Lord's | July 13 | 19 | | | 2Ct | 1-38 |

**BATTING AVERAGES - Including fielding**

| | Matches | Inns | NO | Runs | HS | Avge | 100s | 50s | Ct | St |
|---|---|---|---|---|---|---|---|---|---|---|
| Cornhill Test Matches | 6 | 9 | 1 | 135 | 55 * | 16.87 | - | 1 | 1 | - |
| Britannic Assurance | 11 | 16 | 1 | 325 | 60 | 21.66 | - | 2 | - | - |
| Other First-Class | 1 | 1 | 0 | 39 | 39 | 39.00 | - | - | 1 | - |
| **ALL FIRST-CLASS** | 18 | 26 | 2 | 499 | 60 | 20.79 | - | 3 | 2 | - |
| Texaco Trophy | 3 | 1 | 0 | 8 | 8 | 8.00 | - | - | 4 | - |
| Refuge Assurance | 11 | 9 | 3 | 105 | 41 * | 17.50 | - | - | 1 | - |
| NatWest Trophy | 2 | 2 | 1 | 17 | 11 | 17.00 | - | - | 1 | - |
| Benson & Hedges Cup | 7 | 2 | 0 | 31 | 19 | 15.50 | - | - | 5 | - |
| **ALL ONE-DAY** | 23 | 14 | 4 | 161 | 41 * | 16.10 | - | - | 11 | - |

**BOWLING AVERAGES**

| | Overs | Mdns | Runs | Wkts | Avge | Best | 5wI | 10wM |
|---|---|---|---|---|---|---|---|---|
| Cornhill Test Matches | 233.5 | 71 | 572 | 30 | 19.06 | 7-70 | 1 | - |
| Britannic Assurance | 394.2 | 95 | 1127 | 39 | 28.89 | 6-88 | 2 | - |
| Other First-Class | 29 | 7 | 81 | 4 | 20.25 | 3-62 | - | - |
| **ALL FIRST-CLASS** | 657.1 | 173 | 1780 | 73 | 24.38 | 7-70 | 3 | - |
| Texaco Trophy | 33 | 7 | 98 | 3 | 32.66 | 2-26 | - | |
| Refuge Assurance | 84 | 5 | 369 | 12 | 30.75 | 3-27 | - | |

| | | | | | | | |
|---|---|---|---|---|---|---|---|
| NatWest Trophy | 22 | 5 | 62 | 0 | - | - | - |
| Benson & Hedges Cup | 73.1 | 13 | 235 | 14 | 16.78 | 4-15 | - |
| **ALL ONE-DAY** | 212.1 | 30 | 764 | 29 | 26.34 | 4-15 | - |

## S.J.DENNIS - *Glamorgan*

| Opposition | Venue | Date | Batting | | | Fielding | Bowling |
|---|---|---|---|---|---|---|---|
| **BRITANNIC ASSURANCE** | | | | | | | |
| Warwickshire | Swansea | May 16 | 0 | & | 3 | | 0-49 |
| **OTHER FIRST-CLASS** | | | | | | | |
| Oxford U | The Parks | April 17 | | | | | 3-31 |
| Cambridge U | Fenner's | June 18 | | | | | 0-18 |
| **REFUGE ASSURANCE** | | | | | | | |
| Somerset | Taunton | May 12 | 3 | | | 1Ct | 1-36 |
| Warwickshire | Swansea | May 19 | 6 | | | 1Ct | 0-46 |
| Lancashire | Old Trafford | June 9 | | | | | 0-13 |
| **BENSON & HEDGES CUP** | | | | | | | |
| Hampshire | Southampton | May 2 | 50 | | | | 0-29 |
| Notts | Cardiff | May 4 | 5 | | | | 0-41 |
| Yorkshire | Cardiff | May 7 | | | | | 0-49 |
| **OTHER ONE-DAY** | | | | | | | |
| For Yorkshiremen | | | | | | | |
| Yorkshire | Scarborough | Sept 7 | | | | | 1-49 |

**BATTING AVERAGES - Including fielding**

| | Matches | Inns | NO | Runs | HS | Avge | 100s | 50s | Ct | St |
|---|---|---|---|---|---|---|---|---|---|---|
| Britannic Assurance | 1 | 2 | 0 | 3 | 3 | 1.50 | - | - | - | - |
| Other First-Class | 2 | 0 | 0 | 0 | 0 | - | - | - | - | - |
| **ALL FIRST-CLASS** | 3 | 2 | 0 | 3 | 3 | 1.50 | - | - | - | - |
| Refuge Assurance | 3 | 2 | 0 | 9 | 6 | 4.50 | - | - | 2 | - |
| Benson & Hedges Cup | 3 | 2 | 0 | 55 | 50 | 27.50 | - | 1 | - | - |
| Other One-Day | 1 | 0 | 0 | 0 | 0 | - | - | - | - | - |
| **ALL ONE-DAY** | 7 | 4 | 0 | 64 | 50 | 16.00 | - | 1 | 2 | - |

**BOWLING AVERAGES**

| | Overs | Mdns | Runs | Wkts | Avge | Best | 5wI | 10wM |
|---|---|---|---|---|---|---|---|---|
| Britannic Assurance | 12 | 1 | 49 | 0 | - | - | - | - |
| Other First-Class | 24.3 | 8 | 49 | 3 | 16.33 | 3-31 | - | - |
| **ALL FIRST-CLASS** | 36.3 | 9 | 98 | 3 | 32.66 | 3-31 | - | - |
| Refuge Assurance | 18 | 0 | 95 | 1 | 95.00 | 1-36 | - | |
| Benson & Hedges Cup | 33 | 3 | 119 | 0 | - | - | - | |
| Other One-Day | 9 | 0 | 49 | 1 | 49.00 | 1-49 | - | |
| **ALL ONE-DAY** | 60 | 3 | 263 | 2 | 131.50 | 1-36 | - | |

## J.DERRICK - *Glamorgan*

| Opposition | Venue | Date | Batting | Fielding | Bowling |
|---|---|---|---|---|---|
| **OTHER FIRST-CLASS** | | | | | |
| Cambridge U | Fenner's | June 18 | 12 * | 1Ct | 0-16 |
| **REFUGE ASSURANCE** | | | | | |
| Essex | Pontypridd | June 2 | 25 | | |
| Lancashire | Old Trafford | June 9 | 4 * | | 1-17 |
| Middlesex | Cardiff | June 16 | 5 | | 4-25 |
| Yorkshire | Headingley | June 30 | 5 | | 0-37 |
| **NATWEST TROPHY** | | | | | |
| Durham | Darlington | June 26 | | | 1-59 |

**BATTING AVERAGES - Including fielding**

| | Matches | Inns | NO | Runs | HS | Avge | 100s | 50s | Ct | St |
|---|---|---|---|---|---|---|---|---|---|---|
| Other First-Class | 1 | 1 | 1 | 12 | 12 * | - | - | - | 1 | - |
| **ALL FIRST-CLASS** | 1 | 1 | 1 | 12 | 12 * | - | - | - | 1 | - |

# D · PLAYER RECORDS

| | | | | | | | | | |
|---|---|---|---|---|---|---|---|---|---|
| Refuge Assurance | 4 | 4 | 1 | 39 | 25 | 13.00 | - | - | - | - |
| NatWest Trophy | 1 | 0 | 0 | 0 | 0 | - | - | - | - | - |
| ALL ONE-DAY | 5 | 4 | 1 | 39 | 25 | 13.00 | - | - | - | - |

## BOWLING AVERAGES
| | Overs | Mdns | Runs | Wkts | Avge | Best | 5wI | 10wM |
|---|---|---|---|---|---|---|---|---|
| Other First-Class | 7 | 3 | 16 | 0 | - | - | - | - |
| ALL FIRST-CLASS | 7 | 3 | 16 | 0 | - | - | - | - |
| Refuge Assurance | 14.2 | 0 | 79 | 5 | 15.80 | 4-25 | - | |
| NatWest Trophy | 12 | 0 | 59 | 1 | 59.00 | 1-59 | - | |
| ALL ONE-DAY | 26.2 | 0 | 138 | 6 | 23.00 | 4-25 | - | |

## G.R.DILLEY - *Worcestershire*

| Opposition | Venue | Date | Batting | Fielding | Bowling |
|---|---|---|---|---|---|
| **BRITANNIC ASSURANCE** | | | | | |
| Lancashire | Worcester | May 9 | 0 & 0 | 1Ct | 5-91 & 3-64 |
| Glamorgan | Worcester | May 31 | 0 * | | 4-60 & 1-31 |
| Sussex | Hove | June 14 | | | 0-32 & 1-25 |
| Notts | Worcester | June 18 | 2 | 1Ct | 2-46 & 0-12 |
| Yorkshire | Headingley | July 2 | | | 0-61 |
| Hampshire | Portsmouth | July 16 | 0 & 15 * | | 3-50 |
| Kent | Worcester | July 23 | | | |
| Gloucs | Cheltenham | July 26 | 0 & 14 | 1Ct | 4-45 & 4-39 |
| Warwickshire | Worcester | Aug 2 | | | 3-56 & 2-23 |
| Surrey | Worcester | Aug 16 | 5 * | | 1-30 & 2-87 |
| **OTHER FIRST-CLASS** | | | | | |
| West Indies | Worcester | May 15 | 0 * | | 2-68 & 0-3 |
| **REFUGE ASSURANCE** | | | | | |
| Warwickshire | Edgbaston | May 26 | | | 2-48 |
| Middlesex | Worcester | Aug 25 | | | 0-24 |
| **NATWEST TROPHY** | | | | | |
| Bedfordshire | Bedford | June 26 | | | 1-12 |
| Glamorgan | Worcester | July 11 | 7 * | 1Ct | 1-35 |
| **BENSON & HEDGES CUP** | | | | | |
| Derbyshire | Worcester | May 4 | | | 2-57 |
| Northants | Northampton | May 7 | | | 4-35 |
| Kent | Worcester | May 29 | | | 1-72 |
| Essex | Chelmsford | June 12 | | | 2-17 |
| Lancashire | Lord's | July 13 | | | 2-19 |

### BATTING AVERAGES - Including fielding
| | Matches | Inns | NO | Runs | HS | Avge | 100s | 50s | Ct | St |
|---|---|---|---|---|---|---|---|---|---|---|
| Britannic Assurance | 10 | 10 | 4 | 37 | 15 * | 6.16 | - | - | 3 | - |
| Other First-Class | 1 | 1 | 1 | 0 | 0 * | - | - | - | - | - |
| ALL FIRST-CLASS | 11 | 11 | 5 | 37 | 15 * | 6.16 | - | - | 3 | - |
| Refuge Assurance | 2 | 0 | 0 | 0 | 0 | - | - | - | - | - |
| NatWest Trophy | 2 | 1 | 1 | 7 | 7 * | - | - | - | 1 | - |
| Benson & Hedges Cup | 5 | 0 | 0 | 0 | 0 | - | - | - | - | - |
| ALL ONE-DAY | 9 | 1 | 1 | 7 | 7 * | - | - | - | 1 | - |

### BOWLING AVERAGES
| | Overs | Mdns | Runs | Wkts | Avge | Best | 5wI | 10wM |
|---|---|---|---|---|---|---|---|---|
| Britannic Assurance | 281 | 56 | 752 | 35 | 21.48 | 5-91 | 1 | - |
| Other First-Class | 24.2 | 6 | 71 | 2 | 35.50 | 2-68 | - | - |
| ALL FIRST-CLASS | 305.2 | 62 | 823 | 37 | 22.24 | 5-91 | 1 | - |
| Refuge Assurance | 12 | 0 | 72 | 2 | 36.00 | 2-48 | - | |
| NatWest Trophy | 18 | 3 | 47 | 2 | 23.50 | 1-12 | - | |
| Benson & Hedges Cup | 49.2 | 4 | 200 | 11 | 18.18 | 4-35 | - | |
| ALL ONE-DAY | 79.2 | 7 | 319 | 15 | 21.26 | 4-35 | - | |

## S.B.DIXON - *Norfolk*

| Opposition | Venue | Date | Batting | Fielding | Bowling |
|---|---|---|---|---|---|
| **NATWEST TROPHY** | | | | | |
| Gloucs | Bristol | June 26 | 0 | | |

### BATTING AVERAGES - Including fielding
| | Matches | Inns | NO | Runs | HS | Avge | 100s | 50s | Ct | St |
|---|---|---|---|---|---|---|---|---|---|---|
| NatWest Trophy | 1 | 1 | 0 | 0 | 0 | 0.00 | - | - | - | - |
| ALL ONE-DAY | 1 | 1 | 0 | 0 | 0 | 0.00 | - | - | - | - |

### BOWLING AVERAGES
Did not bowl

## N.P.DOBBS - *Lincolnshire*

| Opposition | Venue | Date | Batting | Fielding | Bowling |
|---|---|---|---|---|---|
| **NATWEST TROPHY** | | | | | |
| Notts | Trent Bridge | June 26 | 0 * | | |

### BATTING AVERAGES - Including fielding
| | Matches | Inns | NO | Runs | HS | Avge | 100s | 50s | Ct | St |
|---|---|---|---|---|---|---|---|---|---|---|
| NatWest Trophy | 1 | 1 | 1 | 0 | 0 * | - | - | - | - | - |
| ALL ONE-DAY | 1 | 1 | 1 | 0 | 0 * | - | - | - | - | - |

### BOWLING AVERAGES
Did not bowl

## M.C.DOBSON - *Kent*

| Opposition | Venue | Date | Batting | Fielding | Bowling |
|---|---|---|---|---|---|
| **OTHER FIRST-CLASS** | | | | | |
| Oxford U | The Parks | June 18 | 13 * & 50 | 1Ct | 0-17 |

### BATTING AVERAGES - Including fielding
| | Matches | Inns | NO | Runs | HS | Avge | 100s | 50s | Ct | St |
|---|---|---|---|---|---|---|---|---|---|---|
| Other First-Class | 1 | 2 | 1 | 63 | 50 | 63.00 | - | 1 | 1 | - |
| ALL FIRST-CLASS | 1 | 2 | 1 | 63 | 50 | 63.00 | - | 1 | 1 | - |

### BOWLING AVERAGES
| | Overs | Mdns | Runs | Wkts | Avge | Best | 5wI | 10wM |
|---|---|---|---|---|---|---|---|---|
| Other First-Class | 8 | 1 | 17 | 0 | - | - | - | - |
| ALL FIRST-CLASS | 8 | 1 | 17 | 0 | - | - | - | - |

## A.I.C.DODEMAIDE - *Sussex*

| Opposition | Venue | Date | Batting | Fielding | Bowling |
|---|---|---|---|---|---|
| **BRITANNIC ASSURANCE** | | | | | |
| Middlesex | Hove | May 22 | 3 | 1Ct | 1-63 & 1-30 |
| Glamorgan | Cardiff | May 25 | 12 & 100 * | | 0-57 |
| Lancashire | Old Trafford | May 31 | 20 & 0 | | 1-21 |
| Kent | Tunbridge W | June 7 | 37 * | 1Ct | 2-25 & 0-27 |
| Worcestershire | Hove | June 14 | 35 * | 1Ct | 2-45 |
| Warwickshire | Coventry | June 18 | 27 | 1Ct | 2-60 |
| Essex | Horsham | June 21 | 27 * | | 2-43 |
| Surrey | Arundel | July 2 | 1 & 2 | | 3-108 |
| Derbyshire | Derby | July 5 | 2 & 9 * | | 0-59 & 1-21 |
| Somerset | Hove | July 16 | 27 * | | 4-90 & 0-46 |
| Leicestershire | Hove | July 19 | 12 * | 1Ct | 1-29 & 0-34 |
| Gloucs | Cheltenham | July 23 | 0 | | 5-130 |
| Northants | Eastbourne | Aug 2 | 28 & 1 | 2Ct | 1-52 & 3-45 |
| Notts | Eastbourne | Aug 6 | 2 & 0 * | | 3-71 |
| Yorkshire | Midd'brough | Aug 9 | 11 | | 4-67 & 1-36 |

# PLAYER RECORDS

**D**

| | | | | | | |
|---|---|---|---|---|---|---|
| Hampshire | Bournemouth | Aug 20 | 12 | | | 2-71 & 0-47 |
| Surrey | The Oval | Aug 28 | 23 & 48 | | | 3-104 |
| Kent | Hove | Sept 3 | 23 * & 25 | | | 3-64 & 4-87 |
| Gloucs | Hove | Sept 17 | 72 & 22 | | | 1-34 & 2-17 |

**OTHER FIRST-CLASS**
For Victoria

| | | | | | | |
|---|---|---|---|---|---|---|
| Essex | Chelmsford | Sept 23 | 21 & 0 | 1Ct | 2-54 |

**REFUGE ASSURANCE**

| | | | | | |
|---|---|---|---|---|---|
| Warwickshire | Edgbaston | April 21 | | 1Ct | 0-20 |
| Glamorgan | Swansea | May 26 | 9 | | 0-10 |
| Hampshire | Basingstoke | June 9 | 0 | | 0-20 |
| Worcestershire | Hove | June 16 | | | |
| Derbyshire | Derby | July 7 | | | 0-25 |
| Surrey | The Oval | July 14 | 17 * | | 1-32 |
| Leicestershire | Hove | July 21 | 18 | | 0-19 |
| Notts | Hove | July 28 | 31 * | | 1-35 |
| Northants | Eastbourne | Aug 4 | 8 | | 2-22 |
| Yorkshire | Midd'brough | Aug 11 | 7 | 1Ct | 2-48 |
| Kent | Hove | Aug 25 | 6 * | 1Ct | 1-29 |

**NATWEST TROPHY**

| | | | | | |
|---|---|---|---|---|---|
| Scotland | Edinburgh | June 26 | 32 * | | 2-12 |
| Essex | Hove | July 11 | 27 * | 1Ct | 0-52 |

**BENSON & HEDGES CUP**

| | | | | |
|---|---|---|---|---|
| Leicestershire | | April 25 | | 1-17 |

**OTHER ONE-DAY**
For Rest of World

| | | | | | |
|---|---|---|---|---|---|
| England XI | Jesmond | July 31 | | | 2-66 |
| England XI | Jesmond | Aug 1 | 6 * | 1Ct | 1-60 |

For Sussex

| | | | | | |
|---|---|---|---|---|---|
| Kent | Hove | Sept 7 | 12 | | 0-12 |
| Gloucs | Hove | Sept 9 | 1 | | 1-30 |

For Victoria

| | | | | |
|---|---|---|---|---|
| Essex | Chelmsford | Sept 22 | | 1-40 |

**BATTING AVERAGES - Including fielding**

| | Matches | Inns | NO | Runs | HS | Avge | 100s | 50s | Ct | St |
|---|---|---|---|---|---|---|---|---|---|---|
| Britannic Assurance | 19 | 28 | 9 | 581 | 100 * | 30.57 | 1 | 1 | 7 | - |
| Other First-Class | 1 | 2 | 0 | 21 | 21 | 10.50 | - | - | 1 | - |
| ALL FIRST-CLASS | 20 | 30 | 9 | 602 | 100 * | 28.66 | 1 | 1 | 8 | - |
| Refuge Assurance | 11 | 8 | 3 | 96 | 31 * | 19.20 | - | - | 3 | - |
| NatWest Trophy | 2 | 2 | 2 | 59 | 32 * | - | - | - | 1 | - |
| Benson & Hedges Cup | 1 | 0 | 0 | 0 | 0 | - | - | - | - | - |
| Other One-Day | 5 | 3 | 1 | 19 | 12 | 9.50 | - | - | 1 | - |
| ALL ONE-DAY | 19 | 13 | 6 | 174 | 32 * | 24.85 | - | - | 5 | - |

**BOWLING AVERAGES**

| | Overs | Mdns | Runs | Wkts | Avge | Best | 5wI | 10wM |
|---|---|---|---|---|---|---|---|---|
| Britannic Assurance | 555 | 110 | 1583 | 52 | 30.44 | 5-130 | 1 | - |
| Other First-Class | 24 | 6 | 54 | 2 | 27.00 | 2-54 | - | - |
| ALL FIRST-CLASS | 579 | 116 | 1637 | 54 | 30.31 | 5-130 | 1 | - |
| Refuge Assurance | 70 | 5 | 260 | 7 | 37.14 | 2-22 | - | |
| NatWest Trophy | 21 | 3 | 64 | 2 | 32.00 | 2-12 | - | |
| Benson & Hedges Cup | 7 | 3 | 17 | 1 | 17.00 | 1-17 | - | |
| Other One-Day | 45 | 3 | 208 | 5 | 41.60 | 2-66 | - | |
| ALL ONE-DAY | 143 | 14 | 549 | 15 | 36.60 | 2-12 | - | |

## A.A.DONALD - *Warwickshire*

| Opposition | Venue | Date | Batting | Fielding | Bowling |
|---|---|---|---|---|---|
| **BRITANNIC ASSURANCE** | | | | | |
| Lancashire | Edgbaston | April 27 | | | 0-58 |
| Yorkshire | Headingley | May 9 | 11 * & 0 | | 5-42 & 5-54 |
| Glamorgan | Swansea | May 16 | 2 * | | 5-38 & 5-36 |
| Essex | Chelmsford | May 22 | 12 & 4 | 1Ct | 3-52 & 0-27 |
| Gloucs | Edgbaston | May 25 | 2 * | 1Ct | 1-27 & 5-33 |
| Yorkshire | Edgbaston | May 31 | 0 | 2Ct | 4-28 & 2-47 |
| Kent | Tunbridge W | June 4 | 0 * | | 1-22 |
| Somerset | Edgbaston | June 7 | | | 0-20 |
| Sussex | Coventry | June 18 | 4 | 1Ct | 1-8 & 5-48 |

| | | | | | |
|---|---|---|---|---|---|
| Notts | Trent Bridge | June 21 | 5 | | 0-1 & 1-31 |
| Derbyshire | Edgbaston | June 28 | 0 * & 0 * | 1Ct | 0-53 & 2-51 |
| Middlesex | Edgbaston | July 2 | 4 | 1Ct | 0-43 & 3-46 |
| Hampshire | Portsmouth | July 19 | 8 * | 1Ct | 1-41 & 3-32 |
| Lancashire | Old Trafford | July 23 | 1 | | 0-50 |
| Leicestershire | Leicester | July 26 | 1 * | | 3-64 & 4-59 |
| Worcestershire | Worcester | Aug 2 | 18 & 12 | 1Ct | 2-90 |
| Northants | Northampton | Aug 9 | | | 2-82 |
| Glamorgan | Edgbaston | Aug 20 | | | 2-68 & 0-2 |
| Worcestershire | Edgbaston | Aug 28 | 0 | 1Ct | 0-51 & 2-27 |
| Northants | Edgbaston | Sept 10 | | | 3-55 & 6-69 |
| Somerset | Taunton | Sept 17 | 4 & 8 * | | 6-84 & 1-95 |

**REFUGE ASSURANCE**

| | | | | | |
|---|---|---|---|---|---|
| Sussex | Edgbaston | April 21 | | 1Ct | 2-7 |
| Notts | Trent Bridge | April 28 | 7 | | 0-41 |
| Glamorgan | Swansea | May 19 | | | 0-43 |
| Worcestershire | Edgbaston | May 26 | | 1Ct | 1-43 |
| Somerset | Edgbaston | June 2 | | | 0-21 |
| Essex | Chelmsford | July 7 | | | 2-30 |
| Middlesex | Edgbaston | July 14 | | | 2-44 |
| Gloucs | Edgbaston | Aug 18 | | 1Ct | 1-35 |

**NATWEST TROPHY**

| | | | | | |
|---|---|---|---|---|---|
| Yorkshire | Edgbaston | June 26 | | | 4-16 |
| Hertfordshire | Edgbaston | July 11 | | | 1-40 |
| Somerset | Edgbaston | July 31 | 2 * | | 1-35 |
| Hampshire | Edgbaston | Aug 14 | 1 | | 0-41 |

**BENSON & HEDGES CUP**

| | | | | | |
|---|---|---|---|---|---|
| Essex | Edgbaston | April 25 | 6 * | | 2-78 |
| Somerset | Edgbaston | May 2 | | | 4-55 |
| Middlesex | Lord's | May 4 | 2 * | 1Ct | 0-32 |
| Surrey | The Oval | May 7 | | | 2-55 |
| Yorkshire | Headingley | May 29 | 0 | | 3-46 |

**BATTING AVERAGES - Including fielding**

| | Matches | Inns | NO | Runs | HS | Avge | 100s | 50s | Ct | St |
|---|---|---|---|---|---|---|---|---|---|---|
| Britannic Assurance | 21 | 21 | 9 | 96 | 18 | 8.00 | - | - | 10 | - |
| ALL FIRST-CLASS | 21 | 21 | 9 | 96 | 18 | 8.00 | - | - | 10 | - |
| Refuge Assurance | 8 | 1 | 0 | 7 | 7 | 7.00 | - | - | 3 | - |
| NatWest Trophy | 4 | 2 | 1 | 3 | 2 * | 3.00 | - | - | - | - |
| Benson & Hedges Cup | 5 | 3 | 2 | 8 | 6 * | 8.00 | - | - | 1 | - |
| ALL ONE-DAY | 17 | 6 | 3 | 18 | 7 | 6.00 | - | - | 4 | - |

**BOWLING AVERAGES**

| | Overs | Mdns | Runs | Wkts | Avge | Best | 5wI | 10wM |
|---|---|---|---|---|---|---|---|---|
| Britannic Assurance | 522.3 | 91 | 1634 | 83 | 19.68 | 6-69 | 8 | 2 |
| ALL FIRST-CLASS | 522.3 | 91 | 1634 | 83 | 19.68 | 6-69 | 8 | 2 |
| Refuge Assurance | 58 | 1 | 264 | 8 | 33.00 | 2-7 | - | |
| NatWest Trophy | 42 | 4 | 132 | 6 | 22.00 | 4-16 | - | |
| Benson & Hedges Cup | 49 | 2 | 266 | 11 | 24.18 | 4-55 | - | |
| ALL ONE-DAY | 149 | 7 | 662 | 25 | 26.48 | 4-16 | - | |

## B.T.P.DONELAN - *Sussex*

| Opposition | Venue | Date | Batting | Fielding | Bowling |
|---|---|---|---|---|---|
| **BRITANNIC ASSURANCE** | | | | | |
| Somerset | Taunton | April 27 | | | 2-39 |
| Middlesex | Hove | May 22 | 27 * | | 0-54 & 1-50 |
| Glamorgan | Cardiff | May 25 | 17 & 22 | | 0-78 |
| Leicestershire | Hove | July 19 | | | 2-96 & 6-92 |
| Gloucs | Cheltenham | July 23 | 28 * | | 0-15 |
| Northants | Eastbourne | Aug 2 | 17 * & 2 | 1Ct | 2-35 & 2-80 |
| Notts | Eastbourne | Aug 6 | 32 | | 0-106 |
| Yorkshire | Midd'brough | Aug 9 | 59 | 1Ct | 0-32 & 3-43 |
| Hampshire | Bournemouth | Aug 20 | 7 * | | 2-82 & 0-47 |
| Surrey | The Oval | Aug 28 | 4 & 36 | | 3-64 |
| Kent | Hove | Sept 3 | 61 & 2 | 1Ct | 1-52 & 0-61 |
| Gloucs | Hove | Sept 17 | 9 & 30 * | | 4-74 & 6-62 |

**OTHER FIRST-CLASS**

| | | | | | |
|---|---|---|---|---|---|
| Cambridge U | Hove | June 29 | | | |

# D  PLAYER RECORDS

### REFUGE ASSURANCE

| | | | | | |
|---|---|---|---|---|---|
| Gloucs | Hove | May 19 | 19 | 1Ct | 1-35 |
| Kent | Hove | Aug 25 | | | 0-23 |

### BENSON & HEDGES CUP

| | | | | | |
|---|---|---|---|---|---|
| Kent | Canterbury | May 2 | 8* | | 0-54 |

### OTHER ONE-DAY
For D of Norfolk

| | | | | | |
|---|---|---|---|---|---|
| West Indies | Arundel | May 12 | 1 | | 3-41 |

For Sussex

| | | | | | |
|---|---|---|---|---|---|
| Kent | Hove | Sept 7 | 45* | 1Ct | 1-14 |
| Gloucs | Hove | Sept 9 | 24 | | 0-41 |

### BATTING AVERAGES - Including fielding

| | Matches | Inns | NO | Runs | HS | Avge | 100s | 50s | Ct | St |
|---|---|---|---|---|---|---|---|---|---|---|
| Britannic Assurance | 12 | 15 | 5 | 353 | 61 | 35.30 | - | 2 | 3 | - |
| Other First-Class | 1 | 0 | 0 | 0 | 0 | - | - | - | - | - |
| ALL FIRST-CLASS | 13 | 15 | 5 | 353 | 61 | 35.30 | - | 2 | 3 | - |
| Refuge Assurance | 2 | 1 | 0 | 19 | 19 | 19.00 | - | - | 1 | - |
| Benson & Hedges Cup | 1 | 1 | 1 | 8 | 8* | - | - | - | - | - |
| Other One-Day | 3 | 3 | 1 | 70 | 45* | 35.00 | - | - | 1 | - |
| ALL ONE-DAY | 6 | 5 | 2 | 97 | 45* | 32.33 | - | - | 2 | - |

### BOWLING AVERAGES

| | Overs | Mdns | Runs | Wkts | Avge | Best | 5wI | 10wM |
|---|---|---|---|---|---|---|---|---|
| Britannic Assurance | 426.3 | 112 | 1162 | 34 | 34.17 | 6-62 | 2 | 1 |
| Other First-Class | | | | | | | | |
| ALL FIRST-CLASS | 426.3 | 112 | 1162 | 34 | 34.17 | 6-62 | 2 | 1 |
| Refuge Assurance | 15 | 1 | 58 | 1 | 58.00 | 1-35 | - | |
| Benson & Hedges Cup | 11 | 0 | 54 | 0 | - | - | - | |
| Other One-Day | 25.2 | 2 | 96 | 4 | 24.00 | 3-41 | - | |
| ALL ONE-DAY | 51.2 | 3 | 208 | 5 | 41.60 | 3-41 | - | |

## K.DONOHUE - *Devon*

| Opposition | Venue | Date | Batting | Fielding | Bowling |
|---|---|---|---|---|---|

### NATWEST TROPHY

| | | | | | |
|---|---|---|---|---|---|
| Essex | Exmouth | June 26 | 4 | | 2-34 |

### BATTING AVERAGES - Including fielding

| | Matches | Inns | NO | Runs | HS | Avge | 100s | 50s | Ct | St |
|---|---|---|---|---|---|---|---|---|---|---|
| NatWest Trophy | 1 | 1 | 0 | 4 | 4 | 4.00 | - | - | - | - |
| ALL ONE-DAY | 1 | 1 | 0 | 4 | 4 | 4.00 | - | - | - | - |

### BOWLING AVERAGES

| | Overs | Mdns | Runs | Wkts | Avge | Best | 5wI | 10wM |
|---|---|---|---|---|---|---|---|---|
| NatWest Trophy | 12 | 3 | 34 | 2 | 17.00 | 2-34 | - | |
| ALL ONE-DAY | 12 | 3 | 34 | 2 | 17.00 | 2-34 | - | |

## P.R.DOWNTON - *Middlesex*

| Opposition | Venue | Date | Batting | Fielding | Bowling |
|---|---|---|---|---|---|

### BRITANNIC ASSURANCE

| | | | | | |
|---|---|---|---|---|---|
| Yorkshire | Lord's | April 27 | | 4Ct | |
| Sussex | Lord's | May 9 | 51* & 38 | 3Ct | |
| Sussex | Hove | May 22 | 24* | 1Ct,1St | |

### OTHER FIRST-CLASS

| | | | | | |
|---|---|---|---|---|---|
| MCC | Lord's | April 16 | 32 | 1Ct | |
| West Indies | Lord's | May 18 | 23 & 21 | 2Ct | |

### REFUGE ASSURANCE

| | | | | | |
|---|---|---|---|---|---|
| Gloucs | Bristol | April 21 | | 1Ct,2St | |
| Surrey | Lord's | April 28 | 5 | | |
| Sussex | Hove | May 12 | 3 | | |

### BENSON & HEDGES CUP

| | | | | | |
|---|---|---|---|---|---|
| Somerset | Taunton | April 23 | | 3Ct,1St | |
| Surrey | Lord's | April 25 | 35* | 1Ct | |
| Essex | Chelmsford | May 2 | 58 | 2Ct | |
| Warwickshire | Lord's | May 4 | 41 | 1Ct | |

### BATTING AVERAGES - Including fielding

| | Matches | Inns | NO | Runs | HS | Avge | 100s | 50s | Ct | St |
|---|---|---|---|---|---|---|---|---|---|---|
| Britannic Assurance | 3 | 3 | 2 | 113 | 51* | 113.00 | - | 1 | 8 | 1 |
| Other First-Class | 2 | 3 | 0 | 76 | 32 | 25.33 | - | - | 3 | - |
| ALL FIRST-CLASS | 5 | 6 | 2 | 189 | 51* | 47.25 | - | 1 | 11 | 1 |
| Refuge Assurance | 3 | 2 | 0 | 8 | 5 | 4.00 | - | - | 1 | 2 |
| Benson & Hedges Cup | 4 | 3 | 1 | 134 | 58 | 67.00 | - | 1 | 7 | 1 |
| ALL ONE-DAY | 7 | 5 | 1 | 142 | 58 | 35.50 | - | 1 | 8 | 3 |

### BOWLING AVERAGES
Did not bowl

## P.J.L.DUJON - *West Indies*

| Opposition | Venue | Date | Batting | Fielding | Bowling |
|---|---|---|---|---|---|

### CORNHILL TEST MATCHES

| | | | | | |
|---|---|---|---|---|---|
| England | Headingley | June 6 | 6 & 33 | 6Ct | |
| England | Lord's | June 20 | 20 | 2Ct | |
| England | Trent Bridge | July 4 | 19 | 3Ct | |
| England | Edgbaston | July 25 | 6 | 4Ct | |
| England | The Oval | Aug 8 | 0 & 5 | 2Ct | |

### OTHER FIRST-CLASS

| | | | | | |
|---|---|---|---|---|---|
| Worcestershire | Worcester | May 15 | 0 | | |
| Leicestershire | Leicester | June 1 | 9* | 2Ct | |
| Northants | Northampton | June 15 | 82 | | |
| Hampshire | Southampton | June 29 | 68 | 2Ct | |
| Kent | Canterbury | July 20 | 22 | | |
| Essex | Chelmsford | Aug 3 | 142* & 27* | | |

### TEXACO TROPHY

| | | | | | |
|---|---|---|---|---|---|
| England | Edgbaston | May 23 | 5 | 2Ct | |
| England | Old Trafford | May 25 | 21 | 1Ct | |
| England | Lord's | May 27 | 0 | 1Ct | |

### OTHER ONE-DAY

| | | | | | |
|---|---|---|---|---|---|
| D of Norfolk | Arundel | May 12 | 21* | 2Ct | |
| Wales | Brecon | July 15 | 19 | 1Ct | |

### BATTING AVERAGES - Including fielding

| | Matches | Inns | NO | Runs | HS | Avge | 100s | 50s | Ct | St |
|---|---|---|---|---|---|---|---|---|---|---|
| Cornhill Test Matches | 5 | 7 | 0 | 89 | 33 | 12.71 | - | - | 17 | - |
| Other First-Class | 6 | 7 | 3 | 350 | 142* | 87.50 | 1 | 2 | 4 | - |
| ALL FIRST-CLASS | 11 | 14 | 3 | 439 | 142* | 39.90 | 1 | 2 | 21 | - |
| Texaco Trophy | 3 | 3 | 0 | 26 | 21 | 8.66 | - | - | 4 | - |
| Other One-Day | 2 | 2 | 1 | 40 | 21* | 40.00 | - | - | 3 | - |
| ALL ONE-DAY | 5 | 5 | 1 | 66 | 21* | 16.50 | - | - | 7 | - |

### BOWLING AVERAGES
Did not bowl

## P.G.DUTHIE - *Scotland*

| Opposition | Venue | Date | Batting | Fielding | Bowling |
|---|---|---|---|---|---|

### OTHER FIRST-CLASS

| | | | | | |
|---|---|---|---|---|---|
| Ireland | Dublin | June 22 | 0 | 1Ct | 2-80 & 0-35 |

### NATWEST TROPHY

| | | | | | |
|---|---|---|---|---|---|
| Sussex | Edinburgh | June 26 | 19 | | 2-42 |

### BATTING AVERAGES - Including fielding

| | Matches | Inns | NO | Runs | HS | Avge | 100s | 50s | Ct | St |
|---|---|---|---|---|---|---|---|---|---|---|
| Other First-Class | 1 | 1 | 0 | 0 | 0 | 0.00 | - | - | 1 | - |

# PLAYER RECORDS                                        D

| | | | | | | | | | |
|---|---|---|---|---|---|---|---|---|---|
| ALL FIRST-CLASS | 1 | 1 | 0 | 0 | 0 | 0.00 | - | - | 1 | - |
| NatWest Trophy | 1 | 1 | 0 | 19 | 19 | 19.00 | - | - | - | - |
| ALL ONE-DAY | 1 | 1 | 0 | 19 | 19 | 19.00 | - | - | - | - |

**BOWLING AVERAGES**

| | Overs | Mdns | Runs | Wkts | Avge | Best | 5wI | 10wM |
|---|---|---|---|---|---|---|---|---|
| Other First-Class | 47 | 15 | 115 | 2 | 57.50 | 2-80 | - | - |
| ALL FIRST-CLASS | 47 | 15 | 115 | 2 | 57.50 | 2-80 | - | - |
| NatWest Trophy | 12 | 2 | 42 | 2 | 21.00 | 2-42 | - | |
| ALL ONE-DAY | 12 | 2 | 42 | 2 | 21.00 | 2-42 | - | |

# A.J.DUTTON - *Staffordshire*

| Opposition | Venue | Date | Batting | Fielding | Bowling |
|---|---|---|---|---|---|
| **NATWEST TROPHY** | | | | | |
| Northants | Stone | June 26 | 12 | | 0-54 |

**BATTING AVERAGES - Including fielding**

| | Matches | Inns | NO | Runs | HS | Avge | 100s | 50s | Ct | St |
|---|---|---|---|---|---|---|---|---|---|---|
| NatWest Trophy | 1 | 1 | 0 | 12 | 12 | 12.00 | - | - | - | - |
| ALL ONE-DAY | 1 | 1 | 0 | 12 | 12 | 12.00 | - | - | - | - |

**BOWLING AVERAGES**

| | Overs | Mdns | Runs | Wkts | Avge | Best | 5wI | 10wM |
|---|---|---|---|---|---|---|---|---|
| NatWest Trophy | 12 | 0 | 54 | 0 | - | - | - | |
| ALL ONE-DAY | 12 | 0 | 54 | 0 | - | - | - | |

# E

# PLAYER RECORDS

## M.A.EALHAM - *Kent*

| Opposition | Venue | Date | Batting | | Fielding | Bowling |
|---|---|---|---|---|---|---|
| **BRITANNIC ASSURANCE** | | | | | | |
| Middlesex | Canterbury | Aug 28 | 34 | | 1Ct | 2-47 & 2-11 |
| Sussex | Hove | Sept 3 | 26 & | 0 | | 5-39 & 0-80 |
| Leicestershire | Canterbury | Sept 17 | 0 & | 36 | 2Ct | 1-32 & 5-65 |
| **OTHER FIRST-CLASS** | | | | | | |
| Oxford U | The Parks | June 18 | 2 * & | 37 | | 2-38 & 0-42 |
| **REFUGE ASSURANCE** | | | | | | |
| Middlesex | Southgate | June 2 | 6 * | | | 2-56 |
| Surrey | Canterbury | Aug 4 | 2 | | | 2-25 |
| Notts | Trent Bridge | Aug 11 | 18 | | | 3-36 |
| Northants | Canterbury | Aug 18 | 3 | | | 0-26 |
| Sussex | Hove | Aug 25 | 17 | | | 0-35 |
| **BENSON & HEDGES CUP** | | | | | | |
| Sussex | Canterbury | May 2 | | | 1Ct | 1-46 |
| Scotland | Glasgow | May 7 | 0 * | | 1Ct | 0-32 |
| **OTHER ONE-DAY** | | | | | | |
| Sussex | Hove | Sept 7 | 12 | | | 3-32 |

**BATTING AVERAGES - Including fielding**

| | Matches | Inns | NO | Runs | HS | Avge | 100s | 50s | Ct | St |
|---|---|---|---|---|---|---|---|---|---|---|
| Britannic Assurance | 3 | 5 | 0 | 96 | 36 | 19.20 | - | - | 3 | - |
| Other First-Class | 1 | 2 | 1 | 39 | 37 | 39.00 | - | - | - | - |
| ALL FIRST-CLASS | 4 | 7 | 1 | 135 | 37 | 22.50 | - | - | 3 | - |
| Refuge Assurance | 5 | 5 | 1 | 46 | 18 | 11.50 | - | - | - | - |
| Benson & Hedges Cup | 2 | 1 | 1 | 0 | 0* | - | - | - | 2 | - |
| Other One-Day | 1 | 1 | 0 | 12 | 12 | 12.00 | - | - | - | - |
| ALL ONE-DAY | 8 | 7 | 2 | 58 | 18 | 11.60 | - | - | 2 | - |

**BOWLING AVERAGES**

| | Overs | Mdns | Runs | Wkts | Avge | Best | 5wI | 10wM |
|---|---|---|---|---|---|---|---|---|
| Britannic Assurance | 98.1 | 20 | 274 | 15 | 18.26 | 5-39 | 2 | - |
| Other First-Class | 20 | 4 | 80 | 2 | 40.00 | 2-38 | - | - |
| ALL FIRST-CLASS | 118.1 | 24 | 354 | 17 | 20.82 | 5-39 | 2 | - |
| Refuge Assurance | 38 | 0 | 178 | 7 | 25.42 | 3-36 | - | |
| Benson & Hedges Cup | 19 | 1 | 78 | 1 | 78.00 | 1-46 | - | |
| Other One-Day | 10 | 1 | 32 | 3 | 10.66 | 3-32 | - | |
| ALL ONE-DAY | 67 | 2 | 288 | 11 | 26.18 | 3-32 | - | |

## D.E.EAST - *Essex*

| Opposition | Venue | Date | Batting | Fielding | Bowling |
|---|---|---|---|---|---|
| **REFUGE ASSURANCE** | | | | | |
| Surrey | The Oval | May 26 | 2 | | |
| **OTHER ONE-DAY** | | | | | |
| Durham | Scarborough | Aug 31 | | 4Ct | |
| Yorkshire | Scarburgh | Sept 2 | 6 | 1Ct | |

**BATTING AVERAGES - Including fielding**

| | Matches | Inns | NO | Runs | HS | Avge | 100s | 50s | Ct | St |
|---|---|---|---|---|---|---|---|---|---|---|
| Refuge Assurance | 1 | 1 | 0 | 2 | 2 | 2.00 | - | - | - | - |
| Other One-Day | 2 | 1 | 0 | 6 | 6 | 6.00 | - | - | 5 | - |
| ALL ONE-DAY | 3 | 2 | 0 | 8 | 6 | 4.00 | - | - | 5 | - |

**BOWLING AVERAGES**
Did not bowl

## K.ECCLESHARF - *League CC XI*

| Opposition | Venue | Date | Batting | Fielding | Bowling |
|---|---|---|---|---|---|
| **OTHER ONE-DAY** | | | | | |
| West Indies | Trowbridge | June 28 | | | 0-33 |

**BATTING AVERAGES - Including fielding**

| | Matches | Inns | NO | Runs | HS | Avge | 100s | 50s | Ct | St |
|---|---|---|---|---|---|---|---|---|---|---|
| Other One-Day | 1 | 0 | 0 | 0 | 0 | - | - | - | - | - |
| ALL ONE-DAY | 1 | 0 | 0 | 0 | 0 | - | - | - | - | - |

**BOWLING AVERAGES**

| | Overs | Mdns | Runs | Wkts | Avge | Best | 5wI | 10wM |
|---|---|---|---|---|---|---|---|---|
| Other One-Day | 3 | 0 | 33 | 0 | - | - | - | - |
| ALL ONE-DAY | 3 | 0 | 33 | 0 | - | - | - | - |

## G.EDMUNDS - *Shropshire*

| Opposition | Venue | Date | Batting | Fielding | Bowling |
|---|---|---|---|---|---|
| **NATWEST TROPHY** | | | | | |
| Leicestershire | Leicester | June 26 | 3 * | | 0-40 |

**BATTING AVERAGES - Including fielding**

| | Matches | Inns | NO | Runs | HS | Avge | 100s | 50s | Ct | St |
|---|---|---|---|---|---|---|---|---|---|---|
| NatWest Trophy | 1 | 1 | 1 | 3 | 3* | - | - | - | - | - |
| ALL ONE-DAY | 1 | 1 | 1 | 3 | 3* | - | - | - | - | - |

**BOWLING AVERAGES**

| | Overs | Mdns | Runs | Wkts | Avge | Best | 5wI | 10wM |
|---|---|---|---|---|---|---|---|---|
| NatWest Trophy | 12 | 0 | 40 | 0 | - | - | - | - |
| ALL ONE-DAY | 12 | 0 | 40 | 0 | - | - | - | - |

## J.H.EDWARDS - *Devon*

| Opposition | Venue | Date | Batting | Fielding | Bowling |
|---|---|---|---|---|---|
| **NATWEST TROPHY** | | | | | |
| Essex | Exmouth | June 26 | 0 | | |

**BATTING AVERAGES - Including fielding**

| | Matches | Inns | NO | Runs | HS | Avge | 100s | 50s | Ct | St |
|---|---|---|---|---|---|---|---|---|---|---|
| NatWest Trophy | 1 | 1 | 0 | 0 | 0 | 0.00 | - | - | - | - |
| ALL ONE-DAY | 1 | 1 | 0 | 0 | 0 | 0.00 | - | - | - | - |

**BOWLING AVERAGES**
Did not bowl

## W.G.EDWARDS - *Wales*

| Opposition | Venue | Date | Batting | Fielding | Bowling |
|---|---|---|---|---|---|
| **OTHER ONE-DAY** | | | | | |
| West Indies | Brecon | July 15 | 19 * | | 2-61 |

**BATTING AVERAGES - Including fielding**

| | Matches | Inns | NO | Runs | HS | Avge | 100s | 50s | Ct | St |
|---|---|---|---|---|---|---|---|---|---|---|
| Other One-Day | 1 | 1 | 1 | 19 | 19* | - | - | - | - | - |
| ALL ONE-DAY | 1 | 1 | 1 | 19 | 19* | - | - | - | - | - |

**BOWLING AVERAGES**

| | Overs | Mdns | Runs | Wkts | Avge | Best | 5wI | 10wM |
|---|---|---|---|---|---|---|---|---|
| Other One-Day | 11 | 0 | 61 | 2 | 30.50 | 2-61 | - | |
| ALL ONE-DAY | 11 | 0 | 61 | 2 | 30.50 | 2-61 | - | |

# PLAYER RECORDS

## R.M.ELLCOCK - *Middlesex*

| Opposition | Venue | Date | Batting | Fielding | Bowling |
|---|---|---|---|---|---|
| **BRITANNIC ASSURANCE** | | | | | |
| Sussex | Hove | May 22 | | | 0-28 & 0-29 |
| Somerset | Taunton | May 25 | 26 * | | 4-60 & 2-50 |
| Leicestershire | Uxbridge | June 7 | | | 1-22 |
| **OTHER FIRST-CLASS** | | | | | |
| Cambridge U | Fenner's | May 15 | | 1Ct | 0-11 & 1-4 |
| **REFUGE ASSURANCE** | | | | | |
| Sussex | Hove | May 12 | | | 0-25 |
| Kent | Southgate | June 2 | 8 * | | 1-33 |
| **BENSON & HEDGES CUP** | | | | | |
| Essex | Chelmsford | May 2 | 0 | | 1-55 |

**BATTING AVERAGES - Including fielding**

| | Matches | Inns | NO | Runs | HS | Avge | 100s | 50s | Ct | St |
|---|---|---|---|---|---|---|---|---|---|---|
| Britannic Assurance | 3 | 1 | 1 | 26 | 26* | - | - | - | - | - |
| Other First-Class | 1 | 0 | 0 | 0 | 0 | - | - | - | 1 | - |
| ALL FIRST-CLASS | 4 | 1 | 1 | 26 | 26* | - | - | - | 1 | - |
| Refuge Assurance | 2 | 1 | 1 | 8 | 8* | - | - | - | - | - |
| Benson & Hedges Cup | 1 | 1 | 0 | 0 | 0 | 0.00 | - | - | - | - |
| ALL ONE-DAY | 3 | 2 | 1 | 8 | 8* | 8.00 | - | - | - | - |

**BOWLING AVERAGES**

| | Overs | Mdns | Runs | Wkts | Avge | Best | 5wI | 10wM |
|---|---|---|---|---|---|---|---|---|
| Britannic Assurance | 50 | 9 | 189 | 7 | 27.00 | 4-60 | - | - |
| Other First-Class | 12 | 6 | 15 | 1 | 15.00 | 1-4 | - | - |
| ALL FIRST-CLASS | 62 | 15 | 204 | 8 | 25.50 | 4-60 | - | - |
| Refuge Assurance | 11 | 0 | 58 | 1 | 58.00 | 1-33 | - | |
| Benson & Hedges Cup | 10 | 0 | 55 | 1 | 55.00 | 1-55 | - | |
| ALL ONE-DAY | 21 | 0 | 113 | 2 | 56.50 | 1-33 | - | |

## M.T.ELLIS - *Norfolk*

| Opposition | Venue | Date | Batting | Fielding | Bowling |
|---|---|---|---|---|---|
| **NATWEST TROPHY** | | | | | |
| Gloucs | Bristol | June 26 | 0 | 1Ct | 2-33 |

**BATTING AVERAGES - Including fielding**

| | Matches | Inns | NO | Runs | HS | Avge | 100s | 50s | Ct | St |
|---|---|---|---|---|---|---|---|---|---|---|
| NatWest Trophy | 1 | 1 | 0 | 0 | 0 | 0.00 | - | - | 1 | - |
| ALL ONE-DAY | 1 | 1 | 0 | 0 | 0 | 0.00 | - | - | 1 | - |

**BOWLING AVERAGES**

| | Overs | Mdns | Runs | Wkts | Avge | Best | 5wI | 10wM |
|---|---|---|---|---|---|---|---|---|
| NatWest Trophy | 12 | 4 | 33 | 2 | 16.50 | 2-33 | - | |
| ALL ONE-DAY | 12 | 4 | 33 | 2 | 16.50 | 2-33 | - | |

## R.M.ELLISON - *Kent*

| Opposition | Venue | Date | Batting | | Fielding | Bowling |
|---|---|---|---|---|---|---|
| **BRITANNIC ASSURANCE** | | | | | | |
| Hampshire | Southampton | April 27 | 1 | | | |
| Surrey | The Oval | May 9 | 50 | | 1Ct | 1-25 & 1-47 |
| Essex | Folkestone | May 16 | 0 & | 7 | | 4-125 |
| Notts | Trent Bridge | May 22 | 5 & | 13 | | 2-85 & 1-22 |
| Derbyshire | Canterbury | May 25 | 16 | | 1Ct | 0-17 |
| Middlesex | Lord's | May 31 | 7 & | 60 | 1Ct | 4-39 & 5-77 |
| Warwickshire | Tunbridge W | June 4 | 0 | | | 7-33 & 0-72 |
| Sussex | Tunbridge W | June 7 | 4 & | 23 * | | 0-72 |
| Yorkshire | Harrogate | June 14 | | | | 1-51 |

| | | | | | | |
|---|---|---|---|---|---|---|
| Lancashire | Old Trafford | June 21 | | 19 * | 1Ct | 1-47 |
| Surrey | Canterbury | Aug 2 | 0 & | 5 * | 1Ct | 2-43 & 3-102 |
| Hampshire | Canterbury | Aug 6 | 61 * & | 19 * | | 1-47 & 1-13 |
| Leicestershire | Leicester | Aug 9 | 13 & | 7 * | 1Ct | 0-53 & 0-37 |
| Middlesex | Canterbury | Aug 28 | 33 | | 2Ct | 2-88 & 4-40 |
| Sussex | Hove | Sept 3 | 17 * & | 1 | | 1-68 & 0-59 |
| Leicestershire | Canterbury | Sept 17 | 13 & | 23 | | 4-93 & 0-20 |
| **OTHER FIRST-CLASS** | | | | | | |
| West Indies | Canterbury | July 20 | 14 & | 4 | 2Ct | 2-55 & 0-50 |
| **REFUGE ASSURANCE** | | | | | | |
| Worcestershire | Worcester | April 21 | 12 * | | | 0-47 |
| Hampshire | Southampton | May 12 | 24 * | | | 0-25 |
| Essex | Folkestone | May 19 | 15 * | | | 2-37 |
| Derbyshire | Canterbury | May 26 | 8 * | | | 2-46 |
| Yorkshire | Scarborough | June 16 | 14 | | | 1-60 |
| Lancashire | Old Trafford | June 23 | | | | |
| Notts | Trent Bridge | Aug 11 | 29 * | | 1Ct | 2-29 |
| Northants | Canterbury | Aug 18 | 0 | | 1Ct | 0-28 |
| **BENSON & HEDGES CUP** | | | | | | |
| Leicestershire | Canterbury | April 23 | | | | 0-44 |
| Lancashire | Old Trafford | April 25 | 6 | | | 1-45 |
| Sussex | Canterbury | May 2 | 7 * | | 1Ct | 2-19 |
| Scotland | Glasgow | May 7 | 15 | | | 2-42 |
| Worcestershire | Worcester | May 29 | 6 | | | 0-49 |
| **OTHER ONE-DAY** | | | | | | |
| Sussex | Hove | Sept 7 | 0 * | | | 0-7 |

**BATTING AVERAGES - Including fielding**

| | Matches | Inns | NO | Runs | HS | Avge | 100s | 50s | Ct | St |
|---|---|---|---|---|---|---|---|---|---|---|
| Britannic Assurance | 16 | 24 | 7 | 397 | 61* | 23.35 | - | 3 | 8 | - |
| Other First-Class | 1 | 2 | 0 | 18 | 14 | 9.00 | - | - | 2 | - |
| ALL FIRST-CLASS | 17 | 26 | 7 | 415 | 61* | 21.84 | - | 3 | 10 | - |
| Refuge Assurance | 8 | 7 | 5 | 102 | 29* | 51.00 | - | - | 2 | - |
| Benson & Hedges Cup | 5 | 4 | 1 | 34 | 15 | 11.33 | - | - | 1 | - |
| Other One-Day | 1 | 1 | 1 | 0 | 0* | - | - | - | - | - |
| ALL ONE-DAY | 14 | 12 | 7 | 136 | 29* | 27.20 | - | - | 3 | - |

**BOWLING AVERAGES**

| | Overs | Mdns | Runs | Wkts | Avge | Best | 5wI | 10wM |
|---|---|---|---|---|---|---|---|---|
| Britannic Assurance | 457.1 | 99 | 1375 | 45 | 30.55 | 7-33 | 2 | - |
| Other First-Class | 27 | 3 | 105 | 2 | 52.50 | 2-55 | - | - |
| ALL FIRST-CLASS | 484.1 | 102 | 1480 | 47 | 31.48 | 7-33 | 2 | - |
| Refuge Assurance | 52 | 1 | 272 | 7 | 38.85 | 2-29 | - | |
| Benson & Hedges Cup | 52 | 7 | 199 | 5 | 39.80 | 2-19 | - | |
| Other One-Day | 1.4 | 0 | 7 | 0 | - | - | - | |
| ALL ONE-DAY | 105.4 | 8 | 478 | 12 | 39.83 | 2-19 | - | |

## J.E.EMBUREY - *Middlesex*

| Opposition | Venue | Date | Batting | | Fielding | Bowling |
|---|---|---|---|---|---|---|
| **BRITANNIC ASSURANCE** | | | | | | |
| Yorkshire | Lord's | April 27 | | | | 1-55 |
| Sussex | Lord's | May 9 | 14 & | 17 | | 3-64 & 0-10 |
| Sussex | Hove | May 22 | | 5 * | 1Ct | 1-76 & 7-71 |
| Somerset | Taunton | May 25 | 17 | | 2Ct | 0-32 & 2-66 |
| Kent | Lord's | May 31 | 5 & | 13 | 1Ct | 0-4 & 2-60 |
| Gloucs | Bristol | June 4 | 6 & | 74 | | 3-50 & 0-11 |
| Leicestershire | Uxbridge | June 7 | 24 | | 3Ct | 1-43 & 4-59 |
| Glamorgan | Cardiff | June 14 | | 47 | 3Ct | 0-24 & 0-31 |
| Yorkshire | Sheffield | June 21 | | 1 | | 0-54 & 3-35 |
| Essex | Lord's | June 28 | | 46 | 1Ct | 0-33 & 0-50 |
| Warwickshire | Edgbaston | July 2 | 0 & | 13 | 1Ct | 1-37 & 0-56 |
| Northants | Uxbridge | July 16 | 16 * | | 1Ct | 2-110 & 0-21 |
| Lancashire | Uxbridge | July 19 | 4 & | 27 | | 4-96 & 1-49 |
| Notts | Lord's | July 26 | 34 | | 1Ct | 1-22 & 2-86 |
| Derbyshire | Lord's | Aug 9 | | | 2Ct | 1-52 & 4-96 |
| Surrey | The Oval | Aug 20 | 59 | | 1Ct | 1-79 & 3-78 |
| Worcestershire | Worcester | Aug 23 | 4 & | 55 * | | 2-76 |
| Kent | Canterbury | Aug 28 | 20 & | 11 | 1Ct | 1-11 & 0-53 |
| Notts | Trent Bridge | Sept 3 | 21 & | 7 | | 4-90 & 4-38 |
| Surrey | Lord's | Sept 10 | 6 & | 2 | 3Ct | 4-25 & 2-41 |

# E

# PLAYER RECORDS

| Essex | Chelmsford | Sept 17 | 1 & 37 | | 0-87 |
|---|---|---|---|---|---|

## OTHER FIRST-CLASS

| | | | | | | |
|---|---|---|---|---|---|---|
| MCC | Lord's | April 16 | 4 | | | 0-38 |
| Cambridge U | Fenner's | May 15 | | 1 * | 2Ct | 2-17 |
| West Indies | Lord's | May 18 | 29 & 10 | | 2Ct | 2-84 |

## REFUGE ASSURANCE

| | | | | | |
|---|---|---|---|---|---|
| Gloucs | Bristol | April 21 | | | 4-39 |
| Surrey | Lord's | April 28 | 16 * | | 0-44 |
| Sussex | Hove | May 12 | 2 * | | 2-18 |
| Somerset | Taunton | May 26 | | | 5-23 |
| Kent | Southgate | June 2 | 5 | | 2-48 |
| Leicestershire | Uxbridge | June 9 | 2 | 1Ct | 2-39 |
| Glamorgan | Cardiff | June 16 | 20 * | | 1-33 |
| Notts | Trent Bridge | June 23 | | | 4-38 |
| Yorkshire | Lord's | July 7 | 15 | | 3-34 |
| Warwickshire | Edgbaston | July 14 | 33 * | | 0-44 |
| Lancashire | Lord's | July 21 | 2 | 1Ct | 0-28 |
| Hampshire | Lord's | Aug 4 | | | 2-21 |
| Derbyshire | Lord's | Aug 11 | 7 | | 1-39 |
| Essex | Colchester | Aug 18 | 8 | | 1-37 |
| Worcestershire | Worcester | Aug 25 | 32 | | 1-43 |

## NATWEST TROPHY

| | | | | | |
|---|---|---|---|---|---|
| Ireland | Dublin | June 26 | 1 | | 0-13 |
| Somerset | Taunton | July 11 | 2 | | 2-52 |

## BENSON & HEDGES CUP

| | | | | | |
|---|---|---|---|---|---|
| Somerset | Taunton | April 23 | | | 5-37 |
| Surrey | Lord's | April 25 | 9 | 1Ct | 0-43 |
| Essex | Chelmsford | May 2 | 6 | | 3-40 |
| Warwickshire | Lord's | May 4 | 23 | 2Ct | 1-47 |

## OTHER ONE-DAY
For England XI

| | | | | | |
|---|---|---|---|---|---|
| Rest of World | Jesmond | July 31 | | | 2-57 |
| Rest of World | Jesmond | Aug 1 | 5 | 1Ct | 0-48 |

## BATTING AVERAGES - Including fielding

| | Matches | Inns | NO | Runs | HS | Avge | 100s | 50s | Ct | St |
|---|---|---|---|---|---|---|---|---|---|---|
| Britannic Assurance | 21 | 29 | 3 | 586 | 74 | 22.53 | - | 3 | 21 | - |
| Other First-Class | 3 | 4 | 1 | 44 | 29 | 14.66 | - | - | 4 | - |
| ALL FIRST-CLASS | 24 | 33 | 4 | 630 | 74 | 21.72 | - | 3 | 25 | - |
| Refuge Assurance | 15 | 11 | 4 | 142 | 33 * | 20.28 | - | - | 2 | - |
| NatWest Trophy | 2 | 2 | 0 | 3 | 2 | 1.50 | - | - | - | - |
| Benson & Hedges Cup | 4 | 3 | 0 | 38 | 23 | 12.66 | - | - | 3 | - |
| Other One-Day | 2 | 1 | 0 | 5 | 5 | 5.00 | - | - | 1 | - |
| ALL ONE-DAY | 23 | 17 | 4 | 188 | 33 * | 14.46 | - | - | 6 | - |

## BOWLING AVERAGES

| | Overs | Mdns | Runs | Wkts | Avge | Best | 5wI | 10wM |
|---|---|---|---|---|---|---|---|---|
| Britannic Assurance | 855.5 | 228 | 2031 | 64 | 31.73 | 7-71 | 1 | - |
| Other First-Class | 50.4 | 18 | 139 | 4 | 34.75 | 2-17 | - | - |
| ALL FIRST-CLASS | 906.3 | 246 | 2170 | 68 | 31.91 | 7-71 | 1 | - |
| Refuge Assurance | 114 | 6 | 528 | 28 | 18.85 | 5-23 | 1 | |
| NatWest Trophy | 24 | 7 | 65 | 2 | 32.50 | 2-52 | - | |
| Benson & Hedges Cup | 44 | 3 | 167 | 9 | 18.55 | 5-37 | 1 | |
| Other One-Day | 19 | 2 | 105 | 2 | 52.50 | 2-57 | - | |
| ALL ONE-DAY | 201 | 18 | 865 | 41 | 21.09 | 5-23 | 2 | |

# B.G.EVANS - *Hertfordshire*

| Opposition | Venue | Date | Batting | Fielding | Bowling |
|---|---|---|---|---|---|

## NATWEST TROPHY

| | | | | | |
|---|---|---|---|---|---|
| Warwickshire | Edgbaston | July 11 | 7 | | |

## BATTING AVERAGES - Including fielding

| | Matches | Inns | NO | Runs | HS | Avge | 100s | 50s | Ct | St |
|---|---|---|---|---|---|---|---|---|---|---|
| NatWest Trophy | 1 | 1 | 0 | 7 | 7 | 7.00 | - | - | - | - |
| ALL ONE-DAY | 1 | 1 | 0 | 7 | 7 | 7.00 | - | - | - | - |

## BOWLING AVERAGES
Did not bowl

# K.P.EVANS - *Nottinghamshire*

| Opposition | Venue | Date | Batting | Fielding | Bowling |
|---|---|---|---|---|---|

## BRITANNIC ASSURANCE

| | | | | | |
|---|---|---|---|---|---|
| Leicestershire | Trent Bridge | May 9 | 22 | | 5-52 & 4-83 |
| Yorkshire | Headingley | May 16 | 7 * & 3 * | | 0-44 & 1-24 |
| Leicestershire | Leicester | May 25 | 6 * | 2Ct | 3-72 & 1-42 |
| Hampshire | Trent Bridge | May 31 | 16 | 1Ct | 1-21 & 1-36 |
| Surrey | The Oval | June 4 | | | 2-71 & 0-34 |
| Gloucs | Gloucester | June 14 | 2 * | 1Ct | 0-39 & 0-35 |
| Worcestershire | Worcester | June 18 | 56 * | | 0-37 & 1-69 |
| Warwickshire | Trent Bridge | June 21 | | 17 * | 1-91 |
| Northants | Well'borough | July 19 | 1 | 1Ct | 2-65 & 0-15 |
| Yorkshire | Worksop | July 23 | | 6 | 4-56 & 0-9 |
| Middlesex | Lord's | July 26 | 0 & 28 * | 1Ct | 2-44 & 0-69 |
| Sussex | Eastbourne | Aug 6 | 37 | | 0-22 & 0-12 |
| Essex | Trent Bridge | Aug 9 | 32 & 22 | | 5-66 & 3-51 |
| Somerset | Trent Bridge | Aug 16 | 14 & 7 | | 3-105 & 1-24 |

## OTHER FIRST-CLASS

| | | | | | |
|---|---|---|---|---|---|
| Oxford U | The Parks | April 27 | 13 | | |

## REFUGE ASSURANCE

| | | | | | |
|---|---|---|---|---|---|
| Lancashire | Old Trafford | April 21 | | | 3-46 |
| Warwickshire | Trent Bridge | April 28 | 14 * | | 0-16 |
| Glamorgan | Cardiff | May 5 | | | 1-54 |
| Essex | Trent Bridge | May 12 | 3 | | 2-54 |
| Leicestershire | Leicester | May 26 | | | 0-51 |
| Somerset | Trent Bridge | June 9 | | | 1-40 |
| Gloucs | Gloucester | June 16 | | 1Ct | 1-34 |
| Middlesex | Trent Bridge | June 23 | 6 | | 0-26 |
| Surrey | The Oval | June 30 | | | 2-43 |
| Hampshire | Trent Bridge | July 14 | 4 * | | 1-52 |
| Northants | Well'borough | July 21 | 8 | | 3-41 |
| Sussex | Hove | July 28 | | | 2-50 |
| Worcestershire | Trent Bridge | Aug 4 | | | 0-35 |
| Kent | Trent Bridge | Aug 11 | | | 1-49 |
| Yorkshire | Scarborough | Aug 18 | 12 * | | 1-47 |
| Derbyshire | Trent Bridge | Aug 25 | | | 0-41 |

## NATWEST TROPHY

| | | | | | |
|---|---|---|---|---|---|
| Gloucs | Bristol | July 11 | 2 | | 0-51 |
| Hampshire | Southampton | July 31 | 20 | 1Ct | 0-31 |

## BENSON & HEDGES CUP

| | | | | | |
|---|---|---|---|---|---|
| Yorkshire | Trent Bridge | April 25 | | | 2-50 |
| Glamorgan | Cardiff | May 4 | 5 * | | 4-43 |
| Min Counties | Trent Bridge | May 7 | 1 * | 1Ct | 0-39 |

## BATTING AVERAGES - Including fielding

| | Matches | Inns | NO | Runs | HS | Avge | 100s | 50s | Ct | St |
|---|---|---|---|---|---|---|---|---|---|---|
| Britannic Assurance | 14 | 17 | 7 | 276 | 56 * | 27.60 | - | 1 | 6 | - |
| Other First-Class | 1 | 1 | 0 | 13 | 13 | 13.00 | - | - | - | - |
| ALL FIRST-CLASS | 15 | 18 | 7 | 289 | 56 * | 26.27 | - | 1 | 6 | - |
| Refuge Assurance | 16 | 6 | 3 | 47 | —14 * | 15.66 | - | - | 1 | - |
| NatWest Trophy | 2 | 2 | 0 | 22 | 20 | 11.00 | - | - | 1 | - |
| Benson & Hedges Cup | 3 | 2 | 2 | 6 | 5 * | - | - | - | 1 | - |
| ALL ONE-DAY | 21 | 10 | 5 | 75 | 20 | 15.00 | - | - | 3 | - |

## BOWLING AVERAGES

| | Overs | Mdns | Runs | Wkts | Avge | Best | 5wI | 10wM |
|---|---|---|---|---|---|---|---|---|
| Britannic Assurance | 425 | 89 | 1278 | 40 | 31.95 | 5-52 | 2 | - |
| Other First-Class | | | | | | | | |
| ALL FIRST-CLASS | 425 | 89 | 1278 | 40 | 31.95 | 5-52 | 2 | - |
| Refuge Assurance | 118 | 2 | 679 | 18 | 37.72 | 3-41 | - | |
| NatWest Trophy | 23 | 3 | 82 | 0 | | | - | |
| Benson & Hedges Cup | 32 | 2 | 132 | 6 | 22.00 | 4-43 | - | |
| ALL ONE-DAY | 173 | 7 | 893 | 24 | 37.20 | 4-43 | - | |

# PLAYER RECORDS

## R.A.EVANS - *Minor Counties*

| Opposition | Venue | Date | Batting | Fielding | Bowling |
|---|---|---|---|---|---|
| **BENSON & HEDGES CUP** | | | | | |
| Glamorgan | Trowbridge | April 23 | 5 | | 0-35 |
| Hampshire | Trowbridge | April 25 | 5* | | 0-47 |
| Yorkshire | Headingley | May 2 | | | 0-37 |
| **OTHER ONE-DAY** | | | | | |
| For England Am. XI | | | | | |
| Sri Lanka | Wolv'hampton | July 24 | 5 | | 2-31 |

### BATTING AVERAGES - Including fielding

| | Matches | Inns | NO | Runs | HS | Avge | 100s | 50s | Ct | St |
|---|---|---|---|---|---|---|---|---|---|---|
| Benson & Hedges Cup | 3 | 2 | 1 | 10 | 5* | 10.00 | - | - | - | - |
| Other One-Day | 1 | 1 | 0 | 5 | 5 | 5.00 | - | - | - | - |
| ALL ONE-DAY | 4 | 3 | 1 | 15 | 5* | 7.50 | - | - | - | - |

### BOWLING AVERAGES

| | Overs | Mdns | Runs | Wkts | Avge | Best | 5wI | 10wM |
|---|---|---|---|---|---|---|---|---|
| Benson & Hedges Cup | 30 | 1 | 119 | 0 | - | - | - | |
| Other One-Day | 6 | 1 | 31 | 2 | 15.50 | 2-31 | - | |
| ALL ONE-DAY | 36 | 2 | 150 | 2 | 75.00 | 2-31 | - | |

# F

# PLAYER RECORDS

## N.H.FAIRBROTHER - *Lancashire & England*

| Opposition | Venue | Date | Batting | | | Fielding | Bowling |
|---|---|---|---|---|---|---|---|
| **BRITANNIC ASSURANCE** | | | | | | | |
| Warwickshire | Edgbaston | April 27 | 121 | | | 1Ct | |
| Worcestershire | Worcester | May 9 | 109 | & | 10 | 5Ct | |
| Sussex | Old Trafford | May 31 | 22 | & | 7* | 1Ct | |
| Hampshire | Basingstoke | June 4 | 25 | | | 1Ct | |
| Leicestershire | Leicester | June 18 | 0 | & | 7 | 4Ct | |
| Kent | Old Trafford | June 21 | 24 | | | 1Ct | |
| Glamorgan | Liverpool | June 28 | 107* | | | | |
| Somerset | Taunton | July 2 | 109 | & | 102* | 1Ct | |
| Notts | Trent Bridge | July 16 | 54 | & | 10 | | |
| Middlesex | Uxbridge | July 19 | 53 | | | 1Ct | |
| Warwickshire | Old Trafford | July 23 | 6* | | | | |
| Yorkshire | Old Trafford | Aug 2 | 32 | | | 1Ct | |
| Northants | Lytham | Aug 6 | 13* | & | 38 | | |
| Derbyshire | Derby | Aug 16 | 33 | & | 72 | | |
| Worcestershire | Blackpool | Aug 20 | 44 | & | 0 | | |
| Essex | Old Trafford | Aug 23 | 1 | | | 1Ct | |
| Notts | Old Trafford | Aug 28 | 0 | & | 12 | 1Ct | |

| **OTHER FIRST-CLASS** | | | | | | | |
|---|---|---|---|---|---|---|---|
| Cambridge U | Fenner's | April 13 | 23 | & | 25* | | |
| For MCC | | | | | | | |
| Middlesex | Lord's | April 16 | 5 | | | 1Ct | |

| **TEXACO TROPHY** | | | | | |
|---|---|---|---|---|---|
| West Indies | Edgbaston | May 23 | 4 | 1Ct |
| West Indies | Old Trafford | May 25 | 5* | |
| West Indies | Lord's | May 27 | 113 | 1Ct |

| **REFUGE ASSURANCE** | | | | | |
|---|---|---|---|---|---|
| Notts | Old Trafford | April 21 | 4 | |
| Northants | Old Trafford | April 28 | 39* | |
| Worcestershire | Worcester | May 12 | 46 | 1Ct |
| Sussex | Old Trafford | June 2 | 12 | 1Ct |
| Glamorgan | Old Trafford | June 9 | | |
| Warwickshire | Edgbaston | June 16 | 20 | 1Ct |
| Kent | Old Trafford | June 23 | 31* | |
| Somerset | Taunton | July 5 | 12* | |
| Leicestershire | Leicester | July 7 | 18 | |
| Middlesex | Lord's | July 21 | 0 | 1Ct |
| Hampshire | Southampton | July 28 | 37 | |
| Yorkshire | Old Trafford | Aug 4 | 39 | 1Ct |
| Gloucs | Bristol | Aug 11 | 43* | |
| Surrey | Old Trafford | Aug 18 | 62 | |
| Essex | Old Trafford | Aug 25 | 52* | |
| Northants | Old Trafford | Sept 1 | 6 | 1Ct |
| Worcestershire | Old Trafford | Sept 15 | 30 | |

| **NATWEST TROPHY** | | | | |
|---|---|---|---|---|
| Dorset | Bournemouth | June 26 | 68 | |
| Hampshire | Southampton | July 11 | 24 | |

| **BENSON & HEDGES CUP** | | | | | |
|---|---|---|---|---|---|
| Scotland | Forfar | April 23 | 22* | 1Ct |
| Kent | Old Trafford | April 25 | 46 | 2Ct |
| Leicestershire | Leicester | May 4 | 53* | |
| Sussex | Old Trafford | May 7 | 50 | 1Ct |
| Northants | Old Trafford | May 29 | 13 | 1Ct |
| Yorkshire | Old Trafford | June 16 | 40 | |
| Worcestershire | Lord's | July 13 | 1 | |

| **OTHER ONE-DAY** | | | | |
|---|---|---|---|---|
| For England XI | | | | |
| Rest of World | Jesmond | July 31 | 21 | |
| Rest of World | Jesmond | Aug 1 | 0 | 1Ct |
| For England A | | | | |
| Sri Lanka | Old Trafford | Aug 14 | 66 | 1Ct |

### BATTING AVERAGES - Including fielding

| | Matches | Inns | NO | Runs | HS | Avge | 100s | 50s | Ct | St |
|---|---|---|---|---|---|---|---|---|---|---|
| Britannic Assurance | 17 | 26 | 5 | 1011 | 121 | 48.14 | 5 | 3 | 18 | - |
| Other First-Class | 2 | 3 | 1 | 53 | 25* | 26.50 | - | - | 1 | - |
| | | | | | | | | | | |
| ALL FIRST-CLASS | 19 | 29 | 6 | 1064 | 121 | 46.26 | 5 | 3 | 19 | - |
| | | | | | | | | | | |
| Texaco Trophy | 3 | 3 | 1 | 122 | 113 | 61.00 | 1 | - | 2 | - |
| Refuge Assurance | 17 | 16 | 5 | 451 | 62 | 41.00 | - | 2 | 6 | - |
| NatWest Trophy | 2 | 2 | 0 | 92 | 68 | 46.00 | - | 1 | - | - |
| Benson & Hedges Cup | 7 | 7 | 2 | 225 | 53* | 45.00 | - | 2 | 5 | - |
| Other One-Day | 3 | 3 | 0 | 87 | 66 | 29.00 | - | 1 | 2 | - |
| | | | | | | | | | | |
| ALL ONE-DAY | 32 | 31 | 8 | 977 | 113 | 42.47 | 1 | 6 | 15 | - |

### BOWLING AVERAGES
Did not bowl

## P.FARBRACE - *Middlesex*

| Opposition | Venue | Date | Batting | | | Fielding | Bowling |
|---|---|---|---|---|---|---|---|
| **BRITANNIC ASSURANCE** | | | | | | | |
| Somerset | Taunton | May 25 | 6 | | | 7Ct | |
| Kent | Lord's | May 31 | 0 | & | 7* | 4Ct | |
| Gloucs | Bristol | June 4 | 5 | & | 0* | 0Ct,1St | |
| Leicestershire | Uxbridge | June 7 | | | | 2Ct,2St | |
| Glamorgan | Cardiff | June 14 | | | 0 | 2Ct | |
| Yorkshire | Sheffield | June 21 | 36* | & | 11 | 2Ct | |
| Essex | Lord's | June 28 | | | 4 | 2Ct | 1-64 |
| Warwickshire | Edgbaston | July 2 | 24 | & | 11* | 2Ct | |
| Northants | Uxbridge | July 16 | | | | 3Ct,1St | |
| Lancashire | Uxbridge | July 19 | 42 | & | 19 | 2Ct,1St | |
| Notts | Lord's | July 26 | 20 | | | 4Ct | |
| Hampshire | Lord's | Aug 2 | 1 | | | 4Ct,1St | |
| Derbyshire | Lord's | Aug 9 | | | 50 | 1Ct,1St | |
| Surrey | The Oval | Aug 20 | 3 | | | | |
| Worcestershire | Worcester | Aug 23 | 18 | & | 11 | 2Ct | |
| Kent | Canterbury | Aug 28 | 0 | & | 0 | 5Ct | |
| Notts | Trent Bridge | Sept 3 | 3 | | | 0Ct,1St | |
| Surrey | Lord's | Sept 10 | 0 | & | 26 | | |
| Essex | Chelmsford | Sept 17 | 12* | & | 8 | 2Ct | |

| **OTHER FIRST-CLASS** | | | | | |
|---|---|---|---|---|---|
| For Middlesex | | | | | |
| Cambridge U | Fenner's | May 15 | 9 | 2Ct |

| **REFUGE ASSURANCE** | | | | | |
|---|---|---|---|---|---|
| Somerset | Taunton | May 26 | | 2Ct,2St |
| Kent | Southgate | June 2 | 6 | 3Ct |
| Leicestershire | Uxbridge | June 9 | 14* | 1Ct,1St |
| Glamorgan | Cardiff | June 16 | 3 | 0Ct,1St |
| Notts | Trent Bridge | June 23 | | 0Ct,1St |
| Yorkshire | Lord's | July 7 | | |
| Warwickshire | Edgbaston | July 14 | 4 | |
| Lancashire | Lord's | July 21 | 26* | 1Ct |
| Hampshire | Lord's | Aug 4 | | 1Ct,1St |
| Derbyshire | Lord's | Aug 11 | 0 | |
| Essex | Colchester | Aug 18 | 5 | 1Ct |
| Worcestershire | Worcester | Aug 25 | 9* | |

| **NATWEST TROPHY** | | | | | |
|---|---|---|---|---|---|
| Ireland | Dublin | June 26 | 13* | 1Ct,1St |
| Somerset | Taunton | July 11 | 7 | |

### BATTING AVERAGES - Including fielding

| | Matches | Inns | NO | Runs | HS | Avge | 100s | 50s | Ct | St |
|---|---|---|---|---|---|---|---|---|---|---|
| Britannic Assurance | 19 | 26 | 5 | 317 | 50 | 15.09 | - | 1 | 44 | 8 |
| Other First-Class | 1 | 1 | 0 | 9 | 9 | 9.00 | - | - | 2 | - |
| | | | | | | | | | | |
| ALL FIRST-CLASS | 20 | 27 | 5 | 326 | 50 | 14.81 | - | 1 | 46 | 8 |
| | | | | | | | | | | |
| Refuge Assurance | 12 | 8 | 3 | 67 | 26* | 13.40 | - | - | 9 | 6 |
| NatWest Trophy | 2 | 2 | 1 | 20 | 13* | 20.00 | - | - | 1 | 1 |
| | | | | | | | | | | |
| ALL ONE-DAY | 14 | 10 | 4 | 87 | 26* | 14.50 | - | - | 10 | 7 |

### BOWLING AVERAGES

| | Overs | Mdns | Runs | Wkts | Avge | Best | 5wI | 10wM |
|---|---|---|---|---|---|---|---|---|
| Britannic Assurance | 4.1 | 0 | 64 | 1 | 64.00 | 1-64 | - | - |
| Other First-Class | | | | | | | | |
| | | | | | | | | |
| ALL FIRST-CLASS | 4.1 | 0 | 64 | 1 | 64.00 | 1-64 | - | - |
| | | | | | | | | |
| Refuge Assurance | | | | | | | | |
| NatWest Trophy | | | | | | | | |
| | | | | | | | | |
| ALL ONE-DAY | | | | | | | | |

# PLEAYER RECORDS — F

## M.A.FELL - *Lincolnshire*

| Opposition | Venue | Date | Batting | Fielding | Bowling |
|---|---|---|---|---|---|
| **NATWEST TROPHY** | | | | | |
| Notts | Trent Bridge | June 26 | 39 | 1Ct | 0-49 |

**BATTING AVERAGES - Including fielding**

| | Matches | Inns | NO | Runs | HS | Avge | 100s | 50s | Ct | St |
|---|---|---|---|---|---|---|---|---|---|---|
| NatWest Trophy | 1 | 1 | 0 | 39 | 39 | 39.00 | - | - | 1 | - |
| ALL ONE-DAY | 1 | 1 | 0 | 39 | 39 | 39.00 | - | - | 1 | - |

**BOWLING AVERAGES**

| | Overs | Mdns | Runs | Wkts | Avge | Best | 5wI | 10wM |
|---|---|---|---|---|---|---|---|---|
| NatWest Trophy | 10 | 0 | 49 | 0 | - | - | - | |
| ALL ONE-DAY | 10 | 0 | 49 | 0 | - | - | - | |

## M.A.FELTHAM - *Surrey*

| Opposition | Venue | Date | Batting | Fielding | Bowling |
|---|---|---|---|---|---|
| **BRITANNIC ASSURANCE** | | | | | |
| Lancashire | The Oval | May 22 | 20 | | 3-64 & 1-58 |
| Notts | The Oval | June 4 | | | 1-42 |
| Leicestershire | Leicester | June 14 | 2 | 1Ct | 3-91 & 0-22 |
| Essex | The Oval | July 5 | 28 | | 0-69 |
| Yorkshire | Guildford | July 19 | 6 | 1Ct | 4-64 & 0-20 |
| Glamorgan | The Oval | July 26 | 38 * & 3 | | 1-58 & 1-77 |
| Kent | Canterbury | Aug 2 | 0 & 10 * | | 2-64 & 1-15 |
| Warwickshire | Edgbaston | Aug 6 | 69 * & 14 * | 1Ct | 4-41 & 3-28 |
| Northants | Northampton | Aug 23 | 16 | | 1-68 |
| Sussex | The Oval | Aug 28 | 37 | | 3-63 & 1-36 |
| Hampshire | The Oval | Sept 3 | 20 & 24 | | 4-36 & 1-11 |
| Middlesex | Lord's | Sept 10 | 25 & 15 | | 0-48 & 1-21 |
| **OTHER FIRST-CLASS** | | | | | |
| Cambridge U | Fenner's | May 18 | 0 * & 48 | 1Ct | 0-57 & 0-22 |
| **REFUGE ASSURANCE** | | | | | |
| Essex | The Oval | May 26 | | | 1-22 |
| Worcestershire | Worcester | June 2 | 23 * | | 1-51 |
| Derbyshire | Chesterfield | June 9 | 19 | | 0-33 |
| Leicestershire | Leicester | June 16 | 11 | | 1-23 |
| Notts | The Oval | June 30 | 14 * | | 0-43 |
| Sussex | The Oval | July 14 | | 1Ct | 3-44 |
| Yorkshire | The Oval | July 21 | 12 * | 1Ct | 0-41 |
| Glamorgan | The Oval | July 28 | 7 | 1Ct | 3-60 |
| Hampshire | The Oval | Aug 25 | 7 | | 0-20 |
| **NATWEST TROPHY** | | | | | |
| Kent | The Oval | July 11 | | | 1-46 |
| **BENSON & HEDGES CUP** | | | | | |
| Essex | The Oval | April 23 | 4 | 1Ct | 2-45 |
| Somerset | Taunton | May 4 | 2 | | 1-58 |
| **OTHER ONE-DAY** | | | | | |
| Warwickshire | Harrogate | June 12 | 32 * | | 2-33 |
| Durham | Harrogate | June 13 | | | 1-9 |

**BATTING AVERAGES - Including fielding**

| | Matches | Inns | NO | Runs | HS | Avge | 100s | 50s | Ct | St |
|---|---|---|---|---|---|---|---|---|---|---|
| Britannic Assurance | 12 | 16 | 4 | 327 | 69 * | 27.25 | - | 1 | 3 | - |
| Other First-Class | 1 | 2 | 1 | 48 | 48 | 48.00 | - | - | 1 | - |
| ALL FIRST-CLASS | 13 | 18 | 5 | 375 | 69 * | 28.84 | - | 1 | 4 | - |
| Refuge Assurance | 9 | 7 | 3 | 93 | 23 * | 23.25 | - | - | 3 | - |
| NatWest Trophy | 1 | 0 | 0 | 0 | 0 | - | - | - | - | - |
| Benson & Hedges Cup | 2 | 2 | 0 | 6 | 4 | 3.00 | - | - | 1 | - |
| Other One-Day | 2 | 1 | 1 | 32 | 32 * | - | - | - | - | - |
| ALL ONE-DAY | 14 | 10 | 4 | 131 | 32 * | 21.83 | - | - | 4 | - |

**BOWLING AVERAGES**

| | Overs | Mdns | Runs | Wkts | Avge | Best | 5wI | 10wM |
|---|---|---|---|---|---|---|---|---|
| Britannic Assurance | 328 | 56 | 996 | 35 | 28.45 | 4-36 | - | - |
| Other First-Class | 21 | 1 | 79 | 0 | - | - | - | - |
| ALL FIRST-CLASS | 349 | 57 | 1075 | 35 | 30.71 | 4-36 | - | - |
| Refuge Assurance | 65.1 | 2 | 337 | 9 | 37.44 | 3-44 | - | |
| NatWest Trophy | 10 | 1 | 46 | 1 | 46.00 | 1-46 | - | |
| Benson & Hedges Cup | 21.2 | 1 | 103 | 3 | 34.33 | 2-45 | - | |
| Other One-Day | 15 | 3 | 42 | 3 | 14.00 | 2-33 | - | |
| ALL ONE-DAY | 111.3 | 7 | 528 | 16 | 33.00 | 3-44 | - | |

## N.A.FELTON - *Northamptonshire*

| Opposition | Venue | Date | Batting | Fielding | Bowling |
|---|---|---|---|---|---|
| **BRITANNIC ASSURANCE** | | | | | |
| Derbyshire | Derby | April 27 | 9 | | |
| Essex | Northampton | May 9 | 0 & 5 | | |
| Leicestershire | Northampton | May 16 | 31 * & 25 | 1Ct | |
| Glamorgan | Cardiff | May 22 | 13 & 3 | | |
| Yorkshire | Headingley | May 25 | 43 & 32 | | |
| Derbyshire | Northampton | May 31 | 15 & 37 | 1Ct | |
| Worcestershire | Northampton | June 4 | 40 & 47 | | |
| Hampshire | Northampton | June 21 | 1 & 38 * | | |
| Gloucs | Luton | June 28 | 0 & 4 | | |
| Kent | Maidstone | July 2 | 0 | | |
| Leicestershire | Leicester | July 5 | 28 | 2Ct | |
| Middlesex | Uxbridge | July 16 | 55 & 6 | 1Ct | |
| Notts | Well'borough | July 19 | 0 & 1 | | |
| Somerset | Northampton | July 23 | 4 & 2 | | 0-66 |
| **OTHER FIRST-CLASS** | | | | | |
| Cambridge U | Fenner's | April 16 | 12 & 26 * | | |
| West Indies | Northampton | June 15 | 20 | | |
| **REFUGE ASSURANCE** | | | | | |
| Worcestershire | Northampton | May 19 | 65 | | |
| Yorkshire | Headingley | May 26 | 9 | | |
| Hampshire | Northampton | June 2 | 69 | | |
| Gloucs | Moreton | June 9 | | | |
| Somerset | Luton | June 30 | 10 | | |
| Surrey | Tring | July 7 | 4 | | |
| Notts | Well'borough | July 21 | 37 | 2Ct | |
| Derbyshire | Derby | July 28 | 4 | | |
| Sussex | Eastbourne | Aug 4 | 5 | 2Ct | |
| **NATWEST TROPHY** | | | | | |
| Staffordshire | Stone | June 26 | 11 | | |
| Leicestershire | Northampton | July 11 | 54 | 1Ct | |
| **BENSON & HEDGES CUP** | | | | | |
| Derbyshire | Derby | April 23 | 23 | 1Ct | |
| Gloucs | Bristol | May 2 | 22 | | |
| Combined U | Northampton | May 4 | 20 | | |
| Worcestershire | Northampton | May 7 | 10 | 1Ct | |
| Lancashire | Old Trafford | May 29 | 44 | | |

**BATTING AVERAGES - Including fielding**

| | Matches | Inns | NO | Runs | HS | Avge | 100s | 50s | Ct | St |
|---|---|---|---|---|---|---|---|---|---|---|
| Britannic Assurance | 14 | 25 | 2 | 439 | 55 | 19.08 | - | 1 | 5 | - |
| Other First-Class | 2 | 3 | 1 | 58 | 26 * | 29.00 | - | - | - | - |
| ALL FIRST-CLASS | 16 | 28 | 3 | 497 | 55 | 19.88 | - | 1 | 5 | - |
| Refuge Assurance | 9 | 8 | 0 | 203 | 69 | 25.37 | - | 2 | 4 | - |
| NatWest Trophy | 2 | 2 | 0 | 65 | 54 | 32.50 | - | 1 | 1 | - |
| Benson & Hedges Cup | 5 | 5 | 0 | 119 | 44 | 23.80 | - | - | 2 | - |
| ALL ONE-DAY | 16 | 15 | 0 | 387 | 69 | 25.80 | - | 3 | 7 | - |

**BOWLING AVERAGES**

| | Overs | Mdns | Runs | Wkts | Avge | Best | 5wI | 10wM |
|---|---|---|---|---|---|---|---|---|
| Britannic Assurance | 6 | 0 | 66 | 0 | - | - | - | - |
| Other First-Class | | | | | | | | |
| ALL FIRST-CLASS | 6 | 0 | 66 | 0 | - | - | - | - |
| Refuge Assurance | | | | | | | | |
| NatWest Trophy | | | | | | | | |
| Benson & Hedges Cup | | | | | | | | |
| ALL ONE-DAY | | | | | | | | |

## F

# PLAYER RECORDS

## N.C.W.FENTON - *Cambridge University*

| Opposition | Venue | Date | Batting | Fielding | Bowling |
|---|---|---|---|---|---|
| **OTHER FIRST-CLASS** | | | | | |
| Leicestershire | Fenner's | May 22 | 7 * | | 0-95 |

**BATTING AVERAGES - Including fielding**

| | Matches | Inns | NO | Runs | HS | Avge | 100s | 50s | Ct | St |
|---|---|---|---|---|---|---|---|---|---|---|
| Other First-Class | 1 | 1 | 1 | 7 | 7 * | - | - | - | - | - |
| ALL FIRST-CLASS | 1 | 1 | 1 | 7 | 7 * | - | - | - | - | - |

**BOWLING AVERAGES**

| | Overs | Mdns | Runs | Wkts | Avge | Best | 5wI | 10wM |
|---|---|---|---|---|---|---|---|---|
| Other First-Class | 25 | 5 | 95 | 0 | - | - | - | - |
| ALL FIRST-CLASS | 25 | 5 | 95 | 0 | - | - | - | - |

## M.G.FIELD-BUSS - *Nottinghamshire*

| Opposition | Venue | Date | Batting | Fielding | Bowling |
|---|---|---|---|---|---|
| **BRITANNIC ASSURANCE** | | | | | |
| Middlesex | Lord's | July 26 | 25 | | 1-73 |
| Derbyshire | Trent Bridge | Aug 23 | 16 | 1Ct | 0-55 & 0-59 |
| **OTHER FIRST-CLASS** | | | | | |
| Oxford U | The Parks | April 27 | | | |
| **REFUGE ASSURANCE** | | | | | |
| Yorkshire | Scarborough | Aug 18 | 0 * | | 2-22 |
| Derbyshire | Trent Bridge | Aug 25 | | | 2-43 |
| Worcestershire | Trent Bridge | Sept 1 | 0 * | | 1-42 |

**BATTING AVERAGES - Including fielding**

| | Matches | Inns | NO | Runs | HS | Avge | 100s | 50s | Ct | St |
|---|---|---|---|---|---|---|---|---|---|---|
| Britannic Assurance | 2 | 2 | 0 | 41 | 25 | 20.50 | - | - | 1 | - |
| Other First-Class | 1 | 0 | 0 | 0 | 0 | | - | - | - | - |
| ALL FIRST-CLASS | 3 | 2 | 0 | 41 | 25 | 20.50 | - | - | 1 | - |
| Refuge Assurance | 3 | 2 | 2 | 0 | 0 * | - | - | - | - | - |
| ALL ONE-DAY | 3 | 2 | 2 | 0 | 0 * | - | - | - | - | - |

**BOWLING AVERAGES**

| | Overs | Mdns | Runs | Wkts | Avge | Best | 5wI | 10wM |
|---|---|---|---|---|---|---|---|---|
| Britannic Assurance | 53 | 11 | 187 | 1 | 187.00 | 1-73 | - | - |
| Other First-Class | | | | | | | | |
| ALL FIRST-CLASS | 53 | 11 | 187 | 1 | 187.00 | 1-73 | - | - |
| Refuge Assurance | 24 | 1 | 107 | 5 | 21.40 | 2-22 | - | |
| ALL ONE-DAY | 24 | 1 | 107 | 5 | 21.40 | 2-22 | - | |

## R.J.FINNEY - *Norfolk*

| Opposition | Venue | Date | Batting | Fielding | Bowling |
|---|---|---|---|---|---|
| **NATWEST TROPHY** | | | | | |
| Gloucs | Bristol | June 26 | 27 | | |

**BATTING AVERAGES - Including fielding**

| | Matches | Inns | NO | Runs | HS | Avge | 100s | 50s | Ct | St |
|---|---|---|---|---|---|---|---|---|---|---|
| NatWest Trophy | 1 | 1 | 0 | 27 | 27 | 27.00 | - | - | - | - |
| ALL ONE-DAY | 1 | 1 | 0 | 27 | 27 | 27.00 | - | - | - | - |

**BOWLING AVERAGES**
Did not bowl

## J.D.FITTON - *Lancashire*

| Opposition | Venue | Date | Batting | Fielding | Bowling |
|---|---|---|---|---|---|
| **BRITANNIC ASSURANCE** | | | | | |
| Northants | Lytham | Aug 6 | | 60 | 1-106 |
| Worcestershire | Blackpool | Aug 20 | 1 & | 9 * | 0-63 & 1-74 |
| Essex | Old Trafford | Aug 23 | 36 | | 1-7 & 1-42 |
| Notts | Old Trafford | Aug 28 | 7 & | 1 | 1-37 & 0-39 |
| Yorkshire | Scarborough | Sept 3 | 33 & | 34 | 0-95 & 1-113 |
| Surrey | Old Trafford | Sept 17 | 5 & | 15 | 0-26 & 2-89 |
| **OTHER FIRST-CLASS** | | | | | |
| Cambridge U | Fenner's | April 13 | | | 1-60 & 1-2 |
| Oxford U | The Parks | June 7 | | 16 | 2-42 & 0-34 |
| **REFUGE ASSURANCE** | | | | | |
| Northants | Old Trafford | Sept 1 | 14 * | | 1-31 |
| Worcestershire | Old Trafford | Sept 15 | 8 | | 2-67 |
| **BENSON & HEDGES CUP** | | | | | |
| Leicestershire | Leicester | May 4 | | | 1-47 |

**BATTING AVERAGES - Including fielding**

| | Matches | Inns | NO | Runs | HS | Avge | 100s | 50s | Ct | St |
|---|---|---|---|---|---|---|---|---|---|---|
| Britannic Assurance | 6 | 10 | 1 | 201 | 60 | 22.33 | - | 1 | - | - |
| Other First-Class | 2 | 1 | 0 | 16 | 16 | 16.00 | - | - | - | - |
| ALL FIRST-CLASS | 8 | 11 | 1 | 217 | 60 | 21.70 | - | 1 | - | - |
| Refuge Assurance | 2 | 2 | 1 | 22 | 14 * | 22.00 | - | - | - | - |
| Benson & Hedges Cup | 1 | 0 | 0 | 0 | 0 | - | - | - | - | - |
| ALL ONE-DAY | 3 | 2 | 1 | 22 | 14 * | 22.00 | - | - | - | - |

**BOWLING AVERAGES**

| | Overs | Mdns | Runs | Wkts | Avge | Best | 5wI | 10wM |
|---|---|---|---|---|---|---|---|---|
| Britannic Assurance | 187.1 | 30 | 691 | 8 | 86.37 | 2-89 | - | - |
| Other First-Class | 50 | 9 | 138 | 4 | 34.50 | 2-42 | - | - |
| ALL FIRST-CLASS | 237.1 | 39 | 829 | 12 | 69.08 | 2-42 | - | - |
| Refuge Assurance | 16 | 0 | 98 | 3 | 32.66 | 2-67 | - | - |
| Benson & Hedges Cup | 11 | 0 | 47 | 1 | 47.00 | 1-47 | | |
| ALL ONE-DAY | 27 | 0 | 145 | 4 | 36.25 | 2-67 | - | - |

## D.W.FLEMING - *Victoria*

| Opposition | Venue | Date | Batting | Fielding | Bowling |
|---|---|---|---|---|---|
| **OTHER FIRST-CLASS** | | | | | |
| Essex | Chelmsford | Sept 23 | 8 | | 2-88 |
| **OTHER ONE-DAY** | | | | | |
| Durham | Durham U. | Sept 16 | | | 0-24 |
| Essex | Chelmsford | Sept 22 | | 1Ct | 2-40 |

**BATTING AVERAGES - Including fielding**

| | Matches | Inns | NO | Runs | HS | Avge | 100s | 50s | Ct | St |
|---|---|---|---|---|---|---|---|---|---|---|
| Other First-Class | 1 | 1 | 0 | 8 | 8 | 8.00 | - | - | - | - |
| ALL FIRST-CLASS | 1 | 1 | 0 | 8 | 8 | 8.00 | - | - | - | - |
| Other One-Day | 2 | 0 | 0 | 0 | 0 | | - | - | 1 | - |
| ALL ONE-DAY | 2 | 0 | 0 | 0 | 0 | | - | - | 1 | - |

**BOWLING AVERAGES**

| | Overs | Mdns | Runs | Wkts | Avge | Best | 5wI | 10wM |
|---|---|---|---|---|---|---|---|---|
| Other First-Class | 25 | 5 | 88 | 2 | 44.00 | 2-88 | - | - |
| ALL FIRST-CLASS | 25 | 5 | 88 | 2 | 44.00 | 2-88 | - | - |
| Other One-Day | 16 | 0 | 64 | 2 | 32.00 | 2-40 | - | |
| ALL ONE-DAY | 16 | 0 | 64 | 2 | 32.00 | 2-40 | - | |

# PLANER RECORDS

# PLAYER RECORDS

**F**

## M.V.FLEMING - *Kent*

| Opposition | Venue | Date | Batting | | | Fielding | Bowling |
|---|---|---|---|---|---|---|---|
| **BRITANNIC ASSURANCE** | | | | | | | |
| Notts | Trent Bridge | May 22 | 40 | & | 27 | 1Ct | 1-38 |
| Derbyshire | Canterbury | May 25 | 33 | & | 10 | | |
| Warwickshire | Tunbridge W | June 4 | 42 | | | 1Ct | 0-27 |
| Sussex | Tunbridge W | June 7 | 0 | & | 4 | 2Ct | 0-39 |
| Yorkshire | Harrogate | June 14 | | | | | 3-28 |
| Lancashire | Old Trafford | June 21 | | | 64 | 1Ct | |
| Northants | Maidstone | July 2 | 3 | & | 15 * | 1Ct | |
| Glamorgan | Maidstone | July 5 | 4 | & | 1 * | 3Ct | 3-40 |
| Essex | Southend | July 16 | 4 | | | | 0-27 & 2-45 |
| Worcestershire | Worcester | July 23 | | | | | |
| Somerset | Taunton | July 26 | 54 | & | 59 | 1Ct | 0-18 |
| Surrey | Canterbury | Aug 2 | 113 | & | 3 | 1Ct | 1-12 & 0-18 |
| Hampshire | Canterbury | Aug 6 | 12 | & | 23 | 1Ct | 2-18 & 0-24 |
| Leicestershire | Leicester | Aug 9 | 0 | & | 58 | 1Ct | 0-20 |
| Gloucs | Canterbury | Aug 20 | 0 | & | 0 | | |
| Middlesex | Canterbury | Aug 28 | 30 | & | 23 * | | 0-65 |
| Sussex | Hove | Sept 3 | 69 | & | 20 | 1Ct | 0-51 & 0-9 |
| Leicestershire | Canterbury | Sept 17 | 19 | & | 4 | | 0-14 & 0-5 |
| **OTHER FIRST-CLASS** | | | | | | | |
| Oxford U | The Parks | June 18 | 60 | | | | 2-25 |
| West Indies | Canterbury | July 20 | 7 | & | 116 | | 2-50 |
| **REFUGE ASSURANCE** | | | | | | | |
| Worcestershire | Worcester | April 21 | 26 | | | | 0-56 |
| Hampshire | Southampton | May 12 | 19 | | | | 0-33 |
| Essex | Folkestone | May 19 | 51 | | | | 1-40 |
| Derbyshire | Canterbury | May 26 | 35 | | | | 1-44 |
| Middlesex | Southgate | June 2 | 2 | | | 1Ct | 2-58 |
| Lancashire | Old Trafford | June 23 | 44 | | | 2Ct | 1-31 |
| Gloucs | Canterbury | June 30 | 13 | | | | 0-25 |
| Glamorgan | Maidstone | July 7 | 2 | | | 1Ct | 2-45 |
| Leicestershire | Canterbury | July 14 | 5 | | | | 3-41 |
| Somerset | Taunton | July 28 | 20 | | | 1Ct | 4-45 |
| Surrey | Canterbury | Aug 4 | 15 | | | | 2-37 |
| Notts | Trent Bridge | Aug 11 | 9 | | | | 0-36 |
| Northants | Canterbury | Aug 18 | 18 | | | | 1-46 |
| Sussex | Hove | Aug 25 | 77 | | | | 0-39 |
| **NATWEST TROPHY** | | | | | | | |
| Cambs | Canterbury | June 26 | 35 * | | | | 1-6 |
| Surrey | The Oval | July 11 | 21 | | | | 0-38 |
| **BENSON & HEDGES CUP** | | | | | | | |
| Leicestershire | Canterbury | April 23 | 8 | | | | 2-52 |
| Lancashire | Old Trafford | April 25 | 8 | | | | 0-9 |
| Sussex | Canterbury | May 2 | 0 | | | | 1-41 |
| Scotland | Glasgow | May 7 | 52 | | | | 1-23 |
| Worcestershire | Worcester | May 29 | 22 | | | | 1-45 |
| **OTHER ONE-DAY** | | | | | | | |
| Sussex | Hove | Sept 7 | 8 | | | | 1-27 |

### BATTING AVERAGES - Including fielding

| | Matches | Inns | NO | Runs | HS | Avge | 100s | 50s | Ct | St |
|---|---|---|---|---|---|---|---|---|---|---|
| Britannic Assurance | 18 | 29 | 3 | 734 | 113 | 28.23 | 1 | 5 | 14 | - |
| Other First-Class | 2 | 3 | 0 | 183 | 116 | 61.00 | 1 | 1 | - | - |
| ALL FIRST-CLASS | 20 | 32 | 3 | 917 | 116 | 31.62 | 2 | 6 | 14 | - |
| Refuge Assurance | 14 | 14 | 0 | 336 | 77 | 24.00 | - | 2 | 5 | - |
| NatWest Trophy | 2 | 2 | 1 | 56 | 35 * | 56.00 | - | - | - | - |
| Benson & Hedges Cup | 5 | 5 | 0 | 90 | 52 | 18.00 | - | 1 | - | - |
| Other One-Day | 1 | 1 | 0 | 8 | 8 | 8.00 | - | - | - | - |
| ALL ONE-DAY | 22 | 22 | 1 | 490 | 77 | 23.33 | - | 3 | 5 | - |

### BOWLING AVERAGES

| | Overs | Mdns | Runs | Wkts | Avge | Best | 5wI | 10wM |
|---|---|---|---|---|---|---|---|---|
| Britannic Assurance | 184 | 41 | 498 | 12 | 41.50 | 3-28 | - | - |
| Other First-Class | 30 | 5 | 75 | 4 | 18.75 | 2-25 | - | - |
| ALL FIRST-CLASS | 214 | 46 | 573 | 16 | 35.81 | 3-28 | - | - |
| Refuge Assurance | 102.3 | 1 | 576 | 17 | 33.88 | 4-45 | - | |
| NatWest Trophy | 12.2 | 1 | 44 | 1 | 44.00 | 1-6 | - | |
| Benson & Hedges Cup | 44 | 0 | 170 | 5 | 34.00 | 2-52 | - | |
| Other One-Day | 5 | 0 | 27 | 1 | 27.00 | 1-27 | - | |

---

| ALL ONE-DAY | 163.5 | 2 | 817 | 24 | 34.04 | 4-45 | - |
|---|---|---|---|---|---|---|---|

## I.FLETCHER - *Somerset & Combined Universities*

| Opposition | Venue | Date | Batting | | | Fielding | Bowling |
|---|---|---|---|---|---|---|---|
| **BRITANNIC ASSURANCE** | | | | | | | |
| Hampshire | Southampton | Aug 28 | 56 | & | 2 * | | |
| **BENSON & HEDGES CUP** | | | | | | | |
| Northants | Northampton | May 4 | 9 | | | 1Ct | |

### BATTING AVERAGES - Including fielding

| | Matches | Inns | NO | Runs | HS | Avge | 100s | 50s | Ct | St |
|---|---|---|---|---|---|---|---|---|---|---|
| Britannic Assurance | 1 | 2 | 1 | 58 | 56 | 58.00 | - | 1 | - | - |
| ALL FIRST-CLASS | 1 | 2 | 1 | 58 | 56 | 58.00 | - | 1 | - | - |
| Benson & Hedges Cup | 1 | 1 | 0 | 9 | 9 | 9.00 | - | - | 1 | - |
| ALL ONE-DAY | 1 | 1 | 0 | 9 | 9 | 9.00 | - | - | 1 | - |

### BOWLING AVERAGES
Did not bowl

## S.D.FLETCHER - *Yorkshire*

| Opposition | Venue | Date | Batting | | | Fielding | Bowling |
|---|---|---|---|---|---|---|---|
| **BRITANNIC ASSURANCE** | | | | | | | |
| Warwickshire | Headingley | May 9 | 1 | & | 5 | | 4-70 & 1-36 |
| Notts | Headingley | May 16 | 1 | | | | 1-53 & 0-15 |
| Northants | Headingley | May 25 | 2 | | | | 2-41 & 0-28 |
| Warwickshire | Edgbaston | May 31 | 4 * | & | 8 | | 6-70 & 0-27 |
| Kent | Harrogate | June 14 | | | | | |
| Middlesex | Sheffield | June 21 | | | | 1Ct | 0-12 & 0-32 |
| Worcestershire | Headingley | July 2 | | | | 2Ct | 2-36 |
| Hampshire | Southampton | July 5 | | | | | 1-57 & 0-5 |
| Derbyshire | Scarborough | July 16 | | | | | 1-33 & 0-20 |
| Surrey | Guildford | July 19 | 6 | & | 9 * | | 0-44 & 1-31 |
| Notts | Worksop | July 23 | 2 | | | | 0-16 |
| Northants | Northampton | Aug 28 | 5 | & | 5 | 2Ct | 1-78 & 0-34 |
| **OTHER FIRST-CLASS** | | | | | | | |
| Oxford U | The Parks | June 4 | | | | | 0-27 |
| **REFUGE ASSURANCE** | | | | | | | |
| Hampshire | Southampton | April 21 | 1 | | | 2Ct | 1-44 |
| Essex | Chelmsford | April 28 | 11 * | | | | 1-37 |
| Warwickshire | Headingley | May 12 | | | | 1Ct | 3-47 |
| Leicestershire | Leicester | May 19 | | | | | 1-34 |
| Northants | Headingley | May 26 | | | | | 1-31 |
| Derbyshire | Chesterfield | June 2 | | | | | 1-17 |
| Kent | Scarborough | June 16 | | | | | 2-23 |
| Worcestershire | Sheffield | June 23 | | | | | 3-26 |
| Glamorgan | Headingley | June 30 | | | | 2Ct | 1-31 |
| Middlesex | Lord's | July 7 | | | | | 2-43 |
| Gloucs | Scarborough | July 14 | 3 * | | | 1Ct | 1-42 |
| Surrey | The Oval | July 21 | | | | | 1-51 |
| **NATWEST TROPHY** | | | | | | | |
| Warwickshire | Edgbaston | June 26 | 9 | | | | 0-15 |
| **BENSON & HEDGES CUP** | | | | | | | |
| Notts | Trent Bridge | April 25 | 2 * | | | | 0-40 |
| Min Counties | Headingley | May 2 | | | | 2Ct | 0-26 |
| Hampshire | Headingley | May 4 | | | | | 1-11 |
| Glamorgan | Cardiff | May 7 | | | | 1Ct | 2-69 |
| Warwickshire | Headingley | May 29 | | | | | 1-11 |
| Lancashire | Old Trafford | June 16 | 1 | | | 1Ct | 4-51 |
| **OTHER ONE-DAY** | | | | | | | |
| For Yorkshire | | | | | | | |
| Yorkshiremen | Scarborough | Sept 7 | | | | | 1-54 |

# F    PLAYER RECORDS

## BATTING AVERAGES - Including fielding

| | Matches | Inns | NO | Runs | HS | | Avge | 100s | 50s | Ct | St |
|---|---|---|---|---|---|---|---|---|---|---|---|
| Britannic Assurance | 12 | 11 | 2 | 48 | 9 | * | 5.33 | - | - | 5 | - |
| Other First-Class | 1 | 0 | 0 | 0 | 0 | | | - | - | - | - |
| ALL FIRST-CLASS | 13 | 11 | 2 | 48 | 9 | * | 5.33 | - | - | 5 | - |
| Refuge Assurance | 12 | 3 | 2 | 15 | 11 | * | 15.00 | - | - | 6 | - |
| NatWest Trophy | 1 | 1 | 0 | 9 | 9 | | 9.00 | - | - | - | - |
| Benson & Hedges Cup | 6 | 2 | 1 | 3 | 2 | * | 3.00 | - | - | 4 | - |
| Other One-Day | 1 | 0 | 0 | 0 | 0 | | | - | - | - | - |
| ALL ONE-DAY | 20 | 6 | 3 | 27 | 11 | * | 9.00 | - | - | 10 | - |

## BOWLING AVERAGES

| | Overs | Mdns | Runs | Wkts | Avge | Best | 5wI | 10wM |
|---|---|---|---|---|---|---|---|---|
| Britannic Assurance | 230.1 | 45 | 738 | 20 | 36.90 | 6-70 | 1 | - |
| Other First-Class | 8 | 0 | 27 | 0 | - | - | - | - |
| ALL FIRST-CLASS | 238.1 | 45 | 765 | 20 | 38.25 | 6-70 | 1 | - |
| Refuge Assurance | 80 | 2 | 426 | 18 | 23.66 | 3-26 | - | |
| NatWest Trophy | 5 | 0 | 15 | 0 | - | - | - | |
| Benson & Hedges Cup | 49.2 | 6 | 208 | 8 | 26.00 | 4-51 | - | |
| Other One-Day | 10 | 0 | 54 | 1 | 54.00 | 1-54 | - | |
| ALL ONE-DAY | 144.2 | 8 | 703 | 27 | 26.03 | 4-51 | - | |

## G.I.FOLEY - *League CC XI*

| Opposition | Venue | Date | Batting | Fielding | Bowling |
|---|---|---|---|---|---|
| **OTHER ONE-DAY** | | | | | |
| West Indies | Trowbridge | June 28 | 36 | | |

### BATTING AVERAGES - Including fielding

| | Matches | Inns | NO | Runs | HS | Avge | 100s | 50s | Ct | St |
|---|---|---|---|---|---|---|---|---|---|---|
| Other One-Day | 1 | 1 | 0 | 36 | 36 | 36.00 | - | - | - | - |
| ALL ONE-DAY | 1 | 1 | 0 | 36 | 36 | 36.00 | - | - | - | - |

### BOWLING AVERAGES
Did not bowl

## N.A.FOLLAND - *Devon & Minor Counties*

| Opposition | Venue | Date | Batting | Fielding | Bowling |
|---|---|---|---|---|---|
| **NATWEST TROPHY** | | | | | |
| Essex | Exmouth | June 26 | 55 | 2Ct | |
| **BENSON & HEDGES CUP** | | | | | |
| Glamorgan | Trowbridge | April 23 | 45 | | |
| Hampshire | Trowbridge | April 25 | 0 | | |
| Yorkshire | Headingley | May 2 | 54 | 1Ct | |
| Notts | Trent Bridge | May 7 | 100 * | 1Ct | |

### BATTING AVERAGES - Including fielding

| | Matches | Inns | NO | Runs | HS | | Avge | 100s | 50s | Ct | St |
|---|---|---|---|---|---|---|---|---|---|---|---|
| NatWest Trophy | 1 | 1 | 0 | 55 | 55 | | 55.00 | - | 1 | 2 | - |
| Benson & Hedges Cup | 4 | 4 | 1 | 199 | 100 | * | 66.33 | 1 | 1 | 2 | - |
| ALL ONE-DAY | 5 | 5 | 1 | 254 | 100 | * | 63.50 | 1 | 2 | 4 | - |

### BOWLING AVERAGES
Did not bowl

## N.G.FOLLAND - *Bedfordshire*

| Opposition | Venue | Date | Batting | Fielding | Bowling |
|---|---|---|---|---|---|
| **NATWEST TROPHY** | | | | | |
| Worcestershire | Bedford | June 26 | 10 | | |

## BATTING AVERAGES - Including fielding

| | Matches | Inns | NO | Runs | HS | Avge | 100s | 50s | Ct | St |
|---|---|---|---|---|---|---|---|---|---|---|
| NatWest Trophy | 1 | 1 | 0 | 10 | 10 | 10.00 | - | - | - | - |
| ALL ONE-DAY | 1 | 1 | 0 | 10 | 10 | 10.00 | - | - | - | - |

## BOWLING AVERAGES
Did not bowl

## I.FOLLEY - *Derbyshire*

| Opposition | Venue | Date | Batting | | | Fielding | Bowling |
|---|---|---|---|---|---|---|---|
| **BRITANNIC ASSURANCE** | | | | | | | |
| Somerset | Derby | May 22 | 0 | & | 3 | | 1-107 |
| Kent | Canterbury | May 25 | 0 | & | 17 * | | 0-40 & 0-70 |
| Notts | Trent Bridge | Aug 23 | | | | 2Ct | 1-60 & 0-73 |
| **OTHER FIRST-CLASS** | | | | | | | |
| West Indies | Derby | June 12 | | | 0 | | 1-67 & 0-52 |
| **REFUGE ASSURANCE** | | | | | | | |
| Surrey | Chesterfield | June 9 | | | | | 0-28 |
| Notts | Trent Bridge | Aug 25 | | | 6 * | | 0-26 |

### BATTING AVERAGES - Including fielding

| | Matches | Inns | NO | Runs | HS | | Avge | 100s | 50s | Ct | St |
|---|---|---|---|---|---|---|---|---|---|---|---|
| Britannic Assurance | 3 | 4 | 1 | 20 | 17 | * | 6.66 | - | - | 2 | - |
| Other First-Class | 1 | 1 | 0 | 0 | 0 | | 0.00 | - | - | - | - |
| ALL FIRST-CLASS | 4 | 5 | 1 | 20 | 17 | * | 5.00 | - | - | 2 | - |
| Refuge Assurance | 2 | 1 | 1 | 6 | 6 | * | | - | - | - | - |
| ALL ONE-DAY | 2 | 1 | 1 | 6 | 6 | * | | - | - | - | - |

### BOWLING AVERAGES

| | Overs | Mdns | Runs | Wkts | Avge | Best | 5wI | 10wM |
|---|---|---|---|---|---|---|---|---|
| Britannic Assurance | 106 | 12 | 350 | 2 | 175.00 | 1-60 | - | - |
| Other First-Class | 21 | 2 | 119 | 1 | 119.00 | 1-67 | - | - |
| ALL FIRST-CLASS | 127 | 14 | 469 | 3 | 156.33 | 1-60 | - | - |
| Refuge Assurance | 8 | 0 | 54 | 0 | - | - | - | - |
| ALL ONE-DAY | 8 | 0 | 54 | 0 | - | - | - | - |

## A.FORDHAM - *Northamptonshire*

| Opposition | Venue | Date | Batting | | | Fielding | Bowling |
|---|---|---|---|---|---|---|---|
| **BRITANNIC ASSURANCE** | | | | | | | |
| Derbyshire | Derby | April 27 | 131 | | | | |
| Essex | Northampton | May 9 | 90 | & | 47 | | |
| Leicestershire | Northampton | May 16 | 1 | & | 42 | 1Ct | |
| Glamorgan | Cardiff | May 22 | 13 | & | 3 | | |
| Yorkshire | Headingley | May 25 | 33 | & | 33 | | |
| Derbyshire | Northampton | May 31 | 4 | & | 105 | 1Ct | |
| Worcestershire | Northampton | June 4 | 13 | & | 60 | 1Ct | 0-14 |
| Hampshire | Northampton | June 21 | 13 | & | 40 * | | |
| Gloucs | Luton | June 28 | 1 | & | 24 | 1Ct | |
| Kent | Maidstone | July 2 | | | 38 | | |
| Leicestershire | Leicester | July 5 | 116 | | | | |
| Middlesex | Uxbridge | July 16 | 85 | & | 4 | | |
| Notts | Well'borough | July 19 | 12 | & | 9 | | |
| Somerset | Northampton | July 23 | 73 | & | 84 | | 1-42 |
| Sussex | Eastbourne | Aug 2 | 0 | & | 14 | | |
| Lancashire | Lytham | Aug 6 | 10 | | | 2Ct | 0-18 |
| Warwickshire | Northampton | Aug 9 | 66 | & | 44 * | | 0-4 |
| Essex | Colchester | Aug 16 | 29 | & | 18 | | |
| Surrey | Northampton | Aug 23 | 28 | & | 25 | 1Ct | |
| Yorkshire | Northampton | Aug 28 | 165 | & | 44 | 1Ct | |
| Gloucs | Bristol | Sept 3 | 96 | & | 90 | | |
| Warwickshire | Edgbaston | Sept 10 | 6 | & | 16 | | |
| **OTHER FIRST-CLASS** | | | | | | | |
| Cambridge U | Fenner's | April 16 | 81 | | | | |
| West Indies | Northampton | June 15 | 34 * | | | | |

# PLAYER RECORDS

**F**

## REFUGE ASSURANCE

| | | | | |
|---|---|---|---|---|
| Glamorgan | Cardiff | April 21 | 3 | |
| Lancashire | Old Trafford | April 28 | 12 | |
| Leicestershire | Northampton | May 12 | 40 | |
| Worcestershire | Northampton | May 19 | 13 | |
| Yorkshire | Headingley | May 26 | 76 | |
| Hampshire | Northampton | June 2 | 41 | 3Ct |
| Gloucs | Moreton | June 9 | | |
| Somerset | Luton | June 30 | 67 | |
| Surrey | Tring | July 7 | 49 | |
| Notts | Well'borough | July 21 | 8 | |
| Derbyshire | Derby | July 28 | 7 | |
| Sussex | Eastbourne | Aug 4 | 20 | |
| Essex | Northampton | Aug 11 | 73 | |
| Kent | Canterbury | Aug 18 | 30 | |
| Warwickshire | Northampton | Aug 25 | 16 | |
| Lancashire | Old Trafford | Sept 1 | 54 | |

## NATWEST TROPHY

| | | | | |
|---|---|---|---|---|
| Staffordshire | Stone | June 26 | 56 | 1-3 |
| Leicestershire | Northampton | July 11 | 132 * | |
| Glamorgan | Northampton | July 31 | 71 | |
| Surrey | The Oval | Aug 14 | 29 | |

## BENSON & HEDGES CUP

| | | | | |
|---|---|---|---|---|
| Derbyshire | Derby | April 23 | 1 | |
| Gloucs | Bristol | May 2 | 0 | |
| Combined U | Northampton | May 4 | 93 * | |
| Worcestershire | Northampton | May 7 | 70 | 1Ct |
| Lancashire | Old Trafford | May 29 | 19 | |

### BATTING AVERAGES - Including fielding

| | Matches | Inns | NO | Runs | HS | Avge | 100s | 50s | Ct | St |
|---|---|---|---|---|---|---|---|---|---|---|
| Britannic Assurance | 22 | 40 | 2 | 1725 | 165 | 45.39 | 4 | 8 | 8 | - |
| Other First-Class | 2 | 2 | 1 | 115 | 81 | 115.00 | - | 1 | - | - |
| ALL FIRST-CLASS | 24 | 42 | 3 | 1840 | 165 | 47.17 | 4 | 9 | 8 | - |
| Refuge Assurance | 16 | 15 | 0 | 509 | 76 | 33.93 | - | 4 | 3 | - |
| NatWest Trophy | 4 | 4 | 1 | 288 | 132 * | 96.00 | 1 | 2 | - | - |
| Benson & Hedges Cup | 5 | 5 | 1 | 183 | 93 * | 45.75 | - | 2 | 1 | - |
| ALL ONE-DAY | 25 | 24 | 2 | 980 | 132 * | 44.54 | 1 | 8 | 4 | - |

### BOWLING AVERAGES

| | Overs | Mdns | Runs | Wkts | Avge | Best | 5wI | 10wM |
|---|---|---|---|---|---|---|---|---|
| Britannic Assurance | 13 | 0 | 78 | 1 | 78.00 | 1-42 | - | - |
| Other First-Class | | | | | | | | |
| ALL FIRST-CLASS | 13 | 0 | 78 | 1 | 78.00 | 1-42 | - | - |
| Refuge Assurance | | | | | | | | |
| NatWest Trophy | 1.3 | 0 | 3 | 1 | 3.00 | 1-3 | - | |
| Benson & Hedges Cup | | | | | | | | |
| ALL ONE-DAY | 1.3 | 0 | 3 | 1 | 3.00 | 1-3 | - | |

## D.J.FOSTER - *Glamorgan*

| Opposition | Venue | Date | Batting | Fielding | Bowling |
|---|---|---|---|---|---|

### BRITANNIC ASSURANCE

| | | | | | |
|---|---|---|---|---|---|
| Somerset | Taunton | May 9 | 6 * | | 6-84 & 3-63 |
| Warwickshire | Swansea | May 16 | 0 & 0 | | 2-73 & 0-17 |
| Northants | Cardiff | May 22 | | | 2-53 & 1-23 |
| Derbyshire | Chesterfield | June 7 | 0 & 13 * | 2Ct | 2-102 & 1-27 |
| Hampshire | Swansea | Aug 9 | 0 | | 2-39 |
| Yorkshire | Headingley | Aug 16 | | | 1-48 & 1-27 |
| Worcestershire | Cardiff | Sept 10 | 0 & 12 * | | 0-99 |
| Hampshire | Southampton | Sept 17 | 4 * | 1Ct | 1-62 & 2-36 |

### OTHER FIRST-CLASS

| | | | | | |
|---|---|---|---|---|---|
| Oxford U | The Parks | April 17 | | | 1-61 |

### REFUGE ASSURANCE

| | | | | | |
|---|---|---|---|---|---|
| Surrey | The Oval | July 28 | 0 * | 1Ct | 0-39 |
| Gloucs | Swansea | Aug 4 | 0 | | 2-16 |
| Hampshire | Ebbw Vale | Aug 11 | | | 1-27 |
| Derbyshire | Checkley | Aug 18 | 2 * | | 3-30 |

### BATTING AVERAGES - Including fielding

| | Matches | Inns | NO | Runs | HS | Avge | 100s | 50s | Ct | St |
|---|---|---|---|---|---|---|---|---|---|---|
| Britannic Assurance | 8 | 9 | 3 | 35 | 13 * | 5.83 | - | - | 3 | - |
| Other First-Class | 1 | 0 | 0 | 0 | 0 | | - | - | - | - |
| ALL FIRST-CLASS | 9 | 9 | 3 | 35 | 13 * | 5.83 | - | - | 3 | - |
| Refuge Assurance | 4 | 3 | 2 | 2 | 2 * | 2.00 | - | - | 1 | - |
| ALL ONE-DAY | 4 | 3 | 2 | 2 | 2 * | 2.00 | - | - | 1 | - |

### BOWLING AVERAGES

| | Overs | Mdns | Runs | Wkts | Avge | Best | 5wI | 10wM |
|---|---|---|---|---|---|---|---|---|
| Britannic Assurance | 210.5 | 34 | 753 | 24 | 31.37 | 6-84 | 1 | - |
| Other First-Class | 13 | 1 | 61 | 1 | 61.00 | 1-61 | | |
| ALL FIRST-CLASS | 223.5 | 35 | 814 | 25 | 32.56 | 6-84 | 1 | - |
| Refuge Assurance | 26 | 0 | 112 | 6 | 18.66 | 3-30 | - | |
| ALL ONE-DAY | 26 | 0 | 112 | 6 | 18.66 | 3-30 | - | |

## J.FOSTER - *Shropshire*

| Opposition | Venue | Date | Batting | Fielding | Bowling |
|---|---|---|---|---|---|

### NATWEST TROPHY

| | | | | | |
|---|---|---|---|---|---|
| Leicestershire | Leicester | June 26 | 10 | | |

### BATTING AVERAGES - Including fielding

| | Matches | Inns | NO | Runs | HS | Avge | 100s | 50s | Ct | St |
|---|---|---|---|---|---|---|---|---|---|---|
| NatWest Trophy | 1 | 1 | 0 | 10 | 10 | 10.00 | - | - | - | - |
| ALL ONE-DAY | 1 | 1 | 0 | 10 | 10 | 10.00 | - | - | - | - |

### BOWLING AVERAGES

Did not bowl

## N.A.FOSTER - *Essex*

| Opposition | Venue | Date | Batting | Fielding | Bowling |
|---|---|---|---|---|---|

### BRITANNIC ASSURANCE

| | | | | | |
|---|---|---|---|---|---|
| Surrey | Chelmsford | April 27 | | | 2-61 |
| Northants | Northampton | May 9 | 63 | 2Ct | 1-78 & 3-44 |
| Kent | Folkestone | May 16 | 38 | 1Ct | 1-98 & 2-57 |
| Warwickshire | Chelmsford | May 22 | 2 | | 5-80 & 3-49 |
| Gloucs | Bristol | May 31 | 39 | 1Ct | 1-13 & 5-54 |
| Leicestershire | Ilford | June 4 | 8 | 1Ct | 2-42 & 0-53 |
| Worcestershire | Ilford | June 7 | 32 & 6 | | 3-102 & 1-27 |
| Sussex | Horsham | June 21 | 107 * | 1Ct | 2-39 |
| Middlesex | Lord's | June 28 | | 1Ct | 1-62 & 4-36 |
| Hampshire | Chelmsford | July 2 | 12 * & 10 | | 5-45 & 2-38 |
| Surrey | The Oval | July 5 | 0 | | 2-52 & 0-17 |
| Kent | Southend | July 16 | 33 | | 1-58 |
| Derbyshire | Derby | Aug 6 | 19 & 24 | | 3-57 & 0-41 |
| Notts | Trent Bridge | Aug 9 | 12 & 15 * | 1Ct | 3-69 & 2-39 |
| Northants | Colchester | Aug 16 | 41 * | | 0-21 & 0-17 |
| Yorkshire | Colchester | Aug 20 | 4 | | 2-97 & 0-46 |
| Lancashire | Old Trafford | Aug 23 | | 1Ct | 8-99 & 0-16 |
| Derbyshire | Chelmsford | Sept 3 | 6 | 1Ct | 3-69 & 2-39 |
| Leicestershire | Leicester | Sept 10 | 3 | 1Ct | 5-86 & 3-71 |
| Middlesex | Chelmsford | Sept 17 | | | 4-18 & 6-104 |

### OTHER FIRST-CLASS

| | | | | | |
|---|---|---|---|---|---|
| Cambridge U | Fenner's | April 19 | 2 | | 4-29 & 2-32 |
| Victoria | Chelmsford | Sept 23 | 37 | | 4-63 & 1-14 |

### REFUGE ASSURANCE

| | | | | | |
|---|---|---|---|---|---|
| Surrey | The Oval | May 26 | 27 * | | 1-22 |
| Glamorgan | Pontypridd | June 2 | | | |
| Worcestershire | Ilford | June 9 | 5 | | 3-28 |
| Warwickshire | Chelmsford | July 7 | 16 * | | 0-19 |
| Gloucs | Cheltenham | July 28 | 29 * | 1Ct | 0-24 |
| Northants | Northampton | Aug 11 | 57 | | 1-45 |
| Middlesex | Colchester | Aug 18 | 14 * | | 1-23 |

# F | PLAYER RECORDS

## NATWEST TROPHY

| | | | | | |
|---|---|---|---|---|---|
| Devon | Exmouth | June 26 | | | 1-17 |
| Sussex | Hove | July 11 | 10* | | 1-53 |
| Surrey | The Oval | July 31 | 9 | 1Ct | 2-57 |

## BENSON & HEDGES CUP

| | | | | | |
|---|---|---|---|---|---|
| Surrey | The Oval | April 23 | | | 1-26 |
| Warwickshire | Edgbaston | April 25 | | | 2-52 |
| Middlesex | Chelmsford | May 2 | 39* | | 2-28 |
| Somerset | Chelmsford | May 7 | | | 1-41 |
| Hampshire | Chelmsford | May 29 | 5 | | 1-24 |
| Worcestershire | Chelmsford | June 12 | 16 | | 0-14 |

## BATTING AVERAGES - Including fielding

| | Matches | Inns | NO | Runs | HS | Avge | 100s | 50s | Ct | St |
|---|---|---|---|---|---|---|---|---|---|---|
| Britannic Assurance | 20 | 20 | 4 | 474 | 107* | 29.62 | 1 | 1 | 11 | - |
| Other First-Class | 2 | 2 | 0 | 39 | 37 | 19.50 | - | - | - | - |
| ALL FIRST-CLASS | 22 | 22 | 4 | 513 | 107* | 28.50 | 1 | 1 | 11 | - |
| Refuge Assurance | 7 | 6 | 4 | 148 | 57 | 74.00 | - | 1 | 1 | - |
| NatWest Trophy | 3 | 2 | 1 | 19 | 10* | 19.00 | - | - | 1 | - |
| Benson & Hedges Cup | 6 | 3 | 1 | 60 | 39* | 30.00 | - | - | - | - |
| ALL ONE-DAY | 16 | 11 | 6 | 227 | 57 | 45.40 | - | 1 | 2 | - |

## BOWLING AVERAGES

| | Overs | Mdns | Runs | Wkts | Avge | Best | 5wI | 10wM |
|---|---|---|---|---|---|---|---|---|
| Britannic Assurance | 693.5 | 163 | 2000 | 91 | 21.97 | 8-99 | 7 | 1 |
| Other First-Class | 63.3 | 22 | 138 | 11 | 12.54 | 4-29 | - | - |
| ALL FIRST-CLASS | 757.2 | 185 | 2138 | 102 | 20.96 | 8-99 | 7 | 1 |
| Refuge Assurance | 41 | 1 | 161 | 6 | 26.83 | 3-28 | - | |
| NatWest Trophy | 31.5 | 6 | 127 | 4 | 31.75 | 2-57 | - | |
| Benson & Hedges Cup | 61 | 8 | 185 | 7 | 26.42 | 2-28 | - | |
| ALL ONE-DAY | 133.5 | 15 | 473 | 17 | 27.82 | 3-28 | - | |

## A.R.FOTHERGILL - *Durham & Minor Counties*

| Opposition | Venue | Date | Batting | Fielding | Bowling |
|---|---|---|---|---|---|

### NATWEST TROPHY

| | | | | | |
|---|---|---|---|---|---|
| Glamorgan | Darlington | June 26 | 24 | 2Ct | |

### BENSON & HEDGES CUP

| | | | | | |
|---|---|---|---|---|---|
| Glamorgan | Trowbridge | April 23 | 0 | 2Ct | |
| Hampshire | Trowbridge | April 25 | 5 | | |
| Yorkshire | Headingley | May 2 | 15* | | |
| Notts | Trent Bridge | May 7 | 4 | | |

### OTHER ONE-DAY
For Durham

| | | | | | |
|---|---|---|---|---|---|
| Leicestershire | Harrogate | June 11 | | | |
| Surrey | Harrogate | June 13 | 13 | | |
| Sri Lanka | Chester-le-S | July 26 | 2 | | |
| Essex | Scarborough | Aug 31 | 1 | 1Ct | |
| Victoria | Durham U. | Sept 16 | | | |

## BATTING AVERAGES - Including fielding

| | Matches | Inns | NO | Runs | HS | Avge | 100s | 50s | Ct | St |
|---|---|---|---|---|---|---|---|---|---|---|
| NatWest Trophy | 1 | 1 | 0 | 24 | 24 | 24.00 | - | - | 2 | - |
| Benson & Hedges Cup | 4 | 4 | 1 | 24 | 15* | 8.00 | - | - | 2 | - |
| Other One-Day | 5 | 3 | 0 | 16 | 13 | 5.33 | - | - | 1 | - |
| ALL ONE-DAY | 10 | 8 | 1 | 64 | 24 | 9.14 | - | - | 5 | - |

## BOWLING AVERAGES
Did not bowl

## G.FOWLER - *Lancashire*

| Opposition | Venue | Date | Batting | | Fielding | Bowling |
|---|---|---|---|---|---|---|

### BRITANNIC ASSURANCE

| | | | | | | | |
|---|---|---|---|---|---|---|---|
| Warwickshire | Edgbaston | April 27 | 35 | | | | |
| Worcestershire | Worcester | May 9 | 80 | & | 1 | | |
| Derbyshire | Old Trafford | May 16 | 10 | & | 103* | 1Ct | |
| Surrey | The Oval | May 22 | 113 | & | 5 | | |
| Sussex | Old Trafford | May 31 | 32 | & | 36 | | |
| Hampshire | Basingstoke | June 4 | 57 | & | 40* | | |
| Leicestershire | Leicester | June 18 | 23 | & | 5 | | |
| Kent | Old Trafford | June 21 | 27 | | | | |
| Glamorgan | Liverpool | June 28 | 4 | | | | |
| Somerset | Taunton | July 2 | 14 | & | 0 | | |
| Notts | Trent Bridge | July 16 | 22 | & | 34 | | |
| Middlesex | Uxbridge | July 19 | 2 | & | 34 | | |
| Warwickshire | Old Trafford | July 23 | | | | | |
| Yorkshire | Old Trafford | Aug 2 | 9 | & | 4 | | 1-41 |
| Northants | Lytham | Aug 6 | 24 | & | 24 | | |
| Gloucs | Bristol | Aug 9 | 23 | & | 4 | | |
| Worcestershire | Blackpool | Aug 20 | 12 | & | 19 | | |
| Essex | Old Trafford | Aug 23 | 43 | & | 26 | | |

### OTHER FIRST-CLASS

| | | | | | | | |
|---|---|---|---|---|---|---|---|
| Cambridge U | Fenner's | April 13 | 63 | & | 25 | 1Ct | |

### REFUGE ASSURANCE

| | | | | | | | |
|---|---|---|---|---|---|---|---|
| Notts | Old Trafford | April 21 | 36 | | | | |
| Northants | Old Trafford | April 28 | 52 | | | 1Ct | |
| Worcestershire | Worcester | May 12 | 27 | | | | |
| Derbyshire | Derby | May 19 | 59 | | | | |
| Sussex | Old Trafford | June 2 | 22 | | | | |
| Glamorgan | Old Trafford | June 9 | 38* | | | | |
| Warwickshire | Edgbaston | June 16 | 26 | | | 1Ct | |
| Kent | Old Trafford | June 23 | 46 | | | | |
| Somerset | Taunton | July 5 | 20 | | | | |
| Leicestershire | Leicester | July 7 | 49 | | | | |
| Middlesex | Lord's | July 21 | 1 | | | | |
| Hampshire | Southampton | July 28 | 38 | | | | |
| Yorkshire | Old Trafford | Aug 4 | 39 | | | | |
| Gloucs | Bristol | Aug 11 | 15 | | | | |
| Surrey | Old Trafford | Aug 18 | 12 | | | | |
| Essex | Old Trafford | Aug 25 | 41 | | | | |
| Worcestershire | Old Trafford | Sept 15 | 51 | | | | |

### NATWEST TROPHY

| | | | | | | | |
|---|---|---|---|---|---|---|---|
| Dorset | Bournemouth | June 26 | 9 | | | | |
| Hampshire | Southampton | July 11 | 71 | | | | |

### BENSON & HEDGES CUP

| | | | | | | | |
|---|---|---|---|---|---|---|---|
| Scotland | Forfar | April 23 | 45 | | | | |
| Kent | Old Trafford | April 25 | 1 | | | | |
| Leicestershire | Leicester | May 4 | 17 | | | | |
| Sussex | Old Trafford | May 7 | 136 | | | | |
| Northants | Old Trafford | May 29 | 9 | | | 1Ct | |
| Yorkshire | Old Trafford | June 16 | 58 | | | | |
| Worcestershire | Lord's | July 13 | 54 | | | 1Ct | |

## BATTING AVERAGES - Including fielding

| | Matches | Inns | NO | Runs | HS | Avge | 100s | 50s | Ct | St |
|---|---|---|---|---|---|---|---|---|---|---|
| Britannic Assurance | 18 | 31 | 2 | 865 | 113 | 29.82 | 2 | 2 | 1 | - |
| Other First-Class | 1 | 2 | 0 | 88 | 63 | 44.00 | - | 1 | 1 | - |
| ALL FIRST-CLASS | 19 | 33 | 2 | 953 | 113 | 30.74 | 2 | 3 | 2 | - |
| Refuge Assurance | 17 | 17 | 1 | 572 | 59 | 35.75 | - | 3 | 2 | - |
| NatWest Trophy | 2 | 2 | 0 | 80 | 71 | 40.00 | - | 1 | - | - |
| Benson & Hedges Cup | 7 | 7 | 0 | 320 | 136 | 45.71 | 1 | 2 | 2 | - |
| ALL ONE-DAY | 26 | 26 | 1 | 972 | 136 | 38.88 | 1 | 6 | 4 | - |

## BOWLING AVERAGES

| | Overs | Mdns | Runs | Wkts | Avge | Best | 5wI | 10wM |
|---|---|---|---|---|---|---|---|---|
| Britannic Assurance | 7 | 0 | 41 | 1 | 41.00 | 1-41 | - | - |
| Other First-Class | | | | | | | | |
| ALL FIRST-CLASS | 7 | 0 | 41 | 1 | 41.00 | 1-41 | - | - |
| Refuge Assurance | | | | | | | | |
| NatWest Trophy | | | | | | | | |
| Benson & Hedges Cup | | | | | | | | |
| ALL ONE-DAY | | | | | | | | |

# PLAYER RECORDS | F

## A.G.J.FRASER - *Essex*

| Opposition | Venue | Date | Batting | Fielding | Bowling |
|---|---|---|---|---|---|
| **BRITANNIC ASSURANCE** | | | | | |
| Sussex | Horsham | June 21 | 52 * | | 0-13 |
| Hampshire | Chelmsford | July 2 | | 23 | 0-31 |
| Glamorgan | Cardiff | July 23 | | | |
| **REFUGE ASSURANCE** | | | | | |
| Warwickshire | Chelmsford | July 7 | | | 0-33 |
| Gloucs | Cheltenham | July 28 | | 1Ct | 1-21 |

**BATTING AVERAGES - Including fielding**

| | Matches | Inns | NO | Runs | HS | Avge | 100s | 50s | Ct | St |
|---|---|---|---|---|---|---|---|---|---|---|
| Britannic Assurance | 3 | 2 | 1 | 75 | 52 * | 75.00 | - | 1 | - | - |
| ALL FIRST-CLASS | 3 | 2 | 1 | 75 | 52 * | 75.00 | - | 1 | - | - |
| Refuge Assurance | 2 | 0 | 0 | 0 | 0 | - | - | - | 1 | - |
| ALL ONE-DAY | 2 | 0 | 0 | 0 | 0 | - | - | - | 1 | - |

**BOWLING AVERAGES**

| | Overs | Mdns | Runs | Wkts | Avge | Best | 5wI | 10wM |
|---|---|---|---|---|---|---|---|---|
| Britannic Assurance | 19 | 5 | 44 | 0 | - | - | - | - |
| ALL FIRST-CLASS | 19 | 5 | 44 | 0 | - | - | - | - |
| Refuge Assurance | 14 | 0 | 54 | 1 | 54.00 | 1-21 | - | |
| ALL ONE-DAY | 14 | 0 | 54 | 1 | 54.00 | 1-21 | - | |

## A.R.C.FRASER - *Middlesex*

| Opposition | Venue | Date | Batting | Fielding | Bowling |
|---|---|---|---|---|---|
| **BRITANNIC ASSURANCE** | | | | | |
| Kent | Lord's | May 31 | 12 | 1Ct | 4-24 & 1-47 |
| Gloucs | Bristol | June 4 | 0 | 1Ct | 1-14 & 0-6 |
| **REFUGE ASSURANCE** | | | | | |
| Sussex | Hove | May 12 | | 1Ct | 1-34 |
| Kent | Southgate | June 2 | 8 * | | 1-44 |

**BATTING AVERAGES - Including fielding**

| | Matches | Inns | NO | Runs | HS | Avge | 100s | 50s | Ct | St |
|---|---|---|---|---|---|---|---|---|---|---|
| Britannic Assurance | 2 | 2 | 0 | 12 | 12 | 6.00 | - | - | 2 | - |
| ALL FIRST-CLASS | 2 | 2 | 0 | 12 | 12 | 6.00 | - | - | 2 | - |
| Refuge Assurance | 2 | 1 | 1 | 8 | 8 * | - | - | - | 1 | - |
| ALL ONE-DAY | 2 | 1 | 1 | 8 | 8 * | - | - | - | 1 | - |

**BOWLING AVERAGES**

| | Overs | Mdns | Runs | Wkts | Avge | Best | 5wI | 10wM |
|---|---|---|---|---|---|---|---|---|
| Britannic Assurance | 39.5 | 12 | 91 | 6 | 15.16 | 4-24 | - | - |
| ALL FIRST-CLASS | 39.5 | 12 | 91 | 6 | 15.16 | 4-24 | - | - |
| Refuge Assurance | 16 | 0 | 78 | 2 | 39.00 | 1-34 | - | |
| ALL ONE-DAY | 16 | 0 | 78 | 2 | 39.00 | 1-34 | - | |

## B.N.FRENCH - *Nottinghamshire*

| Opposition | Venue | Date | Batting | Fielding | Bowling |
|---|---|---|---|---|---|
| **BRITANNIC ASSURANCE** | | | | | |
| Leicestershire | Trent Bridge | May 9 | 9 & 1 | 3Ct | |
| Yorkshire | Headingley | May 16 | | 3Ct | |
| Kent | Trent Bridge | May 22 | 12 & 1 | 2Ct,1St | |
| Leicestershire | Leicester | May 25 | 0 | 3Ct | |
| Hampshire | Trent Bridge | May 31 | 21 | 1Ct,1St | |
| Gloucs | Gloucester | June 14 | | 2Ct | |
| Worcestershire | Worcester | June 18 | | 3Ct | |
| Warwickshire | Trent Bridge | June 21 | | 0Ct,1St | |
| Glamorgan | Cardiff | July 2 | 3 | 1Ct,1St | |
| Lancashire | Trent Bridge | July 16 | 26 | 3Ct,1St | |
| Northants | Well'borough | July 19 | 2 | 1Ct | |
| Yorkshire | Worksop | July 23 | 11 | 3Ct | |
| Middlesex | Lord's | July 26 | 58 * & 2 | 3Ct | |
| Sussex | Eastbourne | Aug 6 | 10 | 2Ct,1St | |
| Essex | Trent Bridge | Aug 9 | 2 & 35 | 5Ct,1St | 0-11 |
| Somerset | Trent Bridge | Aug 16 | 0 * & 0 | 3Ct | |
| Derbyshire | Trent Bridge | Aug 23 | 9 * | 1Ct | |
| Lancashire | Old Trafford | Aug 28 | 6 & 65 | 5Ct | |
| Middlesex | Trent Bridge | Sept 3 | 3 & 0 | 3Ct,1St | |
| Derbyshire | Derby | Sept 10 | 3 | 4Ct | 1-37 |
| Worcestershire | Trent Bridge | Sept 17 | 36 * | 3Ct | |
| **REFUGE ASSURANCE** | | | | | |
| Lancashire | Old Trafford | April 21 | | 1Ct | |
| Warwickshire | Trent Bridge | April 28 | | 0Ct,1St | |
| Glamorgan | Cardiff | May 5 | 8 * | | |
| Essex | Trent Bridge | May 12 | 9 | 3Ct | |
| Leicestershire | Leicester | May 26 | 16 * | 3Ct | |
| Somerset | Trent Bridge | June 9 | 5 * | 1Ct | |
| Gloucs | Gloucester | June 16 | | | |
| Middlesex | Trent Bridge | June 23 | 17 * | | |
| Surrey | The Oval | June 30 | | | |
| Hampshire | Trent Bridge | July 14 | 1 * | | |
| Northants | Well'borough | July 21 | 26 | 2Ct | |
| Sussex | Hove | July 28 | | 3Ct | |
| Worcestershire | Trent Bridge | Aug 4 | 4 * | 1Ct | |
| Kent | Trent Bridge | Aug 11 | 12 | | |
| Yorkshire | Scarborough | Aug 18 | 8 | 1Ct | |
| Derbyshire | Trent Bridge | Aug 25 | | 1Ct | |
| Worcestershire | Trent Bridge | Sept 1 | 31 | 1Ct | |
| **NATWEST TROPHY** | | | | | |
| Lincolnshire | Trent Bridge | June 26 | | 3Ct | |
| Gloucs | Bristol | July 11 | 1 | 4Ct | |
| Hampshire | Southampton | July 31 | 7 | | |
| **BENSON & HEDGES CUP** | | | | | |
| Hampshire | Southampton | April 23 | 37 * | 1Ct | |
| Yorkshire | Trent Bridge | April 25 | | 1Ct | |
| Glamorgan | Cardiff | May 4 | | 1Ct | |
| Min Counties | Trent Bridge | May 7 | | | |

**BATTING AVERAGES - Including fielding**

| | Matches | Inns | NO | Runs | HS | Avge | 100s | 50s | Ct | St |
|---|---|---|---|---|---|---|---|---|---|---|
| Britannic Assurance | 21 | 24 | 4 | 315 | 65 | 15.75 | - | 2 | 54 | 8 |
| ALL FIRST-CLASS | 21 | 24 | 4 | 315 | 65 | 15.75 | - | 2 | 54 | 8 |
| Refuge Assurance | 17 | 11 | 6 | 137 | 31 | 27.40 | - | - | 17 | 1 |
| NatWest Trophy | 3 | 2 | 0 | 8 | 7 | 4.00 | - | - | 7 | - |
| Benson & Hedges Cup | 4 | 1 | 1 | 37 | 37 * | - | - | - | 3 | - |
| ALL ONE-DAY | 24 | 14 | 7 | 182 | 37 * | 26.00 | - | - | 27 | 1 |

**BOWLING AVERAGES**

| | Overs | Mdns | Runs | Wkts | Avge | Best | 5wI | 10wM |
|---|---|---|---|---|---|---|---|---|
| Britannic Assurance | 14 | 4 | 48 | 1 | 48.00 | 1-37 | - | - |
| ALL FIRST-CLASS | 14 | 4 | 48 | 1 | 48.00 | 1-37 | - | - |
| Refuge Assurance | | | | | | | | |
| NatWest Trophy | | | | | | | | |
| Benson & Hedges Cup | | | | | | | | |
| ALL ONE-DAY | | | | | | | | |

## N.FRENCH - *England Amateur XI*

| Opposition | Venue | Date | Batting | Fielding | Bowling |
|---|---|---|---|---|---|
| **OTHER ONE-DAY** | | | | | |
| Sri Lanka | Wolv'hampton | July 24 | 4 | | 0-28 |

**BATTING AVERAGES - Including fielding**

| | Matches | Inns | NO | Runs | HS | Avge | 100s | 50s | Ct | St |
|---|---|---|---|---|---|---|---|---|---|---|
| Other One-Day | 1 | 1 | 0 | 4 | 4 | 4.00 | - | - | - | - |
| ALL ONE-DAY | 1 | 1 | 0 | 4 | 4 | 4.00 | - | - | - | - |

| F | | PLAYER RECORDS |
|---|---|---|

## BOWLING AVERAGES

| | Overs | Mdns | Runs | Wkts | Avge | Best | 5wI | 10wM |
|---|---|---|---|---|---|---|---|---|
| Other One-Day | 8 | 2 | 28 | 0 | - | - | - | |
| ALL ONE-DAY | 8 | 2 | 28 | 0 | - | - | - | |

## M.FROST - *Glamorgan*

| Opposition | Venue | Date | Batting | Fielding | Bowling |
|---|---|---|---|---|---|
| **BRITANNIC ASSURANCE** | | | | | |
| Leicestershire | Leicester | April 27 | 0 | | 0-16 |
| Somerset | Taunton | May 9 | | | 2-56 & 2-52 |
| Sussex | Cardiff | May 25 | | | 3-45 & 2-75 |
| Worcestershire | Worcester | May 31 | 0 | 1Ct | 4-67 & 3-87 |
| Somerset | Swansea | June 4 | | | 2-81 |
| Derbyshire | Chesterfield | June 7 | 8 * & 0 | | 4-84 & 0-72 |
| Middlesex | Cardiff | June 14 | | | 1-24 & 4-55 |
| Leicestershire | Neath | June 21 | | | 1-20 |
| Notts | Cardiff | July 2 | 2 * | | 1-58 & 1-59 |
| Kent | Maidstone | July 5 | 0 | | 1-65 & 1-52 |
| Gloucs | Cheltenham | July 19 | 0 * | | 4-44 & 7-99 |
| Essex | Cardiff | July 23 | | | 1-58 |
| Hampshire | Swansea | Aug 9 | | 6 | 3-56 |
| Yorkshire | Headingley | Aug 16 | | | 1-55 & 1-12 |
| Warwickshire | Edgbaston | Aug 20 | | | 0-35 & 1-75 |
| Gloucs | Abergavenny | Aug 28 | | | 2-82 & 2-30 |
| Worcestershire | Cardiff | Sept 10 | 0 & 2 * | | 3-72 & 0-6 |
| Hampshire | Southampton | Sept 17 | 1 | | 3-89 & 1-47 |
| **OTHER FIRST-CLASS** | | | | | |
| Oxford U | The Parks | April 17 | | | 3-29 |
| West Indies | Swansea | July 16 | 0 * | | 1-111 |
| **REFUGE ASSURANCE** | | | | | |
| Northants | Cardiff | April 21 | | | 1-24 |
| Leicestershire | Leicester | April 28 | | 1Ct | 0-48 |
| Notts | Cardiff | May 5 | | | 1-41 |
| Somerset | Taunton | May 12 | | | 3-35 |
| Warwickshire | Swansea | May 19 | 0 * | | 3-42 |
| Sussex | Swansea | May 26 | 0 * | | 2-46 |
| Lancashire | Old Trafford | June 9 | | | 0-9 |
| Middlesex | Cardiff | June 16 | | | 0-20 |
| Yorkshire | Headingley | June 30 | | 1Ct | 2-53 |
| Derbyshire | Checkley | Aug 18 | 2 | 1Ct | 2-39 |
| **NATWEST TROPHY** | | | | | |
| Durham | Darlington | June 26 | | 2Ct | 1-45 |
| Worcestershire | Worcester | July 11 | | 1Ct | 1-58 |
| Northants | Northampton | July 31 | 3 | | 0-34 |
| **BENSON & HEDGES CUP** | | | | | |
| Min Counties | Trowbridge | April 23 | | | 1-45 |
| Hampshire | Southampton | May 2 | 0 | | 1-50 |
| . Notts | Cardiff | May 4 | 0 * | | 3-38 |
| Yorkshire | Cardiff | May 7 | | | 0-44 |

## BATTING AVERAGES - Including fielding

| | Matches | Inns | NO | Runs | HS | Avge | 100s | 50s | Ct | St |
|---|---|---|---|---|---|---|---|---|---|---|
| Britannic Assurance | 18 | 11 | 4 | 19 | 8* | 2.71 | - | - | 1 | - |
| Other First-Class | 2 | 1 | 1 | 0 | 0* | | - | - | - | - |
| ALL FIRST-CLASS | 20 | 12 | 5 | 19 | 8* | 2.71 | - | - | 1 | - |
| Refuge Assurance | 10 | 3 | 2 | 2 | 2 | 2.00 | - | - | 3 | - |
| NatWest Trophy | 3 | 1 | 0 | 3 | 3 | 3.00 | - | - | 3 | - |
| Benson & Hedges Cup | 4 | 2 | 1 | 0 | 0* | 0.00 | - | - | - | - |
| ALL ONE-DAY | 17 | 6 | 3 | 5 | 3 | 1.66 | - | - | 6 | - |

## BOWLING AVERAGES

| | Overs | Mdns | Runs | Wkts | Avge | Best | 5wI | 10wM |
|---|---|---|---|---|---|---|---|---|
| Britannic Assurance | 497.2 | 84 | 1728 | 61 | 28.32 | 7-99 | 1 | 1 |
| Other First-Class | 36 | 6 | 140 | 4 | 35.00 | 3-29 | - | - |
| ALL FIRST-CLASS | 533.2 | 90 | 1868 | 65 | 28.73 | 7-99 | 1 | 1 |
| Refuge Assurance | 70 | 2 | 357 | 14 | 25.50 | 3-35 | - | |
| NatWest Trophy | 31 | 2 | 137 | 2 | 68.50 | 1-45 | - | |
| Benson & Hedges Cup | 40 | 6 | 177 | 5 | 35.40 | 3-38 | - | |
| ALL ONE-DAY | 141 | 10 | 671 | 21 | 31.95 | 3-35 | - | |

# PLAYER RECORDS

G

## N.T.GADSBY - *Cambridgeshire*

| Opposition | Venue | Date | Batting | Fielding | Bowling |
|---|---|---|---|---|---|
| **NATWEST TROPHY** | | | | | |
| Kent | Canterbury | June 26 | 15 | | |

**BATTING AVERAGES - Including fielding**

| | Matches | Inns | NO | Runs | HS | Avge | 100s | 50s | Ct | St |
|---|---|---|---|---|---|---|---|---|---|---|
| NatWest Trophy | 1 | 1 | 0 | 15 | 15 | 15.00 | - | - | - | - |
| ALL ONE-DAY | 1 | 1 | 0 | 15 | 15 | 15.00 | - | - | - | - |

**BOWLING AVERAGES**
Did not bowl

## N.J.C.GANDON - *Lincolnshire*

| Opposition | Venue | Date | Batting | Fielding | Bowling |
|---|---|---|---|---|---|
| **NATWEST TROPHY** | | | | | |
| Notts | Trent Bridge | June 26 | 0 | | |

**BATTING AVERAGES - Including fielding**

| | Matches | Inns | NO | Runs | HS | Avge | 100s | 50s | Ct | St |
|---|---|---|---|---|---|---|---|---|---|---|
| NatWest Trophy | 1 | 1 | 0 | 0 | 0 | 0.00 | - | - | - | - |
| ALL ONE-DAY | 1 | 1 | 0 | 0 | 0 | 0.00 | - | - | - | - |

**BOWLING AVERAGES**
Did not bowl

## P.J.GARNER - *England Amateur XI*

| Opposition | Venue | Date | Batting | Fielding | Bowling |
|---|---|---|---|---|---|
| **OTHER ONE-DAY** | | | | | |
| Sri Lanka | Wolv'hampton | July 24 | 0 | | 2-17 |

**BATTING AVERAGES - Including fielding**

| | Matches | Inns | NO | Runs | HS | Avge | 100s | 50s | Ct | St |
|---|---|---|---|---|---|---|---|---|---|---|
| Other One-Day | 1 | 1 | 0 | 0 | 0 | 0.00 | - | - | - | - |
| ALL ONE-DAY | 1 | 1 | 0 | 0 | 0 | 0.00 | - | - | - | - |

**BOWLING AVERAGES**

| | Overs | Mdns | Runs | Wkts | Avge | Best | 5wI | 10wM |
|---|---|---|---|---|---|---|---|---|
| Other One-Day | 3 | 0 | 17 | 2 | 8.50 | 2-17 | - | |
| ALL ONE-DAY | 3 | 0 | 17 | 2 | 8.50 | 2-17 | - | |

## M.A.GARNHAM - *Essex*

| Opposition | Venue | Date | Batting | Fielding | Bowling |
|---|---|---|---|---|---|
| **BRITANNIC ASSURANCE** | | | | | |
| Surrey | Chelmsford | April 27 | | 3Ct | |
| Northants | Northampton | May 9 | 1 | 4Ct | |
| Kent | Folkestone | May 16 | 57 | 2Ct | |
| Warwickshire | Chelmsford | May 22 | 46 * | 6Ct | |
| Gloucs | Bristol | May 31 | 14 | 5Ct | |
| Leicestershire | Ilford | June 4 | 63 & 12 * | 3Ct | |
| Worcestershire | Ilford | June 7 | 68 | 1Ct | |
| Sussex | Horsham | June 21 | 41 | 1Ct | |
| Middlesex | Lord's | June 28 | 91 * | 3Ct | |
| Hampshire | Chelmsford | July 2 | 8 & 14 | 3Ct | 0-39 |
| Surrey | The Oval | July 5 | 2 * & 6 | 1Ct | |
| Kent | Southend | July 16 | 16 | 2Ct | |
| Somerset | Southend | July 19 | 14 | 2Ct | |
| Glamorgan | Cardiff | July 23 | | | |
| Derbyshire | Derby | Aug 6 | 15 & 0 | 4Ct | |
| Notts | Trent Bridge | Aug 9 | 6 & 9 | 4Ct | |
| Northants | Colchester | Aug 16 | 16 | 3Ct | |
| Yorkshire | Colchester | Aug 20 | 68 | 4Ct | |
| Lancashire | Old Trafford | Aug 23 | 0 * | 2Ct | |
| Derbyshire | Chelmsford | Sept 3 | 117 | 2Ct | |
| Leicestershire | Leicester | Sept 10 | 123 | 1Ct | |
| Middlesex | Chelmsford | Sept 17 | 24 * | 2Ct | |
| **OTHER FIRST-CLASS** | | | | | |
| Cambridge U | Fenner's | April 19 | 102 * | 2Ct | |
| West Indies | Chelmsford | Aug 3 | 12 & 8 * | | |
| Victoria | Chelmsford | Sept 23 | 33 | 2Ct | |
| **REFUGE ASSURANCE** | | | | | |
| Yorkshire | Chelmsford | April 28 | | 4Ct | |
| Notts | Trent Bridge | May 12 | 4 | 0Ct,1St | |
| Kent | Folkestone | May 19 | 14 | 0Ct,1St | |
| Glamorgan | Pontypridd | June 2 | | 2Ct | |
| Worcestershire | Ilford | June 9 | 1 | | |
| Hampshire | Chelmsford | June 16 | 0 * | | |
| Derbyshire | Chelmsford | June 30 | 1 * | 1Ct | |
| Warwickshire | Chelmsford | July 7 | 8 | 1Ct,1St | |
| Somerset | Southend | July 21 | | | |
| Gloucs | Cheltenham | July 28 | 18 * | 1Ct | |
| Northants | Northampton | Aug 11 | 9 | | |
| Middlesex | Colchester | Aug 18 | | 1Ct | |
| Lancashire | Old Trafford | Aug 25 | 12 | | |
| **NATWEST TROPHY** | | | | | |
| Devon | Exmouth | June 26 | | 2Ct | |
| Sussex | Hove | July 11 | 12 * | | |
| Surrey | The Oval | July 31 | 9 | 1Ct | |
| **BENSON & HEDGES CUP** | | | | | |
| Surrey | The Oval | April 23 | 6 * | | |
| Warwickshire | Edgbaston | April 25 | | 1Ct | |
| Middlesex | Chelmsford | May 2 | 8 | 0Ct,1St | |
| Somerset | Chelmsford | May 7 | | 4Ct | |
| Hampshire | Chelmsford | May 29 | 11 | 2Ct | |
| Worcestershire | Chelmsford | June 12 | 2 | | |
| **OTHER ONE-DAY** | | | | | |
| Durham | Scarborough | Aug 31 | 5 * | | |
| Yorkshire | Scarborough | Sept 2 | 61 * | 1Ct | |
| Victoria | Chelmsford | Sept 22 | 23 | | |

**BATTING AVERAGES - Including fielding**

| | Matches | Inns | NO | Runs | HS | Avge | 100s | 50s | Ct | St |
|---|---|---|---|---|---|---|---|---|---|---|
| Britannic Assurance | 22 | 25 | 6 | 831 | 123 | 43.73 | 2 | 5 | 58 | - |
| Other First-Class | 3 | 4 | 2 | 155 | 102 * | 77.50 | 1 | - | 4 | - |
| ALL FIRST-CLASS | 25 | 29 | 8 | 986 | 123 | 46.95 | 3 | 5 | 62 | - |
| Refuge Assurance | 13 | 9 | 3 | 67 | 18 * | 11.16 | - | - | 10 | 3 |
| NatWest Trophy | 3 | 2 | 1 | 21 | 12 * | 21.00 | - | - | 3 | - |
| Benson & Hedges Cup | 6 | 4 | 1 | 27 | 11 | 9.00 | - | - | 7 | 1 |
| Other One-Day | 3 | 3 | 2 | 89 | 61 * | 89.00 | - | 1 | 1 | - |
| ALL ONE-DAY | 25 | 18 | 7 | 204 | 61 * | 18.54 | - | 1 | 21 | 4 |

**BOWLING AVERAGES**

| | Overs | Mdns | Runs | Wkts | Avge | Best | 5wI | 10wM |
|---|---|---|---|---|---|---|---|---|
| Britannic Assurance | 4 | 0 | 39 | 0 | - | - | - | - |
| Other First-Class | | | | | | | | |
| ALL FIRST-CLASS | 4 | 0 | 39 | 0 | - | - | - | . |
| Refuge Assurance | | | | | | | | |
| NatWest Trophy | | | | | | | | |
| Benson & Hedges Cup | | | | | | | | |
| Other One-Day | | | | | | | | |
| ALL ONE-DAY | | | | | | | | |

## M.W.GATTING - *Middlesex*

| Opposition | Venue | Date | Batting | Fielding | Bowling |
|---|---|---|---|---|---|
| **BRITANNIC ASSURANCE** | | | | | |
| Yorkshire | Lord's | April 27 | 25 * | 1Ct | |
| Sussex | Lord's | May 9 | 19 & 4 | 1Ct | |
| Sussex | Hove | May 22 | 117 * & 31 | | |
| Somerset | Taunton | May 25 | 180 | | |

# G      PLAYER RECORDS

| | | | | | | | |
|---|---|---|---|---|---|---|---|
| Kent | Lord's | May 31 | 34 | & | 32 | 3Ct | |
| Gloucs | Bristol | June 4 | 15 | & | 68* | | |
| Leicestershire | Uxbridge | June 7 | 6 | | | 1Ct | |
| Glamorgan | Cardiff | June 14 | 13 | & | 96* | | |
| Yorkshire | Sheffield | June 21 | 82 | | | | |
| Essex | Lord's | June 28 | 138*& | | 11* | | |
| Northants | Uxbridge | July 16 | 100* | | | | |
| Lancashire | Uxbridge | July 19 | 41 | & | 3 | 1Ct | |
| Notts | Lord's | July 26 | 5 | & | 143* | 1Ct | |
| Hampshire | Lord's | Aug 2 | 0 | & | 85 | 2Ct | |
| Derbyshire | Lord's | Aug 9 | 215*& | | 2* | 1Ct | |
| Surrey | The Oval | Aug 20 | 50 | & | 40* | 1Ct | |
| Worcestershire | Worcester | Aug 23 | 9 | & | 120 | 1Ct | 0-15 |
| Kent | Canterbury | Aug 28 | 174 | & | 9 | | 0-13 |
| Notts | Trent Bridge | Sept 3 | 91 | & | 14 | | |
| Surrey | Lord's | Sept 10 | 8 | & | 29 | | |
| Essex | Chelmsford | Sept 17 | 0 | & | 35 | | 0-62 |

**OTHER FIRST-CLASS**

| | | | | | | | |
|---|---|---|---|---|---|---|---|
| West Indies | Lord's | May 18 | 8 | & | 5 | 1Ct | 0-9 |

**REFUGE ASSURANCE**

| | | | | | |
|---|---|---|---|---|---|
| Gloucs | Bristol | April 21 | 111 | | |
| Surrey | Lord's | April 28 | 22 | | |
| Sussex | Hove | May 12 | 25 | 1Ct | |
| Somerset | Taunton | May 26 | 65* | 1Ct | |
| Kent | Southgate | June 2 | 15 | | |
| Leicestershire | Uxbridge | June 9 | 16 | 1Ct | |
| Glamorgan | Cardiff | June 16 | 8 | 1Ct | |
| Notts | Trent Bridge | June 23 | 61 | 1Ct | |
| Yorkshire | Lord's | July 7 | 14 | | |
| Warwickshire | Edgbaston | July 14 | 33 | | |
| Lancashire | Lord's | July 21 | 7 | | 0-32 |
| Hampshire | Lord's | Aug 4 | 58 | | 0-27 |
| Derbyshire | Lord's | Aug 11 | 22 | | 2-34 |
| Essex | Colchester | Aug 18 | 8 | | 0-26 |
| Worcestershire | Worcester | Aug 25 | 60* | | |

**NATWEST TROPHY**

| | | | | | |
|---|---|---|---|---|---|
| Ireland | Dublin | June 26 | 65 | | 1-8 |
| Somerset | Taunton | July 11 | 85 | 2Ct | |

**BENSON & HEDGES CUP**

| | | | | |
|---|---|---|---|---|
| Somerset | Taunton | April 23 | 112 | |
| Surrey | Lord's | April 25 | 34 | |
| Essex | Chelmsford | May 2 | 6 | 1Ct |
| Warwickshire | Lord's | May 4 | 17 | |

**BATTING AVERAGES - Including fielding**

| | Matches | Inns | NO | Runs | HS | Avge | 100s | 50s | Ct | St |
|---|---|---|---|---|---|---|---|---|---|---|
| Britannic Assurance | 21 | 37 | 11 | 2044 | 215* | 78.61 | 8 | 6 | 13 | - |
| Other First-Class | 1 | 2 | 0 | 13 | 8 | 6.50 | - | - | 1 | - |
| ALL FIRST-CLASS | 22 | 39 | 11 | 2057 | 215* | 73.46 | 8 | 6 | 14 | - |
| Refuge Assurance | 15 | 15 | 2 | 525 | 111 | 40.38 | 1 | 4 | 5 | - |
| NatWest Trophy | 2 | 2 | 0 | 150 | 85 | 75.00 | - | 2 | 2 | - |
| Benson & Hedges Cup | 4 | 4 | 0 | 169 | 112 | 42.25 | 1 | - | 1 | - |
| ALL ONE-DAY | 21 | 21 | 2 | 844 | 112 | 44.42 | 2 | 6 | 8 | - |

**BOWLING AVERAGES**

| | Overs | Mdns | Runs | Wkts | Avge | Best | 5wI | 10wM |
|---|---|---|---|---|---|---|---|---|
| Britannic Assurance | 28 | 4 | 90 | 0 | - | - | - | - |
| Other First-Class | 2.2 | 1 | 9 | 0 | - | - | - | - |
| ALL FIRST-CLASS | 30.2 | 5 | 99 | 0 | - | - | - | - |
| Refuge Assurance | 24.5 | 0 | 119 | 2 | 59.50 | 2-34 | - | |
| NatWest Trophy | 1 | 0 | 8 | 1 | 8.00 | 1-8 | - | |
| Benson & Hedges Cup | | | | | | | | |
| ALL ONE-DAY | 25.5 | 0 | 127 | 3 | 42.33 | 2-34 | - | |

## P.S.GERRANS - *Oxford University*

| Opposition | Venue | Date | Batting | Fielding | Bowling |
|---|---|---|---|---|---|
| **OTHER FIRST-CLASS** | | | | | |
| Lancashire | The Parks | June 7 | 17* | | 0-21 & 1-52 |
| Kent | The Parks | June 18 | 14 & 4 | | 0-84 & 0-13 |
| Cambridge U | Lord's | July 2 | | | 2-73 & 2-65 |

**BATTING AVERAGES - Including fielding**

| | Matches | Inns | NO | Runs | HS | Avge | 100s | 50s | Ct | St |
|---|---|---|---|---|---|---|---|---|---|---|
| Other First-Class | 3 | 3 | 1 | 35 | 17* | 17.50 | - | - | - | - |
| ALL FIRST-CLASS | 3 | 3 | 1 | 35 | 17* | 17.50 | - | - | - | - |

**BOWLING AVERAGES**

| | Overs | Mdns | Runs | Wkts | Avge | Best | 5wI | 10wM |
|---|---|---|---|---|---|---|---|---|
| Other First-Class | 77.3 | 12 | 308 | 5 | 61.60 | 2-65 | - | - |
| ALL FIRST-CLASS | 77.3 | 12 | 308 | 5 | 61.60 | 2-65 | - | - |

## M.J.GERRARD - *Gloucestershire*

| Opposition | Venue | Date | Batting | Fielding | Bowling |
|---|---|---|---|---|---|
| **BRITANNIC ASSURANCE** | | | | | |
| Derbyshire | Gloucester | June 18 | 3*& 0 | | 1-46 & 0-14 |
| Leicestershire | Hinckley | July 2 | | | 0-24 |
| Sussex | Cheltenham | July 23 | 2 | | 2-25 |
| Worcestershire | Cheltenham | July 26 | 0*& 0* | 1Ct | 0-72 & 0-21 |
| Lancashire | Bristol | Aug 9 | | 1Ct | 0-19 & 1-21 |
| Kent | Canterbury | Aug 20 | 0 | | 1-35 |
| Somerset | Bristol | Sept 10 | 2*& 42 | | 0-64 & 0-14 |
| **OTHER FIRST-CLASS** | | | | | |
| Sri Lanka | Bristol | Aug 6 | 0* | | 4-20 & 6-40 |
| **REFUGE ASSURANCE** | | | | | |
| Kent | Canterbury | June 30 | 7 | | 1-52 |
| Essex | Cheltenham | July 28 | 3 | | 1-42 |
| Glamorgan | Swansea | Aug 4 | 4 | | 1-35 |
| Lancashire | Bristol | Aug 11 | 3* | | 0-35 |
| **NATWEST TROPHY** | | | | | |
| Notts | Bristol | July 11 | | | 0-10 |
| **OTHER ONE-DAY** | | | | | |
| Somerset | Hove | Sept 8 | 0 | | 2-18 |
| Sussex | Hove | Sept 9 | | 1Ct | 1-38 |

**BATTING AVERAGES - Including fielding**

| | Matches | Inns | NO | Runs | HS | Avge | 100s | 50s | Ct | St |
|---|---|---|---|---|---|---|---|---|---|---|
| Britannic Assurance | 7 | 8 | 4 | 49 | 42 | 12.25 | - | - | 2 | - |
| Other First-Class | 1 | 1 | 1 | 0 | 0* | - | - | - | - | - |
| ALL FIRST-CLASS | 8 | 9 | 5 | 49 | 42 | 12.25 | - | - | 2 | - |
| Refuge Assurance | 4 | 4 | 1 | 17 | 7 | 5.66 | - | - | - | - |
| NatWest Trophy | 1 | 0 | 0 | 0 | 0 | - | - | - | - | - |
| Other One-Day | 2 | 1 | 0 | 0 | 0 | 0.00 | - | - | 1 | - |
| ALL ONE-DAY | 7 | 5 | 1 | 17 | 7 | 4.25 | - | - | 1 | - |

**BOWLING AVERAGES**

| | Overs | Mdns | Runs | Wkts | Avge | Best | 5wI | 10wM |
|---|---|---|---|---|---|---|---|---|
| Britannic Assurance | 106.4 | 16 | 355 | 5 | 71.00 | 2-25 | - | - |
| Other First-Class | 25.1 | 4 | 60 | 10 | 6.00 | 6-40 | 1 | 1 |
| ALL FIRST-CLASS | 131.5 | 20 | 415 | 15 | 27.66 | 6-40 | 1 | 1 |
| Refuge Assurance | 29 | 3 | 164 | 3 | 54.66 | 1-35 | - | |
| NatWest Trophy | 2 | 0 | 10 | 0 | - | - | - | |
| Other One-Day | 18 | 0 | 56 | 3 | 18.66 | 2-18 | - | |
| ALL ONE-DAY | 49 | 3 | 230 | 6 | 38.33 | 2-18 | - | |

## E.S.H.GIDDINS - *Sussex*

| Opposition | Venue | Date | Batting | Fielding | Bowling |
|---|---|---|---|---|---|
| **BRITANNIC ASSURANCE** | | | | | |
| Middlesex | Lord's | May 9 | 14* | | 1-43 & 0-49 |
| Hampshire | Hove | May 16 | | | 0-65 & 1-29 |
| **REFUGE ASSURANCE** | | | | | |
| Warwickshire | Edgbaston | April 21 | | | 0-19 |

# PLAYER RECORDS

**G**

| | | | | | |
|---|---|---|---|---|---|
| Middlesex | Hove | May 12 | | 0-19 | |

### BENSON & HEDGES CUP

| | | | | | |
|---|---|---|---|---|---|
| Lancashire | Old Trafford | May 7 | 0 | 1-46 | |

### BATTING AVERAGES - Including fielding

| | Matches | Inns | NO | Runs | HS | Avge | 100s | 50s | Ct | St |
|---|---|---|---|---|---|---|---|---|---|---|
| Britannic Assurance | 2 | 1 | 1 | 14 | 14* | - | - | - | - | |
| ALL FIRST-CLASS | 2 | 1 | 1 | 14 | 14* | - | - | - | - | |
| Refuge Assurance | 2 | 0 | 0 | 0 | 0 | - | - | - | - | |
| Benson & Hedges Cup | 1 | 1 | 0 | 0 | 0 | 0.00 | - | - | - | - |
| ALL ONE-DAY | 3 | 1 | 0 | 0 | 0 | 0.00 | - | - | - | - |

### BOWLING AVERAGES

| | Overs | Mdns | Runs | Wkts | Avge | Best | 5wI | 10wM |
|---|---|---|---|---|---|---|---|---|
| Britannic Assurance | 56.2 | 6 | 186 | 2 | 93.00 | 1-29 | - | - |
| ALL FIRST-CLASS | 56.2 | 6 | 186 | 2 | 93.00 | 1-29 | - | - |
| Refuge Assurance | 7 | 0 | 38 | 0 | - | - | - | |
| Benson & Hedges Cup | 8 | 2 | 46 | 1 | 46.00 | 1-46 | - | |
| ALL ONE-DAY | 15 | 2 | 84 | 1 | 84.00 | 1-46 | - | |

## M.I.GIDLEY - *Leicestershire*

| Opposition | Venue | Date | Batting | | | Fielding | Bowling |
|---|---|---|---|---|---|---|---|
| **BRITANNIC ASSURANCE** | | | | | | | |
| Warwickshire | Leicester | July 26 | 10 | & | 1 | 1Ct | 1-79 |
| Somerset | Weston | Aug 2 | 1 | & | 4* | | 0-33 & 0-15 |
| Derbyshire | Leicester | Aug 28 | 80 | & | 0 | | 2-58 |
| Essex | Leicester | Sept 10 | 6 | & | 5 | 2Ct | 0-56 |
| **OTHER FIRST-CLASS** | | | | | | | |
| Cambridge U | Fenner's | May 22 | | | | | 0-11 & 1-33 |
| West Indies | Leicester | June 1 | 0* | | | 1Ct | 0-38 |
| **REFUGE ASSURANCE** | | | | | | | |
| Kent | Canterbury | July 14 | 2 | | | | |
| Hampshire | Bournemouth | Aug 18 | 12* | | | | 0-33 |

### BATTING AVERAGES - Including fielding

| | Matches | Inns | NO | Runs | HS | Avge | 100s | 50s | Ct | St |
|---|---|---|---|---|---|---|---|---|---|---|
| Britannic Assurance | 4 | 8 | 1 | 107 | 80 | 15.28 | - | 1 | 3 | - |
| Other First-Class | 2 | 1 | 1 | 0 | 0* | - | - | - | 1 | - |
| ALL FIRST-CLASS | 6 | 9 | 2 | 107 | 80 | 15.28 | - | 1 | 4 | - |
| Refuge Assurance | 2 | 2 | 1 | 14 | 12* | 14.00 | - | - | - | - |
| ALL ONE-DAY | 2 | 2 | 1 | 14 | 12* | 14.00 | - | - | - | - |

### BOWLING AVERAGES

| | Overs | Mdns | Runs | Wkts | Avge | Best | 5wI | 10wM |
|---|---|---|---|---|---|---|---|---|
| Britannic Assurance | 79.4 | 18 | 241 | 3 | 80.33 | 2-58 | - | - |
| Other First-Class | 28 | 11 | 82 | 1 | 82.00 | 1-33 | - | - |
| ALL FIRST-CLASS | 107.4 | 29 | 323 | 4 | 80.75 | 2-58 | - | - |
| Refuge Assurance | 4 | 0 | 33 | 0 | - | - | - | |
| ALL ONE-DAY | 4 | 0 | 33 | 0 | - | - | - | |

## D.R.GILBERT - *Gloucestershire*

| Opposition | Venue | Date | Batting | | | Fielding | Bowling |
|---|---|---|---|---|---|---|---|
| **BRITANNIC ASSURANCE** | | | | | | | |
| Worcestershire | Worcester | April 27 | 16 | | | | 1-78 |
| Hampshire | Bristol | May 9 | 20 | | | 1Ct | 3-57 & 3-51 |
| Yorkshire | Sheffield | May 22 | | | | 1Ct | 2-80 & 0-18 |
| Warwickshire | Edgbaston | May 25 | 7 | & | 19 | | 0-64 |
| Middlesex | Bristol | June 4 | 14 | | | | 3-49 & 2-22 |
| Hampshire | Southampton | June 7 | | | | | 2-46 |
| Notts | Gloucester | June 14 | 8 | | | | 3-18 & 1-20 |
| Derbyshire | Gloucester | June 18 | 13 | & | 15 | | 1-84 & 0-31 |
| Somerset | Bath | June 21 | 7 | | | | 0-27 |
| Northants | Luton | June 28 | 3 | | | | 1-43 |
| Surrey | Guildford | July 16 | 15 | | | | 0-64 & 0-60 |
| Glamorgan | Cheltenham | July 19 | 2* | & | 17 | | 0-37 & 2-45 |
| Sussex | Cheltenham | July 23 | 28* | | | | 3-78 |
| Worcestershire | Cheltenham | July 26 | 17 | & | 2 | 1Ct | 3-72 & 4-59 |
| Lancashire | Bristol | Aug 9 | | | | | 2-46 & 2-44 |
| Kent | Canterbury | Aug 20 | 4* | & | 22* | 1Ct | 8-55 & 1-50 |
| Glamorgan | Abergavenny | Aug 28 | 2 | & | 16* | 1Ct | 1-85 & 0-31 |
| Northants | Bristol | Sept 3 | 7* | & | 2 | | 1-48 & 0-45 |
| Somerset | Bristol | Sept 10 | 28 | & | 0 | | 3-78 |
| Sussex | Hove | Sept 17 | 0 | & | 8 | | 1-73 & 2-37 |
| **OTHER FIRST-CLASS** | | | | | | | |
| West Indies | Bristol | July 31 | 6* | | | | 1-56 & 1-38 |
| Sri Lanka | Bristol | Aug 6 | 5 | | | | 4-53 & 3-23 |
| **REFUGE ASSURANCE** | | | | | | | |
| Middlesex | Bristol | April 21 | 0 | | | | 0-47 |
| Worcestershire | Bristol | May 5 | 10* | | | | 0-38 |
| Surrey | The Oval | May 12 | | | | | 2-27 |
| Sussex | Hove | May 19 | 0* | | | | 0-27 |
| Hampshire | Swindon | May 26 | | | | | 1-51 |
| Northants | Moreton | June 9 | | | | | |
| Notts | Gloucester | June 16 | | | | | 0-39 |
| Yorkshire | Scarborough | July 14 | | | | 1Ct | 0-41 |
| Derbyshire | Cheltenham | July 21 | 7 | | | | 1-49 |
| Warwickshire | Edgbaston | Aug 18 | 0 | | | | 0-35 |
| Leicestershire | Leicester | Aug 25 | | | | | 2-37 |
| **NATWEST TROPHY** | | | | | | | |
| Notts | Bristol | July 11 | | | | 1Ct | 2-41 |
| **BENSON & HEDGES CUP** | | | | | | | |
| Combined U | Bristol | April 23 | 1 | | | | 1-34 |
| Worcestershire | Worcester | April 25 | 16 | | | | 0-36 |
| Northants | Bristol | May 2 | | | | | 1-31 |
| Derbyshire | Derby | May 7 | 8 | | | | 1-37 |
| **OTHER ONE-DAY** | | | | | | | |
| West Indies | Bristol | May 14 | | | | | 1-36 |

### BATTING AVERAGES - Including fielding

| | Matches | Inns | NO | Runs | HS | Avge | 100s | 50s | Ct | St |
|---|---|---|---|---|---|---|---|---|---|---|
| Britannic Assurance | 20 | 26 | 6 | 292 | 28* | 14.60 | - | - | 5 | - |
| Other First-Class | 2 | 2 | 1 | 11 | 6* | 11.00 | - | - | - | - |
| ALL FIRST-CLASS | 22 | 28 | 7 | 303 | 28* | 14.42 | - | - | 5 | - |
| Refuge Assurance | 11 | 5 | 2 | 17 | 10* | 5.66 | - | - | 1 | - |
| NatWest Trophy | 1 | 0 | 0 | 0 | 0 | - | - | | 1 | - |
| Benson & Hedges Cup | 4 | 3 | 0 | 25 | 16 | 8.33 | - | - | - | - |
| Other One-Day | 1 | 0 | 0 | 0 | 0 | - | - | - | - | |
| ALL ONE-DAY | 17 | 8 | 2 | 42 | 16 | 7.00 | - | - | 2 | - |

### BOWLING AVERAGES

| | Overs | Mdns | Runs | Wkts | Avge | Best | 5wI | 10wM |
|---|---|---|---|---|---|---|---|---|
| Britannic Assurance | 602.2 | 131 | 1695 | 55 | 30.81 | 8-55 | 1 | - |
| Other First-Class | 46.3 | 6 | 170 | 9 | 18.88 | 4-53 | - | - |
| ALL FIRST-CLASS | 648.5 | 137 | 1865 | 64 | 29.14 | 8-55 | 1 | - |
| Refuge Assurance | 77.4 | 1 | 391 | 6 | 65.16 | 2-27 | - | |
| NatWest Trophy | 12 | 0 | 41 | 2 | 20.50 | 2-41 | - | |
| Benson & Hedges Cup | 44 | 5 | 138 | 3 | 46.00 | 1-31 | - | |
| Other One-Day | 11 | 0 | 36 | 1 | 36.00 | 1-36 | - | |
| ALL ONE-DAY | 144.4 | 6 | 606 | 12 | 50.50 | 2-27 | - | |

## J.D.GLENDENEN - *Durham*

| Opposition | Venue | Date | Batting | Fielding | Bowling |
|---|---|---|---|---|---|
| **NATWEST TROPHY** | | | | | |
| Glamorgan | Darlington | June 26 | 109 | | |
| **OTHER ONE-DAY** | | | | | |
| Sri Lanka | Chester-le-S | July 26 | 15 | 1Ct | |
| Essex | Scarborough | Aug 31 | 0 | 1Ct | |

# G

# PLAYER RECORDS

| Victoria | Durham U. | Sept 16 | 69 * |
|---|---|---|---|

**BATTING AVERAGES - Including fielding**

|  | Matches | Inns | NO | Runs | HS | Avge | 100s | 50s | Ct | St |
|---|---|---|---|---|---|---|---|---|---|---|
| NatWest Trophy | 1 | 1 | 0 | 109 | 109 | 109.00 | 1 | - | - | - |
| Other One-Day | 3 | 3 | 1 | 84 | 69 * | 42.00 | - | 1 | 2 | - |
| ALL ONE-DAY | 4 | 4 | 1 | 193 | 109 | 64.33 | 1 | 1 | 2 | - |

**BOWLING AVERAGES**

Did not bowl

## D.J.GOLDSMITH - *Buckinghamshire*

| Opposition | Venue | Date | Batting | Fielding | Bowling |
|---|---|---|---|---|---|
| **NATWEST TROPHY** | | | | | |
| Somerset | Bath | June 26 | 2 * | | |

**BATTING AVERAGES - Including fielding**

|  | Matches | Inns | NO | Runs | HS | Avge | 100s | 50s | Ct | St |
|---|---|---|---|---|---|---|---|---|---|---|
| NatWest Trophy | 1 | 1 | 1 | 2 | 2 * | - | - | - | - | - |
| ALL ONE-DAY | 1 | 1 | 1 | 2 | 2 * | - | - | - | - | - |

**BOWLING AVERAGES**

Did not bowl

## S.C.GOLDSMITH - *Derbyshire*

| Opposition | Venue | Date | Batting | | | Fielding | Bowling |
|---|---|---|---|---|---|---|---|
| **BRITANNIC ASSURANCE** | | | | | | | |
| Surrey | Derby | June 21 | | 73 * | | 1Ct | 1-41 |
| Warwickshire | Edgbaston | June 28 | 49 & | 19 | | | 2-18 |
| Sussex | Derby | July 5 | 35 & | 6 | | | 1-35 & 1-41 |
| Yorkshire | Scarborough | July 16 | 37 & | 4 | | | 3-42 |
| Worcestershire | Kidd'minster | July 19 | 10 | | | | 1-23 |
| Hampshire | Chesterfield | July 23 | | 10 | | | 0-22 & 1-11 |
| Essex | Derby | Aug 6 | 3 & | 60 * | | 1Ct | |
| Middlesex | Lord's | Aug 9 | 1 & | 6 | | | 0-102 & 3-62 |
| Lancashire | Derby | Aug 16 | | 20 | | | 2-40 |
| Leicestershire | Derby | Aug 20 | 0 & | 20 | | | 1-31 |
| Notts | Trent Bridge | Aug 23 | | 29 * | | | 1-37 |
| Leicestershire | Leicester | Aug 28 | 0 & | 9 | | | 0-7 |
| Essex | Chelmsford | Sept 3 | 18 & | 37 | | | |
| Notts | Derby | Sept 10 | 0 & | 6 | | | 0-39 |
| Yorkshire | Chesterfield | Sept 17 | 1 & | 30 | | | 0-25 |
| **OTHER FIRST-CLASS** | | | | | | | |
| Sri Lanka | Derby | Aug 2 | 127 | | | | 1-31 |
| **REFUGE ASSURANCE** | | | | | | | |
| Surrey | Chesterfield | June 9 | | | | | 3-48 |
| Essex | Chelmsford | June 30 | 4 | | | 1Ct | 0-46 |
| Sussex | Derby | July 7 | 42 | | | 2Ct | 2-33 |
| Worcestershire | Worcester | July 9 | 4 | | | | 0-33 |
| Gloucs | Cheltenham | July 21 | 67 * | | | | 0-12 |
| Northants | Derby | July 28 | 5 | | | | 0-55 |
| Warwickshire | Edgbaston | Aug 4 | 10 | | | | 2-45 |
| Middlesex | Lord's | Aug 11 | | | | | 0-62 |
| Glamorgan | Checkley | Aug 18 | 31 | | | 1Ct | 0-11 |
| Notts | Trent Bridge | Aug 25 | 2 | | | | |
| **OTHER ONE-DAY** | | | | | | | |
| Yorkshire | Scarborough | Sept 1 | 21 | | | | 0-53 |

**BATTING AVERAGES - Including fielding**

|  | Matches | Inns | NO | Runs | HS | Avge | 100s | 50s | Ct | St |
|---|---|---|---|---|---|---|---|---|---|---|
| Britannic Assurance | 15 | 25 | 3 | 483 | 73 * | 21.95 | - | 2 | 2 | - |
| Other First-Class | 1 | 1 | 0 | 127 | 127 | 127.00 | 1 | - | - | - |
| ALL FIRST-CLASS | 16 | 26 | 3 | 610 | 127 | 26.52 | 1 | 2 | 2 | - |
| Refuge Assurance | 10 | 8 | 1 | 165 | 67 * | 23.57 | - | 1 | 4 | - |
| Other One-Day | 1 | 1 | 0 | 21 | 21 | 21.00 | - | - | - | - |
| ALL ONE-DAY | 11 | 9 | 1 | 186 | 67 * | 23.25 | - | 1 | 4 | - |

**BOWLING AVERAGES**

|  | Overs | Mdns | Runs | Wkts | Avge | Best | 5wI | 10wM |
|---|---|---|---|---|---|---|---|---|
| Britannic Assurance | 174 | 28 | 576 | 17 | 33.88 | 3-42 | - | - |
| Other First-Class | 13 | 4 | 31 | 1 | 31.00 | 1-31 | - | - |
| ALL FIRST-CLASS | 187 | 32 | 607 | 18 | 33.72 | 3-42 | - | - |
| Refuge Assurance | 60 | 3 | 345 | 7 | 49.28 | 3-48 | - | - |
| Other One-Day | 7 | 0 | 53 | 0 | - | - | - | - |
| ALL ONE-DAY | 67 | 3 | 398 | 7 | 56.85 | 3-48 | - | |

## G.A.GOOCH - *Essex & England*

| Opposition | Venue | Date | Batting | | Fielding | Bowling |
|---|---|---|---|---|---|---|
| **CORNHILL TEST MATCHES** | | | | | | |
| West Indies | Headingley | June 6 | 34 & | 154 * | 3Ct | |
| West Indies | Lord's | June 20 | 37 | | | 0-3 |
| West Indies | Trent Bridge | July 4 | 68 & | 13 | | |
| West Indies | Edgbaston | July 25 | 45 & | 40 | | 0-11 |
| West Indies | The Oval | Aug 8 | 60 & | 29 | 3Ct | |
| Sri Lanka | Lord's | Aug 22 | 38 & | 174 | | |
| **BRITANNIC ASSURANCE** | | | | | | |
| Surrey | Chelmsford | April 27 | 3 | | 1Ct | |
| Northants | Northampton | May 9 | 45 & | 22 | | 0-8 |
| Kent | Folkestone | May 16 | 7 | | | 2-21 |
| Gloucs | Bristol | May 31 | 1 | | | |
| Middlesex | Lord's | June 28 | 47 & | 106 | 1Ct | |
| Kent | Southend | July 16 | 0 & | 27 | 1Ct | 0-81 |
| Somerset | Southend | July 19 | 79 & | 97 | 1Ct | |
| Northants | Colchester | Aug 16 | 173 | | | |
| Derbyshire | Chelmsford | Sept 3 | 44 | | | 2-16 |
| Leicestershire | Leicester | Sept 10 | 68 & | 18 * | 4Ct | 0-29 |
| Middlesex | Chelmsford | Sept 17 | 259 | | 3Ct | |
| **OTHER FIRST-CLASS** | | | | | | |
| Cambridge U | Fenner's | April 19 | 101 * | | 2Ct | |
| West Indies | Chelmsford | Aug 3 | 66 & | 25 * | 1Ct | 0-46 |
| Victoria | Chelmsford | Sept 23 | 31 | | 2Ct | |
| **TEXACO TROPHY** | | | | | | |
| West Indies | Edgbaston | May 23 | 0 | | 1Ct | 1-17 |
| West Indies | Old Trafford | May 25 | 54 | | | 1-51 |
| West Indies | Lord's | May 27 | 11 | | 1Ct | 1-9 |
| **REFUGE ASSURANCE** | | | | | | |
| Yorkshire | Chelmsford | April 28 | 59 * | | | 3-25 |
| Notts | Trent Bridge | May 12 | 41 | | 1Ct | 2-36 |
| Kent | Folkestone | May 19 | 0 | | 1Ct | 1-43 |
| Glamorgan | Pontypridd | June 2 | | | 1Ct | 0-11 |
| Hampshire | Chelmsford | June 16 | 50 | | | |
| Derbyshire | Chelmsford | June 30 | 56 | | | 0-36 |
| Somerset | Southend | July 21 | 107 | | | 0-24 |
| Middlesex | Colchester | Aug 18 | 45 | | | |
| **NATWEST TROPHY** | | | | | | |
| Devon | Exmouth | June 26 | 57 | | | 1-9 |
| Sussex | Hove | July 11 | 95 | | | 0-28 |
| Surrey | The Oval | July 31 | 50 | | | 2-30 |
| **BENSON & HEDGES CUP** | | | | | | |
| Surrey | The Oval | April 23 | 34 | | 1Ct | 1-52 |
| Warwickshire | Edgbaston | April 25 | 26 | | | 2-54 |
| Middlesex | Chelmsford | May 2 | 29 | | | 0-41 |
| Somerset | Chelmsford | May 7 | 72 | | 1Ct | 2-19 |
| Hampshire | Chelmsford | May 29 | 29 | | 1Ct | 2-42 |
| Worcestershire | Chelmsford | June 12 | 12 | | | 0-27 |
| **OTHER ONE-DAY** | | | | | | |
| Durham | Scarborough | Aug 31 | 0 | | | 1-34 |
| Yorkshire | Scarburgh | Sept 2 | 22 | | 1Ct | 0-21 |
| Victoria | Chelmsford | Sept 22 | 0 | | | 0-36 |

**BATTING AVERAGES - Including fielding**

|  | Matches | Inns | NO | Runs | HS | Avge | 100s | 50s | Ct | St |
|---|---|---|---|---|---|---|---|---|---|---|
| Cornhill Test Matches | 6 | 11 | 1 | 692 | 174 | 69.20 | 2 | 2 | 6 | - |
| Britannic Assurance | 11 | 16 | 1 | 996 | 259 | 66.40 | 3 | 3 | 11 | - |
| Other First-Class | 3 | 4 | 2 | 223 | 101 * | 111.50 | 1 | 1 | 5 | - |
| ALL FIRST-CLASS | 20 | 31 | 4 | 1911 | 259 | 70.77 | 6 | 6 | 22 | - |

# PLAYER RECORDS     G

| | | | | | | | | | |
|---|---|---|---|---|---|---|---|---|---|
| Texaco Trophy | 3 | 3 | 0 | 65 | 54 | 21.66 | - | 1 | 2 - |
| Refuge Assurance | 8 | 7 | 1 | 358 | 107 | 59.66 | 1 | 3 | 3 - |
| NatWest Trophy | 3 | 3 | 0 | 202 | 95 | 67.33 | - | 3 | - - |
| Benson & Hedges Cup | 6 | 6 | 0 | 202 | 72 | 33.66 | - | 1 | 3 - |
| Other One-Day | 3 | 3 | 0 | 22 | 22 | 7.33 | - | - | 1 - |
| ALL ONE-DAY | 23 | 22 | 1 | 849 | 107 | 40.42 | 1 | 8 | 9 - |

### BOWLING AVERAGES

| | Overs | Mdns | Runs | Wkts | Avge | Best | 5wI | 10wM |
|---|---|---|---|---|---|---|---|---|
| Cornhill Test Matches | 8 | 1 | 14 | 0 | - | - | - | - |
| Britannic Assurance | 42.1 | 17 | 155 | 4 | 38.75 | 2-16 | - | - |
| Other First-Class | 13 | 4 | 46 | 0 | - | - | - | - |
| ALL FIRST-CLASS | 63.1 | 22 | 215 | 4 | 53.75 | 2-16 | - | - |
| Texaco Trophy | 18 | 1 | 77 | 3 | 25.66 | 1-9 | - | |
| Refuge Assurance | 43 | 2 | 175 | 6 | 29.16 | 3-25 | - | |
| NatWest Trophy | 18 | 3 | 67 | 3 | 22.33 | 2-30 | - | |
| Benson & Hedges Cup | 56 | 2 | 235 | 7 | 33.57 | 2-19 | - | |
| Other One-Day | 21 | 0 | 91 | 1 | 91.00 | 1-34 | - | |
| ALL ONE-DAY | 156 | 8 | 645 | 20 | 32.25 | 3-25 | - | |

## A.L.GORAM - *Scotland*

| Opposition | Venue | Date | Batting | Fielding | Bowling |
|---|---|---|---|---|---|
| **OTHER FIRST-CLASS** | | | | | |
| Ireland | Dublin | June 22 | 5 | | 1-16 & 1-46 |
| **NATWEST TROPHY** | | | | | |
| Sussex | Edinburgh | June 26 | 21 | 1Ct | 2-42 |

### BATTING AVERAGES - Including fielding

| | Matches | Inns | NO | Runs | HS | Avge | 100s | 50s | Ct | St |
|---|---|---|---|---|---|---|---|---|---|---|
| Other First-Class | 1 | 1 | 0 | 5 | 5 | 5.00 | - | - | - | - |
| ALL FIRST-CLASS | 1 | 1 | 0 | 5 | 5 | 5.00 | - | - | - | - |
| NatWest Trophy | 1 | 1 | 0 | 21 | 21 | 21.00 | - | - | 1 | - |
| ALL ONE-DAY | 1 | 1 | 0 | 21 | 21 | 21.00 | - | - | 1 | - |

### BOWLING AVERAGES

| | Overs | Mdns | Runs | Wkts | Avge | Best | 5wI | 10wM |
|---|---|---|---|---|---|---|---|---|
| Other First-Class | 23 | 6 | 62 | 2 | 31.00 | 1-16 | - | - |
| ALL FIRST-CLASS | 23 | 6 | 62 | 2 | 31.00 | 1-16 | - | - |
| NatWest Trophy | 12 | 1 | 42 | 2 | 21.00 | 2-42 | - | |
| ALL ONE-DAY | 12 | 1 | 42 | 2 | 21.00 | 2-42 | - | |

## D.GOUGH - *Yorkshire*

| Opposition | Venue | Date | Batting | Fielding | Bowling |
|---|---|---|---|---|---|
| **BRITANNIC ASSURANCE** | | | | | |
| Gloucs | Sheffield | May 22 | 26 | 1Ct | 1-54 & 0-28 |
| Warwickshire | Edgbaston | May 31 | 24 & 25 | | 1-85 & 0-24 |
| Kent | Harrogate | June 14 | | | |
| Middlesex | Sheffield | June 21 | 2* | | 1-13 & 0-26 |
| Worcestershire | Headingley | July 2 | 2 | | 0-14 |
| Hampshire | Southampton | July 5 | 32 | | 1-86 |
| Derbyshire | Scarborough | July 16 | 1 | | 1-25 & 0-17 |
| Lancashire | Old Trafford | Aug 2 | 9 | 1Ct | 0-51 & 0-23 |
| Somerset | Taunton | Aug 23 | | | 3-99 & 0-25 |
| Northants | Northampton | Aug 28 | 22 & 72 | | 1-87 & 0-29 |
| Lancashire | Scarborough | Sept 3 | 60* & 5* | 1Ct | 1-79 & 5-41 |
| Derbyshire | Chesterfield | Sept 17 | 0 & 27 | | 1-31 & 0-53 |
| **OTHER FIRST-CLASS** | | | | | |
| Oxford U | The Parks | June 4 | | | 2-55 |
| **REFUGE ASSURANCE** | | | | | |
| Leicestershire | Leicester | May 19 | 72* | | 1-26 |
| Northants | Headingley | May 26 | 13 | | 0-21 |
| Derbyshire | Chesterfield | June 2 | 0 | | 0-20 |
| Kent | Scarborough | June 16 | 0 | 1Ct | 2-32 |
| Worcestershire | Sheffield | June 23 | | 1Ct | 0-29 |
| Glamorgan | Headingley | June 30 | | | 1-26 |
| Middlesex | Lord's | July 7 | | | 1-35 |
| Gloucs | Scarborough | July 14 | 7 | | 1-35 |
| Sussex | Midd'brough | Aug 11 | 7 | 1Ct | 1-47 |
| Somerset | Taunton | Aug 25 | 6 | 1Ct | 0-45 |
| **NATWEST TROPHY** | | | | | |
| Warwickshire | Edgbaston | June 26 | 2 | | 0-18 |
| **BENSON & HEDGES CUP** | | | | | |
| Lancashire | Old Trafford | June 16 | 1 | | 2-41 |
| **OTHER ONE-DAY** | | | | | |
| Essex | Scarborough | Sept 2 | | | 2-46 |
| Yorkshiremen | Scarborough | Sept 7 | 11 | | 2-34 |
| World XI | Scarborough | Sept 8 | 0 | | 3-33 |

### BATTING AVERAGES - Including fielding

| | Matches | Inns | NO | Runs | HS | Avge | 100s | 50s | Ct | St |
|---|---|---|---|---|---|---|---|---|---|---|
| Britannic Assurance | 12 | 14 | 3 | 307 | 72 | 27.90 | - | 2 | 3 | - |
| Other First-Class | 1 | 0 | 0 | 0 | 0 | - | - | - | - | - |
| ALL FIRST-CLASS | 13 | 14 | 3 | 307 | 72 | 27.90 | - | 2 | 3 | - |
| Refuge Assurance | 10 | 7 | 1 | 105 | 72* | 17.50 | - | 1 | 4 | - |
| NatWest Trophy | 1 | 1 | 0 | 2 | 2 | 2.00 | - | - | - | - |
| Benson & Hedges Cup | 1 | 1 | 0 | 1 | 1 | 1.00 | - | - | - | - |
| Other One-Day | 3 | 2 | 0 | 11 | 11 | 5.50 | - | - | - | - |
| ALL ONE-DAY | 15 | 11 | 1 | 119 | 72* | 11.90 | - | 1 | 4 | - |

### BOWLING AVERAGES

| | Overs | Mdns | Runs | Wkts | Avge | Best | 5wI | 10wM |
|---|---|---|---|---|---|---|---|---|
| Britannic Assurance | 252 | 52 | 890 | 16 | 55.62 | 5-41 | 1 | - |
| Other First-Class | 18 | 3 | 55 | 2 | 27.50 | 2-55 | - | - |
| ALL FIRST-CLASS | 270 | 55 | 945 | 18 | 52.50 | 5-41 | 1 | - |
| Refuge Assurance | 60.2 | 1 | 316 | 7 | 45.14 | 2-32 | - | |
| NatWest Trophy | 8 | 2 | 18 | 0 | - | - | - | |
| Benson & Hedges Cup | 8 | 0 | 41 | 2 | 20.50 | 2-41 | - | |
| Other One-Day | 29 | 2 | 113 | 7 | 16.14 | 3-33 | - | |
| ALL ONE-DAY | 105.2 | 5 | 488 | 16 | 30.50 | 3-33 | - | |

## I.J.GOULD - *Sussex*

| Opposition | Venue | Date | Batting | Fielding | Bowling |
|---|---|---|---|---|---|
| **REFUGE ASSURANCE** | | | | | |
| Warwickshire | Edgbaston | April 21 | 21 | | |

### BATTING AVERAGES - Including fielding

| | Matches | Inns | NO | Runs | HS | Avge | 100s | 50s | Ct | St |
|---|---|---|---|---|---|---|---|---|---|---|
| Refuge Assurance | 1 | 1 | 0 | 21 | 21 | 21.00 | - | - | - | - |
| ALL ONE-DAY | 1 | 1 | 0 | 21 | 21 | 21.00 | - | - | - | - |

### BOWLING AVERAGES
Did not bowl

## M.R.GOULDSTONE - *Bedfordshire*

| Opposition | Venue | Date | Batting | Fielding | Bowling |
|---|---|---|---|---|---|
| **NATWEST TROPHY** | | | | | |
| Worcestershire | Bedford | June 26 | 2 | | |

### BATTING AVERAGES - Including fielding

| | Matches | Inns | NO | Runs | HS | Avge | 100s | 50s | Ct | St |
|---|---|---|---|---|---|---|---|---|---|---|
| NatWest Trophy | 1 | 1 | 0 | 2 | 2 | 2.00 | - | - | - | - |
| ALL ONE-DAY | 1 | 1 | 0 | 2 | 2 | 2.00 | - | - | - | - |

# G

# PLAYER RECORDS

## BOWLING AVERAGES
Did not bowl

## J.W.GOVAN - *Scotland*

| Opposition | Venue | Date | Batting | Fielding | Bowling |
|---|---|---|---|---|---|
| **OTHER FIRST-CLASS** | | | | | |
| Ireland | Dublin | June 22 | 1 | 1Ct | 0-29 & 1-47 |
| **BENSON & HEDGES CUP** | | | | | |
| Lancashire | Forfar | April 23 | 18 | | 1-26 |
| Leicestershire | Leicester | May 2 | 10 | | 0-50 |
| Sussex | Hove | May 4 | 9 | 1Ct | 0-52 |
| Kent | Glasgow | May 7 | 23 | 1Ct | 1-63 |

### BATTING AVERAGES - Including fielding

| | Matches | Inns | NO | Runs | HS | Avge | 100s | 50s | Ct | St |
|---|---|---|---|---|---|---|---|---|---|---|
| Other First-Class | 1 | 1 | 0 | 1 | 1 | 1.00 | - | - | 1 | - |
| ALL FIRST-CLASS | 1 | 1 | 0 | 1 | 1 | 1.00 | - | - | 1 | - |
| Benson & Hedges Cup | 4 | 4 | 0 | 60 | 23 | 15.00 | - | - | 2 | - |
| ALL ONE-DAY | 4 | 4 | 0 | 60 | 23 | 15.00 | - | - | 2 | - |

### BOWLING AVERAGES

| | Overs | Mdns | Runs | Wkts | Avge | Best | 5wI | 10wM |
|---|---|---|---|---|---|---|---|---|
| Other First-Class | 24 | 5 | 76 | 1 | 76.00 | 1-47 | - | - |
| ALL FIRST-CLASS | 24 | 5 | 76 | 1 | 76.00 | 1-47 | - | - |
| Benson & Hedges Cup | 42 | 4 | 191 | 2 | 95.50 | 1-26 | - | |
| ALL ONE-DAY | 42 | 4 | 191 | 2 | 95.50 | 1-26 | - | |

## D.I.GOWER - *Hampshire*

| Opposition | Venue | Date | Batting | | Fielding | Bowling |
|---|---|---|---|---|---|---|
| **BRITANNIC ASSURANCE** | | | | | | |
| Kent | Southampton | April 27 | 11 | | 1Ct | |
| Gloucs | Bristol | May 9 | 14 & | 3 | | |
| Sussex | Hove | May 16 | 15 & | 13* | | |
| Surrey | Bournemouth | May 25 | 29 & | 3 | 1Ct | |
| Notts | Trent Bridge | May 31 | 10 & | 44 | 2Ct | |
| Lancashire | Basingstoke | June 4 | | 14 | 1Ct | |
| Gloucs | Southampton | June 7 | 28 | | | |
| Somerset | Bath | June 18 | 69 & | 18* | | |
| Northants | Northampton | June 21 | 22 | | 1Ct | |
| Essex | Chelmsford | July 2 | 23 & | 52* | | |
| Yorkshire | Southampton | July 5 | 49 | | | |
| Worcestershire | Portsmouth | July 16 | 77 | | 2Ct | |
| Warwickshire | Portsmouth | July 19 | 43 & | 18 | 1Ct | |
| Derbyshire | Chesterfield | July 23 | 3 & | 0* | | |
| Middlesex | Lord's | Aug 2 | 40 & | 80* | 1Ct | |
| Kent | Canterbury | Aug 6 | 36 & | 40 | 2Ct | |
| Glamorgan | Swansea | Aug 9 | 47 | | | |
| Leicestershire | Bournemouth | Aug 16 | 11 & | 16 | | |
| Sussex | Bournemouth | Aug 20 | 51 & | 58 | | |
| Somerset | Southampton | Aug 28 | 73 & | 15 | 1Ct | |
| Surrey | The Oval | Sept 3 | 7 & | 3 | | |
| Glamorgan | Southampton | Sept 17 | 59 & | 38 | | 0-4 |
| **OTHER FIRST-CLASS** | | | | | | |
| West Indies | Southampton | June 29 | 10 | | | |
| **REFUGE ASSURANCE** | | | | | | |
| Yorkshire | Southampton | April 21 | 45 | | | |
| Derbyshire | Derby | May 5 | 37 | | | |
| Kent | Southampton | May 12 | 3 | | | |
| Somerset | Bournemouth | May 19 | 8 | | | |
| Gloucs | Swindon | May 26 | 2 | | | |
| Sussex | Basingstoke | June 9 | 0 | | 3Ct | |
| Essex | Chelmsford | June 16 | | | | |
| Worcestershire | Southampton | July 7 | 16 | | 1Ct | |

## NATWEST TROPHY

| | | | | | |
|---|---|---|---|---|---|
| Berkshire | Reading | June 26 | | | |
| Lancashire | Southampton | July 11 | 54* | | |
| Notts | Southampton | July 31 | 19 | | |
| Warwickshire | Edgbaston | Aug 14 | | | |
| Surrey | Lord's | Sept 7 | 9 | | |

## BENSON & HEDGES CUP

| | | | | | |
|---|---|---|---|---|---|
| Notts | Southampton | April 23 | 5 | | |
| Min Counties | Trowbridge | April 25 | 6 | | |
| Glamorgan | Southampton | May 2 | 63 | 1Ct | |
| Yorkshire | Headingley | May 4 | 5 | | |
| Essex | Chelmsford | May 29 | 18 | | |

### BATTING AVERAGES - Including fielding

| | Matches | Inns | NO | Runs | HS | Avge | 100s | 50s | Ct | St |
|---|---|---|---|---|---|---|---|---|---|---|
| Britannic Assurance | 22 | 37 | 5 | 1132 | 80* | 35.37 | - | 8 | 13 | - |
| Other First-Class | 1 | 1 | 0 | 10 | 10 | 10.00 | - | - | - | - |
| ALL FIRST-CLASS | 23 | 38 | 5 | 1142 | 80* | 34.60 | - | 8 | 13 | - |
| Refuge Assurance | 8 | 7 | 0 | 111 | 45 | 15.85 | - | - | 4 | - |
| NatWest Trophy | 5 | 3 | 1 | 82 | 54* | 41.00 | - | 1 | - | - |
| Benson & Hedges Cup | 5 | 5 | 0 | 97 | 63 | 19.40 | - | 1 | 1 | - |
| ALL ONE-DAY | 18 | 15 | 1 | 290 | 63 | 20.71 | - | 2 | 5 | - |

### BOWLING AVERAGES

| | Overs | Mdns | Runs | Wkts | Avge | Best | 5wI | 10wM |
|---|---|---|---|---|---|---|---|---|
| Britannic Assurance | 0.1 | 0 | 4 | 0 | - | - | - | - |
| Other First-Class | | | | | | | | |
| ALL FIRST-CLASS | 0.1 | 0 | 4 | 0 | - | - | - | - |
| Refuge Assurance | | | | | | | | |
| NatWest Trophy | | | | | | | | |
| Benson & Hedges Cup | | | | | | | | |
| ALL ONE-DAY | | | | | | | | |

## J.M.H.GRAHAM-BROWN - *Dorset*

| Opposition | Venue | Date | Batting | Fielding | Bowling |
|---|---|---|---|---|---|
| **NATWEST TROPHY** | | | | | |
| Lancashire | Bournemouth | June 26 | 18 | | |

### BATTING AVERAGES - Including fielding

| | Matches | Inns | NO | Runs | HS | Avge | 100s | 50s | Ct | St |
|---|---|---|---|---|---|---|---|---|---|---|
| NatWest Trophy | 1 | 1 | 0 | 18 | 18 | 18.00 | - | - | - | - |
| ALL ONE-DAY | 1 | 1 | 0 | 18 | 18 | 18.00 | - | - | - | - |

### BOWLING AVERAGES
Did not bowl

## D.A.GRAVENEY - *Somerset*

| Opposition | Venue | Date | Batting | | Fielding | Bowling |
|---|---|---|---|---|---|---|
| **BRITANNIC ASSURANCE** | | | | | | |
| Sussex | Taunton | April 27 | 4* | | | 0-0 |
| Glamorgan | Taunton | May 9 | 0* & | 17 | | 4-89 & 2-110 |
| Derbyshire | Derby | May 22 | | | | 0-31 & 5-68 |
| Middlesex | Taunton | May 25 | 1 | | 1Ct | 1-111 |
| Glamorgan | Swansea | June 4 | | | | 0-53 |
| Warwickshire | Edgbaston | June 7 | | | | 3-114 |
| Hampshire | Bath | June 18 | 0* | | | 1-49 & 0-70 |
| Gloucs | Bath | June 21 | | | 1Ct | 0-6 |
| Surrey | The Oval | June 28 | 0* | | 1Ct | 2-30 |
| Lancashire | Taunton | July 2 | | | 2Ct | 0-61 |
| Sussex | Hove | July 16 | 7* | | | 0-38 |
| Northants | Northampton | July 23 | | | | 0-22 & 3-111 |
| Kent | Taunton | July 26 | | 4 | 1Ct | 7-105 & 2-88 |
| Leicestershire | Weston | Aug 2 | | | 1Ct | 1-39 & 2-71 |
| Worcestershire | Weston | Aug 6 | | | | 2-54 & 3-87 |
| Notts | Trent Bridge | Aug 16 | | | | 2-46 & 1-60 |
| Yorkshire | Taunton | Aug 23 | 7 | | 1Ct | 1-58 & 3-61 |

# PLAYER RECORDS

| | | | | | | |
|---|---|---|---|---|---|---|
| Hampshire | Southampton | Aug 28 | | 2Ct | 0-31 & 4-141 |
| Worcestershire | Worcester | Sept 3 | 1 & 0* | | 0-85 |
| Warwickshire | Taunton | Sept 17 | 2* & 8 | | 2-73 & 2-79 |

**OTHER FIRST-CLASS**

| | | | | | |
|---|---|---|---|---|---|
| West Indies | Taunton | May 29 | 8 | | 1-68 & 1-51 |

**REFUGE ASSURANCE**

| | | | | | |
|---|---|---|---|---|---|
| Surrey | The Oval | April 21 | 4* | | |
| Sussex | Taunton | April 28 | | | 1-33 |
| Glamorgan | Taunton | May 12 | | | 2-39 |
| Warwickshire | Edgbaston | June 2 | | | |
| Notts | Trent Bridge | June 9 | | | 0-20 |
| Derbyshire | Derby | June 16 | 2* | | 2-37 |
| Northants | Luton | June 30 | | | 1-23 |
| Kent | Taunton | July 28 | 14* | | 3-21 |
| Worcestershire | Worcester | Aug 18 | | 1Ct | 1-36 |
| Yorkshire | Taunton | Aug 25 | | | 1-44 |

**NATWEST TROPHY**

| | | | | | |
|---|---|---|---|---|---|
| Bucks | Bath | June 26 | | 1Ct | 1-24 |
| Middlesex | Taunton | July 11 | | | 1-24 |
| Warwickshire | Edgbaston | July 31 | | | 1-44 |

**BENSON & HEDGES CUP**

| | | | | | |
|---|---|---|---|---|---|
| Middlesex | Taunton | April 23 | 3* | | 0-33 |

**BATTING AVERAGES - Including fielding**

| | Matches | Inns | NO | Runs | HS | Avge | 100s | 50s | Ct | St |
|---|---|---|---|---|---|---|---|---|---|---|
| Britannic Assurance | 20 | 13 | 7 | 51 | 17 | 8.50 | - | - | 10 | - |
| Other First-Class | 1 | 1 | 0 | 8 | 8 | 8.00 | - | - | - | - |
| ALL FIRST-CLASS | 21 | 14 | 7 | 59 | 17 | 8.42 | - | - | 10 | - |
| Refuge Assurance | 10 | 3 | 3 | 20 | 14* | - | - | - | 1 | - |
| NatWest Trophy | 3 | 0 | 0 | 0 | 0 | - | - | - | 1 | - |
| Benson & Hedges Cup | 1 | 1 | 1 | 3 | 3* | - | - | - | - | - |
| ALL ONE-DAY | 14 | 4 | 4 | 23 | 14* | - | - | - | 2 | - |

**BOWLING AVERAGES**

| | Overs | Mdns | Runs | Wkts | Avge | Best | 5wI | 10wM |
|---|---|---|---|---|---|---|---|---|
| Britannic Assurance | 673.2 | 147 | 2041 | 53 | 38.50 | 7-105 | 2 | - |
| Other First-Class | 35 | 5 | 119 | 2 | 59.50 | 1-51 | - | - |
| ALL FIRST-CLASS | 708.2 | 152 | 2160 | 55 | 39.27 | 7-105 | 2 | - |
| Refuge Assurance | 60 | 2 | 253 | 11 | 23.00 | 3-21 | - | |
| NatWest Trophy | 31 | 5 | 92 | 3 | 30.66 | 1-24 | - | |
| Benson & Hedges Cup | 7 | 0 | 33 | 0 | - | - | - | |
| ALL ONE-DAY | 98 | 7 | 378 | 14 | 27.00 | 3-21 | - | |

# A.P.GRAYSON - *Yorkshire*

| Opposition | Venue | Date | Batting | Fielding | Bowling |
|---|---|---|---|---|---|

**OTHER FIRST-CLASS**

| | | | | | |
|---|---|---|---|---|---|
| Oxford U | The Parks | June 4 | 18* | 1Ct | 1-3 |
| Sri Lanka | Headingley | July 27 | 0 | | 0-53 |

**REFUGE ASSURANCE**

| | | | | | |
|---|---|---|---|---|---|
| Surrey | The Oval | July 21 | | | 1-32 |

**BATTING AVERAGES - Including fielding**

| | Matches | Inns | NO | Runs | HS | Avge | 100s | 50s | Ct | St |
|---|---|---|---|---|---|---|---|---|---|---|
| Other First-Class | 2 | 2 | 1 | 18 | 18* | 18.00 | - | - | 1 | - |
| ALL FIRST-CLASS | 2 | 2 | 1 | 18 | 18* | 18.00 | - | - | 1 | - |
| Refuge Assurance | 1 | 0 | 0 | 0 | 0 | - | - | - | - | - |
| ALL ONE-DAY | 1 | 0 | 0 | 0 | 0 | - | - | - | - | - |

**BOWLING AVERAGES**

| | Overs | Mdns | Runs | Wkts | Avge | Best | 5wI | 10wM |
|---|---|---|---|---|---|---|---|---|
| Other First-Class | 27 | 10 | 56 | 1 | 56.00 | 1-3 | - | - |
| ALL FIRST-CLASS | 27 | 10 | 56 | 1 | 56.00 | 1-3 | - | - |
| Refuge Assurance | 5 | 0 | 32 | 1 | 32.00 | 1-32 | - | |

---

| | | | | | | | |
|---|---|---|---|---|---|---|---|
| ALL ONE-DAY | 5 | 0 | 32 | 1 | 32.00 | 1-32 | - |

# C.R.GREEN - *Minor Counties*

| Opposition | Venue | Date | Batting | Fielding | Bowling |
|---|---|---|---|---|---|

**BENSON & HEDGES CUP**

| | | | | | |
|---|---|---|---|---|---|
| Glamorgan | Trowbridge | April 23 | 0* | | 2-55 |
| Hampshire | Trowbridge | April 25 | | | 0-35 |

**BATTING AVERAGES - Including fielding**

| | Matches | Inns | NO | Runs | HS | Avge | 100s | 50s | Ct | St |
|---|---|---|---|---|---|---|---|---|---|---|
| Benson & Hedges Cup | 2 | 1 | 1 | 0 | 0* | - | - | - | - | - |
| ALL ONE-DAY | 2 | 1 | 1 | 0 | 0* | - | - | - | - | - |

**BOWLING AVERAGES**

| | Overs | Mdns | Runs | Wkts | Avge | Best | 5wI | 10wM |
|---|---|---|---|---|---|---|---|---|
| Benson & Hedges Cup | 20.5 | 0 | 90 | 2 | 45.00 | 2-55 | - | |
| ALL ONE-DAY | 20.5 | 0 | 90 | 2 | 45.00 | 2-55 | - | |

# S.J.GREEN - *Warwickshire*

| Opposition | Venue | Date | Batting | Fielding | Bowling |
|---|---|---|---|---|---|

**BRITANNIC ASSURANCE**

| | | | | | |
|---|---|---|---|---|---|
| Somerset | Edgbaston | June 7 | 77* | | |

**REFUGE ASSURANCE**

| | | | | | |
|---|---|---|---|---|---|
| Glamorgan | Swansea | May 19 | 2 | | |
| Lancashire | Edgbaston | June 16 | 5 | | |

**OTHER ONE-DAY**

| | | | | | |
|---|---|---|---|---|---|
| Surrey | Harrogate | June 12 | 0 | 2Ct | |

**BATTING AVERAGES - Including fielding**

| | Matches | Inns | NO | Runs | HS | Avge | 100s | 50s | Ct | St |
|---|---|---|---|---|---|---|---|---|---|---|
| Britannic Assurance | 1 | 1 | 1 | 77 | 77* | - | - | 1 | - | - |
| ALL FIRST-CLASS | 1 | 1 | 1 | 77 | 77* | - | - | 1 | - | - |
| Refuge Assurance | 2 | 2 | 0 | 7 | 5 | 3.50 | - | - | - | - |
| Other One-Day | 1 | 1 | 0 | 0 | 0 | 0.00 | - | - | 2 | - |
| ALL ONE-DAY | 3 | 3 | 0 | 7 | 5 | 2.33 | - | - | 2 | - |

**BOWLING AVERAGES**
Did not bowl

# K.GREENFIELD - *Sussex*

| Opposition | Venue | Date | Batting | Fielding | Bowling |
|---|---|---|---|---|---|

**BRITANNIC ASSURANCE**

| | | | | | |
|---|---|---|---|---|---|
| Somerset | Taunton | April 27 | | 2Ct | |
| Middlesex | Lord's | May 9 | 5 | 4Ct | |
| Hampshire | Hove | May 16 | 1 & 0 | | |
| Hampshire | Bournemouth | Aug 20 | 22 & 0 | 3Ct | |
| Surrey | The Oval | Aug 28 | 21 & 8 | | |
| Kent | Hove | Sept 3 | 22 & 0 | 4Ct | |
| Gloucs | Hove | Sept 17 | 64 & 13 | 2Ct | |

**OTHER FIRST-CLASS**

| | | | | | |
|---|---|---|---|---|---|
| Cambridge U | Hove | June 29 | 127* | | |
| Sri Lanka | Hove | Aug 17 | 7 & 104 | | 0-30 |

**REFUGE ASSURANCE**

| | | | | | |
|---|---|---|---|---|---|
| Warwickshire | Edgbaston | April 21 | | | |
| Somerset | Taunton | April 28 | 5 | | 0-29 |
| Middlesex | Hove | May 12 | 32* | | 0-37 |
| Gloucs | Hove | May 19 | 5 | | 0-13 |
| Glamorgan | Swansea | May 26 | 38 | | |
| Lancashire | Old Trafford | June 2 | 6 | | 0-16 |

## G — PLAYER RECORDS

| | | | | | |
|---|---|---|---|---|---|
| Hampshire | Basingstoke | June 9 | 78 * | | |
| Worcestershire | Hove | June 16 | 4 * | | |
| Derbyshire | Derby | July 7 | 53 | | |
| Surrey | The Oval | July 14 | 22 | | |
| Leicestershire | Hove | July 21 | 13 | | |
| Notts | Hove | July 28 | 0 | | |
| Northants | Eastbourne | Aug 4 | 57 | | 0-29 |
| Yorkshire | Midd'brough | Aug 11 | 2 | | 0-30 |
| Kent | Hove | Aug 25 | 26 | 1Ct | |

**BENSON & HEDGES CUP**

| | | | | | |
|---|---|---|---|---|---|
| Leicestershire | Hove | April 25 | 0 * | 3Ct | 1-35 |
| Lancashire | Old Trafford | May 7 | 33 | | 0-54 |

**OTHER ONE-DAY**

| | | | | | |
|---|---|---|---|---|---|
| Kent | Hove | Sept 7 | 5 | | 1-2 |
| Gloucs | Hove | Sept 9 | 26 | | 1-44 |

**BATTING AVERAGES - Including fielding**

| | Matches | Inns | NO | Runs | HS | Avge | 100s | 50s | Ct | St |
|---|---|---|---|---|---|---|---|---|---|---|
| Britannic Assurance | 7 | 11 | 0 | 156 | 64 | 14.18 | - | 1 | 15 | - |
| Other First-Class | 2 | 3 | 1 | 238 | 127 * | 119.00 | 2 | - | - | - |
| ALL FIRST-CLASS | 9 | 14 | 1 | 394 | 127 * | 30.30 | 2 | 1 | 15 | - |
| Refuge Assurance | 15 | 14 | 3 | 341 | 78 * | 31.00 | - | 3 | 1 | - |
| Benson & Hedges Cup | 2 | 2 | 1 | 33 | 33 | 33.00 | - | - | 3 | - |
| Other One-Day | 2 | 2 | 0 | 31 | 26 | 15.50 | - | - | - | - |
| ALL ONE-DAY | 19 | 18 | 4 | 405 | 78 * | 28.92 | - | 3 | 4 | - |

**BOWLING AVERAGES**

| | Overs | Mdns | Runs | Wkts | Avge | Best | 5wI | 10wM |
|---|---|---|---|---|---|---|---|---|
| Britannic Assurance | | | | | | | | |
| Other First-Class | 6 | 0 | 30 | 0 | - | - | - | - |
| ALL FIRST-CLASS | 6 | 0 | 30 | 0 | - | - | - | - |
| Refuge Assurance | 25.3 | 0 | 154 | 0 | - | - | - | - |
| Benson & Hedges Cup | 18 | 0 | 89 | 1 | 89.00 | 1-35 | - | |
| Other One-Day | 8 | 0 | 46 | 2 | 23.00 | 1-2 | - | |
| ALL ONE-DAY | 51.3 | 0 | 289 | 3 | 96.33 | 1-2 | - | |

## C.G.GREENIDGE - *West Indies*

| Opposition | Venue | Date | Batting | Fielding | Bowling |
|---|---|---|---|---|---|
| **OTHER FIRST-CLASS** | | | | | |
| Worcestershire | Worcester | May 15 | 26 & 12 * | 1Ct | |
| Middlesex | Lord's | May 18 | 26 & 8 | | |
| For West Indies XI | | | | | |
| World XI | Scarborough | Aug 28 | 14 & 55 * | 2Ct | 1-7 |
| **TEXACO TROPHY** | | | | | |
| England | Edgbaston | May 23 | 23 | | |
| England | Old Trafford | May 25 | 4 | | |
| **OTHER ONE-DAY** | | | | | |
| D of Norfolk | Arundel | May 12 | 22 | | |

**BATTING AVERAGES - Including fielding**

| | Matches | Inns | NO | Runs | HS | Avge | 100s | 50s | Ct | St |
|---|---|---|---|---|---|---|---|---|---|---|
| Other First-Class | 3 | 6 | 2 | 141 | 55 * | 35.25 | - | 1 | 3 | - |
| ALL FIRST-CLASS | 3 | 6 | 2 | 141 | 55 * | 35.25 | - | 1 | 3 | - |
| Texaco Trophy | 2 | 2 | 0 | 27 | 23 | 13.50 | - | - | - | - |
| Other One-Day | 1 | 1 | 0 | 22 | 22 | 22.00 | - | - | - | - |
| ALL ONE-DAY | 3 | 3 | 0 | 49 | 23 | 16.33 | - | - | - | - |

**BOWLING AVERAGES**

| | Overs | Mdns | Runs | Wkts | Avge | Best | 5wI | 10wM |
|---|---|---|---|---|---|---|---|---|
| Other First-Class | 2 | 0 | 7 | 1 | 7.00 | 1-7 | - | - |
| ALL FIRST-CLASS | 2 | 0 | 7 | 1 | 7.00 | 1-7 | - | - |
| Texaco Trophy | | | | | | | | |
| Other One-Day | | | | | | | | |
| ALL ONE-DAY | | | | | | | | |

## S.GREENSWORD - *Minor Counties*

| Opposition | Venue | Date | Batting | Fielding | Bowling |
|---|---|---|---|---|---|
| **BENSON & HEDGES CUP** | | | | | |
| Glamorgan | Trowbridge | April 23 | 3 | | 2-31 |
| Hampshire | Trowbridge | April 25 | | | 1-35 |
| Yorkshire | Headingley | May 2 | | | 2-21 |
| Notts | Trent Bridge | May 7 | | 1Ct | 0-28 |

**BATTING AVERAGES - Including fielding**

| | Matches | Inns | NO | Runs | HS | Avge | 100s | 50s | Ct | St |
|---|---|---|---|---|---|---|---|---|---|---|
| Benson & Hedges Cup | 4 | 1 | 0 | 3 | 3 | 3.00 | - | - | 1 | - |
| ALL ONE-DAY | 4 | 1 | 0 | 3 | 3 | 3.00 | - | - | 1 | - |

**BOWLING AVERAGES**

| | Overs | Mdns | Runs | Wkts | Avge | Best | 5wI | 10wM |
|---|---|---|---|---|---|---|---|---|
| Benson & Hedges Cup | 38 | 8 | 115 | 5 | 23.00 | 2-21 | - | |
| ALL ONE-DAY | 38 | 8 | 115 | 5 | 23.00 | 2-21 | - | |

## I.A.GREIG - *Surrey*

| Opposition | Venue | Date | Batting | Fielding | Bowling |
|---|---|---|---|---|---|
| **BRITANNIC ASSURANCE** | | | | | |
| Essex | Chelmsford | April 27 | 0 | | 2-25 |
| Kent | The Oval | May 9 | 25 & 44 | | 0-23 |
| Lancashire | The Oval | May 22 | 21 | | 0-13 |
| Hampshire | Bournemouth | May 25 | 4 & 61 | | 1-47 & 0-26 |
| Notts | The Oval | June 4 | | | 0-9 |
| Leicestershire | Leicester | June 14 | 27 * | | |
| Derbyshire | Derby | June 21 | 5 & 27 | | |
| Somerset | The Oval | June 28 | 0 | | 0-20 |
| Sussex | Arundel | July 2 | 27 | 1Ct | 3-30 & 1-23 |
| Essex | The Oval | July 5 | 20 & 9 | | 0-43 |
| Gloucs | Guildford | July 16 | 23 * | | 0-25 |
| Glamorgan | The Oval | July 26 | 4 & 0 | | 0-38 & 1-49 |
| Kent | Canterbury | Aug 2 | 8 * & 22 | 3Ct | 0-11 |
| Warwickshire | Edgbaston | Aug 6 | 22 & 52 | | |
| Worcestershire | Worcester | Aug 16 | 38 * & 72 | 1Ct | 0-12 |
| Middlesex | The Oval | Aug 20 | 9 & 4 | | |
| Sussex | The Oval | Aug 28 | 25 | | |
| Hampshire | The Oval | Sept 3 | 5 & 11 | 1Ct | 1-4 |
| Middlesex | Lord's | Sept 10 | 24 & 4 | 1Ct | |
| **OTHER FIRST-CLASS** | | | | | |
| Cambridge U | Fenner's | May 18 | 0 & 17 | | 1-22 & 0-6 |
| **REFUGE ASSURANCE** | | | | | |
| Somerset | The Oval | April 21 | 30 | | |
| Middlesex | Lord's | April 28 | 68 * | | 2-30 |
| Gloucs | The Oval | May 12 | 5 | 1Ct | 0-16 |
| Worcestershire | Worcester | June 2 | | 1Ct | 0-16 |
| Derbyshire | Chesterfield | June 9 | 24 | | 3-10 |
| Leicestershire | Leicester | June 16 | 2 | | |
| Notts | The Oval | June 30 | 3 | | |
| Sussex | The Oval | July 14 | | | |
| Yorkshire | The Oval | July 21 | 15 | | 0-16 |
| Glamorgan | The Oval | July 28 | 5 | | 1-21 |
| Kent | Canterbury | Aug 4 | | | 0-21 |
| Lancashire | Old Trafford | Aug 18 | 0 * | 2Ct | |
| Hampshire | The Oval | Aug 25 | 10 | | |
| **NATWEST TROPHY** | | | | | |
| Essex | The Oval | July 31 | 20 | | |
| Northants | The Oval | Aug 14 | 8 | | |
| Hampshire | Lord's | Sept 7 | 7 * | | |
| **BENSON & HEDGES CUP** | | | | | |
| Essex | The Oval | April 23 | 47 | 1Ct | |
| Middlesex | Lord's | April 25 | 38 | | |
| Somerset | Taunton | May 4 | 4 | | |
| Warwickshire | The Oval | May 7 | 4 | 1Ct | 2-26 |
| **OTHER ONE-DAY** | | | | | |
| Durham | Harrogate | June 13 | 3 * | | |

# PLAYER RECORDS | G

**BATTING AVERAGES - Including fielding**

| | Matches | Inns | NO | Runs | HS | Avge | 100s | 50s | Ct | St |
|---|---|---|---|---|---|---|---|---|---|---|
| Britannic Assurance | 19 | 29 | 4 | 593 | 72 | 23.72 | - | 3 | 7 | - |
| Other First-Class | 1 | 2 | 0 | 17 | 17 | 8.50 | - | - | - | - |
| ALL FIRST-CLASS | 20 | 31 | 4 | 610 | 72 | 22.59 | - | 3 | 7 | - |
| Refuge Assurance | 13 | 10 | 2 | 162 | 68 * | 20.25 | - | 1 | 4 | - |
| NatWest Trophy | 3 | 3 | 1 | 35 | 20 | 17.50 | - | - | - | - |
| Benson & Hedges Cup | 4 | 4 | 0 | 93 | 47 | 23.25 | - | - | 2 | - |
| Other One-Day | 1 | 1 | 1 | 3 | 3 * | - | - | - | - | - |
| ALL ONE-DAY | 21 | 18 | 4 | 293 | 68 * | 20.92 | - | 1 | 6 | - |

**BOWLING AVERAGES**

| | Overs | Mdns | Runs | Wkts | Avge | Best | 5wI | 10wM |
|---|---|---|---|---|---|---|---|---|
| Britannic Assurance | 154.2 | 31 | 398 | 9 | 44.22 | 3-30 | - | - |
| Other First-Class | 11.1 | 3 | 28 | 1 | 28.00 | 1-22 | - | - |
| ALL FIRST-CLASS | 165.3 | 34 | 426 | 10 | 42.60 | 3-30 | - | - |
| Refuge Assurance | 29.5 | 0 | 146 | 6 | 24.33 | 3-10 | - | |
| NatWest Trophy | | | | | | | | |
| Benson & Hedges Cup | 9.2 | 0 | 26 | 2 | 13.00 | 2-26 | - | |
| Other One-Day | | | | | | | | |
| ALL ONE-DAY | 39.1 | 0 | 172 | 8 | 21.50 | 3-10 | - | |

---

# F.A.GRIFFITH - Derbyshire

| Opposition | Venue | Date | Batting | Fielding | Bowling |
|---|---|---|---|---|---|
| **BRITANNIC ASSURANCE** | | | | | |
| Surrey | Derby | June 21 | 1 | | 1-16 & 1-42 |
| **OTHER FIRST-CLASS** | | | | | |
| For Derbyshire | | | | | |
| West Indies | Derby | June 12 | 6 & 4 | | 0-39 & 0-28 |
| **REFUGE ASSURANCE** | | | | | |
| Surrey | Chesterfield | June 9 | | | 0-24 |
| Somerset | Derby | June 16 | 6 | | 3-37 |
| Sussex | Derby | July 7 | 12 * | | 0-49 |
| Worcestershire | Worcester | July 9 | 9 | | 0-22 |
| Northants | Derby | July 28 | 20 | | |

**BATTING AVERAGES - Including fielding**

| | Matches | Inns | NO | Runs | HS | Avge | 100s | 50s | Ct | St |
|---|---|---|---|---|---|---|---|---|---|---|
| Britannic Assurance | 1 | 1 | 0 | 1 | 1 | 1.00 | - | - | - | - |
| Other First-Class | 1 | 2 | 0 | 10 | 6 | 5.00 | - | - | - | - |
| ALL FIRST-CLASS | 2 | 3 | 0 | 11 | 6 | 3.66 | - | - | - | - |
| Refuge Assurance | 5 | 4 | 1 | 47 | 20 | 15.66 | - | - | - | - |
| ALL ONE-DAY | 5 | 4 | 1 | 47 | 20 | 15.66 | - | - | - | - |

**BOWLING AVERAGES**

| | Overs | Mdns | Runs | Wkts | Avge | Best | 5wI | 10wM |
|---|---|---|---|---|---|---|---|---|
| Britannic Assurance | 15 | 2 | 58 | 2 | 29.00 | 1-16 | - | - |
| Other First-Class | 16 | 4 | 67 | 0 | - | - | - | - |
| ALL FIRST-CLASS | 31 | 6 | 125 | 2 | 62.50 | 1-16 | - | - |
| Refuge Assurance | 23 | 0 | 132 | 3 | 44.00 | 3-37 | - | |
| ALL ONE-DAY | 23 | 0 | 132 | 3 | 44.00 | 3-37 | - | |

---

# A.D.GRIFFITHS - Wales

| Opposition | Venue | Date | Batting | Fielding | Bowling |
|---|---|---|---|---|---|
| **OTHER ONE-DAY** | | | | | |
| West Indies | Brecon | July 15 | 8 * | 1Ct | 2-51 |

**BATTING AVERAGES - Including fielding**

| | Matches | Inns | NO | Runs | HS | Avge | 100s | 50s | Ct | St |
|---|---|---|---|---|---|---|---|---|---|---|
| Other One-Day | 1 | 1 | 1 | 8 | 8 * | - | - | - | 1 | - |
| ALL ONE-DAY | 1 | 1 | 1 | 8 | 8 * | - | - | - | 1 | - |

**BOWLING AVERAGES**

| | Overs | Mdns | Runs | Wkts | Avge | Best | 5wI | 10wM |
|---|---|---|---|---|---|---|---|---|
| Other One-Day | 11 | 1 | 51 | 2 | 25.50 | 2-51 | - | |
| ALL ONE-DAY | 11 | 1 | 51 | 2 | 25.50 | 2-51 | | |

---

# C.GUPTE - Oxford University

| Opposition | Venue | Date | Batting | Fielding | Bowling |
|---|---|---|---|---|---|
| **OTHER FIRST-CLASS** | | | | | |
| Hampshire | The Parks | April 13 | 15 & 0 | | 0-24 |
| Glamorgan | The Parks | April 17 | 1 | | |
| Notts | The Parks | April 27 | | | 2-41 |
| Gloucs | The Parks | June 15 | 55 * | 1Ct | 0-22 |
| Worcestershire | The Parks | May 25 | 0 & 15 | | |
| Yorkshire | The Parks | June 4 | 48 | | 1-33 |
| Lancashire | The Parks | June 7 | 23 & 43 | | |
| Cambridge U | Lord's | July 2 | | 1Ct | |

**BATTING AVERAGES - Including fielding**

| | Matches | Inns | NO | Runs | HS | Avge | 100s | 50s | Ct | St |
|---|---|---|---|---|---|---|---|---|---|---|
| Other First-Class | 8 | 9 | 1 | 200 | 55 * | 25.00 | - | 1 | 2 | - |
| ALL FIRST-CLASS | 8 | 9 | 1 | 200 | 55 * | 25.00 | - | 1 | 2 | - |

**BOWLING AVERAGES**

| | Overs | Mdns | Runs | Wkts | Avge | Best | 5wI | 10wM |
|---|---|---|---|---|---|---|---|---|
| Other First-Class | 24.1 | 3 | 120 | 3 | 40.00 | 2-41 | - | - |
| ALL FIRST-CLASS | 24.1 | 3 | 120 | 3 | 40.00 | 2-41 | - | - |

---

# A.P.GURUSINHA - Sri Lanka

| Opposition | Venue | Date | Batting | Fielding | Bowling |
|---|---|---|---|---|---|
| **CORNHILL TEST MATCHES** | | | | | |
| England | Lord's | Aug 22 | 4 & 34 | | |
| **OTHER FIRST-CLASS** | | | | | |
| Yorkshire | Headingley | July 27 | 98 | | |
| Worcestershire | Worcester | July 30 | 44 & 0 | 1Ct | 0-8 |
| Derbyshire | Derby | Aug 2 | 46 | | 0-6 |
| Gloucs | Bristol | Aug 6 | 0 & 36 | | 2-16 |
| Sussex | Hove | Aug 17 | 29 & 1 | 1Ct | 0-11 |
| **OTHER ONE-DAY** | | | | | |
| England Am. XI | Wolv'hampton | July 24 | 9 | | |
| | | | | 1Ct | 1-23 |
| Durham | Chester-le-S | July 26 | 1 | | 0-8 |
| England A | Old Trafford | Aug 14 | 12 | | 0-44 |
| England A | Old Trafford | Aug 15 | 10 | | 0-11 |

**BATTING AVERAGES - Including fielding**

| | Matches | Inns | NO | Runs | HS | Avge | 100s | 50s | Ct | St |
|---|---|---|---|---|---|---|---|---|---|---|
| Cornhill Test Matches | 1 | 2 | 0 | 38 | 34 | 19.00 | - | - | - | - |
| Other First-Class | 5 | 8 | 0 | 254 | 98 | 31.75 | - | 1 | 2 | - |
| ALL FIRST-CLASS | 6 | 10 | 0 | 292 | 98 | 29.20 | - | 1 | 2 | - |
| Other One-Day | 4 | 4 | 0 | 32 | 12 | 8.00 | - | - | 1 | - |
| ALL ONE-DAY | 4 | 4 | 0 | 32 | 12 | 8.00 | - | - | 1 | - |

**BOWLING AVERAGES**

| | Overs | Mdns | Runs | Wkts | Avge | Best | 5wI | 10wM |
|---|---|---|---|---|---|---|---|---|
| Cornhill Test Matches | | | | | | | | |
| Other First-Class | 18 | 5 | 41 | 2 | 20.50 | 2-16 | - | - |
| ALL FIRST-CLASS | 18 | 5 | 41 | 2 | 20.50 | 2-16 | - | - |
| Other One-Day | 17 | 1 | 86 | 1 | 86.00 | 1-23 | - | |
| ALL ONE-DAY | 17 | 1 | 86 | 1 | 86.00 | 1-23 | - | |

## H | PLAYER RECORDS

## N.HACKETT - *Staffordshire*

| Opposition | Venue | Date | Batting | Fielding | Bowling |
|---|---|---|---|---|---|
| **NATWEST TROPHY** | | | | | |
| Northants | Stone | June 26 | 0 | | 3-45 |

**BATTING AVERAGES - Including fielding**

| | Matches | Inns | NO | Runs | HS | Avge | 100s | 50s | Ct | St |
|---|---|---|---|---|---|---|---|---|---|---|
| NatWest Trophy | 1 | 1 | 0 | 0 | 0 | 0.00 | - | - | - | - |
| ALL ONE-DAY | 1 | 1 | 0 | 0 | 0 | 0.00 | - | - | - | - |

**BOWLING AVERAGES**

| | Overs | Mdns | Runs | Wkts | Avge | Best | 5wI | 10wM |
|---|---|---|---|---|---|---|---|---|
| NatWest Trophy | 12 | 0 | 45 | 3 | 15.00 | 3-45 | - | |
| ALL ONE-DAY | 12 | 0 | 45 | 3 | 15.00 | 3-45 | - | |

## D.A.HAGAN - *Oxford University*

| Opposition | Venue | Date | Batting | Fielding | Bowling |
|---|---|---|---|---|---|
| **OTHER FIRST-CLASS** | | | | | |
| Notts | The Parks | April 27 | | | |

**BATTING AVERAGES - Including fielding**

| | Matches | Inns | NO | Runs | HS | Avge | 100s | 50s | Ct | St |
|---|---|---|---|---|---|---|---|---|---|---|
| Other First-Class | 1 | 0 | 0 | 0 | 0 | - | - | - | - | - |
| ALL FIRST-CLASS | 1 | 0 | 0 | 0 | 0 | - | - | - | - | - |

**BOWLING AVERAGES**
Did not bowl

## D.J.HAGGO - *Scotland*

| Opposition | Venue | Date | Batting | Fielding | Bowling |
|---|---|---|---|---|---|
| **OTHER FIRST-CLASS** | | | | | |
| Ireland | Dublin | June 22 | 25 | 0Ct,1St | |
| **NATWEST TROPHY** | | | | | |
| Sussex | Edinburgh | June 26 | 1 | 2Ct,2St | |
| **BENSON & HEDGES CUP** | | | | | |
| Lancashire | Forfar | April 23 | 22* | 1Ct | |
| Leicestershire | Leicester | May 2 | 10* | 1Ct | |
| Sussex | Hove | May 4 | 1 | 0Ct,2St | |
| Kent | Glasgow | May 7 | 25 | 0Ct,1St | |

**BATTING AVERAGES - Including fielding**

| | Matches | Inns | NO | Runs | HS | Avge | 100s | 50s | Ct | St |
|---|---|---|---|---|---|---|---|---|---|---|
| Other First-Class | 1 | 1 | 0 | 25 | 25 | 25.00 | - | - | - | 1 |
| ALL FIRST-CLASS | 1 | 1 | 0 | 25 | 25 | 25.00 | - | - | - | 1 |
| NatWest Trophy | 1 | 1 | 0 | 1 | 1 | 1.00 | - | - | 2 | 2 |
| Benson & Hedges Cup | 4 | 4 | 2 | 58 | 25 | 29.00 | - | - | 2 | 3 |
| ALL ONE-DAY | 5 | 5 | 2 | 59 | 25 | 19.66 | - | - | 4 | 5 |

**BOWLING AVERAGES**
Did not bowl

## J.R.HALL - *Dorset*

| Opposition | Venue | Date | Batting | Fielding | Bowling |
|---|---|---|---|---|---|
| **NATWEST TROPHY** | | | | | |
| Lancashire | Bournemouth | June 26 | 14 | | 1-16 |

**BATTING AVERAGES - Including fielding**

| | Matches | Inns | NO | Runs | HS | Avge | 100s | 50s | Ct | St |
|---|---|---|---|---|---|---|---|---|---|---|
| NatWest Trophy | 1 | 1 | 0 | 14 | 14 | 14.00 | - | - | - | - |
| ALL ONE-DAY | 1 | 1 | 0 | 14 | 14 | 14.00 | - | - | - | - |

**BOWLING AVERAGES**

| | Overs | Mdns | Runs | Wkts | Avge | Best | 5wI | 10wM |
|---|---|---|---|---|---|---|---|---|
| NatWest Trophy | 4 | 0 | 16 | 1 | 16.00 | 1-16 | - | |
| ALL ONE-DAY | 4 | 0 | 16 | 1 | 16.00 | 1-16 | - | |

## J.W.HALL - *Sussex*

| Opposition | Venue | Date | Batting | Fielding | Bowling |
|---|---|---|---|---|---|
| **BRITANNIC ASSURANCE** | | | | | |
| Somerset | Taunton | April 27 | 117* | 1Ct | |
| Middlesex | Lord's | May 9 | 18 & 18* | 1Ct | |
| Hampshire | Hove | May 16 | 65 & 40 | 1Ct | |
| Middlesex | Hove | May 22 | 3 & 41 | | |
| Glamorgan | Cardiff | May 25 | 3 & 7 | | |
| Lancashire | Old Trafford | May 31 | 4 & 92 | | |
| Kent | Tunbridge W | June 7 | 5 & 11 | 1Ct | |
| Worcestershire | Hove | June 14 | 55 & 7 | 1Ct | |
| Warwickshire | Coventry | June 18 | 0 & 17 | | |
| Essex | Horsham | June 21 | 9 | | |
| Derbyshire | Derby | July 5 | 2 & 8 | 1Ct | |
| Yorkshire | Midd'brough | Aug 9 | 28 | | |
| Kent | Hove | Sept 3 | 41 & 52 | 1Ct | |
| Gloucs | Hove | Sept 17 | 25 & 17 | 1Ct | |
| **OTHER FIRST-CLASS** | | | | | |
| Cambridge U | Hove | June 29 | 1 | | |
| **REFUGE ASSURANCE** | | | | | |
| Somerset | Taunton | April 28 | 50 | | |
| Middlesex | Hove | May 12 | 34 | | |
| Gloucs | Hove | May 19 | 12 | | |
| **BENSON & HEDGES CUP** | | | | | |
| Leicestershire | Hove | April 25 | 43 | | |
| Kent | Canterbury | May 2 | 8 | | |
| Scotland | Hove | May 4 | 28 | | |
| Lancashire | Old Trafford | May 7 | 71 | | |
| **OTHER ONE-DAY** | | | | | |
| Kent | Hove | Sept 7 | 2 | | |
| Gloucs | Hove | Sept 9 | 24 | 1Ct | |

**BATTING AVERAGES - Including fielding**

| | Matches | Inns | NO | Runs | HS | Avge | 100s | 50s | Ct | St |
|---|---|---|---|---|---|---|---|---|---|---|
| Britannic Assurance | 14 | 25 | 2 | 685 | 117* | 29.78 | 1 | 4 | 8 | - |
| Other First-Class | 1 | 1 | 0 | 1 | 1 | 1.00 | - | - | - | - |
| ALL FIRST-CLASS | 15 | 26 | 2 | 686 | 117* | 28.58 | 1 | 4 | 8 | - |
| Refuge Assurance | 3 | 3 | 0 | 96 | 50 | 32.00 | - | 1 | - | - |
| Benson & Hedges Cup | 4 | 4 | 0 | 150 | 71 | 37.50 | - | 1 | - | - |
| Other One-Day | 2 | 2 | 0 | 26 | 24 | 13.00 | - | - | 1 | - |
| ALL ONE-DAY | 9 | 9 | 0 | 272 | 71 | 30.22 | - | 2 | 1 | - |

**BOWLING AVERAGES**
Did not bowl

## J.C.HALLETT - *Somerset & Combined Universities*

| Opposition | Venue | Date | Batting | Fielding | Bowling |
|---|---|---|---|---|---|
| **BRITANNIC ASSURANCE** | | | | | |
| Essex | Southend | July 19 | 4 | 2Ct | 2-52 & 0-36 |
| Northants | Northampton | July 23 | | 1Ct | 1-14 & 1-20 |
| Leicestershire | Weston | Aug 2 | | | 1-29 & 0-6 |
| Worcestershire | Weston | Aug 6 | | | 0-36 & 0-34 |
| Notts | Trent Bridge | Aug 16 | | 1Ct | 0-44 & 2-50 |

# PLANER RECORDS

**H**

| Yorkshire | Taunton | Aug 23 | 1 * | | | 0-42 & 0-26 |
|---|---|---|---|---|---|---|
| Worcestershire | Worcester | Sept 3 | 11 | & | 4 | 3-154 |
| Gloucs | Bristol | Sept 10 | 15 | | | 2-71 & 0-23 |

**REFUGE ASSURANCE**

| Lancashire | Taunton | July 5 | | 1Ct | 1-33 |
|---|---|---|---|---|---|
| Essex | Southend | July 21 | | | 1-22 |
| Kent | Taunton | July 28 | 1 | | 1-25 |
| Leicestershire | Weston | Aug 4 | | | 0-29 |
| Worcestershire | Worcester | Aug 18 | | | 0-57 |
| Yorkshire | Taunton | Aug 25 | | | 2-32 |

**NATWEST TROPHY**

| Warwickshire | Edgbaston | July 31 | | 0-31 |
|---|---|---|---|---|

**BENSON & HEDGES CUP**

| Gloucs | Bristol | April 23 | 0 | | 1-32 |
|---|---|---|---|---|---|
| Derbyshire | The Parks | April 25 | | 1Ct | 0-43 |
| Worcestershire | Fenner's | May 2 | 5 | | 3-36 |
| Northants | Northampton | May 4 | | | 2-38 |

**OTHER ONE-DAY**

| Gloucs | Hove | Sept 8 | 3 * | 0-59 |
|---|---|---|---|---|

**BATTING AVERAGES - Including fielding**

| | Matches | Inns | NO | Runs | HS | Avge | 100s | 50s | Ct | St |
|---|---|---|---|---|---|---|---|---|---|---|
| Britannic Assurance | 8 | 5 | 1 | 35 | 15 | 8.75 | - | - | 4 | - |
| ALL FIRST-CLASS | 8 | 5 | 1 | 35 | 15 | 8.75 | - | - | 4 | - |
| Refuge Assurance | 6 | 1 | 0 | 1 | 1 | 1.00 | - | - | 1 | - |
| NatWest Trophy | 1 | 0 | 0 | 0 | 0 | - | - | - | - | - |
| Benson & Hedges Cup | 4 | 2 | 0 | 5 | 5 | 2.50 | - | - | 1 | - |
| Other One-Day | 1 | 1 | 1 | 3 | 3 * | - | - | - | - | - |
| ALL ONE-DAY | 12 | 4 | 1 | 9 | 5 | 3.00 | - | - | 2 | - |

**BOWLING AVERAGES**

| | Overs | Mdns | Runs | Wkts | Avge | Best | 5wI | 10wM |
|---|---|---|---|---|---|---|---|---|
| Britannic Assurance | 178.3 | 31 | 637 | 12 | 53.08 | 3-154 | - | - |
| ALL FIRST-CLASS | 178.3 | 31 | 637 | 12 | 53.08 | 3-154 | - | - |
| Refuge Assurance | 40 | 0 | 198 | 5 | 39.60 | 2-32 | - | |
| NatWest Trophy | 12 | 1 | 31 | 0 | - | - | - | |
| Benson & Hedges Cup | 43.1 | 0 | 149 | 6 | 24.83 | 3-36 | - | |
| Other One-Day | 10 | 0 | 59 | 0 | - | - | - | |
| ALL ONE-DAY | 105.1 | 1 | 437 | 11 | 39.72 | 3-36 | - | |

## N.G.HAMES - *Buckinghamshire*

| Opposition | Venue | Date | Batting | Fielding | Bowling |
|---|---|---|---|---|---|

**NATWEST TROPHY**

| Somerset | Bath | June 26 | 11 | 1Ct | |
|---|---|---|---|---|---|

**BATTING AVERAGES - Including fielding**

| | Matches | Inns | NO | Runs | HS | Avge | 100s | 50s | Ct | St |
|---|---|---|---|---|---|---|---|---|---|---|
| NatWest Trophy | 1 | 1 | 0 | 11 | 11 | 11.00 | - | - | 1 | - |
| ALL ONE-DAY | 1 | 1 | 0 | 11 | 11 | 11.00 | - | - | 1 | - |

**BOWLING AVERAGES**
Did not bowl

## T.HANCOCK - *Gloucestershire*

| Opposition | Venue | Date | Batting | Fielding | Bowling |
|---|---|---|---|---|---|

**BRITANNIC ASSURANCE**

| Lancashire | Bristol | Aug 9 | 17 * | | | 2Ct |
|---|---|---|---|---|---|---|
| Somerset | Bristol | Sept 10 | 12 | & | 0 | 3Ct |
| Sussex | Hove | Sept 17 | 51 | & | 3 | |

**OTHER FIRST-CLASS**

| West Indies | Bristol | July 31 | 1 | & | 7 * | 1Ct |
|---|---|---|---|---|---|---|
| Sri Lanka | Bristol | Aug 6 | 1 | & | 1 | 1Ct |

**REFUGE ASSURANCE**

| Northants | Moreton | June 9 | | |
|---|---|---|---|---|
| Kent | Canterbury | June 30 | 0 | |
| Essex | Cheltenham | July 28 | 0 | |
| Warwickshire | Edgbaston | Aug 18 | 20 | |
| Leicestershire | Leicester | Aug 25 | | 1Ct |

**OTHER ONE-DAY**

| Somerset | Hove | Sept 8 | 23 |
|---|---|---|---|
| Sussex | Hove | Sept 9 | 59 |

**BATTING AVERAGES - Including fielding**

| | Matches | Inns | NO | Runs | HS | Avge | 100s | 50s | Ct | St |
|---|---|---|---|---|---|---|---|---|---|---|
| Britannic Assurance | 3 | 5 | 1 | 83 | 51 | 20.75 | - | 1 | 5 | - |
| Other First-Class | 2 | 4 | 1 | 10 | 7 * | 3.33 | - | - | 2 | - |
| ALL FIRST-CLASS | 5 | 9 | 2 | 93 | 51 | 13.28 | - | 1 | 7 | - |
| Refuge Assurance | 5 | 3 | 0 | 20 | 20 | 6.66 | - | - | 1 | - |
| Other One-Day | 2 | 2 | 0 | 82 | 59 | 41.00 | - | 1 | - | - |
| ALL ONE-DAY | 7 | 5 | 0 | 102 | 59 | 20.40 | - | 1 | 1 | - |

**BOWLING AVERAGES**
Did not bowl

## R.HANLEY - *Sussex*

| Opposition | Venue | Date | Batting | Fielding | Bowling |
|---|---|---|---|---|---|

**BRITANNIC ASSURANCE**

| Surrey | The Oval | Aug 28 | 19 | & | 0 |
|---|---|---|---|---|---|

**OTHER FIRST-CLASS**

| Cambridge U | Hove | June 29 | | |
|---|---|---|---|---|

**REFUGE ASSURANCE**

| Kent | Hove | Aug 25 | 2 | 1Ct |
|---|---|---|---|---|

**BATTING AVERAGES - Including fielding**

| | Matches | Inns | NO | Runs | HS | Avge | 100s | 50s | Ct | St |
|---|---|---|---|---|---|---|---|---|---|---|
| Britannic Assurance | 1 | 2 | 0 | 19 | 19 | 9.50 | - | - | - | - |
| Other First-Class | 1 | 0 | 0 | 0 | 0 | - | - | - | - | - |
| ALL FIRST-CLASS | 2 | 2 | 0 | 19 | 19 | 9.50 | - | - | - | - |
| Refuge Assurance | 1 | 1 | 0 | 2 | 2 | 2.00 | - | - | 1 | - |
| ALL ONE-DAY | 1 | 1 | 0 | 2 | 2 | 2.00 | - | - | 1 | - |

**BOWLING AVERAGES**
Did not bowl

## A.R.HANSFORD - *Combined Universities*

| Opposition | Venue | Date | Batting | Fielding | Bowling |
|---|---|---|---|---|---|

**BENSON & HEDGES CUP**

| Gloucs | Bristol | April 23 | 0 | | 0-21 |
|---|---|---|---|---|---|
| Derbyshire | The Parks | April 25 | | | 1-55 |
| Worcestershire | Fenner's | May 2 | 13 * | | 0-31 |
| Northants | Northampton | May 4 | | | 0-18 |

**BATTING AVERAGES - Including fielding**

| | Matches | Inns | NO | Runs | HS | Avge | 100s | 50s | Ct | St |
|---|---|---|---|---|---|---|---|---|---|---|
| Benson & Hedges Cup | 4 | 2 | 1 | 13 | 13 * | 13.00 | - | - | - | - |
| ALL ONE-DAY | 4 | 2 | 1 | 13 | 13 * | 13.00 | - | - | - | - |

**BOWLING AVERAGES**

| | Overs | Mdns | Runs | Wkts | Avge | Best | 5wI | 10wM |
|---|---|---|---|---|---|---|---|---|
| Benson & Hedges Cup | 32.5 | 3 | 125 | 1 | 125.00 | 1-55 | - | |
| ALL ONE-DAY | 32.5 | 3 | 125 | 1 | 125.00 | 1-55 | - | |

| H | PLAYER RECORDS |
|---|---|

## R.J.HARDEN - *Somerset*

| Opposition | Venue | Date | Batting | | | Fielding | Bowling |
|---|---|---|---|---|---|---|---|
| **BRITANNIC ASSURANCE** | | | | | | | |
| Sussex | Taunton | April 27 | 19 | | | 1Ct | |
| Glamorgan | Taunton | May 9 | 73 | & | 26 | 3Ct | |
| Derbyshire | Derby | May 22 | 134 | & | 23 | 2Ct | |
| Middlesex | Taunton | May 25 | 0 | & | 58 * | | |
| Glamorgan | Swansea | June 4 | 15 | | | | 0-28 |
| Warwickshire | Edgbaston | June 7 | 20 | | | 1Ct | |
| Hampshire | Bath | June 18 | | | 13 | 1Ct | |
| Gloucs | Bath | June 21 | 49 | | | | |
| Surrey | The Oval | June 28 | 13 | | | 1Ct | |
| Lancashire | Taunton | July 2 | 29 * | & | 12 | 2Ct | 2-70 |
| Sussex | Hove | July 16 | 34 | & | 27 * | 1Ct | |
| Essex | Southend | July 19 | 20 | & | 45 | 1Ct | |
| Northants | Northampton | July 23 | | | 59 * | | 1-13 |
| Kent | Taunton | July 26 | 54 | & | 57 | | |
| Leicestershire | Weston | Aug 2 | 64 | | | 2Ct | |
| Worcestershire | Weston | Aug 6 | 0 | & | 74 * | 1Ct | |
| Notts | Trent Bridge | Aug 16 | 101 | & | 38 | | |
| Yorkshire | Taunton | Aug 23 | 13 | & | 24 * | 1Ct | |
| Hampshire | Southampton | Aug 28 | 0 | & | 62 | | 0-11 |
| Worcestershire | Worcester | Sept 3 | 3 | & | 8 | | |
| Gloucs | Bristol | Sept 10 | 1 | & | 1 * | 2Ct | |
| Warwickshire | Taunton | Sept 17 | 5 | & | 68 | | |
| **OTHER FIRST-CLASS** | | | | | | | |
| West Indies | Taunton | May 29 | 7 | & | 6 | 2Ct | |
| Sri Lanka | Taunton | Aug 10 | 100 * | | | | |
| **REFUGE ASSURANCE** | | | | | | | |
| Surrey | The Oval | April 21 | 2 | | | | |
| Sussex | Taunton | April 28 | 15 | | | | |
| Glamorgan | Taunton | May 12 | 40 | | | | |
| Hampshire | Bournemouth | May 19 | 5 | | | | |
| Middlesex | Taunton | May 26 | 35 | | | | |
| Warwickshire | Edgbaston | June 2 | 13 | | | | |
| Notts | Trent Bridge | June 9 | 79 * | | | 1Ct | |
| Derbyshire | Derby | June 16 | 4 | | | | |
| Northants | Luton | June 30 | 1 | | | | |
| Lancashire | Taunton | July 5 | 25 | | | | |
| Essex | Southend | July 21 | 13 | | | | |
| Kent | Taunton | July 28 | 46 | | | | |
| Leicestershire | Weston | Aug 4 | 4 | | | | |
| Worcestershire | Worcester | Aug 18 | 31 | | | | |
| Yorkshire | Taunton | Aug 25 | 29 | | | | |
| **NATWEST TROPHY** | | | | | | | |
| Bucks | Bath | June 26 | 20 | | | 1Ct | |
| Middlesex | Taunton | July 11 | 39 | | | | |
| Warwickshire | Edgbaston | July 31 | 10 | | | | |
| **BENSON & HEDGES CUP** | | | | | | | |
| Middlesex | Taunton | April 23 | 3 | | | | |
| Warwickshire | Edgbaston | May 2 | 21 | | | | |
| Surrey | Taunton | May 4 | 1 | | | | |
| Essex | Chelmsford | May 7 | 1 | | | | |
| **OTHER ONE-DAY** | | | | | | | |
| Gloucs | Hove | Sept 8 | 31 | | | | |

### BATTING AVERAGES - Including fielding

| | Matches | Inns | NO | Runs | HS | Avge | 100s | 50s | Ct | St |
|---|---|---|---|---|---|---|---|---|---|---|
| Britannic Assurance | 22 | 36 | 7 | 1242 | 134 | 42.82 | 2 | 9 | 19 | - |
| Other First-Class | 2 | 3 | 1 | 113 | 100 * | 56.50 | 1 | - | 2 | - |
| ALL FIRST-CLASS | 24 | 39 | 8 | 1355 | 134 | 43.71 | 3 | 9 | 21 | - |
| Refuge Assurance | 15 | 15 | 1 | 342 | 79 * | 24.42 | - | 1 | 1 | - |
| NatWest Trophy | 3 | 3 | 0 | 69 | 39 | 23.00 | - | - | 1 | - |
| Benson & Hedges Cup | 4 | 4 | 0 | 26 | 21 | 6.50 | - | - | - | - |
| Other One-Day | 1 | 1 | 0 | 31 | 31 | 31.00 | - | - | - | - |
| ALL ONE-DAY | 23 | 23 | 1 | 468 | 79 * | 21.27 | - | 1 | 2 | - |

### BOWLING AVERAGES

| | Overs | Mdns | Runs | Wkts | Avge | Best | 5wI | 10wM |
|---|---|---|---|---|---|---|---|---|
| Britannic Assurance | 23.5 | 0 | 122 | 3 | 40.66 | 2-70 | - | - |
| Other First-Class | | | | | | | | |
| ALL FIRST-CLASS | 23.5 | 0 | 122 | 3 | 40.66 | 2-70 | - | - |

Refuge Assurance
NatWest Trophy
Benson & Hedges Cup
Other One-Day

ALL ONE-DAY

## J.J.E.HARDY - *Gloucestershire*

| Opposition | Venue | Date | Batting | | | Fielding | Bowling |
|---|---|---|---|---|---|---|---|
| **BRITANNIC ASSURANCE** | | | | | | | |
| Yorkshire | Sheffield | May 22 | 21 * | & | 32 * | | |
| Warwickshire | Edgbaston | May 25 | 0 | & | 0 | | |
| Middlesex | Bristol | June 4 | 15 | | | | |
| Hampshire | Southampton | June 7 | | | 52 | | |
| Notts | Gloucester | June 14 | 10 | & | 31 | | |
| Derbyshire | Gloucester | June 18 | 0 | & | 13 | | |
| Somerset | Bath | June 21 | 9 | | | | |
| Northants | Luton | June 28 | 0 | & | 12 | | |
| Leicestershire | Hinckley | July 2 | 35 | | | | |
| Lancashire | Bristol | Aug 9 | 12 | | | | |
| **REFUGE ASSURANCE** | | | | | | | |
| Worcestershire | Bristol | May 5 | 20 | | | | |
| Hampshire | Swindon | May 26 | | | | | |
| Notts | Gloucester | June 16 | 42 | | | | |
| Kent | Canterbury | June 30 | 1 | | | | |
| Yorkshire | Scarborough | July 14 | 10 | | | 1Ct | |
| Derbyshire | Cheltenham | July 21 | 54 | | | | |
| Lancashire | Bristol | Aug 11 | 20 | | | 1Ct | |
| Warwickshire | Edgbaston | Aug 18 | 13 | | | | |
| Leicestershire | Leicester | Aug 25 | 11 * | | | | |
| **NATWEST TROPHY** | | | | | | | |
| Norfolk | Bristol | June 26 | 70 | | | | |
| Notts | Bristol | July 11 | 23 | | | | |
| **BENSON & HEDGES CUP** | | | | | | | |
| Derbyshire | Derby | May 7 | 6 | | | | |

### BATTING AVERAGES - Including fielding

| | Matches | Inns | NO | Runs | HS | Avge | 100s | 50s | Ct | St |
|---|---|---|---|---|---|---|---|---|---|---|
| Britannic Assurance | 10 | 15 | 2 | 242 | 52 | 18.61 | - | 1 | - | - |
| ALL FIRST-CLASS | 10 | 15 | 2 | 242 | 52 | 18.61 | - | 1 | - | - |
| Refuge Assurance | 9 | 8 | 1 | 171 | 54 | 24.42 | - | 1 | 2 | - |
| NatWest Trophy | 2 | 2 | 0 | 93 | 70 | 46.50 | - | 1 | - | - |
| Benson & Hedges Cup | 1 | 1 | 0 | 6 | 6 | 6.00 | - | - | - | - |
| ALL ONE-DAY | 12 | 11 | 1 | 270 | 70 | 27.00 | - | 2 | 2 | - |

### BOWLING AVERAGES
Did not bowl

## R.A.HARPER - *League CC XI & West Indies XI*

| Opposition | Venue | Date | Batting | | | Fielding | Bowling |
|---|---|---|---|---|---|---|---|
| **OTHER FIRST-CLASS** | | | | | | | |
| For West Indies XI | | | | | | | |
| World XI | Scarborough | Aug 28 | 63 * | & | 24 * | | 1-77 |
| **OTHER ONE-DAY** | | | | | | | |
| For League CC XI | | | | | | | |
| West Indies | Trowbridge | June 28 | 18 | | | | 0-27 |

### BATTING AVERAGES - Including fielding

| | Matches | Inns | NO | Runs | HS | Avge | 100s | 50s | Ct | St |
|---|---|---|---|---|---|---|---|---|---|---|
| Other First-Class | 1 | 2 | 2 | 87 | 63 * | - | - | 1 | - | - |
| ALL FIRST-CLASS | 1 | 2 | 2 | 87 | 63 * | - | - | 1 | - | - |
| Other One-Day | 1 | 1 | 0 | 18 | 18 | 18.00 | - | - | - | - |

# PLAYER RECORDS

# H

| | | | | | | | | | |
|---|---|---|---|---|---|---|---|---|---|
| ALL ONE-DAY | 1 | 1 | 0 | 18 | 18 | 18.00 | - | - | - - |

**BOWLING AVERAGES**

| | Overs | Mdns | Runs | Wkts | Avge | Best | 5wI | 10wM |
|---|---|---|---|---|---|---|---|---|
| Other First-Class | 17 | 1 | 77 | 1 | 77.00 | 1-77 | - | - |
| ALL FIRST-CLASS | 17 | 1 | 77 | 1 | 77.00 | 1-77 | - | - |
| Other One-Day | 5 | 0 | 27 | 0 | - | - | - | |
| ALL ONE-DAY | 5 | 0 | 27 | 0 | - | - | - | |

## A.W.HARRIS - *Wales*

| Opposition | Venue | Date | Batting | Fielding | Bowling |
|---|---|---|---|---|---|
| **OTHER ONE-DAY** | | | | | |
| West Indies | Brecon | July 15 | 4 | | |

**BATTING AVERAGES - Including fielding**

| | Matches | Inns | NO | Runs | HS | Avge | 100s | 50s | Ct | St |
|---|---|---|---|---|---|---|---|---|---|---|
| Other One-Day | 1 | 1 | 0 | 4 | 4 | 4.00 | - | - | - | - |
| ALL ONE-DAY | 1 | 1 | 0 | 4 | 4 | 4.00 | - | - | - | - |

**BOWLING AVERAGES**
Did not bowl

## G.A.R.HARRIS - *Hertfordshire*

| Opposition | Venue | Date | Batting | Fielding | Bowling |
|---|---|---|---|---|---|
| **NATWEST TROPHY** | | | | | |
| Warwickshire | Edgbaston | July 11 | | | 0-17 |

**BATTING AVERAGES - Including fielding**

| | Matches | Inns | NO | Runs | HS | Avge | 100s | 50s | Ct | St |
|---|---|---|---|---|---|---|---|---|---|---|
| NatWest Trophy | 1 | 0 | 0 | 0 | 0 | | - | - | - | - |
| ALL ONE-DAY | 1 | 0 | 0 | 0 | 0 | | - | - | - | - |

**BOWLING AVERAGES**

| | Overs | Mdns | Runs | Wkts | Avge | Best | 5wI | 10wM |
|---|---|---|---|---|---|---|---|---|
| NatWest Trophy | 4 | 1 | 17 | 0 | - | - | - | |
| ALL ONE-DAY | 4 | 1 | 17 | 0 | - | - | - | |

## G.D.HARRISON - *Ireland*

| Opposition | Venue | Date | Batting | Fielding | Bowling |
|---|---|---|---|---|---|
| **OTHER FIRST-CLASS** | | | | | |
| Scotland | Dublin | June 22 | 77 & 21 | 1Ct | 0-50 & 1-43 |
| **NATWEST TROPHY** | | | | | |
| Middlesex | Dublin | June 26 | 9 | 1Ct | 0-27 |
| **OTHER ONE-DAY** | | | | | |
| West Indies | Downpatrick | July 13 | 2* | | 0-30 |

**BATTING AVERAGES - Including fielding**

| | Matches | Inns | NO | Runs | HS | Avge | 100s | 50s | Ct | St |
|---|---|---|---|---|---|---|---|---|---|---|
| Other First-Class | 1 | 2 | 0 | 98 | 77 | 49.00 | - | 1 | 1 | - |
| ALL FIRST-CLASS | 1 | 2 | 0 | 98 | 77 | 49.00 | - | 1 | 1 | - |
| NatWest Trophy | 1 | 1 | 0 | 9 | 9 | 9.00 | - | - | 1 | - |
| Other One-Day | 1 | 1 | 1 | 2 | 2* | | - | - | - | - |
| ALL ONE-DAY | 2 | 2 | 1 | 11 | 9 | 11.00 | - | - | 1 | - |

**BOWLING AVERAGES**

| | Overs | Mdns | Runs | Wkts | Avge | Best | 5wI | 10wM |
|---|---|---|---|---|---|---|---|---|
| Other First-Class | 26 | 6 | 93 | 1 | 93.00 | 1-43 | - | - |
| ALL FIRST-CLASS | 26 | 6 | 93 | 1 | 93.00 | 1-43 | - | - |
| NatWest Trophy | 5 | 0 | 27 | 0 | - | - | - | |
| Other One-Day | 7 | 0 | 30 | 0 | - | - | - | |
| ALL ONE-DAY | 12 | 0 | 57 | 0 | - | - | - | |

## P.J.HARTLEY - *Yorkshire*

| Opposition | Venue | Date | Batting | | Fielding | Bowling |
|---|---|---|---|---|---|---|
| **BRITANNIC ASSURANCE** | | | | | | |
| Middlesex | Lord's | April 27 | 1 | | | 0-0 |
| Warwickshire | Headingley | May 9 | 0 & | 21 | | 3-47 & 3-53 |
| Notts | Headingley | May 16 | 24 | | | 3-46 & 0-27 |
| Gloucs | Sheffield | May 22 | | | | 0-45 & 0-18 |
| Northants | Headingley | May 25 | 0 | | | 0-35 & 3-34 |
| Warwickshire | Edgbaston | May 31 | 0 & | 14* | | 2-82 & 0-36 |
| Middlesex | Sheffield | June 21 | | | | 0-27 & 5-32 |
| Worcestershire | Headingley | July 2 | 0* | | | 3-70 |
| Hampshire | Southampton | July 5 | 26 | | 1Ct | 4-82 & 0-3 |
| Derbyshire | Scarborough | July 16 | 50* | | | 2-72 & 0-14 |
| Surrey | Guildford | July 19 | 35*& | 0 | | 0-56 & 1-33 |
| Notts | Worksop | July 23 | 7* | | | 0-15 & 1-75 |
| Lancashire | Old Trafford | Aug 2 | 6* | | | 1-72 & 1-28 |
| Leicestershire | Leicester | Aug 6 | 2 | | | 1-78 & 0-7 |
| Sussex | Midd'brough | Aug 9 | 17 & | 10 | | 2-128 |
| Glamorgan | Headingley | Aug 16 | 8*& | 6 | | 0-26 & 0-8 |
| Essex | Colchester | Aug 20 | 33* | | | 0-34 & 1-52 |
| Northants | Northampton | Aug 28 | 19*& | 4 | 1Ct | 6-151 & 0-27 |
| Lancashire | Scarborough | Sept 3 | | | | 5-100 & 1-36 |
| Derbyshire | Chesterfield | Sept 17 | 5 & | 34* | 1Ct | 2-45 & 0-57 |
| **REFUGE ASSURANCE** | | | | | | |
| Hampshire | Southampton | April 21 | 8 | | | 2-36 |
| Warwickshire | Headingley | May 12 | 0* | | | 0-41 |
| Leicestershire | Leicester | May 19 | 2 | | | 1-43 |
| Northants | Headingley | May 26 | 5 | | 1Ct | 0-47 |
| Derbyshire | Chesterfield | June 2 | 0 | | | 3-6 |
| Worcestershire | Sheffield | June 23 | 11 | | | 1-28 |
| Glamorgan | Headingley | June 30 | | | | 1-24 |
| Middlesex | Lord's | July 7 | | | | 0-46 |
| Gloucs | Scarborough | July 14 | 1 | | | 0-33 |
| Surrey | The Oval | July 21 | | | | 1-25 |
| Lancashire | Old Trafford | Aug 4 | | | 1Ct | 1-29 |
| Sussex | Midd'brough | Aug 11 | 5* | | | 2-16 |
| Notts | Scarborough | Aug 18 | | | | 1-42 |
| **NATWEST TROPHY** | | | | | | |
| Warwickshire | Edgbaston | June 26 | 6* | | | 0-19 |
| **BENSON & HEDGES CUP** | | | | | | |
| Notts | Trent Bridge | April 25 | 13 | | | 1-56 |
| Hampshire | Headingley | May 4 | 1 | | | 2-7 |
| Glamorgan | Cardiff | May 7 | | | | 1-47 |
| Warwickshire | Headingley | May 29 | 1* | | 1Ct | 1-19 |
| Lancashire | Old Trafford | June 16 | 0 | | | 0-56 |
| **OTHER ONE-DAY** | | | | | | |
| Derbyshire | Scarborough | Sept 1 | | | | 1-45 |
| Essex | Scarborough | Sept 2 | | | | 0-50 |
| Yorkshiremen | Scarborough | Sept 7 | 7 | | | 1-32 |

**BATTING AVERAGES - Including fielding**

| | Matches | Inns | NO | Runs | HS | Avge | 100s | 50s | Ct | St |
|---|---|---|---|---|---|---|---|---|---|---|
| Britannic Assurance | 20 | 24 | 10 | 322 | 50* | 23.00 | - | 1 | 3 | - |
| ALL FIRST-CLASS | 20 | 24 | 10 | 322 | 50* | 23.00 | - | 1 | 3 | - |
| Refuge Assurance | 13 | 8 | 2 | 32 | 11 | 5.33 | - | - | 2 | - |
| NatWest Trophy | 1 | 1 | 1 | 6 | 6* | | - | - | - | - |
| Benson & Hedges Cup | 5 | 4 | 1 | 15 | 13 | 5.00 | - | - | 1 | - |
| Other One-Day | 3 | 1 | 0 | 7 | 7 | 7.00 | - | - | - | - |
| ALL ONE-DAY | 22 | 14 | 4 | 60 | 13 | 6.00 | - | - | 3 | - |

**BOWLING AVERAGES**

| | Overs | Mdns | Runs | Wkts | Avge | Best | 5wI | 10wM |
|---|---|---|---|---|---|---|---|---|
| Britannic Assurance | 522.3 | 100 | 1751 | 50 | 35.02 | 6-151 | 3 | - |
| ALL FIRST-CLASS | 522.3 | 100 | 1751 | 50 | 35.02 | 6-151 | 3 | - |

## H — PLAYER RECORDS

| | | | | | | |
|---|---|---|---|---|---|---|
| Refuge Assurance | 92.2 | 3 | 416 | 13 | 32.00 | 3-6 - |
| NatWest Trophy | 8 | 1 | 19 | 0 | - | - - |
| Benson & Hedges Cup | 46 | 5 | 185 | 5 | 37.00 | 2-7 - |
| Other One-Day | 27 | 1 | 127 | 2 | 63.50 | 1-32 - |
| ALL ONE-DAY | 173.2 | 10 | 747 | 20 | 37.35 | 3-6 - |

## A.R.HARWOOD - *Buckinghamshire*

| Opposition | Venue | Date | Batting | Fielding | Bowling |
|---|---|---|---|---|---|
| **NATWEST TROPHY** | | | | | |
| Somerset | Bath | June 26 | 4 | | |

**BATTING AVERAGES - Including fielding**

| | Matches | Inns | NO | Runs | HS | Avge | 100s | 50s | Ct | St |
|---|---|---|---|---|---|---|---|---|---|---|
| NatWest Trophy | 1 | 1 | 0 | 4 | 4 | 4.00 | - | - | - | - |
| ALL ONE-DAY | 1 | 1 | 0 | 4 | 4 | 4.00 | - | - | - | - |

**BOWLING AVERAGES**
Did not bowl

## U.C.HATHURUSINGHE - *Sri Lanka*

| Opposition | Venue | Date | Batting | Fielding | Bowling |
|---|---|---|---|---|---|
| **CORNHILL TEST MATCHES** | | | | | |
| England | Lord's | Aug 22 | 66 & 25 | | 1-40 |
| **OTHER FIRST-CLASS** | | | | | |
| Worcestershire | Worcester | July 30 | 0 & 0 | | |
| Derbyshire | Derby | Aug 2 | 74* | | |
| Gloucs | Bristol | Aug 6 | 0 & 11 | 1Ct | 0-6 |
| Somerset | Taunton | Aug 10 | 19 & 67 | 1Ct | 0-43 |
| Sussex | Hove | Aug 17 | 18 & 31 | | 2-18 & 0-3 |
| **OTHER ONE-DAY** | | | | | |
| England Am. | Wolv'hampton | July 24 | 28 | | 0-10 |
| England A | Old Trafford | Aug 15 | 33 | | |

**BATTING AVERAGES - Including fielding**

| | Matches | Inns | NO | Runs | HS | Avge | 100s | 50s | Ct | St |
|---|---|---|---|---|---|---|---|---|---|---|
| Cornhill Test Matches | 1 | 2 | 0 | 91 | 66 | 45.50 | - | 1 | - | - |
| Other First-Class | 5 | 9 | 1 | 220 | 74* | 27.50 | - | 2 | 2 | - |
| ALL FIRST-CLASS | 6 | 11 | 1 | 311 | 74* | 31.10 | - | 3 | 2 | - |
| Other One-Day | 2 | 2 | 0 | 61 | 33 | 30.50 | - | - | - | - |
| ALL ONE-DAY | 2 | 2 | 0 | 61 | 33 | 30.50 | - | - | - | - |

**BOWLING AVERAGES**

| | Overs | Mdns | Runs | Wkts | Avge | Best | 5wI | 10wM |
|---|---|---|---|---|---|---|---|---|
| Cornhill Test Matches | 17 | 6 | 40 | 1 | 40.00 | 1-40 | - | - |
| Other First-Class | 22.3 | 4 | 70 | 2 | 35.00 | 2-18 | - | - |
| ALL FIRST-CLASS | 39.3 | 10 | 110 | 3 | 36.66 | 2-18 | - | - |
| Other One-Day | 3 | 0 | 10 | 0 | - | - | | |
| ALL ONE-DAY | 3 | 0 | 10 | 0 | - | - | | |

## A.N.HAYHURST - *Somerset*

| Opposition | Venue | Date | Batting | Fielding | Bowling |
|---|---|---|---|---|---|
| **BRITANNIC ASSURANCE** | | | | | |
| Sussex | Taunton | April 27 | 32 | | 0-20 |
| Derbyshire | Derby | May 22 | 116 & 12 | | 0-5 |
| Middlesex | Taunton | May 25 | 0 & 26 | 2Ct | 0-34 |
| Glamorgan | Swansea | June 4 | 1 | | 0-49 |
| Warwickshire | Edgbaston | June 7 | 18 & 8 | 1Ct | 1-67 & 0-26 |
| Hampshire | Bath | June 18 | 32 & 12 | | 1-30 & 0-45 |
| Gloucs | Bath | June 21 | 172* | | 0-11 |
| Surrey | The Oval | June 28 | 9 | | |
| Lancashire | Taunton | July 2 | 29 & 22* | | 0-39 & 0-0 |
| Sussex | Hove | July 16 | 12 & 0 | | 2-67 |
| Essex | Southend | July 19 | 11 & 0 | | 0-2 & 1-9 |
| Northants | Northampton | July 23 | 29 & 23 | 1Ct | 0-25 & 1-33 |
| Kent | Taunton | July 26 | 1 & 5 | | 0-17 |
| Leicestershire | Weston | Aug 2 | 71 & 26* | 1Ct | 0-17 |
| Worcestershire | Weston | Aug 6 | 40 & 13 | | 1-18 & 0-15 |
| Notts | Trent Bridge | Aug 16 | 33 & 100* | | 1-48 & 1-37 |
| Yorkshire | Taunton | Aug 23 | 21 & 9* | | 0-35 & 0-10 |
| Worcestershire | Worcester | Sept 3 | | | 0-56 |
| **OTHER FIRST-CLASS** | | | | | |
| West Indies | Taunton | May 29 | 22 & 5 | | 2-42 & 0-23 |
| **REFUGE ASSURANCE** | | | | | |
| Surrey | The Oval | April 21 | 1 | 1Ct | 0-47 |
| Sussex | Taunton | April 28 | 26* | | 0-25 |
| Hampshire | Bournemouth | May 19 | | | 1-44 |
| Middlesex | Taunton | May 26 | 19 | | 1-17 |
| Warwickshire | Edgbaston | June 2 | 12* | | |
| Notts | Trent Bridge | June 9 | 27 | | 1-33 |
| Derbyshire | Derby | June 16 | 18* | | 1-23 |
| Northants | Luton | June 30 | 2 | 1Ct | 0-4 |
| Lancashire | Taunton | July 5 | 2* | | 0-15 |
| Essex | Southend | July 21 | | | 0-35 |
| Leicestershire | Weston | Aug 4 | 35 | | |
| Worcestershire | Worcester | Aug 18 | 7* | | 3-38 |
| Yorkshire | Taunton | Aug 25 | 14 | | 2-27 |
| **NATWEST TROPHY** | | | | | |
| Bucks | Bath | June 26 | 5 | | 1-28 |
| Middlesex | Taunton | July 11 | 58 | | 2-49 |
| Warwickshire | Edgbaston | July 31 | 91* | 1Ct | 5-60 |
| **BENSON & HEDGES CUP** | | | | | |
| Middlesex | Taunton | April 23 | 32 | | 0-18 |
| Warwickshire | Edgbaston | May 2 | 70 | 1Ct | |

**BATTING AVERAGES - Including fielding**

| | Matches | Inns | NO | Runs | HS | Avge | 100s | 50s | Ct | St |
|---|---|---|---|---|---|---|---|---|---|---|
| Britannic Assurance | 18 | 30 | 5 | 883 | 172* | 35.32 | 3 | 1 | 5 | - |
| Other First-Class | 1 | 2 | 0 | 27 | 22 | 13.50 | - | - | - | - |
| ALL FIRST-CLASS | 19 | 32 | 5 | 910 | 172* | 33.70 | 3 | 1 | 5 | - |
| Refuge Assurance | 13 | 11 | 5 | 163 | 35 | 27.16 | - | - | 2 | - |
| NatWest Trophy | 3 | 3 | 1 | 154 | 91* | 77.00 | - | 2 | 1 | - |
| Benson & Hedges Cup | 2 | 2 | 0 | 102 | 70 | 51.00 | - | 1 | 1 | - |
| ALL ONE-DAY | 18 | 16 | 6 | 419 | 91* | 41.90 | - | 3 | 4 | - |

**BOWLING AVERAGES**

| | Overs | Mdns | Runs | Wkts | Avge | Best | 5wI | 10wM |
|---|---|---|---|---|---|---|---|---|
| Britannic Assurance | 191.3 | 30 | 715 | 9 | 79.44 | 2-67 | - | - |
| Other First-Class | 14 | 2 | 65 | 2 | 32.50 | 2-42 | - | - |
| ALL FIRST-CLASS | 205.3 | 32 | 780 | 11 | 70.90 | 2-42 | - | - |
| Refuge Assurance | 61.3 | 0 | 308 | 9 | 34.22 | 3-38 | | |
| NatWest Trophy | 35.3 | 4 | 137 | 8 | 17.12 | 5-60 | 1 | |
| Benson & Hedges Cup | 5.1 | 0 | 18 | 0 | - | - | | |
| ALL ONE-DAY | 102.1 | 4 | 463 | 17 | 27.23 | 5-60 | 1 | |

## D.L.HAYNES - *West Indies*

| Opposition | Venue | Date | Batting | Fielding | Bowling |
|---|---|---|---|---|---|
| **CORNHILL TEST MATCHES** | | | | | |
| England | Headingley | June 6 | 7 & 19 | | |
| England | Lord's | June 20 | 60 & 4* | 1Ct | |
| England | Trent Bridge | July 4 | 18 & 57* | | |
| England | Edgbaston | July 25 | 32 & 8 | | |
| England | The Oval | Aug 8 | 75* & 43 | 1Ct | |
| **OTHER FIRST-CLASS** | | | | | |
| Somerset | Taunton | May 29 | 1 & 16* | | |
| Derbyshire | Derby | June 12 | 31 & 0 | 1Ct | |
| Northants | Northampton | June 15 | 60 | | |

# PLAYER RECORDS

| | | | | | |
|---|---|---|---|---|---|
| Hampshire | Southampton | June 29 | 44 | | 1Ct |
| Glamorgan | Swansea | July 16 | 45 | | |
| Kent | Canterbury | July 20 | 4 & 4 | | |
| Gloucs | Bristol | July 31 | 151 | | |
| Essex | Chelmsford | Aug 3 | 23 * & 19 | | |

**OTHER ONE-DAY**

| | | | | | |
|---|---|---|---|---|---|
| Gloucs | Bristol | May 14 | 101 | | |
| Ireland | Downpatrick | July 13 | 14 * | | 1-14 |

**BATTING AVERAGES - Including fielding**

| | Matches | Inns | NO | Runs | HS | Avge | 100s | 50s | Ct | St |
|---|---|---|---|---|---|---|---|---|---|---|
| Cornhill Test Matches | 5 | 10 | 3 | 323 | 75 * | 46.14 | - | 3 | 2 | - |
| Other First-Class | 8 | 12 | 2 | 398 | 151 | 39.80 | 1 | 1 | 2 | - |
| ALL FIRST-CLASS | 13 | 22 | 5 | 721 | 151 | 42.41 | 1 | 4 | 4 | - |
| Other One-Day | 2 | 2 | 1 | 115 | 101 | 115.00 | 1 | - | - | - |
| ALL ONE-DAY | 2 | 2 | 1 | 115 | 101 | 115.00 | 1 | - | - | - |

**BOWLING AVERAGES**

| | Overs | Mdns | Runs | Wkts | Avge | Best | 5wI | 10wM |
|---|---|---|---|---|---|---|---|---|
| Cornhill Test Matches | | | | | | | | |
| Other First-Class | | | | | | | | |
| ALL FIRST-CLASS | | | | | | | | |
| Other One-Day | 3 | 0 | 14 | 1 | 14.00 | 1-14 | - | |
| ALL ONE-DAY | 3 | 0 | 14 | 1 | 14.00 | 1-14 | - | |

## G.R.HAYNES - *Worcestershire*

| Opposition | Venue | Date | Batting | Fielding | Bowling |
|---|---|---|---|---|---|

**BRITANNIC ASSURANCE**

| | | | | | |
|---|---|---|---|---|---|
| Notts | Worcester | June 18 | 13 * & 16 | | 0-55 & 0-27 |
| Kent | Worcester | July 23 | | | |
| Somerset | Worcester | Sept 3 | 6 | | 0-0 |

**OTHER FIRST-CLASS**

| | | | | | |
|---|---|---|---|---|---|
| Sri Lanka | Worcester | July 30 | 16 | 2Ct | |

**BATTING AVERAGES - Including fielding**

| | Matches | Inns | NO | Runs | HS | Avge | 100s | 50s | Ct | St |
|---|---|---|---|---|---|---|---|---|---|---|
| Britannic Assurance | 3 | 3 | 1 | 35 | 16 | 17.50 | - | - | - | - |
| Other First-Class | 1 | 1 | 0 | 16 | 16 | 16.00 | - | - | 2 | - |
| ALL FIRST-CLASS | 4 | 4 | 1 | 51 | 16 | 17.00 | - | - | 2 | - |

**BOWLING AVERAGES**

| | Overs | Mdns | Runs | Wkts | Avge | Best | 5wI | 10wM |
|---|---|---|---|---|---|---|---|---|
| Britannic Assurance | 19.2 | 2 | 82 | 0 | - | - | - | - |
| Other First-Class | | | | | | | | |
| ALL FIRST-CLASS | 19.2 | 2 | 82 | 0 | - | - | - | - |

## D.W.HEADLEY - *Middlesex*

| Opposition | Venue | Date | Batting | Fielding | Bowling |
|---|---|---|---|---|---|

**BRITANNIC ASSURANCE**

| | | | | | |
|---|---|---|---|---|---|
| Yorkshire | Lord's | April 27 | | | 5-46 |
| Sussex | Lord's | May 9 | 2 & 3 | | 2-96 & 0-19 |
| Northants | Uxbridge | July 16 | | | 0-74 |
| Notts | Lord's | July 26 | 19 * | 1Ct | 2-61 & 1-82 |
| Hampshire | Lord's | Aug 2 | 26 & 76 | 1Ct | 0-45 & 1-50 |
| Derbyshire | Lord's | Aug 9 | | | 0-42 & 0-23 |
| Surrey | The Oval | Aug 20 | 4 | | 3-65 & 4-69 |
| Worcestershire | Worcester | Aug 23 | 0 & 0 | 1Ct | 3-67 |
| Kent | Canterbury | Aug 28 | 26 & 14 | 1Ct | 5-100 & 0-112 |
| Surrey | Lord's | Sept 10 | 2 & 7 | | 0-70 & 0-6 |
| Essex | Chelmsford | Sept 17 | 1 & 22 | | 2-153 |

**OTHER FIRST-CLASS**

| | | | | | |
|---|---|---|---|---|---|
| MCC | Lord's | April 16 | 0 | 1Ct | 1-78 |

**REFUGE ASSURANCE**

| | | | | | |
|---|---|---|---|---|---|
| Gloucs | Bristol | April 21 | | | 0-38 |
| Surrey | Lord's | April 28 | | | 0-41 |
| Warwickshire | Edgbaston | July 14 | | | 0-28 |
| Lancashire | Lord's | July 21 | | | 0-29 |
| Hampshire | Lord's | Aug 4 | | | 0-16 |
| Derbyshire | Lord's | Aug 11 | 4 | | 0-18 |
| Essex | Colchester | Aug 18 | 6 * | | 0-56 |
| Worcestershire | Worcester | Aug 25 | | | 1-70 |

**NATWEST TROPHY**

| | | | | | |
|---|---|---|---|---|---|
| Somerset | Taunton | July 11 | 11 * | | 0-51 |

**BENSON & HEDGES CUP**

| | | | | | |
|---|---|---|---|---|---|
| Somerset | Taunton | April 23 | | | 0-48 |
| Surrey | Lord's | April 25 | 26 | | 1-54 |
| Essex | Chelmsford | May 2 | 2 | | 1-34 |
| Warwickshire | Lord's | May 4 | 2 | 1Ct | 1-44 |

**BATTING AVERAGES - Including fielding**

| | Matches | Inns | NO | Runs | HS | Avge | 100s | 50s | Ct | St |
|---|---|---|---|---|---|---|---|---|---|---|
| Britannic Assurance | 11 | 14 | 1 | 202 | 76 | 15.53 | - | 1 | 4 | - |
| Other First-Class | 1 | 1 | 0 | 0 | 0 | 0.00 | - | - | 1 | - |
| ALL FIRST-CLASS | 12 | 15 | 1 | 202 | 76 | 14.42 | - | 1 | 5 | - |
| Refuge Assurance | 8 | 2 | 1 | 10 | 6 * | 10.00 | - | - | - | - |
| NatWest Trophy | 1 | 1 | 1 | 11 | 11 * | - | - | - | - | - |
| Benson & Hedges Cup | 4 | 3 | 0 | 30 | 26 | 10.00 | - | - | 1 | - |
| ALL ONE-DAY | 13 | 6 | 2 | 51 | 26 | 12.75 | - | - | 1 | - |

**BOWLING AVERAGES**

| | Overs | Mdns | Runs | Wkts | Avge | Best | 5wI | 10wM |
|---|---|---|---|---|---|---|---|---|
| Britannic Assurance | 309.2 | 44 | 1180 | 28 | 42.14 | 5-46 | 2 | - |
| Other First-Class | 20.1 | 7 | 78 | 1 | 78.00 | 1-78 | - | - |
| ALL FIRST-CLASS | 329.3 | 51 | 1258 | 29 | 43.37 | 5-46 | 2 | - |
| Refuge Assurance | 56 | 0 | 296 | 1 | 296.00 | 1-70 | - | |
| NatWest Trophy | 12 | 0 | 51 | 0 | - | - | - | |
| Benson & Hedges Cup | 42.1 | 4 | 180 | 3 | 60.00 | 1-34 | - | |
| ALL ONE-DAY | 110.1 | 4 | 527 | 4 | 131.75 | 1-34 | - | |

## G.T.HEADLEY - *Berkshire*

| Opposition | Venue | Date | Batting | Fielding | Bowling |
|---|---|---|---|---|---|

**NATWEST TROPHY**

| | | | | | |
|---|---|---|---|---|---|
| Hampshire | Reading | June 26 | 12 | | 0-19 |

**BATTING AVERAGES - Including fielding**

| | Matches | Inns | NO | Runs | HS | Avge | 100s | 50s | Ct | St |
|---|---|---|---|---|---|---|---|---|---|---|
| NatWest Trophy | 1 | 1 | 0 | 12 | 12 | 12.00 | - | - | - | - |
| ALL ONE-DAY | 1 | 1 | 0 | 12 | 12 | 12.00 | - | - | - | - |

**BOWLING AVERAGES**

| | Overs | Mdns | Runs | Wkts | Avge | Best | 5wI | 10wM |
|---|---|---|---|---|---|---|---|---|
| NatWest Trophy | 4 | 0 | 19 | 0 | - | - | - | - |
| ALL ONE-DAY | 4 | 0 | 19 | 0 | - | - | - | - |

## N.J.HEATON - *League CC XI*

| Opposition | Venue | Date | Batting | Fielding | Bowling |
|---|---|---|---|---|---|

**OTHER ONE-DAY**

| | | | | | |
|---|---|---|---|---|---|
| West Indies | Trowbridge | June 28 | 44 | | |

**BATTING AVERAGES - Including fielding**

| | Matches | Inns | NO | Runs | HS | Avge | 100s | 50s | Ct | St |
|---|---|---|---|---|---|---|---|---|---|---|
| Other One-Day | 1 | 1 | 0 | 44 | 44 | 44.00 | - | - | - | - |
| ALL ONE-DAY | 1 | 1 | 0 | 44 | 44 | 44.00 | - | - | - | - |

# H

# PLAYER RECORDS

## BOWLING AVERAGES
Did not bowl

## W.K.HEGG - *Lancashire*

| Opposition | Venue | Date | Batting | | | Fielding | Bowling |
|---|---|---|---|---|---|---|---|
| **BRITANNIC ASSURANCE** | | | | | | | |
| Warwickshire | Edgbaston | April 27 | | | | 1Ct | |
| Worcestershire | Worcester | May 9 | 0 | & | 27 * | 4Ct | |
| Derbyshire | Old Trafford | May 16 | 13 | | | 1Ct | |
| Surrey | The Oval | May 22 | 3 | & | 27 | 2Ct | |
| Sussex | Old Trafford | May 31 | 86 | | | 2Ct | |
| Hampshire | Basingstoke | June 4 | 69 | | | 2Ct | |
| Leicestershire | Leicester | June 18 | 23 | & | 4 * | | |
| Kent | Old Trafford | June 21 | 45 | | | 3Ct | |
| Glamorgan | Liverpool | June 28 | 6 | & | 11 * | 1Ct | |
| Somerset | Taunton | July 2 | 0 * & | | 17 | 1Ct,1St | |
| Notts | Trent Bridge | July 16 | 0 | & | 1 | 3Ct | |
| Middlesex | Uxbridge | July 19 | 5 | | | 1Ct | |
| Yorkshire | Old Trafford | Aug 2 | 19 | | | 2Ct | |
| Northants | Lytham | Aug 6 | | | 37 | 1Ct,1St | |
| Gloucs | Bristol | Aug 9 | 13 | & | 16 | 2Ct | |
| Derbyshire | Derby | Aug 16 | 30 | & | 37 * | 1Ct | |
| Worcestershire | Blackpool | Aug 20 | 10 | & | 21 * | 1Ct | |
| Essex | Old Trafford | Aug 23 | 30 | | | 2Ct | |
| Notts | Old Trafford | Aug 28 | 33 | & | 40 | 1Ct | |
| Yorkshire | Scarborough | Sept 3 | | | 2 | 2Ct,1St | |
| Surrey | Old Trafford | Sept 17 | 97 | & | 36 * | 5Ct | |

| OTHER FIRST-CLASS | | | | | | |
|---|---|---|---|---|---|---|
| Cambridge U | Fenner's | April 13 | 26 * | | 4Ct | |

| REFUGE ASSURANCE | | | | | |
|---|---|---|---|---|---|
| Notts | Old Trafford | April 21 | 7 | | |
| Northants | Old Trafford | April 28 | | 1Ct | |
| Worcestershire | Worcester | May 12 | | 3Ct | |
| Derbyshire | Derby | May 19 | 11 * | | |
| Sussex | Old Trafford | June 2 | | | |
| Glamorgan | Old Trafford | June 9 | | | |
| Warwickshire | Edgbaston | June 16 | 2 * | 1Ct | |
| Kent | Old Trafford | June 23 | | 2Ct | |
| Somerset | Taunton | July 5 | | 2Ct | |
| Leicestershire | Leicester | July 7 | | 1Ct | |
| Middlesex | Lord's | July 21 | 47 * | 2Ct | |
| Hampshire | Southampton | July 28 | 42 * | 3Ct | |
| Yorkshire | Old Trafford | Aug 4 | 27 * | 1Ct | |
| Gloucs | Bristol | Aug 11 | | 1Ct | |
| Surrey | Old Trafford | Aug 18 | 7 | 2Ct | |
| Essex | Old Trafford | Aug 25 | | 2Ct | |
| Northants | Old Trafford | Sept 1 | | 1Ct,1St | |
| Worcestershire | Old Trafford | Sept 15 | 9 | | |

| NATWEST TROPHY | | | | | |
|---|---|---|---|---|---|
| Dorset | Bournemouth | June 26 | | 2Ct | |
| Hampshire | Southampton | July 11 | 7 | 2Ct | |

| BENSON & HEDGES CUP | | | | | |
|---|---|---|---|---|---|
| Scotland | Forfar | April 23 | | 2Ct | |
| Kent | Old Trafford | April 25 | | 1Ct | |
| Leicestershire | Leicester | May 4 | | 1Ct | |
| Sussex | Old Trafford | May 7 | | 1Ct | |
| Northants | Old Trafford | May 29 | | | |
| Yorkshire | Old Trafford | June 16 | 0 | 1Ct | |
| Worcestershire | Lord's | July 13 | 13 * | | |

### BATTING AVERAGES - Including fielding
| | Matches | Inns | NO | Runs | HS | Avge | 100s | 50s | Ct | St |
|---|---|---|---|---|---|---|---|---|---|---|
| Britannic Assurance | 21 | 31 | 7 | 758 | 97 | 31.58 | - | 3 | 39 | 3 |
| Other First-Class | 1 | 1 | 1 | 26 | 26 * | - | - | - | 4 | - |
| ALL FIRST-CLASS | 22 | 32 | 8 | 784 | 97 | 32.66 | - | 3 | 43 | 3 |
| Refuge Assurance | 18 | 8 | 5 | 152 | 47 * | 50.66 | - | - | 22 | 1 |
| NatWest Trophy | 2 | 1 | 0 | 7 | 7 | 7.00 | - | - | 4 | - |
| Benson & Hedges Cup | 7 | 2 | 1 | 13 | 13 * | 13.00 | - | - | 6 | - |
| ALL ONE-DAY | 27 | 11 | 6 | 172 | 47 * | 34.40 | - | - | 32 | 1 |

### BOWLING AVERAGES
Did not bowl

## E.E.HEMMINGS - *Nottinghamshire*

| Opposition | Venue | Date | Batting | | | Fielding | Bowling |
|---|---|---|---|---|---|---|---|
| **BRITANNIC ASSURANCE** | | | | | | | |
| Leicestershire | Trent Bridge | May 9 | 15 * | | | | 0-20 & 0-56 |
| Yorkshire | Headingley | May 16 | | | | 1Ct | 3-37 & 3-59 |
| Kent | Trent Bridge | May 22 | | | 8 | 1Ct | 4-70 & 0-31 |
| Hampshire | Trent Bridge | May 31 | 25 | | | | 0-75 & 2-59 |
| Surrey | The Oval | June 4 | | | | | 1-109 & 1-29 |
| Glamorgan | Cardiff | July 2 | 4 | | | 1Ct | 0-19 & 0-65 |
| Lancashire | Trent Bridge | July 16 | 0 | | | | 3-50 & 6-46 |
| Northants | Well'borough | July 19 | 10 | | | | 0-6 |
| Yorkshire | Worksop | July 23 | | | 13 | | 2-102 |
| Middlesex | Lord's | July 26 | 5 | | | | 2-30 & 0-24 |
| Sussex | Eastbourne | Aug 6 | | | | | 3-88 & 0-77 |
| Essex | Trent Bridge | Aug 9 | 2 | & | 1 | | 1-16 & 0-54 |
| Somerset | Trent Bridge | Aug 16 | | | 0 * | | 0-81 |
| Lancashire | Old Trafford | Aug 28 | 6 | & | 29 * | | 1-76 & 5-75 |
| Middlesex | Trent Bridge | Sept 3 | 23 * & | | 2 | | 2-144 & 3-98 |
| Worcestershire | Trent Bridge | Sept 17 | 0 | | | 1Ct | 1-44 & 3-81 |

| REFUGE ASSURANCE | | | | | |
|---|---|---|---|---|---|
| Lancashire | Old Trafford | April 21 | | 1Ct | 2-21 |
| Warwickshire | Trent Bridge | April 28 | | | 4-26 |
| Glamorgan | Cardiff | May 5 | | 1Ct | 0-27 |
| Essex | Trent Bridge | May 12 | 2 * | 1Ct | 2-29 |
| Leicestershire | Leicester | May 26 | | | 2-21 |
| Somerset | Trent Bridge | June 9 | | 1Ct | 1-33 |
| Gloucs | Gloucester | June 16 | | | 0-39 |
| Middlesex | Trent Bridge | June 23 | 0 | | 0-30 |
| Surrey | The Oval | June 30 | | | 1-36 |
| Hampshire | Trent Bridge | July 14 | | 1Ct | 1-35 |
| Northants | Well'borough | July 21 | 17 | | 0-38 |
| Sussex | Hove | July 28 | | 1Ct | 1-34 |
| Worcestershire | Trent Bridge | Aug 4 | | | 0-60 |
| Kent | Trent Bridge | Aug 11 | | 1Ct | 0-46 |
| Worcestershire | Trent Bridge | Sept 1 | 9 | | 0-13 |

| NATWEST TROPHY | | | | | |
|---|---|---|---|---|---|
| Lincolnshire | Trent Bridge | June 26 | | | 1-40 |
| Gloucs | Bristol | July 11 | 17 * | | 1-27 |
| Hampshire | Southampton | July 31 | 5 * | | 0-68 |

| BENSON & HEDGES CUP | | | | | |
|---|---|---|---|---|---|
| Hampshire | Southampton | April 23 | 9 | | 2-49 |
| Yorkshire | Trent Bridge | April 25 | | | 0-52 |
| Glamorgan | Cardiff | May 4 | | | 1-46 |
| Min Counties | Trent Bridge | May 7 | | | 1-54 |

| OTHER ONE-DAY | | | | | |
|---|---|---|---|---|---|
| For World XI | | | | | |
| Yorkshire | Scarborough | Sept 8 | 21 * | | 1-45 |

### BATTING AVERAGES - Including fielding
| | Matches | Inns | NO | Runs | HS | Avge | 100s | 50s | Ct | St |
|---|---|---|---|---|---|---|---|---|---|---|
| Britannic Assurance | 16 | 16 | 4 | 143 | 29 * | 11.91 | - | - | 4 | - |
| ALL FIRST-CLASS | 16 | 16 | 4 | 143 | 29 * | 11.91 | - | - | 4 | - |
| Refuge Assurance | 15 | 4 | 1 | 28 | 17 | 9.33 | - | - | 7 | - |
| NatWest Trophy | 3 | 2 | 2 | 22 | 17 * | - | - | - | - | - |
| Benson & Hedges Cup | 4 | 1 | 0 | 9 | 9 | 9.00 | - | - | - | - |
| Other One-Day | 1 | 1 | 1 | 21 | 21 * | - | - | - | - | - |
| ALL ONE-DAY | 23 | 8 | 4 | 80 | 21 * | 20.00 | - | - | 7 | - |

### BOWLING AVERAGES
| | Overs | Mdns | Runs | Wkts | Avge | Best | 5wI | 10wM |
|---|---|---|---|---|---|---|---|---|
| Britannic Assurance | 638.3 | 171 | 1721 | 46 | 37.41 | 6-46 | 2 | - |
| ALL FIRST-CLASS | 638.3 | 171 | 1721 | 46 | 37.41 | 6-46 | 2 | - |
| Refuge Assurance | 112.1 | 4 | 488 | 14 | 34.85 | 4-26 | - | |
| NatWest Trophy | 33 | 3 | 135 | 2 | 67.50 | 1-27 | - | |
| Benson & Hedges Cup | 44 | 4 | 201 | 4 | 50.25 | 2-49 | - | |
| Other One-Day | 10 | 0 | 45 | 1 | 45.00 | 1-45 | - | |
| ALL ONE-DAY | 199.1 | 11 | 869 | 21 | 41.38 | 4-26 | - | |

# PLAYER RECORDS

## D.L.HEMP - *Glamorgan*

| Opposition | Venue | Date | Batting | Fielding | Bowling |
|---|---|---|---|---|---|
| **BRITANNIC ASSURANCE** | | | | | |
| Hampshire | Southampton | Sept 17 | 8 & 4 * | | |
| **REFUGE ASSURANCE** | | | | | |
| Surrey | The Oval | July 28 | 7 | | |

**BATTING AVERAGES - Including fielding**

| | Matches | Inns | NO | Runs | HS | Avge | 100s | 50s | Ct | St |
|---|---|---|---|---|---|---|---|---|---|---|
| Britannic Assurance | 1 | 2 | 1 | 12 | 8 | 12.00 | - | - | - | - |
| ALL FIRST-CLASS | 1 | 2 | 1 | 12 | 8 | 12.00 | - | - | - | - |
| Refuge Assurance | 1 | 1 | 0 | 7 | 7 | 7.00 | - | - | - | - |
| ALL ONE-DAY | 1 | 1 | 0 | 7 | 7 | 7.00 | - | - | - | - |

**BOWLING AVERAGES**
Did not bowl

## P.W.HENDERSON - *Durham*

| Opposition | Venue | Date | Batting | Fielding | Bowling |
|---|---|---|---|---|---|
| **OTHER ONE-DAY** | | | | | |
| Leicestershire | Harrogate | June 11 | | | |
| Essex | Scarborough | Aug 31 | 1 | 1Ct | 1-72 |

**BATTING AVERAGES - Including fielding**

| | Matches | Inns | NO | Runs | HS | Avge | 100s | 50s | Ct | St |
|---|---|---|---|---|---|---|---|---|---|---|
| Other One-Day | 2 | 1 | 0 | 1 | 1 | 1.00 | - | - | 1 | - |
| ALL ONE-DAY | 2 | 1 | 0 | 1 | 1 | 1.00 | - | - | 1 | - |

**BOWLING AVERAGES**

| | Overs | Mdns | Runs | Wkts | Avge | Best | 5wI | 10wM |
|---|---|---|---|---|---|---|---|---|
| Other One-Day | 10 | 0 | 72 | 1 | 72.00 | 1-72 | - | |
| ALL ONE-DAY | 10 | 0 | 72 | 1 | 72.00 | 1-72 | - | |

## O.HENRY - *Scotland*

| Opposition | Venue | Date | Batting | Fielding | Bowling |
|---|---|---|---|---|---|
| **OTHER FIRST-CLASS** | | | | | |
| For Scotland | | | | | |
| Ireland | Dublin | June 22 | 22 | | 0-42 & 1-43 |
| **NATWEST TROPHY** | | | | | |
| Sussex | Edinburgh | June 26 | 12 | 1Ct | 1-34 |
| **BENSON & HEDGES CUP** | | | | | |
| Lancashire | Forfar | April 23 | 8 | | 0-19 |
| Leicestershire | Leicester | May 2 | 22 | | 0-43 |
| Sussex | Hove | May 4 | 32 | | 1-31 |
| Kent | Glasgow | May 7 | 18 | 2Ct | 0-50 |

**BATTING AVERAGES - Including fielding**

| | Matches | Inns | NO | Runs | HS | Avge | 100s | 50s | Ct | St |
|---|---|---|---|---|---|---|---|---|---|---|
| Other First-Class | 1 | 1 | 0 | 22 | 22 | 22.00 | - | - | - | - |
| ALL FIRST-CLASS | 1 | 1 | 0 | 22 | 22 | 22.00 | - | - | - | - |
| NatWest Trophy | 1 | 1 | 0 | 12 | 12 | 12.00 | - | - | 1 | - |
| Benson & Hedges Cup | 4 | 4 | 0 | 80 | 32 | 20.00 | - | - | 2 | - |
| ALL ONE-DAY | 5 | 5 | 0 | 92 | 32 | 18.40 | - | - | 3 | - |

**BOWLING AVERAGES**

| | Overs | Mdns | Runs | Wkts | Avge | Best | 5wI | 10wM |
|---|---|---|---|---|---|---|---|---|
| Other First-Class | 41 | 13 | 85 | 1 | 85.00 | 1-43 | - | - |
| ALL FIRST-CLASS | 41 | 13 | 85 | 1 | 85.00 | 1-43 | - | - |

| | | | | | | | | |
|---|---|---|---|---|---|---|---|---|
| NatWest Trophy | 12 | 2 | 34 | 1 | 34.00 | 1-34 | - | |
| Benson & Hedges Cup | 39 | 2 | 143 | 1 | 143.00 | 1-31 | - | |
| ALL ONE-DAY | 51 | 4 | 177 | 2 | 88.50 | 1-31 | - | |

## P.N.HEPWORTH - *Leicestershire*

| Opposition | Venue | Date | Batting | Fielding | Bowling |
|---|---|---|---|---|---|
| **BRITANNIC ASSURANCE** | | | | | |
| Glamorgan | Leicester | April 27 | 29 * | | |
| Notts | Trent Bridge | May 9 | 0 & 37 | 1Ct | 1-31 |
| Northants | Northampton | May 16 | 15 & 23 | | 0-2 |
| Notts | Leicester | May 25 | 21 & 56 | 2Ct | 1-8 |
| Essex | Ilford | June 4 | 12 & 7 | 1Ct | |
| Middlesex | Uxbridge | June 7 | 32 & 8 | | 0-20 |
| Surrey | Leicester | June 14 | 0 & 30 | 2Ct | |
| Lancashire | Leicester | June 18 | 0 * & 25 | 1Ct | |
| Glamorgan | Neath | June 21 | 21 | | |
| Worcestershire | Worcester | June 28 | 19 | | |
| Gloucs | Hinckley | July 2 | 35 | 1Ct | 1-19 |
| Sussex | Hove | July 19 | 7 & 56 | | 0-12 & 2-62 |
| Warwickshire | Leicester | July 26 | 15 & 32 | 1Ct | 0-18 |
| Somerset | Weston | Aug 2 | 30 & 4 | 1Ct | 0-11 & 0-5 |
| Yorkshire | Leicester | Aug 6 | 40 * | 1Ct | 2-29 |
| Kent | Leicester | Aug 9 | 8 | 2Ct | 0-13 |
| Hampshire | Bournemouth | Aug 16 | 4 & 43 * | | 0-1 & 0-20 |
| Derbyshire | Derby | Aug 20 | 18 | | |
| Derbyshire | Leicester | Aug 28 | 22 & 7 | 1Ct | 2-57 |
| Essex | Leicester | Sept 10 | 115 & 17 | 1Ct | 0-30 & 1-12 |
| Kent | Canterbury | Sept 17 | 97 & 30 | 2Ct | 0-3 & 3-51 |
| **OTHER FIRST-CLASS** | | | | | |
| Cambridge U | Fenner's | May 22 | 115 | 1Ct | 1-36 & 0-23 |
| West Indies | Leicester | June 1 | 68 & 21 | 1Ct | |
| **REFUGE ASSURANCE** | | | | | |
| Glamorgan | Leicester | April 28 | 5 | | |
| Northants | Northampton | May 12 | 17 * | | 1-26 |
| Yorkshire | Leicester | May 19 | | | |
| Notts | Leicester | May 26 | 0 | | 2-33 |
| Middlesex | Uxbridge | June 9 | 1 | 1Ct | |
| Sussex | Hove | July 21 | 2 | | 2-43 |
| Somerset | Weston | Aug 4 | | | |
| Gloucs | Leicester | Aug 25 | 31 | | 1-38 |
| **BENSON & HEDGES CUP** | | | | | |
| Sussex | Hove | April 25 | 33 | | |
| Scotland | Leicester | May 2 | | | 4-39 |
| Lancashire | Leicester | May 4 | 9 | 1Ct | 1-44 |
| **OTHER ONE-DAY** | | | | | |
| For Yorkshiremen | | | | | |
| Yorkshire | Scarborough | Sept 7 | 1 | | |

**BATTING AVERAGES - Including fielding**

| | Matches | Inns | NO | Runs | HS | Avge | 100s | 50s | Ct | St |
|---|---|---|---|---|---|---|---|---|---|---|
| Britannic Assurance | 21 | 35 | 4 | 915 | 115 | 29.51 | 1 | 3 | 17 | - |
| Other First-Class | 2 | 3 | 0 | 204 | 115 | 68.00 | 1 | 1 | 2 | - |
| ALL FIRST-CLASS | 23 | 38 | 4 | 1119 | 115 | 32.91 | 2 | 4 | 19 | - |
| Refuge Assurance | 8 | 6 | 1 | 56 | 31 | 11.20 | - | - | 1 | - |
| Benson & Hedges Cup | 3 | 2 | 0 | 42 | 33 | 21.00 | - | - | 1 | - |
| Other One-Day | 1 | 1 | 0 | 1 | 1 | 1.00 | - | - | - | - |
| ALL ONE-DAY | 12 | 9 | 1 | 99 | 33 | 12.37 | - | - | 2 | - |

**BOWLING AVERAGES**

| | Overs | Mdns | Runs | Wkts | Avge | Best | 5wI | 10wM |
|---|---|---|---|---|---|---|---|---|
| Britannic Assurance | 102.2 | 20 | 404 | 13 | 31.07 | 3-51 | - | - |
| Other First-Class | 17 | 0 | 59 | 1 | 59.00 | 1-36 | - | - |
| ALL FIRST-CLASS | 119.2 | 20 | 463 | 14 | 33.07 | 3-51 | - | - |
| Refuge Assurance | 27 | 1 | 140 | 6 | 23.33 | 2-33 | - | |
| Benson & Hedges Cup | 20 | 2 | 83 | 5 | 16.60 | 4-39 | - | |
| Other One-Day | | | | | | | | |
| ALL ONE-DAY | 47 | 3 | 223 | 11 | 20.27 | 4-39 | - | |

| H | PLAYER RECORDS |
|---|---|

## P.A.W.HESELTINE - *Durham*

| Opposition | Venue | Date | Batting | Fielding | Bowling |
|---|---|---|---|---|---|
| **NATWEST TROPHY** | | | | | |
| Glamorgan | Darlington | June 26 | 5* | | 1-37 |
| **OTHER ONE-DAY** | | | | | |
| Leicestershire | Harrogate | June 11 | | | |
| Surrey | Harrogate | June 13 | 2 | | 0-57 |

**BATTING AVERAGES - Including fielding**

| | Matches | Inns | NO | Runs | HS | Avge | 100s | 50s | Ct | St |
|---|---|---|---|---|---|---|---|---|---|---|
| NatWest Trophy | 1 | 1 | 1 | 5 | 5* | - | - | - | - | - |
| Other One-Day | 2 | 1 | 0 | 2 | 2 | 2.00 | - | - | - | - |
| ALL ONE-DAY | 3 | 2 | 1 | 7 | 5* | 7.00 | - | - | - | - |

**BOWLING AVERAGES**

| | Overs | Mdns | Runs | Wkts | Avge | Best | 5wI | 10wM |
|---|---|---|---|---|---|---|---|---|
| NatWest Trophy | 12 | 1 | 37 | 1 | 37.00 | 1-37 | - | |
| Other One-Day | 7 | 0 | 57 | 0 | - | - | - | |
| ALL ONE-DAY | 19 | 1 | 94 | 1 | 94.00 | 1-37 | - | |

## P.J.HESELTINE - *Lincolnshire*

| Opposition | Venue | Date | Batting | Fielding | Bowling |
|---|---|---|---|---|---|
| **NATWEST TROPHY** | | | | | |
| Notts | Trent Bridge | June 26 | 2 | | |

**BATTING AVERAGES - Including fielding**

| | Matches | Inns | NO | Runs | HS | Avge | 100s | 50s | Ct | St |
|---|---|---|---|---|---|---|---|---|---|---|
| NatWest Trophy | 1 | 1 | 0 | 2 | 2 | 2.00 | - | - | - | - |
| ALL ONE-DAY | 1 | 1 | 0 | 2 | 2 | 2.00 | - | - | - | - |

**BOWLING AVERAGES**
Did not bowl

## G.A.HICK - *Worcestershire & England*

| Opposition | Venue | Date | Batting | Fielding | Bowling |
|---|---|---|---|---|---|
| **CORNHILL TEST MATCHES** | | | | | |
| West Indies | Headingley | June 6 | 6 & 6 | 2Ct | |
| West Indies | Lord's | June 20 | | 1Ct | 2-77 |
| West Indies | Trent Bridge | July 4 | 43 & 0 | 1Ct | 0-18 |
| West Indies | Edgbaston | July 25 | 19 & 1 | 4Ct | 0-0 |
| **BRITANNIC ASSURANCE** | | | | | |
| Gloucs | Worcester | April 27 | 14 | 1Ct | 0-10 |
| Lancashire | Worcester | May 9 | 57 & 0 | 3Ct | |
| Glamorgan | Worcester | May 31 | 50 & 0 | 1Ct | |
| Sussex | Hove | June 14 | 186 & 28* | 1Ct | 0-8 |
| Leicestershire | Worcester | June 28 | 0 & 24 | | 0-10 |
| Hampshire | Portsmouth | July 16 | 15 & 141 | 1Ct | 1-85 |
| Derbyshire | Kidd'minster | July 19 | 24 & 3 | 1Ct | |
| Warwickshire | Worcester | Aug 2 | 4 | 1Ct | |
| Somerset | Weston | Aug 6 | 10 & 24 | 2Ct | 0-0 |
| Surrey | Worcester | Aug 16 | 145 & 85 | | 0-30 |
| Lancashire | Blackpool | Aug 20 | 12 & 15* | 1Ct | 1-33 & 0-47 |
| Middlesex | Worcester | Aug 23 | 30 | | 1-33 |
| Warwickshire | Edgbaston | Aug 28 | 0 & 13 | 1Ct | |
| Somerset | Worcester | Sept 3 | 11 | 3Ct | 0-42 |
| Glamorgan | Cardiff | Sept 10 | 4 | | 5-42 |
| Notts | Trent Bridge | Sept 17 | 17 & 63 | | 0-39 |
| **OTHER FIRST-CLASS** | | | | | |
| For MCC | | | | | |
| Middlesex | Lord's | April 16 | 58 | 1Ct | 0-18 |
| For Worcestershire | | | | | |
| West Indies | Worcester | May 15 | 11 | | |

| Opposition | Venue | Date | Batting | Fielding | Bowling |
|---|---|---|---|---|---|
| **TEXACO TROPHY** | | | | | |
| West Indies | Edgbaston | May 23 | 14 | | |
| West Indies | Old Trafford | May 25 | 29 | | |
| West Indies | Lord's | May 27 | 86* | | |
| **REFUGE ASSURANCE** | | | | | |
| Kent | Worcester | April 21 | 8 | 1Ct | |
| Gloucs | Bristol | May 5 | | | |
| Lancashire | Worcester | May 12 | 5 | | 2-42 |
| Northants | Northampton | May 19 | 47 | | 0-17 |
| Sussex | Hove | June 16 | | | 1-5 |
| Leicestershire | Worcester | June 30 | 84 | | 0-19 |
| Glamorgan | Worcester | July 21 | 34* | | |
| Notts | Trent Bridge | Aug 4 | 109 | 1Ct | |
| Somerset | Worcester | Aug 18 | 11 | | |
| Middlesex | Worcester | Aug 25 | 65 | | 1-20 |
| Notts | Trent Bridge | Sept 1 | 33 | | 5-35 |
| Lancashire | Old Trafford | Sept 15 | 37 | 1Ct | |
| **NATWEST TROPHY** | | | | | |
| Bedfordshire | Bedford | June 26 | 0 | 1Ct | 0-11 |
| Glamorgan | Worcester | July 11 | 10 | | |
| **BENSON & HEDGES CUP** | | | | | |
| Gloucs | Worcester | April 25 | 56 | 3Ct | |
| Combined U | Fenner's | May 2 | 55 | | |
| Derbyshire | Worcester | May 4 | 6 | 1Ct | |
| Northants | Northampton | May 7 | 4 | | |
| Kent | Worcester | May 29 | 84* | 1Ct | |
| Essex | Chelmsford | June 12 | 4* | | |
| Lancashire | Lord's | July 13 | 88 | 3Ct | |
| **OTHER ONE-DAY** | | | | | |
| For England A | | | | | |
| Sri Lanka | Old Trafford | Aug 14 | 5 | | 2-18 |
| Sri Lanka | Old Trafford | Aug 15 | 1 | | 1-38 |

**BATTING AVERAGES - Including fielding**

| | Matches | Inns | NO | Runs | HS | Avge | 100s | 50s | Ct | St |
|---|---|---|---|---|---|---|---|---|---|---|
| Cornhill Test Matches | 4 | 7 | 0 | 75 | 43 | 10.71 | - | - | 8 | - |
| Britannic Assurance | 16 | 27 | 2 | 975 | 186 | 39.00 | 3 | 4 | 16 | - |
| Other First-Class | 2 | 2 | 0 | 69 | 58 | 34.50 | - | 1 | 1 | - |
| ALL FIRST-CLASS | 22 | 36 | 2 | 1119 | 186 | 32.91 | 3 | 5 | 25 | - |
| Texaco Trophy | 3 | 3 | 1 | 129 | 86* | 64.50 | - | 1 | - | - |
| Refuge Assurance | 12 | 10 | 1 | 433 | 109 | 48.11 | 1 | 2 | 3 | - |
| NatWest Trophy | 2 | 2 | 0 | 10 | 10 | 5.00 | - | - | 1 | - |
| Benson & Hedges Cup | 7 | 7 | 2 | 297 | 88 | 59.40 | - | 4 | 8 | - |
| Other One-Day | 2 | 2 | 0 | 6 | 5 | 3.00 | - | - | - | - |
| ALL ONE-DAY | 26 | 24 | 4 | 875 | 109 | 43.75 | 1 | 7 | 12 | - |

**BOWLING AVERAGES**

| | Overs | Mdns | Runs | Wkts | Avge | Best | 5wI | 10wM |
|---|---|---|---|---|---|---|---|---|
| Cornhill Test Matches | 24 | 5 | 95 | 2 | 47.50 | 2-77 | - | - |
| Britannic Assurance | 123.4 | 29 | 379 | 8 | 47.37 | 5-42 | 1 | - |
| Other First-Class | 4 | 0 | 18 | 0 | - | - | - | - |
| ALL FIRST-CLASS | 151.4 | 34 | 492 | 10 | 49.20 | 5-42 | 1 | - |
| Texaco Trophy | | | | | | | | |
| Refuge Assurance | 27.2 | 1 | 138 | 9 | 15.33 | 5-35 | 1 | |
| NatWest Trophy | 5 | 2 | 11 | 0 | | | | |
| Benson & Hedges Cup | | | | | | | | |
| Other One-Day | 13 | 1 | 56 | 3 | 18.66 | 2-18 | - | |
| ALL ONE-DAY | 45.2 | 4 | 205 | 12 | 17.08 | 5-35 | 1 | |

## S.G.HINKS - *Kent*

| Opposition | Venue | Date | Batting | Fielding | Bowling |
|---|---|---|---|---|---|
| **BRITANNIC ASSURANCE** | | | | | |
| Essex | Folkestone | May 16 | 6 & 40 | 1Ct | |
| Notts | Trent Bridge | May 22 | 61* | | |
| Northants | Maidstone | July 2 | 1 & 7 | 1Ct | |
| Glamorgan | Maidstone | July 5 | 5 & 55* | 1Ct | |
| Essex | Southend | July 16 | 8 | | |
| Worcestershire | Worcester | July 23 | | 1Ct | |
| Somerset | Taunton | July 26 | 39 & 0 | | |
| Surrey | Canterbury | Aug 2 | 5 & 9 | 2Ct | |

# PLAYER RECORDS

# H

## OTHER FIRST-CLASS

| | | | | | |
|---|---|---|---|---|---|
| West Indies | Canterbury | July 20 | 8 | & | 31 |

## REFUGE ASSURANCE

| | | | |
|---|---|---|---|
| Essex | Folkestone | May 19 | 25 |
| Leicestershire | Canterbury | July 14 | 35 |
| Somerset | Taunton | July 28 | 11 |
| Surrey | Canterbury | Aug 4 | 18 |
| Notts | Trent Bridge | Aug 11 | 10 | 1Ct |

## NATWEST TROPHY

| | | | |
|---|---|---|---|
| Surrey | The Oval | July 11 | 34 |

## BATTING AVERAGES - Including fielding

| | Matches | Inns | NO | Runs | HS | Avge | 100s | 50s | Ct | St |
|---|---|---|---|---|---|---|---|---|---|---|
| Britannic Assurance | 8 | 12 | 2 | 236 | 61 * | 23.60 | - | 2 | 6 | - |
| Other First-Class | 1 | 2 | 0 | 39 | 31 | 19.50 | - | - | - | - |
| ALL FIRST-CLASS | 9 | 14 | 2 | 275 | 61 * | 22.91 | - | 2 | 6 | - |
| Refuge Assurance | 5 | 5 | 0 | 99 | 35 | 19.80 | - | - | 1 | - |
| NatWest Trophy | 1 | 1 | 0 | 34 | 34 | 34.00 | - | - | - | - |
| ALL ONE-DAY | 6 | 6 | 0 | 133 | 35 | 22.16 | - | - | 1 | - |

## BOWLING AVERAGES
Did not bowl

## P.D.B.HOARE - *Bedfordshire*

| Opposition | Venue | Date | Batting | Fielding | Bowling |
|---|---|---|---|---|---|

### NATWEST TROPHY

| | | | |
|---|---|---|---|
| Worcestershire | Bedford | June 26 | 0 |

### BATTING AVERAGES - Including fielding

| | Matches | Inns | NO | Runs | HS | Avge | 100s | 50s | Ct | St |
|---|---|---|---|---|---|---|---|---|---|---|
| NatWest Trophy | 1 | 1 | 0 | 0 | 0 | 0.00 | - | - | - | - |
| ALL ONE-DAY | 1 | 1 | 0 | 0 | 0 | 0.00 | - | - | - | - |

### BOWLING AVERAGES
Did not bowl

## G.D.HODGSON - *Gloucestershire*

| Opposition | Venue | Date | Batting | Fielding | Bowling |
|---|---|---|---|---|---|

### BRITANNIC ASSURANCE

| | | | | | | |
|---|---|---|---|---|---|---|
| Worcestershire | Worcester | April 27 | 65 | | | |
| Hampshire | Bristol | May 9 | 26 | & | 8 | |
| Yorkshire | Sheffield | May 22 | 54 | & | 20 | 1Ct |
| Warwickshire | Edgbaston | May 25 | 27 | & | 16 | |
| Essex | Bristol | May 31 | 3 | & | 40 | |
| Middlesex | Bristol | June 4 | 16 | & | 15 * | 1Ct |
| Hampshire | Southampton | June 7 | 89 | | | 1Ct |
| Notts | Gloucester | June 14 | 11 | & | 57 | |
| Derbyshire | Gloucester | June 18 | 12 | & | 22 | |
| Somerset | Bath | June 21 | 30 | | | |
| Northants | Luton | June 28 | 1 | & | 60 | |
| Leicestershire | Hinckley | July 2 | 7 | | | 1Ct |
| Surrey | Guildford | July 16 | 34 | & | 21 | |
| Glamorgan | Cheltenham | July 19 | 29 | & | 0 | 2Ct |
| Sussex | Cheltenham | July 23 | 46 | | | 1Ct |
| Worcestershire | Cheltenham | July 26 | 12 | & | 71 | |
| Kent | Canterbury | Aug 20 | 60 | & | 26 | |
| Glamorgan | Abergavenny | Aug 28 | 38 | & | 4 | |
| Northants | Bristol | Sept 3 | 15 | & | 1 | |
| Somerset | Bristol | Sept 10 | 29 | & | 6 | |
| Sussex | Hove | Sept 17 | 3 | & | 16 | |

### OTHER FIRST-CLASS

| | | | | | |
|---|---|---|---|---|---|
| Oxford U | The Parks | June 15 | 105 | | 1Ct |
| West Indies | Bristol | July 31 | 6 * | | |

### NATWEST TROPHY

| | | | | |
|---|---|---|---|---|
| Norfolk | Bristol | June 26 | 7 | 1Ct |

## BENSON & HEDGES CUP

| | | | | |
|---|---|---|---|---|
| Combined U | Bristol | April 23 | 7 | |
| Worcestershire | Worcester | April 25 | 9 | 1Ct |
| Northants | Bristol | May 2 | 3 | |

### BATTING AVERAGES - Including fielding

| | Matches | Inns | NO | Runs | HS | Avge | 100s | 50s | Ct | St |
|---|---|---|---|---|---|---|---|---|---|---|
| Britannic Assurance | 21 | 37 | 1 | 990 | 89 | 27.50 | - | 7 | 7 | - |
| Other First-Class | 2 | 2 | 1 | 111 | 105 | 111.00 | 1 | - | 1 | - |
| ALL FIRST-CLASS | 23 | 39 | 2 | 1101 | 105 | 29.75 | 1 | 7 | 8 | - |
| NatWest Trophy | 1 | 1 | 0 | 7 | 7 | 7.00 | - | - | 1 | - |
| Benson & Hedges Cup | 3 | 3 | 0 | 19 | 9 | 6.33 | - | - | 1 | - |
| ALL ONE-DAY | 4 | 4 | 0 | 26 | 9 | 6.50 | - | - | 2 | - |

### BOWLING AVERAGES
Did not bowl

## C.HOEY - *Ireland*

| Opposition | Venue | Date | Batting | Fielding | Bowling |
|---|---|---|---|---|---|

### OTHER FIRST-CLASS

| | | | | | |
|---|---|---|---|---|---|
| Scotland | Dublin | June 22 | | 1 * | 0-47 & 3-38 |

### NATWEST TROPHY

| | | | | | |
|---|---|---|---|---|---|
| Middlesex | Dublin | June 26 | | 26 * | 0-33 |

### OTHER ONE-DAY

| | | | | |
|---|---|---|---|---|
| West Indies | Downpatrick | July 13 | | 2-63 |

### BATTING AVERAGES - Including fielding

| | Matches | Inns | NO | Runs | HS | Avge | 100s | 50s | Ct | St |
|---|---|---|---|---|---|---|---|---|---|---|
| Other First-Class | 1 | 1 | 1 | 1 | 1 * | - | - | - | - | - |
| ALL FIRST-CLASS | 1 | 1 | 1 | 1 | 1 * | - | - | - | - | - |
| NatWest Trophy | 1 | 1 | 1 | 26 | 26 * | - | - | - | 1 | - |
| Other One-Day | 1 | 0 | 0 | 0 | 0 | - | - | - | - | - |
| ALL ONE-DAY | 2 | 1 | 1 | 26 | 26 * | - | - | - | 1 | - |

### BOWLING AVERAGES

| | Overs | Mdns | Runs | Wkts | Avge | Best | 5wI | 10wM |
|---|---|---|---|---|---|---|---|---|
| Other First-Class | 25.2 | 7 | 85 | 3 | 28.33 | 3-38 | - | - |
| ALL FIRST-CLASS | 25.2 | 7 | 85 | 3 | 28.33 | 3-38 | - | - |
| NatWest Trophy | 12 | 3 | 33 | 0 | | | - | |
| Other One-Day | 12 | 1 | 63 | 2 | 31.50 | 2-63 | - | |
| ALL ONE-DAY | 24 | 4 | 96 | 2 | 48.00 | 2-63 | - | |

## P.C.L.HOLLOWAY - *Warwickshire & Combined Universities*

| Opposition | Venue | Date | Batting | Fielding | Bowling |
|---|---|---|---|---|---|

### BRITANNIC ASSURANCE

| | | | | | | |
|---|---|---|---|---|---|---|
| Lancashire | Old Trafford | July 23 | 26 * | | | 1Ct |
| Leicestershire | Leicester | July 26 | 89 * | | | 4Ct |
| Worcestershire | Worcester | Aug 2 | 16 | & | 41 | 1Ct |
| Northants | Northampton | Aug 9 | 74 * | | | 1Ct |
| Glamorgan | Edgbaston | Aug 20 | 4 * | & | 0 | |
| Worcestershire | Edgbaston | Aug 28 | 6 | & | 7 * | 2Ct |

### REFUGE ASSURANCE

| | | | |
|---|---|---|---|
| Sussex | Edgbaston | April 21 | |
| Essex | Chelmsford | July 7 | 8 |
| Derbyshire | Edgbaston | Aug 4 | | 1Ct |
| Leicestershire | Leicester | Aug 11 | 25 * | 1Ct |
| Northants | Northampton | Aug 25 | 34 * |

### NATWEST TROPHY

| | | | | |
|---|---|---|---|---|
| Somerset | Edgbaston | July 31 | 2 | 2Ct,1St |

# H — PLAYER RECORDS

## BENSON & HEDGES CUP
For Combined Universities

| | | | | |
|---|---|---|---|---|
| Gloucs | Bristol | April 23 | 0 | 3Ct |
| Derbyshire | The Parks | April 25 | 27 | |
| Worcestershire | Fenner's | May 2 | 22 | |
| Northants | Northampton | May 4 | 10 | 1Ct |

### BATTING AVERAGES - Including fielding

| | Matches | Inns | NO | Runs | HS | Avge | 100s | 50s | Ct | St |
|---|---|---|---|---|---|---|---|---|---|---|
| Britannic Assurance | 6 | 9 | 5 | 263 | 89* | 65.75 | - | 2 | 9 | - |
| ALL FIRST-CLASS | 6 | 9 | 5 | 263 | 89* | 65.75 | - | 2 | 9 | - |
| Refuge Assurance | 5 | 3 | 2 | 67 | 34* | 67.00 | - | - | 2 | - |
| NatWest Trophy | 1 | 1 | 0 | 2 | 2 | 2.00 | - | - | 2 | 1 |
| Benson & Hedges Cup | 4 | 4 | 0 | 59 | 27 | 14.75 | - | - | 4 | - |
| ALL ONE-DAY | 10 | 8 | 2 | 128 | 34* | 21.33 | - | - | 8 | 1 |

### BOWLING AVERAGES
Did not bowl

## B.L.HOLMES - *League CC XI*

| Opposition | Venue | Date | Batting | Fielding | Bowling |
|---|---|---|---|---|---|
| **OTHER ONE-DAY** | | | | | |
| West Indies | Trowbridge | June 28 | | | 1-35 |

### BATTING AVERAGES - Including fielding

| | Matches | Inns | NO | Runs | HS | Avge | 100s | 50s | Ct | St |
|---|---|---|---|---|---|---|---|---|---|---|
| Other One-Day | 1 | 0 | 0 | 0 | 0 | - | - | - | - | - |
| ALL ONE-DAY | 1 | 0 | 0 | 0 | 0 | - | - | - | - | - |

### BOWLING AVERAGES

| | Overs | Mdns | Runs | Wkts | Avge | Best | 5wI | 10wM |
|---|---|---|---|---|---|---|---|---|
| Other One-Day | 7 | 0 | 35 | 1 | 35.00 | 1-35 | - | |
| ALL ONE-DAY | 7 | 0 | 35 | 1 | 35.00 | 1-35 | - | |

## G.C.HOLMES - *Glamorgan*

| Opposition | Venue | Date | Batting | Fielding | Bowling |
|---|---|---|---|---|---|
| **BRITANNIC ASSURANCE** | | | | | |
| Leicestershire | Leicester | April 27 | 18 | | |
| Somerset | Taunton | May 9 | 2 & 25* | | |
| Warwickshire | Swansea | May 16 | 54 & 1 | 1Ct | |
| Northants | Cardiff | May 22 | 21 | | |
| Sussex | Cardiff | May 25 | 0 | | |
| Worcestershire | Worcester | May 31 | 15 | | |
| **OTHER FIRST-CLASS** | | | | | |
| Oxford U | The Parks | April 17 | | | |
| **REFUGE ASSURANCE** | | | | | |
| Northants | Cardiff | April 21 | 13* | | 0-24 |
| Leicestershire | Leicester | April 28 | 72 | | |
| Notts | Cardiff | May 5 | | | |
| Somerset | Taunton | May 12 | 33 | | |
| Warwickshire | Swansea | May 19 | 46 | | |
| Sussex | Swansea | May 26 | 5 | 2Ct | |
| Lancashire | Old Trafford | June 9 | 50* | | |
| Middlesex | Cardiff | June 16 | 15 | 1Ct | |
| Yorkshire | Headingley | June 30 | 6 | | |
| **BENSON & HEDGES CUP** | | | | | |
| Min Counties | Trowbridge | April 23 | 34 | | |
| Hampshire | Southampton | May 2 | 1 | | |
| Notts | Cardiff | May 4 | 22 | | |
| Yorkshire | Cardiff | May 7 | 35* | | |

### BATTING AVERAGES - Including fielding

| | Matches | Inns | NO | Runs | HS | Avge | 100s | 50s | Ct | St |
|---|---|---|---|---|---|---|---|---|---|---|
| Britannic Assurance | 6 | 8 | 1 | 136 | 54 | 19.42 | - | 1 | 1 | - |
| Other First-Class | 1 | 0 | 0 | 0 | 0 | - | - | - | - | - |
| ALL FIRST-CLASS | 7 | 8 | 1 | 136 | 54 | 19.42 | - | 1 | 1 | - |
| Refuge Assurance | 9 | 8 | 2 | 240 | 72 | 40.00 | - | 2 | 3 | - |
| Benson & Hedges Cup | 4 | 4 | 1 | 92 | 35* | 30.66 | - | - | - | - |
| ALL ONE-DAY | 13 | 12 | 3 | 332 | 72 | 36.88 | - | 2 | 3 | - |

### BOWLING AVERAGES

| | Overs | Mdns | Runs | Wkts | Avge | Best | 5wI | 10wM |
|---|---|---|---|---|---|---|---|---|
| Britannic Assurance | | | | | | | | |
| Other First-Class | | | | | | | | |
| ALL FIRST-CLASS | | | | | | | | |
| Refuge Assurance | 1.5 | 0 | 24 | 0 | - | - | - | |
| Benson & Hedges Cup | | | | | | | | |
| ALL ONE-DAY | 1.5 | 0 | 24 | 0 | - | - | - | |

## A.M.HOOPER - *Cambridge University*

| Opposition | Venue | Date | Batting | Fielding | Bowling |
|---|---|---|---|---|---|
| **OTHER FIRST-CLASS** | | | | | |
| Derbyshire | Fenner's | May 9 | 21 & 48* | | 1-35 & 0-15 |
| Middlesex | Fenner's | May 15 | 2 & 0 | | 0-28 & 0-16 |
| Surrey | Fenner's | May 18 | 47 & 125 | | 0-14 |
| Leicestershire | Fenner's | May 22 | 10 & 92 | | 0-32 |
| Glamorgan | Fenner's | June 18 | 14 | | 1-30 |
| Sussex | Hove | June 29 | 6 | | 0-17 |
| Oxford U | Lord's | July 2 | 89 & 4 | | |

### BATTING AVERAGES - Including fielding

| | Matches | Inns | NO | Runs | HS | Avge | 100s | 50s | Ct | St |
|---|---|---|---|---|---|---|---|---|---|---|
| Other First-Class | 7 | 12 | 1 | 458 | 125 | 41.63 | 1 | 2 | - | - |
| ALL FIRST-CLASS | 7 | 12 | 1 | 458 | 125 | 41.63 | 1 | 2 | - | - |

### BOWLING AVERAGES

| | Overs | Mdns | Runs | Wkts | Avge | Best | 5wI | 10wM |
|---|---|---|---|---|---|---|---|---|
| Other First-Class | 43 | 6 | 187 | 2 | 93.50 | 1-30 | - | - |
| ALL FIRST-CLASS | 43 | 6 | 187 | 2 | 93.50 | 1-30 | - | - |

## C.L.HOOPER - *West Indies*

| Opposition | Venue | Date | Batting | Fielding | Bowling |
|---|---|---|---|---|---|
| **CORNHILL TEST MATCHES** | | | | | |
| England | Headingley | June 6 | 0 & 5 | 4Ct | 0-11 |
| England | Lord's | June 20 | 111 & 1* | | 1-10 |
| England | Trent Bridge | July 4 | 11 | 2Ct | 0-10 |
| England | Edgbaston | July 25 | 31 & 55* | 1Ct | 0-2 & 0-26 |
| England | The Oval | Aug 8 | 3 & 54 | 2Ct | 1-78 |
| **OTHER FIRST-CLASS** | | | | | |
| Worcestershire | Worcester | May 15 | 42 | 1Ct | |
| Middlesex | Lord's | May 18 | 42 & 16 | 1Ct | 1-12 |
| Somerset | Taunton | May 29 | 123 & 48* | 1Ct | 1-38 & 3-27 |
| Derbyshire | Derby | June 12 | 82 & 95* | | 3-50 & 4-49 |
| Northants | Northampton | June 15 | 49* | | |
| Hampshire | Southampton | June 29 | 196 | 2Ct | 2-36 & 0-28 |
| Glamorgan | Swansea | July 16 | 80 | 1Ct | 1-36 & 0-22 |
| Kent | Canterbury | July 20 | 61*& 54* | 1Ct | 0-19 & 1-46 |
| Gloucs | Bristol | July 31 | 111* | 1Ct | 3-55 & 3-43 |
| Essex | Chelmsford | Aug 3 | 12 | 2Ct | 2-33 & 0-47 |
| World XI | Scarborough | Aug 28 | 164*& 55 | 1Ct | 5-94 & 0-47 |
| **TEXACO TROPHY** | | | | | |
| England | Edgbaston | May 23 | 10 | | 2-18 |
| England | Old Trafford | May 25 | 48 | | 1-44 |
| England | Lord's | May 27 | 26 | | 0-36 |
| **OTHER ONE-DAY** | | | | | |
| D of Norfolk | Arundel | May 12 | 1 | 1Ct | 2-13 |
| Gloucs | Bristol | May 14 | 22* | 1Ct | 3-36 |
| League CC XI | Trowbridge | June 28 | | 1Ct | 0-22 |

# PLAYER RECORDS

| | | | | | |
|---|---|---|---|---|---|
| Ireland | Downpatrick | July 13 | 26 * | | 2-52 |
| Wales | Brecon | July 15 | 88 | | 1-27 |
| For World XI | | | | | |
| Yorkshire | Scarborough | Sept 8 | 30 | | 3-12 |

### BATTING AVERAGES - Including fielding

| | Matches | Inns | NO | Runs | HS | Avge | 100s | 50s | Ct | St |
|---|---|---|---|---|---|---|---|---|---|---|
| Cornhill Test Matches | 5 | 9 | 2 | 271 | 111 | 38.71 | 1 | 2 | 9 | - |
| Other First-Class | 11 | 16 | 7 | 1230 | 196 | 136.66 | 4 | 6 | 11 | - |
| ALL FIRST-CLASS | 16 | 25 | 9 | 1501 | 196 | 93.81 | 5 | 8 | 20 | - |
| Texaco Trophy | 3 | 3 | 0 | 84 | 48 | 28.00 | - | - | - | - |
| Other One-Day | 6 | 5 | 2 | 167 | 88 | 55.66 | - | 1 | 3 | - |
| ALL ONE-DAY | 9 | 8 | 2 | 251 | 88 | 41.83 | - | 1 | 3 | - |

### BOWLING AVERAGES

| | Overs | Mdns | Runs | Wkts | Avge | Best | 5wI | 10wM |
|---|---|---|---|---|---|---|---|---|
| Cornhill Test Matches | 64 | 13 | 137 | 2 | 68.50 | 1-10 | - | - |
| Other First-Class | 272.2 | 58 | 700 | 29 | 24.13 | 5-94 | 1 | - |
| ALL FIRST-CLASS | 336.2 | 71 | 837 | 31 | 27.00 | 5-94 | 1 | - |
| Texaco Trophy | 15.5 | 0 | 98 | 3 | 32.66 | 2-18 | - | |
| Other One-Day | 60 | 14 | 162 | 11 | 14.72 | 3-12 | - | |
| ALL ONE-DAY | 75.5 | 14 | 260 | 14 | 18.57 | 3-12 | - | |

## I.J.HOUSEMAN - *Yorkshire*

| Opposition | Venue | Date | Batting | Fielding | Bowling |
|---|---|---|---|---|---|
| **OTHER FIRST-CLASS** | | | | | |
| Sri Lanka | Headingley | July 27 | | | 1-52 |

### BATTING AVERAGES - Including fielding

| | Matches | Inns | NO | Runs | HS | Avge | 100s | 50s | Ct | St |
|---|---|---|---|---|---|---|---|---|---|---|
| Other First-Class | 1 | 0 | 0 | 0 | 0 | - | - | - | - | - |
| ALL FIRST-CLASS | 1 | 0 | 0 | 0 | 0 | - | - | - | - | - |

### BOWLING AVERAGES

| | Overs | Mdns | Runs | Wkts | Avge | Best | 5wI | 10wM |
|---|---|---|---|---|---|---|---|---|
| Other First-Class | 21 | 4 | 52 | 1 | 52.00 | 1-52 | - | - |
| ALL FIRST-CLASS | 21 | 4 | 52 | 1 | 52.00 | 1-52 | - | - |

## D.P.HUGHES - *Lancashire*

| Opposition | Venue | Date | Batting | | | Fielding | Bowling |
|---|---|---|---|---|---|---|---|
| **BRITANNIC ASSURANCE** | | | | | | | |
| Surrey | The Oval | May 22 | 20 * & | 5 | | 2Ct | 1-16 |
| Sussex | Old Trafford | May 31 | 1 | | | 1Ct | |
| Hampshire | Basingstoke | June 4 | 4 | | | | |
| Leicestershire | Leicester | June 18 | 51 | | | 1Ct | |
| Kent | Old Trafford | June 21 | 25 * | | | | |
| Somerset | Taunton | July 2 | | | | | 1-86 & 1-90 |
| Notts | Trent Bridge | July 16 | 1 * & | 4 | | | 0-28 |
| Middlesex | Uxbridge | July 19 | 0 | | | | 2-7 & 0-18 |
| **REFUGE ASSURANCE** | | | | | | | |
| Derbyshire | Derby | May 19 | | | | 2Ct | |
| Sussex | Old Trafford | June 2 | | | | 1Ct | |
| Glamorgan | Old Trafford | June 9 | | | | | |
| Warwickshire | Edgbaston | June 16 | | | | | 0-33 |
| Kent | Old Trafford | June 23 | | | | | |
| Middlesex | Lord's | July 21 | 4 * | | | | |
| **NATWEST TROPHY** | | | | | | | |
| Dorset | Bournemouth | June 26 | | | | 3Ct | |
| Hampshire | Southampton | July 11 | 5 * | | | | 0-5 |
| **BENSON & HEDGES CUP** | | | | | | | |
| Northants | Old Trafford | May 29 | | | | 1Ct | |
| Yorkshire | Old Trafford | June 16 | 1 * | | | | |

### BATTING AVERAGES - Including fielding

| | Matches | Inns | NO | Runs | HS | Avge | 100s | 50s | Ct | St |
|---|---|---|---|---|---|---|---|---|---|---|
| Britannic Assurance | 8 | 9 | 3 | 111 | 51 | 18.50 | - | 1 | 4 | - |
| ALL FIRST-CLASS | 8 | 9 | 3 | 111 | 51 | 18.50 | - | 1 | 4 | - |
| Refuge Assurance | 6 | 1 | 1 | 4 | 4 * | - | - | - | 3 | - |
| NatWest Trophy | 2 | 1 | 1 | 5 | 5 * | - | - | - | 3 | - |
| Benson & Hedges Cup | 2 | 1 | 1 | 1 | 1 * | - | - | - | 1 | - |
| ALL ONE-DAY | 10 | 3 | 3 | 10 | 5 * | - | - | - | 7 | - |

### BOWLING AVERAGES

| | Overs | Mdns | Runs | Wkts | Avge | Best | 5wI | 10wM |
|---|---|---|---|---|---|---|---|---|
| Britannic Assurance | 85.2 | 21 | 245 | 5 | 49.00 | 2-7 | - | - |
| ALL FIRST-CLASS | 85.2 | 21 | 245 | 5 | 49.00 | 2-7 | - | - |
| Refuge Assurance | 6 | 0 | 33 | 0 | | - | - | - |
| NatWest Trophy | 0.5 | 0 | 5 | 0 | | - | - | - |
| Benson & Hedges Cup | | | | | | | | |
| ALL ONE-DAY | 6.5 | 0 | 38 | 0 | | - | - | - |

## J.G.HUGHES - *Northamptonshire*

| Opposition | Venue | Date | Batting | Fielding | Bowling |
|---|---|---|---|---|---|
| **BRITANNIC ASSURANCE** | | | | | |
| Yorkshire | Headingley | May 25 | | | 1-43 |

### BATTING AVERAGES - Including fielding

| | Matches | Inns | NO | Runs | HS | Avge | 100s | 50s | Ct | St |
|---|---|---|---|---|---|---|---|---|---|---|
| Britannic Assurance | 1 | 0 | 0 | 0 | 0 | - | - | - | - | - |
| ALL FIRST-CLASS | 1 | 0 | 0 | 0 | 0 | - | - | - | - | - |

### BOWLING AVERAGES

| | Overs | Mdns | Runs | Wkts | Avge | Best | 5wI | 10wM |
|---|---|---|---|---|---|---|---|---|
| Britannic Assurance | 12 | 1 | 43 | 1 | 43.00 | 1-43 | - | - |
| ALL FIRST-CLASS | 12 | 1 | 43 | 1 | 43.00 | 1-43 | - | - |

## M.G.HUGHES - *Victoria*

| Opposition | Venue | Date | Batting | | | Fielding | Bowling |
|---|---|---|---|---|---|---|---|
| **OTHER FIRST-CLASS** | | | | | | | |
| Essex | Chelmsford | Sept 23 | 60 * & | 12 * | | | 1-85 |
| **OTHER ONE-DAY** | | | | | | | |
| Durham | Durham U. | Sept 16 | | | | | 0-23 |
| Essex | Chelmsford | Sept 22 | | | | | 5-41 |

### BATTING AVERAGES - Including fielding

| | Matches | Inns | NO | Runs | HS | Avge | 100s | 50s | Ct | St |
|---|---|---|---|---|---|---|---|---|---|---|
| Other First-Class | 1 | 2 | 2 | 72 | 60 * | - | - | 1 | - | - |
| ALL FIRST-CLASS | 1 | 2 | 2 | 72 | 60 * | - | - | 1 | - | - |
| Other One-Day | 2 | 0 | 0 | 0 | 0 | - | - | - | - | - |
| ALL ONE-DAY | 2 | 0 | 0 | 0 | 0 | - | - | - | - | - |

### BOWLING AVERAGES

| | Overs | Mdns | Runs | Wkts | Avge | Best | 5wI | 10wM |
|---|---|---|---|---|---|---|---|---|
| Other First-Class | 30.3 | 7 | 85 | 1 | 85.00 | 1-85 | - | - |
| ALL FIRST-CLASS | 30.3 | 7 | 85 | 1 | 85.00 | 1-85 | - | - |
| Other One-Day | 14.5 | 1 | 64 | 5 | 12.80 | 5-41 | 1 | |
| ALL ONE-DAY | 14.5 | 1 | 64 | 5 | 12.80 | 5-41 | 1 | |

# H PLAYER RECORDS

## S.P.HUGHES - *Middlesex*

| Opposition | Venue | Date | Batting | Fielding | Bowling |
|---|---|---|---|---|---|
| **BRITANNIC ASSURANCE** | | | | | |
| Kent | Lord's | May 31 | 1 | | 2-46 & 0-95 |
| Yorkshire | Sheffield | June 21 | | 0 * 1Ct | 2-44 & 1-1 |
| Essex | Lord's | June 28 | | 2 1Ct | 0-71 & 0-13 |
| **OTHER FIRST-CLASS** | | | | | |
| Cambridge U | Fenner's | May 15 | | | 0-29 & 0-25 |
| West Indies | Lord's | May 18 | 5 & 3 * | | 1-64 |
| **REFUGE ASSURANCE** | | | | | |
| Surrey | Lord's | April 28 | | | 2-46 |
| Sussex | Hove | May 12 | | | 1-39 |
| Somerset | Taunton | May 26 | | | 2-42 |
| Leicestershire | Uxbridge | June 9 | 4 | | 2-29 |
| Glamorgan | Cardiff | June 16 | 4 | | 1-23 |
| Notts | Trent Bridge | June 23 | | | 0-35 |
| **NATWEST TROPHY** | | | | | |
| Ireland | Dublin | June 26 | 0 * | | 2-24 |

**BATTING AVERAGES - Including fielding**

| | Matches | Inns | NO | Runs | HS | Avge | 100s | 50s | Ct | St |
|---|---|---|---|---|---|---|---|---|---|---|
| Britannic Assurance | 3 | 3 | 1 | 3 | 2 | 1.50 | - | - | 2 | - |
| Other First-Class | 2 | 2 | 1 | 8 | 5 | 8.00 | - | - | - | - |
| ALL FIRST-CLASS | 5 | 5 | 2 | 11 | 5 | 3.66 | - | - | 2 | - |
| Refuge Assurance | 6 | 2 | 0 | 8 | 4 | 4.00 | - | - | - | - |
| NatWest Trophy | 1 | 1 | 1 | 0 | 0 * | - | - | - | - | - |
| ALL ONE-DAY | 7 | 3 | 1 | 8 | 4 | 4.00 | - | - | - | - |

**BOWLING AVERAGES**

| | Overs | Mdns | Runs | Wkts | Avge | Best | 5wI | 10wM |
|---|---|---|---|---|---|---|---|---|
| Britannic Assurance | 70.5 | 14 | 270 | 5 | 54.00 | 2-44 | - | - |
| Other First-Class | 37 | 11 | 118 | 1 | 118.00 | 1-64 | - | - |
| ALL FIRST-CLASS | 107.5 | 25 | 388 | 6 | 64.66 | 2-44 | - | - |
| Refuge Assurance | 47 | 3 | 214 | 8 | 26.75 | 2-29 | - | |
| NatWest Trophy | 11 | 2 | 24 | 2 | 12.00 | 2-24 | - | |
| ALL ONE-DAY | 58 | 5 | 238 | 10 | 23.80 | 2-24 | - | |

## T.C.HUGHES - *Wales*

| Opposition | Venue | Date | Batting | Fielding | Bowling |
|---|---|---|---|---|---|
| **OTHER ONE-DAY** | | | | | |
| West Indies | Brecon | July 15 | 3 | | |

**BATTING AVERAGES - Including fielding**

| | Matches | Inns | NO | Runs | HS | Avge | 100s | 50s | Ct | St |
|---|---|---|---|---|---|---|---|---|---|---|
| Other One-Day | 1 | 1 | 0 | 3 | 3 | 3.00 | - | - | - | - |
| ALL ONE-DAY | 1 | 1 | 0 | 3 | 3 | 3.00 | - | - | - | - |

**BOWLING AVERAGES**
Did not bowl

## M.I.HUMPHRIES - *Staffordshire*

| Opposition | Venue | Date | Batting | Fielding | Bowling |
|---|---|---|---|---|---|
| **NATWEST TROPHY** | | | | | |
| Northants | Stone | June 26 | 0 | | |

**BATTING AVERAGES - Including fielding**

| | Matches | Inns | NO | Runs | HS | Avge | 100s | 50s | Ct | St |
|---|---|---|---|---|---|---|---|---|---|---|
| NatWest Trophy | 1 | 1 | 0 | 0 | 0 | 0.00 | - | - | - | - |
| ALL ONE-DAY | 1 | 1 | 0 | 0 | 0 | 0.00 | - | - | - | - |

**BOWLING AVERAGES**
Did not bowl

## A.J.HUNT - *Gloucestershire*

| Opposition | Venue | Date | Batting | Fielding | Bowling |
|---|---|---|---|---|---|
| **OTHER FIRST-CLASS** | | | | | |
| Sri Lanka | Bristol | Aug 6 | 3 & 12 | 1Ct | |

**BATTING AVERAGES - Including fielding**

| | Matches | Inns | NO | Runs | HS | Avge | 100s | 50s | Ct | St |
|---|---|---|---|---|---|---|---|---|---|---|
| Other First-Class | 1 | 2 | 0 | 15 | 12 | 7.50 | - | - | 1 | - |
| ALL FIRST-CLASS | 1 | 2 | 0 | 15 | 12 | 7.50 | - | - | 1 | - |

**BOWLING AVERAGES**
Did not bowl

## M.HUSSAIN - *England Amateur XI*

| Opposition | Venue | Date | Batting | Fielding | Bowling |
|---|---|---|---|---|---|
| **OTHER ONE-DAY** | | | | | |
| Sri Lanka | Wolv'hampton | July 24 | 0 | | 0-18 |

**BATTING AVERAGES - Including fielding**

| | Matches | Inns | NO | Runs | HS | Avge | 100s | 50s | Ct | St |
|---|---|---|---|---|---|---|---|---|---|---|
| Other One-Day | 1 | 1 | 0 | 0 | 0 | 0.00 | - | - | - | - |
| ALL ONE-DAY | 1 | 1 | 0 | 0 | 0 | 0.00 | - | - | - | - |

**BOWLING AVERAGES**

| | Overs | Mdns | Runs | Wkts | Avge | Best | 5wI | 10wM |
|---|---|---|---|---|---|---|---|---|
| Other One-Day | 6.3 | 1 | 18 | 0 | - | - | - | |
| ALL ONE-DAY | 6.3 | 1 | 18 | 0 | - | - | - | |

## N.HUSSAIN - *Essex*

| Opposition | Venue | Date | Batting | Fielding | Bowling |
|---|---|---|---|---|---|
| **BRITANNIC ASSURANCE** | | | | | |
| Surrey | Chelmsford | April 27 | 19 * | 1Ct | |
| Northants | Northampton | May 9 | 17 | 2Ct | |
| Kent | Folkestone | May 16 | 72 | 2Ct | |
| Warwickshire | Chelmsford | May 22 | 55 | 2Ct | |
| Gloucs | Bristol | May 31 | 67 | 2Ct | |
| Leicestershire | Ilford | June 4 | 9 & 38 * | | |
| Worcestershire | Ilford | June 7 | 8 | 1Ct | 0-9 |
| Sussex | Horsham | June 21 | 20 | | |
| Middlesex | Lord's | June 28 | 0 | 1Ct | |
| Hampshire | Chelmsford | July 2 | 29 *& 52 | 1Ct | |
| Surrey | The Oval | July 5 | 128 & 36 | 1Ct | |
| Kent | Southend | July 16 | 0 | 2Ct | |
| Somerset | Southend | July 19 | 88 & 0 * | 2Ct | |
| Glamorgan | Cardiff | July 23 | 6 * | 1Ct | |
| Derbyshire | Derby | Aug 6 | 0 & 12 | 1Ct | |
| Notts | Trent Bridge | Aug 9 | 13 & 64 | 1Ct | |
| Northants | Colchester | Aug 16 | | 3Ct | |
| Yorkshire | Colchester | Aug 20 | 1 *& 5 | | |
| Lancashire | Old Trafford | Aug 23 | 65 * | | 0-41 |
| Derbyshire | Chelmsford | Sept 3 | 35 | 4Ct | |
| Leicestershire | Leicester | Sept 10 | 196 | 4Ct | |
| Middlesex | Chelmsford | Sept 17 | 57 | 3Ct | |
| **OTHER FIRST-CLASS** | | | | | |
| For MCC | | | | | |
| Middlesex | Lord's | April 16 | 47 * | 1Ct | |
| For Essex | | | | | |
| West Indies | Chelmsford | Aug 3 | 28 & 41 | 1Ct | |
| Victoria | Chelmsford | Sept 23 | 5 | 2Ct | |

# PLAYER RECORDS

**H**

## REFUGE ASSURANCE

| | | | | |
|---|---|---|---|---|
| Yorkshire | Chelmsford | April 28 | | |
| Notts | Trent Bridge | May 12 | 45 | |
| Kent | Folkestone | May 19 | 48 | |
| Surrey | The Oval | May 26 | 22 | |
| Glamorgan | Pontypridd | June 2 | | |
| Worcestershire | Ilford | June 9 | 22 * | 1Ct |
| Hampshire | Chelmsford | June 16 | 10 | |
| Derbyshire | Chelmsford | June 30 | 15 | 1Ct |
| Warwickshire | Chelmsford | July 7 | 17 * | |
| Somerset | Southend | July 21 | 33 * | 1Ct |
| Gloucs | Cheltenham | July 28 | 44 | |
| Northants | Northampton | Aug 11 | 0 | |
| Middlesex | Colchester | Aug 18 | 0 | 1Ct |
| Lancashire | Old Trafford | Aug 25 | 0 | |

## NATWEST TROPHY

| | | | | |
|---|---|---|---|---|
| Devon | Exmouth | June 26 | | 1Ct |
| Sussex | Hove | July 11 | 97 | 1Ct |
| Surrey | The Oval | July 31 | 17 | 2Ct |

## BENSON & HEDGES CUP

| | | | | |
|---|---|---|---|---|
| Surrey | The Oval | April 23 | 1 | |
| Warwickshire | Edgbaston | April 25 | 2 * | 2Ct |
| Middlesex | Chelmsford | May 2 | 0 | |
| Somerset | Chelmsford | May 7 | | |
| Hampshire | Chelmsford | May 29 | 17 | |
| Worcestershire | Chelmsford | June 12 | 26 | |

## OTHER ONE-DAY

For England A

| | | | |
|---|---|---|---|
| Sri Lanka | Old Trafford | Aug 15 | 22 |

For Essex

| | | | |
|---|---|---|---|
| Durham | Scarborough | Aug 31 | 81 * |
| Yorkshire | Scarborugh | Sept 2 | 16 |
| Victoria | Chelmsford | Sept 22 | 36 |

## BATTING AVERAGES - Including fielding

| | Matches | Inns | NO | Runs | HS | Avge | 100s | 50s | Ct | St |
|---|---|---|---|---|---|---|---|---|---|---|
| Britannic Assurance | 22 | 29 | 7 | 1233 | 196 | 56.04 | 3 | 8 | 34 | - |
| Other First-Class | 3 | 4 | 1 | 121 | 47 * | 40.33 | - | - | 4 | - |
| ALL FIRST-CLASS | 25 | 33 | 8 | 1354 | 196 | 54.16 | 3 | 8 | 38 | - |
| Refuge Assurance | 14 | 12 | 3 | 256 | 48 | 28.44 | - | - | 4 | - |
| NatWest Trophy | 3 | 2 | 0 | 114 | 97 | 57.00 | - | 1 | 4 | - |
| Benson & Hedges Cup | 6 | 5 | 1 | 46 | 26 | 11.50 | - | - | 2 | - |
| Other One-Day | 4 | 4 | 1 | 155 | 81 * | 51.66 | - | 1 | - | - |
| ALL ONE-DAY | 27 | 23 | 5 | 571 | 97 | 31.72 | - | 2 | 10 | - |

## BOWLING AVERAGES

| | Overs | Mdns | Runs | Wkts | Avge | Best | 5wI | 10wM |
|---|---|---|---|---|---|---|---|---|
| Britannic Assurance | 8.3 | 0 | 50 | 0 | - | - | - | - |
| Other First-Class | | | | | | | | |
| ALL FIRST-CLASS | 8.3 | 0 | 50 | 0 | - | - | - | - |
| Refuge Assurance | | | | | | | | |
| NatWest Trophy | | | | | | | | |
| Benson & Hedges Cup | | | | | | | | |
| Other One-Day | | | | | | | | |
| ALL ONE-DAY | | | | | | | | |

## I.J.F.HUTCHINSON - *Middlesex*

| Opposition | Venue | Date | Batting | | | Fielding | Bowling |
|---|---|---|---|---|---|---|---|

### BRITANNIC ASSURANCE

| | | | | | | | |
|---|---|---|---|---|---|---|---|
| Yorkshire | Lord's | April 27 | 1 | | | | |
| Sussex | Lord's | May 9 | 5 | & | 3 | 1Ct | |
| Sussex | Hove | May 22 | 125 | & | 46 | 1Ct | 0-9 |
| Somerset | Taunton | May 25 | 2 | | | 2Ct | |
| Kent | Lord's | May 31 | 22 | & | 1 | 2Ct | 0-1 |
| Gloucs | Bristol | June 4 | 114 | & | 0 | 1Ct | |
| Leicestershire | Uxbridge | June 7 | 12 | & | 29 * | 2Ct | |
| Glamorgan | Cardiff | June 14 | 9 | & | 5 | | |
| Yorkshire | Sheffield | June 21 | 21 | & | 0 | 1Ct | |
| Essex | Lord's | June 28 | 4 | & | 3 | 1Ct | 0-1 |
| Warwickshire | Edgbaston | July 2 | 5 | & | 30 | | |

## OTHER FIRST-CLASS

| | | | | | | | |
|---|---|---|---|---|---|---|---|
| MCC | Lord's | April 16 | 70 | | | | |
| Cambridge U | Fenner's | May 15 | 92 | | | 3Ct | |
| West Indies | Lord's | May 18 | 37 | & | 20 | | 1-18 |

## REFUGE ASSURANCE

| | | | | | |
|---|---|---|---|---|---|
| Somerset | Taunton | May 26 | 20 | | |
| Leicestershire | Uxbridge | June 9 | 0 | | 1-10 |
| Glamorgan | Cardiff | June 16 | 42 | | |
| Notts | Trent Bridge | June 23 | 25 | 1Ct | |
| Yorkshire | Lord's | July 7 | 17 | 1Ct | |

## NATWEST TROPHY

| | | | | | |
|---|---|---|---|---|---|
| Ireland | Dublin | June 26 | 23 | 2Ct | 0-17 |
| Somerset | Taunton | July 11 | 17 | | |

## BENSON & HEDGES CUP

| | | | |
|---|---|---|---|
| Warwickshire | Lord's | May 4 | 8 |

## BATTING AVERAGES - Including fielding

| | Matches | Inns | NO | Runs | HS | Avge | 100s | 50s | Ct | St |
|---|---|---|---|---|---|---|---|---|---|---|
| Britannic Assurance | 11 | 20 | 1 | 437 | 125 | 23.00 | 2 | - | 11 | - |
| Other First-Class | 3 | 4 | 0 | 219 | 92 | 54.75 | - | 2 | 3 | - |
| ALL FIRST-CLASS | 14 | 24 | 1 | 656 | 125 | 28.52 | 2 | 2 | 14 | - |
| Refuge Assurance | 5 | 5 | 0 | 104 | 42 | 20.80 | - | - | 2 | - |
| NatWest Trophy | 2 | 2 | 0 | 40 | 23 | 20.00 | - | - | 2 | - |
| Benson & Hedges Cup | 1 | 1 | 0 | 8 | 8 | 8.00 | - | - | - | - |
| ALL ONE-DAY | 8 | 8 | 0 | 152 | 42 | 19.00 | - | - | 4 | - |

## BOWLING AVERAGES

| | Overs | Mdns | Runs | Wkts | Avge | Best | 5wI | 10wM |
|---|---|---|---|---|---|---|---|---|
| Britannic Assurance | 6 | 0 | 11 | 0 | - | - | - | - |
| Other First-Class | 6 | 0 | 18 | 1 | 18.00 | 1-18 | - | - |
| ALL FIRST-CLASS | 12 | 0 | 29 | 1 | 29.00 | 1-18 | - | - |
| Refuge Assurance | 2 | 0 | 10 | 1 | 10.00 | 1-10 | - | - |
| NatWest Trophy | 2 | 0 | 17 | 0 | | | | |
| Benson & Hedges Cup | | | | | | | | |
| ALL ONE-DAY | 4 | 0 | 27 | 1 | 27.00 | 1-10 | - | - |

## S.HUTTON - *Durham*

| Opposition | Venue | Date | Batting | Fielding | Bowling |
|---|---|---|---|---|---|

### OTHER ONE-DAY

| | | | |
|---|---|---|---|
| Essex | Scarborough | Aug 31 | 0 |
| Victoria | Durham U. | Sept 16 | 55 |

## BATTING AVERAGES - Including fielding

| | Matches | Inns | NO | Runs | HS | Avge | 100s | 50s | Ct | St |
|---|---|---|---|---|---|---|---|---|---|---|
| Other One-Day | 2 | 2 | 0 | 55 | 55 | 27.50 | - | 1 | - | - |
| ALL ONE-DAY | 2 | 2 | 0 | 55 | 55 | 27.50 | - | 1 | - | - |

## BOWLING AVERAGES

Did not bowl

# I PLAYER RECORDS

## A.P.IGGLESDEN - *Kent*

| Opposition | Venue | Date | Batting | Fielding | Bowling |
|---|---|---|---|---|---|
| **BRITANNIC ASSURANCE** | | | | | |
| Hampshire | Southampton | April 27 | 7 | | 0-34 |
| Surrey | The Oval | May 9 | 5 | | 3-59 & 2-31 |
| Essex | Folkestone | May 16 | 1 | 1Ct | 1-113 |
| Notts | Trent Bridge | May 22 | | | 1-60 & 0-48 |
| Derbyshire | Canterbury | May 25 | 1 | 1Ct | 0-50 & 1-22 |
| Warwickshire | Tunbridge W | June 4 | 10 | 1Ct | 0-13 & 3-69 |
| Sussex | Tunbridge W | June 7 | 16 * | | 4-68 & 2-22 |
| Yorkshire | Harrogate | June 14 | | | 0-33 |
| Lancashire | Old Trafford | June 21 | | 1 | 3-75 |
| Northants | Maidstone | July 2 | 0 | | 5-36 |
| Glamorgan | Maidstone | July 5 | 2 | | 1-64 & 0-23 |
| Essex | Southend | July 16 | 12 * | | 1-35 & 4-36 |
| Worcestershire | Worcester | July 23 | | | 0-11 |
| Somerset | Taunton | July 26 | 15 | | 0-51 & 4-45 |
| Surrey | Canterbury | Aug 2 | 5 | | 2-51 & 2-81 |
| Hampshire | Canterbury | Aug 6 | 1 | | 1-43 & 0-10 |
| Gloucs | Canterbury | Aug 20 | 13 & 0 * | | 4-46 & 3-47 |
| Middlesex | Canterbury | Aug 28 | 11 | | 1-12 |
| **OTHER FIRST-CLASS** | | | | | |
| West Indies | Canterbury | July 20 | 1 * | 1Ct | 1-20 & 1-43 |
| **REFUGE ASSURANCE** | | | | | |
| Worcestershire | Worcester | April 21 | 1 | | 4-59 |
| Hampshire | Southampton | May 12 | 1 * | 1Ct | 3-33 |
| Essex | Folkestone | May 19 | | | 3-34 |
| Derbyshire | Canterbury | May 26 | | | 0-32 |
| Middlesex | Southgate | June 2 | | | 2-37 |
| Yorkshire | Scarborough | June 16 | 0 | | 0-31 |
| Lancashire | Old Trafford | June 23 | | | 1-34 |
| Gloucs | Canterbury | June 30 | | | 2-18 |
| Glamorgan | Maidstone | July 7 | | | 1-38 |
| Leicestershire | Canterbury | July 14 | | | 0-27 |
| Somerset | Taunton | July 28 | 3 * | | 3-38 |
| Surrey | Canterbury | Aug 4 | | 1Ct | 0-32 |
| Northants | Canterbury | Aug 18 | | | 2-27 |
| Sussex | Hove | Aug 25 | 13 * | 1Ct | 2-21 |
| **NATWEST TROPHY** | | | | | |
| Cambs | Canterbury | June 26 | | 1Ct | 4-29 |
| **BENSON & HEDGES CUP** | | | | | |
| Leicestershire | Canterbury | April 23 | | 1Ct | 3-32 |
| Lancashire | Old Trafford | April 25 | 3 | | 0-48 |
| Sussex | Canterbury | May 2 | | | 2-35 |
| Scotland | Glasgow | May 7 | | | 3-24 |
| Worcestershire | Worcester | May 29 | 26 * | | 2-85 |

### BATTING AVERAGES - Including fielding

| | Matches | Inns | NO | Runs | HS | Avge | 100s | 50s | Ct | St |
|---|---|---|---|---|---|---|---|---|---|---|
| Britannic Assurance | 18 | 16 | 3 | 100 | 16 * | 7.69 | - | - | 3 | - |
| Other First-Class | 1 | 1 | 1 | 1 | 1 * | - | - | - | 1 | - |
| ALL FIRST-CLASS | 19 | 17 | 4 | 101 | 16 * | 7.76 | - | - | 4 | - |
| Refuge Assurance | 14 | 5 | 3 | 18 | 13 * | 9.00 | - | - | 3 | - |
| NatWest Trophy | 1 | 0 | 0 | 0 | 0 | - | - | - | 1 | - |
| Benson & Hedges Cup | 5 | 2 | 1 | 29 | 26 * | 29.00 | - | - | 1 | - |
| ALL ONE-DAY | 20 | 7 | 4 | 47 | 26 * | 15.66 | - | - | 5 | - |

### BOWLING AVERAGES

| | Overs | Mdns | Runs | Wkts | Avge | Best | 5wI | 10wM |
|---|---|---|---|---|---|---|---|---|
| Britannic Assurance | 449 | 86 | 1288 | 48 | 26.83 | 5-36 | 1 | - |
| Other First-Class | 22 | 8 | 63 | 2 | 31.50 | 1-20 | - | - |
| ALL FIRST-CLASS | 471 | 94 | 1351 | 50 | 27.02 | 5-36 | 1 | - |
| Refuge Assurance | 109 | 6 | 461 | 23 | 20.04 | 4-59 | - | |
| NatWest Trophy | 9.2 | 1 | 29 | 4 | 7.25 | 4-29 | - | |
| Benson & Hedges Cup | 50.5 | 7 | 224 | 10 | 22.40 | 3-24 | - | |
| ALL ONE-DAY | 169.1 | 14 | 714 | 37 | 19.29 | 4-29 | - | |

## IJAZ AHMED - *Durham*

| Opposition | Venue | Date | Batting | Fielding | Bowling |
|---|---|---|---|---|---|
| **NATWEST TROPHY** | | | | | |
| Glamorgan | Darlington | June 26 | 10 | | 0-79 |
| **OTHER ONE-DAY** | | | | | |
| Leicestershire | Harrogate | June 11 | 20 | | |
| For Rest of World | | | | | |
| England XI | Jesmond | July 31 | 46 | 1Ct | |
| England XI | Jesmond | Aug 1 | 39 | | |

### BATTING AVERAGES - Including fielding

| | Matches | Inns | NO | Runs | HS | Avge | 100s | 50s | Ct | St |
|---|---|---|---|---|---|---|---|---|---|---|
| NatWest Trophy | 1 | 1 | 0 | 10 | 10 | 10.00 | - | - | - | - |
| Other One-Day | 3 | 3 | 0 | 105 | 46 | 35.00 | - | - | 1 | - |
| ALL ONE-DAY | 4 | 4 | 0 | 115 | 46 | 28.75 | - | - | 1 | - |

### BOWLING AVERAGES

| | Overs | Mdns | Runs | Wkts | Avge | Best | 5wI | 10wM |
|---|---|---|---|---|---|---|---|---|
| NatWest Trophy | 11 | 0 | 79 | 0 | - | - | - | |
| Other One-Day | | | | | | | | |
| ALL ONE-DAY | 11 | 0 | 79 | 0 | - | - | - | |

## R.K.ILLINGWORTH - *Worcestershire & England*

| Opposition | Venue | Date | Batting | Fielding | Bowling |
|---|---|---|---|---|---|
| **CORNHILL TEST MATCHES** | | | | | |
| West Indies | Trent Bridge | July 4 | 13 & 13 | 1Ct | 3-110 & 0-5 |
| West Indies | Edgbaston | July 25 | 0 * & 5 * | | 1-75 & 0-23 |
| **BRITANNIC ASSURANCE** | | | | | |
| Gloucs | Worcester | April 27 | | | 0-40 |
| Lancashire | Worcester | May 9 | 34 & 56 * | | 0-45 |
| Glamorgan | Worcester | May 31 | 26 & 13 | 1Ct | 0-2 |
| Essex | Ilford | June 7 | 19 | | 0-51 & 1-1 |
| Sussex | Hove | June 14 | 1 * | | 1-32 & 0-21 |
| Leicestershire | Worcester | June 28 | 17 * | | 0-64 & 0-10 |
| Hampshire | Portsmouth | July 16 | 0 | | 1-94 |
| Derbyshire | Kidd'minster | July 19 | 31 & 21 | 1Ct | 5-64 & 1-7 |
| Warwickshire | Worcester | Aug 2 | 21 | | 1-32 |
| Somerset | Weston | Aug 6 | 24 & 9 | | 1-37 & 1-7 |
| Surrey | Worcester | Aug 16 | 9 & 0 | | 3-30 & 1-39 |
| Lancashire | Blackpool | Aug 20 | 29 | | 5-49 & 2-82 |
| Middlesex | Worcester | Aug 23 | 16 | | 0-9 & 0-90 |
| Warwickshire | Edgbaston | Aug 28 | 3 & 4 | 1Ct | 0-3 & 1-22 |
| Somerset | Worcester | Sept 3 | 36 | | 0-46 |
| Glamorgan | Cardiff | Sept 10 | 44 | 1Ct | 0-8 & 0-15 |
| Notts | Trent Bridge | Sept 17 | 20 & 9 * | | 2-71 |
| **OTHER FIRST-CLASS** | | | | | |
| For MCC | | | | | |
| Middlesex | Lord's | April 16 | | | 1-46 |
| For Worcestershire | | | | | |
| West Indies | Worcester | May 15 | 4 | 2Ct | 1-62 |
| Sri Lanka | Worcester | July 30 | 47 * | 1Ct | 1-7 & 5-43 |
| **TEXACO TROPHY** | | | | | |
| West Indies | Edgbaston | May 23 | 9 * | 1Ct | 1-20 |
| West Indies | Old Trafford | May 25 | | 1Ct | 0-42 |
| West Indies | Lord's | May 27 | | 2Ct | 2-53 |
| **REFUGE ASSURANCE** | | | | | |
| Kent | Worcester | April 21 | | | 0-32 |
| Gloucs | Bristol | May 5 | | 1Ct | 2-37 |
| Lancashire | Worcester | May 12 | 24 * | 1Ct | 2-26 |
| Northants | Northampton | May 19 | | | 5-49 |
| Surrey | Worcester | June 2 | | | |
| Essex | Ilford | June 9 | 25 * | | 0-45 |
| Sussex | Hove | June 16 | | | 0-40 |
| Yorkshire | Sheffield | June 23 | 17 * | 2Ct | 1-30 |
| Leicestershire | Worcester | June 30 | | | 2-19 |
| Glamorgan | Worcester | July 21 | | | 1-38 |
| Notts | Trent Bridge | Aug 4 | | 1Ct | 2-30 |

# PLACE RECORDS

# PLAYER RECORDS   I

| | | | | | |
|---|---|---|---|---|---|
| Somerset | Worcester | Aug 18 | | | 0-45 |
| Middlesex | Worcester | Aug 25 | | | 0-18 |
| Notts | Trent Bridge | Sept 1 | 24 | | 0-26 |
| Lancashire | Old Trafford | Sept 15 | | 1Ct | 1-38 |

**NATWEST TROPHY**

| | | | | | |
|---|---|---|---|---|---|
| Bedfordshire | Bedford | June 26 | | 1Ct | 1-12 |
| Glamorgan | Worcester | July 11 | 10 | 1Ct | 1-47 |

**BENSON & HEDGES CUP**

| | | | | | |
|---|---|---|---|---|---|
| Gloucs | Worcester | April 25 | | | 0-21 |
| Combined U | Fenner's | May 2 | | | 0-28 |
| Northants | Northampton | May 7 | | 1Ct | 0-52 |
| Kent | Worcester | May 29 | 1 * | | 2-50 |
| Essex | Chelmsford | June 12 | | | |
| Lancashire | Lord's | July 13 | 17 * | 1Ct | 0-38 |

**OTHER ONE-DAY**
For England A

| | | | | | |
|---|---|---|---|---|---|
| Sri Lanka | Old Trafford | Aug 14 | | 1Ct | 2-31 |
| Sri Lanka | Old Trafford | Aug 15 | 10 * | 1Ct | 0-36 |
| For Yorkshiremen | | | | | |
| Yorkshire | Scarborough | Sept 7 | 7 * | 1Ct | 2-49 |

**BATTING AVERAGES - Including fielding**

| | Matches | Inns | NO | Runs | HS | Avge | 100s | 50s | Ct | St |
|---|---|---|---|---|---|---|---|---|---|---|
| Cornhill Test Matches | 2 | 4 | 2 | 31 | 13 | 15.50 | - | - | 1 | - |
| Britannic Assurance | 17 | 23 | 4 | 442 | 56 * | 23.26 | - | 1 | 4 | - |
| Other First-Class | 3 | 2 | 1 | 51 | 47 * | 51.00 | - | - | 3 | - |
| ALL FIRST-CLASS | 22 | 29 | 7 | 524 | 56 * | 23.81 | - | 1 | 8 | - |
| Texaco Trophy | 3 | 1 | 1 | 9 | 9 * | - | - | - | 4 | - |
| Refuge Assurance | 15 | 4 | 3 | 90 | 25 * | 90.00 | - | - | 6 | - |
| NatWest Trophy | 2 | 1 | 0 | 10 | 10 | 10.00 | - | - | 2 | - |
| Benson & Hedges Cup | 6 | 2 | 2 | 18 | 17 * | - | - | - | 2 | - |
| Other One-Day | 3 | 2 | 2 | 17 | 10 * | - | - | - | 3 | - |
| ALL ONE-DAY | 29 | 10 | 8 | 144 | 25 * | 72.00 | - | - | 17 | - |

**BOWLING AVERAGES**

| | Overs | Mdns | Runs | Wkts | Avge | Best | 5wI | 10wM |
|---|---|---|---|---|---|---|---|---|
| Cornhill Test Matches | 56.4 | 10 | 213 | 4 | 53.25 | 3-110 | - | - |
| Britannic Assurance | 430.4 | 132 | 971 | 26 | 37.34 | 5-49 | 2 | - |
| Other First-Class | 63.5 | 13 | 158 | 8 | 19.75 | 5-43 | 1 | - |
| ALL FIRST-CLASS | 551.1 | 155 | 1342 | 38 | 35.31 | 5-43 | 3 | - |
| Texaco Trophy | 32 | 3 | 115 | 3 | 38.33 | 2-53 | - | |
| Refuge Assurance | 100 | 4 | 473 | 16 | 29.56 | 5-49 | 1 | |
| NatWest Trophy | 16 | 2 | 59 | 2 | 29.50 | 1-12 | - | |
| Benson & Hedges Cup | 49 | 2 | 189 | 2 | 94.50 | 2-50 | - | |
| Other One-Day | 30 | 0 | 116 | 4 | 29.00 | 2-31 | - | |
| ALL ONE-DAY | 227 | 11 | 952 | 27 | 35.25 | 5-49 | 1 | |

# M.C.ILOTT - *Essex*

| Opposition | Venue | Date | Batting | Fielding | Bowling |
|---|---|---|---|---|---|
| **OTHER FIRST-CLASS** | | | | | |
| Cambridge U | Fenner's | April 19 | | | 1-32 & 2-30 |
| **REFUGE ASSURANCE** | | | | | |
| Yorkshire | Chelmsford | April 28 | | 1Ct | 2-26 |
| Notts | Trent Bridge | May 12 | 0 | | 1-28 |
| **BENSON & HEDGES CUP** | | | | | |
| Surrey | The Oval | April 23 | | | 3-34 |
| Middlesex | Chelmsford | May 2 | | | 1-32 |
| Somerset | Chelmsford | May 7 | | | 1-35 |

**BATTING AVERAGES - Including fielding**

| | Matches | Inns | NO | Runs | HS | Avge | 100s | 50s | Ct | St |
|---|---|---|---|---|---|---|---|---|---|---|
| Other First-Class | 1 | 0 | 0 | 0 | 0 | - | - | - | - | - |
| ALL FIRST-CLASS | 1 | 0 | 0 | 0 | 0 | - | - | - | - | - |
| Refuge Assurance | 2 | 1 | 0 | 0 | 0 | 0.00 | - | - | 1 | - |
| Benson & Hedges Cup | 3 | 0 | 0 | 0 | 0 | - | - | - | - | - |
| ALL ONE-DAY | 5 | 1 | 0 | 0 | 0 | 0.00 | - | - | 1 | - |

**BOWLING AVERAGES**

| | Overs | Mdns | Runs | Wkts | Avge | Best | 5wI | 10wM |
|---|---|---|---|---|---|---|---|---|
| Other First-Class | 21.4 | 7 | 62 | 3 | 20.66 | 2-30 | - | - |
| ALL FIRST-CLASS | 21.4 | 7 | 62 | 3 | 20.66 | 2-30 | - | - |
| Refuge Assurance | 14 | 1 | 54 | 3 | 18.00 | 2-26 | - | |
| Benson & Hedges Cup | 31 | 6 | 101 | 5 | 20.20 | 3-34 | - | |
| ALL ONE-DAY | 45 | 7 | 155 | 8 | 19.37 | 3-34 | - | |

# M.J.INGHAM - *League CC XI*

| Opposition | Venue | Date | Batting | Fielding | Bowling |
|---|---|---|---|---|---|
| **OTHER ONE-DAY** | | | | | |
| West Indies | Trowbridge | June 28 | 48 * | | |

**BATTING AVERAGES - Including fielding**

| | Matches | Inns | NO | Runs | HS | Avge | 100s | 50s | Ct | St |
|---|---|---|---|---|---|---|---|---|---|---|
| Other One-Day | 1 | 1 | 1 | 48 | 48 * | - | - | - | - | - |
| ALL ONE-DAY | 1 | 1 | 1 | 48 | 48 * | - | - | - | - | - |

**BOWLING AVERAGES**
Did not bowl

# R.IRANI - *Lancashire*

| Opposition | Venue | Date | Batting | Fielding | Bowling |
|---|---|---|---|---|---|
| **OTHER FIRST-CLASS** | | | | | |
| Oxford U | The Parks | June 7 | 31 * | | 0-50 & 0-32 |

**BATTING AVERAGES - Including fielding**

| | Matches | Inns | NO | Runs | HS | Avge | 100s | 50s | Ct | St |
|---|---|---|---|---|---|---|---|---|---|---|
| Other First-Class | 1 | 1 | 1 | 31 | 31 * | - | - | - | - | - |
| ALL FIRST-CLASS | 1 | 1 | 1 | 31 | 31 * | - | - | - | - | - |

**BOWLING AVERAGES**

| | Overs | Mdns | Runs | Wkts | Avge | Best | 5wI | 10wM |
|---|---|---|---|---|---|---|---|---|
| Other First-Class | 32.2 | 5 | 82 | 0 | - | - | - | - |
| ALL FIRST-CLASS | 32.2 | 5 | 82 | 0 | - | - | - | - |

## J | PLAYER RECORDS

### P.B.JACKSON - *Ireland*

| Opposition | Venue | Date | Batting | Fielding | Bowling |
|---|---|---|---|---|---|
| **OTHER ONE-DAY** | | | | | |
| West Indies | Downpatrick | July 13 | | 1Ct | |

**BATTING AVERAGES - Including fielding**

| | Matches | Inns | NO | Runs | HS | Avge | 100s | 50s | Ct | St |
|---|---|---|---|---|---|---|---|---|---|---|
| Other One-Day | 1 | 0 | 0 | 0 | 0 | - | - | - | 1 | - |
| ALL ONE-DAY | 1 | 0 | 0 | 0 | 0 | - | - | - | 1 | - |

**BOWLING AVERAGES**
Did not bowl

### P.W.JACKSON - *Victoria*

| Opposition | Venue | Date | Batting | Fielding | Bowling |
|---|---|---|---|---|---|
| **OTHER FIRST-CLASS** | | | | | |
| Essex | Chelmsford | Sept 23 | 4 | | 2-50 |
| **OTHER ONE-DAY** | | | | | |
| Durham | Durham U. | Sept 16 | | | 2-29 |
| Essex | Chelmsford | Sept 22 | | | 2-45 |

**BATTING AVERAGES - Including fielding**

| | Matches | Inns | NO | Runs | HS | Avge | 100s | 50s | Ct | St |
|---|---|---|---|---|---|---|---|---|---|---|
| Other First-Class | 1 | 1 | 0 | 4 | 4 | 4.00 | - | - | - | - |
| ALL FIRST-CLASS | 1 | 1 | 0 | 4 | 4 | 4.00 | - | - | - | - |
| Other One-Day | 2 | 0 | 0 | 0 | 0 | - | - | - | - | - |
| ALL ONE-DAY | 2 | 0 | 0 | 0 | 0 | - | - | - | - | - |

**BOWLING AVERAGES**

| | Overs | Mdns | Runs | Wkts | Avge | Best | 5wI | 10wM |
|---|---|---|---|---|---|---|---|---|
| Other First-Class | 18 | 11 | 50 | 2 | 25.00 | 2-50 | - | - |
| ALL FIRST-CLASS | 18 | 11 | 50 | 2 | 25.00 | 2-50 | - | - |
| Other One-Day | 17 | 3 | 74 | 4 | 18.50 | 2-29 | - | |
| ALL ONE-DAY | 17 | 3 | 74 | 4 | 18.50 | 2-29 | - | |

### K.D.JAMES - *Hampshire*

| Opposition | Venue | Date | Batting | | | Fielding | Bowling |
|---|---|---|---|---|---|---|---|
| **BRITANNIC ASSURANCE** | | | | | | | |
| Kent | Southampton | April 27 | | | | | 0-59 |
| Gloucs | Bristol | May 9 | 3 | & | 34 | | 4-72 & 0-24 |
| Sussex | Hove | May 16 | 17 * & | | 6 * | | 2-61 & 0-19 |
| Surrey | Bournemouth | May 25 | 29 | & | 39 * | | 2-44 & 0-10 |
| Notts | Trent Bridge | May 31 | 21 * & | | 2 * | | 0-28 & 2-27 |
| Lancashire | Basingstoke | June 4 | | | 14 | 1Ct | 2-50 & 0-18 |
| Gloucs | Southampton | June 7 | 14 | | | | 0-30 |
| Somerset | Bath | June 18 | 75 * | | | | 0-18 & 1-21 |
| Northants | Northampton | June 21 | 18 | | | | 0-59 |
| Essex | Chelmsford | July 2 | 51 | & | 45 | | 1-36 & 1-20 |
| Yorkshire | Southampton | July 5 | 134 * | | | | 1-20 |
| Worcestershire | Portsmouth | July 16 | 84 | | | | 0-5 & 0-54 |
| Warwickshire | Portsmouth | July 19 | 7 | & | 19 | 1Ct | 2-39 & 1-33 |
| Derbyshire | Chesterfield | July 23 | 101 | & | 1 | | 2-12 |
| Middlesex | Lord's | Aug 2 | 36 | & | 7 | 1Ct | 4-32 & 0-17 |
| Kent | Canterbury | Aug 6 | 7 | & | 15 | | 0-35 & 2-44 |
| Glamorgan | Swansea | Aug 9 | 32 | | | | 3-27 |
| Leicestershire | Bournemouth | Aug 16 | 45 | & | 72 | | 2-56 & 0-6 |
| Sussex | Bournemouth | Aug 20 | 68 | & | 50 * | | 0-12 |
| Somerset | Southampton | Aug 28 | 25 | & | 10 | 1Ct | 1-67 & 0-17 |
| Surrey | The Oval | Sept 3 | 1 | & | 42 * | 1Ct | 1-37 & 1-22 |
| Glamorgan | Southampton | Sept 17 | 49 | & | 43 | 3Ct | 2-78 & 0-10 |

### OTHER FIRST-CLASS

| Opposition | Venue | Date | Batting | Fielding | Bowling |
|---|---|---|---|---|---|
| Oxford U | The Parks | April 13 | 47 | 1Ct | 2-25 & 1-33 |
| West Indies | Southampton | June 29 | 11 * | | 1-77 |

### REFUGE ASSURANCE

| Opposition | Venue | Date | Batting | Fielding | Bowling |
|---|---|---|---|---|---|
| Yorkshire | Southampton | April 21 | | | 3-24 |
| Derbyshire | Derby | May 5 | 12 | | 2-29 |
| Kent | Southampton | May 12 | 58 * | | 2-31 |
| Somerset | Bournemouth | May 19 | 16 | | 1-43 |
| Gloucs | Swindon | May 26 | 8 | | 0-25 |
| Worcestershire | Southampton | July 7 | 3 | 1Ct | 0-14 |
| Notts | Trent Bridge | July 14 | 28 * | | 0-11 |
| Warwickshire | Portsmouth | July 21 | 21 | | 1-38 |
| Lancashire | Southampton | July 28 | 10 | | |
| Middlesex | Lord's | Aug 4 | 9 | 1Ct | 0-16 |
| Glamorgan | Ebbw Vale | Aug 11 | 8 | | 0-30 |
| Leicestershire | Bournemouth | Aug 18 | 2 | 1Ct | 1-23 |
| Surrey | The Oval | Aug 25 | 1 | | 1-20 |

### NATWEST TROPHY

| Opposition | Venue | Date | Batting | Fielding | Bowling |
|---|---|---|---|---|---|
| Berkshire | Reading | June 26 | | | 0-14 |
| Warwickshire | Edgbaston | Aug 14 | | | 1-50 |
| Surrey | Lord's | Sept 7 | 0 | 1Ct | 0-33 |

### BENSON & HEDGES CUP

| Opposition | Venue | Date | Batting | Fielding | Bowling |
|---|---|---|---|---|---|
| Notts | Southampton | April 23 | | | 0-55 |
| Essex | Chelmsford | May 29 | 2 | | 1-45 |

**BATTING AVERAGES - Including fielding**

| | Matches | Inns | NO | Runs | HS | Avge | 100s | 50s | Ct | St |
|---|---|---|---|---|---|---|---|---|---|---|
| Britannic Assurance | 22 | 35 | 9 | 1216 | 134 * | 46.76 | 2 | 6 | 8 | - |
| Other First-Class | 2 | 2 | 1 | 58 | 47 | 58.00 | - | - | 1 | - |
| ALL FIRST-CLASS | 24 | 37 | 10 | 1274 | 134 * | 47.18 | 2 | 6 | 9 | - |
| Refuge Assurance | 13 | 12 | 2 | 176 | 58 * | 17.60 | - | 1 | 3 | - |
| NatWest Trophy | 3 | 1 | 0 | 0 | 0 | 0.00 | - | - | 1 | - |
| Benson & Hedges Cup | 2 | 1 | 0 | 2 | 2 | 2.00 | - | - | - | - |
| ALL ONE-DAY | 18 | 14 | 2 | 178 | 58 * | 14.83 | - | 1 | 4 | - |

**BOWLING AVERAGES**

| | Overs | Mdns | Runs | Wkts | Avge | Best | 5wI | 10wM |
|---|---|---|---|---|---|---|---|---|
| Britannic Assurance | 396.5 | 85 | 1219 | 37 | 32.94 | 4-32 | - | - |
| Other First-Class | 46 | 14 | 135 | 4 | 33.75 | 2-25 | - | - |
| ALL FIRST-CLASS | 442.5 | 99 | 1354 | 41 | 33.02 | 4-32 | - | - |
| Refuge Assurance | 66 | 3 | 304 | 11 | 27.63 | 3-24 | - | |
| NatWest Trophy | 22 | 3 | 97 | 1 | 97.00 | 1-50 | - | |
| Benson & Hedges Cup | 22 | 0 | 100 | 1 | 100.00 | 1-45 | - | |
| ALL ONE-DAY | 110 | 6 | 501 | 13 | 38.53 | 3-24 | - | |

### S.P.JAMES - *Glamorgan*

| Opposition | Venue | Date | Batting | | | Fielding | Bowling |
|---|---|---|---|---|---|---|---|
| **BRITANNIC ASSURANCE** | | | | | | | |
| Warwickshire | Swansea | May 16 | 5 | & | 14 | 1Ct | |
| Northants | Cardiff | May 22 | 15 | & | 11 * | 1Ct | |
| Notts | Cardiff | July 2 | 1 | & | 42 | | |
| Essex | Cardiff | July 23 | | | 16 | | |
| Surrey | The Oval | July 26 | 70 | & | 24 | 1Ct | |
| Hampshire | Swansea | Aug 9 | | | 20 | 1Ct | |
| Warwickshire | Edgbaston | Aug 20 | 4 | & | 11 * | 2Ct | |
| Gloucs | Abergavenny | Aug 28 | 66 | | | 1Ct | |
| Worcestershire | Cardiff | Sept 10 | 47 * & | | 30 | | |
| Hampshire | Southampton | Sept 17 | 31 | & | 22 | 1Ct | |
| **OTHER FIRST-CLASS** | | | | | | | |
| West Indies | Swansea | July 16 | 8 | & | 24 | | |
| **REFUGE ASSURANCE** | | | | | | | |
| Gloucs | Swansea | Aug 4 | 23 | | | 1Ct | |
| Hampshire | Ebbw Vale | Aug 11 | 11 | | | | |

**BATTING AVERAGES - Including fielding**

| | Matches | Inns | NO | Runs | HS | Avge | 100s | 50s | Ct | St |
|---|---|---|---|---|---|---|---|---|---|---|
| Britannic Assurance | 10 | 17 | 3 | 429 | 70 | 30.64 | - | 2 | 8 | - |
| Other First-Class | 1 | 2 | 0 | 32 | 24 | 16.00 | - | - | - | - |

# PLANYER RECORDS   J

| | | | | | | | | | |
|---|---|---|---|---|---|---|---|---|---|
| ALL FIRST-CLASS | 11 | 19 | 3 | 461 | 70 | 28.81 | - | 2 | 8 | - |
| Refuge Assurance | 2 | 2 | 0 | 34 | 23 | 17.00 | - | - | 1 | - |
| ALL ONE-DAY | 2 | 2 | 0 | 34 | 23 | 17.00 | - | - | 1 | - |

**BOWLING AVERAGES**
Did not bowl

## P.W.JARVIS - *Yorkshire*

| Opposition | Venue | Date | Batting | Fielding | Bowling |
|---|---|---|---|---|---|
| **BRITANNIC ASSURANCE** | | | | | |
| Middlesex | Lord's | April 27 | 22 * | | 2-25 |
| Notts | Headingley | May 16 | 31 | | 0-37 & 2-49 |
| Gloucs | Sheffield | May 22 | 37 * | | 1-25 |
| Derbyshire | Chesterfield | Sept 17 | 2 & 22 | | 4-28 & 3-71 |
| **REFUGE ASSURANCE** | | | | | |
| Hampshire | Southampton | April 21 | 4 | | 0-27 |
| Essex | Chelmsford | April 28 | 5 | | 0-39 |
| Warwickshire | Headingley | May 12 | 9 | | 2-37 |
| **BENSON & HEDGES CUP** | | | | | |
| Notts | Trent Bridge | April 25 | 3 * | | 1-34 |
| Min Counties | Headingley | May 2 | | | 2-27 |
| Hampshire | Headingley | May 4 | 0 | | 2-13 |
| Glamorgan | Cardiff | May 7 | | | 1-57 |
| Warwickshire | Headingley | May 29 | 12 * | | 0-11 |
| **OTHER ONE-DAY** | | | | | |
| Yorkshiremen | Scarborough | Sept 7 | | | 1-33 |
| World XI | Scarborough | Sept 8 | 1 * | | 1-46 |

**BATTING AVERAGES - Including fielding**

| | Matches | Inns | NO | Runs | HS | Avge | 100s | 50s | Ct | St |
|---|---|---|---|---|---|---|---|---|---|---|
| Britannic Assurance | 4 | 5 | 2 | 114 | 37 * | 38.00 | - | - | - | - |
| ALL FIRST-CLASS | 4 | 5 | 2 | 114 | 37 * | 38.00 | - | - | - | - |
| Refuge Assurance | 3 | 3 | 0 | 18 | 9 | 6.00 | - | - | - | - |
| Benson & Hedges Cup | 5 | 3 | 2 | 15 | 12 * | 15.00 | - | - | - | - |
| Other One-Day | 2 | 1 | 1 | 1 | 1 * | - | - | - | - | - |
| ALL ONE-DAY | 10 | 7 | 3 | 34 | 12 * | 8.50 | - | - | - | - |

**BOWLING AVERAGES**

| | Overs | Mdns | Runs | Wkts | Avge | Best | 5wI | 10wM |
|---|---|---|---|---|---|---|---|---|
| Britannic Assurance | 95 | 26 | 235 | 12 | 19.58 | 4-28 | - | - |
| ALL FIRST-CLASS | 95 | 26 | 235 | 12 | 19.58 | 4-28 | - | - |
| Refuge Assurance | 23 | 3 | 103 | 2 | 51.50 | 2-37 | - | |
| Benson & Hedges Cup | 44.2 | 9 | 142 | 6 | 23.66 | 2-13 | - | |
| Other One-Day | 20 | 3 | 79 | 2 | 39.50 | 1-33 | - | |
| ALL ONE-DAY | 87.2 | 15 | 324 | 10 | 32.40 | 2-13 | - | |

## JAVED MIANDAD - *World XI*

| Opposition | Venue | Date | Batting | Fielding | Bowling |
|---|---|---|---|---|---|
| **OTHER FIRST-CLASS** | | | | | |
| West Indies XI | Scarborough | Aug 28 | 88 & 22 | 1Ct | |

**BATTING AVERAGES - Including fielding**

| | Matches | Inns | NO | Runs | HS | Avge | 100s | 50s | Ct | St |
|---|---|---|---|---|---|---|---|---|---|---|
| Other First-Class | 1 | 2 | 0 | 110 | 88 | 55.00 | - | 1 | 1 | - |
| ALL FIRST-CLASS | 1 | 2 | 0 | 110 | 88 | 55.00 | - | 1 | 1 | - |

**BOWLING AVERAGES**
Did not bowl

## S.T.JAYASURIYA - *Sri Lanka*

| Opposition | Venue | Date | Batting | Fielding | Bowling |
|---|---|---|---|---|---|
| **CORNHILL TEST MATCHES** | | | | | |
| England | Lord's | Aug 22 | 11 & 66 | | 0-1 |
| **OTHER FIRST-CLASS** | | | | | |
| Yorkshire | Headingley | July 27 | 94 | | 0-8 |
| Worcestershire | Worcester | July 30 | 20 & 78 | | |
| Gloucs | Bristol | Aug 6 | 3 & 30 | | |
| Somerset | Taunton | Aug 10 | 33 & 37 * | | 0-35 & 0-2 |
| Sussex | Hove | Aug 17 | 100 * & 10 | | 0-4 & 0-3 |
| **OTHER ONE-DAY** | | | | | |
| England Am. | Wolv'hampton | July 24 | 57 * | 3Ct | 4-39 |
| Durham | Chester-le-S | July 26 | 22 | 1Ct | 3-26 |
| England A | Old Trafford | Aug 14 | 4 | | 1-43 |
| England A | Old Trafford | Aug 15 | 35 | 1Ct | 1-40 |

**BATTING AVERAGES - Including fielding**

| | Matches | Inns | NO | Runs | HS | Avge | 100s | 50s | Ct | St |
|---|---|---|---|---|---|---|---|---|---|---|
| Cornhill Test Matches | 1 | 2 | 0 | 77 | 66 | 38.50 | - | 1 | - | - |
| Other First-Class | 5 | 9 | 2 | 405 | 100 * | 57.85 | 1 | 2 | - | - |
| ALL FIRST-CLASS | 6 | 11 | 2 | 482 | 100 * | 53.55 | 1 | 3 | - | - |
| Other One-Day | 4 | 4 | 1 | 118 | 57 * | 39.33 | - | 1 | 5 | - |
| ALL ONE-DAY | 4 | 4 | 1 | 118 | 57 * | 39.33 | - | 1 | 5 | - |

**BOWLING AVERAGES**

| | Overs | Mdns | Runs | Wkts | Avge | Best | 5wI | 10wM |
|---|---|---|---|---|---|---|---|---|
| Cornhill Test Matches | 1 | 0 | 1 | 0 | - | - | - | - |
| Other First-Class | 11.5 | 2 | 52 | 0 | - | - | - | - |
| ALL FIRST-CLASS | 12.5 | 2 | 53 | 0 | - | - | - | - |
| Other One-Day | 38.4 | 1 | 148 | 9 | 16.44 | 4-39 | - | |
| ALL ONE-DAY | 38.4 | 1 | 148 | 9 | 16.44 | 4-39 | - | |

## M.JEAN-JACQUES - *Derbyshire*

| Opposition | Venue | Date | Batting | Fielding | Bowling |
|---|---|---|---|---|---|
| **BRITANNIC ASSURANCE** | | | | | |
| Northants | Derby | April 27 | | | 1-81 |
| Somerset | Derby | May 22 | 28 & 2 | | 1-62 & 2-87 |
| Kent | Canterbury | May 25 | 0 & 3 | | 4-54 & 0-54 |
| Northants | Northampton | May 31 | 0 & 0 * | | 1-50 & 0-49 |
| **OTHER FIRST-CLASS** | | | | | |
| Cambridge U | Fenner's | May 9 | 2 | | 3-34 & 0-25 |
| **REFUGE ASSURANCE** | | | | | |
| Leicestershire | Leicester | April 21 | | | 0-13 |
| Lancashire | Derby | May 19 | 23 | | 2-56 |
| Kent | Canterbury | May 26 | 0 | 1Ct | 0-55 |

**BATTING AVERAGES - Including fielding**

| | Matches | Inns | NO | Runs | HS | Avge | 100s | 50s | Ct | St |
|---|---|---|---|---|---|---|---|---|---|---|
| Britannic Assurance | 4 | 6 | 1 | 33 | 28 | 6.60 | - | - | - | - |
| Other First-Class | 1 | 1 | 0 | 2 | 2 | 2.00 | - | - | - | - |
| ALL FIRST-CLASS | 5 | 7 | 1 | 35 | 28 | 5.83 | - | - | - | - |
| Refuge Assurance | 3 | 2 | 0 | 23 | 23 | 11.50 | - | - | 1 | - |
| ALL ONE-DAY | 3 | 2 | 0 | 23 | 23 | 11.50 | - | - | 1 | - |

**BOWLING AVERAGES**

| | Overs | Mdns | Runs | Wkts | Avge | Best | 5wI | 10wM |
|---|---|---|---|---|---|---|---|---|
| Britannic Assurance | 113.4 | 18 | 437 | 9 | 48.55 | 4-54 | - | - |
| Other First-Class | 27.5 | 8 | 59 | 3 | 19.66 | 3-34 | - | - |
| ALL FIRST-CLASS | 141.3 | 26 | 496 | 12 | 41.33 | 4-54 | - | - |
| Refuge Assurance | 18 | 1 | 124 | 2 | 62.00 | 2-56 | - | |

# J PLAYER RECORDS

| ALL ONE-DAY | 18 | 1 | 124 | 2 | 62.00 | 2-56 | - |
|---|---|---|---|---|---|---|---|

## A.C.JELFS - Lincolnshire

| Opposition | Venue | Date | Batting | Fielding | Bowling |
|---|---|---|---|---|---|
| **NATWEST TROPHY** | | | | | |
| Notts | Trent Bridge | June 26 | 25 | | 0-51 |

**BATTING AVERAGES - Including fielding**

| | Matches | Inns | NO | Runs | HS | Avge | 100s | 50s | Ct | St |
|---|---|---|---|---|---|---|---|---|---|---|
| NatWest Trophy | 1 | 1 | 0 | 25 | 25 | 25.00 | - | - | - | - |
| ALL ONE-DAY | 1 | 1 | 0 | 25 | 25 | 25.00 | - | - | - | - |

**BOWLING AVERAGES**

| | Overs | Mdns | Runs | Wkts | Avge | Best | 5wI | 10wM |
|---|---|---|---|---|---|---|---|---|
| NatWest Trophy | 9 | 1 | 51 | 0 | - | - | - | - |
| ALL ONE-DAY | 9 | 1 | 51 | 0 | - | - | - | - |

## R.H.J.JENKINS - Cambridge University & Combined Universities

| Opposition | Venue | Date | Batting | Fielding | Bowling |
|---|---|---|---|---|---|
| **OTHER FIRST-CLASS** | | | | | |
| Northants | Fenner's | April 16 | 20 | | 1-71 & 0-17 |
| Essex | Fenner's | April 19 | 5 & 0 | 1Ct | 0-61 & 0-53 |
| Middlesex | Fenner's | May 15 | 10 | | 0-39 & 2-46 |
| Glamorgan | Fenner's | June 18 | 0 | 1Ct | 1-55 & 1-47 |
| Sussex | Hove | June 29 | 3 | | 1-71 |
| Oxford U | Lord's | July 2 | 9 & 17* | | 0-29 & 1-25 |
| **BENSON & HEDGES CUP** | | | | | |
| For Combined Universities | | | | | |
| Gloucs | Bristol | April 23 | 0* | 1Ct | 0-35 |
| Derbyshire | The Parks | April 25 | | | 1-58 |
| Worcestershire | Fenner's | May 2 | 9 | 1Ct | 0-23 |
| Northants | Northampton | May 4 | | | 0-25 |

**BATTING AVERAGES - Including fielding**

| | Matches | Inns | NO | Runs | HS | Avge | 100s | 50s | Ct | St |
|---|---|---|---|---|---|---|---|---|---|---|
| Other First-Class | 6 | 8 | 1 | 64 | 20 | 9.14 | - | - | 2 | - |
| ALL FIRST-CLASS | 6 | 8 | 1 | 64 | 20 | 9.14 | - | - | 2 | - |
| Benson & Hedges Cup | 4 | 2 | 1 | 9 | 9 | 9.00 | - | - | 2 | - |
| ALL ONE-DAY | 4 | 2 | 1 | 9 | 9 | 9.00 | - | - | 2 | - |

**BOWLING AVERAGES**

| | Overs | Mdns | Runs | Wkts | Avge | Best | 5wI | 10wM |
|---|---|---|---|---|---|---|---|---|
| Other First-Class | 150 | 20 | 514 | 7 | 73.42 | 2-46 | - | - |
| ALL FIRST-CLASS | 150 | 20 | 514 | 7 | 73.42 | 2-46 | - | - |
| Benson & Hedges Cup | 26 | 1 | 141 | 1 | 141.00 | 1-58 | - | - |
| ALL ONE-DAY | 26 | 1 | 141 | 1 | 141.00 | 1-58 | - | - |

## T.E.JESTY - Lancashire

| Opposition | Venue | Date | Batting | Fielding | Bowling |
|---|---|---|---|---|---|
| **OTHER FIRST-CLASS** | | | | | |
| Oxford U | The Parks | June 7 | 4* & 122* | | |

**BATTING AVERAGES - Including fielding**

| | Matches | Inns | NO | Runs | HS | Avge | 100s | 50s | Ct | St |
|---|---|---|---|---|---|---|---|---|---|---|
| Other First-Class | 1 | 2 | 2 | 126 | 122* | - | 1 | - | - | - |
| ALL FIRST-CLASS | 1 | 2 | 2 | 126 | 122* | - | 1 | - | - | - |

## A.N.JOHNSON - Shropshire

| Opposition | Venue | Date | Batting | Fielding | Bowling |
|---|---|---|---|---|---|
| **NATWEST TROPHY** | | | | | |
| Leicestershire | Leicester | June 26 | 20 | | |

**BATTING AVERAGES - Including fielding**

| | Matches | Inns | NO | Runs | HS | Avge | 100s | 50s | Ct | St |
|---|---|---|---|---|---|---|---|---|---|---|
| NatWest Trophy | 1 | 1 | 0 | 20 | 20 | 20.00 | - | - | - | - |
| ALL ONE-DAY | 1 | 1 | 0 | 20 | 20 | 20.00 | - | - | - | - |

**BOWLING AVERAGES**
Did not bowl

## P.JOHNSON - Nottinghamshire

| Opposition | Venue | Date | Batting | Fielding | Bowling |
|---|---|---|---|---|---|
| **BRITANNIC ASSURANCE** | | | | | |
| Leicestershire | Trent Bridge | May 9 | 37 & 57* | 1Ct | |
| Yorkshire | Headingley | May 16 | 31 & 7 | | |
| Kent | Trent Bridge | May 22 | 38* & 65 | | |
| Leicestershire | Leicester | May 25 | 24 & 20 | 1Ct | |
| Hampshire | Trent Bridge | May 31 | 16 & 0 | 1Ct | |
| Surrey | The Oval | June 4 | 8* | | |
| Gloucs | Gloucester | June 14 | 0 & 6 | 1Ct | |
| Worcestershire | Worcester | June 18 | 22 & 34* | | 1-26 |
| Warwickshire | Trent Bridge | June 21 | 12 | 1Ct | |
| Glamorgan | Cardiff | July 2 | 8 & 77* | | |
| Lancashire | Trent Bridge | July 16 | 71 | | |
| Northants | Well'borough | July 19 | 81 | 1Ct | |
| Yorkshire | Worksop | July 23 | 13 | | |
| Middlesex | Lord's | July 26 | 34 & 105 | | |
| Sussex | Eastbourne | Aug 6 | 52 | | |
| Essex | Trent Bridge | Aug 9 | 124 & 0 | 1Ct | |
| Somerset | Trent Bridge | Aug 16 | 71* & 19 | 1Ct | 1-36 |
| Derbyshire | Trent Bridge | Aug 23 | 58 & 33 | | |
| Lancashire | Old Trafford | Aug 28 | 11 & 114 | 2Ct | |
| Middlesex | Trent Bridge | Sept 3 | 52 & 0 | 1Ct | |
| Derbyshire | Derby | Sept 10 | 0 | | |
| Worcestershire | Trent Bridge | Sept 17 | 57 | 1Ct | |
| **OTHER FIRST-CLASS** | | | | | |
| Oxford U | The Parks | April 27 | 97* | | |
| **REFUGE ASSURANCE** | | | | | |
| Lancashire | Old Trafford | April 21 | | 2Ct | |
| Warwickshire | Trent Bridge | April 28 | 80 | | |
| Glamorgan | Cardiff | May 5 | 22 | | |
| Essex | Trent Bridge | May 12 | 55 | 1Ct | |
| Leicestershire | Leicester | May 26 | 46 | | |
| Somerset | Trent Bridge | June 9 | 31 | | |
| Gloucs | Gloucester | June 16 | 52* | | |
| Middlesex | Trent Bridge | June 23 | 9 | | |
| Surrey | The Oval | June 30 | 0 | 1Ct | |
| Hampshire | Trent Bridge | July 14 | 31 | | |
| Northants | Well'borough | July 21 | 0 | 1Ct | |
| Sussex | Hove | July 28 | 20 | | |
| Worcestershire | Trent Bridge | Aug 4 | 18 | | |
| Kent | Trent Bridge | Aug 11 | 3 | | |
| Yorkshire | Scarborough | Aug 18 | 0 | | |
| Derbyshire | Trent Bridge | Aug 25 | | 1Ct | |
| Worcestershire | Trent Bridge | Sept 1 | 3 | | |
| **NATWEST TROPHY** | | | | | |
| Lincolnshire | Trent Bridge | June 26 | 48 | | |
| Gloucs | Bristol | July 11 | 18 | | |
| Hampshire | Southampton | July 31 | 0 | | |
| **BENSON & HEDGES CUP** | | | | | |
| Hampshire | Southampton | April 23 | 24 | | |
| Yorkshire | Trent Bridge | April 25 | 4 | 1Ct | |
| Glamorgan | Cardiff | May 4 | 14 | | |

# PLASTER RECORDS

# PLAYER RECORDS

| | | | | |
|---|---|---|---|---|
| Min Counties | Trent Bridge | May 7 | 102 * | |

**OTHER ONE-DAY**
For England A

| | | | | |
|---|---|---|---|---|
| Sri Lanka | Old Trafford | Aug 14 | 32 | |
| Sri Lanka | Old Trafford | Aug 15 | 22 | 1Ct |

**BATTING AVERAGES - Including fielding**

| | Matches | Inns | NO | Runs | HS | Avge | 100s | 50s | Ct | St |
|---|---|---|---|---|---|---|---|---|---|---|
| Britannic Assurance | 22 | 36 | 6 | 1357 | 124 | 45.23 | 3 | 10 | 12 | - |
| Other First-Class | 1 | 1 | 1 | 97 | 97 * | | - | - | 1 | - |
| | | | | | | | | | | |
| ALL FIRST-CLASS | 23 | 37 | 7 | 1454 | 124 | 48.46 | 3 | 11 | 12 | - |
| | | | | | | | | | | |
| Refuge Assurance | 17 | 15 | 1 | 370 | 80 | 26.42 | - | 3 | 6 | - |
| NatWest Trophy | 3 | 3 | 0 | 66 | 48 | 22.00 | - | - | - | - |
| Benson & Hedges Cup | 4 | 4 | 1 | 144 | 102 * | 48.00 | 1 | - | 1 | - |
| Other One-Day | 2 | 2 | 0 | 54 | 32 | 27.00 | - | - | 1 | - |
| | | | | | | | | | | |
| ALL ONE-DAY | 26 | 24 | 2 | 634 | 102 * | 28.81 | 1 | 3 | 8 | - |

**BOWLING AVERAGES**

| | Overs | Mdns | Runs | Wkts | Avge | Best | 5wI | 10wM |
|---|---|---|---|---|---|---|---|---|
| Britannic Assurance | 12.2 | 1 | 62 | 2 | 31.00 | 1-26 | - | - |
| Other First-Class | | | | | | | | |
| | | | | | | | | |
| ALL FIRST-CLASS | 12.2 | 1 | 62 | 2 | 31.00 | 1-26 | - | - |
| | | | | | | | | |
| Refuge Assurance | | | | | | | | |
| NatWest Trophy | | | | | | | | |
| Benson & Hedges Cup | | | | | | | | |
| Other One-Day | | | | | | | | |
| | | | | | | | | |
| ALL ONE-DAY | | | | | | | | |

## S.W.JOHNSON - *Cambridge University*

| Opposition | Venue | Date | Batting | Fielding | Bowling |
|---|---|---|---|---|---|
| **OTHER FIRST-CLASS** | | | | | |
| Lancashire | Fenner's | April 13 | 14 | | 1-88 & 0-38 |
| Northants | Fenner's | April 16 | 20 | | 0-76 & 0-42 |
| Essex | Fenner's | April 19 | 4 * & 18 * | 2Ct | 0-33 & 0-69 |
| Derbyshire | Fenner's | May 9 | 18 | | 1-66 & 0-25 |
| Middlesex | Fenner's | May 15 | 4 * | 1Ct | 0-37 & 0-28 |
| Glamorgan | Fenner's | June 18 | 0 | | 1-34 |
| Oxford U | Lord's | July 2 | 7 | | 0-47 & 0-25 |

**BATTING AVERAGES - Including fielding**

| | Matches | Inns | NO | Runs | HS | Avge | 100s | 50s | Ct | St |
|---|---|---|---|---|---|---|---|---|---|---|
| Other First-Class | 7 | 8 | 3 | 85 | 20 | 17.00 | - | - | 3 | - |
| | | | | | | | | | | |
| ALL FIRST-CLASS | 7 | 8 | 3 | 85 | 20 | 17.00 | - | - | 3 | - |

**BOWLING AVERAGES**

| | Overs | Mdns | Runs | Wkts | Avge | Best | 5wI | 10wM |
|---|---|---|---|---|---|---|---|---|
| Other First-Class | 131.1 | 17 | 608 | 3 | 202.66 | 1-34 | - | - |
| | | | | | | | | |
| ALL FIRST-CLASS | 131.1 | 17 | 608 | 3 | 202.66 | 1-34 | - | - |

## A.N.JONES - *Sussex*

| Opposition | Venue | Date | Batting | Fielding | Bowling |
|---|---|---|---|---|---|
| **BRITANNIC ASSURANCE** | | | | | |
| Somerset | Taunton | April 27 | | | 1-28 |
| Middlesex | Lord's | May 9 | 6 | | 1-48 & 4-65 |
| Hampshire | Hove | May 16 | | 1Ct | 0-64 & 0-42 |
| Glamorgan | Cardiff | May 25 | 3 | | 2-92 |
| Lancashire | Old Trafford | May 31 | 28 & 1 | | 2-86 & 1-38 |
| Kent | Tunbridge W | June 7 | | | 2-41 & 2-56 |
| Worcestershire | Hove | June 14 | | | 0-48 |
| Warwickshire | Coventry | June 18 | | 4 * | 3-97 |
| Essex | Horsham | June 21 | | | 2-110 |
| Surrey | Arundel | July 2 | 14 * & 0 * | | 2-94 |
| Derbyshire | Derby | July 5 | 6 | | 2-67 & 2-36 |
| Somerset | Hove | July 16 | | | 1-73 & 0-66 |

| Opposition | Venue | Date | Batting | Fielding | Bowling |
|---|---|---|---|---|---|
| Leicestershire | Hove | July 19 | | | 2-20 & 0-23 |
| Gloucs | Cheltenham | July 23 | | | 5-84 |
| Northants | Eastbourne | Aug 2 | | 7 * | 3-36 & 0-19 |
| Notts | Eastbourne | Aug 6 | 9 | | 1-32 |
| Yorkshire | Midd'brough | Aug 9 | 1 | | 5-46 & 4-41 |
| Hampshire | Bournemouth | Aug 20 | 7 | | 3-46 & 0-37 |
| Surrey | The Oval | Aug 28 | 4 * & 19 | | 0-83 |
| Kent | Hove | Sept 3 | 8 & 1 | | 0-57 & 0-64 |
| Gloucs | Hove | Sept 17 | 1 | | 3-68 & 0-22 |

**OTHER FIRST-CLASS**

| | | | | | |
|---|---|---|---|---|---|
| Cambridge U | Hove | June 29 | | | 1-9 |
| Sri Lanka | Hove | Aug 17 | 9 * | | 1-30 & 1-50 |

**REFUGE ASSURANCE**

| Opposition | Venue | Date | Batting | Fielding | Bowling |
|---|---|---|---|---|---|
| Warwickshire | Edgbaston | April 21 | | 1Ct | 2-13 |
| Somerset | Taunton | April 28 | 0 * | | 2-49 |
| Middlesex | Hove | May 12 | | | 0-23 |
| Gloucs | Hove | May 19 | 0 * | 1Ct | 3-25 |
| Glamorgan | Swansea | May 26 | 2 | 1Ct | 0-11 |
| Lancashire | Old Trafford | June 2 | 6 * | 1Ct | 3-39 |
| Hampshire | Basingstoke | June 9 | 3 * | 1Ct | 3-33 |
| Worcestershire | Hove | June 16 | | | |
| Derbyshire | Derby | July 7 | | | 2-55 |
| Surrey | The Oval | July 14 | 0 * | | 0-25 |
| Leicestershire | Hove | July 21 | | | 5-32 |
| Notts | Hove | July 28 | | | 1-45 |
| Northants | Eastbourne | Aug 4 | | | 1-28 |
| Yorkshire | Midd'brough | Aug 11 | 7 * | | 0-21 |
| Kent | Hove | Aug 25 | | | 0-49 |

**NATWEST TROPHY**

| | | | | | |
|---|---|---|---|---|---|
| Scotland | Edinburgh | June 26 | 0 * | | 0-30 |
| Essex | Hove | July 11 | | | 2-46 |

**BENSON & HEDGES CUP**

| | | | | | |
|---|---|---|---|---|---|
| Leicestershire | Hove | April 25 | | | 3-33 |
| Kent | Canterbury | May 2 | | | 1-41 |
| Scotland | Hove | May 4 | 0 * | | 3-43 |

**BATTING AVERAGES - Including fielding**

| | Matches | Inns | NO | Runs | HS | Avge | 100s | 50s | Ct | St |
|---|---|---|---|---|---|---|---|---|---|---|
| Britannic Assurance | 21 | 17 | 5 | 119 | 28 | 9.91 | - | - | 1 | - |
| Other First-Class | 2 | 1 | 1 | 9 | 9 * | | - | - | - | - |
| | | | | | | | | | | |
| ALL FIRST-CLASS | 23 | 18 | 6 | 128 | 28 | 10.66 | - | - | 1 | - |
| | | | | | | | | | | |
| Refuge Assurance | 15 | 7 | 6 | 18 | 7 * | 18.00 | - | - | 5 | - |
| NatWest Trophy | 2 | 1 | 1 | 0 | 0 * | | - | - | - | - |
| Benson & Hedges Cup | 3 | 1 | 1 | 0 | 0 * | | - | - | - | - |
| | | | | | | | | | | |
| ALL ONE-DAY | 20 | 9 | 8 | 18 | 7 * | 18.00 | - | - | 5 | - |

**BOWLING AVERAGES**

| | Overs | Mdns | Runs | Wkts | Avge | Best | 5wI | 10wM |
|---|---|---|---|---|---|---|---|---|
| Britannic Assurance | 502.2 | 68 | 1829 | 53 | 34.50 | 5-46 | 2 | - |
| Other First-Class | 25 | 6 | 89 | 3 | 29.66 | 1-9 | - | - |
| | | | | | | | | |
| ALL FIRST-CLASS | 527.2 | 74 | 1918 | 56 | 34.25 | 5-46 | 2 | - |
| | | | | | | | | |
| Refuge Assurance | 81.2 | 5 | 448 | 22 | 20.36 | 5-32 | 1 | |
| NatWest Trophy | 12 | 0 | 76 | 2 | 38.00 | 2-46 | - | |
| Benson & Hedges Cup | 30.4 | 4 | 117 | 7 | 16.71 | 3-33 | - | |
| | | | | | | | | |
| ALL ONE-DAY | 124 | 9 | 641 | 31 | 20.67 | 5-32 | 1 | |

## C.JONES - *Oxford University*

| Opposition | Venue | Date | Batting | Fielding | Bowling |
|---|---|---|---|---|---|
| **OTHER FIRST-CLASS** | | | | | |
| Kent | The Parks | June 18 | 4 & 23 | | |

**BATTING AVERAGES - Including fielding**

| | Matches | Inns | NO | Runs | HS | Avge | 100s | 50s | Ct | St |
|---|---|---|---|---|---|---|---|---|---|---|
| Other First-Class | 1 | 2 | 0 | 27 | 23 | 13.50 | - | - | - | - |
| | | | | | | | | | | |
| ALL FIRST-CLASS | 1 | 2 | 0 | 27 | 23 | 13.50 | - | - | - | - |

**BOWLING AVERAGES**
Did not bowl

| J | PLAYER RECORDS |
|---|---|

## D.M.JONES - *Victoria*

| Opposition | Venue | Date | Batting | Fielding | Bowling |
|---|---|---|---|---|---|
| **OTHER FIRST-CLASS** | | | | | |
| Essex | Chelmsford | Sept 23 | 25 & 9 | | |
| **OTHER ONE-DAY** | | | | | |
| Durham | Durham U. | Sept 16 | 29 | | |
| Essex | Chelmsford | Sept 22 | 86 * | | |

**BATTING AVERAGES - Including fielding**

| | Matches | Inns | NO | Runs | HS | Avge | 100s | 50s | Ct | St |
|---|---|---|---|---|---|---|---|---|---|---|
| Other First-Class | 1 | 2 | 0 | 34 | 25 | 17.00 | - | - | - | - |
| ALL FIRST-CLASS | 1 | 2 | 0 | 34 | 25 | 17.00 | - | - | - | - |
| Other One-Day | 2 | 2 | 1 | 115 | 86 * | 115.00 | - | 1 | - | - |
| ALL ONE-DAY | 2 | 2 | 1 | 115 | 86 * | 115.00 | - | 1 | - | - |

**BOWLING AVERAGES**
Did not bowl

## G.W.JONES - *Cambridge University*

| Opposition | Venue | Date | Batting | Fielding | Bowling |
|---|---|---|---|---|---|
| **OTHER FIRST-CLASS** | | | | | |
| Lancashire | Fenner's | April 13 | 1 & 0 | | |
| Northants | Fenner's | April 16 | 5 | | |
| Leicestershire | Fenner's | May 22 | 0 & 13 * | | |

**BATTING AVERAGES - Including fielding**

| | Matches | Inns | NO | Runs | HS | Avge | 100s | 50s | Ct | St |
|---|---|---|---|---|---|---|---|---|---|---|
| Other First-Class | 3 | 5 | 1 | 19 | 13 * | 4.75 | - | - | - | - |
| ALL FIRST-CLASS | 3 | 5 | 1 | 19 | 13 * | 4.75 | - | - | - | - |

**BOWLING AVERAGES**
Did not bowl

## J.B.R.JONES - *Shropshire*

| Opposition | Venue | Date | Batting | Fielding | Bowling |
|---|---|---|---|---|---|
| **NATWEST TROPHY** | | | | | |
| Leicestershire | Leicester | June 26 | 1 | | |

**BATTING AVERAGES - Including fielding**

| | Matches | Inns | NO | Runs | HS | Avge | 100s | 50s | Ct | St |
|---|---|---|---|---|---|---|---|---|---|---|
| NatWest Trophy | 1 | 1 | 0 | 1 | 1 | 1.00 | - | - | - | - |
| ALL ONE-DAY | 1 | 1 | 0 | 1 | 1 | 1.00 | - | - | - | - |

**BOWLING AVERAGES**
Did not bowl

## J.H.JONES - *Berkshire*

| Opposition | Venue | Date | Batting | Fielding | Bowling |
|---|---|---|---|---|---|
| **NATWEST TROPHY** | | | | | |
| Hampshire | Reading | June 26 | | | 0-9 |

**BATTING AVERAGES - Including fielding**

| | Matches | Inns | NO | Runs | HS | Avge | 100s | 50s | Ct | St |
|---|---|---|---|---|---|---|---|---|---|---|
| NatWest Trophy | 1 | 0 | 0 | 0 | 0 | - | - | - | - | - |
| ALL ONE-DAY | 1 | 0 | 0 | 0 | 0 | - | - | - | - | - |

**BOWLING AVERAGES**

| | Overs | Mdns | Runs | Wkts | Avge | Best | 5wI | 10wM |
|---|---|---|---|---|---|---|---|---|
| NatWest Trophy | 3 | 0 | 9 | 0 | - | - | - | - |

# PLER RECORDS

# PLAYER RECORDS

**K**

## R.S.KALUWITHARANA - *Sri Lanka*

| Opposition | Venue | Date | Batting | Fielding | Bowling |
|---|---|---|---|---|---|
| **OTHER FIRST-CLASS** | | | | | |
| Yorkshire | Headingley | July 27 | 31 | | |
| Worcestershire | Worcester | July 30 | 0 & 34 | 1Ct | |
| Gloucs | Bristol | Aug 6 | 8 & 0 | 1Ct | |
| **OTHER ONE-DAY** | | | | | |
| England Am. | Wolv'hampton | July 24 | | 1Ct,1St | |
| Durham | Chester-le-S | July 26 | 2 | 1Ct,1St | |

**BATTING AVERAGES - Including fielding**

| | Matches | Inns | NO | Runs | HS | Avge | 100s | 50s | Ct | St |
|---|---|---|---|---|---|---|---|---|---|---|
| Other First-Class | 3 | 5 | 0 | 73 | 34 | 14.60 | - | - | 2 | - |
| ALL FIRST-CLASS | 3 | 5 | 0 | 73 | 34 | 14.60 | - | - | 2 | - |
| Other One-Day | 2 | 1 | 0 | 2 | 2 | 2.00 | - | - | 2 | 2 |
| ALL ONE-DAY | 2 | 1 | 0 | 2 | 2 | 2.00 | - | - | 2 | 2 |

**BOWLING AVERAGES**
Did not bowl

## KAPIL DEV - *World XI*

| Opposition | Venue | Date | Batting | Fielding | Bowling |
|---|---|---|---|---|---|
| **OTHER FIRST-CLASS** | | | | | |
| West Indies XI | Scarborough | Aug 28 | 22 & 5 * | 1Ct | 0-23 & 2-42 |

**BATTING AVERAGES - Including fielding**

| | Matches | Inns | NO | Runs | HS | Avge | 100s | 50s | Ct | St |
|---|---|---|---|---|---|---|---|---|---|---|
| Other First-Class | 1 | 2 | 1 | 27 | 22 | 27.00 | - | - | 1 | - |
| ALL FIRST-CLASS | 1 | 2 | 1 | 27 | 22 | 27.00 | - | - | 1 | - |

**BOWLING AVERAGES**

| | Overs | Mdns | Runs | Wkts | Avge | Best | 5wI | 10wM |
|---|---|---|---|---|---|---|---|---|
| Other First-Class | 13 | 0 | 65 | 2 | 32.50 | 2-42 | - | - |
| ALL FIRST-CLASS | 13 | 0 | 65 | 2 | 32.50 | 2-42 | - | - |

## M.KEECH - *Middlesex*

| Opposition | Venue | Date | Batting | Fielding | Bowling |
|---|---|---|---|---|---|
| **BRITANNIC ASSURANCE** | | | | | |
| Sussex | Hove | May 22 | 0 * & 27 | | 0-0 |
| Somerset | Taunton | May 25 | 51 | 1Ct | 0-0 |
| Gloucs | Bristol | June 4 | 8 & 2 | | 0-9 |
| Leicestershire | Uxbridge | June 7 | 16 | | 0-7 |
| Yorkshire | Sheffield | June 21 | 30 & 9 | | |
| Warwickshire | Edgbaston | July 2 | 26 & 11 | | |
| Northants | Uxbridge | July 16 | 31 | | |
| Lancashire | Uxbridge | July 19 | 35 & 0 | | |
| Notts | Lord's | July 26 | 32 & 58 * | | |
| Hampshire | Lord's | Aug 2 | 0 | | |
| Derbyshire | Lord's | Aug 9 | 0 | 1Ct | |
| Surrey | The Oval | Aug 20 | 18 | 2Ct | |
| Worcestershire | Worcester | Aug 23 | 1 & 4 | | |
| Essex | Chelmsford | Sept 17 | 3 & 0 | | |
| **OTHER FIRST-CLASS** | | | | | |
| Cambridge U | Fenner's | May 15 | 12 * & 46 | | 0-20 |
| **REFUGE ASSURANCE** | | | | | |
| Surrey | Lord's | April 28 | 36 | 1Ct | |
| Sussex | Hove | May 12 | 38 | | |
| Somerset | Taunton | May 26 | 49 * | | |
| Kent | Southgate | June 2 | 4 | | |
| Leicestershire | Uxbridge | June 9 | 20 | | |
| Notts | Trent Bridge | June 23 | 14 * | 1Ct | |

---

| Yorkshire | Lord's | July 7 | 5 | | |
|---|---|---|---|---|---|
| Warwickshire | Edgbaston | July 14 | 4 | | |
| Lancashire | Lord's | July 21 | 16 | | |
| Hampshire | Lord's | Aug 4 | 0 * | | |
| Derbyshire | Lord's | Aug 11 | 2 | | |
| Worcestershire | Worcester | Aug 25 | 7 | | |
| **BENSON & HEDGES CUP** | | | | | |
| Essex | Chelmsford | May 2 | 37 | 1Ct | |
| Warwickshire | Lord's | May 4 | 47 | | |

**BATTING AVERAGES - Including fielding**

| | Matches | Inns | NO | Runs | HS | Avge | 100s | 50s | Ct | St |
|---|---|---|---|---|---|---|---|---|---|---|
| Britannic Assurance | 14 | 22 | 2 | 362 | 58 * | 18.10 | - | 2 | 4 | - |
| Other First-Class | 1 | 2 | 1 | 58 | 46 | 58.00 | - | - | - | - |
| ALL FIRST-CLASS | 15 | 24 | 3 | 420 | 58 * | 20.00 | - | 2 | 4 | - |
| Refuge Assurance | 12 | 12 | 3 | 195 | 49 * | 21.66 | - | - | 2 | - |
| Benson & Hedges Cup | 2 | 2 | 0 | 84 | 47 | 42.00 | - | - | 1 | - |
| ALL ONE-DAY | 14 | 14 | 3 | 279 | 49 * | 25.36 | - | - | 3 | - |

**BOWLING AVERAGES**

| | Overs | Mdns | Runs | Wkts | Avge | Best | 5wI | 10wM |
|---|---|---|---|---|---|---|---|---|
| Britannic Assurance | 11 | 6 | 16 | 0 | - | - | - | - |
| Other First-Class | 3 | 0 | 20 | 0 | - | - | - | - |
| ALL FIRST-CLASS | 14 | 6 | 36 | 0 | - | - | - | - |
| Refuge Assurance | | | | | | | | |
| Benson & Hedges Cup | | | | | | | | |
| ALL ONE-DAY | | | | | | | | |

## D.J.M.KELLEHER - *Kent*

| Opposition | Venue | Date | Batting | Fielding | Bowling |
|---|---|---|---|---|---|
| **OTHER FIRST-CLASS** | | | | | |
| Oxford U | The Parks | June 18 | 10 & 29 * | | 3-25 & 0-22 |

**BATTING AVERAGES - Including fielding**

| | Matches | Inns | NO | Runs | HS | Avge | 100s | 50s | Ct | St |
|---|---|---|---|---|---|---|---|---|---|---|
| Other First-Class | 1 | 2 | 1 | 39 | 29 * | 39.00 | - | - | - | - |
| ALL FIRST-CLASS | 1 | 2 | 1 | 39 | 29 * | 39.00 | - | - | - | - |

**BOWLING AVERAGES**

| | Overs | Mdns | Runs | Wkts | Avge | Best | 5wI | 10wM |
|---|---|---|---|---|---|---|---|---|
| Other First-Class | 26 | 5 | 47 | 3 | 15.66 | 3-25 | - | - |
| ALL FIRST-CLASS | 26 | 5 | 47 | 3 | 15.66 | 3-25 | - | - |

## S.A.KELLETT - *Yorkshire*

| Opposition | Venue | Date | Batting | Fielding | Bowling |
|---|---|---|---|---|---|
| **BRITANNIC ASSURANCE** | | | | | |
| Middlesex | Lord's | April 27 | 42 | | |
| Warwickshire | Headingley | May 9 | 8 & 17 | 1Ct | |
| Notts | Headingley | May 16 | 41 & 0 | 2Ct | |
| Gloucs | Sheffield | May 22 | 26 | 1Ct | |
| Northants | Headingley | May 25 | 53 & 5 | 1Ct | |
| Warwickshire | Edgbaston | May 31 | 30 & 0 | 1Ct | |
| Kent | Harrogate | June 14 | 5 | | |
| Middlesex | Sheffield | June 21 | 13 & 18 | 1Ct | |
| Worcestershire | Headingley | July 2 | 36 * | | |
| Hampshire | Southampton | July 5 | 56 * | | |
| Derbyshire | Scarborough | July 16 | 36 | 1Ct | |
| Surrey | Guildford | July 19 | 6 & 13 | 1Ct | |
| Notts | Worksop | July 23 | 9 | 1Ct | |
| Lancashire | Old Trafford | Aug 2 | 81 & 1 * | | |
| Leicestershire | Leicester | Aug 6 | 3 | 1Ct | 0-3 |
| Sussex | Midd'brough | Aug 9 | 66 & 8 | 2Ct | |
| Glamorgan | Headingley | Aug 16 | 34 & 16 | | |
| Essex | Colchester | Aug 20 | 58 & 41 | 2Ct | |

| Somerset | Taunton | Aug 23 | 67 & 1 | | 0-4 |
|---|---|---|---|---|---|
| Northants | Northampton | Aug 28 | 36 & 3 | | |
| Lancashire | Scarborough | Sept 3 | 7 & 5 | | |
| Derbyshire | Chesterfield | Sept 17 | 125 *& 26 | 2Ct | |

**OTHER FIRST-CLASS**

| Oxford U | The Parks | June 4 | 20 & 63 | | |
|---|---|---|---|---|---|
| Sri Lanka | Headingley | July 27 | 82 & 109 * | 2Ct | |

**REFUGE ASSURANCE**

| Warwickshire | Headingley | May 12 | 17 | 2Ct | |
|---|---|---|---|---|---|
| Derbyshire | Chesterfield | June 2 | 0 * | | |
| Lancashire | Old Trafford | Aug 4 | 0 | | |
| Sussex | Midd'brough | Aug 11 | 13 | | |
| Notts | Scarborough | Aug 18 | 26 | | |
| Somerset | Taunton | Aug 25 | 10 | | 0-16 |

**BENSON & HEDGES CUP**

| Min Counties | Headingley | May 2 | | |
|---|---|---|---|---|
| Hampshire | Headingley | May 4 | 0 * | |
| Glamorgan | Cardiff | May 7 | | |
| Warwickshire | Headingley | May 29 | 44 | |
| Lancashire | Old Trafford | June 16 | 2 | |

**OTHER ONE-DAY**

| Derbyshire | Scarborough | Sept 1 | 13 | 0-22 |
|---|---|---|---|---|
| Essex | Scarborough | Sept 2 | 10 * | 0-24 |
| Yorkshiremen | Scarborough | Sept 7 | 26 * | |
| World XI | Scarborough | Sept 8 | 9 | 0-35 |

**BATTING AVERAGES - Including fielding**

| | Matches | Inns | NO | Runs | HS | Avge | 100s | 50s | Ct | St |
|---|---|---|---|---|---|---|---|---|---|---|
| Britannic Assurance | 22 | 36 | 4 | 992 | 125 * | 31.00 | 1 | 6 | 17 | - |
| Other First-Class | 2 | 4 | 1 | 274 | 109 * | 91.33 | 1 | 2 | 2 | - |
| ALL FIRST-CLASS | 24 | 40 | 5 | 1266 | 125 * | 36.17 | 2 | 8 | 19 | - |
| Refuge Assurance | 6 | 6 | 1 | 66 | 26 | 13.20 | - | - | 2 | - |
| Benson & Hedges Cup | 5 | 3 | 1 | 46 | 44 | 23.00 | - | - | - | - |
| Other One-Day | 4 | 4 | 2 | 58 | 26 * | 29.00 | - | - | - | - |
| ALL ONE-DAY | 15 | 13 | 4 | 170 | 44 | 18.88 | - | - | 2 | - |

**BOWLING AVERAGES**

| | Overs | Mdns | Runs | Wkts | Avge | Best | 5wI | 10wM |
|---|---|---|---|---|---|---|---|---|
| Britannic Assurance | 4 | 0 | 7 | 0 | - | - | - | - |
| Other First-Class | | | | | | | | |
| ALL FIRST-CLASS | 4 | 0 | 7 | 0 | - | - | - | - |
| Refuge Assurance | 3 | 0 | 16 | 0 | - | - | - | - |
| Benson & Hedges Cup | | | | | | | | |
| Other One-Day | 14 | 1 | 81 | 0 | - | - | - | - |
| ALL ONE-DAY | 17 | 1 | 97 | 0 | - | - | - | - |

## N.M.KENDRICK - *Surrey*

| Opposition | Venue | Date | Batting | Fielding | Bowling |
|---|---|---|---|---|---|
| **BRITANNIC ASSURANCE** | | | | | |
| Middlesex | Lord's | Sept 10 | 6 *& 11 | | 0-34 & 2-54 |
| Lancashire | Old Trafford | Sept 17 | 17 & 24 | 1Ct | 5-120 & 5-54 |

**BATTING AVERAGES - Including fielding**

| | Matches | Inns | NO | Runs | HS | Avge | 100s | 50s | Ct | St |
|---|---|---|---|---|---|---|---|---|---|---|
| Britannic Assurance | 2 | 4 | 1 | 58 | 24 | 19.33 | - | - | 1 | - |
| ALL FIRST-CLASS | 2 | 4 | 1 | 58 | 24 | 19.33 | - | - | 1 | - |

**BOWLING AVERAGES**

| | Overs | Mdns | Runs | Wkts | Avge | Best | 5wI | 10wM |
|---|---|---|---|---|---|---|---|---|
| Britannic Assurance | 105 | 26 | 262 | 12 | 21.83 | 5-54 | 2 | 1 |
| ALL FIRST-CLASS | 105 | 26 | 262 | 12 | 21.83 | 5-54 | 2 | 1 |

## G.J.KERSEY - *Kent*

| Opposition | Venue | Date | Batting | Fielding | Bowling |
|---|---|---|---|---|---|
| **BRITANNIC ASSURANCE** | | | | | |
| Surrey | The Oval | May 9 | 27 * | 5Ct | |
| **OTHER FIRST-CLASS** | | | | | |
| Oxford U | The Parks | June 18 | | 2Ct | |

**BATTING AVERAGES - Including fielding**

| | Matches | Inns | NO | Runs | HS | Avge | 100s | 50s | Ct | St |
|---|---|---|---|---|---|---|---|---|---|---|
| Britannic Assurance | 1 | 1 | 1 | 27 | 27 * | - | - | - | 5 | - |
| Other First-Class | 1 | 0 | 0 | 0 | 0 | - | - | - | 2 | - |
| ALL FIRST-CLASS | 2 | 1 | 1 | 27 | 27 * | - | - | - | 7 | - |

**BOWLING AVERAGES**
Did not bowl

## R.KINGSHOTT - *Norfolk*

| Opposition | Venue | Date | Batting | Fielding | Bowling |
|---|---|---|---|---|---|
| **NATWEST TROPHY** | | | | | |
| Gloucs | Bristol | June 26 | 4 * | | 0-46 |

**BATTING AVERAGES - Including fielding**

| | Matches | Inns | NO | Runs | HS | Avge | 100s | 50s | Ct | St |
|---|---|---|---|---|---|---|---|---|---|---|
| NatWest Trophy | 1 | 1 | 1 | 4 | 4 * | - | - | - | - | - |
| ALL ONE-DAY | 1 | 1 | 1 | 4 | 4 * | - | - | - | - | - |

**BOWLING AVERAGES**

| | Overs | Mdns | Runs | Wkts | Avge | Best | 5wI | 10wM |
|---|---|---|---|---|---|---|---|---|
| NatWest Trophy | 12 | 0 | 46 | 0 | - | - | - | - |
| ALL ONE-DAY | 12 | 0 | 46 | 0 | - | - | - | - |

## S.KIRNON - *Glamorgan*

| Opposition | Venue | Date | Batting | Fielding | Bowling |
|---|---|---|---|---|---|
| **REFUGE ASSURANCE** | | | | | |
| Surrey | The Oval | July 28 | 0 | | 2-48 |

**BATTING AVERAGES - Including fielding**

| | Matches | Inns | NO | Runs | HS | Avge | 100s | 50s | Ct | St |
|---|---|---|---|---|---|---|---|---|---|---|
| Refuge Assurance | 1 | 1 | 0 | 0 | 0 | 0.00 | - | - | - | - |
| ALL ONE-DAY | 1 | 1 | 0 | 0 | 0 | 0.00 | - | - | - | - |

**BOWLING AVERAGES**

| | Overs | Mdns | Runs | Wkts | Avge | Best | 5wI | 10wM |
|---|---|---|---|---|---|---|---|---|
| Refuge Assurance | 8 | 0 | 48 | 2 | 24.00 | 2-48 | - | |
| ALL ONE-DAY | 8 | 0 | 48 | 2 | 24.00 | 2-48 | - | |

## N.V.KNIGHT - *Essex & Combined Universities*

| Opposition | Venue | Date | Batting | Fielding | Bowling |
|---|---|---|---|---|---|
| **BRITANNIC ASSURANCE** | | | | | |
| Derbyshire | Derby | Aug 6 | 4 & 24 | 1Ct | |
| Notts | Trent Bridge | Aug 9 | 31 & 42 | | |
| Yorkshire | Colchester | Aug 20 | 60 | 2Ct | |
| Lancashire | Old Trafford | Aug 23 | 37 & 101 * | | 0-32 |
| Derbyshire | Chelmsford | Sept 3 | 28 | 2Ct | |
| Middlesex | Chelmsford | Sept 17 | 61 | | |

# PLAYER RECORDS

**K**

## OTHER FIRST-CLASS

Victoria   Chelmsford   Sept 23   53

## REFUGE ASSURANCE

Northants    Northampton    Aug 11    31*    1Ct
Lancashire   Old Trafford   Aug 25    0      1Ct

## BENSON & HEDGES CUP

For Combined Universities

Gloucs           Bristol        April 23   36   3Ct
Derbyshire       The Parks      April 25   5    1Ct
Worcestershire   Fenner's       May 2      9
Northants        Northampton    May 4      12   1Ct   0-4

## OTHER ONE-DAY

Durham       Scarborough   Aug 31    12   2Ct
Yorkshire    Scarborough   Sept 2    0
Victoria     Chelmsford    Sept 22   10

## BATTING AVERAGES - Including fielding

|                     | Matches | Inns | NO | Runs | HS   | Avge  | 100s | 50s | Ct | St |
|---------------------|---------|------|----|------|------|-------|------|-----|----|----|
| Britannic Assurance | 6       | 9    | 1  | 388  | 101* | 48.50 | 1    | 2   | 5  | -  |
| Other First-Class   | 1       | 1    | 0  | 53   | 53   | 53.00 | -    | 1   | -  | -  |
| ALL FIRST-CLASS     | 7       | 10   | 1  | 441  | 101* | 49.00 | 1    | 3   | 5  | -  |
| Refuge Assurance    | 2       | 2    | 1  | 31   | 31*  | 31.00 | -    | -   | 2  | -  |
| Benson & Hedges Cup | 4       | 4    | 0  | 62   | 36   | 15.50 | -    | -   | 5  | -  |
| Other One-Day       | 3       | 3    | 0  | 22   | 12   | 7.33  | -    | -   | 2  | -  |
| ALL ONE-DAY         | 9       | 9    | 1  | 115  | 36   | 14.37 | -    | -   | 9  | -  |

## BOWLING AVERAGES

|                     | Overs | Mdns | Runs | Wkts | Avge | Best | 5wI | 10wM |
|---------------------|-------|------|------|------|------|------|-----|------|
| Britannic Assurance | 5     | 0    | 32   | 0    | -    | -    | -   | -    |
| Other First-Class   |       |      |      |      |      |      |     |      |
| ALL FIRST-CLASS     | 5     | 0    | 32   | 0    | -    | -    | -   | -    |
| Refuge Assurance    |       |      |      |      |      |      |     |      |
| Benson & Hedges Cup | 1     | 0    | 4    | 0    | -    | -    | -   | -    |
| Other One-Day       |       |      |      |      |      |      |     |      |
| ALL ONE-DAY         | 1     | 0    | 4    | 0    | -    | -    | -   | -    |

# K.M.KRIKKEN - *Derbyshire*

| Opposition | Venue | Date | Batting | Fielding | Bowling |
|------------|-------|------|---------|----------|---------|

## BRITANNIC ASSURANCE

| Opposition | Venue | Date | Batting | Fielding | Bowling |
|------------|-------|------|---------|----------|---------|
| Northants | Derby | April 27 | | 1Ct | |
| Lancashire | Old Trafford | May 16 | 10 | 2Ct | |
| Somerset | Derby | May 22 | 46 * & 30 * | 4Ct | |
| Kent | Canterbury | May 25 | 1 & 18 | 1Ct | |
| Northants | Northampton | May 31 | 37 & 46 | 5Ct | |
| Glamorgan | Chesterfield | June 7 | 40 | 5Ct | |
| Gloucs | Gloucester | June 18 | 23 & 1 * | 4Ct | |
| Surrey | Derby | June 21 | 13 | | |
| Warwickshire | Edgbaston | June 28 | 13 & 14 | 5Ct | |
| Sussex | Derby | July 5 | 18 & 27 * | 3Ct | |
| Yorkshire | Scarborough | July 16 | 13 & 16 * | | |
| Worcestershire | Kidd'minster | July 19 | 32 | 4Ct | |
| Hampshire | Chesterfield | July 23 | 1 | 2Ct | |
| Essex | Derby | Aug 6 | 9 & 3 | 5Ct | |
| Middlesex | Lord's | Aug 9 | 40 * & 27 | 0Ct,1St | |
| Lancashire | Derby | Aug 16 | 17 * | 1Ct,2St | |
| Leicestershire | Derby | Aug 20 | 0 & 24 | 1Ct | |
| Notts | Trent Bridge | Aug 23 | 5 * | 3Ct | |
| Leicestershire | Leicester | Aug 28 | 9 & 65 | 4Ct | |
| Essex | Chelmsford | Sept 3 | 19 & 56 | | |
| Notts | Derby | Sept 10 | 3 & 1 | 2Ct | |
| Yorkshire | Chesterfield | Sept 17 | 0 & 0 | 3Ct | |

## OTHER FIRST-CLASS

| Opposition | Venue | Date | Batting | Fielding | Bowling |
|------------|-------|------|---------|----------|---------|
| Cambridge U | Fenner's | May 9 | 11 | 3Ct | |
| West Indies | Derby | June 12 | 6 & 3 | | |

## REFUGE ASSURANCE

| Opposition | Venue | Date | Batting | Fielding | Bowling |
|------------|-------|------|---------|----------|---------|
| Essex | Chelmsford | June 30 | 44 * | 2Ct | |
| Sussex | Derby | July 7 | | | |
| Worcestershire | Worcester | July 9 | 0 | 1Ct | |
| Gloucs | Cheltenham | July 21 | | 3Ct | |

Middlesex    Lord's         Aug 11           2Ct,1St
Glamorgan    Checkley       Aug 18    8      1Ct,2St
Notts        Trent Bridge   Aug 25    15

## OTHER ONE-DAY

For D of Norfolk

West Indies    Arundel       May 12    7*    1Ct

For Derbyshire

Yorkshire      Scarborough   Sept 1    26    1Ct,1St

## BATTING AVERAGES - Including fielding

|                     | Matches | Inns | NO | Runs | HS  | Avge  | 100s | 50s | Ct | St |
|---------------------|---------|------|----|------|-----|-------|------|-----|----|----|
| Britannic Assurance | 22      | 35   | 8  | 677  | 65  | 25.07 | -    | 2   | 55 | 3  |
| Other First-Class   | 2       | 3    | 0  | 20   | 11  | 6.66  | -    | -   | 3  | -  |
| ALL FIRST-CLASS     | 24      | 38   | 8  | 697  | 65  | 23.23 | -    | 2   | 58 | 3  |
| Refuge Assurance    | 7       | 4    | 1  | 67   | 44* | 22.33 | -    | -   | 9  | 3  |
| Other One-Day       | 2       | 2    | 1  | 33   | 26  | 33.00 | -    | -   | 2  | 1  |
| ALL ONE-DAY         | 9       | 6    | 2  | 100  | 44* | 25.00 | -    | -   | 11 | 4  |

## BOWLING AVERAGES

Did not bowl

# D.S.B.P.KURUPPU - *Sri Lanka*

| Opposition | Venue | Date | Batting | Fielding | Bowling |
|------------|-------|------|---------|----------|---------|

## CORNHILL TEST MATCHES

| Opposition | Venue | Date | Batting | Fielding | Bowling |
|------------|-------|------|---------|----------|---------|
| England | Lord's | Aug 22 | 5 & 21 | | |

## OTHER FIRST-CLASS

| Opposition | Venue | Date | Batting | Fielding | Bowling |
|------------|-------|------|---------|----------|---------|
| Yorkshire | Headingley | July 27 | 19 | 1Ct | |
| Worcestershire | Worcester | July 30 | 9 & 4 | | |
| Derbyshire | Derby | Aug 2 | 76 | 1Ct | |
| Gloucs | Bristol | Aug 6 | 17 & 10 | 1Ct | |
| Somerset | Taunton | Aug 10 | 86 & 77 | | |
| Sussex | Hove | Aug 17 | 6 & 59 | | |

## OTHER ONE-DAY

| Opposition | Venue | Date | Batting | Fielding | Bowling |
|------------|-------|------|---------|----------|---------|
| England Am. | Wolv'hampton | July 24 | 11* | 1Ct | |
| Durham | Chester-le-S | July 26 | 53 | | |
| England A | Old Trafford | Aug 14 | 3 | | |
| England A | Old Trafford | Aug 15 | 0 | 1Ct | |

## BATTING AVERAGES - Including fielding

|                      | Matches | Inns | NO | Runs | HS | Avge  | 100s | 50s | Ct | St |
|----------------------|---------|------|----|------|----|-------|------|-----|----|----|
| Cornhill Test Matches | 1      | 2    | 0  | 26   | 21 | 13.00 | -    | -   | -  | -  |
| Other First-Class    | 6       | 10   | 0  | 363  | 86 | 36.30 | -    | 4   | 3  | -  |
| ALL FIRST-CLASS      | 7       | 12   | 0  | 389  | 86 | 32.41 | -    | 4   | 3  | -  |
| Other One-Day        | 4       | 4    | 1  | 67   | 53 | 22.33 | -    | 1   | 2  | -  |
| ALL ONE-DAY          | 4       | 4    | 1  | 67   | 53 | 22.33 | -    | 1   | 2  | -  |

## BOWLING AVERAGES

Did not bowl

## L    PLAYER RECORDS

### A.J.LAMB - *Northamptonshire & England*

| Opposition | Venue | Date | Batting | | Fielding | Bowling |
|---|---|---|---|---|---|---|
| **CORNHILL TEST MATCHES** | | | | | | |
| West Indies | Headingley | June 6 | 11 & | 0 | 4Ct | |
| West Indies | Lord's | June 20 | 1 | | 3Ct | |
| West Indies | Trent Bridge | July 4 | 13 & | 29 | | |
| West Indies | Edgbaston | July 25 | 9 & | 25 | | |
| **BRITANNIC ASSURANCE** | | | | | | |
| Derbyshire | Derby | April 27 | 74 * | | | |
| Essex | Northampton | May 9 | 24 & | 61 | | |
| Derbyshire | Northampton | May 31 | 8 & | 9 | 3Ct | |
| Gloucs | Luton | June 28 | 3 & | 51 | 1Ct | |
| Middlesex | Uxbridge | July 16 | 1 & | 12 * | | |
| Notts | Well'borough | July 19 | 33 & | 2 | | |
| Sussex | Eastbourne | Aug 2 | 13 & | 32 | 1Ct | |
| Lancashire | Lytham | Aug 6 | 125 | | 1Ct | 2-29 |
| Warwickshire | Northampton | Aug 9 | 35 | | 1Ct | |
| Essex | Colchester | Aug 16 | 9 & | 4 | 2Ct | |
| Surrey | Northampton | Aug 23 | 194 | | | |
| Yorkshire | Northampton | Aug 28 | 109 | | 1Ct | |
| Gloucs | Bristol | Sept 3 | 16 & | 82 | 2Ct | |
| Warwickshire | Edgbaston | Sept 10 | 74 & | 22 | 1Ct | |
| **OTHER FIRST-CLASS** | | | | | | |
| West Indies | Northampton | June 15 | | | 1Ct | |
| **TEXACO TROPHY** | | | | | | |
| West Indies | Edgbaston | May 23 | 18 | | | |
| West Indies | Old Trafford | May 25 | 62 | | | |
| **REFUGE ASSURANCE** | | | | | | |
| Glamorgan | Cardiff | April 21 | 2 | | 1Ct | |
| Lancashire | Old Trafford | April 28 | 13 | | | |
| Leicestershire | Northampton | May 12 | 23 | | | |
| Worcestershire | Northampton | May 19 | 1 | | 1Ct | |
| Hampshire | Northampton | June 2 | 61 | | 1Ct | |
| Somerset | Luton | June 30 | 3 | | | |
| Notts | Well'borough | July 21 | 2 | | 1Ct | |
| Sussex | Eastbourne | Aug 4 | 35 | | | |
| Essex | Northampton | Aug 11 | 36 | | | |
| Kent | Canterbury | Aug 18 | 30 | | | |
| Warwickshire | Northampton | Aug 25 | 4 | | | |
| Lancashire | Old Trafford | Sept 1 | 2 | | 1Ct | |
| **NATWEST TROPHY** | | | | | | |
| Staffordshire | Stone | June 26 | 31 | | | |
| Leicestershire | Northampton | July 11 | | | | |
| Glamorgan | Northampton | July 31 | 29 | | 1Ct | |
| Surrey | The Oval | Aug 14 | 24 | | | |
| **BENSON & HEDGES CUP** | | | | | | |
| Derbyshire | Derby | April 23 | 45 | | | |
| Gloucs | Bristol | May 2 | 0 | | 1Ct | |
| Combined U | Northampton | May 4 | 34 | | | |
| Worcestershire | Northampton | May 7 | 23 | | | |
| Lancashire | Old Trafford | May 29 | 48 | | 1Ct | |

**BATTING AVERAGES - Including fielding**

| | Matches | Inns | NO | Runs | HS | Avge | 100s | 50s | Ct | St |
|---|---|---|---|---|---|---|---|---|---|---|
| Cornhill Test Matches | 4 | 7 | 0 | 88 | 29 | 12.57 | - | - | 7 | - |
| Britannic Assurance | 14 | 23 | 2 | 993 | 194 | 47.28 | 3 | 5 | 13 | - |
| Other First-Class | 1 | 0 | 0 | 0 | 0 | - | - | - | 1 | - |
| ALL FIRST-CLASS | 19 | 30 | 2 | 1081 | 194 | 38.60 | 3 | 5 | 21 | - |
| Texaco Trophy | 2 | 2 | 0 | 80 | 62 | 40.00 | - | 1 | - | - |
| Refuge Assurance | 12 | 12 | 0 | 212 | 61 | 17.66 | - | 1 | 5 | - |
| NatWest Trophy | 4 | 3 | 0 | 84 | 31 | 28.00 | - | - | 1 | - |
| Benson & Hedges Cup | 5 | 5 | 0 | 150 | 48 | 30.00 | - | - | 2 | - |
| ALL ONE-DAY | 23 | 22 | 0 | 526 | 62 | 23.90 | - | 2 | 8 | - |

**BOWLING AVERAGES**

| | Overs | Mdns | Runs | Wkts | Avge | Best | 5wI | 10wM |
|---|---|---|---|---|---|---|---|---|
| Cornhill Test Matches | | | | | | | | |
| Britannic Assurance | 3.4 | 0 | 29 | 2 | 14.50 | 2-29 | - | |
| Other First-Class | | | | | | | | |
| ALL FIRST-CLASS | 3.4 | 0 | 29 | 2 | 14.50 | 2-29 | - | |
| Texaco Trophy | | | | | | | | |

Refuge Assurance
NatWest Trophy
Benson & Hedges Cup

ALL ONE-DAY

### C.B.LAMBERT - *West Indies*

| Opposition | Venue | Date | Batting | | Fielding | Bowling |
|---|---|---|---|---|---|---|
| **CORNHILL TEST MATCHES** | | | | | | |
| England | The Oval | Aug 8 | 39 & | 14 | 2Ct | 1-4 |
| **OTHER FIRST-CLASS** | | | | | | |
| Leicestershire | Leicester | June 1 | 4 & | 51 | | |
| Derbyshire | Derby | June 12 | 5 & | 4 | 2Ct | |
| Glamorgan | Swansea | July 16 | 99 | | | |
| Gloucs | Bristol | July 31 | 30 * & | 8 | | 0-0 |
| Essex | Chelmsford | Aug 3 | 116 & | 82 * | | |
| For West Indies XI | | | | | | |
| World XI | Scarborough | Aug 28 | 80 & | 19 | 1Ct | 2-33 |
| **OTHER ONE-DAY** | | | | | | |
| League CC XI | Trowbridge | June 28 | 101 * | | | |
| Ireland | Downpatrick | July 13 | 105 | | | |

**BATTING AVERAGES - Including fielding**

| | Matches | Inns | NO | Runs | HS | Avge | 100s | 50s | Ct | St |
|---|---|---|---|---|---|---|---|---|---|---|
| Cornhill Test Matches | 1 | 2 | 0 | 53 | 39 | 26.50 | - | - | 2 | - |
| Other First-Class | 6 | 11 | 2 | 498 | 116 | 55.33 | 1 | 4 | 3 | - |
| ALL FIRST-CLASS | 7 | 13 | 2 | 551 | 116 | 50.09 | 1 | 4 | 5 | - |
| Other One-Day | 2 | 2 | 1 | 206 | 105 | 206.00 | 2 | - | - | - |
| ALL ONE-DAY | 2 | 2 | 1 | 206 | 105 | 206.00 | 2 | - | - | - |

**BOWLING AVERAGES**

| | Overs | Mdns | Runs | Wkts | Avge | Best | 5wI | 10wM |
|---|---|---|---|---|---|---|---|---|
| Cornhill Test Matches | 0.4 | 0 | 4 | 1 | 4.00 | 1-4 | - | - |
| Other First-Class | 11 | 3 | 33 | 2 | 16.50 | 2-33 | - | - |
| ALL FIRST-CLASS | 11.4 | 3 | 37 | 3 | 12.33 | 2-33 | - | - |

Other One-Day

ALL ONE-DAY

### D.J.LAMPITT - *League CC XI*

| Opposition | Venue | Date | Batting | Fielding | Bowling |
|---|---|---|---|---|---|
| **OTHER ONE-DAY** | | | | | |
| West Indies | Trowbridge | June 28 | 22 | 1Ct | |

**BATTING AVERAGES - Including fielding**

| | Matches | Inns | NO | Runs | HS | Avge | 100s | 50s | Ct | St |
|---|---|---|---|---|---|---|---|---|---|---|
| Other One-Day | 1 | 1 | 0 | 22 | 22 | 22.00 | - | - | 1 | - |
| ALL ONE-DAY | 1 | 1 | 0 | 22 | 22 | 22.00 | - | - | 1 | - |

**BOWLING AVERAGES**
Did not bowl

### S.R.LAMPITT - *Worcestershire*

| Opposition | Venue | Date | Batting | Fielding | Bowling |
|---|---|---|---|---|---|
| **BRITANNIC ASSURANCE** | | | | | |
| Gloucs | Worcester | April 27 | | | 2-75 |
| Glamorgan | Worcester | May 31 | 19 | | 2-37 & 1-38 |
| Northants | Northampton | June 4 | 18 * | | 0-33 & 2-74 |
| Essex | Ilford | June 7 | 58 * | | 2-44 & 0-6 |
| Sussex | Hove | June 14 | | | 0-24 & 0-31 |

# PLAYER RECORDS | L

| | | | | | |
|---|---|---|---|---|---|
| Notts | Worcester | June 18 | 1 & 50* | | 3-97 & 1-14 |
| Leicestershire | Worcester | June 28 | | 1Ct | 2-42 & 0-40 |
| Yorkshire | Headingley | July 2 | 28 | | 1-57 |
| Derbyshire | Kidd'minster | July 19 | 17*& 93 | 1Ct | 1-82 |
| Kent | Worcester | July 23 | | | |
| Gloucs | Cheltenham | July 26 | 12 & 21 | | 2-72 & 1-35 |
| Warwickshire | Worcester | Aug 2 | 0 | | 0-38 |
| Somerset | Weston | Aug 6 | 7 | | 2-70 & 0-8 |
| Surrey | Worcester | Aug 16 | 3 & 5* | 1Ct | 1-25 & 5-70 |
| Lancashire | Blackpool | Aug 20 | 25 | | 1-33 & 0-21 |
| Middlesex | Worcester | Aug 23 | 35 | | 4-53 |
| Somerset | Worcester | Sept 3 | 4 | | 5-78 |
| Glamorgan | Cardiff | Sept 10 | 31 | 1Ct | 1-36 & 1-39 |
| Notts | Trent Bridge | Sept 17 | 17 & 3 | 1Ct | 5-86 |

### OTHER FIRST-CLASS
| | | | | | |
|---|---|---|---|---|---|
| West Indies | Worcester | May 15 | 3 | 1Ct | 0-81 & 0-13 |
| Oxford U | The Parks | May 25 | 23 | | 4-39 & 5-85 |
| Sri Lanka | Worcester | July 30 | 50* | | 2-50 & 0-17 |

### REFUGE ASSURANCE
| | | | | | |
|---|---|---|---|---|---|
| Kent | Worcester | April 21 | | | 2-42 |
| Lancashire | Worcester | May 12 | | | 0-26 |
| Northants | Northampton | May 19 | | | 1-44 |
| Warwickshire | Edgbaston | May 26 | 0* | | 0-32 |
| Surrey | Worcester | June 2 | | | |
| Essex | Ilford | June 9 | 4 | | 0-29 |
| Sussex | Hove | June 16 | | | 0-35 |
| Yorkshire | Sheffield | June 23 | 1 | | 2-27 |
| Leicestershire | Worcester | June 30 | | 1Ct | 0-35 |
| Hampshire | Southampton | July 7 | | 1Ct | 1-52 |
| Derbyshire | Worcester | July 9 | | | 0-57 |
| Notts | Trent Bridge | Aug 4 | | | 1-46 |
| Somerset | Worcester | Aug 18 | | | 0-29 |
| Middlesex | Worcester | Aug 25 | | | 3-23 |

### NATWEST TROPHY
| | | | | | |
|---|---|---|---|---|---|
| Bedfordshire | Bedford | June 26 | | | 1-4 |
| Glamorgan | Worcester | July 11 | 7 | | 1-61 |

### BENSON & HEDGES CUP
| | | | | | |
|---|---|---|---|---|---|
| Gloucs | Worcester | April 25 | | 1Ct | 4-46 |
| Combined U | Fenner's | May 2 | | | 1-29 |
| Derbyshire | Worcester | May 4 | | | 3-46 |
| Kent | Worcester | May 29 | | | 2-59 |
| Essex | Chelmsford | June 12 | | | 1-31 |

### BATTING AVERAGES - Including fielding
| | Matches | Inns | NO | Runs | HS | Avge | 100s | 50s | Ct | St |
|---|---|---|---|---|---|---|---|---|---|---|
| Britannic Assurance | 19 | 20 | 5 | 447 | 93 | 29.80 | - | 3 | 5 | - |
| Other First-Class | 3 | 3 | 1 | 76 | 50* | 38.00 | - | 1 | 1 | - |
| ALL FIRST-CLASS | 22 | 23 | 6 | 523 | 93 | 30.76 | - | 4 | 6 | - |
| Refuge Assurance | 14 | 3 | 1 | 5 | 4 | 2.50 | - | - | 2 | - |
| NatWest Trophy | 2 | 1 | 0 | 7 | 7 | 7.00 | - | - | - | - |
| Benson & Hedges Cup | 5 | 0 | 0 | 0 | 0 | | - | - | 1 | - |
| ALL ONE-DAY | 21 | 4 | 1 | 12 | 7 | 4.00 | - | - | 3 | - |

### BOWLING AVERAGES
| | Overs | Mdns | Runs | Wkts | Avge | Best | 5wI | 10wM |
|---|---|---|---|---|---|---|---|---|
| Britannic Assurance | 422.4 | 74 | 1358 | 45 | 30.17 | 5-70 | 3 | - |
| Other First-Class | 81 | 10 | 285 | 11 | 25.90 | 5-85 | 1 | - |
| ALL FIRST-CLASS | 503.4 | 84 | 1643 | 56 | 29.33 | 5-70 | 4 | - |
| Refuge Assurance | 84 | 1 | 477 | 10 | 47.70 | 3-23 | - | |
| NatWest Trophy | 12.4 | 1 | 65 | 2 | 32.50 | 1-4 | - | |
| Benson & Hedges Cup | 48.1 | 4 | 211 | 11 | 19.18 | 4-46 | - | |
| ALL ONE-DAY | 144.5 | 6 | 753 | 23 | 32.73 | 4-46 | - | |

# B.C.LARA - *West Indies*

| Opposition | Venue | Date | Batting | Fielding | Bowling |
|---|---|---|---|---|---|

### OTHER FIRST-CLASS
| | | | | | |
|---|---|---|---|---|---|
| Worcestershire | Worcester | May 15 | 26 | 1Ct | |
| Somerset | Taunton | May 29 | 93 & 50 | 1Ct | |
| Leicestershire | Leicester | June 1 | 3 & 26 | 1Ct | 0-14 |
| Derbyshire | Derby | June 12 | 1 & 20 | | 0-2 |

| | | | | | |
|---|---|---|---|---|---|
| Northants | Northampton | June 15 | 4 | | 0-9 |
| Hampshire | Southampton | June 29 | 75 | | |
| Glamorgan | Swansea | July 16 | 6 | 1Ct | 0-11 |
| Kent | Canterbury | July 20 | 19 & 18 | 5Ct | |
| For West Indies XI | | | | | |
| World XI | Scarborough | Aug 28 | 2 & 1 | | 0-23 |

### TEXACO TROPHY
| | | | | | |
|---|---|---|---|---|---|
| England | Lord's | May 27 | 23 | | |

### OTHER ONE-DAY
| | | | | | |
|---|---|---|---|---|---|
| D of Norfolk | Arundel | May 12 | 15 | | |
| Gloucs | Bristol | May 14 | 30 | | |
| League CC XI | Trowbridge | June 28 | | | 1-53 |
| Ireland | Downpatrick | July 13 | 4 | 1Ct | 0-13 |
| Wales | Brecon | July 15 | 82 | | 2-29 |

### BATTING AVERAGES - Including fielding
| | Matches | Inns | NO | Runs | HS | Avge | 100s | 50s | Ct | St |
|---|---|---|---|---|---|---|---|---|---|---|
| Other First-Class | 9 | 14 | 0 | 344 | 93 | 24.57 | - | 3 | 9 | - |
| ALL FIRST-CLASS | 9 | 14 | 0 | 344 | 93 | 24.57 | - | 3 | 9 | - |
| Texaco Trophy | 1 | 1 | 0 | 23 | 23 | 23.00 | - | - | - | - |
| Other One-Day | 5 | 4 | 0 | 131 | 82 | 32.75 | - | 1 | 1 | - |
| ALL ONE-DAY | 6 | 5 | 0 | 154 | 82 | 30.80 | - | 1 | 1 | - |

### BOWLING AVERAGES
| | Overs | Mdns | Runs | Wkts | Avge | Best | 5wI | 10wM |
|---|---|---|---|---|---|---|---|---|
| Other First-Class | 11 | 1 | 59 | 0 | - | - | - | - |
| ALL FIRST-CLASS | 11 | 1 | 59 | 0 | - | - | - | - |
| Texaco Trophy | | | | | | | | |
| Other One-Day | 25 | 4 | 95 | 3 | 31.66 | 2-29 | - | |
| ALL ONE-DAY | 25 | 4 | 95 | 3 | 31.66 | 2-29 | - | |

# W.LARKINS - *Northamptonshire*

| Opposition | Venue | Date | Batting | Fielding | Bowling |
|---|---|---|---|---|---|

### BRITANNIC ASSURANCE
| | | | | | |
|---|---|---|---|---|---|
| Essex | Northampton | May 9 | 0 & 27 | | |
| Leicestershire | Northampton | May 16 | 39* | 1Ct | |
| Somerset | Northampton | July 23 | 4*& 19 | | |
| Sussex | Eastbourne | Aug 2 | 34 & 45 | 1Ct | |
| Lancashire | Lytham | Aug 6 | 10 | | |
| Warwickshire | Northampton | Aug 9 | 3 & 28* | 1Ct | 0-2 |
| Yorkshire | Northampton | Aug 28 | 5 & 62* | | |
| Gloucs | Bristol | Sept 3 | 0*& 4* | 2Ct | |
| Warwickshire | Edgbaston | Sept 10 | 75 & 10 | 1Ct | |

### REFUGE ASSURANCE
| | | | | | |
|---|---|---|---|---|---|
| Leicestershire | Northampton | May 12 | 5 | | |
| Notts | Well'borough | July 21 | 63 | | |
| Derbyshire | Derby | July 28 | 2 | | |
| Sussex | Eastbourne | Aug 4 | 43 | 1Ct | |
| Essex | Northampton | Aug 11 | 108 | | |
| Kent | Canterbury | Aug 18 | 56 | | |
| Warwickshire | Northampton | Aug 25 | 66 | | |
| Lancashire | Old Trafford | Sept 1 | 20 | 1Ct | |

### NATWEST TROPHY
| | | | | | |
|---|---|---|---|---|---|
| Glamorgan | Northampton | July 31 | 8 | | |
| Surrey | The Oval | Aug 14 | 31 | 2Ct | |

### BATTING AVERAGES - Including fielding
| | Matches | Inns | NO | Runs | HS | Avge | 100s | 50s | Ct | St |
|---|---|---|---|---|---|---|---|---|---|---|
| Britannic Assurance | 9 | 16 | 6 | 365 | 75 | 36.50 | - | 2 | 6 | - |
| ALL FIRST-CLASS | 9 | 16 | 6 | 365 | 75 | 36.50 | - | 2 | 6 | - |
| Refuge Assurance | 8 | 8 | 0 | 363 | 108 | 45.37 | 1 | 3 | 2 | - |
| NatWest Trophy | 2 | 2 | 0 | 39 | 31 | 19.50 | - | - | 2 | - |
| ALL ONE-DAY | 10 | 10 | 0 | 402 | 108 | 40.20 | 1 | 3 | 4 | - |

### BOWLING AVERAGES
| | Overs | Mdns | Runs | Wkts | Avge | Best | 5wI | 10wM |
|---|---|---|---|---|---|---|---|---|
| Britannic Assurance | 6 | 4 | 2 | 0 | - | - | - | - |

## L — PLAYER RECORDS

| ALL FIRST-CLASS | 6 | 4 | 2 | 0 | - | - | - | - | - |
|---|---|---|---|---|---|---|---|---|---|

Refuge Assurance
NatWest Trophy

ALL ONE-DAY

## M.LATHWELL - *Somerset*

| Opposition | Venue | Date | Batting | | Fielding | Bowling |
|---|---|---|---|---|---|---|
| **BRITANNIC ASSURANCE** | | | | | | |
| Worcestershire | Worcester | Sept 3 | 4 & 43 | | | 0-55 |
| **OTHER FIRST-CLASS** | | | | | | |
| Sri Lanka | Taunton | Aug 10 | 16 | | | 0-15 & 1-29 |
| **REFUGE ASSURANCE** | | | | | | |
| Kent | Taunton | July 28 | 15 | | | |
| Leicestershire | Weston | Aug 4 | 20 | | 1Ct | 0-19 |
| **NATWEST TROPHY** | | | | | | |
| Warwickshire | Edgbaston | July 31 | 16 | | | |

**BATTING AVERAGES - Including fielding**

| | Matches | Inns | NO | Runs | HS | Avge | 100s | 50s | Ct | St |
|---|---|---|---|---|---|---|---|---|---|---|
| Britannic Assurance | 1 | 2 | 0 | 47 | 43 | 23.50 | - | - | - | - |
| Other First-Class | 1 | 1 | 0 | 16 | 16 | 16.00 | - | - | - | - |
| ALL FIRST-CLASS | 2 | 3 | 0 | 63 | 43 | 21.00 | - | - | - | - |
| Refuge Assurance | 2 | 2 | 0 | 35 | 20 | 17.50 | - | - | 1 | - |
| NatWest Trophy | 1 | 1 | 0 | 16 | 16 | 16.00 | - | - | - | - |
| ALL ONE-DAY | 3 | 3 | 0 | 51 | 20 | 17.00 | - | - | 1 | - |

**BOWLING AVERAGES**

| | Overs | Mdns | Runs | Wkts | Avge | Best | 5wI | 10wM |
|---|---|---|---|---|---|---|---|---|
| Britannic Assurance | 17 | 6 | 55 | 0 | - | - | - | - |
| Other First-Class | 11 | 3 | 44 | 1 | 44.00 | 1-29 | - | - |
| ALL FIRST-CLASS | 28 | 9 | 99 | 1 | 99.00 | 1-29 | - | - |
| Refuge Assurance | 4 | 0 | 19 | 0 | - | - | - | - |
| NatWest Trophy | | | | | | | | |
| ALL ONE-DAY | 4 | 0 | 19 | 0 | - | - | - | - |

## D.V.LAWRENCE - *Gloucestershire & England*

| Opposition | Venue | Date | Batting | | Fielding | Bowling |
|---|---|---|---|---|---|---|
| **CORNHILL TEST MATCHES** | | | | | | |
| West Indies | Trent Bridge | July 4 | 4 & 34 | | | 2-116 & 1-61 |
| West Indies | The Oval | Aug 8 | 9 | | | 2-67 & 5-106 |
| Sri Lanka | Lord's | Aug 22 | 3 | | | 2-61 & 2-83 |
| **BRITANNIC ASSURANCE** | | | | | | |
| Worcestershire | Worcester | April 27 | 23 | | | 0-50 |
| Hampshire | Bristol | May 9 | 0 | | | 6-77 & 5-52 |
| Essex | Bristol | May 31 | 3 & 10 | | | 4-111 |
| Middlesex | Bristol | June 4 | 8 | | | 3-44 & 2-35 |
| Hampshire | Southampton | June 7 | | | | 1-38 |
| Notts | Gloucester | June 14 | 41 | | | 1-18 & 2-37 |
| Somerset | Bath | June 21 | 19 | | | 3-69 |
| Northants | Luton | June 28 | 2 & 36* | | 1Ct | 6-67 & 0-0 |
| Surrey | Guildford | July 16 | 19 | | | 1-42 & 3-51 |
| Glamorgan | Cheltenham | July 19 | 6 & 0 | | 1Ct | 4-62 & 2-38 |
| Worcestershire | Cheltenham | July 26 | 1 & 17 | | | 2-60 & 4-80 |
| Glamorgan | Abergavenny | Aug 28 | 66 & 44 | | | 1-63 & 0-23 |
| Northants | Bristol | Sept 3 | 24 & 4 | | | 4-64 & 2-65 |
| Somerset | Bristol | Sept 10 | 30 & 0 | | | 3-106 |
| Sussex | Hove | Sept 17 | 22 & 8 | | 2Ct | 1-44 |

**TEXACO TROPHY**

| West Indies | Lord's | May 27 | | | 4-67 |
|---|---|---|---|---|---|
| **REFUGE ASSURANCE** | | | | | |
| Middlesex | Bristol | April 21 | 9 | | 0-52 |
| Worcestershire | Bristol | May 5 | 0 | | 0-42 |
| Sussex | Hove | May 19 | 0 | | 1-30 |
| Northants | Moreton | June 9 | | | |
| Notts | Gloucester | June 16 | 9* | 1Ct | 1-35 |
| Yorkshire | Scarborough | July 14 | 38* | | 4-27 |
| Derbyshire | Cheltenham | July 21 | 13 | | 3-51 |
| Glamorgan | Swansea | Aug 4 | 13 | | 2-48 |
| **NATWEST TROPHY** | | | | | |
| Norfolk | Bristol | June 26 | 2* | | 5-17 |
| Notts | Bristol | July 11 | 5* | | 2-48 |
| **BENSON & HEDGES CUP** | | | | | |
| Combined U | Bristol | April 23 | 23 | | 6-20 |
| Worcestershire | Worcester | April 25 | 10 | | 2-35 |
| Northants | Bristol | May 2 | | | 4-44 |
| Derbyshire | Derby | May 7 | 18* | | 1-38 |
| **OTHER ONE-DAY** | | | | | |
| West Indies | Bristol | May 14 | | | 1-47 |

**BATTING AVERAGES - Including fielding**

| | Matches | Inns | NO | Runs | HS | Avge | 100s | 50s | Ct | St |
|---|---|---|---|---|---|---|---|---|---|---|
| Cornhill Test Matches | 3 | 4 | 0 | 50 | 34 | 12.50 | - | - | - | - |
| Britannic Assurance | 15 | 22 | 1 | 383 | 66 | 18.23 | - | 1 | 4 | - |
| ALL FIRST-CLASS | 18 | 26 | 1 | 433 | 66 | 17.32 | - | 1 | 4 | - |
| Texaco Trophy | 1 | 0 | 0 | 0 | 0 | - | - | - | - | - |
| Refuge Assurance | 8 | 7 | 2 | 82 | 38* | 16.40 | - | - | 1 | - |
| NatWest Trophy | 2 | 2 | 2 | 7 | 5* | - | - | - | - | - |
| Benson & Hedges Cup | 4 | 3 | 1 | 51 | 23 | 25.50 | - | - | - | - |
| Other One-Day | 1 | 0 | 0 | 0 | 0 | - | - | - | - | - |
| ALL ONE-DAY | 16 | 12 | 5 | 140 | 38* | 20.00 | - | - | 1 | - |

**BOWLING AVERAGES**

| | Overs | Mdns | Runs | Wkts | Avge | Best | 5wI | 10wM |
|---|---|---|---|---|---|---|---|---|
| Cornhill Test Matches | 116.2 | 17 | 494 | 14 | 35.28 | 5-106 | 1 | - |
| Britannic Assurance | 398.5 | 62 | 1296 | 60 | 21.60 | 6-67 | 3 | 1 |
| ALL FIRST-CLASS | 515.1 | 79 | 1790 | 74 | 24.18 | 6-67 | 4 | 1 |
| Texaco Trophy | 11 | 1 | 67 | 4 | 16.75 | 4-67 | - | |
| Refuge Assurance | 55 | 1 | 285 | 11 | 25.90 | 4-27 | - | |
| NatWest Trophy | 21 | 3 | 65 | 7 | 9.28 | 5-17 | 1 | |
| Benson & Hedges Cup | 44 | 7 | 137 | 13 | 10.53 | 6-20 | 1 | |
| Other One-Day | 11 | 2 | 47 | 1 | 47.00 | 1-47 | - | |
| ALL ONE-DAY | 142 | 14 | 601 | 36 | 16.69 | 6-20 | 2 | |

## D.A.LEATHERDALE - *Worcestershire*

| Opposition | Venue | Date | Batting | | Fielding | Bowling |
|---|---|---|---|---|---|---|
| **BRITANNIC ASSURANCE** | | | | | | |
| Somerset | Worcester | Sept 3 | 157 | | 1Ct | |
| Glamorgan | Cardiff | Sept 10 | 24 | | | |
| Notts | Trent Bridge | Sept 17 | 31 & 7 | | 1Ct | |
| **OTHER FIRST-CLASS** | | | | | | |
| Oxford U | The Parks | May 25 | 94 | | 2Ct | 0-6 |
| Sri Lanka | Worcester | July 30 | 66 | | | |
| **REFUGE ASSURANCE** | | | | | | |
| Warwickshire | Edgbaston | May 26 | 12 | | | |
| Surrey | Worcester | June 2 | 0* | | | |
| Yorkshire | Sheffield | June 23 | 15 | | 1Ct | |
| Lancashire | Old Trafford | Sept 15 | 0 | | | |
| **OTHER ONE-DAY** | | | | | | |
| For Yorkshiremen | | | | | | |
| Yorkshire | Scarborough | Sept 7 | 13 | | | 1-35 |

**BATTING AVERAGES - Including fielding**

| | Matches | Inns | NO | Runs | HS | Avge | 100s | 50s | Ct | St |
|---|---|---|---|---|---|---|---|---|---|---|
| Britannic Assurance | 3 | 4 | 0 | 219 | 157 | 54.75 | 1 | - | 2 | - |
| Other First-Class | 2 | 2 | 0 | 160 | 94 | 80.00 | - | 2 | 2 | - |

# PLAYER RECORDS L

| | | | | | | | | | |
|---|---|---|---|---|---|---|---|---|---|
| ALL FIRST-CLASS | 5 | 6 | 0 | 379 | 157 | 63.16 | 1 | 2 4 | - |
| | | | | | | | | | |
| Refuge Assurance | 4 | 4 | 1 | 27 | 15 | 9.00 | - | - 1 | - |
| Other One-Day | 1 | 1 | 0 | 13 | 13 | 13.00 | - | - - | - |
| | | | | | | | | | |
| ALL ONE-DAY | 5 | 5 | 1 | 40 | 15 | 10.00 | - | - 1 | - |

**BOWLING AVERAGES**

| | Overs | Mdns | Runs | Wkts | Avge | Best | 5wI | 10wM |
|---|---|---|---|---|---|---|---|---|
| Britannic Assurance | | | | | | | | |
| Other First-Class | 2 | 0 | 6 | 0 | - | - | - | - |
| | | | | | | | | |
| ALL FIRST-CLASS | 2 | 0 | 6 | 0 | - | - | - | - |
| | | | | | | | | |
| Refuge Assurance | | | | | | | | |
| Other One-Day | 10 | 0 | 35 | 1 | 35.00 | 1-35 | - | |
| | | | | | | | | |
| ALL ONE-DAY | 10 | 0 | 35 | 1 | 35.00 | 1-35 | - | |

## R.P.LEFEBVRE - *Somerset*

| Opposition | Venue | Date | Batting | Fielding | Bowling |
|---|---|---|---|---|---|
| **BRITANNIC ASSURANCE** | | | | | |
| Sussex | Taunton | April 27 | 16 | | 0-50 |
| Glamorgan | Taunton | May 9 | 39 & 1 | 1Ct | 0-51 & 0-49 |
| Derbyshire | Derby | May 22 | 12 * & 8 | 3Ct | 3-51 & 0-42 |
| Warwickshire | Edgbaston | June 7 | | | 0-57 & 1-26 |
| Hampshire | Bath | June 18 | | 4 | 2-66 & 0-12 |
| Gloucs | Bath | June 21 | 5 * | | 0-52 |
| Surrey | The Oval | June 28 | 93 | 1Ct | 0-8 |
| Lancashire | Taunton | July 2 | 23 * | | 2-48 & 3-54 |
| Sussex | Hove | July 16 | 14 | | 0-55 |
| Essex | Southend | July 19 | 0 | | 1-72 & 0-30 |
| Northants | Northampton | July 23 | | | 2-39 & 0-58 |
| Worcestershire | Weston | Aug 6 | 100 | | 0-11 |
| Hampshire | Southampton | Aug 28 | 12 | | 0-52 & 1-29 |
| Gloucs | Bristol | Sept 10 | 13 | | 1-64 & 2-20 |
| Warwickshire | Taunton | Sept 17 | 6 & 15 | 1Ct | 0-27 & 0-25 |
| **OTHER FIRST-CLASS** | | | | | |
| West Indies | Taunton | May 29 | 5 & 0 * | | 0-27 |
| **REFUGE ASSURANCE** | | | | | |
| Surrey | The Oval | April 21 | 15 * | | 1-27 |
| Sussex | Taunton | April 28 | 4 | | 3-29 |
| Glamorgan | Taunton | May 12 | 3 | 1Ct | 3-30 |
| Hampshire | Bournemouth | May 19 | | | 1-35 |
| Middlesex | Taunton | May 26 | 11 | 1Ct | 0-39 |
| Warwickshire | Edgbaston | June 2 | 4 | | |
| Notts | Trent Bridge | June 9 | 4 | | 1-25 |
| Derbyshire | Derby | June 16 | 13 | 1Ct | 1-28 |
| Northants | Luton | June 30 | 24 | | 0-25 |
| Lancashire | Taunton | July 5 | 2 | | 0-35 |
| Essex | Southend | July 21 | 0 | 1Ct | 2-40 |
| Kent | Taunton | July 28 | 27 | | 3-30 |
| Leicestershire | Weston | Aug 4 | | | 0-24 |
| **NATWEST TROPHY** | | | | | |
| Bucks | Bath | June 26 | | 1Ct | 1-30 |
| Middlesex | Taunton | July 11 | 13 | | 2-32 |
| Warwickshire | Edgbaston | July 31 | 21 * | | 3-27 |
| **BENSON & HEDGES CUP** | | | | | |
| Middlesex | Taunton | April 23 | 5 | | 0-22 |
| Warwickshire | Edgbaston | May 2 | 2 | | 1-59 |
| Surrey | Taunton | May 4 | 21 * | 1Ct | 3-44 |
| Essex | Chelmsford | May 7 | 23 * | | 0-25 |
| **OTHER ONE-DAY** | | | | | |
| Gloucs | Hove | Sept 8 | 2 | 1Ct | 3-31 |

**BATTING AVERAGES - Including fielding**

| | Matches | Inns | NO | Runs | HS | Avge | 100s | 50s | Ct | St |
|---|---|---|---|---|---|---|---|---|---|---|
| Britannic Assurance | 15 | 16 | 3 | 361 | 100 | 27.76 | 1 | 1 | 6 | - |
| Other First-Class | 1 | 2 | 1 | 5 | 5 | 5.00 | - | - | - | - |
| | | | | | | | | | | |
| ALL FIRST-CLASS | 16 | 18 | 4 | 366 | 100 | 26.14 | 1 | 1 | 6 | - |
| | | | | | | | | | | |
| Refuge Assurance | 13 | 11 | 1 | 107 | 27 | 10.70 | - | - | 4 | - |
| NatWest Trophy | 3 | 2 | 1 | 34 | 21 * | 34.00 | - | - | 1 | - |
| Benson & Hedges Cup | 4 | 4 | 2 | 51 | 23 * | 25.50 | - | - | 1 | - |

| | | | | | | | | | |
|---|---|---|---|---|---|---|---|---|---|
| Other One-Day | 1 | 1 | 0 | 2 | 2 | 2.00 | - | - 1 | - |
| ALL ONE-DAY | 21 | 18 | 4 | 194 | 27 | 13.85 | - | - 7 | - |

**BOWLING AVERAGES**

| | Overs | Mdns | Runs | Wkts | Avge | Best | 5wI | 10wM |
|---|---|---|---|---|---|---|---|---|
| Britannic Assurance | 353 | 71 | 1048 | 18 | 58.22 | 3-51 | - | - |
| Other First-Class | 12 | 3 | 27 | 0 | - | - | | |
| | | | | | | | | |
| ALL FIRST-CLASS | 365 | 74 | 1075 | 18 | 59.72 | 3-51 | - | |
| | | | | | | | | |
| Refuge Assurance | 87 | 5 | 367 | 15 | 24.46 | 3-29 | - | |
| NatWest Trophy | 36 | 7 | 89 | 6 | 14.83 | 3-27 | - | |
| Benson & Hedges Cup | 38 | 6 | 150 | 4 | 37.50 | 3-44 | - | |
| Other One-Day | 7 | 0 | 31 | 3 | 10.33 | 3-31 | - | |
| | | | | | | | | |
| ALL ONE-DAY | 168 | 18 | 637 | 28 | 22.75 | 3-27 | - | |

## D.S.LEHMANN - *Victoria*

| Opposition | Venue | Date | Batting | Fielding | Bowling |
|---|---|---|---|---|---|
| **OTHER FIRST-CLASS** | | | | | |
| Essex | Chelmsford | Sept 23 | 15 & 8 | | |
| **OTHER ONE-DAY** | | | | | |
| Durham | Durham U. | Sept 16 | 55 * | | |
| Essex | Chelmsford | Sept 22 | 5 | 2Ct | |

**BATTING AVERAGES - Including fielding**

| | Matches | Inns | NO | Runs | HS | Avge | 100s | 50s | Ct | St |
|---|---|---|---|---|---|---|---|---|---|---|
| Other First-Class | 1 | 2 | 0 | 23 | 15 | 11.50 | - | - | - | - |
| | | | | | | | | | | |
| ALL FIRST-CLASS | 1 | 2 | 0 | 23 | 15 | 11.50 | - | - | - | - |
| | | | | | | | | | | |
| Other One-Day | 2 | 2 | 1 | 60 | 55 * | 60.00 | - | 1 | 2 | - |
| | | | | | | | | | | |
| ALL ONE-DAY | 2 | 2 | 1 | 60 | 55 * | 60.00 | - | 1 | 2 | - |

**BOWLING AVERAGES**
Did not bowl

## R.J.LEIPER - *England Amateur XI*

| Opposition | Venue | Date | Batting | Fielding | Bowling |
|---|---|---|---|---|---|
| **OTHER ONE-DAY** | | | | | |
| Sri Lanka | Wolv'hampton | July 24 | 22 | 1Ct | |

**BATTING AVERAGES - Including fielding**

| | Matches | Inns | NO | Runs | HS | Avge | 100s | 50s | Ct | St |
|---|---|---|---|---|---|---|---|---|---|---|
| Other One-Day | 1 | 1 | 0 | 22 | 22 | 22.00 | - | - | 1 | - |
| | | | | | | | | | | |
| ALL ONE-DAY | 1 | 1 | 0 | 22 | 22 | 22.00 | - | - | 1 | - |

**BOWLING AVERAGES**
Did not bowl

## N.J.LENHAM - *Sussex*

| Opposition | Venue | Date | Batting | Fielding | Bowling |
|---|---|---|---|---|---|
| **BRITANNIC ASSURANCE** | | | | | |
| Hampshire | Hove | May 16 | 35 & 8 | | 0-14 |
| Middlesex | Hove | May 22 | 11 & 32 | | 0-11 |
| Glamorgan | Cardiff | May 25 | 21 & 11 | | |
| Lancashire | Old Trafford | May 31 | 0 & 18 | | |
| Kent | Tunbridge W | June 7 | 137 & 1 | 2Ct | |
| Worcestershire | Hove | June 14 | 4 * & 21 | | 0-25 |
| Warwickshire | Coventry | June 18 | 16 * & 20 | | |
| Essex | Horsham | June 21 | 60 | 1Ct | |
| Surrey | Arundel | July 2 | 15 & 5 | | 0-10 |
| Derbyshire | Derby | July 5 | 48 & 13 | 1Ct | |
| Somerset | Hove | July 16 | 106 | 2Ct | 2-5 |

**L**

# PLAYER RECORDS

| | | | Batting | | | Fielding | Bowling |
|---|---|---|---|---|---|---|---|
| Leicestershire | Hove | July 19 | 193 | & | 4 | 1Ct | |
| Gloucs | Cheltenham | July 23 | | | 46 | 2Ct | 0-14 |
| Northants | Eastbourne | Aug 2 | 75 | & | 6 | | |
| Notts | Eastbourne | Aug 6 | 85 | & | 26 | | |
| Yorkshire | Midd'brough | Aug 9 | 0 | | | | |
| Hampshire | Bournemouth | Aug 20 | 8 | & | 1 | 1Ct | |
| Surrey | The Oval | Aug 28 | 2* | | | 1Ct | |

**OTHER FIRST-CLASS**

| | | | | | | | |
|---|---|---|---|---|---|---|---|
| Sri Lanka | Hove | Aug 17 | 61 | & | 2 | | |

**REFUGE ASSURANCE**

| | | | | | |
|---|---|---|---|---|---|
| Warwickshire | Edgbaston | April 21 | 3 | | |
| Gloucs | Hove | May 19 | 12 | 1Ct | |
| Glamorgan | Swansea | May 26 | 13 | | |
| Lancashire | Old Trafford | June 2 | 24* | | |
| Hampshire | Basingstoke | June 9 | 9 | | |
| Worcestershire | Hove | June 16 | 8 | | |
| Derbyshire | Derby | July 7 | 11 | | 1-19 |
| Surrey | The Oval | July 14 | 11 | | 1-12 |
| Leicestershire | Hove | July 21 | 10 | | 0-24 |
| Notts | Hove | July 28 | 21 | | 1-8 |
| Yorkshire | Midd'brough | Aug 11 | 64 | 1Ct | |
| Kent | Hove | Aug 25 | 86 | | |

**NATWEST TROPHY**

| | | | | |
|---|---|---|---|---|
| Scotland | Edinburgh | June 26 | 66 | 2-25 |
| Essex | Hove | July 11 | 19 | 1-35 |

**BATTING AVERAGES - Including fielding**

| | Matches | Inns | NO | Runs | HS | Avge | 100s | 50s | Ct | St |
|---|---|---|---|---|---|---|---|---|---|---|
| Britannic Assurance | 18 | 31 | 3 | 1028 | 193 | 36.71 | 3 | 3 | 11 | - |
| Other First-Class | 1 | 2 | 0 | 63 | 61 | 31.50 | - | 1 | - | - |
| ALL FIRST-CLASS | 19 | 33 | 3 | 1091 | 193 | 36.36 | 3 | 4 | 11 | - |
| Refuge Assurance | 12 | 12 | 1 | 272 | 86 | 24.72 | - | 2 | 2 | - |
| NatWest Trophy | 2 | 2 | 0 | 85 | 66 | 42.50 | - | 1 | - | - |
| ALL ONE-DAY | 14 | 14 | 1 | 357 | 86 | 27.46 | - | 3 | 2 | - |

**BOWLING AVERAGES**

| | Overs | Mdns | Runs | Wkts | Avge | Best | 5wI | 10wM |
|---|---|---|---|---|---|---|---|---|
| Britannic Assurance | 29 | 5 | 79 | 2 | 39.50 | 2-5 | - | - |
| Other First-Class | | | | | | | | |
| ALL FIRST-CLASS | 29 | 5 | 79 | 2 | 39.50 | 2-5 | - | - |
| Refuge Assurance | 8 | 0 | 63 | 3 | 21.00 | 1-8 | - | |
| NatWest Trophy | 18 | 1 | 60 | 3 | 20.00 | 2-25 | - | |
| ALL ONE-DAY | 26 | 1 | 123 | 6 | 20.50 | 2-25 | - | |

## J.K.LEVER - *Duchess of Norfolk's XI*

| Opposition | Venue | Date | Batting | Fielding | Bowling |
|---|---|---|---|---|---|

**OTHER ONE-DAY**

| | | | | | |
|---|---|---|---|---|---|
| West Indies | Arundel | May 12 | | | 0-33 |

**BATTING AVERAGES - Including fielding**

| | Matches | Inns | NO | Runs | HS | Avge | 100s | 50s | Ct | St |
|---|---|---|---|---|---|---|---|---|---|---|
| Other One-Day | 1 | 0 | 0 | 0 | 0 | - | - | - | - | - |
| ALL ONE-DAY | 1 | 0 | 0 | 0 | 0 | - | - | - | - | - |

**BOWLING AVERAGES**

| | Overs | Mdns | Runs | Wkts | Avge | Best | 5wI | 10wM |
|---|---|---|---|---|---|---|---|---|
| Other One-Day | 10 | 3 | 33 | 0 | - | - | - | - |
| ALL ONE-DAY | 10 | 3 | 33 | 0 | - | - | - | - |

## P.J.LEWINGTON - *Berkshire*

| Opposition | Venue | Date | Batting | Fielding | Bowling |
|---|---|---|---|---|---|

**NATWEST TROPHY**

| | | | | | |
|---|---|---|---|---|---|
| Hampshire | Reading | June 26 | | | 0-26 |

**BATTING AVERAGES - Including fielding**

| | Matches | Inns | NO | Runs | HS | Avge | 100s | 50s | Ct | St |
|---|---|---|---|---|---|---|---|---|---|---|
| NatWest Trophy | 1 | 0 | 0 | 0 | 0 | | | | | |
| ALL ONE-DAY | 1 | 0 | 0 | 0 | 0 | | | | | |

**BOWLING AVERAGES**

| | Overs | Mdns | Runs | Wkts | Avge | Best | 5wI | 10wM |
|---|---|---|---|---|---|---|---|---|
| NatWest Trophy | 5 | 0 | 26 | 0 | - | - | - | |
| ALL ONE-DAY | 5 | 0 | 26 | 0 | - | - | - | |

## C.C.LEWIS - *Leicestershire & England*

| Opposition | Venue | Date | Batting | | | Fielding | Bowling |
|---|---|---|---|---|---|---|---|

**CORNHILL TEST MATCHES**

| | | | | | | | |
|---|---|---|---|---|---|---|---|
| West Indies | Edgbaston | July 25 | 13 | & | 65 | 2Ct | 6-111 & 0-45 |
| West Indies | The Oval | Aug 8 | 47* | | | 1Ct | 0-10 & 0-35 |
| Sri Lanka | Lord's | Aug 22 | 11 | | | 1Ct | 0-29 & 2-31 |

**BRITANNIC ASSURANCE**

| | | | | | | | |
|---|---|---|---|---|---|---|---|
| Glamorgan | Leicester | April 27 | | | | 1Ct | 5-35 & 0-8 |
| Northants | Northampton | May 16 | 12 | & | 8* | | 2-38 & 0-41 |
| Surrey | Leicester | June 14 | 46 | | | | 0-17 & 4-45 |
| Lancashire | Leicester | June 18 | 9 | | | 1Ct | 5-60 & 0-3 |
| Glamorgan | Neath | June 21 | | | | | 1-90 |
| Worcestershire | Worcester | June 28 | 68 | | | | 3-40 & 3-39 |
| Gloucs | Hinckley | July 2 | 73 | | | | 1-36 |
| Northants | Leicester | July 5 | 8 | & | 3 | | |
| Sussex | Hove | July 19 | 15 | & | 21 | 1Ct | 3-106 & 1-24 |
| Somerset | Weston | Aug 2 | 7 | & | 43 | | 3-22 & 1-10 |
| Hampshire | Bournemouth | Aug 16 | 34 | | | 1Ct | 1-42 & 1-72 |
| Essex | Leicester | Sept 10 | 49 | & | 17 | | 3-101 |

**OTHER FIRST-CLASS**

| | | | | | |
|---|---|---|---|---|---|
| West Indies | Leicester | June 1 | 72 | 1Ct | 1-60 & 2-63 |

**TEXACO TROPHY**

| | | | | | |
|---|---|---|---|---|---|
| West Indies | Edgbaston | May 23 | 0 | 2Ct | 1-41 |
| West Indies | Old Trafford | May 25 | | | 3-62 |

**REFUGE ASSURANCE**

| | | | | | |
|---|---|---|---|---|---|
| Derbyshire | Leicester | April 21 | 1 | | 0-21 |
| Glamorgan | Leicester | April 28 | 8 | 1Ct | 2-33 |
| Northants | Northampton | May 12 | 6 | 1Ct | 0-26 |
| Yorkshire | Leicester | May 19 | 27 | | 1-46 |
| Middlesex | Uxbridge | June 9 | 10 | | 2-14 |
| Surrey | Leicester | June 16 | 7 | 1Ct | 2-14 |
| Worcestershire | Worcester | June 30 | 28 | | 1-37 |
| Lancashire | Leicester | July 7 | 9 | | 0-33 |
| Kent | Canterbury | July 14 | 8 | | 3-25 |
| Sussex | Hove | July 21 | 36 | 1Ct | 2-33 |
| Somerset | Weston | Aug 4 | 18* | | 1-31 |
| Hampshire | Bournemouth | Aug 18 | 16 | | 1-28 |

**NATWEST TROPHY**

| | | | | | |
|---|---|---|---|---|---|
| Shropshire | Leicester | June 26 | | 2Ct | 3-28 |
| Northants | Northampton | July 11 | 6 | | 0-32 |

**BENSON & HEDGES CUP**

| | | | | | |
|---|---|---|---|---|---|
| Kent | Canterbury | April 23 | 5 | | 3-62 |
| Sussex | Hove | April 25 | 8 | | 0-53 |

**OTHER ONE-DAY**

| | | | | | |
|---|---|---|---|---|---|
| Durham | Harrogate | June 11 | | | 1-17 |

For England XI

| | | | | | |
|---|---|---|---|---|---|
| Rest of World | Jesmond | July 31 | 89* | | 0-40 |
| Rest of World | Jesmond | Aug 1 | 12 | | 2-52 |

**BATTING AVERAGES - Including fielding**

| | Matches | Inns | NO | Runs | HS | Avge | 100s | 50s | Ct | St |
|---|---|---|---|---|---|---|---|---|---|---|
| Cornhill Test Matches | 3 | 4 | 1 | 136 | 65 | 45.33 | - | 1 | 4 | - |
| Britannic Assurance | 12 | 15 | 1 | 413 | 73 | 29.50 | - | 2 | 4 | - |
| Other First-Class | 1 | 1 | 0 | 72 | 72 | 72.00 | - | 1 | 1 | - |
| ALL FIRST-CLASS | 16 | 20 | 2 | 621 | 73 | 34.50 | - | 4 | 9 | - |
| Texaco Trophy | 2 | 1 | 0 | 0 | 0 | 0.00 | - | - | 2 | - |
| Refuge Assurance | 12 | 12 | 1 | 174 | 36 | 15.81 | - | - | 4 | - |
| NatWest Trophy | 2 | 1 | 0 | 6 | 6 | 6.00 | - | - | 2 | - |
| Benson & Hedges Cup | 2 | 2 | 0 | 13 | 8 | 6.50 | - | - | - | - |

# PLAYER RECORDS — L

| | Matches | Inns | NO | Runs | HS | Avge | 100s | 50s | Ct | St |
|---|---|---|---|---|---|---|---|---|---|---|
| Other One-Day | 3 | 2 | 1 | 101 | 89 * | 101.00 | - | 1 | - | - |
| ALL ONE-DAY | 21 | 18 | 2 | 294 | 89 * | 18.37 | - | 1 | 8 | - |

### BOWLING AVERAGES

| | Overs | Mdns | Runs | Wkts | Avge | Best | 5wI | 10wM |
|---|---|---|---|---|---|---|---|---|
| Cornhill Test Matches | 107 | 39 | 261 | 8 | 32.62 | 6-111 | 1 | - |
| Britannic Assurance | 330.4 | 83 | 829 | 37 | 22.40 | 5-35 | 2 | - |
| Other First-Class | 34 | 5 | 123 | 3 | 41.00 | 2-63 | - | - |
| ALL FIRST-CLASS | 471.4 | 127 | 1213 | 48 | 25.27 | 6-111 | 3 | - |
| Texaco Trophy | 22 | 3 | 103 | 4 | 25.75 | 3-62 | - | |
| Refuge Assurance | 91.2 | 10 | 341 | 15 | 22.73 | 3-25 | - | |
| NatWest Trophy | 21 | 2 | 60 | 3 | 20.00 | 3-28 | - | |
| Benson & Hedges Cup | 22 | 0 | 115 | 3 | 38.33 | 3-62 | - | |
| Other One-Day | 29 | 2 | 109 | 3 | 36.33 | 2-52 | - | |
| ALL ONE-DAY | 185.2 | 17 | 728 | 28 | 26.00 | 3-25 | - | |

## D.A.LEWIS - *Ireland*

| Opposition | Venue | Date | Batting | Fielding | Bowling |
|---|---|---|---|---|---|
| **OTHER FIRST-CLASS** | | | | | |
| Scotland | Dublin | June 22 | 14 & 44 | | 0-23 & 1-40 |
| **NATWEST TROPHY** | | | | | |
| Middlesex | Dublin | June 26 | 25 | | 4-47 |
| **OTHER ONE-DAY** | | | | | |
| West Indies | Downpatrick | July 13 | 41 * | | 1-78 |

### BATTING AVERAGES - Including fielding

| | Matches | Inns | NO | Runs | HS | Avge | 100s | 50s | Ct | St |
|---|---|---|---|---|---|---|---|---|---|---|
| Other First-Class | 1 | 2 | 0 | 58 | 44 | 29.00 | - | - | - | - |
| ALL FIRST-CLASS | 1 | 2 | 0 | 58 | 44 | 29.00 | - | - | - | - |
| NatWest Trophy | 1 | 1 | 0 | 25 | 25 | 25.00 | - | - | - | - |
| Other One-Day | 1 | 1 | 1 | 41 | 41 * | - | - | - | - | - |
| ALL ONE-DAY | 2 | 2 | 1 | 66 | 41 * | 66.00 | - | - | - | - |

### BOWLING AVERAGES

| | Overs | Mdns | Runs | Wkts | Avge | Best | 5wI | 10wM |
|---|---|---|---|---|---|---|---|---|
| Other First-Class | 16 | 1 | 63 | 1 | 63.00 | 1-40 | - | - |
| ALL FIRST-CLASS | 16 | 1 | 63 | 1 | 63.00 | 1-40 | - | - |
| NatWest Trophy | 10 | 0 | 47 | 4 | 11.75 | 4-47 | - | |
| Other One-Day | 15 | 2 | 78 | 1 | 78.00 | 1-78 | - | |
| ALL ONE-DAY | 25 | 2 | 125 | 5 | 25.00 | 4-47 | - | |

## J.J.B.LEWIS - *Essex*

| Opposition | Venue | Date | Batting | Fielding | Bowling |
|---|---|---|---|---|---|
| **BRITANNIC ASSURANCE** | | | | | |
| Warwickshire | Chelmsford | May 22 | 48 | 1Ct | |
| **OTHER FIRST-CLASS** | | | | | |
| Victoria | Chelmsford | Sept 23 | 25 | | |
| **REFUGE ASSURANCE** | | | | | |
| Lancashire | Old Trafford | Aug 25 | 19 | | |
| **OTHER ONE-DAY** | | | | | |
| Victoria | Chelmsford | Sept 22 | 0 | | |

### BATTING AVERAGES - Including fielding

| | Matches | Inns | NO | Runs | HS | Avge | 100s | 50s | Ct | St |
|---|---|---|---|---|---|---|---|---|---|---|
| Britannic Assurance | 1 | 1 | 0 | 48 | 48 | 48.00 | - | - | 1 | - |
| Other First-Class | 1 | 1 | 0 | 25 | 25 | 25.00 | - | - | - | - |
| ALL FIRST-CLASS | 2 | 2 | 0 | 73 | 48 | 36.50 | - | - | 1 | - |
| Refuge Assurance | 1 | 1 | 0 | 19 | 19 | 19.00 | - | - | - | - |
| Other One-Day | 1 | 1 | 0 | 0 | 0 | 0.00 | - | - | - | - |
| ALL ONE-DAY | 2 | 2 | 0 | 19 | 19 | 9.50 | - | - | - | - |

### BOWLING AVERAGES
Did not bowl

## V.B.LEWIS - *Dorset*

| Opposition | Venue | Date | Batting | Fielding | Bowling |
|---|---|---|---|---|---|
| **NATWEST TROPHY** | | | | | |
| Lancashire | Bournemouth | June 26 | 4 | 1Ct | |

### BATTING AVERAGES - Including fielding

| | Matches | Inns | NO | Runs | HS | Avge | 100s | 50s | Ct | St |
|---|---|---|---|---|---|---|---|---|---|---|
| NatWest Trophy | 1 | 1 | 0 | 4 | 4 | 4.00 | - | - | 1 | - |
| ALL ONE-DAY | 1 | 1 | 0 | 4 | 4 | 4.00 | - | - | 1 | - |

### BOWLING AVERAGES
Did not bowl

## M.G.LICKLEY - *Berkshire*

| Opposition | Venue | Date | Batting | Fielding | Bowling |
|---|---|---|---|---|---|
| **NATWEST TROPHY** | | | | | |
| Hampshire | Reading | June 26 | 13 | | 0-9 |

### BATTING AVERAGES - Including fielding

| | Matches | Inns | NO | Runs | HS | Avge | 100s | 50s | Ct | St |
|---|---|---|---|---|---|---|---|---|---|---|
| NatWest Trophy | 1 | 1 | 0 | 13 | 13 | 13.00 | - | - | - | - |
| ALL ONE-DAY | 1 | 1 | 0 | 13 | 13 | 13.00 | - | - | - | - |

### BOWLING AVERAGES

| | Overs | Mdns | Runs | Wkts | Avge | Best | 5wI | 10wM |
|---|---|---|---|---|---|---|---|---|
| NatWest Trophy | 2 | 0 | 9 | 0 | - | - | - | |
| ALL ONE-DAY | 2 | 0 | 9 | 0 | - | - | - | |

## D.C.G.LIGERTWOOD - *Hertfordshire*

| Opposition | Venue | Date | Batting | Fielding | Bowling |
|---|---|---|---|---|---|
| **NATWEST TROPHY** | | | | | |
| Warwickshire | Edgbaston | July 11 | 37 * | | |

### BATTING AVERAGES - Including fielding

| | Matches | Inns | NO | Runs | HS | Avge | 100s | 50s | Ct | St |
|---|---|---|---|---|---|---|---|---|---|---|
| NatWest Trophy | 1 | 1 | 1 | 37 | 37 * | - | - | - | - | - |
| ALL ONE-DAY | 1 | 1 | 1 | 37 | 37 * | - | - | - | - | - |

### BOWLING AVERAGES
Did not bowl

## N.J.LLONG - *Kent*

| Opposition | Venue | Date | Batting | Fielding | Bowling |
|---|---|---|---|---|---|
| **BRITANNIC ASSURANCE** | | | | | |
| Notts | Trent Bridge | May 22 | 0 & 42 * | 1Ct | 0-12 & 0-16 |
| Derbyshire | Canterbury | May 25 | 11 & 1 * | 1Ct | |
| Leicestershire | Canterbury | Sept 17 | 0 & 0 | 1Ct | |
| **OTHER FIRST-CLASS** | | | | | |
| Oxford U | The Parks | June 18 | 9 | 1Ct | |

# L PLAYER RECORDS

## REFUGE ASSURANCE

| | | | | |
|---|---|---|---|---|
| Essex | Folkestone | May 19 | 5 | |
| Yorkshire | Scarborough | June 16 | 23 | |
| Sussex | Hove | Aug 25 | 8 | 0-17 |

## OTHER ONE-DAY
For Kent

| | | | | |
|---|---|---|---|---|
| Sussex | Hove | Sept 7 | 3 | 1-23 |

### BATTING AVERAGES - Including fielding

| | Matches | Inns | NO | Runs | HS | Avge | 100s | 50s | Ct | St |
|---|---|---|---|---|---|---|---|---|---|---|
| Britannic Assurance | 3 | 6 | 2 | 54 | 42* | 13.50 | - | - | 3 | - |
| Other First-Class | 1 | 1 | 0 | 9 | 9 | 9.00 | - | - | 1 | - |
| ALL FIRST-CLASS | 4 | 7 | 2 | 63 | 42* | 12.60 | - | - | 4 | - |
| Refuge Assurance | 3 | 3 | 0 | 36 | 23 | 12.00 | - | - | - | - |
| Other One-Day | 1 | 1 | 0 | 3 | 3 | 3.00 | - | - | - | - |
| ALL ONE-DAY | 4 | 4 | 0 | 39 | 23 | 9.75 | - | - | - | - |

### BOWLING AVERAGES

| | Overs | Mdns | Runs | Wkts | Avge | Best | 5wI | 10wM |
|---|---|---|---|---|---|---|---|---|
| Britannic Assurance | 5 | 1 | 28 | 0 | - | - | - | - |
| Other First-Class | | | | | | | | |
| ALL FIRST-CLASS | 5 | 1 | 28 | 0 | - | - | - | - |
| Refuge Assurance | 3 | 0 | 17 | 0 | - | - | | |
| Other One-Day | 10 | 1 | 23 | 1 | 23.00 | 1-23 | - | |
| ALL ONE-DAY | 13 | 1 | 40 | 1 | 40.00 | 1-23 | - | |

## B.J.LLOYD - *Wales*

| Opposition | Venue | Date | Batting | Fielding | Bowling |
|---|---|---|---|---|---|
| **OTHER ONE-DAY** | | | | | |
| West Indies | Brecon | July 15 | 23 | | 0-59 |

### BATTING AVERAGES - Including fielding

| | Matches | Inns | NO | Runs | HS | Avge | 100s | 50s | Ct | St |
|---|---|---|---|---|---|---|---|---|---|---|
| Other One-Day | 1 | 1 | 0 | 23 | 23 | 23.00 | - | - | - | - |
| ALL ONE-DAY | 1 | 1 | 0 | 23 | 23 | 23.00 | - | - | - | - |

### BOWLING AVERAGES

| | Overs | Mdns | Runs | Wkts | Avge | Best | 5wI | 10wM |
|---|---|---|---|---|---|---|---|---|
| Other One-Day | 11 | 0 | 59 | 0 | - | - | - | |
| ALL ONE-DAY | 11 | 0 | 59 | 0 | - | - | - | |

## G.D.LLOYD - *Lancashire*

| Opposition | Venue | Date | Batting | | | Fielding | Bowling |
|---|---|---|---|---|---|---|---|
| **BRITANNIC ASSURANCE** | | | | | | | |
| Worcestershire | Worcester | May 9 | 24 | & | 1 | 2Ct | |
| Derbyshire | Old Trafford | May 16 | 20 | | | | |
| Surrey | The Oval | May 22 | 0 | & | 20 | 1Ct | |
| Sussex | Old Trafford | May 31 | 45 | & | 8 | | |
| Hampshire | Basingstoke | June 4 | 8 | | | | |
| Leicestershire | Leicester | June 18 | 0 | & | 13 | | |
| Kent | Old Trafford | June 21 | 32 | | | 2Ct | |
| Warwickshire | Old Trafford | July 23 | 96 | | | | |
| Yorkshire | Old Trafford | Aug 2 | 31 | | | | 1-57 |
| Northants | Lytham | Aug 6 | 28 | & | 79 | | |
| Gloucs | Bristol | Aug 9 | 20 | & | 8 | | |
| Derbyshire | Derby | Aug 16 | 85 | & | 4 | | |
| Worcestershire | Blackpool | Aug 20 | 19 | & | 58 | | |
| Essex | Old Trafford | Aug 23 | 3 | | | | |
| Notts | Old Trafford | Aug 28 | 25 | & | 22 | 3Ct | |
| Yorkshire | Scarborough | Sept 3 | 51 | & | 3 | 1Ct | |
| Surrey | Old Trafford | Sept 17 | 2 | & | 15 | 1Ct | |
| **OTHER FIRST-CLASS** | | | | | | | |
| Cambridge U | Fenner's | April 13 | 70 | & | 39 | 1Ct | |

## REFUGE ASSURANCE

| | | | | |
|---|---|---|---|---|
| Notts | Old Trafford | April 21 | 2 | |
| Northants | Old Trafford | April 28 | 71 | |
| Worcestershire | Worcester | May 12 | 79* | |
| Derbyshire | Derby | May 19 | 26 | |
| Sussex | Old Trafford | June 2 | 22 | |
| Glamorgan | Old Trafford | June 9 | 4* | |
| Warwickshire | Edgbaston | June 16 | 50 | 1Ct |
| Kent | Old Trafford | June 23 | 18 | |
| Somerset | Taunton | July 5 | 78* | |
| Leicestershire | Leicester | July 7 | 33 | |
| Middlesex | Lord's | July 21 | 5 | 1Ct |
| Hampshire | Southampton | July 28 | 9 | |
| Yorkshire | Old Trafford | Aug 4 | 21 | |
| Gloucs | Bristol | Aug 11 | 25* | 1Ct |
| Surrey | Old Trafford | Aug 18 | 11 | |
| Essex | Old Trafford | Aug 25 | 23 | |
| Northants | Old Trafford | Sept 1 | 10 | |
| Worcestershire | Old Trafford | Sept 15 | 32 | 1Ct |

## NATWEST TROPHY

| | | | | |
|---|---|---|---|---|
| Hampshire | Southampton | July 11 | 39 | |

## BENSON & HEDGES CUP

| | | | | |
|---|---|---|---|---|
| Leicestershire | Leicester | May 4 | 1* | |
| Sussex | Old Trafford | May 7 | 6* | |
| Worcestershire | Lord's | July 13 | 10 | |

### BATTING AVERAGES - Including fielding

| | Matches | Inns | NO | Runs | HS | Avge | 100s | 50s | Ct | St |
|---|---|---|---|---|---|---|---|---|---|---|
| Britannic Assurance | 17 | 28 | 0 | 720 | 96 | 25.71 | - | 5 | 10 | - |
| Other First-Class | 1 | 2 | 0 | 109 | 70 | 54.50 | - | 1 | 1 | - |
| ALL FIRST-CLASS | 18 | 30 | 0 | 829 | 96 | 27.63 | - | 6 | 11 | - |
| Refuge Assurance | 18 | 18 | 4 | 519 | 79* | 37.07 | - | 4 | 4 | - |
| NatWest Trophy | 1 | 1 | 0 | 39 | 39 | 39.00 | - | - | - | - |
| Benson & Hedges Cup | 3 | 3 | 2 | 17 | 10 | 17.00 | - | - | - | - |
| ALL ONE-DAY | 22 | 22 | 6 | 575 | 79* | 35.93 | - | 4 | 4 | - |

### BOWLING AVERAGES

| | Overs | Mdns | Runs | Wkts | Avge | Best | 5wI | 10wM |
|---|---|---|---|---|---|---|---|---|
| Britannic Assurance | 10 | 0 | 57 | 1 | 57.00 | 1-57 | - | - |
| Other First-Class | | | | | | | | |
| ALL FIRST-CLASS | 10 | 0 | 57 | 1 | 57.00 | 1-57 | - | - |
| Refuge Assurance | | | | | | | | |
| NatWest Trophy | | | | | | | | |
| Benson & Hedges Cup | | | | | | | | |
| ALL ONE-DAY | | | | | | | | |

## T.A.LLOYD - *Warwickshire*

| Opposition | Venue | Date | Batting | | | Fielding | Bowling |
|---|---|---|---|---|---|---|---|
| **BRITANNIC ASSURANCE** | | | | | | | |
| Lancashire | Edgbaston | April 27 | 19 | | | | |
| Yorkshire | Headingley | May 9 | 56 | & | 15 | 2Ct | |
| Glamorgan | Swansea | May 16 | 29 | | | | |
| Essex | Chelmsford | May 22 | 10 | & | 22 | | |
| Gloucs | Edgbaston | May 25 | 38 | | | 1Ct | 0-0 |
| Yorkshire | Edgbaston | May 31 | 2 | & | 13* | | |
| Kent | Tunbridge W | June 4 | 34 | & | 97 | 1Ct | |
| Somerset | Edgbaston | June 7 | 62 | & | 53* | | 0-0 |
| Sussex | Coventry | June 18 | 83 | | | | |
| Notts | Trent Bridge | June 21 | 4 | | | | 0-6 |
| Derbyshire | Edgbaston | June 28 | 20 | & | 16 | | |
| Middlesex | Edgbaston | July 2 | 14 | & | 82 | 1Ct | |
| Hampshire | Portsmouth | July 19 | 11 | & | 10 | | |
| Leicestershire | Leicester | July 26 | 20 | | | 1Ct | |
| Worcestershire | Worcester | Aug 2 | 0 | & | 1 | | |
| Surrey | Edgbaston | Aug 6 | 15 | & | 17 | | 0-20 |
| Northants | Northampton | Aug 9 | 26 | | | | |
| Glamorgan | Edgbaston | Aug 20 | 86 | & | 0 | | |
| Worcestershire | Edgbaston | Aug 28 | 7 | & | 13 | 3Ct | |
| Northants | Edgbaston | Sept 10 | 53 | & | 61 | 1Ct | |
| Somerset | Taunton | Sept 17 | 69 | & | 18 | | |

# PLANER RECORDS L

## REFUGE ASSURANCE

| | | | | |
|---|---|---|---|---|
| Sussex | Edgbaston | April 21 | 7* | |
| Notts | Trent Bridge | April 28 | 45 | |
| Yorkshire | Headingley | May 12 | 38 | 1Ct |
| Worcestershire | Edgbaston | May 26 | 34 | 1Ct |
| Somerset | Edgbaston | June 2 | | |
| Lancashire | Edgbaston | June 16 | 16 | |
| Essex | Chelmsford | July 7 | 1 | |
| Middlesex | Edgbaston | July 14 | 44* | 1Ct |
| Hampshire | Portsmouth | July 21 | 24 | |
| Derbyshire | Edgbaston | Aug 4 | 45 | 1Ct |
| Leicestershire | Leicester | Aug 11 | 39 | |
| Gloucs | Edgbaston | Aug 18 | 56* | |
| Northants | Northampton | Aug 25 | 24 | |

## NATWEST TROPHY

| | | | | |
|---|---|---|---|---|
| Yorkshire | Edgbaston | June 26 | | |
| Hertfordshire | Edgbaston | July 11 | | |
| Somerset | Edgbaston | July 31 | 78 | |
| Hampshire | Edgbaston | Aug 14 | 18 | |

## BENSON & HEDGES CUP

| | | | | |
|---|---|---|---|---|
| Essex | Edgbaston | April 25 | 58 | 1Ct |
| Somerset | Edgbaston | May 2 | 40 | 2Ct |
| Middlesex | Lord's | May 4 | 0 | |
| Surrey | The Oval | May 7 | 32 | |
| Yorkshire | Headingley | May 29 | 24 | |

## OTHER ONE-DAY

| | | | | | |
|---|---|---|---|---|---|
| Surrey | Harrogate | June 12 | 46 | | 3-47 |

## BATTING AVERAGES - Including fielding

| | Matches | Inns | NO | Runs | HS | Avge | 100s | 50s | Ct | St |
|---|---|---|---|---|---|---|---|---|---|---|
| Britannic Assurance | 21 | 35 | 2 | 1076 | 97 | 32.60 | - | 10 | 10 | - |
| ALL FIRST-CLASS | 21 | 35 | 2 | 1076 | 97 | 32.60 | - | 10 | 10 | - |
| Refuge Assurance | 13 | 12 | 3 | 373 | 56* | 41.44 | - | 1 | 4 | - |
| NatWest Trophy | 4 | 2 | 0 | 96 | 78 | 48.00 | - | 1 | - | - |
| Benson & Hedges Cup | 5 | 5 | 0 | 154 | 58 | 30.80 | - | 1 | 3 | - |
| Other One-Day | 1 | 1 | 0 | 46 | 46 | 46.00 | - | - | - | - |
| ALL ONE-DAY | 23 | 20 | 3 | 669 | 78 | 39.35 | - | 3 | 7 | - |

## BOWLING AVERAGES

| | Overs | Mdns | Runs | Wkts | Avge | Best | 5wI | 10wM |
|---|---|---|---|---|---|---|---|---|
| Britannic Assurance | 16 | 13 | 26 | 0 | - | - | - | - |
| ALL FIRST-CLASS | 16 | 13 | 26 | 0 | - | - | - | - |
| Refuge Assurance | | | | | | | | |
| NatWest Trophy | | | | | | | | |
| Benson & Hedges Cup | | | | | | | | |
| Other One-Day | 11 | 0 | 47 | 3 | 15.66 | 3-47 | - | |
| ALL ONE-DAY | 11 | 0 | 47 | 3 | 15.66 | 3-47 | - | |

# J.W.LLOYDS - Gloucestershire

| Opposition | Venue | Date | Batting | Fielding | Bowling |
|---|---|---|---|---|---|

## BRITANNIC ASSURANCE

| Opposition | Venue | Date | Batting | Fielding | Bowling |
|---|---|---|---|---|---|
| Worcestershire | Worcester | April 27 | 4 | | 0-30 |
| Hampshire | Bristol | May 9 | 48 | 2Ct | 0-15 & 0-39 |
| Yorkshire | Sheffield | May 22 | | | 0-48 & 2-32 |
| Warwickshire | Edgbaston | May 25 | 22* & 0 | | 1-55 |
| Essex | Bristol | May 31 | 4 & 56 | 1Ct | 0-35 |
| Middlesex | Bristol | June 4 | 2 | | 0-8 & 0-26 |
| Hampshire | Southampton | June 7 | 67 | 1Ct | 0-25 |
| Notts | Gloucester | June 14 | 18 & 3* | | 0-15 & 0-62 |
| Derbyshire | Gloucester | June 18 | 69 & 7 | 1Ct | 2-81 |
| Somerset | Bath | June 21 | 2 | | 1-69 |
| Northants | Luton | June 28 | 26 & 1 | 1Ct | 2-35 & 6-94 |
| Leicestershire | Hinckley | July 2 | 6* | 3Ct | 2-93 |
| Surrey | Guildford | July 16 | 10 | | 2-67 & 0-58 |
| Glamorgan | Cheltenham | July 19 | 24 & 61 | | 3-27 & 0-56 |
| Sussex | Cheltenham | July 23 | 8 | | 1-26 |
| Worcestershire | Cheltenham | July 26 | 19 & 21 | 4Ct | 2-48 & 0-25 |
| Lancashire | Bristol | Aug 9 | 12 | 2Ct | 0-2 |
| Kent | Canterbury | Aug 20 | 8 & 67* | | |
| Glamorgan | Abergavenny | Aug 28 | 50 & 12 | | 0-28 & 0-24 |
| Northants | Bristol | Sept 3 | 59 & 13 | 2Ct | 1-20 & 2-86 |
| Somerset | Bristol | Sept 10 | 3 & 23 | | 3-106 |
| Sussex | Hove | Sept 17 | 4 & 0 | 4Ct | 0-60 & 3-98 |

## OTHER FIRST-CLASS

| Opposition | Venue | Date | Batting | Fielding | Bowling |
|---|---|---|---|---|---|
| Oxford U | The Parks | June 15 | | | 0-11 |
| West Indies | Bristol | July 31 | 71* & 3* | | 1-112 & 0-34 |

## REFUGE ASSURANCE

| | | | | | |
|---|---|---|---|---|---|
| Middlesex | Bristol | April 21 | 11 | | |
| Surrey | The Oval | May 12 | | 1Ct | |
| Sussex | Hove | May 19 | 7 | 1Ct | |
| Hampshire | Swindon | May 26 | | 1Ct | 2-47 |
| Northants | Moreton | June 9 | | | |
| Notts | Gloucester | June 16 | 15 | | 0-5 |
| Kent | Canterbury | June 30 | 4 | | |
| Yorkshire | Scarborough | July 14 | 42* | 1Ct | 0-23 |
| Derbyshire | Cheltenham | July 21 | 0 | | |
| Essex | Cheltenham | July 28 | 12 | | |
| Glamorgan | Swansea | Aug 4 | 20 | | |
| Lancashire | Bristol | Aug 11 | 5 | | |

## NATWEST TROPHY

| | | | | | |
|---|---|---|---|---|---|
| Norfolk | Bristol | June 26 | 4 | | 0-3 |
| Notts | Bristol | July 11 | 13* | 2Ct | 0-36 |

## BENSON & HEDGES CUP

| | | | | | |
|---|---|---|---|---|---|
| Combined U | Bristol | April 23 | 19 | 1Ct | 3-14 |
| Worcestershire | Worcester | April 25 | 24 | 1Ct | |
| Northants | Bristol | May 2 | | | |

## OTHER ONE-DAY

| | | | | | |
|---|---|---|---|---|---|
| West Indies | Bristol | May 14 | 45* | 1Ct | 0-12 |
| Somerset | Hove | Sept 8 | 26 | 1Ct | 1-46 |
| Sussex | Hove | Sept 9 | 15 | | 1-46 |

## BATTING AVERAGES - Including fielding

| | Matches | Inns | NO | Runs | HS | Avge | 100s | 50s | Ct | St |
|---|---|---|---|---|---|---|---|---|---|---|
| Britannic Assurance | 22 | 33 | 4 | 729 | 69 | 25.13 | - | 7 | 21 | - |
| Other First-Class | 2 | 2 | 2 | 74 | 71* | - | - | 1 | - | - |
| ALL FIRST-CLASS | 24 | 35 | 6 | 803 | 71* | 27.69 | - | 8 | 21 | - |
| Refuge Assurance | 12 | 9 | 1 | 116 | 42* | 14.50 | - | - | 4 | - |
| NatWest Trophy | 2 | 2 | 1 | 17 | 13* | 17.00 | - | - | 2 | - |
| Benson & Hedges Cup | 3 | 2 | 0 | 43 | 24 | 21.50 | - | - | 2 | - |
| Other One-Day | 3 | 3 | 1 | 86 | 45* | 43.00 | - | - | 2 | - |
| ALL ONE-DAY | 20 | 16 | 3 | 262 | 45* | 20.15 | - | - | 10 | - |

## BOWLING AVERAGES

| | Overs | Mdns | Runs | Wkts | Avge | Best | 5wI | 10wM |
|---|---|---|---|---|---|---|---|---|
| Britannic Assurance | 510.2 | 121 | 1493 | 33 | 45.24 | 6-94 | 1 | - |
| Other First-Class | 31 | 1 | 157 | 1 | 157.00 | 1-112 | - | - |
| ALL FIRST-CLASS | 541.2 | 122 | 1650 | 34 | 48.52 | 6-94 | 1 | - |
| Refuge Assurance | 12 | 0 | 75 | 2 | 37.50 | 2-47 | - | - |
| NatWest Trophy | 14 | 1 | 39 | 0 | - | - | - | - |
| Benson & Hedges Cup | 9 | 2 | 14 | 3 | 4.66 | 3-14 | - | - |
| Other One-Day | 22 | 1 | 104 | 2 | 52.00 | 1-46 | - | - |
| ALL ONE-DAY | 57 | 4 | 232 | 7 | 33.14 | 3-14 | - | - |

# A.L.LOGIE - West Indies

| Opposition | Venue | Date | Batting | Fielding | Bowling |
|---|---|---|---|---|---|

## CORNHILL TEST MATCHES

| Opposition | Venue | Date | Batting | Fielding | Bowling |
|---|---|---|---|---|---|
| England | Headingley | June 6 | 6 & 3 | 1Ct | |
| England | Lord's | June 20 | 5 | | |
| England | Trent Bridge | July 4 | 78 | 1Ct | |
| England | Edgbaston | July 25 | 28 | 2Ct | |

## OTHER FIRST-CLASS

| Opposition | Venue | Date | Batting | Fielding | Bowling |
|---|---|---|---|---|---|
| Middlesex | Lord's | May 18 | 60 & 1 | 1Ct | |
| Somerset | Taunton | May 29 | 48 | | |
| Leicestershire | Leicester | June 1 | 32 & 10 | 1Ct | |
| Derbyshire | Derby | June 12 | 3* & 9 | | |
| Northants | Northampton | June 15 | 19 | | |
| Glamorgan | Swansea | July 16 | 8 | | |
| Kent | Canterbury | July 20 | 70 & 26 | 1Ct | |

## L — PLAYER RECORDS

| | | | | | |
|---|---|---|---|---|---|
| Gloucs | Bristol | July 31 | 27 | | |

**TEXACO TROPHY**

| | | | | |
|---|---|---|---|---|
| England | Edgbaston | May 23 | 18 | |
| England | Old Trafford | May 25 | 24 | |
| England | Lord's | May 27 | 82 | |

**OTHER ONE-DAY**

| | | | | | |
|---|---|---|---|---|---|
| D of Norfolk | Arundel | May 12 | 61 | 2Ct | |
| Gloucs | Bristol | May 14 | 12* | | |
| League CC XI | Trowbridge | June 28 | | 1Ct | |
| Ireland | Downpatrick | July 13 | 118 | | |
| Wales | Brecon | July 15 | 2* | 1Ct | 1-20 |

**BATTING AVERAGES - Including fielding**

| | Matches | Inns | NO | Runs | HS | Avge | 100s | 50s | Ct | St |
|---|---|---|---|---|---|---|---|---|---|---|
| Cornhill Test Matches | 4 | 5 | 0 | 120 | 78 | 24.00 | - | 1 | 4 | - |
| Other First-Class | 8 | 12 | 1 | 313 | 70 | 28.45 | - | 2 | 3 | - |
| ALL FIRST-CLASS | 12 | 17 | 1 | 433 | 78 | 27.06 | - | 3 | 7 | - |
| Texaco Trophy | 3 | 3 | 0 | 124 | 82 | 41.33 | - | 1 | - | - |
| Other One-Day | 5 | 4 | 2 | 193 | 118 | 96.50 | 1 | 1 | 4 | - |
| ALL ONE-DAY | 8 | 7 | 2 | 317 | 118 | 63.40 | 1 | 2 | 4 | - |

**BOWLING AVERAGES**

| | Overs | Mdns | Runs | Wkts | Avge | Best | 5wI | 10wM |
|---|---|---|---|---|---|---|---|---|
| Cornhill Test Matches | | | | | | | | |
| Other First-Class | | | | | | | | |
| ALL FIRST-CLASS | | | | | | | | |
| Texaco Trophy | | | | | | | | |
| Other One-Day | 3 | 0 | 20 | 1 | 20.00 | 1-20 | - | |
| ALL ONE-DAY | 3 | 0 | 20 | 1 | 20.00 | 1-20 | - | |

## J.I.LONGLEY - *Kent & Combined Universities*

| Opposition | Venue | Date | Batting | Fielding | Bowling |
|---|---|---|---|---|---|
| **REFUGE ASSURANCE** | | | | | |
| Sussex | Hove | Aug 25 | 1 | 1Ct | |
| **BENSON & HEDGES CUP** | | | | | |
| For Combined Universities | | | | | |
| Gloucs | Bristol | April 23 | 1 | | |
| Derbyshire | The Parks | April 25 | 6 | | |
| Worcestershire | Fenner's | May 2 | 47 | 1Ct | |
| Northants | Northampton | May 4 | 9 | | |
| **OTHER ONE-DAY** | | | | | |
| Sussex | Hove | Sept 7 | 40 | | |

**BATTING AVERAGES - Including fielding**

| | Matches | Inns | NO | Runs | HS | Avge | 100s | 50s | Ct | St |
|---|---|---|---|---|---|---|---|---|---|---|
| Refuge Assurance | 1 | 1 | 0 | 1 | 1 | 1.00 | - | - | 1 | - |
| Benson & Hedges Cup | 4 | 4 | 0 | 63 | 47 | 15.75 | - | - | 1 | - |
| Other One-Day | 1 | 1 | 0 | 40 | 40 | 40.00 | - | - | - | - |
| ALL ONE-DAY | 6 | 6 | 0 | 104 | 47 | 17.33 | - | - | 2 | - |

**BOWLING AVERAGES**
Did not bowl

## G.J.LORD - *Worcestershire*

| Opposition | Venue | Date | Batting | | Fielding | Bowling |
|---|---|---|---|---|---|---|
| **BRITANNIC ASSURANCE** | | | | | | |
| Gloucs | Worcester | April 27 | 29 | | 1Ct | |
| Lancashire | Worcester | May 9 | 12 & | 0 | 1Ct | |
| Glamorgan | Worcester | May 31 | 0 & | 8 | | |
| Northants | Northampton | June 4 | 55 & | 38 | | |
| Essex | Ilford | June 7 | 85 & | 0 | | |

| Leicestershire | Worcester | June 28 | 43 & | 64 | | |
|---|---|---|---|---|---|---|
| Yorkshire | Headingley | July 2 | | 0 | | |
| Hampshire | Portsmouth | July 16 | 2 & | 0 | | |
| Derbyshire | Kidd'minster | July 19 | 3 & | 17 | | |

**OTHER FIRST-CLASS**

| | | | | |
|---|---|---|---|---|
| West Indies | Worcester | May 15 | 1 | |
| Oxford U | The Parks | May 25 | 21 | |

**BATTING AVERAGES - Including fielding**

| | Matches | Inns | NO | Runs | HS | Avge | 100s | 50s | Ct | St |
|---|---|---|---|---|---|---|---|---|---|---|
| Britannic Assurance | 9 | 16 | 0 | 356 | 85 | 22.25 | - | 3 | 2 | - |
| Other First-Class | 2 | 2 | 0 | 22 | 21 | 11.00 | - | - | - | - |
| ALL FIRST-CLASS | 11 | 18 | 0 | 378 | 85 | 21.00 | - | 3 | 2 | - |

**BOWLING AVERAGES**
Did not bowl

## J.D.LOVE - *Lincolnshire & Minor Counties*

| Opposition | Venue | Date | Batting | Fielding | Bowling |
|---|---|---|---|---|---|
| **NATWEST TROPHY** | | | | | |
| Notts | Trent Bridge | June 26 | 24 | | |
| **BENSON & HEDGES CUP** | | | | | |
| Glamorgan | Trowbridge | April 23 | 81 | | |
| Hampshire | Trowbridge | April 25 | 75 | | |
| Yorkshire | Headingley | May 2 | 80* | | |

**BATTING AVERAGES - Including fielding**

| | Matches | Inns | NO | Runs | HS | Avge | 100s | 50s | Ct | St |
|---|---|---|---|---|---|---|---|---|---|---|
| NatWest Trophy | 1 | 1 | 0 | 24 | 24 | 24.00 | - | - | - | - |
| Benson & Hedges Cup | 3 | 3 | 1 | 236 | 81 | 118.00 | - | 3 | - | - |
| ALL ONE-DAY | 4 | 4 | 1 | 260 | 81 | 86.66 | - | 3 | - | - |

**BOWLING AVERAGES**
Did not bowl

## G.E.LOVEDAY - *Berkshire*

| Opposition | Venue | Date | Batting | Fielding | Bowling |
|---|---|---|---|---|---|
| **NATWEST TROPHY** | | | | | |
| Hampshire | Reading | June 26 | 14 | | |

**BATTING AVERAGES - Including fielding**

| | Matches | Inns | NO | Runs | HS | Avge | 100s | 50s | Ct | St |
|---|---|---|---|---|---|---|---|---|---|---|
| NatWest Trophy | 1 | 1 | 0 | 14 | 14 | 14.00 | - | - | - | - |
| ALL ONE-DAY | 1 | 1 | 0 | 14 | 14 | 14.00 | - | - | - | - |

**BOWLING AVERAGES**
Did not bowl

## D.J.LOVELL - *Durham*

| Opposition | Venue | Date | Batting | Fielding | Bowling |
|---|---|---|---|---|---|
| **OTHER ONE-DAY** | | | | | |
| Essex | Scarborough | Aug 31 | 32 | | 1-72 |

**BATTING AVERAGES - Including fielding**

| | Matches | Inns | NO | Runs | HS | Avge | 100s | 50s | Ct | St |
|---|---|---|---|---|---|---|---|---|---|---|
| Other One-Day | 1 | 1 | 0 | 32 | 32 | 32.00 | - | - | - | - |
| ALL ONE-DAY | 1 | 1 | 0 | 32 | 32 | 32.00 | - | - | - | - |

**BOWLING AVERAGES**

| | Overs | Mdns | Runs | Wkts | Avge | Best | 5wI | 10wM |
|---|---|---|---|---|---|---|---|---|
| Other One-Day | 10 | 0 | 72 | 1 | 72.00 | 1-72 | - | |

# PLAYER RECORDS

# L

| | | | | | | | | |
|---|---|---|---|---|---|---|---|---|
| ALL ONE-DAY | 10 | 0 | 72 | 1 | 72.00 | 1-72 | - | |

---

## G.LOVELL - *Oxford University*

| Opposition | Venue | Date | Batting | Fielding | Bowling |
|---|---|---|---|---|---|
| **OTHER FIRST-CLASS** | | | | | |
| Hampshire | The Parks | April 13 | 18 & 41 | | 0-36 |
| Glamorgan | The Parks | April 17 | 17 | | |
| Notts | The Parks | April 27 | | | 1-13 |
| Gloucs | The Parks | June 15 | 49 | | 0-11 |
| Worcestershire | The Parks | May 25 | 8 & 7 | 2Ct | 0-53 |
| Yorkshire | The Parks | June 4 | 2 | 1Ct | 0-28 |
| Lancashire | The Parks | June 7 | 1 & 16 * | | |
| Kent | The Parks | June 18 | 17 & 29 | | |
| Cambridge U | Lord's | July 2 | 15 * & 30 * | 3Ct | |

**BATTING AVERAGES - Including fielding**

| | Matches | Inns | NO | Runs | HS | Avge | 100s | 50s | Ct | St |
|---|---|---|---|---|---|---|---|---|---|---|
| Other First-Class | 9 | 13 | 3 | 250 | 49 | 25.00 | - | - | 6 | - |
| ALL FIRST-CLASS | 9 | 13 | 3 | 250 | 49 | 25.00 | - | - | 6 | - |

**BOWLING AVERAGES**

| | Overs | Mdns | Runs | Wkts | Avge | Best | 5wI | 10wM |
|---|---|---|---|---|---|---|---|---|
| Other First-Class | 32 | 3 | 141 | 1 | 141.00 | 1-13 | - | - |
| ALL FIRST-CLASS | 32 | 3 | 141 | 1 | 141.00 | 1-13 | - | - |

---

## W.G.LOVELL - *Essex*

| Opposition | Venue | Date | Batting | Fielding | Bowling |
|---|---|---|---|---|---|
| **REFUGE ASSURANCE** | | | | | |
| Lancashire | Old Trafford | Aug 25 | | | 0-34 |
| **OTHER ONE-DAY** | | | | | |
| Yorkshire | Scarborough | Sept 2 | | | 1-38 |

**BATTING AVERAGES - Including fielding**

| | Matches | Inns | NO | Runs | HS | Avge | 100s | 50s | Ct | St |
|---|---|---|---|---|---|---|---|---|---|---|
| Refuge Assurance | 1 | 0 | 0 | 0 | 0 | - | - | - | - | - |
| Other One-Day | 1 | 0 | 0 | 0 | 0 | - | - | - | - | - |
| ALL ONE-DAY | 2 | 0 | 0 | 0 | 0 | - | - | - | - | - |

**BOWLING AVERAGES**

| | Overs | Mdns | Runs | Wkts | Avge | Best | 5wI | 10wM |
|---|---|---|---|---|---|---|---|---|
| Refuge Assurance | 6 | 0 | 34 | 0 | - | - | - | - |
| Other One-Day | 9 | 0 | 38 | 1 | 38.00 | 1-38 | - | - |
| ALL ONE-DAY | 15 | 0 | 72 | 1 | 72.00 | 1-38 | - | - |

---

## M.J.LOWREY - *Cambridge University*

| Opposition | Venue | Date | Batting | Fielding | Bowling |
|---|---|---|---|---|---|
| **OTHER FIRST-CLASS** | | | | | |
| Lancashire | Fenner's | April 13 | 43 & 2 * | | 0-8 & 1-67 |
| Northants | Fenner's | April 16 | 51 | | 1-34 |
| Essex | Fenner's | April 19 | 0 & 9 | | 0-42 |
| Derbyshire | Fenner's | May 9 | 2 & 4 * | 1Ct | 0-61 & 1-46 |
| Middlesex | Fenner's | May 15 | 0 & 9 | | 0-24 |
| Surrey | Fenner's | May 18 | 2 & 21 | | 3-31 & 0-63 |
| Leicestershire | Fenner's | May 22 | 32 & 30 | 1Ct | 2-62 |
| Glamorgan | Fenner's | June 18 | 4 | | |
| Sussex | Hove | June 29 | | | 1-58 |
| Oxford U | Lord's | July 2 | 25 & 0 | | |

**BATTING AVERAGES - Including fielding**

| | Matches | Inns | NO | Runs | HS | Avge | 100s | 50s | Ct | St |
|---|---|---|---|---|---|---|---|---|---|---|
| Other First-Class | 10 | 16 | 2 | 234 | 51 | 16.71 | - | 1 | 2 | - |

---

| | | | | | | | | | |
|---|---|---|---|---|---|---|---|---|---|
| ALL FIRST-CLASS | 10 | 16 | 2 | 234 | 51 | 16.71 | - | 1 | 2 | - |

**BOWLING AVERAGES**

| | Overs | Mdns | Runs | Wkts | Avge | Best | 5wI | 10wM |
|---|---|---|---|---|---|---|---|---|
| Other First-Class | 136 | 17 | 496 | 9 | 55.11 | 3-31 | - | - |
| ALL FIRST-CLASS | 136 | 17 | 496 | 9 | 55.11 | 3-31 | - | - |

---

## M.B.LOYE - *Northamptonshire*

| Opposition | Venue | Date | Batting | Fielding | Bowling |
|---|---|---|---|---|---|
| **BRITANNIC ASSURANCE** | | | | | |
| Worcestershire | Northampton | June 4 | 3 * | 1Ct | |

**BATTING AVERAGES - Including fielding**

| | Matches | Inns | NO | Runs | HS | Avge | 100s | 50s | Ct | St |
|---|---|---|---|---|---|---|---|---|---|---|
| Britannic Assurance | 1 | 1 | 1 | 3 | 3 * | - | - | - | 1 | - |
| ALL FIRST-CLASS | 1 | 1 | 1 | 3 | 3 * | - | - | - | 1 | - |

**BOWLING AVERAGES**
Did not bowl

---

## M.A.LYNCH - *Surrey*

| Opposition | Venue | Date | Batting | Fielding | Bowling |
|---|---|---|---|---|---|
| **BRITANNIC ASSURANCE** | | | | | |
| Essex | Chelmsford | April 27 | 11 | 2Ct | |
| Hampshire | Bournemouth | May 25 | 0 & 30 | 2Ct | |
| Yorkshire | Guildford | July 19 | 13 | | |
| Warwickshire | Edgbaston | Aug 6 | 10 & 1 | 2Ct | |
| Middlesex | The Oval | Aug 20 | 141 * & 0 | | |
| Northants | Northampton | Aug 23 | 14 & 1 | | |
| Sussex | The Oval | Aug 28 | 0 | 2Ct | |
| Hampshire | The Oval | Sept 3 | 51 & 3 | 3Ct | 0-13 |
| Middlesex | Lord's | Sept 10 | 0 & 12 | 2Ct | |
| Lancashire | Old Trafford | Sept 17 | 30 & 25 | | 0-16 |
| **REFUGE ASSURANCE** | | | | | |
| Somerset | The Oval | April 21 | 9 | | |
| Middlesex | Lord's | April 28 | 5 | | |
| Essex | The Oval | May 26 | 85 | 1Ct | |
| Worcestershire | Worcester | June 2 | 18 * | 2Ct | |
| Derbyshire | Chesterfield | June 9 | 10 | | |
| Leicestershire | Leicester | June 16 | 1 | | |
| Notts | The Oval | June 30 | 33 | | |
| Northants | Tring | July 7 | 55 | 1Ct | |
| Sussex | The Oval | July 14 | 6 | | |
| Yorkshire | The Oval | July 21 | 97 | | |
| Glamorgan | The Oval | July 28 | 28 | 1Ct | |
| Kent | Canterbury | Aug 4 | 17 * | | |
| Lancashire | Old Trafford | Aug 18 | 37 | 1Ct | |
| Hampshire | The Oval | Aug 25 | 32 | | 0-6 |
| **NATWEST TROPHY** | | | | | |
| Kent | The Oval | July 11 | 48 | | |
| Essex | The Oval | July 31 | 6 | 2Ct | |
| Northants | The Oval | Aug 14 | 2 | 1Ct | 0-28 |
| Hampshire | Lord's | Sept 7 | 10 | | |
| **BENSON & HEDGES CUP** | | | | | |
| Essex | The Oval | April 23 | 0 | | |
| Middlesex | Lord's | April 25 | 20 | | |
| **OTHER ONE-DAY** | | | | | |
| Warwickshire | Harrogate | June 12 | 2 | | |
| Durham | Harrogate | June 13 | 1 | 1Ct | |

**BATTING AVERAGES - Including fielding**

| | Matches | Inns | NO | Runs | HS | Avge | 100s | 50s | Ct | St |
|---|---|---|---|---|---|---|---|---|---|---|
| Britannic Assurance | 10 | 17 | 1 | 342 | 141 * | 21.37 | 1 | 1 | 13 | - |
| ALL FIRST-CLASS | 10 | 17 | 1 | 342 | 141 * | 21.37 | 1 | 1 | 13 | - |

| L | **PLAYER RECORDS** |
|---|---|

| | | | | | | | | | | | |
|---|---|---|---|---|---|---|---|---|---|---|---|
| Refuge Assurance | 14 | 14 | 2 | 433 | 97 | 36.08 | - | 3 | 6 | - |
| NatWest Trophy | 4 | 4 | 0 | 66 | 48 | 16.50 | - | - | 3 | - |
| Benson & Hedges Cup | 2 | 2 | 0 | 20 | 20 | 10.00 | - | - | - | - |
| Other One-Day | 2 | 2 | 0 | 3 | 2 | 1.50 | - | - | 1 | - |
| ALL ONE-DAY | 22 | 22 | 2 | 522 | 97 | 26.10 | - | 3 | 10 | - |

**BOWLING AVERAGES**

| | Overs | Mdns | Runs | Wkts | Avge | Best | 5wI | 10wM |
|---|---|---|---|---|---|---|---|---|
| Britannic Assurance | 9 | 1 | 29 | 0 | - | - | - | - |
| ALL FIRST-CLASS | 9 | 1 | 29 | 0 | - | - | - | - |
| Refuge Assurance | 0.4 | 0 | 6 | 0 | - | - | - | - |
| NatWest Trophy | 10 | 1 | 28 | 0 | - | - | - | - |
| Benson & Hedges Cup | | | | | | | | |
| Other One-Day | | | | | | | | |
| ALL ONE-DAY | 10.4 | 1 | 34 | 0 | - | - | - | - |

## R.J.LYONS - *Cambridge University*

| Opposition | Venue | Date | Batting | Fielding | Bowling |
|---|---|---|---|---|---|

**OTHER FIRST-CLASS**

| Opposition | Venue | Date | Batting | Fielding | Bowling |
|---|---|---|---|---|---|
| Essex | Fenner's | April 19 | 20 & 18 | | 1-26 |

**BATTING AVERAGES - Including fielding**

| | Matches | Inns | NO | Runs | HS | Avge | 100s | 50s | Ct | St |
|---|---|---|---|---|---|---|---|---|---|---|
| Other First-Class | 1 | 2 | 0 | 38 | 20 | 19.00 | - | - | - | - |
| ALL FIRST-CLASS | 1 | 2 | 0 | 38 | 20 | 19.00 | - | - | - | - |

**BOWLING AVERAGES**

| | Overs | Mdns | Runs | Wkts | Avge | Best | 5wI | 10wM |
|---|---|---|---|---|---|---|---|---|
| Other First-Class | 4 | 0 | 26 | 1 | 26.00 | 1-26 | - | - |
| ALL FIRST-CLASS | 4 | 0 | 26 | 1 | 26.00 | 1-26 | - | - |

# PLAYER RECORDS — M

## J.MACAULEY - *League CC XI*

| Opposition | Venue | Date | Batting | Fielding | Bowling |
|---|---|---|---|---|---|
| **OTHER ONE-DAY** | | | | | |
| West Indies | Trowbridge | June 28 | | | |

### BATTING AVERAGES - Including fielding

| | Matches | Inns | NO | Runs | HS | Avge | 100s | 50s | Ct | St |
|---|---|---|---|---|---|---|---|---|---|---|
| Other One-Day | 1 | 0 | 0 | 0 | 0 | - | - | - | - | - |
| ALL ONE-DAY | 1 | 0 | 0 | 0 | 0 | - | - | - | - | - |

### BOWLING AVERAGES
Did not bowl

## R.MACDONALD - *Oxford University & Combined Universities*

| Opposition | Venue | Date | Batting | Fielding | Bowling |
|---|---|---|---|---|---|
| **OTHER FIRST-CLASS** | | | | | |
| Hampshire | The Parks | April 13 | 20 & 5 * | | 2-81 |
| Glamorgan | The Parks | April 17 | 4 | | 0-15 |
| Notts | The Parks | April 27 | | | 0-55 |
| Gloucs | The Parks | June 15 | | | 3-66 |
| Worcestershire | The Parks | May 25 | 8 & 3 * | | 2-103 |
| Yorkshire | The Parks | June 4 | 1 * | | 0-48 |
| Cambridge U | Lord's | July 2 | | | 2-73 & 1-16 |
| **BENSON & HEDGES CUP** | | | | | |
| For Combined Universities | | | | | |
| Gloucs | Bristol | April 23 | 5 | | 6-36 |
| Derbyshire | The Parks | April 25 | 1 * | | 0-90 |
| Worcestershire | Fenner's | May 2 | 12 * | | 1-31 |
| Northants | Northampton | May 4 | | | 1-59 |

### BATTING AVERAGES - Including fielding

| | Matches | Inns | NO | Runs | HS | Avge | 100s | 50s | Ct | St |
|---|---|---|---|---|---|---|---|---|---|---|
| Other First-Class | 7 | 6 | 3 | 41 | 20 | 13.66 | - | - | - | - |
| ALL FIRST-CLASS | 7 | 6 | 3 | 41 | 20 | 13.66 | - | - | - | - |
| Benson & Hedges Cup | 4 | 3 | 2 | 18 | 12 * | 18.00 | - | - | - | - |
| ALL ONE-DAY | 4 | 3 | 2 | 18 | 12 * | 18.00 | - | - | - | - |

### BOWLING AVERAGES

| | Overs | Mdns | Runs | Wkts | Avge | Best | 5wI | 10wM |
|---|---|---|---|---|---|---|---|---|
| Other First-Class | 157 | 48 | 457 | 10 | 45.70 | 3-66 | - | - |
| ALL FIRST-CLASS | 157 | 48 | 457 | 10 | 45.70 | 3-66 | - | - |
| Benson & Hedges Cup | 36 | 1 | 216 | 8 | 27.00 | 6-36 | 1 | |
| ALL ONE-DAY | 36 | 1 | 216 | 8 | 27.00 | 6-36 | 1 | |

## A.J.MACK - *Minor Counties*

| Opposition | Venue | Date | Batting | Fielding | Bowling |
|---|---|---|---|---|---|
| **BENSON & HEDGES CUP** | | | | | |
| Glamorgan | Trowbridge | April 23 | | 1Ct | 0-49 |
| Hampshire | Trowbridge | April 25 | | | 0-48 |
| Yorkshire | Headingley | May 2 | | | 0-32 |

### BATTING AVERAGES - Including fielding

| | Matches | Inns | NO | Runs | HS | Avge | 100s | 50s | Ct | St |
|---|---|---|---|---|---|---|---|---|---|---|
| Benson & Hedges Cup | 3 | 0 | 0 | 0 | 0 | - | - | - | 1 | - |
| ALL ONE-DAY | 3 | 0 | 0 | 0 | 0 | - | - | - | 1 | - |

### BOWLING AVERAGES

| | Overs | Mdns | Runs | Wkts | Avge | Best | 5wI | 10wM |
|---|---|---|---|---|---|---|---|---|
| Benson & Hedges Cup | 30 | 6 | 129 | 0 | - | - | - | - |
| ALL ONE-DAY | 30 | 6 | 129 | 0 | - | - | - | - |

## N.R.C.MACLAURIN - *Hertfordshire*

| Opposition | Venue | Date | Batting | Fielding | Bowling |
|---|---|---|---|---|---|
| **NATWEST TROPHY** | | | | | |
| Warwickshire | Edgbaston | July 11 | 3 | | 0-20 |

### BATTING AVERAGES - Including fielding

| | Matches | Inns | NO | Runs | HS | Avge | 100s | 50s | Ct | St |
|---|---|---|---|---|---|---|---|---|---|---|
| NatWest Trophy | 1 | 1 | 0 | 3 | 3 | 3.00 | - | - | - | - |
| ALL ONE-DAY | 1 | 1 | 0 | 3 | 3 | 3.00 | - | - | - | - |

### BOWLING AVERAGES

| | Overs | Mdns | Runs | Wkts | Avge | Best | 5wI | 10wM |
|---|---|---|---|---|---|---|---|---|
| NatWest Trophy | 2 | 0 | 20 | 0 | - | - | - | |
| ALL ONE-DAY | 2 | 0 | 20 | 0 | - | - | - | |

## K.H.MACLEAY - *Somerset*

| Opposition | Venue | Date | Batting | Fielding | Bowling |
|---|---|---|---|---|---|
| **BRITANNIC ASSURANCE** | | | | | |
| Derbyshire | Derby | May 22 | 26 * & 11 | | 3-40 & 0-60 |
| Middlesex | Taunton | May 25 | 19 & 9 * | | 1-54 |
| Glamorgan | Swansea | June 4 | 8 * | | 2-71 |
| Warwickshire | Edgbaston | June 7 | | 1Ct | 1-67 & 1-22 |
| Hampshire | Bath | June 18 | 8 | | 1-30 & 1-17 |
| Gloucs | Bath | June 21 | 5 | | 2-48 |
| Surrey | The Oval | June 28 | 57 | | 2-25 |
| Lancashire | Taunton | July 2 | 36 | 2Ct | 2-42 & 1-39 |
| Sussex | Hove | July 16 | 20 & 2 * | | 3-83 |
| Essex | Southend | July 19 | 6 & 7 | | 2-72 & 1-32 |
| Northants | Northampton | July 23 | 21 * | | 0-33 |
| Kent | Taunton | July 26 | 2 * & 10 | | 0-5 |
| Gloucs | Bristol | Sept 10 | 31 | 1Ct | 2-28 |
| Warwickshire | Taunton | Sept 17 | 63 & 47 | 1Ct | 0-39 |
| **OTHER FIRST-CLASS** | | | | | |
| West Indies | Taunton | May 29 | 15 & 14 | | 0-32 & 0-33 |
| **REFUGE ASSURANCE** | | | | | |
| Glamorgan | Taunton | May 12 | 2 | 1Ct | 1-30 |
| Hampshire | Bournemouth | May 19 | | | 1-16 |
| Middlesex | Taunton | May 26 | 19 | 1Ct | 1-28 |
| Warwickshire | Edgbaston | June 2 | 1 * | | |
| Notts | Trent Bridge | June 9 | 2 | 1Ct | 3-31 |
| Derbyshire | Derby | June 16 | 9 | | 1-31 |
| Northants | Luton | June 30 | 12 * | | 1-24 |
| Lancashire | Taunton | July 5 | 1 | | 1-25 |
| Essex | Southend | July 21 | 10 * | | 0-67 |
| **NATWEST TROPHY** | | | | | |
| Bucks | Bath | June 26 | | | 2-35 |
| Middlesex | Taunton | July 11 | 25 * | 1Ct | 1-32 |
| **OTHER ONE-DAY** | | | | | |
| Gloucs | Hove | Sept 8 | 29 | | 1-47 |

### BATTING AVERAGES - Including fielding

| | Matches | Inns | NO | Runs | HS | Avge | 100s | 50s | Ct | St |
|---|---|---|---|---|---|---|---|---|---|---|
| Britannic Assurance | 14 | 19 | 6 | 388 | 63 | 29.84 | - | 2 | 5 | - |
| Other First-Class | 1 | 2 | 0 | 29 | 15 | 14.50 | - | - | - | - |
| ALL FIRST-CLASS | 15 | 21 | 6 | 417 | 63 | 27.80 | - | 2 | 5 | - |
| Refuge Assurance | 9 | 8 | 3 | 56 | 19 | 11.20 | - | - | 3 | - |
| NatWest Trophy | 2 | 1 | 1 | 25 | 25 * | - | - | - | 1 | - |
| Other One-Day | 1 | 1 | 0 | 29 | 29 | 29.00 | - | - | - | - |
| ALL ONE-DAY | 12 | 10 | 4 | 110 | 29 | 18.33 | - | - | 4 | - |

### BOWLING AVERAGES

| | Overs | Mdns | Runs | Wkts | Avge | Best | 5wI | 10wM |
|---|---|---|---|---|---|---|---|---|
| Britannic Assurance | 266.3 | 51 | 807 | 25 | 32.28 | 3-40 | - | - |

# M PLAYER RECORDS

| | | | | | | | |
|---|---|---|---|---|---|---|---|
| Other First-Class | 18 | 3 | 65 | 0 | - | - | - |
| ALL FIRST-CLASS | 284.3 | 54 | 872 | 25 | 34.88 | 3-40 | - |
| Refuge Assurance | 63 | 1 | 252 | 9 | 28.00 | 3-31 | - |
| NatWest Trophy | 24 | 1 | 67 | 3 | 22.33 | 2-35 | - |
| Other One-Day | 9 | 0 | 47 | 1 | 47.00 | 1-47 | - |
| ALL ONE-DAY | 96 | 2 | 366 | 13 | 28.15 | 3-31 | - |

## MADAN LAL - *World XI*

| Opposition | Venue | Date | Batting | Fielding | Bowling |
|---|---|---|---|---|---|

**OTHER FIRST-CLASS**

| | | | | | |
|---|---|---|---|---|---|
| West Indies XI | Scarborough | Aug 28 | 9 & 16 | 2Ct | 1-25 & 0-22 |

**BATTING AVERAGES - Including fielding**

| | Matches | Inns | NO | Runs | HS | Avge | 100s | 50s | Ct | St |
|---|---|---|---|---|---|---|---|---|---|---|
| Other First-Class | 1 | 2 | 0 | 25 | 16 | 12.50 | - | - | 2 | - |
| ALL FIRST-CLASS | 1 | 2 | 0 | 25 | 16 | 12.50 | - | - | 2 | - |

**BOWLING AVERAGES**

| | Overs | Mdns | Runs | Wkts | Avge | Best | 5wI | 10wM |
|---|---|---|---|---|---|---|---|---|
| Other First-Class | 9 | 0 | 47 | 1 | 47.00 | 1-25 | - | - |
| ALL FIRST-CLASS | 9 | 0 | 47 | 1 | 47.00 | 1-25 | - | - |

## M.A.W.R.MADURASINGHE - *Sri Lanka*

| Opposition | Venue | Date | Batting | Fielding | Bowling |
|---|---|---|---|---|---|

**OTHER FIRST-CLASS**

| | | | | | |
|---|---|---|---|---|---|
| Yorkshire | Headingley | July 27 | 17* | | 1-67 & 1-75 |
| Gloucs | Bristol | Aug 6 | 4 & 6* | 1Ct | 1-13 |
| Somerset | Taunton | Aug 10 | 1 | | 1-64 & 1-33 |

**OTHER ONE-DAY**

| | | | | | |
|---|---|---|---|---|---|
| England Am.<br>For Sri Lanka | Wolv'hampton | July 24 | | | 3-26 |
| Durham<br>For Sri Lanka | Chester-le-S | July 26 | 0 | | 0-34 |
| England A<br>For Sri Lanka | Old Trafford | Aug 14 | 5* | 1Ct | 1-41 |
| England A | Old Trafford | Aug 15 | | 1Ct | 0-49 |

**BATTING AVERAGES - Including fielding**

| | Matches | Inns | NO | Runs | HS | Avge | 100s | 50s | Ct | St |
|---|---|---|---|---|---|---|---|---|---|---|
| Other First-Class | 3 | 4 | 2 | 28 | 17* | 14.00 | - | - | 1 | - |
| ALL FIRST-CLASS | 3 | 4 | 2 | 28 | 17* | 14.00 | - | - | 1 | - |
| Other One-Day | 4 | 2 | 1 | 5 | 5* | 5.00 | - | - | 2 | - |
| ALL ONE-DAY | 4 | 2 | 1 | 5 | 5* | 5.00 | - | - | 2 | - |

**BOWLING AVERAGES**

| | Overs | Mdns | Runs | Wkts | Avge | Best | 5wI | 10wM |
|---|---|---|---|---|---|---|---|---|
| Other First-Class | 82 | 15 | 252 | 5 | 50.40 | 1-13 | - | - |
| ALL FIRST-CLASS | 82 | 15 | 252 | 5 | 50.40 | 1-13 | - | - |
| Other One-Day | 43.1 | 6 | 150 | 4 | 37.50 | 3-26 | - |
| ALL ONE-DAY | 43.1 | 6 | 150 | 4 | 37.50 | 3-26 | - |

## J.N.MAGUIRE - *Leicestershire*

| Opposition | Venue | Date | Batting | Fielding | Bowling |
|---|---|---|---|---|---|

**BRITANNIC ASSURANCE**

| | | | | | | |
|---|---|---|---|---|---|---|
| Glamorgan | Leicester | April 27 | | | | 2-35 & 0-4 |
| Notts | Trent Bridge | May 9 | 33 & | 0 | | 4-92 & 0-34 |
| Northants | Northampton | May 16 | 0* | | | 0-42 & 4-69 |
| Notts | Leicester | May 25 | 0 & | 0 | 2Ct | 2-105 & 3-90 |
| Essex | Ilford | June 4 | 21 | | | 6-85 & 1-72 |
| Middlesex | Uxbridge | June 7 | 2 & | 1* | | 1-70 & 0-15 |
| Surrey | Leicester | June 14 | 5 | | | 0-22 & 1-45 |
| Lancashire | Leicester | June 18 | | 5 | 1Ct | 0-51 & 3-13 |
| Glamorgan | Neath | June 21 | | | | 2-77 |
| Worcestershire | Worcester | June 28 | | | | 2-61 & 1-65 |
| Gloucs | Hinckley | July 2 | | 2* | | 1-75 |
| Northants | Leicester | July 5 | 4 | | | 4-57 |
| Sussex | Hove | July 19 | | 11* | | 2-85 & 0-40 |
| Warwickshire | Leicester | July 26 | 2 & | 18 | | 1-85 |
| Somerset | Weston | Aug 2 | 0* | | | 0-62 & 0-5 |
| Yorkshire | Leicester | Aug 6 | | | | 1-3 & 0-53 |
| Kent | Leicester | Aug 9 | 0 | | | 7-57 & 0-85 |
| Hampshire | Bournemouth | Aug 16 | | | | 1-52 & 2-65 |
| Derbyshire | Derby | Aug 20 | 26 | | | 0-37 & 2-30 |
| Derbyshire | Leicester | Aug 28 | 44* & | 20 | 1Ct | 5-67 & 1-62 |
| Essex | Leicester | Sept 10 | 9* & | 16 | | 3-157 |
| Kent | Canterbury | Sept 17 | 17 & | 1 | 3Ct | 4-39 & 3-59 |

**OTHER FIRST-CLASS**

| | | | | | | |
|---|---|---|---|---|---|---|
| Cambridge U | Fenner's | May 22 | | | | 1-38 & 0-47 |
| West Indies | Leicester | June 1 | | | | 5-44 & 2-86 |

**REFUGE ASSURANCE**

| | | | | | |
|---|---|---|---|---|---|
| Derbyshire | Leicester | April 21 | | 1Ct | 0-25 |
| Glamorgan | Leicester | April 28 | 2* | | 3-31 |
| Northants | Northampton | May 12 | | | 0-48 |
| Yorkshire | Leicester | May 19 | | | 2-46 |
| Notts | Leicester | May 26 | | | 1-30 |
| Middlesex | Uxbridge | June 9 | 0* | | 2-16 |
| Surrey | Leicester | June 16 | 0 | | 2-20 |
| Worcestershire | Worcester | June 30 | | | 1-28 |
| Lancashire | Leicester | July 7 | | | 2-33 |
| Kent | Canterbury | July 14 | 0* | | 0-30 |
| Sussex | Hove | July 21 | 0* | 1Ct | 2-34 |
| Somerset | Weston | Aug 4 | | | 1-42 |
| Warwickshire | Leicester | Aug 11 | | 1Ct | 1-20 |
| Hampshire | Bournemouth | Aug 18 | | | 3-44 |
| Gloucs | Leicester | Aug 25 | 0* | | 1-58 |

**NATWEST TROPHY**

| | | | | | |
|---|---|---|---|---|---|
| Shropshire | Leicester | June 26 | | | 0-49 |
| Northants | Northampton | July 11 | | | 0-45 |

**BENSON & HEDGES CUP**

| | | | | | |
|---|---|---|---|---|---|
| Kent | Canterbury | April 23 | 2 | | 1-59 |
| Sussex | Hove | April 25 | 35 | | 0-43 |
| Scotland | Leicester | May 2 | | 1Ct | 0-25 |
| Lancashire | Leicester | May 4 | 0 | | 1-27 |

**OTHER ONE-DAY**

| | | | | | |
|---|---|---|---|---|---|
| Durham | Harrogate | June 11 | | 1Ct | 1-27 |

**BATTING AVERAGES - Including fielding**

| | Matches | Inns | NO | Runs | HS | Avge | 100s | 50s | Ct | St |
|---|---|---|---|---|---|---|---|---|---|---|
| Britannic Assurance | 22 | 24 | 7 | 237 | 44* | 13.94 | - | - | 7 | - |
| Other First-Class | 2 | 0 | 0 | 0 | 0 | | | | | |
| ALL FIRST-CLASS | 24 | 24 | 7 | 237 | 44* | 13.94 | - | - | 7 | - |
| Refuge Assurance | 15 | 6 | 5 | 2 | 2* | 2.00 | - | - | 3 | - |
| NatWest Trophy | 2 | 0 | 0 | 0 | 0 | | | | | |
| Benson & Hedges Cup | 4 | 3 | 0 | 37 | 35 | 12.33 | - | - | 1 | - |
| Other One-Day | 1 | 0 | 0 | 0 | 0 | | | | 1 | |
| ALL ONE-DAY | 22 | 9 | 5 | 39 | 35 | 9.75 | - | - | 5 | - |

**BOWLING AVERAGES**

| | Overs | Mdns | Runs | Wkts | Avge | Best | 5wI | 10wM |
|---|---|---|---|---|---|---|---|---|
| Britannic Assurance | 730.5 | 160 | 2222 | 69 | 32.20 | 7-57 | 3 | - |
| Other First-Class | 55.1 | 8 | 215 | 8 | 26.87 | 5-44 | 1 | - |
| ALL FIRST-CLASS | 786 | 168 | 2437 | 77 | 31.64 | 7-57 | 4 | - |
| Refuge Assurance | 113.3 | 7 | 505 | 21 | 24.04 | 3-31 | - | - |
| NatWest Trophy | 23 | 1 | 94 | 0 | - | - | - | - |
| Benson & Hedges Cup | 37 | 7 | 154 | 2 | 77.00 | 1-27 | - | |
| Other One-Day | 7 | 0 | 27 | 1 | 27.00 | 1-27 | - | |
| ALL ONE-DAY | 180.3 | 15 | 780 | 24 | 32.50 | 3-31 | - | |

# PLAYER RECORDS

# M

## R.S.MAHANAMA - *Sri Lanka*

| Opposition | Venue | Date | Batting | Fielding | Bowling |
|---|---|---|---|---|---|

### CORNHILL TEST MATCHES
| | | | | | |
|---|---|---|---|---|---|
| England | Lord's | Aug 22 | 2 & 15 | 3Ct | |

### OTHER FIRST-CLASS
| | | | | | |
|---|---|---|---|---|---|
| Yorkshire | Headingley | July 27 | 0 | 1Ct | |
| Derbyshire | Derby | Aug 2 | 14 | 2Ct | |
| Gloucs | Bristol | Aug 6 | 26 & 0 | 1Ct | |
| Somerset | Taunton | Aug 10 | 0 | 1Ct | |
| Sussex | Hove | Aug 17 | 24 & 65 | 1Ct | |

### OTHER ONE-DAY
| | | | | | |
|---|---|---|---|---|---|
| England Am. | Wolv'hampton | July 24 | 26 | | |
| Durham | Chester-le-S | July 26 | 67 | 1Ct | |
| England A | Old Trafford | Aug 14 | 73 | | |
| England A | Old Trafford | Aug 15 | 44 | | |

### BATTING AVERAGES - Including fielding
| | Matches | Inns | NO | Runs | HS | Avge | 100s | 50s | Ct | St |
|---|---|---|---|---|---|---|---|---|---|---|
| Cornhill Test Matches | 1 | 2 | 0 | 17 | 15 | 8.50 | - | - | 3 | - |
| Other First-Class | 5 | 7 | 0 | 129 | 65 | 18.42 | - | 1 | 6 | - |
| ALL FIRST-CLASS | 6 | 9 | 0 | 146 | 65 | 16.22 | - | 1 | 9 | - |
| Other One-Day | 4 | 4 | 0 | 210 | 73 | 52.50 | - | 2 | 1 | - |
| ALL ONE-DAY | 4 | 4 | 0 | 210 | 73 | 52.50 | - | 2 | 1 | - |

### BOWLING AVERAGES
Did not bowl

## B.J.M.MAHER - *Derbyshire*

| Opposition | Venue | Date | Batting | Fielding | Bowling |
|---|---|---|---|---|---|

### OTHER FIRST-CLASS
| | | | | | |
|---|---|---|---|---|---|
| Sri Lanka | Derby | Aug 2 | 5 | | |

### REFUGE ASSURANCE
| | | | | | |
|---|---|---|---|---|---|
| Northants | Derby | July 28 | 0* | 2Ct | |
| Warwickshire | Edgbaston | Aug 4 | 4 | | |

### BATTING AVERAGES - Including fielding
| | Matches | Inns | NO | Runs | HS | Avge | 100s | 50s | Ct | St |
|---|---|---|---|---|---|---|---|---|---|---|
| Other First-Class | 1 | 1 | 0 | 5 | 5 | 5.00 | - | - | - | - |
| ALL FIRST-CLASS | 1 | 1 | 0 | 5 | 5 | 5.00 | - | - | - | - |
| Refuge Assurance | 2 | 2 | 1 | 4 | 4 | 4.00 | - | - | 2 | - |
| ALL ONE-DAY | 2 | 2 | 1 | 4 | 4 | 4.00 | - | - | 2 | - |

### BOWLING AVERAGES
Did not bowl

## D.E.MALCOLM - *Derbyshire & England*

| Opposition | Venue | Date | Batting | Fielding | Bowling |
|---|---|---|---|---|---|

### CORNHILL TEST MATCHES
| | | | | | |
|---|---|---|---|---|---|
| West Indies | Headingley | June 6 | 5* & 4 | | 0-69 & 1-26 |
| West Indies | Lord's | June 20 | 0 | 1Ct | 1-76 & 1-9 |

### BRITANNIC ASSURANCE
| | | | | | |
|---|---|---|---|---|---|
| Lancashire | Old Trafford | May 16 | | | 3-47 & 1-38 |
| Kent | Canterbury | May 25 | 2 & 18 | | 2-54 & 2-87 |
| Northants | Northampton | May 31 | 6 & 5 | | 4-76 & 4-99 |
| Warwickshire | Edgbaston | June 28 | 15 | | 1-86 & 5-45 |
| Sussex | Derby | July 5 | 0 | | 3-79 & 1-29 |
| Yorkshire | Scarborough | July 16 | 6* | | 2-86 |
| Worcestershire | Kidd'minster | July 19 | 0 & 4 | | 3-57 & 0-90 |
| Hampshire | Chesterfield | July 23 | 5 | | 2-84 |
| Essex | Derby | Aug 6 | 10 | | 0-18 & 4-84 |

| | | | | | |
|---|---|---|---|---|---|
| Middlesex | Lord's | Aug 9 | 4 | | 0-95 |
| Leicestershire | Derby | Aug 20 | 5* & 4 | | 2-117 |

### REFUGE ASSURANCE
| | | | | | |
|---|---|---|---|---|---|
| Leicestershire | Leicester | April 21 | | | 2-39 |
| Hampshire | Derby | May 5 | | | 1-35 |
| Lancashire | Derby | May 19 | 11 | | 2-51 |
| Kent | Canterbury | May 26 | 4* | | 2-34 |
| Yorkshire | Chesterfield | June 2 | | 2Ct | 1-19 |
| Somerset | Derby | June 16 | 3* | | 2-41 |
| Essex | Chelmsford | June 30 | 18 | | 3-43 |
| Worcestershire | Worcester | July 9 | 2* | | 1-57 |
| Middlesex | Lord's | Aug 11 | 0 | | 1-65 |

### BENSON & HEDGES CUP
| | | | | | |
|---|---|---|---|---|---|
| Northants | Derby | April 23 | 14 | | 1-42 |
| Combined U | The Parks | April 25 | 15 | | 2-14 |
| Worcestershire | Worcester | May 4 | 8 | | 0-46 |
| Gloucs | Derby | May 7 | | | 2-49 |

### OTHER ONE-DAY
For England XI
| | | | | | |
|---|---|---|---|---|---|
| Rest of World | Jesmond | July 31 | | | 0-61 |
| Rest of World | Jesmond | Aug 1 | 0* | | 3-61 |

### BATTING AVERAGES - Including fielding
| | Matches | Inns | NO | Runs | HS | Avge | 100s | 50s | Ct | St |
|---|---|---|---|---|---|---|---|---|---|---|
| Cornhill Test Matches | 2 | 3 | 1 | 9 | 5* | 4.50 | - | - | 1 | - |
| Britannic Assurance | 11 | 14 | 2 | 84 | 18 | 7.00 | - | - | - | - |
| ALL FIRST-CLASS | 13 | 17 | 3 | 93 | 18 | 6.64 | - | - | 1 | - |
| Refuge Assurance | 9 | 6 | 3 | 38 | 18 | 12.66 | - | - | 2 | - |
| Benson & Hedges Cup | 4 | 3 | 0 | 37 | 15 | 12.33 | - | - | - | - |
| Other One-Day | 2 | 1 | 1 | 0 | 0* | - | - | - | - | - |
| ALL ONE-DAY | 15 | 10 | 4 | 75 | 18 | 12.50 | - | - | 2 | - |

### BOWLING AVERAGES
| | Overs | Mdns | Runs | Wkts | Avge | Best | 5wI | 10wM |
|---|---|---|---|---|---|---|---|---|
| Cornhill Test Matches | 42.3 | 3 | 180 | 3 | 60.00 | 1-9 | - | - |
| Britannic Assurance | 346.2 | 50 | 1271 | 39 | 32.59 | 5-45 | 1 | - |
| ALL FIRST-CLASS | 388.5 | 53 | 1451 | 42 | 34.54 | 5-45 | 1 | - |
| Refuge Assurance | 66 | 2 | 384 | 15 | 25.60 | 3-43 | - | |
| Benson & Hedges Cup | 39 | 3 | 151 | 5 | 30.20 | 2-14 | - | |
| Other One-Day | 20 | 0 | 122 | 3 | 40.66 | 3-61 | - | |
| ALL ONE-DAY | 125 | 5 | 657 | 23 | 28.56 | 3-43 | - | |

## N.A.MALLENDER - *Somerset*

| Opposition | Venue | Date | Batting | Fielding | Bowling |
|---|---|---|---|---|---|

### BRITANNIC ASSURANCE
| | | | | | |
|---|---|---|---|---|---|
| Sussex | Taunton | April 27 | 15 | | 1-33 |
| Glamorgan | Taunton | May 9 | 19 & 4 | | 1-58 & 0-75 |
| Derbyshire | Derby | May 22 | | | 3-52 & 1-37 |
| Middlesex | Taunton | May 25 | 6 | | 3-82 |
| Glamorgan | Swansea | June 4 | | 1Ct | 1-42 |
| Warwickshire | Edgbaston | June 7 | | | 0-29 & 1-40 |
| Hampshire | Bath | June 18 | 0 | | 4-68 & 0-11 |
| Gloucs | Bath | June 21 | | | 6-43 |
| Surrey | The Oval | June 28 | 12* | | 2-44 |
| Lancashire | Taunton | July 2 | | | 0-42 & 1-6 |
| Worcestershire | Worcester | Sept 3 | 6 & 14 | | 5-80 |
| Gloucs | Bristol | Sept 10 | 13* | | 2-44 & 3-60 |
| Warwickshire | Taunton | Sept 17 | 6 & 13* | 13* | 6-68 & 2-55 |

### REFUGE ASSURANCE
| | | | | | |
|---|---|---|---|---|---|
| Surrey | The Oval | April 21 | 0 | | 0-38 |
| Sussex | Taunton | April 28 | | | 0-37 |
| Glamorgan | Taunton | May 12 | | | 0-29 |
| Hampshire | Bournemouth | May 19 | | | 2-21 |
| Middlesex | Taunton | May 26 | 6* | | 0-36 |
| Warwickshire | Edgbaston | June 2 | | | |
| Notts | Trent Bridge | June 9 | 5* | | 0-41 |
| Derbyshire | Derby | June 16 | 0 | | 0-13 |
| Northants | Luton | June 30 | 13* | | 1-31 |

# M PLAYER RECORDS

## NATWEST TROPHY

| | | | | | |
|---|---|---|---|---|---|
| Bucks | Bath | June 26 | | | 3-23 |

## BENSON & HEDGES CUP

| | | | | | |
|---|---|---|---|---|---|
| Middlesex | Taunton | April 23 | 1 | | 1-45 |
| Warwickshire | Edgbaston | May 2 | 1 | | 1-47 |
| Surrey | Taunton | May 4 | | 1Ct | 0-54 |
| Essex | Chelmsford | May 7 | 2* | | 1-35 |

## OTHER ONE-DAY

| | | | | | |
|---|---|---|---|---|---|
| Gloucs | Hove | Sept 8 | 6 | 1Ct | 1-17 |

### For Yorkshiremen

| | | | | | |
|---|---|---|---|---|---|
| Yorkshire | Scarborough | Sept 7 | | 1Ct | 0-16 |

## BATTING AVERAGES - Including fielding

| | Matches | Inns | NO | Runs | HS | Avge | 100s | 50s | Ct | St |
|---|---|---|---|---|---|---|---|---|---|---|
| Britannic Assurance | 13 | 11 | 3 | 108 | 19 | 13.50 | - | - | 1 | - |
| ALL FIRST-CLASS | 13 | 11 | 3 | 108 | 19 | 13.50 | - | - | 1 | - |
| Refuge Assurance | 9 | 5 | 3 | 24 | 13* | 12.00 | - | - | - | - |
| NatWest Trophy | 1 | 0 | 0 | 0 | 0 | - | - | - | - | - |
| Benson & Hedges Cup | 4 | 3 | 1 | 4 | 2* | 2.00 | - | - | 1 | - |
| Other One-Day | 2 | 1 | 0 | 6 | 6 | 6.00 | - | - | 2 | - |
| ALL ONE-DAY | 16 | 9 | 4 | 34 | 13* | 6.80 | - | - | 3 | - |

## BOWLING AVERAGES

| | Overs | Mdns | Runs | Wkts | Avge | Best | 5wI | 10wM |
|---|---|---|---|---|---|---|---|---|
| Britannic Assurance | 349.5 | 76 | 969 | 42 | 23.07 | 6-43 | 3 | - |
| ALL FIRST-CLASS | 349.5 | 76 | 969 | 42 | 23.07 | 6-43 | 3 | - |
| Refuge Assurance | 59 | 1 | 246 | 3 | 82.00 | 2-21 | - | |
| NatWest Trophy | 12 | 4 | 23 | 3 | 7.66 | 3-23 | - | |
| Benson & Hedges Cup | 41 | 3 | 181 | 3 | 60.33 | 1-35 | - | |
| Other One-Day | 14 | 3 | 33 | 1 | 33.00 | 1-17 | - | |
| ALL ONE-DAY | 126 | 11 | 483 | 10 | 48.30 | 3-23 | - | |

# MANINDER SINGH - *World XI*

| Opposition | Venue | Date | Batting | Fielding | Bowling |
|---|---|---|---|---|---|
| **OTHER FIRST-CLASS** | | | | | |
| West Indies XI | Scarborough | Aug 28 | 0 | | 2-122 & 2-86 |
| **OTHER ONE-DAY** | | | | | |
| Yorkshire | Scarborough | Sept 8 | | 1Ct | 1-25 |

## BATTING AVERAGES - Including fielding

| | Matches | Inns | NO | Runs | HS | Avge | 100s | 50s | Ct | St |
|---|---|---|---|---|---|---|---|---|---|---|
| Other First-Class | 1 | 1 | 0 | 0 | 0 | 0.00 | - | - | - | - |
| ALL FIRST-CLASS | 1 | 1 | 0 | 0 | 0 | 0.00 | - | - | - | - |
| Other One-Day | 1 | 0 | 0 | 0 | 0 | | - | - | 1 | - |
| ALL ONE-DAY | 1 | 0 | 0 | 0 | 0 | | - | - | 1 | - |

## BOWLING AVERAGES

| | Overs | Mdns | Runs | Wkts | Avge | Best | 5wI | 10wM |
|---|---|---|---|---|---|---|---|---|
| Other First-Class | 44 | 5 | 208 | 4 | 52.00 | 2-86 | - | - |
| ALL FIRST-CLASS | 44 | 5 | 208 | 4 | 52.00 | 2-86 | - | - |
| Other One-Day | 6 | 0 | 25 | 1 | 25.00 | 1-25 | - | |
| ALL ONE-DAY | 6 | 0 | 25 | 1 | 25.00 | 1-25 | - | |

# S.V.MANJREKAR - *World XI & Rest of World*

| Opposition | Venue | Date | Batting | Fielding | Bowling |
|---|---|---|---|---|---|
| **OTHER FIRST-CLASS** | | | | | |
| For World XI | | | | | |
| West Indies XI | Scarborough | Aug 28 | 45 & 154* | | |
| **OTHER ONE-DAY** | | | | | |
| For Rest of World | | | | | |
| England XI | Jesmond | July 31 | 100 | | |
| England XI | Jesmond | Aug 1 | 14 | | |

## BATTING AVERAGES - Including fielding

| | Matches | Inns | NO | Runs | HS | Avge | 100s | 50s | Ct | St |
|---|---|---|---|---|---|---|---|---|---|---|
| Other First-Class | 1 | 2 | 1 | 199 | 154* | 199.00 | 1 | - | - | - |
| ALL FIRST-CLASS | 1 | 2 | 1 | 199 | 154* | 199.00 | 1 | - | - | - |
| Other One-Day | 2 | 2 | 0 | 114 | 100 | 57.00 | 1 | - | - | - |
| ALL ONE-DAY | 2 | 2 | 0 | 114 | 100 | 57.00 | 1 | - | - | - |

## BOWLING AVERAGES
Did not bowl

# S.A.MARSH - *Kent*

| Opposition | Venue | Date | Batting | Fielding | Bowling |
|---|---|---|---|---|---|
| **BRITANNIC ASSURANCE** | | | | | |
| Hampshire | Southampton | April 27 | | | |
| Essex | Folkestone | May 16 | 18 & 36 | 1Ct | |
| Notts | Trent Bridge | May 22 | 10 & 11 | 5Ct | |
| Derbyshire | Canterbury | May 25 | 3 | 3Ct,1St | |
| Middlesex | Lord's | May 31 | 6 & 108* | 9Ct | |
| Warwickshire | Tunbridge W | June 4 | 0 | 1Ct | 0-28 |
| Sussex | Tunbridge W | June 7 | 50 & 26 | 2Ct | |
| Yorkshire | Harrogate | June 14 | | 1Ct | |
| Lancashire | Old Trafford | June 21 | 3 | 1Ct | |
| Northants | Maidstone | July 2 | 14 | 2Ct | |
| Glamorgan | Maidstone | July 5 | 0 | 4Ct | |
| Essex | Southend | July 16 | 83 | 3Ct | |
| Worcestershire | Worcester | July 23 | | 1Ct | |
| Somerset | Taunton | July 26 | 113* & 28* | 1Ct,1St | |
| Surrey | Canterbury | Aug 2 | 20* & 3 | 2Ct | |
| Hampshire | Canterbury | Aug 6 | 73 & 2 | 6Ct,1St | |
| Leicestershire | Leicester | Aug 9 | 1 & 39* | 6Ct,1St | |
| Gloucs | Canterbury | Aug 20 | 30 & 36 | 5Ct | |
| Middlesex | Canterbury | Aug 28 | 5 | 5Ct | |
| Sussex | Hove | Sept 3 | 19 & 0 | 1Ct | |
| Leicestershire | Canterbury | Sept 17 | 69 & 17 | 2Ct | |
| **OTHER FIRST-CLASS** | | | | | |
| Oxford U | The Parks | June 18 | 57 | 1Ct | |
| West Indies | Canterbury | July 20 | 22 & 8 | 4Ct | |
| **REFUGE ASSURANCE** | | | | | |
| Worcestershire | Worcester | April 21 | 27 | | |
| Essex | Folkestone | May 19 | 7 | 3Ct | |
| Derbyshire | Canterbury | May 26 | 0 | 1Ct | |
| Middlesex | Southgate | June 2 | 2 | 1Ct | |
| Yorkshire | Scarborough | June 16 | 3 | | |
| Lancashire | Old Trafford | June 23 | 4* | | |
| Gloucs | Canterbury | June 30 | 24* | | |
| Glamorgan | Maidstone | July 7 | | | |
| Leicestershire | Canterbury | July 14 | 59 | 1Ct | |
| Somerset | Taunton | July 28 | 3 | 2Ct,1St | |
| Surrey | Canterbury | Aug 4 | 28* | 1Ct | |
| Notts | Trent Bridge | Aug 11 | 56 | | |
| Northants | Canterbury | Aug 18 | 52 | | |
| Sussex | Hove | Aug 25 | 4 | | |
| **NATWEST TROPHY** | | | | | |
| Cambs | Canterbury | June 26 | | 2Ct | |
| Surrey | The Oval | July 11 | 15 | 1Ct | |

# PLAYER RECORDS

**M**

### BENSON & HEDGES CUP

| | | | | |
|---|---|---|---|---|
| Leicestershire | Canterbury | April 23 | 23 * | 2Ct |
| Lancashire | Old Trafford | April 25 | 71 | 2Ct |
| Worcestershire | Worcester | May 29 | 24 | 1Ct |

### OTHER ONE-DAY
For England A

| | | | | |
|---|---|---|---|---|
| Sri Lanka | Old Trafford | Aug 14 | 26 * | 2Ct |
| Sri Lanka | Old Trafford | Aug 15 | 28 * | 1Ct |
| For Kent | | | | |
| Sussex | Hove | Sept 7 | 3 | 1Ct |

### BATTING AVERAGES - Including fielding

| | Matches | Inns | NO | Runs | HS | Avge | 100s | 50s | Ct | St |
|---|---|---|---|---|---|---|---|---|---|---|
| Britannic Assurance | 21 | 29 | 5 | 823 | 113 * | 34.29 | 2 | 4 | 61 | 4 |
| Other First-Class | 2 | 3 | 0 | 87 | 57 | 29.00 | - | 1 | 5 | - |
| ALL FIRST-CLASS | 23 | 32 | 5 | 910 | 113 * | 33.70 | 2 | 5 | 66 | 4 |
| Refuge Assurance | 14 | 13 | 3 | 269 | 59 | 26.90 | - | 3 | 9 | 1 |
| NatWest Trophy | 2 | 1 | 0 | 15 | 15 | 15.00 | - | - | 3 | - |
| Benson & Hedges Cup | 3 | 3 | 1 | 118 | 71 | 59.00 | - | 1 | 5 | - |
| Other One-Day | 3 | 3 | 2 | 57 | 28 * | 57.00 | - | - | 4 | - |
| ALL ONE-DAY | 22 | 20 | 6 | 459 | 71 | 32.78 | - | 4 | 21 | 1 |

### BOWLING AVERAGES

| | Overs | Mdns | Runs | Wkts | Avge | Best | 5wI | 10wM |
|---|---|---|---|---|---|---|---|---|
| Britannic Assurance | 5 | 0 | 28 | 0 | - | - | - | - |
| Other First-Class | | | | | | | | |
| ALL FIRST-CLASS | 5 | 0 | 28 | 0 | - | - | - | - |
| Refuge Assurance | | | | | | | | |
| NatWest Trophy | | | | | | | | |
| Benson & Hedges Cup | | | | | | | | |
| Other One-Day | | | | | | | | |
| ALL ONE-DAY | | | | | | | | |

# D.MARSHALL - *Lincolnshire*

| Opposition | Venue | Date | Batting | Fielding | Bowling |
|---|---|---|---|---|---|
| **NATWEST TROPHY** | | | | | |
| Notts | Trent Bridge | June 26 | | | 0-48 |

### BATTING AVERAGES - Including fielding

| | Matches | Inns | NO | Runs | HS | Avge | 100s | 50s | Ct | St |
|---|---|---|---|---|---|---|---|---|---|---|
| NatWest Trophy | 1 | 0 | 0 | 0 | 0 | | | | | |
| ALL ONE-DAY | 1 | 0 | 0 | 0 | 0 | - | - | - | - | - |

### BOWLING AVERAGES

| | Overs | Mdns | Runs | Wkts | Avge | Best | 5wI | 10wM |
|---|---|---|---|---|---|---|---|---|
| NatWest Trophy | 12 | 0 | 48 | 0 | | | | |
| ALL ONE-DAY | 12 | 0 | 48 | 0 | - | - | - | - |

# M.D.MARSHALL - *West Indies*

| Opposition | Venue | Date | Batting | | | Fielding | Bowling |
|---|---|---|---|---|---|---|---|
| **CORNHILL TEST MATCHES** | | | | | | | |
| England | Headingley | June 6 | 0 | & | 1 | | 3-46 & 3-58 |
| England | Lord's | June 20 | 25 | | | | 2-78 |
| England | Trent Bridge | July 4 | 67 | | | | 2-54 & 2-49 |
| England | Edgbaston | July 25 | 6 * | | | | 4-33 & 2-53 |
| England | The Oval | Aug 8 | 0 | & | 17 | | 1-62 & 1-9 |
| **OTHER FIRST-CLASS** | | | | | | | |
| Middlesex | Lord's | May 18 | 19 | | | | 0-31 & 0-17 |
| Somerset | Taunton | May 29 | 14 | | | | 2-35 & 1-35 |
| Derbyshire | Derby | June 12 | | | | | 1-27 & 1-22 |
| Glamorgan | Swansea | July 16 | 46 * | | | | 2-34 |
| Gloucs | Bristol | July 31 | | | 1 | | 1-57 & 0-6 |
| For West Indies XI | | | | | | | |
| World XI | Scarborough | Aug 28 | | | | | 2-76 |

### TEXACO TROPHY

| | | | | |
|---|---|---|---|---|
| England | Edgbaston | May 23 | 17 | 2-32 |
| England | Old Trafford | May 25 | 22 | 0-45 |
| England | Lord's | May 27 | 13 | 1-49 |

### OTHER ONE-DAY

| | | | | |
|---|---|---|---|---|
| Gloucs | Bristol | May 14 | | 1-32 |
| League CC XI | Trowbridge | June 28 | | 0-15 |
| Wales | Brecon | July 15 | 1Ct | |

### BATTING AVERAGES - Including fielding

| | Matches | Inns | NO | Runs | HS | Avge | 100s | 50s | Ct | St |
|---|---|---|---|---|---|---|---|---|---|---|
| Cornhill Test Matches | 5 | 7 | 1 | 116 | 67 | 19.33 | - | 1 | - | - |
| Other First-Class | 6 | 4 | 1 | 80 | 46 * | 26.66 | - | - | - | - |
| ALL FIRST-CLASS | 11 | 11 | 2 | 196 | 67 | 21.77 | - | 1 | - | - |
| Texaco Trophy | 3 | 3 | 0 | 52 | 22 | 17.33 | - | - | - | - |
| Other One-Day | 3 | 0 | 0 | 0 | 0 | | - | - | 1 | - |
| ALL ONE-DAY | 6 | 3 | 0 | 52 | 22 | 17.33 | - | - | 1 | - |

### BOWLING AVERAGES

| | Overs | Mdns | Runs | Wkts | Avge | Best | 5wI | 10wM |
|---|---|---|---|---|---|---|---|---|
| Cornhill Test Matches | 172.1 | 36 | 442 | 20 | 22.10 | 4-33 | - | - |
| Other First-Class | 110 | 21 | 340 | 10 | 34.00 | 2-34 | - | - |
| ALL FIRST-CLASS | 282.1 | 57 | 782 | 30 | 26.06 | 4-33 | - | - |
| Texaco Trophy | 32 | 2 | 126 | 3 | 42.00 | 2-32 | - | |
| Other One-Day | 16 | 4 | 47 | 1 | 47.00 | 1-32 | - | |
| ALL ONE-DAY | 48 | 6 | 173 | 4 | 43.25 | 2-32 | - | |

# P.J.MARTIN - *Lancashire*

| Opposition | Venue | Date | Batting | Fielding | Bowling |
|---|---|---|---|---|---|
| **BRITANNIC ASSURANCE** | | | | | |
| Hampshire | Basingstoke | June 4 | 1 * | 1Ct | 0-20 & 1-60 |
| Leicestershire | Leicester | June 18 | 2 * | 1Ct | 0-23 & 1-17 |
| Kent | Old Trafford | June 21 | 21 * | | 1-79 |
| Glamorgan | Liverpool | June 28 | | | 0-55 & 0-57 |
| Somerset | Taunton | July 2 | | | 1-42 & 0-25 |
| Middlesex | Uxbridge | July 19 | 0 | | 2-65 & 1-43 |
| Warwickshire | Old Trafford | July 23 | | 1Ct | 3-40 |
| Yorkshire | Old Trafford | Aug 2 | | 1Ct | 1-41 & 0-1 |
| Northants | Lytham | Aug 6 | | 5 * | 2-87 |
| Gloucs | Bristol | Aug 9 | 1 * & | 0 | 4-97 |
| Derbyshire | Derby | Aug 16 | | 6 * | 0-78 & 2-102 |
| Worcestershire | Blackpool | Aug 20 | 17 | | 4-30 & 0-14 |
| Essex | Old Trafford | Aug 23 | 0 | | 1-47 & 0-34 |
| Yorkshire | Scarborough | Sept 3 | | 29 | 3-71 & 0-8 |
| Surrey | Old Trafford | Sept 17 | 0 * & | 3 * | 4-57 & 2-69 |
| **OTHER FIRST-CLASS** | | | | | |
| Oxford U | The Parks | June 7 | | 1Ct | 2-47 & 1-14 |
| **REFUGE ASSURANCE** | | | | | |
| Glamorgan | Old Trafford | June 9 | | | 0-19 |
| Kent | Old Trafford | June 23 | | | 1-20 |
| Somerset | Taunton | July 5 | | | 0-32 |
| Leicestershire | Leicester | July 7 | | | 2-38 |
| Gloucs | Bristol | Aug 11 | | | 0-28 |
| Essex | Old Trafford | Aug 25 | | | 0-37 |
| **NATWEST TROPHY** | | | | | |
| Dorset | Bournemouth | June 26 | | | 2-19 |
| **OTHER ONE-DAY** | | | | | |
| For England A | | | | | |
| Sri Lanka | Old Trafford | Aug 15 | | | 1-18 |

### BATTING AVERAGES - Including fielding

| | Matches | Inns | NO | Runs | HS | Avge | 100s | 50s | Ct | St |
|---|---|---|---|---|---|---|---|---|---|---|
| Britannic Assurance | 15 | 13 | 8 | 85 | 29 | 17.00 | - | - | 4 | - |
| Other First-Class | 1 | 0 | 0 | 0 | 0 | | - | - | 1 | - |
| ALL FIRST-CLASS | 16 | 13 | 8 | 85 | 29 | 17.00 | - | - | 5 | - |
| Refuge Assurance | 6 | 0 | 0 | 0 | 0 | | - | - | - | - |
| NatWest Trophy | 1 | 0 | 0 | 0 | 0 | | - | - | - | - |

357

# M PLAYER RECORDS

| | | | | | | | | | |
|---|---|---|---|---|---|---|---|---|---|
| Other One-Day | 1 | 0 | 0 | 0 | 0 | - | - | - | - |
| ALL ONE-DAY | 8 | 0 | 0 | 0 | 0 | - | - | - | - |

## BOWLING AVERAGES

| | Overs | Mdns | Runs | Wkts | Avge | Best | 5wI | 10wM |
|---|---|---|---|---|---|---|---|---|
| Britannic Assurance | 422.4 | 99 | 1262 | 33 | 38.24 | 4-30 | - | - |
| Other First-Class | 32 | 8 | 61 | 3 | 20.33 | 2-47 | - | - |
| ALL FIRST-CLASS | 454.4 | 107 | 1323 | 36 | 36.75 | 4-30 | - | - |
| Refuge Assurance | 39 | 1 | 174 | 3 | 58.00 | 2-38 | - | |
| NatWest Trophy | 12 | 2 | 19 | 2 | 9.50 | 2-19 | - | |
| Other One-Day | 6 | 1 | 18 | 1 | 18.00 | 1-18 | - | |
| ALL ONE-DAY | 57 | 4 | 211 | 6 | 35.16 | 2-19 | - | |

## D.J.R.MARTINDALE - *Nottinghamshire*

| Opposition | Venue | Date | Batting | Fielding | Bowling |
|---|---|---|---|---|---|
| **OTHER FIRST-CLASS** | | | | | |
| Oxford U | The Parks | April 27 | 4 * | | |

### BATTING AVERAGES - Including fielding

| | Matches | Inns | NO | Runs | HS | Avge | 100s | 50s | Ct | St |
|---|---|---|---|---|---|---|---|---|---|---|
| Other First-Class | 1 | 1 | 1 | 4 | 4 * | - | - | - | - | - |
| ALL FIRST-CLASS | 1 | 1 | 1 | 4 | 4 * | - | - | - | - | - |

### BOWLING AVERAGES
Did not bowl

## D.R.MARTYN - *Leicestershire*

| Opposition | Venue | Date | Batting | Fielding | Bowling |
|---|---|---|---|---|---|
| **OTHER FIRST-CLASS** | | | | | |
| West Indies | Leicester | June 1 | 35 & 60 * | | |

### BATTING AVERAGES - Including fielding

| | Matches | Inns | NO | Runs | HS | Avge | 100s | 50s | Ct | St |
|---|---|---|---|---|---|---|---|---|---|---|
| Other First-Class | 1 | 2 | 1 | 95 | 60 * | 95.00 | - | 1 | - | - |
| ALL FIRST-CLASS | 1 | 2 | 1 | 95 | 60 * | 95.00 | - | 1 | - | - |

### BOWLING AVERAGES
Did not bowl

## R.J.MARU - *Hampshire*

| Opposition | Venue | Date | Batting | Fielding | Bowling |
|---|---|---|---|---|---|
| **BRITANNIC ASSURANCE** | | | | | |
| Kent | Southampton | April 27 | | 1Ct | 1-86 |
| Gloucs | Bristol | May 9 | | | 3-95 & 0-30 |
| Sussex | Hove | May 16 | | 2Ct | 1-15 & 2-53 |
| Surrey | Bournemouth | May 25 | 36 & 23 | 2Ct | 0-1 & 3-65 |
| Notts | Trent Bridge | May 31 | | | 1-52 & 0-58 |
| Lancashire | Basingstoke | June 4 | 5 * | 2Ct | 1-69 & 0-8 |
| Gloucs | Southampton | June 7 | 20 | | 1-48 |
| Somerset | Bath | June 18 | 2 | | 0-60 & 1-22 |
| Northants | Northampton | June 21 | 0 * | 2Ct | 3-48 & 0-19 |
| Essex | Chelmsford | July 2 | 14 & 0 | 3Ct | 1-101 |
| Yorkshire | Southampton | July 5 | 36 | 2Ct | 2-79 |
| Worcestershire | Portsmouth | July 16 | 27 | 4Ct | 0-4 & 0-44 |
| Warwickshire | Portsmouth | July 19 | 2 & 6 | 3Ct | 0-3 |
| Derbyshire | Chesterfield | July 23 | 4 | | 2-48 |
| Middlesex | Lord's | Aug 2 | 0 | 2Ct | 0-36 & 0-42 |
| Kent | Canterbury | Aug 6 | 10 & 21 * | | 0-58 |
| Sussex | Bournemouth | Aug 20 | 34 | 1Ct | 1-38 & 0-2 |
| Somerset | Southampton | Aug 28 | 1 & 3 | | 1-78 & 1-62 |
| Surrey | The Oval | Sept 3 | 7 & 6 | 3Ct | 3-47 & 0-7 |

| | | | | | | | | |
|---|---|---|---|---|---|---|---|---|
| Glamorgan | Southampton | Sept 17 | 19 & 1 | | 2Ct | 5-128 & 1-28 |

| Opposition | Venue | Date | Batting | Fielding | Bowling |
|---|---|---|---|---|---|
| **OTHER FIRST-CLASS** | | | | | |
| Oxford U | The Parks | April 13 | | 1Ct | 4-17 & 2-47 |
| West Indies | Southampton | June 29 | 23 | 1Ct | 0-43 |

| | | | | | |
|---|---|---|---|---|---|
| **REFUGE ASSURANCE** | | | | | |
| Notts | Trent Bridge | July 14 | | | 1-27 |
| Warwickshire | Portsmouth | July 21 | 17 | 2Ct | 0-15 |
| Lancashire | Southampton | July 28 | | | 1-31 |
| Middlesex | Lord's | Aug 4 | | | 0-19 |
| Glamorgan | Ebbw Vale | Aug 11 | 33 * | 1Ct | 0-12 |
| Leicestershire | Bournemouth | Aug 18 | 3 * | | 0-32 |
| Surrey | The Oval | Aug 25 | 10 | 1Ct | 1-34 |

| | | | | | |
|---|---|---|---|---|---|
| **NATWEST TROPHY** | | | | | |
| Lancashire | Southampton | July 11 | | 1Ct | 0-37 |
| Notts | Southampton | July 31 | | 1Ct | 1-42 |
| Warwickshire | Edgbaston | Aug 14 | | | 2-20 |
| Surrey | Lord's | Sept 7 | 1 * | 1Ct | 0-23 |

### BATTING AVERAGES - Including fielding

| | Matches | Inns | NO | Runs | HS | Avge | 100s | 50s | Ct | St |
|---|---|---|---|---|---|---|---|---|---|---|
| Britannic Assurance | 20 | 25 | 3 | 369 | 61 | 16.77 | - | 1 | 29 | - |
| Other First-Class | 2 | 1 | 0 | 23 | 23 | 23.00 | - | - | 2 | - |
| ALL FIRST-CLASS | 22 | 26 | 3 | 392 | 61 | 17.04 | - | 1 | 31 | - |
| Refuge Assurance | 7 | 4 | 2 | 63 | 33 * | 31.50 | - | - | 4 | - |
| NatWest Trophy | 4 | 1 | 1 | 1 | 1 * | - | - | - | 3 | - |
| ALL ONE-DAY | 11 | 5 | 3 | 64 | 33 * | 32.00 | - | - | 7 | - |

### BOWLING AVERAGES

| | Overs | Mdns | Runs | Wkts | Avge | Best | 5wI | 10wM |
|---|---|---|---|---|---|---|---|---|
| Britannic Assurance | 570.1 | 159 | 1534 | 34 | 45.11 | 5-128 | 1 | - |
| Other First-Class | 55 | 19 | 107 | 6 | 17.83 | 4-17 | - | - |
| ALL FIRST-CLASS | 625.1 | 178 | 1641 | 40 | 41.02 | 5-128 | 1 | - |
| Refuge Assurance | 36 | 1 | 170 | 3 | 56.66 | 1-27 | - | |
| NatWest Trophy | 42 | 7 | 122 | 3 | 40.66 | 2-20 | - | |
| ALL ONE-DAY | 78 | 8 | 292 | 6 | 48.66 | 2-20 | - | |

## D.E.MATTOCKS - *Norfolk*

| Opposition | Venue | Date | Batting | Fielding | Bowling |
|---|---|---|---|---|---|
| **NATWEST TROPHY** | | | | | |
| Gloucs | Bristol | June 26 | 1 | | |

### BATTING AVERAGES - Including fielding

| | Matches | Inns | NO | Runs | HS | Avge | 100s | 50s | Ct | St |
|---|---|---|---|---|---|---|---|---|---|---|
| NatWest Trophy | 1 | 1 | 0 | 1 | 1 | 1.00 | - | - | - | - |
| ALL ONE-DAY | 1 | 1 | 0 | 1 | 1 | 1.00 | - | - | - | - |

### BOWLING AVERAGES
Did not bowl

## M.P.MAYNARD - *Glamorgan*

| Opposition | Venue | Date | Batting | Fielding | Bowling |
|---|---|---|---|---|---|
| **BRITANNIC ASSURANCE** | | | | | |
| Leicestershire | Leicester | April 27 | 41 | | |
| Somerset | Taunton | May 9 | 85 & 133 * | | |
| Sussex | Cardiff | May 25 | 127 | | |
| Worcestershire | Worcester | May 31 | 5 & 33 * | | |
| Somerset | Swansea | June 4 | 39 | 1Ct | |
| Derbyshire | Chesterfield | June 7 | 8 & 8 | | |
| Middlesex | Cardiff | June 14 | 0 & 9 * | 1Ct | |
| Leicestershire | Neath | June 21 | 61 | | |
| Lancashire | Liverpool | June 28 | 89 & 43 * | | |
| Notts | Cardiff | July 2 | 2 & 204 | | |
| Kent | Maidstone | July 5 | 59 & 16 | 1Ct | |
| Gloucs | Cheltenham | July 19 | 129 & 126 | 3Ct | |

# PLAYER RECORDS

# M

| | | | | | | |
|---|---|---|---|---|---|---|
| Essex | Cardiff | July 23 | 38 | | | |
| Surrey | The Oval | July 26 | 75 & 103 * | | | |
| Hampshire | Swansea | Aug 9 | 4 | 1Ct | | 0-34 |
| Yorkshire | Headingley | Aug 16 | 21 | | | |
| Warwickshire | Edgbaston | Aug 20 | 24 & 0 | 1Ct | | |
| Gloucs | Abergavenny | Aug 28 | 2 | 2Ct | | |
| Worcestershire | Cardiff | Sept 10 | 0 & 21 | 1Ct | | |
| Hampshire | Southampton | Sept 17 | 243 & 18 | 3Ct | | |

## OTHER FIRST-CLASS

| | | | | | |
|---|---|---|---|---|---|
| Oxford U | The Parks | April 17 | | 1Ct | |
| Cambridge U | Fenner's | June 18 | 21 & 1 | 1Ct | |
| West Indies | Swansea | July 16 | 8 & 7 * | 2Ct | |

## REFUGE ASSURANCE

| | | | | | |
|---|---|---|---|---|---|
| Northants | Cardiff | April 21 | 13 | | |
| Leicestershire | Leicester | April 28 | 2 | | |
| Notts | Cardiff | May 5 | 57 * | | |
| Somerset | Taunton | May 12 | 19 | | |
| Sussex | Swansea | May 26 | 0 | 1Ct | |
| Essex | Pontypridd | June 2 | 6 | | |
| Lancashire | Old Trafford | June 9 | 19 | | |
| Middlesex | Cardiff | June 16 | 25 | 2Ct | |
| Yorkshire | Headingley | June 30 | 44 | | |
| Kent | Maidstone | July 7 | 23 | | |
| Worcestershire | Worcester | July 21 | 15 | 1Ct | 0-2 |
| Surrey | The Oval | July 28 | 51 | 1Ct | |
| Gloucs | Swansea | Aug 4 | 81 | 2Ct | |
| Hampshire | Ebbw Vale | Aug 11 | 2 | 2Ct | |
| Derbyshire | Checkley | Aug 18 | 101 | | |

## NATWEST TROPHY

| | | | | |
|---|---|---|---|---|
| Durham | Darlington | June 26 | 151 * | |
| Worcestershire | Worcester | July 11 | 78 * | |
| Northants | Northampton | July 31 | 27 | |

## BENSON & HEDGES CUP

| | | | | |
|---|---|---|---|---|
| Min Counties | Trowbridge | April 23 | 7 | |
| Hampshire | Southampton | May 2 | 6 | |
| Notts | Cardiff | May 4 | 62 | 2Ct |
| Yorkshire | Cardiff | May 7 | 19 | |

## BATTING AVERAGES - Including fielding

| | Matches | Inns | NO | Runs | HS | Avge | 100s | 50s | Ct | St |
|---|---|---|---|---|---|---|---|---|---|---|
| Britannic Assurance | 20 | 32 | 5 | 1766 | 243 | 65.40 | 7 | 5 | 14 | - |
| Other First-Class | 3 | 4 | 1 | 37 | 21 | 12.33 | - | - | 4 | - |
| ALL FIRST-CLASS | 23 | 36 | 6 | 1803 | 243 | 60.10 | 7 | 5 | 18 | - |
| Refuge Assurance | 15 | 15 | 1 | 458 | 101 | 32.71 | 1 | 3 | 9 | - |
| NatWest Trophy | 3 | 3 | 2 | 256 | 151 * | 256.00 | 1 | 1 | - | - |
| Benson & Hedges Cup | 4 | 4 | 0 | 94 | 62 | 23.50 | - | 1 | 2 | - |
| ALL ONE-DAY | 22 | 22 | 3 | 808 | 151 * | 42.52 | 2 | 5 | 11 | - |

## BOWLING AVERAGES

| | Overs | Mdns | Runs | Wkts | Avge | Best | 5wI | 10wM |
|---|---|---|---|---|---|---|---|---|
| Britannic Assurance | 4.5 | 0 | 34 | 0 | - | - | - | - |
| Other First-Class | | | | | | | | |
| ALL FIRST-CLASS | 4.5 | 0 | 34 | 0 | - | - | - | - |
| Refuge Assurance | 1 | 0 | 2 | 0 | - | - | - | |
| NatWest Trophy | | | | | | | | |
| Benson & Hedges Cup | | | | | | | | |
| ALL ONE-DAY | 1 | 0 | 2 | 0 | - | - | - | |

# M.J.McCAGUE - Kent

| Opposition | Venue | Date | Batting | Fielding | Bowling |
|---|---|---|---|---|---|

## BRITANNIC ASSURANCE

| | | | | | |
|---|---|---|---|---|---|
| Middlesex | Lord's | May 31 | 11 & 21 * | | 1-21 & 1-18 |
| Warwickshire | Tunbridge W | June 4 | 18 | 1Ct | 0-23 & 1-51 |
| Sussex | Tunbridge W | June 7 | 2 & 0 * | | 0-44 & 3-38 |
| Yorkshire | Harrogate | June 14 | | | 1-55 |
| Northants | Maidstone | July 2 | 10 & 7 | | 0-26 |
| Glamorgan | Maidstone | July 5 | 28 | | 3-36 & 0-5 |
| Essex | Southend | July 16 | 16 | | 0-47 & 0-25 |
| Leicestershire | Leicester | Aug 9 | 29 | | 6-88 & 0-4 |

## REFUGE ASSURANCE

| | | | | | |
|---|---|---|---|---|---|
| Derbyshire | Canterbury | May 26 | 5 * | | 4-51 |
| Yorkshire | Scarborough | June 16 | 13 | | 1-53 |
| Lancashire | Old Trafford | June 23 | | | 0-43 |
| Gloucs | Canterbury | June 30 | | | 3-39 |
| Glamorgan | Maidstone | July 7 | | | 0-42 |
| Leicestershire | Canterbury | July 14 | 17 * | 1Ct | 2-37 |
| Somerset | Taunton | July 28 | 4 | | 0-42 |
| Notts | Trent Bridge | Aug 11 | 0 | | 1-42 |

## NATWEST TROPHY

| | | | | | |
|---|---|---|---|---|---|
| Surrey | The Oval | July 11 | 9 | | 0-47 |

## BENSON & HEDGES CUP

| | | | | | |
|---|---|---|---|---|---|
| Leicestershire | Canterbury | April 23 | | | 2-53 |
| Lancashire | Old Trafford | April 25 | 12 | | 2-32 |

## BATTING AVERAGES - Including fielding

| | Matches | Inns | NO | Runs | HS | Avge | 100s | 50s | Ct | St |
|---|---|---|---|---|---|---|---|---|---|---|
| Britannic Assurance | 8 | 10 | 2 | 142 | 29 | 17.75 | - | - | 1 | - |
| ALL FIRST-CLASS | 8 | 10 | 2 | 142 | 29 | 17.75 | - | - | 1 | - |
| Refuge Assurance | 8 | 5 | 2 | 39 | 17 * | 13.00 | - | - | 1 | - |
| NatWest Trophy | 1 | 1 | 0 | 9 | 9 | 9.00 | - | - | - | - |
| Benson & Hedges Cup | 2 | 1 | 0 | 12 | 12 | 12.00 | - | - | - | - |
| ALL ONE-DAY | 11 | 7 | 2 | 60 | 17 * | 12.00 | - | - | 1 | - |

## BOWLING AVERAGES

| | Overs | Mdns | Runs | Wkts | Avge | Best | 5wI | 10wM |
|---|---|---|---|---|---|---|---|---|
| Britannic Assurance | 153.3 | 23 | 481 | 16 | 30.06 | 6-88 | 1 | - |
| ALL FIRST-CLASS | 153.3 | 23 | 481 | 16 | 30.06 | 6-88 | 1 | - |
| Refuge Assurance | 59 | 0 | 349 | 11 | 31.72 | 4-51 | - | - |
| NatWest Trophy | 7 | 0 | 47 | 0 | - | - | - | - |
| Benson & Hedges Cup | 18 | 2 | 85 | 4 | 21.25 | 2-32 | - | - |
| ALL ONE-DAY | 84 | 2 | 481 | 15 | 32.06 | 4-51 | - | - |

# E.McCRAY - Derbyshire

| Opposition | Venue | Date | Batting | Fielding | Bowling |
|---|---|---|---|---|---|

## BRITANNIC ASSURANCE

| | | | | | |
|---|---|---|---|---|---|
| Gloucs | Gloucester | June 18 | 37 | 1Ct | 0-41 & 0-12 |

## OTHER FIRST-CLASS

| | | | | | |
|---|---|---|---|---|---|
| Sri Lanka | Derby | Aug 2 | 31 | | 0-34 |

## REFUGE ASSURANCE

| | | | | | |
|---|---|---|---|---|---|
| Northants | Derby | July 28 | 18 | | 3-38 |
| Warwickshire | Edgbaston | Aug 4 | 1 | | 1-37 |
| Glamorgan | Checkley | Aug 18 | 1 | | 4-49 |
| Notts | Trent Bridge | Aug 25 | 2 | | 0-42 |

## OTHER ONE-DAY

| | | | | | |
|---|---|---|---|---|---|
| Yorkshire | Scarborough | Sept 1 | 0 | | 0-42 |

## BATTING AVERAGES - Including fielding

| | Matches | Inns | NO | Runs | HS | Avge | 100s | 50s | Ct | St |
|---|---|---|---|---|---|---|---|---|---|---|
| Britannic Assurance | 1 | 1 | 0 | 37 | 37 | 37.00 | - | - | 1 | - |
| Other First-Class | 1 | 1 | 0 | 31 | 31 | 31.00 | - | - | - | - |
| ALL FIRST-CLASS | 2 | 2 | 0 | 68 | 37 | 34.00 | - | - | 1 | - |
| Refuge Assurance | 4 | 4 | 0 | 22 | 18 | 5.50 | - | - | - | - |
| Other One-Day | 1 | 1 | 0 | 0 | 0 | 0.00 | - | - | - | - |
| ALL ONE-DAY | 5 | 5 | 0 | 22 | 18 | 4.40 | - | - | - | - |

## BOWLING AVERAGES

| | Overs | Mdns | Runs | Wkts | Avge | Best | 5wI | 10wM |
|---|---|---|---|---|---|---|---|---|
| Britannic Assurance | 25 | 10 | 53 | 0 | - | - | - | - |
| Other First-Class | 17 | 6 | 34 | 0 | - | - | - | - |
| ALL FIRST-CLASS | 42 | 16 | 87 | 0 | - | - | - | - |
| Refuge Assurance | 32 | 0 | 166 | 8 | 20.75 | 4-49 | - | - |
| Other One-Day | 10 | 1 | 42 | 0 | - | - | - | - |

# M      PLAYER RECORDS

| ALL ONE-DAY | 42 | 1 | 208 | 8 | 26.00 | 4-49 | - |
|---|---|---|---|---|---|---|---|

## P.McCRUM - *Ireland*

| Opposition | Venue | Date | Batting | Fielding | Bowling |
|---|---|---|---|---|---|
| **NATWEST TROPHY** | | | | | |
| Middlesex | Dublin | June 26 | 16 | | 3-31 |

### BATTING AVERAGES - Including fielding

| | Matches | Inns | NO | Runs | HS | Avge | 100s | 50s | Ct | St |
|---|---|---|---|---|---|---|---|---|---|---|
| NatWest Trophy | 1 | 1 | 0 | 16 | 16 | 16.00 | - | - | - | - |
| ALL ONE-DAY | 1 | 1 | 0 | 16 | 16 | 16.00 | - | - | - | - |

### BOWLING AVERAGES

| | Overs | Mdns | Runs | Wkts | Avge | Best | 5wI | 10wM |
|---|---|---|---|---|---|---|---|---|
| NatWest Trophy | 10 | 1 | 31 | 3 | 10.33 | 3-31 | - | |
| ALL ONE-DAY | 10 | 1 | 31 | 3 | 10.33 | 3-31 | - | |

## P.D.McKEOWN - *Lincolnshire*

| Opposition | Venue | Date | Batting | Fielding | Bowling |
|---|---|---|---|---|---|
| **NATWEST TROPHY** | | | | | |
| Notts | Trent Bridge | June 26 | 1* | | 3-52 |

### BATTING AVERAGES - Including fielding

| | Matches | Inns | NO | Runs | HS | Avge | 100s | 50s | Ct | St |
|---|---|---|---|---|---|---|---|---|---|---|
| NatWest Trophy | 1 | 1 | 1 | 1 | 1* | - | - | - | - | - |
| ALL ONE-DAY | 1 | 1 | 1 | 1 | 1* | - | - | - | - | - |

### BOWLING AVERAGES

| | Overs | Mdns | Runs | Wkts | Avge | Best | 5wI | 10wM |
|---|---|---|---|---|---|---|---|---|
| NatWest Trophy | 12 | 0 | 52 | 3 | 17.33 | 3-52 | - | |
| ALL ONE-DAY | 12 | 0 | 52 | 3 | 17.33 | 3-52 | - | |

## K.W.McLEOD - *League CC XI*

| Opposition | Venue | Date | Batting | Fielding | Bowling |
|---|---|---|---|---|---|
| **OTHER ONE-DAY** | | | | | |
| West Indies | Trowbridge | June 28 | | | 0-32 |

### BATTING AVERAGES - Including fielding

| | Matches | Inns | NO | Runs | HS | Avge | 100s | 50s | Ct | St |
|---|---|---|---|---|---|---|---|---|---|---|
| Other One-Day | 1 | 0 | 0 | 0 | 0 | - | - | - | - | - |
| ALL ONE-DAY | 1 | 0 | 0 | 0 | 0 | - | - | - | - | - |

### BOWLING AVERAGES

| | Overs | Mdns | Runs | Wkts | Avge | Best | 5wI | 10wM |
|---|---|---|---|---|---|---|---|---|
| Other One-Day | 5 | 0 | 32 | 0 | - | - | - | - |
| ALL ONE-DAY | 5 | 0 | 32 | 0 | - | - | - | - |

## K.T.MEDLYCOTT - *Surrey*

| Opposition | Venue | Date | Batting | | Fielding | Bowling |
|---|---|---|---|---|---|---|
| **BRITANNIC ASSURANCE** | | | | | | |
| Kent | The Oval | May 9 | 4 & | 1 | 1Ct | 4-103 |
| Lancashire | The Oval | May 22 | 66 | | | 1-19 & 1-17 |
| Hampshire | Bournemouth | May 25 | 45 & | 0 | 1Ct | 0-28 |
| Notts | The Oval | June 4 | | | | 1-84 |
| Leicestershire | Leicester | June 14 | | 3 | | 1-11 & 2-46 |
| Derbyshire | Derby | June 21 | 18 | | | 2-102 |

## G.D.MENDIS - *Lancashire*

| Opposition | Venue | Date | Batting | | Fielding | Bowling |
|---|---|---|---|---|---|---|
| **BRITANNIC ASSURANCE** | | | | | | |
| Warwickshire | Edgbaston | April 27 | 113 | | | |
| Worcestershire | Worcester | May 9 | 9 & | 14 | | |
| Derbyshire | Old Trafford | May 16 | 7 & | 1 | | |
| Surrey | The Oval | May 22 | 15 & | 8 | 1Ct | |
| Sussex | Old Trafford | May 31 | 13 & | 39 | 1Ct | |
| Hampshire | Basingstoke | June 4 | 13 & | 39* | | |
| Leicestershire | Leicester | June 18 | 37 & | 26 | 1Ct | |
| Kent | Old Trafford | June 21 | 5 | | | |
| Glamorgan | Liverpool | June 28 | 15 & | 18* | | |
| Somerset | Taunton | July 2 | 31 & | 1 | | |
| Notts | Trent Bridge | July 16 | 29 & | 50 | | |
| Middlesex | Uxbridge | July 19 | 43 & | 2 | 1Ct | |
| Warwickshire | Old Trafford | July 23 | 119 | | 1Ct | |
| Yorkshire | Old Trafford | Aug 2 | 10 & | 59* | | |
| Northants | Lytham | Aug 6 | 4 & | 19 | | |
| Gloucs | Bristol | Aug 9 | 18 & | 44 | | |
| Derbyshire | Derby | Aug 16 | 65 & | 12 | | |
| Worcestershire | Blackpool | Aug 20 | 47 & | 47 | 1Ct | |
| Essex | Old Trafford | Aug 23 | 49 & | 30* | | |
| Notts | Old Trafford | Aug 28 | 7 & | 0 | | |
| Yorkshire | Scarborough | Sept 3 | 114 & | 6 | 1Ct | |
| Surrey | Old Trafford | Sept 17 | 19 & | 26 | | |
| **OTHER FIRST-CLASS** | | | | | | |
| Cambridge U | Fenner's | April 13 | 44 & | 127* | 1Ct | |
| **REFUGE ASSURANCE** | | | | | | |
| Notts | Old Trafford | April 21 | 34 | | | |
| Worcestershire | Worcester | May 12 | 31 | | | |

### (Right column continuation — G.D.MENDIS)

| Opposition | Venue | Date | Batting | | Fielding | Bowling |
|---|---|---|---|---|---|---|
| Somerset | The Oval | June 28 | 52 | | | 2-97 |
| Sussex | Arundel | July 2 | 20 | | | 4-56 |
| Essex | The Oval | July 5 | 20 & | 0* | | 0-89 & 0-40 |
| Gloucs | Guildford | July 16 | | 0 | 1Ct | 1-47 & 0-4 |
| Yorkshire | Guildford | July 19 | | 30* | 2Ct | 2-87 & 2-59 |
| Glamorgan | The Oval | July 26 | 5 & | 28 | | 2-105 & 2-100 |
| Kent | Canterbury | Aug 2 | 4 & | 24 | | 2-119 & 2-18 |
| Worcestershire | Worcester | Aug 16 | 4 & | 57 | | 1-95 & 2-54 |
| Middlesex | The Oval | Aug 20 | 59 & | 40 | 1Ct | 2-90 & 1-24 |
| Northants | Northampton | Aug 23 | | 4 | | 1-62 |
| Sussex | The Oval | Aug 28 | 4 | | | 0-8 & 0-0 |
| Hampshire | The Oval | Sept 3 | 0 & | 25 | | 0-5 |
| **OTHER FIRST-CLASS** | | | | | | |
| Cambridge U | Fenner's | May 18 | 2 & | 109 | | 5-36 & 6-98 |
| **REFUGE ASSURANCE** | | | | | | |
| Essex | The Oval | May 26 | | | 1Ct | |
| Northants | Tring | July 7 | 9 | | 1Ct | |
| **OTHER ONE-DAY** | | | | | | |
| Warwickshire | Harrogate | June 12 | 5 | | | 1-55 |
| Durham | Harrogate | June 13 | | | | 1-29 |

### BATTING AVERAGES - Including fielding

| | Matches | Inns | NO | Runs | HS | Avge | 100s | 50s | Ct | St |
|---|---|---|---|---|---|---|---|---|---|---|
| Britannic Assurance | 18 | 25 | 2 | 513 | 66 | 22.30 | - | 4 | 6 | - |
| Other First-Class | 1 | 2 | 0 | 111 | 109 | 55.50 | 1 | - | - | - |
| ALL FIRST-CLASS | 19 | 27 | 2 | 624 | 109 | 24.96 | 1 | 4 | 6 | - |
| Refuge Assurance | 2 | 1 | 0 | 9 | 9 | 9.00 | - | - | 2 | - |
| Other One-Day | 2 | 1 | 0 | 5 | 5 | 5.00 | - | - | - | - |
| ALL ONE-DAY | 4 | 2 | 0 | 14 | 9 | 7.00 | - | - | 2 | - |

### BOWLING AVERAGES

| | Overs | Mdns | Runs | Wkts | Avge | Best | 5wI | 10wM |
|---|---|---|---|---|---|---|---|---|
| Britannic Assurance | 458.5 | 98 | 1569 | 38 | 41.28 | 4-56 | - | - |
| Other First-Class | 51.5 | 17 | 134 | 11 | 12.18 | 6-98 | 2 | 1 |
| ALL FIRST-CLASS | 510.4 | 115 | 1703 | 49 | 34.75 | 6-98 | 2 | 1 |
| Refuge Assurance | | | | | | | | |
| Other One-Day | 17 | 1 | 84 | 2 | 42.00 | 1-29 | - | |
| ALL ONE-DAY | 17 | 1 | 84 | 2 | 42.00 | 1-29 | - | |

# PLAYER RECORDS

## M

| | | | | |
|---|---|---|---|---|
| Derbyshire | Derby | May 19 | 0 | 1Ct |
| Glamorgan | Old Trafford | June 9 | 11 | |
| Kent | Old Trafford | June 23 | 44 | |
| Somerset | Taunton | July 5 | 79 | |
| Leicestershire | Leicester | July 7 | 13 | |
| Hampshire | Southampton | July 28 | 5 | 1Ct |
| Yorkshire | Old Trafford | Aug 4 | 39 | |
| Gloucs | Bristol | Aug 11 | 23 | |
| Surrey | Old Trafford | Aug 18 | 0 | 1Ct |
| Essex | Old Trafford | Aug 25 | 24 | |
| Northants | Old Trafford | Sept 1 | 23 | |
| Worcestershire | Old Trafford | Sept 15 | 18 | |

### NATWEST TROPHY
| | | | | |
|---|---|---|---|---|
| Dorset | Bournemouth | June 26 | 5 | 1Ct |
| Hampshire | Southampton | July 11 | 50 | |

### BENSON & HEDGES CUP
| | | | | |
|---|---|---|---|---|
| Scotland | Forfar | April 23 | 63 | |
| Kent | Old Trafford | April 25 | 22 | 3Ct |
| Leicestershire | Leicester | May 4 | 36 | |
| Sussex | Old Trafford | May 7 | 31 | 1Ct |
| Northants | Old Trafford | May 29 | 125 * | |
| Yorkshire | Old Trafford | June 16 | 75 | |
| Worcestershire | Lord's | July 13 | 14 | |

### BATTING AVERAGES - Including fielding
| | Matches | Inns | NO | Runs | HS | Avge | 100s | 50s | Ct | St |
|---|---|---|---|---|---|---|---|---|---|---|
| Britannic Assurance | 22 | 41 | 4 | 1223 | 119 | 33.05 | 3 | 3 | 7 | - |
| Other First-Class | 1 | 2 | 1 | 171 | 127 * | 171.00 | 1 | - | 1 | - |
| | | | | | | | | | | |
| ALL FIRST-CLASS | 23 | 43 | 5 | 1394 | 127 * | 36.68 | 4 | 3 | 8 | - |
| | | | | | | | | | | |
| Refuge Assurance | 14 | 14 | 0 | 344 | 79 | 24.57 | - | 1 | 3 | - |
| NatWest Trophy | 2 | 2 | 0 | 55 | 50 | 27.50 | - | 1 | 1 | - |
| Benson & Hedges Cup | 7 | 7 | 1 | 366 | 125 * | 61.00 | 1 | 2 | 4 | - |
| | | | | | | | | | | |
| ALL ONE-DAY | 23 | 23 | 1 | 765 | 125 * | 34.77 | 1 | 4 | 8 | - |

### BOWLING AVERAGES
Did not bowl

---

# D.J.M.MERCER - *Berkshire*

| Opposition | Venue | Date | Batting | Fielding | Bowling |
|---|---|---|---|---|---|
| **NATWEST TROPHY** | | | | | |
| Hampshire | Reading | June 26 | 11 | | |

### BATTING AVERAGES - Including fielding
| | Matches | Inns | NO | Runs | HS | Avge | 100s | 50s | Ct | St |
|---|---|---|---|---|---|---|---|---|---|---|
| NatWest Trophy | 1 | 1 | 0 | 11 | 11 | 11.00 | - | - | - | - |
| | | | | | | | | | | |
| ALL ONE-DAY | 1 | 1 | 0 | 11 | 11 | 11.00 | - | - | - | - |

### BOWLING AVERAGES
Did not bowl

---

# T.A.MERRICK - *Kent*

| Opposition | Venue | Date | Batting | | Fielding | Bowling |
|---|---|---|---|---|---|---|
| **BRITANNIC ASSURANCE** | | | | | | |
| Hampshire | Southampton | April 27 | 9 * | | | 4-37 |
| Surrey | The Oval | May 9 | 36 | | | 2-51 & 2-59 |
| Essex | Folkestone | May 16 | 8 & | 4 * | | 2-109 |
| Notts | Trent Bridge | May 22 | 4 | | 1Ct | 1-78 & 2-67 |
| Derbyshire | Canterbury | May 25 | 13 * | | 1Ct | 4-55 & 3-60 |
| Middlesex | Lord's | May 31 | 4 | | | 3-61 & 0-38 |
| Warwickshire | Tunbridge W | June 4 | 25 * | | | 2-14 & 0-42 |
| Sussex | Tunbridge W | June 7 | 10 & | 1 | | 0-36 |
| Lancashire | Old Trafford | June 21 | | 4 | | 3-88 |
| Northants | Maidstone | July 2 | 18 | | 1Ct | 0-39 |
| Glamorgan | Maidstone | July 5 | 5 | | | 0-39 & 3-26 |
| Worcestershire | Worcester | July 23 | | | | 2-35 |
| Somerset | Taunton | July 26 | 5 & | 2 | | 2-60 & 2-73 |
| Surrey | Canterbury | Aug 2 | 4 & | 4 * | | 0-33 & 3-86 |
| Hampshire | Canterbury | Aug 6 | 0 | | | 4-67 & 1-54 |

| | | | | | |
|---|---|---|---|---|---|
| Leicestershire | Leicester | Aug 9 | 6 * | | 1-43 & 0-32 |
| Gloucs | Canterbury | Aug 20 | 12 & 18 | | 2-41 & 1-85 |
| Sussex | Hove | Sept 3 | 6 | | 2-81 & 7-99 |

### OTHER FIRST-CLASS
| | | | | | | |
|---|---|---|---|---|---|---|
| West Indies | Canterbury | July 20 | | 6 | 1Ct | 1-48 & 2-51 |

### REFUGE ASSURANCE
| | | | | | |
|---|---|---|---|---|---|
| Worcestershire | Worcester | April 21 | 1 | | 0-38 |
| Hampshire | Southampton | May 12 | 4 | | 1-56 |
| Essex | Folkestone | May 19 | | | 1-39 |
| Middlesex | Southgate | June 2 | | | 1-41 |
| Yorkshire | Scarborough | June 16 | 0 * | | 0-48 |
| Gloucs | Canterbury | June 30 | | | 1-16 |
| Glamorgan | Maidstone | July 7 | | | 0-29 |
| Leicestershire | Canterbury | July 14 | | | 1-38 |
| Somerset | Taunton | July 28 | 13 * | | 1-33 |
| Surrey | Canterbury | Aug 4 | 2 * | | 0-47 |
| Notts | Trent Bridge | Aug 11 | | | 0-36 |
| Northants | Canterbury | Aug 18 | 3 * | | 0-42 |

### NATWEST TROPHY
| | | | | | |
|---|---|---|---|---|---|
| Cambs | Canterbury | June 26 | | 1Ct | 3-27 |
| Surrey | The Oval | July 11 | 0 | 1Ct | 0-47 |

### BENSON & HEDGES CUP
| | | | | | |
|---|---|---|---|---|---|
| Leicestershire | Canterbury | April 23 | | | 2-34 |
| Lancashire | Old Trafford | April 25 | 22 * | | 1-30 |
| Sussex | Canterbury | May 2 | | | 0-53 |
| Scotland | Glasgow | May 7 | 4 * | 1Ct | 2-31 |
| Worcestershire | Worcester | May 29 | 0 | | 1-59 |

### BATTING AVERAGES - Including fielding
| | Matches | Inns | NO | Runs | HS | Avge | 100s | 50s | Ct | St |
|---|---|---|---|---|---|---|---|---|---|---|
| Britannic Assurance | 18 | 22 | 6 | 198 | 36 | 12.37 | - | - | 3 | - |
| Other First-Class | 1 | 1 | 0 | 6 | 6 | 6.00 | - | - | 1 | - |
| | | | | | | | | | | |
| ALL FIRST-CLASS | 19 | 23 | 6 | 204 | 36 | 12.00 | - | - | 4 | - |
| | | | | | | | | | | |
| Refuge Assurance | 12 | 6 | 4 | 23 | 13 * | 11.50 | - | - | - | - |
| NatWest Trophy | 2 | 1 | 0 | 0 | 0 | 0.00 | - | - | 2 | - |
| Benson & Hedges Cup | 5 | 3 | 2 | 26 | 22 * | 26.00 | - | - | 1 | - |
| | | | | | | | | | | |
| ALL ONE-DAY | 19 | 10 | 6 | 49 | 22 * | 12.25 | - | - | 3 | - |

### BOWLING AVERAGES
| | Overs | Mdns | Runs | Wkts | Avge | Best | 5wI | 10wM |
|---|---|---|---|---|---|---|---|---|
| Britannic Assurance | 517 | 100 | 1688 | 58 | 29.10 | 7-99 | 1 | - |
| Other First-Class | 22 | 1 | 99 | 3 | 33.00 | 2-51 | - | - |
| | | | | | | | | |
| ALL FIRST-CLASS | 539 | 101 | 1787 | 61 | 29.29 | 7-99 | 1 | - |
| | | | | | | | | |
| Refuge Assurance | 89.2 | 3 | 463 | 6 | 77.16 | 1-16 | - | |
| NatWest Trophy | 21 | 4 | 74 | 3 | 24.66 | 3-27 | - | |
| Benson & Hedges Cup | 50 | 2 | 207 | 6 | 34.50 | 2-31 | - | |
| | | | | | | | | |
| ALL ONE-DAY | 160.2 | 9 | 744 | 15 | 49.60 | 3-27 | - | |

---

# R.P.MERRIMAN - *Cambridgeshire*

| Opposition | Venue | Date | Batting | Fielding | Bowling |
|---|---|---|---|---|---|
| **NATWEST TROPHY** | | | | | |
| Kent | Canterbury | June 26 | 0 | | |

### BATTING AVERAGES - Including fielding
| | Matches | Inns | NO | Runs | HS | Avge | 100s | 50s | Ct | St |
|---|---|---|---|---|---|---|---|---|---|---|
| NatWest Trophy | 1 | 1 | 0 | 0 | 0 | 0.00 | - | - | - | - |
| | | | | | | | | | | |
| ALL ONE-DAY | 1 | 1 | 0 | 0 | 0 | 0.00 | - | - | - | - |

### BOWLING AVERAGES
Did not bowl

# M PLAYER RECORDS

## W.G.MERRY - Hertfordshire

| Opposition | Venue | Date | Batting | Fielding | Bowling |
|---|---|---|---|---|---|
| **NATWEST TROPHY** | | | | | |
| Warwickshire | Edgbaston | July 11 | 7* | | 0-18 |

**BATTING AVERAGES - Including fielding**

| | Matches | Inns | NO | Runs | HS | Avge | 100s | 50s | Ct | St |
|---|---|---|---|---|---|---|---|---|---|---|
| NatWest Trophy | 1 | 1 | 1 | 7 | 7* | - | - | - | - | - |
| ALL ONE-DAY | 1 | 1 | 1 | 7 | 7* | - | - | - | - | - |

**BOWLING AVERAGES**

| | Overs | Mdns | Runs | Wkts | Avge | Best | 5wI | 10wM |
|---|---|---|---|---|---|---|---|---|
| NatWest Trophy | 5 | 1 | 18 | 0 | | | | |
| ALL ONE-DAY | 5 | 1 | 18 | 0 | - | - | - | - |

## A.A.METCALFE - Yorkshire

| Opposition | Venue | Date | Batting | | | Fielding | Bowling |
|---|---|---|---|---|---|---|---|
| **BRITANNIC ASSURANCE** | | | | | | | |
| Middlesex | Lord's | April 27 | 18 | | | | |
| Warwickshire | Headingley | May 9 | 52 | & | 1 | 1Ct | |
| Notts | Headingley | May 16 | 22 | & | 28 | | |
| Gloucs | Sheffield | May 22 | 15 | & | 47 | | |
| Northants | Headingley | May 25 | 27 | & | 53 | 2Ct | |
| Warwickshire | Edgbaston | May 31 | 44 | & | 26 | 1Ct | |
| Kent | Harrogate | June 14 | 10 | | | | |
| Middlesex | Sheffield | June 21 | 61 | & | 3 | | |
| Worcestershire | Headingley | July 2 | 13 | | | | |
| Hampshire | Southampton | July 5 | 6 | | | | |
| Derbyshire | Scarborough | July 16 | 8 | | | 2Ct | |
| Surrey | Guildford | July 19 | 6 | & | 2 | | |
| Notts | Worksop | July 23 | 29 | & | 20* | 2Ct | |
| Lancashire | Old Trafford | Aug 2 | 30 | & | 113* | | |
| Leicestershire | Leicester | Aug 6 | 0 | & | 2 | | 0-23 |
| Sussex | Midd'brough | Aug 9 | 1 | & | 36 | | |
| Glamorgan | Headingley | Aug 16 | 123 | & | 26 | | |
| Essex | Colchester | Aug 20 | 22 | & | 4 | 2Ct | |
| Somerset | Taunton | Aug 23 | 6 | & | 62 | 1Ct | |
| Northants | Northampton | Aug 28 | 66 | & | 42 | | |
| Lancashire | Scarborough | Sept 3 | 2 | & | 2 | 1Ct | |
| Derbyshire | Chesterfield | Sept 17 | 28 | & | 4 | | |
| **OTHER FIRST-CLASS** | | | | | | | |
| Oxford U | The Parks | June 4 | 27 | & | 62 | | |
| Sri Lanka | Headingley | July 27 | 26 | & | 35 | | |
| **REFUGE ASSURANCE** | | | | | | | |
| Hampshire | Southampton | April 21 | 7 | | | | |
| Essex | Chelmsford | April 28 | 3 | | | | |
| Warwickshire | Headingley | May 12 | 27 | | | | |
| Leicestershire | Leicester | May 19 | 5 | | | | |
| Northants | Headingley | May 26 | 33 | | | | |
| Derbyshire | Chesterfield | June 2 | 0 | | | | |
| Kent | Scarborough | June 16 | 20 | | | | |
| Worcestershire | Sheffield | June 23 | 0 | | | | |
| Glamorgan | Headingley | June 30 | 96 | | | | |
| Middlesex | Lord's | July 7 | 116 | | | 1Ct | |
| Gloucs | Scarborough | July 14 | 11 | | | | |
| Surrey | The Oval | July 21 | 31 | | | | |
| Lancashire | Old Trafford | Aug 4 | 41 | | | 1Ct | |
| Sussex | Midd'brough | Aug 11 | 68 | | | 1Ct | |
| Notts | Scarborough | Aug 18 | 33 | | | | |
| Somerset | Taunton | Aug 25 | 49 | | | | |
| **NATWEST TROPHY** | | | | | | | |
| Warwickshire | Edgbaston | June 26 | 8 | | | | |
| **BENSON & HEDGES CUP** | | | | | | | |
| Notts | Trent Bridge | April 25 | 20 | | | 1Ct | |
| Min Counties | Headingley | May 2 | 92* | | | | |
| Hampshire | Headingley | May 4 | 37 | | | | |
| Glamorgan | Cardiff | May 7 | 84 | | | | |
| Warwickshire | Headingley | May 29 | 3 | | | | |
| Lancashire | Old Trafford | June 16 | 114 | | | | |

| Opposition | Venue | Date | Batting | Fielding | Bowling |
|---|---|---|---|---|---|
| **OTHER ONE-DAY** | | | | | |
| Derbyshire | Scarborough | Sept 1 | 61 | 1Ct | |
| Essex | Scarborough | Sept 2 | 21 | | |
| Yorkshiremen | Scarborough | Sept 7 | 67 | 1Ct | |
| World XI | Scarborough | Sept 8 | 42 | | |

**BATTING AVERAGES - Including fielding**

| | Matches | Inns | NO | Runs | HS | Avge | 100s | 50s | Ct | St |
|---|---|---|---|---|---|---|---|---|---|---|
| Britannic Assurance | 22 | 39 | 2 | 1060 | 123 | 28.64 | 2 | 5 | 12 | - |
| Other First-Class | 2 | 4 | 0 | 150 | 62 | 37.50 | - | 1 | - | - |
| ALL FIRST-CLASS | 24 | 43 | 2 | 1210 | 123 | 29.51 | 2 | 6 | 12 | - |
| Refuge Assurance | 16 | 16 | 0 | 540 | 116 | 33.75 | 1 | 2 | 3 | - |
| NatWest Trophy | 1 | 1 | 0 | 8 | 8 | 8.00 | - | - | - | - |
| Benson & Hedges Cup | 6 | 6 | 1 | 350 | 114 | 70.00 | 1 | 2 | 1 | - |
| Other One-Day | 4 | 4 | 0 | 191 | 67 | 47.75 | - | 2 | 2 | - |
| ALL ONE-DAY | 27 | 27 | 1 | 1089 | 116 | 41.88 | 2 | 6 | 6 | - |

**BOWLING AVERAGES**

| | Overs | Mdns | Runs | Wkts | Avge | Best | 5wI | 10wM |
|---|---|---|---|---|---|---|---|---|
| Britannic Assurance | 3 | 0 | 23 | 0 | | | | |
| Other First-Class | | | | | | | | |
| ALL FIRST-CLASS | 3 | 0 | 23 | 0 | - | - | - | - |
| Refuge Assurance | | | | | | | | |
| NatWest Trophy | | | | | | | | |
| Benson & Hedges Cup | | | | | | | | |
| Other One-Day | | | | | | | | |
| ALL ONE-DAY | | | | | | | | |

## C.P.METSON - Glamorgan

| Opposition | Venue | Date | Batting | | | Fielding | Bowling |
|---|---|---|---|---|---|---|---|
| **BRITANNIC ASSURANCE** | | | | | | | |
| Leicestershire | Leicester | April 27 | 0 | | | | |
| Somerset | Taunton | May 9 | 24 | | | 8Ct | |
| Warwickshire | Swansea | May 16 | 28 | & | 57 | 3Ct,1St | |
| Northants | Cardiff | May 22 | 24 | | | 6Ct | |
| Sussex | Cardiff | May 25 | | | | 3Ct | |
| Worcestershire | Worcester | May 31 | 8 | | | 1Ct | |
| Somerset | Swansea | June 4 | 21* | & | 0 | 1Ct | |
| Derbyshire | Chesterfield | June 7 | 34 | & | 7 | 7Ct | |
| Middlesex | Cardiff | June 14 | 49 | | | 4Ct | |
| Leicestershire | Neath | June 21 | 14 | | | | |
| Lancashire | Liverpool | June 28 | | | | 3Ct | |
| Notts | Cardiff | July 2 | 4 | | | 1Ct | |
| Kent | Maidstone | July 5 | 84 | | | 3Ct | |
| Gloucs | Cheltenham | July 19 | 5 | & | 16 | 7Ct | |
| Essex | Cardiff | July 23 | | | 19* | | |
| Surrey | The Oval | July 26 | 5 | | | 1Ct | |
| Hampshire | Swansea | Aug 9 | | | 10 | 2Ct | |
| Yorkshire | Headingley | Aug 16 | | | | 2Ct | |
| Warwickshire | Edgbaston | Aug 20 | 47 | | | 3Ct | |
| Gloucs | Abergavenny | Aug 28 | 26* | | | 5Ct,1St | |
| Worcestershire | Cardiff | Sept 10 | 0 | & | 10 | 5Ct | |
| Hampshire | Southampton | Sept 17 | 19 | | | 2Ct | |
| **OTHER FIRST-CLASS** | | | | | | | |
| Oxford U | The Parks | April 17 | | | | 6Ct | |
| West Indies | Swansea | July 16 | 27 | & | 5 | 0Ct,1St | |
| **REFUGE ASSURANCE** | | | | | | | |
| Northants | Cardiff | April 21 | | | | 1Ct | |
| Leicestershire | Leicester | April 28 | 1* | | | 1Ct | |
| Somerset | Taunton | May 12 | 4 | | | 2Ct | |
| Warwickshire | Swansea | May 19 | 12* | | | 2Ct | |
| Sussex | Swansea | May 26 | 2 | | | | |
| Essex | Pontypridd | June 2 | 6* | | | | |
| Lancashire | Old Trafford | June 9 | | | | | |
| Middlesex | Cardiff | June 16 | 7 | | | | |
| Yorkshire | Headingley | June 30 | | | | | |
| Kent | Maidstone | July 7 | | | | | |
| Worcestershire | Worcester | July 21 | | | | | |
| Surrey | The Oval | July 28 | 18* | | | 2Ct | |
| Gloucs | Swansea | Aug 4 | 7 | | | 1Ct | |
| Hampshire | Ebbw Vale | Aug 11 | 20 | | | 1Ct,1St | |
| Derbyshire | Checkley | Aug 18 | 20 | | | 2Ct,1St | |

# PLAYER RECORDS



**NATWEST TROPHY**

| | | | | | |
|---|---|---|---|---|---|
| Durham | Darlington | June 26 | | | |
| Worcestershire | Worcester | July 11 | | 1Ct | |
| Northants | Northampton | July 31 | 9 | 2Ct | |

**BENSON & HEDGES CUP**

| | | | | | |
|---|---|---|---|---|---|
| Min Counties | Trowbridge | April 23 | 0 | | |

**BATTING AVERAGES - Including fielding**

| | Matches | Inns | NO | Runs | HS | Avge | 100s | 50s | Ct | St |
|---|---|---|---|---|---|---|---|---|---|---|
| Britannic Assurance | 22 | 24 | 3 | 511 | 84 | 24.33 | - | 2 | 67 | 2 |
| Other First-Class | 2 | 2 | 0 | 32 | 27 | 16.00 | - | - | 6 | 1 |
| ALL FIRST-CLASS | 24 | 26 | 3 | 543 | 84 | 23.60 | - | 2 | 73 | 3 |
| Refuge Assurance | 15 | 10 | 4 | 97 | 20 | 16.16 | - | - | 12 | 2 |
| NatWest Trophy | 3 | 1 | 0 | 9 | 9 | 9.00 | - | - | 3 | - |
| Benson & Hedges Cup | 1 | 1 | 0 | 0 | 0 | 0.00 | - | - | - | - |
| ALL ONE-DAY | 19 | 12 | 4 | 106 | 20 | 13.25 | - | - | 15 | 2 |

**BOWLING AVERAGES**

Did not bowl

## T.C.MIDDLETON - *Hampshire*

| Opposition | Venue | Date | Batting | Fielding | Bowling |
|---|---|---|---|---|---|
| **BRITANNIC ASSURANCE** | | | | | |
| Kent | Southampton | April 27 | 15 | 1Ct | |
| Notts | Trent Bridge | May 31 | 26 & 63 | | |
| Lancashire | Basingstoke | June 4 | 25 * & 16 | | |
| Gloucs | Southampton | June 7 | 27 | | |
| Somerset | Bath | June 18 | 35 & 102 | 1Ct | |
| Northants | Northampton | June 21 | 25 | | |
| Essex | Chelmsford | July 2 | 31 & 3 | 1Ct | |
| Derbyshire | Chesterfield | July 23 | 3 & 11 | 2Ct | |
| Middlesex | Lord's | Aug 2 | 23 & 32 | 2Ct | 1-36 |
| Kent | Canterbury | Aug 6 | 66 & 26 | 1Ct | 2-41 |
| Glamorgan | Swansea | Aug 9 | 20 | 1Ct | |
| Leicestershire | Bournemouth | Aug 16 | 22 & 20 | 2Ct | |
| Sussex | Bournemouth | Aug 20 | 6 & 36 | 1Ct | |
| Somerset | Southampton | Aug 28 | 24 & 49 | 1Ct | |
| Surrey | The Oval | Sept 3 | 6 & 3 | 1Ct | |
| Glamorgan | Southampton | Sept 17 | 8 & 43 | | |
| **OTHER FIRST-CLASS** | | | | | |
| Oxford U | The Parks | April 13 | 2 | 1Ct | |
| West Indies | Southampton | June 29 | 20 & 76 * | | |
| **REFUGE ASSURANCE** | | | | | |
| Yorkshire | Southampton | April 21 | 22 | | |
| Gloucs | Swindon | May 26 | 36 | | |
| Northants | Northampton | June 2 | 56 | | |
| Sussex | Basingstoke | June 9 | 8 | | |
| Glamorgan | Ebbw Vale | Aug 11 | 32 | | |
| Leicestershire | Bournemouth | Aug 18 | 8 | | |
| **NATWEST TROPHY** | | | | | |
| Surrey | Lord's | Sept 7 | 78 | | |
| **BENSON & HEDGES CUP** | | | | | |
| Notts | Southampton | April 23 | 60 | 1Ct | |
| Min Counties | Trowbridge | April 25 | 40 | | |
| Glamorgan | Southampton | May 2 | 54 | 2Ct | |
| Yorkshire | Headingley | May 4 | 2 | | |

**BATTING AVERAGES - Including fielding**

| | Matches | Inns | NO | Runs | HS | Avge | 100s | 50s | Ct | St |
|---|---|---|---|---|---|---|---|---|---|---|
| Britannic Assurance | 16 | 28 | 1 | 766 | 102 | 28.37 | 1 | 2 | 14 | - |
| Other First-Class | 2 | 3 | 1 | 98 | 76 * | 49.00 | - | 1 | 1 | - |
| ALL FIRST-CLASS | 18 | 31 | 2 | 864 | 102 | 29.79 | 1 | 3 | 15 | - |
| Refuge Assurance | 6 | 6 | 0 | 162 | 56 | 27.00 | - | 1 | - | - |
| NatWest Trophy | 1 | 1 | 0 | 78 | 78 | 78.00 | - | 1 | - | - |
| Benson & Hedges Cup | 4 | 4 | 0 | 156 | 60 | 39.00 | - | 2 | 3 | - |
| ALL ONE-DAY | 11 | 11 | 0 | 396 | 78 | 36.00 | - | 4 | 3 | - |

**BOWLING AVERAGES**

| | Overs | Mdns | Runs | Wkts | Avge | Best | 5wI | 10wM |
|---|---|---|---|---|---|---|---|---|
| Britannic Assurance | 12 | 2 | 77 | 3 | 25.66 | 2-41 | - | - |
| Other First-Class | | | | | | | | |
| ALL FIRST-CLASS | 12 | 2 | 77 | 3 | 25.66 | 2-41 | - | - |
| Refuge Assurance | | | | | | | | |
| NatWest Trophy | | | | | | | | |
| Benson & Hedges Cup | | | | | | | | |
| ALL ONE-DAY | | | | | | | | |

## E.T.MILBURN - *Gloucestershire*

| Opposition | Venue | Date | Batting | Fielding | Bowling |
|---|---|---|---|---|---|
| **OTHER FIRST-CLASS** | | | | | |
| Oxford U | The Parks | June 15 | | | 0-29 |
| **REFUGE ASSURANCE** | | | | | |
| Essex | Cheltenham | July 28 | 21 | | |
| Glamorgan | Swansea | Aug 4 | 13 | 1Ct | |
| Lancashire | Bristol | Aug 11 | 0 | | |

**BATTING AVERAGES - Including fielding**

| | Matches | Inns | NO | Runs | HS | Avge | 100s | 50s | Ct | St |
|---|---|---|---|---|---|---|---|---|---|---|
| Other First-Class | 1 | 0 | 0 | 0 | 0 | - | - | - | - | - |
| ALL FIRST-CLASS | 1 | 0 | 0 | 0 | 0 | - | - | - | - | - |
| Refuge Assurance | 3 | 3 | 0 | 34 | 21 | 11.33 | - | - | 1 | - |
| ALL ONE-DAY | 3 | 3 | 0 | 34 | 21 | 11.33 | - | - | 1 | - |

**BOWLING AVERAGES**

| | Overs | Mdns | Runs | Wkts | Avge | Best | 5wI | 10wM |
|---|---|---|---|---|---|---|---|---|
| Other First-Class | 7 | 1 | 29 | 0 | - | - | - | - |
| ALL FIRST-CLASS | 7 | 1 | 29 | 0 | - | - | - | - |
| Refuge Assurance | | | | | | | | |
| ALL ONE-DAY | | | | | | | | |

## D.J.MILLNS - *Leicestershire*

| Opposition | Venue | Date | Batting | Fielding | Bowling |
|---|---|---|---|---|---|
| **BRITANNIC ASSURANCE** | | | | | |
| Glamorgan | Leicester | April 27 | | | 3-41 & 0-15 |
| Notts | Trent Bridge | May 9 | 26 * & 0 * | 1Ct | 1-86 & 1-23 |
| Northants | Northampton | May 16 | 14 | 1Ct | 0-45 & 2-45 |
| Notts | Leicester | May 25 | 2 * & 0 | | 0-69 & 3-70 |
| Essex | Ilford | June 4 | 23 * | 1Ct | 2-73 & 1-49 |
| Middlesex | Uxbridge | June 7 | 44 & 10 | 1Ct | 2-95 & 0-18 |
| Surrey | Leicester | June 14 | 3 | | 1-25 & 2-43 |
| Lancashire | Leicester | June 18 | 3 | | 2-99 & 3-45 |
| Glamorgan | Neath | June 21 | | | 0-14 |
| Northants | Leicester | July 5 | 0 & 31 * | | 3-70 |
| Warwickshire | Leicester | July 26 | 6 & 24 * | | 3-106 |
| Somerset | Weston | Aug 2 | 23 | 1Ct | 2-43 & 0-4 |
| Yorkshire | Leicester | Aug 6 | | | 1-33 & 6-59 |
| Kent | Leicester | Aug 9 | 11 & 6 * | 2Ct | 2-27 & 0-61 |
| Hampshire | Bournemouth | Aug 16 | | | 2-48 & 2-65 |
| Derbyshire | Derby | Aug 20 | 17 | | 9-37 & 3-54 |
| Derbyshire | Leicester | Aug 28 | 12 & 0 | 1Ct | 1-63 & 0-68 |
| Essex | Leicester | Sept 10 | 28 & 0 | | 0-96 |
| Kent | Canterbury | Sept 17 | 20 * & 3 | 1Ct | 5-65 & 0-61 |
| **OTHER FIRST-CLASS** | | | | | |
| West Indies | Leicester | June 1 | | | 1-64 & 0-78 |
| **REFUGE ASSURANCE** | | | | | |
| Northants | Northampton | May 12 | | 1Ct | 1-36 |
| Yorkshire | Leicester | May 19 | | | 1-38 |
| Notts | Leicester | May 26 | 20 * | 1Ct | 1-30 |
| Middlesex | Uxbridge | June 9 | 5 | 1Ct | 1-27 |

## M PLAYER RECORDS

| | | | | | |
|---|---|---|---|---|---|
| Surrey | Leicester | June 16 | 7 | | 0-18 |
| Worcestershire | Worcester | June 30 | | | 0-28 |
| Lancashire | Leicester | July 7 | | 1Ct | 0-21 |
| Kent | Canterbury | July 14 | 13 | | 0-41 |
| Sussex | Hove | July 21 | 10* | | 0-24 |
| Warwickshire | Leicester | Aug 11 | | | 2-20 |
| Hampshire | Bournemouth | Aug 18 | | | 2-33 |
| Gloucs | Leicester | Aug 25 | 4 | | 0-36 |

**NATWEST TROPHY**

| | | | | |
|---|---|---|---|---|
| Shropshire | Leicester | June 26 | | 2-27 |
| Northants | Northampton | July 11 | | 0-60 |

**BENSON & HEDGES CUP**

| | | | | | |
|---|---|---|---|---|---|
| Sussex | Hove | April 25 | 11* | | 0-39 |
| Scotland | Leicester | May 2 | | 1Ct | 1-25 |
| Lancashire | Leicester | May 4 | | | 0-37 |

**OTHER ONE-DAY**

| | | | | |
|---|---|---|---|---|
| Durham | Harrogate | June 11 | | 0-32 |

**BATTING AVERAGES - Including fielding**

| | Matches | Inns | NO | Runs | HS | Avge | 100s | 50s | Ct | St |
|---|---|---|---|---|---|---|---|---|---|---|
| Britannic Assurance | 19 | 24 | 8 | 306 | 44 | 19.12 | - | - | 9 | - |
| Other First-Class | 1 | 0 | 0 | 0 | 0 | - | - | - | - | - |
| ALL FIRST-CLASS | 20 | 24 | 8 | 306 | 44 | 19.12 | - | - | 9 | - |
| Refuge Assurance | 12 | 6 | 2 | 59 | 20* | 14.75 | - | - | 4 | - |
| NatWest Trophy | 2 | 0 | 0 | 0 | 0 | - | - | - | - | - |
| Benson & Hedges Cup | 3 | 1 | 1 | 11 | 11* | - | - | - | 1 | - |
| Other One-Day | 1 | 0 | 0 | 0 | 0 | - | - | - | - | - |
| ALL ONE-DAY | 18 | 7 | 3 | 70 | 20* | 17.50 | - | - | 5 | - |

**BOWLING AVERAGES**

| | Overs | Mdns | Runs | Wkts | Avge | Best | 5wI | 10wM |
|---|---|---|---|---|---|---|---|---|
| Britannic Assurance | 522.4 | 93 | 1815 | 62 | 29.27 | 9-37 | 3 | 1 |
| Other First-Class | 27.3 | 2 | 142 | 1 | 142.00 | 1-64 | - | - |
| ALL FIRST-CLASS | 550.1 | 95 | 1957 | 63 | 31.06 | 9-37 | 3 | 1 |
| Refuge Assurance | 77 | 2 | 352 | 8 | 44.00 | 2-20 | - | |
| NatWest Trophy | 21 | 4 | 87 | 2 | 43.50 | 2-27 | - | |
| Benson & Hedges Cup | 23 | 3 | 101 | 1 | 101.00 | 1-25 | - | |
| Other One-Day | 5 | 0 | 32 | 0 | | | | |
| ALL ONE-DAY | 126 | 9 | 572 | 11 | 52.00 | 2-20 | - | |

## R.A.MILNE - Cambridgeshire

| Opposition | Venue | Date | Batting | Fielding | Bowling |
|---|---|---|---|---|---|
| **NATWEST TROPHY** | | | | | |
| Kent | Canterbury | June 26 | 0 | | |

**BATTING AVERAGES - Including fielding**

| | Matches | Inns | NO | Runs | HS | Avge | 100s | 50s | Ct | St |
|---|---|---|---|---|---|---|---|---|---|---|
| NatWest Trophy | 1 | 1 | 0 | 0 | 0 | 0.00 | - | - | - | - |
| ALL ONE-DAY | 1 | 1 | 0 | 0 | 0 | 0.00 | - | - | - | - |

**BOWLING AVERAGES**
Did not bowl

## J.D.MOIR - Scotland

| Opposition | Venue | Date | Batting | Fielding | Bowling |
|---|---|---|---|---|---|
| **NATWEST TROPHY** | | | | | |
| Sussex | Edinburgh | June 26 | 11* | | 1-47 |
| **BENSON & HEDGES CUP** | | | | | |
| Lancashire | Forfar | April 23 | | | 0-26 |
| Leicestershire | Leicester | May 2 | 6* | | 0-16 |
| Sussex | Hove | May 4 | | | 2-47 |
| Kent | Glasgow | May 7 | 2* | | 0-57 |

**BATTING AVERAGES - Including fielding**

| | Matches | Inns | NO | Runs | HS | Avge | 100s | 50s | Ct | St |
|---|---|---|---|---|---|---|---|---|---|---|
| NatWest Trophy | 1 | 1 | 1 | 11 | 11* | - | - | - | - | - |
| Benson & Hedges Cup | 4 | 2 | 2 | 8 | 6* | - | - | - | - | - |
| ALL ONE-DAY | 5 | 3 | 3 | 19 | 11* | - | - | - | - | - |

**BOWLING AVERAGES**

| | Overs | Mdns | Runs | Wkts | Avge | Best | 5wI | 10wM |
|---|---|---|---|---|---|---|---|---|
| NatWest Trophy | 11 | 1 | 47 | 1 | 47.00 | 1-47 | - | |
| Benson & Hedges Cup | 40 | 11 | 146 | 2 | 73.00 | 2-47 | - | |
| ALL ONE-DAY | 51 | 12 | 193 | 3 | 64.33 | 2-47 | - | |

## A.J.MOLES - Warwickshire

| Opposition | Venue | Date | Batting | | | Fielding | Bowling |
|---|---|---|---|---|---|---|---|
| **BRITANNIC ASSURANCE** | | | | | | | |
| Lancashire | Edgbaston | April 27 | 51 | | | 1Ct | 1-14 |
| Yorkshire | Headingley | May 9 | 0 | & | 73 | 1Ct | |
| Glamorgan | Swansea | May 16 | 55 | & | 45 | | |
| Essex | Chelmsford | May 22 | 23 | & | 6 | | |
| Gloucs | Edgbaston | May 25 | 133 | & | 2* | | |
| Yorkshire | Edgbaston | May 31 | 17 | & | 73 | 2Ct | |
| Kent | Tunbridge W | June 4 | 3 | & | 48 | | 0-6 |
| Somerset | Edgbaston | June 7 | 16 | & | 16 | | 0-10 |
| Sussex | Coventry | June 18 | 28 | | | | |
| Notts | Trent Bridge | June 21 | 57 | | | | 0-5 |
| Derbyshire | Edgbaston | June 28 | 40 | & | 1 | | |
| Middlesex | Edgbaston | July 2 | 38 | & | 27 | 1Ct | |
| Hampshire | Portsmouth | July 19 | 1 | & | 15 | 1Ct | |
| Lancashire | Old Trafford | July 23 | 9 | | | | |
| Leicestershire | Leicester | July 26 | 5 | | | 1Ct | |
| Worcestershire | Worcester | Aug 2 | 9 | & | 21 | | |
| Surrey | Edgbaston | Aug 6 | 59 | & | 37 | | |
| Northants | Northampton | Aug 9 | 71 | & | 57* | 1Ct | 0-30 |
| Glamorgan | Edgbaston | Aug 20 | 65 | & | 10 | 1Ct | |
| Worcestershire | Edgbaston | Aug 28 | 26 | & | 56 | | |
| Northants | Edgbaston | Sept 10 | 18 | & | 8 | 1Ct | |
| Somerset | Taunton | Sept 17 | 26 | & | 1 | | |
| **REFUGE ASSURANCE** | | | | | | | |
| Notts | Trent Bridge | April 28 | 0 | | | | 0-24 |
| Yorkshire | Headingley | May 12 | 67 | | | | |
| Glamorgan | Swansea | May 19 | 93* | | | | |
| Worcestershire | Edgbaston | May 26 | 39 | | | | |
| Somerset | Edgbaston | June 2 | | | | | |
| Lancashire | Edgbaston | June 16 | 7 | | | | |
| Essex | Chelmsford | July 7 | 53 | | | 1Ct | |
| Middlesex | Edgbaston | July 14 | 38 | | | | |
| Hampshire | Portsmouth | July 21 | 13 | | | 1Ct | |
| Derbyshire | Edgbaston | Aug 4 | 44 | | | 1Ct | |
| Leicestershire | Leicester | Aug 11 | 1 | | | 1Ct | |
| Gloucs | Edgbaston | Aug 18 | 26 | | | | |
| Northants | Northampton | Aug 25 | 4 | | | 2Ct | |
| **NATWEST TROPHY** | | | | | | | |
| Yorkshire | Edgbaston | June 26 | 30 | | | | |
| Hertfordshire | Edgbaston | July 11 | 62* | | | | |
| Somerset | Edgbaston | July 31 | 13 | | | 1Ct | |
| Hampshire | Edgbaston | Aug 14 | 4 | | | | |
| **BENSON & HEDGES CUP** | | | | | | | |
| Essex | Edgbaston | April 25 | 19 | | | 1Ct | 1-19 |
| Somerset | Edgbaston | May 2 | 65 | | | | |
| Middlesex | Lord's | May 4 | 51 | | | | |
| Surrey | The Oval | May 7 | 21 | | | 3Ct | |
| Yorkshire | Headingley | May 29 | 10 | | | | |

**BATTING AVERAGES - Including fielding**

| | Matches | Inns | NO | Runs | HS | Avge | 100s | 50s | Ct | St |
|---|---|---|---|---|---|---|---|---|---|---|
| Britannic Assurance | 22 | 39 | 2 | 1246 | 133 | 33.67 | 1 | 10 | 10 | - |
| ALL FIRST-CLASS | 22 | 39 | 2 | 1246 | 133 | 33.67 | 1 | 10 | 10 | - |
| Refuge Assurance | 13 | 12 | 1 | 385 | 93* | 35.00 | - | 3 | 6 | - |
| NatWest Trophy | 4 | 4 | 1 | 109 | 62* | 36.33 | - | 1 | 1 | - |
| Benson & Hedges Cup | 5 | 5 | 0 | 166 | 65 | 33.20 | - | 2 | 4 | - |
| ALL ONE-DAY | 22 | 21 | 2 | 660 | 93* | 34.73 | - | 6 | 11 | - |

# PLER RECORDS

**M**

## BOWLING AVERAGES

| | Overs | Mdns | Runs | Wkts | Avge | Best | 5wI | 10wM |
|---|---|---|---|---|---|---|---|---|
| Britannic Assurance | 33 | 13 | 65 | 1 | 65.00 | 1-14 | - | - |
| ALL FIRST-CLASS | 33 | 13 | 65 | 1 | 65.00 | 1-14 | - | - |
| Refuge Assurance | 4 | 0 | 24 | 0 | - | - | - | |
| NatWest Trophy | | | | | | | | |
| Benson & Hedges Cup | 4 | 1 | 19 | 1 | 19.00 | 1-19 | - | |
| ALL ONE-DAY | 8 | 1 | 43 | 1 | 43.00 | 1-19 | - | |

## R.R.MONTGOMERIE - *Northamptonshire & Oxford University*

| Opposition | Venue | Date | Batting | Fielding | Bowling |
|---|---|---|---|---|---|
| **BRITANNIC ASSURANCE** | | | | | |
| Surrey | Northampton | Aug 23 | 2 & 7 | 2Ct | |
| **OTHER FIRST-CLASS** | | | | | |
| For Oxford U | | | | | |
| Hampshire | The Parks | April 13 | 10 & 88 | 1Ct | |
| Glamorgan | The Parks | April 17 | 0 | | |
| Notts | The Parks | April 27 | | 1Ct | |
| Gloucs | The Parks | June 15 | 8 | 1Ct | |
| Worcestershire | The Parks | May 25 | 0 & 10 | 1Ct | |
| Yorkshire | The Parks | June 4 | 54 | 1Ct | |
| Lancashire | The Parks | June 7 | 24 & 3 | 1Ct | |
| Cambridge U | Lord's | July 2 | 50 *& 53 * | 1Ct | |

### BATTING AVERAGES - Including fielding

| | Matches | Inns | NO | Runs | HS | Avge | 100s | 50s | Ct | St |
|---|---|---|---|---|---|---|---|---|---|---|
| Britannic Assurance | 1 | 2 | 0 | 9 | 7 | 4.50 | - | - | 2 | - |
| Other First-Class | 8 | 11 | 2 | 300 | 88 | 33.33 | - | 4 | 7 | - |
| ALL FIRST-CLASS | 9 | 13 | 2 | 309 | 88 | 28.09 | - | 4 | 9 | - |

### BOWLING AVERAGES
Did not bowl

## T.M.MOODY - *Worcestershire*

| Opposition | Venue | Date | Batting | Fielding | Bowling |
|---|---|---|---|---|---|
| **BRITANNIC ASSURANCE** | | | | | |
| Gloucs | Worcester | April 27 | 82 * | 1Ct | |
| Lancashire | Worcester | May 9 | 0 & 135 | 2Ct | |
| Glamorgan | Worcester | May 31 | 0 & 118 | 3Ct | |
| Northants | Northampton | June 4 | 71 & 14 * | 1Ct | |
| Essex | Ilford | June 7 | 10 & 181 * | 3Ct | |
| Sussex | Hove | June 14 | 73 | | 0-4 |
| Notts | Worcester | June 18 | 107 & 96 | 3Ct | 0-4 |
| Leicestershire | Worcester | June 28 | 25 & 13 | | 0-7 |
| Yorkshire | Headingley | July 2 | 6 | | |
| Hampshire | Portsmouth | July 16 | 10 & 25 | 1Ct | |
| Derbyshire | Kidd'minster | July 19 | 51 & 29 | | |
| Kent | Worcester | July 23 | 30 * | | |
| Gloucs | Cheltenham | July 26 | 31 & 80 | 6Ct | |
| Warwickshire | Worcester | Aug 2 | 210 | 1Ct | |
| Somerset | Weston | Aug 6 | 77 & 12 | 1Ct | 0-6 |
| Surrey | Worcester | Aug 16 | 37 & 17 | 1Ct | |
| Lancashire | Blackpool | Aug 20 | 1 | 3Ct | |
| Middlesex | Worcester | Aug 23 | 135 | 3Ct | 0-4 |
| Warwickshire | Edgbaston | Aug 28 | 91 & 3 | | |
| **OTHER FIRST-CLASS** | | | | | |
| West Indies | Worcester | May 15 | 11 | 1Ct | |
| Oxford U | The Parks | May 25 | 20 | 3Ct | 1-19 |
| Sri Lanka | Worcester | July 30 | 86 | 3Ct | 0-3 |
| **REFUGE ASSURANCE** | | | | | |
| Kent | Worcester | April 21 | 160 | | 1-38 |
| Gloucs | Bristol | May 5 | 128 * | | |
| Lancashire | Worcester | May 12 | 50 | | |
| Northants | Northampton | May 19 | 100 | 1Ct | |
| Warwickshire | Edgbaston | May 26 | 45 | | |

| Opposition | Venue | Date | Batting | Fielding | Bowling |
|---|---|---|---|---|---|
| Surrey | Worcester | June 2 | 62 | | |
| Essex | Ilford | June 9 | 0 | | |
| Sussex | Hove | June 16 | | | |
| Yorkshire | Sheffield | June 23 | 19 | | |
| Leicestershire | Worcester | June 30 | 9 | | |
| Hampshire | Southampton | July 7 | 66 | | |
| Derbyshire | Worcester | July 9 | 1 | | |
| Glamorgan | Worcester | July 21 | 58 | | |
| Notts | Trent Bridge | Aug 4 | 0 | | |
| Somerset | Worcester | Aug 18 | 91 | | |
| Middlesex | Worcester | Aug 25 | 128 * | 1Ct | |
| Notts | Trent Bridge | Sept 1 | 9 | 1Ct | |
| **NATWEST TROPHY** | | | | | |
| Bedfordshire | Bedford | June 26 | 42 * | 1Ct | |
| Glamorgan | Worcester | July 11 | 37 | | |
| **BENSON & HEDGES CUP** | | | | | |
| Gloucs | Worcester | April 25 | 21 | 1Ct | 2-22 |
| Combined U | Fenner's | May 2 | 50 | | |
| Derbyshire | Worcester | May 4 | 110 * | | |
| Northants | Northampton | May 7 | 17 | 1Ct | |
| Kent | Worcester | May 29 | 100 | | |
| Essex | Chelmsford | June 12 | 72 * | | |
| Lancashire | Lord's | July 13 | 12 | | |

### BATTING AVERAGES - Including fielding

| | Matches | Inns | NO | Runs | HS | Avge | 100s | 50s | Ct | St |
|---|---|---|---|---|---|---|---|---|---|---|
| Britannic Assurance | 19 | 31 | 4 | 1770 | 210 | 65.55 | 6 | 8 | 30 | - |
| Other First-Class | 3 | 3 | 0 | 117 | 86 | 39.00 | - | 1 | 7 | - |
| ALL FIRST-CLASS | 22 | 34 | 4 | 1887 | 210 | 62.90 | 6 | 9 | 37 | - |
| Refuge Assurance | 17 | 16 | 2 | 926 | 160 | 66.14 | 4 | 5 | 3 | - |
| NatWest Trophy | 2 | 2 | 1 | 79 | 42 * | 79.00 | - | - | 1 | - |
| Benson & Hedges Cup | 7 | 7 | 2 | 382 | 110 * | 76.40 | 2 | 2 | 2 | - |
| ALL ONE-DAY | 26 | 25 | 5 | 1387 | 160 | 69.35 | 6 | 7 | 6 | - |

### BOWLING AVERAGES

| | Overs | Mdns | Runs | Wkts | Avge | Best | 5wI | 10wM |
|---|---|---|---|---|---|---|---|---|
| Britannic Assurance | 8.4 | 3 | 25 | 0 | - | - | - | - |
| Other First-Class | 18 | 8 | 22 | 1 | 22.00 | 1-19 | - | - |
| ALL FIRST-CLASS | 26.4 | 11 | 47 | 1 | 47.00 | 1-19 | - | - |
| Refuge Assurance | 5 | 0 | 38 | 1 | 38.00 | 1-38 | - | |
| NatWest Trophy | | | | | | | | |
| Benson & Hedges Cup | 6 | 0 | 22 | 2 | 11.00 | 2-22 | | |
| ALL ONE-DAY | 11 | 0 | 60 | 3 | 20.00 | 2-22 | - | |

## P.MOORES - *Sussex*

| Opposition | Venue | Date | Batting | Fielding | Bowling |
|---|---|---|---|---|---|
| **BRITANNIC ASSURANCE** | | | | | |
| Somerset | Taunton | April 27 | 69 | 2Ct | |
| Middlesex | Lord's | May 9 | 8 & 86 * | 5Ct | |
| Hampshire | Hove | May 16 | 16 | | |
| Middlesex | Hove | May 22 | 9 | 0Ct,1St | |
| Glamorgan | Cardiff | May 25 | 28 | 1Ct | |
| Lancashire | Old Trafford | May 31 | 33 & 51 | 4Ct | |
| Kent | Tunbridge W | June 7 | 1 * | 4Ct | |
| Worcestershire | Hove | June 14 | | 1Ct | |
| Warwickshire | Coventry | June 18 | 14 | 1Ct | |
| Essex | Horsham | June 21 | 10 | 2Ct | |
| Surrey | Arundel | July 2 | 8 & 14 | 2Ct,1St | |
| Derbyshire | Derby | July 5 | 19 | 4Ct | |
| Somerset | Hove | July 16 | 17 * | 2Ct | |
| Leicestershire | Hove | July 19 | | 0Ct,1St | |
| Gloucs | Cheltenham | July 23 | 6 | 3Ct | |
| Northants | Eastbourne | Aug 2 | 7 & 5 | 1Ct,1St | |
| Notts | Eastbourne | Aug 6 | 12 | 3Ct | |
| Yorkshire | Midd'brough | Aug 9 | 9 | 8Ct | |
| Hampshire | Bournemouth | Aug 20 | 1 | 2Ct | |
| Surrey | The Oval | Aug 28 | 54 & 7 | 2Ct | |
| Kent | Hove | Sept 3 | 8 & 0 | 3Ct,1St | |
| Gloucs | Hove | Sept 17 | 69 & 51 | 2Ct | |
| **OTHER FIRST-CLASS** | | | | | |
| Sri Lanka | Hove | Aug 17 | 102 | 3Ct | |

# PLEADER RECORDS

## M     PLAYER RECORDS

### REFUGE ASSURANCE

| | | | | |
|---|---|---|---|---|
| Somerset | Taunton | April 28 | 12 | 3Ct |
| Middlesex | Hove | May 12 | 25 | |
| Gloucs | Hove | May 19 | 6 | |
| Glamorgan | Swansea | May 26 | 34 | 2Ct |
| Lancashire | Old Trafford | June 2 | 4 | 1Ct |
| Hampshire | Basingstoke | June 9 | 33 | 1Ct |
| Worcestershire | Hove | June 16 | | |
| Derbyshire | Derby | July 7 | | |
| Surrey | The Oval | July 14 | 2 | |
| Leicestershire | Hove | July 21 | 4 * | 3Ct |
| Notts | Hove | July 28 | 7 * | 1Ct |
| Northants | Eastbourne | Aug 4 | 0 | 2Ct,1St |
| Yorkshire | Midd'brough | Aug 11 | 15 | 1Ct |
| Kent | Hove | Aug 25 | 11 | 1Ct |

### NATWEST TROPHY

| | | | | |
|---|---|---|---|---|
| Scotland | Edinburgh | June 26 | 26 | 1Ct |
| Essex | Hove | July 11 | 4 | 1Ct |

### BENSON & HEDGES CUP

| | | | | |
|---|---|---|---|---|
| Leicestershire | Hove | April 25 | | 2Ct |
| Kent | Canterbury | May 2 | 20 | 2Ct |
| Scotland | Hove | May 4 | 9 | 1Ct |
| Lancashire | Old Trafford | May 7 | 2 | 1Ct |

### OTHER ONE-DAY

| | | | | |
|---|---|---|---|---|
| Kent | Hove | Sept 7 | 25 | 1Ct |
| Gloucs | Hove | Sept 9 | 66 | 1Ct,2St |

### BATTING AVERAGES - Including fielding

| | Matches | Inns | NO | Runs | HS | Avge | 100s | 50s | Ct | St |
|---|---|---|---|---|---|---|---|---|---|---|
| Britannic Assurance | 22 | 27 | 3 | 612 | 86 * | 25.50 | - | 6 | 53 | 5 |
| Other First-Class | 1 | 1 | 0 | 102 | 102 | 102.00 | 1 | - | 3 | - |
| ALL FIRST-CLASS | 23 | 28 | 3 | 714 | 102 | 28.56 | 1 | 6 | 56 | 5 |
| Refuge Assurance | 14 | 12 | 2 | 153 | 34 | 15.30 | | | 15 | 1 |
| NatWest Trophy | 2 | 2 | 0 | 30 | 26 | 15.00 | - | - | 2 | - |
| Benson & Hedges Cup | 4 | 3 | 0 | 31 | 20 | 10.33 | - | - | 6 | - |
| Other One-Day | 2 | 2 | 0 | 91 | 66 | 45.50 | - | 1 | 2 | 2 |
| ALL ONE-DAY | 22 | 19 | 2 | 305 | 66 | 17.94 | - | 1 | 25 | 3 |

### BOWLING AVERAGES
Did not bowl

## H.MORRIS - *Glamorgan & England*

| Opposition | Venue | Date | Batting | | Fielding | Bowling |
|---|---|---|---|---|---|---|
| **CORNHILL TEST MATCHES** | | | | | | |
| West Indies | Edgbaston | July 25 | 3 & | 1 | | |
| West Indies | The Oval | Aug 8 | 44 & | 2 | 1Ct | |
| Sri Lanka | Lord's | Aug 22 | 42 & | 23 | 2Ct | |
| **BRITANNIC ASSURANCE** | | | | | | |
| Leicestershire | Leicester | April 27 | 11 & | 15 * | | |
| Somerset | Taunton | May 9 | 141 & | 39 | | |
| Warwickshire | Swansea | May 16 | 11 & | 6 | 2Ct | |
| Northants | Cardiff | May 22 | 132 & | 88 * | | |
| Sussex | Cardiff | May 25 | 156 * | | 1Ct | |
| Worcestershire | Worcester | May 31 | 8 & | 74 * | 1Ct | |
| Somerset | Swansea | June 4 | | 84 | | |
| Derbyshire | Chesterfield | June 7 | 50 & | 51 | 3Ct | |
| Middlesex | Cardiff | June 14 | 48 & | 15 | | |
| Leicestershire | Neath | June 21 | 35 | | | |
| Lancashire | Liverpool | June 28 | 35 & | 28 | | |
| Kent | Maidstone | July 5 | 40 & | 11 | | |
| Gloucs | Cheltenham | July 19 | 6 & | 84 | 1Ct | |
| Yorkshire | Headingley | Aug 16 | 156 *& | 2 * | | |
| Gloucs | Abergavenny | Aug 28 | 85 & | 50 * | 2Ct | |
| Worcestershire | Cardiff | Sept 10 | 2 & | 7 | 2Ct | |
| Hampshire | Southampton | Sept 17 | 131 | | 1Ct | |
| **OTHER FIRST-CLASS** | | | | | | |
| For MCC | | | | | | |
| Middlesex | Lord's | April 16 | 44 | | 1Ct | |
| For Glamorgan | | | | | | |
| Cambridge U | Fenner's | June 18 | 10 & | 33 | | |
| West Indies | Swansea | July 16 | 0 & | 0 | | |

### REFUGE ASSURANCE

| | | | | |
|---|---|---|---|---|
| Northants | Cardiff | April 21 | 2 | 1Ct |
| Leicestershire | Leicester | April 28 | 62 | |
| Notts | Cardiff | May 5 | 46 | 1Ct |
| Somerset | Taunton | May 12 | 27 | 1Ct |
| Warwickshire | Swansea | May 19 | 39 | 1Ct |
| Sussex | Swansea | May 26 | 24 | |
| Essex | Pontypridd | June 2 | 3 | |
| Lancashire | Old Trafford | June 9 | 66 | |
| Middlesex | Cardiff | June 16 | 75 | |
| Yorkshire | Headingley | June 30 | 20 | |
| Kent | Maidstone | July 7 | 32 | 2Ct |
| Worcestershire | Worcester | July 21 | 16 | |
| Derbyshire | Checkley | Aug 18 | 21 | |

### NATWEST TROPHY

| | | | | |
|---|---|---|---|---|
| Durham | Darlington | June 26 | 126 * | 1Ct |
| Worcestershire | Worcester | July 11 | 40 | |
| Northants | Northampton | July 31 | 37 | |

### BENSON & HEDGES CUP

| | | | | |
|---|---|---|---|---|
| Min Counties | Trowbridge | April 23 | 1 | |
| Hampshire | Southampton | May 2 | 3 | |
| Notts | Cardiff | May 4 | 3 | |
| Yorkshire | Cardiff | May 7 | 36 | |

### BATTING AVERAGES - Including fielding

| | Matches | Inns | NO | Runs | HS | Avge | 100s | 50s | Ct | St |
|---|---|---|---|---|---|---|---|---|---|---|
| Cornhill Test Matches | 3 | 6 | 0 | 115 | 44 | 19.16 | - | - | 3 | - |
| Britannic Assurance | 17 | 30 | 7 | 1601 | 156 * | 69.60 | 5 | 8 | 13 | - |
| Other First-Class | 3 | 5 | 0 | 87 | 44 | 17.40 | - | - | 1 | - |
| ALL FIRST-CLASS | 23 | 41 | 7 | 1803 | 156 * | 53.02 | 5 | 8 | 17 | - |
| Refuge Assurance | 13 | 13 | 0 | 433 | 75 | 33.30 | - | 3 | 6 | - |
| NatWest Trophy | 3 | 3 | 1 | 203 | 126 * | 101.50 | 1 | - | 1 | - |
| Benson & Hedges Cup | 4 | 4 | 0 | 43 | 36 | 10.75 | - | - | - | - |
| ALL ONE-DAY | 20 | 20 | 1 | 679 | 126 * | 35.73 | 1 | 3 | 7 | - |

### BOWLING AVERAGES
Did not bowl

## J.MORRIS - *Oxford University*

| Opposition | Venue | Date | Batting | | Fielding | Bowling |
|---|---|---|---|---|---|---|
| **OTHER FIRST-CLASS** | | | | | | |
| Worcestershire | The Parks | May 25 | 15 & | 28 | 1Ct | |
| Yorkshire | The Parks | June 4 | 0 | | | |
| Kent | The Parks | June 18 | 19 & | 1 | 2Ct | |

### BATTING AVERAGES - Including fielding

| | Matches | Inns | NO | Runs | HS | Avge | 100s | 50s | Ct | St |
|---|---|---|---|---|---|---|---|---|---|---|
| Other First-Class | 3 | 5 | 0 | 63 | 28 | 12.60 | - | - | 3 | - |
| ALL FIRST-CLASS | 3 | 5 | 0 | 63 | 28 | 12.60 | - | - | 3 | - |

### BOWLING AVERAGES
Did not bowl

## J.E.MORRIS - *Derbyshire*

| Opposition | Venue | Date | Batting | | Fielding | Bowling |
|---|---|---|---|---|---|---|
| **BRITANNIC ASSURANCE** | | | | | | |
| Northants | Derby | April 27 | | | | |
| Lancashire | Old Trafford | May 16 | 53 | | | |
| Somerset | Derby | May 22 | 43 & | 91 | | |
| Kent | Canterbury | May 25 | 10 & | 17 | | |
| Northants | Northampton | May 31 | 87 & | 4 | | |
| Glamorgan | Chesterfield | June 7 | 0 & | 122 * | 2Ct | |
| Gloucs | Gloucester | June 18 | 30 & | 0 | | |
| Surrey | Derby | June 21 | 14 & | 12 | 1Ct | 0-30 |
| Warwickshire | Edgbaston | June 28 | 24 & | 99 | 1Ct | |
| Sussex | Derby | July 5 | 76 & | 14 | | |
| Yorkshire | Scarborough | July 16 | 25 & | 59 | | |
| Worcestershire | Kidd'minster | July 19 | 97 | | 1Ct | |

| | | | | | | | | |
|---|---|---|---|---|---|---|---|---|
| Hampshire | Chesterfield | July 23 | | | 35 | | | |
| Essex | Derby | Aug 6 | 35 | & | 36 | | | |
| Middlesex | Lord's | Aug 9 | 45 | *& | 0 | | | |
| Notts | Trent Bridge | Aug 23 | 63 | & | 0 | | | |
| Leicestershire | Leicester | Aug 28 | 37 | & | 17 | 1Ct | | |
| Essex | Chelmsford | Sept 3 | 0 | & | 42 | 1Ct | | |
| Notts | Derby | Sept 10 | 39 | & | 28 | | | |
| Yorkshire | Chesterfield | Sept 17 | 13 | & | 0 | | | |

### OTHER FIRST-CLASS

| | | | | | |
|---|---|---|---|---|---|
| Cambridge U | Fenner's | May 9 | 131 | | 1Ct |

### REFUGE ASSURANCE

| | | | | |
|---|---|---|---|---|
| Leicestershire | Leicester | April 21 | 26 | |
| Hampshire | Derby | May 5 | 32 | |
| Kent | Canterbury | May 26 | 11 | |
| Yorkshire | Chesterfield | June 2 | 0 | |
| Somerset | Derby | June 16 | 27 | |
| Essex | Chelmsford | June 30 | 46 | |
| Sussex | Derby | July 7 | 6 | |
| Worcestershire | Worcester | July 9 | 51 | 0-7 |
| Gloucs | Cheltenham | July 21 | 21 | 1Ct |
| Northants | Derby | July 28 | 40 | 1Ct |
| Warwickshire | Edgbaston | Aug 4 | 17 | |

### BENSON & HEDGES CUP

| | | | | |
|---|---|---|---|---|
| Northants | Derby | April 23 | 0 | 1Ct |
| Combined U | The Parks | April 25 | 71 | 0-14 |
| Worcestershire | Worcester | May 4 | 18 | |
| Gloucs | Derby | May 7 | 0 | |

### OTHER ONE-DAY

For D of Norfolk

| | | | |
|---|---|---|---|
| West Indies | Arundel | May 12 | 98 |

For England XI

| | | | |
|---|---|---|---|
| Rest of World | Jesmond | July 31 | 42 |
| Rest of World | Jesmond | Aug 1 | 107 | 1Ct |

For Derbyshire

| | | | |
|---|---|---|---|
| Yorkshire | Scarborough | Sept 1 | 16 |

For World XI

| | | | |
|---|---|---|---|
| Yorkshire | Scarborough | Sept 8 | 5 |

### BATTING AVERAGES - Including fielding

| | Matches | Inns | NO | Runs | HS | Avge | 100s | 50s | Ct | St |
|---|---|---|---|---|---|---|---|---|---|---|
| Britannic Assurance | 20 | 35 | 2 | 1267 | 122* | 38.39 | 1 | 8 | 7 | - |
| Other First-Class | 1 | 1 | 0 | 131 | 131 | 131.00 | 1 | - | 1 | - |
| ALL FIRST-CLASS | 21 | 36 | 2 | 1398 | 131 | 41.11 | 2 | 8 | 8 | - |
| Refuge Assurance | 11 | 11 | 0 | 277 | 51 | 25.18 | - | 1 | 2 | - |
| Benson & Hedges Cup | 4 | 4 | 0 | 89 | 71 | 22.25 | - | 1 | 1 | - |
| Other One-Day | 5 | 5 | 0 | 268 | 107 | 53.60 | 1 | 1 | 1 | - |
| ALL ONE-DAY | 20 | 20 | 0 | 634 | 107 | 31.70 | 1 | 3 | 4 | - |

### BOWLING AVERAGES

| | Overs | Mdns | Runs | Wkts | Avge | Best | 5wI | 10wM |
|---|---|---|---|---|---|---|---|---|
| Britannic Assurance | 2 | 0 | 30 | 0 | - | - | - | - |
| Other First-Class | | | | | | | | |
| ALL FIRST-CLASS | 2 | 0 | 30 | 0 | - | - | - | - |
| Refuge Assurance | 0.3 | 0 | 7 | 0 | - | - | - | - |
| Benson & Hedges Cup | 4 | 0 | 14 | 0 | - | - | - | - |
| Other One-Day | | | | | | | | |
| ALL ONE-DAY | 4.3 | 0 | 21 | 0 | - | - | - | - |

---

# M.J.MORRIS - *Cambridge University*

| Opposition | Venue | Date | Batting | | | Fielding | Bowling |
|---|---|---|---|---|---|---|---|
| **OTHER FIRST-CLASS** | | | | | | | |
| Lancashire | Fenner's | April 13 | 0 | & | 0 | 1Ct | |
| Northants | Fenner's | April 16 | 0 | | | | |
| Essex | Fenner's | April 19 | 2 | & | 15 | | |
| Derbyshire | Fenner's | May 9 | 17 | | | | 0-15 |
| Middlesex | Fenner's | May 15 | 2 | & | 0 | 1Ct | |
| Leicestershire | Fenner's | May 22 | 60 | & | 22 | | |
| Glamorgan | Fenner's | June 18 | | | 20 | | |
| Sussex | Hove | June 29 | | | | | |

---

| | | | | | |
|---|---|---|---|---|---|
| Oxford U | Lord's | July 2 | 6 | & | 27 |

### BATTING AVERAGES - Including fielding

| | Matches | Inns | NO | Runs | HS | Avge | 100s | 50s | Ct | St |
|---|---|---|---|---|---|---|---|---|---|---|
| Other First-Class | 9 | 13 | 0 | 171 | 60 | 13.15 | - | 1 | 2 | - |
| ALL FIRST-CLASS | 9 | 13 | 0 | 171 | 60 | 13.15 | - | 1 | 2 | - |

### BOWLING AVERAGES

| | Overs | Mdns | Runs | Wkts | Avge | Best | 5wI | 10wM |
|---|---|---|---|---|---|---|---|---|
| Other First-Class | 3 | 1 | 15 | 0 | - | - | - | - |
| ALL FIRST-CLASS | 3 | 1 | 15 | 0 | - | - | - | - |

---

# R.E.MORRIS - *Oxford University & Combined Universities*

| Opposition | Venue | Date | Batting | | | Fielding | Bowling |
|---|---|---|---|---|---|---|---|
| **OTHER FIRST-CLASS** | | | | | | | |
| Hampshire | The Parks | April 13 | 5 | & | 0 | | |
| Glamorgan | The Parks | April 17 | 30 | | | | |
| Notts | The Parks | April 27 | | | | | |
| Gloucs | The Parks | June 15 | 6 | | | | |
| Yorkshire | The Parks | June 4 | 2 | | | 1Ct | 2-82 & 0-19 |
| Lancashire | The Parks | June 7 | 15 | & | 50* | | |
| Kent | The Parks | June 18 | 2 | & | 37 | 1Ct | 0-28 |
| Cambridge U | Lord's | July 2 | 71 | & | 18 | 1Ct | |

### BENSON & HEDGES CUP

For Combined Universities

| | | | |
|---|---|---|---|
| Gloucs | Bristol | April 23 | 19 |
| Derbyshire | The Parks | April 25 | 12 |
| Worcestershire | Fenner's | May 2 | 6 |
| Northants | Northampton | May 4 | 7 |

### BATTING AVERAGES - Including fielding

| | Matches | Inns | NO | Runs | HS | Avge | 100s | 50s | Ct | St |
|---|---|---|---|---|---|---|---|---|---|---|
| Other First-Class | 8 | 11 | 1 | 236 | 71 | 23.60 | - | 2 | 3 | - |
| ALL FIRST-CLASS | 8 | 11 | 1 | 236 | 71 | 23.60 | - | 2 | 3 | - |
| Benson & Hedges Cup | 4 | 4 | 0 | 44 | 19 | 11.00 | - | - | - | - |
| ALL ONE-DAY | 4 | 4 | 0 | 44 | 19 | 11.00 | - | - | - | - |

### BOWLING AVERAGES

| | Overs | Mdns | Runs | Wkts | Avge | Best | 5wI | 10wM |
|---|---|---|---|---|---|---|---|---|
| Other First-Class | 24 | 3 | 129 | 2 | 64.50 | 2-82 | - | - |
| ALL FIRST-CLASS | 24 | 3 | 129 | 2 | 64.50 | 2-82 | - | - |
| Benson & Hedges Cup | | | | | | | | |
| ALL ONE-DAY | | | | | | | | |

---

# D.K.MORRISON - *World XI*

| Opposition | Venue | Date | Batting | Fielding | Bowling |
|---|---|---|---|---|---|
| **OTHER FIRST-CLASS** | | | | | |
| West Indies XI | Scarborough | Aug 28 | 1 | 2Ct | 2-82 & 0-31 |

### BATTING AVERAGES - Including fielding

| | Matches | Inns | NO | Runs | HS | Avge | 100s | 50s | Ct | St |
|---|---|---|---|---|---|---|---|---|---|---|
| Other First-Class | 1 | 1 | 0 | 1 | 1 | 1.00 | - | - | 2 | - |
| ALL FIRST-CLASS | 1 | 1 | 0 | 1 | 1 | 1.00 | - | - | 2 | - |

### BOWLING AVERAGES

| | Overs | Mdns | Runs | Wkts | Avge | Best | 5wI | 10wM |
|---|---|---|---|---|---|---|---|---|
| Other First-Class | 17 | 2 | 113 | 2 | 56.50 | 2-82 | - | - |
| ALL FIRST-CLASS | 17 | 2 | 113 | 2 | 56.50 | 2-82 | - | - |

# M | PLAYER RECORDS

## O.H.MORTENSEN - *Derbyshire*

| Opposition | Venue | Date | Batting | Fielding | Bowling |
|---|---|---|---|---|---|
| **BRITANNIC ASSURANCE** | | | | | |
| Northants | Derby | April 27 | | | 1-62 |
| Lancashire | Old Trafford | May 16 | | 1Ct | 4-46 & 1-19 |
| Somerset | Derby | May 22 | 1 & 1 | | 1-36 & 4-47 |
| Northants | Northampton | May 31 | 1 * & 0 * | 2Ct | 5-57 & 2-59 |
| Glamorgan | Chesterfield | June 7 | 7 | | 3-40 & 0-9 |
| Gloucs | Gloucester | June 18 | | 1Ct | 1-28 & 4-66 |
| Surrey | Derby | June 21 | | | 4-43 |
| Warwickshire | Edgbaston | June 28 | 0 * | | 3-36 & 2-33 |
| Yorkshire | Scarborough | July 16 | 0 | | 1-86 |
| Worcestershire | Kidd'minster | July 19 | 0 * | | 1-29 & 6-101 |
| Hampshire | Chesterfield | July 23 | | 0 * | 4-50 |
| Essex | Derby | Aug 6 | 2 * | | 2-53 & 1-30 |
| Middlesex | Lord's | Aug 9 | | 7 * | 0-50 & 1-12 |
| Lancashire | Derby | Aug 16 | | | 2-48 & 0-35 |
| Leicestershire | Derby | Aug 20 | 0 & 0 * | | 1-59 |
| Notts | Trent Bridge | Aug 23 | | | 2-63 & 1-34 |
| Essex | Chelmsford | Sept 3 | 0 & 5 * | | 1-73 |
| Notts | Derby | Sept 10 | 8 | | 0-21 & 0-14 |
| **OTHER FIRST-CLASS** | | | | | |
| Cambridge U | Fenner's | May 9 | 0 | 1Ct | 0-37 & 0-8 |
| **REFUGE ASSURANCE** | | | | | |
| Leicestershire | Leicester | April 21 | | | 2-36 |
| Hampshire | Derby | May 5 | | | 1-27 |
| Lancashire | Derby | May 19 | 1 * | | 1-41 |
| Kent | Canterbury | May 26 | | | 1-42 |
| Essex | Chelmsford | June 30 | 3 * | 1Ct | 0-22 |
| Northants | Derby | July 28 | | | 1-19 |
| Warwickshire | Edgbaston | Aug 4 | 1 * | | 1-41 |
| Middlesex | Lord's | Aug 11 | | 1Ct | 3-29 |
| Glamorgan | Checkley | Aug 18 | 7 * | | 2-36 |
| Notts | Trent Bridge | Aug 25 | 1 * | 1Ct | 0-24 |
| **BENSON & HEDGES CUP** | | | | | |
| Northants | Derby | April 23 | 4 * | | 2-16 |
| Combined U | The Parks | April 25 | | | 2-16 |
| Worcestershire | Worcester | May 4 | 2 | | 1-47 |
| Gloucs | Derby | May 7 | | | 1-36 |
| **OTHER ONE-DAY** | | | | | |
| For D of Norfolk | | | | | |
| West Indies | Arundel | May 12 | 1 * | | 1-32 |

### BATTING AVERAGES - Including fielding

| | Matches | Inns | NO | Runs | HS | Avge | 100s | 50s | Ct | St |
|---|---|---|---|---|---|---|---|---|---|---|
| Britannic Assurance | 18 | 16 | 9 | 32 | 8 | 4.57 | - | - | 4 | - |
| Other First-Class | 1 | 1 | 0 | 0 | 0 | 0.00 | - | - | 1 | - |
| ALL FIRST-CLASS | 19 | 17 | 9 | 32 | 8 | 4.00 | - | - | 5 | - |
| Refuge Assurance | 10 | 5 | 5 | 13 | 7 * | - | - | - | 3 | - |
| Benson & Hedges Cup | 4 | 2 | 1 | 6 | 4 * | 6.00 | - | - | - | - |
| Other One-Day | 1 | 1 | 1 | 1 | 1 * | - | - | - | - | - |
| ALL ONE-DAY | 15 | 8 | 7 | 20 | 7 * | 20.00 | - | - | 3 | - |

### BOWLING AVERAGES

| | Overs | Mdns | Runs | Wkts | Avge | Best | 5wI | 10wM |
|---|---|---|---|---|---|---|---|---|
| Britannic Assurance | 535.1 | 138 | 1339 | 58 | 23.08 | 6-101 | 2 | - |
| Other First-Class | 24 | 5 | 45 | 0 | - | - | - | - |
| ALL FIRST-CLASS | 559.1 | 143 | 1384 | 58 | 23.86 | 6-101 | 2 | - |
| Refuge Assurance | 80 | 7 | 317 | 12 | 26.41 | 3-29 | - | |
| Benson & Hedges Cup | 40 | 10 | 115 | 6 | 19.16 | 2-16 | - | |
| Other One-Day | 10 | 1 | 32 | 1 | 32.00 | 1-32 | - | |
| ALL ONE-DAY | 130 | 18 | 464 | 19 | 24.42 | 3-29 | - | |

## M.D.MOXON - *Yorkshire*

| Opposition | Venue | Date | Batting | Fielding | Bowling |
|---|---|---|---|---|---|
| **BRITANNIC ASSURANCE** | | | | | |
| Middlesex | Lord's | April 27 | 15 | | |
| Warwickshire | Headingley | May 9 | 14 & 57 | 2Ct | 1-17 |
| Notts | Headingley | May 16 | 2 & 36 | | |
| Gloucs | Sheffield | May 22 | 65 & 55 | | |
| Northants | Headingley | May 25 | 108 & 42 | 1Ct | 1-10 |
| Warwickshire | Edgbaston | May 31 | 37 & 27 | | |
| Kent | Harrogate | June 14 | 90 | | |
| Worcestershire | Headingley | July 2 | 26 | 1Ct | |
| Hampshire | Southampton | July 5 | 68 | 1Ct | |
| Derbyshire | Scarborough | July 16 | 44 | 4Ct | |
| Surrey | Guildford | July 19 | 73 & 68 | 1Ct | |
| Notts | Worksop | July 23 | 0 & 25 * | | |
| Lancashire | Old Trafford | Aug 2 | 0 & 30 | 1Ct | |
| Leicestershire | Leicester | Aug 6 | 22 & 12 | | |
| Sussex | Midd'brough | Aug 9 | 33 & 0 | 1Ct | |
| Glamorgan | Headingley | Aug 16 | 80 & 0 | | |
| Essex | Colchester | Aug 20 | 200 & 66 | 1Ct | |
| Somerset | Taunton | Aug 23 | 34 & 91 | | |
| Northants | Northampton | Aug 28 | 12 & 55 | 1Ct | |
| Lancashire | Scarborough | Sept 3 | 4 & 115 | 1Ct | |
| Derbyshire | Chesterfield | Sept 17 | 50 & 13 | 2Ct | |
| **REFUGE ASSURANCE** | | | | | |
| Hampshire | Southampton | April 21 | 15 | 1Ct | |
| Essex | Chelmsford | April 28 | 6 | | 0-7 |
| Warwickshire | Headingley | May 12 | 39 | | 0-14 |
| Leicestershire | Leicester | May 19 | 8 | | |
| Northants | Headingley | May 26 | 31 | 1Ct | 1-34 |
| Derbyshire | Chesterfield | June 2 | 20 | | |
| Kent | Scarborough | June 16 | 3 * | | |
| Glamorgan | Headingley | June 30 | 52 | | |
| Middlesex | Lord's | July 7 | 64 | 1Ct | |
| Gloucs | Scarborough | July 14 | 6 | | |
| Surrey | The Oval | July 21 | 129 * | 1Ct | |
| Lancashire | Old Trafford | Aug 4 | 76 | 1Ct | |
| Sussex | Midd'brough | Aug 11 | 112 | | |
| Somerset | Taunton | Aug 25 | 0 | 1Ct | |
| **NATWEST TROPHY** | | | | | |
| Warwickshire | Edgbaston | June 26 | 2 | 1Ct | |
| **BENSON & HEDGES CUP** | | | | | |
| Notts | Trent Bridge | April 25 | 95 | | |
| Min Counties | Headingley | May 2 | 65 | | |
| Hampshire | Headingley | May 4 | 24 | 1Ct | |
| Glamorgan | Cardiff | May 7 | 141 * | | |
| Warwickshire | Headingley | May 29 | 30 | 3Ct | 5-31 |
| Lancashire | Old Trafford | June 16 | 15 | 1Ct | 0-30 |
| **OTHER ONE-DAY** | | | | | |
| For England XI | | | | | |
| Rest of World | Jesmond | July 31 | 5 | 1Ct | |
| Rest of World | Jesmond | Aug 1 | 40 | | |
| For England A | | | | | |
| Sri Lanka | Old Trafford | Aug 14 | 49 | 2Ct | |
| Sri Lanka | Old Trafford | Aug 15 | 32 | 2Ct | |
| For Yorkshire | | | | | |
| Derbyshire | Scarborough | Sept 1 | 63 | | |
| Essex | Scarborough | Sept 2 | 32 | 1Ct | |
| Yorkshiremen | Scarborough | Sept 7 | 34 | 1Ct | |
| World XI | Scarborough | Sept 8 | 18 | 1Ct | |

### BATTING AVERAGES - Including fielding

| | Matches | Inns | NO | Runs | HS | Avge | 100s | 50s | Ct | St |
|---|---|---|---|---|---|---|---|---|---|---|
| Britannic Assurance | 21 | 37 | 1 | 1669 | 200 | 46.36 | 3 | 12 | 17 | - |
| ALL FIRST-CLASS | 21 | 37 | 1 | 1669 | 200 | 46.36 | 3 | 12 | 17 | - |
| Refuge Assurance | 14 | 14 | 2 | 561 | 129 * | 46.75 | 2 | 3 | 6 | - |
| NatWest Trophy | 1 | 1 | 0 | 2 | 2 | 2.00 | - | - | 1 | - |
| Benson & Hedges Cup | 6 | 6 | 1 | 370 | 141 * | 74.00 | 1 | 2 | 5 | - |
| Other One-Day | 8 | 8 | 0 | 273 | 63 | 34.12 | - | 1 | 8 | - |
| ALL ONE-DAY | 29 | 29 | 3 | 1206 | 141 * | 46.38 | 3 | 6 | 20 | - |

### BOWLING AVERAGES

| | Overs | Mdns | Runs | Wkts | Avge | Best | 5wI | 10wM |
|---|---|---|---|---|---|---|---|---|
| Britannic Assurance | 11 | 2 | 27 | 2 | 13.50 | 1-10 | - | - |

# PLConflicting... 

| | | | | | | | | |
|---|---|---|---|---|---|---|---|---|
| ALL FIRST-CLASS | 11 | 2 | 27 | 2 | 13.50 | 1-10 | - | - |
| Refuge Assurance | 11.3 | 0 | 55 | 1 | 55.00 | 1-34 | - | |
| NatWest Trophy | | | | | | | | |
| Benson & Hedges Cup | 13 | 0 | 61 | 5 | 12.20 | 5-31 | 1 | |
| Other One-Day | | | | | | | | |
| ALL ONE-DAY | 24.3 | 0 | 116 | 6 | 19.33 | 5-31 | 1 | |

## MUDASSAR NAZAR - *World XI & Rest of World*

| Opposition | Venue | Date | Batting | Fielding | Bowling |
|---|---|---|---|---|---|
| OTHER FIRST-CLASS | | | | | |
| For World XI | | | | | |
| West Indies XI | Scarborough | Aug 28 | 3 | 1Ct | |
| OTHER ONE-DAY | | | | | |
| For Rest of World | | | | | |
| England XI | Jesmond | July 31 | 31 | | |
| England XI | Jesmond | Aug 1 | 12 | | 0-15 |

### BATTING AVERAGES - Including fielding

| | Matches | Inns | NO | Runs | HS | Avge | 100s | 50s | Ct | St |
|---|---|---|---|---|---|---|---|---|---|---|
| Other First-Class | 1 | 1 | 0 | 3 | 3 | 3.00 | - | - | 1 | - |
| ALL FIRST-CLASS | 1 | 1 | 0 | 3 | 3 | 3.00 | - | - | 1 | - |
| Other One-Day | 2 | 2 | 0 | 43 | 31 | 21.50 | - | - | - | - |
| ALL ONE-DAY | 2 | 2 | 0 | 43 | 31 | 21.50 | - | - | - | - |

### BOWLING AVERAGES

| | Overs | Mdns | Runs | Wkts | Avge | Best | 5wI | 10wM |
|---|---|---|---|---|---|---|---|---|
| Other First-Class | | | | | | | | |
| ALL FIRST-CLASS | | | | | | | | |
| Other One-Day | 2 | 0 | 15 | 0 | - | - | - | |
| ALL ONE-DAY | 2 | 0 | 15 | 0 | - | - | - | |

## A.D.MULLALLY - *Leicestershire*

| Opposition | Venue | Date | Batting | Fielding | Bowling |
|---|---|---|---|---|---|
| BRITANNIC ASSURANCE | | | | | |
| Glamorgan | Leicester | April 27 | | | 0-40 & 0-4 |
| Yorkshire | Leicester | Aug 6 | | | 1-35 & 0-20 |
| REFUGE ASSURANCE | | | | | |
| Derbyshire | Leicester | April 21 | | 1Ct | 2-31 |
| Somerset | Weston | Aug 4 | | 1Ct | 2-19 |
| BENSON & HEDGES CUP | | | | | |
| Kent | Canterbury | April 23 | 5 | | 1-45 |
| Sussex | Hove | April 25 | 1 | | 0-63 |
| Lancashire | Leicester | May 4 | | | 0-26 |

### BATTING AVERAGES - Including fielding

| | Matches | Inns | NO | Runs | HS | Avge | 100s | 50s | Ct | St |
|---|---|---|---|---|---|---|---|---|---|---|
| Britannic Assurance | 2 | 0 | 0 | 0 | 0 | - | - | - | - | - |
| ALL FIRST-CLASS | 2 | 0 | 0 | 0 | 0 | - | - | - | - | - |
| Refuge Assurance | 2 | 0 | 0 | 0 | 0 | - | - | - | 2 | - |
| Benson & Hedges Cup | 3 | 2 | 0 | 6 | 5 | 3.00 | - | - | - | - |
| ALL ONE-DAY | 5 | 2 | 0 | 6 | 5 | 3.00 | - | - | 2 | - |

### BOWLING AVERAGES

| | Overs | Mdns | Runs | Wkts | Avge | Best | 5wI | 10wM |
|---|---|---|---|---|---|---|---|---|
| Britannic Assurance | 37.4 | 10 | 99 | 1 | 99.00 | 1-35 | - | - |
| ALL FIRST-CLASS | 37.4 | 10 | 99 | 1 | 99.00 | 1-35 | - | - |

| | | | | | | | | |
|---|---|---|---|---|---|---|---|---|
| Refuge Assurance | 16 | 1 | 50 | 4 | 12.50 | 2-19 | - | |
| Benson & Hedges Cup | 33 | 2 | 134 | 1 | 134.00 | 1-45 | - | |
| ALL ONE-DAY | 49 | 3 | 184 | 5 | 36.80 | 2-19 | - | |

## T.A.MUNTON - *Warwickshire*

| Opposition | Venue | Date | Batting | | | Fielding | Bowling |
|---|---|---|---|---|---|---|---|
| BRITANNIC ASSURANCE | | | | | | | |
| Lancashire | Edgbaston | April 27 | 0 * | | | | 0-83 |
| Yorkshire | Headingley | May 9 | 31 & | 2 | | 1Ct | 4-57 & 2-65 |
| Glamorgan | Swansea | May 16 | 6 & | 6 | | 1Ct | 1-43 & 1-41 |
| Essex | Chelmsford | May 22 | 14 & | 10 | | 1Ct | 2-75 |
| Gloucs | Edgbaston | May 25 | 3 | | | 1Ct | 1-25 & 1-51 |
| Yorkshire | Edgbaston | May 31 | 28 | | | | 6-53 |
| Kent | Tunbridge W | June 4 | 6 | | | | 0-66 |
| Somerset | Edgbaston | June 7 | | | | | 1-52 & 0-13 |
| Sussex | Coventry | June 18 | 5 * | | | 1Ct | 0-36 |
| Notts | Trent Bridge | June 21 | 25 | | | 1Ct | 0-12 & 0-26 |
| Derbyshire | Edgbaston | June 28 | 3 & | 5 | | 2Ct | 5-77 & 2-60 |
| Middlesex | Edgbaston | July 2 | 8 * | | | | 8-89 & 3-38 |
| Hampshire | Portsmouth | July 19 | 14 | | | | 2-80 & 1-28 |
| Lancashire | Old Trafford | July 23 | 3 | | | | 0-34 |
| Leicestershire | Leicester | July 26 | | | | | 5-32 & 4-46 |
| Worcestershire | Worcester | Aug 2 | 12 & | 0 | | | 1-87 |
| Surrey | Edgbaston | Aug 6 | 1 * & | 4 | | 3Ct | 3-40 & 0-46 |
| Northants | Northampton | Aug 9 | 17 * | | | 1Ct | 4-85 |
| Glamorgan | Edgbaston | Aug 20 | | | | | 1-38 & 0-18 |
| Worcestershire | Edgbaston | Aug 28 | 5 * | | | 1Ct | 7-59 & 3-32 |
| Northants | Edgbaston | Sept 10 | | | | 1Ct | 1-99 |
| Somerset | Taunton | Sept 17 | 6 * & | 12 * | | | 1-52 & 1-57 |
| OTHER FIRST-CLASS | | | | | | | |
| For MCC | | | | | | | |
| Middlesex | Lord's | April 16 | | | | | 2-68 |
| REFUGE ASSURANCE | | | | | | | |
| Sussex | Edgbaston | April 21 | | | | | 0-16 |
| Notts | Trent Bridge | April 28 | 3 * | | | 1Ct | 2-35 |
| Yorkshire | Headingley | May 12 | | | | | 1-17 |
| Glamorgan | Swansea | May 19 | | | | | 1-15 |
| Worcestershire | Edgbaston | May 26 | | | | | 2-20 |
| Lancashire | Edgbaston | June 16 | | | | | 0-20 |
| Essex | Chelmsford | July 7 | | | | | 0-34 |
| Middlesex | Edgbaston | July 14 | | | | | 0-33 |
| Hampshire | Portsmouth | July 21 | | | | 1Ct | 1-21 |
| Derbyshire | Edgbaston | Aug 4 | | | | | 1-29 |
| Leicestershire | Leicester | Aug 11 | 0 * | | | | 0-27 |
| Gloucs | Edgbaston | Aug 18 | | | | | 5-28 |
| Northants | Northampton | Aug 25 | 10 * | | | | 0-38 |
| NATWEST TROPHY | | | | | | | |
| Yorkshire | Edgbaston | June 26 | | | | 1Ct | 1-21 |
| Hertfordshire | Edgbaston | July 11 | | | | 1Ct | 0-22 |
| Somerset | Edgbaston | July 31 | 1 | | | | 2-42 |
| Hampshire | Edgbaston | Aug 14 | 5 | | | | 0-26 |
| BENSON & HEDGES CUP | | | | | | | |
| Essex | Edgbaston | April 25 | 6 | | | | 1-40 |
| Somerset | Edgbaston | May 2 | | | | 1Ct | 1-48 |
| Middlesex | Lord's | May 4 | 2 * | | | | 1-27 |
| Surrey | The Oval | May 7 | | | | | 4-35 |
| Yorkshire | Headingley | May 29 | 10 | | | | 2-37 |
| OTHER ONE-DAY | | | | | | | |
| Surrey | Harrogate | June 12 | 13 * | | | 1Ct | 1-41 |

### BATTING AVERAGES - Including fielding

| | Matches | Inns | NO | Runs | HS | Avge | 100s | 50s | Ct | St |
|---|---|---|---|---|---|---|---|---|---|---|
| Britannic Assurance | 22 | 25 | 8 | 226 | 31 | 13.29 | - | - | 14 | - |
| Other First-Class | 1 | 0 | 0 | 0 | 0 | - | - | - | - | - |
| ALL FIRST-CLASS | 23 | 25 | 8 | 226 | 31 | 13.29 | - | - | 14 | - |
| Refuge Assurance | 13 | 3 | 3 | 13 | 10 * | - | - | - | 2 | - |
| NatWest Trophy | 4 | 2 | 0 | 6 | 5 | 3.00 | - | - | 2 | - |
| Benson & Hedges Cup | 5 | 3 | 1 | 18 | 10 | 9.00 | - | - | 1 | - |
| Other One-Day | 1 | 1 | 1 | 13 | 13 * | - | - | - | 1 | - |
| ALL ONE-DAY | 23 | 9 | 5 | 50 | 13 * | 12.50 | - | - | 6 | - |

# M      PLAYER RECORDS

## BOWLING AVERAGES

|  | Overs | Mdns | Runs | Wkts | Avge | Best | 5wI | 10wM |
|---|---|---|---|---|---|---|---|---|
| Britannic Assurance | 662 | 177 | 1795 | 71 | 25.28 | 8-89 | 5 | 2 |
| Other First-Class | 31.1 | 7 | 68 | 2 | 34.00 | 2-68 | - | - |
| ALL FIRST-CLASS | 693.1 | 184 | 1863 | 73 | 25.52 | 8-89 | 5 | 2 |
| Refuge Assurance | 90 | 6 | 333 | 13 | 25.61 | 5-28 | 1 | |
| NatWest Trophy | 41 | 7 | 111 | 3 | 37.00 | 2-42 | - | |
| Benson & Hedges Cup | 51.4 | 5 | 187 | 9 | 20.77 | 4-35 | - | |
| Other One-Day | 7 | 0 | 41 | 1 | 41.00 | 1-41 | - | |
| ALL ONE-DAY | 189.4 | 18 | 672 | 26 | 25.84 | 5-28 | 1 | |

## M.MURALITHARAN - *Sri Lanka*

| Opposition | Venue | Date | Batting | Fielding | Bowling |
|---|---|---|---|---|---|
| **OTHER FIRST-CLASS** | | | | | |
| Worcestershire | Worcester | July 30 | 22 * & 0 | 1Ct | 0-98 |
| Gloucs | Bristol | Aug 6 | 0 & 5 | | |
| Sussex | Hove | Aug 17 | | 1Ct | 0-43 & 0-69 |
| **OTHER ONE-DAY** | | | | | |
| England Am. | Wolv'hampton | July 24 | | | 2-30 |

### BATTING AVERAGES - Including fielding

|  | Matches | Inns | NO | Runs | HS | Avge | 100s | 50s | Ct | St |
|---|---|---|---|---|---|---|---|---|---|---|
| Other First-Class | 3 | 4 | 1 | 27 | 22 * | 9.00 | - | - | 2 | - |
| ALL FIRST-CLASS | 3 | 4 | 1 | 27 | 22 * | 9.00 | - | - | 2 | - |
| Other One-Day | 1 | 0 | 0 | 0 | 0 | - | - | - | - | - |
| ALL ONE-DAY | 1 | 0 | 0 | 0 | 0 | - | - | - | - | - |

### BOWLING AVERAGES

|  | Overs | Mdns | Runs | Wkts | Avge | Best | 5wI | 10wM |
|---|---|---|---|---|---|---|---|---|
| Other First-Class | 70.1 | 8 | 210 | 0 | - | - | - | - |
| ALL FIRST-CLASS | 70.1 | 8 | 210 | 0 | - | - | - | - |
| Other One-Day | 11 | 0 | 30 | 2 | 15.00 | 2-30 | - | |
| ALL ONE-DAY | 11 | 0 | 30 | 2 | 15.00 | 2-30 | - | |

## A.J.MURPHY - *Surrey*

| Opposition | Venue | Date | Batting | Fielding | Bowling |
|---|---|---|---|---|---|
| **BRITANNIC ASSURANCE** | | | | | |
| Essex | Chelmsford | April 27 | 2 | | 1-57 |
| Kent | The Oval | May 9 | 11 & 18 | | 3-98 |
| Hampshire | Bournemouth | May 25 | 9 & 1 * | | 2-56 & 1-103 |
| Notts | The Oval | June 4 | | | 0-56 & 0-21 |
| Leicestershire | Leicester | June 14 | | | 1-67 & 1-53 |
| Derbyshire | Derby | June 21 | 7 | | 1-29 & 0-35 |
| Somerset | The Oval | June 28 | | 1Ct | 2-84 |
| Sussex | Arundel | July 2 | | | 1-50 & 0-34 |
| Essex | The Oval | July 5 | 1 * | | 2-52 & 5-63 |
| Gloucs | Guildford | July 16 | | | 1-108 & 0-14 |
| Yorkshire | Guildford | July 19 | | 2 * | 2-66 & 2-30 |
| Glamorgan | The Oval | July 26 | | | 1-33 |
| Kent | Canterbury | Aug 2 | 7 & 0 | 1Ct | 0-35 & 2-41 |
| Warwickshire | Edgbaston | Aug 6 | 0 | | 1-32 & 0-30 |
| Worcestershire | Worcester | Aug 16 | 1 & 2 * | 1Ct | 0-91 |
| Middlesex | The Oval | Aug 20 | 2 * & 7 * | | 0-21 & 1-2 |
| Northants | Northampton | Aug 23 | 0 | 1Ct | 2-103 |
| Hampshire | The Oval | Sept 3 | 0 & 0 | | 0-33 & 1-67 |
| Lancashire | Old Trafford | Sept 17 | 0 * & 1 * | | 0-65 & 2-38 |
| **REFUGE ASSURANCE** | | | | | |
| Somerset | The Oval | April 21 | | | 0-21 |
| Middlesex | Lord's | April 28 | | | 0-31 |
| Gloucs | The Oval | May 12 | 1 * | | 3-45 |
| Essex | The Oval | May 26 | | | 3-28 |
| Worcestershire | Worcester | June 2 | | | 2-58 |
| Derbyshire | Chesterfield | June 9 | 0 * | | 1-35 |

| Leicestershire | Leicester | June 16 | 5 * | | 3-15 |
|---|---|---|---|---|---|
| Notts | The Oval | June 30 | | | 0-26 |
| Northants | Tring | July 7 | | | 2-26 |
| Sussex | The Oval | July 14 | | | 2-36 |
| Yorkshire | The Oval | July 21 | | | 0-46 |
| Lancashire | Old Trafford | Aug 18 | | | 1-45 |
| Hampshire | The Oval | Aug 25 | | 1Ct | 1-32 |
| **NATWEST TROPHY** | | | | | |
| Kent | The Oval | July 11 | | | 1-27 |
| Essex | The Oval | July 31 | 0 * | | 1-30 |
| Northants | The Oval | Aug 14 | 1 * | | 0-45 |
| Hampshire | Lord's | Sept 7 | | | 1-56 |
| **BENSON & HEDGES CUP** | | | | | |
| Essex | The Oval | April 23 | 0 * | | 0-46 |
| Middlesex | Lord's | April 25 | | | 2-23 |
| Somerset | Taunton | May 4 | | | 1-48 |
| Warwickshire | The Oval | May 7 | | 1 | 1-34 |
| **OTHER ONE-DAY** | | | | | |
| Warwickshire | Harrogate | June 12 | | | 1-48 |

### BATTING AVERAGES - Including fielding

|  | Matches | Inns | NO | Runs | HS | Avge | 100s | 50s | Ct | St |
|---|---|---|---|---|---|---|---|---|---|---|
| Britannic Assurance | 19 | 20 | 8 | 71 | 18 | 5.91 | - | - | 4 | - |
| ALL FIRST-CLASS | 19 | 20 | 8 | 71 | 18 | 5.91 | - | - | 4 | - |
| Refuge Assurance | 13 | 3 | 3 | 6 | 5 * | - | - | - | 1 | - |
| NatWest Trophy | 4 | 2 | 2 | 1 | 1 * | - | - | - | - | - |
| Benson & Hedges Cup | 4 | 2 | 1 | 1 | 1 | 1.00 | - | - | - | - |
| Other One-Day | 1 | 0 | 0 | 0 | 0 | - | - | - | - | - |
| ALL ONE-DAY | 22 | 7 | 6 | 8 | 5 * | 8.00 | - | - | 1 | - |

### BOWLING AVERAGES

|  | Overs | Mdns | Runs | Wkts | Avge | Best | 5wI | 10wM |
|---|---|---|---|---|---|---|---|---|
| Britannic Assurance | 546.4 | 118 | 1667 | 35 | 47.62 | 5-63 | 1 | - |
| ALL FIRST-CLASS | 546.4 | 118 | 1667 | 35 | 47.62 | 5-63 | 1 | - |
| Refuge Assurance | 97 | 7 | 444 | 18 | 24.66 | 3-15 | - | |
| NatWest Trophy | 40.2 | 5 | 158 | 3 | 52.66 | 1-27 | - | |
| Benson & Hedges Cup | 41 | 4 | 151 | 4 | 37.75 | 2-23 | - | |
| Other One-Day | 10 | 1 | 48 | 1 | 48.00 | 1-48 | - | |
| ALL ONE-DAY | 188.2 | 17 | 801 | 26 | 30.80 | 3-15 | - | |

# PLAYER RECORDS N

## P.A.NEALE - *Worcestershire*

| Opposition | Venue | Date | Batting | | | Fielding | Bowling |
|---|---|---|---|---|---|---|---|
| **BRITANNIC ASSURANCE** | | | | | | | |
| Gloucs | Worcester | April 27 | 29 | | | | |
| Lancashire | Worcester | May 9 | 4 | & | 11 | 2Ct | |
| Glamorgan | Worcester | May 31 | 12 | & | 7 | | |
| Northants | Northampton | June 4 | 7 | & | 4* | | |
| Essex | Ilford | June 7 | 28 | | | | |
| Sussex | Hove | June 14 | 28 | | | | |
| Notts | Worcester | June 18 | 46* | & | 18 | | 1-81 |
| Leicestershire | Worcester | June 28 | 69* | & | 0* | 1Ct | 0-5 |
| Yorkshire | Headingley | July 2 | 10 | | | | |
| Hampshire | Portsmouth | July 16 | 15 | & | 49 | | |
| Derbyshire | Kidd'minster | July 19 | 0 | & | 42 | | |
| Kent | Worcester | July 23 | | | | | |
| Gloucs | Cheltenham | July 26 | 0 | & | 6 | 2Ct | |
| **OTHER FIRST-CLASS** | | | | | | | |
| West Indies | Worcester | May 15 | 34 | | | | |
| **REFUGE ASSURANCE** | | | | | | | |
| Kent | Worcester | April 21 | 5* | | | 1Ct | |
| Gloucs | Bristol | May 5 | | | | | |
| Lancashire | Worcester | May 12 | 39 | | | | |
| Northants | Northampton | May 19 | 19* | | | 1Ct | |
| Surrey | Worcester | June 2 | 5 | | | | |
| Essex | Ilford | June 9 | 39 | | | | |
| Sussex | Hove | June 16 | | | | 1Ct | |
| Yorkshire | Sheffield | June 23 | 2 | | | | |
| Leicestershire | Worcester | June 30 | 18* | | | | |
| Hampshire | Southampton | July 7 | 12* | | | | |
| Derbyshire | Worcester | July 9 | | | | | |
| **NATWEST TROPHY** | | | | | | | |
| Bedfordshire | Bedford | June 26 | | | | | |
| Glamorgan | Worcester | July 11 | 8 | | | | |
| **BENSON & HEDGES CUP** | | | | | | | |
| Gloucs | Worcester | April 25 | 48* | | | | |
| Combined U | Fenner's | May 2 | 8* | | | | |
| Derbyshire | Worcester | May 4 | | | | | |
| Northants | Northampton | May 7 | 52* | | | | |
| Kent | Worcester | May 29 | 47 | | | 3Ct | |
| Essex | Chelmsford | June 12 | | | | 1Ct | |
| Lancashire | Lord's | July 13 | 4 | | | 2Ct | |

**BATTING AVERAGES - Including fielding**

| | Matches | Inns | NO | Runs | HS | Avge | 100s | 50s | Ct | St |
|---|---|---|---|---|---|---|---|---|---|---|
| Britannic Assurance | 13 | 20 | 4 | 385 | 69* | 24.06 | - | 1 | 5 | - |
| Other First-Class | 1 | 1 | 0 | 34 | 34 | 34.00 | - | - | - | - |
| **ALL FIRST-CLASS** | 14 | 21 | 4 | 419 | 69* | 24.64 | - | 1 | 5 | - |
| Refuge Assurance | 11 | 8 | 4 | 139 | 39 | 34.75 | - | - | 3 | - |
| NatWest Trophy | 2 | 1 | 0 | 8 | 8 | 8.00 | - | - | - | - |
| Benson & Hedges Cup | 7 | 5 | 3 | 159 | 52* | 79.50 | - | 1 | 6 | - |
| **ALL ONE-DAY** | 20 | 14 | 7 | 306 | 52* | 43.71 | - | 1 | 9 | - |

**BOWLING AVERAGES**

| | Overs | Mdns | Runs | Wkts | Avge | Best | 5wI | 10wM |
|---|---|---|---|---|---|---|---|---|
| Britannic Assurance | 17.5 | 1 | 86 | 1 | 86.00 | 1-81 | - | - |
| Other First-Class | | | | | | | | |
| **ALL FIRST-CLASS** | 17.5 | 1 | 86 | 1 | 86.00 | 1-81 | - | - |
| Refuge Assurance | | | | | | | | |
| NatWest Trophy | | | | | | | | |
| Benson & Hedges Cup | | | | | | | | |
| **ALL ONE-DAY** | | | | | | | | |

## A.NEEDHAM - *Hertfordshire*

| Opposition | Venue | Date | Batting | Fielding | Bowling |
|---|---|---|---|---|---|
| **NATWEST TROPHY** | | | | | |
| Warwickshire | Edgbaston | July 11 | 4 | | 0-25 |

---

**BATTING AVERAGES - Including fielding**

| | Matches | Inns | NO | Runs | HS | Avge | 100s | 50s | Ct | St |
|---|---|---|---|---|---|---|---|---|---|---|
| NatWest Trophy | 1 | 1 | 0 | 4 | 4 | 4.00 | - | - | - | - |
| **ALL ONE-DAY** | 1 | 1 | 0 | 4 | 4 | 4.00 | - | - | - | - |

**BOWLING AVERAGES**

| | Overs | Mdns | Runs | Wkts | Avge | Best | 5wI | 10wM |
|---|---|---|---|---|---|---|---|---|
| NatWest Trophy | 12 | 4 | 25 | 0 | | - | - | - |
| **ALL ONE-DAY** | 12 | 4 | 25 | 0 | | - | - | - |

## A.N.NELSON - *Ireland*

| Opposition | Venue | Date | Batting | Fielding | Bowling |
|---|---|---|---|---|---|
| **OTHER FIRST-CLASS** | | | | | |
| Scotland | Dublin | June 22 | | 1Ct | 0-49 & 4-30 |
| **NATWEST TROPHY** | | | | | |
| Middlesex | Dublin | June 26 | 8* | | 1-39 |
| **OTHER ONE-DAY** | | | | | |
| West Indies | Downpatrick | July 13 | | | 0-73 |

**BATTING AVERAGES - Including fielding**

| | Matches | Inns | NO | Runs | HS | Avge | 100s | 50s | Ct | St |
|---|---|---|---|---|---|---|---|---|---|---|
| Other First-Class | 1 | 0 | 0 | 0 | 0 | | - | - | 1 | - |
| **ALL FIRST-CLASS** | 1 | 0 | 0 | 0 | 0 | | - | - | 1 | - |
| NatWest Trophy | 1 | 1 | 1 | 8 | 8* | | - | - | - | - |
| Other One-Day | 1 | 0 | 0 | 0 | 0 | | - | - | - | - |
| **ALL ONE-DAY** | 2 | 1 | 1 | 8 | 8* | | - | - | - | - |

**BOWLING AVERAGES**

| | Overs | Mdns | Runs | Wkts | Avge | Best | 5wI | 10wM |
|---|---|---|---|---|---|---|---|---|
| Other First-Class | 27 | 6 | 79 | 4 | 19.75 | 4-30 | - | - |
| **ALL FIRST-CLASS** | 27 | 6 | 79 | 4 | 19.75 | 4-30 | - | - |
| NatWest Trophy | 11 | 3 | 39 | 1 | 39.00 | 1-39 | - | |
| Other One-Day | 14 | 2 | 73 | 0 | | - | | |
| **ALL ONE-DAY** | 25 | 5 | 112 | 1 | 112.00 | 1-39 | - | |

## M.NEWELL - *Nottinghamshire*

| Opposition | Venue | Date | Batting | Fielding | Bowling |
|---|---|---|---|---|---|
| **OTHER FIRST-CLASS** | | | | | |
| Oxford U | The Parks | April 27 | 91 | | |
| **REFUGE ASSURANCE** | | | | | |
| Northants | Well'borough | July 21 | 12 | | |
| **BENSON & HEDGES CUP** | | | | | |
| Hampshire | Southampton | April 23 | 18 | | |

**BATTING AVERAGES - Including fielding**

| | Matches | Inns | NO | Runs | HS | Avge | 100s | 50s | Ct | St |
|---|---|---|---|---|---|---|---|---|---|---|
| Other First-Class | 1 | 1 | 0 | 91 | 91 | 91.00 | - | 1 | - | - |
| **ALL FIRST-CLASS** | 1 | 1 | 0 | 91 | 91 | 91.00 | - | 1 | - | - |
| Refuge Assurance | 1 | 1 | 0 | 12 | 12 | 12.00 | - | - | - | - |
| Benson & Hedges Cup | 1 | 1 | 0 | 18 | 18 | 18.00 | - | - | - | - |
| **ALL ONE-DAY** | 2 | 2 | 0 | 30 | 18 | 15.00 | - | - | - | - |

**BOWLING AVERAGES**
Did not bowl

# N    PLAYER RECORDS

## P.G.NEWMAN - *Staffordshire*

| Opposition | Venue | Date | Batting | Fielding | Bowling |
|---|---|---|---|---|---|
| **NATWEST TROPHY** | | | | | |
| Northants | Stone | June 26 | 28 | | 1-29 |

**BATTING AVERAGES - Including fielding**

| | Matches | Inns | NO | Runs | HS | Avge | 100s | 50s | Ct | St |
|---|---|---|---|---|---|---|---|---|---|---|
| NatWest Trophy | 1 | 1 | 0 | 28 | 28 | 28.00 | - | - | - | - |
| ALL ONE-DAY | 1 | 1 | 0 | 28 | 28 | 28.00 | - | - | - | - |

**BOWLING AVERAGES**

| | Overs | Mdns | Runs | Wkts | Avge | Best | 5wI | 10wM |
|---|---|---|---|---|---|---|---|---|
| NatWest Trophy | 12 | 3 | 29 | 1 | 29.00 | 1-29 | - | |
| ALL ONE-DAY | 12 | 3 | 29 | 1 | 29.00 | 1-29 | - | |

## P.J.NEWPORT - *Worcestershire*

| Opposition | Venue | Date | Batting | | Fielding | Bowling |
|---|---|---|---|---|---|---|
| **BRITANNIC ASSURANCE** | | | | | | |
| Gloucs | Worcester | April 27 | | | | 1-85 |
| Lancashire | Worcester | May 9 | 5 & | 3 | | 0-106 & 4-58 |
| Glamorgan | Worcester | May 31 | 16 & | 2 * | | 2-32 & 0-31 |
| Northants | Northampton | June 4 | 15 | | 1Ct | 2-49 & 1-77 |
| Essex | Ilford | June 7 | 12 | | | 2-76 & 0-16 |
| Sussex | Hove | June 14 | | | | 0-18 & 3-32 |
| Notts | Worcester | June 18 | | 48 | | 0-79 |
| Leicestershire | Worcester | June 28 | | | | 4-70 & 0-48 |
| Yorkshire | Headingley | July 2 | | 44 | | 3-76 |
| Hampshire | Portsmouth | July 16 | 12 | | 1Ct | 1-60 |
| Derbyshire | Kidd'minster | July 19 | 6 & | 18 * | | 2-80 |
| Kent | Worcester | July 23 | | | | |
| Gloucs | Cheltenham | July 26 | 48 & | 24 * | | 1-44 & 0-24 |
| Warwickshire | Worcester | Aug 2 | 26 * | | | 3-59 & 1-26 |
| Somerset | Weston | Aug 6 | | 8 * | | 2-90 & 0-25 |
| Surrey | Worcester | Aug 16 | 2 * | | 1Ct | 0-30 & 1-64 |
| Lancashire | Blackpool | Aug 20 | 22 * | | | 0-32 & 0-19 |
| Middlesex | Worcester | Aug 23 | 4 | | | 1-35 & 4-51 |
| Warwickshire | Edgbaston | Aug 28 | 12 & | 0 * | | 3-36 & 3-51 |
| Somerset | Worcester | Sept 3 | 1 * | | | 2-40 & 2-67 |
| Glamorgan | Cardiff | Sept 10 | 0 | | 1Ct | 4-44 & 0-27 |
| Notts | Trent Bridge | Sept 17 | 8 & | 4 | | 2-83 |
| **OTHER FIRST-CLASS** | | | | | | |
| West Indies | Worcester | May 15 | 0 | | | 2-110 & 0-20 |
| Oxford U | The Parks | May 25 | 13 | | | 4-27 & 1-43 |
| Sri Lanka | Worcester | July 30 | | | | 3-51 & 2-49 |
| **REFUGE ASSURANCE** | | | | | | |
| Gloucs | Bristol | May 5 | | | | 1-47 |
| Lancashire | Worcester | May 12 | 11 * | | | 0-32 |
| Warwickshire | Edgbaston | May 26 | 0 | | 1Ct | 1-25 |
| Surrey | Worcester | June 2 | | | | 0-27 |
| Essex | Ilford | June 9 | 3 * | | 1Ct | 0-28 |
| Sussex | Hove | June 16 | | | | 0-70 |
| Yorkshire | Sheffield | June 23 | 17 * | | | 1-29 |
| Leicestershire | Worcester | June 30 | | | | 1-37 |
| Hampshire | Southampton | July 7 | | | 1Ct | 2-53 |
| Derbyshire | Worcester | July 9 | | | 2Ct | 0-23 |
| Glamorgan | Worcester | July 21 | | | | 2-43 |
| Notts | Trent Bridge | Aug 4 | | | | 1-38 |
| Somerset | Worcester | Aug 18 | | | | 1-18 |
| Middlesex | Worcester | Aug 25 | | | | 0-24 |
| Notts | Trent Bridge | Sept 1 | | | | 0-52 |
| Lancashire | Old Trafford | Sept 15 | | | 2Ct | 0-30 |
| **NATWEST TROPHY** | | | | | | |
| Bedfordshire | Bedford | June 26 | | | | |
| **BENSON & HEDGES CUP** | | | | | | |
| Gloucs | Worcester | April 25 | | | 1Ct | 1-30 |
| Combined U | Fenner's | May 2 | | | | 2-36 |
| Derbyshire | Worcester | May 4 | | | 1Ct | 1-36 |
| Northants | Northampton | May 7 | | | 2Ct | 0-64 |
| Kent | Worcester | May 29 | | | | 1-38 |
| Lancashire | Lord's | July 13 | 2 | | | 2-38 |

---

### OTHER ONE-DAY
For World XI

| Yorkshire | Scarborough | Sept 8 | 5 * | | 3-39 |
|---|---|---|---|---|---|

**BATTING AVERAGES - Including fielding**

| | Matches | Inns | NO | Runs | HS | Avge | 100s | 50s | Ct | St |
|---|---|---|---|---|---|---|---|---|---|---|
| Britannic Assurance | 22 | 24 | 9 | 340 | 48 | 22.66 | - | - | 4 | - |
| Other First-Class | 3 | 2 | 0 | 13 | 13 | 6.50 | - | - | - | - |
| ALL FIRST-CLASS | 25 | 26 | 9 | 353 | 48 | 20.76 | - | - | 4 | - |
| Refuge Assurance | 16 | 4 | 3 | 31 | 17 * | 31.00 | - | - | 7 | - |
| NatWest Trophy | 1 | 0 | 0 | 0 | 0 | | - | - | - | - |
| Benson & Hedges Cup | 6 | 1 | 0 | 2 | 2 | 2.00 | - | - | 4 | - |
| Other One-Day | 1 | 1 | 1 | 5 | 5 * | | - | - | - | - |
| ALL ONE-DAY | 24 | 6 | 4 | 38 | 17 * | 19.00 | - | - | 11 | - |

**BOWLING AVERAGES**

| | Overs | Mdns | Runs | Wkts | Avge | Best | 5wI | 10wM |
|---|---|---|---|---|---|---|---|---|
| Britannic Assurance | 609.4 | 115 | 1840 | 54 | 34.07 | 4-44 | - | |
| Other First-Class | 103 | 23 | 300 | 12 | 25.00 | 4-27 | - | |
| ALL FIRST-CLASS | 712.4 | 138 | 2140 | 66 | 32.42 | 4-27 | - | |
| Refuge Assurance | 106.2 | 1 | 576 | 10 | 57.60 | 2-43 | | |
| NatWest Trophy | | | | | | | | |
| Benson & Hedges Cup | 66 | 5 | 242 | 7 | 34.57 | 2-36 | | |
| Other One-Day | 9 | 1 | 39 | 3 | 13.00 | 3-39 | | |
| ALL ONE-DAY | 181.2 | 7 | 857 | 20 | 42.85 | 3-39 | - | |

## M.C.J.NICHOLAS - *Hampshire*

| Opposition | Venue | Date | Batting | | Fielding | Bowling |
|---|---|---|---|---|---|---|
| **BRITANNIC ASSURANCE** | | | | | | |
| Kent | Southampton | April 27 | 5 * | | 1Ct | 1-38 |
| Gloucs | Bristol | May 9 | 9 & | 31 | | 0-15 & 0-12 |
| Sussex | Hove | May 16 | 23 | | | 0-40 & 0-5 |
| Surrey | Bournemouth | May 25 | 0 & | 14 | 1Ct | |
| Notts | Trent Bridge | May 31 | 107 *& | 29 | | 0-47 |
| Lancashire | Basingstoke | June 4 | 14 *& | 19 | 1Ct | 0-21 & 0-13 |
| Somerset | Bath | June 18 | 23 & | 28 | | 3-25 |
| Northants | Northampton | June 21 | 1 | | | |
| Essex | Chelmsford | July 2 | 1 & | 0 | | |
| Yorkshire | Southampton | July 5 | 16 | | | |
| Worcestershire | Portsmouth | July 16 | 9 | | 1Ct | |
| Warwickshire | Portsmouth | July 19 | 0 & | 5 | 1Ct | |
| Derbyshire | Chesterfield | July 23 | 2 | | 1Ct | |
| Middlesex | Lord's | Aug 2 | 4 & | 0 | | |
| Kent | Canterbury | Aug 6 | 33 & | 15 | 1Ct | 0-18 |
| Glamorgan | Swansea | Aug 9 | 4 & | 50 * | | |
| Leicestershire | Bournemouth | Aug 16 | 73 *& | 19 | 1Ct | 0-36 |
| Sussex | Bournemouth | Aug 20 | 55 & | 10 * | | |
| Somerset | Southampton | Aug 28 | 27 *& | 90 * | | 0-18 |
| Surrey | The Oval | Sept 3 | 4 & | 13 * | | |
| **OTHER FIRST-CLASS** | | | | | | |
| Oxford U | The Parks | April 13 | 7 | | 1Ct | |
| West Indies | Southampton | June 29 | 37 & | 59 * | 1Ct | |
| **REFUGE ASSURANCE** | | | | | | |
| Yorkshire | Southampton | April 21 | 22 * | | | |
| Derbyshire | Derby | May 5 | 23 | | | |
| Kent | Southampton | May 12 | 43 | | | |
| Somerset | Bournemouth | May 19 | 43 | | | |
| Gloucs | Swindon | May 26 | 45 | | | 0-42 |
| Northants | Northampton | June 2 | 1 | | 1Ct | |
| Sussex | Basingstoke | June 9 | 23 | | | |
| Essex | Chelmsford | June 16 | | | | |
| Worcestershire | Southampton | July 7 | 2 | | 1Ct | |
| Notts | Trent Bridge | July 14 | 32 | | | |
| Warwickshire | Portsmouth | July 21 | 4 | | | |
| Lancashire | Southampton | July 28 | 65 * | | 1Ct | |
| Middlesex | Lord's | Aug 4 | 50 * | | | |
| Glamorgan | Ebbw Vale | Aug 11 | 29 | | | |
| Leicestershire | Bournemouth | Aug 18 | 56 | | 1Ct | |
| Surrey | The Oval | Aug 25 | 24 * | | | |
| **NATWEST TROPHY** | | | | | | |
| Berkshire | Reading | June 26 | | | | 0-9 |

# PLANNER RECORDS

## PLAYER RECORDS — N

| | | | | | |
|---|---|---|---|---|---|
| Lancashire | Southampton | July 11 | | | |
| Notts | Southampton | July 31 | 24 * | 1Ct | |
| Warwickshire | Edgbaston | Aug 14 | | 1Ct | |

**BENSON & HEDGES CUP**

| | | | | | |
|---|---|---|---|---|---|
| Notts | Southampton | April 23 | 50 | | |
| Min Counties | Trowbridge | April 25 | . | | |
| Glamorgan | Southampton | May 2 | 15 * | | 2-27 |
| Yorkshire | Headingley | May 4 | 0 | | |
| Essex | Chelmsford | May 29 | 22 * | | |

**BATTING AVERAGES - Including fielding**

| | Matches | Inns | NO | Runs | HS | Avge | 100s | 50s | Ct | St |
|---|---|---|---|---|---|---|---|---|---|---|
| Britannic Assurance | 20 | 34 | 9 | 723 | 107 * | 28.92 | 1 | 4 | 8 | - |
| Other First-Class | 2 | 3 | 1 | 103 | 59 * | 51.50 | - | 1 | 2 | - |
| ALL FIRST-CLASS | 22 | 37 | 10 | 826 | 107 * | 30.59 | 1 | 5 | 10 | - |
| Refuge Assurance | 16 | 15 | 4 | 462 | 65 * | 42.00 | - | 3 | 4 | - |
| NatWest Trophy | 4 | 1 | 1 | 24 | 24 * | - | - | - | 2 | - |
| Benson & Hedges Cup | 5 | 4 | 2 | 87 | 50 | 43.50 | - | 1 | - | - |
| ALL ONE-DAY | 25 | 20 | 7 | 573 | 65 * | 44.07 | - | 4 | 6 | - |

**BOWLING AVERAGES**

| | Overs | Mdns | Runs | Wkts | Avge | Best | 5wI | 10wM |
|---|---|---|---|---|---|---|---|---|
| Britannic Assurance | 67.5 | 6 | 288 | 4 | 72.00 | 3-25 | - | - |
| Other First-Class | | | | | | | | |
| ALL FIRST-CLASS | 67.5 | 6 | 288 | 4 | 72.00 | 3-25 | - | - |
| Refuge Assurance | 5 | 0 | 42 | 0 | - | - | - | |
| NatWest Trophy | 2 | 0 | 9 | 0 | - | - | - | |
| Benson & Hedges Cup | 4 | 0 | 27 | 2 | 13.50 | 2-27 | - | |
| ALL ONE-DAY | 11 | 0 | 78 | 2 | 39.00 | 2-27 | - | - |

# N.G.NICHOLSON - *Durham*

| Opposition | Venue | Date | Batting | Fielding | Bowling |
|---|---|---|---|---|---|
| **OTHER ONE-DAY** | | | | | |
| Leicestershire | Harrogate | June 11 | 16 | | |
| Surrey | Harrogate | June 13 | 0 | | |

**BATTING AVERAGES - Including fielding**

| | Matches | Inns | NO | Runs | HS | Avge | 100s | 50s | Ct | St |
|---|---|---|---|---|---|---|---|---|---|---|
| Other One-Day | 2 | 2 | 0 | 16 | 16 | 8.00 | - | - | - | - |
| ALL ONE-DAY | 2 | 2 | 0 | 16 | 16 | 8.00 | - | - | - | - |

**BOWLING AVERAGES**
Did not bowl

# P.A.NIXON - *Leicestershire*

| Opposition | Venue | Date | Batting | Fielding | Bowling |
|---|---|---|---|---|---|
| **BRITANNIC ASSURANCE** | | | | | |
| Worcestershire | Worcester | June 28 | | 1Ct | |
| Gloucs | Hinckley | July 2 | 31 | 1Ct,1St | |
| Northants | Leicester | July 5 | 5 & 9 | 4Ct | |
| **OTHER FIRST-CLASS** | | | | | |
| West Indies | Leicester | June 1 | 9 * | 2Ct | |
| **REFUGE ASSURANCE** | | | | | |
| Worcestershire | Worcester | June 30 | 17 | | |
| Sussex | Hove | July 21 | 5 | 3Ct | |

**BATTING AVERAGES - Including fielding**

| | Matches | Inns | NO | Runs | HS | Avge | 100s | 50s | Ct | St |
|---|---|---|---|---|---|---|---|---|---|---|
| Britannic Assurance | 3 | 3 | 0 | 45 | 31 | 15.00 | - | - | 6 | 1 |
| Other First-Class | 1 | 1 | 1 | 9 | 9 * | - | - | - | 2 | - |
| ALL FIRST-CLASS | 4 | 4 | 1 | 54 | 31 | 18.00 | - | - | 8 | 1 |
| Refuge Assurance | 2 | 2 | 0 | 22 | 17 | 11.00 | - | - | 3 | - |

| ALL ONE-DAY | 2 | 2 | 0 | 22 | 17 | 11.00 | - | - | 3 | - |

**BOWLING AVERAGES**
Did not bowl

# W.M.NOON - *Northamptonshire*

| Opposition | Venue | Date | Batting | Fielding | Bowling |
|---|---|---|---|---|---|
| **BRITANNIC ASSURANCE** | | | | | |
| Glamorgan | Cardiff | May 22 | 10 & 0 | | |
| Yorkshire | Headingley | May 25 | 0 | | |
| Surrey | Northampton | Aug 23 | 8 * & 14 | 2Ct | |
| Yorkshire | Northampton | Aug 28 | 10 * | 2Ct | |
| Gloucs | Bristol | Sept 3 | 36 | 3Ct | |
| Warwickshire | Edgbaston | Sept 10 | 5 & 13 | 4Ct | |
| **REFUGE ASSURANCE** | | | | | |
| Yorkshire | Headingley | May 26 | 8 * | | |
| Notts | Well'borough | July 21 | 4 | 1Ct | |
| Warwickshire | Northampton | Aug 25 | | 2Ct,1St | |
| Lancashire | Old Trafford | Sept 1 | | | |

**BATTING AVERAGES - Including fielding**

| | Matches | Inns | NO | Runs | HS | Avge | 100s | 50s | Ct | St |
|---|---|---|---|---|---|---|---|---|---|---|
| Britannic Assurance | 6 | 9 | 2 | 96 | 36 | 13.71 | - | - | 11 | - |
| ALL FIRST-CLASS | 6 | 9 | 2 | 96 | 36 | 13.71 | - | - | 11 | - |
| Refuge Assurance | 4 | 2 | 1 | 12 | 8 * | 12.00 | - | - | 3 | 1 |
| ALL ONE-DAY | 4 | 2 | 1 | 12 | 8 * | 12.00 | - | - | 3 | 1 |

**BOWLING AVERAGES**
Did not bowl

# N.P.NORMAN - *Cambridgeshire*

| Opposition | Venue | Date | Batting | Fielding | Bowling |
|---|---|---|---|---|---|
| **NATWEST TROPHY** | | | | | |
| Kent | Canterbury | June 26 | 2 | | |

**BATTING AVERAGES - Including fielding**

| | Matches | Inns | NO | Runs | HS | Avge | 100s | 50s | Ct | St |
|---|---|---|---|---|---|---|---|---|---|---|
| NatWest Trophy | 1 | 1 | 0 | 2 | 2 | 2.00 | - | - | - | - |
| ALL ONE-DAY | 1 | 1 | 0 | 2 | 2 | 2.00 | - | - | - | - |

**BOWLING AVERAGES**
Did not bowl

# J.A.NORTH - *Sussex*

| Opposition | Venue | Date | Batting | Fielding | Bowling |
|---|---|---|---|---|---|
| **BRITANNIC ASSURANCE** | | | | | |
| Somerset | Taunton | April 27 | 15 | | 3-54 |
| Middlesex | Lord's | May 9 | 0 | | 3-65 & 2-55 |
| Hampshire | Hove | May 16 | 63 * & 22 | 1Ct | 2-114 & 0-39 |
| Hampshire | Bournemouth | Aug 20 | 22 | | 1-55 & 1-18 |
| Surrey | The Oval | Aug 28 | 0 & 0 | | 2-107 |
| **OTHER FIRST-CLASS** | | | | | |
| Cambridge U | Hove | June 29 | | | |
| Sri Lanka | Hove | Aug 17 | 41 | | 2-43 & 4-47 |
| **REFUGE ASSURANCE** | | | | | |
| Warwickshire | Edgbaston | April 21 | 1 * | 1Ct | 0-12 |
| Somerset | Taunton | April 28 | 5 | | 2-39 |
| Gloucs | Hove | May 19 | 14 | 1Ct | 0-44 |
| Northants | Eastbourne | Aug 4 | 18 | | |
| Yorkshire | Midd'brough | Aug 11 | 6 | 2Ct | 3-38 |
| Kent | Hove | Aug 25 | 6 | 1Ct | 3-29 |

## N PLAYER RECORDS

### BENSON & HEDGES CUP

| | | | | |
|---|---|---|---|---|
| Leicestershire | Hove | April 25 | | 1-41 |
| Kent | Canterbury | May 2 | 13 | 1-30 |
| Scotland | Hove | May 4 | 22 | 0-57 |
| Lancashire | Old Trafford | May 7 | 9 | 2-80 |

### BATTING AVERAGES - Including fielding

| | Matches | Inns | NO | Runs | HS | Avge | 100s | 50s | Ct | St |
|---|---|---|---|---|---|---|---|---|---|---|
| Britannic Assurance | 5 | 7 | 1 | 122 | 63* | 20.33 | - | 1 | 1 | - |
| Other First-Class | 2 | 1 | 0 | 41 | 41 | 41.00 | - | - | - | - |
| ALL FIRST-CLASS | 7 | 8 | 1 | 163 | 63* | 23.28 | - | 1 | 1 | - |
| Refuge Assurance | 6 | 6 | 1 | 50 | 18 | 10.00 | - | - | 5 | - |
| Benson & Hedges Cup | 4 | 3 | 0 | 44 | 22 | 14.66 | - | - | - | - |
| ALL ONE-DAY | 10 | 9 | 1 | 94 | 22 | 11.75 | - | - | 5 | - |

### BOWLING AVERAGES

| | Overs | Mdns | Runs | Wkts | Avge | Best | 5wI | 10wM |
|---|---|---|---|---|---|---|---|---|
| Britannic Assurance | 129 | 20 | 507 | 14 | 36.21 | 3-54 | - | - |
| Other First-Class | 27.3 | 6 | 90 | 6 | 15.00 | 4-47 | - | - |
| ALL FIRST-CLASS | 156.3 | 26 | 597 | 20 | 29.85 | 4-47 | - | - |
| Refuge Assurance | 27 | 1 | 162 | 8 | 20.25 | 3-29 | - | |
| Benson & Hedges Cup | 41 | 1 | 208 | 4 | 52.00 | 2-80 | - | |
| ALL ONE-DAY | 68 | 2 | 370 | 12 | 30.83 | 3-29 | - | |

# PLAYER RECORDS O

## S.P.O'DONNELL - *Victoria*

| Opposition | Venue | Date | Batting | | | Fielding | Bowling |
|---|---|---|---|---|---|---|---|
| **OTHER FIRST-CLASS** | | | | | | | |
| Essex | Chelmsford | Sept 23 | 12 | & | 5 | | 1-47 |
| **OTHER ONE-DAY** | | | | | | | |
| Durham | Durham U. | Sept 16 | 14* | | | 1Ct | 0-37 |
| Essex | Chelmsford | Sept 22 | 71* | | | | 0-39 |

**BATTING AVERAGES - Including fielding**

| | Matches | Inns | NO | Runs | HS | Avge | 100s | 50s | Ct | St |
|---|---|---|---|---|---|---|---|---|---|---|
| Other First-Class | 1 | 2 | 0 | 17 | 12 | 8.50 | - | - | - | - |
| ALL FIRST-CLASS | 1 | 2 | 0 | 17 | 12 | 8.50 | - | - | - | - |
| Other One-Day | 2 | 2 | 2 | 85 | 71* | - | - | 1 | 1 | - |
| ALL ONE-DAY | 2 | 2 | 2 | 85 | 71* | - | - | 1 | 1 | - |

**BOWLING AVERAGES**

| | Overs | Mdns | Runs | Wkts | Avge | Best | 5wI | 10wM |
|---|---|---|---|---|---|---|---|---|
| Other First-Class | 13 | 6 | 47 | 1 | 47.00 | 1-47 | - | - |
| ALL FIRST-CLASS | 13 | 6 | 47 | 1 | 47.00 | 1-47 | - | - |
| Other One-Day | 13 | 0 | 76 | 0 | - | - | - | - |
| ALL ONE-DAY | 13 | 0 | 76 | 0 | - | - | - | - |

## T.J.G.O'GORMAN - *Derbyshire*

| Opposition | Venue | Date | Batting | | | Fielding | Bowling |
|---|---|---|---|---|---|---|---|
| **BRITANNIC ASSURANCE** | | | | | | | |
| Northants | Derby | April 27 | | | | | |
| Lancashire | Old Trafford | May 16 | 148 | | | 1Ct | |
| Somerset | Derby | May 22 | 23 | & | 7 | 1Ct | |
| Kent | Canterbury | May 25 | 36 | & | 7 | 1Ct | |
| Northants | Northampton | May 31 | 4 | & | 14 | 1Ct | |
| Glamorgan | Chesterfield | June 7 | 15 | & | 2* | 2Ct | |
| Gloucs | Gloucester | June 18 | 73 | & | 3 | | |
| Surrey | Derby | June 21 | 2 | & | 38 | 2Ct | 1-17 |
| Warwickshire | Edgbaston | June 28 | 5 | & | 37 | 2Ct | |
| Sussex | Derby | July 5 | 32 | & | 19 | 1Ct | |
| Yorkshire | Scarborough | July 16 | 0 | & | 0 | 1Ct | |
| Worcestershire | Kidd'minster | July 19 | 78 | | | 2Ct | |
| Hampshire | Chesterfield | July 23 | | | 42 | | |
| Essex | Derby | Aug 6 | 25 | & | 28 | 2Ct | |
| Middlesex | Lord's | Aug 9 | 16 | & | 38 | | |
| Lancashire | Derby | Aug 16 | 2 | & | 24 | 1Ct | 0-42 |
| Leicestershire | Derby | Aug 20 | 6 | & | 13 | 2Ct | |
| Notts | Trent Bridge | Aug 23 | 51* | & | 0 | | |
| Leicestershire | Leicester | Aug 28 | 0 | & | 33 | | |
| Essex | Chelmsford | Sept 3 | 7 | & | 16 | 1Ct | |
| Notts | Derby | Sept 10 | 34* | & | 108* | 1Ct | |
| Yorkshire | Chesterfield | Sept 17 | 0 | & | 74 | | |
| **OTHER FIRST-CLASS** | | | | | | | |
| Cambridge U | Fenner's | May 9 | 14 | & | 14 | | |
| West Indies | Derby | June 12 | 4 | & | 23 | | |
| Sri Lanka | Derby | Aug 2 | 1 | | | | |
| **REFUGE ASSURANCE** | | | | | | | |
| Leicestershire | Leicester | April 21 | 10* | | | | |
| Hampshire | Derby | May 5 | 22 | | | | |
| Lancashire | Derby | May 19 | 5 | | | | |
| Kent | Canterbury | May 26 | 41 | | | | |
| Yorkshire | Chesterfield | June 2 | | | | 1Ct | |
| Surrey | Chesterfield | June 9 | 49* | | | | |
| Somerset | Derby | June 16 | 31 | | | | |
| Essex | Chelmsford | June 30 | 3 | | | | |
| Sussex | Derby | July 7 | 3 | | | | |
| Worcestershire | Worcester | July 9 | 4 | | | 1Ct | |
| Gloucs | Cheltenham | July 21 | 16 | | | 2Ct | |
| Northants | Derby | July 28 | 38 | | | 2Ct | |
| Warwickshire | Edgbaston | Aug 4 | 32 | | | | |
| Middlesex | Lord's | Aug 11 | 12 | | | | |
| Glamorgan | Checkley | Aug 18 | 11 | | | 1Ct | |

---

| | | | |
|---|---|---|---|
| Notts | Trent Bridge | Aug 25 | 16 |

| Opposition | Venue | Date | Batting | Fielding | Bowling |
|---|---|---|---|---|---|
| **BENSON & HEDGES CUP** | | | | | |
| Northants | Derby | April 23 | 49 | | |
| Combined U | The Parks | April 25 | | | 0-1 |
| Worcestershire | Worcester | May 4 | 6 | | |
| Gloucs | Derby | May 7 | 23* | 1Ct | |
| **OTHER ONE-DAY** | | | | | |
| For D of Norfolk | | | | | |
| West Indies | Arundel | May 12 | 13 | | |
| For Derbyshire | | | | | |
| Yorkshire | Scarborough | Sept 1 | 93 | | |

**BATTING AVERAGES - Including fielding**

| | Matches | Inns | NO | Runs | HS | Avge | 100s | 50s | Ct | St |
|---|---|---|---|---|---|---|---|---|---|---|
| Britannic Assurance | 22 | 39 | 4 | 1060 | 148 | 30.28 | 2 | 4 | 21 | - |
| Other First-Class | 3 | 5 | 0 | 56 | 23 | 11.20 | | | | |
| ALL FIRST-CLASS | 25 | 44 | 4 | 1116 | 148 | 27.90 | 2 | 4 | 21 | - |
| Refuge Assurance | 16 | 15 | 2 | 293 | 49* | 22.53 | - | - | 7 | - |
| Benson & Hedges Cup | 4 | 3 | 1 | 78 | 49 | 39.00 | - | - | 1 | - |
| Other One-Day | 2 | 2 | 0 | 106 | 93 | 53.00 | - | 1 | - | - |
| ALL ONE-DAY | 22 | 20 | 3 | 477 | 93 | 28.05 | - | 1 | 8 | - |

**BOWLING AVERAGES**

| | Overs | Mdns | Runs | Wkts | Avge | Best | 5wI | 10wM |
|---|---|---|---|---|---|---|---|---|
| Britannic Assurance | 15 | 0 | 59 | 1 | 59.00 | 1-17 | - | - |
| Other First-Class | | | | | | | | |
| ALL FIRST-CLASS | 15 | 0 | 59 | 1 | 59.00 | 1-17 | - | - |
| Refuge Assurance | | | | | | | | |
| Benson & Hedges Cup | 1 | 0 | 1 | 0 | - | - | - | - |
| Other One-Day | | | | | | | | |
| ALL ONE-DAY | 1 | 0 | 1 | 0 | - | - | - | - |

## M.W.C.OLLEY - *Cambridgeshire*

| Opposition | Venue | Date | Batting | Fielding | Bowling |
|---|---|---|---|---|---|
| **NATWEST TROPHY** | | | | | |
| Kent | Canterbury | June 26 | 20* | 1Ct | |

**BATTING AVERAGES - Including fielding**

| | Matches | Inns | NO | Runs | HS | Avge | 100s | 50s | Ct | St |
|---|---|---|---|---|---|---|---|---|---|---|
| NatWest Trophy | 1 | 1 | 1 | 20 | 20* | - | - | - | 1 | - |
| ALL ONE-DAY | 1 | 1 | 1 | 20 | 20* | - | - | - | 1 | - |

**BOWLING AVERAGES**
Did not bowl

## J.M.E.OPPENHEIMER - *Oxford University*

| Opposition | Venue | Date | Batting | Fielding | Bowling |
|---|---|---|---|---|---|
| **OTHER FIRST-CLASS** | | | | | |
| Notts | The Parks | April 27 | | | 1-75 |
| Gloucs | The Parks | June 15 | | | 0-33 |
| Lancashire | The Parks | June 7 | | | 0-35 & 2-85 |
| Kent | The Parks | June 18 | 0* | 1Ct | 2-51 & 1-47 |
| Cambridge U | Lord's | July 2 | | | 1-48 & 1-11 |

**BATTING AVERAGES - Including fielding**

| | Matches | Inns | NO | Runs | HS | Avge | 100s | 50s | Ct | St |
|---|---|---|---|---|---|---|---|---|---|---|
| Other First-Class | 5 | 1 | 1 | 0 | 0* | - | - | - | 1 | - |
| ALL FIRST-CLASS | 5 | 1 | 1 | 0 | 0* | - | - | - | 1 | - |

**BOWLING AVERAGES**

| | Overs | Mdns | Runs | Wkts | Avge | Best | 5wI | 10wM |
|---|---|---|---|---|---|---|---|---|
| Other First-Class | 107 | 18 | 385 | 8 | 48.12 | 2-51 | - | - |

# O          PLAYER RECORDS

| | | | | | | | | |
|---|---|---|---|---|---|---|---|---|
| ALL FIRST-CLASS | 107 | 18 | 385 | 8 | 48.12 | 2-51 | - | - |

## T.M.ORRELL - *Lancashire*

| Opposition | Venue | Date | Batting | Fielding | Bowling |
|---|---|---|---|---|---|
| **OTHER FIRST-CLASS** | | | | | |
| Oxford U | The Parks | June 7 | 5 & 16 | | |

**BATTING AVERAGES - Including fielding**

| | Matches | Inns | NO | Runs | HS | Avge | 100s | 50s | Ct | St |
|---|---|---|---|---|---|---|---|---|---|---|
| Other First-Class | 1 | 2 | 0 | 21 | 16 | 10.50 | - | - | - | - |
| ALL FIRST-CLASS | 1 | 2 | 0 | 21 | 16 | 10.50 | - | - | - | - |

**BOWLING AVERAGES**
Did not bowl

## D.P.OSTLER - *Warwickshire*

| Opposition | Venue | Date | Batting | Fielding | Bowling |
|---|---|---|---|---|---|
| **BRITANNIC ASSURANCE** | | | | | |
| Lancashire | Edgbaston | April 27 | 9 | 1Ct | |
| Yorkshire | Headingley | May 9 | 28 & 1 | | |
| Glamorgan | Swansea | May 16 | 10 & 12 * | | |
| Essex | Chelmsford | May 22 | 94 * & 7 | | |
| Gloucs | Edgbaston | May 25 | 42 & 6 * | | |
| Yorkshire | Edgbaston | May 31 | 77 & 7 | | |
| Kent | Tunbridge W | June 4 | 7 & 120 * | | |
| Somerset | Edgbaston | June 7 | 59 & 40 | | |
| Sussex | Coventry | June 18 | 9 | | |
| Notts | Trent Bridge | June 21 | 14 | | |
| Derbyshire | Edgbaston | June 28 | 9 & 0 | | |
| Middlesex | Edgbaston | July 2 | 17 & 48 * | 4Ct | |
| Hampshire | Portsmouth | July 19 | 20 & 12 | 3Ct | |
| Lancashire | Old Trafford | July 23 | 9 & 32 | | |
| Leicestershire | Leicester | July 26 | 65 | 2Ct | |
| Worcestershire | Worcester | Aug 2 | 55 & 0 | 2Ct | |
| Surrey | Edgbaston | Aug 6 | 27 & 25 | 3Ct | |
| Northants | Northampton | Aug 9 | 1 & 65 | 1Ct | 0-7 |
| Glamorgan | Edgbaston | Aug 20 | 35 & 56 | 1Ct | |
| Worcestershire | Edgbaston | Aug 28 | 7 & 41 | 1Ct | |
| Northants | Edgbaston | Sept 10 | 68 & 13 | | |
| Somerset | Taunton | Sept 17 | 79 & 58 | 3Ct | |
| **REFUGE ASSURANCE** | | | | | |
| Sussex | Edgbaston | April 21 | 15 | 1Ct | |
| Notts | Trent Bridge | April 28 | 16 | | |
| Yorkshire | Headingley | May 12 | 14 * | | |
| Glamorgan | Swansea | May 19 | 55 | 1Ct | |
| Worcestershire | Edgbaston | May 26 | 48 | | |
| Somerset | Edgbaston | June 2 | | | |
| Lancashire | Edgbaston | June 16 | 7 | | |
| Essex | Chelmsford | July 7 | 4 | | |
| Middlesex | Edgbaston | July 14 | | | |
| Hampshire | Portsmouth | July 21 | 4 | | |
| Derbyshire | Edgbaston | Aug 4 | 62 * | | |
| Leicestershire | Leicester | Aug 11 | 2 | | |
| Gloucs | Edgbaston | Aug 18 | | | |
| Northants | Northampton | Aug 25 | 26 | | |
| **NATWEST TROPHY** | | | | | |
| Yorkshire | Edgbaston | June 26 | 34 * | | |
| Hertfordshire | Edgbaston | July 11 | | | |
| Somerset | Edgbaston | July 31 | 10 | | |
| Hampshire | Edgbaston | Aug 14 | 3 | | |
| **BENSON & HEDGES CUP** | | | | | |
| Essex | Edgbaston | April 25 | 45 | | |
| Somerset | Edgbaston | May 2 | 12 | | |
| Middlesex | Lord's | May 4 | 7 | 1Ct | |
| Surrey | The Oval | May 7 | 28 | 1Ct | |
| Yorkshire | Headingley | May 29 | 8 | | |
| **OTHER ONE-DAY** | | | | | |
| Surrey | Harrogate | June 12 | 0 | | |

**BATTING AVERAGES - Including fielding**

| | Matches | Inns | NO | Runs | HS | Avge | 100s | 50s | Ct | St |
|---|---|---|---|---|---|---|---|---|---|---|
| Britannic Assurance | 22 | 40 | 5 | 1284 | 120 * | 36.68 | 1 | 10 | 21 | - |
| ALL FIRST-CLASS | 22 | 40 | 5 | 1284 | 120 * | 36.68 | 1 | 10 | 21 | - |
| Refuge Assurance | 14 | 11 | 2 | 253 | 62 * | 28.11 | - | 2 | 2 | - |
| NatWest Trophy | 4 | 3 | 1 | 47 | 34 * | 23.50 | - | - | - | - |
| Benson & Hedges Cup | 5 | 5 | 0 | 100 | 45 | 20.00 | - | - | 2 | - |
| Other One-Day | 1 | 1 | 0 | 0 | 0 | 0.00 | - | - | - | - |
| ALL ONE-DAY | 24 | 20 | 3 | 400 | 62 * | 23.52 | - | 2 | 4 | - |

**BOWLING AVERAGES**

| | Overs | Mdns | Runs | Wkts | Avge | Best | 5wI | 10wM |
|---|---|---|---|---|---|---|---|---|
| Britannic Assurance | 2 | 1 | 7 | 0 | - | - | - | - |
| ALL FIRST-CLASS | 2 | 1 | 7 | 0 | - | - | - | - |
| Refuge Assurance | | | | | | | | |
| NatWest Trophy | | | | | | | | |
| Benson & Hedges Cup | | | | | | | | |
| Other One-Day | | | | | | | | |
| ALL ONE-DAY | | | | | | | | |

## P.J.OXLEY - *Berkshire*

| Opposition | Venue | Date | Batting | Fielding | Bowling |
|---|---|---|---|---|---|
| **NATWEST TROPHY** | | | | | |
| Hampshire | Reading | June 26 | 18 | | |

**BATTING AVERAGES - Including fielding**

| | Matches | Inns | NO | Runs | HS | Avge | 100s | 50s | Ct | St |
|---|---|---|---|---|---|---|---|---|---|---|
| NatWest Trophy | 1 | 1 | 0 | 18 | 18 | 18.00 | - | - | - | - |
| ALL ONE-DAY | 1 | 1 | 0 | 18 | 18 | 18.00 | - | - | - | - |

**BOWLING AVERAGES**
Did not bowl

# PLAYER RECORDS

P

## G.R.PARKER - *Victoria*

| Opposition | Venue | Date | Batting | Fielding | Bowling |
|---|---|---|---|---|---|
| **OTHER FIRST-CLASS** | | | | | |
| Essex | Chelmsford | Sept 23 | 0 & 1 | | |
| **OTHER ONE-DAY** | | | | | |
| Durham | Durham U. | Sept 16 | | | |
| Essex | Chelmsford | Sept 22 | | | |

**BATTING AVERAGES - Including fielding**

| | Matches | Inns | NO | Runs | HS | Avge | 100s | 50s | Ct | St |
|---|---|---|---|---|---|---|---|---|---|---|
| Other First-Class | 1 | 2 | 0 | 1 | 1 | 0.50 | - | - | - | - |
| ALL FIRST-CLASS | 1 | 2 | 0 | 1 | 1 | 0.50 | - | - | - | - |
| Other One-Day | 2 | 0 | 0 | 0 | 0 | | - | - | - | - |
| ALL ONE-DAY | 2 | 0 | 0 | 0 | 0 | | - | - | - | - |

**BOWLING AVERAGES**
Did not bowl

## P.W.G.PARKER - *Sussex*

| Opposition | Venue | Date | Batting | Fielding | Bowling |
|---|---|---|---|---|---|
| **BRITANNIC ASSURANCE** | | | | | |
| Somerset | Taunton | April 27 | 11 | | |
| Glamorgan | Cardiff | May 25 | 95 & 9 | | |
| Lancashire | Old Trafford | May 31 | 11 & 17 | | |
| Kent | Tunbridge W | June 7 | 20 & 8 | 2Ct | |
| Worcestershire | Hove | June 14 | 56 * | | 0-10 |
| Warwickshire | Coventry | June 18 | 23 | 1Ct | |
| Essex | Horsham | June 21 | 2 | 1Ct | |
| Surrey | Arundel | July 2 | 26 & 4 | | |
| Derbyshire | Derby | July 5 | 7 & 20 | 1Ct | |
| Somerset | Hove | July 16 | 7 | 1Ct | |
| Leicestershire | Hove | July 19 | 33 & 55 | 1Ct | |
| Gloucs | Cheltenham | July 23 | 13 | | |
| Northants | Eastbourne | Aug 2 | 6 & 18 | | |
| Notts | Eastbourne | Aug 6 | 24 & 2 | | |
| Kent | Hove | Sept 3 | 2 & 111 | | |
| Gloucs | Hove | Sept 17 | 3 & 24 | 1Ct | |
| **REFUGE ASSURANCE** | | | | | |
| Somerset | Taunton | April 28 | 3 | 1Ct | |
| Middlesex | Hove | May 12 | 33 | | |
| Glamorgan | Swansea | May 26 | 32 | 2Ct | |
| Lancashire | Old Trafford | June 2 | 28 | | |
| Hampshire | Basingstoke | June 9 | 1 | | |
| Worcestershire | Hove | June 16 | 14 | | |
| Derbyshire | Derby | July 7 | 27 | | |
| Surrey | The Oval | July 14 | 60 | | |
| Leicestershire | Hove | July 21 | 104 | 1Ct | |
| Notts | Hove | July 28 | 4 | | |
| Northants | Eastbourne | Aug 4 | 1 | 1Ct | |
| **NATWEST TROPHY** | | | | | |
| Scotland | Edinburgh | June 26 | 12 | 2Ct | |
| Essex | Hove | July 11 | 17 | | |
| **BENSON & HEDGES CUP** | | | | | |
| Leicestershire | Hove | April 25 | 87 | 1Ct | |
| Kent | Canterbury | May 2 | 1 | | |
| Scotland | Hove | May 4 | 35 | | |
| **OTHER ONE-DAY** | | | | | |
| Kent | Hove | Sept 7 | 1 | | |
| Gloucs | Hove | Sept 9 | 15 | | |

**BATTING AVERAGES - Including fielding**

| | Matches | Inns | NO | Runs | HS | Avge | 100s | 50s | Ct | St |
|---|---|---|---|---|---|---|---|---|---|---|
| Britannic Assurance | 16 | 26 | 1 | 607 | 111 | 24.28 | 1 | 3 | 8 | - |
| ALL FIRST-CLASS | 16 | 26 | 1 | 607 | 111 | 24.28 | 1 | 3 | 8 | - |
| Refuge Assurance | 11 | 11 | 0 | 307 | 104 | 27.90 | 1 | 1 | 5 | - |
| NatWest Trophy | 2 | 2 | 0 | 29 | 17 | 14.50 | - | - | 2 | - |
| Benson & Hedges Cup | 3 | 3 | 0 | 123 | 87 | 41.00 | - | 1 | 1 | - |
| Other One-Day | 2 | 2 | 0 | 16 | 15 | 8.00 | - | - | - | - |
| ALL ONE-DAY | 18 | 18 | 0 | 475 | 104 | 26.38 | 1 | 2 | 8 | - |

**BOWLING AVERAGES**

| | Overs | Mdns | Runs | Wkts | Avge | Best | 5wI | 10wM |
|---|---|---|---|---|---|---|---|---|
| Britannic Assurance | 2 | 0 | 10 | 0 | - | - | - | - |
| ALL FIRST-CLASS | 2 | 0 | 10 | 0 | - | - | - | - |
| Refuge Assurance | | | | | | | | |
| NatWest Trophy | | | | | | | | |
| Benson & Hedges Cup | | | | | | | | |
| Other One-Day | | | | | | | | |
| ALL ONE-DAY | | | | | | | | |

## R.J.PARKS - *Hampshire*

| Opposition | Venue | Date | Batting | Fielding | Bowling |
|---|---|---|---|---|---|
| **REFUGE ASSURANCE** | | | | | |
| Worcestershire | Southampton | July 7 | | | |
| Middlesex | Lord's | Aug 4 | 6 | 1Ct | |
| Leicestershire | Bournemouth | Aug 18 | 8 | | |

**BATTING AVERAGES - Including fielding**

| | Matches | Inns | NO | Runs | HS | Avge | 100s | 50s | Ct | St |
|---|---|---|---|---|---|---|---|---|---|---|
| Refuge Assurance | 3 | 2 | 0 | 14 | 8 | 7.00 | - | - | 1 | - |
| ALL ONE-DAY | 3 | 2 | 0 | 14 | 8 | 7.00 | - | - | 1 | - |

**BOWLING AVERAGES**
Did not bowl

## G.J.PARSONS - *Leicestershire*

| Opposition | Venue | Date | Batting | Fielding | Bowling |
|---|---|---|---|---|---|
| **BRITANNIC ASSURANCE** | | | | | |
| Derbyshire | Leicester | Aug 28 | 0 & 10 * | | 2-44 & 1-45 |
| Kent | Canterbury | Sept 17 | 63 & 5 | | 0-27 |
| **REFUGE ASSURANCE** | | | | | |
| Warwickshire | Leicester | Aug 11 | | | 2-28 |
| Gloucs | Leicester | Aug 25 | 9 | 1Ct | 0-23 |

**BATTING AVERAGES - Including fielding**

| | Matches | Inns | NO | Runs | HS | Avge | 100s | 50s | Ct | St |
|---|---|---|---|---|---|---|---|---|---|---|
| Britannic Assurance | 2 | 4 | 1 | 78 | 63 | 26.00 | - | 1 | - | - |
| ALL FIRST-CLASS | 2 | 4 | 1 | 78 | 63 | 26.00 | - | 1 | - | - |
| Refuge Assurance | 2 | 1 | 0 | 9 | 9 | 9.00 | - | - | 1 | - |
| ALL ONE-DAY | 2 | 1 | 0 | 9 | 9 | 9.00 | - | - | 1 | - |

**BOWLING AVERAGES**

| | Overs | Mdns | Runs | Wkts | Avge | Best | 5wI | 10wM |
|---|---|---|---|---|---|---|---|---|
| Britannic Assurance | 40 | 10 | 116 | 3 | 38.66 | 2-44 | - | - |
| ALL FIRST-CLASS | 40 | 10 | 116 | 3 | 38.66 | 2-44 | - | - |
| Refuge Assurance | 13 | 0 | 51 | 2 | 25.50 | 2-28 | - | |
| ALL ONE-DAY | 13 | 0 | 51 | 2 | 25.50 | 2-28 | - | |

## T.PARTON - *Shropshire*

| Opposition | Venue | Date | Batting | Fielding | Bowling |
|---|---|---|---|---|---|
| **NATWEST TROPHY** | | | | | |
| Leicestershire | Leicester | June 26 | 17 | | |

| P | PLAYER RECORDS |
|---|---|

### BATTING AVERAGES - Including fielding

|  | Matches | Inns | NO | Runs | HS | Avge | 100s | 50s | Ct | St |
|---|---|---|---|---|---|---|---|---|---|---|
| NatWest Trophy | 1 | 1 | 0 | 17 | 17 | 17.00 | - | - | - | - |
| ALL ONE-DAY | 1 | 1 | 0 | 17 | 17 | 17.00 | - | - | - | - |

### BOWLING AVERAGES
Did not bowl

## A.S.PATEL - *Durham*

| Opposition | Venue | Date | Batting | Fielding | Bowling |
|---|---|---|---|---|---|
| **NATWEST TROPHY** | | | | | |
| Glamorgan | Darlington | June 26 | 25 | | 0-18 |

### BATTING AVERAGES - Including fielding

|  | Matches | Inns | NO | Runs | HS | Avge | 100s | 50s | Ct | St |
|---|---|---|---|---|---|---|---|---|---|---|
| NatWest Trophy | 1 | 1 | 0 | 25 | 25 | 25.00 | - | - | - | - |
| ALL ONE-DAY | 1 | 1 | 0 | 25 | 25 | 25.00 | - | - | - | - |

### BOWLING AVERAGES

|  | Overs | Mdns | Runs | Wkts | Avge | Best | 5wI | 10wM |
|---|---|---|---|---|---|---|---|---|
| NatWest Trophy | 3 | 0 | 18 | 0 | - | - | - | |
| ALL ONE-DAY | 3 | 0 | 18 | 0 | - | - | - | |

## M.M.PATEL - *Kent*

| Opposition | Venue | Date | Batting | Fielding | Bowling |
|---|---|---|---|---|---|
| **BRITANNIC ASSURANCE** | | | | | |
| Somerset | Taunton | July 26 | 0 | 1Ct | 2-75 & 1-61 |
| Leicestershire | Leicester | Aug 9 | 43 | | 2-4 & 1-93 |
| Gloucs | Canterbury | Aug 20 | 4 & 3 | | 3-33 & 1-25 |
| Sussex | Hove | Sept 3 | 8 | | 1-31 & 2-68 |
| Leicestershire | Canterbury | Sept 17 | 0 * & 18 * | 1Ct | 0-13 & 0-55 |
| **OTHER ONE-DAY** | | | | | |
| Sussex | Hove | Sept 7 | 1 | | 1-13 |

### BATTING AVERAGES - Including fielding

|  | Matches | Inns | NO | Runs | HS | Avge | 100s | 50s | Ct | St |
|---|---|---|---|---|---|---|---|---|---|---|
| Britannic Assurance | 5 | 7 | 2 | 76 | 43 | 15.20 | - | - | 2 | - |
| ALL FIRST-CLASS | 5 | 7 | 2 | 76 | 43 | 15.20 | - | - | 2 | - |
| Other One-Day | 1 | 1 | 0 | 1 | 1 | 1.00 | - | - | - | - |
| ALL ONE-DAY | 1 | 1 | 0 | 1 | 1 | 1.00 | - | - | - | - |

### BOWLING AVERAGES

|  | Overs | Mdns | Runs | Wkts | Avge | Best | 5wI | 10wM |
|---|---|---|---|---|---|---|---|---|
| Britannic Assurance | 183.2 | 43 | 458 | 13 | 35.23 | 3-33 | - | - |
| ALL FIRST-CLASS | 183.2 | 43 | 458 | 13 | 35.23 | 3-33 | - | - |
| Other One-Day | 10 | 5 | 13 | 1 | 13.00 | 1-13 | - | |
| ALL ONE-DAY | 10 | 5 | 13 | 1 | 13.00 | 1-13 | - | |

## B.M.W.PATTERSON - *Scotland*

| Opposition | Venue | Date | Batting | Fielding | Bowling |
|---|---|---|---|---|---|
| **OTHER FIRST-CLASS** | | | | | |
| Ireland | Dublin | June 22 | 108 & 6 | | |
| **NATWEST TROPHY** | | | | | |
| Sussex | Edinburgh | June 26 | 4 | | |
| **BENSON & HEDGES CUP** | | | | | |
| Lancashire | Forfar | April 23 | 2 | | |

| Leicestershire | Leicester | May 2 | 12 |
|---|---|---|---|
| Sussex | Hove | May 4 | 0 |
| Kent | Glasgow | May 7 | 23 |

### BATTING AVERAGES - Including fielding

|  | Matches | Inns | NO | Runs | HS | Avge | 100s | 50s | Ct | St |
|---|---|---|---|---|---|---|---|---|---|---|
| Other First-Class | 1 | 2 | 0 | 114 | 108 | 57.00 | 1 | - | - | - |
| ALL FIRST-CLASS | 1 | 2 | 0 | 114 | 108 | 57.00 | 1 | - | - | - |
| NatWest Trophy | 1 | 1 | 0 | 4 | 4 | 4.00 | - | - | - | - |
| Benson & Hedges Cup | 4 | 4 | 0 | 37 | 23 | 9.25 | - | - | - | - |
| ALL ONE-DAY | 5 | 5 | 0 | 41 | 23 | 8.20 | - | - | - | - |

### BOWLING AVERAGES
Did not bowl

## B.P.PATTERSON - *West Indies*

| Opposition | Venue | Date | Batting | Fielding | Bowling |
|---|---|---|---|---|---|
| **CORNHILL TEST MATCHES** | | | | | |
| England | Headingley | June 6 | 5 * & 0 * | | 3-67 & 0-52 |
| England | Edgbaston | July 25 | 3 | | 1-39 & 5-81 |
| England | The Oval | Aug 8 | 2 & 1 * | 1Ct | 2-87 & 2-63 |
| **OTHER FIRST-CLASS** | | | | | |
| Worcestershire | Worcester | May 15 | | | 3-49 |
| Middlesex | Lord's | May 18 | | 1Ct | 5-88 & 1-29 |
| Leicestershire | Leicester | June 1 | | | 1-75 & 0-15 |
| Northants | Northampton | June 15 | | | 0-2 |
| Hampshire | Southampton | June 29 | | | 1-19 |
| Glamorgan | Swansea | July 16 | | | 1-61 & 0-14 |
| Kent | Canterbury | July 20 | | 1Ct | 4-70 & 3-57 |
| Gloucs | Bristol | July 31 | | 1Ct | 0-28 & 0-16 |
| **TEXACO TROPHY** | | | | | |
| England | Edgbaston | May 23 | | | 2-38 |
| England | Old Trafford | May 25 | | | 1-39 |
| England | Lord's | May 27 | 2 * | | 1-62 |
| **OTHER ONE-DAY** | | | | | |
| D of Norfolk | Arundel | May 12 | | | 2-23 |
| Ireland | Downpatrick | July 13 | | | 0-14 |
| Wales | Brecon | July 15 | | | 3-17 |

### BATTING AVERAGES - Including fielding

|  | Matches | Inns | NO | Runs | HS | Avge | 100s | 50s | Ct | St |
|---|---|---|---|---|---|---|---|---|---|---|
| Cornhill Test Matches | 3 | 5 | 3 | 11 | 5 * | 5.50 | - | - | 1 | - |
| Other First-Class | 8 | 0 | 0 | 0 | 0 | - | - | - | 3 | - |
| ALL FIRST-CLASS | 11 | 5 | 3 | 11 | 5 * | 5.50 | - | - | 4 | - |
| Texaco Trophy | 3 | 1 | 1 | 2 | 2 * | - | - | - | - | - |
| Other One-Day | 3 | 0 | 0 | 0 | 0 | - | - | - | - | - |
| ALL ONE-DAY | 6 | 1 | 1 | 2 | 2 * | - | - | - | - | - |

### BOWLING AVERAGES

|  | Overs | Mdns | Runs | Wkts | Avge | Best | 5wI | 10wM |
|---|---|---|---|---|---|---|---|---|
| Cornhill Test Matches | 117.3 | 20 | 389 | 13 | 29.92 | 5-81 | 1 | - |
| Other First-Class | 170 | 48 | 523 | 19 | 27.52 | 5-88 | 1 | - |
| ALL FIRST-CLASS | 287.3 | 68 | 912 | 32 | 28.50 | 5-81 | 2 | - |
| Texaco Trophy | 31 | 3 | 139 | 4 | 34.75 | 2-38 | - | |
| Other One-Day | 20 | 4 | 54 | 5 | 10.80 | 3-17 | - | |
| ALL ONE-DAY | 51 | 7 | 193 | 9 | 21.44 | 3-17 | - | |

## T.J.T.PATTERSON - *Ireland*

| Opposition | Venue | Date | Batting | Fielding | Bowling |
|---|---|---|---|---|---|
| **OTHER FIRST-CLASS** | | | | | |
| Scotland | Dublin | June 22 | 73 * & 3 | | |

# PLAYER RECORDS

## NATWEST TROPHY

| | | | | |
|---|---|---|---|---|
| Middlesex | Dublin | June 26 | 5 | 2Ct |

## OTHER ONE-DAY

| | | | |
|---|---|---|---|
| West Indies | Downpatrick | July 13 | 8 |

### BATTING AVERAGES - Including fielding

| | Matches | Inns | NO | Runs | HS | Avge | 100s | 50s | Ct | St |
|---|---|---|---|---|---|---|---|---|---|---|
| Other First-Class | 1 | 2 | 1 | 76 | 73* | 76.00 | - | 1 | - | - |
| ALL FIRST-CLASS | 1 | 2 | 1 | 76 | 73* | 76.00 | - | 1 | - | - |
| NatWest Trophy | 1 | 1 | 0 | 5 | 5 | 5.00 | - | - | 2 | - |
| Other One-Day | 1 | 1 | 0 | 8 | 8 | 8.00 | - | - | - | - |
| ALL ONE-DAY | 2 | 2 | 0 | 13 | 8 | 6.50 | - | - | 2 | - |

### BOWLING AVERAGES
Did not bowl

## R.M.PEARSON - *Cambridge University & Combined Universities*

| Opposition | Venue | Date | Batting | Fielding | Bowling |
|---|---|---|---|---|---|
| **OTHER FIRST-CLASS** | | | | | |
| Lancashire | Fenner's | April 13 | 2 | | 3-124 & 0-76 |
| Northants | Fenner's | April 16 | 0 | | 1-115 & 0-5 |
| Essex | Fenner's | April 19 | 0 & 15 | | 0-77 & 2-88 |
| Derbyshire | Fenner's | May 9 | 21 | 1Ct | 1-92 & 4-84 |
| Middlesex | Fenner's | May 15 | | 4* | 1-56 & 1-10 |
| Surrey | Fenner's | May 18 | 3 & 1 | | 0-46 & 2-73 |
| Leicestershire | Fenner's | May 22 | 13 | | 0-103 |
| Glamorgan | Fenner's | June 18 | 1 | 1Ct | 0-35 & 0-27 |
| Sussex | Hove | June 29 | | | 0-35 |
| Oxford U | Lord's | July 2 | 0 & 10 | | 0-28 & 0-24 |

### BENSON & HEDGES CUP
For Combined Universities

| | | | | | |
|---|---|---|---|---|---|
| Worcestershire | Fenner's | May 2 | | | 0-24 |

### BATTING AVERAGES - Including fielding

| | Matches | Inns | NO | Runs | HS | Avge | 100s | 50s | Ct | St |
|---|---|---|---|---|---|---|---|---|---|---|
| Other First-Class | 10 | 12 | 1 | 70 | 21 | 6.36 | - | - | 2 | - |
| ALL FIRST-CLASS | 10 | 12 | 1 | 70 | 21 | 6.36 | - | - | 2 | - |
| Benson & Hedges Cup | 1 | 0 | 0 | 0 | 0 | | - | - | - | - |
| ALL ONE-DAY | 1 | 0 | 0 | 0 | 0 | | - | - | - | - |

### BOWLING AVERAGES

| | Overs | Mdns | Runs | Wkts | Avge | Best | 5wI | 10wM |
|---|---|---|---|---|---|---|---|---|
| Other First-Class | 332 | 59 | 1098 | 15 | 73.20 | 4-84 | - | - |
| ALL FIRST-CLASS | 332 | 59 | 1098 | 15 | 73.20 | 4-84 | - | - |
| Benson & Hedges Cup | 6 | 0 | 24 | 0 | - | - | - | - |
| ALL ONE-DAY | 6 | 0 | 24 | 0 | - | - | - | - |

## A.L.PENBERTHY - *Northamptonshire*

| Opposition | Venue | Date | Batting | Fielding | Bowling |
|---|---|---|---|---|---|
| **BRITANNIC ASSURANCE** | | | | | |
| Leicestershire | Northampton | May 16 | 0 | 1Ct | 0-10 & 0-43 |
| Glamorgan | Cardiff | May 22 | 7 & 2 | | 2-37 & 1-49 |
| Yorkshire | Headingley | May 25 | 2* & 4 | | 1-54 & 0-32 |
| Derbyshire | Northampton | May 31 | 0 & 1* | 1Ct | 0-2 & 0-18 |
| Worcestershire | Northampton | June 4 | | | 3-97 & 0-27 |
| Hampshire | Northampton | June 21 | 3 | | 1-37 |
| Sussex | Eastbourne | Aug 2 | 26 & 8 | 2Ct | 0-22 & 1-9 |
| Lancashire | Lytham | Aug 6 | 38 | | |
| Warwickshire | Northampton | Aug 9 | 52 | 1Ct | 0-16 & 0-21 |
| Surrey | Northampton | Aug 23 | 0 | 1Ct | 3-37 & 0-4 |
| Yorkshire | Northampton | Aug 28 | 41 | | 1-16 |

## OTHER FIRST-CLASS

| | | | | | |
|---|---|---|---|---|---|
| Cambridge U | Fenner's | April 16 | 2* | | 2-24 |

## REFUGE ASSURANCE

| | | | | | |
|---|---|---|---|---|---|
| Lancashire | Old Trafford | April 28 | | 1Ct | |
| Leicestershire | Northampton | May 12 | 22* | | 2-20 |
| Worcestershire | Northampton | May 19 | 41* | | 0-35 |
| Yorkshire | Headingley | May 26 | 6 | 1Ct | 1-43 |
| Hampshire | Northampton | June 2 | | | 1-45 |
| Gloucs | Moreton | June 9 | | | |
| Kent | Canterbury | Aug 18 | | | 0-21 |
| Warwickshire | Northampton | Aug 25 | | | 1-1 |

## BENSON & HEDGES CUP

| | | | | | |
|---|---|---|---|---|---|
| Combined U | Northampton | May 4 | | | 2-22 |
| Lancashire | Old Trafford | May 29 | | 3 | 0-43 |

### BATTING AVERAGES - Including fielding

| | Matches | Inns | NO | Runs | HS | Avge | 100s | 50s | Ct | St |
|---|---|---|---|---|---|---|---|---|---|---|
| Britannic Assurance | 11 | 14 | 2 | 184 | 52 | 15.33 | - | 1 | 6 | - |
| Other First-Class | 1 | 1 | 1 | 2 | 2* | - | - | - | - | - |
| ALL FIRST-CLASS | 12 | 15 | 3 | 186 | 52 | 15.50 | - | 1 | 6 | - |
| Refuge Assurance | 8 | 3 | 2 | 69 | 41* | 69.00 | - | - | 2 | - |
| Benson & Hedges Cup | 2 | 1 | 0 | 3 | 3 | 3.00 | - | - | - | - |
| ALL ONE-DAY | 10 | 4 | 2 | 72 | 41* | 36.00 | - | - | 2 | - |

### BOWLING AVERAGES

| | Overs | Mdns | Runs | Wkts | Avge | Best | 5wI | 10wM |
|---|---|---|---|---|---|---|---|---|
| Britannic Assurance | 163.4 | 26 | 531 | 13 | 40.84 | 3-37 | - | - |
| Other First-Class | 10.4 | 3 | 24 | 2 | 12.00 | 2-24 | - | - |
| ALL FIRST-CLASS | 174.2 | 29 | 555 | 15 | 37.00 | 3-37 | - | - |
| Refuge Assurance | 32 | 2 | 165 | 5 | 33.00 | 2-20 | - | |
| Benson & Hedges Cup | 17 | 3 | 65 | 2 | 32.50 | 2-22 | - | |
| ALL ONE-DAY | 49 | 5 | 230 | 7 | 32.85 | 2-20 | - | |

## C.PENN - *Kent*

| Opposition | Venue | Date | Batting | Fielding | Bowling |
|---|---|---|---|---|---|
| **BRITANNIC ASSURANCE** | | | | | |
| Hampshire | Southampton | April 27 | 37 | | 0-6 |
| Surrey | The Oval | May 9 | 39 | 1Ct | 4-48 & 4-50 |
| Essex | Folkestone | May 16 | 2* & 2* | | 0-99 |
| Notts | Trent Bridge | May 22 | 13 & 8* | 1Ct | 1-63 & 3-64 |
| Derbyshire | Canterbury | May 25 | 19 | | 2-48 & 3-31 |
| Middlesex | Lord's | May 31 | 10* | | 1-19 |
| Yorkshire | Harrogate | June 14 | | 1Ct | 0-14 |
| Lancashire | Old Trafford | June 21 | 12 | 1Ct | 2-62 |
| Northants | Maidstone | July 2 | 1 | | 5-43 |
| Glamorgan | Maidstone | July 5 | 21 | 1Ct | 2-46 & 1-49 |
| Essex | Southend | July 16 | 52 | | 0-36 & 1-18 |
| Worcestershire | Worcester | July 23 | | | 0-14 |
| Surrey | Canterbury | Aug 2 | 0 & 0 | | 4-36 & 1-70 |
| Hampshire | Canterbury | Aug 6 | 3 | | 0-33 & 1-32 |
| Gloucs | Canterbury | Aug 20 | 16 & 35 | 1Ct | 1-41 & 1-10 |
| Middlesex | Canterbury | Aug 28 | 0 | | 5-105 & 4-44 |
| Leicestershire | Canterbury | Sept 17 | 2 & 27 | | 5-90 & 1-45 |

## OTHER FIRST-CLASS

| | | | | | |
|---|---|---|---|---|---|
| West Indies | Canterbury | July 20 | 9 & 3 | | 0-46 & 0-61 |

## REFUGE ASSURANCE

| | | | | | |
|---|---|---|---|---|---|
| Lancashire | Old Trafford | June 23 | | 1Ct | 1-56 |

## NATWEST TROPHY

| | | | | | |
|---|---|---|---|---|---|
| Cambs | Canterbury | June 26 | | | 1-14 |
| Surrey | The Oval | July 11 | 20* | | 1-55 |

### BATTING AVERAGES - Including fielding

| | Matches | Inns | NO | Runs | HS | Avge | 100s | 50s | Ct | St |
|---|---|---|---|---|---|---|---|---|---|---|
| Britannic Assurance | 17 | 20 | 4 | 299 | 52 | 18.68 | - | 1 | 6 | - |
| Other First-Class | 1 | 2 | 0 | 12 | 9 | 6.00 | - | - | - | - |
| ALL FIRST-CLASS | 18 | 22 | 4 | 311 | 52 | 17.27 | - | 1 | 6 | - |
| Refuge Assurance | 1 | 0 | 0 | 0 | 0 | - | - | - | 1 | - |

# P — PLAYER RECORDS

| | | | | | | | | | | |
|---|---|---|---|---|---|---|---|---|---|---|
| NatWest Trophy | 2 | 1 | 1 | 20 | 20* | - | - | - | - | - |
| ALL ONE-DAY | 3 | 1 | 1 | 20 | 20* | - | - | - | 1 | - |

**BOWLING AVERAGES**

| | Overs | Mdns | Runs | Wkts | Avge | Best | 5wI | 10wM |
|---|---|---|---|---|---|---|---|---|
| Britannic Assurance | 407.4 | 79 | 1216 | 52 | 23.38 | 5-43 | 3 | - |
| Other First-Class | 22 | 3 | 107 | 0 | - | - | - | - |
| ALL FIRST-CLASS | 429.4 | 82 | 1323 | 52 | 25.44 | 5-43 | 3 | - |
| Refuge Assurance | 6 | 0 | 56 | 1 | 56.00 | 1-56 | - | |
| NatWest Trophy | 18 | 4 | 69 | 2 | 34.50 | 1-14 | - | |
| ALL ONE-DAY | 24 | 4 | 125 | 3 | 41.66 | 1-14 | - | |

## B.S.PERCY - *Buckinghamshire*

| Opposition | Venue | Date | Batting | Fielding | Bowling |
|---|---|---|---|---|---|
| **NATWEST TROPHY** | | | | | |
| Somerset | Bath | June 26 | 13 | | 1-2 |

**BATTING AVERAGES - Including fielding**

| | Matches | Inns | NO | Runs | HS | Avge | 100s | 50s | Ct | St |
|---|---|---|---|---|---|---|---|---|---|---|
| NatWest Trophy | 1 | 1 | 0 | 13 | 13 | 13.00 | - | - | - | - |
| ALL ONE-DAY | 1 | 1 | 0 | 13 | 13 | 13.00 | - | - | - | - |

**BOWLING AVERAGES**

| | Overs | Mdns | Runs | Wkts | Avge | Best | 5wI | 10wM |
|---|---|---|---|---|---|---|---|---|
| NatWest Trophy | 3 | 2 | 2 | 1 | 2.00 | 1-2 | - | |
| ALL ONE-DAY | 3 | 2 | 2 | 1 | 2.00 | 1-2 | - | |

## D.PFAFF - *Oxford University*

| Opposition | Venue | Date | Batting | Fielding | Bowling |
|---|---|---|---|---|---|
| **OTHER FIRST-CLASS** | | | | | |
| Hampshire | The Parks | April 13 | 48* & 50 | | |
| Glamorgan | The Parks | April 17 | 16 | | |
| Notts | The Parks | April 27 | | | 0-6 |
| Gloucs | The Parks | June 15 | | | |
| Worcestershire | The Parks | May 25 | 46 & 11 | 1Ct | |
| Yorkshire | The Parks | June 4 | 40* | 1Ct | |
| Lancashire | The Parks | June 7 | 20 | | |
| Cambridge U | Lord's | July 2 | | 1Ct | |

**BATTING AVERAGES - Including fielding**

| | Matches | Inns | NO | Runs | HS | Avge | 100s | 50s | Ct | St |
|---|---|---|---|---|---|---|---|---|---|---|
| Other First-Class | 8 | 7 | 2 | 231 | 50 | 46.20 | - | 1 | 3 | - |
| ALL FIRST-CLASS | 8 | 7 | 2 | 231 | 50 | 46.20 | - | 1 | 3 | - |

**BOWLING AVERAGES**

| | Overs | Mdns | Runs | Wkts | Avge | Best | 5wI | 10wM |
|---|---|---|---|---|---|---|---|---|
| Other First-Class | 2 | 0 | 6 | 0 | - | - | - | - |
| ALL FIRST-CLASS | 2 | 0 | 6 | 0 | - | - | - | - |

## I.L.PHILIP - *Scotland*

| Opposition | Venue | Date | Batting | Fielding | Bowling |
|---|---|---|---|---|---|
| **OTHER FIRST-CLASS** | | | | | |
| Ireland | Dublin | June 22 | 116* & 7 | 1Ct | |
| **NATWEST TROPHY** | | | | | |
| Sussex | Edinburgh | June 26 | 9 | 1Ct | |
| **BENSON & HEDGES CUP** | | | | | |
| Lancashire | Forfar | April 23 | 0 | 1Ct | |

| | | | |
|---|---|---|---|
| Leicestershire | Leicester | May 2 | 35 |
| Sussex | Hove | May 4 | 2 |
| Kent | Glasgow | May 7 | 2 | 1Ct |

**BATTING AVERAGES - Including fielding**

| | Matches | Inns | NO | Runs | HS | Avge | 100s | 50s | Ct | St |
|---|---|---|---|---|---|---|---|---|---|---|
| Other First-Class | 1 | 2 | 1 | 123 | 116* | 123.00 | 1 | - | 1 | - |
| ALL FIRST-CLASS | 1 | 2 | 1 | 123 | 116* | 123.00 | 1 | - | 1 | - |
| NatWest Trophy | 1 | 1 | 0 | 9 | 9 | 9.00 | - | - | 1 | - |
| Benson & Hedges Cup | 4 | 4 | 0 | 39 | 35 | 9.75 | - | - | 2 | - |
| ALL ONE-DAY | 5 | 5 | 0 | 48 | 35 | 9.60 | - | - | 3 | - |

**BOWLING AVERAGES**
Did not bowl

## W.N.PHILLIPS - *Victoria*

| Opposition | Venue | Date | Batting | Fielding | Bowling |
|---|---|---|---|---|---|
| **OTHER FIRST-CLASS** | | | | | |
| Essex | Chelmsford | Sept 23 | 2 & 11 | | |
| **OTHER ONE-DAY** | | | | | |
| Durham | Durham U. | Sept 16 | 72 | | |
| Essex | Chelmsford | Sept 22 | 23 | | |

**BATTING AVERAGES - Including fielding**

| | Matches | Inns | NO | Runs | HS | Avge | 100s | 50s | Ct | St |
|---|---|---|---|---|---|---|---|---|---|---|
| Other First-Class | 1 | 2 | 0 | 13 | 11 | 6.50 | - | - | - | - |
| ALL FIRST-CLASS | 1 | 2 | 0 | 13 | 11 | 6.50 | - | - | - | - |
| Other One-Day | 2 | 2 | 0 | 95 | 72 | 47.50 | - | 1 | - | - |
| ALL ONE-DAY | 2 | 2 | 0 | 95 | 72 | 47.50 | - | 1 | - | - |

**BOWLING AVERAGES**
Did not bowl

## R.A.PICK - *Nottinghamshire*

| Opposition | Venue | Date | Batting | Fielding | Bowling |
|---|---|---|---|---|---|
| **BRITANNIC ASSURANCE** | | | | | |
| Leicestershire | Trent Bridge | May 9 | 0 | 1Ct | 2-75 & 3-89 |
| Yorkshire | Headingley | May 16 | | | 3-76 & 1-38 |
| Kent | Trent Bridge | May 22 | 11* | | 1-44 & 2-48 |
| Leicestershire | Leicester | May 25 | | 1Ct | 5-66 & 2-66 |
| Hampshire | Trent Bridge | May 31 | 4 | | 1-43 |
| Gloucs | Gloucester | June 14 | | | 4-61 & 0-22 |
| Worcestershire | Worcester | June 18 | | | 1-36 & 1-60 |
| Warwickshire | Trent Bridge | June 21 | | | 1-77 |
| Glamorgan | Cardiff | July 2 | 0 | 1Ct | 3-54 & 1-60 |
| Lancashire | Trent Bridge | July 16 | 20* | | 1-31 & 1-44 |
| Northants | Well'borough | July 19 | 46 | 1Ct | 3-74 & 5-17 |
| Yorkshire | Worksop | July 23 | | 4 | 1Ct | 1-50 & 0-17 |
| Middlesex | Lord's | July 26 | 5 | | 2-54 & 1-76 |
| Sussex | Eastbourne | Aug 6 | | | 0-20 & 0-17 |
| Essex | Trent Bridge | Aug 9 | 14 & 5* | | 0-62 & 1-40 |
| Somerset | Trent Bridge | Aug 16 | | 1Ct | 0-79 & 2-24 |
| Derbyshire | Trent Bridge | Aug 23 | 0* | 1Ct | 1-41 & 1-50 |
| Lancashire | Old Trafford | Aug 28 | 1 | | 4-75 & 3-37 |
| Middlesex | Trent Bridge | Sept 3 | 14 & 1 | | 5-86 & 0-19 |
| Derbyshire | Derby | Sept 10 | 3* | | 2-53 & 0-69 |
| Worcestershire | Trent Bridge | Sept 17 | 14 | | 0-16 & 1-19 |
| **OTHER FIRST-CLASS** | | | | | |
| For MCC | | | | | |
| Middlesex | Lord's | April 16 | | | 2-95 |
| For Notts | | | | | |
| Oxford U | The Parks | April 27 | | | |
| **REFUGE ASSURANCE** | | | | | |
| Leicestershire | Leicester | May 26 | | | 0-20 |
| Surrey | The Oval | June 30 | | | 0-24 |

# PLAYER RECORDS   P

| | | | | | |
|---|---|---|---|---|---|
| Hampshire | Trent Bridge | July 14 | | | 2-27 |
| Northants | Well'borough | July 21 | 2* | | 1-37 |
| Sussex | Hove | July 28 | | | 0-30 |
| Worcestershire | Trent Bridge | Aug 4 | | | 1-34 |
| Kent | Trent Bridge | Aug 11 | | | 1-32 |
| Yorkshire | Scarborough | Aug 18 | | 1Ct | 1-35 |
| Derbyshire | Trent Bridge | Aug 25 | | | 1-34 |
| Worcestershire | Trent Bridge | Sept 1 | | | 2-35 |

### NATWEST TROPHY

| | | | | | |
|---|---|---|---|---|---|
| Lincolnshire | Trent Bridge | June 26 | | | 0-10 |
| Gloucs | Bristol | July 11 | | 1Ct | 3-41 |
| Hampshire | Southampton | July 31 | 0* | | 1-60 |

### BENSON & HEDGES CUP

| | | | | | |
|---|---|---|---|---|---|
| Hampshire | Southampton | April 23 | 25* | | 1-61 |
| Min Counties | Trent Bridge | May 7 | | | 1-36 |

### OTHER ONE-DAY
For England A

| | | | | |
|---|---|---|---|---|
| Sri Lanka | Old Trafford | Aug 14 | | 1-23 |
| Sri Lanka | Old Trafford | Aug 15 | | 1-31 |

### BATTING AVERAGES - Including fielding

| | Matches | Inns | NO | Runs | HS | Avge | 100s | 50s | Ct | St |
|---|---|---|---|---|---|---|---|---|---|---|
| Britannic Assurance | 21 | 16 | 5 | 142 | 46 | 12.90 | - | - | 7 | - |
| Other First-Class | 2 | 0 | 0 | 0 | 0 | - | - | - | - | - |
| ALL FIRST-CLASS | 23 | 16 | 5 | 142 | 46 | 12.90 | - | - | 7 | - |
| Refuge Assurance | 10 | 1 | 1 | 2 | 2* | - | - | - | 1 | - |
| NatWest Trophy | 3 | 1 | 1 | 0 | 0* | - | - | - | 1 | - |
| Benson & Hedges Cup | 2 | 1 | 1 | 25 | 25* | - | - | - | - | - |
| Other One-Day | 2 | 0 | 0 | 0 | 0 | - | - | - | - | - |
| ALL ONE-DAY | 17 | 3 | 3 | 27 | 25* | - | - | - | 2 | - |

### BOWLING AVERAGES

| | Overs | Mdns | Runs | Wkts | Avge | Best | 5wI | 10wM |
|---|---|---|---|---|---|---|---|---|
| Britannic Assurance | 623.4 | 113 | 1985 | 65 | 30.53 | 5-17 | 3 | - |
| Other First-Class | 27 | 4 | 95 | 2 | 47.50 | 2-95 | - | - |
| ALL FIRST-CLASS | 650.4 | 117 | 2080 | 67 | 31.04 | 5-17 | 3 | - |
| Refuge Assurance | 75 | 2 | 308 | 9 | 34.22 | 2-27 | - | |
| NatWest Trophy | 30 | 4 | 111 | 4 | 27.75 | 3-41 | - | |
| Benson & Hedges Cup | 22 | 1 | 97 | 2 | 48.50 | 1-36 | - | |
| Other One-Day | 17.5 | 2 | 54 | 2 | 27.00 | 1-23 | - | |
| ALL ONE-DAY | 144.5 | 9 | 570 | 17 | 33.52 | 3-41 | - | |

## C.S.PICKLES - Yorkshire

| Opposition | Venue | Date | Batting | Fielding | Bowling |
|---|---|---|---|---|---|

### BRITANNIC ASSURANCE

| Opposition | Venue | Date | Batting | Fielding | Bowling |
|---|---|---|---|---|---|
| Warwickshire | Headingley | May 9 | 10 & 1 | | 0-59 & 2-8 |
| Kent | Harrogate | June 14 | | | |
| Middlesex | Sheffield | June 21 | 22*& 51 | | 1-18 & 1-24 |
| Worcestershire | Headingley | July 2 | 4 | | 0-25 |
| Surrey | Guildford | July 19 | 1 & 2 | 1Ct | 0-35 & 0-13 |
| Lancashire | Old Trafford | Aug 2 | 50 | | 0-30 & 0-4 |
| Leicestershire | Leicester | Aug 6 | 0 | | 0-45 & 0-9 |
| Sussex | Midd'brough | Aug 9 | 48 & 33 | | 0-51 |
| Glamorgan | Headingley | Aug 16 | 28 & 34* | | 0-28 |
| Essex | Colchester | Aug 20 | 0 | | 0-21 & 0-19 |
| Somerset | Taunton | Aug 23 | 0*& 0 | | 1-43 & 1-36 |

### REFUGE ASSURANCE

| Opposition | Venue | Date | Batting | Fielding | Bowling |
|---|---|---|---|---|---|
| Derbyshire | Chesterfield | June 2 | 0 | 2Ct | 0-25 |
| Kent | Scarborough | June 16 | 0 | | 2-51 |
| Worcestershire | Sheffield | June 23 | 30* | | 3-12 |
| Glamorgan | Headingley | June 30 | 8* | | 0-11 |
| Middlesex | Lord's | July 7 | | | 1-13 |
| Gloucs | Scarborough | July 14 | 7 | | 3-30 |
| Surrey | The Oval | July 21 | | | 0-48 |
| Lancashire | Old Trafford | Aug 4 | 1* | 2Ct | 3-49 |
| Sussex | Midd'brough | Aug 11 | 1 | 2Ct | 0-57 |
| Notts | Scarborough | Aug 18 | 15* | | 2-35 |
| Somerset | Taunton | Aug 25 | 16 | | 0-30 |

### NATWEST TROPHY

| | | | | | |
|---|---|---|---|---|---|
| Warwickshire | Edgbaston | June 26 | 12 | 1Ct | 1-30 |

### BENSON & HEDGES CUP

| | | | | | |
|---|---|---|---|---|---|
| Min Counties | Headingley | May 2 | | | 2-49 |

### OTHER ONE-DAY

| | | | | | |
|---|---|---|---|---|---|
| Derbyshire | Scarborough | Sept 1 | 10* | | 5-50 |
| Essex | Scarborugh | Sept 2 | 10* | | 1-57 |

### BATTING AVERAGES - Including fielding

| | Matches | Inns | NO | Runs | HS | Avge | 100s | 50s | Ct | St |
|---|---|---|---|---|---|---|---|---|---|---|
| Britannic Assurance | 11 | 16 | 3 | 284 | 51 | 21.84 | - | 2 | 2 | - |
| ALL FIRST-CLASS | 11 | 16 | 3 | 284 | 51 | 21.84 | - | 2 | 2 | - |
| Refuge Assurance | 11 | 9 | 4 | 78 | 30* | 15.60 | - | - | 6 | - |
| NatWest Trophy | 1 | 1 | 0 | 12 | 12 | 12.00 | - | - | 1 | - |
| Benson & Hedges Cup | 1 | 0 | 0 | 0 | 0 | - | - | - | - | - |
| Other One-Day | 2 | 2 | 2 | 20 | 10* | - | - | - | - | - |
| ALL ONE-DAY | 15 | 12 | 6 | 110 | 30* | 18.33 | - | - | 7 | - |

### BOWLING AVERAGES

| | Overs | Mdns | Runs | Wkts | Avge | Best | 5wI | 10wM |
|---|---|---|---|---|---|---|---|---|
| Britannic Assurance | 138 | 19 | 468 | 6 | 78.00 | 2-8 | - | - |
| ALL FIRST-CLASS | 138 | 19 | 468 | 6 | 78.00 | 2-8 | - | - |
| Refuge Assurance | 63 | 0 | 361 | 14 | 25.78 | 3-12 | - | |
| NatWest Trophy | 10.3 | 2 | 30 | 1 | 30.00 | 1-30 | - | |
| Benson & Hedges Cup | 11 | 0 | 49 | 2 | 24.50 | 2-49 | - | |
| Other One-Day | 20 | 2 | 107 | 6 | 17.83 | 5-50 | 1 | |
| ALL ONE-DAY | 104.3 | 4 | 547 | 23 | 23.78 | 5-50 | 1 | |

## A.R.K.PIERSON - Warwickshire

| Opposition | Venue | Date | Batting | Fielding | Bowling |
|---|---|---|---|---|---|

### BRITANNIC ASSURANCE

| Opposition | Venue | Date | Batting | Fielding | Bowling |
|---|---|---|---|---|---|
| Lancashire | Edgbaston | April 27 | | | 0-49 |
| Essex | Chelmsford | May 22 | 1 & 14* | | 3-45 |
| Lancashire | Old Trafford | July 23 | 3* | | 1-67 |
| Leicestershire | Leicester | July 26 | 35 | 1Ct | 0-38 |
| Worcestershire | Worcester | Aug 2 | 2*& 0* | | 0-80 |

### REFUGE ASSURANCE

| Opposition | Venue | Date | Batting | Fielding | Bowling |
|---|---|---|---|---|---|
| Yorkshire | Headingley | May 12 | | | 1-35 |
| Glamorgan | Swansea | May 19 | | | 0-11 |
| Worcestershire | Edgbaston | May 26 | | | 1-45 |

### BENSON & HEDGES CUP

| | | | | | |
|---|---|---|---|---|---|
| Yorkshire | Headingley | May 29 | 3* | | 0-7 |

### BATTING AVERAGES - Including fielding

| | Matches | Inns | NO | Runs | HS | Avge | 100s | 50s | Ct | St |
|---|---|---|---|---|---|---|---|---|---|---|
| Britannic Assurance | 5 | 6 | 4 | 55 | 35 | 27.50 | - | - | 1 | - |
| ALL FIRST-CLASS | 5 | 6 | 4 | 55 | 35 | 27.50 | - | - | 1 | - |
| Refuge Assurance | 3 | 0 | 0 | 0 | 0 | - | - | - | - | - |
| Benson & Hedges Cup | 1 | 1 | 1 | 3 | 3* | - | - | - | - | - |
| ALL ONE-DAY | 4 | 1 | 1 | 3 | 3* | - | - | - | - | - |

### BOWLING AVERAGES

| | Overs | Mdns | Runs | Wkts | Avge | Best | 5wI | 10wM |
|---|---|---|---|---|---|---|---|---|
| Britannic Assurance | 73 | 11 | 279 | 4 | 69.75 | 3-45 | - | - |
| ALL FIRST-CLASS | 73 | 11 | 279 | 4 | 69.75 | 3-45 | - | - |
| Refuge Assurance | 16 | 1 | 91 | 2 | 45.50 | 1-35 | - | |
| Benson & Hedges Cup | 2 | 0 | 7 | 0 | - | - | - | |
| ALL ONE-DAY | 18 | 1 | 98 | 2 | 49.00 | 1-35 | - | |

# P    PLAYER RECORDS

## A.C.S.PIGOTT - *Sussex*

| Opposition | Venue | Date | Batting | | | Fielding | Bowling |
|---|---|---|---|---|---|---|---|
| **BRITANNIC ASSURANCE** | | | | | | | |
| Somerset | Taunton | April 27 | 5* | | | | 3-36 |
| Middlesex | Lord's | May 9 | 65 | | | | 5-37 & 4-52 |
| Hampshire | Hove | May 16 | 0 | & | 13* | | 1-77 & 0-36 |
| Middlesex | Hove | May 22 | | | 6 | | 1-48 & 0-11 |
| Lancashire | Old Trafford | May 31 | 1 | & | 4 | | 2-88 & 0-38 |
| Kent | Tunbridge W | June 7 | | | | 1Ct | 4-75 & 0-25 |
| Worcestershire | Hove | June 14 | | | | | 2-69 |
| Warwickshire | Coventry | June 18 | | | 2 | | 1-75 |
| Essex | Horsham | June 21 | 26 | | | | 2-61 |
| Surrey | Arundel | July 2 | 26 | & | 12* | | 0-77 |
| Derbyshire | Derby | July 5 | 29* | | | 1Ct | 1-62 & 0-36 |
| Somerset | Hove | July 16 | | | | | 0-50 |
| Gloucs | Cheltenham | July 23 | | | 1 | | 0-13 |
| Notts | Eastbourne | Aug 6 | 12 | | | | 2-66 |
| Hampshire | Bournemouth | Aug 20 | 10 | | | 1Ct | 1-34 & 2-51 |
| Surrey | The Oval | Aug 28 | 0 | & | 18* | | 2-69 |
| Kent | Hove | Sept 3 | 5 | & | 26 | 1Ct | 2-56 & 0-44 |
| Gloucs | Hove | Sept 17 | 30 | & | 0 | 1Ct | 0-7 |
| **OTHER FIRST-CLASS** | | | | | | | |
| Sri Lanka | Hove | Aug 17 | 29 | | | | 0-61 & 1-48 |
| **REFUGE ASSURANCE** | | | | | | | |
| Warwickshire | Edgbaston | April 21 | 5 | | | | 3-11 |
| Somerset | Taunton | April 28 | 14 | | | | 1-30 |
| Middlesex | Hove | May 12 | 10 | | | | 0-28 |
| Gloucs | Hove | May 19 | 7 | | | | 3-40 |
| Glamorgan | Swansea | May 26 | 2 | | | 1Ct | 3-26 |
| Lancashire | Old Trafford | June 2 | 5 | | | | 1-21 |
| Hampshire | Basingstoke | June 9 | 4 | | | 1Ct | 5-30 |
| Worcestershire | Hove | June 16 | | | | | |
| Derbyshire | Derby | July 7 | 4* | | | 1Ct | 3-44 |
| Surrey | The Oval | July 14 | 14 | | | | 0-43 |
| Leicestershire | Hove | July 21 | 1* | | | | 2-35 |
| Notts | Hove | July 28 | 2 | | | | 0-47 |
| Northants | Eastbourne | Aug 4 | 0 | | | | 0-23 |
| Yorkshire | Midd'brough | Aug 11 | 4 | | | 1Ct | 3-57 |
| Kent | Hove | Aug 25 | 1* | | | 1Ct | 3-26 |
| **NATWEST TROPHY** | | | | | | | |
| Scotland | Edinburgh | June 26 | 7 | | | | 2-25 |
| Essex | Hove | July 11 | 0 | | | | 1-40 |
| **BENSON & HEDGES CUP** | | | | | | | |
| Leicestershire | Hove | April 25 | | | | 1Ct | 3-29 |
| Kent | Canterbury | May 2 | 16 | | | | 1-41 |
| Scotland | Hove | May 4 | 2 | | | 2Ct | 1-34 |
| Lancashire | Old Trafford | May 7 | 29 | | | | 0-71 |
| **OTHER ONE-DAY** | | | | | | | |
| Kent | Hove | Sept 7 | 0 | | | 1Ct | 2-18 |
| Gloucs | Hove | Sept 9 | 0 | | | 1Ct | 1-50 |

**BATTING AVERAGES - Including fielding**

| | Matches | Inns | NO | Runs | HS | Avge | 100s | 50s | Ct | St |
|---|---|---|---|---|---|---|---|---|---|---|
| Britannic Assurance | 18 | 21 | 5 | 291 | 65 | 18.18 | - | 1 | 5 | - |
| Other First-Class | 1 | 1 | 0 | 29 | 29 | 29.00 | - | - | - | - |
| ALL FIRST-CLASS | 19 | 22 | 5 | 320 | 65 | 18.82 | - | 1 | 5 | - |
| Refuge Assurance | 15 | 14 | 3 | 73 | 14 | 6.63 | - | - | 5 | - |
| NatWest Trophy | 2 | 2 | 0 | 7 | 7 | 3.50 | - | - | - | - |
| Benson & Hedges Cup | 4 | 3 | 0 | 47 | 29 | 15.66 | - | - | 3 | - |
| Other One-Day | 2 | 2 | 0 | 0 | 0 | 0.00 | - | - | 2 | - |
| ALL ONE-DAY | 23 | 21 | 3 | 127 | 29 | 7.05 | - | - | 10 | - |

**BOWLING AVERAGES**

| | Overs | Mdns | Runs | Wkts | Avge | Best | 5wI | 10wM |
|---|---|---|---|---|---|---|---|---|
| Britannic Assurance | 415.3 | 92 | 1293 | 35 | 36.94 | 5-37 | 1 | - |
| Other First-Class | 28.5 | 6 | 109 | 1 | 109.00 | 1-48 | - | - |
| ALL FIRST-CLASS | 444.2 | 98 | 1402 | 36 | 38.94 | 5-37 | 1 | - |
| Refuge Assurance | 95.5 | 2 | 461 | 27 | 17.07 | 5-30 | 1 | |
| NatWest Trophy | 19.5 | 1 | 65 | 3 | 21.66 | 2-25 | - | |
| Benson & Hedges Cup | 41.4 | 4 | 175 | 5 | 35.00 | 3-29 | - | |
| Other One-Day | 17 | 1 | 68 | 3 | 22.66 | 2-18 | - | |

## K.J.PIPER - *Warwickshire*

| | | | | | | | |
|---|---|---|---|---|---|---|---|
| ALL ONE-DAY | 174.2 | 8 | 769 | 38 | 20.23 | 5-30 | 1 |

| Opposition | Venue | Date | Batting | | | Fielding | Bowling |
|---|---|---|---|---|---|---|---|
| **BRITANNIC ASSURANCE** | | | | | | | |
| Lancashire | Edgbaston | April 27 | 6 | | | | |
| Yorkshire | Headingley | May 9 | 8 | & | 3 | 1Ct | |
| Glamorgan | Swansea | May 16 | 21 | & | 5* | 4Ct | |
| Essex | Chelmsford | May 22 | 4 | & | 11 | 4Ct | |
| Gloucs | Edgbaston | May 25 | 29 | | | 7Ct | |
| Yorkshire | Edgbaston | May 31 | 19 | | | 3Ct | |
| Kent | Tunbridge W | June 4 | 0 | | | 3Ct | |
| Somerset | Edgbaston | June 7 | | | | 2Ct | |
| Sussex | Coventry | June 18 | 41 | | | 5Ct | |
| Notts | Trent Bridge | June 21 | 55 | | | 2Ct | |
| Derbyshire | Edgbaston | June 28 | 9 | & | 1 | 3Ct | |
| Middlesex | Edgbaston | July 2 | 4 | | | 1Ct | |
| Hampshire | Portsmouth | July 19 | 6 | & | 31* | 5Ct | |
| Surrey | Edgbaston | Aug 6 | 5 | & | 2 | 1Ct | |
| Northants | Edgbaston | Sept 10 | 1 | & | 23* | 4Ct | |
| Somerset | Taunton | Sept 17 | 35 | & | 30 | 3Ct | |
| **REFUGE ASSURANCE** | | | | | | | |
| Notts | Trent Bridge | April 28 | 1 | | | 2Ct | |
| Yorkshire | Headingley | May 12 | 1* | | | 0Ct,1St | |
| Glamorgan | Swansea | May 19 | 0* | | | 1Ct | |
| Worcestershire | Edgbaston | May 26 | 15* | | | 1Ct | |
| Somerset | Edgbaston | June 2 | | | | | |
| Lancashire | Edgbaston | June 16 | | | | 1Ct | |
| Middlesex | Edgbaston | July 14 | | | | 0Ct,1St | |
| Hampshire | Portsmouth | July 21 | | | | 1Ct,1St | |
| Gloucs | Edgbaston | Aug 18 | | | | 1Ct | |
| **NATWEST TROPHY** | | | | | | | |
| Yorkshire | Edgbaston | June 26 | | | | 2Ct | |
| Hertfordshire | Edgbaston | July 11 | | | | 2Ct | |
| Hampshire | Edgbaston | Aug 14 | 1 | | | | |
| **BENSON & HEDGES CUP** | | | | | | | |
| Somerset | Edgbaston | May 2 | 6* | | | | |
| Middlesex | Lord's | May 4 | 7 | | | 3Ct | |
| Surrey | The Oval | May 7 | 11* | | | 1Ct | |
| Yorkshire | Headingley | May 29 | 11 | | | 1Ct | |

**BATTING AVERAGES - Including fielding**

| | Matches | Inns | NO | Runs | HS | Avge | 100s | 50s | Ct | St |
|---|---|---|---|---|---|---|---|---|---|---|
| Britannic Assurance | 16 | 23 | 3 | 349 | 55 | 17.45 | - | 1 | 48 | - |
| ALL FIRST-CLASS | 16 | 23 | 3 | 349 | 55 | 17.45 | - | 1 | 48 | - |
| Refuge Assurance | 9 | 4 | 3 | 17 | 15* | 17.00 | - | - | 7 | 3 |
| NatWest Trophy | 3 | 1 | 0 | 1 | 1 | 1.00 | - | - | 4 | - |
| Benson & Hedges Cup | 4 | 4 | 2 | 35 | 11* | 17.50 | - | - | 5 | - |
| ALL ONE-DAY | 16 | 9 | 5 | 53 | 15* | 13.25 | - | - | 16 | 3 |

**BOWLING AVERAGES**
Did not bowl

## S.G.PLUMB - *Norfolk & Minor Counties*

| Opposition | Venue | Date | Batting | Fielding | Bowling |
|---|---|---|---|---|---|
| **NATWEST TROPHY** | | | | | |
| Gloucs | Bristol | June 26 | 11 | | 1-36 |
| **BENSON & HEDGES CUP** | | | | | |
| For Minor Counties | | | | | |
| Glamorgan | Trowbridge | April 23 | 23 | | 0-15 |
| Hampshire | Trowbridge | April 25 | 23* | | |
| Yorkshire | Headingley | May 2 | 0 | | 0-3 |
| Notts | Trent Bridge | May 7 | 52 | | 0-33 |

**BATTING AVERAGES - Including fielding**

| | Matches | Inns | NO | Runs | HS | Avge | 100s | 50s | Ct | St |
|---|---|---|---|---|---|---|---|---|---|---|
| NatWest Trophy | 1 | 1 | 0 | 11 | 11 | 11.00 | - | - | - | - |

# PLAYER RECORDS P

| | | | | | | | | |
|---|---|---|---|---|---|---|---|---|
| Benson & Hedges Cup | 4 | 4 | 1 | 98 | 52 | 32.66 | - 1 | - - |
| ALL ONE-DAY | 5 | 5 | 1 | 109 | 52 | 27.25 | - 1 | - - |

## BOWLING AVERAGES

| | Overs | Mdns | Runs | Wkts | Avge | Best | 5wI 10wM |
|---|---|---|---|---|---|---|---|
| NatWest Trophy | 12 | 0 | 36 | 1 | 36.00 | 1-36 | - |
| Benson & Hedges Cup | 9 | 0 | 51 | 0 | - | - | - |
| ALL ONE-DAY | 21 | 0 | 87 | 1 | 87.00 | 1-36 | - |

# P.POLLARD - *Nottinghamshire*

| Opposition | Venue | Date | Batting | | | Fielding | Bowling |
|---|---|---|---|---|---|---|---|
| **BRITANNIC ASSURANCE** | | | | | | | |
| Leicestershire | Trent Bridge | May 9 | 45 | & | 0 | 3Ct | |
| Yorkshire | Headingley | May 16 | 2 | & | 40 | 2Ct | |
| Kent | Trent Bridge | May 22 | 16 | & | 48 | 1Ct | |
| Leicestershire | Leicester | May 25 | 7* | & | 33 | | |
| Hampshire | Trent Bridge | May 31 | 100 | & | 0 | 1Ct | |
| Surrey | The Oval | June 4 | 62 | & | 1 | | |
| Gloucs | Gloucester | June 14 | 3 | & | 0 | 1Ct | |
| Worcestershire | Worcester | June 18 | 18 | & | 13 | | |
| Warwickshire | Trent Bridge | June 21 | 8* | & | 38 | | |
| Glamorgan | Cardiff | July 2 | 26 | & | 33 | 2Ct | |
| Lancashire | Trent Bridge | July 16 | 145 | | | 2Ct | |
| Northants | Well'borough | July 19 | 52 | | | 1Ct | |
| Yorkshire | Worksop | July 23 | 8 | & | 35 | 1Ct | |
| Middlesex | Lord's | July 26 | 11 | & | 42 | 3Ct | |
| Sussex | Eastbourne | Aug 6 | 13 | | | 2Ct | |
| Essex | Trent Bridge | Aug 9 | 56 | & | 16 | | |
| Somerset | Trent Bridge | Aug 16 | 63 | & | 25 | | 0-29 |
| Derbyshire | Trent Bridge | Aug 23 | 7 | & | 2 | | |
| Lancashire | Old Trafford | Aug 28 | 43 | & | 12 | 1Ct | |
| Middlesex | Trent Bridge | Sept 3 | 26 | & | 18 | | |
| Derbyshire | Derby | Sept 10 | 123 | & | 35* | 1Ct | 1-46 |
| Worcestershire | Trent Bridge | Sept 17 | 10 | | | | |
| **OTHER FIRST-CLASS** | | | | | | | |
| Oxford U | The Parks | April 27 | 20 | | | | |
| **REFUGE ASSURANCE** | | | | | | | |
| Northants | Well'borough | July 21 | 6 | | | 1Ct | |
| Sussex | Hove | July 28 | 30* | | | | |
| Worcestershire | Trent Bridge | Aug 4 | 73 | | | | |
| Kent | Trent Bridge | Aug 11 | 56* | | | 1Ct | |
| Yorkshire | Scarborough | Aug 18 | 53 | | | | |
| Derbyshire | Trent Bridge | Aug 25 | | | | | |
| Worcestershire | Trent Bridge | Sept 1 | 50 | | | | |
| **NATWEST TROPHY** | | | | | | | |
| Hampshire | Southampton | July 31 | 6 | | | | |

## BATTING AVERAGES - Including fielding

| | Matches | Inns | NO | Runs | HS | Avge | 100s | 50s | Ct | St |
|---|---|---|---|---|---|---|---|---|---|---|
| Britannic Assurance | 22 | 40 | 3 | 1235 | 145 | 33.37 | 3 | 4 | 21 | - |
| Other First-Class | 1 | 1 | 0 | 20 | 20 | 20.00 | - | - | - | - |
| ALL FIRST-CLASS | 23 | 41 | 3 | 1255 | 145 | 33.02 | 3 | 4 | 21 | - |
| Refuge Assurance | 7 | 6 | 2 | 268 | 73 | 67.00 | - | 4 | 2 | - |
| NatWest Trophy | 1 | 1 | 0 | 6 | 6 | 6.00 | - | - | - | - |
| ALL ONE-DAY | 8 | 7 | 2 | 274 | 73 | 54.80 | - | 4 | 2 | - |

## BOWLING AVERAGES

| | Overs | Mdns | Runs | Wkts | Avge | Best | 5wI | 10wM |
|---|---|---|---|---|---|---|---|---|
| Britannic Assurance | 23.5 | 8 | 75 | 1 | 75.00 | 1-46 | - | - |
| Other First-Class | | | | | | | | |
| ALL FIRST-CLASS | 23.5 | 8 | 75 | 1 | 75.00 | 1-46 | - | - |
| Refuge Assurance | | | | | | | | |
| NatWest Trophy | | | | | | | | |
| ALL ONE-DAY | | | | | | | | |

# J.C.POOLEY - *Middlesex*

| Opposition | Venue | Date | Batting | | | Fielding | Bowling |
|---|---|---|---|---|---|---|---|
| **BRITANNIC ASSURANCE** | | | | | | | |
| Yorkshire | Lord's | April 27 | 3 | | | | |
| Warwickshire | Edgbaston | July 2 | 18 | & | 2 | 1Ct | |
| Northants | Uxbridge | July 16 | 20 | | | 1Ct | |
| Lancashire | Uxbridge | July 19 | 5 | & | 5 | 2Ct | |
| Notts | Lord's | July 26 | 11 | & | 58 | | |
| Hampshire | Lord's | Aug 2 | 4 | & | 27 | | |
| Derbyshire | Lord's | Aug 9 | 88 | & | 29 | | |
| Surrey | The Oval | Aug 20 | 20 | & | 1 | 1Ct | |
| Worcestershire | Worcester | Aug 23 | 8 | & | 28 | 1Ct | |
| Kent | Canterbury | Aug 28 | 11 | & | 14 | 1Ct | |
| Notts | Trent Bridge | Sept 3 | 2 | & | 36 | 1Ct | |
| **OTHER FIRST-CLASS** | | | | | | | |
| MCC | Lord's | April 16 | 17 | | | | |
| **REFUGE ASSURANCE** | | | | | | | |
| Surrey | Lord's | April 28 | 42 | | | | |
| Derbyshire | Lord's | Aug 11 | 109 | | | | |
| Essex | Colchester | Aug 18 | 12 | | | | |
| Worcestershire | Worcester | Aug 25 | 22 | | | | |
| **BENSON & HEDGES CUP** | | | | | | | |
| Somerset | Taunton | April 23 | 2 | | | | |
| Surrey | Lord's | April 25 | 8 | | | | |
| Essex | Chelmsford | May 2 | 1 | | | | |

## BATTING AVERAGES - Including fielding

| | Matches | Inns | NO | Runs | HS | Avge | 100s | 50s | Ct | St |
|---|---|---|---|---|---|---|---|---|---|---|
| Britannic Assurance | 11 | 20 | 0 | 390 | 88 | 19.50 | - | 2 | 8 | - |
| Other First-Class | 1 | 1 | 0 | 17 | 17 | 17.00 | - | - | - | - |
| ALL FIRST-CLASS | 12 | 21 | 0 | 407 | 88 | 19.38 | - | 2 | 8 | - |
| Refuge Assurance | 4 | 4 | 0 | 185 | 109 | 46.25 | 1 | - | - | - |
| Benson & Hedges Cup | 3 | 3 | 0 | 11 | 8 | 3.66 | - | - | - | - |
| ALL ONE-DAY | 7 | 7 | 0 | 196 | 109 | 28.00 | 1 | - | - | - |

## BOWLING AVERAGES
Did not bowl

# L.POTTER - *Leicestershire*

| Opposition | Venue | Date | Batting | | | Fielding | Bowling |
|---|---|---|---|---|---|---|---|
| **BRITANNIC ASSURANCE** | | | | | | | |
| Glamorgan | Leicester | April 27 | | | | | 0-1 |
| Notts | Trent Bridge | May 9 | 6 | & | 0 | 1Ct | 0-29 & 0-34 |
| Northants | Northampton | May 16 | 10 | & | 22 | | 2-14 |
| Notts | Leicester | May 25 | 44 | & | 64 | 1Ct | 1-37 |
| Essex | Ilford | June 4 | 85 | & | 37 | 2Ct | 0-66 & 2-63 |
| Middlesex | Uxbridge | June 7 | 41 | & | 2 | | |
| Surrey | Leicester | June 14 | 10 | & | 14* | 1Ct | 0-0 & 1-72 |
| Lancashire | Leicester | June 18 | | | 10 | 3Ct | |
| Glamorgan | Neath | June 21 | | | | | 1-46 |
| Worcestershire | Worcester | June 28 | 15 | & | 16* | 1Ct | 0-29 |
| Gloucs | Hinckley | July 2 | | | 1 | | 1-31 |
| Northants | Leicester | July 5 | 4 | & | 0 | | 0-53 |
| Sussex | Hove | July 19 | 89 | & | 0 | | 0-51 & 1-48 |
| Warwickshire | Leicester | July 26 | 8 | & | 44 | | 1-58 |
| Somerset | Weston | Aug 2 | 22 | & | 43* | | 2-52 & 1-13 |
| Yorkshire | Leicester | Aug 6 | | | | 2Ct | 0-20 |
| Kent | Leicester | Aug 9 | 61 | & | 37 | 1Ct | 1-16 & 1-90 |
| Hampshire | Bournemouth | Aug 16 | 14 | | | 1Ct | 2-59 & 1-56 |
| Derbyshire | Derby | Aug 20 | 25 | | | 1Ct | 0-1 |
| Derbyshire | Leicester | Aug 28 | 24 | & | 64 | 2Ct | 0-32 & 1-69 |
| Essex | Leicester | Sept 10 | 0 | & | 45 | | 4-116 & 0-13 |
| Kent | Canterbury | Sept 17 | 0 | & | 42 | 1Ct | 0-36 & 3-32 |
| **OTHER FIRST-CLASS** | | | | | | | |
| Cambridge U | Fenner's | May 22 | 73* | | | 3Ct | 1-27 & 1-27 |
| West Indies | Leicester | June 1 | 53 | & | 2 | 1Ct | 0-47 |
| **REFUGE ASSURANCE** | | | | | | | |
| Derbyshire | Leicester | April 21 | 12 | | | | 1-37 |

# P PLAYER RECORDS

| | | | | | |
|---|---|---|---|---|---|
| Glamorgan | Leicester | April 28 | 45 | | |
| Northants | Northampton | May 12 | 33 | | |
| Yorkshire | Leicester | May 19 | 40 * | | |
| Notts | Leicester | May 26 | 42 * | | 0-17 |
| Surrey | Leicester | June 16 | 9 | | |
| Worcestershire | Worcester | June 30 | 31 * | | |
| Lancashire | Leicester | July 7 | 1 | 1Ct | |
| Kent | Canterbury | July 14 | 19 | 2Ct | 0-20 |
| Sussex | Hove | July 21 | 59 | | |
| Somerset | Weston | Aug 4 | 13 * | | |
| Warwickshire | Leicester | Aug 11 | 15 | 1Ct | |
| Hampshire | Bournemouth | Aug 18 | 2 | | |
| Gloucs | Leicester | Aug 25 | 53 | | |

**NATWEST TROPHY**

| | | | | | |
|---|---|---|---|---|---|
| Shropshire | Leicester | June 26 | 25 * | | |
| Northants | Northampton | July 11 | 57 | | 1-32 |

**BENSON & HEDGES CUP**

| | | | | | |
|---|---|---|---|---|---|
| Kent | Canterbury | April 23 | 6 | | |
| Sussex | Hove | April 25 | 2 | 1Ct | |
| Scotland | Leicester | May 2 | 3 * | | 0-42 |
| Lancashire | Leicester | May 4 | 54 | | |

**OTHER ONE-DAY**

| | | | | |
|---|---|---|---|---|
| Durham | Harrogate | June 11 | 0 * | |

**BATTING AVERAGES - Including fielding**

| | Matches | Inns | NO | Runs | HS | Avge | 100s | 50s | Ct | St |
|---|---|---|---|---|---|---|---|---|---|---|
| Britannic Assurance | 22 | 34 | 3 | 899 | 89 | 29.00 | - | 5 | 17 | - |
| Other First-Class | 2 | 3 | 1 | 128 | 73 * | 64.00 | - | 2 | 4 | - |
| ALL FIRST-CLASS | 24 | 37 | 4 | 1027 | 89 | 31.12 | - | 7 | 21 | - |
| Refuge Assurance | 14 | 14 | 4 | 374 | 59 | 37.40 | - | 2 | 4 | - |
| NatWest Trophy | 2 | 2 | 1 | 82 | 57 | 82.00 | - | 1 | - | - |
| Benson & Hedges Cup | 4 | 4 | 1 | 65 | 54 | 21.66 | - | 1 | 1 | - |
| Other One-Day | 1 | 1 | 1 | 0 | 0 * | - | - | - | - | - |
| ALL ONE-DAY | 21 | 21 | 7 | 521 | 59 | 37.21 | - | 4 | 5 | - |

**BOWLING AVERAGES**

| | Overs | Mdns | Runs | Wkts | Avge | Best | 5wI | 10wM |
|---|---|---|---|---|---|---|---|---|
| Britannic Assurance | 418.2 | 93 | 1237 | 26 | 47.57 | 4-116 | - | - |
| Other First-Class | 39 | 12 | 101 | 2 | 50.50 | 1-27 | - | - |
| ALL FIRST-CLASS | 457.2 | 105 | 1338 | 28 | 47.78 | 4-116 | - | - |
| Refuge Assurance | 11 | 0 | 74 | 1 | 74.00 | 1-37 | - | |
| NatWest Trophy | 6 | 1 | 32 | 1 | 32.00 | 1-32 | - | |
| Benson & Hedges Cup | 9 | 0 | 42 | 0 | - | - | - | |
| Other One-Day | | | | | | | | |
| ALL ONE-DAY | 26 | 1 | 148 | 2 | 74.00 | 1-32 | - | |

## P.J.PRICHARD - *Essex*

| Opposition | Venue | Date | Batting | | | Fielding | Bowling |
|---|---|---|---|---|---|---|---|
| **BRITANNIC ASSURANCE** | | | | | | | |
| Surrey | Chelmsford | April 27 | 45 * | | | | |
| Northants | Northampton | May 9 | 190 | | | 1Ct | |
| Kent | Folkestone | May 16 | 53 | | | | |
| Warwickshire | Chelmsford | May 22 | 5 | & | 12 * | | |
| Gloucs | Bristol | May 31 | 10 | | | | |
| Leicestershire | Ilford | June 4 | 10 | & | 50 | | |
| Worcestershire | Ilford | June 7 | 9 | & | 0 * | 1Ct | 0-52 |
| Sussex | Horsham | June 21 | 13 | | | | |
| Middlesex | Lord's | June 28 | 129 | & | 0 | | |
| Hampshire | Chelmsford | July 2 | 3 | & | 38 | 1Ct | 1-28 |
| Surrey | The Oval | July 5 | 3 | & | 14 | 3Ct | |
| Kent | Southend | July 16 | 122 | & | 14 | | 0-78 |
| Somerset | Southend | July 19 | 0 | & | 8 | 1Ct | |
| Glamorgan | Cardiff | July 23 | 22 * | | | | |
| Derbyshire | Derby | Aug 6 | 20 | & | 11 | 1Ct | |
| Notts | Trent Bridge | Aug 9 | 25 | & | 38 | | |
| Northants | Colchester | Aug 16 | 2 | | | 4Ct | |
| Yorkshire | Colchester | Aug 20 | 128 | & | 8 | 1Ct | |
| Derbyshire | Chelmsford | Sept 3 | 27 | | | 2Ct | |
| Leicestershire | Leicester | Sept 10 | 9 | & | 2 * | 2Ct | |
| Middlesex | Chelmsford | Sept 17 | 11 | | | | |

**OTHER FIRST-CLASS**

| | | | | | | |
|---|---|---|---|---|---|---|
| Cambridge U | Fenner's | April 19 | 55 * | & | 18 * | |
| West Indies | Chelmsford | Aug 3 | 5 | & | 13 | |
| Victoria | Chelmsford | Sept 23 | 2 | | | 2Ct |

**REFUGE ASSURANCE**

| | | | | |
|---|---|---|---|---|
| Yorkshire | Chelmsford | April 28 | | |
| Notts | Trent Bridge | May 12 | 15 | 1Ct |
| Kent | Folkestone | May 19 | 25 | |
| Surrey | The Oval | May 26 | 4 | 1Ct |
| Glamorgan | Pontypridd | June 2 | | 1Ct |
| Worcestershire | Ilford | June 9 | 36 | |
| Hampshire | Chelmsford | June 16 | 34 | |
| Derbyshire | Chelmsford | June 30 | 40 | 1Ct |
| Warwickshire | Chelmsford | July 7 | 5 | |
| Somerset | Southend | July 21 | 22 | 1Ct |
| Gloucs | Cheltenham | July 28 | 0 | 1Ct |
| Northants | Northampton | Aug 11 | 13 | 1Ct |
| Middlesex | Colchester | Aug 18 | 54 * | |

**NATWEST TROPHY**

| | | | | |
|---|---|---|---|---|
| Devon | Exmouth | June 26 | 27 * | |
| Sussex | Hove | July 11 | 0 | 1Ct |
| Surrey | The Oval | July 31 | 11 | |

**BENSON & HEDGES CUP**

| | | | | |
|---|---|---|---|---|
| Surrey | The Oval | April 23 | 10 | 1Ct |
| Warwickshire | Edgbaston | April 25 | 38 | 1Ct |
| Middlesex | Chelmsford | May 2 | 31 | 1Ct |
| Somerset | Chelmsford | May 7 | 12 * | |
| Hampshire | Chelmsford | May 29 | 2 | |
| Worcestershire | Chelmsford | June 12 | 18 | |

**OTHER ONE-DAY**

| | | | | |
|---|---|---|---|---|
| Durham | Scarborough | Aug 31 | 1 | 1Ct |
| Yorkshire | Scarborugh | Sept 2 | 42 | |
| Victoria | Chelmsford | Sept 22 | 12 | |

**BATTING AVERAGES - Including fielding**

| | Matches | Inns | NO | Runs | HS | Avge | 100s | 50s | Ct | St |
|---|---|---|---|---|---|---|---|---|---|---|
| Britannic Assurance | 21 | 33 | 5 | 1031 | 190 | 36.82 | 4 | 2 | 17 | - |
| Other First-Class | 3 | 5 | 2 | 93 | 55 * | 31.00 | - | 1 | 2 | - |
| ALL FIRST-CLASS | 24 | 38 | 7 | 1124 | 190 | 36.25 | 4 | 3 | 19 | - |
| Refuge Assurance | 13 | 11 | 1 | 248 | 54 * | 24.80 | - | 1 | 7 | - |
| NatWest Trophy | 3 | 3 | 1 | 38 | 27 * | 19.00 | - | - | 1 | - |
| Benson & Hedges Cup | 6 | 6 | 1 | 111 | 38 | 22.20 | - | - | 3 | - |
| Other One-Day | 3 | 3 | 0 | 55 | 42 | 18.33 | - | - | 1 | - |
| ALL ONE-DAY | 25 | 23 | 3 | 452 | 54 * | 22.60 | - | 1 | 12 | - |

**BOWLING AVERAGES**

| | Overs | Mdns | Runs | Wkts | Avge | Best | 5wI | 10wM |
|---|---|---|---|---|---|---|---|---|
| Britannic Assurance | 13.3 | 0 | 158 | 1 | 158.00 | 1-28 | - | - |
| Other First-Class | | | | | | | | |
| ALL FIRST-CLASS | 13.3 | 0 | 158 | 1 | 158.00 | 1-28 | - | - |
| Refuge Assurance | | | | | | | | |
| NatWest Trophy | | | | | | | | |
| Benson & Hedges Cup | | | | | | | | |
| Other One-Day | | | | | | | | |
| ALL ONE-DAY | | | | | | | | |

## A.P.PRIDGEON - *Shropshire*

| Opposition | Venue | Date | Batting | Fielding | Bowling |
|---|---|---|---|---|---|
| **NATWEST TROPHY** | | | | | |
| Leicestershire | Leicester | June 26 | 4 | | 0-21 |

**BATTING AVERAGES - Including fielding**

| | Matches | Inns | NO | Runs | HS | Avge | 100s | 50s | Ct | St |
|---|---|---|---|---|---|---|---|---|---|---|
| NatWest Trophy | 1 | 1 | 0 | 4 | 4 | 4.00 | - | - | - | - |
| ALL ONE-DAY | 1 | 1 | 0 | 4 | 4 | 4.00 | - | - | - | - |

**BOWLING AVERAGES**

| | Overs | Mdns | Runs | Wkts | Avge | Best | 5wI | 10wM |
|---|---|---|---|---|---|---|---|---|
| NatWest Trophy | 10.5 | 7 | 21 | 0 | - | - | - | - |

# PLAYER RECORDS

**P**

ALL ONE-DAY    10.5    7    21    0    -    -    -

## D.R.PRINGLE - *Essex & England*

| Opposition | Venue | Date | Batting | Fielding | Bowling |
|---|---|---|---|---|---|
| **CORNHILL TEST MATCHES** | | | | | |
| West Indies | Headingley | June 6 | 16 & 27 | 1Ct | 2-14 & 2-38 |
| West Indies | Lord's | June 20 | 35 | | 5-100 |
| West Indies | Trent Bridge | July 4 | 0 & 3 | | 2-71 & 0-20 |
| West Indies | Edgbaston | July 25 | 2 & 45 | | 1-48 & 0-31 |
| **BRITANNIC ASSURANCE** | | | | | |
| Surrey | Chelmsford | April 27 | | 1Ct | 2-74 |
| Northants | Northampton | May 9 | 68 & 37 * | 1Ct | 5-70 & 1-51 |
| Kent | Folkestone | May 16 | 5 | | 2-56 & 2-25 |
| Gloucs | Bristol | May 31 | 24 | | 2-17 & 0-4 |
| Middlesex | Lord's | June 28 | 0 * | | 0-44 & 3-38 |
| Kent | Southend | July 16 | | 27 | 2-74 & 0-4 |
| Somerset | Southend | July 19 | 25 * | | 0-55 & 0-40 |
| Northants | Colchester | Aug 16 | 5 | | 0-14 & 2-26 |
| Lancashire | Old Trafford | Aug 23 | | | 1-44 & 1-24 |
| Derbyshire | Chelmsford | Sept 3 | 78 * | 1Ct | 0-44 & 0-20 |
| Leicestershire | Leicester | Sept 10 | 45 * | | 1-78 & 1-22 |
| Middlesex | Chelmsford | Sept 17 | 14 * | 1Ct | 3-25 & 2-38 |
| **OTHER FIRST-CLASS** | | | | | |
| Cambridge U | Fenner's | April 19 | 52 | 3Ct | 1-18 & 1-4 |
| West Indies | Chelmsford | Aug 3 | 31 * | | 2-48 & 1-29 |
| Victoria | Chelmsford | Sept 23 | 68 | 1Ct | 0-0 |
| **TEXACO TROPHY** | | | | | |
| West Indies | Edgbaston | May 23 | 1 | | 0-22 |
| West Indies | Old Trafford | May 25 | | 1Ct | 2-52 |
| West Indies | Lord's | May 27 | | | 0-56 |
| **REFUGE ASSURANCE** | | | | | |
| Yorkshire | Chelmsford | April 28 | | | 2-28 |
| Notts | Trent Bridge | May 12 | 28 | 1Ct | 2-45 |
| Kent | Folkestone | May 19 | 9 | 1Ct | 1-41 |
| Glamorgan | Pontypridd | June 2 | | | 1-26 |
| Hampshire | Chelmsford | June 16 | 17 | | |
| Derbyshire | Chelmsford | June 30 | 4 | | 1-49 |
| Somerset | Southend | July 21 | 27 * | | 0-29 |
| Northants | Northampton | Aug 11 | 6 | | 3-43 |
| Middlesex | Colchester | Aug 18 | 34 | 1Ct | 1-6 |
| Lancashire | Old Trafford | Aug 25 | 51 * | | 1-34 |
| **NATWEST TROPHY** | | | | | |
| Devon | Exmouth | June 26 | | | 3-21 |
| Sussex | Hove | July 11 | 2 | 1Ct | 2-54 |
| Surrey | The Oval | July 31 | 19 | | 2-52 |
| **BENSON & HEDGES CUP** | | | | | |
| Surrey | The Oval | April 23 | 25 | 1Ct | 1-25 |
| Warwickshire | Edgbaston | April 25 | 9 * | | 5-51 |
| Middlesex | Chelmsford | May 2 | 36 * | | 1-32 |
| Somerset | Chelmsford | May 7 | | | 3-31 |
| Hampshire | Chelmsford | May 29 | 3 | | 2-36 |
| Worcestershire | Chelmsford | June 12 | 4 | | 0-16 |
| **OTHER ONE-DAY** | | | | | |
| Victoria | Chelmsford | Sept 22 | 51 | | 2-50 |

**BATTING AVERAGES - Including fielding**

| | Matches | Inns | NO | Runs | HS | Avge | 100s | 50s | Ct | St |
|---|---|---|---|---|---|---|---|---|---|---|
| Cornhill Test Matches | 4 | 7 | 0 | 128 | 45 | 18.28 | - | - | 1 | - |
| Britannic Assurance | 12 | 11 | 6 | 328 | 78 * | 65.60 | - | 2 | 4 | - |
| Other First-Class | 3 | 3 | 1 | 151 | 68 | 75.50 | - | 2 | 4 | - |
| ALL FIRST-CLASS | 19 | 21 | 7 | 607 | 78 * | 43.35 | - | 4 | 9 | - |
| Texaco Trophy | 3 | 1 | 0 | 1 | 1 | 1.00 | - | - | 1 | - |
| Refuge Assurance | 10 | 8 | 2 | 176 | 51 * | 29.33 | - | 1 | 3 | - |
| NatWest Trophy | 3 | 2 | 0 | 21 | 19 | 10.50 | - | - | 1 | - |
| Benson & Hedges Cup | 6 | 5 | 2 | 77 | 36 * | 25.66 | - | - | 1 | - |
| Other One-Day | 1 | 1 | 0 | 51 | 51 | 51.00 | - | 1 | - | - |
| ALL ONE-DAY | 23 | 17 | 4 | 326 | 51 * | 25.07 | - | 2 | 6 | - |

**BOWLING AVERAGES**

| | Overs | Mdns | Runs | Wkts | Avge | Best | 5wI | 10wM |
|---|---|---|---|---|---|---|---|---|
| Cornhill Test Matches | 128.1 | 33 | 322 | 12 | 26.83 | 5-100 | 1 | - |
| Britannic Assurance | 359.4 | 95 | 887 | 30 | 29.56 | 5-70 | 1 | - |
| Other First-Class | 46 | 17 | 99 | 5 | 19.80 | 2-48 | - | - |
| ALL FIRST-CLASS | 533.5 | 145 | 1308 | 47 | 27.83 | 5-70 | 2 | - |
| Texaco Trophy | 27 | 2 | 130 | 2 | 65.00 | 2-52 | - | |
| Refuge Assurance | 62.4 | 2 | 301 | 12 | 25.08 | 3-43 | - | |
| NatWest Trophy | 34 | 3 | 127 | 7 | 18.14 | 3-21 | - | |
| Benson & Hedges Cup | 56.2 | 6 | 191 | 12 | 15.91 | 5-51 | 1 | |
| Other One-Day | 10 | 0 | 50 | 2 | 25.00 | 2-50 | - | |
| ALL ONE-DAY | 190 | 13 | 799 | 35 | 22.82 | 5-51 | 1 | |

## N.J.PRINGLE - *Somerset*

| Opposition | Venue | Date | Batting | Fielding | Bowling |
|---|---|---|---|---|---|
| **BRITANNIC ASSURANCE** | | | | | |
| Kent | Taunton | July 26 | 7 & 17 | 1Ct | |
| **OTHER FIRST-CLASS** | | | | | |
| Sri Lanka | Taunton | Aug 10 | 1 & 20 | | |
| **REFUGE ASSURANCE** | | | | | |
| Lancashire | Taunton | July 5 | 7 | | |
| Essex | Southend | July 21 | 1 | | |

**BATTING AVERAGES - Including fielding**

| | Matches | Inns | NO | Runs | HS | Avge | 100s | 50s | Ct | St |
|---|---|---|---|---|---|---|---|---|---|---|
| Britannic Assurance | 1 | 2 | 0 | 24 | 17 | 12.00 | - | - | 1 | - |
| Other First-Class | 1 | 2 | 0 | 21 | 20 | 10.50 | - | - | - | - |
| ALL FIRST-CLASS | 2 | 4 | 0 | 45 | 20 | 11.25 | - | - | 1 | - |
| Refuge Assurance | 2 | 2 | 0 | 8 | 7 | 4.00 | - | - | - | - |
| ALL ONE-DAY | 2 | 2 | 0 | 8 | 7 | 4.00 | - | - | - | - |

**BOWLING AVERAGES**
Did not bowl

## C.S.PRITCHARD - *Devon*

| Opposition | Venue | Date | Batting | Fielding | Bowling |
|---|---|---|---|---|---|
| **NATWEST TROPHY** | | | | | |
| Essex | Exmouth | June 26 | 0 | | |

**BATTING AVERAGES - Including fielding**

| | Matches | Inns | NO | Runs | HS | Avge | 100s | 50s | Ct | St |
|---|---|---|---|---|---|---|---|---|---|---|
| NatWest Trophy | 1 | 1 | 0 | 0 | 0 | 0.00 | - | - | - | - |
| ALL ONE-DAY | 1 | 1 | 0 | 0 | 0 | 0.00 | - | - | - | - |

**BOWLING AVERAGES**
Did not bowl

## A.C.PUDDLE - *Wales*

| Opposition | Venue | Date | Batting | Fielding | Bowling |
|---|---|---|---|---|---|
| **OTHER ONE-DAY** | | | | | |
| West Indies | Brecon | July 15 | 16 | | |

**BATTING AVERAGES - Including fielding**

| | Matches | Inns | NO | Runs | HS | Avge | 100s | 50s | Ct | St |
|---|---|---|---|---|---|---|---|---|---|---|
| Other One-Day | 1 | 1 | 0 | 16 | 16 | 16.00 | - | - | - | - |
| ALL ONE-DAY | 1 | 1 | 0 | 16 | 16 | 16.00 | - | - | - | - |

**BOWLING AVERAGES**
Did not bowl

| P | PLAYER RECORDS |
|---|----------------|

## A.J.PUGH - *Devon*

| Opposition | Venue | Date | Batting | Fielding | Bowling |
|------------|-------|------|---------|----------|---------|
| **NATWEST TROPHY** | | | | | |
| Essex | Exmouth | June 26 | 0 | | |

**BATTING AVERAGES - Including fielding**

| | Matches | Inns | NO | Runs | HS | Avge | 100s | 50s | Ct | St |
|---|---------|------|----|----|----|------|------|-----|----|----|
| NatWest Trophy | 1 | 1 | 0 | 0 | 0 | 0.00 | - | - | - | - |
| ALL ONE-DAY | 1 | 1 | 0 | 0 | 0 | 0.00 | - | - | - | - |

**BOWLING AVERAGES**
Did not bowl

## R.A.PYMAN - *Cambridge University & Dorset*

| Opposition | Venue | Date | Batting | Fielding | Bowling |
|------------|-------|------|---------|----------|---------|
| **OTHER FIRST-CLASS** | | | | | |
| Surrey | Fenner's | May 18 | 6 & 0 | 1Ct | 2-74 & 1-52 |
| Leicestershire | Fenner's | May 22 | 6 & 8* | | 1-90 |
| **NATWEST TROPHY** | | | | | |
| For Dorset | | | | | |
| Lancashire | Bournemouth | June 26 | 1 | | 0-41 |

**BATTING AVERAGES - Including fielding**

| | Matches | Inns | NO | Runs | HS | Avge | 100s | 50s | Ct | St |
|---|---------|------|----|----|----|------|------|-----|----|----|
| Other First-Class | 2 | 4 | 1 | 20 | 8* | 6.66 | - | - | 1 | - |
| ALL FIRST-CLASS | 2 | 4 | 1 | 20 | 8* | 6.66 | - | - | 1 | - |
| NatWest Trophy | 1 | 1 | 0 | 1 | 1 | 1.00 | - | - | - | - |
| ALL ONE-DAY | 1 | 1 | 0 | 1 | 1 | 1.00 | - | - | - | - |

**BOWLING AVERAGES**

| | Overs | Mdns | Runs | Wkts | Avge | Best | 5wI | 10wM |
|---|-------|------|------|------|------|------|-----|------|
| Other First-Class | 65 | 15 | 216 | 4 | 54.00 | 2-74 | - | - |
| ALL FIRST-CLASS | 65 | 15 | 216 | 4 | 54.00 | 2-74 | - | - |
| NatWest Trophy | 12 | 2 | 41 | 0 | - | - | - | - |
| ALL ONE-DAY | 12 | 2 | 41 | 0 | - | - | - | - |

# PLAYER RECORDS

## N.V.RADFORD - *Worcestershire*

| Opposition | Venue | Date | Batting | Fielding | Bowling |
|---|---|---|---|---|---|
| **BRITANNIC ASSURANCE** | | | | | |
| Gloucs | Worcester | April 27 | | | 2-94 |
| Glamorgan | Worcester | May 31 | 0 | | 2-42 & 0-45 |
| Northants | Northampton | June 4 | | 1Ct | 2-61 & 0-53 |
| Essex | Ilford | June 7 | 7 * | | 6-76 & 3-19 |
| Sussex | Hove | June 14 | | | 0-22 & 1-32 |
| Notts | Worcester | June 18 | | 2 | 1-20 |
| Leicestershire | Worcester | June 28 | | | 0-48 & 1-55 |
| Hampshire | Portsmouth | July 16 | 6 * | | 0-72 |
| Derbyshire | Kidd'minster | July 19 | 19 & 45 | 2Ct | 1-61 |
| Warwickshire | Worcester | Aug 2 | 10 * | | 2-55 & 0-18 |
| Somerset | Weston | Aug 6 | 32 * & 0 | | 2-105 & 1-25 |
| Lancashire | Blackpool | Aug 20 | 11 | | 0-21 & 1-24 |
| Middlesex | Worcester | Aug 23 | 0 * | | 2-45 & 3-46 |
| Warwickshire | Edgbaston | Aug 28 | 0 * & 0 | 1Ct | 2-14 & 1-54 |
| Somerset | Worcester | Sept 3 | | | 7-43 & 1-85 |
| Glamorgan | Cardiff | Sept 10 | 20 | | 4-29 & 0-16 |
| Notts | Trent Bridge | Sept 17 | 1 & 4 | | 1-83 |
| **REFUGE ASSURANCE** | | | | | |
| Kent | Worcester | April 21 | | 1Ct | 3-46 |
| Gloucs | Bristol | May 5 | | | 2-37 |
| Northants | Northampton | May 19 | | | 3-31 |
| Warwickshire | Edgbaston | May 26 | 1 * | | 1-42 |
| Surrey | Worcester | June 2 | | | |
| Essex | Ilford | June 9 | 5 | | 2-67 |
| Sussex | Hove | June 16 | | | 1-11 |
| Yorkshire | Sheffield | June 23 | 12 | 1Ct | 1-33 |
| Leicestershire | Worcester | June 30 | | | 1-48 |
| Hampshire | Southampton | July 7 | | 1Ct | 1-37 |
| Derbyshire | Worcester | July 9 | | | 3-16 |
| Glamorgan | Worcester | July 21 | | 2Ct | 1-37 |
| Notts | Trent Bridge | Aug 4 | | 1Ct | 1-25 |
| Somerset | Worcester | Aug 18 | 20 * | | 0-63 |
| Notts | Trent Bridge | Sept 1 | | | 0-36 |
| Lancashire | Old Trafford | Sept 15 | | 1Ct | 5-42 |
| **NATWEST TROPHY** | | | | | |
| Bedfordshire | Bedford | June 26 | | | 7-19 |
| Glamorgan | Worcester | July 11 | 15 * | | 0-35 |
| **BENSON & HEDGES CUP** | | | | | |
| Gloucs | Worcester | April 25 | | | 3-40 |
| Combined U | Fenner's | May 2 | | | 3-22 |
| Derbyshire | Worcester | May 4 | | 1Ct | 2-36 |
| Kent | Worcester | May 29 | | | 2-57 |
| Essex | Chelmsford | June 12 | | 1Ct | 3-41 |
| Lancashire | Lord's | July 13 | 25 * | | 3-48 |

### BATTING AVERAGES - Including fielding

| | Matches | Inns | NO | Runs | HS | Avge | 100s | 50s | Ct | St |
|---|---|---|---|---|---|---|---|---|---|---|
| Britannic Assurance | 17 | 16 | 6 | 157 | 45 | 15.70 | - | - | 4 | - |
| ALL FIRST-CLASS | 17 | 16 | 6 | 157 | 45 | 15.70 | - | - | 4 | - |
| Refuge Assurance | 16 | 4 | 2 | 38 | 20 * | 19.00 | - | - | 7 | - |
| NatWest Trophy | 2 | 1 | 1 | 15 | 15 * | - | - | - | - | - |
| Benson & Hedges Cup | 6 | 1 | 1 | 25 | 25 * | - | - | - | 2 | - |
| ALL ONE-DAY | 24 | 6 | 4 | 78 | 25 * | 39.00 | - | - | 9 | - |

### BOWLING AVERAGES

| | Overs | Mdns | Runs | Wkts | Avge | Best | 5wI | 10wM |
|---|---|---|---|---|---|---|---|---|
| Britannic Assurance | 434.1 | 92 | 1363 | 46 | 29.63 | 7-43 | 2 | - |
| ALL FIRST-CLASS | 434.1 | 92 | 1363 | 46 | 29.63 | 7-43 | 2 | - |
| Refuge Assurance | 108 | 3 | 571 | 25 | 22.84 | 5-42 | 1 | |
| NatWest Trophy | 22 | 4 | 54 | 7 | 7.71 | 7-19 | 1 | |
| Benson & Hedges Cup | 61.5 | 13 | 244 | 16 | 15.25 | 3-22 | - | |
| ALL ONE-DAY | 191.5 | 20 | 869 | 48 | 18.10 | 7-19 | 2 | |

## C.P.RAMANAYAKE - *Sri Lanka*

| Opposition | Venue | Date | Batting | Fielding | Bowling |
|---|---|---|---|---|---|
| **CORNHILL TEST MATCHES** | | | | | |
| England | Lord's | Aug 22 | 0 & 34 * | 1Ct | 2-75 & 0-86 |
| **OTHER FIRST-CLASS** | | | | | |
| Yorkshire | Headingley | July 27 | 25 | | 2-23 & 0-36 |
| Worcestershire | Worcester | July 30 | 8 & 4 | | 1-84 |
| Derbyshire | Derby | Aug 2 | 41 * | | 3-84 |
| Somerset | Taunton | Aug 10 | 38 | | 0-65 & 0-24 |
| Sussex | Hove | Aug 17 | | 2 | 3-83 & 1-34 |
| **OTHER ONE-DAY** | | | | | |
| England Am. | Wolv'hampton | July 24 | | | 0-23 |
| Durham | Chester-le-S | July 26 | 9 | 1Ct | 1-16 |
| England A | Old Trafford | Aug 14 | 3 | | 1-22 |
| England A | Old Trafford | Aug 15 | 2 | | 0-31 |

### BATTING AVERAGES - Including fielding

| | Matches | Inns | NO | Runs | HS | Avge | 100s | 50s | Ct | St |
|---|---|---|---|---|---|---|---|---|---|---|
| Cornhill Test Matches | 1 | 2 | 1 | 34 | 34 * | 34.00 | - | - | 1 | - |
| Other First-Class | 5 | 6 | 1 | 118 | 41 * | 23.60 | - | - | - | - |
| ALL FIRST-CLASS | 6 | 8 | 2 | 152 | 41 * | 25.33 | - | - | 1 | - |
| Other One-Day | 4 | 3 | 0 | 14 | 9 | 4.66 | - | - | 1 | - |
| ALL ONE-DAY | 4 | 3 | 0 | 14 | 9 | 4.66 | - | - | 1 | - |

### BOWLING AVERAGES

| | Overs | Mdns | Runs | Wkts | Avge | Best | 5wI | 10wM |
|---|---|---|---|---|---|---|---|---|
| Cornhill Test Matches | 44 | 7 | 161 | 2 | 80.50 | 2-75 | - | - |
| Other First-Class | 122 | 22 | 433 | 10 | 43.30 | 3-83 | - | - |
| ALL FIRST-CLASS | 166 | 29 | 594 | 12 | 49.50 | 3-83 | - | - |
| Other One-Day | 30 | 7 | 92 | 2 | 46.00 | 1-16 | - | |
| ALL ONE-DAY | 30 | 7 | 92 | 2 | 46.00 | 1-16 | - | |

## M.R.RAMPRAKASH - *Middlesex & England*

| Opposition | Venue | Date | Batting | Fielding | Bowling |
|---|---|---|---|---|---|
| **CORNHILL TEST MATCHES** | | | | | |
| West Indies | Headingley | June 6 | 27 & 27 | 2Ct | |
| West Indies | Lord's | June 20 | 24 | | |
| West Indies | Trent Bridge | July 4 | 13 & 21 | 1Ct | |
| West Indies | Edgbaston | July 25 | 29 & 25 | | |
| West Indies | The Oval | Aug 8 | 25 & 19 | 1Ct | |
| Sri Lanka | Lord's | Aug 22 | 0 | | |
| **BRITANNIC ASSURANCE** | | | | | |
| Yorkshire | Lord's | April 27 | 0 | | |
| Sussex | Lord's | May 9 | 65 & 119 | | |
| Kent | Lord's | May 31 | 1 & 0 | | |
| Glamorgan | Cardiff | June 14 | 16 * & 0 | | |
| Essex | Lord's | June 28 | 70 * & 12 | | |
| Northants | Uxbridge | July 16 | 25 | | 1-0 |
| Lancashire | Uxbridge | July 19 | 5 & 56 | | 0-9 |
| Hampshire | Lord's | Aug 2 | 79 & 28 * | 1Ct | 0-16 |
| Kent | Canterbury | Aug 28 | 87 & 5 | | |
| Notts | Trent Bridge | Sept 3 | 110 & 83 * | 1Ct | |
| Surrey | Lord's | Sept 10 | 85 & 12 | | |
| Essex | Chelmsford | Sept 17 | 0 & 19 | | |
| **OTHER FIRST-CLASS** | | | | | |
| MCC | Lord's | April 16 | 28 | | 0-4 |
| Cambridge U | Fenner's | May 15 | 0 | | 0-11 & 0-36 |
| West Indies | Lord's | May 18 | 38 & 21 | | 0-12 |
| **TEXACO TROPHY** | | | | | |
| West Indies | Old Trafford | May 25 | 6 * | | |
| West Indies | Lord's | May 27 | 0 * | | |
| **REFUGE ASSURANCE** | | | | | |
| Gloucs | Bristol | April 21 | 111 * | 1Ct | |
| Sussex | Hove | May 12 | 62 * | | 2-32 |

# R PLAYER RECORDS

| | | | | | | |
|---|---|---|---|---|---|---|
| Kent | Southgate | June 2 | 47 | 1Ct | | 0-27 |
| Glamorgan | Cardiff | June 16 | 18 | | | 0-12 |
| Warwickshire | Edgbaston | July 14 | 11 | | | |
| Lancashire | Lord's | July 21 | 6 | | | |
| Hampshire | Lord's | Aug 4 | 68 | | | |
| Essex | Colchester | Aug 18 | 59 | 1Ct | | |

**NATWEST TROPHY**

| | | | | | |
|---|---|---|---|---|---|
| Ireland | Dublin | June 26 | 32 | | 2-15 |
| Somerset | Taunton | July 11 | 25 | | 0-31 |

**BENSON & HEDGES CUP**

| | | | | | |
|---|---|---|---|---|---|
| Somerset | Taunton | April 23 | 78* | 1Ct | |
| Surrey | Lord's | April 25 | 2 | 1Ct | |
| Essex | Chelmsford | May 2 | 33 | | |
| Warwickshire | Lord's | May 4 | 7 | 1Ct | |

**BATTING AVERAGES - Including fielding**

| | Matches | Inns | NO | Runs | HS | Avge | 100s | 50s | Ct | St |
|---|---|---|---|---|---|---|---|---|---|---|
| Cornhill Test Matches | 6 | 10 | 0 | 210 | 29 | 21.00 | - | - | 4 | - |
| Britannic Assurance | 12 | 22 | 4 | 877 | 119 | 48.72 | 2 | 7 | 2 | - |
| Other First-Class | 3 | 4 | 0 | 87 | 38 | 21.75 | - | - | - | - |
| ALL FIRST-CLASS | 21 | 36 | 4 | 1174 | 119 | 36.68 | 2 | 7 | 6 | - |
| Texaco Trophy | 2 | 2 | 2 | 6 | 6* | - | - | - | - | - |
| Refuge Assurance | 8 | 8 | 2 | 382 | 111* | 63.66 | 1 | 3 | 3 | - |
| NatWest Trophy | 2 | 2 | 0 | 57 | 32 | 28.50 | - | - | - | - |
| Benson & Hedges Cup | 4 | 4 | 1 | 120 | 78* | 40.00 | - | 1 | 3 | - |
| ALL ONE-DAY | 16 | 16 | 5 | 565 | 111* | 51.36 | 1 | 4 | 6 | - |

**BOWLING AVERAGES**

| | Overs | Mdns | Runs | Wkts | Avge | Best | 5wI | 10wM |
|---|---|---|---|---|---|---|---|---|
| Cornhill Test Matches | | | | | | | | |
| Britannic Assurance | 5 | 1 | 25 | 1 | 25.00 | 1-0 | - | - |
| Other First-Class | 14 | 2 | 63 | 0 | - | - | - | - |
| ALL FIRST-CLASS | 19 | 3 | 88 | 1 | 88.00 | 1-0 | - | - |
| Texaco Trophy | | | | | | | | |
| Refuge Assurance | 12 | 0 | 71 | 2 | 35.50 | 2-32 | - | |
| NatWest Trophy | 13 | 1 | 46 | 2 | 23.00 | 2-15 | - | |
| Benson & Hedges Cup | | | | | | | | |
| ALL ONE-DAY | 25 | 1 | 117 | 4 | 29.25 | 2-15 | - | |

## D.J.RAMSHAW - *Victoria*

| Opposition | Venue | Date | Batting | Fielding | Bowling |
|---|---|---|---|---|---|

**OTHER FIRST-CLASS**

| | | | | |
|---|---|---|---|---|
| Essex | Chelmsford | Sept 23 | 11 & 0 | |

**OTHER ONE-DAY**

| | | | | |
|---|---|---|---|---|
| Essex | Chelmsford | Sept 22 | 71 | |

**BATTING AVERAGES - Including fielding**

| | Matches | Inns | NO | Runs | HS | Avge | 100s | 50s | Ct | St |
|---|---|---|---|---|---|---|---|---|---|---|
| Other First-Class | 1 | 2 | 0 | 11 | 11 | 5.50 | - | - | - | - |
| ALL FIRST-CLASS | 1 | 2 | 0 | 11 | 11 | 5.50 | - | - | - | - |
| Other One-Day | 1 | 1 | 0 | 71 | 71 | 71.00 | - | 1 | - | - |
| ALL ONE-DAY | 1 | 1 | 0 | 71 | 71 | 71.00 | - | 1 | - | - |

**BOWLING AVERAGES**
Did not bowl

## D.W.RANDALL - *Nottinghamshire*

| Opposition | Venue | Date | Batting | Fielding | Bowling |
|---|---|---|---|---|---|

**BRITANNIC ASSURANCE**

| | | | | | |
|---|---|---|---|---|---|
| Leicestershire | Trent Bridge | May 9 | 104 | 1Ct | |
| Yorkshire | Headingley | May 16 | 37*& 7 | | |
| Kent | Trent Bridge | May 22 | 12 & 64* | 1Ct | |
| Leicestershire | Leicester | May 25 | 45 & 35 | 1Ct | |
| Hampshire | Trent Bridge | May 31 | 13 & 48* | | |
| Surrey | The Oval | June 4 | | | |
| Gloucs | Gloucester | June 14 | 9*& 85* | | |
| Worcestershire | Worcester | June 18 | 9 & 42* | 1Ct | |
| Warwickshire | Trent Bridge | June 21 | 21 | | |
| Glamorgan | Cardiff | July 2 | 20 & 112* | | |
| Lancashire | Trent Bridge | July 16 | 120 | 1Ct | |
| Northants | Well'borough | July 19 | 45 | | |
| Yorkshire | Worksop | July 23 | 65 | 1Ct | |
| Middlesex | Lord's | July 26 | 34 & 8 | | |
| Sussex | Eastbourne | Aug 6 | 26 | 2Ct | |
| Essex | Trent Bridge | Aug 9 | 6 & 44 | | |
| Somerset | Trent Bridge | Aug 16 | 13 & 73* | | |
| Derbyshire | Trent Bridge | Aug 23 | 76 & 143* | 1Ct | |
| Lancashire | Old Trafford | Aug 28 | 0 & 39 | 2Ct | |
| Middlesex | Trent Bridge | Sept 3 | 121 & 25 | 1Ct | |
| Derbyshire | Derby | Sept 10 | 27 | 3Ct | 1-19 |
| Worcestershire | Trent Bridge | Sept 17 | 39 | | |

**REFUGE ASSURANCE**

| | | | | | |
|---|---|---|---|---|---|
| Lancashire | Old Trafford | April 21 | 49 | | |
| Warwickshire | Trent Bridge | April 28 | 32 | | |
| Glamorgan | Cardiff | May 5 | 24 | | |
| Essex | Trent Bridge | May 12 | 19 | | |
| Leicestershire | Leicester | May 26 | 83* | | |
| Somerset | Trent Bridge | June 9 | 39 | 1Ct | |
| Gloucs | Gloucester | June 16 | 27 | | |
| Middlesex | Trent Bridge | June 23 | 37 | | |
| Surrey | The Oval | June 30 | 67 | | |
| Hampshire | Trent Bridge | July 14 | 83 | | |
| Northants | Well'borough | July 21 | 48 | | |
| Sussex | Hove | July 28 | 22 | 1Ct | |
| Worcestershire | Trent Bridge | Aug 4 | 50 | | |
| Kent | Trent Bridge | Aug 11 | 16 | 1Ct | |
| Yorkshire | Scarborough | Aug 18 | 10 | | |
| Derbyshire | Trent Bridge | Aug 25 | 67 | 1Ct | |
| Worcestershire | Trent Bridge | Sept 1 | 45 | | |

**NATWEST TROPHY**

| | | | | |
|---|---|---|---|---|
| Lincolnshire | Trent Bridge | June 26 | 25 | |
| Gloucs | Bristol | July 11 | 46 | |
| Hampshire | Southampton | July 31 | 95 | |

**BENSON & HEDGES CUP**

| | | | | |
|---|---|---|---|---|
| Hampshire | Southampton | April 23 | 5 | 1Ct |
| Yorkshire | Trent Bridge | April 25 | 86 | 1Ct |
| Glamorgan | Cardiff | May 4 | 14 | 2Ct |
| Min Counties | Trent Bridge | May 7 | 84 | 1Ct |

**OTHER ONE-DAY**
For World XI

| | | | | |
|---|---|---|---|---|
| Yorkshire | Scarborough | Sept 8 | 24 | |

**BATTING AVERAGES - Including fielding**

| | Matches | Inns | NO | Runs | HS | Avge | 100s | 50s | Ct | St |
|---|---|---|---|---|---|---|---|---|---|---|
| Britannic Assurance | 22 | 34 | 9 | 1567 | 143* | 62.68 | 5 | 5 | 15 | - |
| ALL FIRST-CLASS | 22 | 34 | 9 | 1567 | 143* | 62.68 | 5 | 5 | 15 | - |
| Refuge Assurance | 17 | 17 | 1 | 718 | 83* | 44.87 | - | 5 | 4 | - |
| NatWest Trophy | 3 | 3 | 0 | 166 | 95 | 55.33 | - | 1 | - | - |
| Benson & Hedges Cup | 4 | 4 | 0 | 189 | 86 | 47.25 | - | 2 | 5 | - |
| Other One-Day | 1 | 1 | 0 | 24 | 24 | 24.00 | - | - | - | - |
| ALL ONE-DAY | 25 | 25 | 1 | 1097 | 95 | 45.70 | - | 8 | 9 | - |

**BOWLING AVERAGES**

| | Overs | Mdns | Runs | Wkts | Avge | Best | 5wI | 10wM |
|---|---|---|---|---|---|---|---|---|
| Britannic Assurance | 4 | 0 | 19 | 1 | 19.00 | 1-19 | - | - |
| ALL FIRST-CLASS | 4 | 0 | 19 | 1 | 19.00 | 1-19 | - | - |
| Refuge Assurance | | | | | | | | |
| NatWest Trophy | | | | | | | | |
| Benson & Hedges Cup | | | | | | | | |
| Other One-Day | | | | | | | | |
| ALL ONE-DAY | | | | | | | | |

# PLAYER RECORDS

**R**

## J.D.RATCLIFFE - *Warwickshire*

| Opposition | Venue | Date | Batting | | | Fielding | Bowling |
|---|---|---|---|---|---|---|---|
| **BRITANNIC ASSURANCE** | | | | | | | |
| Yorkshire | Headingley | May 9 | 13 | & | 5 | 1Ct | |
| Yorkshire | Edgbaston | May 31 | 68 | & | 44 | 3Ct | |
| Kent | Tunbridge W | June 4 | 13 | & | 33 | 1Ct | |
| Somerset | Edgbaston | June 7 | 29 | & | 0 | | |
| Sussex | Coventry | June 18 | 10 | | | | |
| Notts | Trent Bridge | June 21 | 47 | | | | |
| Derbyshire | Edgbaston | June 28 | 15 | & | 3 | | |
| Middlesex | Edgbaston | July 2 | 5 | & | 94 | 1Ct | |
| Hampshire | Portsmouth | July 19 | 52 | & | 77 | 3Ct | |
| Lancashire | Old Trafford | July 23 | 0 | & | 51 * | 1Ct | |
| Leicestershire | Leicester | July 26 | 7 | | | | |
| Worcestershire | Worcester | Aug 2 | 48 | & | 28 | | |
| Surrey | Edgbaston | Aug 6 | 1 | & | 9 | | |
| Northants | Northampton | Aug 9 | 21 | & | 12 | | 0-14 |
| Worcestershire | Edgbaston | Aug 28 | 22 | & | 25 | 2Ct | |
| Northants | Edgbaston | Sept 10 | 6 | & | 70 | 1Ct | |
| Somerset | Taunton | Sept 17 | 61 | & | 84 | 2Ct | |

| Opposition | Venue | Date | Batting | Fielding | Bowling |
|---|---|---|---|---|---|
| **REFUGE ASSURANCE** | | | | | |
| Derbyshire | Edgbaston | Aug 4 | 1 | | |
| **NATWEST TROPHY** | | | | | |
| Yorkshire | Edgbaston | June 26 | 26 | | |
| Hertfordshire | Edgbaston | July 11 | 68 * | | |
| **BENSON & HEDGES CUP** | | | | | |
| Surrey | The Oval | May 7 | 29 | | |
| **OTHER ONE-DAY** | | | | | |
| Surrey | Harrogate | June 12 | 42 | | |

### BATTING AVERAGES - Including fielding

| | Matches | Inns | NO | Runs | HS | Avge | 100s | 50s | Ct | St |
|---|---|---|---|---|---|---|---|---|---|---|
| Britannic Assurance | 17 | 31 | 1 | 953 | 94 | 31.76 | - | 8 | 15 | - |
| ALL FIRST-CLASS | 17 | 31 | 1 | 953 | 94 | 31.76 | - | 8 | 15 | - |
| Refuge Assurance | 1 | 1 | 0 | 1 | 1 | 1.00 | - | - | - | - |
| NatWest Trophy | 2 | 2 | 1 | 94 | 68 * | 94.00 | - | 1 | - | - |
| Benson & Hedges Cup | 1 | 1 | 0 | 29 | 29 | 29.00 | - | - | - | - |
| Other One-Day | 1 | 1 | 0 | 42 | 42 | 42.00 | - | - | - | - |
| ALL ONE-DAY | 5 | 5 | 1 | 166 | 68 * | 41.50 | - | 1 | - | - |

### BOWLING AVERAGES

| | Overs | Mdns | Runs | Wkts | Avge | Best | 5wI | 10wM |
|---|---|---|---|---|---|---|---|---|
| Britannic Assurance | 3 | 1 | 14 | 0 | - | - | - | - |
| ALL FIRST-CLASS | 3 | 1 | 14 | 0 | - | - | - | - |
| Refuge Assurance | | | | | | | | |
| NatWest Trophy | | | | | | | | |
| Benson & Hedges Cup | | | | | | | | |
| Other One-Day | | | | | | | | |
| ALL ONE-DAY | | | | | | | | |

## R.J.RATNAYAKE - *Sri Lanka*

| Opposition | Venue | Date | Batting | | | Fielding | Bowling |
|---|---|---|---|---|---|---|---|
| **CORNHILL TEST MATCHES** | | | | | | | |
| England | Lord's | Aug 22 | 52 | & | 17 | 1Ct | 5-69 & 0-91 |
| **OTHER FIRST-CLASS** | | | | | | | |
| Yorkshire | Headingley | July 27 | 68 * | | | 1Ct | 2-61 & 0-6 |
| Derbyshire | Derby | Aug 2 | | | | | 2-94 |
| Gloucs | Bristol | Aug 6 | 27 | & | 29 | 1Ct | 6-97 & 2-29 |

| Opposition | Venue | Date | Batting | Fielding | Bowling |
|---|---|---|---|---|---|
| **OTHER ONE-DAY** | | | | | |
| Durham | Chester-le-S | July 26 | 10 | | 1-12 |
| England A | Old Trafford | Aug 14 | 0 | | 1-28 |
| England A | Old Trafford | Aug 15 | 26 * | | 1-10 |

### BATTING AVERAGES - Including fielding

| | Matches | Inns | NO | Runs | HS | Avge | 100s | 50s | Ct | St |
|---|---|---|---|---|---|---|---|---|---|---|
| Cornhill Test Matches | 1 | 2 | 0 | 69 | 52 | 34.50 | - | 1 | 1 | - |
| Other First-Class | 3 | 3 | 1 | 124 | 68 * | 62.00 | - | 1 | 2 | - |
| ALL FIRST-CLASS | 4 | 5 | 1 | 193 | 68 * | 48.25 | - | 2 | 3 | - |
| Other One-Day | 3 | 3 | 1 | 36 | 26 * | 18.00 | - | - | - | - |
| ALL ONE-DAY | 3 | 3 | 1 | 36 | 26 * | 18.00 | - | - | - | - |

### BOWLING AVERAGES

| | Overs | Mdns | Runs | Wkts | Avge | Best | 5wI | 10wM |
|---|---|---|---|---|---|---|---|---|
| Cornhill Test Matches | 53 | 8 | 160 | 5 | 32.00 | 5-69 | 1 | - |
| Other First-Class | 84.3 | 7 | 287 | 12 | 23.91 | 6-97 | 1 | - |
| ALL FIRST-CLASS | 137.3 | 15 | 447 | 17 | 26.29 | 6-97 | 2 | - |
| Other One-Day | 20 | 3 | 50 | 3 | 16.66 | 1-10 | - | - |
| ALL ONE-DAY | 20 | 3 | 50 | 3 | 16.66 | 1-10 | - | - |

## M.P.REA - *Ireland*

| Opposition | Venue | Date | Batting | | | Fielding | Bowling |
|---|---|---|---|---|---|---|---|
| **OTHER FIRST-CLASS** | | | | | | | |
| Scotland | Dublin | June 22 | 27 | & | 12 | | |
| **NATWEST TROPHY** | | | | | | | |
| Middlesex | Dublin | June 26 | 3 | | | 1Ct | |

### BATTING AVERAGES - Including fielding

| | Matches | Inns | NO | Runs | HS | Avge | 100s | 50s | Ct | St |
|---|---|---|---|---|---|---|---|---|---|---|
| Other First-Class | 1 | 2 | 0 | 39 | 27 | 19.50 | - | - | - | - |
| ALL FIRST-CLASS | 1 | 2 | 0 | 39 | 27 | 19.50 | - | - | - | - |
| NatWest Trophy | 1 | 1 | 0 | 3 | 3 | 3.00 | - | - | 1 | - |
| ALL ONE-DAY | 1 | 1 | 0 | 3 | 3 | 3.00 | - | - | 1 | - |

### BOWLING AVERAGES
Did not bowl

## M.J.RECORD - *Devon*

| Opposition | Venue | Date | Batting | Fielding | Bowling |
|---|---|---|---|---|---|
| **NATWEST TROPHY** | | | | | |
| Essex | Exmouth | June 26 | 8 * | | 0-32 |

### BATTING AVERAGES - Including fielding

| | Matches | Inns | NO | Runs | HS | Avge | 100s | 50s | Ct | St |
|---|---|---|---|---|---|---|---|---|---|---|
| NatWest Trophy | 1 | 1 | 1 | 8 | 8 * | - | - | - | - | - |
| ALL ONE-DAY | 1 | 1 | 1 | 8 | 8 * | - | - | - | - | - |

### BOWLING AVERAGES

| | Overs | Mdns | Runs | Wkts | Avge | Best | 5wI | 10wM |
|---|---|---|---|---|---|---|---|---|
| NatWest Trophy | 6 | 0 | 32 | 0 | - | - | - | - |
| ALL ONE-DAY | 6 | 0 | 32 | 0 | - | - | - | - |

## D.A.REEVE - *Warwickshire & England*

| Opposition | Venue | Date | Batting | | | Fielding | Bowling |
|---|---|---|---|---|---|---|---|
| **BRITANNIC ASSURANCE** | | | | | | | |
| Lancashire | Edgbaston | April 27 | 20 * | | | | 1-42 |
| Yorkshire | Headingley | May 9 | 5 | & | 24 | 1Ct | 1-6 & 1-14 |
| Glamorgan | Swansea | May 16 | 1 | | | | 3-30 |
| Essex | Chelmsford | May 22 | 4 | & | 20 | 1Ct | 1-58 & 0-13 |
| Yorkshire | Edgbaston | May 31 | 99 * | | | 1Ct | 1-44 & 1-22 |

# R PLAYER RECORDS

| | | | | | | |
|---|---|---|---|---|---|---|
| Kent | Tunbridge W | June 4 | 7 & | 66 * | | 6-73 |
| Somerset | Edgbaston | June 7 | 82 & | 3 * | | 1-67 & 0-0 |
| Sussex | Coventry | June 18 | 56 | | | 0-2 & 1-10 |
| Notts | Trent Bridge | June 21 | 70 * | | | 0-21 |
| Derbyshire | Edgbaston | June 28 | 66 & | 66 | 1Ct | 1-55 & 1-25 |
| Hampshire | Portsmouth | July 19 | 3 & | 14 | 2Ct | 4-46 & 4-27 |
| Lancashire | Old Trafford | July 23 | 88 & | 12 * | | 0-29 |
| Leicestershire | Leicester | July 26 | 67 | | 1Ct | 0-7 & 0-9 |
| Worcestershire | Worcester | Aug 2 | 97 & | 0 | | 3-67 |
| Surrey | Edgbaston | Aug 6 | 25 & | 7 | | 4-54 & 0-23 |
| Northants | Northampton | Aug 9 | 65 | | | 1-55 |
| Glamorgan | Edgbaston | Aug 20 | 40 & | 55 * | | |
| Worcestershire | Edgbaston | Aug 28 | 13 & | 29 | 1Ct | 3-13 |
| Northants | Edgbaston | Sept 10 | 24 & | 64 | | 2-72 & 2-10 |
| Somerset | Taunton | Sept 17 | 11 & | 57 | 1Ct | 1-27 & 2-36 |

**TEXACO TROPHY**

| | | | | | |
|---|---|---|---|---|---|
| West Indies | Lord's | May 27 | | | 0-43 |

**REFUGE ASSURANCE**

| | | | | | |
|---|---|---|---|---|---|
| Sussex | Edgbaston | April 21 | 10 | | 0-18 |
| Notts | Trent Bridge | April 28 | 17 | | |
| Yorkshire | Headingley | May 12 | 2 | | 0-40 |
| Glamorgan | Swansea | May 19 | 2 | | 2-45 |
| Somerset | Edgbaston | June 2 | | | 1-60 |
| Lancashire | Edgbaston | June 16 | 100 | | 1-38 |
| Essex | Chelmsford | July 7 | 2 | | 0-24 |
| Middlesex | Edgbaston | July 14 | | | 0-32 |
| Hampshire | Portsmouth | July 21 | 44 * | | 2-27 |
| Derbyshire | Edgbaston | Aug 4 | 38 | 1Ct | 4-18 |
| Leicestershire | Leicester | Aug 11 | 2 | | 1-24 |
| Gloucs | Edgbaston | Aug 18 | | 1Ct | |
| Northants | Northampton | Aug 25 | 43 | | 0-26 |

**NATWEST TROPHY**

| | | | | | |
|---|---|---|---|---|---|
| Yorkshire | Edgbaston | June 26 | 7 | 2Ct | 1-17 |
| Hertfordshire | Edgbaston | July 11 | | | 2-19 |
| Somerset | Edgbaston | July 31 | 25 | 2Ct | 0-54 |
| Hampshire | Edgbaston | Aug 14 | 57 * | 1Ct | 0-11 |

**BENSON & HEDGES CUP**

| | | | | | |
|---|---|---|---|---|---|
| Essex | Edgbaston | April 25 | 80 | | 0-64 |
| Somerset | Edgbaston | May 2 | 19 | 1Ct | 3-43 |
| Middlesex | Lord's | May 4 | 12 | 1Ct | 3-48 |
| Surrey | The Oval | May 7 | 13 | | 4-43 |
| Yorkshire | Headingley | May 29 | 0 | 1Ct | 0-35 |

**OTHER ONE-DAY**

| | | | | | |
|---|---|---|---|---|---|
| Surrey | Harrogate | June 12 | 48 | | 0-29 |

**BATTING AVERAGES - Including fielding**

| | Matches | Inns | NO | Runs | HS | Avge | 100s | 50s | Ct | St |
|---|---|---|---|---|---|---|---|---|---|---|
| Britannic Assurance | 20 | 33 | 7 | 1260 | 99 * | 48.46 | - | 14 | 9 | - |
| ALL FIRST-CLASS | 20 | 33 | 7 | 1260 | 99 * | 48.46 | - | 14 | 9 | - |
| Texaco Trophy | 1 | 0 | 0 | 0 | 0 | - | - | - | - | - |
| Refuge Assurance | 13 | 10 | 1 | 260 | 100 | 28.88 | 1 | - | 2 | - |
| NatWest Trophy | 4 | 3 | 1 | 89 | 57 * | 44.50 | - | 1 | 5 | - |
| Benson & Hedges Cup | 5 | 5 | 0 | 124 | 80 | 24.80 | - | 1 | 3 | - |
| Other One-Day | 1 | 1 | 0 | 48 | 48 | 48.00 | - | - | - | - |
| ALL ONE-DAY | 24 | 19 | 2 | 521 | 100 | 30.64 | 1 | 2 | 10 | - |

**BOWLING AVERAGES**

| | Overs | Mdns | Runs | Wkts | Avge | Best | 5wI | 10wM |
|---|---|---|---|---|---|---|---|---|
| Britannic Assurance | 402.1 | 117 | 957 | 45 | 21.26 | 6-73 | 1 | - |
| ALL FIRST-CLASS | 402.1 | 117 | 957 | 45 | 21.26 | 6-73 | 1 | - |
| Texaco Trophy | 11 | 1 | 43 | 0 | - | - | - | |
| Refuge Assurance | 70.1 | 2 | 352 | 11 | 32.00 | 4-18 | - | |
| NatWest Trophy | 35.5 | 7 | 101 | 3 | 33.66 | 2-19 | - | |
| Benson & Hedges Cup | 51.5 | 0 | 233 | 10 | 23.30 | 4-43 | - | |
| Other One-Day | 9 | 2 | 29 | 0 | - | - | - | |
| ALL ONE-DAY | 177.5 | 12 | 758 | 24 | 31.58 | 4-18 | - | |

## G.N.REIFER - *Scotland*

| Opposition | Venue | Date | Batting | Fielding | Bowling |
|---|---|---|---|---|---|
| **NATWEST TROPHY** | | | | | |
| Sussex | Edinburgh | June 26 | 13 | | 1-40 |
| **BENSON & HEDGES CUP** | | | | | |
| Lancashire | Forfar | April 23 | 25 | 1Ct | 0-27 |
| Leicestershire | Leicester | May 2 | 31 | 1Ct | 1-36 |
| Sussex | Hove | May 4 | 76 | | 0-30 |
| Kent | Glasgow | May 7 | 9 | 1Ct | 0-16 |

**BATTING AVERAGES - Including fielding**

| | Matches | Inns | NO | Runs | HS | Avge | 100s | 50s | Ct | St |
|---|---|---|---|---|---|---|---|---|---|---|
| NatWest Trophy | 1 | 1 | 0 | 13 | 13 | 13.00 | - | - | - | - |
| Benson & Hedges Cup | 4 | 4 | 0 | 141 | 76 | 35.25 | - | 1 | 3 | - |
| ALL ONE-DAY | 5 | 5 | 0 | 154 | 76 | 30.80 | - | 1 | 3 | - |

**BOWLING AVERAGES**

| | Overs | Mdns | Runs | Wkts | Avge | Best | 5wI | 10wM |
|---|---|---|---|---|---|---|---|---|
| NatWest Trophy | 8 | 0 | 40 | 1 | 40.00 | 1-40 | - | |
| Benson & Hedges Cup | 29.2 | 4 | 109 | 1 | 109.00 | 1-36 | - | |
| ALL ONE-DAY | 37.2 | 4 | 149 | 2 | 74.50 | 1-36 | - | |

## P.R.REIFFEL - *Rest of World*

| Opposition | Venue | Date | Batting | Fielding | Bowling |
|---|---|---|---|---|---|
| **OTHER ONE-DAY** | | | | | |
| England XI | Jesmond | July 31 | | | 1-59 |
| England XI | Jesmond | Aug 1 | | | 3-61 |

**BATTING AVERAGES - Including fielding**

| | Matches | Inns | NO | Runs | HS | Avge | 100s | 50s | Ct | St |
|---|---|---|---|---|---|---|---|---|---|---|
| Other One-Day | 2 | 0 | 0 | 0 | 0 | - | - | - | - | - |
| ALL ONE-DAY | 2 | 0 | 0 | 0 | 0 | - | - | - | - | - |

**BOWLING AVERAGES**

| | Overs | Mdns | Runs | Wkts | Avge | Best | 5wI | 10wM |
|---|---|---|---|---|---|---|---|---|
| Other One-Day | 18 | 0 | 120 | 4 | 30.00 | 3-61 | - | |
| ALL ONE-DAY | 18 | 0 | 120 | 4 | 30.00 | 3-61 | - | |

## P.J.RENDELL - *Combined Universities*

| Opposition | Venue | Date | Batting | Fielding | Bowling |
|---|---|---|---|---|---|
| **BENSON & HEDGES CUP** | | | | | |
| Gloucs | Bristol | April 23 | 0 | | |
| Derbyshire | The Parks | April 25 | 8 | 1Ct | 1-55 |

**BATTING AVERAGES - Including fielding**

| | Matches | Inns | NO | Runs | HS | Avge | 100s | 50s | Ct | St |
|---|---|---|---|---|---|---|---|---|---|---|
| Benson & Hedges Cup | 2 | 2 | 0 | 8 | 8 | 4.00 | - | - | 1 | - |
| ALL ONE-DAY | 2 | 2 | 0 | 8 | 8 | 4.00 | - | - | 1 | - |

**BOWLING AVERAGES**

| | Overs | Mdns | Runs | Wkts | Avge | Best | 5wI | 10wM |
|---|---|---|---|---|---|---|---|---|
| Benson & Hedges Cup | 6 | 0 | 55 | 1 | 55.00 | 1-55 | - | |
| ALL ONE-DAY | 6 | 0 | 55 | 1 | 55.00 | 1-55 | - | |

# PLAYER RECORDS

R

## G.D.REYNOLDS - *Dorset*

| Opposition | Venue | Date | Batting | Fielding | Bowling |
|---|---|---|---|---|---|
| **NATWEST TROPHY** | | | | | |
| Lancashire | Bournemouth | June 26 | 22 | | |

### BATTING AVERAGES - Including fielding

| | Matches | Inns | NO | Runs | HS | Avge | 100s | 50s | Ct | St |
|---|---|---|---|---|---|---|---|---|---|---|
| NatWest Trophy | 1 | 1 | 0 | 22 | 22 | 22.00 | - | - | - | - |
| ALL ONE-DAY | 1 | 1 | 0 | 22 | 22 | 22.00 | - | - | - | - |

### BOWLING AVERAGES
Did not bowl

## S.J.RHODES - *Worcestershire*

| Opposition | Venue | Date | Batting | | | Fielding | Bowling |
|---|---|---|---|---|---|---|---|
| **BRITANNIC ASSURANCE** | | | | | | | |
| Gloucs | Worcester | April 27 | | | | 1Ct,1St | |
| Lancashire | Worcester | May 9 | 67 | & | 6 | | |
| Glamorgan | Worcester | May 31 | 5 | & | 66 * | 1Ct | |
| Northants | Northampton | June 4 | 56 * | | | 3Ct | |
| Essex | Ilford | June 7 | 64 | | | 2Ct | |
| Sussex | Hove | June 14 | 77 | & | 10 | 2Ct | |
| Notts | Worcester | June 18 | 0 | & | 17 | 3Ct | |
| Leicestershire | Worcester | June 28 | 36 | | | 3Ct | |
| Yorkshire | Headingley | July 2 | | | 4 | 0Ct,1St | |
| Hampshire | Portsmouth | July 16 | 0 | & | 46 * | 3Ct | |
| Derbyshire | Kidd'minster | July 19 | 15 | & | 90 | 2Ct,1St | |
| Kent | Worcester | July 23 | | | | 3Ct | |
| Gloucs | Cheltenham | July 26 | 2 | & | 10 | 3Ct | |
| Warwickshire | Worcester | Aug 2 | 48 | | | 2Ct,1St | |
| Somerset | Weston | Aug 6 | 53 * | & | 26 | 1Ct,2St | 0-30 |
| Surrey | Worcester | Aug 16 | 12 | & | 23 * | 2Ct | |
| Lancashire | Blackpool | Aug 20 | 48 | | | 1Ct | |
| Middlesex | Worcester | Aug 23 | 0 | | | 6Ct | |
| Warwickshire | Edgbaston | Aug 28 | 4 | & | 7 | 3Ct,1St | |
| Somerset | Worcester | Sept 3 | 58 | | | 3Ct | |
| Glamorgan | Cardiff | Sept 10 | 19 | & | 33 * | 5Ct | |
| Notts | Trent Bridge | Sept 17 | 5 | & | 0 | 2Ct | |
| **OTHER FIRST-CLASS** | | | | | | | |
| For MCC | | | | | | | |
| Middlesex | Lord's | April 16 | | | | 1Ct | |
| For Worcestershire | | | | | | | |
| Sri Lanka | Worcester | July 30 | 35 | | | 5Ct,1St | |
| **REFUGE ASSURANCE** | | | | | | | |
| Kent | Worcester | April 21 | | | | | |
| Gloucs | Bristol | May 5 | | | | 1Ct | |
| Warwickshire | Edgbaston | May 26 | 1 | | | | |
| Surrey | Worcester | June 2 | | | | | |
| Essex | Ilford | June 9 | 0 | | | | |
| Sussex | Hove | June 16 | | | | | |
| Yorkshire | Sheffield | June 23 | 0 | | | | |
| Leicestershire | Worcester | June 30 | | | | 0Ct,1St | |
| Hampshire | Southampton | July 7 | | | | 1Ct | |
| Derbyshire | Worcester | July 9 | | | | 0Ct,1St | |
| Glamorgan | Worcester | July 21 | | | | | |
| Notts | Trent Bridge | Aug 4 | | | | | |
| Somerset | Worcester | Aug 18 | 0 | | | | |
| Middlesex | Worcester | Aug 25 | 11 * | | | 1Ct,1St | |
| Notts | Trent Bridge | Sept 1 | 47 * | | | 0Ct,1St | |
| Lancashire | Old Trafford | Sept 15 | 105 | | | | |
| **NATWEST TROPHY** | | | | | | | |
| Bedfordshire | Bedford | June 26 | 10 | | | | |
| Glamorgan | Worcester | July 11 | 41 | | | | |
| **BENSON & HEDGES CUP** | | | | | | | |
| Gloucs | Worcester | April 25 | | | | 1Ct | |
| Combined U | Fenner's | May 2 | | | | 2Ct | |
| Derbyshire | Worcester | May 4 | | | | 1Ct | |
| Northants | Northampton | May 7 | 13 * | | | 1Ct | |
| Kent | Worcester | May 29 | 8 | | | 0Ct,1St | |
| Essex | Chelmsford | June 12 | | | | 4Ct | |
| Lancashire | Lord's | July 13 | 13 | | | 1Ct | |

## OTHER ONE-DAY
For Yorkshiremen

| | Venue | Date | Batting | Fielding | Bowling |
|---|---|---|---|---|---|
| Yorkshire | Scarborough | Sept 7 | 56 | 1Ct | |
| For World XI | | | | | |
| Yorkshire | Scarborough | Sept 8 | 55 | 1Ct | |

### BATTING AVERAGES - Including fielding

| | Matches | Inns | NO | Runs | HS | Avge | 100s | 50s | Ct | St |
|---|---|---|---|---|---|---|---|---|---|---|
| Britannic Assurance | 22 | 32 | 6 | 907 | 90 | 34.88 | - | 8 | 48 | 7 |
| Other First-Class | 2 | 1 | 0 | 35 | 35 | 35.00 | - | - | 6 | 1 |
| ALL FIRST-CLASS | 24 | 33 | 6 | 942 | 90 | 34.88 | - | 8 | 54 | 8 |
| Refuge Assurance | 16 | 7 | 2 | 164 | 105 | 32.80 | 1 | - | 3 | 4 |
| NatWest Trophy | 2 | 2 | 0 | 51 | 41 | 25.50 | - | - | - | - |
| Benson & Hedges Cup | 7 | 3 | 1 | 34 | 13 * | 17.00 | - | - | 10 | 1 |
| Other One-Day | 2 | 2 | 0 | 111 | 56 | 55.50 | - | 2 | 2 | - |
| ALL ONE-DAY | 27 | 14 | 3 | 360 | 105 | 32.72 | 1 | 2 | 15 | 5 |

### BOWLING AVERAGES

| | Overs | Mdns | Runs | Wkts | Avge | Best | 5wI | 10wM |
|---|---|---|---|---|---|---|---|---|
| Britannic Assurance | 1 | 0 | 30 | 0 | - | - | - | - |
| Other First-Class | | | | | | | | |
| ALL FIRST-CLASS | 1 | 0 | 30 | 0 | - | - | - | - |
| Refuge Assurance | | | | | | | | |
| NatWest Trophy | | | | | | | | |
| Benson & Hedges Cup | | | | | | | | |
| Other One-Day | | | | | | | | |
| ALL ONE-DAY | | | | | | | | |

## K.G.RICE - *Devon*

| Opposition | Venue | Date | Batting | Fielding | Bowling |
|---|---|---|---|---|---|
| **NATWEST TROPHY** | | | | | |
| Essex | Exmouth | June 26 | 15 | | |

### BATTING AVERAGES - Including fielding

| | Matches | Inns | NO | Runs | HS | Avge | 100s | 50s | Ct | St |
|---|---|---|---|---|---|---|---|---|---|---|
| NatWest Trophy | 1 | 1 | 0 | 15 | 15 | 15.00 | - | - | - | - |
| ALL ONE-DAY | 1 | 1 | 0 | 15 | 15 | 15.00 | - | - | - | - |

### BOWLING AVERAGES
Did not bowl

## I.V.A.RICHARDS - *West Indies*

| Opposition | Venue | Date | Batting | | | Fielding | Bowling |
|---|---|---|---|---|---|---|---|
| **CORNHILL TEST MATCHES** | | | | | | | |
| England | Headingley | June 6 | 73 | & | 3 | | 0-5 |
| England | Lord's | June 20 | 63 | | | 1Ct | |
| England | Trent Bridge | July 4 | 80 | | | 1Ct | 0-1 |
| England | Edgbaston | July 25 | 22 | & | 73 * | 1Ct | |
| England | The Oval | Aug 8 | 2 | & | 60 | 1Ct | |
| **OTHER FIRST-CLASS** | | | | | | | |
| Worcestershire | Worcester | May 15 | 131 | | | | |
| Middlesex | Lord's | May 18 | 28 | & | 28 * | 2Ct | |
| Leicestershire | Leicester | June 1 | 45 | & | 39 * | | 1-32 |
| Northants | Northampton | June 15 | 47 | | | | |
| Hampshire | Southampton | June 29 | 15 * | | | | 0-13 |
| Kent | Canterbury | July 20 | 29 | & | 56 | 2Ct | 0-43 |
| Essex | Chelmsford | Aug 3 | | | 23 | 1Ct | 1-49 & 0-18 |
| **TEXACO TROPHY** | | | | | | | |
| England | Edgbaston | May 23 | 30 | | | | |
| England | Old Trafford | May 25 | 78 | | | | |
| England | Lord's | May 27 | 37 | | | 1Ct | |
| **OTHER ONE-DAY** | | | | | | | |
| D of Norfolk | Arundel | May 12 | 17 | | | | 1-5 |

391

# R | PLAYER RECORDS

| | | | | | | | | |
|---|---|---|---|---|---|---|---|---|
| League CC XI | Trowbridge | June 28 | | | | | 1-27 | |
| Wales | Brecon | July 15 | | 68 | | 2Ct | 2-34 | |

## BATTING AVERAGES - Including fielding

| | Matches | Inns | NO | Runs | HS | Avge | 100s | 50s | Ct | St |
|---|---|---|---|---|---|---|---|---|---|---|
| Cornhill Test Matches | 5 | 8 | 1 | 376 | 80 | 53.71 | - | 5 | 4 | - |
| Other First-Class | 7 | 10 | 3 | 441 | 131 | 63.00 | 1 | 1 | 5 | - |
| ALL FIRST-CLASS | 12 | 18 | 4 | 817 | 131 | 58.35 | 1 | 6 | 9 | - |
| Texaco Trophy | 3 | 3 | 0 | 145 | 78 | 48.33 | - | 1 | 1 | - |
| Other One-Day | 3 | 2 | 0 | 85 | 68 | 42.50 | - | 1 | 2 | - |
| ALL ONE-DAY | 6 | 5 | 0 | 230 | 78 | 46.00 | - | 2 | 3 | - |

## BOWLING AVERAGES

| | Overs | Mdns | Runs | Wkts | Avge | Best | 5wI | 10wM |
|---|---|---|---|---|---|---|---|---|
| Cornhill Test Matches | 5 | 1 | 6 | 0 | - | - | - | - |
| Other First-Class | 42 | 8 | 155 | 2 | 77.50 | 1-32 | - | - |
| ALL FIRST-CLASS | 47 | 9 | 161 | 2 | 80.50 | 1-32 | - | - |
| Texaco Trophy | | | | | | | | |
| Other One-Day | 19.4 | 0 | 66 | 4 | 16.50 | 2-34 | - | |
| ALL ONE-DAY | 19.4 | 0 | 66 | 4 | 16.50 | 2-34 | - | |

## R.B.RICHARDSON - *West Indies*

| Opposition | Venue | Date | Batting | | | Fielding | Bowling |
|---|---|---|---|---|---|---|---|
| **CORNHILL TEST MATCHES** | | | | | | | |
| England | Headingley | June 6 | 29 | & | 68 | | |
| England | Lord's | June 20 | 57 | & | 1 | 1Ct | |
| England | Trent Bridge | July 4 | 43 | & | 52 * | | |
| England | Edgbaston | July 25 | 104 | & | 0 | 2Ct | |
| England | The Oval | Aug 8 | 20 | & | 121 | 1Ct | |
| **OTHER FIRST-CLASS** | | | | | | | |
| Worcestershire | Worcester | May 15 | 6 | | | | |
| Middlesex | Lord's | May 18 | 7 | & | 10 * | 1Ct | |
| Somerset | Taunton | May 29 | 7 | & | 91 * | 1Ct | |
| Leicestershire | Leicester | June 1 | 63 | & | 135 * | 1Ct | |
| Derbyshire | Derby | June 12 | 114 | & | 48 * | 1Ct | |
| Hampshire | Southampton | June 29 | 33 | | | 1Ct | |
| Glamorgan | Swansea | July 16 | 109 | | | 3Ct | |
| Gloucs | Bristol | July 31 | 119 | & | 48 | | 0-6 |
| Essex | Chelmsford | Aug 3 | 5 | | | | |
| For West Indies XI | | | | | | | |
| World XI | Scarborough | Aug 28 | 15 | & | 98 | 2Ct | 0-36 |
| **TEXACO TROPHY** | | | | | | | |
| England | Edgbaston | May 23 | 3 | | | 4Ct | |
| England | Old Trafford | May 25 | 13 | | | | |
| England | Lord's | May 27 | 41 | | | | |
| **OTHER ONE-DAY** | | | | | | | |
| D of Norfolk | Arundel | May 12 | 5 | | | | 0-4 |
| Gloucs | Bristol | May 14 | 25 | | | | |
| League CC XI | Trowbridge | June 28 | 11 * | | | | |
| Wales | Brecon | July 15 | 22 | | | 1Ct | |

## BATTING AVERAGES - Including fielding

| | Matches | Inns | NO | Runs | HS | Avge | 100s | 50s | Ct | St |
|---|---|---|---|---|---|---|---|---|---|---|
| Cornhill Test Matches | 5 | 10 | 1 | 495 | 121 | 55.00 | 2 | 3 | 4 | - |
| Other First-Class | 10 | 16 | 4 | 908 | 135 * | 75.66 | 4 | 3 | 10 | - |
| ALL FIRST-CLASS | 15 | 26 | 5 | 1403 | 135 * | 66.81 | 6 | 6 | 14 | - |
| Texaco Trophy | 3 | 3 | 0 | 57 | 41 | 19.00 | - | - | 4 | - |
| Other One-Day | 4 | 4 | 1 | 63 | 25 | 21.00 | - | - | 1 | - |
| ALL ONE-DAY | 7 | 7 | 1 | 120 | 41 | 20.00 | - | - | 5 | - |

## BOWLING AVERAGES

| | Overs | Mdns | Runs | Wkts | Avge | Best | 5wI | 10wM |
|---|---|---|---|---|---|---|---|---|
| Cornhill Test Matches | | | | | | | | |
| Other First-Class | 10 | 2 | 42 | 0 | - | - | - | - |
| ALL FIRST-CLASS | 10 | 2 | 42 | 0 | - | - | - | - |

| | | | | | | | | |
|---|---|---|---|---|---|---|---|---|
| Texaco Trophy | | | | | | | | |
| Other One-Day | 1 | 0 | 4 | 0 | - | - | - | - |
| ALL ONE-DAY | 1 | 0 | 4 | 0 | - | - | - | - |

## D.RIPLEY - *Northamptonshire*

| Opposition | Venue | Date | Batting | | | Fielding | Bowling |
|---|---|---|---|---|---|---|---|
| **BRITANNIC ASSURANCE** | | | | | | | |
| Derbyshire | Derby | April 27 | | | | | |
| Essex | Northampton | May 9 | 30 | & | 15 | 6Ct,1St | |
| Leicestershire | Northampton | May 16 | | | 20 | 2Ct | |
| Glamorgan | Cardiff | May 22 | 49 | & | 32 * | | |
| Yorkshire | Headingley | May 25 | | | 8 | 2Ct | |
| Derbyshire | Northampton | May 31 | 53 * | & | 0 * | 5Ct,1St | |
| Worcestershire | Northampton | June 4 | | | 27 * | 3Ct | |
| Hampshire | Northampton | June 21 | 13 | | | 2Ct | |
| Gloucs | Luton | June 28 | 34 | & | 8 * | 3Ct | |
| Kent | Maidstone | July 2 | | | 7 | 2Ct | |
| Leicestershire | Leicester | July 5 | 0 | | | 4Ct | |
| Middlesex | Uxbridge | July 16 | 43 * | | | 2Ct | |
| Notts | Well'borough | July 19 | 8 | & | 6 | 1Ct | |
| Somerset | Northampton | July 23 | | | 0 | 1Ct | |
| Sussex | Eastbourne | Aug 2 | 22 | & | 11 * | 1Ct | |
| Lancashire | Lytham | Aug 6 | 6 * | | | 2Ct | |
| Warwickshire | Northampton | Aug 9 | 5 | | | | |
| Essex | Colchester | Aug 16 | 17 | & | 15 | 1Ct | |
| **OTHER FIRST-CLASS** | | | | | | | |
| Cambridge U | Fenner's | April 16 | | | 38 * | 3Ct | |
| West Indies | Northampton | June 15 | | | | 1Ct | |
| **REFUGE ASSURANCE** | | | | | | | |
| Glamorgan | Cardiff | April 21 | 14 | | | | |
| Lancashire | Old Trafford | April 28 | | | | 1Ct | |
| Leicestershire | Northampton | May 12 | | | | 2Ct | |
| Worcestershire | Northampton | May 19 | 0 | | | | |
| Yorkshire | Headingley | May 26 | 10 | | | 2Ct | |
| Hampshire | Northampton | June 2 | | | | | |
| Gloucs | Moreton | June 9 | | | | | |
| Somerset | Luton | June 30 | | | 6 * | 1Ct | |
| Surrey | Tring | July 7 | 13 | | | | |
| Derbyshire | Derby | July 28 | 14 | | | | |
| Sussex | Eastbourne | Aug 4 | | | | | |
| Essex | Northampton | Aug 11 | | | 0 * | 2Ct | |
| Kent | Canterbury | Aug 18 | | | | | |
| **NATWEST TROPHY** | | | | | | | |
| Staffordshire | Stone | June 26 | | | | 1Ct | |
| Leicestershire | Northampton | July 11 | | | | 1Ct | |
| Glamorgan | Northampton | July 31 | 10 * | | | | |
| Surrey | The Oval | Aug 14 | 3 | | | 1Ct | |
| **BENSON & HEDGES CUP** | | | | | | | |
| Derbyshire | Derby | April 23 | | | | 3Ct | |
| Gloucs | Bristol | May 2 | 36 * | | | 0Ct,1St | |
| Combined U | Northampton | May 4 | | | | 3Ct | |
| Worcestershire | Northampton | May 7 | 5 | | | | |
| Lancashire | Old Trafford | May 29 | 6 * | | | 1Ct | |

## BATTING AVERAGES - Including fielding

| | Matches | Inns | NO | Runs | HS | Avge | 100s | 50s | Ct | St |
|---|---|---|---|---|---|---|---|---|---|---|
| Britannic Assurance | 18 | 24 | 8 | 429 | 53 * | 26.81 | - | 1 | 37 | 2 |
| Other First-Class | 2 | 1 | 1 | 38 | 38 * | - | - | - | 4 | - |
| ALL FIRST-CLASS | 20 | 25 | 9 | 467 | 53 * | 29.18 | - | 1 | 41 | 2 |
| Refuge Assurance | 13 | 7 | 2 | 57 | 14 | 11.40 | - | - | 8 | - |
| NatWest Trophy | 4 | 2 | 1 | 13 | 10 * | 13.00 | - | - | 3 | - |
| Benson & Hedges Cup | 5 | 3 | 2 | 47 | 36 * | 47.00 | - | - | 7 | 1 |
| ALL ONE-DAY | 22 | 12 | 5 | 117 | 36 * | 16.71 | - | - | 18 | 1 |

## BOWLING AVERAGES
Did not bowl

# PLAYER RECORDS

**R**

## A.R.ROBERTS - *Northamptonshire*

| Opposition | Venue | Date | Batting | | Fielding | Bowling |
|---|---|---|---|---|---|---|
| **BRITANNIC ASSURANCE** | | | | | | |
| Glamorgan | Cardiff | May 22 | 17 * & | 13 * | | 0-56 |
| Yorkshire | Headingley | May 25 | | 9 * | | 0-36 & 1-45 |
| Worcestershire | Northampton | June 4 | | | 2Ct | 0-43 |
| Gloucs | Luton | June 28 | 18 * | | 1Ct | 4-63 |
| Kent | Maidstone | July 2 | | 11 | | 0-0 |
| Leicestershire | Leicester | July 5 | 6 * | | | 2-42 |
| Middlesex | Uxbridge | July 16 | 10 | | | 0-26 |
| Lancashire | Lytham | Aug 6 | | | | 0-0 & 6-72 |
| Warwickshire | Northampton | Aug 9 | 36 * | | | 0-49 & 1-44 |
| Essex | Colchester | Aug 16 | 12 * & | 17 * | | 2-107 |
| Surrey | Northampton | Aug 23 | 11 | | 2Ct | 1-41 & 2-73 |
| Yorkshire | Northampton | Aug 28 | 9 | | 1Ct | 2-40 & 2-90 |
| Gloucs | Bristol | Sept 3 | 48 | | 1Ct | 0-41 & 3-48 |
| Warwickshire | Edgbaston | Sept 10 | 20 * & | 7 | | 3-116 |
| **REFUGE ASSURANCE** | | | | | | |
| Worcestershire | Northampton | May 19 | 14 | | | 1-36 |
| Yorkshire | Headingley | May 26 | | | | 0-15 |
| Hampshire | Northampton | June 2 | | | 1Ct | 3-26 |
| Lancashire | Old Trafford | Sept 1 | | | | 2-41 |

**BATTING AVERAGES - Including fielding**

| | Matches | Inns | NO | Runs | HS | Avge | 100s | 50s | Ct | St |
|---|---|---|---|---|---|---|---|---|---|---|
| Britannic Assurance | 14 | 15 | 9 | 244 | 48 | 40.66 | - | - | 7 | - |
| ALL FIRST-CLASS | 14 | 15 | 9 | 244 | 48 | 40.66 | - | - | 7 | - |
| Refuge Assurance | 4 | 1 | 0 | 14 | 14 | 14.00 | - | - | 1 | - |
| ALL ONE-DAY | 4 | 1 | 0 | 14 | 14 | 14.00 | - | - | 1 | - |

**BOWLING AVERAGES**

| | Overs | Mdns | Runs | Wkts | Avge | Best | 5wI | 10wM |
|---|---|---|---|---|---|---|---|---|
| Britannic Assurance | 331.5 | 72 | 1032 | 29 | 35.58 | 6-72 | 1 | - |
| ALL FIRST-CLASS | 331.5 | 72 | 1032 | 29 | 35.58 | 6-72 | 1 | - |
| Refuge Assurance | 21 | 0 | 118 | 6 | 19.66 | 3-26 | - | |
| ALL ONE-DAY | 21 | 0 | 118 | 6 | 19.66 | 3-26 | - | |

## B.ROBERTS - *Derbyshire*

| Opposition | Venue | Date | Batting | | Fielding | Bowling |
|---|---|---|---|---|---|---|
| **OTHER FIRST-CLASS** | | | | | | |
| Cambridge U | Fenner's | May 9 | 36 * & | 44 * | 1Ct | |
| **REFUGE ASSURANCE** | | | | | | |
| Leicestershire | Leicester | April 21 | 0 | | | |
| Hampshire | Derby | May 5 | 12 | | | 1-34 |
| Lancashire | Derby | May 19 | 8 | | | |
| Kent | Canterbury | May 26 | 15 | | 1Ct | |
| Yorkshire | Chesterfield | June 2 | 9 | | | 1-27 |
| **BENSON & HEDGES CUP** | | | | | | |
| Northants | Derby | April 23 | 2 | | 1Ct | 0-26 |
| Combined U | The Parks | April 25 | | | 1Ct | 1-11 |
| Worcestershire | Worcester | May 4 | 24 | | | 1-32 |
| Gloucs | Derby | May 7 | 49 | | | |

**BATTING AVERAGES - Including fielding**

| | Matches | Inns | NO | Runs | HS | Avge | 100s | 50s | Ct | St |
|---|---|---|---|---|---|---|---|---|---|---|
| Other First-Class | 1 | 2 | 2 | 80 | 44 * | - | - | - | 1 | - |
| ALL FIRST-CLASS | 1 | 2 | 2 | 80 | 44 * | - | - | - | 1 | - |
| Refuge Assurance | 5 | 5 | 0 | 44 | 15 | 8.80 | - | - | 1 | - |
| Benson & Hedges Cup | 4 | 3 | 0 | 75 | 49 | 25.00 | - | - | 2 | - |
| ALL ONE-DAY | 9 | 8 | 0 | 119 | 49 | 14.87 | - | - | 3 | - |

**BOWLING AVERAGES**

| | Overs | Mdns | Runs | Wkts | Avge | Best | 5wI | 10wM |
|---|---|---|---|---|---|---|---|---|
| Other First-Class | | | | | | | | |

---

**ALL FIRST-CLASS**

| | | | | | | | |
|---|---|---|---|---|---|---|---|
| Refuge Assurance | 10 | 1 | 61 | 2 | 30.50 | 1-27 | - |
| Benson & Hedges Cup | 13 | 1 | 69 | 2 | 34.50 | 1-11 | - |
| ALL ONE-DAY | 23 | 2 | 130 | 4 | 32.50 | 1-11 | - |

## M.J.ROBERTS - *Buckinghamshire & Minor Counties*

| Opposition | Venue | Date | Batting | Fielding | Bowling |
|---|---|---|---|---|---|
| **NATWEST TROPHY** | | | | | |
| Somerset | Bath | June 26 | 21 | | |
| **BENSON & HEDGES CUP** | | | | | |
| For Minor Counties | | | | | |
| Glamorgan | Trowbridge | April 23 | 40 | 1Ct | |
| Hampshire | Trowbridge | April 25 | 4 | 1Ct | |
| Yorkshire | Headingley | May 2 | 6 | | |
| Notts | Trent Bridge | May 7 | 1 | | |

**BATTING AVERAGES - Including fielding**

| | Matches | Inns | NO | Runs | HS | Avge | 100s | 50s | Ct | St |
|---|---|---|---|---|---|---|---|---|---|---|
| NatWest Trophy | 1 | 1 | 0 | 21 | 21 | 21.00 | - | - | - | - |
| Benson & Hedges Cup | 4 | 4 | 0 | 51 | 40 | 12.75 | - | - | 2 | - |
| ALL ONE-DAY | 5 | 5 | 0 | 72 | 40 | 14.40 | - | - | 2 | - |

**BOWLING AVERAGES**
Did not bowl

## M.L.ROBERTS - *Glamorgan*

| Opposition | Venue | Date | Batting | Fielding | Bowling |
|---|---|---|---|---|---|
| **OTHER FIRST-CLASS** | | | | | |
| For Glamorgan | | | | | |
| Cambridge U | Fenner's | June 18 | | 1Ct,2St | |
| **REFUGE ASSURANCE** | | | | | |
| Notts | Cardiff | May 5 | | 1Ct | |
| **BENSON & HEDGES CUP** | | | | | |
| Hampshire | Southampton | May 2 | 1 | 1Ct | |
| Notts | Cardiff | May 4 | 0 | 1Ct | |
| Yorkshire | Cardiff | May 7 | 1 * | | |

**BATTING AVERAGES - Including fielding**

| | Matches | Inns | NO | Runs | HS | Avge | 100s | 50s | Ct | St |
|---|---|---|---|---|---|---|---|---|---|---|
| Other First-Class | 1 | 0 | 0 | 0 | 0 | - | - | - | 1 | 2 |
| ALL FIRST-CLASS | 1 | 0 | 0 | 0 | 0 | - | - | - | 1 | 2 |
| Refuge Assurance | 1 | 0 | 0 | 0 | 0 | - | - | - | 1 | - |
| Benson & Hedges Cup | 3 | 3 | 1 | 2 | 1 * | 1.00 | - | - | 2 | - |
| ALL ONE-DAY | 4 | 3 | 1 | 2 | 1 * | 1.00 | - | - | 3 | - |

**BOWLING AVERAGES**
Did not bowl

## N.G.ROBERTS - *Wales*

| Opposition | Venue | Date | Batting | Fielding | Bowling |
|---|---|---|---|---|---|
| **OTHER ONE-DAY** | | | | | |
| West Indies | Brecon | July 15 | 16 | | 0-48 |

**BATTING AVERAGES - Including fielding**

| | Matches | Inns | NO | Runs | HS | Avge | 100s | 50s | Ct | St |
|---|---|---|---|---|---|---|---|---|---|---|
| Other One-Day | 1 | 1 | 0 | 16 | 16 | 16.00 | - | - | - | - |

# R | PLAYER RECORDS

| ALL ONE-DAY | 1 | 1 | 0 | 16 | 16 | 16.00 | - | - | - | - |
|---|---|---|---|---|---|---|---|---|---|---|

## BOWLING AVERAGES

| | Overs | Mdns | Runs | Wkts | Avge | Best | 5wI | 10wM |
|---|---|---|---|---|---|---|---|---|
| Other One-Day | 3 | 0 | 48 | 0 | - | - | - | - |
| ALL ONE-DAY | 3 | 0 | 48 | 0 | - | - | - | - |

## J.D.ROBINSON - *Surrey*

| Opposition | Venue | Date | Batting | Fielding | Bowling |
|---|---|---|---|---|---|
| **BRITANNIC ASSURANCE** | | | | | |
| Essex | Chelmsford | April 27 | 15 | | 0-15 |
| Gloucs | Guildford | July 16 | 20 | | 0-19 |
| Northants | Northampton | Aug 23 | 0 * & 22 | | 1-58 |
| Lancashire | Old Trafford | Sept 17 | 79 & 50 | | 1-18 |
| **REFUGE ASSURANCE** | | | | | |
| Somerset | The Oval | April 21 | 55 * | 1Ct | |
| Middlesex | Lord's | April 28 | 26 | 1Ct | 0-34 |
| Gloucs | The Oval | May 12 | 50 | | 0-40 |
| Essex | The Oval | May 26 | 2 * | | 1-28 |
| Worcestershire | Worcester | June 2 | | | 0-33 |
| Derbyshire | Chesterfield | June 9 | 17 | | 0-9 |
| Leicestershire | Leicester | June 16 | 22 | | 1-20 |
| Notts | The Oval | June 30 | 6 | | 0-14 |
| Northants | Tring | July 7 | 11 | | 1-26 |
| Sussex | The Oval | July 14 | | | 1-39 |
| Yorkshire | The Oval | July 21 | 16 | | 0-26 |
| Glamorgan | The Oval | July 28 | 8 | | 2-32 |
| Kent | Canterbury | Aug 4 | 7 * | 1Ct | 1-26 |
| Lancashire | Old Trafford | Aug 18 | 0 | | 0-41 |
| Hampshire | The Oval | Aug 25 | 33 | 1Ct | 2-34 |
| **NATWEST TROPHY** | | | | | |
| Kent | The Oval | July 11 | | | 3-46 |
| Essex | The Oval | July 31 | 47 | | 1-48 |
| Northants | The Oval | Aug 14 | 0 | | 0-15 |
| Hampshire | Lord's | Sept 7 | 3 * | | 0-43 |
| **BENSON & HEDGES CUP** | | | | | |
| Middlesex | Lord's | April 25 | 4 | 1Ct | 2-31 |
| Somerset | Taunton | May 4 | 35 | | |
| Warwickshire | The Oval | May 7 | 38 | 1Ct | 1-29 |
| **OTHER ONE-DAY** | | | | | |
| Warwickshire | Harrogate | June 12 | 3 | | 4-28 |
| Durham | Harrogate | June 13 | 0 | | 1-31 |

### BATTING AVERAGES - Including fielding

| | Matches | Inns | NO | Runs | HS | Avge | 100s | 50s | Ct | St |
|---|---|---|---|---|---|---|---|---|---|---|
| Britannic Assurance | 4 | 6 | 1 | 186 | 79 | 37.20 | - | 2 | - | - |
| ALL FIRST-CLASS | 4 | 6 | 1 | 186 | 79 | 37.20 | - | 2 | - | - |
| Refuge Assurance | 15 | 13 | 3 | 253 | 55 * | 25.30 | - | 2 | 4 | - |
| NatWest Trophy | 4 | 3 | 1 | 50 | 47 | 25.00 | - | - | - | - |
| Benson & Hedges Cup | 3 | 3 | 0 | 77 | 38 | 25.66 | - | - | 2 | - |
| Other One-Day | 2 | 2 | 0 | 3 | 3 | 1.50 | - | - | - | - |
| ALL ONE-DAY | 24 | 21 | 4 | 383 | 55 * | 22.52 | - | 2 | 6 | - |

### BOWLING AVERAGES

| | Overs | Mdns | Runs | Wkts | Avge | Best | 5wI | 10wM |
|---|---|---|---|---|---|---|---|---|
| Britannic Assurance | 28 | 3 | 110 | 2 | 55.00 | 1-18 | - | - |
| ALL FIRST-CLASS | 28 | 3 | 110 | 2 | 55.00 | 1-18 | - | - |
| Refuge Assurance | 88.1 | 3 | 402 | 9 | 44.66 | 2-32 | - | |
| NatWest Trophy | 40 | 4 | 152 | 4 | 38.00 | 3-46 | - | |
| Benson & Hedges Cup | 19.2 | 3 | 60 | 3 | 20.00 | 2-31 | - | |
| Other One-Day | 15 | 1 | 59 | 5 | 11.80 | 4-28 | - | |
| ALL ONE-DAY | 162.3 | 11 | 673 | 21 | 32.04 | 4-28 | - | |

## M.A.ROBINSON - *Yorkshire*

| Opposition | Venue | Date | Batting | Fielding | Bowling |
|---|---|---|---|---|---|
| **BRITANNIC ASSURANCE** | | | | | |
| Middlesex | Lord's | April 27 | 8 | | 1-16 |
| Warwickshire | Headingley | May 9 | 0 & 0 * | | 1-40 & 1-42 |
| Notts | Headingley | May 16 | 0 * | | 0-42 & 2-30 |
| Gloucs | Sheffield | May 22 | | 1Ct | 0-24 & 1-19 |
| Northants | Headingley | May 25 | 1 * | | 0-29 & 1-28 |
| Warwickshire | Edgbaston | May 31 | 0 & 0 | | 1-70 & 0-35 |
| Notts | Worksop | July 23 | 0 | | 1-17 & 0-42 |
| Lancashire | Old Trafford | Aug 2 | 4 | 1Ct | 3-43 & 0-34 |
| Leicestershire | Leicester | Aug 6 | | | 1-59 & 0-11 |
| Sussex | Midd'brough | Aug 9 | 1 * & 0 | | 2-118 |
| Glamorgan | Headingley | Aug 16 | | | 0-42 & 0-1 |
| Essex | Colchester | Aug 20 | | 1Ct | 2-36 & 1-62 |
| Somerset | Taunton | Aug 23 | | | 1-77 & 1-40 |
| Northants | Northampton | Aug 28 | 3 & 0 | 1Ct | 1-58 & 1-27 |
| Lancashire | Scarborough | Sept 3 | | | 1-84 |
| **OTHER FIRST-CLASS** | | | | | |
| Oxford U | The Parks | June 4 | | | 0-44 |
| Sri Lanka | Headingley | July 27 | | | 2-71 |
| **REFUGE ASSURANCE** | | | | | |
| Hampshire | Southampton | April 21 | 2 * | | 0-45 |
| Essex | Chelmsford | April 28 | | | 0-25 |
| Leicestershire | Leicester | May 19 | | | 0-20 |
| Northants | Headingley | May 26 | | | 2-24 |
| Derbyshire | Chesterfield | June 2 | | | 0-33 |
| Surrey | The Oval | July 21 | | | 4-33 |
| Lancashire | Old Trafford | Aug 4 | | | 1-48 |
| Sussex | Midd'brough | Aug 11 | | 1Ct | 1-27 |
| Notts | Scarborough | Aug 18 | | | 2-46 |
| Somerset | Taunton | Aug 25 | 2 | | 1-48 |
| **BENSON & HEDGES CUP** | | | | | |
| Notts | Trent Bridge | April 25 | | | 1-52 |
| Min Counties | Headingley | May 2 | | | 1-33 |
| Lancashire | Old Trafford | June 16 | 1 * | | 2-43 |
| **OTHER ONE-DAY** | | | | | |
| Essex | Scarborough | Sept 2 | | | 0-21 |
| World XI | Scarborough | Sept 8 | 1 | | 0-14 |

### BATTING AVERAGES - Including fielding

| | Matches | Inns | NO | Runs | HS | Avge | 100s | 50s | Ct | St |
|---|---|---|---|---|---|---|---|---|---|---|
| Britannic Assurance | 15 | 13 | 4 | 17 | 8 | 1.88 | - | - | 4 | - |
| Other First-Class | 2 | 0 | 0 | 0 | 0 | - | - | - | - | - |
| ALL FIRST-CLASS | 17 | 13 | 4 | 17 | 8 | 1.88 | - | - | 4 | - |
| Refuge Assurance | 10 | 2 | 1 | 4 | 2 * | 4.00 | - | - | 1 | - |
| Benson & Hedges Cup | 3 | 1 | 1 | 1 | 1 * | - | - | - | - | - |
| Other One-Day | 2 | 1 | 0 | 1 | 1 | 1.00 | - | - | - | - |
| ALL ONE-DAY | 15 | 4 | 2 | 6 | 2 * | 3.00 | - | - | 1 | - |

### BOWLING AVERAGES

| | Overs | Mdns | Runs | Wkts | Avge | Best | 5wI | 10wM |
|---|---|---|---|---|---|---|---|---|
| Britannic Assurance | 377.1 | 78 | 1126 | 23 | 48.95 | 3-43 | - | - |
| Other First-Class | 39 | 7 | 115 | 2 | 57.50 | 2-71 | - | - |
| ALL FIRST-CLASS | 416.1 | 85 | 1241 | 25 | 49.64 | 3-43 | - | - |
| Refuge Assurance | 64.5 | 3 | 349 | 11 | 31.72 | 4-33 | - | - |
| Benson & Hedges Cup | 31 | 3 | 128 | 4 | 32.00 | 2-43 | - | - |
| Other One-Day | 15 | 1 | 35 | 0 | - | - | - | - |
| ALL ONE-DAY | 110.5 | 7 | 512 | 15 | 34.13 | 4-33 | - | - |

## P.E.ROBINSON - *Yorkshire*

| Opposition | Venue | Date | Batting | Fielding | Bowling |
|---|---|---|---|---|---|
| **BRITANNIC ASSURANCE** | | | | | |
| Middlesex | Lord's | April 27 | 10 | | |
| Warwickshire | Headingley | May 9 | 0 & 33 | 2Ct | |
| Notts | Headingley | May 16 | 57 & 53 * | 1Ct | |

# PLAYER RECORDS

| | | | | | | | |
|---|---|---|---|---|---|---|---|
| Gloucs | Sheffield | May 22 | 31 & | 6 * | | 0-5 & 0-14 | |
| Northants | Headingley | May 25 | 5 & | 21 | 1Ct | | |
| Warwickshire | Edgbaston | May 31 | 16 & | 93 | 1Ct | | |
| Kent | Harrogate | June 14 | 0 | | | | |
| Middlesex | Sheffield | June 21 | 33 & | 0 | | | |
| Worcestershire | Headingley | July 2 | 57 | | | | |
| Hampshire | Southampton | July 5 | 25 | | 2Ct | | |
| Derbyshire | Scarborough | July 16 | 2 | | 2Ct | | |
| Surrey | Guildford | July 19 | 74 & | 17 | 2Ct | | |
| Notts | Worksop | July 23 | 3 | | 3Ct | | |
| Lancashire | Old Trafford | Aug 2 | 58 & | 44 | | | |
| Leicestershire | Leicester | Aug 6 | 7 *& | 9 | | 0-30 | |
| Sussex | Midd'brough | Aug 9 | 8 & | 10 | 3Ct | | |
| Glamorgan | Headingley | Aug 16 | 51 & | 8 | | | |
| Essex | Colchester | Aug 20 | 0 & | 35 * | | | |
| Somerset | Taunton | Aug 23 | 22 *& | 4 | | | |
| Northants | Northampton | Aug 28 | 30 & | 34 | 1Ct | | |
| Lancashire | Scarborough | Sept 3 | 189 & | 79 * | | | |
| Derbyshire | Chesterfield | Sept 17 | 12 & | 0 | 1Ct | | |

## OTHER FIRST-CLASS

| | | | | |
|---|---|---|---|---|
| Oxford U | The Parks | June 4 | 35 *& | 22 |
| Sri Lanka | Headingley | July 27 | 100 | 1Ct |

## REFUGE ASSURANCE

| | | | | |
|---|---|---|---|---|
| Hampshire | Southampton | April 21 | 15 | |
| Essex | Chelmsford | April 28 | 20 | |
| Warwickshire | Headingley | May 12 | 3 | |
| Leicestershire | Leicester | May 19 | 2 | |
| Northants | Headingley | May 26 | 2 | |
| Derbyshire | Chesterfield | June 2 | 57 * | 1Ct |
| Kent | Scarborough | June 16 | 11 | 1Ct |
| Worcestershire | Sheffield | June 23 | 10 | 2Ct |
| Glamorgan | Headingley | June 30 | 21 * | 1Ct |
| Middlesex | Lord's | July 7 | 3 * | 1Ct |
| Gloucs | Scarborough | July 14 | 64 | 1Ct |
| Surrey | The Oval | July 21 | | |
| Lancashire | Old Trafford | Aug 4 | 9 | |
| Sussex | Midd'brough | Aug 11 | 13 | |
| Notts | Scarborough | Aug 18 | 32 | 1Ct |
| Somerset | Taunton | Aug 25 | 39 | 1Ct |

## NATWEST TROPHY

| | | | |
|---|---|---|---|
| Warwickshire | Edgbaston | June 26 | 40 |

## BENSON & HEDGES CUP

| | | | | |
|---|---|---|---|---|
| Notts | Trent Bridge | April 25 | 0 | |
| Min Counties | Headingley | May 2 | 11 * | |
| Hampshire | Headingley | May 4 | 43 | 3Ct |
| Glamorgan | Cardiff | May 7 | | |
| Warwickshire | Headingley | May 29 | 29 | |
| Lancashire | Old Trafford | June 16 | 9 | |

## OTHER ONE-DAY

| | | | | |
|---|---|---|---|---|
| Derbyshire | Scarborough | Sept 1 | 5 | 1Ct |
| Essex | Scarborugh | Sept 2 | 41 | 1Ct |
| Yorkshiremen | Scarborough | Sept 7 | 24 | |
| World XI | Scarborough | Sept 8 | 15 | 1Ct |

## BATTING AVERAGES - Including fielding

| | Matches | Inns | NO | Runs | HS | Avge | 100s | 50s | Ct | St |
|---|---|---|---|---|---|---|---|---|---|---|
| Britannic Assurance | 22 | 38 | 6 | 1136 | 189 | 35.50 | 1 | 8 | 19 | - |
| Other First-Class | 2 | 3 | 1 | 157 | 100 | 78.50 | 1 | - | 1 | - |
| | | | | | | | | | | |
| ALL FIRST-CLASS | 24 | 41 | 7 | 1293 | 189 | 38.02 | 2 | 8 | 20 | - |
| | | | | | | | | | | |
| Refuge Assurance | 16 | 15 | 3 | 301 | 64 | 25.08 | - | 2 | 9 | - |
| NatWest Trophy | 1 | 1 | 0 | 40 | 40 | 40.00 | - | - | - | - |
| Benson & Hedges Cup | 6 | 5 | 1 | 92 | 43 | 23.00 | - | - | 3 | - |
| Other One-Day | 4 | 4 | 0 | 85 | 41 | 21.25 | - | - | 3 | - |
| | | | | | | | | | | |
| ALL ONE-DAY | 27 | 25 | 4 | 518 | 64 | 24.66 | - | 2 | 15 | - |

## BOWLING AVERAGES

| | Overs | Mdns | Runs | Wkts | Avge | Best | 5wI | 10wM |
|---|---|---|---|---|---|---|---|---|
| Britannic Assurance | 10 | 1 | 49 | 0 | - | - | - | - |
| Other First-Class | | | | | | | | |
| | | | | | | | | |
| ALL FIRST-CLASS | 10 | 1 | 49 | 0 | - | - | - | - |
| | | | | | | | | |
| Refuge Assurance | | | | | | | | |
| NatWest Trophy | | | | | | | | |
| Benson & Hedges Cup | | | | | | | | |
| Other One-Day | | | | | | | | |
| | | | | | | | | |
| ALL ONE-DAY | | | | | | | | |

# R.T.ROBINSON - *Nottinghamshire*

| Opposition | Venue | Date | Batting | | | Fielding | Bowling |
|---|---|---|---|---|---|---|---|
| **BRITANNIC ASSURANCE** | | | | | | | |
| Leicestershire | Trent Bridge | May 9 | 13 & | 68 * | | 1Ct | |
| Yorkshire | Headingley | May 16 | 25 & | 2 | | | |
| Kent | Trent Bridge | May 22 | 85 & | 16 | | | |
| Leicestershire | Leicester | May 25 | 101 & | 1 | | 1Ct | |
| Hampshire | Trent Bridge | May 31 | 48 & | 95 * | | | |
| Surrey | The Oval | June 4 | | 6 * | | | |
| Gloucs | Gloucester | June 14 | 28 & | 0 | | | |
| Worcestershire | Worcester | June 18 | 12 & | 89 * | | | 1-30 |
| Warwickshire | Trent Bridge | June 28 | | 39 | | 1Ct | |
| Glamorgan | Cardiff | July 2 | 91 * | | | | |
| Lancashire | Trent Bridge | July 16 | 2 | | | 3Ct | |
| Northants | Well'borough | July 19 | 43 | | | 1Ct | |
| Yorkshire | Worksop | July 23 | 0 *& | 0 | | 2Ct | |
| Middlesex | Lord's | July 26 | 20 & | 62 | | 1Ct | |
| Sussex | Eastbourne | Aug 6 | 95 | | | 2Ct | |
| Essex | Trent Bridge | Aug 9 | 6 & | 0 | | 3Ct | |
| Somerset | Trent Bridge | Aug 16 | 49 & | 44 | | 1Ct | |
| Derbyshire | Trent Bridge | Aug 23 | 53 & | 67 | | | |
| Lancashire | Old Trafford | Aug 28 | 44 & | 59 * | | 2Ct | |
| Middlesex | Trent Bridge | Sept 3 | 34 & | 20 | | | |
| Derbyshire | Derby | Sept 10 | 145 & | 31 * | | | 0-9 |
| Worcestershire | Trent Bridge | Sept 17 | 180 | | | | |
| **REFUGE ASSURANCE** | | | | | | | |
| Lancashire | Old Trafford | April 21 | 29 * | | | 1Ct | |
| Warwickshire | Trent Bridge | April 28 | 3 | | | 1Ct | |
| Glamorgan | Cardiff | May 5 | 10 | | | | |
| Essex | Trent Bridge | May 12 | 25 | | | | |
| Leicestershire | Leicester | May 26 | 8 | | | 1Ct | |
| Somerset | Trent Bridge | June 9 | 15 | | | | |
| Gloucs | Gloucester | June 16 | 24 * | | | | |
| Middlesex | Trent Bridge | June 23 | 23 | | | 1Ct | |
| Surrey | The Oval | June 30 | 3 * | | | 1Ct | |
| Hampshire | Trent Bridge | July 14 | 7 | | | | |
| Northants | Well'borough | July 21 | 35 | | | | |
| Sussex | Hove | July 28 | 10 | | | | |
| Worcestershire | Trent Bridge | Aug 4 | 8 | | | | |
| Kent | Trent Bridge | Aug 11 | 30 | | | | |
| Yorkshire | Scarborough | Aug 18 | 23 | | | | |
| Derbyshire | Trent Bridge | Aug 25 | 25 * | | | 1Ct | |
| **NATWEST TROPHY** | | | | | | | |
| Lincolnshire | Trent Bridge | June 26 | 124 | | | 1Ct | |
| Gloucs | Bristol | July 11 | 48 | | | | |
| Hampshire | Southampton | July 31 | 25 | | | | |
| **BENSON & HEDGES CUP** | | | | | | | |
| Hampshire | Southampton | April 23 | 54 | | | | |
| Yorkshire | Trent Bridge | April 25 | 27 | | | | |
| Glamorgan | Cardiff | May 4 | 116 | | | | |
| Min Counties | Trent Bridge | May 7 | 42 | | | 1Ct | |

## BATTING AVERAGES - Including fielding

| | Matches | Inns | NO | Runs | HS | Avge | 100s | 50s | Ct | St |
|---|---|---|---|---|---|---|---|---|---|---|
| Britannic Assurance | 22 | 37 | 8 | 1673 | 180 | 57.69 | 3 | 10 | 18 | - |
| | | | | | | | | | | |
| ALL FIRST-CLASS | 22 | 37 | 8 | 1673 | 180 | 57.69 | 3 | 10 | 18 | - |
| | | | | | | | | | | |
| Refuge Assurance | 16 | 16 | 4 | 278 | 35 | 23.16 | - | - | 6 | - |
| NatWest Trophy | 3 | 3 | 0 | 197 | 124 | 65.66 | 1 | - | 1 | - |
| Benson & Hedges Cup | 4 | 4 | 0 | 239 | 116 | 59.75 | 1 | 1 | 1 | - |
| | | | | | | | | | | |
| ALL ONE-DAY | 23 | 23 | 4 | 714 | 124 | 37.57 | 2 | 1 | 8 | - |

## BOWLING AVERAGES

| | Overs | Mdns | Runs | Wkts | Avge | Best | 5wI | 10wM |
|---|---|---|---|---|---|---|---|---|
| Britannic Assurance | 8 | 0 | 39 | 1 | 39.00 | 1-30 | - | - |
| | | | | | | | | |
| ALL FIRST-CLASS | 8 | 0 | 39 | 1 | 39.00 | 1-30 | - | - |
| | | | | | | | | |
| Refuge Assurance | | | | | | | | |
| NatWest Trophy | | | | | | | | |
| Benson & Hedges Cup | | | | | | | | |
| | | | | | | | | |
| ALL ONE-DAY | | | | | | | | |

# R  PLAYER RECORDS

## A.G.ROBSON - *Surrey*

| Opposition | Venue | Date | Batting | Fielding | Bowling |
|---|---|---|---|---|---|
| **BRITANNIC ASSURANCE** | | | | | |
| Essex | Chelmsford | April 27 | 0 | | 0-31 |
| Kent | The Oval | May 9 | 0 & 3 | | 1-72 |
| **REFUGE ASSURANCE** | | | | | |
| Kent | Canterbury | Aug 4 | | | 2-40 |
| Lancashire | Old Trafford | Aug 18 | | | 2-46 |
| Hampshire | The Oval | Aug 25 | | | 3-42 |

**BATTING AVERAGES - Including fielding**

| | Matches | Inns | NO | Runs | HS | Avge | 100s | 50s | Ct | St |
|---|---|---|---|---|---|---|---|---|---|---|
| Britannic Assurance | 2 | 3 | 0 | 3 | 3 | 1.00 | - | - | - | - |
| ALL FIRST-CLASS | 2 | 3 | 0 | 3 | 3 | 1.00 | - | - | - | - |
| Refuge Assurance | 3 | 0 | 0 | 0 | 0 | - | - | - | - | - |
| ALL ONE-DAY | 3 | 0 | 0 | 0 | 0 | - | - | - | - | - |

**BOWLING AVERAGES**

| | Overs | Mdns | Runs | Wkts | Avge | Best | 5wI | 10wM |
|---|---|---|---|---|---|---|---|---|
| Britannic Assurance | 39 | 14 | 103 | 1 | 103.00 | 1-72 | - | - |
| ALL FIRST-CLASS | 39 | 14 | 103 | 1 | 103.00 | 1-72 | - | - |
| Refuge Assurance | 24 | 0 | 128 | 7 | 18.28 | 3-42 | - | |
| ALL ONE-DAY | 24 | 0 | 128 | 7 | 18.28 | 3-42 | - | |

## P.M.ROEBUCK - *Somerset*

| Opposition | Venue | Date | Batting | Fielding | Bowling |
|---|---|---|---|---|---|
| **BRITANNIC ASSURANCE** | | | | | |
| Sussex | Taunton | April 27 | 18 | | 0-54 |
| Glamorgan | Taunton | May 9 | 101 & 64 | | 0-13 & 0-12 |
| Derbyshire | Derby | May 22 | 0 & 8* | | 3-37 |
| Middlesex | Taunton | May 25 | 91* & 49 | | 1-11 |
| Glamorgan | Swansea | June 4 | 7 | | 0-22 |
| Warwickshire | Edgbaston | June 7 | 60 & 20* | | |
| Hampshire | Bath | June 18 | 4 & 12 | | |
| Gloucs | Bath | June 21 | 15 | | |
| Surrey | The Oval | June 28 | 47 | 1Ct | 0-7 |
| Lancashire | Taunton | July 2 | 46 & 52 | | 1-42 & 0-16 |
| Sussex | Hove | July 16 | 22 & 55 | 1Ct | 1-39 |
| Essex | Southend | July 19 | 38 & 11 | | 0-25 |
| Northants | Northampton | July 23 | 32 | | |
| Leicestershire | Weston | Aug 2 | 4 & 14 | 1Ct | 3-10 |
| Worcestershire | Weston | Aug 6 | 11 & 6 | | 0-17 |
| Yorkshire | Taunton | Aug 23 | 31 & 2 | | 0-4 |
| **OTHER FIRST-CLASS** | | | | | |
| West Indies | Taunton | May 29 | 10 & 3 | 1Ct | 0-6 |
| **REFUGE ASSURANCE** | | | | | |
| Glamorgan | Taunton | May 12 | | | 1-11 |
| Hampshire | Bournemouth | May 19 | | | |
| Middlesex | Taunton | May 26 | 2 | | 1-47 |
| Derbyshire | Derby | June 16 | 45 | 1Ct | 4-11 |
| Northants | Luton | June 30 | 0 | | 3-15 |
| Lancashire | Taunton | July 5 | 20 | | 0-26 |
| Essex | Southend | July 21 | 41 | | 0-38 |
| Kent | Taunton | July 28 | 34 | 1Ct | 0-56 |
| Leicestershire | Weston | Aug 4 | 10 | | 2-32 |
| **NATWEST TROPHY** | | | | | |
| Bucks | Bath | June 26 | 63* | 1Ct | |
| Middlesex | Taunton | July 11 | 31 | 1Ct | 1-43 |
| Warwickshire | Edgbaston | July 31 | 5 | | 0-19 |
| **BENSON & HEDGES CUP** | | | | | |
| Middlesex | Taunton | April 23 | 61 | | |
| Warwickshire | Edgbaston | May 2 | 11 | | 0-22 |
| Surrey | Taunton | May 4 | 0 | | 0-41 |
| Essex | Chelmsford | May 7 | 2 | | |

**BATTING AVERAGES - Including fielding**

| | Matches | Inns | NO | Runs | HS | Avge | 100s | 50s | Ct | St |
|---|---|---|---|---|---|---|---|---|---|---|
| Britannic Assurance | 16 | 27 | 3 | 820 | 101 | 34.16 | 1 | 5 | 3 | - |
| Other First-Class | 1 | 2 | 0 | 13 | 10 | 6.50 | - | - | 1 | - |
| ALL FIRST-CLASS | 17 | 29 | 3 | 833 | 101 | 32.03 | 1 | 5 | 4 | - |
| Refuge Assurance | 9 | 7 | 0 | 152 | 45 | 21.71 | - | - | 2 | - |
| NatWest Trophy | 3 | 3 | 1 | 99 | 63* | 49.50 | - | 1 | 2 | - |
| Benson & Hedges Cup | 4 | 4 | 0 | 74 | 61 | 18.50 | - | 1 | - | - |
| ALL ONE-DAY | 16 | 14 | 1 | 325 | 63* | 25.00 | - | 2 | 4 | - |

**BOWLING AVERAGES**

| | Overs | Mdns | Runs | Wkts | Avge | Best | 5wI | 10wM |
|---|---|---|---|---|---|---|---|---|
| Britannic Assurance | 128 | 32 | 309 | 9 | 34.33 | 3-10 | - | - |
| Other First-Class | 2 | 1 | 6 | 0 | - | - | - | - |
| ALL FIRST-CLASS | 130 | 33 | 315 | 9 | 35.00 | 3-10 | - | - |
| Refuge Assurance | 49.4 | 3 | 236 | 11 | 21.45 | 4-11 | - | |
| NatWest Trophy | 14 | 0 | 62 | 1 | 62.00 | 1-43 | - | |
| Benson & Hedges Cup | 13 | 0 | 63 | 0 | - | - | - | |
| ALL ONE-DAY | 76.4 | 3 | 361 | 12 | 30.08 | 4-11 | - | |

## C.J.ROGERS - *Norfolk*

| Opposition | Venue | Date | Batting | Fielding | Bowling |
|---|---|---|---|---|---|
| **NATWEST TROPHY** | | | | | |
| Gloucs | Bristol | June 26 | 2 | | |

**BATTING AVERAGES - Including fielding**

| | Matches | Inns | NO | Runs | HS | Avge | 100s | 50s | Ct | St |
|---|---|---|---|---|---|---|---|---|---|---|
| NatWest Trophy | 1 | 1 | 0 | 2 | 2 | 2.00 | - | - | - | - |
| ALL ONE-DAY | 1 | 1 | 0 | 2 | 2 | 2.00 | - | - | - | - |

**BOWLING AVERAGES**
Did not bowl

## P.W.ROMAINES - *Gloucestershire*

| Opposition | Venue | Date | Batting | Fielding | Bowling |
|---|---|---|---|---|---|
| **BRITANNIC ASSURANCE** | | | | | |
| Glamorgan | Cheltenham | July 19 | 28 & 0 | | |
| Sussex | Cheltenham | July 23 | 4 | | |
| Worcestershire | Cheltenham | July 26 | 3 & 0 | 1Ct | |
| **REFUGE ASSURANCE** | | | | | |
| Middlesex | Bristol | April 21 | 13 | | |
| Worcestershire | Bristol | May 5 | 27* | | |
| Surrey | The Oval | May 12 | 5* | 1Ct | |
| Sussex | Hove | May 19 | 2 | | |
| Hampshire | Swindon | May 26 | | | |
| Northants | Moreton | June 9 | | | |
| **BENSON & HEDGES CUP** | | | | | |
| Derbyshire | Derby | May 7 | 22 | 1Ct | |
| **OTHER ONE-DAY** | | | | | |
| West Indies | Bristol | May 14 | 11 | 1Ct | |

**BATTING AVERAGES - Including fielding**

| | Matches | Inns | NO | Runs | HS | Avge | 100s | 50s | Ct | St |
|---|---|---|---|---|---|---|---|---|---|---|
| Britannic Assurance | 3 | 5 | 0 | 35 | 28 | 7.00 | - | - | 1 | - |
| ALL FIRST-CLASS | 3 | 5 | 0 | 35 | 28 | 7.00 | - | - | 1 | - |
| Refuge Assurance | 6 | 4 | 2 | 47 | 27* | 23.50 | - | - | 1 | - |
| Benson & Hedges Cup | 1 | 1 | 0 | 22 | 22 | 22.00 | - | - | 1 | - |
| Other One-Day | 1 | 1 | 0 | 11 | 11 | 11.00 | - | - | 1 | - |
| ALL ONE-DAY | 8 | 6 | 2 | 80 | 27* | 20.00 | - | - | 3 | - |

# PLAYER RECORDS

**R**

## BOWLING AVERAGES
Did not bowl

## G.D.ROSE - *Somerset*

| Opposition | Venue | Date | Batting | | | Fielding | Bowling |
|---|---|---|---|---|---|---|---|
| **BRITANNIC ASSURANCE** | | | | | | | |
| Sussex | Taunton | April 27 | 13 | | | | 1-90 |
| Glamorgan | Taunton | May 9 | 24 | & | 2 | 1Ct | 2-89 & 0-28 |
| Derbyshire | Derby | May 22 | 37 | & | 32 | 1Ct | 1-43 & 1-44 |
| Middlesex | Taunton | May 25 | 17 | | | 1Ct | 1-14 |
| Glamorgan | Swansea | June 4 | | | | | 2-31 |
| Kent | Taunton | July 26 | 3 | & | 0 | | 1-52 |
| Leicestershire | Weston | Aug 2 | 14 | | | | 2-24 & 0-7 |
| Worcestershire | Weston | Aug 6 | 12 | & | 24 * | | 2-58 & 0-15 |
| Notts | Trent Bridge | Aug 16 | 31 | | | 1Ct | 0-51 & 0-28 |
| Yorkshire | Taunton | Aug 23 | 105 * | | | | 2-29 & 0-28 |
| Hampshire | Southampton | Aug 28 | 20 | | | | 2-78 & 0-32 |
| Worcestershire | Worcester | Sept 3 | 4 | & | 58 | | 0-55 |
| Gloucs | Bristol | Sept 10 | 106 | | | 2Ct | 2-46 & 0-17 |
| Warwickshire | Taunton | Sept 17 | 10 | & | 55 | 2Ct | 0-70 & 4-77 |
| **OTHER FIRST-CLASS** | | | | | | | |
| Sri Lanka | Taunton | Aug 10 | | | 23 * | | 2-41 & 0-28 |
| **REFUGE ASSURANCE** | | | | | | | |
| Surrey | The Oval | April 21 | 2 | | | | 2-30 |
| Sussex | Taunton | April 28 | 50 | | | 2Ct | 2-40 |
| Glamorgan | Taunton | May 12 | 59 | | | | 1-43 |
| Hampshire | Bournemouth | May 19 | 11 * | | | | 1-31 |
| Middlesex | Taunton | May 26 | 0 | | | | 0-18 |
| Warwickshire | Edgbaston | June 2 | 2 | | | | |
| Derbyshire | Derby | June 16 | 17 | | | | |
| Northants | Luton | June 30 | 2 | | | | |
| Kent | Taunton | July 28 | 0 | | | | 0-25 |
| Leicestershire | Weston | Aug 4 | 0 * | | | | 1-33 |
| Worcestershire | Worcester | Aug 18 | 14 | | | | 0-49 |
| Yorkshire | Taunton | Aug 25 | 3 | | | | 2-21 |
| **NATWEST TROPHY** | | | | | | | |
| Bucks | Bath | June 26 | | | | | |
| Warwickshire | Edgbaston | July 31 | 3 | | | | 0-40 |
| **BENSON & HEDGES CUP** | | | | | | | |
| Middlesex | Taunton | April 23 | 11 | | | | 0-31 |
| Warwickshire | Edgbaston | May 2 | 2 | | | | 0-38 |
| Surrey | Taunton | May 4 | 23 | | | | 2-48 |
| Essex | Chelmsford | May 7 | 1 | | | | 1-55 |

### BATTING AVERAGES - Including fielding

| | Matches | Inns | NO | Runs | HS | Avge | 100s | 50s | Ct | St |
|---|---|---|---|---|---|---|---|---|---|---|
| Britannic Assurance | 14 | 19 | 2 | 567 | 106 | 33.35 | 2 | 2 | 8 | - |
| Other First-Class | 1 | 1 | 1 | 23 | 23 * | - | - | - | - | - |
| ALL FIRST-CLASS | 15 | 20 | 3 | 590 | 106 | 34.70 | 2 | 2 | 8 | - |
| Refuge Assurance | 12 | 12 | 2 | 160 | 59 | 16.00 | - | 2 | 2 | - |
| NatWest Trophy | 2 | 1 | 0 | 3 | 3 | 3.00 | - | - | - | - |
| Benson & Hedges Cup | 4 | 4 | 0 | 37 | 23 | 9.25 | - | - | - | - |
| ALL ONE-DAY | 18 | 17 | 2 | 200 | 59 | 13.33 | - | 2 | 2 | - |

### BOWLING AVERAGES

| | Overs | Mdns | Runs | Wkts | Avge | Best | 5wI | 10wM |
|---|---|---|---|---|---|---|---|---|
| Britannic Assurance | 307 | 51 | 1006 | 23 | 43.73 | 4-77 | - | - |
| Other First-Class | 16 | 2 | 69 | 2 | 34.50 | 2-41 | - | - |
| ALL FIRST-CLASS | 323 | 53 | 1075 | 25 | 43.00 | 4-77 | - | - |
| Refuge Assurance | 54.1 | 0 | 290 | 9 | 32.22 | 2-21 | - | |
| NatWest Trophy | 7 | 0 | 40 | 0 | - | - | - | |
| Benson & Hedges Cup | 38.5 | 2 | 172 | 3 | 57.33 | 2-48 | - | |
| ALL ONE-DAY | 100 | 2 | 502 | 12 | 41.83 | 2-21 | - | |

## M.A.ROSEBERRY - *Middlesex*

| Opposition | Venue | Date | Batting | | | Fielding | Bowling |
|---|---|---|---|---|---|---|---|
| **BRITANNIC ASSURANCE** | | | | | | | |
| Sussex | Lord's | May 9 | 18 | & | 0 | | |
| Sussex | Hove | May 22 | 25 | & | 47 | 2Ct | |
| Somerset | Taunton | May 25 | 7 | | | | 0-2 |
| Kent | Lord's | May 31 | 2 | & | 16 | | |
| Gloucs | Bristol | June 4 | 17 | & | 7 | | 0-5 |
| Leicestershire | Uxbridge | June 7 | 119 * | & | 44 * | 2Ct | |
| Glamorgan | Cardiff | June 14 | 40 * | & | 37 | 1Ct | |
| Yorkshire | Sheffield | June 21 | 12 | & | 29 | 1Ct | |
| Essex | Lord's | June 28 | 24 | & | 19 | 1Ct | 0-21 |
| Warwickshire | Edgbaston | July 2 | 27 | & | 15 | 2Ct | |
| Northants | Uxbridge | July 16 | 47 | | | | |
| Lancashire | Uxbridge | July 19 | 63 | & | 65 | | |
| Notts | Lord's | July 26 | 2 | & | 4 | | |
| Hampshire | Lord's | Aug 2 | 47 | & | 38 | 1Ct | |
| Derbyshire | Lord's | Aug 9 | 28 | & | 15 | 3Ct | |
| Surrey | The Oval | Aug 20 | 2 | & | 51 | 4Ct | |
| Worcestershire | Worcester | Aug 23 | 36 | & | 15 | | |
| Kent | Canterbury | Aug 28 | 18 | & | 5 | | |
| Notts | Trent Bridge | Sept 3 | 9 | & | 56 | | |
| Surrey | Lord's | Sept 10 | 53 | & | 62 | | |
| Essex | Chelmsford | Sept 17 | 2 | & | 99 | | 0-8 |
| **OTHER FIRST-CLASS** | | | | | | | |
| MCC | Lord's | April 16 | 98 | | | 1Ct | |
| Cambridge U | Fenner's | May 15 | 123 * | | | 1Ct | 0-27 |
| West Indies | Lord's | May 18 | 45 | & | 23 | 1Ct | |
| **REFUGE ASSURANCE** | | | | | | | |
| Gloucs | Bristol | April 21 | 2 | | | 1Ct | |
| Sussex | Hove | May 12 | 21 | | | | |
| Somerset | Taunton | May 26 | 30 | | | | |
| Kent | Southgate | June 2 | 79 | | | 1Ct | |
| Leicestershire | Uxbridge | June 9 | 1 | | | | |
| Glamorgan | Cardiff | June 16 | 6 | | | | |
| Notts | Trent Bridge | June 23 | 3 | | | 1Ct | |
| Yorkshire | Lord's | July 7 | 106 * | | | | |
| Warwickshire | Edgbaston | July 14 | 17 | | | 1Ct | |
| Lancashire | Lord's | July 21 | 42 | | | 1Ct | |
| Hampshire | Lord's | Aug 4 | 5 | | | 1Ct | |
| Derbyshire | Lord's | Aug 11 | 63 | | | 1Ct | |
| Essex | Colchester | Aug 18 | 2 | | | | |
| Worcestershire | Worcester | Aug 25 | 6 | | | | |
| **NATWEST TROPHY** | | | | | | | |
| Ireland | Dublin | June 26 | 6 | | | 1Ct | 0-20 |
| Somerset | Taunton | July 11 | 44 | | | 1Ct | |
| **BENSON & HEDGES CUP** | | | | | | | |
| Somerset | Taunton | April 23 | | | | | |

### BATTING AVERAGES - Including fielding

| | Matches | Inns | NO | Runs | HS | Avge | 100s | 50s | Ct | St |
|---|---|---|---|---|---|---|---|---|---|---|
| Britannic Assurance | 21 | 40 | 3 | 1222 | 119 * | 33.02 | 1 | 7 | 17 | - |
| Other First-Class | 3 | 4 | 1 | 289 | 123 * | 96.33 | 1 | 1 | 3 | - |
| ALL FIRST-CLASS | 24 | 44 | 4 | 1511 | 123 * | 37.77 | 2 | 8 | 20 | - |
| Refuge Assurance | 14 | 14 | 1 | 383 | 106 * | 29.46 | 1 | 2 | 7 | - |
| NatWest Trophy | 2 | 2 | 0 | 50 | 44 | 25.00 | - | - | 2 | - |
| Benson & Hedges Cup | 1 | 0 | 0 | 0 | 0 | - | - | - | - | - |
| ALL ONE-DAY | 17 | 16 | 1 | 433 | 106 * | 28.86 | 1 | 2 | 9 | - |

### BOWLING AVERAGES

| | Overs | Mdns | Runs | Wkts | Avge | Best | 5wI | 10wM |
|---|---|---|---|---|---|---|---|---|
| Britannic Assurance | 9 | 1 | 36 | 0 | - | - | - | - |
| Other First-Class | 5 | 0 | 27 | 0 | - | - | - | - |
| ALL FIRST-CLASS | 14 | 1 | 63 | 0 | - | - | - | - |
| Refuge Assurance | | | | | | | | |
| NatWest Trophy | 2 | 0 | 20 | 0 | - | - | - | - |
| Benson & Hedges Cup | | | | | | | | |
| ALL ONE-DAY | 2 | 0 | 20 | 0 | - | - | - | - |

# R — PLAYER RECORDS

## P.ROSHIER - England Amateur XI

| Opposition | Venue | Date | Batting | Fielding | Bowling |
|---|---|---|---|---|---|
| **OTHER ONE-DAY** | | | | | |
| Sri Lanka | Wolv'hampton | July 24 | 1 | | 0-2 |

**BATTING AVERAGES - Including fielding**

| | Matches | Inns | NO | Runs | HS | Avge | 100s | 50s | Ct | St |
|---|---|---|---|---|---|---|---|---|---|---|
| Other One-Day | 1 | 1 | 0 | 1 | 1 | 1.00 | - | - | - | - |
| ALL ONE-DAY | 1 | 1 | 0 | 1 | 1 | 1.00 | - | - | - | - |

**BOWLING AVERAGES**

| | Overs | Mdns | Runs | Wkts | Avge | Best | 5wI | 10wM |
|---|---|---|---|---|---|---|---|---|
| Other One-Day | 1.1 | 0 | 2 | 0 | - | - | - | |
| ALL ONE-DAY | 1.1 | 0 | 2 | 0 | - | - | - | |

## T.G.ROSHIER - Buckinghamshire

| Opposition | Venue | Date | Batting | Fielding | Bowling |
|---|---|---|---|---|---|
| **NATWEST TROPHY** | | | | | |
| Somerset | Bath | June 26 | 32 | | 1-40 |

**BATTING AVERAGES - Including fielding**

| | Matches | Inns | NO | Runs | HS | Avge | 100s | 50s | Ct | St |
|---|---|---|---|---|---|---|---|---|---|---|
| NatWest Trophy | 1 | 1 | 0 | 32 | 32 | 32.00 | - | - | - | - |
| ALL ONE-DAY | 1 | 1 | 0 | 32 | 32 | 32.00 | - | - | - | - |

**BOWLING AVERAGES**

| | Overs | Mdns | Runs | Wkts | Avge | Best | 5wI | 10wM |
|---|---|---|---|---|---|---|---|---|
| NatWest Trophy | 12 | 1 | 40 | 1 | 40.00 | 1-40 | - | |
| ALL ONE-DAY | 12 | 1 | 40 | 1 | 40.00 | 1-40 | | |

## A.B.RUSSELL - Scotland

| Opposition | Venue | Date | Batting | Fielding | Bowling |
|---|---|---|---|---|---|
| **OTHER FIRST-CLASS** | | | | | |
| Ireland | Dublin | June 22 | 16 | | 0-10 |
| **NATWEST TROPHY** | | | | | |
| Sussex | Edinburgh | June 26 | 0 | | 2-20 |
| **BENSON & HEDGES CUP** | | | | | |
| Lancashire | Forfar | April 23 | 31 | | |
| Leicestershire | Leicester | May 2 | 2 | | |
| Sussex | Hove | May 4 | 45 | 2Ct | |
| Kent | Glasgow | May 7 | 0 | | 4-42 |

**BATTING AVERAGES - Including fielding**

| | Matches | Inns | NO | Runs | HS | Avge | 100s | 50s | Ct | St |
|---|---|---|---|---|---|---|---|---|---|---|
| Other First-Class | 1 | 1 | 0 | 16 | 16 | 16.00 | - | - | - | - |
| ALL FIRST-CLASS | 1 | 1 | 0 | 16 | 16 | 16.00 | - | - | - | - |
| NatWest Trophy | 1 | 1 | 0 | 0 | 0 | 0.00 | - | - | - | - |
| Benson & Hedges Cup | 4 | 4 | 0 | 78 | 45 | 19.50 | - | - | 2 | - |
| ALL ONE-DAY | 5 | 5 | 0 | 78 | 45 | 15.60 | - | - | 2 | - |

**BOWLING AVERAGES**

| | Overs | Mdns | Runs | Wkts | Avge | Best | 5wI | 10wM |
|---|---|---|---|---|---|---|---|---|
| Other First-Class | 5 | 2 | 10 | 0 | - | - | - | - |
| ALL FIRST-CLASS | 5 | 2 | 10 | 0 | - | - | - | - |
| NatWest Trophy | 5 | 0 | 20 | 2 | 10.00 | 2-20 | - | |
| Benson & Hedges Cup | 7 | 0 | 42 | 4 | 10.50 | 4-42 | - | |
| ALL ONE-DAY | 12 | 0 | 62 | 6 | 10.33 | 4-42 | - | |

## M.J.RUSSELL - Oxford University

| Opposition | Venue | Date | Batting | Fielding | Bowling |
|---|---|---|---|---|---|
| **OTHER FIRST-CLASS** | | | | | |
| Hampshire | The Parks | April 13 | 13 & 0 | | |
| Worcestershire | The Parks | May 25 | 0 & 25 | | |
| Kent | The Parks | June 18 | 23 & 30 | | 4-31 |

**BATTING AVERAGES - Including fielding**

| | Matches | Inns | NO | Runs | HS | Avge | 100s | 50s | Ct | St |
|---|---|---|---|---|---|---|---|---|---|---|
| Other First-Class | 3 | 6 | 0 | 91 | 30 | 15.16 | - | - | - | - |
| ALL FIRST-CLASS | 3 | 6 | 0 | 91 | 30 | 15.16 | - | - | - | - |

**BOWLING AVERAGES**

| | Overs | Mdns | Runs | Wkts | Avge | Best | 5wI | 10wM |
|---|---|---|---|---|---|---|---|---|
| Other First-Class | 8 | 2 | 31 | 4 | 7.75 | 4-31 | - | - |
| ALL FIRST-CLASS | 8 | 2 | 31 | 4 | 7.75 | 4-31 | - | - |

## R.C.RUSSELL - Gloucestershire & England

| Opposition | Venue | Date | Batting | Fielding | Bowling |
|---|---|---|---|---|---|
| **CORNHILL TEST MATCHES** | | | | | |
| West Indies | Headingley | June 6 | 5 & 4 | 1Ct | |
| West Indies | Lord's | June 20 | 46 | 1Ct | |
| West Indies | Trent Bridge | July 4 | 3 & 3 | 2Ct | |
| West Indies | Edgbaston | July 25 | 12 & 0 | 1Ct | |
| Sri Lanka | Lord's | Aug 22 | 17 & 12 * | 3Ct | |
| **BRITANNIC ASSURANCE** | | | | | |
| Worcestershire | Worcester | April 27 | 64 | | |
| Hampshire | Bristol | May 9 | 111 | 4Ct | |
| Essex | Bristol | May 31 | 26 & 3 | 2Ct | |
| Notts | Gloucester | June 14 | 5 | 1Ct | |
| Northants | Luton | June 28 | 34 * & 20 * | 4Ct | 0-10 |
| Surrey | Guildford | July 16 | 0 | 6Ct | |
| Glamorgan | Cheltenham | July 19 | 21 & 79 * | 6Ct | |
| Lancashire | Bristol | Aug 9 | 15 | 4Ct | |
| Glamorgan | Abergavenny | Aug 28 | 15 & 39 | 3Ct,1St | |
| Northants | Bristol | Sept 3 | 12 & 0 | 3Ct,1St | |
| Somerset | Bristol | Sept 10 | 0 & 8 | 3Ct | |
| Sussex | Hove | Sept 17 | 11 & 1 | 1Ct | |
| **OTHER FIRST-CLASS** | | | | | |
| Oxford U | The Parks | June 15 | | | |
| West Indies | Bristol | July 31 | 35 & 2 | 1Ct,1St | 1-4 |
| Sri Lanka | Bristol | Aug 6 | 2 & 22 * | 3Ct | |
| **TEXACO TROPHY** | | | | | |
| West Indies | Edgbaston | May 23 | 1 | 2Ct | |
| West Indies | Old Trafford | May 25 | | 1Ct | |
| West Indies | Lord's | May 27 | | 1Ct | |
| **REFUGE ASSURANCE** | | | | | |
| Middlesex | Bristol | April 21 | 12 | | |
| Worcestershire | Bristol | May 5 | 4 | | |
| Surrey | The Oval | May 12 | 11 | 4Ct | |
| Sussex | Hove | May 19 | 42 | 2Ct,1St | |
| Notts | Gloucester | June 16 | 7 * | | |
| Kent | Canterbury | June 30 | 22 | 2Ct | |
| Yorkshire | Scarborough | July 14 | 29 | 2Ct | |
| Derbyshire | Cheltenham | July 21 | 7 | 3Ct | |
| Glamorgan | Swansea | Aug 4 | 40 | 2Ct | |
| Lancashire | Bristol | Aug 11 | 12 | | |
| Warwickshire | Edgbaston | Aug 18 | 28 | | |
| **NATWEST TROPHY** | | | | | |
| Norfolk | Bristol | June 26 | 23 | 2Ct,1St | |
| Notts | Bristol | July 11 | 25 | 3Ct | |
| **BENSON & HEDGES CUP** | | | | | |
| Combined U | Bristol | April 23 | 25 | 1Ct | |
| Worcestershire | Worcester | April 25 | 51 | 1Ct | |
| Northants | Bristol | May 2 | 0 * | 1Ct | |
| Derbyshire | Derby | May 7 | 9 | 1Ct | |

# PLAYER RECORDS

R

## OTHER ONE-DAY

| | | | | |
|---|---|---|---|---|
| West Indies | Bristol | May 14 | 21 | 2Ct |
| Somerset | Hove | Sept 8 | 15 | 1Ct |
| Sussex | Hove | Sept 9 | 74 | 1Ct |

## BATTING AVERAGES - Including fielding

| | Matches | Inns | NO | Runs | HS | Avge | 100s | 50s | Ct | St |
|---|---|---|---|---|---|---|---|---|---|---|
| Cornhill Test Matches | 5 | 9 | 1 | 102 | 46 | 12.75 | - | - | 8 | - |
| Britannic Assurance | 12 | 19 | 3 | 464 | 111 | 29.00 | 1 | 2 | 37 | 2 |
| Other First-Class | 3 | 4 | 1 | 61 | 35 | 20.33 | - | - | 4 | 1 |
| | | | | | | | | | | |
| ALL FIRST-CLASS | 20 | 32 | 5 | 627 | 111 | 23.22 | 1 | 2 | 49 | 3 |
| | | | | | | | | | | |
| Texaco Trophy | 3 | 1 | 0 | 1 | 1 | 1.00 | - | - | 4 | - |
| Refuge Assurance | 11 | 11 | 1 | 214 | 42 | 21.40 | - | - | 15 | 1 |
| NatWest Trophy | 2 | 2 | 0 | 48 | 25 | 24.00 | - | - | 5 | 1 |
| Benson & Hedges Cup | 4 | 4 | 1 | 85 | 51 | 28.33 | - | 1 | 4 | - |
| Other One-Day | 3 | 3 | 0 | 110 | 74 | 36.66 | - | 1 | 4 | - |
| | | | | | | | | | | |
| ALL ONE-DAY | 23 | 21 | 2 | 458 | 74 | 24.10 | - | 2 | 32 | 2 |

## BOWLING AVERAGES

| | Overs | Mdns | Runs | Wkts | Avge | Best | 5wI | 10wM |
|---|---|---|---|---|---|---|---|---|
| Cornhill Test Matches | | | | | | | | |
| Britannic Assurance | 0.3 | 0 | 10 | 0 | - | - | - | - |
| Other First-Class | 0.5 | 0 | 4 | 1 | 4.00 | 1-4 | - | - |
| | | | | | | | | |
| ALL FIRST-CLASS | 1.2 | 0 | 14 | 1 | 14.00 | 1-4 | - | - |

Texaco Trophy
Refuge Assurance
NatWest Trophy
Benson & Hedges Cup
Other One-Day

ALL ONE-DAY

# S

# PLAYER RECORDS

## SALIM MALIK - *Essex*

| Opposition | Venue | Date | Batting | | | Fielding | Bowling |
|---|---|---|---|---|---|---|---|
| **BRITANNIC ASSURANCE** | | | | | | | |
| Surrey | Chelmsford | April 27 | 0 | | | | |
| Northants | Northampton | May 9 | 24 | & | 37 * | 2Ct | 2-26 & 0-3 |
| Kent | Folkestone | May 16 | 173 | | | 1Ct | 2-13 & 0-17 |
| Warwickshire | Chelmsford | May 22 | 21 | & | 26 | 1Ct | 0-3 |
| Gloucs | Bristol | May 31 | 163 | | | 2Ct | |
| Leicestershire | Ilford | June 4 | 215 | & | 74 | | |
| Worcestershire | Ilford | June 7 | 37 | | | | 1-19 & 0-11 |
| Sussex | Horsham | June 21 | 40 | | | | |
| Middlesex | Lord's | June 28 | 8 | & | 12 * | 1Ct | |
| Hampshire | Chelmsford | July 2 | 12 | & | 66 | 2Ct | 1-42 |
| Surrey | The Oval | July 5 | 185 * | & | 59 * | 1Ct | 0-3 |
| Kent | Southend | July 16 | 8 * | & | 51 | | 0-8 |
| Somerset | Southend | July 19 | 102 | & | 35 * | 1Ct | 0-46 |
| Glamorgan | Cardiff | July 23 | | | | 1Ct | |
| Derbyshire | Derby | Aug 6 | 15 | & | 27 | 2Ct | |
| Notts | Trent Bridge | Aug 9 | 18 | & | 74 | 2Ct | |
| Northants | Colchester | Aug 16 | 0 | | | 2Ct | 3-26 |
| Yorkshire | Colchester | Aug 20 | 11 * | & | 56 | | 2-97 |
| Lancashire | Old Trafford | Aug 23 | 11 * | & | 70 * | 1Ct | 0-11 |
| Derbyshire | Chelmsford | Sept 3 | 165 | | | 2Ct | 2-21 & 2-48 |
| Leicestershire | Leicester | Sept 10 | 16 | | | | 0-18 & 0-29 |
| Middlesex | Chelmsford | Sept 17 | 80 | | | 1Ct | 0-32 |
| **OTHER FIRST-CLASS** | | | | | | | |
| Cambridge U | Fenner's | April 19 | 40 | & | 32 | 3Ct | |
| West Indies | Chelmsford | Aug 3 | 9 | | | | |
| **REFUGE ASSURANCE** | | | | | | | |
| Yorkshire | Chelmsford | April 28 | 48 * | | | | |
| Notts | Trent Bridge | May 12 | 6 | | | | |
| Kent | Folkestone | May 19 | 37 | | | | |
| Surrey | The Oval | May 26 | 12 | | | 1Ct | 0-12 |
| Worcestershire | Ilford | June 9 | 89 | | | 3Ct | |
| Derbyshire | Chelmsford | June 30 | 36 | | | 1Ct | |
| Warwickshire | Chelmsford | July 7 | 64 | | | 1Ct | 1-25 |
| Somerset | Southend | July 21 | 41 | | | | |
| Gloucs | Cheltenham | July 28 | 27 | | | | |
| Northants | Northampton | Aug 11 | 58 | | | | 0-34 |
| Middlesex | Colchester | Aug 18 | 33 | | | | |
| **NATWEST TROPHY** | | | | | | | |
| Devon | Exmouth | June 26 | 6 * | | | 2Ct | |
| Sussex | Hove | July 11 | 23 | | | 2Ct | 0-34 |
| Surrey | The Oval | July 31 | 26 | | | | |
| **BENSON & HEDGES CUP** | | | | | | | |
| Surrey | The Oval | April 23 | 90 * | | | | 1-7 |
| Warwickshire | Edgbaston | April 25 | 72 | | | 1Ct | |
| Middlesex | Chelmsford | May 2 | 3 | | | | |
| Somerset | Chelmsford | May 7 | 12 * | | | | |
| Hampshire | Chelmsford | May 29 | 38 | | | | |
| Worcestershire | Chelmsford | June 12 | 2 | | | | |
| **OTHER ONE-DAY** | | | | | | | |
| Durham | Scarborough | Aug 31 | 108 | | | | |

**BATTING AVERAGES - Including fielding**

| | Matches | Inns | NO | Runs | HS | Avge | 100s | 50s | Ct | St |
|---|---|---|---|---|---|---|---|---|---|---|
| Britannic Assurance | 22 | 33 | 9 | 1891 | 215 | 78.79 | 6 | 8 | 22 | - |
| Other First-Class | 2 | 3 | 0 | 81 | 40 | 27.00 | - | - | 3 | - |
| ALL FIRST-CLASS | 24 | 36 | 9 | 1972 | 215 | 73.03 | 6 | 8 | 25 | - |
| Refuge Assurance | 11 | 11 | 1 | 451 | 89 | 45.10 | - | 3 | 6 | - |
| NatWest Trophy | 3 | 3 | 1 | 55 | 26 | 27.50 | - | - | 4 | - |
| Benson & Hedges Cup | 6 | 6 | 2 | 217 | 90 * | 54.25 | - | 2 | 1 | - |
| Other One-Day | 1 | 1 | 0 | 108 | 108 | 108.00 | 1 | - | - | - |
| ALL ONE-DAY | 21 | 21 | 4 | 831 | 108 | 48.88 | 1 | 5 | 11 | - |

**BOWLING AVERAGES**

| | Overs | Mdns | Runs | Wkts | Avge | Best | 5wI | 10wM |
|---|---|---|---|---|---|---|---|---|
| Britannic Assurance | 118.2 | 10 | 473 | 15 | 31.53 | 3-26 | - | - |
| Other First-Class | | | | | | | | |
| ALL FIRST-CLASS | 118.2 | 10 | 473 | 15 | 31.53 | 3-26 | - | - |
| Refuge Assurance | 18.2 | 1 | 71 | 1 | 71.00 | 1-25 | - | |
| NatWest Trophy | 6 | 0 | 34 | 0 | - | - | - | |

| Benson & Hedges Cup | 2 | 0 | 7 | 1 | 7.00 | 1-7 | - |
|---|---|---|---|---|---|---|---|
| Other One-Day | | | | | | | |
| ALL ONE-DAY | 26.2 | 1 | 112 | 2 | 56.00 | 1-7 | - |

## I.D.K.SALISBURY - *Sussex*

| Opposition | Venue | Date | Batting | | | Fielding | Bowling |
|---|---|---|---|---|---|---|---|
| **BRITANNIC ASSURANCE** | | | | | | | |
| Somerset | Taunton | April 27 | | | | 1Ct | 1-64 |
| Middlesex | Lord's | May 9 | 19 | | | 2Ct | 0-24 & 0-22 |
| Hampshire | Hove | May 16 | 10 * | | | 1Ct | 2-107 & 2-46 |
| Middlesex | Hove | May 22 | | 5 | | | 0-62 & 1-62 |
| Glamorgan | Cardiff | May 25 | 0 | | | | 1-85 |
| Lancashire | Old Trafford | May 31 | 0 | & | 17 | | 1-88 & 2-15 |
| Kent | Tunbridge W | June 7 | | | | | 0-24 & 5-40 |
| Worcestershire | Hove | June 14 | | | | | 1-168 |
| Warwickshire | Coventry | June 18 | | 0 | | | |
| Essex | Horsham | June 21 | 0 * | | | | 0-42 |
| Surrey | Arundel | July 2 | 17 | & | 4 | 1Ct | 2-52 |
| Derbyshire | Derby | July 5 | 9 | & | 34 | 2Ct | 3-17 |
| Somerset | Hove | July 16 | | | | | 2-43 & 1-22 |
| Leicestershire | Hove | July 19 | | | | 1Ct | 3-130 & 4-92 |
| Gloucs | Cheltenham | July 23 | | | | | 0-8 |
| Northants | Eastbourne | Aug 2 | 10 * & | 0 | | 1Ct | 3-35 & 3-66 |
| Notts | Eastbourne | Aug 6 | 19 * | | | 1Ct | 1-118 |
| Yorkshire | Midd'brough | Aug 9 | 3 | | | 2Ct | 0-54 & 1-36 |
| Kent | Hove | Sept 3 | 0 * & | 1 * | | | 4-101 & 2-102 |
| Gloucs | Hove | Sept 17 | 0 * & | 31 * | | | 0-50 & 2-62 |
| **OTHER FIRST-CLASS** | | | | | | | |
| Cambridge U | Hove | June 29 | | | | | |
| Sri Lanka | Hove | Aug 17 | 9 * | | | | 1-89 & 0-75 |
| **REFUGE ASSURANCE** | | | | | | | |
| Warwickshire | Edgbaston | April 21 | | | | | 0-11 |
| Somerset | Taunton | April 28 | 2 | | | | 1-16 |
| Middlesex | Hove | May 12 | 2 * | | | | 0-23 |
| Gloucs | Hove | May 19 | 14 | | | | 1-36 |
| Glamorgan | Swansea | May 26 | 4 | | | | 3-10 |
| Lancashire | Old Trafford | June 2 | 0 | | | 1Ct | 0-24 |
| Hampshire | Basingstoke | June 9 | 2 | | | 1Ct | 2-33 |
| Worcestershire | Hove | June 16 | | | | | |
| Derbyshire | Derby | July 7 | | | | | 0-34 |
| Surrey | The Oval | July 14 | 8 | | | | 0-52 |
| Leicestershire | Hove | July 21 | | | | | 0-34 |
| Notts | Hove | July 28 | | | | | 1-22 |
| Northants | Eastbourne | Aug 4 | 6 * | | | | 2-43 |
| Yorkshire | Midd'brough | Aug 11 | 23 | | | | 0-50 |
| Kent | Hove | Aug 25 | | | | | 0-11 |
| **NATWEST TROPHY** | | | | | | | |
| Scotland | Edinburgh | June 26 | 4 | | | | 1-36 |
| Essex | Hove | July 11 | 14 * | | | | 1-40 |
| **BENSON & HEDGES CUP** | | | | | | | |
| Leicestershire | Hove | April 25 | | | | | 1-32 |
| Kent | Canterbury | May 2 | 17 * | | | | 3-40 |
| Scotland | Hove | May 4 | 5 | | | | 1-44 |
| Lancashire | Old Trafford | May 7 | 10 | | | 1Ct | 1-33 |
| **OTHER ONE-DAY** | | | | | | | |
| For England XI | | | | | | | |
| Rest of World | Jesmond | July 31 | | | | 1Ct | 1-72 |
| Rest of World | Jesmond | Aug 1 | 5 | | | | 1-75 |
| For Sussex | | | | | | | |
| Kent | Hove | Sept 7 | 15 | | | | 2-45 |
| Gloucs | Hove | Sept 9 | | 6 * | | | 1-32 |

**BATTING AVERAGES - Including fielding**

| | Matches | Inns | NO | Runs | HS | Avge | 100s | 50s | Ct | St |
|---|---|---|---|---|---|---|---|---|---|---|
| Britannic Assurance | 20 | 20 | 7 | 179 | 34 | 13.76 | - | - | 12 | - |
| Other First-Class | 2 | 1 | 1 | 9 | 9 * | - | - | - | - | - |
| ALL FIRST-CLASS | 22 | 21 | 8 | 188 | 34 | 14.46 | - | - | 12 | - |
| Refuge Assurance | 15 | 9 | 2 | 61 | 23 | 8.71 | - | - | 2 | - |
| NatWest Trophy | 2 | 2 | 1 | 18 | 14 * | 18.00 | - | - | - | - |
| Benson & Hedges Cup | 4 | 3 | 1 | 32 | 17 * | 16.00 | - | - | 2 | - |
| Other One-Day | 4 | 3 | 1 | 26 | 15 | 13.00 | - | - | 1 | - |

# PLAYER RECORDS

| ALL ONE-DAY | 25 | 17 | 5 | 137 | 23 | 11.41 | - | - | 5 | - |
|---|---|---|---|---|---|---|---|---|---|---|

## BOWLING AVERAGES

| | Overs | Mdns | Runs | Wkts | Avge | Best | 5wI | 10wM |
|---|---|---|---|---|---|---|---|---|
| Britannic Assurance | 605.2 | 144 | 1837 | 47 | 39.08 | 5-40 | 1 | - |
| Other First-Class | 33 | 4 | 164 | 1 | 164.00 | 1-89 | - | - |
| ALL FIRST-CLASS | 638.2 | 148 | 2001 | 48 | 41.68 | 5-40 | 1 | - |
| Refuge Assurance | 82.1 | 4 | 399 | 10 | 39.90 | 3-10 | - | |
| NatWest Trophy | 21 | 1 | 76 | 2 | 38.00 | 1-36 | - | |
| Benson & Hedges Cup | 41 | 3 | 149 | 6 | 24.83 | 3-40 | - | |
| Other One-Day | 36 | 2 | 224 | 5 | 44.80 | 2-45 | - | |
| ALL ONE-DAY | 180.1 | 10 | 848 | 23 | 36.87 | 3-10 | - | |

## G.SALMOND - Scotland

| Opposition | Venue | Date | Batting | Fielding | Bowling |
|---|---|---|---|---|---|

**OTHER FIRST-CLASS**

| Ireland | Dublin | June 22 | 66 | 1Ct | |
|---|---|---|---|---|---|

**NATWEST TROPHY**

| Sussex | Edinburgh | June 26 | 1 | | |
|---|---|---|---|---|---|

**BENSON & HEDGES CUP**

| Lancashire | Forfar | April 23 | 6 | | |
|---|---|---|---|---|---|
| Sussex | Hove | May 4 | 24 | | |
| Kent | Glasgow | May 7 | 4 | | |

### BATTING AVERAGES - Including fielding

| | Matches | Inns | NO | Runs | HS | Avge | 100s | 50s | Ct | St |
|---|---|---|---|---|---|---|---|---|---|---|
| Other First-Class | 1 | 1 | 0 | 66 | 66 | 66.00 | - | 1 | 1 | - |
| ALL FIRST-CLASS | 1 | 1 | 0 | 66 | 66 | 66.00 | - | 1 | 1 | - |
| NatWest Trophy | 1 | 1 | 0 | 1 | 1 | 1.00 | - | - | - | - |
| Benson & Hedges Cup | 3 | 3 | 0 | 34 | 24 | 11.33 | - | - | - | - |
| ALL ONE-DAY | 4 | 4 | 0 | 35 | 24 | 8.75 | - | - | - | - |

### BOWLING AVERAGES
Did not bowl

## G.D.SANDFORD - Bedfordshire

| Opposition | Venue | Date | Batting | Fielding | Bowling |
|---|---|---|---|---|---|

**NATWEST TROPHY**

| Worcestershire | Bedford | June 26 | 0 | | |
|---|---|---|---|---|---|

### BATTING AVERAGES - Including fielding

| | Matches | Inns | NO | Runs | HS | Avge | 100s | 50s | Ct | St |
|---|---|---|---|---|---|---|---|---|---|---|
| NatWest Trophy | 1 | 1 | 0 | 0 | 0 | 0.00 | - | - | - | - |
| ALL ONE-DAY | 1 | 1 | 0 | 0 | 0 | 0.00 | - | - | - | - |

### BOWLING AVERAGES
Did not bowl

## D.SANDIFORD - Oxford University

| Opposition | Venue | Date | Batting | Fielding | Bowling |
|---|---|---|---|---|---|

**OTHER FIRST-CLASS**

| Hampshire | The Parks | April 13 | 0 & 10 | 1Ct | |
|---|---|---|---|---|---|
| Glamorgan | The Parks | April 17 | 32 | | |
| Notts | The Parks | April 27 | | 2Ct | |
| Gloucs | The Parks | June 15 | | 1Ct | |
| Worcestershire | The Parks | May 25 | 1 & 0 | 1Ct,1St | |
| Yorkshire | The Parks | June 4 | 83 | | |
| Lancashire | The Parks | June 7 | 0 | 2Ct | |
| Kent | The Parks | June 18 | 28 & 35 * | 1Ct | |

---

| Cambridge U | Lord's | July 2 | | 3Ct | |
|---|---|---|---|---|---|

### BATTING AVERAGES - Including fielding

| | Matches | Inns | NO | Runs | HS | Avge | 100s | 50s | Ct | St |
|---|---|---|---|---|---|---|---|---|---|---|
| Other First-Class | 9 | 9 | 1 | 189 | 83 | 23.62 | - | 1 | 11 | 1 |
| ALL FIRST-CLASS | 9 | 9 | 1 | 189 | 83 | 23.62 | - | 1 | 11 | 1 |

### BOWLING AVERAGES
Did not bowl

## N.F.SARGEANT - Surrey

| Opposition | Venue | Date | Batting | Fielding | Bowling |
|---|---|---|---|---|---|

**BRITANNIC ASSURANCE**

| Essex | Chelmsford | April 27 | 11 | 1Ct | |
|---|---|---|---|---|---|
| Kent | The Oval | May 9 | 24 * & 23 * | 2Ct | |
| Lancashire | The Oval | May 22 | 10 | 3Ct | |
| Hampshire | Bournemouth | May 25 | 4 & 17 | 5Ct | |
| Notts | The Oval | June 4 | | 1Ct | |
| Leicestershire | Leicester | June 14 | 0 | 4Ct,1St | |
| Derbyshire | Derby | June 21 | 4 | | |
| Somerset | The Oval | June 28 | 16 * | 1Ct | |
| Sussex | Arundel | July 2 | 4 | 4Ct | |
| Essex | The Oval | July 5 | 14 | 3Ct | |
| Gloucs | Guildford | July 16 | 1 | | 1-88 |
| Yorkshire | Guildford | July 19 | 3 | | |
| Glamorgan | The Oval | July 26 | 32 & 3 * | 2Ct,2St | |
| Kent | Canterbury | Aug 2 | 0 & 34 | 1Ct | |
| Warwickshire | Edgbaston | Aug 6 | 7 | 2Ct | |
| Worcestershire | Worcester | Aug 16 | 3 & 11 | 4Ct | |
| Middlesex | The Oval | Aug 20 | 37 & 19 | 3Ct,1St | |
| Northants | Northampton | Aug 23 | 5 | 4Ct | |
| Middlesex | Lord's | Sept 10 | 2 & 19 | 3Ct | |
| Lancashire | Old Trafford | Sept 17 | 10 & 49 | 0Ct,1St | |

**OTHER FIRST-CLASS**

| Cambridge U | Fenner's | May 18 | 29 | 3Ct,3St | |
|---|---|---|---|---|---|

**REFUGE ASSURANCE**

| Essex | The Oval | May 26 | | 1Ct | |
|---|---|---|---|---|---|
| Hampshire | The Oval | Aug 25 | 13 * | | |

### BATTING AVERAGES - Including fielding

| | Matches | Inns | NO | Runs | HS | Avge | 100s | 50s | Ct | St |
|---|---|---|---|---|---|---|---|---|---|---|
| Britannic Assurance | 20 | 27 | 4 | 362 | 49 | 15.73 | - | - | 43 | 5 |
| Other First-Class | 1 | 1 | 0 | 29 | 29 | 29.00 | - | - | 3 | 3 |
| ALL FIRST-CLASS | 21 | 28 | 4 | 391 | 49 | 16.29 | - | - | 46 | 8 |
| Refuge Assurance | 2 | 1 | 1 | 13 | 13 * | - | - | - | 1 | - |
| ALL ONE-DAY | 2 | 1 | 1 | 13 | 13 * | - | - | - | 1 | - |

### BOWLING AVERAGES

| | Overs | Mdns | Runs | Wkts | Avge | Best | 5wI | 10wM |
|---|---|---|---|---|---|---|---|---|
| Britannic Assurance | 5 | 0 | 88 | 1 | 88.00 | 1-88 | - | - |
| Other First-Class | | | | | | | | |
| ALL FIRST-CLASS | 5 | 0 | 88 | 1 | 88.00 | 1-88 | - | - |
| Refuge Assurance | | | | | | | | |
| ALL ONE-DAY | | | | | | | | |

## D.G.SAVAGE - Norfolk

| Opposition | Venue | Date | Batting | Fielding | Bowling |
|---|---|---|---|---|---|

**NATWEST TROPHY**

| Gloucs | Bristol | June 26 | 1 | | |
|---|---|---|---|---|---|

### BATTING AVERAGES - Including fielding

| | Matches | Inns | NO | Runs | HS | Avge | 100s | 50s | Ct | St |
|---|---|---|---|---|---|---|---|---|---|---|
| NatWest Trophy | 1 | 1 | 0 | 1 | 1 | 1.00 | - | - | - | - |

# S PLAYER RECORDS

| | Matches | Inns | NO | Runs | HS | Avge | 100s | 50s | Ct | St |
|---|---|---|---|---|---|---|---|---|---|---|
| ALL ONE-DAY | 1 | 1 | 0 | 1 | 1 | 1.00 | - | - | - | - |

**BOWLING AVERAGES**
Did not bowl

## S.SAWNEY - *Dorset*

| Opposition | Venue | Date | Batting | Fielding | Bowling |
|---|---|---|---|---|---|
| **NATWEST TROPHY** | | | | | |
| Lancashire | Bournemouth | June 26 | 8 | | 0-15 |

**BATTING AVERAGES - Including fielding**

| | Matches | Inns | NO | Runs | HS | Avge | 100s | 50s | Ct | St |
|---|---|---|---|---|---|---|---|---|---|---|
| NatWest Trophy | 1 | 1 | 0 | 8 | 8 | 8.00 | - | - | - | - |
| ALL ONE-DAY | 1 | 1 | 0 | 8 | 8 | 8.00 | - | - | - | - |

**BOWLING AVERAGES**

| | Overs | Mdns | Runs | Wkts | Avge | Best | 5wI | 10wM |
|---|---|---|---|---|---|---|---|---|
| NatWest Trophy | 2.2 | 0 | 15 | 0 | - | - | - | |
| ALL ONE-DAY | 2.2 | 0 | 15 | 0 | - | - | - | |

## M.SAXELBY - *Nottinghamshire*

| Opposition | Venue | Date | Batting | Fielding | Bowling |
|---|---|---|---|---|---|
| **BRITANNIC ASSURANCE** | | | | | |
| Yorkshire | Headingley | May 16 | 17 & 16 | | 0-9 |
| Leicestershire | Leicester | May 25 | 44 & 3 * | | 0-24 & 0-20 |
| Surrey | The Oval | June 4 | | | 0-49 & 0-96 |
| Derbyshire | Trent Bridge | Aug 23 | 9 & 28 | | 0-54 & 0-3 |
| Lancashire | Old Trafford | Aug 28 | 5 & 1 | | 1-17 |
| Derbyshire | Derby | Sept 10 | 13 | | 3-41 & 0-110 |
| **OTHER FIRST-CLASS** | | | | | |
| Oxford U | The Parks | April 27 | 13 | | |
| **REFUGE ASSURANCE** | | | | | |
| Lancashire | Old Trafford | April 21 | | | 0-37 |
| Warwickshire | Trent Bridge | April 28 | 0 | | 0-20 |
| Glamorgan | Cardiff | May 5 | 19 | | 1-36 |
| Essex | Trent Bridge | May 12 | 20 | | 2-28 |
| Leicestershire | Leicester | May 26 | 2 | | 4-29 |
| Somerset | Trent Bridge | June 9 | 27 | | 2-31 |
| Gloucs | Gloucester | June 16 | | 1Ct | 1-18 |
| Middlesex | Trent Bridge | June 23 | 22 | | 0-21 |
| Surrey | The Oval | June 30 | | | 0-28 |
| Hampshire | Trent Bridge | July 14 | 24 | 1Ct | |
| Northants | Well'borough | July 21 | 2 | | 0-46 |
| Sussex | Hove | July 28 | 23 * | | 2-26 |
| Worcestershire | Trent Bridge | Aug 4 | 12 | | 0-47 |
| Kent | Trent Bridge | Aug 11 | 1 | | 3-40 |
| Yorkshire | Scarborough | Aug 18 | 55 | | 0-30 |
| Derbyshire | Trent Bridge | Aug 25 | | | 1-38 |
| Worcestershire | Trent Bridge | Sept 1 | 1 | 2Ct | 2-41 |
| **NATWEST TROPHY** | | | | | |
| Lincolnshire | Trent Bridge | June 26 | 6 * | 1Ct | 2-42 |
| Hampshire | Southampton | July 31 | 36 | | 1-48 |
| **BENSON & HEDGES CUP** | | | | | |
| Hampshire | Southampton | April 23 | 32 | | 0-39 |
| Yorkshire | Trent Bridge | April 25 | | | 0-43 |
| Glamorgan | Cardiff | May 4 | 5 | | 1-36 |

**BATTING AVERAGES - Including fielding**

| | Matches | Inns | NO | Runs | HS | Avge | 100s | 50s | Ct | St |
|---|---|---|---|---|---|---|---|---|---|---|
| Britannic Assurance | 6 | 9 | 1 | 136 | 44 | 17.00 | - | - | - | - |
| Other First-Class | 1 | 1 | 0 | 13 | 13 | 13.00 | - | - | - | - |
| ALL FIRST-CLASS | 7 | 10 | 1 | 149 | 44 | 16.55 | - | - | - | - |
| Refuge Assurance | 17 | 13 | 1 | 208 | 55 | 17.33 | - | 1 | 4 | - |
| NatWest Trophy | 2 | 2 | 1 | 42 | 36 | 42.00 | - | - | 1 | - |
| Benson & Hedges Cup | 3 | 2 | 0 | 37 | 32 | 18.50 | - | - | - | - |
| ALL ONE-DAY | 22 | 17 | 2 | 287 | 55 | 19.13 | - | 1 | 5 | - |

**BOWLING AVERAGES**

| | Overs | Mdns | Runs | Wkts | Avge | Best | 5wI | 10wM |
|---|---|---|---|---|---|---|---|---|
| Britannic Assurance | 97.2 | 17 | 423 | 4 | 105.75 | 3-41 | | |
| Other First-Class | | | | | | | | |
| ALL FIRST-CLASS | 97.2 | 17 | 423 | 4 | 105.75 | 3-41 | - | - |
| Refuge Assurance | 108 | 3 | 516 | 18 | 28.66 | 4-29 | - | |
| NatWest Trophy | 18.4 | 1 | 90 | 3 | 30.00 | 2-42 | - | |
| Benson & Hedges Cup | 26 | 1 | 118 | 1 | 118.00 | 1-36 | - | |
| ALL ONE-DAY | 152.4 | 5 | 724 | 22 | 32.90 | 4-29 | - | |

## C.W.SCOTT - *Nottinghamshire*

| Opposition | Venue | Date | Batting | Fielding | Bowling |
|---|---|---|---|---|---|
| **BRITANNIC ASSURANCE** | | | | | |
| Surrey | The Oval | June 4 | | 3Ct | |
| **OTHER FIRST-CLASS** | | | | | |
| Oxford U | The Parks | April 27 | | | |

**BATTING AVERAGES - Including fielding**

| | Matches | Inns | NO | Runs | HS | Avge | 100s | 50s | Ct | St |
|---|---|---|---|---|---|---|---|---|---|---|
| Britannic Assurance | 1 | 0 | 0 | 0 | 0 | - | - | - | 3 | - |
| Other First-Class | 1 | 0 | 0 | 0 | 0 | - | - | - | - | - |
| ALL FIRST-CLASS | 2 | 0 | 0 | 0 | 0 | - | - | - | 3 | - |

**BOWLING AVERAGES**
Did not bowl

## R.J.SCOTT - *Gloucestershire*

| Opposition | Venue | Date | Batting | Fielding | Bowling |
|---|---|---|---|---|---|
| **BRITANNIC ASSURANCE** | | | | | |
| Worcestershire | Worcester | April 27 | 127 | | |
| Hampshire | Bristol | May 9 | 29 & 0 | | 0-17 |
| Yorkshire | Sheffield | May 22 | 17 & 14 | | |
| Warwickshire | Edgbaston | May 25 | 0 & 0 | 1Ct | |
| Essex | Bristol | May 31 | 13 & 15 | | |
| Middlesex | Bristol | June 4 | 14 & 0 | 1Ct | 1-29 & 0-14 |
| Somerset | Bath | June 21 | 34 * | | 1-67 |
| Northants | Luton | June 28 | 17 & 50 | 1Ct | 0-0 & 0-50 |
| Leicestershire | Hinckley | July 2 | 51 | | 2-36 |
| Surrey | Guildford | July 16 | 63 & 47 | | 0-22 & 0-4 |
| Glamorgan | Cheltenham | July 19 | 0 & 122 | 1Ct | 0-32 & 0-19 |
| Sussex | Cheltenham | July 23 | 18 | 1Ct | |
| Worcestershire | Cheltenham | July 26 | 10 & 6 | | 2-39 & 0-16 |
| Kent | Canterbury | Aug 20 | 17 & 30 | | 0-22 |
| Glamorgan | Abergavenny | Aug 28 | 21 & 10 | | 1-59 |
| Northants | Bristol | Sept 3 | 11 & 8 | 1Ct | 0-10 & 1-15 |
| Sussex | Hove | Sept 17 | 8 & 11 | | 3-51 & 3-43 |
| **OTHER FIRST-CLASS** | | | | | |
| Oxford U | The Parks | June 15 | 49 | | |
| West Indies | Bristol | July 31 | 9 & 19 | | 1-48 |
| Sri Lanka | Bristol | Aug 6 | 8 | | 0-21 |
| **REFUGE ASSURANCE** | | | | | |
| Middlesex | Bristol | April 21 | 44 | | 0-23 |
| Worcestershire | Bristol | May 5 | 32 | | 0-11 |
| Surrey | The Oval | May 12 | 2 | | 1-52 |
| Sussex | Hove | May 19 | 44 | | |
| Hampshire | Swindon | May 26 | 77 | | |
| Northants | Moreton | June 9 | 0 * | | |
| Notts | Gloucester | June 16 | 1 | | |
| Kent | Canterbury | June 30 | 58 | | 0-24 |
| Yorkshire | Scarborough | July 14 | 31 | | 2-26 |
| Derbyshire | Cheltenham | July 21 | 17 | | 1-48 |
| Essex | Cheltenham | July 28 | 11 | | 1-23 |
| Glamorgan | Swansea | Aug 4 | 2 | | 0-29 |
| Warwickshire | Edgbaston | Aug 18 | 1 | | 1-29 |

# PLAYER RECORDS  S

| Leicestershire | Leicester | Aug 25 | 56 | | 2-38 |

**NATWEST TROPHY**

| Norfolk | Bristol | June 26 | 11 | | 4-22 |
| Notts | Bristol | July 11 | 0 | | 2-32 |

**BENSON & HEDGES CUP**

| Combined U | Bristol | April 23 | 29 | | |
| Worcestershire | Worcester | April 25 | 10 | | 1-42 |
| Northants | Bristol | May 2 | 46 | | 0-15 |
| Derbyshire | Derby | May 7 | 14 | | 0-24 |

**OTHER ONE-DAY**

| West Indies | Bristol | May 14 | 2 | | |
| Somerset | Hove | Sept 8 | 12 | | 0-24 |
| Sussex | Hove | Sept 9 | 1 | | |

**BATTING AVERAGES - Including fielding**

| | Matches | Inns | NO | Runs | HS | Avge | 100s | 50s | Ct | St |
|---|---|---|---|---|---|---|---|---|---|---|
| Britannic Assurance | 17 | 30 | 1 | 763 | 127 | 26.31 | 2 | 3 | 6 | - |
| Other First-Class | 3 | 4 | 0 | 85 | 49 | 21.25 | - | - | - | - |
| ALL FIRST-CLASS | 20 | 34 | 1 | 848 | 127 | 25.69 | 2 | 3 | 6 | - |
| Refuge Assurance | 14 | 14 | 1 | 376 | 77 | 28.92 | - | 3 | - | - |
| NatWest Trophy | 2 | 2 | 0 | 11 | 11 | 5.50 | - | - | - | - |
| Benson & Hedges Cup | 4 | 4 | 0 | 99 | 46 | 24.75 | - | - | - | - |
| Other One-Day | 3 | 3 | 0 | 15 | 12 | 5.00 | - | - | - | - |
| ALL ONE-DAY | 23 | 23 | 1 | 501 | 77 | 22.77 | - | 3 | - | - |

**BOWLING AVERAGES**

| | Overs | Mdns | Runs | Wkts | Avge | Best | 5wI | 10wM |
|---|---|---|---|---|---|---|---|---|
| Britannic Assurance | 175 | 38 | 545 | 14 | 38.92 | 3-43 | - | - |
| Other First-Class | 24 | 2 | 69 | 1 | 69.00 | 1-48 | - | - |
| ALL FIRST-CLASS | 199 | 40 | 614 | 15 | 40.93 | 3-43 | - | - |
| Refuge Assurance | 62 | 2 | 303 | 8 | 37.87 | 2-26 | - | - |
| NatWest Trophy | 22.2 | 3 | 54 | 6 | 9.00 | 4-22 | - | - |
| Benson & Hedges Cup | 16.5 | 0 | 81 | 1 | 81.00 | 1-42 | - | - |
| Other One-Day | 4 | 0 | 24 | 0 | | - | - | - |
| ALL ONE-DAY | 105.1 | 5 | 462 | 15 | 30.80 | 4-22 | - | - |

# T.J.A.SCRIVEN - *Buckinghamshire*

| Opposition | Venue | Date | Batting | Fielding | Bowling |
|---|---|---|---|---|---|

**NATWEST TROPHY**

| Somerset | Bath | June 26 | 0 | | 1-32 |

**BATTING AVERAGES - Including fielding**

| | Matches | Inns | NO | Runs | HS | Avge | 100s | 50s | Ct | St |
|---|---|---|---|---|---|---|---|---|---|---|
| NatWest Trophy | 1 | 1 | 0 | 0 | 0 | 0.00 | - | - | - | - |
| ALL ONE-DAY | 1 | 1 | 0 | 0 | 0 | 0.00 | - | - | - | - |

**BOWLING AVERAGES**

| | Overs | Mdns | Runs | Wkts | Avge | Best | 5wI | 10wM |
|---|---|---|---|---|---|---|---|---|
| NatWest Trophy | 8 | 1 | 32 | 1 | 32.00 | 1-32 | - | |
| ALL ONE-DAY | 8 | 1 | 32 | 1 | 32.00 | 1-32 | - | |

# A.C.SEYMOUR - *Essex*

| Opposition | Venue | Date | Batting | Fielding | Bowling |
|---|---|---|---|---|---|

**BRITANNIC ASSURANCE**

| Worcestershire | Ilford | June 7 | 67 & | 3 | | 0-27 |
| Sussex | Horsham | June 21 | 9 | | 1Ct |
| Hampshire | Chelmsford | July 2 | 50 & | 23 | |
| Surrey | The Oval | July 5 | 5 & | 10* | 1Ct |
| Glamorgan | Cardiff | July 23 | 157 | | |
| Derbyshire | Derby | Aug 6 | 22 & | 0 | 1Ct |
| Notts | Trent Bridge | Aug 9 | 13 & | 19 | 2Ct |
| Yorkshire | Colchester | Aug 20 | 27 & | 9 | 2Ct |
| Lancashire | Old Trafford | Aug 23 | 28 & | 12 | |

**OTHER FIRST-CLASS**

| West Indies | Chelmsford | Aug 3 | 74 & | 5 | |

**REFUGE ASSURANCE**

| Worcestershire | Ilford | June 9 | 20 | | |
| Hampshire | Chelmsford | June 16 | | | |
| Gloucs | Cheltenham | July 28 | 1 | | 1Ct |
| Northants | Northampton | Aug 11 | 0 | | |
| Lancashire | Old Trafford | Aug 25 | 25 | | |

**NATWEST TROPHY**

| Surrey | The Oval | July 31 | 0 | | 1Ct |

**BATTING AVERAGES - Including fielding**

| | Matches | Inns | NO | Runs | HS | Avge | 100s | 50s | Ct | St |
|---|---|---|---|---|---|---|---|---|---|---|
| Britannic Assurance | 9 | 16 | 1 | 454 | 157 | 30.26 | 1 | 2 | 7 | - |
| Other First-Class | 1 | 2 | 0 | 79 | 74 | 39.50 | - | 1 | - | - |
| ALL FIRST-CLASS | 10 | 18 | 1 | 533 | 157 | 31.35 | 1 | 3 | 7 | - |
| Refuge Assurance | 5 | 4 | 0 | 46 | 25 | 11.50 | - | - | 1 | - |
| NatWest Trophy | 1 | 1 | 0 | 0 | 0 | 0.00 | - | - | 1 | - |
| ALL ONE-DAY | 6 | 5 | 0 | 46 | 25 | 9.20 | - | - | 2 | - |

**BOWLING AVERAGES**

| | Overs | Mdns | Runs | Wkts | Avge | Best | 5wI | 10wM |
|---|---|---|---|---|---|---|---|---|
| Britannic Assurance | 4 | 0 | 27 | 0 | | - | - | - |
| Other First-Class | | | | | | | | |
| ALL FIRST-CLASS | 4 | 0 | 27 | 0 | | - | - | - |
| Refuge Assurance | | | | | | | | |
| NatWest Trophy | | | | | | | | |
| ALL ONE-DAY | | | | | | | | |

# J.H.SHACKLETON - *Dorset*

| Opposition | Venue | Date | Batting | Fielding | Bowling |
|---|---|---|---|---|---|

**NATWEST TROPHY**

| Lancashire | Bournemouth | June 26 | 0* | | 0-16 |

**BATTING AVERAGES - Including fielding**

| | Matches | Inns | NO | Runs | HS | Avge | 100s | 50s | Ct | St |
|---|---|---|---|---|---|---|---|---|---|---|
| NatWest Trophy | 1 | 1 | 1 | 0 | 0* | - | - | - | - | - |
| ALL ONE-DAY | 1 | 1 | 1 | 0 | 0* | - | - | - | - | - |

**BOWLING AVERAGES**

| | Overs | Mdns | Runs | Wkts | Avge | Best | 5wI | 10wM |
|---|---|---|---|---|---|---|---|---|
| NatWest Trophy | 12 | 5 | 16 | 0 | | - | - | - |
| ALL ONE-DAY | | | | | | | | |

# N.SHAHID - *Essex*

| Opposition | Venue | Date | Batting | Fielding | Bowling |
|---|---|---|---|---|---|

**BRITANNIC ASSURANCE**

| Surrey | Chelmsford | April 27 | | | |
| Warwickshire | Chelmsford | May 22 | 11 | | 1Ct |
| Leicestershire | Ilford | June 4 | 0 & | 4 | 5Ct |
| Worcestershire | Ilford | June 7 | 15 & | 22* | |
| Sussex | Horsham | June 21 | 0 | | |
| Surrey | The Oval | July 5 | 0 & | 12 | |
| Glamorgan | Cardiff | July 23 | | | |

**OTHER FIRST-CLASS**

| Cambridge U | Fenner's | April 19 | 83 | | 1Ct |

**REFUGE ASSURANCE**

| Yorkshire | Chelmsford | April 28 | | | |
| Notts | Trent Bridge | May 12 | 1 | | |
| Kent | Folkestone | May 19 | 27 | | |
| Surrey | The Oval | May 26 | 16 | | |
| Glamorgan | Pontypridd | June 2 | | | |

## S — PLAYER RECORDS

| | | | | |
|---|---|---|---|---|
| Worcestershire | Ilford | June 9 | | 1Ct |
| Hampshire | Chelmsford | June 16 | 17 * | |
| Derbyshire | Chelmsford | June 30 | 6 | |
| Warwickshire | Chelmsford | July 7 | | |
| Somerset | Southend | July 21 | | 1Ct |
| Gloucs | Cheltenham | July 28 | 36 | 1Ct |

**NATWEST TROPHY**

| | | | | |
|---|---|---|---|---|
| Sussex | Hove | July 11 | | 1Ct |

**BENSON & HEDGES CUP**

| | | | | |
|---|---|---|---|---|
| Surrey | The Oval | April 23 | 8 | |
| Warwickshire | Edgbaston | April 25 | | |
| Middlesex | Chelmsford | May 2 | 0 | 1Ct |
| Somerset | Chelmsford | May 7 | | |
| Hampshire | Chelmsford | May 29 | 42 | |
| Worcestershire | Chelmsford | June 12 | 1 | |

**BATTING AVERAGES - Including fielding**

| | Matches | Inns | NO | Runs | HS | Avge | 100s | 50s | Ct | St |
|---|---|---|---|---|---|---|---|---|---|---|
| Britannic Assurance | 7 | 8 | 1 | 64 | 22 * | 9.14 | - | - | 6 | - |
| Other First-Class | 1 | 1 | 0 | 83 | 83 | 83.00 | - | 1 | 1 | - |
| ALL FIRST-CLASS | 8 | 9 | 1 | 147 | 83 | 18.37 | - | 1 | 7 | - |
| Refuge Assurance | 11 | 6 | 1 | 103 | 36 | 20.60 | - | - | 3 | - |
| NatWest Trophy | 1 | 0 | 0 | 0 | 0 | - | - | - | 1 | - |
| Benson & Hedges Cup | 6 | 4 | 0 | 51 | 42 | 12.75 | - | - | 1 | - |
| ALL ONE-DAY | 18 | 10 | 1 | 154 | 42 | 17.11 | - | - | 5 | - |

**BOWLING AVERAGES**
Did not bowl

## K.SHARP - Yorkshire

| Opposition | Venue | Date | Batting | Fielding | Bowling |
|---|---|---|---|---|---|
| **REFUGE ASSURANCE** | | | | | |
| Hampshire | Southampton | April 21 | 41 | 1Ct | |
| Essex | Chelmsford | April 28 | 37 | | |
| **BENSON & HEDGES CUP** | | | | | |
| Notts | Trent Bridge | April 25 | 0 | | |

**BATTING AVERAGES - Including fielding**

| | Matches | Inns | NO | Runs | HS | Avge | 100s | 50s | Ct | St |
|---|---|---|---|---|---|---|---|---|---|---|
| Refuge Assurance | 2 | 2 | 0 | 78 | 41 | 39.00 | - | - | 1 | - |
| Benson & Hedges Cup | 1 | 1 | 0 | 0 | 0 | 0.00 | - | - | - | - |
| ALL ONE-DAY | 3 | 3 | 0 | 78 | 41 | 26.00 | - | - | 1 | - |

**BOWLING AVERAGES**
Did not bowl

## M.SHARP - Lancashire

| Opposition | Venue | Date | Batting | Fielding | Bowling |
|---|---|---|---|---|---|
| **OTHER FIRST-CLASS** | | | | | |
| Oxford U | The Parks | June 7 | | | 1-21 |

**BATTING AVERAGES - Including fielding**

| | Matches | Inns | NO | Runs | HS | Avge | 100s | 50s | Ct | St |
|---|---|---|---|---|---|---|---|---|---|---|
| Other First-Class | 1 | 0 | 0 | 0 | 0 | - | - | - | - | - |
| ALL FIRST-CLASS | 1 | 0 | 0 | 0 | 0 | - | - | - | - | - |

**BOWLING AVERAGES**

| | Overs | Mdns | Runs | Wkts | Avge | Best | 5wI | 10wM |
|---|---|---|---|---|---|---|---|---|
| Other First-Class | 15 | 7 | 21 | 1 | 21.00 | 1-21 | - | - |
| ALL FIRST-CLASS | 15 | 7 | 21 | 1 | 21.00 | 1-21 | - | - |

## R.J.SHASTRI - Glamorgan

| Opposition | Venue | Date | Batting | | | Fielding | Bowling |
|---|---|---|---|---|---|---|---|
| **BRITANNIC ASSURANCE** | | | | | | | |
| Leicestershire | Leicester | April 27 | 0 | | | | 0-6 |
| Somerset | Taunton | May 9 | 37 | & | 68 | | 0-5 |
| Warwickshire | Swansea | May 16 | 5 | & | 31 | | 1-25 |
| Northants | Cardiff | May 22 | 50 | | | | 0-16 |
| Sussex | Cardiff | May 25 | 26 | | | 1Ct | |
| Worcestershire | Worcester | May 31 | 84 * | & | 28 | | |
| Somerset | Swansea | June 4 | | | 8 | | |
| Derbyshire | Chesterfield | June 7 | 2 | & | 1 | | |
| Middlesex | Cardiff | June 14 | 33 | & | 25 * | | |
| Leicestershire | Neath | June 21 | 107 | | | | |
| Lancashire | Liverpool | June 28 | 133 * | & | 58 * | | 0-11 |
| Notts | Cardiff | July 2 | 0 | & | 7 | | 0-27 |
| Kent | Maidstone | July 5 | 4 | | | 1Ct | 0-2 |
| Gloucs | Cheltenham | July 19 | 22 | & | 4 | 1Ct | 0-30 |
| Essex | Cardiff | July 23 | | | 70 * | | |
| Surrey | The Oval | July 26 | 38 | | | 1Ct | 3-78 |
| Hampshire | Swansea | Aug 9 | | | 44 * | 1Ct | |
| Yorkshire | Headingley | Aug 16 | 41 | | | 2Ct | 1-111 & 3-18 |
| Warwickshire | Edgbaston | Aug 20 | 80 * | & | 39 * | 1Ct | 4-73 & 5-71 |
| Gloucs | Abergavenny | Aug 28 | 0 | | | | 4-74 & 3-73 |
| Worcestershire | Cardiff | Sept 10 | 10 | & | 1 | | 3-63 & 0-21 |
| **OTHER FIRST-CLASS** | | | | | | | |
| Cambridge U | Fenner's | June 18 | 52 * | | | 1Ct | 4-20 |
| **REFUGE ASSURANCE** | | | | | | | |
| Northants | Cardiff | April 21 | 64 * | | | | 0-31 |
| Leicestershire | Leicester | April 28 | 5 | | | | 1-38 |
| Somerset | Taunton | May 12 | 27 | | | | 0-13 |
| Warwickshire | Swansea | May 19 | 32 | | | 1Ct | 0-21 |
| Sussex | Swansea | May 26 | 14 | | | 1Ct | |
| Essex | Pontypridd | June 2 | 22 | | | | |
| Middlesex | Cardiff | June 16 | 4 | | | | |
| Yorkshire | Headingley | June 30 | 4 | | | | |
| Kent | Maidstone | July 7 | 90 * | | | | 0-35 |
| Worcestershire | Worcester | July 21 | 22 | | | 1Ct | 1-29 |
| Gloucs | Swansea | Aug 4 | 6 | | | | 1-15 |
| Hampshire | Ebbw Vale | Aug 11 | 36 | | | | 3-26 |
| Derbyshire | Checkley | Aug 18 | 16 | | | | 1-33 |
| **NATWEST TROPHY** | | | | | | | |
| Durham | Darlington | June 26 | 26 | | | 1Ct | |
| Northants | Northampton | July 31 | 25 | | | 1Ct | 2-60 |
| **BENSON & HEDGES CUP** | | | | | | | |
| Min Counties | Trowbridge | April 23 | 138 * | | | 1Ct | 0-36 |
| Notts | Cardiff | May 4 | 16 | | | | 1-40 |
| Yorkshire | Cardiff | May 7 | 7 | | | | 1-48 |

**BATTING AVERAGES - Including fielding**

| | Matches | Inns | NO | Runs | HS | Avge | 100s | 50s | Ct | St |
|---|---|---|---|---|---|---|---|---|---|---|
| Britannic Assurance | 21 | 31 | 8 | 1056 | 133 * | 45.91 | 2 | 6 | 8 | - |
| Other First-Class | 1 | 1 | 1 | 52 | 52 * | - | - | 1 | 1 | - |
| ALL FIRST-CLASS | 22 | 32 | 9 | 1108 | 133 * | 48.17 | 2 | 7 | 9 | - |
| Refuge Assurance | 13 | 13 | 2 | 342 | 90 * | 31.09 | - | 2 | 3 | - |
| NatWest Trophy | 2 | 2 | 0 | 51 | 26 | 25.50 | - | - | 2 | - |
| Benson & Hedges Cup | 3 | 3 | 1 | 161 | 138 * | 80.50 | 1 | - | 1 | - |
| ALL ONE-DAY | 18 | 18 | 3 | 554 | 138 * | 36.93 | 1 | 2 | 6 | - |

**BOWLING AVERAGES**

| | Overs | Mdns | Runs | Wkts | Avge | Best | 5wI | 10wM |
|---|---|---|---|---|---|---|---|---|
| Britannic Assurance | 288.5 | 80 | 704 | 27 | 26.07 | 5-71 | 1 | - |
| Other First-Class | 19 | 8 | 20 | 4 | 5.00 | 4-20 | - | - |
| ALL FIRST-CLASS | 307.5 | 88 | 724 | 31 | 23.35 | 5-71 | 1 | - |
| Refuge Assurance | 51 | 1 | 241 | 7 | 34.42 | 3-26 | - | - |
| NatWest Trophy | 12 | 0 | 60 | 2 | 30.00 | 2-60 | - | - |
| Benson & Hedges Cup | 32 | 1 | 124 | 2 | 62.00 | 1-40 | - | - |
| ALL ONE-DAY | 95 | 2 | 425 | 11 | 38.63 | 3-26 | - | - |

# PLAYER RECORDS

## A.D.SHAW - *Wales*

| Opposition | Venue | Date | Batting | Fielding | Bowling |
|---|---|---|---|---|---|
| **OTHER ONE-DAY** | | | | | |
| West Indies | Brecon | July 15 | 0 | 2Ct,2St | |

### BATTING AVERAGES - Including fielding

| | Matches | Inns | NO | Runs | HS | Avge | 100s | 50s | Ct | St |
|---|---|---|---|---|---|---|---|---|---|---|
| Other One-Day | 1 | 1 | 0 | 0 | 0 | 0.00 | - | - | 2 | 2 |
| ALL ONE-DAY | 1 | 1 | 0 | 0 | 0 | 0.00 | - | - | 2 | 2 |

### BOWLING AVERAGES
Did not bowl

## D.SHAW - *Berkshire*

| Opposition | Venue | Date | Batting | Fielding | Bowling |
|---|---|---|---|---|---|
| **NATWEST TROPHY** | | | | | |
| Hampshire | Reading | June 26 | 1* | | 0-17 |

### BATTING AVERAGES - Including fielding

| | Matches | Inns | NO | Runs | HS | Avge | 100s | 50s | Ct | St |
|---|---|---|---|---|---|---|---|---|---|---|
| NatWest Trophy | 1 | 1 | 1 | 1 | 1* | - | - | - | - | - |
| ALL ONE-DAY | 1 | 1 | 1 | 1 | 1* | - | - | - | - | - |

### BOWLING AVERAGES

| | Overs | Mdns | Runs | Wkts | Avge | Best | 5wI | 10wM |
|---|---|---|---|---|---|---|---|---|
| NatWest Trophy | 3.2 | 0 | 17 | 0 | - | - | - | - |
| ALL ONE-DAY | 3.2 | 0 | 17 | 0 | - | - | - | - |

## K.J.SHINE - *Hampshire*

| Opposition | Venue | Date | Batting | Fielding | Bowling |
|---|---|---|---|---|---|
| **BRITANNIC ASSURANCE** | | | | | |
| Gloucs | Southampton | June 7 | 0 | | 1-67 |
| Northants | Northampton | June 21 | | | 1-66 & 0-13 |
| Essex | Chelmsford | July 2 | 0 | 1Ct | 1-34 & 3-68 |
| Yorkshire | Southampton | July 5 | | | 0-41 |
| Worcestershire | Portsmouth | July 16 | 1 | | 5-43 & 4-91 |
| Warwickshire | Portsmouth | July 19 | 1 & 0 | | 2-63 & 2-68 |
| Derbyshire | Chesterfield | July 23 | 0 | | 0-34 |
| Middlesex | Lord's | Aug 2 | 4* | 1Ct | 2-70 & 0-48 |
| Kent | Canterbury | Aug 6 | 2* | | 3-75 & 0-23 |
| Glamorgan | Swansea | Aug 9 | 0* | | 5-58 |
| Leicestershire | Bournemouth | Aug 16 | | 8* | 0-66 & 1-46 |
| Sussex | Bournemouth | Aug 20 | 16* | | 0-32 & 1-19 |
| Somerset | Southampton | Aug 28 | 0* & 16* | | 2-91 & 0-17 |
| Surrey | The Oval | Sept 3 | 1 & 25 | | 1-65 & 3-52 |
| Glamorgan | Southampton | Sept 17 | 3* & 3 | | 0-84 & 0-16 |
| **OTHER FIRST-CLASS** | | | | | |
| West Indies | Southampton | June 29 | 12 | | 1-104 |
| **REFUGE ASSURANCE** | | | | | |
| Lancashire | Southampton | July 28 | | | 2-35 |
| Middlesex | Lord's | Aug 4 | | | 1-22 |
| Glamorgan | Ebbw Vale | Aug 11 | 2* | | 1-17 |
| Leicestershire | Bournemouth | Aug 18 | | | 1-28 |

### BATTING AVERAGES - Including fielding

| | Matches | Inns | NO | Runs | HS | Avge | 100s | 50s | Ct | St |
|---|---|---|---|---|---|---|---|---|---|---|
| Britannic Assurance | 15 | 17 | 8 | 80 | 25 | 8.88 | - | - | 2 | - |
| Other First-Class | 1 | 1 | 0 | 12 | 12 | 12.00 | - | - | - | - |
| ALL FIRST-CLASS | 16 | 18 | 8 | 92 | 25 | 9.20 | - | - | 2 | - |
| Refuge Assurance | 4 | 1 | 1 | 2 | 2* | - | - | - | - | - |
| ALL ONE-DAY | 4 | 1 | 1 | 2 | 2* | - | - | - | - | - |

## BOWLING AVERAGES

| | Overs | Mdns | Runs | Wkts | Avge | Best | 5wI | 10wM |
|---|---|---|---|---|---|---|---|---|
| Britannic Assurance | 316.5 | 44 | 1350 | 37 | 36.48 | 5-43 | 2 | - |
| Other First-Class | 27 | 4 | 104 | 1 | 104.00 | 1-104 | - | - |
| ALL FIRST-CLASS | 343.5 | 48 | 1454 | 38 | 38.26 | 5-43 | 2 | - |
| Refuge Assurance | 27 | 0 | 102 | 5 | 20.40 | 2-35 | - | |
| ALL ONE-DAY | 27 | 0 | 102 | 5 | 20.40 | 2-35 | - | |

## A.SIDEBOTTOM - *Yorkshire*

| Opposition | Venue | Date | Batting | Fielding | Bowling |
|---|---|---|---|---|---|
| **OTHER FIRST-CLASS** | | | | | |
| Sri Lanka | Headingley | July 27 | 18* | 1Ct | 1-26 |
| **REFUGE ASSURANCE** | | | | | |
| Hampshire | Southampton | April 21 | 7* | | 1-42 |
| Essex | Chelmsford | April 28 | 6 | | 0-26 |
| Warwickshire | Headingley | May 12 | 1* | | 0-22 |
| Leicestershire | Leicester | May 19 | 10 | 1Ct | 1-25 |
| **BENSON & HEDGES CUP** | | | | | |
| Hampshire | Headingley | May 4 | | | 4-19 |
| Glamorgan | Cardiff | May 7 | | 1Ct | 0-22 |
| Warwickshire | Headingley | May 29 | | | 0-11 |
| **OTHER ONE-DAY** | | | | | |
| Derbyshire | Scarborough | Sept 1 | | | 1-26 |

### BATTING AVERAGES - Including fielding

| | Matches | Inns | NO | Runs | HS | Avge | 100s | 50s | Ct | St |
|---|---|---|---|---|---|---|---|---|---|---|
| Other First-Class | 1 | 1 | 1 | 18 | 18* | - | - | - | 1 | - |
| ALL FIRST-CLASS | 1 | 1 | 1 | 18 | 18* | - | - | - | 1 | - |
| Refuge Assurance | 4 | 4 | 2 | 24 | 10 | 12.00 | - | - | 1 | - |
| Benson & Hedges Cup | 3 | 0 | 0 | 0 | 0 | - | - | - | 1 | - |
| Other One-Day | 1 | 0 | 0 | 0 | 0 | | | | | |
| ALL ONE-DAY | 8 | 4 | 2 | 24 | 10 | 12.00 | - | - | 2 | - |

### BOWLING AVERAGES

| | Overs | Mdns | Runs | Wkts | Avge | Best | 5wI | 10wM |
|---|---|---|---|---|---|---|---|---|
| Other First-Class | 11 | 4 | 26 | 1 | 26.00 | 1-26 | - | - |
| ALL FIRST-CLASS | 11 | 4 | 26 | 1 | 26.00 | 1-26 | - | - |
| Refuge Assurance | 32 | 0 | 115 | 2 | 57.50 | 1-25 | - | |
| Benson & Hedges Cup | 31 | 11 | 52 | 4 | 13.00 | 4-19 | - | |
| Other One-Day | 5 | 0 | 26 | 1 | 26.00 | 1-26 | - | |
| ALL ONE-DAY | 68 | 11 | 193 | 7 | 27.57 | 4-19 | - | |

## M.L.SIMMONS - *Berkshire*

| Opposition | Venue | Date | Batting | Fielding | Bowling |
|---|---|---|---|---|---|
| **NATWEST TROPHY** | | | | | |
| Hampshire | Reading | June 26 | 9* | | |

### BATTING AVERAGES - Including fielding

| | Matches | Inns | NO | Runs | HS | Avge | 100s | 50s | Ct | St |
|---|---|---|---|---|---|---|---|---|---|---|
| NatWest Trophy | 1 | 1 | 1 | 9 | 9* | - | - | - | - | - |
| ALL ONE-DAY | 1 | 1 | 1 | 9 | 9* | - | - | - | - | - |

### BOWLING AVERAGES
Did not bowl

# S          PLAYER RECORDS

## P.V.SIMMONS - *West Indies*

| Opposition | Venue | Date | Batting | | | Fielding | Bowling |
|---|---|---|---|---|---|---|---|
| **CORNHILL TEST MATCHES** | | | | | | | |
| England | Headingley | June 6 | 38 | & | 0 | 1Ct | |
| England | Lord's | June 20 | 33 | & | 2 | 1Ct | |
| England | Trent Bridge | July 4 | 12 | & | 1 | 2Ct | |
| England | Edgbaston | July 25 | 28 | & | 16 | | 0-7 |
| England | The Oval | Aug 8 | 15 | & | 36 | | |
| **OTHER FIRST-CLASS** | | | | | | | |
| Worcestershire | Worcester | May 15 | 134 | & | 24 * | | 0-35 |
| Middlesex | Lord's | May 18 | 136 | & | 5 | | 0-21 & 2-34 |
| Somerset | Taunton | May 29 | 10 | & | 51 | | 1-16 |
| Leicestershire | Leicester | June 1 | 42 | & | 0 | 1Ct | 1-45 & 0-6 |
| Northants | Northampton | June 15 | 29 | | | | |
| Hampshire | Southampton | June 29 | 0 | | | 1Ct | 0-3 |
| Kent | Canterbury | July 20 | 77 | & | 107 | 1Ct | |
| Gloucs | Bristol | July 31 | 26 | & | 72 | 1Ct | 0-12 |
| Essex | Chelmsford | Aug 3 | 51 | & | 40 | 2Ct | 2-84 |
| For West Indies XI | | | | | | | |
| World XI | Scarborough | Aug 28 | 24 | & | 22 | 3Ct | 0-44 & 2-39 |
| **TEXACO TROPHY** | | | | | | | |
| England | Edgbaston | May 23 | 4 | | | | 0-10 |
| England | Old Trafford | May 25 | 28 | | | | 0-30 |
| England | Lord's | May 27 | 5 | | | | 0-21 |
| **OTHER ONE-DAY** | | | | | | | |
| D of Norfolk | Arundel | May 12 | 40 | | | | 0-52 |
| Gloucs | Bristol | May 14 | 2 | | | | 0-40 |
| League CC XI | Trowbridge | June 28 | 70 | | | | 2-44 |
| Ireland | Downpatrick | July 13 | 50 | | | 1Ct | |
| Wales | Brecon | July 15 | 64 | | | | |

### BATTING AVERAGES - Including fielding

| | Matches | Inns | NO | Runs | HS | Avge | 100s | 50s | Ct | St |
|---|---|---|---|---|---|---|---|---|---|---|
| Cornhill Test Matches | 5 | 10 | 0 | 181 | 38 | 18.10 | - | - | 4 | - |
| Other First-Class | 10 | 18 | 1 | 850 | 136 | 50.00 | 3 | 4 | 9 | - |
| ALL FIRST-CLASS | 15 | 28 | 1 | 1031 | 136 | 38.18 | 3 | 4 | 13 | - |
| Texaco Trophy | 3 | 3 | 0 | 37 | 28 | 12.33 | - | - | - | - |
| Other One-Day | 5 | 5 | 0 | 226 | 70 | 45.20 | - | 3 | 1 | - |
| ALL ONE-DAY | 8 | 8 | 0 | 263 | 70 | 32.87 | - | 3 | 1 | - |

### BOWLING AVERAGES

| | Overs | Mdns | Runs | Wkts | Avge | Best | 5wI | 10wM |
|---|---|---|---|---|---|---|---|---|
| Cornhill Test Matches | 3 | 0 | 7 | 0 | - | - | - | - |
| Other First-Class | 97 | 23 | 339 | 8 | 42.37 | 2-34 | - | - |
| ALL FIRST-CLASS | 100 | 23 | 346 | 8 | 43.25 | 2-34 | - | - |
| Texaco Trophy | 9 | 0 | 61 | 0 | - | - | - | - |
| Other One-Day | 29 | 0 | 136 | 2 | 68.00 | 2-44 | - | - |
| ALL ONE-DAY | 38 | 0 | 197 | 2 | 98.50 | 2-44 | - | - |

## R.W.SLADDIN - *Derbyshire*

| Opposition | Venue | Date | Batting | | | Fielding | Bowling |
|---|---|---|---|---|---|---|---|
| **BRITANNIC ASSURANCE** | | | | | | | |
| Yorkshire | Scarborough | July 16 | 7 | & | 8 * | | 2-112 |
| Hampshire | Chesterfield | July 23 | 4 | | | | 0-44 & 1-18 |
| Lancashire | Derby | Aug 16 | | | | 2Ct | 3-93 & 1-23 |
| Notts | Trent Bridge | Aug 23 | | | | 1Ct | 4-118 & 2-118 |
| Leicestershire | Leicester | Aug 28 | 4 * | | | 1Ct | 2-29 & 3-60 |
| Essex | Chelmsford | Sept 3 | 8 * | & | 18 | 1Ct | 5-186 |
| Yorkshire | Chesterfield | Sept 17 | 7 | & | 12 | 1Ct | 0-53 & 3-27 |
| **OTHER FIRST-CLASS** | | | | | | | |
| Sri Lanka | Derby | Aug 2 | 0 * | | | | 1-84 |
| **OTHER ONE-DAY** | | | | | | | |
| Yorkshire | Scarborough | Sept 1 | | | 1 * | | 2-45 |

### BATTING AVERAGES - Including fielding

| | Matches | Inns | NO | Runs | HS | Avge | 100s | 50s | Ct | St |
|---|---|---|---|---|---|---|---|---|---|---|
| Britannic Assurance | 7 | 8 | 3 | 68 | 18 | 13.60 | - | - | 6 | - |
| Other First-Class | 1 | 1 | 1 | 0 | 0 * | - | - | - | - | - |
| ALL FIRST-CLASS | 8 | 9 | 4 | 68 | 18 | 13.60 | - | - | 6 | - |
| Other One-Day | 1 | 1 | 1 | 1 | 1 * | - | - | - | - | - |
| ALL ONE-DAY | 1 | 1 | 1 | 1 | 1 * | - | - | - | - | - |

### BOWLING AVERAGES

| | Overs | Mdns | Runs | Wkts | Avge | Best | 5wI | 10wM |
|---|---|---|---|---|---|---|---|---|
| Britannic Assurance | 315.5 | 76 | 881 | 26 | 33.88 | 5-186 | 1 | - |
| Other First-Class | 53 | 25 | 84 | 1 | 84.00 | 1-84 | - | - |
| ALL FIRST-CLASS | 368.5 | 101 | 965 | 27 | 35.74 | 5-186 | 1 | - |
| Other One-Day | 10 | 0 | 45 | 2 | 22.50 | 2-45 | - | - |
| ALL ONE-DAY | 10 | 0 | 45 | 2 | 22.50 | 2-45 | - | - |

## P.R.SLEEP - *World XI & Rest of World*

| Opposition | Venue | Date | Batting | | | Fielding | Bowling |
|---|---|---|---|---|---|---|---|
| **OTHER FIRST-CLASS** | | | | | | | |
| For World XI | | | | | | | |
| West Indies XI | Scarborough | Aug 28 | 37 | & | 13 | 1Ct,1St | |
| **OTHER ONE-DAY** | | | | | | | |
| For Rest of World | | | | | | | |
| England XI | Jesmond | July 31 | 12 * | | | | 1-65 |
| England XI | Jesmond | Aug 1 | | | | | 1-48 |

### BATTING AVERAGES - Including fielding

| | Matches | Inns | NO | Runs | HS | Avge | 100s | 50s | Ct | St |
|---|---|---|---|---|---|---|---|---|---|---|
| Other First-Class | 1 | 2 | 0 | 50 | 37 | 25.00 | - | - | 1 | 1 |
| ALL FIRST-CLASS | 1 | 2 | 0 | 50 | 37 | 25.00 | - | - | 1 | 1 |
| Other One-Day | 2 | 1 | 1 | 12 | 12 * | - | - | - | - | - |
| ALL ONE-DAY | 2 | 1 | 1 | 12 | 12 * | - | - | - | - | - |

### BOWLING AVERAGES

| | Overs | Mdns | Runs | Wkts | Avge | Best | 5wI | 10wM |
|---|---|---|---|---|---|---|---|---|
| Other First-Class | | | | | | | | |
| ALL FIRST-CLASS | | | | | | | | |
| Other One-Day | 22 | 1 | 113 | 2 | 56.50 | 1-48 | - | |
| ALL ONE-DAY | 22 | 1 | 113 | 2 | 56.50 | 1-48 | - | |

## G.C.SMALL - *Warwickshire*

| Opposition | Venue | Date | Batting | | | Fielding | Bowling |
|---|---|---|---|---|---|---|---|
| **BRITANNIC ASSURANCE** | | | | | | | |
| Lancashire | Edgbaston | April 27 | 2 | | | 1Ct | 2-67 |
| Yorkshire | Headingley | May 9 | 58 | & | 10 * | | 0-27 & 0-26 |
| Glamorgan | Swansea | May 16 | 31 | | | 1Ct | 1-35 & 1-34 |
| Essex | Chelmsford | May 22 | 1 | & | 11 | | 0-34 & 1-41 |
| Gloucs | Edgbaston | May 25 | 3 | | | | 3-46 & 0-34 |
| Yorkshire | Edgbaston | May 31 | 0 | | | 2Ct | 2-34 & 0-33 |
| Kent | Tunbridge W | June 4 | 5 | | | | 1-68 |
| Somerset | Edgbaston | June 7 | | | | | 0-27 & 1-26 |
| Sussex | Coventry | June 18 | 25 | | | | 0-7 & 4-36 |
| Notts | Trent Bridge | June 21 | 4 | | | | 1-14 |
| Derbyshire | Edgbaston | June 28 | 19 | & | 7 | 1Ct | 4-36 & 0-51 |
| Middlesex | Edgbaston | July 2 | 24 | & | 3 * | | 1-47 & 3-23 |
| Hampshire | Portsmouth | July 19 | 17 | & | 12 * | | 3-45 & 1-50 |
| Lancashire | Old Trafford | July 23 | 0 | | | | 0-18 |
| Leicestershire | Leicester | July 26 | 14 | | | | 1-34 & 2-52 |
| Worcestershire | Worcester | Aug 2 | 6 | & | 13 | | 0-72 |
| Surrey | Edgbaston | Aug 6 | 8 | & | 6 | | 1-38 & 2-05 |
| Glamorgan | Edgbaston | Aug 20 | 4 | & | 45 * | | 0-25 & 3-24 |

# PLAYER RECORDS

**S**

| | | | | | |
|---|---|---|---|---|---|
| Worcestershire | Edgbaston | Aug 28 | 0 & | 4 * | 3-20 & 1-45 |
| Northants | Edgbaston | Sept 10 | 31 * & | 7 * | 1-83 & 2-69 |

### REFUGE ASSURANCE

| | | | | | |
|---|---|---|---|---|---|
| Sussex | Edgbaston | April 21 | | | 0-8 |
| Notts | Trent Bridge | April 28 | 1 | | 1-37 |
| Yorkshire | Headingley | May 12 | | 1Ct | 1-29 |
| Glamorgan | Swansea | May 19 | | | 2-33 |
| Worcestershire | Edgbaston | May 26 | | | 0-32 |
| Somerset | Edgbaston | June 2 | | | 1-39 |
| Lancashire | Edgbaston | June 16 | | 1Ct | 2-60 |
| Hampshire | Portsmouth | July 21 | | | 1-33 |
| Leicestershire | Leicester | Aug 11 | 0 | | 2-25 |
| Northants | Northampton | Aug 25 | 3 | 1Ct | 0-26 |

### NATWEST TROPHY

| | | | | | |
|---|---|---|---|---|---|
| Yorkshire | Edgbaston | June 26 | | | 3-28 |
| Hertfordshire | Edgbaston | July 11 | | | 1-25 |
| Somerset | Edgbaston | July 31 | 3 | | 2-26 |
| Hampshire | Edgbaston | Aug 14 | 2 | | 0-32 |

### BENSON & HEDGES CUP

| | | | | | |
|---|---|---|---|---|---|
| Essex | Edgbaston | April 25 | 2 | 1Ct | 0-43 |
| Somerset | Edgbaston | May 2 | | | 0-52 |
| Middlesex | Lord's | May 4 | 1 | | 1-55 |
| Yorkshire | Headingley | May 29 | 2 | | 0-43 |

### OTHER ONE-DAY

| | | | | | |
|---|---|---|---|---|---|
| Surrey | Harrogate | June 12 | 15 | | 3-16 |

### BATTING AVERAGES - Including fielding

| | Matches | Inns | NO | Runs | HS | Avge | 100s | 50s | Ct | St |
|---|---|---|---|---|---|---|---|---|---|---|
| Britannic Assurance | 20 | 29 | 7 | 370 | 58 | 16.81 | - | 1 | 5 | - |
| ALL FIRST-CLASS | 20 | 29 | 7 | 370 | 58 | 16.81 | - | 1 | 5 | - |
| Refuge Assurance | 10 | 3 | 0 | 4 | 3 | 1.33 | - | - | 3 | - |
| NatWest Trophy | 4 | 2 | 0 | 5 | 5 | 2.50 | - | - | - | - |
| Benson & Hedges Cup | 4 | 3 | 0 | 5 | 2 | 1.66 | - | - | 1 | - |
| Other One-Day | 1 | 1 | 0 | 15 | 15 | 15.00 | - | - | - | - |
| ALL ONE-DAY | 19 | 9 | 0 | 29 | 15 | 3.22 | - | - | 4 | - |

### BOWLING AVERAGES

| | Overs | Mdns | Runs | Wkts | Avge | Best | 5wI | 10wM |
|---|---|---|---|---|---|---|---|---|
| Britannic Assurance | 498 | 126 | 1347 | 45 | 29.93 | 4-36 | - | - |
| ALL FIRST-CLASS | 498 | 126 | 1347 | 45 | 29.93 | 4-36 | - | - |
| Refuge Assurance | 65 | 3 | 322 | 10 | 32.20 | 2-25 | - | |
| NatWest Trophy | 45 | 13 | 111 | 6 | 18.50 | 3-28 | - | |
| Benson & Hedges Cup | 44 | 2 | 193 | 1 | 193.00 | 1-55 | - | |
| Other One-Day | 7 | 1 | 16 | 3 | 5.33 | 3-16 | - | |
| ALL ONE-DAY | 161 | 19 | 642 | 20 | 32.10 | 3-16 | - | |

# A.SMITH - *Wales*

| Opposition | Venue | Date | Batting | Fielding | Bowling |
|---|---|---|---|---|---|

### OTHER ONE-DAY

| | | | | | |
|---|---|---|---|---|---|
| West Indies | Brecon | July 15 | 1 | | 1-57 |

### BATTING AVERAGES - Including fielding

| | Matches | Inns | NO | Runs | HS | Avge | 100s | 50s | Ct | St |
|---|---|---|---|---|---|---|---|---|---|---|
| Other One-Day | 1 | 1 | 0 | 1 | 1 | 1.00 | - | - | - | - |
| ALL ONE-DAY | 1 | 1 | 0 | 1 | 1 | 1.00 | - | - | - | - |

### BOWLING AVERAGES

| | Overs | Mdns | Runs | Wkts | Avge | Best | 5wI | 10wM |
|---|---|---|---|---|---|---|---|---|
| Other One-Day | 11 | 1 | 57 | 1 | 57.00 | 1-57 | - | |
| ALL ONE-DAY | 11 | 1 | 57 | 1 | 57.00 | 1-57 | - | |

# A.M.SMITH - *Gloucestershire*

| Opposition | Venue | Date | Batting | Fielding | Bowling |
|---|---|---|---|---|---|

### BRITANNIC ASSURANCE

| | | | | | | |
|---|---|---|---|---|---|---|
| Worcestershire | Worcester | April 27 | 3 * | | | 0-34 |
| Hampshire | Bristol | May 9 | 3 | | | 0-50 & 0-22 |
| Yorkshire | Sheffield | May 22 | | | | 1-55 & 0-19 |
| Warwickshire | Edgbaston | May 25 | 0 & | 22 | | 3-71 & 1-3 |
| Essex | Bristol | May 31 | 9 & | 4 | | 1-68 |
| Hampshire | Southampton | June 7 | | | | 3-54 |
| Notts | Gloucester | June 14 | 2 | | | 0-30 |
| Derbyshire | Gloucester | June 18 | 0 & | 15 | | 3-71 & 3-21 |
| Somerset | Bath | June 21 | 0 | | | 1-53 |
| Northants | Luton | June 28 | 1 | | | 1-41 & 0-8 |
| Leicestershire | Hinckley | July 2 | | | | 4-41 |
| Surrey | Guildford | July 16 | | | | 0-30 & 4-70 |
| Glamorgan | Cheltenham | July 19 | 1 & | 0 * | | 2-56 & 1-71 |

### OTHER FIRST-CLASS

| | | | | | |
|---|---|---|---|---|---|
| West Indies | Bristol | July 31 | | | 0-46 & 1-69 |

### REFUGE ASSURANCE

| | | | | | |
|---|---|---|---|---|---|
| Middlesex | Bristol | April 21 | 0 * | | 0-36 |
| Surrey | The Oval | May 12 | | | 0-3 |
| Sussex | Hove | May 19 | 1 * | 1Ct | 3-16 |
| Hampshire | Swindon | May 26 | | | 3-47 |
| Northants | Moreton | June 9 | | | |
| Notts | Gloucester | June 16 | | | 0-29 |
| Kent | Canterbury | June 30 | 0 * | | 2-35 |
| Yorkshire | Scarborough | July 14 | | | 3-41 |
| Derbyshire | Cheltenham | July 21 | 2 * | | 0-47 |
| Essex | Cheltenham | July 28 | 15 * | | 0-23 |
| Lancashire | Bristol | Aug 11 | 4 | | 1-10 |
| Warwickshire | Edgbaston | Aug 18 | 5 * | | 0-39 |
| Leicestershire | Leicester | Aug 25 | | 2Ct | 3-52 |

### NATWEST TROPHY

| | | | | | |
|---|---|---|---|---|---|
| Norfolk | Bristol | June 26 | | | 1-14 |
| Notts | Bristol | July 11 | | | 1-49 |

### BENSON & HEDGES CUP

| | | | | | |
|---|---|---|---|---|---|
| Combined U | Bristol | April 23 | 8 | 1Ct | |
| Worcestershire | Worcester | April 25 | 3 * | | 1-30 |
| Northants | Bristol | May 2 | | | 0-26 |
| Derbyshire | Derby | May 7 | 1 * | | 1-39 |

### OTHER ONE-DAY

| | | | | | |
|---|---|---|---|---|---|
| Sussex | Hove | Sept 9 | 1 | | 3-38 |

### BATTING AVERAGES - Including fielding

| | Matches | Inns | NO | Runs | HS | Avge | 100s | 50s | Ct | St |
|---|---|---|---|---|---|---|---|---|---|---|
| Britannic Assurance | 13 | 13 | 2 | 60 | 22 | 5.45 | - | - | - | - |
| Other First-Class | 1 | 0 | 0 | 0 | 0 | | - | - | - | - |
| ALL FIRST-CLASS | 14 | 13 | 2 | 60 | 22 | 5.45 | - | - | - | - |
| Refuge Assurance | 13 | 7 | 6 | 27 | 15 * | 27.00 | - | - | 3 | - |
| NatWest Trophy | 2 | 0 | 0 | 0 | 0 | | - | - | - | - |
| Benson & Hedges Cup | 4 | 3 | 2 | 12 | 8 | 12.00 | - | - | 1 | - |
| Other One-Day | 1 | 1 | 0 | 1 | 1 | 1.00 | - | - | - | - |
| ALL ONE-DAY | 20 | 11 | 8 | 40 | 15 * | 13.33 | - | - | 4 | - |

### BOWLING AVERAGES

| | Overs | Mdns | Runs | Wkts | Avge | Best | 5wI | 10wM |
|---|---|---|---|---|---|---|---|---|
| Britannic Assurance | 284.2 | 51 | 868 | 28 | 31.00 | 4-41 | - | - |
| Other First-Class | 26 | 4 | 115 | 1 | 115.00 | 1-69 | - | - |
| ALL FIRST-CLASS | 310.2 | 55 | 983 | 29 | 33.89 | 4-41 | - | - |
| Refuge Assurance | 66.4 | 2 | 378 | 15 | 25.20 | 3-16 | - | |
| NatWest Trophy | 16 | 2 | 63 | 2 | 31.50 | 1-14 | - | |
| Benson & Hedges Cup | 33 | 2 | 95 | 2 | 47.50 | 1-30 | - | |
| Other One-Day | 10 | 0 | 38 | 3 | 12.66 | 3-38 | - | |
| ALL ONE-DAY | 125.4 | 6 | 574 | 22 | 26.09 | 3-16 | - | |

## S — PLAYER RECORDS

## B.F.SMITH - *Leicestershire*

| Opposition | Venue | Date | Batting | | Fielding | Bowling |
|---|---|---|---|---|---|---|
| **BRITANNIC ASSURANCE** | | | | | | |
| Notts | Leicester | May 25 | 43 & | 43 | | |
| Essex | Ilford | June 4 | 20 & | 41 * | | 1-5 |
| Middlesex | Uxbridge | June 7 | 54 & | 17 | | 0-1 |
| Surrey | Leicester | June 14 | 24 | | 1Ct | |
| Lancashire | Leicester | June 18 | | 13 | | 0-20 |
| Glamorgan | Neath | June 21 | | | | |
| Worcestershire | Worcester | June 28 | 71 & | 8 * | | |
| Gloucs | Hinckley | July 2 | | 29 | | |
| Northants | Leicester | July 5 | 12 & | 47 | | |
| Sussex | Hove | July 19 | 17 & | 19 | 1Ct | |
| Kent | Leicester | Aug 9 | 27 & | 19 * | 1Ct | 0-45 |
| Derbyshire | Derby | Aug 20 | 51 | | | |
| Kent | Canterbury | Sept 17 | 6 & | 24 | | |
| **OTHER FIRST-CLASS** | | | | | | |
| Cambridge U | Fenner's | May 22 | 47 * | | | 0-20 & 0-0 |
| West Indies | Leicester | June 1 | 13 & | 29 * | | |
| **REFUGE ASSURANCE** | | | | | | |
| Northants | Northampton | May 12 | 16 | | | |
| Yorkshire | Leicester | May 19 | 20 * | | | |
| Notts | Leicester | May 26 | 2 | | | 0-15 |
| Middlesex | Uxbridge | June 9 | 33 | | | |
| Surrey | Leicester | June 16 | 12 | | 1Ct | |
| Worcestershire | Worcester | June 30 | 30 * | | | |
| Lancashire | Leicester | July 7 | 26 | | | |
| Kent | Canterbury | July 14 | 21 | | 1Ct | |
| Sussex | Hove | July 21 | 0 | | | |
| Somerset | Weston | Aug 4 | 22 | | | |
| Warwickshire | Leicester | Aug 11 | 21 * | | | |
| Gloucs | Leicester | Aug 25 | 23 | | | |
| **NATWEST TROPHY** | | | | | | |
| Shropshire | Leicester | June 26 | | | | |
| Northants | Northampton | July 11 | 6 | | | |
| **OTHER ONE-DAY** | | | | | | |
| Durham | Harrogate | June 11 | 2 * | | | |

**BATTING AVERAGES - Including fielding**

| | Matches | Inns | NO | Runs | HS | Avge | 100s | 50s | Ct | St |
|---|---|---|---|---|---|---|---|---|---|---|
| Britannic Assurance | 13 | 20 | 3 | 585 | 71 | 34.41 | - | 3 | 3 | - |
| Other First-Class | 2 | 3 | 2 | 89 | 47 * | 89.00 | - | - | - | - |
| ALL FIRST-CLASS | 15 | 23 | 5 | 674 | 71 | 37.44 | - | 3 | 3 | - |
| Refuge Assurance | 12 | 12 | 3 | 226 | 33 | 25.11 | - | - | 2 | - |
| NatWest Trophy | 2 | 1 | 0 | 6 | 6 | 6.00 | - | - | - | - |
| Other One-Day | 1 | 1 | 1 | 2 | 2 * | - | - | - | - | - |
| ALL ONE-DAY | 15 | 14 | 4 | 234 | 33 | 23.40 | - | - | 2 | - |

**BOWLING AVERAGES**

| | Overs | Mdns | Runs | Wkts | Avge | Best | 5wI | 10wM |
|---|---|---|---|---|---|---|---|---|
| Britannic Assurance | 7 | 0 | 71 | 1 | 71.00 | 1-5 | - | - |
| Other First-Class | 6 | 2 | 20 | 0 | - | - | - | - |
| ALL FIRST-CLASS | 13 | 2 | 91 | 1 | 91.00 | 1-5 | - | - |
| Refuge Assurance | 3 | 0 | 15 | 0 | - | - | - | - |
| NatWest Trophy | | | | | | | | |
| Other One-Day | | | | | | | | |
| ALL ONE-DAY | 3 | 0 | 15 | 0 | - | - | - | |

## C.L.SMITH - *Hampshire*

| Opposition | Venue | Date | Batting | | Fielding | Bowling |
|---|---|---|---|---|---|---|
| **BRITANNIC ASSURANCE** | | | | | | |
| Kent | Southampton | April 27 | 19 | | | |
| Gloucs | Bristol | May 9 | 125 & | 24 | | |
| Sussex | Hove | May 16 | 145 & | 101 | | |
| Surrey | Bournemouth | May 25 | 55 & | 47 | 1Ct | |
| Notts | Trent Bridge | May 31 | 22 & | 0 | | 0-31 |
| Lancashire | Basingstoke | June 4 | 22 & | 51 | | 0-3 |
| Gloucs | Southampton | June 7 | 61 | | | |
| Somerset | Bath | June 18 | 2 & | 65 | | 0-1 |
| Northants | Northampton | June 21 | 85 | | 1Ct | |
| Essex | Chelmsford | July 2 | 44 & | 93 | 1Ct | |
| Yorkshire | Southampton | July 5 | 112 & | 2 * | | 0-0 |
| Worcestershire | Portsmouth | July 16 | 87 | | | |
| Derbyshire | Chesterfield | July 23 | 114 & | 16 * | | |
| Kent | Canterbury | Aug 6 | 10 & | 2 | | 0-28 |
| Glamorgan | Swansea | Aug 9 | 0 & | 49 * | | |
| **OTHER FIRST-CLASS** | | | | | | |
| Oxford U | The Parks | April 13 | 200 | | 1Ct | |
| **REFUGE ASSURANCE** | | | | | | |
| Yorkshire | Southampton | April 21 | 86 | | | |
| Derbyshire | Derby | May 5 | 29 | | 1Ct | |
| Kent | Southampton | May 12 | 40 | | 1Ct | |
| Somerset | Bournemouth | May 19 | 47 | | | |
| Northants | Northampton | June 2 | 19 | | | |
| Worcestershire | Southampton | July 7 | 114 | | | |
| Warwickshire | Portsmouth | July 21 | 2 | | | |
| Lancashire | Southampton | July 28 | 60 | | 1Ct | |
| **NATWEST TROPHY** | | | | | | |
| Berkshire | Reading | June 26 | | | 1Ct | |
| Lancashire | Southampton | July 11 | 66 | | | |
| Notts | Southampton | July 31 | 105 * | | | |
| Warwickshire | Edgbaston | Aug 14 | 23 | | | |
| **BENSON & HEDGES CUP** | | | | | | |
| Notts | Southampton | April 23 | 121 * | | | |
| Min Counties | Trowbridge | April 25 | 78 * | | | |
| Glamorgan | Southampton | May 2 | 142 | | | |
| Yorkshire | Headingley | May 4 | 1 | | 1Ct | |
| Essex | Chelmsford | May 29 | 71 | | | |

**BATTING AVERAGES - Including fielding**

| | Matches | Inns | NO | Runs | HS | Avge | 100s | 50s | Ct | St |
|---|---|---|---|---|---|---|---|---|---|---|
| Britannic Assurance | 15 | 26 | 3 | 1353 | 145 | 58.82 | 5 | 7 | 3 | - |
| Other First-Class | 1 | 1 | 0 | 200 | 200 | 200.00 | 1 | - | 1 | - |
| ALL FIRST-CLASS | 16 | 27 | 3 | 1553 | 200 | 64.70 | 6 | 7 | 4 | - |
| Refuge Assurance | 8 | 8 | 0 | 397 | 114 | 49.62 | 1 | 2 | 3 | - |
| NatWest Trophy | 4 | 3 | 1 | 194 | 105 * | 97.00 | 1 | 1 | 1 | - |
| Benson & Hedges Cup | 5 | 5 | 2 | 413 | 142 | 137.66 | 2 | 2 | 1 | - |
| ALL ONE-DAY | 17 | 16 | 3 | 1004 | 142 | 77.23 | 4 | 5 | 5 | - |

**BOWLING AVERAGES**

| | Overs | Mdns | Runs | Wkts | Avge | Best | 5wI | 10wM |
|---|---|---|---|---|---|---|---|---|
| Britannic Assurance | 19 | 3 | 63 | 0 | - | - | - | - |
| Other First-Class | | | | | | | | |
| ALL FIRST-CLASS | 19 | 3 | 63 | 0 | - | - | - | |
| Refuge Assurance | | | | | | | | |
| NatWest Trophy | | | | | | | | |
| Benson & Hedges Cup | | | | | | | | |
| ALL ONE-DAY | | | | | | | | |

## D.M.SMITH - *Sussex*

| Opposition | Venue | Date | Batting | | Fielding | Bowling |
|---|---|---|---|---|---|---|
| **BRITANNIC ASSURANCE** | | | | | | |
| Somerset | Taunton | April 27 | 53 | | 2Ct | |
| Middlesex | Lord's | May 9 | 90 | | | |
| Hampshire | Hove | May 16 | 82 & | 5 | | |
| Middlesex | Hove | May 22 | 126 * & | 28 | | |
| Glamorgan | Cardiff | May 25 | 61 & | 0 | 1Ct | |
| Lancashire | Old Trafford | May 31 | 40 & | 2 | 1Ct | |
| Kent | Tunbridge W | June 7 | 48 & | 17 | 2Ct | |
| Worcestershire | Hove | June 14 | 67 * & | 5 | | 0-15 |
| Warwickshire | Coventry | June 18 | 7 * & | 0 | | |
| Surrey | Arundel | July 2 | 29 & | 46 | | |
| Derbyshire | Derby | July 5 | 43 & | 16 | | |
| Somerset | Hove | July 16 | 38 | | | |
| Leicestershire | Hove | July 19 | 3 & | 50 | 2Ct | |
| Gloucs | Cheltenham | July 23 | | 65 * | 1Ct | |

# PLADER

# PLAYER RECORDS S

| Northants | Eastbourne | Aug 2 | 67 & 39 | 1Ct |
| Notts | Eastbourne | Aug 6 | 10 & 46 | |
| Yorkshire | Midd'brough | Aug 9 | 11 | 1Ct |
| Hampshire | Bournemouth | Aug 20 | 10 & 16 * | 1Ct |
| Surrey | The Oval | Aug 28 | 10 & 0 | 1Ct |

**OTHER FIRST-CLASS**

| Sri Lanka | Hove | Aug 17 | 8 & 100 * | |

**REFUGE ASSURANCE**

| Warwickshire | Edgbaston | April 21 | 23 | 1Ct |
| Somerset | Taunton | April 28 | 48 | |
| Gloucs | Hove | May 19 | 40 | |
| Derbyshire | Derby | July 7 | 78 | |
| Surrey | The Oval | July 14 | 19 | 2Ct |

**NATWEST TROPHY**

| Scotland | Edinburgh | June 26 | 40 | |
| Essex | Hove | July 11 | 62 | 1Ct |

**BENSON & HEDGES CUP**

| Leicestershire | Hove | April 25 | 76 | |
| Kent | Canterbury | May 2 | 4 | 1Ct |
| Scotland | Hove | May 4 | 102 | 1Ct |
| Lancashire | Old Trafford | May 7 | 27 | |

**BATTING AVERAGES - Including fielding**

| | Matches | Inns | NO | Runs | HS | Avge | 100s | 50s | Ct | St |
|---|---|---|---|---|---|---|---|---|---|---|
| Britannic Assurance | 19 | 33 | 5 | 1130 | 126 * | 40.35 | 1 | 8 | 14 | - |
| Other First-Class | 1 | 2 | 1 | 108 | 100 * | 108.00 | 1 | - | - | - |
| ALL FIRST-CLASS | 20 | 35 | 6 | 1238 | 126 * | 42.69 | 2 | 8 | 14 | - |
| Refuge Assurance | 5 | 5 | 0 | 208 | 78 | 41.60 | - | 1 | 3 | - |
| NatWest Trophy | 2 | 2 | 0 | 102 | 62 | 51.00 | - | 1 | 1 | - |
| Benson & Hedges Cup | 4 | 4 | 0 | 209 | 102 | 52.25 | 1 | 1 | 2 | - |
| ALL ONE-DAY | 11 | 11 | 0 | 519 | 102 | 47.18 | 1 | 3 | 6 | - |

**BOWLING AVERAGES**

| | Overs | Mdns | Runs | Wkts | Avge | Best | 5wI | 10wM |
|---|---|---|---|---|---|---|---|---|
| Britannic Assurance | 2 | 0 | 15 | 0 | - | - | - | - |
| Other First-Class | | | | | | | | |
| ALL FIRST-CLASS | 2 | 0 | 15 | 0 | - | - | - | - |
| Refuge Assurance | | | | | | | | |
| NatWest Trophy | | | | | | | | |
| Benson & Hedges Cup | | | | | | | | |
| ALL ONE-DAY | | | | | | | | |

# D.M.SMITH - *Hertfordshire*

| Opposition | Venue | Date | Batting | Fielding | Bowling |
|---|---|---|---|---|---|

**NATWEST TROPHY**

| Warwickshire | Edgbaston | July 11 | 15 | | 0-15 |

**BATTING AVERAGES - Including fielding**

| | Matches | Inns | NO | Runs | HS | Avge | 100s | 50s | Ct | St |
|---|---|---|---|---|---|---|---|---|---|---|
| NatWest Trophy | 1 | 1 | 0 | 15 | 15 | 15.00 | - | - | - | - |
| ALL ONE-DAY | 1 | 1 | 0 | 15 | 15 | 15.00 | - | - | - | - |

**BOWLING AVERAGES**

| | Overs | Mdns | Runs | Wkts | Avge | Best | 5wI | 10wM |
|---|---|---|---|---|---|---|---|---|
| NatWest Trophy | 3 | 0 | 15 | 0 | - | - | - | - |
| ALL ONE-DAY | 3 | 0 | 15 | 0 | - | - | - | - |

# G.SMITH - *Warwickshire*

| Opposition | Venue | Date | Batting | Fielding | Bowling |
|---|---|---|---|---|---|

**OTHER ONE-DAY**

| Surrey | Harrogate | June 12 | 1 * | | 0-24 |

**BATTING AVERAGES - Including fielding**

| | Matches | Inns | NO | Runs | HS | Avge | 100s | 50s | Ct | St |
|---|---|---|---|---|---|---|---|---|---|---|
| Other One-Day | 1 | 1 | 1 | 1 | 1 * | - | - | - | - | - |
| ALL ONE-DAY | 1 | 1 | 1 | 1 | 1 * | - | - | - | - | - |

**BOWLING AVERAGES**

| | Overs | Mdns | Runs | Wkts | Avge | Best | 5wI | 10wM |
|---|---|---|---|---|---|---|---|---|
| Other One-Day | 9 | 0 | 24 | 0 | - | - | - | - |
| ALL ONE-DAY | 9 | 0 | 24 | 0 | - | - | - | - |

# I.SMITH - *Glamorgan*

| Opposition | Venue | Date | Batting | Fielding | Bowling |
|---|---|---|---|---|---|

**BRITANNIC ASSURANCE**

| Leicestershire | Leicester | April 27 | 39 | | |
| Somerset | Taunton | May 9 | 6 | 3Ct | |
| Warwickshire | Swansea | May 16 | 28 & 29 | 2Ct | |
| Northants | Cardiff | May 22 | 13 | | 0-10 & 0-2 |
| Sussex | Cardiff | May 25 | 12 * | | 1-7 & 0-28 |
| Worcestershire | Worcester | May 31 | 14 | 1Ct | 1-41 |
| Somerset | Swansea | June 4 | 33 * & 11 | | 0-7 |
| Derbyshire | Chesterfield | June 7 | 4 & 7 | 1Ct | 1-37 |

**OTHER FIRST-CLASS**

| Oxford U | The Parks | April 17 | | | 1-24 |
| Cambridge U | Fenner's | June 18 | 47 & 2 | | |

**REFUGE ASSURANCE**

| Northants | Cardiff | April 21 | 6 | | |
| Leicestershire | Leicester | April 28 | 27 * | | 0-7 |
| Notts | Cardiff | May 5 | 28 * | | 2-49 |
| Somerset | Taunton | May 12 | 34 * | | |
| Warwickshire | Swansea | May 19 | 41 | | |
| Sussex | Swansea | May 26 | 8 | | 2-35 |
| Essex | Pontypridd | June 2 | 8 | | |
| Lancashire | Old Trafford | June 9 | 23 | | |
| Middlesex | Cardiff | June 16 | 22 | 2Ct | |
| Yorkshire | Headingley | June 30 | 23 | | 0-25 |
| Worcestershire | Worcester | July 21 | 24 | 1Ct | 0-42 |

**NATWEST TROPHY**

| Durham | Darlington | June 26 | | 1Ct | 3-60 |
| Worcestershire | Worcester | July 11 | | | |

**BENSON & HEDGES CUP**

| Min Counties | Trowbridge | April 23 | 2 | | 0-18 |
| Hampshire | Southampton | May 2 | 51 | | 1-51 |
| Notts | Cardiff | May 4 | 36 | 1Ct | |
| Yorkshire | Cardiff | May 7 | 1 | | |

**BATTING AVERAGES - Including fielding**

| | Matches | Inns | NO | Runs | HS | Avge | 100s | 50s | Ct | St |
|---|---|---|---|---|---|---|---|---|---|---|
| Britannic Assurance | 8 | 11 | 2 | 196 | 39 | 21.77 | - | - | 7 | - |
| Other First-Class | 2 | 2 | 0 | 49 | 47 | 24.50 | - | - | - | - |
| ALL FIRST-CLASS | 10 | 13 | 2 | 245 | 47 | 22.27 | - | - | 7 | - |
| Refuge Assurance | 11 | 11 | 3 | 244 | 41 | 30.50 | - | - | 3 | - |
| NatWest Trophy | 2 | 0 | 0 | 0 | 0 | - | - | - | 1 | - |
| Benson & Hedges Cup | 4 | 4 | 0 | 90 | 51 | 22.50 | - | 1 | 1 | - |
| ALL ONE-DAY | 17 | 15 | 3 | 334 | 51 | 27.83 | - | 1 | 5 | - |

**BOWLING AVERAGES**

| | Overs | Mdns | Runs | Wkts | Avge | Best | 5wI | 10wM |
|---|---|---|---|---|---|---|---|---|
| Britannic Assurance | 36.1 | 7 | 132 | 3 | 44.00 | 1-7 | - | - |
| Other First-Class | 6 | 1 | 24 | 1 | 24.00 | 1-24 | - | - |
| ALL FIRST-CLASS | 42.1 | 8 | 156 | 4 | 39.00 | 1-7 | - | - |
| Refuge Assurance | 28 | 0 | 158 | 4 | 39.50 | 2-35 | - | |
| NatWest Trophy | 9 | 0 | 60 | 3 | 20.00 | 3-60 | - | |
| Benson & Hedges Cup | 10 | 0 | 69 | 1 | 69.00 | 1-51 | - | |
| ALL ONE-DAY | 47 | 0 | 287 | 8 | 35.87 | 3-60 | - | - |

## S PLAYER RECORDS

### N.M.K.SMITH - *Warwickshire*

| Opposition | Venue | Date | Batting | Fielding | Bowling |
|---|---|---|---|---|---|
| **BRITANNIC ASSURANCE** | | | | | |
| Surrey | Edgbaston | Aug 6 | 5 & 40 * | | 1-3 |
| Northants | Northampton | Aug 9 | 70 | | 1-50 & 0-2 |
| Glamorgan | Edgbaston | Aug 20 | 6 & 17 | | 1-68 & 0-0 |
| Northants | Edgbaston | Sept 10 | 50 * & 18 | | 3-50 & 0-31 |
| Somerset | Taunton | Sept 17 | 2 & 1 | | 0-38 & 2-79 |
| **REFUGE ASSURANCE** | | | | | |
| Sussex | Edgbaston | April 21 | 1 | | 1-14 |
| Notts | Trent Bridge | April 28 | 8 | 1Ct | 1-30 |
| Somerset | Edgbaston | June 2 | | | |
| Lancashire | Edgbaston | June 16 | 4 * | 1Ct | |
| Essex | Chelmsford | July 7 | 38 * | | 0-27 |
| Middlesex | Edgbaston | July 14 | | 1Ct | 1-11 |
| Hampshire | Portsmouth | July 21 | 8 * | 1Ct | 2-24 |
| Derbyshire | Edgbaston | Aug 4 | 14 * | | 1-50 |
| Leicestershire | Leicester | Aug 11 | 15 | | 1-27 |
| Gloucs | Edgbaston | Aug 18 | | | 0-33 |
| Northants | Northampton | Aug 25 | 39 | | 3-52 |
| **NATWEST TROPHY** | | | | | |
| Somerset | Edgbaston | July 31 | 38 | | 1-20 |
| Hampshire | Edgbaston | Aug 14 | 0 | | 1-17 |
| **BENSON & HEDGES CUP** | | | | | |
| Essex | Edgbaston | April 25 | 23 | | 0-32 |

**BATTING AVERAGES - Including fielding**

| | Matches | Inns | NO | Runs | HS | Avge | 100s | 50s | Ct | St |
|---|---|---|---|---|---|---|---|---|---|---|
| Britannic Assurance | 5 | 9 | 2 | 209 | 70 | 29.85 | - | 2 | - | - |
| ALL FIRST-CLASS | 5 | 9 | 2 | 209 | 70 | 29.85 | - | 2 | - | - |
| Refuge Assurance | 11 | 8 | 4 | 127 | 39 | 31.75 | - | - | 4 | - |
| NatWest Trophy | 2 | 2 | 0 | 38 | 38 | 19.00 | - | - | - | - |
| Benson & Hedges Cup | 1 | 1 | 0 | 23 | 23 | 23.00 | - | - | - | - |
| ALL ONE-DAY | 14 | 11 | 4 | 188 | 39 | 26.85 | - | - | 4 | - |

**BOWLING AVERAGES**

| | Overs | Mdns | Runs | Wkts | Avge | Best | 5wI | 10wM |
|---|---|---|---|---|---|---|---|---|
| Britannic Assurance | 111 | 32 | 321 | 8 | 40.12 | 3-50 | - | - |
| ALL FIRST-CLASS | 111 | 32 | 321 | 8 | 40.12 | 3-50 | - | - |
| Refuge Assurance | 53.3 | 0 | 268 | 10 | 26.80 | 3-52 | - | |
| NatWest Trophy | 13 | 1 | 37 | 2 | 18.50 | 1-17 | - | |
| Benson & Hedges Cup | 4 | 0 | 32 | 0 | | | - | |
| ALL ONE-DAY | 70.3 | 1 | 337 | 12 | 28.08 | 3-52 | - | |

### P.A.SMITH - *Warwickshire*

| Opposition | Venue | Date | Batting | Fielding | Bowling |
|---|---|---|---|---|---|
| **BRITANNIC ASSURANCE** | | | | | |
| Lancashire | Edgbaston | April 27 | 27 | | 1-40 |
| Yorkshire | Headingley | May 9 | 38 & 0 | | 0-20 & 1-26 |
| Glamorgan | Swansea | May 16 | 37 & 6 | 2Ct | 0-16 & 0-9 |
| Essex | Chelmsford | May 22 | 43 & 2 | | 0-22 |
| Gloucs | Edgbaston | May 25 | 1 | | 5-28 & 4-28 |
| Yorkshire | Edgbaston | May 31 | 11 & 9 * | | 1-29 & 1-37 |
| Kent | Tunbridge W | June 4 | 7 & 2 | | 1-38 |
| Sussex | Coventry | June 18 | 11 | | 0-6 & 0-15 |
| Notts | Trent Bridge | June 21 | 7 | | 0-10 & 0-20 |
| Derbyshire | Edgbaston | June 28 | 5 & 13 | | 0-39 & 0-17 |
| Middlesex | Edgbaston | July 2 | 68 & 0 | | 0-6 |
| Hampshire | Portsmouth | July 19 | 7 & 27 | | 0-38 & 0-14 |
| Lancashire | Old Trafford | July 23 | 24 | | |
| Glamorgan | Edgbaston | Aug 20 | 50 & 16 | | 1-55 |
| **REFUGE ASSURANCE** | | | | | |
| Sussex | Edgbaston | April 21 | 44 | | |
| Notts | Trent Bridge | April 28 | 15 | 1Ct | 2-36 |
| Yorkshire | Headingley | May 12 | 75 | | 3-43 |
| Glamorgan | Swansea | May 19 | 0 | | 3-42 |

| | | | | | |
|---|---|---|---|---|---|
| Worcestershire | Edgbaston | May 26 | 16 | | 2-45 |
| Somerset | Edgbaston | June 2 | | 1Ct | 4-21 |
| Lancashire | Edgbaston | June 16 | 49 | | 1-51 |
| Essex | Chelmsford | July 7 | 3 | | 1-24 |
| Middlesex | Edgbaston | July 14 | | | 3-33 |
| Hampshire | Portsmouth | July 21 | 10 | | 1-29 |
| Leicestershire | Leicester | Aug 11 | 38 | | 0-14 |
| Gloucs | Edgbaston | Aug 18 | | | 1-27 |
| Northants | Northampton | Aug 25 | 2 | | 0-39 |
| **NATWEST TROPHY** | | | | | |
| Yorkshire | Edgbaston | June 26 | 2 * | | 1-32 |
| Hertfordshire | Edgbaston | July 11 | | 1Ct | 2-24 |
| Somerset | Edgbaston | July 31 | 26 | | 0-41 |
| Hampshire | Edgbaston | Aug 14 | 14 | | 0-19 |
| **BENSON & HEDGES CUP** | | | | | |
| Essex | Edgbaston | April 25 | 3 | | 0-21 |
| Somerset | Edgbaston | May 2 | 5 | 1Ct | 0-18 |
| Middlesex | Lord's | May 4 | 34 | | 3-28 |
| Surrey | The Oval | May 7 | 17 | | |
| Yorkshire | Headingley | May 29 | 3 | | 1-41 |

**BATTING AVERAGES - Including fielding**

| | Matches | Inns | NO | Runs | HS | Avge | 100s | 50s | Ct | St |
|---|---|---|---|---|---|---|---|---|---|---|
| Britannic Assurance | 14 | 23 | 1 | 411 | 68 | 18.68 | - | 2 | 2 | - |
| ALL FIRST-CLASS | 14 | 23 | 1 | 411 | 68 | 18.68 | - | 2 | 2 | - |
| Refuge Assurance | 13 | 10 | 0 | 252 | 75 | 25.20 | - | 1 | 2 | - |
| NatWest Trophy | 4 | 3 | 1 | 42 | 26 | 21.00 | - | - | 1 | - |
| Benson & Hedges Cup | 5 | 5 | 0 | 62 | 34 | 12.40 | - | - | 1 | - |
| ALL ONE-DAY | 22 | 18 | 1 | 356 | 75 | 20.94 | - | 1 | 4 | - |

**BOWLING AVERAGES**

| | Overs | Mdns | Runs | Wkts | Avge | Best | 5wI | 10wM |
|---|---|---|---|---|---|---|---|---|
| Britannic Assurance | 157.1 | 31 | 513 | 15 | 34.20 | 5-28 | 1 | |
| ALL FIRST-CLASS | 157.1 | 31 | 513 | 15 | 34.20 | 5-28 | 1 | |
| Refuge Assurance | 77.3 | 1 | 404 | 21 | 19.23 | 4-21 | - | |
| NatWest Trophy | 35.2 | 3 | 116 | 3 | 38.66 | 2-24 | - | |
| Benson & Hedges Cup | 28 | 3 | 108 | 4 | 27.00 | 3-28 | - | |
| ALL ONE-DAY | 140.5 | 7 | 628 | 28 | 22.42 | 4-21 | - | |

### P.J.SMITH - *Victoria*

| Opposition | Venue | Date | Batting | Fielding | Bowling |
|---|---|---|---|---|---|
| **OTHER ONE-DAY** | | | | | |
| Durham | Durham U. | Sept 16 | | | 0-29 |

**BATTING AVERAGES - Including fielding**

| | Matches | Inns | NO | Runs | HS | Avge | 100s | 50s | Ct | St |
|---|---|---|---|---|---|---|---|---|---|---|
| Other One-Day | 1 | 0 | 0 | 0 | 0 | - | - | - | - | - |
| ALL ONE-DAY | 1 | 0 | 0 | 0 | 0 | - | - | - | - | - |

**BOWLING AVERAGES**

| | Overs | Mdns | Runs | Wkts | Avge | Best | 5wI | 10wM |
|---|---|---|---|---|---|---|---|---|
| Other One-Day | 4.1 | 0 | 29 | 0 | - | - | - | |
| ALL ONE-DAY | 4.1 | 0 | 29 | 0 | - | - | - | |

### R.A.SMITH - *Hampshire & England*

| Opposition | Venue | Date | Batting | Fielding | Bowling |
|---|---|---|---|---|---|
| **CORNHILL TEST MATCHES** | | | | | |
| West Indies | Headingley | June 6 | 54 & 0 | 1Ct | |
| West Indies | Lord's | June 20 | 148 * | | |
| West Indies | Trent Bridge | July 4 | 64 * & 15 | 1Ct | |
| West Indies | The Oval | Aug 8 | 109 & 26 | | |
| Sri Lanka | Lord's | Aug 22 | 4 & 63 * | 1Ct | |

# PLANER RECORDS

**S**

**BRITANNIC ASSURANCE**

| | | | | | | | | |
|---|---|---|---|---|---|---|---|---|
| Gloucs | Bristol | May 9 | 31 | & | 74 | | |
| Sussex | Hove | May 16 | 68 | & | 16 | 1Ct | |
| Surrey | Bournemouth | May 25 | 33 | & | 29 | 4Ct | |
| Notts | Trent Bridge | May 31 | 46 | & | 60 | | |
| Warwickshire | Portsmouth | July 19 | 19 | & | 0 | | |
| Middlesex | Lord's | Aug 2 | 55 | & | 57 | | 1-55 |
| Leicestershire | Bournemouth | Aug 16 | 61 | & | 39 | | 0-22 |
| Somerset | Southampton | Aug 28 | 81 | & | 107 | 2Ct | |
| Surrey | The Oval | Sept 3 | 12 | & | 21 | 3Ct | |
| Glamorgan | Southampton | Sept 17 | 14 | & | 29 | 2Ct | 2-20 |

**OTHER FIRST-CLASS**

| | | | |
|---|---|---|---|
| West Indies | Southampton | June 29 | 62 * |

**REFUGE ASSURANCE**

| | | | | |
|---|---|---|---|---|
| Somerset | Bournemouth | May 19 | 1 | |
| Gloucs | Swindon | May 26 | 16 | 1Ct |
| Northants | Northampton | June 2 | 2 | |
| Essex | Chelmsford | June 16 | | |
| Notts | Trent Bridge | July 14 | 9 | 1Ct |
| Middlesex | Lord's | Aug 4 | 14 | |
| Leicestershire | Bournemouth | Aug 18 | 75 | |

**NATWEST TROPHY**

| | | | |
|---|---|---|---|
| Berkshire | Reading | June 26 | 43 * |
| Lancashire | Southampton | July 11 | 79 * |
| Notts | Southampton | July 31 | 67 |
| Warwickshire | Edgbaston | Aug 14 | 64 * |
| Surrey | Lord's | Sept 7 | 78 |

**BENSON & HEDGES CUP**

| | | | | |
|---|---|---|---|---|
| Essex | Chelmsford | May 29 | 35 | 1Ct |

**BATTING AVERAGES - Including fielding**

| | Matches | Inns | NO | Runs | HS | Avge | 100s | 50s | Ct | St |
|---|---|---|---|---|---|---|---|---|---|---|
| Cornhill Test Matches | 5 | 9 | 3 | 483 | 148 * | 80.50 | 2 | 3 | 3 | - |
| Britannic Assurance | 10 | 20 | 0 | 852 | 107 | 42.60 | 1 | 7 | 12 | - |
| Other First-Class | 1 | 1 | 1 | 62 | 62 * | - | - | 1 | - | - |
| ALL FIRST-CLASS | 16 | 30 | 4 | 1397 | 148 * | 53.73 | 3 | 11 | 15 | - |
| Refuge Assurance | 7 | 6 | 0 | 117 | 75 | 19.50 | - | 1 | 2 | - |
| NatWest Trophy | 5 | 5 | 3 | 331 | 79 * | 165.50 | - | 4 | - | - |
| Benson & Hedges Cup | 1 | 1 | 0 | 35 | 35 | 35.00 | - | - | 1 | - |
| ALL ONE-DAY | 13 | 12 | 3 | 483 | 79 * | 53.66 | - | 5 | 3 | - |

**BOWLING AVERAGES**

| | Overs | Mdns | Runs | Wkts | Avge | Best | 5wI | 10wM |
|---|---|---|---|---|---|---|---|---|
| Cornhill Test Matches | | | | | | | | |
| Britannic Assurance | 18 | 3 | 97 | 3 | 32.33 | 2-20 | - | - |
| Other First-Class | | | | | | | | |
| ALL FIRST-CLASS | 18 | 3 | 97 | 3 | 32.33 | 2-20 | - | - |
| Refuge Assurance | | | | | | | | |
| NatWest Trophy | | | | | | | | |
| Benson & Hedges Cup | | | | | | | | |
| ALL ONE-DAY | | | | | | | | |

# S.G.SMYTH - *Ireland*

| Opposition | Venue | Date | Batting | Fielding | Bowling |
|---|---|---|---|---|---|

**OTHER FIRST-CLASS**

| | | | | | | |
|---|---|---|---|---|---|---|
| Scotland | Dublin | June 22 | 14 | & | 7 * | 0-7 |

**OTHER ONE-DAY**

| | | | |
|---|---|---|---|
| West Indies | Downpatrick | July 13 | 18 |

**BATTING AVERAGES - Including fielding**

| | Matches | Inns | NO | Runs | HS | Avge | 100s | 50s | Ct | St |
|---|---|---|---|---|---|---|---|---|---|---|
| Other First-Class | 1 | 2 | 1 | 21 | 14 | 21.00 | - | - | - | - |
| ALL FIRST-CLASS | 1 | 2 | 1 | 21 | 14 | 21.00 | - | - | - | - |
| Other One-Day | 1 | 1 | 0 | 18 | 18 | 18.00 | - | - | - | - |
| ALL ONE-DAY | 1 | 1 | 0 | 18 | 18 | 18.00 | - | - | - | - |

**BOWLING AVERAGES**

| | Overs | Mdns | Runs | Wkts | Avge | Best | 5wI | 10wM |
|---|---|---|---|---|---|---|---|---|
| Other First-Class | 1 | 0 | 7 | 0 | - | - | - | - |
| ALL FIRST-CLASS | 1 | 0 | 7 | 0 | - | - | - | - |
| Other One-Day | | | | | | | | |
| ALL ONE-DAY | | | | | | | | |

# N.J.SPEAK - *Lancashire*

| Opposition | Venue | Date | Batting | | | Fielding | Bowling |
|---|---|---|---|---|---|---|---|

**BRITANNIC ASSURANCE**

| | | | | | | | |
|---|---|---|---|---|---|---|---|
| Warwickshire | Edgbaston | April 27 | 37 * | | | | 1-0 |
| Derbyshire | Old Trafford | May 16 | 0 | & | 3 | 1Ct | |
| Surrey | The Oval | May 22 | 6 | & | 6 | 2Ct | |
| Leicestershire | Leicester | June 18 | 26 | & | 0 | 1Ct | |
| Kent | Old Trafford | June 21 | 24 | | | 1Ct | |
| Glamorgan | Liverpool | June 28 | 38 | & | 17 | | |
| Somerset | Taunton | July 2 | 56 | & | 49 | 1Ct | |
| Notts | Trent Bridge | July 16 | 0 | & | 38 | | |
| Middlesex | Uxbridge | July 19 | 11 | & | 25 * | | |
| Northants | Lytham | Aug 6 | 13 | | | | |
| Gloucs | Bristol | Aug 9 | 29 | & | 16 | | |
| Derbyshire | Derby | Aug 16 | 32 | & | 39 | | |
| Worcestershire | Blackpool | Aug 20 | 10 | & | 45 | | |
| Essex | Old Trafford | Aug 23 | 15 | & | 2 | | |
| Notts | Old Trafford | Aug 28 | 9 | & | 11 | 1Ct | |
| Yorkshire | Scarborough | Sept 3 | 73 | & | 11 | | |
| Surrey | Old Trafford | Sept 17 | 153 | & | 12 | | |

**OTHER FIRST-CLASS**

| | | | | | | |
|---|---|---|---|---|---|---|
| Oxford U | The Parks | June 7 | 30 * | & | 8 | 1Ct |

**REFUGE ASSURANCE**

| | | | | |
|---|---|---|---|---|
| Somerset | Taunton | July 5 | | |
| Leicestershire | Leicester | July 7 | 27 * | 2Ct |
| Hampshire | Southampton | July 28 | 8 | |
| Gloucs | Bristol | Aug 11 | | |
| Essex | Old Trafford | Aug 25 | 0 | 1Ct |
| Northants | Old Trafford | Sept 1 | 94 * | |
| Worcestershire | Old Trafford | Sept 15 | 26 | |

**BENSON & HEDGES CUP**

| | | | |
|---|---|---|---|
| Scotland | Forfar | April 23 | |

**BATTING AVERAGES - Including fielding**

| | Matches | Inns | NO | Runs | HS | Avge | 100s | 50s | Ct | St |
|---|---|---|---|---|---|---|---|---|---|---|
| Britannic Assurance | 17 | 31 | 2 | 806 | 153 | 27.79 | 1 | 2 | 7 | - |
| Other First-Class | 1 | 2 | 1 | 38 | 30 * | 38.00 | - | - | 1 | - |
| ALL FIRST-CLASS | 18 | 33 | 3 | 844 | 153 | 28.13 | 1 | 2 | 8 | - |
| Refuge Assurance | 7 | 5 | 2 | 155 | 94 * | 51.66 | - | 1 | 3 | - |
| Benson & Hedges Cup | 1 | 0 | 0 | 0 | 0 | | - | - | - | - |
| ALL ONE-DAY | 8 | 5 | 2 | 155 | 94 * | 51.66 | - | 1 | 3 | - |

**BOWLING AVERAGES**

| | Overs | Mdns | Runs | Wkts | Avge | Best | 5wI | 10wM |
|---|---|---|---|---|---|---|---|---|
| Britannic Assurance | 0.1 | 0 | 0 | 1 | 0.00 | 1-0 | - | - |
| Other First-Class | | | | | | | | |
| ALL FIRST-CLASS | 0.1 | 0 | 0 | 1 | 0.00 | 1-0 | - | - |
| Refuge Assurance | | | | | | | | |
| Benson & Hedges Cup | | | | | | | | |
| ALL ONE-DAY | | | | | | | | |

# M.P.SPEIGHT - *Sussex*

| Opposition | Venue | Date | Batting | Fielding | Bowling |
|---|---|---|---|---|---|

**BRITANNIC ASSURANCE**

| | | | |
|---|---|---|---|
| Middlesex | Lord's | May 9 | 5 |

## S | PLAYER RECORDS

| | | | | | |
|---|---|---|---|---|---|
| Middlesex | Hove | May 22 | 40 & 0 | | |
| Essex | Horsham | June 21 | 6 | | |
| Surrey | Arundel | July 2 | 42 & 15 | | |
| Derbyshire | Derby | July 5 | 60 & 56 | | |
| Somerset | Hove | July 16 | 67 | | |
| Leicestershire | Hove | July 19 | 64 & 18 | 1Ct | |
| Gloucs | Cheltenham | July 23 | 26 | 2Ct | |
| Northants | Eastbourne | Aug 2 | 89 & 22 | | |
| Notts | Eastbourne | Aug 6 | 10 & 37* | | |
| Yorkshire | Midd'brough | Aug 9 | 7 | 1Ct | |
| Hampshire | Bournemouth | Aug 20 | 8 | 1Ct | |

**OTHER FIRST-CLASS**

| | | | | |
|---|---|---|---|---|
| Cambridge U | Hove | June 29 | 149 | 1Ct |
| Sri Lanka | Hove | Aug 17 | 33 | |

**REFUGE ASSURANCE**

| | | | | |
|---|---|---|---|---|
| Middlesex | Hove | May 12 | 15 | 1Ct |
| Glamorgan | Swansea | May 26 | 47 | |
| Lancashire | Old Trafford | June 2 | 39 | 1Ct |
| Hampshire | Basingstoke | June 9 | 7 | 1Ct |
| Worcestershire | Hove | June 16 | 106* | |
| Derbyshire | Derby | July 7 | 3 | |
| Surrey | The Oval | July 14 | 9 | |
| Leicestershire | Hove | July 21 | 4 | 1Ct |
| Notts | Hove | July 28 | 44 | |
| Northants | Eastbourne | Aug 4 | 2 | |
| Yorkshire | Midd'brough | Aug 11 | 19 | 1Ct |

**NATWEST TROPHY**

| | | | |
|---|---|---|---|
| Scotland | Edinburgh | June 26 | 20 |
| Essex | Hove | July 11 | 48 |

**BENSON & HEDGES CUP**

| | | | |
|---|---|---|---|
| Kent | Canterbury | May 2 | 35 |
| Scotland | Hove | May 4 | 6 |
| Lancashire | Old Trafford | May 7 | 1 |

**BATTING AVERAGES - Including fielding**

| | Matches | Inns | NO | Runs | HS | Avge | 100s | 50s | Ct | St |
|---|---|---|---|---|---|---|---|---|---|---|
| Britannic Assurance | 12 | 18 | 1 | 572 | 89 | 33.64 | - | 5 | 5 | - |
| Other First-Class | 2 | 2 | 0 | 182 | 149 | 91.00 | 1 | - | 1 | - |
| ALL FIRST-CLASS | 14 | 20 | 1 | 754 | 149 | 39.68 | 1 | 5 | 6 | - |
| Refuge Assurance | 11 | 11 | 1 | 295 | 106* | 29.50 | 1 | - | 5 | - |
| NatWest Trophy | 2 | 2 | 0 | 68 | 48 | 34.00 | - | - | - | - |
| Benson & Hedges Cup | 3 | 3 | 0 | 42 | 35 | 14.00 | - | - | - | - |
| ALL ONE-DAY | 16 | 16 | 1 | 405 | 106* | 27.00 | 1 | - | 5 | - |

**BOWLING AVERAGES**
Did not bowl

## R.A.SPIERS - *Staffordshire*

| Opposition | Venue | Date | Batting | Fielding | Bowling |
|---|---|---|---|---|---|
| **NATWEST TROPHY** | | | | | |
| Northants | Stone | June 26 | 13* | | 0-65 |

**BATTING AVERAGES - Including fielding**

| | Matches | Inns | NO | Runs | HS | Avge | 100s | 50s | Ct | St |
|---|---|---|---|---|---|---|---|---|---|---|
| NatWest Trophy | 1 | 1 | 1 | 13 | 13* | - | - | - | - | - |
| ALL ONE-DAY | 1 | 1 | 1 | 13 | 13* | - | - | - | - | - |

**BOWLING AVERAGES**

| | Overs | Mdns | Runs | Wkts | Avge | Best | 5wI | 10wM |
|---|---|---|---|---|---|---|---|---|
| NatWest Trophy | 10 | 1 | 65 | 0 | - | - | | |
| ALL ONE-DAY | 10 | 1 | 65 | 0 | - | - | | |

## D.M.STAMP - *Norfolk*

| Opposition | Venue | Date | Batting | Fielding | Bowling |
|---|---|---|---|---|---|
| **NATWEST TROPHY** | | | | | |
| Gloucs | Bristol | June 26 | 6 | 2Ct | |

**BATTING AVERAGES - Including fielding**

| | Matches | Inns | NO | Runs | HS | Avge | 100s | 50s | Ct | St |
|---|---|---|---|---|---|---|---|---|---|---|
| NatWest Trophy | 1 | 1 | 0 | 6 | 6 | 6.00 | - | - | 2 | - |
| ALL ONE-DAY | 1 | 1 | 0 | 6 | 6 | 6.00 | - | - | 2 | - |

**BOWLING AVERAGES**
Did not bowl

## N.A.STANLEY - *Northamptonshire*

| Opposition | Venue | Date | Batting | Fielding | Bowling |
|---|---|---|---|---|---|
| **BRITANNIC ASSURANCE** | | | | | |
| Sussex | Eastbourne | Aug 2 | 6 & 36 | | |
| Lancashire | Lytham | Aug 6 | 132 | | |
| Warwickshire | Northampton | Aug 9 | 62 | 1Ct | 0-16 |
| Essex | Colchester | Aug 16 | 0 & 23 | | |
| Surrey | Northampton | Aug 23 | 18 & 16 | 1Ct | 0-3 |
| Yorkshire | Northampton | Aug 28 | 34 | 2Ct | |
| Gloucs | Bristol | Sept 3 | 27 & 30 | 1Ct | |
| Warwickshire | Edgbaston | Sept 10 | 32 & 54 | | |

**BATTING AVERAGES - Including fielding**

| | Matches | Inns | NO | Runs | HS | Avge | 100s | 50s | Ct | St |
|---|---|---|---|---|---|---|---|---|---|---|
| Britannic Assurance | 8 | 13 | 0 | 470 | 132 | 36.15 | 1 | 2 | 5 | - |
| ALL FIRST-CLASS | 8 | 13 | 0 | 470 | 132 | 36.15 | 1 | 2 | 5 | - |

**BOWLING AVERAGES**

| | Overs | Mdns | Runs | Wkts | Avge | Best | 5wI | 10wM |
|---|---|---|---|---|---|---|---|---|
| Britannic Assurance | 10 | 2 | 19 | 0 | - | - | | - |
| ALL FIRST-CLASS | 10 | 2 | 19 | 0 | - | - | | - |

## J.STANWORTH - *Lancashire*

| Opposition | Venue | Date | Batting | Fielding | Bowling |
|---|---|---|---|---|---|
| **BRITANNIC ASSURANCE** | | | | | |
| Warwickshire | Old Trafford | July 23 | | 1Ct,1St | |
| **OTHER FIRST-CLASS** | | | | | |
| Oxford U | The Parks | June 7 | | 1Ct | |

**BATTING AVERAGES - Including fielding**

| | Matches | Inns | NO | Runs | HS | Avge | 100s | 50s | Ct | St |
|---|---|---|---|---|---|---|---|---|---|---|
| Britannic Assurance | 1 | 0 | 0 | 0 | 0 | - | - | - | 1 | 1 |
| Other First-Class | 1 | 0 | 0 | 0 | 0 | - | - | - | 1 | - |
| ALL FIRST-CLASS | 2 | 0 | 0 | 0 | 0 | - | - | - | 2 | 1 |

**BOWLING AVERAGES**
Did not bowl

## R.STAPLES - *West Indies XI*

| Opposition | Venue | Date | Batting | Fielding | Bowling |
|---|---|---|---|---|---|
| **OTHER FIRST-CLASS** | | | | | |
| World XI | Scarborough | Aug 28 | 40 & 56 | 2Ct | 0-56 |

# PLAYER RECORDS

S

## BATTING AVERAGES - Including fielding

| | Matches | Inns | NO | Runs | HS | Avge | 100s | 50s | Ct | St |
|---|---|---|---|---|---|---|---|---|---|---|
| Other First-Class | 1 | 2 | 0 | 96 | 56 | 48.00 | - | 1 | 2 | - |
| ALL FIRST-CLASS | 1 | 2 | 0 | 96 | 56 | 48.00 | - | 1 | 2 | - |

## BOWLING AVERAGES

| | Overs | Mdns | Runs | Wkts | Avge | Best | 5wI | 10wM |
|---|---|---|---|---|---|---|---|---|
| Other First-Class | 8 | 1 | 56 | 0 | - | - | - | - |
| ALL FIRST-CLASS | 8 | 1 | 56 | 0 | - | - | - | - |

# M.G.STEAR - *Berkshire*

| Opposition | Venue | Date | Batting | Fielding | Bowling |
|---|---|---|---|---|---|
| **NATWEST TROPHY** | | | | | |
| Hampshire | Reading | June 26 | | | 0-11 |

## BATTING AVERAGES - Including fielding

| | Matches | Inns | NO | Runs | HS | Avge | 100s | 50s | Ct | St |
|---|---|---|---|---|---|---|---|---|---|---|
| NatWest Trophy | 1 | 0 | 0 | 0 | 0 | - | - | - | - | - |
| ALL ONE-DAY | 1 | 0 | 0 | 0 | 0 | - | - | - | - | - |

## BOWLING AVERAGES

| | Overs | Mdns | Runs | Wkts | Avge | Best | 5wI | 10wM |
|---|---|---|---|---|---|---|---|---|
| NatWest Trophy | 3 | 0 | 11 | 0 | - | - | - | |
| ALL ONE-DAY | 3 | 0 | 11 | 0 | - | - | - | |

# R.D.STEMP - *Worcestershire*

| Opposition | Venue | Date | Batting | Fielding | Bowling |
|---|---|---|---|---|---|
| **BRITANNIC ASSURANCE** | | | | | |
| Northants | Northampton | June 4 | | | 0-34 |
| Notts | Worcester | June 18 | 15 * | | 0-13 |
| Yorkshire | Headingley | July 2 | 0 | | 4-62 |
| Kent | Worcester | July 23 | | | |
| Gloucs | Cheltenham | July 26 | 3 * & | 0 * | 4-85 |
| Somerset | Weston | Aug 6 | | 0 * | 1-28 & 2-23 |
| Glamorgan | Cardiff | Sept 10 | 3 | | 0-6 & 4-74 |
| Notts | Trent Bridge | Sept 17 | 1 * & | 8 | 0-57 |
| **OTHER FIRST-CLASS** | | | | | |
| Oxford U | The Parks | May 25 | | | 2-9 & 0-34 |
| **REFUGE ASSURANCE** | | | | | |
| Warwickshire | Edgbaston | May 26 | | 1Ct | 1-22 |
| Hampshire | Southampton | July 7 | | | 0-33 |
| Derbyshire | Worcester | July 9 | | 1Ct | 3-18 |
| Glamorgan | Worcester | July 21 | | | 1-16 |

## BATTING AVERAGES - Including fielding

| | Matches | Inns | NO | Runs | HS | Avge | 100s | 50s | Ct | St |
|---|---|---|---|---|---|---|---|---|---|---|
| Britannic Assurance | 8 | 8 | 5 | 30 | 15 * | 10.00 | - | - | - | - |
| Other First-Class | 1 | 0 | 0 | 0 | 0 | - | - | - | - | - |
| ALL FIRST-CLASS | 9 | 8 | 5 | 30 | 15 * | 10.00 | - | - | - | - |
| Refuge Assurance | 4 | 0 | 0 | 0 | 0 | - | - | - | 2 | - |
| ALL ONE-DAY | 4 | 0 | 0 | 0 | 0 | - | - | - | 2 | - |

## BOWLING AVERAGES

| | Overs | Mdns | Runs | Wkts | Avge | Best | 5wI | 10wM |
|---|---|---|---|---|---|---|---|---|
| Britannic Assurance | 141.1 | 30 | 382 | 15 | 25.46 | 4-62 | - | - |
| Other First-Class | 31 | 13 | 43 | 2 | 21.50 | 2-9 | - | - |
| ALL FIRST-CLASS | 172.1 | 43 | 425 | 17 | 25.00 | 4-62 | - | - |
| Refuge Assurance | 22 | 1 | 89 | 5 | 17.80 | 3-18 | - | |
| ALL ONE-DAY | 22 | 1 | 89 | 5 | 17.80 | 3-18 | | |

# F.D.STEPHENSON - *Nottinghamshire*

| Opposition | Venue | Date | Batting | | Fielding | Bowling |
|---|---|---|---|---|---|---|
| **BRITANNIC ASSURANCE** | | | | | | |
| Leicestershire | Trent Bridge | May 9 | 28 | | | 3-52 & 3-33 |
| Yorkshire | Headingley | May 16 | | 24 * | | 4-84 & 0-50 |
| Kent | Trent Bridge | May 22 | 1 & | 2 | | 0-44 & 0-26 |
| Leicestershire | Leicester | May 25 | 16 * & | 3 * | | 0-33 & 3-53 |
| Hampshire | Trent Bridge | May 31 | 22 | | | 2-23 & 2-57 |
| Surrey | The Oval | June 4 | | | 1Ct | 0-51 & 0-8 |
| Gloucs | Gloucester | June 14 | | | | 3-51 & 0-10 |
| Worcestershire | Worcester | June 18 | 11 | | 1Ct | 2-16 & 5-74 |
| Warwickshire | Trent Bridge | June 21 | | | | 0-17 |
| Glamorgan | Cardiff | July 2 | 22 | | 1Ct | 4-40 & 1-66 |
| Lancashire | Trent Bridge | July 16 | 0 | | | 2-56 & 0-32 |
| Northants | Well'borough | July 19 | 1 | | | 5-61 & 5-27 |
| Yorkshire | Worksop | July 23 | | 10 | | 3-57 & 0-19 |
| Middlesex | Lord's | July 26 | 14 & | 11 * | | 4-59 & 1-71 |
| Sussex | Eastbourne | Aug 6 | 0 * | | | 3-26 & 0-29 |
| Essex | Trent Bridge | Aug 9 | 0 & | 58 | 1Ct | 2-46 & 2-90 |
| Somerset | Trent Bridge | Aug 16 | 44 & | 9 | 1Ct | 4-73 & 0-23 |
| Derbyshire | Trent Bridge | Aug 23 | 24 & | 10 * | | 2-44 & 2-62 |
| Lancashire | Old Trafford | Aug 28 | 24 & | 6 | 1Ct | 0-62 & 1-55 |
| Middlesex | Sept 3 | | 0 & | 19 * | | 0-50 & 0-18 |
| Derbyshire | Derby | Sept 10 | 45 | | | 2-61 & 1-112 |
| Worcestershire | Trent Bridge | Sept 17 | 19 | | | 5-63 & 2-26 |
| **REFUGE ASSURANCE** | | | | | | |
| Lancashire | Old Trafford | April 21 | | | | 2-41 |
| Warwickshire | Trent Bridge | April 28 | 36 * | | | 3-17 |
| Glamorgan | Cardiff | May 5 | 15 | | | 0-42 |
| Essex | Trent Bridge | May 12 | 13 | | | 3-33 |
| Leicestershire | Leicester | May 26 | | | | 0-30 |
| Somerset | Trent Bridge | June 9 | 0 | | | 1-26 |
| Gloucs | Gloucester | June 16 | | | | 2-25 |
| Middlesex | Trent Bridge | June 23 | 27 | | | 3-20 |
| Surrey | The Oval | June 30 | | | | 2-27 |
| Hampshire | Trent Bridge | July 14 | 21 | | | 0-32 |
| Northants | Well'borough | July 21 | 19 | | | 5-31 |
| Sussex | Hove | July 28 | | | 1Ct | 2-36 |
| Worcestershire | Trent Bridge | Aug 4 | 18 * | | | 1-26 |
| Kent | Trent Bridge | Aug 11 | 15 * | | 1Ct | 3-48 |
| Yorkshire | Scarborough | Aug 18 | 0 | | | 1-39 |
| Derbyshire | Trent Bridge | Aug 25 | | | | 2-13 |
| Worcestershire | Trent Bridge | Sept 1 | 0 | | 1Ct | 2-39 |
| **NATWEST TROPHY** | | | | | | |
| Lincolnshire | Trent Bridge | June 26 | | | | 1-10 |
| Gloucs | Bristol | July 11 | 1 | | | 1-46 |
| Hampshire | Southampton | July 31 | 7 | | | 0-43 |
| **BENSON & HEDGES CUP** | | | | | | |
| Hampshire | Southampton | April 23 | 14 | | | 0-56 |
| Yorkshire | Trent Bridge | April 25 | | | | 5-30 |
| Glamorgan | Cardiff | May 4 | 4 * | | 1Ct | 2-46 |
| Min Counties | Trent Bridge | May 7 | 1 | | | 0-3 |

## BATTING AVERAGES - Including fielding

| | Matches | Inns | NO | Runs | HS | Avge | 100s | 50s | Ct | St |
|---|---|---|---|---|---|---|---|---|---|---|
| Britannic Assurance | 22 | 27 | 7 | 423 | 58 | 21.15 | - | 1 | 6 | - |
| ALL FIRST-CLASS | 22 | 27 | 7 | 423 | 58 | 21.15 | - | 1 | 6 | - |
| Refuge Assurance | 17 | 11 | 3 | 164 | 36 * | 20.50 | - | - | 3 | - |
| NatWest Trophy | 3 | 2 | 0 | 8 | 7 | 4.00 | - | - | - | - |
| Benson & Hedges Cup | 4 | 3 | 1 | 19 | 14 | 9.50 | - | - | 1 | - |
| ALL ONE-DAY | 24 | 16 | 4 | 191 | 36 * | 15.91 | - | - | 4 | - |

## BOWLING AVERAGES

| | Overs | Mdns | Runs | Wkts | Avge | Best | 5wI | 10wM |
|---|---|---|---|---|---|---|---|---|
| Britannic Assurance | 719.1 | 158 | 2010 | 78 | 25.76 | 5-27 | 4 | 1 |
| ALL FIRST-CLASS | 719.1 | 158 | 2010 | 78 | 25.76 | 5-27 | 4 | 1 |
| Refuge Assurance | 129.2 | 11 | 525 | 32 | 16.40 | 5-31 | 1 | |
| NatWest Trophy | 29 | 0 | 99 | 2 | 49.50 | 1-10 | - | |
| Benson & Hedges Cup | 37 | 9 | 135 | 7 | 19.28 | 5-30 | 1 | |
| ALL ONE-DAY | 195.2 | 20 | 759 | 41 | 18.51 | 5-30 | 2 | |

# S | PLAYER RECORDS

## J.P.STEPHENSON - Essex

| Opposition | Venue | Date | Batting | | | Fielding | Bowling |
|---|---|---|---|---|---|---|---|
| **BRITANNIC ASSURANCE** | | | | | | | |
| Surrey | Chelmsford | April 27 | 85 | | | | |
| Northants | Northampton | May 9 | 11 | & | 1 | | |
| Kent | Folkestone | May 16 | 45 | | | | 0-3 |
| Warwickshire | Chelmsford | May 22 | 79 | & | 40 * | | 0-6 |
| Gloucs | Bristol | May 31 | 38 | | | | |
| Leicestershire | Ilford | June 4 | 24 | & | 16 | | |
| Worcestershire | Ilford | June 7 | 0 | & | 4 | 1Ct | 0-9 & 0-27 |
| Sussex | Horsham | June 21 | 2 | | | 1Ct | 0-16 |
| Middlesex | Lord's | June 28 | 2 | & | 38 | | 1-16 |
| Hampshire | Chelmsford | July 2 | 17 | & | 5 | 1Ct | 0-2 |
| Surrey | The Oval | July 5 | 0 | & | 18 | | |
| Kent | Southend | July 16 | 113 * | & | 19 | | |
| Somerset | Southend | July 19 | 70 | & | 11 | | 1-8 |
| Glamorgan | Cardiff | July 23 | 76 | | | | 2-50 |
| Derbyshire | Derby | Aug 6 | 14 | & | 35 | | 3-86 |
| Notts | Trent Bridge | Aug 9 | 4 | & | 14 | | 3-20 |
| Northants | Colchester | Aug 16 | 0 | | | 2Ct | |
| Yorkshire | Colchester | Aug 20 | 116 | & | 97 | | 2-19 & 0-24 |
| Lancashire | Old Trafford | Aug 23 | 5 | & | 85 | 1Ct | |
| Derbyshire | Chelmsford | Sept 3 | 14 | | | | |
| Leicestershire | Leicester | Sept 10 | 113 | & | 5 | | 0-0 |
| Middlesex | Chelmsford | Sept 17 | 18 | | | | 0-10 |
| **OTHER FIRST-CLASS** | | | | | | | |
| Cambridge U | Fenner's | April 19 | 16 * | & | 84 | | 4-30 |
| West Indies | Chelmsford | Aug 3 | 0 | & | 33 | 1Ct | 0-37 & 0-26 |
| Victoria | Chelmsford | Sept 23 | 54 | | | | 1-10 |
| **REFUGE ASSURANCE** | | | | | | | |
| Yorkshire | Chelmsford | April 28 | 32 | | | | 0-19 |
| Notts | Trent Bridge | May 12 | 29 | | | 1Ct | |
| Kent | Folkestone | May 19 | 4 | | | 1Ct | |
| Surrey | The Oval | May 26 | 64 | | | | 0-16 |
| Glamorgan | Pontypridd | June 2 | | | | | 1-8 |
| Worcestershire | Ilford | June 9 | 67 | | | 1Ct | 3-17 |
| Hampshire | Chelmsford | June 16 | 38 | | | | |
| Derbyshire | Chelmsford | June 30 | 27 | | | 1Ct | |
| Warwickshire | Chelmsford | July 7 | 60 | | | | 4-17 |
| Somerset | Southend | July 21 | 10 | | | | 2-49 |
| Gloucs | Cheltenham | July 28 | 0 | | | | 3-31 |
| Northants | Northampton | Aug 11 | 12 | | | 2Ct | 0-20 |
| Middlesex | Colchester | Aug 18 | 44 | | | | |
| Lancashire | Old Trafford | Aug 25 | 12 | | | 1Ct | 0-17 |
| **NATWEST TROPHY** | | | | | | | |
| Devon | Exmouth | June 26 | 57 | | | | |
| Sussex | Hove | July 11 | 1 | | | | 0-8 |
| Surrey | The Oval | July 31 | 59 | | | | 0-28 |
| **BENSON & HEDGES CUP** | | | | | | | |
| Surrey | The Oval | April 23 | 73 | | | 3Ct | 0-6 |
| Warwickshire | Edgbaston | April 25 | 142 | | | | 0-25 |
| Middlesex | Chelmsford | May 2 | 23 | | | | 1-17 |
| Somerset | Chelmsford | May 7 | 60 | | | | 0-9 |
| Hampshire | Chelmsford | May 29 | 38 | | | 1Ct | |
| Worcestershire | Chelmsford | June 12 | 13 | | | | |
| **OTHER ONE-DAY** | | | | | | | |
| Durham | Scarborough | Aug 31 | 107 | | | | 1-39 |
| Yorkshire | Scarborugh | Sept 2 | 57 | | | | 1-43 |
| Victoria | Chelmsford | Sept 22 | 49 | | | | 0-15 |

**BATTING AVERAGES - Including fielding**

| | Matches | Inns | NO | Runs | HS | Avge | 100s | 50s | Ct | St |
|---|---|---|---|---|---|---|---|---|---|---|
| Britannic Assurance | 22 | 36 | 2 | 1234 | 116 | 36.29 | 3 | 6 | 6 | - |
| Other First-Class | 3 | 5 | 1 | 187 | 84 | 46.75 | - | 2 | 1 | - |
| ALL FIRST-CLASS | 25 | 41 | 3 | 1421 | 116 | 37.39 | 3 | 8 | 7 | - |
| Refuge Assurance | 14 | 13 | 0 | 399 | 67 | 30.69 | - | 3 | 7 | - |
| NatWest Trophy | 3 | 3 | 0 | 117 | 59 | 39.00 | - | 2 | - | - |
| Benson & Hedges Cup | 6 | 6 | 0 | 349 | 142 | 58.16 | 1 | 2 | 4 | - |
| Other One-Day | 3 | 3 | 0 | 213 | 107 | 71.00 | 1 | 1 | - | - |
| ALL ONE-DAY | 26 | 25 | 0 | 1078 | 142 | 43.12 | 2 | 8 | 11 | - |

**BOWLING AVERAGES**

| | Overs | Mdns | Runs | Wkts | Avge | Best | 5wI | 10wM |
|---|---|---|---|---|---|---|---|---|
| Britannic Assurance | 77.4 | 14 | 296 | 12 | 24.66 | 3-20 | - | - |
| Other First-Class | 29 | 5 | 103 | 5 | 20.60 | 4-30 | - | - |
| ALL FIRST-CLASS | 106.4 | 19 | 399 | 17 | 23.47 | 4-30 | - | - |
| Refuge Assurance | 51 | 2 | 194 | 13 | 14.92 | 4-17 | - | |
| NatWest Trophy | 6 | 0 | 36 | 0 | - | - | - | |
| Benson & Hedges Cup | 11 | 0 | 57 | 1 | 57.00 | 1-17 | - | |
| Other One-Day | 18.2 | 0 | 97 | 2 | 48.50 | 1-39 | - | |
| ALL ONE-DAY | 86.2 | 2 | 384 | 16 | 24.00 | 4-17 | - | |

## M.G.STEPHENSON - Cambridgeshire

| Opposition | Venue | Date | Batting | Fielding | Bowling |
|---|---|---|---|---|---|
| **NATWEST TROPHY** | | | | | |
| Kent | Canterbury | June 26 | 2 | 1Ct | 0-19 |

**BATTING AVERAGES - Including fielding**

| | Matches | Inns | NO | Runs | HS | Avge | 100s | 50s | Ct | St |
|---|---|---|---|---|---|---|---|---|---|---|
| NatWest Trophy | 1 | 1 | 0 | 2 | 2 | 2.00 | - | - | 1 | - |
| ALL ONE-DAY | 1 | 1 | 0 | 2 | 2 | 2.00 | - | - | 1 | - |

**BOWLING AVERAGES**

| | Overs | Mdns | Runs | Wkts | Avge | Best | 5wI | 10wM |
|---|---|---|---|---|---|---|---|---|
| NatWest Trophy | 5.4 | 4 | 19 | 0 | - | - | - | - |
| ALL ONE-DAY | 5.4 | 4 | 19 | 0 | - | - | - | - |

## M.E.STEVENS - Berkshire

| Opposition | Venue | Date | Batting | Fielding | Bowling |
|---|---|---|---|---|---|
| **NATWEST TROPHY** | | | | | |
| Hampshire | Reading | June 26 | | | |

**BATTING AVERAGES - Including fielding**

| | Matches | Inns | NO | Runs | HS | Avge | 100s | 50s | Ct | St |
|---|---|---|---|---|---|---|---|---|---|---|
| NatWest Trophy | 1 | 0 | 0 | 0 | 0 | - | - | - | - | - |
| ALL ONE-DAY | 1 | 0 | 0 | 0 | 0 | - | - | - | - | - |

**BOWLING AVERAGES**

Did not bowl

## A.J.STEWART - Surrey & England

| Opposition | Venue | Date | Batting | | | Fielding | Bowling |
|---|---|---|---|---|---|---|---|
| **CORNHILL TEST MATCHES** | | | | | | | |
| West Indies | The Oval | Aug 8 | 31 | & | 38 * | 4Ct | |
| Sri Lanka | Lord's | Aug 22 | 113 * | & | 43 | | |
| **BRITANNIC ASSURANCE** | | | | | | | |
| Essex | Chelmsford | April 27 | 19 | | | | |
| Kent | The Oval | May 9 | 7 | & | 12 | | |
| Lancashire | The Oval | May 22 | 62 | & | 67 * | 3Ct | |
| Notts | The Oval | June 4 | 30 | & | 37 * | | |
| Leicestershire | Leicester | June 14 | 17 * | & | 13 | 1Ct | |
| Derbyshire | Derby | June 21 | 5 | & | 10 * | | |
| Somerset | The Oval | June 28 | | | 3 | | |
| Sussex | Arundel | July 2 | 71 | | | 3Ct | 0-3 |
| Essex | The Oval | July 5 | 33 | & | 83 * | | |
| Gloucs | Guildford | July 16 | 109 | & | 1 | | 0-9 |
| Yorkshire | Guildford | July 19 | 53 * | & | 36 | | |
| Glamorgan | The Oval | July 26 | 34 | & | 29 | 1Ct | 0-10 |
| Kent | Canterbury | Aug 2 | 10 | & | 32 | 1Ct | 0-12 |
| Worcestershire | Worcester | Aug 16 | 9 | & | 57 | 1Ct | |
| Sussex | The Oval | Aug 28 | 47 | | | 4Ct | |
| Hampshire | The Oval | Sept 3 | 8 | & | 0 | 4Ct | |
| Lancashire | Old Trafford | Sept 17 | 14 | & | 28 | 2Ct | |

# PLAYER RECORDS

## REFUGE ASSURANCE

| | | | | |
|---|---|---|---|---|
| Somerset | The Oval | April 21 | 14 | 3Ct |
| Middlesex | Lord's | April 28 | 71 | |
| Gloucs | The Oval | May 12 | 9 | |
| Worcestershire | Worcester | June 2 | | |
| Derbyshire | Chesterfield | June 9 | 60 | 1Ct |
| Leicestershire | Leicester | June 16 | 13 | 1Ct |
| Notts | The Oval | June 30 | 1 | |
| Northants | Tring | July 7 | 1 | 3Ct |
| Sussex | The Oval | July 14 | 84 * | 3Ct,1St |
| Yorkshire | The Oval | July 21 | 5 | 1Ct |
| Glamorgan | The Oval | July 28 | 3 | |
| Kent | Canterbury | Aug 4 | 64 | 1Ct |
| Lancashire | Old Trafford | Aug 18 | 16 | |

## NATWEST TROPHY

| | | | | |
|---|---|---|---|---|
| Kent | The Oval | July 11 | 76 * | 2Ct |
| Essex | The Oval | July 31 | 35 | 2Ct |
| Northants | The Oval | Aug 14 | 34 | 1Ct |
| Hampshire | Lord's | Sept 7 | 61 | 1Ct |

## BENSON & HEDGES CUP

| | | | | |
|---|---|---|---|---|
| Essex | The Oval | April 23 | 30 | 1Ct |
| Middlesex | Lord's | April 25 | 55 | 2Ct |
| Somerset | Taunton | May 4 | 110 * | |
| Warwickshire | The Oval | May 7 | 0 | |

## OTHER ONE-DAY

| | | | | |
|---|---|---|---|---|
| Warwickshire | Harrogate | June 12 | 61 | 1Ct,1St |
| Durham | Harrogate | June 13 | 0 | 1Ct,1St |

## BATTING AVERAGES - Including fielding

| | Matches | Inns | NO | Runs | HS | Avge | 100s | 50s | Ct | St |
|---|---|---|---|---|---|---|---|---|---|---|
| Cornhill Test Matches | 2 | 4 | 2 | 225 | 113 * | 112.50 | 1 | - | 4 | - |
| Britannic Assurance | 17 | 30 | 6 | 936 | 109 | 39.00 | 1 | 6 | 20 | - |
| ALL FIRST-CLASS | 19 | 34 | 8 | 1161 | 113 * | 44.65 | 2 | 6 | 24 | - |
| Refuge Assurance | 13 | 12 | 1 | 341 | 84 * | 31.00 | - | 4 | 13 | 1 |
| NatWest Trophy | 4 | 4 | 1 | 206 | 76 * | 68.66 | - | 2 | 6 | - |
| Benson & Hedges Cup | 4 | 4 | 1 | 195 | 110 * | 65.00 | 1 | 1 | 3 | - |
| Other One-Day | 2 | 2 | 0 | 61 | 61 | 30.50 | - | 1 | 2 | 2 |
| ALL ONE-DAY | 23 | 22 | 3 | 803 | 110 * | 42.26 | 1 | 8 | 24 | 3 |

## BOWLING AVERAGES

| | Overs | Mdns | Runs | Wkts | Avge | Best | 5wI | 10wM |
|---|---|---|---|---|---|---|---|---|
| Cornhill Test Matches | | | | | | | | |
| Britannic Assurance | 7 | 0 | 34 | 0 | - | - | - | - |
| ALL FIRST-CLASS | 7 | 0 | 34 | 0 | - | - | - | - |
| Refuge Assurance | | | | | | | | |
| NatWest Trophy | | | | | | | | |
| Benson & Hedges Cup | | | | | | | | |
| Other One-Day | | | | | | | | |
| ALL ONE-DAY | | | | | | | | |

# D.B.STORER - Lincolnshire

| Opposition | Venue | Date | Batting | Fielding | Bowling |
|---|---|---|---|---|---|

## NATWEST TROPHY

| | | | | | |
|---|---|---|---|---|---|
| Notts | Trent Bridge | June 26 | 28 | 1Ct | 1-17 |

## BATTING AVERAGES - Including fielding

| | Matches | Inns | NO | Runs | HS | Avge | 100s | 50s | Ct | St |
|---|---|---|---|---|---|---|---|---|---|---|
| NatWest Trophy | 1 | 1 | 0 | 28 | 28 | 28.00 | - | - | 1 | - |
| ALL ONE-DAY | 1 | 1 | 0 | 28 | 28 | 28.00 | - | - | 1 | - |

## BOWLING AVERAGES

| | Overs | Mdns | Runs | Wkts | Avge | Best | 5wI | 10wM |
|---|---|---|---|---|---|---|---|---|
| NatWest Trophy | 5 | 0 | 17 | 1 | 17.00 | 1-17 | - | |
| ALL ONE-DAY | 5 | 0 | 17 | 1 | 17.00 | 1-17 | - | |

## S

# P.M.SUCH - Essex

| Opposition | Venue | Date | Batting | Fielding | Bowling |
|---|---|---|---|---|---|

## BRITANNIC ASSURANCE

| | | | | | |
|---|---|---|---|---|---|
| Northants | Northampton | May 9 | 2 * | | 0-37 & 2-8 |
| Kent | Folkestone | May 16 | 23 * | | 0-20 & 2-19 |
| Leicestershire | Ilford | June 4 | 0 * | | 0-55 & 0-8 |
| Middlesex | Lord's | June 28 | | | 0-22 |
| Surrey | The Oval | July 5 | | | 2-87 & 2-91 |
| Somerset | Southend | July 19 | | | 2-46 & 3-23 |
| Northants | Colchester | Aug 16 | | | 3-46 & 3-54 |
| Yorkshire | Colchester | Aug 20 | | 0 * | 1-52 |
| Lancashire | Old Trafford | Aug 23 | | | 1-14 |
| Derbyshire | Chelmsford | Sept 3 | | | 0-30 & 0-57 |
| Leicestershire | Leicester | Sept 10 | 2 | | 1Ct | 0-21 & 2-53 |

## OTHER FIRST-CLASS

| | | | | | |
|---|---|---|---|---|---|
| Cambridge U | Fenner's | April 19 | | | 2-5 & 1-21 |
| West Indies | Chelmsford | Aug 3 | 4 | 2Ct | 1-76 & 2-56 |
| Victoria | Chelmsford | Sept 23 | | | 2-25 & 3-7 |

## REFUGE ASSURANCE

| | | | | | |
|---|---|---|---|---|---|
| Yorkshire | Chelmsford | April 28 | | 1Ct | 0-29 |
| Notts | Trent Bridge | May 12 | 2 * | | 2-45 |
| Kent | Folkestone | May 19 | | | 2-22 |
| Surrey | The Oval | May 26 | 1 * | | 0-46 |
| Glamorgan | Pontypridd | June 2 | | | |
| Worcestershire | Ilford | June 9 | | | 0-38 |
| Hampshire | Chelmsford | June 16 | | | |
| Derbyshire | Chelmsford | June 30 | | | 4-30 |
| Warwickshire | Chelmsford | July 7 | | | 0-33 |
| Somerset | Southend | July 21 | | | 1-32 |
| Gloucs | Cheltenham | July 28 | | | 2-41 |
| Northants | Northampton | Aug 11 | 1 * | 1Ct | 1-67 |
| Middlesex | Colchester | Aug 18 | | | 1-40 |

## NATWEST TROPHY

| | | | | | |
|---|---|---|---|---|---|
| Devon | Exmouth | June 26 | | | 2-29 |
| Sussex | Hove | July 11 | | | 1-36 |
| Surrey | The Oval | July 31 | | 0 * | 2-37 |

## BENSON & HEDGES CUP

| | | | | | |
|---|---|---|---|---|---|
| Surrey | The Oval | April 23 | | | 2-52 |
| Warwickshire | Edgbaston | April 25 | | 1Ct | 0-47 |
| Middlesex | Chelmsford | May 2 | | | 1-34 |
| Somerset | Chelmsford | May 7 | | | 1-34 |
| Hampshire | Chelmsford | May 29 | 4 | | 0-40 |
| Worcestershire | Chelmsford | June 12 | 1 * | | 0-25 |

## OTHER ONE-DAY

For England A

| | | | | | |
|---|---|---|---|---|---|
| Sri Lanka | Old Trafford | Aug 14 | | 1Ct | 2-29 |
| Sri Lanka | Old Trafford | Aug 15 | | | 1-49 |

For Essex

| | | | | | |
|---|---|---|---|---|---|
| Durham | Scarborough | Aug 31 | | | 2-33 |
| Yorkshire | Scarburgh | Sept 2 | 0 * | 1Ct | 1-53 |
| Victoria | Chelmsford | Sept 22 | 0 | | 0-41 |

## BATTING AVERAGES - Including fielding

| | Matches | Inns | NO | Runs | HS | Avge | 100s | 50s | Ct | St |
|---|---|---|---|---|---|---|---|---|---|---|
| Britannic Assurance | 11 | 5 | 4 | 27 | 23 * | 27.00 | - | - | 1 | - |
| Other First-Class | 3 | 1 | 0 | 4 | 4 | 4.00 | - | - | 2 | - |
| ALL FIRST-CLASS | 14 | 6 | 4 | 31 | 23 * | 15.50 | - | - | 3 | - |
| Refuge Assurance | 13 | 3 | 3 | 4 | 2 * | - | - | - | 2 | - |
| NatWest Trophy | 3 | 1 | 1 | 0 | 0 * | - | - | - | - | - |
| Benson & Hedges Cup | 6 | 2 | 1 | 5 | 4 | 5.00 | - | - | 1 | - |
| Other One-Day | 5 | 2 | 1 | 0 | 0 * | 0.00 | - | - | 2 | - |
| ALL ONE-DAY | 27 | 8 | 6 | 9 | 4 | 4.50 | - | - | 5 | - |

## BOWLING AVERAGES

| | Overs | Mdns | Runs | Wkts | Avge | Best | 5wI | 10wM |
|---|---|---|---|---|---|---|---|---|
| Britannic Assurance | 290 | 75 | 743 | 23 | 32.30 | 3-23 | - | - |
| Other First-Class | 80.1 | 26 | 190 | 11 | 17.27 | 3-7 | - | - |
| ALL FIRST-CLASS | 370.1 | 101 | 933 | 34 | 27.44 | 3-7 | - | - |
| Refuge Assurance | 86 | 3 | 423 | 13 | 32.53 | 4-30 | - | - |
| NatWest Trophy | 36 | 2 | 102 | 5 | 20.40 | 2-29 | - | - |
| Benson & Hedges Cup | 58 | 4 | 232 | 4 | 58.00 | 2-52 | - | - |
| Other One-Day | 52 | 4 | 205 | 6 | 34.16 | 2-29 | - | - |

## S | PLAYER RECORDS

| | | | | | | |
|---|---|---|---|---|---|---|
| ALL ONE-DAY | 232 | 13 | 962 | 28 | 34.35 | 4-30 - |

---

## D.SURRIDGE - *Hertfordshire*

| Opposition | Venue | Date | Batting | Fielding | Bowling |
|---|---|---|---|---|---|
| **NATWEST TROPHY** | | | | | |
| Warwickshire | Edgbaston | July 11 | | | 0-15 |

**BATTING AVERAGES - Including fielding**

| | Matches | Inns | NO | Runs | HS | Avge | 100s | 50s | Ct | St |
|---|---|---|---|---|---|---|---|---|---|---|
| NatWest Trophy | 1 | 0 | 0 | 0 | 0 | - | - | - | - | - |
| ALL ONE-DAY | 1 | 0 | 0 | 0 | 0 | - | - | - | - | - |

**BOWLING AVERAGES**

| | Overs | Mdns | Runs | Wkts | Avge | Best | 5wI | 10wM |
|---|---|---|---|---|---|---|---|---|
| NatWest Trophy | 4 | 1 | 15 | 0 | - | - | - | |
| ALL ONE-DAY | 4 | 1 | 15 | 0 | - | - | - | |

---

## I.G.SWALLOW - *Somerset*

| Opposition | Venue | Date | Batting | Fielding | Bowling |
|---|---|---|---|---|---|
| **BRITANNIC ASSURANCE** | | | | | |
| Sussex | Taunton | April 27 | 4 | 1Ct | 3-43 |
| Glamorgan | Taunton | May 9 | 1 & 41* | | 1-47 & 1-62 |
| Leicestershire | Weston | Aug 2 | 13* | | 0-41 & 2-45 |
| Notts | Trent Bridge | Aug 16 | 8* | 2Ct | 1-67 & 0-49 |
| **REFUGE ASSURANCE** | | | | | |
| Sussex | Taunton | April 28 | 4* | | 0-16 |
| **BENSON & HEDGES CUP** | | | | | |
| Warwickshire | Edgbaston | May 2 | 3 | | 1-58 |
| Surrey | Taunton | May 4 | | 1Ct | 1-31 |
| Essex | Chelmsford | May 7 | 2 | | 0-22 |
| **OTHER ONE-DAY** | | | | | |
| For Yorkshiremen | | | | | |
| Yorkshire | Scarborough | Sept 7 | 2* | | 0-47 |

**BATTING AVERAGES - Including fielding**

| | Matches | Inns | NO | Runs | HS | Avge | 100s | 50s | Ct | St |
|---|---|---|---|---|---|---|---|---|---|---|
| Britannic Assurance | 4 | 5 | 3 | 67 | 41* | 33.50 | - | - | 3 | - |
| ALL FIRST-CLASS | 4 | 5 | 3 | 67 | 41* | 33.50 | - | - | 3 | - |
| Refuge Assurance | 1 | 1 | 1 | 4 | 4* | - | - | - | - | - |
| Benson & Hedges Cup | 3 | 2 | 0 | 5 | 3 | 2.50 | - | - | 1 | - |
| Other One-Day | 1 | 1 | 1 | 2 | 2* | - | - | - | - | - |
| ALL ONE-DAY | 5 | 4 | 2 | 11 | 4* | 5.50 | - | - | 1 | - |

**BOWLING AVERAGES**

| | Overs | Mdns | Runs | Wkts | Avge | Best | 5wI | 10wM |
|---|---|---|---|---|---|---|---|---|
| Britannic Assurance | 100.1 | 16 | 354 | 8 | 44.25 | 3-43 | - | - |
| ALL FIRST-CLASS | 100.1 | 16 | 354 | 8 | 44.25 | 3-43 | - | - |
| Refuge Assurance | 3 | 0 | 16 | 0 | - | - | - | |
| Benson & Hedges Cup | 24 | 1 | 111 | 2 | 55.50 | 1-31 | - | |
| Other One-Day | 8 | 0 | 47 | 0 | - | - | - | |
| ALL ONE-DAY | 35 | 1 | 174 | 2 | 87.00 | 1-31 | - | |

---

## R.G.SWAN - *Scotland*

| Opposition | Venue | Date | Batting | Fielding | Bowling |
|---|---|---|---|---|---|
| **OTHER FIRST-CLASS** | | | | | |
| Ireland | Dublin | June 22 | 15 | 1Ct | |

---

| | | | | |
|---|---|---|---|---|
| **NATWEST TROPHY** | | | | |
| Sussex | Edinburgh | June 26 | 45 | |
| **BENSON & HEDGES CUP** | | | | |
| Leicestershire | Leicester | May 2 | 55 | |

**BATTING AVERAGES - Including fielding**

| | Matches | Inns | NO | Runs | HS | Avge | 100s | 50s | Ct | St |
|---|---|---|---|---|---|---|---|---|---|---|
| Other First-Class | 1 | 1 | 0 | 15 | 15 | 15.00 | - | - | 1 | - |
| ALL FIRST-CLASS | 1 | 1 | 0 | 15 | 15 | 15.00 | - | - | 1 | - |
| NatWest Trophy | 1 | 1 | 0 | 45 | 45 | 45.00 | - | - | - | - |
| Benson & Hedges Cup | 1 | 1 | 0 | 55 | 55 | 55.00 | - | 1 | - | - |
| ALL ONE-DAY | 2 | 2 | 0 | 100 | 55 | 50.00 | - | 1 | - | - |

**BOWLING AVERAGES**
Did not bowl

---

## R.SWANN - *Bedfordshire*

| Opposition | Venue | Date | Batting | Fielding | Bowling |
|---|---|---|---|---|---|
| **NATWEST TROPHY** | | | | | |
| Worcestershire | Bedford | June 26 | 7 | | 0-12 |

**BATTING AVERAGES - Including fielding**

| | Matches | Inns | NO | Runs | HS | Avge | 100s | 50s | Ct | St |
|---|---|---|---|---|---|---|---|---|---|---|
| NatWest Trophy | 1 | 1 | 0 | 7 | 7 | 7.00 | - | - | - | - |
| ALL ONE-DAY | 1 | 1 | 0 | 7 | 7 | 7.00 | - | - | - | - |

**BOWLING AVERAGES**

| | Overs | Mdns | Runs | Wkts | Avge | Best | 5wI | 10wM |
|---|---|---|---|---|---|---|---|---|
| NatWest Trophy | 4 | 0 | 12 | 0 | - | - | - | |
| ALL ONE-DAY | 4 | 0 | 12 | 0 | - | - | - | |

---

## S.A.SYLVESTER - *Middlesex*

| Opposition | Venue | Date | Batting | Fielding | Bowling |
|---|---|---|---|---|---|
| **BRITANNIC ASSURANCE** | | | | | |
| Glamorgan | Cardiff | June 14 | 0 | 1Ct | 0-80 & 0-18 |

**BATTING AVERAGES - Including fielding**

| | Matches | Inns | NO | Runs | HS | Avge | 100s | 50s | Ct | St |
|---|---|---|---|---|---|---|---|---|---|---|
| Britannic Assurance | 1 | 1 | 0 | 0 | 0 | 0.00 | - | - | 1 | - |
| ALL FIRST-CLASS | 1 | 1 | 0 | 0 | 0 | 0.00 | - | - | 1 | - |

**BOWLING AVERAGES**

| | Overs | Mdns | Runs | Wkts | Avge | Best | 5wI | 10wM |
|---|---|---|---|---|---|---|---|---|
| Britannic Assurance | 20 | 2 | 98 | 0 | - | - | - | - |
| ALL FIRST-CLASS | 20 | 2 | 98 | 0 | - | - | - | - |

# PLAYER RECORDS

**T**

## C.J.TAVARE - *Somerset*

| Opposition | Venue | Date | Batting | | | Fielding | Bowling |
|---|---|---|---|---|---|---|---|
| **BRITANNIC ASSURANCE** | | | | | | | |
| Sussex | Taunton | April 27 | 25 | | | | |
| Glamorgan | Taunton | May 9 | 8 | & | 9 | 2Ct | |
| Derbyshire | Derby | May 22 | 13 | & | 26 | 4Ct | |
| Middlesex | Taunton | May 25 | 22 | & | 18 | | |
| Glamorgan | Swansea | June 4 | 162 | | | 3Ct | |
| Warwickshire | Edgbaston | June 7 | | | 13 * | | |
| Hampshire | Bath | June 18 | 49 * & | | 27 | | |
| Gloucs | Bath | June 21 | 4 | | | 1Ct | |
| Surrey | The Oval | June 28 | 18 | | | | |
| Lancashire | Taunton | July 2 | | | 50 | | |
| Sussex | Hove | July 16 | 134 | | | | |
| Essex | Southend | July 19 | 0 | & | 20 | 1Ct | |
| Northants | Northampton | July 23 | 65 * | | | | |
| Kent | Taunton | July 26 | 72 | & | 100 | 1Ct | |
| Leicestershire | Weston | Aug 2 | 17 | & | 20 * | | |
| Worcestershire | Weston | Aug 6 | 10 | & | 11 | 2Ct | |
| Notts | Trent Bridge | Aug 16 | 47 | & | 50 | | |
| Yorkshire | Taunton | Aug 23 | 27 | & | 18 | 2Ct | |
| Hampshire | Southampton | Aug 28 | 66 | & | 15 * | 1Ct | |
| Worcestershire | Worcester | Sept 3 | 39 * & | | 59 | | |
| Gloucs | Bristol | Sept 10 | 183 | | | 2Ct | |
| Warwickshire | Taunton | Sept 17 | 0 | & | 85 | 1Ct | |
| **OTHER FIRST-CLASS** | | | | | | | |
| West Indies | Taunton | May 29 | 10 | & | 109 * | | |
| **REFUGE ASSURANCE** | | | | | | | |
| Surrey | The Oval | April 21 | 0 | | | 1Ct | |
| Sussex | Taunton | April 28 | 15 | | | | |
| Glamorgan | Taunton | May 12 | 46 | | | 1Ct | |
| Hampshire | Bournemouth | May 19 | 75 * | | | 1Ct | |
| Middlesex | Taunton | May 26 | 65 | | | | |
| Warwickshire | Edgbaston | June 2 | 59 | | | | |
| Notts | Trent Bridge | June 9 | 16 | | | 1Ct | |
| Derbyshire | Derby | June 16 | 3 | | | 1Ct | |
| Northants | Luton | June 30 | 23 | | | | |
| Lancashire | Taunton | July 5 | 57 | | | 1Ct | |
| Essex | Southend | July 21 | 34 | | | | |
| Kent | Taunton | July 28 | 19 | | | 1Ct | |
| Leicestershire | Weston | Aug 4 | 41 | | | | |
| Worcestershire | Worcester | Aug 18 | 24 | | | | |
| Yorkshire | Taunton | Aug 25 | 65 * | | | | |
| **NATWEST TROPHY** | | | | | | | |
| Bucks | Bath | June 26 | 25 | | | | |
| Middlesex | Taunton | July 11 | 59 | | | | |
| Warwickshire | Edgbaston | July 31 | 43 | | | 3Ct | |
| **BENSON & HEDGES CUP** | | | | | | | |
| Middlesex | Taunton | April 23 | 1 | | | | |
| Warwickshire | Edgbaston | May 2 | 53 | | | | |
| Surrey | Taunton | May 4 | 39 | | | 2Ct | |
| Essex | Chelmsford | May 7 | 46 | | | | |

**BATTING AVERAGES - Including fielding**

| | Matches | Inns | NO | Runs | HS | Avge | 100s | 50s | Ct | St |
|---|---|---|---|---|---|---|---|---|---|---|
| Britannic Assurance | 22 | 35 | 6 | 1482 | 183 | 51.10 | 4 | 7 | 20 | - |
| Other First-Class | 1 | 2 | 1 | 119 | 109 * | 119.00 | 1 | - | - | - |
| ALL FIRST-CLASS | 23 | 37 | 7 | 1601 | 183 | 53.36 | 5 | 7 | 20 | - |
| Refuge Assurance | 15 | 15 | 2 | 542 | 75 * | 41.69 | - | 5 | 7 | - |
| NatWest Trophy | 3 | 3 | 0 | 127 | 59 | 42.33 | - | 1 | 3 | - |
| Benson & Hedges Cup | 4 | 4 | 0 | 139 | 53 | 34.75 | - | 1 | 2 | - |
| ALL ONE-DAY | 22 | 22 | 2 | 808 | 75 * | 40.40 | - | 7 | 12 | - |

**BOWLING AVERAGES**
Did not bowl

## C.W.TAYLOR - *Middlesex*

| Opposition | Venue | Date | Batting | | | Fielding | Bowling |
|---|---|---|---|---|---|---|---|
| **BRITANNIC ASSURANCE** | | | | | | | |
| Yorkshire | Lord's | April 27 | | | | | 1-57 |
| Kent | Lord's | May 31 | 21 | | | | 3-35 & 3-61 |
| Gloucs | Bristol | June 4 | 11 | | | 1Ct | 0-15 & 1-1 |
| Leicestershire | Uxbridge | June 7 | | | | | 2-84 |
| Warwickshire | Edgbaston | July 2 | 4 | & | 12 | | 2-44 & 3-43 |
| Hampshire | Lord's | Aug 2 | 11 | | | 1Ct | 2-65 & 0-20 |
| Derbyshire | Lord's | Aug 9 | | | | | 1-55 |
| **REFUGE ASSURANCE** | | | | | | | |
| Gloucs | Bristol | April 21 | | | | 1Ct | 1-20 |
| Surrey | Lord's | April 28 | | | | | 1-50 |
| Yorkshire | Lord's | July 7 | | | | 1Ct | 0-37 |
| Hampshire | Lord's | Aug 4 | | | | 1Ct | 1-14 |
| Essex | Colchester | Aug 18 | 3 | | | 1Ct | 0-32 |

**BATTING AVERAGES - Including fielding**

| | Matches | Inns | NO | Runs | HS | Avge | 100s | 50s | Ct | St |
|---|---|---|---|---|---|---|---|---|---|---|
| Britannic Assurance | 7 | 5 | 0 | 59 | 21 | 11.80 | - | - | 2 | - |
| ALL FIRST-CLASS | 7 | 5 | 0 | 59 | 21 | 11.80 | - | - | 2 | - |
| Refuge Assurance | 5 | 1 | 0 | 3 | 3 | 3.00 | - | - | 4 | - |
| ALL ONE-DAY | 5 | 1 | 0 | 3 | 3 | 3.00 | - | - | 4 | - |

**BOWLING AVERAGES**

| | Overs | Mdns | Runs | Wkts | Avge | Best | 5wI | 10wM |
|---|---|---|---|---|---|---|---|---|
| Britannic Assurance | 147 | 29 | 480 | 18 | 26.66 | 3-35 | - | - |
| ALL FIRST-CLASS | 147 | 29 | 480 | 18 | 26.66 | 3-35 | - | - |
| Refuge Assurance | 27.2 | 0 | 153 | 3 | 51.00 | 1-14 | - | |
| ALL ONE-DAY | 27.2 | 0 | 153 | 3 | 51.00 | 1-14 | - | |

## J.P.TAYLOR - *Northamptonshire*

| Opposition | Venue | Date | Batting | | | Fielding | Bowling |
|---|---|---|---|---|---|---|---|
| **BRITANNIC ASSURANCE** | | | | | | | |
| Derbyshire | Derby | April 27 | | | | | |
| Essex | Northampton | May 9 | 5 * & | | 0 | 1Ct | 0-101 & 1-43 |
| Leicestershire | Northampton | May 16 | | | 3 | | 3-72 & 5-42 |
| Glamorgan | Cardiff | May 22 | 2 | | | | 1-37 & 0-49 |
| Hampshire | Northampton | June 21 | 3 | | | | 1-27 |
| Gloucs | Luton | June 28 | 0 | | | 1Ct | 3-31 & 0-37 |
| Kent | Maidstone | July 2 | | | 0 * | 1Ct | 2-37 & 0-54 |
| Leicestershire | Leicester | July 5 | | | | | 2-37 & 0-54 |
| Notts | Well'borough | July 19 | 4 | & | 2 | | 2-68 |
| Sussex | Eastbourne | Aug 2 | 3 * & | | 0 * | 1Ct | 0-37 & 1-33 |
| Lancashire | Lytham | Aug 6 | | | | | 1-33 & 1-54 |
| **OTHER FIRST-CLASS** | | | | | | | |
| Cambridge U | Fenner's | April 16 | | | | | 3-56 |
| West Indies | Northampton | June 15 | | | | | 0-36 |
| **REFUGE ASSURANCE** | | | | | | | |
| Glamorgan | Cardiff | April 21 | 2 * | | | | 2-27 |
| Lancashire | Old Trafford | April 28 | | | | | 2-27 |
| Leicestershire | Northampton | May 12 | | | | | 1-32 |
| Worcestershire | Northampton | May 19 | 5 | | | | 0-48 |
| Somerset | Luton | June 30 | | | | 1Ct | 0-22 |
| Surrey | Tring | July 7 | 16 | | | | 2-18 |
| Notts | Well'borough | July 21 | 1 * | | | | 2-45 |
| Derbyshire | Derby | July 28 | 0 | | | | 2-24 |
| Sussex | Eastbourne | Aug 4 | | | | | 2-25 |
| Essex | Northampton | Aug 11 | | | | | 2-33 |
| **NATWEST TROPHY** | | | | | | | |
| Staffordshire | Stone | June 26 | | | | | 2-11 |
| Leicestershire | Northampton | July 11 | | | | | 2-50 |
| Glamorgan | Northampton | July 31 | | | | 1Ct | 2-34 |
| Surrey | The Oval | Aug 14 | 3 * | | | | 2-37 |

| **T** | **PLAYER RECORDS** |

**BENSON & HEDGES CUP**

| | | | | | |
|---|---|---|---|---|---|
| Derbyshire | Derby | April 23 | | | 1-14 |
| Gloucs | Bristol | May 2 | 1* | 1Ct | 1-25 |
| Combined U | Northampton | May 4 | | | 0-37 |
| Worcestershire | Northampton | May 7 | 1* | | 2-30 |

**BATTING AVERAGES - Including fielding**

| | Matches | Inns | NO | Runs | HS | Avge | 100s | 50s | Ct | St |
|---|---|---|---|---|---|---|---|---|---|---|
| Britannic Assurance | 11 | 11 | 4 | 22 | 5* | 3.14 | - | - | 4 | - |
| Other First-Class | 2 | 0 | 0 | 0 | 0 | - | - | - | - | - |
| ALL FIRST-CLASS | 13 | 11 | 4 | 22 | 5* | 3.14 | - | - | 4 | - |
| Refuge Assurance | 10 | 5 | 2 | 24 | 16 | 8.00 | - | - | 1 | - |
| NatWest Trophy | 4 | 1 | 1 | 3 | 3* | - | - | - | 1 | - |
| Benson & Hedges Cup | 4 | 2 | 2 | 2 | 1* | - | - | - | 1 | - |
| ALL ONE-DAY | 18 | 8 | 5 | 29 | 16 | 9.66 | - | - | 3 | - |

**BOWLING AVERAGES**

| | Overs | Mdns | Runs | Wkts | Avge | Best | 5wI | 10wM |
|---|---|---|---|---|---|---|---|---|
| Britannic Assurance | 267.2 | 45 | 828 | 24 | 34.50 | 5-42 | 1 | - |
| Other First-Class | 28 | 5 | 92 | 3 | 30.66 | 3-56 | - | - |
| ALL FIRST-CLASS | 295.2 | 50 | 920 | 27 | 34.07 | 5-42 | 1 | - |
| Refuge Assurance | 74 | 7 | 301 | 15 | 20.06 | 2-18 | - | |
| NatWest Trophy | 42 | 6 | 132 | 8 | 16.50 | 2-11 | - | |
| Benson & Hedges Cup | 42 | 9 | 106 | 4 | 26.50 | 2-30 | - | |
| ALL ONE-DAY | 158 | 22 | 539 | 27 | 19.96 | 2-11 | - | |

# N.R.TAYLOR - *Kent*

| Opposition | Venue | Date | Batting | Fielding | Bowling |
|---|---|---|---|---|---|

**BRITANNIC ASSURANCE**

| | | | | | |
|---|---|---|---|---|---|
| Hampshire | Southampton | April 27 | 3 | 1Ct | |
| Surrey | The Oval | May 9 | 8 | 1Ct | |
| Essex | Folkestone | May 16 | 26 & 4 | | |
| Notts | Trent Bridge | May 22 | 45 & 0 | 3Ct | |
| Derbyshire | Canterbury | May 25 | 24 & 146 | | |
| Middlesex | Lord's | May 31 | 46 & 64 | 1Ct | |
| Warwickshire | Tunbridge W | June 4 | 4 | | |
| Sussex | Tunbridge W | June 7 | 52 & 58 | 1Ct | 0-26 |
| Yorkshire | Harrogate | June 14 | | 1Ct | |
| Lancashire | Old Trafford | June 21 | 33 | | |
| Northants | Maidstone | July 2 | 18 & 26 | 2Ct | |
| Glamorgan | Maidstone | July 5 | 77 | | |
| Essex | Southend | July 16 | 50 | 1Ct | |
| Worcestershire | Worcester | July 23 | | | |
| Somerset | Taunton | July 26 | 0 & 23 | 1Ct | |
| Surrey | Canterbury | Aug 2 | 5 & 35 | 1Ct | |
| Hampshire | Canterbury | Aug 6 | 24 & 59* | 1Ct | |
| Leicestershire | Leicester | Aug 9 | 18 & 150 | | |
| Gloucs | Canterbury | Aug 20 | 17* & 109 | | |
| Middlesex | Canterbury | Aug 28 | 17 & 101 | | |
| Sussex | Hove | Sept 3 | 111 & 203* | | |
| Leicestershire | Canterbury | Sept 17 | 59 & 32 | | |

**OTHER FIRST-CLASS**

| | | | | | |
|---|---|---|---|---|---|
| West Indies | Canterbury | July 20 | 138* & 21 | | |

**REFUGE ASSURANCE**

| | | | | | |
|---|---|---|---|---|---|
| Worcestershire | Worcester | April 21 | 62 | | |
| Hampshire | Southampton | May 12 | 2 | | |
| Essex | Folkestone | May 19 | 4 | | |
| Derbyshire | Canterbury | May 26 | 56 | | |
| Middlesex | Southgate | June 2 | 66 | | |
| Yorkshire | Scarborough | June 16 | 41 | | |
| Lancashire | Old Trafford | June 23 | 10 | | |
| Gloucs | Canterbury | June 30 | 39 | | |
| Glamorgan | Maidstone | July 7 | 82* | | |
| Leicestershire | Canterbury | July 14 | 0 | | |
| Somerset | Taunton | July 28 | 36 | | |
| Surrey | Canterbury | Aug 4 | 29 | 1Ct | |
| Notts | Trent Bridge | Aug 11 | 38 | | |
| Northants | Canterbury | Aug 18 | 2 | | |

**NATWEST TROPHY**

| | | | | | |
|---|---|---|---|---|---|
| Cambs | Canterbury | June 26 | 2 | | |
| Surrey | The Oval | July 11 | 44 | | |

**BENSON & HEDGES CUP**

| | | | | | |
|---|---|---|---|---|---|
| Leicestershire | Canterbury | April 23 | 1 | 2Ct | |
| Lancashire | Old Trafford | April 25 | 9 | | |
| Sussex | Canterbury | May 2 | 21 | | |
| Scotland | Glasgow | May 7 | 110 | | |
| Worcestershire | Worcester | May 29 | 89* | | |

**BATTING AVERAGES - Including fielding**

| | Matches | Inns | NO | Runs | HS | Avge | 100s | 50s | Ct | St |
|---|---|---|---|---|---|---|---|---|---|---|
| Britannic Assurance | 22 | 34 | 3 | 1647 | 203* | 53.12 | 6 | 7 | 14 | - |
| Other First-Class | 1 | 2 | 1 | 159 | 138* | 159.00 | 1 | - | - | - |
| ALL FIRST-CLASS | 23 | 36 | 4 | 1806 | 203* | 56.43 | 7 | 7 | 14 | - |
| Refuge Assurance | 14 | 14 | 1 | 467 | 82* | 35.92 | - | 4 | 1 | - |
| NatWest Trophy | 2 | 2 | 0 | 46 | 44 | 23.00 | - | - | - | - |
| Benson & Hedges Cup | 5 | 5 | 1 | 230 | 110 | 57.50 | 1 | 1 | 2 | - |
| ALL ONE-DAY | 21 | 21 | 2 | 743 | 110 | 39.10 | 1 | 5 | 3 | - |

**BOWLING AVERAGES**

| | Overs | Mdns | Runs | Wkts | Avge | Best | 5wI | 10wM |
|---|---|---|---|---|---|---|---|---|
| Britannic Assurance | 3 | 0 | 26 | 0 | - | - | - | - |
| Other First-Class | | | | | | | | |
| ALL FIRST-CLASS | 3 | 0 | 26 | 0 | - | - | - | - |
| Refuge Assurance | | | | | | | | |
| NatWest Trophy | | | | | | | | |
| Benson & Hedges Cup | | | | | | | | |
| ALL ONE-DAY | | | | | | | | |

# N.R.TAYLOR - *Dorset & Minor Counties*

| Opposition | Venue | Date | Batting | Fielding | Bowling |
|---|---|---|---|---|---|

**NATWEST TROPHY**

| | | | | | |
|---|---|---|---|---|---|
| Lancashire | Bournemouth | June 26 | 10 | | 2-25 |

**BENSON & HEDGES CUP**
For Minor Counties

| | | | | | |
|---|---|---|---|---|---|
| Glamorgan | Trowbridge | April 23 | 1* | | 2-33 |
| Hampshire | Trowbridge | April 25 | | | 0-41 |
| Yorkshire | Headingley | May 2 | | | 0-36 |
| Notts | Trent Bridge | May 7 | | | 1-63 |

**BATTING AVERAGES - Including fielding**

| | Matches | Inns | NO | Runs | HS | Avge | 100s | 50s | Ct | St |
|---|---|---|---|---|---|---|---|---|---|---|
| NatWest Trophy | 1 | 1 | 0 | 10 | 10 | 10.00 | - | - | - | - |
| Benson & Hedges Cup | 4 | 1 | 1 | 1 | 1* | - | - | - | - | - |
| ALL ONE-DAY | 5 | 2 | 1 | 11 | 10 | 11.00 | - | - | - | - |

**BOWLING AVERAGES**

| | Overs | Mdns | Runs | Wkts | Avge | Best | 5wI | 10wM |
|---|---|---|---|---|---|---|---|---|
| NatWest Trophy | 12 | 2 | 25 | 2 | 12.50 | 2-25 | - | |
| Benson & Hedges Cup | 41.2 | 10 | 173 | 3 | 57.66 | 2-33 | - | |
| ALL ONE-DAY | 53.2 | 12 | 198 | 5 | 39.60 | 2-25 | - | |

# S.R.TENDULKAR - *World XI & Rest of World*

| Opposition | Venue | Date | Batting | Fielding | Bowling |
|---|---|---|---|---|---|

**OTHER FIRST-CLASS**
For World XI

| | | | | | |
|---|---|---|---|---|---|
| West Indies XI | Scarborough | Aug 28 | 61 & 14 | | 0-20 & 0-15 |

**OTHER ONE-DAY**
For Rest of World

| | | | | | |
|---|---|---|---|---|---|
| England XI | Jesmond | July 31 | 54 | | |
| England XI | Jesmond | Aug 1 | 102 | | |

# PLAYER RECORDS

**T**

## BATTING AVERAGES - Including fielding

| | Matches | Inns | NO | Runs | HS | Avge | 100s | 50s | Ct | St |
|---|---|---|---|---|---|---|---|---|---|---|
| Other First-Class | 1 | 2 | 0 | 75 | 61 | 37.50 | - | 1 | - | - |
| ALL FIRST-CLASS | 1 | 2 | 0 | 75 | 61 | 37.50 | - | 1 | - | - |
| Other One-Day | 2 | 2 | 0 | 156 | 102 | 78.00 | 1 | 1 | - | - |
| ALL ONE-DAY | 2 | 2 | 0 | 156 | 102 | 78.00 | 1 | 1 | - | - |

## BOWLING AVERAGES

| | Overs | Mdns | Runs | Wkts | Avge | Best | 5wI | 10wM |
|---|---|---|---|---|---|---|---|---|
| Other First-Class | 4 | 0 | 35 | 0 | - | - | - | - |
| ALL FIRST-CLASS | 4 | 0 | 35 | 0 | - | - | - | - |
| Other One-Day | | | | | | | | |
| ALL ONE-DAY | | | | | | | | |

# L.TENNANT - *Leicestershire*

| Opposition | Venue | Date | Batting | Fielding | Bowling |
|---|---|---|---|---|---|
| **BRITANNIC ASSURANCE** | | | | | |
| Notts | Trent Bridge | May 9 | 13 & 8 | | 3-65 & 0-22 |
| Northants | Northampton | May 16 | 12 | | 0-24 & 0-9 |
| Notts | Leicester | May 25 | 12 & 8* | | 1-40 |
| Sussex | Hove | July 19 | 23* & 7 | | 0-54 |
| Warwickshire | Leicester | July 26 | 11* & 0 | | 1-82 |
| **OTHER FIRST-CLASS** | | | | | |
| Cambridge U | Fenner's | May 22 | | | 4-54 & 3-43 |
| **REFUGE ASSURANCE** | | | | | |
| Glamorgan | Leicester | April 28 | | | 0-30 |
| Sussex | Hove | July 21 | 0 | | 0-26 |

## BATTING AVERAGES - Including fielding

| | Matches | Inns | NO | Runs | HS | Avge | 100s | 50s | Ct | St |
|---|---|---|---|---|---|---|---|---|---|---|
| Britannic Assurance | 5 | 9 | 3 | 94 | 23* | 15.66 | - | - | - | - |
| Other First-Class | 1 | 0 | 0 | 0 | 0 | - | - | - | - | - |
| ALL FIRST-CLASS | 6 | 9 | 3 | 94 | 23* | 15.66 | - | - | - | - |
| Refuge Assurance | 2 | 1 | 0 | 0 | 0 | 0.00 | - | - | - | - |
| ALL ONE-DAY | 2 | 1 | 0 | 0 | 0 | 0.00 | - | - | - | - |

## BOWLING AVERAGES

| | Overs | Mdns | Runs | Wkts | Avge | Best | 5wI | 10wM |
|---|---|---|---|---|---|---|---|---|
| Britannic Assurance | 69 | 12 | 296 | 5 | 59.20 | 3-65 | - | - |
| Other First-Class | 30 | 8 | 97 | 7 | 13.85 | 4-54 | - | - |
| ALL FIRST-CLASS | 99 | 20 | 393 | 12 | 32.75 | 4-54 | - | - |
| Refuge Assurance | 9 | 0 | 56 | 0 | - | - | - | - |
| ALL ONE-DAY | 9 | 0 | 56 | 0 | - | - | - | - |

# V.P.TERRY - *Hampshire*

| Opposition | Venue | Date | Batting | Fielding | Bowling |
|---|---|---|---|---|---|
| **BRITANNIC ASSURANCE** | | | | | |
| Gloucs | Bristol | May 9 | 18 & 5 | 1Ct | |
| Sussex | Hove | May 16 | 171 & 55 | 2Ct | |
| Surrey | Bournemouth | May 25 | 8 & 17 | 1Ct | |
| Lancashire | Basingstoke | June 4 | 52 | 1Ct | |
| Gloucs | Southampton | June 7 | 19 | | |
| Somerset | Bath | June 18 | 43 & 10* | 1Ct | |
| Northants | Northampton | June 21 | 22 | 1Ct | |
| Essex | Chelmsford | July 2 | 14 & 12 | 2Ct | |
| Yorkshire | Southampton | July 5 | 13 & 6* | | |
| Worcestershire | Portsmouth | July 16 | 87 | 3Ct | |
| Warwickshire | Portsmouth | July 19 | 124 & 18 | 2Ct | |
| Middlesex | Lord's | Aug 2 | 25 & 39 | 1Ct | |
| Kent | Canterbury | Aug 6 | 26 & 7 | 1Ct | |
| Leicestershire | Bournemouth | Aug 16 | 10 & 79 | | |
| Sussex | Bournemouth | Aug 20 | 4 & 42 | 3Ct | |
| Somerset | Southampton | Aug 28 | 86 & 31 | | |
| Surrey | The Oval | Sept 3 | 30 & 2 | 4Ct | |
| Glamorgan | Southampton | Sept 17 | 81 & 70 | | |
| **OTHER FIRST-CLASS** | | | | | |
| Oxford U | The Parks | April 13 | 4* | 1Ct | |
| West Indies | Southampton | June 29 | 12 & 2 | | |
| **REFUGE ASSURANCE** | | | | | |
| Derbyshire | Derby | May 5 | 5 | | |
| Kent | Southampton | May 12 | 1 | 1Ct | |
| Somerset | Bournemouth | May 19 | 6 | | |
| Gloucs | Swindon | May 26 | 123 | | |
| Northants | Northampton | June 2 | 14 | | |
| Sussex | Basingstoke | June 9 | 42 | 1Ct | |
| Essex | Chelmsford | June 16 | | | |
| Worcestershire | Southampton | July 7 | 42* | | |
| Notts | Trent Bridge | July 14 | 61 | 1Ct | |
| Warwickshire | Portsmouth | July 21 | 27 | | |
| Lancashire | Southampton | July 28 | 1 | 1Ct | |
| Middlesex | Lord's | Aug 4 | 34 | | |
| Glamorgan | Ebbw Vale | Aug 11 | 24 | | |
| Leicestershire | Bournemouth | Aug 18 | 20 | 1Ct | |
| Surrey | The Oval | Aug 25 | 8 | | |
| **NATWEST TROPHY** | | | | | |
| Berkshire | Reading | June 26 | 42* | | |
| Lancashire | Southampton | July 11 | 47 | 1Ct | |
| Notts | Southampton | July 31 | 26 | 1Ct | |
| Warwickshire | Edgbaston | Aug 14 | 62* | 2Ct | |
| Surrey | Lord's | Sept 7 | 32 | | |
| **BENSON & HEDGES CUP** | | | | | |
| Essex | Chelmsford | May 29 | 10 | | |

## BATTING AVERAGES - Including fielding

| | Matches | Inns | NO | Runs | HS | Avge | 100s | 50s | Ct | St |
|---|---|---|---|---|---|---|---|---|---|---|
| Britannic Assurance | 18 | 32 | 2 | 1226 | 171 | 40.86 | 2 | 7 | 23 | - |
| Other First-Class | 2 | 3 | 1 | 18 | 12 | 9.00 | - | - | 1 | - |
| ALL FIRST-CLASS | 20 | 35 | 3 | 1244 | 171 | 38.87 | 2 | 7 | 24 | - |
| Refuge Assurance | 15 | 14 | 1 | 408 | 123 | 31.38 | 1 | 1 | 5 | - |
| NatWest Trophy | 5 | 5 | 2 | 209 | 62* | 69.66 | - | 1 | 4 | - |
| Benson & Hedges Cup | 1 | 1 | 0 | 10 | 10 | 10.00 | - | - | - | - |
| ALL ONE-DAY | 21 | 20 | 3 | 627 | 123 | 36.88 | 1 | 2 | 9 | - |

## BOWLING AVERAGES
Did not bowl

# D.R.THOMAS - *Norfolk & Minor Counties*

| Opposition | Venue | Date | Batting | Fielding | Bowling |
|---|---|---|---|---|---|
| **NATWEST TROPHY** | | | | | |
| Gloucs | Bristol | June 26 | 2 | | 1-58 |
| **BENSON & HEDGES CUP** | | | | | |
| For Minor Counties | | | | | |
| Yorkshire | Headingley | May 2 | 6 | | 0-49 |
| Notts | Trent Bridge | May 7 | 0 | | 1-61 |

## BATTING AVERAGES - Including fielding

| | Matches | Inns | NO | Runs | HS | Avge | 100s | 50s | Ct | St |
|---|---|---|---|---|---|---|---|---|---|---|
| NatWest Trophy | 1 | 1 | 0 | 2 | 2 | 2.00 | - | - | - | - |
| Benson & Hedges Cup | 2 | 2 | 0 | 6 | 6 | 3.00 | - | - | - | - |
| ALL ONE-DAY | 3 | 3 | 0 | 8 | 6 | 2.66 | - | - | - | - |

## BOWLING AVERAGES

| | Overs | Mdns | Runs | Wkts | Avge | Best | 5wI | 10wM |
|---|---|---|---|---|---|---|---|---|
| NatWest Trophy | 12 | 0 | 58 | 1 | 58.00 | 1-58 | - | |
| Benson & Hedges Cup | 22 | 1 | 110 | 1 | 110.00 | 1-61 | - | |
| ALL ONE-DAY | 34 | 1 | 168 | 2 | 84.00 | 1-58 | - | |

# T
# PLAYER RECORDS

## J.G.THOMAS - *Northamptonshire*

| Opposition | Venue | Date | Batting | Fielding | Bowling |
|---|---|---|---|---|---|
| **BRITANNIC ASSURANCE** | | | | | |
| Derbyshire | Derby | April 27 | | | |
| Essex | Northampton | May 9 | 43 & 11 | | 5-146 & 1-25 |
| Leicestershire | Northampton | May 16 | 36 * | | 5-62 & 0-44 |
| Glamorgan | Cardiff | May 22 | 2 & 0 | 1Ct | 0-61 & 0-44 |
| Yorkshire | Headingley | May 25 | 0 | 1Ct | 3-48 & 0-9 |
| Derbyshire | Northampton | May 31 | 64 & 9 | | 4-62 & 0-44 |
| Hampshire | Northampton | June 21 | 8 | 1Ct | 0-37 |
| Kent | Maidstone | July 2 | 10 | | 2-35 & 0-38 |
| Leicestershire | Leicester | July 5 | 22 * | | 3-21 & 1-64 |
| Somerset | Northampton | July 23 | 1 * | | 0-89 |
| **OTHER FIRST-CLASS** | | | | | |
| Cambridge U | Fenner's | April 16 | | | 2-21 |
| West Indies | Northampton | June 15 | | | 2-87 |
| **REFUGE ASSURANCE** | | | | | |
| Glamorgan | Cardiff | April 21 | 5 | 1Ct | 0-27 |
| Lancashire | Old Trafford | April 28 | | | 1-47 |
| Leicestershire | Northampton | May 12 | | 1Ct | 1-42 |
| Worcestershire | Northampton | May 19 | 34 | | 1-36 |
| Yorkshire | Headingley | May 26 | 30 * | | 1-37 |
| Hampshire | Northampton | June 2 | | | 2-20 |
| Gloucs | Moreton | June 9 | | | |
| **BENSON & HEDGES CUP** | | | | | |
| Derbyshire | Derby | April 23 | 4 * | | 5-29 |
| Gloucs | Bristol | May 2 | 3 | | 1-22 |
| Combined U | Northampton | May 4 | | | 1-30 |
| Worcestershire | Northampton | May 7 | 3 | | 0-38 |
| Lancashire | Old Trafford | May 29 | 9 | | 2-54 |

### BATTING AVERAGES - Including fielding

| | Matches | Inns | NO | Runs | HS | Avge | 100s | 50s | Ct | St |
|---|---|---|---|---|---|---|---|---|---|---|
| Britannic Assurance | 10 | 12 | 3 | 206 | 64 | 22.88 | - | 1 | 3 | - |
| Other First-Class | 2 | 0 | 0 | 0 | 0 | | - | - | - | - |
| ALL FIRST-CLASS | 12 | 12 | 3 | 206 | 64 | 22.88 | - | 1 | 3 | - |
| Refuge Assurance | 7 | 3 | 1 | 69 | 34 | 34.50 | - | - | 2 | - |
| Benson & Hedges Cup | 5 | 4 | 1 | 19 | 9 | 6.33 | - | - | - | - |
| ALL ONE-DAY | 12 | 7 | 2 | 88 | 34 | 17.60 | - | - | 2 | - |

### BOWLING AVERAGES

| | Overs | Mdns | Runs | Wkts | Avge | Best | 5wI | 10wM |
|---|---|---|---|---|---|---|---|---|
| Britannic Assurance | 248.4 | 34 | 829 | 24 | 34.54 | 5-62 | 2 | - |
| Other First-Class | 30 | 6 | 108 | 4 | 27.00 | 2-21 | - | - |
| ALL FIRST-CLASS | 278.4 | 40 | 937 | 28 | 33.46 | 5-62 | 2 | - |
| Refuge Assurance | 39 | 0 | 209 | 6 | 34.83 | 2-20 | - | - |
| Benson & Hedges Cup | 49.3 | 5 | 173 | 9 | 19.22 | 5-29 | 1 | |
| ALL ONE-DAY | 88.3 | 5 | 382 | 15 | 25.46 | 5-29 | 1 | |

## K.O.THOMAS - *Cambridgeshire*

| Opposition | Venue | Date | Batting | Fielding | Bowling |
|---|---|---|---|---|---|
| **NATWEST TROPHY** | | | | | |
| Kent | Canterbury | June 26 | 2 | | 0-22 |

### BATTING AVERAGES - Including fielding

| | Matches | Inns | NO | Runs | HS | Avge | 100s | 50s | Ct | St |
|---|---|---|---|---|---|---|---|---|---|---|
| NatWest Trophy | 1 | 1 | 0 | 2 | 2 | 2.00 | - | - | - | - |
| ALL ONE-DAY | 1 | 1 | 0 | 2 | 2 | 2.00 | - | - | - | - |

### BOWLING AVERAGES

| | Overs | Mdns | Runs | Wkts | Avge | Best | 5wI | 10wM |
|---|---|---|---|---|---|---|---|---|
| NatWest Trophy | 4 | 0 | 22 | 0 | | | | |
| ALL ONE-DAY | 4 | 0 | 22 | 0 | - | - | - | - |

## P.D.THOMAS - *Bedfordshire*

| Opposition | Venue | Date | Batting | Fielding | Bowling |
|---|---|---|---|---|---|
| **NATWEST TROPHY** | | | | | |
| Worcestershire | Bedford | June 26 | 4 | | |

### BATTING AVERAGES - Including fielding

| | Matches | Inns | NO | Runs | HS | Avge | 100s | 50s | Ct | St |
|---|---|---|---|---|---|---|---|---|---|---|
| NatWest Trophy | 1 | 1 | 0 | 4 | 4 | 4.00 | - | - | - | - |
| ALL ONE-DAY | 1 | 1 | 0 | 4 | 4 | 4.00 | - | - | - | - |

### BOWLING AVERAGES
Did not bowl

## N.E.THOMPSON - *Ireland*

| Opposition | Venue | Date | Batting | Fielding | Bowling |
|---|---|---|---|---|---|
| **OTHER FIRST-CLASS** | | | | | |
| Scotland | Dublin | June 22 | 21 * & 0 | | 0-52 & 0-15 |
| **NATWEST TROPHY** | | | | | |
| Middlesex | Dublin | June 26 | 14 | | 1-30 |
| **OTHER ONE-DAY** | | | | | |
| West Indies | Downpatrick | July 13 | | 1Ct | 0-74 |

### BATTING AVERAGES - Including fielding

| | Matches | Inns | NO | Runs | HS | Avge | 100s | 50s | Ct | St |
|---|---|---|---|---|---|---|---|---|---|---|
| Other First-Class | 1 | 2 | 1 | 21 | 21 * | 21.00 | - | - | - | - |
| ALL FIRST-CLASS | 1 | 2 | 1 | 21 | 21 * | 21.00 | - | - | - | - |
| NatWest Trophy | 1 | 1 | 0 | 14 | 14 | 14.00 | - | - | - | - |
| Other One-Day | 1 | 0 | 0 | 0 | 0 | | - | - | 1 | - |
| ALL ONE-DAY | 2 | 1 | 0 | 14 | 14 | 14.00 | - | - | 1 | - |

### BOWLING AVERAGES

| | Overs | Mdns | Runs | Wkts | Avge | Best | 5wI | 10wM |
|---|---|---|---|---|---|---|---|---|
| Other First-Class | 29.3 | 6 | 67 | 0 | - | - | - | - |
| ALL FIRST-CLASS | 29.3 | 6 | 67 | 0 | - | - | - | - |
| NatWest Trophy | 12 | 3 | 30 | 1 | 30.00 | 1-30 | | |
| Other One-Day | 12 | 1 | 74 | 0 | - | - | | |
| ALL ONE-DAY | 24 | 4 | 104 | 1 | 104.00 | 1-30 | | |

## G.P.THORPE - *Surrey*

| Opposition | Venue | Date | Batting | Fielding | Bowling |
|---|---|---|---|---|---|
| **BRITANNIC ASSURANCE** | | | | | |
| Essex | Chelmsford | April 27 | 0 | | 0-18 |
| Kent | The Oval | May 9 | 6 & 40 | 1Ct | |
| Hampshire | Bournemouth | May 25 | 25 & 58 | | 1-38 |
| Notts | The Oval | June 4 | 19 * | | |
| Leicestershire | Leicester | June 14 | 24 | | |
| Derbyshire | Derby | June 21 | 3 & 1 | | |
| Somerset | The Oval | June 28 | 2 | 2Ct | |
| Sussex | Arundel | July 2 | 56 * | | |
| Essex | The Oval | July 5 | 28 & 2 | 1Ct | 0-18 & 0-20 |
| Gloucs | Guildford | July 16 | 0 * & 33 | | 0-5 |
| Yorkshire | Guildford | July 19 | 22 | | 0-8 |
| Glamorgan | The Oval | July 26 | 74 * & 106 * | | 0-10 |
| Kent | Canterbury | Aug 2 | 7 & 25 | | 0-29 |
| Warwickshire | Edgbaston | Aug 6 | 6 & 17 | | |
| Worcestershire | Worcester | Aug 16 | 22 & 30 | 1Ct | |
| Middlesex | The Oval | Aug 20 | 0 & 40 | | |
| Northants | Northampton | Aug 23 | 51 * & 116 * | | |
| Sussex | The Oval | Aug 28 | 177 | 1Ct | 0-11 |
| Hampshire | The Oval | Sept 3 | 0 & 8 | | |
| Middlesex | Lord's | Sept 10 | 117 & 4 | 2Ct | |

# PLAYER RECORDS

| Lancashire | Old Trafford | Sept 17 | 11 & 34 | |
|---|---|---|---|---|

**OTHER FIRST-CLASS**
For MCC

| Middlesex | Lord's | April 16 | 37 * | | 2-48 |
|---|---|---|---|---|---|

For Surrey

| Cambridge U | Fenner's | May 18 | 1 * & 1 | | 1-37 |
|---|---|---|---|---|---|

**REFUGE ASSURANCE**

| Somerset | The Oval | April 21 | 8 | | 3-21 |
|---|---|---|---|---|---|
| Middlesex | Lord's | April 28 | 2 | | 0-16 |
| Gloucs | The Oval | May 12 | 47 | | 0-10 |
| Essex | The Oval | May 26 | 29 * | | 0-17 |
| Worcestershire | Worcester | June 2 | | | |
| Derbyshire | Chesterfield | June 9 | 1 | | |
| Leicestershire | Leicester | June 16 | 28 | | |
| Notts | The Oval | June 30 | 34 | | |
| Northants | Tring | July 7 | 50 | | 0-14 |
| Sussex | The Oval | July 14 | | 1Ct | |
| Yorkshire | The Oval | July 21 | 4 | | |
| Glamorgan | The Oval | July 28 | 58 | 1Ct | |
| Kent | Canterbury | Aug 4 | 54 | | |
| Lancashire | Old Trafford | Aug 18 | 115 * | | |
| Hampshire | The Oval | Aug 25 | 1 | | |

**NATWEST TROPHY**

| Kent | The Oval | July 11 | 20 * | | 0-0 |
|---|---|---|---|---|---|
| Essex | The Oval | July 31 | 2 | | |
| Northants | The Oval | Aug 14 | 23 | 1Ct | |
| Hampshire | Lord's | Sept 7 | 93 | | |

**BENSON & HEDGES CUP**

| Essex | The Oval | April 23 | 3 | | 0-16 |
|---|---|---|---|---|---|
| Middlesex | Lord's | April 25 | 40 | 1Ct | |
| Somerset | Taunton | May 4 | 41 | | 0-19 |
| Warwickshire | The Oval | May 7 | 28 | | |

**OTHER ONE-DAY**

| Warwickshire | Harrogate | June 12 | 44 | | 0-17 |
|---|---|---|---|---|---|
| Durham | Harrogate | June 13 | 21 | | |

**BATTING AVERAGES - Including fielding**

| | Matches | Inns | NO | Runs | HS | Avge | 100s | 50s | Ct | St |
|---|---|---|---|---|---|---|---|---|---|---|
| Britannic Assurance | 21 | 35 | 7 | 1164 | 177 | 41.57 | 4 | 4 | 8 | - |
| Other First-Class | 2 | 3 | 2 | 39 | 37 * | 39.00 | - | - | - | - |
| ALL FIRST-CLASS | 23 | 38 | 9 | 1203 | 177 | 41.48 | 4 | 4 | 8 | - |
| Refuge Assurance | 15 | 13 | 2 | 431 | 115 * | 39.18 | 1 | 3 | 2 | - |
| NatWest Trophy | 4 | 4 | 1 | 138 | 93 | 46.00 | - | 1 | 1 | - |
| Benson & Hedges Cup | 4 | 4 | 0 | 112 | 41 | 28.00 | - | - | 1 | - |
| Other One-Day | 2 | 2 | 0 | 65 | 44 | 32.50 | - | - | - | - |
| ALL ONE-DAY | 25 | 23 | 3 | 746 | 115 * | 37.30 | 1 | 4 | 4 | - |

**BOWLING AVERAGES**

| | Overs | Mdns | Runs | Wkts | Avge | Best | 5wI | 10wM |
|---|---|---|---|---|---|---|---|---|
| Britannic Assurance | 39 | 5 | 157 | 1 | 157.00 | 1-38 | - | - |
| Other First-Class | 25 | 5 | 85 | 3 | 28.33 | 2-48 | - | - |
| ALL FIRST-CLASS | 64 | 10 | 242 | 4 | 60.50 | 2-48 | - | - |
| Refuge Assurance | 12 | 0 | 78 | 3 | 26.00 | 3-21 | - | |
| NatWest Trophy | 0.1 | 0 | 0 | 0 | - | - | - | |
| Benson & Hedges Cup | 8 | 0 | 35 | 0 | - | - | - | |
| Other One-Day | 2 | 0 | 17 | 0 | - | - | - | |
| ALL ONE-DAY | 22.1 | 0 | 130 | 3 | 43.33 | 3-21 | - | |

# P.W.THRELFALL - *Sussex*

| Opposition | Venue | Date | Batting | Fielding | Bowling |
|---|---|---|---|---|---|

**OTHER FIRST-CLASS**

| Cambridge U | Hove | June 29 | | | 2-10 |
|---|---|---|---|---|---|

**BATTING AVERAGES - Including fielding**

| | Matches | Inns | NO | Runs | HS | Avge | 100s | 50s | Ct | St |
|---|---|---|---|---|---|---|---|---|---|---|
| Other First-Class | 1 | 0 | 0 | 0 | 0 | - | - | - | - | - |
| ALL FIRST-CLASS | 1 | 0 | 0 | 0 | 0 | - | - | - | - | - |

**BOWLING AVERAGES**

| | Overs | Mdns | Runs | Wkts | Avge | Best | 5wI | 10wM |
|---|---|---|---|---|---|---|---|---|
| Other First-Class | 4 | 1 | 10 | 2 | 5.00 | 2-10 | - | - |
| ALL FIRST-CLASS | 4 | 1 | 10 | 2 | 5.00 | 2-10 | - | - |

# G.E.THWAITES - *Cambridge University*

| Opposition | Venue | Date | Batting | Fielding | Bowling |
|---|---|---|---|---|---|

**OTHER FIRST-CLASS**

| Essex | Fenner's | April 19 | 19 & 6 | | |
|---|---|---|---|---|---|
| Derbyshire | Fenner's | May 9 | 32 | 1Ct | |
| Surrey | Fenner's | May 18 | 7 & 4 | 1Ct | |

**BATTING AVERAGES - Including fielding**

| | Matches | Inns | NO | Runs | HS | Avge | 100s | 50s | Ct | St |
|---|---|---|---|---|---|---|---|---|---|---|
| Other First-Class | 3 | 5 | 0 | 68 | 32 | 13.60 | - | - | 2 | - |
| ALL FIRST-CLASS | 3 | 5 | 0 | 68 | 32 | 13.60 | - | - | 2 | - |

**BOWLING AVERAGES**
Did not bowl

# J.K.TIERNEY - *Devon*

| Opposition | Venue | Date | Batting | Fielding | Bowling |
|---|---|---|---|---|---|

**NATWEST TROPHY**

| Essex | Exmouth | June 26 | 26 | | 0-23 |
|---|---|---|---|---|---|

**BATTING AVERAGES - Including fielding**

| | Matches | Inns | NO | Runs | HS | Avge | 100s | 50s | Ct | St |
|---|---|---|---|---|---|---|---|---|---|---|
| NatWest Trophy | 1 | 1 | 0 | 26 | 26 | 26.00 | - | - | - | - |
| ALL ONE-DAY | 1 | 1 | 0 | 26 | 26 | 26.00 | - | - | - | - |

**BOWLING AVERAGES**

| | Overs | Mdns | Runs | Wkts | Avge | Best | 5wI | 10wM |
|---|---|---|---|---|---|---|---|---|
| NatWest Trophy | 6 | 0 | 23 | 0 | - | - | - | - |
| ALL ONE-DAY | 6 | 0 | 23 | 0 | - | - | - | - |

# H.P.TILLEKARATNE - *Sri Lanka*

| Opposition | Venue | Date | Batting | Fielding | Bowling |
|---|---|---|---|---|---|

**CORNHILL TEST MATCHES**

| England | Lord's | Aug 22 | 20 & 16 | 1Ct | |
|---|---|---|---|---|---|

**OTHER FIRST-CLASS**

| Derbyshire | Derby | Aug 2 | | 2Ct | |
|---|---|---|---|---|---|
| Gloucs | Bristol | Aug 6 | 9 & 0 | 2Ct | |
| Somerset | Taunton | Aug 10 | | | |
| Sussex | Hove | Aug 17 | 30 & 80 * | 4Ct | |

**OTHER ONE-DAY**

| England A | Old Trafford | Aug 14 | 3 | 1Ct,1St | |
|---|---|---|---|---|---|
| England A | Old Trafford | Aug 15 | 5 | 1Ct,1St | 0-27 |

**BATTING AVERAGES - Including fielding**

| | Matches | Inns | NO | Runs | HS | Avge | 100s | 50s | Ct | St |
|---|---|---|---|---|---|---|---|---|---|---|
| Cornhill Test Matches | 1 | 2 | 0 | 36 | 20 | 18.00 | - | - | 1 | - |
| Other First-Class | 4 | 4 | 1 | 119 | 80 * | 39.66 | - | 1 | 8 | - |
| ALL FIRST-CLASS | 5 | 6 | 1 | 155 | 80 * | 31.00 | - | 1 | 9 | - |
| Other One-Day | 2 | 2 | 0 | 8 | 5 | 4.00 | - | - | 2 | 2 |
| ALL ONE-DAY | 2 | 2 | 0 | 8 | 5 | 4.00 | - | - | 2 | 2 |

**BOWLING AVERAGES**

| | Overs | Mdns | Runs | Wkts | Avge | Best | 5wI | 10wM |
|---|---|---|---|---|---|---|---|---|

# T | PLAYER RECORDS

| | | | | | | |
|---|---|---|---|---|---|---|
| Cornhill Test Matches | | | | | | |
| Other First-Class | | | | | | |
| ALL FIRST-CLASS | | | | | | |
| Other One-Day | 7 | 0 | 27 | 0 | - | - - |
| ALL ONE-DAY | 7 | 0 | 27 | 0 | - | - - |

| | | | | | | |
|---|---|---|---|---|---|---|
| Other First-Class | 56 | 18 | 121 | 7 | 17.28 | 4-69 - - |
| ALL FIRST-CLASS | 161 | 39 | 413 | 18 | 22.94 | 4-69 - - |
| Refuge Assurance | 14 | 0 | 107 | 2 | 53.50 | 1-23 - |
| ALL ONE-DAY | 14 | 0 | 107 | 2 | 53.50 | 1-23 - |

## S.P.TITCHARD - *Lancashire*

| Opposition | Venue | Date | Batting | Fielding | Bowling |
|---|---|---|---|---|---|
| **BRITANNIC ASSURANCE** | | | | | |
| Somerset | Taunton | July 2 | 53 & 0 | 3Ct | |
| Notts | Trent Bridge | July 16 | 46 & 23 | 1Ct | |
| Warwickshire | Old Trafford | July 23 | 15 * | 1Ct | |
| Gloucs | Bristol | Aug 9 | 20 & 20 | 1Ct | |
| Notts | Old Trafford | Aug 28 | 135 & 77 | | |
| Yorkshire | Scarborough | Sept 3 | 35 & 22 | 1Ct | |
| Surrey | Old Trafford | Sept 17 | 1 & 17 | | |
| **OTHER FIRST-CLASS** | | | | | |
| Oxford U | The Parks | June 7 | 39 & 43 | 1Ct | |
| **REFUGE ASSURANCE** | | | | | |
| Northants | Old Trafford | Sept 1 | 13 | | |

**BATTING AVERAGES - Including fielding**

| | Matches | Inns | NO | Runs | HS | Avge | 100s | 50s | Ct | St |
|---|---|---|---|---|---|---|---|---|---|---|
| Britannic Assurance | 7 | 13 | 1 | 464 | 135 | 38.66 | 1 | 2 | 7 | - |
| Other First-Class | 1 | 2 | 0 | 82 | 43 | 41.00 | - | - | 1 | - |
| ALL FIRST-CLASS | 8 | 15 | 1 | 546 | 135 | 39.00 | 1 | 2 | 8 | - |
| Refuge Assurance | 1 | 1 | 0 | 13 | 13 | 13.00 | - | - | - | - |
| ALL ONE-DAY | 1 | 1 | 0 | 13 | 13 | 13.00 | - | - | - | - |

**BOWLING AVERAGES**
Did not bowl

## C.M.TOLLEY - *Worcestershire*

| Opposition | Venue | Date | Batting | Fielding | Bowling |
|---|---|---|---|---|---|
| **BRITANNIC ASSURANCE** | | | | | |
| Lancashire | Worcester | May 9 | 18 * & 18 | | 1-45 |
| Lancashire | Blackpool | Aug 20 | 36 | | 2-30 & 2-27 |
| Middlesex | Worcester | Aug 23 | 14 | | 3-40 & 0-37 |
| Warwickshire | Edgbaston | Aug 28 | 7 & 1 | 1Ct | 1-14 & 1-21 |
| Somerset | Worcester | Sept 3 | 24 * | 1Ct | 0-19 |
| Glamorgan | Cardiff | Sept 10 | 15 & 4 * | | 1-29 & 0-30 |
| **OTHER FIRST-CLASS** | | | | | |
| Oxford U | The Parks | May 25 | 7 * | | 0-10 & 0-18 |
| Sri Lanka | Worcester | July 30 | | 1Ct | 4-69 & 3-24 |
| **REFUGE ASSURANCE** | | | | | |
| Leicestershire | Worcester | June 30 | | | 0-41 |
| Middlesex | Worcester | Aug 25 | | 1Ct | 0-11 |
| Notts | Trent Bridge | Sept 1 | | 1Ct | 1-23 |
| Lancashire | Old Trafford | Sept 15 | | | 1-32 |

**BATTING AVERAGES - Including fielding**

| | Matches | Inns | NO | Runs | HS | Avge | 100s | 50s | Ct | St |
|---|---|---|---|---|---|---|---|---|---|---|
| Britannic Assurance | 6 | 9 | 3 | 137 | 36 | 22.83 | - | - | 2 | - |
| Other First-Class | 2 | 1 | 1 | 7 | 7 * | - | - | - | 1 | - |
| ALL FIRST-CLASS | 8 | 10 | 4 | 144 | 36 | 24.00 | - | - | 3 | - |
| Refuge Assurance | 4 | 0 | 0 | 0 | 0 | - | - | - | 2 | - |
| ALL ONE-DAY | 4 | 0 | 0 | 0 | 0 | - | - | - | 2 | - |

**BOWLING AVERAGES**

| | Overs | Mdns | Runs | Wkts | Avge | Best | 5wI | 10wM |
|---|---|---|---|---|---|---|---|---|
| Britannic Assurance | 105 | 21 | 292 | 11 | 26.54 | 3-40 | - | - |

## T.D.TOPLEY - *Essex*

| Opposition | Venue | Date | Batting | Fielding | Bowling |
|---|---|---|---|---|---|
| **BRITANNIC ASSURANCE** | | | | | |
| Surrey | Chelmsford | April 27 | 29 | | 5-71 |
| Northants | Northampton | May 9 | 30 | | 1-63 & 0-54 |
| Kent | Folkestone | May 16 | 37 | | 3-98 & 0-16 |
| Warwickshire | Chelmsford | May 22 | 4 | | 1-60 & 2-60 |
| Gloucs | Bristol | May 31 | 50 * | 1Ct | 4-34 & 1-35 |
| Leicestershire | Ilford | June 4 | 2 | | 5-58 & 2-33 |
| Worcestershire | Ilford | June 7 | 3 & 7 | | 3-77 & 0-44 |
| Hampshire | Chelmsford | July 2 | | 33 * 2Ct | 3-59 & 1-38 |
| Surrey | The Oval | July 5 | | 17 | 1-34 & 0-14 |
| Kent | Southend | July 16 | | 5 1Ct | 1-64 |
| Somerset | Southend | July 19 | 16 * | 1Ct | 0-26 & 0-17 |
| Glamorgan | Cardiff | July 23 | | 1Ct | 0-50 |
| Derbyshire | Derby | Aug 6 | 11 & 9 | 1Ct | 5-79 & 0-65 |
| Notts | Trent Bridge | Aug 9 | 50 & 0 * | 1Ct | 3-92 & 1-72 |
| Northants | Colchester | Aug 16 | 7 | 1Ct | 1-20 |
| Yorkshire | Colchester | Aug 20 | | 3 1Ct | 2-86 & 3-47 |
| Lancashire | Old Trafford | Aug 23 | | 2Ct | 1-60 & 0-27 |
| Leicestershire | Leicester | Sept 10 | 7 | | 3-91 & 0-6 |
| Middlesex | Chelmsford | Sept 17 | | 2Ct | 1-70 |
| **OTHER FIRST-CLASS** | | | | | |
| Cambridge U | Fenner's | April 19 | | 1Ct | 2-19 & 0-28 |
| **REFUGE ASSURANCE** | | | | | |
| Yorkshire | Chelmsford | April 28 | | | 0-18 |
| Notts | Trent Bridge | May 12 | | 1 | 0-35 |
| Kent | Folkestone | May 19 | | 3 * | 2-41 |
| Surrey | The Oval | May 26 | | 3 | 1-28 |
| Glamorgan | Pontypridd | June 2 | | | 1-16 |
| Worcestershire | Ilford | June 9 | | 1Ct | 1-65 |
| Hampshire | Chelmsford | June 16 | | | |
| Derbyshire | Chelmsford | June 30 | | 1 | 1-29 |
| Warwickshire | Chelmsford | July 7 | | | 0-44 |
| Somerset | Southend | July 21 | | | 3-36 |
| Gloucs | Cheltenham | July 28 | | | 3-35 |
| Northants | Northampton | Aug 11 | | 4 | 2-57 |
| Middlesex | Colchester | Aug 18 | | 1Ct | 3-36 |
| Lancashire | Old Trafford | Aug 25 | 38 * | | 3-29 |
| **NATWEST TROPHY** | | | | | |
| Devon | Exmouth | June 26 | | | 1-21 |
| Sussex | Hove | July 11 | | | 3-38 |
| Surrey | The Oval | July 31 | 7 | | 2-44 |
| **BENSON & HEDGES CUP** | | | | | |
| Warwickshire | Edgbaston | April 25 | | | 0-57 |
| Hampshire | Chelmsford | May 29 | 6 * | 1Ct | 4-41 |
| Worcestershire | Chelmsford | June 12 | 1 | | 0-26 |
| **OTHER ONE-DAY** | | | | | |
| Durham | Scarborough | Aug 31 | | | 0-15 |
| Yorkshire | Scarburgh | Sept 2 | 18 | | 1-24 |
| Victoria | Chelmsford | Sept 22 | 17 | | 0-46 |

**BATTING AVERAGES - Including fielding**

| | Matches | Inns | NO | Runs | HS | Avge | 100s | 50s | Ct | St |
|---|---|---|---|---|---|---|---|---|---|---|
| Britannic Assurance | 19 | 19 | 4 | 320 | 50 * | 21.33 | - | 2 | 14 | - |
| Other First-Class | 1 | 0 | 0 | 0 | 0 | - | - | - | 1 | - |
| ALL FIRST-CLASS | 20 | 19 | 4 | 320 | 50 * | 21.33 | - | 2 | 15 | - |
| Refuge Assurance | 14 | 6 | 2 | 50 | 38 * | 12.50 | - | - | 2 | - |
| NatWest Trophy | 3 | 1 | 0 | 7 | 7 | 7.00 | - | - | - | - |
| Benson & Hedges Cup | 3 | 2 | 1 | 7 | 6 * | 7.00 | - | - | 1 | - |
| Other One-Day | 3 | 2 | 0 | 35 | 18 | 17.50 | - | - | - | - |
| ALL ONE-DAY | 23 | 11 | 3 | 99 | 38 * | 12.37 | - | - | 3 | - |

# PLANER RECORDS

## PLAYER RECORDS

**T**

## BOWLING AVERAGES

|  | Overs | Mdns | Runs | Wkts | Avge | Best | 5wI | 10wM |
|---|---|---|---|---|---|---|---|---|
| Britannic Assurance | 484.3 | 83 | 1720 | 53 | 32.45 | 5-58 | 3 | - |
| Other First-Class | 14 | 3 | 47 | 2 | 23.50 | 2-19 | - | - |
| ALL FIRST-CLASS | 498.3 | 86 | 1767 | 55 | 32.12 | 5-58 | 3 | - |
| Refuge Assurance | 95.5 | 5 | 469 | 20 | 23.45 | 3-29 | - | |
| NatWest Trophy | 34 | 6 | 103 | 6 | 17.16 | 3-38 | - | |
| Benson & Hedges Cup | 28 | 4 | 124 | 4 | 31.00 | 4-41 | - | |
| Other One-Day | 23 | 3 | 85 | 1 | 85.00 | 1-24 | - | |
| ALL ONE-DAY | 180.5 | 18 | 781 | 31 | 25.19 | 4-41 | - | |

## G.T.J.TOWNSEND - *Somerset*

| Opposition | Venue | Date | Batting | Fielding | Bowling |
|---|---|---|---|---|---|
| **BRITANNIC ASSURANCE** | | | | | |
| Notts | Trent Bridge | Aug 16 | 20 & 1 | | |
| Hampshire | Southampton | Aug 28 | 29 & 18 | 2Ct | |
| **OTHER FIRST-CLASS** | | | | | |
| Sri Lanka | Taunton | Aug 10 | 53 | 1Ct | |
| **REFUGE ASSURANCE** | | | | | |
| Worcestershire | Worcester | Aug 18 | 27 | | |
| Yorkshire | Taunton | Aug 25 | 27 | 1Ct | |
| **OTHER ONE-DAY** | | | | | |
| Gloucs | Hove | Sept 8 | 4 | | |

### BATTING AVERAGES - Including fielding

|  | Matches | Inns | NO | Runs | HS | Avge | 100s | 50s | Ct | St |
|---|---|---|---|---|---|---|---|---|---|---|
| Britannic Assurance | 2 | 4 | 0 | 68 | 29 | 17.00 | - | - | 2 | - |
| Other First-Class | 1 | 1 | 0 | 53 | 53 | 53.00 | - | 1 | 1 | - |
| ALL FIRST-CLASS | 3 | 5 | 0 | 121 | 53 | 24.20 | - | 1 | 3 | - |
| Refuge Assurance | 2 | 2 | 0 | 54 | 27 | 27.00 | - | - | 1 | - |
| Other One-Day | 1 | 1 | 0 | 4 | 4 | 4.00 | - | - | - | - |
| ALL ONE-DAY | 3 | 3 | 0 | 58 | 27 | 19.33 | - | - | 1 | - |

### BOWLING AVERAGES
Did not bowl

## T.M.TREMLETT - *Hampshire*

| Opposition | Venue | Date | Batting | Fielding | Bowling |
|---|---|---|---|---|---|
| **BRITANNIC ASSURANCE** | | | | | |
| Glamorgan | Swansea | Aug 9 | 2 | | 1-39 |
| **REFUGE ASSURANCE** | | | | | |
| Sussex | Basingstoke | June 9 | 8 | | 0-33 |
| Essex | Chelmsford | June 16 | | | 1-30 |
| Warwickshire | Portsmouth | July 21 | 5 * | | 1-27 |

### BATTING AVERAGES - Including fielding

|  | Matches | Inns | NO | Runs | HS | Avge | 100s | 50s | Ct | St |
|---|---|---|---|---|---|---|---|---|---|---|
| Britannic Assurance | 1 | 1 | 0 | 2 | 2 | 2.00 | - | - | - | - |
| ALL FIRST-CLASS | 1 | 1 | 0 | 2 | 2 | 2.00 | - | - | - | - |
| Refuge Assurance | 3 | 2 | 1 | 13 | 8 | 13.00 | - | - | - | - |
| ALL ONE-DAY | 3 | 2 | 1 | 13 | 8 | 13.00 | - | - | - | - |

### BOWLING AVERAGES

|  | Overs | Mdns | Runs | Wkts | Avge | Best | 5wI | 10wM |
|---|---|---|---|---|---|---|---|---|
| Britannic Assurance | 10 | 3 | 39 | 1 | 39.00 | 1-39 | - | - |
| ALL FIRST-CLASS | 10 | 3 | 39 | 1 | 39.00 | 1-39 | - | - |
| Refuge Assurance | 22.1 | 0 | 90 | 2 | 45.00 | 1-27 | - | |
| ALL ONE-DAY | 22.1 | 0 | 90 | 2 | 45.00 | 1-27 | - | |

## H.R.J.TRUMP - *Somerset*

| Opposition | Venue | Date | Batting | Fielding | Bowling |
|---|---|---|---|---|---|
| **BRITANNIC ASSURANCE** | | | | | |
| Middlesex | Taunton | May 25 | 5 | | 2-113 |
| Glamorgan | Swansea | June 4 | | | 0-24 |
| Hampshire | Bath | June 18 | 0 * | 1Ct | 0-40 & 2-69 |
| Gloucs | Bath | June 21 | | | 2-15 |
| Lancashire | Taunton | July 2 | | 1Ct | 3-47 & 0-45 |
| Sussex | Hove | July 16 | 30 * | | 0-58 |
| Essex | Southend | July 19 | 0 * | 1Ct | 0-102 & 0-9 |
| Kent | Taunton | July 26 | | 1 * | 1-87 & 2-91 |
| Leicestershire | Weston | Aug 2 | 0 | 1Ct | 6-107 & 0-82 |
| Worcestershire | Weston | Aug 6 | 12 * | | 0-69 & 6-48 |
| Notts | Trent Bridge | Aug 16 | 1 | 1Ct | 2-41 & 1-87 |
| Yorkshire | Taunton | Aug 23 | 0 | 1Ct | 2-53 & 2-71 |
| Hampshire | Southampton | Aug 28 | 16 * | 1Ct | 6-121 & 2-132 |
| Worcestershire | Worcester | Sept 3 | 2 & 0 | | 0-75 |
| Gloucs | Bristol | Sept 10 | 0 | 2Ct | 0-12 & 5-64 |
| Warwickshire | Taunton | Sept 17 | 8 & 4 | 2Ct | 2-95 & 1-69 |
| **OTHER FIRST-CLASS** | | | | | |
| West Indies | Taunton | May 29 | 20 * & 9 | 1Ct | 2-69 & 0-86 |
| Sri Lanka | Taunton | Aug 10 | | | 2-54 & 0-78 |
| **REFUGE ASSURANCE** | | | | | |
| Notts | Trent Bridge | June 9 | | | 1-22 |
| Lancashire | Taunton | July 5 | 2 * | | 0-59 |
| Essex | Southend | July 21 | | 1Ct | 1-39 |
| Kent | Taunton | July 28 | 19 | | 2-58 |
| Leicestershire | Weston | Aug 4 | | | 0-30 |
| Worcestershire | Worcester | Aug 18 | | 1Ct | 2-31 |
| Yorkshire | Taunton | Aug 25 | | 1Ct | 1-38 |
| **NATWEST TROPHY** | | | | | |
| Middlesex | Taunton | July 11 | 1 | | 0-33 |
| **OTHER ONE-DAY** | | | | | |
| Gloucs | Hove | Sept 8 | 18 * | | 3-41 |

### BATTING AVERAGES - Including fielding

|  | Matches | Inns | NO | Runs | HS | Avge | 100s | 50s | Ct | St |
|---|---|---|---|---|---|---|---|---|---|---|
| Britannic Assurance | 16 | 15 | 6 | 79 | 30 * | 8.77 | - | - | 11 | - |
| Other First-Class | 2 | 2 | 1 | 29 | 20 * | 29.00 | - | - | 1 | - |
| ALL FIRST-CLASS | 18 | 17 | 7 | 108 | 30 * | 10.80 | - | - | 12 | - |
| Refuge Assurance | 7 | 2 | 1 | 21 | 19 | 21.00 | - | - | 3 | - |
| NatWest Trophy | 1 | 1 | 0 | 1 | 1 | 1.00 | - | - | - | - |
| Other One-Day | 1 | 1 | 1 | 18 | 18 * | - | - | - | - | - |
| ALL ONE-DAY | 9 | 4 | 2 | 40 | 19 | 20.00 | - | - | 3 | - |

### BOWLING AVERAGES

|  | Overs | Mdns | Runs | Wkts | Avge | Best | 5wI | 10wM |
|---|---|---|---|---|---|---|---|---|
| Britannic Assurance | 570.3 | 102 | 1826 | 47 | 38.85 | 6-48 | 4 | - |
| Other First-Class | 66.5 | 9 | 287 | 4 | 71.75 | 2-54 | - | - |
| ALL FIRST-CLASS | 637.2 | 111 | 2113 | 51 | 41.43 | 6-48 | 4 | - |
| Refuge Assurance | 54 | 1 | 277 | 7 | 39.57 | 2-31 | - | |
| NatWest Trophy | 6 | 0 | 33 | 0 | | | | |
| Other One-Day | 10 | 0 | 41 | 3 | 13.66 | 3-41 | - | |
| ALL ONE-DAY | 70 | 1 | 351 | 10 | 35.10 | 3-41 | - | |

## P.C.R.TUFNELL - *Middlesex & England*

| Opposition | Venue | Date | Batting | Fielding | Bowling |
|---|---|---|---|---|---|
| **CORNHILL TEST MATCHES** | | | | | |
| West Indies | The Oval | Aug 8 | 2 | | 6-25 & 1-150 |
| Sri Lanka | Lord's | Aug 22 | 0 | 1Ct | 0-23 & 5-94 |
| **BRITANNIC ASSURANCE** | | | | | |
| Yorkshire | Lord's | April 27 | | | 1-45 |
| Sussex | Lord's | May 9 | 0 & 8 * | | 0-35 & 0-31 |
| Sussex | Hove | May 22 | | 1Ct | 0-111 & 2-69 |
| Somerset | Taunton | May 25 | 9 | | 2-35 & 1-108 |

## T     PLAYER RECORDS

| | | | | | |
|---|---|---|---|---|---|
| Gloucs | Bristol | June 4 | 4 | 1Ct | 6-34 & 0-19 |
| Leicestershire | Uxbridge | June 7 | | | 2-57 & 6-82 |
| Glamorgan | Cardiff | June 14 | 6 | | 3-76 & 1-25 |
| Yorkshire | Sheffield | June 21 | 1* | | 1-62 & 2-59 |
| Essex | Lord's | June 28 | 4 | 1Ct | 2-35 & 2-16 |
| Warwickshire | Edgbaston | July 2 | 0 & 2 | | 0-26 & 1-61 |
| Northants | Uxbridge | July 16 | | 2Ct | 4-95 & 2-21 |
| Lancashire | Uxbridge | July 19 | 24* & 1 | | 2-94 & 1-32 |
| Notts | Lord's | July 26 | 1 | | 0-25 |
| Hampshire | Lord's | Aug 2 | 17 | | 7-116 & 4-112 |
| Kent | Canterbury | Aug 28 | 31* & 4 | | 0-31 & 2-70 |
| Notts | Trent Bridge | Sept 3 | 6 | 2Ct | 4-137 & 5-30 |
| Surrey | Lord's | Sept 10 | 1 & 1 | | 2-52 & 5-17 |

**OTHER FIRST-CLASS**

| | | | | | |
|---|---|---|---|---|---|
| MCC | Lord's | April 16 | 34 | | 0-15 |
| Cambridge U | Fenner's | May 15 | 14* | 1Ct | 2-13 & 4-14 |
| West Indies | Lord's | May 18 | 14* & 26 | | 0-67 |

**REFUGE ASSURANCE**

| | | | | | |
|---|---|---|---|---|---|
| Surrey | Lord's | April 28 | | | 3-28 |

**NATWEST TROPHY**

| | | | | | |
|---|---|---|---|---|---|
| Somerset | Taunton | July 11 | 8 | | 1-29 |

**BENSON & HEDGES CUP**

| | | | | | |
|---|---|---|---|---|---|
| Somerset | Taunton | April 23 | | 1Ct | 1-41 |
| Surrey | Lord's | April 25 | 1 | | 3-50 |
| Essex | Chelmsford | May 2 | 0* | | 0-37 |
| Warwickshire | Lord's | May 4 | 18 | | 0-59 |

**BATTING AVERAGES - Including fielding**

| | Matches | Inns | NO | Runs | HS | Avge | 100s | 50s | Ct | St |
|---|---|---|---|---|---|---|---|---|---|---|
| Cornhill Test Matches | 2 | 2 | 0 | 2 | 2 | 1.00 | - | - | 1 | - |
| Britannic Assurance | 17 | 18 | 4 | 120 | 31* | 8.57 | - | - | 7 | - |
| Other First-Class | 3 | 4 | 2 | 88 | 34 | 44.00 | - | - | 1 | - |
| ALL FIRST-CLASS | 22 | 24 | 6 | 210 | 34 | 11.66 | - | - | 9 | - |
| Refuge Assurance | 1 | 0 | 0 | 0 | 0 | - | - | - | - | - |
| NatWest Trophy | 1 | 1 | 0 | 8 | 8 | 8.00 | - | - | - | - |
| Benson & Hedges Cup | 4 | 3 | 1 | 19 | 18 | 9.50 | - | - | 1 | - |
| ALL ONE-DAY | 6 | 4 | 1 | 27 | 18 | 9.00 | - | - | 1 | - |

**BOWLING AVERAGES**

| | Overs | Mdns | Runs | Wkts | Avge | Best | 5wI | 10wM |
|---|---|---|---|---|---|---|---|---|
| Cornhill Test Matches | 102 | 25 | 292 | 12 | 24.33 | 6-25 | 2 | - |
| Britannic Assurance | 733.4 | 199 | 1818 | 70 | 25.97 | 7-116 | 5 | 1 |
| Other First-Class | 68 | 30 | 109 | 6 | 18.16 | 4-14 | - | - |
| ALL FIRST-CLASS | 903.4 | 254 | 2219 | 88 | 25.21 | 7-116 | 7 | 1 |
| Refuge Assurance | 8 | 0 | 28 | 3 | 9.33 | 3-28 | - | |
| NatWest Trophy | 12 | 2 | 29 | 1 | 29.00 | 1-29 | - | |
| Benson & Hedges Cup | 39 | 0 | 187 | 4 | 46.75 | 3-50 | - | |
| ALL ONE-DAY | 59 | 2 | 244 | 8 | 30.50 | 3-28 | - | |

## D.R.TURNER - *Minor Counties*

| Opposition | Venue | Date | Batting | Fielding | Bowling |
|---|---|---|---|---|---|
| **BENSON & HEDGES CUP** | | | | | |
| Notts | Trent Bridge | May 7 | 15 | | |

**BATTING AVERAGES - Including fielding**

| | Matches | Inns | NO | Runs | HS | Avge | 100s | 50s | Ct | St |
|---|---|---|---|---|---|---|---|---|---|---|
| Benson & Hedges Cup | 1 | 1 | 0 | 15 | 15 | 15.00 | - | - | - | - |
| ALL ONE-DAY | 1 | 1 | 0 | 15 | 15 | 15.00 | - | - | - | - |

**BOWLING AVERAGES**
Did not bowl

## G.J.TURNER - *Oxford University & Combined Universities*

| Opposition | Venue | Date | Batting | | Fielding | Bowling |
|---|---|---|---|---|---|---|
| **OTHER FIRST-CLASS** | | | | | | |
| Hampshire | The Parks | April 13 | 9 & 11 | | 1Ct | 2-105 |
| Glamorgan | The Parks | April 17 | 94 | | | |
| Notts | The Parks | April 27 | | | | 1-92 |
| Gloucs | The Parks | June 15 | 1* | | | 0-36 |
| Worcestershire | The Parks | May 25 | 24 & 99 | | | 2-106 |
| Yorkshire | The Parks | June 4 | 10 | | | 0-91 & 0-16 |
| Lancashire | The Parks | June 7 | 101* | | | 1-61 |
| Cambridge U | Lord's | July 2 | | | | 3-32 & 0-25 |
| **BENSON & HEDGES CUP** | | | | | | |
| For Combined Universities | | | | | | |
| Gloucs | Bristol | April 23 | 8 | | | 2-18 |
| Derbyshire | The Parks | April 25 | 70* | | | 1-61 |
| Worcestershire | Fenner's | May 2 | 12 | | | |
| Northants | Northampton | May 4 | 80* | | | 0-41 |

**BATTING AVERAGES - Including fielding**

| | Matches | Inns | NO | Runs | HS | Avge | 100s | 50s | Ct | St |
|---|---|---|---|---|---|---|---|---|---|---|
| Other First-Class | 8 | 8 | 2 | 349 | 101* | 58.16 | 1 | 2 | 1 | - |
| ALL FIRST-CLASS | 8 | 8 | 2 | 349 | 101* | 58.16 | 1 | 2 | 1 | - |
| Benson & Hedges Cup | 4 | 4 | 2 | 170 | 80* | 85.00 | - | 2 | - | - |
| ALL ONE-DAY | 4 | 4 | 2 | 170 | 80* | 85.00 | - | 2 | - | - |

**BOWLING AVERAGES**

| | Overs | Mdns | Runs | Wkts | Avge | Best | 5wI | 10wM |
|---|---|---|---|---|---|---|---|---|
| Other First-Class | 169 | 36 | 564 | 9 | 62.66 | 3-32 | - | - |
| ALL FIRST-CLASS | 169 | 36 | 564 | 9 | 62.66 | 3-32 | - | - |
| Benson & Hedges Cup | 30.4 | 4 | 120 | 3 | 40.00 | 2-18 | - | - |
| ALL ONE-DAY | 30.4 | 4 | 120 | 3 | 40.00 | 2-18 | - | - |

## I.J.TURNER - *Hampshire*

| Opposition | Venue | Date | Batting | | Fielding | Bowling |
|---|---|---|---|---|---|---|
| **BRITANNIC ASSURANCE** | | | | | | |
| Somerset | Bath | June 18 | 0 | | | 0-47 & 1-17 |
| Yorkshire | Southampton | July 5 | | | 1Ct | 3-67 |
| Derbyshire | Chesterfield | July 23 | 6* | | | 4-28 |
| Glamorgan | Swansea | Aug 9 | 39* | | 1Ct | |
| Leicestershire | Bournemouth | Aug 16 | 1 & | 1* | | 2-69 & 0-32 |
| Sussex | Bournemouth | Aug 20 | 6 | | 1Ct | 2-33 & 0-3 |
| Somerset | Southampton | Aug 28 | 0 & | 3 | | 1-114 & 1-70 |
| Glamorgan | Southampton | Sept 17 | 3 & | 28* | | 0-109 & 0-48 |

**BATTING AVERAGES - Including fielding**

| | Matches | Inns | NO | Runs | HS | Avge | 100s | 50s | Ct | St |
|---|---|---|---|---|---|---|---|---|---|---|
| Britannic Assurance | 8 | 10 | 4 | 87 | 39* | 14.50 | - | - | 3 | - |
| ALL FIRST-CLASS | 8 | 10 | 4 | 87 | 39* | 14.50 | - | - | 3 | - |

**BOWLING AVERAGES**

| | Overs | Mdns | Runs | Wkts | Avge | Best | 5wI | 10wM |
|---|---|---|---|---|---|---|---|---|
| Britannic Assurance | 238.5 | 65 | 637 | 14 | 45.50 | 4-28 | - | - |
| ALL FIRST-CLASS | 238.5 | 65 | 637 | 14 | 45.50 | 4-28 | - | - |

**T**

## R.J.TURNER - *Somerset & Cambridge University*

| Opposition | Venue | Date | Batting | Fielding | Bowling |
|---|---|---|---|---|---|
| **OTHER FIRST-CLASS** | | | | | |
| For Cambridge U | | | | | |
| Lancashire | Fenner's | April 13 | 43 | 2Ct,1St | |
| Northants | Fenner's | April 16 | 0 * | | |
| Middlesex | Fenner's | May 15 | 69 * & 38 | | |
| Surrey | Fenner's | May 18 | 35 & 3 | 2Ct | |
| Leicestershire | Fenner's | May 22 | 10 & 4 | 1Ct | |
| Glamorgan | Fenner's | June 18 | 2 | 4Ct | |
| Sussex | Hove | June 29 | 0 * | | |
| Oxford U | Lord's | July 2 | 27 & 0 | | |
| For Somerset | | | | | |
| Sri Lanka | Taunton | Aug 10 | 18 * | 3Ct | |

**BATTING AVERAGES - Including fielding**

| | Matches | Inns | NO | Runs | HS | Avge | 100s | 50s | Ct | St |
|---|---|---|---|---|---|---|---|---|---|---|
| Other First-Class | 9 | 13 | 4 | 249 | 69 * | 27.66 | - | 1 | 12 | 1 |
| ALL FIRST-CLASS | 9 | 13 | 4 | 249 | 69 * | 27.66 | - | 1 | 12 | 1 |

**BOWLING AVERAGES**
Did not bowl

## S.TURNER - *Cambridgeshire*

| Opposition | Venue | Date | Batting | Fielding | Bowling |
|---|---|---|---|---|---|
| **NATWEST TROPHY** | | | | | |
| Kent | Canterbury | June 26 | 7 | | 0-23 |

**BATTING AVERAGES - Including fielding**

| | Matches | Inns | NO | Runs | HS | Avge | 100s | 50s | Ct | St |
|---|---|---|---|---|---|---|---|---|---|---|
| NatWest Trophy | 1 | 1 | 0 | 7 | 7 | 7.00 | - | - | - | - |
| ALL ONE-DAY | 1 | 1 | 0 | 7 | 7 | 7.00 | - | - | - | - |

**BOWLING AVERAGES**

| | Overs | Mdns | Runs | Wkts | Avge | Best | 5wI | 10wM |
|---|---|---|---|---|---|---|---|---|
| NatWest Trophy | 12 | 3 | 23 | 0 | - | - | - | |
| ALL ONE-DAY | 12 | 3 | 23 | 0 | - | - | - | |

## R.G.TWOSE - *Warwickshire*

| Opposition | Venue | Date | Batting | Fielding | Bowling |
|---|---|---|---|---|---|
| **BRITANNIC ASSURANCE** | | | | | |
| Gloucs | Edgbaston | May 25 | 41 | | |
| Somerset | Edgbaston | June 7 | 1 * | | 1-27 |
| **REFUGE ASSURANCE** | | | | | |
| Sussex | Edgbaston | April 21 | 0 * | 1Ct | |
| Yorkshire | Headingley | May 12 | 1 | | 0-23 |
| Worcestershire | Edgbaston | May 26 | 26 * | 1Ct | 0-9 |
| Somerset | Edgbaston | June 2 | | | |
| Derbyshire | Edgbaston | Aug 4 | | | 0-17 |
| **BENSON & HEDGES CUP** | | | | | |
| Surrey | The Oval | May 7 | 5 | | |
| **OTHER ONE-DAY** | | | | | |
| Surrey | Harrogate | June 12 | 16 | | 0-5 |

**BATTING AVERAGES - Including fielding**

| | Matches | Inns | NO | Runs | HS | Avge | 100s | 50s | Ct | St |
|---|---|---|---|---|---|---|---|---|---|---|
| Britannic Assurance | 2 | 2 | 1 | 42 | 41 | 42.00 | - | - | - | - |
| ALL FIRST-CLASS | 2 | 2 | 1 | 42 | 41 | 42.00 | - | - | - | - |
| Refuge Assurance | 5 | 3 | 2 | 27 | 26 * | 27.00 | - | - | 2 | - |

| Benson & Hedges Cup | 1 | 1 | 0 | 5 | 5 | 5.00 | - | - | - | - |
| Other One-Day | 1 | 1 | 0 | 16 | 16 | 16.00 | - | - | - | - |
| ALL ONE-DAY | 7 | 5 | 2 | 48 | 26 * | 16.00 | - | - | 2 | - |

**BOWLING AVERAGES**

| | Overs | Mdns | Runs | Wkts | Avge | Best | 5wI | 10wM |
|---|---|---|---|---|---|---|---|---|
| Britannic Assurance | 9 | 0 | 27 | 1 | 27.00 | 1-27 | - | - |
| ALL FIRST-CLASS | 9 | 0 | 27 | 1 | 27.00 | 1-27 | - | - |
| Refuge Assurance | 8 | 0 | 49 | 0 | - | - | - | |
| Benson & Hedges Cup | | | | | | | | |
| Other One-Day | 1 | 0 | 5 | 0 | - | - | - | |

## U                    PLAYER RECORDS

## S.D.UDAL - *Hampshire*

| Opposition | Venue | Date | Batting | Fielding | Bowling |
|---|---|---|---|---|---|
| **OTHER FIRST-CLASS** | | | | | |
| West Indies | Southampton | June 29 | 0 | | 2-117 |
| **REFUGE ASSURANCE** | | | | | |
| Yorkshire | Southampton | April 21 | | | 1-27 |
| Derbyshire | Derby | May 5 | 6 | | 1-26 |
| Kent | Southampton | May 12 | | 2Ct | 0-47 |
| Somerset | Bournemouth | May 19 | 4 * | | 1-33 |
| Gloucs | Swindon | May 26 | | | 1-57 |
| Northants | Northampton | June 2 | 13 | | 2-47 |
| Sussex | Basingstoke | June 9 | 3 | 1Ct | 1-40 |
| Essex | Chelmsford | June 16 | | | 1-41 |
| Worcestershire | Southampton | July 7 | | | 1-47 |
| Notts | Trent Bridge | July 14 | | | 2-42 |
| Warwickshire | Portsmouth | July 21 | | | 0-23 |
| Lancashire | Southampton | July 28 | | | 1-30 |
| Middlesex | Lord's | Aug 4 | | | 0-29 |
| Glamorgan | Ebbw Vale | Aug 11 | 23 | | 3-40 |
| Leicestershire | Bournemouth | Aug 18 | 1 * | 1Ct | 1-46 |
| Surrey | The Oval | Aug 25 | 16 * | | 1-19 |
| **NATWEST TROPHY** | | | | | |
| Berkshire | Reading | June 26 | | | 2-14 |
| Lancashire | Southampton | July 11 | | 1Ct | 3-47 |
| Notts | Southampton | July 31 | | | 0-54 |
| Warwickshire | Edgbaston | Aug 14 | | 1Ct | 1-30 |
| Surrey | Lord's | Sept 7 | | | 0-46 |
| **BENSON & HEDGES CUP** | | | | | |
| Notts | Southampton | April 23 | | | 3-48 |
| Min Counties | Trowbridge | April 25 | | | 0-50 |
| Glamorgan | Southampton | May 2 | | 1Ct | 2-33 |
| Yorkshire | Headingley | May 4 | 1 | 1Ct | 1-17 |
| Essex | Chelmsford | May 29 | 9 | | 3-41 |

### BATTING AVERAGES - Including fielding

| | Matches | Inns | NO | Runs | HS | Avge | 100s | 50s | Ct | St |
|---|---|---|---|---|---|---|---|---|---|---|
| Other First-Class | 1 | 1 | 0 | 0 | 0 | 0.00 | - | - | - | - |
| ALL FIRST-CLASS | 1 | 1 | 0 | 0 | 0 | 0.00 | - | - | - | - |
| Refuge Assurance | 16 | 7 | 3 | 66 | 23 | 16.50 | - | - | 4 | - |
| NatWest Trophy | 5 | 0 | 0 | 0 | 0 | - | - | - | 2 | - |
| Benson & Hedges Cup | 5 | 2 | 0 | 10 | 9 | 5.00 | - | - | 2 | - |
| ALL ONE-DAY | 26 | 9 | 3 | 76 | 23 | 12.66 | - | - | 8 | - |

### BOWLING AVERAGES

| | Overs | Mdns | Runs | Wkts | Avge | Best | 5wI | 10wM |
|---|---|---|---|---|---|---|---|---|
| Other First-Class | 22 | 3 | 117 | 2 | 58.50 | 2-117 | - | - |
| ALL FIRST-CLASS | 22 | 3 | 117 | 2 | 58.50 | 2-117 | - | - |
| Refuge Assurance | 119.2 | 6 | 594 | 17 | 34.94 | 3-40 | - | |
| NatWest Trophy | 50 | 3 | 191 | 6 | 31.83 | 3-47 | - | |
| Benson & Hedges Cup | 55 | 9 | 189 | 9 | 21.00 | 3-41 | - | |
| ALL ONE-DAY | 224.2 | 18 | 974 | 32 | 30.43 | 3-40 | - | |

# PLAYER RECORDS

**V**

## A.P.VAN TROOST - *Somerset*

| Opposition | Venue | Date | Batting | Fielding | Bowling |
|---|---|---|---|---|---|
| **BRITANNIC ASSURANCE** | | | | | |
| Surrey | The Oval | June 28 | | | 1-55 |
| Northants | Northampton | July 23 | | 1Ct | 0-24 & 2-52 |
| Kent | Taunton | July 26 | 0 * | | 1-41 & 2-25 |
| Hampshire | Southampton | Aug 28 | | | 0-42 & 0-28 |

**BATTING AVERAGES - Including fielding**

| | Matches | Inns | NO | Runs | HS | Avge | 100s | 50s | Ct | St |
|---|---|---|---|---|---|---|---|---|---|---|
| Britannic Assurance | 4 | 1 | 1 | 0 | 0* | - | - | - | 1 | - |
| ALL FIRST-CLASS | 4 | 1 | 1 | 0 | 0* | - | - | - | 1 | - |

**BOWLING AVERAGES**

| | Overs | Mdns | Runs | Wkts | Avge | Best | 5wI | 10wM |
|---|---|---|---|---|---|---|---|---|
| Britannic Assurance | 86.4 | 12 | 267 | 6 | 44.50 | 2-25 | - | - |
| ALL FIRST-CLASS | 86.4 | 12 | 267 | 6 | 44.50 | 2-25 | - | - |

## J.N.VILJOEN - *Cambridge University*

| Opposition | Venue | Date | Batting | Fielding | Bowling |
|---|---|---|---|---|---|
| **OTHER FIRST-CLASS** | | | | | |
| Derbyshire | Fenner's | May 9 | 1 * | | 0-65 & 1-34 |

**BATTING AVERAGES - Including fielding**

| | Matches | Inns | NO | Runs | HS | Avge | 100s | 50s | Ct | St |
|---|---|---|---|---|---|---|---|---|---|---|
| Other First-Class | 1 | 1 | 1 | 1 | 1* | - | - | - | - | - |
| ALL FIRST-CLASS | 1 | 1 | 1 | 1 | 1* | - | - | - | - | - |

**BOWLING AVERAGES**

| | Overs | Mdns | Runs | Wkts | Avge | Best | 5wI | 10wM |
|---|---|---|---|---|---|---|---|---|
| Other First-Class | 22 | 2 | 99 | 1 | 99.00 | 1-34 | - | - |
| ALL FIRST-CLASS | 22 | 2 | 99 | 1 | 99.00 | 1-34 | - | - |

## D.A.VINCENT - *Ireland*

| Opposition | Venue | Date | Batting | Fielding | Bowling |
|---|---|---|---|---|---|
| **OTHER ONE-DAY** | | | | | |
| West Indies | Downpatrick | July 13 | 16 | | |

**BATTING AVERAGES - Including fielding**

| | Matches | Inns | NO | Runs | HS | Avge | 100s | 50s | Ct | St |
|---|---|---|---|---|---|---|---|---|---|---|
| Other One-Day | 1 | 1 | 0 | 16 | 16 | 16.00 | - | - | - | - |
| ALL ONE-DAY | 1 | 1 | 0 | 16 | 16 | 16.00 | - | - | - | - |

**BOWLING AVERAGES**
Did not bowl

## M.F.VOSS - *Hertfordshire*

| Opposition | Venue | Date | Batting | Fielding | Bowling |
|---|---|---|---|---|---|
| **NATWEST TROPHY** | | | | | |
| Warwickshire | Edgbaston | July 11 | 2 | | |

**BATTING AVERAGES - Including fielding**

| | Matches | Inns | NO | Runs | HS | Avge | 100s | 50s | Ct | St |
|---|---|---|---|---|---|---|---|---|---|---|
| NatWest Trophy | 1 | 1 | 0 | 2 | 2 | 2.00 | - | - | - | - |
| ALL ONE-DAY | 1 | 1 | 0 | 2 | 2 | 2.00 | - | - | - | - |

**BOWLING AVERAGES**
Did not bowl

# W

# PLAYER RECORDS

## J.R.WAKE - *Bedfordshire*

| Opposition | Venue | Date | Batting | Fielding | Bowling |
|---|---|---|---|---|---|
| **NATWEST TROPHY** | | | | | |
| Worcestershire | Bedford | June 26 | 2 | 1Ct | |

**BATTING AVERAGES - Including fielding**

| | Matches | Inns | NO | Runs | HS | Avge | 100s | 50s | Ct | St |
|---|---|---|---|---|---|---|---|---|---|---|
| NatWest Trophy | 1 | 1 | 0 | 2 | 2 | 2.00 | - | - | 1 | - |
| ALL ONE-DAY | 1 | 1 | 0 | 2 | 2 | 2.00 | - | - | 1 | - |

**BOWLING AVERAGES**
Did not bowl

## V.DE C.WALCOTT - *League CC XI*

| Opposition | Venue | Date | Batting | Fielding | Bowling |
|---|---|---|---|---|---|
| **OTHER ONE-DAY** | | | | | |
| West Indies | Trowbridge | June 28 | | | 0-19 |

**BATTING AVERAGES - Including fielding**

| | Matches | Inns | NO | Runs | HS | Avge | 100s | 50s | Ct | St |
|---|---|---|---|---|---|---|---|---|---|---|
| Other One-Day | 1 | 0 | 0 | 0 | 0 | - | - | - | - | - |
| ALL ONE-DAY | 1 | 0 | 0 | 0 | 0 | - | - | - | - | - |

**BOWLING AVERAGES**

| | Overs | Mdns | Runs | Wkts | Avge | Best | 5wI | 10wM |
|---|---|---|---|---|---|---|---|---|
| Other One-Day | 3 | 0 | 19 | 0 | - | - | - | |
| ALL ONE-DAY | 3 | 0 | 19 | 0 | - | - | - | |

## A.WALKER - *Northants*

| Opposition | Venue | Date | Batting | Fielding | Bowling |
|---|---|---|---|---|---|
| **BRITANNIC ASSURANCE** | | | | | |
| Derbyshire | Northampton | May 31 | 8 | 2Ct | 1-42 & 1-27 |
| Worcestershire | Northampton | June 4 | | | 1-62 & 0-20 |
| Gloucs | Bristol | Sept 3 | 13 | | 3-84 & 0-26 |
| Warwickshire | Edgbaston | Sept 10 | 6 & 8 * | | 0-35 |
| **REFUGE ASSURANCE** | | | | | |
| Leicestershire | Northampton | May 12 | | 1Ct | 0-31 |
| Worcestershire | Northampton | May 19 | 6 | 1Ct | 1-38 |
| Yorkshire | Headingley | May 26 | | | 1-27 |
| Hampshire | Northampton | June 2 | | | 1-24 |
| Gloucs | Moreton | June 9 | | | 0-0 |
| Somerset | Luton | June 30 | | | 2-7 |
| Surrey | Tring | July 7 | 4 | 1Ct | 1-14 |
| Notts | Well'borough | July 21 | 2 | | 2-24 |
| Derbyshire | Derby | July 28 | 5 | 2Ct | 0-36 |
| Sussex | Eastbourne | Aug 4 | | 1Ct | 1-26 |
| Essex | Northampton | Aug 11 | | | 1-30 |
| Kent | Canterbury | Aug 18 | | | 1-27 |
| Warwickshire | Northampton | Aug 25 | | | 1-24 |
| Lancashire | Old Trafford | Sept 1 | | | 0-27 |
| **NATWEST TROPHY** | | | | | |
| Staffordshire | Stone | June 26 | | | 1-18 |
| Leicestershire | Northampton | July 11 | | | 0-40 |
| Glamorgan | Northampton | July 31 | | | 2-39 |
| Surrey | The Oval | Aug 14 | 11 | | 1-32 |
| **BENSON & HEDGES CUP** | | | | | |
| Lancashire | Old Trafford | May 29 | 0* | | 1-33 |

**BATTING AVERAGES - Including fielding**

| | Matches | Inns | NO | Runs | HS | Avge | 100s | 50s | Ct | St |
|---|---|---|---|---|---|---|---|---|---|---|
| Britannic Assurance | 4 | 4 | 1 | 35 | 13 | 11.66 | - | - | 2 | - |
| ALL FIRST-CLASS | 4 | 4 | 1 | 35 | 13 | 11.66 | - | - | 2 | - |

| | Matches | Inns | NO | Runs | HS | Avge | 100s | 50s | Ct | St |
|---|---|---|---|---|---|---|---|---|---|---|
| Refuge Assurance | 14 | 4 | 0 | 17 | 6 | 4.25 | - | - | 6 | - |
| NatWest Trophy | 4 | 1 | 0 | 11 | 11 | 11.00 | - | - | - | - |
| Benson & Hedges Cup | 1 | 1 | 1 | 0 | 0* | | - | - | - | - |
| ALL ONE-DAY | 19 | 6 | 1 | 28 | 11 | 5.60 | - | - | 6 | - |

**BOWLING AVERAGES**

| | Overs | Mdns | Runs | Wkts | Avge | Best | 5wI | 10wM |
|---|---|---|---|---|---|---|---|---|
| Britannic Assurance | 103 | 20 | 296 | 6 | 49.33 | 3-84 | - | - |
| ALL FIRST-CLASS | 103 | 20 | 296 | 6 | 49.33 | 3-84 | - | - |
| Refuge Assurance | 98.5 | 8 | 335 | 12 | 27.91 | 2-7 | - | |
| NatWest Trophy | 42 | 6 | 129 | 4 | 32.25 | 2-39 | - | |
| Benson & Hedges Cup | 9 | 1 | 33 | 1 | 33.00 | 1-33 | - | |
| ALL ONE-DAY | 149.5 | 15 | 497 | 17 | 29.23 | 2-7 | - | - |

## R.B.WALLER - *Cambridge University*

| Opposition | Venue | Date | Batting | Fielding | Bowling |
|---|---|---|---|---|---|
| **OTHER FIRST-CLASS** | | | | | |
| Lancashire | Fenner's | April 13 | 2 | | 1-84 & 0-23 |
| Northants | Fenner's | April 16 | 4 * | 1Ct | 1-75 |
| Glamorgan | Fenner's | June 18 | 0 * | | 1-9 & 3-31 |
| Sussex | Hove | June 29 | | | 0-92 |
| Oxford U | Lord's | July 2 | 6 * | | 1-33 & 0-16 |

**BATTING AVERAGES - Including fielding**

| | Matches | Inns | NO | Runs | HS | Avge | 100s | 50s | Ct | St |
|---|---|---|---|---|---|---|---|---|---|---|
| Other First-Class | 5 | 4 | 3 | 12 | 6* | 12.00 | - | - | 1 | - |
| ALL FIRST-CLASS | 5 | 4 | 3 | 12 | 6* | 12.00 | - | - | 1 | - |

**BOWLING AVERAGES**

| | Overs | Mdns | Runs | Wkts | Avge | Best | 5wI | 10wM |
|---|---|---|---|---|---|---|---|---|
| Other First-Class | 85.2 | 16 | 363 | 7 | 51.85 | 3-31 | - | - |
| ALL FIRST-CLASS | 85.2 | 16 | 363 | 7 | 51.85 | 3-31 | - | - |

## C.A.WALSH - *West Indies*

| Opposition | Venue | Date | Batting | Fielding | Bowling |
|---|---|---|---|---|---|
| **CORNHILL TEST MATCHES** | | | | | |
| England | Headingley | June 6 | 3 & 9 | | 1-31 & 1-61 |
| England | Lord's | June 20 | 10 | | 1-90 |
| England | Trent Bridge | July 4 | 12 | | 1-75 & 4-64 |
| England | Edgbaston | July 25 | 18 | | 2-43 & 1-20 |
| England | The Oval | Aug 8 | 0 & 14 | | 3-91 & 1-18 |
| **OTHER FIRST-CLASS** | | | | | |
| Worcestershire | Worcester | May 15 | | | 3-64 |
| Middlesex | Lord's | May 18 | 0 * | | 2-63 & 4-39 |
| Leicestershire | Leicester | June 1 | | | 1-60 & 0-18 |
| Northants | Northampton | June 15 | | | 0-13 |
| Hampshire | Southampton | June 29 | | | 2-41 & 0-22 |
| Kent | Canterbury | July 20 | | | 1-45 & 1-57 |
| **TEXACO TROPHY** | | | | | |
| England | Edgbaston | May 23 | 29 * | | 2-34 |
| England | Old Trafford | May 25 | 1 * | | 0-56 |
| England | Lord's | May 27 | 0 | | 0-50 |
| **OTHER ONE-DAY** | | | | | |
| Ireland | Downpatrick | July 13 | | | 0-13 |

**BATTING AVERAGES - Including fielding**

| | Matches | Inns | NO | Runs | HS | Avge | 100s | 50s | Ct | St |
|---|---|---|---|---|---|---|---|---|---|---|
| Cornhill Test Matches | 5 | 7 | 0 | 66 | 18 | 9.42 | - | - | - | - |
| Other First-Class | 6 | 1 | 1 | 0 | 0* | | - | - | - | - |
| ALL FIRST-CLASS | 11 | 8 | 1 | 66 | 18 | 9.42 | - | - | - | - |
| Texaco Trophy | 3 | 3 | 2 | 30 | 29 * | 30.00 | - | - | - | - |
| Other One-Day | 1 | 0 | 0 | 0 | 0 | - | - | - | - | - |

# PLAYER RECORDS

**W**

| ALL ONE-DAY | 4 | 3 | 2 | 30 | 29 * | 30.00 | - | - | - |

## BOWLING AVERAGES
| | Overs | Mdns | Runs | Wkts | Avge | Best | 5wI | 10wM |
|---|---|---|---|---|---|---|---|---|
| Cornhill Test Matches | 187 | 42 | 493 | 15 | 32.86 | 4-64 | - | - |
| Other First-Class | 137.5 | 33 | 422 | 14 | 30.14 | 4-39 | - | - |
| ALL FIRST-CLASS | 324.5 | 75 | 915 | 29 | 31.55 | 4-39 | - | - |
| Texaco Trophy | 33 | 1 | 140 | 2 | 70.00 | 2-34 | - | |
| Other One-Day | 6 | 2 | 13 | 0 | - | - | - | |
| ALL ONE-DAY | 39 | 3 | 153 | 2 | 76.50 | 2-34 | - | |

## WAQAR YOUNIS - *Surrey*

| Opposition | Venue | Date | Batting | Fielding | Bowling |
|---|---|---|---|---|---|
| **BRITANNIC ASSURANCE** | | | | | |
| Lancashire | The Oval | May 22 | 9 * | 1Ct | 5-57 & 6-65 |
| Hampshire | Bournemouth | May 25 | 16 * & | 4 * | 6-66 & 5-70 |
| Notts | The Oval | June 4 | | | 0-54 & 1-12 |
| Leicestershire | Leicester | June 14 | 2 * | | 5-57 & 0-9 |
| Derbyshire | Derby | June 21 | 17 | | 2-11 & 3-66 |
| Somerset | The Oval | June 28 | | | 1-86 |
| Sussex | Arundel | July 2 | | | 3-69 & 3-42 |
| Gloucs | Guildford | July 16 | 2 * | | 7-87 & 0-15 |
| Yorkshire | Guildford | July 19 | 31 | | 2-54 & 6-40 |
| Glamorgan | The Oval | July 26 | 0 | | 4-75 |
| Kent | Canterbury | Aug 2 | 8 & | 9 | 6-72 & 2-26 |
| Warwickshire | Edgbaston | Aug 6 | 22 | | 5-47 & 4-50 |
| Worcestershire | Worcester | Aug 16 | 15 & | 7 | 4-78 & 3-56 |
| Middlesex | The Oval | Aug 20 | 4 & | 0 | 1Ct | 5-61 & 0-8 |
| Sussex | The Oval | Aug 28 | 3 * | | 1Ct | 4-52 & 0-51 |
| Hampshire | The Oval | Sept 3 | 1 * & | 27 * | 6-45 & 6-47 |
| Middlesex | Lord's | Sept 10 | 0 & | 0 | 5-53 & 4-42 |
| **OTHER FIRST-CLASS** | | | | | |
| Cambridge U | Fenner's | May 18 | | 1Ct | 0-28 & 0-5 |
| **REFUGE ASSURANCE** | | | | | |
| Somerset | The Oval | April 21 | | | 4-30 |
| Middlesex | Lord's | April 28 | | 1Ct | 1-41 |
| Gloucs | The Oval | May 12 | 8 | | 1-43 |
| Essex | The Oval | May 26 | | | 3-27 |
| Worcestershire | Worcester | June 2 | | | 1-36 |
| Derbyshire | Chesterfield | June 9 | 0 | | 0-23 |
| Leicestershire | Leicester | June 16 | 1 | 1Ct | 1-10 |
| Notts | The Oval | June 30 | 0 | | 2-33 |
| Northants | Tring | July 7 | 1 | | 3-37 |
| Sussex | The Oval | July 14 | | | 0-36 |
| Yorkshire | The Oval | July 21 | 0 * | | 1-34 |
| Kent | Canterbury | Aug 4 | | | 4-21 |
| **NATWEST TROPHY** | | | | | |
| Kent | The Oval | July 11 | | | 3-51 |
| Essex | The Oval | July 31 | 26 | | 4-37 |
| Northants | The Oval | Aug 14 | 4 | | 5-40 |
| Hampshire | Lord's | Sept 7 | | | 1-43 |
| **BENSON & HEDGES CUP** | | | | | |
| Essex | The Oval | April 23 | 5 * | | 0-63 |
| Middlesex | Lord's | April 25 | 3 | | 1-32 |
| Somerset | Taunton | May 4 | | 1Ct | 3-29 |
| Warwickshire | The Oval | May 7 | 0 * | | 0-16 |

## BATTING AVERAGES - Including fielding
| | Matches | Inns | NO | Runs | HS | Avge | 100s | 50s | Ct | St |
|---|---|---|---|---|---|---|---|---|---|---|
| Britannic Assurance | 17 | 20 | 8 | 177 | 31 | 14.75 | - | - | 3 | - |
| Other First-Class | 1 | 0 | 0 | 0 | 0 | - | - | - | 1 | - |
| ALL FIRST-CLASS | 18 | 20 | 8 | 177 | 31 | 14.75 | - | - | 4 | - |
| Refuge Assurance | 12 | 6 | 1 | 10 | 8 | 2.00 | - | - | 2 | - |
| NatWest Trophy | 4 | 2 | 0 | 30 | 26 | 15.00 | - | - | - | - |
| Benson & Hedges Cup | 4 | 3 | 2 | 8 | 5 * | 8.00 | - | - | 1 | - |
| ALL ONE-DAY | 20 | 11 | 3 | 48 | 26 | 6.00 | - | - | 3 | - |

## BOWLING AVERAGES
| | Overs | Mdns | Runs | Wkts | Avge | Best | 5wI | 10wM |
|---|---|---|---|---|---|---|---|---|
| Britannic Assurance | 570.1 | 109 | 1623 | 113 | 14.36 | 7-87 | 13 | 3 |

---

| Other First-Class | 11.5 | 3 | 33 | 0 | - | - | - | - |
| ALL FIRST-CLASS | 582 | 112 | 1656 | 113 | 14.65 | 7-87 | 13 | 3 |
| Refuge Assurance | 88.4 | 8 | 371 | 21 | 17.66 | 4-21 | - | |
| NatWest Trophy | 44.3 | 5 | 171 | 13 | 13.15 | 5-40 | 1 | |
| Benson & Hedges Cup | 35.4 | 2 | 140 | 4 | 35.00 | 3-29 | - | |
| ALL ONE-DAY | 168.5 | 15 | 682 | 38 | 17.94 | 5-40 | 1 | |

## D.M.WARD - *Surrey*

| Opposition | Venue | Date | Batting | Fielding | Bowling |
|---|---|---|---|---|---|
| **BRITANNIC ASSURANCE** | | | | | |
| Essex | Chelmsford | April 27 | 30 | | |
| Kent | The Oval | May 9 | 40 & | 23 | |
| Lancashire | The Oval | May 22 | 43 & | 17 * | |
| Hampshire | Bournemouth | May 25 | 22 & | 18 | 1Ct |
| Notts | The Oval | June 4 | 52 * | | |
| Leicestershire | Leicester | June 14 | 60 | | |
| Derbyshire | Derby | June 21 | 26 & | 94 * | |
| Somerset | The Oval | June 28 | 71 | | 1Ct |
| Sussex | Arundel | July 2 | 7 | | |
| Essex | The Oval | July 5 | 98 & | 54 | 1Ct |
| Gloucs | Guildford | July 16 | 40 * & | 80 | 1Ct | 2-66 |
| Yorkshire | Guildford | July 19 | 18 * & | 3 | |
| Glamorgan | The Oval | July 26 | 5 & | 71 | |
| Kent | Canterbury | Aug 2 | 53 & | 35 | |
| Warwickshire | Edgbaston | Aug 6 | 11 & | 14 | |
| Worcestershire | Worcester | Aug 16 | 14 & | 1 | |
| Middlesex | The Oval | Aug 20 | 9 & | 43 | |
| Northants | Northampton | Aug 23 | 5 & | 28 | 1Ct |
| Sussex | The Oval | Aug 28 | 44 | | 1Ct |
| Hampshire | The Oval | Sept 3 | 0 & | 1 | 1Ct |
| Middlesex | Lord's | Sept 10 | 0 & | 23 | |
| Lancashire | Old Trafford | Sept 17 | 0 & | 151 | 2Ct |
| **OTHER FIRST-CLASS** | | | | | |
| Cambridge U | Fenner's | May 18 | 66 & | 2 * | 1Ct |
| **REFUGE ASSURANCE** | | | | | |
| Somerset | The Oval | April 21 | 51 | | |
| Middlesex | Lord's | April 28 | 7 | | 1Ct |
| Gloucs | The Oval | May 12 | 3 | | |
| Essex | The Oval | May 26 | 5 | | 1Ct |
| Worcestershire | Worcester | June 2 | | | |
| Derbyshire | Chesterfield | June 9 | 15 | | |
| Leicestershire | Leicester | June 16 | 19 | | 1Ct |
| Notts | The Oval | June 30 | 4 | | |
| Northants | Tring | July 7 | 3 | | 1Ct |
| Sussex | The Oval | July 14 | 51 * | | 1Ct |
| Yorkshire | The Oval | July 21 | 56 | | |
| Glamorgan | The Oval | July 28 | 0 | | 1Ct |
| Kent | Canterbury | Aug 4 | 22 | | |
| Lancashire | Old Trafford | Aug 18 | 3 | | |
| Hampshire | The Oval | Aug 25 | 29 | | |
| **NATWEST TROPHY** | | | | | |
| Kent | The Oval | July 11 | 55 | | |
| Essex | The Oval | July 31 | 62 | | |
| Northants | The Oval | Aug 14 | 4 | | |
| Hampshire | Lord's | Sept 7 | 43 | | |
| **BENSON & HEDGES CUP** | | | | | |
| Essex | The Oval | April 23 | 41 | | |
| Middlesex | Lord's | April 25 | 46 | | |
| Somerset | Taunton | May 4 | 28 | | |
| Warwickshire | The Oval | May 7 | 5 | | |
| **OTHER ONE-DAY** | | | | | |
| Warwickshire | Harrogate | June 12 | 16 | | 1Ct |
| Durham | Harrogate | June 13 | 51 | | 1-8 |

## BATTING AVERAGES - Including fielding
| | Matches | Inns | NO | Runs | HS | Avge | 100s | 50s | Ct | St |
|---|---|---|---|---|---|---|---|---|---|---|
| Britannic Assurance | 22 | 38 | 5 | 1304 | 151 | 39.51 | 1 | 9 | 9 | - |
| Other First-Class | 1 | 2 | 1 | 68 | 66 | 68.00 | - | 1 | 1 | - |
| ALL FIRST-CLASS | 23 | 40 | 6 | 1372 | 151 | 40.35 | 1 | 10 | 10 | - |
| Refuge Assurance | 15 | 14 | 1 | 268 | 56 | 20.61 | - | 3 | 6 | - |

| NatWest Trophy | 4 | 4 | 0 | 164 | 62 | 41.00 | - | 2 | - | - |
|---|---|---|---|---|---|---|---|---|---|---|
| Benson & Hedges Cup | 4 | 4 | 0 | 120 | 46 | 30.00 | - | - | - | - |
| Other One-Day | 2 | 2 | 0 | 67 | 51 | 33.50 | - | 1 | 1 | - |
| ALL ONE-DAY | 25 | 24 | 1 | 619 | 62 | 26.91 | - | 6 | 7 | - |

**BOWLING AVERAGES**

| | Overs | Mdns | Runs | Wkts | Avge | Best | 5wI | 10wM |
|---|---|---|---|---|---|---|---|---|
| Britannic Assurance | 7.5 | 0 | 66 | 2 | 33.00 | 2-66 | - | - |
| Other First-Class | | | | | | | | |
| ALL FIRST-CLASS | 7.5 | 0 | 66 | 2 | 33.00 | 2-66 | - | - |
| Refuge Assurance | | | | | | | | |
| NatWest Trophy | | | | | | | | |
| Benson & Hedges Cup | | | | | | | | |
| Other One-Day | 1 | 0 | 8 | 1 | 8.00 | 1-8 | - | |
| ALL ONE-DAY | 1 | 0 | 8 | 1 | 8.00 | 1-8 | - | |

## M.WARD - *Lancashire*

| Opposition | Venue | Date | Batting | Fielding | Bowling |
|---|---|---|---|---|---|
| OTHER FIRST-CLASS | | | | | |
| Oxford U | The Parks | June 7 | | | 0-6 |

**BATTING AVERAGES - Including fielding**

| | Matches | Inns | NO | Runs | HS | Avge | 100s | 50s | Ct | St |
|---|---|---|---|---|---|---|---|---|---|---|
| Other First-Class | 1 | 0 | 0 | 0 | 0 | - | - | - | - | - |
| ALL FIRST-CLASS | 1 | 0 | 0 | 0 | 0 | - | - | - | - | - |

**BOWLING AVERAGES**

| | Overs | Mdns | Runs | Wkts | Avge | Best | 5wI | 10wM |
|---|---|---|---|---|---|---|---|---|
| Other First-Class | 2 | 0 | 6 | 0 | - | - | - | - |
| ALL FIRST-CLASS | 2 | 0 | 6 | 0 | - | - | - | - |

## T.R.WARD - *Kent*

| Opposition | Venue | Date | Batting | | | Fielding | Bowling |
|---|---|---|---|---|---|---|---|
| BRITANNIC ASSURANCE | | | | | | | |
| Hampshire | Southampton | April 27 | 35 | | | | |
| Surrey | The Oval | May 9 | 17 | | | | |
| Essex | Folkestone | May 16 | 141 | | | | |
| Middlesex | Lord's | May 31 | 12 | & | 4 | | |
| Warwickshire | Tunbridge W | June 4 | 5 | | | | |
| Sussex | Tunbridge W | June 7 | 13 | & | 2 | | |
| Yorkshire | Harrogate | June 14 | | | | | |
| Lancashire | Old Trafford | June 21 | | | 37 | 3Ct | 0-8 |
| Northants | Maidstone | July 2 | 31 | & | 18 | | |
| Glamorgan | Maidstone | July 5 | 110 | & | 109 | | 0-6 |
| Essex | Southend | July 16 | 53 | & | 88 * | 2Ct | |
| Worcestershire | Worcester | July 23 | | | | | |
| Somerset | Taunton | July 26 | 31 | & | 0 | | |
| Surrey | Canterbury | Aug 2 | 6 | & | 26 | | 1-20 |
| Hampshire | Canterbury | Aug 6 | 65 | & | 50 | 1Ct | |
| Leicestershire | Leicester | Aug 9 | 1 | & | 41 | | 0-6 |
| Gloucs | Canterbury | Aug 20 | 0 | & | 48 | 1Ct | |
| Middlesex | Canterbury | Aug 28 | 51 | & | 235 * | 1Ct | |
| Sussex | Hove | Sept 3 | 51 | & | 38 | | |
| Leicestershire | Canterbury | Sept 17 | 38 | & | 13 | 1Ct | |
| OTHER FIRST-CLASS | | | | | | | |
| Oxford U | The Parks | June 18 | 122 | | | | |
| West Indies | Canterbury | July 20 | 0 | & | 2 | 1Ct | |
| REFUGE ASSURANCE | | | | | | | |
| Worcestershire | Worcester | April 21 | 40 | | | | |
| Hampshire | Southampton | May 12 | 2 | | | | |
| Derbyshire | Canterbury | May 26 | 14 | | | 1Ct | |
| Middlesex | Southgate | June 2 | 55 | | | | |
| Yorkshire | Scarborough | June 16 | 16 | | | 1Ct | |
| Lancashire | Old Trafford | June 23 | 62 * | | | | |
| Gloucs | Canterbury | June 30 | 0 | | | 1Ct | |

| Glamorgan | Maidstone | July 7 | 33 * | |
|---|---|---|---|---|
| Leicestershire | Canterbury | July 14 | 15 | 1Ct |
| Somerset | Taunton | July 28 | 56 | 1Ct |
| Surrey | Canterbury | Aug 4 | 27 | |
| Notts | Trent Bridge | Aug 11 | 15 | |
| Northants | Canterbury | Aug 18 | 9 | |
| Sussex | Hove | Aug 25 | 3 | |

**NATWEST TROPHY**

| Cambs | Canterbury | June 26 | 20 | |
|---|---|---|---|---|
| Surrey | The Oval | July 11 | 55 | |

**BENSON & HEDGES CUP**

| Leicestershire | Canterbury | April 23 | 87 | |
|---|---|---|---|---|
| Lancashire | Old Trafford | April 25 | 1 | 1Ct |
| Sussex | Canterbury | May 2 | 38 | |
| Scotland | Glasgow | May 7 | 29 | 1Ct |
| Worcestershire | Worcester | May 29 | 10 | |

**OTHER ONE-DAY**

For England A
| Sri Lanka | Old Trafford | Aug 14 | 5 | 1Ct |
|---|---|---|---|---|
| Sri Lanka | Old Trafford | Aug 15 | 78 | |

For Kent
| Sussex | Hove | Sept 7 | 2 | |
|---|---|---|---|---|

**BATTING AVERAGES - Including fielding**

| | Matches | Inns | NO | Runs | HS | Avge | 100s | 50s | Ct | St |
|---|---|---|---|---|---|---|---|---|---|---|
| Britannic Assurance | 20 | 31 | 2 | 1369 | 235 * | 47.20 | 4 | 6 | 9 | - |
| Other First-Class | 2 | 3 | 0 | 124 | 122 | 41.33 | 1 | - | 1 | - |
| ALL FIRST-CLASS | 22 | 34 | 2 | 1493 | 235 * | 46.65 | 5 | 6 | 10 | - |
| Refuge Assurance | 14 | 14 | 2 | 347 | 62 * | 28.91 | - | 3 | 5 | - |
| NatWest Trophy | 2 | 2 | 0 | 75 | 55 | 37.50 | - | 1 | - | - |
| Benson & Hedges Cup | 5 | 5 | 0 | 165 | 87 | 33.00 | - | 1 | 2 | - |
| Other One-Day | 3 | 3 | 0 | 85 | 78 | 28.33 | - | 1 | 1 | - |
| ALL ONE-DAY | 24 | 24 | 2 | 672 | 87 | 30.54 | - | 6 | 8 | - |

**BOWLING AVERAGES**

| | Overs | Mdns | Runs | Wkts | Avge | Best | 5wI | 10wM |
|---|---|---|---|---|---|---|---|---|
| Britannic Assurance | 17 | 4 | 40 | 1 | 40.00 | 1-20 | - | - |
| Other First-Class | | | | | | | | |
| ALL FIRST-CLASS | 17 | 4 | 40 | 1 | 40.00 | 1-20 | - | - |
| Refuge Assurance | | | | | | | | |
| NatWest Trophy | | | | | | | | |
| Benson & Hedges Cup | | | | | | | | |
| Other One-Day | | | | | | | | |
| ALL ONE-DAY | | | | | | | | |

## T.W.WARD - *Devon*

| Opposition | Venue | Date | Batting | Fielding | Bowling |
|---|---|---|---|---|---|
| NATWEST TROPHY | | | | | |
| Essex | Exmouth | June 26 | 1 | | 0-35 |

**BATTING AVERAGES - Including fielding**

| | Matches | Inns | NO | Runs | HS | Avge | 100s | 50s | Ct | St |
|---|---|---|---|---|---|---|---|---|---|---|
| NatWest Trophy | 1 | 1 | 0 | 1 | 1 | 1.00 | - | - | - | - |
| ALL ONE-DAY | 1 | 1 | 0 | 1 | 1 | 1.00 | - | - | - | - |

**BOWLING AVERAGES**

| | Overs | Mdns | Runs | Wkts | Avge | Best | 5wI | 10wM |
|---|---|---|---|---|---|---|---|---|
| NatWest Trophy | 10.4 | 4 | 35 | 0 | - | - | - | - |
| ALL ONE-DAY | 10.4 | 4 | 35 | 0 | - | - | - | - |

# PLAYER RECORDS

**W**

## S.J.S.WARKE - *Ireland*

| Opposition | Venue | Date | Batting | Fielding | Bowling |
|---|---|---|---|---|---|
| **OTHER FIRST-CLASS** | | | | | |
| Scotland | Dublin | June 22 | 32 & 78 | | |
| **NATWEST TROPHY** | | | | | |
| Middlesex | Dublin | June 26 | 3 | 1Ct | |
| **OTHER ONE-DAY** | | | | | |
| West Indies | Downpatrick | July 13 | 44 | | |

**BATTING AVERAGES - Including fielding**

| | Matches | Inns | NO | Runs | HS | Avge | 100s | 50s | Ct | St |
|---|---|---|---|---|---|---|---|---|---|---|
| Other First-Class | 1 | 2 | 0 | 110 | 78 | 55.00 | - | 1 | - | - |
| ALL FIRST-CLASS | 1 | 2 | 0 | 110 | 78 | 55.00 | - | 1 | - | - |
| NatWest Trophy | 1 | 1 | 0 | 3 | 3 | 3.00 | - | - | 1 | - |
| Other One-Day | 1 | 1 | 0 | 44 | 44 | 44.00 | - | - | - | - |
| ALL ONE-DAY | 2 | 2 | 0 | 47 | 44 | 23.50 | - | - | 1 | - |

**BOWLING AVERAGES**
Did not bowl

## S.WARLEY - *Oxford University*

| Opposition | Venue | Date | Batting | Fielding | Bowling |
|---|---|---|---|---|---|
| **OTHER FIRST-CLASS** | | | | | |
| Glamorgan | The Parks | April 17 | 3 | | |
| Kent | The Parks | June 18 | 11 & 1 | 1Ct | |

**BATTING AVERAGES - Including fielding**

| | Matches | Inns | NO | Runs | HS | Avge | 100s | 50s | Ct | St |
|---|---|---|---|---|---|---|---|---|---|---|
| Other First-Class | 2 | 3 | 0 | 15 | 11 | 5.00 | - | - | 1 | - |
| ALL FIRST-CLASS | 2 | 3 | 0 | 15 | 11 | 5.00 | - | - | 1 | - |

**BOWLING AVERAGES**
Did not bowl

## S.N.WARMAN - *Lincolnshire*

| Opposition | Venue | Date | Batting | Fielding | Bowling |
|---|---|---|---|---|---|
| **NATWEST TROPHY** | | | | | |
| Notts | Trent Bridge | June 26 | 28 | | |

**BATTING AVERAGES - Including fielding**

| | Matches | Inns | NO | Runs | HS | Avge | 100s | 50s | Ct | St |
|---|---|---|---|---|---|---|---|---|---|---|
| NatWest Trophy | 1 | 1 | 0 | 28 | 28 | 28.00 | - | - | - | - |
| ALL ONE-DAY | 1 | 1 | 0 | 28 | 28 | 28.00 | - | - | - | - |

**BOWLING AVERAGES**
Did not bowl

## A.E.WARNER - *Derbyshire*

| Opposition | Venue | Date | Batting | Fielding | Bowling |
|---|---|---|---|---|---|
| **BRITANNIC ASSURANCE** | | | | | |
| Northants | Derby | April 27 | | | 0-60 |
| Lancashire | Old Trafford | May 16 | 0 | | 2-20 & 0-28 |
| Somerset | Derby | May 22 | 31 & 1 | | 1-68 |
| Glamorgan | Chesterfield | June 7 | 19 & 3 | | 4-42 & 1-36 |
| Gloucs | Gloucester | June 18 | | | 3-35 & 1-53 |
| Warwickshire | Edgbaston | June 28 | 0 & 13 * | | 1-35 & 1-13 |
| Sussex | Derby | July 5 | 6 | 1Ct | 1-32 |
| Worcestershire | Kidd'minster | July 19 | 15 | 1Ct | 3-75 & 0-40 |
| Leicestershire | Derby | Aug 20 | 10 & 8 | | 2-99 |
| Notts | Trent Bridge | Aug 23 | 5 | | 1-49 & 1-32 |
| Leicestershire | Leicester | Aug 28 | 46 & 6 | | 2-76 & 2-55 |
| Essex | Chelmsford | Sept 3 | 25 & 28 | | 0-87 |
| Notts | Derby | Sept 10 | 7 & 8 * | | 0-23 & 0-4 |
| Yorkshire | Chesterfield | Sept 17 | 25 & 33 * | 1Ct | 3-52 & 2-52 |
| **OTHER FIRST-CLASS** | | | | | |
| Cambridge U | Fenner's | May 9 | 53 | | 4-60 |
| West Indies | Derby | June 12 | 7 & 9 | 1Ct | 0-52 & 2-26 |
| Sri Lanka | Derby | Aug 2 | 52 | | 0-11 |
| **REFUGE ASSURANCE** | | | | | |
| Hampshire | Derby | May 5 | 22 * | 2Ct | 2-34 |
| Lancashire | Derby | May 19 | 16 | | 0-70 |
| Yorkshire | Chesterfield | June 2 | 23 | 1Ct | 1-27 |
| Surrey | Chesterfield | June 9 | | | 1-52 |
| Somerset | Derby | June 16 | 12 | 1Ct | 1-34 |
| Essex | Chelmsford | June 30 | 12 | | 3-38 |
| Sussex | Derby | July 7 | 8 | | 0-56 |
| Worcestershire | Worcester | July 9 | 21 | | 1-10 |
| Gloucs | Cheltenham | July 21 | 8 | | 2-36 |
| Northants | Derby | July 28 | 16 * | | 1-21 |
| Glamorgan | Checkley | Aug 18 | 51 | | 0-51 |
| **BENSON & HEDGES CUP** | | | | | |
| Northants | Derby | April 23 | 0 | | 1-25 |
| Combined U | The Parks | April 25 | 35 * | | 0-14 |
| Worcestershire | Worcester | May 4 | 4 | | 1-34 |
| Gloucs | Derby | May 7 | 0 * | | 2-57 |

**BATTING AVERAGES - Including fielding**

| | Matches | Inns | NO | Runs | HS | Avge | 100s | 50s | Ct | St |
|---|---|---|---|---|---|---|---|---|---|---|
| Britannic Assurance | 14 | 20 | 3 | 289 | 46 | 17.00 | - | - | 3 | - |
| Other First-Class | 3 | 4 | 0 | 121 | 53 | 30.25 | - | 2 | 1 | - |
| ALL FIRST-CLASS | 17 | 24 | 3 | 410 | 53 | 19.52 | - | 2 | 4 | - |
| Refuge Assurance | 11 | 10 | 2 | 189 | 51 | 23.62 | - | 1 | 4 | - |
| Benson & Hedges Cup | 4 | 4 | 2 | 39 | 35 * | 19.50 | - | - | - | - |
| ALL ONE-DAY | 15 | 14 | 4 | 228 | 51 | 22.80 | - | 1 | 4 | - |

**BOWLING AVERAGES**

| | Overs | Mdns | Runs | Wkts | Avge | Best | 5wI | 10wM |
|---|---|---|---|---|---|---|---|---|
| Britannic Assurance | 390.4 | 92 | 1066 | 31 | 34.38 | 4-42 | - | - |
| Other First-Class | 56 | 9 | 149 | 6 | 24.83 | 4-60 | - | - |
| ALL FIRST-CLASS | 446.4 | 101 | 1215 | 37 | 32.83 | 4-42 | - | - |
| Refuge Assurance | 76.5 | 2 | 429 | 12 | 35.75 | 3-38 | - | |
| Benson & Hedges Cup | 37.3 | 6 | 130 | 4 | 32.50 | 2-57 | - | |
| ALL ONE-DAY | 114.2 | 8 | 559 | 16 | 34.93 | 3-38 | - | |

## WASIM AKRAM - *Lancashire*

| Opposition | Venue | Date | Batting | Fielding | Bowling |
|---|---|---|---|---|---|
| **BRITANNIC ASSURANCE** | | | | | |
| Warwickshire | Edgbaston | April 27 | | 2Ct | 1-33 |
| Worcestershire | Worcester | May 9 | 17 & 24 | | 1-69 & 4-89 |
| Derbyshire | Old Trafford | May 16 | 15 | | 1-90 |
| Surrey | The Oval | May 22 | 19 & 3 | | 1-84 & 0-37 |
| Sussex | Old Trafford | May 31 | 37 | 1Ct | 4-76 & 4-86 |
| Hampshire | Basingstoke | June 4 | 122 | | 0-10 & 5-48 |
| Leicestershire | Leicester | June 18 | 0 & 20 * | | 1-7 & 5-61 |
| Kent | Old Trafford | June 21 | 42 | | 6-86 |
| Somerset | Taunton | July 2 | 39 & 2 | | 0-7 |
| Notts | Trent Bridge | July 16 | 1 & 18 | | 5-117 |
| Middlesex | Uxbridge | July 19 | 63 & 15 * | 1Ct | 5-63 & 6-66 |
| Warwickshire | Old Trafford | July 23 | | | 1-86 |
| Yorkshire | Old Trafford | Aug 2 | 14 | 1Ct | 5-91 & 0-9 |
| Gloucs | Bristol | Aug 9 | 7 & 13 | | 1-36 |
| **REFUGE ASSURANCE** | | | | | |
| Notts | Old Trafford | April 21 | 12 | | 0-54 |
| Northants | Old Trafford | April 28 | 6 | | 0-33 |
| Worcestershire | Worcester | May 12 | 7 * | | 1-56 |
| Derbyshire | Derby | May 19 | 18 | | 1-42 |

# W     PLAYER RECORDS

| | | | | | |
|---|---|---|---|---|---|
| Sussex | Old Trafford | June 2 | 14 | 1Ct | 0-22 |
| Glamorgan | Old Trafford | June 9 | | | 2-46 |
| Warwickshire | Edgbaston | June 16 | 38 | | 0-51 |
| Kent | Old Trafford | June 23 | 16* | | 2-40 |
| Somerset | Taunton | July 5 | | | 2-30 |
| Leicestershire | Leicester | July 7 | 8* | | 0-40 |
| Middlesex | Lord's | July 21 | 10 | | 1-30 |
| Hampshire | Southampton | July 28 | 0 | | 0-35 |
| Yorkshire | Old Trafford | Aug 4 | 1 | | 0-32 |
| Gloucs | Bristol | Aug 11 | | 1Ct | 1-25 |
| Surrey | Old Trafford | Aug 18 | 38 | | 2-49 |
| Essex | Old Trafford | Aug 25 | 11* | | 1-35 |

**NATWEST TROPHY**

| | | | | | |
|---|---|---|---|---|---|
| Dorset | Bournemouth | June 26 | 11* | | 3-40 |
| Hampshire | Southampton | July 11 | 29 | | 1-46 |

**BENSON & HEDGES CUP**

| | | | | | |
|---|---|---|---|---|---|
| Scotland | Forfar | April 23 | | | 0-32 |
| Kent | Old Trafford | April 25 | 45* | | 0-49 |
| Sussex | Old Trafford | May 7 | 6* | | 4-18 |
| Northants | Old Trafford | May 29 | | | 3-57 |
| Yorkshire | Old Trafford | June 16 | 6 | | 1-32 |
| Worcestershire | Lord's | July 13 | 14 | | 3-58 |

**OTHER ONE-DAY**
For Rest of World

| | | | | | |
|---|---|---|---|---|---|
| England XI | Jesmond | July 31 | 7 | | 1-21 |
| England XI | Jesmond | Aug 1 | 6 | | 1-49 |

**BATTING AVERAGES - Including fielding**

| | Matches | Inns | NO | Runs | HS | Avge | 100s | 50s | Ct | St |
|---|---|---|---|---|---|---|---|---|---|---|
| Britannic Assurance | 14 | 19 | 2 | 471 | 122 | 27.70 | 1 | 1 | 5 | - |
| ALL FIRST-CLASS | 14 | 19 | 2 | 471 | 122 | 27.70 | 1 | 1 | 5 | - |
| Refuge Assurance | 16 | 13 | 4 | 179 | 38 | 19.88 | - | - | 2 | - |
| NatWest Trophy | 2 | 2 | 1 | 40 | 29 | 40.00 | - | - | - | - |
| Benson & Hedges Cup | 6 | 4 | 2 | 71 | 45* | 35.50 | - | - | - | - |
| Other One-Day | 2 | 2 | 0 | 13 | 7 | 6.50 | - | - | - | - |
| ALL ONE-DAY | 26 | 21 | 7 | 303 | 45* | 21.64 | - | - | 2 | - |

**BOWLING AVERAGES**

| | Overs | Mdns | Runs | Wkts | Avge | Best | 5wI | 10wM |
|---|---|---|---|---|---|---|---|---|
| Britannic Assurance | 429.3 | 99 | 1251 | 56 | 22.33 | 6-66 | 7 | 1 |
| ALL FIRST-CLASS | 429.3 | 99 | 1251 | 56 | 22.33 | 6-66 | 7 | 1 |
| Refuge Assurance | 117.5 | 1 | 620 | 13 | 47.69 | 2-30 | - | |
| NatWest Trophy | 23.3 | 2 | 86 | 4 | 21.50 | 3-40 | - | |
| Benson & Hedges Cup | 61 | 5 | 246 | 11 | 22.36 | 4-18 | - | |
| Other One-Day | 18.1 | 4 | 70 | 2 | 35.00 | 1-21 | - | |
| ALL ONE-DAY | 220.3 | 12 | 1022 | 30 | 34.06 | 4-18 | - | |

## A.WASSON - *World XI*

| Opposition | Venue | Date | Batting | Fielding | Bowling |
|---|---|---|---|---|---|
| **OTHER FIRST-CLASS** | | | | | |
| West Indies XI | Scarborough | Aug 28 | 23 & 10 | 1Ct | 1-106 & 3-114 |

**BATTING AVERAGES - Including fielding**

| | Matches | Inns | NO | Runs | HS | Avge | 100s | 50s | Ct | St |
|---|---|---|---|---|---|---|---|---|---|---|
| Other First-Class | 1 | 2 | 0 | 33 | 23 | 16.50 | - | - | 1 | - |
| ALL FIRST-CLASS | 1 | 2 | 0 | 33 | 23 | 16.50 | - | - | 1 | - |

**BOWLING AVERAGES**

| | Overs | Mdns | Runs | Wkts | Avge | Best | 5wI | 10wM |
|---|---|---|---|---|---|---|---|---|
| Other First-Class | 49 | 4 | 220 | 4 | 55.00 | 3-114 | - | - |
| ALL FIRST-CLASS | 49 | 4 | 220 | 4 | 55.00 | 3-114 | - | - |

## S.N.V.WATERTON - *England Amateur XI*

| Opposition | Venue | Date | Batting | Fielding | Bowling |
|---|---|---|---|---|---|
| **OTHER ONE-DAY** | | | | | |
| Sri Lanka | Wolv'hampton | July 24 | 19 | | |

**BATTING AVERAGES - Including fielding**

| | Matches | Inns | NO | Runs | HS | Avge | 100s | 50s | Ct | St |
|---|---|---|---|---|---|---|---|---|---|---|
| Other One-Day | 1 | 1 | 0 | 19 | 19 | 19.00 | - | - | - | - |
| ALL ONE-DAY | 1 | 1 | 0 | 19 | 19 | 19.00 | - | - | - | - |

**BOWLING AVERAGES**
Did not bowl

## S.L.WATKIN - *Glamorgan & England*

| Opposition | Venue | Date | Batting | Fielding | Bowling |
|---|---|---|---|---|---|
| **CORNHILL TEST MATCHES** | | | | | |
| West Indies | Headingley | June 6 | 2 & | 0 | 2-55 & 3-38 |
| West Indies | Lord's | June 20 | 6 | | 0-60 |
| **BRITANNIC ASSURANCE** | | | | | |
| Leicestershire | Leicester | April 27 | 13* | | 0-29 |
| Somerset | Taunton | May 9 | 25* | | 2-120 & 5-63 |
| Warwickshire | Swansea | May 16 | 1* & | 2* | 3-53 & 1-31 |
| Northants | Cardiff | May 22 | 5* | | 3-30 & 6-55 |
| Sussex | Cardiff | May 25 | | | 2-52 & 1-59 |
| Worcestershire | Worcester | May 31 | 10 | 2Ct | 4-40 & 2-61 |
| Middlesex | Cardiff | June 14 | 13* | | 1-35 & 1-82 |
| Lancashire | Liverpool | June 28 | | | 2-71 & 2-40 |
| Notts | Cardiff | July 2 | 15 | | 5-59 & 0-47 |
| Kent | Maidstone | July 5 | 7* | | 2-76 & 0-63 |
| Gloucs | Cheltenham | July 19 | 15 & | 5* | 5-49 & 1-89 |
| Essex | Cardiff | July 23 | | | 0-75 |
| Surrey | The Oval | July 26 | 3 | | 1-14 |
| Hampshire | Swansea | Aug 9 | | 5 | 3-57 |
| Yorkshire | Headingley | Aug 16 | | | 3-64 & 0-34 |
| Warwickshire | Edgbaston | Aug 20 | | | 2-68 & 1-46 |
| Gloucs | Abergavenny | Aug 28 | 4 | | 0-51 & 2-73 |
| Hampshire | Southampton | Sept 17 | 0 | | 3-70 & 3-92 |
| **OTHER FIRST-CLASS** | | | | | |
| For MCC | | | | | |
| Middlesex | Lord's | April 16 | | | 2-88 |
| For Glamorgan | | | | | |
| West Indies | Swansea | July 16 | 5 | | 1-86 |
| **REFUGE ASSURANCE** | | | | | |
| Northants | Cardiff | April 21 | | | 3-30 |
| Leicestershire | Leicester | April 28 | | | 2-28 |
| Notts | Cardiff | May 5 | | 1Ct | 0-33 |
| Warwickshire | Swansea | May 19 | 0 | | 0-27 |
| Sussex | Swansea | May 26 | 0 | | 2-44 |
| Essex | Pontypridd | June 2 | | | |
| Middlesex | Cardiff | June 16 | 2 | | 3-34 |
| Yorkshire | Headingley | June 30 | 14 | | 1-40 |
| Kent | Maidstone | July 7 | | | 0-48 |
| Gloucs | Swansea | Aug 4 | 6 | | 1-11 |
| Hampshire | Ebbw Vale | Aug 11 | 2 | | 2-37 |
| Derbyshire | Checkley | Aug 18 | 31* | | 2-50 |
| **NATWEST TROPHY** | | | | | |
| Durham | Darlington | June 26 | | | 2-41 |
| Worcestershire | Worcester | July 11 | | | 0-35 |
| Northants | Northampton | July 31 | 5* | 1Ct | 2-40 |
| **BENSON & HEDGES CUP** | | | | | |
| Min Counties | Trowbridge | April 23 | 5* | | 3-28 |
| Hampshire | Southampton | May 2 | 15 | | 0-69 |
| Notts | Cardiff | May 4 | 5 | | 1-42 |
| Yorkshire | Cardiff | May 7 | | | 1-51 |

**BATTING AVERAGES - Including fielding**

| | Matches | Inns | NO | Runs | HS | Avge | 100s | 50s | Ct | St |
|---|---|---|---|---|---|---|---|---|---|---|
| Cornhill Test Matches | 2 | 3 | 0 | 8 | 6 | 2.66 | - | - | - | - |
| Britannic Assurance | 18 | 15 | 8 | 123 | 25* | 17.57 | - | - | 2 | - |
| Other First-Class | 2 | 1 | 0 | 5 | 5 | 5.00 | - | - | - | - |

# PLAYER RECORDS

**W**

| | | | | | | | | | | |
|---|---|---|---|---|---|---|---|---|---|---|
| ALL FIRST-CLASS | 22 | 19 | 8 | 136 | 25* | 12.36 | - | - | 2 | - |
| Refuge Assurance | 12 | 7 | 1 | 55 | 31* | 9.16 | - | - | 1 | - |
| NatWest Trophy | 3 | 1 | 1 | 5 | 5* | - | - | - | 1 | - |
| Benson & Hedges Cup | 4 | 3 | 1 | 25 | 15 | 12.50 | - | - | - | - |
| ALL ONE-DAY | 19 | 11 | 3 | 85 | 31* | 10.62 | - | - | 2 | - |

## BOWLING AVERAGES

| | Overs | Mdns | Runs | Wkts | Avge | Best | 5wI | 10wM |
|---|---|---|---|---|---|---|---|---|
| Cornhill Test Matches | 36 | 4 | 153 | 5 | 30.60 | 3-38 | - | - |
| Britannic Assurance | 639.5 | 137 | 1848 | 66 | 28.00 | 6-55 | 4 | - |
| Other First-Class | 53 | 14 | 174 | 3 | 58.00 | 2-88 | - | - |
| ALL FIRST-CLASS | 728.5 | 155 | 2175 | 74 | 29.39 | 6-55 | 4 | - |
| Refuge Assurance | 83 | 4 | 382 | 16 | 23.87 | 3-30 | - | |
| NatWest Trophy | 36 | 2 | 116 | 4 | 29.00 | 2-40 | - | |
| Benson & Hedges Cup | 44 | 7 | 190 | 5 | 38.00 | 3-28 | - | |
| ALL ONE-DAY | 163 | 13 | 688 | 25 | 27.52 | 3-28 | - | |

# S.G.WATKINS - *Wales*

| Opposition | Venue | Date | Batting | Fielding | Bowling |
|---|---|---|---|---|---|
| **OTHER ONE-DAY** | | | | | |
| West Indies | Brecon | July 15 | 3 | | 1-74 |

## BATTING AVERAGES - Including fielding

| | Matches | Inns | NO | Runs | HS | Avge | 100s | 50s | Ct | St |
|---|---|---|---|---|---|---|---|---|---|---|
| Other One-Day | 1 | 1 | 0 | 3 | 3 | 3.00 | - | - | - | - |
| ALL ONE-DAY | 1 | 1 | 0 | 3 | 3 | 3.00 | - | - | - | - |

## BOWLING AVERAGES

| | Overs | Mdns | Runs | Wkts | Avge | Best | 5wI | 10wM |
|---|---|---|---|---|---|---|---|---|
| Other One-Day | 8 | 0 | 74 | 1 | 74.00 | 1-74 | - | |
| ALL ONE-DAY | 8 | 0 | 74 | 1 | 74.00 | 1-74 | - | |

# M.WATKINSON - *Lancashire*

| Opposition | Venue | Date | Batting | | | Fielding | Bowling |
|---|---|---|---|---|---|---|---|
| **BRITANNIC ASSURANCE** | | | | | | | |
| Warwickshire | Edgbaston | April 27 | 30 | | | | |
| Worcestershire | Worcester | May 9 | 12 | & | 6 | | 2-22 |
| Surrey | The Oval | May 22 | 55 | & | 114* | | 3-82 & 1-37 |
| Sussex | Old Trafford | May 31 | 41 | & | 2* | 1Ct | 2-64 & 4-95 |
| Hampshire | Basingstoke | June 4 | 6 | | | | 1-11 & 2-48 |
| Leicestershire | Leicester | June 18 | 12 | & | 6 | | 3-47 |
| Kent | Old Trafford | June 21 | 52 | | | 1Ct | 0-36 |
| Glamorgan | Liverpool | June 28 | 20* | & | 21 | 1Ct | 1-84 & 0-8 |
| Somerset | Taunton | July 2 | 13 | & | 30 | | 1-70 & 1-85 |
| Notts | Trent Bridge | July 16 | 18 | & | 0 | 1Ct | 2-67 |
| Middlesex | Uxbridge | July 19 | 35 | & | 21 | 1Ct | 0-41 & 2-40 |
| Warwickshire | Old Trafford | July 23 | | | | | 3-58 & 1-61 |
| Yorkshire | Old Trafford | Aug 2 | 21 | | | 1Ct | 1-93 & 0-5 |
| Gloucs | Bristol | Aug 9 | 9 | & | 0 | 1Ct | 3-140 |
| Derbyshire | Derby | Aug 16 | 25 | & | 3 | | 0-46 & 0-21 |
| Worcestershire | Blackpool | Aug 20 | 0 | & | 51 | | 1-81 & 0-48 |
| Essex | Old Trafford | Aug 23 | 20 | | | 1Ct | 1-49 & 1-65 |
| Notts | Old Trafford | Aug 28 | 20 | & | 27 | | 4-55 & 1-165 |
| Yorkshire | Scarborough | Sept 3 | 0 | & | 17 | | 1-117 & 4-85 |
| Surrey | Old Trafford | Sept 17 | 21 | & | 5 | | 4-45 & 1-145 |
| **OTHER FIRST-CLASS** | | | | | | | |
| Cambridge U | Fenner's | April 13 | 10 | & | 35* | | 2-52 & 0-5 |
| **REFUGE ASSURANCE** | | | | | | | |
| Notts | Old Trafford | April 21 | 25 | | | | 0-40 |
| Northants | Old Trafford | April 28 | 4 | | | | 0-53 |
| Derbyshire | Derby | May 19 | 82 | | | | 1-36 |
| Sussex | Old Trafford | June 2 | 83 | | | 2Ct | 3-27 |
| Glamorgan | Old Trafford | June 9 | | | | | 0-43 |
| Warwickshire | Edgbaston | June 16 | 7 | | | | 1-37 |
| Kent | Old Trafford | June 23 | 6 | | | 1Ct | 1-34 |

| | | | | | |
|---|---|---|---|---|---|
| Somerset | Taunton | July 5 | | | 1-42 |
| Leicestershire | Leicester | July 7 | 31 | | 2-33 |
| Middlesex | Lord's | July 21 | 2 | | 1-21 |
| Hampshire | Southampton | July 28 | 25 | | 3-34 |
| Yorkshire | Old Trafford | Aug 4 | 4 | | 1-51 |
| Gloucs | Bristol | Aug 11 | | 1Ct | 2-20 |
| Surrey | Old Trafford | Aug 18 | 9 | | 1-48 |
| Essex | Old Trafford | Aug 25 | 3 | 1Ct | 2-34 |
| Northants | Old Trafford | Sept 1 | 0 | | 2-47 |
| Worcestershire | Old Trafford | Sept 15 | 34 | | 1-44 |
| **NATWEST TROPHY** | | | | | |
| Dorset | Bournemouth | June 26 | 5 | | 2-10 |
| Hampshire | Southampton | July 11 | 7 | | 1-62 |
| **BENSON & HEDGES CUP** | | | | | |
| Scotland | Forfar | April 23 | 15* | | 2-30 |
| Kent | Old Trafford | April 25 | 22* | | 3-42 |
| Northants | Old Trafford | May 29 | 32* | | 1-46 |
| Yorkshire | Old Trafford | June 16 | 12 | | 5-49 |
| Worcestershire | Lord's | July 13 | 13 | 1Ct | 1-54 |
| **OTHER ONE-DAY** | | | | | |
| For England A | | | | | |
| Sri Lanka | Old Trafford | Aug 14 | 25* | | 2-21 |
| Sri Lanka | Old Trafford | Aug 15 | 2 | | 1-35 |

## BATTING AVERAGES - Including fielding

| | Matches | Inns | NO | Runs | HS | Avge | 100s | 50s | Ct | St |
|---|---|---|---|---|---|---|---|---|---|---|
| Britannic Assurance | 20 | 33 | 3 | 713 | 114* | 23.76 | 1 | 3 | 8 | - |
| Other First-Class | 1 | 2 | 1 | 45 | 35* | 45.00 | - | - | - | - |
| ALL FIRST-CLASS | 21 | 35 | 4 | 758 | 114* | 24.45 | 1 | 3 | 8 | - |
| Refuge Assurance | 17 | 14 | 0 | 315 | 83 | 22.50 | - | 2 | 5 | - |
| NatWest Trophy | 2 | 2 | 0 | 12 | 7 | 6.00 | - | - | - | - |
| Benson & Hedges Cup | 5 | 5 | 3 | 94 | 32* | 47.00 | - | - | 1 | - |
| Other One-Day | 2 | 2 | 1 | 27 | 25* | 27.00 | - | - | - | - |
| ALL ONE-DAY | 26 | 23 | 4 | 448 | 83 | 23.57 | - | 2 | 6 | - |

## BOWLING AVERAGES

| | Overs | Mdns | Runs | Wkts | Avge | Best | 5wI | 10wM |
|---|---|---|---|---|---|---|---|---|
| Britannic Assurance | 603.2 | 107 | 2116 | 51 | 41.49 | 4-45 | - | - |
| Other First-Class | 26 | 9 | 57 | 2 | 28.50 | 2-52 | - | - |
| ALL FIRST-CLASS | 629.2 | 116 | 2173 | 53 | 41.00 | 4-45 | - | - |
| Refuge Assurance | 122 | 1 | 644 | 22 | 29.27 | 3-27 | - | |
| NatWest Trophy | 22 | 7 | 72 | 3 | 24.00 | 2-10 | - | |
| Benson & Hedges Cup | 54.4 | 4 | 221 | 12 | 18.41 | 5-49 | 1 | |
| Other One-Day | 17 | 2 | 56 | 3 | 18.66 | 2-21 | - | |
| ALL ONE-DAY | 215.4 | 14 | 993 | 40 | 24.82 | 5-49 | 1 | |

# J.R.WEAVER - *Shropshire*

| Opposition | Venue | Date | Batting | Fielding | Bowling |
|---|---|---|---|---|---|
| **NATWEST TROPHY** | | | | | |
| Leicestershire | Leicester | June 26 | 6 | | |

## BATTING AVERAGES - Including fielding

| | Matches | Inns | NO | Runs | HS | Avge | 100s | 50s | Ct | St |
|---|---|---|---|---|---|---|---|---|---|---|
| NatWest Trophy | 1 | 1 | 0 | 6 | 6 | 6.00 | - | - | - | - |
| ALL ONE-DAY | 1 | 1 | 0 | 6 | 6 | 6.00 | - | - | - | - |

## BOWLING AVERAGES
Did not bowl

# P.N.WEEKES - *Middlesex*

| Opposition | Venue | Date | Batting | | | Fielding | Bowling |
|---|---|---|---|---|---|---|---|
| **BRITANNIC ASSURANCE** | | | | | | | |
| Surrey | The Oval | Aug 20 | 86 | | | 2Ct | 1-30 & 2-18 |
| Worcestershire | Worcester | Aug 23 | 57* | & | 48 | 1Ct | 3-57 |

| Kent | Canterbury | Aug 28 | 4 & 2 | | 0-34 |
| Notts | Trent Bridge | Sept 3 | 31 & 10 | 1Ct | 0-24 & 0-4 |
| Surrey | Lord's | Sept 10 | 0 & 6 | | |
| Essex | Chelmsford | Sept 17 | 5 & 0 | 1Ct | 1-21 |

**REFUGE ASSURANCE**

| Gloucs | Bristol | April 21 | | 1Ct | |
| Surrey | Lord's | April 28 | 3 | | |
| Somerset | Taunton | May 26 | | 1Ct | 0-42 |
| Leicestershire | Uxbridge | June 9 | 20 | | 1-45 |
| Glamorgan | Cardiff | June 16 | 1 | 1Ct | 1-40 |
| Notts | Trent Bridge | June 23 | | 1Ct | 2-20 |
| Yorkshire | Lord's | July 7 | 32* | | 0-36 |
| Warwickshire | Edgbaston | July 14 | 16 | | 0-50 |
| Lancashire | Lord's | July 21 | 26* | | 0-8 |
| Hampshire | Lord's | Aug 4 | | | 3-27 |
| Derbyshire | Lord's | Aug 11 | 13 | 1Ct | |
| Essex | Colchester | Aug 18 | 0 | | 1-42 |
| Worcestershire | Worcester | Aug 25 | 4 | 1Ct | 1-63 |

**NATWEST TROPHY**

| Ireland | Dublin | June 26 | 7 | | 1-30 |

**BENSON & HEDGES CUP**

| Surrey | Lord's | April 25 | 0 | 1Ct | |

**BATTING AVERAGES - Including fielding**

| | Matches | Inns | NO | Runs | HS | Avge | 100s | 50s | Ct | St |
|---|---|---|---|---|---|---|---|---|---|---|
| Britannic Assurance | 6 | 11 | 1 | 249 | 86 | 24.90 | - | 2 | 5 | - |
| ALL FIRST-CLASS | 6 | 11 | 1 | 249 | 86 | 24.90 | - | 2 | 5 | - |
| Refuge Assurance | 13 | 9 | 2 | 115 | 32* | 16.42 | - | - | 6 | - |
| NatWest Trophy | 1 | 1 | 0 | 7 | 7 | 7.00 | - | - | - | - |
| Benson & Hedges Cup | 1 | 1 | 0 | 0 | 0 | 0.00 | - | - | 1 | - |
| ALL ONE-DAY | 15 | 11 | 2 | 122 | 32* | 13.55 | - | - | 7 | - |

**BOWLING AVERAGES**

| | Overs | Mdns | Runs | Wkts | Avge | Best | 5wI | 10wM |
|---|---|---|---|---|---|---|---|---|
| Britannic Assurance | 56.4 | 12 | 188 | 7 | 26.85 | 3-57 | - | - |
| ALL FIRST-CLASS | 56.4 | 12 | 188 | 7 | 26.85 | 3-57 | - | - |
| Refuge Assurance | 70.2 | 2 | 373 | 9 | 41.44 | 3-27 | - | |
| NatWest Trophy | 12 | 1 | 30 | 1 | 30.00 | 1-30 | - | |
| Benson & Hedges Cup | | | | | | | | |
| ALL ONE-DAY | 82.2 | 3 | 403 | 10 | 40.30 | 3-27 | - | |

# S.J.WEEKS - *Durham*

| Opposition | Venue | Date | Batting | Fielding | Bowling |
|---|---|---|---|---|---|

**OTHER ONE-DAY**

| Leicestershire | Harrogate | June 11 | 4 | | |
| Surrey | Harrogate | June 13 | 1 | | |

**BATTING AVERAGES - Including fielding**

| | Matches | Inns | NO | Runs | HS | Avge | 100s | 50s | Ct | St |
|---|---|---|---|---|---|---|---|---|---|---|
| Other One-Day | 2 | 2 | 0 | 5 | 4 | 2.50 | - | - | - | - |
| ALL ONE-DAY | 2 | 2 | 0 | 5 | 4 | 2.50 | - | - | - | - |

**BOWLING AVERAGES**

Did not bowl

# A.P.WELLS - *Sussex*

| Opposition | Venue | Date | Batting | Fielding | Bowling |
|---|---|---|---|---|---|

**BRITANNIC ASSURANCE**

| Somerset | Taunton | April 27 | 3 | | |
| Middlesex | Lord's | May 9 | 120 | | |
| Hampshire | Hove | May 16 | 49 & 83* | | |
| Middlesex | Hove | May 22 | 137 & 2 | 1Ct | |
| Glamorgan | Cardiff | May 25 | 0 & 153* | | |
| Lancashire | Old Trafford | May 31 | 6 & 40 | | |
| Kent | Tunbridge W | June 7 | 107 & 0 | 1Ct | |
| Worcestershire | Hove | June 14 | 20 | | 1-21 |
| Warwickshire | Coventry | June 18 | 11 | | |
| Essex | Horsham | June 21 | 26 | 1Ct | |
| Surrey | Arundel | July 2 | 20 & 77 | | |
| Somerset | Hove | July 16 | 159 | | |
| Leicestershire | Hove | July 19 | 12 & 33* | 1Ct | |
| Gloucs | Cheltenham | July 23 | 7 | | |
| Northants | Eastbourne | Aug 2 | 0 & 11 | 2Ct | |
| Notts | Eastbourne | Aug 6 | 6 & 73 | | |
| Yorkshire | Midd'brough | Aug 9 | 253* | | |
| Hampshire | Bournemouth | Aug 20 | 76 & 18* | | |
| Surrey | The Oval | Aug 28 | 28 & 3 | 1Ct | |
| Kent | Hove | Sept 3 | 74 & 162 | | |
| Gloucs | Hove | Sept 17 | 7 & 1 | | |

**OTHER FIRST-CLASS**

| Sri Lanka | Hove | Aug 17 | 0 & 7* | | |

**REFUGE ASSURANCE**

| Warwickshire | Edgbaston | April 21 | 8 | | |
| Somerset | Taunton | April 28 | 38 | 1Ct | |
| Middlesex | Hove | May 12 | 10 | 2Ct | |
| Gloucs | Hove | May 19 | 3 | | |
| Glamorgan | Swansea | May 26 | 5 | | |
| Lancashire | Old Trafford | June 2 | 1 | | |
| Hampshire | Basingstoke | June 9 | 1 | 1Ct | |
| Worcestershire | Hove | June 16 | 58 | | |
| Leicestershire | Hove | July 21 | 36 | | |
| Notts | Hove | July 28 | 33 | | |
| Northants | Eastbourne | Aug 4 | 38 | | |
| Yorkshire | Midd'brough | Aug 11 | 30 | | |
| Kent | Hove | Aug 25 | 28 | | |

**NATWEST TROPHY**

| Scotland | Edinburgh | June 26 | 8 | | |
| Essex | Hove | July 11 | 40 | | |

**BENSON & HEDGES CUP**

| Leicestershire | Hove | April 25 | 23* | | |
| Kent | Canterbury | May 2 | 66 | 1Ct | |
| Scotland | Hove | May 4 | 0 | | |
| Lancashire | Old Trafford | May 7 | 7 | | |

**OTHER ONE-DAY**

| Kent | Hove | Sept 7 | 2 | | |
| Gloucs | Hove | Sept 9 | 13 | | |

**BATTING AVERAGES - Including fielding**

| | Matches | Inns | NO | Runs | HS | Avge | 100s | 50s | Ct | St |
|---|---|---|---|---|---|---|---|---|---|---|
| Britannic Assurance | 21 | 34 | 5 | 1777 | 253* | 61.27 | 7 | 5 | 7 | - |
| Other First-Class | 1 | 2 | 1 | 7 | 7* | 7.00 | - | - | - | - |
| ALL FIRST-CLASS | 22 | 36 | 6 | 1784 | 253* | 59.46 | 7 | 5 | 7 | - |
| Refuge Assurance | 13 | 13 | 0 | 289 | 58 | 22.23 | - | 1 | 4 | - |
| NatWest Trophy | 2 | 2 | 0 | 48 | 40 | 24.00 | - | - | - | - |
| Benson & Hedges Cup | 4 | 4 | 1 | 96 | 66 | 32.00 | - | 1 | 1 | - |
| Other One-Day | 2 | 2 | 0 | 15 | 13 | 7.50 | - | - | - | - |
| ALL ONE-DAY | 21 | 21 | 1 | 448 | 66 | 22.40 | - | 2 | 5 | - |

**BOWLING AVERAGES**

| | Overs | Mdns | Runs | Wkts | Avge | Best | 5wI | 10wM |
|---|---|---|---|---|---|---|---|---|
| Britannic Assurance | 5 | 1 | 21 | 1 | 21.00 | 1-21 | - | - |
| Other First-Class | | | | | | | | |
| ALL FIRST-CLASS | 5 | 1 | 21 | 1 | 21.00 | 1-21 | - | - |
| Refuge Assurance | | | | | | | | |
| NatWest Trophy | | | | | | | | |
| Benson & Hedges Cup | | | | | | | | |
| Other One-Day | | | | | | | | |
| ALL ONE-DAY | | | | | | | | |

# PLAYER RECORDS W

## C.M.WELLS - Sussex

| Opposition | Venue | Date | Batting | Fielding | Bowling |
|---|---|---|---|---|---|
| **BRITANNIC ASSURANCE** | | | | | |
| Kent | Tunbridge W | June 7 | 3 & 30 * | | 2-48 & 1-25 |
| Worcestershire | Hove | June 14 | 0 | | 0-77 |
| Warwickshire | Coventry | June 18 | 24 | | 3-42 |
| Essex | Horsham | June 21 | 7 | | 1-37 |
| Surrey | Arundel | July 2 | 4 & 1 | 1Ct | 0-39 |
| Derbyshire | Derby | July 5 | 38 & 14 * | 1Ct | 7-42 & 0-33 |
| Somerset | Hove | July 16 | 12 | | 0-56 & 0-14 |
| Leicestershire | Hove | July 19 | 31 * & 14 * | | |
| Northants | Eastbourne | Aug 2 | 12 & 20 * | | 1-19 & 0-22 |
| Yorkshire | Midd'brough | Aug 9 | 42 | | 1-30 & 0-4 |
| Kent | Hove | Sept 3 | 76 & 34 | | 0-43 & 0-30 |
| Gloucs | Hove | Sept 17 | 64 & 25 | | 2-37 |
| **OTHER FIRST-CLASS** | | | | | |
| Cambridge U | Hove | June 29 | 52 * | | |
| Sri Lanka | Hove | Aug 17 | 0 | 1Ct | 0-46 |
| **REFUGE ASSURANCE** | | | | | |
| Lancashire | Old Trafford | June 2 | 3 | 1Ct | 1-31 |
| Hampshire | Basingstoke | June 9 | 16 | | 0-32 |
| Worcestershire | Hove | June 16 | | | |
| Derbyshire | Derby | July 7 | 34 * | | 0-35 |
| Surrey | The Oval | July 14 | 10 | | 0-26 |
| Leicestershire | Hove | July 21 | 7 | | 0-36 |
| Notts | Hove | July 28 | 28 | | 0-23 |
| Northants | Eastbourne | Aug 4 | 24 * | | 0-22 |
| Yorkshire | Midd'brough | Aug 11 | 6 | | 0-23 |
| **NATWEST TROPHY** | | | | | |
| Scotland | Edinburgh | June 26 | 0 | | 3-16 |
| Essex | Hove | July 11 | 11 | | 1-39 |
| **OTHER ONE-DAY** | | | | | |
| Kent | Hove | Sept 7 | 3 | | |
| Gloucs | Hove | Sept 9 | 15 | | |

### BATTING AVERAGES - Including fielding

| | Matches | Inns | NO | Runs | HS | Avge | 100s | 50s | Ct | St |
|---|---|---|---|---|---|---|---|---|---|---|
| Britannic Assurance | 12 | 19 | 5 | 451 | 76 | 32.21 | - | 2 | 2 | - |
| Other First-Class | 2 | 2 | 1 | 52 | 52 * | 52.00 | - | 1 | 1 | - |
| ALL FIRST-CLASS | 14 | 21 | 6 | 503 | 76 | 33.53 | - | 3 | 3 | - |
| Refuge Assurance | 9 | 8 | 2 | 128 | 34 * | 21.33 | - | - | 1 | - |
| NatWest Trophy | 2 | 2 | 0 | 11 | 11 | 5.50 | - | - | - | - |
| Other One-Day | 2 | 2 | 0 | 18 | 15 | 9.00 | - | - | - | - |
| ALL ONE-DAY | 13 | 12 | 2 | 157 | 34 * | 15.70 | - | - | 1 | - |

### BOWLING AVERAGES

| | Overs | Mdns | Runs | Wkts | Avge | Best | 5wI | 10wM |
|---|---|---|---|---|---|---|---|---|
| Britannic Assurance | 216.4 | 60 | 598 | 18 | 33.22 | 7-42 | 1 | - |
| Other First-Class | 14 | 2 | 46 | 0 | - | - | - | - |
| ALL FIRST-CLASS | 230.4 | 62 | 644 | 18 | 35.77 | 7-42 | 1 | - |
| Refuge Assurance | 53 | 0 | 228 | 1 | 228.00 | 1-31 | - | |
| NatWest Trophy | 21 | 3 | 55 | 4 | 13.75 | 3-16 | - | |
| Other One-Day | | | | | | | | |
| ALL ONE-DAY | 74 | 3 | 283 | 5 | 56.60 | 3-16 | - | |

## V.J.WELLS - Kent

| Opposition | Venue | Date | Batting | Fielding | Bowling |
|---|---|---|---|---|---|
| **BRITANNIC ASSURANCE** | | | | | |
| Hampshire | Canterbury | Aug 6 | 1 & 28 | 1Ct | |
| Leicestershire | Leicester | Aug 9 | 0 | | |
| **OTHER FIRST-CLASS** | | | | | |
| Oxford U | The Parks | June 18 | 58 | | 1-24 & 3-21 |
| **REFUGE ASSURANCE** | | | | | |
| Hampshire | Southampton | May 12 | 8 | | |

### BENSON & HEDGES CUP

| Opposition | Venue | Date | Batting | Fielding | Bowling |
|---|---|---|---|---|---|
| Sussex | Canterbury | May 2 | 25 | | |
| Scotland | Glasgow | May 7 | 7 | 2Ct | |

### BATTING AVERAGES - Including fielding

| | Matches | Inns | NO | Runs | HS | Avge | 100s | 50s | Ct | St |
|---|---|---|---|---|---|---|---|---|---|---|
| Britannic Assurance | 2 | 3 | 0 | 29 | 28 | 9.66 | - | - | 1 | - |
| Other First-Class | 1 | 1 | 0 | 58 | 58 | 58.00 | - | 1 | - | - |
| ALL FIRST-CLASS | 3 | 4 | 0 | 87 | 58 | 21.75 | - | 1 | 1 | - |
| Refuge Assurance | 1 | 1 | 0 | 8 | 8 | 8.00 | - | - | - | - |
| Benson & Hedges Cup | 2 | 2 | 0 | 32 | 25 | 16.00 | - | - | 2 | - |
| ALL ONE-DAY | 3 | 3 | 0 | 40 | 25 | 13.33 | - | - | 2 | - |

### BOWLING AVERAGES

| | Overs | Mdns | Runs | Wkts | Avge | Best | 5wI | 10wM |
|---|---|---|---|---|---|---|---|---|
| Britannic Assurance | | | | | | | | |
| Other First-Class | 22.4 | 8 | 45 | 4 | 11.25 | 3-21 | - | - |
| ALL FIRST-CLASS | 22.4 | 8 | 45 | 4 | 11.25 | 3-21 | - | - |
| Refuge Assurance | | | | | | | | |
| Benson & Hedges Cup | | | | | | | | |
| ALL ONE-DAY | | | | | | | | |

## M.J.WESTON - Worcestershire

| Opposition | Venue | Date | Batting | Fielding | Bowling |
|---|---|---|---|---|---|
| **BRITANNIC ASSURANCE** | | | | | |
| Northants | Northampton | June 4 | 9 | | 1-27 |
| Essex | Ilford | June 7 | 5 | | |
| **OTHER FIRST-CLASS** | | | | | |
| Oxford U | The Parks | May 25 | 1 | 1Ct | 0-25 |
| **REFUGE ASSURANCE** | | | | | |
| Kent | Worcester | April 21 | | 1Ct | 0-26 |
| Gloucs | Bristol | May 5 | | 2Ct | 1-24 |
| Lancashire | Worcester | May 12 | 4 | | 0-30 |
| Northants | Northampton | May 19 | 1 * | | 0-36 |
| Warwickshire | Edgbaston | May 26 | 51 | | 0-28 |
| Surrey | Worcester | June 2 | 27 | | 0-16 |
| Essex | Ilford | June 9 | 4 | 1Ct | 1-37 |
| Sussex | Hove | June 16 | | | 1-33 |
| Yorkshire | Sheffield | June 23 | 13 | | 1-21 |
| Hampshire | Southampton | July 7 | 0 * | | 1-21 |
| Derbyshire | Worcester | July 9 | | | 0-24 |
| Glamorgan | Worcester | July 21 | | | 0-17 |
| Notts | Trent Bridge | Aug 4 | | | 0-22 |
| Somerset | Worcester | Aug 18 | 30 * | | 0-22 |
| Middlesex | Worcester | Aug 25 | 0 | | 2-27 |
| Notts | Trent Bridge | Sept 1 | 18 | | 1-28 |
| Lancashire | Old Trafford | Sept 15 | 14 * | | 2-25 |
| **BENSON & HEDGES CUP** | | | | | |
| Northants | Northampton | May 7 | 30 | | 1-41 |

### BATTING AVERAGES - Including fielding

| | Matches | Inns | NO | Runs | HS | Avge | 100s | 50s | Ct | St |
|---|---|---|---|---|---|---|---|---|---|---|
| Britannic Assurance | 2 | 2 | 0 | 14 | 9 | 7.00 | - | - | - | - |
| Other First-Class | 1 | 1 | 0 | 1 | 1 | 1.00 | - | - | 1 | - |
| ALL FIRST-CLASS | 3 | 3 | 0 | 15 | 9 | 5.00 | - | - | 1 | - |
| Refuge Assurance | 17 | 11 | 4 | 162 | 51 | 23.14 | - | 1 | 4 | - |
| Benson & Hedges Cup | 1 | 1 | 0 | 30 | 30 | 30.00 | - | - | - | - |
| ALL ONE-DAY | 18 | 12 | 4 | 192 | 51 | 24.00 | - | 1 | 4 | - |

### BOWLING AVERAGES

| | Overs | Mdns | Runs | Wkts | Avge | Best | 5wI | 10wM |
|---|---|---|---|---|---|---|---|---|
| Britannic Assurance | 5 | 1 | 27 | 1 | 27.00 | 1-27 | - | - |
| Other First-Class | 7 | 1 | 25 | 0 | - | - | - | - |
| ALL FIRST-CLASS | 12 | 2 | 52 | 1 | 52.00 | 1-27 | - | - |
| Refuge Assurance | 113.1 | 4 | 437 | 10 | 43.70 | 2-25 | - | - |
| Benson & Hedges Cup | 11 | 0 | 41 | 1 | 41.00 | 1-41 | - | - |

# W

# PLAYER RECORDS

ALL ONE-DAY    124.1    4    478    11    43.45    2-25    -

## W.P.C.WESTON - *Worcestershire*

| Opposition | Venue | Date | Batting | Fielding | Bowling |
|---|---|---|---|---|---|
| **BRITANNIC ASSURANCE** | | | | | |
| Somerset | Worcester | Sept 3 | 5 | | |
| Notts | Trent Bridge | Sept 17 | 8 & 15 | | |

**BATTING AVERAGES - Including fielding**

| | Matches | Inns | NO | Runs | HS | Avge | 100s | 50s | Ct | St |
|---|---|---|---|---|---|---|---|---|---|---|
| Britannic Assurance | 2 | 3 | 0 | 28 | 15 | 9.33 | - | - | - | - |
| ALL FIRST-CLASS | 2 | 3 | 0 | 28 | 15 | 9.33 | - | - | - | - |

**BOWLING AVERAGES**
Did not bowl

## J.J.WHITAKER - *Leicestershire*

| Opposition | Venue | Date | Batting | Fielding | Bowling |
|---|---|---|---|---|---|
| **BRITANNIC ASSURANCE** | | | | | |
| Glamorgan | Leicester | April 27 | | | |
| Notts | Trent Bridge | May 9 | 15 & 86 | | |
| Northants | Northampton | May 16 | 33 & 99 | 2Ct | |
| Notts | Leicester | May 25 | 65 & 14 | | |
| Essex | Ilford | June 4 | 0 & 12 | | |
| Middlesex | Uxbridge | June 7 | 35 & 16 | | |
| Surrey | Leicester | June 14 | 44 & 43 * | | |
| Lancashire | Leicester | June 18 | 28 | 1Ct | |
| Glamorgan | Neath | June 21 | 2 * | | |
| Worcestershire | Worcester | June 28 | 10 & 23 | | |
| Gloucs | Hinckley | July 2 | 30 | | |
| Northants | Leicester | July 5 | 0 & 74 | | |
| Sussex | Hove | July 19 | 0 & 5 | | |
| Warwickshire | Leicester | July 26 | 23 & 12 | | |
| Somerset | Weston | Aug 2 | 5 & 16 | 1Ct | |
| Yorkshire | Leicester | Aug 6 | 31 * | 2Ct | |
| Kent | Leicester | Aug 9 | 36 & 70 | 1Ct | 0-14 |
| Hampshire | Bournemouth | Aug 16 | 10 | 1Ct | |
| Derbyshire | Derby | Aug 20 | 47 | | |
| Derbyshire | Leicester | Aug 28 | 12 & 85 | 3Ct | |
| Essex | Leicester | Sept 10 | 105 & 83 | 1Ct | |
| Kent | Canterbury | Sept 17 | 15 & 58 | 2Ct | |
| **OTHER FIRST-CLASS** | | | | | |
| Cambridge U | Fenner's | May 22 | 47 | | |
| **REFUGE ASSURANCE** | | | | | |
| Derbyshire | Leicester | April 21 | 22 | 1Ct | |
| Glamorgan | Leicester | April 28 | 73 | | |
| Northants | Northampton | May 12 | 34 | | |
| Yorkshire | Leicester | May 19 | 31 | | |
| Notts | Leicester | May 26 | 10 | | |
| Surrey | Leicester | June 16 | 19 | | |
| Worcestershire | Worcester | June 30 | 63 | 1Ct | |
| Lancashire | Leicester | July 7 | 88 | 1Ct | |
| Kent | Canterbury | July 14 | 48 | | |
| Sussex | Hove | July 21 | 17 | | |
| Somerset | Weston | Aug 4 | 85 | | |
| Warwickshire | Leicester | Aug 11 | 29 | 1Ct | |
| Hampshire | Bournemouth | Aug 18 | 1 | 1Ct | |
| Gloucs | Leicester | Aug 25 | 30 | 1Ct | |
| **NATWEST TROPHY** | | | | | |
| Shropshire | Leicester | June 26 | 39 | | |
| Northants | Northampton | July 11 | 94 * | | |
| **BENSON & HEDGES CUP** | | | | | |
| Kent | Canterbury | April 23 | 100 | | |
| Sussex | Hove | April 25 | 2 | | |
| Scotland | Leicester | May 2 | 84 | | |
| Lancashire | Leicester | May 4 | 1 | | |

## OTHER ONE-DAY
For Yorkshiremen

| | | | |
|---|---|---|---|
| Yorkshire | Scarborough | Sept 7 | 24 |

**BATTING AVERAGES - Including fielding**

| | Matches | Inns | NO | Runs | HS | Avge | 100s | 50s | Ct | St |
|---|---|---|---|---|---|---|---|---|---|---|
| Britannic Assurance | 22 | 36 | 3 | 1242 | 105 | 37.63 | 1 | 8 | 14 | - |
| Other First-Class | 1 | 1 | 0 | 47 | 47 | 47.00 | - | - | - | - |
| ALL FIRST-CLASS | 23 | 37 | 3 | 1289 | 105 | 37.91 | 1 | 8 | 14 | - |
| Refuge Assurance | 14 | 14 | 0 | 550 | 88 | 39.28 | - | 4 | 6 | - |
| NatWest Trophy | 2 | 2 | 1 | 133 | 94 * | 133.00 | - | 1 | - | - |
| Benson & Hedges Cup | 4 | 4 | 0 | 187 | 100 | 46.75 | 1 | 1 | - | - |
| Other One-Day | 1 | 1 | 0 | 24 | 24 | 24.00 | - | - | - | - |
| ALL ONE-DAY | 21 | 21 | 1 | 894 | 100 | 44.70 | 1 | 6 | 6 | - |

**BOWLING AVERAGES**

| | Overs | Mdns | Runs | Wkts | Avge | Best | 5wI | 10wM |
|---|---|---|---|---|---|---|---|---|
| Britannic Assurance | 1 | 0 | 14 | 0 | - | - | - | - |
| Other First-Class | | | | | | | | |
| ALL FIRST-CLASS | 1 | 0 | 14 | 0 | - | - | - | - |
| Refuge Assurance | | | | | | | | |
| NatWest Trophy | | | | | | | | |
| Benson & Hedges Cup | | | | | | | | |
| Other One-Day | | | | | | | | |
| ALL ONE-DAY | | | | | | | | |

## C.WHITE - *Yorkshire*

| Opposition | Venue | Date | Batting | Fielding | Bowling |
|---|---|---|---|---|---|
| **REFUGE ASSURANCE** | | | | | |
| Kent | Scarborough | June 16 | 3 | | |
| Worcestershire | Sheffield | June 23 | 9 | | |
| Notts | Scarborough | Aug 18 | 37 | 1Ct | |

**BATTING AVERAGES - Including fielding**

| | Matches | Inns | NO | Runs | HS | Avge | 100s | 50s | Ct | St |
|---|---|---|---|---|---|---|---|---|---|---|
| Refuge Assurance | 3 | 3 | 0 | 49 | 37 | 16.33 | - | - | 1 | - |
| ALL ONE-DAY | 3 | 3 | 0 | 49 | 37 | 16.33 | - | - | 1 | - |

**BOWLING AVERAGES**
Did not bowl

## G.WHITE - *Somerset*

| Opposition | Venue | Date | Batting | Fielding | Bowling |
|---|---|---|---|---|---|
| **OTHER FIRST-CLASS** | | | | | |
| Sri Lanka | Taunton | Aug 10 | 42 | | 1-30 |

**BATTING AVERAGES - Including fielding**

| | Matches | Inns | NO | Runs | HS | Avge | 100s | 50s | Ct | St |
|---|---|---|---|---|---|---|---|---|---|---|
| Other First-Class | 1 | 1 | 0 | 42 | 42 | 42.00 | - | - | - | - |
| ALL FIRST-CLASS | 1 | 1 | 0 | 42 | 42 | 42.00 | - | - | - | - |

**BOWLING AVERAGES**

| | Overs | Mdns | Runs | Wkts | Avge | Best | 5wI | 10wM |
|---|---|---|---|---|---|---|---|---|
| Other First-Class | 6 | 1 | 30 | 1 | 30.00 | 1-30 | - | - |
| ALL FIRST-CLASS | 6 | 1 | 30 | 1 | 30.00 | 1-30 | - | |

# PLAYER RECORDS

**W**

## P.WHITTICASE - *Leicestershire*

| Opposition | Venue | Date | Batting | | | Fielding | Bowling |
|---|---|---|---|---|---|---|---|
| **BRITANNIC ASSURANCE** | | | | | | | |
| Glamorgan | Leicester | April 27 | | | | 3Ct | |
| Notts | Trent Bridge | May 9 | 9 | & | 0 | 5Ct | |
| Northants | Northampton | May 16 | 73 | | | 2Ct | |
| Notts | Leicester | May 25 | 1 | & | 1 | 2Ct | |
| Essex | Ilford | June 4 | 21 | | | 2Ct | |
| Middlesex | Uxbridge | June 7 | 9 | & | 0 | 1Ct | |
| Surrey | Leicester | June 14 | 32 * | | | 2Ct | |
| Lancashire | Leicester | June 18 | | | 51 * | 1Ct | |
| Glamorgan | Neath | June 21 | | | | 2Ct | |
| Sussex | Hove | July 19 | 29 | & | 5 | | |
| Warwickshire | Leicester | July 26 | 2 | & | 17 | 2Ct,1St | |
| Somerset | Weston | Aug 2 | 52 | & | 9 | 3Ct,1St | |
| Yorkshire | Leicester | Aug 6 | | | | 1Ct | |
| Kent | Leicester | Aug 9 | 2 * | | | | |
| Hampshire | Bournemouth | Aug 16 | 114 * | | | 1Ct | |
| Derbyshire | Derby | Aug 20 | 93 | | | 8Ct | |
| Derbyshire | Leicester | Aug 28 | 0 | & | 33 | 4Ct | |
| Essex | Leicester | Sept 10 | 10 | & | 21 * | | |
| Kent | Canterbury | Sept 17 | 27 | & | 9 | 3Ct | |

**OTHER FIRST-CLASS**

| | | | | | | | |
|---|---|---|---|---|---|---|---|
| Cambridge U | Fenner's | May 22 | | | | 2Ct,1St | |

**REFUGE ASSURANCE**

| | | | | | |
|---|---|---|---|---|---|
| Derbyshire | Leicester | April 21 | 0 * | | |
| Glamorgan | Leicester | April 28 | 8 | | |
| Northants | Northampton | May 12 | 0 | | |
| Yorkshire | Leicester | May 19 | 24 | 1Ct | |
| Notts | Leicester | May 26 | 0 | 2Ct | |
| Middlesex | Uxbridge | June 9 | 1 | | |
| Surrey | Leicester | June 16 | 2 | | |
| Lancashire | Leicester | July 7 | 14 * | | |
| Kent | Canterbury | July 14 | 9 | 1Ct | |
| Somerset | Weston | Aug 4 | | 2Ct | |
| Warwickshire | Leicester | Aug 11 | 16 * | | |
| Hampshire | Bournemouth | Aug 18 | 17 | | |
| Gloucs | Leicester | Aug 25 | 17 | 1Ct | |

**NATWEST TROPHY**

| | | | | | |
|---|---|---|---|---|---|
| Shropshire | Leicester | June 26 | | 2Ct | |
| Northants | Northampton | July 11 | | | |

**BENSON & HEDGES CUP**

| | | | | | |
|---|---|---|---|---|---|
| Kent | Canterbury | April 23 | 2 | | |
| Sussex | Hove | April 25 | 31 | | |
| Scotland | Leicester | May 2 | | 1Ct,1St | |
| Lancashire | Leicester | May 4 | 34 * | | |

**OTHER ONE-DAY**
For Leicestershire

| | | | | | |
|---|---|---|---|---|---|
| Durham | Harrogate | June 11 | | | |

**BATTING AVERAGES - Including fielding**

| | Matches | Inns | NO | Runs | HS | Avge | 100s | 50s | Ct | St |
|---|---|---|---|---|---|---|---|---|---|---|
| Britannic Assurance | 19 | 25 | 5 | 620 | 114 * | 31.00 | 1 | 4 | 42 | 2 |
| Other First-Class | 1 | 0 | 0 | 0 | 0 | - | - | - | 2 | 1 |
| ALL FIRST-CLASS | 20 | 25 | 5 | 620 | 114 * | 31.00 | 1 | 4 | 44 | 3 |
| Refuge Assurance | 13 | 12 | 3 | 108 | 24 | 12.00 | - | - | 7 | - |
| NatWest Trophy | 2 | 0 | 0 | 0 | 0 | - | - | - | 2 | - |
| Benson & Hedges Cup | 4 | 3 | 1 | 67 | 34 * | 33.50 | - | - | 1 | 1 |
| Other One-Day | 1 | 0 | 0 | 0 | 0 | - | - | - | - | - |
| ALL ONE-DAY | 20 | 15 | 4 | 175 | 34 * | 15.90 | - | - | 10 | 1 |

**BOWLING AVERAGES**
Did not bowl

## K.I.W.WIJEGUNAWARDENE - *Sri Lanka*

| Opposition | Venue | Date | Batting | Fielding | Bowling |
|---|---|---|---|---|---|
| **CORNHILL TEST MATCHES** | | | | | |
| England | Lord's | Aug 22 | 6 * & 4 | | 0-36 & 0-13 |

### OTHER FIRST-CLASS

| | | | | | |
|---|---|---|---|---|---|
| Worcestershire | Worcester | July 30 | 26 & 6 * | | 4-112 |
| Derbyshire | Derby | Aug 2 | | | 4-97 |
| Somerset | Taunton | Aug 10 | 10 | | 1-109 & 2-35 |
| Sussex | Hove | Aug 17 | | 0 | 4-111 & 0-24 |

### OTHER ONE-DAY

| | | | | | |
|---|---|---|---|---|---|
| England Am. | Wolv'hampton | July 24 | 1 | | 0-33 |
| England A | Old Trafford | Aug 14 | 27 | | 0-39 |

**BATTING AVERAGES - Including fielding**

| | Matches | Inns | NO | Runs | HS | Avge | 100s | 50s | Ct | St |
|---|---|---|---|---|---|---|---|---|---|---|
| Cornhill Test Matches | 1 | 2 | 1 | 10 | 6 * | 10.00 | - | - | - | - |
| Other First-Class | 4 | 4 | 1 | 42 | 26 | 14.00 | - | - | - | - |
| ALL FIRST-CLASS | 5 | 6 | 2 | 52 | 26 | 13.00 | - | - | - | - |
| Other One-Day | 2 | 2 | 0 | 28 | 27 | 14.00 | - | - | - | - |
| ALL ONE-DAY | 2 | 2 | 0 | 28 | 27 | 14.00 | - | - | - | - |

**BOWLING AVERAGES**

| | Overs | Mdns | Runs | Wkts | Avge | Best | 5wI | 10wM |
|---|---|---|---|---|---|---|---|---|
| Cornhill Test Matches | 12 | 1 | 49 | 0 | - | - | - | - |
| Other First-Class | 112.3 | 13 | 488 | 15 | 32.53 | 4-97 | - | - |
| ALL FIRST-CLASS | 124.3 | 14 | 537 | 15 | 35.80 | 4-97 | - | - |
| Other One-Day | 11 | 0 | 72 | 0 | - | - | - | - |
| ALL ONE-DAY | 11 | 0 | 72 | 0 | - | - | - | - |

## C.WILKINSON - *Leicestershire*

| Opposition | Venue | Date | Batting | | | Fielding | Bowling |
|---|---|---|---|---|---|---|---|
| **BRITANNIC ASSURANCE** | | | | | | | |
| Notts | Trent Bridge | May 9 | 41 | & | 16 | 1Ct | 2-80 & 0-17 |
| Essex | Ilford | June 4 | 0 | | | | 0-96 & 0-18 |
| Middlesex | Uxbridge | June 7 | 0 | & | 8 | | 1-41 & 0-10 |
| Glamorgan | Neath | June 21 | | | | 1Ct | 4-106 |
| Worcestershire | Worcester | June 28 | | | | 1Ct | 0-49 & 0-33 |
| Gloucs | Hinckley | July 2 | | | 10 | | 0-41 |
| Northants | Leicester | July 5 | 0 | | | | 0-33 |
| Yorkshire | Leicester | Aug 6 | | | | | 0-35 |
| Kent | Leicester | Aug 9 | 0 | | | | 0-23 & 2-52 |
| Hampshire | Bournemouth | Aug 16 | | | | 3Ct | 0-51 |
| Derbyshire | Derby | Aug 20 | 31 * | | | | 1-34 & 4-59 |
| Derbyshire | Leicester | Aug 28 | 6 | & | 22 | 1Ct | 2-59 & 2-81 |
| Kent | Canterbury | Sept 17 | 2 | & | 2 * | | 1-43 & 1-13 |

**OTHER FIRST-CLASS**

| | | | | | |
|---|---|---|---|---|---|
| Cambridge U | Fenner's | May 22 | | | 2-26 & 1-9 |

**REFUGE ASSURANCE**

| | | | | | |
|---|---|---|---|---|---|
| Derbyshire | Leicester | April 21 | 3 * | | 1-28 |
| Glamorgan | Leicester | April 28 | | | 0-39 |
| Northants | Northampton | May 12 | 0 * | | 2-50 |
| Yorkshire | Leicester | May 19 | | | 2-31 |
| Notts | Leicester | May 26 | 2 | | 1-27 |
| Middlesex | Uxbridge | June 9 | 35 * | 1Ct | 0-18 |
| Surrey | Leicester | June 16 | 0 * | | 1-25 |
| Worcestershire | Worcester | June 30 | | | 0-46 |
| Lancashire | Leicester | July 7 | | 1Ct | 0-19 |
| Somerset | Weston | Aug 4 | | | 1-35 |
| Warwickshire | Leicester | Aug 11 | | 1Ct | 1-32 |
| Hampshire | Bournemouth | Aug 18 | | | 0-32 |
| Gloucs | Leicester | Aug 25 | 12 * | | 1-55 |

**NATWEST TROPHY**

| | | | | | |
|---|---|---|---|---|---|
| Shropshire | Leicester | June 26 | | | 3-16 |
| Northants | Northampton | July 11 | | | 0-46 |

**BENSON & HEDGES CUP**

| | | | | | |
|---|---|---|---|---|---|
| Kent | Canterbury | April 23 | 9 * | 1Ct | 0-58 |
| Scotland | Leicester | May 2 | | 1Ct | 3-46 |
| Lancashire | Leicester | May 4 | 19 * | | 0-26 |

**OTHER ONE-DAY**

| | | | | | |
|---|---|---|---|---|---|
| Durham | Harrogate | June 11 | | | 1-37 |

# W | PLAYER RECORDS

## BATTING AVERAGES - Including fielding

| | Matches | Inns | NO | Runs | HS | Avge | 100s | 50s | Ct | St |
|---|---|---|---|---|---|---|---|---|---|---|
| Britannic Assurance | 13 | 13 | 2 | 138 | 41 | 12.54 | - | - | 7 | - |
| Other First-Class | 1 | 0 | 0 | 0 | 0 | - | - | - | - | - |
| ALL FIRST-CLASS | 14 | 13 | 2 | 138 | 41 | 12.54 | - | - | 7 | - |
| Refuge Assurance | 13 | 6 | 5 | 52 | 35* | 52.00 | - | - | 3 | - |
| NatWest Trophy | 2 | 0 | 0 | 0 | 0 | - | - | - | - | - |
| Benson & Hedges Cup | 3 | 2 | 2 | 28 | 19* | - | - | - | 2 | - |
| Other One-Day | 1 | 0 | 0 | 0 | 0 | - | - | - | - | - |
| ALL ONE-DAY | 19 | 8 | 7 | 80 | 35* | 80.00 | - | - | 5 | - |

## BOWLING AVERAGES

| | Overs | Mdns | Runs | Wkts | Avge | Best | 5wI | 10wM |
|---|---|---|---|---|---|---|---|---|
| Britannic Assurance | 293 | 56 | 974 | 20 | 48.70 | 4-59 | - | - |
| Other First-Class | 22 | 8 | 35 | 3 | 11.66 | 2-26 | - | - |
| ALL FIRST-CLASS | 315 | 64 | 1009 | 23 | 43.87 | 4-59 | - | - |
| Refuge Assurance | 88.3 | 1 | 437 | 10 | 43.70 | 2-31 | - | |
| NatWest Trophy | 16.5 | 5 | 62 | 3 | 20.66 | 3-16 | - | |
| Benson & Hedges Cup | 31 | 3 | 130 | 3 | 43.33 | 3-46 | - | |
| Other One-Day | 7 | 1 | 37 | 1 | 37.00 | 1-37 | - | |
| ALL ONE-DAY | 143.2 | 10 | 666 | 17 | 39.17 | 3-16 | - | |

## P.WILLEY - Leicestershire

| Opposition | Venue | Date | Batting | Fielding | Bowling |
|---|---|---|---|---|---|
| **BRITANNIC ASSURANCE** | | | | | |
| Glamorgan | Leicester | April 27 | | 1Ct | |
| Notts | Trent Bridge | May 9 | 24 & 0 | | 0-15 |
| Northants | Northampton | May 16 | 0 & 26 | 2Ct | 0-4 |
| Notts | Leicester | May 25 | 2 & 6 | | 0-40 & 0-28 |
| Essex | Ilford | June 4 | 11 & 3* | | 0-23 |
| Middlesex | Uxbridge | June 7 | 42* & 26 | 1Ct | 1-37 & 0-11 |
| Surrey | Leicester | June 14 | 18 | | 0-19 & 0-50 |
| Lancashire | Leicester | June 18 | 0 | | 2-15 |
| Worcestershire | Worcester | June 28 | 0* | 1Ct | 1-19 & 0-14 |
| Gloucs | Hinckley | July 2 | 6 | | 1-87 |
| Northants | Leicester | July 5 | 9 & 19* | | 0-79 |
| Sussex | Hove | July 19 | 14* & 11 | 1Ct | |
| **REFUGE ASSURANCE** | | | | | |
| Derbyshire | Leicester | April 21 | 1 | 1Ct | 0-33 |
| Glamorgan | Leicester | April 28 | 27 | | 0-25 |
| Northants | Northampton | May 12 | 27 | | 1-19 |
| Yorkshire | Leicester | May 19 | 16 | | 0-26 |
| Notts | Leicester | May 26 | 12 | | 0-17 |
| Middlesex | Uxbridge | June 9 | 10 | | 1-22 |
| Surrey | Leicester | June 16 | 17 | 1Ct | 4-17 |
| Worcestershire | Worcester | June 30 | | | 0-24 |
| Lancashire | Leicester | July 7 | 12* | | 1-30 |
| Kent | Canterbury | July 14 | 31 | | 1-25 |
| **NATWEST TROPHY** | | | | | |
| Shropshire | Leicester | June 26 | 6 | | 0-27 |
| Northants | Northampton | July 11 | 28 | | 0-29 |
| **BENSON & HEDGES CUP** | | | | | |
| Kent | Canterbury | April 23 | 36 | | 0-33 |
| Sussex | Hove | April 25 | 4 | | 1-34 |
| Scotland | Leicester | May 2 | 0 | | 0-15 |
| Lancashire | Leicester | May 4 | 29 | | 1-29 |
| **OTHER ONE-DAY** | | | | | |
| Durham | Harrogate | June 11 | | 1Ct | 0-32 |

## BATTING AVERAGES - Including fielding

| | Matches | Inns | NO | Runs | HS | Avge | 100s | 50s | Ct | St |
|---|---|---|---|---|---|---|---|---|---|---|
| Britannic Assurance | 12 | 18 | 5 | 217 | 42* | 16.69 | - | - | 6 | - |
| ALL FIRST-CLASS | 12 | 18 | 5 | 217 | 42* | 16.69 | - | - | 6 | - |
| Refuge Assurance | 10 | 9 | 1 | 153 | 31 | 19.12 | - | - | 2 | - |
| NatWest Trophy | 2 | 2 | 0 | 34 | 28 | 17.00 | - | - | - | - |
| Benson & Hedges Cup | 4 | 4 | 0 | 69 | 36 | 17.25 | - | - | - | - |
| Other One-Day | 1 | 0 | 0 | 0 | 0 | - | - | - | 1 | - |

## ALL ONE-DAY

| | | | | | | | | | | |
|---|---|---|---|---|---|---|---|---|---|---|
| ALL ONE-DAY | 17 | 15 | 1 | 256 | 36 | 18.28 | - | - | 3 | - |

## BOWLING AVERAGES

| | Overs | Mdns | Runs | Wkts | Avge | Best | 5wI | 10wM |
|---|---|---|---|---|---|---|---|---|
| Britannic Assurance | 157.4 | 36 | 441 | 5 | 88.20 | 2-15 | - | - |
| ALL FIRST-CLASS | 157.4 | 36 | 441 | 5 | 88.20 | 2-15 | - | - |
| Refuge Assurance | 60 | 2 | 238 | 8 | 29.75 | 4-17 | - | |
| NatWest Trophy | 19 | 3 | 56 | 0 | | | | |
| Benson & Hedges Cup | 36.5 | 4 | 111 | 2 | 55.50 | 1-29 | - | |
| Other One-Day | 5 | 0 | 32 | 0 | | | | |
| ALL ONE-DAY | 120.5 | 9 | 437 | 10 | 43.70 | 4-17 | - | |

## D.WILLIAMS - West Indies

| Opposition | Venue | Date | Batting | Fielding | Bowling |
|---|---|---|---|---|---|
| **OTHER FIRST-CLASS** | | | | | |
| Middlesex | Lord's | May 18 | 35 | 3Ct | |
| Somerset | Taunton | May 29 | 14* | 3Ct | |
| Derbyshire | Derby | June 12 | | 1Ct,2St | |
| Glamorgan | Swansea | July 16 | 6 | 6Ct | |
| Gloucs | Bristol | July 31 | 4 | 4Ct,1St | |
| Essex | Chelmsford | Aug 3 | 24 | 5Ct | |
| For West Indies XI | | | | | |
| World XI | Scarborough | Aug 28 | 19 | 1Ct | |
| **OTHER ONE-DAY** | | | | | |
| Gloucs | Bristol | May 14 | | | |
| League CC XI | Trowbridge | June 28 | | 0Ct,1St | |
| Ireland | Downpatrick | July 13 | | 1Ct | |

## BATTING AVERAGES - Including fielding

| | Matches | Inns | NO | Runs | HS | Avge | 100s | 50s | Ct | St |
|---|---|---|---|---|---|---|---|---|---|---|
| Other First-Class | 7 | 6 | 1 | 102 | 35 | 20.40 | - | - | 23 | 3 |
| ALL FIRST-CLASS | 7 | 6 | 1 | 102 | 35 | 20.40 | - | - | 23 | 3 |
| Other One-Day | 3 | 0 | 0 | 0 | 0 | - | - | - | 1 | 1 |
| ALL ONE-DAY | 3 | 0 | 0 | 0 | 0 | - | - | - | 1 | 1 |

## BOWLING AVERAGES
Did not bowl

## G.D.WILLIAMS - Staffordshire

| Opposition | Venue | Date | Batting | Fielding | Bowling |
|---|---|---|---|---|---|
| **NATWEST TROPHY** | | | | | |
| Northants | Stone | June 26 | 7 | | 0-41 |

## BATTING AVERAGES - Including fielding

| | Matches | Inns | NO | Runs | HS | Avge | 100s | 50s | Ct | St |
|---|---|---|---|---|---|---|---|---|---|---|
| NatWest Trophy | 1 | 1 | 0 | 7 | 7 | 7.00 | - | - | - | - |
| ALL ONE-DAY | 1 | 1 | 0 | 7 | 7 | 7.00 | - | - | - | - |

## BOWLING AVERAGES

| | Overs | Mdns | Runs | Wkts | Avge | Best | 5wI | 10wM |
|---|---|---|---|---|---|---|---|---|
| NatWest Trophy | 12 | 0 | 41 | 0 | | | | |
| ALL ONE-DAY | 12 | 0 | 41 | 0 | | | | |

## N.F.WILLIAMS - Middlesex

| Opposition | Venue | Date | Batting | Fielding | Bowling |
|---|---|---|---|---|---|
| **BRITANNIC ASSURANCE** | | | | | |
| Sussex | Lord's | May 9 | 0 & 28 | | 3-91 & 0-20 |
| Sussex | Hove | May 22 | | | 1-65 & 0-20 |
| Somerset | Taunton | May 25 | 41 | | 4-46 & 0-2 |

# PLAYER RECORDS — W

| | | | | | |
|---|---|---|---|---|---|
| Kent | Lord's | May 31 | 0 & 8 | | 0-39 & 1-66 |
| Leicestershire | Uxbridge | June 7 | 19* | 1Ct | 4-79 & 0-31 |
| Glamorgan | Cardiff | June 14 | 0 | 1Ct | 1-79 |
| Yorkshire | Sheffield | June 21 | 0* & 5 | | 1-53 & 1-23 |
| Essex | Lord's | June 28 | 0 | | 1-89 & 0-4 |
| Warwickshire | Edgbaston | July 2 | 77 & 3 | | 3-73 & 1-42 |
| Lancashire | Uxbridge | July 19 | 0 & 5* | | 1-60 & 0-18 |
| Notts | Lord's | July 26 | 9 | 1Ct | 5-89 & 1-42 |
| Worcestershire | Worcester | Aug 23 | 15 & 0 | 1Ct | 1-36 |
| Kent | Canterbury | Aug 28 | 1 & 5 | | 3-52 & 1-87 |
| Notts | Trent Bridge | Sept 3 | 7 | | 2-47 & 0-4 |
| Surrey | Lord's | Sept 10 | 18 & 26 | | 3-52 & 1-25 |
| Essex | Chelmsford | Sept 17 | 23 & 6 | | 2-140 |

**OTHER FIRST-CLASS**

| | | | | | |
|---|---|---|---|---|---|
| MCC | Lord's | April 16 | 29 | | 2-70 |
| West Indies | Lord's | May 18 | 5 & 21 | 1Ct | 2-82 & 2-42 |

**REFUGE ASSURANCE**

| | | | | | |
|---|---|---|---|---|---|
| Gloucs | Bristol | April 21 | | 1Ct | 1-26 |
| Sussex | Hove | May 12 | | 1Ct | 0-18 |
| Somerset | Taunton | May 26 | | 1Ct | 1-40 |
| Kent | Southgate | June 2 | 27 | 1Ct | 1-55 |
| Leicestershire | Uxbridge | June 9 | 1 | | 0-40 |
| Glamorgan | Cardiff | June 16 | 11 | | 1-32 |
| Notts | Trent Bridge | June 23 | | 1Ct | 1-25 |
| Yorkshire | Lord's | July 7 | | | 0-47 |
| Warwickshire | Edgbaston | July 14 | 7* | | 1-34 |
| Lancashire | Lord's | July 21 | | | 0-23 |
| Derbyshire | Lord's | Aug 11 | 2* | | 1-24 |
| Worcestershire | Worcester | Aug 25 | | 1Ct | 1-44 |

**NATWEST TROPHY**

| | | | | | |
|---|---|---|---|---|---|
| Ireland | Dublin | June 26 | 6 | 1Ct | 1-11 |
| Somerset | Taunton | July 11 | 3 | | 0-32 |

**BENSON & HEDGES CUP**

| | | | | | |
|---|---|---|---|---|---|
| Somerset | Taunton | April 23 | | | 1-26 |
| Surrey | Lord's | April 25 | 6 | | 1-37 |
| Essex | Chelmsford | May 2 | 1 | | 2-19 |
| Warwickshire | Lord's | May 4 | 3 | 1Ct | 1-41 |

**BATTING AVERAGES - Including fielding**

| | Matches | Inns | NO | Runs | HS | Avge | 100s | 50s | Ct | St |
|---|---|---|---|---|---|---|---|---|---|---|
| Britannic Assurance | 16 | 24 | 3 | 296 | 77 | 14.09 | - | 1 | 4 | - |
| Other First-Class | 2 | 3 | 0 | 55 | 29 | 18.33 | - | - | 1 | - |
| ALL FIRST-CLASS | 18 | 27 | 3 | 351 | 77 | 14.62 | - | 1 | 5 | - |
| Refuge Assurance | 12 | 5 | 2 | 48 | 27 | 16.00 | - | - | 6 | - |
| NatWest Trophy | 2 | 2 | 0 | 9 | 6 | 4.50 | - | - | 1 | - |
| Benson & Hedges Cup | 4 | 3 | 0 | 10 | 6 | 3.33 | - | - | 1 | - |
| ALL ONE-DAY | 18 | 10 | 2 | 67 | 27 | 8.37 | - | - | 8 | - |

**BOWLING AVERAGES**

| | Overs | Mdns | Runs | Wkts | Avge | Best | 5wI | 10wM |
|---|---|---|---|---|---|---|---|---|
| Britannic Assurance | 477.2 | 89 | 1474 | 41 | 35.95 | 5-89 | 1 | - |
| Other First-Class | 47.3 | 10 | 194 | 6 | 32.33 | 2-42 | - | - |
| ALL FIRST-CLASS | 524.5 | 99 | 1668 | 47 | 35.48 | 5-89 | 1 | - |
| Refuge Assurance | 83 | 2 | 408 | 8 | 51.00 | 1-24 | - | |
| NatWest Trophy | 12 | 2 | 43 | 1 | 43.00 | 1-11 | - | |
| Benson & Hedges Cup | 44 | 8 | 123 | 5 | 24.60 | 2-19 | - | |
| ALL ONE-DAY | 139 | 12 | 574 | 14 | 41.00 | 2-19 | - | |

## R.C.WILLIAMS - *Gloucestershire*

| Opposition | Venue | Date | Batting | Fielding | Bowling |
|---|---|---|---|---|---|
| **BRITANNIC ASSURANCE** | | | | | |
| Derbyshire | Gloucester | June 18 | 0 & 13 | | 1-81 |
| **OTHER ONE-DAY** | | | | | |
| Somerset | Hove | Sept 8 | 6 | 1Ct | 0-19 |
| Sussex | Hove | Sept 9 | 16 | | 2-29 |

**BATTING AVERAGES - Including fielding**

| | Matches | Inns | NO | Runs | HS | Avge | 100s | 50s | Ct | St |
|---|---|---|---|---|---|---|---|---|---|---|
| Britannic Assurance | 1 | 2 | 0 | 13 | 13 | 6.50 | - | - | - | - |
| ALL FIRST-CLASS | 1 | 2 | 0 | 13 | 13 | 6.50 | - | - | - | - |
| Other One-Day | 2 | 2 | 0 | 22 | 16 | 11.00 | - | - | 1 | - |
| ALL ONE-DAY | 2 | 2 | 0 | 22 | 16 | 11.00 | - | - | 1 | - |

**BOWLING AVERAGES**

| | Overs | Mdns | Runs | Wkts | Avge | Best | 5wI | 10wM |
|---|---|---|---|---|---|---|---|---|
| Britannic Assurance | 26 | 4 | 81 | 1 | 81.00 | 1-81 | - | - |
| ALL FIRST-CLASS | 26 | 4 | 81 | 1 | 81.00 | 1-81 | - | - |
| Other One-Day | 12 | 1 | 48 | 2 | 24.00 | 2-29 | - | |
| ALL ONE-DAY | 12 | 1 | 48 | 2 | 24.00 | 2-29 | - | |

## R.C.J.WILLIAMS - *Gloucestershire*

| Opposition | Venue | Date | Batting | Fielding | Bowling |
|---|---|---|---|---|---|
| **BRITANNIC ASSURANCE** | | | | | |
| Yorkshire | Sheffield | May 22 | | 0Ct,1St | |
| Warwickshire | Edgbaston | May 25 | 8 & 0 | 1Ct | |
| Middlesex | Bristol | June 4 | 0 | 5Ct | |
| Hampshire | Southampton | June 7 | | 2Ct | |
| Derbyshire | Gloucester | June 18 | 8 & 55* | 1Ct,2St | |
| Somerset | Bath | June 21 | 8 | 2Ct | |
| Leicestershire | Hinckley | July 2 | 5* | 1Ct | |
| Sussex | Cheltenham | July 23 | 5 | | |
| Worcestershire | Cheltenham | July 26 | 2 & 0 | 2Ct | |
| Kent | Canterbury | Aug 20 | 0 & 4 | 4Ct | |
| **REFUGE ASSURANCE** | | | | | |
| Hampshire | Swindon | May 26 | | | |
| Leicestershire | Leicester | Aug 25 | | | |

**BATTING AVERAGES - Including fielding**

| | Matches | Inns | NO | Runs | HS | Avge | 100s | 50s | Ct | St |
|---|---|---|---|---|---|---|---|---|---|---|
| Britannic Assurance | 10 | 12 | 2 | 95 | 55* | 9.50 | - | 1 | 18 | 3 |
| ALL FIRST-CLASS | 10 | 12 | 2 | 95 | 55* | 9.50 | - | 1 | 18 | 3 |
| Refuge Assurance | 2 | 0 | 0 | 0 | 0 | - | - | - | - | - |
| ALL ONE-DAY | 2 | 0 | 0 | 0 | 0 | - | - | - | - | - |

**BOWLING AVERAGES**

Did not bowl

## R.G.WILLIAMS - *Northamptonshire*

| Opposition | Venue | Date | Batting | Fielding | Bowling |
|---|---|---|---|---|---|
| **BRITANNIC ASSURANCE** | | | | | |
| Derbyshire | Derby | April 27 | 11* | | |
| Leicestershire | Northampton | May 16 | 4* | | 2-29 & 0-3 |
| Middlesex | Uxbridge | July 16 | 0 | | 1-64 |
| Notts | Well'borough | July 19 | 12 & 0 | | 0-6 |
| Somerset | Northampton | July 23 | 3 | | 0-32 |
| Sussex | Eastbourne | Aug 2 | 22 & 35 | | 0-66 & 0-5 |
| Essex | Colchester | Aug 16 | 19 & 17 | 1Ct | 1-51 |
| **OTHER FIRST-CLASS** | | | | | |
| Cambridge U | Fenner's | April 16 | 101* | | 0-3 |
| **REFUGE ASSURANCE** | | | | | |
| Glamorgan | Cardiff | April 21 | 66* | | 1-27 |
| Lancashire | Old Trafford | April 28 | 16* | | 0-22 |
| Leicestershire | Northampton | May 12 | 8 | | 0-32 |
| Gloucs | Moreton | June 9 | | | |
| Surrey | Tring | July 7 | 0 | | 1-28 |
| Notts | Well'borough | July 21 | 10 | | 2-22 |
| Derbyshire | Derby | July 28 | 28* | | 2-22 |
| Sussex | Eastbourne | Aug 4 | | 1Ct | 2-32 |
| Essex | Northampton | Aug 11 | | 1Ct | 1-65 |
| Kent | Canterbury | Aug 18 | | | 1-46 |
| Warwickshire | Northampton | Aug 25 | | | 2-42 |
| Lancashire | Old Trafford | Sept 1 | 13* | 1Ct | 0-22 |

# W PLAYER RECORDS

## NATWEST TROPHY

| | | | | | |
|---|---|---|---|---|---|
| Leicestershire | Northampton | July 11 | | 1Ct | 0-24 |
| Glamorgan | Northampton | July 31 | 6 | 1Ct | 0-41 |
| Surrey | The Oval | Aug 14 | 1 | 1Ct | 2-34 |

## BENSON & HEDGES CUP

| | | | | | |
|---|---|---|---|---|---|
| Derbyshire | Derby | April 23 | 22 | 1Ct | |
| Gloucs | Bristol | May 2 | 29 | | 1-31 |
| Combined U | Northampton | May 4 | 17* | | 1-44 |
| Worcestershire | Northampton | May 7 | 28* | | 0-34 |

## BATTING AVERAGES - Including fielding

| | Matches | Inns | NO | Runs | HS | Avge | 100s | 50s | Ct | St |
|---|---|---|---|---|---|---|---|---|---|---|
| Britannic Assurance | 7 | 10 | 2 | 123 | 35 | 15.37 | - | - | 1 | - |
| Other First-Class | 1 | 1 | 1 | 101 | 101* | - | 1 | - | - | - |
| ALL FIRST-CLASS | 8 | 11 | 3 | 224 | 101* | 28.00 | 1 | - | 1 | - |
| Refuge Assurance | 12 | 7 | 4 | 141 | 66* | 47.00 | - | 1 | 3 | - |
| NatWest Trophy | 3 | 2 | 0 | 7 | 6 | 3.50 | - | - | 3 | - |
| Benson & Hedges Cup | 4 | 4 | 2 | 96 | 29 | 48.00 | - | - | 1 | - |
| ALL ONE-DAY | 19 | 13 | 6 | 244 | 66* | 34.85 | - | 1 | 7 | - |

## BOWLING AVERAGES

| | Overs | Mdns | Runs | Wkts | Avge | Best | 5wI | 10wM |
|---|---|---|---|---|---|---|---|---|
| Britannic Assurance | 87.3 | 17 | 256 | 4 | 64.00 | 2-29 | - | - |
| Other First-Class | 4 | 2 | 3 | 0 | | | - | - |
| ALL FIRST-CLASS | 91.3 | 19 | 259 | 4 | 64.75 | 2-29 | - | - |
| Refuge Assurance | 70 | 0 | 360 | 12 | 30.00 | 2-22 | - | |
| NatWest Trophy | 36 | 4 | 99 | 2 | 49.50 | 2-34 | - | |
| Benson & Hedges Cup | 33 | 2 | 109 | 2 | 54.50 | 1-31 | - | |
| ALL ONE-DAY | 139 | 6 | 568 | 16 | 35.50 | 2-22 | - | |

## A.WILLOWS - *Dorset*

| Opposition | Venue | Date | Batting | Fielding | Bowling |
|---|---|---|---|---|---|

### NATWEST TROPHY

| | | | | |
|---|---|---|---|---|
| Lancashire | Bournemouth | June 26 | 14 | |

## BATTING AVERAGES - Including fielding

| | Matches | Inns | NO | Runs | HS | Avge | 100s | 50s | Ct | St |
|---|---|---|---|---|---|---|---|---|---|---|
| NatWest Trophy | 1 | 1 | 0 | 14 | 14 | 14.00 | - | - | - | - |
| ALL ONE-DAY | 1 | 1 | 0 | 14 | 14 | 14.00 | - | - | - | - |

## BOWLING AVERAGES
Did not bowl

## B.WOOD - *Oxford University*

| Opposition | Venue | Date | Batting | Fielding | Bowling |
|---|---|---|---|---|---|

### OTHER FIRST-CLASS

| | | | | | |
|---|---|---|---|---|---|
| Hampshire | The Parks | April 13 | 0 | | 0-41 |
| Glamorgan | The Parks | April 17 | 2* | | 0-19 |
| Notts | The Parks | April 27 | | | 0-74 |
| Gloucs | The Parks | June 15 | | | 0-53 |
| Worcestershire | The Parks | May 25 | 0 & 0 | | 2-79 |
| Yorkshire | The Parks | June 4 | 6 | | 2-85 & 0-37 |
| Lancashire | The Parks | June 7 | | | 1-23 & 1-52 |
| Kent | The Parks | June 18 | 0 | | 1-77 & 1-60 |
| Cambridge U | Lord's | July 2 | | | 2-41 & 2-24 |

## BATTING AVERAGES - Including fielding

| | Matches | Inns | NO | Runs | HS | Avge | 100s | 50s | Ct | St |
|---|---|---|---|---|---|---|---|---|---|---|
| Other First-Class | 9 | 6 | 1 | 8 | 6 | 1.60 | - | - | - | - |
| ALL FIRST-CLASS | 9 | 6 | 1 | 8 | 6 | 1.60 | - | - | - | - |

## BOWLING AVERAGES

| | Overs | Mdns | Runs | Wkts | Avge | Best | 5wI | 10wM |
|---|---|---|---|---|---|---|---|---|
| Other First-Class | 187.5 | 34 | 665 | 12 | 55.41 | 2-24 | - | - |
| ALL FIRST-CLASS | 187.5 | 34 | 665 | 12 | 55.41 | 2-24 | - | - |

## J.WOOD - *Durham*

| Opposition | Venue | Date | Batting | Fielding | Bowling |
|---|---|---|---|---|---|

### NATWEST TROPHY

| | | | | | |
|---|---|---|---|---|---|
| Glamorgan | Darlington | June 26 | 1 | | 0-82 |

### OTHER ONE-DAY

| | | | | | |
|---|---|---|---|---|---|
| Leicestershire | Harrogate | June 11 | | | 1-10 |
| Surrey | Harrogate | June 13 | 2 | | 2-28 |
| Sri Lanka | Chester-le-S | July 26 | 8 | | 2-31 |
| Essex | Scarborough | Aug 31 | 30 | | 0-66 |
| Victoria | Durham U. | Sept 16 | | 1Ct | 0-71 |

## BATTING AVERAGES - Including fielding

| | Matches | Inns | NO | Runs | HS | Avge | 100s | 50s | Ct | St |
|---|---|---|---|---|---|---|---|---|---|---|
| NatWest Trophy | 1 | 1 | 0 | 1 | 1 | 1.00 | - | - | - | - |
| Other One-Day | 5 | 3 | 0 | 40 | 30 | 13.33 | - | - | 1 | - |
| ALL ONE-DAY | 6 | 4 | 0 | 41 | 30 | 10.25 | - | - | 1 | - |

## BOWLING AVERAGES

| | Overs | Mdns | Runs | Wkts | Avge | Best | 5wI | 10wM |
|---|---|---|---|---|---|---|---|---|
| NatWest Trophy | 10 | 0 | 82 | 0 | | | | |
| Other One-Day | 40.1 | 5 | 206 | 5 | 41.20 | 2-28 | | |
| ALL ONE-DAY | 50.1 | 5 | 288 | 5 | 57.60 | 2-28 | | |

## J.R.WOOD - *Hampshire*

| Opposition | Venue | Date | Batting | Fielding | Bowling |
|---|---|---|---|---|---|

### BRITANNIC ASSURANCE

| | | | | | |
|---|---|---|---|---|---|
| Kent | Southampton | April 27 | 25 | | 0-17 |
| Yorkshire | Southampton | July 5 | 0 | | |

### REFUGE ASSURANCE

| | | | | |
|---|---|---|---|---|
| Yorkshire | Southampton | April 21 | 14 | 1Ct |
| Derbyshire | Derby | May 5 | 19 | |
| Kent | Southampton | May 12 | 18 | 1Ct |
| Sussex | Basingstoke | June 9 | 39 | |
| Essex | Chelmsford | June 16 | | |
| Worcestershire | Southampton | July 7 | 54 | |
| Notts | Trent Bridge | July 14 | 11 | |
| Warwickshire | Portsmouth | July 21 | 19 | |
| Lancashire | Southampton | July 28 | 10 | |
| Middlesex | Lord's | Aug 4 | 17 | |
| Surrey | The Oval | Aug 25 | 3 | |

### BENSON & HEDGES CUP

| | | | | |
|---|---|---|---|---|
| Notts | Southampton | April 23 | 0 | 1Ct |
| Min Counties | Trowbridge | April 25 | 70* | |
| Glamorgan | Southampton | May 2 | 6 | 1Ct |
| Yorkshire | Headingley | May 4 | 14 | 1Ct |

## BATTING AVERAGES - Including fielding

| | Matches | Inns | NO | Runs | HS | Avge | 100s | 50s | Ct | St |
|---|---|---|---|---|---|---|---|---|---|---|
| Britannic Assurance | 2 | 2 | 0 | 25 | 25 | 12.50 | - | - | - | - |
| ALL FIRST-CLASS | 2 | 2 | 0 | 25 | 25 | 12.50 | - | - | - | - |
| Refuge Assurance | 11 | 10 | 0 | 204 | 54 | 20.40 | - | 1 | 2 | - |
| Benson & Hedges Cup | 4 | 4 | 1 | 90 | 70* | 30.00 | - | 1 | 3 | - |
| ALL ONE-DAY | 15 | 14 | 1 | 294 | 70* | 22.61 | - | 2 | 5 | - |

## BOWLING AVERAGES

| | Overs | Mdns | Runs | Wkts | Avge | Best | 5wI | 10wM |
|---|---|---|---|---|---|---|---|---|
| Britannic Assurance | 6 | 0 | 17 | 0 | | | - | - |
| ALL FIRST-CLASS | 6 | 0 | 17 | 0 | | | - | - |
| Refuge Assurance | | | | | | | | |
| Benson & Hedges Cup | | | | | | | | |
| ALL ONE-DAY | | | | | | | | |

# PLATER RECORDS

# PLAYER RECORDS

**W**

## M.C.WOODMAN - *Devon*

| Opposition | Venue | Date | Batting | Fielding | Bowling |
|---|---|---|---|---|---|
| **NATWEST TROPHY** | | | | | |
| Essex | Exmouth | June 26 | 8 | | 0-24 |

**BATTING AVERAGES - Including fielding**

| | Matches | Inns | NO | Runs | HS | Avge | 100s | 50s | Ct | St |
|---|---|---|---|---|---|---|---|---|---|---|
| NatWest Trophy | 1 | 1 | 0 | 8 | 8 | 8.00 | - | - | - | - |
| ALL ONE-DAY | 1 | 1 | 0 | 8 | 8 | 8.00 | - | - | - | - |

**BOWLING AVERAGES**

| | Overs | Mdns | Runs | Wkts | Avge | Best | 5wI | 10wM |
|---|---|---|---|---|---|---|---|---|
| NatWest Trophy | 10 | 4 | 24 | 0 | - | | - | - |
| ALL ONE-DAY | 10 | 4 | 24 | 0 | - | | - | - |

## P.B.WORMWALD - *Shropshire*

| Opposition | Venue | Date | Batting | Fielding | Bowling |
|---|---|---|---|---|---|
| **NATWEST TROPHY** | | | | | |
| Leicestershire | Leicester | June 26 | 9 | | 1-18 |

**BATTING AVERAGES - Including fielding**

| | Matches | Inns | NO | Runs | HS | Avge | 100s | 50s | Ct | St |
|---|---|---|---|---|---|---|---|---|---|---|
| NatWest Trophy | 1 | 1 | 0 | 9 | 9 | 9.00 | - | - | - | - |
| ALL ONE-DAY | 1 | 1 | 0 | 9 | 9 | 9.00 | - | - | - | - |

**BOWLING AVERAGES**

| | Overs | Mdns | Runs | Wkts | Avge | Best | 5wI | 10wM |
|---|---|---|---|---|---|---|---|---|
| NatWest Trophy | 8 | 1 | 18 | 1 | 18.00 | 1-18 | - | |
| ALL ONE-DAY | 8 | 1 | 18 | 1 | 18.00 | 1-18 | - | |

## T.N.WREN - *Kent*

| Opposition | Venue | Date | Batting | Fielding | Bowling |
|---|---|---|---|---|---|
| **OTHER FIRST-CLASS** | | | | | |
| Oxford U | The Parks | June 18 | | | 3-14 & 1-34 |
| **REFUGE ASSURANCE** | | | | | |
| Sussex | Hove | Aug 25 | 0* | | 1-33 |

**BATTING AVERAGES - Including fielding**

| | Matches | Inns | NO | Runs | HS | Avge | 100s | 50s | Ct | St |
|---|---|---|---|---|---|---|---|---|---|---|
| Other First-Class | 1 | 0 | 0 | 0 | 0 | - | - | - | - | - |
| ALL FIRST-CLASS | 1 | 0 | 0 | 0 | 0 | - | - | - | - | - |
| Refuge Assurance | 1 | 1 | 1 | 0 | 0* | - | - | - | - | - |
| ALL ONE-DAY | 1 | 1 | 1 | 0 | 0* | - | - | - | - | - |

**BOWLING AVERAGES**

| | Overs | Mdns | Runs | Wkts | Avge | Best | 5wI | 10wM |
|---|---|---|---|---|---|---|---|---|
| Other First-Class | 19.3 | 3 | 48 | 4 | 12.00 | 3-14 | - | - |
| ALL FIRST-CLASS | 19.3 | 3 | 48 | 4 | 12.00 | 3-14 | - | - |
| Refuge Assurance | 5 | 0 | 33 | 1 | 33.00 | 1-33 | - | |
| ALL ONE-DAY | 5 | 0 | 33 | 1 | 33.00 | 1-33 | - | |

## A.J.WRIGHT - *Gloucestershire*

| Opposition | Venue | Date | Batting | | | Fielding | Bowling |
|---|---|---|---|---|---|---|---|
| **BRITANNIC ASSURANCE** | | | | | | | |
| Worcestershire | Worcester | April 27 | 30 | | | | |
| Hampshire | Bristol | May 9 | 15 | & | 61* | 2Ct | |
| Yorkshire | Sheffield | May 22 | 100* | & | 0 | 1Ct | |
| Warwickshire | Edgbaston | May 25 | 24 | & | 2 | | |
| Essex | Bristol | May 31 | 22 | & | 8 | 1Ct | |
| Middlesex | Bristol | June 4 | 9 | & | 35* | | |
| Hampshire | Southampton | June 7 | | | 17 | 1Ct | |
| Notts | Gloucester | June 14 | 34 | & | 45* | 1Ct | |
| Derbyshire | Gloucester | June 18 | 13 | & | 20 | | |
| Somerset | Bath | June 21 | 0 | | | | |
| Northants | Luton | June 28 | 14 | & | 20 | | |
| Leicestershire | Hinckley | July 2 | 63 | | | 2Ct | |
| Surrey | Guildford | July 16 | 101* | & | 29 | | |
| Glamorgan | Cheltenham | July 19 | 0 | & | 4 | 1Ct | |
| Sussex | Cheltenham | July 23 | 70 | | | 1Ct | |
| Worcestershire | Cheltenham | July 26 | 120 | & | 52 | 2Ct | |
| Lancashire | Bristol | Aug 9 | 85 | | | 1Ct | |
| Kent | Canterbury | Aug 20 | 47 | & | 45 | 1Ct | |
| Glamorgan | Abergavenny | Aug 28 | 89 | & | 83 | | 0-4 |
| Northants | Bristol | Sept 3 | 42 | & | 52 | | |
| Somerset | Bristol | Sept 10 | 16 | & | 11 | 1Ct | |
| Sussex | Hove | Sept 17 | 31 | & | 68* | 1Ct | |
| **OTHER FIRST-CLASS** | | | | | | | |
| Oxford U | The Parks | June 15 | | | | | |
| West Indies | Bristol | July 31 | 12 | & | 60 | 1Ct | |
| Sri Lanka | Bristol | Aug 6 | 47 | | | 2Ct | |
| **REFUGE ASSURANCE** | | | | | | | |
| Middlesex | Bristol | April 21 | 1 | | | 1Ct | |
| Worcestershire | Bristol | May 5 | 23 | | | | |
| Surrey | The Oval | May 12 | 71 | | | 1Ct | |
| Sussex | Hove | May 19 | 20 | | | 1Ct | |
| Hampshire | Swindon | May 26 | 60* | | | | |
| Northants | Moreton | June 9 | | | | | |
| Notts | Gloucester | June 16 | 4 | | | | |
| Kent | Canterbury | June 30 | 24 | | | | |
| Yorkshire | Scarborough | July 14 | 41 | | | | |
| Derbyshire | Cheltenham | July 21 | 19 | | | | |
| Essex | Cheltenham | July 28 | 10 | | | | |
| Glamorgan | Swansea | Aug 4 | 23 | | | | |
| Lancashire | Bristol | Aug 11 | 33 | | | | |
| Warwickshire | Edgbaston | Aug 18 | 56 | | | | |
| Leicestershire | Leicester | Aug 25 | 29 | | | | |
| **NATWEST TROPHY** | | | | | | | |
| Norfolk | Bristol | June 26 | 56 | | | | |
| Notts | Bristol | July 11 | 11 | | | | |
| **BENSON & HEDGES CUP** | | | | | | | |
| Combined U | Bristol | April 23 | 13 | | | | |
| Worcestershire | Worcester | April 25 | 36 | | | | |
| Northants | Bristol | May 2 | 81 | | | | |
| Derbyshire | Derby | May 7 | 45 | | | | |
| **OTHER ONE-DAY** | | | | | | | |
| West Indies | Bristol | May 14 | 78* | | | | |
| Somerset | Hove | Sept 8 | 57 | | | | |
| Sussex | Hove | Sept 9 | 3 | | | | |

**BATTING AVERAGES - Including fielding**

| | Matches | Inns | NO | Runs | HS | Avge | 100s | 50s | Ct | St |
|---|---|---|---|---|---|---|---|---|---|---|
| Britannic Assurance | 22 | 38 | 6 | 1477 | 120 | 46.15 | 3 | 9 | 16 | - |
| Other First-Class | 3 | 3 | 0 | 119 | 60 | 39.66 | - | 1 | 3 | - |
| ALL FIRST-CLASS | 25 | 41 | 6 | 1596 | 120 | 45.60 | 3 | 10 | 19 | - |
| Refuge Assurance | 15 | 14 | 1 | 414 | 71 | 31.84 | - | 3 | 3 | - |
| NatWest Trophy | 2 | 2 | 0 | 67 | 56 | 33.50 | - | 1 | - | - |
| Benson & Hedges Cup | 4 | 4 | 0 | 175 | 81 | 43.75 | - | 1 | - | - |
| Other One-Day | 3 | 3 | 1 | 138 | 78* | 69.00 | - | 2 | - | - |
| ALL ONE-DAY | 24 | 23 | 2 | 794 | 81 | 37.81 | - | 7 | 3 | - |

**BOWLING AVERAGES**

| | Overs | Mdns | Runs | Wkts | Avge | Best | 5wI | 10wM |
|---|---|---|---|---|---|---|---|---|
| Britannic Assurance | 0.3 | 0 | 4 | 0 | - | - | - | - |
| Other First-Class | | | | | | | | |

| W | PLAYER RECORDS |
|---|---|

ALL FIRST-CLASS    0.3    0    4    0    -    -    -    -

Refuge Assurance
NatWest Trophy
Benson & Hedges Cup
Other One-Day

ALL ONE-DAY

## J.WRIGHT - *England Amateur XI*

| Opposition | Venue | Date | Batting | Fielding | Bowling |
|---|---|---|---|---|---|
| **OTHER ONE-DAY** | | | | | |
| Sri Lanka | Wolv'hampton | July 24 | 26 | | 0-9 |

**BATTING AVERAGES - Including fielding**

| | Matches | Inns | NO | Runs | HS | Avge | 100s | 50s | Ct | St |
|---|---|---|---|---|---|---|---|---|---|---|
| Other One-Day | 1 | 1 | 0 | 26 | 26 | 26.00 | - | - | - | - |
| ALL ONE-DAY | 1 | 1 | 0 | 26 | 26 | 26.00 | - | - | - | - |

**BOWLING AVERAGES**

| | Overs | Mdns | Runs | Wkts | Avge | Best | 5wI | 10wM |
|---|---|---|---|---|---|---|---|---|
| Other One-Day | 3 | 0 | 9 | 0 | - | - | - | |
| ALL ONE-DAY | 3 | 0 | 9 | 0 | - | - | - | |

## N.P.G.WRIGHT - *Hertfordshire*

| Opposition | Venue | Date | Batting | Fielding | Bowling |
|---|---|---|---|---|---|
| **NATWEST TROPHY** | | | | | |
| Warwickshire | Edgbaston | July 11 | 6 | | 0-9 |

**BATTING AVERAGES - Including fielding**

| | Matches | Inns | NO | Runs | HS | Avge | 100s | 50s | Ct | St |
|---|---|---|---|---|---|---|---|---|---|---|
| NatWest Trophy | 1 | 1 | 0 | 6 | 6 | 6.00 | - | - | - | - |
| ALL ONE-DAY | 1 | 1 | 0 | 6 | 6 | 6.00 | - | - | - | - |

**BOWLING AVERAGES**

| | Overs | Mdns | Runs | Wkts | Avge | Best | 5wI | 10wM |
|---|---|---|---|---|---|---|---|---|
| NatWest Trophy | 0.4 | 0 | 9 | 0 | - | - | - | |
| ALL ONE-DAY | 0.4 | 0 | 9 | 0 | - | - | - | |

## S.C.WUNDKE - *League CC XI*

| Opposition | Venue | Date | Batting | Fielding | Bowling |
|---|---|---|---|---|---|
| **OTHER ONE-DAY** | | | | | |
| West Indies | Trowbridge | June 28 | 2 * | | 0-42 |

**BATTING AVERAGES - Including fielding**

| | Matches | Inns | NO | Runs | HS | Avge | 100s | 50s | Ct | St |
|---|---|---|---|---|---|---|---|---|---|---|
| Other One-Day | 1 | 1 | 1 | 2 | 2* | - | - | - | - | - |
| ALL ONE-DAY | 1 | 1 | 1 | 2 | 2* | - | - | - | - | - |

**BOWLING AVERAGES**

| | Overs | Mdns | Runs | Wkts | Avge | Best | 5wI | 10wM |
|---|---|---|---|---|---|---|---|---|
| Other One-Day | 8 | 0 | 42 | 0 | - | - | - | |
| ALL ONE-DAY | 8 | 0 | 42 | 0 | - | - | - | |

# PLEDGE RECORDS

## G.YATES - *Lancashire*

| Opposition | Venue | Date | Batting | | | Fielding | Bowling |
|---|---|---|---|---|---|---|---|
| **BRITANNIC ASSURANCE** | | | | | | | |
| Warwickshire | Edgbaston | April 27 | | | | | 3-47 |
| Worcestershire | Worcester | May 9 | 4 | & | 0 | | 0-80 & 0-24 |
| Derbyshire | Old Trafford | May 16 | 19 * | | | | 3-69 |
| Surrey | The Oval | May 22 | 0 | & | 12 | | 3-95 & 1-27 |
| Sussex | Old Trafford | May 31 | 1 * | | | 1Ct | 2-40 & 1-45 |
| Hampshire | Basingstoke | June 4 | 15 | | | | 0-27 |
| Glamorgan | Liverpool | June 28 | | | | 1Ct | 1-109 & 0-66 |
| Somerset | Taunton | July 2 | 0 | & | 27 * | 1Ct | 0-59 & 3-83 |
| Notts | Trent Bridge | July 16 | 1 | & | 0 * | | 0-137 |
| Middlesex | Uxbridge | July 19 | 0 * | | | 1Ct | 1-60 & 0-42 |
| Warwickshire | Old Trafford | July 23 | | | | | 2-60 & 0-36 |
| Yorkshire | Old Trafford | Aug 2 | 10 * | | | 1Ct | 1-17 & 0-88 |
| Northants | Lytham | Aug 6 | 28 * | & | 0 | 1Ct | 1-89 |
| Gloucs | Bristol | Aug 9 | 3 | & | 15 * | | 0-84 |
| Derbyshire | Derby | Aug 16 | 4 * | & | 7 | 1Ct | 0-72 & 0-53 |
| Worcestershire | Blackpool | Aug 20 | 29 * | | | | 2-39 & 0-67 |
| Essex | Old Trafford | Aug 23 | 6 | & | 100 * | | 0-20 & 0-48 |
| Notts | Old Trafford | Aug 28 | 0 | & | 11 * | | 2-47 & 0-40 |
| **OTHER FIRST-CLASS** | | | | | | | |
| Cambridge U | Fenner's | April 13 | 11 * | | | | 3-39 & 0-24 |
| Oxford U | The Parks | June 7 | | | 12 | 1Ct | 1-55 & 1-26 |
| **REFUGE ASSURANCE** | | | | | | | |
| Northants | Old Trafford | April 28 | | | | | 0-20 |
| Worcestershire | Worcester | May 12 | | | | | 2-45 |
| Kent | Old Trafford | June 23 | | | | | 0-18 |
| Hampshire | Southampton | July 28 | | | | | 0-42 |
| **BENSON & HEDGES CUP** | | | | | | | |
| Kent | Old Trafford | April 25 | | | | 1Ct | |
| Leicestershire | Leicester | May 4 | | | | | 0-35 |
| Sussex | Old Trafford | May 7 | | | | | 2-50 |

### BATTING AVERAGES - Including fielding

| | Matches | Inns | NO | Runs | HS | Avge | 100s | 50s | Ct | St |
|---|---|---|---|---|---|---|---|---|---|---|
| Britannic Assurance | 18 | 24 | 12 | 292 | 100 * | 24.33 | 1 | - | 7 | - |
| Other First-Class | 2 | 2 | 1 | 23 | 12 | 23.00 | - | - | 1 | - |
| ALL FIRST-CLASS | 20 | 26 | 13 | 315 | 100 * | 24.23 | 1 | - | 8 | - |
| Refuge Assurance | 4 | 0 | 0 | 0 | 0 | - | - | - | - | - |
| Benson & Hedges Cup | 3 | 0 | 0 | 0 | 0 | - | - | - | 1 | - |
| ALL ONE-DAY | 7 | 0 | 0 | 0 | 0 | - | - | - | 1 | - |

### BOWLING AVERAGES

| | Overs | Mdns | Runs | Wkts | Avge | Best | 5wI | 10wM |
|---|---|---|---|---|---|---|---|---|
| Britannic Assurance | 529.4 | 97 | 1770 | 26 | 68.07 | 3-47 | - | - |
| Other First-Class | 61.2 | 20 | 144 | 5 | 28.80 | 3-39 | - | - |
| ALL FIRST-CLASS | 591 | 117 | 1914 | 31 | 61.74 | 3-39 | - | - |
| Refuge Assurance | 20 | 1 | 125 | 2 | 62.50 | 2-45 | - | |
| Benson & Hedges Cup | 22 | 3 | 85 | 2 | 42.50 | 2-50 | - | |
| ALL ONE-DAY | 42 | 4 | 210 | 4 | 52.50 | 2-45 | - | |

# THE BULL COMPUTER
# UNDER-19
# INTERNATIONALS

# ONE-DAY INTERNATIONALS

## HEADLINES

### The Bull Computer
### Under-19
### Internationals

### 6th August - 12th September

The visit of a powerful Australian under-19 side was the centrepiece of a long season of representative youth cricket, again sponsored by Bull Computers as part of the Development of Excellence scheme. Although the Australians held the upper hand for most of the three-match Test series, England's youngsters, under the leadership of John Crawley, gained much credit by emerging with a one-all draw. A remarkable victory at Chelmsford and a determined rearguard at Old Trafford showed the character of the side and will have provided invaluable experience for England's most talented under-19 cricketers.

The opening match at Leicester had seen a comprehensive Australian victory by 10 wickets, the first two days proving a nightmare for the England team: Australia raced to 525 for seven declared, then dismissed the home side for 117, but at least the second innings provided more encouragement, the English batsmen hinting at better things to come by reaching 415. Damien Martyn (179) and Mike Kasporwicz (nine for 95 in the match) took the individual honours for Australia.

The Australian batsmen were again in high-scoring mood at Chelmsford, Blewett and Gilchrist hitting 100s in the first innings and Martyn a marathon 181 not out in the second, but the English spinners, Pearson and Bainbridge, played such an effective containing role that when the Australians declared at the end of the third day, England still retained an outside hope of victory, needing to score 401 in a full day's play. A steady start was capitalised upon by Crawley, who led by example in compiling his first 100 in youth Tests and sharing a thrilling fifth-wicket stand of 134 with Irani. Then Welch and Rollins held their nerve to bring England victory by four wickets. Not only did England's youngsters gain some long overdue compensation for Australia's famous Headingley victory in 1948, but they also ended a run of a 17 Tests without victory against Australia at both full and under-19 level.

Old Trafford brought an equally satisfying rearguard action, after the home side had been forced to follow on 180 runs behind on first innings. Three English batsmen hit 100s. Irani brought some respectability to the first innings with an unbeaten 106, and then Weston and Crawley added second-innings centuries as they shared a second-wicket stand of 178. The English captain became the first to score 1000 runs in youth Tests during his 121, but it was Weston's 146 which finally ensured that England achieved a lead beyond Australia's reach. Spinners from each side gained full reward for marathon spells, Pearson claiming match figures of 11 for 212 for England, Castle responding with 11 for 190 for Australia.

Australia had earlier begun their tour with comfortable victories in both one-day matches, but the English had, against the odds, proved able to compete on level terms in the Test matches.

---

## ENGLAND vs. AUSTRALIA
at Lord's on 6th August 1991
Toss : England. Umpires : H.D.Bird and N.T.Plews
Australia won by 9 runs

### AUSTRALIA
| | | |
|---|---|---:|
| G.Blewett | c Bainbridge b Irani | 24 |
| G.Hayne | not out | 112 |
| D.Martyn * | st Shaw b Smith | 37 |
| K.Roberts | b Smith | 18 |
| A.Gilchrist + | b Broadhurst | 65 |
| M.Fraser | run out | 0 |
| C.Linhart | not out | 0 |
| G.Barr | | |
| M.Kasprowicz | | |
| S.Cook | | |
| D.Castle | | |
| Extras | (lb 15,w 12) | 27 |
| TOTAL | (55 overs)(for 5 wkts) | 283 |

### ENGLAND
| | | |
|---|---|---:|
| R.J.Warren | run out | 5 |
| M.B.Loye | c Gilchrist b Cook | 3 |
| J.P.Crawley * | b Blewett | 89 |
| B.F.Smith | c Roberts b Castle | 23 |
| M.Lathwell | b Castle | 26 |
| W.P.C.Weston | c Roberts b Cook | 44 |
| R.Irani | st Gilchrist b Blewett | 34 |
| G.Welch | run out | 0 |
| A.D.Shaw + | b Kasprowicz | 22 |
| M.Bainbridge | not out | 17 |
| M.Broadhurst | not out | 1 |
| Extras | (lb 5,w 2,nb 3) | 10 |
| TOTAL | (55 overs)(for 9 wkts) | 274 |

| ENGLAND | O | M | R | W | | FALL OF WICKETS | |
|---|---|---|---|---|---|---|---|
| | | | | | | AUS | ENG |
| Broadhurst | 11 | 0 | 85 | 1 | | | |
| Irani | 9 | 0 | 43 | 1 | 1st | 61 | 6 |
| Welch | 10 | 0 | 51 | 0 | 2nd | 127 | 28 |
| Bainbridge | 11 | 1 | 40 | 0 | 3rd | 158 | 73 |
| Smith | 11 | 0 | 37 | 2 | 4th | 274 | 125 |
| Lathwell | 3 | 0 | 12 | 0 | 5th | 275 | 169 |
| | | | | | 6th | | 227 |
| AUSTRALIA | O | M | R | W | 7th | | 228 |
| Kasprowicz | 6 | 0 | 27 | 1 | 8th | | 235 |
| Cook | 9 | 2 | 58 | 2 | 9th | | 273 |
| Barr | 11 | 1 | 54 | 0 | 10th | | |
| Castle | 11 | 0 | 42 | 2 | | | |
| Blewett | 11 | 0 | 42 | 2 | | | |
| Fraser | 7 | 0 | 46 | 0 | | | |

---

## ENGLAND vs. AUSTRALIA
at Trent Bridge on 8th August 1991
Toss : England. Umpires : H.D.Bird and N.T.Plews
Australia won by 5 wickets

### ENGLAND
| | | |
|---|---|---:|
| R.J.Warren | c Barr b Kasprowicz | 1 |
| M.B.Loye | c Hayne b Cook | 3 |
| J.P.Crawley * | st Gilchrist b Blewett | 20 |
| B.F.Smith | c Hayne b Barr | 8 |
| M.Lathwell | c Gilchrist b Cook | 31 |
| W.P.C.Weston | run out | 5 |
| R.Irani | b Barr | 31 |
| G.Welch | c Blewett b Kasprowicz | 55 |
| A.D.Shaw + | run out | 0 |
| M.Bainbridge | b Kasprowicz | 3 |
| M.Broadhurst | not out | 6 |
| Extras | (b 1,lb 3,w 15,nb 1) | 20 |
| TOTAL | (52.1 overs) | 183 |

### AUSTRALIA
| | | |
|---|---|---:|
| G.Blewett | b Broadhurst | 19 |
| G.Hayne | c Shaw b Welch | 22 |
| D.Martyn * | b Welch | 43 |
| K.Roberts | c Lathwell b Smith | 11 |
| A.Gilchrist + | not out | 48 |
| M.Fraser | c Weston b Bainbridge | 3 |
| C.Linhart | not out | 20 |
| G.Barr | | |
| M.Kasprowicz | | |
| S.Cook | | |
| D.Castle | | |
| Extras | (b 1,lb 6,w 10,nb 2) | 19 |
| TOTAL | (46 overs)(for 5 wkts) | 185 |

| AUSTRALIA | O | M | R | W | | FALL OF WICKETS | |
|---|---|---|---|---|---|---|---|
| | | | | | | ENG | AUS |
| Kasprowicz | 9.1 | 4 | 11 | 3 | 1st | 7 | 33 |
| Cook | 11 | 2 | 37 | 2 | 2nd | 9 | 80 |
| Barr | 11 | 1 | 39 | 2 | 3rd | 43 | 96 |
| Blewett | 10 | 1 | 66 | 1 | 4th | 45 | 122 |
| Castle | 11 | 3 | 26 | 0 | 5th | 67 | 132 |
| | | | | | 6th | 97 | |
| ENGLAND | O | M | R | W | 7th | 143 | |
| Broadhurst | 11 | 1 | 46 | 1 | 8th | 145 | |
| Irani | 8 | 0 | 39 | 0 | 9th | 167 | |
| Welch | 9 | 2 | 34 | 2 | 10th | 183 | |
| Bainbridge | 11 | 3 | 31 | 1 | | | |
| Smith | 7 | 1 | 28 | 1 | | | |

# TEST MATCHES

## ENGLAND vs. AUSTRALIA
at Leicester on 16th, 17th, 18th August 1991
Toss : Australia.  Umpires : J.W.Holder and M.J.Kitchen
Australia won by 10 wickets

### AUSTRALIA

|  | | | | |
|---|---|---|---|---|
| G.Blewett | lbw b Welch | 34 | not out | 5 |
| G.Hayne | c Crawley b Irani | 21 | not out | 4 |
| D.Martyn * | c Lathwell b Chapple | 179 | | |
| K.Roberts | c Lathwell b Irani | 8 | | |
| A.Gilchrist + | b Welch | 54 | | |
| M.Foster | c Irani b Chapple | 132 | | |
| M.Fraser | run out | 7 | | |
| M.Kasprowicz | not out | 63 | | |
| D.Castle | | | | |
| S.Cook | | | | |
| A.Littlejohn | | | | |
| Extras | (b 13,lb 5,w 8,nb 1) | 27 | | 0 |
| TOTAL | (for 7 wkts dec) | 525 | (for 0 wkts) | 9 |

### ENGLAND

|  | | | | |
|---|---|---|---|---|
| T.A.Radford | b Castle | 26 | (8) c sub b Kasprowicz | 0 |
| W.P.C.Weston | c Gilchrist b Kasprowicz | 30 | lbw b Castle | 93 |
| J.P.Crawley * | b Kasprowicz | 9 | (4) c Hayne b Castle | 57 |
| B.F.Smith | c Foster b Castle | 4 | (5) lbw b Kasprowicz | 54 |
| M.Lathwell | lbw b Kasprowicz | 0 | (1) c Martyn b Castle | 29 |
| R.Irani | b Kasprowicz | 1 | c sub b Kasprowicz | 61 |
| G.Welch | c Roberts b Cook | 10 | c Fraser b Kasprowicz | 48 |
| G.Chapple | not out | 9 | (9) st Gilchrist b Blewett | 13 |
| M.Bainbridge | c Gilchrist b Cook | 13 | (10) not out | 14 |
| A.D.Shaw + | c Fraser b Cook | 0 | (3) c Castle b Cook | 22 |
| M.Broadhurst | c Martyn b Cook | 4 | b Kasprowicz | 4 |
| Extras | (lb 3,w 1,nb 7) | 11 | (b 2,lb 11,w 7) | 20 |
| TOTAL | | 117 | | 415 |

| ENGLAND | O | M | R | W | O | M | R | W |
|---|---|---|---|---|---|---|---|---|
| Broadhurst | 27 | 3 | 123 | 0 | 0.5 | 0 | 9 | 0 |
| Chapple | 18.5 | 1 | 81 | 2 | | | | |
| Welch | 18 | 2 | 87 | 2 | | | | |
| Irani | 21 | 4 | 89 | 2 | | | | |
| Bainbridge | 28 | 6 | 74 | 0 | | | | |
| Smith | 3 | 0 | 15 | 0 | | | | |
| Lathwell | 9 | 2 | 38 | 0 | | | | |

| AUSTRALIA | O | M | R | W | O | M | R | W |
|---|---|---|---|---|---|---|---|---|
| Kasprowicz | 17 | 4 | 33 | 4 | 20.2 | 8 | 62 | 5 |
| Cook | 14.3 | 6 | 16 | 4 | 16 | 4 | 58 | 1 |
| Littlejohn | 10 | 2 | 24 | 0 | 17 | 3 | 64 | 0 |
| Blewett | 5 | 0 | 18 | 0 | 17 | 3 | 60 | 1 |
| Castle | 16 | 10 | 23 | 2 | 29 | 12 | 87 | 3 |
| Fraser | | | | | 17 | 3 | 71 | 0 |

**FALL OF WICKETS**

| | AUS | ENG | ENG | AUS |
|---|---|---|---|---|
| 1st | 66 | 61 | 46 | |
| 2nd | 79 | 71 | 110 | |
| 3rd | 113 | 76 | 197 | |
| 4th | 228 | 76 | 238 | |
| 5th | 370 | 76 | 304 | |
| 6th | 388 | 82 | 344 | |
| 7th | 525 | 98 | 346 | |
| 8th | | 112 | 375 | |
| 9th | | 113 | 399 | |
| 10th | | 117 | 415 | |

---

## ENGLAND vs. AUSTRALIA
at Chelmsford on 27th, 28th, 29th, 30th August 1991
Toss : Australia.  Umpires : D.J.Constant and B.J.Meyer
England won by 4 wickets

### AUSTRALIA

|  | | | | |
|---|---|---|---|---|
| G.Blewett | c Welch b Broadhurst | 164 | b Welch | 0 |
| G.Hayne | c Loye b Broadhurst | 22 | lbw b Pearson | 47 |
| D.Martyn * | c Rollins b Broadhurst | 13 | not out | 181 |
| K.Roberts | lbw b Pearson | 18 | lbw b Pearson | 65 |
| A.Gilchrist + | c Bainbridge b Irani | 106 | not out | 23 |
| G.Barr | b Broadhurst | 0 | | |
| M.Foster | not out | 26 | | |
| M.Kasprowicz | c Smith b Pearson | 10 | | |
| D.Castle | | | | |
| S.Godwin | | | | |
| S.Cook | | | | |
| Extras | (b 2,lb 4,w 1,nb 9) | 16 | (b 12,lb 4,nb 6) | 22 |
| TOTAL | (for 7 wkts dec) | 375 | (for 3 wkts dec) | 338 |

### ENGLAND

|  | | | | |
|---|---|---|---|---|
| W.P.C.Weston | c Hayne b Cook | 16 | c Gilchrist b Godwin | 45 |
| M.B.Loye | c Gilchrist b Kasprowicz | 19 | c & b Cook | 5 |
| M.Bainbridge | c Hayne b Cook | 26 | | |
| J.P.Crawley * | c Gilchrist b Barr | 9 | lbw b Kasprowicz | 130 |
| B.F.Smith | c Foster b Cook | 77 | (3) b Barr | 16 |
| M.Lathwell | c Foster b Castle | 38 | (5) c Gilchrist b Castle | 45 |
| R.Irani | b Kasprowicz | 56 | (6) run out | 73 |
| G.Welch | c Blewett b Cook | 53 | (7) not out | 46 |
| R.J.Rollins + | b Kasprowicz | 2 | (8) not out | 12 |
| R.M.Pearson | b Kasprowicz | 0 | | |
| M.Broadhurst | not out | 2 | | |
| Extras | (lb 3,nb 12) | 15 | (b 1,lb 13,w 4,nb 14) | 32 |
| TOTAL | | 313 | (for 6 wkts) | 404 |

| ENGLAND | O | M | R | W | O | M | R | W |
|---|---|---|---|---|---|---|---|---|
| Broadhurst | 20 | 2 | 85 | 4 | 14 | 2 | 74 | 0 |
| Welch | 14 | 1 | 68 | 0 | 15 | 3 | 48 | 1 |
| Bainbridge | 28 | 7 | 91 | 0 | 48 | 17 | 97 | 0 |
| Pearson | 22.4 | 2 | 69 | 2 | 61 | 19 | 103 | 2 |
| Irani | 12 | 4 | 44 | 1 | | | | |
| Smith | 4 | 1 | 12 | 0 | | | | |

| AUSTRALIA | O | M | R | W | O | M | R | W |
|---|---|---|---|---|---|---|---|---|
| Kasprowicz | 28.5 | 4 | 77 | 4 | 25 | 3 | 94 | 1 |
| Cook | 19 | 3 | 75 | 4 | 13 | 2 | 55 | 1 |
| Godwin | 15 | 2 | 51 | 0 | 16 | 3 | 68 | 1 |
| Barr | 12 | 2 | 55 | 1 | 20.3 | 5 | 71 | 1 |
| Castle | 24 | 7 | 52 | 1 | 24 | 4 | 88 | 1 |
| Blewett | | | | | 3 | 0 | 14 | 0 |

**FALL OF WICKETS**

| | AUS | ENG | AUS | ENG |
|---|---|---|---|---|
| 1st | 47 | 21 | 13 | 29 |
| 2nd | 65 | 46 | 199 | 55 |
| 3rd | 107 | 67 | 265 | 89 |
| 4th | 319 | 113 | | 187 |
| 5th | 326 | 187 | | 321 |
| 6th | 356 | 203 | | 373 |
| 7th | 375 | 297 | | |
| 8th | | 304 | | |
| 9th | | 304 | | |
| 10th | | 313 | | |

---

## ENGLAND vs. AUSTRALIA
at Old Trafford on 9th, 10th, 11th, 12th September 1991
Toss : Australia.  Umpires : J.H.Hampshire and B.Leadbeater
Match drawn

### AUSTRALIA

|  | | | | |
|---|---|---|---|---|
| G.Blewett | b Pearson | 78 | c Weston b Pearson | 42 |
| G.Hayne | c Rollins b Broadhurst | 3 | st Rollins b Pearson | 51 |
| D.Martyn * | c Crawley b Bainbridge | 31 | not out | 62 |
| M.Foster | b Pearson | 45 | run out | 9 |
| A.Gilchrist + | b Pearson | 45 | run out | 28 |
| M.Fraser | lbw b Welch | 23 | c Crawley b Pearson | 2 |
| C.Linhart | c Weston b Pearson | 88 | lbw b Pearson | 13 |
| G.Barr | not out | 113 | run out | 2 |
| D.Castle | st Rollins b Pearson | 6 | not out | 0 |
| S.Cook | c Welch b Pearson | 6 | | |
| A.Littlejohn | c Welch b Pearson | 3 | | |
| Extras | (b 7,lb 9,w 2,nb 17) | 35 | (b 6,lb 5,w 1,nb 2) | 14 |
| TOTAL | | 476 | (for 7 wkts) | 223 |

### ENGLAND

|  | | | | |
|---|---|---|---|---|
| W.P.C.Weston | c Hayne b Castle | 36 | c Littlejohn b Fraser | 146 |
| M.B.Loye | c Gilchrist b Castle | 8 | c & b Blewett | 11 |
| J.P.Crawley * | c & b Fraser | 35 | c Martyn b Fraser | 121 |
| B.F.Smith | c Castle b Fraser | 6 | c Hayne b Castle | 29 |
| M.Lathwell | b Castle | 27 | c Martyn b Fraser | 66 |
| R.Irani | not out | 106 | c Barr b Littlejohn | 1 |
| G.Welch | c Fraser b Castle | 14 | c Foster b Castle | 6 |
| R.J.Rollins + | c Gilchrist b Fraser | 5 | b Castle | 0 |
| M.Bainbridge | lbw b Castle | 9 | b Castle | 14 |
| R.M.Pearson | run out | 5 | c & b Castle | 0 |
| M.Broadhurst | b Castle | 20 | not out | 2 |
| Extras | (b 12,lb 7,w 2,nb 4) | 25 | (b 18,lb 12,w 5,nb 2) | 37 |
| TOTAL | | 296 | | 433 |

| ENGLAND | O | M | R | W | O | M | R | W |
|---|---|---|---|---|---|---|---|---|
| Broadhurst | 21 | 1 | 87 | 1 | 4 | 0 | 38 | 0 |
| Welch | 17 | 2 | 52 | 1 | 3 | 0 | 15 | 0 |
| Lathwell | 6 | 1 | 37 | 0 | | | | |
| Irani | 9 | 2 | 42 | 0 | 2 | 0 | 19 | 0 |
| Bainbridge | 43 | 12 | 96 | 1 | 24 | 3 | 74 | 0 |
| Pearson | 54 | 14 | 146 | 7 | 26 | 5 | 66 | 4 |

| AUSTRALIA | O | M | R | W | O | M | R | W |
|---|---|---|---|---|---|---|---|---|
| Cook | 6 | 1 | 16 | 0 | | | | |
| Littlejohn | 3 | 0 | 12 | 0 | 15 | 2 | 58 | 1 |
| Barr | 15 | 2 | 42 | 0 | 18 | 3 | 67 | 0 |
| Castle | 37.2 | 15 | 87 | 6 | 60 | 26 | 103 | 5 |
| Fraser | 29 | 7 | 103 | 3 | 53.4 | 22 | 140 | 3 |
| Blewett | 4 | 1 | 17 | 0 | 14 | 4 | 35 | 1 |

**FALL OF WICKETS**

| | AUS | ENG | ENG | AUS |
|---|---|---|---|---|
| 1st | 37 | 37 | 24 | 94 |
| 2nd | 111 | 92 | 202 | 101 |
| 3rd | 141 | 98 | 261 | 118 |
| 4th | 217 | 98 | 382 | 171 |
| 5th | 238 | 140 | 385 | 180 |
| 6th | 261 | 168 | 405 | 206 |
| 7th | 447 | 201 | 406 | 209 |
| 8th | 462 | 239 | 423 | |
| 9th | 472 | 255 | 427 | |
| 10th | 476 | 296 | 433 | |